Statistical Record of Hispanic Americans

ISSN 1082-0507

Statistical Record of Hispanic Americans

Second Edition

Marlita A. Reddy, Editor

Gale Research Inc.
An International Thomson Publishing Company

I(T)P
Changing the Way the World Learns

NEW YORK • LONDON • BONN • BOSTON • DETROIT • MADRID
MELBOURNE • MEXICO CITY • PARIS • SINGAPORE • TOKYO
TORONTO • WASHINGTON • ALBANY NY • BELMONT CA • CINCINNATI OH

Marlita A. Reddy, *Editor*

Editorial Code and Data, Inc. Staff

Arsen J. Darnay, *Senior Editor*
Helen S. Fisher, Robert S. Lazich, and Susan M. Turner, *Contributing Editors*
Gary Alampi, *Programmer Analyst*
Nancy Ratliff and Sherae R. Carroll, *Data Entry Associates*

Gale Research Inc. Staff

Mark Mikula, *Developmental Editor*
Neil Schlager, *Managing Editor, Multicultural Team*

Mary Beth Trimper, *Production Director*
Shanna Heilveil, *Production Assistant*
Cynthia Baldwin, *Product Design Manager*
C.J. Jonik, *Desktop Publisher*
Sherrell L. Hobbs, *Graphic Artist*
Bernadette M. Gornie, *Cover Design*

∞™ This book is printed on acid-free paper that meets the minimum requirements of American National Standard for Information Sciences—Permanence Paper for Printed Library Materials, ANSI Z39.48-1984.

This book is printed on recycled paper that meets Environmental Protection Agency standards.

Library of Congress Catalog Card Number 93-78367
ISBN 0-8103-6422-0
ISSN 1082-0507
Printed in the United States of America

I(T)P™ Gale Research Inc., an International Thomson Publishing Company.
ITP logo is a trademark under license.

10 9 8 7 6 5 4 3 2 1

TABLE OF CONTENTS

CHAPTER 1 - DEMOGRAPHICS continued:

CHAPTER 1 - DEMOGRAPHICS continued:

CHAPTER 1 - DEMOGRAPHICS continued:

CHAPTER 2 - THE FAMILY continued:

CHAPTER 3 - EDUCATION continued:

CHAPTER 3 - EDUCATION continued:

CHAPTER 3 - EDUCATION continued:

CHAPTER 5 - HEALTH AND HEALTH CARE continued:

CHAPTER 6 - SOCIAL AND ECONOMIC CONDITIONS continued:

CHAPTER 6 - SOCIAL AND ECONOMIC CONDITIONS continued:

CHAPTER 6 - SOCIAL AND ECONOMIC CONDITIONS continued:

CHAPTER 7 - BUSINESS AND INDUSTRY continued:

CHAPTER 7 - BUSINESS AND INDUSTRY continued:

CHAPTER 7 - BUSINESS AND INDUSTRY continued:

CHAPTER 8 - GOVERNMENT AND POLITICS continued:

INTRODUCTION

Statistical Record of Hispanic Americans, 2nd Edition (*SRHA-2*) brings together in one convenient volume a wide range of statistical information on Hispanics drawn from governmental, public, and private sources.

Given the size and importance of this ethnic group, it is surprising to find that comprehensive statistical characterizations of Hispanics are difficult to find. Most data are scattered, embedded in subject- or theme-oriented presentations, and difficult to access. The first edition of *SRHA* was conceived as the first step toward a genuinely thorough statistical profiling of Hispanics living in the U.S. Because of overwhelmingly favorable user comments received about the first edition, *SRHA-2* retains the look and feel of the original, while providing updated statistics in all subject areas.

Hispanics in America constitute a large and growing minority with distinct cultural, linguistic, and economic characteristics. At present about 9% of the total U.S. population, Hispanics are rapidly becoming the largest single minority. According to projections made by the Bureau of the Census, that situation will be reached by 2020. In the intervening years, the Hispanic American population is making a significant contribution to total population growth.[1] This phe-

1 U.S. Bureau of the Cenus, Current Population Reports, P25-1092, *Population Projections of the United States, by Age, Sex, Race, and Hispanic Origin: 1992 to 2050.* U.S. Government Printing Office, Washington, DC, 1992.

nomenon is well known to leaders and analysts in politics, government, education, business, and other sectors. It is our hope that *SRHA-2* will continue to be of use to all interested parties in understanding Hispanics more fully by way of the numerical/quantitative perspective which this compilation presents.

Who are the Hispanics?

The U.S. Census Bureau defines a Hispanic as "a person of Mexican, Puerto Rican, Cuban, Central or South American or other Spanish-speaking culture or origin, regardless of race."[2] A variety of sources used in this book report data on the Hispanic population and may or may not separate data by race. These sources also vary in whether or not they subcategorize Hispanic sub-groups (e.g. Cubans, Puerto Ricans, etc.). No attempt has been made to conform either the data or the terms used throughout *SRHA-2* to a uniform pattern. Wherever possible, the definition of Hispanics used by the originator of a table is reproduced in the source note of that table.

Scope and Coverage

SRHA-2 provides up-to-date information on persons of Hispanic origin living in the U.S. Data are presented on the entire spectrum of Hispanic American experience—to the extent that it lends itself to statistical quantification and some group or agency has collected statistical data. Subject matter includes demographics, families and housing, education, culture, health and welfare, social conditions, governance and politics, law and criminal justice, and economic activities.

Sources

The data found in *SRHA-2* are drawn largely—but not exclusively—from governmental sources. Data were obtained from the major statistical programs operated by the federal Departments of Commerce, Labor, Health and Human Services, Housing and Urban Development, Education, State, Defense, and Justice; in most cases several bureaus or agencies within these departments provided data. Other federal sources included independent agencies, the U.S. Congress and its agencies, and special commissions. Federal data were augmented by data from newspapers and the trade press; some of these sources cite state-level data. Valuable materials were also obtained from associations and religious bodies.

A listing of sources is provided in the *Listing of Sources* beginning on pg. 1037.

2 U.S. Census Bureau, op. cit.

Arrangement of Data

Data in *SRHA* are arranged into chapters. Within each chapter, information is further divided topics. Topics and tables are shown in an order which attempts to place the most general information first, followed by more specific information.
The following chapter arrangement gives *SRHA* its basic organization:

- Chapter 1 - Demographics
- Chapter 2 - The Family
- Chapter 3 - Education
- Chapter 4 - Culture
- Chapter 5 - Health and Health Care
- Chapter 6 - Social and Economic Conditions
- Chapter 7 - Business and Industry
- Chapter 8 - Government
- Chapter 9 - Law and Law Enforcement

The *Table of Contents* provides a general overview of the book. It is divided by chapter and topic and lists each table by number and title.

A source listing follows the chapters as *Appendix I - Sources*. The *Keyword Index* provides additional access through keywords to subjects, concepts, and names.

Acknowledgments

The original edition of *SRHA* was compiled with the advice of Dr. Lucinda Hart-Gonzalez of Research, Evaluation & Development, Foreign Service Institute, U.S. Department of State; Dr. Jorge Del Pinal, Chief, Hispanic and Ethnic Statistics Branch, Bureau of the Census; and Dr. Harry Pachon, National Director, National Association of Latino Elected and Appointed Officials. These individuals graciously consented to serve as an advisory panel in the initial phases of this project. The editors would also like to express thanks to the many individuals in the federal government, associations, and publishers who helped in the compilation of *SRHA* by providing reports, data, references, and permissions. The monumental task of rendering many hundreds of tables into machine-readable form fell to Nancy Ratliff and Sherae Carroll who, as usual, met the challenge and contributed to timely performance. Special thanks to Mark

Mikula, developmental editor, Gale Research, for his help throughout the compilation of this material.

Suggestions and Comments

The editors welcome suggestions and comments on the improvement of *Statistical Record of Hispanic Americans*. Ideas relating to content, scope, coverage, presentation—indeed on any aspect of *SRHA*—should be addressed to:

The Editors
Statistical Record of Hispanic Americans, 2nd Edition
Gale Research Inc.
835 Penobscot Building
Detroit, MI 48226

GUIDE TO CHAPTERS AND CONTENTS

This section presents a discussion of *SRHA*'s nine chapters. The intent is to provide some comment on the main sources consulted, to highlight issues and limitations of the data presented, and to provide a brief summary of the more important contents of each chapter.

Chapter 1 - Demographics

Data for this chapter were drawn from the most recent 1990 Census of Population (not yet fully released by the government) and various Current Population Reports.

Population

This section contains current population data on the Hispanic population (including sub-groups) largely from the 1990 Census. Please note that the designation "Hispanic" refers to persons of Hispanic origin *regardless of race*. Tables in which race and ethnicity are considered separately are specified in the legends (e.g. *White non-Hispanic* or *Black non-Hispanic*) In the remainder of the tables, each Hispanic person is typically counted twice—once as a Hispanic and once as a White, Black, or person of other race. This is important to keep in mind when making comparisons between Hispanics and other groups.

In 1990 there were 22.4 million Hispanics in the U.S. The states with the largest Hispanic population were California (7.7 million), Texas (4.3 million), New York (2.2 million), and

Florida (1.6 million). The remaining states all reported having fewer than one million persons of Hispanic origin. The states with the highest *concentration* of Hispanics were New Mexico (38.2%), California (25.8%), and Texas (25.5%). The remaining states all reported having Hispanic populations of less than a 25% of total. Population statistics are also presented at the Metropolitan Statistical Area (MSA), county, and city levels.

As of March 1993 the Hispanic population had grown to as estimated 22.8 million. Hispanics are about 9% of the total population. The majority of this group were Mexican by origin (64%), Puerto Rican (11%), Cuban (5%), or had origin in other countries (20%).

The median age of the Hispanic population in 1993 was 26.7 years; for the total U.S. population, median age was 33.6 years. A larger percentage of Hispanics were below the age of 16—31.3% of Hispanics than for the U.S. population (23.8%).

A variety of statistical displays on population are presented in this chapter by sub-group as well as for the total Hispanic population.

Population Trends

This section contains population trends and projections for the Hispanic population and its subgroups in the U.S. from 1970 to 2080.

The Hispanic population is growing at a much faster rate than the non-Hispanic White population or African Americans. Between 1992 and 2000, Hispanics will contribute 37% of the nation's growth (while being, currently, just 9% of the total population). Projections show that the contribution to growth will be 43% between 2000 and 2014 and 57% from 2030 to 2050.[1] The data for these projections are in this section. Projections are for the U.S., by age.

Immigration

From 1981 to 1990 the immigration of legal aliens and refugees from Latin America remained in the area of about 33% of total. In 1993, legal immigration brought more than 238,000 people to the United States from Mexico and Central and South America; total immigration for all countries of origin was about 900,000. Hispanics represent the second largest immigrant group, with Mexicans accounting for 14% of all persons admitted in 1993. The largest single immi-

1 *Population Projections of the United States, by Age, Sex, Race, and Hispanic Origin: 1992 to 2050,* P25-1092, November 1992..

grant group comes from Asia. Trends in immigration have held fairly steady over the last decade. This section presents detailed statistics for immigration classified by immigration status.

Chapter 2 - The Family

In 1993 about 80% of the 6.6 million households of Hispanic origin were families; the corresponding figure for the nation as a whole was 71%. About 69% of the families (24%) were headed by married couples, slightly lower than in the general population (78%). Detailed family characteristics are presented in this chapter by Hispanic sub-group.

Hispanic families tended to be larger than those of the general population: 3.8 persons per family versus 3.2 persons in the U.S. as a whole.

Family income tended to be lower than the general population. In 1992 *Median* income for Hispanic families was $23,912 ($36,811 for the U.S.). *Average* income for Hispanic families was $30,322, well below the U.S. mean of $44,483. This income gap has widened by more than $1,000 since 1990. About 26% of Hispanic families lived below the poverty line in 1993. Statistical data are presented by Hispanic sub-group. Additional information on income can be found in the chapter entitled *Social and Economic Conditions*.

Other topics in this chapter include marriage, divorce, work experience, and child care.

Chapter 3 - Education

This chapter presents statistical data from a wide variety of sources on the state of education of Hispanic children and adults in the U.S.

While social and economic factors, such as level of income, can affect the educational performance of all children, the Hispanic population faces a unique challenge in education: persons of Hispanic origin are more likely than non-Hispanics to be raised speaking Spanish; the children in these families are less likely to hear English at home and are more likely to have limited English proficiency.[2] For additional information on this subject, please consult *The Condition of Bilingual Education in the Nation: a Report to the Congress and the President* (U.S. Department of Education, June 30, 1991).

---

2 U.S. Department of Education, National Center for Education Statistics. *The Condition of Eduction, 1992.* Washington, D.C., 1992.

As the Hispanic population in the U.S. has increased, so has its representation in the school systems. In Fall 1992 just under 43 million persons were enrolled in public schools. At that time, Hispanic children made up about 20% of public school enrollment.[3] For persons 25 years and older in 1993, slightly more than half had completed at least four years of high school, nearly 13% had completed at least a year of college, and nearly 7% had completed bachelor's degrees.

In the 1991-92 academic year 40,761 Hispanic persons received baccalaureates, about 4% of all bachelors degrees conferred. The most baccaluareates were awarded in business and management (45%), social sciences (14%), and education (8%).

Hispanic students received 9,358 masters degrees (3% of total) in 1992; the majority were awarded in education (30%), business and management (21%), and public affairs (8%).

At the doctoral level, 811 degrees were awarded to Hispanic students (2% of total); these degrees were awarded primarily in education (23%), psychology (13%), and biological/life sciences (11%).

Chapter 4 - Culture

While cultural issues are not generally quantifiable, this chapter has been included to present statistical information on the area of language, religion, sports, voluntarism, and perceived social standing. Most of the material is on language.

Language

In 1990, near 14% of 230 million Americans (1990 Census) spoke a language other than English; and more than half those using a different language communicated in Spanish.

In the 1991-92 academic year in New York, about 66% of students with limited English proficiency spoke Spanish as their native language.[4] Data are presented for 1980 through 1990 for selected populations and areas of the U.S.

---

3 U.S. Department of Education, National Center for Education Statistics, *Digest of Education Statistics, 1994.* Washington, D.C., 1994.

4 For information on the impact of limited English proficiency on education, please consult *The Condition of Bilingual Education*, op. cit.

Chapter 5 - Health and Health Care

This chapter provides detailed information on vital statistics, the health concerns of Hispanics, health care received, and health insurance.

Births

In 1991, there were more than 600,000 births to women of Hispanic origin, representing about 14% of total registered births. The rate of births to teenage mothers was about 17%, as compared to about 13% for the general population. The percentage born to teenagers was slightly higher for Puerto Ricans (22%) and lower for those of Cuban origin (7%).

Hispanic mothers tended to receive prenatal care later than the general population; about 61% received prenatal care in the first trimester and 11% received prenatal care in the third trimester or not at all. A notable exception to this pattern is seen in the Cuban population, in which more than 85% of mothers received early prenatal care. This figure is only lower that for Japanese mothers whose early prenatal care rate is 88%. The figures for the general population were 76% and 7%, respectively (1989). Babies born with low birth-weight accounted for about 6% for Hispanic births, lower than the rate for the general population in 1989 (7%). This figure was slightly higher for Puerto Ricans (9.5%).

Deaths

Limited data are available on the mortality rate of Hispanics. A study presented in 1988 showed that in 15 states Hispanic mortality rates were lower than rates for the non-Hispanic population for all causes of death.[5] Cuban American mortality rates tended to be the lowest of all the subgroups. Leading causes of death from chronic diseases were heart disorders, cerebrovascular diseases, and cancer.

Health Concerns

According to the U.S. Department of Health and Human Services, Hispanic Americans are less likely than non-Hispanics to receive preventive medical examinations. Nearly 15% of Hispanics have had no diagnostic tests (vs. 9.7% of non-Hispanics). According to National Health Inter-

5 U.S. Department of Health and Human Services, Public Health Service, Health Resources and Services Administration, *Health Status of Minorities and Low-Income Groups: Third Edition*, 1989.

view Surveys, from 1978-80, Mexican Americans had the lowest physician visit rate of all groups studied.[6]

About 45% of Hispanics (22%) spent at least one month without health insurance coverage in 1991; this compares with figures of 21% for non-Hispanic whites and 36% for non-Hispanic blacks. Of those Hispanics with coverage, 68% had private health insurance (84% of the general population). Around 11% of Hispanics with health insurance had continuous coverage. 61% of insured Hispanics had private insurance or were covered by Champus, Veterans', and other military programs throughout the year. Detailed information on health status and health insurance are presented in this chapter.

Chapter 6 - Social and Economic Conditions

Unemployment of Hispanic persons age 16 years and older (all races) was 11.9% in 1992. Nearly 16 million Hispanics participated in the U.S. civilian labor force. Unemployment by origin varied: Mexican - 11.7%; Puerto Rican - 14.4%; Cuban - 7.3%.

Employment of Hispanics was nearly 9.0 million in 1991. Of these, 25% worked in technical, sales and administrative support occupations. The smallest participation was in the farming and forestry occupations (less than 6%). Detailed data are presented for all industries and by Hispanic subgroup.

The median annual income for Hispanic American families in 1993 was $22,859 ($30,874 for families of all races). In that year, approximately 26% of Hispanic families were living below the poverty level; the figure for all races was 12%.

There were about 6.6 million Hispanic households in the U.S. in March of 1993 representing an increase of about 65% since 1980. Hispanics were less likely than non-Hispanics to own their homes, with about 40% of households owned or being bought, as compared to 65% for non-Hispanics. Detailed statistics are presented on household characteristics, housing tenure, and housing amenities.

---

6 U.S. Department of Health, op. cit.

Chapter 7 - Business and Industry

This chapter presents information on Hispanics both as business owners and executives and as consumers. The data come from the U.S. Census Bureau and a variety of private sources.

Minority-Owned and Hispanic-Owned Firms

In 1987 there were more than 1.2 million minority-owned firms in the United States. These firms constituted 8.9% of all U.S. firms and 3.9% of all sales and receipts for U.S. firms. Hispanic-owned firms represented 34.8% of minority firms and 33.0% of those sales and receipts. With average sales and receipts of $58,554, Hispanic-owned firms were below average as compared to all minority firms ($64,000) and well below average as compared to all U.S. firms ($146,000). In terms of growth, Hispanic-owned business have shown an 80% increase in number of firms since 1982 (64% for all minority firms) and an 110% increase in receipts (126% for all minority firms).

For all firms in the U.S., the largest concentration of minority firms is in the service industries and the largest concentration of sales and receipts is in the retail industry. This does not hold true for Hispanic-owned firms. The largest grouping of Hispanic firms (34%) is engaged in the construction sector; and the largest Hispanic share of total U.S. sales and receipts was in agriculture, forestry, and fishing (also 34%).

Overall, minority-owned firms tend to be concentrated in a few states. California, Texas, New York, and Florida are home to more than half of minority firms in the U.S. and account for about 59% of minority firm receipts. Similarly, more than three-quarters of Hispanic-owned firms are located in the same four states and account for about 76% of Hispanic firm receipts.

Like most minority-owned businesses, Hispanic firms tend to be propietorships rather than partnerships or corporations.

Consumer Affairs

Demographic data are one of the crucial pieces of information used in the marketing of products and services in the U.S. As the Hispanic population increases, so does its importance as a market segment. This section provides information on this market, including market shares and consumer preferences within the Hispanic market.

Chapter 8 - Government

This chapter presents statistics from a variety of sources on voting, political affiliation, and goverment employment.

Voting and Politics

At the time of the 1992 elections, nearly 15 million Hispanics age 18 and older resided in the U.S. Of these persons, 35% were reported registered to vote and 83% of those reported as registered also reported actually voting (28.9% of the 15 million). Detailed information on registration and voting, as well as information on political affiliation are shown in this chapter.

Government Representation

According to the Census Bureau and the National Association of Latino Elected and Appointed Officials[7], about 37% of Hispanic elected officials serve in the education sector and another 32% serve in municipal offices. Detailed statistical information on Hispanic representation in the government sector is shown in this chapter, as well as employment at the local, state, and federal levels. The federal information includes Hispanic participation in the U.S. military.

Chapter 9 - Law and Law Enforcement

This chapter presents statistics from the U.S. Department of Justice and other private sources on Hispanics and the justice system, including incarceration figures, victimization data, and representation in the law enforcement sector.

Incarceration

Only limited information is available on the Hispanic origin of criminal offenders. According to the Department of Justice, Hispanics represented 14% of jail inmates in the U.S. in 1992. The most recent figure for State prisons was in 1991, when Hispanics represented 14.2% of females and 16.8% of males. Data for additional years are presented in this chapter, as well as information on sentencing, time served, parole, etc.

---

7 *USA TODAY*, March 3, 1992, p. 13A. From the *National Roster of Hispanic Elected Officians*, the National Association of Latino Elected and Appointed Officians, 3409 Garnet Street, Los Angeles, CA 90023.

Victimization

From 1976-86, the rate of violent crimes inflicted upon Hispanics age 12 and older was 39.6 per 1,000 persons. This compared with a rate of 35.3 per 1,000 for the non-Hispanic U.S. population. For the period from 1976-1986, the rate for household crimes was also higher for Hispanics, with a rate of 265.6 for Hispanics versus 204.5 for non-Hispanics. The victimization rate for crimes of theft was lower for Hispanics (74.9) than for non-Hispanics (80.3). Detailed statistics on Hispanics as victims of crime in the U.S. are shown in this chapter.

Law Enforcement Representation

About 6% of all U.S. law enforcement officers were Hispanics in 1988. In 1990, Hispanics held 7% of correctional officer positions in jails, 5% in State prisons, and 6% in the juvenile system. Detailed information on Hispanics in law enforcement is presented for major cities and by state.

The summary in this section merely highlights information available in *SRHA* and the sources used in its compilation. For additional information, the reader should also consult the source notes to individual tables.

Statistical Record of Hispanic Americans

Chapter 1
DEMOGRAPHICS

Geographic Mobility

★1★

Geographic Mobility, by Race/Ethnicity, 1990-1991

Data show percent distribution of an estimated 41.5 million movers.

Race/ethnicity	Percent
Hispanic[1]	23.4
Black	18.4
White	16.6

Source: Miner, Betsy. "Tough times have people staying put." *USA TODAY* (18 November 1992), p. 11A. Primary source: Bureau of the Census. *Note:* 1. Hispanics can be of any race.

★2★

Geographic Mobility

Detailed Geographic Mobility, 1991-92

The number, in thousands, and percent distribution of movers and nonmovers age one and older, are shown, for each race/ethnicity and sex, from March 1991 to March 1992.

Detailed mobility	All races			White			Black			Hispanic[1]		
	Total	Male	Female	Total	Male	Female	Total	Male	Female	Total	Male	Female
Total population												
Total, 1 year and over	247,380	120,436	126,944	207,030	101,315	105,715	30,773	14,423	16,350	21,544	10,788	10,756
MSAs												
Central cities	74,649	35,703	38,947	53,657	25,865	27,792	17,139	7,944	9,195	11,227	5,518	5,709
Balance	118,176	58,057	60,119	104,897	51,644	53,253	8,910	4,280	4,630	8,864	4,527	4,337
Outside MSAs	54,555	26,676	27,879	48,476	23,806	24,670	4,725	2,199	2,526	1,452	743	709
Same house (nonmovers)												
MSAs												
Central cities	58,952	27,952	31,000	42,281	20,192	22,089	13,686	6,306	7,380	8,549	4,165	4,385
Balance	99,269	48,588	50,681	88,831	43,583	45,248	7,001	3,342	3,659	6,793	3,446	3,347
Outside MSAs	46,359	22,546	23,813	41,344	20,204	21,140	3,919	1,814	2,105	1,143	582	561

[Continued]

★2★

Detailed Geographic Mobility, 1991-92

[Continued]

Detailed mobility	All races Total	All races Male	All races Female	White Total	White Male	White Female	Black Total	Black Male	Black Female	Hispanic[1] Total	Hispanic[1] Male	Hispanic[1] Female
Movers within same MSA												
Total	24,424	12,047	12,377	19,211	9,557	9,654	4,128	1,933	2,194	3,612	1,843	1,769
Within central city	9,426	4,563	4,863	6,390	3,152	3,239	2,548	1,171	1,377	1,779	899	881
Between central cities	392	216	177	296	173	123	71	28	43	87	45	42
Within balance	9,605	4,742	4,863	8,409	4,153	4,256	800	372	428	1,072	558	514
Central city to balance	3,373	1,680	1,693	2,731	1,369	1,363	514	256	258	495	249	246
Balance to central city	1,627	846	782	1,384	710	674	195	107	88	179	93	88
Movers between MSAs												
Total	7,256	3,665	3,591	5,835	2,961	2,873	991	495	496	689	352	338
Between central cities	1,811	913	899	1,325	679	647	368	184	184	267	132	135
Between balance	2,421	1,245	1,175	2,070	1,068	1,002	226	115	110	155	88	67
Central city to balance	1,863	927	937	1,467	737	730	263	125	138	164	84	81
Balance to central city	1,160	580	580	972	478	494	135	71	64	103	48	55
Movers from outside MSAs to MSAs												
Total	1,793	884	909	1,600	781	820	131	73	58	92	53	38
To central cities	735	349	385	634	293	340	77	43	34	69	37	23
To balances of MSAs	1,058	535	523	967	487	479	54	30	24	23	16	6
Movers from MSAs to outside MSAs												
Total	1,720	876	845	1,582	804	778	97	47	50	92	40	52
From central cities	697	359	338	602	308	294	67	36	31	43	19	24
From balances of MSAs	1,023	517	506	980	496	484	29	11	19	49	21	28
Movers, outside MSAs at both dates												
Total	6,352	3,172	3,180	5,478	2,746	2,732	678	320	357	201	110	91
Within same county	4,594	2,279	2,315	3,907	1,949	1,958	535	245	290	180	98	82
To different county	1,758	893	865	1,571	797	774	142	76	67	21	12	8
Movers from abroad												
Total	1,255	706	549	868	488	381	143	91	52	372	197	176
To central cities of MSAs	546	284	262	375	189	186	59	33	25	193	100	93
To balance of MSAs	586	340	246	422	247	175	53	40	13	163	86	77
To outside MSAs	124	82	42	71	52	20	31	17	14	16	10	5

Source: Hansen, Kristin A. U.S. Bureau of the Census. *Geographic Mobility: March 1991 to March 1992.* Current Population Reports, P20-473. Washington, DC: U.S. Government Printing Office, 1993, pp. 82-89. *Notes:* A dash (-) represents or rounds to zero. 1. Persons of Hispanic origin may be of any race.

★3★

Geographic Mobility

Detailed Geographic Mobility, by Employment Status, 1991-92

The number, in thousands, of movers and nonmovers is shown, by race/ethnicity, sex, and mobility, from March 1991 to March 1992.

Characteristic	Total	Same house (nonmovers)	Different house in United States: Total	Same county	Different county: Total	Same state	Different state: Total	Same region: Total	Same division	Different division	Different region	Movers from abroad
ALL RACES												
Both sexes												
Persons 16 years and over	191,862	159,162	31,660	20,003	11,656	6,155	5,501	3,004	1,932	1,072	2,496	1,041
Civilian labor force	125,452	101,293	23,595	15,282	8,313	4,553	3,760	2,086	1,305	782	1,673	564

[Continued]

★3★

Detailed Geographic Mobility, by Employment Status, 1991-92

[Continued]

Characteristic	Total	Same house (nonmovers)	Different house in United States									Movers from abroad
			Total	Same county	Different county							
					Total	Same state	Different state					
							Total	Same region			Different region	
								Total	Same division	Different division		
Employed	115,724	94,354	20,904	13,678	7,226	4,042	3,184	1,765	1,115	650	1,419	467
Unemployed	9,728	6,939	2,691	1,604	1,087	511	575	321	190	132	254	98
Armed Forces	841	447	294	135	159	28	131	61	42	19	70	100
Not in labor force	65,568	57,421	7,771	4,586	3,185	1,575	1,610	857	585	271	754	376
Male												
Persons 16 years and over	92,038	75,760	15,675	9,829	5,847	3,049	2,797	1,505	957	548	1,293	602
Civilian labor force	68,209	54,792	13,070	8,370	4,699	2,537	2,163	1,152	709	443	1,011	347
Employed	62,191	50,430	11,475	7,422	4,053	2,219	1,835	968	609	360	866	286
Unemployed	6,018	4,362	1,595	949	646	318	328	184	101	83	144	61
Armed Forces	801	424	278	131	147	28	119	54	40	14	65	98
Not in labor force	23,029	20,544	2,328	1,327	1,001	485	516	298	207	91	217	157
Female												
Persons 16 years and over	99,824	83,401	15,984	10,175	5,809	3,106	2,703	1,500	975	525	1,204	439
Civilian labor force	57,244	46,501	10,525	6,912	3,613	2,016	1,597	934	595	339	663	218
Employed	53,533	43,924	9,429	6,256	3,173	1,823	1,349	797	506	290	553	181
Unemployed	3,710	2,577	1,096	655	441	193	248	138	89	49	110	37
Armed Forces	41	23	16	4	12	-	12	7	2	6	5	2
Not in labor force	42,540	36,877	5,444	3,259	2,184	1,090	1,095	558	378	180	536	219
HISPANIC[1]												
Both sexes												
Persons 16 years and over	15,161	11,647	3,217	2,437	780	470	310	144	73	71	166	297
Civilian labor force	9,940	7,440	2,318	1,787	531	333	199	105	49	57	94	182
Employed	8,820	6,645	2,019	1,563	455	300	155	82	41	42	73	156
Unemployed	1,120	795	300	224	76	33	43	23	8	15	20	26
Armed Forces	56	30	18	6	11	1	10	1	1	-	9	7
Not in labor force	5,165	4,176	881	644	237	136	101	38	24	14	63	108
Male												
Persons 16 years and over	7,555	5,690	1,700	1,283	417	238	179	84	37	47	95	165
Civilian labor force	5,971	4,374	1,480	1,140	340	206	134	72	28	44	62	117
Employed	5,240	3,841	1,299	1,004	295	185	110	60	25	36	50	99
Unemployed	731	533	181	136	45	21	24	12	3	8	13	17
Armed Forces	56	30	18	6	11	1	10	1	1	-	9	7
Not in labor force	1,527	1,285	202	136	66	31	35	11	7	3	24	41
Female												
Persons 16 years and over	7,607	5,957	1,517	1,154	363	232	131	60	37	23	70	132
Civilian labor force	3,969	3,066	838	647	191	127	64	33	20	12	31	65
Employed	3,580	2,804	719	559	160	115	45	22	16	6	24	57
Unemployed	389	262	119	88	31	12	19	11	5	6	8	8
Armed Forces	-	-	-	-	-	-	-	-	-	-	-	-
Not in labor force	3,638	2,891	679	508	172	105	67	27	16	11	40	68

Source: Hansen, Kristin A. U.S. Bureau of the Census. *Geographic Mobility: March 1991 to March 1992.* Current Population Reports, P20-473. Washington, DC: U.S. Government Printing Office, 1993, pp. 15-16. *Notes:* A dash (-) represents zero or rounds to zero. 1. Persons of Hispanic origin may be of any race.

★4★

Geographic Mobility

Geographic Mobility of Families Living Below Poverty, by Current Residence and Residence One Year Ago, 1992

Numbers of families are shown in thousands.

Characteristic	All races			White			Black			Hispanic origin[1]		
	Total	Below poverty level		Total	Below poverty level		Total	Below poverty level		Total	Below poverty level	
		Number	Percent of total		Number	Percent of total		Number	Percent of total		Number	Percent of total
PERSONS IN FAMILIES												
Total	211,552	26,931	12.7	176,050	17,036	9.7	26,623	8,538	32.1	19,613	5,450	27.8
Moved within U.S.	30,830	6,705	21.7	24,552	4,227	17.2	4,773	2,076	43.5	3,994	1,528	38.2
Now in Northeast	3,675	681	18.5	3,068	475	15.5	443	167	37.8	422	164	38.8
Was in:												
Northeast	3,445	660	19.2	2,860	456	15.9	431	166	38.6	414	161	38.9
Midwest	33	-	(B)	31	-	(B)	-	-	(B)	-	-	(B)
South	150	16	11.0	133	15	11.5	12	1	(B)	7	2	(B)
West	47	5	(B)	45	4	(B)	-	-	(B)	1	-	(B)
Now in Midwest	7,005	1,381	19.7	5,844	893	15.3	982	436	44.5	337	163	48.3
Was in:												
Northeast	94	19	20.0	80	18	22.6	4	-	(B)	4	4	(B)
Midwest	6,343	1,246	19.6	5,240	779	14.9	941	421	44.7	311	150	48.2
South	307	57	18.5	278	52	18.8	25	4	(B)	5	-	(B)
West	262	59	22.5	246	44	17.7	11	11	(B)	16	9	(B)
Now in South	11,820	2,8812	24.4	8,595	1,531	17.8	2,853	1,250	43.8	1,213	439	36.2
Was in:												
Northeast	318	57	18.0	248	33	13.4	52	14	(B)	50	24	(B)
Midwest	283	50	17.6	236	38	16.0	33	6	(B)	15	4	(B)
South	10,919	2,730	25.0	7,858	1,425	18.1	2,739	1,222	44.6	1,106	397	35.9
West	300	45	15.0	253	34	13.5	30	8	(B)	42	15	(B)
Now in West	8,330	1,762	21.1	7,046	1,329	18.9	495	222	44.9	2,022	762	37.7
Was in:												
Northeast	57	2	(B)	55	-	(B)	2	2	(B)	-	-	(B)
Midwest	139	13	9.7	125	12	9.8	6	-	(B)	8	1	(B)
South	394	50	12.7	335	26	7.7	38	20	(B)	41	18	(B)
West	7,741	1,696	21.9	6,531	1,291	19.8	449	200	44.6	1,973	743	37.6
Moved from outside U.S.	1,055	384	36.4	757	276	36.5	42	10	(B)	335	176	52.4
Did not move	179,667	19,842	11.0	150,741	12,534	8.3	21,808	6,452	29.6	15,284	3,746	24.5
Northeast	38,297	3,695	9.6	33,188	2,443	7.4	3,830	1,126	29.4	2,395	773	32.3
Midwest	43,382	4,194	9.7	38,152	2,595	6.8	4,481	1,484	33.1	1,065	220	20.7
South	61,469	8,134	13.2	48,231	4,394	9.1	11,882	3,587	30.2	4,731	1,088	23.0
West	36,519	3,819	10.5	31,170	3,102	10.0	1,616	255	15.8	7,093	1,665	23.5
PERSONS IN MARRIED-COUPLE FAMILIES												
Total	168,520	12,436	7.4	148,088	9,736	6.6	13,322	1,885	14.1	14,271	3,021	21.2
Moved within U.S.	21,909	2,639	12.0	18,791	2,050	10.9	2,067	409	19.8	2,687	822	30.6
Now in Northeast	2,479	169	6.8	2,217	145	6.5	154	3	2.1	226	52	23.0
Was in:												
Northeast	2,289	160	7.0	2,045	135	6.6	143	3	2.3	222	50	22.3
Midwest	31	-	(B)	29	-	(B)	-	-	(B)	-	-	(B)
South	125	10	7.6	110	10	8.7	11	-	(B)	4	2	(B)
West	33	-	(B)	33	-	(B)	-	-	(B)	-	-	(B)
Now in Midwest	5,042	508	10.1	4,551	381	8.4	379	101	26.7	217	85	39.1
Was in:												
Northeast	81	6	7.7	68	6	(B)	4	-	(B)	4	4	(B)
Midwest	4,511	444	9.8	4,058	331	8.2	354	92	25.9	198	76	38.5
South	240	31	12.9	228	31	13.6	11	-	(B)	2	-	(B)
West	210	26	12.5	196	13	6.5	10	10	(B)	12	4	(B)
Now in South	8,215	1,149	14.0	6,697	848	12.7	1,278	250	19.6	890	297	33.4
Was in:												
Northeast	248	32	12.9	207	22	10.5	27	3	(B)	41	16	(B)
Midwest	227	25	11.1	194	19	9.8	18	-	(B)	5	-	(B)
South	7,503	1,072	14.3	6,083	788	13.0	1,222	247	20.2	827	280	33.8
West	237	19	8.2	212	19	9.1	11	-	(B)	16	1	(B)
Now in West	6,174	814	13.2	5,326	675	12.7	256	54	21.2	1,355	388	28.6
Was in:												
Northeast	52	-	(B)	52	-	(B)	-	-	9B)	-	-	(B)
Midwest	125	7	5.6	112	6	5.2	6	-	(B)	8	1	(B)
South	354	26	7.4	314	17	5.5	20	4	(B)	34	11	(B)

[Continued]

★4★

Geographic Mobility of Families Living Below Poverty, by Current Residence and Residence One Year Ago, 1992

[Continued]

Characteristic	All races			White			Black			Hispanic origin[1]		
	Total	Below poverty level		Total	Below poverty level		Total	Below poverty level		Total	Below poverty level	
		Number	Percent of total		Number	Percent of total		Number	Percent of total		Number	Percent of total
West	5,643	781	13.8	4,847	652	13.5	230	50	21.7	1,313	376	28.6
Moved from outside U.S.	867	285	32.8	624	212	34.0	26	2	(B)	244	109	44.5
Did not move	145,743	9,512	6.5	128,673	7,474	5.8	11,229	1,474	13.1	11,340	2,090	18.4
Northeast	30,688	1,489	4.9	27,683	1,174	4.2	1,903	232	12.2	1,364	197	14.5
Midwest	35,456	1,867	5.3	32,929	1,559	4.7	1,945	247	12.7	829	133	16.0
South	49,647	4,013	8.1	42,091	2,970	7.1	6,426	945	14.7	3,790	780	20.6
West	29,952	2,143	7.2	25,970	1,771	6.8	955	50	5.3	5,356	980	18.3
PERSONS IN FAMILIES WITH FEMALE HOUSEHOLDER, NO SPOUSE PRESENT												
Total	34,855	13,153	37.7	21,680	6,402	29.6	11,927	6,312	52.9	4,089	2,076	50.8
Moved within U.S.	7,243	3,696	51.0	4,447	1,933	43.5	2,445	1,577	64.5	975	616	63.2
Now in Northeast	973	490	50.3	675	314	46.5	267	164	61.5	167	103	61.5
Was in:												
Northeast	942	481	51.1	645	306	47.4	266	163	61.3	164	103	62.5
Midwest	1	-	(B)	1	-	(B)	-	-	(B)	-	-	(B)
South	19	5	(B)	17	4	(B)	1	1	(B)	3	-	(B)
West	11	4	(B)	11	4	(B)	-	-	(B)	-	-	(B)
Now in Midwest	1,608	771	48.0	1,009	433	42.9	544	311	57.2	97	66	68.3
Was in:												
Northeast	11	11	(B)	11	11	(B)	-	-	(B)	-	-	(B)
Midwest	1,525	724	47.5	940	388	41.3	534	310	58.0	90	62	68.9
South	41	16	(B)	30	16	(B)	8	-	(B)	3	-	(B)
West	30	20	(B)	29	19	(B)	2	2	(B)	4	4	(B)
Now in South	3,064	1,603	52.3	1,530	614	40.1	1,420	945	66.6	247	121	49.1
Was in:												
Northeast	48	23	(B)	28	12	(B)	20	12	(B)	8	7	(B)
Midwest	48	24	(B)	33	18	(B)	15	6	(B)	10	4	(B)
South	2,921	1,532	52.5	1,443	571	39.5	1,366	920	67.4	215	97	45.2
West	47	25	(B)	24	14	(B)	19	8	(B)	14	13	(B)
Now in West	1,598	831	52.0	1,233	572	46.4	215	156	72.7	463	326	70.3
Was in:												
Northeast	4	2	(B)	2	-	(B)	2	2	(B)	-	-	(B)
Midwest	7	3	(B)	6	3	(B)	-	-	(B)	-	-	(B)
South	40	24	(B)	20	9	(B)	18	15	(B)	7	7	(B)
West	1,548	803	51.9	1,205	561	463.6	195	139	71.4	456	318	68.8
Moved from outside U.S.	117	61	52.5	86	42	48.4	10	9	(B)	46	34	(B)
Did not move	27,495	9,396	34.2	17,127	4,428	25.9	9,471	4,727	49.9	3,068	1,426	46.5
Northeast	6,178	2,030	32.9	4,327	1,137	26.3	1,723	859	49.8	929	558	60.1
Midwest	6,471	2,137	33.0	4,064	917	22.6	2,288	1,174	51.3	164	73	44.8
South	9,986	3,838	38.4	4,942	1,285	26.0	4,892	2,497	51.0	722	264	36.5
West	4,860	1,391	28.6	3,794	1,089	28.7	568	197	34.7	1,254	351	42.3

Source: U.S. Bureau of the Census. Current Population Reports, Series P60-185, *Poverty in the United States: 1992.* Washington, D.C., U.S. Government Printing Office, 1993, pp. 66-67. *Notes:* A dash (-) represents zero or rounds to zero. A (B) indicates base was less than 75,000 or not applicable. NA means not available. 1. Persons of Hispanic origin may be of any race.

★5★

Geographic Mobility

Geographic Mobility of Persons Living Below Poverty, 1992

Figures are shown, by geographic region and race/ethnicity, for persons one year old and older.

Geographic region	All races			White			Black			Hispanic origin[1]		
	Total (000)	Below poverty level: Number (000)	Below poverty level: Percent of total	Total (000)	Below poverty level: Number (000)	Below poverty level: Percent of total	Total (000)	Below poverty level: Number (000)	Below poverty level: Percent of total	Total (000)	Below poverty level: Number (000)	Below poverty level: Percent of total
Persons 1 Year Old And Over												
Total	249,964	35,833	14.3	208,634	23,886	11.4	31,256	10,241	32.8	22,201	6,432	29.0
Moved within U.S.	40,706	9,216	22.6	32,891	6,227	18.9	5,897	2,452	41.6	4,823	1,847	38.3
Now in Northeast	5,060	990	19.6	4,274	721	16.9	561	207	36.8	501	189	37.7
Was in:												
Northeast	4,746	954	20.1	3,993	691	17.3	542	203	37.4	492	187	37.9
Midwest	48	3	(B)	43	2	(B)	2	-	(B)	-	-	(B)
South	203	27	13.4	178	23	12.7	16	4	(B)	7	2	(B)
West	62	5	(B)	60	5	(B)	-	-	(B)	1	-	(B)
Now in Midwest	9,475	1,973	20.8	8,026	1,393	17.4	1,209	510	42.2	418	186	44.4
Was in:												
Northeast	131	31	23.3	113	30	26.6	9	-	(B)	6	4	(B)
Midwest	8,634	1,792	20.8	7,273	1,240	17.0	1,152	490	42.5	384	170	44.3
South	375	78	20.7	335	69	20.6	33	9	(B)	8	-	(B)
West	335	72	21.5	306	55	17.8	15	11	(B)	22	12	(B)
Now in South	15,158	3,769	24.9	11,163	2,158	19.3	3,516	1,473	41.9	1,472	545	37.0
Was in:												
Northeast	412	69	16.7	321	38	12.0	71	21	(B)	62	28	(B)
Midwest	360	71	19.7	304	52	17.0	40	12	(B)	19	4	(B)
South	14,012	3,564	25.4	10,230	2,016	19.7	3,365	1,429	42.5	1,343	496	36.9
West	373	65	17.3	308	51	16.7	40	10	(B)	48	18	(B)
Now in West	11,013	2,485	22.6	9,428	1,956	20.7	612	263	43.1	2,432	927	38.1
Was in:												
Northeast	104	6	5.7	99	4	4.2	2	2	(B)	-	-	(B)
Midwest	199	26	13.1	179	23	12.9	13	2	(B)	11	1	(B)
South	466	63	13.5	397	36	9.1	47	21	(B)	45	20	(B)
West	10,244	2,390	23.3	8,753	1,892	21.6	550	238	43.3	2,375	905	38.1
Moved from outside U.S.	1,305	631	40.7	931	388	41.7	56	13	(B)	414	241	58.2
Did not move	207,953	26,086	12.5	174,812	17,271	9.9	25,303	7,775	30.7	16,964	4,344	25.6
Northeast	44,645	4,969	11.1	38,646	3,403	8.8	4,588	1,401	30.5	2,732	891	32.6
Midwest	50,295	5.742	11.4	44,247	3,834	8.7	5,194	1,750	33.7	1,169	241	20.6
South	70,354	10,379	14.8	55,299	5,919	10.7	13,594	4,281	31.5	5,210	1,284	24.6
West	42,659	4,996	11.7	36,620	4,114	11.2	1,927	343	17.8	7,854	1,929	24.6

Source: U.S. Bureau of the Census. *Poverty in the United States: 1992.* Current Population Reports, Series P60-185, Washington, D.C., U.S. Government Printing Office, 1993, p. 66. *Notes:* A dash (-) stands for zero or rounds to zero. A (B) stands for base less than 75,000 or not applicable. 1. Persons of Hispanic origin may be of any race.

★6★

Geographic Mobility

Geographic Mobility of Persons Living Below Poverty, by Current Residence and Residence One Year Ago, 1992

Numbers of householders are shown in thousands.

Characteristic	All races			White			Black			Hispanic origin[1]		
	Total	Below poverty level		Total	Below poverty level		Total	Below poverty level		Total	Below poverty level	
		Number	Percent of total		Number	Percent of total		Number	Percent of total		Number	Percent of total
FAMILY HOUSEHOLDERS												
Total	68,144	7,960	11.7	57,858	5,160	8.9	7,888	2,435	30.9	5,318	1,395	26.2
Moved within U.S.	9,688	2,044	21.1	7,817	1,309	16.7	1,423	612	43.0	1,110	404	36.4
Now in Northeast	1,218	219	17.9	1,038	165	15.9	134	43	32.3	137	48	35.0
Was in:												
Northeast	1,152	211	18.3	976	157	16.1	131	43	32.8	135	47	35.1
Midwest	8	-	(B)	8	-	(B)	-	-	(B)	-	-	(B)
South	47	6	(B)	42	6	(B)	2	-	(B)	2	1	(B)
West	12	2	(B)	12	2	(B)	-	-	(B)	-	-	(B)
Now in Midwest	2,236	437	19.5	1,889	283	15.0	295	140	47.3	95	41	43.4
Was in:												
Northeast	30	5	(B)	28	5	(B)	-	-	(B)	2	2	(B)
Midwest	2,046	399	19.5	1,716	253	14.7	283	133	47.0	89	39	43.3
South	85	14	16.7	75	11	(B)	8	3	(B)	2	-	(B)
West	76	19	24.5	71	14	(B)	4	4	(B)	3	1	(B)
Now in South	3,728	886	23.8	2,771	494	17.8	849	358	42.2	334	117	35.0
Was in:												
Northeast	100	18	17.5	77	6	8.4	13	2	(B)	13	6	(B)
Midwest	97	14	14.2	82	11	14.1	10	1	(B)	5	1	(B)
South	3,457	841	24.3	2,549	467	18,3	819	353	43.1	307	106	34.5
West	74	13	(B)	63	9	(B)	7	2	(B)	9	4	(B)
Now in West	2,506	503	20.1	2,120	367	17.3	146	71	48.9	544	198	36.3
Was in:												
Northeast	18	1	(B)	17	-	(B)	1	1	(B)	-	-	(B)
Midwest	42	6	(B)	41	5	(B)	1	-	(B)	-	-	(B)
South	121	18	14.7	106	9	8.1	7	7	(B)	11	7	(B)
West	2,325	478	20.6	1,956	353	18.1	137	64	46.6	533	191	35.8
Moved from outside U.S.	279	97	34.8	200	64	31.9	16	6	(B)	65	38	(B)
Did not move	58,177	5,819	10.0	49,841	3,787	7.6	6,449	1,816	28.2	4,143	953	23.0
Northeast	12,210	1,128	9.2	10,759	782	7.3	1,106	309	27.9	730	229	31.4
Midwest	14,053	1,221	8.7	12,541	776	6.2	1,319	417	31.6	299	57	19.2
South	20,189	2,408	11.9	16,324	1,356	8.3	3,507	1,008	28.7	1,312	272	20.7
West	11,725	1,062	9.1	10,217	872	8.5	517	82	15.8	1,802	394	21.9
HOUSEHOLDERS IN MARRIED-COUPLE FAMILIES												
Total	53,171	3,318	6.2	47,601	2,631	5.5	3,748	486	13.0	3,674	680	18.5
Moved within U.S.	6,666	687	10.3	5,794	535	9.2	584	102	17.5	704	193	27.4
Now in Northeast	793	41	5.2	718	34	4.7	45	2	(B)	67	10	(B)
Was in:												
Northeast	737	37	5.0	666	30	4.4	42	2	(B)	65	10	(B)
Midwest	8	-	(B)	8	-	(B)	-	-	(B)	-	-	(B)
South	38	4	(B)	35	4	(B)	2	-	(B)	1	1	(B)
West	10	-	(B)	10	-	(B)	-	-	(B)	-	-	(B)
Now in Midwest	1,543	132	8.5	1,416	98	7.0	100	26	26.4	54	17	(B)
Was in:												
Northeast	27	2	(B)	25	2	(B)	-	-	(B)	2	2	(B)
Midwest	1,388	116	8.4	1,270	86	6.8	94	24	25.7	49	15	(B)
South	66	7	(B)	63	7	(B)	3	-	(B)	-	-	(B)
West	62	6	(B)	58	3	(B)	2	2	(B)	3	1	(B)
Now in South	2,533	320	12.6	2,099	247	11.8	368	56	15.2	238	75	31.4
Was in:												
Northeast	77	11	14.0	64	4	(B)	6	-	(B)	10	4	(B)
Midwest	79	6	7.2	66	4	(B)	7	-	(B)	2	-	(B)
South	2,319	300	12.9	1,918	235	12.2	350	56	16.0	224	71	31.8
West	57	4	(B)	50	4	(B)	4	-	(B)	2	-	(B)
Now in West	1,797	194	10.8	1,562	156	10.0	72	18	(B)	345	90	26.2
Was in:												
Northeast	17	-	(B)	17	-	(B)	-	-	(B)	-	-	(B)
Midwest	38	2	(B)	37	1	(B)	1	-	(B)	-	-	(B)
South	110	8	7.4	102	5	4.6	1	1	(B)	7	3	(B)
West	1,632	185	11.3	1,407	150	10.7	69	17	(B)	338	88	25.9

[Continued]

★6★

Geographic Mobility of Persons Living Below Poverty, by Current Residence and Residence One Year Ago, 1992

[Continued]

Characteristic	All races			White			Black			Hispanic origin[1]		
	Total	Below poverty level		Total	Below poverty level		Total	Below poverty level		Total	Below poverty level	
		Number	Percent of total		Number	Percent of total		Number	Percent of total		Number	Percent of total
Moved from outside U.S.	223	64	28.6	156	42	26.8	12	2	(B)	39	17	(B)
Did not move	46,281	2,567	5.5	41,650	2,054	4.9	3,152	382	12.1	2,930	470	16.1
Northeast	9,556	428	4.5	8,738	350	4.0	530	56	10.6	396	52	13.0
Midwest	11,252	478	4.2	10,564	403	3.8	543	59	10.9	219	28	13.0
South	16,076	1,126	7.0	14,005	849	6.1	1,788	249	13.9	1,011	182	18.0
West	9,397	535	5.7	8,342	452	5.4	291	18	6.2	1,304	208	16.0
HOUSEHOLDERS IN FAMILIES WITH FEMALE HOUSEHOLDER, NO SPOUSE PRESENT												
Total	11,947	4,171	34.9	7,848	2,202	28.1	3,680	1,835	49.8	1,238	604	48.8
Moved within U.S.	2,416	1,214	50.3	1,540	674	43.8	756	479	63.4	290	177	60.9
Now in Northeast	344	170	49.6	255	126	49.5	80	41	51.5	58	33	(B)
Was in:												
Northeast	336	167	49.6	247	122	49.5	80	41	51.5	58	33	(B)
Midwest	-	-	(B)	-	-	(B)	-	-	(B)	-	-	(B)
South	5	2	(B)	5	2	(B)	-	-	(B)	-	-	(B)
West	2	2	(B)	2	2	(B)	-	-	(B)	-	-	(B)
Now in Midwest	565	261	46.2	367	148	40.4	179	105	58.6	31	17	(B)
Was in:												
Northeast	3	3	(B)	3	3	(B)	-	-	(B)	-	-	(B)
Midwest	540	247	45.6	349	136	39.1	175	103	58.9	29	17	(B)
South	11	3	(B)	7	3	(B)	2	-	(B)	2	-	(B)
West	11	8	(B)	9	7	(B)	2	2	(B)	-	-	(B)
Now in South	992	518	52.2	526	218	41.5	432	287	66.4	67	33	(B)
Was in:												
Northeast	9	4	(B)	5	2	(B)	4	2	(B)	2	2	(B)
Midwest	15	7	(B)	12	6	(B)	3	1	(B)	4	1	(B)
South	956	498	52.0	501	205	40.8	423	282	66.6	58	26	(B)
West	11	9	(B)	7	5	(B)	2	2	(B)	4	4	(B)
Now in West	516	265	51.3	392	181	46.3	64	46	(B)	134	93	69.4
Was in:												
Northeast	1	1	(B)	-	-	(B)	1	1	(B)	-	-	(B)
Midwest	1	-	(B)	1	-	(B)	-	-	(B)	-	-	(B)
South	10	10	(B)	5	4	(B)	6	6	(B)	4	4	(B)
West	504	254	50.4	387	177	45.8	58	40	(B)	130	89	68.4
Moved from outside U.S.	37	22	(B)	27	13	(B)	4	4	(B)	12	10	(B)
Did not move	9,494	2,935	30.9	6,281	1,516	24.1	2,920	1,351	46.3	935	418	44.7
Northeast	2,129	640	30.1	1,579	390	24.7	509	239	47.0	297	171	57.6
Midwest	2,218	665	30.0	1,504	324	21.6	680	331	48.6	55	24	(B)
South	3,435	1,187	34.6	1,844	455	24.7	1,536	717	46.7	224	75	33.4
West	1,712	442	25.8	1,354	346	25.6	195	63	32.2	359	147	41.1

Source: U.S. Bureau of the Census. Current Population Reports, Series P60-185, *Poverty in the United States: 1992.* Washington, D.C., U.S. Government Printing Office, 1993, pp. 68-69. *Notes:* A dash (-) represents zero or rounds to zero. A (B) indicates base was less than 75,000 or not applicable. 1. Persons of Hispanic origin may be of any race.

★7★

Geographic Mobility

Geographic Mobility of Unrelated Individuals Living Below Poverty, by Current Residence and Residence One Year Ago, 1992

Numbers of persons are shown in thousands.

Characteristic	All races			White			Black			Hispanic origin[1]		
	Total	Below poverty level		Total	Below poverty level		Total	Below poverty level		Total	Below poverty level	
		Number	Percent of total		Number	Percent of total		Number	Percent of total		Number	Percent of total
UNRELATED INDIVIDUALS												
Total	36,734	7,991	21.8	31,176	6,087	19.5	4,431	1,584	35.8	2,278	777	34.1
Moved within U.S.	9,448	2,274	24.1	7,963	1,786	22.4	1,008	361	33.2	735	260	35.3
Now in Northeast	1,337	287	21.5	1,165	225	19.4	114	39	34.2	71	19	(B)
Was in:												
Northeast	1,254	272	21.7	1,092	215	19.7	108	36	33.8	70	19	(B)
Midwest	15	3	(B)	12	2	(B)	2	-	(B)	-	-	(B)
South	53	11	(B)	45	7	(B)	5	3	(B)	-	-	(B)
West	15	1	(B)	15	1	(B)	-	-	(B)	-	-	(B)
Now in Midwest	2,398	548	22.8	2,117	459	21.7	222	71	31.9	76	18	23.7
Was in:												
Northeast	37	12	(B)	32	12	(B)	5	-	(B)	2	-	(B)
Midwest	2,225	506	22.8	1,972	425	21.5	206	67	32.4	70	18	(B)
South	68	21	(B)	57	17	(B)	8	4	(B)	3	-	(B)
West	68	9	(B)	55	6	(B)	3	-	(B)	1	-	(B)
Now in South	3,186	809	25.4	2,447	563	23.0	636	209	32.9	236	95	40.5
Was in:												
Northeast	93	12	12.4	72	5	(B)	20	6	(B)	10	4	(B)
Midwest	78	21	27.2	69	14	(B)	7	6	(B)	4	-	(B)
South	2,948	757	25.7	2,252	527	23.4	605	194	32.1	215	88	40.9
West	67	20	(B)	55	17	(B)	5	2	(B)	6	4	(B)
Now in West	2,527	630	24.9	2,234	539	24.1	115	41	36.0	352	127	36.1
Was in:												
Northeast	47	4	(B)	44	4	(B)	-	-	(B)	-	-	(B)
Midwest	59	12	(B)	52	10	(B)	7	2	(B)	3	-	(B)
South	72	13	(B)	62	10	(B)	9	1	(B)	4	2	(B)
West	2,348	600	25.6	2,076	514	24.7	99	38	38.3	346	125	36.2
Moved from outside U.S.	236	141	59.5	162	106	65.4	14	3	(B)	70	59	(B)
Did not move	27,050	5,577	20.6	23,050	4,194	18.2	3,329	1,220	36.7	1,472	459	31.2
Northeast	6,151	1,191	19.4	5,306	895	16.9	717	257	35.9	319	105	33.0
Midwest	6,580	1,335	20.3	5,804	1,063	18.3	685	240	35.0	89	14	15.3
South	8,511	2,046	24.0	6,774	1,377	20.3	1,634	644	39.4	412	151	36.5
West	5,808	1,004	17.3	5,166	858	16.6	293	79	27.0	651	189	29.1

Source: U.S. Bureau of the Census. Current Population Reports, Series P60-185, *Poverty in the United States: 1992.* Washington, D.C., U.S. Government Printing Office, 1993, p. 67. *Notes:* A dash (-) represents zero or rounds to zero. A (B) indicates base was less than 75,000 or not applicable. 1. Persons of Hispanic origin may be of any race.

★8★

Geographic Mobility

Reasons for Move and Choice of Current Residence in Housing Units With a Hispanic Householder, 1991

Numbers are shown in thousands.

Reason for moving	Total occupied units	Tenure		Housing unit characteristics				Household characteristics		
		Owner	Renter	New construction 4 yrs	Mobile homes	Physical problems: Severe	Physical problems: Moderate	Elderly (65+)	Moved in past year	Below poverty level
RESPONDENT MOVED DURING PAST YEAR										
Total	1,760	249	1,511	112	46	69	146	55	1,714	511
Reasons for leaving previous unit[1]										
Private displacement	82	7	75	8	1	-	9	2	78	14
Owner to move into unit	15	-	15	-	1	-	-	2	15	3
To be converted to condominium or cooperative	3	-	3	-	-	-	-	-	3	-
Closed for repairs	7	-	7	-	-	-	-	-	7	-
Other	38	7	31	5	-	-	6	-	34	7
Not reported	19	-	19	3	-	-	2	-	19	4
Government displacement	25	2	23	-	-	-	8	-	25	7
Government wanted building or land	3	-	2	-	-	-	3	-	3	-
Unit unfit for occupancy	2	-	2	-	-	-	-	-	2	2
Other	11	-	11	-	-	-	2	-	11	2
Not reported	8	2	6	-	-	-	2	-	8	2
Disaster loss (fire, flood, etc.)	5	-	5	-	-	-	-	-	5	5
New job or job transfer	150	28	122	14	2	-	5	-	139	29
To be closer to work/school/other	177	9	157	11	4	6	13	2	177	18
Other, financial/employment related	103	7	96	5	2	12	6	8	98	36
To establish own household	241	26	215	10	4	10	17	6	238	72
Needed larger house or apartment	268	35	233	19	4	4	19	7	268	70
Married	30	9	21	8	2	-	-	-	28	6
Widowed, divorced, or separated	74	14	60	-	5	1	2	4	66	25
Other, family/person related	177	15	162	8	7	12	20	13	154	70
Wanted better home	301	29	272	21	3	7	23	4	301	86
Change from owner to renter	9	-	9	-	-	-	-	-	9	-
Change from renter to owner	51	51	-	6	-	-	-	2	51	5
Wanted lower rent or maintenance	166	8	157	6	3	3	21	5	166	57
Other housing related reasons	135	26	109	12	15	6	15	8	133	42
Other	260	35	225	22	2	11	37	6	260	71
Not reported	55	10	45	-	2	6	4	6	49	26
Choice of present home[1]										
Financial reasons	704	112	592	44	26	30	50	25	693	211
Room layout/design	254	52	22	31	-	3	5	5	252	49
Kitchen	38	8	30	3	-	-	3	-	38	3
Size	323	55	268	38	3	8	18	2	321	75
Exterior appearance	90	24	66	12	-	-	-	2	88	20
Yard/trees/view	99	31	67	7	-	-	7	-	95	10
Quality of construction	67	17	49	19	-	-	2	-	67	12
Only one available	268	18	250	3	8	11	45	9	266	101
Other	501	57	444	34	8	18	49	15	485	113

Source: U.S. Department of Housing and Urban Development. Office of Policy Development and Research. *Current Housing Reports, American Housing Survey for the United States in 1991,* Washington, DC: U.S. Government Printing Office, April 1993, p. 274. *Notes:* 1. Figures may not add to total because more than one category may apply to unit.

★9★

Geographic Mobility

Central City Geographic Mobility, by Years of School Completed, 1991-92

The number, in thousands, of movers and nonmovers is shown, by Hispanic origin of person, years of school completed, and detailed mobility, from March 1991 to March 1992.

Characteristic	Total	Same house (nonmovers)	Different house in United States									Movers from abroad
					Different county							
							Different state					
								Same region				
			Total	Same county	Total	Same state	Total	Total	Same division	Different division	Different region	
Family households of all races												
All households												
Householders 15 to 54 years old	46,742	37,744	8,766	5,831	2,935	1,545	1,390	745	465	281	645	233
No own children under 18	14,989	12,315	2,602	1,634	968	487	481	253	134	118	229	72
With own children under 18	31,753	25,429	6,164	4,197	1,966	1,058	908	493	330	162	416	161
Under 6 only	8,209	5,730	2,415	1,664	751	400	350	171	120	51	179	65
Under 6 and 6 to 17	7,054	5,709	1,314	915	399	200	199	114	73	42	85	31
6 to 17 only	16,489	13,989	2,435	1,618	817	458	359	207	137	69	152	65
Married-couple households												
Householders 15 to 54 years old	35,511	29,556	5,750	3,603	2,147	1,084	1,063	545	336	209	519	205
No own children under 18	11,901	9,805	2,035	1,228	807	386	421	209	108	101	212	61
With own children under 18	23,610	19,752	3,715	2,375	1,340	698	642	335	227	108	307	143
Under 6 only	6,346	4,737	1,557	1,019	539	281	258	126	93	33	131	52
Under 6 and 6 to 17	5,486	4,587	868	570	298	140	158	87	53	34	71	31
6 to 17 only	11,778	10,428	1,290	786	504	277	227	122	82	41	104	60
Single-parent households												
Householders 15 to 54 years old	11,231	8,187	3,016	2,228	788	461	326	201	129	72	126	28
No own children under 18	3,088	2,510	567	406	161	101	60	43	26	17	17	11
With own children under 18	8,143	5,677	2,449	1,823	626	360	266	157	103	54	109	17
Under 6 only	1,863	993	857	645	212	119	93	45	27	18	47	13
Under 6 and 6 to 17	1,569	1,122	446	345	101	60	41	27	20	7	14	-
6 to 17 only	4,711	3,561	1,145	832	314	181	132	85	56	29	48	5
Female single-parent households												
Householders 15 to 54 years old	8,941	6,464	2,454	1,835	618	359	260	152	102	51	107	24
No own children under 18	1,998	1,650	341	255	86	55	31	22	11	11	9	7
With own children under 18	6,943	4,813	2,113	1,581	532	303	228	130	91	39	98	17
Under 6 only	1,521	796	713	541	172	91	81	40	26	14	41	13
Under 6 and 6 to 17	1,414	1,001	414	322	91	56	35	21	16	5	14	-
6 to 17 only	4,008	3,017	986	718	269	156	113	70	49	21	43	5
Hispanic family householders[1]												
All Households												
Householders 15 to 54 years old	4,173	3,165	964	729	235	134	101	43	22	21	58	44
No own children under 18	960	736	214	155	59	31	28	14	2	12	14	10
With own children under 18	3,213	2,430	750	574	176	103	73	29	20	9	44	33
Under 6 only	821	541	268	201	67	37	30	14	9	5	16	12
Under 6 and 6 to 17	947	703	239	190	49	32	17	5	5	-	12	5
6 to 17 only	1,445	1,186	243	183	60	34	26	10	6	3	16	16
Married-couple households												
Householders 15 to 54 years old	2,817	2,158	623	465	159	86	73	27	14	13	46	35
No own children under 18	583	436	138	99	39	19	21	8	-	8	12	8
With own children under 18	2,234	1,722	485	366	119	67	52	19	14	5	33	27
Under 6 only	621	420	193	147	46	26	20	11	8	3	9	8

[Continued]

★9★

Central City Geographic Mobility, by Years of School Completed, 1991-92

[Continued]

Characteristic	Total	Same house (nonmovers)	Different house in United States										Movers from abroad
			Total	Same county	Different county								
					Total	Same state	Different state						
							Total	Same region			Different region		
								Total	Same division	Different division			
Under 6 and 6 to 17	688	521	161	125	36	22	14	2	2	-	12		5
6 to 17 only	926	781	131	94	38	20	18	6	3	2	12		14
Single-parent households													
Householders 15 to 54 years old	1,357	1,007	341	264	76	48	28	16	8	8	12		8
No own children under 18	377	299	76	56	20	12	7	6	2	4	1		2
With own children under 18	979	708	265	208	57	36	21	10	6	4	11		6
Under 6 only	201	121	75	54	21	11	10	3	1	2	7		5
Under 6 and 6 to 17	260	182	78	65	13	10	3	3	3	-	-		-
6 to 17 only	519	406	112	89	22	15	8	4	3	1	4		1
Female single-parent households													
Householders 15 to 54 years old	1,033	768	259	202	57	38	19	10	6	4	10		7
No own children under 18	201	169	31	21	10	7	3	2	-	2	1		1
With own children under 18	832	598	228	181	47	31	16	8	6	2	8		6
Under 6 only	159	92	62	47	15	9	6	1	-	1	5		5
Under 6 and 6 to 17	232	159	73	59	13	10	3	3	3	-	-		-
6 to 17 only	442	348	94	75	19	12	7	4	3	1	3		1

Source: Hansen, Kristin A. U.S. Bureau of the Census. *Geographic Mobility: March 1991 to March 1992.* Current Population Reports, P20-473. Washington, DC: U.S. Government Printing Office, 1993, pp. 31-32. *Notes:* A dash (-) represents zero or rounds to zero. 1. Persons of Hispanic origin may be of any race.

Immigration

★10★

Immigrants Admitted from Top Fifteen Countries of Birth, 1993

Data show number of persons admitted as legalization immigrants under the Immigration Reform and Control Act (IRCA) and as non-legalization immigrants. A legalization applicant is an alien who has been continuously in the U.S. unlawfully since January 1, 1982. That person must also have either 1) entered the country illegally before that date; or 2) have been a temporary visitor, with a visit authorization expiring before January 1, 1982 or with the Government's knowledge of unlawful status before that date. Mexico was the leading source of immigrants overall and accounted for more than 70 percent of IRCA legalization.

Country of birth	Rank	Total		Non-legalization		IRCA legalization[1]	
		Number	Percent	Number	Percent	Number	Percent
All countries		904,292	100.0	880,014	100.0	24,278	100.0
Mexico	1	126,561	14.0	109,027	12.4	17,534	72.2
China, Mainland	2	65,578	7.3	65,552	7.4	26	.1
Philippines	3	63,457	7.0	63,189	7.2	268	1.1

[Continued]

★ 10 ★

Immigrants Admitted from Top Fifteen Countries of Birth, 1993

[Continued]

Country of birth	Rank	Total		Non-legalization		IRCA legalization[1]	
		Number	Percent	Number	Percent	Number	Percent
Vietnam	4	59,614	6.6	59,613	6.8	1	[2]
Soviet Union	5	58,571	6.5	58,568	6.7	3	[2]
Dominican Republic	6	45,420	5.0	44,886	5.1	534	2.2
India	7	40,121	4.4	40,021	4.5	100	.4
Poland	8	27,846	3.1	27,729	3.2	117	.5
El Salvador	9	26,818	3.0	25,517	2.9	1,301	5.4
United Kingdom	10	18,783	2.1	18,712	2.1	71	.3
Korea	11	18,026	2.0	17,949	2.0	77	.3
Jamaica	12	17,241	1.9	16,969	1.9	272	1.1
Canada	13	17,156	1.9	17,081	1.9	75	.3
Iran	14	14,841	1.6	14,700	1.7	141	.6
Taiwan	15	14,329	1.6	14,309	1.6	20	.1
Other		289,930	32.1	286,192	32.5	3,738	15.4

Source: U.S. Immigration and Naturalization Service, *Statistical Yearbook of the Immigration and Naturalization Service, 1993*, U.S. Government Printing Office, Washington, DC, 1994, p. 21. *Notes:* 1. IRCA stands for Immigration Reform and Control Act. 2. Rounds to less than 0.5 percent.

★ 11 ★

Immigration

Immigrants Admitted, by Age, Sex, and Selected Country of Birth, 1993 - I

Data show number of immigrants admitted during fiscal year 1993.

Age and sex	All countries	Canada	China, Mainland	Colombia	Cuba	Dominican Republic	Ecuador	El Salvador	Germany	Guatemala
Total	904,292	17,156	65,578	12,819	13,666	45,420	7,324	26,818	7,312	11,870
Under 5 years	39,111	1,070	1,067	754	212	3,268	411	425	335	699
5-9 years	62,949	1,532	2,549	772	472	3,901	656	1,155	411	700
10-14 years	78,157	1,535	2,618	1,229	483	4,552	902	4,653	289	1,852
15-19 years	95,514	1,391	2,429	1,177	821	5,382	1,033	6,607	365	2,332
20-24 years	96,237	1,455	3,129	989	902	4,884	737	2,994	1,269	1,213
25-29 years	122,787	2,328	8,492	1,825	1,265	7,146	910	3,428	1,726	1,394
30-34 years	108,815	2,415	13,408	1,882	1,243	5,212	754	2,683	1,075	1,258
35-39 years	78,887	1,999	10,330	1,361	981	3,665	557	1,641	617	851
40-44 years	56,100	1,377	5,443	804	1,180	2,300	376	1,035	375	594
45-49 years	41,378	904	4,211	524	1,410	1,401	246	631	308	341
50-54 years	31,484	495	2,592	415	1,305	1,076	197	396	219	228
55-59 years	28,246	286	2,603	337	1,001	863	167	386	116	152
60-64 years	24,758	157	2,423	295	857	721	162	295	60	98
65-69 years	19,400	102	2,124	206	602	533	100	219	40	78
70-74 years	11,131	63	1,248	117	422	273	56	153	40	43
75-79 years	5,347	28	554	82	251	163	40	75	20	17
80 years and over	3,888	19	335	48	259	79	20	42	46	20
Unknown age	103	-	23	2	-	1	-	-	1	-
Male	424,475	8,431	33,013	5,260	7,248	21,942	3,304	12,507	2,309	5,588
Under 5 years	19,550	554	416	386	116	1,647	222	224	161	371

[Continued]

★ 11 ★

Immigrants Admitted, by Age, Sex, and Selected Country of Birth, 1993 - I

[Continued]

Age and sex	All countries	Canada	China, Mainland	Colombia	Cuba	Dominican Republic	Ecuador	El Salvador	Germany	Guatemala
5-9 years	32,092	772	1,323	397	257	1,958	336	576	214	370
10-14 years	40,286	767	1,421	627	260	2,272	463	2,393	158	939
15-19 years	48,672	731	1,253	601	403	2,603	517	3,346	106	1,196
20-24 years	41,829	607	994	371	480	2,172	311	1,497	124	644
25-29 years	54,859	1,063	3,751	716	759	3,628	422	1,572	360	632
30-34 years	51,845	1,195	7,280	713	708	2,592	318	1,095	379	510
35-39 years	37,413	946	5,727	490	560	1,822	219	641	278	334
40-44 years	25,560	695	2,861	283	645	1,045	136	374	162	220
45-49 years	19,388	494	2,322	190	794	623	95	226	134	122
50-54 years	13,889	245	1,318	122	713	437	64	126	111	88
55-59 years	11,916	166	1,148	105	530	352	55	133	58	62
60-64 years	10,318	83	1,052	102	415	30	54	112	30	37
65-69 years	8,110	51	1,051	63	278	236	44	74	17	26
70-74 years	4,841	36	638	47	170	120	20	66	9	20
75-79 years	2,284	21	279	23	88	66	20	35	2	6
80 years and over	1,565	5	168	23	72	38	8	17	6	11
Unknown age	58	-	11	1	-	1	-	-	-	-
Female	479,771	8,724	32,552	7,559	6,417	23,477	4,020	14,310	5,003	6,282
Under 5 years	19,561	516	651	368	96	1,621	189	201	174	328
5-9 years	30,855	760	1,226	375	215	1,943	320	579	197	330
10-14 years	37,866	768	1,196	602	223	2,279	439	2,259	131	913
15-19 years	46,838	660	1,176	576	418	2,779	516	3,261	259	1,136
20-24 years	54,403	848	2,134	618	422	2,712	426	1,497	1,145	569
25-29 years	67,922	1,265	4,738	1,109	506	3,518	488	1,856	1,366	762
30-34 years	56,962	1,220	6,122	1,169	535	2,620	436	1,588	696	748
35-39 years	41,472	1,053	4,603	871	421	1,843	338	1,000	339	517
40-44 years	30,534	681	2,581	521	535	1,255	540	661	213	374
45-49 years	21,986	410	1,889	334	615	778	151	405	174	219
50-54 years	17,594	250	1,274	293	592	639	133	270	108	140
55-59 years	16,330	120	1,455	232	471	511	112	253	58	90
60-64 years	14,438	74	1,370	193	442	391	108	183	30	61
65-69 years	11,290	51	1,073	143	324	297	56	145	23	52
70-74 years	6,289	27	610	70	252	153	36	87	31	23
75-79 years	3,063	7	275	59	163	97	20	40	18	11
80 years and over	2,323	14	167	25	187	41	12	25	40	9
Unknown age	45	-	12	1	-	-	-	-	1	-
Unknown sex	46	1	13	-	1	1	-	1	-	-
Percent distribution	100.0	100.0	100.0	100.0	100.0	100.0	100.0	100.0	100.0	100.0
Male	46.9	49.1	50.3	41.0	53.0	48.3	45.1	46.6	31.6	47.1
Female	53.1	50.9	49.6	59.0	47.0	51.7	54.9	53.4	68.4	52.9
Median age	28.3	28.6	34.6	29.2	41.9	25.5	24.5	20.8	27.8	21.2
Male	27.8	28.9	35.0	26.9	40.6	25.4	21.5	19.6	30.4	19.7
Female	28.7	28.3	34.1	30.5	43.6	25.5	26.2	22.4	27.0	23.9

Source: U.S. Immigration and Naturalization Service, *Statistical Yearbook of the Immigration and Naturalization Service, 1993,* U.S. Government Printing Office, Washington, DC, 1994, pp. 53-55. *Note:* A dash (-) represents zero.

★ 12 ★

Immigration

Immigrants Admitted, by Age, Sex, and Selected Country of Birth, 1993 - II

Data show number of immigrants admitted during fiscal year 1993.

Age and sex	All countries	Guyana	Haiti	Hong Kong	India	Iran	Ireland	Honduras	Jamaica	Korea	Mexico
Total	904,292	8,384	10,094	9,161	40,121	14,841	13,590	7,306	17,241	18,026	126,561
Under 5 years	39,111	278	367	507	1,932	196	260	378	703	2,350	4,247
5-9 years	62,949	499	361	697	1,944	640	299	603	1,492	726	12,857
10-14 years	78,157	901	1,467	1,029	2,337	897	275	1,035	2,100	1,395	14,743
15-19 years	95,514	1,097	2,008	1,171	2,827	762	905	1,168	2,278	1,477	19,914
20-24 years	96,237	642	989	513	4,401	833	4,404	818	1,447	1,199	18,543
25-29 years	122,787	689	978	1,192	7,189	1,634	3,556	947	1,912	2,127	18,592
30-34 years	108,815	740	920	1,343	4,620	1,828	1,789	816	2,033	2,117	11,898
35-39 years	78,887	709	695	1,005	3,079	1,429	855	528	1,440	1,851	7,566
40-44 years	56,100	673	478	820	2,402	1,091	457	337	1,033	1,194	5,184
45-49 years	41,378	516	311	358	1,936	867	333	174	810	1,019	3,918
50-54 years	31,484	484	275	181	1,931	787	225	128	619	685	2,919
55-59 years	28,246	457	316	157	1,929	950	153	125	450	539	2,252
60-64 years	24,758	336	328	76	1,659	1,076	49	91	390	516	1,682
65-69 years	19,400	211	293	56	1,148	928	13	72	240	357	1,071
70-74 years	11,131	97	171	38	652	569	8	51	152	251	607
75-79 years	5,347	34	86	10	283	212	5	25	87	145	293
80 years and over	3,888	21	50	7	149	141	4	10	54	78	260
Unknown age	103	-	1	1	-	1	-	-	1	-	15
Male	424,475	3,862	4,484	4,407	18,822	6,930	7,384	3,158	8,343	7,545	58,780
Under 5 years	19,550	131	173	258	965	99	133	175	370	1,173	2,164
5-9 years	32,092	254	171	350	998	326	166	308	774	385	6,545
10-14 years	40,286	453	738	532	1,209	501	141	512	1,019	738	7,560
15-19 years	48,672	510	991	610	1,382	392	492	572	1,157	769	10,465
20-24 years	41,829	237	456	219	941	315	2,315	353	673	321	9,089
25-29 years	54,859	323	439	519	3,440	654	1,940	393	957	540	8,173
30-34 years	51,845	336	437	643	2,613	854	1,024	312	1,066	797	4,973
35-39 years	37,413	329	304	486	1,580	675	499	204	746	817	3,017
40-44 years	25,560	320	182	370	1,215	521	258	114	476	502	1,938
45-49 years	19,388	239	120	161	882	433	184	60	364	489	1,368
50-54 years	13,889	222	88	91	825	296	112	47	263	335	1,044
55-59 years	11,916	2041	83	79	866	367	77	36	178	202	815
60-64 years	10,318	157	94	36	801	503	31	27	135	175	659
65-69 years	8,110	94	90	24	544	462	5	19	78	126	432
70-74 years	4,841	34	59	19	328	331	3	15	44	99	280
75-79 years	2,284	12	36	4	152	123	3	9	27	44	138
80 years and over	1,565	10	22	5	81	77	1	2	15	33	110
Unknown age	58	-	1	1	-	1	-	-	1	-	10
Female	479,771	4,522	5,609	4,754	21,296	7,908	6,206	4,148	8,898	10,480	67,778
Under 5 years	19,561	147	194	249	967	97	127	203	333	1,177	2,083
5-9 years	30,855	245	190	347	946	313	133	295	718	341	6,312
10-14 years	37,866	448	729	497	1,128	396	134	523	1,081	657	7,183
15-19 years	46,838	587	1,016	561	1,445	370	413	596	1,121	708	9,448
20-24 years	54,403	405	533	294	3,163	518	2,089	465	774	877	9,453
25-29 years	67,922	366	539	673	3,748	980	1,616	554	955	1,587	10,419
30-34 years	56,962	404	483	700	2,007	973	765	504	967	1,320	6,925
35-39 years	41,472	380	391	519	1,498	754	356	324	694	1,034	4,549
40-44 years	30,534	353	296	450	1,187	570	199	223	557	692	3,245
45-49 years	21,986	277	191	197	1,053	434	149	114	446	530	2,550

[Continued]

★ 12 ★

Immigrants Admitted, by Age, Sex, and Selected Country of Birth, 1993 - II

[Continued]

Age and sex	All countries	Guyana	Haiti	Hong Kong	India	Iran	Ireland	Honduras	Jamaica	Korea	Mexico
50-54 years	17,594	262	187	90	1,106	491	113	81	356	350	1,875
55-59 years	16,330	256	233	78	1,063	583	76	89	272	337	1,437
60-64 years	14,438	179	234	40	858	573	18	64	255	341	1,023
65-69 years	11,290	117	203	32	604	466	8	53	162	231	639
70-74 years	6,289	63	112	19	324	237	5	36	108	152	324
75-79 years	6,063	22	50	6	131	89	2	16	60	101	155
80 years and over	2,323	11	28	2	68	64	3	8	39	45	150
Unknown age	45	-	-	-	-	-	-	-	-	-	5
Unknown sex	46	-	1	-	3	3	-	-	-	1	3
Percent distribution	100.0	100.0	100.0	100.0	100.0	100.0	100.0	100.0	100.0	100.0	100.0
Male	46.9	46.1	44.4	48.1	46.9	46.7	54.3	43.2	48.4	41.9	46.4
Female	53.1	53.9	55.6	51.9	53.1	53.3	45.7	56.8	51.6	58.1	53.6
Median age	28.3	30.6	24.2	28.2	29.8	37.1	25.7	22.8	26.8	29.4	23.1
Male	27.8	30.4	21.4	27.7	30.7	37.4	25.9	20.1	26.2	28.8	21.3
Female	28.7	30.8	26.4	28.5	28.8	36.9	25.5	24.9	27.4	29.6	24.7

Source: U.S. Immigration and Naturalization Service, *Statistical Yearbook of the Immigration and Naturalization Service, 1993,* U.S. Government Printing Office, Washington, DC, 1994, pp. 53-55. *Note:* A dash (-) represents zero.

★ 13 ★

Immigration

Immigrants Admitted, by Age, Sex, and Selected Country of Birth, 1993 - III

Data show number of immigrants admitted during fiscal year 1993.

Age and sex	All countries	Pakistan	Peru	Philippines	Poland	Soviet Union	Taiwan	United Kingdom	Vietnam	Other
Total	904,292	8,927	10,447	63,457	27,846	58,571	14,329	18,783	59,614	169,030
Under 5 years	39,111	778	495	2,448	1,470	3,451	364	716	2,155	7,775
5-9 years	62,949	677	600	4,260	1,928	5,540	695	1,145	4,093	11,745
10-14 years	78,157	668	1,012	5,435	2,426	4,754	1,416	1,159	4,248	12,747
15-19 years	95,514	808	1,196	6,533	3,071	4,029	1,234	1,040	7,786	14,673
20-24 years	96,237	900	898	4,831	2,730	3,779	577	2,097	10,867	18,494
25-29 years	122,787	1,210	1,160	7,021	3,041	4,154	1,848	3,682	6,077	27,264
30-34 years	108,815	965	1,151	7,577	3,006	5,295	2,970	3,074	3,652	23,091
35-39 years	78,887	667	915	5,770	2,993	4,868	1,842	1,931	3,333	15,409
40-44 years	56,100	474	655	3,845	2,619	4,490	1,421	1,443	3,862	10,138
45-49 years	41,378	398	444	2,779	1,675	2,948	548	1,116	3,851	7,401
50-54 years	31,484	352	327	2,501	1,092	2,385	368	581	3,168	5,553
55-59 years	28,246	371	419	2,753	838	2,950	328	344	2,449	4,555
60-64 years	24,758	291	396	2,982	499	2,946	301	177	1,917	3,978
65-69 years	19,400	218	332	2,545	257	3,162	220	111	1,098	3,064
70-74 years	11,131	88	251	1,375	108	1,843	118	72	610	1,655
75-79 years	5,347	39	118	543	51	1,010	58	45	274	799
80 years and over	3,888	22	78	257	41	945	21	49	160	673

[Continued]

★ 13 ★

Immigrants Admitted, by Age, Sex, and Selected Country of Birth, 1993 - III

[Continued]

Age and sex	All countries	Pakistan	Peru	Philippines	Poland	Soviet Union	Taiwan	United Kingdom	Vietnam	Other
Unknown age	103	1	-	2	1	22	-	1	14	16
Male	424,475	4,301	4,595	25,363	13,229	27,797	6,264	9,680	28,508	81,421
Under 5 years	19,550	403	235	1,261	721	1,732	204	332	1,056	3,868
5-9 years	32,092	368	307	2,195	980	2,779	341	556	2,136	5,950
10-14 years	40,286	343	503	2,718	1,245	2,500	780	612	2,193	6,689
15-19 years	48,672	430	600	3,274	1,601	2,089	574	516	4,091	7,401
20-24 years	41,829	286	370	1,557	1,238	1,785	244	871	5,527	7,832
25-29 years	54,859	554	491	2,036	1,338	1,901	560	1,808	2,938	12,952
30-34 years	51,845	513	479	2,930	1,464	2,438	1,288	1,668	1,460	11,760
35-39 years	37,413	340	388	2,376	1,408	2,353	823	1,071	1,190	7,790
40-44 years	25,560	251	276	1,590	1,208	2,148	612	823	1,363	4,972
45-49 years	19,388	171	204	1,084	797	1,488	269	659	1,879	3,537
50-54 years	13,889	131	115	945	468	1,074	158	323	1,644	2,484
55-59 years	11,916	182	140	984	367	1,287	132	201	1,151	1,959
60-64 years	10,318	134	152	925	212	1,329	97	106	921	1,609
65-69 years	8,110	110	146	755	98	1,312	97	65	508	1,305
70-74 years	4,841	49	110	438	45	780	52	30	268	731
75-79 years	2,284	20	48	192	20	423	24	23	122	324
80 years and over	1,565	16	31	102	19	367	9	16	52	249
Unknown age	58	-	-	1	-	12	-	-	9	9
Female	479,771	4,626	5,852	38,094	14,617	30,767	8,065	9,102	31,103	87,602
Under 5 years	19,561	375	260	1,187	749	1,719	160	384	1,099	3,907
5-9 years	30,855	309	293	2,065	948	2,760	354	589	1,957	5,795
10-14 years	37,866	325	509	2,717	1,181	2,254	636	547	2,055	6,056
15-19 years	46,838	378	596	3,259	1,470	1,939	660	524	3,695	7,271
20-24 years	54,403	614	528	3,274	1,492	1,994	333	1,226	5,339	10,661
25-29 years	67,922	656	669	4,985	1,703	2,253	1,288	1,874	3,139	14,310
30-34 years	56,962	452	672	4,647	1,542	2,857	1,682	1,406	2,191	11,331
35-39 years	41,472	327	527	3,394	1,585	2,514	1,019	860	2,143	7,619
40-44 years	30,534	223	379	2,255	1,411	2,340	809	620	2,499	5,165
45-49 years	21,986	227	240	1,695	878	1,460	279	456	1,971	3,864
50-54 years	17,594	221	212	1,556	624	1,310	210	258	1,524	3,069
55-59 years	16,330	189	279	1,769	471	1,663	196	143	1,298	2,596
60-64 years	14,438	157	244	2,057	287	1,616	204	71	996	2,369
65-69 years	11,290	108	186	1,790	159	1,850	123	46	590	1,759
70-74 years	6,289	39	141	937	63	1,063	66	42	342	924
75-79 years	3,063	19	70	351	31	587	34	22	152	475
80 years and over	2,323	6	47	155	22	578	12	33	108	424
Unknown age	45	1	-	1	1	10	-	1	5	7
Unknown sex	46	-	-	-	-	7	-	1	3	7
Percent distribution	100.0	100.0	100.0	100.0	100.0	100.0	100.0	100.0	100.0	100.0
Male	46.9	48.2	44.0	40.0	47.5	47.5	43.7	51.5	47.8	48.2

[Continued]

★ 13 ★

Immigrants Admitted, by Age, Sex, and Selected Country of Birth, 1993 - III

[Continued]

Age and sex	All countries	Pakistan	Peru	Philippines	Poland	Soviet Union	Taiwan	United Kingdom	Vietnam	Other
Female	53.1	51.8	56.0	60.0	52.5	52.5	56.3	48.5	52.2	51.8
Median age	28.3	27.7	29.4	30.8	28.8	33.4	31.6	29.4	25.5	28.5
Male	27.8	28.2	27.9	29.3	28.1	32.4	31.7	30.4	24.2	28.5
Female	28.7	27.2	30.5	31.7	29.3	34.4	31.5	28.4	27.0	28.5

Source: U.S. Immigration and Naturalization Service, *Statistical Yearbook of the Immigration and Naturalization Service, 1993*, U.S. Government Printing Office, Washington, DC, 1994, pp. 53-55. *Note:* A dash (-) represents zero.

★ 14 ★

Immigration

Immigrants Admitted, by Major Occupational Group and Selected Country of Birth, 1993

Approximately 36 percent of all immigrants admitted in fiscal year 1993 reported having some occupation. Distribution of immigrants by major occupational group is shown in percent.

Region and country of birth	Total	Occupation: Total	Professional specialty and technical	Executive, administrative and managerial	Sales	Administrative support	Precision production, craft, and repair	Operator, fabricator and laborer	Farming, forestry, and fishing	Service	No occupation or not reported[1]
All countries	904,292	325,611	78,905	30,855	14,436	23,667	27,669	71,679	21,814	56,586	578,681
North America	301,380	112,107	10,073	4,837	4,894	6,466	10,495	41,065	9,440	24,837	189,273
Canada	17,156	7,348	2,916	2,022	431	663	318	372	66	560	9,808
Mexico	126,561	47,201	1,159	703	1,895	1,572	4,791	21,478	6,980	8,623	79,360
Caribbean	99,438	36,334	4,943	1,498	1,662	2,959	4,078	11,060	2,018	8,116	63,104
Antigua-Barbuda	554	233	37	12	14	17	20	17	4	112	321
Bahamas	686	220	68	21	15	21	16	31	3	45	466
Barbados	1,184	509	73	38	23	40	25	33	3	274	675
Cuba	13,666	6,025	422	138	197	311	282	3,968	22	685	7,641
Dominica	683	295	40	9	12	18	19	26	19	152	388
Dominican Republic	45,420	15,533	2,161	751	893	1,118	2,383	5,782	1,119	1,326	29,887
Grenada	827	384	62	17	9	25	29	32	3	207	443
Haiti	10,094	2,800	441	112	184	228	659	306	490	380	7,294
Jamaica	17,241	7,217	959	182	175	880	316	514	308	3,883	10,024
St. Kitts-Nevis	544	221	31	6	7	15	15	25	2	120	323
St. Lucia	634	258	30	13	7	13	22	19	11	143	376
St. Vincent & Grenadines	657	285	48	11	6	20	25	15	5	155	372
Trinidad & Tobago	6,577	2,100	510	160	104	235	247	269	22	553	4,477
Other Caribbean	671	254	61	28	16	18	20	23	7	81	417
Central America	58,162	21,194	1,047	602	904	1,272	1,307	8,152	376	7,534	36,968
Belize	1,035	369	60	17	23	47	48	68	8	98	666
Costa Rica	1,368	428	52	35	12	25	36	193	9	66	940
El Salvador	26,818	10,672	129	70	502	363	370	3,849	149	5,240	16,146
Guatemala	11,870	3,958	244	97	118	221	281	1,962	134	901	7,912
Honduras	7,306	2,245	182	130	51	141	307	914	40	480	5,061
Nicaragua	7,086	2,768	221	160	155	290	229	1,061	30	622	4,318
Panama	2,679	754	159	93	43	185	36	105	6	127	1,925
Other North America	63	30	8	12	2	-	1	3	-	4	33
South America	53,921	18,075	3,599	1,585	1,008	1,690	1,797	4,991	741	2,934	35,846
Argentina	2,824	1,175	475	177	58	151	109	93	14	98	1,649
Bolivia	1,545	488	104	34	12	42	47	61	7	181	1,057
Brazil	4,604	1,491	486	241	67	98	87	150	41	321	3,113
Chile	1,778	631	198	87	29	81	64	76	5	91	1,147
Colombia	12,819	4,575	673	242	169	157	183	2,672	46	433	8,244
Ecuador	7,324	2,294	262	98	222	319	488	392	60	453	5,030

[Continued]

★ 14 ★

Immigrants Admitted, by Major Occupational Group and Selected Country of Birth, 1993

[Continued]

Region and country of birth	Total	Occupation									No occupation or not reported[1]
		Total	Professional specialty and technical	Executive, administrative and managerial	Sales	Administrative support	Precision production, craft, and repair	Operator, fabricator and laborer	Farming, forestry, and fishing	Service	
Guyana	8,384	2,605	439	183	108	325	387	465	214	484	5,779
Paraguay	668	95	23	4	3	4	22	8	5	26	573
Peru	10,447	3,630	577	296	303	406	354	925	71	698	6,817
Uruguay	568	245	43	27	10	21	42	47	5	50	323
Venezuela	2,743	791	292	195	25	83	11	93	3	89	1,952
Other South America	217	55	27	1	2	3	3	9	-	10	162
Europe	158,254	62,698	20,066	6,328	2,388	5,883	7,561	9,390	1,622	9,460	95,556
Albania	1,400	536	38	4	11	7	51	241	10	174	864
Austria	549	251	101	55	6	32	12	17	1	27	298
Belgium	657	277	123	83	9	21	8	10	-	23	380
Bulgaria	1,029	374	176	26	11	14	28	61	2	56	655
Czechoslovakia	1,000	415	187	37	12	42	33	42	3	59	585
Denmark	735	340	109	97	21	26	14	17	8	48	395
Finland	544	248	99	60	9	22	16	8	3	31	296
France	2,864	1,262	463	324	40	136	58	41	4	96	1,602
Germany	7,312	3,306	960	518	198	610	168	188	8	656	4,006
Greece	1,884	681	238	60	22	24	98	90	35	114	1,203
Hungary	1,091	422	200	45	17	22	38	43	3	54	669
Ireland	13,590	9,781	2,284	1,028	486	1,494	1,202	1,300	223	1,764	3,809
Italy	2,487	1,018	290	233	39	69	70	122	6	189	1,469
Latvia	668	188	55	13	11	18	11	42	-	38	480
Lithuania	529	182	90	7	9	10	17	29	-	20	347
Netherlands	1,430	721	305	188	30	60	19	29	5	85	709
Norway	608	255	96	63	9	18	11	14	11	33	353
Poland	27,846	15,605	5,909	165	416	1,119	3,679	2,076	1,096	1,145	12,241
Portugal	2,081	778	60	43	15	36	163	207	97	157	1,303
Romania	5,601	1,905	487	54	68	89	216	610	5	376	3,696
Soviet Union, former	58,571	11,982	3,423	412	434	806	861	3,445	17	2,584	46,589
Armenia	6,287	509	86	11	46	30	56	221	-	59	5,778
Azerbaijan	2,943	886	130	15	29	42	67	336	1	266	2,057
Belarus	4,702	918	227	23	32	62	85	261	-	228	3,784
Moldova	2,646	575	160	16	20	56	63	130	-	130	2,071
Russia	12,079	2,992	1,183	155	107	240	124	594	4	585	9,087
Ukraine	18,316	3,954	1,085	135	138	289	299	1,156	5	847	14,362
Uzbekistan	2,664	406	117	7	18	23	33	118	1	89	2,258
Other republics	1,565	359	104	13	13	16	19	110	2	82	1,206
Unknown republic	7,369	1,383	331	37	31	48	115	519	4	298	5,986
Spain	1,388	574	260	80	25	66	35	37	4	67	814
Sweden	1,393	604	251	164	23	49	17	22	2	76	789
Switzerland	972	456	182	122	12	42	28	16	2	52	516
United Kingdom	18,783	9,337	3,205	2,303	413	979	596	550	40	1,251	9,446
Yugoslavia	2,809	1,053	422	115	38	56	103	115	36	168	1,756
Other Europe	433	147	53	29	4	16	9	18	1	17	286
Asia	358,049	119,290	40,755	16,352	5,231	8,490	7,228	14,680	10,039	16,515	238,759
Afghanistan	2,964	697	82	42	107	39	47	89	3	288	2,267
Bangladesh	3,291	719	257	72	161	35	4	37	73	80	2,572
Burma	849	339	90	45	36	36	40	23	1	68	510
Cambodia	1,639	471	26	12	27	20	63	159	55	109	1,168
China, Mainland	65,578	26,076	11,056	2,898	684	1,919	796	2,661	3,292	2,770	39,502
Hong Kong	9,161	3,977	1,259	1,160	143	671	261	117	2	364	5,184
India	40,121	14,013	7,973	2,237	378	882	204	195	1,195	949	26,108
Indonesia	1,767	689	232	176	56	85	25	11	4	100	1,078
Iran	14,841	4,260	1,387	706	382	388	453	341	38	565	10,581
Iraq	4,072	929	207	77	66	51	72	226	21	209	3,143
Israel	4,494	1,622	682	257	162	130	120	92	16	163	2,872
Japan	6,908	2,524	648	865	132	286	41	29	16	507	4,384
Jordan	4,741	1,315	327	171	128	79	92	226	77	215	3,426
Korea	18,026	4,190	1,662	754	167	517	185	369	101	435	13,836
Kuwait	1,129	268	92	52	22	17	7	22	1	55	861
Laos	7,285	975	31	8	12	13	77	598	65	171	6,310
Lebanon	5,465	1,932	564	335	156	126	254	143	73	281	3,533
Malaysia	2,026	1,061	468	250	30	102	40	17	7	147	965

[Continued]

★ 14 ★

Immigrants Admitted, by Major Occupational Group and Selected Country of Birth, 1993

[Continued]

Region and country of birth	Total	Occupation									No occupation or not reported[1]
		Total	Professional specialty and technical	Executive, administrative and managerial	Sales	Administrative support	Precision production, craft, and repair	Operator, fabricator and laborer	Farming, forestry, and fishing	Service	
Pakistan	8,927	2,488	824	509	102	125	25	56	177	670	6,439
Philippines	63,457	21,500	7,974	3,190	587	1,546	1,120	1,589	1,745	3,749	41,957
Saudi Arabia	616	70	30	15	1	5	4	7	-	8	546
Singapore	798	338	157	97	18	31	4	4	1	26	460
Sri Lanka	1,109	570	292	99	20	60	11	14	5	69	539
Syria	2,933	825	282	97	64	36	129	72	35	110	2,108
Taiwan	14,329	6,056	2,919	1,789	244	683	61	49	50	261	8,273
Thailand	6,654	1,111	254	92	233	154	75	50	51	202	5,543
Turkey	2,204	758	212	121	48	51	111	71	11	133	1,446
Vietnam	59,614	18,302	591	126	1,042	360	2,879	6,685	2,888	3,731	41,312
Yemen	1,793	802	13	9	8	6	4	718	28	16	991
Other Asia	1,258	413	164	91	15	37	24	10	8	64	845
Africa	27,783	11,104	3,544	1,326	802	950	429	1,401	151	2,501	16,679
Cape Verde	936	165	10	1	4	6	21	102	1	20	771
Egypt	3,556	1,442	626	281	97	98	30	74	25	211	2,114
Ethiopia	5,276	1,946	192	71	205	148	55	594	8	673	3,330
Ghana	1,604	598	196	27	35	59	91	36	25	129	1,006
Kenya	1,065	488	180	90	36	64	17	27	4	70	577
Liberia	1,050	337	103	29	20	27	8	53	7	90	713
Morocco	1,176	552	95	76	47	40	34	40	2	218	624
Nigeria	4,448	2,021	966	136	129	148	36	125	37	444	2,427
Sierra Leone	690	251	88	12	12	35	4	14	6	80	439
Somalia	1,088	320	32	19	23	29	9	93	3	112	768
South Africa	2,197	976	470	249	52	92	40	22	6	45	1,221
Sudan	714	200	35	31	21	11	5	40	1	56	514
Tanzania	426	195	67	51	10	34	9	7	2	15	231
Uganda	415	239	74	47	11	30	14	18	2	43	176
Other Africa	3,142	1,374	410	206	100	129	56	156	22	295	1,768
Oceania	4,900	2,335	867	427	113	188	159	152	90	339	2,565
Australia	2,320	1,145	528	262	58	93	49	40	16	99	1,175
Fiji	854	385	36	32	20	51	44	30	26	146	469
New Zealand	1,052	578	277	120	28	24	45	26	15	43	474
Other Oceania	674	227	26	13	7	20	21	56	33	51	447
Unknown or not reported	5	2	1	-	-	-	-	-	1	-	3

Source: U.S. Immigration and Naturalization Service, *Statistical Yearbook of the Immigration and Naturalization Service, 1993*, U.S. Government Printing Office, Washington, DC, 1994, pp. 68-69. *Notes:* A dash (-) represents zero 1. Includes homemakers, students, unemployed or retired persons, and others not reporting or with an unknown occupation.

★ 15 ★

Immigration

Immigrants Admitted, by Selected Metropolitan Statistical Area of Intended Residence and Selected Country of Birth, 1993 - I

The leading MSAs (metropolitan statistical areas) of intended residence for immigrants admitted in fiscal year 1993 were New York, NY; Los Angeles-Long Beach, CA; Chicago, IL; Miami, FL; and Washington, DC-MD-VA.

MSA[1]	All countries	Canada	China, Mainland	Colombia	Cuba	Dominican Republic	El Salvador	Ecuador	Germany	Guatemala
Total	904,292	17,156	65,578	12,819	13,666	45,420	26,818	7,324	7,312	11,870
New York, NY	128,434	582	11,998	3,034	271	25,689	1,144	3,728	311	801
Los Angeles-Long Beach, CA	106,703	748	4,508	420	240	54	10,542	350	328	5,260
Chicago, IL	44,121	421	2,599	286	96	82	258	300	301	715
Miami, FL	30,464	247	381	1,938	10,292	1,626	295	337	115	310

[Continued]

★ 15 ★

Immigrants Admitted, by Selected Metropolitan Statistical Area of Intended Residence and Selected Country of Birth, 1993 - I

[Continued]

MSA[1]	All countries	Canada	China, Mainland	Colombia	Cuba	Dominican Republic	El Salvador	Ecuador	Germany	Guatemala
Washington, DC-MD-VA	27,427	259	2,057	308	35	421	3,589	132	181	501
Orange County, CA	24,921	303	526	92	15	10	494	45	92	338
Houston, TX	22,634	394	1,577	287	46	52	2,829	51	84	295
San Francisco, CA	21,054	184	3,626	44	59	5	1,211	19	141	256
Boston-Lawrence-Lowell-Brockton, MA	20,414	315	2,586	210	41	2,138	300	41	143	211
San Jose, CA	19,473	195	1,558	35	12	8	170	10	85	52
San Diego, CA	16,931	241	365	51	9	6	94	10	103	52
Oakland, CA	16,087	230	1,801	44	24	12	322	10	84	107
Newark, NJ	13,551	145	511	715	158	675	330	416	67	148
Bergen-Passaic, NJ	12,931	58	381	736	43	1,970	135	227	42	73
Philadelphia, PA-NJ	12,842	199	1,218	99	14	182	27	32	98	51
Nassau-Suffolk, NY	11,601	93	679	473	15	939	1,504	218	52	198
Seattle-Bellevue-Everett, WA	11,509	357	1,028	21	15	4	21	11	84	16
Riverside-San Bernardino, CA	11,187	192	235	40	25	13	304	33	62	243
Dallas, TX	10,959	218	669	68	30	10	437	14	68	137
Detroit, MI	9,816	637	677	24	1	10	7	8	110	13
Jersey City, NJ	8,754	12	336	441	535	1,456	362	511	9	96
Fort Lauderdale, FL	8,124	521	137	494	204	191	83	84	91	50
Atlanta, GA	8,031	266	711	105	27	37	50	7	94	22
Middlesex-Somerset-Hunterdon, NJ	7,371	79	818	126	23	762	41	56	36	50
Honolulu, HI	6,880	175	732	4	-	2	2	2	38	1
Fresno, CA	6,780	14	60	6	3	-	68	4	10	18
Sacramento, CA	6,746	78	383	17	2	2	47	4	41	14
Minneapolis-St. Paul, MN-WI	6,349	219	814	72	-	4	16	11	39	14
Phoenix-Mesa, AZ	5,918	313	273	23	11	9	71	6	72	64
Portland-Vancouver, OR-WA	5,800	135	413	14	1	5	16	3	59	41
El Paso, TX	5,410	9	26	5	2	4	10	1	51	25
San Juan, PR	4,981	4	34	64	70	4,443	15	9	5	6
Baltimore, MD	4,539	92	470	23	9	23	54	6	67	29
Tampa-St. Petersburg-Clearwater, FL	4,529	396	158	121	309	93	32	28	82	31
Orlando, FL	4,505	207	174	191	101	133	33	32	60	24
Denver, CO	4,459	154	292	18	4	1	19	4	41	11
McAllen-Edinburg-Mission, TX	4,322	21	11	1	2	-	12	-	6	7
West Palm Beach-Boca Raton, FL	4,302	233	186	160	198	100	32	43	81	33
Bridgeport-Stamford-Norwalk-Danbury, CT	4,201	146	150	198	21	106	44	73	41	54
Hartford, CT	4,014	76	276	75	2	65	15	9	16	6
Fort Worth-Arlington, TX	3,996	97	157	18	4	6	49	1	27	23
Ventura, CA	3,968	75	54	8	7	-	79	7	25	63
Cleveland-Lorain-Elyria, OH	3,819	126	438	20	2	7	3	-	38	7
San Antonio, TX	3,397	62	162	20	1	6	45	9	56	30
Providence-Warwick-Pawtucket, RI	3,060	61	223	178	-	579	24	22	20	200
Las Vegas, NV	2,836	75	99	19	155	12	118	7	33	52
Austin-San Marcos, TX	2,757	56	423	21	4	2	76	5	24	4
St. Louis, MO-IL	2,745	85	461	16	6	2	3	4	42	12
Salinas, CA	2,725	11	38	7	1	-	44	1	29	2
Stockton-Lodi, CA	2,571	33	72	4	4	-	7	-	3	8
Other MSA	138,241	5,372	15,085	1,091	351	1,098	986	296	2,460	871
Non-MSA	44,861	1,931	2,932	331	166	2,366	349	87	1,162	225
Unknown	242	4	-	3	-	-	-	-	3	-

Source: U.S. Immigration and Naturalization Service, *Statistical Yearbook of the Immigration and Naturalization Service, 1993*, U.S. Government Printing Office, Washington, DC, 1994, pp. 64-66. *Notes:* A dash (-) represents zero. 1. Ranked by the number of immigrants.

★ 16 ★

Immigration

Immigrants Admitted, by Selected Metropolitan Statistical Area of Intended Residence and Selected Country of Birth, 1993 - II

The leading MSAs (metropolitan statistical areas) of intended residence for immigrants admitted in fiscal year 1993 were New York, NY; Los Angeles-Long Beach, CA; Chicago, IL; Miami, FL; and Washington, DC-MD-VA.

MSA[1]	All countries	Guyana	Haiti	Honduras	Hong Kong	India	Iran	Ireland	Jamaica	Korea	Laos
Total	904,292	8,384	10,094	7,306	9,161	40,121	14,841	13,590	17,241	18,026	7,285
New York, NY	128,434	5,817	3,325	1,487	1,438	3,880	510	3,636	7,149	1,594	15
Los Angeles-Long Beach, CA	106,703	54	40	944	1,220	1,828	5,721	374	168	3,526	74
Chicago, IL	44,121	21	84	181	272	3,750	221	717	272	733	48
Miami, FL	30,464	125	1,925	1,143	56	152	75	73	1,424	45	1
Washington, DC-MD-VA	27,427	260	129	207	165	1,568	911	222	569	1,073	59
Orange County, CA	24,921	14	3	65	153	733	907	126	19	793	59
Houston, TX	22,634	27	17	391	238	1,267	339	65	81	241	16
San Francisco, CA	21,054	5	13	45	1,152	377	248	758	13	228	6
Boston-Lawrence-Lowell-Brockton, MA	20,414	29	781	177	297	722	157	1,845	353	121	26
San Jose, CA	19,473	7	-	31	375	1,951	560	127	14	398	40
San Diego, CA	16,931	18	3	29	69	180	365	89	22	151	171
Oakland, CA	16,087	19	4	25	567	1,287	353	141	43	196	174
Newark, NJ	13,551	375	768	126	83	818	49	218	470	148	-
Bergen-Passaic, NJ	12,931	65	31	60	49	892	88	304	351	573	1
Philadelphia, PA-NJ	12,842	44	100	46	150	1,067	89	390	381	458	41
Nassau-Suffolk, NY	11,601	220	273	129	128	735	224	533	494	172	-
Seattle-Bellevue-Everett, WA	11,509	1	3	14	235	352	149	101	8	359	151
Riverside-San Bernardino, CA	11,187	12	6	74	51	348	174	28	23	215	53
Dallas, TX	10,959	15	5	92	60	682	304	48	26	220	36
Detroit, MI	9,816	4	5	14	47	889	93	46	65	182	80
Jersey City, NJ	8,754	179	56	192	34	829	12	125	26	50	-
Fort Lauderdale, FL	8,124	135	740	101	58	147	55	146	1,401	46	2
Atlanta, GA	8,031	52	17	22	42	562	200	115	148	243	49
Middlesex-Somerset-Hunterdon, NJ	7,371	60	13	53	120	1,450	31	86	92	113	-
Honolulu, HI	6,880	-	-	1	241	21	10	16	2	375	37
Fresno, CA	6,780	1	3	15	35	355	43	9	2	13	1,638
Sacramento, CA	6,746	-	1	4	112	309	101	40	15	118	366
Minneapolis-St. Paul, MN-WI	6,349	66	4	23	64	198	70	46	27	178	679
Phoenix-Mesa, AZ	5,918	10	2	31	58	212	76	38	6	122	3
Portland-Vancouver, OR-WA	5,800	4	1	9	71	134	95	29	9	164	63
El Paso, TX	5,410	-	1	10	10	16	7	6	3	33	-
San Juan, PR	4,981	6	6	6	2	4	1	1	2	1	-
Baltimore, MD	4,539	39	5	18	55	388	130	89	144	267	1
Tampa-St. Petersburg-Clearwater, FL	4,529	32	35	59	25	193	73	92	143	47	26
Orlando, FL	4,505	106	158	29	21	173	63	57	338	23	10
Denver, CO	4,459	-	-	2	39	103	61	28	11	114	32
McAllen-Edinburg-Mission, TX	4,322	-	-	11	1	6	-	-	1	3	-
West Palm Beach-Boca Raton, FL	4,302	28	577	52	32	102	38	71	412	13	1
Bridgeport-Stamford-Norwalk-Danbury, CT	4,201	30	259	31	24	219	20	140	266	29	7
Hartford, CT	4,014	84	13	1	13	218	33	79	500	25	26
Fort Worth-Arlington, TX	3,996	4	-	14	19	232	67	13	7	45	38
Ventura, CA	3,968	-	2	5	19	87	80	25	2	54	2
Cleveland-Lorain-Elyria, OH	3,819	12	-	13	21	277	33	36	39	58	4
San Antonio, TX	3,397	1	-	43	26	90	40	12	-	40	4
Providence-Warwick-Pawtucket, RI	3,060	3	33	13	24	43	9	49	17	24	67
Las Vegas, NV	2,836	6	2	39	22	53	24	24	23	61	6
Austin-San Marcos, TX	2,757	3	1	36	36	161	57	22	2	36	-
St. Louis, MO-IL	2,745	4	5	8	25	172	43	30	24	64	1
Salinas, CA	2,725	-	-	11	13	43	9	8	-	48	-
Stockton-Lodi, CA	2,571	-	-	-	41	152	7	-	3	14	174
Other MSA	138,241	287	503	922	819	8,012	1,594	1,833	1,299	2,982	2,527

[Continued]

★ 16 ★

Immigrants Admitted, by Selected Metropolitan Statistical Area of Intended Residence and Selected Country of Birth, 1993 - II

[Continued]

MSA[1]	All countries	Guyana	Haiti	Honduras	Hong Kong	India	Iran	Ireland	Jamaica	Korea	Laos
Non-MSA	44,861	100	142	252	234	1,682	222	483	332	1,189	471
Unknown	242	-	-	-	-	-	-	1	-	8	-

Source: U.S. Immigration and Naturalization Service, *Statistical Yearbook of the Immigration and Naturalization Service, 1993*, U.S. Government Printing Office, Washington, DC, 1994, pp. 64-66. *Notes:* A dash (-) represents zero. 1. Ranked by the number of immigrants.

★ 17 ★

Immigration

Immigrants Admitted, by Selected Metropolitan Statistical Area of Intended Residence and Selected Country of Birth, 1993 - III

The leading MSAs (metropolitan statistical areas) of intended residence for immigrants admitted in fiscal year 1993 were New York, NY; Los Angeles-Long Beach, CA; Chicago, IL; Miami, FL; and Washington, DC-MD-VA.

MSA[1]	All countries	Mexico	Pakistan	Peru	Philippines	Poland	Soviet Union	Taiwan	United Kingdom	Vietnam	Other
Total	904,292	126,561	8,927	10,447	63,457	27,846	58,571	14,329	18,783	59,614	161,745
New York, NY	128,434	1,683	1,618	1,713	4,254	5,310	12,351	879	1,478	675	22,064
Los Angeles-Long Beach, CA	106,703	25,132	456	813	8,677	333	10,679	3,548	1,285	4,997	14,384
Chicago, IL	44,121	8,568	844	185	2,710	10,602	2,319	387	531	791	5,927
Miami, FL	30,464	337	132	1,077	434	56	390	46	240	55	7,228
Washington, DC-MD-VA	27,427	310	651	740	1,450	112	668	417	510	1,821	8,102
Orange County, CA	24,921	5,657	144	178	1,227	111	174	886	344	8,482	2,931
Houston, TX	22,634	5,997	558	111	817	58	242	438	369	2,510	3,237
San Francisco, CA	21,054	1,181	96	211	3,333	69	2,088	372	527	1,232	3,555
Boston-Lawrence-Lowell-Brockton, MA	20,414	79	99	111	338	259	2,114	235	650	1,490	4,546
San Jose, CA	19,473	1,514	188	83	2,193	60	600	1,160	390	5,095	2,562
San Diego, CA	16,931	5,425	30	71	3,558	93	610	190	322	1,551	3,053
Oakland, CA	16,087	1,503	182	188	2,847	80	439	498	356	1,430	3,121
Newark, NJ	13,551	69	105	534	1,216	1,078	693	263	244	233	2,896
Bergen-Passaic, NJ	12,931	158	110	893	911	1,586	439	149	166	25	2,415
Philadelphia, PA-NJ	12,842	150	153	56	530	457	2,273	141	601	1,274	2,521
Nassau-Suffolk, NY	11,601	101	288	286	368	822	139	151	213	80	2,074
Seattle-Bellevue-Everett, WA	11,509	220	53	38	1,223	144	1,691	224	203	2,301	2,482
Riverside-San Bernardino, CA	11,187	4,771	123	75	1,159	38	107	210	157	783	1,633
Dallas, TX	10,959	3,140	142	48	305	57	391	258	239	1,092	2,148
Detroit, MI	9,816	173	170	7	320	527	929	76	240	111	4,351
Jersey City, NJ	8,754	72	98	362	1,090	318	93	61	61	129	1,209
Fort Lauderdale, FL	8,124	120	58	335	148	65	138	36	357	89	2,092
Atlanta, GA	8,031	333	83	76	227	71	483	144	297	1,365	2,183
Middlesex-Somerset-Hunterdon, NJ	7,371	51	149	166	640	406	276	265	167	88	1,154
Honolulu, HI	6,880	23	7	6	3,425	2	17	127	71	476	1,067
Fresno, CA	6,780	2,781	35	2	149	4	125	3	53	99	1,232
Sacramento, CA	6,746	572	113	21	660	27	1,534	89	121	840	1,115
Minneapolis-St. Paul, MN-WI	6,349	93	39	24	135	66	887	69	174	704	1,614
Phoenix-Mesa, AZ	5,918	2,254	21	26	219	47	194	81	167	603	906
Portland-Vancouver, OR-WA	5,800	291	15	25	245	22	1,605	46	90	1,050	1,145
El Paso, TX	5,410	4,954	4	4	64	-	18	6	10	5	126
San Juan, PR	4,981	29	-	31	1	-	-	1	5	-	235
Baltimore, MD	4,539	49	86	54	289	72	513	90	167	136	1,174
Tampa-St. Petersburg-Clearwater, FL	4,529	179	17	74	202	104	82	17	328	452	1,099
Orlando, FL	4,505	168	57	87	222	21	61	62	372	693	1,126
Denver, CO	4,459	1,130	15	54	153	55	517	49	118	581	853
McAllen-Edinburg-Mission, TX	4,322	4,150	-	1	39	1	-	3	2	-	44

[Continued]

★ 17 ★

Immigrants Admitted, by Selected Metropolitan Statistical Area of Intended Residence and Selected Country of Birth, 1993 - III

[Continued]

MSA[1]	All countries	Mexico	Pakistan	Peru	Philippines	Poland	Soviet Union	Taiwan	United Kingdom	Vietnam	Other
West Palm Beach-Boca Raton, FL	4,302	161	29	61	123	59	76	32	211	65	1,093
Bridgeport-Stamford-Norwalk-Danbury, CT	4,201	68	58	92	123	331	215	17	267	124	1,048
Hartford, CT	4,014	25	59	155	58	897	308	18	92	248	622
Fort Worth-Arlington, TX	3,996	1,329	51	16	76	14	33	72	61	843	680
Ventura, CA	3,968	2,070	19	42	489	19	41	58	99	132	405
Cleveland-Lorain-Elyria, OH	3,819	31	26	12	111	140	1,207	55	93	91	919
San Antonio, TX	3,397	2,005	11	22	138	19	50	35	62	100	308
Providence-Warwick-Pawtucket, RI	3,060	23	5	26	75	85	339	6	27	16	869
Las Vegas, NV	2,836	709	20	14	459	19	26	32	64	90	573
Austin-San Marcos, TX	2,757	728	15	14	62	16	35	65	91	224	538
St. Louis, MO-IL	2,745	60	48	25	139	23	395	33	80	430	505
Salinas, CA	2,725	1,853	-	9	299	3	39	9	18	63	167
Stockton-Lodi, CA	2,571	649	66	7	470	7	9	10	38	408	385
Other MSA	138,241	21,363	1,337	927	8,910	2,431	8,937	1,795	4,651	12,778	26,724
Non-MSA	44,861	12,067	244	258	6,081	650	981	415	1,297	960	7,252
Unknown	242	3	-	1	157	-	1	-	7	1	53

Source: U.S. Immigration and Naturalization Service, *Statistical Yearbook of the Immigration and Naturalization Service, 1993,* U.S. Government Printing Office, Washington, DC, 1994, pp. 64-66. *Notes:* A dash (-) represents zero. 1. Ranked by the number of immigrants.

★ 18 ★

Immigration

Immigrants Admitted, by Selected Port of Entry and Selected Country of Birth, 1993

Data show the number of new arrivals at each port during fiscal year 1993. The most active ports overall were New York, Los Angeles, and El Paso.

Region and country of birth	All ports	Chicago, IL	El Paso, TX	Los Angeles, CA	Miami, FL	New York, NY	San Francisco, CA	San Diego, CA	Seattle, WA	Other
All countries	536,294	25,989	71,902	72,590	42,804	13,902	140,680	43,683	24,054	100,690
North America	229,689	1,302	69,396	18,564	22,746	5,644	47,736	1,834	23,889	38,578
Canada	8,010	162	9	154	117	26	1,053	55	3	6,431
Mexico	100,570	317	69,071	185	91	35	252	69	23,718	6,832
Caribbean	73,481	33	209	34	14,004	5,557	41,071	9	10	12,554
Antigua-Barbuda	364	1	-	-	29	2	129	-	-	203
Bahamas	318	6	-	-	269	-	12	-	-	31
Barbados	825	-	-	2	113	1	525	1	-	183
Cuba	1,873	1	174	5	1,607	8	25	-	7	46
Dominica	532	1	-	-	26	2	98	-	-	405
Dominican Republic	41,478	2	14	5	2,846	5,327	25,069	5	1	8,209
Grenada	589	-	-	-	54	-	317	-	-	218
Haiti	8,195	2	20	2	3,762	8	4,234	-	1	166
Jamaica	13,416	16	-	15	4,219	198	7,644	2	1	1,321
St. Kitts-Nevis	382	1	-	-	14	-	51	-	-	316
St. Lucia	457	-	-	-	37	-	83	-	-	337
St. Vincent & Grenadines	476	1	-	1	53	1	260	-	-	160
Trinidad & Tobago	4,194	2	-	4	906	3	2,513	-	-	766
Other Caribbean	382	-	1	-	69	7	111	1	-	193
Central America	47,598	790	104	18,187	8,533	26	5,356	1,701	158	12,743
Belize	794	3	11	221	251	-	39	3	14	252
Costa Rica	885	12	-	135	448	-	105	16	2	167

[Continued]

★ 18 ★

Immigrants Admitted, by Selected Port of Entry and Selected Country of Birth, 1993

[Continued]

Region and country of birth	All ports	Chicago, IL	El Paso, TX	Los Angeles, CA	Miami, FL	New York, NY	San Francisco, CA	San Diego, CA	Seattle, WA	Other
El Salvador	24,207	136	29	10,829	1,675	3	2,683	1,293	63	7,496
Guatemala	10,412	531	25	5,477	1,189	10	888	201	61	2,030
Honduras	6,307	15	21	935	2,122	9	1,379	39	6	1,781
Nicaragua	3,197	10	11	562	1,853	2	52	145	12	550
Panama	1,796	83	7	28	995	2	210	4	-	467
Other North America	30	-	3	4	1	-	4	-	-	18
South America	39,571	107	58	2,348	17,014	91	18,326	84	26	1,517
Argentina	1,477	9	9	338	698	3	359	5	6	50
Bolivia	1,184	3	1	33	1,105	-	17	4	1	20
Brazil	1,955	63	7	240	676	6	627	-	1	335
Chile	1,020	1	1	141	627	1	178	4	2	65
Colombia	9,697	10	17	372	4,320	20	4,698	1	9	250
Ecuador	6,342	11	1	310	1,227	8	4,596	3	2	184
Guyana	7,539	-	-	8	479	12	6,759	-	-	281
Paraguay	569	-	-	15	374	-	171	-	-	9
Peru	8,005	5	18	847	6,584	27	334	65	5	120
Uruguay	364	1	-	27	121	1	198	-	-	16
Venezuela	1,294	4	4	16	736	13	343	2	-	176
Other South America	125	-	-	1	67	-	46	-	-	11
Europe	64,423	13,255	134	3,197	1,538	5,176	24,582	1,604	20	14,917
Albania	184	28	-	-	-	1	136	-	-	19
Austria	207	19	2	27	15	5	61	10	-	68
Belgium	265	33	-	14	9	11	76	6	-	116
Bulgaria	355	46	-	16	2	24	200	14	-	53
Czechoslovakia	442	53	-	37	14	23	179	13	-	123
Denmark	318	31	-	66	10	41	71	11	1	87
Finland	260	18	-	18	31	5	135	7	-	46
France	1,147	45	8	149	68	104	256	78	1	438
Germany	3,703	314	22	281	93	313	440	102	1	2,137
Greece	890	87	2	35	13	9	493	21	-	230
Hungary	448	24	-	65	16	32	187	9	1	114
Ireland	12,484	447	-	462	282	230	6,648	515	1	3,899
Italy	1,114	63	3	109	56	6	595	14	2	266
Latvia	72	10	1	8	1	4	37	5	-	6
Lithuania	160	42	-	6	6	16	65	1	-	24
Netherlands	512	28	2	53	30	15	107	17	-	260
Norway	258	11	-	25	4	69	50	8	-	91
Poland	24,315	10,533	6	267	245	2,996	9,404	71	1	792
Portugal	1,597	3	-	8	7	462	452	2	1	662
Romania	1,002	216	3	111	7	15	498	24	-	128
Soviet Union, former	2,629	215	18	223	42	83	1,287	168	2	591
Armenia	88	-	7	54	-	1	14	5	-	7
Azerbaijan	28	2	-	7	-	-	13	3	-	3
Belarus	102	17	-	8	2	5	49	12	-	9
Moldova	50	2	-	7	-	1	36	-	-	4
Russia	1,203	102	4	65	16	32	509	94	-	381
Ukraine	621	45	4	27	9	19	379	25	2	111
Uzbekistan	85	4	1	5	-	5	61	4	-	5
Other republics	83	3	-	17	2	1	37	4	-	19
Unknown republic	369	40	2	33	13	19	189	21	-	52
Spain	621	14	6	30	83	52	217	10	2	207
Sweden	562	131	1	73	17	84	122	22	-	112
Switzerland	387	42	1	67	19	10	98	19	-	131
United Kingdom	8,774	463	17	932	441	510	1,999	439	5	3,968
Yugoslavia	1,577	336	42	106	25	55	717	16	2	278
Other Europe	140	3	-	9	2	1	52	2	-	71

[Continued]

★ 18 ★

Immigrants Admitted, by Selected Port of Entry and Selected Country of Birth, 1993

[Continued]

Region and country of birth	All ports	Chicago, IL	El Paso, TX	Los Angeles, CA	Miami, FL	New York, NY	San Francisco, CA	San Diego, CA	Seattle, WA	Other
Asia	189,379	10,742	2,252	46,642	1,225	2,610	44,481	39,336	113	41,978
Afghanistan	573	15	34	72	1	17	282	67	-	85
Bangladesh	2,747	44	-	463	40	65	1,797	44	-	294
Burma	605	17	4	247	2	3	96	189	-	47
Cambodia	484	4	1	211	-	4	86	81	-	97
China, Mainland	24,014	1,163	34	4,351	102	110	7,794	7,474	42	2,944
Hong Kong	6,691	251	1	1,333	36	74	1,420	2,466	-	1,110
India	27,771	3,470	16	3,304	221	706	11,516	2,968	3	5,567
Indonesia	1,199	25	-	725	5	3	123	208	-	110
Iran	6,493	280	1,584	1,680	169	309	762	347	8	1,354
Iraq	1,865	272	58	226	7	15	507	66	9	705
Israel	1,976	70	44	343	71	13	1,159	45	-	231
Japan	3,236	176	1	1,163	6	64	401	500	8	917
Jordan	3,216	531	8	300	6	77	1,552	106	2	544
Korea	12,375	760	15	3,952	130	21	2,536	969	1	3,991
Kuwait	511	76	10	72	8	11	246	14	2	72
Laos	302	5	2	159	-	1	25	37	-	73
Lebanon	3,374	277	357	592	108	105	904	50	6	975
Malaysia	853	23	2	427	4	12	180	134	1	70
Pakistan	6,957	606	2	533	101	191	4,300	337	-	887
Philippines	46,273	2,011	10	13,638	13	64	3,771	13,438	24	13,304
Saudi Arabia	347	36	5	30	10	13	171	15	1	66
Singapore	307	15	-	83	3	9	56	87	-	54
Sri Lanka	528	7	3	167	2	86	95	25	-	143
Syria	1,603	140	25	459	20	38	568	28	-	325
Taiwan	7,112	168	19	3,409	30	200	893	1,412	4	977
Thailand	1,978	114	4	845	3	2	206	339	-	465
Turkey	1,154	59	3	157	17	331	304	36	-	247
Vietnam	22,342	52	7	7,489	10	12	1,232	7,600	1	5,939
Yemen	1,670	25	-	45	2	38	1,253	108	1	198
Other Asia	823	50	3	167	8	16	246	146	-	187
Africa	11,107	572	62	993	276	368	5,502	294	5	3,035
Cape Verde	669	-	-	-	-	-	561	-	1	107
Egypt	2,144	70	1	350	33	28	1,333	42	-	287
Ethiopia	830	55	11	100	11	17	138	64	1	433
Ghana	1,063	70	4	48	2	25	522	15	-	377
Kenya	544	72	-	39	12	37	171	17	-	196
Liberia	385	13	15	3	3	60	230	3	1	57
Morocco	388	10	1	22	15	11	263	7	1	58
Nigeria	1,894	117	3	102	48	16	1,109	29	-	470
Sierra Leone	326	2	-	18	6	24	132	1	-	143
Somalia	144	10	11	2	1	4	53	4	-	59
South Africa	980	48	-	168	102	31	368	32	1	230
Sudan	93	5	8	10	1	-	33	3	-	33
Tanzania	301	27	-	38	5	13	95	11	-	112
Uganda	199	20	-	8	2	17	49	8	-	95
Other Africa	1,147	53	8	85	35	85	445	58	-	378
Oceania	2,125	11	-	846	5	13	53	531	1	665
Australia	802	6	-	432	5	11	45	22	1	280
Fiji	683	3	-	143	-	1	2	481	-	53
New Zealand	334	2	-	170	-	1	3	5	-	153
Other Oceania	306	-	-	101	-	-	3	23	-	179

Source: U.S. Immigration and Naturalization Service, *Statistical Yearbook of the Immigration and Naturalization Service, 1993,* U.S. Government Printing Office, Washington, DC, 1994, pp. 58-59. *Note:* A dash (-) represents zero.

★ 19 ★

Immigration

Immigrants Admitted, by State of Intended Residence and Selected Country of Birth, 1993 - I

The leading states of immigrants' intended residence have remained unchanged since 1971: California, New York, Texas, Florida, New Jersey, and Illinois. These six states were the intended homes of more than 70 percent of immigrants admitted in fiscal year 1993.

State of intended residence	All countries	Canada	China, Mainland	Colombia	Cuba	Dominican Republic	Ecuador	El Salvador	Germany	Guatemala
Total	904,292	17,156	65,578	12,819	13,666	45,420	7,324	26,818	7,312	11,870
Alabama	2,298	72	378	8	-	2	7	14	95	12
Alaska	1,286	87	56	10	-	18	-	5	23	2
Arizona	9,778	395	416	38	13	9	6	102	137	82
Arkansas	1,312	29	150	7	3	-	2	25	39	12
California	260,090	2,520	13,700	805	407	126	504	13,739	1,125	6,548
Colorado	6,650	242	638	29	4	6	10	34	171	19
Connecticut	10,966	291	763	344	28	229	118	68	91	78
Delaware	1,132	33	152	8	3	12	1	6	17	5
District of Columbia	3,608	21	239	18	3	159	13	719	19	49
Florida	61,423	2,293	1,572	3,075	11,264	2,250	548	519	668	502
Georgia	10,213	339	937	129	29	51	12	62	238	23
Hawaii	8,528	224	745	7	-	2	2	4	64	2
Idaho	1,270	74	132	8	-	-	2	2	24	11
Illinois	46,744	490	3,170	302	97	86	302	267	253	732
Indiana	4,539	226	929	28	4	10	3	6	86	34
Iowa	2,626	81	495	15	1	6	2	6	48	9
Kansas	3,225	66	452	6	3	2	3	22	77	13
Kentucky	2,182	149	334	14	3	4	5	5	139	11
Louisiana	3,725	75	411	28	30	26	18	36	82	68
Maine	838	147	85	5	-	13	2	5	32	4
Maryland	16,899	238	1,730	167	35	213	73	1,294	162	246
Massachusetts	25,011	426	3,002	263	51	2,233	59	332	184	232
Michigan	14,913	954	1,574	56	13	46	10	11	214	49
Minnesota	7,438	306	911	89	1	5	14	18	76	23
Mississippi	906	38	184	8	1	1	2	1	39	4
Missouri	4,644	122	792	21	19	7	7	12	92	17
Montana	509	125	75	3	-	-	1	-	25	1
Nebraska	1,980	27	252	7	2	-	2	26	32	9
Nevada	4,045	118	164	29	156	13	8	178	43	73
New Hampshire	1,263	72	150	22	-	69	8	4	39	4
New Jersey	50,285	437	2,548	2,170	783	5,176	1,265	923	225	485
New Mexico	3,409	42	167	26	67	3	2	16	55	46
New York	151,209	1,391	13,958	3,674	315	26,799	3,988	2,711	521	1,089
North Carolina	6,892	517	849	62	7	23	22	42	203	30
North Dakota	601	90	59	-	-	-	-	1	8	3
Ohio	10,703	423	1,846	44	11	23	5	11	171	23
Oklahoma	2,942	59	317	17	4	4	3	17	97	29
Oregon	7,250	212	676	19	5	8	3	28	114	54
Pennsylvania	16,964	390	1,877	171	24	195	64	49	203	81
Rhode Island	3,168	65	227	179	-	581	22	24	21	200
South Carolina	2,195	140	276	33	1	16	3	7	75	8
South Dakota	543	28	35	-	-	1	3	1	15	1
Tennessee	4,287	282	473	14	2	3	1	17	116	16
Texas	67,380	1,143	3,606	458	97	103	92	3,642	515	565
Utah	3,266	239	546	24	-	9	14	25	40	28
Vermont	709	124	83	3	-	1	1	-	20	1
Virginia	16,451	250	1,133	179	14	80	59	1,686	218	248
Washington	17,147	798	1,313	40	17	5	14	40	197	34
West Virginia	689	32	113	4	-	8	1	2	21	6

[Continued]

★ 19 ★

Immigrants Admitted, by State of Intended Residence and Selected Country of Birth, 1993 - I

[Continued]

State of intended residence	All countries	Canada	China, Mainland	Colombia	Cuba	Dominican Republic	Ecuador	El Salvador	Germany	Guatemala
Wisconsin	5,168	144	691	31	5	5	3	15	88	26
Wyoming	263	31	53	-	-	2	-	-	14	4
U.S. territories and possessions										
Guam	3,072	3	70	-	-	-	-	-	5	-
Northern Mariana Is.	158	-	10	-	-	-	-	-	1	-
Puerto Rico	7,614	9	62	118	144	6,462	15	38	23	19
Virgin Islands	1,610	23	2	1	-	315	-	-	8	-
Armed services posts	236	1	-	3	-	-	-	-	2	-
Other or unknown	40	3	-	-	-	-	-	1	2	-

Source: U.S. Immigration and Naturalization Service, *Statistical Yearbook of the Immigration and Naturalization Service, 1993,* U.S. Government Printing Office, Washington, DC, 1994, pp. 60-62. *Note:* A dash (-) represents zero.

★ 20 ★

Immigration

Immigrants Admitted, by State of Intended Residence and Selected Country of Birth, 1993 - II

The leading states of immigrants' intended residence have remained unchanged since 1971: California, New York, Texas, Florida, New Jersey, and Illinois. These six states were the intended homes of more than 70 percent of immigrants admitted in fiscal year 1993.

State of intended residence	All countries	Guyana	Haiti	Hong Kong	India	Iran	Ireland	Honduras	Jamaica	Korea	Mexico
Total	904,292	8,384	10,094	9,161	40,121	14,841	13,590	7,306	17,241	18,026	126,561
Alabama	2,298	2	2	2	303	54	14	13	22	76	67
Alaska	1,286	-	1	-	26	7	9	7	5	101	48
Arizona	9,778	10	6	68	290	92	63	47	13	160	4,719
Arkansas	1,312	4	-	7	84	16	26	7	10	36	115
California	260,090	133	75	3,884	8,674	8,816	1,833	1,308	340	5,929	63,221
Colorado	6,650	4	1	46	144	73	52	31	14	178	1,688
Connecticut	10,966	146	287	55	624	80	306	40	907	91	136
Delaware	1,132	10	28	14	129	8	12	2	35	93	53
District of Columbia	3,608	59	35	17	46	40	44	30	106	33	33
Florida	61,423	488	3,724	250	1,138	377	594	1,467	4,079	293	1,832
Georgia	10,213	61	20	56	752	214	147	44	177	322	606
Hawaii	8,528	-	1	251	28	11	19	2	2	390	39
Idaho	1,270	2	1	8	17	10	7	5	1	16	494
Illinois	46,744	22	87	286	3,991	255	743	192	284	841	8,911
Indiana	4,539	14	5	37	406	77	38	8	20	114	486
Iowa	2,626	1	2	30	89	16	15	15	2	117	186
Kansas	3,225	6	2	19	153	84	14	18	5	66	560
Kentucky	2,182	5	3	14	131	31	59	6	3	84	73
Louisiana	3,725	13	9	15	160	34	35	329	20	35	116
Maine	838	-	7	4	18	2	20	3	7	10	7
Maryland	16,899	214	108	148	1,291	519	175	93	544	772	187
Massachusetts	25,011	42	795	314	907	195	2,152	187	450	179	99
Michigan	14,913	7	8	81	1,283	144	77	34	75	386	400
Minnesota	7,438	68	5	74	236	82	64	28	27	237	192
Mississippi	906	-	1	8	86	12	8	9	4	16	31

[Continued]

★ 20 ★

Immigrants Admitted, by State of Intended Residence and Selected Country of Birth, 1993 - II

[Continued]

State of intended residence	All countries	Guyana	Haiti	Hong Kong	India	Iran	Ireland	Honduras	Jamaica	Korea	Mexico
Missouri	4,644	9	6	31	271	74	41	26	37	78	182
Montana	509	-	3	-	10	-	2	2	1	28	12
Nebraska	1,980	-	1	7	58	15	9	3	1	62	225
Nevada	4,045	6	2	31	88	43	33	45	24	77	1,049
New Hampshire	1,263	-	7	17	78	9	61	1	5	27	19
New Jersey	50,285	710	970	355	4,725	221	1,012	480	1,138	1,069	462
New Mexico	3,409	1	1	7	90	39	12	13	-	28	2,010
New York	151,209	6,082	3,643	1,625	5,338	799	4,411	1,691	7,992	2,022	1,911
North Carolina	6,892	37	9	30	526	87	78	47	26	233	341
North Dakota	601	-	-	4	16	6	1	1	-	13	13
Ohio	10,703	28	3	82	877	143	157	38	71	240	151
Oklahoma	2,942	2	2	2	178	111	12	11	10	90	574
Oregon	7,250	4	-	80	1261	97	34	15	8	199	901
Pennsylvania	16,964	32	96	177	1,397	139	470	78	397	518	220
Rhode Island	3,168	3	33	26	43	10	67	14	18	29	23
South Carolina	2,195	10	10	38	198	30	36	7	11	53	66
South Dakota	543	1	-	1	18	3	1	-	1	22	7
Tennessee	4,287	4	4	29	332	90	35	14	11	115	125
Texas	67,380	64	31	412	2,808	871	204	690	134	759	31,773
Utah	3,266	3	3	18	103	44	16	10	6	49	297
Vermont	709	-	3	6	27	2	19	2	2	21	6
Virginia	16,451	43	14	110	958	539	146	120	122	761	278
Washington	17,147	4	14	263	426	170	128	24	17	637	1,108
West Virginia	689	3	-	1	101	11	11	3	8	22	19
Wisconsin	5,168	8	3	46	236	36	57	22	30	110	356
Wyoming	263	-	-	1	6	1	4	-	-	8	36
U.S. territories and possessions											
Guam	3,072	-	-	61	15	1	2	1	-	169	3
Northern Mariana Is.	158	-	-	1	-	-	-	-	-	2	-
Puerto Rico	7,614	9	15	11	17	1	1	20	5	2	60
Virgin Islands	1,610	9	8	1	14	-	3	3	14	-	1
Armed services posts	236	-	-	-	-	-	1	-	-	8	2
Other or unknown	40	1	-	-	-	-	-	-	-	-	32

Source: U.S. Immigration and Naturalization Service, *Statistical Yearbook of the Immigration and Naturalization Service, 1993,* U.S. Government Printing Office, Washington, DC, 1994, pp. 60-62. *Note:* A dash (-) represents zero.

★21★

Immigration

Immigrants Admitted, by State of Intended Residence and Selected Country of Birth, 1993 - III

The leading states of immigrants' intended residence have remained unchanged since 1971: California, New York, Texas, Florida, New Jersey, and Illinois. These six states were the intended homes of more than 70 percent of immigrants admitted in fiscal year 1993.

State of intended residence	All countries	Pakistan	Peru	Philippines	Poland	Soviet Union	Taiwan	United Kingdom	Vietnam	Other
Total	904,292	8,927	10,447	63,457	27,846	58,571	14,329	18,783	59,614	169,030
Alabama	2,298	34	20	88	5	64	55	101	226	562
Alaska	1,286	-	17	411	61	76	12	24	16	264
Arizona	9,778	37	37	345	71	269	100	256	808	1,189
Arkansas	1,312	8	5	95	3	25	32	142	129	301
California	260,090	1,630	1,789	27,614	888	16,886	7,157	4,041	25,429	40,969
Colorado	6,650	18	62	239	101	594	76	228	651	1,297
Connecticut	10,966	138	299	286	1,490	744	50	481	454	2,342
Delaware	1,132	22	9	64	11	37	27	51	13	277
District of Columbia	3,608	24	60	123	8	57	12	48	453	1,140
Florida	61,423	349	1,737	1,930	672	1,113	291	2,136	1,384	14,878
Georgia	10,213	98	99	369	77	515	165	424	1,599	2,648
Hawaii	8,528	8	8	4,672	3	20	132	83	481	1,328
Idaho	1,270	6	22	50	8	81	6	37	73	173
Illinois	46,744	884	209	2,842	10,651	2,381	429	607	923	6,507
Indiana	4,539	67	18	200	104	248	108	173	182	908
Iowa	2,626	6	9	95	26	110	43	52	661	488
Kansas	3,225	33	18	117	14	187	40	65	616	564
Kentucky	2,182	33	13	127	13	164	26	77	245	411
Louisiana	3,725	41	24	165	10	60	30	129	846	880
Maine	838	5	2	53	16	57	6	46	97	185
Maryland	16,899	303	292	1,007	120	933	365	400	666	4,604
Massachusetts	25,011	134	146	425	682	2,691	267	810	1,915	5,839
Michigan	14,913	222	20	497	615	1,195	170	407	729	5,636
Minnesota	7,438	50	25	201	77	942	90	199	812	2,586
Mississippi	906	8	3	94	11	7	15	48	90	177
Missouri	4,644	67	35	274	41	497	78	131	810	867
Montana	509	2	2	41	2	47	4	16	7	100
Nebraska	1,980	7	10	65	16	157	31	49	615	292
Nevada	4,045	30	29	723	21	36	43	86	121	776
New Hampshire	1,263	27	3	49	17	76	20	97	90	292
New Jersey	50,285	619	2,073	4,637	3,887	1,875	927	950	937	9,226
New Mexico	3,409	14	9	88	9	39	22	102	229	272
New York	151,209	2,056	2,062	4,905	6,517	14,345	1,135	2,059	1,759	26,411
North Carolina	6,892	59	36	290	62	261	124	369	749	1,773
North Dakota	601	1	2	21	6	106	3	23	105	119
Ohio	10,703	120	44	414	192	1,866	219	334	481	2,686
Oklahoma	2,942	14	27	140	12	23	30	75	575	507
Oregon	7,250	20	35	341	33	1,527	54	128	1,070	1,424
Pennsylvania	16,964	181	111	549	542	2,920	175	729	1,637	3,542
Rhode Island	3,168	5	28	86	86	343	6	39	17	973
South Carolina	2,195	21	23	186	23	70	31	178	136	509
South Dakota	543	4	3	38	8	95	1	14	44	198
Tennessee	4,287	53	13	177	42	217	87	190	457	1,368
Texas	67,380	836	251	2,031	174	808	980	970	5,173	8,190

[Continued]

★ 21 ★

Immigrants Admitted, by State of Intended Residence and Selected Country of Birth, 1993 - III

[Continued]

State of intended residence	All countries	Pakistan	Peru	Philippines	Poland	Soviet Union	Taiwan	United Kingdom	Vietnam	Other
Utah	3,266	34	77	82	27	255	56	120	395	746
Vermont	709	1	2	9	4	45	12	33	157	125
Virginia	16,451	461	471	1,390	78	525	196	484	1,300	4,588
Washington	17,147	67	70	1,834	179	2,678	268	318	3,080	3,404
West Virginia	689	26	9	60	1	8	9	23	41	146
Wisconsin	5,168	27	29	172	129	290	65	141	116	2,287
Wyoming	263	11	-	13	1	6	2	14	-	56
U.S. territories and possessions										
Guam	3,072	5	3	2,430	-	-	46	16	14	228
Northern Mariana Is.	158	-	-	136	-	-	-	-	-	8
Puerto Rico	7,614	-	45	6	-	-	1	8	-	523
Virgin Islands	1,610	1	1	4	-	-	-	15	-	1,187
Armed services posts	236	-	1	157	-	-	-	7	1	53
Other or unknown	40	-	-	-	-	-	-	-	-	1

Source: U.S. Immigration and Naturalization Service, *Statistical Yearbook of the Immigration and Naturalization Service, 1993,* U.S. Government Printing Office, Washington, DC, 1994, pp. 60-62. *Note:* A dash (-) represents zero.

★ 22 ★

Immigration

Immigration, by Region and Selected Country of Birth, FY 1983-93

Data show number of immigrants admitted in each fiscal year. Mexico accounted for the highest percentage of immigrant admissions in 1993, with 14 percent of the overall total.

Region and country of birth	1983	1984	1985	1986	1987	1988	1989	1990	1991	1992	1993
All countries	559,763	543,903	570,009	601,708	601,516	643,025	1,090,924	1,536,483	1,827,167	973,977	904,292
North America	168,487	166,706	182,045	207,714	216,550	250,009	607,398	957,558	1,210,981	384,047	301,380
Canada	11,390	10,791	11,385	11,039	11,876	11,783	12,151	16,812	13,504	15,205	17,156
Mexico	59,079	57,557	61,077	66,533	72,351	95,039	405,172	679,068	946,167	213,802	126,561
Caribbean	73,306	74,265	83,281	101,632	102,899	112,357	88,932	115,351	140,139	97,413	99,438
Antigua-Barbuda	2,008	953	957	812	874	837	979	1,319	944	619	554
Bahamas, The	505	499	533	570	556	1,283	861	1,378	1,062	641	686
Barbados	1,849	1,577	1,625	1,595	1,665	1,455	1,616	1,745	1,460	1,091	1,184
Cuba	8,978	10,599	20,334	33,114	28,916	17,558	10,046	10,645	10,349	11,791	13,666
Dominica	546	442	540	564	740	611	748	963	9821	809	683
Dominican Republic	22,058	23,147	23,787	26,175	24,858	27,189	26,723	42,195	41,405	41,969	45,420
Grenada	1,154	980	934	1,045	1,098	842	1,046	1,294	979	848	827
Haiti	8,424	9,839	10,165	12,666	14,819	34,806	13,658	20,324	47,527	11,002	10,094
Jamaica	19,535	19,811	18,923	19,595	23,148	20,966	24,523	25,013	23,828	18,915	17,241
St. Kitts & Nevis	2,773	1,648	769	573	589	660	795	896	830	626	544
St. Lucia	662	484	499	502	496	606	709	833	766	654	634
St. Vincent & Grenadines	767	695	693	635	746	634	892	973	828	687	657
Trinidad & Tobago	3,156	2,900	2,831	2,891	3,543	3,947	5,394	6,740	8,407	7,008	6,577
Other Caribbean	891	680	691	895	851	963	942	1,033	792	753	671

[Continued]

★ 22 ★

Immigration, by Region and Selected Country of Birth, FY 1983-93

[Continued]

Region and country of birth	1983	1984	1985	1986	1987	1988	1989	1990	1991	1992	1993
Central America	24,601	24,088	26,302	28,380	29,296	30,715	101,034	146,202	111,093	57,558	58,162
Belize	1,585	1,492	1,353	1,385	1,354	1,497	2,217	3,867	2,377	1,020	1,035
Costa Rica	1,182	1,473	1,281	1,356	1,391	1,351	1,985	2,840	2,341	1,480	1,368
El Salvador	8,596	8,787	10,156	10,929	10,693	12,045	57,878	80,173	47,351	26,191	26,818
Guatemala	4,090	3,937	4,389	5,158	5,739	5,723	19,049	32,303	25,527	10,521	11,870
Honduras	3,619	3,405	3,726	4,532	4,751	4,302	7,593	12,024	11,451	6,552	7,306
Nicaragua	2,983	2,718	2,786	2,826	3,294	3,311	8,830	11,562	17,842	8,949	7,086
Panama	2,546	2,276	2,611	2,194	2,084	2,486	3,482	3,433	4,204	2,845	2,679
Other North America	111	5	-	130	128	115	109	125	78	69	63
South America	36,087	37,460	39,058	41,874	44,385	41,007	58,926	85,819	79,934	55,308	53,921
Argentina	2,029	2,141	1,844	2,187	2,106	2,371	3,301	5,437	3,889	3,877	2,824
Bolivia	823	918	1,006	1,079	1,170	1,038	1,805	2,843	3,006	1,510	1,545
Brazil	1,503	1,847	2,272	2,332	2,505	2,699	3,332	4,191	8,133	4,755	4,604
Chile	1,970	1,912	1,992	2,243	2,140	2,137	3,037	4,049	2,842	1,937	1,778
Colombia	9,658	11,020	11,982	11,408	11,700	10,322	15,214	24,189	19,702	13,201	12,819
Ecuador	4,243	4,164	4,482	4,516	4,641	4,716	7,532	12,476	9,958	7,286	7,324
Guyana	8,980	8,412	8,531	10,367	11,384	8,747	10,789	11,362	11,666	9,064	8,384
Paraguay	187	167	170	190	291	483	529	704	538	514	668
Peru	4,384	4,368	4,181	4,895	5,901	5,936	10,175	15,726	16,237	9,868	10,447
Uruguay	681	712	790	699	709	612	948	1,457	1,161	716	568
Venezuela	1,508	1,721	1,714	1,854	1,694	1,791	2,099	3,142	2,622	2,340	2,743
Other South America	121	78	94	104	144	155	165	243	180	240	217
Europe	58,867	64,076	63,043	62,512	61,174	64,797	82,891	112,401	135,234	145,392	158,254
Albania	22	32	45	53	62	82	71	78	142	682	1,400
Austria	433	442	419	463	483	514	501	675	589	701	549
Belgium	538	537	538	620	636	581	548	682	525	780	657
Bulgaria	201	225	249	221	205	217	265	428	623	1,049	1,029
Czechoslovakia	946	1,218	1,222	1,118	1,357	1,482	992	1,412	1,156	1,181	1,000
Denmark	513	512	478	554	537	558	593	666	601	764	735
Finland	311	264	290	322	331	390	325	369	333	525	544
France	2,061	2,135	2,187	2,518	2,513	2,524	2,598	2,849	2,450	3,288	2,864
Germany	6,725	6,747	7,109	6,991	7,210	6,645	6,708	7,388	6,509	9,888	7,312
Greece	2,997	2,865	2,579	2,512	2,653	2,458	2,491	2,742	2,079	1,858	1,884
Hungary	632	825	1,009	1,006	994	1,227	1,193	1,655	1,534	1,304	1,091
Ireland	1,101	1,223	1,397	1,839	3,060	5,058	6,961	10,333	4,767	12,226	13,590
Italy	3,225	3,130	3,214	3,089	2,784	2,949	2,910	3,287	2,619	2,592	2,487
Latvia	31	37	25	26	23	31	57	45	86	419	668
Lithuania	41	45	39	49	37	47	63	67	157	353	529
Netherlands	1,152	1,242	1,217	1,261	1,230	1,187	1,193	1,424	1,283	1,586	1,430
Norway	409	375	361	354	326	397	482	524	486	665	608
Poland	6,427	9,466	9,464	8,481	7,519	9,507	15,101	20,537	19,199	25,504	27,846
Portugal	3,231	3,779	3,781	3,766	3,912	3,199	3,758	4,035	4,524	2,748	2,081
Romania	2,543	4,004	5,188	5,198	3,837	3,875	4,573	4,647	8,096	6,500	5,601
Soviet Union	5,214	6,088	3,521	2,588	2,384	2,949	11,128	25,524	56,980	43,614	58,571
Spain	1,507	1,393	1,413	1,591	1,578	1,483	1,550	1,886	1,849	1,631	1,388
Sweden	870	974	1,076	1,098	1,057	1,156	1,078	1,196	1,080	1,463	1,393
Switzerland	680	620	729	677	759	751	788	845	696	1,023	972
United Kingdom	14,830	13,949	13,408	13,657	13,497	13,228	14,090	15,928	13,903	19,973	18,783
Yugoslavia	1,382	1,569	1,662	2,011	1,827	1,841	2,496	2,828	2,713	2,604	2,809
Other Europe	845	380	423	449	363	361	378	351	255	471	433

[Continued]

★ 22 ★

Immigration, by Region and Selected Country of Birth, FY 1983-93

[Continued]

Region and country of birth	1983	1984	1985	1986	1987	1988	1989	1990	1991	1992	1993
Asia	277,697	256,272	264,691	268,248	257,684	264,465	312,149	338,581	358,533	356,955	358,047
Afghanistan	2,566	3,222	2,794	2,831	2,424	2,873	3,232	3,187	2,879	2,685	2,964
Bangladesh	787	823	1,146	1,634	1,649	1,325	2,180	4,252	10,676	3,740	3,291
Burma	723	719	990	863	941	803	1,170	1,120	946	816	849
Cambodia	18,120	11,856	13,563	13,501	12,460	9,629	6,076	5,179	3,251	2,573	1,639
China, Mainland	25,777	23,363	24,787	25,106	25,841	28,717	32,272	31,815	33,025	38,907	65,578
Hong Kong	5,948	5,465	5,171	5,021	4,706	8,546	9,740	9,393	10,427	10,452	9,161
India	25,451	24,964	26,026	26,227	27,803	26,268	31,175	30,667	45,064	36,755	40,121
Indonesia	952	1,113	1,269	1,183	1,254	1,342	1,513	3,498	2,223	2,916	1,767
Iran	11,163	13,807	16,071	16,505	14,426	15,246	21,243	24,977	19,569	13,233	14,841
Iraq	2,343	2,930	1,951	1,323	1,072	1,022	1,516	1,756	1,494	4,111	4,072
Israel	3,239	3,066	3,113	3,790	3,699	3,640	4,244	4,664	4,181	5,104	4,494
Japan	4,092	4,043	4,086	3,959	4,174	4,512	4,849	5,734	5,049	11,028	6,908
Jordan	2,718	2,438	2,998	3,081	3,125	3,232	3,921	4,449	4,259	4,036	4,741
Korea	33,339	33,042	35,253	35,776	35,849	34,703	34,222	32,301	26,518	19,359	18,026
Kuwait	344	437	503	496	507	599	710	691	861	989	1,129
Laos	23,662	12,279	9,133	7,842	6,828	10,667	12,524	10,446	9,950	8,696	7,285
Lebanon	2,941	3,203	3,385	3,994	4,367	4,910	5,716	5,634	6,009	5,838	5,465
Macau	246	260	271	243	254	183	246	301	267	320	334
Malaysia	852	879	939	886	1,016	1,250	1,506	1,867	1,860	2,235	2,026
Pakistan	4,807	5,509	5,744	5,994	6,319	5,438	8,000	9,729	20,355	10,214	8,927
Philippines	41,546	42,768	47,978	52,558	50,060	50,697	57,034	63,756	63,596	61,022	63,457
Saudi Arabia	170	208	228	275	294	338	381	518	552	584	616
Singapore	362	377	460	480	469	492	566	620	535	774	798
Sri Lanka	472	554	553	596	630	634	757	976	1,377	1,081	1,109
Syria	1,683	1,724	1,581	1,604	1,669	2,183	2,675	2,972	2,837	2,940	2,933
Taiwan	16,698	12,478	14,895	13,424	11,931	9,670	13,974	15,151	13,274	16,344	14,329
Thailand	5,875	4,885	5,239	6,204	6,733	6,888	9,332	8,914	7,397	7,090	6,654
Turkey	2,263	1,793	1,691	1,753	1,596	1,642	2,007	2,468	2,528	2,488	2,204
Vietnam	37,560	37,236	31,895	29,993	24,231	25,789	37,739	48,792	55,307	77,735	59,614
Yemen	507	331	435	480	727	619	966	1,945	1,547	2,056	1,793
Other Asia	491	500	543	626	630	608	663	809	720	834	922
Africa	15,084	15,540	17,117	17,463	17,724	18,882	25,166	35,893	36,179	27,086	27,783
Algeria	201	197	202	183	172	199	230	302	269	407	360
Cameroon	92	145	123	130	132	157	187	380	452	236	262
Cape Verde	594	591	627	760	657	921	1,118	907	973	757	936
Egypt	2,600	2,642	2,802	2,989	3,377	3,016	3,717	4,117	5,602	3,576	3,556
Ethiopia	2,643	2,461	3,362	2,737	2,156	2,571	3,389	4,336	5,127	4,602	5,276
Ghana	976	1,050	1,041	1,164	1,120	1,239	2,045	4,466	3,330	1,867	1,604
Kenya	710	753	735	719	698	773	910	1,297	1,185	953	1,065
Liberia	518	585	618	618	622	769	1,175	2,004	1,292	999	1,050
Libya	221	206	242	195	183	198	210	268	314	286	343
Morocco	479	506	570	646	635	715	984	1,200	1,601	1,316	1,176
Nigeria	2,354	2,337	2,846	2,976	3,278	3,343	5,213	8,843	7,912	4,551	4,448
Senegal	71	59	91	91	92	130	141	537	869	337	178
Sierre Leone	319	368	371	323	453	571	939	1,290	951	693	690
Somalia	83	90	139	139	197	183	228	227	458	500	1,088
South Africa	1,261	1,246	1,210	1,566	1,741	1,832	1,899	1,990	1,854	2,516	2,197
Sudan	128	199	271	230	198	217	272	306	679	675	714
Tanzania	364	418	395	370	385	388	507	635	500	352	426
Uganda	332	369	3041	401	357	343	393	674	538	437	415
Zimbabwe	193	200	222	221	252	216	230	272	261	296	308

[Continued]

★ 22 ★

Immigration, by Region and Selected Country of Birth, FY 1983-93

[Continued]

Region and country of birth	1983	1984	1985	1986	1987	1988	1989	1990	1991	1992	1993
Other Africa	945	1,118	949	1,005	1,019	1,101	1,379	1,792	2,012	1,730	1,691
Oceania	3,515	3,818	4,054	3,894	3,993	3,839	4,360	6,182	6,236	5,169	4,902
Australia	1,273	1,308	1,362	1,354	1,253	1,356	1,546	1,754	1,678	2,238	2,320
Fiji	712	901	980	972	1,205	1,028	968	1,353	1,349	807	854
New Zealand	606	595	679	610	591	668	789	829	793	967	1,052
Tonga	481	555	669	510	545	434	646	1,375	1,685	703	348
Other Oceania	443	459	364	448	399	353	411	871	731	454	328
Unknown or not reported	26	31	1	3	6	23	34	49	70	18	5
Born on board ship	-	-	-	-	-	3	-	-	-	2	-

Source: U.S. Immigration and Naturalization Service, *Statistical Yearbook of the Immigration and Naturalization Service, 1993*, U.S. Government Printing Office, Washington, DC, 1994, pp. 30-31. *Note:* A dash (-) represents zero.

★ 23 ★

Immigration

Immigration, by Region and Selected Country of Last Residence, 1820-1993 - I

Data show immigration in fiscal years for which ending date may vary.

Region and country of last residence[1]	1820	1821-30	1831-40	1841-50	1851-60	1861-70	1871-80	1881-90
All countries	8,385	143,439	599,125	1,713,251	2,598,214	2,314,824	2,812,191	5,246,613
Europe	7,690	98,797	495,681	1,597,442	2,452,577	2,065,141	2,271,925	4,735,484
Austria-Hungary	[2]	[2]	[2]	[2]	[2]	7,800	72,969	353,719
Austria	[2]	[2]	[2]	[2]	[2]	7,124[3]	63,009	226,038
Hungary	[2]	[2]	[2]	[2]	[2]	484[3]	9,960	127,681
Belgium	1	27	22	5,074	4,738	6,734	7,221	20,177
Czechoslovakia	[4]	[4]	[4]	[4]	[4]	[4]	[4]	[4]
Denmark	20	169	1,063	539	3,749	17,094	31,771	88,132
France	371	8,497	45,575	77,262	76,358	35,986	72,206	50,464
Germany	968	6,761	152,454	434,626	951,667	787,468	718,182	1,452,970
Greece	-	20	49	16	31	72	210	2,308
Ireland[5]	3,614	50,724	207,381	780,719	914,119	435,778	736,871	655,482
Italy	30	409	2,253	1,870	9,231	11,725	55,759	307,309
Netherlands	49	1,078	1,412	8,251	10,789	9,102	16,541	53,701
Norway-Sweden	3	91	1,201	13,903	20,931	109,298	211,245	568,362
Norway	[6]	[6]	[6]	[6]	[6]	[6]	95,323	176,586
Sweden	[6]	[6]	[6]	[6]	[6]	[6]	115,922	391,776
Poland	5	16	369	105	1,164	2,027	12,970	51,806
Portugal	35	145	829	550	1,055	2,658	14,082	16,978
Romania	[7]	[7]	[7]	[7]	[7]	[7]	11[7]	6,348
Soviet Union	14	75	277	551	457	2,512	39,284	213,282
Spain	139	2,477	2,125	2,209	9,298	6,697	5,266	4,419
Switzerland	31	3,226	4,821	4,644	25,011	23,286	28,293	81,988
United Kingdom[5,8]	2,410	25,079	75,810	267,044	423,974	606,896	548,043	807,357

[Continued]

★ 23 ★

Immigration, by Region and Selected Country of Last Residence, 1820-1993 - I

[Continued]

Region and country of last residence[1]	1820	1821-30	1831-40	1841-50	1851-60	1861-70	1871-80	1881-90
Yugoslavia	[9]	[9]	[9]	[9]	[9]	[9]	[9]	[9]
Other Europe	-	3	40	79	5	8	1,001	682
Asia	6	30	55	141	41,538	64,759	124,160	69,942
China[10]	1	2	8	35	41,397	64,301	123,201	61,711
Hong Kong	[11]	[11]	[11]	[11]	[11]	[11]	[11]	[11]
India	1	8	39	36	43	69	163	269
Iran	[12]	[12]	[12]	[12]	[12]	[12]	[12]	[12]
Israel	[13]	[13]	[13]	[13]	[13]	[13]	[13]	[13]
Japan	[14]	[14]	[14]	[14]	[14]	186	149	2,270
Korea	[15]	[15]	[15]	[15]	[15]	[15]	[15]	[15]
Philippines	[16]	[16]	[16]	[16]	[16]	[16]	[16]	[16]
Turkey	1	20	7	59	83	131	404	3,782
Vietnam	[11]	[11]	[11]	[11]	[11]	[11]	[11]	[11]
Other Asia	3	-	1	11	15	72	243	1,910
North-America	387	11,564	33,424	62,469	74,720	166,607	404,044	426,967
Canada & Newfoundland[17,18]	209	2,277	13,624	41,723	59,309	153,878	383,640	393,304
Mexico[18]	1	4,817	6,599	3,271	3,078	2,191	5,162	1,913[19]
Caribbean	164	3,834	12,301	13,526	10,660	9,046	13,957	29,042
Cuba	[12]	[12]	[12]	[12]	[12]	[12]	[12]	[12]
Dominican Republic	[20]	[20]	[20]	[20]	[20]	[20]	[20]	[20]
Haiti	[20]	[20]	[20]	[20]	[20]	[20]	[20]	[20]
Jamaica	[21]	[21]	[21]	[21]	[21]	[21]	[21]	[21]
Other Caribbean	164	3,834	12,301	13,528	10,660	9,046	13,957	29,042
Central America	2	105	44	368	449	95	157	404
El Salvador	[20]	[20]	[20]	[20]	[20]	[20]	[20]	[20]
Other Central America	2	105	44	368	449	95	157	404
South America	11	531	856	3,579	1,224	1,397	1,128	2,304
Argentina	[20]	[20]	[20]	[20]	[20]	[20]	[20]	[20]
Colombia	[20]	[20]	[20]	[20]	[20]	[20]	[20]	[20]
Ecuador	[20]	[20]	[20]	[20]	[20]	[20]	[20]	[20]
Other South America	11	531	856	3,579	1,224	1,397	1,128	2,304
Other America	[22]	[22]	[22]	[22]	[22]	[22]	[22]	[22]

[Continued]

★ 23 ★

Immigration, by Region and Selected Country of Last Residence, 1820-1993 - I

[Continued]

Region and country of last residence[1]	1820	1821-30	1831-40	1841-50	1851-60	1861-70	1871-80	1881-90
Africa	1	16	54	55	210	312	358	857
Oceania	1	2	9	29	158	214	10,914	12,574
Not specified[22]	300	33,030	69,902	53,115	29,011	17,791	790	789

Source: U.S. Immigration and Naturalization Service, *Statistical Yearbook of the Immigration and Naturalization Service, 1993*, U.S. Government Printing Office, Washington, DC, 1994, pp. 26-29. *Notes:* A dash (-) represents zero. From 1820-67, figures represent alien passengers arrived at seaports; from 1868-97, immigrant aliens arrived; from 1892-94 and 1898-1990, immigrant aliens admitted for permanent residence. From 1892-1903, aliens entering by cabin class were not counted as immigrants. Land arrivals were not completely enumerated until 1908. 1. Data for years prior to 1906 relate to country whence alien came; data from 1906-79 and 1984-90 are for country of last permanent residence, and data for 1980-83 refer to country of birth. Because of changes in boundaries, changes in lists of countries, and lack of data for specified countries for various periods, data for certain countries, especially for the total period 1820-1990, are not comparable throughout. Data for specified countries are included with countries to which they belonged prior to World War I. 2. Data for Austria and Hungary not reported until 1861. 3. Data for Austria and Hungary not reported separately for all years during the period. 4. No data available for Czechoslovakia until 1920. 5. Prior to 1926, data for Northern Ireland included in Ireland. 6. Data for Norway and Sweden not reported separately until 1871. 7. No data available for Romania until 1880. 8. Since 1925, data for United Kingdom refer to England, Scotland, Wales, and Northern Ireland. 9. In 1920, a separate enumeration was made for the Kingdom of Serbs, Croats, and Slovenes. Since 1922, the Serb, Croat, and Slovene Kingdom recorded as Yugoslavia. 10. Beginning in 1957, China includes Taiwan. 11. Data not reported separately until 1952. 12. Data not reported separately until 1925. 13. Data not reported separately until 1949. 14. No data available for Japan until 1861. 15. Data not reported separately until 1948. 16. Prior to 1934, Philippines recorded as insular travel. 17. Prior to 1920, Canada and Newfoundland recorded as British North America. From 1820-98, figures include all British North America possessions. 18. Land arrivals not completely enumerated until 1908. 19. No data available for Mexico from 1886-93. 20. Data not reported separately until 1932. 21. Data for Jamaica not collected until 1953. In prior years, consolidated under British West Indies, which is included in "Other Caribbean." 22. Included in countries "Not specified" until 1925. 23. From 1899-1919, data for Poland included in Austria-Hungary, Germany, and the Soviet Union. 24. From 1938-45 Austria included in Germany. 25. Includes 32,897 persons returning to their homes in the United States.

★ 24 ★

Immigration

Immigration, by Region and Selected Country of Last Residence, 1820-1993 - II

Data show immigration in fiscal years for which ending date may vary.

Region and country of last residence[1]	1891-1900	1901-10	1911-20	1921-30	1931-40	1941-50	1951-60	1961-70
All countries	3,687,564	8,795,386	5,735,811	4,107,209	528,431	1,035,039	2,515,479	3,321,677
Europe	3,555,352	8,056,040	4,321,887	2,463,194	347,566	621,147	1,325,727	1,123,492
Austria-Hungary	592,707[23]	2,145,266[23]	896,342[23]	63,548	11,424	28,329	103,743	26,022
Austria	234,081[3]	668,209[3]	453,649	32,868	3,563[24]	24,860[24]	67,106	20,621
Hungary	181,288[3]	808,511[3]	442,693	30,680	7,861	3,469	36,637	5,401
Belgium	18,167	41,635	33,746	15,846	4,817	12,189	18,575	9,192
Czechoslovakia	[4]	[4]	3,426[4]	102,194	14,393	8,347	918	3,273
Denmark	50,231	65,285	41,983	32,430	2,559	5,393	10,984	9,201
France	30,770	73,379	61,897	49,610	12,623	38,809	51,121	45,237
Germany	505,152[23]	341,498[23]	143,945[23]	412,202	114,058[24]	226,578[24]	477,765	190,796
Greece	15,979	167,519	184,201	51,084	9,119	8,973	47,608	85,969
Ireland[5]	388,416	339,065	146,181	211,234	10,973	19,789	48,362	32,966
Italy	651,893	2,045,877	1,109,524	455,315	68,028	57,661	185,491	214,111
Netherlands	26,758	48,262	43,718	26,948	7,150	14,860	52,277	30,606
Norway-Sweden	321,281	440,039	161,469	165,780	8,700	20,765	44,632	32,600
Norway	95,015	190,505	66,395	68,531	4,740	10,100	22,935	15,484
Sweden	226,266	249,534	95,074	97,249	3,960	10,665	21,697	17,116

[Continued]

★ 24 ★

Immigration, by Region and Selected Country of Last Residence, 1820-1993 - II

[Continued]

Region and country of last residence[1]	1891-1900	1901-10	1911-20	1921-30	1931-40	1941-50	1951-60	1961-70
Poland	96,720[23]	[23]	4,813[23]	227,734	17,026	7,571	9,985	53,539
Portugal	27,508	69,149	89,732	29,994	3,329	7,423	19,588	76,065
Romania	12,750	53,008	13,311	67,646	3,871	1,076	1,039	2,531
Soviet Union	505,290[23]	1,597,306[23]	921,201[23]	61,742	1,370	571	671	2,465
Spain	8,731	27,935	68,611	28,958	3,258	2,898	7,894	44,659
Switzerland	31,179	34,922	23,091	29,676	5,512	10,547	17,675	18,453
United Kingdom[5,8]	271,538	525,950	341,408	339,570	31,572	139,306	202,824	213,822
Yugoslavia	[9]	[9]	1,888[9]	49,064	5,835	1,576	8,225	20,381
Other Europe	282	39,945	31,400	42,619	11,949	8,486	16,350	11,604
Asia	74,862	323,543	247,236	112,059	16,595	37,028	153,249	427,642
China[10]	14,799	20,605	21,278	29,907	4,928	16,709	9,657	34,764
Hong Kong	[11]	[11]	[11]	[11]	[11]	[11]	15,541[11]	75,007
India	68	4,713	2,082	1,886	496	1,761	1,973	27,189
Iran	[12]	[12]	[12]	241[12]	195	1,380	3,388	10,339
Israel	[13]	[13]	[13]	[13]	[13]	476[13]	25,476	29,602
Japan	25,942	129,797	83,837	33,462	1,948	1,555	46,250	39,988
Korea	[15]	[15]	[15]	[15]	[15]	107[15]	6,231	34,526
Philippines	[16]	[16]	[16]	[16]	528[16]	4,691	19,307	98,376
Turkey	30,425	157,369	134,066	33,824	1,065	798	3,519	10,142
Vietnam	[11]	[11]	[11]	[11]	[11]	[11]	335[11]	4,340
Other Asia	3,628	11,059	5,973	12,739	7,435	9,551	21,572	63,369
North-America	38,972	361,888	1,143,671	1,516,716	160,037	354,804	996,944	1,716,374
Canada & Newfoundland[17,18]	3,311	179,226	742,185	924,515	108,527	171,718	377,952	413,310
Mexico[18]	971[19]	49,642	219,004	459,287	22,319	60,589	299,811	453,937
Caribbean	33,066	107,548	123,424	74,899	15,502	49,725	123,091	470,213
Cuba	[12]	[12]	[12]	15,901[12]	9,571	26,313	78,948	208,536
Dominican Republic	[20]	[20]	[20]	[20]	1,150[20]	5,627	9,897	93,292
Haiti	[20]	[20]	[20]	[20]	191[20]	911	4,442	34,499
Jamaica	[21]	[21]	[21]	[21]	[21]	[21]	8,869[21]	74,906
Other Caribbean	33,066	107,548	123,424	58,998	4,590	16,874	20,935[21]	58,980
Central America	549	8,192	17,159	15,769	5,861	21,665	44,751	101,330
El Salvador	[20]	[20]	[20]	[20]	673[20]	5,132	5,895	14,992
Other Central America	549	8,192	17,159	15,769	5,188	16,533	38,856	86,338
South America	1,075	17,280	41,899	42,215	7,803	21,831	91,628	257,940
Argentina	[20]	[20]	[20]	[20]	1,349[20]	3,338	19,486	49,721
Colombia	[20]	[20]	[20]	[20]	1,223[20]	3,858	18,048	72,028
Ecuador	[20]	[20]	[20]	[20]	337[20]	2,417	9,841	36,780
Other South America	1,075	17,280	41,899	42,215	4,894	12,218	44,253	99,425
Other America	[22]	[22]	[22]	31[22]	25	29,276	59,711	19,630

[Continued]

★ 24 ★

Immigration, by Region and Selected Country of Last Residence, 1820-1993 - II

[Continued]

Region and country of last residence[1]	1891-1900	1901-10	1911-20	1921-30	1931-40	1941-50	1951-60	1961-70
Africa	350	7,368	8,443	6,286	1,750	7,367	14,092	28,954
Oceania	3,965	13,024	13,427	8,726	2,483	14,551	12,976	25,122
Not specified[22]	14,063	33,523[25]	1,147	228	-	142	12,491	93

Source: U.S. Immigration and Naturalization Service, *Statistical Yearbook of the Immigration and Naturalization Service, 1993,* U.S. Government Printing Office, Washington, DC, 1994, pp. 26-29. *Notes:* A dash (-) represents zero. From 1820-67, figures represent alien passengers arrived at seaports; from 1868-97, immigrant aliens arrived; from 1892-94 and 1898-1990, immigrant aliens admitted for permanent residence. From 1892-1903, aliens entering by cabin class were not counted as immigrants. Land arrivals were not completely enumerated until 1908. 1. Data for years prior to 1906 relate to country whence alien came; data from 1906-79 and 1984-90 are for country of last permanent residence, and data for 1980-83 refer to country of birth. Because of changes in boundaries, changes in lists of countries, and lack of data for specified countries for various periods, data for certain countries, especially for the total period 1820-1990, are not comparable throughout. Data for specified countries are included with countries to which they belonged prior to World War I. 2. Data for Austria and Hungary not reported until 1861. 3. Data for Austria and Hungary not reported separately for all years during the period. 4. No data available for Czechoslovakia until 1920. 5. Prior to 1926, data for Northern Ireland included in Ireland. 6. Data for Norway and Sweden not reported separately until 1871. 7. No data available for Romania until 1880. 8. Since 1925, data for United Kingdom refer to England, Scotland, Wales, and Northern Ireland. 9. In 1920, a separate enumeration was made for the Kingdom of Serbs, Croats, and Slovenes. Since 1922, the Serb, Croat, and Slovene Kingdom recorded as Yugoslavia. 10. Beginning in 1957, China includes Taiwan. 11. Data not reported separately until 1952. 12. Data not reported separately until 1925. 13. Data not reported separately until 1949. 14. No data available for Japan until 1861. 15. Data not reported separately until 1948. 16. Prior to 1934, Philippines recorded as insular travel. 17. Prior to 1920, Canada and Newfoundland recorded as British North America. From 1820-98, figures include all British North America possessions. 18. Land arrivals not completely enumerated until 1908. 19. No data available for Mexico from 1886-93. 20. Data not reported separately until 1932. 21. Data for Jamaica not collected until 1953. In prior years, consolidated under British West Indies, which is included in "Other Caribbean." 22. Included in countries "Not specified" until 1925. 23. From 1899-1919, data for Poland included in Austria-Hungary, Germany, and the Soviet Union. 24. From 1938-45 Austria included in Germany. 25. Includes 32,897 persons returning to their homes in the United States.

★ 25 ★

Immigration

Immigration, by Region and Selected Country of Last Residence, 1820-1993 - III

Data show immigration in fiscal years for which ending date may vary.

Region and country of last residence[1]	1971-80	1981-90	1988	1989	1990	1991	1992	1993	Total 174 years 1820-1993
All countries	4,493,314	7,338,062	643,025	1,090,924	1,536,483	1,827,167	973,977	904,292	60,699,450
Europe	800,368	761,550	71,854	94,338	124,026	146,671	153,260	165,711	37,566,702
Austria-Hungary	16,028	24,885	3,200	3,586	4,733	4,455	3,934	2,914	4,354,085
Austria	9,478	18,340	2,493	2,845	3,774	3,511	2,895	1,880	1,837,232[3]
Hungary	6,550	6,545	707	741	959	944	1,039	1,034	1,670,777[3]
Belgium	5,329	7,066	706	705	827	701	957	776	212,990
Czechoslovakia	6,023	7,227	744	526	578	625	874	792	148,092
Denmark	4,439	5,370	561	617	674	629	769	762	372,572
France	25,069	32,353	3,637	4,101	4,265	3,978	4,492	3,959	800,016
Germany	74,414	91,961	9,748	10,419	12,152	10,887	12,875	9,965	7,117,192
Greece	92,369	38,377	4,690	4,588	3,887	2,929	2,168	2,460	711,461
Ireland[5]	11,490	31,969	5,121	6,983	9,740	4,608	12,035	13,396	4,755,172
Italy	129,368	67,254	5,332	11,089	16,246	30,316	11,962	3,899	5,419,285
Netherlands	10,492	12,238	1,152	1,253	1,515	1,303	1,687	1,542	378,764
Norway-Sweden	10,472	15,182	1,669	1,809	1,930	1,796	2,296	2,253	2,152,299
Norway	3,941	4,164	446	556	552	554	790	713	803,281[6]
Sweden	6,531	11,018	1,223	1,253	1,378	1,242	1,506	1,540	1,288,763[6]
Poland	37,234	83,252	7,298	13,279	18,364	17,106	24,491	27,288	675,221
Portugal	101,710	40,431	3,290	3,861	4,066	4,576	2,774	2,075	510,686

[Continued]

★ 25 ★

Immigration, by Region and Selected Country of Last Residence, 1820-1993 - III

[Continued]

Region and country of last residence[1]	1971-80	1981-90	1988	1989	1990	1991	1992	1993	Total 174 years 1820-1993
Romania	12,393	30,857	2,915	3,535	3,496	6,786	4,907	4,517	221,051
Soviet Union	38,961	57,677	1,408	4,570	14,779	31,557	37,069	59,949	3,572,281
Spain	39,141	20,433	1,972	2,179	2,744	2,663	2,041	1,791	291,643
Switzerland	8,235	8,849	920	1,072	1,288	1,003	1,303	1,263	363,008
United Kingdom[5,8]	137,374	159,173	14,667	16,961	19,054	16,768	21,924	20,422	5,178,264
Yugoslavia	30,540	18,762	2,039	2,464	2,778	2,802	2,741	2,781	144,595
Other Europe	9,287	8,234	785	741	910	1,183	1,961	2,907	188,025
Asia	1,588,178	2,738,157	254,745	296,420	321,879	342,157	344,802	345,425	7,051,564
China[10]	124,326	346,747	34,300	39,284	40,639	23,995	29,554	57,775	1,025,700
Hong Kong	113,467	98,215	11,817	15,257	14,367	15,895	16,802	14,026	348,953[11]
India	164,134	250,786	25,312	28,599	28,809	42,707	34,841	38,653	571,917
Iran	45,136	116,172	9,846	13,027	14,905	9,927	6,995	8,908	202,681[12]
Israel	37,713	44,273	4,444	5,494	5,906	5,116	5,938	5,216	153,810[13]
Japan	49,775	47,085	5,085	5,454	6,431	5,600	11,735	7,673	487,252[14]
Korea	267,638	333,746	34,151	33,016	30,964	25,430	18,734	17,320	703,732[15]
Philippines	354,987	548,764	61,017	66,119	71,279	68,750	63,478	63,406	1,222,287[16]
Turkey	13,399	23,233	2,200	2,538	3,205	3,466	3,203	3,487	422,483
Vietnam	172,820	280,782	12,856	13,174	14,755	14,847	31,172	31,894	536,190[11]
Other Asia	244,783	648,354	53,717	74,458	90,619	126,424	122,350	97,067	1,376,559
North-America	1,982,735	3,615,225	294,906	672,639	1,050,527	1,297,580	445,194	361,476	15,171,798
Canada & Newfoundland[17,18]	169,939	156,938	15,821	18,294	24,642	19,931	21,541	23,898	4,360,955
Mexico[18]	640,294	1,655,843	95,170	405,660	680,186	947,923	214,128	126,642	5,177,422
Caribbean	741,126	872,051	110,949	87,597	112,635	138,591	95,945	98,185	3,035,898
Cuba	264,863	144,578	16,610	9,523	9,436	9,474	10,890	12,976	782,050[12]
Dominican Republic	148,135	252,035	27,195	26,744	42,136	41,422	41,948	45,464	638,970[20]
Haiti	56,335	138,379	34,858	13,341	19,869	47,046	10,756	9,899	302,458[20]
Jamaica	137,577	208,148	20,474	23,572	23,667	22,977	18,280	16,761	487,518[21]
Other Caribbean	134,216	128,911	11,812	14,417	17,527	17,672	14,071	13,085	824,902
Central America	134,640	468,088	31,311	101,273	146,243	110,820	57,849	58,666	1,046,963
El Salvador	34,436	213,539	12,043	57,628	79,601	46,923	26,077	26,794	374,461[20]
Other Central America	100,204	254,549	19,268	43,645	66,642	63,897	31,772	31,872	672,502
South America	295,741	461,847	41,646	59,812	86,821	80,308	55,725	54,077	1,440,413
Argentina	29,897	27,327	2,556	3,766	5,953	4,231	4,083	2,972	142,404[20]
Colombia	77,347	122,849	10,153	14,918	23,783	19,272	12,885	12,597	340,107[20]
Ecuador	50,077	56,315	4,736	7,587	12,474	9,962	7,322	7,400	180,451[20]
Other South America	138,420	255,356	24,201	33,541	44,611	46,843	31,435	31,108	777,451
Other America	995	458	9	3	-	7	6	8	110,147

[Continued]

★ 25 ★

Immigration, by Region and Selected Country of Last Residence, 1820-1993 - III

[Continued]

Region and country of last residence[1]	1971-80	1981-90	1988	1989	1990	1991	1992	1993	Total 174 years 1820-1993
Africa	80,779	176,893	17,124	22,485	32,797	33,542	24,707	25,532	417,926
Oceania	41,242	45,205	4,324	4,956	6,804	7,061	5,994	6,144	223,821
Not specified[22]	12	1,032	72	86	450	156	20	4	267,639

Source: U.S. Immigration and Naturalization Service, *Statistical Yearbook of the Immigration and Naturalization Service, 1993,* U.S. Government Printing Office, Washington, DC, 1994, pp. 26-29. *Notes:* A dash (-) represents zero. From 1820-67, figures represent alien passengers arrived at seaports; from 1868-97, immigrant aliens arrived; from 1892-94 and 1898-1990, immigrant aliens admitted for permanent residence. From 1892-1903, aliens entering by cabin class were not counted as immigrants. Land arrivals were not completely enumerated until 1908. 1. Data for years prior to 1906 relate to country whence alien came; data from 1906-79 and 1984-90 are for country of last permanent residence, and data for 1980-83 refer to country of birth. Because of changes in boundaries, changes in lists of countries, and lack of data for specified countries for various periods, data for certain countries, especially for the total period 1820-1990, are not comparable throughout. Data for specified countries are included with countries to which they belonged prior to World War I. 2. Data for Austria and Hungary not reported until 1861. 3. Data for Austria and Hungary not reported separately for all years during the period. 4. No data available for Czechoslovakia until 1920. 5. Prior to 1926, data for Northern Ireland included in Ireland. 6. Data for Norway and Sweden not reported separately until 1871. 7. No data available for Romania until 1880. 8. Since 1925, data for United Kingdom refer to England, Scotland, Wales, and Northern Ireland. 9. In 1920, a separate enumeration was made for the Kingdom of Serbs, Croats, and Slovenes. Since 1922, the Serb, Croat, and Slovene Kingdom recorded as Yugoslavia. 10. Beginning in 1957, China includes Taiwan. 11. Data not reported separately until 1952. 12. Data not reported separately until 1925. 13. Data not reported separately until 1949. 14. No data available for Japan until 1861. 15. Data not reported separately until 1948. 16. Prior to 1934, Philippines recorded as insular travel. 17. Prior to 1920, Canada and Newfoundland recorded as British North America. From 1820-98, figures include all British North America possessions. 18. Land arrivals not completely enumerated until 1908. 19. No data available for Mexico from 1886-93. 20. Data not reported separately until 1932. 21. Data for Jamaica not collected until 1953. In prior years, consolidated under British West Indies, which is included in "Other Caribbean." 22. Included in countries "Not specified" until 1925. 23. From 1899-1919, data for Poland included in Austria-Hungary, Germany, and the Soviet Union. 24. From 1938-45 Austria included in Germany. 25. Includes 32,897 persons returning to their homes in the United States.

★ 26 ★

Immigration

Immigration, by Relative/Occupational Preferences, 1993

According to the Immigration Act of 1990, there are nine categories among which immigrant preference visas are distributed. This act, which increased the number of categories from six, took effect in fiscal year 1992. The present categories of preference for family-sponsored admission are: First Preference—unmarried sons and daughters of U.S. citizens; Second Preference—spouses, children, and unmarried sons and daughters of permanent resident aliens; Third Preference—married sons and daughters of U.S. citizens; and Fourth Preference—brothers and sisters of U.S. citizens. The present categories of preference for employment-sponsored admission are: First Preference—priority workers (persons of extraordinary ability, outstanding professors and researchers, and certain multinational executives and managers); Second Preference—professionals with advanced degrees or aliens with exceptional ability; Third Preference—skilled workers, professionals (without advanced degrees), and needed unskilled workers; Fourth Preference—special immigrants; and Fifth Preference—employment creation immigrants (investors).

Region and foreign state chargeability	Total	Family-sponsored preferences					Employment-based preferences					
		Total	First pref.	Second pref.	Third pref.	Fourth pref.	Total	First pref.	Second pref.	Third pref.	Fourth pref.	Fifth pref.
All countries	373,788	266,776	12,819	128,308	23,385	62,264	147,012	21,112	29,468	87,689	8,158	583
North America	78,187	55,718	6,972	26,747	6,752	15,247	22,469	4,177	2,024	14,163	2,071	34
Canada	9,482	1,505	356	181	563	405	7,977	3,534	1,355	2,880	189	19
Mexico	17,483	13,370	2,427	1,935	2,423	6,585	4,113	351	244	2,891	612	15
Caribbean	34,258	30,738	3,403	17,932	3,012	6,391	3,520	170	316	2,313	721	-
Antigua-Barbuda	228	186	36	64	10	76	42	-	-	36	6	-
Barbados	555	423	98	132	40	153	132	4	6	105	17	-
Cuba	1,224	1,200	287	123	519	281	24	3	-	6	15	-
Dominica	306	280	21	149	24	86	26	3	3	20	-	-

[Continued]

★ 26 ★

Immigration, by Relative/Occupational Preferences, 1993

[Continued]

Region and foreign state chargeability	Total	Family-sponsored preferences					Employment-based preferences					
		Total	First pref.	Second pref.	Third pref.	Fourth pref.	Total	First pref.	Second pref.	Third pref.	Fourth pref.	Fifth pref.
Dominican Republic	17,344	16,906	1,476	12,061	907	2,462	438	78	23	143	194	-
Grenada	371	299	29	122	20	128	72	-	5	65	2	-
Haiti	2,318	2,0410	259	1,041	131	579	308	5	19	133	151	-
Jamaica	7,883	6,844	789	3,35	734	2,016	1,039	26	108	766	139	-
St. Kitts & Nevis	252	219	37	84	39	59	33	-	-	28	5	-
St. Lucia	269	237	37	65	22	113	32	1	-	26	5	-
St. Vincent & Grenadines	317	226	20	116	15	75	91	-	2	76	13	-
Trinidad & Tobago	2,993	1,814	287	636	546	345	1,179	42	141	837	159	-
Other Caribbean	198	94	27	34	15	18	104	8	9	72	15	-
Central America	16,964	10,105	786	6,699	754	1,866	6,859	122	109	6,079	549	-
Belize	358	290	54	91	58	87	68	1	4	51	12	-
Costa Rica	363	234	29	100	23	82	129	23	8	62	36	-
El Salvador	8,406	4,521	140	3,787	128	466	3,885	12	15	3,729	129	-
Guatemala	3,978	2,175	123	1,336	178	538	1,803	16	31	1,576	180	-
Honduras	2,038	1,711	225	977	135	374	327	7	4	287	29	-
Nicaragua	1,165	779	103	322	147	207	386	1	25	286	74	-
Panama	656	395	112	86	85	112	261	62	22	88	89	-
South America	21,216	13,080	979	4,834	1,841	5,426	8,136	1,292	1,006	5,221	609	8
Argentina	1,448	300	31	113	66	90	1,148	216	271	617	51	3
Bolivia	676	218	30	91	19	78	458	15	30	402	11	-
Brazil	1,646	297	29	144	54	70	1,349	443	210	541	150	5
Chile	772	371	41	122	54	154	401	93	71	190	47	-
Colombia	4,485	3,205	254	1,434	319	1,198	1,280	113	98	964	105	-
Ecuador	2,609	1,858	117	1,009	182	550	742	31	32	661	27	-
Guyana	4,680	4,124	275	907	719	2,223	556	16	30	480	30	-
Peru	3,489	2,235	165	787	319	964	1,254	168	125	884	77	-
Uruguay	242	95	4	36	18	37	147	21	16	99	11	-
Venezuela	1,012	337	29	164	91	53	675	173	113	299	90	-
Other South America	157	40	4	27	-	9	117	3	10	94	10	-
Europe	30,024	10,701	1,149	1,823	4,662	3,067	19,323	7,038	3,617	7,842	756	70
Belgium	314	19	5	3	2	9	295	118	78	84	15	-
Bulgaria	338	77	10	11	53	3	261	91	88	73	9	-
Czechoslovakia	283	114	21	18	74	1	169	49	58	56	6	-
Denmark	264	12	6	2	2	2	252	120	39	90	3	-
Finland	192	14	3	6	3	2	178	98	27	43	9	1
France	1,109	164	28	62	30	44	945	388	203	314	39	1
Germany	1,710	236	52	59	58	67	1,474	644	296	476	41	17
Greece	553	237	28	27	27	155	316	58	106	142	10	-
Hungary	428	79	14	22	37	6	349	95	132	102	20	-
Ireland	548	170	62	43	28	37	378	87	73	182	36	-
Italy	864	173	22	44	25	82	691	219	101	323	41	7
Netherlands	662	91	3	37	15	36	571	205	127	223	12	4
Poland	7,567	5,897	491	788	3,585	1,033	1,670	185	327	1,088	69	1
Portugal	1,390	852	7	176	52	617	538	36	39	445	10	8
Portugal	1,130	666	7	152	17	490	464	22	20	412	8	2
Macau	260	186	-	24	35	127	74	14	19	33	2	6
Romania	658	223	38	51	114	20	435	56	96	215	68	-
Soviet Union	1,688	179	52	32	76	19	1,509	750	303	392	60	4

[Continued]

★ 26 ★

Immigration, by Relative/Occupational Preferences, 1993

[Continued]

Region and foreign state chargeability	Total	Family-sponsored preferences					Employment-based preferences					
		Total	First pref.	Second pref.	Third pref.	Fourth pref.	Total	First pref.	Second pref.	Third pref.	Fourth pref.	Fifth pref.
Spain	420	79	5	24	4	46	341	104	59	134	43	1
Sweden	593	54	11	30	2	11	539	272	98	153	14	2
Switzerland	427	41	9	12	12	8	386	176	71	127	10	2
United Kingdom	8,260	1,392	191	280	297	624	6,868	2,913	1,035	2,736	173	11
Yugoslavia	1,134	427	50	59	94	224	707	218	155	275	50	9
Other Europe	622	171	41	37	72	21	451	156	106	169	18	2
Asia	134,710	70,543	3,360	20,778	9,808	36,597	64,167	7,374	21,492	30,708	4,133	460
Afghanistan	210	147	16	53	60	18	63	12	1	42	8	-
Bangladesh	1,502	1,053	21	379	49	604	449	54	186	181	28	-
Burma	522	441	16	86	90	249	81	1	20	55	5	-
China, Mainland	24,726	12,590	154	3,275	3,055	6,106	12,136	1,776	6,556	3,658	70	76
Hong Kong	5,774	3,434	53	555	351	2,475	2,340	353	537	1,327	66	57
India	24,462	14,002	58	3,506	1,224	9,214	10,460	1,036	5,152	3,904	350	18
Indonesia	524	204	8	52	22	122	320	45	85	170	15	5
Iran	3,902	1,318	44	584	143	547	2,584	133	519	1,894	33	5
Iraq	970	765	27	50	103	585	205	30	38	100	26	11
Israel	2,545	375	46	83	107	139	2,170	246	432	1,341	148	3
Japan	3,047	239	14	127	43	55	2,808	1,128	417	1,190	71	2
Jordan	1,456	1,118	32	305	215	566	338	40	77	206	15	-
Korea	9,378	4,093	102	1,416	449	2,126	5,285	602	723	3,100	824	36
Kuwait	401	213	7	60	36	110	188	15	60	100	6	7
Lebanon	2,374	1,306	47	533	306	420	1,068	87	231	712	35	3
Malaysia	1,105	184	3	62	15	104	921	68	229	584	40	-
Pakistan	4,960	3,605	29	718	210	2,648	1,355	218	339	686	109	3
Philippines	26,296	14,373	1,562	6,742	1,592	4,477	11,923	455	2,469	6,997	1,990	12
Singapore	435	63	4	24	6	29	372	51	119	176	26	-
Sri Lanka	773	275	5	54	29	187	498	64	166	245	23	-
Syria	1,181	606	28	232	143	203	575	31	117	399	25	3
Taiwan	9,794	3,282	98	781	339	2,064	6,512	802	2,701	2,687	113	209
Thailand	1,145	731	71	274	31	355	414	18	58	288	46	4
Turkey	676	151	11	43	23	74	525	41	113	359	11	1
Vietnam	4,937	4,807	492	566	871	2,878	130	12	20	79	15	4
Yemen	703	687	349	97	210	31	16	1	1	10	4	-
Other Asia	912	481	63	121	86	211	431	55	126	218	31	1
Africa	8,080	3,457	299	1,451	194	1,513	4,623	710	1,080	2,319	503	11
Cape Verde	491	486	18	405	2	61	5	3	-	2	-	-
Egypt	1,442	712	13	238	58	403	730	114	168	391	57	-
Ethiopia	316	176	22	144	1	9	140	23	20	53	44	-
Ghana	427	238	84	98	12	44	189	15	75	62	37	-
Kenya	623	432	4	65	23	340	191	19	44	92	36	-
Liberia	226	123	49	53	11	10	103	12	12	40	39	-
Nigeria	,237	146	20	115	2	9	1,091	133	320	521	112	5
Sierre Leone	265	170	29	124	2	15	95	7	17	59	12	-
South Africa	1,333	167	32	31	33	71	1,166	238	214	643	69	2
Tanzania	308	230	-	9	9	212	78	9	16	44	9	-
Uganda	272	196	-	12	4	180	76	11	25	38	2	-
Other Africa	1,140	381	28	157	37	159	759	126	169	374	86	4

[Continued]

★ 26 ★

Immigration, by Relative/Occupational Preferences, 1993

[Continued]

Region and foreign state chargeability	Total	Family-sponsored preferences					Employment-based preferences					
		Total	First pref.	Second pref.	Third pref.	Fourth pref.	Total	First pref.	Second pref.	Third pref.	Fourth pref.	Fifth pref.
Oceania	2,194	752	60	150	128	414	1,442	523	249	584	86	-
Australia	997	65	20	12	31	2	932	410	187	279	56	-
Fiji	495	452	5	81	67	299	43	6	3	34	-	-
New Zealand	511	56	17	8	17	14	455	106	59	270	20	-
Other Oceania	191	179	18	49	13	99	12	1	-	1	10	-
No country limitation	99,377	72,525	-	72,525	-	-	26,852	-	-	26,852	-	-

Source: U.S. Immigration and Naturalization Service, *Statistical Yearbook of the Immigration and Naturalization Service, 1993,* U.S. Government Printing Office, Washington, DC, 1994, pp. 40-41. *Note:* A dash (-) represents zero.

★ 27 ★

Immigration

Immigration, by Selected Class of Admission, 1993

Region and country of birth	Total	Family sponsored preferences	Employment based preferences	Immediate relatives of U.S. citizens				Refugee and asylee adjust.	Diversity transitions	IRCA[1] legalization	Legalization dependents	Other[2]
				Total	Spouses	Children	Parents					
All countries	904,292	226,776	147,012	225,059	145,843	46,788	62,428	127,343	33,468	24,278	55,344	35,012
North America	301,380	107,680	21,989	83,517	51,211	18,951	13,355	15,926	787	21,571	47,077	2,833
Canada	17,156	1,729	7,854	6,338	5,095	1,029	214	8	764	75	45	343
Mexico	126,561	33,044	3,710	31,525	20,401	6,129	4,995	29	10	17,534	39,243	1,466
Caribbean	99,438	47,827	3,588	32,473	18,506	8,084	5,883	11,700	9	1,595	1,832	414
Bahamas	686	163	101	337	233	90	14	4	2	53	19	7
Barbados	1,184	557	131	455	300	81	74	-	-	18	15	8
Cuba	13,666	1,327	23	653	291	155	207	11,603	-	16	-	44
Dominica	683	374	28	236	135	48	53	4	-	18	21	2
Dominican Republic	45,420	26,741	427	16,493	9,815	4,167	2,511	18	1	534	1,080	126
Grenada	827	370	75	328	206	54	68	-	-	20	31	3
Haiti	10,094	5,629	305	3,497	1,394	910	1,193	68	-	484	10	87
Jamaica	17,241	9,121	1,043	6,293	3,520	1,609	1,164	3	1	272	444	64
St. Lucia	634	312	33	257	141	66	50	-	-	19	12	1
St. Vincent & Grenadines	657	297	94	242	136	52	54	-	-	10	14	-
Trinidad & Tobago	6,577	2,228	1,178	2,903	1,879	679	345	-	3	65	156	44
Other Caribbean	1,769	708	150	779	456	173	150	-	2	72	30	28
Central America	58,162	25,066	6,827	13,156	7,195	3,708	2,253	4,188	4	2,365	5,957	599
Belize	1,035	468	65	332	181	92	59	-	-	67	81	22
Costa Rica	1,368	339	135	734	489	183	62	29	-	45	61	25
El Salvador	26,818	12,818	3,833	3,554	1,827	764	963	811	-	1,301	4,393	108
Guatemala	11,870	6,282	1,808	2,228	1,082	839	307	210	1	601	674	66
Honduras	7,306	3,010	335	3,009	1,605	1,026	378	165	-	172	583	32
Nicaragua	7,086	1,564	383	1,613	952	374	287	2,892	-	144	162	328
Panama	2,679	585	268	1,686	1,059	430	197	81	3	35	3	18
Other North America	63	14	10	25	14	1	10	1	-	2	-	11
South America	53,921	18,312	8,239	22,416	12,412	4,942	5,062	461	313	885	2,953	342
Argentina	2,824	394	1,168	873	600	87	186	4	280	49	37	19
Bolivia	1,545	388	443	584	253	204	127	6	-	22	81	21
Brazil	4,604	507	1,394	2,549	1,919	503	127	11	12	48	51	32
Chile	1,778	445	397	806	516	155	135	17	1	28	66	18
Colombia	12,819	4,333	1,294	5,949	3,491	1,372	1,086	63	2	307	787	84
Ecuador	7,324	3,177	758	2,175	1,191	443	541	25	1	145	1,000	43
Guyana	8,384	5,318	555	2,346	868	308	1,170	4	-	47	102	12
Peru	10,447	3,009	1,263	4,990	2,428	1,068	1,494	176	2	171	760	76
Uruguay	568	118	148	232	151	23	58	4	1	26	30	9
Venezuela	2,743	539	698	1,272	833	325	114	135	12	41	23	23

[Continued]

★ 27 ★

Immigration, by Selected Class of Admission, 1993

[Continued]

Region and country of birth	Total	Family sponsored preferences	Employment based preferences	Immediate relatives of U.S. citizens				Refugee and asylee adjust.	Diver-sity transi-tions	IRCA[1] legali-zation	Legali-zation depen-dents	Other[2]
				Total	Spouses	Children	Parents					
Other South America	885	84	121	640	162	454	24	16	2	1	16	5
Europe	158,254	12,182	19,165	34,012	25,286	4,917	3,809	53,195	30,593	334	712	8,061
Albania	1,400	64	-	105	58	27	20	1,198	32	-	-	1
Austria	549	41	142	290	261	15	14	54	13	1	1	7
Belgium	657	22	295	302	251	31	20	2	28	3	1	4
Bulgaria	1,029	79	259	356	154	158	44	303	1	-	-	31
Czechoslovakia	1,000	116	176	505	389	63	53	119	80	2	-	2
Denmark	735	24	244	421	392	25	4	1	38	2	-	5
France	2,864	196	933	1,549	1,371	114	64	15	107	8	1	55
Germany	7,312	311	1,478	5,167	4,388	594	185	82	177	12	12	73
Greece	1,884	302	309	945	689	89	167	39	1	24	6	258
Hungary	1,091	85	359	509	336	110	63	80	49	2	-	7
Ireland	13,590	205	370	709	626	61	22	-	12,221	15	11	59
Italy	2,487	247	681	1,375	1,120	79	176	32	97	15	17	23
Netherlands	1,430	74	565	733	667	31	35	7	37	2	2	10
Norway	608	22	146	392	341	41	10	-	45	2	-	1
Poland	27,846	6,572	1,674	3,405	1,895	700	810	731	14,806	117	477	64
Portugal	2,081	832	447	676	479	61	136	4	1	16	88	17
Romania	5,601	294	444	1,165	607	236	322	3,654	3	1	1	39
Soviet Union, former	58,571	265	1,534	3,714	1,592	1,448	674	45,900	28	3	4	7,123
Armenia	6,267	32	53	119	87	19	13	329	-	-	-	5,754
Azerbaijan	2,943	4	32	38	21	3	14	2,790	-	-	-	79
Belarus	4,702	4	26	132	39	39	54	4,480	2	-	-	58
Moldova	2,646	5	36	41	20	4	17	2,546	-	-	1	17
Russia	12,079	95	910	1,804	786	901	117	8,965	4	-	-	301
Ukraine	18,316	54	207	814	279	311	224	16,977	5	-	2	257
Uzbekistan	2,664	14	42	89	41	15	33	2,475	-	-	-	44
Other republics	1,565	15	70	126	78	29	19	1,212	-	-	-	142
Unknown republic	7,369	42	158	551	241	127	183	6,126	17	3	1	471
Spain	1,388	111	329	859	713	74	72	37	7	7	25	13
Sweden	1,393	65	538	732	685	33	14	1	45	3	-	9
Switzerland	972	50	383	466	438	22	6	3	56	-	1	13
United Kingdom	18,783	1,604	6,801	7,561	6,509	663	389	7	2,542	71	35	162
Yugoslavia	2,809	520	179	1,414	811	155	448	77	8	25	24	22
Other Europe	2,174	81	339	662	514	87	61	849	171	3	6	63
Asia	358,049	83,315	91,479	101,144	46,697	16,330	38,117	51,783	1,566	1,008	4,247	23,507
Afghanistan	2,964	210	67	431	201	31	199	2,233	-	17	3	3
Bangladesh	3,291	1,420	437	1,026	408	97	521	7	-	40	344	17
Burma	849	446	87	237	122	8	107	78	-	-	1	-
Cambodia	1,639	126	26	454	177	41	236	808	-	-	-	225
China, Mainland	65,578	12,603	38,509	12,052	4,156	954	6,942	1,153	28	26	429	778
Hong Kong	9,161	5,126	2,457	1,207	833	171	203	90	19	11	35	216
India	40,121	16,381	10,439	10,827	4,111	687	6,029	103	13	100	2,073	185
Indonesia	1,767	270	333	474	316	34	124	16	649	5	6	14
Iran	14,841	2,056	2,876	4,817	1,558	125	3,134	3,875	14	141	67	995
Iraq	4,072	823	211	1,146	403	32	711	1,856	2	8	-	26
Israel	4,494	403	2,176	1,806	1,346	161	299	20	9	22	10	48
Japan	6,908	416	2,795	2,832	2,524	190	118	3	780	25	18	39
Jordan	4,741	1,450	335	2,848	1,657	239	952	42	-	18	2	46
Korea	18,026	5,254	5,243	7,091	3,139	2,251	1,701	1	3	77	229	128
Kuwait	1,129	300	216	493	451	36	6	114	2	-	2	2
Laos	7,285	129	10	585	255	99	231	6,547	-	1	-	13
Lebanon	5,465	1,492	1,101	2,406	1,338	134	934	204	-	58	10	194
Malaysia	2,026	274	936	718	596	32	90	37	9	4	30	18
Pakistan	8,927	4,181	1,324	2,701	1,449	270	982	185	2	98	340	96
Philippines	63,457	16,143	11,882	32,225	15,765	8,215	8,245	122	8	268	466	2,343
Singapore	798	101	382	304	2563	29	22	-	3	-	-	8
Sri Lanka	1,109	290	499	248	145	16	87	62	-	4	3	3
Syria	2,933	624	579	1,172	669	24	479	115	1	23	2	417
Taiwan	14,329	4,564	6,912	2,652	1,434	333	885	1	3	20	109	68
Thailand	6,654	947	428	1,440	953	304	183	3,724	1	27	43	44
Turkey	2,204	214	523	1,132	767	76	289	79	3	9	20	224
Vietnam	59,614	5,692	118	6,241	1,074	849	4,318	30,249	2	1	-	17,311

[Continued]

★27★

Immigration, by Selected Class of Admission, 1993

[Continued]

Region and country of birth	Total	Family sponsored preferences	Employment based preferences	Immediate relatives of U.S. citizens				Refugee and asylee adjust.	Diver-sity transi-tions	IRCA[1] legali-zation	Legali-zation depen-dents	Other[2]
				Total	Spouses	Children	Parents					
Yemen	1,793	684	17	1,079	235	815	29	9	-	1	-	3
Other Asia	1,874	696	561	500	362	77	61	50	15	4	5	43
Africa	27,783	4,429	4,719	11,571	8,224	1,443	1,904	5,944	178	379	337	226
Cape Verde	936	489	5	437	244	121	72	-	1	3	1	-
Egypt	3,556	890	718	1,770	1,133	93	544	35	7	21	25	90
Ethiopia	5,276	252	149	1,096	618	174	304	3,725	-	36	1	17
Ghana	1,604	452	190	740	440	192	108	35	2	44	139	2
Kenya	1,065	394	209	385	326	36	43	42	2	10	11	12
Liberia	1,050	147	107	507	196	193	118	239	-	40	3	7
Morocco	1,176	66	149	946	824	25	97	3	7	2	1	2
Nigeria	4,448	596	1,086	2,483	2,031	248	204	14	4	121	103	41
Sierra Leone	690	167	94	406	261	85	60	2	1	12	1	7
South Africa	2,197	201	1,185	727	518	78	131	37	26	7	3	11
Sudan	714	18	64	181	158	4	19	443	-	6	-	2
Other Africa	5,071	757	763	1,893	1,495	194	204	1,369	128	77	49	35
Oceania	4,900	858	1,421	2,399	2,013	205	181	34	31	96	18	43
Australia	2,320	107	913	1,244	1,133	102	9	2	25	9	1	19
Fiji	854	479	39	293	166	15	112	31	1	4	3	4
New Zealand	1,052	59	447	528	485	32	11	-	5	4	-	9
Tonga	348	163	1	115	79	7	29	-	-	48	14	7
Other Oceania	326	50	21	219	150	49	20	1	-	31	-	4
Unknown or not reported	5	-	-	-	-	-	-	-	-	5	-	-

Source: U.S. Immigration and Naturalization Service, *Statistical Yearbook of the Immigration and Naturalization Service, 1993*, U.S. Government Printing Office, Washington, DC, 1994, pp. 44-45. *Notes:* A dash (-) represents zero. 1. IRCA stands for Immigration Reform and Control Act. 2. Includes persons entering under the Amerasian, former H-1 registered nurse, Cuban/Haitian entrant, Soviet and Indochinese parolee, and 1972 Registry provisions.

★28★

Immigration

Immigrant Status Under the Marriage Fraud Amendments of 1986, by Selected Status, 1993

The Immigration Marriage Fraud Amendments of 1986 were devised to deter immigration-related marriage fraud. They are also known as Public Law 99-639. The major stipulation of this law is that aliens that immigrate on the basis of a marriage of less than two years are "conditional immigrants." In order to remove this conditional status, an alien must petition the INS (Immigration and Naturalization Service) within the 90 days preceding the two-year anniversary of receiving conditional status. At that time, if validity of marriage cannot be proven, the conditional status is terminated and the alien becomes deportable. This table shows the status of immigrants in this process as of fiscal year 1993.

Region and country of birth	Total cases processed	Conditional status removals[1]	Status terminated[2]				Administra-tively closed[3]
			Total	For cause[4]	Failure to show[5]	Failure to file[6]	
All countries	91,258	81,810	7,591	508	741	6,342	1,857
North America	26,415	23,708	2,191	182	278	1,731	516
Canada	3,473	3,068	308	6	23	279	97
Mexico	9,583	8,804	645	63	71	511	134

[Continued]

★ 28 ★

Immigrant Status Under the Marriage Fraud Amendments of 1986, by Selected Status, 1993

[Continued]

Region and country of birth	Total cases processed	Conditional status removals[1]	Status terminated[2]				Administratively closed[3]
			Total	For cause[4]	Failure to show[5]	Failure to file[6]	
Caribbean	9,283	8,249	857	102	138	617	177
Antigua-Barbuda	85	75	10	3	1	6	-
Bahamas	148	128	18	1	-	17	2
Barbados	212	190	20	-	2	18	2
Dominican Republic	4,752	4,247	416	62	70	284	89
Grenada	91	83	6	-	3	3	2
Haiti	456	405	40	5	5	30	11
Jamaica	1,953	1,731	174	19	33	122	48
St. Lucia	116	96	16	3	-	13	4
St. Vincent & Grenadines	86	73	10	-	1	9	3
Trinidad & Tobago	1,044	938	94	6	16	72	12
Other Caribbean	340	283	53	3	7	43	4
Central America	4,068	3,580	380	11	46	323	108
Belize	106	97	7	-	-	7	2
Costa Rica	362	298	52	1	8	43	12
El Salvador	862	770	76	2	12	62	16
Guatemala	578	520	41	5	4	32	17
Honduras	781	708	57	2	11	44	16
Nicaragua	502	471	28	-	8	20	3
Panama	877	716	119	1	3	115	42
Other North America	8	7	1	-	-	1	-
South America	7,800	6,933	731	35	73	623	136
Argentina	555	497	57	-	3	54	1
Bolivia	180	153	22	1	3	18	5
Brazil	1,304	1,175	117	3	13	101	12
Chile	383	324	53	-	3	50	6
Colombia	1,840	1,622	183	12	24	147	35
Ecuador	719	637	71	2	8	61	11
Guyana	650	571	49	3	6	40	30
Peru	1,349	1,227	104	10	9	85	18
Uruguay	112	95	14	-	-	14	3
Venezuela	596	535	50	4	3	43	11
Other South America	112	97	11	-	1	10	4
Europe	18,562	15,980	2,258	62	127	2,069	324
Austria	209	183	25	1	1	23	1
Belgium	198	173	23	1	-	22	2
Bulgaria	80	75	5	-	-	5	-
Czechoslovakia	191	175	15	3	1	11	1
Denmark	325	278	41	1	1	39	6
Finland	147	128	16	1	-	15	3
France	1,043	884	149	1	13	135	10

[Continued]

★ 28 ★

Immigrant Status Under the Marriage Fraud Amendments of 1986, by Selected Status, 1993

[Continued]

Region and country of birth	Total cases processed	Conditional status removals[1]	Status terminated[2]				Administratively closed[3]
			Total	For cause[4]	Failure to show[5]	Failure to file[6]	
Germany	3,243	2,536	627	6	22	599	80
Greece	633	515	107	3	6	98	11
Hungary	275	247	21	1	3	17	7
Ireland	866	793	963	1	5	57	10
Italy	833	710	114	2	7	105	9
Netherlands	522	449	66	1	1	64	7
Norway	244	197	39	1	3	35	8
Poland	1,251	1,144	72	8	4	60	35
Portugal	482	416	60	1	4	55	6
Romania	401	366	30	3	1	26	5
Soviet Union	864	810	51	3	6	42	3
Spain	494	398	87	-	7	80	9
Sweden	487	425	58	2	4	52	4
Switzerland	294	245	43	1	3	39	6
United Kingdom	4,658	4,111	458	11	28	419	89
Yugoslavia	701	616	75	10	7	58	10
Other Europe	107	92	13	-	-	13	2
Asia	31,530	29,026	1,761	152	171	1,438	743
Afghanistan	101	93	7	-	-	7	1
Bangladesh	130	121	6	2	3	1	3
Burma	100	97	3	-	-	3	-
China, Mainland	2,972	2,842	79	6	8	65	51
Cyprus	83	72	10	-	-	10	1
Hong Kong	694	664	21	3	3	15	9
India	2,858	2,697	107	19	10	78	54
Indonesia	247	226	19	1	2	16	2
Iran	1,022	936	66	8	15	43	20
Iraq	178	168	7	-	1	6	3
Israel	1,139	990	135	7	8	120	14
Japan	1,693	1,516	147	3	8	136	30
Jordan	1,144	1,024	99	7	9	83	21
Korea	2,979	2,590	217	11	18	188	172
Kuwait	294	278	11	3	-	8	5
Laos	172	167	2	-	1	1	3
Lebanon	1,012	936	62	7	3	52	14
Malaysia	507	474	25	-	4	21	8
Pakistan	841	753	54	5	7	42	34
Philippines	9,370	8,761	398	48	44	306	211
Saudi Arabia	106	91	14	2	2	10	1
Singapore	173	161	9	1	-	8	3
Sri Lanka	95	91	2	-	-	2	2
Syria	510	462	42	7	4	31	6

[Continued]

★28★

Immigrant Status Under the Marriage Fraud Amendments of 1986, by Selected Status, 1993

[Continued]

Region and country of birth	Total cases processed	Conditional status removals[1]	Status terminated[2]				Administratively closed[3]
			Total	For cause[4]	Failure to show[5]	Failure to file[6]	
Taiwan	1,087	1,010	47	1	4	42	30
Thailand	799	702	76	4	7	65	21
Turkey	590	526	53	5	4	44	11
Victnam	409	376	27	2	4	21	6
Yemen	83	71	8	-	1	7	4
Other Asia	142	131	8	-	1	7	3
Africa	5,417	4,863	454	72	83	299	100
Algeria	99	94	4	-	-	4	1
Cameroon	111	98	11	2	4	5	2
Cape Verde	120	106	11	2	4	5	3
Egypt	760	683	67	2	7	58	10
Ethiopia	255	236	17	2	3	12	2
Ghana	278	259	14	2	4	8	5
Ivory Coast	140	128	10	1	4	5	2
Kenya	194	159	25	6	2	17	10
Liberia	210	173	34	15	4	15	3
Morocco	671	632	35	2	3	30	4
Nigeria	1,246	1,107	113	27	19	67	26
Sierra Leone	223	188	34	8	11	15	1
South Africa	339	312	20	-	2	18	7
Sudan	96	90	4	-	2	2	2
Other Africa	675	598	55	3	14	38	22
Oceania	1,498	1,297	180	5	9	166	21
Australia	758	631	115	1	4	110	12
Fiji	186	170	15	3	4	8	1
New Zealand	391	350	34	-	1	33	7
Other Oceania	163	146	16	1	-	15	1
Unknown	36	3	16	-	-	16	17

Source: U.S. Immigration and Naturalization Service, *Statistical Yearbook of the Immigration and Naturalization Service, 1993*, U.S. Government Printing Office, Washington, DC, 1994, pp. 70-71. *Notes:* A dash (-) represents zero. 1. Refers to removals of conditions on permanent resident status, established by the Marriage Fraud Amendments of 1986. 2. Refers to termination of conditional status, rendering the alien deportable. 3. Includes aliens who naturalized, died, emigrated, or were misclassified as conditional immigrants. 4. Refers to applications denied after an INS interview or because the alien was ineligible for removal of conditional status. 5. Refers to aliens who applied for removal of conditional status but failed to appear for the interview. 6. Refers to aliens who failed to apply for removal of conditional status.

★ 29 ★

Immigration

Aliens Deported, 1985-93

From the source: "[Deportation is] the formal removal of an alien from the United States when the presence of that alien is deemed inconsistent with the public welfare. Deportation is ordered by an immigration judge without any punishment being imposed or contemplated. Data for a fiscal year cover the deportations verified during that year. Airlines, ship companies, or port officials provide the Immigration and Naturalization Service with the departure data on aliens who are deported." The number of aliens deported is shown, by region and country of nationality, for fiscal years 1985-93.

Region and country of nationality	1985	1986	1987	1988	1989	1990	1991	1992	1993
All countries	21,334	22,225	22,233	22,963	30,346	26,091	28,759	38,202	36,686
North America	18,635	19,038	19,679	20,718	27,610	23,259	25,994	34,759	33,459
Canada	293	244	227	244	259	249	254	277	227
Mexico	11,684	11,001	13,070	12,926	14,994	14,750	19,776	26,351	25,501
Caribbean	575	653	725	1,151	1,559	2,137	1,701	2,422	2,415
Bahamas, The	15	26	20	39	36	40	37	60	54
Barbados	15	6	4	4	17	17	19	19	27
Dominica	5	10	12	14	53	60	29	31	30
Dominican Republic	190	196	279	541	641	949	706	1,065	1,118
Haiti	62	145	98	151	135	213	168	164	154
Jamaica	219	219	253	328	565	740	608	921	852
Trinidad & Tobago	30	29	35	44	66	75	80	104	120
Other Caribbean	39	22	24	30	46	43	54	58	60
Central America	6,083	7,140	5,657	6,397	10,798	6,123	4,263	5,709	5,316
Belize	73	88	89	77	86	126	83	97	114
Costa Rica	51	55	42	44	45	34	43	41	35
El Salvador	3,218	3,481	2,508	2,780	3,984	2,470	1,496	1,937	1,952
Guatemala	1,761	2,260	1,858	2,080	3,525	1,642	1,058	1,396	1,273
Honduras	785	1,041	1,030	1,322	2,953	1,626	1,259	1,838	1,614
Nicaragua	145	166	87	35	121	122	254	296	227
Panama	50	49	43	59	84	103	70	104	101
South America	1,342	1,769	1,433	1,270	1,537	1,387	1,345	1,757	1,589
Brazil	19	94	77	60	120	62	57	54	38
Chile	23	36	20	21	34	25	33	25	42
Colombia	857	1,133	966	850	978	951	909	1,205	1,091
Ecuador	144	167	107	89	101	76	94	107	88
Guyana	26	20	18	27	40	52	56	102	78
Peru	124	140	108	90	125	97	96	125	152
Venezuela	39	48	35	47	54	49	40	66	40
Other South America	110	131	102	86	85	75	60	73	60
Europe	332	375	334	279	383	409	439	601	644
France	20	30	29	23	29	30	26	29	42
Germany	42	38	39	34	42	36	31	54	86
Italy	9	12	16	7	17	21	27	43	41
Netherlands	10	12	6	4	10	15	7	12	23
Poland	8	12	13	15	26	39	71	93	60
Portugal	8	32	17	6	21	16	25	39	42

[Continued]

★29★

Aliens Deported, 1985-93

[Continued]

Region and country of nationality	1985	1986	1987	1988	1989	1990	1991	1992	1993
United Kingdom	119	120	105	97	125	140	152	166	217
Other Europe	116	119	109	93	113	112	100	165	133
Asia	525	618	392	389	428	547	448	559	510
China	35	31	15	16	19	14	13	32	33
India	46	68	39	31	21	50	27	42	35
Iran	72	98	36	27	25	31	17	43	42
Israel	16	21	26	17	27	30	32	41	43
Japan	33	29	18	16	28	87	92	21	28
Jordan	23	28	23	25	27	26	11	37	30
Korea	40	29	15	35	37	20	18	27	25
Lebanon	17	22	21	22	18	28	20	27	35
Pakistan	35	65	42	36	40	41	33	40	38
Philippines	110	121	78	78	105	98	87	125	116
Other Asia	98	106	79	86	81	122	98	124	85
Africa	401	360	344	270	339	329	270	388	405
Ghana	40	30	18	8	17	19	10	15	24
Niger	19	17	35	48	84	97	63	57	34
Nigeria	218	225	216	140	151	138	124	202	229
Other Africa	124	88	75	74	87	75	73	114	118
Oceania	79	63	45	27	33	31	37	40	40
Stateless or not reported	20	2	6	10	16	129	226	98	39

Source: U.S. Immigration and Naturalization Service, *Statistical Yearbook of the Immigration and Naturalization Service, 1993*, U.S. Government Printing Office, Washington, DC, 1994, p. 165. *Note:* A dash (-) represents zero.

★30★

Immigration

Aliens Deported, by Cause, 1993

The number of aliens deported is shown, by cause and region and nationality, for fiscal year 1993.

Region and country of nationality	Total	Convictions for criminal or narcotics violations	Related to criminal or narcotics violations	Entered without inspection	Violation of of nonimmigrant status	Other	Unknown
All countries	36,686	18,870	1,163	14,456	658	1,429	110
North America	33,459	17,099	1,109	13,659	188	1,312	92
Canada	227	110	39	50	11	17	-
Mexico	25,501	13,552	988	9,639	109	1,137	76

[Continued]

★30★

Aliens Deported, by Cause, 1993

[Continued]

Region and country of nationality	Total	Convictions for criminal or narcotics violations	Related to criminal or narcotics violations	Entered without inspection	Violation of of nonimmigrant status	Other	Unknown
Caribbean	2,415	1,886	47	363	43	71	5
Bahamas, The	54	38	3	11	2	-	-
Barbados	27	24	1	1	-	1	-
Dominica	30	20	-	9	1	-	-
Dominican Republic	1,118	847	16	216	8	29	2
Haiti	154	127	4	16	5	2	-
Jamaica	852	686	16	90	21	36	3
Trinidad & Tobago	120	99	5	9	5	2	-
Other Caribbean	60	45	2	11	1	1	-
Central America	5,316	1,551	35	3,607	25	87	11
Belize	114	64	1	45	1	3	-
Costa Rica	35	17	-	14	3	1	-
El Salvador	1,952	730	17	1,158	5	35	7
Guatemala	1,273	290	7	951	7	17	1
Honduras	1,614	274	8	1,300	3	29	-
Nicaragua	227	94	-	125	4	1	3
Panama	101	82	2	14	2	1	-
South America	1,589	1,021	30	419	71	43	5
Brazil	38	11	1	13	13	-	-
Chile	42	24	1	13	2	1	1
Colombia	1,091	765	20	247	31	27	1
Ecuador	88	41	-	41	4	1	1
Guyana	78	53	4	9	3	8	1
Peru	152	81	2	59	5	5	-
Venezuela	40	21	-	13	5	1	-
Other South America	60	25	2	24	8	-	1
Europe	644	255	9	162	193	24	1
France	42	13	1	12	15	1	-
Germany	86	29	1	16	37	3	-
Italy	41	15	1	16	8	1	-
Netherlands	23	6	1	3	9	4	-
Poland	60	6	-	24	29	1	-
Portugal	42	34	1	3	3	1	-
United Kingdom	217	97	4	50	59	6	1
Other Europe	133	55	-	38	33	7	-
Asia	510	224	10	127	112	27	10
China	33	11	1	15	6	-	-
India	35	13	-	13	6	3	-
Iran	42	23	-	5	9	4	1

[Continued]

★ 30 ★

Aliens Deported, by Cause, 1993

[Continued]

Region and country of nationality	Total	Convictions for criminal or narcotics violations	Related to criminal or narcotics violations	Entered without inspection	Violation of of nonimmigrant status	Other	Unknown
Israel	43	17	-	15	8	2	1
Japan	28	8	-	8	10	1	1
Jordan	30	9	-	10	9	1	1
Korea	25	16	1	2	5	1	-
Lebanon	35	21	2	4	7	1	-
Pakistan	38	20	1	9	5	2	1
Philippines	116	52	3	24	26	7	4
Other Asia	85	34	2	22	21	5	1
Africa	405	240	2	67	76	19	1
Ghana	24	14	-	8	2	-	-
Niger	34	17	-	4	12	1	-
Nigeria	229	154	2	26	33	14	-
Other Africa	118	55	-	29	29	4	1
Oceania	40	14	1	5	17	2	1
Stateless or not reported	39	17	2	17	1	2	-

Source: U.S. Immigration and Naturalization Service, *Statistical Yearbook of the Immigration and Naturalization Service, 1993*, U.S. Government Printing Office, Washington, DC, 1994, p. 167. *Note:* A dash (-) represents zero.

★ 31 ★

Immigration

Aliens Excluded, 1988-93

From the source: "[Exclusion is] the formal denial of an alien's entry into the United States. The exclusion of the alien is made by an immigration judge after an exclusion hearing. Data for a fiscal year cover exclusions verified during that fiscal year. Airlines, ship companies, or port officials provide the Immigration and Naturalization Service with the departure data on aliens who are excluded." The number of aliens excluded each year is shown, by region and country of nationality.

Region and country of nationality	1988	1989	1990	1991	1992	1993
All countries	2,686	3,829	3,674	4,117	4,927	4,411
North America	1,649	2,510	2,469	2,971	3,202	2,899
Canada	139	406	422	558	751	488
Mexico	481	600	656	1,103	1,164	1,277
Caribbean	955	1,396	1,252	1,125	948	967
Bahamas, The	8	12	6	10	7	12
Cuba	12	89	69	98	106	108

[Continued]

★ 31 ★

Aliens Excluded, 1988-93

[Continued]

Region and country of nationality	1988	1989	1990	1991	1992	1993
Dominica	8	22	17	21	14	11
Dominican Republic	281	383	342	411	278	499
Haiti	431	707	617	385	285	155
Jamaica	192	144	152	154	200	155
Trinidad & Tobago	8	12	18	35	39	13
Other Caribbean	15	27	31	11	19	14
Central America	68	107	139	185	338	167
Belize	4	11	7	8	9	16
El Salvador	24	30	50	58	134	65
Guatemala	8	13	21	50	122	47
Honduras	11	32	22	46	39	20
Nicaragua	2	5	4	7	7	10
Other Central America	19	16	35	16	27	9
Other North America	6	1	-	-	1	-
South America	278	279	368	462	481	419
Bolivia	10	4	7	13	11	23
Brazil	27	28	96	109	113	58
Colombia	193	156	119	177	159	189
Ecuador	15	25	35	56	61	42
Guyana	5	32	55	41	41	43
Peru	11	13	20	28	70	48
Other South America	17	21	36	38	26	16
Europe	103	147	145	162	187	135
France	6	7	5	6	5	10
Germany	15	13	16	12	11	11
Greece	1	7	10	5	7	8
Italy	10	15	12	16	22	11
Poland	8	9	15	17	31	10
United Kingdom	12	36	21	46	45	38
Yugoslavia	4	11	6	5	10	10
Other Europe	47	49	60	55	56	37
Asia	497	714	518	362	777	645
Bangladesh	64	106	49	31	54	46
China, Mainland	26	46	15	27	36	50
India	65	113	78	53	140	215
Indonesia	-	1	3	2	4	12
Iran	12	14	13	18	6	12
Japan	26	39	43	18	10	9
Jordan	7	5	10	3	7	9
Korea	9	7	18	8	15	17
Lebanon	22	14	17	16	13	35
Pakistan	114	182	124	57	280	95
Philippines	86	86	51	34	90	46
Sri Lanka	15	27	49	44	67	40
Taiwan	6	5	6	11	4	11

[Continued]

★ 31 ★

Aliens Excluded, 1988-93

[Continued]

Region and country of nationality	1988	1989	1990	1991	1992	1993
Other Asia	45	69	42	40	51	48
Africa	119	144	138	118	251	279
Ghana	31	55	47	40	53	75
Ivory Coast	-	-	1	2	5	11
Liberia	4	5	7	2	9	20
Niger	18	35	25	21	19	11
Nigeria	29	25	24	19	98	102
Other Africa	37	24	34	34	67	60
Oceania	15	11	11	22	19	32
New Zealand	1	2	1	5	4	10
Other Oceania	14	9	10	17	15	22
Unknown or not reported	25	24	25	20	10	2

Source: U.S. Immigration and Naturalization Service, *Statistical Yearbook of the Immigration and Naturalization Service, 1993,* U.S. Government Printing Office, Washington, DC, 1994, p. 161. *Notes:* A dash (-) represents zero. There are a number of opportunities for an alien to withdraw a request for admission to the United States prior to the formal exclusion process before an immigration judge. In fiscal year 1990, 280,307 aliens withdrew during the primary inspection process. Another 608,451 aliens withdrew during secondary inspection. Only 10,921 aliens continued their cases before an immigration judge. Of this latter group, 2,845 aliens were formally excluded.

★ 32 ★

Immigration

Aliens Expelled, 1993

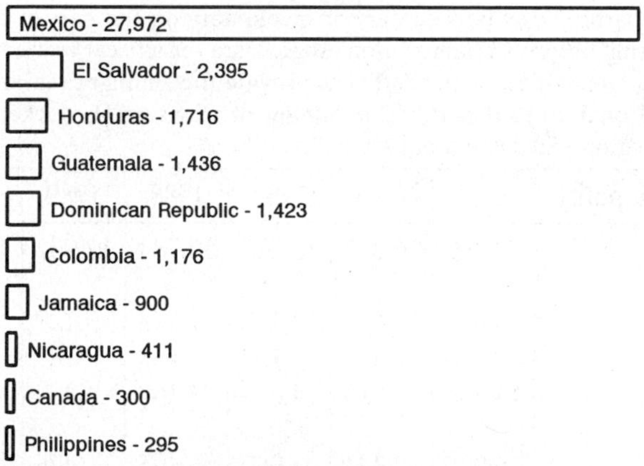

Chart shows data from column 1.

From the source: "In 1993 the INS expelled aliens from 131 countries; 20 countries had more than 100 expulsions each. Mexican nationals accounted for more than 66.6 percent of all expulsions under docket control. The top 10 nationalities accounted for 90.5 percent of all removals."

Country	Number expelled	Percent of total
Mexico	27,972	66.6
El Salvador	2,395	5.7
Honduras	1,716	4.1
Guatemala	1,436	3.4
Dominican Republic	1,423	3.4
Colombia	1,176	2.8
Jamaica	900	2.1
Nicaragua	411	1.0
Canada	300	0.7
Philippines	295	0.7

Source: U.S. Immigration and Naturalization Service, *Statistical Yearbook of the Immigration and Naturalization Service, 1993,* U.S. Government Printing Office, Washington, DC, 1994, p. 156.

★33★

Immigration

Aliens Under Docket Control Required to Depart, 1985-93

From the source: "[Required departure is] the directed departure of an alien from the United States without an order of deportation. The departure may be voluntary or involuntary on the part of the alien, and may or may not have been preceded by a hearing before an immigration judge. Data for a fiscal year cover the required departures in that fiscal year. Airlines, ship companies, or port officials provide the Immigration and Naturalization Service with the departure data on aliens required to depart." The number of aliens under docket control required to depart in each fiscal year is shown, by region and country of nationality.

Region and country of nationality	1985	1986	1987	1988	1989	1990	1991	1992	1993
All countries	39,499	26,373	15,268	10,783	12,902	11,341	6,865	7,030	5,306
North America	26,930	17,968	10,157	7,568	8,127	8,084	4,687	4,986	3,885
Canada	493	350	187	168	187	123	96	105	73
Mexico	14,756	9,916	4,879	4,160	4,399	4,897	2,455	3,004	2,471
Caribbean	6,935	3,341	989	495	476	438	435	395	413
Cuba	29	31	18	18	10	10	19	9	16
Dominican Republic	2,109	993	293	230	188	237	239	263	305
Jamaica	1,290	603	234	103	136	108	91	70	48
Trinidad & Tobago	335	135	75	21	29	21	33	23	20
Other Caribbean	3,172	1,579	369	123	113	62	53	30	24
Central America	4,746	4,361	4,102	2,745	3,065	2,626	1,701	1,482	928
El Salvador	2,445	2,435	2,531	1,544	1,400	1,082	595	546	443
Guatemala	1,130	1,045	952	795	1,009	836	389	345	163
Honduras	551	442	285	211	356	317	216	170	102
Nicaragua	235	232	217	130	207	301	414	366	184
Panama	124	61	30	12	33	30	32	16	15
Other Central America	261	146	87	53	60	60	55	39	21
South America	5,146	3,137	1,732	774	820	598	382	398	265
Bolivia	105	79	57	26	22	19	12	16	21
Brazil	196	121	102	55	111	115	58	46	29
Chile	122	120	59	22	41	25	14	15	18
Colombia	2,491	1,555	808	346	275	215	115	135	85
Ecuador	694	377	193	82	75	44	34	41	29
Peru	455	363	272	137	168	78	63	57	38
Venezuela	93	53	38	26	41	37	21	29	17
Other South America	990	469	203	80	87	65	65	59	28
Europe	2,426	1,685	987	783	982	847	737	622	382
Bulgaria	-	2	1	1	1	4	10	15	21
France	133	86	72	57	153	74	48	45	24
Germany	126	121	66	72	95	61	42	31	18
Poland	277	232	174	120	122	207	266	225	105
Romania	8	10	7	6	4	5	10	13	24
United Kingdom	761	478	220	180	193	175	110	90	65
Yugoslavia	106	102	83	81	61	54	45	23	17
Other Europe	1,015	654	364	266	353	267	206	180	108

[Continued]

★33★

Aliens Under Docket Control Required to Depart, 1985-93

[Continued]

Region and country of nationality	1985	1986	1987	1988	1989	1990	1991	1992	1993
Asia	3,963	2,814	1,814	1,263	2,091	1,217	729	727	587
China, Mainland	555	305	156	97	108	42	45	78	46
India	504	321	193	129	123	65	44	40	59
Iran	309	295	212	78	140	62	53	45	43
Israel	144	110	73	61	92	61	41	51	19
Japan	377	204	165	158	252	243	112	58	31
Jordan	44	42	29	25	50	42	21	32	26
Korea	290	188	90	73	118	101	61	40	39
Malaysia	30	32	14	21	28	29	25	17	16
Pakistan	310	154	88	64	90	35	21	38	23
Philippines	592	550	381	244	323	231	115	173	179
Thailand	150	77	56	39	58	27	27	27	15
Other Asia	658	536	357	274	709	279	164	128	91
Africa	803	532	385	234	612	332	168	189	96
Egypt	104	64	26	20	28	17	10	18	23
Nigeria	226	166	95	49	43	25	9	27	19
Other Africa	473	302	264	165	541	290	149	144	54
Oceania	206	211	124	84	106	87	55	52	46
Stateless or not reported	25	26	69	77	164	176	107	56	45

Source: U.S. Immigration and Naturalization Service, *Statistical Yearbook of the Immigration and Naturalization Service, 1993,* U.S. Government Printing Office, Washington, DC, 1994, p. 162.

★34★

Immigration

Aliens Under Docket Control Required to Depart, by Cause, 1993

From the source: "[Required departure is] the directed departure of an alien from the United States without an order of deportation. The departure may be voluntary or involuntary on the part of the alien, and may or may not have been preceded by a hearing before an immigration judge. Data for a fiscal year cover the required departures in that fiscal year. Airlines, ship companies, or port officials provide the Immigration and Naturalization Service with the departure data on aliens required to depart." The number of aliens under docket control required to depart in fiscal year 1993 is shown, by cause and region and selected country of nationality.

Region and country of nationality	Total	Convictions for criminal or narcotics violations	Related to criminal or narcotics violations	Entered without inspection	Violation of nonimmigrant status	Other	Unknown
All countries	5,306	120	22	3,991	919	153	101
North America	3,885	86	20	3,360	259	95	65
Canada	73	2	10	12	36	13	-
Mexico	2,471	53	7	2,182	143	63	23

[Continued]

★ 34 ★

Aliens Under Docket Control Required to Depart, by Cause, 1993

[Continued]

Region and country of nationality	Total	Convictions for criminal or narcotics violations	Related to criminal or narcotics violations	Entered without inspection	Violation of nonimmigrant status	Other	Unknown
Caribbean	413	19	2	320	35	6	31
Cuba	16	-	-	5	2	-	9
Dominican Republic	305	10	1	273	6	4	11
Jamaica	48	7	1	20	10	1	9
Trinidad & Tobago	20	-	-	11	8	-	1
Other Caribbean	24	2	-	11	9	1	1
Central America	928	12	1	846	45	13	11
El Salvador	443	4	-	425	5	4	5
Guatemala	163	2	1	146	8	3	3
Honduras	102	1	-	87	10	4	-
Nicaragua	184	3	-	170	8	1	2
Panama	15	2	-	4	9	-	-
Other Central America	21	-	-	14	5	1	1
South America	265	9	-	187	58	5	6
Bolivia	21	-	-	11	9	1	-
Brazil	29	-	-	19	10	-	-
Chile	18	-	-	10	8	-	-
Colombia	85	6	-	66	9	3	1
Ecuador	29	1	-	21	6	-	1
Peru	38	-	-	29	8	1	-
Venezuela	17	-	-	13	2	-	2
Other South America	28	2	-	18	6	-	2
Europe	382	10	-	153	192	16	11
Bulgaria	21	-	-	12	9	-	-
France	24	-	-	9	14	1	-
Germany	18	-	-	6	9	3	-
Poland	105	1	-	52	52	-	-
Romania	24	-	-	9	15	-	-
United Kingdom	65	5	-	12	37	7	4
Yugoslavia	17	1	-	12	1	1	2
Other Europe	108	3	-	41	55	4	5
Asia	587	11	2	203	327	31	13
China, Mainland	46	-	-	20	22	3	1
India	59	4	1	19	30	3	2
Iran	43	1	-	16	24	2	-
Israel	19	1	-	13	5	-	-
Japan	31	-	-	9	21	1	-
Jordan	26	1	-	8	16	-	1
Korea	39	-	-	16	19	3	1
Malaysia	16	1	-	5	10	-	-

[Continued]

★34★

Aliens Under Docket Control Required to Depart, by Cause, 1993

[Continued]

Region and country of nationality	Total	Convictions for criminal or narcotics violations	Related to criminal or narcotics violations	Entered without inspection	Violation of nonimmigrant status	Other	Unknown
Pakistan	23	1	-	8	11	2	1
Philippines	179	-	1	48	116	11	3
Thailand	15	-	-	1	12	1	1
Other Asia	91	2	-	40	41	5	3
Africa	96	1	-	35	53	3	4
Egypt	23	-	-	8	13	1	1
Nigeria	19	-	-	5	13	1	-
Other Africa	54	1	-	22	27	1	3
Oceania	46	2	-	16	24	2	2
Stateless or not reported	45	1	-	37	6	1	-

Source: U.S. Immigration and Naturalization Service, *Statistical Yearbook of the Immigration and Naturalization Service, 1993,* U.S. Government Printing Office, Washington, DC, 1994, p. 163. *Note:* A dash (-) represents zero.

★35★

Immigration

Asylum Cases Filed, 1993

The number of cases filed with Immigration and Naturalization Service officers in fiscal year 1993 is shown, by selected nationality.

Nationality	Applications pending beginning of year[1]	Applications received during year	Applications reopened during year	Applications granted during year	Individuals granted asylum during year	Applications denied during year	Applications otherwise closed during year	Applications pending end of year
All nationalities	233,709	143,118	1,048	5,012	7,464	17,979	11,237	333,647
Afghanistan	711	219	5	44	70	65	24	802
Albania	230	318	-	18	30	17	12	501
Armenia	464	923	6	17	28	84	36	1,256
Bangladesh	1,178	3,764	12	22	33	123	140	4,669
Brazil	90	494	1	2	2	27	18	538
Bulgaria	1,720	429	17	47	75	327	102	1,690
Burma	330	163	5	32	42	10	11	445
Cameroon	356	232	2	25	26	51	44	470
China	4,429	14,433	32	245	336	254	568	17,827
Colombia	775	1,290	13	17	36	141	104	1,816
Croatia	33	361	-	8	9	18	8	360
Cuba	4,435	2,674	25	240	319	245	1,129	5,520
Czechoslovakia	190	184	-	2	2	23	9	340
Ecuador	159	530	3	2	3	11	18	661
Egypt	608	463	18	12	28	44	33	1,000
El Salvador	46,017	14,554	62	63	74	1,346	795	58,429

[Continued]

★35★

Asylum Cases Filed, 1993

[Continued]

Nationality	Applications pending beginning of year[1]	Applications received during year	Applications reopened during year	Applications granted during year	Individuals granted asylum during year	Applications denied during year	Applications otherwise closed during year	Applications pending end of year
Ethiopia	3,076	1,200	25	285	352	339	118	3,559
Fiji	1,031	263	9	33	70	225	37	1,008
Gambia	145	311	2	-	-	14	46	398
Ghana	651	1,597	3	14	14	52	48	2,137
Guatemala	70,344	34,045	153	13	172	1,958	1,768	100,683
Guyana	152	377	2	-	-	14	25	492
Haiti	5,639	10,858	50	549	636	1,774	444	13,780
Honduras	2,421	2,780	25	28	32	401	366	4,431
Hungary	364	92	1	2	2	41	19	395
India	3,629	5,657	41	306	357	985	485	7,551
Iran	2,483	557	21	222	347	156	138	2,545
Iraq	486	173	3	60	101	38	25	539
Israel	380	306	-	16	30	42	35	593
Ivory Coast	162	379	3	2	2	23	18	501
Jamaica	66	440	-	1	3	11	28	466
Jordan	806	294	5	23	35	112	52	918
Laos	1,768	480	6	65	79	338	82	1,769
Lebanon	1,517	508	4	37	65	158	69	1,765
Liberia	4,347	846	31	160	247	276	160	4,628
Mali	210	577	2	-	-	14	40	735
Mexico	717	6,390	7	-	-	501	744	5,869
Nicaragua	22,558	3,038	142	166	291	2,082	721	22,769
Pakistan	3,666	4,511	25	126	176	906	496	6,674
Panama	362	38	2	3	6	15	8	376
Peru	1,597	3,135	15	139	241	397	119	4,092
Philippines	4,983	3,932	54	41	58	888	522	7,518
Poland	2,435	849	4	2	3	203	113	2,970
Romania	4,860	1,111	27	169	258	773	186	4,870
Russia	1,347	3,234	13	184	233	204	81	4,125
Senegal	166	293	3	1	2	19	34	408
Sierra Leone	688	534	7	20	22	226	42	941
Somalia	600	131	4	88	121	26	29	592
Soviet Union[2]	7,281	320	69	361	588	671	268	6,370
Sri Lanka	405	169	5	13	16	37	24	505
Sudan	544	243	4	95	133	30	35	631
Syria	872	805	3	226	638	79	51	1,324
Trinidad	171	416	5	-	-	23	18	551
Turkey	263	287	4	4	4	16	14	520
Ukraine	315	996	3	45	54	74	22	1,173
Yemen	292	371	-	1	1	31	22	609
Yugoslavia	3,595	2,221	29	301	496	296	150	5,098
Other	4,590	7,323	36	295	466	725	484	10,445

Source: U.S. Immigration and Naturalization Service, *Statistical Yearbook of the Immigration and Naturalization Service, 1993*, U.S. Government Printing Office, Washington, DC, 1994, p. 85. *Notes:* A dash (-) represents zero. 1. The total number of applications pending at the beginning of fiscal year 1993 is higher than the 219,014 reported at the end of fiscal year 1992 because some cases were added late to the data base. 2. Some pending claims filed by persons from the former Soviet Union were recoded under the new Soviet republics.

★36★

Immigration

Asylum Grantees, 1987-93

The number of grantees given asylum by Immigration and Naturalization Service district directors and asylum officers is shown by selected nationality, for 1987-93.

Nationality	1987	1988	1989	1990	1991	1992[1]	1993
All nationalities	5,093	7,340	9,229	5,672	2,908	3,959	7,464
Afghanistan	24	50	23	24	46	90	70
Bulgaria	4	14	17	26	22	44	75
China, Mainland	27	90	150	679	348	277	336
Cuba	73	36	107	229	124	214	319
El Salvador	39	149	443	260	185	110	74
Ethiopia	205	570	517	382	405	347	352
Guatemala	7	42	102	65	49	94	172
Haiti	-	8	11	3	1	120	636
Hungary	14	40	33	20	5	1	2
India	-	4	4	-	13	78	357
Iran	1,346	1,107	723	256	232	231	347
Iraq	16	25	17	21	26	70	101
Laos	2	4	7	38	36	56	79
Lebanon	48	73	76	86	67	81	65
Liberia	7	5	20	10	53	209	247
Libya	115	79	39	23	6	14	22
Nicaragua	2,213	3,725	5,092	2,277	703	341	291
Pakistan	7	51	23	11	11	83	176
Panama	-	47	318	251	3	3	6
Peru	1	1	24	27	20	113	241
Poland	558	488	329	39	6	2	58
Romania	137	398	650	204	50	156	258
Russia	-	-	-	-	-	51	233
Somalia	14	79	128	204	117	122	121
Soviet Union	33	47	127	264	142	381	588
Sri Lanka	-	1	4	10	4	44	16
Sudan	-	-	-	8	31	73	133
Syria	67	36	28	63	9	16	638
Yugoslavia	17	6	4	14	3	72	496
Other	119	165	213	178	191	466	955

Source: U.S. Immigration and Naturalization Service, *Statistical Yearbook of the Immigration and Naturalization Service, 1993*, U.S. Government Printing Office, Washington, DC, 1994, p. 84. *Notes:* A dash (-) represents zero. 1. The 3,959 individuals known to have been granted asylum were in the 2,470 cases in the data system. An additional 1,179 cases were granted asylum, but the number of individuals covered and their nationalities are unknown.

★37★

Immigration

Border Patrol Activities, 1987-93

Activities and accomplishments	1987	1988	1989	1990	1991	1992	1993
Persons apprehended	1,168,861	980,522	906,535	1,123,223	1,152,667	1,221,904	1,281,721
Deportable aliens located	1,158,030	969,214	891,147	1,103,353	1,132,933	1,199,560	1,263,490
Mexican aliens	1,123,725	928,278	830,985	1,054,849	1,095,122	1,168,946	1,230,124
Working in agriculture	15,862	3,333	2,592	4,661	4,707	5,488	5,393
Working in trades, crafts industry, and service	15,097	9,969	5,686	7,544	8,095	7,165	7,403
Welfare/seeking employment	996,873	838,242	727,400	865,739	978,807	1,065,159	1,117,414
Canadian aliens	4,814	4,237	5,297	5,746	6,666	6,167	5,249
All others	29,491	36,699	54,865	42,758	31,145	24,447	28,117
Smugglers of aliens located	11,560	10,373	13,794	21,901	18,826	17,237	15,266
Aliens located who were smuggled into the United States	59,268	50,122	50,638	71,049	64,170	69,538	80,835
Seizures (conveyances)	7,512	6,643	10,789	17,275	14,261	11,391	10,995
Value of seizures (dollars)	590,638,336	721,213,999	1,212,724,491	843,562,055	950,199,178	1,247,938,634	1,382,898,517
Narcotics	582,395,375	700,523,810	1,191,505,131	797,768,179	910,146,141	216,833,993	1,337,766,371
Other	8,242,961	20,690,189	21,219,360	45,793,876	40,053,037	31,104,641	45,132,146

Source: U.S. Immigration and Naturalization Service, *Statistical Yearbook of the Immigration and Naturalization Service, 1993,* U.S. Government Printing Office, Washington, DC, 1994, p. 171. *Notes:* Data on aliens previously expelled, aliens with previous criminal records located, conveyances examined, and persons questioned shown in previous *Yearbooks* are not available starting with fiscal year 1990.

★38★

Immigration

Deportable Aliens Located, by Status at Entry, 1993

From the source: "[A deportable alien is] an alien in the United States subject to any of the five grounds of deportation specified in the Immigration and Nationality Act. This includes any alien illegally in the United States, regardless of whether the alien entered the country illegally or entered legally but subsequently violated the terms of his or her visa." The number of deportable aliens located in fiscal year 1993 is shown, by status at entry and selected country of nationality.

Region and country of nationality	All located	Visitor	Crewman	Student	Temporary worker		Immigrant	Stowaway	TWOV[1]	Entry without inspection	Other
					Agriculture	Other					
All countries	1,327,259	15,902	894	1,080	273	147	9,854	293	50	1,294,256	4,510
North America	1,308,669	8,977	454	137	243	64	7,842	146	24	1,288,389	2,393
Belize	267	73	1	1	-	-	36	-	-	147	9
Canada	5,684	2,035	17	17	7	9	133	-	1	3,323	142
Costa Rica	211	71	4	1	-	-	24	6	-	100	5
Cuba	1,316	11	5	1	-	1	273	4	1	457	563
Dominican Republic	7,064	215	57	15	3	6	950	55	8	5,689	66
El Salvador	7,820	96	5	2	-	-	158	-	3	7,531	25
Guatemala	6,696	163	11	4	1	-	91	-	-	6,419	7
Haiti	709	72	96	4	1	3	132	2	-	317	82
Honduras	4,914	152	93	6	-	-	63	9	1	4,579	11
Jamaica	1,961	450	57	15	107	12	884	39	4	268	125
Mexico	1,269,294	5,062	24	50	114	31	4,705	17	-	1,258,009	1,282
Nicaragua	1,567	88	54	3	-	-	36	-	1	1,373	12
Panama	212	66	6	4	-	-	71	13	-	41	11
Trinidad & Tobago	371	157	6	3	-	-	136	-	-	43	26
Other North America	583	266	18	11	10	2	150	1	5	93	27

[Continued]

★ 38 ★

Deportable Aliens Located, by Status at Entry, 1993

[Continued]

Region and country of nationality	All located	Visitor	Crewman	Student	Temporary worker: Agriculture	Temporary worker: Other	Immigrant	Stowaway	TWOV[1]	Entry without inspection	Other
South America	4,989	1,387	119	69	2	4	657	105	17	2,460	169
Argentina	151	85	-	11	-	-	15	-	-	32	8
Brazil	406	192	2	9	-	1	15	-	1	177	9
Colombia	2,082	572	52	24	1	-	328	83	8	941	73
Ecuador	1,055	88	19	2	-	-	87	10	-	844	5
Guyana	218	22	11	3	-	-	122	7	-	26	27
Peru	556	189	17	8	1	2	46	1	7	257	28
Venezuela	196	107	2	7	-	-	14	3	-	60	3
Other South America	325	132	16	5	-	1	30	1	1	123	16
Europe	2,653	1,415	122	39	6	9	373	15	2	397	275
France	111	72	6	4	-	2	5	-	-	14	8
Germany	226	133	9	8	-	1	29	-	-	18	28
Ireland	62	32	1	1	2	-	5	-	-	13	8
Italy	137	57	7	2	-	-	39	-	-	14	18
Poland	369	267	1	3	-	1	22	3	-	55	17
Portugal	114	29	3	-	-	-	69	-	-	12	1
United Kingdom	567	341	19	12	2	4	84	-	-	52	53
Yugoslavia	100	28	8	-	-	-	19	1	-	33	11
Other Europe	967	456	68	9	2	1	101	11	2	186	131
Asia	8,159	2,908	180	551	16	62	727	11	6	2,715	983
China, Mainland	1,767	130	10	179	1	9	46	2	2	1,274	114
India	749	256	20	31	2	1	39	1	-	368	31
Iran	299	111	-	44	-	8	39	-	-	79	18
Israel	219	152	1	9	-	-	11	-	1	32	13
Japan	75	38	3	16	-	2	3	-	-	8	5
Jordan	197	110	1	53	-	-	23	-	-	5	5
Korea	198	64	13	10	2	4	57	-	2	34	12
Lebanon	191	98	-	32	-	1	23	-	-	29	8
Pakistan	1,269	733	5	38	1	1	21	1	-	419	50
Philippines	774	334	81	21	8	32	178	2	1	52	65
Vietnam	345	5	-	-	-	1	127	1	-	33	178
Other Asia	2,076	877	46	118	2	3	160	4	-	382	484
Africa	2,498	1,015	16	266	6	6	221	16	-	274	678
Liberia	93	44	-	7	1	-	9	3	-	23	6
Nigeria	681	289	6	137	2	-	103	4	-	83	57
Other Africa	1,724	682	10	122	3	6	109	9	-	168	615
Oceania	283	195	1	18	-	2	34	-	1	21	11
Unknown or not reported	8	5	2	-	-	-	-	-	-	-	1

Source: U.S. Immigration and Naturalization Service, *Statistical Yearbook of the Immigration and Naturalization Service, 1993*, U.S. Government Printing Office, Washington, DC, 1994, p. 159. *Notes:* A dash (-) represents zero. 1. TWOV stands for transit without visa.

★ 39 ★

Immigration

Expected Immigration to the U.S. as Refugees, by Geographic Region, 1993

The United States expected to admit 122,000 immigrants as refugees in 1993.

Geographic region	Expected refugees
East Asia	52,000
Former Soviet Union	50,000
Southeast Asia	7,000
Africa	7,000
Latin American/Caribbean	3,500
Eastern Europe	1,500
Unallocated	1,000

Source: Tan, Evelyn D. "Immigrants may find more of a promised land." *USA TODAY* (17 November 1992), p. 7A. Primary source: State Department.

★ 40 ★

Immigration

Immigrant-Orphans Adopted by U.S. Citizens, by Age, Sex, and Selected Country of Birth, 1993

Data are shown for fiscal year 1993. From the source: "For immigration purposes, [an orphan is] a child whose parents have died or disappeared, or who has been abandoned or otherwise separated from both parents. An orphan may also be a child whose sole surviving parent is incapable of providing that child with proper care and who has, in writing, irrevocably released the child for emigration and adoption. In order to qualify as an immediate relative, the orphan must be under the age of 16 at the time a petition is filed on his or her behalf. To enter the United States, an orphan must have been adopted abroad by a U.S. citizen or be coming to the U.S. for adoption by a citizen."

Region and country of birth	Total	Sex		Age				
		Male	Female	Under 1 year	1 to 4 years	5 to 9 years	Over 9 years	Unknown
All countries	7,348	3,361	3,987	4,099	2,231	680	337	1
Europe	1,521	694	827	332	840	301	48	-
Bulgaria	126	54	72	1	72	50	3	-
Hungary	54	20	34	16	20	17	1	-
Latvia	17	7	10	4	9	4	-	-
Lithuania	23	16	7	12	9	2	-	-
Poland	70	34	36	24	25	12	9	-
Romania	88	44	44	8	56	15	9	-
Soviet Union	1,107	498	609	257	630	195	25	-
Russia	695	313	382	147	397	130	21	-
Ukraine	248	119	129	74	140	33	1	-
Other republics	62	25	37	17	35	10	-	-

[Continued]

★ 40 ★

Immigrant-Orphans Adopted by U.S. Citizens, by Age, Sex, and Selected Country of Birth, 1993

[Continued]

Region and country of birth	Total	Sex		Age				
		Male	Female	Under 1 year	1 to 4 years	5 to 9 years	Over 9 years	Unknown
Unknown republics	102	41	61	19	58	22	3	-
United Kingdom	7	4	3	-	5	2	-	-
Yugoslavia	17	11	6	6	7	3	1	-
Other Europe	12	6	6	4	7	1	-	-
Asia	3,163	1,379	1,784	2,187	619	185	171	1
Bangladesh	8	1	7	4	2	-	2	-
China, Mainland	330	11	319	248	69	10	3	-
Hong Kong	27	15	12	11	10	3	3	-
India	342	109	233	105	166	48	23	-
Japan	59	32	27	35	24	-	-	-
Korea	1,765	877	888	1,612	121	27	5	-
Lebanon	24	17	7	22	-	-	2	-
Nepal	14	3	11	7	6	1	-	-
Pakistan	12	6	6	10	1	-	1	-
Philippines	358	205	153	69	126	56	106	1
Taiwan	31	15	16	18	9	3	1	-
Thailand	65	37	28	4	37	13	11	-
Vietnam	105	39	66	34	40	22	9	-
Other Asia	23	12	11	8	8	2	5	-
Africa	59	21	38	11	23	11	14	-
Ethiopia	29	9	20	2	10	7	10	-
Kenya	6	4	2	1	3	1	1	-
Other Africa	24	8	16	8	10	3	3	-
Oceania	1	-	1	-	-	1	-	-
North America	1,133	566	567	552	402	106	73	-
Canada	7	1	6	1	4	1	1	-
Mexico	97	53	44	32	37	15	13	-
Caribbean	150	54	96	41	46	26	37	-
Dominican Republic	39	15	24	27	7	3	2	-
Haiti	49	21	28	9	19	13	8	-
Jamaica	48	14	34	3	13	7	25	-
Other Caribbean	14	4	10	2	7	3	2	-
Central America	878	458	420	478	314	64	22	-
Costa Rica	48	26	22	10	13	22	3	-
El Salvador	97	44	53	44	41	11	1	-
Guatemala	512	274	238	366	124	17	5	-
Honduras	183	96	87	43	125	8	7	-
Panama	24	10	14	9	9	3	3	-
Other Central America	14	8	6	6	2	3	3	-
Other North America	1	-	1	-	1	-	-	-

[Continued]

★ 40 ★

Immigrant-Orphans Adopted by U.S. Citizens, by Age, Sex, and Selected Country of Birth, 1993

[Continued]

Region and country of birth	Total	Sex		Age				
		Male	Female	Under 1 year	1 to 4 years	5 to 9 years	Over 9 years	Unknown
South America	1,471	701	770	1,017	347	76	31	-
Bolivia	123	58	65	88	29	4	2	-
Brazil	178	96	82	115	25	28	10	-
Chile	61	28	33	15	42	4	-	-
Colombia	416	205	211	303	70	30	13	-
Ecuador	48	28	20	7	34	6	1	-
Paraguay	405	192	213	312	91	2	-	-
Peru	230	87	143	175	51	1	3	-
Other South America	10	7	3	2	5	1	2	-

Source: U.S. Immigration and Naturalization Service, *Statistical Yearbook of the Immigration and Naturalization Service, 1993*, U.S. Government Printing Office, Washington, DC, 1994, p. 57. *Note:* A dash (-) represents zero.

★ 41 ★

Immigration

Immigrants Admitted Who Were Adjusted to Permanent Resident Status, by Selected Status at Entry, 1993

From the source: "[Adjustment to Immigrant Status is a] procedure allowing certain aliens already in the United States to apply for immigrant status. Aliens admitted to the United States in a nonimmigrant or other category may have their status changed to that of lawful permanent resident if they are eligible to receive an immigrant visa and one is available. In such cases, the alien is counted as an immigrant as of the date of adjustment, even though that alien may have been in the United States for an extended period of time." Data show number of adjustments made in fiscal year 1993.

Region and country of birth	Total	Visitors for business	Visitors for pleasure	Students[1]	Temporary workers[1]	Exchange visitors[1]	Fiances(ees)[2]	Intracompany transferees[1]	Refugees and parolees	Entered without inspection	Other and unknown
All countries	367,998	4,140	83,352	37,866	38,854	10,293	7,893	9,421	128,560	24,831	22,788
North America	71,691	697	26,676	1,530	2,973	184	1,289	2,278	7,201	22,854	6,009
Canada	9,146	62	2,811	485	1,432	103	477	1,942	168	62	1,604
Mexico	25,991	138	6,073	196	302	15	418	154	192	17,215	1,288
Caribbean	25,957	408	13,991	605	1,100	37	252	115	6,058	1,412	1,979
Bahamas, The	368	6	238	38	28	-	2	5	2	14	35
Barbados	359	8	257	21	33	-	5	2	3	6	24
Cuba	11,793	15	4,384	7	1	-	4	1	5,879	257	1,245
Dominica	151	7	104	7	6	-	1	3	-	14	9
Dominican Republic	3,942	170	2,755	69	146	11	108	63	23	494	103
Grenada	238	6	183	15	11	-	-	-	-	8	15
Haiti	1,899	28	1,124	56	14	1	9	3	119	391	154
Jamaica	3,825	99	2,441	170	566	19	86	8	21	164	251
St. Lucia	177	4	131	7	10	1	3	-	2	8	11
St. Vincent & Grenadines	181	5	138	9	15	-	1	1	1	3	8
Trinidad & Tobago	2,383	45	1,801	149	234	4	22	22	6	28	72
Other Caribbean	641	15	435	57	36	1	11	7	2	25	52
Central America	10,564	89	3,791	242	134	29	142	66	780	4,163	1,128
Belize	241	3	135	14	1	-	1	-	4	57	26
Costa Rica	483	10	325	21	10	2	28	9	16	30	32
El Salvador	2,611	10	320	33	26	-	7	5	177	1,722	311
Guatemala	1,458	14	494	21	29	10	22	2	55	695	116
Honduras	999	19	575	43	18	1	34	2	25	209	73
Nicaragua	3,889	17	1,410	32	6	12	8	3	454	1,437	510

[Continued]

★ 41 ★

Immigrants Admitted Who Were Adjusted to Permanent Resident Status, by Selected Status at Entry, 1993

[Continued]

Region and country of birth	Total	Visitors for business	Visitors for pleasure	Students[1]	Temporary workers[1]	Exchange visitors[1]	Fiances(ees)[2]	Intracompany transferees[1]	Refugees and parolees	Entered without inspection	Other and unknown
Panama	883	16	532	78	44	4	42	45	49	13	60
Other North America	33	-	10	2	5	-	-	1	3	2	10
South America	14,350	305	8,391	1,118	,551	212	427	709	186	652	799
Argentina	1,347	23	539	96	355	76	16	109	13	18	102
Bolivia	361	8	230	43	23	2	5	11	1	13	25
Brazil	2,649	58	1,436	246	315	33	152	240	23	28	118
Chile	758	23	404	69	102	18	24	41	6	11	60
Colombia	3,122	73	2,039	198	202	19	107	61	37	259	127
Ecuador	982	17	649	51	40	3	26	18	10	115	53
Guyana	845	16	578	41	83	4	19	9	5	27	63
Peru	2,442	52	1,527	141	176	41	49	105	58	151	142
Uruguay	204	8	105	14	20	2	3	13	1	14	24
Venezuela	1,449	23	771	199	211	13	17	100	31	14	70
Other South America	191	4	113	20	24	1	9	2	1	2	15
Europe	93,831	586	13,928	1,913	6,359	1,615	1,502	3,073	57,405	210	7,240
Albania	1,216	-	36	-	-	-	2	-	1,105	1	72
Austria	342	9	139	19	47	12	9	26	57	-	24
Belgium	392	4	103	29	103	17	11	61	7	2	55
Bulgaria	674	8	202	14	81	62	9	3	261	-	34
Czechoslovakia	558	4	257	22	68	21	31	20	105	1	29
Denmark	417	9	135	27	110	16	16	38	3	-	63
France	1,717	21	500	153	325	87	75	169	49	5	333
Germany	3,609	54	1,236	214	392	124	197	254	161	14	963
Greece	994	8	320	143	119	26	23	17	294	13	31
Hungary	643	2	289	30	144	38	21	28	63	2	26
Ireland	1,106	17	378	75	319	80	27	115	9	1	85
Italy	1,373	32	571	87	138	46	50	58	41	5	345
Netherlands	918	8	238	77	252	41	39	137	13	3	110
Norway	350	8	113	66	54	15	16	13	7	-	58
Poland	3,531	24	1,811	102	435	116	125	33	631	67	187
Portugal	484	16	303	35	20	8	48	17	4	12	21
Romania	4,599	19	791	24	123	19	47	5	3,245	11	315
Soviet Union, former	55,942	137	2,039	70	562	379	156	49	50,296	6	2,248
Armenia	6,199	5	93	1	7	12	2	-	6,073	-	6
Azerbaijan	2,915	2	31	-	15	8	1	1	2,774	-	83
Belarus	4,600	-	75	-	10	8	1	2	4,300	-	204
Moldova	2,596	3	43	3	3	1	1	1	2,346	-	195
Russia	10,876	80	866	43	368	268	99	41	8,706	2	403
Ukraine	17,695	22	474	12	72	38	22	-	16,253	4	798
Uzbekistan	2,579	1	59	2	8	5	5	-	2,255	-	244
Other republics	1,482	7	83	5	22	12	6	-	1,298	-	49
Unknown republic	7,000	17	315	4	57	27	19	4	6,291	-	266
Spain	767	12	330	101	91	25	25	42	27	5	109
Sweden	831	11	215	78	163	29	31	182	18	3	101
Switzerland	585	6	155	47	124	33	27	84	15	1	93
United Kingdom	10,009	155	2,853	349	2,383	284	458	1,643	137	28	1,719
Yugoslavia	1,232	12	598	78	211	94	33	24	30	29	123
Other Europe	1,542	10	316	73	95	43	26	55	827	1	96
Asia	168,670	2,098	28,065	30,939	25,718	7,851	4,172	2,714	58,779	916	7,418
Afghanistan	2,391	7	139	14	2	1	12	6	1,741	132	337
Bangladesh	544	8	143	158	141	18	4	3	7	35	27
Burma	244	6	106	30	21	4	9	3	46	1	18
Cambodia	1,155	1	69	5	1	-	27	-	1,021	-	31
China, Mainland	41,564	560	3,770	19,513	7,939	6,541	417	436	853	105	1,430
Hong Kong	2,470	50	581	682	644	21	30	274	117	6	65
India	12,350	283	3,023	1,789	5,750	554	201	249	89	114	298
Indonesia	568	9	191	158	86	8	42	30	14	2	28
Iran	8,348	81	2,351	860	250	64	125	66	4,005	74	472
Iraq	2,207	9	188	67	48	4	35	5	1,753	5	93
Israel	2,518	35	1,206	227	636	136	22	73	25	9	149
Japan	3,672	35	516	685	600	55	222	307	51	13	1,188
Jordan	1,525	34	852	409	87	7	28	12	40	12	44

[Continued]

★ 41 ★

Immigrants Admitted Who Were Adjusted to Permanent Resident Status, by Selected Status at Entry, 1993

[Continued]

Region and country of birth	Total	Visitors for business	Visitors for pleasure	Students[1]	Temporary workers[1]	Exchange visitors[1]	Fiances(ees)[2]	Intracompany transferees[1]	Refugees and parolees	Entered without inspection	Other and unknown
Korea	5,651	155	2,193	1,257	774	45	240	221	38	53	675
Kuwait	618	8	193	228	90	5	11	5	54	-	24
Laos	6,983	3	407	10	1	-	18	1	6,482	1	60
Lebanon	2,091	35	900	354	199	85	71	47	237	49	114
Malaysia	1,173	10	332	354	318	12	33	42	43	1	28
Pakistan	1,970	33	688	366	287	51	49	64	135	85	212
Philippines	17,184	469	6,433	364	5,180	65	2,107	312	1,100	174	980
Singapore	491	8	115	127	142	2	21	51	8	-	17
Sri Lanka	581	11	119	117	199	33	10	13	25	6	48
Syria	1,330	11	474	204	57	27	49	11	419	17	61
Taiwan	7,217	170	1,703	2,402	1,824	82	42	403	18	3	570
Thailand	4,676	36	410	177	79	1	146	10	3,764	8	45
Turkey	1,050	10	387	148	129	9	21	14	286	6	40
Vietnam	37,272	12	313	30	30	7	169	11	36,378	3	319
Yemen	123	4	75	23	4	2	2	1	5	-	7
Other Asia	704	5	188	181	200	12	9	44	25	2	38
Africa	16,676	380	5,207	2,197	1,590	348	370	319	4,942	168	1,155
Cape Verde	267	2	240	4	-	-	15	3	-	1	2
Egypt	1,412	35	791	104	219	35	25	34	78	14	77
Ethiopia	4,446	16	646	280	33	11	19	13	3,084	25	319
Ghana	541	27	226	81	54	16	42	1	20	33	41
Kenya	521	11	106	191	73	11	14	17	44	3	51
Liberia	665	15	320	66	14	4	4	-	166	5	71
Morocco	788	17	372	223	36	58	4	12	5	1	40
Nigeria	2,554	132	1,084	531	405	86	111	22	28	40	115
Sierra Leone	364	16	230	58	19	5	8	1	7	1	19
South Africa	1,217	17	321	107	464	49	23	147	22	2	65
Sudan	621	5	109	56	12	3	5	4	399	1	27
Other Africa	3,280	87	762	496	261	70	80	65	1,089	42	328
Oceania	2,775	74	1,085	169	663	83	133	328	47	27	166
Australia	1,518	44	523	80	406	58	84	241	17	1	64
Fiji	171	3	113	17	6	1	11	7	6	4	3
New Zealand	718	16	235	34	243	24	33	78	11	-	44
Tonga	142	4	83	9	3	-	1	-	2	14	26
Other Oceania	226	7	131	29	5	-	4	2	11	8	29
Unknown or not reported	5	-	-	-	-	-	-	-	-	4	1

Source: U.S. Immigration and Naturalization Service, *Statistical Yearbook of the Immigration and Naturalization Service, 1993*, U.S. Government Printing Office, Washington, DC, 1994, pp. 48-49. *Notes:* A dash (-) represents zero. 1. Includes spouses and children. 2. Includes children.

★ 42 ★

Immigration

International Refugee Ceilings Imposed by the U.S., 1993

From the source: "At the beginning of each fiscal year, the President, after consultation with Congress to review the worldwide refugee situation, determines the number of refugees in need of resettlement who are of special humanitarian concern to the United States. The President then establishes the authorized number of admissions for that fiscal year. During the year, changes in the need for resettlement may require revisions in the overall limit on refugee admission or reallocation among areas of the world. The admission ceiling of 132,000 for 1993 was established and later reallocated among the following geographic regions."

Geographic region	Initial ceilings	Final ceilings
Africa	7,000	7,000
East Asia	52,000	51,000
Eastern Europe	1,500	2,725
Soviet Union	50,000	49,775
Latin American/Caribbean	3,500	4,500
Near East/South Asia	7,000	7,000
Unallocated, funded	1,000	-
Unallocated, unfunded	10,000	10,000

Source: U.S. Immigration and Naturalization Service, *Statistical Yearbook of the Immigration and Naturalization Service, 1993,* U.S. Government Printing Office, Washington, DC, 1994, p. 72. *Note:* A dash (-) stands for zero.

★ 43 ★

Immigration

Legal Alien Immigrants and Refugees, 1970-88

Numbers of immigrants are shown in thousands.

Year (July 1 to June 30)	All regions[1]	Latin America	Africa	Asia	Europe	North America	Oceania	U.S.S.R.
1987-88[2]	586	215	19	267	64	13	4	3
1986-87	555	211	17	252	57	11	4	2
1985-86	573	206	17	271	60	11	4	3
1984-85	550	190	17	264	59	12	4	4
1983-84	538	191	16	253	58	11	4	6
1982-83	509	182	14	238	52	11	3	8
1981-82	591	201	15	292	55	11	4	13
1980-81	670	257	15	312	60	12	4	10
1979-80	732	286	14	344	60	14	4	9
1978-79	486	177	12	215	60	14	4	3
1977-78	486	205	11	172	69	18	4	6
1976-77	389	132	9	167	62	10	4	6
1975-76	403	131	8	180	64	8	4	8
1974-75	468	144	7	233	69	8	3	5

[Continued]

★ 43 ★

Legal Alien Immigrants and Refugees, 1970-88

[Continued]

Year (July 1 to June 30)	All regions[1]	Latin America	Africa	Asia	Europe	North America	Oceania	U.S.S.R.
1973-74	390	161	6	131	80	8	3	1
1972-73	389	152	7	124	91	9	3	1
1971-72	387	156	7	121	89	11	3	1
1970-71	397	174	7	103	96	13	3	1

Source: Hollmann, Frederick W. U.S. Department of Commerce. Bureau of the Census. *United States Population Estimates, by Age, Sex, Race, and Hispanic Origin: 1980 to 1988.* Current Population Reports, Population Estimates and Projections, Series P-25, No. 1045. Washington, DC: The Bureau, January 1990, p. 27. Primary source: Unpublished data supplied by the Immigration and Naturalization Service, consistent with *Annual Report: Immigration and Naturalization Service*, 1970 through 1978; *Statistical Yearbook of the Immigration and Naturalization Service* for 1979 through 1987; *Immigration Statistics: Fiscal Year 1988 - Advance Report*; Office of Refugee Resettlement, *Report to Congress: Refugee Resettlement Program*, 1981 through 1988, and unpublished data supplied by the Office of Refugee Resettlement. *Notes:* Regions are United Nations macro-regions, as described in the United Nations, *Demographic Yearbook, 1984*. Immigrants from Mexico are included with Latin America, but not North America. Temporary residents from Cuba, Haiti, and Southeast Asia adjusting to permanent resident status are excluded from the tally for America, Asia, and all regions, but parolees and refugees from these areas are included at time of arrival. 1. A small number of immigrants of unknown place of birth or born aboard ship are included. 2. For 1987-88, the number of immigrants is provisional. The distribution of immigrants by region of birth is based on final data for years ending September 30, 1987 and September 30, 1988 (available since the population estimates were completed) supplied by the Immigration and Naturalization Service.

★ 44 ★

Immigration

Legal Alien Immigrants and Refugees, by Region of Birth, 1970-88

Numbers of immigrants are shown in thousands.

Region of birth	July 1, 1970 to June 30, 1976		July 1, 1976 to June 30, 1982		July 1, 1982 to June 30, 1988	
	Number	Percent	Number	Percent	Number	Percent
All regions[1]	2,434	100.0	3,355	100.0	3,311	100.0
Latin America	917	37.7	1,258	37.5	1,195	36.1
Cuba and Haiti	140	5.8	216	6.4	86	2.6
Other Caribbean	218	9.0	297	8.9	335	10.1
Mexico	376	15.4	405	12.1	375	11.3
Central America	54	2.2	120	3.6	161	4.9
South America	128	5.3	220	6.5	237	7.2
Africa	41	1.7	76	2.3	101	3.0
Western Africa	10	0.4	23	0.7	35	1.1
Eastern Africa	9	0.4	17	0.5	29	0.9
Northern Africa	18	0.7	23	0.7	25	0.8
Middle Africa	1	0.0	2	0.1	2	0.1
Southern Africa	3	0.1	11	0.3	9	0.3
Asia	892	36.7	1,502	44.8	1,545	46.7
East Asia	306	12.6	387	11.5	506	15.3
Cambodia, Laos, and Vietnam	151	6.2	502	15.0	289	8.7
Other Eastern South Asia	229	9.4	291	8.7	343	10.3
Middle South Asia	126	5.2	211	6.3	304	9.2
Western South Asia	80	3.3	110	3.3	104	3.1

[Continued]

★ 44 ★

Legal Alien Immigrants and Refugees, by Region of Birth, 1970-88

[Continued]

Region of birth	July 1, 1970 to June 30, 1976		July 1, 1976 to June 30, 1982		July 1, 1982 to June 30, 1988	
	Number	Percent	Number	Percent	Number	Percent
Europe	489	20.1	366	10.9	351	10.6
Eastern Europe	50	2.1	52	1.5	89	2.7
Northern Europe	85	3.5	104	3.1	110	3.3
Southern Europe	290	11.9	145	4.3	77	2.3
Western Europe	64	2.6	66	2.0	75	2.3
North America	57	2.3	80	2.4	70	2.1
Oceania	19	0.8	25	0.7	23	0.7
U.S.S.R.	18	0.8	48	1.4	26	0.8

Source: Hollmann, Frederick W. U.S. Department of Commerce. Bureau of the Census. *United States Population Estimates, by Age, Sex, Race, and Hispanic Origin: 1980 to 1988.* Current Population Reports, Population Estimates and Projections, Series P-25, No. 1045. Washington, DC: The Bureau, January 1990, p. 28. Primary source: Unpublished data supplied by the Immigration and Naturalization Service, consistent with *Annual Report: Immigration and Naturalization Service*, 1970 through 1978; *Statistical Yearbook of the Immigration and Naturalization Service* for 1979 through 1987; *Immigration Statistics: Fiscal Year 1988 - Advance Report*; Office of Refugee Resettlement, *Report to Congress: Refugee Resettlement Program*, 1981 through 1988, and unpublished data supplied by the Office of Refugee Resettlement. *Notes:* Regions are United Nations micro-regions and macro-regions, as described in the United Nations, *Demographic Yearbook, 1984*, except for the separation of Cambodia, Laos, and Vietnam from Eastern South Asia, and the separation of Cuba and Haiti from the Caribbean. Immigrants from the United Kingdom are included with Northern Europe, but not Western Europe. Temporary residents from Cuba, Haiti, and Southeast Asia adjusting to permanent resident status are excluded from the tally for Latin America and Asia, but parolees and refugees from these areas are included at time of arrival. 1. Includes a small number of immigrants of unknown place of birth or born aboard ship.

★ 45 ★

Immigration

Median Years of Residence, by Year of Naturalization, 1960-93

Median number of years is shown, by region of birth, for selected fiscal years. According to naturalization law, the majority of aliens naturalizing must have resided in the U.S. as lawful permanent residents for a minimum of five years.

Region of birth	1993	1985	1980	1975	1970	1965	1960
Persons naturalized	9	8	8	7	8	7	8
Europe	13	9	10	8	9	7	7
Asia	7	7	7	6	6	6	6
Africa	7	7	7	6	6	6	6
Oceania	9	8	8	7	9	8	10
North America	15	13	11	9	7	9	10
South America	10	8	9	10	7	7	7

Source: U.S. Immigration and Naturalization Service, *Statistical Yearbook of the Immigration and Naturalization Service, 1993*, U.S. Government Printing Office, Washington, DC, 1994, p. 126.

★ 46 ★

Immigration

Net Civilian Immigration, 1980-88

Numbers of persons are shown in thousands for each year.

Source of immigration	1980	1981	1982	1983	1984	1985	1986	1987	1988[1]
Net civilian immigration	845	718	626	605	615	650	660	689	667[2]
Net arrivals from Puerto Rico	11	21	44	40	31	39	35	30	37
Legal alien immigrants[3]	482	500	470	478	492	519	524	548	516
Cuban parolees and entrants	128	-	-	-	-	-	-	-	-
Southeast Asian refugees	155	121	61	43	53	49	42	36	39
Haitian refugees	11	8	-	-	-	-	-	-	-
Net arrival of other civilian U.S. citizens	37	27	11	4	-1	4	18	35	35
Net undocumented immigration[4]	150	200	200	200	200	200	200	200	200
Emigration of legal residents[4]	129	160	160	160	160	160	160	160	160

Source: Hollmann, Frederick W. U.S. Department of Commerce. Bureau of the Census. *United States Population Estimates, by Age, Sex, Race, and Hispanic Origin: 1980 to 1988.* Current Population Reports, Population Estimates and Projections, Series P-25, No. 1045. Washington, DC: The Bureau, January 1990, p. 25. Primary source: Unpublished data supplied by the Immigration and Naturalization Service, consistent with *Statistical Yearbook of the Immigration and Naturalization Service* for 1980 through 1987; Office of Refugee Resettlement, *Report to Congress: Refugee Resettlement Program,* 1981 through 1988, and unpublished data supplied by the Office of Refugee Resettlement; unpublished data supplied by the Department of Defense, the U.S. Office of Personnel Management, and the Puerto Rico Planning Board. *Notes:* - represents zero. 1. For all sources except Southeast Asian refugees, the second half of calendar year 1988 is projected on the basis of the year ending June 30, 1988. The number of Southeast Asian refugees is based on provisional monthly tallies provided by the Office of Refugee Resettlement. 2. Southeast Asian refugees in 1988 include a small number of Amerasian arrivals. 3. Temporary residents from Cuba, Haiti, and Southeast Asia adjusting to permanent resident status are excluded from the number of legal immigrants; these persons are included in their year of arrival in the three subsequent categories in the table. 4. Net undocumented immigration was assumed constant at 200,000 per year after April 1, 1980; zero for the first three months of 1980. Emigration was assumed to be 160,000 per year after April 1, 1980; 36,000 per year for the first three months of 1980.

★ 47 ★

Immigration

Non-Legalization Immigrants Admitted from Top Fifteen Countries of Birth, 1992-93

Data show changes in levels of non-legalization immigration for the top 15 countries of birth in fiscal year 1993. Immigration from Mexico increased by 19.4 percent due to increases in the numbers of legalization dependents and spouses of U.S. citizens.

Country of birth	Rank	1993	1992	Change	
				Number	Percent
All countries		880,014	810,635	69,379	8.6
Mexico	1	109,027	91,332	17,695	19.4
China, Mainland	2	65,552	38,735	26,817	69.2
Philippines	3	63,189	59,179	4,010	6.8
Vietnam	4	59,613	77,728	-18,115	-23.3
Soviet Union	5	58,568	43,590	14,978	34.4
Dominican Republic	6	44,886	40,840	4,046	9.9
India	7	40,021	34,629	5,392	15.6
Poland	8	27,729	24,837	2,892	11.6
El Salvador	9	25,517	21,110	4,407	20.9

[Continued]

★ 47 ★

Non-Legalization Immigrants Admitted from Top Fifteen Countries of Birth, 1992-93

[Continued]

Country of birth	Rank	1993	1992	Change	
				Number	Percent
United Kingdom	10	18,712	19,757	-1,045	-5.3
Korea	11	17,949	18,983	-1,034	-5.4
Canada	12	17,081	14,958	2,123	14.2
Jamaica	13	16,969	16,820	149	.9
Iran	14	14,700	12,808	1,892	14.8
Taiwan	15	14,309	16,232	-1,923	-11.8
Other		286,1192	279,097	7,095	2.5

Source: U.S. Immigration and Naturalization Service, *Statistical Yearbook of the Immigration and Naturalization Service, 1993,* U.S. Government Printing Office, Washington, DC, 1994, p. 22.

★ 48 ★

Immigration

Nonimmigrants Admitted as Temporary Workers, Exchange Visitors, and Intracompany Transferees, 1993 - I

Numbers of immigrants are shown, by selected country of citizenship, for 1993. Letters and numbers in parentheses represent code designations for their respective classes of immigrant admission, as specified by the U.S. Department of State Visa Office.

Region and country of citizenship	Total	Registered nurses (H1A)	Workers with specialty occupations (H1B)	Other temporary workers (H2)		Industrial trainees (H3)	Exchange visitors (J1)	Intracompany transferees (L1)
				Agricultural (H2A)	Non-agricultural (H2B)			
All countries	462,602	6,437	93,069	16,257	15,038	3,135	197,545	82,781
Europe	206,811	956	35,660	41	1,421	1,499	116,537	37,622
Albania	278	-	4	-	23	-	249	1
Austria	2,865	2	411	-	53	24	1,570	571
Belgium	3,526	9	715	-	81	19	1,752	874
Bulgaria	1,088	1	134	-	-	10	804	30
Czechoslovakia	1,912	1	138	-	9	13	1,582	51
Denmark	4,954	9	567	2	78	14	3,459	664
Estonia	325	-	14	-	6	7	288	2
Finland	3,789	3	469	-	100	73	2,309	778
France	23,334	5	4,206	1	34	242	12,705	4,962
Germany	31,047	11	3,539	-	139	184	21,105	5,168
Greece	1,840	-	563	-	5	3	1,035	111
Hungary	2,247	-	290	-	1	5	1,789	82
Iceland	621	-	83	-	-	2	487	45
Ireland	8,781	215	1,045	2	41	35	6,071	934
Italy	9,102	1	1,817	-	22	101	5,102	1,323
Latvia	266	-	18	-	1	4	196	1
Liechtenstein	25	-	4	-	-	-	8	10
Lithuania	248	-	24	-	-	-	202	14
Luxembourg	142	-	44	-	-	1	50	46
Malta	62	-	8	-	-	-	39	11
Netherlands	8,978	15	2,009	-	180	84	4,563	1,840
Norway	3,902	7	475	-	32	28	2,683	444
Poland	3,979	5	713	20	39	30	2,597	105
Portugal	868	1	128	-	10	5	519	183

[Continued]

★ 48 ★

Nonimmigrants Admitted as Temporary Workers, Exchange Visitors, and Intracompany Transferees, 1993 - I

[Continued]

Region and country of citizenship	Total	Registered nurses (H1A)	Workers with specialty occupations (H1B)	Other temporary workers (H2) Agricultural (H2A)	Other temporary workers (H2) Non-agricultural (H2B)	Industrial trainees (H3)	Exchange visitors (J1)	Intracompany transferees (L1)
Romania	808	-	115	-	-	11	605	30
Soviet Union	12,223	2	1,380	2	40	166	7,949	566
Spain	9,380	2	1,290	4	9	66	6,438	779
Sweden	9,028	4	1,266	1	124	18	4,862	2,486
Switzerland	5,147	6	837	-	125	133	2,679	1,244
United Kingdom	54,994	655	13,063	9	247	212	22,242	14,222
Yugoslavia	1,039	2	290	-	22	9	587	45
Other Europe	13	-	1	-	-	-	11	-
Asia	112,220	4,508	34,347	33	4,213	1,142	38,918	24,465
Afghanistan	31	-	6	-	-	-	12	11
Bangladesh	543	1	145	-	1	2	348	12
Burma	27	-	13	-	-	-	10	-
Cambodia	18	-	1	-	-	1	7	1
China[1]	13,585	29	2,749	9	236	91	6,636	3,029
Cyprus	635	-	83	-	-	-	544	7
Hong Kong	1,462	23	541	-	6	1	367	323
India	17,191	103	11,411	4	45	27	3,218	1,235
Indonesia	1,358	-	175	-	2	16	1,030	113
Iran	403	3	161	-	-	-	166	56
Iraq	66	-	37	-	-	-	9	13
Israel	5,413	10	1,874	1	12	21	2,583	586
Japan	38,447	13	8,496	6	1,337	834	10,746	16,080
Jordan	729	4	243	-	2	-	426	50
Korea	6,999	39	1,252	3	1,121	50	2,939	1,223
Kuwait	139	-	35	-	-	-	79	23
Lebanon	1,132	4	442	-	3	-	550	85
Malaysia	1,815	4	604	-	37	4	867	284
Nepal	228	-	32	1	-	2	182	4
Oman	605	-	5	-	-	-	597	2
Pakistan	2,620	6	703	-	1	6	1,766	87
Philippines	11,834	4,258	4,045	9	1,378	36	1,177	664
Qatar	116	-	5	-	-	-	111	-
Saudi Arabia	606	-	44	-	7	5	438	110
Singapore	1,040	-	364	-	6	5	332	284
Sri Lanka	512	1	161	-	3	-	279	30
Syria	475	-	110	-	-	-	345	5
Thailand	1,616	10	136	-	14	18	1,202	59
Turkey	2,145	-	454	-	1	23	1,565	75
United Arab Emirates	101	-	7	-	-	-	92	1
Vietnam	125	-	3	-	-	-	115	1
Yemen	95	-	6	-	-	-	87	1
Other Asia	109	-	4	-	1	-	93	11
Africa	11,364	211	2,354	1	33	51	7,212	656
Algeria	201	-	55	-	-	1	123	19
Angola	15	-	3	-	-	-	7	3
Burundi	73	-	1	-	-	-	54	-
Cameroon	158	-	37	-	-	1	97	5
Congo	55	-	1	-	1	-	39	1
Egypt	2,234	1	330	-	3	5	1,744	104
Ethiopia	228	1	63	-	-	-	115	34
Gambia, The	59	-	5	-	-	-	49	1
Ghana	501	10	58	-	2	2	307	4

[Continued]

★ 48 ★

Nonimmigrants Admitted as Temporary Workers, Exchange Visitors, and Intracompany Transferees, 1993 - I

[Continued]

Region and country of citizenship	Total	Registered nurses (H1A)	Workers with specialty occupations (H1B)	Other temporary workers (H2)		Industrial trainees (H3)	Exchange visitors (J1)	Intracompany transferees (L1)
				Agricultural (H2A)	Non-agricultural (H2B)			
Guinea	115	-	3	-	-	2	103	1
Ivory Coast	184	-	14	-	-	2	135	1
Kenya	447	1	102	-	-	2	318	13
Liberia	46	1	19	-	-	2	17	3
Malawi	70	-	5	-	-	-	60	4
Mali	89	-	5	-	-	1	71	3
Mauritania	16	-	2	-	-	-	10	-
Mauritius	53	-	6	-	1	-	41	1
Morocco	675	-	62	-	1	7	513	20
Namibia	69	1	4	-	-	-	60	1
Niger	26	-	-	-	-	-	22	-
Nigeria	1,084	132	326	-	1	1	411	79
Rwanda	56	-	2	-	-	-	52	-
Senegal	255	-	48	-	-	-	159	16
Sierra Leone	71	-	22	-	-	1	48	-
Somalia	18	-	8	-	-	-	7	-
South Africa	2,682	57	966	-	16	21	1,173	290
Sudan	96	1	29	-	-	-	60	4
Tanzania	262	2	21	1	1	-	226	1
Tunisia	262	-	33	-	6	2	213	7
Uganda	182	1	30	-	-	-	132	2
Zaire	145	-	19	-	1	1	51	14
Zambia	114	-	16	-	-	-	92	3
Zimbabwe	272	3	54	-	-	-	175	14
Other Africa	551	-	5	-	-	-	528	8
Oceania	13,403	390	3,157	111	376	46	5,094	3,517
Australia	9,810	183	2,528	23	242	37	3,532	2,771
Fiji	68	-	11	-	-	-	48	8
New Zealand	3,411	207	611	88	134	9	1,431	735
Tonga	30	-	-	-	-	-	19	1
Western Samoa	15	-	2	-	-	-	5	-
Other Oceania	69	-	5	-	-	-	59	2
North America	85,685	324	9,286	15,769	8,408	266	15,183	9,712
Canada	39,726	45	3,346	448	3,946	69	5,774	6,140
Mexico	23,169	33	3,271	7,159	3,108	113	4,187	2,161
Caribbean	16,702	238	1,830	8,151	1,208	50	1,757	580
Antigua	118	-	44	-	1	1	44	-
Aruba	21	1	10	-	-	-	2	8
Bahamas, The	345	44	133	1	2	6	101	37
Barbados	282	9	79	-	2	4	112	63
Bermuda	65	-	44	-	6	4	8	3
British Virgin Is.	17	-	1	-	-	-	6	-
Cayman Islands	14	-	3	-	-	-	8	1
Cuba	21	-	3	-	-	-	2	1
Dominica	2,208	1	293	22	358	18	259	131
Dominican Republic	1,073	-	232	8	149	10	114	81
Grenada	57	-	9	-	-	-	47	-
Haiti	348	2	51	-	3	-	154	24
Jamaica	10,974	117	477	8,119	660	4	547	102
Montserrat	17	-	6	-	-	-	5	-
Netherlands Antilles	51	-	25	-	9	1	11	3
St. Kitts & Nevis	44	-	15	-	1	-	21	-

[Continued]

★ 48 ★

Nonimmigrants Admitted as Temporary Workers, Exchange Visitors, and Intracompany Transferees, 1993 - I

[Continued]

Region and country of citizenship	Total	Registered nurses (H1A)	Workers with specialty occupations (H1B)	Other temporary workers (H2)		Industrial trainees (H3)	Exchange visitors (J1)	Intracompany transferees (L1)
				Agricultural (H2A)	Non-agricultural (H2B)			
St. Lucia	60	1	3	-	-	-	53	1
St. Vincent & Grenadines	66	2	5	-	-	-	49	4
Trinidad & Tobago	911	61	392	1	17	2	111	119
Other Caribbean	10	-	5	-	-	-	3	2
Central America	6,076	8	839	11	146	34	3,453	831
Belize	256	5	13	-	-	1	215	16
Costa Rica	1,371	-	158	3	11	13	843	283
El Salvador	931	-	129	-	6	3	448	104
Guatemala	995	1	90	1	29	-	565	136
Honduras	1,014	-	133	-	47	10	626	21
Nicaragua	400	-	22	-	5	5	314	25
Panama	1,109	2	294	7	48	2	442	246
Other North America	12	-	-	-	-	-	12	-
South America	30,185	39	7,971	293	504	112	12,509	6,642
Argentina	4,388	2	1,572	1	42	13	1,579	977
Bolivia	538	-	113	-	-	1	349	38
Brazil	10,302	4	1,955	-	18	38	5,030	2,706
Chile	1,892	2	516	44	33	7	817	428
Colombia	3,624	6	980	-	94	17	1,332	566
Ecuador	1,003	-	244	-	31	1	539	142
Guyana	240	16	90	-	12	-	61	36
Paraguay	181	-	26	-	2	-	137	13
Peru	2,283	7	802	246	86	11	532	492
Suriname	50	-	16	-	1	1	20	8
Uruguay	402	-	85	1	1	1	250	52
Venezuela	5,282	2	1,572	1	184	22	1,863	1,184
Stateless	74	1	20	-	-	-	27	11
Unknown	2,860	8	274	9	83	19	2,065	156

Source: U.S. Immigration and Naturalization Service, *Statistical Yearbook of the Immigration and Naturalization Service, 1993,* U.S. Government Printing Office, Washington, DC, 1994, pp. 110-115. *Notes:* A dash (-) represents zero. 1. Includes Mainland China and Taiwan. The number of nonimmigrant visas issued in fiscal year 1993 for Mainland China were: 6 H1As, 1,025 H1Bs, 9 H2As, 319 H2Bs, 44 H3s, 4,588 J1s, and 2,610 L1s, 15 O1s, 2 O2s, 214 P2s, 178 P3s, 27 Q1s, and 1 R1. The number of nonimmigrant visas issued to Taiwan were: 19 H1As, 592 H1Bs, no H2As, 2 H2Bs, 9 H3s, 1,058 J1s, 201 L1s, 10 O1s, no O2s, 22 P1s, 198 P3s, 1 Q1, and 29 R1s. (SOURCE: U.S. Department of State, Bureau of Consular Affairs, Visa Office) 2. Entries began in April, 1992.

★ 49 ★

Immigration

Nonimmigrants Admitted as Temporary Workers, Exchange Visitors, and Intracompany Transferees, 1993 - II

Numbers of immigrants are shown, by selected country of citizenship, for 1993. Letters and numbers in parentheses represent code designations for their respective classes of immigrant admission, as specified by the U.S. Department of State Visa Office.

Region and country of citizenship	Total	Workers with extraordinary ability or achievement	Workers accompanying and assisting in performance of O1 workers (O2)[2]	Internationally recognized athletes or entertainers (P1)[2]	Artists or entertainers in reciprocal exchange programs (P2)[2]	Artists or entertainers in culturally unique programs (P3)[2]	Workers in international cultural exchange programs (Q1)[2]	Workers in religious occupations (R1)[2]	U.S.-Canada Free-Trade Agreement workers (TC)
All countries	462,602	3,128	977	17,205	423	4,103	1,006	4,460	17,038
Europe	206,811	2,026	398	7,435	80	1,162	716	1,258	-
Albania	278	1	-	-	-	-	-	-	
Austria	2,865	46	3	171	1	6	-	7	-
Belgium	3,526	7	-	59	1	1	-	8	-
Bulgaria	1,088	7	-	98	-	1	-	3	-
Czechoslovakia	1,912	22	4	63	-	21	-	8	-
Denmark	4,954	25	5	113	-	2	1	15	-
Estonia	325	7	-	1	-	-	-	-	-
Finland	3,789	11	-	15	4	8	1	18	-
France	23,334	201	39	551	2	43	241	102	-
Germany	31,047	191	47	354	10	80	93	126	-
Greece	1,840	12	18	45	4	36	-	8	-
Hungary	2,247	21	-	33	-	19	-	7	-
Iceland	621	3	-	1	-	-	-	-	-
Ireland	8,781	27	6	233	4	56	2	110	-
Italy	9,102	147	32	297	2	23	96	139	-
Latvia	266	2	-	6	3	35	-	-	-
Liechtenstein	25	3	-	-	-	-	-	-	-
Lithuania	248	3	-	1	-	-	-	4	-
Luxembourg	142	-	-	1	-	-	-	-	-
Malta	62	-	-	-	-	-	-	4	-
Netherlands	8,978	66	3	152	1	16	-	49	-
Norway	3,902	24	-	15	1	11	173	9	-
Poland	3,979	29	2	332	8	35	-	64	-
Portugal	868	1	3	8	1	2	-	7	-
Romania	808	3	2	24	-	9	-	9	-
Soviet Union	12,223	165	18	1,397	7	467	5	59	-
Spain	9,380	89	30	427	5	129	-	112	-
Sweden	9,028	69	-	161	-	7	-	30	-
Switzerland	5,147	46	3	26	-	18	1	29	-
United Kingdom	54,994	782	179	2,839	26	113	101	304	-
Yugoslavia	1,039	15	4	12	-	24	2	27	-
Other Europe	13	1	-	-	-	-	-	-	-
Asia	112,220	249	264	978	52	1,651	81	1,319	-
Afghanistan	31	-	-	-	-	1	-	1	-
Bangladesh	543	1	10	1	-	11	-	11	-
Burma	27	-	-	-	-	-	-	4	-
Cambodia	18	-	-	-	-	-	-	8	-
China[1]	13,585	34	9	263	4	388	29	79	-
Cyprus	635	-	-	-	-	1	-	-	-
Hong Kong	1,462	21	65	61	1	31	10	12	-
India	17,191	13	46	93	4	597	3	392	-
Indonesia	1,358	1	1	1	-	-	1	18	-
Iran	403	1	-	-	1	9	-	6	-
Iraq	66	1	-	5	-	-	-	1	-
Israel	5,413	25	3	185	1	30	2	80	-
Japan	38,447	83	74	191	6	377	22	182	-
Jordan	729	1	-	-	1	-	-	2	-
Korea	6,999	22	40	80	2	102	-	126	-
Kuwait	139	-	-	-	-	-	1	1	-
Lebanon	1,132	14	4	8	10	4	-	8	-
Malaysia	1,815	1	-	2	-	4	-	8	-
Nepal	228	-	-	-	-	2	-	5	-
Oman	605	1	-	-	-	-	-	-	-
Pakistan	2,620	-	-	4	-	37	-	10	-

[Continued]

★ 49 ★

Nonimmigrants Admitted as Temporary Workers, Exchange Visitors, and Intracompany Transferees, 1993 - II

[Continued]

Region and country of citizenship	Total	Workers with extraordinary ability or achievement	Workers accompanying and assisting in performance of O1 workers (O2)[2]	Internationally recognized athletes or entertainers (P1)[2]	Artists or entertainers in reciprocal exchange programs (P2)[2]	Artists or entertainers in culturally unique programs (P3)[2]	Workers in international cultural exchange programs (Q1)[2]	Workers in religious occupations (R1)[2]	U.S.-Canada Free-Trade Agreement workers (TC)
Philippines	11,834	16	8	54	14	8	2	165	-
Qatar	116	-	-	-	-	-	-	-	-
Saudi Arabia	606	-	-	1	1	-	-	-	-
Singapore	1,040	-	-	3	3	30	1	12	-
Sri Lanka	512	-	-	-	2	6	10	20	-
Syria	475	5	4	3	1	-	-	2	-
Thailand	1,616	3	4	14	-	-	-	160	-
Turkey	2,145	6	-	7	-	11	-	3	-
United Arab Emirates	101	-	-	-	1	-	-	-	-
Vietnam	125	-	-	1	-	2	-	3	-
Yemen	95	-	-	1	-	-	-	-	-
Other Asia	109	-	-	-	-	-	-	-	-
Africa	11,364	49	3	262	21	275	74	162	-
Algeria	201	-	-	3	-	-	-	-	-
Angola	15	-	-	2	-	-	-	-	-
Burundi	73	1	-	17	-	-	-	-	-
Cameroon	158	1	-	14	-	2	-	1	-
Congo	55	-	-	3	-	10	-	-	-
Egypt	2,234	7	1	16	-	-	3	20	-
Ethiopia	228	-	-	-	1	4	-	10	-
Gambia, The	59	1	-	-	-	1	-	2	-
Ghana	501	2	-	3	-	97	2	14	-
Guinea	115	-	-	4	-	2	-	-	-
Ivory Coast	184	-	-	2	-	27	-	3	-
Kenya	447	1	-	2	-	-	-	8	-
Liberia	46	1	-	-	-	1	-	2	-
Malawi	70	-	-	-	-	-	-	1	-
Mali	89	-	-	-	-	9	-	-	-
Mauritania	16	-	-	-	-	4	-	-	-
Mauritius	53	-	-	4	-	-	-	-	-
Morocco	675	3	-	6	-	7	55	1	-
Namibia	69	2	-	-	-	-	-	1	-
Niger	26	-	-	-	-	4	-	-	-
Nigeria	1,084	1	-	38	1	49	-	45	-
Rwanda	56	-	-	1	-	-	-	1	-
Senegal	255	1	-	6	19	3	-	3	-
Sierra Leone	71	-	-	-	-	-	-	-	-
Somalia	18	2	-	-	-	-	-	1	-
South Africa	2,682	20	2	84	-	20	12	21	-
Sudan	96	-	-	1	-	-	-	1	-
Tanzania	262	-	-	6	-	-	-	4	-
Tunisia	262	-	-	1	-	-	-	-	-
Uganda	182	-	-	1	-	9	2	5	-
Zaire	145	-	-	30	-	20	-	9	-
Zambia	114	-	-	1	-	1	-	1	-
Zimbabwe	272	6	-	8	-	5	-	7	-
Other Africa	551	-	-	9	-	-	-	1	-
Oceania	13,403	144	43	317	4	32	11	161	-
Australia	9,810	123	28	228	4	8	10	93	-
Fiji	68	-	-	-	-	-	-	1	-
New Zealand	3,411	21	15	89	-	24	-	47	-
Tonga	30	-	-	-	-	-	-	10	-
Western Samoa	15	-	-	-	-	-	-	8	-
Other Oceania	69	-	-	-	-	-	1	2	-
North America	85,685	444	204	6,908	194	679	116	1,154	17,038
Canada	39,726	244	85	1,668	152	125	50	596	17,038
Mexico	23,169	121	77	2,512	32	77	65	253	-

[Continued]

★ 49 ★

Nonimmigrants Admitted as Temporary Workers, Exchange Visitors, and Intracompany Transferees, 1993 - II

[Continued]

Region and country of citizenship	Total	Workers with extraordinary ability or achievement	Workers accompanying and assisting in performance of O1 workers (O2)[2]	Internationally recognized athletes or entertainers (P1)[2]	Artists or entertainers in reciprocal exchange programs (P2)[2]	Artists or entertainers in culturally unique programs (P3)[2]	Workers in international cultural exchange programs (Q1)[2]	Workers in religious occupations (R1)[2]	U.S.-Canada Free-Trade Agreement workers (TC)
Caribbean	16,702	54	33	2,228	2	375	-	196	-
Antigua	118	-	-	18	-	5	-	5	-
Aruba	21	-	-	-	-	-	-	-	-
Bahamas, The	345	1	-	7	-	-	-	13	-
Barbados	282	-	-	2	-	4	-	7	-
Bermuda	65	-	-	-	-	-	-	-	-
British Virgin Islands	17	-	-	-	-	-	-	10	-
Cayman Islands	14	-	-	-	-	-	-	2	-
Cuba	21	6	5	1	-	2	-	1	-
Dominica	2,208	15	6	918	1	32	-	54	-
Dominican Republic	1,073	12	11	423	-	7	26	-	
Grenada	57	-	-	-	-	-	-	1	-
Haiti	348	1	-	67	-	34	-	12	-
Jamaica	10,974	18	11	649	-	250	-	20	-
Montserrat	17	-	-	4	-	1	-	1	-
Netherland Antilles	51	-	-	-	-	-	-	2	-
St. Kitts & Nevis	44	-	-	2	-	-	-	5	-
St. Lucia	60	-	-	-	1	-	-	1	-
St. Vincent & Grenadines	66	-	-	4	-	1	-	1	-
Trinidad & Tobago	911	1	-	133	-	39	-	35	-
Other Caribbean	10	-	-	-	-	-	-	-	-
Central America	6,076	25	9	500	8	102	1	109	-
Belize	256	1	-	2	-	-	-	3	-
Costa Rica	1,371	1	-	20	2	9	-	28	-
El Salvador	931	7	-	197	4	4	1	28	-
Guatemala	995	-	2	112	2	43	-	14	-
Honduras	1,014	1	-	142	-	23	-	11	-
Nicaragua	400	2	5	4	-	2	-	16	-
Panama	1,109	13	2	23	-	21	-	9	-
Other North America	12	-	-	-	-	-	-	-	-
South America	30,185	192	58	1,187	44	265	2	367	-
Argentina	4,388	59	9	59	12	15	-	48	-
Bolivia	538	4	-	5	-	9	-	19	-
Brazil	10,302	34	11	290	3	129	-	84	-
Chile	1,892	7	3	17	1	-	-	17	-
Colombia	3,624	11	13	509	4	17	2	73	-
Ecuador	1,003	-	-	2	2	15	-	27	-
Guyana	240	-	1	-	-	18	-	6	-
Paraguay	181	-	-	-	-	1	-	2	-
Peru	2,283	1	1	18	-	39	-	48	-
Suriname	50	-	-	-	-	-	-	4	-
Uruguay	402	4	-	2	1	-	-	5	-
Venezuela	5,282	72	20	285	21	22	-	34	-
Stateless	74	3	-	7	-	2	-	2	-
Unknown	2,860	21	17	111	28	36	6	37	-

Source: U.S. Immigration and Naturalization Service, *Statistical Yearbook of the Immigration and Naturalization Service, 1993,* U.S. Government Printing Office, Washington, DC, 1994, pp. 110-115. *Notes:* A dash (-) represents zero. 1. Includes Mainland China and Taiwan. The number of nonimmigrant visas issued in fiscal year 1993 for Mainland China were: 6 H1As, 1,025 H1Bs, 9 H2As, 319 H2Bs, 44 H3s, 4,588 J1s, and 2,610 L1s, 15 O1s, 2 O2s, 214 P2s, 178 P3s, 27 Q1s, and 1 R1. The number of nonimmigrant visas issued to Taiwan were: 19 H1As, 592 H1Bs, no H2As, 2 H2Bs, 9 H3s, 1,058 J1s, 201 L1s, 10 O1s, no O2s, 22 P1s, 198 P3s, 1 Q1, and 29 R1s. (SOURCE: U.S. Department of State, Bureau of Consular Affairs, Visa Office) 2. Entries began in April, 1992.

★ 50 ★

Immigration

Nonimmigrants Admitted, by Age, 1993

Data show number of nonimmigrants admitted in fiscal year 1993, by selected country of citizenship.

Region and country of citizenship	All ages	Under 15 years	15-19 years	20-24 years	25-34 years	35-44 years	45-64 years	65 years and over	Unknown
All countries	21,446,993	1,807,569	1,067,730	2,068,236	5,438,509	4,249,534	5,602,645	1,183,458	29,312
North America	3,255,057	361,204	176,326	274,598	817,877	720,782	720,893	168,845	7,532
Canada	98,439	8,459	5,968	12,913	31,760	22,037	15,996	1,122	184
Mexico	1,567,937	182,691	89,950	140,025	390,627	329,004	350,727	80,926	3,987
Caribbean	1,033,727	108,445	49,619	79,533	266,238	244,330	230,183	53,333	2,046
Antigua	23,550	2,650	1,257	2,666	6,505	5,423	4,283	729	37
Aruba	9,073	955	353	567	2,090	2,339	2,498	254	17
Bahamas, The	282,996	34,549	15,561	29,324	82,086	57,725	54,835	8,144	772
Barbados	52,753	6,281	2,720	3,876	13,649	12,784	11,353	2,007	83
Cayman Islands	21,637	2,967	1,405	2,497	5,383	4,538	4,126	703	18
Cuba	23,543	178	165	365	1,057	1,921	10,479	9,346	32
Dominica	111,656	12,449	6,123	8,180	25,799	27,227	26,072	5,580	226
Dominican Republic	95,867	9,406	4,691	7,471	24,571	22,879	21,753	4,939	157
Grenada	9,436	914	399	984	2,860	2,115	1,708	436	20
Haiti	49,510	3,277	1,337	1,956	10,157	15,429	13,443	3,796	115
Jamaica	190,916	17,288	8,150	10,410	53,803	53,409	38,941	8,581	334
Netherlands Antilles	19,844	2,414	998	1,334	4,302	5,136	5,045	599	16
St. Kitts and Nevis	11,760	1,286	596	980	3,404	3,239	1,855	370	30
St. Lucia	13,955	1,143	571	1,437	4,456	3,440	2,465	423	20
St. Vincent and Grenadines	7,202	556	277	732	2,310	1,909	1,189	216	13
Trinidad & Tobago	90,167	9,744	3,743	4,438	18,569	20,517	26,597	6,442	117
Turks & Caicos Islands	6,875	956	432	881	1,809	1,501	1,065	221	10
Other Caribbean	12,987	1,432	841	1,435	3,428	2,799	2,476	547	29
Central America	554,879	61,605	30,770	42,119	129,239	125,398	130,972	33,461	1,315
Belize	18,485	2,232	925	1,939	4,991	4,095	3,456	818	29
Costa Rica	114,362	13,451	6,898	8,175	27,602	26,381	25,863	5,752	240
El Salvador	96,049	10,083	5,193	7,395	22,575	21,725	22,844	5,984	250
Guatemala	137,649	17,751	8,113	11,038	30,773	29,507	31,326	8,785	356
Honduras	73,932	6,707	3,222	6,008	18,931	19,258	16,692	2,944	170
Nicaragua	47,175	4,526	2,271	2,559	10,144	10,993	12,549	3,970	163
Panama	67,227	6,855	4,148	5,005	14,223	13,439	18,242	5,208	107
Other North America	75	4	19	8	13	13	15	3	-
South America	2,027,114	240,544	136,887	132,677	424,334	453,706	522,536	112,608	3,822
Argentina	372,366	42,868	27,569	24,295	68,405	77,080	107,613	23,842	694
Bolivia	28,536	2,986	2,095	2,130	6,216	6,460	7,179	1,410	60
Brazil	548,978	64,974	47,115	31,199	111,836	129,980	137,881	25,217	776
Chile	125,869	12,770	5,831	7,550	26,632	31,280	34,896	6,624	196
Colombia	222,769	28,091	12,532	12,674	50,480	50,786	54,394	12,945	867
Ecuador	89,102	11,378	6,044	6,833	18,470	19,451	21,345	5,368	213
Guyana	14,288	1,229	488	779	3,496	4,455	3,233	592	16
Paraguay	13,310	1,507	849	985	3,287	2,951	3,135	565	31
Peru	163,724	14,125	7,959	14,090	38,197	35,044	42,580	11,431	298
Uruguay	37,917	2,731	1,796	2,156	7,767	8,160	11,915	3,320	72
Venezuela	404,346	57,411	24,429	29,559	88,219	86,660	96,462	21,012	594
Other South America	5,909	474	180	427	1,329	1,399	1,813	282	5
Europe	9,263,004	721,620	473,264	767,527	2,281,918	1,780,672	2,664,229	565,244	8,530
Austria	178,603	9,841	8,396	21,285	48,308	33,280	48,853	8,526	114

[Continued]

★ 50 ★

Nonimmigrants Admitted, by Age, 1993

[Continued]

Region and country of citizenship	All ages	Under 15 years	15-19 years	20-24 years	25-34 years	35-44 years	45-64 years	65 years and over	Unknown
Belgium	180,318	10,968	9,381	14,435	45,309	38,819	51,071	10,180	155
Bulgaria	10,280	661	782	1,014	2,315	2,713	2,338	449	8
Czechoslovakia	28,377	1,508	2,293	3,315	6,100	5,849	7,455	1,816	41
Denmark	118,576	6,678	8,958	12,621	26,454	21,299	35,801	6,646	119
Finland	83,460	5,894	5,478	5,631	18,607	18,517	25,091	4,171	71
France	896,433	66,093	77,668	78,958	209,091	178,883	233,427	51,624	689
Germany	1,887,420	111,548	89,796	158,472	519,775	337,901	563,737	104,866	1,325
Greece	66,660	3,571	2,437	4,758	14,767	12,760	21,495	6,710	162
Hungary	35,061	2,266	2,620	3,430	6,493	7,905	9,807	2,483	57
Iceland	20,047	2,075	1,095	1,986	4,325	4,083	5,368	1,092	23
Ireland	167,494	14,034	6,928	18,065	43,740	29,963	43,992	10,352	420
Italy	630,286	25,464	28,480	64,003	207,915	114,571	160,049	29,193	611
Luxembourg	11,994	868	603	934	3,150	2,417	3,357	652	13
Netherlands	436,631	23,075	16,008	37,073	118,488	87,486	128,515	25,604	382
Norway	117,311	7,388	6,714	10,989	25,473	23,630	35,996	6,990	131
Poland	55,429	3,896	3,469	4,518	10,966	12,538	15,232	4,739	71
Portugal	66,984	4,298	3,374	5,183	15,591	14,706	18,689	4,984	159
Romania	14,152	890	606	835	2,680	3,368	4,194	1,521	58
Soviet Union	127,546	7,950	8,923	8,500	28,705	33,464	36,151	3,724	129
Spain	349,127	20,443	27,504	31,654	98,147	70,088	85,940	14,836	515
Sweden	250,446	16,871	15,284	23,773	51,852	46,231	82,010	14,063	362
Switzerland	315,566	18,535	12,401	33,054	86,115	56,469	90,060	18,688	244
United Kingdom	3,173,079	354,063	131,103	218,722	677,766	614,875	945,019	228,929	2,602
Yugoslavia	23,726	1,526	1,950	2,403	5,220	5,107	6,140	1,340	40
Other Europe	17,998	1,216	1,013	1,916	4,566	3,750	4,442	1,066	29
Asia	5,864,415	397,558	234,104	791,665	1,669,735	1,081,011	1,408,736	274,250	7,356
Bangladesh	13,454	1,813	854	1,387	3,171	3,160	2,729	303	37
China[1]	558,648	35,926	11,740	29,417	145,197	133,248	165,100	37,073	947
Hong Kong	128,226	8,561	6,277	14,005	37,069	28,517	26,473	7,143	181
India	162,113	11,502	3,968	14,136	46,334	29,697	44,988	11,189	299
Indonesia	60,671	4,619	4,779	7,443	13,652	12,456	15,705	1,904	113
Iran	27,767	2,815	890	1,281	5,611	5,071	8,399	3,527	173
Israel	199,434	17,436	9,761	17,527	33,695	43,153	60,585	16,944	333
Japan	3,610,305	214,555	156,033	612,134	1,091,771	577,583	813,859	141,585	2,785
Jordan	19,235	2,070	997	1,884	4,658	3,468	5,235	849	74
Korea	447,346	33,483	10,909	31,349	111,096	101,658	132,197	25,992	662
Kuwait	16,160	3,505	1,069	1,920	4,382	3,103	1,911	216	54
Lebanon	22,913	1,779	803	2,095	6,457	3,922	6,252	1,520	85
Malaysia	60,036	5,013	2,529	8,319	16,444	14,321	11,749	1,573	88
Pakistan	41,507	5,606	2,406	4,092	9,367	8,012	10,450	1,484	90
Philippines	205,311	17,020	6,587	13,272	58,269	52,358	44,754	12,576	475
Saudi Arabia	52,536	12,604	2,618	5,245	16,077	9,137	5,909	704	242
Singapore	59,696	5,123	,065	5,413	19,777	15,062	10,718	1,451	87
Sri Lanka	9,900	907	283	882	2,581	2,226	2,484	522	15
Syria	10,712	964	470	894	2,539	1,829	3,079	875	62
Thailand	70,058	4,891	3,630	6,867	17,938	16,692	17,523	2,273	244
Turkey	47,639	2,325	2,677	5,675	12,903	9,197	11,975	2,774	113
United Arab Emirates	7,958	1,275	772	1,828	2,424	947	559	82	71
Other Asia	32,790	3,766	1,987	4,600	8,323	6,194	6,103	1,691	126

[Continued]

★ 50 ★

Nonimmigrants Admitted, by Age, 1993

[Continued]

Region and country of citizenship	All ages	Under 15 years	15-19 years	20-24 years	25-34 years	35-44 years	45-64 years	65 years and over	Unknown
Africa	222,945	19,604	9,209	16,807	56,938	56,479	54,141	9,205	562
Egypt	32,911	3,047	1,198	1,893	7,039	7,536	10,143	1,978	77
Ethiopia	6,783	508	387	549	1,338	1,441	2,123	382	55
Ghana	7,483	428	233	427	2,076	2,270	1,845	186	18
Kenya	7,423	683	425	948	1,852	1,670	1,659	169	17
Morocco	12,964	970	672	1,310	3,842	2,947	2,807	365	51
Nigeria	23,890	2,299	711	1,003	6,497	7,022	5,796	525	37
South Africa	66,295	6,845	2,960	5,105	15,795	14,745	16,539	4,229	77
Other Africa	65,196	4,824	2,623	5,572	18,499	18,848	13,229	1,371	230
Oceania	632,080	54,199	28,779	67,617	143,742	123,726	174,402	38,933	682
Australia	450,490	38,933	20,830	49,391	101,268	87,899	124,350	27,319	500
New Zealand	145,356	10,980	5,562	14,445	33,992	28,053	41,997	10,216	111
Pacific Island Trust Territory	21,035	2,781	1,836	2,398	4,834	4,318	4,157	671	40
Other Oceania	15,199	1,505	551	1,383	3,648	3,456	3,898	727	31
Stateless	20,053	693	398	1,131	2,554	3,377	8,191	3,674	35
Unknown	162,325	12,147	8,763	16,214	41,411	29,781	42,517	10,699	793

Source: U.S. Immigration and Naturalization Service, *Statistical Yearbook of the Immigration and Naturalization Service, 1993*, U.S. Government Printing Office, Washington, DC, 1994, pp. 120-121. *Notes:* A dash (-) represents zero. Includes arrivals under the Visa Waiver Pilot program. Excludes the following cases of admission processed in the Nonimmigrant Information System: for all countries—123,628 parolees, 26,435 withdrawals and stowaways, and 113,152 refugees. 1. Includes Mainland China and Taiwan. A total of 446,204 nonimmigrant visas were issued to these two countries in fiscal year 1993: 269,345 to Taiwan and 176,859 to Mainland China. (SOURCE: U.S. Department of State, Bureau of Consular Affairs, Visa Office.).

★ 51 ★

Immigration

Nonimmigrants Admitted, by Port of Entry, 1993 - I

Data show number of nonimmigrants admitted at each port in fiscal year 1993, by selected country of citizenship.

Region and country of citizenship	All ports	Agana	Atlanta	Boston	Chicago	Dallas	Honolulu	Houston
All countries	21,446,993	688,782	488,796	495,420	907,451	401,966	2,041,052	451,092
North America	3,255,057	327	31,148	4,227	80,557	166,974	2,694	240,161
Canada	98,439	78	663	2,085	4,125	2,2344	730	744
Mexico	1,567,937	126	19,882	785	69,664	149,372	1,281	178,679
Caribbean	1,033,727	65	9,906	1,032	1,101	1,083	261	1,194
Antigua	23,550	3	3	14	12	12	3	4
Aruba	9,073	4	172	12	7	6	2	217
Bahamas, The	282,996	-	4,403	66	142	262	22	334
Barbados	52,753	-	23	86	77	44	14	6
Cayman Islands	21,637	-	288	10	6	4	7	217
Cuba	23,543	-	13	5	30	44	2	140
Dominica	111,656	1	27	23	49	115	10	30
Dominican Republic	95,867	2	32	41	172	132	45	27
Grenada	9,436	4	2	13	16	9	8	4

[Continued]

★51★

Nonimmigrants Admitted, by Port of Entry, 1993 - I

[Continued]

Region and country of citizenship	All ports	Agana	Atlanta	Boston	Chicago	Dallas	Honolulu	Houston
Haiti	49,510	2	36	134	126	136	2	14
Jamaica	190,916	21	2,875	167	238	141	46	70
Netherlands Antilles	19,844	17	1,612	24	17	16	4	17
St. Kitts & Nevis	11,760	-	5	8	9	3	2	-
St. Lucia	13,955	-	2	19	12	15	1	5
St. Vincent & Grenadines	7,202	-	7	12	11	5	3	1
Trinidad & Tobago	90,167	6	101	122	124	102	52	90
Turks & Caicos Islands	6,875	4	12	5	3	5	2	2
Other Caribbean	12,987	1	293	271	50	32	36	16
Central America	554,879	58	694	325	5,664	14,172	422	59,544
Belize	18,485	5	11	10	47	27	18	4,826
Costa Rica	114,362	5	180	53	673	5,877	131	6,222
El Salvador	96,049	11	95	75	631	363	97	12,374
Guatemala	137,649	3	123	65	3,669	7,240	65	14,448
Honduras	73,932	10	138	38	162	211	20	12,538
Nicaragua	47,175	5	31	23	121	190	16	3,622
Panama	67,227	19	116	61	361	264	75	5,514
Other North America	75	-	3	-	3	3	-	-
South America	2,027,114	284	6,598	2,389	12,458	8,661	3,199	12,095
Argentina	372,366	25	643	341	2,191	1,477	713	950
Bolivia	28,536	4	46	32	215	297	32	165
Brazil	548,978	77	627	679	5,851	1,879	1,044	780
Chile	125,869	17	431	295	925	774	256	491
Colombia	222,769	21	309	294	759	849	369	1,228
Ecuador	89,102	20	120	90	335	311	126	3,046
Guyana	14,288	7	42	32	34	15	6	23
Paraguay	13,310	3	12	8	77	92	74	14
Peru	163,724	73	244	161	867	1,959	247	508
Uruguay	37,917	5	177	43	461	164	83	110
Venezuela	404,346	32	3,908	397	736	830	247	4,777
Other South America	5,909	-	39	17	7	14	2	3
Europe	9,263,004	7,317	398,621	437,709	570,038	164,729	98,433	162,963
Austria	178,603	162	7,757	5,084	10,671	2,606	1,709	1,559
Belgium	180,318	72	7,570	9,339	21,016	9,248	458	3,960
Bulgaria	10,280	3	244	114	649	53	15	63
Czechoslovakia	28,377	5	1,246	734	2,514	568	76	231
Denmark	118,576	133	2,486	3,208	7,689	1,278	1,101	1,847
Finland	83,460	77	1,297	1,051	3,435	442	354	1,007
France	896,433	580	24,050	40,536	47,194	25,008	9,732	37,493
Germany	1,887,420	730	138,072	72,134	138,213	42,112	25,241	16,547
Greece	66,660	40	1,500	4,732	5,264	722	87	1,455
Hungary	35,061	17	1,489	850	1,5632	700	116	329
Iceland	20,047	-	53	115	69	43	43	38
Ireland	167,494	62	11,362	20,458	5,801	1,012	1,514	1,443

[Continued]

★ 51 ★

Nonimmigrants Admitted, by Port of Entry, 1993 - I

[Continued]

Region and country of citizenship	All ports	Agana	Atlanta	Boston	Chicago	Dallas	Honolulu	Houston
Italy	630,286	269	6,112	21,057	41,397	4,467	1,670	6,596
Luxembourg	11,994	1	318	349	592	342	36	77
Netherlands	436,631	205	25,787	19,454	17,268	2,790	2,595	11,292
Norway	117,311	59	1,315	1,906	4,367	454	666	2,949
Poland	55,429	4	1,656	752	12,147	802	97	458
Portugal	66,984	126	431	8,223	823	392	1,304	359
Romania	14,152	3	350	194	2,217	208	20	68
Soviet Union	127,546	57	1,613	1,005	8,178	1,027	170	1,779
Spain	349,127	82	14,134	3,734	5,301	17,760	405	3,945
Sweden	250,446	230	3,540	4,079	32,144	1,365	2,043	2,524
Switzerland	315,566	375	26,865	14,638	31,948	1,989	2,951	2,625
United Kingdom	3,173,079	3,922	117,690	202,780	164,973	48,905	45,789	63,636
Yugoslavia	23,726	97	1,239	712	2,799	256	96	450
Other Europe	17,998	6	445	471	1,837	180	145	233
Asia	5,864,415	656,273	41,706	29,910	213,380	54,559	1,746,781	20,276
Bangladesh	13,454	9	177	308	529	137	94	186
China[1]	558,648	20,603	777	1,234	17,014	2,782	87,085	1,063
Hong Kong	128,226	3,690	235	394	4,070	1,464	17,103	160
India	162,113	306	5,370	5,119	10,245	2,695	1,136	3,781
Indonesia	60,671	753	826	514	1,739	293	7,319	211
Iran	27,767	8	810	885	1,832	619	93	663
Israel	199,434	33	4,240	4,917	5,237	872	475	1,022
Japan	3,610,305	550,100	21,398	3,941	119,610	39,769	1,531,994	2,762
Jordan	19,235	2	502	516	2,509	196	24	591
Korea	447,346	62,614	412	727	22,599	667	72,571	633
Kuwait	16,160	-	286	731	1,084	318	41	238
Lebanon	22,913	-	443	1,326	1,482	186	35	743
Malaysia	60,036	301	269	607	1,588	261	5,618	273
Pakistan	41,507	18	663	945	2,339	481	163	1,625
Philippines	205,311	16,690	418	863	7,881	587	8,228	708
Saudi Arabia	52,536	5	807	1,560	1,462	416	139	2,117
Singapore	59,696	416	162	450	2,257	177	8,647	191
Sri Lanka	9,900	57	125	275	353	49	330	225
Syria	10,712	2	152	334	917	144	7	262
Thailand	70,058	536	236	576	2,586	159	4,839	141
Turkey	47,639	10	2,431	2,018	2,695	1,275	134	1,211
United Arab Emirates	7,958	-	296	431	1,067	271	33	617
Other Asia	32,790	120	671	1,239	2,285	741	673	853
Africa	222,945	125	5,221	8,369	8,731	2,769	669	4,518
Egypt	32,911	5	758	1,052	1,318	254	42	724
Ethiopia	6,783	2	313	248	406	265	10	126
Ghana	7,483	14	249	357	404	112	19	162
Kenya	7,423	-	318	571	671	169	15	156
Morocco	12,964	2	219	331	224	105	16	131

[Continued]

★51★

Nonimmigrants Admitted, by Port of Entry, 1993 - I

[Continued]

Region and country of citizenship	All ports	Agana	Atlanta	Boston	Chicago	Dallas	Honolulu	Houston
Nigeria	23,890	11	913	782	916	497	18	1,285
South Africa	66,295	35	1,091	2,096	2,124	649	405	759
Other Africa	65,196	56	1,360	2,932	2,668	718	144	1,175
Oceania	632,080	21,526	1,475	8,023	5,967	1,734	186,102	7,606
Australia	450,490	6,775	1,150	7,167	4,453	1,428	122,956	5,027
New Zealand	145,356	1,201	314	839	1,482	290	48,532	2,549
Pacific Island Trust Territories	21,035	12,543	1	1	4	3	8,282	8
Other Oceania	15,199	1,007	10	16	28	13	6,332	22
Stateless	20,053	10	102	109	730	155	188	26
Unknown	162,325	2,920	3,925	4,684	15,590	2,385	2,986	3,447

Source: U.S. Immigration and Naturalization Service, *Statistical Yearbook of the Immigration and Naturalization Service, 1993*, U.S. Government Printing Office, Washington, DC, 1994, pp. 116-117. *Notes:* A dash (-) represents zero. Includes arrivals under the Visa Waiver Pilot program. Excludes the following classes of admission processed in the Nonimmigrant Information System: for all countries—123,628 parolees, 26,435 withdrawals and stowaways, and 113,152 refugees. 1. Includes Mainland China and Taiwan. A total of 446,204 nonimmigrant visas were issued to these two countries in fiscal year 1993: 269,345 to Taiwan and 176,859 to Mainland China.

★52★

Immigration

Nonimmigrants Admitted, by Port of Entry, 1993 - II

Data show number of nonimmigrants admitted at each port in fiscal year 1993, by selected country of citizenship.

Region and country of citizenship	All ports	Los Angeles	Miami	Newark	New York	Orlando	San Francisco	Washington DC	Other[2]
All countries	21,446,993	2,591,295	3,726,158	635,949	3,279,858	882,155	1,016,898	527,039	3,313,082
North America	3,255,057	370,695	1,011,251	29,493	272,837	93,267	54,568	19,064	877,794
Canada	98,439	2,544	3,141	814	4,483	478	1,841	985	73,384
Mexico	1,567,937	305,428	163,444	14,369	83,459	76,301	45,089	10,967	449,091
Caribbean	1,033,727	1,484	508,392	13,683	167,162	12,515	447	674	314,728
Antigua	23,550	20	3,042	36	3,529	4	3	3	16,862
Aruba	9,073	18	2,889	117	165	613	4	-	2,847
Bahamas, The	282,996	111	161,260	1,362	905	9,491	44	89	104,505
Barbados	52,753	103	13,955	65	13,677	30	14	56	24,603
Cayman Islands	21,637	24	18,544	9	182	13	4	5	2,324
Cuba	23,543	41	22,433	34	413	22	19	22	325
Dominica	111,656	52	44,297	4,741	20,961	44	29	25	41,252
Dominican Republic	95,867	132	29,111	5,008	24,838	21	63	39	36,204
Grenada	9,436	40	2,089	28	2,582	16	1	17	4,607
Haiti	49,510	38	29,866	199	10,539	86	6	92	8,234
Jamaica	190,916	457	124,388	1,483	45,782	1,910	98	160	13,080
Netherlands Antilles	19,844	17	8,723	221	515	84	18	9	8,550
St. Kitts & Nevis	11,760	23	683	28	498	3	-	3	10,495
St. Lucia	13,955	14	2,579	24	3,060	5	7	10	8,202
St. Vincent & Grenadines	7,202	34	1,627	20	2,031	1	12	7	3,431

[Continued]

★ 52 ★

Nonimmigrants Admitted, by Port of Entry, 1993 - II

[Continued]

Region and country of citizenship	All ports	Los Angeles	Miami	Newark	New York	Orlando	San Francisco	Washington DC	Other[2]
Trinidad & Tobago	90,167	253	35,605	172	36,696	140	95	123	16,486
Turks & Caicos Islands	6,875	5	6,245	9	36	16	1	2	528
Other Caribbean	12,987	102	1,056	127	753	16	29	12	10,193
Central America	554,879	61,238	336,265	612	17,720	3,969	7,190	6,438	40,568
Belize	18,485	1,256	9,405	44	190	7	271	89	2,279
Costa Rica	114,362	9,635	75,771	103	4,191	3,426	929	990	6,176
El Salvador	96,049	20,632	43,265	90	4,833	71	3,305	3,062	7,145
Guatemala	137,649	23,897	70,086	130	4,088	151	747	1,874	11,063
Honduras	73,932	2,537	47,671	67	2,217	138	915	164	7,106
Nicaragua	47,175	2,324	37,845	57	308	98	409	82	2,044
Panama	67,227	957	52,222	121	1,893	78	614	177	4,755
Other North America	75	1	9	15	13	4	1	-	23
South America	2,027,114	98,240	1,385,406	5,409	267,264	70,293	6,788	20,660	127,370
Argentina	372,366	15,597	276,440	914	48,687	846	1,108	4,260	18,174
Bolivia	28,536	700	23,981	67	876	37	103	197	1,784
Brazil	548,978	47,687	313,201	1,718	91,913	45,212	2,757	12,283	23,270
Chile	125,869	5,745	97,606	380	8,583	637	797	814	8,118
Colombia	222,769	7,353	172,283	572	25,640	321	504	461	11,806
Ecuador	89,102	2,368	65,812	274	13,646	103	170	191	2,490
Guyana	14,288	37	4,403	159	5,896	79	11	61	3,483
Paraguay	13,310	622	10,237	15	1,556	16	49	32	503
Peru	163,724	14,881	129,622	396	4,005	442	459	511	9,349
Uruguay	37,917	1,894	24,157	207	7,132	110	207	1,165	2,002
Venezuela	404,346	1,298	262,491	683	59,128	22,483	593	671	46,072
Other South America	5,909	58	5,173	24	202	7	30	14	319
Europe	9,263,004	817,823	1,170,631	502,027	1,893,235	696,055	348,270	358,795	1,636,358
Austria	178,603	19,997	33,146	3,442	53,353	4,257	9,203	4,487	21,170
Belgium	180,318	8,608	13,820	4,306	54,343	2,524	6,301	21,437	17,316
Bulgaria	10,280	386	253	960	5,980	31	143	473	913
Czechoslovakia	28,377	2,000	1,647	1,272	10,223	399	699	973	5,790
Denmark	118,576	15,355	12,306	21,771	20,203	2,459	4,571	3,036	21,133
Finland	83,460	3,968	21,121	3,286	33,238	424	3,943	1,281	8,536
France	896,433	74,513	95,966	72,012	192,326	9,433	35,524	43,448	188,618
Germany	1,887,420	192,925	274,996	100,445	307,078	52,911	118,501	86,504	321,011
Greece	66,660	2,940	5,192	787	31,319	1,035	1,289	2,567	7,731
Hungary	35,061	3,289	2,510	5,089	10,493	1,028	879	1,985	4,755
Iceland	20,047	191	783	156	6,914	4,671	102	42	6,827
Ireland	167,494	9,177	17,987	3,329	54,849	10,012	4,544	2,836	23,108
Italy	630,286	54,887	134,557	8,800	249,238	4,718	11,382	25,999	59,137
Luxembourg	11,994	1,189	1,411	170	2,607	1,257	984	603	2,058
Netherlands	436,631	43,847	74,494	9,261	77,734	12,334	16,336	13,792	109,442
Norway	117,311	9,805	10,762	40,195	19,831	2,599	2,627	1,298	18,478
Poland	55,429	1,915	1,940	4,687	19,865	533	737	1,698	8,138
Portugal	66,984	2,663	9,341	9,822	23,680	684	1,510	675	6,951
Romania	14,152	819	518	244	7,505	77	208	473	1,248
Soviet Union	127,546	4,286	7,166	1,416	66,828	226	10,852	12,863	10,080
Spain	349,127	17,386	85,395	26,572	117,840	4,743	4,178	16,928	30,724
Sweden	250,446	21,862	26,422	57,418	43,220	4,316	5,881	3,466	41,936
Switzerland	315,566	38,577	38,719	3,995	82,786	8,342	10,951	12,747	38,058
United Kingdom	3,173,079	284,591	296,722	120,177	386,824	565,975	96,024	97,734	677,337

[Continued]

★ 52 ★

Nonimmigrants Admitted, by Port of Entry, 1993 - II

[Continued]

Region and country of citizenship	All ports	Los Angeles	Miami	Newark	New York	Orlando	San Francisco	Washington DC	Other[2]
Yugoslavia	23,726	1,744	1,957	975	8,135	277	502	827	3,660
Other Europe	17,998	903	1,500	1,440	6,823	790	399	623	2,203
Asia	5,864,415	1,005,536	99,915	70,801	680,453	14,801	578,204	93,871	557,949
Bangladesh	13,454	2,400	321	473	6,901	55	260	794	810
China[1]	558,648	186,179	7,652	9,743	42,208	371	105,166	2,577	74,194
Hong Kong	128,226	27,973	1,958	726	8,428	528	32,983	278	28,236
India	162,113	15,912	8,834	5,579	61,361	1,869	10,166	8,289	21,451
Indonesia	60,671	26,912	966	318	5,636	226	8,085	838	6,035
Iran	27,767	6,347	751	1,029	4,412	179	1,787	2,072	6,280
Israel	199,434	12,759	16,430	1,844	128,910	1,296	1,852	2,800	16,747
Japan	3,610,305	445,400	37,446	29,684	216,342	3,636	299,830	50,100	258,293
Jordan	19,235	1,222	603	274	9,139	143	443	1,105	1,966
Korea	447,346	124,944	6,526	1,401	68,820	215	25,927	1,182	58,108
Kuwait	16,160	822	929	217	8,255	436	452	1,076	1,275
Lebanon	22,913	2,326	1,388	1,051	6,287	214	416	1,568	5,448
Malaysia	60,036	31,105	869	529	5,113	403	6,497	541	6,062
Pakistan	41,507	2,496	984	2,532	23,242	289	844	1,533	3,353
Philippines	205,311	53,366	5,488	1,338	18,665	589	53,624	1,342	35,524
Saudi Arabia	52,536	3,100	1,352	410	28,058	1,657	539	8,127	2,787
Singapore	59,696	19,761	653	644	7,012	242	12,945	293	5,846
Sri Lanka	9,900	1,732	511	878	2,641	87	492	555	1,590
Syria	10,712	1,004	290	386	5,074	74	163	546	1,357
Thailand	70,058	30,594	647	447	4,062	134	12,240	1,083	11,778
Turkey	47,639	3,653	3,750	9,877	11,074	964	1,127	3,009	4,411
United Arab Emirates	7,958	704	271	544	829	204	146	1,057	1,488
Other Asia	32,790	4,825	1,296	877	7,984	990	2,220	3,106	4,910
Africa	222,945	11,344	18,081	7,572	106,947	2,565	3,308	17,488	25,238
Egypt	32,911	2,178	980	817	18,565	366	334	2,137	3,381
Ethiopia	6,783	602	88	169	1,548	18	294	1,943	751
Ghana	7,483	305	278	378	3,150	50	76	913	1,016
Kenya	7,423	482	327	246	2,108	126	171	860	1,203
Morocco	12,964	437	563	441	7,834	120	109	454	1,978
Nigeria	23,890	906	1,037	742	12,550	220	312	1,834	1,867
South Africa	66,295	4,248	11,924	1,672	30,499	1,104	1,168	1,327	7,194
Other Africa	65,196	2,186	2,884	3,107	30,693	561	844	8,020	7,848
Oceania	632,080	267,856	12,288	13,481	31,746	1,621	17,312	9,255	46,088
Australia	450,490	200,255	9,753	10,329	26,995	1,272	12,167	6,080	34,683
New Zealand	145,356	62,564	2,405	3,123	4,590	312	3,749	3,127	10,279
Pacific Island Trust Territories	21,035	7	11	11	10	1	17	5	131
Other Oceania	15,199	5,030	119	18	151	36	1,379	43	995
Stateless	20,053	1,943	177	137	919	110	1,577	97	13,773
Unknown	162,325	17,858	28,409	7,029	26,457	3,443	6,871	7,809	28,512

Source: U.S. Immigration and Naturalization Service, *Statistical Yearbook of the Immigration and Naturalization Service, 1993*, U.S. Government Printing Office, Washington, DC, 1994, pp. 118-119. *Notes:* A dash (-) represents zero. Includes arrivals under the Visa Waiver Pilot program. Excludes the following classes of admission processed in the Nonimmigrant Information System: for all countries—123,628 parolees, 26,435 withdrawals and stowaways, and 113,152 refugees. 1. Includes Mainland China and Taiwan. A total of 446,204 nonimmigrant visas were issued to these two countries in fiscal year 1993: 269,345 to Taiwan and 176,859 to Mainland China. 2. Includes unknown port of entry.

★ 53 ★

Immigration

Nonimmigrants Admitted, by Selected Class of Admission, 1981-93

Data show number of nonimmigrants admitted each year, in thousands, by selected country of last residence, for selected years from 1981 to 1993.

Region and country of last residence	All classes[1] (in thousands)					Visitors for pleasure (in thousands)				
	1981	1985	1990[2]	1992[2]	1993[2]	1981	1985	1990[2]	1992[2]	1993[2]
All countries	11,757	9,540	17,574	20,794	21,447	9,515	6,609	13,418	16,450	16,900
North America	2,817	2,189	3,245	3,442	3,605	2,480	1,664	2,463	2,605	2,701
Canada	135	154	216	275	276	75	79	119	166	160
Mexico	1,768	945	1,348	1,585	1,621	1,634	773	1,061	1,238	1,256
Caribbean	614	774	1,231	1,077	1,144	526	584	963	844	881
Antigua-Barbuda	9	12	25	26	26	7	9	16	18	17
Aruba	Z	Z	14	16	20	Z	Z	10	13	17
Bahamas, The	172	231	345	303	309	163	211	332	286	282
Barbados	19	24	47	44	56	15	17	34	32	41
Bermuda	4	8	8	9	8	3	5	6	6	5
British Virgin Islands	4	5	16	17	18	3	4	8	10	10
Cayman Islands	5	24	38	38	38	4	18	31	30	31
Cuba	7	10	34	25	23	5	8	33	23	21
Dominica	19	6	16	15	13	16	4	11	10	9
Dominican Republic	78	87	189	182	197	65	57	137	135	145
Grenada	3	3	6	7	9	2	1	4	5	6
Guadeloupe	9	5	8	8	8	8	4	6	7	7
Haiti	43	79	72	42	39	30	56	57	34	31
Jamaica	112	126	213	166	189	93	74	132	101	117
Netherlands Antilles	27	38	48	52	53	23	27	31	38	39
St. Lucia	4	4	11	13	14	3	2	7	8	9
Trinidad & Tobago	81	90	99	82	87	70	71	81	65	69
Turks & Caicos Islands	4	6	9	10	10	3	4	7	8	8
Other Caribbean	16	16	33	23	27	12	12	20	15	16
Central America	300	316	449	505	563	245	228	320	357	403
Belize	11	11	18	18	21	8	8	12	12	13
Costa Rica	43	58	86	104	121	36	41	62	75	88
El Salvador	39	50	66	74	88	33	38	46	52	64
Guatemala	83	71	124	127	140	74	53	91	93	103
Honduras	47	55	80	76	75	32	37	52	46	45
Nicaragua	25	17	16	37	45	20	14	13	29	34
Panama	52	54	59	68	73	42	38	43	51	55
Other North America	1	Z	Z	Z	Z	Z	Z	Z	Z	Z
South America	1,449	832	1,343	1,846	2,033	1,256	606	1,016	1,423	1,593
Argentina	227	89	175	356	370	206	66	136	302	312
Bolivia	23	17	21	29	28	18	10	14	19	18
Brazil	201	200	393	498	561	164	148	300	380	446
Chile	62	40	75	107	122	48	28	54	79	91
Colombia	206	164	164	189	217	173	123	122	140	162
Ecuador	82	53	75	92	91	71	42	57	72	70
Guyana	11	11	10	11	10	8	7	6	6	6
Paraguay	8	6	9	13	14	6	3	6	9	10

[Continued]

★ 53 ★

Nonimmigrants Admitted, by Selected Class of Admission, 1981-93

[Continued]

Region and country of last residence	All classes[1] (in thousands)					Visitors for pleasure (in thousands)				
	1981	1985	1990[2]	1992[2]	1993[2]	1981	1985	1990[2]	1992[2]	1993[2]
Peru	72	59	124	140	152	60	44	97	92	102
Suriname	6	8	12	13	6	5	6	10	10	4
Uruguay	21	10	21	30	36	17	7	16	23	28
Venezuela	530	173	264	369	425	481	122	199	291	343
Other South America	Z	Z	Z	Z	Z	Z	Z	Z	Z	Z
Europe	4,537	3,129	6,875	8,453	8,874	3,601	2,048	5,383	6,979	7,341
Austria	58	48	108	152	167	49	34	87	131	145
Belgium	118	67	137	172	189	91	39	95	131	147
Bulgaria	1	2	7	6	9	1	1	5	3	4
Czechoslovakia	5	6	16	26	27	3	4	12	17	18
Denmark	62	59	105	108	109	45	36	75	80	80
Finland	42	37	107	95	76	31	24	83	75	56
France	441	358	742	833	863	341	226	566	667	697
Germany[3]	754	[3]	[3]	1,705	1,890	618	[3]	[3]	1,487	1,664
Germany, East	[3]	5	7	[3]	[3]	[3]	3	5	[3]	[3]
Germany, West	[3]	537	1,186	[3]	[3]	[3]	373	969	[3]	[3]
Greece	66	51	61	60	61	37	34	43	44	44
Hungary	13	13	23	27	34	10	10	15	18	23
Iceland	11	8	14	16	19	9	5	10	12	15
Ireland	102	73	108	123	137	88	55	81	99	111
Italy	264	240	402	598	581	189	155	308	508	491
Luxembourg	5	5	10	13	16	4	3	8	11	13
Netherlands	217	139	291	349	380	165	82	214	272	301
Norway	84	71	114	112	112	50	41	80	80	79
Poland	41	46	72	58	50	34	40	55	38	32
Portugal	33	26	40	48	54	23	18	30	36	42
Romania	6	5	15	15	13	3	3	10	9	7
Soviet Union	10	6	86	105	124	4	2	53	50	47
Spain	144	103	245	351	326	109	64	183	295	272
Sweden	174	121	299	282	240	135	71	230	222	177
Switzerland	183	155	296	329	338	150	110	236	276	282
United Kingdom	1,669	923	2,338	2,830	3,020	1,388	598	1,899	2,395	2,564
Yugoslavia	29	22	36	21	17	21	15	23	12	10
Other Europe	6	6	10	18	22	4	1	3	12	16
Asia	2,290	2,627	4,937	5,816	5,667	1,704	1,866	3,830	4,699	4,502
Bangladesh	4	4	6	9	12	2	2	4	6	8
China[4]	111	183	329	426	513	53	83	187	249	289
Cyprus	3	5	7	7	7	2	2	4	4	4
Hong Kong	75	101	176	200	196	54	64	111	142	141
India	88	85	125	127	125	57	52	75	68	63
Indonesia	21	32	47	53	58	11	19	28	30	33
Iran	17	40	18	14	13	12	33	16	11	11
Iraq	6	2	6	1	1	4	1	4	Z	Z
Israel	131	115	175	171	191	102	80	128	124	142

[Continued]

★ 53 ★

Nonimmigrants Admitted, by Selected Class of Admission, 1981-93

[Continued]

Region and country of last residence	All classes[1] (in thousands)					Visitors for pleasure (in thousands)				
	1981	1985	1990[2]	1992[2]	1993[2]	1981	1985	1990[2]	1992[2]	1993[2]
Japan	1,372	1,555	3,298	3,870	3,536	1,155	1,277	2,846	3,486	3,178
Jordan	17	14	19	14	13	8	7	13	9	9
Korea	77	91	235	355	399	29	26	120	230	270
Kuwait	15	22	18	16	20	8	10	12	10	13
Lebanon	26	19	13	11	12	16	12	10	7	8
Malaysia	33	40	44	50	51	21	19	27	30	29
Pakistan	28	28	41	36	34	18	17	27	23	21
Philippines	100	107	143	176	177	60	59	76	94	95
Saudi Arabia	57	60	53	63	69	27	31	33	40	45
Singapore	27	37	54	67	70	19	23	32	42	42
Syria	8	7	8	8	8	5	5	6	6	6
Thailand	21	28	45	60	70	12	15	25	37	44
Turkey	18	16	34	37	41	11	9	20	23	25
United Arab Emirates	6	11	12	13	17	3	6	7	8	10
Other Asia	35	24	31	35	34	18	14	15	20	19
Africa	225	177	186	193	209	130	101	105	112	127
Egypt	34	27	27	27	28	21	16	16	16	16
Kenya	6	6	8	8	8	4	3	4	4	4
Liberia	6	6	5	2	1	4	4	4	1	1
Morocco	8	7	11	10	11	5	4	7	6	7
Nigeria	54	44	22	22	21	25	25	11	11	11
Senegal	3	3	5	5	5	1	1	2	2	2
South Africa	61	40	40	56	73	45	26	26	40	54
Other Africa	52	45	67	62	61	23	22	34	32	33
Oceania	379	365	679	702	660	315	282	562	581	534
Australia	230	255	466	506	475	188	195	380	416	381
Fiji	5	6	6	6	6	4	4	4	5	4
New Zealand[5]	109	90	177	149	138	95	74	153	127	117
Other Oceania	34	14	31	41	40	27	9	25	33	33
Unknown or not reported	60	221	308	342	400	30	40	60	51	101

Source: U.S. Immigration and Naturalization Service, *Statistical Yearbook of the Immigration and Naturalization Service, 1993*, U.S. Government Printing Office, Washington, DC, 1994, pp. 102-103. *Notes:* A (Z) indicates less than 500 arrivals. Totals may not add due to rounding. 1. Excludes classes of admission processed as nonimmigrants in the following years: for all countries—1985 - 64,487 parolees, 3,239 withdrawals and stowaways, and 68,044 refugees; 1990 - 90,265 parolees, 19,984 withdrawals and stowaways, and 110,197 refugees; 1992 - 137,478 parolees, 25,839 withdrawals and stowaways, and 123,010 refugees; 1993 - 123,628 parolees, 26,435 withdrawals and stowaways, and 113,152 refugees. 2. Includes arrivals under the Visa Waiver Pilot program. 3. Prior to fiscal year 1982 and after fiscal year 1990, data for East and West Germany are included in Germany. 4. Includes Mainland China and Taiwan. 5. Prior to fiscal year 1985, data for Niue are included in New Zealand.

★ 54 ★

Immigration

Nonimmigrants Admitted, by Selected Class of Admission, 1993 - I

Data show number of nonimmigrants admitted in each class in fiscal year 1993, by selected country of citizenship.

Region and country of citizenship	All classes[1,2]	Foreign government officials[3]	Temporary visitors for business[2]	Temporary visitors for pleasure[2]	Transit aliens[4]	Treaty traders and investors[3]	Students	Spouses and children of students	Temporary workers and trainees	Spouses and children of temp. workers and trainees
All countries	21,446,993	102,173	2,961,775	16,900,459	337,018	144,880	257,430	33,379	165,238	39,764
North America	3,255,057	12,744	602,385	2,411,265	81,620	3,698	30,469	2,122	43,752	3,738
Canada	98,439	609	16,672	13,245	609	3,103	11,659	672	10,774	1,892
Mexico	1,567,937	3,260	299,182	1,210,266	16,253	134	8,875	935	16,821	1,102
Caribbean	1,033,727	5,110	176,795	793,006	30,855	178	6,991	318	14,365	518
Antigua	23,550	176	6,933	15,544	546	3	168	5	74	5
Aruba	9,073	3	1,377	7,542	17	10	56	2	11	6
Bahamas, The	282,996	1,072	19,262	259,103	653	12	2,229	105	207	57
Barbados	52,753	628	11,888	38,761	655	9	282	12	107	29
Cayman Islands	21,637	-	3,498	17,909	60	-	146	5	5	-
Cuba	23,543	176	1,396	21,548	107	6	6	-	18	7
Dominica	111,656	467	22,667	82,681	2,744	24	365	29	1,718	134
Dominican Republic	95,867	355	17,119	65,554	11,041	26	218	26	878	60
Grenada	9,436	133	1,847	5,937	1,333	2	75	-	10	2
Haiti	49,510	84	7,768	39,139	1,676	2	218	3	170	8
Jamaica	190,916	1,220	50,677	118,283	7,745	25	1,174	46	10,325	108
Netherlands Antilles	19,844	3	4,070	15,398	29	39	235	11	37	2
St. Kitts & Nevis	11,760	121	3,432	7,804	276	-	72	1	23	2
St. Lucia	13,955	142	4,078	8,869	672	-	84	1	6	-
St. Vincent & Grenadines	7,202	95	1,594	4,585	755	-	71	4	13	5
Trinidad & Tobago	90,167	421	14,873	70,271	2,006	18	927	47	681	82
Turks & Caicos Islands	6,875	-	890	5,904	40	1	34	-	3	-
Other Caribbean	12,987	14	3,426	8,174	500	1	631	21	79	11
Central America	554,879	3,765	109,726	394,698	33,901	283	2,944	197	1,792	226
Belize	18,485	125	4,905	11,798	1,163	2	167	5	25	3
Costa Rica	114,362	542	23,713	83,229	4,031	138	463	56	245	63
El Salvador	93,049	650	17,508	68,760	7,232	15	337	15	379	17
Guatemala	137,649	885	28,947	100,787	5,046	19	365	59	294	35
Honduras	73,932	848	15,258	44,295	11,537	67	508	30	367	37
Nicaragua	47,175	197	7,642	35,531	2,832	8	182	18	61	7
Panama	67,227	518	11,753	50,298	2,060	34	922	14	421	64
Other North America	75	-	10	50	2	-	-	-	-	-
South America	2,027,114	13,872	305,828	1,560,844	73,953	2,556	12,999	2,011	11,034	2,953
Argentina	372,366	2,397	46,797	308,142	4,586	832	1,112	164	1,832	481
Bolivia	28,536	325	5,638	17,517	3,091	193	492	21	151	30
Brazil	548,978	2,202	76,508	431,768	17,355	173	3,277	591	2,566	917
Chile	125,869	1,321	24,342	91,999	3,286	37	442	139	647	185
Colombia	222,769	2,336	41,237	163,260	6,402	938	2,133	184	1,726	279
Ecuador	89,102	1,219	14,021	67,958	3,046	11	1,016	70	322	79
Guyana	14,288	161	3,896	8,245	1,211	1	149	2	143	63
Paraguay	13,310	272	2,134	9,262	875	127	162	23	31	4
Peru	163,724	1,003	21,852	105,746	28,924	39	1,114	95	1,259	255
Uruguay	37,917	481	6,257	28,644	967	4	87	47	100	37
Venezuela	404,346	2,136	61,727	324,409	3,891	105	2,944	675	2,235	620
Other South America	5,909	19	1,419	3,894	319	96	71	-	22	3
Europe	9,263,004	30,547	1,210,020	7,571,555	55,451	19,120	45,677	2,814	52,652	11,111
Austria	178,603	487	19,171	152,453	761	937	631	20	724	101
Belgium	180,318	543	31,466	140,063	260	1,075	555	41	900	246
Bulgaria	10,280	115	2,427	4,620	644	2	695	110	254	162
Czechoslovakia	28,377	196	5,142	19,416	688	5	346	44	279	82
Denmark	118,576	457	23,097	84,478	1,850	1,107	779	24	831	204
Finland	83,460	539	15,579	60,089	457	476	667	87	702	243
France	896,433	3,915	126,484	718,063	2,229	6,325	4,688	271	5,667	1,135
Germany	1,887,420	3,700	170,820	1,648,637	2,822	10,814	5,942	240	4,774	876
Greece	66,660	734	7,996	46,985	5,632	38	2,349	78	694	59
Hungary	35,061	271	5,836	24,252	565	2	562	65	376	189
Iceland	20,047	104	2,306	15,901	16	2	477	234	89	27
Ireland	167,494	390	22,384	132,415	1,331	140	584	35	1,776	182
Italy	630,286	1,871	74,562	529,677	4,541	3,756	2,171	131	2,677	372
Luxembourg	11,994	57	1,289	10,358	11	18	41	1	46	2

[Continued]

★ 54 ★

Nonimmigrants Admitted, by Selected Class of Admission, 1993 - I

[Continued]

Region and country of citizenship	All classes[1,2]	Foreign government officials[3]	Temporary visitors for business[2]	Temporary visitors for pleasure[2]	Transit aliens[4]	Treaty traders and investors[3]	Students	Spouses and children of students	Temporary workers and trainees	Spouses and children of temp. workers and trainees
Netherlands	436,631	797	76,106	341,373	1,659	2,151	1,470	68	2,575	403
Norway	117,311	511	24,214	81,015	2,792	1,245	1,811	94	775	110
Poland	55,429	484	8,107	36,690	3,425	7	749	77	1,277	573
Portugal	66,984	402	8,863	51,382	3,970	11	475	24	166	20
Romania	14,152	346	2,131	7,756	2,009	6	356	112	173	135
Soviet Union	127,546	2,069	53,620	48,289	2,828	19	2,153	341	3,708	1,100
Spain	349,127	1,779	37,389	288,596	1,416	1,809	5,422	140	2,163	246
Sweden	250,446	707	51,551	181,307	1,041	303	2,960	65	1,680	358
Switzerland	315,566	818	36,246	266,044	241	2,232	2,216	130	1,224	280
United Kingdom	3,173,079	8,886	397,748	2,653,974	11,336	16,456	6,205	280	18,530	3,741
Yugoslavia	23,726	73	2,490	15,562	2,528	182	980	51	407	209
Other Europe	17,998	296	2,996	12,160	399	2	393	51	185	56
Asia	5,864,415	31,933	676,644	4,577,575	110,175	88,655	157,355	25,176	48,837	19,292
Bangladesh	13,454	179	1,666	8,755	149	1	1,425	148	183	96
China[5]	558,648	1,052	157,014	318,426	17,500	4,933	29,860	7,362	3,920	1,689
Hong Kong	128,226	38	22,973	92,092	5,170	67	5,842	96	772	84
India	162,113	872	31,107	80,979	7,438	51	12,826	1,266	12,738	5,082
Indonesia	60,671	1,212	9,961	34,028	5,856	16	6,679	464	215	78
Iran	27,767	1	2,261	23,267	137	118	534	109	181	84
Israel	199,434	2,949	35,316	145,086	690	4,279	1,296	228	2,244	1,046
Japan	3,610,305	9,478	225,753	3,185,409	6,741	70,635	40,492	2,797	11,621	5,328
Jordan	19,235	770	2,944	12,367	171	4	1,400	164	253	110
Korea	447,346	2,187	81,984	300,777	13,763	6,311	22,286	6,567	2,837	771
Kuwait	16,160	975	2,198	10,051	48	4	1,705	842	37	21
Lebanon	22,913	242	3,710	15,621	558	5	800	41	497	111
Malaysia	60,036	594	14,010	34,055	1,513	20	6,263	613	664	120
Pakistan	41,507	441	5,882	25,358	631	631	3,498	257	767	358
Philippines	205,311	1,819	25,038	111,589	43,561	1,072	1,179	57	9,993	3,820
Saudi Arabia	52,536	4,022	7,116	33,933	342	10	2,933	2,716	58	19
Singapore	59,696	1,220	16,255	37,073	776	33	2,530	146	424	92
Sri Lanka	9,900	150	1,992	5,099	594	3	787	54	203	75
Syria	10,712	169	1,328	7,050	858	-	370	59	125	59
Thailand	70,058	1,268	13,538	43,708	1,959	287	6,732	122	355	35
Turkey	47,639	517	9,519	28,648	1,113	166	3,667	154	505	97
United Arab Emirates	7,958	969	1,052	3,776	7	2	1,537	462	8	-
Other Asia	32,790	809	4,027	20,428	600	7	2,714	452	237	117
Africa	222,945	7,084	50,051	130,019	3,703	92	7,067	863	3,496	1,248
Egypt	32,911	2,529	6,812	18,247	540	14	700	194	386	211
Ethiopia	6,783	62	834	4,605	54	4	424	51	79	5
Ghana	7,483	140	1,715	3,806	243	1	295	37	190	27
Kenya	7,423	146	1,438	3,593	151	6	994	95	116	43
Morocco	12,964	586	1,924	8,624	167	4	511	9	142	9
Nigeria	23,890	399	8,088	12,112	266	3	536	88	594	230
South Africa	66,295	443	12,953	47,536	419	25	671	107	1,219	583
Other Africa	65,196	2,779	16,287	31,496	1,863	35	2,936	282	770	140
Oceania	632,080	4,845	95,581	503,365	5,567	287	2,177	180	4,792	1,186
Australia	450,490	4,257	73,383	353,156	3,113	257	1,346	104	3,507	937
New Zealand	145,356	420	19,888	119,347	365	28	438	57	1,245	244
Pacific Island Trust Territory	21,035	14	777	19,930	103	-	186	9	1	1
Other Oceania	15,199	154	1,533	10,932	1,986	2	207	10	39	4
Stateless	20,053	1	2,208	17,034	561	-	131	8	36	3
Unknown	162,325	1,147	19,058	128,802	5,988	472	1,555	205	639	233

Source: U.S. Immigration and Naturalization Service, *Statistical Yearbook of the Immigration and Naturalization Service, 1993*, U.S. Government Printing Office, Washington, DC, 1994, pp. 104-107. *Notes:* A dash (-) represents zero. 1. Excludes the following classes of admission processed in the Nonimmigrant Information System: for all countries—123,628 parolees, 26,435 withdrawals and stowaways, and 113,152 refugees. 2. Includes arrivals under the Visa Waiver Pilot program. 3. Includes spouses and unmarried minor (or dependent) children. 4. Includes foreign government officials and their spouses and unmarried minor (or dependent) children in transit. 5. Includes Mainland China and Taiwan. A total of 446,204 nonimmigrant visas were issued to these countries in fiscal year 1993: 269,345 to Taiwan and 176,859 to Mainland China. (SOURCE: U.S. Department of State, Bureau of Consular Affairs, Visa Office.) 6. Includes minor children of fiances(ees).

★ 55 ★

Immigration

Nonimmigrants Admitted, by Selected Class of Admission, 1993 - II

Data show number of nonimmigrants admitted in each class in fiscal year 1993, by selected country of citizenship.

Region and country of citizenship	All classes[1,2]	Intl. represent-atives[3]	Represent-atives of foreign information media	Exchange visitors	Spouses and children of exchange visitors	Fiances(ees) of U.S. citizens[6]	Intra-company transferees	Spouses and children of intracompany transferees	NATO officials[3]	U.S.-Canada Free-Trade Agreement workers	Unknown
All countries	21,446,993	72,834	21,088	197,545	42,911	9,390	82,781	49,642	8,896	19,452	338
North America	3,255,057	7,007	969	15,183	2,804	1,437	9,712	6,032	602	19,452	66
Canada	98,439	1,670	118	5,774	992	569	6,140	3,999	489	19,452	1
Mexico	1,567,937	1,233	478	4,187	1,180	380	2,161	1,404	56	-	30
Caribbean	1,033,727	2,109	267	1,757	178	311	580	332	32	-	25
Antigua	23,550	47	4	44	-	-	-	1	-	-	-
Aruba	9,073	-	39	2	-	-	8	-	-	-	-
Bahamas, The	282,996	94	3	101	21	12	37	12	2	-	14
Barbados	52,753	160	2	112	7	5	63	32	1	-	-
Cayman Islands	21,637	2	1	8	1	-	1	-	-	-	1
Cuba	23,543	246	13	2	1	13	1	3	-	-	-
Dominica	111,656	157	41	359	33	54	131	49	3	-	-
Dominican Republic	95,867	185	35	114	27	66	81	73	5	-	4
Grenada	9,436	46	-	47	1	-	-	3	-	-	-
Haiti	49,510	224	4	154	9	16	24	8	3	-	-
Jamaica	190,916	427	26	547	34	111	102	56	6	-	4
Netherlands Antilles	19,844	2	3	11	-	-	3	1	-	-	-
St. Kitts & Nevis	11,760	6	1	21	-	-	-	-	-	-	1
St. Lucia	13,955	41	1	53	3	2	1	-	2	-	-
St. Vincent & Grenadines	7,202	20	1	49	3	1	4	1	1	-	-
Trinidad & Tobago	90,167	448	7	111	35	28	119	84	8	-	1
Turks & Caicos Islands	6,875	-	-	2	-	-	1	-	-	-	-
Other Caribbean	12,987	4	86	20	3	3	4	9	1	-	-
Central America	554,879	1,994	106	3,453	454	177	831	297	25	-	10
Belize	18,485	30	-	215	22	3	16	5	-	-	1
Costa Rica	114,362	397	39	843	155	28	283	131	5	-	1
El Salvador	93,049	495	22	448	35	16	104	13	3	-	-
Guatemala	137,649	295	13	565	98	25	136	67	8	-	5
Honduras	73,932	234	10	626	41	39	21	11	3	-	-
Nicaragua	47,175	295	1	314	36	13	25	11	2	-	-
Panama	67,227	248	21	442	67	53	246	59	4	-	3
Other North America	75	1	-	12	-	-	-	-	-	-	-
South America	2,027,114	12,987	1,279	12,509	3,164	465	6,642	3,879	88	-	51
Argentina	372,366	2,143	268	1,579	495	15	977	527	12	-	7
Bolivia	28,536	600	15	349	51	6	38	16	2	-	1
Brazil	548,978	2,502	320	5,030	1,141	121	2,706	1,753	31	-	17
Chile	125,869	1,591	148	817	235	28	428	218	5	-	1
Colombia	222,769	1,599	127	1,332	183	129	566	323	7	-	8
Ecuador	89,102	473	27	539	68	38	142	66	4	-	3
Guyana	14,288	283	5	61	5	22	36	4	1	-	-
Paraguay	13,310	160	49	137	39	8	13	14	-	-	-
Peru	163,724	1,839	111	532	161	76	492	214	3	-	9
Uruguay	37,917	828	54	250	65	2	52	36	6	-	-
Venezuela	404,346	933	155	1,863	720	19	1,184	708	17	-	5
Other South America	5,909	36	-	20	1	1	8	-	-	-	-
Europe	9,263,004	26,436	11,253	116,537	12,796	1,891	37,622	19,928	7,478	-	116
Austria	178,603	497	242	1,570	201	11	571	220	5	-	1
Belgium	180,318	1,141	256	1,752	224	16	874	580	323	-	3
Bulgaria	10,280	153	30	804	195	15	30	23	1	-	-
Czechoslovakia	28,377	104	89	1,582	259	49	51	42	1	-	2
Denmark	118,576	636	146	3,459	251	16	664	265	312	-	-
Finland	83,460	491	149	2,309	350	22	778	520	1	-	1
France	896,433	4,435	1,031	12,705	1,185	90	4,962	3,190	40	-	18
Germany	1,887,420	2,600	2,070	21,105	1,699	205	5,168	2,563	3,360	-	25
Greece	66,660	397	108	1,035	134	30	111	28	252	-	-
Hungary	35,061	314	155	1,789	521	18	82	62	2	-	-
Iceland	20,047	118	10	487	193	7	45	29	1	-	1
Ireland	167,494	505	172	6,071	154	42	934	365	9	-	5
Italy	630,286	1,618	705	5,102	660	53	1,323	639	419	-	9
Luxembourg	11,994	36	17	50	2	-	46	15	5	-	-
Netherlands	436,631	1,437	329	4,563	410	51	1,840	967	424	-	8
Norway	117,311	545	193	2,683	348	12	444	240	277	-	2
Poland	55,429	374	170	2,597	577	149	105	66	-	-	2
Portugal	66,984	337	98	519	87	43	183	86	318	-	-
Romania	14,152	247	50	605	122	63	30	11	-	-	-
Soviet Union	127,546	2,158	242	7,949	1,828	308	566	366	2	-	-
Spain	349,127	1,058	600	6,438	712	39	779	395	141	-	5
Sweden	250,446	1,041	376	4,862	400	38	2,486	1,264	2	-	5
Switzerland	315,566	538	269	2,679	663	22	1,244	706	9	-	5
United Kingdom	3,173,079	5,138	3,607	22,242	1,351	526	14,222	7,244	1,569	-	24
Yugoslavia	23,726	308	106	587	122	44	45	29	3	-	-
Other Europe	17,998	210	33	993	148	22	39	13	2	-	-

[Continued]

★55★

Nonimmigrants Admitted, by Selected Class of Admission, 1993 - II

[Continued]

Region and country of citizenship	All classes[1,2]	Intl. representatives[3]	Representatives of foreign information media	Exchange visitors	Spouses and children of exchange visitors	Fiances(ees) of U.S. citizens[6]	Intra-company transferees	Spouses and children of intracompany transferees	NATO officials[3]	U.S.-Canada Free-Trade Agreement workers	Unknown
Asia	5,864,415	14,794	6,490	38,918	21,155	4,916	24,465	17,328	624	-	83
Bangladesh	13,454	381	6	348	87	6	12	12	-	-	-
China[5]	558,648	1,066	302	6,636	3,887	731	3,029	1,210	25	-	6
Hong Kong	128,226	69	44	367	36	33	323	211	7	-	2
India	162,113	2,816	73	3,218	1,349	217	1,235	839	4	-	3
Indonesia	60,671	344	56	1,030	448	37	113	131	1	-	2
Iran	27,767	452	4	166	183	154	56	57	1	-	2
Israel	199,434	512	131	2,583	1,953	42	586	473	12	-	8
Japan	3,610,305	1,517	4,789	10,746	6,473	269	16,080	12,152	4	-	21
Jordan	19,235	249	28	426	186	62	50	50	1	-	-
Korea	447,346	522	628	2,939	3,257	249	1,223	1,022	10	-	13
Kuwait	16,160	122	2	79	42	1	23	8	2	-	-
Lebanon	22,913	378	50	550	111	92	85	62	-	-	-
Malaysia	60,036	410	23	867	373	21	284	205	1	-	-
Pakistan	41,507	882	14	1,766	757	61	87	109	3	-	5
Philippines	205,311	2,454	78	1,177	182	2,296	664	309	13	-	10
Saudi Arabia	52,536	140	5	438	614	-	110	78	2	-	-
Singapore	59,696	113	9	332	153	16	284	238	-	-	2
Sri Lanka	9,900	484	5	279	110	12	30	18	1	-	4
Syria	10,712	117	4	345	158	59	5	3	-	-	3
Thailand	70,058	339	75	1,202	146	183	59	46	2	-	2
Turkey	47,639	512	144	1,565	350	27	75	50	530	-	-
United Arab Emirates	7,958	38	3	92	10	-	1	-	1	-	-
Other Asia	32,790	877	17	1,767	290	348	51	45	4	-	-
Africa	222,945	8,630	229	7,212	1,598	377	656	599	14	-	7
Egypt	32,911	710	67	1,744	496	34	104	118	4	-	1
Ethiopia	6,783	447	1	115	36	20	34	10	-	-	2
Ghana	7,483	617	4	307	53	44	4	-	-	-	-
Kenya	7,423	428	1	318	68	7	13	6	-	-	-
Morocco	12,964	352	27	513	38	26	20	11	1	-	-
Nigeria	23,890	682	28	411	150	131	79	92	-	-	1
South Africa	66,295	238	46	1,173	287	26	290	275	3	-	1
Other Africa	65,196	5,156	55	2,631	470	89	112	87	6	-	2
Oceania	632,080	1,879	692	5,094	974	177	3,517	1,731	24	-	12
Australia	450,490	1,202	593	3,532	768	121	2,771	1,415	21	-	7
New Zealand	145,356	543	88	1,431	180	40	735	306	1	-	-
Pacific Island Trust Territory	21,035	6	-	-	-	-	-	3	-	-	5
Other Oceania	15,199	128	11	131	26	16	11	7	2	-	-
Stateless	20,053	8	-	27	18	5	11	2	-	-	-
Unknown	162,325	1,093	176	2,065	402	122	156	143	66	-	3

Source: U.S. Immigration and Naturalization Service, *Statistical Yearbook of the Immigration and Naturalization Service, 1993*, U.S. Government Printing Office, Washington, DC, 1994, pp. 104-107. *Notes:* A dash (-) represents zero. 1. Excludes the following classes of admission processed in the Nonimmigrant Information System: for all countries—123,628 parolees, 26,435 withdrawals and stowaways, and 113,152 refugees. 2. Includes arrivals under the Visa Waiver Pilot program. 3. Includes spouses and unmarried minor (or dependent) children. 4. Includes foreign government officials and their spouses and unmarried minor (or dependent) children in transit. 5. Includes Mainland China and Taiwan. A total of 446,204 nonimmigrant visas were issued to these countries in fiscal year 1993: 269,345 to Taiwan and 176,859 to Mainland China. (SOURCE: U.S. Department of State, Bureau of Consular Affairs, Visa Office.) 6. Includes minor children of fiances(ees).

★56★

Immigration

Percent Distribution of Immigrants Admitted, by Geographic Region, 1955-1993

Data are shown for periods of fiscal years.

Region	1955-93	1955-64	1965-74	1975-84	1985-90	1991	1992	1993
All regions	100.0	100.0	100.0	100.0	100.0	100.0	100.0	100.0
Europe	20.0	50.2	29.8	13.4	8.9	7.4	14.9	17.5
North and West	8.9	28.6	11.0	5.2	4.0	1.8	5.3	5.4

[Continued]

★ 56 ★

Percent Distribution of Immigrants Admitted, by Geographic Region, 1955-1993

[Continued]

Region	1955-93	1955-64	1965-74	1975-84	1985-90	1991	1992	1993
South and East	11.1	21.6	18.7	8.1	4.9	5.6	9.6	12.1
Asia	29.7	7.7	22.4	43.3	33.8	19.6	36.6	39.6
Africa	2.1	.7	1.5	2.4	2.6	2.0	2.8	3.1
Oceania	.6	.4	.7	.8	.5	.3	.5	.5
North America	41.7	35.9	39.6	33.6	48.0	66.3	39.4	33.3
Caribbean	12.7	7.0	18.0	15.1	12.0	7.7	10.0	11.0
Central America	4.6	2.4	2.5	3.7	7.2	6.1	5.9	6.4
Other North America	24.4	26.4	19.0	14.8	28.8	52.5	23.5	15.9
South America	5.9	5.1	6.0	6.6	6.2	4.4	5.7	6.0

Source: U.S. Immigration and Naturalization Service, *Statistical Yearbook of the Immigration and Naturalization Service, 1993,* U.S. Government Printing Office, Washington, DC, 1994, p. 20.

★ 57 ★

Immigration

Percent Distribution of Legal Immigrants and Refugees, by Region of Birth: 1970 to 1988

Distribution of immigrants and refugees is shown in percent, by country of origin.

Year (July 1 to June 30)	All regions	Latin America	Africa	Asia	Europe	North America	Oceania	U.S.S.R.
1987-88	100.0	36.6	3.3	45.6	11.0	2.2	0.7	0.5
1986-87	100.0	38.0	3.1	45.4	10.3	2.0	0.7	0.4
1985-86	100.0	36.0	3.0	47.2	10.5	2.0	0.7	0.5
1984-85	100.0	34.5	3.1	48.0	10.8	2.1	0.7	0.7
1983-84	100.0	35.5	2.9	47.0	10.7	2.1	0.7	1.1
1982-83	100.0	35.8	2.8	46.7	10.2	2.2	0.7	1.5
1981-82	100.0	34.0	2.5	49.4	9.3	1.9	0.7	2.3
1980-81	100.0	38.3	2.3	46.5	8.9	1.8	0.6	1.5
1979-80	100.0	39.1	1.9	47.0	8.2	2.0	0.6	1.3
1978-79	100.0	36.3	2.6	44.3	12.3	2.9	0.9	0.6
1977-78	100.0	42.3	2.3	35.4	14.1	3.7	0.9	1.3
1976-77	100.0	33.9	2.4	42.8	16.0	2.5	1.0	1.4
1975-76	100.0	32.6	1.9	44.6	15.9	2.0	0.9	2.1
1974-75	100.0	30.7	1.4	49.8	14.7	1.6	0.7	1.1
1973-74	100.0	41.2	1.6	33.5	20.5	2.0	0.8	0.3
1972-73	100.0	39.2	1.7	32.0	23.5	2.4	0.8	0.4

[Continued]

★57★

Percent Distribution of Legal Immigrants and Refugees, by Region of Birth: 1970 to 1988

[Continued]

Year (July 1 to June 30)	All regions	Latin America	Africa	Asia	Europe	North America	Oceania	U.S.S.R.
1971-72	100.0	40.1	1.7	31.2	22.9	2.8	0.8	0.3
1970-71	100.0	43.8	1.7	26.1	24.1	3.4	0.7	0.2

Source: Hollmann, Frederick W. U.S. Department of Commerce. Bureau of the Census. *United States Population Estimates, by Age, Sex, Race, and Hispanic Origin: 1980 to 1988*. Current Population Reports, Population Estimates and Projections, Series P-25, No. 1045. Washington, DC: The Bureau, January 1990, p. 27. Primary source: Unpublished data supplied by the Immigration and Naturalization Service, consistent with *Annual Report: Immigration and Naturalization Service*, 1970 through 1978; *Statistical Yearbook of the Immigration and Naturalization Service* for 1979 through 1987; *Immigration Statistics: Fiscal Year 1988 - Advance Report*; Office of Refugee Resettlement, *Report to Congress: Refugee Resettlement Program*, 1981 through 1988, and unpublished data supplied by the Office of Refugee Resettlement.

★58★

Immigration

Persons Naturalized, 1984-93

The number of persons naturalized each fiscal year is shown, by selected country of former allegiance, from 1984 to 1993. In general, immigrants from Western Europe and the Western Hemisphere are less likely to become naturalized citizens than are immigrants from other parts of the world.

Region and country of former allegiance	1984	1985	1986	1987	1988	1989	1990	1991	1992	1993
All countries	197,023	244,717	280,623	227,008	242,063	233,777	270,101	308,058	240,252	314,681
North America	54,808	61,761	73,899	54,794	65,096	61,954	64,730	71,838	56,710	87,781
Canada	3,403	3,824	3,787	2,919	2,947	2,922	3,644	4,441	4,067	6,662
Mexico	14,575	23,042	27,807	21,999	22,085	18,520	17,564	22,066	12,880	23,630
Caribbean	30,833	26,899	32,442	21,751	31,110	31,952	34,320	34,025	32,272	47,061
Antigua-Barbuda	200	225	178	205	550	490	339	478	376	439
Barbados	804	885	1,036	794	896	931	970	852	669	855
Cuba	15,756	10,487	13,818	6,738	11,228	9,514	10,291	9,554	7,763	15,109
Dominica	110	205	165	266	421	436	399	550	308	285
Dominican Republic	4,875	5,887	5,980	4,257	5,842	6,454	5,984	6,368	8,464	12,274
Grenada	294	267	250	290	360	413	459	456	421	552
Haiti	2,592	2,545	2,608	1,936	2,350	3,692	5,009	4,436	3,993	5,202
Jamaica	4,666	4,809	6,563	5,196	6,441	6,455	6,762	6,838	6,765	7,976
St. Kitts & Nevis	83	68	75	154	325	405	265	699	307	372
St. Lucia	69	69	66	221	281	249	204	286	194	236
St. Vincent & Grenadines	113	106	103	205	250	263	279	324	254	328
Trinidad and Tobago	1,192	1,280	1,476	1,427	2,079	2,552	3,198	3,033	2,602	3,293
Other Caribbean	79	66	124	62	87	98	161	151	156	140
Central America	5,997	7,996	9,863	8,125	8,954	8,560	9,202	11,306	7,491	10,398
Belize	138	265	366	316	426	373	389	499	304	381
Costa Rica	663	819	968	658	726	676	589	792	547	672
El Salvador	1,380	2,119	2,628	2,428	2,291	2,001	2,410	3,653	2,056	3,057
Guatemala	968	1,408	1,841	1,490	1,358	1,281	1,280	1,832	1,086	1,682

[Continued]

★ 58 ★

Persons Naturalized, 1984-93

[Continued]

Region and country of former allegiance	1984	1985	1986	1987	1988	1989	1990	1991	1992	1993
Honduras	1,063	1,219	1,400	964	1,229	1,167	1,259	1,306	1,248	1,713
Nicaragua	762	965	1,343	1,118	1,363	1,271	1,520	1,732	1,100	1,500
Panama	1,023	1,201	1,317	1,151	1,561	1,791	1,755	1,492	1,150	1,393
South America	13,092	15,227	16,925	13,945	16,972	16,503	19,548	20,928	19,982	26,464
Argentina	1,235	1,456	1,593	1,194	1,288	1,246	1,466	1,850	1,237	1,611
Bolivia	319	484	514	401	448	424	471	519	423	571
Brazil	488	655	615	466	553	564	574	583	579	922
Chile	915	1,213	1,242	955	1,040	887	866	920	713	862
Colombia	3,543	4,136	5,156	4,006	5,021	4,736	5,540	5,513	6,439	9,976
Ecuador	1,458	1,739	1,870	1,519	1,774	1,671	2,052	2,215	1,857	2,703
Guyana	2,844	2,628	2,784	2,694	3,535	3,654	4,306	4,826	4,717	4,938
Peru	1,451	1,969	2,180	1,844	2,255	2,267	2,829	3,088	2,633	3,274
Uruguay	406	458	337	379	406	381	433	400	371	577
Venezuela	326	348	468	373	490	521	751	747	730	829
Other South America	107	141	166	114	162	152	160	167	183	201
Europe	197,023	244,717	280,623	227,008	242,063	233,777	270,101	308,058	240,252	314,681
Czechoslovakia	410	480	697	699	775	949	916	843	676	629
France	1,003	1,145	1,147	975	950	940	1,091	1,413	1,124	1,239
Germany	3,023	3,352	3,248	2,315	2,363	2,196	2,395	2,197	1,901	2,554
Greece	3,068	4,283	2,750	2,083	2,239	2,768	2,270	1,820	1,769	2,135
Hungary	859	845	824	661	683	580	743	814	608	624
Ireland	682	911	991	813	827	787	742	746	738	1,079
Italy	3,576	3,816	3,110	2,601	2,852	2,492	2,453	1,976	1,618	3,495
Netherlands	492	585	569	485	449	410	410	508	378	471
Poland	2,117	2,939	3,140	2,731	4,145	5,002	5,972	5,493	4,681	5,551
Portugal	2,907	3,579	4,177	3,518	3,236	2,698	2,491	1,848	1,884	3,978
Romania	1,131	1,400	1,816	1,909	2,060	2,190	2,914	3,471	2,457	2,699
Soviet Union	4,038	8,935	9,370	7,276	5,304	3,020	2,847	2,822	1,648	2,763
Spain	735	710	658	487	616	490	535	436	462	615
Sweden	122	164	127	121	107	129	166	208	186	228
Switzerland	209	309	285	225	254	246	302	357	310	393
United Kingdom	7,631	8,833	8,609	7,102	7,042	7,865	8,286	9,935	7,800	10,158
Yugoslavia	1,675	1,908	1,758	1,495	1,484	1,342	1,640	1,642	1,452	2,198
Other Europe	1,220	1,405	1,322	1,036	965	975	1,091	1,279	1,089	1,353
Asia	87,261	113,084	134,695	113,392	114,849	111,488	124,675	160,367	121,965	145,318
Afghanistan	82	154	297	528	905	1,051	1,141	1,392	1,047	1,539
Bangladesh	275	337	296	334	419	496	696	874	967	942
Burma	477	855	888	634	532	479	597	827	454	469
Cambodia	512	860	1,847	2,816	3,132	3,234	3,525	4,786	2,749	3,149
China, Mainland	9,143	11,743	11,151	9,208	10,509	11,664	13,563	16,783	13,488	16,851
India	8,294	10,357	10,017	8,659	9,983	9,833	11,499	12,961	13,413	16,506
Indonesia	330	489	538	425	384	352	350	603	309	408
Iran	2,268	3,431	4,569	4,277	4,970	4,485	5,973	10,411	6,778	7,029

[Continued]

★ 58 ★

Persons Naturalized, 1984-93

[Continued]

Region and country of former allegiance	1984	1985	1986	1987	1988	1989	1990	1991	1992	1993
Iraq	1,043	1,571	1,659	1,316	1,397	1,387	1,855	1,641	1,196	1,522
Israel	1,851	2,117	2,300	1,740	1,815	1,703	2,102	2,789	2,376	2,609
Japan	1,108	1,053	1,011	752	1,041	727	736	938	621	989
Jordan	1,264	1,628	1,819	1,700	1,834	1,872	2,408	2,493	2,297	2,678
Korea	14,019	16,824	18,037	14,233	13,012	11,301	10,500	12,266	8,297	9,611
Kuwait	29	44	111	94	119	198	247	301	299	344
Laos	968	1,616	3,426	3,159	3,480	3,463	3,329	3,594	3,052	3,945
Lebanon	2,439	2,964	3,011	2,350	2,262	2,213	2,797	3,570	2,881	3,402
Malaysia	230	305	315	336	323	362	426	477	388	418
Pakistan	1,690	1,950	2,285	1,976	2,174	2,443	3,330	3,670	3,350	3,777
Philippines	23,487	28,954	31,002	25,296	24,580	24,802	25,936	33,714	28,579	33,864
Sri Lanka	247	267	238	236	230	298	335	464	333	445
Syria	732	902	1,096	890	1,097	908	1,146	1,480	1,200	1,312
Taiwan	2,758	3,407	4,501	4,033	5,716	5,779	6,895	10,876	6,408	7,384
Thailand	1,396	1,518	1,750	1,327	1,308	1,167	1,145	1,379	962	1,169
Turkey	845	932	1,019	980	1,242	1,085	1,214	1,349	1,124	1,229
Vietnam	11,039	18,060	30,840	25,469	21,636	19,357	22,027	29,603	18,357	22,427
Yemen	235	300	254	229	317	349	419	590	528	706
Other Asia	500	446	418	395	432	480	484	536	512	594
Africa	4,276	5,305	6,334	5,956	7,122	7,209	8,770	10,230	9,628	11,293
Egypt	1,556	1,803	1,888	1,731	1,960	1,638	1,945	2,644	2,098	2,045
Ethiopia	150	258	474	714	1,142	1,246	1,370	1,453	1,505	1,858
Ghana	246	284	497	434	617	567	714	669	692	722
Kenya	162	212	225	197	186	202	257	273	237	307
Liberia	67	108	109	159	224	229	283	356	359	455
Morocco	173	185	253	239	274	243	320	365	396	482
Nigeria	109	166	211	159	274	932	1,415	1,775	1,862	2,378
Sierra Leone	62	62	66	96	117	137	163	194	187	292
South Africa	809	954	1,296	884	746	687	697	883	650	830
Other Africa	942	1,273	1,315	1,343	1,582	1,328	1,606	1,618	1,642	1,924
Oceania	709	869	1,057	902	779	868	881	1,045	891	1,208
Australia	154	166	180	115	76	81	110	116	140	230
Fiji	156	317	368	377	353	436	374	477	398	544
Other Oceania	399	386	509	410	350	351	397	452	353	434
U.S. possessions	-	22	13	3	31	52	52	53	51	76
Stateless or not reported	1,979	2,850	3,102	1,484	863	624	14,181	5,789	244	409

Source: U.S. Immigration and Naturalization Service, *Statistical Yearbook of the Immigration and Naturalization Service, 1993*, U.S. Government Printing Office, Washington, DC, 1994, pp. 138-139. *Note:* A dash (-) represents zero.

★ 59 ★

Immigration

Persons Naturalized, by Major Occupation Group, 1993

The number of persons naturalized in fiscal year 1993 is shown, by major occupation group and selected country of former allegiance. In general people in high status occupations, such as medicine and engineering, are more likely to become naturalized citizens.

Region and country of former allegiance	Total	Occupation									No occupation or not reported[1]
		Total	Professional speciality	Executive, administrative, and managerial	Sales	Administrative support	Precision production, craft and repair	Operators, fabricators, and laborers	Farming, forestry, and fishing	Service	
All countries	314,681	175,036	27,954	24,047	15,379	34,926	15,353	27,893	1,735	27,749	139,645
North America	87,751	45,296	4,892	5,422	3,809	10,123	4,761	8,477	582	7,230	42,455
Canada	6,662	4,110	1,088	774	379	697	298	471	36	367	2,552
Mexico	23,630	13,948	742	2,284	1,026	1,817	1,769	3,960	431	1,919	9,682
Caribbean	47,061	21,667	2,456	1,761	1,913	6,204	2,125	3,270	86	3,852	25,394
Antigua-Barbuda	439	265	32	16	16	86	43	18	1	53	174
Bahamas, The	140	93	18	6	6	22	13	8	-	20	47
Barbados	855	383	48	23	15	152	46	40	2	57	472
Cuba	15,109	6,193	498	659	783	1,167	693	1,280	22	1,091	8,916
Dominica	285	175	22	12	22	4	26	17	2	25	110
Dominican Republic	12,274	4,805	317	334	453	1,753	351	826	15	756	7,469
Grenada	552	212	24	15	12	94	24	11	2	30	340
Haiti	5,202	2,682	322	117	138	726	201	511	21	646	2,520
Jamaica	7,976	4,690	851	383	312	1,398	467	396	14	869	3,286
St. Kitts and Nevis	372	248	24	21	28	60	53	20	2	40	124
St. Lucia	236	142	18	7	19	37	16	18	1	26	94
St. Vincent and Grenadines	328	121	19	6	6	46	15	5	-	24	207
Trinidad and Tobago	3,293	1,658	263	162	103	614	177	120	4	215	1,635
Central America	10,398	5,571	606	603	491	1,405	569	776	29	1,092	4,827
Belize	381	183	22	37	8	54	19	15	2	26	198
Costa Rica	672	337	50	40	30	76	31	48	4	58	335
El Salvador	3,057	1,781	184	139	138	432	167	264	10	447	1,276
Guatemala	1,682	904	79	165	64	179	88	165	8	156	778
Honduras	1,713	801	62	78	65	197	97	127	3	172	912
Nicaragua	1,500	865	111	96	115	243	72	94	1	133	635
Panama	1,393	700	98	48	71	224	95	63	1	100	693
South America	26,464	13,600	1,837	1,511	1,179	3,665	1,167	2,071	34	2,136	12,864
Argentina	1,611	913	188	135	88	180	67	100	3	152	698
Bolivia	571	342	85	40	35	64	21	25	-	72	229
Brazil	922	488	77	70	41	128	38	63	2	69	434
Chile	862	503	102	66	38	97	42	78	2	78	359
Colombia	9,976	5,095	584	546	477	1,185	460	965	13	865	4,881
Ecuador	2,703	1,382	119	152	100	466	129	252	1	163	1,321
Guyana	4,938	2,020	219	152	141	926	182	146	5	249	2,918
Paraguay	175	77	26	7	3	11	8	6	-	16	98
Peru	3,274	1,975	248	249	172	454	161	319	6	366	1,299
Uruguay	577	343	42	3	26	74	34	74	1	59	234
Venezuela	829	449	144	60	55	75	25	43	1	46	380
Other South America	26	13	3	1	3	5	-	-	-	1	13
Europe	42,162	24,724	4,305	4,424	1,689	4,443	2,372	4,193	181	3,117	17,438
Austria	199	114	20	28	8	14	14	8	-	22	85
Belgium	193	115	27	21	8	19	13	12	2	13	78
Bulgaria	165	99	18	12	14	10	14	13	-	18	66
Czechoslovakia	629	398	93	46	22	48	49	83	3	54	231
Denmark	162	96	25	25	12	15	4	8	2	5	66
France	1,239	672	161	142	68	129	30	42	6	94	567
Germany	2,554	1,433	237	262	158	288	133	143	10	202	1,121
Greece	2,135	1,150	151	280	72	174	121	139	5	208	985
Hungary	624	404	87	49	21	49	55	81	-	62	220
Ireland	1,079	615	143	91	40	134	56	83	5	63	464
Italy	3,495	1,962	211	267	107	470	270	344	6	287	1,533
Netherlands	471	273	58	59	23	54	16	27	6	30	198
Norway	129	86	18	14	6	18	8	11	4	7	43
Poland	5,551	3,664	503	1,086	151	404	46	691	11	372	1,887
Portugal	3,978	2,642	148	174	111	321	304	1,211	73	300	1,336
Romania	2,699	1,510	301	190	77	205	203	284	7	243	1,189
Soviet Union	2,763	1,414	336	206	100	332	96	198	6	140	1,349
Spain	615	281	64	23	23	57	24	38	3	49	334
Sweden	228	115	32	26	15	17	5	7	-	13	113
Switzerland	393	233	65	49	26	48	12	10	-	23	160
United Kingdom	10,158	5,981	1,439	1,073	545	1,401	344	477	26	676	4,177
Yugoslavia	2,198	1,201	129	251	61	185	132	235	4	204	997
Other Europe	505	266	39	50	21	51	23	48	2	32	239
Asia	145,318	82,356	14,911	11,429	7,860	15,050	6,614	11,784	896	13,812	62,962
Afghanistan	1,539	888	115	106	128	155	64	143	2	175	651
Bangladesh	942	503	118	64	59	106	13	57	-	86	439

[Continued]

★ 59 ★

Persons Naturalized, by Major Occupation Group, 1993

[Continued]

Region and country of former allegiance	Total	Occupation									No occupation or not reported[1]
		Total	Professional speciality	Executive, administrative, and managerial	Sales	Administrative support	Precision production, craft and repair	Operators, fabricators, and laborers	Farming, forestry, and fishing	Service	
Burma	469	287	46	34	21	71	39	37	-	39	182
Cambodia	3,149	1,813	141	162	121	252	189	614	11	323	1,336
China, Mainland	16,851	8,721	983	1,098	632	1,755	928	992	16	2,317	8,130
Cyprus	188	98	23	24	7	17	7	5	1	14	90
India	16,506	10,322	3,263	2,048	939	1,891	283	1,099	46	753	6,184
Indonesia	408	236	59	28	22	48	9	21	-	49	172
Iran	7,029	4,521	1,399	854	546	655	225	311	14	517	2,508
Iraq	1,522	753	101	216	129	80	42	101	4	80	769
Israel	2,609	1,315	306	259	193	230	79	104	11	133	1,294
Japan	989	520	79	88	66	100	23	53	9	102	469
Jordan	2,678	1,445	184	434	210	162	87	154	3	211	1,233
Korea	9,611	4,829	524	1,215	636	870	332	465	23	764	4,782
Kuwait	344	200	32	57	29	25	9	19	-	29	144
Laos	3,945	2,568	172	120	113	302	429	1,033	28	371	1,377
Lebanon	3,402	1,973	424	378	266	241	148	244	6	266	1,429
Malaysia	418	272	79	55	20	53	12	18	-	35	146
Pakistan	3,777	2,019	407	417	300	401	76	217	6	195	1,758
Philippines	33,864	19,688	3,388	1,741	1,546	4,502	1,872	2,149	564	3,926	14,176
Saudi Arabia	139	61	10	16	11	4	3	40	-	7	78
Singapore	157	108	38	17	10	24	2	6	-	11	49
Sri Lanka	445	295	104	55	21	68	13	14	1	19	150
Syria	1,312	720	141	165	95	70	60	112	4	73	592
Taiwan	7,384	4,229	1,352	781	392	834	103	206	16	545	3,155
Thailand	1,169	694	110	89	63	127	58	84	2	161	475
Turkey	1,229	704	156	123	82	108	58	83	3	91	525
Vietnam	22,427	12,356	1,139	743	1,181	1,847	1,437	3,402	124	2,483	10,071
Yemen	706	158	6	29	15	42	11	28	2	25	548
Other Asia	110	60	12	13	7	10	3	3	-	12	50
Africa	11,293	7,956	1,830	1,145	761	1,410	323	1,216	24	1,247	3,337
Algeria	120	79	27	11	7	10	6	8	-	10	41
Cape Verde	216	156	14	3	3	13	15	92	-	16	60
Egypt	2,045	1,228	273	223	125	225	44	146	2	190	817
Ethiopia	1,858	1,413	228	151	165	224	70	278	3	294	445
Ghana	722	520	123	57	24	112	20	86	3	95	202
Kenya	307	202	63	36	24	42	1	18	2	16	105
Liberia	455	341	75	34	30	70	18	37	-	77	114
Libya	142	87	19	17	15	4	8	14	-	10	55
Morocco	482	313	40	39	30	58	17	41	3	85	169
Nigeria	2,378	1,871	503	261	173	305	55	301	2	271	507
Sierra Leone	292	230	57	38	12	51	4	25	1	42	62
Somalia	130	98	17	16	14	15	4	22	-	10	32
South Africa	830	524	180	96	51	108	19	28	3	39	306
Sudan	129	86	18	19	11	12	5	7	-	14	43
Tanzania	187	120	25	24	14	34	6	14	1	2	67
Tunisia	123	78	24	16	3	8	10	8	-	9	45
Uganda	133	92	15	17	13	25	4	11	-	7	41
Zimbabwe	118	84	28	18	9	10	1	7	-	11	34
Other Africa	626	434	101	69	38	84	16	73	4	49	192
Oceania	1,284	833	123	84	64	202	84	122	9	145	451
Australia	230	137	50	17	10	28	5	12	2	13	93
Fiji	544	368	23	28	32	100	44	57	4	80	176
New Zealand	178	112	35	23	10	22	6	11	-	5	66
Tuvalu	2	2	1	-	-	-	-	-	-	1	-
Western Samoa	131	82	7	5	6	19	8	19	1	17	49
Other Oceania	199	132	7	11	6	33	21	23	2	29	67
Stateless	225	147	28	13	11	18	17	19	9	32	78
Not reported	184	124	28	19	6	15	15	11	-	30	60

Source: U.S. Immigration and Naturalization Service, *Statistical Yearbook of the Immigration and Naturalization Service, 1993*, U.S. Government Printing Office, Washington, DC, 1994, pp. 146-147. *Notes:* A dash (-) represents zero. 1. Includes homemakers, students, unemployed or retired persons, and others not reporting or with an unknown occupation.

★ 60 ★

Immigration

Persons Naturalized, by Selected Country of Former Allegiance, Age, and Sex, 1993 - I

The number of persons naturalized in fiscal year 1993 is shown, by age, sex, and selected country of former allegiance. The likelihood of a person becoming a naturalized citizen of the U.S. decreases as age increases. Very low rates of naturalization for elderly immigrants may also reflect their higher death rates.

Age and sex	All countries	Canada	China, Mainland	Colombia	Cuba	Dominican Republic	Guyana	Haiti	India	Iran
Total	314,681	6,662	16,851	9,976	15,109	12,274	4,938	5,202	16,506	7,029
Under 18 years	8,854	170	393	192	41	302	183	66	602	95
18-19 years	6,812	91	464	104	104	219	111	42	580	87
20-24 years	31,357	323	2,070	561	748	1,238	547	350	2,029	485
25-29 years	37,957	417	1,769	868	1,010	1,722	775	689	2,268	847
30-34 years	47,913	587	2,212	1,493	1,0725	2,005	724	973	2,721	1,537
35-39 years	45,436	669	2,081	1,324	817	1,867	737	1,167	2,448	1,504
40-44 years	33,471	767	1,531	1,138	835	1,301	568	741	2,041	1,021
45-49 years	23,969	919	1,218	1,043	752	763	354	384	1,495	580
50-54 years	18,854	880	78	948	1,183	704	289	278	861	326
55-59 years	17,165	636	931	819	1,887	697	226	215	582	227
60-64 years	14,664	537	1,110	671	2,170	612	179	140	380	126
65-69 years	12,979	348	986	426	1,936	394	124	88	288	94
70-74 years	8,642	201	736	220	1,237	228	70	42	123	60
75-79 years	4,314	79	369	110	748	152	34	12	55	26
80 years and over	2,273	38	202	59	568	69	17	15	27	14
Not reported	21	-	1	-	1	1	-	-	6	-
Male	155,910	2,768	7,468	4,348	7,035	4,737	2,217	2,661	8,727	4,396
Under 18 years	4,428	70	200	110	22	152	68	30	288	54
18-19 years	3,244	51	208	55	44	84	50	16	249	37
20-24 years	15,032	158	964	263	350	453	223	147	908	242
25-29 years	18,572	210	602	409	466	663	330	317	1,046	469
30-34 years	24,405	263	782	715	542	757	324	487	1,521	1,035
35-39 years	23,259	294	914	568	385	753	340	660	1,453	996
40-44 years	16,741	299	706	476	430	501	284	423	1,087	703
45-49 years	11,483	360	599	433	374	320	174	215	800	338
50-54 years	8,461	336	400	398	502	272	124	139	480	190
55-59 years	7,591	248	441	343	783	273	103	101	341	134
60-64 years	6,783	206	551	300	1,033	243	99	61	225	81
65-69 years	7,106	148	475	165	962	129	46	44	186	52
70-74 years	5,096	77	368	65	571	76	28	16	77	37
75-79 years	2,56	33	170	35	322	36	18	3	42	18
80 years and over	1,130	15	88	13	248	24	6	2	20	10
Not reported	13	-	-	-	1	1	-	-	4	-
Female	157,980	3,873	9,363	5,616	8,050	7,504	2,708	2,527	7,757	2,628
Under 18 years	4,228	99	190	81	18	150	114	36	308	40
18-19 years	3,543	40	254	49	60	135	60	25	329	50
20-24 years	16,278	165	1,106	296	398	784	321	201	1,117	242
25-29 years	19,334	206	1,165	459	540	1,055	442	372	1,219	378
30-34 years	23,445	323	1,430	777	529	1,244	400	482	1,199	501
35-39 years	22,110	371	1,167	756	430	1,106	396	507	995	508
40-44 years	16,643	466	823	659	399	798	284	315	952	317

[Continued]

★ 60 ★

Persons Naturalized, by Selected Country of Former Allegiance, Age, and Sex, 1993 - I

[Continued]

Age and sex	All countries	Canada	China, Mainland	Colombia	Cuba	Dominican Republic	Guyana	Haiti	India	Iran
45-49 years	12,427	558	617	608	376	439	179	169	692	242
50-54 years	10,335	541	376	549	681	428	164	138	381	135
55-59 years	9,537	387	489	475	1,100	422	122	113	240	93
60-64 years	7,840	327	557	371	1,135	368	80	78	155	45
65-69 years	5,850	200	509	261	972	264	77	44	102	42
70-74 years	3,529	122	368	154	666	150	42	25	46	23
75-79 years	1,741	45	198	75	426	116	16	9	13	8
80 years and over	1,134	23	113	46	320	45	11	13	7	4
Not reported	6	-	1	-	-	-	-	-	2	-
Unknown sex	791	21	20	12	24	33	13	14	22	5
Percent distribution	100.0	100.0	100.0	100.0	100.0	100.0	100.0	100.0	100.0	100.0
Male	49.5	41.5	44.3	43.6	46.6	38.6	44.9	51.2	52.9	62.5
Female	50.2	58.1	55.6	56.3	53.3	61.1	54.8	48.6	47.0	37.4
Unknown	.3	.3	.1	.1	.2	.3	.3	.3	.1	.1
Median age	37.6	46.6	38.7	41.9	57.7	36.6	35.7	37.0	35.2	36.5
Male	37.6	45.5	40.5	40.6	57.6	36.6	36.4	37.5	36.2	36.8
Female	37.7	47.3	37.3	42.9	57.8	36.7	35.2	36.5	33.7	36.0

Source: U.S. Immigration and Naturalization Service, *Statistical Yearbook of the Immigration and Naturalization Service, 1993,* U.S. Government Printing Office, Washington, DC, 1994, pp. 150-151. *Note:* A dash (-) represents zero.

★ 61 ★

Immigration

Persons Naturalized, by Selected Country of Former Allegiance, Age, and Sex, 1993 - II

The number of persons naturalized in fiscal year 1993 is shown, by age, sex, and selected country of former allegiance. The likelihood of a person becoming a naturalized citizen of the U.S. decreases as age increases. Very low rates of naturalization for elderly immigrants may also reflect their higher death rates.

Age and sex	All countries	Jamaica	Korea	Mexico	Philippines	Poland	Portugal	Taiwan	United Kingdom	Vietnam	Other
Total	314,681	7,976	9,611	23,630	33,864	5,551	3,978	7,384	10,158	22,427	95,555
Under 18 years	8,854	159	726	235	937	138	53	304	319	676	3,263
18-19 years	6,812	104	466	316	359	110	80	272	226	1,352	1,725
20-24 years	31,357	677	1,763	2,243	2,097	326	366	841	1,134	5,177	8,382
25-29 years	37,957	1,200	1,295	2,806	3,811	463	456	503	1,241	3,669	12,148
30-34 years	47,913	1,275	1,532	3,149	4,721	834	531	1,286	1,299	3,195	16,767
35-39 years	45,436	1,285	1,261	2,842	4,665	1,114	495	2,042	1,255	2,764	15,099
40-44 years	33,471	957	775	2,350	3,046	870	421	1,242	1,093	2,088	10,686
45-49 years	23,969	731	586	1,732	2,079	497	276	383	982	1,158	8,037
50-54 years	18,854	541	338	1,902	1,467	335	300	192	830	739	5,963
55-59 years	17,165	392	299	2,095	1,270	275	369	102	735	529	4,879
60-64 years	14,664	291	217	1,695	1,290	213	299	76	474	441	3,743
65-69 years	12,979	177	162	1,061	3,325	197	192	66	304	283	2,528

[Continued]

★ 61 ★

Persons Naturalized, by Selected Country of Former Allegiance, Age, and Sex, 1993 - II

[Continued]

Age and sex	All countries	Jamaica	Korea	Mexico	Philippines	Poland	Portugal	Taiwan	United Kingdom	Vietnam	Other
70-74 years	8,642	109	106	700	2,866	110	92	45	162	187	1,348
75-79 years	4,314	56	54	285	1,522	40	29	20	60	109	554
80 years and over	2,273	22	30	217	409	29	19	10	43	60	425
Not reported	21	-	1	2	-	-	-	-	1	-	8
Male	155,910	3,388	4,208	11,838	16,955	2,709	2,008	3,467	4,524	12,548	49,908
Under 18 years	4,428	80	309	117	462	68	32	163	157	337	1,709
18-19 years	3,244	49	256	128	181	54	28	158	111	674	811
20-24 years	15,032	278	898	999	964	149	180	443	541	2,756	4,116
25-29 years	18,572	515	548	1,576	1,434	224	220	186	625	2,226	6,506
30-34 years	24,405	539	516	1,888	1,744	425	259	470	589	1,949	9,600
35-39 years	23,259	515	462	1,576	1,777	564	255	974	596	1,509	8,668
40-44 years	16,741	421	287	1,202	1,160	468	208	623	529	1,161	5,773
45-49 years	11,483	322	294	816	829	250	150	181	405	650	3,973
50-54 years	8,461	238	175	803	581	152	155	104	296	436	2,680
55-59 years	7,591	164	163	880	504	113	186	52	271	298	2,193
60-64 years	6,783	117	110	785	597	91	158	32	174	224	1,696
65-69 years	7,106	62	91	470	2,626	73	107	35	124	148	1,163
70-74 years	5,096	59	65	377	2,440	45	48	31	61	96	559
75-79 years	2,56	22	23	119	1,330	20	17	11	25	54	268
80 years and over	1,130	7	10	101	326	13	5	4	19	30	189
Not reported	13	-	1	1	-	-	-	-	1	-	4
Female	157,980	4,563	5,301	11,754	16,863	2,833	1,966	3,904	5,596	9,843	45,331
Under 18 years	4,228	76	325	116	462	69	21	136	152	324	1,484
18-19 years	3,543	55	205	188	177	56	52	112	114	674	908
20-24 years	16,278	398	861	1,239	1,126	177	186	397	591	2,419	4,254
25-29 years	19,334	679	745	1,226	2,376	237	236	316	610	1,441	5,632
30-34 years	23,445	736	1,013	1,252	2,976	409	272	815	704	1,244	7,139
35-39 years	22,110	765	793	1,262	2,885	550	239	1,068	655	1,250	6,407
40-44 years	16,643	535	481	1,144	1,880	400	211	617	563	924	4,875
45-49 years	12,427	406	288	915	1,248	245	126	201	575	507	4,036
50-54 years	10,335	301	159	1,097	883	182	145	88	533	303	3,251
55-59 years	9,537	227	135	1,215	764	162	182	50	463	231	2,667
60-64 years	7,840	173	106	906	693	122	141	44	299	216	2,024
65-69 years	5,850	115	71	589	697	123	85	31	178	135	1,355
70-74 years	3,529	48	41	323	425	65	44	14	100	90	783
75-79 years	1,741	34	31	165	191	20	12	9	35	55	283
80 years and over	1,134	15	20	116	80	16	14	6	24	30	231
Not reported	6	-	-	1	-	-	-	-	-	-	2
Unknown sex	791	25	102	38	46	9	4	13	38	36	316
Percent distribution	100.0	100.0	100.0	100.0	100.0	100.0	100.0	100.0	100.0	100.0	100.0
Male	49.5	42.5	43.8	50.1	50.1	48.8	50.5	47.0	44.5	56.0	52.2
Female	50.2	57.2	55.2	49.7	49.8	51.0	49.4	52.9	55.1	43.9	47.4
Unknown	.3	.3	1.1	.2	.1	.2	.1	.2	.4	.2	.3

[Continued]

★61★

Persons Naturalized, by Selected Country of Former Allegiance, Age, and Sex, 1993 - II

[Continued]

Age and sex	All countries	Jamaica	Korea	Mexico	Philippines	Poland	Portugal	Taiwan	United Kingdom	Vietnam	Other
Median age	37.6	37.1	31.8	40.5	40.5	39.1	40.1	36.2	38.4	30.5	36.8
Male	37.6	37.1	30.8	38.8	49.4	38.8	40.7	36.6	37.0	30.7	36.2
Female	37.7	37.1	32.5	42.5	37.2	39.3	39.5	35.7	39.8	30.3	37.5

Source: U.S. Immigration and Naturalization Service, *Statistical Yearbook of the Immigration and Naturalization Service, 1993*, U.S. Government Printing Office, Washington, DC, 1994, pp. 150-151. *Note:* A dash (-) represents zero.

★62★

Immigration

Persons Naturalized, by Selected Metropolitan Residence, 1993 - I

The number of persons naturalized in fiscal year 1993 is shown, by selected country of former allegiance and selected metropolitan statistical area (MSA) of residence.

MSA[1]	All countries	Canada	China, Mainland	Colombia	Cuba	Dominican Republic	Guyana	Haiti	India	Iran
Total	314,681	6,662	16,851	9,976	15,109	12,274	4,938	5,202	16,506	7,029
New York, NY	47,370	223	4,003	2,644	618	7,649	3,316	2,337	1,342	317
Los Angeles-Long Beach, CA	19,854	180	1,360	212	351	25	25	16	414	1,210
Miami, FL	17,222	65	63	1,571	10,001	573	70	757	46	44
Chicago, IL	16,529	109	728	336	25	67	15	57	1,654	161
Washington, DC-MD-VA	13,601	187	567	256	69	108	240	90	1,099	689
Houston, TX	9,797	105	370	341	133	30	31	15	704	227
San Francisco, CA	8,558	94	2,462	28	8	2	5	7	142	195
San Jose, CA	7,539	57	488	12	21	-	7	-	401	334
Oakland, CA	6,601	90	932	36	9	5	8	7	435	195
Philadelphia, PA-NJ	5,748	108	268	131	28	38	27	80	670	75
Dallas, TX	5,505	105	143	101	74	11	19	4	404	228
San Diego, CA	5,166	94	104	29	4	4	3	2	63	182
Boston-Lawrence-Lowell-Brockton, MA	5,096	163	663	86	20	252	20	241	248	105
Orange County, CA	4,900	75	128	40	55	3	1	-	156	269
Newark, NJ	4,820	49	81	393	268	215	197	323	337	34
Nassau-Suffolk, NY	4,707	73	155	344	44	218	123	213	395	204
Detroit, MI	4,666	250	122	18	9	2	9	3	394	55
Bergen-Passaic, NJ	4,343	26	55	548	124	387	42	20	354	59
Honolulu, HI	4,279	36	407	8	1	5	5	2	11	4
Jersey City, NJ	4,219	3	21	327	1,150	498	90	23	293	10
Lincoln, NE	4,085	1	-	1	-	-	-	-	7	1
Seattle-Bellevue-Everett, WA	4,062	194	327	21	3	3	2	2	137	131
Atlanta, GA	3,302	114	75	139	74	23	43	22	283	135
Sacramento, CA	3,044	41	313	12	2	-	-	2	143	97
Fort Lauderdale, FL	3,018	124	52	388	255	73	74	252	36	25
Baltimore, MD	2,484	44	106	37	9	16	24	14	277	129
Hartford, CT	2,462	317	50	48	23	16	62	8	108	30
Middlesex-Somerset-Hunterdon, NJ	2,457	20	89	96	49	194	35	12	573	20
Riverside-San Bernardino, CA	2,223	29	44	17	29	3	5	3	98	51
Bridgeport-Stamford-Norwalk-Danbury, CT	2,190	120	52	173	26	40	3	158	121	32
Fort Worth-Arlington, TX	2,104	36	31	37	10	4	4	4	132	47
San Antonio, TX	1,828	15	24	31	11	8	1	1	48	29
Denver, CO	1,789	97	44	11	6	2	-	3	65	71

[Continued]

★62★

Persons Naturalized, by Selected Metropolitan Residence, 1993 - I

[Continued]

MSA[1]	All countries	Canada	China, Mainland	Colombia	Cuba	Dominican Republic	Guyana	Haiti	India	Iran
Portland-Vancouver, OR-WA	1,694	87	117	14	13	-	-	1	36	57
Providence-Warwick-Pawtucket, RI	1,679	30	32	74	10	146	3	17	33	11
Minneapolis-St. Paul, MN-WI	1,660	76	65	9	3	1	55	1	65	28
Orlando, FL	1,571	40	34	135	79	58	49	62	63	51
Stockton-Lodi, CA	1,436	6	86	2	1	1	-	-	73	8
Cleveland-Lorain-Elyria, OH	1,374	51	60	8	7	5	3	3	113	21
Phoenix-Mesa, AZ	1,357	99	108	23	3	2	2	2	62	52
Las Vegas, NV	1,343	54	56	20	74	-	-	1	23	25
Tampa-St. Petersburg-Clearwater, FL	1,327	75	29	75	200	25	15	10	37	27
New Orleans, LA	1,315	12	32	45	85	-	10	6	70	15
Fresno, CA	1,219	12	44	3	-	-	2	-	150	24
Vallejo-Fairfield-Napa, CA	1,219	17	29	3	4	2	1	4	54	14
West Palm Beach-Boca Raton, FL	1,208	41	17	92	232	15	15	120	45	14
Austin-San Marcos, TX	1,044	24	24	17	5	2	4	-	70	50
New Haven-Waterbury-Meriden, CT	1,026	99	40	29	7	17	25	6	47	13
San Juan, PR	1,002	1	25	60	111	674	1	4	3	-
Monmouth-Ocean, NJ	910	23	56	21	9	15	9	26	118	13
Other MSA	41,525	1,715	1,351	603	241	262	181	193	3,163	1,051
Non-MSA	14,429	950	303	202	227	529	40	49	661	148
Unknown	773	6	16	69	61	46	17	19	30	12

Source: U.S. Immigration and Naturalization Service, *Statistical Yearbook of the Immigration and Naturalization Service, 1993,* U.S. Government Printing Office, Washington, DC, 1994, pp. 144-145. *Notes:* A dash (-) represents zero. 1. Ranked by the number of persons naturalized.

★63★

Immigration

Persons Naturalized, by Selected Metropolitan Residence, 1993 - II

The number of persons naturalized in fiscal year 1993 is shown, by selected country of former allegiance and selected metropolitan statistical area (MSA) of residence.

MSA[1]	All countries	Jamaica	Korea	Mexico	Philippines	Poland	Portugal	Taiwan	United Kingdom	Vietnam	Other
Total	314,681	7,976	9,611	26,630	33,864	5,551	3,978	7,384	10,158	22,427	95,555
New York, NY	47,370	3,134	968	130	1,233	601	163	607	1,296	435	16,354
Los Angeles-Long Beach, CA	19,854	48	1,111	2,252	3,433	93	34	1,192	575	1,788	5,535
Miami, FL	17,222	691	6	44	123	14	9	12	76	17	3,040
Chicago, IL	16,529	122	737	3,491	1,506	1,495	7	198	262	455	4,876
Washington, DC-MD-VA	13,601	390	845	94	932	74	46	330	428	1,107	6,050
Houston, TX	9,797	102	115	2,312	405	52	4	273	252	1,803	2,523
San Francisco, CA	8,558	5	118	159	1,839	34	38	244	619	736	1,823
San Jose, CA	7,539	1	151	241	1,292	53	60	696	249	2,306	1,170
Oakland, CA	6,601	10	125	242	1,492	69	41	297	347	730	1,531
Philadelphia, PA-NJ	5,748	219	353	23	411	215	54	144	269	570	2,065
Dallas, TX	5,505	17	224	951	256	60	5	267	168	645	1,823
San Diego, CA	5,166	12	47	939	1,699	70	13	69	115	624	1,093
Boston-Lawrence-Lowell-Brockton, MA	5,096	90	61	14	83	61	282	92	288	511	1,816
Orange County, CA	4,900	2	311	353	461	22	2	362	106	1,534	1,020
Newark, NJ	4,820	183	70	16	296	135	356	106	118	44	1,599
Nassau-Suffolk, NY	4,707	255	97	15	204	89	50	119	194	47	1,868
Detroit, MI	4,666	29	97	61	287	225	1	77	126	86	2,815
Bergen-Passaic, NJ	4,343	155	188	17	264	162	24	50	105	11	1,752

[Continued]

★ 63 ★

Persons Naturalized, by Selected Metropolitan Residence, 1993 - II

[Continued]

MSA[1]	All countries	Jamaica	Korea	Mexico	Philippines	Poland	Portugal	Taiwan	United Kingdom	Vietnam	Other
Honolulu, HI	4,279	10	286	29	2,478	8	9	59	134	247	540
Jersey City, NJ	4,219	11	33	9	334	64	97	15	23	45	1,173
Lincoln, NE	4,085	-	4	1	4,014	2	-	1	1	22	30
Seattle-Bellevue-Everett, WA	4,062	10	259	23	758	79	5	145	211	607	1,145
Atlanta, GA	3,302	117	187	49	97	33	6	113	140	291	1,361
Sacramento, CA	3,044	9	71	189	445	28	19	45	113	642	873
Fort Lauderdale, FL	3,018	681	10	15	70	27	5	7	69	38	817
Baltimore, MD	2,484	78	256	6	198	63	6	72	131	93	925
Hartford, CT	2,462	348	22	4	36	337	252	5	78	87	631
Middlesex-Somerset-Hunterdon, NJ	2,457	40	48	7	156	77	30	150	84	51	726
Riverside-San Bernardino, CA	2,223	10	94	416	427	8	5	97	49	191	647
Bridgeport-Stamford-Norwalk-Danbury, CT	2,190	132	19	9	46	56	197	3	138	55	810
Fort Worth-Arlington, TX	2,104	8	36	293	87	11	1	85	67	427	784
San Antonio, TX	1,828	12	42	1,092	104	20	-	16	43	67	264
Denver, CO	1,789	5	90	236	86	44	2	28	78	316	605
Portland-Vancouver, OR-WA	1,694	4	128	25	152	14	4	41	80	277	644
Providence-Warwick-Pawtucket, RI	1,679	2	7	6	45	12	720	-	31	22	478
Minneapolis-St. Paul, MN-WI	1,660	9	46	17	57	14	3	20	53	248	890
Orlando, FL	1,571	102	22	16	105	11	3	27	45	142	527
Stockton-Lodi, CA	1,436	2	2	199	305	2	86	8	20	206	429
Cleveland-Lorain-Elyria, OH	1,374	31	17	13	46	58	-	16	55	50	817
Phoenix-Mesa, AZ	1,357	3	32	221	100	28	2	45	52	104	417
Las Vegas, NV	1,343	6	60	198	300	10	6	19	58	71	362
Tampa-St. Petersburg-Clearwater, FL	1,327	31	12	18	77	38	1	11	56	130	462
New Orleans, LA	1,315	6	10	19	70	4	-	13	22	349	547
Fresno, CA	1,219	1	6	371	82	1	20	6	16	78	403
Vallejo-Fairfield-Napa, CA	1,219	3	18	79	677	8	6	13	29	44	216
West Palm Beach-Boca Raton, FL	1,208	91	6	18	23	10	1	8	39	38	383
Austin-San Marcos, TX	1,044	6	34	174	41	4	2	66	43	148	330
New Haven-Waterbury-Meriden, CT	1,026	50	15	3	37	61	109	4	46	30	390
San Juan, PR	1,002	1	-	4	-	-	-	2	6	1	109
Monmouth-Ocean, NJ	910	33	12	7	72	15	30	35	54	20	342
Other MSA	41,525	515	1,581	5,645	3,518	744	1,058	878	1,846	3,334	13,646
Non-MSA	14,429	129	508	2,847	2,476	126	82	187	643	492	3,830
Unknown	773	15	14	20	129	12	22	9	12	15	249

Source: U.S. Immigration and Naturalization Service, *Statistical Yearbook of the Immigration and Naturalization Service, 1993,* U.S. Government Printing Office, Washington, DC, 1994, pp. 144-145. *Notes:* A dash (-) represents zero. 1. Ranked by the number of persons naturalized.

★ 64 ★

Immigration

Persons Naturalized, by Selected Naturalization Provisions, 1993

The number of persons naturalized in fiscal year 1993 is shown, by selected provisions and by selected country of former allegiance.

Region and country of former allegiance	Total naturalized	General provisions	Special provisions					Not reported
			Total	Married to U.S. citizen	Children of U.S. parents	Military	Other	
All countries	314,681	273,857	36,423	22,392	6,759	7,069	203	4,401
North America	87,751	82,167	4,520	3,041	1,050	410	19	1,064
Canada	6,662	6,025	521	373	118	27	3	116
Mexico	23,630	22,363	1,086	776	192	114	4	181

[Continued]

★ 64 ★

Persons Naturalized, by Selected Naturalization Provisions, 1993

[Continued]

Region and country of former allegiance	Total naturalized	General provisions	Special provisions					Not reported
			Total	Married to U.S. citizen	Children of U.S. parents	Military	Other	
Caribbean	47,061	44,676	1,873	1,179	494	192	8	512
Antigua-Barbuda	439	416	16	11	2	3	-	7
Bahamas, The	140	114	23	12	5	6	-	3
Barbados	855	789	49	26	12	11	-	17
Cuba	15,109	14,905	110	68	27	14	1	94
Dominica	285	273	12	9	1	1	1	-
Dominican Republic	12,274	11,366	758	496	241	18	3	150
Grenada	552	521	20	10	6	4	-	11
Haiti	5,202	4,948	183	140	31	11	1	71
Jamaica	7,976	7,416	445	244	119	80	2	115
St. Kitts and Nevis	372	340	25	12	6	7	-	7
St. Lucia	236	220	14	10	3	1	-	2
St. Vincent and Grenadines	328	298	22	12	7	3	-	8
Trinidad and Tobago	3,293	3,070	196	129	34	33	-	27
Central America	10,398	9,103	1,040	713	246	77	4	255
Belize	381	350	28	17	7	4	-	3
Costa Rica	672	600	53	33	18	2	-	19
El Salvador	3,057	2,752	261	200	39	18	4	44
Guatemala	1,682	1,486	162	82	71	9	-	34
Honduras	1,713	1,520	155	101	49	5	-	38
Nicaragua	1,500	1,353	133	97	28	8	-	14
Panama	1,393	1,042	248	183	34	31	-	103
South America	26,464	23,813	2,260	1,668	495	90	7	391
Argentina	1,611	1,476	115	94	18	3	-	20
Bolivia	571	504	61	46	12	3	-	6
Brazil	922	736	156	99	51	6	-	30
Chile	862	747	91	66	19	5	1	24
Colombia	9,976	9,254	641	472	147	20	2	81
Ecuador	2,703	2,559	123	84	25	13	1	21
Guyana	4,938	4,474	337	217	103	15	2	127
Paraguay	175	121	36	16	19	1	-	18
Peru	3,274	2,694	532	443	71	17	1	48
Uruguay	577	541	25	22	1	2	-	11
Venezuela	829	686	138	104	29	5	-	5
Other South America	26	21	5	5	-	-	-	-
Europe	42,162	37,769	3,582	2,678	790	97	17	811
Austria	199	178	16	10	5	1	-	5
Belgium	193	158	29	23	4	2	-	6
Bulgaria	165	139	25	18	7	-	-	1
Czechoslovakia	629	586	33	23	7	3	-	10
Denmark	162	144	17	14	3	-	-	1
France	1,239	1,086	127	100	24	3	-	26

[Continued]

★ 64 ★

Persons Naturalized, by Selected Naturalization Provisions, 1993

[Continued]

Region and country of former allegiance	Total naturalized	General provisions	Special provisions					Not reported
			Total	Married to U.S. citizen	Children of U.S. parents	Military	Other	
Germany	2,554	2,246	241	185	37	17	2	67
Greece	2,135	1,885	208	173	32	2	1	42
Hungary	624	542	67	60	4	3	-	15
Ireland	1,079	967	81	69	6	5	1	31
Italy	3,495	3,277	143	115	22	6	-	75
Netherlands	471	424	38	33	2	2	1	9
Norway	129	112	12	8	3	1	-	5
Poland	5,551	5,037	435	333	97	4	1	79
Portugal	3,978	3,854	101	60	39	2	-	23
Romania	2,699	2,311	303	111	191	1	-	85
Soviet Union	2,763	2,542	135	94	41	-	-	86
Spain	615	560	48	41	4	3	-	7
Sweden	228	199	26	21	5	-	-	3
Switzerland	393	346	40	35	5	-	-	7
United Kingdom	10,158	8,781	1,184	918	218	39	9	193
Yugoslavia	2,198	1,953	225	200	24	1	-	20
Other Europe	505	442	48	34	10	2	2	15
Asia	145,318	119,243	24,081	13,264	4,238	6,443	136	1,994
Afghanistan	1,539	1,472	51	30	21	-	-	16
Bangladesh	942	765	173	129	38	5	1	4
Burma	469	418	39	38	1	-	-	12
Cambodia	3,149	3,030	85	30	50	2	3	34
China, Mainland	16,851	14,753	1,934	1,604	306	3	21	164
Cyprus	188	145	43	41	2	-	-	-
India	16,506	14,760	1,593	1,023	551	11	8	153
Indonesia	408	326	76	61	15	-	-	6
Iran	7,029	6,511	471	397	71	2	1	47
Iraq	1,522	1,293	214	192	22	-	-	15
Israel	2,609	2,037	520	436	82	2	-	52
Japan	989	879	90	60	24	3	3	20
Jordan	2,678	1,954	689	578	107	3	1	35
Korea	9,611	8,046	1,257	712	520	20	5	308
Kuwait	344	206	129	112	17	-	-	9
Laos	3,945	3,771	138	39	95	4	-	36
Lebanon	3,402	2,491	873	785	86	2	-	38
Malaysia	418	302	110	86	23	1	-	6
Pakistan	3,777	3,108	606	461	143	1	1	63
Philippines	33,864	21,353	12,038	4,886	706	6,359	87	473
Saudi Arabia	139	67	64	30	33	1	-	8
Singapore	157	123	33	30	3	-	-	1
Sri Lanka	445	398	42	39	3	-	-	5
Syria	1,312	980	325	289	35	-	1	7
Taiwan	7,384	6,421	835	615	218	1	1	128
Thailand	1,169	925	196	100	89	7	-	48

[Continued]

★ 64 ★

Persons Naturalized, by Selected Naturalization Provisions, 1993

[Continued]

Region and country of former allegiance	Total naturalized	General provisions	Special provisions					Not reported
			Total	Married to U.S. citizen	Children of U.S. parents	Military	Other	
Turkey	1,229	1,006	209	189	19	1	-	14
Vietnam	22,427	21,379	787	210	559	15	3	261
Yemen	706	251	427	39	388	-	-	28
Other Asia	110	73	34	23	11	-	-	3
Africa	11,293	9,399	1,799	1,619	155	19	6	95
Algeria	120	94	24	23	1	-	-	2
Cape Verde	216	193	20	16	4	-	-	3
Egypt	2,045	1,518	492	442	49	1	-	35
Ethiopia	1,858	1,780	72	52	19	1	-	6
Ghana	722	609	112	100	11	-	1	1
Kenya	307	271	33	25	7	1	-	3
Liberia	455	387	65	64	1	-	-	3
Libya	142	118	21	20	1	-	-	3
Morocco	482	279	199	195	2	2	-	4
Nigeria	2,378	2,011	360	338	14	8	-	7
Sierra Leone	292	259	32	32	-	-	-	1
Somalia	130	102	28	25	1	2	-	-
South Africa	830	707	119	92	24	1	2	4
Sudan	129	84	37	32	5	-	-	8
Tanzania	187	167	15	14	-	1	-	5
Tunisia	123	93	29	26	4	4	4	4
Uganda	133	122	10	10	-	-	-	1
Zimbabwe	118	106	12	10	2	-	-	-
Other Africa	626	499	119	103	13	1	2	8
Oceania	1,284	1,126	139	95	19	8	17	19
Australia	230	211	18	12	5	1	-	1
Fiji	544	481	56	45	10	1	-	7
New Zealand	178	157	20	17	1	2	-	1
Tuvalu	2	1	1	1	-	-	-	-
Western Samoa	131	108	17	10	2	2	3	6
Other Oceania	199	168	27	10	1	2	14	4
Stateless	225	204	20	14	6	-	-	1
Not reported	184	136	22	13	6	2	1	26

Source: U.S. Immigration and Naturalization Service, *Statistical Yearbook of the Immigration and Naturalization Service, 1993*, U.S. Government Printing Office, Washington, DC, 1994, pp. 136-137. *Note:* A dash (-) represents zero.

★ 65 ★

Immigration

Persons Naturalized, by State of Residence, 1993 - I

The number of persons naturalized in fiscal year 1993 is shown, by state of residence and country of former allegiance.

State of residence	All countries	Canada	China, Mainland	Colombia	Cuba	Dominican Republic	Guyana	Haiti	India	Iran
Total	314,681	6,662	16,851	9,976	15,109	12,274	4,938	5,202	16,506	7,029
Alabama	719	31	27	8	-	3	4	4	96	41
Alaska	530	21	5	11	3	10	1	1	10	5
Arizona	2,548	134	122	27	4	3	2	3	87	60
Arkansas	405	10	4	-	6	-	-	-	24	13
California	68,100	791	6,176	427	504	52	61	44	2,544	2,720
Colorado	2,732	149	73	16	8	7	3	4	100	107
Connecticut	6,125	601	159	252	61	77	90	178	295	80
Delaware	423	10	14	4	4	2	6	7	66	14
District of Columbia	773	3	54	16	3	24	38	12	11	15
Florida	26,628	499	252	2,361	10,899	773	256	1,256	330	197
Georgia	4,185	153	106	157	80	30	52	25	387	152
Hawaii	4,960	48	415	10	1	6	5	2	11	5
Idaho	255	12	12	1	2	-	-	1	4	6
Illinois	17,394	135	759	352	257	69	20	60	1,760	189
Indiana	1,395	63	77	7	7	3	4	4	179	30
Iowa	578	26	14	4	1	-	15	-	48	15
Kansas	1,085	38	31	19	3	-	1	1	86	40
Kentucky	534	20	19	12	4	1	3	2	47	32
Louisiana	2,016	22	52	64	99	1	20	6	140	31
Maine	584	368	14	3	1	2	-	-	7	4
Maryland	9,864	167	466	186	58	79	210	87	1,021	476
Massachusetts	6,574	221	697	108	23	281	25	247	297	129
Michigan	6,091	334	185	30	15	7	15	4	535	98
Minnesota	1,921	93	84	11	4	1	55	1	74	33
Mississippi	426	12	14	1	-	-	4	-	51	8
Missouri	1,379	35	54	18	4	6	7	5	129	34
Montana	165	35	11	4	2	-	-	-	1	-
Nebraska	4,411	10	4	3	-	-	-	-	34	6
Nevada	1,518	57	66	20	75	1	-	2	29	32
New Hampshire	387	72	14	7	3	7	-	1	25	13
New Jersey	18,495	171	356	1,450	1,610	1,354	375	446	1,895	156
New Mexico	665	29	18	12	3	4	1	5	22	24
New York	55,519	562	4,312	3,063	678	7,926	3,470	2,587	2,038	564
North Carolina	2,397	115	44	63	15	15	14	8	274	69
North Dakota	159	31	5	5	-	-	-	-	15	-
Ohio	3,382	147	160	25	12	12	9	10	385	74
Oklahoma	1,092	26	28	11	3	5	5	-	59	57
Oregon	2,146	130	155	16	16	1	-	1	52	72
Pennsylvania	7,236	160	304	152	37	60	35	84	822	114
Rhode Island	1,720	33	35	75	10	146	3	18	34	11
South Carolina	675	28	68	19	2	1	1	3	56	9
South Dakota	85	7	-	-	-	-	-	-	4	2
Tennessee	1,039	53	31	16	2	1	13	3	107	60
Texas	26,403	335	630	577	252	69	66	28	1,515	628
Utah	950	76	39	8	4	5	1	-	18	53

[Continued]

★ 65 ★

Persons Naturalized, by State of Residence, 1993 - I

[Continued]

State of residence	All countries	Canada	China, Mainland	Colombia	Cuba	Dominican Republic	Guyana	Haiti	India	Iran
Vermont	221	99	12	-	1	1	-	-	10	1
Virginia	7,141	119	224	112	19	31	24	21	472	360
Washington	5,741	349	375	38	10	6	6	2	183	155
West Virginia	205	4	4	3	-	-	-	-	40	10
Wisconsin	6	-	-	-	-	-	-	-	-	-
Wyoming	43	-	2	-	-	-	-	-	4	3
U.S. territories and possessions										
Guam	1,131	3	12	2	1	-	-	2	4	1
Northern Mariana Islands	32	-	-	-	-	-	-	-	-	-
Puerto Rico	1,852	2	44	116	241	1,116	2	6	5	2
Virgin Islands	752	4	1	1	-	30	1	1	12	-
Other or unknown	889	9	12	73	62	49	15	20	52	19

Source: U.S. Immigration and Naturalization Service, *Statistical Yearbook of the Immigration and Naturalization Service, 1993,* U.S. Government Printing Office, Washington, DC, 1994, pp. 142-143. *Note:* A dash (-) represents zero.

★ 66 ★

Immigration

Persons Naturalized, by State of Residence, 1993 - II

The number of persons naturalized in fiscal year 1993 is shown, by state of residence and country of former allegiance.

State of residence	All countries	Jamaica	Korea	Mexico	Philippines	Poland	Portugal	Taiwan	United Kingdom	Vietnam	Other
Total	314,681	7,976	9,611	23,630	33,864	5,551	3,978	7,384	10,158	22,427	95,555
Alabama	719	12	48	18	50	6	-	28	36	42	265
Alaska	530	6	62	21	200	7	2	7	8	16	134
Arizona	2,548	4	66	983	155	38	3	55	79	141	582
Arkansas	405	-	9	13	36	7	-	8	10	69	196
California	68,100	123	2,188	7,281	13,125	426	793	3,119	2,411	9,156	16,159
Colorado	2,732	13	155	357	149	74	3	56	138	370	950
Connecticut	6,125	541	59	19	146	478	582	13	314	177	2,003
Delaware	423	12	16	8	35	4	1	16	46	12	146
District of Columbia	773	51	7	5	57	1	2	-	27	13	434
Florida	26,628	1,673	108	141	670	133	30	83	444	516	6,010
Georgia	4,185	149	279	76	187	37	6	135	183	345	1,646
Hawaii	4,960	10	302	35	3,035	10	9	62	145	252	597
Idaho	255	1	5	56	19	3	3	2	18	19	91
Illinois	17,394	127	780	3,592	1,585	1,490	8	204	300	506	5,201
Indiana	1,395	12	41	187	88	36	2	21	54	62	518
Iowa	578	1	34	32	21	5	1	26	10	134	191
Kansas	1,085	4	42	118	71	7	2	44	28	145	405
Kentucky	534	16	42	10	51	19	-	17	35	39	165
Louisiana	2,016	14	28	35	108	7	1	32	37	505	814
Maine	584	3	9	1	20	3	3	3	26	22	95
Maryland	9,864	386	671	54	723	109	35	347	380	443	3,966
Massachusetts	6,574	115	81	18	103	124	816	110	337	607	2,235

[Continued]

★ 66 ★

Persons Naturalized, by State of Residence, 1993 - II

[Continued]

State of residence	All countries	Jamaica	Korea	Mexico	Philippines	Poland	Portugal	Taiwan	United Kingdom	Vietnam	Other
Michigan	6,091	37	190	94	350	267	2	119	187	228	3,394
Minnesota	1,921	9	60	39	66	25	3	20	60	291	992
Mississippi	426	4	17	14	43	2	-	13	15	91	137
Missouri	1,379	18	40	67	140	25	1	43	50	151	552
Montana	165	-	17	5	18	4	-	4	14	7	43
Nebraska	4,411	1	24	36	4,053	8	1	10	23	41	157
Nevada	1,518	6	71	208	362	10	6	27	67	83	396
New Hampshire	387	3	13	3	14	11	8	20	31	23	119
New Jersey	18,495	478	414	66	1,319	512	553	412	469	256	6,203
New Mexico	665	5	14	196	35	6	1	24	32	53	181
New York	55,519	3,517	1,160	175	1,590	842	231	799	1,736	610	19,659
North Carolina	2,397	28	80	33	145	37	1	76	151	215	1,014
North Dakota	159	2	8	5	19	3	1	-	6	11	48
Ohio	3,382	44	77	54	135	99	3	51	169	133	1,783
Oklahoma	1,092	8	49	116	73	5	1	13	42	210	381
Oregon	2,146	2	160	69	182	19	4	52	106	319	790
Pennsylvania	7,236	222	433	32	363	272	63	167	365	748	2,803
Rhode Island	1,720	2	8	8	51	14	734	-	33	22	485
South Carolina	675	6	32	9	91	10	1	16	39	47	237
South Dakota	85	3	8	4	23	4	1	1	4	2	22
Tennessee	1,039	11	56	18	62	6	1	37	62	64	436
Texas	26,403	174	539	8,968	1,117	156	15	775	656	3,454	6,449
Utah	950	3	37	64	46	15	1	13	41	110	416
Vermont	221	1	6	1	8	3	-	4	26	2	46
Virginia	7,141	67	507	56	793	48	17	75	255	887	3,054
Washington	5,741	21	456	169	1,035	91	5	183	282	739	1,636
West Virginia	205	-	8	4	22	-	-	7	9	2	92
Wisconsin	6	-	-	-	-	-	-	-	-	1	5
Wyoming	43	-	1	8	8	-	-	1	1	1	14
U.S. territories and possessions											
Guam	1,131	3	66	2	945	-	-	21	9	9	51
Northern Mariana Islands	32	-	2	-	27	-	-	-	-	-	3
Puerto Rico	1,852	2	-	22	1	-	-	2	8	2	281
Virgin Islands	752	10	-	1	5	-	1	-	123	1	561
Other or unknown	889	16	26	26	89	33	21	11	21	23	312

Source: U.S. Immigration and Naturalization Service, *Statistical Yearbook of the Immigration and Naturalization Service, 1993,* U.S. Government Printing Office, Washington, DC, 1994, pp. 142-143. *Note:* A dash (-) represents zero.

★67★

Immigration

Projected Annual Amount of Net Immigration, by Age Group and Race/Ethnicity, 1982 to 2080

Numbers are shown in thousands and do not sum to totals because persons of Hispanic origin may be of any race.

Age	Total	Spanish origin	White non-Hispanic	Black	Other races
Total	450.0	143.2	139.0	55.7	123.6
Under 18 years	139.3	43.3	48.5	18.3	32.4
18 to 24 years	76.9	34.7	15.2	9.5	20.1
25 to 44 years	176.0	51.3	60.6	20.7	47.9
45 to 64 years	49.3	11.1	16.1	6.0	17.0
65 years and over	8.2	2.9	-1.6	1.3	5.8

Source: Spencer, Gregory. U.S. Bureau of the Census. *Current Population Reports*, Series P-25, No. 995, *Projections of the Hispanic Population: 1983 to 2080*. Washington, D.C.: The Bureau, 1986, p. 18. Primary source: Current Population Reports, Series P-25, No. 952, appendix table C; and unpublished data.

★68★

Immigration

Refugee Applications and Admissions, 1983-93

The number of approvals are shown, by geographic area of chargeability, for fiscal years 1986-93. This number decreased five percent between 1992 and 1993.

Geographic area of chargeability	1986	1987	1988	1989[1]	1990[1]	1991[1]	1992[1]	1993[1]
Authorized admissions	67,000	70,000	87,500	104,500	110,000	116,000	123,500	116,000
Africa	3,000	2,000	3,000	2,000	3,500	4,900	6,000	7,000
East Asia	45,500	40,500	38,000	38,000	36,800	38,500	33,500	36,000
Eastern Europe & Soviet Union	9,500	12,300	30,000	50,000	58,300	53,500	64,000	51,500
Latin America & Caribbean	3,000	1,000	3,500	3,500	2,400	3,100	3,000	3,500
Near East	6,000	10,200	9,000	7,000	6,000	6,000	6,000	7,000
Unallocated reserve	NA	NA	4,000	4,000	4,000	10,000	11,000	11,000
Approvals	52,081	61,529	80,282	95,505	99,697	107,962	115,330	106,026
Africa	1,329	1,974	1,304	1,825	3,318	4,430	5,667	6,813
East Asia	35,193	37,082	41,450	35,196	30,613	33,560	31,751	38,314
Eastern Europe & Soviet Union	9,515	12,290	26,645	48,620	58,951	62,582	68,131	52,090
Latin America & Caribbean	47	99	2,452	2,848	1,863	2,263	4,121	3,991
Near East	5,997	10,084	8,431	7,016	4,952	5,127	5,660	4,818
Admissions[2]	58,329	66,803	80,382	101,072	110,197	100,229	123,010	113,152
Africa	1,279	2,068	1,708	1,998	3,585	4,564	6,152	7,098
East Asia	41,673	40,046	35,160	36,989	37,192	37,063	36,518	38,494
Eastern Europe & Soviet Union	9,270	12,450	28,906	48,416	57,081	46,726	65,230	50,844
Latin America & Caribbean	48	902	4,319	5,033	5,786	5,107	5,372	6,153

[Continued]

★68★

Refugee Applications and Admissions, 1983-93

[Continued]

Geographic area of chargeability	1986	1987	1988	1989[1]	1990[1]	1991[1]	1992[1]	1993[1]
Near East	6,059	10,619	9,486	7,699	5,636	5,895	8,834	7,847
Unknown	-	718	803	937	917	874	904	2,716

Source: U.S. Immigration and Naturalization Service, *Statistical Yearbook of the Immigration and Naturalization Service, 1993,* U.S. Government Printing Office, Washington, DC, 1994, p. 80. *Notes:* A dash (-) represents zero. NA stands for not applicable. Beginning in 1987, refugee admission data were compiled through the Nonimmigrant Information System. Since the system collects all entries of persons with nonimmigrant status, initial arrivals of refugees may be overstated. 1. The authorized admission levels for 1989, 1990, 1991, 1992, and 1993 were 116,500, 125,000, 131,000, 142,000, and 132,000 respectively, including 12,000 Amerasians in 1989 and 15,000 in both 1990 and 1991, 18,500 in 1992, and 16,000 in 1993. Since Amerasians enter the United States on immigrant visas, they are not included as refugee arrivals in the INS' data. As a result, the authorized admission levels for 1989, 1990, 1991, 1992, and 1993 for East Asia have been reduced accordingly. 2. Admissions may be higher than approvals because of the arrival of persons approved in previous years.

★69★

Immigration

Refugee Arrivals, by Selected Nationality, 1987-93

Number of arrivals is shown for each fiscal year indicated.

Nationality	1987	1988	1989	1990	1991	1992	1993
All nationalities	66,803	80,382	101,072	110,197	100,229	123,010	113,152
Afghanistan	3,241	2,380	1,991	1,835	1,690	1,841	1,536
Albania	49	74	44	103	1,354	1,195	484
Bulgaria	110	147	110	352	621	152	48
Cambodia	1,772	2,802	2,110	2,347	183	233	156
China[1]	416	162	210	133	192	1,229	269
Cuba	314	3,006	3,742	3,980	3,910	4,001	3,205
Czechoslovakia	373	247	257	246	175	36	13
El Salvador	74	60	74	136	110	259	1,006
Ethiopia	1,858	1,539	1,750	3,255	3,889	2,981	2,722
Ghana	7	17	12	17	35	191	11
Hungary	690	810	1,071	295	25	18	10
Iran	7,075	6,920	5,466	3,603	2,833	2,037	1,302
Iraq	186	37	115	73	812	3,466	4,561
Laos	15,508	14,561	12,779	8,667	9,212	7,964	6,853
Liberia	7	10	13	11	38	899	1,034
Nicaragua	486	1,155	1,053	1,239	883	361	346
Poland	3,734	3,670	3,792	1,883	573	249	115
Romania	3,203	2,953	3,369	4,625	4,803	1,664	382
Somalia	4	13	68	52	305	1,690	2,802
South Africa	69	35	22	39	17	10	14
Soviet Union	3,652	20,533	39,076	49,385	39,116	61,631	49,559
Sudan	3	-	6	8	31	134	229
Uganda	27	33	52	31	115	92	27
Vietnam	22,320	17,626	21,865	26,023	27,441	26,921	30,920

[Continued]

★ 69 ★

Refugee Arrivals, by Selected Nationality, 1987-93

[Continued]

Nationality	1987	1988	1989	1990	1991	1992	1993
Yugoslavia	578	400	619	130	35	123	59
Other	1,047	1,192	1,406	1,729	1,831	3,633	5,489

Source: U.S. Immigration and Naturalization Service, *Statistical Yearbook of the Immigration and Naturalization Service, 1993*, U.S. Government Printing Office, Washington, DC, 1994, p. 81. *Notes:* A dash (-) represents zero. Beginning in 1987, refugee admission data were compiled through the Nonimmigrant Information System. Since the system collects all entries of persons with nonimmigrant status, initial arrivals of refugees may be overstated. 1. Data for Mainland China and Taiwan are included in China.

★ 70 ★

Immigration

Refugee-Status Applications, 1993

Refugee-status applications made in fiscal year 1993 are shown, by geographic area and selected country of chargeability. The overall number of applications filed decreased five percent from the previous fiscal year. The number of applications approved also decreased, from 115,330 in 1992 to 106,026 in 1993. The leading countries approved were the former Soviet Union, Vietnam, and Laos—these, and Haiti, were also the top applicants.

Geographic area and country of chargeability	Applications pending beginning of year	Applications filed during year	Applications approved during year	Applications denied during year	Applications otherwise closed during year	Applications pending end of year
All countries	15,028	127,676	106,026	20,280	5,107	11,291
Latin America	139	10,920	3,991	6,928	96	44
Cuba	122	3,493	2,740	753	81	41
Haiti	4	7,421	1,246	6,175	4	-
Nicaragua	13	6	5	-	11	3
Africa	6,361	10,634	6,813	2,656	1,180	6,346
Angola	13	2	-	-	2	13
Ethiopia	2,887	1,384	2,779	573	406	513
Liberia	793	1,211	793	744	54	413
Mozambique	17	4	-	8	2	11
Somalia	1,519	6,940	2,758	1,062	265	4,374
South Africa	13	15	7	2	6	13
Sudan	312	924	243	130	100	763
Uganda	351	24	21	29	285	40
Zaire	434	106	201	104	57	178
Other Africa	22	24	11	4	3	28
East Asia	101	43,397	38,314	5,057	21	106
Burma	-	251	89	162	-	-
Cambodia	1	5	5	-	-	1
Laos	1	7,004	6,927	77	-	1
Vietnam	99	36,137	31,293	4,818	21	104

[Continued]

★ 70 ★

Refugee-Status Applications, 1993

[Continued]

Geographic area and country of chargeability	Applications pending beginning of year	Applications filed during year	Applications approved during year	Applications denied during year	Applications otherwise closed during year	Applications pending end of year
Eastern Europe and Soviet Union	2,756	55,671	52,090	2,781	1,567	1,989
Albania	864	653	413	462	494	148
Bosnia-Herzegovina	-	903	302	-	80	521
Bulgaria	87	36	31	6	43	43
Czechoslovakia	50	2	3	-	27	22
Hungary	18	2	-	-	9	11
Poland	638	40	54	-	286	338
Romania	653	300	227	163	206	357
Soviet Union[1]	446	53,735	51,060	2,150	422	549
Near East	5,671	7,054	4,818	2,858	2,243	2,806
Afghanistan	2,234	486	1,248	330	1,048	94
Iran	1,109	2,175	1,159	1,174	417	534
Iraq	2,327	4,381	2,410	1,346	778	2,174
Other	1	12	1	8	-	4

Source: U.S. Immigration and Naturalization Service, *Statistical Yearbook of the Immigration and Naturalization Service, 1993,* U.S. Government Printing Office, Washington, DC, 1994, p. 79. *Notes:* A dash (-) represents zero. 1. The Washington Processing Center, which handles the administrative processing of potential applicants residing in the former Soviet Union, received 84,826 pre-application questionnaires in fiscal year 1993.

★ 71 ★

Immigration

Refugees Granted Lawful Permanent Resident Status, by Calendar Year of Entry, 1993

Numbers of grantees in fiscal year 1993 are shown, by selected country of birth.

Region and country of birth	Total	1992	1991	1990	1989	1988	1987	1986	Before 1986	Unknown or not reported
All countries	115,539	34,086	63,034	10,708	3,670	1,494	529	374	1,577	67
North America	11,348	1,311	6,381	1,969	776	280	45	65	502	19
Caribbean	11,111	1,265	6,309	1,905	760	265	43	63	498	3
Cuba	11,083	1,253	6,305	1,900	754	265	43	63	498	2
Other Caribbean	28	12	4	5	6	-	-	-	-	1
Central America	220	45	64	61	14	15	2	2	2	15
El Salvador	11	3	5	-	1	-	-	-	2	-
Guatemala	5	2	-	2	-	-	-	-	-	1
Nicaragua	103	23	33	32	4	5	1	1	-	4
Other Central America	101	17	26	27	9	10	1	1	-	10
Other North America	17	1	8	3	2	-	-	-	2	1

[Continued]

★ 71 ★

Refugees Granted Lawful Permanent Resident Status, by Calendar Year of Entry, 1993

[Continued]

Region and country of birth	Total	1992	1991	1990	1989	1988	1987	1986	Before 1986	Unknown or not reported
South America	266	50	101	57	16	2	1	3	4	32
Europe	51,665	14,028	32,520	3,702	887	28	82	32	176	10
Albania	1,186	371	755	41	7	2	2	1	6	1
Bulgaria	225	37	156	29	-	-	-	-	3	-
Latvia	470	162	276	21	8	-	1	-	2	-
Lithuania	217	65	135	8	6	1	-	-	2	-
Poland	529	46	27	89	44	40	26	15	52	-
Romania	3,095	588	1,999	346	86	28	14	7	27	-
Soviet Union	45,373	12,670	28,708	3,066	699	128	29	3	62	8
Other Europe	570	89	274	102	37	29	10	6	22	1
Asia	47,833	17,035	21,704	4,645	1,928	971	396	265	883	6
Afghanistan	1,296	493	644	103	14	13	13	5	11	-
Cambodia	791	88	61	161	135	57	13	43	233	-
China, Mainland	78	16	48	9	1	1	2	-	1	-
Iran	2,988	754	1,577	323	172	89	38	15	20	-
Iraq	1,769	862	889	12	1	-	2	-	3	-
Laos	6,471	843	2,739	1,230	810	426	177	75	169	2
Lebanon	9	3	5	1	-	-	-	-	-	-
Pakistan	83	37	29	8	2	4	2	-	1	-
Thailand	3,722	711	1,674	640	311	215	55	39	74	3
Vietnam	30,233	13,128	13,881	2,080	463	157	90	84	349	1
Other Asia	393	100	157	78	19	9	4	4	22	-
Africa	4,424	1,660	2,327	335	63	13	5	9	12	-
Ethiopia	2,913	815	1,774	254	43	7	5	9	6	-
Liberia	111	108	3	-	-	-	-	-	-	-
Somalia	644	545	91	8	-	-	-	-	-	-
Sudan	373	106	213	43	9	-	-	-	2	-
Other Africa	383	86	246	30	11	6	-	-	4	-
Oceania	3	2	1	-	-	-	-	-	-	-

Source: U.S. Immigration and Naturalization Service, *Statistical Yearbook of the Immigration and Naturalization Service, 1993,* U.S. Government Printing Office, Washington, DC, 1994, p. 82. *Note:* A dash (-) represents zero.

★ 72 ★

Immigration

Refugees and Asylees Granted Lawful Permanent Resident Status, 1984-93

From the source: "In order to adjust to lawful permanent resident status, a refugee must reside in the United States for one year in refugee status....The number of refugees adjusting to lawful permanent resident status increased by nine percent from 1992 to 1993." Number of grantees in each fiscal year is shown, by selected country of birth.

Region and country of birth	1984	1985	1986	1987	1988	1989	1990	1991	1992	1993
All countries	92,127	95,040	104,383	91,840	81,719	84,288	97,364	139,079	117,037	127,343
North America	5,146	15,667	31,086	27,677	11,912	6,740	9,910	21,317	15,962	15,926
Caribbean	4,599	15,090	30,356	26,850	10,907	5,272	7,700	8,005	9,969	11,700
Cuba	4,560	15,080	30,333	26,817	10,846	5,245	7,668	7,953	9,919	11,603
Other Caribbean	39	10	23	33	61	27	32	52	50	97
Central America	512	556	682	785	964	1,416	2,143	13,221	5,959	4,188
El Salvador	112	166	289	172	170	198	245	1,249	743	811
Guatemala	32	7	18	13	37	33	58	296	169	210
Honduras	30	14	37	36	71	58	66	133	105	165
Nicaragua	319	347	324	555	645	1,075	1,694	11,233	4,668	2,892
Other Central America	19	22	14	9	41	52	80	310	274	110
Other North America	35	21	48	42	41	52	67	91	34	38
South America	178	124	195	155	260	175	264	320	442	461
Europe	16,068	14,008	11,868	9,684	11,418	18,348	33,111	62,946	42,721	53,195
Albania	26	39	43	44	66	55	64	75	539	1,198
Bulgaria	140	141	134	117	129	126	178	311	562	303
Czechoslovakia	936	958	841	1,075	1,164	640	883	659	319	119
Estonia	-	-	-	2	1	-	5	9	155	125
Latvia	6	1	1	1	9	8	6	34	315	493
Lithuania	1	5	1	1	8	5	11	75	157	228
Poland	5,601	4,813	3,949	3,357	4,242	3,842	3,903	4,205	1,512	731
Romania	3,226	4,426	4,308	2,959	3,028	3,338	3,186	4,276	4,971	3,654
Soviet Union	5,206	2,638	1,654	1,242	1,642	9,264	23,186	51,551	33,504	45,900
Other Europe	926	987	937	886	1,129	1,070	1,689	1,751	687	444
Asia	68,399	62,035	58,685	52,600	56,006	56,751	51,867	49,762	53,422	51,783
Afghanistan	3,032	2,555	2,600	2,141	2,597	2,606	2,144	2,100	2,082	2,233
Cambodia	11,663	13,365	13,300	12,206	9,255	5,648	4,719	2,550	1,695	808
China, Mainland	643	728	618	540	588	500	330	620	884	1,153
Iran	3,544	5,420	6,022	5,559	6,895	8,167	8,649	8,515	3,093	3,875
Iraq	1,862	951	367	310	268	191	141	193	365	1,856
Kuwait	7	7	5	-	4	4	4	11	13	114
Laos	12,094	8,921	7,556	6,560	10,348	12,033	9,824	9,127	8,026	6,547
Lebanon	43	34	41	24	29	116	118	318	140	204
Pakistan	30	59	68	65	101	142	157	166	129	185
Philippines	338	323	459	386	429	361	290	249	221	122
Syria	89	59	23	34	67	273	393	252	96	115
Thailand	2,216	2,349	3,240	3,751	3,587	4,347	4,077	3,603	4,048	3,724
Vietnam	32,033	26,775	23,930	20,617	21,407	21,883	20,537	21,543	32,155	30,249
Other Asia	805	489	456	407	431	480	484	515	475	598

[Continued]

★ 72 ★

Refugees and Asylees Granted Lawful Permanent Resident Status, 1984-93

[Continued]

Region and country of birth	1984	1985	1986	1987	1988	1989	1990	1991	1992	1993
Africa	2,322	3,201	2,547	1,719	2,121	2,269	2,212	4,731	4,480	5,944
Ethiopia	2,018	2,762	2,102	1,425	1,723	1,784	1,682	3,582	3,268	3,725
Liberia	1	2	2	7	6	7	26	42	25	239
Libya	17	31	27	37	54	71	84	175	143	172
Somalia	16	23	14	15	20	33	38	282	330	885
Sudan	66	180	121	83	80	97	60	184	369	443
Zaire	6	23	56	23	23	20	14	57	72	109
Other Africa	198	180	225	129	215	257	308	409	273	371
Oceania	5	5	1	3	1	1	-	1	9	34
Born on board ship	-	-	-	-	-	-	-	-	1	-
Unknown or not reported	9	-	1	2	1	4	-	2	-	-

Source: U.S. Immigration and Naturalization Service, *Statistical Yearbook of the Immigration and Naturalization Service, 1993,* U.S. Government Printing Office, Washington, DC, 1994, p. 90. *Notes:* A dash (-) represents zero. Data on refugees and asylees granted lawful permanent resident status for fiscal year 1987-88 have been adjusted. The data no longer include Cuban/Haitian entrants granted immigrant status.

★ 73 ★

Immigration

Refugees and Asylees Granted Lawful Permanent Resident Status, by Selected Area of Residence, 1993 - I

The number of refugees and asylees in fiscal year 1993 is shown, by selected country of birth and metropolitan statistical area (MSA) of residence.

MSA[1]	All countries	Afghanistan	Albania	Cambodia	China, Mainland	Cuba	El Salvador	Ethiopia	Iran
Total	127,343	2,233	1,198	808	1,153	11,603	811	3,725	3,875
New York, NY	14,158	434	415	18	354	198	15	64	242
Miami, FL	11,398	-	3	2	11	8,880	20	13	7
Los Angeles-Long Beach, CA	10,475	153	9	131	112	179	119	196	2,359
Orange County, CA	6,252	101	-	36	12	11	4	31	101
San Jose, CA	4,448	69	-	27	26	10	36	192	154
Seattle-Bellevue-Everett, WA	4,328	32	9	76	18	15	-	420	13
Chicago, IL	3,767	3	96	14	31	72	21	94	50
Boston-Lawrence-Lowell-Brockton, MA	3,426	5	84	76	15	25	10	88	10
San Francisco, CA	3,029	2	7	2	75	59	120	76	33
San Diego, CA	2,936	86	8	7	6	6	11	234	68
Philadelphia, PA-NJ	2,908	7	16	18	20	10	2	52	4
Sacramento, CA	2,876	19	-	2	5	2	1	7	6
Portland-Vancouver, OR-WA	2,721	31	1	10	8	1	-	50	7
Fresno, CA	2,702	-	-	26	9	2	13	18	9
Washington, DC-MD-VA	2,539	247	1	22	27	26	140	486	117
Oakland, CA	2,517	543	-	22	31	20	67	123	34
Minneapolis-St. Paul, MN-WI	2,456	12	-	15	10	-	5	167	11

[Continued]

★ 73 ★

Refugees and Asylees Granted Lawful Permanent Resident Status, by Selected Area of Residence, 1993 - I

[Continued]

MSA[1]	All countries	Afghanistan	Albania	Cambodia	China, Mainland	Cuba	El Salvador	Ethiopia	Iran
Houston, TX	1,853	-	-	9	29	41	31	101	20
Detroit, MI	1,776	2	144	-	1	-	-	6	11
Dallas, TX	1,672	11	6	-	8	26	17	199	57
Atlanta, GA	1,594	12	2	8	7	21	2	243	23
Cleveland-Lorain-Elyria, OH	1,314	-	6	4	2	2	-	8	6
Newark, NJ	1,031	38	23	-	6	120	1	15	7
Denver, CO	1,000	17	2	15	11	4	-	59	12
Riverside-San Bernardino, CA	894	34	-	5	4	21	8	8	18
Rochester, NY	820	-	-	2	1	19	-	39	-
Phoenix-Mesa, AZ	765	33	7	3	-	10	22	28	19
Fort Worth-Arlington, TX	719	7	-	-	3	4	1	9	12
St. Louis, MO-IL	707	13	13	-	3	5	-	47	14
Stockton-Lodi, CA	663	7	-	41	1	4	1	3	-
Tampa-St. Petersburg-Clearwater, FL	663	-	30	7	3	272	1	9	3
Jersey City, NJ	615	-	1	-	5	425	7	10	2
Fort Lauderdale, FL	566	-	1	-	6	157	5	1	12
Baltimore, MD	534	1	-	-	6	6	7	5	30
Bergen-Passaic, NJ	534	21	47	-	7	28	1	18	17
Milwaukee-Waukesha, WI	533	-	13	-	3	2	-	5	5
Hartford, CT	520	5	31	-	3	1	-	3	4
Jacksonville, FL	520	1	55	2	-	4	-	21	5
Merced, CA	515	-	-	-	-	-	2	-	-
Nashville, TN	513	24	-	-	9	-	-	19	4
Visalia-Tulare-Porterville, CA	500	-	-	-	2	-	1	1	-
Tacoma, WA	484	-	-	26	1	-	-	3	-
Buffalo-Niagara Falls, NY	476	1	3	-	7	-	-	16	4
Springfield, MA	471	-	1	1	2	-	-	2	-
Kansas City, MO-KS	466	-	10	3	1	10	-	23	15
Charlotte-Gastonia-Rock Hill, NC-SC	441	-	-	10	1	4	-	19	4
Columbus, OH	437	9	7	3	4	2	-	33	6
Lincoln, NE	431	6	-	-	-	-	-	-	-
Orlando, FL	419	-	5	-	3	84	-	7	1
Salt Lake City-Ogden, UT	418	-	1	3	5	-	-	3	5
Other MSA	17,305	237	121	153	216	670	99	423	304
Non-MSA	2,237	10	20	9	23	145	20	28	30
Unknown	1	-	-	-	-	-	-	-	-

Source: U.S. Immigration and Naturalization Service, *Statistical Yearbook of the Immigration and Naturalization Service, 1993*, U.S. Government Printing Office, Washington, DC, 1994, pp. 92-93. *Notes:* A dash (-) represents zero. 1. Ranked by the number of refugees and asylees.

★ 74 ★

Immigration

Refugees and Asylees Granted Lawful Permanent Resident Status, by Selected Area of Residence, 1993 - II

The number of refugees and asylees in fiscal year 1993 is shown, by selected country of birth and metropolitan statistical area (MSA) of residence.

MSA[1]	All countries	Iraq	Laos	Nicaragua	Romania	Somalia	Soviet Union	Thailand	Vietnam	Other
Total	127,343	1,856	6,547	2,892	3,654	885	45,900	3,724	30,249	6,230
New York, NY	14,158	5	13	20	315	13	11,267	1	231	552
Miami, FL	11,398	-	1	1,444	2	-	340	1	20	654
Los Angeles-Long Beach, CA	10,475	35	50	273	144	28	3,999	53	2,243	392
Orange County, CA	6,252	17	46	3	248	16	122	17	5,424	63
San Jose, CA	4,448	20	23	79	20	23	499	15	3,120	135
Seattle-Bellevue-Everett, WA	4,328	-	133	6	239	24	1,601	76	1,399	267
Chicago, IL	3,767	100	33	6	628	9	2,038	8	273	291
Boston-Lawrence-Lowell-Brockton, MA	3,426	11	19	5	21	36	1,846	41	960	174
San Francisco, CA	3,029	4	4	272	12	-	1,888	4	321	150
San Diego, CA	2,936	462	150	15	11	298	544	47	812	171
Philadelphia, PA-NJ	2,908	2	34	11	47	13	2,007	30	534	101
Sacramento, CA	2,876	7	359	21	115	-	1,515	276	445	96
Portland-Vancouver, OR-WA	2,721	8	48	1	265	12	1,563	12	629	75
Fresno, CA	2,702	-	1,611	5	-	6	72	875	48	8
Washington, DC-MD-VA	2,539	24	18	124	19	116	284	6	612	270
Oakland, CA	2,517	6	161	78	90	20	355	109	705	153
Minneapolis-St. Paul, MN-WI	2,456	6	618	3	16	20	823	330	361	56
Houston, TX	1,853	7	5	37	45	4	185	-	1,207	132
Detroit, MI	1,776	374	75	2	129	13	832	56	31	100
Dallas, TX	1,672	276	22	25	45	21	340	1	507	111
Atlanta, GA	1,594	-	36	6	48	49	418	8	623	88
Cleveland-Lorain-Elyria, OH	1,314	-	3	2	59	9	1,124	-	45	44
Newark, NJ	1,031	1	-	8	20	3	617	-	71	101
Denver, CO	1,000	-	28	2	28	3	441	16	273	89
Riverside-San Bernardino, CA	894	12	48	32	108	-	70	24	465	37
Rochester, NY	820	-	23	2	9	-	519	6	149	51
Phoenix-Mesa, AZ	765	8	2	6	109	7	168	1	275	67
Fort Worth-Arlington, TX	719	78	24	-	1	-	15	3	538	24
St. Louis, MO-IL	707	9	-	2	14	7	349	-	185	46
Stockton-Lodi, CA	663	6	169	2	-	-	5	144	260	20
Tampa-St. Petersburg-Clearwater, FL	663	-	17	-	6	-	63	5	204	43
Jersey City, NJ	615	-	-	12	4	-	64	-	61	24
Fort Lauderdale, FL	566	-	-	20	122	-	120	-	42	80
Baltimore, MD	534	-	-	-	7	8	393	-	31	40
Bergen-Passaic, NJ	534	-	-	3	11	1	330	-	3	47
Milwaukee-Waukesha, WI	533	1	163	11	-	1	205	66	39	19
Hartford, CT	520	1	6	1	14	7	276	1	135	32
Jacksonville, FL	520	6	-	2	38	-	250	2	64	70
Merced, CA	515	-	285	-	-	-	-	227	1	-
Nashville, TN	513	209	41	-	8	22	69	6	52	50
Visalia-Tulare-Porterville, CA	500	-	270	-	-	-	-	225	1	-
Tacoma, WA	484	2	13	-	-	-	204	16	190	29
Buffalo-Niagara Falls, NY	476	-	1	1	20	-	337	-	57	29
Springfield, MA	471	2	-	-	-	-	351	-	100	12
Kansas City, MO-KS	466	2	23	1	2	10	225	2	117	22
Charlotte-Gastonia-Rock Hill, NC-SC	441	-	26	6	10	4	97	11	233	16
Columbus, OH	437	-	8	-	2	-	279	1	40	43
Lincoln, NE	431	-	5	-	-	-	64	1	338	17
Orlando, FL	419	-	7	6	2	-	51	-	229	24

[Continued]

★ 74 ★

Refugees and Asylees Granted Lawful Permanent Resident Status, by Selected Area of Residence, 1993 - II

[Continued]

MSA[1]	All countries	Iraq	Laos	Nicaragua	Romania	Somalia	Soviet Union	Thailand	Vietnam	Other
Salt Lake City-Ogden, UT	418	-	8	-	-	-	204	2	170	17
Other MSA	17,305	139	1,520	287	531	62	5,776	862	4,924	981
Non-MSA	2,237	13	398	50	70	20	695	137	452	117
Unknown	1	-	-	-	-	-	1	-	-	-

Source: U.S. Immigration and Naturalization Service, *Statistical Yearbook of the Immigration and Naturalization Service, 1993,* U.S. Government Printing Office, Washington, DC, 1994, pp. 92-93. *Notes:* A dash (-) represents zero. 1. Ranked by the number of refugees and asylees.

Population

★ 75 ★

Population Distribution, 1980 and 1986-89

Data include Armed Forces overseas.

Percent distribution, by race/ethnicity	1989	1988	1987	1986	1980
All races	100.0	100.0	100.0	100.0	100.0
White	84.1	84.3	84.5	84.7	85.9
Black	12.4	12.3	12.2	12.2	11.8
Hispanic origin	8.3	8.1	7.9	7.7	6.5
Other races	3.5	3.4	3.2	3.1	2.3

Source: Hollmann, Frederick W. U.S. Department of Commerce. Bureau of the Census. *United States Population Estimates, by Age, Sex, Race, and Hispanic Origin: 1980 to 1988.* Current Population Reports, Population Estimates and Projections, Series P-25, No. 1045. Washington, DC: The Bureau, January 1990, p. 2.

★76★

Population

Population Distribution, by Age Group and Race/ Ethnicity, 1990

Age group	White	Black	Hispanic	Asian/Pacific Islander	American Indian	Other races
0 to 9	74.8	15.0	12.6	3.3	1.1	5.9
10 to 19	75.1	15.1	11.6	3.3	1.1	5.4
20 to 29	77.3	13.1	11.5	3.3	0.8	5.5
30 to 39	79.9	12.0	8.9	3.3	0.8	4.0
40 to 49	82.9	10.4	7.1	3.1	0.7	2.9
50 to 59	84.4	10.1	6.4	2.6	0.6	2.3
60 to 69	87.4	8.8	4.8	1.9	0.5	1.5
70 to 79	89.3	7.9	3.5	1.4	0.4	0.9
80 or older	90.4	7.5	3.2	1.0	0.3	0.8
All ages	80.3	12.1	9.0	2.9	0.8	3.9

Source: American Demographics (October 1991), p. 29. Primary source: 1990 Census. *Notes:* Hispanics may be of any race; therefore, the percentages do not total to 100.

★77★

Population

Population Distribution, by Reported Ancestry of Ethnic Group, 1990

The U.S. Census in 1990 asked people to identify their "ancestry of ethnic origin." Because the Bureau asked separate questions about race and Hispanic origin, it counted most Hispanics, Asians and Blacks under "other," which makes up 27.51% of the population.

Ethnicity	Percent
German	23.31
Irish	15.59
English	13.13
Italian	5.92
Mexican	5.43
American	5.25
French	4.16
Polish	3.77
Dutch	2.50
Scotch-Irish	2.26
Scottish	2.17
Swedish	1.88
Norwegian	1.56
Russian	1.19
French-Canadian	1.14
Puerto Rican	1.10
Welsh	0.82

[Continued]

★77★

Population Distribution, by Reported Ancestry of Ethnic Group, 1990

[Continued]

Ethnicity	Percent
Slovak	0.76
Danish	0.66
Chinese	0.66
Czech	0.65
Hungarian	0.64
Filipino	0.57
Portuguese	0.46
West Indian	0.46
Greek	0.45
Swiss	0.42
Cuban	0.42
Spaniard/Spanish	0.39
Austrian	0.35
Japanese	0.34
Lithuanian	0.33
Asian Indian	0.33
Korean	0.32
Ukrainian	0.30
Finnish	0.26
Vietnamese	0.25
Salvadoran	0.23
Canadian	0.23
Dominican	0.22
Sub-Sahara African	0.20
Yugoslavian	0.20
Belgian	0.16
Colombian	0.15
Romanian	0.15

Source: Usdansky, Margaret L. "Old ethnic influences still play in cities." *USA TODAY* (4 August 1992), p. 9A.

★78★

Population

Resident Population 65 Years of Age or Older

Estimates, by age and sex, 1980 and 1986-89. Numbers are shown in thousands.

Date and age	Total[1]			White			Black			Hispanic origin[2]		
	Total	Male	Female	Total	Male	Female	Total	Male	Female	Total	Male	Female
July 1, 1989												
65 years and over	30,984	12,636	18,348	27,822	11,347	16,475	2,555	1,025	1,529	1,073	447	626
65 to 69 years	10,170	4,631	5,538	9,029	4,130	4,899	916	402	515	401	181	220
65 years	2,175	1,001	1,174	1,921	888	1,033	204	91	113	93	42	50
66 years	2,045	935	1,111	1,812	832	981	187	82	104	87	40	47

[Continued]

★ 78 ★

Resident Population 65 Years of Age or Older

[Continued]

Date and age	Total[1]			White			Black			Hispanic origin[2]		
	Total	Male	Female	Total	Male	Female	Total	Male	Female	Total	Male	Female
67 years	2,089	954	1,135	1,857	852	1,005	186	81	104	81	36	44
68 years	1,987	905	1,082	1,781	815	966	164	71	93	74	33	41
69 years	1,874	837	1,037	1,657	743	914	176	75	101	67	29	38
70 to 74 years	8,012	3,464	4,549	7,193	3,120	4,074	661	274	386	264	110	153
70 years	1,741	772	969	1,552	690	862	154	66	88	61	26	35
71 years	1,708	751	956	1,541	680	861	134	57	77	55	23	32
72 years	1,619	700	918	1,457	632	824	131	54	76	51	21	30
73 years	1,487	632	855	1,338	571	767	120	48	71	49	20	29
74 years	1,458	608	850	1,306	546	760	123	49	74	47	19	28
75 to 79 years	6,033	2,385	3,648	5,430	2,147	3,282	486	187	299	197	77	120
75 years	1,376	566	811	1,237	510	727	113	44	68	45	18	27
76 years	1,297	521	776	1,165	468	697	106	41	65	43	17	26
77 years	1,212	476	735	1,089	428	661	98	38	61	40	16	24
78 years	1,120	432	688	1,009	389	620	89	34	55	36	14	22
79 years	1,028	391	637	930	353	577	79	30	50	33	13	20
80 to 84 years	3,728	1,306	2,422	3,409	1,189	2,220	256	91	165	121	46	74
80 years	921	338	583	832	304	528	72	27	45	30	11	18
81 years	815	290	526	750	265	485	51	18	33	26	10	16
82 years	720	253	467	661	231	430	47	17	30	24	9	15
83 years	669	228	441	614	208	406	44	15	29	21	8	13
84 years	603	198	405	552	181	371	42	14	28	19	7	12
85 to 89 years	1,962	588	1,374	1,791	531	1,260	142	45	97	63	23	40
85 years	515	164	351	470	148	322	37	12	25	17	6	11
86 years	448	137	311	408	124	285	32	10	22	15	5	9
87 years	387	114	272	353	103	250	28	9	19	13	5	8
88 years	332	95	237	303	86	217	24	7	17	10	4	7
89 years	281	78	203	257	70	187	20	6	14	8	3	5
90 to 94 years	790	195	594	719	174	544	61	17	43	20	7	14
90 years	234	62	171	213	56	157	17	5	12	6	2	4
91 years	190	48	142	174	43	130	14	4	10	5	2	3
92 years	151	36	115	138	32	106	12	3	8	4	1	3
93 years	117	26	91	107	23	84	9	2	7	3	1	2
94 years	97	23	74	87	20	67	9	3	6	3	1	2
95 to 99 years	229	53	176	200	46	155	25	7	18	6	2	4
95 years	77	19	59	69	16	52	8	2	6	2	1	1
96 years	58	14	44	51	12	39	6	2	5	2	1	1
97 years	42	10	32	37	8	28	5	1	4	1	0	1
98 years	30	7	23	25	5	20	4	1	3	1	0	1
99 years	22	5	17	19	4	15	3	1	2	1	0	0
100 years and over	61	13	48	50	10	41	9	3	6	1	0	1
July 1, 1988												
65 years and over	30,374	12,355	18,018	27,312	11,107	16,205	2,499	1,002	1,497	1,021	426	596
65 to 69 years	9,992	4,544	5,448	8,890	4,060	4,830	894	390	503	375	169	207
65 years	2,121	974	1,147	1,873	864	1,009	201	89	112	88	40	48
66 years	2,113	970	1,143	1,887	871	1,017	182	80	102	82	37	45

[Continued]

★ 78 ★

Resident Population 65 Years of Age or Older

[Continued]

Date and age	Total[1]			White			Black			Hispanic origin[2]		
	Total	Male	Female	Total	Male	Female	Total	Male	Female	Total	Male	Female
67 years	2,045	935	1,109	1,822	838	984	181	79	102	75	34	41
68 years	1,894	858	1,037	1,697	771	926	159	69	90	68	30	38
69 years	1,819	807	1,013	1,611	717	894	171	73	98	62	27	35
70 to 74 years	7,914	3,405	4,509	7,113	3,070	4,043	652	269	383	255	106	149
70 years	1,756	779	977	1,573	700	873	150	64	86	57	24	32
71 years	1,657	722	936	1,494	652	842	132	56	76	53	22	31
72 years	1,574	679	895	1,414	612	802	130	54	76	50	21	30
73 years	1,481	626	855	1,336	567	769	118	47	71	49	20	29
74 years	1,446	600	846	1,297	539	757	122	49	73	47	19	28
75 to 79 years	5,907	2,323	3,584	5,322	2,092	3,230	476	183	293	190	75	115
75 years	1,357	556	802	1,220	500	720	112	44	68	44	18	27
76 years	1,272	509	764	1,144	457	687	105	41	64	41	16	25
77 years	1,183	462	721	1,065	416	649	96	37	59	38	15	23
78 years	1,092	418	674	985	377	609	87	33	54	35	14	21
79 years	1,002	379	624	908	342	566	77	29	48	31	12	19
80 to 84 years	3,619	1,260	2,359	3,312	1,147	2,165	249	89	160	117	45	71
80 years	897	327	570	811	294	517	70	26	44	28	11	17
81 years	792	280	513	729	256	473	50	18	32	26	10	16
82 years	698	244	455	642	223	419	46	16	29	23	9	14
83 years	648	219	429	596	201	395	43	15	28	21	8	13
84 years	583	191	393	534	174	360	41	14	27	19	7	12
85 to 89 years	1,908	571	1,337	1,743	516	1,227	138	44	94	58	22	37
85 years	499	158	341	455	142	313	36	12	24	16	6	10
86 years	435	133	302	398	120	277	31	10	21	14	5	9
87 years	378	112	266	345	101	244	27	9	19	12	4	7
88 years	323	93	231	296	84	212	23	7	16	9	3	6
89 years	272	75	197	249	68	181	20	6	14	7	3	5
90 to 94 years	768	192	576	700	172	529	60	17	42	19	7	13
90 years	225	59	166	206	53	152	16	5	12	6	2	4
91 years	182	46	137	167	41	126	13	4	10	4	2	3
92 years	144	34	111	132	30	102	11	3	8	4	1	2
93 years	120	29	91	109	26	83	10	3	7	3	1	2
94 years	96	24	73	87	21	66	9	2	6	3	1	2
95 to 99 years	215	50	165	188	42	146	23	6	17	6	2	4
95 years	74	18	56	66	16	50	7	2	5	2	1	1
96 years	54	13	42	48	11	37	5	1	4	2	0	1
97 years	38	9	30	33	7	26	4	1	3	1	0	1
98 years	28	6	21	24	5	19	3	1	2	1	0	1
99 years	21	5	16	18	4	14	3	1	2	1	0	0
100 years and over	52	11	41	44	8	35	7	2	5	1	0	1
July 1, 1987												
65 years and over	29,841	12,119	17,721	26,874	10,909	15,965	2,446	981	1,465	973	405	567
65 to 69 years	9,888	4,494	5,394	8,825	4,029	4,797	870	379	491	350	157	193
65 years	2,190	1,010	1,179	1,949	904	1,046	197	87	109	83	38	45
66 years	2,070	952	1,118	1,853	857	996	177	78	99	76	35	42

[Continued]

★ 78 ★

Resident Population 65 Years of Age or Older

[Continued]

Date and age	Total[1]			White			Black			Hispanic origin[2]		
	Total	Male	Female	Total	Male	Female	Total	Male	Female	Total	Male	Female
67 years	1,952	888	1,064	1,738	794	943	176	77	99	70	31	39
68 years	1,841	829	1,013	1,652	746	906	154	67	88	63	28	35
69 years	1,834	814	1,020	1,633	728	906	166	71	96	58	25	33
70 to 74 years	7,786	3,333	4,453	7,000	3,004	3,995	647	266	381	250	103	146
70 years	1,706	750	957	1,528	673	855	148	63	85	54	23	31
71 years	1,613	701	913	1,453	633	820	132	55	76	52	22	30
72 years	1,569	673	896	1,412	608	804	129	53	76	50	21	29
73 years	1,470	618	852	1,327	560	767	117	47	71	48	20	28
74 years	1,428	590	837	1,280	530	750	122	49	73	46	19	27
75 to 79 years	5,780	2,264	3,516	5,214	2,039	3,175	465	180	285	182	73	109
75 years	1,334	544	790	1,200	490	710	110	44	67	43	17	26
76 years	1,245	495	749	1,121	446	675	102	40	62	40	16	24
77 years	1,156	450	706	1,042	405	638	93	36	57	36	14	22
78 years	1,067	407	660	964	367	598	84	32	52	33	13	20
79 years	978	368	611	887	332	555	75	28	47	30	12	18
80 to 84 years	3,522	1,222	2,299	3,225	1,113	2,112	244	88	157	113	44	69
80 years	874	318	556	791	286	506	68	25	43	27	11	16
81 years	771	271	500	710	248	462	49	18	31	25	10	15
82 years	679	236	443	625	216	409	45	16	29	23	9	14
83 years	630	212	417	579	194	385	42	15	28	20	8	12
84 years	567	185	382	520	169	351	40	14	27	18	7	11
85 to 89 years	1,864	559	1,305	1,705	505	1,200	134	44	91	53	20	33
85 years	487	154	333	445	139	306	35	12	23	16	6	10
86 years	427	131	296	391	119	272	31	10	21	13	5	8
87 years	370	110	260	338	99	239	27	9	18	10	4	7
88 years	315	91	225	289	82	207	23	7	15	8	3	5
89 years	264	73	191	242	66	176	19	6	13	6	2	4
90 to 94 years	754	191	563	688	171	516	58	17	41	19	6	12
90 years	217	57	160	199	51	148	16	5	11	5	2	3
91 years	176	44	132	161	39	122	13	4	9	4	1	3
92 years	148	38	110	135	34	101	12	4	8	4	1	2
93 years	120	30	90	109	27	82	10	3	7	3	1	2
94 years	93	23	70	84	20	64	8	2	6	2	1	2
95 to 99 years	204	48	156	179	41	138	21	6	15	6	2	4
95 years	70	17	53	63	15	48	6	2	5	2	1	1
96 years	50	12	39	45	10	35	5	1	4	1	0	1
97 years	36	8	28	32	7	25	4	1	3	1	0	1
98 years	27	6	20	23	5	18	3	1	2	1	0	1
99 years	20	5	15	17	4	13	2	1	2	1	0	0
100 years and over	44	9	35	37	7	31	6	2	4	1	0	1
July 1, 1986												
65 years and over	29,174	11,820	17,354	26,299	10,647	15,653	2,394	960	1,434	927	387	540
65 to 69 years	9,662	4,377	5,285	8,636	3,928	4,707	850	369	480	327	145	181
65 years	2,146	992	1,154	1,914	890	1,025	191	85	107	77	35	42
66 years	1,978	906	1,073	1,769	814	956	173	76	97	71	32	39

[Continued]

★ 78 ★

Resident Population 65 Years of Age or Older

[Continued]

Date and age	Total[1]			White			Black			Hispanic origin[2]		
	Total	Male	Female	Total	Male	Female	Total	Male	Female	Total	Male	Female
67 years	1,899	859	1,040	1,693	769	924	171	74	96	64	29	36
68 years	1,856	836	1,020	1,673	756	917	151	65	86	59	26	33
69 years	1,783	784	999	1,586	700	886	164	70	95	55	24	31
70 to 74 years	7,672	3,272	4,401	6,901	2,950	3,951	641	263	378	245	102	144
70 years	1,661	728	933	1,485	653	832	147	62	85	53	22	31
71 years	1,606	694	912	1,449	628	821	130	54	76	51	21	30
72 years	1,555	664	891	1,401	600	801	128	52	76	49	20	29
73 years	1,449	608	842	1,309	550	758	116	46	70	47	19	28
74 years	1,401	577	824	1,258	519	739	120	48	72	45	18	26
75 to 79 years	5,640	2,200	3,440	5,094	1,982	3,112	453	176	278	173	70	103
75 years	1,303	530	774	1,174	477	697	107	43	65	41	17	24
76 years	1,215	482	734	1,096	433	662	99	39	61	38	15	22
77 years	1,128	437	691	1,019	393	626	91	35	56	34	14	20
78 years	1,040	395	645	941	356	585	82	31	51	31	13	19
79 years	952	357	596	864	322	542	73	28	45	29	12	17
80 to 84 years	3,422	1,185	2,237	3,135	1,079	2,056	239	86	153	109	43	66
80 years	849	308	542	770	277	493	67	25	42	27	11	16
81 years	749	263	487	690	241	450	48	17	31	24	10	15
82 years	659	228	431	606	209	397	44	16	28	22	9	13
83 years	611	206	406	562	188	374	41	15	27	20	8	12
84 years	553	181	372	507	165	342	39	13	26	17	7	10
85 to 89 years	1,812	544	1,268	1,660	492	1,168	130	43	87	48	18	30
85 years	477	151	325	436	137	299	34	12	23	14	5	9
86 years	417	128	288	382	116	265	30	10	20	12	4	7
87 years	359	107	252	329	97	232	26	8	17	9	3	6
88 years	305	87	217	280	79	201	22	7	15	7	3	5
89 years	255	70	185	234	63	171	18	6	12	6	2	4
90 to 94 years	736	190	547	672	171	501	57	17	40	18	6	12
90 years	209	55	155	192	49	143	15	5	10	5	2	3
91 years	178	47	131	162	42	120	14	4	9	4	2	3
92 years	146	38	108	133	34	99	12	3	8	4	1	2
93 years	115	29	86	105	26	79	9	3	7	3	1	2
94 years	88	21	67	80	19	61	7	2	5	2	1	2
95 to 99 years	193	46	147	170	40	131	19	5	14	5	2	4
95 years	65	15	50	59	13	45	6	2	4	2	1	1
96 years	48	11	37	42	10	33	5	1	3	1	0	1
97 years	35	8	26	30	7	23	4	1	3	1	0	1
98 years	26	7	19	22	5	17	3	1	2	1	0	0
99 years	20	5	15	17	4	13	2	1	2	0	0	0
100 years and over	36	6	30	31	5	26	5	1	3	1	0	1

Source: Hollmann, Frederick W. U.S. Department of Commerce. Bureau of the Census. *United States Population Estimates, by Age, Sex, Race, and Hispanic Origin: 1980 to 1988.* Current Population Reports, Population Estimates and Projections, Series P-25, No. 1045. Washington, DC: The Bureau, January 1990, pp. 22-23. *Notes:* 1. Includes groups not shown in table. 2. Persons of Hispanic origin may be of any race.

★ 79 ★

Population

Urban/Rural Residence Distribution, by Hispanic Origin, 1991

Urban/rural residence	Total population	Hispanic origin population	Non-Hispanic population	Mexican origin	Puerto Rican origin	Cuban origin	Central and South American origin	Other Hispanic origin
Percent	100.0	100.0	100.0	100.0	100.0	100.0	100.0	100.0
Urban	74.0	91.8	72.8	90.5	95.2	95.7	97.0	84.9
Rural, non-farm	24.2	7.5	25.4	8.6	4.7	4.3	3.0	13.9
Rural, farm	1.7	0.6	1.8	0.9	0.1	0.0	0.0	1.2

Source: U.S. Bureau of the Census, *The Hispanic Population in the United States: March 1991.* Current Population Reports, Series P-20, No. 455, Washington, DC: U.S. Government Printing Office, 1991, pp. 16-17.

★ 80 ★

Population

Minority Populations, by State, 1990

	Hispanic	African American	American Indian[1]	Asian or Pacific Islander	Total combined non-white population[2]
California	7,687,938	2,092,446	184,065	2,710,353	12,674,802
Texas	4,339,905	1,976,360	52,803	303,825	6,672,893
New York	2,214,026	2,569,126	50,540	666,843	5,500,535
Florida	1,574,143	1,701,103	32,910	146,159	3,454,315
Illinois	904,446	1,673,703	18,213	275,568	2,871,930
New Jersey	739,861	984,845	12,490	264,341	2,001,537
Georgia	108,922	1,737,165	12,621	73,725	1,932,433
North Carolina	76,726	1,449,142	78,930	50,593	1,655,391
Michigan	201,596	1,282,744	52,571	102,506	1,639,417
Virginia	160,288	1,153,133	14,347	154,183	1,481,951
Pennsylvania	232,262	1,072,459	13,505	134,056	1,452,282
Maryland	125,102	1,177,823	12,143	136,619	1,451,687
Louisiana	93,044	1,291,470	17,539	39,302	1,441,355
Ohio	139,696	1,147,440	19,137	89,195	1,395,468
South Carolina	30,551	1,035,947	8,004	21,304	1,095,806
Alabama	24,629	1,017,713	16,221	21,217	1,079,780
Arizona	688,338	104,809	190,091	51,530	1,034,768
Mississippi	15,931	911,891	8,316	12,543	948,681
Tennessee	32,741	774,925	9,685	30,938	848,289
Hawaii	81,390	25,916	4,001	646,404	757,711
New Mexico	579,224	27,642	128,068	12,587	747,521
Massachusetts	287,549	274,464	10,545	140,338	712,896
Missouri	61,702	545,527	18,873	40,087	666,189
Washington	214,570	146,000	76,397	203,668	640,635
Colorado	424,302	128,057	22,068	56,773	631,200
Oklahoma	86,160	231,462	246,631	32,366	596,619

[Continued]

★ 80 ★

Minority Populations, by State, 1990

[Continued]

	Hispanic	African American	American Indian[1]	Asian or Pacific Islander	Total combined non-white population[2]
Indiana	98,788	428,612	11,999	36,618	576,017
Connecticut	213,116	260,840	5,950	49,114	529,020
Dist. of Columbia	32,710	395,213	1,252	10,734	439,909
Wisconsin	93,194	241,697	37,769	52,284	424,944
Arkansas	19,876	372,762	12,393	12,144	417,175
Kentucky	21,984	261,360	5,518	17,201	306,063
Kansas	93,670	140,761	20,363	30,814	285,608
Minnesota	53,884	93,040	48,251	76,229	271,404
Oregon	112,707	44,982	35,749	67,422	260,860
Nevada	124,419	76,503	17,480	35,897	254,299
Alaska	17,803	21,799	84,594	18,730	142,926
Delaware	15,820	111,011	1,938	8,854	137,623
Nebraska	36,969	56,711	11,719	12,026	117,425
Iowa	32,647	47,493	6,765	24,926	111,831
Rhode Island	45,752	34,283	3,629	17,584	101,248
Utah	49,489	7,060	12,654	21,132	90,335
Idaho	52,927	3,211	12,418	9,053	77,609
West Virginia	8,489	55,986	2,363	7,252	74,090
Montana	12,174	2,242	46,475	4,123	65,014
South Dakota	5,252	3,176	49,648	3,013	61,089
Wyoming	25,751	3,426	8,857	2,622	40,656
North Dakota	4,665	3,451	25,590	3,345	37,051
New Hampshire	11,333	6,749	2,042	9,197	29,321
Maine	6,829	4,937	5,898	6,505	24,169
Vermont	3,661	1,868	1,651	3,159	10,339

Source: "Ranking of total combined non-white population of states, 1990," *Black Issues in Higher Education*, (29 August 1991), p. 47. Primary source: *1990 Census of Population and Housing*, P.L. 94-171 Redistricting Data. *Notes:* 1. Includes Eskimo and Aleut populations. 2. Excludes other (non-white) race populations. This "Other Race" category was excluded to enable comparisons to 1980 census compilations. Nationally, nearly 10 million persons listed their race as "Other."

★ 81 ★

Population

Hispanic Population Distribution, by Age Group, Sex, and Ethnicity, 1991

Numbers are shown in thousands. Data are U.S. Census Bureau estimates.

Characteristic	Total population	Non-Hispanic population	Hispanic origin population	Mexican origin	Puerto Rican origin	Cuban origin	Central and South American origin	Other Hispanic origin
Age								
Total	248,886	227,448	21,437	13,421	2,382	1,055	2,951	1,628
Percent	100.0	100.0	100.0	100.0	100.0	100.0	100.0	100.0
Under 5 years	7.8	7.4	11.1	11.9	11.0	5.6	10.8	8.5

[Continued]

★ 81 ★

Hispanic Population Distribution, by Age Group, Sex, and Ethnicity, 1991

[Continued]

Characteristic	Total population	Non-Hispanic population	Hispanic origin population	Mexican origin	Puerto Rican origin	Cuban origin	Central and South American origin	Other Hispanic origin
5 to 9 years	7.4	7.2	9.6	10.7	9.3	4.5	7.9	7.5
10 to 14 years	7.1	6.9	9.1	9.4	10.7	4.1	9.0	7.4
15 to 19 years	6.8	6.6	8.5	9.1	8.6	5.3	7.0	8.6
20 to 24 years	7.2	7.0	9.5	10.4	7.4	6.2	9.2	7.4
25 to 29 years	8.3	8.2	9.9	10.2	8.9	8.2	10.6	8.7
30 to 34 years	8.9	8.8	9.8	9.6	9.3	8.8	11.5	9.3
35 to 39 years	8.2	8.3	7.5	6.6	9.2	8.3	9.0	8.5
40 to 44 years	7.3	7.5	6.2	5.8	6.1	7.0	7.3	6.9
45 to 49 years	5.7	5.8	4.4	4.1	5.0	4.8	5.3	4.7
50 to 54 years	4.6	4.7	3.7	3.0	3.8	8.7	4.1	4.8
55 to 59 years	4.3	4.4	3.1	2.5	3.7	6.4	3.3	4.2
60 to 64 years	4.3	4.4	2.7	2.4	2.2	7.3	2.1	4.4
65 to 69 years	4.1	4.3	2.1	1.9	1.7	4.7	1.4	3.0
70 to 74 years	3.3	3.4	1.4	1.1	1.5	4.1	0.7	3.1
75 to 79 years	2.3	2.5	0.9	0.7	0.7	3.1	0.5	1.7
80 to 84 years	1.5	1.5	0.5	0.5	0.5	1.8	0.2	0.7
85 years and over	1.0	1.0	0.2	0.1	0.3	1.0	0.2	0.6
16 years and over	76.4	77.2	68.5	66.3	66.3	85.3	70.8	74.8
18 years and over	73.8	74.6	65.1	62.6	63.3	82.8	68.1	70.8
21 years and over	69.6	70.5	60.0	57.0	59.1	79.3	63.9	66.8
55 years and over	20.7	21.6	10.9	9.3	10.6	28.4	8.4	17.6
65 years and over	12.1	12.8	5.1	4.4	4.7	14.7	3.0	9.0
75 years and over	4.8	5.1	1.7	1.3	1.5	6.0	0.9	2.9
Median age (years)	33.0	33.8	26.2	24.3	20.7	39.9	27.9	31.0
Sex								
Percent	100.0	100.0	100.0	100.0	100.0	100.0	100.0	100.0
Male	48.7	48.6	50.2	51.2	47.3	50.7	48.3	48.9
Female	51.3	51.4	49.8	48.8	52.7	49.3	51.7	51.1

Source: U.S. Bureau of the Census, *The Hispanic Population in the United States: March 1991.* Current Population Reports, Series P-20, No. 455, Washington, DC: U.S. Government Printing Office, 1991, pp. 10-11.

★ 82 ★

Population

Hispanic Population and Percent Distribution, by Ethnic Group and Geographic Region, 1990

Data are shown as of April 1 for persons who reported single and multiple ancestry groups. Persons who reported a multiple ancestry group may be included in more than one category. Major classifications of ancestry groups do not represent strict geographic or cultural definitions.

	Population (number)					Percent distribution by region			
	Total	North-east	Mid-west	South	West	North-east	Midwest	South	West
Cuban	859,739	157,247	29,269	594,106	79,117	18.0	3.0	69.0	9.0
Dominican	505,690	436,478	6,083	53,021	10,108	86.0	1.0	10.0	2.0
Hispanic	1,113,259	149,104	61,715	347,411	555,029	13.0	6.0	31.0	50.0
Mexican	11,586,983	142,829	1,021,049	3,774,379	6,648,726	1.0	9.0	33.0	57.0
Puerto Rican	1,955,323	1,289,858	209,974	293,124	162,367	66.0	11.0	15.0	8.0
Salvadoran	499,153	66,537	8,709	114,707	309,200	13.0	2.0	23.0	62.0
Spanish	2,024,004	331,319	158,061	614,708	919,916	16.0	8.0	30.0	45.0

Source: U.S. Bureau of the Census. *Statistical Abstract of the United States, 1994 on CD-ROM.* [machine-readable datafiles] Washington, DC: U.S. Government Printing Office, 1994. Primary source: U.S. Bureau of the Census, 1990 Census of Population, Supplementary Reports, Detailed Ancestry Groups for States (1990 CP-S-1-2).

★ 83 ★

Population

Hispanic Population, by Geographic Region, State and Ethnicity, 1990

Numbers are shown in thousands.

Region, division, and state	Hispanic origin[1]				
	Total	Mexican	Puerto Rican	Cuban	Other Hispanic
United States	22,354	13,496	2,728	1,044	5,086
Northeast	3,754	175	1,872	184	1,524
Northeast	568	29	316	16	207
Maine	7	2	1	(Z)	3
New Hampshire	11	2	3	1	5
Vermont	4	1	1	(Z)	2
Massachusetts	288	13	151	8	116
Rhode Island	46	2	13	1	29
Connecticut	213	8	147	6	51
Middle Atlantic	3,186	146	1,556	167	1,317
New York	2,214	93	1,087	74	960
New Jersey	740	29	320	85	306
Pennsylvania	232	24	149	7	52

[Continued]

★ 83 ★

Hispanic Population, by Geographic Region, State and Ethnicity, 1990

[Continued]

Region, division, and state	Hispanic origin[1] Total	Mexican	Puerto Rican	Cuban	Other Hispanic
Midwest	1,727	1,153	258	37	279
East North Central	1,438	944	244	30	220
Ohio	140	58	46	4	32
Indiana	99	67	14	2	16
Illinois	904	624	146	18	116
Michigan	202	138	19	5	40
Wisconsin	93	58	19	2	15
West North Central	289	209	14	6	60
Minnesota	54	35	3	2	14
Iowa	33	24	1	(Z)	7
Missouri	62	38	4	2	17
North Dakota	5	3	(Z)	(Z)	1
South Dakota	5	3	(Z)	(Z)	1
Nebraska	37	30	1	(Z)	6
Kansas	94	76	4	1	13
South	6,767	4,344	406	735	1,282
South Atlantic	2,133	315	338	702	778
Delaware	16	3	8	1	4
Maryland	125	18	18	6	83
District of Columbia	33	3	2	1	26
Virginia	160	33	24	6	97
West Virginia	8	3	1	(Z)	5
North Carolina	77	33	15	4	26
South Carolina	31	11	6	2	11
Georgia	109	49	17	8	34
Florida	1,574	161	247	674	492
East South Central	95	39	13	5	39
Kentucky	22	9	4	1	9
Tennessee	33	14	4	2	13
Alabama	25	10	4	1	10
Mississippi	16	7	1	(Z)	7
West South Central	4,539	3,990	55	28	466
Arkansas	20	12	1	(Z)	6
Louisiana	93	23	6	9	55
Oklahoma	86	63	5	1	17
Texas	4,340	3,891	43	18	388
West	10,106	7,824	192	88	2,002
Mountain	1,992	1,440	26	12	514
Montana	12	8	(Z)	(Z)	3
Idaho	53	43	1	(Z)	9
Wyoming	26	19	(Z)	(Z)	7
Colorado	424	282	7	2	133

[Continued]

★83★

Hispanic Population, by Geographic Region, State and Ethnicity, 1990

[Continued]

Region, division, and state	Hispanic origin[1] Total	Mexican	Puerto Rican	Cuban	Other Hispanic
New Mexico	579	329	3	1	247
Arizona	688	616	8	2	62
Utah	85	57	2	(Z)	25
Nevada	124	85	4	6	29
Pacific	8,114	6,384	166	76	1,488
Washington	215	156	9	2	47
Oregon	113	86	3	1	23
California	7,688	6,119	126	72	1,371
Alaska	18	9	2	(Z)	6
Hawaii	81	14	26	1	41

Source: U.S. Bureau of the Census. *Statistical Abstract of the United States: 1992,* (112th edition). Washington, DC: U.S. Government Printing Office, 1992, pp. 24-25. Primary source: U.S. Bureau of the Census, press release CB91-215. *Notes:* A (Z) stands for less than 500. 1. Persons of Hispanic origin may be of any race.

★84★

Population

Hispanic Population, by Race and State, 1990

State	Total population	Hispanic population: Total Number	Total %	White	Black	American Indian	Asian	Other
U.S. total	248,709,873	22,354,059	9.0	11,557,774	769,767	165,461	305,303	9,555,754
Alabama	4,040,587	24,629	0.6	15,630	2,992	285	580	5,142
Alaska	550,043	17,803	3.2	8,770	652	1,104	998	6,279
Arizona	3,665,228	688,338	18.8	337,001	5,715	13,436	3,676	328,510
Arkansas	2,350,725	19,876	0.8	11,662	1,150	380	386	6,298
California	29,760,021	7,687,938	25.8	3,495,201	116,355	58,099	135,306	3,882,977
Colorado	3,294,394	424,302	12.9	246,529	5,089	5,708	3,089	163,887
Connecticut	3,287,116	213,116	6.5	105,169	13,429	704	1,584	92,230
Delaware	666,168	15,820	2.4	7,002	1,449	81	203	7,085
District of Columbia	606,900	32,710	5.4	13,536	4,391	214	480	14,089
Florida	12,937,926	1,574,143	12.2	1,273,959	58,431	3,425	8,143	230,185
Georgia	6,478,216	108,922	1.7	56,723	9,400	727	2,056	40,016
Hawaii	1,108,229	81,390	7.3	21,972	1,279	1,098	38,832	18,209
Idaho	1,006,749	52,927	5.3	21,790	159	1,362	312	29,304
Illinois	11,430,602	904,446	7.9	402,770	20,570	3,623	9,743	467,740
Indiana	5,544,159	98,788	1.8	55,458	3,480	721	999	38,130
Iowa	2,776,755	32,647	1.2	19,250	597	584	550	11,666
Kansas	2,477,574	93,670	3.8	41,462	2,315	1,602	936	47,355
Kentucky	3,685,296	21,984	0.6	13,810	1,547	251	611	5,765

[Continued]

★ 84 ★

Hispanic Population, by Race and State, 1990

[Continued]

State	Total population	Hispanic population						
		Total		White	Black	American Indian	Asian	Other
		Number	%					
Louisiana	4,219,973	93,044	2.2	63,116	7,811	1,002	1,797	19,318
Maine	1,227,928	6,829	0.6	5,003	201	100	178	1,347
Maryland	4,781,468	125,102	2.6	67,855	12,076	829	3,100	41,242
Massachusetts	6,016,425	287,549	4.8	125,082	25,666	1,696	3,054	132,051
Michigan	9,295,297	201,596	2.2	106,135	8,962	3,067	2,477	80,955
Minnesota	4,375,099	53,884	1.2	29,129	1,904	1,658	1,657	19,536
Mississippi	2,573,216	15,931	0.6	9,263	3,166	209	473	2,820
Missouri	5,117,073	61,702	1.2	37,763	2,681	962	1,190	19,106
Montana	799,065	12,174	1.5	7,233	139	1,204	136	3,462
Nebraska	1,578,385	36,969	2.3	20,463	693	691	396	14,726
Nevada	1,201,833	124,419	10.4	66,338	2,268	2,157	2,230	51,426
New Hampshire	1,109,252	11,333	1.0	7,949	449	92	146	2,697
New Jersey	7,730,188	739,861	9.6	411,499	51,980	2,480	8,180	265,722
New Mexico	1,515,069	579,224	38.2	381,864	2,568	6,287	1,537	186,968
New York	17,990,455	2,214,026	12.3	925,066	289,929	12,111	26,917	960,003
North Carolina	6,628,637	76,726	1.2	37,364	7,181	1,225	1,573	29,383
North Dakota	638,800	4,665	0.7	2,550	73	327	117	1,598
Ohio	10,847,115	139,696	1.3	77,134	7,386	1,221	1,984	51,971
Oklahoma	3,145,585	86,160	2.7	35,924	2,339	5,789	1,197	40,911
Oregon	2,842,321	112,707	4.0	57,055	1,196	2,747	1,847	49,862
Pennsylvania	11,881,643	232,262	2.0	98,143	17,336	1,228	3,382	112,173
Rhode Island	1,003,464	45,752	4.6	21,266	4,578	442	741	18,725
South Carolina	3,486,703	30,551	0.9	16,918	3,937	242	1,078	8,376
South Dakota	696,004	5,252	0.8	2,727	82	927	110	1,406
Tennessee	4,877,185	32,741	0.7	20,437	3,110	354	901	7,939
Texas	16,986,510	4,339,905	25.5	2,483,082	45,272	13,074	15,634	1,782,843
Utah	1,722,850	84,597	4.9	44,591	708	1,535	881	36,882
Vermont	562,758	3,661	0.7	2,904	83	45	56	573
Virginia	6,187,358	160,288	2.6	90,089	9,861	935	4,870	54,533
Washington	4,866,692	214,570	4.4	87,315	3,801	5,086	7,290	111,078
West Virginia	1,793,477	8,489	0.5	6,627	309	95	207	1,251
Wisconsin	4,891,769	93,194	1.9	47,846	2,842	1,618	1,299	39,589
Wyoming	453,588	25,751	5.7	14,350	180	622	184	10,415

Source: U.S. Bureau of the Census, *1990 Census of Population and Housing, Summary Tape File 1C, United States Summary,* February 1992.

★85★

Population

Hispanic Population, by State and Ethnicity, 1990

State	Total population	Hispanic population					
		Total Number	Total %	Mexicans	Puerto Ricans	Cubans	Other Hispanic
U.S. total	248,709,873	22,354,059	9.00	13,495,938	2,727,754	1,043,932	5,086,435
Alabama	4,040,587	24,629	0.60	9,509	3,553	1,463	10,104
Alaska	550,043	17,803	3.20	9,321	1,938	277	6,267
Arizona	3,665,228	688,338	18.80	616,195	8,256	2,079	61,808
Arkansas	2,350,725	19,876	0.80	12,496	1,176	494	5,710
California	29,760,021	7,687,938	25.80	6,118,996	126,417	71,977	1,370,548
Colorado	3,294,394	424,302	12.90	282,478	7,225	2,058	132,541
Connecticut	3,287,116	213,116	6.50	8,393	146,842	6,386	51,495
Delaware	666,168	15,820	2.40	3,083	8,257	728	3,752
District of Columbia	606,900	32,710	5.40	2,981	2,204	1,241	26,284
Florida	12,937,926	1,574,143	12.20	161,499	247,010	674,052	491,582
Georgia	6,478,216	108,922	1.70	49,182	17,443	7,818	34,479
Hawaii	1,108,229	81,390	7.30	14,367	25,778	558	40,687
Idaho	1,006,749	52,927	5.30	43,213	665	164	8,885
Illinois	11,430,602	904,446	7.90	623,688	146,059	18,204	116,495
Indiana	5,544,159	98,788	1.80	66,736	14,021	1,853	16,178
Iowa	2,776,755	32,647	1.20	24,386	1,270	488	6,503
Kansas	2,477,574	93,670	3.80	75,798	3,570	1,403	12,899
Kentucky	3,685,296	21,984	0.60	8,692	3,682	1,075	8,535
Louisiana	4,219,973	93,044	2.20	23,452	6,180	8,569	54,843
Maine	1,227,928	6,829	0.60	2,153	1,250	350	3,076
Maryland	4,781,468	125,102	2.60	18,434	17,528	6,367	82,773
Massachusetts	6,016,425	287,549	4.80	12,703	151,193	8,106	115,547
Michigan	9,295,297	201,596	2.20	138,312	18,538	5,157	39,589
Minnesota	4,375,099	53,884	1.20	34,691	3,286	1,539	14,368
Mississippi	2,573,216	15,931	0.60	6,718	1,304	497	7,412
Missouri	5,117,073	61,702	1.20	38,274	3,959	2,108	17,361
Montana	799,065	12,174	1.50	8,362	437	124	3,251
Nebraska	1,578,385	36,969	2.30	29,665	1,159	480	5,665
Nevada	1,201,833	124,419	10.40	85,287	4,272	5,988	28,872
New Hampshire	1,109,252	11,333	1.00	2,362	3,299	578	5,094
New Jersey	7,730,188	739,861	9.60	28,759	320,133	85,378	305,591
New Mexico	1,515,069	579,224	38.20	328,836	2,635	903	246,850
New York	17,990,455	2,214,026	12.30	93,244	1,086,601	74,345	959,836
North Carolina	6,628,637	76,726	1.20	32,670	14,620	3,723	25,713
North Dakota	638,800	4,665	0.70	2,878	386	63	1,338
Ohio	10,847,115	139,696	1.30	57,815	45,853	3,559	32,469
Oklahoma	3,145,585	86,160	2.70	63,226	4,693	1,043	17,198
Oregon	2,842,321	112,707	4.00	85,632	2,764	1,333	22,978
Pennsylvania	11,881,643	232,262	2.00	24,220	148,988	7,485	51,569
Rhode Island	1,003,464	45,752	4.60	2,437	13,016	840	29,459
South Carolina	3,486,703	30,551	0.90	11,028	6,423	1,652	11,448
South Dakota	696,004	5,252	0.80	3,438	377	44	1,393
Tennessee	4,877,185	32,741	0.70	13,879	4,292	2,012	12,558
Texas	16,986,510	4,339,905	25.50	3,890,820	42,981	18,195	387,909

[Continued]

★ 85 ★

Hispanic Population, by State and Ethnicity, 1990

[Continued]

State	Total population	Hispanic population					
		Total		Mexicans	Puerto Ricans	Cubans	Other Hispanic
		Number	%				
Utah	1,722,850	84,597	4.90	56,842	2,181	456	25,118
Vermont	562,758	3,661	0.70	725	659	168	2,109
Virginia	6,187,358	160,288	2.60	33,044	23,698	6,268	97,278
Washington	4,866,692	214,570	4.40	155,864	9,345	2,281	47,080
West Virginia	1,793,477	8,489	0.50	2,810	897	261	4,521
Wisconsin	4,891,769	93,194	1.90	57,615	19,116	1,679	14,784
Wyoming	453,588	25,751	5.70	18,730	325	63	6,633

Source: U.S. Bureau of the Census, *1990 Census of Population and Housing, Summary Tape File 1C, United States Summary,* February 1992.

★ 86 ★

Population

Hispanic Population - Top 15 States, by Ethnic Origin, 1990

State	Total Population	Hispanic population					
		Total		Mexicans	Puerto Ricans	Cubans	Other Hispanic
		Number	%				
U.S. Total	218,949,852	14,666,121	6.70	7,376,942	2,601,337	971,955	3,715,887
California	29,760,021	7,687,938	25.80	6,118,996	126,417	71,977	1,370,548
Texas	16,986,510	4,339,905	25.50	3,890,820	42,981	18,195	387,909
New York	17,990,455	2,214,026	12.30	93,244	1,086,601	74,345	959,836
Florida	12,937,926	1,574,143	12.20	161,499	247,010	674,052	491,582
Illinois	11,430,602	904,446	7.90	623,688	146,059	18,204	116,495
New Jersey	7,730,188	739,861	9.60	28,759	320,133	85,378	305,591
Massachusetts	6,016,425	287,549	4.80	12,703	151,193	8,106	115,547
Pennsylvania	11,881,643	232,262	2.00	24,220	148,988	7,485	51,569
Washington	4,866,692	214,570	4.40	155,864	9,345	2,281	47,080
Michigan	9,295,297	201,596	2.20	138,312	18,538	5,157	39,589
Virginia	6,187,358	160,288	2.60	33,044	23,698	6,268	97,278
Ohio	10,847,115	139,696	1.30	57,815	45,853	3,559	32,469
Maryland	4,781,468	125,102	2.60	18,434	17,528	6,367	82,773
Georgia	6,478,216	108,922	1.70	49,182	17,443	7,818	34,479
Indiana	5,544,159	98,788	1.80	66,736	14,021	1,853	16,178

Source: U.S. Bureau of the Census, *1990 Census of Population and Housing, Summary Tape File 1C, United States Summary,* February 1992.

★87★

Population

Hispanic Population in U.S. Southwest Border States and Counties, by Ethnicity, 1980

State and county	All persons	Hispanic origin			Non-Hispanic origin
		Total	Mexican	Other Hispanic	
Total, border States	41,918,202	8,445,036	6,984,363	1,460,673	33,473,166
Percent	100.0	100.0	100.0	100.0	100.0
All border counties	9.6	17.2	18.9	8.8	7.6
All non-border counties	90.4	82.8	81.1	91.2	92.4
California	23,667,902	4,541,300	3,613,167	928,133	19,126,602
Percent	100.0	100.0	100.0	100.0	100.0
Border counties	8.3	7.2	7.7	5.3	8.5
San Diego	7.9	6.0	6.3	5.1	8.3
Imperial	0.4	1.1	1.4	0.2	0.2
Non-border counties	91.7	92.8	92.3	94.7	91.5
Arizona	2,718,215	444,102	397,940	46,162	2,274,113
Percent	100.0	100.0	100.0	100.0	100.0
Border counties	26.8	40.3	40.8	35.7	24.1
Cochise	3.2	5.1	5.3	4.2	2.8
Pima	19.6	25.1	25.0	25.7	18.5
Santa Cruz	0.8	3.4	3.6	2.0	0.2
Yuma	3.3	6.6	7.0	3.9	2.7
Non-border counties	73.2	59.7	59.2	64.3	75.9
New Mexico	1,302,894	477,051	228,706	248,345	825,843
Percent	100.0	100.0	100.0	100.0	100.0
Border counties	9.1	12.4	22.4	3.2	7.1
Dona Ana	7.4	10.5	18.8	2.8	5.6
Hidalgo	0.5	0.6	1.2	0.0	0.4
Luna	1.2	1.3	2.4	0.3	1.1
Non-border counties	90.9	87.6	77.6	96.8	92.9
Texas	14,229,191	2,982,583	2,744,550	238,033	11,246,608
Percent	100.0	100.0	100.0	100.0	100.0
Border counties	8.5	29.7	30.3	22.9	2.9
El Paso	3.4	10.0	10.3	6.3	1.6
Webb	0.7	3.0	3.1	1.9	0.1
Hidalgo	2.0	7.7	8.1	3.6	0.5
Cameron	1.5	5.4	5.0	9.9	0.4

[Continued]

★ 87 ★

Hispanic Population in U.S. Southwest Border States and Counties, by Ethnicity, 1980

[Continued]

State and county	All persons	Hispanic origin			Non-Hispanic origin
		Total	Mexican	Other Hispanic	
Other counties	0.9	3.6	3.8	1.2	0.3
Non-border counties	91.5	70.3	69.7	77.1	97.1

Source: U.S. Bureau of the Census, *The Hispanic Population of the Southwest Borderland*. Current Population Reports, Series P-23, No. 172, Washington, DC: U.S. Government Printing Office, 1991, p. 25.

★ 88 ★

Population

Proportions of Hispanic Population in the U.S. Southwest Border States and Counties, 1980

Area	Total population	Hispanic population	
		Number	Percent
United States	226,545,805	14,603,683	6.4
Non-border states	184,627,603	6,158,647	3.3
Border states	41,918,202	8,445,036	20.1
All border counties	4,009,079	1,449,156	36.1
All non-border counties	37,909,123	6,995,880	18.5
California	23,667,902	4,541,300	19.2
Border counties	1,953,956	325,956	16.7
San Diego	1,861,846	274,530	14.7
Imperial	92,110	51,426	55.8
Non-border counties	21,713,946	4,215,344	19.4
Arizona	2,718,215	444,102	16.3
Border counties	728,142	178,985	24.6
Cochise	85,686	22,848	26.7
Pima	531,443	111,378	21.0
Santa Cruz	20,459	15,229	74.4
Yuma	90,554	29,530	32.6
Non-border counties	1,990,073	265,117	13.3
New Mexico	1,302,894	477,051	36.6
Border counties	117,974	59,191	50.2
Dona Ana	96,340	50,171	52.1
Hidalgo	6,049	2,849	47.1
Luna	15,585	6,171	39.6
Non-border counties	1,184,920	417,860	35.3

[Continued]

★ 88 ★

Proportions of Hispanic Population in the U.S. Southwest Border States and Counties, 1980

[Continued]

Area	Total population	Hispanic population	
		Number	Percent
Texas	14,229,191	2,982,583	21.0
Border counties	1,209,007	885,024	73.2
El Paso	479,899	297,196	61.9
Hudspeth	2,728	1,589	58.2
Culberson	3,315	2,101	63.4
Jeff Davis	1,647	777	47.2
Presidio	5,188	3,989	76.9
Brewster	7,573	3,262	43.1
Terrell	1,595	691	43.3
Valverde	35,910	22,612	63.0
Kinney	2,279	1,310	57.5
Maverick	31,398	28,366	90.3
Dimmitt	11,367	8,869	78.0
Webb	99,258	90,823	91.5
Zapata	6,628	5,042	76.1
Starr	27,266	26,409	96.9
Hidalgo	283,229	230,287	81.3
Cameron	209,727	161,701	77.1
Non-border counties	13,020,184	2,097,559	16.1

Source: U.S. Bureau of the Census, *The Hispanic Population of the Southwest Borderland.* Current Population Reports, Series P-23, No. 172, Washington, DC: U.S. Government Printing Office, 1991, p. 24.

★ 89 ★

Population

U.S. Southwest Border Population Distribution, by Age Group, Sex, and Population Group, 1980

Characteristic	United States	Total, border states	Border states			
			Border county areas		Non-border county areas	
			Hispanic	Non-Hispanic	Hispanic	Non-Hispanic
Age						
Total persons	226,545,805	41,918,202	1,449,156	2,559,923	6,995,880	30,913,243
Percent	100.0	100.0	100.0	100.0	100.0	100.0
Under 15 years	22.6	23.0	34.1	19.0	33.0	20.5
15-24 years	18.7	19.1	21.6	20.2	22.3	18.2
25-34 years	16.4	17.6	15.5	17.7	18.0	17.6
35-44 years	11.3	11.6	9.8	11.0	10.3	12.0
45-54 years	10.0	9.7	8.2	9.6	7.5	10.3
55-64 years	9.6	8.9	5.6	10.3	4.8	9.9
65 years old and over	11.3	10.0	5.3	12.2	4.1	11.4
Median age	30.0	29.4	22.1	30.8	22.6	31.2

[Continued]

★ 89 ★

U.S. Southwest Border Population Distribution, by Age Group, Sex, and Population Group, 1980

[Continued]

Characteristic	United States	Total, border states	Border states			
			Border county areas		Non-border county areas	
			Hispanic	Non-Hispanic	Hispanic	Non-Hispanic
Sex						
Percent	100.0	100.0	100.0	100.0	100.0	100.0
Male	48.6	49.3	48.5	50.5	50.6	48.9
Female	51.4	50.7	51.5	49.5	49.4	51.1
Ratio (male/female)	94.6	97.2	94.2	102.0	102.4	95.7

Source: U.S. Bureau of the Census, *The Hispanic Population of the Southwest Borderland.* Current Population Reports, Series P-23, No. 172, Washington, DC: U.S. Government Printing Office, 1991, p. 19. *Notes:* For the purposes of this report, the U.S. Census Bureau included the following counties: San Diego, and Imperial counties, in California; Cochise, Pima, Santa Cruz, and Yuma counties, in Arizona; Dona Ana, Hidalgo, and Luna counties, in New Mexico; El Paso, Hudspeth, Culberson, Jeff Davis, Presidio, Brewster, Terrell, Valverde, Kinney, Maverick, Dimmit, Webb, Zapata, Starr, Hidalgo, and Cameron counties, in Texas.

★ 90 ★

Population

U.S. Southwest Border State Populations, by Place of Birth, 1980

Place of birth	United States	Total, border states	Border states			
			Border county areas		Non-border county areas	
			Hispanic	Non-Hispanic	Hispanic	Non-Hispanic
Total persons	226,545,805	41,918,202	1,449,156	2,559,923	6,995,880	30,913,243
Native born	212,465,899	37,266,745	1,042,295	2,381,013	5,042,762	28,800,675
Percent	93.8	88.9	71.9	93.0	72.1	93.2
Born in state	63.9	52.4	60.9	32.4	60.1	51.9
Born in different state	28.9	35.6	9.5	59.3	10.6	40.5
Born abroad	0.9	0.9	1.5	1.3	1.4	0.7
Foreign born	14,079,906	4,651,457	406,861	178,910	1,953,118	2,112,568
Percent	6.2	11.1	28.1	7.0	27.9	6.8

Source: U.S. Bureau of the Census, *The Hispanic Population of the Southwest Borderland.* Current Population Reports, Series P-23, No. 172, Washington, DC: U.S. Government Printing Office, 1991, p. 20. *Notes:* For this report, the U.S. Census Bureau included the following border counties: San Diego, and Imperial counties, in California; Cochise, Pima, Santa Cruz, and Yuma counties, in Arizona; Dona Ana, Hidalgo, and Luna counties, in New Mexico; El Paso, Hudspeth, Culberson, Jeff Davis, Presidio, Brewster, Terrell, Valerde, Kinney, Maverick, Dimmit, Webb, Zapata, Starr, Hidalgo, and Cameron counties, in Texas.

★ 91 ★

Population

Population of Hispanics by MSA in 1990 - I: A-K

Metropolitan Statistical Area	Total area population	Hispanic population										
		Ethnic origin						Race				
		Total	% of area's population	Mexican	Puerto Rican	Cuban	Other	White	Black	American Indian/ Eskimo/ Aleut	Asian/ Pacific Islander	Other
Abilene, TX MSA	119,655	17,511	14.6	15,500	274	39	1,698	7,282	211	84	107	9,827
Albany, GA MSA	112,561	928	0.8	402	146	37	343	485	194	16	35	198
Albany - Schenectady - Troy, NY MSA	874,304	15,840	1.8	1,240	8,148	590	5,862	9,390	1,436	90	248	4,676
Albuquerque, NM MSA	480,577	178,310	37.1	94,433	1,148	479	82,250	101,480	1,337	2,105	694	72,694
Alexandria, LA MSA	131,556	1,526	1.2	761	157	63	545	1,057	138	36	29	266
Allentown - Bethlehem - Easton, PA - NJ MSA	686,688	28,885	4.2	1,605	20,792	579	5,909	12,735	1,038	94	177	14,841
Altoona, PA MSA	130,542	431	0.3	112	98	8	213	315	17	3	8	88
Amarillo, TX MSA	187,547	25,390	13.5	21,689	167	71	3,463	10,276	246	232	159	14,477
Anchorage, AK MSA	226,338	9,258	4.1	4,606	1,134	167	3,351	4,568	418	443	483	3,346
Anderson, IN MSA	130,669	885	0.7	523	101	43	218	527	47	13	8	290
Anderson, SC MSA	145,196	559	0.4	205	117	23	214	371	54	10	6	118
Anniston, AL MSA	116,034	1,282	1.1	491	435	42	314	719	102	5	55	401
Appleton - Oshkosh - Neenah, WI MSA	315,121	2,280	0.7	1,497	150	53	580	1,378	23	49	80	750
Asheville, NC MSA	174,821	1,173	0.7	421	175	102	475	862	57	7	20	227
Athens, GA MSA	156,267	2,011	1.3	740	223	129	919	1,306	99	20	63	523
Atlanta, GA MSA	2,833,511	57,169	2	23,077	8,083	5,804	20,205	32,332	4,498	330	943	19,066
Atlantic City, NJ MSA	319,416	17,972	5.6	1,160	11,900	530	4,382	7,760	1,441	93	257	8,421
Augusta, GA - SC MSA	396,809	5,620	1.4	1,868	1,882	207	1,663	2,859	539	49	178	1,995
Austin, TX MSA	781,572	159,942	20.5	141,004	2,131	670	16,137	69,359	2,628	679	731	86,545
Bakersfield, CA MSA	543,477	151,995	28	134,995	2,044	294	14,662	37,587	1,280	1,406	1,662	110,060
Baltimore, MD MSA	2,382,172	30,160	1.3	6,007	7,672	1,783	14,698	18,270	4,075	323	917	6,575
Bangor, ME MSA	88,745	509	0.6	119	103	34	253	359	14	10	12	114
Baton Rouge, LA MSA	528,264	7,532	1.4	1,988	471	822	4,251	5,536	563	49	124	1,260
Battle Creek, MI MSA	135,982	2,583	1.9	1,942	145	25	471	1,438	125	37	24	959
Beaumont - Port Arthur, TX MSA	361,226	15,241	4.2	11,752	226	173	3,090	8,884	693	66	218	5,380
Bellingham, WA MSA	127,780	3,718	2.9	2,724	115	26	853	2,016	27	175	44	1,456
Benton Harbor, MI MSA	161,378	2,683	1.7	1,382	413	100	788	1,461	184	34	55	949
Billings, MT MSA	113,419	3,158	2.8	2,501	66	14	577	1,853	46	149	8	1,102
Biloxi - Gulfport, MS MSA	197,125	3,488	1.8	1,268	528	208	1,484	2,448	214	41	140	645
Binghamton, NY MSA	264,497	2,845	1.1	431	1,104	146	1,164	1,806	217	21	45	756
Birmingham, AL MSA	907,810	3,989	0.4	1,585	384	299	1,721	2,683	376	33	85	812
Bismarck, ND MSA	83,831	435	0.5	192	15	7	221	219	1	65	25	125
Bloomington, IN MSA	108,978	1,367	1.3	583	144	53	587	938	46	14	41	328
Bloomington - Normal, IL MSA	129,180	1,671	1.3	997	188	70	416	901	78	23	15	654
Boise City, ID MSA	205,775	5,556	2.7	3,346	129	41	2,040	3,768	34	135	58	1,561
Boston - Lawrence - Salem, MA - NH CMSA	4,171,643	193,199	4.6	10,069	78,774	6,797	97,559	85,916	21,011	1,244	2,397	82,631
Bradenton, FL MSA	211,707	9,424	4.5	6,006	1,271	452	1,695	5,760	429	62	35	3,138
Bremerton, WA MSA	189,731	6,169	3.3	3,299	565	97	2,208	3,213	134	220	684	1,918
Brownsville - Harlingen, TX MSA	260,120	212,995	81.9	200,811	444	196	11,544	169,070	258	229	148	43,290
Bryan - College Station, TX MSA	121,862	16,713	13.7	14,256	251	142	2,064	7,727	263	51	65	8,607
Buffalo - Niagara Falls, NY CMSA	1,189,288	24,347	2	2,405	16,017	543	5,382	11,227	1,743	285	222	10,870
Burlington, NC MSA	108,213	736	0.7	324	90	47	275	460	59	7	5	205
Burlington, VT MSA	131,439	1,171	0.9	216	179	53	723	907	35	13	21	195
Canton, OH MSA	394,106	2,854	0.7	745	249	76	1,784	2,273	158	30	22	371
Casper, WY MSA	61,226	2,252	3.7	1,662	43	2	545	1,435	20	42	12	743
Cedar Rapids, IA MSA	168,767	1,591	0.9	988	86	30	487	1,077	46	30	28	410
Champaign - Urbana - Rantoul, IL MSA	173,025	3,485	2	1,265	289	127	1,804	1,746	144	32	137	1,426
Charleston, SC MSA	506,875	7,512	1.5	2,774	1,702	393	2,643	4,289	770	55	447	1,951
Charleston, WV MSA	250,454	1,042	0.4	359	153	36	494	762	56	9	43	172
Charlotte - Gastonia - Rock Hill, NC - SC MSA	1,162,093	10,671	0.9	3,797	1,402	792	4,680	6,568	915	123	282	2,783
Charlottesville, VA MSA	131,107	1,384	1.1	379	173	84	748	993	71	4	29	287
Chattanooga, TN - GA MSA	433,210	2,539	0.6	830	339	170	1,200	1,639	188	22	73	617
Cheyenne, WY MSA	73,142	7,310	10	5,126	153	20	2,011	3,870	105	58	73	3,204
Chicago - Gary - Lake County, IL - IN - WI CMSA	8,065,633	893,422	11.1	616,293	152,480	17,334	107,315	393,777	20,086	3,317	9,101	467,141
Chico, CA MSA	182,120	13,606	7.5	10,758	277	67	2,504	6,958	123	295	209	6,021
Cincinnati - Hamilton, OH - KY - IN CMSA	1,744,124	9,376	0.5	3,342	1,288	606	4,140	6,405	748	119	350	1,754
Clarksville - Hopkinsville, TN - KY MSA	169,439	5,567	3.3	2,070	1,888	129	1,480	2,319	517	50	162	2,519
Cleveland - Akron - Lorain, OH CMSA	2,759,823	52,997	1.9	9,135	32,940	1,125	9,797	27,486	3,014	356	540	21,601
Colorado Springs, CO MSA	397,014	34,473	8.7	20,573	2,626	277	10,997	18,939	994	601	568	13,371
Columbia, MO MSA	112,379	1,226	1.1	492	108	53	573	780	71	20	36	319
Columbia, SC MSA	453,331	5,949	1.3	1,560	1,918	375	2,096	2,950	827	35	143	1,994
Columbus, GA - AL MSA	243,072	7,388	3	1,822	2,923	206	2,437	3,198	774	52	185	3,179
Columbus, OH MSA	1,377,419	11,363	0.8	3,723	2,144	674	4,822	6,820	1,047	149	517	2,830
Corpus Christi, TX MSA	349,894	181,860	52	167,292	573	349	13,646	113,617	850	438	474	66,481

[Continued]

★ 91 ★

Population of Hispanics by MSA in 1990 - I: A-K

[Continued]

Metropolitan Statistical Area	Total area population	Hispanic population - Ethnic origin: Total	Ethnic origin: % of area's population	Ethnic origin: Mexican	Ethnic origin: Puerto Rican	Ethnic origin: Cuban	Ethnic origin: Other	Race: White	Race: Black	Race: American Indian/ Eskimo/ Aleut	Race: Asian/ Pacific Islander	Race: Other
Cumberland, MD - WV MSA	101,643	420	0.4	83	72	12	253	311	27	2	23	57
Dallas - Fort Worth, TX CMSA	3,885,415	518,917	13.4	445,566	8,236	4,507	60,608	216,281	10,633	2,777	3,713	285,513
Danville, VA MSA	108,711	515	0.5	159	68	21	267	268	138	8	12	89
Davenport - Rock Island - Moline, IA - IL MSA	350,861	13,134	3.7	11,482	254	96	1,302	7,350	319	108	82	5,275
Dayton - Springfield, OH MSA	951,270	7,254	0.8	2,956	1,308	430	2,560	4,715	578	100	193	1,668
Daytona Beach, FL MSA	370,712	14,840	4	4,654	5,992	981	3,213	9,271	470	59	102	4,938
Decatur, AL MSA	131,556	686	0.5	374	82	29	201	476	47	9	4	150
Decatur, IL MSA	117,206	540	0.5	281	48	18	193	359	40	7	4	130
Denver - Boulder, CO CMSA	1,848,319	226,200	12.2	152,243	3,707	1,516	68,734	125,728	3,580	3,161	1,987	91,744
Des Moines, IA MSA	392,928	6,614	1.7	5,016	223	136	1,239	4,026	183	98	143	2,164
Detroit - Ann Arbor, MI CMSA	4,665,236	90,947	1.9	54,563	11,654	2,759	21,971	52,659	5,036	1,235	1,506	30,511
Dothan, AL MSA	130,964	1,679	1.3	551	443	61	624	955	134	8	49	533
Dubuque, IA MSA	86,403	437	0.5	200	50	20	167	290	3	9	1	134
Duluth, MN - WI MSA	239,971	1,153	0.5	530	135	41	447	743	24	79	16	291
Eau Claire, WI MSA	137,543	611	0.4	243	66	26	276	377	8	24	28	174
El Paso, TX MSA	591,610	411,619	69.6	391,847	4,007	454	15,311	301,199	1,585	956	665	107,214
Elkhart - Goshen, IN MSA	156,198	2,932	1.9	1,996	443	25	468	1,804	60	29	16	1,023
Elmira, NY MSA	95,195	1,441	1.5	118	640	40	643	570	332	22	41	476
Enid, OK MSA	56,735	1,086	1.9	783	38	8	257	497	18	63	33	475
Erie, PA MSA	275,572	3,364	1.2	517	2,195	63	589	1,702	296	21	37	1,308
Eugene - Springfield, OR MSA	282,912	6,852	2.4	4,374	328	71	2,079	4,407	67	190	138	2,050
Evansville, IN - KY MSA	278,990	1,321	0.5	556	147	90	528	959	70	16	36	240
Fargo - Moorhead, ND - MN MSA	153,296	1,879	1.2	1,430	36	5	408	907	8	42	29	893
Fayetteville, NC MSA	274,566	13,298	4.8	4,297	4,935	360	3,706	5,012	1,280	217	281	6,508
Fayetteville - Springdale, AR MSA	113,409	1,526	1.3	1,000	86	36	404	1,019	20	34	16	437
Fitchburg - Leominster, MA MSA	102,797	7,312	7.1	387	5,401	63	1,461	4,084	312	21	58	2,837
Flint, MI MSA	430,459	8,877	2.1	6,809	459	145	1,464	4,818	550	214	78	3,217
Florence, AL MSA	131,327	500	0.4	229	41	12	218	369	41	4	3	83
Florence, SC MSA	114,344	508	0.4	257	52	18	181	249	140	4	27	88
Fort Collins - Loveland, CO MSA	186,136	12,227	6.6	8,745	169	66	3,247	6,758	71	219	98	5,081
Fort Myers - Cape Coral, Fl MSA	335,113	15,094	4.5	5,068	5,155	1,124	3,747	10,195	669	69	118	4,043
Fort Pierce, FL MSA	251,071	10,680	4.3	4,358	2,226	877	3,219	6,036	622	82	75	3,865
Fort Smith, AR - OK MSA	175,911	2,120	1.2	1,252	150	114	604	1,217	71	99	94	639
Fort Walton Beach, FL MSA	143,776	4,427	3.1	1,344	1,272	405	1,406	2,958	172	39	187	1,071
Fort Wayne, IN MSA	363,811	6,268	1.7	4,562	374	140	1,192	3,146	270	61	114	2,677
Fresno, CA MSA	667,490	236,634	35.5	217,080	1,216	239	18,099	84,244	2,112	2,049	3,129	145,100
Gadsden, AL MSA	99,840	331	0.3	174	23	15	119	196	17	8	18	92
Gainesville, FL MSA	204,111	7,205	3.5	737	1,697	1,740	3,031	5,383	361	36	93	1,332
Glens Falls, NY MSA	118,539	1,789	1.5	180	807	106	696	1,001	341	22	16	409
Grand Forks, ND MSA	70,683	1,053	1.5	668	119	27	239	638	33	46	32	304
Grand Rapids, MI MSA	688,399	22,631	3.3	15,530	2,859	987	3,255	9,636	942	324	209	11,520
Great Falls, MT MSA	77,691	1,398	1.8	863	105	22	408	776	43	151	41	387
Greeley, CO MSA	131,821	27,502	20.9	22,981	67	28	4,426	15,270	58	192	70	11,912
Green Bay, WI MSA	194,594	1,525	0.8	984	136	40	365	752	20	193	29	531
Greensboro - Winston-Salem - High Point, NC MSA	942,091	7,096	0.8	3,050	862	535	2,649	4,031	689	84	153	2,139
Greenville - Spartanburg, SC MSA	640,861	5,120	0.8	1,707	774	345	2,294	3,390	319	54	146	1,211
Hagerstown, MD MSA	121,393	905	0.7	270	248	39	348	503	121	25	21	235
Harrisburg - Lebanon - Carlisle, PA MSA	587,986	10,239	1.7	1,235	6,511	405	2,088	4,668	940	68	152	4,411
Hartford - New Britain - Middletown, CT CMSA	1,085,837	75,627	7	2,066	58,220	2,056	13,285	30,959	5,577	225	485	38,381
Hickory - Morganton, NC MSA	221,700	1,449	0.7	598	171	62	618	860	70	10	27	482
Honolulu, HI MSA	836,231	56,884	6.8	10,820	17,068	413	28,583	14,756	1,158	732	26,418	13,820
Houma - Thibodaux, LA MSA	182,842	2,625	1.4	870	112	127	1,516	1,899	128	139	59	400
Houston - Galveston - Brazoria, TX CMSA	3,711,043	772,295	20.8	625,929	10,092	8,281	127,993	359,471	15,679	2,346	5,307	389,492
Huntington - Ashland, WV - KY - OH MSA	312,529	1,274	0.4	351	128	163	632	991	73	14	36	160
Huntsville, AL MSA	238,912	2,984	1.2	1,147	603	159	1,075	1,863	290	37	92	702
Indianapolis, IN MSA	1,249,822	11,084	0.9	6,005	1,266	454	3,359	6,879	838	128	264	2,975
Iowa City, IA MSA	96,119	1,435	1.5	649	130	69	587	944	38	15	29	409
Jackson, MI MSA	149,756	2,303	1.5	1,713	162	36	392	1,274	161	28	12	828
Jackson, MS MSA	395,396	1,944	0.5	762	129	100	953	1,067	454	24	52	347
Jackson, TN MSA	77,982	376	0.5	129	48	7	192	204	105	2	8	57
Jacksonville, FL MSA	906,727	22,479	2.5	4,623	6,747	2,491	8,618	14,447	1,670	164	993	5,205
Jacksonville, NC MSA	149,838	8,035	5.4	3,227	2,420	312	2,076	3,049	671	72	254	3,989
Jamestown - Dunkirk, NY	141,895	4,055	2.9	163	3,282	54	556	1,875	108	24	39	2,009

[Continued]

★91★

Population of Hispanics by MSA in 1990 - I: A-K

[Continued]

Metropolitan Statistical Area	Total area population	Hispanic population: Ethnic origin: Total	% of area's population	Mexican	Puerto Rican	Cuban	Other	Race: White	Black	American Indian/ Eskimo/ Aleut	Asian/ Pacific Islander	Other
Janesville-Beloit, WI MSA	139,510	1,754	1.3	1,300	92	36	326	1,015	45	13	53	628
Johnson City-Kingsport-Bristol, TN-VA MSA	436,047	1,690	0.4	696	207	111	676	1,293	26	26	37	308
Johnstown, PA MSA	241,247	1,216	0.5	565	180	60	411	958	53	8	16	181
Joplin, MO MSA	134,910	1,150	0.9	737	95	7	311	806	7	44	33	260
Kalamazoo, MI MSA	223,411	3,950	1.8	2,644	243	158	905	1,946	211	64	44	1,685
Kankakee, IL MSA	96,255	1,946	2	1,493	93	43	317	986	106	10	26	818
Kansas City, MO-KS MSA	1,566,280	45,227	2.9	34,569	1,680	1,508	7,470	23,337	1,599	561	634	19,096
Killeen-Temple, TX MSA	255,301	31,238	12.2	21,859	5,197	156	4,026	13,555	1,417	216	516	15,534
Knoxville, TN MSA	604,816	3,232	0.5	1,199	369	205	1,459	2,314	138	36	89	655
Kokomo, IN MSA	96,946	1,178	1.2	800	87	33	258	792	33	13	15	325

Source: U.S. Bureau of the Census, *1990 Census of Population and Housing, Summary Tape File 1C on CD-ROM, United States Summary,* February, 1992.

★92★

Population

Population of Hispanics by MSA in 1990 - II: L-Y

Metropolitan Statistical Area	Total area population	Hispanic population: Ethnic origin: Total	% of area's population	Mexican	Puerto Rican	Cuban	Other	Race: White	Black	American Indian/ Eskimo/ Aleut	Asian/ Pacific Islander	Other
La Crosse, WI MSA	97,904	640	0.7	202	57	69	312	365	33	8	122	112
Lafayette, LA MSA	208,740	3,115	1.5	1,078	167	162	1,708	2,250	283	22	42	518
Lafayette-West Lafayette, IN MSA	130,598	2,078	1.6	1,100	280	74	624	1,289	24	18	37	710
Lake Charles, LA MSA	168,134	1,847	1.1	922	117	64	744	1,259	180	25	22	361
Lakeland-Winter Haven, FL MSA	405,382	16,600	4.1	8,668	3,408	1,398	3,126	10,220	885	79	148	5,268
Lancaster, PA MSA	422,822	15,639	3.7	723	12,826	205	1,885	4,917	891	43	119	9,669
Lansing-East Lansing, MI MSA	432,674	16,963	3.9	13,041	705	455	2,762	7,548	564	220	165	8,466
Laredo, TX MSA	133,239	125,069	93.9	119,039	230	153	5,647	86,230	88	157	87	38,507
Las Cruces, NM MSA	135,510	76,448	56.4	68,995	347	59	7,047	68,276	204	204	151	7,613
Las Vegas, NV MSA	741,459	82,904	11.2	55,317	3,411	5,640	18,536	43,783	1,880	902	1,560	34,779
Lawrence, KS MSA	81,798	2,138	2.6	1,297	122	49	670	1,138	50	141	40	769
Lawton, OK MSA	111,486	6,923	6.2	3,830	1,625	72	1,396	2,479	361	341	186	3,556
Lewiston-Auburn, ME MSA	88,141	559	0.6	205	99	21	234	387	21	4	15	132
Lexington-Fayette, KY MSA	348,428	3,117	0.9	1,163	368	226	1,360	2,084	262	33	47	691
Lima, OH MSA	154,340	1,483	1	933	119	30	401	902	78	32	38	433
Lincoln, NE MSA	213,641	3,938	1.8	2,788	154	114	882	2,142	76	117	32	1,571
Little Rock-North Little Rock, AR MSA	513,117	4,164	0.8	2,303	358	118	1,385	2,701	240	61	85	1,077
Longview-Marshall, TX MSA	162,431	5,053	3.1	4,356	52	44	601	2,005	180	30	20	2,818
Los Angeles-Anaheim-Riverside, CA CMSA	14,531,529	4,779,118	32.9	3,751,278	62,008	57,864	907,968	2,158,798	72,187	27,903	64,081	2,456,149
Louisville, KY-IN MSA	952,662	5,765	0.6	2,114	838	361	2,452	3,731	541	45	172	1,276
Lubbock, TX MSA	222,636	51,011	22.9	46,479	246	74	4,212	24,623	508	93	106	25,681
Lynchburg, VA MSA	142,199	923	0.6	327	114	60	422	545	131	9	21	217
Macon-Warner Robins, GA MSA	281,103	2,832	1	1,265	432	225	910	1,551	360	21	63	837
Madison, WI MSA	367,085	5,744	1.6	2,992	585	251	1,916	3,560	208	79	120	1,777
Manchester, NH MSA	147,809	2,415	1.6	443	830	60	1,082	1,557	78	16	31	733
Mansfield, OH MSA	126,137	903	0.7	545	79	19	260	634	67	6	6	190
Mcallen-Edinburg-Mission, TX MSA	383,545	326,972	85.2	311,425	555	241	14,751	232,599	288	439	241	93,405
Medford, OR MSA	146,389	5,949	4.1	4,524	101	33	1,291	3,231	21	141	43	2,513
Melbourne-Titusville-Palm Bay, FL MSA	398,978	12,261	3.1	1,899	4,544	1,458	4,360	9,115	593	96	185	2,272
Memphis, TN-AR-MS MSA	981,747	7,986	0.8	3,557	787	705	2,937	4,348	1,381	56	247	1,954
Merced, CA MSA	178,403	58,107	32.6	52,826	467	53	4,761	23,579	634	381	1,019	32,494
Miami-Fort Lauderdale, FL CMSA	3,192,582	1,061,846	33.3	30,468	99,760	587,950	343,668	912,646	35,149	1,307	2,988	109,756
Midland, TX MSA	106,611	22,780	21.4	21,146	64	27	1,543	12,478	265	67	51	9,919
Milwaukee-Racine, WI CMSA	1,607,183	60,340	3.8	36,080	16,411	798	7,051	28,730	2,242	829	520	28,019
Minneapolis-St. Paul, MN-WI MSA	2,464,124	37,448	1.5	23,096	2,644	1,276	10,432	20,257	1,718	1,223	1,382	12,868
Mobile, AL MSA	476,923	4,186	0.9	1,310	390	208	2,278	2,958	411	54	84	679
Modesto, CA MSA	370,522	80,897	21.8	70,901	1,097	164	8,735	35,992	341	565	1,077	42,922
Monroe, LA MSA	142,191	1,194	0.8	741	65	20	368	825	100	22	14	233
Montgomery, AL MSA	292,517	2,124	0.7	792	377	166	789	1,250	345	20	62	447
Muncie, IN MSA	119,659	853	0.7	460	73	19	301	499	54	21	24	255
Muskegon, MI MSA	158,983	3,623	2.3	2,803	224	50	546	1,886	173	102	19	1,443
Naples, FL MSA	152,099	20,734	13.6	12,984	1,565	2,625	3,560	14,373	1,216	75	88	4,982

[Continued]

★ 92 ★

Population of Hispanics by MSA in 1990 - II: L-Y

[Continued]

Metropolitan Statistical Area	Total area population	Hispanic population: Ethnic origin: Total	% of area's population	Mexican	Puerto Rican	Cuban	Other	Race: White	Black	American Indian/ Eskimo/ Aleut	Asian/ Pacific Islander	Other
Nashville, TN MSA	985,026	7,665	0.8	3,446	847	481	2,891	4,921	619	124	250	1,751
New Bedford, MA MSA	175,641	7,347	4.2	225	5,028	68	2,026	3,691	607	43	17	2,989
New Haven - Meriden, CT MSA	530,180	32,907	6.2	1,538	24,623	744	6,002	16,344	2,075	89	213	14,186
New London - Norwich, CT - RI MSA	266,819	8,517	3.2	1,053	4,914	185	2,365	4,145	537	89	247	3,499
New Orleans, LA MSA	1,238,816	53,226	4.3	7,536	3,050	6,259	36,381	36,059	3,758	284	1,115	12,010
New York - Northern New Jersey - Long Island, NY - NJ - CT CMSA	18,087,251	2,777,951	15.4	106,159	1,290,135	154,942	1,226,715	1,264,816	322,043	13,259	32,751	1,145,082
Norfolk - Virginia Beach - Newport News, VA MSA	1,396,107	32,329	2.3	9,051	9,899	1,364	12,015	15,982	3,824	337	2,212	9,974
Ocala, FL MSA	194,833	5,860	3	935	2,527	566	1,832	4,233	302	22	49	1,254
Odessa, TX MSA	118,934	37,315	31.4	34,479	85	43	2,708	16,487	166	105	64	20,493
Oklahoma City, OK MSA	958,839	34,152	3.6	25,921	1,389	388	6,454	14,462	1,000	1,886	627	16,177
Olympia, WA MSA	161,238	4,873	3	2,680	633	100	1,460	2,854	103	184	302	1,430
Omaha, NE - IA MSA	618,262	16,371	2.6	12,522	815	313	2,721	9,225	551	245	267	6,083
Orlando, FL MSA	1,072,748	96,418	9	10,490	51,847	10,412	23,669	65,318	3,870	273	1,015	25,942
Owensboro, KY MSA	87,189	312	0.4	120	39	8	145	251	13	4	11	33
Panama City, FL MSA	126,994	2,256	1.8	726	519	228	783	1,566	101	46	64	479
Parkersburg - Marietta, WV - OH MSA	149,169	479	0.3	184	69	11	215	389	8	4	3	75
Pascagoula, MS MSA	115,243	1,060	0.9	408	162	41	449	799	69	5	28	159
Pensacola, FL MSA	344,406	6,236	1.8	1,955	1,232	422	2,627	4,018	329	93	367	1,429
Peoria, IL MSA	339,172	3,642	1.1	2,412	224	86	920	2,260	152	24	48	1,158
Philadelphia - Wilmington - Trenton, PA - NJ - DE - MD CMSA	5,899,345	225,868	3.8	15,858	155,688	7,421	46,901	81,935	20,815	1,041	3,124	118,953
Phoenix, AZ MSA	2,122,101	345,498	16.3	304,566	4,833	1,183	34,916	162,344	3,414	5,747	2,298	171,695
Pine Bluff, AR MSA	85,487	427	0.5	226	43	9	149	172	106	7	5	137
Pittsburgh - Beaver Valley, PA CMSA	2,242,798	12,852	0.6	4,083	2,117	477	6,175	9,450	1,162	169	188	1,883
Pittsfield, MA MSA	79,250	770	1	102	164	34	470	506	52	24	23	165
Portland, ME MSA	215,281	1,257	0.6	302	216	87	652	958	62	18	49	170
Portland - Vancouver, OR - WA CMSA	1,477,895	49,921	3.4	34,941	1,531	989	12,460	27,161	946	1,197	1,253	19,364
Portsmouth - Dover - Rochester, NH - ME MSA	223,578	1,994	0.9	602	457	113	822	1,450	54	26	48	416
Poughkeepsie, NY MSA	259,462	9,765	3.8	893	5,043	458	3,371	6,403	1,230	37	65	2,030
Providence - Pawtucket - Fall River, RI - MA CMSA	1,141,510	47,467	4.2	2,345	13,622	815	30,685	22,837	4,537	428	712	18,953
Provo - Orem, UT MSA	263,590	8,488	3.2	4,785	266	80	3,357	4,540	15	155	94	3,684
Pueblo, CO MSA	123,051	44,090	35.8	29,016	260	35	14,779	28,922	224	377	124	14,443
Raleigh - Durham, NC MSA	735,480	9,019	1.2	3,262	1,355	605	3,797	5,074	859	67	163	2,856
Rapid City, SD MSA	81,343	1,777	2.2	1,189	154	9	425	887	39	317	49	485
Reading, PA MSA	336,523	17,174	5.1	2,068	12,969	276	1,861	7,174	789	68	412	8,731
Redding, CA MSA	147,036	5,652	3.8	3,816	176	33	1,627	3,976	36	308	74	1,258
Reno, NV MSA	254,667	22,959	9	16,117	547	244	6,051	12,679	266	541	554	8,919
Richland - Kennewick - Pasco, WA MSA	150,033	19,940	13.3	17,806	142	48	1,944	6,187	90	115	114	13,434
Richmond - Petersburg, VA MSA	865,640	9,327	1.1	2,408	2,365	642	3,912	5,066	1,285	75	298	2,603
Roanoke, VA MSA	224,477	1,359	0.6	431	253	80	595	897	150	11	46	255
Rochester, MN MSA	106,470	970	0.9	437	68	37	428	625	21	15	80	229
Rochester, NY MSA	1,002,410	31,238	3.1	1,844	21,732	1,151	6,511	13,029	2,658	139	288	15,124
Rockford, IL MSA	283,719	9,836	3.5	7,715	394	250	1,477	4,959	209	48	90	4,530
Sacramento, CA MSA	1,481,102	172,374	11.6	135,067	4,861	923	31,523	86,094	3,429	2,992	4,981	74,878
Saginaw - Bay City - Midland, MI MSA	399,320	17,715	4.4	15,306	278	145	1,986	7,615	603	242	91	9,164
St. Cloud, MN MSA	190,921	910	0.5	399	70	44	397	594	7	27	31	251
St. Joseph, MO MSA	83,083	1,709	2.1	1,445	23	21	220	1,145	20	40	14	490
St. Louis, MO - IL MSA	2,444,099	26,014	1.1	13,059	2,283	1,071	9,601	18,076	1,588	322	545	5,483
Salem, OR MSA	278,024	21,027	7.6	18,092	303	132	2,500	8,849	101	367	219	11,491
Salinas - Seaside - Monterey, CA MSA	355,660	119,570	33.6	105,637	2,427	232	11,274	40,842	1,343	893	2,491	74,001
Salt Lake City - Ogden, UT MSA	1,072,227	61,964	5.8	42,077	1,719	338	17,830	32,635	663	929	679	27,058
San Angelo, TX MSA	98,458	25,501	25.9	23,339	290	23	1,849	11,891	181	93	47	13,289
San Antonio, TX MSA	1,302,099	620,290	47.6	567,478	6,853	1,339	44,620	401,669	3,550	1,863	1,678	211,530
San Diego, CA MSA	2,498,016	510,781	20.4	438,721	12,163	2,862	57,035	238,975	9,408	5,016	13,167	244,215
San Francisco - Oakland - San Jose, CA CMSA	6,253,311	970,403	15.5	669,043	33,720	7,639	260,001	504,552	19,003	9,175	34,724	402,949
Santa Barbara - Santa Maria - Lompoc, CA MSA	369,608	98,199	26.6	86,615	974	738	9,872	41,152	1,023	1,225	1,379	53,420
Santa Fe, NM MSA	117,043	50,947	43.5	16,939	148	101	33,759	34,537	118	552	81	15,659
Sarasota, FL MSA	277,776	5,882	2.1	1,740	1,163	1,072	1,907	4,741	218	12	36	875
Savannah, GA MSA	242,622	2,951	1.2	870	846	199	1,036	1,574	448	24	80	825
Scranton - Wilkes-Barre, PA MSA	734,175	5,640	0.8	697	2,305	320	2,318	4,125	268	41	86	1,120
Seattle - Tacoma, WA CMSA	2,559,164	75,555	3	41,346	6,274	1,504	26,431	40,068	2,852	2,325	4,966	25,344
Sharon, PA MSA	121,003	506	0.4	132	98	17	259	393	24	7	12	70
Sheboygan, WI MSA	103,877	1,668	1.6	1,288	67	19	294	942	18	33	62	613
Sherman - Denison, TX MSA	95,021	2,795	2.9	2,296	69	22	408	1,282	54	34	21	1,404
Shreveport, LA MSA	334,341	4,394	1.3	2,551	309	110	1,424	2,913	490	75	61	855
Sioux City, IA - NE MSA	115,018	3,728	3.2	3,221	77	26	404	1,640	43	227	52	1,766
Sioux Falls, SD MSA	123,809	648	0.5	325	33	5	285	407	15	35	25	166
South Bend - Mishawaka, IN MSA	247,052	5,201	2.1	3,704	313	92	1,092	2,529	237	29	37	2,369
Spokane, WA MSA	361,364	6,994	1.9	4,241	451	112	2,190	4,313	133	323	217	2,008
Springfield, IL MSA	189,550	1,311	0.7	626	141	52	492	979	67	9	21	235
Springfield, MO MSA	240,593	1,991	0.8	1,043	199	62	687	1,421	37	43	41	449
Springfield, MA MSA	529,519	47,635	9	812	41,556	410	4,857	15,305	2,229	123	224	29,754
State College, PA MSA	123,786	1,350	1.1	207	476	72	595	897	75	8	24	346
Steubenville - Weirton, OH - WV MSA	142,523	710	0.5	238	59	33	380	557	7	12	15	119

[Continued]

★92★

Population of Hispanics by MSA in 1990 - II: L-Y

[Continued]

Metropolitan Statistical Area	Total area population	Hispanic population										
		Ethnic origin						Race				
		Total	% of area's population	Mexican	Puerto Rican	Cuban	Other	White	Black	American Indian/ Eskimo/ Aleut	Asian/ Pacific Islander	Other
Stockton, CA MSA	480,628	112,673	23.4	98,889	1,715	214	11,855	70,403	2,303	1,278	3,916	34,773
Syracuse, NY MSA	659,864	8,926	1.4	1,226	4,313	336	3,051	5,129	889	119	175	2,614
Tallahassee, FL MSA	233,598	5,679	2.4	1,188	1,132	1,202	2,157	3,645	416	33	78	1,507
Tampa - St. Petersburg - Clearwater, FL MSA	2,067,959	139,248	6.7	26,041	34,986	32,205	46,016	108,215	4,231	444	862	25,496
Terre Haute, IN MSA	130,812	1,063	0.8	432	91	209	331	647	124	21	6	265
Texarkana, TX - Texarkana, AR MSA	120,132	1,644	1.4	1,109	72	111	352	1,113	124	15	12	380
Toledo, OH MSA	614,128	20,382	3.3	16,883	621	226	2,652	9,702	627	155	128	9,770
Topeka, KS MSA	160,976	7,785	4.8	6,609	313	94	769	3,939	307	176	76	3,287
Tucson, AZ MSA	666,880	163,262	24.5	147,547	1,764	628	13,323	70,057	1,340	3,325	736	87,804
Tulsa, OK MSA	708,954	14,534	2.1	9,513	1,078	363	3,580	7,787	535	921	188	5,103
Tuscaloosa, AL MSA	150,522	948	0.6	353	106	59	430	597	105	12	36	198
Tyler, TX MSA	151,309	8,986	5.9	7,879	102	28	977	3,823	283	42	15	4,823
Utica - Rome, NY MSA	316,633	6,174	1.9	648	3,892	107	1,527	3,139	1,029	45	87	1,874
Victoria, TX MSA	74,361	25,372	34.1	23,530	142	41	1,659	15,416	268	67	32	9,589
Visalia - Tulare - Porterville, CA MSA	311,921	120,893	38.8	113,416	724	75	6,678	34,552	313	764	851	84,413
Waco, TX MSA	189,123	23,643	12.5	21,309	263	103	1,968	11,593	484	91	61	11,414
Washington, DC - MD - VA MSA	3,923,574	224,786	5.7	29,002	19,645	9,097	167,042	118,800	14,912	1,042	4,566	85,466
Waterbury, CT MSA	221,629	16,384	7.4	312	12,876	260	2,936	8,235	928	45	61	7,115
Waterloo - Cedar Falls, IA MSA	146,611	984	0.7	618	56	31	279	603	27	13	27	314
Wausau, WI MSA	115,400	470	0.4	200	32	14	224	262	2	13	70	123
West Palm Beach - Boca Raton - Delray Beach, FL MSA	863,518	66,613	7.7	15,228	12,366	16,339	22,680	48,829	4,396	183	328	12,877
Wheeling, WV - OH MSA	159,301	569	0.4	187	47	10	325	491	20	7	8	43
Wichita, KS MSA	485,270	19,793	4.1	16,267	587	294	2,645	8,619	578	387	228	9,981
Wichita Falls, TX MSA	122,378	10,555	8.6	9,063	328	53	1,111	4,300	235	90	73	5,857
Williamsport, PA MSA	118,710	641	0.5	172	224	34	211	447	37	8	15	134
Wilmington, NC MSA	120,284	924	0.8	294	170	91	369	607	114	9	4	190
Worcester, MA MSA	436,905	20,009	4.6	742	14,148	537	4,582	8,656	1,075	139	192	9,947
Yakima, WA MSA	188,823	45,114	23.9	41,048	115	50	3,901	7,367	153	710	255	36,629
York, PA MSA	417,848	6,381	1.5	1,183	3,925	147	1,126	2,710	492	35	55	3,089
Youngstown - Warren, OH MSA	492,619	7,400	1.5	1,286	4,409	124	1,581	4,083	553	48	36	2,680
Yuba City, CA MSA	122,643	17,320	14.1	14,681	316	32	2,291	5,998	150	260	623	10,289
Yuma, AZ MSA	106,895	43,388	40.6	41,374	316	62	1,636	22,551	280	251	205	20,101

Source: U.S. Bureau of the Census, *1990 Census of Population and Housing, Summary Tape File 1C on CD-ROM, United States Summary,* February, 1992.

★93★

Population

Metropolitan Statistical Area Populations Close to the Mexican Border, by Hispanic and Non-Hispanic Origin, 1970-85 - I

Metropolitan statistical area	Hispanic origin						
	1970	1980[1]	1985[2]	Change, 1970-80		Change, 1980-85	
				Number	Percent	Number	Percent
United States	9,072,000	14,251,000	17,517,000	5,532,000	57.0	2,914,000	22.9
All MSAs	7,500,000	12,687,000	15,699,000	5,187,000	69.2	3,012,000	23.7
Total selected MSAs	686,000	1,225,000	1,501,000	539,000	78.6	276,000	22.5
Tucson, AZ	64,000	112,000	132,000	48,000	75.0	20,000	17.9
San Diego, CA	121,000	274,000	358,000	153,000	126.4	84,000	30.7
Las Cruces, NM[3]	30,000	51,000	65,000	21,000	70.0	14,000	27.5
El Paso, TX	182,000	300,000	360,000	118,000	64.8	60,000	20.0
Laredo, TX	57,000	92,000	110,000	35,000	61.4	18,000	19.6

[Continued]

★93★

Metropolitan Statistical Area Populations Close to the Mexican Border, by Hispanic and Non-Hispanic Origin, 1970-85 - I

[Continued]

Metropolitan statistical area	Hispanic origin						
	1970	1980[1]	1985[2]	Change, 1970-80 Number	Change, 1970-80 Percent	Change, 1980-85 Number	Change, 1980-85 Percent
McAllen-Pharr-Edinburg, TX	132,000	232,000	281,000	100,000	75.8	49,000	21.1
Brownsville-Harlingen-San Benito, TX	100,000	164,000	195,000	64,000	64.0	31,000	18.9

Source: U.S. Bureau of the Census, *The Hispanic Population of the Southwest Borderland*. Current Population Reports, Series P-23, No. 172, Washington, DC: U.S. Government Printing Office, 1991, p. 16. *Notes:* 1. Shows modified 1980 census counts. See note 2 below. 2. Estimates of Hispanics for 1985 were derived by using 1980 census counts modified to correct census Hispanic reporting errors. These errors were relatively minor, however, in the above areas. See: U.S. Bureau of the Census, *Current Population Reports: Population Estimates by Race and Hispanic Origin, for States, Metropolitan Areas, and Selected Counties: 1980 to 1985*, Series P-25, No. 1040-RD-1, U.S. Government Printing Office, Washington, D.C., 1989. 3. The Las Cruces area was not constituted SMSA in 1970; hence total for that year is for Las Cruces county.

★94★

Population

Metropolitan Statistical Area Populations Close to the Mexican Border, by Hispanic and Non-Hispanic Origin, 1970-85 - II

Metropolitan statistical area	Non-Hispanic origin						
	1970	1980	1985	Change, 1970-80 Number	Change, 1970-80 Percent	Change, 1980-85 Number	Change, 1980-85 Percent
United States	194,140,000	212,291,000	221,181,000	18,151,000	9.3	8,890,000	4.2
All MSAs	131,919,000	159,768,000	166,982,000	27,849,000	21.1	7,214,000	4.5
Total selected MSAs	1,847,000	2,337,000	2,608,000	490,000	26.5	271,000	11.6
Tucson, AZ	288,000	419,000	453,000	131,000	45.5	34,000	8.1
San Diego	1,237,000	1,588,000	1,774,000	351,000	28.4	186,000	11.7
Las Cruces, NM[3]	40,000	46,000	54,000	6,000	15.0	8,000	17.4
El Paso, TX	177,000	180,000	186,000	3,000	1.7	6,000	3.3
Laredo, TX	16,000	7,000	8,000	(9,000)	-56.3	1,000	14.3
McAllen-Pharr-Edinburg, TX	50,000	51,000	75,000	1,000	2.0	24,000	47.1
Brownsville-Harlingen-San Benito, TX	40,000	46,000	57,000	6,000	15.0	11,000	23.9

Source: U.S. Bureau of the Census, *The Hispanic Population of the Southwest Borderland*. Current Population Reports, Series P-23, No. 172, Washington, DC: U.S. Government Printing Office, 1991, p. 16. *Notes:* 1. Shows modified 1980 census counts. See note 2 below. 2. Estimates of Hispanics for 1985 were derived by using 1980 census counts modified to correct census Hispanic reporting errors. These errors were relatively minor, however, in the above areas. See: U.S. Bureau of the Census, *Current Population Reports: Population Estimates by Race and Hispanic Origin, for States, Metropolitan Areas, and Selected Counties: 1980 to 1985*, Series P-25, No. 1040-RD-1, U.S. Government Printing Office, Washington, D.C., 1989. 3. The Las Cruces area was not constituted SMSA in 1970; hence total for that year is for Las Cruces county.

★ 95 ★

Population

Top MSAs for Hispanic Population

Metropolitan Area	Number of Hispanics	Percent of total metro. population
Los Angeles, Anaheim, Riverside, CA CMSA	4,779,000	32.9
New York-Northern New Jersey-Long Island, NY-NJ-CT CMSA	2,778,000	15.4
Miami-Fort Lauderdale, FL CMSA	1,062,000	33.3
San Francisco-Oakland-San Jose, CA CMSA	970,000	15.5
Chicago-Gary-Lake County, IL-IN-WI CMSA	893,000	11.1
Houston-Galveston-Brazoria, TX CMSA	772,000	20.8
San Antonio, TX MSA	620,000	47.6
Dallas-Fort Worth, TX CMSA	519,000	13.4
San Diego, CA MSA	511,000	20.4
El Paso, TX MSA	412,000	69.6
Phoenix, AZ MSA	345,000	16.3
McAllen-Edinburg-Mission, TX MSA	327,000	85.2
Fresno, CA MSA	237,000	35.5
Denver-Boulder, CO CMSA	226,000	12.2
Philadelphia-Wilmington-Trenton, PA-NJ-DE-MD CMSA	226,000	3.8
Washington, DC-MD-VA MSA	225,000	5.7
Brownsville-Harlingen, TX MSA	213,000	81.9
Boston-Lawrence-Salem, MA-NH CMSA	193,000	4.6
Corpus Christi, TX MSA	182,000	52.0
Albuquerque, NM MSA	178,000	37.1
Sacramento, CA MSA	172,000	11.6
Austin, TX MSA	160,000	20.5
Bakersfield, CA MSA	152,000	28.0
Tampa-St. Petersburg-Clearwater, FL MSA	139,000	6.7
Laredo, TX MSA	125,000	93.9
Visalia-Tulare-Porterville, CA MSA	121,000	38.8
Salinas-Seaside-Monterey, CA MSA	120,000	33.6
Stockton, CA MSA	113,000	23.4

Source: U.S. Bureau of the Census. *Statistical Abstract of the United States: 1992*, (112th edition). Washington, DC: U.S. Government Printing Ofice, 1992, p. 33. Primary source: U.S. Bureau of the Census, press release CB91-229. *Note:* 1. Persons of Hispanic origin may be of any race.

★96★

Population

Top 50 MSAs for Colombian Population, 1990

Figures show the 50 MSAs (metropolitan statistical areas) in the United States with the largest percentage of persons of Colombian origin.

MSA	% of total population	Rank
Miami-Fort Lauderdale, FL	2.0649	1
New York-Northern New Jersey-Long Island, NY-NJ-CT	0.8765	2
Providence-Pawtucket-Fall River, RI-MA	0.4525	3
Orlando, FL	0.4388	4
West Palm Beach-Boca Raton-Delray Beach, FL	0.3882	5
Houston-Galveston-Brazoria, TX	0.2875	6
Los Angeles-Anaheim-Riverside, CA	0.2092	7
Washington, DC-MD-VA	0.2036	8
Tampa-Saint Petersburg-Clearwater, FL	0.2026	9
Atlantic City, NJ	0.1985	10
Gainesville, FL	0.1950	11
Tallahassee, FL	0.1901	12
Boston-Lawrence-Salem, MA-NH	0.1843	13
Naples, FL	0.1736	14
Anchorage, AK	0.1728	15
Poughkeepsie, NY	0.1692	16
Ocala, FL	0.1601	17
Hartford-New Britain-Middletown, CT	0.1580	18
Fort Myers-Cape Coral, FL	0.1435	19
Las Vegas, NV	0.1351	20
Fort Pierce, FL	0.1338	21
Melbourne-Titusville-Palm Bay, FL	0.1271	22
Chicago-Gary-Lake County, IL-IN-WI	0.1198	23
Worcester, MA	0.1188	24
Atlanta, GA	0.1160	25
Manchester, NH	0.1150	26
Lawton, OK	0.1112	27
Daytona Beach, FL	0.1033	28
Allentown-Bethlehem-Easton, PA-NJ	0.1005	29
Fitchburg-Leominster, MA	0.1002	30
New Haven-Meriden, CT	0.1000	31
San Francisco-Oakland-San Jose, CA	0.0989	32
Greenville-Spartanburg, SC	0.0972	33
San Diego, CA	0.0965	34
Salinas-Seaside-Monterey, CA	0.0964	35
Reno, NV	0.0915	36
Lancaster, PA	0.0906	37
Waterbury, CT	0.0902	38
Lexington-Fayette, KY	0.0898	39
Jacksonville, FL	0.0886	40
Springfield, MA	0.0867	41
Rochester, MN	0.0855	42

[Continued]

★ 96 ★

Top 50 MSAs for Colombian Population, 1990

[Continued]

MSA	% of total population	Rank
Philadelphia - Wilmington - Trenton, PA - NJ - DE - MD	0.0826	43
New Orleans, LA	0.0814	44
Lafayette, LA	0.0776	45
Terre Haute, IN	0.0734	46
Scranton - Wilkes-Barre, PA	0.0711	47
Burlington, VT	0.0708	48
Dallas - Fort Worth, TX	0.0691	49
Austin, TX	0.0681	50

Source: Fisher, Helen S. (ed.). *Gale City & Metro Rankings Reporter.* Detroit, MI: Gale Research Inc., 1994, p. 77. Published with permission. U.S. Bureau of the Census, Data User Services Division, *1990 Census of Population and Housing,* Summary Tape File 3C, United States Summary, CD- ROM, February 1992.

★ 97 ★

Population

Top 50 MSAs for Cuban Population, 1990

Figures show the 50 MSAs (metropolitan statistical areas) in the United States with the largest percentage of persons of Cuban origin.

MSA	% of total population	Rank
Miami - Fort Lauderdale, FL	18.3701	1
West Palm Beach - Boca Raton - Delray Beach, FL	2.0052	2
Naples, FL	1.8363	3
Tampa - Saint Petersburg - Clearwater, FL	1.6409	4
Orlando, FL	0.9406	5
New York - Northern New Jersey - Long Island, NY - NJ - CT	0.8804	6
Las Vegas, NV	0.8257	7
Gainesville, FL	0.7898	8
Tallahassee, FL	0.6032	9
New Orleans, LA	0.4670	10
Los Angeles - Anaheim - Riverside, CA	0.4150	11
Fort Pierce, FL	0.3808	12
Sarasota, FL	0.3445	13
Daytona Beach, FL	0.3391	14
Ocala, FL	0.3326	15
Lakeland - Winter Haven, FL	0.3313	16
Fort Myers - Cape Coral, FL	0.3271	17
Melbourne - Titusville - Palm Bay, FL	0.3128	18
Fort Walton Beach, FL	0.2671	19
Jacksonville, FL	0.2639	20

[Continued]

★97★

Top 50 MSAs for Cuban Population, 1990

[Continued]

MSA	% of total population	Rank
Jacksonville, NC	0.2496	21
Houston - Galveston - Brazoria, TX	0.2394	22
Washington, DC - MD - VA	0.2346	23
Panama City, FL	0.2173	24
Bradenton, FL	0.2121	25
Atlanta, GA	0.2113	26
Chicago - Gary - Lake County, IL - IN - WI	0.2106	27
Hartford - New Britain - Middletown, CT	0.1859	28
Atlantic City, NJ	0.1759	29
Poughkeepsie, NY	0.1673	30
Boston - Lawrence - Salem, MA - NH	0.1565	31
New Haven - Meriden, CT	0.1562	32
Laredo, TX	0.1471	33
Fayetteville, NC	0.1424	34
Anchorage, AK	0.1401	35
Dallas - Fort Worth, TX	0.1341	36
Grand Rapids, MI	0.1341	36
Rochester, NY	0.1319	37
Philadelphia - Wilmington - Trenton, PA - NJ - DE - MD	0.1307	38
Worcester, MA	0.1305	39
Bryan - College Station, TX	0.1297	40
San Francisco - Oakland - San Jose, CA	0.1283	41
La Crosse, WI	0.1277	42
Austin, TX	0.1244	43
Pensacola, FL	0.1243	44
San Diego, CA	0.1225	45
Savannah, GA	0.1216	46
Tuscaloosa, AL	0.1216	46
Santa Barbara - Santa Maria - Lompoc, CA	0.1193	47
Glens Falls, NY	0.1173	48

Source: Fisher, Helen S. (ed.). *Gale City & Metro Rankings Reporter*. Detroit, MI: Gale Research Inc., 1994, p. 72. Published with permission. U.S. Bureau of the Census, Data User Services Division, *1990 Census of Population and Housing*, Summary Tape File 3C, United States Summary, CD- ROM, February 1992.

★98★

Population

Top 50 MSAs for Dominican Population, 1990

Figures show the 50 MSAs (metropolitan statistical areas) in the United States with the largest percentage of persons of Dominican [Republic] origin.

MSA	% of total population	Rank
New York - Northern New Jersey - Long Island, NY - NJ - CT	2.24446	1
Miami - Fort Lauderdale, FL	0.84458	2
Providence - Pawtucket - Fall River, RI - MA	0.81829	3
Boston - Lawrence - Salem, MA - NH	0.69602	4
Orlando, FL	0.24983	5
Waterbury, CT	0.19853	6
Atlantic City, NJ	0.17782	7
Poughkeepsie, NY	0.16611	8
Anchorage, AK	0.14006	9
West Palm Beach - Boca Raton - Delray Beach, FL	0.13376	10
Worcester, MA	0.13366	11
New Bedford, MA	0.12692	12
Fitchburg - Leominster, MA	0.12452	13
Killeen - Temple, TX	0.11947	14
Washington, DC - MD - VA	0.11941	15
Glens Falls, NY	0.11895	16
Allentown - Bethlehem - Easton, PA - NJ	0.10849	17
Elmira, NY	0.10820	18
Jacksonville, NC	0.10745	19
Springfield, MA	0.09538	20
Hartford - New Britain - Middletown, CT	0.09218	21
Reading, PA	0.09212	22
Sarasota, FL	0.08100	23
Albany - Schenectady - Troy, NY	0.08052	24
Tampa - Saint Petersburg - Clearwater, FL	0.07640	25
Binghamton, NY	0.07599	26
Jamestown - Dunkirk, NY	0.07541	27
Lawton, OK	0.07445	28
Rochester, NY	0.07392	29
Manchester, NH	0.07304	30
Philadelphia - Wilmington - Trenton, PA - NJ - DE - MD	0.06077	31
Utica - Rome, NY	0.05937	32
Fayetteville, NC	0.05900	33
Lancaster, PA	0.05842	34
Pittsfield, MA	0.05803	35
Ocala, FL	0.05595	36
Fort Pierce, FL	0.05218	37
New London - Norwich, CT - RI	0.05097	38
Las Vegas, NV	0.05071	39
Colorado Springs, CO	0.04886	40
Lewiston - Auburn, ME	0.04655	41
Melbourne - Titusville - Palm Bay, FL	0.04537	42

[Continued]

★ 98 ★

Top 50 MSAs for Dominican Population, 1990

[Continued]

MSA	% of total population	Rank
New Haven - Meriden, CT	0.04451	43
Jacksonville, FL	0.04312	44
Salinas - Seaside - Monterey, CA	0.04274	45
Norfolk - Virginia Beach - Newport News, VA	0.04169	46
Tallahassee, FL	0.04152	47
Clarksville - Hopkinsville, TN - KY	0.03836	48
Charleston, SC	0.03827	49
Buffalo - Niagara Falls, NY	0.03801	50

Source: Fisher, Helen S. (ed.). *Gale City & Metro Rankings Reporter.* Detroit, MI: Gale Research Inc., 1994, p. 72. Published with permission. U.S. Bureau of the Census, Data User Services Division, *1990 Census of Population and Housing,* Summary Tape File 3C, United States Summary, CD- ROM, February 1992.

★ 99 ★

Population

Top 50 MSAs for Ecuadorian Population, 1990

Figures show the 50 MSAs (metropolitan statistical areas) in the United States with the largest percentage of persons of Ecuadorian origin.

MSA	% of total population	Rank
New York - Northern New Jersey - Long Island, NY - NJ - CT	0.65061	1
Miami - Fort Lauderdale, FL	0.33399	2
Los Angeles - Anaheim - Riverside, CA	0.15928	3
Fitchburg - Leominster, MA	0.13911	4
Washington, DC - MD - VA	0.12025	5
Chicago - Gary - Lake County, IL - IN - WI	0.10541	6
West Palm Beach - Boca Raton - Delray Beach, FL	0.08813	7
Orlando, FL	0.08492	8
New Haven - Meriden, CT	0.06903	9
Poughkeepsie, NY	0.06591	10
Santa Barbara - Santa Maria - Lompoc, CA	0.05438	11
Allentown - Bethlehem - Easton, PA - NJ	0.05403	12
Daytona Beach, FL	0.05341	13
Waterbury, CT	0.05053	14
Sarasota, FL	0.04824	15
Houston - Galveston - Brazoria, TX	0.04718	16
Tampa - Saint Petersburg - Clearwater, FL	0.04700	17
Fayetteville, NC	0.04516	18
Boston - Lawrence - Salem, MA - NH	0.04351	19
New Orleans, LA	0.04262	20

[Continued]

★ 99 ★

Top 50 MSAs for Ecuadorian Population, 1990

[Continued]

MSA	% of total population	Rank
Providence - Pawtucket - Fall River, RI - MA	0.04240	21
Fort Myers - Cape Coral, FL	0.04237	22
Columbus, GA - AL	0.04196	23
Bryan - College Station, TX	0.04103	24
Ocala, FL	0.03901	25
Fort Pierce, FL	0.03704	26
Worcester, MA	0.03662	27
Charlotte - Gastonia - Rock Hill, NC - SC	0.03614	28
Pensacola, FL	0.03513	29
Bakersfield, CA	0.03422	30
San Francisco - Oakland - San Jose, CA	0.03421	31
Melbourne - Titusville - Palm Bay, FL	0.03409	32
Atlantic City, NJ	0.03381	33
Provo - Orem, UT	0.03339	34
Gainesville, FL	0.03283	35
Jacksonville, NC	0.03137	36
Texarkana, TX - Texarkana, AR	0.02997	37
San Diego, CA	0.02962	38
New London - Norwich, CT - RI	0.02886	39
Las Vegas, NV	0.02819	40
El Paso, TX	0.02603	41
Syracuse, NY	0.02576	42
Hartford - New Britain - Middletown, CT	0.02542	43
Iowa City, IA	0.02497	44
Wichita, KS	0.02493	45
Yuma, AZ	0.02339	46
Columbia, SC	0.02338	47
Brownsville - Harlingen, TX	0.02307	48
South Bend - Mishawaka, IN	0.02307	48
Abilene, TX	0.02173	49

Source: Fisher, Helen S. (ed.). *Gale City & Metro Rankings Reporter*. Detroit, MI: Gale Research Inc., 1994, p. 78. Published with permission. U.S. Bureau of the Census, Data User Services Division, *1990 Census of Population and Housing*, Summary Tape File 3C, United States Summary, CD- ROM, February 1992.

★ 100 ★

Population

Top 50 MSAs for Guatemalan Population, 1990

Figures show the 50 MSAs (metropolitan statistical areas) in the United States with the largest percentage of persons of Guatemalan origin.

MSA	% of total population	Rank
Los Angeles - Anaheim - Riverside, CA	0.96101	1
Providence - Pawtucket - Fall River, RI - MA	0.38904	2
Miami - Fort Lauderdale, FL	0.28854	3
Washington, DC - MD - VA	0.23948	4
San Francisco - Oakland - San Jose, CA	0.21034	5
Santa Barbara - Santa Maria - Lompoc, CA	0.20508	6
Reno, NV	0.19908	7
Chicago - Gary - Lake County, IL - IN - WI	0.19562	8
Brownsville - Harlingen, TX	0.18953	9
Naples, FL	0.18606	10
New Orleans, LA	0.16637	11
Houston - Galveston - Brazoria, TX	0.16615	12
New York - Northern New Jersey - Long Island, NY - NJ - CT	0.15707	13
West Palm Beach - Boca Raton - Delray Beach, FL	0.15298	14
Boston - Lawrence - Salem, MA - NH	0.15250	15
Santa Fe, NM	0.14866	16
Fort Pierce, FL	0.13940	17
Fort Myers - Cape Coral, FL	0.11608	18
San Diego, CA	0.10408	19
Bakersfield, CA	0.09936	20
Albuquerque, NM	0.08802	21
Visalia - Tulare - Porterville, CA	0.07951	22
Greeley, CO	0.07889	23
Modesto, CA	0.07449	24
Dallas - Fort Worth, TX	0.06681	25
Fresno, CA	0.06592	26
Orlando, FL	0.06451	27
Las Vegas, NV	0.06271	28
San Antonio, TX	0.06236	29
Medford, OR	0.06216	30
Waco, TX	0.06186	31
Bradenton, FL	0.05574	32
Phoenix, AZ	0.05240	33
Portland - Vancouver, OR - WA	0.05102	34
El Paso, TX	0.04547	35
Merced, CA	0.04540	36
Corpus Christi, TX	0.04458	37
Salt Lake City - Ogden, UT	0.04430	38
Bloomington, IN	0.04405	39
Iowa City, IA	0.04057	40
Provo - Orem, UT	0.04021	41
Salinas - Seaside - Monterey, CA	0.03993	42
Anchorage, AK	0.03976	43

[Continued]

★ 100 ★

Top 50 MSAs for Guatemalan Population, 1990

[Continued]

MSA	% of total population	Rank
Stockton, CA	0.03912	44
Austin, TX	0.03851	45
Sacramento, CA	0.03801	46
Columbus, GA-AL	0.03703	47
Tucson, AZ	0.03464	48
Elkhart-Goshen, IN	0.03201	49
Allentown-Bethlehem-Easton, PA-NJ	0.03160	50

Source: Fisher, Helen S. (ed.). *Gale City & Metro Rankings Reporter.* Detroit, MI: Gale Research Inc., 1994, p. 69. Published with permission. U.S. Bureau of the Census, Data User Services Division, *1990 Census of Population and Housing,* Summary Tape File 3C, United States Summary, CD- ROM, February 1992.

★ 101 ★

Population

Top 50 MSAs for Honduran Population, 1990

Figures show the 50 MSAs (metropolitan statistical areas) in the United States with the largest percentage of persons of Honduran origin.

MSA	% of total population	Rank
New Orleans, LA	0.78301	1
Miami-Fort Lauderdale, FL	0.61687	2
New York-Northern New Jersey-Long Island, NY-NJ-CT	0.18626	3
Los Angeles-Anaheim-Riverside, CA	0.17494	4
Houston-Galveston-Brazoria, TX	0.16157	5
Brownsville-Harlingen, TX	0.15262	6
Naples, FL	0.09402	7
Washington, DC-MD-VA	0.08984	8
Boston-Lawrence-Salem, MA-NH	0.07989	9
Salinas-Seaside-Monterey, CA	0.07620	10
Tyler, TX	0.07204	11
Tampa-Saint Petersburg-Clearwater, FL	0.07152	12
Bradenton, FL	0.06518	13
West Palm Beach-Boca Raton-Delray Beach, FL	0.06253	14
Beaumont-Port Arthur, TX	0.06063	15
Orlando, FL	0.05975	16
Iowa City, IA	0.05826	17
McAllen-Edinburg-Mission, TX	0.05553	18
Dallas-Fort Worth, TX	0.05021	19
Manchester, NH	0.04869	20
Melbourne-Titusville-Palm Bay, FL	0.04762	21
Bryan-College Station, TX	0.04759	22

[Continued]

★ 101 ★

Top 50 MSAs for Honduran Population, 1990

[Continued]

MSA	% of total population	Rank
Columbus, GA-AL	0.04525	23
Killeen-Temple, TX	0.04426	24
Jacksonville, NC	0.04138	25
Baton Rouge, LA	0.04070	26
Chicago-Gary-Lake County, IL-IN-WI	0.04032	27
Austin, TX	0.03992	28
San Diego, CA	0.03799	29
San Francisco-Oakland-San Jose, CA	0.03748	30
San Antonio, TX	0.03656	31
Ocala, FL	0.03644	32
Reno, NV	0.03495	33
Poughkeepsie, NY	0.03469	34
Sarasota, FL	0.03456	35
El Paso, TX	0.03262	36
Tuscaloosa, AL	0.03255	37
Clarksville-Hopkinsville, TN-KY	0.03246	38
Tallahassee, FL	0.03211	39
Fresno, CA	0.03116	40
Gainesville, FL	0.03038	41
Fort Walton Beach, FL	0.02991	42
Sioux City, IA-NE	0.02956	43
Las Vegas, NV	0.02954	44
Waterbury, CT	0.02888	45
Benton Harbor, MI	0.02850	46
Fargo-Moorhead, ND-MN	0.02740	47
Visalia-Tulare-Porterville, CA	0.02725	48
Shreveport, LA	0.02722	49
Charleston, SC	0.02703	50

Source: Fisher, Helen S. (ed.). *Gale City & Metro Rankings Reporter*. Detroit, MI: Gale Research Inc., 1994, p. 70. Published with permission. U.S. Bureau of the Census, Data User Services Division, *1990 Census of Population and Housing*, Summary Tape File 3C, United States Summary, CD- ROM, February 1992.

★ 102 ★

Population

Top 50 MSAs for Mexican Population, 1990

Figures show the 50 MSAs (metropolitan statistical areas) in the United States with the largest percentage of persons of Mexican origin.

MSA	% of total population	Rank
Laredo, TX	90.810	1
McAllen - Edinburg - Mission, TX	82.266	2
Brownsville - Harlingen, TX	77.695	3
El Paso, TX	66.654	4
Las Cruces, NM	51.486	5
Corpus Christi, TX	48.289	6
San Antonio, TX	43.926	7
Yuma, AZ	40.016	8
Visalia - Tulare - Porterville, CA	36.341	9
Fresno, CA	32.786	10
Victoria, TX	31.703	11
Odessa, TX	29.652	12
Merced, CA	29.571	13
Salinas - Seaside - Monterey, CA	29.255	14
Los Angeles - Anaheim - Riverside, CA	25.713	15
Bakersfield, CA	25.165	16
San Angelo, TX	23.970	17
Pueblo, CO	23.719	18
Santa Barbara - Santa Maria - Lompoc, CA	23.477	19
Tucson, AZ	22.079	20
Yakima, WA	21.914	21
Lubbock, TX	20.997	22
Stockton, CA	20.226	23
Midland, TX	19.656	24
Albuquerque, NM	19.526	25
Modesto, CA	19.107	26
Austin, TX	18.131	27
Greeley, CO	17.569	28
San Diego, CA	17.362	29
Houston - Galveston - Brazoria, TX	16.790	30
Phoenix, AZ	14.418	31
Santa Fe, NM	14.282	32
Abilene, TX	12.646	33
Richland - Kennewick - Pasco, WA	11.979	34
Yuba City, CA	11.600	35
Bryan - College Station, TX	11.580	36
Amarillo, TX	11.519	37
Dallas - Fort Worth, TX	11.311	38
Waco, TX	11.171	39
San Francisco - Oakland - San Jose, CA	10.354	40
Sacramento, CA	8.938	41
Killeen - Temple, TX	8.317	42
Denver - Boulder, CO	8.142	43
Naples, FL	8.125	44
Wichita Falls, TX	7.630	45

[Continued]

★ 102 ★

Top 50 MSAs for Mexican Population, 1990

[Continued]

MSA	% of total population	Rank
Chicago - Gary - Lake County, IL - IN - WI	7.523	46
Las Vegas, NV	7.226	47
Cheyenne, WY	7.115	48
Salem, OR	6.378	49
Reno, NV	6.040	50

Source: Fisher, Helen S. (ed.). *Gale City & Metro Rankings Reporter.* Detroit, MI: Gale Research Inc., 1994, p. 76. Published with permission. U.S. Bureau of the Census, Data User Services Division, *1990 Census of Population and Housing,* Summary Tape File 3C, United States Summary, CD- ROM, February 1992.

★ 103 ★

Population

Top 50 MSAs for Nicaraguan Population, 1990

Figures show the 50 MSAs (metropolitan statistical areas) in the United States with the largest percentage of persons of Nicaraguan origin.

MSA	% of total population	Rank
Miami - Fort Lauderdale, FL	2.36238	1
San Francisco - Oakland - San Jose, CA	0.48712	2
New Orleans, LA	0.33968	3
Los Angeles - Anaheim - Riverside, CA	0.27508	4
Abilene, TX	0.24738	5
Washington, DC - MD - VA	0.20390	6
Merced, CA	0.14518	7
West Palm Beach - Boca Raton - Delray Beach, FL	0.14383	8
Brownsville - Harlingen, TX	0.10764	9
Las Vegas, NV	0.10412	10
Beaumont - Port Arthur, TX	0.10409	11
Modesto, CA	0.10256	12
Gainesville, FL	0.10142	13
Houston - Galveston - Brazoria, TX	0.09668	14
Santa Fe, NM	0.08800	15
Baton Rouge, LA	0.08178	16
Austin, TX	0.07933	17
New York - Northern New Jersey - Long Island, NY - NJ - CT	0.07778	18
Bryan - College Station, TX	0.06483	19
Sacramento, CA	0.06347	20
Stockton, CA	0.06013	21
Salinas - Seaside - Monterey, CA	0.05286	22
Orlando, FL	0.04819	23
Richland - Kennewick - Pasco, WA	0.04732	24

[Continued]

★ 103 ★

Top 50 MSAs for Nicaraguan Population, 1990

[Continued]

MSA	% of total population	Rank
San Antonio, TX	0.04715	25
Cumberland, MD - WV	0.04526	26
Monroe, LA	0.04431	27
Laredo, TX	0.03828	28
Albuquerque, NM	0.03766	29
Dallas - Fort Worth, TX	0.03462	30
Bakersfield, CA	0.03422	31
San Diego, CA	0.03379	32
Fayetteville, NC	0.03314	33
Columbia, MO	0.03292	34
Billings, MT	0.03262	35
Atlantic City, NJ	0.03225	36
Jacksonville, NC	0.03203	37
Reno, NV	0.03181	38
New Haven - Meriden, CT	0.03150	39
Tampa - Saint Petersburg - Clearwater, FL	0.03134	40
Lawton, OK	0.03050	41
Santa Barbara - Santa Maria - Lompoc, CA	0.03003	42
Jamestown - Dunkirk, NY	0.02960	43
McAllen - Edinburg - Mission, TX	0.02920	44
Corpus Christi, TX	0.02801	45
Anchorage, AK	0.02783	46
Yuma, AZ	0.02619	47
Rochester, NY	0.02474	48
Tucson, AZ	0.02459	49
Naples, FL	0.02433	50

Source: Fisher, Helen S. (ed.). *Gale City & Metro Rankings Reporter.* Detroit, MI: Gale Research Inc., 1994, p. 70. Published with permission. U.S. Bureau of the Census, Data User Services Division, *1990 Census of Population and Housing,* Summary Tape File 3C, United States Summary, CD- ROM, February 1992.

★ 104 ★

Population

Top 50 MSAs for Panamanian Population, 1990

Figures show the 50 MSAs (metropolitan statistical areas) in the United States with the largest percentage of persons of Panamanian origin.

MSA	% of total population	Rank
Fayetteville, NC	0.36421	1
Killeen - Temple, TX	0.29690	2
Columbus, GA - AL	0.25383	3
Miami - Fort Lauderdale, FL	0.24660	4
Clarksville - Hopkinsville, TN - KY	0.23312	5

[Continued]

★ 104 ★

Top 50 MSAs for Panamanian Population, 1990

[Continued]

MSA	% of total population	Rank
Lawton, OK	0.21976	6
Colorado Springs, CO	0.19596	7
Jacksonville, NC	0.17886	8
Salinas - Seaside - Monterey, CA	0.15998	9
New York - Northern New Jersey - Long Island, NY - NJ - CT	0.14984	10
Fort Walton Beach, FL	0.14954	11
Rapid City, SD	0.12171	12
El Paso, TX	0.10581	13
Washington, DC - MD - VA	0.09632	14
Orlando, FL	0.09536	15
Norfolk - Virginia Beach - Newport News, VA	0.08703	16
Dothan, AL	0.08094	17
Yuma, AZ	0.07578	18
Augusta, GA - SC	0.07434	19
Olympia, WA	0.07256	20
Tampa - Saint Petersburg - Clearwater, FL	0.06722	21
San Diego, CA	0.06617	22
Austin, TX	0.06269	23
San Antonio, TX	0.06267	24
Melbourne - Titusville - Palm Bay, FL	0.06216	25
Columbia, SC	0.05559	26
San Francisco - Oakland - San Jose, CA	0.05351	27
Bremerton, WA	0.05323	28
Huntsville, AL	0.05274	29
Fort Collins - Loveland, CO	0.05265	30
Los Angeles - Anaheim - Riverside, CA	0.05218	31
Pensacola, FL	0.04936	32
Tallahassee, FL	0.04837	33
Albuquerque, NM	0.04578	34
New Orleans, LA	0.04553	35
Las Vegas, NV	0.04532	36
Poughkeepsie, NY	0.04509	37
Sarasota, FL	0.04320	38
Honolulu, HI	0.04090	39
Bloomington, IN	0.03946	40
Rochester, MN	0.03945	41
Abilene, TX	0.03844	42
Champaign - Urbana - Rantoul, IL	0.03814	43
Richmond - Petersburg, VA	0.03754	44
Savannah, GA	0.03751	45
Jacksonville, FL	0.03739	46
Glens Falls, NY	0.03712	47
Biloxi - Gulfport, MS	0.03653	48

[Continued]

★ 104 ★

Top 50 MSAs for Panamanian Population, 1990

[Continued]

MSA	% of total population	Rank
Fort Myers - Cape Coral, FL	0.03611	49
Gainesville, FL	0.03478	50

Source: Fisher, Helen S. (ed.). *Gale City & Metro Rankings Reporter.* Detroit, MI: Gale Research Inc., 1994, p. 71. Published with permission. U.S. Bureau of the Census, Data User Services Division, *1990 Census of Population and Housing,* Summary Tape File 3C, United States Summary, CD- ROM, February 1992.

★ 105 ★

Population

Top 50 MSAs for Peruvian Population, 1990

Figures show the 50 MSAs (metropolitan statistical areas) in the United States with the largest percentage of persons of Peruvian origin.

MSA	% of total population	Rank
Miami - Fort Lauderdale, FL	0.64130	1
New York - Northern New Jersey - Long Island, NY - NJ - CT	0.31195	2
Washington, DC - MD - VA	0.29613	3
Hartford - New Britain - Middletown, CT	0.20380	4
Los Angeles - Anaheim - Riverside, CA	0.20162	5
San Francisco - Oakland - San Jose, CA	0.19829	6
Athens, GA	0.13950	7
West Palm Beach - Boca Raton - Delray Beach, FL	0.09264	8
Provo - Orem, UT	0.08953	9
Salinas - Seaside - Monterey, CA	0.08885	10
Sarasota, FL	0.08352	11
Anchorage, AK	0.08350	12
Orlando, FL	0.08035	13
Houston - Galveston - Brazoria, TX	0.07418	14
Champaign - Urbana - Rantoul, IL	0.06935	15
San Diego, CA	0.06425	16
Gainesville, FL	0.06026	17
Salt Lake City - Ogden, UT	0.06025	18
Boston - Lawrence - Salem, MA - NH	0.05763	19
Santa Barbara - Santa Maria - Lompoc, CA	0.05736	20
Naples, FL	0.05391	21
Tucson, AZ	0.05383	22
Chicago - Gary - Lake County, IL - IN - WI	0.05373	23
Poughkeepsie, NY	0.05357	24
Melbourne - Titusville - Palm Bay, FL	0.05339	25
Denver - Boulder, CO	0.05335	26
Bakersfield, CA	0.05281	27

[Continued]

★ 105 ★

Top 50 MSAs for Peruvian Population, 1990

[Continued]

MSA	% of total population	Rank
Las Cruces, NM	0.05166	28
Sacramento, CA	0.05118	29
Tampa - Saint Petersburg - Clearwater, FL	0.04826	30
Dallas - Fort Worth, TX	0.04630	31
Atlanta, GA	0.04623	32
Providence - Pawtucket - Fall River, RI - MA	0.04582	33
Bryan - College Station, TX	0.04513	34
Manchester, NH	0.04463	35
Modesto, CA	0.04426	36
Fort Pierce, FL	0.04421	37
Lawrence, KS	0.04401	38
Reno, NV	0.04359	39
Fort Collins - Loveland, CO	0.04298	40
Yuba City, CA	0.04240	41
Las Vegas, NV	0.04140	42
Stockton, CA	0.03995	43
Seattle - Tacoma, WA	0.03943	44
New Haven - Meriden, CT	0.03942	45
Springfield, MA	0.03909	46
Fort Myers - Cape Coral, FL	0.03879	47
Austin, TX	0.03800	48
El Paso, TX	0.03769	49
Jacksonville, NC	0.03537	50

Source: Fisher, Helen S. (ed.). *Gale City & Metro Rankings Reporter.* Detroit, MI: Gale Research Inc., 1994, p. 78-79. Published with permission. U.S. Bureau of the Census, Data User Services Division, *1990 Census of Population and Housing,* Summary Tape File 3C, United States Summary, CD- ROM, February 1992.

★ 106 ★

Population

Top 50 MSAs for Puerto Rican Population, 1990

Data show the 50 MSAs (metropolitan statistical areas) in te United States with the largest percentage of Puerto Rican persons.

MSA	% of total population	Rank
Springfield, MA	7.613	1
New York - Northern New Jersey - Long Island, NY - NJ - CT	6.834	2
Waterbury, CT	5.614	3
Hartford - New Britain - Middletown, CT	5.215	4
Fitchburg - Leominster, MA	5.129	5
Orlando, FL	4.820	6
New Haven - Meriden, CT	4.215	7

[Continued]

★ 106 ★

Top 50 MSAs for Puerto Rican Population, 1990

[Continued]

MSA	% of total population	Rank
Atlantic City, NJ	3.842	8
Reading, PA	3.815	9
Worcester, MA	3.203	10
Miami - Fort Lauderdale, FL	2.965	11
Allentown - Bethlehem - Easton, PA - NJ	2.934	12
Lancaster, PA	2.904	13
New Bedford, MA	2.649	14
Philadelphia - Wilmington - Trenton, PA - NJ - DE - MD	2.538	15
Jamestown - Dunkirk, NY	2.307	16
Rochester, NY	2.034	17
Killeen - Temple, TX	2.004	18
Honolulu, HI	1.936	19
Poughkeepsie, NY	1.910	20
Chicago - Gary - Lake County, IL - IN - WI	1.900	21
New London - Norwich, CT - RI	1.860	22
Boston - Lawrence - Salem, MA - NH	1.804	23
Fort Myers - Cape Coral, FL	1.746	24
Fayetteville, NC	1.660	25
Jacksonville, NC	1.654	26
Tampa - Saint Petersburg - Clearwater, FL	1.632	27
Lawton, OK	1.579	28
Daytona Beach, FL	1.573	29
West Palm Beach - Boca Raton - Delray Beach, FL	1.430	30
Buffalo - Niagara Falls, NY	1.322	31
Ocala, FL	1.301	32
Utica - Rome, NY	1.259	33
Naples, FL	1.210	34
Melbourne - Titusville - Palm Bay, FL	1.199	35
Cleveland - Akron - Lorain, OH	1.198	36
Providence - Pawtucket - Fall River, RI - MA	1.152	37
Columbus, GA - AL	1.140	38
Clarksville - Hopkinsville, TN - KY	1.115	39
Harrisburg - Lebanon - Carlisle, PA	1.065	40
Milwaukee - Racine, WI	0.955	41
Albany - Schenectady - Troy, NY	0.933	42
Fort Pierce, FL	0.899	43
York, PA	0.886	44
Fort Walton Beach, FL	0.836	45
Youngstown - Warren, OH	0.823	46
Elmira, NY	0.818	47
Gainesville, FL	0.802	48

[Continued]

★ 106 ★

Top 50 MSAs for Puerto Rican Population, 1990

[Continued]

MSA	% of total population	Rank
Erie, PA	0.785	49
Jacksonville, FL	0.768	50

Source: Fisher, Helen S. (ed.). *Gale City & Metro Rankings Reporter.* Detroit, MI: Gale Research Inc., 1994, p. 76. Published with permission. U.S. Bureau of the Census, Data User Services Division, *1990 Census of Population and Housing,* Summary Tape File 3C, United States Summary, CD- ROM, February 1992.

★ 107 ★

Population

Top 50 MSAs for Salvadoran Population, 1990

Figures show the 50 MSAs (metropolitan statistical areas) in the United States with the largest percentage of persons of Salvadoran origin.

MSA	% of total population	Rank
Los Angeles - Anaheim - Riverside, CA	1.89098	1
Washington, DC - MD - VA	1.32260	2
Houston - Galveston - Brazoria, TX	1.09066	3
San Francisco - Oakland - San Jose, CA	0.83856	4
Reno, NV	0.42722	5
New York - Northern New Jersey - Long Island, NY - NJ - CT	0.35205	6
Brownsville - Harlingen, TX	0.34292	7
Salinas - Seaside - Monterey, CA	0.32053	8
Dallas - Fort Worth, TX	0.29657	9
Miami - Fort Lauderdale, FL	0.28560	10
Las Vegas, NV	0.27945	11
Bakersfield, CA	0.25889	12
Fresno, CA	0.23731	13
Boston - Lawrence - Salem, MA - NH	0.20953	14
Merced, CA	0.15751	15
Sherman - Denison, TX	0.15260	16
Santa Barbara - Santa Maria - Lompoc, CA	0.14421	17
Austin, TX	0.14061	18
Richland - Kennewick - Pasco, WA	0.13664	19
Modesto, CA	0.13360	20
Visalia - Tulare - Porterville, CA	0.13273	21
Worcester, MA	0.10734	22
Sacramento, CA	0.10391	23
West Palm Beach - Boca Raton - Delray Beach, FL	0.10237	24
Stockton, CA	0.09820	25
Bryan - College Station, TX	0.09683	26
Tucson, AZ	0.09387	27

[Continued]

★ 107 ★

Top 50 MSAs for Salvadoran Population, 1990

[Continued]

MSA	% of total population	Rank
New Orleans, LA	0.09009	28
Chico, CA	0.08731	29
Laredo, TX	0.08631	30
San Diego, CA	0.08435	31
Providence - Pawtucket - Fall River, RI - MA	0.07937	32
Chicago - Gary - Lake County, IL - IN - WI	0.07645	33
San Antonio, TX	0.07403	34
Jacksonville, NC	0.07141	35
McAllen - Edinburg - Mission, TX	0.06753	36
Phoenix, AZ	0.06479	37
Victoria, TX	0.06455	38
Provo - Orem, UT	0.06411	39
Tallahassee, FL	0.06164	40
Yuma, AZ	0.06081	41
Atlantic City, NJ	0.06011	42
Pittsfield, MA	0.05803	43
Odessa, TX	0.05802	44
Las Cruces, NM	0.05608	45
Albuquerque, NM	0.05369	46
Yakima, WA	0.05349	47
Salt Lake City - Ogden, UT	0.05195	48
Santa Fe, NM	0.05041	49
Atlanta, GA	0.04856	50

Source: Fisher, Helen S. (ed.). *Gale City & Metro Rankings Reporter*. Detroit, MI: Gale Research Inc., 1994, p. 71. Published with permission. U.S. Bureau of the Census, Data User Services Division, *1990 Census of Population and Housing*, Summary Tape File 3C, United States Summary, CD- ROM, February 1992.

★ 108 ★

Population

Racial/Ethnic Diversity, by County, 1990

The counties where proportions of Hispanics, non-Hispanic whites, non-Hispanic blacks, and non-Hispanic other races are nearest to being equal are shown for 1990.

County	Rank	State
Queens County	1	New York
San Francisco County	2	California
Los Angeles County	3	California
Kings County	4	New York
Alameda County	5	California
New York County	6	New York
Bronx County	7	New York
Hudson County	8	New Jersey

[Continued]

★ 108 ★

Racial/Ethnic Diversity, by County, 1990

[Continued]

County	Rank	State
Fort Bend County	9	Texas
Cibola County	10	New Mexico
Harris County	11	Texas
Robeson County	12	North Carolina
Solano County	13	California
Essex County	14	New Jersey
Dade County	15	Florida
Sandoval County	16	New Mexico
Monterey County	17	California
Fresno County	18	California
San Joaquin County	19	California
Santa Clara County	20	California
San Mateo County	21	California
Cook County	22	Illinois
Merced County	23	California
Hoke County	24	North Carolina
Chattahoochee County	25	Georgia
Kings County	26	California
Dallas County	27	Texas
Suffolk County	28	Massachusetts
Hendry County	29	Florida
Matagorda County	30	Texas
Graham County	31	Arizona
Denver County	32	Colorado
San Juan County	33	New Mexico
San Bernardino County	34	California
Socorro County	35	New Mexico
Aleutians West Census Area	36	Alaska
Passaic County	37	New Jersey
Pinal County	38	Arizona
Alexandria (city)	39	Virginia
Waller County	40	Texas
Coldwell County	41	Texas
San Diego County	42	California
Liberty County	43	Georgia
Prince Georges County	44	Maryland
Wharton County	45	Texas
Philadelphia County	46	Pennsylvania
Bell County	47	Texas
Otero County	48	New Mexico
Union County	49	New Jersey
Coconino County	50	Arizona

Source: Edmondson, Brad. "American diversity." *American Demographics Desk Reference*, July 1991, p. 21. Primary source: 1990 U.S. Census.

★ 109 ★

Population

U.S. Southwest Border County Populations, by Place of Birth, 1980

State/county	Total	Percent				
		Native born	Born in state	Born in different state	Born abroad	Foreign born
California						
San Diego	274,530	62.5	46.3	13.8	2.3	37.5
Imperial	51,426	56.9	49.0	6.6	1.3	43.1
Arizona						
Cochise	22,848	73.0	56.2	14.0	2.7	27.0
Pima	111,378	83.6	67.1	15.0	1.5	16.4
Santa Cruz	15,229	53.2	45.3	5.2	2.7	46.8
Yuma	29,530	60.7	43.1	16.3	1.3	39.3
New Mexico						
Dona Ana	50,171	82.6	58.6	23.5	0.6	17.4
Hidalgo	2,849	82.8	64.9	17.9	0.6	17.2
Luna	6,171	81.2	66.6	14.0	0.6	18.8
Texas						
El Paso	297,196	70.7	60.0	8.9	1.8	29.3
Hudspeth	1,589	64.8	54.6	6.5	3.7	35.2
Culberson	2,101	82.6	80.9	1.5	0.2	17.4
Jeff Davis	777	91.9	85.3	4.5	2.1	8.1
Presidio	3,989	80.3	75.1	4.7	0.5	19.7
Brewster	3,262	91.8	89.7	1.7	0.4	8.2
Terrell	691	87.6	85.2	2.0	0.3	8.2
Valverde	22,612	71.0	63.8	5.3	1.9	29.0
Kinney	1,310	75.6	70.7	3.6	1.4	24.4
Maverick	28,366	60.1	51.2	6.6	2.2	39.9
Dimmitt	8,869	87.4	76.3	10.8	0.3	12.6
Webb	90,823	77.8	72.0	4.7	1.2	22.2
Zapata	5,042	78.1	74.4	3.7	0.0	21.9
Starr	26,409	77.9	72.5	4.6	0.8	22.1
Hildalgo	230,287	76.3	69.7	5.8	0.9	23.7
Cameron	161,701	76.5	70.7	4.7	1.1	23.5

Source: U.S. Bureau of the Census, *The Hispanic Population of the Southwest Borderland.* Current Population Reports, Series P-23, No. 172, Washington, DC: U.S. Government Printing Office, 1991, pp. 26-28.

★ 110 ★

Population

Hispanic Population in Cities With 100,000 or More Inhabitants, 1990: Abilene - New York

Numbers are shown in thousands.

City	Total (000)	Percent Hispanic
Abilene, TX	107	15.5
Akron, OH	223	0.7
Albany, NY	101	3.1
Albuquerque, NM	385	34.5
Alexandria, VA	111	9.7
Allentown, PA	105	11.7
Amarillo, TX	158	14.7
Anaheim, CA	266	31.4
Anchorage, AK[1]	226	4.1
Ann Arbor, MI	110	2.6
Arlington, VA[2]	171	13.5
Arlington, TX	262	8.9
Atlanta, GA	394	1.9
Aurora, CO	222	6.6
Austin, TX	466	23.0
Bakersfield, CA	175	20.5
Baltimore, MD	736	1.0
Baton Rouge, LA	220	1.6
Beaumont, TX	114	4.3
Berkeley, CA	103	8.4
Boise City, ID	126	2.7
Boston, MA	574	10.8
Bridgeport, CT	142	26.5
Buffalo, NY	328	4.9
Cedar Rapids, IA	109	1.1
Charlotte, NC	396	1.4
Chattanooga, TN	152	0.6
Chesapeake, VA	152	1.3
Chicago, IL	2,784	19.6
Chula Vista, CA	135	37.3
Cincinnati, OH	364	0.7
Citrus Heights, CA	107	6.9
Cleveland, OH	506	4.6
Colorado Springs, CO	281	9.1
Columbus, GA	179	3.0
Columbus, OH	633	1.1
Concord, CA	111	11.5
Corpus Christi, TX	257	50.4
Dallas, TX	1,007	20.9
Dayton, OH	182	0.7
Denver, CO	468	23.0
Des Moines, IA	193	2.4
Detroit, MI	1,028	2.8
Durham, NC	137	1.2
East Los Angeles, CA	126	94.7

[Continued]

★ 110 ★

Hispanic Population in Cities With 100,000 or More Inhabitants, 1990: Abilene - New York

[Continued]

City	Total (000)	Percent Hispanic
Elizabeth, NJ	110	39.1
El Monte, CA	106	72.5
El Paso, TX	515	69.0
Erie, PA	109	2.4
Escondido, CA	109	23.4
Eugene, OR	113	2.7
Evansville, IN	126	0.6
Flint, MI	141	2.9
Fort Lauderdale, FL	149	7.2
Fort Wayne, IN	173	2.7
Fort Worth, TX	448	19.5
Fremont, CA	173	13.3
Fresno, CA	354	29.9
Fullerton, CA	114	21.3
Garden Grove, CA	143	23.5
Garland, TX	181	11.6
Gary, IN	117	5.7
Glendale, AZ	148	15.5
Glendale, CA	180	21.0
Grand Rapids, MI	189	5.0
Greensboro, NC	184	1.0
Hampton, VA	134	2.0
Hartford, CT	140	31.6
Hayward, CA	111	23.9
Hialeah, FL	188	87.6
Hollywood, FL	122	11.9
Honolulu, HI	365	4.6
Houston, TX	1,631	27.6
Huntington Beach, CA	182	11.2
Huntsville, AL	160	1.2
Independence, MO	112	2.0
Indianapolis, IN	731	1.1
Inglewood, CA	110	38.5
Irvine, CA	110	6.3
Irving, TX	155	16.3
Jackson, MS	197	0.4
Jacksonville, FL	635	2.6
Jersey City, NJ	229	24.2
Kansas City, KS	150	7.1
Kansas City, MO	435	3.9
Knoxville, TN	165	0.7
Lakewood, CO	126	9.1
Lansing, MI	127	7.9
Laredo, TX	123	93.9
Las Vegas, NV	258	12.5

[Continued]

★ 110 ★

Hispanic Population in Cities With 100,000 or More Inhabitants, 1990: Abilene - New York

[Continued]

City	Total (000)	Percent Hispanic
Lexington-Fayette, KY[3]	225	1.1
Lincoln, NE	192	2.0
Little Rock, AR	176	0.8
Livonia, MI	101	1.3
Long Beach, CA	429	23.6
Los Angeles, CA	3,485	39.9
Louisville, KY	269	0.7
Lowell, MA	103	10.1
Lubbock, TX	186	22.5
Macon, GA	107	0.6
Madison, WI	191	2.0
Memphis, TN	610	0.7
Mesa, AZ	288	10.9
Mesquite, TX	101	8.8
Metairie, LA	149	6.2
Miami, FL	359	62.5
Milwaukee, WI	628	6.3
Minneapolis, MN	368	2.1
Mobile, AL	196	1.0
Modesto, CA	165	16.3
Montgomery, AL	187	0.8
Moreno Valley, CA	119	22.9
Nashville-Davidson, TN	488	0.9
Newark, NJ	275	26.1
New Haven, CT	130	13.2
New Orleans, LA	497	3.5
Newport News, VA	170	2.8
New York, NY	7, 323	24.4
Bronx Borough	1,204	43.5
Brooklyn Borough	2,301	20.1
Manhattan Borough	1,488	26.0
Queens Borough	1,952	19.5
Staten Island Borough	379	8.0

Source: U.S. Bureau of the Census. *Statistical Abstract of the United States: 1992,* (112th edition). Washington, DC: U.S. Government Printing Office, 1992, p. 35. Primary source: U.S. Bureau of the Census, *Census of Population: 1970,* vol. I, chapters A and B; *1980 Census of Population,* vol. 1, chapters A and B; *1990 Census of Population and Housing, Summary Population and Housing Characteristics,* (CPH-1). *Notes:* Hispanic persons may be of any race. 1. Anchorage City consolidated with Anchorage Borough September 15, 1975. 2. Data represent the census designated place as delineated by State and local authorities. 3. Lexington and Fayette County consolidated January 1, 1974.

★ 111 ★

Population

Hispanic Population in Cities With 100,000 or More Inhabitants, 1990: Norfolk - Yonkers

Numbers are shown in thousands.

City	Total (000)	Percent Hispanic
Norfolk, VA	261	2.9
Oakland, CA	372	13.9
Oceanside, CA	128	22.6
Oklahoma City, OK	445	5.0
Omaha, NE	336	3.1
Ontario, CA	133	41.7
Orange, CA	111	22.8
Orlando, FL	165	8.7
Overland Park, KS	112	2.0
Oxnard, CA	142	54.4
Paradise, NV	125	10.5
Pasadena, CA	132	27.3
Pasadena, TX	119	28.8
Paterson, NJ	141	41.0
Peoria, IL	114	1.6
Philadelphia, PA	1,586	5.6
Phoenix, AZ	983	20.0
Pittsburgh, PA	370	0.9
Plano, TX	129	6.2
Pomona, CA	132	51.3
Portland, OR	437	3.2
Portsmouth, VA	104	1.3
Providence, RI	161	15.5
Raleigh, NC	208	1.4
Rancho Cucamonga, CA	101	20.0
Reno, NV	134	11.1
Richmond, VA	203	0.9
Riverside, CA	227	26.0
Rochester, NY	232	8.7
Rockford, IL	139	4.2
Sacramento, CA	369	16.2
St. Louis, MO	397	1.3
St. Paul, MN	272	4.2
St. Petersburg, FL	239	2.6
Salem, OR	108	6.1
Salinas, CA	109	50.6
Salt Lake City, UT	160	9.7
San Antonio, TX	936	55.6
San Bernardino, CA	164	34.6
San Diego, CA	1,111	20.7
San Francisco, CA	724	13.9
San Jose, CA	782	26.6
Santa Ana, CA	294	65.2
Santa Clarita, CA	111	13.4
Santa Rosa, CA	113	9.5

[Continued]

★ 111 ★

Hispanic Population in Cities With 100,000 or More Inhabitants, 1990: Norfolk - Yonkers

[Continued]

City	Total (000)	Percent Hispanic
Savannah, GA	138	1.4
Scottsdale, AZ	130	4.8
Seattle, WA	516	3.6
Shreveport, LA	199	1.1
Simi Valley, CA	100	12.7
Sioux Falls, SD	101	0.6
South Bend, IN	106	3.4
Spokane, WA	177	2.1
Springfield, IL	105	0.8
Springfield, MA	157	16.9
Springfield, MO	140	1.0
Stamford, CT	108	9.8
Sterling Heights, MI	118	1.1
Stockton, CA	211	25.0
Sunnyvale, CA	117	13.2
Syracuse, NY	164	2.9
Tacoma, WA	177	3.8
Tallahassee, FL	125	3.0
Tampa, FL	280	15.0
Tempe, AZ	142	10.9
Thousand Oaks, CA	104	9.6
Toledo, OH	333	4.0
Topeka, KS	120	5.8
Torrance, CA	133	10.1
Tucson, AZ	405	29.3
Tulsa, OK	367	2.6
Vallejo, CA	109	10.8
Virginia Beach, VA	393	3.1
Waco, TX	104	16.3
Warren, MI	145	1.1
Washington, DC	607	5.4
Waterbury, CT	109	13.4
Wichita, KS	304	5.0
Winston-Salem, NC	143	0.9
Worcester, MA	170	9.6
Yonkers, NY	188	16.7

Source: U.S. Bureau of the Census. *Statistical Abstract of the United States: 1992,* (112th edition). Washington, DC: U.S. Government Printing Office, 1992, p. 35. Primary source: U.S. Bureau of the Census, *Census of Population: 1970,* vol. I, chapters A and B; *1980 Census of Population,* vol. 1, chapters A and B; *1990 Census of Population and Housing, Summary Population and Housing Characteristics,* (CPH-1). *Note:* Hispanic persons may be of any race.

★ 112 ★

Population

Los Angeles: Hispanics as a Percentage of Total Population, 1980 and 1990

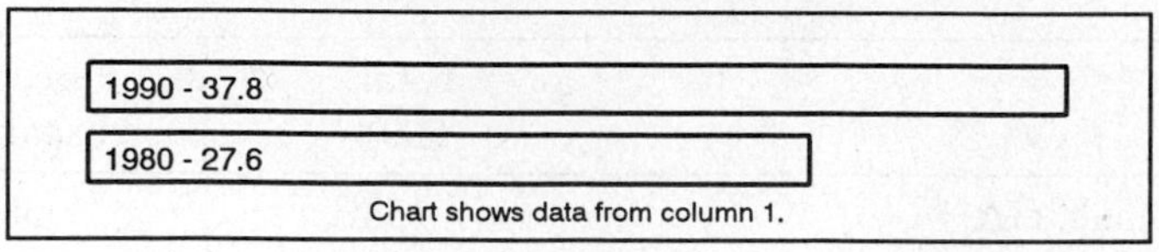

Year	Percent of population in Los Angeles	Total percent of U.S.
1980	27.6	[1]
1990	37.8	8.4

Source: Sanchez, Sandra. "Hispanics in L.A.: we suffered too." *USA TODAY* (7 May 1992), p. 3A. Census Bureau *Notes:* 1980 census classified "Spanish" only, 1990 recognizes all Hispanics. 1. Data not given by source.

★ 113 ★

Population

Los Angeles: Population Distribution, by Race/Ethnicity and Region

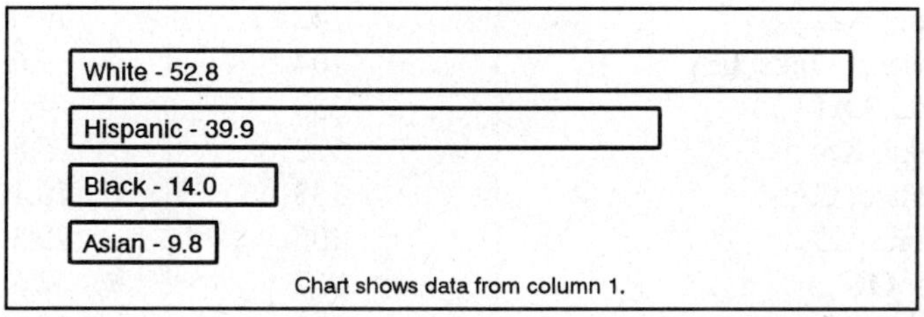

Percent distributions are shown; chart shows data for the city as a whole.

Race/ethnicity	L.A. Region Percent Distribution		
	City as a whole	South Central	Koreatown
White	52.8	10.5	25.4
Hispanic[1]	39.9	45.1	67.9
Black	14.0	55.5	5.0
Asian	9.8	11	26.5

Source: Goodavage, Maria. "Curfew arrests fuel rage in L.A." *USA TODAY* (11 May 1992), p. 3-A. Primary source: U.S. Census Bureau *Note:* 1. Hispanics may be of any race.

★ 114 ★

Population

Los Angeles: Population, by Selected Minority, 1980 and 1990

Numbers are shown in thousands.

Race/ethnicity	1980	1990
Hispanic	816.1	1,391.4
Black	505.2	487.7
Asian/Pacific Islander	196.2	341.8

Source: Reinhold, Robert. "A terrible chain of events reveals Los Angeles without its makeup." *The New York Times* (3 May 1992), p. 10. Primary source: U.S. Census Bureau.

★ 115 ★

Population

Los Angeles: Selected Social Characteristics, by Race/ Ethnicity

Black and white data exclude Hispanic respondents.

Characteristic	Percent		
	Latino	Black	White
Population in L.A. County	38.0	11.0	41.0
Traditional households (two parents with children)	43.0	14.0	16.0
Low birth-weight babies	5.3	13.0	5.5
On welfare	6.0	35.0	12.0
Males in labor force	80.6	66.7	76.2
Life expectancy (in years)	79.4	68.7	75.1

Source: Meyer, Michael. "Los Angeles 2010: a Latino subcontinent." *Newsweek* (9 November 1992), p. 32. Primary source: U.S. Census, UCLA School of Medicine Center for the Study of Latino Health.

★ 116 ★

Population

New York City: Population Distribution, by Race/ Ethnicity, 1980 and 1987

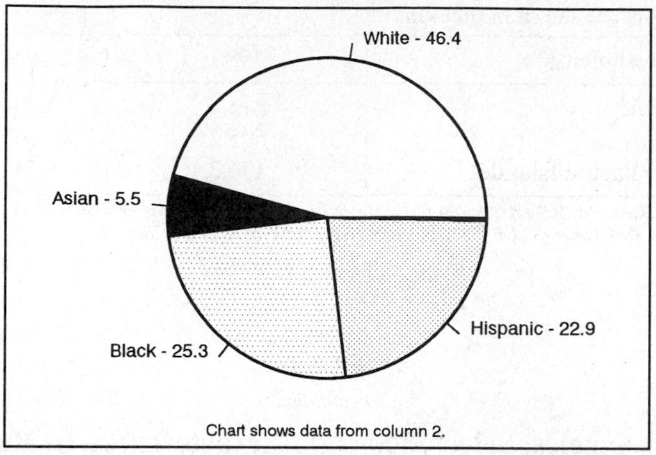

Chart shows data for 1987.

Race/ethnicity	Percent distribution	
	1980	1987
White	52.6	46.4
Black	24.0	25.3
Hispanic	19.9	22.9
Asian	3.5	5.5

Source: Mouat, Lucia. "New York City - a vibrant but troubled metropolis." *Christian Science Monitor* (6 November 1991), p. 11. Primary source: The New York Times; N.Y.C. Human Resources Administration; U.S. Bureau of Labor Statistics.

Population Trends

★ 117 ★

Average Rate of Population Change, 1980 to 1989

Total population includes Armed Forces overseas. Rates are per 1,000 mid-period population.

Race and Hispanic origin	Net change	Natural increase	Births	Deaths	Net civilian immigration
All races					
1985-89	9.8	7.0	15.8	8.7	2.7
1980-84[1]	10.1	7.1	15.7	8.6	2.9
Hispanic origin[2]					
1985-89	34.2	18.7	23.1	4.4	15.5
1980-84[1]	38.4	18.7	22.9	4.2	19.6
White					
1985-89	7.5	5.7	14.7	9.0	1.8
1980-84[1]	7.8	5.9	14.7	8.8	1.9
Black					
1985-89	15.0	13.0	21.4	8.5	2.1
1980-84[1]	15.1	12.9	21.2	8.3	2.2
Other races					
1985-89	48.6	18.9	22.1	3.2	29.7
1980-84[1]	61.0	20.1	23.3	3.2	40.9

Source: Hollmann, Frederick W. U.S. Department of Commerce. Bureau of the Census. *United States Population Estimates, by Age, Sex, Race, and Hispanic Origin: 1980 to 1988.* Current Population Reports, Population Estimates and Projections, Series P-25, No. 1045. Washington, DC: The Bureau, January 1990, p. 4. *Notes:* 1. 1980-84 refers to the period from April 1, 1980, through December 31, 1984. 1985-89 refers to January 1, 1985, through December 31, 1989. 2. Persons of Hispanic origin may be of any race.

★ 118 ★

Population Trends

Changes in Population, 1980 to 1989

Numbers are shown in thousands and include Armed Forces overseas.

Race/ethnicity	Population on July 1		Population change, 1980-89		Average annual percent change
	1989	1980	Number	Percent	
Total, all ages	248,762	227,757	21,005	9.2	1.0
Hispanic origin[1]	20,528	14,803	5,724	38.7	3.6
White	209,326	195,571	13,755	7.0	0.8
Black	30,788	26,903	3,885	14.4	1.5

[Continued]

★ 118 ★

Changes in Population, 1980 to 1989

[Continued]

Race/ethnicity	Population on July 1		Population change, 1980-89		Average annual percent change
	1989	1980	Number	Percent	
American Indian, Eskimo, or Aleut[2]	1,737	1,429	308	21.6	2.2
Asian or Pacific Islander[2]	6,881	3,834	3,047	79.5	6.5

Source: Hollmann, Frederick W. U.S. Department of Commerce. Bureau of the Census. *United States Population Estimates, by Age, Sex, Race, and Hispanic Origin: 1980 to 1988.* Current Population Reports, Population Estimates and Projections, Series P-25, No. 1045. Washington, DC: The Bureau, January 1990, p. 2. *Notes:* 1. Persons of Hispanic origin may be of any race. 2. Resident population.

★ 119 ★

Population Trends

Fastest Growing Counties for Hispanics, 1980-90

Counties with Hispanic populations of 5,000 or more in 1990 are ranked, by percent change in Hispanic population, for 1980-90.

County, state	State	Rank	1980 Hispanic population	1990 Hispanic population	Percent change 1980-90
Osceola County	Florida	1	1,089	12,866	1,081.5
Gwinnett County	Georgia	2	1,424	8,470	494.8
Seminole County	Florida	3	5,157	18,606	260.8
Volusia County	Florida	4	4,124	14,840	259.8
St. Lucie County	Florida	5	1,743	5,952	241.5
Cobb County	Georgia	6	2,839	9,403	231.2
Orange County	Florida	7	19,726	64,946	229.2
Montgomery County	Texas	8	4,288	13,237	208.7
Prince William County	Virginia	9	3,195	9,662	202.4
Denton County	Texas	10	6,396	19,013	197.3
Manatee County	Florida	11	3,185	9,424	195.9
Marion County	Florida	12	2,012	5,860	191.3
Essex County	Massachusetts	13	16,922	48,440	186.3
Johnson County	Texas	14	2,771	7,457	169.1
Broward County	Florida	15	40,314	108,439	169.0
Alexandria (city)	Virginia	16	4,042	10,778	166.7
Fairfax County	Virginia	17	19,523	51,874	165.7
Lee County	Florida	18	5,717	15,094	164.0
Arlington County	Virginia	19	8,863	23,089	160.5
Hillsborough County	New Hampshire	20	2,223	5,696	156.2
Providence County	Rhode Island	21	15,935	40,569	154.6
Collin County	Texas	22	7,187	18,158	152.7
Somerset County	New Jersey	23	4,080	10,187	149.7
Riverside County	California	24	124,419	307,514	147.2
Washoe County	Nevada	25	9,349	22,959	145.6
Montgomery County	Maryland	26	22,789	55,684	144.3
Finney County	Kansas	27	3,459	8,353	141.5
Tehama County	California	28	2,126	5,124	141.0

[Continued]

★ 119 ★

Fastest Growing Counties for Hispanics, 1980-90

[Continued]

County, state	State	Rank	1980 Hispanic population	1990 Hispanic population	Percent change 1980-90
Hendry County	Florida	29	2,389	5,757	141.0
Clark County	Nevada	30	35,088	82,904	136.3
Virginia Beach (city)	Virginia	31	5,160	12,137	135.2
Palm Beach County	Florida	32	28,504	66,613	133.7
Worcester County	Massachusetts	33	14,217	32,940	131.7
Brevard County	Flordia	34	5,336	12,261	129.8
San Bernardino County	California	35	165,865	378,582	128.3
Wake County	North Carolina	36	2,386	5,396	126.1
Washington County	Oregon	37	6,418	14,401	124.4
Collier County	Florida	38	9,255	20,734	124.0
Mendocino County	California	39	3,686	8,248	123.8
Smith County	Texas	40	4,035	8,986	122.7
Oneida County	New York	41	2,619	5,804	121.6
El Dorado County	California	42	3,910	8,777	121.1
Colusa County	California	43	2,493	5,424	117.6
Plymouth County	Massachusetts	44	4,429	9,571	116.1
Lehigh County	Pennsylvania	45	7,028	15,001	113.4
Atlantic County	New Jersey	46	7,590	16,117	112.3
Franklin County	Washington	47	5,411	11,316	109.1
DeKalb County	Georgia	48	7,469	15,619	109.1
Prince Georges County	Maryland	49	14,421	29,983	107.9
Tarrant County	Texas	50	67,637	139,879	106.8

Source: Edmondson, Brad. "Hispanic America." *American Demographics Desk Reference*, July 1991, p. 15. Primary source: 1990 U.S. Census.

★ 120 ★

Population Trends

Hispanic Population Growth Compared With Other Groups, 1980-90

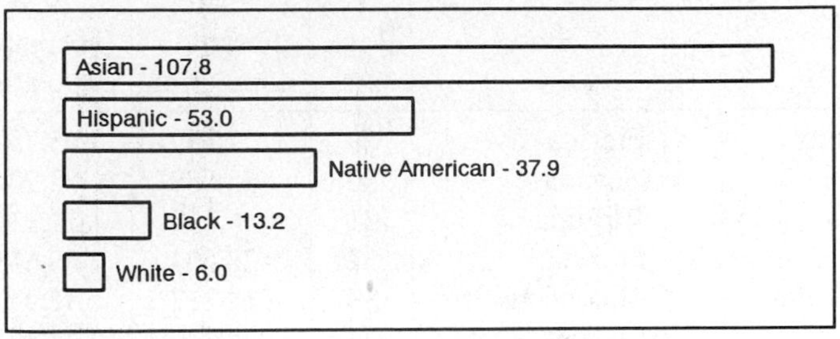

Race/ethnicity	Population increase (%)
Asian	107.8
Hispanic[1]	53.0
Native American	37.9
Black	13.2
White	6.0

Source: USA TODAY (10 December 1992), p. 11A. Primary source: U.S. Census Bureau. *Note:* 1. Hispanics may be of any race.

★ 121 ★

Population Trends

Hispanic Population Growth Compared With Other Racial/Ethnic Groups, 1980-90

Race/ethnicity	1990		1980		Change, 1980-90	
	Number (000)	Percent	Number (000)	Percent	Number (000)	Percent
All persons	226,546	100.0	248,710	100.0	22,164	9.8
Hispanic origin						
Hispanic origin[2]	14,609	6.4	22,354	9.0	7,745	53.0
Mexican	8,740	3.9	13,496	5.4	4,755	54.4
Puerto Rican	2,014	0.9	2,728	1.1	714	35.4
Cuban	803	0.4	1,044	0.4	241	30.0
Other Hispanic[1]	3,051	1.3	5,086	2.0	2,035	66.7
Not of Hispanic origin	211,937	93.6	226,356	91.0	14,419	6.8
Race						
White	188,372	83.1	199,686	80.3	11,314	6.0
Black	26,495	11.7	29,986	12.1	3,491	13.2
American Indian, Eskimo, or Aleut	1,420	0.6	1,959	0.8	539	37.9

[Continued]

★ 121 ★

Hispanic Population Growth Compared With Other Racial/Ethnic Groups, 1980-90

[Continued]

Race/ethnicity	1990		1980		Change, 1980-90	
	Number (000)	Percent	Number (000)	Percent	Number (000)	Percent
American Indian	1,364	0.6	1,878	0.8	514	37.7
Eskimo	42	(Z)	57	(Z)	15	35.6
Aleut	14	(Z)	24	(Z)	10	67.5
Asian or Pacific Islander	3,500[1]	1.5	7,274	2.9	3,773	107.8
Chinese	806	0.4	1,645	0.7	839	104.1
Filipino	775	0.3	1,407	0.6	632	81.6
Japanese	701	0.3	848	0.3	147	20.9
Asian Indian	362	0.2	815	0.3	454	125.6
Korean	355	0.2	799	0.3	444	125.3
Vietnamese	262	0.1	615	0.2	353	134.8
Hawaiian	167	0.1	211	0.1	44	26.5
Samoan	42	(Z)	63	(Z)	21	50.1
Guamanian	32	(Z)	49	(Z)	17	53.4
Other Asian or Pacific Islander	(NA)	(NA)	822	0.3	(NA)	(NA)
Other race	6,758	3.0	9,805	3.9	3,047	45.1

Source: U.S. Bureau of the Census. *Statistical Abstract of the United States: 1992,* (112th edition). Washington, DC: U.S. Government Printing Office, 1992, p. 17. Primary source: U.S. Bureau of the Census, press release CB91-216. *Notes:* (NA) indicates that data were not available. (Z) stands for less than 0.05 percent. 1. Not entirely comparable with 1990 counts. The 1990 count shown here which is based on 100-percent tabulations includes only the nine specific Asian or Pacific Islander groups listed separately in the 1980 race item. The 1980 total Asian or Pacific Islander population of 3,726,440 from sample tabulations is comparable to the 1990 count; these figures include groups not listed separately in the race item on the 1980 census form. 2. Persons of Hispanic origin may be of any race.

★ 122 ★

Population Trends

New York City: Population Trends, 1980-90

New York City's overall population grew 3% to 7.3 million from 1980 to 1990.

Race/ethnicity	1980	1990	Percent change
Hispanic[1]	1,406,024	1,783,511	26.8
White	3,668,945	3,163,125	14.5
Black	1,784,337	2,102,512	26.8
Asian	231,501	512,719	121.5

Source: Usdansky, Margaret L. "NYC in 'dumps' after losing gains of '80." *USA TODAY* (16 April 1992), p. 3A. Primary source: USA TODAY research; Census Bureau. *Note:* 1. Hispanics can be of any race.

★ 123 ★

Population Trends

Population Changes, 1980-90

U.S. population including Armed Forces overseas. Numbers in thousands.

January 1-December 31	Population at beginning of year	Percent change	Net change[1]	Components of change during period				Rate per 1,000 mid-year population				
				Natural increase	Births	Deaths[2]	Net civilian immigration	Net change	Natural increase	Births	Deaths	Net civilian immigration
Total												
1990	250,122	(NA)	(NA)	(NA)	(NA)	(NA)	(NA)	(NA)	(NA)	(NA)	(NA)	(NA)
1989	247,617	1.01	2,505	1,822	3,977	2,155	682	10.1	7.3	16.0	8.7	2.7
1988	245,208	0.98	2,409	1,742	3,913	2,171	667	9.8	7.1	15.9	8.8	2.7
1987	242,841	0.97	2,367	1,686	3,809	2,124	683	9.7	6.9	15.6	8.7	2.8
1986	240,532	0.96	2,309	1,651	3,757	2,106	658	9.6	6.8	15.5	8.7	2.7
1985	238,207	0.98	2,325	1,673	3,761	2,087	650	9.7	7.0	15.7	8.7	2.7
1984	235,961	0.95	2,246	1,629	3,669	2,040	615	9.5	6.9	15.5	8.6	2.6
1983	233,736	0.95	2,224	1,619	3,639	2,020	605	9.5	6.9	15.5	8.6	2.6
1982	231,405	1.01	2,332	1,705	3,681	1,975	626	10.0	7.3	15.8	8.5	2.7
1981	229,033	1.04	2,371	1,651	3,629	1,979	718	10.3	7.2	15.8	8.6	3.1
1980 (from April 1)	227,061	0.87	1,972	1,280	2,743	1,463	691	11.5	7.5	16.0	8.6	4.0
Hispanic origin[3]												
1990	20,859	(NA)	(NA)	(NA)	(NA)	(NA)	(NA)	(NA)	(NA)	(NA)	(NA)	(NA)
1989	20,198	3.27	661	379	470	92	282	32.2	18.4	22.9	4.5	13.8
1988	19,537	3.38	661	368	456	88	293	33.3	18.5	23.0	4.4	14.7
1987	18,871	3.53	666	359	444	84	306	34.7	18.7	23.1	4.4	15.9
1986	18,215	3.60	656	352	433	81	304	35.4	19.0	23.4	4.4	16.4
1985	17,573	3.65	642	336	413	77	306	35.9	18.8	23.1	4.3	17.1
1984	16,972	3.54	602	316	389	74	286	34.8	18.3	22.5	4.3	16.6
1983	16,371	3.67	601	307	377	71	295	36.1	18.4	22.6	4.2	17.7
1982	15,773	3.79	598	305	373	68	292	37.2	19.0	23.2	4.2	18.2
1981	15,149	4.12	624	295	360	64	328	40.3	19.1	23.3	4.2	21.2
1980 (from April 1)	14,630	3.55	519	214	261	46	305	46.5	19.2	23.3	4.1	27.3
White												
1990	210,221	(NA)	(NA)	(NA)	(NA)	(NA)	(NA)	(NA)	(NA)	(NA)	(NA)	(NA)
1989	208,604	0.78	1,617	1,234	3,105	1,872	383	7.7	5.9	14.8	8.9	1.8
1988	207,024	0.76	1,580	1,197	3,084	1,887	383	7.6	5.8	14.8	9.1	1.8
1987	205,490	0.75	1,534	1,149	2,992	1,843	386	7.4	5.6	14.5	8.9	1.9
1986	203,990	0.74	1,501	1,139	2,970	1,831	361	7.3	5.6	14.5	8.9	1.8
1985	202,463	0.75	1,527	1,172	2,991	1,820	353	7.5	5.8	147	9.0	1.7
1984	200,989	0.73	1,474	1,141	2,924	1,782	331	7.3	5.7	14.5	8.8	1.6
1983	199,516	0.74	1,473	1,138	2,904	1,766	334	7.4	5.7	14.5	8.8	1.7
1982	197,960	0.79	1,556	1,213	2,942	1,729	343	7.8	6.1	14.8	8.7	1.7
1981	196,415	0.79	1,545	1,177	2,909	1,732	366	7.8	6.0	14.8	8.8	1.9
1980 (from April 1)	195,086	0.68	1,328	926	2,203	1,277	400	9.0	6.3	15.0	8.7	2.7
Black												
1990	31,047	(NA)	(NA)	(NA)	(NA)	(NA)	(NA)	(NA)	(NA)	(NA)	(NA)	(NA)
1989	30,562	1.59	485	425	681	256	60	15.8	13.8	22.1	8.3	2.0
1988	30,110	1.50	452	391	650	259	60	14.9	12.9	21.4	8.5	2.0
1987	29,656	1.53	454	387	642	255	67	15.2	12.9	21.5	8.5	2.3
1986	29,223	1.48	433	371	621	250	62	14.7	12.6	21.1	8.5	2.1
1985	28,802	1.46	421	264	608	244	58	14.5	12.5	21.0	8.4	2.0
1984	28,391	1.45	410	357	593	236	54	14.4	12.5	20.7	8.3	1.9
1983	27,984	1.46	407	353	586	233	54	14.5	12.5	20.8	8.3	1.9
1982	27,561	1.53	423	366	593	227	57	15.2	13.2	21.3	8.2	2.0
1981	27,133	1.58	429	359	588	229	70	15.7	13.1	21.5	8.4	2.6
1980 (from April 1)	26,803	1.23	330	272	445	173	58	16.3	13.4	22.0	8.6	2.9
Other races												
1990	8,854	(NA)	(NA)	(NA)	(NA)	(NA)	(NA)	(NA)	(NA)	(NA)	(NA)	(NA)
1989	8,451	4.76	402	163	190	27	239	46.5	18.9	22.0	3.1	27.6
1988	8,074	4.67	377	154	179	26	224	45.7	18.6	21.7	3.1	27.1
1987	7,694	4.94	380	150	175	25	230	48.2	19.0	22.3	3.2	29.2
1986	7,319	5.12	375	141	165	24	234	50.0	18.8	22.0	3.2	31.2
1985	6,942	5.43	377	138	161	23	239	52.9	19.3	22.6	3.3	33.6
1984	6,580	5.49	361	131	153	22	230	53.5	19.4	22.6	3.2	34.1
1983	6,236	5.52	344	128	149	21	216	53.8	20.0	23.2	3.2	33.8
1982	5,883	6.00	353	127	146	19	226	58.2	20.9	24.1	3.2	37.3

[Continued]

★ 123 ★

Population Changes, 1980-90

[Continued]

January 1-December 31	Population at beginning of year	Percent change	Net change[1]	Components of change during period				Rate per 1,000 mid-year population				
				Natural increase	Births	Deaths[2]	Net civilian immigration	Net change	Natural increase	Births	Deaths	Net civilian immigration
1981	5,486	7.24	397	115	133	18	282	69.9	20.2	23.4	3.2	49.7
1980 (from April 1)	5,172	6.08	314	82	95	14	233	78.6	20.4	23.8	3.4	58.1

Source: Hollmann, Frederick W. U.S. Department of Commerce. Bureau of the Census. *United States Population Estimates, by Age, Sex, Race, and Hispanic Origin: 1980 to 1988*. Current Population Reports, Population Estimates and Projections, Series P-25, No. 1045. Washington, DC: The Bureau, January 1990, pp. 22. *Notes:* NA stands for not available. 1. Includes estimates of overseas admissions into and discharges from the Armed Forces. 2. Deaths occurring in the United States plus estimated deaths occurring to Armed Forces overseas. 3. Persons of Hispanic origin may be of any race.

★ 124 ★

Population Trends

Population Projections for 2010, by Age Group and Sex

Numbers are shown in thousands.

Age group	1990		2010		Percent change 1990-2010	
	Men	Women	Men	Women	Men	Women
All ages	11,154	11,200	18,887	19,697	69.0	76.0
Under age 5	1,260	1,223	1,665	1,599	32.0	31.0
5 to 14	2,083	2,032	3,358	3,245	61.0	60.0
15 to 24	2,156	2,114	3,191	3,149	48.0	49.0
25 to 34	2,202	2,098	2,885	2,915	31.0	39.0
35 to 44	1,509	1,514	2,820	2,966	87.0	96.0
45 to 54	864	913	2,391	2,545	177.0	179.0
55 to 64	592	653	1,481	1,663	150.0	154.0
65 to 74	349	438	721	941	107.0	115.0
75 and older	139	215	374	675	169.0	214.0

Source: American Demographics (February 1993), p. 59. Primary source: The Urban Institute.

★ 125 ★

Population Trends

Population Projections for 2040

By the middle of the next century minority groups will make up 47% of the U.S. population.

Race/ethnicity	1992 (in millions)	Projected population for 2040 (in millions)
Total	254.9	382.7
Whites	190.6	201.8
Blacks	30.4	57.3
Hispanics[1]	24.1	80.7
Asians	7.9	38.8
Native Americans	1.9	4.1

Source: "California's mix offers a look at the future." *USA TODAY* (4 December 1992), p. 8A. Primary source: U.S. Census Bureau *Note:* 1. Hispanics may be of any race.

★ 126 ★

Population Trends

Population Shifts, 1980-1990

Population is shown in millions.

Race/ethnicity	1980		1990		Pop. Shifts	
	Pop.	% distribution	Pop.	% distribution	Pop.	% Increase
Total population	226.5	100.0	249.9	100.0	23.4	10.0
White	194.7	86.0	210.3	84.0	15.6	8.0
Black	26.7	12.0	31.0	12.0	4.3	16.0
Hispanic[1]	14.6	6.0	21.0	8.0	6.4	44.0
Asian or other races	5.2	2.0	8.6	3.0	3.4	65.0

Source: "Minority customers to become a major marketing target." *Discount Store News* (18 May 1992), p. 100. Primary source: *American Demographics*. *Note:* 1. Hispanics may be of any race.

★ 127 ★

Population Trends

Projections of Hispanic Population, 1995 to 2080

The three "series" listed below are intended to give low, middle, and high estimates. Numbers are shown in millions and include persons in the Armed Forces overseas.

Year	Numbers in millions		
	Lowest series	Middle series	Highest series
1995	21.1	22.6	26.5
2000	23.1	25.2	31.2
2010	26.8	30.8	41.9
2020	30.1	36.5	54.3
2030	32.7	41.9	67.7
2040	34.5	46.7	81.9
2050	35.4	50.8	96.1
2060	35.6	54.2	110.6
2070	35.3	57.2	125.6
2080	34.6	59.6	140.7

Source: U.S. Bureau of the Census. *Projections of the Hispanic Population: 1983 to 2080.* Current Population Reports, Series P-25, No. 995, Washington, DC: U.S. Government Printing Office, 1986, p. 2.

★ 128 ★

Population Trends

Projections of the Median Age of the Hispanic Population, 1995 to 2080

The three "series" listed below are intended to give low, middle, and high estimates. Data include persons in the Armed Forces overseas.

Year	Lowest series	Middle series	Highest series
1995	27.9	27.2	25.9
2000	29.1	28.0	26.2
2010	31.3	29.3	26.7
2020	33.9	31.2	27.7
2030	36.3	33.0	28.8
2050	39.9	36.2	31.6
2080	44.3	40.9	35.9

Source: U.S. Bureau of the Census. *Projections of the Hispanic Population: 1983 to 2080.* Current Population Reports, Series P-25, No. 995, Washington, DC: U.S. Government Printing Office, 1986, p. 2.

★ 129 ★

Population Trends

Projections of the Percent Distribution of the Hispanic Population, by Age Group, 1995 to 2080

The three "series" listed below are intended to give low, middle, and high estimates. Data include persons in the Armed Forces overseas.

Year	Total	Age (years)								
		Under 5	5-13	14-17	18-24	25-34	35-44	45-64	65 +	85 +
Lowest series										
1995	100.0	9.6	17.5	6.9	11.2	16.6	15.6	16.0	6.5	0.6
2000	100.0	8.8	16.3	7.3	11.3	15.3	15.6	18.4	7.1	0.7
2010	100.0	8.1	14.1	6.3	11.4	15.4	13.5	22.7	8.4	0.9
2020	100.0	7.3	13.3	5.8	10.1	15.2	13.9	22.9	11.5	1.2
2030	100.0	6.5	12.2	5.6	9.9	14.1	14.2	22.8	14.8	1.5
2050	100.0	5.3	10.4	4.9	8.9	13.7	13.9	25.1	17.8	2.9
2080	100.0	4.6	8.9	4.2	7.8	12.2	13.3	26.5	22.5	4.0
Middle series										
1995	100.0	10.7	17.9	6.7	11.1	16.5	15.2	15.5	6.3	0.6
2000	100.0	9.9	17.4	7.2	11.0	15.1	15.1	17.6	6.8	0.7
2010	100.0	9.3	15.5	6.7	11.7	14.7	12.9	21.1	8.0	0.9
2020	100.0	8.6	15.0	6.3	10.7	15.2	12.9	20.9	10.6	1.2
2030	100.0	7.8	14.0	6.2	10.5	14.3	13.6	20.3	13.3	1.5
2050	100.0	6.6	12.2	5.5	9.8	14.2	13.5	22.6	15.6	3.0
2080	100.0	5.8	10.6	4.8	8.6	12.6	13.0	24.2	20.4	4.4
Highest series										
1995	100.0	11.8	18.4	6.6	11.6	18.1	14.2	13.8	5.5	0.5
2000	100.0	11.2	18.4	7.1	11.2	16.4	14.7	15.1	5.8	0.6
2010	100.0	10.9	17.3	7.1	12.0	15.1	13.1	18.1	6.5	0.8
2020	100.0	10.4	17.1	6.8	11.3	15.5	12.3	18.5	8.1	1.0
2030	100.0	9.6	16.4	6.8	11.3	14.9	12.9	17.8	10.3	1.3
2050	100.0	8.3	14.7	6.3	10.8	14.8	13.0	19.5	12.5	2.6
2080	100.0	7.4	12.9	5.6	9.6	13.3	12.7	21.4	17.1	4.2

Source: U.S. Bureau of the Census. *Projections of the Hispanic Population: 1983 to 2080.* Current Population Reports, Series P-25, No. 995, Washington, DC: U.S. Government Printing Office, 1986, p. 6.

★ 130 ★

Population Trends

Projections of the Total U.S. Population, by Race/ Ethnicity, 1995 to 2080

Numbers are shown in millions and do not sum to total because persons of Spanish origin may be of any race. Data include persons in the Armed Forces overseas.

Year	Total	Spanish origin	White non-Hispanic	Black	Other races
1995	259.6	22.6	196.2	33.7	8.5
2000	268.0	25.2	198.9	35.8	9.5
2010	283.2	30.8	202.6	40.0	11.7
2020	296.6	36.5	204.5	44.2	13.7
2030	304.8	41.9	202.4	47.6	15.6
2040	308.6	46.7	197.2	50.3	17.3
2050	309.5	50.8	190.8	52.3	18.9
2060	309.7	54.2	184.8	53.7	20.4
2070	310.4	57.2	180.0	54.9	21.9
2080	310.8	59.6	176.0	55.7	23.4

Source: U.S. Bureau of the Census. *Projections of the Hispanic Population: 1983 to 2080*. Current Population Reports, Series P-25, No. 995, Washington, DC: U.S. Government Printing Office, 1986, p. 10. Primary source: Current Population Reports, Series P-25, No. 952, tables 5 and 6; tables 1 and 14; and unpublished data.

★ 131 ★

Population Trends

Projections of the U.S. Population Distribution, by Age Group and Race/Ethnicity, 1995 to 2080

Percentages do not sum to 100 because persons of Hispanic origin may be of any race. Data include persons in the Armed Forces overseas.

Year	All ages	0 to 17	18 to 44	45 to 64	65 and over	85 and over
Spanish origin						
1995	8.7	11.9	9.1	6.7	4.2	3.2
2000	9.4	12.9	9.9	7.3	4.9	3.4
2010	10.9	15.0	11.9	8.4	6.3	4.4
2020	12.3	16.5	13.8	10.0	7.5	6.3
2030	13.7	17.8	15.5	12.0	8.6	7.5
2050	16.4	19.1	18.5	15.5	11.7	9.4
2080	19.2	20.0	20.2	19.6	16.7	14.4
White non-Hispanic						
1995	75.6	68.9	74.2	80.2	85.8	87.6
2000	74.2	67.3	72.5	79.0	84.5	87.0
2010	71.5	63.8	68.9	76.3	81.8	85.6

[Continued]

★ 131 ★

Projections of the U.S. Population Distribution, by Age Group and Race/Ethnicity, 1995 to 2080

[Continued]

Year	All ages	0 to 17	18 to 44	45 to 64	65 and over	85 and over
2020	68.9	61.3	65.8	72.8	79.2	82.0
2030	66.4	59.3	62.9	68.9	76.4	79.5
2050	61.6	57.0	58.1	63.1	69.9	74.5
2080	56.6	54.9	54.9	56.2	60.9	65.0
Black						
1995	13.0	16.4	13.6	10.2	8.3	8.1
2000	13.3	16.9	14.2	10.6	8.5	8.4
2010	14.1	17.7	15.4	12.0	9.1	8.3
2020	14.9	18.3	16.3	13.4	9.9	9.1
2030	15.6	18.6	17.1	14.5	11.3	9.7
2050	16.9	18.8	18.2	16.4	13.7	12.2
2080	17.9	18.5	18.3	18.1	16.8	15.5
Other races						
1995	3.3	3.5	3.6	3.2	2.0	1.2
2000	3.6	3.7	3.9	3.5	2.3	1.4
2010	4.1	4.4	4.5	3.8	3.2	2.0
2020	4.6	4.9	5.0	4.4	3.8	2.9
2030	5.1	5.4	5.4	5.3	4.1	3.8
2050	6.1	6.4	6.4	6.0	5.4	4.4
2080	7.5	7.9	7.9	7.5	6.7	6.0

Source: U.S. Bureau of the Census. *Projections of the Hispanic Population: 1983 to 2080*. Current Population Reports, Series P-25, No. 995, Washington, DC: U.S. Government Printing Office, 1986, p. 16.

★ 132 ★

Population Trends

States With the Largest Hispanic Populations, 1993, 2000, and 2020

From the source: "The Hispanic-origin population is projected to account for one-third of the growth in the Nation's population....The largest share of growth for the Nation's Hispanic population will occur in the West and South. Both regions combined will account for 61 percent of the six million Hispanics added to the Nation during 1993 to 2000." Numbers are shown in thousands of persons as of July 1.

State and year	Population
1993	
California	8,585
Texas	4,901
New York	2,319
Florida	1,803

[Continued]

★ 132 ★

States With the Largest Hispanic Populations, 1993, 2000, and 2020

[Continued]

State and year	Population
Illinois	1,016
2000	
California	10,584
Texas	6,173
New York	2,498
Florida	2,333
Illinois	1,264
2020	
California	17,489
Texas	10,302
Florida	4,173
New York	3,031
Illinois	2,076

Source: Campbell, Paul R. U.S. Bureau of the Census. *Population Projections for States, by Age, Race, and Sex: 1993 to 2020.* Current Population Reports, P25-1111. Washington, DC: U.S. Government Printing Office, 1994, p. xvii. *Note:* 1. Persons of Hispanic origin may be of any race.

★ 133 ★

Population Trends

Trends in U.S. Southwest Border County Populations, by Hispanic and Non-Hispanic Origin, 1970 to 1980

State and county	1970			1980			Percent change, 1970-1980		
	Total	Hispanic	Non-Hispanic	Total	Hispanic	Non-Hispanic	Total	Hispanic	Non-Hispanic
United States	203,211,926	9,072,602	194,139,324	226,545,805	14,603,683	211,942,122	11.5	61.0	9.2
Non-border states	169,275,162	4,289,613	164,985,549	184,627,603	6,158,647	178,468,956	9.1	43.6	8.2
Border states	33,936,764	4,782,989	29,153,775	41,918,202	8,445,036	33,473,166	23.5	76.6	14.8
All border counties	2,861,560	833,284	2,028,276	4,009,079	1,449,156	2,559,923	40.1	73.9	26.2
All non-border counties	31,075,204	3,949,705	27,125,499	37,909,123	6,995,880	30,913,243	22.0	77.1	14.0
California	19,953,134	2,369,231	17,583,903	23,667,902	4,541,300	19,126,602	18.6	91.7	8.8
Border counties	1,432,346	151,579	1,280,767	1,953,956	325,956	1,628,000	36.4	115.0	27.1
San Diego	1,357,854	121,485	1,236,369	1,861,846	274,530	1,587,316	37.1	126.0	28.4
Imperial	74,492	30,094	44,398	92,110	51,426	40,684	23.7	70.9	-8.4
Non-border counties	18,520,788	2,217,652	16,303,136	21,713,946	4,215,344	17,498,602	17.2	90.1	7.3
Arizona	1,770,900	264,770	1,506,130	2,718,215	444,102	2,274,113	53.5	67.7	51.0
Border counties	488,370	106,493	381,877	728,142	178,985	549,157	49.1	68.1	43.8
Cochise	61,910	18,244	43,666	85,686	22,848	62,838	38.4	25.2	43.9
Pima	351,667	64,136	287,531	531,443	111,378	420,065	51.1	73.7	46.1
Santa Cruz	13,966	10,208	3,758	20,459	15,229	5,230	46.5	49.2	39.2

[Continued]

★ 133 ★

Trends in U.S. Southwest Border County Populations, by Hispanic and Non-Hispanic Origin, 1970 to 1980

[Continued]

State and county	1970			1980			Percent change, 1970-1980		
	Total	Hispanic	Non-Hispanic	Total	Hispanic	Non-Hispanic	Total	Hispanic	Non-Hispanic
Yuma	60,827	13,905	46,922	90,554	29,530	61,024	48.9	112.4	30.1
Non-border counties	1,282,530	158,277	1,124,253	1,990,073	265,117	1,724,956	55.2	67.5	53.4
New Mexico	1,016,000	308,340	707,660	1,302,894	477,051	825,843	28.2	54.7	16.7
Border counties	86,213	37,951	48,262	117,974	59,191	58,783	36.8	56.0	21.8
Dona Ana	69,773	30,322	39,451	96,340	50,171	46,169	38.1	65.5	17.0
Hidalgo	4,734	2,286	2,448	6,049	2,849	3,200	27.8	24.6	30.7
Luna	11,706	5,343	6,363	15,585	6,171	9,414	33.1	15.5	47.9
Non-border counties	929,787	270,389	659,398	1,184,920	417,860	767,060	27.4	54.5	16.3
Texas	11,196,730	1,840,648	9,356,082	14,229,191	2,982,583	11,246,608	27.1	62.0	20.2
Border counties	854,631	537,261	317,370	1,209,007	885,024	323,983	41.5	64.7	2.1
El Paso	359,291	181,705	177,586	479,899	297,196	182,703	33.6	63.6	2.9
Hudspeth	2,392	769	1,623	2,728	1,589	1,139	14.0	106.6	-29.8
Culberson	3,429	1,301	2,128	3,315	2,101	1,214	-3.3	61.5	-43.0
Jeff Davis	1,527	642	885	1,647	777	870	7.9	21.0	-1.7
Presidio	4,842	4,359	483	5,188	3,989	1,199	7.1	-8.5	148.2
Brewster	7,780	3,692	4,088	7,573	3,262	4,311	-2.7	-11.6	5.5
Terrell	1,940	1,047	893	1,595	691	904	-17.8	-34.0	1.2
Valverde	27,471	14,888	12,583	35,910	22,612	13,298	30.7	51.9	5.7
Kinney	2,006	1,547	459	2,279	1,310	969	13.6	-15.3	111.1
Maverick	18,093	15,505	2,588	31,398	28,366	3,032	73.5	82.9	17.2
Dimmitt	9,039	6,842	2,197	11,367	8,869	2,498	25.8	29.6	13.7
Webb	72,859	56,530	16,329	99,258	90,823	8,435	36.2	60.7	-48.3
Zapata	4,352	2,720	1,632	6,628	5,042	1,586	52.3	85.4	-2.8
Starr	17,707	14,314	3,393	27,266	26,409	857	54.0	84.5	-74.7
Hidalgo	181,535	131,732	49,803	283,229	230,287	52,942	56.0	74.8	6.3
Cameron	140,368	99,668	40,700	209,727	161,701	48,026	49.4	62.2	18.0
Non-border counties	10,342,099	1,303,387	9,038,712	13,020,184	2,097,559	10,922,625	25.9	60.9	20.8

Source: U.S. Bureau of the Census, *The Hispanic Population of the Southwest Borderland.* Current Population Reports, Series P-23, No. 172, Washington, DC: U.S. Government Printing Office, 1991, p. 23.

Chapter 2
THE FAMILY

Characteristics

★ 134 ★

Families, by Poverty Status, Geographic Region of Residence, and Selected Family Characteristics, 1992 - I

Numbers are shown in thousands of persons, families, as of March of the following year.

Characteristic	All races			White			Black			Hispanic origin[1]		
	Total	Below poverty level		Total	Below poverty level		Total	Below poverty level		Total	Below poverty level	
		Number	Percent of total		Number	Percent of total		Number	Percent of total		Number	Percent of total
ALL FAMILIES												
Total	68,144	7,960	11.7	57,858	5,160	8.9	7,888	2,435	30.9	5,318	1,395	26.2
Residence and Region												
United States												
Metropolitan	52,299	5,907	11.3	43,575	3,644	8.4	6,648	1,968	29.6	4,919	1,278	26.0
Central city	19,336	3,387	17.5	13,966	1,768	12.7	4,382	1,443	32.9	2,761	861	31.2
Not central city	32,964	2,520	7.6	29,609	1,876	6.3	2,266	525	23.2	2,158	417	19.3
Not metropolitan	15,844	2,053	13.0	14,283	1,516	10.6	1,240	467	37.6	399	117	29.4
Northeast	13,478	1,369	10.2	11,839	968	8.2	1,242	353	28.4	884	289	32.7
Metropolitan	11,758	1,203	10.2	10,145	807	8.0	1,233	350	28.4	869	286	32.9
Central city	3,990	773	19.4	2,884	446	15.5	896	292	32.6	648	254	39.2
Not central city	7,768	429	5.5	7,262	361	5.0	336	58	17.3	222	32	14.5
Not metropolitan	1,720	166	9.6	1,694	161	9.5	9	3	(B)	14	3	(B)
Midwest	16,326	1,670	10.2	14,454	1,064	7.4	1,621	561	34.6	400	103	25.6
Metropolitan	11,472	1,177	10.3	9,713	627	6.5	1,567	523	33.4	376	97	25.9
Central city	4,309	792	18.4	2,971	319	10.7	1,226	449	36.7	244	64	26.2
Not central city	7,163	385	5.4	6,742	308	4.6	341	74	21.6	132	33	25.3
Not metropolitan	4,854	493	10.2	4,742	437	9.2	55	38	(B)	24	5	(B)
South	24,040	3,319	13.8	19,184	1,870	9.7	4,361	1,367	31.3	1,676	404	24.1
Metropolitan	17,068	2,182	12.8	13,474	1,172	8.7	3,216	952	29.6	1,501	341	22.7
Central city	6,305	1,153	18.3	4,255	495	11.6	1,907	627	32.9	865	235	27.2
Not central city	10,763	1,030	9.6	9,220	677	7.3	1,310	3285	24.8	636	106	16.7
Not metropolitan	6,972	1,137	16.3	5,709	698	12.2	1,145	416	36.3	176	63	35.8
West	14,299	1,602	11.2	12,381	1,257	10.2	663	153	23.1	2,358	600	25.4
Metropolitan	12,001	1,345	11.2	10,243	1,038	10.1	632	143	22.6	2,173	554	25.5
Central city	4,731	669	14.1	3,857	508	13.2	353	75	21.2	1,004	308	30.7
Not central city	7,270	676	9.3	6,386	530	8.3	279	68	24.4	1,168	246	21.0
Not metropolitan	2,298	257	11.2	2,138	219	10.2	31	10	(B)	185	46	25.0
Division												
New England	3,461	287	8.3	3,277	231	7.1	122	45	36.5	122	51	42.2
Middle Atlantic	10,017	1,081	10.8	8,562	737	8.6	1,120	308	27.5	762	238	31.2
East North Central	11,527	1,184	10.3	10,005	724	7.2	1,355	433	32.0	340	85	25.0
West North Central	4,798	486	10.1	4,450	340	7.6	267	128	48.1	61	18	(B)
South Atlantic	12,352	1,504	12.2	9,620	765	8.0	2,501	706	28.2	617	124	20.0
East South Central	4,340	686	15.8	3,493	393	11.3	820	290	35.4	11	-	(B)
West South Central	7,348	1,129	15.4	6,071	712	11.7	1,040	372	35.7	1,048	280	26.8
Mountain	3,728	386	10.4	3,465	318	9.2	103	23	22.1	427	114	26.6

[Continued]

★ 134 ★

Families, by Poverty Status, Geographic Region of Residence, and Selected Family Characteristics, 1992 - I

[Continued]

Characteristic	All races			White			Black			Hispanic origin[1]		
	Total	Below poverty level		Total	Below poverty level		Total	Below poverty level		Total	Below poverty level	
		Number	Percent of total		Number	Percent of total		Number	Percent of total		Number	Percent of total
Pacific	10,571	1,216	11.5	8,916	939	10.5	560	130	23.3	1,931	486	25.2
FAMILIES WITH RELATED CHILDREN UNDER 18												
Total	35,492	6,269	17.7	28,709	3,926	13.7	5,316	2,075	39.0	3,655	1,184	32.4
Residence and Region												
United States												
Metropolitan	27,406	4,700	17.2	21,648	2,800	12.9	4,491	1,686	37.5	3,362	1,080	32.1
Central city	10,400	2,740	26.3	6,900	1,379	20.0	2,935	1,229	41.9	1,907	735	38.5
Not central city	17,006	1,961	11.5	14,748	1,421	9.6	1,555	457	29.4	1,455	346	23.7
Not metropolitan	8,086	1,569	19.4	7,061	1,126	16.0	826	390	47.2	293	104	35.5
Northeast	6,652	1,068	16.1	5,565	730	13.1	822	305	37.1	599	253	42.3
Metropolitan	5,840	943	16.2	4,772	609	12.8	816	302	37.0	591	251	42.5
Central city	2,069	613	29.6	1,341	344	25.6	598	247	41.3	449	222	49.4
Not central city	3,771	330	8.7	3,431	266	7.7	218	55	25.2	142	29	20.5
Not metropolitan	812	125	15.4	793	120	15.1	6	3	(B)	8	2	(B)
Midwest	8,609	1,359	15.8	7,304	847	11.6	1,148	483	42.1	282	90	31.8
Metropolitan	6,163	982	15.9	4,939	514	10.4	1,106	452	40.9	264	85	32.1
Central city	2,461	658	26.7	1,517	260	17.1	878	383	43.6	178	58	32.6
Not central city	3,702	324	8.8	3,422	255	7.4	227	70	30.7	87	27	31.0
Not metropolitan	2,446	377	15.4	2,365	332	14.1	42	31	(B)	18	5	(B)
South	12,595	2,553	20.3	9,374	1,331	14.2	2,916	1,167	40.0	1,080	326	30.2
Metropolitan	8,952	1,704	19.0	6,551	844	12.9	2,158	820	38.0	950	270	28.5
Central city	3,341	917	27.4	2,021	353	17.5	1,233	541	43.9	538	184	34.1
Not central city	5,611	787	14.0	4,530	491	10.8	925	279	30.1	412	87	21.0
Not metropolitan	3,643	849	23.3	2,823	487	17.3	758	347	45.8	130	56	42.8
West	7,637	1,290	16.9	6,466	1,019	15.8	431	121	28.0	1,694	515	30.4
Metropolitan	6,451	1,071	16.6	5,386	832	15.5	411	111	27.1	1,557	474	30.5
Central city	2,530	551	21.8	2,021	423	20.9	226	58	25.7	743	271	36.5
Not central city	3,922	519	13.2	3,365	410	12.2	184	53	28.9	814	203	24.9
Not metropolitan	1,185	219	18.5	1,080	187	17.3	20	9	(B)	137	41	29.9
Division												
New England	1,682	241	14.3	1,552	191	12.3	91	41	45.1	97	48	49.2
Middle Atlantic	4,969	827	16.6	4,013	538	13.4	731	264	36.1	502	205	40.9
East North Central	6,151	959	15.6	5,093	573	11.2	961	370	38.5	236	73	30.7
West North Central	2,457	400	16.3	2,211	274	12.4	186	113	60.9	45	17	(B)
South Atlantic	6,166	1,144	18.6	4,375	526	12.0	1,660	597	36.0	362	98	27.1
East South Central	2,324	510	22.0	1,771	270	15.3	540	239	44.2	4	-	(B)
West South Central	4,106	898	21.9	3,228	534	16.6	716	331	46.2	715	228	31.9
Mountain	1,953	298	15.3	1,772	248	14.0	79	17	21.5	284	89	31.3
Pacific	5,683	991	17.4	4,694	771	16.4	352	103	29.4	1,410	426	30.2

Source: U.S. Bureau of the Census. *Poverty in the United States: 1992.* Current Population Reports, Series P60-185, U.S. Government Printing Office, Washington, D.C., 1993, p. 137. *Notes:* A dash (-) stands for zero or rounds to zero. A (B) stands for base less than 75,000. 1. Persons of Hispanic origin may be of any race.

★ 135 ★

Characteristics

Families, by Poverty Status, Geographic Region of Residence, and Selected Family Characteristics, 1992 - II

Numbers are shown thousands of families, as of March of the following year.

Characteristic	All races			White			Black			Hispanic origin[1]		
	Total	Below poverty level		Total	Below poverty level		Total	Below poverty level		Total	Below poverty level	
		Number	Percent of total		Number	Percent of total		Number	Percent of total		Number	Percent of total
MARRIED-COUPLE FAMILIES												
Total	53,171	3,318	6.2	47,601	2,631	5.5	3,748	486	13.0	3,674	680	18.5
Residence and Region												
United States												
Metropolitan	40,237	2,239	5.6	35,501	1,722	4.9	3,138	352	11.2	3,355	602	17.9
Central city	13,223	1,083	8.2	10,617	767	7.2	1,876	222	11.8	1,739	361	20.8
Not central city	27,014	1,156	4.3	24,883	955	3.8	1,263	130	10.3	1,616	241	14.9
Not metropolitan	12,934	1,079	8.3	12,100	909	7.5	610	134	22.1	318	79	24.7
Northeast	10,391	487	4.7	9,491	400	4.2	577	58	10.1	474	68	14.4
Metropolitan	8,981	402	4.5	8,104	317	3.9	569	57	10.0	461	65	14.1
Central city	2,575	224	8.7	2,039	152	7.5	377	52	13.7	302	54	17.9
Not central city	6,406	178	2.8	6,065	165	2.7	192	5	2.8	159	11	6.9
Not metropolitan	1,410	85	6.0	1,387	83	6.0	8	1	(B)	14	3	(B)
Midwest	12,827	618	4.8	12,004	506	4.2	648	87	13.5	279	49	17.6
Metropolitan	8,782	357	4.1	8,016	262	3.3	630	79	12.5	261	46	17.7
Central city	2,768	200	7.2	2,254	122	5.4	445	64	14.3	167	29	17.5
Not central city	6,014	157	2.6	5,761	140	2.4	185	15	8.3	94	17	18.1
Not metropolitan	4,045	261	6.5	3,988	244	6.1	17	8	(B)	17	3	(B)
South	18,704	1,458	7.8	16,168	1,106	6.8	2,161	305	14.1	1,267	262	20.7
Metropolitan	13,153	859	6.5	11,271	644	5.7	1,595	183	11.5	1,130	218	19.3
Central city	4,388	382	8.7	3,408	274	8.0	872	92	10.6	628	140	22.3
Not central city	8,765	476	5.4	7,862	370	4.7	723	90	12.5	502	78	15.6
Not metropolitan	5,551	599	10.8	4,898	461	9.4	566	122	21.6	138	44	32.0
West	11,249	759	6.7	9,937	619	6.2	363	36	10.0	1,653	301	18.2
Metropolitan	9,321	622	6.7	8,110	498	6.1	344	34	9.7	1,504	272	18.1
Central city	3,492	277	7.9	2,915	218	7.5	181	14	7.9	642	138	21.4
Not central city	5,829	345	5.9	5,195	280	5.4	163	19	11.7	861	135	15.6
Not metropolitan	1,927	134	7.0	1,827	120	6.6	19	3	(B)	149	29	19.2
Division												
New England	2,733	95	3.5	2,634	84	3.2	51	4	(B)	57	11	(B)
Middle Atlantic	7,658	391	5.1	6,857	316	4.6	526	54	10.3	417	58	13.8
East North Central	8,931	429	4.8	8,259	342	4.1	558	71	12.7	233	38	16.4
West North Central	3,896	188	4.8	3,745	165	4.4	90	16	18.0	45	11	(B)
South Atlantic	9,568	625	6.5	8,158	441	5.4	1,238	162	13.1	471	73	15.5
East South Central	3,326	269	8.1	2,916	207	7.1	390	60	15.5	9	-	(B)
West South Central	5,808	564	9.7	5,094	457	9.0	533	82	15.4	788	189	24.0
Mountain	2,987	187	6.3	2,822	159	5.6	64	8	(B)	293	62	21.1
Pacific	8,262	569	6.9	7,115	460	6.5	299	28	9.4	1,360	239	17.6
MARRIED-COUPLE FAMILIES WITH RELATED CHILDREN UNDER 18												
Total	25,714	2,166	8.4	22,406	1,706	7.6	2,175	335	15.4	2,497	562	22.5
Residence and Region												
United States												
Metropolitan	19,575	1,454	7.4	16,771	1,110	6.6	1,804	240	13.3	2,270	497	21.9
Central city	6,286	717	11.4	4,835	507	10.5	1,030	148	14.3	1,174	303	25.8
Not central city	13,289	737	5.5	11,936	604	5.1	774	93	12.0	1,096	194	17.7
Not metropolitan	6,139	712	11.6	5,634	595	10.6	371	94	25.4	227	65	28.7
Northeast	4,826	292	6.1	4,292	231	5.4	307	41	13.4	298	56	18.8
Metropolitan	4,197	243	5.8	3,680	184	5.0	303	40	13.2	290	54	18.5
Central city	1,162	136	11.7	860	89	10.3	196	35	17.6	193	44	23.0
Not central city	3,035	107	3.5	2,821	95	3.4	106	5	5.1	98	9	9.5
Not metropolitan	628	49	7.8	612	47	7.7	4	1	(B)	8	2	(B)
Midwest	6,217	418	6.7	5,718	350	6.1	386	57	14.8	199	43	21.7
Metropolitan	4,310	241	5.6	3,847	181	4.7	375	53	14.2	186	40	21.8
Central city	1,356	128	9.5	1,051	84	8.0	265	38	14.4	119	25	21.3
Not central city	2,954	113	3.8	2,795	97	3.5	110	15	13.9	67	15	(B)
Not metropolitan	1,907	178	9.3	1,871	169	9.1	11	4	(B)	13	3	(B)
South	9,063	915	10.1	7,558	671	8.9	1,270	217	17.1	820	209	25.5
Metropolitan	6,358	533	8.4	5,245	383	7.3	922	130	14.1	723	173	23.9

[Continued]

★ 135 ★

Families, by Poverty Status, Geographic Region of Residence, and Selected Family Characteristics, 1992 - II

[Continued]

Characteristic	All races			White			Black			Hispanic origin[1]		
	Total	Below poverty level		Total	Below poverty level		Total	Below poverty level		Total	Below poverty level	
		Number	Percent of total		Number	Percent of total		Number	Percent of total		Number	Percent of total
Central city	2,044	243	11.9	1,517	164	10.8	461	68	14.7	384	108	28.1
Not central city	4,314	289	6.7	3,728	219	5.9	461	62	13.5	339	65	19.1
Not metropolitan	2,706	383	14.1	2,312	288	12.4	348	87	25.0	97	37	38.1
West	5,608	540	9.6	4,836	454	9.4	212	20	9.4	1,180	254	21.5
Metropolitan	4,710	437	9.3	3,999	362	9.1	203	17	8.5	1,070	230	21.5
Central city	1,724	209	12.1	1,407	170	12.1	107	7	6.5	478	125	26.2
Not central city	2,986	228	7.6	2,592	192	7.4	96	10	10.6	592	105	17.7
Not metropolitan	898	103	11.4	839	91	10.9	8	3	(B)	110	23	21.4
Division												
New England	1,255	63	5.0	1,196	57	4.7	24	2	(B)	41	9	(B)
Middle Atlantic	3,570	230	6.4	3,094	174	5.6	283	39	13.9	257	47	18.3
East North Central	4,376	288	6.6	3,964	232	5.8	340	48	14.2	16	33	19.8
West North Central	1,842	130	7.1	1,753	118	6.8	46	9	(B)	33	10	(B)
South Atlantic	4,359	369	8.5	3,528	246	7.0	736	114	15.5	272	56	20.8
East South Central	1,636	155	9.5	1,410	113	8.0	215	42	19.6	1	-	(B)
West South Central	3,069	391	12.8	2,619	312	11.9	318	60	18.9	547	153	28.0
Mountain	1,444	124	8.6	1,344	110	8.2	40	2	(B)	194	49	25.3
Pacific	4,164	416	10.0	3,495	344	9.8	171	18	10.3	986	205	20.7

Source: U.S. Bureau of the Census. *Poverty in the United States: 1992.* Current Population Reports, Series P60-185, U.S. Government Printing Office, Washington, D.C., 1993, p. 138. *Notes:* A dash stands for zero or rounds to zero. A (B) stands for base less than 75,000. 1. Persons of Hispanic origin may be of any race.

★ 136 ★

Characteristics

Families, by Poverty Status, Geographic Region of Residence, and Selected Family Characteristics, 1992 - III

Numbers are shown in thousands of families, as of March of the following year.

Characteristic	All races			White			Black			Hispanic origin[1]		
	Total	Below poverty level		Total	Below poverty level		Total	Below poverty level		Total	Below poverty level	
		Number	Percent of total		Number	Percent of total		Number	Percent of total		Number	Percent of total
FAMILIES WITH FEMALE HOUSEHOLDER, NO SPOUSE PRESENT												
Total	11,947	4,171	34.9	7,848	2,202	28.1	3,680	1,835	49.8	1,238	604	48.8
Residence and Region												
United States												
Metropolitan	9,671	3,321	34.3	6,206	1,699	27.4	3,122	1,517	48.6	1,187	579	48.8
Central city	5,043	2,098	41.6	2,584	880	34.0	2,260	1,150	50.9	801	433	54.0
Not central city	4,628	1,223	26.4	3,623	819	22.6	862	367	42.6	386	146	37.9
Not metropolitan	2,276	850	37.3	1,642	504	30.7	558	318	56.9	51	25	(B)
Northeast	2,477	813	32.8	1,837	518	28.2	590	281	47.6	358	207	57.9
Metropolitan	2,236	741	33.1	1,599	449	28.0	588	279	47.5	357	207	58.0
Central city	1,193	518	43.4	690	274	39.9	470	233	49.6	305	186	60.9
Not central city	1,043	223	21.4	910	174	19.1	118	46	39.0	52	21	(B)
Not metropolitan	241	72	30.0	238	70	29.4	2	2	(B)	1	-	(B)
Midwest	2,787	930	33.4	1,872	473	25.3	861	439	51.0	87	43	49.3
Metropolitan	2,178	731	33.6	1,313	314	23.9	826	409	49.5	82	40	49.3
Central city	1,293	540	41.8	568	174	30.6	695	357	51.4	58	33	(B)
Not central city	885	191	21.6	745	140	18.7	132	52	39.4	23	8	(B)
Not metropolitan	608	198	32.6	559	160	28.6	35	30	(B)	5	2	(B)
South	4,446	1,713	38.5	2,387	678	28.4	1,970	1,006	51.1	297	111	37.3
Metropolitan	3,286	1,237	37.6	1,764	488	27.7	1,460	727	49.8	274	100	36.4
Central city	1,640	711	43.4	669	195	29.2	944	503	53.3	180	75	41.9
Not central city	1,646	525	31.9	1,095	293	26.7	517	224	43.4	94	24	25.9
Not metropolitan	1,160	476	41.0	623	190	30.5	509	279	54.7	23	11	(B)
West	2,237	715	32.0	1,752	533	30.4	260	109	42.0	497	244	49.2
Metropolitan	1,970	612	31.1	1,529	449	29.3	247	102	41.2	474	232	48.9
Central city	917	329	35.9	657	235	35.8	152	57	37.3	258	139	53.9

[Continued]

★ 136 ★

Families, by Poverty Status, Geographic Region of Residence, and Selected Family Characteristics, 1992 - III

[Continued]

Characteristic	All races			White			Black			Hispanic origin[1]		
	Total	Below poverty level		Total	Below poverty level		Total	Below poverty level		Total	Below poverty level	
		Number	Percent of total		Number	Percent of total		Number	Percent of total		Number	Percent of total
Not central city	1,053	283	26.9	873	213	24.4	95	45	47.3	217	93	42.9
Not metropolitan	267	103	38.5	222	84	37.9	13	7	(B)	22	12	(B)
Division												
New England	564	175	31.0	496	134	27.1	59	37	(B)	59	38	(B)
Middle Atlantic	1,913	638	33.4	1,341	384	28.6	531	244	45.9	299	169	56.4
East North Central	2,051	664	32.4	1,310	319	24.4	707	336	47.6	75	37	49.5
West North Central	735	266	36.2	563	154	27.4	155	103	66.3	11	5	(B)
South Atlantic	2,330	806	34.6	1,172	286	24.4	1,116	509	45.6	102	40	39.2
East South Central	855	394	46.1	466	171	36.7	385	221	57.3	3	-	(B)
West South Central	1,262	513	40.7	749	221	29.5	469	276	58.9	192	71	36.8
Mountain	551	169	30.7	475	138	29.1	36	14	(B)	90	40	44.9
Pacific	1,686	546	32.4	1,277	395	30.9	224	95	42.5	407	204	50.1
FAMILIES WITH FEMALE HOUSEHOLDER, NO SPOUSE PRESENT, WITH RELATED CHILDREN UNDER 18												
Total	8,230	3,761	45.7	5,060	1,980	39.1	2,898	1,659	57.2	945	543	57.4
Residence and Region												
United States												
Metropolitan	6,647	2,997	45.1	3,953	1,531	38.7	2,476	1,369	55.3	905	517	57.1
Central city	3,573	1,876	52.5	1,677	788	47.0	1,775	1,028	57.9	621	388	62.5
Not central city	3,074	1,121	36.5	2,276	743	32.6	701	341	48.7	284	129	45.5
Not metropolitan	1,583	764	48.2	1,107	449	40.6	422	289	68.6	40	25	(B)
Northeast	1,544	725	46.9	1,048	461	44.0	470	253	53.8	281	188	66.9
Metropolitan	1,400	658	47.0	906	397	43.8	468	251	53.6	280	188	67.1
Central city	806	455	56.4	419	242	57.7	371	207	55.8	239	168	70.2
Not central city	594	203	34.2	487	156	31.9	98	44	45.3	41	20	(B)
Not metropolitan	145	67	46.1	142	64	45.1	2	2	(B)	1	-	(B)
Midwest	2,013	849	42.2	1,271	432	34.0	704	399	56.7	69	38	(B)
Metropolitan	1,599	675	42.2	896	294	32.8	675	372	55.1	66	36	(B)
Central city	986	494	50.1	394	162	41.1	568	323	56.8	52	30	(B)
Not central city	613	181	29.5	502	132	26.3	107	49	45.8	14	5	(B)
Not metropolitan	415	174	42.0	374	138	37.0	29	27	(B)	4	2	(B)
South	3,101	1,536	49.5	1,507	596	39.5	1,529	914	59.8	195	94	48.2
Metropolitan	2,291	1,110	48.5	1,095	431	39.3	1,149	660	57.4	176	83	47.0
Central city	1,152	632	54.8	409	169	41.4	724	451	62.3	124	65	52.1
Not central city	1,139	479	42.0	685	261	38.1	425	209	49.1	53	18	(B)
Not metropolitan	810	426	52.6	413	165	40.1	380	254	66.9	18	11	(B)
West	1,571	651	41.5	1,235	490	39.7	195	93	47.6	400	223	55.6
Metropolitan	1,357	554	40.9	1,056	409	38.7	183	86	47.1	383	211	55.0
Central city	628	296	47.1	454	215	47.2	112	47	42.3	206	125	60.7
Not central city	728	258	35.5	602	194	32.3	71	39	(B)	177	86	48.4
Not metropolitan	214	97	45.3	178	82	45.7	12	6	(B)	17	12	(B)
Division												
New England	351	163	46.5	289	124	42.8	56	36	(B)	52	36	(B)
Middle Atlantic	1,194	561	47.0	759	337	44.5	414	217	52.3	229	152	66.3
East North Central	1,483	607	40.9	884	294	33.2	575	304	52.9	59	33	(B)
West North Central	531	243	45.7	386	138	35.8	129	95	73.8	11	5	(B)
South Atlantic	1,581	722	45.7	696	250	36.0	852	461	54.1	61	33	(B)
East South Central	610	344	56.5	312	150	48.1	295	193	65.5	3	-	(B)
West South Central	910	470	51.6	500	196	39.2	382	260	68.1	131	61	46.6
Mountain	403	155	38.5	339	127	37.4	36	14	(B)	66	33	(B)
Pacific	1,168	496	42.5	896	364	40.6	159	79	49.5	334	190	56.9

Source: U.S. Bureau of the Census. *Poverty in the United States: 1992.* Current Population Reports, Series P60-185, U.S. Government Printing Office, Washington, D.C., 1993, p. 139. *Notes:* A dash (-) stands for zero or rounds to zero. A (B) stands for base less than 75,000. 1. Persons of Hispanic origin may be of any race.

★ 137 ★

Characteristics

Fatherless Families, 1975 and 1990

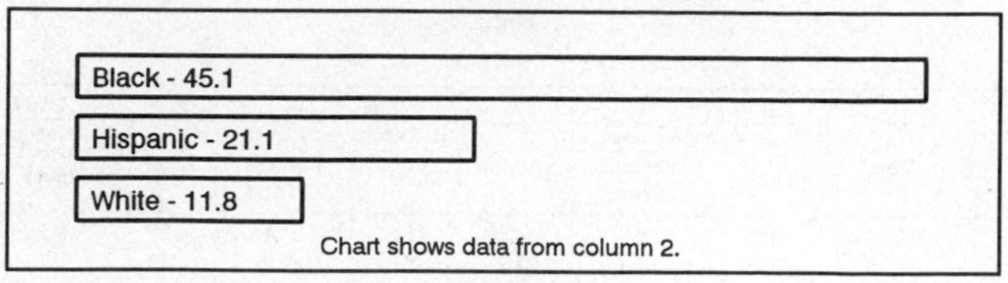

Numbers are shown in percent for each race/ethnicity. Chart shows data for 1990.

Race/ethnicity	1975	1990
Black	35.4	45.1
Hispanic[1]	17.6	21.1
White	9.4	11.8

Source: "Issues 'too critical' for glib debate." *USA TODAY* (21 May 1992), p. 2A. Primary source: U.S. Census Bureau *Note:* 1. Hispanics can be of any race.

★ 138 ★

Characteristics

Fatherless Families, by Race/Ethnicity, 1990

Race/ethnicity	Fatherless families (in millions)
White	20.8
Black	11.9
Hispanic[1]	3.9

Source: "Issues 'too critical' for glib debate." *USA TODAY* (21 May 1992), p. 2A. Primary source: U.S. Census Bureau. *Note:* 1. Hispanics can be of any race.

★ 139 ★

Characteristics

Household Characteristics

Data are shown for March, except as noted. Based on Current Population Survey, except as noted. Includes members of Armed Forces living off post or with their families on post, but excludes all other members of Armed Forces.

Race/ethnicity and household type	Number (thousands)						Percent distribution					
	1970	1980	1990	1991	1992	1993	1970	1980	1990	1991	1992	1993
Total households												
Total[1]	63401	80776	93347	94312	95669	96391	100.0	100.0	100.0	100.0	100.0	100.0
White	56602	70766	80163	80968	81675	82083	89.0	88.0	86.0	86.0	85.0	85.0
Black	6223	8586	10486	10671	11083	11190	10.0	11.0	11.0	11.0	12.0	12.0
Hispanic[2]	2303	3684	5933	6220	6379	6626	4.0	5.0	6.0	7.0	7.0	7.0
Family households												
White, total	46166	52243	56590	56803	57224	57858	100.0	100.0	100.0	100.0	100.0	100.0
Married couple	41029	44751	46981	47014	47124	47601	89.0	86.0	83.0	83.0	82.0	82.0
Male householder[3]	1038	1441	2303	2276	2374	2409	2.0	3.0	4.0	4.0	4.0	4.0
Female householder[3]	4099	6052	7306	7512	7726	7848	9.0	12.0	13.0	13.0	14.0	14.0
Black, total	4856	6184	7470	7471	7716	7888	100.0	100.0	100.0	100.0	100.0	100.0
Married couple	3317	3433	3750	3569	3631	3748	68.0	56.0	50.0	48.0	47.0	48.0
Male householder[3]	181	256	446	472	504	460	4.0	4.0	6.0	6.0	7.0	6.0
Female householder[3]	1358	2495	3275	3430	3582	3680	28.0	40.0	44.0	46.0	46.0	47.0
Asian or Pacific Islander, total[4]	NA	818	1531	1536	1624	1662	NA	100.0	100.0	100.0	100.0	100.0
Married couple	NA	691	1256	1230	1284	1335	NA	84.0	82.0	80.0	79.0	80.0
Male householder[3]	NA	39	86	112	103	95	NA	5.0	6.0	7.0	6.0	6.0
Female householder[3]	NA	88	188	194	237	232	NA	11.0	12.0	13.0	15.0	14.0
Hispanic, total[2]	2004	3029	4840	4981	5177	5318	100.0	100.0	100.0	100.0	100.0	100.0
Married couple	1615	2282	3395	3454	3532	3674	81.0	75.0	70.0	69.0	68.0	69.0
Male householder[3]	82	138	329	342	383	407	4.0	5.0	7.0	7.0	7.0	8.0
Female householder[3]	307	610	1116	1186	1261	1238	15.0	20.0	23.0	24.0	24.0	23.0
Nonfamily households												
White, total	10436	18522	23573	24166	24451	24225	100.0	100.0	100.0	100.0	100.0	100.0
Male householder	3406	7499	9951	10312	10476	10370	33.0	40.0	42.0	43.0	43.0	43.0
Female householder	7030	11023	13622	13853	13975	13856	67.0	60.0	58.0	57.0	57.0	57.0
Black, total	1367	2402	3015	3200	3367	3302	100.0	100.0	100.0	100.0	100.0	100.0
Male householder	564	1146	1313	1531	1594	1484	41.0	48.0	44.0	48.0	47.0	45.0
Female householder	803	1256	1702	1670	1773	1818	59.0	52.0	56.0	52.0	53.0	55.0
Hispanic, total[2]	299	654	1093	1238	1202	1308	100.0	100.0	100.0	100.0	100.0	100.0
Male householder	150	365	587	669	660	691	50.0	56.0	54.0	54.0	55.0	53.0
Female householder	148	289	506	569	542	617	49.0	44.0	46.0	46.0	45.0	47.0

Source: 1994 Statistical Abstract of the United States on CD-ROM [machine-readable datafiles]. CD-8A-94. Washington, DC: U.S. Department of Commerce, Economics and Statistics Administration, Bureau of the Census, Data User Services Division, January 1995. Primary source: U.S. Bureau of the Census, Census of Population: 1970, Persons of Spanish Origin, PC(2)- 1C; and Current Population Reports, P20-477, and earlier reports. *Notes:* NA stands for not available. 1. Includes other races not shown separately. 2. Hispanic persons may be of any race. 1970 data as of April. 3. No spouse present. 4. 1980 data as of April and are from 1980 Census of Population.

★ 140 ★

Characteristics

Marital Status and Size of Families, by Hispanic Origin, March 1993

Data show percent distribution by family characteristic for each ethnic group.

Characteristic	Total population	Hispanic origin population	Non-Hispanic population	Non-Hispanic White population	Hispanic subgroup				
					Mexican origin population	Puerto Rican origin population	Cuban origin population	Central and South American origin population	Other Hispanic origin population
Type of family									
All families	68,144	5,318	62,825	52,855	3,210	653	309	751	395
Percent	100.0	100.0	100.0	100.0	100.0	100.0	100.0	100.0	100.0
Married-couple families	78.0	69.1	78.8	83.5	72.3	53.4	76.1	67.9	66.0
Female householder, no husband present	17.5	23.3	17.0	12.7	19.4	40.5	18.2	24.7	27.7
Male householder, no wife present	4.4	7.7	4.2	3.8	8.4	6.2	5.7	7.4	6.3
Size of Family									
Percent	100.0	100.0	100.0	100.0	100.0	100.0	100.0	100.0	100.0
Two persons	42.0	26.2	43.3	45.2	22.8	31.7	40.3	24.4	36.7
Three persons	23.6	23.5	23.6	23.1	21.8	26.8	29.0	25.5	24.2
Four persons	21.0	23.1	20.8	20.7	22.2	25.5	20.0	26.2	23.1
Five persons	8.9	14.5	8.4	8.0	16.1	11.0	7.6	15.6	11.0
Six persons	3.0	6.8	2.7	2.2	8.5	3.3	2.1	5.7	4.2
Seven or more persons	1.6	5.9	1.2	0.9	8.6	1.7	1.1	2.6	0.9
Mean number of persons	3.16	3.78	3.08	3.02	4.01	3.33	3.06	3.63	3.25

Source: Montgomery, Patricia A. U.S. Bureau of the Census. *The Hispanic Population in the United States: March 1993.* Current Population Reports, Series P20-475. Washington, DC: U.S. Government Printing Office, 1994, pp. 18-19.

★ 141 ★

Characteristics

Marital Status, Fertility, and Household Type in U.S. Southwest Border States and Counties, 1980

Characteristic	United States	Total, border states	Border states			
			Border county areas		Non-border county areas	
			Hispanic	Non-Hispanic	Hispanic	Non-Hispanic
Marital status						
Persons, 15 years and over	175,307,629	32,278,897	954,668	2,073,859	4,686,142	24,564,228
Percent	100.0	100.0	100.0	100.0	100.0	100.0
Single (never married)	26.1	26.1	31.0	26.3	31.0	25.0
Married	60.1	59.6	59.3	59.0	59.3	59.7
Widowed	7.6	6.5	5.0	6.5	4.0	7.1
Divorced	6.2	7.7	4.8	8.2	5.7	8.2
Fertility						
Women, 15 to 44 years	52,878,032	10,020,561	349,662	586,037	1,718,184	7,366,678
Children ever born per 1000 women	1,302	1,303	1,691	1,159	1,659	1,214
Type of household						
Persons in households	220,807,382	40,936,886	1,442,809	2,439,040	6,896,412	30,176,625
Percent	100.0	100.0	100.0	100.0	100.0	100.0

[Continued]

★ 141 ★

Marital Status, Fertility, and Household Type in U.S. Southwest Border States and Counties, 1980

[Continued]

Characteristic	United States	Total, border states	Border states			
			Border county areas		Non-border county areas	
			Hispanic	Non-Hispanic	Hispanic	Non-Hispanic
Family householder	26.8	26.2	22.0	27.8	22.2	27.2
Nonfamily householder	9.6	10.4	4.2	12.4	4.6	11.9
Spouse	22.1	21.6	17.5	22.9	17.7	22.5
Other relative	38.7	38.2	54.5	32.4	51.8	34.7
Non-relative	2.7	3.7	1.8	4.6	3.7	3.7

Source: U.S. Bureau of the Census, *The Hispanic Population of the Southwest Borderland.* Current Population Reports, Series P-23, No. 172, Washington, DC: U.S. Government Printing Office, 1991, p. 19. *Notes:* For the purposes of this report, the U.S. Census Bureau included the following counties: San Diego, and Imperial counties, in California; Cochise, Pima, Santa Cruz, and Yuma counties, in Arizona; Dona Ana, Hidalgo, and Luna counties, in New Mexico; El Paso, Hudspeth, Culberson, Jeff Davis, Presidio, Brewster, Terrell, Valverde, Kinney, Maverick, Dimmit, Webb, Zapata, Starr, Hidalgo, and Cameron counties, in Texas.

★ 142 ★

Characteristics

Married-Couple Households, by Hispanic Origin Status of Husband and Wife, March 1993

Numbers are shown in thousands.

Origin of husband	Total population	Origin of wife							
					Hispanic subgroups				
		Total Hispanic	Non-Hispanic	Non-Hispanic White	Mexican	Puerto Rican	Cuban	Central and South American	Other Hispanic
Total, all persons	53,137	3,784	49,353	43,878	2,401	328	240	532	283
Total Hispanic	3,665	3,144	521	479	2,043	267	199	449	186
Non-Hispanic	49,472	640	48,832	43,399	358	61	41	83	97
Non-Hispanic White	44,066	570	43,496	42,957	312	47	37	80	94
Hispanic subgroups:									
Mexican	2,322	2,028	294	275	1,988	9	4	23	4
Puerto Rican	335	255	80	68	3	232	5	11	4
Cuban	232	209	23	20	3	4	185	15	2
Central and South American	514	457	57	52	38	12	3	398	6
Other Hispanic	262	195	67	64	11	10	2	2	170

Source: Montgomery, Patricia A. U.S. Bureau of the Census. *The Hispanic Population in the United States: March 1993.* Current Population Reports, Series P20-475. Washington, DC: U.S. Government Printing Office, 1994, p. 6.

★ 143 ★

Characteristics

Persons 16 Years Old and Older in Families With Specified Work Experience During Year, 1974-89 - I

Numbers are shown in thousands.

Household relationship	Number of persons 16 years old and over (000)				Percent with work experience during year			
	1974	1979	1984	1989	1974	1979	1984	1989
ALL RACES								
Persons 16 to 64 years	129,322	142,759	150,843	157,958	75.3	77.6	77.6	80.4
In families	116,889	124,129	128,802	132,051	74.3	76.4	76.4	79.2
Householder	46,581	49,850	52,182	54,597	91.2	90.0	87.5	88.1
In families with related children under 18 years	73,857	76,231	74,454	75,290	72.9	76.0	75.8	79.0
Householder	29,846	31,286	31,791	33,041	91.9	91.1	88.8	89.3
In families with related children under 6 years	30,271	29,905	31,683	33,353	70.7	73.8	74.5	77.4
Householder	14,023	14,066	14,989	16,022	92.1	90.8	87.9	87.9
In married couple families	102,114	105,969	107,055	108,229	75.0	77.4	77.7	80.5
Husbands	39,463	40,922	41,473	42,489	94.9	93.9	92.1	92.6
Wives	42,435	43,774	44,346	45,504	56.6	63.2	66.4	71.5
Children	18,844	19,888	19,757	18,460	75.0	75.7	73.6	76.2
Other	1,372	1,384	1,480	1,776	68.3	65.2	67.6	69.0
In married couple families with related children under 18	64,838	64,723	61,528	61,358	74.0	77.5	78.0	81.2
Husbands	24,760	24,760	24,196	24,559	96.9	96.5	95.5	96.0
Wives	25,724	25,513	24,905	25,284	53.7	62.9	66.9	72.5
Children	13,483	13,552	11,433	10,315	71.3	71.3	66.2	69.0
Other	870	896	995	1,201	65.7	61.7	63.2	67.8
In married couple families with related children under 6	26,884	26,019	26,822	27,697	72.2	75.9	77.4	80.4
Husbands	11,877	11,546	11,918	12,290	97.7	97.4	96.2	96.8
Wives	12,416	11,919	12,312	12,667	48.3	58.1	62.4	67.3
Children	2,041	2,021	1,976	1,876	70.7	61.8	61.2	67.0
Other	549	532	615	864	67.3	60.0	63.6	67.8
In female householder family with no spouse present	12,153	15,027	17,688	18,429	68.2	68.3	68.0	70.9
Householder	6,000	7,446	8,671	9,417	67.8	71.9	70.0	73.0
Other	6,153	7,581	9,017	9,011	68.6	64.7	66.0	68.8
In female householder family with no spouse present and related children under 18	8,018	10,187	11,196	11,732	63.6	65.8	63.7	67.1
Householder	4,597	5,824	6,567	7,157	65.1	70.7	67.6	71.3
Children	2,911	3,811	3,915	3,658	60.3	58.6	57.3	59.7
Other	510	552	714	917	69.0	63.7	62.8	63.6
In female householder family with no spouse present and related children under 6	3,108	3,524	4,275	4,880	57.0	57.8	56.5	59.6
Householder	2,011	2,309	2,696	3,203	58.7	60.8	56.6	61.4
Children	809	928	1,166	1,182	49.8	48.9	55.7	54.2
Other	287	287	413	495	65.5	62.2	57.5	60.9

[Continued]

★ 143 ★

Persons 16 Years Old and Older in Families With Specified Work Experience During Year, 1974-89 - I

[Continued]

Household relationship	Number of persons 16 years old and over (000)				Percent with work experience during year			
	1974	1979	1984	1989	1974	1979	1984	1989
In unrelated subfamilies	181	444	707	632	67.2	74.2	71.4	69.1
Unrelated individuals	12,252	18,187	21,334	25,275	84.5	86.2	85.4	87.0
Males	6,322	9,825	11,651	13,938	88.6	90.0	88.3	90.0
Householder	4,511	7,154	8,311	9,535	89.1	90.6	89.3	90.6
Females	5,930	8,361	9,683	11,337	80.1	81.7	81.8	83.4
Householder	4,795	6,434	7,309	8,274	79.5	80.6	81.5	83.1
HISPANIC ORIGIN[1]								
Persons 16 to 64 years	6,280	7,820	10,610	13,132	68.7	72.0	70.0	73.0
In families	5,741	6,927	9,263	11,232	67.3	70.3	68.5	71.4
Householder	2,255	2,785	3,614	4,356	85.1	85.4	80.3	82.8
In families with related children under 18 years	4,386	5,212	6,607	7,870	65.3	68.3	66.6	69.6
Householder	1,759	2,141	2,699	3,185	84.2	84.3	80.2	82.1
In families with related children under 6 years	2,242	2,642	3,329	4,208	64.6	67.5	67.0	68.4
Householder	998	1,208	1,488	1,804	84.2	84.2	80.8	81.3
In married couple families	4,744	5,580	7,108	8,429	69.4	72.5	71.4	73.1
Husbands	1,748	2,085	2,575	3,029	94.3	93.7	91.5	92.2
Wives	1,898	2,166	2,840	3,332	49.8	56.7	58.1	60.0
Children	974	1,155	1,371	1,491	63.6	64.4	64.2	64.8
Other	124	174	322	577	62.9	70.2	58.8	70.1
In married couple families with related children under 18	3,689	4,262	5,199	6,086	68.1	71.2	70.3	72.6
Husbands	1,364	1,593	1,922	2,235	94.8	94.7	93.3	94.2
Wives	1,442	1,629	2,030	2,357	47.1	55.0	56.7	59.2
Children	785	909	987	1,025	61.0	60.0	57.9	58.3
Other	98	130	260	469	61.6	66.1	54.0	68.4
In married couple families with related children under 6	1,940	2,244	2,713	3,382	67.6	70.8	71.3	71.6
Husbands	802	942	1,118	1,309	94.6	94.9	94.7	95.5
Wives	841	945	1,168	1,362	42.8	51.3	54.1	54.0
Children	230	266	251	336	65.4	56.3	55.3	53.9
Other	66	91	177	375	(B)	64.7	59.4	68.5
In female householder family with no spouse present	817	1,044	1,657	2,007	53.9	55.6	53.8	60.2
Householder	431	583	841	1,025	48.6	55.3	51.0	60.1
Other	386	461	815	982	59.9	56.0	56.8	60.3
In female householder family with no spouse present and related children under 18	634	809	1,210	1,438	49.4	51.1	49.5	55.6
Householder	363	492	688	814	45.4	51.7	47.6	55.9
Children	238	264	435	447	51.0	48.8	47.1	52.4

[Continued]

★ 143 ★

Persons 16 Years Old and Older in Families With Specified Work Experience During Year, 1974-89 - I

[Continued]

Household relationship	Number of persons 16 years old and over (000)				Percent with work experience during year			
	1974	1979	1984	1989	1974	1979	1984	1989
Other	33	53	86	177	(B)	(B)	75.8	62.0
In female householder family with no spouse present and related children under 6	283	365	522	682	44.7	45.5	45.0	50.8
Householder	187	247	335	425	39.6	45.3	41.2	49.0
Children	73	86	144	167	(B)	45.1	47.7	54.6
Other	24	32	43	90	(B)	(B)	(B)	52.5
In unrelated subfamilies	17	56	96	108	(B)	(B)	80.5	66.3
Unrelated individuals	522	837	1,250	1,791	83.1	86.4	80.3	83.6
Males	341	508	800	1,177	90.2	92.5	85.0	90.0
Householder	213	318	436	500	90.5	93.2	84.9	90.1
Females	181	329	451	615	69.8	76.8	71.8	71.2
Householder	136	206	302	356	68.5	76.8	72.2	73.5

Source: U.S. Bureau of the Census. *Workers With Low Earnings: 1964 to 1990.* Current Population Reports, Series P-60, No. 178. Washington, DC: U.S. Government Printing Office, 1992, pp. 9-16. *Notes:* A (B) indicates that base was less than 75,000 and is too small for derived measures. 1. Hispanic persons may be of any race.

★ 144 ★

Characteristics

Persons 16 Years Old and Older in Families With Specified Work Experience During Year, 1974-89 - II

Numbers are shown in thousands.

Household relationship	Percent with year-round full-time attachment to labor force				Percent worked year-round, full-time			
	1974	1979	1984	1989	1974	1979	1984	1989
ALL RACES								
Persons 16 to 64 years	49.3	52.4	55.4	57.4	41.7	44.5	45.9	49.8
In families	48.1	50.7	53.5	55.3	40.9	43.4	44.5	48.2
Householder	79.3	78.1	77.4	76.3	69.9	70.0	67.3	68.7
In families with related children under 18 years	45.0	48.1	51.4	53.3	37.9	40.8	42.6	46.1
Householder	81.0	79.9	79.5	77.5	71.1	71.1	68.4	69.2
In families with related children under 6 years	46.6	49.4	52.9	54.0	38.7	41.5	43.2	46.6
Householder	80.5	79.0	77.7	74.6	68.8	68.7	65.6	66.4
In married couple families	49.0	52.0	54.8	56.6	42.1	44.9	46.3	50.1
Husbands	84.8	84.7	84.3	83.8	75.3	76.5	74.0	76.3
Wives	27.2	32.8	38.3	42.7	23.1	27.8	32.4	37.7
Children	23.7	27.9	30.2	29.5	16.0	19.0	20.3	22.2

[Continued]

★ 144 ★

Persons 16 Years Old and Older in Families With Specified Work Experience During Year, 1974-89 - II

[Continued]

Household relationship	Percent with year-round full-time attachment to labor force				Percent worked year-round, full-time			
	1974	1979	1984	1989	1974	1979	1984	1989
Other	45.3	39.3	45.6	43.6	32.7	28.5	32.0	31.2
In married couple families with related children under 18	46.5	49.9	53.4	55.3	39.7	42.9	44.8	48.5
Husbands	88.8	88.9	89.5	88.6	78.7	80.1	77.9	80.1
Wives	21.2	28.1	34.1	38.9	17.6	23.3	28.3	33.7
Children	17.3	20.6	19.7	17.8	11.0	12.8	12.2	11.9
Other	43.3	35.2	43.1	43.6	29.6	25.9	29.5	30.6
In married couple families with related children under 6	48.6	51.9	55.5	57.1	40.9	44.2	46.1	49.9
Husbands	88.9	89.7	89.6	88.6	76.6	78.9	76.5	79.7
Wives	14.9	21.1	27.8	31.7	11.9	16.7	22.3	27.1
Children	20.3	23.1	26.8	28.1	12.6	13.8	15.7	18.4
Other	43.8	32.9	43.6	43.2	29.3	25.2	30.3	29.6
In female householder family with no spouse present	38.8	40.7	44.7	46.0	29.9	31.7	33.4	36.8
Householder	43.8	49.9	52.5	53.7	36.0	41.2	43.1	45.5
Other	33.8	31.6	37.1	37.9	23.9	22.5	24.2	27.8
In female householder family with no spouse present and related children under 18	32.2	36.4	39.7	41.3	23.4	27.7	30.0	32.8
Householder	39.7	47.3	49.7	50.7	31.5	38.4	40.0	42.0
Children	18.3	19.4	22.7	22.4	9.6	11.5	13.6	14.9
Other	43.7	40.1	41.2	43.9	28.6	27.3	27.5	32.8
In female householder family with no spouse present and related children under 6	28.9	30.2	34.8	35.2	20.2	21.1	24.9	27.8
Householder	31.4	33.8	36.0	37.0	23.8	24.9	27.5	30.6
Children	17.9	18.9	30.9	26.8	8.7	11.4	17.8	18.8
Other	42.6	37.1	38.3	43.1	27.2	22.4	27.3	31.5
In unrelated subfamilies	38.2	45.4	39.7	42.2	26.5	33.7	27.5	30.4
Unrelated individuals	60.8	63.8	67.3	68.7	50.1	52.4	55.1	58.8
Males	64.7	68.7	72.0	73.2	51.4	55.6	57.5	61.8
Householder	66.9	71.1	74.8	76.0	53.7	59.4	61.6	65.5
Females	56.7	58.1	61.6	63.2	48.9	48.6	52.3	55.0
Householder	59.0	60.4	64.3	65.0	51.0	51.3	55.6	57.7
HISPANIC ORIGIN[1]								
Persons 16 to 64 years	45.1	48.9	50.6	53.3	35.3	38.5	39.0	43.3
In families	44.1	47.2	49.2	51.6	34.7	37.6	38.0	42.2
Householder	71.9	71.5	70.3	68.9	58.6	59.7	55.8	58.0
In families with related children under 18 years	41.3	44.9	47.3	49.3	32.2	35.6	36.4	40.1
Householder	71.0	70.8	70.6	68.4	57.4	59.2	55.5	57.2

[Continued]

★ 144 ★

Persons 16 Years Old and Older in Families With Specified Work Experience During Year, 1974-89 - II

[Continued]

Household relationship	Percent with year-round full-time attachment to labor force				Percent worked year-round, full-time			
	1974	1979	1984	1989	1974	1979	1984	1989
In families with related children under 6 years	42.0	45.5	48.7	48.2	32.5	35.0	37.2	38.7
Householder	70.4	70.2	70.9	65.8	56.0	56.8	54.7	55.1
In married couple families	46.5	49.5	51.8	53.3	36.9	39.8	40.4	44.3
Husbands	82.8	82.3	83.6	80.9	67.3	69.5	66.6	69.5
Wives	25.0	30.5	34.0	38.2	19.7	24.3	27.5	32.4
Children	23.6	27.2	30.7	33.6	15.9	17.0	19.9	23.5
Other	44.3	41.0	44.4	46.7	33.9	29.7	31.2	34.2
In married couple families with related children under 18	44.4	47.7	50.8	52.0	35.1	38.2	39.3	42.9
Husbands	83.5	83.8	85.8	83.6	67.6	71.0	68.0	71.4
Wives	21.6	27.7	31.9	34.8	17.0	21.7	25.6	29.1
Children	18.9	22.1	24.0	25.8	12.4	12.6	14.7	17.3
Other	41.3	34.4	41.0	45.0	29.7	22.7	27.5	33.2
In married couple families with related children under 6	45.5	48.8	52.3	51.4	35.5	38.1	39.9	41.9
Husbands	83.2	84.1	86.6	83.3	66.3	69.1	66.7	71.0
Wives	16.6	21.8	26.0	28.7	12.7	16.0	20.4	23.4
Children	22.2	23.4	27.6	27.9	13.5	11.7	16.0	15.0
Other	(B)	38.3	44.9	43.4	(B)	22.8	32.9	31.2
In female householder family with no spouse present	28.2	33.8	34.9	39.9	21.0	24.4	26.6	30.7
Householder	29.0	37.5	37.3	42.2	24.5	27.7	29.4	32.4
Other	27.2	29.0	32.4	37.5	17.0	20.2	23.7	29.0
In female householder family with no spouse present and related children under 18	23.4	30.2	30.8	35.2	16.0	20.9	23.3	26.6
Householder	25.4	34.6	34.4	37.3	20.7	24.6	26.6	28.0
Children	17.0	21.5	22.8	25.8	6.1	14.5	16.7	18.5
Other	(B)	(B)	43.2	49.1	(B)	(B)	30.0	40.9
In female householder family with no spouse present and related children under 6	18.4	25.5	29.0	30.3	12.7	16.1	22.2	22.1
Householder	16.4	26.0	27.9	28.4	12.9	16.1	22.1	20.2
Children	(B)	23.5	27.9	32.1	(B)	14.5	21.0	22.6
Other	(B)	(B)	(B)	36.2	(B)	(B)	(B)	29.9
In unrelated subfamilies	(B)	(B)	32.9	31.9	(B)	(B)	24.5	26.1
Unrelated individuals	55.3	63.1	62.7	64.9	42.2	47.1	47.5	51.4
Males	61.0	70.2	66.7	69.9	44.7	49.2	49.6	53.9
Householder	65.3	73.7	71.4	74.2	47.7	54.8	55.8	60.0

[Continued]

★ 144 ★

Persons 16 Years Old and Older in Families With Specified Work Experience During Year, 1974-89 - II

[Continued]

Household relationship	Percent with year-round full-time attachment to labor force				Percent worked year-round, full-time			
	1974	1979	1984	1989	1974	1979	1984	1989
Females	44.5	52.0	55.8	55.2	37.3	43.8	43.7	46.6
Householder	44.6	58.3	59.3	62.0	38.1	49.9	46.9	54.6

Source: U.S. Bureau of the Census. *Workers With Low Earnings: 1964 to 1990.* Current Population Reports, Series P-60, No. 178. Washington, DC: U.S. Government Printing Office, 1992, pp. 9-16. *Notes:* A (B) indicates that base was less than 75,000 and is too small for derived measures. 1. Hispanic persons may be of any race.

★ 145 ★

Characteristics

Proportion of People 65 Years Old or Older Living Alone With No Living Children, 1990

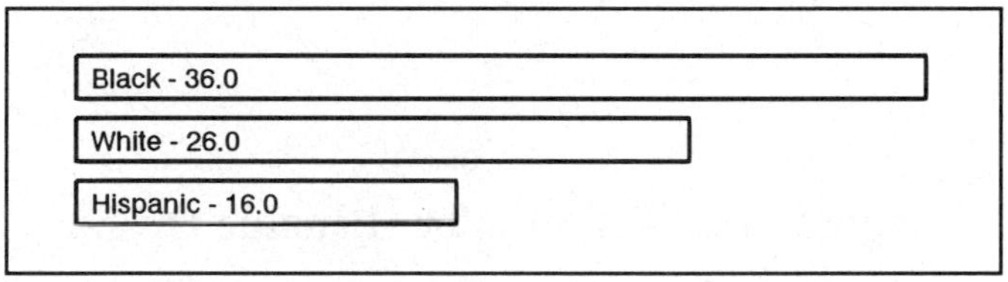

Characteristic	Percent
Hispanic	16.0
White	26.0
Black	36.0

Source: Aging America, Trends and Projections, 1991 Edition. Prepared by the U.S. Senate Special Committee on Aging, the American Association of Retired Persons, the Federal Council on the Aging, and the U.S. Administration on Aging, p. 234. Primary source: Lewin/ICF estimates based on data from the 1984 *Supplement on Aging* and the Brookings/ICF Long-Term Care Financing Model, 1990.

★ 146 ★

Characteristics

Proportion of People 65 Years Old or Older Living Alone With a Child Who Lives Nearby, 1990

Characteristic	Percent
Hispanic	68.0
White	58.0
Black	48.0

Source: Aging America, Trends and Projections, 1991 Edition. Prepared by the U.S. Senate Special Committee on Aging, the American Association of Retired Persons, the Federal Council on the Aging, and the U.S. Administration on Aging, p. 233. Primary source: Lewin/ICF estimates based on data from the 1984 *Supplement on Aging* and the Brookings/ICF Long-Term Care Financing Model, 1990.

★ 147 ★

Characteristics

Single-Parent Families, by Hispanic Origin

Data show percent of each group that are single-parent families.

Hispanic origin	Percent single-parent
Mexican	19.0
Central and South American	26.0
Puerto Rican	43.0
Cuban	19.0
Nation as a whole	17.0

Source: Tharp, Mike, David Whitman, and Betsy Streisand. "Hispanics' tale of two cities." *U.S. News & World Report* (25 May 1992), p. 40. Primary source: U.S. Bureau of the Census.

Child Care

★ 148 ★

Children in Self-Care, 1991

Data show the percentage of children of each race/ethnicity reported to be caring for themselves while their mothers were at work.

Race/ethnicity	5 to 14 years			5 to 11 years			12 to 14 years		
	Number of children	In self-care		Number of children	In self-care		Number of children	In self-care	
		Number	Percent		Number	Percent		Number	Percent
Total	21,220	1,611	7.6	14,913	554	3.7	6,307	1,058	16.8
White	17,393	1,444	8.3	12,141	494	4.1	5,252	950	18.1
Black	2,841	103	3.6	2,087	29	1.4	754	74	9.9
Other	986	64	6.5	685	31	4.6	301	33	11.0
Hispanic origin									
Hispanic	1,733	84	4.8	1,295	35	2.7	439	49	11.2
Non-Hispanic	19,487	1,528	7.8	13,618	519	3.8	5,868	1,009	17.2

Source: Casper, Lynne M., Mary Hawkins, and Martin O'Connell. U.S. Bureau of the Census. *Who's Minding the Kids? Child Care Arrangements: Fall 1991*. Current Population Reports, P70-36. Washington, DC: U.S. Government Printing Office, 1994, p. 31.

★ 149 ★

Child Care

Primary Child Care Arrangements Used by Employed Mothers for Children Under 5 Years Old, 1991 - I

Numbers are shown in thousands.

Characteristic of mother	Number of children	Type of primary child care arrangements						
		Care in child's home by				Care in another home by		
		Father	Grand-parent	Other relative	Non-relative	Grand-parent	Other relative	Non-relative
Total	9,854	1,974	708	313	527	846	443	1,763
White	8,103	1,744	538	210	490	660	297	1,482
Black	1,251	170	95	90	13	153	107	224
Hispanic	989	187	141	26	88	75	67	99
Non-Hispanic	8,865	1,787	567	286	439	771	376	1,664

Source: Casper, Lynne M., Mary Hawkins, and Martin O'Connell. U.S. Bureau of the Census. *Who's Minding the Kids? Child Care Arrangements: Fall 1991*. Current Population Reports, P70-36. Washington, DC: U.S. Government Printing Office, 1994, p. 28. *Note:* A dash (-) stands for zero.

★ 150 ★

Child Care

Primary Child Care Arrangements Used by Employed Mothers for Children Under 5 Years Old, 1991 - II

Numbers are shown in thousands.

Characteristic of mother	Type of primary child care arrangement					
	Day/ group care center	Nursery/ pre-school	School-based activity	Kinder-garten/ grade school	Child cares for self	Mother cares for child[1]
Total	1,553	716	52	105	-	855
White	1,279	536	35	87	-	747
Black	213	108	17	9	-	52
Hispanic	140	77	5	25	-	58
Non-Hispanic	1,412	639	46	80	-	797

Source: Casper, Lynne M., Mary Hawkins, and Martin O'Connell. U.S. Bureau of the Census. *Who's Minding the Kids? Child Care Arrangements: Fall 1991.* Current Population Reports, P70-36. Washington, DC: U.S. Government Printing Office, 1994, p. 28. *Notes:* A dash (-) stands for zero. 1. Includes mothers working at home or away from home.

★ 151 ★

Child Care

Average Hourly Fees Paid for Child Care, 1990

Race/ethnicity	Percentage of programs that charge a fee	Sample size	Average hourly fee (excluding $0 fees)		
			Mean ($)	Standard error ($)	Sample size
Percentage of children who are Hispanic					
Under 25 percent	89.0	1,831	1.62	(0.03)	1,348
25 to 49 percent	78.0	91	1.37	(0.15)	52
50 to 74 percent	66.0	51	1.15	(0.25)	19
75 to 100 percent	53.0	70	0.85	(0.22)	24
Percentage of children who are White					
Under 25 percent	68.0	449	1.14	(0.07)	229
25 to 49 percent	73.0	125	1.26	(0.14)	62
50 to 74 percent	85.0	226	1.59	(0.09)	142
75 to 100 percent	94.0	1,243	1.70	(0.04)	1,010
Percentage of children who are Black					
Under 25 percent	91.0	1,499	1.69	(0.04)	1,148
25 to 49 percent	82.0	168	1.27	(0.11)	98

[Continued]

★ 151 ★

Average Hourly Fees Paid for Child Care, 1990

[Continued]

Race/ethnicity	Percentage of programs that charge a fee	Sample size	Average hourly fee (excluding $0 fees)		
			Mean ($)	Standard error ($)	Sample size
50 to 74 percent	67.0	101	1.25	(0.15)	51
75 to 100 percent	68.0	275	1.11	(0.09)	146

Source: Kisker, Ellen Eliason and others. *A Profile of Child Care Settings: Early Education and Care in 1990, Volume 1.* Prepared under contract for the U.S. Department of Education by Mathematica Policy Research Inc., 1991, pp. 166- 167.

★ 152 ★

Child Care

Weekly Child Care Expenditures, 1991

This table shows characteristics of child care expenditures for families with employed mothers. Data exclude persons with no report of family income in the last four months.

Race/ethnicity	Number (000)	No payments made	Payments made		Weekly child care expenses (dollars)		Hours worked per week		Monthly family income (dollars)		Proportion of income spent on child care per month	
			Number	%	Mean[1]	Std. error	Mean[2]	Std. error	Mean[3]	Std. error	%[4]	Std. error
All employed mothers	19,180	12,564	6,616	34.5	63.3	2.43	37.4	0.39	3,838	109	7.1	0.33
White	15,803	10,302	5,501	34.8	62.4	2.34	36.9	0.43	3,885	116	7.0	0.29
Black	2,447	1,641	806	32.9	53.2	4.49	39.0	1.03	3,179	346	7.3	0.20
Hispanic origin												
Hispanic	1,560	983	577	37.0	62.2	5.79	39.1	0.75	3,306	297	8.4	0.33
Non-Hispanic	17,620	11,581	6,039	34.3	63.2	2.62	37.2	0.43	3,889	116	7.0	0.33

Source: Casper, Lynne M., Mary Hawkins, and Martin O'Connell. U.S. Bureau of the Census. *Who's Minding the Kids? Child Care Arrangements: Fall 1991.* Current Population Reports, P70-36. Washington, DC: U.S. Government Printing Office, 1994, p. 37. *Notes:* 1. Mean expenditures per week among persons making child care payments. 2. Mean number of hours usually worked per week in the last 4 months among persons making child care payments. 3. Mean monthly income for the last 4 months among persons making child care payments. 4. Percent is ratio of average monthly child care payments (prorated from weekly averages) to the average monthly family income for each of the categories shown in the table.

Children

★ 153 ★

Adopted Children: Living Arrangements

Data show number (in thousands) and percent distribution of adopted children, by race/ethnicity and living arrangements, for the summer of 1991.

Characteristics	Number	Percent
Adopted children	1,062	100.0
Race		
White	805	75.8
Black	130	12.2
Other	127	12.0
Hispanic origin[1]		
Hispanic	65	6.1
Not Hispanic	997	93.9
Living arrangements		
Two parents	936	88.1
Two adoptive parents	581	54.7
One adoptive and one biological	324	30.5
One adoptive and one other	31	2.9
One parent	126	11.9
Mother only	110	10.4
Father only	16	1.5

Source: Furukawa, Stacy. U.S. Bureau of the Census. *The Diverse Living Arrangements of Children: Summer 1991.* Current Population Reports, Series P70, No. 38, Washington, DC: U.S. Government Printing Office, 1994, p. 7. *Note:* 1. Persons of Hispanic origin may be of any race.

★ 154 ★

Children

Children Living With Grandparents

Data show number of children (in thousands), by race/ethnicity and relationship to others living in household. Data are shown for summer of 1991.

Living arrangements	All races	White	Black	Hispanic origin[1]
Children living with at least one grandparent	4,737	2,777	1,580	908
Percent of all children under 18 years	7.2	5.3	14.9	12.1
Presence of parents				
Living with both parents	1,459	1,112	118	336

[Continued]

★ 154 ★

Children Living With Grandparents

[Continued]

Living arrangements	All races	White	Black	Hispanic origin[1]
Grandparent is the householder	555	454	63	82
Percent	38.0	40.8	53.4	24.4
Living with mother only	1,876	971	839	396
Grandparent is the householder	1,520	837	651	280
Percent	81.0	86.2	77.6	70.7
Living with father only	303	225	53	76
Grandparent is the householder	255	189	47	65
Percent	84.2	84.0	88.7	85.5
Living with neither parent	1,099	469	570	100
Percent	100.0	100.0	100.0	100.0
Living with both parents	30.8	40.0	7.5	37.0
Living with mother only	39.6	35.0	53.1	43.6
Living with father only	6.4	8.1	3.4	8.4
Living with neither parent	23.2	16.9	36.1	11.0

Source: Furukawa, Stacy. U.S. Bureau of the Census. *The Diverse Living Arrangements of Children: Summer 1991.* Current Population Reports, Series P70, No. 38, Washington, DC: U.S. Government Printing Office, 1994, p. 12. *Note:* 1. Persons of Hispanic origin may be of any race.

★ 155 ★

Children

Children Living With Single Parents and Adults of the Opposite Sex

Data show number (in thousands) and percent distribution of children and their living arrangements, by race/ethnicity and relationship to the adults in the households. Data are shown for summer of 1991.

Living arrangements	All races		White		Black		Hispanic origin[1]	
	Number	Percent	Number	Percent	Number	Percent	Number	Percent
Living with mother only	13,955	100.0	8,503	100.0	4,938	100.0	2,141	100.0
Presence of at least one adult male other than brothers	2,816	20.2	2,023	23.8	696	14.1	458	21.4
Relationship of adult male to child								
Living with at least one								
Relative	1,455	10.4	853	10.0	520	10.5	279	13.0
Nonrelative	1,018	7.3	902	10.6	110	2.2	145	6.8
Relationship unknown	401	2.9	20	3.8	73	1.5	34	1.6
Living with father only	1,793	100.0	1,416	100.0	258	100.0	196	100.0
Presence of at least one adult female other than sisters	661	36.9	500	35.3	121	46.9	131	66.8

[Continued]

★ 155 ★

Children Living With Single Parents and Adults of the Opposite Sex

[Continued]

Living arrangements	All races		White		Black		Hispanic origin[1]	
	Number	Percent	Number	Percent	Number	Percent	Number	Percent
Relationship of adult female to child								
Living with at least one								
Relative	342	19.1	255	18.0	61	23.6	82	41.8
Nonrelative	227	12.7	171	12.1	38	14.7	36	18.4
Relationship unknown	114	6.4	85	6.0	21	8.1	13	6.6

Source: Furukawa, Stacy. U.S. Bureau of the Census. *The Diverse Living Arrangements of Children: Summer 1991.* Current Population Reports, Series P70, No. 38, Washington, DC: U.S. Government Printing Office, 1994, p. 10. *Note:* 1. Persons of Hispanic origin may be of any race.

★ 156 ★

Children

Children Living With Single Parents and Other Adults of the Same Sex

Data show number (in thousands) and percent distribution of children and their living arrangements, by race/ethnicity and relationship to the adults in the households. Data are shown for summer of 1991.

Living arrangements	All races		White		Black		Hispanic origin[1]	
	Number	Percent	Number	Percent	Number	Percent	Number	Percent
Living with mother only	13,955	100.0	8,503	10.0	4,938	100.0	2,141	100.0
Presence of at least one adult female, other than mother or sisters	2,639	18.9	1,429	16.8	1,085	22.0	558	26.1
Relationship of adult female to child								
Living with at least one								
Relative	2,283	16.4	1,146	13.5	1,035	21.0	511	23.9
Nonrelative	289	2.1	237	2.8	13	-	96	4.5
Relationship unknown	181	1.3	138	1.6	36	0.7	31	1.4
Living with father only	1,793	100.0	1,416	100.0	258	100.0	196	100.0
Presence of at least one adult male, other than father or brothers	335	18.7	256	18.1	52	20.2	54	27.6
Relationship of adult male to child								
Living with at least one								
Relative	258	14.4	185	13.1	46	17.8	48	24.5
Nonrelative	50	2.8	43	3.0	7	2.7	-	-
Relationship unknown	34	1.9	28	2.0	6	2.3	6	3.1

Source: Furukawa, Stacy. U.S. Bureau of the Census. *The Diverse Living Arrangements of Children: Summer 1991.* Current Population Reports, Series P70, No. 38, Washington, DC: U.S. Government Printing Office, 1994, p. 10. *Notes:* A dash (-) represents zero or a number that rounds to zero. 1. Persons of Hispanic origin may be of any race.

★ 157 ★

Children

Children Living in Blended Families

Data show number of children (in thousands) living in blended families, by composition of family, and race/ethnicity of child, for summer of 1991.

Living arrangements	All races	White	Black	Hispanic origin[1]
Children living in a blended family	9,807	7,298	2,101	1,016
Percent of all children under 18 years	14.9	14.0	19.9	13.5
Type of blended family				
Stepparent only[2]	2,068	1,848	152	166
Stepsibling only	235	55	173	5
Half-sibling only	4,966	3,271	1,485	593
Stepparent and stepsibling	517	409	62	32
Stepparent and half-sibling	1,794	1,540	176	203
Stepsibling and half-sibling	13	-	13	-
Stepparent, stepsibling, and half-sibling	216	175	40	16
Percent	100.0	100.0	100.0	100.0
Stepparent only[2]	21.1	25.3	7.2	16.3
Stepsibling only	2.4	0.8	8.2	0.5
Half-sibling only	50.6	44.8	70.7	58.4
Stepparent and stepsibling	5.3	5.6	3.0	3.1
Stepparent and half-sibling	18.3	21.1	8.4	20.0
Stepsibling and half-sibling	-	-	0.6	-
Stepparent, stepsibling, and half-sibling	2.2	2.4	1.9	1.6

Source: Furukawa, Stacy. U.S. Bureau of the Census. *The Diverse Living Arrangements of Children: Summer 1991.* Current Population Reports, Series P70, No. 38, Washington, DC: U.S. Government Printing Office, 1994, p. 6. *Notes:* A dash (-) represents zero or a number that rounds to zero. 1. Persons of Hispanic origin may be of any race. 2. Children living with one biological parent and one adoptive parent are considered to live with a stepparent in order to be consistent with survey instructions.

★ 158 ★

Children

Children Living in Extended Families

Data show characteristics of children living in extended families, by race/ethnicity, for the summer of 1991. Numbers are shown in thousands; distribution is shown in percent.

Living arrangements	Children living with one or both parents									
	Total		Two parents		One parent					
					Total		Mother only		Father only	
	Number	Percent	Number	Percent	Number	Percent	Number	Percent	Number	Percent
All races	63,754	100.0	47,826	100.0	15,748	100.0	13,955	100.0	1,793	100.0
Children living in an extended household	7,951	12.5	3,235	6.8	4,716	29.9	4,092	29.3	624	34.8
Relationship of extended household members to child										
Relatives only	5,749	9.0	2,594	5.4	3,155	20.0	2,803	20.1	352	19.6
Nonrelatives only	1,891	3.0	542	1.1	1,349	8.6	1,099	7.9	250	13.9
Both	313	0.5	100	-	213	1.4	191	1.4	22	1.2
White	50,914	100.0	40,995	100.0	8,919	100.0	8,503	100.0	1,416	100.0
Children living in an extended household	5,210	10.2	2,350	5.7	2,861	28.8	2,383	28.0	478	33.8
Relationship of extended household members to child										
Relatives only	3,373	6.6	1,827	4.5	1,546	15.6	1,277	15.0	269	19.0
Nonrelatives only	1,582	3.1	423	1.0	1,159	11.7	960	11.3	199	14.1
Both	255	0.5	100	-	155	1.6	145	1.7	10	0.7
Black	9,600	100.0	4,404	100.0	5,196	100.0	4,938	100.0	258	100.0
Children living in an extended household	2,100	21.9	444	10.1	1,656	31.9	1,550	31.4	106	41.1
Relationship of extended household members to child										
Relatives only	1,861	19.4	389	8.8	1,473	28.3	1,411	28.6	62	24.0
Nonrelatives only	208	2.2	55	1.2	154	3.0	116	2.3	38	14.7
Both	30	-	-	-	30	0.6	23	0.5	7	2.7
Hispanic origin[1]	7,163	100.0	4,826	100.0	2,337	100.0	2,141	100.0	196	100.0
Children living in an extended household	1,795	25.1	858	17.8	937	40.1	820	38.3	117	59.7
Relationship of extended household members to child										
Relatives only	1,357	18.9	649	13.4	708	30.3	626	29.2	82	41.8
Nonrelatives only	279	3.9	144	3.0	136	5.8	100	4.7	36	18.4
Both	160	2.2	65	1.3	95	4.1	95	4.4	-	-

Source: Furukawa, Stacy. U.S. Bureau of the Census. *The Diverse Living Arrangements of Children: Summer 1991.* Current Population Reports, Series P70, No. 38, Washington, DC: U.S. Government Printing Office, 1994, p. 8. *Notes:* A dash (-) represents zero or a number that rounds to zero. 1. Persons of Hispanic origin may be of any race.

★ 159 ★

Children

Children Living in Extended Families, by Type of Relative Present

Data show number of children (in thousands), by race/ethnicity and relatives living in the same household. Data are shown for summer of 1991.

Living arrangements	All races	White	Black	Hispanic origin[1]
Total children in extended families[2]	7,951	5,210	2,100	1,795
Living with at least one relative				
Grandmother and grandfather	1,323	914	280	197
Grandmother only	2,004	1,137	680	532
Grandfather only	312	257	49	79
Uncle	1,506	825	438	513
Aunt	1,567	868	512	542
Nephew	451	196	231	143
Niece	486	182	276	167
Father-in-law	15	5	9	-
Mother-in-law	13	7	-	-
Brother-in-law	32	19	-	4
Sister-in-law	86	64	18	24
Cousin	1,704	788	729	461
Percent	100.0	100.0	100.0	100.0
Grandmother and grandfather	16.6	17.5	13.3	11.0
Grandmother only	25.2	21.8	32.4	29.6
Grandfather only	3.9	4.9	2.3	4.4
Uncle	18.9	15.8	20.9	28.6
Aunt	19.7	16.7	24.4	30.2
Nephew	5.7	3.8	11.0	8.0
Niece	6.1	3.5	13.1	9.3
Father-in-law	-	-	-	-
Mother-in-law	-	-	-	-
Brother-in-law	-	-	-	-
Sister-in-law	1.1	1.2	0.9	1.3
Cousin	21.4	15.1	34.7	25.7

Source: Furukawa, Stacy. U.S. Bureau of the Census. *The Diverse Living Arrangements of Children: Summer 1991.* Current Population Reports, Series P70, No. 38, Washington, DC: U.S. Government Printing Office, 1994, p. 11. *Notes:* A dash (-) represents zero or a number that rounds to zero. 1. Persons of Hispanic origin may be of any race. 2. At least one parent lives in the household.

★ 160 ★

Children

Children Living in Multi-Generational Households

Data show number of children (in thousands) in each type of household, by race/ethnicity. Data are shown for summer of 1991.

Living arrangements	All races	White	Black	Hispanic origin[1]
Children living in multi-generational households	3,775	2,378	1,077	831
Percent of children under 18 years	5.7	4.6	10.2	11.0
With parent and grandparent	3,634	2,304	1,009	808
With parent and own child	127	66	61	23
Other[2]	14	8	7	-

Source: Furukawa, Stacy. U.S. Bureau of the Census. *The Diverse Living Arrangements of Children: Summer 1991.* Current Population Reports, Series P70, No. 38, Washington, DC: U.S. Government Printing Office, 1994, p. 12. *Notes:* A dash (-) represents zero or a number that rounds to zero. 1. Persons of Hispanic origin may be of any race. 2. Children living in four-generation households or with a grandparent and own child.

★ 161 ★

Children

Children Living with Two Parents, by Parental Relationship

Data show the number of children (in thousands) living with both parents, for each type of parental relationship, by race/ethnicity of the child. Data are shown for summer of 1991.

Characteristics of parents	All races	White	Black	Hispanic origin[1]
Children living with two parents	47,826	40,995	4,404	4,826
Biological mother and father	40,553	35,002	3,576	4,129
Biological mother and stepfather	3,672	3,195	351	367
Biological father and stepmother	830	740	40	43
Adoptive mother and father[2]	582	387	103	42
Foster mother and father[3]	195	147	48	-
Other	1,994	1,524	286	245
Percent distribution	100.0	100.0	100.0	100.0
Biological mother and father	84.8	85.4	81.2	85.6
Biological mother and stepfather	7.7	7.8	8.0	7.6
Biological father and stepmother	1.7	1.8	0.9	0.9
Adoptive mother and father[2]	1.2	0.9	2.3	0.9

[Continued]

★ 161 ★

Children Living with Two Parents, by Parental Relationship

[Continued]

Characteristics of parents	All races	White	Black	Hispanic origin[1]
Foster mother and father[3]	-	-	1.1	-
Other	4.2	3.7	6.5	5.1

Source: Furukawa, Stacy. U.S. Bureau of the Census. *The Diverse Living Arrangements of Children: Summer 1991.* Current Population Reports, Series P70, No. 38, Washington, DC: U.S. Government Printing Office, 1994, p. 4. *Notes:* A dash (-) represents zero or a number that rounds to zero. 1. Persons of Hispanic origin may be of any race. 2. Children living with one biological parent and one adoptive parent have been placed in a biological parent/stepparent category. 3. Foster relationships only include official placements by a government agency or representative of a governmental agency.

★ 162 ★

Children

Children in Nuclear Families, Summer 1991

Data show number of children (in thousands) in each category, by race/ethnicity of child and type of relationship for family members.

Living arrangements	All races		White		Black		Hispanic origin[1]	
	Number	Percent	Number	Percent	Number	Percent	Number	Percent
All children under 18 years	65,727	100.0	51,944	100.0	10,571	100.0	7,525	100.0
Presence of parent								
Living with at least one parent	63,574	96.7	50,914	98.0	9,600	90.8	7,163	95.2
Living with at least one stepparent[2]	4,594	7.0	3,972	7.6	431	4.1	418	5.6
Neither parent is present	2,153	3.3	1,030	2.0	971	9.2	362	4.8
Presence of brothers and sisters								
Living with at least one sibling	49,728	75.7	39,607	76.2	7,661	72.5	5,956	79.1
Living with at least one stepsibling	980	1.5	639	1.2	289	2.7	53	0.7
Living with at least one half-sibling	6,989	10.6	4,986	9.6	1,714	16.2	813	10.8
Living with no brothers or sisters	15,999	24.3	12,337	23.8	2,910	27.5	1,569	20.9

Source: Furukawa, Stacy. U.S. Bureau of the Census. *The Diverse Living Arrangements of Children: Summer 1991.* Current Population Reports, Series P70, No. 38, Washington, DC: U.S. Government Printing Office, 1994, p. 5. *Notes:* A dash (-) represents zero or a number that rounds to zero. 1. Persons of Hispanic origin may be of any race. 2. Children living with one biological parent and one adoptive parent are considered to live with a stepparent in order to be consistent with survey instructions.

★ 163 ★

Children

Living Arrangements of Children, Summer 1991

Data show living arrangement of children younger than 18 years of age, by race/ethnicity. Numbers are shown in thousands of persons.

Living arrangements	All races	White	Black	Hispanic origin[1]
Children under 18 years	65,727	51,944	10,571	7,525
Living with				
Two parents	47,826	40,995	4,404	4,826
In a traditional nuclear family[2]	33,403	29,292	2,741	2,846
One parent	15,748	9,919	5,196	2,337
Mother only	13,955	8,503	4,938	2,141
Father only	1,793	1,416	258	196
Grandparents only	1,099	469	570	100
Other	689	385	262	110
Unknown[3]	365	175	138	152
Percent	100.0	100.0	100.0	100.0
Living with				
Two parents	72.8	78.9	41.7	64.1
In a traditional nuclear family[2]	50.8	56.4	25.9	37.8
One parent	24.0	19.1	49.2	31.1
Mother only	21.2	16.4	46.7	28.5
Father only	2.7	2.7	2.4	2.6
Grandparents only	1.7	0.9	5.4	1.3
Other	1.0	0.7	2.5	1.5
Unknown[3]	0.6	0.3	1.3	2.0

Source: Furukawa, Stacy. U.S. Bureau of the Census. *The Diverse Living Arrangements of Children: Summer 1991.* Current Population Reports, Series P70, No. 38, Washington, DC: U.S. Government Printing Office, 1994, p. 3. *Notes:* 1. Persons of Hispanic origin may be of any race. 2. Children in a traditional nuclear family live with both biological parents and, if siblings are present, with full brothers and sisters. No other household members are present. 3. Data on living arrangements are missing for these children.

Divorce

★ 164 ★

Child Support and Alimony, 1989

Data are shown for women with own children under 21 years of age present from absent fathers. For 1989, data are shown for women 15 years old and over as of April 1990. Figures refer to the civilian noninstitutional population. Alimony data are for ever-divorced and currently separated women.

Recipient status of woman	Unit	Total[1]	Age			Race/ethnicity			Current marital status			
			18 to 29 years	30 to 39 years	40 years and over	White	Black	Hispanic[2]	Divorced	Married[3]	Never married	Separated
Child support, 1989												
All women, total	1,000	9,955	3,086	4,175	2,566	6,905	2,770	1,112	3,056	2,531	2,950	1,352
Payments awarded	1,000	5,748	1,408	2,685	1,632	4,661	955	452	2,347	1,999	704	648
Percent of total	Percent	58	46	64	64	68	35	41	77	79	24	48
Supposed to receive child support in 1989	1,000	4,953	1,208	2,413	1,309	4,048	791	364	2,123	1,685	583	527
Percent received payment	Percent	75	76	74	76	77	70	70	77	72	73	80
Mean child support	Dollars	2,995	1,981	3,032	3,903	3,132	2,263	2,965	3,322	2,931	1,888	3,060
Percent of total income	Percent	19	20	18	19	19	16	20	17	20	20	21
Women with incomes below the poverty level in 1989	1,000	3,206	1,531	1,189	434	1,763	1,314	536	820	176	1,590	612
Payments awarded	1,000	1,387	608	568	195	962	384	177	577	127	389	288
Percent of total	Percent	43	40	48	45	55	29	33	70	72	25	47
Supposed to receive child support in 1989	1,000	1,190	507	500	168	827	325	148	525	106	334	221
Percent received payment	Percent	68	68	67	72	68	70	64	66	67	69	74
Mean child support	Dollars	1,889	1,515	2,167	2,316	1,972	1,674	1,824	2,112	2,275	1,553	1,717
Percent of total income	Percent	37	33	36	56	39	32	37	38	52	34	35
Alimony, 1989												
All women, total	1,000	20,610	2,464	6,093	12,051	17,245	2,863	1,499	8,888	7,738	(X)	2,790
Number awarded payments	1,000	3,189	184	610	2,394	2,801	305	171	1,472	1,170	(X)	316
Percent of total	Percent	16	8	10	20	16	11	11	17	15	(X)	11
Supposed to receive payments	1,000	922	85	267	569	787	98	63	567	170	(X)	164
Women with incomes below the poverty level in 1989	1,000	3,692	726	1,206	1,758	2,640	931	477	1,860	420	(X)	1,147
Number awarded payments	1,000	429	60	96	273	340	76	31	223	55	(X)	110
Percent of total	Percent	12	8	8	16	13	8	6	12	13	(X)	10
Supposed to receive payments	1,000	178	43	56	79	149	26	21	112	11	(X)	54

Source: 1994 Statistical Abstract of the United States on CD-ROM [machine-readable datafiles]. CD-8A-94. Washington, DC: U.S. Department of Commerce, Economics and Statistics Administration, Bureau of the Census, Data User Services Division, January 1995. Primary source: U.S. Bureau of the Census, Current Population Reports, P60-173. *Notes:* An (X) stands for not applicable. 1. Includes other items, not shown separately. 2. Hispanic women may be of any race. 3. Remarried women whose previous marriage ended in divorce.

★ 165 ★

Divorce

Divorces and Birth History of Mothers, 1990

Data show percent of mothers 40 to 49 years old divorced after first marriage, by birth history at first marriage and race/ethnicity, as of June 1990.

Birth history	All races	White	Black	Hispanic origin[1]
With a premarital first birth or premaritally conceived/postmarital first birth	43.5	44.9	42.4	31.8
With a postmaritally conceived first birth	32.6	32.3	43.3	24.1

Source: U.S. Bureau of the Census. *Marriage, Divorce, and Remarriage in the 1990's*. Current Population Reports, P23-180. Washington, DC: U.S. Government Printing Office, 1992, p. 8. *Note:* 1. Persons of Hispanic origin may be of any race.

★ 166 ★

Divorce

Remarriage After First Divorce, by Race/Ethnicity

Data show percent of women who remarried after a divorce from a first marriage, by age at divorce and race/ethnicity.

Race and Hispanic origin	Age at divorce				
	All ages	20 to 24	25 to 29	30 to 34	35 to 39
All races	63.1	77.8	67.7	53.5	44.6
White	64.6	78.6	68.5	56.1	47.0
Black	51.4	70.6	60.9	38.63	29.5
Hispanic origin[1]	51.8	68.6	58.3	40.6	24.2

Source: U.S. Bureau of the Census, *Marriage, Divorce, and Remarriage in the 1990's*, Current Population Reports, P23-180. Washington, DC: U.S. Government Printing Office, 1992, p. 8. *Note:* 1. Persons of Hispanic origin may be of any race.

★ 167 ★

Divorce

Women, 50 to 54 Years Old, Who Remarried After Divorce, 1990

Race/ethnicity	Percent who remarried
White	65.4
Hispanic	62.2
Black	50.2

Source: Usdansky, Margaret L. "1990s' wedding bell blues: new report echoes trend of the '70s." *USA TODAY* (9 December 1992), p. 12A. Primary source: The Census Bureau; National Center for Health Statistics.

Income

★ 168 ★

Family Income and Poverty Levels in U.S. Southwest Border Counties, 1980

State/border county	Family income					Poverty	
	Total families	Percent			Median income ($)	Families below poverty	Percentage of all families
		Under $5,000	$5,000 to $24,000	$25,000 and over			
California							
San Diego	55,707	10.6	68.3	21.1	15,004	10,109	18.1
Imperial	10,596	9.7	72.7	17.5	14,130	2,028	19.1
Arizona							
Cochise	5,099	13.5	75.3	11.3	12,694	1,078	21.1
Pima	24,473	11.4	66.5	22.1	16,144	4,191	17.1
Santa Cruz	3,423	8.3	74.9	16.9	13,507	618	18.1
Yuma	6,341	9.6	76.1	14.2	12,700	1,386	21.9
New Mexico							
Dona Ana	11,052	16.9	71.3	11.8	11,451	3,051	27.6
Hidalgo	616	9.4	70.9	19.6	13,150	121	19.6
Luna	1,393	25.2	63.2	11.6	10,139	446	32.0
Texas							
El Paso	65,038	15.5	70.5	14.0	12,222	17,267	26.5
Hudspeth	350	16.9	79.7	3.4	8,987	124	35.4
Culberson	500	15.6	82.6	1.8	9,919	124	24.8
Jeff Davis	191	22.0	67.5	10.5	8,576	58	30.4
Presidio	908	33.1	61.7	5.2	8,727	406	44.7

[Continued]

★ 168 ★

Family Income and Poverty Levels in U.S. Southwest Border Counties, 1980

[Continued]

State/border county	Family income					Poverty	
	Total families	Percent			Median income ($)	Families below poverty	Percentage of all families
		Under $5,000	$5,000 to $24,000	$25,000 and over			
Brewster	708	20.3	77.7	2.0	11,049	185	26.1
Terrell	174	17.2	67.8	14.9	14,079	39	22.4
Valverde	4,935	20.3	73.0	6.7	9,819	1,804	36.6
Kinney	277	30.0	67.5	2.5	8,125	133	48.0
Maverick	6,023	20.5	71.4	8.1	9,882	2,249	37.3
Dimmett	1,996	26.4	65.3	8.3	9,328	832	41.7
Webb	19,661	18.8	66.2	15.0	11,346	6,208	31.6
Zapata	1,203	18.6	68.4	13.0	11,332	368	30.6
Starr	5,762	29.4	62.1	8.5	8,415	2,664	46.2
Hildalgo	48,303	20.8	68.6	10.6	10,418	17,688	36.6
Cameron	34,578	19.3	69.8	10.9	13,781	11,654	33.7

Source: U.S. Bureau of the Census, *The Hispanic Population of the Southwest Borderland.* Current Population Reports, Series P-23, No. 172, Washington, DC: U.S. Government Printing Office, 1991, p. 29-31.

★ 169 ★

Income

Family Income in U.S. Southwest Border States and Counties, 1980

Family income	United States	Total, border states	Border states			
			Border county area		Non-border county area	
			Hispanic	Non-Hispanic	Hispanic	Non-Hispanic
Total families	59,190,133	10,719,569	309,307	676,939	1,530,825	8,202,498
Percent with income	100.0	100.0	100.0	100.0	100.0	100.0
Under $5,000	7.3	7.1	16.0	5.9	11.3	6.1
$5,000 to $9,999	13.1	12.8	23.9	13.1	18.2	11.4
$10,000 to $14,999	14.7	14.3	20.0	15.5	18.9	13.1
$15,000 to $19,999	15.1	14.0	15.1	14.5	16.3	13.5
$20,000 and $24,999	14.3	13.6	10.3	13.7	13.0	13.8
$25,000 or more	35.4	38.1	14.7	37.3	22.3	42.0
Median income (dollars)	$19,917	$20,572	$12,388	$20,334	$15,461	$21,999
Mean income (dollars)	$23,092	$24,327	$14,897	$24,217	$17,764	$25,916

Source: U.S. Bureau of the Census, *The Hispanic Population of the Southwest Borderland.* Current Population Reports, Series P-23, No. 172, Washington, DC: U.S. Government Printing Office, 1991, p. 21. *Notes:* For the purposes of this report, the U.S. Census Bureau included the following counties: San Diego, and Imperial counties, in California; Cochise, Pima, Santa Cruz, and Yuma counties, in Arizona; Dona Ana, Hidalgo, and Luna counties, in New Mexico; El Paso, Hudspeth, Culberson, Jeff Davis, Presidio, Brewster, Terrell, Valverde, Kinney, Maverick, Dimmit, Webb, Zapata, Starr, Hidalgo, and Cameron counties, in Texas.

★ 170 ★

Income

Family Income, by Hispanic Origin, March 1993

Data show distribution of families in each income bracket, by Hispanic origin of family.

Income group	Total population	Hispanic origin population	Non-Hispanic population	Non-Hispanic White population	Hispanic subgroup				
					Mexican origin population	Puerto Rican origin population	Cuban origin population	Central and South American origin population	Other Hispanic origin population
Percent	100.0	100.0	100.0	100.0	100.0	100.0	100.0	100.0	100.0
Less than $10,000	9.6	17.7	8.9	6.2	16.1	27.9	12.1	17.4	18.5
$10,000 to $24,999	22.8	34.3	21.8	20.6	36.2	32.0	29.2	34.4	26.0
$25,000 to $49,999	34.2	31.3	34.4	35.6	32.8	25.6	31.7	30.4	30.3
$50,000 or more	33.4	16.7	34.8	37.5	14.9	14.6	27.0	17.8	25.2
Median income (dollars)	36,811	23,912	38,015	40,420	23,714	20,301	31,015	23,649	28,562
Mean income (dollars)	44,483	30,332	45,681	48,201	29,251	26,618	39,632	30,713	37,262

Source: Montgomery, Patricia A. U.S. Bureau of the Census. *The Hispanic Population in the United States: March 1993.* Current Population Reports, Series P20-475. Washington, DC: U.S. Government Printing Office, 1994, pp. 18-19.

★ 171 ★

Income

Hispanic Families Living Below Poverty Level, by Ethnicity and Family Characteristic, 1990

Data are estimates based on a sample. Numbers are shown in thousands and in percent.

Family characteristic	Total population	Hispanic origin population	Non-Hispanic population	Mexican origin	Puerto Rican origin	Cuban origin	Central and South American origin	Other Hispanic origin
Families	7,098	1,244	5,854	736	235	46	148	79
Percent below poverty level[1]	10.7	25.0	9.5	25.0	37.5	13.8	22.2	19.4
Family householder[2]								
65 years old and over:								
Number	686	69	617	45	10	5	1	7
Percent	6.3	17.0	5.9	19.8	(B)	(B)	(B)	(B)
Not a high school graduate[3]								
Number	3,406	900	2,506	582	154	27	90	46
Percent	23.7	35.7	21.2	33.8	54.4	22.0	33.3	38.7
Female, husband absent:								
Number	3,768	573	3,195	257	175	17	69	55
Percent	33.4	48.3	31.7	45.7	64.4	(B)	39.3	49.1

Source: U.S. Bureau of the Census, *The Hispanic Population in the United States: March 1991.* Current Population Reports, Series P-20, No. 455, Washington, DC: U.S. Government Printing Office, 1991, pp. 18-19. *Notes:* A (B) indicates base too small to show derived measures. 1. Percent of all families of specified origin. 2. Percentages are based on householders with specified characteristics and of specified origin. 3. Householders 25 years old and older.

★ 172 ★

Income

Income Sources of Households Headed by Elderly Women, 1989-91

Data are shown in average number of dollars, for the 88 percent of the surveyed women who reported their income.

	Hispanic	Black	White
Total income before taxes	16,570	11,872	18,932
Social Security, Railroad Retirement	6,370	6,017	8,986
Pensions, annuities	1,697	839	3,299
Interest, dividends	947	71	2,630
Earnings	6,045	4,185	3,656
Public assistance	1,432	718	268
SSI	784	371	82
Welfare	158	112	15
Food stamps	127	142	17
Other public	363	93	154
Regular contribution	80	42	93
Percent receiving income			
Social Security, Railroad Retirement	86.0	93.0	96.0
Pensions, annuities	17.0	15.0	42.0
Interest, dividends	19.0	7.0	44.0
Earnings	36.0	33.0	25.0
Public assistance	39.0	36.0	11.0
SSI	27.0	23.0	5.0
Welfare	4.0	5.0	1.0
Food stamps	21.0	22.0	4.0
Other public	3.0	3.0	5.0
Regular contribution	3.0	4.0	2.0

Source: Schwenk, F.N. Family Economics Research Group. "Income and consumer expenditures of households headed by Hispanic and Black elderly women." *Family Economics Review* Vol. 7, no. 1 (1994), p. 5.

★ 173 ★

Income

Median Household Income, by Type of Household and Race/Ethnicity of Householder, 1992

Data are shown for households, as of March of following year.

Item	All households	Family households				Nonfamily households		
		Total	Married couple	Male householder, wife absent	Female householder, husband absent	Total[1]	Single-person household	
							Male householder	Female householder
Median income (dollars)								
All households	30,786	37,222	42,140	30,492	18,587	17,711	20,011	12,944
White	32,368	39,320	42,820	32,412	21,970	18,479	21,171	13,413
Black	18,660	21,761	34,290	23,439	12,606	12,062	13,369	9,092
Hispanic[2]	22,848	24,926	29,007	21,994	13,994	14,862	16,360	9,136
Number (1,000)								
All households	96,391	68,144	53,171	3,026	11,947	28,247	9,436	14,206
Under $5,000	4,437	2,340	729	108	1,503	2,097	628	1,356
$5,000 to $9,999	9,675	3,761	1,615	212	1,933	5,914	1,554	4,119
$10,000 to $14,999	9,120	4,880	3,054	259	1,567	4,240	1,397	2,500
$15,000 to $19,999	8,473	5,316	3,683	318	1,315	3,157	1,136	1,664
$20,000 to $24,999	7,763	5,254	3,769	305	1,181	2,509	883	1,257
$25,000 to $34,999	14,305	10,253	7,957	535	1,761	4,052	1,477	1,721
$35,000 to $49,999	16,480	13,233	11,186	592	1,454	3,248	1,248	1,023
$50,000 to $74,999	15,490	13,492	12,167	444	881	1,997	719	411
$75,000 and over	10,648	9,614	9,009	254	351	1,034	394	156

Source: U.S. Bureau of the Census. *Statistical Abstract of the United States, 1994 on CD-ROM.* [machine-readable datafiles] Washington, DC: U.S. Government Printing Office, 1994. Primary source: U.S. Bureau of the Census, Current Population Reports, P60-184. *Notes:* 1. Includes other nonfamily households not shown separately. 2. Persons of Hispanic origin may be of any race.

★ 174 ★

Income

Persons and Families Living in Poverty, by Status of Husband in Household, 1973-1991

Numbers are shown in thousands.

Year and characteristic	All persons			Persons in families					
	Total	Below poverty level		All families			Families with female householder, no husband present		
		Number	Percent	Total	Below poverty level		Total	Below poverty level	
					Number	Percent		Number	Percent
All races									
1991	251,179	35,708	14.2	212,716	27,143	12.8	34,790	13,824	39.7
1990	248,644	33,585	13.5	210,967	25,232	12.0	33,795	12,578	37.2

[Continued]

★ 174 ★

Persons and Families Living in Poverty, by Status of Husband in Household, 1973-1991

[Continued]

Year and characteristic	All persons			Persons in families					
	Total	Below poverty level		All families			Families with female householder, no husband present		
				Total	Below poverty level		Total	Below poverty level	
		Number	Percent		Number	Percent		Number	Percent
1989	245,992	31,528	12.8	209,515	24,066	11.5	32,525	11,668	35.9
1988	243,530	31,745	13.0	208,056	24,048	11.6	32,164	11,972	37.2
1987	240,982	32,221	13.4	206,877	24,725	12.0	31,893	12,148	38.1
1986	238,554	32,370	13.6	205,459	24,754	12.0	31,152	11,944	38.3
1985	236,594	33,064	14.0	203,963	25,729	12.6	30,878	11,600	37.6
1984	233,816	33,700	14.4	202,288	26,458	13.1	30,844	11,831	38.4
1983	231,700	35,303	15.2	201,338	27,933	13.9	30,049	12,072	40.2
1982	229,412	34,398	15.0	200,385	27,349	13.6	28,834	11,701	40.6
1981	227,157	31,822	14.0	198,541	24,850	12.5	28,587	11,051	38.7
1980	225,027	29,272	13.0	196,963	22,601	11.5	27,565	10,120	36.7
1979	222,903	26,072	11.7	195,860	19,964	10.2	26,927	9,400	34.9
1978	215,656	24,497	11.4	191,071	19,062	10.0	26,032	9,269	35.6
1977	213,867	24,720	11.6	190,757	19,505	10.2	25,404	9,205	36.2
1976	212,303	24,975	11.8	190,844	19,632	10.3	24,204	9,029	37.3
1975	210,864	25,877	12.3	190,630	20,789	10.9	23,580	8,846	37.5
1974	209,362	23,370	11.2	190,436	18,817	9.9	23,165	8,462	36.5
1973	207,621	22,973	11.1	189,361	18,299	9.7	21,823	8,178	37.5
Hispanic origin[1]									
1991	22,068	6,339	28.7	19,657	5,541	28.2	4,326	2,282	52.7
1990	21,405	6,006	28.1	18,912	5,091	26.9	3,993	2,115	53.0
1989	20,746	5,430	26.2	18,488	4,659	25.2	3,763	1,902	50.6
1988	20,064	5,357	26.7	18,102	4,700	26.0	3,734	2,052	55.0
1987	19,395	5,422	28.0	17,342	4,761	27.5	3,678	2,045	55.6
1986	18,758	5,117	27.3	16,880	4,469	26.5	3,631	1,921	52.9
1985	18,075	5,236	29.0	16,276	4,605	28.3	3,561	1,983	55.7
1984	16,916	4,806	28.4	15,293	4,192	27.4	3,139	1,764	56.2
1983	16,544	4,633	28.0	15,075	4,113	27.3	3,032	1,670	55.1
1982	14,385	4,301	29.9	13,242	3,865	29.2	2,664	1,601	60.1
1981	14,021	3,713	26.5	12,922	3,349	25.9	2,622	1,465	55.9
1980	13,600	3,491	25.7	12,547	3,143	25.1	2,421	1,319	54.5
1979	13,371	2,921	21.8	12,291	2,599	21.1	2,058	1,053	51.2
1978	12,079	2,607	21.6	11,193	2,343	20.9	1,817	1,024	56.4
1977	12,046	2,700	22.4	11,249	2,463	21.9	1,901	1,077	56.7
1976	11,269	2,783	24.7	10,552	2,516	23.8	1,766	1,000	56.6
1975	11,117	2,991	26.9	10,472	2,755	26.3	1,842	1,053	57.2
1974	11,201	2,575	23.0	10,584	2,374	22.4	1,723	915	53.1
1973	10,795	2,366	21.9	10,269	2,209	21.5	1,534	881	57.4
White									
1991	210,121	23,747	11.3	177,613	17,268	9.7	21,604	6,806	31.5

[Continued]

★ 174 ★

Persons and Families Living in Poverty, by Status of Husband in Household, 1973-1991

[Continued]

Year and characteristic	All persons			Persons in families					
				All families			Families with female householder, no husband present		
	Total	Below poverty level		Total	Below poverty level		Total	Below poverty level	
		Number	Percent		Number	Percent		Number	Percent
1990	208,611	22,326	10.7	176,504	15,916	9.0	20,845	6,210	29.8
1989	206,853	20,785	10.0	175,857	15,179	8.6	20,362	5,723	28.1
1988	205,235	20,715	10.1	175,111	15,001	8.6	20,396	5,950	29.2
1987	203,605	21,195	10.4	174,488	15,593	8.9	20,244	5,989	28.6
1986	202,282	22,183	11.0	174,024	16,393	9.4	20,163	6,171	30.6
1985	200,918	22,860	11.4	172,863	17,125	9.9	20,105	5,990	29.8
1984	198,941	22,955	11.5	171,839	17,299	10.1	19,727	5,866	29.7
1983	197,496	23,984	12.1	171,407	18,377	10.7	19,256	6,017	31.2
1982	195,919	23,517	12.0	170,748	18,015	10.6	18,374	5,686	30.9
1981	194,504	21,553	11.1	169,868	16,127	9.5	18,795	5,600	29.8
1980	192,912	19,699	10.2	168,756	14,587	8.6	17,642	4,940	28.0
1979	191,742	17,214	9.0	168,461	12,495	7.4	17,349	4,375	25.2
1978	186,450	16,259	8.7	165,193	12,050	7.3	16,877	4,371	25.9
1977	185,254	16,416	8.9	165,385	12,364	7.5	16,721	4,474	26.8
1976	184,165	16,713	9.1	165,571	12,500	7.5	15,941	4,463	28.0
1975	183,164	17,770	9.7	165,661	13,799	8.3	15,577	4,577	29.4
1974	182,376	15,736	8.6	166,081	12,181	7.3	15,433	4,278	27.7
1973	181,185	15,142	8.4	165,424	11,412	6.9	14,303	4,003	28.0
Black									
1991	31,312	10,242	32.7	26,564	8,504	32.0	11,959	6,557	54.8
1990	30,806	9,837	31.9	26,296	8,160	31.0	11,866	6,005	50.6
1989	30,332	9,302	30.7	25,931	7,704	29.7	11,190	5,530	49.4
1988	29,849	9,356	31.3	25,484	7,650	30.0	10,794	5,601	51.9
1987	29,362	9,520	32.4	25,128	7,848	31.2	10,701	5,789	54.1
1986	28,871	8,983	31.1	24,910	7,410	29.7	10,175	5,473	53.8
1985	28,485	8,926	31.3	24,620	7,504	30.5	10,041	5,342	53.2
1984	28,087	9,490	33.8	24,387	8,104	33.2	10,384	5,666	54.6
1983	27,678	9,882	35.7	24,138	8,376	34.7	10,059	5,736	57.0
1982	27,216	9,697	35.6	23,948	8,355	34.9	9,699	5,698	58.8
1981	26,834	9,173	34.2	23,423	7,780	33.2	9,214	5,222	56.7
1980	26,408	8,579	32.5	23,084	7,190	31.1	9,338	4,984	53.4
1979	25,944	8,050	31.0	22,666	6,800	30.0	9,065	4,816	53.1
1978	24,956	7,625	30.6	22,027	6,493	29.5	8,689	4,712	54.2
1977	24,710	7,726	31.3	21,850	6,667	30.5	8,315	4,595	55.3
1976	24,399	7,595	31.1	21,840	6,576	30.1	7,926	4,415	55.7
1975	24,089	7,545	31.3	21,687	6,533	30.1	7,676	4,168	54.3
1974	23,699	7,182	30.3	21,341	6,255	29.3	7,483	4,116	55.0
1973	23,512	7,388	31.4	21,328	6,560	30.8	7,188	4,064	56.5

Source: U.S. Bureau of the Census. *Poverty in the United States: 1991.* Current Population Reports, Series P60-181, U.S. Government Printing Office, Washington, D.C., 1992, pp. 2-3. *Note:* 1. Persons of Hispanic origin may be of any race.

★ 175 ★

Income

Persons in Families With Work Experience During the Year and Percent With Low Annual Earnings, by Selected Characteristics, 1974-89

This census report defines earnings as low if they are less than the poverty level for a four-person family, working 40 hours a week, 50 weeks per year: $3,144 or $1.57 per hour in 1964; $3,676 or $1.84 per hour in 1969; $4,843 or $2.42 per hour in 1974; $6,905 or $3.45 per hour in 1979; $9,694 or $4.85 per hour in 1984; $11,570 or $5.79 per hour in 1989; $12,195 or $6.10 per hour in 1990. Numbers are shown in thousands.

Characteristics	Number with work experience during year (000)				Percent with low annual earnings			
	1974	1979	1984	1989	1974	1979	1984	1989
ALL RACES								
Persons 16 to 64 years	97,360	110,786	117,089	127,045	40.4	38.9	40.1	39.4
In families	86,884	94,780	98,368	104,611	40.9	40.0	41.4	40.4
Householder	42,502	44,841	45,643	48,101	14.7	15.7	19.8	21.3
In families with related children under 18 years	53,859	57,898	56,438	59,470	43.8	43.1	42.9	42.4
Householder	27,426	28,515	28,245	29,522	14.1	15.9	19.8	22.3
In families with related children under 6 years	21,401	22,070	23,609	25,799	38.6	38.2	39.4	39.2
Householder	12,911	12,777	13,172	14,083	15.4	17.3	21.8	24.4
In married couple families	76,549	82,036	83,174	87,166	39.3	38.2	39.2	38.3
Husbands	37,438	38,410	38,198	39,362	10.8	10.8	14.8	15.5
Wives	24,034	27,669	29,444	32,515	59.6	55.1	51.7	48.2
Children	14,140	15,054	14,532	14,064	79.6	76.0	76.8	76.8
Other	937	902	1,000	1,225	50.4	54.8	57.0	61.1
In married couple families with related children under 18	48,005	50,167	47,974	49,841	41.6	40.9	40.6	40.1
Husbands	23,995	23,890	23,112	23,582	9.0	9.5	13.4	15.0
Wives	13,823	16,060	16,660	18,324	66.5	61.3	56.6	53.1
Children	9,615	9,664	7,573	7,121	86.4	84.2	86.8	87.3
Other	572	554	629	814	53.1	55.7	59.3	61.1
In married couple families with related children under 6	19,419	19,743	20,748	22,263	36.0	35.6	36.5	36.4
Husbands	11,610	11,252	11,469	11,898	10.4	11.0	15.7	17.1
Wives	5,996	6,923	7,678	8,521	72.9	66.4	59.7	55.6
Children	1,443	1,249	1,209	1,258	84.8	80.5	80.4	76.8
Other	369	319	391	586	51.2	57.1	56.7	61.8
In female householder family with no spouse present	8,287	10,262	12,027	13,070	56.5	54.2	56.6	54.2
Householder	4,065	5,354	6,071	6,871	49.4	43.7	43.9	43.5
Other	4,222	4,908	5,956	6,199	63.3	65.8	69.5	65.9
In female householder family with no spouse present and related children under 18	5,098	6,699	7,132	7,872	64.6	59.4	59.3	57.4
Householder	2,991	4,116	4,439	5,104	54.0	47.4	46.7	47.2
Children	1,755	2,231	2,245	2,185	85.4	82.0	83.2	80.5
Other	352	351	448	583	51.3	55.3	64.6	59.8
In female householder family with no spouse present and related children under 6	1,772	2,036	2,414	2,910	66.6	63.0	64.1	59.7

[Continued]

★ 175 ★

Persons in Families With Work Experience During the Year and Percent With Low Annual Earnings, by Selected Characteristics, 1974-89

[Continued]

Characteristics	Number with work experience during year (000)				Percent with low annual earnings			
	1974	1979	1984	1989	1974	1979	1984	1989
Householder	1,180	1,403	1,527	1,967	62.9	58.7	57.0	56.0
Children	403	454	650	641	82.9	78.0	79.8	72.3
Other	188	179	238	302	54.6	59.2	66.0	57.0
In unrelated subfamilies	122	329	505	437	67.5	53.9	60.4	65.9
Unrelated individuals	10,354	15,677	18,216	21,997	35.6	32.2	32.7	34.0
Males	5,603	8,845	10,292	12,537	31.7	27.8	29.6	30.8
Householder	4,018	6,485	7,423	8,636	28.3	23.9	25.1	25.6
Females	4,750	6,832	7,924	9,459	40.1	37.9	36.8	38.1
Householder	3,813	5,187	5,960	6,879	36.0	32.6	31.7	33.1
Years of school completed								
Less than 12 years	28,581	26,280	22,166	21,096	54.3	56.9	61.8	64.6
12 years	38,436	44,244	46,903	49,874	37.6	37.3	41.0	41.2
13 years and over	30,343	40,262	48,020	56,075	30.8	29.0	29.2	28.3
HISPANIC ORIGIN[1]								
Household relationship								
Persons 16 to 64 years	4,312	5,632	7,426	9,587	46.9	46.6	48.4	49.7
In families	3,865	4,871	6,345	8,019	47.0	46.4	47.7	49.6
Householder	1,920	2,378	2,902	3,608	23.7	24.7	29.3	35.4
In families with related children under 18 years	2,864	3,559	4,398	5,476	48.4	46.9	48.1	51.0
Householder	1,480	1,805	2,164	2,616	23.0	24.2	29.3	35.7
In families with related children under 6 years	1,449	1,784	2,232	2,879	46.1	44.9	46.8	51.1
Householder	841	1,017	1,202	1,466	25.3	26.6	31.9	38.5
In married couple families	3,291	4,047	5,076	6,165	44.7	44.3	45.1	46.8
Husbands	1,648	1,954	2,356	2,794	19.1	19.3	23.3	28.1
Wives	945	1,227	1,651	2,000	65.7	62.0	58.2	55.9
Children	619	743	8779	967	80.2	78.2	75.3	73.1
Other	78	122	189	404	47.2	62.5	62.1	68.7
In married couple families with related children under 18	2,512	3,036	3,656	4,418	45.6	44.7	45.4	48.3
Husbands	1,293	1,509	1,793	2,104	17.9	18.2	23.1	28.2
Wives	678	896	1,152	1,395	69.2	64.0	59.8	60.3
Children	479	545	572	598	85.8	82.9	82.1	79.8
Other	60	86	140	321	(B)	66.3	62.0	69.7
In married couple families with related children under 6	1,311	1,588	1,933	2,422	43.8	42.3	44.2	48.3
Husbands	759	895	1,058	1,249	20.8	20.3	26.9	30.6
Wives	360	485	632	735	73.2	67.0	62.9	63.3
Children	151	150	139	182	85.6	82.9	81.1	80.6
Other	42	59	105	256	(B)	(B)	56.2	68.6

[Continued]

★ 175 ★

Persons in Families With Work Experience During the Year and Percent With Low Annual Earnings, by Selected Characteristics, 1974-89

[Continued]

Characteristics	Number with work experience during year (000)				Percent with low annual earnings			
	1974	1979	1984	1989	1974	1979	1984	1989
In female householder family with no spouse present	441	581	892	1,208	65.5	59.3	62.3	59.8
Householder	210	323	429	616	58.2	51.7	53.3	54.7
Other	231	258	463	592	72.1	68.8	70.6	65.0
In female householder family with no spouse present and related children under 18	313	414	598	799	69.6	62.3	65.2	64.4
Householder	165	255	328	455	60.1	54.6	55.5	58.9
Children	122	129	205	235	89.2	77.4	79.0	74.2
Other	27	30	65	109	(B)	(B)	(B)	66.3
In female householder family with no spouse present and related children under 6	127	166	235	347	69.2	69.0	66.8	68.8
Householder	74	112	138	208	(B)	66.5	61.5	68.5
Children	35	39	69	91	(B)	(B)	(B)	69.1
Other	18	15	28	47	(B)	(B)	(B)	(B)
In unrelated subfamilies	13	38	77	72	(B)	(B)	82.5	(B)
Unrelated individuals	434	723	1,004	1,497	45.9	46.9	49.9	49.2
Males	307	470	680	1,059	43.6	43.0	49.7	48.8
Householder	193	296	370	450	36.9	37.8	37.8	40.0
Females	126	253	323	438	51.6	54.0	50.4	50.2
Householder	93	158	218	261	41.8	43.3	44.9	37.5
Years of school completed								
Less than 12 years	2,327	2,674	3,276	4,117	54.8	55.7	60.3	62.1
12 years	1,211	1,787	2,424	3,134	41.5	41.9	43.6	47.0
13 years and over	774	1,170	1,726	2,336	31.9	33.1	32.5	31.6

Source: U.S. Bureau of the Census. *Workers With Low Earnings: 1964 to 1990.* Current Population Reports, Series P-60, No. 178. Washington, DC: U.S. Government Printing Office, 1992, pp. 17-20. *Notes:* A (B) indicates that the base was less than 75,000 and is too small for derived measures. 1. Persons of Hispanic origin may be of any race.

★ 176 ★

Income

Persons in Families With Year-Round, Full-Time Attachment to Labor Force and Percent With Low Annual Earnings, 1974-89

This census report defines earnings as low if they are less than the poverty level for a four-person family, working 40 hours a week, 50 weeks per year: $3,144 or $1.57 per hour in 1964; $3,676 or $1.84 per hour in 1969; $4,843 or $2.42 per hour in 1974; $6,905 or $3.45 per hour in 1979; $9,694 or $4.85 per hour in 1984; $11,570 or $5.79 per hour in 1989; $12,195 or $6.10 per hour in 1990. Numbers are shown in thousands.

Characteristics	Number with year-round, full-time attachment to labor force				Percent with low annual earnings			
	1974	1979	1984	1989	1974	1979	1984	1989
ALL RACES								
Household relationship								
Persons 16 to 64 years	63,738	74,776	83,564	90,722	18.0	18.6	22.9	22.9
In families	56,215	62,968	68,924	73,088	17.6	18.4	23.1	22.6
Householder	36,919	38,946	40,375	41,631	9.0	9.7	14.2	14.6
In families with related children under 18 years	33,215	36,684	38,300	40,117	17.2	18.6	22.6	22.7
Householder	24,186	24,993	25,275	25,600	8.8	9.9	14.6	15.5
In families with related children under 6 years	14,101	14,774	16,749	18,014	15.7	17.2	22.3	22.3
Householder	11,286	11,116	11,646	11,956	9.6	10.9	15.8	16.3
In married couple families	50,063	55,108	58,619	61,289	16.2	16.9	20.8	20.3
Husbands	33,453	34,650	34,981	35,611	7.3	7.6	11.5	11.5
Wives	11,526	14,357	16,992	19,450	30.0	28.5	29.2	27.8
Children	4,463	5,557	5,971	5,454	44.4	42.7	49.0	47.3
Other	621	544	675	774	32.6	35.6	42.7	44.7
In married couple families with related children under 18	30,149	32,281	32,833	33,948	15.4	16.8	20.3	20.4
Husbands	21,992	22,022	21,667	21,751	6.8	7.3	11.4	12.0
Wives	5,451	7,157	8,491	9,833	32.7	31.2	31.2	30.6
Children	2,328	2,786	2,247	1,841	52.9	52.7	59.8	58.9
Other	377	316	429	524	34.6	32.7	46.4	45.4
In married couple families with related children under 6	13,066	13,506	14,891	15,802	13.7	15.3	19.7	20.0
Husbands	10,559	10,352	10,674	10,891	7.8	8.7	13.1	13.6
Wives	1,852	2,512	3,420	4,011	35.9	33.9	32.4	30.6
Children	414	467	529	527	55.0	53.9	58.0	54.4
Other	241	175	268	373	31.1	30.9	43.2	45.9
In female householder family with no spouse present	4,710	6,111	7,900	8,470	31.3	31.0	39.0	35.8
Householder	2,628	3,715	4,554	5,054	28.7	26.6	30.8	30.5
Other	2,081	2,396	3,346	3,416	34.6	37.8	50.1	43.6
In female householder family with no spouse present and related children under 18	2,581	3,712	4,446	4,846	37.5	34.4	39.7	37.2
Householder	1,825	2,753	3,265	3,625	32.0	29.4	33.0	33.0
Children	533	738	887	818	58.9	52.8	60.0	52.3
Other	223	221	294	403	31.0	34.8	52.3	45.0

[Continued]

★ 176 ★

Persons in Families With Year-Round, Full-Time Attachment to Labor Force and Percent With Low Annual Earnings, 1974-89

[Continued]

Characteristics	Number with year-round, full-time attachment to labor force				Percent with low annual earnings			
	1974	1979	1984	1989	1974	1979	1984	1989
In female householder family with no spouse present and related children under 6	899	1,064	1,489	1,716	43.7	40.2	47.3	39.3
Householder	631	782	971	1,186	39.2	37.5	39.3	35.9
Children	145	176	360	317	67.9	53.0	65.6	49.5
Other	122	107	158	214	38.2	38.9	54.7	42.7
In unrelated subfamilies	69	201	281	267	(B)	33.1	35.9	52.0
Unrelated individuals	7,453	11,606	14,359	17,367	20.9	19.4	21.6	23.7
Males	4,088	6,747	8,389	10,207	18.5	17.0	20.7	22.1
Householder	3,016	5,089	6,217	7,247	16.4	14.5	17.5	18.3
Females	3,365	4,859	5,969	7,160	23.8	22.7	22.9	26.0
Householder	2,827	3,888	4,699	5,375	22.0	19.9	20.0	22.0
Years of school completed								
Less than 12 years	16,416	14,989	13,264	12,105	29.1	32.6	41.5	43.6
12 years	26,505	31,322	34,831	37,103	17.8	19.5	26.0	27.0
13 years and over	20,817	28,464	35,469	41,514	9.5	10.2	12.9	13.2
HISPANIC ORIGIN[1]								
Persons 16 to 64 years	2,831	3,821	5,372	6,996	27.6	29.4	34.5	36.8
In families	2,533	3,272	4,556	5,799	26.9	28.1	33.2	36.1
Householder	1,620	1,991	2,542	3,001	17.1	17.3	23.9	27.9
In families with related children under 18 years	1,813	2,339	3,124	3,878	26.2	27.4	33.2	36.3
Householder	1,249	1,517	1,906	2,180	16.4	17.0	24.1	27.8
In families with related children under 6 years	941	1,202	1,623	2,030	25.2	27.6	33.8	36.7
Householder	703	848	1,056	1,187	18.0	19.3	26.6	28.7
In married couple families	2,207	2,761	3,682	4,495	25.2	26.2	30.5	32.9
Husbands	1,447	1,715	2,153	2,450	15.5	14.6	20.3	23.0
Wives	475	660	966	1,274	41.3	40.8	39.4	38.7
Children	229	315	420	502	52.5	53.5	54.3	52.4
Other	55	71	143	270	(B)	(B)	54.1	58.0
In married couple families with related children under 18	1,640	2,032	2,641	3,164	24.6	25.5	30.6	33.5
Husbands	1,140	1,336	1,650	1,869	14.7	14.2	20.3	23.7
Wives	311	451	648	820	43.3	41.7	40.9	41.6
Children	149	200	237	264	58.1	57.2	62.7	57.4
Other	41	45	106	211	(B)	(B)	55.6	58.2
In married couple families with related children under 6	883	1,096	1,420	1,737	24.6	25.6	31.2	34.2
Husbands	667	793	968	1,090	17.3	16.8	23.6	25.0
Wives	139	206	304	390	44.6	42.3	42.7	43.7

[Continued]

★ 176 ★

Persons in Families With Year-Round, Full-Time Attachment to Labor Force and Percent With Low Annual Earnings, 1974-89

[Continued]

Characteristics	Number with year-round, full-time attachment to labor force				Percent with low annual earnings			
	1974	1979	1984	1989	1974	1979	1984	1989
Children	51	62	69	94	(B)	(B)	(B)	64.5
Other	26	35	79	163	(B)	(B)	48.8	56.2
In female householder family with no spouse present	230	353	578	800	40.9	40.4	47.2	45.8
Householder	125	219	314	432	35.8	36.2	42.8	42.7
Other	105	134	265	368	46.9	47.2	52.3	49.4
In female householder family with no spouse present and related children under 18	149	244	373	506	41.6	42.6	50.1	49.6
Householder	92	170	237	304	33.9	38.7	44.6	44.8
Children	40	57	99	115	(B)	(B)	59.9	53.1
Other	16	17	37	87	(B)	(B)	(B)	61.8
In female householder family with no spouse present and related children under 6	52	93	152	207	(B)	52.6	54.0	54.0
Householder	31	64	93	121	(B)	(B)	51.3	51.2
Children	11	20	40	54	(B)	(B)	(B)	(B)
Other	11	9	18	33	(B)	(B)	(B)	(B)
In unrelated subfamilies	9	21	32	35	(B)	(B)	(B)	(B)
Unrelated individuals	289	528	785	1,162	32.2	36.6	41.1	39.7
Males	208	357	533	823	30.6	35.7	42.0	39.8
Householder	139	234	311	371	24.9	30.3	33.9	33.8
Females	80	171	251	339	36.6	38.6	39.3	39.4
Householder	61	120	179	220	(B)	31.9	35.1	28.9
Years of school completed								
Less than 12 years	1,459	1,745	2,282	2,900	35.8	39.1	47.5	50.2
12 years	839	1,254	1,821	2,331	23.7	25.6	30.0	34.1
13 years and over	532	822	1,269	1,765	11.1	14.6	17.6	18.3

Source: U.S. Bureau of the Census. *Workers With Low Earnings: 1964 to 1990.* Current Population Reports, Series P-60, No. 178. Washington, DC: U.S. Government Printing Office, 1992, pp. 21-24. *Notes:* A (B) indicates that the base was less than 75,000 and is too small for derived measures. 1. Persons of Hispanic origin may be of any race.

★ 177 ★

Income

Poverty Rates of Fatherless Families, by Race/Ethnicity, 1990

Race/ethnicity	Percent living below poverty level[1]
Hispanic[2]	53.0
Black	50.6
White	29.8

Source: "Issues 'too critical' for glib debate." *USA TODAY* (21 May 1992), p. 2A. Primary source: U.S. Census Bureau. *Notes:* 1. Poverty level was $13,359 in annual income for a family of four. 2. Hispanics can be of any race.

Marriage

★ 178 ★

Marital Experience of Women, by Race/Ethnicity and Age

Data are shown for women between the ages of 20 and 54 years, for selected years.

Category	All races			White			Black			Hispanic origin[1]		
	1980	1985	1990	1980	1985	1990	1980	1985	1990	1980	1985	1990
Percent ever married												
20 to 24	49.5	43.3	38.5	52.2	46.6	41.3	33.3	23.9	23.5	55.4	56.7	45.8
25 to 29	78.6	74.0	69.0	81.0	77.4	73.2	62.3	53.4	45.0	80.2	78.4	69.6
30 to 34	89.9	85.8	82.2	91.6	88.1	85.6	77.9	70.9	61.1	88.3	88.0	83.0
35 to 39	4.3	91.6	89.4	95.3	93.1	91.4	87.4	80.7	74.9	91.2	91.6	88.9
40 to 44	95.1	94.6	92.0	95.8	95.6	93.4	89.7	86.1	82.1	94.2	90.3	92.8
45 to 49	95.9	94.4	94.4	96.4	95.1	95.1	92.5	88.4	89.7	94.4	91.1	91.7
50 to 54	95.3	95.2	95.5	95.8	95.4	96.1	92.1	93.4	91.9	95.0	92.5	91.8
Percent divorced after first marriage												
20 to 24	14.2	13.9	12.5	14.7	14.4	12.8	10.5	11.0	9.6	9.4	11.0	6.8
25 to 29	20.7	21.0	19.2	21.0	21.5	19.8	20.2	18.2	17.8	13.9	14.8	13.5
30 to 34	26.2	29.3	28.1	25.8	29.0	28.6	31.4	34.4	26.6	21.1	19.2	19.9

[Continued]

★ 178 ★

Marital Experience of Women, by Race/Ethnicity and Age

[Continued]

Category	All races			White			Black			Hispanic origin[1]		
	1980	1985	1990	1980	1985	1990	1980	1985	1990	1980	1985	1990
35 to 39	27.2	32.0	34.1	26.7	32.0	34.6	32.9	34.6	35.8	21.9	26.3	29.7
40 to 44	26.1	32.1	35.8	25.5	32.0	35.2	33.7	36.9	45.1	19.7	22.8	26.6
45 to 49	23.1	29.0	35.2	22.7	28.4	35.5	29.0	36.0	39.8	23.9	24.3	24.6
50 to 54	21.8	25.7	29.5	21.0	24.6	28.5	29.0	33.7	39.2	22.5	21.8	22.9
Percent remarried after divorce												
20 to 24	45.5	44.3	38.1	47.0	46.0	39.3	(B)	(B)	(B)	(B)	(B)	(B)
25 to 29	53.4	55.3	51.8	56.4	58.3	52.8	27.9	25.4	44.4	(B)	50.5	49.5
30 to 34	60.9	61.4	59.6	63.3	64.3	61.4	42.0	41.1	42.0	58.3	44.9	45.9
35 to 39	64.9	63.0	65.0	66.9	64.9	66.5	50.6	44.8	54.0	45.2	57.1	51.2
40 to 44	67.4	64.7	67.1	68.6	67.5	69.5	58.4	45.4	50.3	(B)	50.6	53.9
45 to 49	69.2	67.9	65.9	70.4	69.6	67.2	62.7	54.6	55.0	(B)	78.9	51.0
50 to 54	72.0	68.2	63.0	72.6	68.4	65.4	72.7	64.3	50.2	(B)	(B)	62.2
Percent redivorced after remarriage												
20 to 24	8.5	8.7	13.1	(NA)	(NA)	(NA)	(NA)	(NA)	(NA)	(NA)	(NA)	(NA)
25 to 29	15.6	18.2	17.8	(NA)	(NA)	(NA)	(NA)	(NA)	(NA)	(NA)	(NA)	(NA)
30 to 34	19.1	20.0	22.7	(NA)	(NA)	(NA)	(NA)	(NA)	(NA)	(NA)	(NA)	(NA)
35 to 39	24.7	26.9	28.5	(NA)	(NA)	(NA)	(NA)	(NA)	(NA)	(NA)	(NA)	(NA)
40 to 44	28.4	33.0	30.6	(NA)	(NA)	(NA)	(NA)	(NA)	(NA)	(NA)	(NA)	(NA)
45 to 49	25.1	33.8	36.4	(NA)	(NA)	(NA)	(NA)	(NA)	(NA)	(NA)	(NA)	(NA)
50 to 54	29.0	27.3	34.5	(NA)	(NA)	(NA)	(NA)	(NA)	(NA)	(NA)	(NA)	(NA)

Source: U.S. Bureau of the Census. *Marriage, Divorce, and Remarriage in the 1990's.* Current Population Reports, P23-180. Washington, DC: U.S. Government Printing Office, 1992, p. 3. *Note:* (NA) stands for not available. A (B) stands for base less than 75,000.

★ 179 ★

Marriage

Marital Status of Hispanics, by Ethnicity, March 1993

Numbers are shown in thousands. Data are U.S. Census Bureau estimates.

Marital status	Total population	Hispanic origin population	Non-Hispanic population	Non-Hispanic White population	Mexican origin population	Puerto Rican origin population	Cuban origin population	Central and South American origin population	Other Hispanic origin population
Total, 15 years and over	197,254	16,022	181,233	151,710	9,902	1,656	938	2,288	1,238
Percent	100.0	100.0	100.0	100.0	100.0	100.0	100.0	100.0	100.0
Never married	26.5	32.8	26.0	23.4	33.1	35.7	23.1	34.5	29.8
Married	58.1	56.3	58.3	60.9	57.1	50.2	61.3	57.1	53.6

[Continued]

★ 179 ★

Marital Status of Hispanics, by Ethnicity, March 1993

[Continued]

Marital status	Total population	Hispanic origin population	Non-Hispanic population	Non-Hispanic White population	Mexican origin population	Puerto Rican origin population	Cuban origin population	Central and South American origin population	Other Hispanic origin population
Widowed	6.9	4.1	7.2	7.2	3.6	4.6	7.7	3.3	5.4
Divorced	8.4	6.8	8.6	8.5	6.1	9.6	8.0	5.1	11.1

Source: Montgomery, Patricia A. U.S. Bureau of the Census. *The Hispanic Population in the United States: March 1993.* Current Population Reports, Series P20-475. Washington, DC: U.S. Government Printing Office, 1994, p. 10.

★ 180 ★

Marriage

Marital Status of Persons Age 65 Years or Older, 1989

The number, in thousands, and percent of elderly people are shown, by marital status, race/ethnicity, sex, and age, as of March 1989.

Marital status	65+		65 to 74		75 to 84		85+	
	Men	Women	Men	Women	Men	Women	Men	Women
All races								
Total (thousands)	12,078	16,944	7,880	9,867	3,506	5,669	693	1.408
Percent	100.0	100.0	100.0	100.0	100.0	100.0	100.0	100.0
Never married	4.7	5.0	4.9	4.5	4.6	5.8	3.2	5.6
Married, spouse present	74.3	40.1	78.4	51.4	70.4	28.1	48.2	9.1
Married, spouse absent	2.7	1.6	2.7	1.8	2.3	1.5	4.4	0.9
Widowed	14.0	48.7	8.9	36.6	19.7	61.5	42.1	82.3
Divorced	4.3	4.5	5.1	5.7	2.9	3.0	2.1	2.1
White								
Total (thousands)	10,798	15,204	7,050	8,767	3,136	5,174	612	1,263
Percent	100.0	100.0	100.0	100.0	100.0	100.0	100.0	100.0
Never married	4.6	5.1	4.8	4.5	4.5	6.0	3.1	5.7
Married, spouse present	76.3	41.2	80.6	53.3	72.3	28.7	47.9	8.8
Married, spouse absent	2.1	1.2	2.0	1.3	1.6	1.1	4.8	0.6
Widowed	13.2	48.1	8.1	35.5	19.2	61.0	41.8	82.7
Divorced	3.8	4.4	4.5	5.4	2.4	3.2	2.4	2.2
Black								
Total (thousands)	981	1,455	619	913	300	416	62	126
Percent	100.0	100.0	100.0	100.0	100.0	100.0	100.0	100.0
Never married	4.5	4.5	4.0	4.3	6.0	4.6	[2]	5.7
Married, spouse present	56.0	27.9	58.6	33.4	50.9	20.8	[2]	12.2
Married, spouse absent	8.3	5.8	8.6	6.0	9.2	5.9	[2]	4.2
Widowed	21.4	55.3	17.6	47.1	24.7	66.9	[2]	76.3
Divorced	9.8	6.5	11.1	9.2	9.2	1.9	[2]	1.6
Hispanic origin[1]								
Total (thousands)	447	558	301	350	120	176	26	31
Percent	100.0	100.0	100.0	100.0	100.0	100.0	100.0	100.0

[Continued]

★ 180 ★

Marital Status of Persons Age 65 Years or Older, 1989

[Continued]

Marital status	65+		65 to 74		75 to 84		85+	
	Men	Women	Men	Women	Men	Women	Men	Women
Never married	6.6	8.2	6.4	6.8	6.0	11.0	[2]	[2]
Married, spouse present	65.6	37.6	69.7	47.5	62.8	23.1	[2]	[2]
Married, spouse absent	7.7	2.5	8.5	2.4	6.6	2.9	[2]	[2]
Widowed	15.1	43.6	9.3	33.6	21.4	57.8	[2]	[2]
Divorced	5.0	8.1	6.1	9.7	3.2	5.2	[2]	[2]

Source: Aging America, Trends and Projections, 1991 Edition. Prepared by the U.S. Senate Special Committee on Aging, the American Association of Retired Persons, the Federal Council on the Aging, and the U.S. Administration on Aging, p. 184. Primary source: U.S. Bureau of the Census, *Marital Status and Living Arrangements: March 1989. Current Population Series*, P20-445 (June 1990). *Notes:* Data exclude people in institutions. 1. People of Hispanic origin may be of any race. 2. Base less than 75,000.

★ 181 ★

Marriage

Marital Status of the Population, by Sex, Race, and Hispanic Origin

Data are shown in millions, except percent, as of March, except as noted. Figures refer to persons 18 years old and older and exclude members of Armed Forces except those living off post or with their families on post. Except as noted, data are based on Current Population Surveys.

Marital status, race, and Hispanic origin	Males						Females					
	1970	1980	1990	1991	1992	1993	1970	1980	1990	1991	1992	1993
Total[1]	62.5	75.7	86.9	87.8	88.7	89.7	70.0	83.8	95.0	95.8	96.6	97.4
Never married	11.8	18.0	22.4	22.9	23.2	23.6	9.6	14.3	17.9	18.5	18.6	18.6
Married	47.1	51.8	55.8	55.9	56.2	56.8	47.9	52.8	56.7	56.8	57.1	57.7
Widowed	2.1	2.0	2.3	2.4	2.5	2.5	9.7	10.8	11.5	11.3	11.3	11.2
Divorced	1.6	3.9	6.3	6.6	6.8	6.8	2.7	6.0	8.8	9.2	9.6	9.9
Percent of total	100.0	100.0	100.0	100.0	100.0	100.0	100.0	100.0	100.0	100.0	100.0	100.0
Never married	18.9	23.8	25.8	26.1	26.2	26.3	13.7	17.1	18.9	19.3	19.2	19.1
Married	75.3	68.4	64.3	63.6	63.3	63.4	68.5	63.0	59.7	59.3	59.1	59.2
Widowed	3.3	2.6	2.7	2.7	2.9	2.8	13.9	12.8	12.1	11.8	11.7	11.5
Divorced	2.5	5.2	7.2	7.5	7.6	7.6	3.9	7.1	9.3	9.6	9.9	10.1
Percent standardized for age:[2]												
Never married	16.5	18.7	23.3	24.0	24.4	24.9	12.1	14.5	18.2	19.0	19.2	19.4
Married	77.6	72.9	66.5	65.5	64.9	64.3	70.8	65.9	61.2	60.6	60.2	60.1
Widowed	3.3	2.7	2.7	2.7	2.8	3.1	13.0	12.1	10.8	10.4	10.3	10.0
Divorced	2.6	5.6	7.6	7.8	7.9	7.7	4.1	7.6	9.8	10.0	10.3	10.4
White, total	55.9	66.7	74.8	75.5	76.0	76.6	62.2	72.8	80.6	81.2	81.6	82.1
Never married	10.2	15.0	18.0	18.3	18.4	18.6	8.2	11.4	13.6	13.9	13.8	13.8
Married	42.7	46.7	49.5	49.7	50.0	50.3	43.1	47.1	49.9	50.1	50.3	50.6
Widowed	1.7	1.6	1.9	2.0	2.0	2.0	8.6	9.3	9.8	9.6	9.6	9.5
Divorced	1.3	3.4	5.4	5.6	5.8	5.8	2.3	5.0	7.3	7.6	7.9	8.2
Percent of total	100.0	100.0	100.0	100.0	100.0	100.0	100.0	100.0	100.0	100.0	100.0	100.0

[Continued]

★ 181 ★

Marital Status of the Population, by Sex, Race, and Hispanic Origin

[Continued]

Marital status, race, and Hispanic origin	Males						Females					
	1970	1980	1990	1991	1992	1993	1970	1980	1990	1991	1992	1993
Never married	18.2	22.5	24.1	24.2	24.2	24.3	13.2	15.7	16.9	17.1	16.9	16.8
Married	76.3	70.0	66.2	65.8	65.5	65.7	69.3	64.7	61.9	61.8	61.6	61.6
Widowed	3.1	2.5	2.6	2.6	2.7	2.6	13.8	12.8	12.2	11.8	11.8	11.6
Divorced	2.4	5.0	7.2	7.4	7.6	7.5	3.8	6.8	9.0	9.3	9.6	10.0
Black, total	5.9	7.4	9.1	9.3	9.5	9.6	7.1	9.2	11.2	11.4	11.5	11.7
Never married	1.4	2.5	3.5	3.7	3.8	3.9	1.2	2.5	3.6	3.9	4.0	4.1
Married	3.9	4.1	4.5	4.3	4.4	4.4	4.4	4.5	4.8	4.7	4.7	4.8
Widowed	0.3	0.3	0.3	0.3	0.4	0.4	1.1	1.3	1.4	1.4	1.4	1.4
Divorced	0.2	0.5	0.8	0.9	0.9	0.8	0.4	0.9	1.3	1.3	1.4	1.4
Percent of total	100.0	100.0	100.0	100.0	100.0	100.0	100.0	100.0	100.0	100.0	100.0	100.0
Never married	24.3	34.3	38.4	40.2	40.4	40.8	17.4	27.4	32.5	34.5	35.0	34.9
Married	66.9	54.6	49.2	46.7	46.0	46.1	61.7	48.7	43.0	41.0	40.6	41.1
Widowed	5.2	4.2	3.7	3.6	4.5	4.4	15.8	14.3	12.4	12.7	12.3	12.0
Divorced	3.6	7.0	8.8	9.5	9.1	8.6	5.0	9.5	12.0	11.8	12.2	12.0
Hispanic, total[3]	2.4	3.8	6.7	6.9	7.2	7.4	2.6	4.1	6.8	7.0	7.2	7.5
Never married	0.5	1.0	2.2	2.2	2.3	2.4	0.4	0.9	1.5	1.6	1.7	1.7
Married	1.8	2.5	4.1	4.2	4.3	4.4	1.8	2.6	4.3	4.3	4.4	4.6
Widowed	0.1	0.1	0.1	0.1	0.1	0.1	0.2	0.3	0.4	0.5	0.5	0.5
Divorced	0.1	0.2	0.4	0.4	0.4	0.5	0.1	0.3	0.6	0.6	0.6	0.6
Percent of total	100.0	100.0	100.0	100.0	100.0	100.0	100.0	100.0	100.0	100.0	100.0	100.0
Never married	21.2	27.3	32.1	32.2	32.4	32.5	16.2	21.1	22.5	22.4	23.5	23.3
Married	73.8	67.1	60.9	60.2	60.0	59.7	70.0	64.3	62.4	61.9	60.7	61.1
Widowed	2.3	1.6	1.5	1.5	1.7	1.7	8.7	7.1	6.5	7.1	7.2	7.0
Divorced	2.7	4.0	5.5	6.0	5.9	6.1	5.1	7.6	8.5	8.6	8.7	8.6

Source: U.S. Bureau of the Census. *Statistical Abstract of the United States, 1994 on CD-ROM.* 114th ed. [machine-readable datafiles] Washington, DC: U.S. Government Printing Office, 1994. Primary source: U.S. Bureau of the Census, 1970 Census of Population, vol. I, part 1, and Current Population Reports, P20-468, and earlier reports; and unpublished data. *Notes:* 1. Includes persons of other races, not shown separately. 2. 1960 age distribution used as standard; standardization improves comparability over time by removing effects of changes in age distribution of population. 3. Hispanic persons may be of any race. 1970 data as of April and based on Census of Population.

★ 182 ★

Marriage

Married Couples of Same or Mixed Races and Origins

Data are shown in thousands, as of March, except as noted for persons 15 years old and older. Except as noted, data are based on Current Population Surveys and include members of Armed Forces living off post or with their families on post, but exclude all other members of Armed Forces.

Race/ethnicity of spouses	1970[1]	1980	1990	1992	1993
Married couples, total	44,598	49,714	53,256	53,512	54,199
Race					
Same race couples	43,922	48,264	50,889	50,873	51,437
White/White	40,578	44,910	47,202	47,358	47,782
Black/Black	3,344	3,354	3,687	3,515	3,655
Interracial couples	310	651	964	1,161	1,195
Black/White	65	167	211	246	242
Black husband/White wife	41	122	150	163	182
White husband/Black wife	24	45	61	83	60
White/other race[2]	233	450	720	883	920
Black/other race[2]	12	34	33	32	33
All other couples[2]	366	799	1,401	1,478	1,567
Hispanic origin[3]					
Hispanic/Hispanic	1,368	1,906	3,085	3,297	3,419
Hispanic/other origin (not Hispanic)	584	891	1,193	1,155	1,206
All other couples (not of Hispanic origin)	42,645	46,917	48,979	49,060	49,573

Source: 1994 Statistical Abstract of the United States on CD-ROM [machine-readable datafiles]. CD-8A-94. Washington, DC: U.S. Department of Commerce, Economics and Statistics Administration, Bureau of the Census, Data User Services Division, January 1995. Primary source: U.S. Bureau of the Census, Current Population Reports, P20-468; and unpublished data. *Notes:* 1. As of April and based on Census of Population. 2. Excluding White and Black. 3. Persons of Hispanic origin may be of any race.

★ 183 ★

Marriage

Ratio of Unmarried Men to Unmarried Women

Data show number of unmarried men per 100 unmarried women.

Race/ethnicity	Age			
	25-29	30-34	35-39	40-44
Hispanic	141	125	106	118
White	136	133	119	88
Black	98	77	72	65

Source: Usdansky, Margaret L. " Wedded to the single life: attitudes, economy delaying marriages." *USA TODAY* (17 July 1992), p. 9A. Primary source: Census Bureau.

★ 184 ★

Marriage

Unmarried Men and Women

Percent of men and women who have never been married is shown by age and race/ethnicity.

Race/ethnicity	Age 20-24				Age 30-34			
	Men		Women		Men		Women	
	1970	1991	1970	1991	1970	1991	1970	1991
Hispanic	49.9	74.1	33.4	53.2	11.0	26.5	8.4	19.0
White	54.4	78.2	34.6	60.7	9.2	25.0	5.5	14.7
Black	56.1	87.9	43.5	81.6	9.2	43.7	10.8	43.4

Source: Usdansky, Margaret. "Wedded to the single life: attitudes, economy delaying marriages." *USA TODAY* (17 July 1992), p. 9A. Primary source: Census Bureau.

Chapter 3
EDUCATION

Academic Progress

★ 185 ★

ACT Average Scores, by Race/Ethnicity, 1994

Data show average ACT (American College Testing Assessment) scores for 1994 and percent change from 1993. The ACT is scored on a scale of 1 to 36.

Race/ethnicity	Score	1-yr. chg.
American Indian	18.5	+0.1
Asian	21.7	0.0
Black	17.0	-0.1
Mexican American	18.4	-0.1
Other Hispanic	19.3	0.0
White	21.4	0.0
All students	20.8	+0.1

Source: Chronicle of Higher Education Almanac (7 September 1994), p. A54. Primary source: American College Testing.

★ 186 ★

Academic Progress

Adult Document Literacy Skills, 1992

Data show percent of persons age 16 and older at each proficiency level. Document literacy reflects the knowledge and skills used to process information from documents. A level 1 score of 0 to 225 requires the reader to locate pieces of information based on a literal match. A level 2 score of 225 to 275 requires the reader to match a single piece of information among several distractors. A level 3 score of 276 to 325 requires the reader to integrate multiple pieces of information from one or more documents. A level 4 score of 326 to 375 requires the performance of multiple-feature matches, cycling through documents, and integrating information. A level 5 score of 376 to 500 requires the reader to search through complex displays that contain multiple distractors, to make high-level text-based inferences.

Race/ethnicity	Average score	Percent of adults with proficiency level -				
		1	2	3	4	5
Total	267	23	28	31	15	3
White	280	16	27	34	19	3
Black	230	43	36	18	3	0
Asian or Pacific Islander	245	34	25	28	12	2
American Indian	254	27	37	29	7	0
Hispanic						
Mexican	205	54	25	16	4	0
Cuban	212	48	30	16	4	2
Puerto Rican	215	49	29	18	3	0
Central/South American	206	53	25	16	4	0
Other	254	28	26	32	12	2

Source: U.S. Department of Education. National Center for Education Statistics. Office of Educational Research and Improvement. *Digest of Education Statistics, 1994*. Lanham, MD: Bernan, November 1994, p. 408. U.S. Department of Education, National Center for Education Statistics, National Adult Literacy Survey, *Adult Literacy in America, 1992*, prepared by Educational Testing Service. (This table was prepared February 1994.).

★187★

Academic Progress

Adult Prose Literacy Skills, 1992

Data show percent of persons age 16 and older at each proficiency level. Prose literacy is the ability to understand and use information contained in various kinds of textual material. A level 1 score of 0 to 225 requires the reader to locate a single piece of information in a short text. A level 2 score of 226 to 275 requires the reader to locate a single piece of information in the text with several distractors or to make low-level inferences. A level 3 score of 276 to 325 requires the reader to make literal or synonymous matches between the text and information given in the task, or to make low-level inferences. A level 4 score of 326 to 375 requires the reader to perform multiple-feature matches and to integrate or synthesize information from complex passages. A level 5 score of 376 to 500 requires the reader to search for information in dense text which contains a number of distractors.

Race/ethnicity	Average score	Percent of adults with proficiency level -				
		1	2	3	4	5
Total	272	21	27	32	17	3
White	286	14	25	36	21	4
Black	237	38	37	21	4	0
Asian or Pacific Islander	242	36	25	25	12	2
American Indian	254	25	39	28	7	1
Hispanic						
Mexican	206	54	25	16	5	0
Cuban	211	53	24	17	6	1
Puerto Rican	218	47	32	17	3	0
Central/South American	207	56	22	17	4	0
Other	260	25	27	33	13	2

Source: U.S. Department of Education. National Center for Education Statistics. Office of Educational Research and Improvement. *Digest of Education Statistics, 1994.* Lanham, MD: Bernan, November 1994, p. 408. U.S. Department of Education, National Center for Education Statistics, National Adult Literacy Survey, *Adult Literacy in America, 1992,* prepared by Educational Testing Service. (This table was prepared February 1994.).

★ 188 ★

Academic Progress

Adult Quantitative Literacy Skills, 1992

Data show percent of persons age 16 and older at each proficiency level. Quantitative literacy is the ability to perform numerical operations in everyday life. A level 1 score of 0 to 225 requires the reader to perform a single, relatively simple, arithmetic operation. A level 2 score of 226 to 275 requires the reader to perform a single operation using numbers that are either stated in the task or easily located in the material. A level 3 score of 276 to 325 requires the reader to use two or more numbers to solve the problem. A level 4 score of 326 to 375 requires the reader to perform two or more sequential operations or a single operation in which the quantities are found in different types of displays. A level 5 score of 376 to 500 requires the reader to perform multiple operations sequentially. They must extract the features of the problem from text or rely on background knowledge to determine the quantities or operations needed.

Race/ethnicity	Average score	Percent of adults with proficiency level -				
		1	2	3	4	5
Total	271	22	25	31	17	4
White	287	14	24	35	21	5
Black	224	46	34	17	3	0
Asian or Pacific Islander	256	30	23	27	16	4
American Indian	250	33	32	28	7	1
Hispanic						
Mexican	205	54	25	17	4	0
Cuban	223	46	20	25	6	3
Puerto Rican	212	51	28	17	3	1
Central/South American	203	53	25	18	4	0
Other	246	31	25	31	11	1

Source: U.S. Department of Education. National Center for Education Statistics. Office of Educational Research and Improvement. *Digest of Education Statistics, 1994.* Lanham, MD: Bernan, November 1994, p. 408. U.S. Department of Education, National Center for Education Statistics, National Adult Literacy Survey, *Adult Literacy in America, 1992,* prepared by Educational Testing Service. (This table was prepared February 1994.).

★ 189 ★

Academic Progress

Average Carnegie Units Completed by High School Graduates, by Subject Field and Race/ Ethnicity: 1982 and 1992

The Carnegie unit is a standard of measurement that represents one credit for the completion of a one-year course. Data refer to public high school students.

Subject field	Academic year and race/ethnicity of student											
	1982 graduates						1992 graduates					
	Total	White	Black	Hispanic	Asian	Am. Indian	Total	White	Black	Hispanic	Asian	Am. Indian
Total	21.44	21.51	21.13	21.19	22.18	21.32	23.76	23.83	23.21	23.62	23.45	23.38
English	3.87	3.84	4.06	3.88	3.82	3.92	4.18	4.17	4.20	4.26	4.14	4.09
History/social studies	3.16	3.19	3.09	3.02	3.19	3.22	3.58	3.61	3.59	3.38	3.51	3.63
Mathematics												
Total	2.55	2.59	2.53	2.26	3.14	2.09	3.39	3.38	3.37	3.36	3.65	3.16

[Continued]

★ 189 ★

Average Carnegie Units Completed by High School Graduates, by Subject Field and Race/ Ethnicity: 1982 and 1992

[Continued]

Subject field	Academic year and race/ethnicity of student											
	1982 graduates						1992 graduates					
	Total	White	Black	Hispanic	Asian	Am. Indian	Total	White	Black	Hispanic	Asian	Am. Indian
Less than algebra	0.92	0.80	1.39	1.24	0.74	1.14	0.98	0.87	1.35	1.24	0.74	1.55
Algebra or higher	1.62	1.79	1.14	1.03	2.41	0.95	2.41	2.51	2.02	2.12	2.91	1.61
Science												
Total	2.16	2.24	2.04	1.79	2.59	1.96	2.87	2.93	2.74	2.60	3.22	2.55
General science	0.74	0.73	0.81	0.77	0.51	0.72	0.84	0.83	0.94	0.81	0.73	1.03
Biology	0.93	0.96	0.89	0.79	1.09	0.78	1.19	1.21	1.15	1.16	1.20	0.99
Chemistry	0.34	0.37	0.25	0.16	0.60	0.35	0.58	0.61	0.47	0.47	0.79	0.35
Physics	0.16	0.19	0.09	0.07	0.39	0.11	0.26	0.28	0.18	0.16	0.50	0.18
Foreign languages	0.96	1.02	0.70	0.76	1.89	0.45	1.67	1.70	1.28	1.76	2.43	0.92
Arts	1.45	1.51	1.25	1.30	1.32	1.67	1.62	1.68	1.45	1.44	1.38	1.53
Vocational education[1]	4.64	4.53	4.82	5.26	3.12	5.09	3.76	3.73	3.92	3.79	3.18	4.53
Personal use[2]	2.64	2.59	2.64	2.92	3.10	2.93	2.69	2.63	2.66	3.03	2.93	2.97
Computer science[3]	0.08	0.09	0.08	0.04	0.14	0.04	0.35	0.34	0.38	0.41	0.43	0.25

Source: U.S. Department of Education. National Center for Education Statistics. Office of Educational Research and Improvement. *Digest of Education Statistics, 1994.* Lanham, MD: Bernan, November 1994, p. 133. Primary source: U.S. Department of Education, National Center for Education Statistics. "High School and Beyond," First Followup survey; "1990 High School Transcript Study" and the "National Education Longitudinal Study of 1988," Second Followup survey. (This table was prepared August 1994.) *Notes:* 1. Includes nonoccupational vocational education, vocational general introduction, agriculture, business, marketing, health, occupational home economics, trade and industry, and technical courses. 2. Includes personal and social courses, religion and theology, and courses not included in other subject fields. 3. Computer courses are included in mathematics and vocational categories.

★ 190 ★

Academic Progress

Average Vocational Carnegie Units, by Vocational Category Completed by High School Graduates: 1990 and 1992

Vocational Carnegie Units include: Consumer and homemaking education; General labor market preparation (typewriting 1, introductory industrial arts, work experience/career exploration, general labor market skills); Specific labor market preparation (agriculture/renewable resources, business, marketing and distribution, health occupations, occupational home economics, trade and industry, technical and communications).

	1990 graduates						1992 graduates					
	Total	White	Black	Hispanic	Asian	American Indian	Total	White	Black	Hispanic	Asian	American Indian
Total	4.10	4.13	4.36	4.00	2.89	4.43	3.76	3.73	3.92	3.79	3.18	4.53
General labor market preparation	0.83	0.80	0.96	0.85	0.73	0.84	0.69	0.67	0.74	0.74	0.56	0.56
Consumer and homemaking education	0.57	0.55	0.79	0.54	0.32	0.72	0.54	0.53	0.68	0.46	0.36	0.50
Specific labor market preparation	2.70	2.78	2.62	2.61	1.85	2.87	2.53	2.52	2.52	2.59	2.25	3.37
Agriculture	0.20	0.24	0.06	0.15	0.04	0.36	0.19	0.22	0.12	0.09	0.03	0.20
Business	0.90	0.88	1.08	0.96	0.66	0.96	0.85	0.84	0.93	0.92	0.85	0.75
Marketing	0.16	0.16	0.18	0.19	0.05	0.15	0.13	0.13	0.14	0.13	0.07	0.06
Health	0.04	0.04	0.04	0.02	0.01	-	0.06	0.05	0.08	0.09	0.07	0.06
Occupational home economics	0.17	0.15	0.27	0.27	0.05	0.08	0.18	0.15	0.35	0.21	0.06	0.35
Trade and industrial	0.87	0.94	0.64	0.75	0.73	0.95	0.79	0.80	0.61	0.71	0.88	1.73

[Continued]

★ 190 ★

Average Vocational Carnegie Units, by Vocational Category Completed by High School Graduates: 1990 and 1992

[Continued]

	1990 graduates						1992 graduates					
	Total	White	Black	Hispanic	Asian	American Indian	Total	White	Black	Hispanic	Asian	American Indian
Technical/communications	0.22	0.22	0.23	0.17	0.26	0.16	0.22	0.22	0.20	0.26	0.26	0.12
Other	0.14	0.15	0.12	0.10	0.05	0.21	0.11	0.11	0.09	0.18	0.03	0.06

Source: U.S. Department of Education. National Center for Education Statistics. Office of Educational Research and Improvement. *Digest of Education Statistics, 1994.* Lanham, MD: Bernan, November 1994, p. 134. Primary source: U.S. Department of Education, National Center for Education Statistics. "High School and Beyond," First Followup survey; "1990 High School Transcript Study" and the "National Education Longitudinal Study of 1988," Second Followup survey. (This table was prepared August 1994.) *Notes:* A dash (-) stands for data not available. The Carnegie unit is a standard of measurement that represents one credit for the completion of a one-year course.

★ 191 ★

Academic Progress

Enrollment Trends in Special Education Classes

From the source: "The Individuals with Disabilities Education Act (IDEA) mandates that all children have available to them a free and appropriate education designed to meet their unique needs. Changes in the number and distribution of students with disabilities affect the level of effort required of educators and policymakers to comply with the current law and help them to forecast the need for resources in the future." This table shows the distribution of students in special education, by race/ethnicity of student, for selected school years.

Type of disability, and race/ethnicity	1986	1988	1990
Total			
All conditions	100.0	100.0	100.0
Learning disabilities	46.6	47.5	48.6
Speech impairments	27.5	27.5	26.5
Mental retardation[1]	14.1	14.3	13.6
Serious emotional disturbance	6.9	5.9	6.7
White			
All conditions	66.0	66.7	65.1
Learning disabilities	33.1	34.3	34.0
Speech impairments	20.2	20.5	19.2
Mental retardation[1]	8.2	7.7	7.2
Serious emotional disturbance	4.4	4.2	4.7
Black			
All conditions	18.8	17.5	18.4
Learning disabilities	7.8	7.3	8.1
Speech impairments	4.4	4.0	4.2
Mental retardation[1]	4.7	4.9	4.6
Serious emotional disturbance	1.8	1.3	1.5
Hispanic			
All conditions	8.1	8.8	9.6
Learning disabilities	4.7	4.8	5.4
Speech impairments	2.1	2.1	2.3

[Continued]

★ 191 ★

Enrollment Trends in Special Education Classes

[Continued]

Type of disability, and race/ethnicity	1986	1988	1990
Mental retardation[1]	0.8	1.5	1.5
Serious emotional disturbance	0.5	0.3	0.4

Source: U.S. Department of Education. National Center for Education Statistics. *The Condition of Education 1994.* Washington, DC: U.S. Government Printing Office, 1994, p. 319. Primary source: U.S. Department of Education, Office for Civil Rights, *National Summaries from the Elementary and Secondary School Civil Rights Survey*, various years. *Notes:* 1. Includes both those students classified as Educably Mentally Retarded (EMR) and Trainably Mentally Retarded (TMR).

★ 192 ★

Academic Progress

Enrollment and Completion of Higher Education Programs

From the source: "Among beginning students whose goal in 1989-90 was a vocational certificate, half had completed one by early 1992, and a majority of them were completed within nine months of starting a program. A lower percentage of Hispanic students seeking a certificate completed one than did white students." This table shows completion status for first-time postsecondary students, by degree objective and race/ethnicity of student. Data are shown as of spring 1992.

Student characteristic	Degree objective									
	Vocational certificate			Associate's degree				Bachelor's degree		
	Completed in		Not completed	Completed	Continuously enrolled[1]	Re-enrolled after inter-ruption[1,2]	No re-enrollment after inter-ruption[3]	Continuously enrolled[4]	Re-enrollment after inter-ruption	No re-enrollment after inter-ruption
	Nine months or less	Over nine months								
Total	29.2	21.3	49.5	12.3	19.1	22.5	46.1	56.8	18.9	24.2
Race/ethnicity[5]										
White	29.6	23.1	47.3	12.8	18.5	21.6	47.2	57.6	17.9	24.5
Black	26.4	17.5	56.1	7.9	12.2	27.1	52.9	50.3	23.4	26.3
Hispanic	23.2	9.2	67.6	16.6	27.0	28.0	28.4	46.0	27.7	26.3
Asian	6	6	6	6	6	6	6	68.8	19.3	11.8

Source: U.S. Department of Education. National Center for Education Statistics. *The Condition of Education 1994.* Washington, DC: U.S. GPO, 1994, p. 184. U.S. Department of Education, National Center for Education Statistics, Beginning Postsecondary Student Longitudinal Survey, 1992 (data analysis system). *Notes:* A dash (-) stands for not available. 1. Includes enrollment or re-enrollment toward a bachelor's degree. 2. Re-enrolled toward degree after an interruption, that is, a year with more than four consecutive months not enrolled. However, may not be enrolled at the time of the follow-up survey. 3. Has an interruption in enrollment and has not re-enrolled during the survey period. 4. A small number of bachelor's degree recipients are included in "continuously enrolled." 5. Included in the total but not reported separately are American Indian students. 6. Too few observations for a reliable estimate.

★ 193 ★

Academic Progress

Enrollment in Science and Math Courses

Figures represent percentage of high school students having taken various levels of science and math courses by graduation. Data are shown for in 1982 and 1990, by race/ethnicity of student.

Subject and race/ethnicity	1982	1990	Percent change
Algebra 1			
Asian American	66	72	6.0
Black	57	78	21.0
Hispanic	55	81	26.0
White	66	77	9.0
Algebra 2			
Asian American	56	59	3.0
Black	24	39	15.0
Hispanic	21	39	18.0
White	39	52	13.0
Calculus (regular and AP)[1]			
Asian American	19	34	15.0
Black	2	4	2.0
Hispanic	2	7	5.0
White	8	11	3.0
Biology			
Asian American	82	90	8.0
Black	71	91	20.0
Hispanic	67	90	23.0
White	77	92	15.0
Chemistry			
Asian American	51	64	13.0
Black	21	40	19.0
Hispanic	15	39	24.0
White	34	52	18.0

Source: "HS Science/Math." *Manpower Comments*, September 1993, p. 29. Primary source: Council of Chief State School Officers. *State Indicators of Science and Mathematics Education 1993. Note:* 1. AP stands for Advanced Placement.

★ 194 ★

Academic Progress

High School Completion Rates

From the source: "Among the sophomore class of 1980, white and Asian students were more likely to complete high school on time (by 1982) than black, Hispanic, or American Indian students." This table shows completion rates for the tenth-grade class of 1980, by race/ethnicity of student.

Characteristics	Completed on time (June 1982)	Completed between 1982 and 1986	Completed between 1986 and 1992	Completion rate 1992
Total	83.6	8.3	1.7	93.7
Race/ethnicity[1]				
White	85.7	7.4	1.6	94.7
Black	78.9	11.4	1.9	92.2
Hispanic	72.6	11.9	2.8	87.5
Asian/Pacific Islander	90.8	7.7	0.9	99.4
American Indian	65.4	12.0	4.3	81.7

Source: U.S. Department of Education. National Center for Education Statistics. *The Condition of Education 1994.* Washington, DC: U.S. GPO, 1994, p. 34. Primary source: U.S. Department of Education, National Center for Education Statistics, High School and Beyond (Sophomore Cohort), and National Education Longitudinal Study of 1988 (Student and Dropout Surveys). *Notes:* 1. Not shown separately for the eighth-grade class of 1988 are 434 persons whose race/ethnicity is unknown.

★ 195 ★

Academic Progress

High School Graduates Entering College in the Same Year as Graduation, 1973-92

From the source: "Most college students enroll in college immediately after finishing high school. The percentage of high school graduates enrolled in college the October following graduation is a leading indicator of the total proportion of that year's graduates who will ever enroll in college. The percentage enrolling is a measure of the immediate accessibility of higher education to high school graduates." This table shows the percentage of graduates who were enrolled in college in the October following completion of high school, by race/ethnicity of student.

October	Type of college			Family income			Race/ethnicity[1]		
	Total	2-year	4-year	Low	Middle	High	White	Black	Hispanic
1973	46.6	14.9	31.7	20.3	41.0	64.4	-	-	-
1974	47.6	15.2	32.4	-	-	-	48.7	40.5	53.1
1975	50.7	18.2	32.6	31.2	46.2	64.5	49.1	44.5	52.7
1976	48.8	15.6	33.3	39.1	40.5	63.0	50.3	45.3	53.6
1977	50.6	17.5	33.1	27.7	44.4	66.3	50.1	46.8	48.8
1978	50.1	17.0	331	31.4	44.3	64.2	50.4	47.5	46.1
1979	49.3	17.5	31.8	30.5	43.1	63.4	50.1	45.2	46.3
1980	19.3	19.4	29.9	32.5	42.7	65.2	51.5	44.0	49.6
1981	53.9	20.5	33.5	33.6	49.3	67.6	52.4	40.3	48.7
1982	50.6	19.1	31.5	32.8	41.7	71.7	54.2	38.8	49.4
1983	52.7	19.2	33.5	34.6	45.4	70.2	55.5	38.0	46.7

[Continued]

★ 195 ★

High School Graduates Entering College in the Same Year as Graduation, 1973-92

[Continued]

October	Type of college			Family income			Race/ethnicity[1]		
	Total	2-year	4-year	Low	Middle	High	White	Black	Hispanic
1984	55.2	19.4	35.8	34.5	48.4	74.0	57.9	39.9	49.3
1985	57.7	19.6	38.1	40.2	50.7	74.5	58.6	39.5	46.1
1986	53.8	19.3	34.5	33.9	48.4	71.4	58.5	43.5	42.3
1987	56.8	18.9	37.9	36.9	49.9	74.0	58.8	44.2	45.0
1988	58.9	21.9	37.1	42.5	54.7	72.8	60.1	49.7	48.5
1989	59.6	20.7	38.9	48.1	55.4	70.9	61.6	48.0	52.7
1990	60.1	20.1	40.0	46.7	54.5	76.5	63.0	48.7	52.5
1991	62.5	24.9	37.7	39.5	58.4	78.2	64.2	47.2	52.5
1992	61.9	23.0	38.9	40.9	56.9	80.9	-	-	-

Source: U.S. Department of Education. National Center for Education Statistics. *The Condition of Education 1994.* Washington, DC: U.S. GPO, 1994, p. 40. Primary source: U.S. Department of Commerce, Bureau of the Census, *October Current Population Surveys. Notes:* A dash (-) means not available. 1. Due to small sample sizes for the Black, Hispanic and Other categories, 3-year averages were calculated. The 3-year average for 1991 is the average percentage of graduates enrolled in college in 1990, 1991, and 1992.

★ 196 ★

Academic Progress

Mathematics Course Enrollment

As industry becomes more technically oriented, exposure to mathematics and science is essential in preparing a student for future employment and the rate of student enrollment in such courses can be used to predict the availability of candidates in technical fields. This table shows the percentage of high school graduates who have taken each course.

Mathematics courses (credits)	White	Black	Hispanic	Asian	American Indian
1990					
Any mathematics (1.00)	99.7	98.7	99.8	99.9	100.0
Remedial/below grade level math (1.00)	20.0	35.4	38.3	19.9	37.7
Algebra I (1.00)	77.2	77.6	81.4	71.6	72.2
Algebra II (.50)	52.4	39.0	38.6	59.5	47.3
Geometry (1.00)	67.2	56.3	54.4	72.1	54.5
Trigonometry (0.50)	19.6	14.1	11.0	35.2	15.6
Analysis/pre-calculus (.50)	15.0	6.2	7.3	25.5	8.5
Calculus (1.00)	7.0	2.8	3.9	18.6	6.1
AP Calculus (1.00)	4.3	1.2	3.0	15.6	4.2
Algebra II and geometry (1.50)	47.2	32.9	34.5	53.2	37.8
Algebra II, geometry, and trigonometry (2.0)	13.6	8.1	8.6	21.5	10.3
Algebra II, geometry, trigonometry, and calculus (3.00)	2.3	1.1	1.5	6.5	3.2
1992					
Any mathematics (1.00)	99.7	99.1	99.8	100.0	100.0
Remedial/below grade level math (1.00)	14.6	30.9	24.2	14.5	35.2
Algebra I (1.00)	79.6	78.0	84.4	71.9	80.8
Algebra II (.50)	59.2	40.9	46.9	60.8	42.1

[Continued]

★ 196 ★

Mathematics Course Enrollment

[Continued]

Mathematics courses (credits)	White	Black	Hispanic	Asian	American Indian
Geometry (1.00)	72.6	60.4	62.9	77.1	53.6
Trigonometry (0.50)	22.5	13.0	15.2	31.3	10.0
Analysis/pre-calculus (.50)	17.9	12.6	10.6	33.9	3.0
Calculus (1.00)	10.7	6.9	4.7	20.1	1.4
AP Calculus (1.00)	5.8	2.5	2.2	16.1	1.3
Algebra II and geometry (1.50)	53.1	35.0	41.9	55.5	35.7
Algebra II, geometry, and trigonometry (2.0)	15.9	6.8	10.9	18.2	5.9
Algebra II, geometry, trigonometry, and calculus (3.00)	3.0	0.9	1.2	5.4	0.6

Source: U.S. Department of Education. National Center for Education Statistics. *The Condition of Education 1994.* Washington, DC: U.S. Government Printing Office, 1994, p. 243. U.S. Department of Education, National Center for Education Statistics, *The 1990 High School Transcript Study Tabulations, 1993* (based on the 1987 and 1990 NAEP High School Transcript Studies), High School and Beyond Transcript Study, and the National Education Longitudinal Study Transcripts, 1992. *Note:* AP stands for Advanced Placement.

★ 197 ★

Academic Progress

Mathematics Proficiency, by Race/Ethnicity and Age

Data show the percentage of students at or above each proficiency level in selected years, as measured by the National Assessment of Educational Progress (NAEP).

	9-year-olds[1]				13-year-olds[2]				17-year-olds[2]			
	Simple arithmetic facts	Beginning skills and under-standing	Numerical operations and beginning problem solving	Moderately complex procedures and reasoning	Beginning skills and under-standing	Numerical operations and beginning problem solving	Moderately complex procedures and reasoning	Multi-step problem solving and algebra	Beginning skills and under-standing	Numerical operations and beginning problem solving	Moderately complex procedures and reasoning	Multi-step problem solving and algebra
All students												
1978	97	70	20	1	95	65	18	1	100	92	52	7
1982	97	71	19	1	98	71	17	0	100	93	48	6
1986	98	74	21	1	99	73	16	0	100	96	52	6
1990	99	82	28	1	98	75	17	0	100	96	56	7
1992	99	81	28	1	99	78	19	0	100	97	59	7
White[3]												
1978	98	76	23	1	98	73	21	1	100	96	58	8
1982	98	77	22	1	99	78	21	1	100	96	55	6
1986	99	80	25	1	99	79	19	0	100	98	59	8
1990	100	87	33	2	99	82	21	0	100	98	63	8
1992	100	87	32	1	100	85	23	0	100	98	66	9
Black[3]												
1978	88	42	4	0	80	29	2	0	99	71	17	0
1982	90	46	4	0	90	38	3	0	100	76	17	1
1986	94	53	6	0	95	49	4	0	100	86	21	0
1990	97	60	9	0	95	49	4	0	100	92	33	2
1992	97	60	10	0	95	51	4	0	100	90	30	7
Hispanic												
1978	93	54	9	0	86	36	4	0	99	78	23	1
1982	94	56	8	0	96	52	6	0	100	81	22	1
1986	96	58	7	0	97	56	6	0	99	89	27	1

[Continued]

★ 197 ★

Mathematics Proficiency, by Race/Ethnicity and Age

[Continued]

	9-year-olds[1]				13-year-olds[2]				17-year-olds[2]			
	Simple arithmetic facts	Beginning skills and under-standing	Numerical operations and beginning problem solving	Moderately complex procedures and reasoning	Beginning skills and under-standing	Numerical operations and beginning problem solving	Moderately complex procedures and reasoning	Multi-step problem solving and algebra	Beginning skills and under-standing	Numerical operations and beginning problem solving	Moderately complex procedures and reasoning	Multi-step problem solving and algebra
1990	98	68	11	0	97	57	6	0	100	86	30	2
1992	97	65	12	0	98	63	7	0	100	94	39	1

Source: U.S. Department of Education. National Center for Education Statistics. Office of Educational Research and Improvement. *Digest of Education Statistics, 1994.* Lanham, MD: Bernan, November 1994, p. 122. Primary source: U.S. Department of Education, National Center for Education Statistics, National Assessment of Educational Progress, *NAEP 1992 Trends in Academic Progress,* prepared by Educational Testing Service. (This table was prepared May 1994.) *Notes:* 1. Virtually no students were able to perform multi-step problems and algebra. 2. Virtually all students knew simple arithmetic facts. Data are only for students enrolled in school. 3. Excludes persons of Hispanic origin.

★ 198 ★

Academic Progress

Occupational Goals of High School Seniors in 1992

Data show percent distribution of intended occupations at age 30 for each race/ethnicity.

Expected occupation at age 30	Total	Race/ethnicity				
		White	Black	Hispanic	Asian	American Indian
Total	100.0	100.0	100.0	100.0	100.0	100.0
Craftsperson or operator	3.5	3.7	3.4	2.7	2.4	2.7
Farmer or farm manager	0.9	1.0	0.6	0.7	0.1	[1]
Housewife/homemaker	1.0	1.2	0.4	0.7	0.8	[1]
Laborer or farmworker	0.7	0.7	0.3	0.6	1.2	1.9
Military, police, or security officer	6.6	6.4	7.7	7.4	5.1	10.0
Professional, business, or managerial	50.8	50.0	55.1	47.1	61.3	43.3
Teacher	7.5	8.4	3.7	6.7	3.4	4.8
Business owner	6.0	5.6	6.8	7.7	7.0	6.4
Technical	5.4	5.0	5.5	7.5	6.0	8.2
Salesperson, clerical, or office worker	4.8	4.6	5.3	6.4	4.1	5.2
Service worker	2.4	2.3	3.1	2.5	0.6	5.8
Other employment	10.2	10.8	8.0	9.6	8.0	10.6
Don't know or no plans	0.2	0.2	0.2	0.5	0.2	1.0

Source: U.S. Department of Education. National Center for Education Statistics. Office of Educational Research and Improvement. *Digest of Education Statistics, 1994.* Lanham, MD: Bernan, November 1994, p. 136. *Note:* 1. Less than 0.05 percent.

★ 199 ★

Academic Progress

Percentage of 16 to 24 Year Old Students Enrolled in High School Who Were Employed, by Hours Worked Per Week, 1973-90

Data are shown for the month of October.

Year	All students			Hispanic			White			Black		
	Total[1]	20 or more hours	35 or more hours	Total[1]	20 or more hours	35 or more hours	Total[1]	20 or more hours	35 or more hours	Total[1]	20 or more hours	35 or more hours
1973	36.1	15.4	3.3	25.7	10.0	3.7	41.0	17.5	3.5	13.8	5.7	1.6
1974	35.2	15.1	3.1	23.3	10.7	2.8	40.0	16.9	3.4	16.3	8.1	1.9
1975	32.9	13.0	2.7	21.2	10.1	3.2	37.9	15.0	3.0	12.9	4.7	1.0
1976	33.4	14.3	2.6	20.1	10.8	2.7	38.9	16.6	2.6	12.7	5.2	2.4
1977	35.8	15.7	3.2	24.8	14.1	4.6	41.7	18.1	3.6	12.5	5.7	1.6
1978	38.2	16.2	2.9	28.0	15.9	3.1	43.9	18.4	3.2	16.1	6.8	1.4
1979	38.0	16.2	2.7	22.0	11.1	3.4	44.4	19.0	2.9	14.1	5.0	1.3
1980	35.1	13.3	2.3	24.5	11.6	4.9	40.7	15.2	2.1	13.7	5.7	1.9
1981	32.5	12.0	2.1	23.0	11.3	2.1	38.8	13.9	2.4	11.0	4.8	1.1
1982	29.5	9.7	1.6	15.0	6.2	1.5	35.9	11.8	2.0	8.9	2.4	0.1
1983	28.7	9.8	1.5	20.4	11.2	3.2	35.1	11.7	1.6	6.8	2.4	0.2
1984	31.0	11.5	1.3	23.2	10.5	3.7	36.4	13.1	1.2	13.4	6.1	0.6
1985	31.3	11.9	1.2	16.9	7.8	0.4	37.7	14.2	1.6	14.5	5.2	0.4
1986	34.1	13.7	1.9	25.8	15.8	1.7	40.3	15.7	2.2	14.5	6.5	0.8
1987	34.6	13.4	1.6	22.4	10.5	2.6	40.9	15.4	1.6	17.6	8.3	1.2
1988	35.1	14.2	1.6	23.2	10.3	2.8	40.6	16.0	1.6	19.3	8.2	1.1
1989	37.6	14.8	1.9	27.9	16.9	5.3	43.3	16.4	1.6	21.1	8.0	1.2
1990	32.1	11.9	2.0	24.6	13.2	4.5	38.0	13.6	1.8	16.7	5.0	1.0

Source: U.S. Department of Education. National Center for Education Statistics. *The Condition of Education, 1992.* Washington, DC: Government Printing Office, 1992, p. 120. Primary source: U.S. Department of Commerce, Bureau of the Census, October Current Population Surveys. *Notes:* Numbers have been revised from those previously published. 1. Includes those with a job but not at work during the survey week.

★ 200 ★

Academic Progress

Percentage of Students at or Above Five Reading Levels, 1980, 1990, and 1992

Data show the percentage of students at or above each reading proficiency level, as measured by the National Assessment of Educational Progress (NAEP).

Race/ethnicity and proficiency	9-year-olds[1]			13-year-olds[1]			17-year-olds[1]		
	1980	1990	1992	1980	1990	1992	1980	1990	1992
Total									
Level 150[2]	94.6	90.1	92.3	99.9	99.8	99.5	99.9	99.9	99.8
Level 200[3]	67.7	58.9	62.0	94.8	93.8	92.7	97.2	98.1	97.1
Level 250[4]	17.7	18.4	16.2	60.7	58.7	61.6	80.7	84.1	82.5
Level 300[5]	0.6	1.7	0.7	11.3	11.0	15.3	37.8	41.4	43.2

[Continued]

★ 200 ★

Percentage of Students at or Above Five Reading Levels, 1980, 1990, and 1992

[Continued]

Race/ethnicity and proficiency	9-year-olds[1]			13-year-olds[1]			17-year-olds[1]		
	1980	1990	1992	1980	1990	1992	1980	1990	1992
Level 350[6]	0.0	0.0	0.0	0.2	0.4	0.6	5.3	7.0	6.8
White									
Level 150[2]	97.1	93.5	95.8	100.0	99.9	99.8	100.0	100.0	99.9
Level 200[3]	74.2	66.0	69.3	97.1	96.0	95.9	99.1	98.8	98.6
Level 250[4]	21.0	22.6	19.6	67.8	64.8	68.5	86.9	88.3	88.0
Level 300[5]	0.8	2.2	0.9	13.6	13.3	18.1	43.3	47.5	50.1
Level 350[6]	0.0	0.0	0.0	0.3	0.5	0.8	6.2	8.7	8.3
Black									
Level 150[2]	84.9	76.9	79.6	99.3	99.4	98.7	99.0	99.6	99.1
Level 200[3]	41.3	33.9	36.6	84.1	87.7	82.0	85.6	95.7	91.6
Level 250[4]	4.1	5.2	4.6	30.1	41.7	38.4	44.0	69.1	61.4
Level 300[5]	0.0	0.3	0.0	1.8	4.6	5.7	7.1	19.7	16.9
Level 350[6]	0.0	0.0	0.0	0.0	0.1	0.1	0.2	1.5	1.6
Hispanic									
Level 150[2]	84.5	83.7	83.4	99.7	99.1	98.1	99.8	99.7	99.8
Level 200[3]	41.6	40.9	43.1	86.8	85.8	83.4	93.3	96.3	93.4
Level 250[4]	5.0	5.8	7.2	35.4	37.2	40.9	62.2	75.2	69.2
Level 300[5]	0.0	0.2	0.0	2.3	3.9	6.0	16.5	27.1	27.3
Level 350[6]	0.0	0.0	0.0	0.0	0.1	0.0	1.3	2.4	2.3

Source: U.S. Department of Education. National Center for Education Statistics. Office of Educational Research and Improvement. *Digest of Education Statistics, 1994.* Lanham, MD: Bernan, November 1994, p. 115. Primary source: U.S. Department of Education, National Center for Educational Progress, *The Reading Report Card, 1971-88* and *NAEP 1992 Trends in Academic Progress*, by Educational Testing Service. (This table was prepared April 1994.) *Notes:* A dash (-) stands for data not available. 1. All participants of this age were in school. 2. Able to follow brief written directions and carry out simple, discrete reading tasks. 3. Able to understand, combine ideas, and make inferences based on uncomplicated passages about specific or sequentially related information. 4. Able to search for specific information, interrelate ideas, and make generalizations about literature, science, and social studies materials. 5. Able to find, understand, summarize, and explain relatively complicated literary and informational material. 6. Able to understand the links between ideas even when those links are not explicitly stated and to make appropriate generalizations even when the texts lack clear introductions or explanations.

★ 201 ★

Academic Progress

SAT Average Scores, by Race/Ethnicity, 1994

Data show average SAT (Scholastic Aptitude Test) scores for 1994 and percent change from 1993.

Race/ethnicity	Verbal		Mathematics	
	Score	1-yr. chg.	Score	1-yr. chg.
American Indian	396	-3	441	-6
Asian	416	+1	535	0
Black	352	-1	388	0
Mexican American	372	-2	427	-1
Puerto Rican	367	0	411	+2
Other Hispanic	383	-1	435	+2
White	443	-1	495	+1
Other	425	+3	480	+3
All students	423	-1	479	+1

Source: Chronicle of Higher Education Almanac (1 September 1994), p. 13. Primary source: The College Board.

★ 202 ★

Academic Progress

SAT Scores, by Race/Ethnicity, 1993

From the source: "The Scholastic Aptitude Test (SAT) is the test taken most frequently by college-bound students. It is designed to predict success in the freshman year of college, and to track the performance of groups of students across time....Between 1992 and 1993, average SAT scores improved for all test-takers, both sexes and nearly every racial/ethnic group....In 1993, students from families with the lowest parental education and income levels received the lowest scores overall, while scores increased with higher levels of parental education and income." This table shows average verbal and mathematics scores of college-bound seniors, by parents' highest level of education and race/ethnicity of student.

	Parents' highest education level									
	No high school diploma		High school diploma		Associate's degree		Bachelor's degree		Graduate degree	
	Verbal	Math	Verbal	Math	Verbal	Math	Verbal	Math	Verbal	Math
White	374	422	412	459	422	470	456	509	486	538
Black	308	351	338	374	352	385	377	409	405	436
Mexican American	332	395	373	426	389	437	418	464	435	477
Puerto Rican	323	363	361	396	370	410	382	431	406	455
Other Hispanic	322	377	375	419	388	435	418	466	430	487
Asian American	331	478	377	502	396	501	425	548	484	588
American Indian	328	377	383	431	394	445	418	466	443	491
Other	335	408	387	437	402	450	440	496	481	536

Source: U.S. Department of Education. National Center for Education Statistics. *The Condition of Education 1994.* Washington, DC: U.S. Government Printing Office, 1994, p. 227. Primary source: College Entrance Exam Board, *College Bound Seniors: 1993 Profile of SAT and Achievement Test Takers.*

★ 203 ★

Academic Progress

SAT Takers, by Race/Ethnicity and Sex, 1976-91

Year	Race/ethnicity(%)								Sex(%)	
	Mexican American	Puerto Rican	Other Hispanic	White	Black	Asian American	American Indian	Other	Male	Female
1976	1.0	0.7	-	85.0	8.2	2.2	0.3	2.0	49.5	50.5
1977	1.7	0.8	-	83.9	8.8	2.4	0.4	2.1	48.9	51.1
1978	1.7	1.0	-	83.0	9.0	2.6	0.4	2.3	48.4	51.6
1979	1.6	1.0	-	82.9	8.9	2.8	0.4	2.4	48.3	51.7
1980	1.7	1.1	-	82.1	9.1	3.2	0.5	2.3	48.3	51.7
1981	1.7	1.1	-	81.9	9.0	3.4	0.6	2.2	48.1	51.9
1982	1.8	1.2	-	81.7	8.9	3.8	0.5	2.2	48.2	51.8
1983	1.9	1.2	-	81.1	8.8	4.2	0.5	2.2	48.3	51.7
1984	2.0	1.3	-	80.3	9.1	4.5	0.5	2.3	48.2	51.8
1985	2.2	1.2	-	80.0	8.9	4.8	0.5	2.4	48.3	51.7
1986	-	-	-	-	-	-	-	-	48.1	51.9
1987	2.1	1.0	1.9	78.2	8.7	5.8	1.0	1.2	48.2	51.8
1988	2.2	1.1	1.9	77.0	9.2	6.1	1.2	1.3	48.0	52.0
1989	2.5	1.1	2.1	74.7	9.6	6.8	1.8	1.3	47.9	52.1
1990	2.8	1.2	2.5	73.4	10.0	7.6	1.1	1.5	47.8	52.2
1991	3.0	1.3	2.7	72.0	10.5	8.0	0.8	1.7	47.8	52.2

Source: U.S. Department of Education. National Center for Education Statistics. *The Condition of Education, 1992.* Washington, DC: Government Printing Office, 1992, p. 226. Primary source: College Entrance Examination Board, *National Report: College Bound Seniors,* 1972-1991. *Notes:* A dash (-) indicates that data were not available. The first year for which SAT scores by race/ethnic group are available is 1976. SAT stands for Scholastic Aptitude Test.

★ 204 ★

Academic Progress

Science Course Enrollment, 1982 to 1992

Data show percent of 17-year-old students taking science courses for one or more years.

Academic year and race/ethnicity	Percent taking courses in -						
	Biology	General science	Chemistry	Physical science	Earth and space science	Life science	Physics
1982							
All students	76.0	61.0	31.0	33.0	27.0	27.0	11.0
White, non-Hispanic	78.0	61.0	33.0	32.0	28.0	27.0	11.0
Black, non-Hispanic	66.0	66.0	19.0	34.0	28.0	27.0	12.0
Hispanic	62.0	58.0	13.0	35.0	20.0	31.0	9.0
1986							
All students	83.0	78.0	37.0	41.0	38.0	40.0	10.0
White, non-Hispanic	89.0	84.0	42.0	41.0	38.0	40.0	10.0

[Continued]

★ 204 ★

Science Course Enrollment, 1982 to 1992

[Continued]

Academic year and race/ethnicity	Percent taking courses in - Biology	General science	Chemistry	Physical science	Earth and space science	Life science	Physics
Black, non-Hispanic	84.0	83.0	29.0	45.0	44.0	40.0	18.0
Hispanic	84.0	82.0	24.0	37.0	23.0	41.0	13.0
1990							
All students	85.0	78.0	42.0	41.0	35.0	30.0	13.0
White, non-Hispanic	90.0	84.0	46.0	39.0	34.0	28.0	13.0
Black, non-Hispanic	87.0	76.0	46.0	47.0	35.0	35.0	15.0
Hispanic	79.0	82.0	31.0	55.0	38.0	44.0	17.0
1992							
All students	89.0	81.0	46.0	-	-	-	12.0
White, non-Hispanic	93.0	86.0	52.0	-	-	-	13.0
Black, non-Hispanic	92.0	78.0	36.0	-	-	-	14.0
Hispanic	87.0	79.0	36.0	-	-	-	13.0

Source: U.S. Department of Education. National Center for Education Statistics. Office of Educational Research and Improvement. *Digest of Education Statistics, 1994.* Lanham, MD: Bernan, November 1994, p. 135. Primary source: U.S. Department of Education, National Center for Education Statistics, National Assessment of Educational Progress, *NAEP 1992 Trends in Academic Progress*, prepared by the Educational Testing Service. (This table was prepared March 1994.) *Note:* A dash (-) stands for data not available.

★ 205 ★

Academic Progress

Science Course Enrollment, 1990 and 1992

As industry becomes more technically oriented, exposure to mathematics and science is essential in preparing a student for future employment and the rate of student enrollment in such courses can be used to predict the availability of candidates in technical fields. This table shows the percentage of high school graduates who have taken each course.

Science courses (credits)[1]	White	Black	Hispanic	Asian	American Indian
1990					
Any science (1.00)	99.5	99.0	99.3	99.8	99.5
Biology (1.00)	92.0	91.0	90.3	90.5	91.1
AP/honors biology (1.00)	5.1	3.8	2.4	6.4	3.2
Chemistry (1.00)	52.3	40.3	38.8	64.1	38.6
AP/honors chemistry (1.00)	3.8	2.5	1.2	7.7	4.8
Physics (1.00)	23.1	14.5	13.0	38.4	18.9
AP/honors physics (1.00)	2.1	0.7	1.0	5.9	2.7
Engineering (1.00)	0.1	0.1	0.0	0.0	0.0
Astronomy (1.00)	1.4	0.4	1.1	0.7	2.2
Geology (1.00)	28.3	15.8	14.2	15.6	30.6
Biology and chemistry (2.00)	50.9	39.6	36.8	60.5	37.6
Biology, chemistry, and physics (3.00)	20.7	12.1	10.2	33.8	16.0

[Continued]

★ 205 ★

Science Course Enrollment, 1990 and 1992

[Continued]

Science courses (credits)[1]	White	Black	Hispanic	Asian	American Indian
1992					
Any science (1.00)	99.5	100.0	99.7	100.0	100.0
Biology (1.00)	93.5	92.2	91.2	93.4	84.5
AP/honors biology (1.00)	6.5	3.2	2.4	6.8	5.0
Chemistry (1.00)	58.0	45.9	42.6	67.4	32.9
AP/honors chemistry (1.00)	4.2	2.3	2.5	9.1	1.8
Physics (1.00)	25.9	17.6	15.7	41.6	13.3
AP/honors physics (1.00)	2.9	1.4	2.4	9.2	0.6
Engineering (1.00)	0.3	0.2	0.1	0.5	0.0
Astronomy (1.00)	1.0	0.1	0.1	0.1	0.0
Geology (1.00)	19.3	17.6	11.5	16.6	29.7
Biology and chemistry (2.00)	56.5	44.2	40.5	65.4	31.2
Biology, chemistry, and physics (3.00)	22.6	15.5	12.8	38.2	10.8

Source: U.S. Department of Education. National Center for Education Statistics. *The Condition of Education 1994.* Washington, DC: U.S. Government Printing Office, 1994, p. 243. U.S. Department of Education, National Center for Education Statistics, *The 1990 High School Transcript Study Tabulations, 1993* (based on the 1987 and 1990 NAEP High School Transcript Studies), High School and Beyond Transcript Study, and the National Education Longitudinal Study Transcripts, 1992. *Note:* 1. AP stands for advanced placement.

★ 206 ★

Academic Progress

Science Experiments and Projects

Data show the percentage of students providing affirmative responses to the question "Have you ever done experiments or projects at home or in school with...?" Standard error for each result is shown in parentheses.

Grade and race/ethnicity	Plants or animals	Electricity	Chemicals	Rocks or minerals	Telescope	Thermometer or barometer
Grade 4						
White	58 (1.0)	53 (1.5)	42 (1.0)	51 (1.4)	42 (0.9)	45 (1.3)
Black	53 (1.5)	53 (1.6)	38 (1.8)	47 (1.5)	40 (2.0)	49 (2.0)
Hispanic	57 (1.6)	55 (1.9)	40 (1.5)	47 (1.8)	46 (2.0)	48 (1.8)
Asian/Pacific Islander	64 (3.8)	52 (6.1)	38 (4.7)	48 (5.9)	46 (3.4)	37 (6.0)
American Indian	70 (3.4)	58 (3.6)	39 (4.7)	53 (3.0)	45 (3.9)	57 (3.5)
Male	58 (1.0)	60 (1.4)	41 (1.1)	50 (1.2)	43 (1.1)	46 (1.4)
Female	57 (1.3)	46 (1.5)	41 (1.0)	51 (1.7)	41 (1.0)	46 (1.4)
Total	58 (0.8)	53 (1.2)	41 (0.7)	50 (1.2)	42 (0.8)	46 (1.1)
Grade 8						
White	74 (1.2)	67 (1.4)	65 (1.6)	60 (1.5)	49 (1.1)	56 (1.5)
Black	64 (2.0)	58 (2.5)	57 (2.3)	51 (2.1)	36 (2.3)	47 (2.6)
Hispanic	68 (1.8)	60 (2.3)	55 (1.9)	54 (2.5)	44 (1.7)	49 (2.5)
Asian/Pacific Islander	73 (4.2)	70 (3.0)	64 (3.3)	54 (4.8)	36 (3.3)	46 (5.1)
American Indian	59 (14.4)[1]	60 (7.8)[1]	60 (12.5)[1]	58 (9.2)[1]	49 (5.0)[1]	56 (6.4)[1]
Male	71 (1.2)	75 (1.2)	64 (1.5)	57 (1.4)	49 (1.2)	52 (1.3)
Female	73 (1.5)	54 (1.4)	61 (1.6)	59 (1.6)	45 (1.1)	56 (1.6)
Total	72 (1.1)	65 (1.2)	63 (1.4)	58 (1.3)	47 (0.9)	54 (1.2)

[Continued]

★ 206 ★

Science Experiments and Projects

[Continued]

Grade and race/ethnicity	Plants or animals	Electricity	Chemicals	Rocks or minerals	Telescope	Thermometer or barometer
Grade 12						
White	86 (0.7)	74 (1.1)	83 (0.8)	70 (1.0)	55 (1.0)	71 (1.2)
Black	79 (1.8)	65 (2.0)	77 (1.8)	62 (2.3)	51 (2.3)	63 (1.6)
Hispanic	83 (1.9)	64 (2.2)	76 (1.8)	64 (2.5)	53 (2.4)	63 (2.1)
Asian/Pacific Islander	84 (1.9)	74 (2.3)	81 (5.6)	63 (5.2)	49 (3.6)	74 (2.4)
American Indian	78 (7.0)[1]	72 (9.9)[1]	74 (7.2)[1]	61 (5.2)[1]	42 (8.5)[1]	62 (6.6)[1]
Male	84 (0.9)	82 (0.9)	83 (0.7)	68 (1.2)	56 (1.1)	70 (1.1)
Female	85 (0.8)	63 (1.4)	80 (1.0)	68 (1.3)	52 (1.1)	69 (1.3)
Total	85 (0.7)	72 (1.0)	81 (0.7)	68 (1.0)	54 (0.8)	69 (1.0)

Source: Jones, Lee R., and others. *The 1990 Science Report Card: NAEP's Assessment of Fourth, Eighth, and Twelfth Graders*, Prepared by Educational Testing Service under contract with the National Center for Education Statistics, Office of Educational Research and Improvement, U.S. Department of Education, March 1992, p. 83. *Notes:* 1. Interpret with caution - the nature of the sample does not allow accurate determination of the variability of these estimated statistics.

★ 207 ★

Academic Progress

Science Experiments and Projects Performed and Average Proficiencies of Students

Percent of students reporting the number of projects or experiments done and their average proficiencies based on IRT (item response theory) scaling procedures. Progress is estimated on a scale of 0 to 500. Scores are assigned to five proficiency levels: Level 150—Knows everyday science facts; Level 200—Understands simple scientific principles; Level 250—Applies general scientific information; Level 300—Analyzes scientific procedures and data; and Level 350—Integrates specialized scientific information. Data presented are proficiency scores, not levels.

Grade and race/ethnicity	Five or six		Three or four		One or two		None	
	% of students	Avg. profic.	% of students	Avg. profic.	% of students	Avg. profic.	% of students	Avg. profic.
Grade 4								
White	16 (0.7)	246 (1.3)	44 (0.8)	240 (1.3)	32 (0.9)	243 (1.2)	8 (0.6)	243 (2.0)
Black	11 (0.9)	212 (3.4)	49 (1.6)	203 (2.0)	33 (1.4)	206 (1.6)	8 (0.9)	213 (3.0)
Hispanic	12 (1.2)	216 (3.2)	51 (1.8)	210 (1.6)	31 (1.3)	215 (1.9)	6 (0.6)	215 (4.2)
Asian/Pacific Islander	15 (5.5)	234 (7.9)	41 (3.4)	231 (4.0)	39 (5.5)	236 (6.1)	4 (1.6)	228 (10.9)
American Indian	17 (2.9)	231 (4.4)	56 (4.2)	225 (3.4)	22 (3.7)	224 (6.0)	5 (1.5)	233 (10.7)
Male	16 (0.9)	243 (1.7)	47 (1.1)	230 (1.3)	31 (1.1)	235 (1.5)	6 (0.5)	237 (2.9)
Female	13 (0.8)	235 (2.0)	45 (1.1)	230 (1.4)	34 (1.0)	232 (1.3)	8 (0.8)	234 (2.4)
Total	15 (0.6)	239 (1.2)	46 (0.6)	230 (1.2)	32 (1.1)	234 (1.1)	7 (0.5)	235 (1.7)
Grade 8								
White	38 (1.6)	283 (1.5)	37 (1.0)	272 (1.5)	20 (0.9)	262 (2.1)	5 (0.5)	246 (2.8)
Black	22 (1.9)	246 (3.6)	40 (2.0)	232 (2.4)	32 (1.5)	223 (3.2)	6 (1.1)	216 (6.5)
Hispanic	28 (2.0)	253 (2.8)	40 (1.6)	242 (2.7)	26 (1.7)	234 (2.9)	7 (1.1)	222 (5.0)
Asian/Pacific Islander	29 (3.1)	284 (4.5)	41 (3.2)	270 (4.1)	26 (3.2)	260 (6.1)	5 (1.6)	253 (18.2)
American Indian	34 (10.6)[1]	266 (5.6)[1]	35 (6.0)[1]	251 (10.7)[1]	20 (9.9)[1]	245 (6.0)[1]	11 (3.7)[1]	223 (9.1)[1]
Male	36 (1.5)	278 (1.6)	38 (0.9)	264 (1.8)	20 (0.9)	252 (1.9)	6 (0.5)	239 (4.0)
Female	33 (1.6)	276 (1.8)	37 (1.2)	261 (1.2)	24 (1.0)	248 (2.1)	6 (0.6)	238 (3.1)
Total	35 (1.3)	277 (1.4)	38 (0.9)	262 (1.3)	22 (0.8)	250 (1.6)	6 (0.4)	238 (2.4)
Grade 12								
White	58 (1.3)	311 (1.1)	28 (0.9)	298 (1.9)	10 (0.6)	282 (2.8)	4 (0.4)	270 (3.6)
Black	46 (2.2)	266 (2.8)	34 (1.7)	253 (3.6)	15 (1.3)	243 (3.9)	6 (0.8)	233 (6.7)
Hispanic	46 (2.1)	283 (2.5)	34 (1.7)	270 (5.2)	16 (1.6)	258 (3.8)	4 (0.9)	238 (9.0)
Asian/Pacific Islander	55 (4.1)	316 (8.6)	27 (2.7)	306 (7.3)	15 (2.1)	289 (7.5)	3 (1.2)	274 (32.2)
American Indian	47 (6.9)[1]	288 (6.6)[1]	31 (6.7)[1]	294 (7.0)[1]	12 (7.4)[1]	270 (5.6)[1]	10 (5.3)[1]	268 (7.5)[1]
Male	59 (1.3)	308 (1.6)	27 (1.0)	293 (2.1)	10 (0.7)	277 (2.9)	4 (0.4)	266 (4.4)

[Continued]

★ 207 ★

Science Experiments and Projects Performed and Average Proficiencies of Students

[Continued]

Grade and race/ethnicity	Five or six		Three or four		One or two		None	
	% of students	Avg. profic.	% of students	Avg. profic.	% of students	Avg. profic.	% of students	Avg. profic.
Female	51 (1.5)	299 (1.3)	31 (1.0)	284 (1.8)	13 (0.9)	270 (2.4)	5 (0.4)	256 (3.8)
Total	55 (1.2)	304 (1.2)	29 (0.8)	288 (1.6)	12 (0.6)	273 (2.2)	4 (0.3)	260 (2.9)

Source: Jones, Lee R., and others. *The 1990 Science Report Card: NAEP's Assessment of Fourth, Eighth, and Twelfth Graders*, Prepared by Educational Testing Service under contract with the National Center for Education Statistics, Office of Educational Research and Improvement, U.S. Department of Education, March 1992, p. 84. *Notes:* Achievement results were analyzed using item response theory (IRT) scaling procedures, which allowed the National Assessment of Educational Progress to estimate students' average proficiency on a scale ranging from 0 to 500. The standard errors of the estimated percentages and proficiencies appear in parentheses. It can be said with 95 percent certainty that for each population of interest, the value for the whole population is within plus or minus two standard errors of the estimate for the sample. 1. Interpret with caution - the nature of the sample does not allow accurate determination of the variability of these estimated statistics.

★ 208 ★

Academic Progress

Science Instruction: Frequency Reported by 4th Graders

Frequency of instruction is shown in percent. Proficiency is based on IRT (item response theory) scaling procedures. Progress is estimated on a scale of 0 to 500. Scores are assigned to five proficiency levels: Level 150—Knows everyday science facts; Level 200—Understands simple scientific principles; Level 250—Applies general scientific information; Level 300—Analyzes scientific procedures and data; and Level 350—Integrates specialized scientific information. Data presented are proficiency scores, not levels.

Group	Almost every day		Several times a week		About once a week		Less than once a week		Never	
	% of students	Avg. profic.	% of students	Avg. profic.	% of students	Avg. profic.	% of students	Avg. profic.	% of students	Avg. profic.
White	54 (2.1)	243 (1.1)	22 (1.1)	246 (1.6)	12 (1.1)	242 (1.7)	8 (0.8)	238 (2.2)	5 (0.8)	230 (3.3)
Black	46 (2.9)	209 (1.8)	20 (1.9)	207 (3.0)	17 (1.7)	203 (1.9)	10 (1.1)	201 (4.0)	7 (1.1)	192 (4.0)
Hispanic	44 (3.4)	216 (2.1)	20 (1.5)	213 (2.2)	18 (1.9)	211 (3.0)	9 (1.0)	205 (2.9)	10 (1.4)	203 (4.0)
Asian/Pacific Islander	39 (5.3)	240 (6.5)	24 (2.6)	230 (4.5)	21 (3.2)	230 (4.1)	8 (2.1)	232 (8.8)	9 (4.1)	223 (10.9)
American Indian	51 (5.0)	228 (3.6)	19 (3.0)	229 (6.8)	13 (3.8)	233 (6.9)	10 (3.2)	216 (8.6)	6 (2.8)	201 (7.6)
Male	51 (1.9)	237 (1.3)	22 (1.1)	237 (2.2)	13 (1.1)	232 (1.9)	8 (0.7)	226 (2.7)	6 (0.8)	218 (3.2)
Female	51 (2.2)	234 (1.3)	20 (1.2)	235 (1.6)	15 (1.3)	228 (2.1)	8 (0.8)	227 (2.6)	5 (0.8)	216 (4.4)
Total	51 (1.9)	235 (1.1)	21 (0.9)	236 (1.5)	14 (1.0)	230 (1.5)	8 (0.7)	227 (2.0)	6 (0.7)	217 (2.8)

Source: Jones, Lee R., and others. *The 1990 Science Report Card: NAEP's Assessment of Fourth, Eighth, and Twelfth Graders*, Prepared by Educational Testing Service under contract with the National Center for Education Statistics, Office of Educational Research and Improvement, U.S. Department of Education, March 1992, p. 79. *Notes:* Achievement results were analyzed using item response theory (IRT) scaling procedures, which allowed the National Assessment of Educational Progress to estimate students' average proficiency on a scale ranging from 0 to 500. The standard errors of the estimated percentages and proficiencies appear in parentheses. It can be said with 95 percent certainty that for each population of interest, the value for the whole population is within plus or minus two standard errors of the estimate for the sample.

★ 209 ★

Academic Progress

Science Proficiency of Eighth Graders

Figures shown are based on IRT (item response theory) scaling procedures. Progress is estimated on a scale of 0 to 500.

Characteristic	Race/ethnicity						Sex	
	Hispanic	White	Black	American Indian/ Alaska Native	Asian/Pacific Pacific Islander	Other	Male	Female
Total(%)	10.1 (0.3)	70.8 (0.4)	14.8 (0.4)	1.4 (0.5)	2.7 (0.4)	0.1 (0.0)	50.1 (0.8)	49.9 (0.8)
Score	241.2 (2.1)	272.9 (1.4)	231.0 (2.2)	251.9 (8.5)	270.5 (4.0)	255.1 (12.8)	265.1 (1.6)	261.0 (1.2)
Race/ethnicity								
Hispanic (%)	100.0 (0.0)	0.0 (0.0)	0.0 (0.0)	0.0 (0.0)	0.0 (0.0)	0.0 (0.0)	51.9 (1.6)	48.1 (1.6)
Score	241.2 (2.1)	- (0.0)	- (0.0)	- (0.0)	- (0.0)	- (0.0)	243.1 (3.0)	239.1 (2.5)
White (%)	0.0 (0.0)	100.0 (0.0)	0.0 (0.0)	0.0 (0.0)	0.0 (0.0)	0.0 (0.0)	50.9 (1.0)	49.1 (1.0)
Score	- (0.0)	272.9 (1.4)	- (0.0)	- (0.0)	- (0.0)	- (0.0)	274.4 (1.8)	271.3 (1.4)
Black (%)	0.0 (0.0)	0.0 (0.0)	100.0 (0.0)	0.0 (0.0)	0.0 (0.0)	0.0 (0.0)	45.1 (1.7)	56.9 (1.7)
Score	- (0.0)	- (0.0)	231.0 (2.2)	- (0.0)	- (0.0)	- (0.0)	231.9 (2.9)	230.3 (2.1)
American Indian/ Alaska Native (%)	0.0 (0.0)	0.0 (0.0)	0.0 (0.0)	100.0 (0.0)	0.0 (0.0)	0.0 (0.0)	42.0 (5.4)	58.0 (5.4)
Score	- (0.0)	- (0.0)	- (0.0)	251.9 (8.5)	- (0.0)	- (0.0)	255.2 (10.3)	249.5 (7.8)
Asian/Pacific Islander (%)	0.0 (0.0)	0.0 (0.0)	0.0 (0.0)	0.0 (0.0)	100.0 (0.0)	0.0 (0.0)	52.9 (3.8)	47.1 (3.8)
Score	- (0.0)	- (0.0)	- (0.0)	- (0.0)	270.5 (4.0)	- (0.0)	272.5 (4.7)	268.3 (4.5)
Sex								
Male (%)	10.5 (0.4)	72.0 (0.7)	13.4 (0.6)	1.2 (0.4)	2.9 (0.4)	0.1 (0.0)	100.0 (0.0)	0.0 (0.0)
Score	243.1 (3.0)	274.4 (1.8)	231.9 (2.9)	255.2 (10.3)	272.5 (4.7)	273.9 (12.8)	265.1 (1.6)	- (0.0)
Female (%)	9.8 (0.4)	69.6 (0.7)	16.3 (0.6)	1.6 (0.6)	2.6 (0.5)	0.1 (0.1)	0.0 (0.0)	100.0 (0.0)
Score	239.1 (2.5)	271.3 (1.4)	230.3 (2.1)	249.5 (7.8)	268.3 (4.5)	234.8 (14.5)	- (0.0)	261.0 (1.2)
Region								
Northeast (%)	7.0 (0.9)	76.4 (3.4)	12.3 (2.7)	0.7 (0.4)	3.5 (1.0)	0.1 (0.1)	51.5 (1.8)	48.5 (1.8)
Score	242.1 (6.3)	277.3 (2.7)	232.0 (7.4)	249.8 (19.5)	280.8 (7.8)	226.2 (-)	270.7 (3.6)	267.6 (3.1)
Southeast (%)	3.9 (0.9)	69.1 (2.3)	25.9 (2.3)	0.5 (0.2)	0.6 (0.2)	-	47.5 (1.4)	52.5 (1.4)
Score	242.0 (4.5)	267.2 (1.7)	228.8 (3.3)	258.3 (12.5)	272.3 (6.2)	305.6 (6.4)	259.5 (2.2)	253.3 (2.3)
Central (%)	5.6 (0.9)	78.6 (1.6)	12.8 (1.6)	1.0 (0.3)	1.8 (0.4)	0.2 (0.1)	50.9 (2.0)	49.1 (2.0)
Score	240.2 (4.9)	272.0 (2.2)	230.3 (5.6)	248.0 (11.2)	268.3 (8.3)	240.9 (11.9)	266.1 (2.8)	262.8 (2.3)
West (%)	21.2 (1.2)	61.8 (3.8)	9.3 (2.0)	2.9 (1.6)	4.6 (1.5)	0.1 (0.1)	50.5 (1.0)	49.5 (1.0)
Score	241.1 (2.6)	275.0 (3.8)	236.0 (3.6)	252.5 (18.0)	265.5 (4.7)	274.4 (16.5)	264.7 (3.7)	261.5 (2.4)
Type of community								
Extreme rural (%)	5.7 (1.9)	78.1 (5.3)	10.2 (3.7)	5.4 (4.9)	0.4 (0.3)	0.2 (0.2)	50.8 (2.3)	49.2 (2.3)
Score	237.7 (3.6)	263.1 (5.3)	227.2 (7.4)	246.4 (19.4)	237.5 (30.3)	273.8 (34.3)	258.8 (3.4)	256.0 (5.0)
Disadvantaged urban (%)	22.9 (3.7)	38.8 (6.7)	32.1 (6.2)	1.1 (0.4)	5.0 (1.9)	0.1 (0.1)	52.2 (1.8)	47.8 (1.8)
Score	233.6 (4.7)	263.2 (4.7)	221.2 (4.8)	222.4 (13.4)	257.5 (7.0)	226.2 (-)	242.5 (4.3)	241.8 (4.7)
Advantaged urban (%)	6.4 (0.9)	82.3 (3.4)	6.7 (2.8)	0.4 (0.2)	4.1 (1.3)	0.0 (0.0)	49.2 (1.5)	50.8 (1.5)
Score	270.2 (5.2)	287.0 (3.8)	245.6 (7.8)	280.4 (5.7)	294.5 (7.7)	- (0.0)	286.4 (5.0)	280.5 (4.0)
Other (%)	9.7 (0.8)	72.1 (1.5)	14.5 (1.0)	0.9 (0.2)	2.6 (0.6)	0.1 (0.0)	49.8 (1.0)	50.2 (1.0)
Score	241.1 (3.0)	272.7 (1.3)	233.3 (3.1)	260.2 (6.2)	268.8 (4.0)	253.3 (12.9)	266.2 (1.8)	261.2 (1.5)
Parents' education level								
Less than H.S. (%)	21.2 (1.9)	60.7 (2.7)	15.4 (1.8)	1.3 (0.6)	1.3 (0.5)	0.1 (0.1)	40.4 (2.3)	59.6 (2.3)
Score	236.6 (3.4)	247.9 (2.5)	219.9 (5.3)	246.3 (23.3)	242.3 (12.6)	273.5 (-)	244.8 (3.3)	238.7 (2.8)
Graduated H.S. (%)	9.8 (0.6)	71.4 (1.3)	15.7 (1.0)	1.6 (0.6)	1.4 (0.3)	0.1 (0.1)	50.1 (1.4)	49.9 (1.4)
Score	238.6 (2.7)	263.2 (1.5)	223.6 (2.7)	239.8 (13.7)	261.0 (9.2)	218.8 (10.2)	255.9 (1.8)	252.3 (1.5)

[Continued]

★ 209 ★

Science Proficiency of Eighth Graders

[Continued]

Characteristic	Race/ethnicity						Sex	
	Hispanic	White	Black	American Indian/ Alaska Native	Asian/Pacific Pacific Islander	Other	Male	Female
Some education after H.S. (%)	9.6 (0.9)	72.2 (1.5)	14.5 (1.2)	1.7 (0.6)	2.0 (0.5)	0.0 (0.0)	46.0 (1.4)	54.0 (1.4)
Score	248.6 (2.8)	276.3 (1.7)	240.8 (3.7)	269.9 (16.5)	275.1 (5.8)	- (0.0)	270.3 (2.3)	266.7 (1.5)
Graduated college (%)	5.6 (0.5)	76.5 (1.0)	13.1 (0.8)	1.0 (0.4)	3.7 (0.5)	0.2 (0.1)	52.6 (1.2)	47.4 (1.2)
Score	254.0 (3.5)	284.2 (1.6)	240.6 (3.0)	259.8 (4.4)	280.9 (4.5)	273.0 (12.9)	277.4 (2.0)	275.3 (1.9)
Unknown (%)	22.8 (1.9)	48.8 (1.9)	21.0 (2.0)	1.9 (0.7)	5.3 (1.4)	0.1 (0.2)	57.2 (2.7)	42.8 (2.7)
Score	226.4 (3.9)	250.5 (3.3)	213.4 (4.6)	230.0 (16.5)	245.3 (6.7)	226.2 (-)	240.6 (3.0)	231.0 (2.7)
Type of school								
Public (%)	9.8 (0.4)	70.6 (0.6)	15.6 (0.4)	1.5 (0.5)	2.3 (0.4)	0.1 (0.0)	50.1 (0.8)	49.9 (0.8)
Score	238.3 (2.1)	271.9 (1.5)	229.6 (2.3)	250.9 (8.4)	266.7 (5.1)	252.4 (14.4)	263.5 (1.7)	259.6 (1.4)
Private (%)	12.5 (1.7)	72.1 (3.4)	8.8 (2.1)	0.5 (0.2)	5.9 (1.9)	0.2 (0.1)	50.1 (1.6)	49.9 (1.6)
Score	259.1 (3.5)	279.9 (2.1)	251.5 (4.9)	277.2 (8.6)	282.0 (4.9)	266.7 (19.5)	277.6 (2.4)	272.1 (2.7)
Ability of students in class								
High ability (%)	5.5 (0.8)	78.0 (2.1)	11.4 (1.9)	1.0 (0.4)	4.0 (0.9)	0.1 (0.1)	48.0 (1.9)	52.0 (1.9)
Score	271.6 (5.1)	295.2 (1.9)	258.7 (3.9)	289.2 (15.7)	295.4 (6.9)	242.9 (19.9)	294.3 (2.6)	285.3 (2.1)
Average ability (%)	8.4 (1.1)	77.1 (1.7)	11.5 (1.0)	0.6 (0.2)	2.3 (0.6)	0.2 (0.1)	49.5 (1.4)	50.5 (1.4)
Score	246.0 (3.0)	273.2 (1.6)	237.5 (3.6)	272.6 (5.6)	261.5 (4.9)	228.5 (18.8)	268.4 (2.0)	264.6 (1.5)
Low ability (%)	10.8 (2.1)	62.1 (3.6)	23.8 (3.4)	1.3 (0.6)	1.9 (0.7)	0.1 (0.1)	49.9 (2.6)	50.1 (2.6)
Score	232.2 (4.4)	254.6 (4.0)	221.7 (5.9)	221.7 (23.1)	257.0 (11.9)	273.5 (-)	246.5 (4.9)	241.5 (4.0)
Mixed ability (%)	8.5 (1.2)	72.9 (2.5)	15.7 (2.1)	0.9 (0.3)	1.8 (0.5)	0.2 (0.1)	50.6 (1.4)	49.4 (1.4)
Score	246.0 (3.5)	272.3 (3.2)	229.2 (4.6)	255.0 (6.5)	281.3 (5.3)	270.7 (19.5)	267.3 (2.9)	259.3 (3.1)

Source: Jones, Lee R., and others. *The 1990 Science Report Card: NAEP's Assessment of Fourth, Eighth, and Twelfth Graders*, Prepared by Educational Testing Service under contract with the National Center for Education Statistics, Office of Educational Research and Improvement, U.S. Department of Education, March 1992, p. 153-154. *Notes:* A dash (-) indicates no data were given in the original source. Achievement results were analyzed using item response theory (IRT) scaling procedures, which allowed the National Assessment of Educational Progress to estimate students' average proficiency on a scale ranging from 0 to 500. The standard errors of the estimated proficiencies appear in parentheses. It can be said with 95 percent certainty that for each population of interest, the value for the whole population is within plus or minus two standard errors of the estimate for the sample.

★ 210 ★

Academic Progress

Science Proficiency of Fourth Graders

Figures shown are based on IRT (item response theory) scaling procedures. Progress is estimated on a scale of 0 to 500.

Characteristic	Race/ethnicity						Sex	
	Hispanic	White	Black	American Indian/ Alaska Native	Asian/Pacific Pacific Islander	Other	Male	Female
Total(%)	11.0 (0.3)	70.2 (0.5)	15.2 (0.4)	1.6 (0.3)	1.9 (0.3)	0.1 (0.0)	51.2 (0.7)	48.8 (0.7)
Score	212.0 (1.5)	242.1 (1.0)	205.4 (1.5)	226.1 (2.7)	233.0 (1.5)	223.0 (24.3)	233.8 (1.1)	231.7 (1.0)
Race/ethnicity								
Hispanic (%)	100.0 (0.0)	0.0 (0.0)	0.0 (0.0)	0.0 (0.0)	0.0 (0.0)	0.0 (0.0)	51.9 (1.6)	48.1 (1.6)
Score	212.0 (1.5)	- (0.0)	- (0.0)	- (0.0)	- (0.0)	- (0.0)	213.0 (1.6)	211.0 (1.9)

[Continued]

★ 210 ★

Science Proficiency of Fourth Graders

[Continued]

Characteristic	Race/ethnicity						Sex	
	Hispanic	White	Black	American Indian/ Alaska Native	Asian/Pacific Pacific Islander	Other	Male	Female
White (%)	0.0 (0.0)	100.0 (0.0)	0.0 (0.0)	0.0 (0.0)	0.0 (0.0)	0.0 (0.0)	51.5 (1.0)	48.5 (1.0)
Score	- (0.0)	242.1 (1.0)	- (0.0)	- (0.0)	- (0.0)	- (0.0)	243.2 (1.3)	240.9 (1.1)
Black (%)	0.0 (0.0)	0.0 (0.0)	100.0 (0.0)	0.0 (0.0)	0.0 (0.0)	0.0 (0.0)	48.7 (1.6)	51.3 (1.6)
Score	- (0.0)	- (0.0)	205.4 (1.5)	- (0.0)	- (0.0)	- (0.0)	204.9 (1.8)	205.8 (1.8)
American Indian/ Alaska Native (%)	0.0 (0.0)	0.0 (0.0)	0.0 (0.0)	100.0 (0.0)	0.0 (0.0)	0.0 (0.0)	57.5 (4.2)	42.5 (4.2)
Score	- (0.0)	- (0.0)	- (0.0)	226.1 (2.7)	- (0.0)	- (0.0)	227.1 (3.4)	224.8 (4.0)
Asian/Pacific Islander (%)	0.0 (0.0)	0.0 (0.0)	0.0 (0.0)	0.0 (0.0)	100.0 (0.0)	0.0 (0.0)	51.0 (4.0)	49.0 (4.0)
Score	- (0.0)	- (0.0)	- (0.0)	- (0.0)	233.2 (3.0)	- (0.0)	231.6 (3.2)	234.9 (4.4)
Sex								
Male (%)	11.1 (0.5)	70.7 (0.7)	14.4 (0.5)	1.8 (0.3)	1.9 (0.3)	0.1 (0.0)	100.0 (0.0)	0.0 (0.0)
Score	213.6 (3.2)	243.2 (1.3)	204.9 (1.8)	227.1 (3.4)	231.6 (3.2)	250.3 (3.8)	233.8 (1.1)	- (0.0)
Female (%)	10.8 (0.5)	69.7 (0.7)	16.0 (0.7)	1.4 (0.3)	1.9 (0.3)	0.2 (0.1)	0.0 (0.0)	100.0 (0.0)
Score	211.0 (1.9)	240.9 (1.1)	205.8 (1.8)	224.8 (4.0)	234.9 (4.4)	212.7 (32.7)	- (0.0)	231.7 (1.0)
Region								
Northeast (%)	9.7 (1.0)	73.2 (2.0)	15.3 (1.9)	1.1 (0.3)	0.7 (0.2)	0.0 (0.0)	51.3 (1.4)	48.7 (1.4)
Score	209.9 (3.3)	246.7 (2.1)	199.7 (3.1)	229.2 (5.8)	228.3 (5.3)	- (0.0)	237.9 (3.4)	233.2 (1.7)
Southeast (%)	8.1 (0.9)	63.6 (1.9)	26.5 (1.7)	1.2 (0.3)	0.5 (0.2)	0.1 (0.1)	51.1 (1.7)	48.9 (1.7)
Score	208.7 (8.0)	236.7 (2.7)	208.4 (2.0)	235.7 (5.0)	226.7 (8.0)	187.3 (-)	228.0 (2.7)	225.3 (2.1)
Central (%)	6.4 (0.6)	78.4 (2.0)	12.3 (1.7)	2.0 (0.4)	0.8 (0.2)	0.2 (0.0)	52.7 (1.9)	47.3 (1.9)
Score	217.2 (3.7)	240.9 (1.6)	202.3 (4.2)	221.6 (4.1)	244.3 (11.6)	232.7 (12.7)	235.3 (2.5)	233.2 (2.4)
West (%)	19.0 (1.1)	65.8 (1.9)	7.9 (1.3)	2.1 (0.6)	5.1 (1.2)	0.1 (0.1)	49.7 (1.0)	50.3 (1.0)
Score	212.5 (2.3)	244.0 (1.8)	209.4 (3.1)	229.1 (5.3)	232.8 (3.4)	252.7 (7.7)	234.2 (1.7)	234.6 (2.7)
Type of community								
Extreme rural (%)	6.4 (0.9)	85.6 (2.1)	5.3 (1.7)	2.1 (0.8)	0.3 (0.2)	0.3 (0.3)	54.4 (2.5)	45.6 (2.5)
Score	223.6 (4.5)	237.8 (2.6)	208.7 (5.1)	229.9 (7.2)	243.6 (4.5)	187.3 (-)	236.3 (3.6)	233.5 (2.2)
Disadvantaged urban (%)	23.1 (2.7)	35.3 (4.3)	36.9 (4.6)	1.9 (0.5)	2.6 (0.9)	0.2 (0.2)	53.1 (2.0)	46.9 (2.0)
Score	197.3 (3.5)	231.0 (2.9)	193.7 (2.3)	207.8 (4.1)	213.3 (3.4)	243.1 (-)	210.3 (3.1)	206.5 (2.7)
Advantaged urban (%)	7.7 (0.9)	80.4 (2.7)	6.3 (1.6)	1.1 (0.3)	4.4 (1.7)	0.1 (0.1)	50.3 (2.8)	49.7 (2.8)
Score	233.3 (4.4)	255.7 (2.2)	221.5 (8.3)	243.6 (7.8)	254.4 (10.3)	261.5 (10.3)	251.7 (2.9)	251.6 (2.5)
Other (%)	10.6 (0.5)	70.9 (1.0)	15.2 (0.9)	1.6 (0.3)	1.6 (0.3)	0.1 (0.0)	50.5 (1.0)	49.5 (1.0)
Score	212.8 (1.6)	241.1 (1.0)	208.0 (2.0)	226.5 (3.6)	228.0 (3.8)	234.6 (18.4)	233.9 (1.2)	231.4 (1.1)
Parents' education level								
Less than H.S. (%)	16.4 (2.3)	67.8 (3.4)	12.5 (2.3)	1.8 (0.9)	1.5 (0.7)	0.0 (0.0)	50.3 (3.4)	49.7 (3.4)
Score	204.8 (3.3)	228.4 (2.7)	206.3 (5.3)	209.8 (7.2)	226.4 (11.4)	- (0.0)	222.2 (3.4)	220.6 (2.8)
Graduated H.S. (%)	10.8 (0.9)	69.8 (1.7)	16.8 (1.2)	1.7 (0.5)	0.7 (0.2)	0.2 (0.2)	51.3 (1.7)	48.7 (1.7)
Score	208.2 (3.1)	234.5 (1.5)	201.9 (2.6)	219.4 (6.8)	219.9 (7.0)	187.3 (-)	228.2 (1.8)	223.1 (1.9)
Some education after H.S. (%)	9.3 (1.1)	77.0 (1.6)	10.9 (1.4)	1.3 (0.4)	1.5 (0.5)	0.0 (0.0)	50.8 (2.7)	49.2 (2.7)
Score	220.7 (4.1)	249.6 (1.8)	206.8 (4.5)	231.2 (7.5)	243.3 (8.1)	- (0.0)	243.7 (2.5)	240.1 (2.6)
Graduated college (%)	8.6 (0.5)	71.2 (1.1)	16.6 (0.8)	1.4 (0.3)	2.0 (0.4)	0.1 (0.1)	54.0 (1.3)	46.0 (1.3)
Score	221.8 (2.2)	252.7 (1.2)	210.7 (2.3)	234.4 (5.2)	246.0 (5.1)	246.4 (6.3)	243.0 (1.5)	242.2 (1.4)
Unknown (%)	13.2 (0.6)	68.0 (0.8)	14.3 (0.8)	1.9 (0.4)	2.5 (0.4)	0.1 (0.1)	48.3 (1.1)	51.7 (1.1)
Score	207.0 (2.1)	234.7 (1.0)	201.1 (2.0)	223.9 (4.0)	224.2 (3.2)	233.6 (12.0)	225.8 (1.2)	225.8 (1.1)

[Continued]

★ 210 ★

Science Proficiency of Fourth Graders

[Continued]

Characteristic	Race/ethnicity						Sex	
	Hispanic	White	Black	American Indian/ Alaska Native	Asian/Pacific Pacific Islander	Other	Male	Female
Type of school								
Public (%)	11.4 (0.6)	69.0 (0.6)	16.0 (0.5)	1.7 (0.3)	1.7 (0.2)	0.1 (0.0)	50.9 (0.8)	49.1 (0.8)
Score	210.9 (1.6)	241.3 (1.1)	204.4 (1.5)	225.2 (2.8)	230.4 (3.6)	220.4 (25.3)	232.4 (1.1)	230.4 (1.2)
Private (%)	8.1 (1.3)	79.6 (2.3)	8.3 (1.4)	0.9 (0.3)	3.0 (1.2)	0.1 (0.1)	53.6 (2.2)	46.4 (2.2)
Score	224.3 (4.8)	247.6 (1.9)	221.1 (4.1)	241.1 (4.4)	246.1 (7.1)	268.2 (-)	244.4 (2.7)	242.3 (1.8)

Source: Jones, Lee R., and others. *The 1990 Science Report Card: NAEP's Assessment of Fourth, Eighth, and Twelfth Graders*, Prepared by Educational Testing Service under contract with the National Center for Education Statistics, Office of Educational Research and Improvement, U.S. Department of Education, March 1992, p. 151-152. *Notes:* A dash (-) indicates no data were given in the original source. Achievement results were analyzed using item response theory (IRT) scaling procedures, which allowed the National Assessment of Educational Progress to estimate students' average proficiency on a scale ranging from 0 to 500. The standard errors of the estimated proficiencies appear in parentheses. It can be said with 95 percent certainty that for each population of interest, the value for the whole population is within plus or minus two standard errors of the estimate for the sample.

★ 211 ★

Academic Progress

Science Proficiency of Twelfth Graders

Figures shown are based on IRT (item response theory) scaling procedures. Progress is estimated on a scale of 0 to 500.

Characteristic	Race/ethnicity						Sex	
	Hispanic	White	Black	American Indian/ Alaska Native	Asian/Pacific Pacific Islander	Other	Male	Female
Total(%)	8.2 (0.3)	73.2 (0.4)	14.2 (0.5)	0.7 (0.2)	3.6 (0.2)	0.1 (0.0)	48.2 (0.8)	51.8 (0.8)
Score	272.5 (2.8)	302.5 (1.3)	256.3 (2.4)	285.7 (4.6)	308.2 (7.1)	277.2 (18.1)	298.9 (1.5)	288.6 (1.2)
Race/ethnicity								
Hispanic (%)	100.0 (0.0)	0.0 (0.0)	0.0 (0.0)	0.0 (0.0)	0.0 (0.0)	0.0 (0.0)	49.1 (2.9)	50.9 (2.9)
Score	272.5 (2.8)	- (0.0)	- (0.0)	- (0.0)	- (0.0)	- (0.0)	277.7 (3.1)	267.5 (3.5)
White (%)	0.0 (0.0)	100.0 (0.0)	0.0 (0.0)	0.0 (0.0)	0.0 (0.0)	0.0 (0.0)	49.0 (1.3)	51.0 (1.0)
Score	- (0.0)	302.5 (1.3)	- (0.0)	- (0.0)	- (0.0)	- (0.0)	307.1 (1.5)	298.0 (1.3)
Black (%)	0.0 (0.0)	0.0 (0.0)	100.0 (0.0)	0.0 (0.0)	0.0 (0.0)	0.0 (0.0)	43.3 (2.2)	56.7 (2.2)
Score	- (0.0)	- (0.0)	256.3 (2.4)	- (0.0)	- (0.0)	- (0.0)	261.2 (2.7)	252.6 (2.9)
American Indian/ Alaska Native (%)	0.0 (0.0)	0.0 (0.0)	0.0 (0.0)	100.0 (0.0)	0.0 (0.0)	0.0 (0.0)	56.9 (7.7)	43.1 (7.7)
Score	- (0.0)	- (0.0)	- (0.0)	285.7 (4.6)	- (0.0)	- (0.0)	288.7 (7.1)	281.8 (5.9)
Asian/Pacific Islander (%)	0.0 (0.0)	0.0 (0.0)	0.0 (0.0)	0.0 (0.0)	100.0 (0.0)	0.0 (0.0)	46.0 (2.3)	54.0 (2.3)
Score	- (0.0)	- (0.0)	- (0.0)	- (0.0)	308.2 (7.1)	- (0.0)	315.2 (10.6)	302.3 (5.0)
Sex								
Male (%)	8.4 (0.6)	74.5 (0.9)	12.8 (0.8)	0.8 (0.3)	3.4 (0.2)	0.1 (0.1)	100.0 (0.0)	0.0 (0.0)
Score	277.7 (3.1)	307.1 (1.5)	261.2 (2.7)	288.7 (7.1)	315.2 (10.6)	271.7 (35.7)	298.9 (1.5)	- (0.0)
Female (%)	8.1 (0.5)	72.0 (0.8)	15.6 (0.7)	0.6 (0.3)	3.7 (0.3)	0.1 (0.1)	0.0 (0.0)	100.0 (0.0)
Score	267.5 (3.5)	298.0 (1.3)	252.6 (2.9)	281.8 (5.9)	302.3 (5.0)	284.4 (9.6)	- (0.0)	288.6 (1.2)

[Continued]

★211★

Science Proficiency of Twelfth Graders

[Continued]

Characteristic	Race/ethnicity						Sex	
	Hispanic	White	Black	American Indian/ Alaska Native	Asian/Pacific Pacific Islander	Other	Male	Female
Region								
Northeast (%)	4.8 (1.3)	80.5 (3.0)	11.3 (2.1)	0.1 (0.0)	3.2 (1.2)	0.0 (0.0)	47.8 (1.5)	52.2 (1.5)
Score	269.6 (8.0)	306.9 (2.2)	261.6 (6.1)	280.4 (13.4)	318.5 (9.1)	- (0.0)	305.7 (3.4)	295.4 (3.4)
Southeast (%)	4.4 (1.0)	64.3 (2.4)	29.3 (2.2)	0.6 (0.3)	1.4 (0.6)	0.0 (0.0)	46.4 (1.7)	53.6 (1.7)
Score	268.8 (4.9)	291.1 (3.0)	251.5 (3.1)	296.1 (9.7)	306.3 (8.0)	- (0.0)	281.7 (4.0)	276.2 (2.2)
Central (%)	3.0 (0.7)	84.6 (1.5)	10.0 (1.5)	1.0 (0.6)	1.2 (0.5)	0.2 (0.1)	50.6 (1.9)	49.4 (1.9)
Score	268.5 (5.9)	301.4 (2.5)	251.4 (7.0)	284.8 (7.0)	319.3 (14.8)	282.9 (21.2)	300.7 (2.8)	289.9 (2.4)
West (%)	18.4 (1.1)	63.1 (2.2)	9.7 (1.5)	1.0 (0.4)	7.6 (1.7)	0.2 (0.1)	47.5 (1.1)	52.5 (1.1)
Score	274.3 (3.7)	307.5 (2.7)	266.3 (5.0)	282.8 (9.2)	303.4 (10.3)	272.9 (33.0)	303.4 (3.2)	290.7 (2.9)
Type of community								
Extreme rural (%)	3.8 (1.4)	82.4 (5.4)	10.8 (4.7)	2.0 (1.1)	1.1 (0.4)	0.0 (0.0)	48.6 (2.5)	51.4 (2.5)
Score	269.5 (6.5)	297.0 (3.3)	249.5 (4.1)	277.7 (6.4)	324.5 (13.1)	277.7 (6.4)	294.0 (4.3)	287.6 (4.2)
Disadvantaged urban (%)	24.2 (5.6)	42.9 (10.7)	27.5 (7.0)	0.5 (0.3)	4.6 (1.5)	0.4 (0.3)	46.5 (3.5)	53.5 (3.5)
Score	262.9 (4.1)	295.5 (5.5)	242.2 (5.3)	285.5 (13.7)	295.5 (10.3)	296.6 (12.8)	280.8 (4.1)	266.1 (6.0)
Advantaged urban (%)	6.6 (1.6)	74.4 (6.1)	13.5 (5.4)	0.8 (0.5)	4.7 (1.3)	0.0 (0.0)	47.2 (2.2)	52.8 (2.2)
Score	176.4 (7.0)	313.4 (2.7)	264.2 (11.0)	286.6 (6.9)	312.0 (8.1)	- (0.0)	312.9 (4.2)	296.1 (5.3)
Other (%)	6.2 (0.7)	77.1 (1.5)	12.4 (1.1)	0.5 (0.2)	3.6 (0.6)	0.1 (0.0)	48.6 (1.0)	51.4 (1.0)
Score	279.0 (3.7)	302.5 (1.4)	261.8 (2.8)	290.6 (7.5)	309.7 (10.7)	263.7 (30.4)	300.7 (1.9)	291.8 (1.5)
Parents' education level								
Less than H.S. (%)	27.2 (2.8)	52.9 (4.0)	16.6 (2.2)	0.5 (0.4)	2.6 (0.8)	0.2 (0.2)	37.3 (2.4)	62.7 (2.4)
Score	265.2 (4.1)	276.3 (4.0)	247.8 (4.9)	271.5 (11.5)	301.4 (6.9)	209.5 (-)	276.5 (4.3)	264.6 (2.9)
Graduated H.S. (%)	7.9 (0.5)	71.7 (1.2)	17.4 (1.0)	0.8 (0.4)	2.1 (0.5)	0.0 (0.0)	47.7 (1.6)	52.3 (1.6)
Score	266.0 (3.4)	288.7 (1.5)	243.9 (3.5)	262.9 (9.2)	290.5 (6.2)	264.7 (9.3)	283.3 (2.0)	274.8 (1.6)
Some education after H.S. (%)	6.9 (0.6)	74.9 (1.5)	14.7 (1.0)	1.0 (0.4)	2.5 (1.0)	0.0 (0.0)	48.7 (1.6)	51.3 (1.6)
Score	278.9 (3.4)	302.3 (1.5)	267.0 (3.4)	295.7 (8.2)	294.9 (12.1)	- (0.0)	298.9 (1.7)	291.7 (1.7)
Graduated college (%)	4.7 (0.5)	78.7 (1.0)	10.7 (0.8)	0.5 (0.2)	5.2 (0.4)	0.2 (0.1)	49.9 (1.0)	50.1 (1.0)
Score	287.1 (3.9)	314.5 (1.2)	266.1 (3.1)	298.1 (10.4)	319.7 (6.4)	298.1 (10.4)	313.1 (1.9)	303.3 (1.3)
Unknown (%)	26.0 (4.7)	39.3 (6.1)	29.6 (5.5)	1.1 (1.2)	3.9 (1.5)	0.2 (0.1)	53.3 (5.2)	46.7 (5.2)
Score	253.9 (12.0)	258.3 (7.9)	226.8 (9.8)	267.5 (2.1)	286.2 (11.5)	261.1 (23.1)	260.5 (6.8)	235.9 (6.6)
Type of school								
Public (%)	8.2 (0.4)	72.6 (0.6)	14.7 (0.5)	0.7 (0.3)	3.7 (0.2)	0.1 (0.0)	47.8 (0.8)	52.2 (0.8)
Score	271.6 (2.9)	302.0 (1.4)	254.5 (2.5)	285.3 (4.9)	308.8 (7.5)	277.2 (18.1)	298.4 (1.7)	287.5 (1.3)
Private (%)	8.6 (1.9)	78.1 (2.6)	10.2 (1.7)	0.5 (0.3)	2.6 (0.6)	0.0 (0.0)	51.7 (3.9)	48.3 (3.9)
Score	279.7 (4.9)	306.3 (2.9)	280.8 (6.0)	292.0 (9.3)	300.9 (6.7)	- (0.0)	303.0 (4.2)	299.2 (2.4)
Type of high school program								
General (%)	10.4 (1.1)	71.1 (1.2)	14.0 (1.1)	0.9 (0.4)	3.5 (1.0)	0.2 (0.1)	50.1 (1.0)	49.9 (1.0)
Score	261.2 (2.3)	284.7 (1.6)	245.3 (2.6)	281.0 (6.8)	289.5 (9.5)	266.9 (51.2)	283.0 (2.0)	270.7 (1.7)
Academic/college prep. (%)	6.8 (0.4)	75.8 (0.9)	12.9 (0.7)	0.5 (0.2)	3.9 (0.5)	0.1 (0.0)	45.7 (1.2)	54.3 (1.2)
Score	287.4 (4.0)	316.6 (1.2)	270.3 (2.7)	291.3 (8.2)	321.4 (4.0)	305.4 (9.5)	315.8 (1.7)	302.7 (1.2)

[Continued]

★ 211 ★

Science Proficiency of Twelfth Graders

[Continued]

Characteristic	Race/ethnicity						Sex	
	Hispanic	White	Black	American Indian/ Alaska Native	Asian/Pacific Pacific Islander	Other	Male	Female
Vocational/technical (%)	7.4 (1.2)	67.5 (2.4)	22.2 (2.4)	1.2 (0.4)	1.5 (0.3)	0.2 (0.3)	55.2 (2.7)	44.8 (2.7)
Score	258.2 (7.2)	274.7 (2.8)	235.6 (4.1)	284.5 (11.9)	271.5 (17.4)	251.0 (10.6)	270.7 (3.4)	258.3 (3.2)

Source: Jones, Lee R., and others. *The 1990 Science Report Card: NAEP's Assessment of Fourth, Eighth, and Twelfth Graders*, Prepared by Educational Testing Service under contract with the National Center for Education Statistics, Office of Educational Research and Improvement, U.S. Department of Education, March 1992, p. 155-156. *Notes:* A dash (-) indicates no data were given in the original source. Achievement results were analyzed using item response theory (IRT) scaling procedures, which allowed the National Assessment of Educational Progress to estimate students' average proficiency on a scale ranging from 0 to 500. The standard errors of the estimated proficiencies appear in parentheses. It can be said with 95 percent certainty that for each population of interest, the value for the whole population is within plus or minus two standard errors of the estimate for the sample.

★ 212 ★

Academic Progress

Science and Math: Reasons for High School Senior Enrollment

Data show the percentage of 12th graders who answered either, "somewhat important" or "very important," when presented with each reason for taking a course. Responses are shown, by race/ethnicity of the student, for 1992.

Response	All 12th graders	Race/ethnicity				
		White	Black	Hispanic	Asian	American Indian
Mathematics class						
I am interested in mathematics	74.5	72.9	74.6	80.4	81.9	87.7
I do well in mathematics	77.1	76.4	76.1	79.7	83.6	76.8
I need it for college or trade school	87.2	86.5	89.8	86.5	90.8	90.5
I need it for a job after high school	64.7	62.5	69.7	70.9	66.3	83.9
I need it for advanced placement	53.6	49.6	58.4	62.5	72.6	56.9
Advised to take class by:						
Teacher	65.9	63.6	74.8	71.1	66.7	70.6
Guidance counselor	64.8	60.7	77.8	76.2	64.2	83.0
Parent	71.6	70.5	74.6	74.4	73.3	79.8
Friend	42.2	39.8	51.2	43.7	50.8	56.2
Sibling	30.9	26.3	37.2	43.1	46.2	51.5
Science class						
I am interested in science	78.8	78.5	77.4	78.9	83.6	74.9
I do well in science	80.6	80.1	76.7	86.1	84.2	86.6
I need it for college or trade school	83.3	82.4	86.4	83.5	88.4	88.8
I need it for a job after high school	47.0	44.5	53.2	57.6	51.3	55.9
I need it for advanced placement	50.2	47.1	51.6	59.0	66.8	59.6
Advised to take class by:						
Teacher	58.9	57.6	61.7	63.7	61.0	67.2
Guidance counselor	59.4	56.2	71.4	7.9	59.7	57.9

[Continued]

★ 212 ★

Science and Math: Reasons for High School Senior Enrollment

[Continued]

Response	All 12th graders	Race/ethnicity				
		White	Black	Hispanic	Asian	American Indian
Parent	66.3	65.7	69.1	70.5	64.1	73.8
Friend	43.5	42.9	40.9	44.6	49.7	62.9
Sibling	28.7	25.3	35.0	35.5	44.3	57.6

Source: U.S. Department of Education. National Center for Education Statistics. Office of Educational Research and Improvement. *Digest of Education Statistics, 1994.* Lanham, MD: Bernan, November 1994, p. 136. U.S. Department of Education, National Center for Education Statistics, "National Educational Longitudinal Study of 1988," First and Second Followup surveys. (This table was prepared February 1994.).

★ 213 ★

Academic Progress

Science, Biology, Chemistry, and Physics Proficiency

Data are shown for students in grades 9-12, by race/ethnicity. Proficiencies are based on IRT (item response theory) scaling procedures. Progress is estimated on a scale of 0 to 500.

Subject area and race/ethnicity	One year or more			Less than one year		
	Percent of students	Average proficiency	Average content area proficiency	Percent of students	Average proficiency	Average content area proficiency
Biology						
White	92 (1.2)	306 (1.2)	308 (1.1)	8 (1.2)	270 (2.6)	274 (3.0)
Black	91 (1.2)	259 (2.6)	265 (2.2)	9 (1.2)	233 (5.4)	240 (5.4)
Hispanic	86 (2.7)	281 (2.8)	283 (2.8)	14 (2.7)	246 (5.5)	247 (6.6)
Asian/Pacific Islander	89 (1.6)	311 (6.0)	312 (6.0)	11 (1.6)	297 (13.8)	298 (14.7)
American Indian	74 (10.0)[1]	290 (6.5)[1]	292 (10.0)[1]	26 (10.0)[1]	269 (15.2)[1]	270 (16.7)[1]
Total	91 (1.0)	298 (1.2)	301 (1.1)	9 (1.0)	263 (1.8)	267 (2.1)
Chemistry						
White	56 (1.4)	321 (1.2)	322 (1.6)	44 (1.4)	280 (1.4)	273 (1.8)
Black	49 (3.3)	275 (2.6)	274 (2.9)	51 (3.3)	240 (2.8)	234 (4.1)
Hispanic	48 (3.0)	293 (3.5)	295 (4.5)	52 (3.0)	262 (2.8)	257 (4.1)
Asian/Pacific Islander	80 (7.3)	319 (3.8)	322 (5.1)	20 (7.3)	277 (6.4)	273 (9.4)
American Indian	36 (6.8)[1]	304 (9.5)[1]	306 (8.0)[1]	64 (6.8)[1]	272 (4.8)[1]	267 (5.7)[1]
Total	55 (1.3)	314 (1.2)	314 (1.6)	45 (1.3)	273 (1.3)	266 (1.6)
Physics						
White	29 (1.2)	329 (1.6)	334 (2.1)	71 (1.2)	293 (1.0)	287 (1.3)
Black	24 (2.8)	262 (4.5)	262 (5.7)	76 (2.8)	255 (2.6)	251 (3.5)
Hispanic	26 (1.9)	293 (4.1)	294 (4.9)	74 (1.9)	271 (3.4)	268 (4.4)
Asian/Pacific Islander	56 (5.0)	326 (6.2)	333 (7.8)	44 (5.0)	290 (4.2)	285 (5.7)
American Indian	19 (6.0)[1]	298 (17.8)[1]	304 (17.2)[1]	81 (6.0)[1]	281 (5.2)[1]	276 (4.6)[1]
Total	29 (1.1)	319 (1.6)	323 (2.1)	71 (1.1)	286 (1.0)	280 (1.2)

Source: Jones, Lee R., and others. *The 1990 Science Report Card: NAEP's Assessment of Fourth, Eighth, and Twelfth Graders,* Prepared by Educational Testing Service under contract with the National Center for Education Statistics, Office of Educational Research and Improvement, U.S. Department of Education, March 1992, p. 73. *Notes:* The standard errors of the estimated percentages and proficiencies appear in parentheses. It can be said with 95 percent certainty that for each population of interest, the value for the whole population is within plus or minus two standard errors of the estimate for the sample. 1. Interpret with caution - the nature of the sample does not allow accurate determination of the variability of these estimated statistics.

★214★

Academic Progress

Student Attitudes Toward Science

Responses to the question "Do you like science?" Average proficiencies are based on IRT (item response theory) scaling procedures. Progress is estimated on a scale of 0 to 500. Scores are assigned to five proficiency levels: Level 150—Knows everyday science facts; Level 200—Understands simple scientific principles; Level 250—Applies general scientific information; Level 300—Analyzes scientific procedures and data; and Level 350—Integrates specialized scientific information. Data presented are proficiency scores, not levels.

Grade and race/ethnicity	Yes		No	
	Percent of students	Average proficiency	Percent of students	Average proficiency
Grade 4				
White	81 (0.9)	245 (1.1)	19 (0.9)	231 (1.5)
Black	75 (1.9)	208 (1.7)	25 (1.9)	199 (2.3)
Hispanic	76 (1.4)	217 (1.5)	24 (1.4)	199 (2.5)
Asian/Pacific Islander	78 (5.7)	238 (2.9)	22 (5.7)	217 (4.3)
American Indian	80 (4.1)	230 (3.1)	21 (4.1)	212 (5.1)
Male	81 (1.0)	238 (1.2)	19 (1.0)	218 (2.0)
Female	78 (1.0)	235 (1.2)	22 (1.0)	222 (1.6)
Total	80 (0.8)	237 (1.0)	20 (0.8)	220 (1.4)
Grade 8				
White	67 (1.1)	280 (1.2)	33 (1.1)	258 (1.6)
Black	70 (2.1)	235 (2.3)	30 (2.1)	223 (2.9)
Hispanic	71 (2.1)	245 (2.7)	29 (2.1)	233 (2.9)
Asian/Pacific Islander	70 (4.6)	277 (4.5)	31 (4.6)	256 (5.0)
American Indian	71 (5.9)[1]	254 (12.5)[1]	29 (5.9)[1]	246 (6.8)[1]
Male	72 (1.1)	272 (1.5)	28 (1.1)	248 (2.0)
Female	64 (1.2)	266 (1.5)	36 (1.2)	253 (1.6)
Total	68 (1.0)	269 (1.2)	32 (1.0)	251 (1.4)
Grade 12				
White	66 (0.9)	312 (1.4)	34 (0.9)	284 (1.3)
Black	60 (1.8)	263 (2.9)	40 (1.8)	247 (3.0)
Hispanic	68 (2.3)	279 (3.0)	32 (2.3)	261 (3.9)
Asian/Pacific Islander	69 (3.5)	320 (7.8)	31 (3.5)	284 (5.0)
American Indian	71 (6.5)[1]	298 (5.3)[1]	29 (6.5)[1]	257 (6.0)[1]
Male	74 (0.9)	307 (1.6)	26 (0.9)	275 (1.9)
Female	57 (1.1)	298 (1.3)	43 (1.1)	277 (1.4)
Total	65 (0.7)	303 (1.3)	35 (0.7)	276 (1.2)

Source: Jones, Lee R., and others. *The 1990 Science Report Card: NAEP's Assessment of Fourth, Eighth, and Twelfth Graders*, Prepared by Educational Testing Service under contract with the National Center for Education Statistics, Office of Educational Research and Improvement, U.S. Department of Education, March 1992, p. 81. *Notes:* Achievement results were analyzed using item response theory (IRT) scaling procedures, which allowed the National Assessment of Educational Progress to estimate students' average proficiency on a scale ranging from 0 to 500. The standard errors of the estimated percentages and proficiencies appear in parentheses. It can be said with 95 percent certainty, that for each population of interest, the value for the whole population is within plus or minus two standard errors of the estimate for the sample. 1. Interpret with caution - the nature of the sample does not allow accurate determination of the variability of these estimated statistics.

★ 215 ★

Academic Progress

Students Responding Correctly to Science Items - I

Data show weighted percentages of students responding correctly. Standard deviations are shown in parentheses.

Item description	Grade	Nation	Hispanic	White	Black	Male	Female
Classify a grasshopper	4	82.7 (1.0)	76.0 (2.5)	84.2 (1.1)	81.2 (2.2)	82.7 (1.1)	82.98 (1.3)
Identify cat tracks	4	83.2 (0.8)	76.7 (2.3)	86.2 (0.9)	74.6 (2.1)	81.1 (1.1)	85.5 (1.1)
Graph: Mass of 4 objects	4	90.1 (0.7)	85.6 (1.8)	92.1 (0.8)	83.7 (1.6)	87.3 (1.2)	93.1 (0.7)
Identify a solid	4	76.9 (0.9)	62.4 (2.2)	83.1 (0.9)	59.5 (2.4)	75.3 (1.4)	78.8 (1.3)
Human and dinosaur fossils	4	78.5 (1.0)	69.8 (2.4)	83.7 (1.1)	61.2 (2.2)	77.0 (1.4)	80.1 (1.2)
Which are fossils?	4	61.5 (1.1)	47.3 (2.2)	67.9 (1.4)	43.2 (2.1)	61.7 (1.8)	61.4 (1.3)
Testing growth of seeds	4	61.9 (1.1)	54.3 (2.5)	65.2 (1.5)	53.3 (2.3)	61.7 (1.6)	62.0 (1.7)
Function of lungs	4	83.9 (0.9)	71.9 (2.4)	89.1 (1.0)	70.1 (2.3)	83.7 (1.3)	84.3 (1.2)
Which is not a lever?	4	59.1 (1.3)	46.6 (3.1)	64.5 (1.5)	44.4 (2.5)	63.9 (1.4)	53.6 (1.8)
Closest star to Earth	4	35.5 (1.0)	32.3 (2.5)	36.0 (1.3)	35.5 (2.2)	37.3 (1.5)	33.4 (1.7)
Observing with microscope	4	36.9 (1.1)	27.9 (2.3)	41.3 (1.4)	23.3 (1.8)	42.9 (2.0)	30.3 (1.4)
Use library for weather info	4	45.6 (1.3)	34.7 (2.0)	48.9 (1.7)	41.0 (2.7)	45.2 (1.4)	46.0 (2.0)
Exp: Tablet in hot/cold H_2O	4	42.4 (1.0)	31.4 (2.4)	46.5 (1.2)	30.7 (2.7)	40.9 (1.5)	44.2 (1.5)
Relative speed of light	4	44.5 (1.4)	32.8 (2.5)	49.2 (1.6)	28.7 (3.2)	51.2 (1.6)	37.1 (1.8)
Fridge-slow bacteria growth	4	49.7 (1.1)	39.9 (2.5)	54.1 (1.3)	38.3 (2.2)	49.7 (1.1)	51.0 (1.5)
Exp: Temp pref of g'hoppers	4	25.5 (0.9)	27.1 (2.6)	25.8 (1.2)	23.2 (2.0)	26.2 (1.1)	24.8 (1.2)
Examples of conductors	4	62.0 (1.1)	58.6 (2.4)	66.0 (1.4)	44.9 (2.5)	66.1 (1.3)	57.5 (1.6)
Determine wind direction	4	28.3 (1.1)	25.7 (2.1)	30.6 (1.4)	17.5 (2.0)	25.1 (1.3)	31.8 (1.6)
Causes of winds on Earth	4	35.1 (1.0)	27.3 (2.2)	37.3 (1.3)	28.4 (2.8)	37.1 (1.6)	32.9 (1.5)
Predict order candles go out	4	33.3 (1.1)	24.5 (2.4)	36.7 (1.5)	23.7 (2.1)	37.8 (1.4)	28.2 (1.6)
Balloon shape and volume	4	47.2 (1.0)	35.7 (2.7)	51.5 (1.4)	36.0 (2.4)	46.9 (1.4)	47.6 (1.5)
Determining the age of a tree	4	58.9 (1.4)	40.3 (2.6)	66.7 (1.5)	35.5 (2.7)	61.3 (1.6)	56.3 (1.7)
Garden loses nutrients	4	45.5 (1.2)	28.6 (2.7)	51.8 (1.5)	26.4 (2.2)	46.6 (1.7)	44.4 (1.6)
Life cycle of a butterfly	4	41.2 (1.3)	32.5 (2.9)	45.2 (1.6)	28.3 (2.3)	42.0 (2.0)	40.3 (1.6)

[Continued]

★ 215 ★

Students Responding Correctly to Science Items - I

[Continued]

Item description	Grade	Nation	Hispanic	White	Black	Male	Female
Position of fulcrum	4	61.8 (1.2)	56.6 (2.9)	64.6 (1.4)	53.3 (2.5)	64.4 (1.6)	59.2 (1.6)
Use of a telescope	4	67.9 (0.8)	53.9 (2.6)	73.2 (1.0)	53.8 (2.5)	69.3 (1.3)	66.4 (1.4)
Balloon: volume & temperature	4	42.1 (1.5)	34.3 (2.9)	45.2 (1.9)	32.3 (2.4)	45.1 (2.2)	39.0 (1.7)
Sun is a star	4	58.6 (1.2)	43.0 (2.9)	64.3 (1.3)	42.2 (2.6)	65.1 (1.6)	51.7 (1.5)
Objects that conduct heat	4	48.5 (1.1)	38.9 (2.8)	52.3 (1.4)	35.5 (2.9)	48.7 (1.5)	48.2 (1.5)
Planting to avoid erosion	4	30.5 (1.0)	28.4 (2.7)	31.9 (1.3)	27.0 (2.6)	30.2 (1.6)	30.8 (1.3)
Length of shadows at noon	4	34.1 (1.0)	27.8 (3.3)	37.2 (1.3)	23.4 (2.1)	38.5 (1.5)	29.4 (1.3)
Reading a histogram	4	94.7 (0.5)	89.6 (1.2)	96.6 (0.6)	89.9 (1.6)	92.2 (0.7)	97.3 (0.5)
Relating speed of car/train	4	44.9 (1.0)	37.6 (2.7)	49.2 (1.2)	30.6 (2.2)	48.8 (1.7)	40.8 (1.4)
Classifying objects: shape	4	78.7 (1.0)	67.0 (2.1)	83.1 (1.2)	67.3 (2.8)	76.1 (1.3)	81.5 (1.3)
Survey height of boys/girls	4	48.5 (1.1)	42.0 (2.4)	49.6 (1.3)	48.1 (2.8)	48.0 (1.6)	49.6 (1.3)
Example of a force	4	63.5 (1.0)	50.6 (2.2)	69.0 (1.3)	49.6 (2.7)	61.3 (1.4)	65.8 (1.5)
	8	82.1 (0.7)	71.2 (2.5)	83.4 (0.7)	82.3 (2.6)	78.5 (1.1)	85.6 (1.0)
Fossils show new species	4	68.3 (1.1)	58.8 (2.3)	72.2 (1.4)	58.4 (2.2)	67.1 (1.4)	69.6 (1.2)
	8	83.5 (0.9)	74.1 (2.4)	87.0 (1.1)	74.1 (2.8)	81.7 (1.3)	85.3 (1.1)
Origin of oil/coal	4	22.0 (0.9)	20.6 (1.7)	22.7 (1.2)	18.8 (1.8)	25.3 (1.4)	18.8 (1.3)
	8	50.5 (1.4)	41.7 (3.0)	55.2 (1.6)	34.6 (2.5)	60.1 (1.8)	40.9 (1.6)
Aluminum recycling	4	67.3 (1.4)	50.2 (2.6)	73.9 (1.8)	49.3 (2.3)	68.0 (2.0)	66.5 (1.5)
	8	87.6 (0.7)	78.7 (2.2)	90.4 (0.7)	80.2 (2.5)	87.0 (1.0)	88.3 (0.9)

Source: Jones, Lee R., and others. *The 1990 Science Report Card: NAEP's Assessment of Fourth, Eighth, and Twelfth Graders*, Prepared by Educational Testing Service under contract with the National Center for Education Statistics, Office of Educational Research and Improvement, U.S. Department of Education, March 1992, pp. 160-172.

★ 216 ★

Academic Progress

Students Responding Correctly to Science Items - II

Data show weighted percentages of students responding correctly. Standard deviations are shown in parentheses.

Item description	Grade	Nation	Hispanic	White	Black	Male	Female
Reducing acid rain	4	38.0 (1.1)	26.7 (2.5)	41.4 (1.3)	31.2 (2.2)	39.1 (1.7)	37.0 (1.5)
	8	73.3 (1.1)	62.4 (3.4)	77.3 (1.3)	61.1 (3.2)	75.6 (1.5)	71.1 (1.6)
Major types of rocks	4	49.7 (1.3)	42.9 (2.4)	51.0 (2.0)	48.4 (2.0)	46.6 (1.6)	52.0 (2.0)
	8	61.1 (1.6)	55.7 (3.3)	62.6 (1.8)	59.3 (3.2)	59.5 (1.8)	62.7 (1.8)
Predator skull	4	61.4 (1.0)	51.1 (2.5)	65.6 (1.2)	50.7 (2.3)	66.2 (1.3)	56.7 (1.4)
	8	68.3 (1.1)	59.2 (3.1)	73.2 (1.1)	53.2 (2.8)	75.4 (1.1)	61.1 (1.6)
Graph: hours of darkness	4	36.3 (0.8)	31.6 (2.4)	39.2 (1.1)	26.4 (2.0)	37.1 (1.3)	35.6 (1.3)
	8	71.3 (1.1)	64.2 (2.2)	75.3 (1.2)	57.0 (2.9)	70.4 (1.4)	72.2 (1.5)
Graph: most O_2 produced	4	38.4 (1.0)	25.2 (2.1)	43.2 (1.3)	27.6 (2.1)	41.6 (1.3)	35.3 (1.5)
	8	74.2 (1.0)	65.2 (2.7)	79.7 (1.2)	53.8 (2.1)	73.5 (1.5)	74.9 (1.2)
Calculate distance on map	4	46.1 (1.2)	36.7 (2.7)	51.6 (1.6)	29.5 (2.0)	48.6 (1.7)	43.6 (1.7)
	8	76.2 (1.0)	68.2 (2.3)	80.0 (1.1)	64.4 (2.6)	77.4 (1.3)	75.0 (1.5)
Table: plant growth/light	4	38.3 (1.3)	27.5 (2.2)	43.5 (1.8)	23.6 (2.7)	35.3 (1.7)	41.3 (1.6)
	8	66.8 (0.9)	53.4 (2.7)	71.9 (1.0)	51.1 (3.3)	61.9 (1.7)	71.9 (1.0)
Table: powders X/Y	4	41.9 (1.2)	32.8 (2.1)	45.0 (1.4)	34.3 (2.4)	40.8 (1.6)	43.0 (1.7)
	8	61.4 (0.9)	48.4 (3.3)	63.8 (1.1)	58.3 (2.3)	57.8 (1.5)	64.9 (1.1)
Graph: photosynthesis rate	4	42.5 (1.0)	34.3 (2.1)	46.3 (1.4)	29.6 (2.2)	40.8 (1.6)	44.2 (1.4)
	8	68.8 (1.0)	55.0 (2.5)	72.5 (1.4)	59.7 (2.3)	66.4 (1.7)	71.2 (1.1)
Woodpecker's beak	4	48.8 (1.5)	38.8 (2.7)	52.7 (1.8)	39.4 (2.2)	53.7 (1.9)	44.0 (2.1)
	8	67.9 (1.2)	53.7 (3.1)	73.7 (1.3)	50.2 (3.5)	71.9 (1.5)	63.8 (1.5)
Questions science can't answer	4	37.4 (1.0)	33.9 (2.8)	39.9 (1.3)	29.3 (2.1)	38.3 (1.5)	36.6 (1.4)
	8	66.6 (0.9)	55.4 (2.4)	70.7 (1.1)	54.3 (2.8)	62.5 (1.4)	70.8 (1.2)
Exp: Stronger of 2 magnets	4	34.4 (1.2)	24.8 (2.0)	36.9 (1.5)	30.6 (2.8)	36.6 (1.7)	32.2 (1.6)
	8	60.6 (1.1)	46.2 (2.6)	65.7 (1.1)	45.4 (3.8)	60.4 (1.3)	60.9 (1.8)
Water and erosion	4	31.7 (1.3)	29.5 (2.6)	34.0 (1.5)	21.5 (2.2)	37.0 (1.7)	26.4 (1.4)
	8	52.8 (1.4)	44.0 (3.6)	58.1 (1.7)	32.9 (3.3)	58.8 (1.7)	46.7 (2.0)
Block floating in H_2O/oil	4	28.2 (0.9)	22.2 (1.9)	30.7 (1.3)	21.5 (2.4)	27.5 (1.2)	29.0 (1.5)
	8	38.3 (1.0)	30.7 (2.0)	40.6 (1.1)	33.5 (2.4)	37.6 (1.3)	39.0 (1.5)
Earth's temp and sea level	4	24.9 (1.1)	25.2 (2.2)	24.7 (1.4)	25.7 (2.6)	23.6 (1.6)	26.2 (1.5)
	8	28.1 (1.1)	27.8 (2.1)	28.8 (1.4)	24.0 (2.6)	32.3 (1.7)	23.9 (1.1)
Animals breathe O_2	4	84.3 (0.9)	75.2 (2.3)	88.0 (1.3)	74.4 (1.8)	83.0 (1.3)	85.7 (1.1)
	8	94.5 (0.6)	91.9 (1.5)	96.0 (0.6)	88.6 (1.9)	94.9 (0.8)	94.1 (0.7)

[Continued]

★ 216 ★

Students Responding Correctly to Science Items - II

[Continued]

Item description	Grade	Nation	Hispanic	White	Black	Male	Female
Characteristics of a snake	4	72.7 (1.1)	67.1 (2.2)	75.6 (1.4)	53.2 (2.6)	74.0 (1.4)	71.3 (1.5)
	8	82.0 (0.8)	74.9 (2.1)	83.8 (1.0)	78.5 (1.8)	81.1 (1.1)	82.9 (1.1)
Interpret fossil tracks	4	53.5 (1.0)	44.7 (2.7)	58.8 (1.2)	36.4 (2.3)	56.9 (1.5)	50.0 (1.7)
	8	74.4 (1.2)	64.4 (2.0)	79.4 (1.3)	56.9 (2.6)	76.9 (1.4)	72.0 (1.6)
Seismograph's function	4	56.7 (1.4)	46.8 (3.1)	60.4 (1.8)	46.1 (2.1)	58.3 (1.6)	54.9 (1.8)
	8	82.4 (1.1)	75.4 (2.3)	85.1 (1.4)	73.4 (2.4)	83.4 (1.2)	81.5 (1.6)
Classifying fossils	4	50.0 (1.3)	37.9 (2.1)	54.2 (1.5)	38.2 (2.8)	46.4 (1.6)	53.7 (1.7)
	8	74.0 (1.0)	63.9 (2.4)	77.4 (1.2)	65.2 (3.4)	69.2 (1.9)	78.7 (1.0)
Measuring rate of flow	4	42.7 (1.3)	28.3 (2.4)	47.8 (1.6)	27.5 (2.2)	43.1 (1.4)	42.2 (1.9)
	8	71.4 (0.9)	56.8 (3.3)	75.5 (1.1)	59.6 (2.7)	69.4 (1.7)	73.4 (1.1)
Which mixture is solution?	4	49.5 (1.3)	43.8 (2.9)	50.5 (1.9)	49.1 (2.4)	49.7 (1.4)	49.3 (2.1)
	8	66.9 (1.3)	64.9 (2.6)	67.7 (1.4)	62.9 (2.3)	66.0 (1.6)	67.8 (1.7)
Graph: light preference-moths	4	30.4 (1.0)	21.9 (2.2)	33.5 (1.4)	22.4 (1.8)	29.5 (1.4)	31.3 (1.4)
	8	61.0 (1.3)	54.9 (2.6)	65.0 (1.6)	46.8 (3.4)	57.1 (1.7)	64.8 (1.8)
Graph: number of moths/day	4	29.9 (1.2)	21.3 (2.1)	33.3 (1.3)	21.4 (1.8)	32.1 (1.4)	27.7 (1.4)
	8	58.6 (1.1)	44.9 (3.2)	64.6 (1.3)	38.3 (2.9)	61.6 (1.6)	55.6 (1.3)
Stars and moon	4	47.9 (1.3)	30.7 (2.8)	56.0 (1.7)	21.0 (1.9)	52.2 (1.5)	43.7 (1.8)
	8	72.6 (0.9)	65.4 (3.0)	78.9 (1.0)	46.5 (2.7)	74.1 (1.4)	71.2 (1.5)
Dissolving sugar	4	73.1 (1.2)	63.0 (2.8)	76.8 (1.4)	60.4 (2.4)	72.01 (1.6)	74.1 (1.6)
	8	89.3 (0.9)	85.1 (1.9)	91.4 (1.1)	81.8 (2.5)	88.2 (1.4)	80.4 (0.9)
Stirring sugar sol'n	4	24.0 (1.3)	12.6 (1.9)	28.0 (1.5)	10.4 (1.8)	19.1 (1.3)	28.9 (1.8)
	8	56.4 (1.2)	50.6 (3.0)	60.3 (1.4)	42.3 (2.4)	49.6 (1.7)	63.0 (1.4)
Oceans contain most H_2O	4	76.1 (0.9)	71.7 (2.2)	80.4 (1.2)	59.4 (2.3)	78.9 (1.4)	73.1 (1.3)
	8	85.9 (0.9)	86.9 (1.8)	87.7 (1.1)	76.3 (2.6)	88.1 (0.9)	83.7 (1.1)

Source: Jones, Lee R., and others. *The 1990 Science Report Card: NAEP's Assessment of Fourth, Eighth, and Twelfth Graders*, Prepared by Educational Testing Service under contract with the National Center for Education Statistics, Office of Educational Research and Improvement, U.S. Department of Education, March 1992, pp. 160-172.

★ 217 ★

Academic Progress

Students Responding Correctly to Science Items - III

Data show weighted percentages of students responding correctly. Standard deviations are shown in parentheses.

Item description	Grade	Nation	Hispanic	White	Black	Male	Female
Simple food chain	4	58.9 (1.3)	48.5 (3.0)	64.4 (1.6)	42.3 (2.3)	60.4 (1.6)	57.3 (1.5)
	8	80.4 (1.2)	70.8 (2.4)	85.7 (1.3)	62.1 (3.4)	83.9 (1.2)	76.9 (1.8)
Opinion vs. observation	4	51.1 (1.6)	35.6 (2.1)	57.1 (2.0)	37.5 (3.0)	48.9 (2.0)	53.4 (2.1)
	8	81.2 (1.1)	72.1 (2.5)	85.9 (1.0)	67.3 (3.8)	78.5 (1.1)	84.0 (1.6)
Sound travel through table	4	57.1 (1.2)	48.3 (2.3)	61.5 (1.5)	42.2 (2.1)	52.2 (1.6)	62.2 (1.7)
	8	75.1 (1.1)	74.1 (2.8)	78.2 (1.1)	60.8 (3.6)	72.4 (1.3)	77.9 (1.5)
Liquid expands in thermometer	4	35.7 (1.2)	32.2 (2.4)	39.2 (1.6)	23.4 (1.8)	37.5 (1.7)	34.0 (1.7)
	8	56.6 (1.1)	43.7 (2.5)	62.4 (1.4)	41.6 (3.1)	63.1 (1.3)	50.2 (1.6)
Position of shadow at 2 pm	4	33.8 (1.0)	28.2 (2.2)	36.0 (1.2)	27.2 (1.9)	31.8 (1.3)	35.9 (1.5)
	8	52.1 (1.0)	45.9 (2.8)	55.8 (1.2)	38.2 (2.6)	49.3 (1.5)	55.0 (1.5)
Observation: ducks feeding	4	36.1 (1.0)	30.4 (2.6)	39.0 (1.2)	27.4 (2.4)	37.7 (1.6)	34.4 (1.6)
	8	57.3 (1.2)	40.0 (2.6)	62.6 (1.2)	47.6 (3.2)	55.1 (1.7)	59.6 (1.6)
Steps to identify minerals	4	35.3 (1.1)	30.1 (2.3)	37.3 (1.4)	30.5 (3.0)	34.9 (1.3)	35.8 (1.6)
	8	62.1 (1.3)	47.2 (3.3)	66.5 (1.5)	52.9 (3.6)	59.2 (1.6)	65.1 (1.8)
Battery/bulb	4	3.7 (0.6)	2.2 (1.0)	4.5 (0.8)	0.0 (0.0)	6.3 (1.1)	1.1 (0.4)
	8	11.0 (0.7)	10.3 (1.7)	12.3 (1.0)	6.2 (1.2)	19.7 (1.3)	2.3 (0.3)
Separate iron filings	4	32.3 (1.3)	16.8 (2.3)	38.4 (1.7)	14.0 (2.1)	36.1 (1.6)	28.5 (1.7)
	8	59.9 (1.2)	41.7 (3.5)	67.9 (1.3)	35.1 (2.8)	62.1 (1.6)	57.6 (1.8)
Separate sand/salt	4	0.1 (0.0)	0.0 (0.0)	0.1 (0.1)	0.0 (0.0)	0.1 (0.1)	0.1 (0.1)
	8	3.1 (0.4)	1.3 (0.6)	3.8 (0.5)	0.5 (0.3)	3.7 (0.6)	2.4 (0.5)
Positions of stars	4	55.6 (1.0)	45.5 (2.0)	62.3 (1.1)	31.0 (2.5)	54.4 (1.7)	56.8 (1.5)
	8	72.2 (1.0)	63.9 (2.8)	77.3 (1.1)	54.1 (2.7)	73.4 (1.4)	70.9 (1.5)
	12	82.7 (0.9)	79.8 (2.9)	86.0 (1.0)	67.3 (2.9)	84.2 (1.2)	81.3 (1.3)
Water-freezing temp	4	55.1 (1.4)	49.5 (2.8)	56.4 (1.9)	53.5 (2.5)	53.0 (1.6)	57.3 (1.9)
	8	53.2 (1.2)	50.1 (2.3)	53.2 (1.2)	54.0 (3.4)	54.0 (1.4)	52.3 (1.9)
	12	52.6 (1.3)	49.6 (3.8)	53.9 (1.5)	44.6 (3.0)	55.5 (1.9)	49.9 (1.5)
Fossils and Earth's age	4	61.1 (1.3)	48.2 (2.3)	65.5 (1.6)	49.1 (2.4)	59.4 (1.5)	62.9 (1.7)
	8	80.2 (0.9)	69.8 (2.3)	83.7 (0.9)	71.0 (2.6)	76.9 (1.5)	83.4 (0.9)
	12	89.8 (0.8)	85.3 (2.8)	91.8 (0.8)	82.4 (2.1)	87.8 (1.1)	91.7 (0.8)
Table: properties of sugar	4	58.9 (1.0)	40.0 (2.2)	63.9 (1.3)	43.9 (2.6)	56.3 (1.4)	61.5 (1.6)
	8	83.0 (0.7)	75.8 (2.7)	85.3 (0.9)	77.1 (2.2)	81.5 (1.0)	84.4 (1.1)
	12	87.7 (0.7)	84.3 (1.9)	88.8 (2.4)	82.4 (2.4)	86.3 (1.1)	89.0 (1.0)
Exp: water evaporation	4	56.2 (1.0)	41.8 (2.5)	61.7 (1.3)	40.7 (3.6)	51.7 (1.4)	60.9 (1.9)

[Continued]

★ 217 ★

Students Responding Correctly to Science Items - III

[Continued]

Item description	Grade	Nation	Hispanic	White	Black	Male	Female
	8	76.4 (0.9)	68.7 (2.2)	80.2 (1.0)	62.5 (3.4)	72.3 (1.4)	80.3 (1.0)
	12	89.3 (0.6)	81.5 (2.7)	91.8 (0.8)	79.4 (2.1)	86.5 (1.1)	91.9 (0.7)
Inheritance/cat's tails	4	43.1 (1.2)	30.6 (2.3)	47.7 (1.5)	29.8 (2.4)	42.8 (1.6)	43.4 (1.4)
	8	70.8 (1.1)	59.5 (2.5)	76.8 (1.3)	51.9 (3.1)	71.0 (1.5)	70.5 (1.3)
	12	86.1 (0.8)	80.4 (3.6)	89.9 (0.9)	68.5 (2.4)	84.9 (1.3)	87.2 (0.9)
Dinosaur/fish evolution	4	51.5 (0.9)	44.7 (2.4)	55.0 (1.3)	40.8 (2.9)	54.0 (1.6)	48.9 (1.6)
	8	65.8 (1.2)	62.1 (2.6)	69.1 (1.4)	51.8 (3.8)	69.9 (1.6)	61.7 (1.6)
	12	76.7 (1.0)	79.0 (2.5)	79.7 (1.3)	59.3 (3.4)	80.7 (1.3)	72.9 (1.3)
Continents' positions change	4	42.9 (1.2)	37.9 (2.5)	45.2 (1.7)	36.0 (3.0)	42.5 (1.5)	43.3 (1.7)
	8	63.9 (1.3)	52.9 (3.0)	68.9 (1.3)	47.1 (2.7)	66.4 (1.6)	61.5 (1.3)
	12	73.5 (1.3)	67.0 (3.5)	77.3 (1.5)	55.0 (3.0)	77.3 (1.9)	70.0 (1.5)
Heart and exercise	4	40.4 (1.1)	34.0 (2.2)	42.8 (1.4)	33.7 (2.3)	39.7 (1.5)	41.1 (1.4)
	8	63.1 (1.0)	49.3 (3.5)	68.2 (1.2)	48.6 (2.4)	63.1 (1.3)	63.1 (1.6)
	12	72.9 (1.1)	65.4 (3.6)	76.0 (1.4)	59.7 (3.6)	72.9 (1.5)	73.0 (1.3)
Time between lightning/thunder	4	35.7 (1.2)	27.0 (1.9)	39.7 (1.5)	23.9 (2.1)	37.5 (1.4)	33.8 (1.7)
	8	61.9 (1.0)	44.7 (2.9)	69.4 (1.1)	41.8 (2.6)	63.5 (1.5)	60.4 (1.6)
	12	78.6 (1.1)	60.8 (3.5)	84.4 (1.1)	58.8 (2.9)	80.7 (1.3)	76.6 (1.3)
Direction of sunrise/sunset	4	37.9 (1.0)	26.0 (2.2)	41.0 (1.5)	31.5 (2.4)	39.8 (1.5)	35.9 (1.6)
	8	55.5 (0.9)	38.2 (2.3)	61.7 (1.2)	40.3 (3.5)	60.2 (1.3)	51.0 (1.6)
	12	73.8 (0.9)	48.8 (3.3)	80.4 (0.8)	53.7 (3.6)	78.8 (1.0)	69.1 (1.3)
Cooling and condensation	4	34.7 (1.2)	31.4 (2.2)	34.7 (1.4)	38.3 (2.0)	35.6 (1.7)	33.7 (1.6)
	8	49.3 (1.2)	41.9 (2.8)	52.9 (1.2)	38.1 (3.0)	52.7 (1.5)	45.9 (1.6)
	12	61.7 (1.0)	50.7 (3.8)	65.6 (1.2)	43.3 (2.4)	68.2 (1.3)	55.6 (1.8)
Sci knowledge-observation	4	46.6 (1.3)	34.8 (2.5)	49.8 (1.7)	38.9 (1.8)	44.6 (1.9)	48.7 (1.6)
	8	73.9 (0.8)	62.7 (2.5)	77.6 (1.0)	63.1 (2.7)	69.2 (1.3)	78.6 (1.0)
	12	85.9 (0.9)	84.7 (2.5)	87.5 (1.0)	76.3 (2.4)	82.4 (1.3)	89.1 (1.0)
Table: melting points	4	48.8 (1.1)	39.6 (2.2)	52.7 (1.5)	38.1 (2.9)	51.4 (1.6)	46.3 (1.6)
	8	72.2 (0.8)	61.4 (2.6)	76.4 (1.1)	60.1 (2.5)	75.4 (1.3)	69.0 (1.5)
	12	80.9 (0.9)	72.8 (3.5)	84.6 (1.0)	65.4 (3.0)	83.7 (1.1)	78.3 (1.2)
Energy flow in food web	4	37.1 (1.1)	34.1 (2.2)	38.5 (1.5)	31.8 (2.4)	39.4 (1.7)	34.8 (1.3)
	8	55.6 (1.1)	41.7 (2.6)	59.7 (1.4)	46.6 (2.5)	56.2 (1.4)	55.1 (1.6)
	12	70.5 (0.8)	58.7 (3.1)	74.1 (1.0)	58.3 (3.1)	71.0 (1.3)	70.0 (1.0)

[Continued]

★ 217 ★

Students Responding Correctly to Science Items - III

[Continued]

Item description	Grade	Nation	Hispanic	White	Black	Male	Female
Land/H_2O temp difference	4	34.1 (1.2)	29.3 (2.2)	34.7 (1.5)	35.7 (2.6)	35.7 (1.6)	32.4 (1.7)
	8	46.5 (1.3)	37.8 (3.0)	50.2 (1.5)	35.5 (2.8)	47.7 (1.8)	45.4 (1.5)
	12	59.8 (1.3)	50.1 (3.4)	63.7 (1.5)	46.4 (3.4)	63.7 (1.6)	56.2 (1.4)
Exp: plant fertilizer	4	36.4 (1.2)	26.9 (2.4)	39.2 (1.3)	29.6 (3.0)	35.0 (1.6)	37.9 (1.9)
	8	62.6 (1.1)	53.4 (2.2)	67.0 (1.1)	48.7 (3.7)	62.2 (1.4)	62.9 (1.5)
	12	78.4 (0.9)	71.2 (2.9)	81.5 (1.1)	64.1 (2.7)	77.4 (1.4)	79.4 (1.2)

Source: Jones, Lee R., and others. *The 1990 Science Report Card: NAEP's Assessment of Fourth, Eighth, and Twelfth Graders,* Prepared by Educational Testing Service under contract with the National Center for Education Statistics, Office of Educational Research and Improvement, U.S. Department of Education, March 1992, pp. 160-172.

★ 218 ★

Academic Progress

Students Responding Correctly to Science Items - IV

Data show weighted percentages of students responding correctly. Standard deviations are shown in parentheses.

Item description	Grade	Nation	Hispanic	White	Black	Male	Female
Volcanoes and igneous rocks	4	28.8 (1.1)	27.8 (2.2)	28.8 (1.5)	28.7 (2.4)	31.3 (1.8)	26.2 (1.2)
	8	36.3 (1.1)	28.7 (2.6)	37.8 (1.1)	33.0 (2.7)	36.7 (1.5)	36.0 (1.3)
	12	32.6 (0.8)	24.7 (3.2)	34.4 (0.9)	26.3 (2.8)	34.5 (1.6)	30.8 (1.3)
Hypothesis-ideas to be tested	4	26.7 (1.1)	23.3 (2.7)	27.5 (1.5)	23.1 (2.1)	26.8 (1.5)	26.5 (1.5)
	8	62.8 (1.3)	47.4 (2.7)	67.9 (1.6)	49.6 (3.6)	59.8 (2.0)	65.7 (1.6)
	12	74.5 (0.9)	60.6 (2.7)	78.1 (1.2)	64.9 (2.7)	72.8 (1.3)	76.0 (1.3)
Diagram: Leaf's function	4	19.3 (0.9)	17.9 (2.0)	19.7 (1.1)	17.7 (1.9)	21.1 (1.3)	17.4 (1.4)
	8	23.4 (1.2)	18.3 (1.9)	25.4 (1.3)	16.5 (2.3)	29.4 (1.7)	17.5 (1.3)
	12	29.8 (1.1)	18.0 (3.1)	31.9 (1.2)	22.7 (2.4)	37.1 (1.6)	23.0 (1.4)
Force on rock	4	60.5 (1.2)	46.9 (2.4)	65.3 (1.4)	47.5 (3.2)	66.9 (1.6)	53.7 (1.8)
	8	80.2 (0.9)	70.2 (2.1)	85.1 (1.0)	64.6 (2.6)	85.4 (1.0)	75.1 (1.3)
	12	83.9 (1.0)	83.1 (2.1)	87.7 (0.8)	65.7 (2.1)	87.9 (1.0)	80.1 (1.5)
Light hits mirror	4	35.7 (1.1)	25.6 (2.2)	41.0 (1.3)	18.3 (1.6)	44.2 (1.7)	26.9 (1.5)
	8	62.6 (1.2)	53.1 (2.7)	69.0 (1.3)	37.2 (3.0)	72.7 (1.2)	52.3 (1.8)
	12	65.9 (1.2)	55.4 (3.4)	71.5 (1.3)	43.2 (2.9)	75.1 (1.7)	57.1 (1.4)
Falling glasses	4	32.7 (1.3)	29.9 (2.5)	35.8 (1.7)	21.5 (2.7)	35.7 (1.7)	29.7 (1.7)
	8	40.6 (1.1)	37.9 (2.6)	42.4 (1.1)	35.0 (2.8)	45.2 (1.6)	35.9 (1.6)
	12	41.9 (1.1)	32.8 (3.3)	46.1 (1.3)	25.2 (3.3)	50.6 (1.5)	33.6 (1.5)
Thermometer	4	10.9 (0.7)	6.2 (1.2)	12.9 (0.9)	6.0 (1.1)	12.8 (1.0)	8.8 (0.9)
	8	46.9 (1.2)	36.2 (2.2)	52.1 (1.5)	28.9 (3.0)	49.6 (1.7)	44.2 (1.6)
	12	66.2 (1.1)	56.2 (4.2)	70.2 (1.3)	49.6 (2.1)	71.7 (1.6)	61.1 (1.4)

[Continued]

★ 218 ★

Students Responding Correctly to Science Items - IV

[Continued]

Item description	Grade	Nation	Hispanic	White	Black	Male	Female
Half moon	4	12.1 (1.0)	6.9 (1.2)	14.3 (1.2)	5.4 (1.3)	12.4 (1.2)	11.9 (1.2)
	8	28.9 (0.9)	15.7 (1.6)	33.2 (1.2)	16.5 (2.7)	31.6 (1.1)	26.2 (1.4)
	12	42.2 (1.1)	31.6 (2.9)	47.9 (1.3)	15.4 (2.2)	49.4 (1.4)	35.4 (1.4)
Solar eclipse	4	26.0 (1.2)	15.0 (2.2)	30.9 (1.4)	10.5 (1.5)	33.0 (1.6)	18.8 (1.6)
	8	54.4 (1.2)	41.5 (2.2)	61.3 (1.4)	29.8 (3.1)	63.6 (1.6)	45.1 (1.6)
	12	66.5 (1.3)	57.6 (3.8)	73.0 (1.6)	33.8 (2.7)	78.8 (1.5)	54.9 (1.7)
Cross-section of worm	4	14.7 (0.9)	9.5 (1.8)	16.4 (1.1)	10.4 (1.4)	13.5 (1.1)	15.9 (1.4)
	8	29.1 (1.2)	23.9 (2.3)	31.3 (1.3)	23.7 (3.2)	29.6 (1.3)	28.6 (1.6)
	12	41.6 (1.3)	32.7 (2.8)	44.7 (1.5)	27.1 (2.7)	46.3 (2.0)	37.1 (1.4)
Path of object	4	2.7 (0.5)	3.3 (1.1)	3.1 (0.6)	0.1 (0.1)	3.7 (0.7)	1.7 (0.5)
	8	6.1 (0.5)	3.8 (1.2)	7.0 (0.6)	3.8 (1.5)	9.1 (0.9)	3.0 (0.5)
	12	16.0 (0.6)	9.2 (2.5)	18.5 (0.8)	3.3 (0.9)	22.8 (1.4)	9.6 (0.8)
Path of ball from tube	4	28.2 (1.3)	21.3 (2.1)	31.0 (1.8)	19.3 (1.7)	35.6 (1.9)	20.9 (1.5)
	8	46.6 (1.0)	43.0 (2.5)	50.5 (1.3)	32.1 (3.0)	56.7 (1.5)	36.5 (1.2)
	12	57.8 (1.0)	52.3 (3.0)	61.6 (1.1)	38.7 (3.0)	70.7 (1.3)	45.7 (1.3)
Predator/prey graph	4	11.7 (0.8)	6.1 (1.8)	13.6 (0.9)	5.6 (2.0)	13.2 (1.1)	10.2 (1.2)
	8	42.8 (1.2)	27.5 (2.9)	48.2 (1.6)	23.6 (3.1)	46.6 (1.5)	38.9 (1.4)
	12	64.9 (1.1)	45.8 (3.5)	71.3 (1.0)	35.9 (3.1)	70.5 (1.1)	59.6 (1.4)
Finding cause of a sore throat	4	41.8 (1.1)	35.0 (2.5)	46.7 (1.3)	25.9 (2.3)	36.3 (1.5)	47.5 (1.6)
	8	68.7 (1.0)	56.9 (3.3)	72.4 (1.2)	58.6 (2.8)	62.1 (1.6)	75.5 (1.3)
	12	84.0 (0.7)	76.3 (3.3)	87.3 (0.9)	72.2 (2.2)	79.1 (1.2)	88.6 (0.8)
Plants bend toward light	4	27.3 (1.0)	26.8 (2.5)	28.7 (1.2)	20.5 (2.1)	28.4 (1.6)	26.3 (1.4)
	8	55.1 (1.3)	47.5 (2.8)	60.4 (1.4)	35.3 (3.5)	59.6 (1.7)	50.6 (1.7)
	12	64.4 (1.2)	55.4 (3.6)	69.3 (1.5)	42.3 (3.0)	67.0 (1.6)	62.2 (1.8)
Heights of children compared	8	70.1 (0.9)	59.0 (2.8)	74.4 (1.1)	55.3 (2.6)	68.2 (1.4)	72.0 (1.6)
Best temp for ivy growth	8	46.8 (1.3)	39.7 (3.3)	48.9 (1.5)	39.2 (2.6)	45.5 (1.6)	48.0 (1.6)
Effect of temp on ball's bounce	8	48.8 (1.2)	38.8 (2.0)	52.1 (1.4)	37.9 (2.8)	46.5 (1.6)	51.0 (1.6)
How measure # of snowflakes	8	62.1 (1.0)	54.8 (2.6)	64.4 (1.2)	54.3 (3.1)	59.4 (1.5)	64.8 (1.7)
How report # of snowflakes	8	36.5 (1.1)	32.6 (2.5)	39.1 (1.4)	26.3 (3.3)	36.4 (1.7)	36.5 (1.3)
Cause of ocean tides	8	52.5 (1.5)	38.5 (2.5)	58.3 (1.9)	31.5 (2.8)	58.6 (1.6)	46.4 (2.0)
Meaning of specific heat	8	15.7 (0.6)	14.0 (1.9)	15.8 (0.8)	15.7 (2.4)	18.0 (1.2)	13.4 (0.9)
NRG source for photosynthesis	8	77.8 (1.2)	72.4 (2.4)	80.6 (1.4)	66.4 (3.4)	77.8 (1.6)	77.9 (1.4)

[Continued]

★ 218 ★

Students Responding Correctly to Science Items - IV

[Continued]

Item description	Grade	Nation	Hispanic	White	Black	Male	Female
Mixing red/green light	8	46.8 (1.3)	41.6 (2.6)	47.5 (1.6)	47.6 (3.2)	42.0 (1.8)	51.5 (1.8)
Hypothesis: river's water level	8	37.1 (1.3)	29.5 (2.2)	38.2 (1.5)	37.9 (3.5)	36.0 (1.7)	38.1 (1.7)
Gravity and 2 objects' mass	8	35.7 (1.1)	32.1 (2.4)	37.0 (1.4)	32.8 (2.5)	38.2 (1.5)	33.3 (1.7)
Ice caps not on moon's surface	8	54.2 (1.3)	49.2 (2.3)	58.2 (1.5)	38.7 (3.7)	58.8 (1.6)	49.8 (1.7)
Cause of changing seasons	8	70.7 (1.2)	52.8 (3.3)	74.5 (1.2)	67.7 (3.9)	69.3 (1.6)	72.0 (1.5)
Living/made of cells	8	81.2 (0.8)	77.3 (1.8)	83.7 (0.9)	72.5 (2.8)	79.9 (1.1)	82.5 (1.3)
Exp: Food pref of rabbits	8	46.5 (1.1)	49.3 (2.7)	45.8 (1.4)	47.5 (1.4)	46.6 (1.8)	46.3 (1.4)
Star formation in Japan	8	30.5 (1.0)	32.0 (2.8)	30.3 (1.0)	28.0 (2.0)	31.6 (1.6)	29.3 (1.2)
Best way to survey students	8	43.3 (1.2)	38.2 (2.7)	46.2 (1.4)	31.8 (2.8)	40.2 (1.7)	46.4 (1.5)
Museum habitats	8	68.8 (1.1)	59.1 (2.6)	72.5 (1.6)	55.0 (3.5)	62.6 (1.8)	75.1 (1.5)

Source: Jones, Lee R., and others. *The 1990 Science Report Card: NAEP's Assessment of Fourth, Eighth, and Twelfth Graders*, Prepared by Educational Testing Service under contract with the National Center for Education Statistics, Office of Educational Research and Improvement, U.S. Department of Education, March 1992, pp. 160-172.

★ 219 ★

Academic Progress

Students Responding Correctly to Science Items - V

Data show weighted percentages of students responding correctly. Standard deviations are shown in parentheses.

Item description	Grade	Nation	Hispanic	White	Black	Male	Female
Wolves and caribou	8	37.4 (1.1)	25.1 (2.4)	41.4 (1.3)	22.0 (2.2)	40.4 (1.9)	34.3 (1.4)
Cells, tissues, organs	8	39.3 (1.0)	27.8 (2.4)	43.0 (1.3)	28.3 (2.2)	39.2 (1.5)	39.5 (1.3)
Present energy source in U.S.	8	44.3 (1.0)	26.3 (2.2)	49.0 (1.4)	30.2 (2.6)	46.8 (1.8)	41.7 (1.6)
Acceleration of ball on ramp	8	56.3 (1.0)	46.5 (3.1)	60.7 (1.1)	41.9 (2.9)	59.7 (1.5)	60.7 (1.1)
Predicting snowfall	8	55.6 (1.2)	42.1 (2.6)	60.0 (1.5)	40.9 (2.7)	53.6 (1.9)	57.5 (1.2)
Human error in measuring time	8	37.9 (1.1)	30.8 (2.7)	40.7 (1.3)	28.8 (2.6)	43.0 (1.4)	32.6 (1.4)
Seasonal rainfall graph	8	37.3 (1.0)	29.4 (2.6)	39.7 (1.2)	31.2 (2.6)	37.2 (1.5)	37.5 (1.2)
Object with most inertia	8	39.3 (1.1)	28.3 (2.2)	42.7 (1.2)	28.9 (2.8)	44.0 (1.7)	34.8 (1.2)
	12	50.7 (1.1)	39.6 (4.8)	54.8 (1.3)	35.2 (2.7)	61.3 (1.6)	40.9 (1.5)

[Continued]

★ 219 ★

Students Responding Correctly to Science Items - V

[Continued]

Item description	Grade	Nation	Hispanic	White	Black	Male	Female
Exp: appropriate controls	8	41.2 (1.1)	36.6 (2.1)	43.4 (1.5)	32.2 (2.3)	40.8 (1.4)	41.5 (1.6)
	12	59.4 (1.2)	48.0 (3.6)	654.7 (1.6)	36.8 (2.1)	57.7 (1.9)	61.0 (1.4)
Evidence that light is energy	8	58.9 (1.1)	49.9 (2.5)	62.9 (1.3)	44.2 (3.3)	61.3 (1.5)	56.5 (1.7)
	12	75.0 (1.1)	64.0 (4.2)	78.7 (1.0)	61.8 (3.5)	77.5 (1.6)	72.6 (1.4)
Salt left after evaporation	8	23.6 (0.9)	20.6 (2.2)	24.2 (1.1)	22.0 (2.2)	25.5 (1.6)	21.8 (1.3)
	12	34.6 (1.1)	25.6 (3.2)	37.7 (1.3)	21.3 (2.8)	39.1 (1.4)	30.4 (1.2)
Estimated age of Earth	8	23.8 (1.0)	22.3 (2.4)	25.4 (1.2)	16.0 (2.1)	24.2 (1.5)	23.4 (1.5)
	12	32.3 (1.1)	27.9 (2.6)	34.0 (1.2)	22.2 (2.8)	34.5 (1.8)	30.3 (1.2)
Observing spider and web	8	54.7 (1.2)	40.3 (2.8)	61.2 (1.5)	35.5 (2.4)	54.8 (1.6)	54.5 (1.5)
	12	72.8 (1.3)	56.6 (3.8)	78.6 (1.3)	51.2 (3.9)	74.4 (1.4)	71.4 (1.7)
Exp: Measure vine growth	8	57.6 (1.1)	52.8 (2.6)	60.2 (1.4)	47.9 (2.7)	55.2 (1.4)	60.1 (1.6)
	12	67.0 (1.1)	60.3 (2.8)	68.9 (1.3)	60.5 (3.0)	66.2 (1.6)	67.8 (1.6)
Measure mass with spring scale	8	64.6 (1.1)	49.3 (3.1)	69.0 (1.3)	53.5 (3.3)	62.0 (1.5)	67.2 (1.7)
	12	76.4 (1.0)	69.3 (2.6)	78.5 (1.2)	68.3 (2.8)	77.9 (1.3)	74.9 (1.3)
Exp design: control light	8	72.1 (0.9)	62.9 (3.3)	74.6 (1.2)	66.8 (2.6)	67.6 (1.2)	76.7 (1.2)
	12	80.8 (1.1)	70.4 (3.9)	83.6 (1.2)	71.6 (3.1)	78.5 (1.1)	83.0 (1.6)
Exp design: apply fertilizer	8	50.3 (1.0)	38.3 (3.0)	56.2 (1.3)	30.3 (2.0)	48.1 (1.4)	52.6 (1.8)
	12	68.8 (1.3)	53.1 (3.4)	75.0 (1.3)	43.9 (3.2)	68.3 (1.7)	69.3 (1.6)
Exp design: sample size	8	27.0 (1.1)	17.5 (2.3)	31.0 (1.4)	15.3 (2.3)	31.1 (1.5)	31.0 (1.4)
	12	46.3 (1.4)	27.9 (3.1)	53.3 (1.5)	20.0 (2.6)	53.9 (1.7)	39.0 (1.7)
Hypothesis: salt/container	8	49.7 (1.4)	44.7 (2.7)	52.7 (1.7)	38.0 (2.7)	51.5 (1.5)	47.9 (1.9)
	12	66.5 (0.9)	59.9 (3.2)	68.4 (1.0)	58.9 (2.7)	68.0 (1.5)	65.0 (1.4)
Measure angle of Polaris	8	56.3 (1.3)	53.2 (3.6)	58.9 (1.2)	48.2 (3.5)	53.5 (1.7)	59.2 (1.4)
	12	64.5 (1.0)	61.8 (2.7)	64.7 (1.3)	65.3 (3.2)	62.9 (1.4)	66.1 (1.8)
Earth's temp from core to crust	8	38.3 (1.2)	29.0 (2.9)	44.2 (1.4)	18.5 (2.3)	40.1 (1.6)	36.5 (1.7)
	12	51.3 (1.1)	39.3 (3.7)	56.2 (1.2)	31.5 (2.4)	53.5 (1.6)	49.2 (1.7)
Dinosaur extinction	8	49.0 (1.4)	41.5 (2.4)	51.8 (1.7)	38.5 (2.9)	49.6 (1.8)	48.3 (1.7)
	12	60.2 (1.3)	59.2 (3.3)	63.2 (1.5)	42.1 (2.6)	65.0 (1.7)	55.6 (1.8)
Wet/dry bulb: measure RH	8	37.9 (1.1)	34.4 (2.3)	39.8 (1.4)	30.7 (3.0)	39.5 (1.4)	36.3 (1.9)
	12	53.2 (1.4)	44.5 (3.7)	57.0 (1.7)	38.2 (2.7)	55.5 (1.7)	51.1 (1.7)
Wet/dry bulb: effect of temp	8	39.1 (1.0)	37.2 (3.3)	39.4 (1.3)	40.7 (2.9)	40.4 (1.4)	37.8 (1.4)
	12	49.0 (1.1)	42.2 (2.7)	52.6 (1.3)	33.4 (2.6)	51.2 (1.8)	47.0 (1.5)

[Continued]

★ 219 ★

Students Responding Correctly to Science Items - V

[Continued]

Item description	Grade	Nation	Hispanic	White	Black	Male	Female
Exp: compare eating rates	8	29.2 (0.9)	21.2 (2.1)	31.4 (1.2)	26.3 (2.3)	28.7 (1.3)	29.8 (1.1)
	12	39.9 (1.1)	28.1 (3.0)	43.0 (1.4)	29.7 (2.2)	39.5 (1.4)	40.4 (1.5)
NE wind blows toward SW	8	32.8 (1.0)	24.1 (2.1)	35.6 (1.2)	23.7 (2.0)	38.2 (1.4)	27.3 (1.4)
	12	47.5 (1.3)	34.1 (2.9)	53.2 (1.5)	24.2 (2.5)	54.3 (1.7)	41.0 (1.8)
Diagram of folded mts	8	44.0 (1.7)	35.7 (3.5)	47.5 (2.2)	33.7 (3.2)	47.4 (1.8)	40.5 (2.3)
	12	48.5 (1.2)	46.6 (3.4)	51.1 (1.4)	35.1 (2.2)	53.8 (1.2)	43.4 (1.9)
Exp: Moisture pref of insects	8	41.5 (1.0)	36.7 (2.1)	44.2 (1.2)	31.9 (2.7)	41.5 (1.4)	41.4 (1.3)
	12	57.4 (1.2)	52.6 (3.0)	60.2 (1.4)	45.7 (3.2)	59.1 (1.6)	55.9 (1.5)
Volume of space between rocks	8	38.5 (1.2)	33.3 (2.9)	41.2 (1.5)	27.2 (2.6)	40.4 (1.4)	36.5 (1.8)
	12	53.9 (1.3)	49.9 (3.1)	56.7 (1.5)	37.6 (2.8)	56.8 (1.7)	51.2 (1.7)
Relative age of rock layers	8	26.7 (1.1)	18.5 (2.4)	30.0 (1.4)	16.8 (2.0)	25.3 (1.2)	28.1 (1.7)
	12	38.9 (1.2)	25.7 (3.0)	42.8 (1.3)	22.1 (2.8)	37.6 (1.7)	40.1 (1.5)
Determine best electrolyte	8	20.6 (0.9)	15.8 (2.4)	22.5 (1.1)	13.2 (1.9)	20.5 (1.2)	20.8 (1.4)
	12	28.2 (1.3)	21.6 (3.2)	30.7 (1.5)	17.8 (2.7)	30.6 (1.7)	26.0 (1.5)
Interpret graph: dinosaurs	8	26.7 (1.1)	27.4 (3.4)	26.8 (1.2)	25.2 (3.1)	28.3 (1.6)	24.9 (1.6)
	12	27.8 (1.2)	28.8 (3.8)	28.2 (1.3)	25.1 (2.3)	33.5 (1.7)	22.5 (1.4)

Source: Jones, Lee R., and others. *The 1990 Science Report Card: NAEP's Assessment of Fourth, Eighth, and Twelfth Graders*, Prepared by Educational Testing Service under contract with the National Center for Education Statistics, Office of Educational Research and Improvement, U.S. Department of Education, March 1992, pp. 160-172.

★ 220 ★

Academic Progress

Students Responding Correctly to Science Items - VI

Data show weighted percentages of students responding correctly. Standard deviations are shown in parentheses.

Item description	Grade	Nation	Hispanic	White	Black	Male	Female
Best battery	8	66.5 (1.1)	60.4 (3.0)	68.2 (1.1)	58.5 (3.6)	68.5 (1.3)	64.5 (1.6)
	12	69.6 (1.2)	58.9 (2.7)	71.8 (1.4)	63.0 (3.6)	68.9 (1.7)	70.2 (1.5)
How to use info	8	60.9 (1.6)	47.0 (3.0)	64.4 (1.8)	47.4 (3.0)	59.5 (2.0)	62.4 (1.8)
	12	70.8 (1.3)	59.5 (4.1)	74.5 (1.4)	54.0 (4.6)	69.2 (1.8)	72.2 (1.5)
Energy from battery	8	4.8 (0.9)	0.8 (0.7)	5.3 (1.1)	6.0 (1.3)	5.5 (1.1)	4.0 (1.0)
	12	11.5 (1.1)	10.7 (3.2)	12.8 (1.2)	4.0 (1.4)	16.6 (1.9)	6.7. (0.9)
Temperature graph	8	65.9 (1.3)	55.2 (2.9)	68.8 (1.5)	58.3 (4.1)	64.8 (1.4)	67.0 (2.0)
	12	77.8 (1.2)	64.8 (5.0)	81.0 (1.2)	64.3 (3.2)	80.9 (1.5)	74.9 (1.6)

[Continued]

★ 220 ★

Students Responding Correctly to Science Items - VI

[Continued]

Item description	Grade	Nation	Hispanic	White	Black	Male	Female
Image of retina	8	32.9 (1.0)	25.8 (3.3)	37.2 (1.2)	13.3 (2.0)	40.2 (1.6)	25.7 (1.3)
	12	42.2 (1.3)	32.3 (4.4)	45.4 (1.5)	24.3 (3.8)	53.2 (1.7)	31.8 (1.6)
Earth's crust motion	8	13.8 (0.9)	12.7 (2.0)	15.3 (1.2)	4.7 (1.6)	15.8 (1.2)	11.9 (1.2)
	12	14.8 (0.9)	10.2 (2.8)	15.9 (1.0)	11.0 (2.3)	15.9 (1.2)	13.8 (1.2)
Blood flow in heart	8	15.1 (1.1)	7.9 (1.9)	17.4 (1.4)	7.0 (1.8)	18.2 (1.7)	11.9 (1.2)
	12	24.5 (1.0)	16.6 (3.0)	26.6 (1.2)	13.1 (2.1)	30.9 (1.5)	18.6 (1.2)
Observing a sealed aquarium	8	54.3 (1.1)	49.8 (2.8)	56.9 (1.1)	45.5 (3.2)	54.5 (1.3)	54.0 (1.6)
	12	70.8 (0.9)	60.2 (3.7)	73.8 (1.1)	59.5 (3.1)	71.2 (1.5)	70.5 (1.4)
Tissues and cells	8	57.0 (1.4)	47.9 (2.7)	59.6 (1.8)	48.1 (2.8)	60.1 (1.5)	53.8 (1.7)
	12	63.1 (1.2)	56.3 (3.8)	65.2 (1.5)	54.7 (2.0)	64.6 (1.7)	61.7 (1.4)
Melting crushed ice	8	44.3 (1.1)	34.7 (2.5)	48.8 (1.4)	28.0 (2.3)	48.3 (1.5)	40.3 (1.5)
	12	59.2 (1.2)	49.9 (4.3)	65.0 (1.5)	33.7 (2.8)	66.1 (1.5)	53.1 (1.6)
Sulfur dioxide and acid rain	8	55.3 (1.1)	40.9 (3.3)	58.9 (1.3)	46.2 (2.6)	59.5 (1.6)	51.1 (1.7)
	12	66.6 (1.2)	56.7 (4.5)	70.8 (1.5)	50.6 (2.8)	74.7 (1.4)	59.2 (1.7)
Components of solar system	8	68.9 (1.1)	62.7 (2.3)	72.4 (1.4)	57.7 (2.9)	69.7 (1.7)	68.2 (1.5)
	12	69.3 (1.1)	62.4 (3.4)	71.9 (1.2)	58.2 (3.2)	71.5 (1.5)	67.4 (1.4)
Communicating on the moon	8	58.7 (1.3)	54.5 (3.0)	61.8 (1.6)	45.9 (2.6)	63.4 (1.8)	53.9 (1.5)
	12	67.1 (1.0)	66.1 (3.9)	68.5 (1.3)	57.9 (3.3)	74.3 (1.5)	60.5 (1.4)
Angle of reflection	8	55.4 (1.0)	45.9 (2.0)	59.4 (1.2)	40.6 (2.6)	62.0 (1.6)	48.7 (1.5)
	12	62.5 (1.1)	57.5 (3.2)	66.3 (1.3)	46.1 (2.6)	73.1 (1.6)	52.9 (1.5)
Earth's crust: oldest layers	8	47.7 (1.3)	42.0 (3.1)	51.6 (1.5)	31.9 (3.2)	49.7 (1.8)	45.6 (1.5)
	12	50.7 (1.1)	50.9 (3.9)	53.1 (1.2)	38.5 (2.7)	49.3 (1.6)	51.9 (1.4)
Earth's crust: curved layers	8	41.3 (1.3)	39.7 (2.4)	43.9 (1.5)	31.3 (3.1)	43.4 (1.6)	39.1 (1.5)
	12	44.7 (1.1)	38.3 (2.4)	47.1 (1.2)	34.4 (3.0)	51.3 (1.4)	38.7 (1.5)
Rain and corn growth	8	48.5 (1.2)	38.0 (2.5)	51.5 (1.5)	41.4 (2.6)	50.4 (1.7)	46.6 (1.5)
	12	68.1 (1.1)	60.0 (3.5)	70.9 (1.4)	56.0 (2.1)	69.6 (1.2)	66.7 (1.8)
Meaning of 20% chance of rain	8	19.9 (1.0)	16.3 (1.8)	22.0 (1.4)	12.4 (1.3)	23.6 (1.4)	16.2 (1.2)
	12	40.0 (1.0)	26.2 (2.4)	44.6 (1.2)	23.6 (2.5)	48.0 (1.4)	32.7 (1.4)
Water evaporation	12	37.3 (1.4)	36.6 (4.2)	37.4 (1.6)	35.5 (2.8)	35.8 (2.0)	38.7 (1.7)
Reaction rates during equilib	12	33.5 (1.0)	32.3 (2.9)	33.5 (1.2)	29.7 (2.6)	37.4 (1.7)	29.8 (2.6)
What is accuracy?	12	68.6 (1.2)	58.9 (4.7)	71.2 (1.4)	55.3 (3.9)	64.5 (1.4)	72.4 (1.6)

[Continued]

★ 220 ★

Students Responding Correctly to Science Items - VI

[Continued]

Item description	Grade	Nation	Hispanic	White	Black	Male	Female
Graph: population/adaptation	12	66.8 (1.0)	64.9 (2.7)	68.5 (1.1)	60.2 (3.1)	70.0 (1.5)	64.0 (1.4)
Einstein's $E=MC^2$	12	78.8 (0.9)	68.2 (3.4)	81.1 (1.1)	70.8 (2.6)	81.1 (1.1)	76.9 (1.1)
Inertia of lead-filled box	12	57.4 (0.9)	50.6 (3.3)	61.0 (1.1)	44.0 (2.5)	60.9 (1.5)	54.3 (1.1)
Test predictions w/experiment	12	64.5 (1.1)	52.3 (2.7)	68.4 (1.2)	50.4 (3.3)	59.9 (1.6)	68.7 (1.3)
Heat gas, increase pressure	12	67.2 (0.9)	61.8 (2.7)	70.0 (1.1)	55.1 (3.2)	67.3 (1.3)	67.1 (1.4)
Exp: effect of wt on pendulum	12	48.6 (1.4)	35.3 (3.1)	53.3 (1.7)	30.2 (2.8)	48.9 (2.1)	48.3 (1.5)
Relation of pressure/altitude	12	52.2 (1.4)	49.9 (3.7)	53.7 (1.5)	46.3 (2.9)	53.6 (1.7)	50.9 (1.7)
Which can be tested	12	54.5 (1.3)	45.1 (3.2)	58.3 (1.6)	41.1 (2.9)	53.3 (1.8)	55.6 (1.6)
Graph: greatest solubility	12	72.6 (0.9)	66.8 (2.6)	74.7 (1.0)	63.5 (2.9)	73.6 (1.3)	71.7 (1.4)
Graph: grams to be dissolved	12	51.7 (1.2)	43.1 (2.7)	55.1 (1.5)	35.4 (3.4)	54.3 (1.9)	49.4 (3.4)
Mass increase as iron rusts	12	18.2 (0.9)	16.7 (3.2)	18.6 (1.1)	14.2 (2.6)	22.6 (1.5)	14.1 (1.0)
Exp: test air pollution	12	65.4 (1.2)	54.5 (3.6)	69.3 (1.4)	51.2 (2.3)	65.0 (1.4)	65.8 (1.8)
Diagram: new crust	12	29.2 (1.2)	26.1 (2.9)	30.2 (1.4)	27.8 (2.3)	31.9 (1.4)	26.7 (1.5)
Diagram: subduction	12	51.4 (1.1)	45.6 (2.6)	54.6 (1.2)	38.0 (2.9)	56.8 (1.8)	46.5 (1.4)
Graph: immune system memory	12	36.7 (1.1)	30.8 (3.0)	39.1 (1.4)	27.1 (2.2)	41.4 (1.7)	32.5 (1.1)
Table: pulling objects	12	29.4 (0.9)	23.3 (2.6)	31.9 (1.2)	18.1 (2.3)	35.8 (1.5)	23.6 (1.1)

Source: Jones, Lee R., and others. *The 1990 Science Report Card: NAEP's Assessment of Fourth, Eighth, and Twelfth Graders,* Prepared by Educational Testing Service under contract with the National Center for Education Statistics, Office of Educational Research and Improvement, U.S. Department of Education, March 1992, pp. 160-172.

★ 221 ★

Academic Progress

Students Responding Correctly to Science Items - VII

Data show weighted percentages of students responding correctly. Standard deviations are shown in parentheses.

Item description	Grade	Nation	Hispanic	White	Black	Male	Female
Graph: temp/O_2 consumed	12	43.0 (1.3)	31.3 (3.6)	46.5 (1.4)	30.9 (3.0)	41.6 (1.8)	44.2 (1.4)
Graph: O_2 consumed at 26 C	12	25.1 (0.8)	24.8 (2.9)	25.4 (0.9)	20.9 (2.2)	24.7 (1.6)	25.5 (1.2)
Air movement in high pressure	12	40.5 (1.2)	31.6 (3.1)	43.2 (1.3)	29.8 (2.3)	44.1 (1.9)	37.2 (1.3)
Explosion of star	12	28.8 (1.2)	26.1 (3.6)	31.1 (1.5)	15.4 (2.4)	34.7 (1.8)	23.6 (1.3)
Genetic pedigree/sex-linked	12	17.6 (1.0)	14.2 (3.3)	18.2 (1.2)	14.6 (2.3)	14.7 (1.2)	20.1 (1.5)
Make 1-molar solution	12	22.6 (1.0)	25.5 (3.2)	21.0 (1.1)	28.1 (3.5)	23.1 (1.3)	22.2 (1.3)
Why strawberries appear red	12	37.6 (1.4)	25.3 (4.0)	41.5 (1.7)	21.5 (2.0)	40.8 (2.1)	34.8 (1.8)
Colors in white light	12	59.4 (1.2)	48.4 (3.3)	63.3 (1.5)	44.9 (3.0)	60.6 (1.7)	58.4 (1.4)
Table: electrical conductors	12	70.3 (1.1)	71.6 (2.5)	70.6 (1.3)	66.7 (2.5)	70.5 (1.8)	70.1 (1.1)
Function of plant stem	12	59.9 (1.1)	48.2 (3.6)	66.3 (1.2)	34.5 (3.0)	59.6 (1.7)	60.1 (1.6)
Positions of stars/planets	12	57.6 (1.0)	61.5 (2.8)	57.0 (1.3)	56.8 (2.8)	56.8 (1.4)	58.4 (1.5)
Increase strength of magnet	12	58.3 (1.1)	55.5 (3.3)	59.8 (1.2)	52.4 (2.6)	59.8 (1.4)	56.9 (1.5)
Probability of m/f children	12	50.8 (1.2)	49.1 (3.2)	52.5 (1.4)	42.3 (2.8)	47.7 (1.5)	53.6 (1.8)
Exp: dissolve seltzer	12	43.2 (1.1)	32.8 (3.0)	47.8 (1.2)	26.3 (2.3)	42.5 (1.3)	43.8 (1.6)
Gravity effect on satellites	12	68.1 (1.0)	67.1 (2.9)	69.0 (1.2)	63.3 (2.4)	68.5 (1.6)	67.8 (1.4)
Phylogenic-trees	12	36.2 (0.9)	36.5 (2.2)	37.3 (1.0)	30.6 (2.7)	37.7 (1.5)	34.9 (1.6)
Steps to develop vaccine	12	34.6 (0.8)	29.4 (3.2)	34.9 (1.0)	34.5 (3.0)	33.7 (1.1)	34.9 (1.0)
Answer question w/measurement	12	51.2 (1.3)	47.9 (3.0)	54.0 (1.4)	37.9 (2.8)	51.2 (1.6)	51.3 (1.5)
1-liter samples of gases	12	16.2 (0.9)	20.5 (2.4)	16.0 (1.1)	12.1 (1.9)	17.1 (1.3)	15.3 (1.3)
Graph: temp/energy	12	25.2 (1.0)	24.0 (2.9)	25.0 (1.3)	21.9 (1.9)	27.1 (1.6)	23.6 (1.2)
Ways to measure reaction rate	12	25.4 (1.0)	24.4 (3.1)	25.7 (1.2)	22.7 (1.9)	26.3 (1.6)	24.6 (1.1)
Ratio of liquid/gas density	12	8.9 (0.6)	10.0 (2.3)	8.2 (0.7)	10.8 (2.0)	6.6 (0.8)	10.9 (1.2)
Speed of sound explorers	12	25.2 (1.0)	29.2 (2.7)	24.1 (0.9)	26.4 (2.6)	25.1 (1.3)	25.3 (1.5)
Genetic engineering	12	60.7 (1.7)	55.7 (4.5)	63.3 (1.9)	44.4 (3.8)	56.0 (2.4)	64.8 (2.4)

[Continued]

★ 221 ★

Students Responding Correctly to Science Items - VII

[Continued]

Item description	Grade	Nation	Hispanic	White	Black	Male	Female
New element: repeat exp	12	46.5 (1.5)	49.7 (5.8)	47.7 (1.6)	36.6 (3.1)	47.3 (2.2)	45.7 (1.7)
Table: causes of death	12	57.7 (1.4)	47.4 (5.3)	61.6 (1.7)	42.2 (3.6)	56.7 (1.8)	58.6 (2.3)
Capacitor charge and time	12	15.1 (1.0)	15.8 (4.4)	15.6 (1.2)	10.0 (2.0)	18.0 (1.5)	12.0 (1.2)
Altitude profile	12	16.1 (1.2)	10.7 (2.4)	17.2 (1.3)	5.2 (2.1)	21.3 (1.8)	10.7 (1.1)
Half-life graph	12	23.3 (1.4)	14.7 (4.2)	24.8 (1.4)	5.1 (1.9)	29.2 (2.0)	16.8 (1.6)
Fossils on 2 continents	12	80.7 (0.9)	73.4 (2.8)	83.7 (1.0)	67.4 (3.1)	82.3 (1.2)	79.2 (1.3)
Exp: effect of vitamin K	12	51.6 (1.2)	46.3 (2.8)	55.7 (1.3)	32.3 (2.6)	47.0 (1.6)	55.8 (1.3)
Model of atoms' behavior	12	55.9 (1.1)	39.2 (2.7)	61.2 (1.3)	37.6 (2.7)	53.2 (1.6)	58.4 (1.4)
Diagram: stomach	12	81.1 (1.0)	67.0 (3.3)	85.1 (0.9)	69.0 (2.3)	83.9 (1.5)	78.5 (1.3)
Diagram: source of insulin	12	58.4 (1.1)	53.0 (3.7)	60.5 (1.4)	50.5 (3.3)	59.8 (1.9)	57.1 (1.6)
Specific heat of H_2O/oil	12	26.7 (1.0)	24.9 (3.2)	26.6 (1.1)	26.9 (2.6)	27.7 (1.3)	25.7 (1.4)
Increase greenhouse effect	12	61.2 (1.3)	50.1 (3.2)	65.8 (1.4)	42.0 (2.8)	65.5 (1.6)	57.2 (1.6)
Graph: velocity of 3 objects	12	34.2 (1.5)	30.6 (3.4)	35.2 (1.7)	29.0 (2.9)	37.1 (2.2)	31.5 (1.7)
Graph: cooling of 2 liquids	12	37.8 (1.2)	30.4 (2.8)	40.7 (1.5)	24.7 (2.4)	39.7 (1.7)	36.0 (1.5)
Shadows-north	12	20.8 (0.8)	17.7 (2.4)	22.1 (1.0)	17.4 (2.3)	21.2 (1.1)	20.4 (1.2)
Shadows-label	12	28.7 (1.0)	20.0 (2.5)	31.9 (1.4)	13.0 (2.0)	30.7 (1.2)	26.9 (1.4)
Shadows-length	12	36.5 (1.3)	27.8 (3.8)	41.1 (1.5)	15.4 (2.7)	42.4 (2.0)	31.0 (1.5)
Nuclear power	12	54.6 (1.7)	36.6 (4.7)	58.4 (1.7)	36.2 (4.3)	59.6 (2.1)	49.8 (1.7)
Graph: velocity/time	12	16.5 (0.9)	19.4 (2.8)	15.9 (1.1)	15.9 (1.9)	20.6 (1.4)	13.0 (1.1)
Cause of seasons	12	28.5 (1.2)	22.4 (3.3)	30.1 (1.3)	19.9 (2.9)	33.5 (1.9)	24.1 (1.5)
Poisons in food chains	12	76.6 (1.2)	70.3 (3.3)	79.2 (1.5)	64.7 (3.1)	76.9 (1.6)	76.4 (1.5)
Why publish? share findings	12	83.6 (1.0)	78.0 (3.7)	85.2 (1.3)	77.8 (1.8)	80.9 (1.8)	86.2 (1.3)
Why publish? check findings	12	17.6 (1.0)	75.8 (2.6)	78.5 (1.2)	72.2 (2.7)	76.8 (1.4)	78.2 (1.3)
Why publish? add to knowledge	12	84.6 (0.9)	82.6 (2.6)	87.0 (1.2)	78.9 (2.4)	84.4 (1.3)	84.7 (1.4)

[Continued]

★ 221 ★

Students Responding Correctly to Science Items - VII

[Continued]

Item description	Grade	Nation	Hispanic	White	Black	Male	Female
Ocean currents and climate	12	32.0 (1.2)	26.5 (3.8)	33.9 (1.3)	19.2 (2.2)	36.2 (1.5)	28.2 (1.5)
Light bulbs in series	12	26.1 (1.0)	21.9 (2.9)	28.5 (1.1)	14.4 (2.0)	32.1 (1.5)	20.7 (1.3)
Interpret a chemical formula	12	56.8 (1.1)	50.4 (4.6)	59.2 (1.3)	48.5 (2.4)	56.8 (1.6)	59.2 (1.3)
Analyzing cause of disease	12	49.1 (1.1)	41.9 (4.4)	51.5 (1.2)	38.2 (2.9)	47.5 (1.4)	50.5 (1.6)
Ratio of oxygen/copper	12	49.4 (1.4)	44.1 (2.9)	51.7 (1.6)	37.7 (3.4)	50.1 (1.8)	48.8 (1.9)
Plant experiment control	12	78.9 (1.0)	72.0 (2.5)	81.8 (1.3)	66.7 (2.6)	74.5 (1.3)	82.8 (1.1)
Balancing a chemical equation	12	51.0 (1.7)	39.1 (3.5)	54.2 (1.8)	36.5 (2.7)	48.9 (2.4)	53.8 (1.8)

Source: Jones, Lee R., and others. *The 1990 Science Report Card: NAEP's Assessment of Fourth, Eighth, and Twelfth Graders*, Prepared by Educational Testing Service under contract with the National Center for Education Statistics, Office of Educational Research and Improvement, U.S. Department of Education, March 1992, pp. 160-172.

★ 222 ★

Academic Progress

Students in the Top and Bottom Thirds of Their Classes in Science

Percentages are shown for 1990, by race/ethnicity. Standard error for each result is shown in parentheses.

Academic standing	White	Black	Hispanic	Asian/ Pacific Islander	American Indian
Grade 4					
Top one-third	38 (3.2)	8 (1.8)	15 (2.3)	25 (9.7)	27 (6.0)
Bottom one-third	18 (2.2)	73 (3.9)	53 (3.4)	39 (9.0)	33 (4.7)
Grade 8					
Top one-third	31 (3.5)	11 (2.3)	13 (7.7)	36 (7.7)	15 (11.8)[1]
Bottom one-third	25 (3.4)	69 (4.7)	59 (5.9)	33 (8.5)	59 (26.9)[1]
Grade 12					
Top one-third	41 (3.8)	13 (3.3)	22 (4.4)	37 (15.4)	29 (8.4)[1]
Bottom one-third	16 (3.6)	64 (4.6)	47 (6.8)	17 (5.9)	28 (11.2)[1]

Source: Jones, Lee R., and others. *The 1990 Science Report Card: NAEP's Assessment of Fourth, Eighth, and Twelfth Graders*, Prepared by Educational Testing Service under contract with the National Center for Education Statistics, Office of Educational Research and Improvement, U.S. Department of Education, March 1992, p. 20. *Notes:* Achievement results were analyzed using item response theory (IRT) scaling procedures, which allowed the National Assessment of Educational Progress to estimate students' average proficiency on a scale ranging from 0 to 500. The standard errors of the estimated percentages and proficiencies appear in parentheses. It can be said with 95 percent certainty that for each population of interest, the value for the whole population is within plus or minus two standard errors of the estimate for the sample. 1. Interpret with caution - the nature of the sample does not allow accurate determination of the variability of these estimated statistics.

★ 223 ★

Academic Progress

Students' Average Science Proficiency, by Content Area

Proficiency is based on IRT (item response theory) scaling procedures. Progress is estimated on a scale of 0 to 500. Scores are assigned to five proficiency levels: Level 150—Knows everyday science facts; Level 200—Understands simple scientific principles; Level 250—Applies general scientific information; Level 300—Analyzes scientific procedures and data; and Level 350—Integrates specialized scientific information. Data presented are proficiency scores, not levels.

Grade and race/ethnicity	Distribution of students (percent)	Life sciences	Physical sciences	Earth and space sciences	Nature of science
Grade 4					
White	70 (0.5)	238 (1.0)	245 (1.2)	243 (1.1)	242 (1.1)
Black	15 (0.4)	204 (1.6)	207 (2.0)	204 (1.5)	212 (1.7)
Hispanic	11 (0.3)	209 (1.8)	213 (1.6)	215 (1.6)	212 (1.7)
Asian/Pacific Islander	2 (0.3)	227 (4.1)	238 (3.9)	233 (3.6)	238 (3.5)
American Indian	2 (0.3)	222 (3.8)	229 (4.0)	228 (3.6)	226 (3.8)
Grade 8					
White	71 (0.4)	273 (1.4)	271 (1.4)	276 (1.5)	270 (1.5)
Black	15 (0.4)	233 (2.3)	232 (2.3)	228 (2.6)	230 (2.7)
Hispanic	10 (0.3)	242 (2.4)	241 (2.2)	242 (2.3)	236 (2.4)
Asian/Pacific Islander	3 (0.4)	272 (4.0)	271 (3.9)	270 (4.3)	267 (5.2)
American Indian	1 (0.5)[1]	252 (9.7)[1]	250 (7.8)[1]	257 (7.3)[1]	244 (15.6)[1]
Grade 12					
White	73 (0.4)	305 (1.1)	300 (1.7)	301 (1.3)	307 (1.4)
Black	14 (0.5)	262 (2.0)	253 (3.1)	247 (2.8)	267 (3.0)
Hispanic	8 (0.3)	275 (2.7)	271 (3.2)	270 (2.9)	277 (3.9)
Asian/Pacific Islander	4 (0.2)	309 (7.1)	310 (8.3)	304 (6.6)	312 (6.9)
American Indian	1 (0.2)[1]	287 (4.5)[1]	283 (5.6)[1]	289 (6.1)[1]	283 (9.6)[1]

Source: Jones, Lee R., and others. *The 1990 Science Report Card: NAEP's Assessment of Fourth, Eighth, and Twelfth Graders*, Prepared by Educational Testing Service under contract with the National Center for Education Statistics, Office of Educational Research and Improvement, U.S. Department of Education, March 1992, p. 64. *Notes:* Achievement results were analyzed using item response theory (IRT) scaling procedures, which allowed the National Assessment of Educational Progress to estimate students' average proficiency on a scale ranging from 0 to 500. The standard errors of the estimated percentages and proficiencies appear in parentheses. It can be said with 95 percent certainty that for each population of interest, the value for the whole population is within plus or minus two standard errors of the estimate for the sample. 1. Interpret with caution - the nature of the sample does not allow accurate determination of the variability of these estimated statistics.

★ 224 ★

Academic Progress

Students' Average Science Proficiency, by Race/Ethnicity and Sex

Proficiency levels are based on IRT (item response theory) scaling procedures. Progress is estimated on a scale of 0 to 500.

	Percent	Standard error	Average Proficiency	Standard error
Grade 4				
White				
Male	36	0.7	243	1.3
Female	34	0.7	214	1.1
Black				
Male	7	0.3	205	1.8
Female	8	0.4	206	1.8
Hispanic				
Male	6	0.2	213	1.6
Female	5	0.2	211	1.9
Grade 8				
White				
Male	36	0.8	274	1.8
Female	35	0.7	271	1.4
Black				
Male	7	0.3	232	2.9
Female	8	0.3	230	2.1
Hispanic				
Male	5	0.2	243	3.0
Female	5	0.2	239	2.5
Grade 12				
White				
Male	36	0.8	307	1.5
Female	37	0.7	298	1.3
Black				
Male	6	0.4	261	2.7
Female	8	0.4	253	2.9
Hispanic				
Male	4	0.3	278	3.1
Female	4	0.3	268	3.5

Source: Jones, Lee R., and others. *The 1990 Science Report Card: NAEP's Assessment of Fourth, Eighth, and Twelfth Graders*, Prepared by Educational Testing Service under contract with the National Center for Education Statistics, Office of Educational Research and Improvement, U.S. Department of Education, March 1992, p. 12. *Notes:* It can be said with 95 percent certainty that for each population of interest, the value for the whole population is within plus or minus two standard errors of the estimate for the sample. Data are not presented for Asian/Pacific Islanders or American Indian students because breakdown of these groups by gender resulted in too few students in each category.

★ 225 ★

Academic Progress

Students' Science Proficiency

Students' average proficiency is shown, based on IRT (item response theory) scaling procedures. Progress is estimated on a scale of 0 to 500. Scores are assigned to five proficiency levels: Level 150—Knows everyday science facts; Level 200—Understands simple scientific principles; Level 250—Applies general scientific information; Level 300—Analyzes scientific procedures and data; and Level 350—Integrates specialized scientific information. Data presented are proficiency scores, not levels.

Race/ethnicity	Students		Proficiency	
	Percent distribution	Standard error	Average score	Standard error
Grade 4				
White	70	0.5	242	1.0
Black	15	0.4	205	1.5
Hispanic	11	0.3	212	1.5
Asian/Pacific Islander	2	0.3	233	3.0
American Indian	2	0.3	226	2.7
Grade 8				
White	71	0.4	273	1.4
Black	15	0.4	231	2.2
Hispanic	10	0.3	241	2.1
Asian/Pacific Islander	3	0.4	271	4.0
American Indian	1	0.5[1]	252	8.5[1]
Grade 12				
White	73	0.4	303	1.3
Black	14	0.5	256	2.4
Hispanic	8	0.3	273	2.8
Asian/Pacific Islander	4	0.2	308	7.1
American Indian	1	0.2[1]	286	4.6[1]

Source: Jones, Lee R., and others. *The 1990 Science Report Card: NAEP's Assessment of Fourth, Eighth, and Twelfth Graders,* Prepared by Educational Testing Service under contract with the National Center for Education Statistics, Office of Educational Research and Improvement, U.S. Department of Education, March 1992, p. 10. *Notes:* Achievement results were analyzed using item response theory (IRT) scaling procedures, which allowed the National Assessment of Educational Progress to estimate students' average proficiency on a scale ranging from 0 to 500. It can be said with 95 percent certainty that for each population of interest, the value for the whole population is within plus or minus two standard errors of the estimate for the sample. 1. Interpret with caution-the nature of the sample does not allow accurate determination of the variability of these estimated statistics.

★ 226 ★

Academic Progress

Students' Science Proficiency Levels

Percent of students at or above four proficiency levels based on IRT (item response theory) scaling procedures. Progress is estimated on a scale of 0 to 500. Scores are assigned to five proficiency levels: Level 150—Knows everyday science facts; Level 200—Understands simple scientific principles; Level 250—Applies general scientific information; Level 300—Analyzes scientific procedures and data; and Level 350—Integrates specialized scientific information. Standard error is shown in parentheses.

	Level 200	Level 250	Level 300	Level 350
Grade 4				
White	93 (0.8)	40 (1.6)	1 (0.3)	0 (0.0)
Black	58 (2.7)	5 (1.1)	0 (0.2)	0 (0.2)
Hispanic	66 (2.4)	10 (1.2)	0 (0.0)	0 (0.0)
Asian/Pacific Islander	88 (3.1)	29 (5.2)	2 (1.5)	0 (0.0)
American Indian	81 (5.3)	20 (4.8)	0 (0.0)	0 (0.0)
Grade 8				
White	97 (0.5)	74 (1.3)	23 (1.3)	1 (0.3)
Black	80 (2.5)	31 (2.5)	3 (0.8)	0 (0.1)
Hispanic	87 (1.7)	42 (2.8)	5 (0.9)	0 (0.1)
Asian/Pacific Islander	96 (1.9)	71 (4.8)	23 (4.1)	1 (0.6)
American Indian	92 (2.8)[1]	54 (11.6)[1]	8 (2.8)[1]	0 (0.0)[1]
Grade 12				
White	100 (0.1)	91 (0.8)	53 (1.4)	12 (0.9)
Black	94 (1.4)	57 (3.0)	12 (2.0)	1 (0.6)
Hispanic	98 (0.8)	70 (3.4)	23 (2.9)	3 (1.0)
Asian/Pacific Islander	99 (1.4)	90 (3.2)	60 (7.4)	17 (5.0)
American Indian	100 (0.7)[1]	89 (5.6)[1]	33 (9.3)[1]	2 (0.0)[1]

Source: Jones, Lee R., and others, *The 1990 Science Report Card: NAEP's Assessment of Fourth, Eighth, and Twelfth Graders*, Prepared by Educational Testing Service under contract with the National Center for Education Statistics, Office of Educational Research and Improvement, U.S. Department of Education, March, 1992, p. 52. *Notes:* Achievement results were analyzed using item response theory (IRT) scaling procedures, which allowed the National Assessment of Educational Progress to estimate students' average proficiency on a scale ranging from 0 to 500. The standard errors of the estimated percentages and proficiencies appear in parentheses. It can be said with 95 percent certainty that for each population of interest, the value for the whole population is within plus or minus two standard errors of the estimate for the sample. When the percentage of students is either 0 or 100, the standard error is inestimatable. However, percentages 99.5 percent and greater were rounded to 100 percent and percentages less than 0.5 were rounded to 0 percent. 1. Interpret with caution - the nature of the sample does not allow accurate determination of the variability of these estimated statistics.

★ 227 ★

Academic Progress

U.S. History and Civics Proficiency of Fourth, Eighth and Twelfth Graders, 1988

Data show the percentage of students who were at or above selected levels of proficiency in 1988.

Race/ethnicity	Grade and percent at each proficiency level										
	4th graders[1]			8th graders				12th graders			
	200+[2]	250+[3]	300+[4]	200+[2]	250+[3]	300+[4]	350+[5]	200+[2]	250+[3]	300+[4]	350+[5]
All students	76.0	15.9	0.2	96.0	67.7	12.7	0.1	99.4	88.9	45.9	4.6
White	84.8	19.8	0.3	97.4	75.9	15.7	0.1	99.6	92.7	52.8	5.5
Black	49.0	4.2	[6]	93.2	44.9	3.5	[6]	99.0	77.3	21.2	0.5
Hispanic	54.3	4.2	[6]	91.2	43.8	4.1	[6]	98.4	76.1	23.2	1.4

Source: U.S. Department of Education. National Center for Education Statistics. Office of Educational Research and Improvement. *Digest of Education Statistics, 1994*. Lanham, MD: Bernan, November 1994, p. 120. Primary source: U.S. Department of Education, National Center for Education Statistics, National Assessment of Educational Progress, *The U.S. History Report Card*, prepared by Educational Testing Service. (This table was prepared April 1990.) *Notes:* 1. Virtually no students were able to interpret historical information and ideas. 2. Simple historical facts—knows some historical facts of the type learned from everyday experiences and is able to read simple timelines, graphs and maps. 3. Beginning historical information and interpretation—knows a variety of historical facts of the type learned from historical studies. Developing sense of chronology. 4. Basic historical terms and relationships—Demonstrates broad knowledge of historical terms, facts, regions, and ideas. Some knowledge of content of primary texts in political history. 5. Detailed understanding of historical vocabulary, facts, regions, and ideas. Able to relate social science concepts to historical themes and can evaluate causal relationships. 6. Virtually no students were able to perform at this level.

★ 228 ★

Academic Progress

Writing Proficiency in Fourth, Eighth, and Eleventh Grades, 1984-92

Students' average proficiency is shown, based on IRT (item response theory) scaling procedures. Test scores range from 0 to 500 and represent the average of a respondent's estimated scores on specific writing tasks. The average response method is used to estimate average writing achievement for each participant as if each had performed all 11 writing tasks.

Race/ethnicity	4th graders				8th graders				11th graders			
	1984	1988	1990	1992	1984	1988	1990	1992	1984	1988	1990	1992
All students	203.8	205.7	201.7	207.1	266.7	263.7	256.6	274.4	289.7	291.3	287.1	287.3
White	210.7	214.9	211.0	216.7	271.7	269.1	262.1	279.2	296.8	296.2	292.8	294.1
Black	181.6	173.3	171.4	175.0	247.1	246.0	239.0	258.1	270.3	275.2	268.2	263.2
Hispanic	188.5	190.3	184.1	189.4	246.9	250.4	245.7	265.0	259.1	273.8	276.9	273.6

Source: U.S. Department of Education. National Center for Education Statistics. Office of Educational Research and Improvement. *Digest of Education Statistics, 1994*. Lanham, MD: Bernan, November 1994, p. 118. Primary source: U.S. Department of Education, National Center for Educational Statistics, National Assessment of Educational Progress, *The Writing Report Card, 1984-88* and *NAEP 1992 Trends in Academic Progress*, by Educational Testing Service. (This table was prepared April 1994.).

Dropouts

★ 229 ★

Continuous Attendance and Grade Level Progression Rates

From the source: "Persistent attendance, measured by the proportion of students in consecutive years, is strongly associated with completing high school. Students who do not complete high school face a decreased opportunity for assuming a successful and fully functional place in the American work place and society at large." This table shows continuous attendance and grade progression rates for persons age 15 to 24 years, by race/ethnicity of student. Data are shown for October 1992.

Grade last year	Total	Race/ethnicity		
		White	Black	Hispanic
Continuous attendance rate (percent)[2]				
9-11 average	96.8	97.3	96.3	94.4
9	97.8	98.4	96.5	94.9
10	97.0	97.3	95.7	96.1
11	95.7	96.1	96.7	91.8
12	67.5	68.7	57.4	66.7
13-15 average	84.4	84.8	81.5	78.6
13	83.5	83.8	83.2	78.1
14	80.9	81.4	72.1	82.3
15	90.7	90.8	92.7	[1]
16	41.7	41.6	[1]	[1]
17	65.9	65.6	[1]	[1]
Grade level progression rate (percent)[2]				
9-11 average	98.1	98.8	96.0	96.9
9	97.8	98.7	93.9	98.0
10	98.2	98.9	96.2	96.0
11	98.4	98.8	97.9	96.9
12	95.8	96.3	95.7	90.2
13-15 average	86.9	87.1	89.4	79.9
13	85.9	86.4	85.3	77.3
14	84.4	84.1	93.4	82.3
15	91.5	91.4	93.0	[1]
16	69.0	67.6	[1]	[1]
17	64.1	68.2	[1]	[1]

Source: U.S. Department of Education. National Center for Education Statistics. *The Condition of Education 1994.* Washington, DC: U.S. GPO, 1994, p. 179. Primary source: U.S. Department of Commerce, Bureau of the Census, October Current Population Surveys. *Notes:* 1. Too few sample observations for a reliable estimate. 2. The continuous attendance rate is the percentage of those enrolled the previous October who were enrolled again the following October. The grade level progression rate is the percentage of those enrolled two consecutive Octobers who advanced at least one grade level. At most grade levels, the continuous attendance rate is conceptually similar to the school persistence rate, but is numerically slightly different because of data used to measure grade level the previous October. However, the continuous attendance rate for grade 12 is the percentage of students in grade 12 the previous October who enrolled in college (or in grade 12 again) the following October. Similarly, the continuous attendance rate for grade 16 (4th year of college) is the percentage of students in grade 16 the previous October who enrolled in the 5th year of college (or in the 4th year again) the following October.

★ 230 ★

Dropouts

High School Dropout Rates, 1990-93

Dropout rate is shown as percent of civilian noninstitutional population by age, group, sex, race/ethnicity. Dropouts are persons who are not enrolled in school and who are not high school graduates.

Characteristic	Total, 14 to 34 years	14 and 15 years	16 and 17 years	18 and 19 years	20 and 21 years	22 to 24 years	25 to 29 years	30 to 34 years
October 1990								
All races	11.9	0.9	6.3	14.2	12.8	13.8	13.9	12.9
Male	12.2	0.8	6.6	14.6	13.2	14.0	14.5	13.3
Female	11.6	1.0	6.1	13.8	12.4	13.6	13.4	12.5
White, non-Hispanic	8.3	0.8	5.4	11.1	9.4	9.5	9.2	8.7
Male	8.8	0.7	5.9	11.4	9.6	9.8	9.8	9.4
Female	7.8	1.0	5.0	10.8	9.1	9.1	8.5	8.0
Black, non-Hispanic	14.4	0.7	6.9	16.6	15.6	13.6	19.3	16.7
Male	13.4	0.3	6.3	15.5	12.4	13.2	18.9	16.4
Female	15.1	1.0	7.5	17.6	18.6	13.9	19.6	16.9
Hispanic origin[1]	34.3	1.1	12.9	34.2	31.6	42.8	41.7	42.4
Male	34.8	0.9	13.1	39.4	37.9	41.4	42.6	41.4
Female	33.8	1.3	12.5	29.4	25.0	44.4	40.7	43.5
October 1992								
All races	11.0	0.8	4.9	11.9	13.7	12.5	13.0	12.3
Male	11.5	0.8	3.7	12.2	15.3	13.2	13.9	13.3
Female	10.4	0.9	6.2	11.7	12.1	11.9	12.1	11.3
White, non-Hispanic	7.4	0.8	3.8	8.7	9.8	8.2	8.9	7.8
Male	7.9	0.8	2.9	9.3	11.0	8.5	9.5	8.6
Female	7.0	0.7	4.8	8.1	8.6	7.9	8.2	7.0
Black, non-Hispanic	13.1	0.7	5.6	16.4	17.3	15.3	13.8	16.4
Male	12.3	0.1	4.0	16.4	14.6	14.9	12.4	17.2
Female	13.8	1.2	7.1	16.4	19.7	15.7	14.8	15.8
Hispanic origin[1]	32.2	1.2	11.9	25.3	36.3	38.1	40.0	40.5
Male	35.1	1.9	9.1	25.7	45.8	41.7	44.7	42.4
Female	29.1	0.4	15.0	24.9	27.0	34.4	34.9	38.3
October 1993[2]								
All races	10.6	1.1	4.8	11.8	13.4	12.9	12.1	11.8
Male	11.1	1.0	4.0	12.1	13.9	13.5	13.2	12.7
Female	10.1	1.2	5.7	11.5	12.9	12.3	11.1	10.8
White, non-Hispanic	7.3	0.9	3.9	9.5	9.8	8.4	8.2	7.5
Male	7.8	0.7	3.1	10.1	9.7	9.4	8.7	8.5
Female	6.8	1.1	4.7	8.7	9.9	7.4	7.6	6.6
Black, non-Hispanic	12.5	1.2	4.5	12.8	19.0	17.0	13.3	14.8
Male	12.1	1.0	3.5	10.5	22.8	14.7	15.0	13.7
Female	12.9	1.4	5.5	15.2	15.8	19.1	11.9	15.7
Hispanic origin[1]	30.7	2.4	9.9	28.3	29.0	37.8	38.5	38.9

[Continued]

★ 230 ★

High School Dropout Rates, 1990-93

[Continued]

Characteristic	Total, 14 to 34 years	14 and 15 years	16 and 17 years	18 and 19 years	20 and 21 years	22 to 24 years	25 to 29 years	30 to 34 years
Male	32.0	3.1	8.4	32.2	28.9	39.8	40.8	39.3
Female	29.3	1.8	11.8	25.0	29.0	35.8	35.8	38.5

Source: U.S. Department of Education. National Center for Education Statistics. Office of Educational Research and Improvement. *Digest of Education Statistics, 1994.* Lanham, MD: Bernan, November 1994, p. 111. Primary source: U.S. Department of Commerce, Bureau of the Census, *Current Population Reports,* and unpublished data. (This table was prepared May 1994.) *Notes:* People who received GED credentials are counted as graduates. Data are based upon sample surveys of the civilian noninstitutional population. 1. Includes persons of Hispanic origin. 2. Because of changes in data collection procedures, data may not be comparable with figures for earlier years.

★ 231 ★

Dropouts

High School Dropout and Retention Rates

From the source: "Studies have shown that students who have repeated at least one grade are more likely to become dropouts. Knowledge about how that relationship varies among subgroups of students or by the grade repeated can help schools develop grade retention policies and services for students who have been retained." This table shows dropout and retention rates for persons age 16-24, by race/ethnicity of student and language spoken at home. Data are shown for 1992.

Student characteristic	Percent retained in one or more more grades[1]	Dropout rate[2]		
		Total[3]	Never retained	Retained
Total	11.5	11.0	9.4	19.8
Race/ethnicity[4]				
White	10.5	7.7	6.0	18.8
Black	18.1	13.78	12.0	20.1
Hispanic	10.9	29.4	29.2	24.1
Language at home/English proficiency				
English only	11.9	8.8	7.1	19.5
Non-English language spoken at home[5]	9.3	21.5	21.3	22.3
Speak English very well[6]	10.6	11.2	10.2	18.9
Speak English less than very well	6.9	39.7	40.5	32.1

Source: U.S. Department of Education. National Center for Education Statistics. *The Condition of Education 1994.* Washington, DC: U.S. Government Printing Office, 1994, p. 319. Primary source: U.S. Department of Commerce, Bureau of the Census, Current Population Survey, October 1992. *Notes:* 1. Percentages are based on those who responded to the item on grade retention. 2. The percentage who are not enrolled in school and do not have a high school diploma or equivalency certificate. 3. Included in the total are some for whom whether they repeated is unknown. 4. Not shown separately are non-Hispanics who are neither white nor black. 5. Included but not shown separately are some for whom English language proficiency is unknown. 6. English proficiency is determined using responses to the question asked about those who spoke a language other than English at home: "How well does this person speak English?" Possible responses were "Very well," "Well," "not well," and "Not at all." Persons who responded less than "Very well" were included in the category "Speak English less than very well."

★ 232 ★

Dropouts

High School Dropouts, 1991

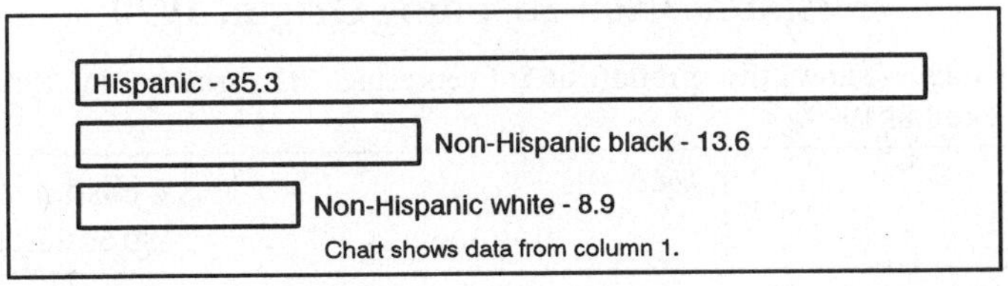

Dropouts are defined as people age 16-24 who have not completed high school and were not enrolled during October 1991[1].

Race/ethnicity	Dropout rate	Percent of total 16-24 population
Hispanic	35.3	11.3
Non-Hispanic white	8.9	70.2
Non-Hispanic black	13.6	14.4

Source: Arocha, Zita. "Stop putting barriers in front of Hispanic kids." *USA TODAY* (22 September 1992), p. 13A. Primary source: National Center for Education Statistics. *Notes:* 1. Not shown separately are non-Hispanics who are neither black nor white, but who are included in the total.

★ 233 ★

Dropouts

New Jersey: Survival to Graduation in Selected Cities, 1990

	Hispanic	
	Males (%)	Females (%)
Camden	24.0	30.0
Newark	35.0	37.0
Jersey City	42.0	41.0

Source: ASPIRA News: National Newsletter of the ASPIRA Association, Inc. Vol. 5, No. 4 (Winter 1991-92), p. 3. Primary source: Public Affairs Focus, September 1991, Public Affairs Institute of New Jersey, Inc.

★234★

Dropouts

New Jersey: Survival to Graduation in Selected Cities, by Hispanic/Non-Hispanic Origin, 1990

Percentages show the proportion of entering 7th graders in 1984 who graduated in 1990.

	Total graduates	Hispanic graduates
Camden	35.4	26.8
Newark	46.7	35.6
Jersey City	47.4	41.6

Source: ASPIRA News: National Newsletter of the ASPIRA Association, Inc. Vol. 5, No. 4 (Winter 1991-92), p. 3. Primary source: Public Affairs Research Institute of New Jersey, Inc., September 1991.

★235★

Dropouts

Trends in High School Dropout Rates, 1967-93

Dropout rate is shown as percentage of civilian noninstitutional population for persons 16-24 years old, by race/ethnicity and sex for the years 1967 through 1993. Data refer to "status" dropouts, which are persons not enrolled in school and are not high school graduates. People who have received GED credentials are counted as graduates.

Year	Total[1]				Men				Women			
	All races	White, non-Hispanic	Black, non-Hispanic	Hispanic	All races	White, non-Hispanic	Black, non-Hispanic	Hispanic	All races	White, non-Hispanic	Black, non-Hispanic	Hispanic
1967[2]	17.0	15.4	28.6	-	16.5	14.7	30.6	-	17.3	16.1	26.9	-
1968[2]	16.2	14.7	27.4	-	15.8	14.4	27.1	-	16.5	15.0	27.6	-
1969[2]	15.2	13.6	26.7	-	14.3	12.6	26.9	-	16.0	14.6	26.7	-
1970[2]	15.0	13.2	27.9	-	14.2	12.2	29.4	-	15.7	14.1	26.6	-
1971[2]	14.7	13.4	23.7	-	14.2	12.6	25.5	-	15.2	14.2	22.1	-
1972	14.6	12.3	21.3	34.3	14.1	11.7	22.3	33.7	15.1	12.8	20.5	34.9
1973	14.1	11.6	22.2	33.5	13.7	11.5	21.5	30.4	14.5	11.8	22.8	36.4
1974	14.3	11.9	21.2	33.0	14.2	12.0	20.1	33.8	14.4	11.8	22.1	32.2
1975	13.9	11.4	22.9	29.2	13.3	11.0	23.0	26.7	14.5	11.8	22.9	31.6
1976	14.1	12.0	20.5	31.4	14.1	12.1	21.2	30.3	14.2	11.8	19.9	32.3
1977	14.1	11.9	19.8	33.0	14.5	12.6	19.5	31.6	13.8	11.2	20.0	34.3
1978	14.2	11.9	20.2	33.3	14.6	12.2	22.5	33.6	13.9	11.6	18.3	33.1
1979	14.6	12.0	21.1	33.8	15.0	12.6	22.4	33.0	14.2	11.5	20.0	34.5
1980	14.1	11.4	19.1	35.2	15.1	12.3	20.8	37.2	13.1	10.5	17.7	33.2
1981	13.9	11.4	18.4	33.2	15.1	12.5	19.9	36.0	12.8	10.2	17.1	30.4
1982	13.9	11.4	18.4	31.7	14.5	12.1	21.2	30.5	13.3	10.9	15.9	32.8
1983	13.7	11.2	18.0	31.6	14.9	12.2	19.9	34.3	12.5	10.1	16.2	29.1
1984	13.1	11.0	15.5	29.8	14.0	12.0	16.8	30.6	12.3	10.1	14.3	29.0
1985	12.6	10.4	15.2	27.6	13.4	11.1	16.1	29.9	11.8	9.8	14.3	25.2
1986	12.2	9.7	14.2	30.1	13.1	10.3	15.0	32.8	11.4	9.1	13.5	27.2
1987	12.7	10.4	14.1	28.6	13.2	10.8	15.0	29.1	12.1	10.0	13.3	28.1
1988	12.9	9.6	14.5	35.8	13.5	10.4	15.0	36.0	12.2	8.9	14.1	35.4
1989	12.6	9.4	13.9	33.0	13.6	10.3	14.9	34.4	11.7	8.5	13.0	31.6

[Continued]

★ 235 ★

Trends in High School Dropout Rates, 1967-93

[Continued]

Year	Total[1]				Men				Women			
	All races	White, non-Hispanic	Black, non-Hispanic	Hispanic	All races	White, non-Hispanic	Black, non-Hispanic	Hispanic	All races	White, non-Hispanic	Black, non-Hispanic	Hispanic
1990	12.1	9.0	13.2	32.4	12.3	9.3	11.9	34.3	11.8	8.7	14.4	30.3
1991	12.5	8.9	13.6	35.3	13.0	8.9	13.5	39.2	11.9	8.9	13.7	31.1
1992[3]	11.0	7.7	13.7	29.4	11.3	8.0	12.5	32.1	10.7	7.5	14.8	26.6
1993[3]	11.0	7.9	13.6	27.5	11.2	8.2	12.6	28.1	10.9	7.7	14.4	26.9

Source: U.S. Department of Education. National Center for Education Statistics. Office of Educational Research and Improvement. *Digest of Education Statistics, 1994.* Lanham, MD: Bernan, November 1994, p. 110. Primary source: U.S. Department of Commerce, Bureau of the Census, Current Population Survey, unpublished tabulations; and U.S. Department of Education, National Center for Education Statistics, *Dropout Rates in the United States.* (This table was prepared May 1994.) *Notes:* A dash (-) indicates that data were not available. 1. "Status" dropouts. 2. White and black include persons of Hispanic origin. 3. Because of changes in data collection procedures, data may not be comparable with figures for earlier years.

★ 236 ★

Dropouts

Trends in the Work Status of High School Dropouts, 1979-93

Numbers are shown in thousands, by work status and race/ethnicity, for 16 to 24 year olds from October 1980 to October 1993.

School year and race/ethnicity	Dropouts		Dropouts in civilian labor force[1]						Not in labor force
					Employed		Unemployed		
	Number	Percent of total	Number	Labor force participation rate	Number	Percent of dropouts	Number	Unemployment rate	
All dropouts									
1979-80 dropouts in October[2]	739	100.0	471	63.7	322	43.6	149	31.6	268
1984-85 dropouts in October[3]	612	100.0	413	67.5	266	43.5	147	35.6	199
1985-86 dropouts in October[4]	562	100.0	359	63.9	259	46.1	100	27.9	203
1986-87 dropouts in October[5]	502	100.0	333	66.4	207	41.2	126	37.8	169
1987-88 dropouts in October[6]	552	100.0	327	59.2	240	43.5	87	26.7	225
1988-89 dropouts in October[7]	446	100.0	292	65.4	210	47.1	82	28.0	154
1989-90 dropouts in October[8]	405	100.0	280	69.0	189	46.7	90	32.3	125
1990-91 dropouts in October[9]	380	100.0	235	61.8	140	36.9	95	40.3	145
1991-92 dropouts in October[10]	406	100.0	242	59.6	147	36.3	95	39.1	164
1992-93 dropouts in October[11]	399	100.0	254	63.8	187	47.0	67	26.3	145
White[12]									
1979-80 dropouts in October[2]	580	78.5	392	67.6	286	49.3	106	27.0	188
1984-85 dropouts in October[3]	458	74.8	330	72.1	214	46.7	116	35.2	128
1988-89 dropouts in October[7]	324	72.6	228	70.6	176	54.3	52	22.9	96
1989-90 dropouts in October[8]	303	74.8	211	69.8	156	51.4	56	26.3	92
1990-91 dropouts in October[9]	273	71.8	177	65.1	109	40.0	68	38.5	96
1991-92 dropouts in October[10]	319	78.6	190	59.7	128	40.3	62	32.5	129
1992-93 dropouts in October[11]	304	76.2	209	68.8	159	52.2	50	24.1	95
Black[12]									
1979-80 dropouts in October[2]	146	19.8	73	50.0	33	22.6	40	[13]	73
1984-85 dropouts in October[3]	132	21.6	69	52.3	39	29.5	30	[13]	63
1988-89 dropouts in October[7]	112	25.1	59	52.2	31	27.7	27	[13]	53
1989-90 dropouts in October[8]	86	21.2	56	65.3	26	29.9	30	[13]	30
1990-91 dropouts in October[9]	98	25.8	54	55.0	28	28.4	26	[13]	44
1991-92 dropouts in October[10]	66	16.3	35	[13]	7	[13]	28	[13]	31
1992-93 dropouts in October[11]	80	20.1	34	42.9	21	26.2	13	[13]	46

[Continued]

★ 236 ★

Trends in the Work Status of High School Dropouts, 1979-93

[Continued]

School year and race/ethnicity	Dropouts		Dropouts in civilian labor force[1]						Not in labor force
					Employed		Unemployed		
	Number	Percent of total	Number	Labor force participa-tion rate	Number	Percent of dropouts	Number	Unemploy-ment rate	
Hispanic[14]									
1979-80 dropouts in October[2]	91	12.3	60	65.9	43	47.3	17	13	31
1984-85 dropouts in October[3]	106	17.3	73	68.9	40	37.7	33	13	33
1988-89 dropouts in October[7]	65	14.6	36	13	26	13	11	13	29
1989-90 dropouts in October[8]	67	16.5	32	13	22	13	10	13	35
1990-91 dropouts in October[9]	61	16.1	48	13	30	13	18	13	13
1991-92 dropouts in October[10]	80	19.7	40	49.9	23	28.4	17	13	40
1992-93 dropouts in October[11]	60	15.0	43	13	28	13	15	13	17

Source: U.S. Department of Education. National Center for Education Statistics. Office of Educational Research and Improvement. *Digest of Education Statistics, 1994.* Lanham, MD: Bernan, November 1994, p. 402. Primary source: U.S. Department of Labor, Bureau of Labor Statistics, *College Enrollment of 1993 High School Graduates.* (This table was prepared June 1994.) *Notes:* Data are based upon sample surveys of the civilian noninstitutional population. Includes dropouts from any grade, including a small number from elementary and middle schools. Percents are only shown when the base is 75,000 or greater. Even though the standard errors are large, smaller estimates are shown to permit users to combine categories in various ways. Because of rounding, details may not add to totals. 1. The labor force includes all employed persons plus those seeking employment. The labor force participation rate is the percentage of persons either employed or seeking employment. 2. Persons who dropped out of school between October 1979 and October 1980. 3. Persons who dropped out of school between October 1984 and October 1985. 4. Persons who dropped out of school between October 1985 and October 1986. 5. Persons who dropped out of school between October 1986 and October 1987. 6. Persons who dropped out of school between October 1987 and October 1988. 7. Persons who dropped out of school between October 1988 and October 1989. 8. Persons who dropped out of school between October 1989 and October 1990. 9. Persons who dropped out of school between October 1990 and October 1991. 10. Persons who dropped out of school between October 1991 and October 1992. 11. Persons who dropped out of school between October 1992 and October 1993. 12. Includes persons of Hispanic origin. 13. Data not shown where base is less than 75,000. 14. Persons of Hispanic origin may be of any race.

Educational Attainment

★ 237 ★

College Completion Rates, by Race/Ethnicity

This table shows results of a study of 534,981 students who enrolled as first-time freshmen on a full-time basis in the Fall of 1984. Percentages reflect how many of the students had graduated from those institutions by Fall of 1990.

Race/ethnicity	Percent of students graduated
Total	53.0
American Indian	29.0
Asian	62.0
Black	31.0
Hispanic	40.0
White	56.0

Source: Cage, Mary Crystal. "Fewer students get bachelor's degrees in 4 years, study finds." *Chronicle of Higher Education* (15 July 1992), p. A29. Primary source: National Collegiate Athletic Association.

★ 238 ★

Educational Attainment

College Enrollment of High School Graduates 1960-91

Numbers are shown in thousands, by race/ethnicity and year.

Year	High school graduates[1]				Enrolled in college[2]							
					Total		White[3]		Black[3,4]		Hispanic[4]	
	Total	White[3]	Black[3,4]	Hispanic[4]	Number	Percent	Number	Percent	Number	Percent	Number	Percent
1960	1,679	1,565	-	-	758	45.1	717	45.8	-	-	-	-
1961	1,763	1,612	-	-	847	48.0	798	49.5	-	-	-	-
1962	1,838	1,660	-	-	900	49.0	840	50.6	-	-	-	-
1963	1,741	1,615	-	-	784	45.0	736	45.6	-	-	-	-
1964	2,145	1,964	-	-	1,037	48.3	967	49.2	-	-	-	-
1965	2,659	2,417	-	-	1,354	50.9	1,249	51.7	-	-	-	-
1966	2,612	2,403	-	-	1,309	50.1	1,243	51.7	-	-	-	-
1967	2,525	2,267	-	-	1,311	51.9	1,202	53.0	-	-	-	-
1968	2,606	2,303	-	-	1,444	55.4	1,304	56.6	-	-	-	-
1969	2,842	2,538	-	-	1,516	53.3	1,402	55.2	-	-	-	-
1970	2,757	2,461	-	-	1,427	51.8	1,280	52.0	-	-	-	-
1971	2,872	2,596	-	-	1,535	53.4	1,402	54.0	-	-	-	-
1972	2,961	2,614	-	-	1,457	49.2	1,292	49.4	-	-	-	-
1973	3,059	2,707	-	-	1,425	46.6	1,302	48.1	-	-	-	-
1974	3,101	2,736	-	-	1,474	47.5	1,288	47.1	-	-	-	-
1975	3,186	2,825	-	-	1,615	50.7	1,446	51.2	-	-	-	-
1976	2,987	2,640	320	152	1,458	48.8	1,291	48.9	134	41.9	80	52.6
1977	3,140	2,768	335	156	1,590	50.6	1,403	50.7	166	49.6	80	51.3
1978	3,161	2,750	352	133	1,584	50.1	1,378	50.1	161	45.7	57	42.9
1979	3,160	2,776	324	154	1,559	49.3	1,376	49.6	147	45.4	69	44.8
1980	3,089	2,682	361	129	1,524	49.3	1,339	49.9	151	41.8	68	52.7
1981	3,053	2,626	359	146	1,646	53.9	1,434	54.6	154	42.9	76	52.1
1982	3,100	2,644	384	174	1,568	50.6	1,376	52.0	140	396.5	75	43.1
1983	2,964	2,496	392	138	1,562	52.7	1,372	55.0	151	38.5	75	54.3
1984	3,012	2,514	438	185	1,662	55.2	1,455	57.9	176	40.2	82	44.3
1985	2,666	2,241	333	141	1,539	57.7	1,332	59.4	141	42.3	72	51.1
1986	2,786	2,307	386	169	1,499	53.8	1,292	56.0	141	36.5	75	44.4
1987	2,647	2,207	337	176	1,503	56.8	1,249	56.6	175	51.9	59	33.5
1988	2,673	2,187	382	179	1,575	58.9	1,328	60.7	172	45.0	102	57.0
1989	2,454	2,051	337	168	1,463	59.6	1,238	60.4	178	52.8	93	55.4
1990	2,355	1,921	341	112	1,410	59.9	1,182	61.5	158	46.3	53	47.3
1991	2,276	1,867	320	154	1,420	62.4	1,207	64.6	146	45.6	88	57.1

[Continued]

★ 238 ★

College Enrollment of High School Graduates 1960-91

[Continued]

Year	High school graduates[1]				Enrolled in college[2]							
					Total		White[3]		Black[3,4]		Hispanic[4]	
	Total	White[3]	Black[3,4]	Hispanic[4]	Number	Percent	Number	Percent	Number	Percent	Number	Percent
1992	2,398	1,900	353	199	1,479	61.7	1,204	63.4	169	47.9	109	54.8
1993	2,338	1,910	302	200	1,464	62.6	1,200	62.8	168	55.6	125	62.5

Source: U.S. Department of Education. National Center for Education Statistics. Office of Educational Research and Improvement. *Digest of Education Statistics, 1994.* Lanham, MD: Bernan, November 1994, p. 187. Primary source: American College Testing Program, unpublished tabulations, 1987 derived from statistics collected by the U.S. Bureau of the Census; and U.S. Department of Labor, College Enrollment of 1993 High School Graduates. (This table was prepared June 1994.) *Notes:* A dash (-) stands for data not available. Data are based upon sample surveys of the civilian population. High school graduate data in this table differ from figures appearing in other tables because of varying survey procedures and coverage. High school graduates include GED recipients. 1. Individuals age 16 to 24 who graduated from high school during the preceding 12 months. 2. Enrollment in college as of October of each year for individuals age 16 to 24 who graduated from high school during the preceding 12 months. 3. Includes persons of Hispanic origin. 4. Due to the small sample size, data are subject to relatively large sampling errors.

★ 239 ★

Educational Attainment

Educational Attainment by State, 1990

Data for persons age 25 and over show the percentage having completed high school and college, by race/ethnicity and state, as of April 1990.

	Percent with high school diploma or higher						Percent with bachelor's degree or higher					
	Total	White[1]	Black[1]	Hispanic[2]	Asian/ Pacific Islander[1]	American Indian/ Alaskan Native[1]	Total	White[1]	Black[1]	Hispanic[2]	Asian/ Pacific Islander[1]	American Indian/ Alaskan Native[1]
United States	75.2	77.9	63.1	49.8	77.5	66.5	20.3	21.5	11.4	9.2	36.6	9.3
Alabama	66.9	70.3	54.6	73.8	78.9	64.9	15.7	17.3	9.3	20.1	43.7	11.6
Alaska	86.6	91.1	88.2	80.4	75.4	63.1	23.0	26.8	14.1	14.6	20.5	4.1
Arizona	78.7	82.4	75.1	51.7	80.2	52.1	20.3	22.2	14.3	6.9	37.5	4.6
Arkansas	66.3	68.6	51.5	59.1	66.4	65.4	13.3	14.1	8.4	11.1	24.6	9.8
California	76.2	81.1	75.6	45.0	77.2	71.4	23.4	25.4	14.8	7.1	34.1	11.1
Colorado	84.4	86.1	80.8	58.3	78.3	73.9	27.0	28.3	17.1	8.6	32.1	12.1
Connecticut	79.2	80.9	67.0	53.5	81.9	68.9	27.2	28.5	12.3	12.1	50.8	12.5
Delaware	77.5	80.3	63.2	60.1	86.1	62.0	21.4	23.0	10.6	16.5	55.9	10.2
District of Columbia	73.1	93.1	63.8	52.6	80.2	66.3	33.3	69.0	15.3	24.0	50.9	17.7
Florida	74.4	77.0	56.4	57.2	77.8	68.2	18.3	19.3	9.8	14.2	33.6	11.5
Georgia	70.9	74.9	58.6	66.2	77.5	71.6	19.3	21.8	11.0	20.5	38.6	12.5
Hawaii	80.1	89.3	94.2	73.9	74.7	84.4	22.9	30.2	15.2	10.3	19.4	17.7
Idaho	79.7	80.9	82.8	43.4	80.3	68.1	17.7	18.0	15.8	6.6	27.6	7.2
Illinois	76.2	79.1	65.2	45.0	83.9	71.4	21.0	22.4	11.4	8.0	49.8	13.4
Indiana	75.6	76.5	65.4	62.6	85.8	65.0	15.6	17.6	9.3	10.8	53.1	8.4
Iowa	80.1	80.3	70.1	64.2	76.4	67.6	16.9	16.7	12.8	13.7	47.3	9.7
Kansas	81.3	82.4	71.0	58.1	73.6	75.4	21.1	21.7	11.6	10.1	39.9	10.8
Kentucky	64.6	64.7	61.7	74.0	77.9	59.8	13.6	13.9	7.7	18.9	44.2	8.0
Louisiana	68.3	74.2	53.1	67.6	68.1	49.1	16.1	18.7	9.1	16.6	31.4	5.5
Maine	78.8	78.9	87.6	83.8	74.3	69.9	18.8	18.8	22.3	23.6	44.9	7.7
Maryland	78.4	80.8	70.6	70.3	84.8	73.4	26.5	28.9	16.1	25.2	50.3	19.7
Massachusetts	80.0	81.2	70.0	52.0	74.1	71.1	27.2	27.7	17.0	13.6	44.9	14.9
Michigan	76.8	78.6	64.9	60.9	83.3	67.8	17.4	18.1	10.1	11.6	54.1	7.6
Minnesota	82.4	82.8	76.2	71.1	69.7	68.2	21.8	21.9	17.5	17.2	33.5	7.7

[Continued]

★ 239 ★

Educational Attainment by State, 1990

[Continued]

	Percent with high school diploma or higher						Percent with bachelor's degree or higher					
	Total	White[1]	Black[1]	Hispanic[2]	Asian/ Pacific Islander[1]	American Indian/ Alaskan Native[1]	Total	White[1]	Black[1]	Hispanic[2]	Asian/ Pacific Islander[1]	American Indian/ Alaskan Native[1]
Mississippi	64.3	71.7	47.3	67.7	68.2	57.4	14.7	17.2	8.8	17.1	35.1	8.1
Missouri	73.9	74.9	65.1	71.0	81.5	65.1	17.8	18.3	11.2	18.0	47.3	11.0
Montana	81.0	81.7	80.9	66.4	78.5	68.1	19.8	20.3	18.4	10.9	32.1	7.9
Nebraska	81.8	82.4	73.2	600	80.0	69.0	18.9	19.2	12.4	9.4	39.5	8.8
Nevada	78.8	80.9	70.8	53.7	74.1	69.8	15.3	15.9	9.0	7.0	21.9	8.0
New Hampshire	82.2	82.2	86.1	78.2	82.7	65.9	24.4	24.2	25.7	25.5	26.1	16.0
New Jersey	76.7	78.6	67.0	53.9	86.8	66.9	24.9	25.8	13.6	10.8	57.1	14.8
New Mexico	75.1	78.6	74.7	59.6	80.8	58.2	20.4	23.4	14.2	8.7	38.7	5.8
New York	76.7	78.5	64.7	50.4	72.4	65.2	23.1	25.3	12.6	9.3	38.7	13.4
North Carolina	70.0	73.1	58.1	71.0	77.9	51.5	17.4	19.3	9.5	17.9	39.3	7.9
North Dakota	76.7	76.9	95.9	75.2	83.7	64.3	18.1	18.3	17.1	15.9	37.8	8.3
Ohio	75.7	76.9	64.6	63.3	83.5	65.3	17.0	17.6	9.1	14.2	53.2	8.3
Oklahoma	74.6	75.7	70.1	55.9	76.1	68.1	17.8	18.7	12.0	10.5	34.7	10.8
Oregon	81.5	82.3	75.0	53.0	79.4	71.0	20.6	20.8	9.1	10.1	32.3	8.3
Pennsylvania	74.7	75.9	63.5	52.2	77.1	67.8	17.9	18.5	10.0	11.8	45.2	12.0
Rhode Island	72.0	73.0	65.9	46.8	59.6	64.5	21.3	21.8	12.7	8.9	30.6	8.3
South Carolina	68.3	73.6	53.3	71.8	77.4	62.5	16.6	19.8	7.6	19.8	34.4	10.9
South Dakota	77.1	77.8	82.2	71.3	74.3	62.5	17.2	17.6	24.1	13.4	33.1	6.8
Tennessee	67.1	68.2	59.4	71.5	79.3	63.1	16.0	16.7	10.2	21.9	42.6	10.5
Texas	72.1	76.2	66.1	44.6	79.1	70.9	20.3	22.6	12.0	7.3	41.3	13.9
Utah	85.1	86.2	77.0	61.0	80.7	59.3	22.3	22.7	15.9	9.1	29.4	6.4
Vermont	80.8	80.8	82.9	84.7	87.1	66.8	24.3	24.2	30.5	28.2	52.1	11.1
Virginia	75.2	78.3	60.3	70.5	82.1	70.7	24.5	27.0	11.1	22.4	40.2	14.7
Washington	83.8	85.0	81.2	56.7	77.3	72.3	22.9	23.3	15.4	11.0	30.2	9.1
West Virginia	66.0	66.0	64.7	70.3	88.8	57.9	12.3	12.2	10.9	17.6	63.3	6.5
Wisconsin	78.6	79.6	61.3	54.1	71.5	66.8	17.7	18.1	8.3	10.0	40.4	5.5
Wyoming	83.0	83.9	81.2	59.3	77.5	68.2	18.8	19.3	9.5	4.8	28.6	6.2

Source: U.S. Department of Education. National Center for Education Statistics. Office of Educational Research and Improvement. *Digest of Education Statistics, 1994.* Lanham, MD: Bernan, November 1994, p. 22. Primary source: U.S. Bureau of the Census, Decennial Census, Minority Economic Profiles, unpublished data. (This table was prepared June 1993.) *Notes:* 1. Includes persons of Hispanic origin. 2. Persons of Hispanic origin may be of any race.

★ 240 ★

Educational Attainment

Educational Attainment of Persons Age 18 and Older, by Race/Ethnicity, 1993

Education level attained	Number of persons			
	Total	White, non-Hispanic	Black, non-Hispanic	Hispanic
Total population[1]	187,135	144,675	21,009	14,913
Elementary level				
Less than 7 years	7,199	2,485	1,174	3,102

[Continued]

★ 240 ★

Educational Attainment of Persons Age 18 and Older, by Race/Ethnicity, 1993

[Continued]

Education level attained	Number of persons			
	Total	White, non-Hispanic	Black, non-Hispanic	Hispanic
7 or 8 years	8,610	6,279	1,007	1,122
High school				
1 to 3 years	18,553	12,464	3,324	2,301
4 years	3,063	1,872	629	440
Graduate	65,140	51,826	7,634	4,027
College				
Some college	35,626	28,371	3,951	2,147
Associate's	11,471	9,400	1,039	629
Bachelor's	25,388	21,512	1,647	833
Master's	8,411	7,267	472	213
First professional	2,247	1,978	76	66
Doctorate	1,427	1,222	56	35

Source: U.S. Department of Education. National Center for Education Statistics. Office of Educational Research and Improvement. *Digest of Education Statistics, 1994.* Lanham, MD: Bernan, November 1994, p. 18. Primary source: U.S. Department of Commerce, Bureau of the Census, Current Population Survey, unpublished data. (This table was prepared May 1994.) *Notes:* A dash (-) stands for data not applicable or not available. Data are based on a sample survey of the noninstitutional population. Although cells with fewer than 75,000 people are subject to relatively wide sampling variation, they are included in the table to permit various types of aggregations. Because of rounding, details may not round to totals. 1. Civilian noninstitutional population.

★ 241 ★

Educational Attainment

Educational Attainment of Persons Age 65 Years or Older, 1989

The median number of years of school completed and the percent of elderly people with a high school education and four or more years of college are shown, by age and sex for each race/ethnicity, as of March 1989.

Measure of educational attainment and age	Total			Hispanic[1]			White			Black		
	Total	Men	Women	Total	Men	Women	Total	Men	Women	Total	Men	Women
Median years of school completed:												
60 to 64	12.4	12.5	12.4	9.3	9.6	8.9	12.5	12.5	12.4	10.7	10.6	10.7
65+	12.1	12.1	12.2	8.0	8.1	8.0	12.2	12.2	12.2	8.5	8.1	8.7
65 to 69	12.3	12.3	12.3	8.4	8.5	8.3	12.4	12.4	12.4	9.5	9.1	9.8
70 to 74	12.2	12.2	12.2	8.0	8.1	7.9	12.3	12.3	12.3	8.4	8.2	8.6
75+	10.9	10.5	11.3	7.1	7.0	7.1	11.6	11.1	11.9	7.8	7.0	8.2
Percent with a high school education:												
60 to 64	66	65	67	34	37	31	69	68	71	39	43	37
65+	55	54	56	28	26	29	58	57	59	25	22	26
65 to 69	63	61	65	33	31	35	67	65	68	31	28	33

[Continued]

★ 241 ★

Educational Attainment of Persons Age 65 Years or Older, 1989

[Continued]

Measure of educational attainment and age	Total			Hispanic[1]			White			Black		
	Total	Men	Women	Total	Men	Women	Total	Men	Women	Total	Men	Women
70 to 74	57	56	58	25	21	29	60	59	62	21	20	22
75+	46	44	48	23	21	24	49	47	50	21	18	23
Percent with 4 or more years of college:												
60 to 64	14	19	10	6	5	7	15	21	10	5	7	4
65+	11	14	9	6	7	5	12	15	10	5	4	5
65 to 69	13	16	10	9	9	9	13	17	10	5	3	6
70 to 74	11	13	9	3	3	3	11	13	10	3	3	3
75+	10	12	9	4	7	3	11	13	9	6	4	6

Source: Aging America, Trends and Projections, 1991 Edition. Prepared by the U.S. Senate Special Committee on Aging, the American Association of Retired Persons, the Federal Council on the Aging, and the U.S. Administration on Aging, p. 192. Primary source: U.S. Bureau of the Census. Unpublished data from the March 1989 *Current Population Survey*. *Note:* 1. People of Hispanic origin may be of any race.

★ 242 ★

Educational Attainment

Educational Attainment, by MSA, March 1993

Data show educational attainment of persons age 25 years and older, by race/ethnicity, in the 15 largest MSAs (metropolitan statistical areas). Numbers are shown in thousands for the noninstitutional population.

Metropolitan area	Total population	High school graduation or more		Completed Bachelor's degree or more	
		Percent	1.6*(s.e.)[1]	Percent	1.6*(s.e.)[1]
Atlanta, GA MSA					
25 years and over	1,981	84.1	2.8	31.3	3.6
White	1,401	85.1	3.2	33.3	4.3
Black	520	80.9	6.8	26.2	7.7
Hispanic origin[2]	44	(B)	(B)	(B)	(B)
Boston-Lawrence-Salem, MA-NH					
25 years and over	2,809	87.0	1.2	34.9	1.6
White	2,629	87.8	1.2	35.2	1.7
Black	90	73.1	10.0	17.1	8.5
Hispanic origin[2]	79	58.8	11.8	14.2	8.4
Chicago-Gary-Lake County, IL-IN-WI CMSA					
25 years and over	5,281	78.6	1.4	25.0	1.5
White	4,079	80.9	1.5	26.8	1.7
Black	1,026	69.6	4.2	14.2	3.2
Hispanic origin[2]	487	45.2	6.5	6.4	3.2
Cleveland-Akron-Lorain, OH CMSA					
25 years and over	1,812	86.0	1.9	21.9	2.3
White	1,517	88.0	2.0	23.1	2.6
Black	266	75.3	7.3	10.5	5.2

[Continued]

★ 242 ★

Educational Attainment, by MSA, March 1993

[Continued]

Metropolitan area	Total population	High school graduation or more		Completed Bachelor's degree or more	
		Percent	1.6*(s.e.)[1]	Percent	1.6*(s.e.)[1]
Hispanic origin[2]	23	(B)	(B)	(B)	(B)
Dallas-Fort Worth, TX CMSA					
25 years and over	2,553	80.9	2.2	27.2	2.5
White	2,018	83.5	2.4	30.4	3.0
Black	401	71.7	7.6	10.7	5.2
Hispanic origin[2]	321	41.1	9.2	7.6	5.0
Detroit-Ann Arbor, MI CMSA					
25 years and over	2,946	81.7	1.6	22.1	1.7
White	2,361	84.6	1.7	23.2	1.9
Black	534	67.9	5.2	14.1	3.9
Hispanic origin[2]	43	(B)	(B)	(B)	(B)
Houston-Galveston-Brazoria, TX CMSA					
25 years and over	2,476	83.3	2.2	30.7	2.7
White	1,907	84.3	2.4	32.0	3.1
Black	430	75.0	7.0	16.6	6.0
Hispanic origin[2]	311	52.8	9.5	12.4	6.3
Los Angeles-Anaheim-Riverside, CA CMSA					
25 years and over	9,480	76.6	1.0	23.6	1.1
White	7,876	74.8	1.2	21.9	1.1
Black	667	81.0	4.3	15.1	3.9
Hispanic origin[2]	2,694	44.2	2.7	5.8	1.3
Miami-Fort Lauderdale, FL CMSA					
25 years and over	2,250	75.4	2.2	21.2	2.1
White	1,828	78.2	2.4	23.2	2.4
Black	374	61.9	7.2	10.2	4.5
Hispanic origin[2]	858	64.1	4.7	17.1	3.7
New York-Northern New Jersey-Long Island, NY-NJ-CT CMSA					
25 years and over	11,666	80.3	.9	27.7	1.0
White	9,284	81.4	.9	29.5	1.1
Black	1,785	74.5	2.8	14.7	2.3
Hispanic origin[2]	1,500	56.1	3.5	8.5	1.9
Philadelphia-Wilmington-Trenton, PA-NJ-DE-MD CMSA					
25 years and over	3,937	79.6	1.6	23.4	1.7
White	3,237	82.1	1.7	25.3	1.9
Black	583	67.8	5.6	9.2	3.4
Hispanic origin[2]	98	63.4	14.0	11.1	9.1
Pittsburgh-Beaver Valley, PA CMSA					
25 years and over	1,666	82.3	2.3	20.5	2.4
White	1,538	82.7	2.4	20.4	2.5
Black	116	75.3	11.5	17.1	10.1
Hispanic origin[2]	7	(B)	(B)	(B)	(B)
San Francisco-Oakland-San Jose, CA CMSA					
25 years and over	4,387	86.3	1.6	33.0	2.2

[Continued]

★ 242 ★

Educational Attainment, by MSA, March 1993

[Continued]

Metropolitan area	Total population	High school graduation or more		Completed Bachelor's degree or more	
		Percent	1.6*(s.e.)[1]	Percent	1.6*(s.e.)[1]
White	3,393	87.1	1.8	33.5	2.5
Black	262	88.3	7.2	14.1	7.7
Hispanic origin[2]	583	59.7	7.3	6.3	3.6
St. Louis, MO-IL MSA					
25 years and over	1,503	80.9	3.5	21.2	3.7
White	1,255	83.6	3.6	23.3	4.1
Black	238	66.3	12.4	9.8	7.8
Hispanic origin[2]	12	(B)	(B)	(B)	(B)
Washington, DC-MD-VA MSA					
25 years and over	2,677	88.0	2.1	38.2	2.1
White	1,868	90.6	2.2	45.2	3.8
Black	632	80.7	-	16.2	-
Hispanic origin[2]	125	67.1	-	33.5	-

Source: Kominski, Robert and Andrea Adams. U.S. Bureau of the Census. *Educational Attainment in the United States: March 1993 and 1992.* Current Population Reports, P20-476. Washington, DC: U.S. Government Printing Office, 1994, pp. 90-92. *Notes:* Based on population estimates of states as of July 1, 1986. Population values shown in this table are derived from the CPS sample, and may not match independently derived estimates of the population. (B) stands for base too small for derived measures. 1. The value of 1.6 times the standard error [1.6*(s.e.)], added and subtracted from the estimated percentage, yields the 90-percent confidence interval. 2. Persons of Hispanic origin may be of any race.

★ 243 ★

Educational Attainment

Educational Attainment, by Race and Ethnicity

Data are shown in percent for persons 25 years old and over. Figures for 1960, 1970, and 1980 are shown as of April 1 and based on sample data from the censuses of population. Other years as of March and based on the Current Population Survey.

Year	Total[1]	White	Black	Asian and Pacific Islander	Hispanic[2]			
					Total[3]	Mexican	Puerto Rican	Cuban
Completed 4 years of high school or more								
1960	41.1	43.2	20.1	NA	NA	NA	NA	NA
1965	49.0	51.3	27.2	NA	NA	NA	NA	NA
1970	52.3	54.5	31.4	NA	32.1	24.2	23.4	43.9
1975	62.5	64.5	42.5	NA	37.9	31.0	28.7	51.7
1980	66.5	68.8	51.2	NA	44.0	37.6	40.1	55.3
1985	73.9	75.5	59.8	NA	47.9	41.9	46.3	51.1
1990	77.6	79.1	66.2	80.4	50.8	44.1	55.5	63.5
1991	78.4	79.9	66.7	81.8	51.3	43.6	58.0	61.0
1992[4]	79.4	80.9	67.7	NA	52.6	45.2	60.5	62.0
1993[4]	80.2	81.5	70.4	NA	53.1	46.2	59.8	62.1

[Continued]

★ 243 ★

Educational Attainment, by Race and Ethnicity

[Continued]

Year	Total[1]	White	Black	Asian and Pacific Islander	Hispanic[2]			
					Total[3]	Mexican	Puerto Rican	Cuban
Completed 4 years of college or more								
1960	7.7	8.1	3.1	NA	NA	NA	NA	NA
1965	9.4	9.9	4.7	NA	NA	NA	NA	NA
1970	10.7	11.3	4.4	NA	4.5	2.5	2.2	11.1
1975	13.9	14.5	6.4	NA	NA	NA	NA	NA
1980	16.2	17.1	8.4	NA	7.6	4.9	5.6	16.2
1985	19.4	20.0	11.1	NA	8.5	5.5	7.0	13.7
1990	21.3	22.0	11.3	39.9	9.2	5.4	9.7	20.2
1991	21.4	22.2	11.5	39.1	9.7	6.2	10.1	18.5
1992[4]	21.4	22.1	11.9	NA	9.3	6.1	8.4	18.4
1993[4]	21.9	22.6	12.2	NA	9.0	5.9	8.0	16.5

Source: U.S. Bureau of the Census. *Statistical Abstract of the United States, 1994 on CD-ROM.* [machine-readable datafiles] Washington, DC: U.S. Government Printing Office, 1994. Primary source: U.S. Bureau of the Census, U.S. Census of Population, U.S. Summary, PC80-1-C1 and Current Population Reports P20-455, P20-459, P20-462, P20- 465RV, P20-475; and unpublished data. *Notes:* NA stands for not available. 1. Includes other races, not shown separately. 2. Persons of Hispanic origin may be of any race. 3. Includes persons of other Hispanic origin, not shown separately. 4. Beginning in 1992, persons who are high school graduates and those with a BA degree or higher.

★ 244 ★

Educational Attainment

Educational Attainment, by Race/Ethnicity and Sex

Data are shown in percent for persons 25 years old and over. Figures for 1960, 1970, and 1980 are shown as of April 1 and based on sample data from the Censuses of Population. Other years are shown as of March and based on the Current Population Survey.

Year	All races[1]		White		Black		Asian/Pacific Islander		Hispanic[2]	
	Male	Female	Male	Female	Male	Female	Male	Female	Male	Female
Completed 4 years of high school or more										
1960	39.5	42.5	41.6	44.7	18.2	21.8	NA	NA	NA	NA
1965	48.0	49.9	50.2	52.2	25.8	28.4	NA	NA	NA	NA
1970	51.9	52.8	54.0	55.0	30.1	32.5	NA	NA	37.9	34.2
1975	63.1	62.1	65.0	64.1	41.6	43.3	NA	NA	39.5	36.7
1980	67.3	65.8	69.6	68.1	50.8	51.5	NA	NA	67.3	65.8
1985	74.4	73.5	76.0	75.1	58.4	60.8	NA	NA	48.5	47.4
1990	77.7	77.5	79.1	79.0	65.8	66.5	84.0	77.2	50.3	51.3
1991	78.5	78.3	79.8	79.9	66.7	66.7	83.8	80.0	51.4	51.2
1992[3]	79.7	79.2	81.1	80.7	67.0	68.2	NA	NA	53.7	51.5
1993[3]	80.5	80.0	81.8	81.3	69.6	71.1	NA	NA	52.9	53.2

[Continued]

★ 244 ★

Educational Attainment, by Race/Ethnicity and Sex

[Continued]

Year	All races[1]		White		Black		Asian/Pacific Islander		Hispanic[2]	
	Male	Female	Male	Female	Male	Female	Male	Female	Male	Female
Completed 4 years of college or more										
1960	9.7	5.8	10.3	6.0	2.8	3.3	NA	NA	NA	NA
1965	12.0	7.1	12.7	7.3	4.9	4.5	NA	NA	NA	NA
1970	13.5	8.1	14.4	8.4	4.2	4.6	NA	NA	7.8	4.3
1975	17.6	10.6	18.4	11.0	6.7	6.2	NA	NA	8.3	4.6
1980	20.1	12.8	21.3	13.3	8.4	8.3	NA	NA	9.4	6.0
1985	23.1	16.0	24.0	16.3	11.2	11.0	NA	NA	9.7	7.3
1990	24.4	18.4	25.3	19.0	11.9	10.8	44.9	35.4	9.8	8.7
1991	24.3	18.8	25.4	19.3	11.4	11.6	43.2	35.5	10.0	9.4
1992[3]	24.3	18.6	25.2	19.1	11.9	12.0	NA	NA	10.2	8.5
1993[3]	24.8	19.2	25.7	19.7	11.9	12.4	NA	NA	9.5	8.5

Source: U.S. Bureau of the Census. *Statistical Abstract of the United States, 1994 on CD-ROM.* 114th ed. [machine-readable datafiles] Washington, DC: U.S. Government Printing Office, 1994. Primary source: U.S. Bureau of the Census, U.S. Census of Population, 1960, 1970, and 1980, vol. 1; and Current Population Reports P20-459, P20-462, P20-475; and unpublished data. *Notes:* NA stands for not available. 1. Includes other races, not shown separately. 2. Persons of Hispanic origin may be of any race. 3. Beginning 1992, persons high school graduates and those with a BA degree or higher.

★ 245 ★

Educational Attainment

Educational Attainment, by Race/Ethnicity, March 1993

Data show percentage of persons of each race/ethnicity who have attained each level of education. Numbers are shown in thousands.

Race/ethnicity	Number of persons	Percentage with -		
		High school diploma or more	Some college or more	Bachelor's degree or more
All persons	162,826	80.2	44.9	21.9
White	139,019	80.5	45.9	22.6
Black	17,786	70.4	34.2	12.2
Other	6,021	79.0	52.4	33.9
Hispanic origin[1]				
Hispanic	12,100	53.1	26.3	9.0
Non-Hispanic	150,726	82.4	46.3	22.9

Source: Kominski, Robert and Andrea Adams. U.S. Bureau of the Census. *Educational Attainment in the United States: March 1993 and 1992.* Current Population Reports, P20-476. Washington, DC: U.S. Government Printing Office, 1994, p. vii. *Note:* 1. Persons of Hispanic origin may be of any race.

★ 246 ★

Educational Attainment

Educational Attainment, by State, March 1993

Data show educational attainment of persons age 25 years and older, by race/ethnicity, in the 25 largest states. Numbers are shown in thousands for the noninstitutional population.

Race, Hispanic origin, and state	Total population	High school graduation or more		Completed bachelor's degree or more	
		Percent	1.6*(s.e.)[1]	Percent	1.6*(s.e.)[1]
Alabama					
25 years and over	2,606	76.0	2.3	14.6	1.9
White	1,971	78.3	2.6	16.8	2.4
Black	623	69.0	6.1	7.3	3.4
Hispanic origin[2]	11	(B)	(B)	(B)	(B)
Arizona					
25 years and over	2,429	83.9	2.0	22.4	2.3
White	2,256	84.5	2.1	23.1	2.4
Black	84	89.6	10.4	12.5	11.3
Hispanic origin[2]	328	52.0	8.6	5.9	4.1
California					
25 years and over	19,689	79.7	.8	25.0	.9
White	16,503	78.9	.9	24.0	1.0
Black	1,162	83.1	3.7	13.5	3.4
Hispanic origin[2]	4,314	47.3	2.6	6.0	1.2
Florida					
25 years and over	9,330	79.6	1.0	19.8	1.0
White	7,988	81.9	1.1	20.6	1.1
Black	1,184	64.2	4.0	12.5	2.8
Hispanic origin[2]	1,205	61.7	4.0	15.9	3.0
Georgia					
25 years and over	4,183	74.7	2.3	21.1	2.2
White	2,959	77.1	2.7	23.0	2.7
Black	1,125	67.6	5.7	16.5	4.5
Hispanic origin[2]	66	(B)	(B)	(B)	(B)
Illinois					
25 years and over	7,587	79.2	1.2	22.1	1.2
White	6,262	80.6	1.3	22.7	1.3
Black	1,135	71.6	3.9	14.7	3.1
Hispanic origin[2]	509	47.8	6.5	6.7	3.3
Indiana					
25 years and over	3,588	79.2	2.3	14.1	2.0
White	3,230	80.7	2.4	14.8	2.1
Black	339	64.8	10.3	4.9	4.6
Hispanic origin[2]	48	(B)	(B)	(B)	(B)
Kentucky					
25 years and over	2,385	73.9	2.4	17.2	2.1
White	2,201	73.6	2.5	17.8	2.2
Black	158	74.8	10.8	4.6	5.2
Hispanic origin[2]	7	(B)	(B)	(B)	(B)
Louisiana					
25 years and over	2,546	73.7	2.6	16.5	2.2
White	1,841	79.0	2.8	19.4	2.7
Black	686	59.4	3.5	8.0	3.6

[Continued]

★ 246 ★

Educational Attainment, by State, March 1993

[Continued]

Race, Hispanic origin, and state	Total population	High school graduation or more		Completed bachelor's degree or more	
		Percent	1.6*(s.e.)[1]	Percent	1.6*(s.e.)[1]
Hispanic origin[2]	41	(B)	(B)	(B)	(B)
Maryland					
25 years and over	3,251	82.6	2.1	26.1	2.5
White	2,393	85.7	2.3	29.0	3.0
Black	815	73.5	5.8	16.5	4.9
Hispanic origin[2]	65	(B)	(B)	(B)	(B)
Massachusetts					
25 years and over	3,959	84.6	1.1	30.0	1.3
White	3,744	85.2	1.1	30.1	1.4
Black	121	71.9	8.7	19.5	7.7
Hispanic origin[2]	109	59.9	10.0	12.3	6.7
Michigan					
25 years and over	5,908	81.5	1.1	19.1	1.1
White	5,076	83.3	1.2	19.6	1.2
Black	742	68.7	4.4	12.7	3.2
Hispanic origin[2]	95	66.4	12.6	17.1	10.0
Minnesota					
25 years and over	2,811	86.0	2.0	23.3	2.4
White	2,713	86.3	2.0	23.2	2.4
Black	66	(B)	(B)	(B)	(B)
Hispanic origin[2]	33	(B)	(B)	(B)	(B)
Missouri					
25 years and over	3,188	80.3	2.3	20.3	2.3
White	2,849	82.2	2.3	21.6	2.5
Black	272	68.9	10.7	8.3	6.4
Hispanic origin[2]	42	(B)	(B)	(B)	(B)
New Jersey					
25 years and over	5,160	82.1	1.1	27.9	1.3
White	4,389	82.9	1.2	28.4	1.4
Black	557	74.0	4.4	14.6	3.6
Hispanic origin[2]	445	60.2	5.5	10.7	3.5
New York					
25 years and over	11,600	80.7	.9	24.2	.9
White	9,515	81.9	.9	25.4	1.0
Black	1,602	74.3	3.0	14.2	2.4
Hispanic origin[2]	1,118	56.0	4.0	7.8	2.2
North Carolina					
25 years and over	4,385	74.8	1.2	18.5	1.1
White	3,361	78.6	1.3	21.3	1.3
Black	943	62.9	3.4	8.9	2.0
Hispanic origin[2]	46	(B)	(B)	(B)	(B)
Ohio					
25 years and over	7,101	82.8	1.1	19.5	1.1
White	6,356	83.4	1.1	20.1	1.2
Black	681	77.2	4.5	11.6	3.4

[Continued]

★ 246 ★

Educational Attainment, by State, March 1993

[Continued]

Race, Hispanic origin, and state	Total population	High school graduation or more		Completed bachelor's degree or more	
		Percent	1.6*(s.e.)[1]	Percent	1.6*(s.e.)[1]
Hispanic origin[2]	48	(B)	(B)	(B)	(B)
Pennsylvania					
25 years and over	8,107	79.8	1.1	18.7	1.1
White	7,414	80.6	1.1	19.1	1.1
Black	560	71.4	5.5	9.7	3.6
Hispanic origin[2]	95	64.2	14.2	16.6	11.0
South Carolina					
25 years and over	2,220	73.3	2.2	16.7	1.9
White	1,604	78.0	2.4	20.3	2.4
Black	592	60.7	5.5	6.7	2.8
Hispanic origin[2]	18	(B)	(B)	(B)	(B)
Tennessee					
25 years and over	3,202	72.0	2.4	14.9	1.9
White	2,642	72.2	2.6	15.5	2.1
Black	521	69.6	6.9	9.6	4.4
Hispanic origin[2]	10	(B)	(B)	(B)	(B)
Texas					
25 years and over	10,777	77.3	1.2	22.1	1.2
White	9,161	77.7	1.3	22.6	1.3
Black	1,253	74.0	4.2	13.1	3.3
Hispanic origin[2]	2,251	48.8	3.6	7.9	1.9
Virginia					
25 years and over	4,026	80.7	1.9	25.8	2.1
White	3,206	82.5	2.1	28.4	2.5
Black	666	70.7	6.3	11.0	4.4
Hispanic origin[2]	73	(B)	(B)	(B)	(B)
Washington					
25 years and over	3,250	88.5	1.7	27.9	2.4
White	3,020	90.1	1.7	28.4	2.5
Black	67	(B)	(B)	(B)	(B)
Hispanic origin[2]	76	76.1	17.5	15.9	15.0
Wisconsin					
25 years and over	3,089	84.8	1.9	20.0	2.1
White	2,918	86.1	1.9	20.7	2.2
Black	139	56.0	14.2	7.6	7.6
Hispanic origin[2]	40	(B)	(B)	(B)	(B)

Source: Kominski, Robert and Andrea Adams. U.S. Bureau of the Census. *Educational Attainment in the United States: March 1993 and 1992*. Current Population Reports, P20-476. Washington, DC: U.S. Government Printing Office, 1994, pp. 84-88. *Notes:* Based on population estimates of states as of July 1, 1986. Population values shown in this table are derived from the CPS sample, and may not match independently derived estimates of the population. (B) stands for base too small for derived measures. 1. The value of 1.6 times the standard error [1.6*(s.e.)], added and subtracted from the estimated percentage, yields the 90-percent confidence interval. 2. Persons of Hispanic origin may be of any race.

★ 247 ★

Educational Attainment

Educational Status of Persons Age 18 and Older, 1990

Data show, in thousands, the number and percent distribution of persons who have attained each level of education, as of Spring 1990.

Sex and race/ethnicity	Total	Not high school graduate[1]	High school graduate only	Some college, no degree or certificate	Vocational certificate	Associate's degree	Bachelor's degree	Master's degree	Professional degree	Doctor's degree
					Number in thousands					
Total population, age 18 and older	182,591	38,012	65,291	33,191	4,973	7,570	22,845	7,599	2,054	1,056
Men	87,240	17,948	29,713	16,099	1,737	3,600	11,769	3,996	1,547	833
Women	95,350	20,065	35,578	17,092	3,236	3,970	11,076	3,603	506	223
White, total[2]	156,385	30,270	56,240	28,608	4,541	6,677	20,381	6,813	1,898	956
Men	75,262	14,425	25,556	14,076	1,588	3,242	10,629	3,552	1,449	744
Women	81,123	15,845	30,684	14,532	2,953	3,435	9,752	3,261	449	212
Black, total[2]	20,401	6,510	7,495	3,534	284	670	1,367	462	46	34
Men	9,158	3,045	3,483	1,441	87	257	581	199	38	28
Women	11,242	3,465	4,012	2,094	197	413	786	262	8	6
Hispanic, total[3]	13,548	5,934	4,091	1,933	208	316	734	245	55	32
Men	6,708	2,950	1,961	976	89	153	388	121	44	27
Women	6,841	2,984	2,130	958	119	163	346	124	11	2
				Percent distribution, by highest degree earned						
Total population, age 18 and older	100.0	20.8	35.8	18.2	2.7	4.1	12.5	4.2	1.1	0.6
Men	100.0	20.6	34.1	18.5	2.0	4.1	13.5	4.6	1.8	1.0
Women	100.0	21.0	37.3	17.9	3.4	4.2	11.6	3.8	0.5	0.2
White, total[2]	100.0	19.4	36.0	18.3	2.9	4.3	13.0	4.4	1.2	0.6
Men	100.0	19.2	34.0	18.7	2.1	4.3	14.1	4.7	1.9	1.0
Women	100.0	19.5	37.8	17.9	3.6	4.2	12.0	4.0	0.6	0.3
Black, total[2]	100.0	31.9	36.7	17.3	1.4	3.3	6.7	2.3	0.2	0.2
Men	100.0	33.2	38.0	15.7	0.9	2.8	6.3	2.2	0.4	0.3
Women	100.0	30.8	35.7	18.6	1.7	3.7	7.0	2.3	0.1	0.1
Hispanic, total[3]	100.0	43.8	30.2	14.3	1.5	2.3	5.4	1.8	0.4	0.2
Men	100.0	44.0	29.2	14.5	1.3	2.3	5.8	1.8	0.7	0.4
Women	100.0	43.6	31.1	14.0	1.7	2.4	5.1	1.8	0.2	0.1

Source: U.S. Department of Education. National Center for Education Statistics. Office of Educational Research and Improvement. *Digest of Education Statistics, 1994.* Lanham, MD: Bernan, November 1994, p. 20. Primary source: U.S. Bureau of the Census, *Current Population Reports*, Series P-70, No. 32, "What's It Worth? Educational Background and Economic Status: Spring 1990." (This table was prepared February 1993.) *Notes:* A dash (-) stands for data not available. Data are based on sample surveys of the civilian noninstitutional population. Because of rounding, details may not add to totals. 1. Some people are still enrolled in high school. 2. Includes persons of Hispanic origin. 3. Persons of Hispanic origin may be of any race.

★ 248 ★

Educational Attainment

High School and College Completion Percentages in Selected Large Metropolitan Areas, 1989

Numbers are in shown thousands.

Metropolitan area	Total population	Completed 4 years of high school	Completed 4 years of college
Chicago-Gary-Lake County, IL-IN-WI CMSA			
White	3,958	80.9	26.0
Black	876	73.5	13.6
Hispanic origin[1]	433	50.3	10.6
Los Angeles-Anaheim-Riverside, CA CMSA			
White	6,911	73.9	23.6
Black	787	86.0	19.9
Hispanic origin[1]	2,226	43.4	6.8
New York-Northern New Jersey-Long Island, NY-NJ-CT CMSA			
White	9,437	79.1	26.1
Black	1,754	68.9	13.7
Hispanic origin[1]	1,454	53.0	9.6
San Francisco-Oakland-San Jose, CA CMSA			
White	3,106	85.9	34.8
Black	200	71.4	20.0
Hispanic origin[1]	446	58.9	11.7

Source: U.S. Bureau of the Census. *Educational Attainment in the United States: March 1989 and 1988.* Current Population Reports, Series P-20, No. 451, Washington, DC: U.S. Government Printing Office, 1991, pp. 96-98. *Notes:* Based on population estimates of metropolitan areas as of July 1, 1986. Population values shown in this table are derived from the CPS sample, and may not match independently derived estimates of the population. 1. Persons of Hispanic origin may be of any race.

★ 249 ★

Educational Attainment

High School and College Completion Trends

Data show the percentage of persons age 25 years and older who had completed at least four years of high school or four years of college in each year. Rates refer to the noninstitutional population.

Year	All races			White			Black[1]			Hispanic origin[2]		
	Both sexes	Male	Female	Both sexes	Male	Female	Both sexes	Male	Female	Both sexes	Male	Female
Completed 4 years of high school or more												
1993	80.2	80.5	80.0	81.5	81.9	81.3	70.4	69.6	71.1	53.1	52.9	53.2
1992[3]	79.4	79.7	79.2	80.9	81.1	80.7	67.7	67.0	68.2	52.6	53.7	51.5
1991	78.4	78.5	78.3	79.9	79.8	79.9	66.7	66.7	66.7	51.3	51.4	51.2
1990	77.6	77.7	77.5	79.1	79.1	79.0	66.2	65.8	66.5	50.8	50.3	51.3
1989	76.9	77.2	76.6	78.4	78.6	78.2	64.6	64.2	65.0	50.9	51.0	50.7
1988	76.2	76.4	76.0	77.7	77.7	77.6	63.5	63.7	63.4	51.0	52.0	50.0
1987	75.6	76.0	75.3	77.0	77.3	76.7	63.4	63.0	63.7	50.9	51.8	50.0
1986	74.7	75.1	74.4	76.2	76.5	75.9	62.3	61.5	63.0	48.5	49.2	47.8
1985	73.9	74.4	73.5	75.5	76.0	75.1	59.8	58.4	60.8	47.9	48.5	47.4
1984	73.3	73.7	73.0	75.0	75.4	74.6	58.5	57.1	59.7	47.1	48.6	45.7
1983	72.1	72.7	71.5	73.8	74.4	73.3	56.8	56.5	57.1	46.2	48.6	44.2
1982	71.0	71.7	70.3	72.8	73.4	72.3	54.9	55.7	54.3	45.9	48.1	44.1
1981	69.7	70.3	69.1	71.6	72.1	71.2	52.9	53.2	52.6	44.5	45.5	43.6
1980	68.6	69.2	68.1	70.5	71.0	70.1	51.2	51.1	51.3	45.3	46.4	44.1
1979	67.7	68.4	67.1	69.7	70.3	69.2	49.4	49.2	49.5	42.0	42.3	41.7
1978	65.9	66.8	65.2	67.9	68.6	67.2	47.6	47.9	47.3	40.8	42.2	39.6
1977	64.9	65.6	64.4	67.0	67.5	66.5	45.5	45.6	45.4	39.6	42.3	37.2
1976	64.1	64.7	63.5	66.1	66.7	65.5	43.8	42.3	45.0	39.3	41.4	37.3
1975	62.5	63.1	62.1	64.5	65.0	64.1	42.5	41.6	43.3	37.9	39.5	36.7
1974	61.2	61.6	60.9	63.3	63.6	63.0	40.8	39.9	41.5	36.5	38.3	34.9
1973	59.8	60.0	59.6	61.9	62.1	61.7	39.2	38.2	40.1	(NA)	(NA)	(NA)
1972	58.2	58.2	58.2	60.4	60.3	60.5	36.6	35.7	37.2	(NA)	(NA)	(NA)
1971	56.4	56.3	56.6	58.6	58.4	58.8	34.7	33.8	35.4	(NA)	(NA)	(NA)
1970	55.2	55.0	55.4	57.4	57.2	57.6	33.7	32.4	34.8	(NA)	(NA)	(NA)
1969	54.0	53.6	54.4	56.3	55.7	56.7	32.3	31.9	32.6	(NA)	(NA)	(NA)
1968	52.6	52.0	53.2	54.9	54.3	55.5	30.1	28.9	31.0	(NA)	(NA)	(NA)
1967	51.1	50.5	51.7	53.4	52.8	53.8	29.5	27.1	31.5	(NA)	(NA)	(NA)
1966	49.9	49.0	50.8	52.2	51.3	53.0	27.8	25.8	29.5	(NA)	(NA)	(NA)
1965	49.0	48.0	49.9	51.3	50.2	52.2	27.2	25.8	28.4	(NA)	(NA)	(NA)
1964	48.0	47.0	48.9	50.3	49.3	51.2	25.7	23.7	27.4	(NA)	(NA)	(NA)
1962	46.3	45.0	47.5	48.7	47.4	49.9	24.8	23.2	26.2	(NA)	(NA)	(NA)
1959	43.7	42.2	45.2	46.1	44.5	47.7	20.7	19.6	21.6	(NA)	(NA)	(NA)
1957	41.6	39.7	43.3	43.2	41.1	45.1	18.4	16.9	19.7	(NA)	(NA)	(NA)
1952	38.8	36.9	40.5	(NA)	(NA)	(NA)	15.0	14.0	15.7	(NA)	(NA)	(NA)
1950	34.3	32.6	36.0	(NA)	(NA)	(NA)	13.7	12.5	14.7	(NA)	(NA)	(NA)
1947	33.1	31.4	34.7	35.0	33.2	36.7	13.6	12.7	14.5	(NA)	(NA)	(NA)
1940	24.5	22.7	26.3	26.1	24.2	28.1	7.7	6.9	8.4	(NA)	(NA)	(NA)
Completed 4 years of college or more												
1993	21.9	24.8	419.2	22.6	25.7	19.7	12.2	11.9	12.4	9.0	9.5	8.5
1992[4]	21.4	24.3	18.6	22.1	25.2	19.1	11.9	11.9	12.0	9.3	10.2	8.5
1991	21.4	24.3	18.8	22.2	25.4	19.3	11.5	11.4	11.6	9.7	10.0	9.4
1990	21.3	24.4	18.4	22.0	25.3	19.0	11.3	11.9	10.8	9.2	9.8	8.7
1989	21.1	24.5	18.1	21.8	25.4	18.5	11.8	11.7	11.9	9.9	11.0	8.8
1988	20.0	24.0	17.0	20.9	25.0	17.3	11.2	11.1	11.4	10.1	12.3	8.1
1987	19.9	23.6	16.5	20.5	24.5	16.9	10.7	11.0	10.4	8.6	9.7	7.5
1986	19.4	23.2	16.1	20.1	24.1	16.4	10.9	11.2	10.7	8.4	9.5	7.4
1985	19.4	23.1	16.0	20.0	24.0	16.3	11.1	11.2	11.0	8.5	9.7	7.3
1984	19.1	22.9	15.7	19.8	23.9	16.0	10.4	10.4	10.4	8.2	9.5	7.0
1983	18.8	23.0	15.1	19.5	24.0	15.4	9.5	10.0	9.2	7.9	9.2	6.8
1982	17.7	21.9	14.0	18.5	23.0	14.4	8.8	9.1	8.5	7.8	9.6	6.2
1981	17.1	21.1	13.4	17.8	22.2	13.8	8.2	8.2	8.2	7.7	9.7	5.9

[Continued]

★ 249 ★

High School and College Completion Trends

[Continued]

Year	All races			White			Black[1]			Hispanic origin[2]		
	Both sexes	Male	Female	Both sexes	Male	Female	Both sexes	Male	Female	Both sexes	Male	Female
1980	17.0	20.9	13.6	17.8	22.1	14.0	7.9	7.7	8.1	7.9	9.7	6.2
1979	16.4	20.4	12.9	17.2	21.4	13.3	7.9	8.3	7.5	6.7	8.2	5.3
1978	15.7	19.7	12.2	16.4	20.7	12.6	7.2	7.3	7.1	7.0	8.6	5.7
1977	15.4	19.2	12.0	16.1	20.2	12.4	7.2	7.0	7.4	6.2	8.1	4.4
1976	14.7	18.6	11.3	15.4	19.6	11.6	6.6	6.3	6.8	6.1	8.6	4.0
1975	13.9	17.6	10.6	14.5	18.4	11.0	6.4	6.7	6.2	6.3	8.3	4.6
1974	13.3	16.9	10.1	14.0	17.7	10.6	5.5	5.7	53	5.5	7.1	4.0
1973	12.6	16.0	9.6	13.1	16.8	9.9	6.0	5.9	6.0	(NA)	(NA)	(NA)
1972	12.0	15.4	9.0	12.6	16.2	9.4	5.1	5.5	4.8	(NA)	(NA)	(NA)
1971	11.4	14.6	8.5	12.0	15.5	8.9	4.5	4.7	4.3	(NA)	(NA)	(NA)
1970	11.0	14.1	8.2	11.6	15.0	8.6	4.5	4.6	4.4	(NA)	(NA)	(NA)
1969	10.7	13.6	8.1	11.2	14.3	8.5	4.6	4.8	4.5	(NA)	(NA)	(NA)
1968	10.5	13.3	8.0	11.0	14.1	8.3	4.3	3.7	4.8	(NA)	(NA)	(NA)
1967	10.1	12.8	7.6	10.6	13.6	7.9	4.0	3.4	4.4	(NA)	(NA)	(NA)
1966	9.8	12.5	7.4	10.4	13.3	7.7	3.8	3.9	3.7	(NA)	(NA)	(NA)
1965	9.4	12.0	7.1	9.9	12.7	7.3	4.7	4.9	4.5	(NA)	(NA)	(NA)
1964	9.1	11.7	6.8	9.6	12.3	7.1	3.9	4.5	3.4	(NA)	(NA)	(NA)
1962	8.9	11.4	6.7	9.5	12.2	7.0	4.0	3.9	4.0	(NA)	(NA)	(NA)
1959	8.1	10.3	6.0	8.6	11.0	6.2	3.3	3.8	2.9	(NA)	(NA)	(NA)
1957	7.6	9.6	5.8	8.0	10.1	6.0	2.9	2.7	3.0	(NA)	(NA)	(NA)
1952	7.0	8.3	5.8	(NA)	(NA)	(NA)	2.4	2.0	2.7	(NA)	(NA)	(NA)
1950	6.2	7.3	5.2	(NA)	(NA)	(NA)	2.3	2.1	2.4	(NA)	(NA)	(NA)
1947	5.4	6.2	4.7	5.7	6.6	4.9	2.5	2.4	2.6	(NA)	(NA)	(NA)
1940	4.6	5.5	3.8	4.9	5.9	4.0	1.3	1.4	1.2	(NA)	(NA)	(NA)

Source: Kominski, Robert and Andrea Adams. U.S. Bureau of the Census. *Educational Attainment in the United States: March 1993 and 1992.* Current Population Reports, P20-476. Washington, DC: U.S. Government Printing Office, 1994, pp. 96-97. Primary source: 1947, and 1952 to 1993 March Current Population Survey (noninstitutional population, excluding members of the Armed forces living in barracks) 1950 Census of Population and 1940 Census of Population (resident population). *Notes:* 1. Data are for black and other races for 1940 to 1962; for 1963 to 1981, data are for black persons only. 2. Persons of Hispanic origin may be of any race. 3. Beginning 1992, high school graduate or more. 4. Beginning 1992, Bachelor's degree or more.

★ 250 ★

Educational Attainment

Highest Degree Earned by Persons Age 18 and Older

Data are shown in thousands of persons, by sex and race/ethnicity, for spring of 1990.

Age, sex, race	Total	Doctorate	Professional	Master's	Bachelor's	Associate's	Vocational	Some college, no degree	High school graduate only	Not a high school graduate
Total, 18 years and over	182,591	1,056	2,054	7,599	22,845	7,570	4,973	33,191	65,291	38,012
White	156,385	956	1,898	6,813	20,381	6,677	4,541	28,608	56,240	30,270
Male	75,262	744	1,449	3,552	10,629	3,242	1,588	14,076	25,556	14,425
Female	81,123	212	449	3,261	9,752	3,435	2,953	14,532	30,684	15,845
Black	20,401	34	46	462	1,367	670	284	3,534	7,495	6,510
Male	9,158	28	38	199	581	257	87	1,441	3,483	3,045
Female	11,242	6	8	262	786	413	197	2,094	4,012	3,465
Hispanic origin[1]	13,548	32	55	245	734	316	208	1,933	4,091	5,934
Male	6,708	27	44	121	388	153	89	976	1,961	2,950
Female	6,841	5	11	124	346	163	119	958	2,130	2,984

Source: U.S. Bureau of the Census. *What's it Worth? Educational Background and Economic Status: Spring 1990.* Current Population Reports, Series P70-32. Washington DC: U.S. Government Printing Office, 1992, p. 13. *Notes:* A dash (-) represents zero or a number which rounds to zero. 1. Persons of Hispanic origin may be of any race.

★ 251 ★

Educational Attainment

Hispanic Educational Attainment, by Age Group and Ethnicity, March 1993

Numbers are shown in thousands. Data are U.S. Census Bureau estimates.

Characteristic	Total population	Hispanic origin population	Non-Hispanic population	Non-Hispanic White population	Hispanic subgroups: Mexican origin population	Puerto Rican origin population	Cuban origin population	Central and South American origin population	Other Hispanic origin
Educational attainment									
Total, 25 years and over	162,826	12,100	150,725	127,601	7,198	1,280	818	1,776	1,029
Percent completed-									
Less than 5th grade education	2.1	11.8	1.3	0.8	15.4	8.2	5.3	7.3	3.8
High school graduate or more	80.2	53.1	82.4	84.1	46.2	59.8	62.1	62.9	68.9
Bachelor's degree or more	21.9	9.0	22.9	23.8	5.9	8.0	16.5	15.2	15.1
Total, 25 to 34 years	41,864	4,277	37,587	30,599	2,702	434	138	694	309
Percent completed-									
Less than 5th grade education	0.9	5.4	0.4	0.3	7.5	1.1	1.0	2.7	1.0
High school graduate or more	86.9	60.4	89.9	91.2	52.7	74.4	84.2	67.8	80.8
Bachelor's degree or more	23.8	9.0	25.5	26.8	5.8	10.4	25.1	13.5	18.0
Total, 35 years and over	120,962	7,823	113,139	97,002	4,496	846	680	1,081	721
Percent completed-									
Less than 5th grade education	2.5	15.3	1.6	1.0	20.2	11.8	6.2	10.2	5.0
High school graduate or more	77.9	49.1	79.9	81.9	42.3	52.4	57.6	59.8	63.8
Bachelor's degree or more	21.2	9.0	22.0	22.8	6.0	6.8	14.7	16.3	13.8

Source: Montgomery, Patricia A. U.S. Bureau of the Census. *The Hispanic Population in the United States: March 1993.* Current Population Reports, Series P20-475. Washington, DC: U.S. Government Printing Office, 1994, p. 10.

★ 252 ★

Educational Attainment

Percentage of Persons 25 to 29 Years Old Who Have Completed 12 or More Years of School, 1971-91

Year	All: Total	All: Male	All: Female	Hispanic: Total	Hispanic: Male	Hispanic: Female	White: Total	White: Male	White: Female	Black: Total	Black: Male	Black: Female
1971	77.7	79.0	76.5	44.8	46.8	43.3	81.7	83.0	80.4	53.9	52.3	55.3
1972	79.8	80.5	79.2	45.9	46.2	45.7	83.4	84.1	82.7	61.1	66.4	45.9
1973	80.2	80.6	79.8	52.0	53.5	50.6	84.1	84.2	83.9	64.7	64.4	64.9
1974	81.9	83.1	80.8	51.3	51.4	51.1	85.5	86.0	85.0	66.4	68.9	64.5
1975	83.1	84.5	81.8	54.8	54.8	55.4	86.6	88.0	85.2	69.4	69.1	69.6
1976	84.7	86.0	83.5	58.8	59.5	58.2	87.7	89.0	86.4	75.4	74.2	76.3
1977	85.4	86.6	84.2	55.4	59.3	52.4	88.6	89.2	88.0	72.2	76.3	68.9
1978	85.3	86.0	84.6	56.6	57.9	55.2	88.5	88.8	88.2	75.3	76.5	74.2
1979	85.6	86.3	84.9	56.0	54.0	57.7	89.2	89.8	88.5	76.4	77.7	75.8
1980	85.4	85.4	85.5	58.4	56.9	60.0	89.2	89.1	89.2	74.9	71.0	78.1
1981	86.3	86.5	86.1	60.4	61.4	59.6	89.8	89.7	89.9	76.3	78.2	74.6
1982	86.2	86.4	86.1	58.4	57.3	59.2	89.1	89.1	89.1	79.2	78.6	79.8
1983	86.0	86.0	86.0	58.9	59.0	58.8	89.3	89.2	89.3	81.0	80.5	81.3
1984	85.9	85.6	86.3	58.3	55.6	60.7	89.4	89.4	89.4	78.7	76.6	80.6
1985	86.1	85.9	86.4	61.1	59.2	62.7	89.5	89.2	89.9	78.3	76.9	79.5

[Continued]

★ 252 ★

Percentage of Persons 25 to 29 Years Old Who Have Completed 12 or More Years of School, 1971-91

[Continued]

Year	All			Hispanic			White			Black		
	Total	Male	Female	Total	Male	Female	Total	Male	Female	Total	Male	Female
1986	86.1	85.9	86.4	56.6	55.9	57.3	89.6	88.8	90.4	82.6	85.6	80.0
1987	86.0	85.5	86.4	58.4	57.1	59.7	89.4	88.9	90.0	83.7	87.2	80.7
1988	85.9	84.7	87.1	63.0	61.3	64.9	89.7	88.4	90.9	83.5	81.9	84.9
1989	85.5	84.5	86.5	60.8	59.8	61.7	89.3	88.2	90.4	79.7	77.1	82.0
1990	85.7	84.4	87.0	58.2	56.6	59.9	90.1	88.6	91.6	81.8	82.0	58.2
1991	85.4	84.9	85.8	55.9	55.7	56.3	89.8	89.2	90.5	80.7	80.4	80.9

Source: U.S. Department of Education. National Center for Education Statistics. *The Condition of Education, 1992.* Washington, DC: U.S. Government Printing Office, 1992, p. 235. Primary source: U.S. Department of Commerce, Bureau of the Census, March Current Population Survey.

★ 253 ★

Educational Attainment

Years of School Completed by Persons 25 Years Old and Older, by Race/Ethnicity and Sex, 1970 and 1991

Characteristic	Population (000)	Percent of population completing-							Median school years completed
		Elementary school			High school		College		
		1 to 4 years	5 to 7 years	8 years	1 to 3 years	4 years	1 to 3 years	4 years or more	
1970, total persons[1]	109,899	5.5	10.0	12.8	19.4	31.1	10.6	10.7	12.1
Hispanic[2]	3,946	19.5	18.6	11.5	18.2	21.1	6.5	4.5	9.1
Male	1,897	19.1	18.0	11.3	18.1	19.9	7.6	5.9	9.3
Female	2,050	19.9	19.2	11.6	18.3	22.3	5.4	3.2	8.9
White	98,246	4.5	9.1	13.0	18.8	32.2	11.1	11.3	12.1
Male	46,527	4.8	9.7	13.3	18.2	28.5	11.1	14.4	12.1
Female	51,718	4.1	8.6	12.8	19.4	35.5	11.1	8.4	12.1
Black	10,375	14.6	18.7	10.5	24.8	21.2	5.9	4.4	9.8
Male	4,714	17.7	19.1	10.2	22.9	20.0	6.0	4.2	9.4
Female	5,661	12.0	18.3	10.8	26.4	22.2	5.8	4.6	10.0
1991, total persons[1]	158,694	2.4	3.8	4.4	11.0	38.6	18.4	21.4	12.7
Hispanic[2]	11,208	12.5	14.8	6.3	15.1	29.3	12.3	9.7	12.0
Male	5,509	12.9	14.8	6.1	14.7	28.5	13.0	10.0	12.1
Female	5,699	12.1	14.7	6.5	15.5	30.1	11.7	9.4	12.0
White	136,299	2.0	3.4	4.5	10.2	39.1	18.6	22.2	12.8
Male	65,394	2.2	3.6	4.5	9.9	36.1	18.4	25.4	12.8
Female	70,905	1.8	3.3	4.5	10.5	41.8	18.8	19.3	12.7
Black	17,096	4.7	6.4	4.1	18.0	37.7	17.5	11.5	12.4

[Continued]

★ 253 ★

Years of School Completed by Persons 25 Years Old and Older, by Race/Ethnicity and Sex, 1970 and 1991

[Continued]

Characteristic	Population (000)	Percent of population completing-							Median school years completed
		Elementary school			High school		College		
		1 to 4 years	5 to 7 years	8 years	1 to 3 years	4 years	1 to 3 years	4 years or more	
Male	7,626	6.5	6.3	4.3	16.3	38.3	17.0	11.4	12.4
Female	9,470	3.3	6.6	3.9	19.4	37.2	17.9	11.6	12.4

Source: U.S. Bureau of the Census. *Statistical Abstract of the United States: 1992,* (112th edition). Washington, DC: U.S. Government Printing Ofice, 1992, p. 144. Primary source: U.S. Bureau of the Census, *U.S. Census Population: 1970,* vols. I and II; and *Current Population Reports,* series P-20, No. 462. *Notes:* 1. Includes other races, not shown separately. 2. Persons of Hispanic origin may be of any race.

Extracurriculars

★ 254 ★

Extracurricular Activities at School

Data show percentage of high school seniors participating in each type of activity in 1992.

Activity	White	Black	Hispanic	Asian	American Indian
Athletics					
Interscholastic team sport	30.8	32.3	25.8	28.3	30.4
Interscholastic individual sport	20.9	21.2	14.9	21.6	20.7
Intramural team sport	22.3	25.8	20.8	24.9	27.9
Intramural individual sport	12.5	16.7	14.0	14.7	18.2
Performing arts					
Cheerleading	7.4	10.6	6.7	5.1	11.9
School band or orchestra	19.6	24.4	16.9	17.7	16.8
School play or musical	16.1	15.9	10.6	13.7	14.0
Student govt./clubs					
Student government	15.4	16.7	14.7	14.6	14.3
Academic honor society	19.6	14.0	12.5	27.2	13.6
School yearbook/newspaper	19.7	14.3	16.8	18.9	21.2
School service clubs	13.6	13.6	14.4	19.3	11.6
School academic clubs	25.8	20.7	22.6	32.3	17.7
School hobby clubs	7.4	6.6	9.1	11.3	10.8
School FTA, FHA, and FFA[1]	17.6	22.5	16.4	8.8	22.1

Source: U.S. Department of Education. National Center for Education Statistics. Office of Educational Research and Improvement. *Digest of Education Statistics, 1994.* Lanham, MD: Bernan, November 1994, p. 138. Primary source: U.S. Department of Education, National Center for Education Statistics, "National Education Longitudinal Study of 1988," First and Second Followup surveys. (This table was prepared March 1994.) *Notes:* 1. FTA stands for Future Teachers of America; FHA stands for Future Homemakers of America; FFA stands for Future Farmers of America.

★ 255 ★

Extracurriculars

Leisure Activity, by Type

Data show the percentage of high school seniors who said they engaged in each activity in 1982 and 1992.

Activity	Total	White	Black	Hispanic	Asian	American Indian
	Percent of 12th graders, 1982					
At least once a week						
Talking with friends	92.7	94.2	89.1	88.9	86.7	91.3
Reading for pleasure	50.4	51.0	53.9	43.1	56.4	50.3
Going on dates	61.3	63.9	51.9	58.1	40.3	54.5
Driving or riding around	62.4	65.2	48.9	60.7	42.4	62.3
Thinking or daydreaming	68.5	71.1	64.6	58.0	62.4	53.9
Talking with parents	83.9	85.6	80.1	78.0	79.8	76.0
Reading front page of newspaper	69.1	69.7	71.9	63.3	73.5	61.8
Five or more weekday hours						
Watches television	11.5	9.4	22.2	13.8	8.1	20.9
	Percent of 12th graders, 1992					
At least once a week						
Use a personal computer	23.7	23.9	23.6	20.9	27.0	23.8
Work on hobbies	40.9	42.0	34.8	39.9	37.8	49.8
Attend religious activities	31.0	31.4	33.7	26.9	30.4	14.6
Attend youth groups	22.4	22.5	23.3	18.5	26.4	22.1
Perform community service	11.3	11.1	12.1	10.9	14.0	9.2
Driving or riding around	73.3	75.7	67.8	66.2	66.7	71.0
Do things with friends	88.1	90.7	79.8	82.4	85.9	77.2
Do things with parent	66.7	68.2	62.0	63.8	63.4	61.2
Talk with other adult	47.7	48.8	44.3	46.2	43.0	44.0
Take music, art, or dance class	10.1	9.9	9.7	9.8	14.0	10.6
Take sports lessons	7.3	7.0	7.4	8.2	9.4	11.6
Play ball or other sport	26.3	27.1	22.9	23.6	28.7	29.4
More than an hour a day						
Reading for pleasure	55.4	56.3	51.0	53.5	54.4	59.3
Plays video games	13.0	11.7	19.9	13.0	13.5	21.1
Five or more weekday hours						
Watches television	8.4	6.4	21.3	9.3	6.4	12.7

Source: U.S. Department of Education. National Center for Education Statistics. Office of Educational Research and Improvement. *Digest of Education Statistics, 1994.* Lanham, MD: Bernan, November 1994, p. 139. Primary source: U.S. Department of Education, National Center for Education Statistics, "National Education Longitudinal Study of 1988," Second Followup survey, and "High School and Beyond," First Followup survey. (This table was prepared April 1994.).

★ 256 ★

Extracurriculars

School-Sponsored Extracurriculars

Data show the percentage of high school seniors who participated in each activity in 1982 and 1992.

Race/ethnicity	Academic clubs, 1992	Athletics		Cheerleading/drill team		Hobby clubs		Music		Vocational clubs	
		1982	1992	1982	1992	1982	1992	1982	1992	1982	1992
All seniors	25.1	50.0	40.0	13.5	7.6	19.5	7.7	27.6	19.8	23.5	17.7
White	25.8	49.8	41.1	13.1	7.4	18.7	7.4	26.7	19.6	21.9	17.6
Black	20.7	51.8	38.9	16.9	10.6	18.5	6.6	34.7	24.4	31.0	22.5
Hispanic	22.6	49.9	32.9	14.1	6.7	23.6	9.1	26.8	16.9	27.5	16.4
Asian	32.3	43.7	42.3	6.3	5.1	26.1	11.3	20.6	17.7	7.0	8.8
American Indian	17.7	52.8	42.5	11.5	11.9	30.3	10.8	26.5	16.8	30.0	22.1

Source: U.S. Department of Education. National Center for Education Statistics. Office of Educational Research and Improvement. *Digest of Education Statistics, 1994.* Lanham, MD: Bernan, November 1994, p. 139. Primary source: U.S. Department of Education, National Center for Education Statistics, "High School and Beyond," First Followup survey, 1980 Sophomore Cohort; and "National Education Longitudinal Study of 1988," Second Followup survey. (This table was prepared April 1994.).

School Enrollment

★ 257 ★

Continuous Enrollment in High School, 1972-92

From the source: "Persistent attendance, measured by the proportion of students enrolled in two consecutive years, is strongly associated with completing high school. Students who do not complete high school face a decreased opportunity for assuming a successful and fully functional place in the American work place and society at large." This table shows the percentage of high school students in grades 10-12, ages 15-24, who were enrolled the previous October and who had either completed high school or were enrolled again in the following October. Data are shown by sex and by race/ethnicity.

October	Total	Male	Female	White	Black	Hispanic	Male			Female		
							White	Black	Hispanic	White	Black	Hispanic
1972	93.9	94.1	94.1	94.7	90.5	88.8	95.0	90.2	88.5	94.4	90.7	89.1
1973	93.7	93.2	94.3	94.5	90.1	90.0	94.0	88.2	92.1	95.0	91.8	88.2
1974	93.3	92.6	94.0	94.2	88.4	90.1	93.4	89.2	87.2	95.1	87.7	92.9
1975	94.2	94.6	93.9	95.0	91.3	89.1	95.3	91.6	89.7	94.6	91.0	88.4
1976	94.1	93.5	94.8	94.4	92.6	92.7	93.7	91.5	92.4	95.1	93.7	92.9
1977	93.5	93.1	93.9	93.9	91.4	92.2	93.4	92.2	90.2	94.4	90.7	94.7
1978	93.3	92.5	94.1	94.2	89.8	87.7	93.6	89.0	84.1	94.9	90.5	91.5
1979	93.3	93.2	93.3	94.0	90.1	90.2	93.6	92.2	89.5	94.3	88.3	90.9
1980	93.9	93.3	94.5	94.8	91.8	88.3	94.3	92.3	82.4	95.2	91.3	93.3
1981	94.1	94.0	94.2	95.2	90.3	89.3	94.8	90.6	89.3	95.5	90.0	89.3
1982	94.5	94.2	94.9	95.3	92.2	90.8	95.1	91.1	90.5	95.4	93.4	91.2
1983	94.8	94.2	95.3	95.6	93.0	89.9	95.3	93.1	86.2	96.0	92.9	93.8
1984	94.9	94.6	95.2	95.6	94.3	88.9	95.2	94.0	87.7	95.9	94.5	89.8
1985	94.8	94.6	95.0	95.7	92.2	90.2	95.4	91.7	90.6	95.9	92.7	90.0
1986	95.3	95.3	95.3	96.3	94.6	88.1	96.2	94.9	87.6	96.3	94.3	88.7

[Continued]

★ 257 ★

Continuous Enrollment in High School, 1972-92

[Continued]

October	Total	Male	Female	White	Black	Hispanic	Male			Female		
							White	Black	Hispanic	White	Black	Hispanic
1987	95.9	95.7	96.2	96.5	93.6	94.6	96.1	93.8	95.2	96.9	93.3	94.0
1988	95.2	94.9	95.6	95.8	94.1	89.6	95.7	93.8	87.7	95.9	94.4	91.8
1989	95.5	95.5	95.5	96.5	92.2	92.2	96.3	93.0	92.2	96.7	91.4	92.3
1990	96.0	96.0	96.1	96.7	95.0	92.1	96.5	95.8	91.3	96.9	94.3	92.8
1991	96.0	96.2	95.8	96.8	94.0	92.7	97.2	94.7	89.9	96.3	93.2	95.4
1992[1]	95.6	96.1	95.1	96.3	95.0	91.8	96.5	96.7	92.4	96.0	93.3	91.0

Source: U.S. Department of Education. National Center for Education Statistics. *The Condition of Education 1994.* Washington, DC: U.S. Government Printing Office, 1994, p. 178. Primary source: U.S. Department of Commerce, Bureau of the Census, October Current Population Surveys; U.S. Department of Education, National Center for Education Statistics, *Dropout Rates in the United States: 1992. Notes:* Data for 1987 through 1990 reflect new editing procedures instituted by the Bureau of the Census for cases involving missing school enrollment items. 1. Beginning in 1992, the Current Population Survey changed the questions used to obtain the educational attainment of respondents.

★ 258 ★

School Enrollment

Elementary and Secondary School Enrollment Distribution by State and Race/Ethnicity, 1986 and 1993

Data show percent distribution of students by race/ethnicity in each state as of the fall semester. The 1986-87 data were derived from the 1986 Elementary and Secondary School Civil Rights sample survey of public school districts. Because of rounding, details may not add to totals.

State	Percent distribution, fall 1986						Percent distribution, fall 1993					
	Total	White[1]	Black[1]	Hispanic	Asian or Pacific Islander	American Indian/ Alaskan Native	Total	White[1]	Black[1]	Hispanic	Asian or Pacific Islander	American Indian/ Alaskan Native
United States	100.0	70.4	16.1	9.9	2.8	0.9	100.0	66.7[2]	16.5[2]	12.3[2]	3.5[2]	1.0[2]
Alabama	100.0	62.0	37.0	0.1	0.4	0.5	100.0	62.7	35.6	0.3	0.6	0.8
Alaska	100.0	65.7	4.3	1.7	3.3	25.1	100.0	66.1	4.7	2.3	4.0	23.0
Arizona	100.0	62.2	4.0	26.4	1.3	6.1	100.0	60.4	4.1	26.9	1.6	7.0
Arkansas	100.0	74.7	24.2	0.4	0.6	0.2	100.0	74.4	23.9	0.7	0.7	0.3
California	100.0	53.7	9.0	27.5	9.1	0.7	100.0	43.4	8.6	36.1	11.0	0.8
Colorado	100.0	78.7	4.5	13.7	2.0	1.0	100.0	74.5	5.4	16.8	2.4	1.0
Connecticut	100.0	77.2	12.1	8.9	1.5	0.2	100.0	73.8	12.9	10.7	2.3	0.2
Delaware	100.0	68.3	27.7	2.5	1.4	0.2	100.0	66.8	28.1	3.2	1.7	0.2
District of Columbia	100.0	4.0	91.1	3.9	0.9	0.1	100.0	4.0	89.1	5.6	1.3	[3]
Florida	100.0	65.4	23.7	9.5	1.2	0.2	100.0	60.3	24.4	13.4	1.6	0.2
Georgia	100.0	60.7	37.9	0.6	0.8	[3]	-	-	-	-	-	-
Hawaii	100.0	23.5	2.3	2.2	71.7	0.3	100.0	23.8	2.7	5.2	68.0	0.3
Idaho	100.0	92.6	0.3	4.9	0.8	1.3	-	-	-	-	-	-
Illinois	100.0	69.8	18.7	9.2	2.3	0.1	100.0	65.1	21.2	10.7	2.8	0.1
Indiana	100.0	88.7	9.0	1.7	0.5	0.1	100.0	86.2	11.0	1.9	0.7	0.1
Iowa	100.0	94.6	3.0	0.9	1.2	0.3	100.0	93.8	2.9	1.5	1.4	0.4
Kansas	100.0	85.6	7.6	4.4	1.9	0.6	100.0	84.1	8.2	5.0	1.8	0.9
Kentucky	100.0	89.2	10.2	0.1	0.5	[3]	99.9	89.7	9.5	0.2	0.5	[3]
Louisiana	100.0	56.5	41.3	0.8	1.1	0.3	100.0	52.2	45.1	1.0	1.2	0.4
Maine	100.0	98.3	0.5	0.2	0.8	0.2	-	-	-	-	-	-

[Continued]

★ 258 ★

Elementary and Secondary School Enrollment Distribution by State and Race/Ethnicity, 1986 and 1993

[Continued]

State	Percent distribution, fall 1986						Percent distribution, fall 1993					
	Total	White[1]	Black[1]	Hispanic	Asian or Pacific Islander	American Indian/ Alaskan Native	Total	White[1]	Black[1]	Hispanic	Asian or Pacific Islander	American Indian/ Alaskan Native
Maryland	100.0	59.7	35.3	1.7	3.1	0.2	100.0	59.8	33.6	2.7	3.7	0.3
Massachusetts	100.0	83.7	7.4	6.0	2.8	0.1	100.0	79.8	8.0	8.5	3.6	0.2
Michigan	100.0	76.4	19.8	1.8	1.2	0.8	100.0	77.8	17.4	2.4	1.3	1.0
Minnesota	100.0	93.9	2.1	0.9	1.7	1.5	100.0	89.8	3.7	1.5	3.2	1.8
Mississippi	100.0	43.9	55.5	0.1	0.4	0.1	100.0	48.3	50.6	0.2	0.5	0.4
Missouri	100.0	83.4	14.9	0.7	0.8	0.2	100.0	82.6	15.5	0.8	0.9	0.2
Montana	100.0	92.7	0.3	0.9	0.5	5.5	100.0	88.0	0.5	1.4	0.7	9.4
Nebraska	100.0	91.4	4.4	2.4	0.8	1.0	100.0	88.9	5.5	3.2	1.1	1.2
Nevada	100.0	77.4	9.6	7.5	3.2	2.3	100.0	72.0	9.1	13.1	3.9	1.9
New Hampshire	100.0	98.0	0.7	0.5	0.8	0.1	100.0	97.0	0.8	1.0	1.0	0.2
New Jersey	100.0	69.1	17.4	10.7	2.7	0.1	100.0	63.7	18.7	12.6	4.9	0.1
New Mexico	100.0	43.1	2.3	45.1	0.8	8.7	100.0	40.9	2.3	45.8	0.9	10.2
New York	100.0	68.4	16.5	12.3	2.7	0.2	100.0	58.9	20.0	16.1	4.6	0.3
North Carolina	100.0	68.4	28.9	0.4	0.6	1.7	100.0	66.1	30.2	1.1	1.0	1.6
North Dakota	100.0	92.4	0.6	1.1	0.8	5.0	100.0	90.8	0.7	0.7	0.7	7.1
Ohio	100.0	83.1	15.0	1.0	0.7	0.1	100.0	83.0	14.6	1.3	1.0	0.1
Oklahoma	100.0	79.0	7.8	1.6	1.0	10.6	100.0	72.6	10.2	3.1	1.2	13.0
Oregon	100.0	89.8	2.2	3.9	2.4	1.7	100.0	87.5	2.4	5.3	3.0	1.8
Pennsylvania	100.0	84.4	12.6	1.8	1.2	0.1	100.0	81.7	13.5	3.1	1.7	0.4
Rhode Island	100.0	87.9	5.6	3.7	2.4	0.3	100.0	82.0	6.6	8.0	3.1	0.4
South Carolina	100.0	54.6	44.5	0.2	0.6	0.1	100.0	57.3	41.4	0.5	0.6	0.2
South Dakota	100.0	90.6	0.5	0.6	0.7	7.6	100.0	86.3	0.7	0.5	0.7	11.9
Tennessee	100.0	76.5	22.6	0.2	0.6	[3]	100.0	75.8	22.9	0.4	0.8	0.1
Texas	100.0	51.0	14.4	32.5	2.0	0.2	100.0	48.4	14.3	34.9	2.2	0.2
Utah	100.0	93.7	0.4	3.0	1.5	1.5	100.0	91.7	0.6	4.3	2.0	1.4
Vermont	100.0	98.4	0.3	0.2	0.6	0.6	100.0	97.7	0.6	0.3	0.6	0.8
Virginia	100.0	72.6	23.7	1.0	2.6	0.1	100.0	68.5	25.5	2.5	3.3	0.2
Washington	100.0	84.5	4.2	3.8	5.1	2.3	100.0	80.7	4.4	6.4	6.0	2.5
West Virginia	100.0	95.9	3.7	0.1	0.3	[3]	100.0	95.4	4.0	0.2	0.4	0.1
Wisconsin	100.0	86.6	8.9	1.9	1.7	1.0	100.0	84.8	8.9	2.8	2.2	1.3
Wyoming	100.0	90.7	0.9	5.9	0.6	1.9	100.0	89.6	0.9	6.1	0.7	2.6
Outlying areas												
American Samoa	-	-	-	-	-	-	100.0	[3]	[3]	[3]	100.0	[3]
Guam	-	-	-	-	-	-	100.0	10.6	2.4	0.5	86.4	0.1
Northern Marianas	-	-	-	-	-	-	100.0	1.3	[3]	[3]	98.7	[3]
Puerto Rico	-	-	-	-	-	-	100.0	[3]	[3]	100.0	[3]	[3]
Virgin Islands	-	-	-	-	-	-	100.0	1.2	84.8	13.6	0.4	[3]

Source: U.S. Department of Education. National Center for Educational Statistics. Office of Educational Research and Improvement. *Digest of Education Statistics, 1994.* Lanham, MD: Bernan, 1994, p. 60. Primary source: U.S. Department of Education, Office for Civil Rights, 1986 State Summaries of Elementary and Secondary School Civil Rights Survey; and National Center for Education Statistics, Common Core Data survey (This table was prepared May 1994.). *Notes:* A dash (-) stands for data not available. 1. Excludes persons of Hispanic origin. 2. Includes estimate for nonresponding states. 3. Less than 0.05 percent.

★ 259 ★

School Enrollment

Enrollment Rates of Five-Year-Olds in Preschool, Kindergarten, and First/Second Grades, 1971-91

From the source: "During the mid-1970s, white and black pre-k enrollment rates were similar. In the 1980s, white pre-k enrollment rates continued to increase, while those of blacks and Hispanics were generally stable. By 1991, average white pre-k enrollment rates were nearly 10 percentage points higher than those of blacks and 20 percentage points higher than those of Hispanics. Yet, black and Hispanic 3- to 4-year-olds were more likely to be enrolled in kindergarten than their white agemates. This table shows 3-year averages for enrollment of 5-year-olds in early elementary education.

Year	Enrolled in pre-k				Enrolled in kindergarten				Enrolled in grades 1 or 2			
	Total	White	Black	Hispanic	Total	White	Black	Hispanic	Total	White	Black	Hispanic
1971	2.1	-	-	-	71.1	-	-	-	10.3	-	-	-
1972	2.0	-	-	-	73.5	-	-	-	10.1	-	-	-
1973	2.3	2.0	3.2	3.2	75.0	75.7	70.6	76.5	10.2	10.0	10.8	10.8
1974	2.7	2.5	4.3	3.0	76.0	77.7	69.2	69.5	10.2	9.4	12.5	12.3
1975	2.8	2.6	3.7	2.5	77.7	79.3	71.4	74.1	10.3	9.3	14.0	10.7
1976	3.0	2.9	3.7	2.6	78.7	80.0	73.8	76.0	9.9	9.0	13.5	9.1
1977	3.0	3.0	3.5	1.6	78.9	79.9	74.6	78.5	10.0	9.5	12.9	8.0
1978	3.5	-	-	-	79.1	-	-	-	9.4	-	-	-
1979	3.4	-	-	-	80.0	-	-	-	8.8	-	-	-
1980	3.4	-	-	-	80.0	-	-	-	8.1	-	-	-
1981	3.2	3.5	3.1	1.7	80.2	81.9	76.1	74.0	7.6	6.2	12.5	10.1
1982	4.1	4.6	3.0	2.7	79.2	80.8	75.1	74.5	7.6	6.1	13.3	9.6
1983	4.4	4.9	3.2	2.5	79.5	80.7	76.0	76.6	7.3	6.1	11.4	10.2
1984	4.9	5.3	3.5	3.3	80.1	81.5	76.5	76.9	7.1	5.9	11.1	10.6
1985	4.4	4.8	3.0	3.1	81.4	82.6	79.4	77.6	6.2	5.0	9.2	9.1
1986	5.4	6.1	2.4	4.6	81.0	81.6	82.4	76.3	5.7	4.6	8.4	8.2
1987	6.1	6.9	2.5	5.3	80.4	81.1	80.6	77.5	5.3	3.9	9.7	7.0
1988	7.1	8.1	3.4	5.9	79.3	80.1	79.1	75.8	5.5	3.9	10.2	7.8
1989	7.7	8.7	5.2	5.2	79.6	80.7	77.6	77.8	5.3	3.6	9.7	7.6
1990	7.6	8.7	5.4	4.4	79.4	80.2	79.1	76.3	5.1	3.8	7.8	8.0
1991	7.5	8.6	5.7	4.3	79.8	80.2	80.3	78.3	5.0	3.8	6.6	7.9

Source: U.S. Department of Education. National Center for Education Statistics. *The Condition of Education 1994.* Washington, DC: U.S. GPO, 1994, p. 170. Primary source: U.S. Department of Commerce, Bureau of the Census, October Current Population Surveys. *Notes:* A dash (-) stands for not available. Due to small sample sizes for the black and Hispanic categories, 3-year averages are calculated. The 3-year average for 1991 is the average percentage enrolled in 1990, 1991, and 1992.

★ 260 ★

School Enrollment

High School Seniors by Program Characteristic, 1982 and 1992

Data show percent of high school seniors reporting enrollment in each curriculum track.

Race/ethnicity	General		College prep or academic		Vocational	
	1982	1992	1982	1992	1982	1992
Total	35.2	45.3	37.9	43.0	26.9	11.7
White	34.8	43.3	40.6	45.7	24.6	11.0
Black	35.1	48.9	33.3	35.6	31.6	15.4
Hispanic	37.4	56.4	24.9	30.6	37.7	13.1
Asian	27.5	40.3	55.9	50.9	16.6	8.8
American Indian	55.3	60.8	19.1	22.6	25.6	16.7

Source: U.S. Department of Education. National Center for Education Statistics. Office of Educational Research and Improvement. *Digest of Education Statistics, 1994.* Lanham, MD: Bernan, November 1994, p. 132. Primary source: U.S. Department of Education, National Center for Education Statistics, "High School and Beyond," First Followup survey; and "National Education Longitudinal Study of 1988," Second Followup survey. (This table was prepared April 1994.).

★ 261 ★

School Enrollment

Los Angeles: Ethnic Distribution of the Student Population

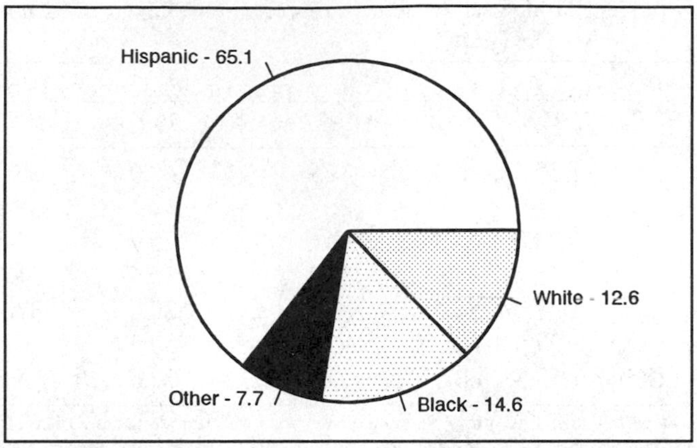

Race/ethnicity	Percent
Hispanic	65.1
White	12.6
Black	14.6
Other	7.7

Source: "Los Angeles schools hobbled and desperate." *The New York Times* (16 February 1993), p. A12. Primary source: Los Angeles Unified School District, United Teachers of Los Angeles.

★ 262 ★

School Enrollment

New Jersey: Hispanic Enrollment in Public Schools for Selected Cities, 1989-90

Districts	Total enrollment, 1989-90	% minority	% Hispanic
Camden	18,999	95.8	35.3
Newark	48,573	90.2	25.6
Jersey City	27,788	87.4	34.4
Trenton	12,351	90.3	18.4
Paterson	21,671	90.2	44.3

Source: ASPIRA News: National Newsletter of the ASPIRA Association, Inc. Vol. 5, No. 4 (Winter 1991-92), p. 3. Primary source: Public Affairs Research Institute of New Jersey, Inc., September 1991.

★ 263 ★

School Enrollment

Percentage of Students in Grades 1 to 12 Who Are Black or Hispanic, by Control of School and Residence, 1970-92

From the source: "Changes in the racial/ethnic composition of students may contribute to a greater degree of heterogeneity of language and culture in our nation's schools. While a variety of language backgrounds and interests of students can enhance the learning environment, it can also create new or increased challenges for the schools. Many minority students come from poor or non-English language backgrounds and may be at greater risk of not succeeding in school than other children."

Year	Total	Public schools			Private schools
		Central cities	Other metropolitan	Non-metropolitan	
1970	-	-	-	-	-
1971	-	-	-	-	-
1972	20.5	42.0	10.6	14.9	9.9
1973	20.3	41.8	10.1	14.6	10.6
1974	21.5	44.0	10.9	16.2	11.5
1975	22.0	44.5	12.0	15.9	10.9
1976	22.4	44.9	13.4	15.3	11.0
1977	21.9	47.0	12.6	15.5	13.1
1978	22.3	47.4	13.3	15.3	11.1
1979	22.7	49.5	14.1	14.4	13.0
1980	-	-	-	-	-
1981	24.6	51.4	15.6	16.0	13.9
1982	24.7	51.0	15.5	16.1	13.9
1983	25.2	51.5	16.6	15.6	13.7
1984	-	-	-	-	12.1
1985	26.8	56.7	18.1	16.8	11.5
1986	27.1	52.4	16.5	18.3	13.8
1987	27.1	51.7	17.5	16.7	14.3
1988	27.4	51.1	18.6	16.9	14.8
1989	27.8	51.8	20.0	15.3	14.1
1990	27.8	52.1	19.5	16.4	14.3
1991	28.1	52.9	19.6	15.9	14.3
1992	28.3	52.6	20.4	15.5	14.9

Source: U.S. Department of Education. National Center for Education Statistics. *The Condition of Education 1994.* Washington, DC: U.S. Government Printing Office, 1994, p. 122. Primary source: U.S. Department of Commerce, Bureau of the Census, *Current Population Reports,* Series P-20, "School Enrollment ...." various years; October Current Population Surveys. *Note:* A dash (-) indicates that data were not available.

★ 264 ★

School Enrollment

Preschool Enrollment, 1970-93

Data are shown as of October, for selected years, for the civilian noninstitutional population. Figures include public and nonpublic nursery school and kindergarten programs. Figures exclude five year olds enrolled in elementary school. Data are based on Current Population Surveys.

Item	1970	1980	1985	1986	1987	1988	1989	1990	1991	1992
Number of children (1,000)										
Population, 3 to 5 years old	10,949	9,284	10,733	10,866	10,872	10,994	11,038	11,207	11,370	11,544
Total enrolled[1]	4,104	4,878	5,865	5,971	5,932	5,977	6,026	6,659	6,334	6,403
Level and control										
Nursery	1,094	1,981	2,477	2,545	2,555	2,621	2,825	3,378	2,824	2,857
Public	332	628	846	829	819	852	930	1,202	996	1,074
Private	762	1,353	1,631	1,715	1,736	1,770	1,894	2,177	1,827	1,784
Kindergarten	3,010	2,897	3,388	3,426	3,377	3,356	3,201	3,281	3,510	3,546
Public	2,498	2,438	2,847	2,859	2,842	2,875	2,704	2,767	2,968	2,996
Private	511	459	541	567	535	481	496	513	543	550
Race										
White	3,443	3,994	4,757	4,851	4,748	4,891	4,911	5,389	5,104	5,137
Black	586	725	919	892	893	814	872	964	928	966
Hispanic origin										
Hispanic[2]	(NA)	370	496	593	587	544	520	642	675	728
Age										
3 years old	454	857	1,035	1,041	1,022	1,028	1,005	1,205	1,075	1,081
4 years old	1,007	1,423	1,765	1,772	1,717	1,768	1,882	2,086	1,993	1,982
5 years old	2,643	2,598	3,065	3,157	3,192	3,183	3,139	3,367	3,266	3,340
Enrollment rate										
Total enrolled[1]	37.5	52.5	54.6	55.0	54.6	54.4	54.6	59.4	55.7	55.5
Race										
White	37.8	52.7	54.7	55.2	54.1	55.4	55.0	59.7	56.2	55.8
Black	34.9	51.8	55.8	54.1	54.2	48.2	54.2	57.8	53.1	55.1
Hispanic origin										
Hispanic[2]	(NA)	43.3	43.3	47.8	45.5	44.2	41.6	49.0	46.4	48.4
Age										
3 years old	12.9	27.3	28.8	28.9	28.6	27.6	27.1	32.6	28.2	27.7
4 years old	27.8	46.3	49.1	49.0	47.7	49.1	51.0	56.0	53.0	52.1
5 years old	69.3	84.7	86.5	86.7	86.1	86.6	86.4	88.8	86.0	87.2

Source: 1994 Statistical Abstract of the United States on CD-ROM [machine-readable datafiles]. CD-8A-94. Washington, DC: U.S. Department of Commerce, Economics and Statistics Administration, Bureau of the Census, Data User Services Division, January 1995. Primary source: U.S. Bureau of the Census, Current Population Reports, P20-474. *Notes:* NA stands for not available. 1. Includes races not shown separately. 2. Persons of Hispanic origin may be of any race. The method of identifying Hispanic children was changed in 1980 from allocation based on status of mother to status reported for each child. The number of Hispanic children using the new method is larger.

★ 265 ★

School Enrollment

Preschool and Kindergarten Enrollment Rates of Three and Four Year Olds, 1971-91

From the source: "Within most population groups, an increasing percentage of children receive pre-k instruction. This instruction contributes to the readiness of children to participate in elementary school. Many policymakers and educators believe that it is important to help children from disadvantaged backgrounds start elementary school on an equal footing with other children by involving them and their parents in prekindergarten programs." These data show preprimary enrollment rates in percent. Figures are 3-year averages.

Year	Enrolled in pre-K				Enrolled in kindergarten			
	Total	White	Black	Hispanic	Total	White	Black	Hispanic
1971	15.4	-	-	-	6.6	-	-	-
1972	16.6	-	-	-	6.6	-	-	-
1973	19.1	19.5	19.0	13.8	6.7	6.1	9.6	7.9
1974	21.3	21.6	21.1	15.6	6.8	6.1	9.5	8.2
1975	23.0	23.6	22.2	15.8	7.5	6.7	10.3	9.1
1976	24.1	24.7	23.9	15.4	7.5	6.6	10.8	7.5
1977	25.4	26.1	25.8	15.4	7.1	6.4	11.0	6.0
1978	27.3	-	-	-	6.5	-	-	-
1979	29.2	-	-	-	6.2	-	-	-
1980	29.7	-	-	-	6.2	-	-	-
1981	30.4	32.3	28.4	18.7	6.0	5.1	9.5	6.3
1982	30.6	32.8	28.7	15.7	6.1	5.4	8.5	7.7
1983	30.7	32.9	28.9	15.3	6.0	5.2	8.8	8.0
1984	31.2	33.6	28.7	17.4	6.4	5.4	10.5	7.7
1985	31.9	34.6	28.6	19.2	6.1	4.8	11.4	7.6
1986	32.4	35.5	27.4	20.3	6.3	4.7	12.1	8.3
1987	32.5	36.1	25.9	18.7	6.0	4.3	10.4	9.1
1988	33.0	36.8	26.7	18.0	5.5	4.1	9.6	7.6
1989	36.0	39.9	30.4	19.6	4.5	3.7	7.5	6.1
1990	36.5	40.3	31.4	21.0	4.8	3.9	7.6	6.7
1991	36.2	40.1	30.8	21.0	5.4	4.2	8.1	8.6

Source: U.S. Department of Education. National Center for Education Statistics. *The Condition of Education 1994.* Washington, DC: U.S. GPO, 1994, p. 169. Primary source: U.S. Department of Commerce, Bureau of the Census, October Current Population Surveys. *Notes:* A dash (-) stands for not available. Due to small sample sizes for the black and Hispanic categories, 3-year averages are calculated. The 3-year average for 1991 is the average percentage enrolled in 1990, 1991, and 1992.

★ 266 ★

School Enrollment

Public School Enrollment Trends by Race/Ethnicity

Percent change in enrollment for 1976 to 1986 is shown for each race/ethnicity.

Race/ethnicity	Percent
White, non-Hispanic	-12.9
Black, non-Hispanic	-2.2
Hispanic	44.7
Asian/Pacific Islander	116.4
American Indian, Aleut, Eskimo	-3.3
Total minority	16.4

Source: U.S. Department of Education. National Center for Education Statistics. Office of Educational Research and Improvement. *The Condition of Education 1991, Volume 1, Elementary and Secondary Education,* 1991, p. 69. Primary source: U.S. Department of Education, Office of Civil Rights, *Directory of Elementary and Secondary School Districts and Schools in Selected Districts*: 1976-1977; and *1984 and 1986 Elementary and Secondary School Civil Rights Survey.*

★ 267 ★

School Enrollment

Public School Enrollment, 1986 and 1992

Percent distribution of enrolled students is shown, by race/ethnicity, for 1986 and for 1992, as reported by States to the Department of Education.

Race/ethnicity	Percent distribution	
	1986	1992[2]
Total U.S.	100.0	100.0
White, non-Hispanic[1]	70.4	66.7
Black, non-Hispanic[1]	16.1	16.5
Hispanic	9.9	12.3
Asian/Pacific Islander	2.8	3.5
American Indian/Alaskan Native	0.9	1.0

Source: U.S. Department of Education. National Center for Education Statistics. Office of Educational Research and Improvement. *Digest of Education Statistics, 1994.* Lanham, MD: Bernan, November 1994, p. 60. Primary source: U.S. Department of Education, Office for Civil Rights, 1986 State Summaries of Elementary and Secondary School Civil Rights Survey; and National Center for Education Statistics, Common Core of Data Survey. (This table was prepared May 1994.) *Notes:* A dash (-) stands for data not available. 1. Excludes persons of Hispanic origin. 2. Data include estimates for non-responding states.

★ 268 ★

School Enrollment

School Enrollment Rates of Mexicans, Hispanics, and Other Groups, 1980-91

Age, race, and Hispanic origin	Enrollment (000)					Rate (%)				
	1980	1985	1989	1990	1991	1980	1985	1989	1990	1991
Total, 3 to 34 years old[1]	57,348	58,013	59,235	60,588	61,276	49.7	48.3	49.1	50.2	50.7
3 and 4 years old	2,280	2,801	2,898	3,292	3,068	36.7	38.9	39.1	44.4	40.5
5 and 6 years old	5,853	6,697	6,990	7,207	7,178	95.7	96.1	95.2	96.5	95.4
7 to 13 years old	23,751	22,849	24,431	25,016	25,445	99.3	99.2	99.3	99.6	99.7
14 and 15 years old	7,282	7,362	6,493	6,555	6,634	98.2	98.1	98.8	99.0	98.8
16 and 17 years old	7,129	6,654	6,254	6,098	6,155	89.0	91.7	92.7	92.5	93.3
18 and 19 years old	3,788	3,716	4,125	4,044	3,969	46.4	51.6	56.0	57.3	59.6
20 and 21 years old	2,515	2,708	2,630	2,852	3,041	31.0	35.3	38.5	39.7	42.0
22 to 24 years old	1,931	2,068	2,207	2,231	2,365	16.3	16.9	19.9	21.0	22.2
25 to 29 years old	1,714	1,942	1,960	2,013	2,045	9.3	9.2	9.3	9.7	10.2
30 to 34 years old	1,105	1,218	1,248	1,281	1,377	6.4	6.1	5.7	5.8	6.2
35 years old and over	1,290	1,766	2,230	2,439	2,620	1.4	1.7	2.0	2.1	2.2
Mexican[2]**, total 3 to 34 years old**	2,698	3,180	3,743	4,017	4,171	49.0	47.5	44.7	46.8	47.7
3 and 4 years old	104	137	148	165	215	27.0	26.0	22.7	27.4	32.3
5 and 6 years old	327	458	553	619	581	93.2	95.3	91.8	94.7	92.1
7 to 13 years old	1,378	1,526	1,768	1,815	1,957	99.5	99.2	98.9	99.7	99.7
14 and 15 years old	361	367	481	499	475	92.1	97.7	95.7	99.5	97.6
16 and 17 years old	257	358	356	403	351	76.1	83.8	85.3	83.8	81.0
18 and 19 years old	113	127	176	213	282	32.0	35.2	36.9	40.9	47.0
20 and 21 years old	55	61	79	121	132	15.6	16.4	14.6	23.6	24.8
22 to 24 years old	40	55	77	70	70	7.5	7.8	8.9	8.3	8.2
25 to 29 years old	41	56	64	64	61	5.4	5.0	5.0	4.9	4.8
30 to 34 years old	22	36	41	47	48	3.3	4.5	3.3	3.6	3.7
35 years old and over	(NA)	(NA)	73	81	89	(NA)	(NA)	2.0	2.1	2.2
White, total 3 to 34 years old	47,673	47,452	47,923	48,899	49,156	48.9	47.8	48.4	49.5	50.0
3 and 4 years old	1,844	2,250	2,370	2,700	2,502	36.3	38.6	39.4	44.9	41.3
5 and 6 years old	4,781	5,437	5,598	5,750	5,727	95.8	96.4	95.2	96.5	95.3
7 to 13 years old	19,585	18,464	19,638	20,076	20,325	99.2	99.3	99.3	99.6	99.6
14 and 15 years old	6,038	6,007	5,197	5,265	5,311	98.3	98.1	98.8	99.1	98.7
16 and 17 years old	5,937	5,449	4,993	4,858	4,902	88.6	91.6	92.3	92.5	93.3
18 and 19 years old	3,199	3,105	3,392	3,271	3,197	46.3	52.4	56.4	57.1	59.7
20 and 21 years old	2,206	2,318	2,208	2,402	2,517	31.9	36.1	39.5	41.0	43.2
22 to 24 years old	1,669	1,744	1,841	1,781	1,910	16.4	17.0	20.0	20.2	21.7
25 to 29 years old	1,473	1,635	1,659	1,706	1,646	9.2	9.2	9.4	9.9	9.9
30 to 34 years old	942	1,043	1,028	1,090	1,119	6.3	6.2	5.6	5.9	6.0
35 years old and over	1,104	1,533	1,956	2,096	2,219	1.3	1.7	2.0	2.1	2.2
Black, total 3 to 34 years old	8,251	8,444	8,707	8,854	9,031	53.9	50.9	51.3	51.9	52.5
3 and 4 years old	371	469	407	452	428	38.2	42.7	38.9	41.6	37.2
5 and 6 years old	904	1,030	1,084	1,129	1,108	95.4	95.7	94.9	96.3	95.8
7 to 13 years old	3,598	3,549	3,761	3,832	3,941	99.4	99.1	99.2	99.8	99.8
14 and 15 years old	1,088	1,106	1,023	1,023	1,032	97.9	97.9	99.4	99.2	99.1

[Continued]

★ 268 ★

School Enrollment Rates of Mexicans, Hispanics, and Other Groups, 1980-91

[Continued]

Age, race, and Hispanic origin	Enrollment (000)					Rate (%)				
	1980	1985	1989	1990	1991	1980	1985	1989	1990	1991
16 and 17 years old	1,047	994	1,033	962	959	90.6	91.7	93.7	91.7	91.7
18 and 19 years old	494	472	541	596	578	45.7	44.1	50.2	55.2	55.6
20 and 21 years old	242	298	309	305	329	23.4	27.7	30.7	28.4	30.0
22 to 24 years old	196	215	253	274	249	13.6	13.7	17.2	20.0	18.2
25 to 29 years old	187	192	168	162	229	8.8	7.4	6.4	6.1	8.7
30 to 34 years old	124	119	130	119	177	6.8	5.1	4.9	4.4	6.5
35 years old and over	186	233	167	238	289	1.8	1.9	1.5	2.1	2.5
Hispanic[2], total 3 to 34 years old	4,263	5,070	5,722	6,073	6,306	49.8	47.7	45.8	47.4	47.9
3 and 4 years old	172	213	202	249	299	28.5	27.0	23.8	29.8	30.6
5 and 6 years old	491	662	785	835	850	94.5	94.5	92.8	94.8	92.4
7 to 13 years old	2,009	2,322	2,637	2,794	2,909	99.2	99.0	98.7	99.4	99.7
14 and 15 years old	568	606	706	739	732	94.3	96.1	96.5	99.0	97.2
16 and 17 years old	454	562	554	592	532	81.8	84.5	86.4	85.4	82.6
18 and 19 years old	226	238	327	329	394	37.8	41.8	44.6	44.1	47.9
20 and 21 years old	111	137	152	213	215	19.5	24.0	18.8	27.2	26.4
22 to 24 years old	93	125	153	121	144	11.7	11.6	12.0	9.9	11.6
25 to 29 years old	84	120	129	130	140	6.9	6.6	6.6	6.3	6.9
30 to 34 years old	54	83	76	72	93	5.1	5.7	3.8	3.6	4.5
35 years old and over	(NA)	(NA)	136	145	148	(NA)	(NA)	2.1	2.1	2.0

Source: U.S. Bureau of the Census. *Statistical Abstract of the United States: 1992,* (112th edition). Washington, DC: U.S. Government Printing Office, 1992, p. 142. Primary source: U.S. Bureau of the Census, *Current Population Reports*, series P-20, No. 460, and earlier reports; and unpublished data. *Notes:* (NA) stands for not available. 1. Includes other races, not shown separately. 2. Persons of Hispanic origin may be of any race.

★ 269 ★

School Enrollment

School Enrollment Rates of Persons 3 to 34 Years Old, 1975 to 1993

Rates are shown in percent, by age group and race/ethnicity, for 1975 to 1993. Data include enrollment in any type of graded public, parochial, or other private school in regular school systems. Included are nursery schools, kindergarten, elementary schools, high schools, colleges, universities, and professional schools. Attendance may be on either a full-time or part-time basis and during the day or night. Enrollments in "special" schools, such as trade schools, business colleges, or correspondence schools, are not included.

Year and age	Percent			
	All races	White, non-Hispanic	Black, non-Hispanic	Hispanic origin
1975				
Total, 3 to 34 years	53.7	53.0	57.7	54.8
3 and 4 years	31.5	31.0	34.4	27.3
5 and 6 years	94.7	95.1	94.4	92.1

[Continued]

★ 269 ★

School Enrollment Rates of Persons 3 to 34 Years Old, 1975 to 1993

[Continued]

Year and age	Percent			
	All races	White, non-Hispanic	Black, non-Hispanic	Hispanic origin
7 to 9 years	99.3	99.4	99.3	99.6
10 to 13 years	99.3	99.3	99.1	99.2
14 and 15 years	98.2	98.5	97.4	95.6
16 and 17 years	89.0	89.5	86.8	86.2
18 and 19 years	46.9	46.8	46.9	44.0
20 and 21 years	31.2	32.1	26.7	27.5
22 to 24 years	16.2	16.4	13.9	14.1
25 to 29 years	10.1	10.1	9.4	8.3
30 to 34 years	6.6	6.6	7.1	5.5
1980				
Total, 3 to 34 years	49.7	48.8	54.0	49.8
3 and 4 years	36.7	37.4	38.2	28.5
5 and 6 years	95.7	95.9	95.5	94.5
7 to 9 years	99.1	99.1	99.4	98.4
10 to 13 years	99.4	99.4	99.4	99.7
14 and 15 years	98.2	98.7	97.9	94.3
16 and 17 years	89.0	89.2	90.7	81.8
18 and 19 years	46.4	47.0	45.8	37.8
20 and 21 years	31.0	33.0	23.3	19.5
22 to 24 years	16.3	16.8	13.6	11.7
25 to 29 years	9.3	9.4	8.8	6.9
30 to 34 years	6.4	6.4	6.9	5.1
1985				
Total, 3 to 34 years	48.3	47.8	50.8	47.7
3 and 4 years	38.9	40.3	42.8	27.0
5 and 6 years	96.1	9.6	95.7	94.5
7 to 9 years	99.1	99.4	98.6	98.4
10 to 13 years	99.3	99.3	99.5	99.4
14 and 15 years	98.1	98.3	98.1	96.1
16 and 17 years	91.7	92.5	91.8	84.5
18 and 19 years	51.6	53.7	43.5	41.8
20 and 21 years	35.3	37.2	27.7	24.0
22 to 24 years	16.9	17.5	13.8	11.6
25 to 29 years	9.2	9.6	7.4	6.6
30 to 34 years	6.1	6.2	5.2	5.7
1990				
Total, 3 to 34 years	50.2	49.8	50.2	47.2
3 and 4 years	44.4	47.2	41.8	30.7
5 and 6 years	96.5	96.7	96.5	94.9
7 to 9 years	99.7	99.7	99.8	99.5
10 to 13 years	99.6	99.7	99.9	99.1
14 and 15 years	99.0	99.0	99.4	99.0
16 and 17 years	92.5	93.5	91.7	85.4
18 and 19 years	57.2	59.1	55.0	44.0

[Continued]

★269★

School Enrollment Rates of Persons 3 to 34 Years Old, 1975 to 1993

[Continued]

Year and age	Percent			
	All races	White, non-Hispanic	Black, non-Hispanic	Hispanic origin
20 and 21 years	39.7	43.1	28.3	27.2
22 to 24 years	21.0	21.9	19.7	9.9
25 to 29 years	9.7	10.4	6.1	6.3
30 to 34 years	5.8	6.2	4.5	3.6
1993				
Total, 3 to 34 years	51.8	51.4	53.5	48.9
3 and 4 years	40.4	43.1	40.1	26.8
5 and 6 years	95.4	95.7	94.5	93.8
7 to 9 years	99.4	99.5	99.0	99.6
10 to 13 years	99.5	99.5	99.8	99.2
14 and 15 years	98.9	99.1	98.5	97.6
16 and 17 years	94.0	95.0	94.9	88.3
18 and 19 years	61.6	63.6	57.4	50.0
20 and 21 years	42.7	46.1	29.9	31.8
22 to 24 years	23.6	24.9	18.0	13.7
25 to 29 years	10.2	10.2	10.0	7.7
30 to 34 years	5.9	6.0	5.3	5.1

Source: U.S. Department of Education. National Center for Education Statistics. Office of Educational Research and Improvement. *Digest of Education Statistics, 1994.* Lanham, MD: Bernan, November 1994, p. 16. Primary source: U.S. Department of Commerce, Bureau of the Census, Current Population Survey, unpublished data. (This table was prepared March 1994.) *Notes:* Data are based upon sample surveys of the civilian noninstitutional population.

★270★

School Enrollment

School Enrollment and Educational Attainment in U.S. Southwest Border States and Counties, 1980

Characteristic	United States	Total, border states	Border states			
			Border county areas		Non-border county areas	
			Hispanic	Non-Hispanic	Hispanic	Non-Hispanic
School enrollment						
Persons, 3 years and over enrolled in school	62,054,304	11,828,637	513,060	687,741	2,257,263	8,370,573
Percent	100.0	100.0	100.0	100.0	100.0	100.0
Nursery school	3.9	4.3	2.8	4.1	3.8	4.6
Kindergarten and elementary school	51.5	49.9	61.2	43.3	60.5	46.9
High school	24.6	23.0	22.9	21.4	23.2	23.2
College	19.9	22.8	13.1	31.1	12.9	25.4
Years of school completed						
Persons, 25 years and over	132,835,687	24,254,185	642,167	1,555,847	3,123,182	18,932,989
Percent	100.0	100.0	100.0	100.0	100.0	100.0
Elementary, 0 to 8 years	18.3	16.5	49.4	8.7	42.5	11.7

[Continued]

★270★

School Enrollment and Educational Attainment in U.S. Southwest Border States and Counties, 1980

[Continued]

Characteristic	United States	Total, border states	Border states			
			Border county areas		Non-border county areas	
			Hispanic	Non-Hispanic	Hispanic	Non-Hispanic
High school, 1 to 4 years	49.9	44.6	33.3	45.2	39.3	45.9
College, 1 or more years	31.9	43.0	17.3	46.1	18.2	42.4

Source: U.S. Bureau of the Census, *The Hispanic Population of the Southwest Borderland*. Current Population Reports, Series P-23, No. 172, Washington, DC: U.S. Government Printing Office, 1991, p. 19. *Notes:* For the purposes of this report, the U.S. Census Bureau included the following counties: San Diego, and Imperial counties, in California; Cochise, Pima, Santa Cruz, and Yuma counties, in Arizona; Dona Ana, Hidalgo, and Luna counties, in New Mexico; El Paso, Hudspeth, Culberson, Jeff Davis, Presidio, Brewster, Terrell, Valverde, Kinney, Maverick, Dimmit, Webb, Zapata, Starr, Hidalgo, and Cameron counties, in Texas.

★271★

School Enrollment

School Enrollment, by Sector

From the source: "Private schools provide alternatives to the public schools. Whether a family chooses a private school for their child will be a function of many factors, including private school tuition levels, family income, the relative value placed on education, satisfaction with public schools, and the availability of public schools (especially at the preschool level). Differences among population subgroups in the proportion of children enrolled in private schools may reflect differences in any of these factors." These data show the racial and ethnic composition of each type of school, as of October of 1982, 1985, and 1991.

School level and type	1982			1985			1991		
	White	Black	Hispanic	White	Black	Hispanic	White	Black	Hispanic
Preschool									
All public	63.4	25.8	6.4	59.9	24.8	12.3	60.4	22.4	13.3
All private	88.0	7.6	2.4	86.2	7.2	3.5	86.9	5.9	3.1
Private, church-related	87.3	8.8	2.6	87.9	6.9	3.3	89.4	3.9	2.8
Private, non-church-related	65.4	23.8	10.8	85.1	7.4	3.7	84.8	7.5	3.3
Kindergarten									
All public	69.2	16.8	10.6	69.4	17.3	9.8	64.1	16.9	14.7
All private	82.0	8.3	6.0	79.4	10.0	8.1	79.0	11.4	4.5
Private, church-related	83.7	6.5	5.8	79.5	9.8	9.5	81.3	9.7	4.8
Private, non-church-related	76.8	13.8	6.6	78.9	10.3	4.4	73.8	15.3	3.8
Elementary									
All public	71.3	16.1	9.3	68.4	17.1	10.9	67.2	16.8	11.9
All private	82.4	6.7	7.6	85.0	4.9	6.4	82.3	6.8	6.7
Private, church-related	81.4	7.0	8.3	85.3	4.3	7.2	82.1	6.7	7.5
Private, non-church-related	89.6	4.8	2.0	83.2	8.6	1.7	83.2	7.2	2.7
Secondary									
All public	73.8	15.8	7.5	72.1	16.0	8.5	68.3	16.7	10.6
All private	86.2	4.8	6.6	87.6	3.9	5.9	84.2	6.1	5.6

[Continued]

★ 271 ★

School Enrollment, by Sector

[Continued]

School level and type	1982			1985			1991		
	White	Black	Hispanic	White	Black	Hispanic	White	Black	Hispanic
Private, church-related	86.3	4.3	6.9	86.7	4.2	6.63	84.4	5.7	6.6
Private, non-church-related	86.0	6.8	5.1	92.2	2.5	3.5	83.8	7.6	2.7

Source: U.S. Department of Education. National Center for Education Statistics. *The Condition of Education 1994.* Washington, DC: U.S. Government Printing Office, 1994, p. 175. U.S. Department of Commerce, Bureau of the Census, October Current Population Surveys. *Notes:* The percentages do not sum to 100 because included among students but not reported separately are those who are not white, black, or Hispanic. Most are Asian, and some are American Indian.

School Environment

★ 272 ★

Alcohol and Drug Use by Students, 1991-92

Data show percentage of students who reported alcohol and/or drug use within the past 12 months, by race/ethnicity and grade of student and location of drug use.

Situation and race/ethnicity	Alcohol Percentage saying one or more times		Marijuana or other illegal drug Percentage saying one or more times	
	8th grade	10th grade	8th grade	10th grade
At a school dance, game, or other school event				
Total	11.0	18.9	3.7	5.6
White	10.4	18.3	3.2	5.6
Black	10.4	19.5	2.6	3.6
Hispanic	16.3	24.4	8.4	8.4
At school during the day				
Total	3.9	7.2	2.5	5.2
White	3.5	6.5	2.2	5.2
Black	3.8	8.1	1.8	2.8
Hispanic	6.2	11.7	5.5	8.3
Near school				
Total	6.4	11.3	3.6	6.2
White	6.4	11.8	3.2	6.5
Black	4.5	7.3	2.1	3.4
Hispanic	10.5	14.0	7.8	8.2

Source: U.S. Department of Education. National Center for Education Statistics. *The Condition of Education 1994.* Washington, DC: U.S. Government Printing Office, 1994, p. 310. Primary source: Johnston, Lloyd D., O'Malley, Patrick, and Bachman, Jerald G., "Selected 1992 Outcome Measures from the Monitoring the Future Study for Goal 6 of the National Education Goals," Institute for Social Research, The University of Michigan, August, 1993.

★ 273 ★

School Environment

Computer Access at Home

Figures show percentage of persons using home computers for various purposes. Data, shown as of October 1993, are based on a sample survey of households and are subject to sampling and nonsampling error.

	Total	White, non-Hispanic	Black, non-Hispanic	Hispanic
Percent with computers at home	27.1	43.3	16.1	15.2
Percent using computers at home	17.6	32.3	10.8	10.3
Distribution of frequency of use per week for persons using computers in the home				
6 or 7 days	14.7	11.9	13.8	13.9
4 or 5 days	17.1	16.0	16.8	21.1
2 or 3 days	33.3	35.8	37.0	39.6
1 day or less	34.9	36.3	32.4	25.5
Percent of persons whose home computer has specific components[1]				
Hard disk	80.7	81.1	73.8	74.7
Printer	75.8	77.6	64.8	73.0
Color monitor	68.2	70.1	68.4	63.0
Fax or modem	38.5	38.0	34.5	32.7
Percent of computer users using specific applications[2]				
Communications[3]	33.5	11.4	14.2	17.2
School assignments	28.3	55.2	53.0	54.9
Education programs	34.6	38.4	50.8	34.7
Games	34.9	55.6	56.3	51.2
Job-related	23.8	5.7	7.4	5.2
Word processing	53.2	42.6	33.9	35.3

Source: U.S. Department of Education. National Center for Education Statistics. Office of Educational Research and Improvement. *Digest of Education Statistics, 1994.* Lanham, MD: Bernan, November 1994, p. 440. U.S. Department of Commerce, Bureau of the Census, Current Population Survey, October 1993, unpublished data. (This table was prepared May 1994.) *Notes:* 1. Data are for the most recently purchased computer for families with more than one computer in their home. 2. Individuals may be counted in more than one computer activity. 3. Includes bulletin boards and electronic mail.

★ 274 ★

School Environment

Computer Access at Home, by Level of Study, 1989 and 1993

Figures are shown, by race/ethnicity and selected level of study. Data are based on a sample survey of households and are subject to sampling and nonsampling error.

	Total	White, non-Hispanic	Black, non-Hispanic	Hispanic	Other
October 1989					
Total	18.8	22.7	7.3	7.5	18.8
Prekindergarten/kindergarten	10.2	12.2	3.7	3.4	9.9
Grades 1 to 8	17.8	22.3	6.8	6.6	16.6
Grades 9 to 12	20.7	25.3	8.5	8.2	21.6
1st to 4th year of college	21.3	23.6	9.1	11.5	23.7
5th year or later of college	33.4	35.6	18.6	27.1	24.7
October 1993					
Total	27.0	32.8	10.9	10.4	28.7
Prekindergarten/kindergarten	15.6	19.4	4.2	5.7	17.0
Grades 1 to 8	24.7	31.4	9.0	7.5	23.2
Grades 9 to 12	28.7	35.9	10.4	9.8	37.0
1st to 4th year of college	32.8	36.0	19.4	22.0	33.0
5th year or later of college	52.6	53.6	48.1	52.2	47.1

Source: U.S. Department of Education. National Center for Education Statistics. Office of Educational Research and Improvement. *Digest of Education Statistics, 1994.* Lanham, MD: Bernan, November 1994, p. 441. Primary source: U.S. Department of Commerce, Bureau of the Census, Current Population Surveys, October 1989 and 1993, unpublished data.

★ 275 ★

School Environment

Computer Access at School, by Level of Study, 1989 and 1993

Figures are shown, by race/ethnicity and selected level of study. Data are based on a sample survey of households and are subject to sampling and nonsampling error.

	Total	White, non-Hispanic	Black, non-Hispanic	Hispanic	Other
October 1989					
Total	42.7	45.7	32.6	34.9	42.7
Prekindergarten/kindergarten	14.7	17.0	7.4	10.1	8.5
Grades 1 to 8	52.3	58.4	35.7	40.2	47.0
Grades 9 to 12	39.2	40.6	36.0	33.6	41.4
1st to 4th year of college	39.2	40.0	35.1	32.4	43.9
5th year or later of college	40.7	39.6	35.2	37.8	58.0
October 1993					
Total	59.0	61.6	51.5	52.3	59.0
Prekindergarten/kindergarten	26.2	29.4	16.5	19.2	23.5
Grades 1 to 8	68.9	73.7	56.5	58.4	65.7
Grades 9 to 12	58.2	59.9	54.5	54.1	57.3

[Continued]

★275★

Computer Access at School, by Level of Study, 1989 and 1993

[Continued]

	Total	White, non-Hispanic	Black, non-Hispanic	Hispanic	Other
1st to 4th year of college	55.2	54.9	56.9	51.9	60.9
5th year or later of college	52.1	49.8	57.9	53.7	69.4

Source: U.S. Department of Education. National Center for Education Statistics. Office of Educational Research and Improvement. *Digest of Education Statistics, 1994.* Lanham, MD: Bernan, November 1994, p. 441. Primary source: U.S. Department of Commerce, Bureau of the Census, Current Population Surveys, October 1989 and 1993, unpublished data.

★276★

School Environment

Computer Use for Homework, by Level of Study, 1989 and 1993

Figures show the percentage of students using computers at home for the completion of school assignments, by race/ethnicity and selected level of study. Data are based on a sample survey of households and are subject to sampling and nonsampling error.

	Total	White, non-Hispanic	Black, non-Hispanic	Hispanic	Other
October 1989					
Total	8.9	10.7	3.4	3.6	9.1
Prekindergarten/kindergarten	0.6	0.6	0.9	-	-
Grades 1 to 8	6.3	7.7	2.7	2.8	5.8
Grades 9 to 12	12.2	15.2	4.0	4.4	13.4
1st to 4th year of college	13.7	15.1	6.2	6.4	15.5
5th year or later of college	23.9	25.5	12.6	24.8	14.8
October 1993					
Total	14.9	18.2	5.7	5.6	16.0
Prekindergarten/kindergarten	0.6	0.8	-	-	1.1
Grades 1 to 8	10.8	13.8	4.0	2.9	9.3
Grades 9 to 12	20.9	26.5	6.9	6.7	27.0
1st to 4th year of college	23.1	25.7	11.5	15.9	23.7
5th year or later of college	36.6	37.8	30.1	36.8	29.2

Source: U.S. Department of Education. National Center for Education Statistics. Office of Educational Research and Improvement. *Digest of Education Statistics, 1994.* Lanham, MD: Bernan, November 1994, p. 441. Primary source: U.S. Department of Commerce, Bureau of the Census, Current Populations Surveys, October 1989 and 1993, unpublished data. *Note:* A dash (-) stands for data not available.

★ 277 ★

School Environment

Drug Exposure in School

Aside from the fact that drug use by youth is a contributing risk factor in their education, the sale of drugs in school is an indication of the overall learning environment. This table shows the percentage of students who were offered drugs in school during the first semester, for 1988, 1990, and 1992. Data are shown by race/ethnicity of the student.

Race/ethnicity	8th graders in 1988		10th graders in 1990		12th graders in 1992	
	Once or twice	More than twice	Once or twice	More than twice	Once or twice	More than twice
All students	6.9	3.1	10.1	6.9	9.5	6.5
Race/ethnicity						
White	6.9	3.1	10.6	7.3	9.7	6.9
Black	5.8	1.8	7.1	3.8	6.5	2.8
Hispanic	8.9	5.3	9.4	7.9	12.2	8.9
Asian	3.5	1.3	8.5	4.9	6.7	4.8
American Indian	11.3	5.1	16.5	8.1	10.8	10.3

Source: U.S. Department of Education. National Center for Education Statistics. *The Condition of Education 1994.* Washington, DC: U.S. Government Printing Office, 1994, p. 310.

★ 278 ★

School Environment

Percentage of High School Seniors Who Reported Using Drugs or Alcohol in the Past Year, 1985-89

Data have been combined for 1985 to 1989.

Type of drug	Mexican American		Puerto Rican/ Latin American		White		Black		Asian American		American Indian	
	Male	Female	Male	Female	Male	Female	Male	Female	Male	Female	Male	Female
Sample size	1,518	1,599	680	712	28,056	29,808	3,688	4,499	982	917	537	531
Percent who used within last 12 months:												
Marijuana	37.3	26.0	30.6	21.3	40.2	36.0	29.8	18.4	19.6	17.1	42.0	44.0
Inhalants[1]	6.0	4.3	5.1	2.9	8.8	5.2	2.6	2.2	4.8	3.2	9.6	4.4
Hallucinogens	5.9	2.2	6.5	2.1	8.3	5.0	1.9	0.6	3.0	2.2	10.0	9.0
LSD	5.2	1.6	3.4	1.1	7.0	3.9	1.3	0.3	2.5	1.9	7.8	7.2
Cocaine	14.7	7.6	15.6	8.2	11.9	9.3	6.1	2.6	5.8	5.7	14.2	15.5
Heroin	0.9	0.4	1.2	0.4	0.7	0.3	0.7	0.4	0.4	0.2	1.5	1.0
Other opiates[2]	3.2	2.1	3.0	1.6	6.5	5.3	1.9	1.2	3.1	2.1	7.4	5.7
Stimulants[2]	11.3	10.1	8.0	5.9	13.6	14.7	4.6	3.1	5.6	7.0	17.0	19.4
Sedatives[2]	4.7	2.7	4.6	2.6	5.3	4.4	2.2	1.2	3.4	2.6	8.8	6.4
Barbiturates[2]	4.1	2.4	4.0	2.5	4.4	3.8	1.9	1.1	2.6	2.3	7.2	6.2
Methaqualone[2]	1.2	0.5	2.3	0.5	2.5	1.4	0.9	0.3	1.5	0.9	4.8	2.2

[Continued]

★ 278 ★

Percentage of High School Seniors Who Reported Using Drugs or Alcohol in the Past Year, 1985-89

[Continued]

Type of drug	Mexican American		Puerto Rican/ Latin American		White		Black		Asian American		American Indian	
	Male	Female	Male	Female	Male	Female	Male	Female	Male	Female	Male	Female
Tranquilizers[2]	2.6	2.1	3.1	4.1	5.8	5.9	1.7	1.4	3.2	1.8	6.9	8.7
Alcohol	82.4	73.6	80.6	77.2	88.3	88.6	72.5	63.9	69.3	67.5	82.0	81.3

Source: U.S. Department of Education. National Center for Education Statistics. *The Condition of Education, 1992.* Washington, DC: U.S. Government Printing Office, 1992, p. 312. Primary source: U.S. Department of Health and Human Services; Alcohol, Drug Abuse, and Mental Health Administration; National Institute on Drug Abuse, *Drug Use Among American High School Students, College Students, and Other Young Adults*, 1991. *Notes:* 1. Respondents represent four-fifths of sample size indicated. 2. Only drug use which was not under a doctor's orders are included here.

★ 279 ★

School Environment

Percentage of High School Seniors Who Reported Using Drugs, Alcohol, or Cigarettes Daily in the Previous Month, 1985-89

Data have been combined for 1985 to 1989.

Type of drug	Mexican American		Puerto Rican/ Latin American		White		Black		Asian American		American Indian	
	Male	Female	Male	Female	Male	Female	Male	Female	Male	Female	Male	Female
Sample size	1,518	1,599	680	712	28,056	29,808	3,688	4,499	982	917	537	531
Percent who used daily in last 30 days												
Marijuana/hashish	4.2	1.1	3.5	0.5	5.1	2.1	2.8	0.9	1.7	0.5	8.2	4.3
Alcohol												
Daily	8.3	2.6	4.0	0.9	7.0	2.8	4.2	0.7	2.3	0.9	10.1	5.4
Five or more drinks in a row/last 2 weeks	45.3	23.6	31.4	14.5	48.1	31.3	24.0	9.3	19.4	10.7	48.1	33.7
Cigarettes	11.6	8.1	13.3	13.3	18.8	22.5	8.6	7.1	9.0	9.4	26.0	33.8
Half-pack or more per day	5.2	2.5	6.1	4.2	12.5	13.3	3.3	2.2	4.4	4.5	18.4	23.4

Source: U.S. Department of Education. National Center for Education Statistics. *The Condition of Education, 1992.* Washington, DC: U.S. Government Printing Office, 1992, p. 313. Primary source: U.S. Department of Health and Human Services; Alcohol, Drug Abuse, and Mental Health Administration; National Institute on Drug Abuse, *Drug Use Among American High School Students, College Students, and Other Young Adults*, 1991.

★ 280 ★

School Environment

Percentage of High School Seniors Who Reported Using Selected Drugs Daily in the Previous Month, 1985-89

Data have been combined for 1985 to 1989.

Type of drug	Mexican American		Puerto Rican/ Latin American		White		Black		Asian American		American Indian	
	Male	Female	Male	Female	Male	Female	Male	Female	Male	Female	Male	Female
Sample size	1,518	1,599	680	712	28,056	29,808	3,688	4,499	982	917	537	531
Percent who used daily in last 30 days:												
Marijuana	22.0	13.6	18.9	9.6	25.0	19.8	18.5	9.9	9.7	8.1	27.6	23.9
Inhalants[1]	2.3	2.1	2.0	0.8	3.4	2.0	1.4	1.4	1.3	0.8	5.2	0.9
Hallucinogens	2.4	0.7	3.0	0.4	3.5	1.7	0.9	0.3	1.5	0.3	3.6	2.7
LSD	1.9	0.3	1.6	0.2	2.8	1.1	0.6	0.2	1.1	0.1	3.1	2.2
Cocaine	8.2	3.0	8.1	2.9	5.6	4.1	2.6	1.3	1.8	2.6	7.3	9.2
Heroin	0.3	0.2	0.9	0.2	0.3	0.1	0.5	0.3	0.1	0.0	1.1	0.4
Other opiates[2]	1.1	0.7	1.5	0.5	2.3	1.9	0.9	0.6	1.6	0.7	4.0	2.4
Stimulants[2]	4.9	4.8	3.1	1.2	5.6	6.0	1.9	1.3	2.1	3.6	8.1	10.3
Sedatives[2]	2.0	0.9	1.8	1.3	2.2	1.7	1.1	0.5	1.9	1.3	4.8	2.6
Barbiturates[2]	1.7	0.8	1.3	1.2	1.8	1.5	0.9	0.5	1.4	1.0	3.7	2.1
Methaqualone[2]	0.6	0.2	0.9	0.1	0.9	0.5	0.5	0.1	0.8	0.6	2.5	0.9
Tranquilizers[2]	0.8	0.9	0.6	1.5	1.9	2.0	0.8	0.5	1.7	0.9	3.1	2.2
Alcohol	65.0	50.5	55.4	43.0	72.3	66.6	49.2	32.8	43.7	34.2	69.0	60.2
Cigarettes	23.8	18.7	22.0	24.7	29.8	34.0	15.6	13.3	16.8	14.3	36.8	43.6

Source: U.S. Department of Education. National Center for Education Statistics. *The Condition of Education, 1992.* Washington, DC: U.S. Government Printing Office, 1992, p. 312. Primary source: U.S. Department of Health and Human Services; Alcohol, Drug Abuse, and Mental Health Administration; National Institute on Drug Abuse, *Drug Use Among American High School Students, College Students, and Other Young Adults*, 1991. *Notes:* 1. Respondents represent four-fifths of sample size indicated. 2. Only drug use which was not under a doctor's orders are included here.

★ 281 ★

School Environment

Percentage of High School Seniors Who Reported Using Selected Drugs in the Past Year, 1985-89

Drug used in past 12 months	Mexican American		Puerto Rican/ Latin American		White		Black		Asian American		American Indian	
	Male	Female	Male	Female	Male	Female	Male	Female	Male	Female	Male	Female
Marijuana/hashish	37.3	26.0	30.6	21.3	40.2	36.0	29.8	18.4	19.6	17.1	42.0	44.0
Cocaine	14.7	7.6	15.6	7.6	11.9	9.3	6.1	2.6	5.8	5.7	14.2	15.5
Alcohol	82.4	73.6	80.6	77.2	88.3	88.6	72.5	63.9	69.3	67.5	82.0	81.3

Source: U.S. Department of Education. National Center for Education Statistics. *The Condition of Education, 1992.* Washington, DC: U.S. Government Printing Office, 1992, p. 118. Primary source: U.S. Department of Health and Human Services, Alcohol, Drug Use and Mental Health Administration, National Institute on Drug Abuse, *Drug Use Among American High School Students, College Students, and Other Young Adults*, 1991.

★ 282 ★

School Environment

Reasons for Attending School

Figures represent percentage of tenth grade students who agree or strongly agree with each statement. Data are shown by race/ethnicity, for 1990.

Reason given	Total	White	Black	Hispanic	Asian	American Indian
Think subjects are interesting	71.0	68.8	79.1	74.5	77.3	81.2
Get a feeling of satisfaction	76.9	74.8	85.8	81.3	79.6	81.6
Nothing else to do	30.3	30.1	29.0	31.1	32.4	31.3
Need education to get a job	96.6	96.5	96.7	96.8	97.1	93.4
To meet friends	82.7	85.5	66.1	80.1	84.9	80.8
Play on a team or belong to a club	53.6	55.3	49.3	45.3	56.3	46.2
Teachers care and expect student to succeed	74.0	72.4	81.6	76.0	74.6	79.4

Source: U.S. Department of Education. National Center for Education Statistics. Office of Educational Research and Improvement. *Digest of Education Statistics, 1994.* Lanham, MD: Bernan, November 1994, p. 144. Primary source: U.S. Department of Education, National Center for Education Statistics, "National Education Longitudinal Survey of 1988," First Followup survey. (This table was prepared February 1993.).

★ 283 ★

School Environment

School Segregation

States with the largest percentage of Hispanics attending schools that have 50 to 100 percent minority populations are shown. Minority could include Asian, Black and Hispanic.

State	Percent
New York	86.1
Illinois	85.0
Texas	84.3
New Jersey	84.1
California	79.1
Rhode Island	77.8
New Mexico	74.4
Connecticut	72.4
Pennsylvania	66.9
Arizona	56.9

Source: De Witt, Karen. "The nation's schools learn a 4th: resegregation." *The New York Times* (19 January 1992), p. E5. Primary source: "Status of School Desegregation: The Next Generation," by Gary Orfield and Franklin Monfort, a report to the National School Boards Association.

★ 284 ★

School Environment

School Violence

Data reflect percentages of each race/ethnicity threatened or injured.

Incident/grade	Hispanic	White	Black
Threatened with a weapon			
Grade 8	22.0	17.0	27.0
Grade 10	17.0	16.0	20.0
Grade 12	15.0	13.0	20.0
Injured with a weapon			
Grade 8	16.0	8.0	15.0
Grade 10	12.0	7.0	11.0
Grade 12	7.0	5.0	10.0

Source: Kelly, Dennis. "When kids are fighting mad: curbing conflict becomes part of the curriculum." *USA TODAY* (18 November 1992), p. 7A. Primary source: University of Michigan.

★ 285 ★

School Environment

Student Opinions on School Environment

Figures represent percentage of 12th graders who agreed or strongly agreed with each statement. Data are shown for 1992.

	Total	White	Black	Hispanic	Asian	American Indian
There is school spirit	71.4	72.1	67.4	71.0	70.7	62.0
Discipline is fair	68.0	68.0	58.6	74.7	75.6	73.0
Teaching is good	85.4	85.1	84.1	88.5	85.5	88.3
Teachers are interested in students	81.6	81.9	78.4	83.7	80.1	83.0
I don't feel safe at this school	10.4	8.6	16.1	14.7	15.8	13.0
Disruptions by other students interfere with my learning	33.1	30.8	38.1	39.8	41.4	40.5
Fights occur between different racial/ethnic groups	22.7	20.9	22.2	31.9	30.5	29.9
There are many gangs in school	16.3	12.5	17.5	36.4	27.2	23.2
Students are graded fairly	78.3	79.5	71.6	77.6	77.3	74.7
There is a lot of cheating on tests and assignments	58.8	59.7	57.1	53.8	63.5	59.8
Some teachers ignore cheating when they see it	30.9	32.7	25.4	26.0	30.7	24.8

Source: U.S. Department of Education. National Center for Education Statistics. Office of Educational Research and Improvement. *Digest of Education Statistics, 1994.* Lanham, MD: Bernan, November 1994, p. 137. Primary source: U.S. Department of Education, National Center for Education Statistics, "National Education Longitudinal Study of 1988." Base Year and First and Second Followup surveys. (This table was prepared February 1994.).

School Personnel

★ 286 ★

Los Angeles: Ethnic Distribution of Teachers

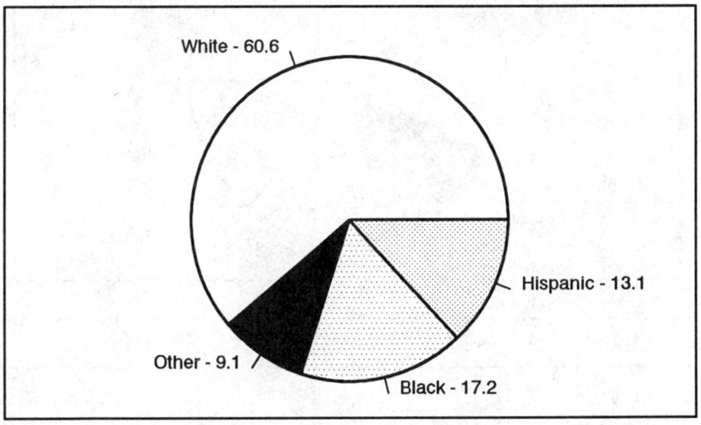

Race/ethnicity	Percent
White	60.6
Black	17.2
Hispanic	13.1
Other	9.1

Source: "Los Angeles schools hobbled and desperate." *The New York Times* (16 February 1993), p. A12. Primary source: Los Angeles Unified School District, United Teachers of Los Angeles.

★ 287 ★

School Personnel

Los Angeles: Ethnic Distribution of the School Board

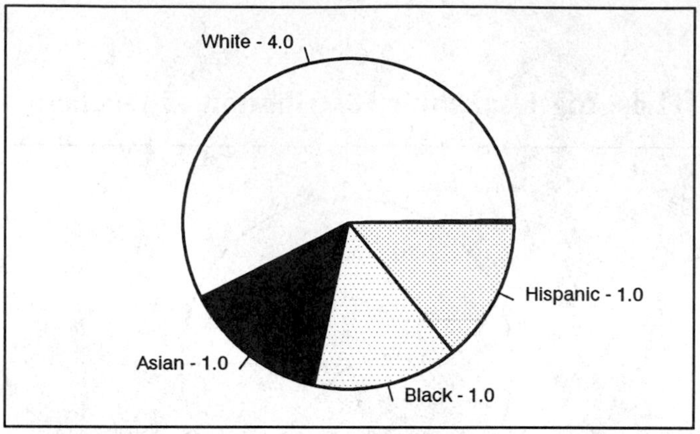

Race/ethnicity	Number
White	4.0
Black	1.0
Hispanic	1.0
Asian	1.0

Source: "Los Angeles schools hobbled and desperate." *The New York Times* (16 February 1993), p. A12. Primary source: Los Angeles Unified School District, United Teachers of Los Angeles.

★ 288 ★

School Personnel

Math Teacher Qualifications

Data show the percentage of eighth graders whose math teachers majored or minored in math in college. Data are shown for 1988.

Students' race/ethnicity	Teacher			
	Major in math/math educ.	Minor in math/math educ.	Major in education	Other major
All students	43.3	27.1	18.2	11.4
White	45.7	27.2	17.7	9.4
Asian	44.1	23.5	15.0	17.5
Black	40.0	26.6	21.5	12.9
Hispanic	33.3	28.5	17.5	20.8
Native American	30.5	23.5	23.4	22.6

Source: National Science Board. *Science & Engineering Indicators—1993* (NSB 93- 1). Washington, DC: U.S. Government Printing Office, 1993, p. 20. Primary source: Research, Evaluation, and Dissemination Division, *Indicators of Science and Mathematics Education 1992*, NSF-95 (Washington, DC: National Science Foundation, 1993).

★ 289 ★

School Personnel

Private School Teachers: Selected Characteristics, 1990-91

Data are shown for the school year, based on a survey and subject to sampling error.

Characteristic	Unit	Age				Sex		Race/ethnicity		
		Under 30 years old	30 to 39 years old	40 to 49 years old	Over 50 years old	Male	Female	White[1]	Black[1]	Hispanic
Total[2]	1,000	68	105	115	67	82	275	329	9	12
Highest degree held:										
Bachelor's	Percent	81.4	65.9	55.4	47.0	51.5	65.0	61.8	72.8	60.6
Master's	Percent	9.8	23.5	33.4	38.7	35.3	24.5	27.3	21.7	22.1
Education specialist	Percent	0.8	2.3	3.7	4.8	4.0	2.6	3.0	1.0	1.7
Doctorate	Percent	0.3	1.1	1.9	4.0	4.2	1.0	1.8	0.9	2.7
Full-time teaching experience:										
Less than 3 years	Percent	51.7	19.7	10.1	7.3	19.8	20.6	20.1	20.1	28.8
3 to 9 years	Percent	48.0	45.4	31.3	10.0	30.7	35.8	34.8	39.1	31.6
10 to 20 years	Percent	0.2	34.8	44.7	27.5	30.4	29.9	30.3	25.4	25.3
20 years or more	Percent	-	0.1	13.8	55.2	19.0	13.7	14.9	15.4	14.2
Full-time teachers	1,000	61	86	98	55	70	231	277	9	9
Earned income	Dol.	18,658	21,334	22,463	24,197	27,196	20,007	21,578	23,094	22,912
Salary	Dol.	16,403	19,190	20,892	21,534	23,003	18,815	19,717	20,333	20,740

Source: 1994 Statistical Abstract of the United States on CD-ROM [machine-readable datafiles]. CD-8A-94. Washington, DC: U.S. Department of Commerce, Economics and Statistics Administration, Bureau of the Census, Data User Services Division, January 1995. Primary source: U.S. National Center for Education Statistics, *Digest of Education Statistics, 1993. Notes:* A dash (-) represents zero. 1. Non-Hispanic. 2. Includes teachers with no degrees and associates degrees, not shown separately.

★ 290 ★

School Personnel

Public School Teachers: Selected Characteristics, 1990-91

Data are shown for the school year, based on a survey and are subject to sampling error. Data exclude prekindergarten teachers.

Characteristic	Unit	Age				Sex		Race/ethnicity			Level of control	
		Under 30 years old	30 to 39 years old	40 to 49 years old	Over 50 years old	Male	Female	White[1]	Black[1]	Hispanic	Elementary	Secondary
Total teachers[2]	1,000	312	731	1,002	514	719	1,840	2,214	212	87	1,331	1,229
Highest degree held:												
Bachelor's	Percent	84.1	56.4	43.8	41.6	44.7	54.7	51.5	50.8	61.0	56.5	46.9
Master's	Percent	14.4	39.1	48.8	49.9	47.0	40.1	42.7	42.1	32.9	38.8	45.7
Education specialist	Percent	1.2	3.4	5.9	5.9	5.3	4.3	4.5	5.0	4.3	4.1	5.1
Doctorate	Percent	-	0.4	1.0	1.4	1.3	0.6	0.7	1.3	0.9	0.5	1.1
Full-time teaching experience:												
Less than 3 years	Percent	41.8	10.2	3.5	1.5	7.8	10.4	9.7	6.5	14.0	10.6	8.7
3 to 9 years	Percent	58.1	38.7	16.3	7.3	19.9	28.4	26.3	20.0	33.4	27.7	24.2
10 to 20 years	Percent	0.1	51.0	49.1	26.0	37.0	39.8	39.0	40.9	39.6	39.2	38.8
20 years or more	Percent	(X)	0.1	31.1	65.2	35.3	21.4	25.1	32.8	13.1	22.5	28.3

[Continued]

★ 290 ★

Public School Teachers: Selected Characteristics, 1990-91

[Continued]

Characteristic	Unit	Age				Sex		Race/ethnicity			Level of control	
		Under 30 years old	30 to 39 years old	40 to 49 years old	Over 50 years old	Male	Female	White[1]	Black[1]	Hispanic	Elementary	Secondary
Full-time teachers	1,000	283	650	925	481	668	1,680	2,021	202	82	1,206	1,142
Earned income	Dol.	24,918	30,108	36,083	38,614	37,874	31,870	33,611	33,539	32,907	31,868	35,384
Salary	Dol.	22,779	27,918	33,690	36,333	33,360	30,476	31,293	31,579	30,743	30,501	32,135
Supplemental contract during school year:												
Teachers receiving	1,000	122	231	313	122	354	435	703	49	25	244	544
Salary	Dol.	1,675	2,045	1,914	2,088	2,663	1,357	1,977	1,664	1,709	1,172	2,276
Supplemental contract during summer:												
Teachers receiving	1,000	54	113	162	64	156	237	321	45	18	169	224
Salary	Dol.	1,615	1,969	2,018	2,294	2,328	1,773	1,935	2,251	2,375	1,829	2,117
Teachers with nonschool employment:												
Teaching/tutoring	1,000	13	30	47	20	39	71	95	8	5	44	66
Education related	1,000	9	18	28	12	31	36	59	5	2	24	43
Not education related	1,000	33	63	91	42	130	99	204	16	5	84	146

Source: *1994 Statistical Abstract of the United States on CD-ROM* [machine-readable datafiles]. CD-8A-94. Washington, DC: U.S. Department of Commerce, Economics and Statistics Administration, Bureau of the Census, Data User Services Division, January 1995. Primary source: U.S. National Center for Education Statistics, *Digest of Education Statistics, 1993*. *Notes:* A dash (-) represents or rounds to zero. An X stands for not applicable. 1. Non-Hispanic. 2. Includes teachers with no degrees and associates degrees, not shown separately.

★ 291 ★

School Personnel

School Teachers and Administrators: Degree Status and Experience of School Teachers, 1990-91

Data are shown for teachers in public and private elementary and secondary schools.

Race/ethnicity	Total[1]	Percent of teachers, by highest degree earned						Percent of teachers, by years of full-time teaching experience			
		No degree	Associate	Bachelor's	Master's	Education specialist	Doctor's	Less than 3	3 to 9	10 to 20	Over 20
Public schools											
Total	2,559,488	0.5	0.2	51.9	42.1	4.6	0.8	9.7	26.0	39.0	25.3
White	2,214,097	0.5	0.2	51.5	42.7	4.5	0.7	9.7	26.3	39.0	25.1
Black	211,640	0.5	0.3	50.8	42.1	5.0	1.3	6.5	20.0	40.9	32.8
Hispanic	86,917	0.7	0.2	61.0	32.9	4.3	0.9	14.0	33.4	39.6	13.1
Asian or Pacific Islander	26,766	0.7	0.1	51.2	31.2	15.3	1.6	12.4	29.8	33.0	24.7
American Indian or Alaskan Native	20,070	0.5	0.5	64.4	30.8	3.7	0.2	15.3	28.1	36.9	20.1
Private schools											
Total	356,285	5.3	1.1	61.9	27.0	2.9	1.8	27.5	36.6	25.0	10.9
White	328,624	5.1	1.1	61.8	27.3	3.0	1.8	27.2	36.6	25.1	11.1
Black	9,462	3.4	0.2	72.8	21.7	1.0	0.9	28.9	43.0	22.5	5.6
Hispanic	11,651	11.1	1.8	60.6	22.1	1.7	2.7	32.4	33.0	22.8	11.9
Asian or Pacific Islander	5,190	4.0	0.9	58.6	26.4	8.9	1.2	24.8	38.7	26.5	10.0

[Continued]

★ 291 ★

School Teachers and Administrators: Degree Status and Experience of School Teachers, 1990-91

[Continued]

Race/ethnicity	Total[1]	Percent of teachers, by highest degree earned						Percent of teachers, by years of full-time teaching experience			
		No degree	Associate	Bachelor's	Master's	Education specialist	Doctor's	Less than 3	3 to 9	10 to 20	Over 20
American Indian or Alaskan Native	1,360	20.1	0.9	50.2	26.3	2.5	0.0	43.4	24.9	24.4	7.3

Source: U.S. Department of Education. National Center for Education Statistics. Office of Educational Research and Improvement. *Digest of Education Statistics, 1994.* Lanham, MD: Bernan, November 1994, p. 67. Primary source: U.S. Department of Education, National Center for Education Statistics, "Schools and Staffing Survey, 1990-91." (This table was prepared July 1993.) *Notes:* Excludes prekindergarten teachers. Details may not add to totals because of survey item nonresponse and rounding. 1. Data are based on a sample survey and may not be strictly comparable with data reported elsewhere. Table reflects count of both full-time and part-time teachers rather than full-time equivalent teachers.

★ 292 ★

School Personnel

School Teachers and Administrators: Degree Status, Experience, and Salary of School Principals, 1990-91

Data are shown for principals in public and private elementary and secondary schools.

Race/ethnicity	Total[1]	Percent of principals, by highest degree earned[2]				Average years of experience			Average annual salary of principals, by length of work		
		Bachelor's	Master's	Education specialist	Doctor's and first professional	As a principal	Other school position	Outside school position	10 months or less	11 months	12 months
						Public schools					
Total	78,889	1.8	60.5	28.2	9.5	9.3	3.8	0.8	$45,126	$48,377	$52,761
White, non-Hispanic	67,794	1.7	60.5	28.6	9.1	9.6	3.7	0.8	44,645	48,184	52,674
Black, non-Hispanic	6,770	0.9	57.8	27.4	13.9	8.3	4.7	0.9	48,589	49,501	53,338
Hispanic	3,097	4.1	67.5	21.6	6.4	7.4	4.6	0.9	49,176	49,220	54,981
Asian or Pacific Islander	529	7.1	64.8	20.6	7.5	6.7	4.5	1.0	50,857	58,652	[3]
American Indian or Alaskan Native	700	6.0	52.8	28.0	13.2	7.7	5.6	0.8	38,374	[3]	46,176
						Private schools					
Total	23,881	26.9	47.4	11.5	6.8	8.7	2.8	2.4	20,591	29,738	30,410
White, non-Hispanic	22,366	26.6	47.9	11.7	6.6	8.7	2.8	2.5	20,481	29,496	30,429
Black, non-Hispanic	643	24.0	44.1	4.7	13.2	6.9	3.6	2.2	[3]	[3]	29,559
Hispanic	607	44.9	36.0	12.8	3.5	7.0	3.2	1.4	[3]	[3]	29,479

Source: U.S. Department of Education. National Center for Education Statistics. Office of Educational Research and Improvement. *Digest of Education Statistics, 1994.* Lanham, MD: Bernan, November 1994, p. 94. Primary source: U.S. Department of Education, National Center for Education Statistics, "Schools and Staffing Survey, 1990-91." (This table was prepared July 1993.) *Notes:* Details may not add to 100 percent because of rounding and survey item nonresponse. 1. Total differs from data appearing in other tables because of varying survey processing procedures and time period coverages. 2. Percentages for those with less than a bachelor's degree are not shown. 3. Too few cases for reliable estimates.

★ 293 ★

School Personnel

School Teachers and Administrators: Salaries and Other Characteristics of School Teachers, 1990-91

Data are shown for teachers in public and private elementary and secondary schools.

Race/ethnicity	Total earned income	Base salary	Number of full-time teachers	School year supplemental contract: Number of teachers	School year supplemental contract: Supplemental salary	Supplemental contract during summer: Number of teachers	Supplemental contract during summer: Supplemental salary	Number of teachers with nonschool employment: Teaching or tutoring	Number of teachers with nonschool employment: Education related	Number of teachers with nonschool employment: Not education related
Public schools										
Total	$33,578	$31,298	2,348,315	788,215	$1,942	393,215	$1,993	109,923	67,072	229,670
Hispanic	32,907	30,743	82,119	25,190	1,709	18,183	2,375	4,874	1,576	4,947
White, non-Hispanic	33,611	31,293	2,021,075	702,746	1,977	321,128	1,935	95,488	58,916	203,859
Black, non-Hispanic	33,539	31,579	201,690	48,905	1,664	45,331	2,251	7,680	5,359	15,920
Asian or Pacific Islander	35,889	33,908	25,208	5,064	1,454	5,859	2,137	910	818	2,175
American Indian or Alaskan Native	30,167	27,322	18,222	6,310	1,567	2,714	1,681	971	403	2,768
Private schools										
Total	21,673	19,783	301,257	60,038	1,712	54,503	1,864	21,438	9,622	31,492
Hispanic	22,912	20,740	9,487	[1]	[1]	1,553	2,320	[1]	[1]	[1]
White, non-Hispanic	21,569	19,709	277,539	56,645	1,695	49,853	1,832	19,742	8,556	29,532
Black, non-Hispanic	23,094	20,333	8,593	[1]	[1]	2,058	1,930	[1]	[1]	[1]
Asian or Pacific Islander	22,795	21,145	4,645	[1]	[1]	867	2,968	[1]	[1]	[1]
American Indian or Alaskan Native	21,373	20,128	994	[1]	[1]	[1]	[1]	[1]	[1]	[1]

Source: U.S. Department of Education. National Center for Education Statistics. Office of Educational Research and Improvement. *Digest of Education Statistics, 1994.* Lanham, MD: Bernan, November 1994, p. 82. Primary source: U.S. Department of Education, National Center for Education Statistics, "School and Staffing Survey, 1990-91." (This table was prepared July 1993.) *Notes:* Details may not add to totals because of rounding, missing values in cells with too few cases, or survey item nonresponse. 1. Too few sample cases (fewer than 30) for a reliable estimate.

★ 294 ★

School Personnel

Student/Science Teacher Ratios, by Race/Ethnicity and Gender

Data show the percent of students taught by teachers of each race/ethnicity or gender. Standard error is shown in parentheses.

Grade 8 student characteristics	Percent of students: Teachers' race/ethnicity: White	Black	Hispanic	Asian/Pacific Islander	Teachers' gender: Male	Female
Race/ethnicity						
White	95 (1.2)	4 (0.8)	1 (0.7)	0 (0.1)	58 (3.3)	43 (3.3)
Black	70 (4.8)	28 (4.7)	1 (0.4)	2 (1.1)	41 (5.7)	59 (5.7)
Hispanic	82 (3.9)	9 (2.1)	6 (3.3)	2 (1.2)	51 (3.1)	49 (3.1)
Asian/Pacific Islander	86 (5.0)	7 (3.5)	1 (1.1)	6 (3.6)	56 (8.9)	45 (8.9)
Sex						
Male	89 (1.7)	8 (1.4)	2 (0.9)	1 (0.4)	55 (3.4)	45 (3.4)

[Continued]

★ 294 ★

Student/Science Teacher Ratios, by Race/Ethnicity and Gender

[Continued]

Grade 8 student characteristics	Percent of students					
	Teachers' race/ethnicity				Teachers' gender	
	White	Black	Hispanic	Asian/Pacific Islander	Male	Female
Female	90 (1.5)	8 (1.1)	2 (0.8)	1 (0.4)	54 (3.1)	46 (3.1)
All students	90 (1.5)	8 (1.2)	2 (0.8)	1 (0.4)	55 (3.0)	45 (3.0)

Source: Jones, Lee R., and others. *The 1990 Science Report Card: NAEP's Assessment of Fourth, Eighth, and Twelfth Graders,* Prepared by Educational Testing Service under contract with the National Center for Education Statistics, Office of Educational Research and Improvement, U.S. Department of Education, March 1992, p. 104. *Notes:* The standard errors of the estimated percentages appear in parentheses. It can be said with 95 percent certainty that for each population of interest, the value for the whole population is within plus or minus two standard errors of the estimate for the sample. When the percentage of students is either 0 or 100, the standard error is inestimatable. However, percentages 99.5 percent and greater were rounded to 100 percent, and percentages less than 0.5 percent were rounded to 0 percent. Data are not presented for American Indian because breakdown by teachers' race/ethnicity resulted in too few students in each category.

Higher Education

★ 295 ★

Bachelor's Degree Conferrals, by Sex and Race/Ethnicity, 1976-92

Distribution of bachelor's degrees awarded in each academic year is shown in percent, by sex and race/ethnicity.

Year and sex of student	Percentage distribution of degrees conferred						
	Total	White, non-Hispanic	Black, non-Hispanic	Hispanic	Asian or Pacific Islander	American Indian/ Alaskan Native	Non-resident alien
1976-77							
Total[1]	100.0	88.0	6.4	2.0	1.5	0.4	1.7
Men	100.0	88.6	5.1	2.1	1.5	0.4	2.3
Women	100.0	87.3	7.9	2.0	1.5	0.4	1.0
1978-79							
Total[2]	100.0	87.3	6.6	2.2	1.7	0.4	1.9
Men	100.0	87.8	5.2	2.2	1.7	0.4	2.7
Women	100.0	86.7	8.0	2.2	1.6	0.4	1.1
1980-81							
Total[3]	100.0	86.4	6.5	2.3	2.0	0.4	2.4
Men	100.0	86.5	5.2	2.3	2.2	0.4	3.5
Women	100.0	86.2	7.8	2.4	1.9	0.4	1.3
1984-85							
Total[4]	100.0	85.3	5.9	2.7	2.6	0.4	3.0
Men	100.0	85.1	4.8	2.6	2.8	0.4	4.2
Women	100.0	85.5	7.0	2.7	2.4	0.5	1.9
1986-87							
Total[5]	100.0	84.9	5.7	2.7	3.3	0.4	3.0

[Continued]

★ 295 ★

Bachelor's Degree Conferrals, by Sex and Race/Ethnicity, 1976-92

[Continued]

Year and sex of student	Percentage distribution of degrees conferred						
	Total	White, non-Hispanic	Black, non-Hispanic	Hispanic	Asian or Pacific Islander	American Indian/ Alaskan Native	Non-resident alien
Men	100.0	84.6	4.7	2.7	3.6	0.4	4.1
Women	100.0	85.2	6.7	2.8	3.0	0.4	1.9
1988-89							
Total[6]	100.0	84.6	5.7	2.9	3.7	0.4	2.7
Men	100.0	84.5	4.6	2.9	4.0	0.4	3.6
Women	100.0	84.7	6.7	3.0	3.4	0.4	1.8
1989-90							
Total[7]	100.0	84.3	5.8	3.1	3.7	0.4	2.5
Men	100.0	84.3	4.7	3.0	4.0	0.4	3.5
Women	100.0	84.3	6.8	3.2	3.5	0.5	1.7
1990-91							
Total[8]	100.0	83.6	6.0	3.4	3.8	0.4	2.7
Men	100.0	83.7	4.9	3.3	4.2	0.4	3.6
Women	100.0	83.5	7.0	3.5	3.6	0.4	1.9
1991-92							
Total[9]	100.0	82.9	6.4	3.6	4.1	0.5	2.5
Men	100.0	83.1	5.2	3.5	4.5	0.4	3.2
Women	100.0	82.7	7.4	3.7	3.8	0.5	1.8

Source: U.S. Department of Education. National Center for Education Statistics. Office of Educational Research and Improvement. *Digest of Education Statistics, 1994.* Lanham, MD: Bernan, November 1994, p. 278. Primary source: U.S. Department of Education, National Center for Education Statistics, "Degrees and Other Formal Awards Conferred" surveys, and Integrated Postsecondary Education Data System (IPEDS), "Completions" surveys. (This table was prepared March 1994.) *Notes:* Some data have been revised from previously published data. 1. Excludes 1,121 men and 528 women whose racial/ethnic group was not available. 2. Excludes 1,279 men and 571 women whose racial/ethnic group was not available. 3. Excludes 258 men and 82 women whose racial/ethnic group was not available. 4. Exclude 6,380 men and 4,786 women whose racial/ethnic group was not available. 5. Reported racial/ethnic distributions of students by level of degree, field of degree, and sex were used to estimate race/ethnicity for students whose race/ethnicity was not reported. 6. Reported racial/ethnic distributions of students by level of degree, field of degree, and sex were used to estimate race/ethnicity for students whose race/ethnicity was not reported. Excludes 1,400 men and 1,005 women whose racial/ethnic group and field of study were not available. 7. Reported racial/ethnic distributions of students by level of degree, field of degree, and sex were used to estimate race/ethnicity for students whose race/ethnicity was not reported. Excludes 1,379 men and 1,334 women whose racial/ethnic group and field of study were not available. 8. Reported racial/ethnic distributions of students by level of degree, field of degree, and sex were used to estimate race/ethnicity for students whose race/ethnicity was not reported. Excludes 7,621 men and 5,637 women whose racial/ethnic group and field of study were not available. 9. Reported racial/ethnic distributions of students by level of degree, field of degree, and sex were used to estimate race/ethnicity for students whose race/ethnicity was not reported. Excludes 3,835 men and 2,885 women whose racial/ethnic group and field of study were not available.

★ 296 ★

Higher Education

Bachelor's Degrees Held by Persons 25 Years Old and Older, by Race/Ethnicity, 1992

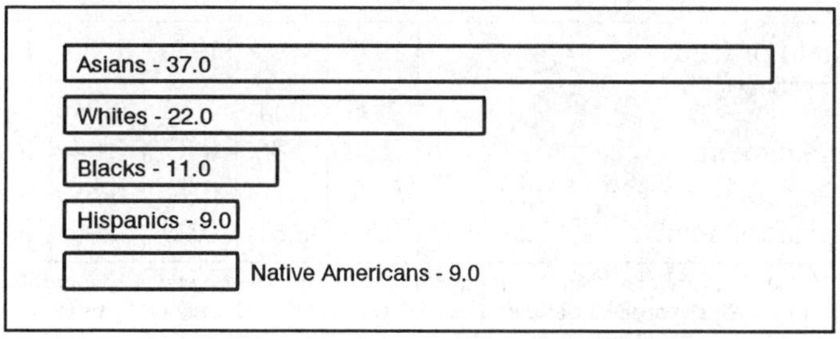

Race/ethnicity	Percent holding a bachelor's degree
Asians	37.0
Whites	22.0
Blacks	11.0
Hispanics	9.0
Native Americans	9.0

Source: USA TODAY (10 December 1992), p. 11A. Primary source: U.S. Census Bureau.

★ 297 ★

Higher Education

Concentration Ratios of Hispanics, at the Bachelor's Degree Level, by Field of Study, 1977-91

From the source: "The minority field concentration ratio is calculated as the percentage of a minority group earning bachelor's degrees who majored in a selected field divided by the percentage of whites earning bachelor's degrees who majored in the same field....Among 1991 bachelor's degree recipients, Hispanics and blacks were more likely than whites to major in the social and behavioral sciences."

Race/ethnicity and field of study	1977	1979	1981	1985	1987	1989	1990	1991
Hispanic concentration ratio								
Humanities and social/behavioral sciences	1.23	1.22	1.20	1.15	1.11	1.14	1.13	1.10
Humanities	1.17	1.15	1.11	1.09	1.10	1.10	1.12	1.06
Social and behavioral sciences	1.29	1.28	1.29	1.20	1.13	1.18	1.14	1.13
Natural and computer sciences and engineering	0.85	0.88	0.91	0.92	1.05	1.05	1.07	1.07
Natural sciences	0.82	0.89	0.94	0.95	0.98	1.01	0.98	1.00
Life sciences	0.89	1.04	1.13	1.25	1.26	1.25	1.18	1.20
Physical sciences	0.71	0.66	0.70	0.64	0.77	0.77	0.70	0.71
Mathematics	0.76	0.76	0.72	0.67	0.62	0.72	0.80	0.79
Computer sciences and engineering	0.90	0.86	0.87	0.91	1.09	1.08	1.12	1.13
Computer and information sciences	0.73	0.84	0.89	0.84	1.11	1.15	1.18	1.26
Engineering	0.92	0.86	0.87	0.94	1.09	1.06	1.11	1.08
Technical/professional	0.89	0.91	0.92	0.95	0.92	0.90	0.90	0.92

[Continued]

★ 297 ★

Concentration Ratios of Hispanics, at the Bachelor's Degree Level, by Field of Study, 1977-91

[Continued]

Race/ethnicity and field of study	1977	1979	1981	1985	1987	1989	1990	1991
Education	1.05	1.11	1.12	1.04	0.89	0.74	0.81	0.86
Business and management	0.84	0.85	0.87	0.94	0.97	0.97	0.93	0.94
Health sciences	0.72	0.76	0.75	0.89	0.75	0.79	0.87	0.85
Other technical/professional	0.84	0.87	0.90	0.96	0.93	0.96	0.94	0.95

Source: U.S. Department of Education. National Center for Education Statistics. *The Condition of Education 1994.* Washington, DC: U.S. GPO, 1994, p. 265. Primary source: U.S. Department of Education, National Center for Education Statistics, *Digest of Education Statistics 1993,* table 255 (based on IPEDS/HEGIS surveys of degrees conferred).

★ 298 ★

Higher Education

Index of the Number of Bachelor's Degrees Conferred and the Number of High School Completions, 1977-90

Percentages are in relation to 1981 conferrals and completions.

Academic year ending	Hispanics			White			Black		
	Degrees		High school	Degrees		High school	Degrees		High school
	Men	Women	completions	Men	Women	completions	Men	Women	completions
1977	94.7	76.4	98.4	107.3	92.1	102.8	102.1	92.6	88.8
1979	95.8	87.8	93.5	102.2	95.8	103.7	100.1	98.4	93.7
1981	100.0	100.0	100.0	100.0	100.0	100.0	100.0	100.0	100.0
1985	114.7	122.2	110.6	99.7	105.0	87.5	93.9	95.3	105.8
1987	119.0	128.2	116.5	100.1	108.5	82.5	91.8	94.2	100.9
1989	129.0	144.8	104.1	100.2	112.8	76.1	91.2	98.7	96.3
1990	137.6	161.6	-	101.8	117.0	-	95.0	104.5	-

Source: U.S. Department of Education. National Center for Education Statistics. *The Condition of Education, 1992.* Washington, DC: U.S. Government Printing Office, 1992, p. 66. Primary source: U.S. Department of Education, National Center for Education Statistics, IPEDS/HEGIS surveys of degrees conferred. U.S. Department of Commerce, Bureau of the Census, October Current Population Survey. *Notes:* A dash (-) indicates that data were not available. High school completions include diplomas and GED credentials. The index of completions is based on a 3-year moving average of the number of completions.

★ 299 ★

Higher Education

Doctoral Degrees Conferred, by Major Field of Study, 1991-92

The number of degrees conferred is shown by major field of study and race/ethnicity for the 1991-92 academic year.

Major field of study	Total	White, non-Hispanic	Black, non-Hispanic	Hispanic	Asian/ Pacific Islander	American Indian/ Alaskan Native	Nonresident alien
All fields, total[1]	1,129,833	936,771	72,326	40,761	46,720	5,176	28,079
Agricultural and natural resources	15,124	13,743	413	296	300	83	289
Architecture and related programs	8,753	7,050	294	407	551	33	418
Area, ethnic, and cultural studies	5,342	3,875	517	355	382	48	165
Biological/life sciences	42,941	33,179	2,428	1,673	4,488	185	988
Business management and administrative svcs.	256,603	209,768	18,304	8,466	10,592	949	8,524
Communications	54,257	46,554	3,970	1,650	1,088	177	818
Communication technologies	720	588	99	14	6	2	11
Computer and information sciences	24,557	17,311	2,147	901	2,140	81	1,977
Construction trades	67	52	11	1	1	1	1
Education	108,006	97,460	5,226	3,116	977	654	573
Engineering	61,206	45,923	2,406	2,087	6,387	186	4,217
Engineering-related technologies	16,190	13,071	1,174	558	794	88	505
English language and literature/letters	54,951	48,543	2,658	1,623	1,447	222	458
Foreign languages and literature	13,903	11,157	427	1,426	480	46	367
Health professions and related sciences	61,720	52,281	4,222	1,765	2,261	332	859
Home economics and vocational home economics	14,898	12,980	868	340	425	67	218
Law and legal studies	2,144	1,835	149	69	67	16	8
Liberal arts and sciences, general studies, and humanities	32,174	26,457	2,670	1,581	817	205	444
Library science	97	85	5	1	2	0	4
Mathematics	14,783	11,906	916	455	868	46	592
Mechanics and repairers	78	70	4	1	1	0	2
Multi/interdisciplinary studies	20,647	16,853	1,290	957	1,056	126	365
Parks, recreation, leisure and fitness studies	8,446	7,679	393	181	85	38	70
Philosophy and religion	7,526	6,559	311	229	276	27	124
Physical sciences and science technologies	16,960	14,044	836	382	1,025	66	607
Precision production trades	378	303	42	2	11	6	14
Protective services	18,855	14,574	2,699	1,075	262	135	110
Psychology	63,513	53,242	4,271	2,827	319	660	
Public administration & services	15,987	12,169	2,369	798	302	174	175
Military sciences	184	149	20	14	0	1	0
Social sciences and history	133,974	110,086	9,188	5,808	5,470	606	2,816
Theological studies/religious vocations	4,729	4,143	159	102	136	21	168
Transportation and material moving	3,598	3,156	174	123	55	28	62
Visual and performing arts	46,522	39,926	1,666	1,478	1,774	208	1,470

Source: U.S. Department of Education. National Center for Education Statistics. Office of Educational Research and Improvement. *Digest of Education Statistics, 1994.* Lanham, MD: Bernan, November 1994, p. 285. Primary source: U.S. Department of Education, National Center for Education Statistics, Integrated Postsecondary Education Data System (IPEDS), "Completions" survey. (This table was prepared April 1994.) *Notes:* To facilitate trend comparisons, certain aggregations have been made of the degree fields as reported in the IPEDS "Completions" survey: "Agriculture and natural resources" includes Agribusiness and agriculture production, Agricultural sciences, and Conservation and renewable natural resources; "Business and management and administrative services" includes Business and management, Business and office, Marketing and distribution, and Consumer and personal services. 1. Reported racial/ethnic distributions of students by level of degree, field of degree, and sex were used to estimate race/ethnicity for students whose race/ethnicity was not reported. Excludes 389 men and 180 women whose racial/ethnic group and field of study were not available.

★ 300 ★

Higher Education

Doctoral Degrees Conferred, by Sex and Race/Ethnicity, 1976-92

Distribution of doctoral degrees awarded in each academic year is shown in percent, by sex and race/ethnicity. This category includes Ph.D., Ed.D., and comparable degrees at the doctoral level but does not include first professional degrees.

Year and sex of student	Percentage distribution of degrees conferred						
	Total	White, non-Hispanic	Black, non-Hispanic	Hispanic	Asian or Pacific Islander	American Indian/ Alaskan Native	Non-resident alien
1976-77							
Total[1]	100.0	81.1	3.8	1.6	2.0	0.3	11.3
Men	100.0	80.0	3.1	1.5	2.2	0.3	13.0
Women	100.0	84.3	6.0	1.7	1.5	0.3	6.2
1978-79							
Total[2]	100.0	80.0	3.9	1.3	2.5	0.3	12.0
Men	100.0	78.5	3.1	1.3	2.8	0.3	14.1
Women	100.0	83.9	5.8	1.6	1.8	0.4	6.6
1980-81							
Total[3]	100.0	78.9	3.9	1.4	2.7	0.4	12.8
Men	100.0	76.6	3.1	1.2	2.9	0.4	15.8
Women	100.0	83.9	5.6	1.7	2.2	0.3	6.2
1984-85							
Total[4]	100.0	74.1	3.6	2.1	3.4	0.4	16.5
Men	100.0	70.5	2.6	2.0	3.8	0.3	20.8
Women	100.0	81.0	5.4	2.2	2.8	0.5	8.1
1986-87							
Total[5]	100.0	71.8	3.1	2.2	3.2	0.3	19.4
Men	100.0	67.1	2.2	2.0	3.6	0.3	24.8
Women	100.0	80.3	4.8	2.6	2.5	0.4	9.4
1988-89							
Total[6]	100.0	69.8	3.0	1.8	3.7	0.2	21.5
Men	100.0	64.3	2.2	1.5	4.2	0.2	27.5
Women	100.0	79.2	4.4	2.1	2.9	0.3	11.1
1989-90							
Total[7]	100.0	67.9	3.0	2.1	3.2	0.3	23.5
Men	100.0	62.3	2.2	1.7	3.6	0.2	30.0
Women	100.0	77.7	4.5	2.6	2.6	0.4	12.2
1990-91							
Total[8]	100.0	65.7	3.1	1.9	3.8	0.3	25.2
Men	100.0	59.9	24	1.6	4.1	0.2	31.9
Women	100.0	75.7	4.4	2.4	3.3	0.3	13.8
1991-92							
Total[9]	100.0	64.4	3.1	2.0	3.9	0.3	26.4

[Continued]

★ 300 ★

Doctoral Degrees Conferred, by Sex and Race/Ethnicity, 1976-92

[Continued]

Year and sex of student	Percentage distribution of degrees conferred						
	Total	White, non-Hispanic	Black, non-Hispanic	Hispanic	Asian or Pacific Islander	American Indian/ Alaskan Native	Non-resident alien
Men	100.0	58.3	2.3	1.8	4.2	0.3	33.1
Women	100.0	74.6	4.3	2.4	3.3	0.4	15.0

Source: U.S. Department of Education. National Center for Education Statistics. Office of Educational Research and Improvement. *Digest of Education Statistics, 1994.* Lanham, MD: Bernan, November 1994, p. 278. Primary source: U.S. Department of Education, National Center for Education Statistics, "Degrees and Other Formal Awards Conferred" surveys, and Integrated Postsecondary Education Data System (IPEDS), "Completions" surveys. (This table was prepared March 1994.) *Notes:* Some data have been revised from previously published data. 1. Excludes 106 men whose racial/ethnic group was not available. 2. Excludes 53 men and 2 women whose racial/ethnic group was not available. 3. Excludes 116 men and 3 women whose racial/ethnic group was not available. 4. Excludes 404 men and 232 women whose racial/ethnic group was not available. 5. Reported racial/ethnic distributions of students by level of degree, field of degree, and sex were used to estimate race/ethnicity for students whose race/ethnicity was not reported. 6. Reported racial/ethnic distributions of students by level of degree, field of degree, and sex were used to estimate race/ethnicity for students whose race/ethnicity was not reported. Excludes 51 men and 10 women whose racial/ethnic group and field of study were not available. 7. Reported racial/ethnic distributions of students by level of degree, field of degree, and sex were used to estimate race/ethnicity for students whose race/ethnicity was not reported. Excludes 153 men and 105 women whose racial/ethnic group and field of study were not available. 8. Reported racial/ethnic distributions of students by level of degree, field of degree, and sex were used to estimate race/ethnicity for students whose race/ethnicity was not reported. Excludes 423 men and 324 women whose racial/ethnic group and field of study were not available. 9. Reported racial/ethnic distributions of students by level of degree, field of degree, and sex were used to estimate race/ethnicity for students whose race/ethnicity was not reported. Excludes 389 men and 180 women whose racial/ethnic group and field of study were not available.

★ 301 ★

Higher Education

Master's Degrees Conferred, by Major Field of Study, 1991-92

The number of degrees conferred is shown by major field of study and race/ethnicity for the 1991-92 academic year.

Major field of study	Total	White, non-Hispanic	Black, non-Hispanic	Hispanic	Asian/ Pacific Islander	American Indian/ Alaskan Native	Nonresident alien
All fields, total[1]	348,682	268,371	18,116	9,358	12,658	1,273 0	38,906
Agricultural and natural resources	3,735	2,546	82	61	74	7	965
Architecture and related programs	3,640	2,530	135	121	191	10	653
Area, ethnic, and cultural studies	1,385	957	91	86	69	16	166
Biological/life sciences	4,785	3,404	156	141	276	13	795
Business management and administrative svcs.	84,642	65,320	3,966	1,944	3,635	220	9,557
Communications	4,180	3,109	258	78	110	15	610
Communications technologies	284	170	18	5	9	0	82
Computer and information sciences	9,530	4,678	334	158	1,171	16	3,173
Education	92,668	78,874	6,444	2,838	1,192	457	2,863
Engineering	24,983	13,640	498	521	2,377	45	7,902
Engineering-related technologies	994	728	52	20	55	6	133
English language and literature/letters	7,450	6,462	220	152	146	37	433
Foreign languages and literature	2,926	1,896	37	280	101	6	606
Health professions and related sciences	23,065	19,220	1,136	559	739	94	1,317
Home economics and vocational home economics	2,412	1,920	121	61	45	6	259
Law and legal studies	2,369	1,253	46	76	77	2	915

[Continued]

★ 301 ★

Master's Degrees Conferred, by Major Field of Study, 1991-92

[Continued]

Major field of study	Total	White, non-Hispanic	Black, non-Hispanic	Hispanic	Asian/ Pacific Islander	American Indian/ Alaskan Native	Nonresident alien
Liberal arts and sciences, general studies, and humanities	2,394	2,057	107	48	36	8	138
Library science	4,893	4,230	159	106	148	8	242
Mathematics	4,011	2,523	84	64	216	4	1,120
Multi/interdisciplinary studies	2,126	1,721	87	60	63	8	187
Parks, recreation, leisure and fitness studies	1,358	1,191	49	32	11	2	73
Philosophy and religion	1,146	931	50	26	39	7	93
Physical sciences and science technologies	5,374	3,296	105	91	318	19	1,545
Precision production trades	0	0	0	0	0	0	0
Protective services	1,249	973	182	35	15	6	38
Psychology	10,215	8,737	562	379	194	41	302
Public administration & services	19,243	15,231	2,001	771	422	124	694
Social sciences and history	12,702	9,034	602	301	396	50	2,319
Theological studies/religious vocations	5,185	4,085	240	116	189	12	543
Transportation and material moving	385	340	22	9	8	3	3
Visual and performing arts	9,353	7,315	272	219	336	31	1,180

Source: U.S. Department of Education. National Center for Education Statistics. Office of Educational Research and Improvement. *Digest of Education Statistics, 1994.* Lanham, MD: Bernan, November 1994, p. 279. Primary source: U.S. Department of Education, National Center for Education Statistics, Integrated Postsecondary Education Data System (IPEDS), "Completions" survey. (This table was prepared April 1994.) *Notes:* To facilitate trend comparisons, certain aggregations have been made of the degree fields as reported in the IPEDS "Completions" survey: "Agriculture and natural resources" includes Agribusiness and agriculture production, Agricultural sciences, and Conservation and renewable natural resources; "Business and management and administrative services" includes Business and management, Business and office, Marketing and distribution, and Consumer and personal services. 1. Reported racial/ethnic distributions of students by level of degree, field of degree, and sex were used to estimate race/ethnicity for students whose race/ethnicity was not reported. Excludes 2,299 men and 1,857 women whose racial/ethnic group and field of study were not available.

★ 302 ★

Higher Education

Master's Degrees Conferred, by Race/Ethnicity, 1976-92

Distribution of degrees awarded in each academic year is shown in percent, by sex and race/ethnicity.

Year and sex of student	Percentage of degrees conferred						
	Total	White, non-Hispanic	Black, non-Hispanic	Hispanic	Asian or Pacific Islander	American Indian/ Alaskan Native	Non-resident alien
1976-77							
Total[1]	100.0	84.0	6.6	1.9	1.6	0.3	5.5
Men	100.0	83.25	4.6	2.0	1.9	0.3	8.1
Women	100.0	85.0	8.9	1.9	1.3	0.3	2.6
1978-79							
Total[2]	100.0	83.0	6.5	1.9	1.8	0.3	6.5
Men	100.0	81.3	4.6	1.8	2.2	0.3	9.8
Women	100.0	84.9	8.4	1.9	1.5	0.3	3.1
1980-81							
Total[3]	100.0	82.0	5.8	2.2	2.1	0.4	7.5

[Continued]

★ 302 ★

Master's Degrees Conferred, by Race/Ethnicity, 1976-92

[Continued]

Year and sex of student	Percentage of degrees conferred						
	Total	White, non-Hispanic	Black, non-Hispanic	Hispanic	Asian or Pacific Islander	American Indian/ Alaskan Native	Non-resident alien
Men	100.0	79.3	4.2	2.1	2.6	0.3	11.4
Women	100.0	84.6	7.4	2.3	1.7	0.4	3.7
1984-85							
Total[4]	100.0	79.7	5.0	2.4	2.8	0.4	9.6
Men	100.0	76.1	3.7	2.2	3.5	0.4	14.1
Women	100.0	83.4	6.2	2.7	2.1	0.5	5.2
1986-87							
Total[5]	100.0	79.1	4.8	2.4	3.0	0.4	10.3
Men	100.0	74.7	3.6	2.4	3.7	0.4	15.2
Women	100.0	83.3	5.9	2.5	2.2	0.4	5.7
1988-89							
Total[6]	100.0	78.4	4.6	2.3	3.3	0.4	11.0
Men	100.0	73.7	3.5	2.2	4.1	0.3	16.2
Women	100.0	82.7	5.5	2.5	2.7	0.4	6.3
1989-90							
Total[7]	100.0	78.1	4.8	2.5	3.3	0.3	11.1
Men	100.0	73.8	3.6	2.3	3.9	0.3	16.0
Women	100.0	81.9	5.8	2.6	2.7	0.4	6.6
1990-91							
Total[8]	100.0	77.7	4.9	2.6	3.4	0.3	11.1
Men	100.0	73.3	3.8	2.4	4.2	0.3	16.1
Women	100.0	81.5	5.9	2.7	2.7	0.4	6.8
1991-92							
Total[9]	100.0	77.0	5.2	2.7	3.6	0.4	11.2
Men	100.0	72.8	3.8	2.6	4.4	0.3	16.1
Women	100.0	80.5	6.4	2.8	3.0	0.4	7.0

Source: U.S. Department of Education. National Center for Education Statistics. Office of Educational Research and Improvement. *Digest of Education Statistics, 1994.* Lanham, MD: Bernan, November 1994, p. 281. Primary source: U.S. Department of Education, National Center for Education Statistics, "Degrees and Other Formal Awards Conferred" surveys, and Integrated Postsecondary Education Data System (IPEDS), "Completions" survey. (This table was prepared March 1994.) *Notes:* Some data have been revised from previously published figures. 1. Excludes 387 men and 175 women whose racial/ethnic group was not available. 2. Excludes 733 men and 91 women whose racial/ethnic group was not available. 3. Excludes 1,377 men and 179 women whose racial/ethnic group was not available. 4. Excludes 3,973 men and 1,857 women whose racial/ethnic group was not available. 5. Reported racial/ethnic distributions of students by level of degree, field of degree, and sex were used to estimate race/ethnicity for students whose race/ethnicity was not reported. 6. Reported racial/ethnic distributions of students by level of degree, field of degree, and sex were used to estimate race/ethnicity for students whose race/ethnicity was not reported. Excludes 482 men and 369 women whose racial/ethnic group and field of study were not available. 7. Reported racial/ethnic distributions of students by level of degree, field of degree, and sex were used to estimate race/ethnicity for students whose race/ethnicity was not reported. Excludes 727 men and 1,109 women whose racial/ethnic group and field of study were not available. 8. Reported racial/ethnic distributions of students by level of degree, field of degree, and sex were used to estimate race/ethnicity for students whose race/ethnicity was not reported. Excludes 4,686 men and 3,837 women whose racial/ethnic group and field of study were not available. 9. Reported racial/ethnic distributions of students by level of degree, field of degree, and sex were used to estimate race/ethnicity for students whose race/ethnicity was not reported. Excludes 2,299 men and 1,857 women whose racial/ethnic group and field of study were not available.

★ 303 ★

Higher Education

Enrollment and College Completion of Recent High School Graduates

Figures show the enrollment and completion status of first-time postsecondary students who enrolled in the 1989-1990 school year. Data are shown for Spring 1992, by race/ethnicity.

	Total	White non-Hispanic	Black non-Hispanic	Hispanic
Vocational certificate				
Number (000)	376	270	55	36
Total	100.0	100.0	100.0	100.0
Completed nine months or less	29.2	29.6	26.4	23.2
Completed in over nine months	21.3	23.1	17.5	9.2
Not completed	49.5	47.3	56.1	67.6
Associate's degree				
Number (000)	708	566	70	52
Total	100.0	100.0	100.0	100.0
Completed	12.3	12.8	7.9	16.6
Continuously enrolled	19.1	18.5	12.2	27.0
Stopped and re-enrolled[1]	22.5	21.6	27.1	28.0
Stopped, no re-enrollment[2]	46.1	47.2	52.9	28.4
Bachelor's degree				
Number (000)	1,162	920	92	76
Total	100.0	100.0	100.0	100.0
Continuously enrolled	56.8	57.6	50.3	46.0
Stopped and re-enrolled[1]	18.9	17.9	23.4	27.7
Stopped, no re-enrollment[2]	24.2	24.5	26.3	26.3

Source: U.S. Department of Education. National Center for Education Statistics. Office of Educational Research and Improvement. *Digest of Education Statistics, 1994.* Lanham, MD: Bernan, November 1994, p. 309. U.S. Department of Education, National Center for Education Statistics, Beginning Postsecondary Student Longitudinal Survey, 1992. (This table was prepared in June 1994.) *Notes:* Data reflect completion and enrollment status by spring 1992 of first-time postsecondary students starting academic year 1989-90. Due to the limited time period covered by the survey, it was inappropriate to calculate bachelor's degree completion rates. Some cells in this table have relatively large standard errors. 1. Includes those students who were not enrolled for more than 4 months out of the year. Some students may not be enrolled at the time of the follow-up survey. 2. Includes those students who stopped enrolling for more than 4 months and did not re-enroll during the survey period.

★ 304 ★

Higher Education

Enrollment in College and Employment Status of High School Graduates 16 to 24 Years Old, 1992-93

Numbers, in thousands, and rates in percent are shown, by employment status and race/ethnicity.

Item	Civilian noninstitutional population			Civilian labor force[1]					Not in labor force
	Number	Percent	Percent of high school graduates	Number	Labor force participation rate	Employed	Unemployed: Number	Unemployed: Unemployment rate	
1992 high school graduates[2]									
Total	2,398	100.0	100.0	1,449	60.4	1,204	245	16.9	949
White[3]	1,900	79.2	79.2	1,193	62.8	1,309	153	12.9	707
Black[3]	353	14.7	14.7	172	48.6	104	68	39.6	181
Hispanic origin[4]	199	8.3	8.3	127	63.8	90	37	28.8	72
Enrolled in college, October 1992									
White[3]	1,204	81.4	50.2	619	51.4	552	67	10.8	585
Black[3]	169	11.4	7.0	58	34.1	35	22	[5]	111
Hispanic origin[4]	109	7.4	4.5	62	57.2	42	21	[5]	47
Not enrolled in college, October 1992									
White[3]	696	75.7	29.0	574	82.5	487	86	15.1	122
Black[3]	184	20.0	7.7	114	62.0	69	46	40.0	70
Hispanic origin[4]	90	9.8	3.8	64	71.8	48	16	[5]	26
1993 high school graduates[6]									
Total	2,338	100.0	100.0	1,413	60.5	1,144	268	19.1	925
White[3]	1,910	81.7	81.7	1,217	63.7	1,002	215	17.7	693
Black[3]	302	12.9	12.9	149	49.2	102	47	31.6	154
Hispanic origin[4]	200	8.6	8.6	131	65.7	86	46	34.8	68
Enrolled in college, October 1993									
White[3]	1,200	82.0	51.3	585	48.7	511	74	12.6	615
Black[3]	168	11.5	7.2	62	37.1	45	17	[5]	106
Hispanic origin[4]	125	8.5	5.3	70	56.2	53	17	[5]	54
Not enrolled in college, October 1993									
White[3]	710	81.3	30.4	632	89.1	491	141	22.4	77
Black[3]	134	15.3	5.7	86	64.3	57	30	34.4	48
Hispanic origin[4]	75	8.6	3.2	61	81.1	33	28	[5]	14

Source: U.S. Department of Education. National Center for Education Statistics. Office of Educational Research and Improvement. *Digest of Education Statistics, 1994.* Lanham, MD: Bernan, November 1994, p. 401. Primary source: U.S. Department of Labor, Bureau of Labor Statistics, *College Enrollment of 1993 High School Graduates*. (This table was prepared June 1994.) *Notes:* A dash (-) indicates data not available or not applicable. Data are based upon sample surveys of the civilian noninstitutional population. Percents are only shown when base is 75,000 or greater. Even though the standard errors are large, smaller estimates are shown to permit users to combine categories in various ways. Because of rounding, details may not add to totals. 1. The labor force includes all employed persons plus those seeking employment. The labor force participation rate is the percentage of persons either employed or seeking employment. 2. Includes persons who graduated from high school between January and October 1992. 3. Includes persons of Hispanic origin. 4. Persons of Hispanic origin may be of any race. 5. Data are not shown where base is less than 75,000. 6. Includes persons who graduated from high school between January and October 1993.

★ 305 ★

Higher Education

Enrollment in Higher Education, 1990

Data are based on enrollments, Fall 1990.

Control and level of institution, and sex	All students	White, non-Hispanic	Black, non-Hispanic	Hispanic	Asian or Pacific Islander	American Indian/Alaskan Native	Race/ethnicity unknown	Nonresident alien
Total[1]	13,711,555	10,436,129	1,206,102	747,863	544,353	100,732	279,788	396,588
4-year	8,530,276	6,593,453	703,845	337,525	334,425	47,160	191,782	322,086
2-year	5,181,279	3,842,676	502,257	410,338	209,928	53,572	88,006	74,502
Public total	10,741,588	8,183,127	942,501	642,066	438,778	89,039	181,310	264,767
4-year	5,803,501	4,507,235	482,658	246,801	233,688	37,713	101,698	193,708
2-year	4,938,087	3,675,892	459,843	395,265	205,090	51,326	79,612	71,059
Private total	2,970,147	2,253,002	263,601	105,797	105,575	11,873	98,478	131,821
4-year	2,726,775	2,086,218	221,187	90,724	100,737	9,447	90,084	128,378
2-year	243,372	166,784	42,414	15,073	4,838	2,426	8,394	3,443

Source: U.S. Department of Education. Office of Educational Research and Improvement. Postsecondary Education Statistics Division. *Trends in Racial/Ethnic Enrollment in Higher Education: Fall 1980 Through Fall 1990*. Washington, DC: U.S. Government Printing Office, p. 11. Primary source: U.S. Department of Education, National Center of Education Statistics, Integrated Postsecondary Education Data System "Fall Enrollment" survey 1990. *Notes:* Fall enrollment represents actual counts reported, or imputed, prior to distribution of "race/ethnicity unknown" category. 1. Total enrollment reflects student counts prior to the distribution of race/ethnicity unknown data. After the distribution procedure, total enrollment dropped slightly (to 13,710,150) due to rounding.

★ 306 ★

Higher Education

Enrollment of Hispanics in Public Affairs Programs, 1981-91

These data show percent distribution of enrollment in NASPAA (National Association of Schools of Public Affairs and Administration) member institutions, percentage of public affairs degrees awarded to Hispanics, and percentage of NASPAA faculty that is of Hispanic origin.

	NASPAA enrollment	Public Affairs Degrees				NASPAA faculty
		A.A.	B.A.	M.P.A.	D.P.A.	
1981	5.0	-	3.2	3.1	2.3	-
1983	4.0	NR	NR	3.7	NR	1.0
1985	4.0	5.3	3.5	3.8	2.4	1.0
1987	4.0	4.0	3.8	3.6	4.5	1.5
1989	4.0	4.8	4.0	3.3	2.4	1.5
1991	7.0	5.0	4.1	3.4	2.6	2.1

Source: Sisneros, Antonio. "Hispanics in the public service in the late twentieth century." *Public Administration Review* 53 no. 1 (January/February 1993), p. 5. Primary source: Characteristics of masters enrollment, NASPAA Correspondence, November 29, 1990; National Center for Education Statistics, *Digest of Education Statistics*, 1985-86; National Center for Education Statistics, *Integrated Postsecondary Education System "Completion" Survey, 1986-87, 1988-89*; National Center for Education statistics, *Completions in Institutions of Higher Education*, 1986-87; National Center for Education Statistics, Vance Grant, Education Information Branch, Telephone interviews, 1981, 1983, 1985, 1989, 1991. *Note:* NR stands for not reported.

★ 307 ★

Higher Education

Enrollment Trends in Higher Education

Total fall enrollment and percent distribution of students, by race and ethnicity, are shown biennially from 1980 through 1990.

Control of institution and race/ethnicity	Number in thousands						Percent distribution					
	1980	1982	1984	1986	1988	1990	1980	1982	1984	1986	1988	1990
All institutions												
Total	12,087	12,388	12,235	12,504	13,043	13,710	100.0	100.0	100.0	100.0	100.0	100.0
Hispanic	472	519	535	618	680	758	3.9	4.2	4.4	4.9	5.2	5.5
White, non-Hispanic	9,833	9,997	9,815	9,921	10,283	10,675	81.4	80.7	80.2	79.3	78.8	77.9
Black, non-Hispanic	1,107	1,101	1,076	1,082	1,130	1,223	9.2	8.9	8.8	8.7	8.7	8.9
Asian or Pacific Islander	286	351	390	448	497	555	2.4	2.8	3.2	3.6	3.8	4.0
American Indian or Alaskan Native	84	88	84	90	93	103	0.7	0.7	0.7	0.7	0.7	0.7
Nonresident alien	305	331	335	345	361	397	2.5	2.7	2.7	2.8	2.8	2.9
Public												
Total	9,456	9,695	9,458	9,714	10,156	10,741	78.2	78.3	77.3	77.7	77.9	78.3
Hispanic	406	446	456	532	587	648	3.4	3.6	3.7	4.3	4.5	4.7
White, non-Hispanic	7,656	7,785	7,543	7,654	7,964	8,340	63.3	62.8	61.6	61.2	61.1	60.8
Black, non-Hispanic	876	873	844	854	881	952	7.2	7.0	6.9	6.8	6.8	6.9
Asian or Pacific Islander	240	296	323	371	406	445	2.0	2.4	2.6	3.0	3.1	3.2
American Indian or Alaskan Native	74	77	72	79	81	90	0.6	0.6	0.6	0.6	0.6	0.7
Nonresident alien	204	219	219	224	238	265	1.7	1.8	1.8	1.8	1.8	1.9
Private												
Total	2,630	2,693	2,777	2,790	2,887	2,970	21.8	21.7	22.7	22.3	22.1	21.7
Hispanic	66	74	79	86	93	110	0.5	0.6	0.6	0.7	0.7	0.8
White, non-Hispanic	2,177	2,212	2,272	2,267	2,319	2,335	18.0	17.9	18.6	18.1	17.8	17.0
Black, non-Hispanic	231	228	232	228	248	271	1.9	1.8	1.9	1.8	1.9	2.0
Asian or Pacific Islander	47	55	67	77	91	109	0.4	0.4	0.5	0.6	0.7	0.8
American Indian or Alaskan Native	10	10	11	11	11	12	0.1	0.1	0.1	0.1	0.1	0.1
Nonresident	101	113	116	120	123	132	0.8	0.9	0.9	1.0	0.9	1.0

Source: U.S. Department of Education. Office of Educational Research and Improvement. Postsecondary Education Statistics Division. *Trends in Racial/Ethnic Enrollment in Higher Education: Fall 1980 Through Fall 1990.* Washington, DC: U.S. Government Printing Office, p. 1. Primary source: U.S. Department of Education, National Center for Education Statistics, Higher Education General Information Survey "Fall Enrollment in Colleges and Universities" (1978-1984) and Integrated Postsecondary Education Data System "Fall Enrollment" surveys 1986, 1988, and 1990, p. 1. *Notes:* Because of underreporting/nonreporting of racial/ethnic data, data prior to 1986 were estimated when possible. Also, due to rounding, detail may not add to totals.

★ 308 ★

Higher Education

Enrollment Trends of High School Seniors in Postsecondary Education, 1960-93

The numbers and percentages of enrolled students in the 12 months preceding each year are shown, by race/ethnicity.

Year	High school graduates[1]				Enrolled in college[2]							
					Total		White[3]		Black[3,4]		Hispanic[4]	
	Total	White[3]	Black[3,4]	Hispanic[4]	Number	Percent	Number	Percent	Number	Percent	Number	Percent
1960	1,679	1,565	-	-	758	45.1	717	45.8	-	-	-	-
1961	1,763	1,612	-	-	847	48.0	798	49.5	-	-	-	-
1962	1,838	1,660	-	-	900	49.0	840	50.6	-	-	-	-
1963	1,741	1,615	-	-	784	45.0	736	45.6	-	-	-	-

[Continued]

★ 308 ★

Enrollment Trends of High School Seniors in Postsecondary Education, 1960-93

[Continued]

Year	High school graduates[1]				Enrolled in college[2]							
					Total		White[3]		Black[3,4]		Hispanic[4]	
	Total	White[3]	Black[3,4]	Hispanic[4]	Number	Percent	Number	Percent	Number	Percent	Number	Percent
1964	2,145	1,964	-	-	1,037	48.3	967	49.2	-	-	-	-
1965	2,659	2,417	-	-	1,354	50.9	1,249	51.7	-	-	-	-
1966	2,612	2,403	-	-	1,309	50.1	1,243	51.7	-	-	-	-
1967	2,525	2,267	-	-	1,311	51.9	1,202	53.0	-	-	-	-
1968	2,606	2,303	-	-	1,444	55.4	1,034	56.6	-	-	-	-
1969	2,842	2,538	-	-	1,516	53.3	1,402	55.2	-	-	-	-
1970	2,757	2,461	-	-	1,427	51.8	1,280	52.0	-	-	-	-
1971	2,872	2,596	-	-	1,535	53.4	1,402	54.0	-	-	-	-
1972	2,961	2,614	-	-	1,457	49.2	1,292	49.4	-	-	-	-
1973	3,059	2,707	-	-	1,425	46.6	1,302	48.1	-	-	-	-
1974	3,101	2,736	-	-	1,474	47.5	1,288	47.1	-	-	-	-
1975	3,186	2,825	-	-	1,615	50.7	1,446	51.2	-	-	-	-
1976	2,987	2,640	320	152	1,458	48.8	1,291	48.9	134	41.9	80	52.6
1977	3,140	2,768	335	156	1,590	50.6	1,403	50.7	166	49.6	80	51.3
1978	3,161	2,750	352	133	1,584	50.1	1,378	50.1	161	45.7	57	42.9
1979	3,160	2,776	324	154	1,559	49.3	1,376	49.6	147	45.4	69	44.8
1980	3,089	2,682	361	129	1,524	49.3	1,339	49.9	151	41.8	68	52.7
1981	3,053	2,626	359	146	1,646	53.9	1,434	54.6	154	42.9	76	52.1
1982	3,100	2,644	384	174	1,568	50.6	1,376	52.0	140	36.5	75	43.1
1983	2,964	2,496	392	138	1,562	52.7	1,372	55.0	151	38.5	75	54.3
1984	3,012	2,514	438	185	1,662	55.2	1,455	57.9	176	40.2	82	44.3
1985	2,666	2,241	333	141	1,539	57.7	1,332	59.4	141	42.3	72	51.1
1986	2,786	2,307	386	169	1,499	53.8	1,292	56.0	141	36.5	75	44.4
1987	2,647	2,207	337	176	1,503	56.8	1,249	56.6	175	51.9	59	33.5
1988	2,673	2,187	382	179	1,575	58.9	1,328	60.7	172	45.0	102	57.0
1989	2,454	2,051	337	168	1,463	59.6	1,238	60.4	178	52.8	93	55.4
1990	2,355	1,921	341	112	1,410	59.9	1,182	61.5	158	46.3	53	47.3
1991	2,276	1,867	320	154	1,420	62.4	1,207	64.6	146	45.6	88	57.1
1992	2,398	1,900	353	199	1,479	61.7	1,204	63.4	169	47.9	109	54.8
1993	2,338	1,910	302	200	1,464	62.6	1,200	62.8	168	55.6	125	62.5

Source: U.S. Department of Education. National Center for Education Statistics. Office of Educational Research and Improvement. *Digest of Education Statistics, 1994.* Lanham, MD: Bernan, November 1994, p. 187. Primary source: American College Testing Program, unpublished tabulations, 1987, derived from statistics collected by the U.S. Bureau of the Census; and U.S. Department of Labor, College Enrollment of 1993 High School Graduates. (This table was prepared June 1994.) *Notes:* A dash (-) stands for data not available. Data are based upon sample surveys of the civilian noninstitutionalized population. High school graduate data in this table differ from figures appearing in other tables because of varying survey procedures and coverage. High school graduates include GED recipients. 1. Individuals age 16 to 24 years who graduated from high school during the preceding 12 months. 2. Enrollment in college as of October of each year for individuals age 16 to 24 who graduated from high school during the preceding 12 months. 3. Includes persons of Hispanic origin. 4. Due to the small sample size, data were subject to relatively large sampling errors.

★ 309 ★

Higher Education

Enrollment Trends of Persons 14 to 34 Years Old in Higher Education Institutions, 1980-93

Numbers are shown, in thousands, by sex, and race/ethnicity.

Characteristic	1980	1983[2]	1984	1985	1986	1987	1988	1989	1990	1991	1992	1993
					Numbers in thousands							
All students[1]	10,181	10,825	10,858	10,863	10,605	10,919	10,937	11,068	11,303	11,589	11,671	11,409
White, non-Hispanic												
Total	8,453	8,741	8,764	8,781	8,284	8,519	8,616	8,786	8,892	8,916	8,883	8,592
Men	4,225	4,477	4,487	4,361	4,158	4,221	4,155	4,220	4,298	4,323	4,207	4,168
Women	4,228	4,265	4,277	4,420	4,126	4,299	4,461	4,565	4,594	4,594	4,676	4,424
Black, non-Hispanic												
Total	996	1,088	1,124	1,036	1,126	1,162	1,096	1,116	1,167	1,190	1,205	1,227
Men	431	488	538	458	484	505	423	425	508	523	467	515
Women	565	600	586	578	642	657	674	690	659	667	738	713
Hispanic origin												
Total	443	523	524	579	677	667	654	640	617	721	816	867
Men	222	232	232	280	331	369	313	311	297	310	349	391
Women	221	270	292	299	346	298	341	330	321	411	468	475
					Percentage distribution							
All students	100.0	100.0	100.0	100.0	100.0	100.0	100.0	100.0	100.0	100.0	100.0	100.0
White, non-Hispanic												
Total	83.0	80.8	80.7	80.8	78.1	78.0	78.8	79.4	78.7	76.9	76.1	75.3
Men	41.5	41.4	41.3	40.1	39.2	638.7	38.0	38.1	38.0	37.3	36.0	36.5
Women	41.5	39.4	39.4	40.7	38.9	39.4	40.8	41.2	40.6	39.6	40.1	38.8
Black, non-Hispanic												
Total	9.8	10.1	10.4	9.5	10.6	10.6	10.0	10.1	10.3	10.3	10.3	10.8
Men	4.2	4.5	5.0	4.2	4.6	4.6	3.9	3.8	4.5	4.5	4.0	4.5
Women	5.5	5.5	5.4	5.3	6.1	6.0	6.2	6.2	5.8	5.8	6.3	6.2
Hispanic origin												
Total	4.4	4.8	4.8	5.3	6.4	6.1	6.0	5.8	5.5	6.2	7.0	7.6
Men	2.2	2.3	2.1	2.6	3.1	3.4	2.9	2.8	2.6	2.7	3.0	3.4
Women	2.2	2.5	2.7	2.8	3.3	2.7	3.1	3.0	2.8	3.5	4.0	4.2

Source: U.S. Department of Education. National Center for Education Statistics. Office of Educational Research and Improvement. *Digest of Education Statistics, 1994.* Lanham, MD: Bernan, November 1994, p. 213. Primary source: U.S. Department of Commerce, Bureau of the Census, *Current Population Reports*, Series P-20, No. 403, and unpublished data. (This table was prepared March 1994.) *Notes:* Data are based upon sample surveys of the civilian noninstitutional population. Because of rounding, details may not add to totals. 1. Totals differ from those shown in other tables. This table presents data collected in sample surveys of households rather than surveys of institutions. Excludes persons age 35 and over. 2. Data for 1983 to 1989 are controlled to 1980 census base.

★ 310 ★

Higher Education

Enrollment Trends of Persons 18 to 24 Years Old in Higher Education Institutions, 1967-93

Figures are shown, by race/ethnicity and year.

Year	All students		White		Black		Hispanic origin	
	Enrollment as a % of 18-24-year-olds	Enrollment as a % of high school graduates	Enrollment as a % of 18-24-year-olds	Enrollment as a % of high school graduates	Enrollment as a % of 18-24-year-olds	Enrollment as a % of high school graduates	Enrollment as a % of 18-24-year-olds	Enrollment as a % of high school graduates
1967[1]	25.5	33.7	26.9	34.5	13.0	23.3	-	-
1968[1]	26.0	34.2	27.5	34.9	14.5	25.2	-	-
1969[1]	27.3	35.0	28.7	35.6	16.0	27.2	-	-
1970[1]	25.7	32.7	27.1	33.2	15.5	26.0	-	-
1971[1]	26.2	33.2	27.2	33.5	18.2	29.2	-	-
1972	25.5	31.1	27.2	31.9	18.3	25.2	13.4	24.1
1973	24.0	28.9	25.5	29.5	15.9	22.5	16.1	27.6
1974	24.6	29.8	25.8	29.9	17.6	24.6	18.0	30.7
1975	26.3	31.4	27.4	31.3	20.4	30.1	20.4	33.0
1976	26.7	32.3	27.6	32.1	22.5	32.1	20.0	34.7
1977	26.1	31.4	27.2	31.3	21.1	29.1	17.2	30.5
1978	25.3	30.0	26.5	30.1	20.1	27.9	15.2	25.9
1979	25.0	29.9	26.3	30.2	19.8	27.5	16.7	27.8
1980	25.7	30.5	27.3	31.0	19.4	26.0	16.1	27.6
1981	26.2	31.3	27.7	31.6	19.9	26.6	16.6	28.5
1982	26.6	31.6	28.1	32.0	19.9	26.5	16.8	27.6
1983	26.2	31.3	28.0	31.8	19.2	25.3	17.3	29.9
1984	27.1	31.8	28.9	32.6	20.3	25.6	17.9	28.8
1985	27.8	32.5	30.0	33.9	19.6	24.5	16.9	25.0
1986	27.9	32.7	29.7	33.3	21.9	26.9	17.6	28.3
1987	29.7	35.4	31.9	36.6	23.0	28.2	17.7	26.6
1988	30.2	36.0	33.1	37.4	21.1	26.8	17.1	29.1
1989	30.9	36.5	34.2	38.3	23.4	28.5	16.0	26.6
1990	32.1	37.7	35.2	39.2	25.3	30.4	16.2	26.8
1991	33.3	39.3	36.8	41.0	23.4	28.2	17.8	31.4
1992	34.4	42.0	37.3	42.8	25.2	33.9	21.3	37.5
1993	34.0	41.6	36.8	42.6	24.5	32.8	21.7	36.1

Source: U.S. Department of Education. National Center for Education Statistics. Office of Educational Research and Improvement. *Digest of Education Statistics, 1994.* Lanham, MD: Bernan, November 1994, p. 189. Primary source: U.S. Department of Commerce, Bureau of the Census, Current Population Survey, unpublished data. (This table was prepared March 1994.) *Notes:* A dash (-) stands for not available. Data are based on sample surveys of the civilian noninstitutionalized population. Some data have been revised from previously published figures. Percentages based on high school graduates for 1992 and 1993 use a slightly different definition of graduation and may not be directly comparable with figures for other years. 1. Data for white and black enrollment include persons of Hispanic origin.

★311★

Higher Education

Enrollment Trends, by Age Group, 1980-88

The number, in thousands, of high school graduates and persons enrolled in college are shown, by race/ethnicity, year and age group.

Age, group and Year	Total population[1] High school graduates	Total population[1] Enrolled in college	Total population[1] % participation rate	Hispanic High school graduates	Hispanic Enrolled in college	Hispanic % participation rate	White, non-Hispanic High school graduates	White, non-Hispanic Enrolled in college	White, non-Hispanic % participation rate	Black, non-Hispanic High school graduates	Black, non-Hispanic Enrolled in college	Black, non-Hispanic % participation rate
18-24 year olds												
1980 (census base)												
1981	23,343	7,575	32.5	1,144	342	29.9	19,029	6,222	32.7	2,628	735	28.0
1982	23,291	7,678	33.0	1,153	337	29.2	18,842	6,272	33.3	2,693	752	27.9
1983	22,988	7,477	32.5	1,110	349	31.4	18,582	6,129	33.0	2,691	726	27.0
1984	22,870	7,591	33.2	1,212	362	29.9	18,214	6,180	33.9	2,832	770	27.2
1985	22,349	7,537	33.7	1,396	375	26.9	17,581	6,142	34.9	2,749	718	26.1
1986	21,766	7,397	34.0	1,506	443	29.4	16,839	5,814	34.5	2,735	782	28.6
1987[2]	21,118	7,693	36.4	1,597	455	28.5	16,162	6,048	37.4	2,669	803	30.1
1988[2]	20,900	7,791	37.3	1,458	450	30.9	16,097	6,229	38.7	2,616	732	28.0
25-34 year olds												
1980 (census base)												
1981	32,675	2,928	9.0	1,423	153	10.8	26,927	2,271	8.4	3,368	344	10.2
1982	33,391	2,988	8.9	1,459	141	9.7	27,364	2,384	8.7	3,493	332	9.5
1983	34,112	3,088	9.1	1,590	155	9.7	27,727	2,416	8.7	3,640	323	8.9
1984	34,915	3,015	8.6	1,588	157	9.9	28,344	2,383	8.4	3,788	306	8.1
1985	35,341	3,064	8.7	1,947	189	9.7	28,288	2,423	8.6	3,869	287	7.4
1986	36,226	2,991	8.3	2,131	222	10.4	28,929	2,305	8.0	3,961	307	7.8
1987[2]	36,522	2,985	8.2	2,285	204	8.9	28,932	2,273	7.9	4,050	332	8.2
1988[2]	36,905	2,963	8.0	2,311	191	8.3	28,948	2,265	7.8	4,328	322	7.4

Source: U.S. Department of Education. Office of Educational Research and Improvement. Postsecondary Education Statistics Division. *Trends in Racial/Ethnic Enrollment in Higher Education: Fall 1978 through Fall 1988,* Washington, DC: U.S. Government Printing Office, 1990, p. 15. Primary source: Department of Commerce, Bureau of the Census, "Current Population Reports," Series P-20, various years. *Notes:* Totals differ from those shown in other tables. This table represents data collected in sample surveys of households rather than surveys of institutions of higher education. The Current Population Survey samples are derived from the decennial censuses of populations. Also, the data for whites and blacks differ from Bureau of the Census reports because Hispanic data have been removed from these groups to allow comparisons of all three racial/ethnic categories. 1. Totals reflected here represent all possible racial/ethnic categories, not just those displayed in table. 2. Unpublished data from the Bureau of the Census.

★312★

Higher Education

Enrollment Trends, by Level of Institution

Total fall enrollment and percent distributions are shown, by race/ethnicity, for 1984-92.

Level of institution and race/ethnicity	Numbers in thousands 1984	1988	1990	1991	1992[2]	Percent distribution by type and control[1] 1984	1988	1990	1991	1992[2]
All institutions	12,233.0	13,043.1	13,818.6	14,359.0	14,491.2	100.0	100.0	100.0	100.0	100.0
White, non-Hispanic	9,814.7	10,283.2	10,722.5	10,989.8	10,870.0	82.5	81.1	79.9	78.8	77.5
Total minority	2,083.8	2,398.8	2,704.7	2,952.8	3,163.6	17.5	18.9	20.1	21.2	22.5
Black, non-Hispanic	1,075.8	1,129.6	1,247.0	1,335.4	1,393.5	9.0	8.9	9.3	9.6	9.9
Hispanic	534.9	680.0	782.4	8966.6	954.4	4.5	5.4	5.8	6.2	6.8
Asian or Pacific Islander	389.5	496.7	572.4	637.2	696.8	63.3	3.9	4.3	4.6	5.0
American Indian or Alaskan Native	83.6	92.5	102.8	113.7	118.8	0.7	0.7	0.8	0.8	0.8
Nonresident alien	334.6	361.2	391.5	416.4	457.6	-	-	-	-	-
4-year institutions	7,706.1	8,175.0	8,578.6	8,707.1	8,768.0	100.0	100.0	100.0	100.0	100.0
White, non-Hispanic	6,300.4	6,581.6	6,768.1	6,791.0	6,746.9	84.9	83.6	82.0	81.2	80.2
Total minority	1,123.6	1,291.8	1,486.1	1,573.3	1,663.8	15.1	16.4	18.0	18.8	19.8
Black, non-Hispanic	617.0	656.3	722.8	757.8	791.5	8.3	8.3	8.8	9.1	9.4

[Continued]

★ 312 ★

Enrollment Trends, by Level of Institution

[Continued]

Level of institution and race/ethnicity	Numbers in thousands 1984	1988	1990	1991	1992[2]	Percent distribution by type and control[1] 1984	1988	1990	1991	1992[2]
Hispanic	246.1	296.0	358.2	382.9	409.9	3.3	3.8	4.3	4.6	4.9
Asian or Pacific Islander	222.4	297.4	357.2	381.5	407.6	3.0	3.8	4.3	4.6	4.8
American Indian or Alaskan Native	38.1	42.1	47.9	51.1	54.9	0.5	0.5	0.6	0.6	0.7
Nonresident alien	282.1	301.5	324.3	342.8	357.2	-	-	-	-	-
2-year institutions[1]	4,526.9	4,868.1	5,240.1	5,651.9	5,723.2	100.0	100.0	100.0	100.0	100.0
White, non-Hispanic	3,514.3	3,701.5	3,954.3	4,198.8	4,123.1	78.5	77.0	76.4	75.3	73.3
Total minority	960.1	1,106.9	1,218.6	1,379.6	1,499.7	21.5	23.0	23.6	24.7	26.7
Black, non-Hispanic	458.7	473.3	524.3	577.6	602.0	10.3	9.8	10.1	10.4	10.7
Hispanic	288.8	383.9	424.2	483.7	544.5	6.5	8.0	8.2	8.7	9.7
Asian or Pacific Islander	167.1	199.3	215.2	255.7	289.2	3.7	4.1	4.2	4.6	5.1
American Indian or Alaskan Native	45.5	50.4	54.9	62.6	64.0	1.0	1.0	1.1	1.1	1.1
Nonresident alien	52.5	59.6	67.1	73.5	100.4	-	-	-	-	-

Source: U.S. Department of Education. National Center for Education Statistics. Office of Educational Research and Improvement. *Digest of Education Statistics, 1994.* Lanham, MD: Bernan, November 1994, p. 207. Primary source: U.S. Department of Education, National Center for Education Statistics, "Fall Enrollment in Colleges and Universities," and Integrated Postsecondary Education Data System "Fall Enrollment" surveys. (This table was prepared March 1994.) *Notes:* A dash (-) stands for not applicable. Because of underreporting/nonreporting of racial/ethnic data, some figures are slightly lower than corresponding data in other tables. Because of rounding, detail may not add to totals. 1. Distribution for U.S. citizens only. 2. Preliminary data.

★ 313 ★

Higher Education

Enrollment Trends, by Level of Study

Fall enrollment and percent distribution are shown biennially from 1980 through 1990.

Level of institution and race/ethnicity	Numbers in thousands 1980	1982	1984	1986	1988	1990	Percent distribution by level of study 1980	1982	1984	1986	1988	1990
Undergraduate enrollment												
Total	10,560	10,875	10,610	10,798	11,304	11,863	100.0	100.0	100.0	100.0	100.0	100.0
White, non-Hispanic	8,556	8,749	8,484	8,558	8,907	9,231	81.0	80.5	80.0	79.3	76.8	77.8
Total minority	1,797	1,907	1,911	2,036	2,192	2,406	17.0	17.5	18.0	18.9	19.4	20.3
Black, non-Hispanic	1,028	1,028	995	996	1,039	1,124	9.7	9.4	9.4	9.2	9.2	9.5
Hispanic	438	485	495	563	631	702	4.1	4.5	4.7	5.2	5.6	5.9
Asian or Pacific Islander	253	313	343	393	437	485	2.4	2.9	3.2	3.6	3.9	4.1
American Indian or Alaskan Native	79	82	78	83	86	95	0.7	0.8	0.7	0.8	0.8	0.8
Nonresident alien	208	220	216	205	205	226	2.0	2.0	2.0	1.9	1.8	1.9
Graduate enrollment												
Total	1,250	1,235	1,344	1,435	1,472	1,574	100.0	100.0	100.0	100.0	100.0	100.0
White, non-Hispanic	1,030	1,002	1,087	1,133	1,153	1,221	82.4	81.1	80.9	78.9	78.4	77.6
Total minority	125	123	141	167	167	187	10.0	10.0	10.5	11.6	11.4	11.9
Black, non-Hispanic	66	61	67	72	76	84	5.3	4.9	5.0	5.0	5.2	5.3
Hispanic	27	27	32	46	39	46	2.2	2.2	2.4	3.2	2.7	2.9
Asian or Pacific Islander	28	30	37	43	46	52	2.2	2.5	2.8	3.0	3.1	3.3
American Indian or Alaskan Native	4	5	5	5	6	6	0.4	0.4	0.4	0.4	0.4	0.4
Nonresident alien	94	108	115	136	151	165	7.5	8.8	8.6	9.5	10.3	10.5
First-professional enrollment												
Total	277	278	278	270	267	274	100.0	100.0	100.0	100.0	100.0	100.0
White, non-Hispanic	248	246	243	231	223	222	89.5	88.5	87.4	85.3	83.6	81.3
Total minority	26	29	32	36	39	46	9.5	10.4	11.4	13.2	14.6	16.7

[Continued]

★313★

Enrollment Trends, by Level of Study

[Continued]

Level of institution and race/ethnicity	Numbers in thousands 1980	1982	1984	1986	1988	1990	Percent distribution by level of study 1980	1982	1984	1986	1988	1990
Black, non-Hispanic	13	13	13	14	14	16	4.6	4.7	4.8	5.2	5.4	5.8
Hispanic	7	7	8	9	9	10	2.4	2.5	2.9	3.4	3.5	3.8
Asian or Pacific Islander	6	6	9	11	14	18	2.2	2.9	3.4	4.2	5.4	6.7
American Indian or Alaskan Native	1	1	1	1	1	1	0.3	0.4	0.4	0.4	0.4	0.4
Nonresident alien	3	3	3	4	5	5	1.0	1.1	1.2	1.5	1.8	2.0

Source: U.S. Department of Education. Office of Educational Research and Improvement. Postsecondary Education Statistics Division. *Trends in Racial/Ethnic Enrollment in Higher Education: Fall 1980 Through Fall 1990.* Washington, DC: U.S. Government Printing Office, p. 4. Primary source: U.S. Department of Education, National Center for Education Statistics, Higher Education General Information Survey "Fall Enrollment in Colleges and Universities" (1978-1984) and Integrated Postsecondary Education Data System "Fall Enrollment" surveys (1986, 1988, and 1990). *Notes:* Because of underreporting/nonreporting of racial/ethnic data, data prior to 1986 were estimated when possible. Also, due to rounding, detail may not add to totals.

★314★

Higher Education

Enrollment Trends, by Sex

Total fall enrollment and percent distribution of students are shown biennially from 1980 through 1990.

Race/ethnicity and sex	Number, in thousands 1980	1982	1984	1986	1988	1990	Percent distribution 1980	1982	1984	1986	1988	1990
All students												
Total	12,087	12,388	12,235	12,504	13,043	13,710	100.0	100.0	100.0	100.0	100.0	100.0
White, non-Hispanic	9,833	9,997	9,815	9,921	10,283	10,675	81.4	80.7	80.2	79.3	78.8	77.9
Black, non-Hispanic	1,107	1,101	1,076	1,082	1,130	1,223	9.2	8.9	8.8	8.7	8.7	8.9
Hispanic	472	519	535	618	680	758	3.9	4.2	4.4	4.9	5.2	5.5
Asian or Pacific Islander	286	351	390	448	497	555	2.4	2.8	3.2	3.6	3.8	4.0
American Indian or Alaskan Native	84	88	84	90	93	103	0.7	0.7	0.7	0.7	0.7	0.7
Nonresident alien	305	331	335	345	361	397	2.5	2.7	2.7	2.8	2.8	2.9
Men												
Total	5,868	5,999	5,859	5,885	5,998	6,239	48.5	48.4	47.9	47.1	46.0	45.5
White, non-Hispanic	4,773	4,830	4,690	4,647	4,712	4,841	39.5	39.0	38.3	37.2	36.1	35.3
Black, non-Hispanic	464	458	437	436	443	476	3.8	3.7	3.6	3.5	3.4	3.5
Hispanic	232	252	254	290	310	344	1.9	2.0	2.1	2.3	2.4	2.5
Asian or Pacific Islander	151	189	210	239	259	287	1.3	1.5	1.7	1.9	2.0	2.1
American Indian or Alaskan Native	38	40	38	39	39	43	0.3	0.3	0.3	0.3	0.3	0.3
Nonresident alien	211	230	231	233	235	248	1.7	1.9	1.9	1.9	1.8	1.8
Women												
Total	6,219	6,389	6,376	6,619	7,045	7,472	51.5	51.6	52.1	52.9	54.0	54.5
White, non-Hispanic	5,060	5,167	5,125	5,273	5,572	5,834	41.9	41.7	41.9	42.2	42.7	42.6
Black, non-Hispanic	643	644	639	646	687	747	5.3	5.2	5.2	5.2	5.3	5.4
Hispanic	240	267	281	328	370	414	2.0	2.2	2.3	2.6	2.8	3.0
Asian or Pacific Islander	135	162	180	209	237	268	1.1	1.3	1.5	1.7	1.8	2.0
Nonresident alien	94	101	104	112	126	149	0.8	0.8	0.9	0.9	1.0	1.1

Source: U.S. Department of Education. Office of Educational Research and Improvement. Postsecondary Education Statistics Division. *Trends in Racial/Ethnic Enrollment in Higher Education: Fall 1980 Through Fall 1990.* Washington, DC: U.S. Government Printing Office, p. 6. Primary source: U.S. Department of Education, National Center for Education Statistics, Higher Education Data System "Fall Enrollment" surveys (1986, 1988, and 1990). *Notes:* Because of underreporting/nonreporting of racial/ethnic data, data prior to 1986 were estimated when possible. Also, due to rounding, detail may not add to totals.

★ 315 ★

Higher Education

Enrollment, by State

Figures show preliminary enrollment data for fall of 1992.

State	Total	White, non-Hispanic	Minority enrollment					Non-resident alien	Percent minority 1992[1]	Percent minority 1991[1]
			Total	Black, non-Hispanic	Hispanic	Asian Pacific Islander	American Indian/ Alsakan Native			
Total	14,491,226	10,870,037	3,163,562	1,393,483	954,422	696,812	118,845	457,627	22.5	21.2
Alabama	230,537	172,209	53,634	49,466	1,428	1,901	839	4,694	23.7	22.6
Alaska	30,902	24,682	5,524	1,143	730	799	2,852	696	18.3	17.5
Arizona	275,599	208,688	59,368	8,616	34,443	7,065	9,244	7,543	22.1	21.0
Arkansas	97,435	79,602	16,127	14,014	511	1,024	578	1,706	16.8	16.3
California	1,977,249	1,115,374	764,039	139,665	315,261	287,194	21,919	97,836	40.7	35.6
Colorado	240,163	197,648	37,075	7,755	20,063	6,616	2,641	5,440	15.8	15.1
Connecticut	165,874	138,151	22,833	11,036	6,448	4,943	406	4,890	14.2	13.1
Delaware	42,763	35,230	6,719	5,156	569	881	113	814	16.0	15.8
District of Columbia	81,909	40,934	31,748	25,156	2,648	3,742	202	9,227	43.7	42.5
Florida	618,285	435,987	165,512	72,750	75,270	15,205	2,287	16,786	27.5	25.8
Georgia	293,162	211,081	75,646	65,261	3,838	5,785	762	6,435	26.4	24.9
Hawaii	61,162	17,075	39,012	1,446	1,229	36,112	225	5,075	69.6	69.1
Idaho	57,798	52,914	3,101	333	1,305	833	630	1,783	5.5	5.3
Illinois	748,033	543,108	186,921	93,641	54,582	36,270	2,428	18,004	25.6	24.9
Indiana[1]	296,912	260,263	28,435	17,466	5,354	4,600	1,015	8,214	9.8	9.4
Iowa	177, 813	158,393	11,316	5,179	2,534	3,051	552	8,104	6.7	5.7
Kansas	169,419	145,577	17,495	7,888	4,185	3,152	2,270	6,347	10.7	10.0
Kentucky	188,320	170,235	15,184	12,026	977	1,589	592	2,901	8.2	7.9
Louisiana	204,379	139,873	59,029	50,181	4,348	3,446	1,054	5,477	29.7	29.3
Maine	57,977	54,777	2,504	666	352	632	854	696	4.4	2.8
Maryland	268,399	188,771	71,088	51,623	5,229	13,254	863	8,659	27.3	25.7
Massachusetts	422,976	342,585	57,645	20,491	15,146	20,299	1,709	22,746	14.4	13.3
Michigan	559,729	460,953	83,289	57,086	9,996	12,060	4,147	15,487	15.3	14.5
Minnesota	272,920	248,519	18,117	5,588	2,919	7,062	2,548	6,284	6.8	6.0
Mississippi	123,754	85,331	36,197	34,496	454	849	398	2,226	29.8	29.9
Missouri	296,617	252,664	36,263	25,484	4,030	5,496	1,253	7,690	12.6	12.0
Montana	39,644	33,501	4,958	133	371	214	4,240	1,185	12.9	9.4
Nebraska	122,603	111,388	8,600	3,820	2,336	1,644	800	2,615	7.2	6.0
Nevada	63,877	50,783	11,659	3,222	4,104	3,338	995	1,435	18.7	17.6
New Hampshire	63,924	59,521	3,425	722	926	1,539	238	978	5.4	4.6
New Jersey	342,446	247,458	81,615	38,001	25,702	17,075	837	13,373	24.8	23.6
New Mexico	99,276	58,534	39,647	2,933	28,577	1,462	5,675	2,095	39.8	38.7
New York	1,069,772	753,717	276,637	128,966	87,712	56,395	3,564	39,418	26.8	26.2
North Carolina	383,453	291,861	85,438	71,533	3,552	7,015	3,338	6,154	22.6	21.6
North Dakota	40,470	35,923	2,824	311	213	281	2,019	1,723	7.3	7.1
Ohio	573,183	490,035	67,296	49,884	6,723	8,862	1,827	15,852	12.1	11.6
Oklahoma	182,105	143,732	31,273	12,843	3,292	3,306	11,832	7,100	17.9	17.1
Oregon	167,415	143,921	17,153	2,651	4,033	8,285	2,184	6,341	10.6	10.0
Pennsylvania	629,832	536,620	76,703	46,317	11,109	17,951	1,326	16,509	12.5	12.1
Rhode Island	79,165	68,636	7,833	2,976	2,295	2,289	273	2,696	10.2	9.2
South Carolina	171,443	128,445	39,892	36,268	1,310	1,917	397	3,106	23.7	22.0
South Dakota[1]	37,596	33,998	2,769	290	146	270	2,063	829	7.5	7.4
Tennessee	242,970	197,783	40,935	35,459	1,969	2,895	612	4,252	17.1	16.9
Texas	938,526	616,515	295,042	89,213	168,644	33,423	3,762	26,969	32.4	30.8
Utah	133,083	119,979	7,461	766	2,905	2,489	1,301	5,643	5.9	5.6
Vermont	37,377	35,108	1,454	429	406	522	97	815	4.0	4.0
Virginia	354,172	273,589	74,099	52,881	5,963	14,128	1,127	6,484	21.3	20.5
Washington	276,484	230,176	40,014	9,350	7,528	18,701	4,435	6,294	14.8	14.3
West Virginia	90,252	83,673	4,819	3,384	451	829	155	1,760	5.4	5.2

[Continued]

★ 315 ★

Enrollment, by State

[Continued]

State	Total	White, non-Hispanic	Minority enrollment: Total	Black, non-Hispanic	Hispanic	Asian Pacific Islander	American Indian/ Alsakan Native	Non-resident alien	Percent minority 1992[1]	Percent minority 1991[1]
Wisconsin	307,902	274,875	26,048	12,354	5,545	5,720	2,499	6,979	8.7	8.2
Wyoming	31,548	28,691	2,243	371	1,150	268	454	614	7.3	6.0

Source: U.S. Department of Education. National Center for Education Statistics. Office of Educational Research and Improvement. *Digest of Education Statistics, 1994.* Lanham, MD: Bernan, November 1994, p. 211. Primary source: U.S. Department of Education, National Center for Education Statistics, Integrated Postsecondary Education Data System (IPEDS), "Fall Enrollment" surveys. (This table was prepared August 1994.) *Notes:* Because of adjustments to underreported and nonreported racial/ethnic data, figures are slightly different from corresponding data in other tables. 1. Percent minority based on U.S. citizen enrollment (total enrollment less enrollment of nonresident aliens). .

★ 316 ★

Higher Education

Fall Enrollment Distribution in Higher Education Institutions, by Year

Distribution of students is shown, for U.S. citizens, by race/ethnicity for selected years.

Race/ethnicity	Percent distribution: 1976	1980	1984	1988	1990	1991	1992[1]
Total	100.0	100.0	100.0	100.0	100.0	100.0	100.0
White, non-Hispanic	84.3	83.5	82.5	81.1	79.9	78.8	77.5
Total minority	15.7	16.5	17.5	18.9	20.1	21.2	22.5
Black, non-Hispanic	9.6	9.4	9.0	8.9	9.3	9.6	9.9
Hispanic	3.6	4.0	4.5	5.4	5.8	6.2	6.8
Asian or Pacific Islander	1.8	2.4	3.3	3.9	4.3	4.6	5.0
American Indian/Alaskan Native	0.7	0.7	0.7	0.7	0.8	0.8	0.8
Men	52.4	48.0	47.3	45.4	45.0	44.8	44.5
White, non-Hispanic	44.7	40.5	39.4	37.2	36.2	35.6	34.8
Total minority	7.7	7.5	7.9	8.3	8.8	9.2	9.7
Black, non-Hispanic	4.4	3.9	3.7	3.5	3.6	3.7	3.8
Hispanic	1.9	2.0	2.1	2.4	2.6	2.8	3.0
Asian or Pacific Islander	1.0	1.3	1.8	2.0	2.2	2.3	2.5
American Indian/Alaskan Native	0.4	0.3	0.3	0.3	0.3	0.3	0.4
Women	47.6	52.0	52.7	54.6	550	55.2	55.5
White, non-Hispanic	39.6	42.9	43.1	43.9	43.7	43.2	42.7
Total minority	8.0	9.0	9.6	10.6	11.4	12.0	12.8
Black, non-Hispanic	5.2	5.5	5.4	5.4	5.7	5.9	6.1
Hispanic	1.6	2.0	2.4	2.9	3.2	3.4	3.8

[Continued]

★316★

Fall Enrollment Distribution in Higher Education Institutions, by Year

[Continued]

Race/ethnicity	Percent distribution						
	1976	1980	1984	1988	1990	1991	1992[1]
Asian or Pacific Islander	0.8	1.1	1.5	1.9	2.1	2.2	2.5
American Indian/Alaskan Native	0.3	0.4	0.4	0.4	0.4	0.5	0.5

Source: U.S. Department of Education. National Center for Education Statistics. Office of Educational Research and Improvement. *Digest of Education Statistics, 1994.* Lanham, MD: Bernan, November 1994, p. 208. Primary source: U.S. Department of Education, National Center for Education Statistics, "Fall Enrollment in Colleges and Universities"; and Integrated Postsecondary Education Data System (IPEDS), "Fall Enrollment" survey. (This Table was prepared March 1994.) *Notes:* Because of underreporting and nonreporting of racial/ethnic data, some figures are slightly lower than corresponding data in other tables. Because of rounding, details may not add to totals. 1. Preliminary data.

★317★

Higher Education

Fall Enrollment in Higher Education Institutions, by Year

Figures are shown, by race/ethnicity and nonresident alien status for selected years.

Race/ethnicity	Number, in thousands						
	1976	1980	1984	1988	1990	1991	1992[1]
Total	10,985.6	12,068.8	12,233.0	13,043.1	13,818.6	14,359.0	14,491.2
White, non-Hispanic	9,076.1	9,833.0	9,814.7	10,283.2	10,722.5	10,989.8	10,870.0
Total minority	1,690.8	1,948.8	2,083.8	2,398.8	2,704.7	2,952.8	3,163.6
Black, non-Hispanic	1,033.0	1,106.8	1,075.8	1,129.6	1,247.0	1,335.4	1,393.5
Hispanic	383.8	471.7	534.9	680.0	782.4	866.6	954.4
Asian or Pacific Islander	197.9	286.4	389.5	496.7	572.4	637.2	696.8
American Indian/Alaskan Native	76.1	83.9	83.6	92.5	102.8	113.7	118.8
Nonresident alien	218.7	305.0	334.6	361.2	391.5	416.4	457.6
Men	5,794.4	5,868.1	5,858.3	5,998.2	6,283.9	6,501.8	6,526.1
White, non-Hispanic	4,813.7	4,772.9	4,689.9	4,771.6	4,861.0	4,962.2	4,882.5
Total minority	826.6	884.4	937.9	1,051.3	1,176.6	1,280.3	1,365.8
Black, non-Hispanic	469.9	463.7	436.8	442.7	484.7	517.0	537.1
Hispanic	209.7	231.6	253.8	310.3	353.9	390.5	427.4
Asian or Pacific Islander	108.4	151.3	210.0	259.2	294.9	325.1	351.3
American Indian/Alaskan Native	38.5	37.8	37.4	9.1	43.1	47.6	50.1
Nonresident alien	154.1	210.8	230.4	235.3	246.3	259.4	277.8
Women	5,191.2	6,218.7	6,374.7	7,044.9	7,534.7	7,857.1	7,965.1
White, non-Hispanic	4,262.4	5,060.1	5,124.7	5,571.6	5,861.5	6,027.6	5,987.6
Total minority	864.2	1,064.4	1,145.8	1,347.4	1,528.1	1,672.5	1,797.7
Black, non-Hispanic	563.1	643.0	639.0	686.9	762.3	818.4	856.4
Hispanic	174.1	240.1	281.2	369.6	428.5	476.0	527.1
Asian or Pacific Islander	89.4	135.2	179.5	237.5	277.5	312.0	345.5

[Continued]

★317★

Fall Enrollment in Higher Education Institutions, by Year

[Continued]

Race/ethnicity	Number, in thousands						
	1976	1980	1984	1988	1990	1991	1992[1]
American Indian/Alaskan Native	37.6	46.1	46.1	53.4	59.7	66.1	68.8
Nonresident alien	64.6	94.2	104.1	125.9	145.2	157.0	179.8

Source: U.S. Department of Education. National Center for Education Statistics. Office of Educational Research and Improvement. *Digest of Education Statistics, 1994.* Lanham, MD: Bernan, November 1994, p. 208. Primary source: U.S. Department of Education, National Center for Education Statistics, "Fall Enrollment in Colleges and Universities"; and Integrated Postsecondary Education Data System (IPEDS), "Fall Enrollment" survey. (This Table was prepared March 1994.) *Notes:* Because of underreporting and nonreporting of racial/ethnic data, some figures are slightly lower than corresponding data in other tables. Because of rounding, details may not add to totals. 1. Preliminary data.

★318★

Higher Education

Highest Degree Completed by Hispanic Persons Age 18 and Older, by Field of Study

Data are shown in thousands of persons for spring of 1990.

Field of degree	Total		Doctorate or professional	Master's	Bachelor's	Associate	Vocational
	Number	Percent					
Hispanic, 18 years and over[1]							
Both sexes	1,590	100	86	245	734	316	208
Agriculture/Forestry	16	1	-	-	12	4	-
Biology	13	1	-	-	10	2	-
Business/Management	281	18	8	42	146	48	37
Economics	22	1	-	-	22	-	-
Education	278	17	4	108	133	27	6
Engineering	107	7	3	9	72	23	-
English/Journalism	12	1	-	-	10	2	-
Home Economics	13	1	-	-	6	7	-
Law	35	2	27	2	-	6	-
Liberal Arts/Humanities	191	12	-	31	114	41	5
Mathematics/Statistics	18	1	-	4	14	-	-
Medicine/Dentistry	40	3	21	7	7	5	-
Nursing/Pharmacy/Technical Health	120	8	2	7	43	30	37
Physical/Earth Sciences	21	1	7	4	7	-	3
Police Science/Law Enforcement	15	1	-	-	15	-	-
Psychology	45	3	6	9	23	6	-
Religion/Theology	13	1	3	4	6	-	-
Social Sciences	57	4	-	3	39	9	6
Vo-tech Studies	182	11	-	-	12	75	94
Other	112	7	6	15	43	30	19

Source: U.S. Bureau of the Census. *What's it Worth? Educational Background and Economic Status: Spring 1990.* Current Population Reports, Series P70-32. Washington DC: U.S. Government Printing Office, 1992, p. 18. *Notes:* - represents zero. 1. Persons of Hispanic origin may be of any race.

★ 319 ★

Higher Education

Primary Care Medical Practice as a Career Choice

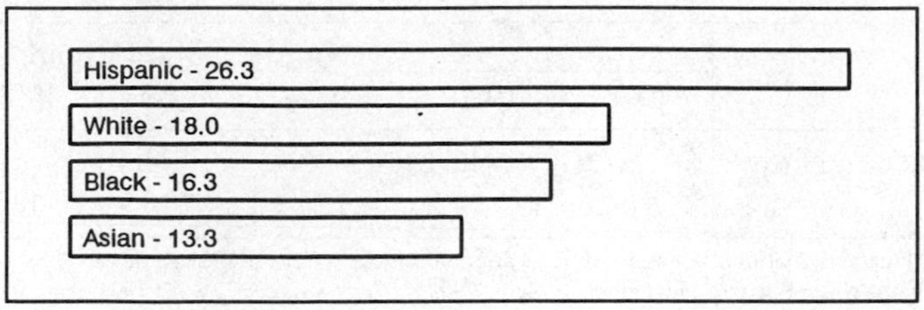

Figures show percentage of medical students of each race/ethnicity who say they would practice primary care rather than other specialties.

Race/ethnicity	Percent
Hispanic	26.3
White	18.0
Black	16.3
Asian	13.3

Source: Hall, Cindy and Stephen Conley. "Choosing primary care careers." *USA TODAY* (22 November 1994), p. 1A. Primary source: U.S. General Accounting Office.

★ 320 ★

Higher Education

Schools With Highest Hispanic Enrollment

Data are shown for four-year co-educational colleges with business schools, with enrollment of over 5,000 students.

College/university	Total students	Hispanic students	Percent Hispanic
UT - Pan American	12,248	10,344	84.4
Texas A&I	6,014	3,540	58.9
UT - El Paso	16,524	9,508	57.5
Florida International	21,999	9,455	43.0
CUNY: Lehman College	10,238	3,712	36.3
UT - San Antonio	15,489	4,687	30.3
Barry University	5,903	1,722	29.2
New Mexico State	14,812	4,039	27.3
Cal State - LA	21,596	5,856	27.1
CUNY: City College	14,090	3,642	25.8

Source: Hispanic (March 1995), p. 42. Hispanic Association of Colleges and Universities, *1991 Annual Report.*

★ 321 ★

Higher Education

Science and Engineering Bachelor's Degrees, 1977-91

Data show number of degrees earned in each field, by race/ethnicity of recipient, for each year.

Race/ethnicity and field	1977	1979	1981	1985	1987	1989	1990	1991
Total								
All degrees	928,228	931,340	946,877	990,877	1,003,532	1,030,171	1,062,151	1,107,997
Science and engineering	374,579	373,431	374,693	355,253	355,873	351,150	360,242	371,658
Natural sciences[1]	98,342	96,186	90,254	75,670	68,929	63,073	62,865	65,401
Math and computer sciences	20,729	20,670	26,406	54,388	56,442	46,277	42,369	40,194
Social and behavioral sciences[2]	205,831	193,775	182,638	147,624	156,079	174,853	190,305	203,877
Engineering	49,677	62,800	75,395	77,571	74,423	66,947	64,703	62,186
Engineering technology	NA	NA	NA	20,533	20,577	20,098	19,150	18,294
	U.S. citizens and permanent residents							
White								
All degrees	807,857	802,665	807,509	826,356	819,477	840,326	856,686	892,363
Science and engineering	323,845	318,819	313,486	290,388	281,588	277,106	280,889	289,253
Natural sciences[1]	88,308	85,403	78,778	63,592	55,898	50,580	49,527	51,113
Math and computer sciences	18,110	17,633	22,013	43,484	42,446	33,998	30,683	28,998
Social and behavioral sciences[2]	175,355	163,132	151,839	122,320	126,753	142,447	153,185	163,980
Engineering	42,072	52,651	60,856	60,992	56,491	50,081	47,494	45,162
Engineering technology	NA	NA	NA	16,673	16,541	16,156	15,251	14,279
Asian								
All degrees	13,907	15,542	18,908	25,562	31,921	37,573	38,027	41,725
Science and engineering	6,558	7,591	9,572	13,454	17,114	19,383	19,698	20,860
Natural sciences[1]	1,935	2,227	2,406	2,880	3,641	3,973	4,308	4,670
Math and computer sciences	479	587	1,061	2,929	3,489	3,287	3,018	2,925
Social and behavioral sciences[2]	2,933	2,919	3,039	3,163	4,394	6,048	6,360	7,045
Engineering	1,211	1,858	3,066	4,482	5,590	6,075	6,012	6,220
Engineering technology	NA	NA	NA	542	807	839	755	768
Black								
All degrees	58,700	60,301	60,729	57,563	55,103	56,837	59,301	65,009
Science and engineering	23,134	23,324	23,767	18,946	18,955	19,273	20,074	21,943
Natural sciences[1]	3,416	3,541	3,561	3,096	2,870	2,756	2,815	3,026
Math and computer sciences	1,073	1,159	1,371	2,913	3,654	3,249	2,967	2,808
Social and behavioral sciences[2]	17,260	16,849	16,386	10,898	10,116	11,201	12,220	13,880
Engineering	1,385	1,775	2,449	2,039	2,315	2,067	2,072	2,229
Engineering technology	NA	NA	NA	1,277	1,269	1,208	1,200	1,227
Hispanic								
All degrees	27,043	29,719	33,167	36,391	38,196	41,361	43,864	49,027
Science and engineering	11,002	12,163	13,107	12,848	13,182	14,177	14,896	16,290
Natural sciences[1]	2,271	2,634	2,958	2,979	2,964	2,849	2,859	3,010
Math and computer sciences	435	495	688	1,380	1,696	1,568	1,498	1,695
Social and behavioral sciences[2]	7,006	7,479	7,641	6,302	5,968	7,199	8,028	9,019
Engineering	1,290	1,555	1,820	2,187	2,554	2,561	2,511	2,566
Engineering technology	NA	NA	NA	525	664	634	784	731

[Continued]

★ 321 ★

Science and Engineering Bachelor's Degrees, 1977-91

[Continued]

Race/ethnicity and field	1977	1979	1981	1985	1987	1989	1990	1991
Native American								
All degrees	3,328	3,410	3,593	4,246	3,866	3,967	4,212	4,486
Science and engineering	1,368	1,411	1,430	1,500	1,409	1,361	1,416	1,519
Natural sciences[1]	338	296	298	313	259	265	262	298
Math and computer sciences	41	52	39	198	164	143	129	123
Social and behavioral sciences[2]	854	899	898	780	776	776	879	940
Engineering	135	164	195	209	210	177	146	158
Engineering technology	NA	NA	NA	103	78	105	69	75
				Foreign citizens				
All degrees	15,744	17,853	22,631	29,258	28,592	26,457	26,553	29,657
Science and engineering	8,486	10,039	13,282	14,249	13,838	12,479	12,489	12,879
Natural sciences[1]	2,042	2,061	2,251	2,132	1,786	1,744	1,736	1,941
Math and computer sciences	583	741	1,233	2,879	3,233	2,678	2,590	3,741
Social and behavioral sciences[2]	2,287	2,473	2,835	3,048	2,930	2,985	3,246	3,741
Engineering	3,574	4,764	6,963	6,190	5,889	5,072	4,917	4,582
Engineering technology	NA	NA	NA	1,277	986	659	727	712

Source: National Science Board. *Science & Engineering Indicators—1993* (NSB 93-1). Washington, DC: U.S. Government Printing Office, 1993, pp. 274-275. Primary source: Science Resources Studies Division, National Science Foundation, *Science and Engineering Degrees, by Race/Ethnicity of Recipients: 1977-91,* Detailed Statistical Tables (Washington, DC: NSF, forthcoming). *Notes:* NA stands for data not available. Data by racial/ethnic group were collected on a biennial schedule until 1990. Data are not available by racial/ethnic group for foreign citizens on temporary visas. Data by racial/ethnic group are collected by broad fields of study only; therefore, these data cannot be adjusted to the exact field taxonomies used by the National Science Foundation. 1. The natural sciences include all physical, environmental, biological, and agricultural sciences. 2. The social and behavioral sciences include psychology, sociology, and other social sciences.

★ 322 ★

Higher Education

Science and Engineering Doctoral Degrees, 1977-91

Data show number of degrees awarded in each field for each year.

Race/ethnicity and field	1977	1979	1981	1985	1987	1989	1990	1991
				Total[1]				
Total								
All degrees	31,716	31,239	31,357	31,297	32,363	34,318	36,057	37,451
Science and engineering	8,016	17,872	18,258	18,935	19,890	21,727	22,857	23,979
Natural sciences[2]	6,622	7,817	7,996	8,437	8,655	9,185	9,766	10,152
Math and computer sciences	1,618	979	960	998	1,190	1,471	1,597	1,837
Social and behavioral sciences[3]	7,135	6,463	6,659	6,223	6,227	6,425	6,507	6,653
Engineering	2,633	2,494	2,528	3,166	3,712	4,544	4,893	5,212
				Total U.S. citizens and permanent residents				
Total								
All degrees	27,487	26,784	26,342	24,694	24,561	25,026	26,581	26,535
Science and engineering	14,889	14,711	14,655	14,065	14,055	14,592	15,346	15,360
Natural sciences[2]	6,427	6,604	6,641	6,634	6,450	6,628	6,942	6,898
Math and computer sciences	769	778	713	631	671	824	825	935

[Continued]

★ 322 ★

Science and Engineering Doctoral Degrees, 1977-91

[Continued]

Race/ethnicity and field	1977	1979	1981	1985	1987	1989	1990	1991
Social and behavioral sciences[3]	5,886	5,712	5,830	5,206	5,021	4,911	5,239	5,169
Engineering	1,799	1,617	1,471	1,594	1,913	2,229	2,340	2,358
White								
All degrees	23,654	22,396	22,470	21,297	21,116	21,569	22,862	22,604
Science and engineering	12,875	12,314	12,573	12,166	12,051	12,501	13,156	12,983
Natural sciences[2]	5,598	5,620	5,771	5,902	5,662	5,800	6,078	5,993
Math and computer sciences	671	658	610	527	548	688	711	758
Social and behavioral sciences[3]	5,177	4,879	5,099	4,549	4,383	4,287	4,531	4,444
Engineering	1,429	1,157	1,093	1,188	1,458	1,726	1,836	1,788
Asian								
All degrees	910	1,102	1,073	1,069	1,167	1,261	1,302	1,491
Science and engineering	745	884	827	809	924	981	1,006	1,157
Natural sciences[2]	342	377	344	346	369	400	411	462
Math and computer sciences	42	55	56	50	67	76	75	122
Social and behavioral sciences[3]	112	146	142	132	161	145	163	172
Engineering	249	306	285	281	327	360	357	401
Black								
All degrees	1,194	1,114	1,110	1,043	907	962	1,046	1,082
Science and engineering	344	347	346	374	319	366	371	431
Natural sciences[2]	85	84	89	100	95	105	98	108
Math and computer sciences	10	12	11	10	13	9	5	19
Social and behavioral sciences[3]	234	231	227	230	186	219	228	249
Engineering	15	20	19	34	25	33	40	55
Hispanic								
All degrees	474	539	526	634	709	694	835	843
Science and engineering	194	231	239	296	357	384	465	478
Natural sciences[2]	74	83	92	107	138	158	196	187
Math and computer sciences	10	12	5	18	15	15	15	20
Social and behavioral sciences[3]	88	112	126	149	170	163	200	212
Engineering	22	24	16	22	34	48	54	59
Native American								
All degrees	66	81	85	96	115	94	96	130
Science and engineering	31	29	28	41	53	53	42	56
Natural sciences[2]	14	6	8	21	20	25	12	27
Math and computer sciences	1	1	1	0	3	2	1	1
Social and behavioral sciences[3]	15	19	15	19	23	19	25	22
Engineering	1	3	4	1	7	7	4	6
	Foreign citizens							
Total								
All degrees	3,448	3,587	3,940	5,228	5,610	6,647	8,074	8,852
Science and engineering	2,675	2,689	2,983	4,048	4,468	5,392	6,555	7,281

[Continued]

★ 322 ★

Science and Engineering Doctoral Degrees, 1977-91

[Continued]

Race/ethnicity and field	1977	1979	1981	1985	1987	1989	1990	1991
Natural sciences[2]	1,079	1,046	1,140	1,518	1,704	1,975	2,531	2,843
Math and computer sciences	170	181	226	327	445	524	695	818
Social and behavioral sciences[3]	651	645	675	784	787	952	1,056	1,147
Engineering	775	817	942	1,419	1,532	1,941	2,273	2,473
	Unknown citizenship							
Total								
All degrees	781	868	1,075	1,375	2,192	2,645	1,402	2,064
Science and engineering	452	472	620	822	1,367	1,743	956	1,338
Natural sciences[2]	170	167	215	285	501	582	293	411
Math and computer sciences	25	20	21	40	74	123	77	84
Social and behavioral sciences[3]	183	225	269	344	525	664	306	462
Engineering	74	60	115	153	267	374	280	381

Source: National Science Board. *Science & Engineering Indicators—1993* (NSB 93-1). Washington, DC: U.S. Government Printing Office, 1993, pp. 286-87. Primary source: Science Resources Studies Division, National Science Foundation, *Science and Engineering Doctorates: 1960-91,* Detailed Statistical Tables NSF 93-301 (Washington, DC: NSF 1993). *Notes:* Data by racial/ethnic group were collected on a biennial schedule until 1990. Data are not available by racial/ethnic group for foreign citizens on temporary visas. Data by racial/ethnic group are collected by broad fields of study only; therefore, these data cannot be adjusted to the exact field taxonomies used by the National Science Foundation. 1. Includes all doctorates awarded to U.S. citizens and permanent residents, temporary residents, and persons whose citizenship is unknown. 2. The natural sciences include all physical, environmental, biological, and agricultural sciences. 3. The social and behavioral sciences include psychology, sociology, and other social sciences.

★ 323 ★

Higher Education

Science and Engineering Graduate Students, by Field and Race/Ethnicity, 1983-91

Data show number of graduate students enrolled in science and engineering programs.

Field	1983	1984	1985	1986	1987	1988	1989	1990	1991
Total enrollment									
Total science and engineering	348,315	350,755	359,554	369,047	373,762	376,821	384,691	395,298	415,240
Natural sciences	103,213	103,784	104,347	105,803	105,485	406,085	107,851	108,486	113,242
Math and computer sciences	40,996	43,269	47,424	49,364	50,661	51,657	51,936	54,155	54,720
Social and behavioral sciences	112,995	110,922	111,623	111,740	113,727	115,920	120,585	125,328	132,871
Engineering	91,111	92,780	96,160	102,140	103,889	103,159	104,319	107,329	114,407
White enrollment									
Total science and engineering	225,313	223,420	224,177	227,998	229,011	229,950	231,001	237,686	245,172
Natural sciences	74,538	74,244	72,170	71,885	69,496	69,169	68,545	68,341	69,989
Math and computer sciences	23,762	23,942	25,367	26,015	26,799	27,653	26,634	27,864	27,119
Social and behavioral sciences	78,318	75,809	76,249	77,017	79,000	80,621	84,244	88,357	93,044
Engineering	48,695	49,425	50,391	53,081	53,716	52,507	51,578	53,124	55,020
Asian enrollment									
Total science and engineering	9,368	10,185	12,024	12,788	14,590	15,182	15,682	17,039	18,217
Natural sciences	2,389	2,535	2,727	2,771	3,061	3,450	3,581	3,874	4,305

[Continued]

★ 323 ★

Science and Engineering Graduate Students, by Field and Race/Ethnicity, 1983-91

[Continued]

Field	1983	1984	1985	1986	1987	1988	1989	1990	1991
Math and computer sciences	1,663	1,816	2,475	2,767	3,232	3,446	3,449	3,679	3,704
Social and behavioral sciences	1,911	2,019	2,010	2,127	2,441	2,370	2,659	2,789	3,005
Engineering	3,405	3,815	4,812	5,123	5,856	5,916	5,993	6,697	7,203
Black enrollment									
Total science and engineering	10,980	10,724	10,534	10,471	10,443	11,216	11,800	12,635	13,696
Natural sciences	1,983	2,004	1,993	1,839	1,821	1,980	2,097	2,137	2,311
Math and computer sciences	967	954	1,017	1,135	1,191	1,247	1,299	1,472	1,605
Social and behavioral sciences	6,637	6,306	6,115	6,024	6,009	6,469	6,765	7,228	7,746
Engineering	1,393	1,460	1,409	1,473	1,422	1,520	1,639	1,798	2,034
Hispanic enrollment									
Total science and engineering	8,901	8,692	8,623	8,659	8,812	9,093	9,464	10,132	11,168
Natural sciences	1,922	1,895	2,097	2,123	2,075	2,230	2,394	2,360	2,576
Math and computer sciences	612	584	743	715	810	845	851	920	978
Social and behavioral sciences	4,926	4,713	4,303	4,218	4,199	4,301	4,508	4,960	5,435
Engineering	1,441	1,500	1,480	1,603	1,728	1,717	1,711	1,892	2,179
Native American enrollment									
Total science and engineering	915	831	740	746	786	926	864	1,048	1,201
Natural sciences	224	207	169	198	183	220	180	251	329
Math and computer sciences	53	70	78	51	75	72	75	63	62
Social and behavioral sciences	457	362	371	366	404	490	485	583	621
Engineering	181	192	122	131	124	144	124	151	189
Foreign citizen enrollment									
Total science and engineering	70,381	72,297	76,853	84,035	88,806	93,849	98,272	101,835	108,408
Natural sciences	18,286	18,853	20,360	22,729	24,487	26,220	28,166	29,478	31,342
Math and computer sciences	10,502	11,552	12,803	13,816	14,857	15,422	16,337	17,356	18,021
Social and behavioral sciences	14,105	14,006	14,836	15,479	16,082	16,878	16,959	17,034	17,726
Engineering	27,488	27,886	28,854	32,011	33,380	35,329	36,810	37,967	41,319

Source: National Science Board. *Science & Engineering Indicators—1993* (NSB 93-1). Washington, DC: U.S. Government Printing Office, 1993, p. 279. Primary source: Science Resources Studies Division, National Science Foundation, *Academic Science and Engineering, Graduate Enrollment and Support, Fall 1991*, Detailed Statistical Tables, NSF 93-309 (Washington, DC: NSF, 1993). *Notes:* The natural sciences include all physical, environmental, biological, and agricultural sciences. The social and behavioral sciences include psychology, sociology, and other social sciences.

★ 324 ★

Higher Education

Science and Engineering Master's Degrees, by Selected Field and Race/Ethnicity, 1977-91

Data show number of degrees earned in each field for each year.

Race/ethnicity and field	1977	1979	1981	1985	1987	1989	1990	1991
Total								
All degrees	318,241	302,075	296,798	287,213	290,532	311,050	324,947	338,498
Science and engineering	83,475	79,785	79,869	80,630	83,515	87,783	89,826	91,126
Natural sciences[1]	16,234	16,350	15,332	14,045	13,461	13,260	12,966	12,713
Math and computer sciences	6,496	6,101	6,787	9,989	11,808	12,829	13,327	12,956
Social and behavioral sciences[2]	44,494	41,824	41,034	35,661	36,189	37,959	39,548	41,450
Engineering	16,251	15,510	1,716	20,935	22,057	23,735	23,985	24,007
Engineering technology	NA	NA	NA	816	883	1,135	1,194	1,188
U.S. citizens and permanent residents								
White								
All degrees	266,109	249,401	241,255	223,649	216,807	230,322	236,874	247,524
Science and engineering	66,661	62,158	60,407	56,101	55,790	56,864	57,606	58,435
Natural sciences[1]	13,405	13,282	12,411	10,559	9,623	9,262	8,722	8,300
Math and computer sciences	5,256	4,625	4,708	6,176	6,729	6,818	7,020	6,705
Social and behavioral sciences[2]	36,556	34,169	33,141	27,180	26,601	27,952	29,005	30,795
Engineering	11,444	10,082	10,147	12,186	12,837	12,832	12,859	12,635
Engineering technology	NA	NA	NA	526	581	802	823	830
Asian								
All degrees	5,145	5,519	6,304	7,805	8,129	10,174	9,994	11,070
Science and engineering	2,021	2,232	2,481	3,543	3,745	4,482	4,393	4,676
Natural sciences[1]	388	469	365	450	464	545	504	532
Math and computer sciences	198	253	376	779	962	1,072	1,125	1,203
Social and behavioral sciences[2]	698	660	661	763	669	873	901	933
Engineering	737	850	1,079	1,551	1,650	1,992	1,863	2,008
Engineering technology	NA	NA	NA	25	46	40	79	60
Black								
All degrees	21,041	19,422	17,152	13,960	13,173	13,455	14,473	15,857
Science and engineering	4,197	4,042	3,695	3,152	3,223	3,151	3,559	3,825
Natural sciences[1]	351	382	351	290	301	238	225	261
Math and computer sciences	200	136	137	233	280	257	302	383
Social and behavioral sciences[2]	3,406	3,278	2,947	2,299	2,239	2,301	2,645	2,783
Engineering	240	246	260	330	403	355	387	398
Engineering technology	NA	NA	NA	37	42	55	44	47
Hispanic								
All degrees	7,071	6,470	7,439	7,730	7,781	8,133	8,495	9,684
Science and engineering	2,078	1,702	2,052	2,231	2,291	2,339	2,321	2,575
Natural sciences[1]	245	227	251	332	310	266	262	281
Math and computer sciences	91	61	102	149	183	178	169	213
Social and behavioral sciences[2]	1,491	1,199	1,414	1,404	1,286	1,427	1,444	1,613
Engineering	251	215	285	346	512	468	446	468
Engineering technology	NA	NA	NA	6	17	10	9	19

[Continued]

★ 324 ★

Science and Engineering Master's Degrees, by Selected Field and Race/Ethnicity, 1977-91

[Continued]

Race/ethnicity and field	1977	1979	1981	1985	1987	1989	1990	1991
Native American								
All degrees	968	999	1,034	1,257	1,049	1,082	1,050	1,125
Science and engineering	225	246	257	313	270	302	258	294
Natural sciences[1]	48	50	33	45	23	41	31	34
Math and computer sciences	15	24	19	48	25	45	13	23
Social and behavioral sciences[2]	139	148	174	173	184	183	179	197
Engineering	23	24	31	47	38	33	35	40
Engineering technology	NA	NA	NA	2	26	2	5	3
Foreign citizens								
All degrees	17,345	19,427	22,058	26,952	28,264	32,123	34,602	37,611
Science and engineering	8,282	9,111	10,468	13,132	13,764	15,949	17,077	17,841
Natural sciences[1]	1,797	1,895	1,864	2,178	2,132	2,504	2,732	2,856
Math and computer sciences	736	937	1,368	2,394	2,903	3,418	3,598	3,878
Social and behavioral sciences[2]	2,204	2,319	2,673	2,866	2,948	3,280	3,508	3,587
Engineering	3,545	3,960	4,563	5,694	5,781	6,747	7,239	7,520
Engineering technology	NA	NA	NA	124	127	131	162	172

Source: National Science Board. *Science & Engineering Indicators—1993* (NSB 93-1). Washington, DC: U.S. Government Printing Office, 1993, pp. 282-83. Primary source: Science Resources Studies Division, National Science Foundation, *Science and Engineering Degrees, by Race/Ethnicity of Recipients: 1977-91,* Detailed Statistical Tables (Washington, DC: NSF, forthcoming). *Notes:* Data by racial/ethnic group were collected on a biennial schedule until 1990. Data are not available by racial/ethnic group for foreign citizens on temporary visas. Data by racial/ethnic group are collected by broad fields of study only; therefore, these data cannot be adjusted to the exact field taxonomies used by the National Science Foundation. NA stands for not available. 1. The natural sciences include all physical, environmental. biological, and agricultural sciences. 2. The social and behavioral sciences include psychology, sociology, and other social sciences.

★ 325 ★

Higher Education

Financial Aid Received by Undergraduates, 1989-90 - I

Figures are shown, by type of aid given and race/ethnicity of student.

Selected student characteristics	Enrollment of under-graduates[1] (000)	Any aid			Grants		
		Total[2]	Federal	Non Federal	Total	Federal	Non Federal
Percent of all undergraduates receiving aid							
All undergraduates	12,600	44.0	30.0	32.3	37.2	21.4	28.4
Race/ethnicity							
White, non-Hispanic	9,410	41.2	26.3	31.2	34.2	17.5	27.2
Black, non-Hispanic	1,142	61.2	50.0	40.5	55.3	42.2	37.0
Hispanic	840	44.2	34.4	31.6	38.7	27.6	28.1
Asian American	575	35.5	25.5	28.2	31.2	20.2	25.9
American Indian	83	51.6	31.8	44.1	46.8	27.5	38.4
Average 1989-90 award for full-time, full-year undergraduates enrolled in fall 1989							
All full-time, full-year undergraduates	3,947	4,732	3,511	2,836	3,095	1,770	2,544
Race/ethnicity							
White, non-Hispanic	3,208	4,597	3,488	2,785	2,976	1,702	2,494
Black, non-Hispanic	301	5,116	3,586	2,902	3,433	1,997	2,668

[Continued]

★ 325 ★

Financial Aid Received by Undergraduates, 1989-90 - I

[Continued]

Selected student characteristics	Enrollment of under-graduates[1] (000)	Any aid			Grants		
		Total[2]	Federal	Non Federal	Total	Federal	Non Federal
Hispanic	189	5,139	3,502	3,002	3,388	1,867	2,698
Asian American	174	5,614	3,650	3,304	3,836	1,886	2,874
American Indian	19	6,299	4,004	3,510	3,921	2,099	2,908
Average 1989-90 award for other undergraduates enrolled in fall 1989							
All other undergraduates[3]	7,285	2,798	2,728	1,577	1,715	1,370	1,324
Race/ethnicity							
White, non-Hispanic	5,465	2,699	2,758	1,544	1,619	1,341	1,282
Black, non-Hispanic	665	3,021	2,580	1,599	1,948	1,396	1,434
Hispanic	556	2,946	2,680	1,490	1,798	1,345	1,287
Asian American	339	3,624	2,904	2,274	2,388	1,654	1,758
American Indian	52	2,945	3,265	1,762	2,131	1,787	1,601

Source: U.S. Department of Education. National Center for Education Statistics. Office of Educational Research and Improvement. *Digest of Education Statistics, 1994.* Lanham, MD: Bernan, November 1994, p. 315-316. Primary source: U.S. Department of Education, National Center for Education Statistics, *National Postsecondary Student Aid Study, 1989-90.* (This table was prepared June 1992.) *Notes:* Because of rounding and/or the fact that some students receive aid from multiple sources, details may not add to totals. Because of rounding and survey nonresponse, row details may not add to totals. Data include undergraduates in noncollegiate and collegiate institutions. 1. Numbers of undergraduates may not equal figures reported in other tables, since these data are based on a sample survey. 2. Includes students who reported they were awarded aid, but did not specify the source or type of aid. 3. Enrollment data include persons whose attendance was not reported.

★ 326 ★

Higher Education

Financial Aid Received by Undergraduates, 1989-90 - II

Figures are shown, by type of aid given and race/ethnicity of student.

Selected student characteristics	Loans			Work study total[3]	Other		
	Total	Federal	Non Federal		Total	Federal	Non Federal
Percent of all undergraduates receiving aid							
All undergraduates	20.4	19.3	2.3	5.4	8.2	1.8	6.5
Race/ethnicity							
White, non-Hispanic	19.1	18.0	2.4	5.2	8.3	1.8	6.7
Black, non-Hispanic	28.2	27.2	2.4	8.4	7.8	2.3	5.7
Hispanic	19.9	19.2	2.4	5.3	7.9	1.6	6.4
Asian American	14.7	13.7	2.0	5.7	6.5	1.2	5.2
American Indian	16.2	15.5	1.5	6.9	11.9	3.4	9.6
Average 1989-90 award for full-time, full-year undergraduates enrolled in fall 1989							
All full-time, full-year undergraduates	2,764	2,660	2,252	1,071	2,091	3,133	1,694
Race/ethnicity							
White, non-Hispanic	2,783	2,671	2,305	1,033	2,028	3,222	1,602
Black, non-Hispanic	2,543	2,501	1,565	1,143	2,442	2,443	2,348
Hispanic	2,755	2,632	2,047	1,252	1,919	3,058	1,606
Asian American	2,915	2,840	2,541	1,296	2,758	3,500	2,584
American Indian	3,361	3,387	1,610	1,182	3,362	4,404	2,893
Average 1989-90 award for other undergraduates enrolled in fall 1989							
All other undergraduates[4]	2,668	2,527	2,004	1,063	1,523	2,783	1,248
Race/ethnicity							
White, non-Hispanic	2,665	2,511	2,066	989	1,537	2,840	1,261
Black, non-Hispanic	2,558	2,521	1,510	1,048	1,609	2,381	1,334
Hispanic	2,789	2,630	1,962	1,280	1,114	3,088	710

[Continued]

★ 326 ★

Financial Aid Received by Undergraduates, 1989-90 - II

[Continued]

Selected student characteristics	Loans			Work study total[3]	Other		
	Total	Federal	Non Federal		Total	Federal	Non Federal
Asian American	2,795	2,568	2,065	1,549	1,902	2,434	1,917
American Indian	3,472	3,094	3,240	1,187	1,188	2,019	1,029

Source: U.S. Department of Education. National Center for Education Statistics. Office of Educational Research and Improvement. *Digest of Education Statistics, 1994.* Lanham, MD: Bernan, November 1994, p. 315-316. Primary source: U.S. Department of Education, National Center for Education Statistics, *National Postsecondary Student Aid Study, 1989-90.* (This table was prepared June 1992.) *Notes:* Because of rounding and/or the fact that some students receive aid from multiple sources, details may not add to totals. Because of rounding and survey nonresponse, row details may not add to totals. Data include undergraduates in noncollegiate and collegiate institutions. 1. Numbers of undergraduates may not equal figures reported in other tables, since these data are based on a sample survey. 2. Includes students who reported they were awarded aid, but did not specify the source or type of aid. 3. Details on Federal and nonfederal Work Study programs were not available. 4. Enrollment data include persons whose attendance was not reported.

★ 327 ★

Higher Education

Financial Aid Recipients, by Race/Ethnicity, 1990-91

Aid received	All students	Race/ethnicity			
		White	Black	Hispanic	Other
Total aid recipients[1]	10,461	8,381	1,128	551	401
Percent with					
One type of aid	66	67	58	67	61
Veterans Assistance	2	2	2	-	2
SEOG/College Work Study	1	1	2	1	-
Pell Grant	7	6	13	17	6
Loan	8	7	9	13	9
Employer assistance/JTPA	32	35	19	21	15
Fellowship/scholarship	8	9	5	7	8
Other type	9	9	8	7	19
Multiple types	34	33	42	33	39
Two types of aid	21	19	30	23	25
Fellowship or scholarship/other	2	2	3	2	-
Loan/other	2	2	2	2	2
Loan/fellowship or scholarship	3	3	1	2	8
Pell/other	2	2	3	1	6
Pell/fellowship or scholarship	1	1	2	2	2
Pell/loan	6	5	13	2	1
Three types of aid	9	9	9	7	9
Loan/fellowship or scholarship/other	1	1	1	1	1
Pell/loan/other	2	2	2	-	3

[Continued]

★ 327 ★

Financial Aid Recipients, by Race/Ethnicity, 1990-91

[Continued]

Aid received	All students	Race/ethnicity White	Black	Hispanic	Other
Pell/loan/fellowship or scholarship	1	1	-	1	-
Four or more types of aid	5	5	3	3	6

Source: Sutterlin, Rebecca and Robert A. Kominski. U.S. Bureau of the Census. *Dollars for Scholars: Postsecondary Costs and Financing, 1990-1991.* Current Population Reports, P70-39, Washington, DC: U.S. Government Printing Office, 1994, p. 9. *Notes:* A dash (-) represents zero. SEOG stands for Supplemental Educational Opportunity Grant. JPTA stands for Job Training Partnership Act. 1. Numbers in thousands.

★ 328 ★

Higher Education

Higher Education Costs, by Race/Ethnicity of Student, 1990-91

Average postsecondary schooling costs are shown in dollars for each level of schooling.

Characteristic	Total	College years 1 to 2	College years 3 to 4	College years 5 or higher	Vocational, technical, business school or other
Race/ethnicity					
White					
Total cost					
Mean	2,691	2,804	3,988	2,524	1,006
Standard error	68	118	152	135	91
Tuition and fees					
Mean	1,662	1,691	2,252	1,749	761
Standard error	45	77	99	95	69
Books and supplies					
Mean	286	316	400	265	108
Standard error	8	12	17	19	14
Room and board					
Mean	3,207	3,276	3,536	2,771	1,823
Standard error	84	118	126	255	351
Black					
Total cost					
Mean	2,552	2,941	3,222	(B)	1,177
Standard error	170	296	310	(B)	258
Tuition and fees					
Mean	1,649	1,922	1,971	(B)	814
Standard error	115	201	202	(B)	182
Books and supplies					
Mean	305	251	430	(B)	188

[Continued]

★ 328 ★

Higher Education Costs, by Race/Ethnicity of Student, 1990-91

[Continued]

Characteristic	Total	College years 1 to 2	College years 3 to 4	College years 5 or higher	Vocational, technical, business school or other
Standard error	31	20	78	(B)	59
Room and board					
Mean	2,834	2,790	(B)	(B)	(B)
Standard error	231	296	(B)	(B)	(B)
Hispanic					
Total cost					
Mean	1,882	1,668	2,802	(B)	1,028
Standard error	162	224	409	(B)	214
Tuition and fees					
Mean	1,275	1,086	1,648	(B)	922
Standard error	125	165	293	(B)	210
Books and supplies					
Mean	252	267	390	(B)	75
Standard error	21	22	66	(B)	17
Room and board					
Mean	(B)	(B)	(B)	(B)	(B)
Standard error	(B)	(B)	(B)	(B)	(B)
Other					
Total cost					
Mean	3,203	2,284	(B)	4,828	(B)
Standard error	353	439	(B)	966	(B)
Tuition and fees					
Mean	1,972	1,384	(B)	2,935	(B)
Standard error	222	262	(B)	607	(B)
Books and supplies					
Mean	367	367	(B)	518	(B)
Standard error	49	75	(B)	167	(B)
Room and board					
Mean	(B)	(B)	(B)	(B)	(B)
Standard error	(B)	(B)	(B)	(B)	(B)

Source: Sutterlin, Rebecca and Robert A. Kominski. U.S. Bureau of the Census. *Dollars for Scholars: Postsecondary Costs and Financing, 1990-1991.* Current Population Reports, P70-39, Washington, DC: U.S. Government Printing Office, 1994, pp. 17-18. *Note:* (B) stands for base is less than 200,000.

★ 329 ★

Higher Education

Percentage of Students 16 to 24 Years Old Enrolled in College Full-Time Who Were Employed, by Hours Worked per Week, 1970-92

From the source: "Although working during the school year leaves less time for students to concentrate on their studies or to participate in extracurricular activities, students may learn things from work experience that are not taught in the classroom....A moderate amount of work—less than 15 hours per week—may be associated with higher completion rates and better grades. A substantial amount of work—20 or more hours per week—may be detrimental to grades and attendance."

October	All students			White			Black			Hispanic		
	Total[1]	20 or more hours	35 or more hours	Total[1]	20 or more hours	35 or more hours	Total[1]	20 or more hours	35 or more hours	Total[1]	20 or more hours	35 or more hours
1970	33.8	14.1	3.7	34.9	14.7	3.9	21.2	8.0	1.8	-	-	-
1971	34.1	14.8	3.7	35.8	15.6	3.8	16.9	6.1	2.5	-	-	-
1972	35.1	15.0	3.4	36.3	15.2	3.2	21.5	12.2	5.8	42.7	21.0	2.5
1973	36.4	16.8	4.4	37.6	17.4	4.3	27.7	14.2	5.8	34.8	13.8	3.3
1974	36.6	17.0	4.7	38.2	17.4	4.7	23.2	13.0	5.0	34.4	15.8	6.8
1975	35.2	16.6	4.6	36.3	17.0	4.6	23.8	13.0	4.7	39.0	17.5	4.5
1976	37.5	16.9	4.0	39.6	17.7	3.9	22.7	11.9	4.7	35.4	14.8	3.1
1977	38.8	18.1	4.2	40.9	18.9	4.0	20.8	10.5	5.3	42.9	23.5	4.6
1978	39.9	19.0	4.7	41.8	19.7	4.7	22.2	11.7	4.7	53.2	26.8	7.4
1979	38.1	18.0	4.0	40.0	18.4	3.9	24.8	13.9	5.4	35.6	20.4	5.2
1980	40.0	17.9	3.8	42.1	18.3	3.8	24.0	12.2	5.1	41.4	26.6	4.5
1981	39.3	18.7	4.2	41.6	19.5	4.1	23.8	11.7	3.8	39.2	21.9	5.9
1982	39.9	18.5	3.1	42.4	19.6	3.0	26.2	12.2	4.3	33.1	14.1	1.6
1983	40.4	18.8	3.8	42.7	19.3	4.0	28.5	16.0	2.2	33.7	20.2	5.6
1984	42.1	21.0	4.2	44.7	22.0	4.3	25.2	14.8	3.2	34.8	19.7	4.1
1985	44.2	21.5	4.3	47.4	22.6	4.4	24.1	16.0	4.9	43.5	23.2	3.5
1986	43.0	21.9	4.3	46.3	23.5	4.7	24.7	14.2	3.9	40.5	22.6	2.1
1987	44.2	22.3	4.3	45.7	22.8	4.0	31.7	15.8	4.3	52.1	31.8	7.6
1988	46.5	24.5	4.7	48.9	25.1	5.0	31.8	18.6	3.3	40.9	28.7	6.7
1989	46.5	25.2	5.4	48.8	25.6	5.6	29.3	18.5	4.3	49.6	33.8	6.0
1990	45.7	24.1	4.8	48.6	25.1	5.2	29.8	17.1	2.8	45.7	28.0	6.7
1991	47.2	25.4	5.6	49.6	26.5	6.0	31.7	19.1	3.4	54.2	30.6	4.3
1992	47.2	25.8	5.5	5.5	27.2	5.9	30.2	1.9	4.4	47.0	29.4	4.7

Source: U.S. Department of Education. National Center for Education Statistics. *The Condition of Education 1994.* Washington, DC: U.S. Government Printing Office, 1994, p. 313. Primary source: U.S. Department of Commerce, Bureau of the Census, October Current Population Surveys. *Notes:* A dash (-) stands for not available. 1. Includes those with a job but not at work during the survey week.

★ 330 ★

Higher Education

Percentage of Students 16 to 24 Years Old Enrolled in College Part-Time Who Were Employed, by Hours Worked per Week, 1970-92

From the source: "Although working during the school year leaves less time for students to concentrate on their studies or to participate in extracurricular activities, students may learn things from work experience that are not taught in the classroom....A moderate amount of work—less than 15 hours per week—may be associated with higher completion rates and better grades. A substantial amount of work—20 or more hours per week—may be detrimental to grades and attendance."

October	All students			White			Black			Hispanic		
	Total[1]	20 or more hours	35 or more hours	Total[1]	20 or more hours	35 or more hours	Total[1]	20 or more hours	35 or more hours	Total[1]	20 or more hours	35 or more hours
1970	82.5	76.2	60.4	83.0	76.6	60.7	78.0	76.0	62.0	-	-	-
1971	83.4	75.0	51.7	83.8	75.2	53.6	79.2	74.0	36.4	-	-	-
1972	84.8	76.1	53.1	84.4	77.1	54.3	73.1	69.2	41.3	91.7	83.3	66.7
1973	85.3	76.8	52.5	76.6	77.9	53.5	70.7	66.7	42.7	92.5	82.5	55.0
1974	84.4	77.2	61.0	85.7	77.8	60.4	74.2	70.8	64.0	80.6	77.4	62.9
1975	80.8	72.1	52.6	82.4	74.1	55.1	76.0	62.5	41.3	68.3	57.1	39.7
1976	84.6	76.1	53.0	85.6	77.4	53.2	72.3	66.0	58.5	81.5	69.2	40.0
1977	83.4	75.3	53.1	86.0	77.4	54.7	65.9	51.1	44.4	77.8	74.1	51.9
1978	86.1	76.6	53.9	88.0	78.3	55.7	65.2	51.7	29.2	82.3	75.9	63.3
1979	86.9	78.8	56.6	89.2	80.0	58.2	73.5	66.3	49.0	75.0	68.3	46.7
1980	85.2	75.7	53.0	87.3	77.6	55.0	72.5	58.8	36.3	76.5	71.6	50.6
1981	85.7	76.0	51.4	87.2	77.8	52.0	75.4	61.0	41.5	84.1	79.7	50.7
1982	81.1	69.7	48.1	84.4	72.3	50.0	62.5	58.1	33.1	80.6	68.9	49.5
1983	81.7	74.8	48.1	86.6	79.2	51.9	49.2	47.5	23.8	74.0	68.0	45.0
1984	84.9	77.7	55.2	87.1	79.3	57.8	67.7	63.4	45.3	89.6	83.1	50.6
1985	85.9	79.0	52.2	87.9	81.7	56.2	71.8	66.4	42.0	85.2	70.4	28.4
1986	87.2	78.0	54.4	90.0	81.0	57.4	77.0	73.8	44.3	81.0	64.3	43.7
1987	85.4	77.4	49.5	87.2	79.2	51.4	70.9	65.8	37.3	86.5	77.4	54.1
1988	88.3	81.6	54.2	90.4	84.5	55.7	78.1	68.6	48.6	83.9	72.9	52.5
1989	87.2	80.8	55.4	89.8	83.2	58.3	73.2	67.5	43.1	85.1	79.3	55.4
1990	83.7	78.7	52.7	86.8	80.5	55.3	76.9	76.3	49.5	81.8	77.7	50.4
1991	85.8	76.3	50.9	89.0	79.1	55.3	66.1	63.4	38.4	80.2	71.0	37.4
1992	83.4	75.0	47.8	87.0	78.4	49.8	77.6	67.1	45.4	73.0	65.5	38.5

Source: U.S. Department of Education. National Center for Education Statistics. *The Condition of Education 1994.* Washington, DC: U.S. Government Printing Office, 1994, p. 315. Primary source: U.S. Department of Commerce, Bureau of the Census, October Current Population Surveys. *Notes:* A dash (-) stands for not available. 1. Includes those with a job but not at work during the survey week.

★ 331 ★

Higher Education

Hispanics on the Tenure Track in Ivy League Schools

School	Total faculty	Hispanic faculty	Percent Hispanic
Columbia	2347	66	2.81
U. of Pennsylvania	900	22	2.44
Harvard	620	13	2.10
Princeton	715	15	2.10

[Continued]

★ 331 ★

Hispanics on the Tenure Track in Ivy League Schools

[Continued]

School	Total faculty	Hispanic faculty	Percent Hispanic
Brown	545	9	1.65
Yale	1445	20	1.38
Dartmouth	1419	19	1.34
Cornell	1581	20	1.27

Source: Hispanic (December 1994), p. 22.

★ 332 ★

Higher Education

Faculty at Institutions of Higher Education, 1991

Figures are shown, by the type of position and race/ethnicity, for both men and women in 1991.

	Total	Race/ethnicity				
		White, non-Hispanic	Black, non-Hispanic	Hispanic	Asian or Pacific Islander	American Indian/ Alaska Native
Men and women, all ranks	520,324	456,222	24,516	11,422	26,510	1,654
Professors	144,341	132,065	3,572	2,038	6,371	295
Associate professors	116,631	103,918	4,942	2,107	5,391	273
Assistant professors	126,344	106,557	7,524	3,246	8,649	368
Instructors	78,082	67,539	5,223	2,326	2,326	462
Lecturers	11,275	9,603	739	397	483	53
Other faculty	43,651	36,540	2,516	1,102	3,290	203
Men, all ranks	355,111	313,205	13,056	7,353	20,481	1,016
Professors	123,173	113,097	2,466	1,654	5,721	235
Associate professors	84,311	75,341	2,924	1,490	4,363	193
Assistant professors	76,129	63,573	3,884	1,964	6,511	197
Instructors	41,124	35,776	2,328	1,421	1,339	260
Lecturers	5,362	4,599	326	183	225	29
Other faculty	25,012	20,819	1,128	641	2,322	102
Women, all ranks	165,213	143,017	11,460	4,069	6,029	638
Professors	21,168	18,968	1,106	384	650	60
Associate professors	32,320	28,577	2,018	617	1,028	80
Assistant professors	50,215	42,984	3,640	1,282	2,138	171
Instructors	36,958	31,763	2,895	1,111	987	202
Lecturers	5,913	5,004	413	214	258	24
Other faculty	18,639	15,721	1,388	461	968	101

Source: U.S. Department of Education. National Center for Education Statistics. Office of Educational Research and Improvement. *Digest of Education Statistics, 1994.* Lanham, MD: Bernan, November 1994, p. 230. Primary source: U.S. Equal Employment Opportunity Commission, EEO-6 *Higher Education Staff Information, 1991.* (This table was prepared Novermber 1991.) *Note:* Data exclude faculty employed by system offices.

★ 333 ★

Higher Education

Full-Time Faculty at Institutions of Higher Education, 1987 - I

Figures are shown, by the type of position and race/ethnicity, for 1987.

Selected characteristics	Number in thousands	Percent total	Public research	Private research	Public doctoral	Private doctoral	Public comprehensive
Total (in thousands)	489	-	96	39	396	15	93
Percent	-	100.0	19.7	8.0	7.3	3.0	19.0
Percent distribution							
Total	-	100.0	100.0	100.0	100.0	100.0	100.0
Race							
White, non-Hispanic	438	89.5	90.4	85.4	92.0	91.3	88.0
Black, non-Hispanic	16	3.2	1.6	6.1	1.8	0.1	3.5
Hispanic	11	2.3	2.4	5.0	1.1	2.2	2.1
Asian	21	4.2	4.8	3.5	4.5	5.9	5.8
American Indian	3	0.7	0.7	[1]	0.6	0.5	0.6

Source: U.S. Department of Education. National Center for Education Statistics. Office of Educational Research and Improvement. *Digest of Education Statistics, 1994.* Lanham, MD: Bernan, November 1994, p. 231. Primary source: U.S. Department of Education, National Center for Education Statistics, National Survey of Postsecondary Faculty (NSOPF), 1988. (This table was prepared June 1990.) *Notes:* Data may not add to totals because of rounding or missing data. A dash (-) stands for not applicable. 1. Less than 0.5 percent.

★ 334 ★

Higher Education

Full-Time Faculty at Institutions of Higher Education, 1987 - II

Figures are shown, by the type of position and race/ethnicity, for 1987.

Selected characteristics	Private comprehensive	Liberal arts	Public 2-year	Private 2-year	Medical	Other
Total (in thousands)	35	39	91	4	25	15
Percent	7.2	8.0	18.7	0.8	5.2	3.0
Percent distribution						
Total	100.0	100.0	100.0	100.0	100.0	100.0
Race						
White, non-Hispanic	91.2	86.9	91.0	94.1	85.3	95.1
Black, non-Hispanic	1.7	8.0	3.0	3.1	3.0	2.3
Hispanic	1.6	1.2	3.5	2.3	[1]	1.6
Asian	4.4	2.7	1.6	0.5	10.3	1.0
American Indian	1.1	1.2	0.9	[1]	1.4	[1]

Source: U.S. Department of Education. National Center for Education Statistics. Office of Educational Research and Improvement. *Digest of Education Statistics, 1994.* Lanham, MD: Bernan, November 1994, p. 231. Primary source: U.S. Department of Education, National Center for Education Statistics, National Survey of Postsecondary Faculty (NSOPF), 1988. (This table was prepared June 1990.) *Notes:* Data may not add to totals because of rounding or missing data. A dash (-) stands for not applicable. 1. Less than 0.5 percent.

★ 335 ★

Higher Education

Full-Time Faculty at Institutions of Higher Education, by Field, 1987-88

Figures are shown, by field and race/ethnicity, for 1987-88.

Faculty characteristics	Number in thousands	All fields	Agricultural and home economics	Business	Education	Engineering	Fine arts	Health	Humanities	Natural sciences	Social sciences	Other
Total, in thousands	489	-	13	37	35	25	32	85	62	84	53	64
Percentage	-	100.0	3.0	7.0	7.0	5.0	7.0	17.0	13.0	17.0	11.0	13.0
Percent distribution												
Total	489	100.0	100.0	100.0	100.0	100.0	100.0	100.0	100.0	100.0	100.0	100.0
Race/ethnicity												
White, non-Hispanic	438	90.0	94.0	88.0	88.0	87.0	92.0	88.0	90.0	91.0	90.0	89.0
Black, non-Hispanic	16	3.0	0.0	4.0	6.0	[1]	3.0	2.0	3.0	2.0	5.0	5.0
Hispanic	11	2.0	3.0	1.0	4.0	2.0	3.0	1.0	5.0	1.0	3.0	2.0
Asian	21	4.0	2.0	6.0	1.0	11.0	1.0	7.0	2.0	6.0	2.0	3.0
American Indian	4	1.0	1.0	1.0	1.0	[1]	[1]	1.0	1.0	[1]	1.0	1.0

Source: U.S. Department of Education. National Center for Education Statistics. Office of Educational Research and Improvement. *Digest of Education Statistics, 1994.* Lanham, MD: Bernan, November 1994, p. 232. Primary source: U.S. Department of Education, National Survey of Postsecondary Faculty (NSOPF), 1987-88. (This table was prepared April 1991.) *Notes:* Because of rounding and survey item nonresponse, details may not add to totals. A dash (-) stands for not applicable. 1. Less than 0.5 percent.

★ 336 ★

Higher Education

Part-Time Faculty at Institutions of Higher Education, 1987 - I

Figures are shown, by the type of position and race/ethnicity, for 1987.

Selected characteristics	Number in thousands	Percent total	Public research	Private research	Public doctoral	Private doctoral	Public comprehensive
Total (in thousands)	174	-	10	9	5	8	22
Percent	-	100.0	6.0	5.0	3.0	5.0	12.0
Percent distribution							
Total	-	100.0	100.0	100.0	100.0	100.0	100.0
White, non-Hispanic	156	90.0	98.0	83.0	94.0	91.0	84.0
Black, non-Hispanic	6	4.0	1.0	12.0	2.0	[1]	2.0
Hispanic	4	3.0	[1]	2.0	2.0	9.0	2.0
Asian	6	3.0	[1]	2.0	[1]	[1]	9.0
American Indian	2	1.0	1.0	2.0	2.0	[1]	4.0

Source: U.S. Department of Education. National Center for Education Statistics. *Digest of Education Statistics 1991.* Washington, DC: U.S. Government Printing Office, November 1991, p. 222. Primary source: U.S. Department of Education, National Center for Education Statistics, National Survey of Postsecondary Faculty (NSOPF), 1988. (This table was prepared June 1990.) *Notes:* Data may not add to totals because of rounding or missing data. A dash (-) stands for not applicable. 1. Less than 0.5 percent.

★ 337 ★

Higher Education

Part-Time Faculty at Institutions of Higher Education, 1987 - II

Figures are shown, by the type of position and race/ethnicity, for 1987.

Selected characteristics	Private comp-rehensive	Liberal arts	Public 2-year	Private 2-year	Medical	Other
Total (in thousands)	10	13	81	2	5	11
Percent	6.0	7.0	46.0	1.0	3.0	6.0
Percent distribution						
Total	100.0	100.0	100.0	100.0	100.0	100.0
White, non-Hispanic	97.0	82.0	92.0	[1]	[1]	97.0
Black, non-Hispanic	[2]	14.0	3.0	[1]	[1]	1.0
Hispanic	3.0	2.0	3.0	[1]	[1]	[2]
Asian	0.0	[2]	2.0	[1]	[1]	1.0
American Indian	[2]	1.0	0.0	[1]	[1]	[2]

Source: U.S. Department of Education. National Center for Education Statistics. *Digest of Education Statistics 1991.* Washington, DC: U.S. Government Printing Office, November 1991, p. 222. Primary source: U.S. Department of Education, National Center for Education Statistics, National Survey of Postsecondary Faculty (NSOPF), 1988. (This table was prepared June 1990.) *Notes:* Data may not add to totals because of rounding or missing data. A dash (-) stands for not applicable. 1. Too few cases for reliable estimate. 2. Less than 0.5 percent.

Chapter 4
CULTURE

Language

★ 338 ★

California: Number of Students Who Speak Limited English in Schools, by the 10 Largest Language Groups, 1987 and 1991

Data are shown for public elementary and secondary schools only.

Language	1987	1991	Percent change
Spanish	449,308	755,359	68.0
Vietnamese	30,906	40,477	31.0
Cantonese	19,761	21,498	9.0
Hmong	10,780	21,060	95.0
Cambodian	15,665	20,055	28.0
Filipino	14,381	18,146	26.0
Korean	10,738	14,932	39.0
Lao	10,283	12,430	21.0
Armenian	2,660	11,399	329.0
Mandarin	7,334	8,386	14.0

Source: SCAN/INFO (September 1992), p. 20. Primary source: *Los Angeles Times*, 9/21/92, p. A11.

★ 339 ★

Language

Hispanic Opinions on Knowledge of English

Should citizens and residents of the United States learn English?

Hispanic ethnicity	Percent	
	Agree or strongly agree	Disagree or strongly disagree
U.S. citizens		
Cuban-American	92.0	8.0
Mexican-American	93.0	7.0
Puerto Rican	91.0	9.0
Non-U.S. citizens		
Cuban	92.0	8.0
Mexican	93.0	7.0

Source: Suro, Robert. "Poll finds Hispanic desire to assimilate." *The New York Times* (15 December 1992), p. A18. Primary source: Latino National Political Survey.

★ 340 ★

Language

Language Ability in U.S. Southwest Border Counties, 1980

State/county	Persons 5 years and over	Percent			
		Speak only English at home	Speak only Spanish at home	Speak English very well	Speak English not well at all
California					
San Diego	243,434	26.7	70.8	52.2	18.6
Imperial	45,604	6.5	93.1	63.8	29.4
Arizona					
Cochise	20,349	13.8	85.4	68.4	17.1
Pima	98,507	19.7	79.6	69.3	10.3
Santa Cruz	13,498	3.6	96.1	69.6	26.5
Yuma	26,012	14.4	85.1	57.5	27.6
New Mexico					
Dona Ana	44,856	10.3	88.6	70.2	18.4
Hidalgo	2,494	8.1	91.9	81.5	10.5
Luna	5,423	8.2	91.8	78.5	13.4
Texas					
El Paso	264,955	6.2	93.6	68.9	24.7
Hudspeth	1,385	0.9	99.0	59.4	39.6
Culberson	1,855	0.2	99.8	75.8	23.9

[Continued]

★ 340 ★

Language Ability in U.S. Southwest Border Counties, 1980

[Continued]

State/county	Persons 5 years and over	Percent			
		Speak only English at home	Speak only Spanish at home	Speak English very well	Speak English not well at all
Jeff Davis	699	6.0	94.0	71.2	22.7
Presidio	3,679	2.3	97.5	63.3	34.2
Brewster	2,970	4.7	95.3	76.2	19.1
Terrell	622	5.6	94.4	73.3	21.1
Valverde	20,139	2.9	97.0	68.5	28.5
Kinney	1,198	4.3	95.4	65.9	29.5
Maverick	25,202	1.2	98.8	60.6	38.2
Dimmitt	7,867	2.2	97.2	69.0	28.2
Webb	81,178	2.4	97.5	70.9	26.6
Zapata	4,463	2.4	97.6	65.7	31.8
Starr	23,679	3.1	96.8	61.7	35.2
Hildalgo	203,304	2.7	97.2	67.8	29.4
Cameron	142,550	3.5	96.3	68.0	28.3

Source: U.S. Bureau of the Census, *The Hispanic Population of the Southwest Borderland.* Current Population Reports, Series P-23, No. 172, Washington, DC: U.S. Government Printing Office, 1991, pp. 22-28. *Notes:* For the purposes of this report, the U.S. Census Bureau included the following counties: San Diego, and Imperial counties, in California; Cochise, Pima, Santa Cruz, and Yuma counties, in Arizona; Dona Ana, Hidalgo, and Luna counties, in New Mexico; El Paso, Hudspeth, Culberson, Jeff Davis, Presidio, Terrell, Valverde, Kinney, Maverick, Dimmit, Webb, Zapata, Starr, Hidalgo, and Cameron counties, in Texas.

★ 341 ★

Language

Language Ability, 1980

Language ability	United States	Total, border states	Border states			
			Border county areas		Non-border county areas	
			Hispanic	Non-Hispanic	Hispanic	Non-Hispanic
Persons, 5 years and over	210,247,455	38,728,052	1,285,922	2,400,611	6,160,352	28,881,167
Percent						
Speak only English at home	89.0	77.4	10.2	90.5	22.3	91.0
Speak language other than English at home	11.0	22.6	89.8	9.5	77.7	9.0
Speak Spanish at home	5.3	16.3	89.1	2.8	76.7	1.3
Speak English very well or well	4.0	12.2	65.0	2.5	56.8	1.1
Speak English not well or not at all	1.3	4.1	24.1	0.3	19.9	0.1

Source: U.S. Bureau of the Census, *The Hispanic Population of the Southwest Borderland.* Current Population Reports, Series P-23, No. 172, Washington, DC: U.S. Government Printing Office, 1991, p. 20. *Notes:* For the purposes of this report, the U.S. Census Bureau included the following counties: San Diego, and Imperial counties, in California; Cochise, Pima, Santa Cruz, and Yuma counties, in Arizona; Dona Ana, Hidalgo, and Luna counties, in New Mexico; El Paso, Hudspeth, Culberson, Jeff Davis, Presidio, Brewster, Terrell, Valverde, Kinney, Maverick, Dimmit, Webb, Zapata, Starr, Hidalgo, and Cameron counties, in Texas.

★ 342 ★

Language

Language Spoken at Home, 1980

Of the 11 million persons who reported speaking Spanish at home, 24 percent reported speaking English "not well" or "not at all"; and 76 percent reported speaking English "very well" or "well." Data are shown for persons three years old and older.

Language	Percent
English	89.0
Spanish	5.0
Speaks English very well or well	76.0
Speaks English not well or not at all	24.0
Italian	1.0
German	1.0
French	1.0
All other languages	3.0

Source: U.S. Bureau of the Census. *The Condition of Hispanics in America Today*. Washington, DC: U.S. Government Printing Office, 1983, p. 8.

★ 343 ★

Language

Language Spoken at Home, 1990

Data are shown for persons five years old and older.

Characteristic	Number
Persons 5 years and over	230,445,777
Speak a language other than English	31,844,979
Do not speak English "very well"	13,982,502
Speak Spanish	17,345,064
Do not speak English "very well"	8,309,995
Speak Asian or Pacific Island language	4,471,621
Do not speak English "very well"	2,420,355

Source: U.S. Bureau of the Census, *Summary Tape File, STF-3A*, 1990.

★ 344 ★

Language

Media Penetration in the Hispanic Market

Data show results of a 1992 survey of 1,200 Hispanic consumers.

Activity	Percent		
	1988	1990	1992
Watch TV (weekday)	96.0	97.0	95.0
Percent of above who watch Spanish TV	74.0	81.0	86.0
Listen to radio (weekday)	88.0	80.0	84.0
Percent of above who listen to Spanish radio	65.0	64.0	74.0
Read any newspaper	85.0	76.0	66.0
Percent of above who read any Spanish newspaper	43.0	38.0	41.0
Read any magazincs	62.0	52.0	40.0
Read any Spanish magazines	24.0	26.0	23.0

Source: "Surveys point to group differences." *Brandweek* (18 July 1994), p. 32. Primary source: Yankelovich Partners and Market Development.

★ 345 ★

Language

Median Number of Days in JTPA (Job Training Partnership Act) Programs, 1988

"Taken as a whole, these data correspond to testimony at the hearings. On the one hand, Hispanics need lengthy training to overcome their English-language and basic skills deficiencies. On the other hand, Hispanics' strong sense of responsibility for their families (especially among the males) virtually mandates that they be employed, or if unemployed, find jobs quickly. Without some income support and childcare, they cannot afford to take the training they need. Thus, and especially for Hispanic men, JTPA may be one other way to find jobs, comparable to the use of friends, relatives or newspaper advertisements. Without the possibility of long-term training, Hispanics may view JTPA as a labor exchange bureau—rather than a training program."

Characteristic	Median number of days in JTPA
Hispanics	67.7
Non-Hispanics	96.5
Limited English proficient	59.6
Non-limited English proficient	94.8

Source: National Commission for Employment Policy. *Training Hispanics: Implications for the JTPA System: Special Report.* January 1990, p. 57. Primary source: U.S. Department of Labor, Office of Strategic Planning and Policy Development, June 1989.

★ 346 ★

Language

Miami: Language Characteristics of Hispanics, 1980-90

Language characteristics	Miami		Florida	
	1980	1990	1980	1990
Percentage of total population	56.0	62.0	9.0	12.0
Percentage reporting English as a second language	64.0	73.0	13.0	17.0
Percentage reporting not speaking English well	30.0	50.0	5.0	8.0

Source: Sharp, Deborah. "Miami's language gap widens: culturally rich but very divided." *USA TODAY* (3 April 1992), p. 3A. Primary source: U.S. Census Bureau.

★ 347 ★

Language

New York: Native Languages of LEP Students, 1991-92

"[Data show] The number of students with limited English proficiency [LEP] who are native speakers of each language in the 1991-1992 school year. There were 133,948 students who were not proficient in English during this period. These languages are the most common of the 120 spoken by students who were not proficient in English."

Language	Number
Spanish	88,894
Chinese	12,921
Haitian Creole	7,166
Russian	5,332
Korean	3,467
Arabic	1,883
Urdu	1,421
Bengali	1,184
Vietnamese	986
French	928
Polish	862
Italian	732
Hindi	683
Albanian	595
Farsi	509

Source: Berger, Joseph. "New York's bilingual bureaucracy assailed as non-English programs cover more pupils." *The New York Times* (4 January 1993), p. A13. Primary source: New York Board of Education.

★ 348 ★

Language

Percentage of Children Eight to Fifteen Years Old Below Modal Grade, by Selected Language Characteristics, 1979 and 1989

Numbers are shown in thousands.

Language characteristic	1979			1989		
	Enrolled in school	Number below modal grade	Percent below modal grade	Enrolled in school	Number below modal grade	Percent below modal grade
All children	26,741	6,650	24.9	25,572	8,863	34.7
Speak language other than English at home						
Total[1]	2,098	734	35.0	2,961	1,075	36.3
Spanish	1,414	557	39.4	1,896	756	39.9
All other European languages	430	88	20.3	278	74	26.7
Asian languages	156	52	33.2	429	120	28.0
All other languages	66	[2]	[2]	222	78	35.2
Limited-English-proficient[3]						
Total	555	291	52.5	830	313	37.7
Spanish	442	230	52.1	576	242	42.1
All other European languages	33	[2]	[2]	73	[2]	[2]
Asian languages	61	[2]	[2]	118	39	32.8
All other languages	19	[2]	[2]	63	[2]	[2]

Source: U.S. Department of Education. National Center for Education Statistics. *The Condition of Education, 1992.* Washington, DC: U.S. Government Printing Office, 1992, p. 22. Primary source: U.S. Department of Commerce, Bureau of the Census, October and November Current Population Survey, 1979 and 1989. *Notes:* Modal grade refers to the grade in which most children of an age are enrolled. For example, modal grade for 8-year-olds in October is third grade; for 13-year-olds it is eighth grade. 1. Includes some children for whom a specific language was not reported. 2. Too few sample observations for a reliable estimate. 3. For the purpose of this indicator, limited English proficiency is derived from a person's own responses to a survey question on English ability. Persons who were reported to speak English less than "very well" were considered to be limited English proficient.

★ 349 ★

Language

Radio Listenership, by Metropolitan Area

Figures represent percentages of persons listening to radio in an average 15-minute period from Spring 1989 to Winter 1990.

Market	Total	Hispanic
Los Angeles	18.3	20.4
New York	19.4	21.2
Miami	19.9	22.6
San Francisco	17.0	17.8
Chicago	18.8	19.7
San Antonio	18.3	19.3
Houston	18.1	18.0
McAllen-Brownsville	18.9	19.8
Anaheim-Santa Ana	17.4	19.3
San Diego	17.2	17.0
El Paso	18.6	19.6

[Continued]

★ 349 ★

Radio Listenership, by Metropolitan Area

[Continued]

Market	Total	Hispanic
Dallas	17.8	18.0
San Jose	16.8	17.9
Phoenix	17.2	18.2
Riverside-San Bernardino	18.1	18.9
Albuquerque	18.1	19.7
Fresno	17.5	19.3
Corpus Christi	18.1	19.4
Sacramento	16.6	16.7
Austin	16.9	18.7

Source: "Firms try to improve Hispanic measurement." *Broadcasting* (20 May 91), p. 42. Katz Hispanic Radio Research, Arbitron Ethnic Composition Spring '89-Winter '90.

★ 350 ★

Language

Spanish-Speaking Employees in Social Security Administration Regional Offices, 1987

SSA regional office	Staff[1]	Spanish-speaking[2]	
		Number	Percent
Atlanta	6,295	334	5.3
Boston	1,836	62	3.4
Chicago	6,559	222	3.4
Dallas	3,828	533	13.9
Denver	1,010	64	6.3
Kansas City	1,779	50	2.8
Philadelphia	3,602	99	2.7
New York	4,860	722	14.8
Seattle	1,316	68	5.2
San Francisco	5,527	861	15.6
Total	36,612	3,015	8.2

Source: U.S. General Accounting Office. Report to the Chairman Select Committee on Aging, House of Representatives, *Social Security Administration: Employment and Services to Hispanics*, GAO/HRD-89-35. Washington, DC: U.S. GAO, January 1989, p. 33. *Notes:* 1. As of September 30, 1987. 2. As of January 29, 1988.

Perceptions

★ 351 ★

Hispanic Opinions of the U.S. Government

Data reflect percentage of Hispanics who believe the government is run...

Citizenship and ethnicity	By the few in their interest	For benefit of all
U.S. citizens		
Cuban-American	36.0	64.0
Mexican-American	51.0	49.0
Puerto Rican	51.0	49.0
Non-Hispanic white	57.0	43.0
Non-U.S. citizens		
Cuban	15.0	85.0
Mexican	16.0	84.0

Source: Suro, Robert. "Poll finds Hispanic desire to assimilate." *The New York Times* (15 December 1992), p. A18. Primary source: Latino National Political Survey.

★ 352 ★

Perceptions

Hispanic Opinions on Abortion, 1992

Conditions under which abortions should be permitted.

Condition	Mexican		Puerto Rican		Cuban	
	Male	Female	Male	Female	Male	Female
None	16.8	23.3	27.0	18.6	11.0	12.0
Rape/incest	31.9	33.3	33.2	39.0	30.1	35.8
Any	38.1	34.1	24.8	31.3	33.9	37.8

Source: Benedetto, Richard. "Hispanics feeling at home: survey shows a solid fit in mainstream." *USA TODAY* (16 December 1992), p. 5A. Primary source: Latino National Political Survey.

★ 353 ★

Perceptions

Hispanic Opinions on Immigration

Statement/ ethnicity	Percent	
	Agree or strongly agree	Disagree or strongly disagree
Immigration preference should be given to Latin Americans		
U.S. citizens		
Cuban-American	30.0	70.0
Mexican-American	38.0	62.0
Puerto Rican	37.0	63.0
Non-U.S. citizen		
Cuban	48.0	52.0
Mexican	74.0	26.0
There are too many immigrants		
U.S. citizens		
Cuban-Americans	66.0	34.0
Mexican-American	75.0	25.0
Puerto Rican	74.0	26.0
Non-Hispanic white	74.0	26.0
Non-U.S. citizen		
Cuban	73.0	27.0
Mexican	84.0	16.0

Source: Suro, Robert. "Poll finds Hispanic desire to assimilate." *The New York Times* (15 December 1992), pp. A1 and A18. Primary source: Latino National Political Survey.

★ 354 ★

Perceptions

How Hispanic Americans Describe Themselves, by Place of Birth

Data are based on a survey which involved face-to-face interviews with 2,817 people in 1989 and 1990. Figures may not add to 100 percent due to rounding.

Origin and place of birth	Percent			
	Place of origin (called themselves Mexican, Puerto Rican, Cuban)	Pan-ethnic names (called themselves Hispanic, Latino, Spanish, Spanish-American, Hispano)	American (called themselves American)	Other
Mexicans				
Born in Mexico	86.0	14.0	-	-
Born in U.S.	62.0	28.0	10.0	-
Puerto Ricans				
Born on the island	85.0	13.0	3.0	-
Born on mainland	57.0	19.0	21.0	3.0
Cubans				
Born in Cuba	83.0	12.0	3.0	-
Born in U.S.	41.0	20.0	39.0	-

Source: Gonzalez, Davis. "What's the problem with 'Hispanic'? Just ask a 'Latino'." *The New York Times* (15 November 1992), p. E6. Primary source: Rodolfo O. de la Garza, one of the authors of the Latino National Political Survey. *Note:* A dash (-) represents zero.

★ 355 ★

Perceptions

Opinions on Coverage of Minorities in Television and Newspapers

Data show percentages of persons of each race/ethnicity that report satisfaction with television and newspaper coverage of their respective groups. Figures are results of a poll conducted in July, 1994.

	National TV	Local TV	Local newspaper
Hispanic Americans	76.0	71.0	72.0
African Americans	58.0	53.0	48.0
Asian Americans	74.0	65.0	61.0

Source: "How are we covered?" *Hispanic* (October 1994), p. 10. Primary source: USA TODAY/CNN/Gallup Poll, July 1994.

★ 356 ★

Perceptions

Perceived Social Standing of Selected Racial Groups: 1964-89

In polls taken in 1964 and 1989, adults nationwide were asked to rate the "social standing" of the following groups in the United States, using a scale in which 1 was the lowest standing and 9 was the highest. The figures shown are averages. The Wisians, a fictitious group, were included in 1989.

Ethnic group	1964	1989	Change
Native white Americans	7.25	7.03	0.22
People of my own ethnic background	6.16	6.57	0.41
British	6.37	6.46	0.09
Protestants	6.59	6.39	0.20
Catholics	6.36	6.33	0.03
French	5.73	6.07	0.34
Irish	5.94	6.05	0.11
Swiss	5.50	6.03	0.53
Swedes	5.41	5.99	0.58
Austrians	5.06	5.94	0.88
Dutch	5.60	5.90	0.30
Norwegians	5.48	5.87	0.39
Scotch	5.73	5.85	0.12
Germans	5.63	5.78	0.15
Southerners	5.25	5.77	0.52
Italians	5.03	5.69	0.66
Danes	5.20	5.63	0.43
French Canadians	5.08	5.62	0.54
Japanese	3.95	5.56	1.61
Jews	4.71	5.55	0.84
People of foreign ancestry	4.84	5.38	0.54
Finns	5.08	5.34	0.26
Greeks	4.31	5.09	0.78
Lithuanians	4.42	4.96	0.54
Spanish-Americans	4.81	4.79	0.02
Chinese	3.44	4.76	1.32
Hungarians	4.57	4.70	0.13
Czechs	4.40	4.64	0.24
Poles	4.54	4.63	0.09
Russians	3.88	4.58	0.70
Latin Americans	4.27	4.42	0.15
American Indians	4.04	4.27	0.23
Negroes[1]	2.75	4.17	1.42
"Wisians"	-	4.12	-
Mexicans	3.00	3.52	0.52
Puerto Ricans	2.91	3.32	0.41
Gypsies	2.29	2.65	0.36

Source: Lewin, Tamar. "Study points to increase in tolerance of ethnicity." *The New York Times* (8 January 1992), p. A10. Primary source: National Opinion Research Center. The 1989 survey included 1,537 adults. *Notes:* 1. Blacks were referred to as Negroes by the National Opinion Research Center in the 1989 survey to conform with the wording in the 1964 survey.

Religion

★ 357 ★

Hispanic Bishops in the United States

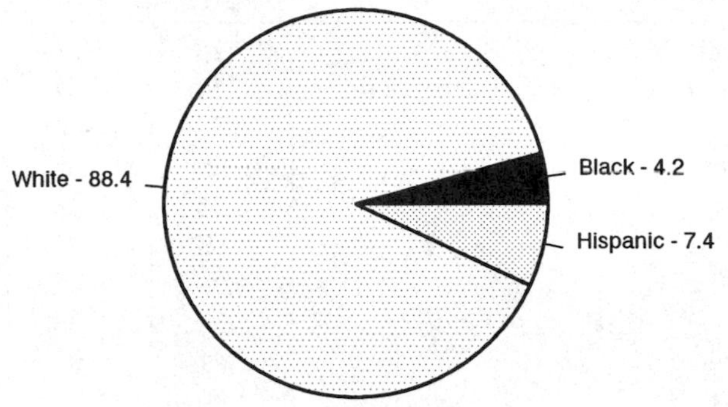

Chart shows data from column 1.

Numbers are shown as percentages. Chart shows U.S. bishops.

Race and ethnicity	U.S. bishops	All U.S. Catholics
White	88.4	58.0
Black	4.2	4.3
Hispanic	7.4	37.7

Source: Parker, Suzy. "USA Snapshots: Catholics in the USA." *USA TODAY* (20 November 1992), p. 1A. Primary source: Catholic Almanac.

Sports and Leisure

★ 358 ★

Golf Participation Rates, by Race/Ethnicity

Race/ethnicity	Number of of golfers (000)	Percentage of golf population	Participation rate (percent)[2]
All golfers	24,796	100	11.9
Hispanics[1]	459	1.9	6.5
White	23,947	96.6	13.2
Black	437	1.8	1.9

[Continued]

★ 358 ★

Golf Participation Rates, by Race/Ethnicity

[Continued]

Race/ethnicity	Number of of golfers (000)	Percentage of golf population	Participation rate (percent)[2]
Asian/Pacific Islander	179	0.07	13.3
Other	233	0.09	8.7

Source: Potter, Jerry. "Minorities try to forge link with golf." *USA TODAY* (21 October 1992), p. 1C. Primary source: National Golf Foundation. *Notes:* 1. Hispanics are not a distinct racial group. Respondents who stated they were of Spanish ethnicity could also identify themselves as any of the racial groupings listed above. 2. Percentages are rounded.

★ 359 ★

Sports and Leisure

Numbers of Sports Teams Who Broadcast Locally in Spanish, by League, 1992

League	Number
National Football League	5
Major League baseball	10
National Basketball Association	7
National Hockey League	0

Source: Galifianakis, Nick. "USA Snaphots: The language of sports." *USA TODAY* (14 January 1993), p. 1C. *USA TODAY* research by John Riley.

Volunteerism

★ 360 ★

Volunteer Workers for Schools and Other Organizations, 1989

Race/ethnicity	Number of volunteers (000)	Percent distribution, by type of organization							
		Total	School or other educational institution	Church or other religious organization	Civic or political organization	Hospital or other health organization	Social or welfare organization	Sports or recreational organization	Other organization
Total	38,042	100.0	15.1	37.4	13.2	10.4	9.9	7.8	6.3
Hispanic[1]	1,289	100.0	18.3	42.2	9.6	8.5	8.9	6.9	5.6
White[2]	34,823	100.0	15.1	36.6	13.5	10.7	9.8	8.0	6.3
Black[2]	2,505	100.0	12.4	50.4	9.6	7.0	10.4	4.6	5.6

Source: U.S. Department of Education. National Center for Education Statistics. *Digest of Education Statistics, 1991.* Washington, DC: U.S. GPO, November 1991, p. 32. Primary source: U.S. Department of Labor, Bureau of Labor Statistics, news release, "Thirty-Eight Million Persons Do Volunteer Work." *Notes:* 1. Persons of Hispanic origin may be of any race. 2. Includes persons of Hispanic origin.

Chapter 5
HEALTH AND HEALTH CARE

AIDS

★361★

AIDS Case Trends for Selected Populations, 1989-92

Data show the number of diagnosed AIDS (acquired immunodeficiency syndrome) cases per year and the target number of cases set as a goal by the Public Health Service in its prevention initiative in improving the health of the U.S. population by the year 2000.

Population	Number of cases (in thousands)				
	1989	1990	1991	1992	Year 2000 target
All persons	49	55	68	87	98
Men who have sex with men	27	30	35	42	48
Black	15	17	22	31	37
Hispanic	8	10	12	15	18

Source: National Center for Health Statistics. *Healthy People 2000 Review. Health, United States, 1992.* Hyattsville, MD: Public Health Service, 1993, p. 119. Primary source: Centers for Disease Control and Prevention, National Center for Infectious Diseases, AIDS Surveillance System.

★ 362 ★

AIDS

AIDS Cases

AIDS cases, by age at diagnosis, sex, and race/ethnicity are shown for selected years from 1985 to 1993. Data based on reporting by State health departments are shown for the United States but do not include the U.S. territories.

Age at diagnosis, sex, race, and Hispanic origin	Percent distribution All years[1]	Number, by year of report									Cases per 100,000 population[2] 12 months ending September 30, 1993
		All years[1]	1985	1987	1988	1989	1990	1991	1992	January-September 1993	
All races	-	328,392	8,189	21,048	30,648	33,511	41,558	43,574	45,603	83,814	37.0
Male											
All males, 13 years and over	100.0	285,063	7,538	19,047	27,049	29,549	36,300	37,530	38,917	70,369	80.2
White, not Hispanic	56.4	160,861	4,787	12,304	16,008	17,470	20,903	20,613	20,763	36,336	54.3
Black, not Hispanic	28.8	82,110	1,704	4,315	7,153	8,031	10,268	11,082	12,107	23,047	244.3
Hispanic	13.7	38,914	987	2,245	3,647	3,714	4,731	5,403	5,540	10,125	125.3
American Indian[3]	0.2	614	7	24	34	60	72	75	97	223	36.9
Asian or Pacific Islander[4]	0.7	1,992	48	131	163	214	255	259	283	540	20.0
13-19 years	0.3	934	31	67	84	90	102	99	94	299	-
20-29 years	18.2	51,845	1,468	3,784	5,449	5,692	6,814	6,459	6,350	12,052	-
30-39 years	46.3	131,858	3,610	8,855	12,581	13,868	16,802	17,332	17,819	32,116	-
40-49 years	24.8	70,729	1,657	4,283	6,105	6,809	8,908	9,628	10,337	18,935	-
50-59 years	7.6	21,657	605	1,474	1,990	2,240	2,651	2,896	3,079	5,289	-
60 years and over	2.8	7,940	167	584	840	850	1,023	1,116	1,238	1,705	-
Female											
All females, 13 years and over	100.0	38,684	522	1,682	3,034	3,370	4,540	5,375	5,942	12,789	13.4
White, not Hispanic	26.6	10,288	141	544	854	948	1,225	1,358	1,454	3,379	4.6
Black, not Hispanic	56.1	21,707	285	894	1,650	1,893	2,539	3,109	3,398	7,171	64.3
Hispanic	16.2	6,285	92	230	497	493	736	859	1,024	2,091	27.0
American Indian[3]	0.3	103	3	3	6	9	10	11	15	43	6.5
Asian or Pacific Islander[4]	0.6	228	1	11	22	17	19	25	37	86	3.1
13-19 years	1.1	418	4	11	23	29	63	55	57	157	-
20-29 years	24.3	9,418	173	480	768	889	1,104	1,223	1,370	2,962	-
30-39 years	47.1	18,224	236	750	1,503	1,615	2,091	2,538	2,715	6,131	-
40-49 years	17.9	6,919	44	229	411	507	788	995	1,245	2,523	-
50-59 years	5.6	2,148	26	92	151	172	275	342	344	681	-
60 years and over	4.0	1,557	39	120	178	158	219	222	211	335	-
Children											
All children, under 13 years	100.0	4,645	129	319	565	592	718	669	744	629	1.7
White, not Hispanic	21.1	979	27	85	149	111	159	146	128	110	0.4
Black, not Hispanic	57.7	2,680	83	160	300	339	384	403	470	380	6.9
Hispanic	20.2	937	19	71	112	135	168	113	137	128	2.6
American Indian[3]	0.3	14	-	2	-	2	3	2	3	2	0.4
Asian or Pacific Islander[4]	0.5	22	-	1	4	3	4	4	1	4	0.2
Under 1 year	39.2	1,820	54	141	190	241	284	247	302	224	-
1-12 years	60.8	2,825	75	178	375	351	434	422	405	-	

Source: National Center for Health Statistics. *Health, United States, 1993.* Hyattsville, MD: Public Health Service, May 1994, p. 143. Primary source: Centers for Disease Control and Prevention, National Center for Infectious Diseases, Division of HIV/AIDS. *Notes:* A dash (-) stands for zero. NA stands for not applicable. The AIDS case reporting definitions were expanded in 1985, 1987, and 1993. Data are updated periodically because of reporting delays and have been updated through September 30, 1993 for all years and are shown as of December 31, 1993. 1. Includes cases prior to 1985. 2. Resident population estimates for 1992 are based on extrapolation from 1990 census counts from the U.S. Bureau of the Census. 3. Includes Aleut and Eskimo. 4. Includes Chinese, Japanese, Filipino, Hawaiian and part Hawaiian, and other Asian or Pacific Islander.

★ 363 ★

AIDS

AIDS Cases by Type of Transmission

AIDS (acquired immunodeficiency syndrome) cases are shown by sex, race/ethnicity, and type of transmission for persons age 13 and older in of the United States. Data do not include residents the U.S. territories. Figures shown for selected years from 1985 to 1993 are based on reporting by State health departments.

Race/ethnicity and transmission category	Percent distribution All years[1]	Number, by year of report								
		All years[1]	1985	1987	1988	1989	1990	1991	1992	January-September 1993
All races	100.0	323,747	8,060	20,729	30,083	32,919	40,840	42,905	44,859	83,185
Men who have sex with men	56.1	181,468	5,419	13,536	17,811	19,632	23,863	12,879	24,116	40,054
Injecting drug use	23.1	74,937	1,392	3,529	6,905	7,203	9,270	10,367	10,755	21,989
Men who have sex with men and injecting drug use	6.3	20,376	592	1,564	2,063	2,237	2,452	2,593	2,605	4,595
Hemophilia/coagulation disorder	0.9	2,926	75	205	295	286	335	311	306	935
Born in Caribbean/African countries	1.2	3,756	138	261	370	367	414	490	448	808
Heterosexual contact[2]	5.9	19,016	144	650	1,193	1,512	2,252	2,743	3,505	6,589
Sex with injecting drug user	3.4	10,858	106	447	865	1,068	1,499	1,692	1,937	2,943
Transfusion[3]	1.8	5,779	170	611	811	718	788	651	642	1,012
Undetermined[4]	4.8	15,489	130	373	635	964	1,466	1,871	2,482	7,203
Race and Hispanic origin										
White, not Hispanic	100.0	171,149	4,928	12,848	16,862	18,418	22,128	21,971	22,217	39,715
Men who have sex with men	73.2	125,351	4,028	10,002	12,735	13,813	16,649	16,155	15,902	26,421
Injecting drug use	10.0	17,119	252	815	1,471	1,691	2,068	2,329	2,503	5,340
Men who have sex with men and injecting drug use	7.0	11,954	376	1,012	1,195	1,337	1,404	1,485	1,441	2,636
Hemophilia/coagulation disorder	1.4	2,397	64	178	240	238	275	251	239	754
Born in Caribbean/African countries	0.0	13	-	1	1	-	1	4	1	4
Heterosexual contact[2]	3.1	5,231	33	210	372	447	664	740	886	1,764
Sex with injecting drug user	1.5	2,505	18	103	214	260	357	373	403	719
Transfusion[3]	2.3	3,916	132	468	603	528	518	411	399	567
Undetermined[4]	3.0	5,168	43	162	245	364	549	596	846	2,229
Black, not Hispanic	100.0	103,817	1,989	5,209	8,803	9,924	12,807	14,191	15,505	30,218
Men who have sex with men	32.9	34,136	792	2,127	3,079	3,589	4,479	4,620	5,022	8,412
Injecting drug use	39.6	41,137	747	1,882	3,754	4,011	5,150	5,762	5,952	12,010
Men who have sex with men and injecting drug use	5.8	5,971	143	388	617	663	778	787	811	1,377
Hemophilia/coagulation disorder	0.3	275	4	11	28	18	28	35	33	110
Born in Caribbean/African countries	3.6	3,713	138	257	365	362	409	483	442	798
Heterosexual contact[2]	10.0	10,421	83	326	577	802	1,203	1,563	2,031	6,633
Sex with injecting drug user	6.0	6,214	64	254	455	604	852	1,017	1,180	1,639
Transfusion[3]	1.1	1,173	26	91	135	123	164	145	145	290
Undetermined[4]	6.7	6,991	56	127	248	356	596	796	1,069	3,588
Hispanic	100.0	45,199	1,079	2,475	4,144	4,207	5,467	6,262	6,564	12,216
Men who have sex with men	43.5	19,676	552	1,261	1,804	1,984	2,441	2,787	2,837	4,620
Injecting drug use	36.1	16,299	386	823	1,654	1,456	2,009	2,222	2,243	4,512
Men who have sex with men and injecting drug use	5.0	2,264	70	151	242	221	249	302	316	519
Hemophilia/coagulation disorder	0.4	198	7	11	22	21	26	20	27	54
Born in Caribbean/African countries	0.0	20	-	3	2	2	4	2	3	4
Heterosexual contact[2]	7.0	3,162	28	111	231	243	371	418	553	1,100
Sex with injecting drug user	4.5	2,051	24	89	188	191	281	291	343	550

[Continued]

★ 363 ★

AIDS Cases by Type of Transmission

[Continued]

Race/ethnicity and transmission category	Percent distribution All years[1]	Number, by year of report All years[1]	1985	1987	1988	1989	1990	1991	1992	January-September 1993
Transfusion[3]	1.2	536	7	38	55	56	79	73	78	126
Undetermined[4]	6.7	3,044	29	77	134	224	288	438	507	1,281
Sex										
Male	100.0	285,063	7,538	19,047	27,049	29,549	36,300	37,530	38,917	70,396
Men who have sex with men	63.7	181,468	5,419	13,536	17,811	19,632	23,863	23,879	24,116	40,054
Injecting drug use	19.6	55,900	1,108	2,691	5,279	5,429	6,993	7,652	7,972	16,006
Men who have sex with men and injecting drug use	7.1	20,376	592	1,564	2,063	2,237	2,452	2,593	2,605	4,595
Hemophilia/coagulation disorder	1.0	2,855	73	201	291	279	326	302	303	910
Born in Caribbean/African countries	0.9	2,596	107	187	263	237	303	324	279	528
Heterosexual contact[2]	2.2	6,169	28	162	328	507	726	889	1,276	2,175
Sex with injecting drug user	1.2	3,317	25	116	227	367	461	515	650	901
Transfusion[3]	1.2	3,496	111	395	487	435	460	408	381	581
Undetermined[4]	4.3	12,203	100	311	527	793	1,177	1,483	1,985	5,547
Female	100.0	38,684	522	1,682	3,034	3,370	4,540	5,375	5,942	12,789
Injecting drug use	49.2	19,037	284	838	1,626	1,774	2,277	2,715	2,783	5,983
Hemophilia/coagulation disorder	0.2	71	2	4	4	7	9	9	3	25
Born in Caribbean/African countries	3.0	1,160	31	74	107	130	111	166	169	280
Heterosexual contact[2]	33.2	12,847	116	488	865	1,005	1,526	1,854	2,229	4,414
Sex with injecting drug user	19.5	7,541	81	331	638	701	1,038	1,177	1,287	2,042
Transfusion[3]	5.9	2,283	59	216	324	283	328	243	261	431
Undetermined[4]	8.5	3,286	30	62	108	171	289	388	497	1,656

Source: National Center for Health Statistics. *Health, United States, 1993.* Hyattsville, MD: Public Health Service, May 1994, pp. 145-146. Primary source: Centers for Disease Control and Prevention, National Center for Health Statistics. Centers for Disease Control and Prevention, National Center for Infectious Diseases, Division of HIV/AIDS. *Notes:* A dash (-) stands for zero. The AIDS case reporting definitions were expanded in 1985, 1987, and 1993. Data are updated periodically because of reporting delays. Data have been updated through September 30, 1993 for all years and are shown as of December 31, 1993. 1. Includes cases prior to 1985. 2. Includes persons who have had heterosexual contact with persons who have human immunodeficiency virus (HIV) infection or are at risk of HIV infection. 3. Receipt of blood transfusion, blood components, or tissue. 4. Includes persons for whom risk information is incomplete (because of death, refusal to be interviewed, or loss to follow-up), persons still under investigation, men reported to have had heterosexual contact with prostitutes, and interviewed persons for whom no specific risk is identified.

★ 364 ★

AIDS

AIDS Deaths, by Type of Transmission and Race/Ethnicity, 1985-93

Data shown for persons age 13 years and older are based on reporting by State health departments and exclude residents of U.S. territories.

Transmission category and race/ethnicity	All years[1] (percent distribution)	Number, by year of death All years[1]	1985	1987	1988	1989	1990	1991	1992	Jan.-Sept. 1993
All races	100.0	195,226	6,598	15,232	19,480	25,668	28,662	32,224	33,875	16,706
Men who have sex with men	58.9	115,015	4,240	9,164	11,505	15,281	16,893	18,758	18,985	9,583
Injecting drug use	22.1	43,110	1,220	3,189	4,429	5,768	6,472	7,484	7,979	3,467
Men who have sex with men and injecting drug use	6.4	12,442	499	1,139	1,282	1,601	1,725	1,854	1,979	984

[Continued]

★ 364 ★

AIDS Deaths, by Type of Transmission and Race/Ethnicity, 1985-93

[Continued]

Transmission category and race/ethnicity	All years[1] (percent distribution)	Number, by year of death								
		All years[1]	1985	1987	1988	1989	1990	1991	1992	Jan.-Sept. 1993
Hemophilia/coagulation disorder	0.9	1,718	78	160	193	224	254	251	257	149
Born in Caribbean/African countries	1.0	1,953	113	197	193	249	214	239	280	109
Heterosexual contact[2]	4.8	9,405	128	468	741	1,079	1,489	1,796	2,141	1,222
Sex with injecting drug user	3.0	5,911	88	331	522	770	991	1,127	1,233	608
Transfusion[3]	2.2	4,292	196	533	612	620	582	559	511	216
Undetermined[4]	3.7	7,291	124	382	525	846	1,033	1,283	1,743	976
Race and Hispanic origin										
White, not Hispanic	100.0	106,849	3,960	8,677	10,661	14,090	15,768	17,344	17,584	8,874
Men who have sex with men	75.6	80,780	3,128	6,498	8,009	10,755	11,956	13,150	12,952	6,591
Injecting drug use	8.6	9,153	223	654	882	1,225	1,398	1,608	1,811	789
Men who have sex with men and injecting drug use	6.8	7,235	311	689	725	893	985	1,077	1,120	587
Hemophilia/coagulation disorder	1.3	1,434	64	137	170	180	212	211	202	121
Born in Caribbean/African countries	0.0	2	-	-	-	-	-	-	2	-
Heterosexual contact[2]	2.5	2,623	32	128	214	310	417	494	606	329
Sex with injecting drug user	1.2	1,329	12	70	109	178	215	252	307	140
Transfusion[3]	2.9	3,054	153	417	466	428	413	374	308	131
Undetermined[4]	2.4	2,568	49	154	195	299	387	430	583	326
Black, not Hispanic	100.0	59,766	1,724	4,411	5,920	7,768	8,709	10,002	11,235	5,495
Men who have sex with men	34.9	20,835	659	1,639	2,184	2,778	2,972	3,342	3,752	1,810
Injecting drug use	40.3	24,084	674	1,743	2,447	3,202	3,620	4,198	4,444	2,050
Men who have sex with men and injecting drug use	6.2	3,719	129	319	396	496	552	559	620	286
Hemophilia/coagulation disorder	0.2	147	7	14	11	21	19	23	31	17
Born in Caribbean/African countries	3.2	1,937	112	196	193	244	214	236	275	109
Heterosexual contact[2]	8.6	5,142	68	270	386	572	813	989	1,182	704
Sex with injecting drug user	5.7	3,414	53	207	294	433	578	666	697	369
Transfusion[3]	1.3	770	26	76	95	124	111	101	128	53
Undetermined[4]	5.2	3,132	49	154	208	331	408	554	803	466
Hispanic	100.0	26,676	874	2,026	2,719	3,548	3,916	4,502	4,696	2,125
Men who have sex with men	45.3	12,090	428	936	1,183	1,578	1,780	2,019	2,038	1,042
Injecting drug use	36.3	9,683	319	786	1,083	1,310	1,430	1,637	1,690	606
Men who have sex with men and injecting drug use	5.2	1,393	58	126	154	200	173	198	223	98
Hemophilia/coagulation disorder	0.4	116	5	7	10	19	19	15	22	8
Born in Caribbean/African countries	0.0	11	1	1	-	3	-	3	2	-
Heterosexual contact[2]	5.8	1,559	28	69	136	184	249	291	338	177
Sex with injecting drug user	4.3	1,136	23	54	116	152	191	201	225	97
Transfusion[3]	1.4	363	11	29	41	53	48	61	62	25
Undetermined[4]	5.5	1,461	24	72	112	201	217	278	321	169
Sex										
Male	100.0	174,556	6,138	13,812	17,482	23,097	25,579	28,540	29,778	14,662
Men who have sex with men	65.9	115,015	4,240	9,164	11,505	15,281	16,893	18,758	18,985	9,583
Injecting drug use	18.7	32,717	977	2,462	3,375	4,451	4,916	5,614	5,961	2,548
Men who have sex with men and injecting drug use	7.1	12,442	499	1,139	1,282	1,601	1,725	1,854	1,979	984
Hemophilia/coagulation disorder	1.0	1,675	72	158	188	220	248	247	251	143

[Continued]

★ 364 ★

AIDS Deaths, by Type of Transmission and Race/Ethnicity, 1985-93

[Continued]

Transmission category and race/ethnicity	All years[1] (percent distribution)	Number, by year of death								
		All years[1]	1985	1987	1988	1989	1990	1991	1992	Jan.-Sept. 1993
Born in Caribbean/African countries	0.8	1,358	90	142	131	162	150	155	184	74
Heterosexual contact[2]	1.7	2,898	30	122	192	316	453	552	730	442
Sex with injecting drug user	1.0	1,705	26	83	139	206	290	332	374	211
Transfusion[3]	1.5	2,631	127	318	372	381	364	336	305	119
Undetermined[4]	3.3	5,820	103	307	437	685	830	1,024	1,383	769
Female	100.0	20,670	460	1,420	1,998	2,571	3,083	3,684	4,097	2,044
Injecting drug use	50.3	10,393	243	727	1,054	1,317	1,556	1,870	2,018	919
Hemophilia/coagulation disorder	0.2	43	6	2	5	4	6	4	6	6
Born in Caribbean/African countries	2.9	595	23	55	62	87	64	84	96	35
Heterosexual contact[2]	31.5	6,507	98	346	549	763	1,036	1,244	1,411	780
Sex with injecting drug user	20.3	4,206	62	248	383	564	701	795	859	397
Transfusion[3]	8.0	1,661	69	215	240	239	218	223	206	97
Undetermined[4]	7.1	1,471	21	75	88	161	203	259	360	207

Source: National Center for Health Statistics. *Health, United States, 1993.* Hyattsville, MD: Public Health Service, May 1994, p. 147. Primary source: U.S. Centers for Disease Control and Prevention, National Center for Infectious Diseases, Division of HIV/AIDS. *Notes:* A dash (-) stands for zero. The AIDS case reporting definitions were expanded in 1985, 1987, and 1993. Data are updated periodically because of reporting delays and have been updated for all years through September 30, 1993. Data as of December 31, 1993, are available in the Centers for Disease Control and Prevention, HIV/AIDS Surveillance Report Year-End edition, February, 1994. 1. Includes cases prior to 1985. 2. Includes persons who have had heterosexual contact with a person with human immunodeficiency virus (HIV) infection or at risk of HIV infection. 3. Receipt of blood transfusion, blood components, or tissue. 4. Includes persons for whom risk information is incomplete (because of death, refusal to be interviewed, or loss to followup), persons still under investigation, men reported only to have had heterosexual contact with prostitutes, and interviewed persons for whom no specific risk is identified.

★ 365 ★

AIDS

AIDS Education of 8th and 10th Graders

Percentages reflect responses to the question "Since the beginning of the 7th grade, have you received instruction in school on AIDS?" Data are based on a 1988 national study of 3,617 eighth and tenth graders.

Response	Hispanic	White	Black	Asian/Pacific Islander	American Indian/Alaskan	Other
Yes	39.4	33.3	40.2	30.2	50.1	38.4
No	32.1	48.7	41.9	39.5	24.8	38.8
Don't remember	28.6	18.0	18.0	30.3	25.1	22.8

Source: Anderson, D. Michael and Christenson, Gregory M. "Ethnic breakdown of AIDS related knowledge and attitudes from the National Adolescent Student Health Survey." *Journal of Health Education* vol. 22, no. 1, (January/February 1991), p. 31. Primary source: *The National Adolescent Student Health Survey: A Report on the Health of America's Youth, 1989.* Third Party Publishing Co., Oakland, CA; American School Health Association, Association for the Advancement of Health Education, Society for Public Health Education, Inc. (Subset of original data).

★366★

AIDS

AIDS Prevention Awareness of 8th and 10th Graders

Percentages reflect results of a 1988 national survey of 3,617 eighth and tenth graders.

Questions/responses	Hispanic	White	Black	Asian/Pacific Islander	American Indian/Alaskan	Other
Does this behavior make infection LESS likely?						
Using condoms (rubbers) during sex:						
Yes[1]	75.0	88.3	84.3	76.4	75.4	74.8
No	14.8	5.6	11.6	14.7	6.4	12.0
Don't know	10.2	6.1	4.0	8.9	18.2	13.3
Not having sex:						
Yes[1]	62.4	79.7	66.5	66.8	65.2	75.4
No	28.2	15.0	26.1	24.3	17.6	19.0
Don't know	9.4	5.4	7.4	8.9	17.3	5.6
Going to the bathroom after having sex:						
Yes	9.7	6.4	16.7	11.7	18.9	18.4
No[1]	57.3	61.8	55.1	52.3	42.9	54.5
Don't know	33.1	31.8	28.3	36.1	38.4	27.0
Washing after having sex:						
Yes	33.5	20.0	41.0	23.1	40.0	20.5
No[1]	36.4	52.5	41.0	49.5	33.1	46.1
Don't know	30.1	27.5	18.1	27.4	26.9	33.4

Source: Anderson, D. Michael and Christenson, Gregory M. "Ethnic breakdown of AIDS related knowledge and attitudes from the National Adolescent Student Health Survey." *Journal of Health Education* vol. 22, no. 1, (January/February 1991), p. 33. Primary source: *The National Adolescent Student Health Survey: A Report on the Health of America's Youth, 1989.* Third Party Publishing Co., Oakland, CA; American School Health Association, Association for the Advancement of Health Education, Society for Public Health Education, Inc. (Subset of original data.) *Note:* 1. Indicates a correct response.

★367★

AIDS

AIDS Risk Awareness of 8th and 10th Graders

Percentages reflect results of a 1988 national survey of 3,617 eighth and tenth graders.

Questions/responses	Hispanic	White	Black	Asian/Pacific Islander	American Indian/Alaskan	Other
Does this behavior make infection MORE likely?						
Having sexual intercourse with someone who has AIDS:						
Yes[1]	87.8	96.8	90.3	86.9	92.2	89.4
No	10.4	2.9	7.2	11.3	3.5	8.6
Don't know	1.8	0.3	2.5	1.8	4.3	2.0

[Continued]

★ 367 ★

AIDS Risk Awareness of 8th and 10th Graders

[Continued]

Questions/responses	Hispanic	White	Black	Asian/Pacific Islander	American Indian/Alaskan	Other
Being in the same classroom with someone who has AIDS:						
Yes	5.0	4.3	5.9	3.8	0.0	5.1
No[1]	75.9	88.2	79.6	84.1	84.2	77.9
Don't know	19.1	7.6	14.5	12.1	15.8	17.0
Having more than one sex partner:						
Yes[1]	75.8	85.0	74.1	75.0	85.3	82.9
No	11.4	7.2	15.4	17.3	10.4	8.1
Don't know	12.9	7.7	10.6	7.7	4.3	9.1
Having sex with someone who has had several sex partners:						
Yes[1]	75.8	86.7	74.4	73.7	82.0	81.7
No	10.4	5.0	12.8	14.9	10.8	7.2
Don't know	13.8	8.3	12.9	11.5	7.2	11.1
A male having sex with another male:						
Yes[1]	73.7	82.4	79.7	74.6	85.9	75.1
No	12.2	7.6	11.4	15.5	8.0	10.3
Don't know	14.1	10.0	8.8	9.9	6.1	14.6
Sharing drug needles:						
Yes[1]	85.9	93.8	86.8	83.3	79.3	80.2
No	10.7	3.3	8.4	14.0	6.4	11.5
Don't know	3.4	2.9	4.8	2.7	14.2	8.3
Donating blood:						
Yes	54.7	43.0	55.0	45.1	49.7	63.9
No[1]	31.3	43.3	27.4	44.8	19.0	28.4
Don't know	14.0	13.7	17.6	10.1	31.3	7.8

Source: Anderson, D. Michael and Christenson, Gregory M. "Ethnic breakdown of AIDS related knowledge and attitudes from the National Adolescent Student Health Survey." *Journal of Health Education* vol. 22, no. 1, (January/February 1991), p. 32. Primary source: *The National Adolescent Student Health Survey: A Report on the Health of America's Youth, 1989.* Third Party Publishing Co., Oakland, CA; American School Health Association, Association for the Advancement of Health Education, Society for Public Health Education, Inc. (Subset of original data.) *Note:* 1. Indicates a correct response.

★ 368 ★

AIDS

AIDS and HIV Cases Among Hispanics, by Sex

Percent distribution of these cases is shown for each patient group, by category of transmission. Figures are based on totals of 361,164 AIDS cases and 55,649 HIV infections reported through December 31, 1993. While AIDS data were reported by all States and the District of Columbia, HIV data were reported only by 26 States legally required to release such figures. Of these States , only four - Arizona, Colorado, Nevada, and New Jersey - have large Hispanic populations; none of the States which comprise over 75% of the U.S. Hispanic population - California, Texas, New York, Florida, Illinois, and New Mexico - report HIV infections.

Sex of patient and transmission method	Percent of cases	
	AIDS	HIV
Male		
Male-male sexual contact	43.0	30.0
IV drug use	38.0	35.0
Heterosexual contact	5.0	7.0
Male-male IV drug use	6.0	5.0
Blood products	1.0	1.0
Hemophilia	0.0	0.0
Risk not identified	8.0	21.0
Female		
Heterosexual contact	44.0	43.0
IV drug use	44.0	28.0
Blood products	3.0	5.0
Hemophilia	0.0	0.0
Risk not identified	9.0	26.0

Source: de Palomo, Frank B. National Council of La Raza. "CDC HIV/AIDS Surveillance Report Adds HIV Cases: Report Lacks Representative Hispanic Data." *NCLR AIDS/SIDA Network News* 5(3): (Fall 1994). Centers for Disease Control. *HIV/AIDS Surveillance Report*, Year-End Edition, vol. 5, no. 4, August 1994.

★ 369 ★

AIDS

AIDS, Basic Knowledge of 8th and 10th Graders

Percentages reflect results of a 1988 national survey of 3,617 eighth and tenth graders.

Questions/responses	Hispanic	White	Black	Asian/Pacific Islander	American Indian/Alaskan	Other
There is no known cure for AIDS:						
True[1]	82.5	88.9	84.0	82.3	73.7	75.8
False	9.0	4.1	6.7	8.4	19.8	7.8
Don't know	8.6	7.0	9.3	9.3	6.6	16.5

[Continued]

★ 369 ★

AIDS, Basic Knowledge of 8th and 10th Graders

[Continued]

Questions/responses	Hispanic	White	Black	Asian/Pacific Islander	American Indian/Alaskan	Other
A test to determine whether a person has the AIDS virus is now available:						
True[1]	76.2	85.0	73.3	84.4	82.5	78.3
False	7.0	5.1	10.7	2.2	9.6	5.6
Don't know	16.8	9.9	16.1	13.4	8.0	16.1
A vaccine that protects people from getting the AIDS virus is available:						
True	14.2	8.5	17.6	8.6	8.8	13.0
False[1]	51.3	66.9	47.0	58.1	56.2	56.2
Don't know	34.5	24.7	35.5	33.4	35.0	30.8
A pregnant woman who has the AIDS virus can give AIDS to her baby:						
True[1]	85.0	80.8	84.3	79.9	62.1	71.7
False	2.5	1.4	2.4	4.4	0.0	1.4
Don't know	12.5	17.8	13.3	15.8	37.9	26.9

Source: Anderson, D. Michael and Christenson, Gregory M. "Ethnic breakdown of AIDS related knowledge and attitudes from the National Adolescent Student Health Survey." *Journal of Health Education* vol. 22, no. 1, (January/February 1991), p. 33. Primary source: *The National Adolescent Student Health Survey: A Report on the Health of America's Youth, 1989.* Third Party Publishing Co., Oakland, CA; American School Health Association, Association for the Advancement of Health Education, Society for Public Health Education, Inc. (Subset of original data.) *Note:* 1. Indicates a correct response.

★ 370 ★

AIDS

Condom Use

Data represent percentage of students who said they had sexual intercourse during the three months prior to the survey and reported using a condom.

Race/ethnicity	Percentage
Hispanic	38.4
White	45.9
Black	47.1

Source: Painter, Kim. "Lifestyles remain a major barrier to condom use." *USA TODAY* (7 July 1992), p. 4D. Primary source: U.S. Youth Risk Behavior Survey, 1990.

★ 371 ★

AIDS

Heterosexual HIV Transmission, by Race/Ethnicity, 1993

Data show rate of HIV (human immunodeficiency virus) transmissions among heterosexuals in the United States in 1993, by race/ethnicity. Figures are based on a total of 9,288 cases reported, of which 6,056 were among women and 3,232 were among men. A disproportionate number of these cases occurred among the black and Hispanic populations.

Race/ethnicity	Rate per 100,000 population
Black, not Hispanic	20.0
Hispanic	10.0
American Indian/Alaskan Native	2.0
Asian/Pacific Islander	1.0
White, not Hispanic	1.0

Source: "Heterosexually Acquired AIDS - United States, 1993." *JAMA*, vol. 271, no. 13 (6 April 1994), p. 975. Primary source: Centers for Disease Control and Prevention. *Morbidity and Mortality Weekly Report* 1994;43:155-160.

Abortion

★ 372 ★

Teen Abortion Distribution, by Race/Ethnicity, 1991

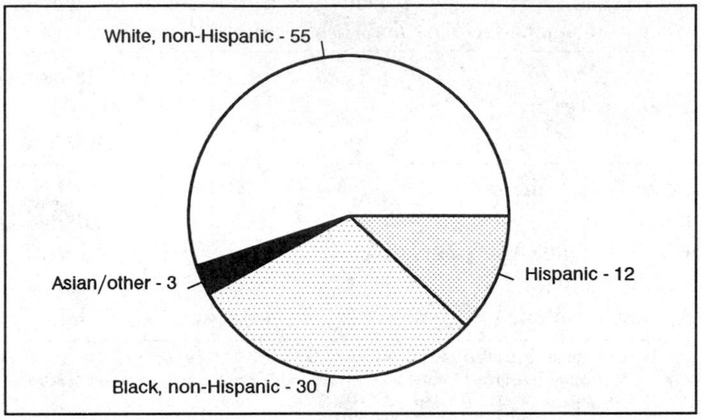

Percentages are shown for states without parental consent laws.

Race/ethnicity	Abortion distribution
White, non-Hispanic	55
Black, non-Hispanic	30
Hispanic	12
Asian/other	3

Source: Hall, Mimi. "Study zeros in on pregnant teens, parents: both sides say new report is a validation of positions." *USA TODAY* (20 October 1992), p. 10A. Primary source: Survey by the Alan Guttmacher Institute, 1991.

Births and Deaths

★ 373 ★

Death Rates for Selected Years, by Race/Ethnicity, Age, and Sex

Race and age	Both sexes			Male			Female		
	1980-82	1985-87	1989-91	1980-82	1985-87	1989-91	1980-82	1985-87	1989-91
	Deaths per 100,000 resident population								
All ages, age adjusted[1]	568.6	544.2	519.9	753.7	715.3	678.7	420.9	407.5	390.9
All ages, crude	863.3	876.7	864.3	955.3	944.1	918.0	776.4	812.7	813.2
1-14 years	38.1	33.9	31.4	44.5	39.8	36.2	31.4	27.7	26.3
15-24 years	107.7	97.8	99.1	159.9	143.4	146.1	54.5	50.9	50.0

[Continued]

★ 373 ★

Death Rates for Selected Years, by Race/Ethnicity, Age, and Sex

[Continued]

Race and age	Both sexes			Male			Female		
	1980-82	1985-87	1989-91	1980-82	1985-87	1989-91	1980-82	1985-87	1989-91
25-44 years	166.4	166.4	178.3	228.5	232.1	252.9	105.7	101.7	104.6
45-64 years	940.2	884.9	805.2	1,243.5	1,149.5	1,035.2	664.8	642.4	592.3
65-74 years	2,929.6	2,828.1	2,650.8	4,005.3	3,785.9	3,492.0	2,106.0	2,087.2	1,994.1
75-84 years	6,482.6	6,308.9	5,979.2	8,567.3	8,364.9	7,821.3	5,254.7	5,097.5	4,873.7
85 years and over	15,404.8	15,618.5	15,231.2	18,262.5	18,386.5	17,898.3	14,189.5	14,520.4	14,198.6
White									
All ages, age adjusted[1]	544.6	519.5	492.5	724.5	684.1	642.7	401.4	388.0	370.3
All ages, crude	881.4	900.2	888.5	966.0	958.3	930.5	800.9	844.7	848.2
1-14 years	35.6	31.2	28.4	41.7	36.8	32.8	29.2	25.3	23.8
15-24 years	104.9	93.9	89.3	155.7	137.2	129.5	52.7	49.0	47.0
25-44 years	146.0	145.5	153.8	199.6	202.6	218.7	92.5	88.1	88.4
45-64 years	886.8	833.7	752.9	1,174.9	1,083.7	966.5	621.6	601.2	551.6
65-74 years	2,864.1	2,755.6	2,574.6	3,939.3	3,698.7	3,397.5	2,038.5	2,020.3	1,925.7
75-84 years	6,464.5	6,267.4	5,931.1	8,594.6	8,341.9	7,775.7	5,222.1	5,051.3	4,824.3
85 years and over	15,658.7	15,814.9	15,367.5	18,609.3	18,696.9	18,113.3	14,423.8	14,692.4	14,321.7
Black									
All ages, age adjusted[1]	808.5	795.6	790.4	1,070.2	1,059.8	1,062.0	604.9	593.8	582.4
All ages, crude	845.3	863.2	873.2	995.5	999.5	1,009.4	710.8	740.5	750.8
1-14 years	53.0	49.2	48.3	61.7	57.3	56.1	44.2	40.9	40.3
15-24 years	127.6	125.7	161.9	191.7	188.9	254.9	66.1	64.1	69.8
25-44 years	334.1	337.4	373.8	485.3	491.5	547.1	204.5	203.4	221.5
45-64 years	1,523.1	1,446.6	1,374.9	2,045.6	1,931.0	1,847.7	1,099.7	1,055.4	994.2
65-74 years	3,811.2	3,854.5	3,734.7	5,034.8	5,149.8	4,962.4	2,928.2	2,947.2	2,880.2
75-84 years	7,080.8	7,193.0	6,962.0	8,862.7	9,275.5	9,087.6	5,968.2	5,968.5	5,767.6
85 years and over	12,917.1	13,956.3	14,336.4	15,240.0	16,200.3	16,740.5	11,771.5	12,934.2	13,312.5
Asian or Pacific Islander[2]									
All ages, age adjusted[1]	298.0	300.2	289.7	391.6	389.3	369.0	214.8	223.1	222.2
All ages, crude	276.9	279.4	279.0	345.6	339.2	329.7	211.6	222.2	230.5
1-14 years	25.5	24.6	22.7	28.3	28.0	25.3	22.6	21.1	20.0
15-24 years	52.0	51.3	50.1	71.4	71.4	70.8	31.6	29.5	28.1
25-44 years	75.7	73.8	76.1	92.9	95.8	100.2	60.2	53.7	53.9
45-64 years	410.5	404.2	380.4	537.3	511.6	468.1	302.5	310.9	303.6
65-74 years	1,516.0	1,504.9	1,458.7	2,087.4	2,036.5	1,952.2	969.9	1,063.5	1,064.7
75-84 years	3,832.7	4,051.2	3,895.6	5,176.0	5,439.1	5,007.3	2,617.7	2,784.3	2,923.4
85 years and over	9,617.6	10,902.5	11,058.3	12,305.2	12,277.8	12,496.9	7,975.6	9,944.1	10,039.5
American Indian or Alaskan Native[3]									
All ages, age adjusted[1]	521.5	459.1	452.6	676.4	590.8	582.6	383.8	344.5	340.6
All ages, crude	453.8	412.1	412.5	553.4	490.1	484.9	356.5	335.7	341.3
1-14 years	48.0	45.2	37.3	57.0	56.3	45.1	38.6	33.7	29.2
15-24 years	186.7	149.9	142.0	276.8	222.2	208.3	94.2	73.3	71.1
25-44 years	289.6	226.5	214.3	400.1	317.6	304.1	84.1	139.6	127.4
45-64 years	846.7	733.5	712.8	1,091.7	911.3	891.5	621.1	569.2	547.8
65-74 years	2,148.9	2,033.4	2,083.4	2,761.2	2,579.8	2,593.2	1,653.7	1,597.7	1,676.5
75-84 years	4,114.0	4,020.8	4,121.2	5,128.3	5,224.7	5,326.9	3,370.9	3,225.9	3,338.2
85 years and over	9,225.3	8,714.0	9,122.4	11,048.4	9,945.4	11,237.3	8,079.3	7,964.7	7,964.5
Hispanic[4]									
All ages, age adjusted[1]	-	-	395.8	-	-	521.3	-	-	284.5

[Continued]

★ 373 ★

Death Rates for Selected Years, by Race/Ethnicity, Age, and Sex

[Continued]

Race and age	Both sexes			Male			Female		
	1980-82	1985-87	1989-91	1980-82	1985-87	1989-91	1980-82	1985-87	1989-91
All ages, crude	-	-	344.2	-	-	401.4	-	-	284.1
1-14 years	-	-	30.2	-	-	34.7	-	-	25.5
15-24 years	-	-	103.3	-	-	156.5	-	-	40.9
25-44 years	-	-	162.2	-	-	242.7	-	-	74.2
45-64 years	-	-	566.8	-	-	746.1	-	-	400.4
65-74 years	-	-	1,874.8	-	-	2,413.5	-	-	1,447.0
75-84 years	-	-	4,282.5	-	-	5,541.8	-	-	3,471.2
85 years and over	-	-	11,021.7	-	-	12,514.5	-	-	10,182.5

Source: National Center for Health Statistics. *Health, United States, 1993.* Hyattsville, MD: Public Health Service, May 1994, p. 101. Primary source: Centers for Disease Control and Prevention, National Center for Health Statistics. Data computed by the Division of Analysis from data compiled by the Division of Vital Statistics and from national population estimates for race groups from the Census Bureau and State or U.S. aggregate population estimates for Hispanics provided by the Census Bureau. *Notes:* The race groups, white, black, Asian or Pacific Islander, and American Indian or Alaskan Native, include persons of Hispanic and non-Hispanic origin. Conversely, persons of Hispanic origin may be of any race. Consistency of race and Hispanic origin identification between the death certificate (source of data for numerator of death rates) and data from the Census Bureau (denominator) is high for individual white, black, and Hispanic persons; however, persons identified as American Indian or Asian in data from the Census Bureau are sometimes misreported as white on the death certificate, causing death rates to be underestimated by 20-30 percent for American Indians and by about 12 percent for Asians. (Sorlie, P.D., Rogot, E., and Johnson, N.J.: Validity of demographic characteristics on the death certificate, *Epidemiology*, 3(2):181-184, 1992.) A dash (-) stands for data not available. 1. Age adjusted by the direct method based on 11 age groups. 2. Interpretation of trends should take into account that the Asian population in the United States more than doubled between 1980 and 1990, primarily due to immigration. 3. Interpretation of trends should take into account that population estimates for American Indians increased by 45 percent between 1980 and 1990, partly due to better enumeration techniques in the 1990 Decennial Census and to the increased tendency for people to identify themselves as American Indian in 1990. 4. Excludes data from States lacking an Hispanic-origin item on their death certificates and from New York. It is estimated that death rates for persons 25-44 years of age are underestimated by about 12-13 percent; other death rates are generally over- or understated by about 5 percent or less due to excluding New York data.

★ 374 ★

Births and Deaths

Deaths Among AIDS Cases

Deaths among AIDS (acquired immunodeficiency syndrome) cases in the United States, but not those of including residents of U.S. territories, are shown for selected years, by age at death, sex, race, and Hispanic origin. Data are based on reporting by State health departments.

Age at death, sex, race, and Hispanic origin	Percent distribution All years[1]	Number, by year of death								
		All years[1]	1985	1987	1988	1989	1990	1991	1992	January-September 1993
All races	NA	197,727	6,704	15,504	19,773	26,005	29,022	32,573	34,228	16,885
Male										
All males, 13 years and over at diagnosis	100.0	174,556	6,138	13,812	17,482	23,097	25,579	28,540	29,778	14,662
White, not Hispanic	58.1	101,443	3,814	8,232	10,106	13,424	14,964	16,424	16,596	8,345
Black, not Hispanic	27.5	48,058	1,497	3,629	4,823	6,314	6,943	7,906	8,839	4,315
Hispanic	13.4	23,309	790	1,841	2,391	3,128	3,428	3,870	4,017	1,810
American Indian[2]	0.2	314	4	22	23	31	39	71	55	53
Asian or Pacific Islander[3]	0.7	1,152	29	76	110	156	169	214	208	117
Age at death										
13-19 years	0.2	389	21	40	37	55	49	58	48	26
20 to 29 years	15.0	26,123	1,129	2,502	3,005	3,635	3,696	3,763	3,726	1,821
30 to 39 years	45.2	78,907	2,810	6,313	7,871	10,498	11,605	12,839	13,262	6,572
40 to 49 years	26.9	47,016	1,386	3,190	4,252	5,970	7,049	8,253	8,958	4,369

[Continued]

★ 374 ★

Deaths Among AIDS Cases

[Continued]

Age at death, sex, race, and Hispanic origin	Percent distribution All years[1]	Number, by year of death								
		All years[1]	1985	1987	1988	1989	1990	1991	1992	January-September 1993
50 to 59 years	9.1	15,825	584	1,201	1,615	2,124	2,296	2,550	2,730	1,371
60 years and over	3.6	6,296	208	566	702	815	884	1,077	1,054	503
Female										
All females, 13 years and over at diagnosis	100.0	20,670	460	1,420	1,998	2,571	3,083	3,684	4,097	2,044
White, not Hispanic	26.2	5,406	146	445	555	666	804	920	988	529
Black, not Hispanic	56.6	11,708	227	782	1,097	1,454	1,766	2,096	2,396	1,180
Hispanic	16.3	3,367	84	185	328	420	488	632	679	315
American Indian[2]	0.2	38	3	2	1	6	5	11	5	3
Asian or Pacific Islander[3]	0.6	115	-	6	16	19	12	21	19	13
Age at death										
13-19 years	0.7	137	5	10	12	13	24	24	20	14
20-29 years	21.4	4,424	128	356	453	551	650	766	750	382
30-39 yeas	46.5	9,602	210	637	954	1,276	1,470	1,642	1,902	920
40-49 years	19.0	3,929	54	194	300	431	571	791	972	471
50-59 years	6.6	1,357	22	92	118	153	193	284	275	157
60 years and over	5.9	1,221	41	131	161	147	175	177	178	100
Children										
All children under 13 years at diagnosis	100.0	2,501	106	272	293	337	360	349	353	179
White, not Hispanic	22.7	568	28	69	68	91	63	77	72	41
Black, not Hispanic	55.6	1,390	60	132	161	168	221	198	210	101
Hispanic	20.6	514	16	68	61	74	72	69	69	33
American Indian[2]	0.4	10	-	2	-	2	1	4	-	1
Asian or Pacific Islander[3]	0.6	16	2	1	3	1	2	1	1	3
Age at death										
Under 1 year	29.6	741	34	84	93	113	109	84	90	25
1 year and over	70.4	1,760	72	188	200	224	251	265	263	154

Source: National Center for Health Statistics. *Health, United States, 1993.* Hyattsville, MD: Public Health Service, May 1994, p. 144. Primary source: Centers for Disease Control and Prevention, National Center for Infectious Diseases, Division of HIV/AIDS. *Notes:* NA stands for not applicable. A dash (-) stands for data not available. The AIDS case reporting definitions were expanded in 1985, 1987, and 1993. Data are updated periodically because of reporting delays and have been updated through September, 1993 for all years. 1. Includes cases prior to 1985. 2. Includes Aleut and Eskimo. 3. Includes Chinese, Japanese, Filipino, Hawaiian and part Hawaiian, and other Asian or Pacific Islander.

★ 375 ★

Births and Deaths

Infant, Neonatal, and Postneonatal Mortality Rates

Infant, neonatal, and postneonatal deaths and mortality rates are shown for selected birth cohorts, by race and Hispanic origin of mother.

Race and Hispanic origin of mother	Birth cohort						
	1960[1]	1983	1984	1985	1986	1987	1985-87
	Infant deaths per 1,000 live births						
All mothers	25.1	10.9	10.4	10.4	10.1	9.8	10.1
White	22.2	9.3	8.9	8.9	8.5	8.2	8.5
Black	42.1	19.2	18.2	18.6	18.2	17.8	18.2
American Indian or Alaskan Native	-	15.2	13.4	13.1	13.9	18.0	13.3
Asian or Pacific Islander	-	8.3	8.9	7.8	7.8	7.3	7.6
Chinese	-	9.5	7.2	5.8	5.9	6.2	6.0
Japanese	-	[5]	[5]	6.0[6]	7.2[6]	6.6[6]	6.6
Filipino	-	8.4	8.5	7.7	7.2	6.6	7.2
Other Asian or Pacific Islander[2]	-	8.3	937	8.6	8.6	7.9	8.3
Hispanic origin[3,4]	-	9.5	9.3	8.8	8.4	8.2	8.5
Mexican American	-	9.1	8.9	8.5	7.9	8.0	8.1
Puerto Rican	-	12.9	12.9	11.1	11.7	9.9	10.9
Cuban	-	7.5[6]	8.1[6]	8.5	7.5[6]	7.1	7.7
Central and South American	-	8.5	8.3	8.0	7.8	7.8	7.8
Other and unknown Hispanic	-	10.6	9.6	9.5	9.2	8.7	9.1
Non-Hispanic white[4]	-	9.2	8.7	8.7	8.4	8.1	8.4
Non-Hispanic black[4]	-	19.1	18.1	18.3	18.0	17.4	17.9
	Neonatal deaths per 1,000 live births						
All mothers	18.4	7.1	6.8	6.8	6.5	6.2	6.6
White	16.9	6.1	5.8	5.8	5.5	5.2	5.5
Black	27.3	12.5	11.9	12.3	11.9	11.8	12.0
American Indian or Alaskan Native	-	7.5	6.4	6.1	6.1	6.2	6.1
Asian or Pacific Islander	-	5.2	5.7	4.8	4.8	4.5	4.7
Chinese	-	5.5	4.4	3.3	3.1	3.7	3.4
Japanese	-	[5]	[5]	3.1[6]	4.7[6]	4.0[6]	3.9
Filipino	-	5.6	5.3	5.1	4.9	4.1	4.7
Other Asian or Pacific Islander[2]	-	5.2	6.5	5.4	5.3	4.9	5.2
Hispanic origin[3,4]	-	6.2	6.2	5.7	5.5	5.3	5.5
Mexican American	-	5.9	5.8	5.4	5.1	5.1	5.2
Puerto Rican	-	8.7	8.6	7.6	7.6	6.7	7.3
Cuban	-	5.0[6]	6.4[6]	6.2	5.1[6]	5.3	5.5
Central and South American	-	5.8	5.9	5.6	5.2	5.0	5.2
Other and unknown Hispanic	-	6.4	6.5	5.6	6.0	5.6	5.7
Non-Hispanic white[4]	-	6.0	5.7	5.7	5.4	5.0	5.4
Non-Hispanic black[4]	-	12.1	11.5	11.9	11.5	11.3	11.6

[Continued]

★375★

Infant, Neonatal, and Postneonatal Mortality Rates

[Continued]

Race and Hispanic origin of mother	Birth cohort						
	1960[1]	1983	1984	1985	1986	1987	1985-87
	Postneonatal deaths per 1,000 live births						
All mothers	6.7	3.8	3.6	3.6	3.6	3.5	3.6
White	5.3	3.2	3.1	3.1	3.0	3.0	3.0
Black	14.8	6.7	6.3	6.3	6.3	6.1	6.2
American Indian or Alaskan Native	-	7.7	7.0	7.0	7.8	6.8	7.2
Asian or Pacific Islander	-	3.1	3.1	2.9	3.0	2.8	2.9
Chinese	-	[5]	[5]	2.5[6]	2.8[6]	2.5[6]	2.6
Japanese	-	[5]	[5]	[5]	2.5[6]	[5]	2.7
Filipino	-	2.8[6]	3.2[6]	2.7[6]	2.3	2.5	2.5
Other Asian or Pacific Islander[2]	-	3.1	3.2	3.1	3.3	3.0	3.2
Hispanic origin[3,4]	-	3.3	3.1	3.2	2.9	2.9	3.0
Mexican American	-	3.2	3.2	3.2	2.8	2.9	2.9
Puerto Rican	-	4.2	4.3	3.5	4.2	3.2	3.6
Cuban	-	[5]	1.7[6]	[5]	2.4[6]	[5]	2.2
Central and South American	-	2.6	2.4	2.4	2.6	2.8	2.6
Other and unknown Hispanic	-	4.2	3.1	3.9	3.2	3.2	3.4
Non-Hispanic white[4]	-	3.2	3.0	3.0	3.0	3.0	3.0
Non-Hispanic black[4]	-	7.0	6.6	6.4	6.5	6.2	6.3

Source: National Center for Health Statistics. *Health, United States, 1993.* Hyattsville, MD: Public Health Service, May 1994, p. 80. Primary source: Centers for Disease Control and Prevention, National Center for Health Statistics. Data computed by the Division of Analysis from data compiled by the Division of Vital Statistics for the National Linked Files of Live Births and Infant Deaths. *Notes:* A dash (-) stands for data not available. 1. Data are shown by race of child in 1960. 2. Includes Hawaiians and part Hawaiians. 3. Includes mothers of all races. 4. Data shown only for States with an Hispanic-origin item on their birth certificates. In 1983-87, 23 States and the District of Columbia included this item. 5. Infant and neonatal mortality rates for groups with fewer than 7,500 births are considered highly unreliable and are not shown. Postneonatal mortality rates for groups with fewer than 15,000 births are considered highly unreliable and are not shown. 6. Infant and neonatal mortality rates for groups with fewer than 10,000 births are considered unreliable. Postneonatal mortality rates for groups with fewer than 20,000 births are considered unreliable.

★376★

Births and Deaths

Live Births per Year, by Race and Hispanic Origin of Mother

Live births in selected years are shown by race and Hispanic origin of the mother. Data are based on the National Vital Statistics System of the Centers for Disease Control and Prevention.

Race and Hispanic origin of mother	Total number of live births								
	1970	1975	1980	1985	1987	1988	1989	1990	1991
All races	3,731,386	3,144,198	3,612,258	3,760,561	3,809,394	3,909,510	4,040,958	4,158,212	4,110,907
White	3,109,956	2,576,818	2,936,351	3,037,913	3,043,828	3,102,083	3,192,355	3,290,273	3,241,273
Black	561,992	496,829	568,080	581,824	611,173	638,562	673,124	684,336	682,602
American Indian or Alaskan Native	22,264	22,690	29,389	34,037	35,322	37,088	39,478	39,051	38,841
Asian or Pacific Islander	-	-	74,355	104,606	116,560	129,035	133,075	141,635	145,372
Chinese	7,044	7,778	11,671	16,405	17,818	21,322	20,982	22,737	22,498
Japanese	7,744	6,725	7,482	8,035	8,054	8,658	6,689	8,674	8,500

[Continued]

★ 376 ★

Live Births per Year, by Race and Hispanic Origin of Mother

[Continued]

Race and Hispanic origin of mother	Total number of live births								
	1970	1975	1980	1985	1987	1988	1989	1990	1991
Filipino	8,066	10,359	13,968	20,058	22,134	23,207	24,585	25,770	26,227
Other Asian or Pacific Islander[1]	-	-	41,234	60,108	68,554	75,848	78,819	84,454	88,147
Hispanic origin (selected States)[2,3]	-	-	307,163	372,814	406,153	449,604	532,249	595,073	632,085
Mexican American	-	-	215,439	242,976	251,189	271,170	327,233	385,640	411,233
Puerto Rican	-	-	33,671	35,147	38,139	46,232	56,229	58,807	59,833
Cuban	-	-	7,163	10,024	9,987	10,189	10,842	11,311	11,058
Central and South American	-	-	21,268	40,985	50,350	57,610	72,443	83,008	86,908
Other and unknown Hispanic	-	-	29,622	43,682	56,488	64,403	65,502	56,307	54,053
Non-Hispanic white (selected States)[2]	-	-	1,245,221	1,394,729	1,399,129	1,664,239	2,526,367	2,626,500	2,589,878
Non-Hispanic black (selected States)[2]	-	-	299,646	336,029	355,644	434,843	611,269	661,701	666,758

Source: National Center for Health Statistics. *Health, United States, 1993.* Hyattsville, MD: Public Health Service, May 1994, p. 68. Primary source: Centers for Disease Control and Prevention, National Center for Health Statistics. Data computed by the Division of Analysis from data compiled by the Division of Vital Statistics. *Notes:* A dash (-) stands for data not available. The race groups, white and black, include persons of Hispanic and non-Hispanic origin. Conversely, persons of Hispanic origin may be of any race. 1. Includes Hawaiians and part Hawaiians. 2. Trend data for Hispanics and non-Hispanics are affected by expansion of the reporting area for an Hispanic-origin item on the birth certificate and by immigration. These two factors affect the numbers of events, composition of the Hispanic population, and maternal and infant health characteristics. The number of States in the reporting area increased from 22 in 1980, to 23 plus the District of Columbia (DC) in 1983, 30 plus DC in 1988, 47 plus DC in 1989, 48 plus DC in 1990, and 49 plus DC in 1991. 3. Includes mothers of all races.

★ 377 ★

Births and Deaths

Live Births, by Race, Type of Hispanic Origin, and Selected Characteristics

Figures represent registered births. Data exclude births to nonresidents of the U.S. and are based on race and Hispanic-origin of mother. Prior to 1990, data are for race of child and are not comparable. Hispanic-origin data are available from only 48 States and DC in 1990. However, approximately 99.6 percent of all births to Hispanic mothers in 1990 occurred in these states.

Race/ethnicity	Number of births (000)		Births to teenage mothers, percent of total		Births to unmarried mothers, percent of total		Percent of mothers beginning prenatal care during: First trimester		Percent of mothers beginning prenatal care during: Third trimester or no care		Percent of births with low birth weight[1]	
	1990	1991	1990	1991	1990	1991	1990	1991	1990	1991	1990	1991
Total	4,158	4,111	12.8	12.9	26.6	28.0	74.2	76.2	6.0	5.8	7.0	7.1
White	3,290	3,241	10.9	11.0	16.9	18.0	77.7	79.5	4.9	4.7	5.7	5.8
Black	684	683	23.1	23.1	66.7	68.2	60.7	61.9	10.9	10.7	13.3	13.6
American Indian, Eskimo, Aleut	39	39	19.5	20.3	53.6	55.3	57.9	59.9	12.9	12.2	6.1	6.2
Asian and Pacific Islander[2]	142	145	5.7	5.8	NA	NA	NA	NA	NA	NA	NA	NA
Filipino	26	26	6.1	6.1	15.9	16.8	77.1	77.1	4.5	5.0	7.3	7.3
Chinese	23	22	1.2	1.1	5.0	5.5	81.3	82.3	3.4	3.4	4.7	5.1
Japanese	9	9	2.9	2.7	9.6	9.8	87.0	87.7	2.9	2.5	6.2	5.9
Hawaiian	6	6	18.4	18.1	45.0	45.0	65.8	68.1	8.7	7.5	7.2	6.7
Hispanic origin[3]	595	623	16.8	17.2	36.7	38.5	60.2	61.0	12.0	11.0	6.1	6.1
Mexican	386	411	17.7	18.1	33.3	35.3	57.8	58.7	13.2	12.2	5.5	5.6
Puerto Rican	59	60	21.7	21.7	55.9	57.5	63.5	65.0	10.6	9.1	9.0	9.4
Cuban	11	11	7.7	7.1	18.2	19.5	84.8	85.4	2.8	2.4	5.7	5.6
Central and South American	83	87	9.0	9.4	41.2	43.1	61.5	63.4	10.9	9.5	5.8	5.9

Source: 1994 Statistical Abstract of the United States on CD-ROM [machine-readable datafiles]. CD-8A-94. Washington, DC: U.S. Department of Commerce, Economics and Statistics Administration, Bureau of the Census, Data User Services Division, January 1995. Primary source: U.S. National Center for Health Statistics; Vital Statistics of the United States, annual; Monthly Vital Statistics Report; and unpublished data. *Notes:* NA stands for not available. 1. Births less than 2,500 grams (5 lbs.- 8 oz.). 2. Includes other races not shown separately. 3. Hispanic persons may be of any race. Includes other types not shown separately.

★ 378 ★

Births and Deaths

Low-Birthweight Live Births per Year, by Race and Hispanic Origin of Mother

Percent of live births that are of low or very low birthweight are shown for selected years from 1970 to 1991.

Birthweight and race and Hispanic origin of mother	Percent of live births[1]								
	1970	1975	1980	1985	1987	1988	1989	1990	1991
Low birthweight (less than 2,500 grams)									
All mothers	7.93	7.38	6.84	6.75	6.90	6.93	7.05	6.97	7.12
White	6.85	6.27	5.72	5.65	5.70	5.67	5.72	5.70	5.80
Black	13.90	13.19	12.69	12.65	12.98	13.26	13.51	13.25	13.55
American Indian or Alaskan Native	7.97	6.41	6.44	5.86	6.15	6.00	6.26	6.11	6.15
Asian or Pacific Islander	-	-	6.68	6.16	6.41	6.31	6.51	6.45	6.54
Chinese	6.67	5.29	5.21	4.98	5.02	4.63	4.89	4.69	5.10
Japanese	9.03	7.47	6.60	6.21	6.49	6.69	6.67	6.16	5.90
Filipino	10.02	8.08	7.40	6.95	7.30	7.15	7.35	7.30	7.31
Other Asian or Pacific Islander[2]	-	-	12.71	12.61	13.10	13.28	13.61	13.32	13.62
Hispanic origin (selected States)[3,4]	-	-	6.12	6.16	6.24	6.17	6.18	6.06	6.15
Mexican American	-	-	5.62	5.77	5.74	5.60	5.60	5.55	5.60
Puerto Rican	-	-	8.95	8.69	9.30	9.42	9.50	8.99	9.42
Cuban	-	-	5.62	6.02	5.89	5.94	5.77	5.67	5.57
Central and South American	-	-	5.76	5.68	5.74	5.58	5.81	5.84	5.87
Other and unknown Hispanic	-	-	6.96	6.83	6.91	6.85	6.74	6.87	7.25
Non-Hispanic white (selected States)[3]	-	-	5.67	5.60	5.63	5.62	5.62	5.61	5.72
Non-Hispanic black (selected States)[3]	-	-	12.71	12.61	13.10	13.28	13.61	13.32	13.62
Very low birthweight (less than 1,500 grams)									
All mothers	1.17	1.16	1.15	1.21	1.24	1.24	1.28	1.27	1.29
White	0.95	0.92	0.90	0.94	0.94	0.93	0.95	0.95	0.96
Black	2.40	2.40	2.48	2.71	2.79	2.86	2.95	2.92	2.96
American Indian or Alaskan Native	0.98	0.95	0.92	1.01	1.13	1.00	1.00	1.01	1.07
Asian or Pacific Islander	-	-	0.92	0.85	0.83	0.84	0.90	0.87	0.85
Chinese	0.80	0.52	0.66	0.57	0.65	0.57	0.61	0.51	0.65
Japanese	1.48	0.89	0.94	0.84	0.80	0.92	0.86	0.73	0.62
Filipino	1.08	0.93	0.99	0.86	0.94	0.91	1.12	1.05	0.97
Other Asian or Pacific Islander[2]	-	-	0.97	0.92	0.84	0.89	0.91	0.92	0.88
Hispanic origin (selected States)[3,4]	-	-	0.98	1.01	1.06	1.01	1.05	1.03	1.02
Mexican American	-	-	0.92	0.97	0.96	0.89	0.94	0.92	0.92
Puerto Rican	-	-	1.29	1.30	1.63	1.61	1.71	1.62	1.66
Cuban	-	-	1.02	1.18	0.97	1.17	1.13	1.20	1.15
Central and South American	-	-	0.99	1.01	1.02	0.97	1.05	1.05	1.02
Other and unknown Hispanic	-	-	1.01	0.96	1.15	1.11	1.04	1.09	1.09

[Continued]

★ 378 ★

Low-Birthweight Live Births per Year, by Race and Hispanic Origin of Mother

[Continued]

Birthweight and race and Hispanic origin of mother	Percent of live births[1]								
	1970	1975	1980	1985	1987	1988	1989	1990	1991
Non-Hispanic white (selected States)[3]	-	-	0.86	0.90	0.91	0.89	0.93	0.93	0.94
Non-Hispanic black (selected States)[3]	-	-	2.46	2.66	2.73	2.82	2.97	2.93	2.97

Source: National Center for Health Statistics. *Health, United States, 1993.* Hyattsville, MD: Public Health Service, May 1994, p. 69. Primary source: Centers for Disease Control and Prevention, National Center for Health Statistics. Data computed by the Division of Analysis from data compiled by the Division of Vital Statistics. *Notes:* A dash (-) stands for data not available. The race groups, white and black, include persons of Hispanic and non-Hispanic origin. Conversely, persons of Hispanic origin can be of any race. 1. Excludes live births with unknown birth weight. Percent based on births with known birth weight. 2. Includes Hawaiians and part Hawaiians. 3. Trend data for Hispanics and non-Hispanics are affected by expansion of the reporting area for an Hispanic-origin item on the birth certificate and by immigration. These two factors affect numbers of events, composition of the Hispanic population, and maternal and infant health characteristics. The number of States in the reporting area increased from 22 in 1980, to 30 plus the District of Columbia (DC) in 1988, 47 plus DC in 1989, 48 plus DC in 1990, and 49 plus DC in 1991. 4. Includes mothers of all races.

★ 379 ★

Births and Deaths

Maternal Age and Marital Status for Live Births, by Race and Hispanic Origin of Mother

Data show percent distribution of live births in selected years according to age, marital status, and race/ethnicity of the mother.

Age, marital status, race, and Hispanic origin of mother	Percent of live births								
	1970	1975	1980	1985	1987	1988	1989	1990	1991
Age of mother less than 18 years									
All mothers	6.3	7.6	5.8	4.7	4.8	4.8	4.8	4.7	4.9
White	4.8	6.0	4.5	3.7	3.7	3.7	3.6	3.6	3.8
Black	14.8	16.3	12.5	10.6	10.7	10.6	10.5	10.1	10.3
American Indian or Alaskan Native	7.5	11.2	9.4	7.6	7.9	7.8	7.5	7.2	7.9
Asian or Pacific Islander	-	-	1.5	1.6	1.8	1.8	2.0	2.1	2.1
Chinese	1.1	0.4	0.3	0.3	0.2	0.3	0.3	0.4	0.3
Japanese	2.0	1.7	1.0	0.9	0.9	0.8	0.9	0.8	1.0
Filipino	3.7	2.4	1.6	1.6	1.8	1.7	1.9	2.0	2.0
Other Asian or Pacific Islander[1]	-	-	1.8	2.1	2.3	2.4	2.6	2.7	2.7
Hispanic origin (selected States)[2,3]	-	-	7.4	6.4	6.6	6.6	6.7	6.6	6.9
Mexican American	-	-	7.7	6.9	7.0	7.0	6.9	6.9	7.2
Puerto Rican	-	-	10.0	8.5	8.7	9.2	9.4	9.4	9.5
Cuban	-	-	3.8	2.2	2.1	2.2	2.7	2.7	2.6
Central and South American	-	-	2.4	2.4	2.7	2.7	3.0	3.2	3.5
Other and unknown Hispanic	-	-	6.5	7.0	7.7	7.6	8.0	8.0	8.3
Non-Hispanic white (selected States)[2]	-	-	4.0	3.2	3.2	3.2	3.0	3.0	3.1
Non-Hispanic black (selected States)[2]	-	-	12.7	10.7	10.7	10.8	10.5	10.2	10.3
Age of mother 18-19 years									
All mothers	11.3	11.3	9.8	8.0	7.6	7.7	8.1	8.1	8.1

[Continued]

★ 379 ★

Maternal Age and Marital Status for Live Births, by Race and Hispanic Origin of Mother

[Continued]

Age, marital status, race, and Hispanic origin of mother	Percent of live births								
	1970	1975	1980	1985	1987	1988	1989	1990	1991
White	10.4	10.3	9.0	7.1	6.8	6.9	7.2	7.3	7.2
Black	16.6	16.9	14.5	12.9	12.2	12.3	12.9	13.0	12.8
American Indian or Alaskan Native	12.8	15.2	14.6	12.4	11.8	11.4	12.1	12.3	12.4
Asian or Pacific Islander	-	-	3.9	3.4	3.3	3.4	3.7	3.7	3.7
Chinese	3.9	1.7	1.0	0.6	0.6	0.5	0.7	0.8	0.8
Japanese	4.1	3.3	2.3	1.9	1.6	1.8	1.8	2.0	1.7
Filipino	7.1	5.0	4.0	3.7	3.4	3.8	4.0	4.1	4.0
Other Asian or Pacific Islander[1]	-	-	4.9	4.2	4.1	4.3	4.6	4.5	4.6
Hispanic origin (selected States)[2,3]	-	-	11.6	10.1	9.7	9.8	10.0	10.2	10.3
Mexican American	-	-	12.0	10.6	10.3	10.3	10.5	10.7	10.9
Puerto Rican	-	-	13.3	12.4	11.8	12.2	12.6	12.6	12.2
Cuban	-	-	9.2	4.9	4.1	3.9	4.3	5.0	4.5
Central and South American	-	-	6.0	5.8	5.3	5.4	5.6	5.9	6.0
Other and unknown Hispanic	-	-	10.8	10.5	10.5	10.8	11.2	11.1	11.4
Non-Hispanic white (selected States)[2]	-	-	8.5	6.6	6.2	6.6	6.5	6.6	6.5
Non-Hispanic black (selected States)[2]	-	-	14.7	12.9	12.2	12.4	13.0	13.0	12.9
Unmarried mothers									
All mothers	10.7	14.3	18.4	22.0	24.5	25.7	27.1	28.0	29.5
White	5.5	7.1	11.2	14.7	16.9	18.0	19.2	20.4	21.8
Black	37.5	49.5	56.1	61.2	63.4	64.7	65.7	66.5	67.9
American Indian or Alaskan Native	22.4	632.7	39.2	46.8	51.1	51.7	52.7	53.6	55.3
Asian or Pacific Islander	-	-	7.3	9.5	11.0	11.5	12.4	13.2	13.9
Chinese	3.0	1.6	2.7	3.0	4.5	3.9	4.2	5.0	5.5
Japanese	4.6	4.6	5.2	7.9	7.9	8.8	9.4	9.6	9.8
Filipino	9.1	6.9	8.6	11.4	12.7	13.6	14.8	15.9	16.8
Other Asian or Pacific Islander[1]	-	-	8.5	10.9	12.4	13.2	14.2	14.9	15.6
Hispanic origin (selected States)[2,3]	-	-	23.6	29.5	32.6	34.0	35.5	36.7	38.5
Mexican American	-	-	20.3	25.7	28.9	30.6	31.7	33.3	35.3
Puerto Rican	-	-	46.3	51.1	53.0	53.3	55.2	55.9	57.5
Cuban	-	-	10.0	16.1	16.1	16.3	17.5	18.2	19.5
Central and South American	-	-	27.1	34.9	37.1	36.4	38.9	41.2	43.1
Other and unknown Hispanic	-	-	22.4	31.1	34.2	35.5	37.0	37.2	37.9
Non-Hispanic white (selected States)[2]	-	-	9.6	12.4	14.3	15.2	16.1	16.9	18.0
Non-Hispanic black (selected States)[2]	-	-	57.3	62.1	64.2	64.8	66.0	66.7	68.2

Source: National Center for Health Statistics. *Health, United States, 1993.* Hyattsville, MD: Public Health Service, May 1994, p. 72. Primary source: Centers for Disease Control and Prevention, National Center for Health Statistics. Data computed by the Division of Analysis from data compiled by the Division of Vital Statistics. *Notes:* A dash (-) stands for data not available. Data for 1970 and 1975 exclude births that occurred in States not reporting marital status. The race groups, white and black, include persons of Hispanic and non-Hispanic origin. Conversely, persons of Hispanic origin may be of any race. 1. Includes Hawaiians and part Hawaiians. 2. Trend data for Hispanics and non-Hispanics are affected by expansion of the reporting area for an Hispanic-origin item on the birth certificate and by immigration. These two factors affect numbers of events, composition of the Hispanic population, and maternal and infant health characteristics. The number of States in the reporting area increased from 22 in 1980, to 30 plus the District of Columbia (DC) in 1988, 47 plus DC in 1989, 48 plus DC in 1990, and 49 plus DC in 1991. 3. Includes mothers of all races.

★ 380 ★

Births and Deaths

Maternal Education for Live Births, by Race and Hispanic Origin

Data show distribution of live births, by educational status of mother, for selected years.

Education and race and Hispanic origin of mother	Percent of live births[1]								
	1970	1975	1980	1985	1987	1988	1989	1990	1991
Education of mother less than 12 years									
All mothers	30.8	28.6	23.7	20.6	20.2	20.4	23.2	23.8	23.9
White	27.1	25.1	20.8	17.8	17.4	17.6	21.6	22.4	22.5
Black	51.2	45.3	36.4	32.6	31.6	31.4	30.4	30.2	30.4
American Indian or Alaskan Native	60.5	52.7	44.2	39.0	38.5	37.9	37.2	36.4	36.3
Asian or Pacific Islander	-	-	21.0	19.4	17.9	17.9	19.5	20.0	19.7
Chinese	23.0	16.5	15.2	15.5	13.5	14.2	14.9	15.8	15.7
Japanese	11.8	9.1	5.0	4.8	3.1	3.5	3.3	3.5	3.0
Filipino	26.4	22.3	16.4	13.9	12.3	11.8	10.2	10.3	10.1
Other Asian or Pacific Islander[2]	-	-	26.4	23.5	21.7	21.7	26.1	26.2	25.5
Hispanic origin (selected states)[3,4]	-	-	51.1	44.5	42.8	42.5	52.8	53.9	54.3
Mexican American	-	-	62.8	59.0	58.4	56.9	61.3	61.4	61.7
Puerto Rican	-	-	55.3	46.6	44.3	45.2	43.7	42.7	41.9
Cuban	-	-	24.1	21.1	18.7	18.1	17.9	17.8	16.7
Central and South American	-	-	41.2	37.0	34.1	31.8	43.6	44.2	44.5
Other and unknown Hispanic	-	-	40.1	36.5	34.3	34.1	34.5	33.3	34.4
Non-Hispanic white (selected states)[3]	-	-	18.3	15.8	15.3	16.7	15.3	15.2	15.0
Non-Hispanic black (selected states)[3]	-	-	37.4	33.5	32.2	31.8	29.9	30.0	30.3
Education of mother 16 years or more									
All mothers	8.6	11.4	14.0	16.7	17.6	17.7	17.4	17.5	18.1
White	9.6	12.7	15.5	18.6	19.8	20.1	19.2	19.3	19.9
Black	2.8	4.3	6.2	7.0	7.1	7.1	7.2	7.2	7.3
American Indian or Alaskan Native	2.7	2.2	3.5	3.7	3.7	3.7	4.3	4.4	4.0
Asian or Pacific Islander	-	-	30.8	30.3	32.0	31.7	31.2	31.0	31.8
Chinese	34.0	37.8	41.5	35.2	36.8	36.4	40.5	40.3	41.7
Japanese	20.7	30.6	36.8	38.1	41.8	42.3	43.6	44.1	45.0
Filipino	28.1	36.6	37.1	35.2	36.9	35.5	36.0	34.5	34.1
Other Asian or Pacific Islander[2]	-	-	25.5	27.1	28.8	28.6	25.3	25.7	27.1
Hispanic origin (selected states)[3,4]	-	-	4.2	6.0	6.6	7.0	5.1	5.1	5.2
Mexican American	-	-	2.2	3.0	3.2	3.7	3.2	3.3	3.3
Puerto Rican	-	-	3.0	4.6	5.4	5.3	6.3	6.5	6.8
Cuban	-	-	11.6	15.0	17.3	18.2	19.2	20.4	21.9
Central and South American	-	-	6.1	8.1	8.8	10.1	8.2	8.6	9.1
Other and unknown Hispanic	-	-	5.5	7.2	7.6	8.0	7.7	8.5	8.2

[Continued]

★ 380 ★

Maternal Education for Live Births, by Race and Hispanic Origin

[Continued]

Education and race and Hispanic origin of mother	Percent of live births[1]								
	1970	1975	1980	1985	1987	1988	1989	1990	1991
Non-Hispanic white (selected states)[3]	-	-	16.4	19.3	20.4	20.4	22.0	22.6	23.3
Non-Hispanic black (selected states)[3]	-	-	5.7	6.7	6.8	6.9	7.2	7.3	7.3

Source: National Center for Health Statistics. *Health, United States, 1993.* Hyattsville, MD: May 1994, p. 71. Centers for Disease Control and Prevention, National Center for Health Statistics: Data computed by the Division of Analysis from data compiled by the Division of Vital Statistics. *Notes:* A dash (-) stands for data not available. Excludes births that occurred in States not reporting education. The race groups, white and black, include persons of Hispanic and non-Hispanic origin. Conversely, persons of Hispanic origin may be of any race. 1. Excludes live births for whom education of mother is not known. 2. Includes Hawaiians and part Hawaiians. 3. Trend data for Hispanics and non-Hispanics are affected by expansion of the reporting area for an Hispanic-origin item on the birth certificate and by immigration. These two factors affect numbers of events, composition of the Hispanic population, and maternal and infant health characteristics. The number of States in the reporting area increased from 22 in 1980, to 30 plus the District of Columbia (DC) in 1988, 47 plus DC in 1989, 48 plus DC in 1990, and 49 plus DC in 1991.

★ 381 ★

Births and Deaths

Projected Fertility Rates, by Race and Age Group

The total fertility rate is the number of births that 1,000 women would have in their lifetime if, at each year of age, they experienced the birth rates occurring in the specified year. Birth rates represent live births per 1,000 women in age group indicated.

Age group	All races[1]			White			Black			Hispanic[2]		
	1993	2000	2010	1993	2000	2010	1993	2000	2010	1993	2000	2010
Total fertility rate	2,074	2,097	2,119	1,973	1,992	2,009	2,470	2,470	2,469	2,900	2,858	2,777
Birth rates:												
10 to 14 years old	1.4	1.5	1.6	0.7	0.8	0.9	4.8	4.8	5.0	2.3	2.3	2.3
15 to 19 years old	60.5	60.2	62.4	50.4	50.4	52.9	114.4	113.7	113.8	99.6	98.2	95.8
20 to 24 years old	117.6	119.3	120.0	109.6	111.3	112.4	161.0	161.2	161.1	180.5	177.7	172.6
25 to 29 years old	118.6	119.6	120.2	117.9	118.4	118.8	112.9	113.1	113.5	149.8	147.6	143.7
30 to 34 years old	80.1	80.3	82.0	80.2	79.8	80.9	67.8	67.4	68.4	95.8	93.8	91.5
35 to 39 years old	31.6	31.5	31.8	31.0	30.7	30.6	28.1	27.7	27.5	43.1	42.1	40.5
40 to 44 years old	5.4	5.5	5.5	5.1	5.2	5.1	5.4	5.3	5.1	9.2	9.0	8.5
45 to 49 years old	0.2	0.3	0.3	0.2	0.2	0.2	0.3	0.3	0.3	0.6	0.5	0.5

Source: 1994 Statistical Abstract of the United States on CD-ROM [machine-readable datafiles]. CD-8A-94. Washington, DC: U.S. Department of Commerce, Economics and Statistics Administration, Bureau of the Census, Data User Services Division, January 1995. Primary source: U.S. Bureau of the Census, Current Population Reports, P25-1104; and unpublished data. *Notes:* 1. Includes races not shown separately. 2. Persons of Hispanic origin may be of any race.

Body Weight

★ 382 ★

Obesity in the U.S., by Sex and Race/Ethnicity

According to data from the National Center for Health Statistics, the percentage of overweight adults in the United States increased 31 percent from 1981 to 1991. Data show the percentage of persons in each group that are at least 20 percent above a person's ideal weight.

Race/ethnicity	Percent	
	Male	Female
White, non-Hispanic	32.3	32.9
Black, non-Hispanic	30.9	48.6
Mexican-American	35.5	46.7

Source: "Report calls a third of U.S. adults obese." *St. Louis Post-Dispatch* (18 July 1994), p. 2A. Primary source: National Center for Health Statistics.

★ 383 ★

Body Weight

Overweight Adults

Data show percentage of the U.S. population age 20 years and older that have been diagnosed in physical examinations as being overweight. Data are shown for selected years and are based on a sample of the civilian noninstitutionalized population.

Sex, age, race and Hispanic origin[1]	Percent of population			
	1960-62	1971-74	1976-80[2]	1988-91
	Percent of population			
20-74 years, age adjusted[3]				
Both sexes	24.4	24.9	25.4	33.3
Male	22.9	23.6	24.0	31.6
Female[4]	25.6	25.9	26.5	35.0
White male	23.1	23.8	24.2	32.0
White female[4]	23.5	24.0	24.4	33.5
Black male	22.2	24.3	25.7	31.5
Black female[4]	41.7	42.9	44.3	49.6
White, non-Hispanic male	-	-	24.1	32.1
White, non-Hispanic female[4]	-	-	23.9	32.4
Black, non-Hispanic male	-	-	25.6	31.5
Black, non-Hispanic female[4]	-	-	44.1	49.5
Mexican-American male	-	-	31.0	39.5
Mexican-American female[4]	-	-	41.4	47.9

[Continued]

★ 383 ★

Overweight Adults

[Continued]

Sex, age, race and Hispanic origin[1]	Percent of population			
	1960-62	1971-74	1976-80[2]	1988-91
20-74 years, crude				
Both sexes	25.5	25.5	25.7	33.7
Male	23.4	24.0	24.2	31.7
Female[4]	27.4	27.0	27.1	35.6
White male	23.7	24.2	24.4	32.4
White female[4]	25.4	25.2	25.1	34.3
Black male	22.5	24.5	25.7	31.2
Black female[4]	43.0	43.2	43.7	49.1
White, non-Hispanic male	-	-	24.4	32.7
White, non-Hispanic female[4]	-	-	24.8	33.3
Black, non-Hispanic male	-	-	25.6	31.2
Black, non-Hispanic female[4]	-	-	43.4	49.1
Mexican- American male	-	-	29.5	35.6
Mexican-American female[4]	-	-	39.1	47.1

Source: National Center for Health Statistics. *Health, United States, 1993.* Hyattsville, MD: Public Health Service, May 1994, p. 166. Primary source: Centers for Disease Control and Prevention, National Center for Health Statistics, Division of Health Examination Statistics: Unpublished data. *Notes:* A dash (-) stands for data not available. Overweight is defined for men as body mass index greater than or equal to 27.8 kilogram/sq. meter, and for women as body mass index greater than or equal to 27.3 kilograms/sq. meter. These cut points were used because they represent the sex-specific 85th percentiles for persons 20-29 years of age in the 1976-80 National Health and Nutrition Examination Survey. Height was measured without shoes; two pounds were deducted from data for 1960-62 to allow for weight of clothing. 1. The race groups, white and black, include persons of Hispanic and non-Hispanic origin. Conversely, persons of Hispanic origin may be of any race. 2. Data for Mexican-Americans are for 1982-84. 3. Age adjusted. 4. Excludes pregnant women.

Cancer

★ 384 ★

Cancer Death Rates Among Cuban Americans

Age-adjusted death rates per 100,000 are shown for selected causes of cancer in persons of age five and older.

Cancer site	Cubans in Cuba 1981[1]	Cuban-born in U.S. 1979-81	All whites in U.S. 1979-81[2]
Men			
Lung (trachea and bronchus)	60.6	58.7	81.8
Colon	11.3	17.6	24.4
Prostate	26.6	22.8	25.9
Stomach	15.3	6.4	9.1
Liver	2.2	6.0	3.4

[Continued]

★ 384 ★

Cancer Death Rates Among Cuban Americans

[Continued]

Cancer site	Cubans in Cuba 1981[1]	Cuban-born in U.S. 1979-81	All whites in U.S. 1979-81[2]
Rectum	3.9	3.6	5.6
Women			
Lung (trachea and bronchus)	18.6	13.5	23.8
Breast	20.4	24.1	30.4
Colon	12.6	16.0	18.5
Stomach	7.0	4.7	4.4
Liver	1.4	3.4	1.8
Rectum	3.8	3.1	3.3
Cervix uteri	5.3	2.4	3.6

Source: Shai, Donna. "Cancer Mortality in Cuba and Among the Cuban-Born in the United States: 1979-81." *Public Health Reports* Vol. 106, No. 1, (January-February 1991), p. 69. *Notes:* 1. From *World Health Statistics Annual 1985*, World Health Organization, Geneva, 1985. 2. From I. Rosenwaike, "Cancer Mortality Among Mexican Immigrants in the United States," *Public Health Reports*, Vol. 103, March/April 1988, pp. 195-201.

Dental Care

★ 385 ★

Dental Visits of Adults

Figures show the percentage of persons age 18 years and older who had visited a dentist in the past 12 months, as of 1990. Data are based on household interviews of the civilian noninstitutionalized population.

Race/ethnicity	Both sexes 18 years and older	Male					Female				
		Total	18-29 years	30-44 years	45-64 years	65 years and older	Total	18-29 years	30-44 years	45-64 years	65 years and older
White	64.1	60.8	59.6	64.8	62.6	50.5	67.2	68.9	75.4	66.6	52.2
Black	51.8	46.0	51.4	48.9	42.5	29.2	56.2	59.1	66.4	53.2	31.1
Hispanic	54.0	47.7	44.3	50.5	53.6	32.1	59.3	55.5	65.8	62.0	42.1
Non-Hispanic	63.3	59.9	59.6	64.0	61.0	49.2	66.3	69.2	74.8	65.1	50.5

Source: Piani, A., and C. Schoenborn. National Center for Health Statistics. *Health Promotion and Disease Prevention: United States, 1990. Vital and Health Statistics* 10(185), 1993, p. 55. *Note:* Denominator for each cell excludes unknowns.

★386★

Dental Care

Tooth Loss of Adults

Data show the percentage of persons age 18 years and older who had lost all of their permanent teeth, as of 1990. Figures are based on survey of the civilian noninstitutionalized population.

Race/ethnicity	Both sexes 18 years and older	Male					Female				
		Total	18-29 years	30-44 years	45-64 years	65 years and older	Total	18-29 years	30-44 years	45-64 years	65 years and older
White	10.8	9.9	1.4	2.8	14.7	31.4	11.7	1.6	3.5	15.2	32.7
Black	9.3	7.6	1.3	3.6	11.9	29.3	10.6	2.9	2.8	13.5	41.5
Hispanic	4.9	4.4	1.1	1.7	10.2	21.8	5.3	1.6	2.0	6.7	33.1
Non-Hispanic	11.0	10.0	1.4	3.1	14.7	31.2	12.0	1.8	3.5	15.5	33.8

Source: Piani, A., and Schoenborn, C. National Center for Health Statistics. *Health Promotion and Disease Prevention: United States, 1990. Vital Health Statistics* 10(185), 1993, p. 56. *Note:* Denominator for each cell excludes unknowns.

Diabetes

★387★

Diabetes Prevalence Among Selected Groups

Figures for each group reflect the likelihood of developing diabetes, as compared to the white, non-Hispanic population.

U.S. population group[1]	Rate relative to whites (percent)
American Indian	2.7
Puerto Rican	2.2
Mexican-American	2.1
African American	1.6
Cuban-American	1.5
White	1.0

Source: Manning, Anita. "Hispanics are at higher risk for diabetes." *USA TODAY* (10 February 1994), sec. D, p. 1. American Diabetes Association, from the Centers for Disease Control and Prevention and other sources.

★ 388 ★

Diabetes

Projects and Funding for Diabetes Research by the U.S. Government, 1991

Type of research and population group	Projects		Funding	
	Number	%	($000)	%
Human (total)[1]				
Hispanic	4	2.0	1,671	5.0
American Indian	46	28.0	7,458	21.0
Black	15	9.0	4,145	11.0
Multiracial[2]	19	12.0	5,965	17.0
White	77	47.0	16,728	46.0
Total	163	100.0	36,089	100.0
Prevention/behavioral				
Hispanic	0	0.0	70[3]	2.0
American Indian	5	36.0	358	8.0
Black	5	36.0	2,048	47.0
Multiracial[2]	1	7.0	258	7.0
White	3	21.0	1,600	37.0
Total	14	100.0	4,361	100.0
Clinical[1]				
Hispanic	1	<1.0	293	1.0
American Indian	35	28.0	6,042	25.0
Black	6	5.0	1,095	4.0
Multiracial[2]	12	10.0	2,559	11.0
White	69	55.0	14,246	58.0
Total	125	100.0	24,357	100.0
Epidemiologic				
Hispanic	3	13.0	1,308	18.0
American Indian	6	26.0	1,058	15.0
Black	4	17.0	1,002	14.0
Multiracial	6	26.0	3,121	44.0
White	4	17.0	666	9.0
Total	23	100.0	7,155	100.0

Source: U.S. General Accounting Office. *Diabetes: Status of the Disease Among American Indians, Blacks and Hispanics*. Washington, DC: U.S. GAO, 1992, p. 13. National Institute of Diabetes and Digestive and Kidney Diseases, 1991 *Notes:* 1. Totals for human and clinical research categories include two projects ($122,000) that were targeted to another population group; the human research for whites includes another type of project ($216,000). 2. Involved only non-white populations. 3. The amount from two multiracial projects that targeted Hispanics.

Diseases

★ 389 ★

Diphtheria Cases, by Race/Ethnicity, 1990-1992

From the source: "Hispanic-specific diphtheria morbidity and mortality data are limited since information collected by ethnicity has only been available since 1990 because of changes in research methodologies....Depsite the low number of recent diphtheria cases, some populations such as Hispanics, Native Americans, and low-income groups are highly vulnerable to contracting diphtheria due to certain existing risk factors."

Race/ethnicity	Number of cases[1]		
	1990	1991	1992
Total population	4	5	4
White	0	1	3
Black	1	0	0
Hispanic[2]	0	1	1
Other	2	2	0
Unknown[3]	1	1	2

Source: Alaniz, Gabriela A. National Council of La Raza. Center for Health Promotion. *NCLR Health Fact Sheet: Childhood Immunization in the Hispanic Community*. Washington, DC: NCLR, June 1994, p. 3. Centers for Disease Control. *Morbidity and Mortality Weekly Report* vol. 41, no. 55, 1992. *Notes:* 1. Race and ethnicity data not available until 1990; only 1990-91 data collected together. 2. Persons of Hispanic origin may be of any race. 3. Unknown race and ethnicity for 1992 calculated separately; figures may not add up to total population.

★ 390 ★

Diseases

Down's Syndrome

According to the Centers for Disease Control and Prevention, Hispanics have the highest rate of occurrence of Down's syndrome than any other ethnic group in the U.S. Down's syndrome is a congenital disorder cause by the genetic transmittance of an extra chromosome. Prevalent characteristics are moderate to severe mental retardation, distinctive physical features, and a life expectancy of usually not more than 35 years. It most frequently occurs in children born to mothers age 35 and older. Data show prevalence over a seven-year period from 1983 to 1990 in a study of 7.8 million births in 17 states and rates for 1983 and 1990.

Race/ethnicity	Rate per 10,000 infants		
	1983-1990	1983	1990
All races	9.2	9.5	8.6
White	9.2	[1]	[1]
Black	7.3	7.1	5.3
Hispanic	11.8	9.4	6.4

Source: "Rate of Down's syndrome highest among Hispanics, CDC finds." *Chicago Tribune* (26 August 1994), sec. 1, p. 4. Primary source: Centers for Disease Control and Prevention. *Notes:* 1. Rates were not cited for individual years 1983 and 1990 but were reported as having been stable.

★ 391 ★

Diseases

Hepatitis B Cases, by Race/Ethnicity, 1990-1992

From the source: "The hepatitis B virus (HBV) infects 300 million persons worldwide, of which 250,000 persons die from hepatitis-associated liver disease each year....HBV infection can cause acute and chronic hepatitis, cancer of the liver, and cirrhosis....In 1992, 2% of cases occurred among children under five years of age. Alaskan Natives, Pacific Islanders, and children of first-generation immigrant mothers from HBV endemic areas had the highest rates of infection."

Race/ethnicity	Number of cases[1]		
	1990	1991	1992
Total population	21,102	18,003	16,126
White	9,358	7,289	6,805
Black	4,597	3,927	3,641
Hispanic[2]	1,450	1,136	1,212
Other	1,127	924	1,080
Unknown[3]	4,570	4,727	10,684

Source: Alaniz, Gabriela A. National Council of La Raza. Center for Health Promotion. *NCLR Health Fact Sheet: Childhood Immunization in the Hispanic Community.* Washington, DC: NCLR, June 1994, p. 8. Centers for Disease Control. *Morbidity and Mortality Weekly Report* vol. 41, no. 55, 1992. *Notes:* 1. Race and ethnicity data not available until 1990; only 1990-91 data collected together. 2. Persons of Hispanic origin may be of any race. 3. Unknown race and ethnicity for 1992 calculated separately; figures may not add up to total population.

★ 392 ★

Diseases

Hib Cases, by Race/Ethnicity, 1991-1992

From the source: "Bacterial meningitis occurs in 60% of Haemophilus influenzae type b (Hib) cases....Young children who have household and day care contacts with persons with Hib disease have an increased risk of infection because they may face prolonged exposure to Hib....Minority children, particularly Hispanics, Blacks, and Native Americans, living in low-income families or with older siblings are at risk for infection with Hib."

Race/ethnicity	Number of cases[1]	
	1991	1992
Total population	2,764	1,412
White	1,368	815
Black	489	235
Hispanic[2]	243	110
Other	61	40
Unknown[3]	585	718

Source: Alaniz, Gabriela A. National Council of La Raza. Center for Health Promotion. *NCLR Health Fact Sheet: Childhood Immunization in the Hispanic Community.* Washington, DC: NCLR, June 1994, p. 7. Centers for Disease Control. *Morbidity and Mortality Weekly Report* vol. 41, no. 55, 1992. *Notes:* 1. Not a reported notifiable disease until 1991; 1991 race/ethnicity data collected together. 2. Persons of Hispanic origin may be of any race. 3. Unknown race and ethnicity for 1992 calculated separately; figures may not add up to total population.

★ 393 ★

Diseases

Measles Cases, by Race/Ethnicity, 1990-1992

From the source: "Measles is increasingly affecting children at a younger age; the median age of children infected with measles has dropped from 12.0 years in 1989 to 4.9 years in 1992....The epidemic resurgence of measles in the United States between 1989 and 1991 disproportionately affected Hispanic and Black preschool-aged children....Recent data indicate that Hispanics were more likely than Blacks to suffer from measles in 1992....Texas, where 19% of U.S. Hispanics live, accounted for 44% of the total measles cases in 1992."

Race/ethnicity	Number of cases[1]		
	1990	1991	1992
Total population	27,786	9,643	2,237
White	7,887	2,528	1,461
Black	3,209	1,328	64
Hispanic[2]	5,226	2,338	996

[Continued]

★ 393 ★

Measles Cases, by Race/Ethnicity, 1990-1992

[Continued]

Race/ethnicity	Number of cases[1]		
	1990	1991	1992
Other	731	498	76
Unknown[3]	10,733	2,961	912

Source: Alaniz, Gabriela A. National Council of La Raza. Center for Health Promotion. *NCLR Health Fact Sheet: Childhood Immunization in the Hispanic Community*. Washington, DC: NCLR, June 1994, p. 9. Centers for Disease Control. *Morbidity and Mortality Weekly Report* vol. 41, no. 55, 1992. *Notes:* 1. Race and ethnicity data not available until 1990; only 1990-91 data collected together. 2. Persons of Hispanic origin may be of any race. 3. Unknown race and ethnicity for 1992 calculated separately; figures may not add up to total population.

★ 394 ★

Diseases

Mumps Cases, by Race/Ethnicity, 1990-1992

From the source: "Mumps is a vaccine-preventable disease that affects mostly children; it can go undetected and untreated, eventually developing into serious complications.... Available data suggest that Hispanics are less likely than Blacks to become infected by mumps. However, it is difficult to determine the extent to which mumps has affected Hispanics since data by race and ethnicity have only been available since 1990."

Race/ethnicity	Number of cases[1]		
	1990	1991	1992
Total population	5,292	4,264	2,572
White	1,791	1,566	1,155
Black	1,228	662	475
Hispanic[2]	296	281	225
Other	69	55	51
Unknown[3]	1,908	1,700	2,029

Source: Alaniz, Gabriela A. National Council of La Raza. Center for Health Promotion. *NCLR Health Fact Sheet: Childhood Immunization in the Hispanic Community*. Washington, DC: NCLR, June 1994, p. 10. Centers for Disease Control. *Morbidity and Mortality Weekly Report* vol. 41, no. 55, 1992. *Notes:* 1. Race and ethnicity data not available until 1990; only 1990-91 data collected together. 2. Persons of Hispanic origin may be of any race. 3. Unknown race and ethnicity for 1992 calculated separately; figures may not add up to total population.

★ 395 ★

Diseases

Pertussis Cases, by Race/Ethnicity, 1990-1992

From the source: "Pertussis is highly contagious, infecting 70-100% of unimmunized individuals living with an infectious person....Children have accounted for the majority of pertussis cases, frequently resulting in hospitalization....Pertussis data for Hispanics are limited since cases have not been routinely reported by race/ethnicity."

Race/ethnicity	Number of cases[1]		
	1990	1991	1992
Total population	4,570	2,719	4,083
White	2,040	1,037	1,566
Black	296	184	234
Hispanic[2]	225	196	558
Other	118	51	88
Unknown[3]	1,894	1,251	4,455

Source: Alaniz, Gabriela A. National Council of La Raza. Center for Health Promotion. *NCLR Health Fact Sheet: Childhood Immunization in the Hispanic Community*. Washington, DC: NCLR, June 1994, p. 5. Centers for Disease Control. *Morbidity and Mortality Weekly Report* vol. 41, no. 55, 1992. *Notes:* 1. Race and ethnicity data not available until 1990; only 1990-91 data collected together. 2. Persons of Hispanic origin may be of any race. 3. Unknown race and ethnicity for 1992 calculated separately; figures may not add up to total population.

★ 396 ★

Diseases

Polio Cases, by Race/Ethnicity, 1990-1992

From the source: "The annual number of polio cases has declined in recent years. There were 34 cases between 1989 and 1992, compared to 48 cases between 1983 and 1987. Polio data for Hispanics are limited because information collected by race or ethnicity has only been available since 1990. Of the reported 17 cases between 1990 and 1992, ten were reported among whites and one among blacks. None were reported to be Hispanic; however race and ethnicity were unknown in six of the cases."

Race/ethnicity	Number of cases[1]		
	1990	1991	1992
Total population	7	6	4
White	7	2	1
Black	0	1	0
Hispanic[2]	0	0	0

[Continued]

★ 396 ★

Polio Cases, by Race/Ethnicity, 1990-1992

[Continued]

Race/ethnicity	Number of cases[1]		
	1990	1991	1992
Other	0	0	0
Unknown[3]	0	3	6

Source: Alaniz, Gabriela A. National Council of La Raza. Center for Health Promotion. *NCLR Health Fact Sheet: Childhood Immunization in the Hispanic Community*. Washington, DC: NCLR, June 1994, p. 12. Centers for Disease Control. *Morbidity and Mortality Weekly Report* vol. 41, no. 55, 1992. *Notes:* 1. Race and ethnicity data not available until 1990; only 1990-91 data collected together. 2. Persons of Hispanic origin may be of any race. 3. Unknown race and ethnicity for 1992 calculated separately; figures may not add up to total population.

★ 397 ★

Diseases

Rubella Cases, by Race/Ethnicity, 1990-1992

From the source: "Rubella has a similar transmission mode, incubation period, and symptoms as measles.... Limited data indicate that Hispanics continue to suffer from rubella despite a reduction in the overall number of cases."

Race/ethnicity	Number of cases[1]		
	1990	1991	1992
Total population	1,125	1,401	160
White	373	980	55
Black	9	15	2
Hispanic[2]	42	24	14
Other	11	9	27
Unknown[3]	690	373	163

Source: Alaniz, Gabriela A. National Council of La Raza. Center for Health Promotion. *NCLR Health Fact Sheet: Childhood Immunization in the Hispanic Community*. Washington, DC: NCLR, June 1994, p. 11. Centers for Disease Control. *Morbidity and Mortality Weekly Report* vol. 41, no. 55, 1992. *Notes:* 1. Race and ethnicity data not available until 1990; only 1990-91 data collected together. 2. Persons of Hispanic origin may be of any race. 3. Unknown race and ethnicity for 1992 calculated separately; figures may not add up to total population.

★ 398 ★

Diseases

Tetanus Cases, by Race/Ethnicity, 1990-1992

From the source: "The incidence and fatality rates of tetanus have decreased throughout the second half of this century....In the last ten years, 26% of tetanus cases resulted in death....National tetanus data for Hispanics are limited - information has only been made available since 1990."

Race/ethnicity	Number of cases[1]		
	1990	1991	1992
Total population	64	57	45
White	38	32	33
Black	14	12	4
Hispanic[2]	6	3	6
Other	1	1	0
Unknown[3]	8	9	19

Source: Alaniz, Gabriela A. National Council of La Raza. Center for Health Promotion. *NCLR Health Fact Sheet: Childhood Immunization in the Hispanic Community.* Washington, DC: NCLR, June 1994, p. 4. Centers for Disease Control. *Morbidity and Mortality Weekly Report* vol. 41, no. 55, 1992. *Notes:* 1. Race and ethnicity data not available until 1990; only 1990-91 race/ethnicity data collected together. 2. Persons of Hispanic origin may be of any race. 3. Unknown race and ethnicity for 1992 calculated separately; figures may not add up to total population.

Examinations

★ 399 ★

Breast Self-Examinations

Data show percentage of women age 18 years and older who knew how to do a breast self-examination and percent of those who both knew how to do a self-examination and did so at least 12 times per year. Data are shown for the United States in 1990.

Characteristic	Percent of women				
	All	Race		Ethnicity	
	women	White	Black	Hispanic	Non-Hispanic
Knew breast self-examination					
Total	88.1	88.8	86.0	74.7	89.2
18-29 years	84.9	85.6	84.8	70.4	87.0
30-44 years	92.7	93.5	92.4	77.9	94.2
45-64 years	90.6	91.2	88.4	78.0	91.5
65 years and older	80.5	81.9	68.3	71.7	80.8
Did breast self-examination					
Total	43.1	42.3	50.9	44.1	43.1
18-29 years	36.6	35.6	43.1	37.7	36.5

[Continued]

★ 399 ★

Breast Self-Examinations

[Continued]

Characteristic	Percent of women				
	All women	Race		Ethnicity	
		White	Black	Hispanic	Non-Hispanic
30-44 years	43.6	42.7	51.3	46.2	43.4
45-64 years	47.1	46.1	55.6	47.1	47.1
65 years and older	45.4	44.3	61.8	53.6	45.1

Source: Piani, A., and C. Schoenborn. National Center for Health Statistics. *Health Promotion and Disease Prevention: United States, 1990. Vital and Health Statistics* 10(185), 1993, p. 31. *Note:* Denominator for each cell excludes unknowns.

★ 400 ★

Examinations

Mammograms

Data show the percentage of women in each age group who have ever had a mammogram, as of 1990. Figures are based on household interviews of the civilian noninstitutionalized population.

Race/ethnicity	Age of woman					
	Total 35 years and older	35-39 years	40-49 years	50-59 years	60-69 years	70 years and older
White	58.9	40.9	65.6	69.2	63.5	50.2
Black	51.3	35.7	56.3	61.9	49.1	49.2
Hispanic	49.4	35.5	50.2	58.3	55.8	48.6
Non-Hispanic	58.2	39.8	65.4	68.5	62.0	50.1

Source: Piani, A., and C. Schoenborn. National Center for Health Statistics. *Health Promotion and Disease Prevention: United States, 1990. Vital Health Statistics* 10(185), 1993, p. 56. *Note:* Denominator for each cell excludes unknowns.

★ 401 ★

Examinations

Pap Smears and Breast Examinations

Data show the percentage of women age 18 years and older who had a pap smear or a breast examination by a medical professional in 1990.

Race/ethnicity	Pap smear					Breast examination				
	Total	18-29 years	30-44 years	45-64 years	65 years and older	Total	18-29 years	30-44 years	45-64 years	65 years and older
All women	50.1	63.9	55.2	43.6	30.4	53.1	62.2	55.6	49.1	42.0
White	49.7	63.5	55.5	43.8	30.4	53.1	61.8	56.1	49.3	42.4
Black	54.3	71.8	55.8	42.6	29.2	55.3	68.4	55.1	48.0	38.0
Hispanic	49.1	55.0	53.8	40.3	24.5	50.4	54.1	52.2	44.6	40.3
Non-Hispanic	50.1	65.1	55.3	43.7	30.6	53.4	63.4	55.9	49.3	42.1

Source: Piani, A., and C. Schoenborn. National Center for Health Statistics. *Health Promotion and Disease Prevention: United States, 1990. Vital Health Statistics* 10(185), 1993, p. 30. *Note:* Denominator for each cell includes unknowns.

Health Insurance

★ 402 ★

Continuous Health Insurance Coverage of Wage and Salary Workers, 1990-92

Data are shown for workers between the ages of 18 and 64 years, in thousands, with 32 months of continuous health insurance coverage.

Health insurance coverage	Both sexes	Male	Female	White		Black	Hispanic origin[1]	Not of Hispanic origin
				Total	Not of Hispanic origin			
Worked full-period, full-time								
All persons	53,372	32,435	20,937	46,172	43,437	5,406	3,228	50,144
Percent	100.0	100.0	100.0	100.0	100.0	100.0	100.0	100.0
Percent distribution								
Covered by private or government health insurance	87.5	87.6	87.4	8.7	90.0	78.3	70.4	88.6
Covered by private health insurance	86.9	86.8	87.1	88.2	89.5	77.0	69.3	88.1
Covered by employer-provided health insurance	67.2	71.0	61.3	68.3	69.3	59.9	55.5	68.0
Worked full-period, full-time								
All persons	4,803	1,080	3,723	4,186	3,941	479	259	4,544
Percent	100.0	100.0	100.0	100.0	100.0	100.0	100.0	100.0

[Continued]

★ 402 ★

Continuous Health Insurance Coverage of Wage and Salary Workers, 1990-92

[Continued]

Health insurance coverage	Both sexes	Male	Female	White		Black	Hispanic origin[1]	Not of Hispanic origin
				Total	Not of Hispanic origin			
Percent distribution								
Covered by private or government health insurance	77.9	67.3	81.0	81.5	83.7	53.6	45.4	79.7
Covered by private health insurance	74.3	60.3	78.4	78.6	81.0	44.2	39.9	76.3
Covered by employer-provided health insurance	19.3	20.3	19.1	20.3	20.6	14.5	14.5	19.6
Workers with one or more work interruptions								
All persons	75,635	29,861	45,773	62,887	57,214	10,052	6,662	68,973
Percent	100.0	100.0	100.0	100.0	100.0	100.0	100.0	100.0
Percent distribution								
Covered by private or government health insurance	62.0	54.1	67.2	63.6	65.9	53.2	41.3	64.0
Covered by private health insurance	52.4	46.6	56.2	56.2	59.0	31.2	27.5	54.8
Covered by employer-provided health insurance	14.9	21.6	10.6	15.6	16.1	12.3	9.9	15.4

Source: Bennefield, Robert L. U.S. Bureau of the Census. *Dynamics of Economic Well-Being: Health Insurance, 1990 to 1992.* Current Population Reports, P70-37. Washington, DC: U.S. Government Printing Office, 1994, p. 16. *Note:* 1. Persons of Hispanic origin may be of any race.

★ 403 ★

Health Insurance

Full-Time Work Force Without Health Insurance, by Sex, Ethnicity, and Selected Industry, 1989

Industry	Proportion uninsured (%)			
	Latino	Anglo	Black	Asian and other
Men				
Agriculture	65.2	23.2	62.2	37.6
Construction	60.1	25.1	42.0	28.8
Durables	26.9	6.7	14.3	12.4
Retail	48.9	18.0	36.3	33.5
Personal services	60.2	17.5	37.8	29.3
Professional	21.4	7.7	15.0	11.0
Women				
Agriculture	66.3	15.6	49.7	47.5
Durables	20.9	7.3	9.3	11.1
Retail	40.5	16.3	28.3	23.4

[Continued]

★ 403 ★

Full-Time Work Force Without Health Insurance, by Sex, Ethnicity, and Selected Industry, 1989

[Continued]

Industry	Proportion uninsured (%)			
	Latino	Anglo	Black	Asian and other
Personal services	58.2	18.0	44.0	27.7
Professional	19.0	7.4	13.6	15.2

Source: Burciaga Valdez, PhD, B. and others. "Insuring Latinos Against the Cost of Illness." *JAMA* Vol. 269, No. 7, p. 892. Primary source: Source of data was March 1990 Current Population Survey.

★ 404 ★

Health Insurance

Health Insurance Coverage Lapses, by Race/Ethnicity

A "spell" without insurance is defined as a period without health insurance coverage, which was preceded by at least one month with coverage. This table shows the median number of months that each group experienced a spell.

Characteristic	Median spell duration	
	1990	1987
All spells	6.0	4.2
Race and Hispanic origin		
White	5.4	4.2
Not of Hispanic origin	4.9	4.1
Black	7.3	4.0
Hispanic[1]	7.2	4.5
Not of Hispanic origin	5.7	4.2

Source: Bennefield, Robert L. U.S. Bureau of the Census. *Dynamics of Economic Well-Being: Health Insurance, 1990 to 1992.* Current Population Reports, P70-37. Washington, DC: U.S. Government Printing Office, 1994, p. 19. *Notes:* These estimates represent those persons observed during the 32-month period of the 1990 panel and 28-month period of the 1987 panel. 1. Persons of Hispanic origin may be of any race.

★ 405 ★

Health Insurance

Health Insurance Coverage Status of Hispanics, by Age Group, Sex, Household Relationship, Work Experience, and Poverty Status, 1992 - I

Numbers are shown in thousands for persons and families as of March, 1993. Coverage status is based on that of each person in the household. Persons of Hispanic origin may be of any race.

Characteristic	Total	Covered by some form of health insurance during all or part of year										Not covered at any time during the year
		Total	Covered by private health insurance			Covered by Medicaid		Covered by Medicare			Covered by CHAMPUS, VA, or military health care	
			Total	Related to current or past employment of relative or self	Related to own current or past employment	Total	Also covered by private insurance	Total	Also covered by private insurance	Also covered by Medicaid		
ALL INCOME LEVELS												
Number												
Both sexes												
Total	22,720	15,323	10,121	8,765	4,246	4,976	528	1,473	379	580	467	7,397
Under 18 years	7,807	5,804	3,279	2,795	12	2,830	342	10	3	8	154	2,003
18 to 24 years	2,813	1,406	951	753	395	463	56	34	4	23	64	1,407
25 to 34 years	4,277	2,569	1,979	1,834	1,387	562	44	68	12	48	75	1,708
35 to 44 years	3,330	2,200	1,825	1,696	1,233	352	34	63	8	31	58	1,130
45 to 54 years	2,037	1,342	1,112	995	738	198	16	73	8	34	29	695
55 to 59 years	680	471	370	317	218	94	12	38	6	23	25	209
60 to 64 years	554	375	245	198	146	95	4	69	10	34	17	180
65 years and over	1,222	1,156	360	178	117	381	20	1,118	329	379	46	66
65 to 74 years	806	758	276	152	94	216	10	723	247	215	39	49
75 years and over	416	399	84	26	22	165	10	394	82	164	8	17
Male												
Total	11,378	7,345	5,126	4,478	2,543	2,110	263	642	181	211	232	4,033
Under 18 years	3,958	2,963	1,709	1,450	10	1,446	189	7	3	5	78	975
18 to 24 years	1,417	609	491	397	217	114	22	9	4	3	32	809
25 to 34 years	2,237	1,148	996	933	834	139	14	22	7	13	28	1,089
35 to 44 years	1,682	1,069	916	852	735	130	10	40	6	20	28	613
45 to 54 years	1,035	656	553	494	436	83	10	46	7	19	17	379
55 to 59 years	292	209	171	149	128	35	6	17	3	9	13	83
60 to 64 years	249	182	129	111	100	37	2	32	7	17	12	67
65 years and over	508	489	162	93	82	127	10	469	144	125	24	19
65 to 74 years	345	333	122	77	68	78	4	317	105	78	19	11
75 years and over	163	156	40	16	13	49	6	152	39	47	5	7
Female												
Total	11,342	7,978	4,995	4,287	1,703	2,865	265	832	199	370	235	3,364
Under 18 years	3,849	2,820	1,570	1,345	2	1,384	153	3	-	3	76	1,028
18 to 24 years	1,396	798	460	356	177	349	34	25	-	20	32	598
25 to 34 years	2,040	1,422	983	901	553	424	30	46	5	36	46	618
35 to 44 years	1,648	1,132	910	844	499	222	24	23	3	11	30	517
45 to 54 years	1,002	685	559	501	302	115	6	27	1	15	13	316
55 to 59 years	387	261	199	168	90	59	6	21	3	14	12	126
60 to 64 years	305	193	116	86	45	58	2	37	2	17	4	112
65 years and over	715	667	189	86	35	255	11	648	184	253	22	47
65 to 74 years	462	424	154	75	26	138	6	406	141	137	19	37
75 years and over	253	243	44	10	9	117	4	242	43	117	3	10
Household relationship												
Total	22,720	15,323	10,121	8,765	4,246	4,976	528	1,473	379	580	467	7,397
65 years and over	1,222	1,156	360	178	117	381	20	1,118	329	379	46	66
In families	20,116	13,829	9,151	7,987	3,502	4,542	500	1,133	300	415	431	6,287
Householder	5,318	3,695	2,609	2,336	2,008	880	79	549	156	190	121	1,623
Under 65 years	4,880	3,271	2,459	2,255	1,942	771	69	145	25	81	102	1,610
65 years and over	438	425	150	81	66	109	10	404	131	109	20	13
Related children under 18 years:												
Under 18 years	7,589	5,682	3,230	2,760	11	2,745	331	10	3	8	151	1,907
Under 6 years	2,870	2,266	1,123	918	-	1,309	174	-	-	-	60	604
6 to 17 years	4,719	3,416	2,107	1,842	11	1,436	156	10	3	8	91	1,303
Own children 18 years and over	1,888	1,088	820	681	390	267	27	54	6	37	28	800
In married-couple families	14,624	10,142	7,656	6,772	2,816	2,321	328	805	258	229	378	4,482
Husbands	3,686	2,588	2,080	1,897	1,581	323	42	379	123	92	104	1,099
Under 65 years	3,364	2,273	1,956	1,822	1,517	261	36	80	14	30	86	1,091
65 years and over	322	314	125	75	64	62	7	299	109	62	18	8
Wives	3,806	2,723	2,193	1,972	876	418	55	290	112	78	117	1,083
Under 65 years	3,561	2,483	2,081	1,908	862	370	49	59	9	29	102	1,079

[Continued]

★ 405 ★

Health Insurance Coverage Status of Hispanics, by Age Group, Sex, Household Relationship, Work Experience, and Poverty Status, 1992 - I

[Continued]

Characteristic	Total	Covered by some form of health insurance during all or part of year										Not covered at any time during the year
		Total	Covered by private health insurance			Covered by Medicaid		Covered by Medicare			Covered by CHAMPUS, VA, or military health care	
			Total	Related to current or past employment of relative or self	Related to own current or past employment	Total	Also covered by private insurance	Total	Also covered by private insurance	Also covered by Medicaid		
65 years and over	245	241	112	65	14	48	6	231	103	48	15	4
Related children under 18 years:												
Under 18 years	5,259	3,848	2,654	2,299	11	1,368	205	4	2	2	135	1,411
Under 6 years	1,988	1,534	936	777	-	704	114	-	-	-	51	453
6 to 17 years	3,271	2,314	1,718	1,523	11	664	91	4	2	2	84	957
Own children 18 years and over	1,194	700	587	489	247	113	17	28	5	15	19	494
In families with female householder, no spouse present	4,207	3,066	1,131	928	494	1,993	154	248	24	154	36	1,141
Householder	1,238	910	369	316	316	525	32	140	20	87	12	328
Under 65 years	1,142	820	353	311	311	479	29	53	5	41	11	322
65 years and over	95	90	16	5	5	46	2	87	15	46	1	5
Related children under 18 years:												
Under 18 years	1,963	1,613	474	382	-	1,245	112	6	-	6	14	351
Under 6 years	710	619	151	113	-	524	56	-	-	-	7	91
6 to 17 years	1,253	994	323	269	-	721	56	6	-	6	6	259
Own children 18 years and over	603	347	202	167	123	146	9	26	1	21	6	256
In unrelated subfamilies	327	168	61	52	18	113	12	6	-	1	-	159
Under 18 years	167	107	42	34	-	76	12	-	-	-	-	61
Under 6 years	80	57	15	10	-	46	4	-	-	-	-	23
6 to 17 years	87	50	27	23	-	31	8	-	-	-	-	37
18 years and over	160	62	20	18	18	36	-	6	-	1	-	98
Unrelated individuals	2,278	1,326	909	725	725	321	17	333	79	164	36	951
Male	1,354	667	523	451	451	112	12	106	25	55	21	687
Under 65 years	1,274	587	503	442	442	75	10	28	7	18	16	687
Living alone	410	256	218	194	194	38	6	13	3	10	7	155
65 years and over	80	80	20	9	9	37	2	78	18	37	4	-
Living alone	70	70	19	9	9	30	1	67	17	30	3	-
Female	924	659	386	274	274	208	5	228	54	109	15	264
Under 65 years	719	458	330	261	261	119	5	29	-	19	12	261
Living alone	340	247	175	143	143	57	-	27	-	17	5	94
65 years and over	205	201	56	13	13	90	-	199	54	90	3	4
Living alone	188	185	55	12	12	81	-	183	53	81	3	3
Work experience												
Male:												
Under 16 years	3,595	2,750	1,555	1,316	1	1,366	181	2	-	2	68	845
16 to 64 years	7,276	4,106	3,409	3,070	2,460	618	72	170	36	83	140	3,170
Worked during year	6,066	3,422	3,112	2,842	2,401	261	47	37	10	7	111	2,644
Year-round, full-time	3,719	2,411	2,309	2,161	1,975	58	11	9	3	2	69	1,309
Not year-round full-time	2,346	1,011	803	682	427	203	36	28	8	5	42	1,336
Did not work	1,210	684	297	227	59	357	24	133	26	76	29	526
65 years and over	508	489	162	93	82	127	10	469	144	125	24	19
Worked during year	86	76	47	31	28	5	2	65	36	4	-	10
Year-round, full-time	30	27	20	18	17	1	1	17	10	1	-	3
Not year-round full-time	56	49	27	13	11	5	1	47	26	5	-	7
Did not work	421	413	114	61	54	121	7	405	109	120	24	8
Female:												
Under 16 years	3,497	2,589	1,423	1,228	1	1,296	146	1	-	1	69	908
16 to 64 years	7,130	4,722	3,374	2,973	1,667	1,314	109	182	14	115	144	2,408
Worked during year	4,170	2,877	2,507	2,270	1,613	394	77	33	8	22	84	1,293
Year-round, full-time	2,131	1,610	1,560	1,474	1,248	61	24	7	3	3	34	521
Not year-round full-time	2,040	1,268	947	796	365	333	53	25	5	18	50	772
Did not work	2,960	1,844	866	703	54	920	32	150	6	93	60	1,115
65 years and over	715	667	198	86	35	255	11	648	184	253	22	47
Worked during year	61	53	30	20	14	2	-	47	24	2	1	8
Year-round, full-time	25	21	17	11	8	-	-	18	13	-	1	4
Not year-round full-time	35	32	13	9	6	2	-	30	11	2	-	4
Did not work	654	614	168	65	21	252	11	601	160	251	21	40

[Continued]

★ 405 ★

Health Insurance Coverage Status of Hispanics, by Age Group, Sex, Household Relationship, Work Experience, and Poverty Status, 1992 - I

[Continued]

Characteristic	Total	Covered by some form of health insurance during all or part of year										Not covered at any time during the year
		Total	Covered by private health insurance			Covered by Medicaid		Covered by Medicare			Covered by CHAMPUS, VA, or military health care	
			Total	Related to current or past employment of relative or self	Related to own current or past employment	Total	Also covered by private insurance	Total	Also covered by private insurance	Also covered by Medicaid		
Percent												
Both sexes												
Total	100.0	67.4	44.5	38.6	18.7	21.9	2.3	6.5	1.7	2.6	2.1	32.6
Under 18 years	100.0	74.3	42.0	35.8	.2	36.2	4.4	.1	-	.1	2.0	25.7
18 to 24 years	100.0	50.0	33.8	26.8	14.0	16.5	2.0	1.2	.2	.8	2.3	50.0
25 to 34 years	100.0	60.1	46.3	42.9	32.4	13.1	1.0	1.6	.3	1.1	1.7	39.9
35 to 44 years	100.0	66.1	54.8	50.9	37.0	10.6	1.0	1.9	.2	.9	1.7	33.9
45 to 54 years	100.0	65.9	54.6	48.8	36.2	9.7	.8	3.6	.4	1.7	1.4	34.1
55 to 59 years	100.0	69.3	54.5	46.6	32.1	13.8	1.7	5.6	.8	3.4	3.7	30.7
60 to 64 years	100.0	67.6	44.3	35.6	26.3	17.2	.8	12.5	1.8	6.1	3.0	32.4
65 years and over	100.0	94.6	29.4	14.6	9.5	31.2	1.6	91.4	26.0	31.0	3.8	5.4
65 to 74 years	100.0	94.0	34.2	18.9	11.7	26.8	1.3	89.7	30.6	26.6	4.8	6.0
75 years and over	100.0	95.9	20.2	6.2	5.4	39.8	2.4	94.9	19.7	39.5	1.8	4.1
Male												
Total	100.0	64.6	45.1	39.4	22.3	18.5	2.3	5.6	1.6	1.9	2.0	35.4
Under 18 years	100.0	75.4	43.2	36.6	.2	36.5	4.8	.2	.1	.1	2.0	24.6
18 to 24 years	100.0	42.9	34.6	28.0	15.3	8.1	1.5	.6	.3	.2	2.3	57.1
25 to 34 years	100.0	51.3	44.5	41.7	37.3	6.2	.6	1.0	.3	.6	1.3	48.7
35 to 44 years	100.0	63.6	54.4	50.7	43.7	7.7	.6	2.4	.3	1.2	1.7	36.4
45 to 54 years	100.0	63.4	53.4	47.7	42.2	8.0	1.0	4.4	.6	1.8	1.6	36.6
55 to 59 years	100.0	71.8	58.8	50.9	43.8	12.0	2.0	5.7	1.0	3.0	4.4	28.4
60 to 64 years	100.0	73.0	51.8	44.7	40.4	14.9	1.0	13.0	2.9	7.0	4.9	27.0
65 years and over	100.0	96.3	31.8	18.2	16.1	24.9	1.9	92.5	28.4	24.7	4.8	3.7
65 to 74 years	100.0	96.7	35.4	22.3	19.8	22.6	1.1	91.9	30.6	22.6	5.6	3.3
75 years and over	100.0	95.6	24.4	9.6	8.3	29.9	3.4	93.7	23.8	29.2	3..0	4.4
Female												
Total	100.0	70.3	44.0	37.6	15.0	25.3	2.3	7.3	1.8	3.3	2.1	29.7
Under 18 years	100.0	73.3	40.8	35.0	.1	36.0	4.0	.4	-	.1	2.0	26.7
18 to 24 years	100.0	57.1	33.0	25.5	12.7	25.0	2.5	1.8	-	1.4	2.3	42.9
25 to 34 years	100.0	69.7	48.2	44.2	27.1	20.8	1.5	2.3	.2	1.7	2.3	30.3
35 to 44 years	100.0	68.7	55.2	51.2	30.3	13.5	1.5	1.4	.2	.7	1.8	31.3
45 to 54 years	100.0	68.4	55.8	50.0	30.1	11.4	.6	2.7	.1	1.5	1.3	31.6
55 to 59 years	100.0	67.5	61.3	43.3	23.2	15.2	1.5	5.5	.7	3.6	3.1	32.5
60 to 64 years	100.0	63.2	38.1	28.3	14.8	19.1	.6	12.1	.8	5.5	1.5	36.8
65 years and over	100.0	93.4	27.7	12.0	4.9	35.7	1.5	90.7	25.8	35.5	3.1	6.6
65 to 74 years	100.0	91.9	33.4	16.3	5.6	30.0	1.3	88.0	30.6	29.6	4.2	8.1
75 years and over	100.0	96.0	17.5	4.0	3.5	46.1	1.7	95.6	17.0	46.1	1.1	4.0

Source: U.S. Bureau of the Census. *Poverty in the United States: 1992*. Current Population Reports, Series P60-185, U.S. Government Printing Office, Washington, D.C., 1993, pp. 168-174. *Notes:* A dash (-) stands for zero or rounds to zero. A (B) indicates that the base was less than 75,000 or data not applicable. CHAMPUS stands for Civilian Health and Medical Program for the Uniformed Services.

★ 406 ★

Health Insurance

Health Insurance Coverage Status of Hispanics, by Age Group, Sex, Household Relationship, Work Experience, and Poverty Status, 1992 - II

Numbers are shown in thousands for persons and families as of March, 1993. Coverage status is based on that of each person in the household. Persons of Hispanic origin may be of any race.

Characteristic	Total	Covered by some form of health insurance during all or part of year										Not covered at any time during the year
		Total	Covered by private health insurance			Covered by Medicaid		Covered by Medicare			Covered by CHAMPUS, VA, or military health care	
			Total	Related to current or past employment of relative or self	Related to own current or past employment	Total	Also covered by private insurance	Total	Also covered by private insurance	Also covered by Medicaid		
ALL INCOME LEVELS (cont.)												
Percent (cont.)												
Household relationship												
Total	100.0	67.4	44.5	38.6	18.7	21.9	2.3	6.5	1.7	2.6	2.1	32.6
65 years and over	100.0	94.6	29.4	14.6	9.5	31.2	1.6	91.4	26.9	31.0	3.8	5.4
In families	100.0	68.7	45.5	39.7	17.4	22.6	2.5	5.6	1.5	2.1	2.1	31.3
Householder	100.0	69.5	49.1	43.9	37.7	16.6	1.5	10.3	2.9	3.6	2.3	30.5
Under 65 years	100.0	67.0	50.4	46.2	39.8	15.8	1.4	3.0	.5	1.7	2.1	33.0
65 years and over	100.0	96.9	34.3	18.5	15.0	24.9	2.2	92.3	30.0	24.8	4.5	3.1
Related children under 18 years:												
Under 18 years	100.0	74.9	42.6	36.4	.1	36.2	4.4	.1	-	.1	2.0	25.1
Under 6 years	100.0	78.9	39.1	32.0	-	45.6	6.1	-	-	-	2.1	21.1
6 to 17 years	100.0	72.4	44.7	39.0	.2	30.4	3.3	.2	.1	.2	1.9	27.6
Own children 18 years and over	100.0	57.6	43.4	36.1	20.6	14.2	1.4	2.9	.3	2.0	1.5	42.4
In married-couple families	100.0	69.4	52.3	46.3	19.3	15.9	2.2	5.5	1.8	1.6	2.6	30.6
Husbands	100.0	70.2	56.4	51.5	42.9	8.8	1.2	10.3	3.3	2.5	2.8	29.6
Under 65 years	100.0	67.6	58.1	54.2	45.1	7.8	1.1	2.4	.4	.9	2.6	32.4
65 years and over	100.0	97.7	38.7	23.3	19.9	19.1	2.0	93.0	34.0	19.1	5.5	2.3
Wives	100.0	71.6	57.6	51.8	23.0	11.0	1.5	7.6	2.9	2.0	3.1	26.4
Under 65 years	100.0	69.7	58.4	53.6	24.2	10.4	1.4	1.7	.3	.8	2.9	30.3
65 years and over	100.0	98.5	45.8	26.4	5.9	19.7	2.5	94.2	42.0	19.7	5.9	1.5
Related children under 18 years:												
Under 18 years	100.0	73.2	50.5	43.7	.2	26.0	3.9	.1	-	-	2.6	26.8
Under 6 years	100.0	77.2	47.1	39.1	-	35.4	5.7	-	-	-	2.6	22.8
6 to 17 years	100.0	70.7	52.5	46.5	.3	20.3	2.8	.1	.1	-	2.6	29.3
Own children 18 years and over	100.0	58.7	49.2	41.0	20.7	9.5	1.4	2.3	.4	1.3	1.6	41.3
In families with female householder, no spouse present	100.0	72.9	26.9	22.1	11.7	47.4	3.7	5.9	.6	3.7	.9	27.1
Householder	100.0	73.5	29.8	25.5	25.5	42.5	2.6	11.3	1.6	7.0	1.0	26.5
Under 65 years	100.0	71.8	30.9	27.3	27.3	41.9	2.6	4.7	.4	3.6	1.0	28.2
65 years and over	100.0	94.4	17.3	4.8	4.8	48.6	2.4	91.4	15.8	48.1	1.4	5.6
Related children under 18 years:												
Under 18 years	100.0	82.1	24.2	19.5	-	63.4	5.7	.3	-	.3	.7	17.9
Under 6 years	100.0	87.2	21.2	16.0	-	73.8	7.9	-	-	-	1.0	12.8
6 to 17 years	100.0	79.3	25.8	21.4	-	57.5	4.5	.5	-	.5	.5	20.7
Own children 18 years and over	100.0	57.5	33.5	27.6	20.5	24.2	1.5	4.2	.2	3.5	1.0	42.5
In unrelated subfamilies	100.0	51.4	18.8	15.9	5.6	34.5	3.6	1.9	-	.3	.1	48.6
Under 18 years	100.0	63.7	25.0	20.2	-	45.7	7.0	-	-	-	.1	36.3
Under 6 years	100.0	71.0	18.4	13.0	-	57.3	4.7	-	-	-	.3	29.0
6 to 17 years	100.0	57.1	31.1	26.7	-	35.1	9.1	-	-	-	-	42.9
18 years and over	100.0	38.5	12.2	11.5	11.5	22.8	-	4.0	-	.6	.1	61.5
Unrelated individuals	100.0	58.2	39.9	31.8	31.8	14.1	.7	14.6	3.5	7.2	1.6	41.8
Male	100.0	49.3	38.6	33.3	33.3	8.3	.9	7.8	1.8	4.1	1.5	50.7
Under 65 years	100.0	46.1	39.5	34.7	34.7	5.9	.8	2.2	.6	1.4	1.3	53.9
Living alone	100.0	62.3	53.2	47.2	47.2	9.2	1.4	3.2	.7	2.5	1.6	37.7
65 years and over	100.0	100.0	24.9	11.6	11.6	46.6	1.9	97.2	22.1	46.6	5.6	-
Living alone	(B)	(B)	(B)	(B)	(B)	(B)	(B)	(B)	(B)	(B)	(B)	(B)
Female	100.0	71.4	41.8	29.6	29.6	22.6	.6	24.7	5.9	11.8	1.6	28.6
Under 65 years	100.0	63.7	45.9	36.3	36.3	16.5	.7	4.0	-	2.7	1.6	36.3
Living alone	100.0	72.5	51.5	42.1	42.1	16.8	-	7.8	.1	5.1	1.6	27.5
65 years and over	100.0	98.1	27.4	6.3	6.3	43.8	-	97.1	26.4	43.8	1.7	1.9
Living alone	100.0	98.5	29.2	6.6	6.6	43.1	-	97.4	28.1	43.1	1.8	1.5

[Continued]

★ 406 ★

Health Insurance Coverage Status of Hispanics, by Age Group, Sex, Household Relationship, Work Experience, and Poverty Status, 1992 - II

[Continued]

Characteristic	Total	Covered by some form of health insurance during all or part of year										Not covered at any time during the year
			Covered by private health insurance			Covered by Medicaid		Covered by Medicare			Covered by CHAMPUS, VA, or military health care	
		Total	Total	Related to current or past employment of relative or self	Related to own current or past employment	Total	Also covered by private insurance	Total	Also covered by private insurance	Also covered by Medicaid		
Work experience												
Male:												
Under 16 years	100.0	76.5	43.3	36.6	-	38.0	5.0	.1	-	.1	1.9	23.5
16 to 64 years	100.0	56.4	46.9	42.2	33.8	8.5	1.0	2.3	.5	1.1	1.9	43.6
Worked during year	100.0	56.4	51.3	46.9	39.6	4.3	.8	.6	.2	.1	1.8	43.6
Year-round, full-time	100.0	64.8	62.1	58.1	53.1	1.6	.3	.2	.1	-	1.9	35.2
Not year-round full-time	100.0	43.1	34.2	29.1	18.2	8.6	1.5	1.2	.3	.2	1.8	56.9
Did not work	100.0	56.6	24.6	18.8	4.8	29.5	2.0	11.0	2.1	6.3	2.4	43.4
65 years and over	100.0	96.3	31.8	18.2	16.1	24.9	1.9	92.5	28.4	24.7	4.8	3.7
Worked during year	100.0	88.3	54.9	36.0	32.5	6.2	2.6	74.8	41.4	6.2	-	11.7
Year-round, full-time	(B)	(B)	(B)	(B)	(B)	(B)	(B)	(B)	(B)	(B)	(B)	(B)
Not year-round full-time	(B)	(B)	(B)	(B)	(B)	(B)	(B)	(B)	(B)	(B)	(B)	(B)
Did not work	100.0	98.0	27.1	14.6	12.8	28.8	1.7	96.1	25.8	28.5	5.7	2.0
Female:												
Under 16 years	100.0	74.0	40.7	35.1	-	37.1	4.2	-	-	-	2.0	26.0
16 to 64 years	100.0	66.2	47.3	41.7	23.4	18.4	1.5	2.6	.2	1.6	2.0	33.8
Worked during year	100.0	69.0	60.1	54.4	38.7	9.4	1.8	.8	.2	.5	2.0	31.0
Year-round, full-time	100.0	75.6	73.2	69.2	58.6	2.8	1.1	.3	.2	.2	1.6	24.4
Not year-round full-time	100.0	62.1	46.4	39.0	17.9	16.3	2.6	1.2	.2	.9	2.4	37.9
Did not work	100.0	62.3	29.3	23.7	1.8	31.1	1.1	5.1	.2	3.2	2.0	37.7
65 years and over	100.0	93.4	27.7	12.0	4.9	35.7	1.5	90.7	25.8	35.5	3.1	6.6
Worked during year	(B)	(B)	(B)	(B)	(B)	(B)	(B)	(B)	(B)	(B)	(B)	(B)
Year-round, full-time	(B)	(B)	(B)	(B)	(B)	(B)	(B)	(B)	(B)	(B)	(B)	(B)
Not year-round full-time	(B)	(B)	(B)	(B)	(B)	(B)	(B)	(B)	(B)	(B)	(B)	(B)
Did not work	100.0	93.9	25.7	10.0	3.3	38.6	1.6	91.8	24.5	38.4	3.2	6.1
BELOW POVERTY LEVEL												
Number												
Both sexes												
Total	6,655	3,913	767	523	193	3,172	174	396	31	253	55	2,742
Under 18 years	3,116	2,208	374	259	5	1,960	133	8	-	8	22	908
18 to 24 years	844	359	83	46	30	278	11	25	-	19	9	485
25 to 34 years	1,076	476	112	82	52	361	12	32	-	23	7	600
35 to 44 years	719	317	94	80	63	221	8	15	1	11	6	402
45 to 54 years	349	157	40	28	22	105	1	27	-	16	3	192
55 to 59 years	137	70	17	11	9	51	2	16	1	12	3	67
60 to 64 years	145	82	19	9	6	52	2	33	3	21	2	63
65 years and over	269	243	28	7	5	145	5	240	25	144	4	25
65 to 74 years	157	139	21	6	3	77	3	138	19	77	4	18
75 years and over	112	104	7	1	1	67	2	103	6	67	-	8
Male												
Total	3,067	1,666	383	283	124	1,313	88	138	12	85	19	1,401
Under 18 years	1,551	1,114	201	145	5	981	70	5	-	5	8	437
18 to 24 years	360	102	41	28	19	62	3	3	-	1	-	258
25 to 34 years	467	135	50	41	35	84	5	7	-	2	2	332
35 to 44 years	328	110	43	40	36	65	2	4	-	4	2	218
45 to 54 years	170	68	22	15	14	38	1	15	-	8	3	102
55 to 59 years	63	23	7	5	5	17	2	5	1	4	-	30
60 to 64 years	50	32	8	5	5	19	2	18	2	13	2	18
65 years and over	88	82	10	4	4	48	3	81	8	48	1	6
65 to 74 years	57	53	6	2	2	28	1	52	5	28	1	4
75 years and over	31	29	4	1	1	20	2	29	4	20	-	1
Female												
Total	3,588	2,247	384	241	69	1,859	85	257	19	168	36	1,341
Under 18 years	1,565	1,094	173	154	-	980	62	3	-	3	14	471
18 to 24 years	484	257	47	18	10	216	8	22	-	17	8	227
25 to 34 years	609	141	61	41	17	277	7	25	-	21	5	268
35 to 44 years	391	207	51	41	26	155	6	11	1	7	3	184
45 to 54 years	178	89	18	13	9	67	-	12	-	8	-	90
55 to 59 years	84	47	10	6	4	33	-	11	-	8	3	37
60 to 64 years	96	50	12	4	1	33	-	14	1	8	-	45
65 years and over	181	161	18	3	1	97	2	159	17	97	2	20
65 to 74 years	100	86	15	3	1	49	2	86	15	49	2	13

[Continued]

★ 406 ★

Health Insurance Coverage Status of Hispanics, by Age Group, Sex, Household Relationship, Work Experience, and Poverty Status, 1992 - II

[Continued]

Characteristic	Total	Covered by some form of health insurance during all or part of year											Not covered at any time during the year
		Total	Covered by private health insurance			Covered by Medicaid		Covered by Medicare			Covered by CHAMPUS, VA, or military health care	
			Total	Related to current or past employment of relative or self	Related to own current or past employment	Total	Also covered by private insurance	Total	Also covered by private insurance	Also covered by Medicaid		
75 years and over	81	75	3	-	-	48	-	74	2	48	-	6
Household relationship												
Total	6,655	3,913	767	523	193	3,172	174	396	31	253	55	2,742
65 years and over	269	243	28	7	545	145	540	240	254	144	4	25
In families	5,655	3,442	663	488	165	2,845	155	226	19	143	40	2,213
Householder	1,395	802	171	135	129	594	20	136	9	82	14	594
Under 65 years	1,324	736	162	132	125	559	18	72	2	48	12	588
65 years and over	72	66	8	4	4	35	1	64	7	35	1	6
Related children under 18 years:												
Under 18 years	2,946	2,121	351	250	4	1,888	124	8	-	8	20	826
Under 6 years	1,223	949	141	89	-	873	66	-	-	-	9	274
6 to 17 years	1,723	1,171	210	161	4	1,015	58	8	-	8	11	552
Own children 18 years and over	333	136	35	26	12	103	2	10	-	10	1	197
In married-couple families	3,136	1,599	422	334	118	1,178	65	134	14	71	24	1,537
Husbands	687	314	107	92	84	175	8	78	6	37	7	373
Under 65 years	638	269	100	91	81	154	7	34	7	16	6	369
65 years and over	50	45	7	4	4	21	1	44	6	21	1	4
Wives	672	294	93	73	20	187	4	46	7	26	6	378
Under 65 years	648	272	86	70	19	175	3	25	1	14	6	376
65 years and over	24	22	7	3	1	12	1	22	7	12	-	3
Related children under 18 years:												
Under 18 years	1,500	924	198	147	4	774	52	2	-	2	11	576
Under 6 years	641	444	86	55	-	390	33	-	-	-	4	196
6 to 17 years	860	480	112	91	4	384	19	2	-	2	8	380
Own children 18 years and over	137	40	19	17	7	21	-	3	-	3	-	97
In families with female householder, no spouse present	2,154	1,682	188	126	34	1,555	82	81	4	65	14	472
Householder	604	461	49	32	32	412	14	58	3	46	6	143
Under 65 years	580	439	47	32	32	397	14	36	1	31	6	142
65 years and over	24	22	2	-	-	15	-	22	2	15	-	2
Related children under 18 years:												
Under 18 years	1,289	1,106	126	89	-	1,044	66	6	-	6	7	184
Under 6 years	510	456	47	28	-	441	31	-	-	-	4	53
6 to 17 years	779	649	79	61	-	603	35	6	-	6	3	130
Own children 18 years and over	177	91	12	5	2	80	1	7	-	7	1	86
In unrelated subfamilies	222	114	19	9	1	101	9	4	-	1	-	108
Under 18 years	127	74	17	8	-	66	9	-	-	-	-	53
Under 6 years	66	44	8	4	-	40	4	-	-	-	-	22
6 to 17 years	61	30	9	5	-	27	5	-	-	-	-	31
18 years and over	95	40	2	1	1	35	-	4	-	1	-	55
Unrelated individuals	777	357	85	26	26	226	10	166	12	109	15	421
Male	382	111	30	13	13	74	6	46	5	35	3	271
Under 65 years	350	79	28	13	13	51	5	14	3	12	3	271
Living alone	72	35	10	5	5	26	2	8	-	8	2	37
65 years and over	32	32	3	-	-	23	2	32	3	23	-	-
Living alone	29	29	2	-	-	20	1	29	2	20	-	-
Female	396	246	55	13	13	152	4	120	7	74	12	150
Under 65 years	292	143	47	13	13	90	4	19	-	12	9	148
Living alone	102	63	14	2	2	39	-	17	-	10	4	39
65 years and over	104	103	8	-	-	62	-	101	7	62	2	1
Living alone	93	93	8	-	-	58	-	92	7	58	2	-
Work experience												
Male:												
Under 16 years	1,433	1,053	186	136	1	934	69	2	-	2	7	379
16 to 64 years	1,546	530	187	143	119	332	17	55	3	35	11	1,016
Worked during year	1,007	286	147	123	112	137	8	6	-	1	5	721

[Continued]

★ 406 ★

Health Insurance Coverage Status of Hispanics, by Age Group, Sex, Household Relationship, Work Experience, and Poverty Status, 1992 - II

[Continued]

Characteristic	Total	Covered by some form of health insurance during all or part of year										Not covered at any time during the year
		Total	Covered by private health insurance			Covered by Medicaid		Covered by Medicare			Covered by CHAMPUS, VA, or military health care	
			Total	Related to current or past employment of relative or self	Related to own current or past employment	Total	Also covered by private insurance	Total	Also covered by private insurance	Also covered by Medicaid		
Year-round, full-time	317	90	75	71	70	16	1	-	-	-	1	226
Not year-round full-time	690	196	72	52	43	121	7	6	-	1	4	494
Did not work	539	244	40	21	7	195	9	48	3	34	6	295
65 years and over	88	82	10	4	4	48	3	81	8	48	1	6
Worked during year	8	5	1	1	1	3	-	4	-	3	-	3
Year-round, full time	1	1	1	1	1	-	-	-	-	-	-	-
Not year-round full-time	7	4	-	-	-	3	-	4	-	3	-	3
Did not work	80	77	8	2	2	45	3	77	8	45	1	3
Female:												
Under 16 years	1,443	1,024	157	106	-	922	58	1	-	1	14	419
16 to 64 years	1,964	1,061	209	131	68	840	25	97	2	71	20	903
Worked during year	645	297	117	78	62	192	22	13	1	10	11	349
Year-round, full-time	130	42	31	29	28	13	3	3	1	1	-	87
Not year-round full-time	516	255	86	49	34	179	19	10	-	9	11	261
Did not work	1,319	765	92	53	5	648	3	84	1	61	9	554
65 years and over	181	161	18	3	1	97	2	159	17	97	2	20
Worked during year	6	4	-	-	-	1	-	4	-	1	-	2
Year-round, full-time	-	-	-	-	-	-	-	-	-	-	-	-
Not year-round full-time	6	4	-	-	-	1	-	4	-	1	-	2
Did not work	175	157	18	3	1	96	2	155	17	96	2	18

Source: U.S. Bureau of the Census. *Poverty in the United States: 1992.* Current Population Reports, Series P60-185, U.S. Government Printing Office, Washington, D.C., 1993, pp. 168-174. *Notes:* A dash (-) stands for zero or rounds to zero. A (B) indicates that the base was less than 75,000 or data not applicable. CHAMPUS stands for Civilian Health and Medical Program for the Uniformed Services.

★ 407 ★

Health Insurance

Health Insurance Coverage Status of Hispanics, by Age Group, Sex, Household Relationship, Work Experience, and Poverty Status, 1992 - III

Numbers are shown in thousands for persons and families as of March, 1993. Coverage status is based on that of each person in the household. Persons of Hispanic origin may be of any race.

Characteristic	Total	Covered by some form of health insurance during all or part of year										Not covered at any time during the year
		Total	Covered by private health insurance			Covered by Medicaid		Covered by Medicare			Covered by CHAMPUS, VA, or military health care	
			Total	Related to current or past employment of relative or self	Related to own current or past employment	Total	Also covered by private insurance	Total	Also covered by private insurance	Also covered by Medicaid		
BELOW POVERTY LEVEL (cont.)												
Percent												
Both sexes												
Total	100.0	58.8	11.5	7.9	2.9	47.7	2.6	5.9	.5	3.8	.8	41.2
Under 18 years	100.0	70.9	12.0	8.3	.2	62.9	4.3	.2	-	.2	.7	29.1
18 to 24 years	100.0	42.5	9.8	5.5	3.5	32.9	1.3	3.0	-	2.2	1.0	57.5
25 to 34 years	100.0	44.2	10.4	7.6	4.8	33.5	1.1	3.0	-	2.1	.6	55.8
35 to 44 years	100.0	44.1	13.1	11.2	8.7	30.7	1.1	2.1	.1	1.5	.8	55.9
45 to 54 years	100.0	45.0	11.5	8.1	6.4	30.1	.3	7.6	-	4.6	.9	55.0
55 to 59 years	100.0	51.3	12.4	8.1	6.9	36.9	1.5	11.5	.4	8.4	2.1	48.7
60 to 64 years	100.0	56.5	13.4	6.5	4.4	35.8	1.7	22.5	2.0	14.7	1.5	43.5
65 years and over	100.0	90.6	10.2	2.6	1.7	53.9	1.7	89.5	9.3	53.7	1.4	9.4
65 to 74 years	100.0	88.7	13.2	3.6	2.1	49.3	2.0	87.6	12.4	49.0	2.4	11.3
75 years and over	100.0	93.3	6.1	1.1	1.1	60.4	1.4	92.2	5.0	60.4	-	6.7
Male												
Total	100.0	54.3	12.5	9.2	4.0	42.8	2.9	4.5	.4	2.8	.6	45.7

[Continued]

★ 407 ★

Health Insurance Coverage Status of Hispanics, by Age Group, Sex, Household Relationship, Work Experience, and Poverty Status, 1992 - III

[Continued]

Characteristic	Total	Covered by some form of health insurance during all or part of year											Not covered at any time during the year
		Total	Covered by private health insurance			Covered by Medicaid		Covered by Medicare			Covered by CHAMPUS, VA, or military health care		
			Total	Related to current or past employment of relative or self	Related to own current or past employment	Total	Also covered by private insurance	Total	Also covered by private insurance	Also covered by Medicaid			
Under 18 years	100.0	71.8	13.0	9.4	.3	63.2	4.5	.3	-	.3	.5		28.2
18 to 24 years	100.0	28.3	11.5	7.7	5.4	17.3	.9	.8	.1	.4	-		71.7
25 to 34 years	100.0	28.9	10.8	8.8	7.6	17.9	1.0	1.4	-	.5	.3		71.1
35 to 44 years	100.0	33.5	13.2	12.1	11.1	19.9	.5	1.3	-	1.2	.8		66.5
45 to 54 years	100.0	39.9	13.1	9.0	7.9	22.0	.6	8.7	-	4.6	1.9		60.1
55 to 59 years	(B)	(B)	(B)	(B)	(B)	(B)	(B)	(B)	(B)	(B)	(B)		(B)
60 to 64 years	(B)	(B)	(B)	(B)	(B)	(B)	(B)	(B)	(B)	(B)	(B)		(B)
65 years and over	100.0	93.6	10.9	4.0	4.0	54.2	2.9	92.2	9.5	54.2	4.5		6.4
65 to 74 years	(B)	(B)	(B)	(B)	(B)	(B)	(B)	(B)	(B)	(B)	(B)		(B)
75 years and over	(B)	(B)	(B)	(B)	(B)	(B)	(B)	(B)	(B)	(B)	(B)		(B)
Female													
Total	100.0	62.6	10.7	6.7	1.9	51.8	2.4	7.2	.5	4.7	1.0		37.4
Under 18 years	100.0	69.9	11.1	7.3	-	62.6	4.0	.2	-	.2	.9		30.1
18 to 24 years	100.0	53.1	8.6	3.8	2.1	44.5	1.6	4.6	-	3.6	1.7		46.9
25 to 34 years	100.0	56.0	10.1	6.7	2.8	45.5	1.2	4.2	.1	3.4	.9		44.0
35 to 44 years	100.0	53.0	13.0	10.5	6.7	39.8	1.6	2.8	.2	1.7	.8		47.0
45 to 54 years	100.0	49.8	9.9	7.3	5.0	37.8	-	6.6	-	4.5	-		50.2
55 to 59 years	100.0	56.2	11.6	7.1	5.1	39.7	-	12.8	-	9.2	3.4		43.8
60 to 64 years	100.0	52.5	12.2	4.4	1.2	34.7	-	14.8	.6	8.7	-		47.5
65 years and over	100.0	89.1	9.9	1.9	.6	53.8	1.1	88.2	9.2	53.5	1.4		10.9
65 to 74 years	100.0	86.5	15.0	3.4	1.1	49.6	2.1	86.0	15.0	49.1	2.5		13.5
75 years and over	100.0	92.3	3.7	-	-	58.9	-	90.8	2.2	58.9	-		7.7
Household relationship													
Total	100.0	58.8	11.5	7.9	2.9	47.7	2.6	5.9	.5	3.8	.8		41.2
65 years and over	100.0	90.6	10.2	2.6	1.7	53.9	1.7	89.5	9.3	53.7	1.4		9.4
In families	100.0	60.9	11.7	8.6	2.9	50.3	2.7	4.0	.3	2.5	.7		39.1
Householder	100.0	57.4	12.2	9.7	9.2	42.6	1.4	9.8	.6	5.9	1.0		42.6
Under 65 years	100.0	55.6	12.3	9.9	9.4	42.2	1.4	5.5	.1	3.6	.9		44.4
65 years and over	(B)	(B)	(B)	(B)	(B)	(B)	(B)	(B)	(B)	(B)	(B)		(B)
Related children under 18 years:													
Under 18 years	100.0	72.0	11.9	8.5	.1	64.1	4.2	.3	-	.3	.7		28.0
Under 6 years	100.0	77.8	11.6	7.2	-	71.4	5.4	-	-	-	.7		22.4
6 to 17 years	100.0	68.0	12.2	9.3	.2	58.9	3.4	.4	-	.4	.6		32.0
Own children 18 years and over	100.0	40.8	10.5	7.7	3.5	30.8	.7	3.1	-	3.1	.2		59.2
In married-couple families	100.0	51.0	13.4	10.6	3.7	37.6	2.1	4.3	.4	2.3	.8		49.0
Husbands	100.0	45.7	15.6	13.8	12.2	25.5	1.2	11.4	.9	5.4	1.0		54.3
Under 65 years	100.0	42.2	15.7	14.3	12.6	24.2	1.2	5.4	.1	2.5	.9		57.8
65 years and over	(B)	(B)	(B)	(B)	(B)	(B)	(B)	(B)	(B)	(B)	(B)		(B)
Wives	100.0	43.7	13.9	10.9	3.0	27.8	.6	6.9	1.1	3.9	.8		56.3
Under 65 years	100.0	42.0	13.3	10.7	3.0	27.0	.5	3.8	.1	2.2	8		56.0
65 years and over	(B)	(B)	(B)	(B)	(B)	(B)	(B)	(B)	(B)	(B)	(B)		(B)
Related children under 18 years:													
Under 18 years	100.0	61.6	13.2	9.8	.3	51.6	3.5	.1	-	.1	.8		38.4
Under 6 years	100.0	89.4	13.5	8.6	-	60.9	5.2	-	-	-	.6		30.6
6 to 17 years	100.0	55.8	13.0	10.6	.5	44.7	2.2	.2	-	.2	.9		44.2
Own children 18 years and over	100.0	29.63	13.8	12.6	5.0	15.5	-	2.5	-	2.5	-		70.7
In families with female householder, no spouse present	100.0	78.1	8.7	5.8	1.6	72.2	3.8	3.7	.2	3.0	.7		21.9
Householder	100.0	76.3	8.1	5.3	5.3	68.2	2.3	9.6	.6	7.6	1.0		23.7
Under 65 years	100.0	75.6	8.0	5.5	5.5	68.4	2.4	6.2	.2	6.4	1.1		24.4
65 years and over	(B)	(B)	(B)	(B)	(B)	(B)	(B)	(B)	(B)	(B)	(B)		(B)
Related children under 18 years:													
Under 18 years	100.0	85.8	9.7	6.9	-	81.0	5.1	.5	-	.5	.6		14.2
Under 6 years	100.0	89.5	9.2	5.5	-	86.5	6.2	-	-	-	.8		10.5
6 to 17 years	100.0	83.3	10.1	7.8	-	77.4	4.5	.8	.1	.8	.4		16.7
Own children 18 years and over	100.0	51.2	6.6	2.7	1.3	45.0	.8	3.9	-	3.9	.4		48.8
In unrelated subfamilies	100.0	51.3	8.4	4.2	.4	45.5	3.9	1.7	-	.4	.2		48.7

[Continued]

★ 407 ★

Health Insurance Coverage Status of Hispanics, by Age Group, Sex, Household Relationship, Work Experience, and Poverty Status, 1992 - III

[Continued]

Characteristic	Total	Covered by some form of health insurance during all or part of year										Not covered at any time during the year
		Total	Covered by private health insurance			Covered by Medicaid		Covered by Medicare			Covered by CHAMPUS, VA, or military health care	
			Total	Related to current or past employment of relative or self	Related to own current or past employment	Total	Also covered by private insurance	Total	Also covered by private insurance	Also covered by Medicaid		
Under 18 years	100.0	58.3	13.0	6.6	-	52.2	6.9	-	-	-	.2	41.7
Under 6 years	(B)	(B)	(B)	(B)	(B)	(B)	(B)	(B)	(B)	(B)	(B)	(B)
6 to 17 years	(B)	(B)	(B)	(B)	(B)	(B)	(B)	(B)	(B)	(B)	(B)	(B)
18 years and over	100.0	42.0	2.2	1.0	1.0	36.6	-	4.0	-	1.0	.2	58.0
Unrelated individuals	100.0	45.9	11.0	3.4	3.4	29.1	1.3	21.3	1.6	14.0	1.9	54.1
Male	100.0	29.0	8.0	3.4	3.4	19.3	1.6	11.9	1.4	9.1	.8	71.0
Under 65 years	100.0	22.5	7.9	3.7	3.7	14.6	1.3	3.9	.8	3.4	.9	77.5
Living alone	(B)	(B)	(B)	(B)	(B)	(B)	(B)	(B)	(B)	(B)	(B)	(B)
65 years and over	(B)	(B)	(B)	(B)	(B)	(B)	(B)	(B)	(B)	(B)	(B)	(B)
Living alone	(B)	(B)	(B)	(B)	(B)	(B)	(B)	(B)	(B)	(B)	(B)	(B)
Female	100.0	62.2	13.9	3.3	3.3	38.5	1.0	30.4	1.7	18.8	3.0	37.8
Under 65 years	100.0	49.1	16.2	4.5	4.5	30.7	1.4	6.5	-	4.1	3.2	50.9
Living alone	100.0	61.9	13.4	2.2	2.2	38.2	-	16.5	-	9.6	3.5	38.1
65 years and over	100.0	98.9	7.7	-	-	60.2	-	97.7	6.5	60.2	2.4	1.1
Living alone	100.0	100.0	8.5	-	-	62.0	-	98.7	7.2	62.0	2.7	-
Work experience												
Male:												
Under 16 years	100.0	73.5	13.0	9.5	.1	65.2	4.8	.2	-	.2	.5	26.5
16 to 64 years	100.0	34.3	12.1	9.3	7.7	21.4	1.1	3.5	.2	2.2	.7	65.7
Worked during year	100.0	28.4	14.6	12.2	11.2	13.6	.8	.6	-	.1	.5	71.6
Year-round, full-time	100.0	28.5	23.7	22.3	22.0	4.9	.3	-	-	-	.3	71.5
Not year-round full-time	100.0	28.4	10.5	7.5	6.2	17.5	1.0	.9	-	.1	.6	71.6
Did not work	100.0	45.2	7.4	3.8	1.3	36.2	1.7	8.9	.6	6.3	1.1	54.8
65 years and over	100.0	93.6	10.9	4.0	4.0	54.2	2.9	92.2	9.5	54.2	1.5	6.4
Worked during year	(B)	(B)	(B)	(B)	(B)	(B)	(B)	(B)	(B)	(B)	(B)	(B)
Year-round, full-time	(B)	(B)	(B)	(B)	(B)	(B)	(B)	(B)	(B)	(B)	(B)	(B)
Not year-round full-time	(B)	(B)	(B)	(B)	(B)	(B)	(B)	(B)	(B)	(B)	(B)	(B)
Did not work	100.0	96.2	10.5	2.9	2.9	56.2	3.2	96.2	10.5	56.2	1.7	3.8
Female:												
Under 16 years	100.0	71.0	10.9	7.4	-	63.9	4.0	.1	-	.1	1.0	29.0
16 to 64 years	100.0	54.0	10.6	6.7	3.4	42.8	1.3	4.9	.1	3.6	1.0	46.0
Worked during year	100.0	46.0	18.1	12.0	9.6	29.8	3.4	2.0	.2	1.5	1.7	54.0
Year-round, full-time	100.0	32.5	23.6	22.3	21.6	9.9	2.4	2.0	.7	.7	-	67.5
Not year-round full-time	100.0	49.4	16.7	9.5	6.6	34.7	3.7	1.9	.1	1.8	2.1	50.6
Did not work	100.0	58.0	7.0	4.0	.4	49.1	.2	6.4	-	4.6	.7	42.0
65 years and over	100.0	89.1	9.9	1.9	.6	53.8	1.1	88.2	9.2	53.5	1.4	10.9
Worked during year	(B)	(B)	(B)	(B)	(B)	(B)	(B)	(B)	(B)	(B)	(B)	(B)
Year-round, full-time	(B)	(B)	(B)	(B)	(B)	(B)	(B)	(B)	(B)	(B)	(B)	(B)
Not year-round full-time	(B)	(B)	(B)	(B)	(B)	(B)	(B)	(B)	(B)	(B)	(B)	(B)
Did not work	100.0	89.8	10.3	1.9	.6	55.0	1.2	88.9	9.6	54.7	1.4	10.2

Source: U.S. Bureau of the Census. *Poverty in the United States: 1992*. Current Population Reports, Series P60-185, U.S. Government Printing Office, Washington, D.C., 1993, pp. 168-174. *Notes:* A dash (-) stands for zero or rounds to zero. A (B) indicates that the base was less than 75,000 or data not applicable. CHAMPUS stands for Civilian Health and Medical Program for the Uniformed Services.

★ 408 ★

Health Insurance

Health Insurance Coverage Status, by Race/Ethnicity, 1992

Data are shown for persons as of the following year for coverage in the year shown. Government health insurance includes Medicare, Medicaid, and military plans.

	Number (mil.)							Percent			
	Total persons	Covered by private or Government health insurance					Not covered by health insurance	Covered by private or Government health insurance			Not covered by health insurance
		Total[1]	Private		Government			Total[1]	Private	Medicaid	
			Total	Group health[2]	Medicare	Medicaid					
1992, total[3]	254.2	216.8	180.8	148.2	33.7	28.6	37.4	85.3	71.1	11.2	14.7
White	212.0	183.1	158.7	129.7	29.6	18.1	28.9	86.4	74.9	8.5	13.6
Black	32.0	25.6	15.7	13.3	3.3	8.9	6.4	79.9	49.0	27.9	20.1
Hispanic origin[4]	22.8	15.3	10.1	8.8	1.5	5.0	7.4	67.5	44.5	21.9	32.5

Source: 1994 Statistical Abstract of the United States on CD-ROM [machine-readable datafiles]. CD-8A-94. Washington, DC: U.S. Department of Commerce, Economics and Statistics Administration, Bureau of the Census, Data User Services Division, January 1995. Primary source: U.S. Bureau of the Census, March 1993 Supplement to the Current Population Survey, unpublished data. *Notes:* 1. Includes other Government insurance, not shown separately. Persons with coverage counted only once in total, even though they may have been covered by more than one type of policy. 2. Related to employment of self or other family members. 3. Includes other races not shown separately. 4. Persons of Hispanic origin may be of any race.

★ 409 ★

Health Insurance

Health Insurance Coverage for HIV Counseling and Testing

Health insurance status is shown for 885,046 clients of publicly funded HIV (human immunodeficiency virus) counseling and testing sites in 1992. Totals may be less than 885,046 because of missing data. These figures are based on analysis of data from 30 State, territorial, and local health departments, funded by the CDC (Centers for Disease Control). About half of the testing on total clients was performed on specimens from persons with no health insurance.

Race/ethnicity	Any insurance		No insurance	
	Number	Percent	Number	Percent
White	268,005	56.0	211,124	44.0
Black	107,199	42.0	149,364	58.0
Hispanic	61,070	46.0	71,673	54.0
Asian or Pacific Islander	3,546	56.0	2,840	44.0
American Indian or Alaska Native	1,990	49.0	2,069	51.0
Other	2,820	46.0	3,346	54.0

Source: Valdiserri, Ronald O., MD, MPH, et al. "Clients without health insurance at publicly funded HIV counseling and testing sites: implications for early intervention." *Public Health Reports* 110, no. 1 (January-February 1995), p. 49.

★ 410 ★

Health Insurance

Health Insurance Coverage in the Nine States With the Largest Latino Nonelderly Populations, 1989

State	Hispanic pop. (000)	Proportion of nonelderly Latino population (%)		
		Uninsured	Medicaid	Other insured[1]
United States	18,422	39.0	11.8	49.2
California	6,944	43.7	11.0	45.3
Texas	3,980	47.6	7.8	44.6
New York	1,727	31.0	26.2	42.8
Florida	1,331	36.5	6.7	56.8
Illinois	828	22.9	12.0	65.2
New Jersey	533	28.1	10.5	61.5
Connecticut	123	13.5	11.5	75.0
Washington	106	23.3	20.3	56.4
Michigan	100	12.5	25.5	62.1

Source: Burciaga Valdez, PH.D., R. and others. "Insuring Latinos against the cost of illness." *JAMA* Vol. 269, No. 7, p. 892. Primary source: Source of data was March 1990 Current Population Survey. *Notes:* 1. Other insured category includes group and individual coverage, as well as some Medicare coverage.

★ 411 ★

Health Insurance

Health Insurance Coverage, by Poverty Status, 1992

Numbers are shown in thousands.

Poverty status, race, and Hispanic origin	Total	Covered by some form of health insurance all or part of year					Not covered
		Total	Private insurance[1]	Medicaid[1]	Medicare[1]	CHAMPUS, VA or military health plan[1]	
Number							
ALL INCOME LEVELS							
Total	253,969	213,613	180,668	28,411	33,663	9,453	37,356
White	211,820	182,989	158,635	18,046	29,591	7,549	28,830
Black	31,916	25,512	15,677	8,860	3,319	1,443	6,404
Hispanic origin[2]	22,720	15,323	10,121	4,976	1,473	467	7,397
INCOME BELOW POVERTY LEVEL							
Total	36,880	26,373	8,101	17,419	4,924	715	10,507
White	24,523	16,930	6,157	10,122	3,603	509	7,593
Black	10,613	8,214	1,580	6,445	1,192	159	2,399
Hispanic origin[2]	6,655	3,913	767	3,172	396	55	2,742

[Continued]

★ 411 ★

Health Insurance Coverage, by Poverty Status, 1992

[Continued]

Poverty status, race, and Hispanic origin	Total	Covered by some form of health insurance all or part of year					Not covered
		Total	Private insurance[1]	Medicaid[1]	Medicare[1]	CHAMPUS, VA or military health plan[1]	
Percent distribution							
ALL INCOME LEVELS							
Total	100.0	85.3	71.1	11.2	13.3	3.7	14.7
White	100.0	86.4	74.9	8.5	14.0	3.6	13.6
Black	100.0	79.9	49.1	27.8	10.4	4.5	20.1
Hispanic origin[2]	100.0	67.4	44.5	21.9	6.5	2.1	32.6
INCOME BELOW POVERTY LEVEL							
Total	100.0	71.5	22.0	47.2	13.4	1.9	28.5
White	100.0	69.0	25.1	41.3	14.7	2.1	31.0
Black	100.0	77.4	14.9	60.7	11.2	1.5	22.6
Hispanic origin[2]	100.0	58.8	11.5	47.7	6.0	0.8	41.2

Source: U.S. Bureau of the Census. *Poverty in the United States: 1992.* Current Population Reports, Series P60-185, U.S. Government Printing Office, Washington, D.C., 1993, p. XIX. *Notes:* CHAMPUS stands for Civilian Health and Medical Program for the Uniformed Services. VA stands for Veterans Administration. 1. Includes those also covered by other insurance. 2. Persons of Hispanic origin may be of any race.

★ 412 ★

Health Insurance

Health Insurance Coverage, by Race/Ethnicity, 1987-89

Data represent persons covered by Government or private health insurance coverage during a 28-month period, beginning October 1986. Figures are based on Survey of Income and Program Participation.

Race/ethnicity	All persons (mil.)	Covered by insurance (mil.)				Percent covered by insurance			
		Government or private			Private	Government or private			Private
		For entire period	For part of the period	No coverage	for entire period	For entire period	For part of the period	No coverage	for entire period
Total[1]	231.0	169.8	52.1	9.1	146.8	73.5	22.6	3.9	63.6
White	195.6	148.2	40.2	7.2	132.6	75.8	20.6	3.7	67.8
Black	27.8	16.7	9.7	1.4	10.5	60.2	34.9	4.9	37.8
Hispanic[2]	17.4	9.3	6.2	1.9	7.0	53.6	35.6	10.7	40.2

Source: 1994 Statistical Abstract of the United States on CD-ROM [machine-readable datafiles]. CD-8A-94. Washington, DC: U.S. Department of Commerce, Economics and Statistics Administration, Bureau of the Census, Data User Services Division, January 1995. Primary source: U.S. Bureau of the Census, Current Population Reports, series P70-17 and P70-29; and unpublished data. *Notes:* 1. Includes other races, not shown separately. 2. Persons of Hispanic origin may be of any race.

★ 413 ★

Health Insurance

Health Insurance Coverage, by Sex and Race/Ethnicity, 1990-92

Data show percent distribution of persons covered in each time period by various types of programs.

Health insurance coverage	Both sexes	Male	Female	White		Black	Hispanic origin[1]	Not of Hispanic origin
				Total	Not of Hispanic origin			
All persons (in thousands)	235,811	113,681	122,131	198,579	182,646	28,982	18,565	217,246
Percent	100.0	100.0	100.0	100.0	100.0	100.0	100.0	100.0
Percent distribution								
Covered by private or government health insurance								
Less than 32 months	25.3	26.6	24.0	23.5	21.2	36.0	48.0	23.3
No months	3.8	4.3	3.3	3.5	2.9	5.1	10.1	3.3
1 to 6 months	2.4	2.7	2.2	2.2	1.9	3.4	6.0	2.1
7 to 12 months	3.0	3.1	2.9	2.7	2.4	5.2	5.9	2.8
13 to 18 months	2.7	2.8	2.6	2.5	2.3	3.9	5.0	2.5
19 to 24 months	4.8	4.7	4.8	4.3	3.9	7.6	9.0	4.4
25 to 30 months	7.5	7.8	7.1	7.1	6.7	9.9	10.8	7.2
31 months	1.1	1.1	1.1	1.2	1.2	0.9	1.1	1.1
32 months	74.7	73.4	76.0	76.5	78.8	64.0	52.0	76.7
Covered by private health insurance								
Less than 32 months	35.4	34.8	35.9	31.6	28.7	58.5	63.9	33.0
No months	11.6	10.7	12.4	9.3	7.6	25.3	28.5	10.2
1 to 6 months	3.6	3.7	3.6	3.1	2.8	6.8	7.3	3.3
7 to 12 months	3.7	3.7	3.7	3.2	2.9	7.4	6.7	3.5
13 to 18 months	2.7	2.8	2.6	2.5	2.3	3.6	4.7	2.5
19 to 24 months	4.9	4.9	4.9	4.6	4.4	6.9	7.1	4.7
25 to 30 months	7.9	8.0	7.7	7.8	7.6	8.2	9.0	7.8
31 months	1.0	1.0	0.9	1.1	1.1	-	0.7	1.0
32 months	64.6	65.2	64.1	68.4	71.3	41.5	36.1	67.0
Covered by Medicaid								
Less than 32 months	95.3	96.7	94.1	97.0	97.6	85.1	89.5	95.8
No months	87.7	90.3	85.3	90.7	92.1	68.8	72.2	89.0
1 to 6 months	2.5	2.2	2.8	2.2	1.9	4.4	5.7	2.2
7 to 12 months	1.8	1.4	2.1	1.5	1.3	3.6	4.1	1.6
13 to 18 months	0.9	0.7	1.1	0.8	0.6	2.0	2.2	0.8
19 to 24 months	1.1	1.0	1.3	0.8	0.7	3.2	2.8	1.0
25 to 30 months	1.1	1.0	1.2	0.9	0.8	2.6	2.1	1.0
31 months	-	-	-	-	-	-	-	-
32 months	4.7	3.3	5.9	3.0	2.4	14.9	10.5	4.2

Source: Bennefield, Robert L. U.S. Bureau of the Census. *Dynamics of Economic Well-Being: Health Insurance, 1990 to 1992.* Current Population Reports, P70-37. Washington, DC: U.S. Government Printing Office, 1994, p. 5. *Note:* 1. Persons of Hispanic origin may be of any race.

★ 414 ★

Health Insurance

Health Insurance Coverage, by Sex and Race/Ethnicity, 1991

This table shows percent distribution of persons covered for each length of time, for various types of coverage plans.

Health insurance coverage	Both sexes	Male	Female	White Total	White Not of Hispanic origin	Black	Hispanic origin[1]	Not of Hispanic origin
All persons (in thousands)	244,658	118,795	125,862	205,468	187,679	30,342	20,756	223,901
Percent	100.0	100.0	100.0	100.0	100.0	100.0	100.0	100.0
Percent distribution								
Covered by private or government health insurance								
Less than 12 months	19.2	20.7	17.8	17.9	15.8	26.6	38.9	17.4
No months	7.0	7.8	6.2	6.5	5.5	9.3	16.8	6.1
1 to 4 months	3.7	4.0	3.3	3.4	2.9	5.3	7.5	3.3
5 to 8 months	4.8	5.0	4.6	4.3	3.8	8.0	9.7	4.3
9 to 11 months	3.8	3.9	3.7	3.7	3.6	4.0	4.9	3.7
12 months	80.8	79.3	82.2	82.1	84.2	73.4	61.1	82.6
1 to 12 months	93.0	92.2	93.8	93.5	94.5	90.7	83.2	93.9
Covered by private health insurance								
Less than 12 months	29.7	29.3	30.0	26.0	23.0	51.2	56.8	27.1
No months	16.4	15.7	17.1	13.6	11.3	33.0	37.3	14.5
1 to 4 months	4.5	4.6	4.3	4.0	3.6	7.5	7.3	4.2
5 to 8 months	5.1	5.2	5.1	4.8	4.4	7.8	8.6	4.8
9 to 11 months	3.6	3.8	3.5	3.7	3.7	2.9	3.7	3.6
12 months	70.3	70.7	70.0	74.0	77.0	48.8	43.2	72.9
1 to 12 months	83.6	84.3	82.9	86.4	88.7	67.0	62.7	85.5
Covered by Medicaid								
Less than 12 months	93.7	95.4	92.2	95.7	96.6	81.7	86.5	94.4
No months	89.2	91.4	87.1	92.0	93.4	71.7	76.4	90.4
1 to 4 months	2.2	2.0	2.3	1.8	1.6	4.5	5.1	1.9
5 to 8 months	1.4	1.1	1.7	1.1	1.0	3.3	3.0	1.3
9 to 11 months	0.9	0.8	1.0	0.8	0.6	2.1	2.1	0.8
12 months	6.3	4.6	7.8	4.3	3.4	18.3	13.5	5.6
1 to 12 months	10.8	8.6	12.9	8.0	6.6	28.3	23.6	9.6

Source: Bennefield, Robert L. U.S. Bureau of the Census. *Dynamics of Economic Well-Being: Health Insurance, 1990 to 1992.* Current Population Reports, P70-37. Washington, DC: U.S. Government Printing Office, 1994, p. 3. *Notes:* Government health insurance includes Medicare, Medicaid, CHAMPUS, and CHAMPVA. Persons in the Armed Forces living off post or with their families on post are also covered by government insurance. 1. Persons of Hispanic origin may be of any race.

★ 415 ★

Health Insurance

Health Insurance - Lack of Coverage, 1989-91

Number of uninsured is shown in millions, by year, for each race/ethnicity.

Year	Hispanics	Whites	Blacks
1989	6.67	19.20	5.84
1990	6.73	20.22	6.09
1991	6.72	20.41	6.51

Source: "Uninsured strain hospitals, hike costs: the working poor often delay treatment." *Detroit Free Press* (10 February 1993), p. 10A. Primary source: Harvard Center for National Health Program Studies based on U.S. Census data.

★ 416 ★

Health Insurance

Medicaid Recipients in 1992

Data are shown in thousands, except percent, and represent number of persons as of March of the following year who were enrolled at any time in the year shown. A person did not have to receive medical care paid for by Medicaid in order to be counted.

Poverty s atus	Total[1]	White	Black	His-panic[2]
Persons covered, total	24,160	15,037	7,753	3,898
Below poverty level	15,175	8,758	5,686	2,686
Above poverty level	8,985	6,279	2,067	1,212
Percent of population covered	9.7	7.2	25.2	18.2
Below poverty level	45.2	39.2	57.8	44.7
Above poverty level	4.2	3.4	9.9	7.9

Source: 1994 Statistical Abstract of the United States on CD-ROM [machine-readable datafiles]. CD-8A-94. Washington, DC: U.S. Department of Commerce, Economics and Statistics Administration, Bureau of the Censu , Data User Services Division, January 1995. Primary source: U.S. Bureau of the Census, Current Population Reports, P60-185, earlier reports; and unpublished data. *Notes:* 1. Includes other races not shown separately. 2. Persons of Hispanic origin may be of any race.

★ 417 ★

Health Insurance

Uninsured Children Under Age 18, 1991

Race/ethnicity	Percent uninsured
All races	12.3
Latino	26.2
White	11.7
Black	14.8

Source: Mide, Susan. "Healing the hurt of homeless kids." *USA TODAY* (23 November 1992), p. 13A. Primary source: March 1992 Census survey; Centers for Disease Control.

Mental Health

★ 418 ★

Psychiatric Patients in Private Care, by Race/Ethnicity, 1990

Data show percent distribution of patients in private psychiatric hospitals. Figures are based on the following total numbers of patients: 30,182 patients in inpatient care; 2,615 persons in residential treatment care programs; 1,439 persons in residential supportive programs; 9,930 patients in partial care programs; and 84,918 patients in outpatient care.

Race/ethnicity	Type of private care				
	Inpatient care	Residential treatment care	Residential supportive care	Partial care	Outpatient care
White	87.3	81.5	91.9	86.7	91.0
Black	11.2	16.4	7.6	12.4	8.1
Native American	0.8	0.5	0.1	0.7	0.4
Asian/Pacific Islander	0.7	1.6	0.3	0.2	0.5
Hispanic	11.3	4.2	2.4	10.6	4.8
Non-Hispanic	88.7	95.8	97.6	89.4	95.2

Source: U.S. Department of Health and Human Services. Center for Mental Health Services. *Mental Health, United States, 1994*. Manderscheid, R.W., and Sonnenschein, M.A., eds. DHHS Pub. No. (SMA)94-3000. Washington, DC: U.S. Government Printing Office, 1994, p. 137. 1990 Inventory of Mental Health Organizations (IMHO), survey and Analysis Branch, Division of State and Community Systems Development, Center for Mental Health Services (CMHS).

★ 419 ★

Mental Health

Psychological Services Sought by Adults

Data show percentage of persons age 18 years and older who had sought help for personal or emotional problems in the past year, as of 1990. Figures are based on household interviews of the civilian noninstitutionalized population.

Race/ethnicity	Both sexes 18 years and older	Male Total	Male 18-29 years	Male 30-44 years	Male 45-64 years	Male 65 years and older	Female Total	Female 18-29 years	Female 30-44 years	Female 45-64 years	Female 65 years and older
White	12.8	8.7	10.1	10.9	8.1	3.0	16.6	20.0	22.4	13.5	6.9
Black	10.2	7.0	6.6	9.0	6.2	3.9	12.7	11.5	17.2	11.8	6.0
Hispanic	10.3	6.2	7.4	6.0	6.3	-	13.9	12.8	16.8	12.6	9.1
Non-Hispanic	12.6	8.7	9.8	11.1	7.9	3.2	16.2	19.3	21.9	13.4	6.7

Source: Piani, A., and C. Schoenborn. National Center for Health Statistics. *Health Promotion and Disease Prevention: United States, 1990. Vital Health Statistics* 10(185), 1993, p. 39. *Note:* Denominator for each cell excludes unknowns.

Nutrition

★ 420 ★

Breakfast Consumption, by Age, Sex, and Race/Ethnicity

Data show percentage of persons age 18 years and older who ate breakfast almost every day in 1990.

Age and sex	All persons[1]	Race: White	Race: Black	Ethnicity: Hispanic	Ethnicity: Non-Hispanic
Both sexes, age 18 and older	56.4	57.8	46.9	52.5	56.7
Male					
Total	54.6	55.6	47.0	52.7	54.8
18-29 years	45.1	45.5	41.6	50.9	44.4
30-44 years	45.1	45.7	38.3	47.2	44.9
45-64 years	59.1	59.4	53.0	57.5	59.2
65 years and older	86.2	87.4	75.8	80.5	86.4
Female					
Total	58.0	59.8	46.7	52.2	58.4
18-29 years	42.7	43.9	37.0	44.1	42.5
30-44 years	49.8	51.6	38.7	47.5	50.0
45-64 years	63.5	64.8	55.0	63.6	63.5
65 years and older	84.8	85.8	73.8	80.4	84.9

Source: Piani, A., and C. Schoenborn. National Center for Health Statistics. *Health Promotion and Disease Prevention: United States, 1990. Vital and Health Statistics* 10(185), 1993, p. 25. *Notes:* Denominator for each cell excludes unknowns. 1. Includes persons with unknown sociodemographic characteristics.

★ 421 ★

Nutrition

Low Snack Consumption, by Age, Sex, and Race/Ethnicity

Data show percentage of persons age 18 years and older who rarely or never ate snacks in 1990.

Age and sex	Percent of persons				
	All persons[1]	Race		Ethnicity	
		White	Black	Hispanic	Non-Hispanic
Both sexes, age 18 and older	25.5	25.8	22.7	29.3	25.2
Male					
Total	25.6	25.9	22.4	29.7	25.3
18-29 years	19.3	19.6	17.0	25.6	18.6
30-44 years	24.4	24.5	20.6	33.4	23.6
45-64 years	29.0	28.9	27.1	30.2	28.9
65 years and older	33.8	34.0	32.8	32.4	33.8
Female					
Total	25.4	25.7	22.9	29.0	25.1
18-29 years	19.7	20.4	15.4	23.4	19.2
30-44 years	22.6	22.4	22.4	26.5	22.2
45-64 years	26.5	26.3	27.3	40.6	25.6
65 years and older	36.5	36.8	33.5	36.3	36.4

Source: Piani, A., and C. Schoenborn. National Center for Health Statistics. *Health Promotion and Disease Prevention: United States, 1990. Vital and Health Statistics* 10(185), 1993, p. 26. *Notes:* Denominator for each cell excludes unknowns. 1. Includes persons with unknown sociodemographic characteristics.

Occupational Safety

★ 422 ★

Deaths from Occupational Injury, by Race/Ethnicity

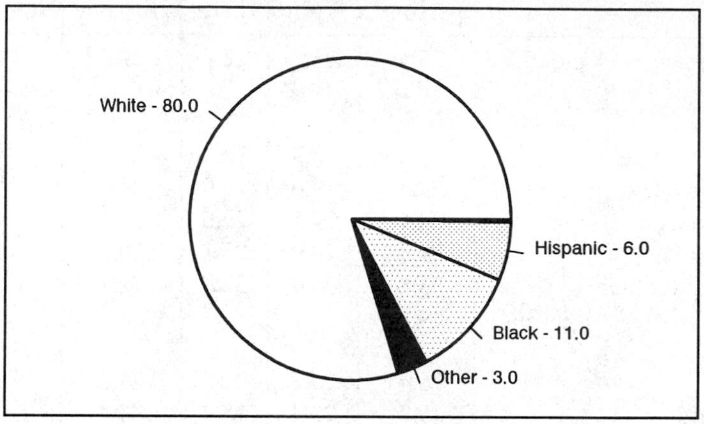

Data show percent distribution of deaths based on a total of 5,714 civilian worker injury deaths in 1989. The total represented a decline of 23% throughout the 1980s.

Race/ethnicity	Percent
White	80.0
Black	11.0
Hispanic	6.0
Other	3.0

Source: "Fatalities decline." *Occupational Hazards* (July 1993), p. 25. Primary source: NIOSH Division of Safety Research.

★ 423 ★

Occupational Safety

Occupational Injuries by Frequency of Occurrence

Data show number and percentage of currently employed persons age 18 or older, by frequency of injuries sustained within the past year. Data are shown for the United States in 1988.

Frequency of work injury	All persons[1]	Race		Ethnicity	
		White	Black	Hispanic	Non-Hispanic
	Number				
All categories	27,408	23,160	3,496	1,674	25,734
	Percent distribution				
Total	100.0	100.0	100.0	100.0	100.0

[Continued]

★ 423 ★

Occupational Injuries by Frequency of Occurrence

[Continued]

Frequency of work injury	All persons[1]	Race		Ethnicity	
		White	Black	Hispanic	Non-Hispanic
None	92.3	92.2	92.7	91.9	92.4
Once in past 12 months	6.2	6.3	5.8	6.9	6.1
More than once in past 12 months	1.0	1.0	0.8	0.7[2]	1.1
Unknown	0.5	0.4	0.8	0.4[2]	0.5

Source: Park, C.H. and others. National Center for Health Statistics. *Health Conditions Among the Currently Employed: United States, 1988. Vital Health Statistics* 10 (186), 1993, p. 29. *Notes:* Percentages are weighted estimates. 1. Includes injuries to persons of races other than black and white. 2. Estimated data—numerator has a relative standard error (RSE) of greater than 30 percent.

★ 424 ★

Occupational Safety

Occupational Injuries, by Type and Effect on Work Status

Data show number and percent distribution of injuries to currently employed persons age 18 years and older in 1988.

Body part affected, type of injury, and work status	All injuries at work[1]	Race		Ethnicity	
		White	Black	Hispanic	Non-Hispanic
			Number		
All categories	2,211	1,893	255	132	2,079
			Percent distribution		
Total	100.0	100.0	100.0	100.0	100.0
Body part injured					
Shoulder	3.7	3.4	4.4[2]	2.8[2]	3.7
Knee	6.5	6.3	10.2	4.9[2]	6.6
Head	3.6	3.4	4.5[2]	2.7[2]	3.7
Eyeball	6.1	6.2	5.4[2]	5.3[2]	6.1
Back	20.3	20.1	25.1	16.5	20.6
Hand, wrist, or finger	28.2	28.9	22.2	33.5	27.8
Foot, toe, or ankle	8.5	8.5	8.0	10.0	8.3
Other	19.6	19.6	17.9	23.8	19.3
Unknown	3.6	3.7	2.3[2]	0.6[2]	3.8
Type of injury					
Burns	4.7	4.6	4.8[2]	4.8[2]	4.7
Contusions or abrasions	12.5	12.2	15.3	15.9	12.2
Fracture	6.6	7.1	2.8[2]	5.7[2]	6.6
Laceration or puncture	20.5	21.0	14.3	24.5	20.2
Strain or sprain	26.4	25.4	32.9	25.0	26.4
Other	22.3	22.9	20.7	18.3	22.6
Unknown	7.1	6.7	9.3	5.8[2]	7.2

[Continued]

★ 424 ★

Occupational Injuries, by Type and Effect on Work Status

[Continued]

Body part affected, type of injury, and work status	All injuries at work[1]	Race		Ethnicity	
		White	Black	Hispanic	Non-Hispanic
Change in work status/activity					
No change	86.4	86.3	88.7	89.6	86.2
Changed employer	3.4	3.5	2.6[2]	3.9[2]	3.3
Changed kind of work only	3.0	2.9	3.9[2]	1.2[2]	3.1
Changed work activity	1.8	2.0	0.7[2]	2.0[2]	1.8
Unknown	5.4	5.4	4.1[2]	3.3[2]	5.6

Source: Park, C.H. and others. National Center for Health Statistics. *Health Conditions Among the Currently Employed: United States, 1988. Vital Health Statistics* 10 (186), 1993, p. 30. *Notes:* Percentages are weighted estimates. 1. Includes injuries to persons of races other than black and white. 2. Estimated data—numerator has a relative standard error (RSE) of greater than 30 percent.

★ 425 ★

Occupational Safety

Physical Work Activity, by Type, 1988

Data show the number and percentage of currently employed persons age 18 years and older, by time spent at specified work activity each day. Hispanic persons were more likely than other groups to be involved in daily work activities that involved at least four hours of bending, twisting or reaching.

Work activity and hours spent	All persons[1]	Race		Ethnicity	
		White	Black	Hispanic	Non-Hispanic
	Number				
All categories	27,408	23,160	3,496	1,674	25,734
	Percent distribution				
Total	100.0	100.0	100.0	100.0	100.0
Repeated strenuous physical activity					
None	67.9	67.6	68.8	63.4	68.2
Less than 2 hours	7.7	8.0	5.1	8.1	7.6
2-3 hours	6.0	6.3	4.5	5.2	6.1
4 or more hours	16.2	16.1	18.8	20.4	15.9
Unknown	2.1	2.0	2.8	2.9	2.1
Repeated bending, twisting, or reaching					
None	54.2	54.5	49.7	46.9	54.7
Less than 2 hours	5.7	5.8	5.2	5.9	5.7
2-3 hours	7.7	7.9	6.6	7.0	7.7
4 or more hours	29.5	29.2	33.8	37.2	29.0
Unknown	2.9	2.7	4.6	3.0	2.9
Bending or twisting of hands or wrists					
None	49.7	49.6	49.4	43.2	50.2
Less than 2 hours	3.0	3.0	2.9	2.8	3.0

[Continued]

★ 425 ★

Physical Work Activity, by Type, 1988

[Continued]

Work activity and hours spent	All persons[1]	Race		Ethnicity	
		White	Black	Hispanic	Non-Hispanic
2-3 hours	5.9	6.0	5.1	5.0	6.0
4 or more hours	38.3	38.5	38.3	45.3	37.8
Unknown	3.1	2.9	4.3	3.6	3.0
Hand operation of vibrating machinery					
None	81.7	81.7	80.4	77.2	82.0
Less than 2 hours	5.2	5.3	4.1	4.8	5.2
2-3 hours	3.7	3.7	3.8	4.2	3.7
4 or more hours	8.0	7.8	9.6	12.6	7.7
Unknown	1.4	1.4	2.1	1.2	1.4

Source: Park, C.H. and others. National Center for Health Statistics. *Health Conditions Among the Currently Employed: United States, 1988. Vital Health Statistics* 10 (186), 1993, p. 19. *Notes:* The percentages shown are weighted national estimates. 1. Includes persons of races other than black and white.

★ 426 ★

Occupational Safety

Selected Ailments in the Workplace

Data show number and percentage of currently employed persons age 18 years and older, who have experienced each health condition during the past year. Data are shown for the United States in 1988. For all groups neck, back, and spine problems were the most prevalent among these ailments.

Health condition	All persons[1]	Race		Ethnicity	
		White	Black	Hispanic	Non-Hispanic
	Number				
All categories	27,408	23,160	3,496	1,674	25,734
	Percent distribution				
Repeated trouble with neck, back, or spine	19.1	19.7	15.2	16.6	19.3
Carpal tunnel syndrome	1.4	1.6	0.7	0.9	1.5
Tendinitis	3.4	3.7	2.1	2.0	3.5
Asthma	2.4	2.4	2.3	1.8	2.4
Chronic bronchitis	1.8	2.0	1.1	1.4	1.9
Deafness	1.5	1.7	0.5	0.5[3]	1.6
Other trouble hearing[2]	6.1	6.6	2.9	2.7	6.3

Source: Park, C.H. and others. National Center for Health Statistics. *Health Conditions Among the Currently Employed: United States, 1988. Vital Health Stat* 10 (186), 1993, p. 31. *Notes:* Percentages are weighted estimates. 1. Includes persons of races other than black and white. 2. Currently occurring in one or both ears. 3. Estimated data—numerator has a relative standard error (RSE) of more than 30 percent.

Organ Donors

★ 427 ★

Organ Donor Distribution, by Race/Ethnicity, 1991

	Kidney	Liver	Pancreas	Heart	Heart/lung	Lung	Multiple organs	All donors
Total (number)	4,272	3,166	1,069	2,148	51	345	3,445	4,532
Percent distribution								
Total	100.0	100.0	100.0	100.0	100.0	100.0	100.0	100.0
Hispanic	7.1	7.8	7.1	8.2	8.2	7.3	7.7	7.5
White	81.1	80.5	83.4	80.3	81.6	79.9	80.7	80.4
Black	9.9	10.0	7.9	9.9	8.2	11.6	9.8	10.2
Asian	0.9	0.9	1.0	0.8	2.0	0.3	0.9	0.9
Other	1.0	0.8	0.6	0.8	0	0.9	0.9	1.0

Source: Richardson, Rod. "Blacks reluctant to donate organs." *Detroit News* (1 March 1993), p. 2A. Primary source: United Network for Organ Sharing.

Pollution

★ 428 ★

Persons Living with Pollution

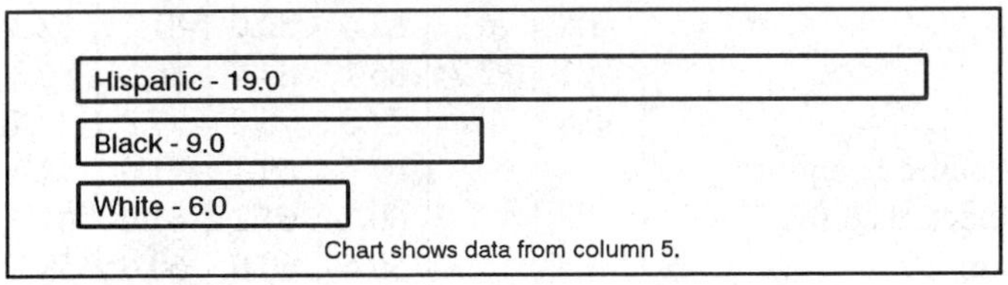

Chart shows data from column 5.

Data show percentage of persons of each race/ethnicity living in areas exposed to each substance.

Race/ethnicity	Dust, soot, and other particles	Carbon monoxide	Ozone	Sulfur dioxide	Lead[1]
White	15.0	34.0	53.0	7.0	6.0
Black	17.0	46.0	62.0	12.0	9.0
Hispanic	34.0	57.0	71.0	6.0	19.0

Source: Suro, Roberto. "Pollution-weary minorities try civil rights tack." *The New York Times* (11 January 1993), sec. A, p. 1. Environmental Protection Agency. *Notes:* 1. Figures refer to percentage of children age 6 months to 5 years in cities with more than one million persons, with high blood levels of lead.

Prenatal Care

★ 429 ★

Prenatal Care for Live Births, by Race and Hispanic Origin of Mother

Data show the percentage of babies born to women obtaining prenatal care in the first trimester and the percentage born to women receiving prenatal care in the third trimester or not all. Data are shown for selected years.

Prenatal care, education, race of mother, and Hispanic origin of mother	Percent of live births[1]								
	1970	1975	1980	1985	1987	1988	1989	1990	1991
Prenatal care began during 1st trimester									
All mothers	68.0	72.4	76.3	76.2	76.0	75.9	75.5	75.8	76.2
White	72.3	75.8	79.2	79.3	79.3	79.3	78.9	79.2	79.5
Black	44.2	55.5	62.4	61.5	60.8	60.7	60.0	60.6	61.9
American Indian or Alaskan Native	38.2	45.4	55.8	57.5	57.6	58.1	57.9	57.9	59.9
Asian or Pacific Islander	-	-	73.7	74.1	75.0	75.5	74.8	75.1	75.3

[Continued]

★ 429 ★

Prenatal Care for Live Births, by Race and Hispanic Origin of Mother

[Continued]

Prenatal care, education, race of mother, and Hispanic origin of mother	Percent of live births[1]								
	1970	1975	1980	1985	1987	1988	1989	1990	1991
Chinese	71.8	76.7	82.6	82.0	81.5	82.3	81.5	81.3	82.3
Japanese	78.1	82.7	86.1	84.7	86.6	86.3	86.2	87.0	87.7
Filipino	60.6	70.6	77.3	76.5	77.9	78.4	77.6	77.1	77.1
Other Asian or Pacific Islander[2]	-	-	67.6	69.7	71.0	71.5	70.8	71.4	71.7
Hispanic origin (selected states)[3,4]	-	-	60.2	61.2	61.0	61.3	59.5	60.2	61.0
Mexican American	-	-	59.6	60.0	60.0	58.3	56.7	57.8	58.7
Puerto Rican	-	-	55.1	58.3	57.4	63.2	62.7	63.5	65.0
Cuban	-	-	82.7	82.5	83.1	83.4	83.2	84.8	85.4
Central and South American	-	-	58.8	60.6	59.1	62.8	60.8	61.5	63.4
Other and unknown Hispanic	-	-	66.4	65.8	65.5	67.3	66.0	66.4	65.6
Non-Hispanic white (selected states)[3]	-	-	81.2	81.4	81.7	81.8	82.7	83.3	83.7
Non-Hispanic black (selected states)[3]	-	-	60.7	60.1	60.0	60.4	59.9	60.7	61.9
Prenatal care began during 3rd trimester or no prenatal care									
All mothers	7.9	6.0	5.1	5.7	6.1	6.1	6.4	6.1	5.8
White	6.3	5.0	4.3	4.8	5.0	5.0	5.2	4.9	4.7
Black	16.6	10.5	8.9	10.2	11.2	11.0	11.9	11.3	10.7
American Indian or Alaskan Native	28.9	22.4	15.2	12.9	13.1	13.2	13.4	12.9	12.2
Asian or Pacific Islander	-	-	6.5	6.5	6.3	5.9	6.1	5.8	5.7
Chinese	6.5	4.4	3.7	4.4	4.2	3.4	3.6	3.4	3.4
Japanese	4.1	2.7	2.1	3.1	2.8	3.3	2.7	2.9	2.5
Filipino	7.2	4.1	4.0	4.8	4.9	4.8	4.7	4.5	5.0
Other Asian or Pacific Islander[2]	-	-	9.0	8.1	7.8	7.3	7.6	7.2	6.8
Hispanic origin (selected states)[3,4]	-	-	12.0	12.4	12.7	12.1	13.0	12.0	11.0
Mexican American	-	-	11.8	12.9	13.0	13.9	14.6	13.2	12.2
Puerto Rican	-	-	16.2	15.5	17.1	10.2	11.3	10.6	9.1
Cuban	-	-	3.9	3.7	3.9	3.6	4.0	2.8	2.4
Central and South American	-	-	13.1	12.5	13.5	9.9	11.9	10.9	9.5
Other and unknown Hispanic	-	-	9.2	9.4	9.3	8.8	9.3	8.5	8.2
Non-Hispanic white (selected states)[3]	-	-	3.5	4.0	4.1	4.1	3.7	3.4	3.2
Non-Hispanic black (selected states)[3]	-	-	9.7	10.9	11.8	11.0	12.0	11.2	10.7

Source: National Center for Health Statistics. *Health, United States, 1993.* Hyattsville, MD: Public Health Service, May 1994, p. 70. Centers for Disease Control and Prevention, National Center for Health Statistics: Data computed by the Division of Analysis from data compiled by the Division of Vital Statistics. *Notes:* A dash (-) stands for data not available. Excludes births that occurred in States not reporting prenatal care. The race groups, white and black, include persons of Hispanic and non-Hispanic origin. Conversely, persons of Hispanic origin may be of any race. 1. Excludes live births for whom trimester prenatal care began is unknown. 2. Includes Hawaiians and part Hawaiians. 3. Trend data for Hispanics and non-Hispanics are affected by expansion of the reporting area for an Hispanic-origin item on the birth certificate and by immigration. These two factors affect numbers of events, composition of the Hispanic population, and maternal and infant health characteristics. The number of States in the reporting area increased from 22 in 1980, to 30 plus the District of Columbia (DC) in 1988, 47 plus DC in 1989, 48 plus DC in 1990, and 49 plus DC in 1991. 4. Includes mothers of all races.

★ 430 ★

Prenatal Care

Smoking During Pregnancy

Data show the percentage of women age 18-44 years who had given birth within the past five years and reported smoking cigarettes in the 12 months preceding the birth. Data shown are for 1990.

Race/ethnicity	Age of mother				
	Total	18-24 years	25-29 years	30-34 years	35-44 years
White	25.3	34.7	27.4	21.2	18.1
Black	19.0	13.1	20.2	25.1	20.6
Hispanic	12.1	11.3	13.4	12.3	11.2
Non-Hispanic	25.5	33.0	27.5	22.2	18.8

Source: Piani, A., and C. Schoenborn. National Center for Health Statistics. *Health Promotion and Disease Prevention: United States, 1990. Vital and Health Statistics* 10(185), 1993, p. 61. *Note:* Denominator for each cell excludes unknowns.

Preventive Care

★ 431 ★

Primary Care Availability for Selected Populations, 1986-91

Data show the percentage of adults with a regular source of clinical preventive services. This health care category includes immunizations, screening for early detection of disease or risk factors, and patient counseling. There was a slight decline in the percentage of persons with a regular care source from 1986 through 1991.

Population	1986	1990	1991	1992	Year 2000 target
All persons age 18 and older	82	78	80	79	95
Hispanic	70	64	64	65	95
Black	80	75	80	77	95
Low-income persons age 18 and older[1]	80	71	72	72	95

Source: National Center for Health Statistics. *Healthy People 2000 Review. Health, United States, 1992.* Hyattsville, MD: Public Health Service, 1993, p. 139. Primary source: Centers for Disease Control and Prevention, National Center for Health Statistics, National Health Interview Survey. *Note:* 1. Low-income is defined as below the poverty threshold.

Substance Abuse

★ 432 ★

Alcohol Use

Figures show alcohol consumption by persons age 18 and older in the United States for 1985 and 1990. Data are shown by sex, race/ethnicity, and age, and are based on household interviews of a sample of the civilian noninstitutionalized population.

Alcohol consumption, race, Hispanic origin, and age	Both sexes		Male		Female	
	1985	1990	1985	1990	1985	1990
Drinking status						
	Percent distribution					
All	100.0	100.0	100.0	100.0	100.0	100.0
Abstainer	26.9	29.7	14.4	16.6	38.0	41.5
Former drinker	7.5	9.6	9.2	11.6	6.1	7.8
Current drinker	65.6	60.7	76.4	71.8	55.9	50.7
	Percent current drinkers among all persons					
All races						
18-44 years	72.8	67.5	82.4	77.1	63.8	58.3
18-24 years	71.8	63.7	79.5	71.7	64.5	56.1
25-44 years	73.2	68.8	83.5	78.9	63.5	59.0
45 years and over	55.5	51.3	67.4	63.8	45.6	40.8
45-64 years	62.2	57.6	72.2	68.4	53.0	47.6
65 years and over	44.3	41.4	58.2	55.6	34.7	31.3
White, non-Hispanic						
18-44 years	76.9	72.7	85.0	80.4	68.9	65.1
18-24 years	77.9	71.5	84.9	77.5	71.0	65.7
25-44 years	76.5	73.1	85.0	81.2	68.2	65.0
45 years and over	57.6	53.8	69.0	65.5	48.2	44.0
45-64 years	65.2	61.0	74.1	70.6	56.9	52.2
65 years and over	45.8	43.3	59.6	57.1	36.2	33.3
Black, non-Hispanic						
18-44 years	59.0	51.5	72.2	68.1	48.2	37.9
45 years and over	41.5	36.0	57.1	51.3	29.9	24.5
Hispanic						
18-44 years	58.7	55.7	73.2	71.3	45.6	42.0
45 years and over	48.5	43.4	64.3	63.3	35.4	27.8
Level of alcohol consumption in past 2 weeks for current drinkers						
	Percent distribution of current drinkers					
All drinking levels	100.0	100.0	100.0	100.0	100.0	100.0
None	21.6	24.1	18.0	20.3	26.1	29.1
Light	37.1	39.4	30.9	33.9	44.7	46.4
Moderate	29.5	27.4	34.0	32.3	24.0	21.1

[Continued]

★ 432 ★

Alcohol Use

[Continued]

Alcohol consumption, race, Hispanic origin, and age	Both sexes 1985	Both sexes 1990	Male 1985	Male 1990	Female 1985	Female 1990
Heavier	11.8	9.1	17.2	13.6	5.3	3.4
	Percent heavier drinkers among current drinkers					
All races						
18-44 years	11.0	8.5	16.6	13.0	4.2	2.8
18-24 years	12.2	8.8	18.3	13.8	5.0	2.7
25-44 years	10.6	8.4	16.0	12.7	3.8	2.9
45 years and over	13.3	10.3	18.2	14.7	7.4	4.6
45-64 years	13.2	9.9	18.1	14.4	7.2	4.1
65 years and over	13.6	11.0	18.4	15.3	7.9	5.5
White, non-Hispanic						
18-44 years	11.2	8.5	17.1	13.2	4.0	2.8
18-24 years	13.3	9.9	20.4	16.0	5.2	3.0
25-44 years	10.4	8.1	16.0	12.4	3.6	2.7
45 years and over	13.4	10.4	18.2	15.0	7.6	4.7
45-64 years	13.2	10.0	18.0	14.6	7.3	4.2
65 years and over	13.9	11.3	18.7	15.8	8.3	5.7
Black, non-Hispanic						
18-44 years	9.6	10.3	13.4	14.7	5.1	3.9
45 years and over	10.3	7.7	16.2	10.1	[1]	[1]
Hispanic						
18-44 years	10.6	7.9	15.2	11.3	[1]	[1]
45 years and over	15.7	12.1	[1]	17.2	[1]	[1]

Source: National Center for Health Statistics. *Health, United States, 1993.* Hyattsville, MD: Public Health Service, May 1994, p. 163. Primary source: Data computed by the Alcohol Epidemiological Data System of the National Institute on Alcohol Abuse and Alcoholism from data in the National Interview Survey compiled by the Division of Health Interview Statistics, National Center for Health Statistics, Centers for Disease Control and Prevention. *Notes:* Abstainers consumed less than 12 drinks in any single year. Former drinkers consumed 12 or more drinks in any single year and at least one drink in the past year. For current drinkers, drinking levels are classified according to the average daily consumption of absolute alcohol (ethanol), in ounces, in the previous 2-week period, assuming 0.5 ounce ethanol per drink, as follows: none; light, .01-.21; moderate, .22-.99; and heavier, 1.00 or more. This corresponds to up to 3, 4-13, and 14 or more drinks per week for light, moderate, and heavier drinkers. 1. Estimates based on fewer than 30 subjects are not shown.

★ 433 ★

Substance Abuse

Alcohol Use in the Past Month

Use by persons age 12 and older in the contiguous United States is shown for selected years based on household interviews. Data are shown by age and race/ethnicity.

Age, sex, race and Hispanic origin	Percent of population									
	1974	1976	1977	1979	1982	1985	1988	1990	1991	1992
12 years and over	54	52	54	60	55	59	53	51	51	48
12-17 years	34	32	31	37	27	31	25	25	20	16
12-13 years	19	19	13	20	10	11	7	8	7	4
14-15 years	32	31	28	36	23	35	23	26	19	15
16-17 years	51	47	52	55	45	46	42	38	35	30

[Continued]

★433★

Alcohol Use in the Past Month

[Continued]

Age, sex, race and Hispanic origin	Percent of population									
	1974	1976	1977	1979	1982	1985	1988	1990	1991	1992
18-25 years	69	69	70	76	68	71	65	63	64	59
26-34 years	68	68	70	70	71	70	64	63	62	61
35 years and over	49	52	50	58	52	57	52	49	49	46
12-17 years										
Male	39	36	37	39	27	34	27	25	22	17
Female	29	29	25	36	27	29	23	24	18	15
White, non-Hispanic	-	-	-	-	-	35	27	28	20	17
Black, non-Hispanic	-	-	-	-	-	21	16	15	20	13
Hispanic	-	-	-	-	-	23	25	19	23	16
18-25 years										
Male	-	79	82	84	75	78	75	74	70	66
Female	-	58	59	68	61	65	57	53	58	53
White, non-Hispanic	-	-	-	-	-	76	69	66	67	63
Black, non-Hispanic	-	-	-	-	-	58	50	59	56	51
Hispanic	-	-	-	-	-	58	61	57	53	53

Source: National Center for Health Statistics. *Health, United States, 1993.* Hyattsville, MD: Public Health Service, May 1994, p. 158. Primary source: National Institute on Drug Abuse National Household Survey on Drug Abuse: Main Findings, 1979, by P.M. Fishburne, H.I. Abelson, and I. Cisin. DHHS Pub. No. (ADM) 80-976. Alcohol, Drug Abuse, and Mental Health Administration. Washington. U.S. Government Printing Office, 1980; National Household Survey on Drug Abuse: Main Findings, 1982, by J.D. Miller et al, DHHS Pub. No. (ADM) 83-1263. Alcohol, Drug Abuse, and Mental Health Administration. Washington, D.C.: U.S. Government Printing Office, 1983; National Household Survey on Drug Abuse: Main Findings, 1985. DHHS Pub. No. (ADM) 88-1586. National Household Survey on Drug Abuse: Main Findings, 1988; National Household Survey on Drug Abuse Main Findings, 1990; National Household Survey on Drug Abuse: Main Findings, 1991; and preliminary estimates from the 1992 National Household Survey on Drug Abuse: Advance Report Number 3. *Notes:* A dash (-) stands for data not available. Estimates of the use of substances from the National Household Survey on Drug Abuse and the Monitoring the Future Study differ because of different methodologies, sampling frames, and tabulation categories. In surveys conducted in 1979 and later years, private answer sheets were used for alcohol questions; prior to 1979 respondents answered questions aloud.

★434★

Substance Abuse

Analgesics Use

Estimates are shown for 1993, by age, sex, and race/ethnicity.

Age/sex	Ever used				Used in past year				Used in past month			
	Total	Hispanic	White	Black	Total	Hispanic	White	Black	Total	Hispanic	White	Black
Percent rate estimates												
Age												
12-17	3.7	3.2	4.1	2.7	2.2	2.1	2.5	1.1	0.7	0.9	0.7	0.6
18-25	8.7	4.4	10.6	4.6	4.1	2.4	5.0	2.3	1.4	1.1	1.8	0.4
26-34	9.0	5.9	10.3	3.4	3.7	2.4	4.2	1.4	1.0	1.0	0.9	0.5
35+	4.4	2.8	4.6	3.5	1.3	1.4	1.4	0.7	0.4	0.5	0.4	0.3
Sex												
Male	6.7	4.2	7.5	3.1	2.2	1.7	2.6	0.9	0.7	0.6	0.8	0.5
Female	4.9	3.6	5.2	3.9	2.2	2.1	2.2	1.4	0.7	0.9	0.7	0.3

[Continued]

★ 434 ★

Analgesics Use

[Continued]

Age/sex	Ever used				Used in past year				Used in past month			
	Total	Hispanic	White	Black	Total	Hispanic	White	Black	Total	Hispanic	White	Black
Total	5.8	3.9	6.3	3.5	2.2	1.9	2.4	0.2	0.7	0.8	0.7	0.4
Population estimates (in thousands)												
Age												
12-17	776	83	603	84	461	55	367	34	147	23	102	19
18-25	2,455	156	2,089	172	1,165	84	983	88	405	39	348	14
26-34	3,341	251	2,781	150	1,384	101	1,123	64	367	42	253	24
35+	5,349	230	4,447	408	1,563	113	1,303	87	498	37	425	36
Sex												
Male	6,632	385	5,678	319	2,222	156	1,973	90	684	58	572	55
Female	5,288	335	4,243	494	2,350	197	1,803	183	733	82	555	39
Total	11,921	720	9,921	814	4,571	353	3,776	273	1,417	140	1,127	93

Source: U.S. Department of Health and Human Services. Public Health Service. Alcohol, Drug Abuse, and Mental Health Administration. *National Household Survey on Drug Abuse: Population Estimates 1993.* DHHS Publication No. (SMA) 94-3017. Bethesda, MD: Department of Health and Human Services, 1994, pp. 77-79. Primary source: Substance Abuse and Mental Health Services Administration, Office of Applied Studies, 1993 National Household Survey on Drug Abuse.

★ 435 ★

Substance Abuse

Cigarette Use

Estimates are shown for 1993, by age, sex, and race/ethnicity.

	Ever used				Used in past year				Used in past month			
	Total	Hispanic	White	Black	Total	Hispanic	White	Black	Total	Hispanic	White	Black
Percent rate estimates												
Age												
12-17	34.5	33.1	37.8	21.2	19.1	18.2	21.6	8.4	9.6	8.4	11.0	4.0
18-25	66.7	57.8	72.9	46.6	38.3	32.9	42.9	21.8	29.0	25.5	32.7	16.3
26-34	74.0	62.5	78.6	66.8	35.1	31.0	36.3	34.3	30.1	24.8	31.1	30.5
35+	77.9	62.3	80.8	71.2	27.4	26.5	27.0	30.3	23.8	21.5	12.4	28.0
Sex												
Male	76.6	67.5	79.8	63.4	32.4	32.5	33.0	27.2	26.2	25.0	26.9	22.7
Female	66.3	47.3	71.5	56.5	26.6	22.8	27.3	26.4	22.3	17.3	22.8	23.9
Total	71.2	57.4	75.5	59.6	29.4	27.6	30.1	26.7	24.2	21.2	24.7	23.4
Population estimates (in thousands)												
Age												
12-17	7,318	853	5,521	658	4,056	469	3,150	260	2,042	216	1,607	124
18-25	18,893	2,067	14,325	1,751	10,862	1,177	8,445	820	8,228	910	6,423	614
26-34	27,532	2,644	21,187	2,934	13,048	1,312	9,771	1,507	11,183	1,049	8,378	1,340
35+	93,776	5,053	77,993	8,367	33,001	2,153	26,050	3,563	28,662	1,745	22,620	3,294
Sex												
Male	76,039	6,246	60,599	6,519	32,227	3,008	25,062	2,796	26,071	2,318	20,410	2,335

[Continued]

★ 435 ★

Cigarette Use

[Continued]

	Ever used				Used in past year				Used in past month			
	Total	Hispanic	White	Black	Total	Hispanic	White	Black	Total	Hispanic	White	Black
Female	71,480	4,371	58,428	7,190	28,739	2,104	22,354	3,355	24,043	1,602	18,617	3,036
Total	147,519	10,617	119,026	31,709	60,966	5,112	47,416	6,151	50,114	3,920	39,027	5,371

Source: U.S. Department of Health and Human Services. Public Health Service. Alcohol, Drug Abuse, and Mental Health Administration. *National Household Survey on Drug Abuse: Population Estimates 1993.* DHHS Publication No. (SMA) 94-3017. Bethesda, MD: Department of Health and Human Services, 1994, pp. 89-91. Primary source: Substance Abuse and Mental Health Services Administration, Office of Applied Studies, 1993 National Household Survey on Drug Abuse.

★ 436 ★

Substance Abuse

Cigarette Use in the Past Month

Use by persons age 12 to 17 years in the contiguous United States is shown for selected years based on household interviews. Data are shown by age and race/ethnicity.

Age, sex, race and Hispanic origin	Percent of population									
	1974	1976	1977	1979	1982	1985	1988	1990	1991	1992
12-17 years	25	23	22	[1]	15	15	12	12	11	10
12-13 years	13	11	10	[1]	[2]	6	3	2	3	2
14-15 years	25	20	22	[1]	10	14	11	14	9	10
16-17 years	38	39	35	[1]	30	25	20	18	21	18
12-17 years										
Male	27	21	23	[1]	16	16	12	12	12	10
Female	24	26	22	[1]	13	15	11	11	10	10
White, non-Hispanic	-	-	-	-	-	17	14	14	13	12
Black, non-Hispanic	-	-	-	-	-	9	5	4	4	3
Hispanic	-	-	-	-	-	11	8	11	9	7

Source: National Center for Health Statistics. *Health, United States, 1993.* Hyattsville, MD: Public Health Service, May 1994, p. 158. Primary source: National Institute on Drug Abuse National Household Survey on Drug Abuse: Main Findings, 1979, by P.M. Fishburne, H.I. Abelson, and I. Cisin. DHHS Pub. No. (ADM) 80-976. Alcohol, Drug Abuse, and Mental Health Administration. Washington, DC: U.S. Government Printing Office, 1980; National Household Survey on Drug Abuse: Main Findings, 1982, by J.D. Miller et al, DHHS Pub. No. (ADM) 83-1263. Alcohol, Drug Abuse, and Mental Health Administration. Washington. U.S. Government Printing Office, 1983; National Household Survey on Drug Abuse: Main Findings, 1985. DHHS Pub. No. (ADM) 88-1586. National Household Survey on Drug Abuse: Main Findings, 1988; National Household Survey on Drug Abuse Main Findings, 1990; National Household Survey on Drug Abuse: Main Findings, 1991; and preliminary estimates from the 1992 National Household Survey on Drug Abuse: Advance Report Number 3. *Notes:* A dash (-) stands for data not available. Estimates of the use of substances from the National Household Survey on Drug Abuse and the Monitoring the Future Study differ because of different methodologies, sampling frames, and tabulation categories. 1. Data not comparable because definitions differ. 2. Relative standard error greater than 30 percent. Estimates with relative standard error greater than 50 percent are not shown.

★ 437 ★

Substance Abuse

Cocaine - Frequency of Use

Estimates are shown for 1993, by age, sex, and race/ethnicity.

	At least once				12 or more times				Once a week or more			
	Total	Hispanic	White	Black	Total	Hispanic	White	Black	Total	Hispanic	White	Black
Percent rate estimates												
Age												
12-17	0.8	1.8	0.7	0.3	0.3	1.1	.01	0.2	0.1	0.3	(X)	0.2
18-25	5.0	6.6	5.3	2.2	1.6	1.5	1.7	1.7	0.6	0.6	0.6	1.1
26-34	4.4	3.6	4.4	5.2	1.0	1.5	0.8	2.3	0.4	0.7	0.2	1.1
35+	1.1	1.6	0.8	2.9	0.5	0.8	0.4	1.3	0.1	0.4	0.1	0.4
Sex												
Male	3.2	4.1	2.9	4.7	1.1	1.4	0.9	2.2	0.4	0.7	0.3	1.0
Female	1.3	2.0	1.2	1.4	0.4	0.8	0.3	0.7	0.1	0.4	(X)	0.6
Total	2.2	3.1	2.0	2.9	0.7	1.1	0.6	1.4	0.2	0.6	0.1	0.6
Population estimates (in thousands)												
Age												
12-17	163	46	99	11	57	28	16	7	16	7	(X)	6
18-25	1,430	236	1,039	82	444	53	327	63	178	21	115	55
26-34	1,629	152	1,187	230	384	64	219	101	138	28	61	48
35+	1,310	132	799	344	600	63	352	149	145	46	49	50
Sex												
Male	3,149	381	2,164	484	1,057	131	699	227	365	65	199	102
Female	1,382	185	959	183	427	77	215	93	111	38	(X)	44
Total	4,530	566	3,123	667	1,484	208	914	320	476	103	227	146

Source: U.S. Department of Health and Human Services. Public Health Service. Alcohol, Drug Abuse, and Mental Health Administration. *National Household Survey on Drug Abuse: Population Estimates 1993.* DHHS Publication No. (SMA) 94-3017. Bethesda, MD: Department of Health and Human Services, 1994, pp. 113-115. Primary source: Substance Abuse and Mental Health Services Administration, Office of Applied Studies, 1993 National Household Survey on Drug Abuse. *Note:* An (X) stands for low precision, no estimate reported.

★ 438 ★

Substance Abuse

Cocaine Abuse

Estimates are shown for 1993, by age, sex, and race/ethnicity.

Age/sex	Ever used				Used in past year				Used in past month			
	Total	Hispanic	White	Black	Total	Hispanic	White	Black	Total	Hispanic	White	Black
Percent rate estimates												
Age												
12-17	1.1	2.5	1.0	0.7	0.8	1.8	0.7	0.3	0.4	1.0	0.3	0.3
18-25	12.5	12.2	13.9	6.7	5.0	6.6	5.3	2.2	1.5	2.1	1.6	1.3
26-34	25.6	18.4	29.0	16.4	4.4	3.6	4.4	5.2	1.0	1.1	0.9	1.8
35+	8.5	6.0	8.6	9.9	1.1	1.6	0.8	2.9	0.4	0.7	0.2	1.4

[Continued]

★ 438 ★

Cocaine Abuse

[Continued]

Age/sex	Ever used				Used in past year				Used in past month			
	Total	Hispanic	White	Black	Total	Hispanic	White	Black	Total	Hispanic	White	Black
Sex												
Male	14.5	11.8	15.2	13.3	3.2	4.1	2.9	4.7	0.9	1.5	0.7	2.0
Female	8.5	7.3	9.0	6.2	1.3	2.0	1.2	1.4	0.4	0.7	0.3	0.7
Total	11.3	9.5	12.0	9.4	2.2	3.1	2.0	2.9	0.6	1.1	0.5	1.3
Population estimates (in thousands)												
Age												
12-17	239	65	147	21	162	46	99	11	83	26	47	10
18-25	3,548	437	2,737	252	1,430	236	1,039	82	429	76	305	48
26-34	9,512	778	7,810	720	1,629	152	1,187	230	362	46	238	78
35+	10,195	485	8,268	1,164	1,310	132	799	344	434	57	179	163
Sex												
Male	14,362	1,093	11,562	1,367	3,149	381	2,164	484	891	143	542	207
Female	9,132	671	7,399	790	1,382	185	959	183	416	62	227	91
Total	23,494	1,765	18,961	2,156	4,530	566	3,123	667	1,307	205	769	298

Source: U.S. Department of Health and Human Services. Public Health Service. Alcohol, Drug Abuse, and Mental Health Administration. *National Household Survey on Drug Abuse: Population Estimates 1993.* DHHS Publication No. (SMA 94-3017. Bethesda, MD: Department of Health and Human Services, 1994, pp. 29-31. Primary source: Substance Abuse and Mental Health Services Administration, Office of Applied Studies, 1993 National Household Survey on Drug Abuse.

★ 439 ★

Substance Abuse

Cocaine Use in the Past Month

Use by persons age 12 years and older in the coterminous United States is shown for selected years based on household interviews. Data are shown by age and race/ethnicity.

Age, sex, race, and Hispanic origin	Percent of population									
	1974	1976	1977	1979	1982	1985	1988	1990	1991	1992
12 years and over	0.2	0.7	1.0	2.4	2.3	2.9	1.5	0.8	0.9	0.6
12-17 years	1.0[1]	1.0[1]	0.8[1]	1.4	1.6	1.5	1.1	0.6	0.4	0.3
18-25 years	3.1	2.0	3.7	9.3	6.8	7.6	4.5	2.2	2.0	1.8
26-34 years	-	-	-	-	3.3	6.1	2.6	1.7	1.8	1.4
35 years and over	-	-	-	-	0.5	0.5	0.4	0.2	0.5	0.2
12-17 years										
Male	-	-	-	-	1.8	2.0	0.9	0.7	0.5	0.2
Female	-	-	-	-	1.5[1]	1.4[1]	1.4	0.4	0.3	0.3
White, non-Hispanic	-	-	-	-	-	1.7	1.3	0.4	0.3[1]	0.1
Black, non-Hispanic	-	-	-	-	-	1.1	0.5	0.7	0.5[1]	0.2
Hispanic	-	-	-	-	-	2.7	1.3	1.9	1.3	1.2
18-25 years										
Male	-	-	-	-	9.1	9.0	6.0	2.8	2.8	2.9

[Continued]

★ 439 ★

Cocaine Use in the Past Month

[Continued]

Age, sex, race, and Hispanic origin	Percent of population									
	1974	1976	1977	1979	1982	1985	1988	1990	1991	1992
Female	-	-	-	-	4.7	6.2	3.0	1.6	1.3	0.8
White, non-Hispanic	-	-	-	-	-	8.0	4.1	1.9	1.7	2.0
Black, non-Hispanic	-	-	-	-	-	6.5	4.3	3.6	3.1	1.4
Hispanic	-	-	-	-	-	6.4	6.7	3.1	2.7	1.8

Source: National Center for Health Statistics. *Health, United States, 1993.* Hyattsville, MD: Public Health Service, May 1994, pp. 158-159. Primary source: National Institute on Drug Abuse National Household Survey on Drug Abuse: Main Findings, 1979, by P.M. Fishburne, H.I. Abelson, and I. Cisin. DHHS Pub. No. (ADM) 80-976. Alcohol, Drug Abuse, and Mental Health Administration. Washington. U.S. Government Printing Office, 1980; National Household Survey on Drug Abuse: Main Findings, 1982, by J.D. Miller et al, DHHS Pub. No. (ADM) 83-1263. Alcohol, Drug Abuse, and Mental Health Administration. Washington, DC: Government Printing Office, 1983; National Household Survey on Drug Abuse: Main Findings, 1985. DHHS Pub. No. (ADM) 88-1586. National Household Survey on Drug Abuse: Main Findings, 1988; National Household Survey on Drug Abuse Main Findings, 1990; National Household Survey on Drug Abuse: Main Findings, 1991; and preliminary estimates from the 1992 National Household Survey on Drug Abuse: Advance Report Number 3. *Notes:* A dash (-) stands for data not available. Estimates of the use of substances from the National Household Survey on Drug Abuse and the Monitoring the Future Study differ because of different methodologies, sampling frames, and tabulation categories. 1. Relative standard error greater than 30 percent. Estimates with relative standard error greater than 50 percent are not shown.

★ 440 ★

Substance Abuse

Crack Abuse

Estimates are shown for 1993, by age, sex, and race/ethnicity.

Age/sex	Ever used				Used in past year				Used in past month			
	Total	Hispanic	White	Black	Total	Hispanic	White	Black	Total	Hispanic	White	Black
Percent rate estimates												
Age												
12-17	0.4	1.2	0.2	0.3	0.2	0.5	0.2	0.3	0.1	0.4	0.1	0.2
18-25	3.5	3.5	4.0	2.1	1.0	1.2	1.0	1.1	0.4	0.7	0.4	0.7
26-34	4.2	3.2	3.8	7.2	1.0	0.7	0.5	3.0	0.3	0.3	0.2	1.1
35+	0.9	0.9	0.7	3.3	0.2	0.2	0.1	1.7	0.1	0.2	(X)	1.2
Sex												
Male	2.6	2.5	2.2	5.3	0.8	0.9	0.5	2.8	0.3	0.5	0.1	1.6
Female	1.1	1.4	1.0	1.9	0.2	0.3	0.1	0.7	0.1	0.1	0.1	0.4
Total	1.8	2.0	1.6	3.4	0.5	0.6	0.3	1.6	0.2	0.3	0.1	0.9
Population estimates (in thousands)												
Age												
12-17	75	30	34	11	50	14	26	9	29	10	13	5
18-25	1,003	127	781	79	294	42	205	40	118	24	69	25
26-34	1,554	136	1,019	318	355	32	142	131	111	13	52	47
35+	1,116	69	1,685	386	297	16	86	195	159	13	(X)	137
Sex												
Male	2,576	235	1,685	547	783	80	354	292	308	49	99	160

[Continued]

★ 440 ★

Crack Abuse

[Continued]

Age/sex	Ever used				Used in past year				Used in past month			
	Total	Hispanic	White	Black	Total	Hispanic	White	Black	Total	Hispanic	White	Black
Female	1,173	126	781	247	213	24	105	84	109	11	44	54
Total	3,749	361	2,465	794	996	103	459	376	417	60	142	214

Source: U.S. Department of Health and Human Services. Public Health Service. Alcohol, Drug Abuse, and Mental Health Administration. *National Household Survey on Drug Abuse: Population Estimates 1993.* DHHS Publication No. (SMA) 94-3017. Bethesda, MD: Department of Health and Human Services, 1994, pp. 35-37. Primary source: Substance Abuse and Mental Health Services Administration, Office of Applied Studies, 1993 National Household Survey on Drug Abuse. *Note:* (X) stands for low precision; no estimate reported.

★ 441 ★

Substance Abuse

Hallucinogen Abuse

Estimates are shown for 1993, by age, sex, and race/ethnicity.

Age/sex	Ever used				Used in past year				Used in past month			
	Total	Hispanic	White	Black	Total	Hispanic	White	Black	Total	Hispanic	White	Black
Percent rate estimates												
Age												
12-17	2.9	4.1	3.1	0.2	2.1	2.4	2.3	0.2	0.5	0.5	0.5	0.1
18-25	12.5	7.8	15.8	1.9	4.9	2.4	6.4	0.6	1.3	0.8	1.5	0.6
26-34	15.9	6.7	19.6	5.3	1.2	0.5	1.5	0.6	0.1	0.2	0.1	0.2
35+	6.6	5.1	7.3	3.1	0.1	(X)	0.1	0.1	(X)	(X)	(X)	(X)
Sex												
Male	11.8	7.3	13.7	4.3	1.7	1.4	2.0	0.3	0.4	0.4	0.4	0.1
Female	5.9	4.5	6.6	1.9	0.6	0.5	0.7	0.2	0.1	0.2	0.1	0.2
Total	8.7	5.9	10.1	3.0	1.2	0.9	1.3	0.3	0.2	0.3	0.3	0.2
Population estimates (in thousands)												
Age												
12-17	620	105	451	5	437	61	336	5	98	14	78	4
18-25	3,547	281	3,107	72	1,380	85	1,251	24	370	27	301	21
26-34	5,900	284	5,283	233	452	20	404	27	44	10	24	10
35+	7,986	415	7,014	369	122	(X)	109	9	(X)	(X)	(X)	(X)
Sex												
Male	11,694	672	10,425	441	1,702	127	1,515	33	392	38	330	11
Female	6,360	413	5,430	238	689	43	585	31	123	15	73	25
Total	18,054	1,085	15,854	679	2,391	170	2,100	65	515	53	403	37

Source: U.S. Department of Health and Human Services. Public Health Service. Alcohol, Drug Abuse, and Mental Health Administration. *National Household Survey on Drug Abuse: Population Estimates 1993.* DHHS Publication No. (SMA) 94-3017. Bethesda, MD: Department of Health and Human Services, 1994, pp. 47-49. Primary source: Substance Abuse and Mental Health Services Administration, Office of Applied Studies, 1993 National Household Survey on Drug Abuse. *Note:* An (X) stands for low precision; no estimate reported.

★ 442 ★

Substance Abuse

Illicit Drug Use

Illicit drugs include marijuana, nonmedical use of psychotherapeutics, inhalants, cocaine, hallucinogens and heroin. Estimates are for 1993.

Age/sex	Ever used				Used in past year				Used in past month			
	Total	Hispanic	White	Black	Total	Hispanic	White	Black	Total	Hispanic	White	Black
Percent rate estimates												
Age												
12-17	17.9	21.6	18.0	14.5	13.6	17.6	13.5	11.0	6.6	9.3	6.3	6.5
18-25	50.9	40.9	56.5	37.8	26.6	21.3	29.7	19.0	13.5	9.8	15.2	10.3
26-34	61.1	44.4	66.9	50.8	17.4	11.7	18.1	19.0	8.5	5.6	8.6	11.2
35+	29.9	23.1	30.7	30.7	6.3	6.8	6.2	7.7	2.8	4.0	2.5	4.0
Sex												
Male	42.4	38.1	43.6	41.4	14.2	15.3	14.0	16.1	7.4	7.4	7.2	9.4
Female	32.4	24.4	34.6	27.1	9.6	9.1	9.8	8.9	4.1	5.1	3.9	4.6
Total	37.2	31.2	38.9	33.5	11.8	12.2	11.8	12.1	5.6	6.2	5.5	6.8
Population estimates (in thousands)												
Age												
12-17	3,794	559	2,624	450	2,877	454	1,972	340	1,400	239	922	203
18-25	14,426	1,463	11,115	1,418	7,525	761	5,834	714	3,816	350	2,996	386
26-34	22,730	1,880	18,023	2,232	6,454	495	4,875	833	3,171	237	2,322	493
35+	36,071	1,874	29,628	3,608	7,581	552	5,960	904	3,318	321	2,455	473
Sex												
Male	42,109	3,522	33,116	4,255	14,105	1,419	10,640	1,661	7,301	680	5,504	966
Female	34,913	2,254	28,274	3,452	10,333	843	8,001	1,131	4,404	468	3,191	588
Total	77,022	5,775	61,390	7,707	24,437	2,263	18,641	2,792	11,705	1,148	8,695	1,555

Source: U.S. Department of Health and Human Services. Public Health Service. Alcohol, Drug Abuse, and Mental Health Administration. *National Household Survey on Drug Abuse: Population Estimates 1993.* DHHS Publication No. (SMA) 94-3017. Bethesda, MD: Department of Health and Human Services, 1994, pp. 17-19. Primary source: Substance Abuse and Mental Health Services Administration, Office of Applied Studies, 1993 National Household Survey on Drug Abuse.

★ 443 ★

Substance Abuse

Inhalant Abuse

Estimates are shown for 1993.

	Ever used				Used in past year				Used in past month			
	Total	Hispanic	White	Black	Total	Hispanic	White	Black	Total	Hispanic	White	Black
Percent rate estimates												
Age												
12-17	5.9	7.7	6.5	1.7	3.6	5.2	3.9	0.7	1.4	2.3	1.6	0.3
18-25	9.9	7.2	12.4	2.0	2.8	2.2	3.4	0.7	1.1	0.8	1.3	0.2
26-34	9.4	5.0	11.5	4.0	0.7	0.2	0.8	0.6	0.4	0.2	0.5	0.1
35+	2.8	3.0	2.8	3.1	0.2	0.3	0.3	0.1	0.1	0.1	0.1	(X)
Sex												
Male	7.4	6.9	8.1	4.8	1.4	1.8	1.6	0.5	0.6	0.7	0.7	0.1

[Continued]

★ 443 ★

Inhalant Abuse

[Continued]

	Ever used				Used in past year				Used in past month			
	Total	Hispanic	White	Black	Total	Hispanic	White	Black	Total	Hispanic	White	Black
Female	3.3	2.9	3.7	1.4	0.6	0.8	0.6	0.3	0.2	0.3	0.3	0.2
Total	5.3	4.9	5.8	2.9	1.0	1.3	1.1	0.4	0.4	0.5	0.5	0.1
Population estimates (in thousands)												
Age												
12-17	1,253	199	947	52	757	135	575	23	305	59	233	11
18-25	2,793	258	2,432	77	793	77	678	28	302	29	261	8
26-34	3,501	213	3,091	177	253	7	220	26	145	7	133	6
35+	3,353	242	2,736	362	290	24	253	13	137	5	130	(X)
Sex												
Male	7,339	643	6,157	495	1,425	170	1,203	46	623	68	544	7
Female	3,561	270	3,050	173	668	74	523	43	266	31	213	20
Total	10,900	912	9,207	668	2,092	244	1,727	90	889	100	757	27

Source: U.S. Department of Health and Human Services. Public Health Service. Alcohol, Drug Abuse, and Mental Health Administration. *National Household Survey on Drug Abuse: Population Estimates 1993.* DHHS Publication No. (SMA) 94-3017. Bethesda, MD: Department of Health and Human Services, 1994, pp. 41-43. Primary source: Substance Abuse and Mental Health Services Administration, Office of Applied Studies, 1993 National Household Survey on Drug Abuse.

★ 444 ★

Substance Abuse

Marijuana Abuse

Estimates are shown for 1993, by age, sex, and race/ethnicity.

Age/sex	Ever used				Used in past year				Used in past month			
	Total	Hispanic	White	Black	Total	Hispanic	White	Black	Total	Hispanic	White	Black
Percent rate estimates												
Age												
12-17	11.7	15.7	11.3	10.9	10.1	13.2	9.8	9.6	4.9	6.7	4.5	5.8
18-25	47.4	39.2	52.9	34.0	22.9	18.9	25.5	16.7	11.1	7.8	12.5	9.2
26-34	59.2	42.3	65.1	49.5	13.8	9.1	14.3	16.2	6.7	4.1	6.8	9.9
35+	26.6	20.3	27.5	27.9	4.0	4.6	3.7	6.5	1.9	2.9	1.7	2.7
Sex												
Male	39.2	34.8	40.7	39.1	11.7	12.7	11.3	14.2	6.0	5.9	5.9	8.2
Female	28.7	21.4	30.8	24.0	6.5	6.4	6.4	7.4	2.8	3.4	2.7	3.4
Total	33.7	28.1	35.6	30.7	9.0	9.6	8.8	10.4	4.3	4.7	4.2	5.6
Population estimates (in thousands)												
Age												
12-17	2,482	404	1,650	338	2,136	340	1,429	297	1,043	172	662	180
18-25	13,414	1,364	10,396	1,278	6,483	674	5,010	626	3,142	279	2,466	347
26-34	22,017	1,792	17,549	2,174	5,144	387	3,851	712	2,504	175	1,826	434
35+	32,010	1,644	26,493	3,283	4,810	371	3,568	766	2,303	239	1,673	323
Sex												
Male	38,974	3,225	30,910	4,017	11,605	1,178	8,601	1,456	5,977	550	4,449	847

[Continued]

★ 444 ★

Marijuana Abuse

[Continued]

Age/sex	Ever used				Used in past year				Used in past month			
	Total	Hispanic	White	Black	Total	Hispanic	White	Black	Total	Hispanic	White	Black
Female	30,949	1,979	25,178	3,055	6,968	594	5,256	945	3,015	315	2,178	436
Total	69,923	5,204	56,088	7,073	18,573	1,772	13,858	2,401	8,992	864	6,627	1,283

Source: U.S. Department of Health and Human Services. Public Health Service. Alcohol, Drug Abuse, and Mental Health Administration. *National Household Survey on Drug Abuse: Population Estimates 1993.* DHHS Publication No. (SMA) 94-3017. Bethesda, MD: Department of Health and Human Services, 1994, pp. 23-25. Primary source: Substance Abuse and Mental Health Services Administration, Office of Applied Studies, 1993 National Household Survey on Drug Abuse.

★ 445 ★

Substance Abuse

Marijuana - Frequency of Use

Estimated use during the past year is shown for 1993, by age, sex, and race/ethnicity.

	At least once				12 or more times				Once a week or more			
	Total	Hispanic	White	Black	Total	Hispanic	White	Black	Total	Hispanic	White	Black
Percent rate estimates												
Age												
12-17	10.1	13.2	9.8	9.6	4.8	5.9	4.7	4.6	2.8	3.3	2.9	2.1
18-25	22.9	18.9	25.5	16.7	10.1	7.8	11.2	8.5	5.9	4.7	6.3	6.2
26-34	13.8	9.1	14.3	16.2	7	4.7	7.2	9.1	3.7	2.3	3.7	5.6
35+	4	4.6	3.7	6.5	2	2.8	1.9	3.4	1.2	1.5	1.1	1.6
Sex												
Male	11.7	12.7	11.3	14.2	6.2	6.3	6.1	8	3.5	3.4	3.5	4.8
Female	6.5	6.4	6.4	7.4	2.6	2.9	2.5	3.5	1.4	1.7	1.3	1.9
Total	9	9.6	8.8	10.4	4.3	4.6	4.2	5.5	2.4	2.6	2.4	3.2
Population estimates (in thousands)												
Age												
12-17	2136	340	1429	297	1029	153	687	142	600	85	425	66
18-25	6483	674	5010	626	2863	279	2205	319	1685	169	1247	234
26-34	5144	387	3851	712	2614	200	1942	402	1365	99	998	344
35+	4810	371	3568	766	2467	224	1809	401	1414	124	1065	192
Sex												
Male	11605	1178	8601	1456	6171	585	4620	819	3513	317	2638	493
Female	6968	594	5256	945	2802	271	2023	444	1551	159	1097	243
Total	18573	1772	13858	2401	8973	856	6643	1263	5064	476	3735	736

Source: U.S. Department of Health and Human Services. Public Health Service. Alcohol, Drug Abuse, and Mental Health Administration. *National Household Survey on Drug Abuse: Population Estimates 1993.* DHHS Publication No. (SMA) 94-3017. Bethesda, MD: Department of Health and Human Services, 1994, pp. 107-109. Primary source: Substance Abuse and Mental Health Services Administration, Office of Applied Studies, 1993 National Household Survey on Drug Abuse.

★ 446 ★

Substance Abuse

Marijuana Use in the Past Month

Use by persons age 12 years and older in the contiguous United States is shown for selected years based on household interviews. Data are shown by age and race/ethnicity.

Age, sex, race and Hispanic origin	Percent of population									
	1974	1976	1977	1979	1982	1985	1988	1990	1991	1992
12 years and over	8	9	10	13	11	9	6	5	5	4
12-17 years	12	12	17	17	12	12	6	5	4	4
12-13 years	[1]	[1]	[1]	4	[1]	[1]	1	[1]	[1]	1
14-15 years	12	13	16	17	8	11	5	5	4	4
16-17 years	20	21	30	28	23	21	12	10	9	8
18-25 years	25	25	27	35	27	22	15	13	13	11
26-34 years	8	11	12	17	17	17	11	9	7	8
35 years and over	[1]	1	1	2	3	2	1	2	2	2
12-17 years										
Male	12	14	20	19	13	13	6	6	5	5
Female	11	11	13	14	10	11	7	4	4	3
White, non-Hispanic	-	-	-	-	-	13	7	6	4	4
Black, non-Hispanic	-	-	-	-	-	8	4	3	4	3
Hispanic	-	-	-	-	-	10	5	4	5	5
18-25 years										
Male	-	31	35	45	36	27	20	17	16	15
Female	-	19	20	26	19	17	11	9	10	8
White, non-Hispanic	-	-	-	-	-	22	16	14	14	12
Black, non-Hispanic	-	-	-	-	-	24	15	13	15	11
Hispanic	-	-	-	-	-	15	14	8	9	8

Source: National Center for Health Statistics. *Health, United States, 1993.* Hyattsville, MD: Public Health Service, May 1994, p. 158. Primary source: National Institute on Drug Abuse National Household Survey on Drug Abuse: Main Findings, 1979, by P.M. Fishburne, H.I. Abelson, and I. Cisin. DHHS Pub. No. (ADM) 80-976. Alcohol, Drug Abuse, and Mental Health Administration. Washington, DC: U.S. Government Printing Office, 1980; National Household Survey on Drug Abuse: Main Findings, 1982, by J.D. Miller et al, DHHS Pub. No. (ADM) 83-1263. Alcohol, Drug Abuse, and Mental Health Administration. Washington, DC: U.S. Government Printing Office, 1983; National Household Survey on Drug Abuse: Main Findings, 1985. DHHS Pub. No. (ADM) 88-1586. National Household Survey on Drug Abuse: Main Findings, 1988; National Household Survey on Drug Abuse Main Findings, 1990; National Household Survey on Drug Abuse: Main Findings, 1991; and preliminary estimates from the 1992 National Household Survey on Drug Abuse: Advance Report Number 3. *Notes:* A dash (-) stands for data not available. Estimates of the use of substances from the National Household Survey on Drug Abuse and the Monitoring the Future Study differ because of different methodologies, sampling frames, and tabulation categories. 1. Relative standard error greater than 30 percent. Estimates with relative standard error greater than 50 percent are not shown.

★ 447 ★

Substance Abuse

Psychotherapeutics Abuse

Psychotherapeutics include nonmedical use of sedatives, tranquilizers, stimulants or analgesics. Estimates are shown for 1993, by age, sex, and race/ethnicity.

	Ever used				Used in past year				Used in past month			
	Total	Hispanic	White	Black	Total	Hispanic	White	Black	Total	Hispanic	White	Black
Percent rate estimates												
Age												
12-17	5.9	5.7	6.6	3.8	3.5	4.1	4.1	1.3	1.2	1.6	1.3	0.7
18-25	14.2	8.5	17.2	6.2	7.2	3.7	9.0	3.2	2.9	2.1	3.5	0.8
26-34	17.2	11.3	20.2	6.6	5.7	3.9	6.4	2.7	1.9	1.3	2.1	1.0
35+	9.4	6.7	9.7	7.3	2.5	2.2	2.5	2.2	0.7	1.0	0.7	1.0
Sex												
Male	12.7	8.8	14.0	6.6	3.9	3.2	4.4	2.1	1.4	1.2	1.6	0.8
Female	9.7	7.1	10.5	6.4	3.7	3.2	3.9	2.5	1.2	1.6	1.1	1.0
Total	11.1	8.0	12.2	6.5	3.8	3.2	4.1	2.3	1.3	1.4	1.3	0.9
Population estimates (in thousands)												
Age												
12-17	1,252	147	957	118	747	106	593	39	264	41	197	21
18-25	4,017	305	3,379	234	2,050	132	1,766	120	813	74	684	31
26-34	6,404	477	5,438	289	2,116	166	1,734	118	709	55	556	44
35+	11,361	545	9,393	854	2,979	182	2,449	253	868	84	666	118
Sex												
Male	12,568	817	10,605	676	3,868	292	3,350	216	1,397	107	1,202	86
Female	10,465	656	8,561	819	4,024	294	3,192	315	1,258	147	900	128
Total	23,034	1,474	19,166	1,495	7,892	587	6,542	531	2,655	254	2,103	214

Source: U.S. Department of Health and Human Services. Public Health Service. Alcohol, Drug Abuse, and Mental Health Administration. *National Household Survey on Drug Abuse: Population Estimates 1993.* DHHS Publication No. (SMA) 94-3017. Bethesda, MD: Department of Health and Human Services, 1994, pp. 53-55. Primary source: Substance Abuse and Mental Health Services Administration, Office of Applied Studies, 1993 National Household Survey on Drug Abuse.

★ 448 ★

Substance Abuse

Reported Crack Cocaine Users in Neighborhoods

Characteristics	Neighborhoods with at least one crack cocaine user (128 neighborhoods, 939 residents)	Neighborhoods with no crack cocaine users[1] (1,404 neighborhoods 7,875 residents)
All	100	100
Race/ethnicity		
White American	35.9	53.5
Hispanic American	33.1	23.9
African American	28.3	20.6
Other	2.7	2.0

Source: Lillie-Blanton, Dr. Marsha PH; James C. Anthony, PH.D.; Charles R. Schuster, PH.D. "Probing the meaning of racial/ethnic group comparisons in crack cocaine smoking." *JAMA* (24 February 1993) Vol. 269, No. 8, p. 996. Primary source: *National Household Survey on Drug Abuse.* *Note:* 1. National Household Survey on Drug Abuse.

★ 449 ★

Substance Abuse

Sedatives Abuse

Estimates are shown for 1993, by age, sex, and race/ethnicity.

Age/sex	Ever used				Used in past year				Used in past month			
	Total	Hispanic	White	Black	Total	Hispanic	White	Black	Total	Hispanic	White	Black
Percent rate estimates												
Age												
12-17	1.4	2.2	1.4	0.9	0.8	0.3	0.8	0.2	0.2	0.4	0.2	0.1
18-25	2.7	2.4	3.1	1.5	1.1	1.1	1.2	0.6	0.6	0.7	0.6	0.6
26-34	4.8	2.2	5.9	1.8	1	0.5	1.1	0.6	0.3	(X)	0.4	0.2
35+	3.6	2.1	3.5	2.9	0.6	0.2	0.7	0.4	0.1	0.1	0.2	(X)
Sex												
Male	4.1	2.4	4.3	2.3	0.7	0.8	0.8	0.6	0.2	0.3	0.3	0.2
Female	2.8	2	3	2	0.8	0.4	0.9	0.2	0.3	0.2	0.3	0.1
Total	3.4	2.2	3.6	2.2	0.8	0.6	0.8	0.4	0.3	0.2	0.3	0.1
Population estimates (in thousands)												
Age												
12-17	297	58	199	27	163	34	120	5	46	11	31	2
18-25	766	85	604	56	308	41	239	22	177	26	123	22

[Continued]

★ 449 ★

Sedatives Abuse

[Continued]

Age/sex	Ever used				Used in past year				Used in past month			
	Total	Hispanic	White	Black	Total	Hispanic	White	Black	Total	Hispanic	White	Black
26-34	1770	91	1577	80	359	20	307	26	129	(X)	115	7
35+	4294	173	3331	337	752	20	655	42	176	6	170	(X)
Sex												
Male	4103	221	3288	242	722	76	577	65	247	26	203	16
Female	3025	286	2423	257	860	39	745	29	281	18	236	15
Total	7127	407	5711	499	1582	115	1321	95	528	44	439	31

Source: U.S. Department of Health and Human Services. Public Health Service. Alcohol, Drug Abuse, and Mental Health Administration. *National Household Survey on Drug Abuse: Population Estimates 1993.* DHHS Publication No. (SMA) 94-3017. Bethesda, MD: Department of Health and Human Services, 1994, pp. 65-67. Primary source: Substance Abuse and Mental Health Services Administration, Office of Applied Studies, 1993 National Household Survey on Drug Abuse. *Note:* An (X) stands for low precision; no estimates reported.

★ 450 ★

Substance Abuse

Smokeless Tobacco Use

Estimates are shown for 1993, by age, sex, and race/ethnicity.

	Ever used				Used in past year				Used in past month			
	Total	Hispanic	White	Black	Total	Hispanic	White	Black	Total	Hispanic	White	Black
Percent rate estimates												
Age												
12-17	8.7	5.1	11.5	1.2	4.8	3.2	6.3	0.4	2.0	0.9	2.7	0.2
18-25	19.7	9.5	25.3	5.2	8.9	2.9	11.8	1.5	6.4	1.9	8.5	1.1
26-34	18.4	7.5	22.8	7.2	5.6	1.4	7.4	0.7	4.4	1.0	5.9	0.2
35+	10.1	5.7	10.9	9.8	2.2	1.3	2.3	2.5	1.9	0.8	1.9	2.5
Sex												
Male	23.7	12.6	27.7	11.0	7.8	3.6	9.3	2.5	5.9	2.1	7.2	2.1
Female	2.7	0.9	2.8	4.5	0.5	0.2	0.4	1.1	0.2	(X)	0.1	1.0
Total	12.8	6.8	14.8	7.4	4.0	1.9	4.7	1.7	2.9	1.1	3.5	1.5
Population estimates (in thousands)												
Age												
12-17	1,851	132	1,673	36	1,019	82	918	11	420	24	391	5
18-25	5,590	340	4,973	195	2,533	105	2,320	55	1,805	68	1,670	40
26-34	6,827	315	6,140	316	2,067	57	1,981	29	1,632	41	1,582	9
35+	12,225	462	10,530	1,155	2,624	105	2,220	296	2,238	63	1,877	296
Sex												
Male	23,554	1,169	21,034	1,126	7,733	334	74,080	256	5,875	193	5,433	219

[Continued]

★ 450 ★

Smokeless Tobacco Use

[Continued]

	Ever used				Used in past year				Used in past month			
	Total	Hispanic	White	Black	Total	Hispanic	White	Black	Total	Hispanic	White	Black
Female	2,939	81	2,282	576	510	16	358	136	220	(X)	86	132
Total	26,493	250	23,316	1,702	8,243	349	7,438	392	6,095	195	5,520	351

Source: U.S. Department of Health and Human Services. Public Health Service. Alcohol, Drug Abuse, and Mental Health Administration. *National Household Survey on Drug Abuse: Population Estimates 1993.* DHHS Publication No. (SMA) 94-3017. Bethesda, MD: Department of Health and Human Services, 1994, pp. 95-97. Primary source: Substance Abuse and Mental Health Services Administration, Office of Applied Studies, 1993 National Household Survey on Drug Abuse. *Note:* An (X) stands for low precision; no estimates reported.

★ 451 ★

Substance Abuse

Stimulant Abuse

Estimates are shown for 1993, by age, sex, and race/ethnicity.

Age/sex	Ever used				Used in past year				Used in past month			
	Total	Hispanic	White	Black	Total	Hispanic	White	Black	Total	Hispanic	White	Black
Percent rate estimates												
Age												
12-17	2.1	2.2	2.5	0.2	1.6	1.8	2.0	0.1	0.5	0.5	0.7	0.1
18-25	6.4	4.4	8.0	1.3	3.0	1.7	3.9	0.5	0.9	0.4	1.1	0.1
26-34	10.5	5.8	12.7	3.2	1.7	1.5	2.0	0.6	0.5	0.2	0.6	0.1
35+	5.3	3.3	5.7	4.2	0.5	0.5	0.4	1.2	0.2	0.1	0.1	0.4
Sex												
Male	7.4	5.0	8.5	3.8	1.5	1.4	1.6	0.8	0.5	0.3	0.6	(X)
Female	4.8	2.9	5.4	2.3	0.9	0.8	0.9	0.8	0.2	0.2	0.2	0.4
Total	6.0	3.9	6.9	3.0	1.1	1.1	1.2	0.8	0.3	0.2	0.4	0.3
Population estimates (in thousands)												
Age												
12-17	436	57	364	8	339	45	291	2	113	14	98	2
18-25	1,816	157	1,583	47	853	60	760	18	251	14	220	5
26-34	3,894	246	3,431	139	630	62	536	27	171	9	159	4
35+	6,378	269	5,452	490	555	44	375	136	183	7	127	49
Sex												
Male	7,351	460	6,417	394	1,449	134	1,233	81	505	27	474	(X)
Female	5,174	269	4,413	290	929	78	729	102	213	17	129	54
Total	12,524	728	10,830	684	2,377	212	1,962	183	719	43	603	59

Source: U.S. Department of Health and Human Services. Public Health Service. Alcohol, Drug Abuse, and Mental Health Administration. *National Household Survey on Drug Abuse: Population Estimates 1993.* DHHS Publication No. (SMA) 94-3017. Bethesda, MD: Department of Health and Human Services, 1994, pp. 59-61. Primary source: Substance Abuse and Mental Health Services Administration, Office of Applied Studies, 1993 National Household Survey on Drug Abuse. *Note:* An (X) stands for low precision; no estimate reported.

★ 452 ★

Substance Abuse

Tranquilizer Abuse

Estimates are shown for 1993, by age, sex, and race/ethnicity.

Age/sex	Ever used				Used in past year				Used in past month			
	Total	Hispanic	White	Black	Total	Hispanic	White	Black	Total	Hispanic	White	Black
Percent rate estimates												
Age												
12-17	1.2	1.1	1.4	0.4	0.7	0.3	0.9	0.2	0.2	0.2	0.3	0.2
18-25	5.4	2.4	7.0	1.2	2.0	1.0	2.5	0.6	0.6	0.5	0.8	0.1
26-34	7.1	3.6	8.4	3.0	1.9	1.0	2.2	1.1	0.5	0.3	0.6	0.5
35+	4.2	3.0	4.5	2.9	1.0	0.6	1.0	0.7	0.1	0.4	0.1	0.3
Sex												
Male	5.0	3.2	5.9	1.9	1.1	0.8	1.3	0.4	0.3	0.2	0.3	0.2
Female	4.1	2.4	4.5	2.6	1.3	0.7	1.5	0.9	0.3	0.5	0.3	0.3
Total	4.6	2.8	5.2	2.3	1.2	0.7	1.4	0.7	0.3	0.4	0.3	0.3
Population estimates (in thousands)												
Age												
12-17	256	29	205	12	151	7	138	6	53	4	43	6
18-25	1,522	85	1,374	44	553	37	494	22	170	18	148	5
26-34	2,635	154	2,272	131	694	40	597	50	183	12	149	21
35+	5,044	245	4,319	338	1,144	52	977	80	165	36	96	33
Sex												
Male	4,990	294	4,458	199	1,126	69	1,012	42	256	22	210	23
Female	4,467	220	3,712	326	1,416	67	1,194	115	316	48	226	42
Total	9,467	513	8,171	525	2,543	136	2,206	158	572	70	436	65

Source: U.S. Department of Health and Human Services. Public Health Service. Alcohol, Drug Abuse, and Mental Health Administration. *National Household Survey on Drug Abuse: Population Estimates 1993.* DHHS Publication No. (SMA) 94-3017. Bethesda, MD: Department of Health and Human Services, 1994, pp. 71-73. Primary source: Substance Abuse and Mental Health Services Administration, Office of Applied Studies, 1993 National Household Survey on Drug Abuse.

Substance Abuse Treatment

★ 453 ★

Alcohol Treatment Program Admissions

State-funded client treatment admissions, by race/ethnicity and state and U.S. territory are shown for fiscal year 1992.

State	White, not of Hispanic origin	Black, not of Hispanic origin	Hispanic	Asian or Pacific Islander	Native American	Other	Not reported	Total
Alabama	5,917	2,335	NA	NA	NA	27	NA	8,279
Alaska	5,135	221	141	40	6,009	37	81	11,664
Arizona	7,160	681	2,647	54	2,472	0	3,973	16,987[1]
Arkansas	6,115	2,281	48	4	49	0	0	8,497[2]
California	37,316	12,404	10,222	690	1,116	0	547	62,295
Colorado	33,461	3,445	14,271	164	3,226	109	0	54,676
Connecticut	8,657	3,148	1,537	NA	NA	81	4,932	18,355
Delaware	2,426	1,075	22	0	4	22	1	3,550
District of Columbia	236	1,980	158	0	13	6	5	2,398
Florida	21,932	4,022	3,232	68	104	125	38,035	67,518
Georgia	20,526	10,410	102	26	33	64	0	31,161
Guam	38	0	1	55	0	1	0	95
Hawaii	1,180	94	158	904	107	65	19	2,527
Idaho	4,501	38	366	15	287	48	0	5,255
Illinois	27,202	10,742	3,319	161	480	289	0	42,193
Indiana	12,896	2,293	116	13	58	137	2,645	18,158
Iowa	17,524	729	448	46	247	46	0	19,040
Kansas	10,684	1,195	966	53	420	388	0	13,706
Kentucky	22,550	1,784	1	0	0	0	289	24,624
Louisiana	6,220	3,594	NA	25	26	NA	NA	9,865
Maine	6,800	36	0	8	104	25	0	6,973
Maryland	12,290	5,386	205	37	73	33	1	18,025
Massachusetts	41,244	4,867	3,034	193	228	2,087	0	51,653
Michigan	38,059	7,562	1,585	29	1,163	99	63	48,560
Minnesota	38,621	4,035	1,941	90	8,800	285	388	54,160
Mississippi	3,746	2,997	0	0	28	0	0	6,771
Missouri	18,807	4,373	125	21	195	48	0	23,569
Montana	4,459	27	101	8	1,317	0	13	5,925
Nebraska	17,972	1,541	0	49	3,343	1,231	2	24,138
Nevada	2,899	319	279	37	209	30	1,237	5,010
New Hampshire	3,931	88	13	4	21	0	0	4,057
New Jersey	15,800	6,464	2,097	98	64	214	13	24,750
New Mexico	4,507	163	3,266	34	2,192	0	152	10,314
New York	54,553	29,424	7,864	133	2,013	760	0	94,747
North Carolina	19,152	9,055	192	10	430	57	74	28,970
North Dakota	3,361	18	0	6	931	26	2	4,344
Ohio	32,830	7,145	737	102	162	98	181	41,255
Oklahoma	8,722	1,279	263	13	1,564	0	0	11,841
Oregon	NA	NA	NA	NA	NA	NA	NA	NA
Pennsylvania	27,294	5,901	973	39	80	4	0	34,291
Puerto Rico	0	0	8,710	0	0	0	0	8,710

[Continued]

★ 453 ★

Alcohol Treatment Program Admissions

[Continued]

State	White, not of Hispanic origin	Black, not of Hispanic origin	Hispanic	Asian or Pacific Islander	Native American	Other	Not reported	Total
Rhode Island	6,132	938	330	25	90	152	0	7,667
South Carolina	13,732	7,034	220	27	40	24	106	21,183
South Dakota	7,043	103	0	0	3,090	155	0	10,391
Tennessee	5,181	1,379	72	6	15	0	17	6,670
Texas	10,968	3,347	5,877	33	175	7	0	20,407
Utah	8,691	378	1,272	74	1,890	150	18	12,473
Vermont	4,953	46	11	12	50	111	0	5,183
Virginia	11,807	3,616	603	62	99	0	923	17,110
Washington	NA	NA	NA	NA	NA	NA	NA	NA
West Virginia	9,812	490	45	9	11	0	0	10,367
Wisconsin	90,338	3,313	1,431	216	2,868	0	0	98,166
Wyoming	NA	NA	NA	NA	NA	NA	NA	NA
Total	775,380	173,795	79,001	3,693	45,896	7,041	53,717	1,138,523
Percent of total	68.1	15.3	6.9	.3	4.0	.6	4.7	100.0

Source: U.S. Department of Health and Human Services. Public Health Service. Substance Abuse and Mental Health Services Administration. Office of Applied Studies. *State Resources and Services Related to Alcohol and Other Drug Problems, Fiscal Year 1992: An Analysis of State Alcohol and Drug Abuse Profile Data.* Prepared by the National Association of State Alcohol and Drug Abuse Directors, Incorporated. DHHS Publication No. (SMA) 94-2092. Rockville, MD: Department of Health and Human Services, 1994, p. 29. Primary source: State Alcohol and Drug Abuse Profile (SADAP), FY 1992; data are included for only those programs that received at least some funds administered by the State Alcohol/Drug Agency during the states' fiscal year (FY) 1992. *Notes:* NA stands for information not available. 1. Figures represent clients "served." 2. Native American category includes American Indian and Alaskan Native (Aleut, Eskimo Indian).

★ 454 ★

Substance Abuse Treatment

Alcohol and Drug Abuse Treatment Programs

Data show number and percent distribution of clients in treatment, by treatment setting and by race/ethnicity of client. Data are current as of September 30, 1991.

Client diagnosis and race/ethnicity	Treatment setting					
	Hospital/ residential setting		Ambulatory setting		All clients	
	Number	Percent	Number	Percent	Number	Percent
Drug abuse clients						
White, not Hispanic	10,215	37.2	96,849	50.5	107,064	48.9
Black, not Hispanic	12,536	45.6	55,800	29.1	68,336	31.2
Hispanic	4,244	15.4	35,391	18.5	39,635	18.1
Asian	151	0.5	1,232	0.6	1,383	0.6
Indian	178	0.6	1,434	0.7	1,612	0.7
Other	147	0.5	941	0.5	1,088	0.5
Subtotal	27,471	100.0	191,647	100.0	219,118	100.0
Unknown[1]	1,229		16,661		17,890	
All clients	28,700		208,308		237,008	
Units reporting	1,937		4,196		5,548	

[Continued]

★ 454 ★

Alcohol and Drug Abuse Treatment Programs

[Continued]

Client diagnosis and race/ethnicity	Treatment setting					
	Hospital/ residential setting		Ambulatory setting		All clients	
	Number	Percent	Number	Percent	Number	Percent
Alcoholism clients						
White, not Hispanic	18,976	67.3	209,644	67.8	228,620	67.8
Black, not Hispanic	5,949	21.1	40,040	12.9	45,989	13.6
Hispanic	2,043	7.2	46,858	15.2	48,901	14.5
Asian	154	0.5	3,768	1.2	3,922	1.2
Indian	994	3.5	7,122	2.3	8,116	2.4
Other	72	0.3	1,771	0.6	1,843	0.5
Subtotal	28,188	100.0	309,203	100.0	337,391	100.0
Unknown[1]	1,642		26,114		27,756	
All clients	29,830		335,317		365,147	
Units reporting	2,681		4,832		6,682	
Clients with both problems						
White, not Hispanic	20,497	54.3	95,990	67.8	116,487	65.0
Black, not Hispanic	10,659	28.3	31,030	21.9	41,689	23.3
Hispanic	5,419	14.4	10,029	7.1	15,448	8.6
Asian	193	0.5	953	0.7	1,146	0.6
Indian	796	2.1	2,941	2.1	3,737	2.1
Other	157	0.4	576	0.4	733	0.4
Subtotal	37,721	100.0	141,519	100.0	179,240	100.0
Unknown[1]	2,899		27,525		30,424	
All clients	40,620		169,044		209,664	
Units reporting	2,546		4,008		5,707	
All clients						
White, not Hispanic	49,688	53.2	402,483	62.7	452,171	61.5
Black, not Hispanic	29,144	31.2	126,870	19.8	156,014	21.2
Hispanic	11,706	12.5	92,278	14.4	103,984	14.1
Asian	498	0.5	5,953	0.9	6,451	0.9
Indian	1,968	2.1	11,497	1.8	13,465	1.8
Other	376	0.4	3,288	0.5	3,664	0.5
Subtotal	93,380	100.0	642,369	100.0	735,749	100.0
Unknown[1]	5,770		70,300		76,070	
All clients	99,150		712,669		811,819	
Units reporting	3,682		6,428		8,928	

Source: U.S. Department of Health and Human Services. Public Health Service. Substance Abuse and Mental Health Services Administration. Office of Applied Studies. *National Drug and Alcoholism Treatment Unit Survey (NDATUS)*, 1991 Main Findings Report. DHHS Publication No. (SMA) 92-2007, 1993, p. 32. Primary source: NIDA and NIAA, 1991 National Drug and Alcoholism Treatment Unit Survey. *Notes:* Sum of units reporting in a hospital/residential setting and units reporting clients in an ambulatory setting does not equal total units, because units may treat clients in both types of setting. Column percentages are based on subtotals, excluding unknowns for race/ethnicity. Percentages may not sum to 100 because of rounding. Excludes 127 units that reported no clients. 1. Where units did not report clients by race/ethnicity, race/ethnicity is classified as "unknown."

★ 455 ★

Substance Abuse Treatment

Alcohol and Drug Treatment Program, by Location

Data show the percent distribution of Hispanic clients by location of treatment units. The vast majority of Hispanic clients received treatment in free-standing non-residential facilities.

Unit location	Hispanic clients		Percent of all clients
	Number	Percent	
Free-standing non-residential	69,518	66.9	52.5
CMHC	9,095	8.7	16.5
Hospital[1]	6,364	6.1	9.6
Correctional	4,239	4.1	4.8
Halfway house	1,158	1.1	1.9
Other residential	8,262	7.9	6.4
Other	1,011	1.0	1.5
Multiple sites	4,337	4.2	6.8
All units	103,984	100.0	100.0

Source: U.S. Department of Health and Human Services. Public Health Service. Substance Abuse and Mental Health Services Administration. Office of Applied Studies. *National Drug and Alcoholism Treatment Unit Survey (NDATUS)*, 1991 Main Findings Report. DHHS Publication No. (SMA) 92-2007, 1993, p. 70. Primary source: NIDA and NIAA, 1991 NDATUS. *Notes:* CMHC stands for community mental health center. 1. General hospitals, alcoholism hospitals, mental/psychiatric hospitals, and other specialized hospitals.

★ 456 ★

Substance Abuse Treatment

Drug Treatment Program Admissions

State-funded client treatment admissions, by race/ethnicity and state and U.S. territory are shown for fiscal year 1992.

State	White, not of Hispanic origin	Black, not of Hispanic origin	Hispanic	Asian or Pacific Islander	Native American	Other	Not reported	Total
Alabama	3,773	3,830	NA	NA	NA	25	NA	7,628
Alaska	1,498	303	65	16	694	7	19	2,602
Arizona	4,512	864	1,605	21	276	0	1,427	8,705[1]
Arkansas	2,626	2,305	21	6	13	0	0	4,971[2]
California	34,940	15,650	18,522	1,338	782	0	906	72,138
Colorado	5,396	1,796	2,200	48	135	28	0	9,603
Connecticut	4,447	3,856	2,311	NA	NA	55	3,159	13,828
Delaware	773	1,505	34	1	3	31	2	2,349
District of Columbia	325	8,114	114	11	22	27	602	9,215
Florida	12,943	13,339	3,358	47	83	119	20	29,909
Georgia	10,142	17,396	73	15	14	36	1	27,677
Guam	6	0	0	22	0	1	5	34
Hawaii	599	46	56	1,069	66	68	0	1,904
Idaho	2,006	19	112	3	73	29	0	2,242
Illinois	11,617	25,235	2,081	126	339	284	0	39,682

[Continued]

★ 456 ★

Drug Treatment Program Admissions

[Continued]

State	White, not of Hispanic origin	Black, not of Hispanic origin	Hispanic	Asian or Pacific Islander	Native American	Other	Not reported	Total
Indiana	3,695	412	35	2	9	46	1,554	5,753
Iowa	2,861	429	62	11	51	14	0	3,428
Kansas	2,446	1,554	98	9	82	93	0	4,282
Kentucky	7,402	1,528	0	0	0	0	74	9,004
Louisiana	5,781	10,261	NA	23	26	NA	NA	16,091
Maine	1,163	18	0	0	21	12	0	1,214
Maryland	5,637	11,615	124	57	41	29	1	17,504
Massachusetts	16,535	9,297	5,066	59	106	1,608	0	32,671
Michigan	13,018	13,496	552	37	220	62	51	27,436
Minnesota	3,587	1,741	164	25	355	69	37	5,978
Mississippi	1,657	2,730	0	0	1	0	0	4,388
Missouri	5,260	5,065	44	11	23	41	0	10,444
Montana	1,475	21	38	3	287	0	0	1,824
Nebraska	1,767	480	0	11	53	85	0	2,396
Nevada	1,872	491	147	28	47	15	263	2,863
New Hampshire	1,658	66	11	3	13	0	0	1,751
New Jersey	9,783	13,283	4,959	75	52	10	0	28,162
New Mexico	1,120	96	831	5	139	0	174	2,365
New York	21,633	21,390	9,751	90	303	531	0	53,698
North Carolina	5,412	8,549	20	4	147	16	24	14,172
North Dakota	182	4	0	0	34	4	9	233
Ohio	14,249	12,075	462	45	87	75	236	27,229
Oklahoma	3,392	1,524	137	8	332	0	0	5,393
Oregon	NA	NA	NA	NA	NA	NA	NA	NA
Pennsylvania	11,534	17,520	2,032	40	21	0	0	31,147
Puerto Rico	0	0	14,886	0	0	0	0	14,886
Rhode Island	3,473	580	331	6	40	76	0	4,506
South Carolina	2,767	4,019	87	6	14	8	60	6,961
South Dakota	568	18	0	0	189	7	1,237	2,019
Tennessee	4,405	1,927	58	5	15	0	17	6,427
Texas	11,011	12,022	6,439	53	84	118	0	29,727
Utah	2,481	130	252	15	60	71	30	3,039
Vermont	822	51	9	1	13	42	0	938
Virginia	9,493	8,027	294	56	64	0	1,596	19,530
Washington	NA	NA	NA	NA	NA	NA	NA	NA
West Virginia	1,147	160	12	15	2	0	0	1,336
Wisconsin	13,090	8,353	1,293	74	307	0	0	23,117
Wyoming	NA	NA	NA	NA	NA	NA	NA	NA

[Continued]

★ 456 ★

Drug Treatment Program Admissions

[Continued]

State	White, not of Hispanic origin	Black, not of Hispanic origin	Hispanic	Asian or Pacific Islander	Native American	Other	Not reported	Total
Total	287,979	263,190	78,746	3,500	5,738	3,742	11,504	654,399
Percent of total	44.0	40.2	12.0	.5	.9	.6	1.8	100.0

Source: U.S. Department of Health and Human Services. Public Health Service. Substance Abuse and Mental Health Services Administration. Office of Applied Studies. *State Resources and Services Related to Alcohol and Other Drug Problems, Fiscal Year 1992: An Analysis of State Alcohol and Drug Abuse Profile Data.* Prepared by the National Association of State Alcohol and Drug Abuse Directors, Incorporated. DHHS Publication No. (SMA) 94-2092. Rockville, MD: Department of Health and Human Services, 1994, p. 35. Primary source: State Alcohol and Drug Abuse Profile (SADAP), FY 1992; data are included for only those programs that received at least some funds administered by the State Alcohol/Drug Agency during the states' fiscal year (FY) 1992. *Notes:* NA stands for information not available. 1. Figures represent clients "served." 2. Native American category includes American Indian and Alaskan Native (Aleut, Eskimo Indian).

★ 457 ★

Substance Abuse Treatment

Drug and Alcohol Treatment Units: Proportion of Hispanic Clients

Percentages of clients with selected characteristics are shown for drug and alcohol treatment units that have high percentages of Hispanic clients. Data are based on analysis of 140 units in which 100% of the clients were of Hispanic origin and 414 units in which 50% or more of the clients were of Hispanic origin. However, units with 100% Hispanic populations accounted for only 6.8% of all Hispanics in treatment and units with 50% or more Hispanics accounted for only 37.2% of all Hispanics in treatment. Data shown are current as of September 30, 1991.

Characteristic	Units with 100% Hispanics	Units with 50% Hispanics[1]	All units
Age			
Under 18	8.8	7.4	5.9
18-20	3.2	4.0	5.2
21-24	13.9	12.4	13.0
25-34	44.8	33.1	35.2
35-44	19.0	27.7	26.7
45-54	7.9	11.1	9.7
55-64	2.2	3.7	3.3
65 & older	0.2	0.7	1.0
Sex			
Male	93.8	79.5	72.5
Female	6.2	20.5	27.5
Special characteristics			
IV drug users[2]	25.6	38.7	23.6

[Continued]

★ 457 ★

Drug and Alcohol Treatment Units: Proportion of Hispanic Clients

[Continued]

Characteristic	Units with 100% Hispanics	Units with 50% Hispanics[1]	All units
HIV positives[3]	10.5	16.2	8.4
Methadone clients[4]	1.5	26.6	12.0

Source: U.S. Department of Health and Human Services. Public Health Service. Substance Abuse and Mental Health Services Administration. Office of Applied Studies. *National Drug and Alcoholism Treatment Unit Survey (NDATUS)*, 1991 Main Findings Report. DHHS Publication No. (SMA) 92-2007, 1993, pp. 69-70. Primary source: NIDA and NIAA, 1991 NDATUS. *Notes:* 1. 29.8 percent of clients in these units were not Hispanic or were of unknown race/ethnicity. 2. Excludes units that did not report data on IV drug users. 3. Excludes units that did not report data on HIV positives. 4. Excludes units that did not report on methadone clients.

★ 458 ★

Substance Abuse Treatment

Drug and Alcohol Treatment by Type of Care

From the the source: "The distribution of Hispanic clients by type of care received is shown [in the table]. Nearly 90 percent of Hispanic clients received ambulatory care, and two thirds received ambulatory outpatient care."

Type of care	Hispanic clients		Percent of all clients
	Number	Percent	
Detoxification (24-hr. care)			
Hospital inpatient	191	0.2	0.2
Free-standing residential	271	0.3	0.3
Rehab/residential (24-hr. care)			
Hospital inpatient	83	0.1	0.1
Short-term	283	0.1	0.7
Long-term	7,944	7.6	5.6
Unspecified (24-hr. care)	2,932	2.8	5.2
Ambulatory (less than 24-hr. care)			
Outpatient	68,709	66.1	53.8
Intensive outpatient	1,178	1.1	1.6
Detox	550	0.5	0.3
Unspecified	21,841	21.0	32.1
All units	103,984	100.0	100.0

Source: U.S. Department of Health and Human Services. Public Health Service. Substance Abuse and Mental Health Services Administration. Office of Applied Studies. *National Drug and Alcoholism Treatment Unit Survey (NDATUS)*, 1991 Main Findings Report. DHHS Publication No. (SMA) 92-2007, 1993, p. 70. Primary source: NIDA and NIAA, 1991 NDATUS.

★ 459 ★

Substance Abuse Treatment

Substance Abuse Treatment Services Available to Hispanics

Availability of selected services to Hispanic clients enrolled in treatment programs is shown. Data reflect services offered as reported by treatment units, and do not necessarily reflect use of those services by clients. Overall, services were less available to Hispanics than to the general client population.

Service provided	Hispanic clients		Percent of all clients
	Number	Percent	
Individual treatment/counseling	94,906	91.2	94.5
Group therapy/counseling	92,820	89.3	94.3
Referral	84,045	80.8	85.6
Family therapy/counseling	62,828	60.4	75.9
Aftercare follow-up	58,710	56.5	71.7
Urine testing	55,122	53.0	61.1
Self-help groups	52,131	50.1	57.9
Treat IV drug users	51,483	49.5	56.0
Outreach	49,111	47.2	52.0
Crisis intervention	43,679	42.0	56.4
Early intervention	35,291	33.9	43.8
Transportation	17,161	16.5	17.2

Source: U.S. Department of Health and Human Services. Public Health Service. Alcohol, Drug Abuse, and Mental Health Administration. *National Household Survey on Drug Abuse: Population Estimates 1993.* DHHS Publication No. (SMA) 94-3017. Bethesda, MD: Department of Health and Human Services, 1994, p. 70. Primary source: NIDA and NIAA, 1991 NDATUS.

Tobacco

★ 460 ★

Cigarette Smoking Among High School Students

Data show the percentage of high school students of each race/ethnicity who report that they smoke frequently.

Race/ethnicity	Percent
White	15.4
Hispanic	6.8
Black	3.1

Source: Baumann, Marty. "USA Snapshots: Which students smoke most." *USA TODAY* (15 July 1992), p. 1D.

★ 461 ★

Tobacco

Cigarette Smoking, by Age, Sex, and Race/Ethnicity

Data show percentage of persons age 18 years and older who currently smoked cigarettes in 1990. Data are based on household surveys of the civilian noninstitutionalized U.S. population.

Age and sex	Percent of persons				
	All	Race		Ethnicity	
	persons[1]	White	Black	Hispanic	Non-Hispanic
Both sexes, age 18 and older	25.5	25.6	26.2	23.0	25.7
Male					
Total	28.4	28.0	32.5	30.9	28.2
18-29 years	28.6	29.1	26.7	28.5	28.6
30-44 years	33.6	33.0	38.8	35.9	33.4
45-64 years	29.3	28.7	36.7	30.2	29.3
65 years and older	14.6	13.7	21.5	19.4	14.4
Female					
Total	22.8	23.4	21.2	16.3	23.4
18-29 years	25.3	27.1	17.9	15.7	26.7
30-44 years	25.8	26.1	27.2	18.6	26.6
45-64 years	24.8	25.4	22.6	18.1	25.3
65 years and older	11.5	11.5	11.1	5.1[2]	11.7

Source: Piani, A., and C. Schoenborn. National Center for Health Statistics. *Health Promotion and Disease Prevention: United States, 1990. Vital and Health Statistics* 10(185), 1993, p. 46. *Notes:* Denominator for each cell excludes unknowns. 1. Includes persons with unknown sociodemographic characteristics. 2. Figure does not meet standard of reliability or precision (more than 30 percent relative standard error in numerator of percent).

★ 462 ★

Tobacco

Respiratory Ailments and Smoking Status

Data show number and percentage of currently employed persons age 18 years and older who had asthma or chronic bronchitis during the past year. Data are shown for persons in the United States in 1988.

Smoking status and respiratory conditions	All persons[1]	Race		Ethnicity	
		White	Black	Hispanic	Non-Hispanic
"Never" smokers					
All "never" smokers (number)	12,847	10,591	1,800	901	11,946
	Percent				
Asthma	2.4	2.4	2.5	1.4[2]	2.5
Chronic bronchitis	1.2	1.3	0.7[2]	1.1[2]	1.2
Asthma or chronic bronchitis	3.3	3.4	3.1	2.5	3.4

[Continued]

★ 462 ★

Respiratory Ailments and Smoking Status

[Continued]

Smoking status and respiratory conditions	All persons[1]	Race		Ethnicity	
		White	Black	Hispanic	Non-Hispanic
Former smokers					
All former smokers (number)	6,020	5,407	506	328	5,692
	Percent				
Asthma	2.8	2.9	3.3[2]	3.0[2]	2.8
Chronic bronchitis	1.8	1.9	1.3[2]	1.5[2]	1.9
Asthma or chronic bronchitis	4.2	4.3	3.2	4.4	4.1
Current smokers					
All current smokers (number)	8,343	7,004	1,152	435	7,908
	Percent				
Asthma	2.0	2.0	2.0	1.8[2]	2.0
Chronic bronchitis	2.8	3.0	1.7	2.2[2]	2.9
Asthma or chronic bronchitis	4.2	4.4	3.2	3.8	4.3

Source: Park, C.H. and others. National Center for Health Statistics. *Health Conditions Among the Currently Employed: United States, 1988. Vital Health Statistics* 10 (186), 1993, p. 34. *Notes:* Percentages are weighted national estimates. 1. Includes persons of races other than black and white. 2. Estimated figure—numerator has a relative standard error (RSE) of more than 30 percent.

★ 463 ★

Tobacco

Smoking Status of the Currently Employed

Data show number and percentage of currently employed persons age 18 years and older, by exposure to smoking. Data are shown for persons in the United States in 1988.

Smoking status and respiratory conditions	All persons[1]	Race		Ethnicity	
		White	Black	Hispanic	Non-Hispanic
	Number				
All categories	27,408	23,160	3,496	1,674	25,734
	Percent distribution				
Total	100.0	100.0	100.0	100.0	100.0
Smoking status					
Never smoked	47.2	46.0	53.4	54.3	46.7
Former smoker	22.3	23.6	14.7	19.6	22.5
Current occasional	0.4	0.4	0.5	0.9[2]	0.4
Other	0.2	0.2	0.2[2]	0.2[2]	0.2
Unknown	0.7	0.7	1.1	0.6[2]	0.7
Number of cigarettes per day					
Never smoked	49.3	48.2	54.6	56.7	48.8

[Continued]

★ 463 ★

Smoking Status of the Currently Employed

[Continued]

Smoking status and respiratory conditions	All persons[1]	Race		Ethnicity	
		White	Black	Hispanic	Non-Hispanic
1-10 cigarettes	13.7	12.5	22.5	21.3	13.2
11-20 cigarettes	20.9	21.7	15.6	13.5	21.4
21 cigarettes or more	14.1	15.6	5.0	6.0	14.7
Unknown	2.0	2.0	2.3	2.4	1.9
Smoking at work					
Smoking allowed					
Causes no discomfort	22.3	22.8	20.4	19.2	22.5
Causes discomfort	16.7	17.1	13.9	16.8	16.7
Smoking not allowed	55.4	54.4	60.6	59.2	55.1
Smoking practice at work unknown or works at home	5.6	5.7	5.1	4.8	5.6

Source: Park, C.H. and others. National Center for Health Statistics. *Health Conditions Among the Currently Employed: United States, 1988. Vital Health Statistics* 10 (186), 1993, p. 32. *Notes:* Percentages are weighted national estimates. 1. Includes persons of races other than black and white. 2. Estimated figure—numerator has a relative standard error (RSE) of more than 30 percent.

Chapter 6
SOCIAL AND ECONOMIC CONDITIONS

Credit and Loans

★ 464 ★

Denial of Conventional Mortgages, 1990

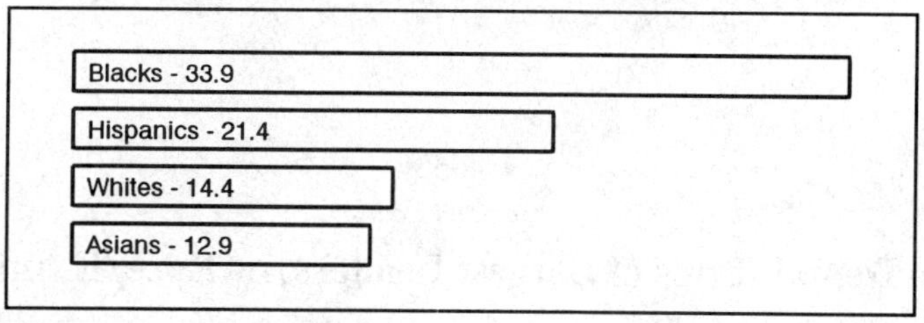

Race/ethnicity	Percent denied
Hispanics	21.4
Asians	12.9
Whites	14.4
Blacks	33.9

Source: "Percent of conventional mortgages denied, 1990," *Time,* Vol. 138, No. 18, November 4, 1991, p. 65. Primary source: The Federal Reserve Board.

★ 465 ★

Credit and Loans

Mortgage Approval and Denial Rates, by Race/Ethnicity and Income, 1991

Percentage of conventional home mortgage applications approved or denied is shown, by race/ethnicity of applicant.

Race/ethnicity	Lower income[1]		Upper income[1]	
	Percent approved	Percent denied	Percent approved	Percent denied
Hispanic	54.0	37.1	68.5	19.8
White	61.7	31.5	81.0	9.7
Black	44.9	48.2	66.0	23.2
American Indian	53.9	38.6	73.4	15.7
Asian	68.5	20.2	74.3	13.6
Joint[2]	59.2	33.2	76.8	12.6
Other	63.0	28.1	70.4	16.6

Source: "Weak economy may be hurting moves to fight mortgage bias, study finds." *Wall Street Journal* (28 October 1992), p. A10. Primary source: Federal Reserve Board *Notes:* 1. Lower income is defined as less than 80% and upper income greater than 120% of median family income for the metropolitan statistical area in which the property is located. 2. White/minority.

★ 466 ★

Credit and Loans

Mortgage Denial Rates of Largest Lenders, by Race/Ethnicity, 1991

Lenders are ranked by number of applications.

Lender	State	Total applications	White rejection rate	Minority to white rejection ratio			
				Hispanic	Black	Asian	Native American
Green Tree Acceptance	MN	144,519	68.71	1.05	1.16	1.06	1.09
Security Pacific Housing Svc.	CA	93,599	54.19	1.09	1.16	0.97	1.12
Norwest Mortgage	IA	65,210	5.23	2.18	2.68	1.22	1.73
American Residential Mortgage	CA	48,854	41.74	1.15	1.02	1.00	1.14
Home Savings of America	CA	36,392	18.69	1.30	1.94	0.99	0.96
Sears Mortgage	IL	35,844	3.03	1.98	2.94	0.96	1.65
Margaretten & Co.	NJ	32,182	5.33	1.16	3.14	1.15	4.79
Bank of America	CA	28,922	31.68	1.63	1.47	1.02	1.29
Great Western Bank	CA	26,951	16.36	1.12	1.55	0.98	1.04
Fleet National Bank	RI	22,368	11.07	1.73	2.48	1.39	1.45
GMAC Mortgage	PA	22,036	6.57	2.48	3.70	1.29	3.23
Imco Realty Services	CA	21,518	11.80	1.78	2.10	1.26	1.84
Oakwood Acceptance	NC	20,643	44.56	1.30	1.36	-	1.12
United Savings Association	TX	19,643	8.81	1.68	1.96	1.13	2.06
The Prudential Home Mortgage	MD	18,192	16.38	1.72	2.53	1.43	1.67
Directors Mortgage Loan	CA	17,372	12.37	1.40	2.23	1.21	2.05
CTX Mortgage	TX	16,671	7.32	1.92	3.15	1.40	1.18

[Continued]

★ 466 ★

Mortgage Denial Rates of Largest Lenders, by Race/Ethnicity, 1991

[Continued]

Lender	State	Total applications	White rejection rate	Minority to white rejection ratio			
				Hispanic	Black	Asian	Native American
World Savings and Loan	CA	16,360	16.24	1.29	1.96	0.72	1.12
Security Pacific Natl. Bank	CA	15,858	14.98	1.53	1.53	1.23	1.53
Washington Mutual Savings	WA	15,439	20.98	2.11	1.58	0.92	2.30

Source: "Persistent gap: blacks can face a host of trying conditions in getting mortgages." *Wall Street Journal* (30 November 1992), p. A5. *Note:* A dash (-) indicates fewer than 50 applications.

★ 467 ★

Credit and Loans

Mortgage Lending Distribution, by Race/Ethnicity: Amounts Approved

Each group's share of total mortgage money is shown in percent based on 1991 data reported to Federal Reserve.

Characteristic	Percent
White[1]	84.5
Asian	5.5
Hispanic	5.2
Black	4.2
Native American	0.6

Source: "Persistent gap: blacks can face a host of trying conditions in getting mortgages." *Wall Street Journal* (30 November 1992), p. A4. *Note:* 1. White includes a small number from "other" races.

★ 468 ★

Credit and Loans

Mortgage Lending Distribution, by Race/Ethnicity: Approved Applications

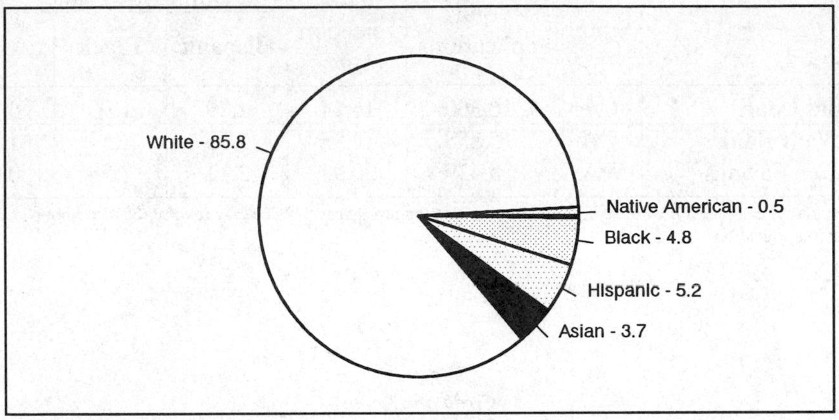

Each group's share of approved loans is shown based on 1991 data reported to Federal Reserve.

Characteristic	Percent
White[1]	85.8
Hispanic	5.2
Black	4.8
Asian	3.7
Native American	0.5

Source: "Persistent gap: blacks can face a host of trying conditions in getting mortgages." *Wall Street Journal* (30 November 1992), p. A4. *Note:* 1. White includes a small number from "other" races.

★ 469 ★

Credit and Loans

Mortgage Lending Distribution, by Race/Ethnicity: Mortgage Applications

Distribution is based on 1991 data reported to Federal Reserve.

Characteristic	Percent
White[1]	84.4
Black	5.9
Hispanic	5.6
Asian	3.5
Native American	0.6

Source: "Persistent gap: blacks can face a host of trying conditions in getting mortgages." *Wall Street Journal* (30 November 1992), p. A4. *Note:* 1. White includes a small number from "other" races.

★ 470 ★

Credit and Loans

Mortgage Lending Distribution, by Race/Ethnicity: U.S. Population

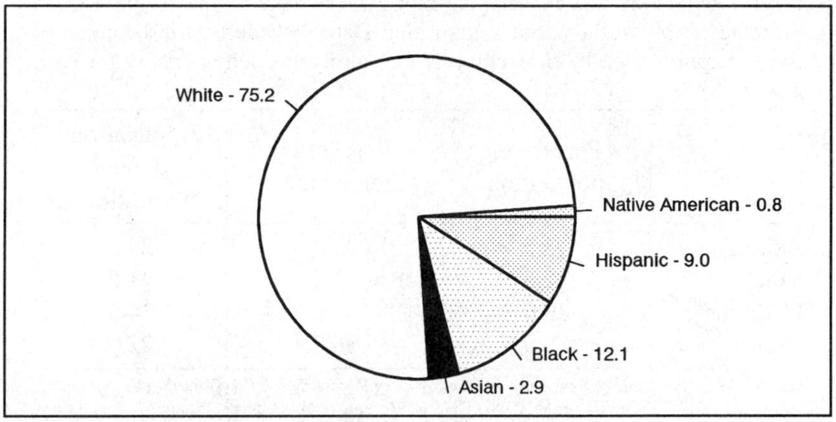

Shares based on 1990 Census data.

Characteristic	Percent
White[1]	75.2
Black	12.1
Hispanic	9.0
Asian	2.9
Native American	0.8

Source: "Persistent gap: blacks can face a host of trying conditions in getting mortgages." *Wall Street Journal* (30 November 1992), p. A4. *Note:* 1. White includes a small number from "other" races.

★ 471 ★

Credit and Loans

Mortgage Loan Denial Rates

In a combined effort to bolster the housing market and end racial bias, federal regulators are encouraging mortgage lenders to make home loans more accessible to the nation's minorities. Data show percent distribution of the U.S. population by race/ethnicity and mortgage characteristics for each group.

	Percent of population	Percent of home loans	Applications denied or withdrawn
Asian	3.0	3.0	24.0
Black	12.0	4.0	41.0
Hispanic[1]	10.0	4.0	34.0
White	83.0	86.0	22.0

Source: Willette, Anne. "New rules help more people qualify." *USA TODAY* (15 November 1994), p. 1B. Primary source: U.S. Census Bureau and Federal Financial Institutions Examination Council. *Note:* 1. Can be any race.

Employment

★ 472 ★

Academic Employment of Doctoral Scientists and Engineers Active in R&D, by Sex and Race/Ethnicity, 1977-91

Data show number of persons employed and active in research and devlopment (R&D) in each field, for each year.

	White	Asian	Black	Hispanic	Native American
Total science & engineering employment					
1979	127,249	4,604	1,263	1,453	243
1981	136,984	6,340	1,689	1,596	217
1989	162,105	9,768	2,579	2,453	365
1991	153,493	15,132	4,223	3,838	348
Total with responsibility for R&D					
1979	82,595	3,630	707	931	176
1981	87,526	4,977	717	1,049	156
1989	122,792	8,572	1,543	2,030	242
1991	114,882	13,105	2,770	3,038	248
Men					
1979	73,583	3,242	533	812	159
1981	76,633	4,342	472	913	141
1989	101,602	7,256	1,013	1,567	191

[Continued]

★ 472 ★

Academic Employment of Doctoral Scientists and Engineers Active in R&D, by Sex and Race/Ethnicity, 1977-91

[Continued]

	White	Asian	Black	Hispanic	Native American
1991	93,316	11,100	1,834	2,422	202
Women					
1979	9,012	388	174	119	[1]
1981	10,893	635	245	136	[1]
1989	21,190	1,316	530	463	51
1991	21,566	2,005	936	616	[1]

Source: National Science Board. *Science & Engineering Indicators—1993* (NSB 93-1). Washington, DC: U.S. Government Printing Office, 1993, pp. 409-411. Primary source: Science Resources Studies Division, National Science Foundation (NSF), *Characteristics of Doctoral Scientists and Engineers: 1991* (Washington, DC: NSF, forthcoming); and NSF, unpublished tabulations. *Notes:* Details cannot be aggregated to totals because of small sample sizes. Data reflect the composition of survey respondents whose field of employment, race/ethnicity, sex, and primary and secondary work responsibilities are known. Data are weighted estimates from sample surveys. Small numbers are subject to especially large variability and may not accurately reflect population patterns. 1. Too few cases in survey to estimate population values.

★ 473 ★

Employment

Academic Employment of Doctoral Scientists and Engineers, by Sex and Race/Ethnicity, 1977-91

Data show number of persons employed in each field, for each year.

	White	Asian	Black	Hispanic	Native American
Total science & engineering employment					
1979	127,249	4,604	1,263	1,453	243
1981	136,984	6,340	1,689	1,596	217
1989	162,105	9,768	2,579	2,453	365
1991	153,493	15,132	4,223	3,838	348
Men					
1979	111,819	4,036	912	1,273	225
1981	119,131	5,494	1,189	1,384	201
1989	132,728	8,217	1,665	1,844	298
1991	122,741	12,634	2,846	3,025	268
Women					
1979	15,430	568	351	180	[1]
1981	17,853	846	500	212	[1]

[Continued]

★ 473 ★

Academic Employment of Doctoral Scientists and Engineers, by Sex and Race/Ethnicity, 1977-91

[Continued]

	White	Asian	Black	Hispanic	Native American
1989	29,377	1,551	914	609	67
1991	30,752	2,498	1,377	813	80

Source: National Science Board. *Science & Engineering Indicators—1993* (NSB 93-1). Washington, DC: U.S. Government Printing Office, 1993, pp. 409-411. Primary source: Science Resources Studies Division, National Science Foundation (NSF), *Characteristics of Doctoral Scientists and Engineers: 1991* (Washington, DC: NSF, forthcoming); and NSF, unpublished tabulations. *Notes:* Details cannot be aggregated to totals because of small sample sizes. Data reflect the composition of survey respondents whose field of employment, race/ethnicity, sex, and primary and secondary work responsibilities are known. Data are weighted estimates from sample surveys. Small numbers are subject to especially large variability and may not accurately reflect population patterns. 1. Too few cases in survey to estimate population values.

★ 474 ★

Employment

Civilian Labor Force Participation of Hispanic Persons, 1992 and 1993

Data are shown for the civilian noninstitutional population, age 16 years old and older, as annual averages of monthly figures.

Item	1992					1993				
	Total	Mexican	Puerto Rican	Cuban	Other Hispanic origin[1]	Total	Mexican	Puerto Rican	Cuban	Other Hispanic origin[1]
Total (1,000)	15,244	9,368	1,628	867	3,381	15,753	9,693	1,676	927	3,457
Percent in labor force:										
Male	80.5	82.0	69.9	73.2	82.5	80.0	81.5	70.6	73.3	81.2
Female	52.6	52.1	47.1	50.3	57.4	52.0	51.9	45.3	47.9	56.7
Employed (1,000)	8,971	5,581	802	488	2,100	9,272	5,805	828	511	2,128
Percent by occupation	100.0	100.0	100.0	100.0	100.0	100.0	100.0	100.0	100.0	100.0
Managerial and professional	13.4	10.8	18.2	25.1	16.0	14.1	11.5	19.1	25.0	16.6
Tech., sales, and admin. support	24.8	23.2	31.8	32.5	24.8	24.9	23.3	32.1	32.9	24.3
Services	20.3	19.2	19.7	12.1	25.2	19.9	19.1	19.9	12.9	23.8
Precision production, craft, and repair	13.4	14.2	11.0	13.0	12.4	13.2	14.4	9.8	10.2	12.0
Operators, fabricators and laborers	22.2	24.4	18.1	15.4	19.6	22.2	23.7	17.9	17.0	20.9
Farming, forestry, and fishing	5.8	8.3	1.1	1.9	1.9	5.8	8.0	1.2	2.2	2.3
Percent of labor force unemployed:										
Male	11.5	11.7	15.6	7.1	10.5	10.4	10.2	14.4	7.8	10.1
Female	11.3	11.7	12.3	8.9	10.5	10.9	11.4	10.8	7.7	10.8

Source: 1994 Statistical Abstract of the United States on CD-ROM [machine-readable datafiles]. CD-8A-94. Washington, DC: U.S. Department of Commerce, Economics and Statistics Administration, Bureau of the Census, Data User Services Division, January 1995. Primary source: U.S. Bureau of Labor Statistics, Employment and Earnings, monthly, January issues. *Note:* 1. Includes Central or South American and other Hispanic origin.

★475★

Employment

Coaches and Assistant Coaches, by Race/Ethnicity

Data show percent distribution in each sports league, by race/ethnicity.

Position and race/ethnicity	NBA 1993-94	NFL 1993	Major league baseball 1994
Head coaches or on-field managers			
White	80.0	89.0	82.0
Black	20.0	7.0	14.0
Latino	0.0	4.0	4.0
Assistant coaches			
White	68.0	76.0	78.0
Black	32.0	23.0	14.0
Latino	0.0	1.0	8.0

Source: Brady, Erik. "Leagues have catching up to do off field." *USA TODAY* (3 August 1994), p. 7C. Primary source: Northeastern University Center for the Study of Sport in Society.

★476★

Employment

Editorial Staff on Leading Newspapers, 1991

Percentage rates are shown for the top 62 U.S. newspapers; there were 538 editorial-staff Hispanics in all, which accounted for 3.5% of the total editorial staff in 1991.

Type of newspaper personnel	Percent of top 62 newspapers
Newsroom managers	2.0
Copy editors	4.0
Reporters/writers	4.0
Photographers/artists	6.0

Source: Stein, M.L. "Concerned about diversity: Hispanic journalists say the slightest percentage increase in the number of Hispanic editorial staffers at newspapers is 'insignificant'." *Editor and Publisher - the Fourth Estate* (9 May 1992), p. 22. Primary source: "Hispanics in the News Media 1992: Still Struggling for Entry," a survey by the National Association of Hispanic Journalists.

★ 477 ★

Employment

Employed Civilians, by Occupation, Sex, Race, and Hispanic Origin, 1983 and 1993

Data are shown for the civilian noninstitutional population 16 years old and older, as an annual average of monthly figures. Figures are based on Current Population Survey. Persons of Hispanic origin may be of any race.

Occupation	1983				1993			
	Total employed (000)	Percent of total			Total employed (000)	Percent of total		
		Female	Black	Hispanic		Female	Black	Hispanic
Total	100,834	43.7	9.3	5.3	119,306	45.8	10.2	7.8
Managerial and professional specialty	23,592	40.9	5.6	2.6	32,280	47.8	6.6	4.0
Executive, administrative, and managerial[1]	10,772	32.4	4.7	2.8	15,376	42.0	6.2	4.5
Officials and administrators, public	417	38.5	8.3	3.8	581	45.2	11.3	4.5
Financial managers	357	38.6	3.5	3.1	529	46.2	4.4	4.2
Personnel and labor relations managers	106	43.9	4.9	2.6	96	60.7	7.9	4.6
Purchasing managers	82	23.6	5.1	1.4	109	34.9	8.0	5.3
Managers, marketing, advertising and public relations	396	21.8	2.7	1.7	496	31.2	3.1	3.5
Administrators, education and related fields	415	41.4	11.3	2.4	635	59.9	13.0	3.8
Managers, medicine and health	91	57.0	5.0	2.0	450	70.5	6.5	4.2
Managers, properties and real estate	305	42.8	5.5	5.2	481	45.7	6.6	6.3
Management-related occupations[1]	2,966	40.3	5.8	3.5	4,155	52.7	7.5	4.6
Accountants and auditors	1,105	38.7	5.5	3.3	1,387	49.2	7.0	4.2
Professional specialty[1]	12,820	48.1	6.4	2.5	16,904	53.2	7.0	3.6
Architects	103	12.7	1.6	1.5	123	18.6	3.1	2.3
Engineers[1]	1,572	5.8	2.7	2.2	1,716	8.6	3.7	3.6
Aerospace engineers	80	6.9	1.5	2.1	83	7.5	2.1	3.9
Chemical engineers	67	6.1	3.0	1.4	58	10.0	2.5	4.9
Civil engineers	211	4.0	1.9	3.2	221	9.4	4.7	3.8
Electrical and electronic	450	6.1	3.4	3.1	533	7.6	4.5	3.4
Industrial engineers	210	11.0	3.3	2.4	201	16.4	3.4	4.4
Mechanical	259	2.8	3.2	1.1	296	5.2	4.4	3.3
Mathematical and computer scientists[1]	463	29.6	5.4	2.6	1,051	32.4	6.0	2.5
Computer systems analysts, scientists	276	27.8	6.2	2.7	769	29.9	5.8	2.4
Operations and systems researchers and analysts	142	31.3	4.9	2.2	236	39.7	6.3	3.0
Natural scientists[1]	357	20.5	2.6	2.1	531	30.1	3.6	1.9
Chemists, except biochemists	98	23.3	4.3	1.2	133	28.8	4.3	3.0
Geologists and geodesists	65	18.0	1.1	2.6	54	14.0	1.0	2.1
Biological and life scientists	55	40.8	2.4	1.8	114	40.4	3.9	1.4
Medical scientists	[2]	[2]	[2]	[2]	82	45.5	5.8	2.5
Health diagnosing occupations[1]	735	13.3	2.7	3.3	909	20.5	3.0	3.9
Physicians	519	15.8	3.2	4.5	605	21.8	3.7	4.6
Dentists	126	6.7	2.4	1.0	152	10.5	1.9	3.0
Health assessment and treating occupations	1,900	85.8	7.1	2.2	2,602	86.4	8.3	3.5
Registered nurses	1,372	95.8	6.7	1.8	1,859	94.4	8.4	3.2
Pharmacists	158	26.7	3.8	2.6	187	38.1	6.1	2.7
Dietitians	71	90.8	21.0	3.7	94	92.8	17.5	6.0
Therapists[1]	247	76.3	7.6	2.7	416	74.9	6.9	4.1
Inhalation therapists	69	69.4	6.5	3.7	92	58.4	10.0	6.9
Physical therapists	55	77.0	9.7	1.5	115	72.5	3.0	5.0
Speech therapists	51	90.5	1.5	-	83	91.8	6.7	1.2
Physicians' assistants	51	36.3	7.7	4.4	[2]	[2]	[2]	[2]
Teachers, college and university	606	36.3	4.4	1.8	772	42.5	4.8	3.1
Teachers, except college and university[1]	3,365	70.9	9.1	2.7	4,397	75.1	8.6	3.6
Prekindergarten and kindergarten	299	98.2	11.8	3.4	501	97.7	11.7	5.0
Elementary school	1,350	83.3	11.1	3.1	1,668	85.9	9.3	3.9
Secondary school	1,209	51.8	7.2	2.3	1,237	57.5	6.9	3.1
Special education	81	82.2	10.2	2.3	286	84.0	10.1	2.3
Counselors, educational and vocational	184	53.1	13.9	3.2	224	67.6	14.3	6.9
Librarians, archivists, and curators	213	84.4	7.8	1.6	223	83.5	6.2	3.8
Librarians	193	87.3	7.9	1.8	195	88.3	7.0	3.5
Social scientists and urban planners[1]	261	46.8	7.1	2.1	399	57.0	5.9	3.0
Economists	98	37.9	6.3	2.7	117	47.6	4.8	3.5
Psychologists	135	57.1	8.6	1.1	241	64.1	7.1	3.1
Social, recreation, and religious workers[1]	831	43.1	12.1	3.8	1,096	50.5	15.6	5.0

[Continued]

★ 477 ★

Employed Civilians, by Occupation, Sex, Race, and Hispanic Origin, 1983 and 1993

[Continued]

Occupation	1983				1993			
	Total employed (000)	Percent of total			Total employed (000)	Percent of total		
		Female	Black	Hispanic		Female	Black	Hispanic
Social workers	407	64.3	18.2	6.3	586	68.9	21.4	6.0
Recreation workers	65	71.9	15.7	2.0	89	75.1	14.8	4.7
Clergy	293	5.6	4.9	1.4	350	11.4	8.7	3.1
Lawyers and judges	651	15.8	2.7	1.0	815	22.8	2.8	2.1
Lawyers	612	15.3	2.6	0.9	777	22.9	2.7	2.1
Writers, artists, entertainers, and athletes[1]	1,544	42.7	4.8	2.9	2,026	46.6	5.3	4.7
Authors	62	46.7	2.1	0.9	139	57.2	2.4	1.9
Technical writers	[2]	[2]	[2]	[2]	63	52.8	2.7	2.3
Designers	393	52.7	3.1	2.7	541	52.6	3.7	4.4
Musicians and composers	155	28.0	7.9	4.4	174	32.8	8.8	5.8
Actors and directors	60	30.8	6.6	3.4	96	38.3	10.4	4.7
Painters, sculptors, craft-artists, and artist printmakers	186	47.4	2.1	2.3	222	48.0	3.5	4.1
Photographers	113	20.7	4.0	3.4	135	26.2	6.5	7.1
Editors and reporters	204	48.4	2.9	2.1	266	48.5	5.0	3.4
Public relations specialists	157	50.1	6.2	1.9	155	59.6	7.0	3.5
Announcers	[2]	[2]	[2]	[2]	[2]	[2]	[2]	[2]
Athletes	58	17.6	9.4	1.7	80	23.9	10.1	3.9
Technical, sales, and administrative support	31,265	64.6	7.6	4.3	36,814	63.8	9.3	6.3
Technicians and related support	3,053	48.2	8.2	3.1	4,014	50.5	9.6	5.0
Health technologists and technicians[1]	1,111	84.3	12.7	3.1	1,522	81.0	12.4	5.8
Clinical laboratory technologists and technicians	255	76.2	10.5	2.9	315	76.1	12.1	6.1
Dental hygienists	66	98.6	1.6	-	76	99.3	0.4	2.0
Health record technologists and technicians	[2]	[2]	[2]	[2]	63	88.8	20.4	5.7
Radiologic technicians	101	71.7	8.6	4.5	146	70.2	8.3	7.0
Licensed practical nurses	443	97.0	17.7	3.1	425	94.6	17.2	3.4
Engineering and related technologists and technicians[1]	822	18.4	6.1	3.5	870	17.8	7.4	4.9
Electrical and electronic technicians	260	12.5	8.2	4.6	297	15.5	7.4	5.6
Drafting occupations	273	17.5	5.5	2.3	244	18.1	6.9	5.9
Surveying and mapping technicians	[2]	[2]	[2]	[2]	73	5.0	4.8	2.8
Science technicians[1]	202	29.1	6.6	2.8	261	37.5	7.2	5.2
Biological technicians	52	37.7	2.9	2.0	85	59.7	6.1	3.8
Chemical technicians	82	26.9	9.5	3.5	74	26.0	7.1	3.9
Technicians, except health, engineering, and science[1]	917	35.3	5.0	2.7	1,361	39.9	8.4	4.0
Airplane pilots and navigators	69	2.1	-	1.6	101	3.9	5.5	2.4
Computer programmers	443	32.5	4.4	2.1	578	31.5	6.7	3.5
Legal assistants	128	74.0	4.3	3.6	254	79.6	8.6	4.9
Sales occupations	11,818	47.5	4.7	3.7	14,245	48.1	6.7	5.9
Supervisors and proprietors	2,958	28.4	3.6	3.4	4,016	36.4	4.4	5.3
Sales representatives, finance and business services[1]	1,853	37.2	2.7	2.2	2,317	40.5	4.7	3.7
Insurance sales	551	25.1	3.8	2.5	583	33.3	5.1	3.8
Real estate sales	570	48.9	1.3	1.5	710	51.4	2.5	4.1
Securities and financial services sales	212	23.6	3.1	1.1	355	28.1	4.1	2.2
Advertising and related sales	124	47.9	4.5	3.3	161	50.8	4.5	3.1
Sales representatives, commodities, except retail	1,442	15.1	2.1	2.2	1,538	21.0	2.9	3.9
Sales workers, retail and personal services	5,511	69.7	6.7	4.8	6,281	64.9	9.7	7.5
Cashiers	2,009	84.4	10.1	5.4	2,581	78.4	13.2	8.7
Sales-related occupations	54	58.7	2.8	1.3	93	60.5	5.3	6.1
Administrative support, including clerical	16,395	79.9	9.6	5.0	18,555	78.8	11.2	6.8
Supervisors	676	53.4	9.3	5.0	778	58.4	11.9	6.8
Computer equipment operators	605	63.9	12.5	6.0	603	61.9	13.8	6.2
Computer operators	597	63.7	12.1	6.0	597	61.9	13.7	6.1
Secretaries, stenographers, and typists[1]	4,861	98.2	7.3	4.5	4,174	96.2	8.9	5.9
Secretaries	3,891	99.0	5.8	4.0	3,586	98.9	7.7	5.8
Typists	906	95.6	13.8	6.4	494	94.3	18.8	7.4
Information clerks	1,174	88.9	8.5	5.5	1,678	88.8	9.3	7.9
Receptionists	602	96.8	7.5	6.6	899	97.2	8.6	7.6

[Continued]

★ 477 ★

Employed Civilians, by Occupation, Sex, Race, and Hispanic Origin, 1983 and 1993

[Continued]

Occupation	1983 Total employed (000)	1983 Percent of total: Female	1983 Black	1983 Hispanic	1993 Total employed (000)	1993 Percent of total: Female	1993 Black	1993 Hispanic
Records processing occupations, except financial[1]	866	82.4	13.9	4.8	908	79.1	14.9	6.6
Order clerks	188	78.1	10.6	4.4	212	78.1	17.1	6.5
Personnel clerks, except payroll and time keeping	64	91.1	14.9	4.6	63	89.2	15.2	3.9
Library clerks	147	81.9	15.4	2.5	146	75.9	11.6	3.4
File clerks	287	83.5	16.7	6.1	288	79.6	15.0	10.4
Records clerks	157	82.8	11.6	5.6	184	77.9	14.3	4.8
Financial records processing[1]	2,457	89.4	4.6	3.7	2,272	89.9	5.4	5.3
Bookkeepers, accounting, and auditing clerks	1,970	91.0	4.3	3.3	1,806	90.9	4.5	4.9
Payroll and time keeping clerks	192	82.2	5.9	5.0	173	88.3	6.6	5.2
Billing clerks	146	88.4	6.2	3.9	160	88.5	8.4	6.6
Cost and rate clerks	96	75.6	5.9	5.3	60	72.9	10.9	9.7
Billing, posting, and calculating machine operators	[2]	[2]	[2]	[2]	72	86.1	12.0	8.2
Duplicating, mail and other office machine operators	68	62.6	16.0	6.1	63	47.8	19.2	9.2
Communications equipment operators	256	89.1	17.0	4.4	208	86.1	20.9	8.0
Telephone operators	244	90.4	17.0	4.3	197	86.9	21.0	7.9
Mail and message distributing occupations	799	31.6	18.1	4.5	953	37.6	19.0	7.4
Postal clerks, except mail carriers	248	36.7	26.2	5.2	297	44.8	26.8	6.8
Mail carrier, postal service	259	17.1	12.5	2.7	333	28.4	12.6	7.0
Mail clerks, except postal service	170	50.0	15.8	5.9	166	51.5	22.5	8.8
Messengers	122	26.2	16.7	5.2	157	29.1	14.2	7.9
Material recording, scheduling, and distributing [3]	1,562	37.5	10.9	6.6	1,852	44.0	14.0	8.3
Dispatchers	157	45.7	11.4	4.3	221	52.7	11.8	5.7
Production coordinators	182	44.0	6.1	2.2	196	50.2	7.8	4.7
Traffic, shipping, and receiving clerks	421	22.6	9.1	11.1	570	30.9	15.1	11.9
Stock and inventory clerks	532	38.7	13.3	5.5	489	43.4	14.5	6.8
Weighers, measurers, and checkers	79	47.2	16.9	5.8	67	45.6	15.9	10.4
Expediters	112	57.5	8.4	4.3	227	67.0	13.9	7.1
Adjusters and investigators	675	69.9	11.1	5.1	1,372	74.0	12.2	6.1
Insurance adjusters, examiners, and investigators	199	65.0	11.5	3.3	372	71.5	12.1	4.0
Investigators and adjusters, except insurance	301	70.1	11.3	4.8	748	76.2	11.2	6.3
Eligibility clerks, social welfare	69	88.7	12.9	9.4	86	84.7	16.2	6.0
Bill and account collectors	106	66.4	8.5	6.5	166	64.3	14.8	9.5
Miscellaneous administrative support[1]	2,397	85.2	12.5	5.9	3,694	82.3	12.4	7.8
General office clerks	648	80.6	12.7	5.2	731	82.0	11.4	9.6
Bank tellers	480	91.0	7.5	4.3	446	88.4	6.9	6.2
Data entry keyers	311	93.6	18.6	5.6	623	82.4	16.4	8.3
Statistical clerks	96	75.7	7.5	3.4	50	78.4	15.4	3.3
Teachers' aides	348	93.7	17.8	12.6	508	92.2	15.7	12.3
Service occupations	13,857	60.1	16.6	6.8	16,522	59.5	17.3	11.2
Private household[1]	980	96.1	27.8	8.5	912	95.1	17.1	21.6
Child care workers	408	96.9	7.9	3.6	345	97.2	9.0	15.0
Cleaners and servants	512	95.8	42.4	11.8	534	94.0	21.6	25.7
Protective service	1,672	12.8	13.6	4.6	2,152	17.2	17.4	6.6
Supervisors, protective service	127	4.7	7.7	3.1	185	7.8	12.2	4.8
Supervisors, police and detectives	58	4.2	9.3	1.2	96	10.3	6.6	6.1
Firefighting and fire prevention	189	1.0	6.7	4.1	208	3.7	7.6	4.5
Firefighting occupations	170	1.0	7.3	3.8	188	3.3	7.5	5.0
Police and detectives	645	9.4	13.1	4.0	923	16.0	18.0	5.4
Police and detectives, public service	412	5.7	9.5	4.4	511	12.0	14.5	5.9
Sheriffs, bailiffs, and other law enforcement officers	87	13.2	11.5	4.0	117	19.5	13.4	4.6
Correctional institution officers	146	17.8	24.0	2.8	295	21.6	25.8	5.0
Guards	711	20.6	17.0	5.6	836	23.9	20.4	8.8
Guards and police, except public service	602	13.0	18.9	6.2	711	17.2	22.6	9.5
Service except private household and protective	11,205	64.0	16.0	6.9	13,457	63.9	17.3	11.2
Food preparation and service occupations[1]	4,860	63.3	10.5	6.8	5,691	58.4	12.8	11.7
Bartenders	338	48.4	2.7	4.4	321	53.3	3.8	3.1
Waiters and waitresses	1,357	87.8	4.1	3.6	1,414	80.0	4.6	7.5

[Continued]

★ 477 ★

Employed Civilians, by Occupation, Sex, Race, and Hispanic Origin, 1983 and 1993

[Continued]

Occupation	1983				1993			
	Total employed (000)	Percent of total			Total employed (000)	Percent of total		
		Female	Black	Hispanic		Female	Black	Hispanic
Cooks	1,452	50.0	15.8	6.5	1,992	44.2	19.0	13.9
Food counter, fountain, and related occupations	326	76.0	9.1	6.7	367	69.2	12.6	8.1
Kitchen workers, food preparation	138	77.0	13.7	8.1	260	75.3	15.0	10.8
Waiters' and waitresses' assistants	364	38.8	12.6	14.2	368	43.7	11.4	18.1
Health service occupations	1,739	89.2	23.5	4.8	2,213	87.4	27.3	7.7
Dental assistants	154	98.1	6.1	5.7	181	97.8	3.4	10.4
Health aides, except nursing	316	86.8	16.5	4.8	312	78.9	22.2	4.7
Nursing aides, orderlies, and attendants	1,269	88.7	27.3	4.7	1,719	87.9	30.7	7.9
Cleaning and building service occupations[1]	2,736	38.8	24.4	9.2	2,959	42.2	22.4	16.2
Maids and housemen	531	81.2	32.3	10.1	661	81.7	27.3	18.6
Janitors and cleaners	2,031	28.6	22.6	8.9	2,086	30.7	21.5	16.1
Personal service occupations[1]	1,870	79.2	11.1	6.0	2,594	80.7	12.9	7.6
Barbers	92	12.9	8.4	12.1	86	22.3	27.5	8.5
Hairdressers and cosmetologists	622	88.7	7.0	5.7	758	90.1	9.4	6.3
Attendants, amusement and recreation facilities	131	40.2	7.1	4.3	161	39.4	7.4	5.8
Public transportation attendants	63	74.3	11.3	5.9	104	80.4	8.8	7.4
Welfare service aides	77	92.5	24.2	10.5	73	82.1	21.2	16.6
Family child care providers	NA	NA	NA	NA	302	99.0	9.4	10.2
Early childhood teachers' assistants	NA	NA	NA	NA	418	96.6	15.7	6.4
Precision production, craft, and repair	12,328	8.1	6.8	6.2	13,326	8.6	7.4	9.2
Mechanics and repairers	4,158	3.0	6.8	5.3	4,416	3.5	7.3	7.9
Mechanics and repairers, except supervisors[1]	3,906	2.8	7.0	5.5	4,196	3.3	7.3	8.1
Vehicle and mobile equipment mechanics/repairers[1]	1,683	0.8	6.9	6.0	1,800	1.0	6.1	9.9
Automobile mechanics	800	0.5	7.8	6.0	854	0.6	6.4	10.8
Aircraft engine mechanics	95	2.5	4.0	7.6	139	4.1	5.1	11.5
Electrical and electronic equipment repairers[1]	674	7.4	7.3	4.5	655	9.5	9.0	5.8
Data processing equipment repairers	98	9.3	6.1	4.5	152	10.7	10.2	5.0
Telephone installers and repairers	247	9.9	7.8	3.7	188	12.5	9.9	3.4
Construction trades	4,289	1.8	6.6	6.0	5,004	1.9	6.5	9.5
Construction trades, except supervisors	3,784	1.9	7.1	6.1	4,269	1.9	7.0	10.2
Carpenters	1,160	1.4	5.0	5.0	1,276	0.9	4.5	7.7
Extractive occupations	196	2.3	3.3	6.0	148	1.8	4.6	7.9
Precision production occupations	3,685	21.5	7.3	7.4	3,758	23.6	8.8	10.5
Operators, fabricators, and laborers	16,091	26.6	14.0	8.3	17,038	24.5	14.9	12.1
Machine operators, assemblers, and inspectors[1]	7,744	42.1	14.0	9.4	7,415	38.7	14.7	13.8
Textile, apparel, and furnishings machine operators[1]	1,414	82.1	18.7	12.5	1,159	74.4	20.8	19.9
Textile sewing machine operators	806	94.0	15.5	14.5	616	85.8	18.5	24.1
Pressing machine operators	141	66.4	27.1	14.2	147	62.7	24.0	20.4
Fabricators, assemblers, and hand working occupations	1,715	33.7	11.3	8.7	1,882	32.7	12.7	12.0
Production inspectors, testers, samplers, and weighers	794	53.8	13.0	7.7	777	52.4	15.0	13.7
Transportation and material moving occupations	4,201	7.8	13.0	5.9	5,004	9.3	14.0	8.6
Motor vehicle operators	2,978	9.2	13.5	6.0	3,825	10.8	14.2	8.9
Trucks, heavy and light	2,195	3.1	12.3	5.7	2,786	4.5	12.3	8.8
Transportation occupations, except motor vehicles	212	2.4	6.7	3.0	170	4.1	10.2	3.1
Material moving equipment operators	1,011	4.8	12.9	6.3	1,009	4.5	13.9	8.5
Industrial truck and tractor operators	369	5.6	19.6	8.2	432	7.3	20.9	12.0
Handlers, equipment cleaners, helpers, and laborers[1]	4,147	16.8	15.1	8.6	4,619	18.3	16.1	12.9
Freight, stock, and material handlers	1,488	15.4	15.3	7.1	1,850	20.7	16.7	9.9
Laborers, except construction	1,024	19.4	16.0	8.6	1,127	17.0	16.7	13.7
Farming, forestry, and fishing	3,700	16.0	7.5	8.2	3,326	15.4	6.3	16.0
Farm operators and managers	1,450	12.1	1.3	0.7	1,170	14.3	0.9	2.4
Other agricultural and related occupations	2,072	19.9	11.7	14.0	1,963	17.0	9.5	24.8
Farm workers	1,149	24.8	11.6	15.9	801	20.0	7.0	28.5

[Continued]

★ 477 ★

Employed Civilians, by Occupation, Sex, Race, and Hispanic Origin, 1983 and 1993

[Continued]

Occupation	1983 Total employed (000)	1983 Percent of total: Female	1983 Percent of total: Black	1983 Percent of total: Hispanic	1993 Total employed (000)	1993 Percent of total: Female	1993 Percent of total: Black	1993 Percent of total: Hispanic
Forestry and logging occupations	126	1.4	12.8	2.1	132	5.9	10.4	11.8
Fishers, hunters, and trappers	53	4.5	1.8	2.5	61	4.4	1.7	4.8

Source: 1994 Statistical Abstract of the United States on CD-ROM [machine-readable datafiles]. CD-8A-94. Washington, DC: U.S. Department of Commerce, Economics and Statistics Administration, Bureau of the Census, Data User Services Division, January 1995. Primary source: U.S. Bureau of Labor Statistics, Employment and Earnings, monthly, January issues. *Notes:* A dash (-) represents or rounds to zero. NA stands for not available. 1. Includes other occupations, not shown separately. 2. Level of total employment below 50,000. 3. Includes clerks.

★ 478 ★

Employment

Employment Distribution and Labor Force Status, by Hispanic Ethnicity, Selected Occupation, and Sex, 1991

Numbers are shown in thousands, except where noted.

Characteristic	Total population	Non-Hispanic population	Hispanic origin population	Mexican origin	Puerto Rican origin	Cuban origin	Central and South American origin	Other Hispanic origin
Labor force status[1]								
Total, 16 years and over	190,216	175,528	14,688	8,900	1,580	900	2,089	1,218
In civilian labor force	124,074	114,569	9,505	5,839	835	577	1,468	786
Percent in civilian labor force	65.2	65.3	64.7	65.6	52.8	64.1	70.3	64.5
Percent unemployed	7.2	6.9	10.0	10.7	10.3	6.4	10.3	6.9
Males, 16 years and over	91,159	83,849	7,310	4,601	694	446	994	575
In civilian labor force	67,701	61,986	5,715	3,663	461	327	837	427
Percent in civilian labor force	74.3	73.9	78.2	79.6	66.4	73.3	84.2	74.3
Percent unemployed	8.1	7.8	10.6	11.7	11.9	5.2	9.9	5.4
Females, 16 years and over	99,057	91,679	7,378	4,299	887	454	1,096	643
In civilian labor force	56,373	52,283	3,791	2,176	374	250	631	359
Percent in civilian labor force	56.9	57.4	51.4	50.6	42.2	55.1	57.6	55.8
Percent unemployed	6.1	5.9	9.2	9.2	8.3	8.0	10.8	8.4
Occupation[1]								
Employed males, 16 years and over	62,246	57,137	5,109	3,236	406	310	753	404
Percent	100.0	100.0	100.0	100.0	100.0	100.0	100.0	100.0
Managerial and professional specialty	26.3	27.6	11.4	8.9	11.8	21.6	12.7	20.5
Technical, sales, and administrative support	20.5	21.0	15.1	13.0	21.2	21.9	17.0	16.3
Service occupations	10.4	9.8	17.1	15.0	21.2	11.9	26.0	17.1
Farming, forestry, and fishing	4.1	3.7	8.6	12.2	2.2	1.0	3.1	2.2
Precision production, craft, and repair	18.8	18.8	18.7	18.8	17.2	22.6	18.1	18.1
Operators, fabricators, and laborers	19.9	19.1	29.1	32.1	26.4	20.6	23.1	25.7
Employed females, 16 years and over	52,941	49,500	3,441	1,976	343	230	564	329
Percent	100.0	100.0	100.0	100.0	100.0	100.0	100.0	100.0
Managerial and professional specialty	27.2	28.0	15.8	14.1	21.6	20.0	14.5	19.8
Technical, sales and administrative support	44.1	44.3	39.8	38.9	47.2	50.0	32.3	42.9
Service occupations	17.6	17.0	26.2	26.9	16.0	16.5	34.9	24.0
Farming, forestry, and fishing	0.9	0.9	1.2	2.0	0.3	-	0.2	0.3

[Continued]

★ 478 ★

Employment Distribution and Labor Force Status, by Hispanic Ethnicity, Selected Occupation, and Sex, 1991

[Continued]

Characteristic	Total population	Non-Hispanic population	Hispanic origin population	Mexican origin	Puerto Rican origin	Cuban origin	Central and South American origin	Other Hispanic origin
Precision production, craft and repair	2.2	2.1	3.0	3.2	2.3	2.6	2.7	2.7
Operators, fabricators, and laborers	8.1	7.6	14.0	14.9	12.2	11.7	15.2	10.3

Source: U.S. Bureau of the Census, *The Hispanic Population in the United States: March 1991.* Current Population Reports, Series P-20, No. 455, Washington, DC: U.S. Government Printing Office, 1991, pp. 12-15. *Notes:* A dash (-) represents or rounds to zero. 1. Data on labor force status and occupation groups shown in this report reflect characteristics of the population for March 1991 and are not adjusted for seasonal change. Data released by the Department of Labor, Bureau of Labor Statistics, may not agree entirely with data shown in this report due to differences in methodological procedures and seasonal adjustment of the data.

★ 479 ★

Employment

Employment Distribution of Hispanics, by Selected Occupation and Geographic Region, 1993 - I

Average annual employment distribution of selected occupations is shown, for persons of Hispanic origin in each geographic region, in 1993.

Occupation	Northeast			Midwest		
	Total	New England	Middle Atlantic	Total	East North Central	West North Central
Total (in thousands)	1,256	162	1,095	708	596	112
Percent	100.0	100.0	100.0	100.0	100.0	100.0
Managerial and professional speciality	15.4	13.8	15.7	11.5	10.8	15.2
Technical, sales, and administrative support	26.0	24.6	26.2	21.8	21.7	22.4
Sales occupations	7.6	5.3	8.0	7.0	6.5	9.6
Administrative support, including clerical	15.7	15.9	15.7	12.9	13.4	10.5
Service occupations	23.4	18.4	24.1	19.5	19.0	22.3
Precision production, craft and repair	10.0	12.0	9.7	14.4	14.2	15.3
Operators, fabricators, and laborers	23.3	29.7	22.4	30.4	32.0	21.8
Farming, forestry, and fishing	1.9	1.5	2.0	2.4	2.3	3.0

Source: U.S. Bureau of Labor Statistics. U.S. Department of Labor. *Geographic Profile of Employment and Unemployment, 1993* (Bulletin 2446). Washington, DC: U.S. Government Printing Office, September 1994, p. 18. *Notes:* Items may not add to totals or compute to displayed percentages because of rounding. 1. Data are not shown when the labor force does not meet BLS publication standards of reliability for the particular area, based on the sample in that area.

★ 480 ★

Employment

Employment Distribution of Hispanics, by Selected Occupation and Geographic Region, 1993 - II

Annual average employment distribution of selected occupations is shown for persons of Hispanic origin in each geographic region in 1993.

Occupation	South				West		
	Total	South Atlantic	East South Central	West South Central	Total	Moun- tain	Pacific
Total (in thousands)	3,161	1,164	-[1]	1,977	4,244	791	3,453
Percent	100.0	100.0	-[1]	100.0	100.0	100.0	100.0
Managerial and professional speciality	17.0	20.0	-[1]	15.1	12.0	15.3	11.2
Technical, sales, and administrative support	26.3	25.7	-[1]	26.8	24.0	28.0	23.1
Sales occupations	10.2	10.5	-[1]	10.0	8.9	10.2	8.6
Administrative support, including clerical	13.7	12.8	-[1]	14.3	13.2	14.9	12.9
Service occupations	18.7	18.9	-[1]	18.6	19.9	19.2	20.1
Precision production, craft and repair	14.2	11.2	-[1]	15.9	13.3	13.9	13.1
Operators, fabricators, and laborers	19.0	17.1	-[1]	20.2	22.7	17.9	23.8
Farming, forestry, and fishing	4.7	7.1	-[1]	3.3	8.2	5.6	8.8

Source: U.S. Bureau of Labor Statistics. U.S. Department of Labor. *Geographic Profile of Employment and Unemployment, 1993* (Bulletin 2446). Washington, DC: U.S. Government Printing Office, September 1994, p. 19. *Notes:* Items may not add to totals or compute to displayed percentages because of rounding. 1. Data are not shown when the labor force base does not meet Bureau of Labor Statistics publication standards of reliability for the particular area, based on the sample in that area.

★ 481 ★

Employment

Employment Distribution of Hispanics, by Selected Occupation, for MSAs in 1993

The percent distribution of Hispanics employed in selected occupations is shown, by Metropolitan Statistical Area (MSA). Data shown are annual averages for 1993.

Geographical Area	Total employed[1]	Private nonagricultural wage and salary workers									Government
		Total[2]	Construction	Manufacturing			Transportation, communications, and public utilities	Trade	Finance, insurance, and real estate	Services[3]	
				Total	Durable goods	Nondurable goods					
Metropolitan areas[4]											
Anaheim-Santa Ana PMSA	100.0	84.7	4.6	28.5	20.7	7.8	1.9	22.6	4.5	22.7	7.2
Bergen-Passaic PMSA	100.0	86.5	2.1	28.5	13.9	14.6	3.8	27.5	3.8	20.7	10.4
Boston PMSA	100.0	86.5	1.2	14.3	5.9	8.4	5.9	20.3	8.3	36.5	10.5
Chicago PMSA	100.0	91.6	3.3	37.2	23.6	13.5	3.9	20.4	5.5	21.2	6.4
Dallas-Fort Worth CMSA	100.0	87.6	13.4	19.3	13.3	5.9	7.5	25.5	4.0	17.6	6.6
Denver-Boulder CMSA	100.0	69.3	7.6	6.5	5.1	1.3	8.8	17.2	6.0	23.2	26.5
Detroit PMSA	100.0	85.7	2.9	34.4	29.0	5.4	7.8	20.5	4.7	15.4	14.1
Houston PMSA	100.0	83.1	14.5	16.9	9.8	7.1	6.4	19.6	5.4	19.3	8.2
Los Angeles-Long Beach PMSA	100.0	85.5	5.4	27.7	13.1	14.7	4.7	22.9	4.3	20.4	9.1
Miami-Hialeah PMSA	100.0	85.5	6.6	13.4	4.7	8.7	9.1	23.5	7.4	25.4	7.6
Nassau-Suffolk PMSA	100.0	82.1	6.2	22.6	14.9	7.7	8.1	14.4	10.5	20.3	13.1
New York PMSA	100.0	79.7	2.5	16.4	6.0	10.6	5.1	18.7	9.4	27.7	15.0
Newark PMSA	100.0	85.0	1.6	31.8	9.9	22.0	9.9	19.1	4.6	17.9	9.7

[Continued]

★ 481 ★

Employment Distribution of Hispanics, by Selected Occupation, for MSAs in 1993

[Continued]

Geographical Area	Total employed[1]	Private nonagricultural wage and salary workers: Total[2]	Construction	Manufacturing: Total	Manufacturing: Durable goods	Manufacturing: Nondurable goods	Transportation, communications, and public utilities	Trade	Finance, insurance, and real estate	Services[3]	Government
Oakland PMSA	100.0	87.1	11.6	16.0	3.7	12.3	8.7	26.3	6.8	17.7	11.1
Philadelphia PMSA	100.0	79.7	3.1	20.9	7.4	13.5	2.1	22.1	5.4	26.2	13.0
Phoenix	100.0	82.3	11.7	22.9	17.7	5.2	3.9	19.0	6.8	18.0	11.8
Portland, Ore. PMSA	100.0	88.3	2.0	19.6	13.6	5.9	1.5	32.2	4.3	28.7	6.3
Providence-Pawtucket-Fall River CMSA	100.0	94.2	.5	61.6	43.8	17.7	1.2	9.4	2.5	19.0	1.1
Riverside-San Bernardino PMSA	100.0	80.3	8.2	21.3	16.6	4.8	10.2	20.3	3.7	16.5	12.1
Salt Lake City-Ogden	100.0	78.7	3.2	21.7	8.0	13.7	6.3	13.6	10.3	18.1	18.6
San Antonio	100.0	75.0	8.0	12.0	6.5	5.5	5.8	22.6	3.2	22.9	18.2
San Diego	100.0	79.5	9.5	16.1	8.6	7.5	3.7	27.9	3.8	18.5	14.8
San Francisco PMSA	100.0	80.4	7.3	12.9	3.2	9.7	5.6	26.1	8.4	20.2	10.0
San Jose PMSA	100.0	82.7	6.4	17.9	14.5	3.4	4.6	17.6	5.8	30.3	14.0
Tampa-St. Petersburg-Clearwater	100.0	78.2	3.9	17.2	7.6	9.7	6.5	26.0	1.6	23.0	14.6
Washington D.C.	100.0	81.0	6.9	1.4	.4	1.0	2.8	25.3	7.5	37.2	8.6
Cities											
Chicago	100.0	90.2	2.5	36.2	22.7	13.4	3.8	18.4	5.6	23.6	7.7
Dallas	100.0	88.7	14.6	17.1	9.1	8.0	2.8	28.5	3.5	21.6	6.1
District of Columbia	100.0	83.8	4.4	5.0	.8	4.2	1.8	29.8	8.4	34.4	14.2
Houston	100.0	84.3	15.1	15.2	9.6	5.6	7.7	18.7	4.1	23.5	6.1
Los Angeles	100.0	87.4	5.1	30.3	11.6	18.7	4.4	22.6	4.0	21.0	7.6
New York	100.0	78.8	2.0	16.2	5.5	10.6	5.5	18.6	9.4	27.1	15.5
Phoenix	100.0	84.3	13.5	19.9	17.0	2.9	5.8	18.6	8.4	18.1	9.1
San Antonio	100.0	75.7	8.5	10.7	5.4	5.3	5.8	22.6	3.7	24.3	17.0
San Diego	100.0	79.4	9.1	10.7	3.4	7.4	7.7	23.4	4.9	23.6	14.7
San Francisco	100.0	86.1	11.4	9.6	1.4	8.2	4.2	30.2	7.4	23.2	7.1

Source: U.S. Bureau of Labor Statistics. U.S. Department of Labor. *Geographic Profile of Employment and Unemployment, 1993* (Bulletin 2446). Washington, DC: U.S. Government Printing Office, September 1994, pp. 123-124. *Notes:* Data for demographic groups are not shown when they do not meet BLS publication standards of reliability for the particular area based on the sample in that area. Items may not add to totals or compute to displayed percentages because of rounding. 1. Includes self-employed and unpaid family workers and mining. 2. Includes mining. 3. Excludes private household workers. 4. All are Metropolitan Statistical Areas (MSAs) except those labeled Consolidated Metropolitan Statistical Areas (CMSAs) or Primary Metropolitan Statistical Areas (PMSAs).

★ 482 ★

Employment

Employment Distribution, by Labor Force Status in U.S. Southwest Border Counties, 1980

State/county	Male, 16 years and over	Percent: In labor force	Percent: In civilian labor force	Percent: Unemployed in civilian force labor force	Females, 16 years and over	Percent: In labor force	Percent: In civilian labor force	Percent: Unemployed in civilian labor force
California								
San Diego	92,189	82.0	71.4	9.3	89,142	49.0	48.6	9.1
Imperial	15,229	74.9	74.6	13.9	16,755	44.9	44.9	11.5
Arizona								
Cochise	6,926	73.1	67.4	14.3	7,739	41.9	41.5	12.1
Pima	34,799	77.5	76.0	9.4	37,497	46.1	46.0	8.7
Santa Cruz	4,323	81.2	80.4	5.1	5,447	44.2	44.2	6.3
Yuma	8,740	82.5	78.7	10.0	8,861	44.3	44.1	17.5
New Mexico								
Dona Ana	15,685	73.0	72.0	9.3	17,019	42.0	41.9	11.2
Hidalgo	830	75.3	75.3	15.4	911	32.3	32.3	3.7
Luna	1,772	72.1	72.1	14.1	2,055	32.8	32.8	18.2

[Continued]

★ 482 ★

Employment Distribution, by Labor Force Status in U.S. Southwest Border Counties, 1980

[Continued]

State/county	Male, 16 years and over	Percent			Females, 16 years and over	Percent		
		In labor force	In civilian labor force	Unemployed in civilian force labor force		In labor force	In civilian labor force	Unemployed in civilian labor force
Texas								
El Paso	86,557	75.4	72.8	9.8	103,145	44.4	44.3	8.6
Hudspeth	490	76.3	76.3	1.1	468	23.1	23.1	8.3
Culberson	613	82.5	82.5	9.3	641	40.6	40.6	3.1
Jeff Davis	267	66.3	66.3	5.6	282	31.2	31.2	1.1
Presidio	1,194	63.6	63.6	5.7	1,424	30.8	30.8	4.8
Brewster	1,084	69.9	69.9	5.4	1,173	50.7	50.7	9.4
Terrell	237	76.4	76.4	2.2	240	35.4	35.4	3.5
Valverde	6,499	72.6	68.2	12.9	7,351	37.4	36.8	10.0
Kinney	426	68.3	68.3	6.9	440	33.0	33.0	13.8
Maverick	7,938	70.9	70.9	15.8	9,312	40.3	40.3	12.9
Dimmett	2,691	66.1	66.1	6.5	2,906	39.0	39.0	11.3
Webb	26,621	72.1	71.9	8.0	31,661	39.7	39.7	6.3
Zapata	1,592	73.0	73.0	10.8	1,681	31.2	31.2	12.4
Starr	7,795	65.0	64.9	13.0	8,793	37.1	37.1	12.6
Hildalgo	64,740	74.3	74.1	9.5	76,054	45.6	45.6	10.2
Cameron	45,311	73.8	73.5	9.5	54,259	44.0	44.0	8.9

Source: U.S. Bureau of the Census, *The Hispanic Population of the Southwest Borderland.* Current Population Reports, Series P-23, No. 172, Washington, DC: U.S. Government Printing Office, 1991, pp. 29-31.

★ 483 ★

Employment

Employment Distribution, by Occupation, and Labor Force Status in U.S. Southwest Border States and Counties, 1980

Characteristic	United States	Total, border states	Border states			
			Border county areas		Non-border county areas	
			Hispanic	Non-Hispanic	Hispanic	Non-Hispanic
Labor force status						
Males, 16 years and over	81,732,090	15,341,158	434,548	1,023,786	2,280,180	11,602,644
In labor force	61,416,203	11,793,536	330,473	766,527	1,829,957	8,866,579
Percent of males 16 and over	75.1	76.9	76.0	74.9	80.3	76.4
In civilian labor force	59,926,488	11,378,554	316,405	629,981	1,806,014	8,626,254
Percent unemployed	6.5	5.6	9.8	6.3	7.8	4.9
Females, 16 years and over	89,482,168	16,206,485	485,256	1,012,148	2,254,826	12,454,255
In labor force	44,668,465	8,356,257	216,328	495,248	1,142,594	6,502,087
Percent of females 16 and over	49.9	51.6	44.6	48.9	50.7	52.2
In civilian labor force	44,523,329	8,316,003	215,728	487,400	1,140,117	6,472,758
Percent unemployed	6.5	5.9	9.4	6.3	9.0	5.1

[Continued]

★ 483 ★

Employment Distribution, by Occupation, and Labor Force Status in U.S. Southwest Border States and Counties, 1980

[Continued]

Characteristic	United States	Total, border states	Border states			
			Border county areas		Non-border county areas	
			Hispanic	Non-Hispanic	Hispanic	Non-Hispanic
Occupation						
Employed persons, 16 years and over	97,639,355	18,573,758	480,810	1,046,957	2,702,779	14,343,212
Percent	100.0	100.0	100.0	100.0	100.0	100.0
Managers and professionals	22.7	23.9	13.2	29.0	10.5	26.4
Technical sales and support	30.3	32.0	26.4	33.5	23.0	33.8
Service occupations	12.9	12.4	15.9	13.0	16.2	11.6
Farming, forestry, fishing	2.9	2.8	7.5	2.1	5.9	2.2
Precision, production, craft and repair	12.9	13.4	14.1	12.4	15.6	13.1
Operators, fabricators, and laborers	18.3	15.3	22.9	10.1	28.7	12.9

Source: U.S. Bureau of the Census, *The Hispanic Population of the Southwest Borderland*. Current Population Reports, Series P-23, No. 172, Washington, DC: U.S. Government Printing Office, 1991, p. 21. *Notes:* For the purposes of this report, the U.S. Census Bureau included the following counties: San Diego, and Imperial counties, in California; Cochise, Pima, Santa Cruz, and Yuma counties, in Arizona; Dona Ana, Hidalgo, and Luna counties, in New Mexico; El Paso, Hudspeth, Culberson, Jeff Davis, Presidio, Terrell, Valverde, Kinney, Maverick, Dimmit, Webb, Zapata, Starr, Hidalgo, and Cameron counties, in Texas.

★ 484 ★

Employment

Employment Distribution, by Occupation, in U.S. Southwest Border Counties, 1980

State/ county	Total employed 16 years and over	Percent					
		Managers and professionals	Technical sales and support	Service occupations	Farm, forest and and fishing	Precision, production craft and repair	Operators, fabricators and laborers
California							
San Diego	99,102	12.9	23.3	19.1	10.0	14.7	20.1
Imperial	16,440	10.0	26.2	15.6	20.7	9.1	18.5
Arizona							
Cochise	6,818	11.0	26.6	19.0	5.7	16.8	20.9
Pima	39,705	14.1	26.1	16.2	2.2	19.8	21.6
Santa Cruz	5,555	16.6	33.1	13.2	4.3	11.5	21.3
Yuma	9,420	9.0	18.6	12.6	28.6	10.7	20.5
New Mexico							
Dona Ana	16,585	12.5	24.9	16.6	9.4	14.1	22.5
Hidalgo	812	10.5	20.2	21.7	6.5	14.0	27.1
Luna	1,648	11.6	27.0	17.5	9.1	13.9	20.9
Texas							
El Paso	98,625	13.1	28.6	14.8	1.4	14.7	27.4
Hudspeth	469	3.8	11.1	14.5	38.4	12.8	19.4

[Continued]

★ 484 ★

Employment Distribution, by Occupation, in U.S. Southwest Border Counties, 1980

[Continued]

State/ county	Total employed 16 years and over	Percent: Managers and professionals	Technical sales and support	Service occupations	Farm, forest and and fishing	Precision, production craft and repair	Operators, fabricators and laborers
Culberson	711	4.6	17.7	31.2	9.8	14.6	21.9
Jeff Davis	254	5.1	15.7	31.5	18.5	9.8	19.3
Presidio	1,134	11.4	25.1	18.6	13.8	11.9	19.2
Brewster	1,256	5.7	24.2	29.5	5.3	13.4	22.0
Terrell	259	3.5	20.5	23.9	4.2	12.4	35.5
Valverde	6,295	13.7	24.9	16.2	5.1	16.7	23.5
Kinney	396	8.1	18.7	14.4	28.5	12.1	18.2
Maverick	8,007	15.4	26.8	12.2	7.1	11.5	27.0
Dimmett	2,668	9.2	22.0	17.8	9.0	16.0	25.9
Webb	29,404	18.7	34.7	13.1	2.3	12.5	18.6
Zapata	1,493	12.7	19.2	17.8	11.6	17.4	21.3
Starr	7,248	15.2	22.5	15.1	18.1	11.3	17.7
Hildalgo	74,609	13.2	25.8	13.9	11.4	12.2	23.4
Cameron	51,897	12.2	27.8	16.1	5.5	13.9	24.4

Source: U.S. Bureau of the Census, *The Hispanic Population of the Southwest Borderland*. Current Population Reports, Series P-23, No. 172, Washington, DC: U.S. Government Printing Office, 1991, pp. 29-31.

★ 485 ★

Employment

Employment Participation Rates and Projections

Data are shown for the civilian noninstitutional population, age 16 years and older, as annual averages of monthly figures. Rates are based on annual average civilian noninstitutional population of each specified group and represent proportion of each specified group in the civilian labor force. Figures are based on Current Population Surveys.

Race/ethnicity and sex	Civilian labor force (mil.)						Participation rate (percent)					
	1990	1991	1992	1993	2000, proj.	2005, proj.	1990	1991	1992	1993	2000, proj.	2005, proj.
Total[1]	124.8	125.3	127.0	128.0	141.8	150.5	66.4	66.0	66.3	66.2	68.2	68.8
White	107.2	107.5	108.5	109.4	118.8	124.8	66.8	66.6	66.7	66.7	68.7	69.3
Male	59.3	59.3	59.8	60.2	63.8	66.0	76.9	76.4	76.4	76.1	76.0	75.3
Female	47.9	48.2	48.7	49.2	55.1	58.8	57.5	57.4	57.8	58.0	61.8	63.6
Black	13.5	13.5	13.9	13.9	16.0	17.4	63.3	62.6	63.3	62.4	65.5	66.2
Male	6.7	6.8	6.9	6.9	7.8	8.3	70.1	69.5	69.7	68.6	70.8	70.5
Female	6.8	6.8	7.0	7.0	8.2	9.0	57.8	57.0	58.0	57.4	61.2	62.6
Hispanic[2]	9.6	9.8	10.1	10.4	14.3	16.6	67.0	66.1	66.5	65.9	68.0	68.4
Male	5.8	5.9	6.1	6.3	8.7	9.6	81.2	80.1	80.5	80.0	80.2	79.5
Female	3.8	3.9	4.0	4.1	5.8	7.0	53.0	52.3	52.6	52.0	55.8	57.3

Source: 1994 Statistical Abstract of the United States on CD-ROM [machine-readable datafiles]. CD-8A-94. Washington, DC: U.S. Department of Commerce, Economics and Statistics Administration, Bureau of the Census, Data User Services Division, January 1995. Primary source: U.S. Bureau of Labor Statistics, Bulletin 2307; Employment and Earnings, monthly, January issues; Monthly Labor Review, November 1993; and unpublished data. *Notes:* 1. Includes other races not shown separately. 2. Persons of Hispanic origin may be of any race.

★ 486 ★

Employment

Employment Status of the Civilian Noninstitutional Population, 1990-93

Data are shown in thousands, except as indicated, as annual averages of monthly figures for the civilian noninstitutional population age 16 years and older. Figures are based on Current Population Surveys.

Race, ethnicity, and year	Civilian non-institutional population	Civilian labor force						Not in labor force	
		Total	Percent of population	Employed	Employment/ population ratio[1]	Unemployed		Number	Percent of population
						Number	Percent of labor force		
Total[2]									
1990	188,049	124,787	66.4	117,914	62.7	6,874	5.5	63,262	33.6
1991	189,765	125,303	66.0	116,877	61.6	8,426	6.7	64,462	34.0
1992	191,576	126,982	66.3	117,598	61.4	9,384	7.4	64,593	33.7
1993	193,550	128,040	66.2	119,306	61.6	8,734	6.8	65,509	33.8
White:									
1990	160,415	107,177	66.8	102,087	63.6	5,091	4.7	53,237	33.2
1991	161,511	107,486	66.6	101,039	62.6	6,447	6.0	54,025	33.4
1992	162,658	108,526	66.7	101,479	62.4	7,047	6.5	54,132	33.3
1993	163,921	109,359	66.7	102,812	62.7	6,547	6.0	54,562	33.3
Black:									
1990	21,300	13,493	63.3	11,966	56.2	1,527	11.3	7,808	36.7
1991	21,615	13,542	62.6	11,863	54.9	1,679	12.4	8,074	37.4
1992	21,958	13,891	63.3	11,933	54.3	1,958	14.1	8,067	36.7
1993	22,329	13,943	62.4	12,146	54.4	1,796	12.9	8,386	37.6
Hispanic:[3]									
1990	14,297	9,576	67.0	8,808	61.6	769	8.0	4,721	33.0
1991	14,770	9,762	66.1	8,799	59.6	963	9.9	5,008	33.9
1992	15,244	10,131	66.5	8,971	58.9	1,160	11.4	5,113	33.5
1993	15,753	10,377	65.9	9,272	58.9	1,104	10.6	5,377	34.1
Mexican:									
1990	8,742	5,970	68.3	5,478	62.7	492	8.2	2,773	31.7
1991	8,947	5,984	66.9	5,363	59.9	621	10.4	2,963	33.1
1992	9,368	6,319	67.5	5,581	59.6	739	11.7	3,049	32.5
1993	9,693	6,499	67.0	5,805	59.9	693	10.7	3,194	33.0
Puerto Rican:									
1990	1,546	859	55.6	780	50.5	79	9.1	687	44.4
1991	1,629	930	57.1	822	50.5	108	11.6	699	42.9
1992	1,628	934	57.4	802	49.2	132	14.1	694	42.6
1993	1,676	950	56.7	828	49.4	122	12.8	725	43.3
Cuban:									
1990	847	552	65.1	512	60.4	40	7.2	295	34.8
1991	849	543	63.9	499	58.8	44	8.1	306	36.0
1992	867	529	61.1	488	56.3	42	7.9	337	38.9
1993	927	554	59.8	511	55.1	43	7.8	373	40.2

Source: 1994 Statistical Abstract of the United States on CD-ROM [machine-readable datafiles]. CD-8A-94. Washington, DC: U.S. Department of Commerce, Economics and Statistics Administration, Bureau of the Census, Data User Services Division, January 1995. Primary source: U.S. Bureau of Labor Statistics, Bulletin 2307; and Employment and Earnings, monthly, January issues. *Notes:* 1. Civilian employed as a percent of the civilian noninstitutional population. 2. Includes other races, not shown separately. 3. Persons of Hispanic origin may be of any race. Includes persons of other Hispanic origin, not shown separately.

★ 487 ★

Employment

Employment Status, 1992-93

Data show employment status of the population, by race/ethnicity, in thousands of persons. Figures are annual averages.

Employment status	Annual average	
	1992	1993
Total		
Civilian noninstitutional population[1]	191,576	193,550
Civilian labor force	126,982	128,040
Participation rate	66.3	66.2
Employed	117,598	119,306
Employment-population ratio[2]	61.4	61.6
Unemployed	9,384	8,734
Unemployment rate	7.4	6.8
Not in labor force	64,593	65,509
White		
Civilian noninstitutional population[1]	162,658	163,921
Civilian labor force	108,526	109,359
Participation rate	66.7	66.7
Employed	101,479	102,812
Employment-population ratio[2]	62.4	62.7
Unemployed	7,047	6,547
Unemployment rate	6.5	6.0
Black		
Civilian noninstitutional population[1]	21,958	22,329
Civilian labor force	13,891	13,943
Participation rate	63.3	62.4
Employed	11,933	12,146
Employment-population ratio[2]	54.3	54.4
Unemployed	1,958	1,796
Unemployment rate	14.1	12.9
Hispanic origin		
Civilian noninstitutional population[1]	15,244	15,753
Civilian labor force	10,131	10,377
Participation rate	66.5	65.9
Employed	8,971	9,272
Employment-population ratio[2]	58.9	58.9
Unemployed	1,160	1,104
Unemployment rate	11.4	10.6

Source: U.S. Bureau of Labor Statistics. *Monthly Labor Review* (January 1995), pp. 80-81. *Notes:* 1. The population figures are not seasonally adjusted. 2. Civilian employment as a percent of the civilian noninstitutional population.

★ 488 ★

Employment

Employment Status, by Sex, Race/Ethnicity, and Age

Data are shown for the civilian noninstitutional population age 16 years and older, as annual averages of monthly figures. Figures are based on Current Population Surveys.

Age and race/ethnicity	Total (000)	Male (000)			Female (000)			Percent of labor force			
								Employed		Unemployed	
		Total	Employed	Unemployed	Total	Employed	Unemployed	Male	Female	Male	Female
All workers[1]	128,040	69,633	64,700	4,932	58,407	54,606	3,801	92.9	93.5	7.1	6.5
16 to 19 years	6,826	3,564	2,836	728	3,261	2,694	568	79.6	82.6	20.4	17.4
20 to 24 years	13,558	7,164	6,356	808	6,393	5,780	613	88.7	90.4	11.3	9.6
25 to 34 years	34,465	19,053	17,734	1,319	15,412	14,373	1,038	93.1	93.3	6.9	6.7
35 to 44 years	34,264	18,537	17,508	1,029	15,727	14,894	833	94.4	94.7	5.6	5.3
45 to 54 years	23,542	12,634	11,997	638	10,907	10,415	492	95.0	95.5	5.0	4.5
55 to 64 years	11,867	6,639	6,294	345	5,228	5,017	211	94.8	96.0	5.2	4.0
65 years and over	3,520	2,041	1,976	65	1,479	1,433	46	96.8	96.9	3.2	3.1
White	109,359	60,150	56,397	3,753	49,208	46,415	2,793	93.8	94.3	6.2	5.7
16 to 19 years	5,831	3,035	2,500	535	2,795	2,387	408	82.4	85.4	17.6	14.6
20 to 24 years	11,360	6,021	5,448	573	5,339	4,921	418	90.5	92.2	9.5	7.8
25 to 34 years	28,996	16,217	15,211	1,006	12,779	12,045	734	93.8	94.3	6.2	5.7
35 to 44 years	29,190	16,043	15,248	795	13,148	12,529	619	95.0	95.3	5.0	4.7
45 to 54 years	20,407	11,099	10,584	516	9,308	8,907	400	95.4	95.7	4.6	4.3
55 to 64 years	10,385	5,861	5,588	274	4,524	4,349	175	95.3	96.1	4.7	3.9
65 years and over	3,189	1,873	1,818	55	1,316	1,277	39	97.1	97.0	2.9	3.0
Black	13,943	6,911	5,957	954	7,031	6,189	842	86.2	88.0	13.8	12.0
16 to 19 years	776	413	247	166	363	227	136	59.8	62.5	40.2	37.5
20 to 24 years	1,689	854	658	196	835	661	174	77.0	79.2	23.0	20.8
25 to 34 years	4,168	2,115	1,854	261	2,053	1,789	264	87.7	87.1	12.3	12.9
35 to 44 years	3,738	1,788	1,600	188	1,950	1,783	167	89.5	91.4	10.5	8.6
45 to 54 years	2,213	1,050	964	85	1,163	1,096	67	91.9	94.2	8.1	5.8
55 to 64 years	1,102	566	515	51	536	508	28	91.0	94.8	9.0	5.2
65 years and over	257	126	119	7	131	126	5	94.4	96.2	5.6	3.8
Hispanic[2]	10,377	6,256	5,603	653	4,120	3,669	451	89.6	89.1	10.4	10.9
16 to 19 years	660	385	285	101	274	202	72	73.8	73.7	26.2	26.3
20 to 24 years	1,456	895	782	113	561	482	79	87.4	85.9	12.6	14.1
25 to 34 years	3,365	2,119	1,930	189	1,246	1,123	123	91.1	90.1	8.9	9.9
35 to 44 years	2,671	1,562	1,424	138	1,109	1,003	106	91.2	90.4	8.8	9.6
45 to 54 years	1,442	842	768	74	600	550	50	91.2	91.7	8.8	8.3
55 to 64 years	646	369	338	31	277	257	20	91.6	92.8	8.4	7.2
65 years and over	137	84	76	8	53	52	1	90.5	98.1	9.5	1.9

Source: 1994 Statistical Abstract of the United States on CD-ROM [machine-readable datafiles]. CD-8A-94. Washington, DC: U.S. Department of Commerce, Economics and Statistics Administration, Bureau of the Census, Data User Services Division, January 1995. Primary source: U.S. Bureau of Labor Statistics, Employment and Earnings, monthly, January issues. *Notes:* 1. Includes other races not shown separately. 2. Persons of Hispanic origin may be of any race.

★ 489 ★

Employment

Employment of Union Members, by Race/Ethnicity, 1983-93

Data shown are annual averages of monthly data and cover employed wage and salary workers age 16 years and older. Figures exclude self-employed workers whose businesses are incorporated although they technically qualify as wage and salary workers.

Race/ethnicity	Employed salary and wage workers											
	Total (000)				Percent union members[1]				Percent represented by unions[2]			
	1983	1991	1992	1993	1983	1991	1992	1993	1983	1991	1992	1993
Total	88,290	102,786	103,688	105,067	20.1	16.1	15.8	15.8	23.3	18.2	17.9	17.7
White	77,046	87,981	88,624	89,643	19.3	15.4	15.1	15.2	22.3	17.4	17.1	17.0
Men	42,168	46,586	46,732	47,186	24.0	18.8	18.2	18.0	26.9	20.6	20.0	19.7
Women	34,877	41,395	41,892	42,458	13.5	11.7	11.7	12.1	16.7	13.8	13.8	14.1
Black	8,979	11,318	11,416	11,612	27.2	21.4	21.3	21.0	31.7	24.4	24.2	23.9
Men	4,477	5,502	5,480	5,588	31.7	24.6	23.9	23.2	36.1	27.7	26.4	25.8
Women	4,502	5,816	5,936	6,024	22.7	18.4	19.0	18.9	27.4	21.2	22.1	22.0
Hispanic[3]	NA	8,193	8,341	8,575	NA	15.6	14.9	15.1	NA	17.7	17.0	16.6
Men	NA	4,860	4,954	5,085	NA	16.9	16.8	16.3	NA	18.6	18.7	17.5
Women	NA	3,333	3,386	3,490	NA	13.5	12.1	13.3	NA	16.2	14.5	15.4

Source: 1994 Statistical Abstract of the United States on CD-ROM [machine-readable datafiles]. CD-8A-94. Washington, DC: U.S. Department of Commerce, Economics and Statistics Administration, Bureau of the Census, Data User Services Division, January 1995. Primary source: U.S. Bureau of Labor Statistics, Employment and Earnings, January issues. *Notes:* NA stands for not available. 1. Members of a labor union or an employee association similar to a labor union. 2. Members of a labor union or an employee association similar to a union as well as workers who report no union affiliation but whose jobs are covered by a union or an employee association contract. 3. Persons of Hispanic origin may be of any race.

★ 490 ★

Employment

Employment, by Geographic Region and Hours Worked, 1993

Data show the number of persons working in each region and distribution of employed persons by hours worked. Numbers are shown in thousands.

Population group and area	Total at work	Hours of work								Average hours	
		1 to 14 hours	15 to 29 hours	30 to 34 hours	35 hours and over					Total	Full-time sched-ules[1]
					Total	35 to 39 hours	40 hours	41 to 48 hours	49 hours and over		
TOTAL											
Northeast	22,457	1,068	2,939	1,639	16,811	2,107	8,565	2,117	4,022	38.6	46.4
New England	6,212	319	843	533	4,517	492	2,191	627	1,207	38.6	47.2
Middle Atlantic	16,245	749	2,096	1,105	12,294	1,615	6,373	1,491	2,815	38.6	46.1
Midwest	28,002	1,504	3,431	2,085	20,982	1,622	9,957	3,230	6,173	39.7	47.7
East North Central	19,356	982	2,354	1,395	14,625	1,130	7,144	2,238	4,114	39.6	47.3
West North Central	8,646	522	1,077	690	6,357	492	2,814	992	2,059	39.9	48.8
South	39,308	1,604	4,465	2,922	30,318	2,390	15,770	4,035	8,123	40.0	47.2
South Atlantic	20,501	814	2,306	1,561	15,821	1,283	8,364	2,041	4,132	39.9	47.1
East South Central	6,668	271	775	495	5,127	434	2,677	697	1,319	39.8	47.0
West South Central	12,139	519	1,384	866	9,370	674	4,728	1,296	2,672	40.3	47.5
West	24,256	1,172	3,105	2,086	17,892	1,294	9,535	2,295	4,768	39.0	47.2

[Continued]

★ 490 ★

Employment, by Geographic Region and Hours Worked, 1993

[Continued]

Population group and area	Total at work	Hours of work								Average hours	
		1 to 14 hours	15 to 29 hours	30 to 34 hours	35 hours and over					Total	Full-time sched-ules[1]
					Total	35 to 39 hours	40 hours	41 to 48 hours	49 hours and over		
Mountain	6,588	340	857	565	4,826	359	2,363	687	1,416	39.4	48.1
Pacific	17,688	832	2,249	1,521	13,066	935	7,172	1,608	3,352	38.9	46.9
White											
Northeast	2,013	49	225	125	1,614	300	995	113	206	38.2	43.8
New England	249	7	31	23	189	19	122	18	31	38.2	45.4
Middle Atlantic	1,763	42	195	102	1,425	281	873	96	175	38.2	43.6
Midwest	2,063	78	253	167	1,565	138	1,025	162	241	38.1	44.9
East North Central	1,732	64	210	135	1,322	119	866	138	200	38.1	44.9
West North Central	331	14	43	32	242	19	159	24	41	37.8	45.3
South	6,633	247	797	546	5,044	479	3,276	480	808	38.3	45.2
South Atlantic	4,067	143	462	333	3,129	292	2,053	290	494	38.5	45.2
East South Central	1,131	47	144	102	838	86	542	80	129	37.7	45.3
West South Central	1,435	56	191	110	1,077	101	681	110	186	38.2	45.2
West	927	39	113	77	698	45	476	60	116	38.0	45.5
Mountain	156	5	18	12	121	9	80	11	21	38.6	44.9
Pacific	771	34	95	65	577	36	397	49	95	37.8	45.6
Black											
Northeast	2,013	49	225	125	1,614	300	995	113	206	38.2	43.8
New England	249	7	31	23	189	19	122	18	31	38.2	45.4
Middle Atlantic	1,763	42	195	102	1,425	281	873	96	175	38.2	43.6
Midwest	2,063	78	253	167	1,565	138	1,025	162	241	38.1	44.9
East North Central	1,732	64	210	135	1,322	119	866	138	200	38.1	44.9
West North Central	331	14	43	32	242	19	159	24	41	37.8	45.3
South	6,633	247	797	546	5,044	479	3,276	480	808	38.3	45.2
South Atlantic	4,067	143	462	333	3,129	292	2,053	290	494	38.5	45.2
East South Central	1,131	47	144	102	838	86	542	80	129	37.7	45.3
West South Central	1,435	56	191	110	1,077	101	681	110	186	38.2	45.2
West	927	39	113	77	698	45	476	60	116	38.0	45.5
Mountain	156	5	18	12	121	9	80	11	21	38.6	44.9
Pacific	771	34	95	65	577	36	397	49	95	37.8	45.6
Hispanic origin											
Northeast	1,201	29	129	73	971	152	570	99	151	38.8	44.1
New England	153	4	18	13	119	13	77	14	15	38.1	44.6
Middle Atlantic	1,048	25	111	60	853	139	493	85	136	38.9	44.1
Midwest	676	18	65	44	549	36	359	69	85	39.3	44.4
East North Central	568	14	51	35	468	28	316	57	67	39.4	44.2
West North Central	108	4	15	8	81	9	44	11	17	38.8	45.4
South	3,024	99	352	254	2,319	198	1,391	264	466	39.1	45.7
South Atlantic	1,115	32	130	84	869	62	568	68	171	39.1	45.1

[Continued]

★ 490 ★

Employment, by Geographic Region and Hours Worked, 1993

[Continued]

Population group and area	Total at work	Hours of work								Average hours	
		1 to 14 hours	15 to 29 hours	30 to 34 hours	35 hours and over					Total	Full-time sched-ules[1]
					Total	35 to 39 hours	40 hours	41 to 48 hours	49 hours and over		
West South Central	1,889	67	220	170	1,432	136	816	194	286	39.0	46.0
West	4,043	154	559	356	2,973	234	1,957	326	457	37.5	44.7
Mountain	755	29	97	70	560	50	343	62	104	38.3	45.7
Pacific	3,287	125	462	286	2,414	184	1,614	264	352	37.4	44.4

Source: U.S. Bureau of Labor Statistics, U.S. Department of Labor. *Geographic Profile of Employment and Unemployment, 1993* (Bulletin 2446). Washington, DC: U.S. Government Printing Office, September 1994, pp. 25-26. *Notes:* Data for demographic groups are not shown when they do not meet BLS publication standards of reliability for the particular area based on the sample in that area. Items may not add to totals or compute to displayed percentages because of rounding. Detail for race and Hispanic origin groups will not add to totals because data for the "other races" group are not presented and Hispanics are included in both the white and black population groups. 1. Refers to persons who worked 35 hours or more during the survey week.

★ 491 ★

Employment

Expected Growth in the Labor Force of Selected Groups, 1990 - 2005

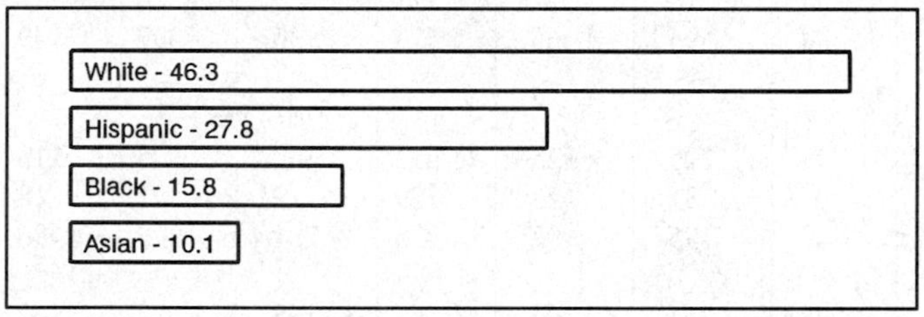

From 1990 to 2005 the labor force is expected to grow by 26 million people.

Race/ethnicity	Percentage of growth
White	46.3
Hispanic	27.8
Black	15.8
Asian	10.1

Source: Greenhouse, Steven. "The coming crisis of the American work force." *The New York Times* (7 June 1992), p. F14. Primary source: Bureau of Labor Statistics.

★ 492 ★

Employment

Farmworkers and Annual Earnings, 1991-92

Data represent average number of persons age 15 years and older in the civilian noninstitutional population who were employed at hired farmwork at any time during the year. Figures are based on Current Population Surveys.

Race/ethnicity	Workers (000)			Median weekly earnings (dol.)[1]		
	1990	1991	1992	1990	1991	1992
All workers	886	884	848	200	210	200
White[2]	540	533	506	201	222	225
Black and other races[2]	85	101	82	175	170	190
Hispanic	260	250	260	213	220	200

Source: 1994 Statistical Abstract of the United States on CD-ROM [machine-readable datafiles]. CD-8A-94. Washington, DC: U.S. Department of Commerce, Economics and Statistics Administration, Bureau of the Census, Data User Services Division, January 1995. Primary source: U.S. Dept. of Agriculture, Economic Research Service, unpublished data. *Notes:* 1. The weekly earnings the farmworker usually earns at his farmwork job before deductions and including any overtime pay or commissions. 2. Excludes persons of Hispanic origin.

★ 493 ★

Employment

Foodservice Employment of Blacks and Hispanics, 1992

Data show blacks and Hispanics as percentage of total foodservice employment in 1992, for each occupation.

	Black	Hispanic[1]
All employed persons (16 and older)	10.1	7.6
Buspersons	14.3	19.0
Cooks	18.5	14.7
Foodservice occupations	13.0	12.2
Kitchen workers	15.9	11.4
Fast food, counter	12.3	8.5
Waiters and waitresses	4.7	7.6
Foodservice supervisors	13.3	6.5
Bartenders	2.7	4.8
Misc. food preparation	17.2	18.9

Source: "The changing face of foodservice: grappling with diversity in the workplace." *Nation's Restaurant News* (20 September 1993), p. 146. Primary source: Bureau of Labor Statistics. *Note:* 1. Persons of Hispanic origin may be of any race.

★ 494 ★

Employment

Full-Time Work of Employed Wage and Salary Workers, 1992 and 1993

Data show number of employees who usually work full-time in each profession, by race/ethnicity.

Occupation	Employment (000)					Proportion of total employment (Percent)		
	Total	White	Black	Hispanic origin	Other	Black	Hispanic origin	Other
					1983			
Total, all occupations	70,976	61,739	7,373	4,127	1,864	10.4	5.8	2.6
Managerial and professional specialty occupations	17,451	15,843	1,100	472	508	6.3	2.7	2.9
Executive, administrative, and managerial	8,117	7,513	424	230	180	5.2	2.8	2.2
Professional specialty occupations	9,334	8,331	676	242	327	7.2	2.6	3.5
Engineers	1,487	1,369	38	33	80	2.6	2.2	5.4
Mathematical and computer scientists	421	380	22	11	19	5.2	2.6	4.5
Natural scientists	318	287	10	6	21	3.1	1.9	6.6
Health-diagnosing occupations	254	215	8	13	31	3.1	5.1	12.2
Health assessment and treating	1,340	1,143	117	31	80	8.7	2.3	6.0
Teachers, college and university	414	382	16	5	16	3.9	1.2	3.9
Teachers, except college and university	2,673	2,378	263	77	32	9.8	2.9	1.2
Lawyers and judges	321	306	9	5	6	2.8	1.6	1.9
Other professional specialties	2,106	1,871	192	60	43	9.1	2.8	2.0
Engineering and science technicians	945	848	65	32	32	6.9	3.4	3.4
All other occupations	52,580	45,048	6,208	3,623	1,324	11.8	6.9	2.5
					1992			
Total, all occupations	84,143	71,630	9,537	6,986	2,976	11.3	8.3	3.5
Managerial and professional specialty occupations	23,247	20,617	1,708	952	922	7.3	4.1	4.0
Executive, administrative, and managerial	11,288	10,205	746	495	337	6.6	4.4	3.0
Professional specialty occupations	11,959	10,467	962	456	530	8.0	3.8	4.4
Engineers	1,594	1,407	64	49	123	4.0	3.1	7.7
Mathematical and computer scientists	861	736	61	28	64	7.1	3.3	7.4
Natural scientists	402	362	11	12	29	2.7	3.0	7.2
Health-diagnosing occupations	341	284	16	19	41	4.7	5.6	12.0
Health assessment and treating	1,791	1,497	189	63	105	10.6	3.5	5.9
Teachers, college and university	495	440	24	13	31	4.8	2.6	6.3
Teachers, except college and university	3,418	3,038	325	123	55	9.5	3.6	1.6
Lawyers and judges	412	384	21	12	7	5.1	2.9	1.7
Other professional specialties	2,645	2,319	251	136	75	9.5	5.1	2.8
Engineering and science technicians	1,044	912	83	49	49	8.0	4.7	4.7
All other occupations	59,852	50,101	7,746	5,985	2,005	12.9	10.0	3.3

Source: National Science Board. *Science & Engineering Indicators—1993* (NSB 93-1). Washington, DC: U.S. Government Printing Office, 1993, p. 322. Primary source: Bureau of Labor Statistics, Current Population Survey, unpublished tabulations. *Note:* Details may not sum to totals because of rounding.

★ 495 ★

Employment

Hispanic Employment Characteristics in Selected States, 1993

Data shown represent the annual average number of persons in each employment category in 1993. Figures for selected states are shown in thousands.

State	Employed						Unemployed	
	Full time			Part time				
	Total	Full-time schedules[1]	Part time for economic reasons, usually work full time	Total	Voluntary[1]	Part time for economic reasons, usually work part time	Looking for full-time work	Looking for part-time work
Arizona	230	219	10	52	30	22	[2]	[2]
California	2,723	2,579	145	592	347	245	411	58
Colorado	123	120	3	28	21	6	[2]	[2]
Connecticut	62	59	2	5	4	2	[2]	[2]
District of Columbia	14	14	1	3	1	2	[2]	[2]
Florida	730	707	22	136	99	37	68	14
Idaho	23	23	1	4	2	1	[2]	[2]
Illinois	388	381	7	45	33	12	32	3
Massachusetts	55	52	3	15	8	7	[2]	[2]
Michigan	58	57	1	11	6	4	[2]	[2]
Nevada	66	64	2	7	4	2	[2]	[2]
New Jersey	298	291	7	32	20	12	43	3
New Mexico	166	161	4	41	29	12	[2]	[2]
New York	614	603	12	98	59	39	94	11
North Carolina	33	32	1	4	3	1	[2]	[2]
Oklahoma	27	26	1	6	3	3	[2]	[2]
Oregon	54	52	2	8	5	3	[2]	[2]
Pennsylvania	54	53	1	9	8	1	[2]	[2]
Rhode Island	20	20	[3]	2	1	1	[2]	[2]
Texas	1,621	1,562	59	302	186	116	153	36
Utah	31	30	1	6	5	2	[2]	[2]
Virginia	72	70	2	18	11	7	[2]	[2]
Wyoming	6	6	[3]	2	1	[3]	[2]	[2]

Source: U.S. Bureau of Labor Statistics. U.S. Department of Labor. *Geographic Profile of Employment and Unemployment, 1993* (Bulletin 2446). Washington, DC: U.S. Government Printing Office, September 1994, p. 55. *Notes:* Items may not add to totals because of rounding. 1. Employed persons with a job but not at work are distributed according to whether they usually work full or part time. 2. Data are not shown when the labor force base does not meet Bureau of Labor Statistics publication standards of reliability for the particular area, based on the sample in that area. 3. Less than 500 persons.

★ 496 ★

Employment

Hispanic Employment Distribution, by Major Industry and Selected State, 1993 - I

Percent distribution of persons employed is shown, by major industry and selected state. Data shown are annual averages for 1993.

State	Total employed[1]		Nonagricultural industries					
			Total[2]	Private nonagricultural wage and salary workers				
				Total[3]	Con-struc-tion	Manufacturing		
	Number (000)	%				Total	Durable goods	Nondurable goods
Arizona	282	100.0	92.1	70.8	9.8	14.5	10.9	3.6
California	3,315	100.0	88.8	73.0	5.3	20.5	10.7	9.8
Colorado	151	100.0	96.8	69.9	8.1	10.4	8.8	1.6
Connecticut	67	100.0	99.3	83.3	1.0	34.6	20.4	14.2
District of Columbia	17	100.0	94.5	79.1	4.2	4.7	.7	4.0
Florida	866	100.0	91.6	76.4	5.4	11.6	4.8	6.8
Hawaii	10	100.0	91.8	58.4	.4	1.7	1.8	[4]
Idaho	27	100.0	78.6	67.6	6.0	33.6	11.3	22.3
Illinois	433	100.0	97.2	89.1	3.0	36.9	23.2	13.7
Maryland	57	100.0	86.1	69.8	2.7	1.7	.8	.9
Massachusetts	70	100.0	97.5	82.9	3.0	24.0	13.9	10.2
Michigan	69	100.0	97.1	78.5	2.1	30.2	25.1	5.1
Nevada	73	100.0	96.2	81.8	8.2	7.1	4.7	2.4
New Jersey	330	100.0	97.3	82.5	2.7	27.3	9.6	17.7
New Mexico	207	100.0	95.7	65.0	8.0	1.7	3.7	3.4
New York	712	100.0	95.5	75.7	2.7	16.2	6.7	9.5
North Carolina	37	100.0	90.6	81.9	4.2	40.8	8.8	32.0
Ohio	32	100.0	96.3	80.9	7.6	29.3	18.6	10.7
Oklahoma	33	100.0	90.4	78.1	6.5	13.6	8.4	5.2
Oregon	62	100.0	80.1	65.9	1.0	19.0	12.3	6.7
Pennsylvania	63	100.0	99.5	79.1	2.8	22.1	5.0	17.1
Rhode Island	22	100.0	100.0	93.9	.5	59.5	41.0	18.5
Texas	1,923	100.0	95.1	73.7	8.1	14.2	7.3	6.9
Utah	37	100.0	91.7	73.3	2.2	22.0	7.9	14.1
Virginia	90	100.0	93.8	75.1	9.1	1.9	.4	1.5
Wyoming	8	100.0	96.1	70.8	9.1	9.8	4.4	5.4

Source: U.S. Bureau of Labor Statistics. U.S. Department of Labor. *Geographic Profile of Employment and Unemployment, 1993* (Bulletin 2446). Washington, DC: U.S. Government Printing Office, September 1994, p. 73. *Notes:* Data for demographic groups are not shown when they do not meet Bureau of Labor Statistics publication standards of reliability for the particular area based on the sample in that area. Items may not add to totals or compute to displayed percentages because of rounding. Detail for race and Hispanic origin groups will not add to totals because data for the "other races" group are not presented and Hispanics are included in both the white and black population groups. 1. Includes private household workers, self-employed and unpaid family workers, and mining. 2. Includes self-employed and unpaid family workers and mining. 3. Includes mining. 4. Less than 500 persons employed or less than 0.05 percent of total employed.

★ 497 ★

Employment

Hispanic Employment Distribution, by Major Industry and Selected State, 1993 - II

Percent distribution of persons employed is shown, by major industry and selected state, for 1993. Data shown are annual averages for 1993.

State	Nonagricultural industries					Agri-culture
	Private nonagricultural wage and salary workers					
	Transportation, communications, and public utilities	Trade	Finance, insurance, and real estate	Services[1]	Government	
Arizona	4.2	22.5	4.2	15.7	14.8	5.7
California	4.4	21.4	4.1	17.3	10.6	7.8
Colorado	6.4	19.1	5.0	20.9	22.8	2.2
Connecticut	2.4	15.1	9.0	21.1	14.7	.1
District of Columbia	1.7	28.1	7.9	32.5	13.4	.3
Florida	7.1	21.5	6.1	24.8	8.8	7.0
Hawaii	7.2	14.7	5.5	28.7	27.2	7.5
Idaho	7.3	9.6	1.8	9.3	8.8	21.4
Illinois	3.8	19.8	5.0	20.5	6.4	1.9
Maryland	5.5	27.9	6.3	25.8	5.7	5.8
Massachusetts	4.0	17.0	5.1	29.8	10.4	.9
Michigan	4.5	23.0	3.9	14.9	13.9	1.6
Nevada	2.7	19.2	2.9	40.7	9.2	3.5
New Jersey	5.7	23.2	4.4	19.1	10.6	1.2
New Mexico	3.8	20.8	4.0	18.6	22.5	2.7
New York	4.9	17.0	8.6	26.3	14.6	1.8
North Carolina	5.3	15.5	1.9	14.1	4.9	9.4
Ohio	3.2	13.2	1.3	26.2	9.1	3.7
Oklahoma	2.4	24.3	1.2	28.7	7.5	9.7
Oregon	.7	20.5	5.3	19.3	11.1	18.1
Pennsylvania	4.0	18.0	5.0	27.1	14.6	.1
Rhode Island	1.3	9.8	2.6	20.3	1.2	[2]
Texas	6.0	22.3	3.6	18.3	15.4	2.8
Utah	5.6	12.0	7.2	19.7	15.5	6.9
Virginia	1.5	21.1	5.1	36.4	9.8	1.4
Wyoming	9.2	20.7	4.5	11.8	16.6	2.9

Source: U.S. Bureau of Labor Statistics. U.S. Department of Labor. *Geographic Profile of Employment and Unemployment, 1993* (Bulletin 2446). Washington, DC: U.S. Government Printing Office, September 1994, p. 73. *Notes:* Data for demographic groups are not shown when they do not meet Bureau of Labor Statistics publication standards of reliability for the particular area based on the sample in that area. Items may not add to totals or compute to displayed percentages because of rounding. Detail for race and Hispanic origin groups will not add to totals because data for the "other races" group are not presented and Hispanics are included in both the white and black population groups. 1. Excludes private household workers. 2. Less than 500 persons employed or less than 0.05 percent of total employed.

★ 498 ★

Employment

Hispanic Employment, by Hours Worked, in Selected States, 1993

Data show number persons working in each schedule category. Figures are shown in thousands of persons.

State	Total at work	Hours of work								Average hours	
		1 to 14 hours	15 to 29 hours	30 to 34 hours	35 hours and over					Total	Full-time schedules[1]
					Total	35 to 39 hours	40 hours	41 to 48 hours	49 hours and over		
Hispanic origin											
Arizona	270	10	35	26	199	19	127	21	32	37.9	44.9
California	3,156	119	446	276	2,314	174	1,553	249	338	37.3	44.4
Colorado	143	4	18	15	106	9	64	12	20	38.2	45.9
Connecticut	64	1	5	4	54	5	33	7	8	39.8	44.5
District of Columbia	17	[2]	2	2	12	1	8	1	2	37.6	44.9
Florida	830	22	93	60	655	44	440	44	126	39.1	44.5
Hawaii	8	[2]	1	[2]	8	[2]	4	1	2	46.4	50.2
Idaho	26	2	3	1	20	3	9	3	5	39.0	46.2
Illinois	414	10	32	24	348	17	247	41	43	39.3	43.6
Maryland	55	2	9	4	40	2	26	4	7	38.8	47.9
Massachusetts	66	2	11	6	46	6	30	5	6	35.9	43.4
Michigan	65	2	7	6	50	4	28	7	11	39.5	46.8
Nevada	70	1	6	4	59	3	44	3	9	39.8	44.2
New Jersey	317	5	27	18	267	34	157	28	47	40.0	44.4
New Mexico	195	10	28	19	139	14	78	17	30	37.9	46.8
New York	680	19	77	37	547	100	315	51	81	38.4	43.7
North Carolina	36	1	3	3	29	3	15	4	8	41.7	47.2
Ohio	30	1	3	2	25	2	15	3	5	40.8	45.9
Oklahoma	31	1	4	2	24	2	15	2	4	38.6	44.2
Oregon	58	2	6	5	45	6	26	6	7	39.0	45.0
Pennsylvania	61	1	8	5	47	5	25	6	9	39.6	47.1
Rhode Island	21	[2]	2	3	16	2	11	1	2	38.3	47.3
Texas	1,838	65	214	166	1,392	132	788	191	282	39.0	46.0
Utah	37	1	5	3	27	2	15	4	6	39.1	47.1
Virginia	83	2	14	8	59	6	31	5	17	39.6	49.3
Wyoming	8	[2]	1	1	5	[2]	3	1	1	38.5	48.2

Source: U.S. Bureau of Labor Statistics. U.S. Department of Labor. *Geographic Profile of Employment and Unemployment, 1993* (Bulletin 2446). Washington, DC: U.S. Government Printing Office, September 1994, p. 78. *Notes:* Data for demographic groups are not shown when they do not meet Bureau of Labor Statistics publication standards of reliability for the particular area based on the sample in that area. Items may not add to totals or compute to displayed percentages because of rounding. 1. Refers to persons who worked 35 hours or more during the survey week. 2. Less than 500 persons or less than 0.05 percent.

★ 499 ★

Employment

Hispanic Migrant Workers, by Ethnicity, 1992

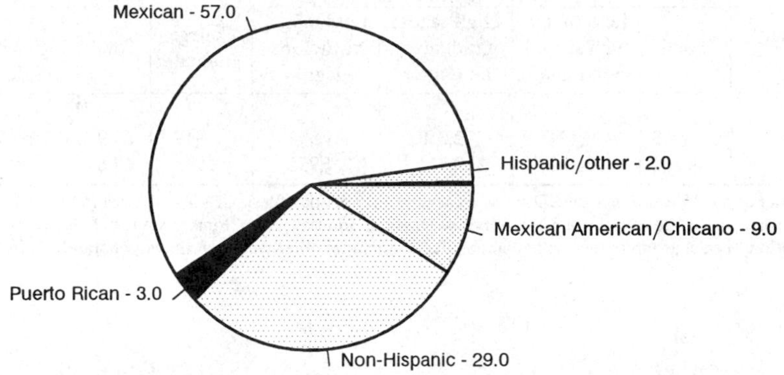

Distribution of workers is shown in percent.

Ethnicity	Percent
Mexican	57.0
Non-Hispanic	29.0
Mexican American/Chicano	9.0
Puerto Rican	3.0
Hispanic/other	2.0

Source: Harney, James and Deborah Sharp. "For farm workers, a harvest of danger." *USA TODAY* (25 February 1992), p. 3A. U.S. Department of Labor; USDA.

★ 500 ★

Employment

Labor Force Characteristics, by Educational Attainment, Sex, Race, and Hispanic Origin

Data shown are annual averages of monthly figures, for civilian noninstitutional population age 25 years and older.

Year, sex, and race/ethnicity	Civilian labor force (000)					Participation rate[1]				
	Total	Less than a high school diploma	High school graduates, no degree	Less than a bachelor's degree	College graduate	Total	Less than a high school diploma	High school graduates, no degree	Less than a bachelor's degree	College graduate
Total:[2]										
1992	106,530	13,191	37,993	27,089	28,257	66.3	40.7	66.2	75.1	81.2
1993	107,657	12,360	37,821	28,413	29,062	66.2	39.7	65.4	75.0	81.0
White:										
1992	91,242	10,543	32,488	23,273	24,938	66.3	40.8	65.4	74.5	80.9
1993	92,168	9,960	32,273	24,345	25,590	66.3	40.1	64.8	74.4	80.8
Black:										
1992	11,422	2,110	4,505	3,004	1,803	65.7	39.7	72.3	80.5	85.6
1993	11,477	1,873	4,492	3,216	1,896	64.7	37.1	69.9	79.7	84.8

[Continued]

★ 500 ★

Labor Force Characteristics, by Educational Attainment, Sex, Race, and Hispanic Origin

[Continued]

Year, sex, and race/ethnicity	Civilian labor force (000)					Participation rate[1]				
	Total	Less than a high school diploma	High school graduates, no degree	Less than a bachelor's degree	College graduate	Total	Less than a high school diploma	High school graduates, no degree	Less than a bachelor's degree	College graduate
Hispanic:[3]										
1992	7,993	3,124	2,358	1,592	919	67.9	55.9	75.2	82.1	83.0
1993	8,261	3,130	2,411	1,756	963	67.6	55.7	73.2	81.6	83.7

Source: 1994 Statistical Abstract of the United States on CD-ROM [machine-readable datafiles]. CD-8A-94. Washington, DC: U.S. Department of Commerce, Economics and Statistics Administration, Bureau of the Census, Data User Services Division, January 1995. Primary source: U.S. Bureau of Labor Statistics, unpublished data. *Notes:* 1. Percent of the civilian population in each group in the civilian labor force. 2. Includes other races, not shown separately. 3. Persons of Hispanic origin may be of any race.

★ 501 ★

Employment

Labor Force Participation, Participation Rates, and Projections, by Sex and Race/Ethnicity, 1986 and 2000

Characteristic	Participation rate (percent)		Number (000)		Percent change
	1986	2000	1986	2000	1986-2000
Hispanics-16 and older	65.4	68.7	8,076	14,086	74.4
Men	81.0	80.4	4,948	8,303	67.8
Women	50.1	56.9	3,128	5,783	84.9
Whites-16 and older	65.5	68.2	101,801	116,701	14.6
Men	76.9	75.3	57,216	62,252	8.8
Women	55.0	61.5	44,585	54,449	22.1
Blacks-16 and older	63.5	66.0	12,684	16,334	28.8
Men	71.2	70.7	6,373	7,926	24.4
Women	57.2	62.1	6,311	8,408	33.2

Source: Business Horizons, (January/February 1990), p. 75. Primary source: Bureau of Labor Statistics, 1987.

★ 502 ★

Employment

Labor Force Projections, 1990-2005

The number and percent of workers projected to enter and leave the United States labor force, from 1990 to 2005, are shown, by race/ethnicity and sex.

Race/ethnicity	Entrants		Leavers	
	1990-2005	Percent	1990-2005	Percent
Total	55,798	100.0	29,851	100.0
Men	28,197	50.5	17,090	57.3
Women	27,601	49.5	12,761	42.7
Hispanic	8,768	15.7	1,556	5.2
Men	5,085	9.1	939	3.1
Women	3,683	6.6	617	2.1
White, non-Hispanic	36,425	65.3	24,423	81.8
Men	17,965	32.2	14,204	47.6
Women	18,460	33.1	10,219	34.2
Black	7,250	13.0	3,144	10.5
Men	3,461	6.2	1,553	5.2
Women	3,789	6.8	1,591	5.2
Asian and Other Races	3,354	6.0	728	2.4
Men	1,686	3.0	395	1.3
Women	1,668	3.0	333	1.1

Source: American Demographics (June 1992), p. 63. Primary source: Bureau of Labor Statistics *Note:* All groups add to total. Numbers may not add up due to rounding.

★ 503 ★

Employment

Leading Newspapers With the Most Hispanic Editorial Staff Members, 1991

On the top 62 U.S. newspapers, there were 538 editorial-staff Hispanics in all, which accounted for 3.5% of the total editorial staff in 1991.

Newspaper	Hispanic editorial staff
Los Angeles Times	55
Miami Herald	27
San Antonio Light	23
New York Times	21
Houston Chronicle	18
Wall Street Journal	17
Dallas Morning News, Riverside (Calif.) Press-Enterprise	17
Chicago Tribune	17

[Continued]

★ 503 ★

Leading Newspapers With the Most Hispanic Editorial Staff Members, 1991

[Continued]

Newspaper	Hispanic editorial staff
Tucson Citizen	16
Fort Worth Star-Telegram	15
San Jose Mercury News	15

Source: Stein, M.L. "Concerned about diversity: Hispanic journalists say the slightest percentage increase in the number of Hispanic editorial staffers at newspapers is 'insignificant'." *Editor and Publisher - the Fourth Estate* (9 May 1992), p. 22. Primary source: "Hispanics in the News Media 1992: Still Struggling for Entry," a survey by the National Association of Hispanic Journalists.

★ 504 ★

Employment

Minority Representation Among Engineers

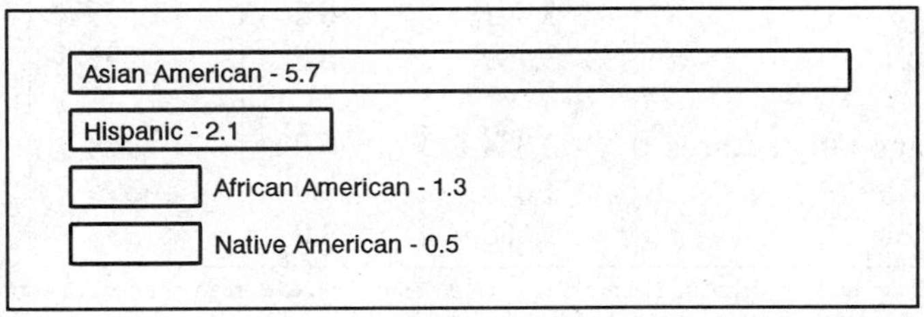

Data show results of a survey of a random sample of members of 22 engineering societies. Distribution by race/ethnicity is shown in percent.

Race/ethnicity	Percent
Asian American	5.7
Hispanic	2.1
African American	1.3
Native American	0.5

Source: Lewin, David. "Washington window: across the gender divide." *Mechanical Engineering* (October 1993), p. 34. Primary source: Society of Women Engineers survey.

★ 505 ★

Employment

Minority Representation in Newspapers, 1993

Minorities made up just over 10 percent of the 53,700 persons who worked at newspapers in 1993. Distribution of minority employees is shown by race/ethnicity.

Race/ethnicity	Percent
African-American	5.0
Hispanic	3.0
Asian	2.0
Native American	0.3
Total	10.49

Source: Atkins, Elizabeth. "Racial bias still widespread in the media, study finds." *Detroit News* (24 July 1994), p. 2A. Primary source: American Society of Newspaper Editors.

★ 506 ★

Employment

Minority Representation in Radio Newsrooms, 1993

Minorities made up 13 percent of the 15,000 persons who worked in radio news in 1993. Distribution of minority employees is shown by race/ethnicity.

Race/ethnicity	Percent
African-American	6.0
Hispanic	4.0
Asian	3.0
Native American	0.2
Total	13.0

Source: Atkins, Elizabeth. "Racial bias still widespread in the media, study finds." *Detroit News* (24 July 1994), p. 2A. Primary source: Radio and Television News Directors of America.

★ 507 ★

Employment

Minority Representation in Television Newsrooms, 1993

Minorities accounted for approximately 19 percent of the 25,000 persons who worked in television newsrooms in 1993. Distribution of minority employees is shown by race/ethnicity.

Race/ethnicity	Percent
African-American	11.0
Hispanic	5.0
Asian	2.0
Native American	0.5
Total	19.0

Source: Atkins, Elizabeth. "Racial bias still widespread in the media, study finds." *Detroit News* (24 July 1994), p. 2A. Primary source: Radio and Television News Directors of America.

★ 508 ★

Employment

Multiple Jobholder Percent Distribution, by Reason for Multiple Employment, 1991

Figures are shown for October 1991.

Characteristics	Total (000)	Percent distribution, by reason								
		Total	To meet regular household expenses	To pay off debts	To save for the future	To get experience or build up a business	To help out a friend or relative	To get extra money to buy something special	Enjoys the work on the second job	Other reasons
Total, 16 years and over	7,183	100.0	31.0	9.1	9.1	8.3	4.6	8.1	16.3	13.4
Men, 16 years and over	4,054	100.0	28.5	8.6	10.4	8.8	3.7	7.7	17.5	15.0
Single	947	100.0	23.4	8.9	12.9	7.5	3.8	11.2	13.8	18.5
Married, spouse present	2,747	100.0	29.0	8.4	9.9	9.1	3.7	6.5	19.3	14.1
Widowed, divorced, or separated	359	100.0	37.5	9.1	7.4	9.4	3.3	7.5	13.3	12.4
Hispanic origin	163	100.0	47.9	7.3	10.3	3.0	2.6	4.3	8.2	16.4
White	3,662	100.0	27.9	8.7	10.4	8.7	3.7	7.2	18.2	15.2
Black	298	100.0	36.9	5.5	10.2	9.2	2.2	13.9	9.6	12.5
Women, 16 years and over	3,129	100.0	34.3	9.9	7.3	7.8	5.8	8.6	14.8	11.4
Single	838	100.0	28.3	18.2	10.2	6.0	4.4	11.1	11.1	10.6
Married, spouse present	1,512	100.0	26.8	6.4	6.1	10.4	7.7	9.4	18.9	14.3
Widowed, divorced, or separated	779	100.0	55.4	7.6	6.8	4.6	3.8	4.4	10.9	6.5
Hispanic origin	113	100.0	55.7	2.8	8.7	11.2	1.0	3.3	6.7	10.5
White	2,787	100.0	33.5	9.3	7.1	8.3	6.2	8.4	15.9	11.5
Black	273	100.0	45.6	17.3	5.6	2.6	1.9	10.4	6.0	10.6

Source: "Multiple Jobholders by Sex, Marital Status, Race, Hispanic Origin, and Reason for Working at More Than One Job," *Bureau of Labor Statistics News*, 28 October 1991, p. 6. *Notes:* Detail for race and Hispanic origin groups will not add to totals because data for the "other races" group are not presented and Hispanics are included in both the white and black population groups.

★ 509 ★

Employment

Multiple Jobholders, 1991

Numbers are shown in thousands or as percent of total, by race/ethnicity and sex, for May 1991.

Race/ethnicity	Both sexes			Men			Women		
	Total employed	Multiple jobholders		Total employed	Multiple jobholders		Total employed	Multiple jobholders	
		Number	Rate[1]		Number	Rate[1]		Number	Rate[1]
Hispanic origin	8,687	275	3.2	5,207	163	3.1	3,480	113	3.2
White	101,017	6,449	6.4	55,655	3,662	6.6	45,362	2,787	6.1
Black	11,687	572	4.9	5,723	298	5.2	5,964	273	4.6

Source: "Multiple jobholders by age, marital status, race, Hispanic origin, and sex, May 1991." *Bureau of Labor Statistics News* (28 October 1991), p. 4. *Notes:* Detail for race and Hispanic origin groups will not add to totals because data for the "other races" group are not presented and Hispanics are included in both the white and black population groups. 1. Multiple jobholders as a percent of all employed persons in specified group.

★ 510 ★

Employment

Multiple Jobholders, by Extent of Work Done at Home on Secondary Job, 1991

Data are shown, by race/ethnicity, for May 1991.

Race/ethnicity	Total multiple jobholders (000)	Persons who did any regularly scheduled work at home on their secondary job		Persons who did all regularly scheduled work at home on their secondary job	
		Number (000)	% of total multiple jobholders	Number (000)	% of total multiple jobholders
Total, 16 years and over	7,183	2,736	38.1	1,178	16.4
Hispanic origin	275	56	20.4	34	12.4
Men	4,054	1,583	39.0	677	16.7
Women	3,129	1,153	36.8	502	16.0
White	6,449	2,556	39.6	1,134	17.6
Black	572	138	24.1	26	4.5

Source: "Multiple jobholders by selected characteristics and extent of work at home on secondary job, May 1991," *Bureau of Labor Statistics News*, (28 October 1991). *Notes:* Detail for race and Hispanic origin groups will not add to totals because data for the "other races" group are not presented and Hispanics are included in both the white and black population groups.

★ 511 ★

Employment

Multiple Jobholders, by Full or Part-Time Work Status, 1991

Numbers are shown in thousands and as percent of total, by race/ethnicity and multiple job work status, for May 1991.

Race/ethnicity	Usually work full time on primary job			Usually work part time on primary job			Percent distribution of multiple jobholders by usual full- or part-time status on both jobs			
	Total employed	Multiple jobholders		Total employed	Multiple jobholders		Total	One full-time job, one part-time job	Two part-time jobs	Two full-time jobs
		Number	Rate[1]		Number	Rate[1]				
Total, 16 years and over	93,988	5,413	5.8	22,638	1,769	7.8	100.0	72.2	23.4	4.4
Hispanic origin	7,227	198	2.7	1,460	78	5.3	100.0	67.3	26.4	6.2
White	81,022	4,801	5.9	19,995	1,648	8.2	100.0	71.2	24.5	4.3
Black	9,736	472	4.9	1,950	99	5.1	100.0	79.4	15.3	5.4

Source: "Multiple jobholders by age, marital status, race, Hispanic origin, and sex, May 1991." *Bureau of Labor Statistics News* (28 October 1991), p. 6. *Notes:* Detail for race and Hispanic origin groups will not add to totals because data for the "other races" group are not presented and Hispanics are included in both the white and black population groups. 1. Multiple jobholders as a percent of all employed persons in specified group.

★ 512 ★

Employment

Percent Changes in Selected Occupations for Hispanics and Blacks, 1980 to 1990

Occupation	Hispanics		Blacks	
	Men	Women	Men	Women
Household cleaners	144.3	155.0	-36.9	-44.6
Construction	81.3	70.0	14.4	16.3
Machine operator	26.2	15.0	-18.4	-8.8

Source: Usdansky, Margaret L. "A new U.S. workforce evolves: job shifts reflect progress of Hispanics and women." *USA TODAY* (29 January 1993), p. 7A. Primary source: U.S. Census Bureau; Bureau of Labor Statistics; *USA TODAY* analysis of Census data.

★ 513 ★

Employment

Percent Changes in Selected Professional Occupations for Hispanics, Whites, and Blacks, 1980 to 1990

Profession	Hispanics		Whites		Blacks	
	Men	Women	Men	Women	Men	Women
Managers/executives	61.4	165.1	12.8	87.4	45.3	120.1
Physicians	41.1	125.8	20.8	119.5	35.8	127.3
Lawyers	45.7	228.4	28.5	160.2	52.4	160.4

Source: Usdansky, Margaret L. "A new U.S. workforce evolves: job shifts reflect progress of Hispanics and women." *USA TODAY* (29 January 1993), p. 7A. Primary source: U.S. Census Bureau; Bureau of Labor Statistics; *USA TODAY* analysis of Census data.

★ 514 ★

Employment

Percent Changes in the Workforce, by Race/Ethnicity and Sex, 1980 to 1990

Characteristic	Men	Women
Hispanics	63.9	72.3
Whites	5.7	21.5
Blacks	29.8	29.8
Asians	105.2	107.2
Native Americans	36.7	56.0
Total workforce	11.8	26.9

Source: Usdansky, Margaret L. "A new U.S. workforce evolves: job shifts reflect progress of Hispanics and women." *USA TODAY* (29 January 1993), p. 7A. Primary source: U.S. Census Bureau; Bureau of Labor Statistics, *USA TODAY* analysis of Census data.

★ 515 ★

Employment

Persons 16 Years Old and Older With Specified Work Experience During Year, 1974-89 - I

Numbers are shown in thousands.

Characteristics	Number of persons 16 years old and over (000)				Percent with work experience during year			
	1974	1979	1984	1989	1974	1979	1984	1989
ALL RACES								
Sex and age								
Both sexes								
16 years and over	150,449	166,953	177,661	187,524	67.4	68.9	68.2	70.3
16 and 17 years	8,299	8,315	7,218	6,629	55.5	54.6	48.3	51.9
18 to 64 years	121,023	134,444	143,626	151,330	76.6	79.0	79.1	81.7
18 to 24 years	25,950	28,883	27,603	25,113	82.5	83.0	80.6	82.1
25 to 34 years	29,682	36,207	40,453	42,793	79.4	84.3	84.6	86.5
35 to 54 years	45,910	47,879	53,422	62,193	76.9	80.5	82.1	85.1
55 to 64 years	19,481	21,476	22,148	21,230	63.9	61.6	59.9	61.4
65 years and over	21,127	24,194	26,818	29,566	19.5	17.4	15.1	16.3
Males								
16 years and over	70,996	79,014	84,206	89,373	82.8	81.1	78.3	79.2
16 and 17 years	4,191	4,211	3,680	3,392	62.4	59.4	49.7	53.2
18 to 64 years	58,083	64,851	69,512	73,647	92.1	91.0	88.8	89.8
18 to 24 years	12,466	14,067	13,454	12,275	90.1	88.9	85.2	86.1
25 to 34 years	14,366	17,642	19,780	21,048	96.7	95.6	94.2	94.6
35 to 54 years	22,075	23,128	25,905	30,323	94.6	94.3	92.7	93.5
55 to 64 years	9,176	10,013	10,374	10,001	81.8	78.0	73.5	73.1
65 years and over	8,722	9,953	11,014	12,334	30.4	25.8	21.8	22.6
Females								
16 years and over	79,453	87,939	93,455	98,152	53.7	57.9	59.1	62.3
16 and 17 years	4,108	4,104	3,538	3,237	48.5	49.7	46.8	50.6
18 to 64 years	62,940	69,594	74,113	77,682	62.3	67.9	70.0	74.0
18 to 24 years	13,484	14,815	14,149	12,837	75.5	77.3	76.2	78.2
25 to 34 years	15,316	18,564	20,674	21,745	63.1	73.5	75.5	78.6
35 to 54 years	23,835	24,752	27,517	31,870	60.6	67.6	72.1	77.2
55 to 64 years	10,305	11,462	11,774	11,230	48.0	47.2	48.0	51.0
65 years and over	12,405	14,241	15,804	17,232	11.8	11.5	10.5	11.8
HISPANIC ORIGIN[1]								
Sex and age								
Both sexes								
16 years and over	6,685	8,394	11,429	14,155	65.5	68.3	66.0	68.7
16 and 17 years	486	544	618	652	40.5	39.0	35.0	32.5
18 to 64 years	5,794	7,276	9,992	12,480	71.0	74.5	72.2	75.1
18 to 24 years	1,457	1,938	2,386	2,716	72.2	75.0	70.7	73.6
25 to 34 years	1,553	2,209	3,070	4,116	71.9	77.5	77.6	79.0
35 to 54 years	2,263	2,485	3,495	4,441	73.5	76.0	73.8	77.9
55 to 64 years	521	643	1,041	1,207	54.4	56.7	54.0	55.3

[Continued]

★ 515 ★

Persons 16 Years Old and Older With Specified Work Experience During Year, 1974-89 - I

[Continued]

Characteristics	Number of persons 16 years old and over (000)				Percent with work experience during year			
	1974	1979	1984	1989	1974	1979	1984	1989
65 years and over	405	574	819	1,024	15.9	17.4	14.2	14.0
Males								
16 years and over	3,192	4,043	5,605	7,013	83.0	83.3	79.1	81.4
16 and 17 years	264	293	321	328	45.7	47.2	39.1	38.1
18 to 64 years	2,741	3,492	4,931	6,218	90.5	90.6	85.9	88.4
18 to 24 years	688	946	1,251	1,412	83.9	86.5	80.0	84.4
25 to 34 years	729	1,071	1,512	2,086	95.3	94.2	92.5	93.1
35 to 54 years	1,091	1,182	1,696	2,183	93.6	94.0	88.9	90.3
55 to 64 years	233	293	471	537	80.4	77.2	70.0	73.5
65 years and over	187	258	353	467	26.8	26.0	20.8	18.8
Females								
16 years and over	3,493	4,351	5,823	7,142	49.4	54.3	53.3	56.3
16 and 17 years	221	250	297	324	34.3	29.4	30.6	26.8
18 to 64 years	3,054	3,785	5,061	6,262	53.6	59.6	58.7	61.9
18 to 24 years	769	992	1,134	1,304	61.8	64.1	60.5	62.0
25 to 34 years	824	1,139	1,558	2,030	51.2	61.9	63.1	64.5
35 to 54 years	1,172	1,303	1,799	2,258	54.8	59.7	59.6	65.9
55 to 64 years	289	350	569	670	33.4	39.5	40.7	40.6
65 years and over	218	316	466	557	6.6	10.4	9.2	10.0
WHITE								
Sex and age								
Both sexes								
16 years and over	132,885	145,671	153,289	160,021	67.9	69.6	69.0	71.1
16 and 17 years	7,050	6,935	5,897	5,314	58.3	59.1	5.2	55.9
18 to 64 years	106,629	116,839	123,185	128,228	77.2	80.0	80.4	83.0
18 to 24 years	22,382	24,523	23,022	20,609	84.7	86.1	84.1	85.6
25 to 34 years	26,013	31,103	34,364	35,842	79.5	85.0	85.9	87.7
35 to 54 years	40,616	41,883	46,171	53,200	77.4	81.1	82.9	86.0
55 to 64 years	17,618	19,330	19,628	18,576	64.1	62.0	60.5	62.3
65 years and over	19,206	21,898	24,206	26,479	19.3	17.3	15.1	16.5
Males								
16 years and over	63,073	69,439	73,180	76,839	83.7	82.2	79.7	80.4
16 and 17 years	3,570	3,531	3,009	2,720	65.2	64.6	55.0	57.6
18 to 64 years	51,610	56,928	60,226	63,084	93.1	92.2	90.5	91.4
18 to 24 years	10,856	12,068	11,303	10,145	91.8	91.3	88.7	89.6
25 to 34 years	12,743	15,335	17,024	17,850	97.2	96.7	95.6	96.0
35 to 54 years	19,692	20,455	22,646	26,260	95.7	95.1	93.8	94.5
55 to 64 years	8,319	9,069	9,253	8,828	82.4	79.2	74.9	74.6
65 years and over	7,893	8,980	9,945	11,035	30.6	25.8	22.0	23.3

[Continued]

★515★

Persons 16 Years Old and Older With Specified Work Experience During Year, 1974-89 - I

[Continued]

Characteristics	Number of persons 16 years old and over (000)				Percent with work experience during year			
	1974	1979	1984	1989	1974	1979	1984	1989
Females								
16 years and over	69,812	76,232	80,109	83,182	53.5	58.1	59.3	62.5
16 and 17 years	3,480	3,404	2,889	2,595	51.3	53.4	51.4	54.1
18 to 64 years	55,019	59,911	62,959	65,144	62.3	68.5	70.8	74.8
18 to 24 years	11,526	12,454	11,719	10,464	77.9	81.1	79.7	81.7
25 to 34 years	13,270	15,768	17,339	17,992	62.5	73.7	76.4	79.4
35 to 54 years	20,924	21,428	23,526	26,940	60.1	57.7	72.3	77.6
55 to 64 years	9,299	10,261	10,375	9,748	47.7	46.9	47.6	51.2
65 years and over	11,313	12,918	14,261	15,444	11.5	11.4	10.2	11.7

Source: U.S. Bureau of the Census. *Workers With Low Earnings: 1964 to 1990.* Current Population Reports, Series P-60, No. 178. Washington, DC: U.S. Government Printing Office, 1992, pp. 9-16. *Note:* 1. Hispanic persons may be of any race.

★516★

Employment

Persons 16 Years Old and Older With Specified Work Experience During Year, 1974-89 - II

Numbers are shown in thousands.

Characteristics	Percent with year-round, full-time attachment to labor force				Percent worked year-round full-time			
	1974	1979	1984	1989	1974	1979	1984	1989
ALL RACES								
Sex and age								
Both sexes								
16 years and over	43.4	45.7	47.8	49.3	36.7	38.8	39.6	42.8
16 and 17 years	4.1	4.6	3.0	2.6	1.3	1.1	.8	.7
18 to 64 years	52.4	55.3	58.0	59.8	44.5	47.2	48.2	52.0
18 to 24 years	37.6	41.5	40.4	39.5	26.2	29.7	27.2	29.8
25 to 34 years	57.7	62.4	66.3	66.7	48.8	52.9	54.6	57.4
35 to 54 years	59.7	62.5	66.3	68.8	53.2	55.9	57.8	61.7
55 to 64 years	46.8	46.0	45.0	43.7	41.7	41.6	39.5	39.2
65 years and over	7.1	6.0	5.1	5.8	6.0	5.0	4.2	5.0
Males								
16 years and over	62.8	62.4	62.7	62.6	53.5	53.7	52.1	54.6
16 and 17 years	5.9	6.1	4.1	3.2	2.1	1.6	1.1	1.0
18 to 64 years	74.4	74.2	74.4	74.4	63.6	64.1	61.8	65.0
18 to 24 years	46.9	50.1	47.6	46.0	31.3	35.4	30.7	34.3
25 to 34 years	84.5	83.4	84.3	82.8	71.4	71.3	68.8	71.2
35 to 54 years	86.4	85.6	85.8	85.2	78.1	77.9	75.6	76.9

[Continued]

★ 516 ★

Persons 16 Years Old and Older With Specified Work Experience During Year, 1974-89 - II

[Continued]

Characteristics	Percent with year-round, full-time attachment to labor force				Percent worked year-round full-time			
	1974	1979	1984	1989	1974	1979	1984	1989
55 to 64 years	67.2	65.2	61.6	58.9	60.5	59.9	54.8	53.3
65 years and over	12.6	9.9	8.4	8.7	10.8	8.4	7.3	7.7
Females								
16 years and over	26.0	30.6	34.4	37.2	21.7	25.3	28.4	32.0
16 and 17 years	2.2	3.0	1.9	2.1	.5	.7	.5	.4
18 to 64 years	32.1	37.8	42.7	46.0	26.8	31.4	35.4	39.7
18 to 24 years	29.1	33.3	33.5	33.4	21.5	24.3	23.8	25.5
25 to 34 years	32.5	42.4	49.1	51.2	27.6	35.5	41.1	43.9
35 to 54 years	34.9	41.0	47.9	53.2	30.1	35.3	41.1	47.1
55 to 64 years	28.7	29.3	30.4	30.2	24.9	25.6	26.0	26.6
65 years and over	3.2	3.2	2.8	3.8	2.6	2.6	2.1	3.1
HISPANIC ORIGIN[1]								
Sex and age								
Both sexes								
16 years and over	42.9	46.1	47.4	49.9	33.5	36.3	36.5	40.5
16 and 17 years	4.6	3.7	4.2	3.8	1.6	1.1	1.3	1.0
18 to 64 years	48.5	52.2	53.5	55.9	38.2	41.3	41.3	45.5
18 to 24 years	34.8	40.8	40.4	42.4	23.7	27.8	26.5	30.6
25 to 34 years	52.8	56.8	60.7	61.4	42.0	44.3	47.1	50.0
35 to 54 years	56.1	60.2	59.7	63.0	46.0	50.9	48.5	53.4
55 to 64 years	40.6	40.3	41.7	40.9	33.1	34.9	33.6	34.4
65 years and over	8.6	8.5	5.9	6.2	5.1	6.3	5.4	4.5
Males								
16 years and over	63.1	63.4	63.5	64.5	49.0	50.1	48.3	52.1
16 and 17 years	6.2	4.6	5.8	5.4	2.0	.9	1.8	1.4
18 to 64 years	71.7	72.1	71.2	71.8	56.1	57.2	54.2	58.2
18 to 24 years	47.9	53.4	52.2	55.3	31.2	34.6	32.1	39.6
25 to 34 years	81.5	78.8	80.9	78.7	63.8	61.8	61.9	63.8
35 to 54 years	81.7	83.6	79.6	79.2	67.5	72.1	64.9	67.0
55 to 64 years	64.0	61.4	60.4	58.6	52.9	53.8	50.0	49.6
65 years and over	17.1	12.7	8.6	8.5	10.7	8.9	8.4	6.9
Females								
16 years and over	24.4	30.0	32.0	35.5	19.4	23.5	25.2	29.1
16 and 17 years	2.7	2.6	2.5	2.2	1.0	1.3	.7	.6
18 to 64 years	27.6	33.9	36.3	40.0	22.0	26.6	28.7	32.9
18 to 24 years	23.1	28.8	27.5	28.3	17.1	21.2	20.4	20.9
25 to 34 years	27.4	36.1	41.0	43.6	22.8	27.9	32.8	35.9
35 to 54 years	32.2	39.0	40.9	47.4	26.0	31.6	33.0	40.3
55 to 64 years	21.6	22.7	26.2	26.8	17.1	19.0	20.0	22.2

[Continued]

★ 516 ★

Persons 16 Years Old and Older With Specified Work Experience During Year, 1974-89 - II

[Continued]

Characteristics	Percent with year-round, full-time attachment to labor force				Percent worked year-round full-time			
	1974	1979	1984	1989	1974	1979	1984	1989
65 years and over	1.3	5.0	3.8	4.1	.3	4.3	3.1	2.6
WHITE								
Sex and age								
Both sexes								
16 years and over	43.6	46.0	48.1	49.7	37.3	39.5	40.2	43.3
16 and 17 years	4.3	5.0	3.3	2.9	1.5	1.3	.9	.9
18 to 64 years	52.8	55.9	58.7	60.7	45.3	48.2	49.2	53.0
18 to 24 years	38.6	43.1	42.0	41.3	27.3	31.4	29.0	31.5
25 to 34 years	57.7	62.8	66.8	67.7	49.3	53.8	55.6	58.6
35 to 54 years	59.9	62.7	66.6	69.1	53.9	56.5	58.4	62.1
55 to 64 years	47.3	46.5	45.4	44.3	42.4	42.3	40.1	39.8
65 years and over	7.2	6.1	4.9	6.0	6.2	5.1	4.2	5.1
Males								
16 years and over	63.7	63.5	63.8	63.8	54.9	55.1	53.6	56.0
16 and 17 years	6.3	6.8	4.6	3.4	2.3	1.8	1.3	1.3
18 to 64 years	75.5	75.5	75.9	76.0	65.2	65.8	63.9	66.8
18 to 24 years	47.6	51.6	49.1	48.1	32.1	37.1	32.6	36.2
25 to 34 years	85.3	84.7	85.7	84.5	72.8	73.0	70.9	73.2
35 to 54 years	87.7	86.7	87.2	86.4	79.9	79.4	77.3	78.5
55 to 64 years	68.0	66.3	63.0	60.1	61.7	61.0	56.4	54.4
65 years and over	12.7	10.2	8.2	9.0	11.2	8.7	7.3	8.0
Females								
16 years and over	25.5	30.0	33.7	36.6	21.5	25.2	28.0	31.6
16 and 17 years	2.3	3.1	1.9	2.5	.6	.7	.4	.6
18 to 64 years	31.5	37.3	42.2	45.8	26.7	31.4	35.2	39.6
18 to 24 years	30.0	34.8	35.2	34.8	22.7	25.9	25.5	26.9
25 to 34 years	31.2	41.4	48.3	51.2	26.7	35.2	40.6	44.2
35 to 54 years	33.8	39.8	46.8	52.2	29.4	34.6	40.2	46.1
55 to 64 years	28.7	28.9	29.8	29.9	25.2	25.7	25.5	26.5
65 years and over	3.3	3.3	2.7	3.7	2.7	2.7	2.1	3.1

Source: U.S. Bureau of the Census. *Workers With Low Earnings: 1964 to 1990.* Current Population Reports, Series P-60, No. 178. Washington, DC: U.S. Government Printing Office, 1992, pp. 9-16. *Note:* 1. Hispanic persons may be of any race.

★ 517 ★

Employment

Persons With Job Accessions, 1987-89

A "job accession" is defined as not having a job in one month but having a job in the following month. This table shows the number of persons (in thousands) who experienced job accessions from 1987-89, by race/ethnicity and age group.

Age	Total persons	White	Black	Hispanic origin[1]
Total	41,485	34,541	5,539	3,263
16 to 24 years	17,470	14,500	2,450	1,438
25 to 34 years	10,463	8,596	1,450	917
35 to 54 years	10,303	8,594	1,302	762
55 years and over	3,250	2,849	337	145

Source: U.S. Bureau of the Census. *Job Creation During the Late 1980's (Data from the Survey of Income and Program Participation).* Current Population Reports, P70, No. 27. Washington, DC: U.S. Government Printing Office, 1992, p. 5. *Note:* 1. Persons of Hispanic origin may be of any race.

★ 518 ★

Employment

Racial/Ethnic Distribution of the U.S. Workforce

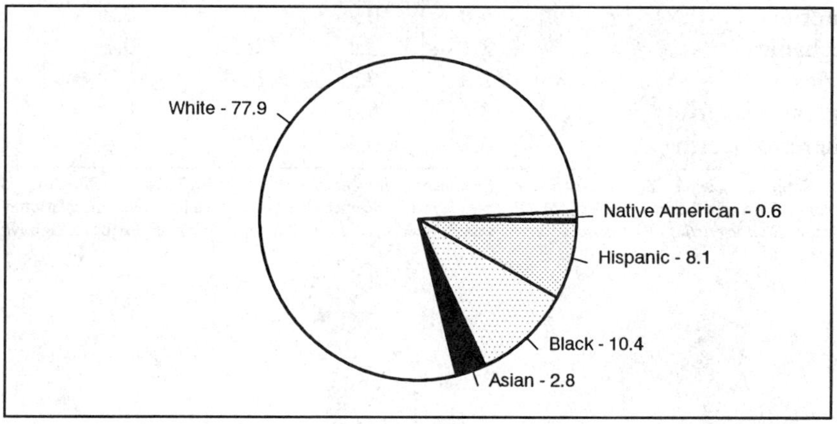

Characteristic	Percent
White	77.9
Black	10.4
Hispanic	8.1
Asian	2.8
Native American	0.6

Source: Usdansky, Margaret L. "A new U.S. workforce evolves: job shifts reflect progress of Hispanics and women." *USA TODAY* (29 January 1993), p. 7A. Primary source: U.S. Census Bureau; Bureau of Labor Statistics; *USA TODAY* analysis of Census data.

★ 519 ★

Employment

Science and Engineering Doctoral Workforce, by Race/Ethnicity and Degree Field, 1991

Data show proportion of the workforce that is made up of each minority, in percent.

	Portion of science & engineering workforce				
	Female	Black	Asian	Native American	Hispanic
Total science and engineering	18.8	2.1	9.8	0.2	1.8
Sciences	21.7	2.2	7.3	0.2	1.8
Physical sciences	8.9	1.1	11.3	0.1	1.7
Mathematics	10.2	1.1	10.7	0.1	2.2
Computer sciences	11.8	0.5	20.3	0.1	1.7
Environmental sciences	9.6	0.2	5.3	0.2	1.0
Life sciences	24.0	1.9	7.8	0.2	1.6
Psychology	38.1	3.1	1.6	0.2	2.0
Social sciences	23.9	4.2	5.6	0.2	2.1
Engineering	3.4	1.2	23.1	0.2	1.9
Aeronautical/astronautical	2.0	1.4	19.3	[1]	1.5
Chemical	3.7	0.8	24.4	[1]	1.2
Civil	3.6	2.4	23.0	0.2	2.0
Electrical/electronic	2.5	1.3	23.3	0.1	1.9
Materials	6.0	0.9	25.2	0.2	3.0
Mechanical	2.1	1.4	26.7	0.1	2.0
Nuclear	2.8	0.3	18.8	[1]	2.8
Systems design	13.4	5.8	15.8	[1]	4.3
Other engineering	3.2	0.3	20.9	0.4	1.5

Source: National Science Board. *Science & Engineering Indicators—1993* (NSB 93-1). Washington, DC: U.S. Government Printing Office, 1993, p. 81. Primary source: Science Resources Studies division, National Science Foundation, *Characteristics of Doctoral Scientists and Engineers: 1991* (Washington, DC: NSF, forthcoming). *Note:* 1. No cases reported.

★ 520 ★

Employment

Work-Related Training Received, Spring 1990

Data show number of persons in thousands, by race/ethnicity.

Characteristic	Total	Race		Hispanic origin[1]
		White	Black	
All persons, 18 to 64	152,815	129,575	17,891	12,463
Persons receiving work training	39,238	33,984	4,241	2,218
Uses training on current or most recent job	26,563	23,595	2,316	1,486

[Continued]

★ 520 ★

Work-Related Training Received, Spring 1990

[Continued]

Characteristic	Total	Race		Hispanic origin[1]
		White	Black	
Location				
Apprenticeship	1,749	1,616	76	114
Business/vo-tech school	10,213	8,659	1,301	537
Community college	4,077	3,722	275	220
Four-year college	2,738	2,488	198	89
High school vo-tech program	2,158	1,875	250	183
Training program at work	13,330	11,774	1,164	598
Military	2,229	1,968	180	139
Correspondence	811	762	31	28
Previous job	1,821	1,636	134	134
Sheltered workshop	392	309	83	5
Vocational rehab center	919	632	275	66
Other	7,598	6,601	780	398
Year of training				
1990	7,348	6,628	564	290
1989	5,207	4,491	575	316
1988	3,364	2,852	432	222
1987	2,666	2,240	337	166
1986	1,801	1,584	157	143
1985 or before	18,852	16,188	2,176	1,081
Program paid for by:				
Self or family	11,540	10,348	914	588
Employer	17,834	16,059	1,379	880
Federal, state, or local government	10,429	8,079	2,010	748
Someone else	1,000	859	99	84
Participated in government sponsored training program[2]	4,479	3,134	1,128	396
Length of training program (average number of weeks)	22	23	21	22

Source: U.S. Bureau of the Census. *What's it Worth? Educational Background and Economic Status: Spring 1990.* Current Population Reports, Series P70-32. Washington DC: U.S. Government Printing Office, 1992, p. 27. *Notes:* 1. Persons of Hispanic origin may be of any race. 2. Includes: Job Training Partnership Act (JTPA), Comprehensive Employment Training Act (CETA), Job Opportunities and Basic Skills (JOBS), Work Incentive Program (WIN), Food Stamps Work Program, Veterans' Training Programs, and other programs sponsored by the Welfare Program and AFDC.

★ 521 ★

Employment

Workers on Flex-Time, 1991

Data are shown in thousands, except percent, as of May for employed persons age 16 years and older who usually work full time and who were at work during the survey reference week. A flexible schedule allows workers to vary the time they begin and end their work day. Figures are based on Current Population Surveys.

Race/ethnicity	All workers			Workers with flexible schedules					
				Number			Percent		
	Total	Male	Female	Total	Male	Female	Total	Male	Female
Total	80,452	46,308	34,145	12,118	7,168	4,950	15.1	15.5	14.5
White	68,795	40,267	28,528	10,630	6,416	4,214	15.5	15.9	14.8
Black	8,943	4,522	4,421	1,083	525	558	12.1	11.6	12.6
Hispanic[1]	6,598	4,172	2,425	702	427	275	10.6	10.2	11.3

Source: 1994 Statistical Abstract of the United States on CD-ROM [machine-readable datafiles]. CD-8A-94. Washington, DC: U.S. Department of Commerce, Economics and Statistics Administration, Bureau of the Census, Data User Services Division, January 1995. Primary source: U.S. Bureau of Labor Statistics, News, USDL 92-491, August 4, 1992; and unpublished data. *Note:* 1. Persons of Hispanic origin may be of any race.

Homelessness

★ 522 ★

Homeless Health Care Recipients, by Race/Ethnicity, 1987

Data show percentages of selected minority patients, based on a total service population of more than 35,000 in 19 cities.

Race/ethnicity	Percent
Black	40.0
Hispanic	11.0
Native American	2.0

Source: Staff Report on Homelessness in the United States, August 1990, p. 16. Prepared by the staff of the U.S. Commission on Security and Cooperation in Europe. Primary source: Health Care for the Homeless centers survey. Only selected minorities are reported here; therefore data do not add to 100.

★ 523 ★

Homelessness

Homeless Population in Major Cities, by Race/ Ethnicity

Data show percentages of selected minority patients, based on a total service population of more than 35,000 in 19 cities.

Race/ethnicity	Percent
Black	40.0
Hispanic	11.0
Native American	2.0

Source: Staff Report on Homelessness in the United States, August 1990, p. 16. Prepared by the staff of the U.S. Commission on Security and Cooperation in Europe. Primary source: Health Care for the Homeless centers survey. Only selected minorities are reported here; therefore data do not add to 100.

★ 524 ★

Homelessness

Homeless Population, by Race/Ethnicity, 1987

As of 1987, an estimated 600,000 people were homeless in the United States. These data show distribution of the homeless by race/ethnicity for each type of family, based on a study of 20 cities.

Race/ethnicity	Men alone	Men with children	Men with adult	Women alone	Women with children	Women with adult
Black	40.0	42.0	24.0	47.0	56.0	29.0
Hispanic	9.0	0.0	15.0	7.0	22.0	0.0
White, not Hispanic	48.0	57.0	56.0	40.0	17.0	66.0
Other	2.0	1.0	5.0	6.0	5.0	6.0

Source: "Counting homelessness." *Social Science and the Citizen* (November/December, 1994), p. 2. The Urban Institute.

Housing

★ 525 ★

Amenities and Deficiencies of Owner-Occupied Housing, 1991

Figures are shown in thousands, by selected housing unit characteristic for selected groups in 1991.

Characteristic	Total occupied units (000)	Housing unit characteristics				Household characteristics				
		New construction 4 yrs.	Mobile homes	Physical problems		Black	Hispanic	Elderly (65+)	Moved in past year	Below poverty level
				Severe	Moderate					
Total units	59,796	3,824	4,532	1,527	2,156	4,635	2,423	15,734	4,204	4,994
Selected amenities[1]										
Porch, deck, balcony or patio	50,333	3,314	3,465	1,231	1,724	3,552	1,927	12,957	3,487	3,899
Not reported	116	9	7	2	3	8	2	37	10	18
Telephone available	58,148	3,696	4,237	1,424	2,015	4,388	2,271	15,381	3,956	4,632
Usable fireplace	24,585	2,234	454	530	455	1,179	743	5,099	1,834	1,106
Separate dining room	32,197	2,249	1,090	727	934	2,483	1,163	7,709	2,244	2,060
With 2 or more living rooms or recreation rooms, etc.	26,213	1,878	637	537	673	1,640	767	5,739	1,778	1,242
Garage or carport included with home	43,555	2,891	1,244	961	1,124	2,443	1,728	11,787	2,942	2,765
Not included	16,207	919	3,286	567	1,032	2,188	690	3,943	1,257	2,229
Offstreet parking included	13,251	863	2,941	476	803	1,576	562	3,051	1,125	1,752
Offstreet parking not reported	65	-	8	4	1	7	-	15	2	6
Garage or carport not reported	34	15	2	-	-	5	5	5	4	-
Cars and trucks available										
No cars, trucks, or vans	2,811	53	240	162	246	624	119	1,955	96	1,008
Other households without cars	3,116	143	389	81	197	145	199	578	223	338
1 car with or without trucks or vans	28,177	1,638	2,615	766	1,085	2,119	1,055	9,373	2,040	2,671
2 cars	19,804	1,602	1,100	409	490	1,342	835	3,326	1,517	805
3 or more cars	5,889	389	187	109	139	405	215	502	328	172
With cars, no trucks or vans	32,144	2,051	2,200	720	927	2,692	1,171	9,900	2,352	2,445
1 truck or van, with or without cars	19,856	1,412	1,633	495	767	1,141	903	3,358	1,403	1,256
2 or more trucks or vans	4,986	309	459	151	216	177	230	521	353	284
Selected deficiencies[1]										
Signs of rats in last 3 months	1,554	62	250	118	413	444	142	400	108	336
Holes in floors	465	6	91	87	229	82	40	111	38	131
Open cracks or holes (interior)	2,016	49	172	190	675	326	136	484	140	369
Broken plaster or peeling paint (interior)	1,808	12	92	165	613	286	114	469	134	354
No electrical wiring	26	10	-	26	-	-	-	4	2	17
Exposed wiring	660	16	49	70	71	78	76	228	47	122
Rooms without electrical outlet	824	24	66	85	94	110	39	272	59	175

Source: U.S. Department of Housing and Urban Development. Office of Policy Development and Research. *Current Housing Reports, American Housing Survey for the United States in 1991,* Washington, DC: U.S. Government Printing Office, April 1993, p. 102. *Notes:* A dash (-) represents zero. 1. Figures may not add to total because more than one category may apply to a unit.

★ 526 ★

Housing

Appliances in Housing Units With a Hispanic Householder, 1991

Numbers are shown in thousands. Data refer to selected equipment that is in working order and for the household's exclusive use. If there are two or more of a specified appliance in the housing unit, the age of the newest is reported.

Characteristics	Total occupied units	Tenure		Housing unit characteristics				Household characteristics		
		Owner	Renter	New construction 4 yrs.	Mobile homes	Physical problems: Severe	Physical problems: Moderate	Elderly (65+)	Moved in past year	Below poverty level
Total	6,239	2,423	3,816	218	208	267	564	669	1,720	1,501
Equipment[1]										
Lacking complete kitchen facilities	117	16	101	2	5	48	58	7	52	38
With complete kitchen (sink, refrigerator and burners)	6,122	2,407	3,716	216	203	219	507	662	1,667	1,463
Kitchen sink	6,168	2,413	3,756	218	208	231	530	662	1,694	1,473
Refrigerator	6,210	2,421	3,790	216	205	249	554	667	1,702	1,489
Less than 5 years old	2,351	983	1,368	166	74	81	173	230	691	514
Age not reported	178	15	163	2	4	6	13	5	94	36
Burners and oven	6,152	2,419	3,733	218	205	222	533	662	1,669	1,471
Less than 5 years old	1,729	750	979	187	45	48	97	154	536	340
Age not reported	225	26	199	4	11	11	8	11	116	67
Burners only	11	3	8	-	2	-	-	-	5	4
Less than 5 years old	5	-	5	-	-	-	-	-	2	2
Age not reported	-	-	-	-	-	-	-	-	-	-
Oven only	11	-	11	-	-	-	11	-	5	-
Less than 5 years old	3	-	3	-	-	-	3	-	3	-
Age not reported	2	-	2	-	-	-	2	-	2	-
Neither burners nor oven	65	-	65	-	-	45	20	7	40	26
Dishwasher	1,990	1,059	931	170	51	46	47	176	562	224
Less than 5 years old	690	378	312	152	22	21	12	50	218	55
Age not reported	94	17	77	5	1	6	3	3	44	16
Washing machine	3,526	2,177	1,349	176	136	117	294	431	620	682
Less than 5 years old	1,545	945	600	127	71	47	123	129	358	290
Age not reported	42	9	33	-	-	3	-	1	21	10
Clothes dryer	2,588	1,765	824	164	87	64	177	301	437	326
Less than 5 years old	1,039	664	375	115	34	29	69	69	262	122
Age not reported	18	7	11	-	-	-	-	1	8	-
Disposal in kitchen sink	2,320	978	1,342	170	26	66	69	206	704	361
Less than 5 years old	918	437	480	158	11	36	29	90	279	121
Age not reported	153	17	137	8	3	5	6	3	78	32
Air conditioning										
Central	2,022	1,043	979	163	78	31	53	205	577	338
1 room unit	1,212	374	838	10	45	62	135	137	305	317
2 room units	407	198	209	3	11	16	71	69	74	86
3 room units or more	146	103	43	2	4	3	36	20	11	20

Source: U.S. Department of Housing and Urban Development. Office of Policy Development and Research. *Current Housing Reports, American Housing Survey for the United States in 1991,* Washington, DC: U.S. Government Printing Office, April 1993, p. 258. *Notes:* A dash (-) represents zero or a percentage which rounds to zero. 1. Figures may not add to total because more than one category may apply to a unit.

★ 527 ★

Housing

Availability of Telephone and Other Items in Selected Spanish-Speaking Countries and the U.S.

Country	Telephones per 100 population,[1] 1987	Daily newspaper circulation, copies per 1,000 population,[2] 1988	Television receivers per 1,000 population,[3] 1989	Radio receivers per 1,000 population,[4] 1989
United States	76.0[5]	259[6]	813.6	2,122
Argentina	11.6	(NA)	219.3	673
Bolivia	2.9[6]	50[5]	98.4	597
Chile	6.5	67	200.6	340
Colombia	8.0	(NA)	108.1	167
Costa Rica	14.7	86	136.1	259
Cuba	5.4	129	203.4	343
Dominican Republic	2.9[8]	42[6]	81.9	168
Ecuador	3.6	64[7]	82.3	314
El Salvador	2.7	45	87.1	403
Guatemala	1.6	(NA)	44.7	64
Honduras	1.2	41	70.3	384
Mexico	9.6[6]	127	126.8	242
Nicaragua	1.6[5]	47[5]	61.4	247
Panama	10.7	69	164.6	222
Paraguay	2.5	(NA)	48.2	169
Peru	3.1[6]	31[10]	94.6	251
Puerto Rico	20.3[6,9]	185	265.7	720
Spain	39.6	82	388.7	304
Uruguay	14.9	(NA)	227.2	600
Venezuela	9.2	186[7]	156.0	432

Source: U.S. Bureau of the Census. *Statistical Abstract of the United States: 1992,* (112th edition). Washington, DC: U.S. Government Printing Ofice, 1992, p. 835. International Telecommunications Union, Geneva, Switzerland, Telecommunication Statistics, and United Nations Educational, Scientific, and Cultural Organization, Paris, France, Statistical Yearbook (copyright); Taiwan, U.S. Bureau of the Census. *Notes:* (NA) stands for not available. 1. As of December 31, except as noted. Comprises public and private telephones installed which can be connected to a central exchange. 2. Publications containing general news and appearing at least 4 times a week, may range in size from a single sheet to 50 or more pages. Circulation data refer to average circulation per issue or number of printed copies per issue and include copies sold outside the country. 3. Estimated number of sets in use. 4. Data cover estimated number of receivers in use, except as noted, and apply to all types of receivers for radio broadcasts to the public, including receivers connected to a radio "redistribution system" but excluding television sets. 5. For 1984. 6. For 1986. 7. For 1982. 8. For 1980. 9. As of March 31. 10. Lima only.

★ 528 ★

Housing

Average Value of Owner-Occupied Housing, by Metro Area, 1990 - I: A-K

Data show total values for owner-occupied housing divided by number of householders in each category. Values are in dollars.

Metropolitan Statistical Area	Avg. value of housing	Avg. value of housing, by race					By Hispanic origin[2]	
		White	Black	American Indian[1]	Asian/ Pacific Islander	Other race	Not Hispanic origin	Hispanic origin
Abilene, TX MSA	54,932	57,489	36,405	46,375	68,483	27,614	57,547	30,769
Albany, GA MSA	67,971	75,130	50,388	52,929	100,096	41,875	68,041	54,483
Albany - Schenectady - Troy, NY MSA	112,731	112,603	97,893	102,363	165,237	106,476	112,731	112,692
Albuquerque, NM MSA	97,686	101,777	80,951	67,359	105,927	73,893	106,292	77,622
Alexandria, LA MSA	60,393	66,128	39,411	47,535	91,958	58,786	60,422	57,321
Allentown - Bethlehem - Easton, PA - NJ MSA	116,736	116,869	97,038	118,313	162,667	77,407	117,137	91,724
Altoona, PA MSA	48,084	48,001	33,586	49,156	143,404	66,286	48,038	70,344
Amarillo, TX MSA	61,952	64,265	35,455	47,267	51,726	36,687	63,698	40,386
Anchorage, AK MSA	120,624	122,136	108,559	97,701	111,298	108,020	120,889	108,543
Anderson, IN MSA	49,472	49,851	40,842	38,500	74,028	43,333	49,499	43,690
Anderson, SC MSA	62,560	64,864	43,525	58,750	95,417	43,214	62,547	67,487
Anniston, AL MSA	56,568	59,382	39,268	50,063	68,704	52,250	56,548	60,965
Appleton - Oshkosh - Neenah, WI MSA	70,453	70,432	87,721	53,521	103,694	66,971	70,471	63,466
Asheville, NC MSA	77,548	79,404	47,884	65,043	83,933	61,731	77,533	81,245
Athens, GA MSA	79,161	83,974	48,479	61,023	110,598	108,900	79,070	93,094
Atlanta, GA MSA	112,264	120,190	71,832	98,017	124,405	96,148	112,231	115,367
Atlantic City, NJ MSA	131,275	136,302	80,612	98,977	129,925	83,205	132,060	94,617
Augusta, GA - SC MSA	74,875	81,732	51,345	64,694	94,609	68,115	74,858	76,708
Austin, TX MSA	94,221	99,596	59,418	86,520	97,985	57,112	98,673	62,683
Bakersfield, CA MSA	95,068	99,544	74,646	85,265	100,239	66,998	99,513	71,503
Baltimore, MD MSA	123,886	132,986	69,611	108,094	162,128	108,418	123,867	126,231
Bangor, ME MSA	88,891	89,035	82,054	57,281	114,476	74,000	88,922	77,095
Baton Rouge, LA MSA	76,146	83,274	52,293	75,596	99,243	69,649	76,087	81,402
Battle Creek, MI MSA	50,887	52,324	34,615	33,412	86,388	33,337	51,026	39,697
Beaumont - Port Arthur, TX MSA	51,436	55,241	35,567	48,238	58,443	37,227	51,732	42,315
Bellingham, WA MSA	111,363	112,140	97,128	70,050	116,130	87,661	111,587	94,730
Benton Harbor, MI MSA	63,557	65,878	36,069	48,955	112,120	51,680	63,619	54,327
Billings, MT MSA	68,982	69,173	59,521	60,589	72,964	48,637	69,203	53,756
Biloxi - Gulfport, MS MSA	64,798	68,275	43,050	66,274	61,528	58,245	64,748	68,994
Binghamton, NY MSA	86,937	86,542	88,228	75,622	133,860	94,286	86,910	92,023
Birmingham, AL MSA	74,893	83,292	43,572	67,322	110,366	67,784	74,844	93,529
Bismarck, ND MSA	66,985	66,863	71,667	62,989	107,476	102,143	66,946	84,394
Bloomington, IN MSA	77,855	77,693	71,478	66,800	109,050	79,063	77,859	77,181
Bloomington - Normal, IL MSA	74,272	74,296	66,035	63,542	108,291	53,060	74,374	59,457
Boise City, ID MSA	81,590	81,742	69,899	75,393	77,475	68,611	81,712	74,955
Boston - Lawrence - Salem, MA - NH CMSA	204,591	204,942	173,117	172,092	226,440	160,402	204,727	188,476
Bradenton, FL MSA	96,563	99,152	52,674	90,660	121,120	68,198	96,702	88,361
Bremerton, WA MSA	114,302	115,649	79,433	88,163	97,874	81,802	114,551	99,914
Brownsville - Harlingen, TX MSA	49,063	51,289	48,856	66,200	74,266	36,348	74,896	40,237
Bryan - College Station, TX MSA	75,976	81,229	42,672	86,429	100,010	46,692	78,236	51,284
Buffalo - Niagara Falls, NY CMSA	81,004	82,357	46,948	54,588	146,294	56,839	81,059	72,992
Burlington, NC MSA	77,078	81,111	51,790	64,146	107,083	76,538	77,082	75,484
Burlington, VT MSA	135,526	135,457	132,371	109,375	154,036	117,969	135,538	133,292
Canton, OH MSA	63,951	64,875	38,762	46,473	135,122	46,142	63,932	66,822
Casper, WY MSA	59,536	59,798	42,253	50,236	59,432	42,451	59,817	47,109
Cedar Rapids, IA MSA	66,964	67,129	51,431	50,357	73,563	52,955	67,013	57,845
Champaign - Urbana - Rantoul, IL MSA	78,669	79,747	55,048	70,735	106,642	70,050	78,655	80,953
Charleston, SC MSA	91,188	100,807	59,404	66,417	85,213	73,030	91,290	79,118
Charleston, WV MSA	65,984	66,211	51,899	61,944	135,493	104,868	65,932	84,865

[Continued]

★ 528 ★

Average Value of Owner-Occupied Housing, by Metro Area, 1990 - I: A-K

[Continued]

Metropolitan Statistical Area	Avg. value of housing	Avg. value of housing, by race					By Hispanic origin[2]	
		White	Black	American Indian[1]	Asian/ Pacific Islander	Other race	Not Hispanic origin	Hispanic origin
Charlotte - Gastonia - Rock Hill, NC - SC MSA	90,413	95,430	55,979	72,089	108,067	83,000	90,396	93,686
Charlottesville, VA MSA	118,189	124,878	61,166	114,643	134,994	132,500	118,185	119,028
Chattanooga, TN - GA MSA	68,819	70,885	46,296	63,900	100,952	71,382	68,816	69,791
Cheyenne, WY MSA	75,787	76,687	64,731	75,877	70,118	57,396	77,125	60,271
Chicago - Gary - Lake County, IL - IN - WI CMSA	128,490	135,569	67,387	99,031	167,363	78,651	130,013	90,197
Chico, CA MSA	108,121	109,233	74,735	81,335	111,385	76,752	108,873	90,059
Cincinnati - Hamilton, OH - KY - IN CMSA	87,556	89,031	60,389	79,991	133,104	105,207	87,507	102,171
Clarksville - Hopkinsville, TN - KY MSA	58,944	61,420	43,452	55,250	72,163	59,794	58,926	60,141
Cleveland - Akron - Lorain, OH CMSA	85,099	88,455	51,009	63,864	126,927	50,593	85,296	65,398
Colorado Springs, CO MSA	95,093	96,705	77,954	75,679	87,232	69,736	96,423	73,553
Columbia, MO MSA	75,696	76,715	48,058	65,938	101,170	64,239	75,728	70,293
Columbia, SC MSA	87,473	95,273	57,603	80,940	101,292	71,357	87,528	80,414
Columbus, GA - AL MSA	66,833	73,564	48,640	55,727	81,541	61,848	66,868	64,409
Columbus, OH MSA	87,150	89,296	58,091	71,922	118,590	77,375	87,157	85,767
Corpus Christi, TX MSA	63,248	67,141	46,112	61,707	79,627	43,131	76,587	45,492
Cumberland, MD - WV MSA	53,348	53,217	40,760	76,833	155,302	74,375	53,304	69,349
Dallas - Fort Worth, TX CMSA	98,491	104,052	61,533	82,293	107,192	57,777	100,807	65,729
Danville, VA MSA	54,153	57,896	40,493	57,500	102,457	52,500	54,157	52,824
Davenport - Rock Island - Moline, IA - IL MSA	56,940	57,360	42,852	45,032	91,986	41,151	57,214	44,934
Dayton - Springfield, OH MSA	76,016	78,548	49,424	63,242	122,664	73,050	75,965	86,732
Daytona Beach, FL MSA	82,311	84,219	50,915	78,108	106,459	67,489	82,461	76,630
Decatur, AL MSA	65,774	67,708	44,796	56,062	100,707	75,000	65,766	68,378
Decatur, IL MSA	53,226	54,310	35,682	54,310	88,773	48,048	53,227	52,875
Denver - Boulder, CO CMSA	104,539	106,559	80,505	86,747	99,781	72,502	106,751	77,327
Des Moines, IA MSA	67,396	68,081	43,152	53,792	70,076	48,404	67,539	53,856
Detroit - Ann Arbor, MI CMSA	85,292	92,621	37,595	63,620	140,754	51,058	85,500	69,256
Dothan, AL MSA	61,429	65,273	40,581	58,793	73,819	60,074	61,372	70,725
Dubuque, IA MSA	59,725	59,700	46,250	44,643	99,500	50,909	59,727	58,967
Duluth, MN - WI MSA	48,131	48,189	45,665	36,995	65,804	61,738	48,139	44,122
Eau Claire, WI MSA	56,768	56,734	73,571	43,548	82,500	54,500	56,754	64,219
El Paso, TX MSA	68,082	70,458	66,179	56,880	78,502	54,844	84,685	56,788
Elkhart - Goshen, IN MSA	70,316	70,949	48,479	54,475	93,212	48,636	70,451	54,772
Elmira, NY MSA	62,147	62,035	51,289	40,263	132,660	47,917	62,146	62,482
Enid, OK MSA	45,696	46,163	29,510	38,376	54,137	29,375	45,837	32,784
Erie, PA MSA	62,789	63,106	41,561	47,195	123,947	42,144	62,843	48,765
Eugene - Springfield, OR MSA	76,085	76,151	77,577	61,886	83,371	64,464	76,159	69,672
Evansville, IN - KY MSA	62,998	63,710	40,538	57,461	102,301	76,855	62,964	74,643
Fargo - Moorhead, ND - MN MSA	70,812	70,794	77,167	59,754	91,929	50,459	70,864	58,344
Fayetteville, NC MSA	71,356	76,395	58,660	54,833	74,049	64,195	71,473	67,520
Fayetteville - Springdale, AR MSA	65,186	65,316	54,246	54,844	75,436	58,281	65,188	65,000
Fitchburg - Leominster, MA MSA	143,704	143,776	129,009	121,964	155,484	134,360	143,798	134,703
Flint, MI MSA	57,597	60,444	40,339	45,986	107,676	43,280	57,743	47,635
Florence, AL MSA	58,591	60,265	42,823	47,356	95,329	59,000	58,563	70,162
Florence, SC MSA	65,784	74,572	43,339	80,735	79,578	62,500	65,774	69,509
Fort Collins - Loveland, CO MSA	95,154	95,502	92,500	78,864	99,385	74,456	95,843	77,288
Fort Myers - Cape Coral, Fl MSA	110,553	112,961	52,753	82,184	139,096	70,332	111,248	83,496
Fort Pierce, FL MSA	115,411	120,047	56,400	77,937	122,186	68,355	116,025	87,960
Fort Smith, AR - OK MSA	54,517	55,846	35,339	41,489	39,833	46,667	54,523	53,632
Fort Walton Beach, FL MSA	85,981	87,625	58,732	67,799	76,543	71,545	86,219	72,919
Fort Wayne, IN MSA	67,898	69,503	40,119	52,437	95,738	43,712	68,085	50,750

[Continued]

★ 528 ★

Average Value of Owner-Occupied Housing, by Metro Area, 1990 - I: A-K

[Continued]

Metropolitan Statistical Area	Avg. value of housing	Avg. value of housing, by race					By Hispanic origin[2]	
		White	Black	American Indian[1]	Asian/ Pacific Islander	Other race	Not Hispanic origin	Hispanic origin
Fresno, CA MSA	99,235	104,476	72,794	85,570	109,431	69,220	106,540	72,686
Gadsden, AL MSA	50,243	52,164	34,218	48,197	78,083	98,214	50,215	65,808
Gainesville, FL MSA	75,870	80,866	46,025	59,367	95,740	65,262	75,799	79,352
Glens Falls, NY MSA	95,619	95,546	87,458	69,000	156,400	82,857	95,650	88,923
Grand Forks, ND MSA	66,536	66,609	63,293	47,542	76,429	46,269	66,600	55,704
Grand Rapids, MI MSA	80,236	81,561	49,072	59,486	87,404	49,712	80,619	56,525
Great Falls, MT MSA	65,260	65,449	63,086	49,322	66,767	49,887	65,317	57,838
Greeley, CO MSA	75,665	76,542	79,635	70,548	81,077	57,459	78,307	57,182
Green Bay, WI MSA	70,032	70,097	73,085	53,317	97,630	56,379	70,072	54,741
Greensboro - Winston-Salem - High Point, NC MSA	85,757	89,426	59,676	68,549	106,916	89,357	85,736	91,118
Greenville - Spartanburg, SC MSA	72,939	76,113	45,997	68,487	93,314	61,689	72,947	71,081
Hagerstown, MD MSA	92,544	92,656	67,807	93,000	128,801	90,250	92,517	102,717
Harrisburg - Lebanon - Carlisle, PA MSA	83,450	84,898	50,702	66,471	102,632	51,168	83,581	64,748
Hartford - New Britain - Middletown, CT CMSA	187,648	188,791	155,008	168,762	204,313	157,425	187,887	171,144
Hickory - Morganton, NC MSA	70,021	71,433	46,176	56,222	74,133	54,659	70,045	62,090
Honolulu, HI MSA	312,624	354,788	273,876	273,192	299,261	254,134	314,309	266,990
Houma - Thibodaux, LA MSA	59,621	61,604	44,549	35,215	83,622	53,423	59,594	61,868
Houston - Galveston - Brazoria, TX CMSA	83,108	91,169	49,516	69,104	87,456	47,543	86,715	53,850
Huntington - Ashland, WV - KY - OH MSA	53,686	53,776	40,391	52,830	114,323	90,464	53,628	85,668
Huntsville, AL MSA	90,667	94,405	63,221	85,728	120,074	78,208	90,656	92,037
Indianapolis, IN MSA	79,512	82,420	49,408	64,725	109,021	62,929	79,541	74,325
Iowa City, IA MSA	90,260	90,008	101,201	74,393	108,143	64,500	90,219	95,440
Jackson, MI MSA	56,312	57,209	34,151	45,767	96,743	37,832	56,426	44,183
Jackson, MS MSA	71,266	82,271	46,145	67,533	98,480	57,436	71,260	72,946
Jackson, TN MSA	61,619	68,298	38,235	48,636	71,019	122,000	61,647	51,867
Jacksonville, FL MSA	83,310	90,137	46,793	71,552	90,289	73,951	83,281	84,904
Jacksonville, NC MSA	69,263	71,314	56,792	73,280	68,466	65,537	69,284	68,367
Jamestown - Dunkirk, NY	56,307	56,455	37,373	44,608	100,921	33,693	56,464	40,396
Janesville - Beloit, WI MSA	57,198	57,635	39,852	49,038	61,745	42,562	57,235	50,611
Johnson City - Kingsport - Bristol, TN - VA MSA	60,322	60,525	43,978	55,679	95,802	70,000	60,289	76,344
Johnstown, PA MSA	47,674	47,699	29,983	40,975	122,993	52,524	47,691	42,060
Joplin, MO MSA	47,611	47,843	30,575	38,027	77,788	48,672	47,614	46,860
Kalamazoo, MI MSA	72,791	74,098	45,406	55,004	110,474	49,364	72,900	61,594
Kankakee, IL MSA	61,764	63,601	39,347	56,667	123,110	48,878	61,746	63,759
Kansas City, MO - KS MSA	77,682	81,113	44,630	64,029	93,923	51,217	78,044	59,329
Killeen - Temple, TX MSA	63,189	65,322	53,622	58,830	65,743	45,745	64,436	50,155
Knoxville, TN MSA	71,479	72,344	49,099	57,745	108,717	79,432	71,453	79,337
Kokomo, IN MSA	58,865	59,246	45,964	56,313	97,331	49,341	58,924	50,623

Source: U.S. Bureau of the Census. *1990 Census of Population and Housing, Summary Tape File 1C on CD-ROM, United States Summary*. February, 1992. *Notes:* 1. Includes Eskimos and Aleuts. 2. Hispanics may be of any race.

★ 529 ★

Housing

Average Value of Owner-Occupied Housing, by Metro Area, 1990 - II: L-Y

Data show total values for owner-occupied housing divided by number of householders in each category. Values are in dollars.

Metropolitan Statistical Area	Avg. value of housing	Avg. value of housing by race					By Hispanic origin[2]	
		White	Black	American Indian[1]	Asian/ Pacific Islander	Other race	Not Hispanic origin	Hispanic origin
La Crosse, WI MSA	65,309	65,225	88,036	62,712	86,708	60,833	65,275	77,806
Lafayette, LA MSA	69,193	74,961	44,664	60,857	79,708	56,925	69,146	73,232
Lafayette - West Lafayette, IN MSA	77,293	76,941	70,630	68,286	119,148	58,444	77,398	62,715
Lake Charles, LA MSA	62,982	67,049	44,630	52,046	95,127	59,589	62,996	61,201
Lakeland - Winter Haven, FL MSA	72,592	75,867	43,760	54,783	88,468	53,835	72,647	70,084
Lancaster, PA MSA	100,721	101,401	65,268	86,810	100,083	59,946	101,124	70,048
Lansing - East Lansing, MI MSA	73,203	73,753	63,292	57,660	109,091	49,985	73,665	54,875
Laredo, TX MSA	60,551	64,515	61,667	48,194	118,113	48,197	105,684	56,711
Las Cruces, NM MSA	77,223	78,295	69,718	70,981	90,322	57,382	91,917	59,190
Las Vegas, NV MSA	111,010	113,930	83,035	93,298	105,437	85,506	112,239	93,594
Lawrence, KS MSA	77,619	78,242	58,066	62,800	98,267	66,007	77,643	76,083
Lawton, OK MSA	59,604	60,806	55,250	48,041	61,910	52,487	59,788	55,238
Lewiston - Auburn, ME MSA	94,404	94,376	105,469	87,361	107,786	82,885	94,434	86,852
Lexington-Fayette, KY MSA	85,359	88,220	49,033	68,220	121,163	75,093	85,330	91,774
Lima, OH MSA	60,254	61,151	38,695	56,403	111,033	50,745	60,279	55,351
Lincoln, NE MSA	70,669	70,800	55,729	63,178	85,415	52,025	70,803	57,982
Little Rock - North Little Rock, AR MSA	70,425	74,639	44,842	62,302	81,720	65,859	70,421	71,221
Longview - Marshall, TX MSA	59,608	64,934	37,013	49,783	82,592	33,962	59,822	42,286
Los Angeles - Anaheim - Riverside, CA CMSA	249,528	261,734	169,181	196,940	270,502	171,953	262,478	186,700
Louisville, KY - IN MSA	69,439	71,887	40,591	55,639	115,202	65,279	69,396	80,161
Lubbock, TX MSA	63,117	66,857	37,411	60,188	101,475	36,414	67,652	37,867
Lynchburg, VA MSA	65,791	70,809	40,479	49,318	87,619	71,618	65,801	62,995
Macon - Warner Robins, GA MSA	68,889	75,102	47,973	60,488	92,556	72,538	68,885	69,515
Madison, WI MSA	89,819	89,845	80,788	83,753	102,524	73,395	89,837	86,577
Manchester, NH MSA	142,387	142,346	125,297	141,848	160,360	132,500	142,469	127,233
Mansfield, OH MSA	57,786	58,812	35,720	44,132	123,893	42,231	57,807	52,098
Mcallen - Edinburg - Mission, TX MSA	45,363	47,554	52,465	52,031	91,197	37,001	75,100	38,558
Medford, OR MSA	89,729	89,892	92,115	81,484	88,824	68,951	89,899	79,135
Melbourne - Titusville - Palm Bay, FL MSA	94,901	96,693	62,242	88,938	109,915	77,651	94,976	91,611
Memphis, TN - AR - MS MSA	80,477	92,944	48,993	75,833	108,944	72,594	80,441	88,963
Merced, CA MSA	103,091	107,113	86,101	88,282	106,431	79,411	108,524	82,626
Miami - Fort Lauderdale, FL CMSA	115,063	123,557	69,151	89,415	116,548	90,154	118,589	105,438
Midland, TX MSA	73,947	78,848	37,694	78,636	84,514	37,766	79,236	38,838
Milwaukee - Racine, WI CMSA	87,832	89,982	47,806	64,233	116,825	53,404	88,235	61,855
Minneapolis - St. Paul, MN - WI MSA	103,387	103,804	81,179	77,398	110,348	80,045	103,495	89,421
Mobile, AL MSA	66,830	73,226	42,789	53,091	75,361	54,173	66,825	67,548
Modesto, CA MSA	136,744	138,768	134,099	124,339	149,695	107,359	140,413	113,722
Monroe, LA MSA	62,426	69,272	38,347	59,500	79,462	41,786	62,453	57,606
Montgomery, AL MSA	72,962	81,880	47,015	64,554	95,038	74,235	72,959	73,609
Muncie, IN MSA	50,052	50,841	31,190	39,380	81,411	41,818	50,090	41,221
Muskegon, MI MSA	53,597	55,657	33,490	38,804	100,990	36,857	53,772	40,030
Naples, FL MSA	172,501	175,909	61,420	81,538	147,227	69,548	177,624	86,840
Nashville, TN MSA	94,334	97,885	63,560	83,710	103,541	85,491	94,328	95,763
New Bedford, MA MSA	149,703	150,690	120,902	109,000	179,478	121,858	149,901	131,353
New Haven - Meriden, CT MSA	196,482	198,523	147,269	175,582	220,572	149,889	196,971	165,223
New London - Norwich, CT - RI MSA	170,920	171,756	134,667	149,242	167,024	143,363	171,121	152,472
New Orleans, LA MSA	84,618	91,643	60,008	68,053	87,241	71,442	84,775	80,151
New York - Northern New Jersey - Long Island, NY - NJ - CT CMSA	223,746	228,375	161,223	175,381	247,298	173,170	224,937	191,564
Norfolk - Virginia Beach - Newport News, VA MSA	102,970	110,888	71,060	90,829	110,748	89,673	103,033	98,238
Ocala, FL MSA	71,973	74,154	50,047	66,848	111,157	66,070	72,002	70,811
Odessa, TX MSA	51,093	54,260	36,687	49,355	79,452	31,373	55,853	33,041
Oklahoma City, OK MSA	64,349	66,019	49,756	53,673	69,294	44,661	64,595	50,989
Olympia, WA MSA	92,286	92,847	84,181	74,916	87,514	78,000	92,449	84,221
Omaha, NE - IA MSA	67,891	69,391	41,714	54,982	78,488	50,073	68,130	53,785
Orlando, FL MSA	103,028	106,681	67,149	91,606	114,820	83,919	103,859	91,061

[Continued]

★ 529 ★

Average Value of Owner-Occupied Housing, by Metro Area, 1990 - II: L-Y

[Continued]

Metropolitan Statistical Area	Avg. value of housing	Avg. value of housing by race					By Hispanic origin[2]	
		White	Black	American Indian[1]	Asian/ Pacific Islander	Other race	Not Hispanic origin	Hispanic origin
Owensboro, KY MSA	57,143	57,681	32,418	35,737	106,286	55,417	57,134	60,951
Panama City, FL MSA	74,017	76,514	44,173	63,205	81,184	60,909	74,078	68,521
Parkersburg - Marietta, WV - OH MSA	57,207	57,080	50,951	42,838	137,840	54,889	57,150	88,474
Pascagoula, MS MSA	60,406	63,604	43,836	52,825	63,913	59,479	60,377	63,968
Pensacola, FL MSA	71,098	74,855	44,439	56,786	70,593	62,797	71,106	70,524
Peoria, IL MSA	59,424	59,876	41,997	44,536	91,625	39,888	59,489	49,156
Philadelphia - Wilmington - Trenton, PA - NJ - DE - MD CMSA	122,258	133,568	54,706	86,588	154,247	49,629	123,159	74,513
Phoenix, AZ MSA	103,487	106,122	75,609	69,339	110,770	65,379	106,764	71,034
Pine Bluff, AR MSA	50,077	57,180	36,166	45,313	81,667	44,318	50,099	42,344
Pittsburgh - Beaver Valley, PA CMSA	66,661	67,510	42,031	57,924	136,625	64,045	66,642	71,437
Pittsfield, MA MSA	133,900	134,139	104,034	114,286	159,884	108,042	133,803	158,203
Portland, ME MSA	139,312	139,458	117,868	115,116	121,522	129,231	139,312	139,246
Portland - Vancouver, OR - WA CMSA	87,100	87,897	57,442	70,445	84,015	67,058	87,259	75,727
Portsmouth - Dover - Rochester, NH - ME MSA	154,747	154,840	137,128	120,951	158,176	152,237	154,746	154,951
Poughkeepsie, NY MSA	161,658	161,605	140,830	136,368	200,584	154,105	161,720	158,025
Providence - Pawtucket - Fall River, RI - MA CMSA	150,788	151,297	115,481	125,941	153,056	119,362	150,950	132,612
Provo - Orem, UT MSA	81,623	81,771	75,417	69,321	77,568	64,442	81,839	67,473
Pueblo, CO MSA	57,293	58,462	48,291	49,907	79,630	45,907	61,254	46,874
Raleigh - Durham, NC MSA	111,165	118,501	70,603	100,120	137,680	101,764	111,149	113,953
Rapid City, SD MSA	63,609	64,027	61,094	43,426	67,586	51,693	63,714	54,226
Reading, PA MSA	90,917	91,844	48,992	78,860	116,629	43,038	91,455	52,045
Redding, CA MSA	104,712	104,945	99,305	87,818	138,197	84,630	104,870	98,568
Reno, NV MSA	137,212	139,254	102,843	85,262	115,165	106,086	138,009	117,202
Richland - Kennewick - Pasco, WA MSA	70,788	71,471	61,427	59,278	88,497	46,670	71,684	50,746
Richmond - Petersburg, VA MSA	95,497	104,158	62,329	75,958	113,449	83,586	95,513	92,981
Roanoke, VA MSA	79,097	81,918	47,038	69,459	110,319	68,241	79,110	75,242
Rochester, MN MSA	85,072	84,936	88,786	64,063	97,947	75,565	85,040	91,327
Rochester, NY MSA	98,400	99,581	70,790	80,321	127,715	65,844	98,621	79,667
Rockford, IL MSA	70,004	71,276	43,093	59,332	89,271	48,793	70,271	53,850
Sacramento, CA MSA	157,753	161,702	115,434	131,399	156,416	113,011	160,273	126,504
Saginaw - Bay City - Midland, MI MSA	57,448	59,175	35,214	49,093	119,476	35,183	57,965	40,698
St. Cloud, MN MSA	69,442	69,394	78,471	71,229	85,750	69,457	69,433	73,269
St. Joseph, MO MSA	48,652	49,077	26,702	33,073	78,342	43,592	48,720	44,600
St. Louis, MO - IL MSA	86,873	90,727	50,123	70,461	149,128	74,552	86,885	85,285
Salem, OR MSA	68,297	68,679	64,256	55,938	66,359	50,582	68,688	54,925
Salinas - Seaside - Monterey, CA MSA	241,836	260,246	165,537	186,799	198,484	140,417	258,485	157,050
Salt Lake City - Ogden, UT MSA	83,240	83,914	64,286	64,460	76,415	58,984	84,040	62,606
San Angelo, TX MSA	58,553	61,789	43,893	55,000	66,787	34,692	63,736	37,209
San Antonio, TX MSA	71,214	76,175	53,632	63,591	80,627	45,099	85,044	49,657
San Diego, CA MSA	224,048	231,999	144,817	169,782	206,688	153,798	229,893	172,117
San Francisco - Oakland - San Jose, CA CMSA	286,393	296,303	185,111	230,953	287,012	211,760	291,516	231,737
Santa Barbara - Santa Maria - Lompoc, CA MSA	280,478	290,974	192,932	215,955	219,763	184,501	292,071	207,078
Santa Fe, NM MSA	143,132	148,524	124,286	97,496	149,303	102,542	161,942	108,654
Sarasota, FL MSA	117,880	119,326	58,954	99,518	147,817	91,560	118,094	102,811
Savannah, GA MSA	80,941	92,286	48,572	80,269	98,040	72,885	80,874	89,801
Scranton - Wilkes-Barre, PA MSA	79,166	78,934	96,180	71,226	137,588	102,427	79,048	107,309
Seattle - Tacoma, WA CMSA	150,916	152,722	110,661	114,124	147,027	121,409	151,213	132,285
Sharon, PA MSA	47,768	48,354	27,093	42,208	110,128	40,000	47,787	38,843
Sheboygan, WI MSA	66,447	66,456	57,500	58,667	82,969	44,621	66,511	54,114
Sherman - Denison, TX MSA	55,591	56,923	33,832	42,994	109,375	41,597	55,619	53,516
Shreveport, LA MSA	66,209	75,050	40,100	58,298	89,610	60,886	66,254	61,457
Sioux City, IA - NE MSA	48,541	48,733	34,252	36,089	50,904	37,233	48,660	36,924
Sioux Falls, SD MSA	66,293	66,330	48,380	48,580	80,804	71,042	66,283	70,702
South Bend - Mishawaka, IN MSA	61,762	63,411	36,876	53,559	93,636	36,949	61,939	44,930
Spokane, WA MSA	68,272	68,507	56,255	55,790	65,517	59,139	68,335	62,382
Springfield, IL MSA	70,297	70,940	48,272	52,331	115,603	96,121	70,268	76,693

[Continued]

★ 529 ★

Average Value of Owner-Occupied Housing, by Metro Area, 1990 - II: L-Y

[Continued]

Metropolitan Statistical Area	Avg. value of housing	Avg. value of housing by race					By Hispanic origin[2]	
		White	Black	American Indian[1]	Asian/ Pacific Islander	Other race	Not Hispanic origin	Hispanic origin
Springfield, MA MSA	138,675	139,591	108,525	117,190	177,095	109,231	138,960	118,706
Springfield, MO MSA	67,205	67,454	42,803	55,840	79,446	58,654	67,230	61,595
State College, PA MSA	85,720	85,242	105,978	76,188	127,456	121,765	85,673	97,208
Steubenville - Weirton, OH - WV MSA	48,578	48,811	36,670	40,309	105,515	49,433	48,550	56,977
Stockton, CA MSA	135,986	140,674	99,897	120,358	125,547	101,927	140,736	107,942
Syracuse, NY MSA	87,161	87,477	67,096	72,081	125,425	78,046	87,184	83,150
Tallahassee, FL MSA	83,379	92,067	50,255	73,173	107,143	81,306	83,328	87,390
Tampa - St. Petersburg - Clearwater, FL MSA	88,560	90,777	54,259	77,022	104,776	70,415	89,018	80,508
Terre Haute, IN MSA	46,986	47,279	29,582	39,250	106,555	67,188	46,958	56,904
Texarkana, TX - Texarkana, AR MSA	53,910	57,861	35,880	47,424	82,676	40,716	53,934	49,390
Toledo, OH MSA	71,701	74,019	41,412	57,019	126,995	42,867	72,176	48,060
Topeka, KS MSA	63,845	65,175	44,622	50,757	98,019	46,123	64,464	47,687
Tucson, AZ MSA	93,196	98,190	69,877	41,960	98,824	60,846	99,040	66,211
Tulsa, OK MSA	69,975	72,607	43,535	53,935	87,040	55,037	70,055	62,906
Tuscaloosa, AL MSA	70,664	76,456	46,865	66,797	99,218	78,462	70,644	77,019
Tyler, TX MSA	71,699	78,784	40,923	55,235	86,571	35,132	72,453	40,502
Utica - Rome, NY MSA	76,456	76,498	58,457	62,224	120,404	67,361	76,443	79,179
Victoria, TX MSA	62,832	66,454	38,950	57,732	109,578	38,968	69,087	42,644
Visalia - Tulare - Porterville, CA MSA	87,483	93,354	66,337	65,690	89,264	63,063	94,731	64,988
Waco, TX MSA	60,362	64,418	36,850	57,875	80,890	35,102	62,276	37,059
Washington, DC - MD - VA MSA	200,545	216,545	129,464	170,216	218,375	156,998	200,790	190,795
Waterbury, CT MSA	165,633	166,542	129,249	165,000	193,246	129,833	165,982	144,942
Waterloo - Cedar Falls, IA MSA	50,781	51,289	35,039	44,958	89,598	40,227	50,789	48,679
Wausau, WI MSA	60,809	60,772	53,000	61,894	75,482	59,000	60,821	54,524
West Palm Beach - Boca Raton - Delray Beach, FL MSA	138,092	143,793	69,416	100,890	135,912	84,844	139,826	105,792
Wheeling, WV - OH MSA	50,601	50,666	33,826	43,250	117,006	48,167	50,592	53,509
Wichita, KS MSA	66,438	67,779	45,863	52,572	73,408	47,230	66,760	52,547
Wichita Falls, TX MSA	55,440	57,619	34,061	44,346	63,909	34,848	56,462	38,134
Williamsport, PA MSA	62,048	62,080	38,366	54,464	125,833	49,167	62,032	67,579
Wilmington, NC MSA	91,859	98,956	49,920	68,613	104,387	78,688	91,871	89,252
Worcester, MA MSA	155,128	154,854	152,646	139,941	191,233	134,025	155,167	148,364
Yakima, WA MSA	62,930	65,989	49,518	49,712	60,950	39,151	65,795	40,552
York, PA MSA	87,627	88,172	51,591	84,548	102,259	60,836	87,680	77,333
Youngstown - Warren, OH MSA	57,831	59,788	32,994	40,848	146,068	32,330	57,992	42,717
Yuba City, CA MSA	93,531	94,866	84,155	76,215	96,282	72,612	94,849	77,995
Yuma, AZ MSA	71,871	75,157	56,531	53,731	90,964	54,572	79,465	55,967

Source: U.S. Bureau of the Census. *1990 Census of Population and Housing, Summary Tape File 1C on CD-ROM, United States Summary*. February, 1992. *Notes:* 1. Includes Eskimos and Aleuts. 2. Hispanics may be of any race.

★ 530 ★

Housing

Average Value of Owner-Occupied Housing, by State, 1990

Data show total values for owner-occupied housing divided by number of householders in each category. Values are shown in dollars.

State	Avg. value of housing	Avg.value of housing by race					By Hispanic origin[2]	
		White	Black	American Indian[1]	Asian/ Pacific Islander	Other race	Not Hispanic origin	Hispanic origin
United States	111,667	113,710	68,572	72,389	209,725	99,818	111,822	108,359
Alabama	64,794	70,125	42,133	54,994	99,121	64,342	64,763	73,011
Alaska	103,739	109,037	103,969	71,973	107,771	101,569	103,781	101,049
Arizona	96,372	100,881	72,755	41,557	106,684	61,444	100,622	65,697
Arkansas	55,138	57,874	35,183	49,558	62,044	48,338	55,141	54,241
California	232,345	240,136	164,284	165,316	258,300	156,919	241,247	175,463
Colorado	95,760	97,372	79,300	74,227	96,517	63,632	98,522	66,072
Connecticut	213,726	215,297	162,700	174,761	240,643	162,386	214,127	188,932
Delaware	120,923	126,064	74,956	92,107	175,642	81,988	121,121	103,894
D.C.	194,317	343,177	118,767	170,047	266,684	168,054	193,819	223,375
Florida	99,224	103,646	58,045	74,636	109,991	82,183	99,225	99,220
Georgia	88,222	95,311	55,680	78,523	115,125	83,635	88,135	98,549
Hawaii	272,857	302,266	258,160	226,611	261,664	216,946	274,904	226,370
Idaho	67,478	67,898	61,452	53,350	68,678	43,083	67,917	50,403
Illinois	103,582	106,006	65,203	79,990	161,566	78,424	103,955	89,490
Indiana	63,940	65,014	43,620	52,166	107,054	47,757	64,053	53,978
Iowa	52,442	52,507	42,059	41,497	74,859	42,053	52,471	47,939
Kansas	62,395	63,226	45,015	47,938	87,623	42,850	62,692	48,810
Kentucky	60,536	61,539	39,670	52,355	109,699	64,452	60,504	70,357
Louisiana	67,775	73,812	46,682	50,949	86,614	64,923	67,678	73,387
Maine	102,743	102,834	102,340	65,827	111,793	96,483	102,734	106,070
Maryland	142,451	149,860	96,477	127,259	197,263	136,551	142,208	159,864
Massachusetts	186,836	187,160	157,211	155,833	220,115	139,772	186,992	168,933
Michigan	73,927	77,464	38,481	51,822	130,038	46,221	74,130	58,916
Minnesota	83,781	83,825	80,408	55,831	106,204	71,985	83,800	80,526
Mississippi	54,735	60,930	38,182	39,988	75,000	55,586	54,717	59,062
Missouri	72,086	73,739	48,657	54,309	123,561	57,474	72,113	68,790
Montana	61,623	62,146	61,571	44,751	64,500	47,277	61,704	51,647
Nebraska	56,707	57,088	42,521	43,837	75,114	41,521	56,860	45,539
Nevada	115,896	118,762	84,217	73,929	107,776	86,814	117,102	95,979
New Hampshire	143,282	143,195	145,158	115,957	165,399	139,088	143,277	144,270
New Jersey	185,294	189,186	119,405	132,853	232,622	125,537	185,965	161,894
New Mexico	82,171	86,859	65,632	47,882	99,256	63,876	89,323	66,946
New York	158,315	157,928	144,396	105,711	228,622	160,400	157,845	176,337
North Carolina	79,714	84,696	52,016	51,454	108,019	71,236	79,707	81,154
North Dakota	53,875	53,998	61,053	40,725	89,678	55,361	53,867	57,081
Ohio	74,966	76,518	50,409	60,387	124,544	50,368	75,056	63,169
Oklahoma	57,240	58,966	43,399	43,865	72,296	40,142	57,382	47,539
Oregon	79,097	79,553	57,621	61,825	81,554	55,540	79,313	65,527
Pennsylvania	88,027	90,918	45,235	71,445	133,951	45,452	88,212	68,079
Rhode Island	153,669	154,332	116,022	125,969	152,865	117,851	153,857	133,161
South Carolina	74,764	81,993	47,823	60,026	91,283	67,318	74,759	75,809

[Continued]

★ 530 ★

Average Value of Owner-Occupied Housing, by State, 1990

[Continued]

State	Avg. value of housing	Avg.value of housing by race					By Hispanic origin[2]	
		White	Black	American Indian[1]	Asian/ Pacific Islander	Other race	Not Hispanic origin	Hispanic origin
South Dakota	49,887	50,189	53,072	32,950	75,392	47,825	49,882	51,398
Tennessee	70,769	73,390	49,567	63,281	103,054	72,585	70,741	78,247
Texas	74,451	79,352	48,560	64,305	91,516	43,642	80,126	47,492
Utah	79,953	80,568	64,446	43,751	76,020	58,152	80,544	61,584
Vermont	110,424	110,379	122,274	82,510	139,633	98,882	110,413	112,844
Virginia	122,603	129,372	70,322	112,604	183,123	137,373	122,221	154,634
Washington	119,679	120,299	103,701	82,362	135,953	69,330	120,249	90,952
West Virginia	55,073	55,330	39,203	49,692	127,326	66,588	55,049	61,557
Wisconsin	71,819	72,245	49,007	50,392	105,047	54,130	71,896	61,863
Wyoming	67,724	68,164	58,697	51,873	71,140	53,119	68,241	55,503

Source: U.S. Bureau of the Census. *1990 Census of Population and Housing, Summary Tape File 1C on CD-ROM, United States Summary.* February, 1992. *Notes:* 1. Includes Eskimos and Aleuts. 2. Hispanics may be of any race.

★ 531 ★

Housing

Costs of Utilities per Month in Housing Units With a Hispanic Householder, 1991

Data show number of persons (in thousands) in each dollar range of utilities costs.

Characteristics	Total occupied units	Tenure		Housing unit characteristics				Household characteristics		
		Owner	Renter	New construction 4 yrs.	Mobile homes	Physical problems: Severe	Physical problems: Moderate	Elderly (65+)	Moved in past year	Below poverty level
Total	6,239	2,423	3,816	218	208	267	564	669	1,720	1,501
Monthly cost paid for electricity										
Electricity used	6,239	2,423	3,816	218	208	267	564	669	1,720	1,501
Less than $25	1,035	257	778	17	16	46	104	148	286	295
$25 to $49	2,057	789	1,269	66	71	73	207	223	563	520
$50 to $74	1,032	515	517	65	50	3	75	105	278	203
$75 to $99	430	258	172	31	16	8	29	38	123	59
$100 to $149	370	248	122	19	14	9	12	24	69	39
$150 to $199	85	55	29	2	3	2	2	15	27	16
$200 or more	41	37	4	2	-	-	2	2	7	2
Median	43	52	38	57	49	39	39	40	42	38
Included in rent, other fee, or obtained free	1,189	265	925	16	38	96	134	114	366	368
Monthly cost paid for piped gas										
Piped gas used	4,779	1,838	2,941	115	105	222	509	503	1,226	1,213
Less than $25	1,999	754	1,246	50	42	86	222	207	468	492
$25 to $49	1,117	566	551	35	20	34	125	118	295	243
$50 to $74	317	152	165	8	14	17	27	31	99	87
$75 to $99	125	82	44	3	1	5	3	24	16	20
$100 to $149	52	29	23	-	-	4	-	14	8	7
$150 to $199	15	13	2	-	-	-	-	-	-	1
$200 or more	30	21	9	-	-	-	8	4	2	8
Median	-25	27	-25	-25	-25	-25	-25	-25	-25	-25

[Continued]

★ 531 ★

Costs of Utilities per Month in Housing Units With a Hispanic Householder, 1991

[Continued]

Characteristics	Total occupied units	Tenure		Housing unit characteristics				Household characteristics		
		Owner	Renter	New construction 4 yrs.	Mobile homes	Physical problems: Severe	Physical problems: Moderate	Elderly (65+)	Moved in past year	Below poverty level
Included in rent, other fee, or obtained free	1,122	220	902	19	28	75	125	105	337	356
Average monthly cost paid for fuel oil										
Fuel oil used	837	170	666	8	4	75	75	87	169	240
Less than $25	71	28	43	5	-	15	4	13	13	7
$25 to $49	66	19	47	-	-	3	2	9	14	20
$50 to $74	34	15	19	2	3	1	-	2	8	2
$75 to $99	37	25	11	-	-	-	2	13	2	5
$100 to $149	46	33	13	-	-	-	-	8	3	2
$150 to $199	8	6	2	-	-	-	-	2	2	-
$200 or more	13	11	2	-	-	-	-	2	1	-
Median	50	81	39	...	...	-25	-25	76	41	39
Included in rent, other fee, or obtained free	562	33	529	1	2	55	67	39	125	204
Monthly costs paid for selected utilities and fuels										
Water paid separately	2,159	1,587	571	95	69	72	204	303	361	357
Median	24	24	22	24	24	24	23	20	24	21
Trash paid separately	1,505	1,064	441	75	45	44	150	195	275	280
Median	14	15	13	17	...	...	-10	15	13	-10
Bottled gas paid separately	201	130	70	8	60	20	17	30	25	46
Median	43	46	26	...	46	...	...	...	...	...
Other fuel paid separately	504	291	213	28	24	7	37	53	132	98
Median	12	11	13	...	...	...	...	18	-10	19

Source: U.S. Department of Housing and Urban Development. Office of Policy Development and Research. *Current Housing Reports, American Housing Survey for the United States in 1991,* Washington, DC: U.S. Government Printing Office, April 1993, p. 278-280. *Notes:* Three dots (...) means not applicable or that the sample was too small. A dash (-) represents zero or a percentage which rounds to zero.

★ 532 ★

Housing

First-Time Owners, Purchase Price, and Major Source of Down Payment in Homes With Hispanic Owners, 1991

Data show number of persons (in thousands) in each category.

Characteristics	Total occupied units	Tenure		Housing unit characteristics				Household characteristics		
		Owner	Renter	New construction 4 yrs.	Mobile homes	Physical problems: Severe	Physical problems: Moderate	Elderly (65+)	Moved in past year	Below poverty level
First-time owners[1]										
First time ever owned	1,331	1,331	...	46	85	42	123	156	90	199
Not first home	997	997	...	76	60	16	70	219	128	91
Not reported	95	95	...	4	10	4	4	19	14	22
Purchase price[2]										
Home purchased or built	2,299	2,299	...	123	144	54	180	373	220	278
Less than $10,000	237	237	...	-	62	13	44	77	24	63
$10,000 to $19,999	336	336	...	5	40	9	48	89	4	54
$20,000 to $29,999	213	213	...	5	19	11	13	35	12	23

[Continued]

★ 532 ★

First-Time Owners, Purchase Price, and Major Source of Down Payment in Homes With Hispanic Owners, 1991

[Continued]

Characteristics	Total occupied units	Tenure		Housing unit characteristics				Household characteristics		
		Owner	Renter	New construction 4 yrs.	Mobile homes	Physical problems: Severe	Physical problems: Moderate	Elderly (65+)	Moved in past year	Below poverty level
$30,000 to $39,999	187	187	...	2	5	2	19	22	23	19
$40,000 to $49,999	190	190	...	8	9	4	7	20	4	14
$50,000 to $59,999	149	149	...	9	6	2	8	14	16	15
$60,000 to $69,999	159	159	...	9	-	3	2	12	20	12
$70,000 to $79,999	122	122	...	10	-	-	-	9	13	10
$80,000 to $99,999	141	141	...	14	-	5	2	15	10	5
$100,000 to $119,999	78	78	...	3	-	-	2	3	10	-
$120,000 to $149,999	108	108	...	15	-	2	5	7	16	4
$150,000 to $199,999	95	95	...	18	-	2	-	10	31	2
$200,000 to $249,999	36	36	...	8	-	-	-	2	4	-
$250,000 to $299,999	32	32	...	7	-	-	7	2	18	-
$300,000 or more	25	25	...	6	-	2	2	-	10	2
Not reported	196	196	...	3	4	-	19	56	6	53
Median	44,193	44,193	...	96,291	12,018	24,561	17,416	19,237	73,306	19,188
Received as inheritance or gift	67	67	...	-	4	5	16	10	-	19
Not reported	57	57	...	2	8	4	2	11	12	15
Major source of down payment[3]										
Home purchased or built	2,299	2,299	...	123	144	54	180	373	220	278
Sale of previous home	483	483	...	41	16	6	28	107	53	36
Savings or cash on hand	1,362	1,362	...	63	95	37	102	181	124	146
Sale of other investment	3	3	...	2	-	-	-	-	3	1
Borrowing, other than mortgage on this property	69	69	...	3	3	4	9	12	4	9
Inheritance or gift	37	37	...	-	3	-	5	5	6	9
Land where building built used for financing	7	7	...	-	2	-	2	2	-	5
Other	75	75	...	4	5	-	10	8	12	20
No down payment	206	206	...	8	17	7	20	48	13	47
Not reported	56	56	...	1	2	-	3	10	5	5

Source: U.S. Department of Housing and Urban Development. Office of Policy Development and Research. *Current Housing Reports, American Housing Survey for the United States in 1991,* Washington, DC: U.S. Government Printing Office, April 1993, p. 284. *Notes:* Three dots (...) means not applicable or that the sample was too small. A dash (-) represents zero or a percentage which rounds to zero. 1. If both the owner and any co-owners have never owned or co-owned another home as a usual place of residence, then the housing unit was reported as the first home ever owned. Previous homes purchased solely as vacation homes or homes purchased for commercial rental purposes are not to be considered usual residences. However, if a previously owned home was originally purchased as a usual residence and later used as a vacation home or for commercial or rental purposes, the home is considered as being owned as a usual residence. 2. The purchase price refers to the price of the house or apartment and lot at the time the property was purchased. Closing costs are excluded from the purchase price, and for mobile homes, the value of the land is excluded. Median purchase price is rounded to the nearest dollar. 3. This item refers to the source of cash used for down payment or outright purchase of the property (house and lot). If more than one source applied, the one providing the largest portion of the down payment or outright purchase was recorded. Sale of previous home was indicated only if the previous home was sold during the 12-month period preceding the acquisition of the present home. Savings, or cash on hand, includes money drawn from savings, such as bank deposits, credit unions, share accounts, savings bonds, certificates of deposit (CDs), money market funds, and IRA or KEOGH accounts. Sale of other investment includes the sale of real property or real estate other than the previous home or from the sale of other investments such as securities (Common and preferred stock, municipal or corporate bonds, mutual funds), dissolved business ventures, etc. Borrowing other than a mortgage on this property was indicated if the present owner borrowed the down payment, even if the property was mortgaged. Money received as a gift regardless of the source was categorized "inheritance or gift." "Land where building built used for financing" means the land on which the structure was built was used as the present owner's equity in the property. Sources of down payment that do not fit any of the above categories were recorded in the "other" category.

★ 533 ★

Housing

Heating Equipment Used in Housing Units With a Hispanic Householder, 1991

Data, shown in thousands, are shown for the main heating equipment and other heating equipment used in addition to the main heating equipment. More than one category of "other heating equipment" could be reported for the same household. Only one type of equipment was reported as the "main heating equipment."

Characteristics	Total occupied units	Tenure		Housing unit characteristics				Household characteristics		
		Owner	Renter	New construction 4 yrs.	Mobile homes	Physical problems: Severe	Physical problems: Moderate	Elderly (65+)	Moved in past year	Below poverty level
Total	6,239	2,423	3,816	218	208	267	564	669	1,720	1,501
Main heating equipment										
Warm-air furnace	2,329	1,183	1,147	125	124	76	62	229	615	445
Steam or hot water system	1,023	177	846	6	-	80	84	101	265	281
Electric heat pump	385	196	188	42	14	9	7	43	130	50
Built-in electric units	407	92	315	27	-	14	9	46	156	83
Floor, wall, or other built-in hot air units without ducts	842	278	564	4	18	22	46	71	223	218
Room heaters with flue	244	85	160	-	3	10	18	33	69	100
Room heaters without flue	290	139	151	-	16	20	271	61	66	96
Portable electric heaters	158	55	103	2	15	10	14	17	32	64
Stoves	135	62	73	-	10	11	8	21	32	58
Fireplaces with inserts	23	20	3	-	-	-	-	2	3	3
Fireplaces without inserts	71	43	29	4	-	-	9	3	18	10
Other	84	32	52	4	-	2	7	18	19	22
None	248	61	186	4	7	15	30	23	92	73
Other heating equipment										
With other heating equipment[1]	1,172	711	462	62	43	45	78	135	231	189
Warm-air furnace	62	42	20	5	7	-	13	11	16	9
Steam or hot water system	3	3	-	-	-	-	-	-	-	-
Electric heat pump	29	10	20	3	-	-	-	3	7	7
Built-in electric units	101	51	50	4	2	1	6	9	13	22
Floor, wall, or other built-in hot air units without ducts	38	22	16	-	1	-	-	6	8	3
Room heaters with flue	38	31	7	-	2	-	-	6	2	3
Room heaters without flue	46	30	16	-	2	-	1	3	10	14
Portable electric heaters	329	150	179	5	20	21	36	39	62	72
Stoves	115	77	38	1	8	6	13	15	14	27
Fireplaces with inserts	88	65	23	7	-	-	5	7	24	5
Fireplaces with no inserts	370	275	95	39	1	8	7	40	77	24
Other	43	28	15	-	5	7	10	6	7	9

Source: U.S. Department of Housing and Urban Development. Office of Policy Development and Research. *Current Housing Reports, American Housing Survey for the United States in 1991,* Washington, DC: U.S. Government Printing Office, April 1993, p. 258. *Notes:* A dash (-) represents zero or a percentage which rounds to zero. 1. Figures may not add to total because more than one category may apply to a unit.

★ 534 ★

Housing

Heating Fuel Used in Housing Units With a Hispanic Householder, 1991

This table shows number of persons (in thousands) using each type of fuel.

Characteristics	Total occupied units	Tenure		Housing unit characteristics				Household characteristics		
		Owner	Renter	New construction 4 yrs.	Mobile homes	Physical problems: Severe	Physical problems: Moderate	Elderly (65+)	Moved in past year	Below poverty level
Total	6,239	2,423	3,816	218	208	267	564	669	1,720	1,501
Main house heating fuel										
Housing units with heating fuel	5,992	2,361	3,630	214	201	252	534	646	1,627	1,429
Electricity	1,607	593	1,014	127	53	37	36	165	531	334
Piped gas	3,239	1,434	1,859	70	84	122	396	348	853	780
Bottled gas	112	61	51	6	44	12	17	17	22	29
Fuel oil	694	131	562	7	4	71	57	82	146	200
Kerosene or other liquid fuel	16	6	9	-	5	-	7	-	5	5
Coal or coke	4	4	-	-	-	-	-	4	-	-
Wood	231	125	106	4	9	11	17	26	52	70
Solar energy	-	-	-	-	-	-	-	-	-	-
Other	36	7	29	-	1	-	5	4	18	11
Other house heating fuels										
With other heating fuels[1]	734	474	260	44	36	18	53	74	139	109
Electricity	280	150	130	10	15	14	36	28	48	54
Piped gas	69	44	25	2	5	-	6	5	11	6
Bottled gas	9	7	1	-	-	-	-	2	-	4
Fuel oil	12	5	7	-	-	-	-	3	3	-
Kerosene or other liquid fuel	35	23	13	-	4	-	3	2	6	7
Coal or coke	4	1	3	-	-	-	1	1	-	1
Wood	327	245	81	33	13	4	10	36	69	35
Solar energy	9	9	-	-	-	-	3	-	2	-
Other	13	8	5	-	-	-	-	-	5	4
Not reported	39	22	17	7	-	2	11	-	12	9

Source: U.S. Department of Housing and Urban Development. Office of Policy Development and Research. *Current Housing Reports, American Housing Survey for the United States in 1991,* Washington, DC: U.S. Government Printing Office, April 1993, p. 260. *Notes:* A dash (-) represents zero or a percentage which rounds to zero. Electricity is generally supplied by means of above ground or underground power lines. Piped gas is gas piped through underground pipes from a central system to serve the neighborhood. Bottled gas is pressurized gas stored in tanks or bottles that are filled or exchanged when empty. Fuel oil is heating oil normally supplied by truck to a tank storage tank for use by the heating system. Kerosene or other liquid fuel includes kerosene, gasoline, alcohol, and other similar combustible liquids. Coal or coke refers to coal or any coal derivative usually delivered by means of truck. Wood refers to the use of wood or wood charcoal, etc., as a fuel. Solar energy refers to the use of energy available from sunlight as a heating fuel source. Other includes briquettes made of pitch and sawdust, coal dust, waste material like corncobs, purchased steam, or any other fuel not listed. 1. Figures may not add to total because more than one category may apply to a unit.

★ 535 ★

Housing

Heating and Electrical Problems in Housing Units With a Hispanic Householder, 1991

This table shows number of persons (in thousands) who experienced each type of equipment failure of heating equipment during the winter prior to interview or whether an electrical problem occurred in the 3 months prior to interview.

Characteristics	Total occupied units	Tenure		Housing unit characteristics				Household characteristics		
		Owner	Renter	New construction 4 yrs.	Mobile homes	Physical problems: Severe	Physical problems: Moderate	Elderly (65+)	Moved in past year	Below poverty level
Total	6,239	2,423	3,816	218	208	267	564	669	1,720	1,501
Heating problems										
With heating equipment and occupied last winter	5,058	2,250	2,808	176	173	227	454	619	722	1,179
Not uncomfortably cold for 24 hours or more last winter	4,527	2,088	2,439	171	153	155	365	558	657	982
Uncomfortably cold for 24 hours or more last winter[1]	514	157	358	5	16	72	89	61	65	189
Equipment breakdowns	207	38	169	3	6	58	31	15	20	85
No breakdowns lasting 6 hours or more	13	1	12	-	-	-	-	2	3	4
1 time lasting 6 hours or more	104	26	78	3	1	5	21	7	14	48
2 times	28	3	25	-	3	2	8	-	-	12
3 times	18	2	16	-	-	18	-	4	-	6
4 times or more	30	3	27	-	2	30	-	2	-	8
Number of times not reported	13	2	12	-	-	2	2	-	3	6
Other causes	349	122	26	5	10	28	66	54	50	121
Utility interruption	42	27	15	-	2	-	7	8	8	5
Inadequate heating capacity	140	43	97	5	2	13	20	18	17	55
Inadequate insulation	49	20	28	-	-	4	13	11	7	21
Other	109	28	81	-	5	12	22	14	16	40
Not reported	10	4	5	-	-	-	4	2	2	-
Reason for discomfort not reported	3	3	-	-	-	-	-	3	-	-
Discomfort not reported	16	6	11	-	4	-	-	-	-	8
Electric fuses and circuit breakers										
With electrical wiring	6,239	2,423	3,816	218	208	267	564	669	1,720	1,501
No fuses or breakers blown in last 3 mo.	5,516	2,150	3,366	182	168	215	469	622	1,528	1,329
With fuses or breakers blown in last 3 mo.	616	259	359	29	40	46	79	40	128	148
1 time	240	125	115	14	18	15	22	23	41	51
2 times	123	58	66	4	9	3	28	6	30	33
3 times	71	24	47	3	8	19	2	-	14	19
4 times or more	107	34	72	2	5	6	25	2	20	25
Number of times not reported	75	18	57	5	-	4	2	9	24	20
Problem not reported or don't know	108	15	93	8	-	6	16	7	63	25

Source: U.S. Department of Housing and Urban Development. Office of Policy Development and Research, *Current Housing Reports, American Housing Survey for the United States in 1991,* Washington, DC: U.S. Government Printing Office, April 1993, p. 262. *Notes:* A dash (-) represents zero or a percentage which rounds to zero. Heating equipment is considered to be broken down if it is not providing heat at its normal heating capacity through some fault in the equipment. Utility interruptions occur when there is a cut off in the gas, electricity, or other fuel supplying the heat. Inadequate heating capacity refers to heating equipment that is providing heat at its normal capacity, but the housing is still too cold for the occupants. Inadequate insulation refers to air drafts through window frames, electrical outlets, or walls that are cold. A blown fuse or tripped breaker switch results in the temporary loss of electricity until the fuse is replaced or the breaker reset. Blown fuses inside major pieces of installed equipment (such as some air conditioners) are counted as blown fuses or tripped breaker switches. 1. Other causes and equipment breakdowns may not add to total as both may be reported.

★ 536 ★

Housing

Home Improvements and Repairs of Owner-Occupied Housing

From the source: "The statistics refer to the 24 months prior to the date of the interview and are restricted to owner occupied units. The data are presented according to whether the repairs, improvements, and alterations cost less than $500 or $500 or more.

	Total occupied units	Tenure		Housing unit characteristics				Household characteristics		
				New construction 4 yrs.	Mobile homes	Physical problems		Elderly (65+)	Moved in past year	Below poverty level
		Owner	Renter			Severe	Moderate			
Total units	2,423	2,423	...	125	155	63	198	395	232	312
Roof replaced (all or part)	453	453	...	2	14	16	49	79	24	70
Mostly done by others	271	271	...	2	4	13	22	55	16	42
Costing $500 or more	296	296	...	-	9	7	32	50	13	32
Additions built	116	116	...	1	15	8	8	9	6	4
Mostly done by others	56	56	...	-	-	-	5	6	2	2
Costing $500 or more	95	95	...	1	11	8	8	7	1	2
Kitchen remodeled or added	265	265	...	-	14	3	42	25	26	25
Mostly done by others	106	106	...	-	6	-	18	15	5	15
Costing $500 or more	153	153	...	-	2	3	13	12	5	1
Bathroom remodeled or added	317	317	...	-	20	10	52	51	26	42
Mostly done by others	134	134	...	-	2	3	8	32	10	17
Costing $500 or more	169	169	...	-	8	9	6	29	7	6
Bathroom remodeled or added not reported	53	53	...	2	7	3	2	11	12	16
Mostly done by others	56	56	...	-	-	-	5	11	2	14
Costing $500 or more	61	61	...	-	-	-	3	3	4	-
Storm doors/windows bought and installed	252	252	...	-	13	5	22	25	13	27
Mostly done by others	106	106	...	-	2	-	3	18	8	8
Costing $500 or more	79	79	...	-	-	-	-	11	3	5
Major equipment replaced or added	188	188	...	2	15	9	7	21	9	15
Costing $500 or more	130	130	...	-	7	7	7	16	1	3
Insulation added	163	163	...	4	12	8	16	15	8	19
Mostly done by others	70	70	...	2	-	5	5	14	5	9
Costing $500 or more	23	23	...	-	-	2	-	3	-	3
Other major work[1]	455	455	...	17	8	12	38	59	48	38
Mostly done by others	254	254	...	7	3	5	15	39	22	20
Other major work not reported	53	53	...	2	7	3	2	11	12	16

Source: U.S. Department of Housing and Urban Development. Office of Policy Development and Research. *Current Housing Reports, American Housing Survey for the United States in 1991*, Washington, DC: U.S. Government Printing Office, April 1993, p. 290. *Notes:* NA stands for not applicable or sample too small. A dash (-) stands for zero or rounds to zero. 1. Includes other major repairs, alterations, or improvements totaling over $500 each.

★ 537 ★

Housing

Household Characteristics and Housing Tenure, by Hispanic Origin, 1991

Numbers are shown in thousands.

Characteristic	Total population	Hispanic origin population	Non-Hispanic population	Mexican origin	Puerto Rican origin	Cuban origin	Central and South American origin	Other Hispanic origin
Households, by type								
All households	94,312	6,220	88,093	3,604	805	425	809	576
Percent	100.0	100.0	100.0	100.0	100.0	100.0	100.0	100.0
Family households	70.3	80.1	69.6	81.7	77.8	78.8	82.5	70.8
Married-couple families	55.3	55.5	55.3	60.0	40.7	60.0	54.5	46.1
Male householder, no wife present	3.1	5.5	2.9	6.1	3.4	3.5	6.4	5.2
Female householder, no husband present	11.9	19.1	11.4	15.6	33.7	15.3	21.5	19.5
Non-family households	29.7	19.9	30.4	18.3	22.2	21.2	17.5	29.2
Male householder	12.9	10.8	13.0	10.4	12.3	8.6	9.0	15.3
Female householder	16.8	9.1	17.3	7.9	10.0	12.6	8.5	13.9
Housing tenure								
Percent	100.0	100.0	100.0	100.0	100.0	100.0	100.0	100.0
Own or buying home	64.0	39.0	65.8	43.5	23.4	47.3	22.2	49.6
Renting	36.0	61.0	34.2	56.5	76.6	52.5	77.8	50.3

Source: U.S. Bureau of the Census. *The Hispanic Population in the United States: March 1991.* Current Population Reports, Series P-20, No. 455, Washington, DC: U.S. Government Printing Office, 1991, pp. 16-17.

★ 538 ★

Housing

Living Arrangements of Elderly Hispanics, 1989

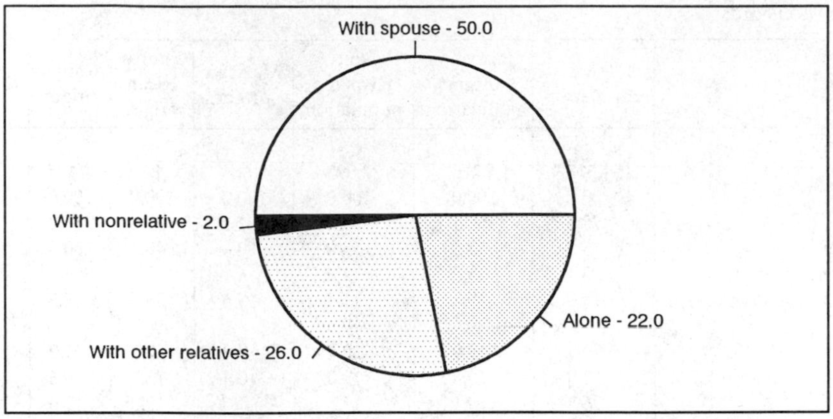

Figures shown in percentages.

Person lives...	Percent
With spouse	50.0
With other relatives	26.0
Alone	22.0
With nonrelative	2.0

Source: Aging America, Trends and Projections, 1991 Edition. Prepared by the U.S. Senate Special Committee on Aging, the American Association of Retired Persons, the Federal Council on the Aging, and the U.S. Administration on Aging, p. 188. Primary source: U.S. Bureau of the Census. "Marital Status and Living Arrangements: March 1989," *Current Population Reports* Series P-20, No. 455, June 1990. *Note:* May not add to 100 percent due to rounding.

★ 539 ★

Housing

Living Arrangements of Persons Age 65 Years or Older, 1989

The number (in thousands) and percent of elderly people are shown by living arrangement, gender and age, as of March 1989.

Living arrangement	65+		65 to 74		75 to 84		85+	
	Men	Women	Men	Women	Men	Women	Men	Women
Hispanic origin[1]								
Total (thousands)	447	557	301	350	120	176	26	31
Percent	100.0	100.0	100.0	100.0	100.0	100.0	100.0	100.0
Living with spouse	65.5	37.7	69.8	47.4	62.5	23.3	[2]	[2]
Living with other relatives	15.2	35.5	12.6	30.0	18.3	43.2	[2]	[2]
Living alone	17.4	25.7	15.0	21.1	19.2	33.5	[2]	[2]
Living with nonrelatives	1.8	1.4	2.7	1.4	0.0	0.6	[2]	[2]
All races								
Total (thousands)	12.078	16.944	7.880	9.867	3.506	5.669	693	1.408
Percent	100.0	100.0	100.0	100.0	100.0	100.0	100.0	100.0

[Continued]

★ 539 ★

Living Arrangements of Persons Age 65 Years or Older, 1989

[Continued]

Living arrangement	65+		65 to 74		75 to 84		85+	
	Men	Women	Men	Women	Men	Women	Men	Women
Living with spouse	74.3	40.1	78.4	51.4	70.4	28.1	48.2	9.1
Living with other relatives	7.7	16.9	6.4	13.5	8.7	19.1	17.3	32.6
Living alone	15.9	40.9	13.3	33.5	18.4	50.5	32.6	54.0
Living with nonrelatives	2.1	2.0	2.0	1.5	2.5	2.3	1.7	4.3
White								
Total (thousands)	10.798	15.204	7.050	8.767	3.136	5.174	612	1.263
Percent	100.0	100.0	100.0	100.0	100.0	100.0	100.0	100.0
Living with spouse	76.3	41.2	80.6	53.3	72.3	28.7	47.9	8.8
Living with other relatives	6.6	15.4	5.3	11.8	7.7	17.5	16.8	31.1
Living alone	15.3	41.4	12.5	33.5	17.9	51.5	33.7	55.5
Living with nonrelatives	1.8	2.0	1.7	1.4	2.0	2.3	1.6	4.6
Black								
Total (thousands)	981	1.455	619	913	300	416	62	126
Percent	100.0	100.0	100.0	100.0	100.0	100.0	100.0	100.0
Living with spouse	56.1	27.9	58.6	33.4	51.0	20.7	[2]	11.9
Living with other relatives	15.6	29.7	15.0	26.4	17.0	32.2	[2]	45.2
Living alone	23.9	39.8	22.8	37.7	24.7	43.5	[2]	42.9
Living with nonrelatives	4.6	2.6	3.7	2.5	7.3	3.6	[2]	0.0

Source: Aging America, Trends and Projections, 1991 Edition. Prepared by the U.S. Senate Special Committee on Aging, the American Association of Retired Persons, the Federal Council on the Aging, and the U.S. Administration on Aging, p. 187. U.S. Bureau of the Census. Marital Status and Living Arrangements: March 1989. Current Population Reports Series. p. 20 *Notes:* Data exclude people in institutions. Percentage distributions may not add to 100.0 due to rounding. 1. People of Hispanic origin may be of any race. 2. Base is less than 75,000.

★ 540 ★

Housing

Monthly Costs in Housing Units With a Hispanic Householder, 1991

Data show number of persons (in thousands) in each cost category. Figures are presented for both owner-occupied and renter-occupied housing units.

Characteristics	Total occupied units	Tenure		Housing unit characteristics				Household characteristics		
		Owner	Renter	New construction 4 yrs.	Mobile homes	Physical problems: Severe	Physical problems: Moderate	Elderly (65+)	Moved in past year	Below poverty level
Total	6,239	2,423	3,816	218	208	267	564	669	1,720	1,501
Monthly housing costs										
Less than $100	147	102	45	9	20	12	21	45	33	89
$100 to $199	630	404	226	4	37	35	109	181	75	267
$200 to $249	322	137	185	10	25	19	53	71	66	116
$250 to $299	320	133	188	-	21	22	44	61	80	99
$300 to $349	406	90	316	2	12	12	37	38	129	122
$350 to $399	414	102	312	11	22	13	36	55	140	154
$400 to $499	403	74	329	5	19	7	49	32	133	99
$450 to $499	432	78	353	5	4	17	3	27	140	90
$500 to $599	781	150	631	11	18	42	53	33	244	155
$600 to $699	520	141	379	20	1	22	44	25	172	81
$700 to $799	412	130	282	22	4	21	17	26	133	40

[Continued]

★ 540 ★

Monthly Costs in Housing Units With a Hispanic Householder, 1991

[Continued]

Characteristics	Total occupied units	Tenure		Housing unit characteristics				Household characteristics		
		Owner	Renter	New construction 4 yrs.	Mobile homes	Physical problems: Severe	Physical problems: Moderate	Elderly (65+)	Moved in past year	Below poverty level
$800 to $999	431	220	211	27	9	14	25	15	130	41
$1,000 to $1,249	256	169	88	17	1	7	11	6	74	14
$1,250 to $1,499	131	107	24	21	-	2	2	4	31	2
$1,500 or more	209	193	16	34	-	4	10	15	57	10
No cash rent	231	...	231	4	8	12	17	20	62	107
Mortgage payment not reported	195	195	...	6	5	6	3	15	21	15
Median (excludes no cash rent)	481	497	477	774	286	463	361	266	509	348
Median monthly housing costs for owners										
Monthly costs including all mortgages plus maintenance costs	520	520	...	958	276	408	251	246	848	204
Monthly costs excluding 2nd and subsequent mortgages and maintenance costs	479	479	...	955	267	408	251	228	814	191
Monthly housing costs as percent of current income[1]										
Less than 5 percent	109	95	15	-	7	5	5	25	12	2
5 to 9 percent	446	355	91	10	34	23	65	58	48	17
10 to 14 percent	465	266	199	12	25	10	33	50	41	25
15 to 19 percent	702	312	391	33	23	42	81	78	159	65
20 to 24 percent	708	295	413	29	21	31	53	50	173	78
25 to 29 percent	625	209	416	26	20	20	60	73	199	94
30 to 34 percent	530	171	359	11	9	11	34	57	149	84
35 to 39 percent	357	90	267	10	3	17	18	41	127	54
40 to 49 percent	601	169	432	25	15	27	63	47	193	171
50 to 59 percent	297	74	223	13	13	15	35	42	118	118
60 to 69 percent	229	32	197	5	2	12	20	29	93	122
70 to 99 percent	324	88	236	11	12	17	34	41	117	201
100 percent or more[2]	332	50	283	20	8	21	36	33	165	269
Zero or negative income	89	24	65	5	3	-	8	8	43	79
No cash rent	231	...	231	4	8	12	17	20	62	107
Mortgage payment not reported	195	195	...	6	5	6	3	15	21	15
Median (excludes 3 previous lines)	28	21	33	28	22	28	28	29	36	55
Median (excludes 4 lines before medians)	27	21	31	27	21	26	26	27	33	46

Source: U.S. Department of Housing and Urban Development. Office of Policy Development and Research. *Current Housing Reports, American Housing Survey for the United States in 1991,* Washington, DC: U.S. Government Printing Office, April 1993, p. 278. *Notes:* Three dots (...) means not applicable or that the sample was too small. A dash (-) represents zero or a percentage which rounds to zero. 1. Beginning in 1989 this item uses current income in its calculation. 2. May reflect a temporary situation, living off savings, or response error.

★ 541 ★

Housing

Neighborhood Conditions of Housing Units With a Hispanic Householder, 1991

From the source: "The statistics presented are based on the respondent's opinion and attitude toward the neighborhood. The respondent defines the neighborhood. The respondent was asked a two-part question: 1) If anything about the neighborhood bothered the respondent and 2) if so, what?....Multiple responses were allowed. The respondent may not have the same opinion as a neighbor about neighborhood conditions. The respondent's opinion may or may not reflect the actual neighborhood situation." Data in this table are shown in thousands of persons.

Characteristics	Total occupied units	Tenure		Housing unit characteristics				Household characteristics		
		Owner	Renter	New construction 4 yrs.	Mobile homes	Physical problems: Severe	Physical problems: Moderate	Elderly (65+)	Moved in past year	Below poverty level
Total	6,239	2,423	3,816	218	208	267	564	669	1,720	1,501
Neighborhood conditions										
With neighborhood	6,119	2,368	3,751	217	204	258	541	642	1,692	1,460
No problems	3,787	1,468	2,319	122	121	109	331	440	1,110	920
With problems[1]	2,308	896	1,412	94	83	146	211	196	573	536
Crime	737	188	549	23	14	52	82	52	154	232
Noise	616	146	470	27	16	42	70	50	182	150
Traffic	424	164	260	13	24	12	43	29	109	81
Litter or housing deterioration	270	119	151	6	2	22	32	23	48	73
Poor city or county services	107	42	65	3	1	10	13	7	19	27
Undesirable commercial, institutional, industrial	114	42	72	2	5	5	12	10	25	14
People	884	304	579	21	31	76	119	55	250	259
Other	380	212	168	30	23	13	36	41	82	65
Type of problem not reported	18	6	12	3	-	-	2	-	8	8
Presence of problems not reported	24	5	19	-	-	3	-	6	9	4

Source: U.S. Department of Housing and Urban Development. Office of Policy Development and Research. *Current Housing Reports, American Housing Survey for the United States in 1991,* Washington, DC: U.S. Government Printing Office, April 1993, p. 266. *Notes:* A dash (-) represents zero or a percentage which rounds to zero. 1. Figures may not add to total because more than one category may apply to unit.

★ 542 ★

Housing

Number and Percentage of Occupied Housing Units, by Ownership/Rental Status and State, 1990

State	Total occupied housing units	All units			Hispanic occupied units		
		Owner occupied	Rented units: Number	Rented units: %	Owner occupied	Rented units: Number	Rented units: %
United States	91,947,410	59,024,811	32,922,599	35.8	2,545,584	3,456,134	57.6
Alabama	1,506,790	1,061,897	444,893	29.5	3,836	3,537	48.0
Alaska	188,915	105,989	82,926	43.9	1,733	2,938	62.9
Arizona	1,368,843	878,561	490,282	35.8	99,840	85,102	46.0
Arkansas	891,179	619,938	271,241	30.4	2,554	2,796	52.3
California	10,381,206	5,773,943	4,607,263	44.4	741,623	1,095,366	59.6
Colorado	1,282,489	798,277	484,212	37.8	66,205	64,499	49.3
Connecticut	1,230,479	807,481	422,998	34.4	15,920	45,660	74.1

[Continued]

★ 542 ★

Number and Percentage of Occupied Housing Units, by Ownership/Rental Status and State, 1990

[Continued]

State	Total occupied housing units	All units			Hispanic occupied units		
		Owner occupied	Rented units		Owner occupied	Rented units	
			Number	%		Number	%
Delaware	247,497	173,813	73,684	29.8	1,983	2,514	55.9
D.C.	249,634	97,108	152,526	61.1	2,141	8,314	79.5
Florida	5,134,869	3,452,160	1,682,709	32.8	257,602	253,247	49.6
Georgia	2,366,615	1,536,759	829,856	35.1	12,119	17,754	59.4
Hawaii	356,267	191,911	164,356	46.1	7,692	12,484	61.9
Idaho	360,723	252,734	107,989	29.9	6,267	7,197	53.5
Illinois	4,202,240	2,699,182	1,503,058	35.8	91,490	138,503	60.2
Indiana	2,065,355	1,450,898	614,457	29.8	15,611	11,960	43.4
Iowa	1,064,325	745,377	318,948	30.0	4,493	4,433	49.7
Kansas	944,726	641,762	302,964	32.1	13,190	12,416	48.5
Kentucky	1,379,782	960,469	419,313	30.4	2,972	3,248	52.2
Louisiana	1,499,269	987,919	511,350	34.1	16,129	13,861	46.2
Maine	465,312	327,888	137,424	29.5	883	997	53.0
Maryland	1,748,991	1,137,296	611,695	35.0	15,881	18,523	53.8
Massachusetts	2,247,110	1,331,493	915,617	40.7	15,296	66,353	81.3
Michigan	3,419,331	2,427,643	991,688	29.0	31,256	24,542	44.0
Minnesota	1,647,853	1,183,673	464,180	28.2	6,559	7,480	53.3
Mississippi	911,374	651,587	259,787	28.5	2,665	2,080	43.8
Missouri	1,961,206	1,348,746	612,460	31.2	10,095	8,349	45.3
Montana	306,163	205,899	100,264	32.7	1,575	1,799	53.3
Nebraska	602,363	400,394	201,969	33.5	5,132	5,385	51.2
Nevada	466,297	255,388	210,909	45.2	14,316	21,342	59.9
New Hampshire	411,186	280,372	130,814	31.8	1,323	1,932	59.4
New Jersey	2,794,711	1,813,381	981,330	35.1	67,210	148,316	68.8
New Mexico	542,709	365,965	176,744	32.6	120,599	58,110	32.5
New York	6,639,322	3,464,436	3,174,886	47.8	113,596	551,483	82.9
North Carolina	2,517,026	1,711,817	805,209	32.0	8,925	12,608	58.6
North Dakota	240,878	157,950	82,928	34.4	374	764	67.1
Ohio	4,087,546	2,758,149	1,329,397	32.5	20,669	20,450	49.7
Oklahoma	1,206,135	821,188	384,947	31.9	10,956	12,525	53.3
Oregon	1,103,313	695,957	407,356	36.9	10,833	17,371	61.6
Pennsylvania	4,495,966	3,176,121	1,319,845	29.4	28,082	37,256	57.0
Rhode Island	377,977	224,792	153,185	40.5	3,009	10,083	77.0
South Carolina	1,258,044	878,704	379,340	30.2	4,096	4,490	52.3
South Dakota	259,034	171,161	87,873	33.9	540	781	59.1
Tennessee	1,853,725	1,261,118	592,607	32.0	4,693	4,956	51.4
Texas	6,070,937	3,695,115	2,375,822	39.1	615,696	542,314	46.8
Utah	537,273	365,979	171,294	31.9	11,247	11,473	50.5
Vermont	210,650	145,368	65,282	31.0	640	507	44.2
Virginia	2,291,830	1,519,521	772,309	33.7	17,917	25,839	59.1
Washington	1,872,431	1,171,580	700,851	37.4	22,485	33,221	59.6
West Virginia	688,557	510,058	178,499	25.9	1,756	1,029	36.9

[Continued]

★ 542 ★

Number and Percentage of Occupied Housing Units, by Ownership/Rental Status and State, 1990

[Continued]

State	Total occupied housing units	All units			Hispanic occupied units		
		Owner occupied	Rented units		Owner occupied	Rented units	
			Number	%		Number	%
Wisconsin	1,822,118	1,215,350	606,768	33.3	9,430	14,735	61.0
Wyoming	168,839	114,544	54,295	32.2	4,450	3,212	41.9

Source: U.S. Bureau of the Census. *1990 Census of Population and Housing, Summary Tape File 1C on CD-ROM, United States Summary*. February, 1992.

★ 543 ★

Housing

Number of Rooms in Housing Units With a Hispanic Householder, 1991

Data are shown in thousands of persons.

Characteristics	Total occupied units	Tenure		Housing unit characteristics				Household characteristics		
		Owner	Renter	New construction 4 yrs.	Mobile homes	Physical problems: Severe	Physical problems: Moderate	Elderly (65+)	Moved in past year	Below poverty level
Total	6,239	2,423	3,816	218	208	267	564	669	1,720	1,501
Rooms[1]										
1 room	86	2	84	-	-	37	20	10	46	27
2 rooms	125	6	119	-	4	9	15	14	65	54
3 rooms	934	57	877	17	25	46	79	123	388	324
4 rooms	1,785	360	1,426	58	86	58	160	149	568	532
5 rooms	1,413	600	814	40	58	48	134	176	336	327
6 rooms	991	668	323	30	26	44	83	117	174	142
7 rooms	506	396	111	38	5	18	52	41	57	58
8 rooms	248	205	43	25	2	5	17	24	59	24
9 rooms	81	64	17	6	1	4	-	5	15	10
10 rooms or more	69	66	3	3	-	-	5	9	11	5
Median	4.6	5.8	4.1	5.3	4.4	4.2	4.6	4.7	4.1	4.2
Bedrooms[2]										
None	154	5	149	-	-	44	30	17	83	52
1	1,228	76	1,152	25	23	58	103	153	504	397
2	2,304	616	1,688	73	111	80	205	247	707	645
3	1,972	1,267	705	77	68	74	174	200	331	326
4 or more	581	459	122	43	6	12	52	52	95	82
Median	2.3	2.9	1.9	2.6	2.2	1.9	2.2	2.2	1.9	2.0
Complete bathrooms[3]										
None	72	14	58	-	4	57	-	8	30	33
1	3,982	1,002	2,980	49	122	156	448	439	1,248	1,177

[Continued]

★ 543 ★

Number of Rooms in Housing Units With a Hispanic Householder, 1991

[Continued]

Characteristics	Total occupied units	Tenure		Housing unit characteristics				Household characteristics		
		Owner	Renter	New construction 4 yrs.	Mobile homes	Physical problems: Severe	Physical problems: Moderate	Elderly (65+)	Moved in past year	Below poverty level
1 and one-half	585	292	293	18	14	23	54	69	117	107
2 or more	1,601	1,115	486	151	67	32	63	152	324	184

Source: U.S. Department of Housing and Urban Development. Office of Policy Development and Research. *Current Housing Reports, American Housing Survey for the United States in 1991*, Washington, DC: U.S. Government Printing Office, April 1993, p. 256. *Notes:* A dash (-) represents zero or a percentage which rounds to zero. 1. The statistics on rooms are for the number of housing units with a specified number of rooms. Counted rooms include whole rooms used for living purposes, such as bedrooms, living rooms, dining rooms, kitchens, recreation rooms, permanently enclosed porches that are suitable for year-round use, lodgers' rooms, and other finished and unfinished rooms. Also included are rooms used for offices by a person living in the unit. The median for rooms is rounded to the nearest tenth. A dining room, to be counted, must be a separate room. It must be separated from adjoining rooms by built-in floor-to-ceiling walls extending at least a few inches from the intersecting walls. Movable or collapsible partitions or partitions consisting solely of shelves or cabinets are not considered built-in-walls. Bathrooms are not counted as rooms and are shown separately. 2. The number of bedrooms in the housing unit is the count of rooms used mainly for sleeping, even if also used for other purposes. Rooms reserved for sleeping, such as guest rooms, even though used infrequently, are counted as bedrooms. On the other hand, rooms used mainly for other purposes, such as living room with a hideaway bed, are not considered bedrooms. A housing unit consisting of only one room, such as a one-room efficiency apartment, is classified by definition as having no bedroom. 3. A housing unit is classified as having a complete bathroom if it has a room with a flush toilet, bathtub or shower, a sink, and hot and cold piped water. All facilities must be in the same room to be a complete bathroom. A half bathroom has either a flush toilet or a bathtub or shower but does not have all the facilities for a complete bathroom.

★ 544 ★

Housing

Persons Per Room and Square Footage Per Person in Housing Units With a Hispanic Householder, 1991

Numbers are shown in thousands.

Characteristics	Total occupied units	Tenure		Housing unit characteristics				Household characteristics		
		Owner	Renter	New construction 4 yrs.	Mobile homes	Physical problems: Severe	Physical problems: Moderate	Elderly (65+)	Moved in past year	Below poverty level
Total	6,239	2,423	3,816	218	208	267	564	669	1,720	1,501
Persons per room[1]										
0.50 or less	2,565	1,229	1,336	107	82	80	187	538	626	477
0.51 to 1.00	2,757	995	1,762	96	98	134	260	117	795	658
1.01 to 1.50	651	154	497	11	15	34	75	11	194	243
1.51 or more	267	45	222	3	12	19	43	2	103	123
Square feet per person[2]										
Single detached and mobile homes	3,052	2,136	916	123	206	103	313	407	559	568
Less than 200	395	198	197	4	57	21	76	24	90	137
200 to 299	486	305	181	9	41	22	55	29	109	105
300 to 399	445	318	126	22	25	5	48	15	81	64
400 to 499	290	211	78	12	13	12	25	16	34	36
500 to 599	244	197	47	9	14	7	13	39	30	29
600 to 699	219	165	54	12	7	8	18	44	45	50
700 to 799	128	107	21	1	7	5	14	33	21	17
800 to 899	121	98	23	6	8	2	14	37	23	13
900 to 999	88	64	24	2	5	2	6	27	13	18
1,000 to 1,499	218	183	34	22	4	5	13	65	24	27
1,500 or more	151	126	25	5	4	2	6	53	25	14

[Continued]

★ 544 ★

Persons Per Room and Square Footage Per Person in Housing Units With a Hispanic Householder, 1991

[Continued]

Characteristics	Total occupied units	Tenure		Housing unit characteristics				Household characteristics		
		Owner	Renter	New construction 4 yrs.	Mobile homes	Physical problems: Severe	Physical problems: Moderate	Elderly (65+)	Moved in past year	Below poverty level
Not reported	268	162	106	19	21	12	23	23	63	57
Median	423	478	321	554	286	344	328	771	361	320

Source: U.S. Department of Housing and Urban Development. Office of Policy Development and Research. *Current Housing Reports, American Housing Survey for the United States in 1991,* Washington, DC: U.S. Government Printing Office, April 1993, p. 256. *Notes:* 1. Persons per room is computed for each occupied housing unit by dividing the number of persons in the unit by the number of rooms in the unit. The figures shown refer, therefore, to the number of housing units having the specified ratio of persons per room. 2. Square feet per person is computed for each single-family detached housing unit and mobile home by dividing the number of persons in the unit by the square footage of the unit. The figures shown refer to the number of housing units having the specified square feet per person. Median square footage is rounded to the nearest foot.

★ 545 ★

Housing

Rent Paid by Lodgers in Units With a Hispanic Householder, 1991

Data show number of persons (in thousands) in each rent category. Figures refer to a regular fixed rent, a set amount of money, billed or charged, that is paid at regular intervals by a lodger (usually weekly or monthly) to a member of the household. Data are restricted to lodgers who are 14 years of age and older, nonrelatives of the householder or any co-owners or co-renters, and not a co-owner or co-renter themselves. Medians for rent paid by lodgers are rounded to the nearest tenth.

Characteristics	Total occupied units	Tenure		Housing unit characteristics				Household characteristics		
		Owner	Renter	New construction 4 yrs.	Mobile homes	Physical problems: Severe	Physical problems: Moderate	Elderly (65+)	Moved in past year	Below poverty level
Total	6,239	2,423	3,816	218	208	267	564	669	1,720	1,501
Rent paid by lodgers										
Lodgers in housing units	92	14	77	5	-	-	12	-	34	7
Less than $100 per month	4	-	4	-	-	-	-	-	2	2
$100 to $199	19	-	19	-	-	-	3	-	9	-
$200 to $299	32	8	24	2	-	-	8	-	6	2
$300 to $399	14	2	12	-	-	-	2	-	4	-
$400 or more per month	15	2	13	3	-	-	-	-	9	3
Not reported	8	3	5	-	-	-	-	-	3	-
Median	261	...	256	...	...	...	...	...	...	...

Source: U.S. Department of Housing and Urban Development. Office of Policy Development and Research. *Current Housing Reports, American Housing Survey for the United States in 1991,* Washington, DC: U.S. Government Printing Office, April 1993, p. 278. *Notes:* Three dots (...) means not applicable or that the sample was too small. A dash (-) represents zero or a percentage which rounds to zero.

★ 546 ★

Housing

Selected Amenities in Housing Units With a Hispanic Householder, 1991

Data show number of housing units (in thousands) that have each feature.

Characteristics	Total occupied units	Tenure		Housing unit characteristics				Household characteristics		
		Owner	Renter	New construction 4 yrs.	Mobile homes	Physical problems: Severe	Physical problems: Moderate	Elderly (65+)	Moved in past year	Below poverty level
Total	6,239	4,423	3,816	218	208	267	564	669	1,720	1,501
Selected amenities[1]										
Porch, deck, balcony, or patio	3,854	1,927	1,926	173	127	103	335	442	963	765
Not reported	7	2	4	-	2	-	-	-	-	4
Telephone available	5,420	2,271	3,149	207	168	213	455	624	1,367	1,176
Usable fireplace	1,051	743	308	102	6	28	46	100	233	69
Separate dining room	2,103	1,163	940	101	37	89	175	239	475	327
With 2 or more living rooms or recreation rooms, etc.	991	767	224	69	12	36	61	120	173	102
Garage or carport included with home	2,887	1,728	1,159	149	54	90	205	343	612	441
Not included	3,336	690	2,646	69	153	177	359	323	1,107	1,059
Offstreet parking included	2,121	562	1,560	69	142	72	220	207	779	648
Offstreet parking not reported	41	-	41	-	1	2	10	7	14	11
Garage or carport not reported	16	5	11	-	-	-	-	2	-	2

Source: U.S. Department of Housing and Urban Development. Office of Policy Development and Research. *Current Housing Reports, American Housing Survey for the United States in 1991,* Washington, DC: U.S. Government Printing Office, April 1993, p. 264. *Notes:* A dash (-) represents zero or a percentage which rounds to zero. Qualifiers for categories shown are as follows: Porch, deck, balcony, or patio—The porch, deck, balcony, or patio must be attached to the sample unit, not just to the building or free standing. Porches may be enclosed or open; Telephone available—A housing unit is classified as having a telephone if there is a telephone for receiving calls available to the occupants of the unit. The telephone may be located outside or inside the housing unit, and one telephone may serve several occupants of several units. The number of housing units with a telephone available, therefore, does not indicate the number of telephones installed in homes; Usable fireplace—Excludes the following: fireplaces that have been blocked off or whose chimneys or flues have been filled; decorative or artificial fireplaces, and Franklin stoves. Free-standing fireplaces are included in this item; Separate dining room—A separate dining room is an area separated from adjoining rooms by a built-in floor-to-ceiling wall extending at least a few inches from its intersecting wall. Built-in walls do not include movable or collapsible partitions or partitions consisting solely of shelves and cabinets; Living rooms, recreation rooms, etc.—Includes family rooms, dens, recreation rooms and/or libraries; Garage or carport—The garage or carport must be on the same property but does not have to be attached to the house. Off-street parking is considered driveway or parking lot privileges that is paid for as part of the rent. 1. Figures may not add to total because more than one category may apply to unit.

★ 547 ★

Housing

Selected Characteristics of Owner-Occupied Housing, 1991

Figures are shown in thousands, by selected housing unit characteristic for selected groups in 1991.

Characteristics	Total occupied units	Tenure		Housing unit characteristic				Household characteristics				
		Owner	Renter	New construction 4 yrs.	Mobile homes	Physical problems: Severe	Physical problems: Moderate	Black	Hispanic	Elderly (65+)	Moved in past year	Below poverty level
Total units	93,147	59,796	33,351	5,147	5,630	2,874	4,531	10,832	6,239	20,348	16,434	12,836
Units in structure												
1, detached	57,485	49,084	8,401	3,041	...	1,600	2,675	5,002	2,846	13,571	5,904	5,797
1, attached	5,442	2,722	2,720	390	...	135	252	1,054	368	1,040	1,331	785
2-4 units	9,490	1,909	7,581	237	...	277	597	1,649	1,023	1,558	2,820	2,037
5-9 units	4,639	398	4,240	260	...	202	192	932	542	628	1,766	1,015
10-19 units	3,993	317	3,676	291	...	138	166	670	413	511	1,649	701
20-49 units	3,118	328	2,790	206	...	147	175	481	476	609	1,131	659
50 or more units	3,350	505	2,845	161	...	147	142	670	363	1,204	878	705
Mobile home or trailer	5,630	4,532	1,098	561	5,630	228	330	374	208	1,227	955	1,136

[Continued]

★ 547 ★

Selected Characteristics of Owner-Occupied Housing, 1991

[Continued]

Characteristics	Total occupied units	Tenure		Housing unit characteristic				Household characteristics				
				New construction 4 yrs.	Mobile homes	Physical problems		Black	Hispanic	Elderly (65+)	Moved in past year	Below poverty level
		Owner	Renter			Severe	Moderate					
Year structure built[1]												
1990-1994	2,041	1,539	501	2,041	292	56	41	147	67	180	1,253	160
1985-1989	8,043	5,433	2,610	3,106	878	199	92	521	424	833	1,804	563
1980-1984	7,290	4,671	2,619	...	917	133	149	674	432	1,035	1,547	842
1975-1979	11,023	7,300	3,724	...	1,241	270	337	952	670	1,725	1,939	1,355
1970-1974	9,982	6,077	3,905	...	1,277	247	368	1,204	646	1,928	1,925	1,459
1960-1969	14,523	9,570	4,953	...	865	447	588	1,704	908	3,364	2,160	1,779
1950-1959	12,512	8,982	3,530	...	133	313	626	1,424	986	3,775	1,449	1,581
1940-1949	7,668	4,742	2,926	...	16	240	721	1,282	725	2,247	1,199	1,386
1930-1939	5,984	3,355	2,629	...	11	265	571	1,083	526	1,490	1,019	1,151
1920-1929	5,062	2,872	2,190	...	-	180	406	805	381	1,357	744	934
1919 or earlier	9,019	5,257	3,762	...	-	525	632	1,038	476	2,415	1,395	1,625
Median	1964	1965	1963	...	1977	1957	1947	1958	1960	1957	1970	1958

Source: U.S. Department of Housing and Urban Development. Office of Policy Development and Research. *Current Housing Reports, American Housing Survey for the United States in 1991,* Washington, DC: U.S. Government Printing Office, April 1993, p. 38. *Notes:* Three dots (...) means not applicable or sample too small. A dash (-) means zero or rounds to zero. 1. For mobile homes, oldest category is 1939 or earlier.

★ 548 ★

Housing

Size of Households, by Hispanic Origin, 1991

Data show what percentage of each ethnic group lives in each household size.

Size of household	Total population	Hispanic origin population	Non-Hispanic population	Non-Hispanic White population	Hispanic subgroup				
					Mexican origin population	Puerto Rican origin population	Cuban origin population	Central and South American origin population	Other Hispanic origin population
Percent	100.0	100.0	100.0	100.0	100.0	100.0	100.0	100.0	100.0
One person	24.5	15.0	25.2	25.5	13.0	18.8	21.0	12.2	23.9
Two persons	32.3	22.3	33.1	34.3	19.6	25.9	31.7	22.0	28.8
Three persons	17.5	19.5	17.4	17.0	18.6	20.3	22.1	21.9	18.9
Four persons	15.5	19.4	15.2	15.1	19.1	21.2	16.5	22.4	16.5
Five persons	6.6	12.1	6.2	5.9	13.5	9.4	6.2	13.8	7.9
Six persons	2.3	6.2	2.0	1.6	8.1	2.8	1.6	5.3	3.2
Seven or more persons	1.3	5.4	1.0	0.7	8.1	1.5	0.8	2.3	0.8
Mean number of persons	2.63	3.41	2.57	2.52	3.78	2.85	2.65	3.25	2.78

Source: Montgomery, Patricia A. U.S. Bureau of the Census. *The Hispanic Population in the United States: March 1993.* Current Population Reports, Series P20-475. Washington, DC: U.S. Government Printing Office, 1994, pp. 16-17.

★ 549 ★

Housing

Source of Water and Sewage Disposal Method in Housing Units With a Hispanic Householder, 1991

Numbers are shown in thousands.

Characteristics	Total occupied units	Tenure		Housing unit characteristics				Household characteristics		
		Owner	Renter	New construction 4 yrs.	Mobile homes	Physical problems: Severe	Physical problems: Moderate	Elderly (65+)	Moved in past year	Below poverty level
Total	6,239	2,423	3,816	218	208	267	564	669	1,720	1,501
Source of water[1]										
Public system or private company	5,861	2,214	3,647	203	159	240	540	619	1,630	1,429
Well serving 1 to 5 units	204	139	65	10	43	15	7	25	36	34
Drilled	184	123	60	10	41	13	6	19	31	26
Dug	9	8	2	-	-	1	1	4	-	6
Not reported	11	8	3	-	2	2	-	2	2	2
Other	174	70	104	5	6	12	17	24	54	39
Means of sewage disposal[2]										
Public sewer	5,693	2,051	3,642	179	133	235	528	596	1,619	1,390
Septic tank, cesspool, chemical toilet	538	372	3,642	179	133	235	528	596	1,619	1,390
Other	9	-	9	-	-	9	-	-	5	4

Source: U.S. Department of Housing and Urban Development. Office of Policy Development and Research. *Current Housing Reports, American Housing Survey for the United States in 1991,* Washington, DC: U.S. Government Printing Office, April 1993, p. 258. *Notes:* A dash (-) represents zero or a percentage which rounds to zero. 1. A public system or private company refers to any source supplying running water to six or more housing units. The water may be supplied by a city, county, water district, or private water company, or it may be obtained from a well that supplies six or more housing units. An individual well that provides water for five or fewer housing units is further classified by whether it is "drilled" or "dug." Water sources such as springs, cisterns, streams, lakes, or bottled water are included in the "other" category. 2. A public sewer is connected to a city, county, sanitary district, neighborhood, or subdivision sewer system. Included are only systems operated by a government body or private organization sewage treatment system serving six or more units. Small sewage treatment plants, which in some localities are called neighborhood septic tanks, are classified as public sewers. A septic tank or cesspool is an underground tank or pit used for disposal of sewage (serving five or fewer units). A chemical toilet, which may be inside or outside the unit, uses chemicals to break down or dissolve sewage. Housing units for which sewage is disposed of in some other way are included in the "other category.

★ 550 ★

Housing

Square Footage and Lot Size of Housing Units With a Hispanic Householder, 1991

Numbers are shown in thousands.

Characteristics	Total occupied units	Tenure		Housing unit characteristics				Household characteristics		
		Owner	Renter	New construction 4 yrs.	Mobile homes	Physical problems: Severe	Physical problems: Moderate	Elderly (65+)	Moved in past year	Below poverty level
Total	6,239	2,423	3,816	218	208	267	564	669	1,720	1,501
Square footage of unit[1]										
Single detached and mobile homes	3,052	2,136	916	123	206	103	313	407	559	568
Less than 500	96	34	62	2	31	2	14	17	42	38
500 to 749	213	93	120	-	46	7	45	35	59	75
750 to 999	401	256	145	5	51	13	72	67	61	104
1,000 to 1,499	920	646	273	20	38	41	76	101	154	186
1,500 to 1,999	582	452	130	26	10	18	54	74	80	62
2,000 to 2,499	285	242	43	32	2	3	17	46	46	21
2,500 to 2,999	110	87	24	11	-	2	5	13	33	11
3,000 to 3,999	105	100	4	5	6	5	2	16	9	7

[Continued]

★ 550 ★

Square Footage and Lot Size of Housing Units With a Hispanic Householder, 1991

[Continued]

Characteristics	Total occupied units	Tenure		Housing unit characteristics				Household characteristics		
		Owner	Renter	New construction 4 yrs.	Mobile homes	Physical problems: Severe	Physical problems: Moderate	Elderly (65+)	Moved in past year	Below poverty level
4,000 or more	71	63	9	3	2	-	5	13	11	6
Not reported	268	162	106	19	21	12	23	23	63	57
Median	1,371	1,467	1,143	1,975	829	1,287	1,090	1,358	1,279	1,104
Lot size[2]										
Less than one-eighth acre	403	312	91	8	43	16	40	72	71	90
One-eighth up to one-quarter acre	681	535	147	30	13	12	82	105	87	102
One-quarter up to one-half acre	326	280	46	22	7	8	38	44	54	37
One-half up to one acre	166	131	35	1	20	12	13	23	25	22
1 to 4 acres	209	165	44	24	33	11	20	25	3	11
5 to 9 acres	28	22	7	4	5	1	2	4	3	4
10 acres or more	50	23	27	5	6	3	2	15	5	14
Don't know	1,479	721	758	36	78	47	134	150	381	370
Not reported	77	55	22	2	-	-	10	12	10	10
Median	.22	.22	.22	.35	.51	.36	.22	.21	.22	.19

Source: U.S. Department of Housing and Urban Development. Office of Policy Development and Research. *Current Housing Reports, American Housing Survey for the United States in 1991,* Washington, DC: U.S. Government Printing Office, April 1993, p. 256. *Notes:* A dash (-) stands for zero or rounds to zero. 1. Housing size is shown for single-family, detached housing units and mobile homes. Excluded from the calculation of square footage are unfinished attics, carports, attached garages, porches that are not protected from the elements (i.e. screened porches), and mobile home hitches. Both finished and unfinished basements are included. Median square footage is rounded to the nearest foot. Square footage is based on the respondent's estimate of the size of the unit. If the respondent did not know the square footage, the interviewer measured the outside dimensions of the unit. Preliminary evaluation indicates that this item is somewhat unreliable. 2. Lot size includes all connecting land that is owned or rented with the home. Excluded are two-or-more unit buildings and two-or-more-unit mobile homes. Median lot size is shown to hundreths of an acre.

★ 551 ★

Housing

Telephone Availability in Households, by Hispanic Origin, 1991

Availability of telephone in household	Total population	Hispanic origin population	Non-Hispanic population	Non-Hispanic White population	Hispanic subgroup: Mexican origin population	Puerto Rican origin population	Cuban origin population	Central and South American origin population	Other Hispanic origin population
Percent	100.0	100.0	100.0	100.0	100.0	100.0	100.0	100.0	100.0
In household	94.2	86.0	94.9	96.2	85.5	81.3	95.1	85.4	90.6
Available in household	1.3	2.0	1.3	1.0	2.4	1.5	0.7	1.4	2.1
Not available	4.4	11.9	3.9	2.7	12.0	17.2	4.1	13.2	7.3

Source: Montgomery, Patricia A. U.S. Bureau of the Census. *The Hispanic Population in the United States: March 1993.* Current Population Reports, Series P20-475. Washington, DC: U.S. Government Printing Office, 1994, pp. 16-17.

★552★

Housing

Value and Gross Rent for Occupied Housing, 1991

Housing units are shown in thousands, by housing unit value and monthly rent for selected racial/ethnic groups in 1991.

Characteristics	Total occupied units	Housing unit characteristics				Household characteristics				
		New construction 4 yrs.	Mobile homes	Physical problems: Severe	Physical problems: Moderate	Black	Hispanic	Elederly (65+)	Moved in past year	Below poverty level
Value										
Total	59,796	3,824	4,532	1,527	2,156	4,635	2,423	15,734	4,204	4,994
Less than $10,000	2,224	28	1,619	104	220	258	96	568	222	531
$10,000 to $19,999	2,691	239	1,395	113	284	365	106	771	207	531
$20,000 to $29,999	2,898	166	663	117	248	446	133	1,000	220	515
$30,000 to $39,999	3,588	101	381	82	271	488	180	1,185	233	570
$40,000 to $49,999	4,574	69	158	139	210	491	183	1,515	259	525
$50,000 to $59,999	4,457	107	111	102	184	521	148	1,370	288	406
$60,000 to $69,999	4,963	150	88	119	153	475	205	1,409	307	350
$70,000 to $79,999	4,495	214	51	128	102	316	147	1,211	268	264
$80,000 to $99,999	7,471	494	33	173	156	462	254	1,767	488	445
$100,000 to $119,999	4,376	351	22	91	65	182	143	1,022	347	227
$120,000 to $149,999	4,906	482	8	97	43	201	167	1,076	407	160
$150,000 to $199,999	5,574	566	-	100	80	244	288	1,226	406	247
$200,000 to $249,999	2,863	330	-	60	47	90	151	628	227	84
$250,000 to $299,999	1,640	1852	-	33	30	47	95	370	118	67
$300,000 or more	3,074	375	5	69	64	48	128	619	214	71
Median	80,015	119,627	14,638	68,919	42,646	55,173	81,128	70,418	84,266	46,652
Monthly housing costs										
Total	33,351	1,323	1,098	1,347	2,376	6,197	3,816	4,613	12,230	7,843
Less than $100	615	9	4	27	50	281	45	124	205	486
$100 to $199	2,252	32	70	149	251	761	226	786	511	1,352
$200 to $249	1,420	16	74	108	237	344	185	327	478	576
$250 to $299	2,003	11	127	137	261	454	188	367	651	666
$300 to $349	2,591	57	153	101	219	519	316	394	937	771
$350 to $399	2,843	35	161	101	211	541	312	346	1,135	655
$400 to $449	3,019	63	111	125	148	570	329	291	1,192	598
$450 to $499	2,861	76	82	87	171	484	353	336	1,074	418
$500 to $599	4,641	208	63	143	284	729	631	450	1,811	580
$600 to $699	3,252	248	19	106	162	466	379	283	1,359	333
$700 to $799	2,078	165	9	41	77	288	282	189	886	182
$800 to $999	1,945	157	10	51	67	209	211	128	810	180
$1,000 to $1,249	765	90	2	23	26	73	88	51	327	51
$1,250 to $1,499	296	33	-	5	5	15	24	28	1224	6
$1,500 or more	244	43	-	6	-	12	16	30	125	22
No cash rent	2,526	80	214	137	204	450	231	484	605	968
Mortgage payment not reported	...	...	...	...	...	...	...	...	...	...
Median (excludes no cash rent)	462	646	354	391	366	398	477	360	483	323

Source: U.S. Department of Housing and Urban Development. Office of Policy Development and Research. *Current Housing Reports, American Housing Survey for the United States in 1991,* Washington, DC: U.S. Government Printing Office, April 1993, p. 120. *Notes:* 1. Beginning with 1989 this item uses current income in its calculation. 2. Figures may not add to total because more than one category may apply to a unit.

★ 553 ★

Housing

Value and Value-Income Ratio of Homes With Hispanic Owners, 1991

Data show number of persons (in thousands) in each value range. The ratio of value to current income was computed by dividing the value of the housing unit by the total current income. The ratio was computed separately and rounded to the nearest tenth.

Characteristics	Total occupied units	Tenure		Housing unit characteristics				Household characteristics		
		Owner	Renter	New construction 4 yrs.	Mobile homes	Physical problems: Severe	Physical problems: Moderate	Elderly (65+)	Moved in past year	Below poverty level
Total	2,423	2,423	...	125	155	63	198	395	232	312
Value										
Less than $10,000	96	96	...	-	71	8	12	12	16	20
$10,000 to $19,999	106	106	...	5	38	9	18	26	4	34
$20,000 to $29,999	133	133	...	3	22	5	32	18	14	30
$30,000 to $39,999	180	180	...	-	10	-	30	22	26	37
$40,000 to $49,999	183	183	...	-	5	10	37	35	11	40
$50,000 to $59,999	148	148	...	7	5	3	12	34	12	24
$60,000 to $69,999	205	205	...	16	-	-	12	21	20	27
$70,000 to $79,999	147	147	...	8	2	8	10	27	7	10
$80,000 to $99,999	254	254	...	21	2	5	2	38	26	33
$100,000 to $119,999	143	143	...	10	-	4	4	28	10	12
$120,000 to $149,999	167	167	...	14	-	-	-	26	21	5
$150,000 to $199,999	288	288	...	15	-	4	7	39	26	20
$200,000 to $249,999	151	151	...	3	-	2	5	25	6	9
$250,000 to $299,999	95	95	..	9	-	2	7	16	18	5
$300,000 or more	128	128	...	15	-	2	9	28	16	5
Median	81,128	81,128	...	105,393	11,797	48,713	41,862	81,212	85,814	48,532
Value-Income ratio[1]										
Less than 1.5	669	669	...	27	122	30	85	61	69	36
1.5 to 1.9	233	233	...	3	6	3	11	17	24	12
2.0 to 2.4	258	258	...	23	12	5	26	26	34	23
2.5 to 2.9	191	191	...	9	5	4	12	10	17	15
3.0 to 3.9	294	294	...	15	3	7	13	57	22	35
4.0 to 4.9	197	197	...	12	3	4	6	39	12	17
5.0 or more	554	554	...	35	4	9	46	176	51	149
Zero or negative income	25	25	...	2	-	-	-	8	2	25
Median	2.6	2.6	...	3.0	-1.5	1.7	2.1	4.6	2.3	5.0+

Source: U.S. Department of Housing and Urban Development. Office of Policy Development and Research. *Current Housing Reports, American Housing Survey for the United States in 1991,* Washington, DC: U.S. Government Printing Office, April 1993, p. 284. *Notes:* Three dots (...) means not applicable or that the sample was too small. A dash (-) represents zero or a percentage which rounds to zero. 1. Beginning in 1989 this item uses current income in its calculation.

★ 554 ★

Housing

Water Supply and Sewage Disposal Problems in Housing Units With a Hispanic Householder, 1991

Numbers are shown in thousands.

Characteristics	Total occupied units	Tenure		Housing unit characteristics				Household characteristics		
		Owner	Renter	New construction 4 yrs.	Mobile homes	Physical problems: Severe	Physical problems: Moderate	Elderly (65+)	Moved in past year	Below poverty level
Total	6,239	2,423	3,816	218	208	267	564	669	1,720	1,501
Water supply stoppage										
With hot and cold piped water	6,210	2,418	3,793	218	206	238	564	665	1,709	1,487
No stoppage in last 3 months	5,839	2,302	3,537	206	183	194	503	630	1,612	1,376
With stoppage in last 3 months	289	89	200	12	18	36	47	24	79	76
No stoppage lasting 6 hours or more	80	25	55	4	4	3	10	5	25	9
1 time lasting 6 hours or more	112	38	74	5	12	5	22	14	26	34
2 times	39	9	30	-	-	15	7	2	7	18
3 times	11	1	10	-	1	10	-	-	3	3
4 times or more	11	3	8	-	-	4	7	-	-	4
Number of times not reported	37	13	24	3	2	-	2	3	17	7
Stoppage not reported	82	26	56	-	4	8	14	11	18	35
Flush toilet breakdowns										
With one or more flush toilets	6,193	2,420	3,774	218	206	221	564	665	1,691	1,483
With at least one working toilet at all times in last 3 months	5,628	2,233	3,395	201	179	16	448	618	1,555	1,266
None working some time in last 3 months	536	178	358	17	26	46	116	47	129	213
No breakdowns lasting 6 hours or more	130	33	96	7	7	2	17	8	33	41
1 time lasting 6 hours or more	250	101	149	9	17	24	49	31	57	95
2 times	67	20	47	-	2	12	4	5	13	40
3 times	14	7	7	2	-	1	13	-	2	2
4 times or more	35	4	31	-	-	4	31	-	9	20
Number of times not reported	40	13	27	-	-	4	2	3	14	16
Breakdowns not reported	29	8	21	-	-	9	-	-	7	5
Sewage disposal breakdowns										
With public sewer	5,693	2,051	3,642	179	133	235	528	596	1,619	1,390
No breakdowns in last 3 months	5,550	1,998	3,552	179	124	225	489	578	1,585	1,337
With breakdowns in last 3 months	143	53	90	-	9	10	39	18	34	53
No breakdowns lasting 6 hours or more	40	19	21	-	-	4	3	4	12	15
1 time lasting 6 hours or more	73	26	47	-	9	2	19	7	17	21
2 times	7	2	5	-	-	-	7	-	5	5
3 times	12	4	9	-	-	5	6	6	-	5
4 times or more	10	2	7	-	-	-	4	-	-	7
With septic tank or cesspool	538	372	166	39	75	24	37	73	95	108
No breakdowns in last 3 months	525	367	158	39	75	24	33	68	94	103
With breakdowns in last 3 months	13	5	8	-	-	-	4	5	2	5
No breakdowns lasting 6 hours or more	-	-	-	-	-	-	-	-	-	-
1 time lasting 6 hours or more	11	5	6	-	-	-	4	3	2	3
2 times	2	-	2	-	-	-	-	2	-	2
3 times	-	-	-	-	-	-	-	-	-	-
4 times or more	-	-	-	-	-	-	-	-	-	-

Source: U.S. Department of Housing and Urban Development. Office of Policy Development and Research. *Current Housing Reports, American Housing Survey for the United States in 1991*, Washington, DC: U.S. Government Printing Office, April 1993, p. 262. *Notes:* A dash (-) represents zero or a percentage which rounds to zero. 1. Water supply stoppage means that the housing unit was completely without running water from its regular source. Completely without running water means that the water system servicing the unit supplied no water at all, that is, no equipment or facility using running water (in kitchen and washer, and other similar items) had water supplied to it, or all were operable. The reason could vary from a stoppage because of a flood or storm, to a broken pipe, to a shutdown of the water system, to a failure to pay the bill, or other reasons. 2. A privy or chemical toilet is not considered a flush toilet. Flush toilets outside the unit are not counted. The statistics on breakdowns of flush toilets are shown for housing units with at least one flush toilet for the household's use only. The flush toilet may be completely unusable because of a faulty flushing mechanism, broken pipes, stopped up soil pipe, lack of water supplied to the flush toilet, or some other reason. 3. Data are limited to housing units in which the means of sewage disposal was a public sewer, septic tank, or cesspool. Breakdowns refer to situations in which the system was completely unusable. Examples include septic tank being pumped because it no longer perked, tank collapsed, tank exploded, sewer main broken, sewer treatment plant not operating as a result of electrical failure or water service interruption, etc.

Income

★ 555 ★

Counties With the Most Affluent Hispanics, 1989

Hispanic households with incomes over $50,000 in 1989 are shown, by county or county equivalents.

County (metropolitan area)	All Hispanic households[1]	Percent affluent
Morris, NJ (Newark)	5,134	44.9
Somerset, NJ (Middlesex-Somerset-Hunterdon)	2,849	43.8
Fairfax, VA (Washington)[2]	13,726	42.7
Suffolk, NY (Nassau-Suffolk)	20,557	42.4
Anne Arundel, MD (Baltimore)	1,731	41.8
Rockland, NY (New York)	4,356	41.0
Bergen, NJ (Bergen-Passaic)	14,834	39.8
Nassau, NY (Nassau-Suffolk)	18,756	39.8
St. Louis, MO (St. Louis)	3,151	36.2
Prince William, VA (Washington)[3]	2,885	35.7
Montgomery, MD (Washington)	15,086	35.2
Montgomery, PA (Philadelphia)	2,196	34.7
Ocean, NJ (Monmouth-Ocean)	3,736	34.6
Baltimore, MD (Baltimore)	2,391	34.4
Dutchess, NY (Poughkeepsie)	2,149	34.3
Oakland, MI (Detroit)	5,095	34.2
Norfolk, MA (Boston-Lawrence-Salem-Lowell-Brockton)	2,152	33.7
San Mateo, CA (San Francisco)	29,029	33.7
Macomb, MI (Detroit)	1,892	33.6
Monmouth, NJ (Monmouth-Ocean)	5,758	33.2

Source: American Demographics (December 1992), p. 40. Primary source: 1990 census. *Notes:* 1. U.S. average is 16.1 %. Includes only counties with Hispanic population of 5,000 or more, Hispanics may be of any race. 2. Includes the independent cities of Fairfax and Falls Church. 3. Includes the independent cities of Manassas and Manassas Park.

★ 556 ★

Income

Family Income Distribution Among Racial/Ethnic Groups, 1990

Percent distribution is shown, by race/ethnicity, within quintiles, in 1990.

Race/ethnicity	Total	Lowest fifth	Second fifth	Middle fifth	Fourth fifth	Highest fifth	Top 5 percent
Total	100.0	100.0	100.0	100.0	100.0	100.0	100.0
Hispanic origin[1]	7.5	13.4	9.1	6.8	4.8	3.3	2.6
White	85.6	73.5	85.4	88.0	90.1	91.3	93.4
Black	11.3	23.2	11.8	9.3	7.2	4.8	2.7

Source: U.S. Bureau of the Census. *Money Income of Households, Families, and Persons in the United States: 1990.* Current Population Reports, P60-174, 1991, pp. 58-59. Primary source: U.S. Bureau of the Census, Current Population Reports, Series P-60, No. 174, 1991. *Note:* 1. Persons of Hispanic origin may be of any race.

★ 557 ★

Income

Family Income Distribution Within Selected Racial/Ethnic Groups, 1990

Percent distribution is shown, by quintile, for each race/ethnicity.

Race/ethnicity	Number (thous.)	Percent distribution						
		Total	Lowest fifth	Second fifth	Middle fifth	Fourth fifth	Highest fifth	Top 5 percent
All families	66,322	100.0	20.0	20.0	20.0	20.0	20.0	5.0
Hispanic origin[1]	4,981	100.0	35.8	24.4	18.2	12.9	8.7	1.7
White	56,803	100.0	17.2	20.0	20.5	21.0	21.3	5.5
Black	7,471	100.0	41.3	21.0	16.5	12.7	8.5	1.2

Source: U.S. Bureau of the Census. *Money Income of Households, Families, and Persons in the United States: 1990.* Current Population Reports, P60-174, 1991, pp. 60-61. Primary source: U.S. Bureau of the Census, Current Population Reports, Series P-60, No. 174, 1991. *Note:* 1. Persons of Hispanic origin may be of any race.

★ 558 ★

Income

Family Income, by Number of Earners, 1990

Figures are shown in thousands, by income characteristics, race/ethnicity, and number of earners in family.

Income characteristics and race/ethnicity	Total	Families having specified number of earners						Mean number of earners
		No earners	One earner	Two earners or more				
				Total	Two earners	Three earners	Four earners or more	
All races								
Total number of families (000)	66,322	9,519	18,215	38,587	29,536	6,598	2,453	1.65
Median income ($)	35,353	15,047	25,878	45,462	42,146	53,721	67,700	1
Standard error ($)	169	244	235	219	226	509	1,112	1
Mean income ($)	42,652	20,239	33,717	52,399	48,919	60,025	73,796	1
Standard error ($)	197	305	361	258	285	633	1,064	1
Income per family member ($)	13,408	8,294	11,158	15,238	15,616	14,560	13,957	1
Standard error ($)	77	156	145	102	125	234	342	1
Hispanic origin[2]								
Total number of families (000)	4,981	694	1,571	2,716	1,948	533	235	1.64
Median income ($)	23,431	7,858	16,795	33,704	30,549	39,738	52,776	1
Standard error ($)	566	362	494	712	827	1,683	3,227	1
Mean income ($)	29,311	9,617	21,264	38,999	35,149	45,490	56,210	1
Standard error ($)	526	462	737	739	796	1,772	2,891	1
Income per family member ($)	7,670	3,042	5,991	9,403	9,4174	9,483	9,198	1
Standard error ($)	185	207	276	269	328	575	766	1
White								
Total number of families (000)	56,803	7,882	15,047	33,873	26,003	5,770	2,100	1.67
Median income ($)	36,915	17,369	27,670	46,261	43,036	54,632	67,753	1
Standard error ($)	178	264	323	231	273	543	1,215	1
Mean income ($)	44,532	22,595	36,054	53,403	50,009	61,103	74,269	1
Standard error ($)	217	351	415	279	309	688	1,171	1
Income per family member ($)	14,291	9,862	12,103	15,851	16,245	15,160	14,418	1
Standard error ($)	87	198	171	114	139	261	384	1
Black								
Total number of families (000)	7,471	1,407	2,591	3,473	2,660	600	213	1.51
Median income ($)	21,423	6,305	16,308	36,741	34,050	43,813	59,983	1
Standard error ($)	381	263	399	569	708	1,761	3,469	1
Mean income ($)	27,554	8,061	19,802	41,234	37,536	50,041	62,636	1
Standard error ($)	419	272	496	645	666	1,815	2,498	1
Income per family member ($)	7,855	2,565	6,193	10,607	10,798	10,311	9,940	1
Standard error ($)	159	123	217	264	316	585	787	1

Source: U.S. Bureau of the Census. *Money Income of Households, Families, and Persons in the United States: 1990.* Current Population Reports, P60-174, 1991, pp. 98-99. Primary source: U.S. Bureau of the Census, Current Population Reports, Series P-60, No. 174, 1991. *Notes:* 1. Not applicable. 2. Persons of Hispanic origin may be of any race.

★ 559 ★

Income

Family Income, by Size of Family, 1990

Figures are shown in thousands, by income characteristics, race/ethnicity, and family size.

Race/ethnicity	Total	Families having specified number of persons						Mean size of family
		Two persons	Three persons	Four persons	Five persons	Six persons	Seven persons or more	
All races								
Total number of families (000)	66,322	27,615	15,298	14,098	5,965	2,060	1,285	3.18
Median income ($)	35,353	30,428	36,644	41,451	39,452	38,378	35,363	1
Standard error ($)	169	244	368	363	586	1,428	1,312	1
Mean income ($)	42,652	38,451	43,194	48,203	46,583	44,988	43,582	1
Standard error ($)	197	297	397	451	658	1,105	1,418	1
Income per family member ($)	13,408	19,023	14,202	12,045	9,347	7,475	5,559	1
Standard error ($)	77	193	174	149	177	244	237	1
Hispanic origin[2]								
Total number of families (000)	4,981	1,229	1,188	1,146	777	342	299	3.82
Median income ($)	23,431	19,230	22,778	25,808	25,727	24,785	30,549	1
Standard error ($)	566	754	1,061	1,335	1,078	2,437	1,928	1
Mean income ($)	29,311	25,189	28,463	31,505	31,239	29,794	35,665	1
Standard error ($)	526	966	1,101	1,177	1,288	1,856	2,205	1
Income per family member ($)	7,670	12,443	9,343	7,820	6,213	4,934	4,557	1
Standard error ($)	185	744	503	393	348	408	379	1
White								
Total number of families (000)	56,803	24,532	12,928	11,951	4,929	1,607	856	3.12
Median income ($)	36,915	31,743	38,858	43,352	41,037	40,387	39,845	1
Standard error ($)	178	253	420	411	594	1,124	2,183	1
Mean income ($)	44,532	40,051	45,644	50,283	48,659	47,122	47,256	1
Standard error ($)	217	323	441	491	733	1,293	1,795	1
Income per family member ($)	14,291	19,887	15,051	12,614	9,774	7,869	6,132	1
Standard error ($)	87	214	198	166	200	289	312	1
Black								
Total number of families (000)	7,471	2,496	1,941	1,598	788	328	319	3.51
Median income ($)	21,423	19,020	20,602	25,758	22,455	26,926	22,501	1
Standard error ($)	381	769	952	1,592	1,474	2,888	1,382	1
Mean income ($)	27,554	23,779	27,207	30,803	30,655	32,985	29,677	1
Standard error ($)	419	604	849	1,022	1,377	1,973	1,994	1
Income per family member ($)	7,855	11,367	8,797	7,533	6,175	5,423	3,734	1
Standard error ($)	159	459	375	328	362	442	321	1

Source: U.S. Bureau of the Census. *Money Income of Households, Families, and Persons in the United States: 1990.* Current Population Reports, P60-174, 1991, pp. 89-95. Primary source: U.S. Bureau of the Census, Current Population Reports, Series P-60, No. 174, 1991. *Notes:* 1. Not applicable. 2. Persons of Hispanic origin may be of any race.

★ 560 ★

Income

Full-Time Workers With Low Annual Earnings, by Race/Ethnicity and Sex, 1974-90

This Census report defines earnings as low if they are less than the poverty level for a four-person family, working 40 hours a week, 50 weeks per year: $3,144 or $1.57 per hour in 1964; $3,676 or $1.84 per hour in 1969; $4,843 or $2.42 per hour in 1974; $6,905 or $3.45 per hour in 1979; $9,694 or $4.85 per hour in 1984; $11,570 or $5.79 per hour in 1989; $12,195 or $6.10 per hour in 1990. Figures are percentages.

Characteristics	1974	1979	1984	1989	1990
Both sexes					
Hispanic origin[1]	18.3	19.7	22.9	27.6	31.4
White	11.4	11.4	13.8	15.7	17.1
Black	18.1	18.5	21.5	21.2	25.3
Males					
Hispanic origin[1]	12.1	13.4	18.7	24.3	28.2
White	6.9	7.2	9.9	11.5	13.0
Black	13.8	14.0	17.5	17.1	22.4
Females					
Hispanic origin[1]	32.6	32.2	30.7	33.6	37.0
White	21.8	19.8	20.7	22.5	23.6
Black	24.5	24.3	25.6	25.5	28.5

Source: U.S. Bureau of the Census. *Workers With Low Earnings: 1964 to 1990.* Current Population Reports, Series P-60, No. 178. Washington, DC: U.S. Government Printing Office, 1992, p. 5. *Note:* 1. Persons of Hispanic origin may be of any race.

★ 561 ★

Income

Full-Time Workers With Low Annual Earnings, by Years of School Completed, 1974-90

This Census report defines earnings as low if they are less than the poverty level for a four-person family, working 40 hours a week, 50 weeks per year: $3,144 or $1.57 per hour in 1964; $3,676 or $1.84 per hour in 1969; $4,843 or $2.42 per hour in 1974; $6,905 or $3.45 per hour in 1979; $9,694 or $4.85 per hour in 1984; $11,570 or $5.79 per hour in 1989; $12,195 or $6.10 per hour in 1990. Figures are percentages.

Characteristics	1974	1979	1984	1989	1990
All races					
Less than 12 years	19.7	21.3	28.1	32.1	36.1
12 years	12.0	13.0	16.7	19.5	21.6
13 years and over	5.4	6.2	8.0	9.3	10.5

[Continued]

★ 561 ★

Full-Time Workers With Low Annual Earnings, by Years of School Completed, 1974-90

[Continued]

Characteristics	1974	1979	1984	1989	1990
Hispanic origin[1]					
Less than 12 years	25.5	27.2	34.6	39.6	48.3
12 years	15.2	17.5	19.3	25.1	27.8
13 years and over	6.4	8.3	9.9	14.1	14.3
White					
Less than 12 years	18.4	19.9	26.6	31.2	35.4
12 years	11.6	12.4	16.0	19.1	20.4
13 years and over	5.4	6.1	7.7	8.9	10.1
Black					
Less than 12 years	26.1	29.4	35.3	36.1	40.1
12 years	16.2	17.6	22.5	22.4	29.5
13 years and over	6.5	8.3	11.3	13.1	14.5

Source: U.S. Bureau of the Census. *Workers With Low Earnings: 1964 to 1990.* Current Population Reports, Series P-60, No. 178. Washington, DC: U.S. Government Printing Office, 1992, p. 6. *Note:* 1. Persons of Hispanic origin may be of any race.

★ 562 ★

Income

Hourly Pay of Persons With Job Accessions, 1987-89

A "job accession" is defined as not having a job in one month but having a job in the following month. This table shows mean hourly pay rates for persons who experienced job accessions and were paid on an hourly basis. Data are shown as of the first job accession of each person.

Race and Hispanic origin	Hourly rate of pay				
	Total	16 to 19 years	20 to 24 years	25 to 34 years	35 and over
All persons	5.63	4.33	5.33	6.33	6.54
White	5.76	4.41	5.44	6.56	6.66
Black	5.05	3.96	4.89	5.29	6.14
Hispanic origin	5.17	4.36	5.36	5.38	5.91

Source: U.S. Bureau of the Census. *Job Creation During the Late 1980's (Data from the Survey of Income and Program Participation).* Current Population Reports, P70, No. 27. Washington, DC: U.S. Government Printing Office, 1992, p. 8.

★ 563 ★

Income

Hourly Workers Paid at or Below Minimum Wage, 1993

Data shown are annual average of monthly figures for employed wage and salary workers, based on Current Population Surveys.

	Number of workers (000)[1]				Percent distribution			Percent of all workers paid hourly rates			Median hourly earnings of workers paid hourly rates[2] (dol.)
	Total paid hourly rates	Number at or below $4.25									
		Total	At $4.25	Below $4.25	Total	At $4.25	Below $4.25	Total	At $4.25	Below $4.25	
Total, 16 years and over[3]	63,316	4,186	2,518	1,668	100.0	100.0	100.0	6.6	4.0	2.6	7.92
White	52,971	3,467	2,036	1,431	83.7	80.9	85.8	6.5	3.8	2.7	8.03
Black	8,078	572	392	180	12.8	15.6	10.8	7.1	4.9	2.2	7.19
Hispanic origin[4]	6,047	544	427	117	9.6	17.0	7.0	9.0	7.1	1.9	6.87

Source: 1994 Statistical Abstract of the United States on CD-ROM [machine-readable datafiles]. CD-8A-94. Washington, DC: U.S. Department of Commerce, Economics and Statistics Administration, Bureau of the Census, Data User Services Division, January 1995. Primary source: U.S. Bureau of Labor Statistics, unpublished data. *Notes:* 1. Excludes the incorporated self-employed. 2. For definition of median, see Guide to Tabular Presentation. 3. Includes races not shown separately. 4. Persons of Hispanic origin may be of any race.

★ 564 ★

Income

Household Income Percent Distribution, by Income Level, 1970-92

Data are shown in (1992) constant dollars for households as of March of following year and are based on Current Population Surveys.

Year	Number of house-holds (000)	Percent distribution							Median income (dollars)
		Under $10,000	$10,000-$14,999	$15,000-$24,999	$25,000-$34,999	$35,000-$49,999	$50,000-$74,999	$75,000 and over	
All households[1]									
1970	64,778	15.5	8.7	17.5	18.5	20.0	14.0	5.9	29,670
1975	72,867	15.5	9.9	17.9	16.4	19.7	14.6	6.3	29,458
1980	82,368	14.7	9.3	17.7	16.1	18.7	15.6	8.0	30,191
1981	83,527	15.2	9.3	18.5	15.4	18.6	15.0	8.0	29,701
1982	83,918	15.4	9.5	17.9	15.7	18.4	14.9	8.2	29,602
1983[2]	85,290	15.2	9.5	17.9	15.6	18.1	15.1	8.5	29,607
1984	86,789	14.9	9.4	17.5	15.3	17.7	15.8	9.4	30,268
1985	88,458	14.9	8.9	17.3	15.2	17.9	16.0	9.8	30,796
1986	89,479	14.6	8.5	16.8	14.8	17.8	16.5	10.9	31,871
1987[3]	91,124	14.3	8.7	16.5	14.5	17.8	16.8	11.4	32,186
1988	92,830	14.1	8.6	16.7	14.4	17.9	16.6	11.7	32,288
1989	93,347	13.5	8.9	16.3	14.6	17.7	16.7	12.4	32,706
1990	94,312	13.8	8.7	16.9	15.1	17.6	16.1	11.7	32,142
1991	95,669	14.5	9.2	17.1	14.8	17.5	15.7	11.2	31,033
1992	96,391	14.6	9.5	16.8	14.8	17.1	16.1	11.0	30,786
White									
1970	57,575	14.2	8.2	16.9	18.8	20.9	14.7	6.3	30,903
1975	64,392	13.6	9.4	17.6	16.7	20.4	15.4	6.8	30,806
1980	71,872	12.9	8.8	17.4	16.3	19.5	16.5	8.6	31,851

[Continued]

★564★

Household Income Percent Distribution, by Income Level, 1970-92

[Continued]

Year	Number of households (000)	Percent distribution							Median income (dollars)
		Under $10,000	$10,000-$14,999	$15,000-$24,999	$25,000-$34,999	$35,000-$49,999	$50,000-$74,999	$75,000 and over	
1981	72,845	13.3	8.8	18.2	15.8	19.3	15.9	8.6	31,381
1982	73,182	13.7	9.0	17.8	16.0	19.0	15.7	8.9	30,991
1983[2]	74,170	13.2	9.0	17.8	16.0	18.8	15.9	9.3	31,039
1984	75,328	13.0	8.9	17.3	15.7	18.5	16.6	10.0	31,931
1985	76,576	13.2	8.5	17.0	15.5	18.5	16.8	10.6	32,478
1986	77,284	12.8	8.0	16.5	15.1	18.5	17.5	11.7	33,507
1987[3]	78,519	12.3	8.2	16.3	14.7	18.5	17.8	12.2	33,912
1988	79,734	12.1	8.1	16.5	14.6	18.7	17.5	12.5	34,133
1989	80,163	11.6	8.5	16.1	14.8	18.3	17.5	13.2	34,403
1990	80,968	11.8	8.4	16.8	15.4	18.2	16.9	12.4	33,525
1991	81,675	12.4	8.9	17.0	15.1	18.1	16.6	12.0	32,519
1992	82,083	12.5	9.1	16.7	15.1	17.7	17.0	11.9	32,368
Black									
1970	6,180	27.9	13.4	22.4	15.5	12.2	7.2	1.5	18,810
1975	7,489	29.0	14.1	20.1	14.6	13.5	7.1	1.6	18,494
1980	8,847	29.0	13.5	20.4	13.8	12.4	8.3	2.5	18,350
1981	8,961	30.6	13.3	20.7	12.9	12.6	7.8	2.1	17,610
1982	8,916	30.5	13.4	19.9	13.7	13.3	7.2	2.0	17,564
1983[2]	9,243	31.0	13.2	20.0	12.6	12.7	8.1	2.5	17,570
1984	9,480	29.8	13.6	19.9	13.1	11.9	8.6	3.3	18,190
1985	9,797	29.0	12.5	20.3	12.8	13.0	9.2	3.1	19,323
1986	9,922	29.6	11.8	18.8	13.5	13.0	9.1	4.2	19,304
1987[3]	10,192	29.9	11.9	18.9	13.5	12.4	8.9	4.6	19,355
1988	10,561	29.4	12.3	18.2	13.0	12.4	10.2	4.5	19,458
1989	10,486	27.8	12.1	18.4	13.5	13.5	9.8	4.8	20,460
1990	10,671	28.9	11.5	18.5	13.4	13.5	9.3	4.9	20,048
1991	11,083	30.3	11.4	18.2	13.4	13.7	9.0	4.0	19,373
1992	11,190	30.5	12.2	18.3	13.2	12.8	8.8	4.2	18,660
Hispanic[4]									
1975	2,948	19.6	13.4	23.8	17.4	16.0	7.5	2.3	22,131
1980	3,906	18.8	12.5	22.5	16.7	15.3	10.6	3.5	23,271
1981	3,980	18.8	11.8	22.1	17.3	16.1	10.3	3.6	23,825
1982	4,085	21.3	13.4	21.2	16.0	14.9	10.0	3.2	22,275
1983[2]	4,666	22.2	12.5	21.3	16.6	13.9	10.0	3.5	22,248
1984	4,883	21.6	12.2	20.2	15.7	15.3	10.8	4.3	22,945
1985	5,213	21.0	13.2	19.9	15.8	15.0	10.6	4.4	22,773
1986	5,418	20.2	11.9	20.5	15.9	15.2	10.9	5.4	23,493
1987[3]	5,642	20.9	12.0	20.0	15.2	15.2	11.3	5.5	23,881
1988	5,910	20.3	10.9	20.9	15.5	15.6	10.9	5.8	24,145
1989	5,933	19.1	11.3	20.4	15.5	15.2	12.6	6.0	24,803
1990	6,220	19.3	12.6	20.0	16.3	16.2	10.0	5.5	23,970

[Continued]

★ 564 ★

Household Income Percent Distribution, by Income Level, 1970-92

[Continued]

Year	Number of house-holds (000)	Percent distribution							Median income (dollars)
		Under $10,000	$10,000-$14,999	$15,000-$24,999	$25,000-$34,999	$35,000-$49,999	$50,000-$74,999	$75,000 and over	
1991	6,379	20.1	11.8	21.3	15.5	15.6	10.3	5.5	23,374
1992	6,626	20.4	12.6	20.8	16.3	14.5	10.5	5.0	22,848

Source: 1994 Statistical Abstract of the United States on CD-ROM [machine-readable datafiles]. CD-8A-94. Washington, DC: U.S. Department of Commerce, Economics and Statistics Administration, Bureau of the Census, Data User Services Division, January 1995. Primary source: U.S. Bureau of the Census, Current Population Reports, P60-184. *Notes:* 1. Includes other races not shown separately. 2. Beginning 1983, data based on revised Hispanic population controls and not directly comparable with prior years. 3. Beginning 1987, data based on revised processing procedures and not directly comparable with prior years. 4. Persons of Hispanic origin may be of any race. Income data for Hispanic origin households are not available prior to 1972.

★ 565 ★

Income

Household Income Quintile Distribution, 1990

Percent distribution is shown, as of March 1991.

Race/ethnicity	Total	Lowest fifth	Second fifth	Middle fifth	Fourth fifth	Highest fifth	Top 5 percent
Total	100.0	100.0	100.0	100.0	100.0	100.0	100.0
Hispanic origin[1]	6.6	9.4	8.0	7.0	5.2	3.4	2.6
White	85.9	76.2	85.2	87.5	89.0	91.3	92.8
Black	11.3	21.3	12.4	9.9	8.0	5.1	3.1

Source: U.S. Bureau of the Census. *Money Income of Households, Families, and Persons in the United States: 1990.* Current Population Reports, P60-174, 1991, p. 19. Primary source: U.S. Bureau of the Census, *Current Population Reports, Series P-60,* No. 174, 1991. *Note:* 1. Persons of Hispanic origin may be of any race.

★ 566 ★

Income

Household Income, by Hispanic Origin, March 1993

Data distribution of persons in each income bracket, by Hispanic origin of householder.

Household income in 1992	Total population	Hispanic origin population	Non-Hispanic population	Non-Hispanic White population	Mexican origin population	Puerto Rican origin population	Cuban origin population	Central and South American origin population	Other Hispanic origin population
Percent	100.0	100.0	100.0	100.0	100.0	100.0	100.0	100.0	100.0
Less than $10,000	14.6	20.4	14.2	11.9	18.4	31.2	19.8	18.1	22.3
10,000 to $24,999	26.3	33.4	25.8	25.2	35.2	30.5	28.6	34.9	26.2
$25,000 to $49,999	31.9	30.7	32.0	32.9	32.4	25.3	27.1	30.8	30.3
$50,000 or more	27.1	15.5	28.0	30.0	14.0	12.9	24.5	16.2	21.2

[Continued]

★ 566 ★

Household Income, by Hispanic Origin, March 1993

[Continued]

Household income in 1992	Total population	Hispanic origin population	Non-Hispanic population	Non-Hispanic White population	Mexican origin population	Puerto Rican origin population	Cuban origin population	Central and South American origin population	Other Hispanic origin population
Median income (dollars)	30,784	22,859	31,447	33,355	22,938	18,999	25,874	22,812	26,086
Mean income (dollars)	39,020	29,102	39,752	41,646	28,448	25,060	35,594	29,682	33,909

Source: Montgomery, Patricia A. U.S. Bureau of the Census. *The Hispanic Population in the United States: March 1993.* Current Population Reports, Series P20-475. Washington, DC: U.S. Government Printing Office, 1994, pp. 16-17.

★ 567 ★

Income

Household Participation in Government Assistance Programs - I

This table shows numbers and percentages of persons participating in government assistance programs in 1992. Data are shown for persons of all races and ethnicities and specifically for persons of Hispanic origin.

Characteristic	Total	In household that received means-tested assistance		In household that received means-tested assistance excluding school lunches		In household that received means-tested cash assistance	
		Number	Percent	Number	Percent	Number	Percent
ALL PERSONS							
All Income Levels							
Both Sexes							
Total	253,968	61,165	24.1	50,355	19.8	28,101	11.1
Under 18 years	66,834	24,350	36.4	18,902	28.3	10,921	16.3
18 to 24 years	24,309	6,434	26.5	5,707	23.5	2,936	12.1
25 to 34 years	41,864	9,624	23.0	7,813	18.7	4,214	10.1
35 to 44 years	40,342	7,609	18.9	5,725	14.2	3,093	7.7
45 to 54 years	28,503	4,268	15.0	3,660	12.8	2,072	7.3
55 to 59 years	10,718	1,658	15.5	1,524	14.2	954	8.9
60 to 64 years	10,529	1,619	15.4	1,518	14.4	903	8.6
65 years and over	30,870	5,602	18.1	5,505	17.8	3,009	9.7
65 to 74 years	18,362	3,065	16.7	3,000	16.3	1,746	9.5
75 years and over	12,508	2,538	20.3	2,506	20.0	1,263	10.1
Male							
Total	123,873	27,863	22.5	22,538	18.2	12,277	9.9
Under 18 years	34,180	12,450	36.4	9,590	28.1	5,513	16.1
18 to 24 years	12,049	2,770	23.0	2,358	19.6	1,099	9.1
25 to 34 years	20,856	4,064	19.5	3,326	15.9	1,658	7.9
35 to 44 years	19,904	3,358	16.9	2,521	12.7	1,327	6.7
45 to 54 years	13,847	1,916	13.8	1,597	11.5	863	6.2
55 to 59 years	5,122	709	13.8	654	12.8	419	8.2
60 to 64 years	5,084	670	13.2	612	12.0	357	7.0
65 years and over	12,832	1,926	15.0	1,881	14.7	1,042	8.1
65 to 74 years	8,114	1,194	14.7	1,164	14.3	697	8.6
75 years and over	4,718	732	15.5	717	15.2	345	7.3

[Continued]

★ 567 ★

Household Participation in Government Assistance Programs - I

[Continued]

Characteristic	Total	In household that received means-tested assistance		In household that received means-tested assistance excluding school lunches		In household that received means-tested cash assistance	
		Number	Percent	Number	Percent	Number	Percent
Female							
Total	130,096	33,302	25.6	27,817	21.4	15,823	12.2
Under 18 years	32,654	11,900	36.4	9,312	28.5	5,408	16.6
18 to 24 years	12,260	3,664	29.9	3,351	27.3	1,836	15.0
25 to 34 years	21,008	5,561	26.5	4,486	21.4	2,556	12.2
35 to 44 years	20,438	4,251	20.8	3,204	15.7	1,764	8.6
45 to 54 years	14,655	2,352	16.1	2,063	14.1	1,209	8.3
55 to 59 years	5,597	949	17.0	871	15.6	525	9.6
60 to 64 years	5,445	949	17.4	906	16.6	547	10.0
65 years and over	18,038	3,676	20.4	3,624	20.1	1,967	10.9
65 to 74 years	10,249	1,871	18.3	1,835	17.9	1,049	10.2
75 years and over	7,790	1,805	23.2	1,789	23.0	918	11.8
Household Relationship							
Total	253,969	61,165	24.1	50,355	19.8	28,101	11.1
65 years and over	30,870	5,602	18.1	5,505	17.8	3,009	9.7
In families	215,515	53,405	24.8	43,017	20.0	24,379	11.3
Householder	68,144	14,541	21.3	12,055	17.7	6,817	10.0
Under 65 years	56,883	12,809	22.5	10,373	18.2	5,757	10.1
65 years and over	11,261	1,732	15.4	1,681	14.9	1,060	9.4
Related children under 18 years	65,691	23,659	36.0	18,327	27.9	10,594	16.1
Under 6 years	23,129	8,828	38.2	7,761	33.6	4,651	20.1
6 to 17 years	42,562	14,831	34.8	10,566	24.8	5,942	14.0
Own children 18 years and over	21,091	5,102	24.2	4,403	20.9	2,747	13.0
In married-couple families	171,514	30,087	17.5	22,645	13.2	10,563	6.2
Husbands	53,171	7,305	13.7	5,724	10.8	2,650	5.0
Under 65 years	43,719	6,261	14.3	4,708	10.8	2,032	4.6
65 years and over	9,451	1,043	11.0	1,016	10.8	618	6.5
Wives	53,171	7,305	13.7	5,724	10.8	2,650	5.0
Under 65 years	45,944	6,590	14.3	5,019	10.9	2,228	4.8
65 years and over	7,227	714	9.9	705	9.7	422	5.8
Related children under 18 years	48,532	12,032	24.8	8,295	17.1	3,572	7.4
Under 6 years	17,180	4,361	25.4	3,539	20.6	1,485	8.6
6 to 17 years	31,352	7,671	24.5	4,755	15.2	2,087	6.7
Own children 18 years and over	13,866	2,410	17.4	2,021	14.6	1,216	8.8
In families with female householder, no spouse present	35,639	20,580	57.7	18,044	50.6	12,455	34.9
Householder	11,947	6,349	53.1	5,558	46.5	3,718	31.1
Under 65 years	10,355	5,752	55.5	4,981	48.1	3,322	32.1
65 years and over	1,592	597	37.5	578	36.3	396	24.9
Related children under 18 years	14,801	10,583	71.5	9,205	62.2	6,534	44.1
Under 6 years	5,051	4,032	79.8	3,813	75.5	2,908	57.6
6 to 17 years	9,749	6,551	67.2	5,392	55.3	3,626	37.2
Own children 18 years and over	6,066	2,430	40.1	2,149	35.4	1,408	23.2
In unrelated subfamilies	1,720	1,014	59.0	827	48.1	511	29.7
Under 18 years	941	592	62.9	482	51.2	304	32.3

[Continued]

★ 567 ★

Household Participation in Government Assistance Programs - I

[Continued]

Characteristic	Total	In household that received means-tested assistance		In household that received means-tested assistance excluding school lunches		In household that received means-tested cash assistance	
		Number	Percent	Number	Percent	Number	Percent
Under 6 years	379	248	65.3	234	61.7	138	36.4
6 to 17 years	562	345	61.3	248	44.1	166	29.5
18 years and over	778	422	54.2	345	44.3	207	26.6
Unrelated individuals	36,734	6,746	18.4	6,510	17.7	3,211	8.7
Male	17,278	3,004	17.4	2,802	16.2	1,422	8.2
Under 65 years	14,923	2,457	16.5	2,255	15.1	1,190	8.0
Living alone	7,521	692	9.2	692	9.2	338	4.5
65 years and over	2,355	548	23.3	548	23.3	233	9.9
Living alone	2,005	443	22.1	443	22.1	169	8.4
Female	19,456	3,742	19.2	3,708	19.1	1,789	9.2
Under 65 years	11,769	1,969	16.7	1,935	16.4	1,048	8.9
Living alone	6,893	1,013	14.7	1,013	14.7	549	8.0
65 years and over	7,686	1,773	23.1	1,773	23.1	741	9.6
Living alone	7,382	1,682	22.8	1,682	22.8	689	9.3
Below Poverty Level							
Both Sexes							
Total	36,880	26,980	73.2	24,552	66.6	15,735	42.7
Under 18 years	14,617	12,810	87.6	11,534	78.9	7,779	53.2
18 to 24 years	4,367	2,803	64.2	2,619	60.0	1,575	36.1
25 to 34 years	5,540	4,116	74.3	3,706	66.9	2,377	42.9
35 to 44 years	3,944	2,765	70.1	2,383	60.4	1,442	36.6
45 to 54 years	2,245	1,400	62.4	1,294	57.6	744	33.1
55 to 59 years	1,073	607	56.5	577	53.7	380	35.4
60 to 64 years	1,112	607	54.6	593	53.3	387	34.8
65 years and over	3,983	1,873	47.0	1,847	46.4	1,051	26.4
65 to 74 years	1,956	983	50.3	967	49.4	590	30.2
75 years and over	2,027	889	43.9	880	43.4	460	22.7
Male							
Total	15,700	11,229	71.5	10,070	64.1	6,309	40.2
Under 18 years	7,343	6,401	87.2	5,751	78.3	3,876	52.8
18 to 24 years	1,714	970	56.6	870	50.7	465	27.1
25 to 34 years	2,050	1,326	64.7	1,170	57.1	647	31.6
35 to 44 years	1,647	1,032	62.7	864	52.5	461	28.0
45 to 54 years	964	578	60.0	525	54.4	290	30.1
55 to 59 years	443	221	49.8	213	48.0	149	33.6
60 to 64 years	397	204	51.4	197	49.7	139	35.0
65 years and over	1,142	497	43.5	481	42.1	282	24.7
65 to 74 years	657	293	44.7	285	43.3	179	27.2
75 years and over	485	204	42.0	196	40.5	103	21.2
Female							
Total	21,180	15,751	74.4	14,481	68.4	9,427	44.5
Under 18 years	7,273	6,408	88.1	5,783	79.5	3,903	53.7
18 to 24 years	2,653	1,833	69.1	1,749	65.9	1,110	41.8
25 to 34 years	3,490	2,790	80.0	2,536	72.7	1,730	49.6

[Continued]

★ 567 ★

Household Participation in Government Assistance Programs - I

[Continued]

Characteristic	Total	In household that received means-tested assistance		In household that received means-tested assistance excluding school lunches		In household that received means-tested cash assistance	
		Number	Percent	Number	Percent	Number	Percent
35 to 44 years	2,297	1,733	75.5	1,519	66.1	981	42.7
45 to 54 years	1,281	822	64.1	769	60.1	454	35.4
55 to 59 years	630	386	61.3	364	57.7	232	36.8
60 to 64 years	715	403	56.3	395	55.2	249	34.8
65 years and over	2,840	1,375	48.4	1,366	48.1	769	27.1
65 to 74 years	1,299	690	53.1	682	52.5	411	31.7
75 years and over	1,542	686	44.5	683	44.3	357	23.2
Household Relationship							
Total	36,880	26,980	73.2	24,552	66.6	15,735	42.7
65 years and over	3,983	1,873	47.0	1,847	46.4	1,051	26.4
In families	27,947	22,637	81.0	20,349	72.8	13,276	47.5
Householder	7,960	6,122	76.9	5,573	70.0	3,679	46.2
Under 65 years	7,081	5,711	80.7	5,179	73.1	3,427	48.4
65 years and over	878	411	46.8	395	44.9	252	28.7
Related children under 18 years	13,876	12,262	88.4	11,051	79.6	7,491	54.0
Under 6 years	5,781	5,111	88.4	4,814	83.3	3,348	57.9
6 to 17 years	8,095	7,152	88.3	6,237	77.1	4,143	51.2
Own children 18 years and over	1,833	1,417	77.3	1,267	69.1	809	44.2
In married-couple families	12,830	9,193	71.7	7,717	60.1	3,732	29.1
Husbands	3,318	2,098	63.2	1,791	54.0	877	26.4
Under 65 years	2,710	1,870	69.0	1,570	57.9	735	27.1
65 years and over	608	228	37.5	221	36.3	142	23.4
Wives	3,318	2,098	63.2	1,791	54.0	877	26.4
Under 65 years	2,896	1,960	67.7	1,655	57.2	793	27.4
65 years and over	423	138	32.7	135	32.0	83	19.7
Related children under 18 years	5,268	4,306	81.8	3,555	67.5	1,677	31.8
Under 6 years	2,198	1,770	80.5	1,556	70.8	720	32.8
6 to 17 years	3,070	2,537	82.6	1,999	65.1	957	31.2
Own children 18 years and over	639	453	70.9	387	60.5	217	33.9
In families with female householder, no spouse present	13,716	12,408	90.5	11,727	85.5	8,952	65.3
Householder	4,171	3,694	88.6	3,489	83.7	2,618	62.8
Under 65 years	3,923	3,528	89.9	3,326	84.8	2,508	63.9
65 years and over	248	166	66.8	164	65.9	110	44.4
Related children under 18 years	8,032	7,484	93.2	7,090	88.3	5,534	68.9
Under 6 years	3,331	3,135	94.1	3,061	91.9	2,487	74.7
6 to 17 years	4,702	4,348	92.5	4,029	85.7	3,047	64.8
Own children 18 years and over	1,069	881	82.4	816	76.4	557	52.1
In unrelated subfamilies	943	730	77.4	639	67.8	423	44.9
Under 18 years	569	457	80.2	397	69.8	265	46.5
Under 6 years	265	205	77.6	194	73.3	122	46.1
6 to 17 years	305	251	82.5	203	66.7	143	46.8
18 years and over	373	273	73.2	242	64.9	158	42.4
Unrelated individuals	7,991	3,613	45.2	3,563	44.6	2,037	25.5

[Continued]

★ 567 ★

Household Participation in Government Assistance Programs - I

[Continued]

Characteristic	Total	In household that received means-tested assistance		In household that received means-tested assistance excluding school lunches		In household that received means-tested cash assistance	
		Number	Percent	Number	Percent	Number	Percent
Male	3,103	1,304	42.0	1,267	40.8	761	24.5
Under 65 years	2,666	1,093	41.0	1,055	39.6	641	24.0
Living alone	1,018	375	36.8	375	36.8	229	22.5
65 years and over	438	211	48.3	211	48.3	120	27.5
Living alone	356	171	47.9	171	47.9	93	26.1
Female	4,888	2,309	47.2	2,297	47.0	1,276	26.1
Under 65 years	2,827	1,319	46.6	1,307	46.2	756	26.8
Living alone	1,303	676	51.9	676	51.9	424	32.5
65 years and over	2,061	990	48.0	990	48.0	519	25.2
Living alone	1,953	943	48.3	943	48.3	492	25.2
HISPANIC ORIGIN							
All Income Levels							
Both Sexes							
Total	22,270	11,405	50.2	8,584	37.8	4,478	19.7
Under 18 years	7,807	5,008	64.2	3,663	46.9	1,961	25.1
18 to 24 years	2,813	1,345	47.8	1,108	39.4	513	18.2
25 to 34 years	4,277	1,848	43.2	1,368	32.0	649	15.2
35 to 44 years	3,330	1,417	42.6	940	28.2	455	13.7
45 to 54 years	2,037	749	36.8	565	27.7	323	15.9
55 to 59 years	680	233	34.3	186	27.4	110	16.2
60 to 64 years	554	221	39.8	194	35.0	110	19.9
65 years and over	1,222	584	47.7	559	45.7	357	29.2
65 to 74 years	806	358	44.4	341	42.3	217	26.9
75 years and over	416	226	54.2	218	52.4	140	33.7
Male							
Total	11,378	5,464	48.0	4,045	35.6	2,012	17.7
Under 18 years	3,958	2,537	64.1	1,861	47.0	983	24.8
18 to 24 years	1,417	638	45.0	494	34.9	204	14.4
25 to 34 years	2,237	862	38.5	635	28.4	267	11.9
35 to 44 years	1,682	665	39.5	444	26.4	202	12.0
45 to 54 years	1,035	373	36.1	268	25.9	152	14.7
55 to 59 years	292	91	31.3	75	25.6	44	15.0
60 to 64 years	249	82	32.8	68	27.4	38	15.2
65 years and over	508	216	42.5	201	39.5	123	24.2
65 to 74 years	345	146	42.2	135	39.1	79	22.8
75 years and over	163	70	43.0	66	40.4	44	27.3
Female							
Total	11,342	5,941	52.4	4,539	40.0	2,465	21.7
Under 18 years	3,849	2,471	64.2	1,803	46.8	978	25.4
18 to 24 years	1,396	707	50.7	614	44.0	309	22.1
25 to 34 years	2,040	986	48.3	732	35.9	382	18.7
35 to 44 years	1,648	752	45.6	497	30.2	253	15.3
45 to 54 years	1,002	376	37.5	297	29.7	171	17.1
55 to 59 years	387	142	36.6	111	28.8	66	17.1

[Continued]

★ 567 ★

Household Participation in Government Assistance Programs - I

[Continued]

Characteristic	Total	In household that received means-tested assistance		In household that received means-tested assistance excluding school lunches		In household that received means-tested cash assistance	
		Number	Percent	Number	Percent	Number	Percent
60 to 64 years	305	139	45.5	126	41.2	72	23.7
65 years and over	715	368	51.5	359	50.2	234	32.7
65 to 74 years	462	212	46.0	207	44.8	138	29.9
75 years and over	253	156	61.4	152	60.0	96	37.8
Household Relationship							
Total	22,720	11,405	50.2	8,584	37.8	4,478	19.7
65 years and over	1,222	584	47.7	559	45.7	357	29.2
In families	20,116	10,407	51.7	7,705	38.3	23,983	19.8
Householder	5,318	2,441	45.9	1,865	35.1	981	18.5
Under 65 years	4,880	2,259	46.3	1,695	34.7	861	17.6
65 years and over	438	182	41.4	170	38.8	120	27.4
Related children under 18 years	7,589	4,848	63.9	3,539	46.6	1,903	25.1
Under 6 years	2,870	1,806	62.9	1,501	52.3	812	28.3
6 to 17 years	4,719	3,042	64.5	2,038	43.2	1,091	23.1
Own children 18 years and over	1,888	878	46.5	681	36.0	387	20.5
In married-couple families	14,642	6,700	45.8	4,518	30.9	1,713	11.7
Husbands	3,686	1,409	38.2	967	26.2	349	9.5
Under 65 years	3,364	1,300	38.6	866	25.7	284	8.4
65 years and over	322	109	33.8	101	31.5	65	20.1
Wives	3,806	1,428	37.5	981	25.8	354	9.3
Under 65 years	3,561	1,354	38.0	906	25.4	305	8.6
65 years and over	245	75	30.6	75	30.6	49	20.1
Related children under 18 years	5,259	2,970	56.5	1,924	36.6	704	13.4
Under 6 years	1,988	1,087	54.7	832	41.8	295	14.8
6 to 17 years	3,271	1,883	57.8	1,092	33.4	409	12.5
Own children 18 years and over	1,194	490	41.0	348	29.2	162	13.5
In families with female householder, no spouse present	4,207	3,108	73.9	2,718	64.6	1,983	47.1
Householder	1,238	864	69.8	760	61.4	549	44.4
Under 65 years	1,142	798	69.8	699	61.2	500	43.8
65 years and over	95	66	69.5	61	64.0	49	51.9
Related children under 18 years	1,963	1,639	83.5	1,437	73.2	1,086	55.3
Under 6 years	710	604	85.1	563	79.3	452	63.6
6 to 17 years	1,253	1,035	82.6	874	69.7	635	50.6
Own children 18 years and over	603	359	59.6	311	51.6	210	34.8
In unrelated subfamilies	327	245	75.0	190	58.1	105	32.1
Under 18 years	167	131	78.3	100	60.0	56	33.7
Under 6 years	80	58	72.5	54	68.2	32	39.8
6 to 17 years	87	73	83.6	46	52.4	25	28.1
18 years and over	160	114	71.5	90	56.1	49	30.3
Unrelated individuals	2,278	752	33.0	689	30.3	390	17.1
Male	1,354	411	30.3	361	26.7	203	15.0
Under 65 years	1,274	361	28.3	311	24.4	175	13.7
Living alone	410	54	13.3	54	13.3	30	7.4

[Continued]

★ 567 ★

Household Participation in Government Assistance Programs - I

[Continued]

Characteristic	Total	In household that received means-tested assistance		In household that received means-tested assistance excluding school lunches		In household that received means-tested cash assistance	
		Number	Percent	Number	Percent	Number	Percent
65 years and over	80	50	62.9	50	62.9	28	35.2
Living alone	70	41	B	41	B	23	B
Female	924	341	37.0	328	35.5	187	20.2
Under 65 years	719	220	30.6	207	28.8	117	16.3
Living alone	340	85	25.0	85	25.0	56	16.6
65 years and over	205	122	59.3	122	59.3	69	33.9
Living alone	188	109	58.0	109	58.0	65	34.8
Below Poverty Level							
Both Sexes							
Total	6,655	5,465	82.1	4,582	68.9	2,642	39.7
Under 18 years	3,116	2,810	90.2	2,342	75.2	1,437	46.1
18 to 24 years	844	606	71.8	535	63.3	264	31.3
25 to 34 years	1,076	825	76.7	669	62.1	374	34.8
35 to 44 years	719	564	78.5	441	61.4	226	31.4
45 to 54 years	349	266	76.1	228	65.5	124	35.7
55 to 59 years	137	90	65.3	77	56.0	57	41.2
60 to 64 years	145	107	73.7	99	68.2	52	36.1
65 years and over	269	197	73.4	191	71.2	107	39.9
65 to 74 years	157	110	69.8	107	67.9	60	38.1
75 years and over	112	88	78.6	85	75.8	47	42.4
Male							
Total	3,067	2,454	80.0	2,021	65.9	1,124	36.6
Under 18 years	1,551	1,398	90.1	1,165	75.1	716	46.2
18 to 24 years	360	235	65.3	197	54.7	84	23.3
25 to 34 years	467	325	69.7	254	54.5	117	25.0
35 to 44 years	328	236	72.0	183	55.8	80	24.5
45 to 54 years	170	122	71.7	98	57.4	51	29.7
55 to 59 years	53	34	B	30	B	23	B
60 to 64 years	50	38	B	33	B	20	B
65 years and over	88	66	75.3	62	70.1	33	37.2
65 to 74 years	57	43	B	40	B	20	B
75 years and over	31	24	B	21	B	13	B
Female							
Total	3,588	3,010	83.9	2,561	71.4	1,518	42.3
Under 18 years	1,565	1,412	90.2	1,177	75.2	721	46.1
18 to 24 years	484	371	76.7	338	69.8	181	37.3
25 to 34 years	609	500	82.1	414	68.0	257	42.2
35 to 44 years	391	328	83.9	258	66.1	145	37.2
45 to 54 years	178	143	80.3	131	73.2	74	41.4
55 to 59 years	84	56	66.1	47	55.5	33	39.6
60 to 64 years	96	69	72.4	66	69.2	33	34.2
65 years and over	181	131	72.5	130	71.7	74	41.2
65 to 74 years	100	67	67.1	66	66.5	40	39.9
75 years and over	81	64	79.2	63	78.1	35	42.8

[Continued]

★ 567 ★

Household Participation in Government Assistance Programs - I

[Continued]

Characteristic	Total	In household that received means-tested assistance		In household that received means-tested assistance excluding school lunches		In household that received means-tested cash assistance	
		Number	Percent	Number	Percent	Number	Percent
Household Relationship							
Total	6,655	5,465	82.1	4,582	68.9	2,642	39.7
65 years and over	269	197	73.4	191	71.2	107	39.9
In families	5,655	4,855	85.8	4,021	71.1	2,305	40.8
Householder	1,395	1,152	82.5	981	70.3	583	41.8
Under 65 years	1,324	1,099	83.0	931	70.4	555	42.0
65 years and over	72	53	B	50	B	28	B
Related children under 18 years	2,946	2,676	90.8	2,231	75.7	1,379	46.8
Under 6 years	1,223	1,078	88.1	960	78.5	595	48.6
6 to 17 years	1,723	1,598	92.7	1,271	73.8	785	45.5
Own children 18 years and over	333	275	82.5	224	67.3	120	36.1
In married-couple families	3,136	2,610	83.2	1,969	62.8	707	22.5
Husbands	687	536	78.0	413	60.0	142	20.6
Under 65 years	638	502	78.7	380	59.7	127	19.9
65 years and over	50	35	B	32	B	15	B
Wives	672	519	77.2	398	59.1	136	20.2
Under 65 years	648	504	77.8	383	59.1	129	19.9
65 years and over	24	15	B	15	B	7	B
Related children under 18 years	1,500	1,320	88.0	996	66.4	381	25.4
Under 6 years	641	534	83.4	438	68.4	162	25.3
6 to 17 years	860	786	91.4	558	64.9	219	25.5
Own children 18 years and over	137	115	84.3	79	57.5	22	16.0
In families with female householder, no spouse present	2,154	2,002	92.9	1,863	86.5	1,456	67.6
Householder	604	550	91.0	514	85.1	399	66.1
Under 65 years	580	531	91.4	496	85.4	386	66.5
65 years and over	24	19	B	19	B	13	B
Related children under 18 years	1,289	1,233	95.7	1,147	89.0	930	72.1
Under 6 years	510	488	95.7	471	92.3	390	76.5
6 to 17 years	779	745	95.6	677	86.8	540	69.3
Own children 18 years and over	177	151	85.2	139	78.3	93	52.7
In unrelated subfamilies	222	177	79.5	148	66.5	92	41.5
Under 18 years	127	108	84.7	89	70.0	55	43.6
Under 6 years	66	52	B	48	B	31	B
6 to 17 years	61	56	B	41	B	25	B
18 years and over	95	69	72.5	59	62.0	37	38.7
Unrelated individuals	777	434	55.8	413	53.2	245	31.5
Male	382	195	51.0	182	47.6	114	29.8
Under 65 years	350	170	48.5	157	44.7	99	28.2
Living alone	72	32	B	32	B	24	B
65 years and over	32	25	B	25	B	15	B
Living alone	29	22	B	22	B	14	B
Female	396	239	60.4	231	58.5	131	33.1
Under 65 years	292	159	54.7	152	52.1	83	28.3
Living alone	102	58	57.2	58	57.2	39	38.3

[Continued]

★ 567 ★

Household Participation in Government Assistance Programs - I

[Continued]

Characteristic	Total	In household that received means-tested assistance		In household that received means-tested assistance excluding school lunches		In household that received means-tested cash assistance	
		Number	Percent	Number	Percent	Number	Percent
65 years and over	104	80	76.6	80	76.6	48	46.6
Living alone	93	71	76.1	71	76.1	45	48.7

Source: U.S. Bureau of the Census. *Poverty in the United States: 1992.* Current Population Reports, Series P60-185, U.S. Government Printing Office, Washington, D.C., 1993, pp. 31-38. *Notes:* (B) stands for base less than 75,000. 1. Persons of Hispanic origin may be of any race.

★ 568 ★

Income

Household Participation in Government Assistance Programs - II

This table shows numbers and percentages of persons participating in government assistance programs in 1992. Data are shown for persons of all races and ethnicities and specifically for persons of Hispanic origin.

Characteristic	In household that received food stamps		In household in which one or more persons covered by Medicaid		Lived in public or subsidized housing	
	Number	Percent	Number	Percent	Number	Percent
ALL PERSONS						
All Income Levels						
Both Sexes						
Total	27,620	10.9	40,364	15.9	10,567	4.2
Under 18 years	12,703	19.0	16,075	24.1	4,350	6.5
18 to 24 years	2,989	12.3	4,697	19.3	1,236	5.1
25 to 34 years	4,402	10.5	6,428	15.4	1,576	3.8
35 to 44 years	3,086	7.6	4,274	10.6	968	2.4
45 to 54 years	1,659	5.8	2,874	10.1	479	1.7
55 to 59 years	653	6.1	1,169	10.9	227	2.1
60 to 64 years	592	5.6	1,093	10.4	262	2.5
65 years and over	1,537	5.0	3,753	12.2	1,469	4.8
65 to 74 years	873	4.8	2,082	11.3	660	3.6
75 years and over	663	5.3	1,671	13.4	809	6.5
Male						
Total	11,989	9.7	18,047	14.6	4,015	3.2
Under 18 years	6,409	18.8	8,133	23.8	2,141	6.3
18 to 24 years	1,132	9.4	1,852	15.4	449	3.7
25 to 34 years	1,597	7.7	2,715	13.0	480	2.3
35 to 44 years	1,242	6.2	1,822	9.2	288	1.4
45 to 54 years	698	5.0	1,245	9.0	176	1.3
55 to 59 years	249	4.9	509	9.9	65	1.3
60 to 64 years	220	4.3	475	9.3	70	1.4

[Continued]

★ 568 ★

Household Participation in Government Assistance Programs - II

[Continued]

Characteristic	In household that received food stamps		In household in which one or more persons covered by Medicaid		Lived in public or subsidized housing	
	Number	Percent	Number	Percent	Number	Percent
65 years and over	443	3.5	1,297	10.1	345	2.7
65 to 74 years	273	3.4	821	10.1	166	2.0
75 years and over	170	3.6	475	10.1	179	3.8
Female						
Total	15,632	12.0	22,317	17.2	6,552	5.0
Under 18 years	6,294	19.3	7,942	24.3	2,209	6.8
18 to 24 years	1,857	15.1	2,846	23.2	787	6.4
25 to 34 years	2,805	13.4	3,714	17.7	1,095	5.2
35 to 44 years	1,844	9.0	2,452	12.0	680	3.3
45 to 54 years	961	6.6	1,630	11.1	303	2.1
55 to 59 years	404	7.2	660	11.8	161	2.9
60 to 64 years	373	6.8	618	11.4	192	3.5
65 years and over	1,093	6.1	2,457	13.6	1,124	6.2
65 to 74 years	601	5.9	1,261	12.3	494	4.8
75 years and over	493	6.3	1,196	15.3	630	8.1
Household Relationship						
Total	27,620	10.9	40,364	15.9	10,567	4.2
65 years and over	1,537	5.0	3,753	12.2	1,469	4.8
In families	24,134	11.2	35,396	16.4	8,303	3.9
Householder	6,611	9.7	9,666	14.2	2,610	3.8
Under 65 years	6,153	10.8	8,415	14.8	2,399	4.2
65 years and over	458	4.1	1,251	11.1	211	1.9
Related children under 18 years	12,317	18.8	15,554	23.7	4,273	6.5
Under 6 years	5,319	23.0	6,943	30.0	1,882	8.1
6 to 17 years	6,998	16.4	8,610	20.2	2,391	5.6
Own children 18 years and over	1,812	8.6	3,668	17.4	592	2.8
In married-couple families	10,028	5.8	17,954	10.5	2,270	1.3
Husbands	2,379	4.5	4,347	8.2	658	1.2
Under 65 years	2,152	4.9	3,646	8.3	536	1.2
65 years and over	226	2.4	701	7.4	122	1.3
Wives	2,379	4.5	4,347	8.2	658	1.2
Under 65 years	2,230	4.9	3,877	8.4	569	1.2
65 years and over	149	2.1	470	6.5	89	1.2
Related children under 18 years	4,432	9.1	6,755	13.9	865	1.8
Under 6 years	1,916	11.2	3,067	17.9	397	2.3
6 to 17 years	2,516	8.0	3,688	11.8	468	1.5
Own children 18 years and over	562	4.1	1,709	12.3	68	.5
In families with female householder, no spouse present	12,863	36.1	15,473	43.4	5,775	16.2
Householder	3,834	32.1	4,671	39.1	1,856	15.5

[Continued]

★ 568 ★

Household Participation in Government Assistance Programs - II

[Continued]

Characteristic	In household that received food stamps		In household in which one or more persons covered by Medicaid		Lived in public or subsidized housing	
	Number	Percent	Number	Percent	Number	Percent
Under 65 years	3,618	34.9	4,199	40.5	1,768	17.1
65 years and over	216	13.6	473	29.7	88	5.5
Related children under 18 years	7,337	49.6	8,059	54.5	3,288	22.2
Under 6 years	3,138	62.1	3,494	69.2	1,418	28.1
6 to 17 years	4,198	43.1	4,566	46.8	1,870	19.2
Own children 18 years and over	1,156	19.1	1,766	29.1	510	8.4
In unrelated subfamilies	565	32.8	749	43.6	93	5.4
Under 18 years	340	36.1	438	46.5	59	6.3
Under 6 years	157	41.5	215	56.7	30	8.0
6 to 17 years	183	32.5	223	39.7	28	5.1
18 years and over	225	28.9	311	40.0	34	4.3
Unrelated individuals	2,922	8.0	4,219	11.5	2,171	5.9
Male	1,315	7.6	1,899	11.0	700	4.1
Under 65 years	1,187	8.0	1,573	10.5	500	3.3
Living alone	284	3.8	375	5.0	274	3.6
65 years and over	127	5.4	327	13.9	200	8.5
Living alone	100	5.0	242	12.1	196	9.8
Female	1,607	8.3	2,319	11.9	1,471	7.6
Under 65 years	1,016	8.6	1,305	11.1	550	4.7
Living alone	580	8.4	594	8.6	425	6.2
65 years and over	591	7.7	1,014	13.2	921	12.0
Living alone	573	7.8	939	12.7	910	12.3
Below Poverty Level						
Both Sexes						
Total	18,930	51.3	20,790	56.4	6,794	18.4
Under 18 years	9,654	66.0	10,204	69.8	3,375	23.1
18 to 24 years	1,899	43.5	2,244	51.4	747	17.1
25 to 34 years	2,912	52.6	3,210	57.9	1,003	18.1
35 to 44 years	1,882	47.7	1,885	47.8	520	13.2
45 to 54 years	907	40.4	989	44.0	258	11.5
55 to 59 years	394	36.7	459	42.8	133	12.4
60 to 64 years	350	31.5	452	40.6	146	13.1
65 years and over	932	23.4	1,348	33.8	611	15.3
65 to 74 years	500	25.6	715	36.6	291	14.9
75 years and over	432	21.3	632	31.2	320	15.8
Male						
Total	7,802	49.7	8,511	54.2	2,423	15.4
Under 18 years	4,842	65.9	5,096	69.4	1,629	22.2
18 to 24 years	611	35.6	723	42.2	199	11.6

[Continued]

★ 568 ★

Household Participation in Government Assistance Programs - II

[Continued]

Characteristic	In household that received food stamps		In household in which one or more persons covered by Medicaid		Lived in public or subsidized housing	
	Number	Percent	Number	Percent	Number	Percent
25 to 34 years	847	41.3	971	47.4	232	11.3
35 to 44 years	646	39.2	627	38.1	124	7.5
45 to 54 years	363	37.6	402	41.7	83	8.6
55 to 59 years	138	31.1	163	36.9	29	6.4
60 to 64 years	119	30.0	173	43.6	24	6.1
65 years and over	236	20.7	356	31.2	104	9.1
65 to 74 years	143	21.7	214	32.5	51	7.8
75 years and over	94	19.3	143	29.4	53	10.8
Female						
Total	11,128	52.5	12,278	58.0	4,371	20.6
Under 18 years	4,812	66.2	5,108	70.2	1,745	24.0
18 to 24 years	1,288	48.6	1,520	57.3	549	20.7
25 to 34 years	2,065	59.2	2,239	64.2	772	22.1
35 to 44 years	1,236	53.8	1,258	54.8	396	17.3
45 to 54 years	544	42.5	587	45.8	175	13.7
55 to 59 years	256	40.6	296	46.9	105	16.6
60 to 64 years	231	32.3	278	38.9	122	17.0
65 years and over	696	24.5	991	34.9	507	17.9
65 to 74 years	358	27.5	502	38.6	240	18.5
75 years and over	338	21.9	490	31.8	267	17.3
Household Relationship						
Total	18,930	51.3	20,790	56.4	6,794	18.4
65 years and over	932	23.4	1,348	33.8	611	15.3
In families	16,449	58.9	17,626	63.1	5,606	20.1
Householder	4,482	56.3	4,795	60.2	1,683	21.1
Under 65 years	4,259	60.1	4,473	63.2	1,622	22.9
65 years and over	223	25.4	322	36.6	61	6.9
Related children under 18 years	9,326	67.2	9,758	70.3	3,302	23.8
Under 6 years	4,089	70.7	4,408	76.2	1,542	26.7
6 to 17 years	5,238	64.7	5,348	66.1	1,760	21.7
Own children 18 years and over	874	47.7	1,034	56.4	304	16.6
In married-couple families	5,773	45.0	6,342	49.4	1,019	7.9
Husbands	1,321	39.8	1,448	43.6	256	7.7
Under 65 years	1,193	44.0	1,274	47.0	223	8.2
65 years and over	128	21.1	174	28.6	33	5.4
Wives	1,321	39.8	1,448	43.6	256	7.7
Under 65 years	1,237	42.7	1,348	46.5	241	8.3
65 years and over	84	19.9	101	23.8	15	3.6
Related children under 18 years	2,778	52.7	2,963	56.3	479	9.1
Under 6 years	1,221	55.6	1,372	62.4	233	10.6
6 to 17 years	1,557	50.7	1,592	51.8	246	8.0

[Continued]

★ 568 ★

Household Participation in Government Assistance Programs - II

[Continued]

Characteristic	In household that received food stamps		In household in which one or more persons covered by Medicaid		Lived in public or subsidized housing	
	Number	Percent	Number	Percent	Number	Percent
Own children 18 years and over	236	36.9	305	47.8	21	3.3
In families with female householder, no spouse present	10,017	73.0	10,464	76.3	4,431	32.3
Householder	2,950	70.7	3,084	73.9	1,374	32.9
Under 65 years	2,855	72.8	2,945	75.1	1,343	34.2
65 years and over	94	38.1	139	56.2	31	12.6
Related children under 18 years	6,229	77.5	6,418	79.9	2,735	34.0
Under 6 years	2,713	81.5	2,850	85.6	1,257	37.7
6 to 17 years	3,515	74.8	3,568	75.9	1,478	31.4
Own children 18 years and over	606	56.7	676	63.2	278	26.0
In unrelated subfamilies	455	48.3	598	63.4	82	8.7
Under 18 years	285	50.1	371	65.1	55	9.6
Under 6 years	131	49.3	181	68.5	30	11.5
6 to 17 years	155	50.8	189	62.1	24	7.9
18 years and over	170	45.4	227	60.8	27	7.3
Unrelated individuals	2,026	25.3	2,567	32.1	1,106	13.8
Male	749	24.1	912	29.4	304	9.8
Under 65 years	662	24.9	777	29.1	235	8.8
Living alone	206	20.3	255	25.1	130	12.8
65 years and over	87	19.9	135	30.9	69	15.7
Living alone	72	20.2	104	29.1	69	19.3
Female	1,276	26.1	1,655	33.9	802	16.4
Under 65 years	799	28.3	974	34.5	349	12.4
Living alone	461	35.3	468	35.9	264	20.2
65 years and over	477	23.1	681	33.0	452	22.0
Living alone	467	23.9	642	32.9	446	22.8
HISPANIC ORIGIN						
All Income Levels						
Both Sexes						
Total	4,922	21.7	7,474	32.9	1,536	6.8
Under 18 years	2,450	31.4	3,259	41.7	689	8.8
18 to 24 years	561	19.9	974	34.6	167	5.9
25 to 34 years	730	17.1	1,223	28.6	225	5.3
35 to 44 years	511	15.3	785	23.6	164	4.9
45 to 54 years	303	14.9	446	21.9	90	4.4
55 to 59 years	90	13.2	158	23.2	23	3.4
60 to 64 years	86	15.4	152	27.4	40	7.3
65 years and over	192	15.7	477	39.0	137	11.2

[Continued]

★ 568 ★

Household Participation in Government Assistance Programs - II

[Continued]

Characteristic	In household that received food stamps		In household in which one or more persons covered by Medicaid		Lived in public or subsidized housing	
	Number	Percent	Number	Percent	Number	Percent
65 to 74 years	108	13.4	287	35.6	75	9.2
75 years and over	84	20.2	190	45.6	63	15.1
Male						
Total	2,212	19.4	3,495	30.7	649	5.7
Under 18 years	1,206	30.5	1,646	41.6	324	8.2
18 to 24 years	220	15.5	416	29.3	66	4.7
25 to 34 years	292	13.1	570	25.5	92	4.1
35 to 44 years	216	12.9	358	21.3	68	4.0
45 to 54 years	149	14.4	218	21.1	35	3.4
55 to 59 years	32	11.0	66	22.5	6	2.0
60 to 64 years	28	11.1	56	22.4	10	4.1
65 years and over	68	13.4	165	32.5	49	9.6
65 to 74 years	40	11.5	107	31.0	32	9.3
75 years and over	28	17.4	58	35.8	17	10.2
Female						
Total	2,710	23.9	3,979	35.1	887	7.8
Under 18 years	1,243	32.3	1,613	41.9	365	9.5
18 to 24 years	341	24.4	558	40.0	101	7.3
25 to 34 years	438	21.4	653	32.0	133	6.5
35 to 44 years	295	17.9	427	25.9	96	5.8
45 to 54 years	154	15.3	228	22.7	55	5.5
55 to 59 years	58	14.9	92	23.8	17	4.5
60 to 64 years	58	19.0	96	31.6	30	9.9
65 years and over	124	17.4	311	43.6	89	12.4
65 to 74 years	68	14.8	180	39.0	43	9.2
75 years and over	56	22.0	132	52.0	46	18.2
Household Relationship						
Total	4,922	21.7	7,474	32.9	1,536	6.8
65 years and over	192	15.7	477	39.0	137	11.2
In families	4,476	22.2	6,772	33.7	1,306	6.5
Householder	1,071	20.1	1,619	30.4	373	7.0
Under 65 years	1,008	20.7	1,472	30.2	340	7.0
65 years and over	63	14.4	147	33.6	33	7.5
Related children under 18 years	2,367	31.2	3,156	41.6	659	8.7
Under 6 years	984	34.3	1,398	48.7	251	8.7
6 to 17 years	1,384	29.3	1,759	37.3	408	8.6
Own children 18 years and over	303	16.0	592	31.3	83	4.4
In married-couple families	2,250	15.4	3,877	26.5	560	3.8
Husbands	459	12.4	813	22.1	142	3.8
Under 65 years	421	12.5	733	21.8	120	3.6

[Continued]

★ 568 ★

Household Participation in Government Assistance Programs - II

[Continued]

Characteristic	In household that received food stamps		In household in which one or more persons covered by Medicaid		Lived in public or subsidized housing	
	Number	Percent	Number	Percent	Number	Percent
65 years and over	38	11.7	81	25.1	22	6.7
Wives	454	11.9	813	21.5	145	3.8
Under 65 years	433	12.2	755	21.2	132	3.7
65 years and over	21	8.7	64	26.1	13	5.3
Related children under 18 years	1,097	20.9	1,668	31.7	245	4.7
Under 6 years	449	22.6	761	38.3	104	5.2
6 to 17 years	649	19.8	907	27.7	141	4.3
Own children 18 years and over	129	10.8	294	24.6	18	1.5
In families with female householder, no spouse present	1,966	46.7	2,487	59.1	689	16.4
Householder	542	43.8	687	55.5	208	16.8
Under 65 years	522	45.7	629	55.1	195	17.1
65 years and over	20	20.8	58	61.1	13	13.2
Related children under 18 years	1,145	58.3	1,332	67.8	389	19.8
Under 6 years	464	65.3	543	76.4	131	18.5
6 to 17 years	681	54.3	789	63.0	258	20.6
Own children 18 years and over	161	26.8	279	46.3	64	10.6
In unrelated subfamilies	115	35.0	166	50.8	33	10.1
Under 18 years	67	39.8	85	50.9	24	14.1
Under 6 years	34	42.1	48	59.8	13	16.9
6 to 17 years	33	37.7	37	42.7	10	11.7
18 years and over	48	30.0	81	50.6	9	5.8
Unrelated individuals	332	14.6	536	23.6	197	8.7
Male	172	12.7	286	21.1	83	6.1
Under 65 years	160	12.6	248	19.5	59	4.7
Living alone	17	4.2	38	9.2	28	6.9
65 years and over	12	14.8	38	47.3	23	29.2
Living alone	11	B	30	B	22	B
Female	159	17.3	251	27.1	115	12.4
Under 65 years	104	14.4	157	21.9	59	8.2
Living alone	49	14.5	57	16.8	40	11.9
65 years and over	56	27.2	94	45.7	56	27.3
Living alone	54	28.5	81	43.1	56	29.8
Below Poverty Level						
Both Sexes						
Total	3,417	51.3	4,075	61.2	1,000	15.0
Under 18 years	1,849	59.3	2,133	68.4	508	16.3
18 to 24 years	359	42.5	471	55.8	99	11.7
25 to 34 years	479	44.5	615	57.1	144	13.3

[Continued]

★ 568 ★

Household Participation in Government Assistance Programs - II

[Continued]

Characteristic	In household that received food stamps		In household in which one or more persons covered by Medicaid		Lived in public or subsidized housing	
	Number	Percent	Number	Percent	Number	Percent
35 to 44 years	338	47.1	373	51.9	90	12.6
45 to 54 years	162	46.4	175	50.2	50	14.3
55 to 59 years	56	40.6	71	51.8	17	12.0
60 to 64 years	60	41.2	75	51.5	26	18.3
65 years and over	115	42.7	162	60.1	67	24.9
65 to 74 years	60	38.0	89	56.9	27	17.3
75 years and over	55	49.4	72	64.7	40	35.7
Male						
Total	1,485	48.4	1,779	58.0	384	12.5
Under 18 years	911	58.8	1,058	68.2	224	14.4
18 to 24 years	124	34.5	164	45.6	29	8.1
25 to 34 years	167	35.7	233	49.8	57	12.2
35 to 44 years	133	40.7	141	43.0	33	9.9
45 to 54 years	72	42.5	79	46.2	14	7.6
55 to 59 years	18	B	28	B	2	B
60 to 64 years	19	B	26	B	7	B
65 years and over	39	44.7	51	57.4	20	22.3
65 to 74 years	24	B	31	B	10	B
75 years and over	15	B	20	B	10	B
Female						
Total	1,932	53.9	2,296	64.0	616	17.2
Under 18 years	937	59.9	1,075	68.7	283	18.1
18 to 24 years	234	48.4	307	63.4	70	14.4
25 to 34 years	312	51.2	382	62.7	87	14.2
35 to 44 years	205	52.5	232	59.4	58	14.8
45 to 54 years	89	50.0	97	54.1	37	20.6
55 to 59 years	38	44.6	43	51.5	15	17.4
60 to 64 years	41	42.8	49	50.8	20	20.6
65 years and over	76	41.8	111	61.5	47	26.2
65 to 74 years	35	35.5	59	58.8	17	17.4
75 years and over	40	49.6	52	64.8	30	37.0
Household Relationship						
Total	3,417	51.3	4,075	61.2	1,000	15.0
65 years and over	115	42.7	162	60.1	67	24.9
In families	3,070	54.3	3,619	64.0	843	14.9
Householder	750	53.8	875	62.7	237	17.0
Under 65 years	717	54.1	836	63.1	225	17.0
65 years and over	34	B	39	B	12	B
Related children under 18 years	1,768	60.0	2,043	69.3	478	16.2
Under 6 years	752	61.5	902	73.7	200	16.4
6 to 17 years	1,017	59.9	1,141	66.2	277	16.1

[Continued]

★ 568 ★

Household Participation in Government Assistance Programs - II

[Continued]

Characteristic	In household that received food stamps		In household in which one or more persons covered by Medicaid		Lived in public or subsidized housing	
	Number	Percent	Number	Percent	Number	Percent
Own children 18 years and over	152	45.5	195	58.6	36	10.9
In married-couple families	1,378	43.9	1,696	54.1	290	9.2
Husbands	279	40.5	347	50.5	72	10.5
Under 65 years	252	39.6	324	50.8	62	9.7
65 years and over	26	B	23	B	10	B
Wives	275	40.9	335	49.8	67	10.0
Under 65 years	262	40.5	323	49.9	64	9.9
65 years and over	13	B	12	B	3	B
Related children under 18 years	717	47.8	876	58.4	138	9.2
Under 6 years	303	47.4	404	63.0	65	10.2
6 to 17 years	414	48.1	472	54.9	73	8.5
Own children 18 years and over	52	38.2	62	45.0	4	3.3
In families with female householder, no spouse present	1,541	71.5	1,754	81.4	512	23.7
Householder	427	70.6	478	79.2	151	24.9
Under 65 years	419	72.2	461	79.5	149	25.6
65 years and over	8	B	17	B	2	B
Related children under 18 years	977	75.8	1,088	84.4	316	24.5
Under 6 years	406	79.6	451	88.4	119	23.3
6 to 17 years	571	73.3	637	81.8	197	25.3
Own children 18 years and over	94	53.2	129	73.2	32	17.9
In unrelated subfamilies	105	47.3	126	56.7	33	14.8
Under 18 years	66	51.6	74	58.0	24	18.6
Under 6 years	33	B	42	B	13	B
6 to 17 years	33	B	32	B	10	B
18 years and over	39	41.4	52	55.0	9	9.8
Unrelated individuals	242	31.1	330	42.4	124	16.0
Male	110	28.7	144	37.8	43	11.3
Under 65 years	99	28.3	121	34.6	34	9.7
Living alone	16	B	26	B	16	B
65 years and over	11	B	23	B	9	B
Living alone	10	B	20	B	9	B
Female	132	33.5	185	46.8	81	20.5
Under 65 years	86	29.6	119	40.7	44	15.1
Living alone	38	37.9	39	38.2	29	28.4
65 years and over	46	44.5	66	63.9	37	35.8
Living alone	45	48.4	58	62.0	37	39.9

Source: U.S. Bureau of the Census. *Poverty in the United States: 1992.* Current Population Reports, Series P60-185, U.S. Government Printing Office, Washington, D.C., 1993, pp. 31-38. *Notes:* (B) stands for base less than 75,000. 1. Persons of Hispanic origin may be of any race.

★ 569 ★

Income

Income Distribution of Females Age 15 and Older, 1990 - I

Numbers are shown in thousands.

Characteristic	Total	With income					
		Total	$1 to $4,999 or less	$5,000 to $9,999	$10,000 to $14,999	$15,000 to $24,999	$25,000 to $34,999
All females	100,680	92,245	26,337	19,563	13,563	17,516	8,707
Race and Hispanic origin							
Hispanic origin[1]	7,559	5,903	2,059	1,502	901	892	346
White	85,012	78,566	22,062	16,358	11,652	15,162	7,547
Black	12,124	10,687	3,455	2,561	1,487	1,793	883
Year round, full-time worker							
All females	31,758	31,734	741	2,501	5,777	11,129	6,564
Race and Hispanic origin							
Hispanic origin[1]	2,108	2,107	59	340	545	695	295
White	26,668	26,647	625	1,982	4,682	9,502	5,578
Black	3,918	3,918	90	427	868	1,368	754

Source: U.S. Bureau of the Census. *Money Income of Households, Families, and Persons in the United States: 1990*. Current Population Reports, P60-174, 1991, pp. 108-111. Primary source: U.S. Bureau of the Census, *Current Population Reports*, Series P-60, No. 174, 1991. *Note:* 1. Persons of Hispanic origin may be of any race.

★ 570 ★

Income

Income Distribution of Females Age 15 and Older, 1990 - II

Numbers are shown in thousands, except where noted.

Characteristic	With income			Median income		Mean income	
	$35,000 to $49,999	$50,000 to $74,999	$75,000 and over	Value (dol.)	Standard error (dol.)	Value (dol.)	Standard error (dol.)
All females	4,457	1,535	565	10,070	71	13,913	73
Race and Hispanic origin							
Hispanic origin[1]	149	43	12	7,532	217	10,587	222
White	3,895	1,382	509	10,317	77	14,138	80
Black	392	83	32	8,328	206	12,049	185
Year round, full-time worker							
All females	3,429	1,136	347	20,591	107	23,392	133
Race and Hispanic origin							
Hispanic origin[1]	128	34	9	16,181	400	18,542	404

[Continued]

★ 570 ★

Income Distribution of Females Age 15 and Older, 1990 - II

[Continued]

Characteristic	With income			Median income		Mean income	
	$35,000 to $49,999	$50,000 to $74,999	$75,000 and over	Value (dol.)	Standard error (dol.)	Value (dol.)	Standard error (dol.)
White	2,958	1,020	300	20,839	115	23,722	147
Black	321	64	27	18,544	369	20,719	325

Source: U.S. Bureau of the Census. *Money Income of Households, Families, and Persons in the United States: 1990.* Current Population Reports, P60-174, 1991, pp. 108-111. Primary source: U.S. Bureau of the Census, *Current Population Reports*, Series P-60, No. 174, 1991. *Note:* 1. Persons of Hispanic origin may be of any race.

★ 571 ★

Income

Income Distribution of Males Age 15 and Older, 1990 - I

Numbers are shown in thousands.

Characteristic	Total	With income					
		Total	$1 to $4,999 or less	$5,000 to $9,999	$10,000 to $14,999	$15,000 to $24,999	$25,000 t0 $34,999
All males	92,840	88,220	10,820	11,312	11,253	19,166	14,185
Race and Hispanic origin							
Hispanic origin[1]	7,502	6,767	1,053	1,353	1,298	1,572	776
White	79,555	76,480	8,539	9,249	9,529	16,679	12,707
Black	10,074	8,820	1,866	1,643	1,323	1,859	1,112
Year round, full-time worker							
All males	49,181	49,172	690	2,088	4,939	12,046	11,054
Race and Hispanic origin							
Hispanic origin[1]	3,708	3,704	72	412	788	1,155	650
White	43,137	43,128	582	1,645	4,007	10,202	9,833
Black	4,363	4,363	81	348	744	1,382	923

Source: U.S. Bureau of the Census. *Money Income of Households, Families, and Persons in the United States: 1990.* Current Population Reports, P60-174, 1991, pp. 108-111. Primary source: U.S. Bureau of the Census, *Current Population Reports*, Series P-60, No. 174, 1991. *Note:* 1. Persons of Hispanic origin may be of any race.

★ 572 ★

Income

Income Distribution of Males Age 15 and Older, 1990 - II

Numbers are shown in thousands, except where noted.

Characteristic	With income						
	$35,000 to $49,999	$50,000 to $74,999	$75,000 and over	Median income		Mean income	
				Value (dol.)	Standard error (dol.)	Value (dol.)	Standard error (dol.)
All males	11,604	6,433	3,446	20,293	102	26,041	137
Race and Hispanic origin							
Hispanic origin[1]	459	184	72	13,470	316	17,452	332
White	10,531	5,973	3,273	21,170	108	27,142	152
Black	716	237	64	12,868	378	16,985	278
Year round, full-time worker							
All males	9,783	5,572	3,001	28,979	197	35,076	203
Race and Hispanic origin							
Hispanic origin[1]	404	164	60	19,358	436	23,377	480
White	8,842	5,165	2,852	30,081	139	36,178	223
Black	628	208	50	21,481	356	24,690	398

Source: U.S. Bureau of the Census. *Money Income of Households, Families, and Persons in the United States: 1990.* Current Population Reports, P60-174, 1991, pp. 108-111. Primary source: U.S. Bureau of the Census, *Current Population Reports*, Series P-60, No. 174, 1991. *Note:* 1. Persons of Hispanic origin may be of any race.

★ 573 ★

Income

Income Distribution, by Annual Earnings, Sex and Hispanic Origin, March 1993

Numbers are shown in thousands, except where noted.

Income characteristic[1]	Total population	Hispanic-origin population	Non-Hispanic population	Non-Hispanic White population	Hispanic subgroup				
					Mexican origin population	Puerto Rican origin population	Cuban origin population	Central and South American origin population	Other Hispanic origin population
EARNINGS OF PERSONS IN 1992									
Males with earnings	72,318	6,176	66,142	56,764	3,997	491	313	905	469
Percent	100.0	100.0	100.0	100.0	100.0	100.0	100.0	100.0	100.0
Less than $10,000	24.2	32.7	23.4	22.0	35.0	24.3	24.6	31.3	29.9
$10,000 to $24,999	30.1	42.0	29.0	28.0	43.0	41.4	38.5	43.6	33.3
$25,000 to $49,999	32.0	21.0	33.0	34.2	18.9	28.4	25.3	20.7	28.4
$50,000 or more	13.7	4.4	14.6	15.8	3.1	6.0	11.6	4.5	8.4
Median earnings (dollars)	22,171	14,706	23,301	24,994	13,622	18,386	18,416	14,358	18,518
Mean earnings (dollars)	27,748	18,488	28,613	29,826	17,050	21,559	25,237	18,628	22,748
Females with earnings	62,050	4,240	57,809	48,613	2,542	424	251	656	367
Percent	100.0	100.0	100.0	100.0	100.0	100.0	100.0	100.0	100.0
Less than $10,000	37.9	46.0	37.3	37.0	49.6	35.9	33.3	48.4	37.8
$10,000 to $24,999	37.9	38.1	37.9	37.7	36.7	42.3	42.0	38.7	38.6
$25,000 to $49,999	21.1	14.5	21.6	22.0	12.7	20.8	23.7	10.5	20.3
$50,000 or more	3.1	1.4	3.2	3.3	1.0	1.0	0.9	2.4	3.4

[Continued]

★ 573 ★

Income Distribution, by Annual Earnings, Sex and Hispanic Origin, March 1993

[Continued]

Income characteristic[1]	Total population	Hispanic-origin population	Non-Hispanic population	Non-Hispanic White population	Hispanic subgroup				
					Mexican origin population	Puerto Rican origin population	Cuban origin population	Central and South American origin population	Other Hispanic origin population
Median earnings (dollars)	13,675	10,813	14,046	14,241	10,098	14,200	14,117	10,249	13,649
Mean earnings (dollars)	16,745	13,587	16,977	17,141	12,588	15,656	16,456	13,170	16,902

Source: Montgomery, Patricia A. U.S. Bureau of the Census. *The Hispanic Population in the United States: March 1993.* Current Population Reports, Series P20-475. Washington, DC: U.S. Government Printing Office, 1994, pp. 12-15. *Note:* 1. For persons 15 years old and over.

★ 574 ★

Income

Income Distribution, by Sex, Income Level, and Race/Ethnicity, 1990

Data are shown for persons 15 years old and over, as of March of following year.

Sex, year, race Hispanic origin	All persons (mil.)	Persons with income									
		Total (mil.)	Percent distribution, by income (1988 dollars)								Median income (dol.)
			1 to 2,499 or less[1]	2,500 to 4,999	5,000 to 9,999	10,000 to 14,999	15,000 to 24,999	25,000 to 49,999	50,000 to 74,999	75,000 to and over	
Male											
Hispanic[2]	7.5	6.8	7.4	8.1	20.0	19.2	23.2	18.3	2.7	1.1	13,470
White	80.0	76.5	6.2	4.9	12.1	12.5	21.8	30.4	7.8	4.3	21.170
Black	10.1	8.8	10.7	10.5	18.6	15.0	21.1	20.7	2.7	0.7	12,868
Female											
Hispanic[2]	7.6	5.9	19.1	15.8	25.4	15.3	15.1	8.4	0.7	0.2	7,532
White	85.0	78.6	16.0	12.0	20.8	14.8	19.3	14.6	1.8	0.6	10,317
Black	12.1	10.7	13.8	18.5	24.0	13.9	16.8	11.9	0.8	0.3	8,328

Source: "Money Income of Persons - Percent Distribution by Income Level and Median Income in Constant (1990) Dollars: 1970 to 1990," *Statistical Abstract of the United States, 1992* (12th edition), p. 453. Primary source: U.S. Bureau of the Census, *Current Population Reports*, Series P-174; and unpublished data. *Notes:* 1. Includes persons with income deficit. 2. Hispanic persons may be of any race.

★ 575 ★

Income

Income, Earnings, and Work Activity of Hispanic Persons, by Educational Status

Data for persons age 18 and older are shown in dollars for spring of 1990.

Educational attainment	Monthly income		Monthly earnings		Months with work activity	
	Mean	Standard error	Mean	Standard error	Mean	Standard error
Hispanic, 18 years and over[1]						
Both sexes	1,078	19	958	19	2.60	0.04
Doctorate	(B)	(B)	(B)	(B)	(B)	(B)
Professional	(B)	(B)	(B)	(B)	(B)	(B)

[Continued]

★ 575 ★

Income, Earnings, and Work Activity of Hispanic Persons, by Educational Status

[Continued]

Educational attainment	Monthly income		Monthly earnings		Months with work activity	
	Mean	Standard error	Mean	Standard error	Mean	Standard error
Master's	2,840	468	2,761	466	3.25	0.22
Bachelor's	1,895	127	1,841	124	3.45	0.10
Associate	1,549	127	1,569	132	3.34	0.16
Vocational	1,314	149	1,149	116	2.89	0.21
Some college, no degree	1,298	49	1,168	47	3.05	0.07
High school graduate only	1,092	29	974	30	2.76	0.05
Not a high school graduate	760	20	625	21	2.14	0.05

Source: U.S. Bureau of the Census. *What's it Worth? Educational Background and Economic Status: Spring 1990.* Current Population Reports, Series P70-32. Washington DC: U.S. Government Printing Office, 1992, p. 15. *Notes:* A (B) stands for base is less than 200,000 persons. 1. Persons of Hispanic origin may be of any race.

★ 576 ★

Income

Mean Earnings of Hispanic Persons, by Sex and Educational Attainment, 1975-92

Mean annual earnings are shown in number of dollars for all workers age 18 years and older.

Earnings year	Total	Standard error	Not a high school graduate	Standard error	High school graduate	Standard error	Some college/ Associates degree	Standard error	Bachelor's degree	Standard error	Advanced degree	Standard error
Hispanic origin[1]												
Male												
1992	18,842	365	13,313	366	19,357	662	23,033	596	33,430	1,957	53,645	2,748
1991	18,516	316	13,133	263	18,582	471	21,974	693	31,699	1,729	45,873	2,549
1990	18,320	332	13,182	276	18,100	455	22,376	831	31,485	1,966	47,479	4,339
1989	18,087	352	13,167	265	17,579	452	22,374	996	32,767	2,536	49,088	4,778
1988	17,357	361	12,836	316	17,446	475	21,631	1,205	26,935	1,807	40,916	4,602
1987	17,048	372	12,823	369	16,774	523	19,414	773	26,581	1,782	39,014	4,410
1986	15,624	305	11,262	313	15,948	476	19,675	962	27,427	1,975	32,538	2,705
1985	15,293	285	11,671	342	15,602	464	18,168	771	24,723	1,723	32,831	2,792
1984	14,957	344	11,441	385	15,763	549	17,261	1,014	23,835	1,878	30,727	3,231
1983	14,265	324	11,353	400	14,584	549	16,626	864	21,911	2,111	28,680	2,681
1982	13,484	339	10,108	392	13,883	488	15,560	845	22,565	2,632	34,474	3,995
1981	13,052	292	10,447	342	13,513	489	15,432	785	19,201	1,928	27,619	3,427
1980	12,310	303	9,825	394	13,108	526	14,331	890	19,224	1,986	24,642	3,439
1979	11,332	268	9,393	378	11,714	448	12,489	714	18,923	2,113	21,299	2,619
1978	10,473	258	8,836	427	10,940	426	11,545	665	16,898	1,861	20,702	2,730
1977	9,655	198	8,192	281	10,386	372	9,924	501	15,189	1,420	19,025	2,291
1976	8,787	195	7,440	272	9,640	345	8,843	508	13,650	1,299	16,184	2,339
1975	8,162	189	6,745	268	8,546	289	8,807	536	12,881	1,142	17,991	2,535
Female												
1992	13,880	304	8,913	334	13,396	435	16,076	669	22,160	1,343	34,551	2,666
1991	13,069	273	4,809	307	13,043	380	15,721	654	20,791	1,377	30,721	2,392
1990	12,516	254	5,093	309	12,109	354	15,245	629	19,378	1,331	27,184	1,824
1989	12,307	266	8,256	401	11,799	365	14,482	629	22,617	1,379	26,700	2,265
1988	11,573	290	7,597	349	11,284	392	14,012	662	19,707	1,171	24,444	3,675
1987	11,234	286	7,350	354	10,627	417	13,929	688	18,003	1,033	26,584	3,436
1986	10,457	231	7,130	338	10,319	332	12,648	547	16,142	1,165	22,071	2,096
1985	9,865	236	6,699	367	9,784	327	11,791	639	15,503	1,098	22,480	2,173
1984	9,150	252	6,438	436	9,492	380	10,848	619	14,404	1,310	18,706	2,355
1983	8,704	NA	6,305	NA	9,261	NA	9,750	NA	13,507	NA	16,817	NA
1982	8,195	233	5,781	373	8,668	374	9,896	605	13,719	1,235	15,244	2,247

[Continued]

★ 576 ★

Mean Earnings of Hispanic Persons, by Sex and Educational Attainment, 1975-92

[Continued]

Earnings year	Total	Standard error	Not a high school graduate	Standard error	High school graduate	Standard error	Some college/ Associates degree	Standard error	Bachelor's degree	Standard error	Advanced degree	Standard error
1981	7,723	215	5,486	364	8,292	342	9,483	563	12,292	1,101	15,503	2,767
1980	6,770	199	5,028	358	6,923	287	8,808	576	10,568	1,177	14,668	2,935
1979	6,255	184	4,675	347	6,708	286	7,069	482	9,168	1,001	13,313	1,905
1978	5,501	173	4,135	377	5,834	273	6,686	507	9,684	1,098	10,908	1,872
1977	4,964	137	3,707	276	5,466	236	5,588	367	9,082	691	10,569	2,119
1976	4,548	132	3,537	273	5,124	229	5,075	373	6,884	826	9,218	1,425
1975	4,152	122	3,233	277	4,708	209	4,790	376	6,226	805	8,067	1,536

Source: Kominski, Robert and Andrea Adams. U.S. Bureau of the Census. *Educational Attainment in the United States: March 1993 and 1992.* Current Population Reports, P20-476. Washington, DC: U.S. Government Printing Office, 1994, p. 101. *Notes:* Prior to 1991, some college/Associate degrees equal 1 to 3 years of college completed; Bachelor's degree equals 4 years of college; Advanced degree equals 5 or more years of college completed. NA stands for not available. 1. May be of any race.

★ 577 ★

Income

Mean Earnings, by Educational Attainment and Race/Ethnicity, March 1993

Data show estimated mean earnings in 1992, by level of education. As is the case with other subgroups of the population, income of Hispanic persons increased in proportion to educational attainment.

	Total (dol.)	Not a high school graduate (dol.)	High school graduate (dol.)	Some college or associate degree (dol.)	Bachelor's degree (dol.)	Advanced degree (dol.)
Total	23,227	12,809	18,737	20,866	32,629	48,653
White	23,932	13,193	19,265	21,357	33,092	49,346
Black	17,416	11,077	15,260	17,768	27,457	39,088
Hispanic origin[1]	16,824	11,836	16,714	19,215	28,260	41,296

Source: Kominski, Robert and Andrea Adams. U.S. Bureau of the Census. *Educational Attainment in the United States: March 1993 and 1992.* Current Population Reports, P20-476. Washington, DC: U.S. Government Printing Office, 1994, p. ix. *Note:* 1. May be of any race.

★ 578 ★

Income

Median Annual Income of Full-Time Local Government Employees, by Race/Ethnicity and Type of Government, 1990

Race/ethnicity and sex	Median annual income ($)			
	County	City	Town	Special districts
Both sexes				
Total	22,066	26,258	27,306	27,209
White	22,145	27,645	27,407	28,270
Black	20,739	22,874	24,510	24,456
Hispanic	22,425	24,620	25,309	25,017
Asian	29,947	32,337	26,726	32,318
American Indian/Alaska Native	20,472	24,376	27,083	30,525
Men				
Total	24,208	28,048	29,317	30,380
White	24,510	29,298	29,426	31,614
Black	21,549	23,391	25,849	27,987
Hispanic	24,356	26,063	27,160	27,935
Asian	31,522	34,031	29,849	35,125
American Indian/Alaska Native	22,057	25,643	28,179	33,322
Women				
Total	20,141	22,711	21,599	22,218
White	19,816	22,707	21,584	23,452
Black	20,244	22,310	22,109	19,096
Hispanic	21,152	22,408	20,673	19,234
Asian	28,762	30,270	22,353	29,861
American Indian/Alaska Native	19,066	22,061	22,857	24,296

Source: U.S. Equal Employment Opportunity Commission. *Job Patterns for Minorities and Women in State and Local Government, 1990.* Washington, DC: U.S. Government Printing Office, 1991, pp. 15, 18, 21, and 24. *Note:* This table includes some units that cross geographical boundaries.

★ 579 ★

Income

Median Annual Income of Full-Time State and Local Government Employees, by Race/Ethnicity, Sex, and Profession, 1990: U.S. Summary

Race/ethnicity and sex	Median annual income ($)				
	Total	Officials/ administrators	Professionals	Technicians	Protective services
Both sexes					
Total	24,499	39,986	31,806	24,955	27,738
White	25,188	40,208	31,936	25,496	27,896
Black	22,011	37,911	29,485	22,806	25,705
Hispanic	23,764	38,071	31,694	24,955	30,719
Asian	31,462	45,315	38,796	28,548	35,104
American Indian/ Alaska Native	22,507	37,349	28,937	23,106	23,562
Men					
Total	27,323	42,457	34,669	28,014	28,265
White	28,166	42,504	34,932	28,353	28,394
Black	23,351	41,081	30,682	25,047	26,155
Hispanic	25,998	41,529	33,932	27,306	31,030
Asian	34,111	45,857	40,653	30,485	35,297
American Indian/ Alaska Native	24,064	40,198	30,334	24,318	24,041
Women					
Total	21,847	35,037	29,724	22,157	23,995
White	22,005	35,007	29,597	22,076	23,411
Black	20,963	35,036	28,901	21,643	24,481
Hispanic	21,578	32,742	29,902	23,074	28,645
Asian	28,962	44,042	37,316	26,705	33,527
American Indian/ Alaska Native	20,453	31,316	27,514	21,264	21,403

Source: U.S. Equal Employment Opportunity Commission. *Job Patterns for Minorities and Women in State and Local Government, 1990.* Washington, DC: U.S. Government Printing Office, 1991, pp.1-7.

★ 580 ★

Income

Median Income of Elderly Men and Women, 1989

Characteristic	Men	Women
Hispanic	8,469	4,992
White	13,391	7,816
Black	8,192	5,059

Source: Aging America, Trends and Projections, 1991 Edition. Prepared by the U.S. Senate Special Committee on Aging, the American Association of Retired Persons, the Federal Council on the Aging, and the U.S. Administration on Aging, p. 52. Primary source: March 1990, Current Population Survey.

★ 581 ★

Income

Median Income of Persons 15 Years Old and Older, by Sex and Race/Ethnicity, 1988-90

Race/ethnicity	1990			1989			1988			Percent change in real median income (1989-90)
	Number with income (000)	Median income Value (dol.)	Median income Standard error (dol.)	Number with income (000)	Median income Value (dol.)	Median income Standard error (dol.)	Number with income (000)	Median income Value (dol.)	Median income Standard error (dol.)	
Male										
All males	88,220	20,293	102	87,454	19,893	122	86,584	18,908	136	-3.2[2]
Race and Hispanic origin										
Hispanic origin[1]	6,767	13,470	315	6,592	13,400	330	6,342	13,030	407	-4.6[2]
White	76,480	21,170	107	75,858	20,863	111	75,247	19,959	135	-3.7[2]
Black	8,820	12,868	378	8,806	12,609	304	8,610	12,044	283	-3.2
Female										
All females	92,245	10,070	71	91,399	9,624	69	90,593	8,884	79	-.7
Race and Hispanic origin										
Hispanic origin[1]	5,903	7,532	217	5,677	7,647	234	5,532	6,990	256	-6.6[2]
White	78,566	10,317	77	77,933	9,812	73	77,493	9,103	85	-.2
Black	10,687	8,328	206	10,577	7,875	238	10,380	7,349	151	.3
Year-round, full-time workers										
Male										
All males	48,351	29,172	199	48,831	28,605	202	48,290	27,342	126	-3.2[2]
Race and Hispanic origin										
Hispanic origin[1]	3,650	19,314	435	3,656	18,570	413	3,608	18,190	582	-1.3
White	42,470	30,186	124	43,054	29,846	198	42,721	28,262	218	-4.0[2]
Black	4,226	21,540	365	4,206	20,706	281	4,108	20,716	362	-1.3
Female										
All females	31,658	20,586	106	31,336	19,643	120	31,306	18,545	132	-.6
Race and Hispanic origin										
Hispanic origin[1]	2,106	16,186	399	2,076	16,006	398	1,971	15,201	540	-4.1
White	26,606	20,840	114	26,246	19,873	132	26,272	18,823	144	-.5
Black	3,902	18,518	367	3,960	17,908	362	3,985	16,867	285	-1.9

Source: U.S. Bureau of the Census. *Money Income of Households, Families, and Persons in the United States: 1990.* Current Population Reports, P60-174, 1991, pp. 104-107. Primary source: U.S. Department of Commerce, Economics and Statistics Administration, Bureau of the Census, *Current Population Reports: Consumer Income,* Series P-60, No. 174, 1991. *Notes:* 1. Persons of Hispanic origin may be of any race. 2. Indicates statistically significant change at the 90-percent confidence level.

★ 582 ★

Income

Median Income of Persons Age 65 Years or Older, 1989

Median income is shown in dollars for each race/ethnicity, by age and sex, in 1989.

Race/ethnicity	Both sexes			Men			Women		
	65+	65 to 69	70+	65+	65 to 69	70+	65+	65 to 69	70+
Hispanic[1]	5,978	6,664	5,715	8,469	10,240	6,816	4,992	4,640	5,112
White	9,838	11,323	9,305	13,391	15,680	12,410	7,816	7,977	7,756
Black	5,772	6,552	5,517	8,192	10,464	7,224	5,059	5,235	5,032
All races	9,420	10,722	8,936	13,024	15,273	12,022	7,508	7,584	7,476

Source: Aging America, Trends and Projections, 1991 Edition. Prepared by the U.S. Senate Special Committee on Aging, the American Association of Retired Persons, the Federal Council on the Aging, and the U.S. Administration on Aging, p. 51. Primary source: Unpublished data from the March 1990 *Current Population Survey*. *Note:* 1. Hispanic people may be of any race.

★ 583 ★

Income

Median Income, by Race/Ethnicity and Sex, 1991

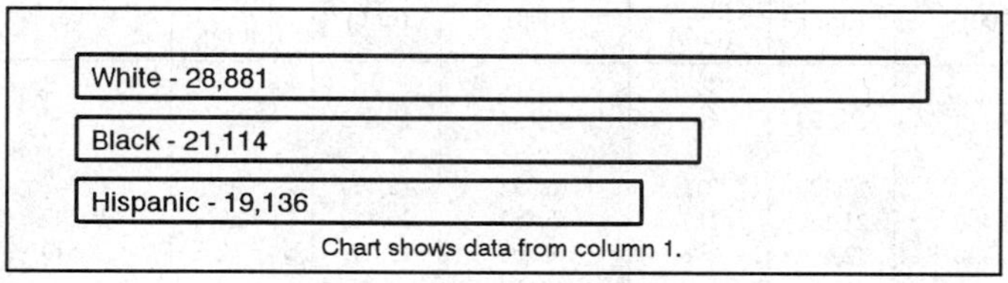

Race/ethnicity	Median income ($)	
	Men	Women
Hispanic[1]	19,136	15,672
White	28,881	20,048
Black	21,114	18,040

Source: Estrich, Susan. "Positive signal for working women." *USA TODAY* (29 April 1992), p. 9A. Primary source: Census Bureau; Equal Employment Opportunity Commission *Note:* 1. Hispanics can be included as black or white.

★584★

Income

Median Monthly Income, by Level of Education and Race/Ethnicity, 1990

Figures are shown in dollars for persons over 18 years old.

Level of education	Hispanic	White	Black
Doctorate	[1]	4,679.00	[1]
Master	2,840.00	3,248.00	2,786.00
Bachelor	1,895.00	2,552.00	2,002.00
Some college	1,298.00	1,595.00	1,204.00
High school	1,092.00	1,405.00	1,009.00
Some high school	760.00	909.00	652.00

Source: Kilborn, Peter T. "Extending jobless benefits is on the table, Reich says." *The New York Times* (28 January 1993), p. 11A. Primary source: 1990 U.S. Census. *Notes:* 1. There were too few black and Hispanic recipients of doctorate degrees to determine monthly income. Hispanics may be of any race.

★585★

Income

Median Net Worth of Elderly Households, 1988

Characteristic	Number
Married couple	124,419
All households	73,471
Men	48,883
Women	47,233
Hispanic	40,371
White	81,648
Black	22,210

Source: Aging America, Trends and Projections, 1991 Edition. Prepared by the U.S. Senate Special Committee on Aging, the American Association of Retired Persons, the Federal Council on the Aging, and the U.S. Administration on Aging, p. 78. Primary source: U.S. Bureau of the Census, "Household Wealth and Asset Ownership: 1988," *Current Population Reports Series P-70, No. 22,* December 1990.

★ 586 ★

Income

Median Weekly Earnings of Full-Time Wage and Salary Workers, 1983-93

Data are shown in current dollars of usual weekly earnings and represent annual averages of quarterly data, based on Current Population Surveys.

	Median weekly earnings (dollars)								
	1983	1985	1987	1988	1989	1990	1991	1992	1993
All workers[1]	313	343	373	385	399	415	430	445	463
White	319	355	383	394	409	427	446	462	478
Male	387	417	450	465	482	497	509	518	531
Female	254	281	307	318	334	355	374	388	403
Black	261	277	301	314	319	329	348	357	370
Male	293	304	326	347	348	360	374	380	392
Female	231	252	275	288	301	308	323	336	349
Hispanic origin[2]	NA	NA	284	290	298	307	315	324	335
Male	NA	NA	306	307	315	322	328	345	352
Female	NA	NA	251	260	269	280	293	303	314

Source: 1994 Statistical Abstract of the United States on CD-ROM [machine-readable datafiles]. CD-8A-94. Washington, DC: U.S. Department of Commerce, Economics and Statistics Administration, Bureau of the Census, Data User Services Division, January 1995. Primary source: U.S. Bureau of Labor Statistics, Bulletin 2307, and Employment and Earnings, January issue. *Notes:* NA stands for not available. 1. Includes other races, not shown separately. 2. Persons of Hispanic origin may be of any race.

★ 587 ★

Income

Median Weekly Earnings of Union Members, by Race/Ethnicity, 1983-93

Data shown are annual averages of monthly data and cover employed wage and salary workers age 16 years and older. Figures exclude self-employed workers whose businesses are incorporated although they technically qualify as wage and salary workers. Data are based on Current Population Surveys.

	Median usual weekly earnings (dol.)[1]							
	Total		Union members[2]		Represented by unions[3]		Not represented by unions	
	1983	1993	1983	1993	1983	1993	1983	1993
Total	313	463	388	575	383	569	288	426
White	319	478	396	589	391	585	295	444
Men	387	531	423	619	421	618	362	505
Women	254	403	314	514	313	510	240	382
Black	261	370	331	490	324	485	222	330
Men	293	392	366	514	360	510	244	345
Women	231	349	292	454	287	447	209	320
Hispanic[4]	NA	335	NA	481	NA	478	NA	311

[Continued]

★ 587 ★

Median Weekly Earnings of Union Members, by Race/Ethnicity, 1983-93

[Continued]

	Median usual weekly earnings (dol.)[1]							
	Total		Union members[2]		Represented by unions[3]		Not represented by unions	
	1983	1993	1983	1993	1983	1993	1983	1993
Men	NA	352	NA	511	NA	509	NA	318
Women	NA	314	NA	413	NA	415	NA	297

Source: 1994 Statistical Abstract of the United States on CD-ROM [machine-readable datafiles]. CD-8A-94. Washington, DC: U.S. Department of Commerce, Economics and Statistics Administration, Bureau of the Census, Data User Services Division, January 1995. Primary source: U.S. Bureau of Labor Statistics, Employment and Earnings, January issues. *Notes:* NA stands for not available. 1. For full-time employed wage and salary workers; 1983 revised since originally published. 2. Members of a labor union or an employee association similar to a labor union. 3. Members of a labor union or an employee association similar to a union as well as workers who report no union affiliation but whose jobs are covered by a union or an employee association contract. 4. Persons of Hispanic origin may be of any race.

★ 588 ★

Income

Minimum Wage Earners, by Race/Ethnicity, 1993

Data show percentage of persons of each race/ethnicity who earned minimum wage, currently $4.25 per hour, in 1993.

Race/ethnicity	Percent
Total	3.1
White	6.5
Black	7.1
Hispanic	9.0

Source: Chavez, Linda. "Minimum Wage Hurts the Poor." *USA TODAY* (8 February 1994), sec. A, p. 11. Primary source: U.S. Bureau of Labor Statistics.

★ 589 ★

Income

Money Income of Households, by Race and Hispanic Origin, 1992

Data are shown for households as of March of following year, based on Current Population Surveys.

Characteristic	All races[1]		White		Black		Hispanic[2]	
	Aggregate income ($ bil.)	Mean income (dol.)	Aggregate income ($ bil.)	Mean income (dol.)	Aggregate income ($ bil.)	Mean income (dol.)	Aggregate income ($ bil.)	Mean income (dol.)
Total	3,761	39,020	3,347	40,780	284	25,409	193	29,102
Age of householder:								
15 to 24 years old	109	21,606	94	23,023	10	13,675	11	18,490
25 to 34 years old	717	36,328	628	38,616	61	22,460	51	27,584
35 to 44 years old	1,012	46,584	891	48,998	80	30,232	54	32,140
45 to 54 years old	870	52,479	776	54,476	64	35,756	41	36,249
55 to 64 years old	535	42,988	480	44,980	38	26,944	23	32,568
65 years old and over	519	24,849	479	25,678	32	16,528	14	19,529
Region:								
Northeast	820	42,189	745	43,691	52	27,904	30	25,818
Midwest	885	37,972	814	39,465	58	24,935	15	30,392
South	1,193	35,740	1,025	38,377	146	24,135	58	28,014
West	863	42,592	764	43,134	29	29,733	89	30,987
Size of household:								
One person	505	21,374	446	22,077	47	16,108	18	17,154
Two persons	1,252	40,146	1,152	41,926	71	24,401	41	27,592
Three persons	777	46,013	687	48,712	62	28,577	39	30,080
Four persons	759	50,821	671	53,243	58	33,888	44	33,881
Five persons	312	49,021	268	51,513	27	31,307	27	33,547
Six persons	104	47,573	83	51,054	14	32,562	13	31,750
Seven or more persons	53	43,606	41	46,763	7	26,727	12	34,864

Source: 1994 Statistical Abstract of the United States on CD-ROM [machine-readable datafiles]. CD-8A-94. Washington, DC: U.S. Department of Commerce, Economics and Statistics Administration, Bureau of the Census, Data User Services Division, January 1995. Primary source: U.S. Bureau of the Census, Current Population Reports, P60-184, and unpublished data. *Notes:* 1. Includes other races not shown separately. 2. Persons of Hispanic origin may be of any race.

★ 590 ★

Income

Pension Plan Coverage of Workers, by Race/Ethnicity, 1992

Data cover workers as of March of following year who had earnings in 1992. Figures are based on Current Population Surveys.

Sex and age	Number with coverage				Percent of civilian workers			
	Total[1]	White	Black	Hispanic[2]	Total[1]	White	Black	Hispanic[2]
Total	53,899	46,628	5,519	2,586	40	40	39	25
Male	30,197	26,607	2,624	1,499	42	43	37	24
Under 65 years old	29,617	26,097	2,572	1,486	43	43	38	24
15 to 24 years old	1,411	1,223	140	91	12	12	10	7

[Continued]

★ 590 ★

Pension Plan Coverage of Workers, by Race/Ethnicity, 1992

[Continued]

Sex and age	Number with coverage				Percent of civilian workers			
	Total[1]	White	Black	Hispanic[2]	Total[1]	White	Black	Hispanic[2]
25 to 44 years old	17,428	15,186	1,628	952	46	47	42	27
45 to 64 years old	10,777	9,688	804	443	54	55	50	36
65 years old and over	579	509	52	14	22	21	31	16
Female	23,703	20,021	2,896	1,087	38	38	41	26
Under 65 years old	23,287	19,657	2,850	1,074	39	39	41	26
15 to 24 years old	1,206	1,044	129	67	11	11	11	8
25 to 44 years old	13,857	11,561	1,796	701	43	43	45	29
45 to 64 years old	8,224	7,052	925	306	48	48	54	34
65 years old and over	416	364	46	12	21	21	26	20

Source: 1994 Statistical Abstract of the United States on CD-ROM [machine-readable datafiles]. CD-8A-94. Washington, DC: U.S. Department of Commerce, Economics and Statistics Administration, Bureau of the Census, Data User Services Division, January 1995. Primary source: U.S. Bureau of the Census, unpublished data. *Notes:* 1. Includes other races, not shown separately. 2. Hispanic persons may be of any race.

★ 591 ★

Income

Persons With Work Experience During the Year and Percent With Low Annual Earnings, by Age Group and Race/Ethnicity, 1974-89

This Census report defines earnings as low if they are less than the poverty level for a four-person family, working 40 hours a week, 50 weeks per year: $3,144 or $1.57 per hour in 1964; $3,676 or $1.84 per hour in 1969; $4,843 or $2.42 per hour in 1974; $6,905 or $3.45 per hour in 1979; $9,694 or $4.85 per hour in 1984; $11,570 or $5.79 per hour in 1989; $12,195 or $6.10 per hour in 1990. Numbers are shown in thousands.

Characteristics	Number with work experience during year (000)				Percent with low annual earnings			
	1974	1979	1984	1989	1974	1979	1984	1989
ALL RACES								
Sex and age								
Both sexes								
16 years and over	101,472	114,993	121,148	131,868	41.6	40.1	41.2	40.4
16 and 17 years	4,606	4,542	3,487	3,442	99.4	99.3	99.5	99.3
18 to 64 years	92,754	106,244	113,603	123,603	37.5	36.3	38.3	37.7
18 to 24 years	21,416	23,969	22,248	20,605	65.7	63.2	71.2	72.9
25 to 34 years	23,556	30,518	34,241	37,016	29.9	29.5	31.9	34.5
35 to 54 years	35,326	38,537	43,837	52,945	27.2	27.1	28.1	27.0
55 to 64 years	12,455	13,220	13,277	13,037	32.0	30.4	33.3	35.0
65 years and over	4,114	4,207	4,059	4,823	69.6	71.7	73.3	67.5
Males								
16 years and over	58,779	64,063	65,960	70,752	27.4	27.2	30.5	30.8
16 and 17 years	2,615	2,502	1,831	1,805	99.0	99.1	99.4	98.8
18 to 64 years	53,513	58,989	61,727	66,154	22.1	22.5	27.1	27.6

[Continued]

★ 591 ★

Persons With Work Experience During the Year and Percent With Low Annual Earnings, by Age Group and Race/Ethnicity, 1974-89

[Continued]

Characteristics	Number with work experience during year (000)				Percent with low annual earnings			
	1974	1979	1984	1989	1974	1979	1984	1989
18 to 24 years	11,238	12,510	11,465	10,573	57.6	55.5	67.2	68.6
25 to 34 years	13,895	16,866	18,628	19,921	14.2	15.7	21.8	25.2
35 to 54 years	20,875	21,801	24,010	28,351	9.6	10.8	14.2	15.2
55 to 64 years	7,505	7,811	7,623	7,310	18.0	17.1	20.5	23.1
65 years and over	2,651	2,573	2,403	2,793	63.9	65.2	66.0	61.9
Females								
16 years and over	42,693	50,929	55,188	61,116	61.1	56.4	54.0	51.6
16 and 17 years	1,991	2,040	1,656	1,637	99.8	99.6	99.5	99.8
18 to 64 years	39,241	47,256	51,876	57,449	58.4	53.6	51.6	49.4
18 to 24 years	10,178	11,459	10,783	10,033	74.7	71.5	75.6	77.4
25 to 34 years	9,661	13,652	15,613	17,095	52.6	46.7	44.0	45.3
35 to 54 years	14,451	16,736	19,827	24,594	52.7	48.3	44.9	40.6
55 to 64 years	4,950	5,410	5,654	5,727	53.3	49.7	50.6	50.3
65 years and over	1,461	1,634	1,656	2,030	79.8	81.9	83.8	75.2
HISPANIC ORIGIN[1]								
Sex and age								
Both sexes								
16 years and over	4,376	5,732	7,543	9,731	47.3	47.0	48.8	50.0
16 and 17 years	197	212	216	212	99.2	98.2	99.0	98.3
18 to 64 years	4,115	5,420	7,210	9,376	44.4	44.6	46.9	48.6
18 to 24 years	1,052	1,454	1,688	1,999	68.5	68.3	72.9	73.3
25 to 34 years	1,116	1,713	2,381	3,250	38.0	37.6	41.2	46.5
35 to 54 years	1,663	1,888	2,580	3,460	33.9	33.1	35.7	38.1
55 to 64 years	284	365	562	667	41.9	42.4	44.0	39.6
65 years and over	64	100	116	144	(B)	68.8	74.4	65.9
Males								
16 years and over	2,651	3,369	4,436	5,711	34.1	35.5	40.7	43.2
16 and 17 years	121	138	125	125	98.7	98.2	99.9	97.1
18 to 64 years	2,480	3,163	4,237	5,498	30.4	32.2	38.4	41.7
18 to 24 years	577	818	1,002	1,191	61.0	62.0	72.1	68.2
25 to 34 years	695	1,008	1,398	1,941	25.3	23.7	33.1	40.4
35 to 54 years	1,021	1,110	1,508	1,971	17.1	18.7	23.2	29.0
55 to 64 years	187	226	330	395	28.1	28.5	27.8	31.1
65 years and over	50	67	74	88	(B)	(B)	(B)	61.6
Females								
16 years and over	1,726	2,363	3,106	4,020	67.5	63.4	60.4	59.6
16 and 17 years	76	74	91	87	100.0	(B)	97.7	100.0
18 to 64 years	1,635	2,257	2,973	3,878	65.7	62.0	59.0	58.5
18 to 24 years	475	636	686	808	77.7	76.3	74.1	80.9

[Continued]

★ 591 ★

Persons With Work Experience During the Year and Percent With Low Annual Earnings, by Age Group and Race/Ethnicity, 1974-89

[Continued]

Characteristics	Number with work experience during year (000)				Percent with low annual earnings			
	1974	1979	1984	1989	1974	1979	1984	1989
25 to 34 years	422	705	983	1,309	58.9	57.6	52.8	55.5
35 to 54 years	642	778	1,072	1,489	60.7	53.7	53.3	50.2
55 to 64 years	96	138	232	272	68.8	65.2	67.2	51.9
65 years and over	14	33	43	56	(B)	(B)	(B)	(B)
WHITE								
Sex and age								
Both sexes								
16 years and over	90,166	101,407	105,818	113,713	40.6	39.3	40.4	39.7
16 and 17 years	4,113	4,098	3,139	2,969	99.3	99.3	99.5	99.1
18 to 64 years	82,344	93,522	99,034	106,372	36.5	35.4	37.3	37.0
18 to 24 years	18,950	21,114	19,371	17,645	65.0	62.2	70.0	72.4
25 to 34 years	20,686	26,452	29,526	31,425	29.2	28.5	30.7	33.3
35 to 54 years	31,417	33,961	38,260	45,727	26.2	26.3	27.5	26.6
55 to 64 years	11,291	11,994	11,877	11,576	30.4	29.2	32.1	34.0
65 years and over	3,709	3,787	3,645	4,372	68.0	70.3	72.6	66.4
Males								
16 years and over	52,788	57,084	58,324	61,764	26.2	25.9	29.1	29.6
16 and 17 years	2,328	2,282	1,654	1,566	98.9	99.0	99.3	98.6
18 to 64 years	48,047	52,489	54,486	57,630	20.8	21.1	25.5	26.3
18 to 24 years	9,969	11,019	10,026	9,092	56.5	54.0	65.6	67.9
25 to 34 years	12,386	14,836	16,275	17,131	13.0	14.2	19.8	23.6
35 to 54 years	18,836	19,453	21,250	24,824	8.6	9.6	13.0	14.0
55 to 64 years	6,856	7,181	6,934	6,583	16.7	16.0	19.3	22.4
65 years and over	2,413	2,313	2,184	2,569	62.6	63.8	65.7	61.0
Females								
16 years and over	37,379	44,323	47,494	51,948	61.0	56.4	54.2	51.8
16 and 17 years	1,786	1,816	1,485	1,403	99.8	99.7	99.7	99.8
18 to 64 years	34,297	41,033	44,548	48,743	58.4	53.7	51.8	49.6
18 to 24 years	8,981	10,095	9,345	8,553	74.4	71.1	74.8	77.2
25 to 34 years	8,300	11,616	13,251	14,293	53.5	46.7	44.2	45.0
35 to 54 years	12,580	14,509	17,009	20,903	52.6	48.7	45.5	41.5
55 to 64 years	4,435	4,813	4,942	4,993	51.5	49.0	50.0	49.3
65 years and over	1,296	1,474	1,461	1,803	78.2	80.6	83.0	74.1

Source: U.S. Bureau of the Census. *Workers With Low Earnings: 1964 to 1990.* Current Population Reports, Series P-60, No. 178. Washington, DC: U.S. Government Printing Office, 1992, pp. 17-20. *Notes:* A (B) indicates that the base was less than 75,000 and is too small for derived measures. 1. Persons of Hispanic origin may be of any race.

★ 592 ★

Income

Persons With Year-Round, Full-Time Attachment to Labor Force and Percent With Low Annual Earnings, by Age Group and Sex, 1974-89

This Census report defines earnings as low if they are less than the poverty level for a four-person family, working 40 hours a week, 50 weeks per year: $3,144 or $1.57 per hour in 1964; $3,676 or $1.84 per hour in 1969; $4,843 or $2.42 per hour in 1974; $6,905 or $3.45 per hour in 1979; $9,694 or $4.85 per hour in 1984; $11,570 or $5.79 per hour in 1989; $12,195 or $6.10 per hour in 1990. Numbers are shown in thousands.

Characteristics	Number with year-round, full-time attachment to labor force (000)				Percent with low annual earnings			
	1974	1979	1984	1989	1974	1979	1984	1989
ALL RACES								
Sex and age								
Both sexes								
16 years and over	65,236	76,225	84,925	92,448	18.5	18.9	23.2	23.1
16 and 17 years	338	380	216	176	93.5	95.6	93.1	90.8
18 to 64 years	63,400	74,396	83,348	90,546	17.6	18.2	22.7	22.7
18 to 24 years	9,765	11,979	11,143	9,925	36.0	36.2	49.1	50.4
25 to 34 years	17,120	22,585	26,823	28,560	13.5	14.6	20.3	23.0
35 to 54 years	27,389	29,946	35,418	42,777	13.6	14.2	17.2	16.8
55 to 64 years	9,125	9,885	9,964	9,284	17.5	16.6	19.4	19.6
65 years and over	1,498	1,449	1,361	1,726	40.4	37.8	40.6	33.6
Males								
16 years and over	44,568	49,339	52,763	55,962	12.7	13.3	18.5	18.3
16 and 17 years	246	256	149	108	92.2	94.6	93.2	87.3
18 to 64 years	43,224	48,094	51,692	54,775	11.6	12.5	18.0	18.0
18 to 24 years	5,842	7,052	6,404	5,644	31.0	31.4	47.1	47.5
25 to 34 years	12,137	14,708	16,669	17,421	9.4	10.6	17.5	19.3
35 to 54 years	19,080	19,805	22,229	25,821	7.2	7.8	11.4	11.6
55 to 64 years	6,165	6,528	6,390	5,889	11.0	10.5	13.3	13.6
65 years and over	1,097	989	921	1,079	39.3	32.8	33.1	28.5
Females								
16 years and over	20,668	26,887	32,162	36,487	30.9	29.3	30.9	30.4
16 and 17 years	92	124	66	68	97.1	97.6	(B)	(B)
18 to 64 years	20,175	26,302	31,656	35,771	30.4	28.6	30.4	30.0
18 to 24 years	3,923	4,927	4,739	4,281	43.3	43.0	51.7	54.2
25 to 34 years	4,983	7,876	10,153	11,139	23.5	22.2	25.1	28.7
35 to 54 years	8,309	10,142	13,189	16,955	28.1	26.5	27.0	24.8
55 to 64 years	2,960	3,357	3,574	3,395	31.2	28.5	30.3	30.0
65 years and over	401	461	439	648	43.3	48.4	56.3	42.1
HISPANIC ORIGIN[1]								
Sex and age								
Both sexes								
16 years and over	2,865	3,869	5,420	7,059	27.8	29.7	34.6	36.8
16 and 17 years	22	20	26	25	(B)	(B)	(B)	(B)
18 to 64 years	2,808	3,801	5,346	6,971	27.0	29.1	34.2	36.6

[Continued]

★ 592 ★

Persons With Year-Round, Full-Time Attachment to Labor Force and Percent With Low Annual Earnings, by Age Group and Sex, 1974-89

[Continued]

Characteristics	Number with year-round, full-time attachment to labor force (000)				Percent with low annual earnings			
	1974	1979	1984	1989	1974	1979	1984	1989
18 to 24 years	507	790	964	1,150	44.5	49.1	58.5	58.0
25 to 34 years	820	1,255	1,862	2,527	24.3	24.7	31.6	36.8
35 to 54 years	1,269	1,496	2,086	2,800	21.2	22.1	25.2	29.0
55 to 64 years	212	259	433	494	30.8	29.3	34.4	29.0
65 years and over	35	49	48	63	(B)	(B)	(B)	(B)
Males								
16 years and over	2,013	2,563	3,559	4,524	21.5	23.1	30.6	33.6
16 and 17 years	16	13	19	18	(B)	(B)	(B)	(B)
18 to 64 years	1,964	2,516	3,510	4,467	20.6	22.5	30.2	33.3
18 to 24 years	330	505	653	781	41.8	46.2	61.6	55.7
25 to 34 years	594	844	1,222	1,642	19.9	17.7	28.6	34.2
35 to 54 years	892	988	1,350	1,730	13.4	14.6	18.0	23.9
55 to 64 years	149	180	284	314	19.4	22.4	23.6	24.3
65 years and over	32	33	31	40	(B)	(B)	(B)	(B)
Females								
16 years and over	852	1,307	1,861	2,534	42.6	42.5	42.1	42.7
16 and 17 years	6	6	7	7	(B)	(B)	(B)	(B)
18 to 64 years	844	1,284	1,836	2,504	42.0	41.8	41.8	42.5
18 to 24 years	178	285	311	370	49.4	54.2	52.1	62.8
25 to 34 years	226	411	639	885	36.0	38.9	37.4	41.7
35 to 54 years	377	508	736	1,070	39.4	36.8	38.4	37.1
55 to 64 years	62	79	149	179	(B)	44.8	55.1	37.2
65 years and over	3	16	18	23	(B)	(B)	(B)	(B)
WHITE								
Sex and age								
Both sexes								
16 years and over	57,995	67,011	73,704	79,507	17.2	17.6	21.7	22.1
16 and 17 years	306	346	193	156	93.1	95.7	93.6	89.7
18 to 64 years	56,314	65,325	72,313	77,774	16.3	16.8	21.3	21.8
18 to 24 years	8,630	10,561	9,677	8,518	34.3	34.7	46.9	49.7
25 to 34 years	15,016	19,527	22,966	24,282	12.3	13.0	18.5	21.7
35 to 54 years	24,336	26,257	30,752	36,750	12.4	12.9	16.1	16.1
55 to 64 years	8,332	8,981	8,918	8,224	16.3	15.3	18.2	18.4
65 years and over	1,375	1,340	1,198	1,577	38.6	36.4	38.7	32.2
Males								
16 years and over	40,198	44,127	46,678	49,056	11.6	12.2	17.0	17.3
16 and 17 years	227	242	137	92	91.5	94.3	92.6	85.2
18 to 64 years	38,970	42,971	45,726	47,965	10.5	11.3	16.5	16.9
18 to 24 years	5,169	6,225	5,555	4,881	29.1	29.5	29.5	46.8

[Continued]

★ 592 ★

Persons With Year-Round, Full-Time Attachment to Labor Force and Percent With Low Annual Earnings, by Age Group and Sex, 1974-89

[Continued]

Characteristics	Number with year-round, full-time attachment to labor force (000)				Percent with low annual earnings			
	1974	1979	1984	1989	1974	1979	1984	1989
25 to 34 years	10,872	12,995	14,591	15,078	8.4	9.3	15.5	18.1
35 to 54 years	17,270	17,734	19,753	22,701	6.4	6.9	10.5	10.7
55 to 64 years	5,659	6,017	5,827	5,305	10.1	9.6	12.5	13.0
65 years and over	1,002	914	815	999	37.2	31.9	32.1	27.3
Females								
16 years and over	17,797	22,884	27,026	30,452	29.9	28.0	30.0	29.9
16 and 17 years	79	105	55	64	97.5	99.0	(B)	(B)
18 to 64 years	17,344	22,354	26,587	29,809	29.3	27.4	29.5	29.5
18 to 24 years	3,462	4,336	4,123	3,638	42.1	42.3	50.2	53.6
25 to 34 years	4,144	6,531	8,374	9,203	22.6	20.4	23.8	27.7
35 to 54 years	7,065	8,522	10,998	14,049	27.0	25.3	26.2	24.7
55 to 64 years	2,673	2,965	3,092	2,919	29.4	26.9	29.0	28.3
65 years and over	373	426	383	578	42.5	46.0	52.9	40.7
BLACK								
Sex and age								
Both sexes								
16 years and over	6,245	7,614	8,874	9,875	29.7	30.5	35.1	31.0
16 and 17 years	30	31	15	19	(B)	(B)	(B)	(B)
18 to 64 years	6,109	7,492	8,727	9,741	28.8	29.9	34.7	30.6
18 to 24 years	1,030	1,205	1,227	1,131	48.8	49.0	66.2	56.5
25 to 34 years	1,798	2,507	3,103	3,330	23.2	26.4	33.9	32.5
35 to 54 years	2,590	3,013	3,586	4,496	23.8	25.0	25.1	22.7
55 to 64 years	691	766	811	785	32.7	30.4	31.9	30.5
65 years and over	107	92	132	114	61.0	55.2	55.3	53.3
Males								
16 years and over	3,744	4,220	4,697	5,123	24.0	25.1	33.1	27.7
16 and 17 years	18	11	9	15	(B)	(B)	(B)	(B)
18 to 64 years	3,639	4,148	4,607	5,051	22.8	24.6	32.9	27.2
18 to 24 years	620	703	714	604	44.9	49.0	68.3	54.3
25 to 34 years	1,069	1,355	1,620	1,771	19.4	21.8	34.5	29.2
35 to 54 years	1,512	1,662	1,847	2,242	15.9	17.4	19.6	19.7
55 to 64 years	438	428	426	433	23.2	21.7	25.0	19.9
65 years and over	86	60	80	57	61.2	(B)	40.2	(B)
Females								
16 years and over	2,502	3,395	4,178	4,752	38.2	37.1	37.3	34.6
16 and 17 years	11	19	6	4	(B)	(B)	(B)	(B)
18 to 64 years	2,470	3,344	4,120	4,691	37.8	36.4	36.7	34.3
18 to 24 years	410	502	512	527	54.6	49.1	63.3	59.0
25 to 34 years	729	1,152	1,483	1,558	28.8	31.9	33.4	36.3

[Continued]

★ 592 ★

Persons With Year-Round, Full-Time Attachment to Labor Force and Percent With Low Annual Earnings, by Age Group and Sex, 1974-89

[Continued]

Characteristics	Number with year-round, full-time attachment to labor force (000)				Percent with low annual earnings			
	1974	1979	1984	1989	1974	1979	1984	1989
35 to 54 years	1,078	1,351	1,740	2,253	34.8	34.3	31.1	25.7
55 to 64 years	253	338	385	352	49.3	41.5	39.5	43.5
65 years and over	21	32	52	57	(B)	(B)	(B)	(B)

Source: U.S. Bureau of the Census. *Workers With Low Earnings: 1964 to 1990.* Current Population Reports, Series P-60, No. 178. Washington, DC: U.S. Government Printing Office, 1992, pp. 21-24. *Notes:* A (B) indicates that the base was less than 75,000 and is too small for derived measures. 1. Persons of Hispanic origin may be of any race.

★ 593 ★

Income

State and Local Government Full-Time Employee Salary, by Sex and Race/Ethnicity

Data, as of June 30, exclude school systems and educational institutions and are based on reports from State governments (44 in 1973, 48 in 1975, 1976, and 1979, 47 in 1977 and 1983, 45 in 1978, 42 in 1980, 49 in 1981 and 1984 through 1987, 50 in 1989-91) and a sample of county, municipal township, and special district jurisdictions employing 15 or more nonelected, nonappointed full-time employees. Data for 1982 and 1988 were not available.

Year and occupation	Median annual salary ($000)			
	White[1]	Minority		
		Total[2]	Black[1]	Hispanic[3]
1973	8.8	7.5	7.4	7.4
1975	10.2	8.8	8.6	8.9
1976	10.7	9.2	9.1	9.4
1977	11.3	9.7	9.5	9.9
1978	12.0	10.4	10.1	10.7
1979	12.8	10.9	10.6	11.4
1980	13.8	11.8	11.5	12.3
1981	16.1	13.5	13.3	14.7
1983	18.5	15.9	15.6	17.3
1984	19.6	17.4	16.5	18.4
1985	20.6	18.4	17.5	19.2
1986	21.5	19.6	18.7	20.2
1987	22.4	20.9	19.3	21.1
1989	24.1	22.1	20.7	22.7
1990	25.2	23.3	22.0	23.8
1991	26.4	23.8	22.7	24.5
Officials/administrators	41.9	41.2	41.6	41.8
Professionals	33.1	30.9	30.4	32.5
Technicians	26.6	23.6	23.3	25.8
Protective service	29.1	28.3	27.1	31.9

[Continued]

★ 593 ★

State and Local Government Full-Time Employee Salary, by Sex and Race/Ethnicity

[Continued]

Year and occupation	Median annual salary ($000)			
	White[1]	Minority		
		Total[2]	Black[1]	Hispanic[3]
Paraprofessionals	20.0	19.6	19.1	20.0
Admin. support	19.6	19.8	19.9	20.1
Skilled craft	25.7	25.6	25.0	26.5
Service/maintenance	20.4	20.5	18.9	20.7

Source: 1994 Statistical Abstract of the United States on CD-ROM [machine-readable datafiles]. CD-8A-94. Washington, DC: U.S. Department of Commerce, Economics and Statistics Administration, Bureau of the Census, Data User Services Division, January 1995. Primary source: U.S. Equal Employment Opportunity Commission, State and Local Government Information Report, annual. *Notes:* 1. Non-Hispanic. 2. Includes other minority groups not shown separately. 3. Persons of Hispanic origin may be of any race.

★ 594 ★

Income

Total Annual Income of Households, by Race/Ethnicity, 1990 - I

Numbers are shown in thousands, as of March 1991.

Race/ethnicity	Total number	Less than $5,000	$5,000 to $9,999	$10,000 to $14,999	$15,000 to $24,999	$25,000 to 34,999	$35,000 to $49,999
All households	94,312	4,901	9,184	8,925	16,723	14,865	16,469
Hispanic origin[1]	6,220	466	849	804	1,312	1,029	923
White	80,968	3,256	7,161	7,460	14,297	13,052	14,572
Black	10,671	1,500	1,786	1,240	2,038	1,436	1,403

Source: U.S. Bureau of the Census. *Money Income of Households, Families, and Persons in the United States: 1990.* Current Population Reports, P60-174, 1991, pp. 17-18. Primary source: U.S. Bureau of the Census, *Current Population Reports*, Series P-60, No. 174, 1991. *Note:* 1. Persons of Hispanic origin may be of any race.

★ 595 ★

Income

Total Annual Income of Households, by Race/Ethnicity, 1990 - II

Numbers are shown in thousands, except where noted, as of March 1991.

Race/ethnicity	$50,000 to $74,999	75,000 to $99,999	$100,000 and over	Median income		Mean income	
				Value (dol.)	Standard error (dol.)	Value (dol.)	Standard error (dol.)
All households	14,061	5,100	4,085	29,943	153	37,403	158
Hispanic origin[1]	568	156	111	22,330	458	27,972	461
White	12,760	4,621	3,791	31,231	143	38,912	174
Black	863	283	122	18,676	426	24,814	335

Source: U.S. Bureau of the Census. *Money Income of Households, Families, and Persons in the United States: 1990.* Current Population Reports, P60-174, 1991, pp. 17-18. Primary source: U.S. Bureau of the Census, *Current Population Reports*, Series P-60, No. 174, 1991. *Note:* 1. Persons of Hispanic origin may be of any race.

★ 596 ★

Income

Total Annual Income of Unrelated Individuals, by Race/Ethnicity, 1990 - I

Numbers are shown in thousands for unrelated individuals (those not residing with) relatives 15 years old and older as of March 1991.

Race/ethnicity	Total	Less than $5,000	$5,000 to $9,999	$10,000 to $14,999	$15,000 t0 24,999	$25,000 to 34,999	$35,000 to 49,999	$50,000 to 74,999	$75,000 to 99,999	$100,000 and over
All unrelated individuals	36,056	4,686	7,556	5,778	8,162	4,948	2,960	1,361	312	292
Hispanic origin[1]	2,254	543	587	400	400	181	88	42	10	1
White	30,833	3,517	6,346	5,018	7,163	4,370	2,596	1,262	296	266
Black	4,244	1,013	1,025	600	787	464	263	66	12	14

Source: U.S. Bureau of the Census. *Money Income of Households, Families, and Persons in the United States: 1990.* Current Population Reports, P60-174, 1991, p. 103. Primary source: U.S. Bureau of the Census, *Current Population Reports*, Series P-60, No. 174, 1991. *Note:* 1. Persons of Hispanic origin may be of any race.

★ 597 ★

Income

Total Annual Income of Unrelated Individuals, by Race/ Ethnicity, 1990 - II

Income is shown for unrelated individuals (those not residing with relatives) 15 years old and older as of March 1991.

Race/ethnicity	Median income		Mean income	
	Value (dol.)	Standard error (dol.)	Value (dol.)	Standard error (dol.)
All unrelated individuals	15,008	147	19,801	166
Hispanic origin[1]	9,968	381	13,315	453
White	15,624	153	20,494	185
Black	10,547	338	14,850	366

Source: U.S. Bureau of the Census. *Money Income of Households, Families, and Persons in the United States: 1990*. Current Population Reports, P60-174, 1991, p. 103. Primary source: U.S. Bureau of the Census, *Current Population Reports*, Series P-60, No. 174, 1991. *Note:* 1. Persons of Hispanic origin may be of any race.

★ 598 ★

Income

Trends in Median Household Income, 1970-92

Data are shown in current and constant (1992) dollars for households, as of March of following year, based on Current Population Surveys.

Year	Median income in current dollars					Median income in constant (1992) dollars				
	All households[1]	White	Black	Asian, Pacific Islander	Hispanic[2]	All households[1]	White	Black	Asian, Pacific Islander	Hispanic[2]
1970	8,734	9,097	5,537	NA	NA	29,670	30,903	18,810	NA	NA
1975	11,800	12,340	7,408	NA	8,865	29,458	30,806	18,494	NA	22,131
1976	12,686	13,289	7,902	NA	9,569	29,964	31,388	18,664	NA	22,602
1977	13,572	14,272	8,422	NA	10,647	30,129	31,683	18,696	NA	23,636
1978	15,064	15,660	9,411	NA	11,803	31,311	32,550	19,561	NA	24,533
1979[3]	16,461	17,259	10,133	NA	13,042	31,209	32,722	19,212	NA	24,727
1980	17,710	18,684	10,764	NA	13,651	30,191	31,851	18,350	NA	23,271
1981	19,074	20,153	11,309	NA	15,300	29,701	31,381	17,610	NA	23,825
1982	20,171	21,117	11,968	NA	15,178	29,602	30,991	17,564	NA	22,275
1983[4]	21,018	22,035	12,473	NA	15,794	29,607	31,039	17,570	NA	22,248
1984	22,415	23,647	13,471	NA	16,992	30,268	31,931	18,190	NA	22,945
1985	23,618	24,908	14,819	NA	17,465	30,796	32,478	19,323	NA	22,773
1986	24,897	26,175	15,080	NA	18,352	31,871	33,507	19,304	NA	23,493
1987[5]	26,061	27,458	15,672	NA	19,336	32,186	33,912	19,355	NA	23,881
1988	27,225	28,781	16,407	32,267	20,359	32,288	34,133	19,458	38,268	24,125
1989	28,906	30,406	18,083	36,102	21,921	32,706	34,403	20,460	40,848	24,803
1990	29,943	31,231	18,676	38,450	22,330	32,142	33,525	20,048	41,274	23,970

[Continued]

★ 598 ★

Trends in Median Household Income, 1970-92

[Continued]

Year	Median income in current dollars					Median income in constant (1992) dollars				
	All households[1]	White	Black	Asian, Pacific Islander	Hispanic[2]	All households[1]	White	Black	Asian, Pacific Islander	Hispanic[2]
1991	30,126	31,569	18,807	36,449	22,691	31,033	32,519	19,373	37,546	23,374
1992	30,786	32,368	18,660	38,153	22,848	30,786	32,368	18,660	38,153	22,848

Source: 1994 Statistical Abstract of the United States on CD-ROM [machine-readable datafiles]. CD-8A-94. Washington, DC: U.S. Department of Commerce, Economics and Statistics Administration, Bureau of the Census, Data User Services Division, January 1995. Primary source: U.S. Bureau of the Census, Current Population Reports, P60-184. *Notes:* NA stands for not available. 1. Includes other races not shown separately. 2. Hispanic persons may be of any race. 3. Population controls based on 1980 census. 4. Beginning 1983, data based on revised Hispanic population controls and not directly comparable with prior years. 5. Beginning 1987, data based on revised processing procedures and not directly comparable with prior years.

★ 599 ★

Income

Weekly Pay of Persons With Job Accessions, 1987-89

A "job accession" is defined as not having a job in one month but having a job in the following month. This table shows mean weekly earnings for persons who experienced job accessions and were paid on a weekly basis. Data are shown as of the first job accession of each person.

Race and Hispanic origin	Weekly earnings ($)				
	Total persons	16 to 19 years	20 to 24 years	25 to 34 years	35 years and over
All persons	336	101	238	325	411
White	354	103	244	348	433
Black	198	(B)	(B)	(B)	(B)
Hispanic origin	334	(B)	(B)	(B)	(B)

Source: U.S. Bureau of the Census. *Job Creation During the Late 1980's (Data from the Survey of Income and Program Participation).* Current Population Reports, P70, No. 27. Washington, DC: U.S. Government Printing Office, 1992, p. 9. *Note:* A (B) stands for base less than 200,000.

★ 600 ★

Income

Who's Who Among Successful Hispanic Americans

Hispanic Business has ranked the net worth of Hispanic Americans. To be included on the list, net worth of the company had to exceed 20 million dollars.

Name	Rank	Company and location	Net worth 1993 ($ mil.)
Joseph Unanue & family	1	Goya Foods, Secaucus, N.J.	330
John Arrillaga	2	Peery/Arrillaga, Palo Alto, CA	320
Roberto Goizueta	3	Coca-Cola, Atlanta	245
Arturo Torres	4	Arturo Torres Ent., San Antonio	105
Amigo & Max Soriano	5	Western Pioneer, Seattle	90
Robert Alvarez	6	Coast Citrus Dist., San Diego	85
Jose Milton	7	J. Milton & Assoc., Hialeah, FL	50
Manuel Medina	8	Terremark, Miami	45
Natan Rok	9	Rok Ent., Miami	45
Daniel Villanueva	10	Villanueva Capital, Los Angeles	45
Carlos Benavides Jr. & III	11	El Potrerito del Lano, Webb, TX	40
Manuel Caldera	12	The Caldera Co., Indian Wells, CA	40
Oscar de la Renta	13	Oscar de la Renta Ltd., New York	40
Gloria & Emilio Estefan	14	Estefan Ent./Miami Sound Machine	40
Abel Holtz	15	Capital Bancorp, Miami	40
Amancio Suarez family	16	Cosmo Communications, Miami	40
Lloyd Chavez	17	Burt on Broadway, Englewood, CA	35
Gedalio Grinberg & family	18	North American Watch, NJ	35
Liberman brothers	19	Liberman Broad., Santa Ana, CA	35
I.E. Lozano & family	20	Lozano Ent., Los Angeles	35
Oscar Porcelli	21	Gaseteria Oil, New York	35
Antonio Sanchez family	22	Sanchez/O'Brien Oil, Laredo, TX	35
Lucie Arnaz & Desi Arnaz Jr.	23	New York and CA	30
Belia Benavides de Munoz	24	Texas property, San Ignacio, TX	30
Francisco Collazo	25	Colsa, Huntsville, AL	30
Frank Fouce	26	Fouce Amusement Ent., Las Vegas	30
Manuel Herran	27	Sedano's markets, Hialeah, FL	30
Javier Uribe	28	1-Day Paint & Body, Torrance, CA	30
Carmelo Velez	29	CTA, Rockville, MD	30
Benjamin & Victor Acevedo	30	Cal-State Lumber Sales, San Diego	25
Alarcon family	31	Spanish Broadcasting, New York	25
Richard Carrion	32	BanPonce, San Juan, Puerto Rico	25
Gilbert Cuellar	33	El Chico, Dallas	25
Salvador Diaz-Verson	34	Diaz-Verson Cap., Columbus, GA	25
Frank Galeana	35	Van Dyke Dodge, Warren, MI	25
Diego Gutierrez family	36	El Nino Feliz, Zapata Co., TX	25
Thomas Marquez	37	Carrington Labs, Irving, TX	25
Felix Sabates	38	Top Sales, Charlotte, NC	25
Frank Sepulveda	39	Handy Andy markets, San Antonio	25
Ernesto Ancira	40	Ancira Ent., San Antonio	20
Ernest Camacho	41	Pacifica Services, Pasadena, Calif.	20
Carlos Manuel de la Cruz	42	Eagle Brands, Miami	20
Angel Echevarria	43	Angel Echavarria Co., Los Angeles	20
Nelson Fernandez family	44	Condal Distributors, New York	20
Lauro Lopez	45	El Huisache, Zapata, Texas	20

[Continued]

★ 600 ★

Who's Who Among Successful Hispanic Americans

[Continued]

Name	Rank	Company and location	Net worth 1993 ($ mil.)
Jorge Mas Canosa	46	Mas Group, Miami	20
Emilio Nicolas	47	Nicolas Comm., San Antonio	20
Frank Parra family	48	Frank Parra Autoplex, Irving Texas	20
Ed Romero	49	Advanced Sciences, Albuquerque	20
Ruiz family	50	Ruiz Food Products, Dinuva, Calif.	20

Source: "Who's who among Hispanic Americans." *USA TODAY* (24 February 1993), p. 6B. Primary source: *Hispanic Business.*

Income Taxes

★ 601 ★

Aggregate Household Income: Total Income, After Taxes Income, and Taxes Paid, 1982-1990

Figures are all in current 1990 dollars.

Year/ethnicity	Total		After taxes		Taxes paid	
	Value ($ bil.)	Standard error ($ bil.)	Value ($ bil.)	Standard error ($ bil.)	Value ($ bil.)	Standard error ($ bil.)
Hispanic origin						
1982	103.6	2.5	84.6	1.9	19.0	0.6
1983	110.0	2.5	91.3	2.0	18.7	0.6
1984	129.8	3.0	106.6	2.3	23.2	0.7
1985	138.2	2.9	113.5	2.2	24.7	0.7
1986	148.8	3.1	122.5	3.2	26.2	0.7
1987	159.7	3.5	132.2	3.6	27.5	0.9
1988	168.2	3.9	139.0	4.0	29.2	1.0
1989	174.0	3.4	144.4	3.5	29.6	0.7
1990	173.1	3.4	144.1	3.4	29.0	0.6
Non-Hispanic origin						
1982	2,659.3	13.1	2,064.2	9.4	595.1	3.7
1983	2,736.9	13.3	2,150.4	9.7	586.5	3.6
1984	2,868.6	15.0	2,247.6	11.0	621.0	4.0
1985	2,984.9	16.1	2,319.8	11.6	665.1	4.5
1986	3,119.2	17.1	2,451.8	17.8	667.4	4.8
1987	3,225.0	17.7	2,557.3	18.3	667.7	4.7
1988	3,309.6	19.7	2,624.3	20.3	685.2	4.9
1989	3,407.2	18.5	2,677.0	19.2	730.2	5.0
1990	3,342.7	18.3	2,640.9	18.7	701.8	4.2

[Continued]

★ 601 ★

Aggregate Household Income: Total Income, After Taxes Income, and Taxes Paid, 1982-1990

[Continued]

Year/ethnicity	Total		After taxes		Taxes paid	
	Value ($ bil.)	Standard error ($ bil.)	Value ($ bil.)	Standard error ($ bil.)	Value ($ bil.)	Standard error ($ bil.)
Total population						
1982	2,762.9	12.9	2,148.8	9.2	614.1	3.7
1983	2,846.8	13.1	2,241.6	9.5	605.2	3.6
1984	2,998.4	14.7	2,354.3	10.8	644.1	3.9
1985	3,123.1	15.8	2,433.3	11.4	689.8	4.4
1986	3,267.9	16.8	2,574.3	17.5	693.6	4.8
1987	3,384.7	17.3	2,689.5	17.9	695.2	4.6
1988	3,477.8	19.3	2,763.3	19.9	714.4	4.8
1989	3,581.2	18.2	2,821.4	18.8	759.8	5.0
1990	3,515.8	17.9	2,785.0	18.4	730.8	4.1

Source: U.S. Bureau of the Census, *The Hispanic Population in the United States: March 1991.* Current Population Reports, Series P-20, No. 455, Washington, DC: U.S. Government Printing Office, 1991, p. 6.

Poverty

★ 602 ★

Child Poverty Rates, 1989

The highest poverty rates, for selected racial/ethnic groups, are shown.

Race/ethnicity	City	Percent of children living in poverty
Hispanics	Erie, PA	69.0
Native Americans	Minneapolis, MN	66.0
Blacks	Erie, PA	62.0
Asians	St. Paul, MN	69.0

Source: Leavitt, Paul. "Child poverty rates on the rise." *USA TODAY* (12 August 1992), p. 3A. Children's Defense Fund.

★ 603 ★

Poverty

Distribution of the Poor by Race and Hispanic Origin: 1966 to 1992

Numbers are shown in thousands, by race/ethnicity.

Year	Total poor		White		Black		Hispanic origin[1]		White, not Hispanic	
	Number	Percent	Number	Percent	Number	Percent	Number	Percent	Number	Percent
1966	28,510	100.0	19,290	67.7	8,867	31.1	(NA)	(NA)	(NA)	(NA)
1967	27,769	100.0	18,983	68.4	8,486	30.6	(NA)	(NA)	(NA)	(NA)
1968	25,389	100.0	17,395	68.5	7,616	30.0	(NA)	(NA)	(NA)	(NA)
1969	24,147	100.0	16,659	69.0	7,095	29.4	(NA)	(NA)	(NA)	(NA)
1970	25,420	100.0	17,484	68.8	7,548	29.7	(NA)	(NA)	(NA)	(NA)
1971	25,559	100.0	17,780	69.6	7,396	28.9	(NA)	(NA)	(NA)	(NA)
1972	24,460	100.0	16,203	66.2	7,710	31.5	(NA)	(NA)	(NA)	(NA)
1973	22,973	100.0	15,142	65.9	7,388	32.2	2,366	10.3	(NA)	(NA)
1974	23,370	100.0	15,736	67.3	7,182	30.7	2,575	11.0	(NA)	(NA)
1975	25,877	100.0	17,770	68.7	7,545	29.2	2,991	11.6	(NA)	(NA)
1976	24,975	100.0	16,713	66.9	7,595	30.4	2,783	11.1	(NA)	(NA)
1977	24,720	100.0	16,416	66.4	7,726	31.3	2,700	10.9	(NA)	(NA)
1978	24,497	100.0	16,259	66.4	7,625	31.1	2,607	10.6	(NA)	(NA)
1979	26,072	100.0	17,214	66.0	8,050	30.9	2,921	11.2	14,419	55.3
1980	29,272	100.0	19,699	67.3	8,579	29.3	3,491	11.9	16,365	55.9
1981	31,822	100.0	21,553	67.7	9,173	28.8	3,713	11.7	17,987	56.5
1982	34,398	100.0	23,517	68.4	9,697	28.2	4,301	12.5	19,362	56.3
1983	35,303	100.0	23,984	67.9	9,882	28.0	4,633	13.1	19,538	55.3
1984	33,700	100.0	22,955	68.1	9,490	28.2	4,806	14.3	18,300	54.3
1985	33,064	100.0	22,860	69.1	8,926	27.0	5,236	15.8	17,839	54.0
1986	32,370	100.0	22,183	68.5	8,983	27.8	5,117	15.8	17,244	53.3
1987	32,221	100.0	21,195	65.8	9,520	29.5	5,422	16.8	16,029	49.7
1988	31,745	100.0	20,715	65.3	9,356	29.5	5,357	16.9	15,565	49.0
1989	31,528	100.0	20,785	65.9	9,302	29.5	5,430	17.2	15,599	49.5
1990	33,585	100.0	22,326	66.5	9,837	29.3	6,006	17.9	16,622	49.5
1991	35,708	100.0	23,747	66.5	10,242	28.7	6,339	17.8	17,741	49.7
1992	36,880	100.0	24,523	66.5	10,613	28.8	6,655	18.0	18,613	50.5

Source: U.S. Bureau of the Census. *Poverty in the United States: 1992.* Current Population Reports, Series P60-185, U.S. Government Printing Office, Washington, D.C., 1993, p. D-5. *Notes:* NA stands for not available. 1. Persons of Hispanic origin may be of any race.

★ 604 ★

Poverty

Families Living in Poverty, by Type of Family and Presence of Related Children, 1972-92

Numbers are shown in thousands of families, as of March of the following year.

Year and characteristic	All families			Married-couple families			Male householder, no spouse present			Female householder, no spouse present		
	Total	Below poverty		Total	Below poverty		Total	Below poverty		Total	Below poverty	
		Number	Percent		Number	Percent		Number	Percent		Number	Percent
ALL RACES												
With & without children under 18 years												
1992	68,144	7,960	11.7	53,171	3,318	6.2	3,026	471	15.6	11,947	4,171	34.9
1991	67,173	7,712	11.5	52,457	3,158	6.0	3,024	393	13.0	11,692	4,161	35.6

[Continued]

★ 604 ★

Families Living in Poverty, by Type of Family and Presence of Related Children, 1972-92

[Continued]

Year and characteristic	All families			Married-couple families			Male householder, no spouse present			Female householder, no spouse present		
	Total	Below poverty		Total	Below poverty		Total	Below poverty		Total	Below poverty	
		Number	Percent		Number	Percent		Number	Percent		Number	Percent
1990	66,322	7,098	10.7	52,147	2,981	5.7	2,907	349	12.0	11,268	3,768	33.4
1989	66,090	6,784	10.3	52,317	2,931	5.6	2,884	348	12.1	10,890	3,504	32.2
1988	65,837	6,874	10.4	52,100	2,897	5.6	2,847	336	11.8	10,890	3,642	33.4
1987	65,204	7,005	10.7	51,675	3,011	5.8	2,833	340	12.0	10,696	3,654	34.2
1986	64,491	7,023	10.9	851,537	3,123	6.1	2,510	287	11.4	10,445	3,613	34.6
1985	63,558	7,223	11.4	50,933	3,438	6.7	2,414	311	12.9	10,211	3,474	34.0
1984	62,706	7,277	11.6	50,350	3,488	6.9	2,228	292	13.1	10,129	3,498	34.5
1983	62,015	7,647	12.3	50,081	3,815	7.6	2,038	268	13.2	9,896	3,564	36.0
1982	61,393	7,512	12.2	49,908	3,789	7.6	2,016	290	14.4	9,469	3,434	36.3
1981	61,019	6,851	11.2	49,630	3,394	6.8	1,986	205	10.3	9,403	3,252	34.6
1980	60,309	6,217	10.3	49,294	3,032	6.2	1,933	213	11.0	9,082	2,972	32.7
1979	59,550	5,461	9.2	49,112	2,640	5.4	1,733	176	10.2	8,705	2,645	30.4
1978	57,804	5,280	9.1	47,692	2,474	5.2	1,654	152	9.2	8,458	2,654	31.4
1977	57,215	5,311	9.3	47,385	2,524	5.3	1,594	177	11.1	8,236	2,610	31.7
1976	56,710	5,311	9.4	47,497	2,606	5.5	1,500	162	10.8	7,713	2,543	33.0
1975	56,245	5,450	9.7	47,318	2,904	6.1	1,445	116	8.0	7,482	2,430	32.5
1974	55,698	4,922	8.8	47,069	2,474	5.3	1,399	125	8.9	7,230	2,324	32.1
1973	55,053	4,828	8.8	46,812	2,482	5.3	1,438	154	10.7	6,804	2,193	32.2
1972	54,373	5,075	9.3	46,314	(NA)	(NA)	1,452	(NA)	(NA)	6,607	2,158	32.7
With children under 18 years												
1992	35,492	6,269	17.7	25,714	2,166	8.4	1,548	342	22.1	8,230	3,761	45.7
1991	34,861	6,170	17.7	25,357	2,106	8.3	1,513	297	19.6	7,991	3,767	47.1
1990	34,503	5,676	16.4	25,410	1,990	7.8	1,386	260	18.8	7,707	3,426	44.5
1989	34,279	5,308	15.5	25,476	1,872	7.3	1,358	246	18.1	7,445	3,190	42.8
1988	34,251	5,373	15.7	25,598	1,847	7.2	1,292	232	18.0	7,361	3,294	44.7
1987	33,996	5,465	16.1	25,464	1,963	7.7	1,316	221	16.8	7,216	3,281	45.5
1986	33,801	5,516	16.3	25,571	2,050	8.0	1,136	202	17.8	7,094	3,264	46.0
1985	33,536	5,586	16.7	25,496	2,258	8.9	1,147	197	17.1	6,892	3,131	45.4
1984	32,942	5,662	17.2	25,038	2,344	9.4	1,072	194	18.1	6,832	3,124	45.7
1983	32,787	5,871	17.9	25,216	2,557	10.1	949	192	20.2	6,622	3,122	47.1
1982	32,565	5,712	17.5	25,276	2,470	9.8	892	184	20.6	6,397	3,059	47.8
1981	32,587	5,191	15.9	25,278	2,199	8.7	822	115	14.0	6,488	2,877	44.3
1980	32,773	4,822	14.7	25,671	1,974	7.7	802	144	18.0	6,299	2,703	42.9
1979	32,397	4,081	12.6	25,615	1,573	6.1	747	116	15.5	6,035	2,392	39.6
1978	31,735	4,060	12.8	25,199	1,495	5.9	699	103	14.7	5,837	2,462	42.2
1977	31,637	4,081	12.9	25,284	1,602	6.3	644	95	14.8	5,709	2,384	41.8
1976	31,434	4,060	12.9	25,515	1,623	6.4	609	94	15.4	5,310	2,343	44.1
1975	31,377	4,172	13.3	25,704	1,855	7.2	554	65	11.7	5,119	2,252	44.0
1974	31,319	3,789	12.1	25,857	1,558	6.0	545	84	15.4	4,917	2,147	43.7
1973	30,977	3,520	11.4	25,983	(NA)	(NA)	397	(NA)	(NA)	4,597	1,987	43.2
1972	30,807	3,621	11.8	26,085	(NA)	(NA)	401	(NA)	(NA)	4,321	1,925	44.5
WHITE												
With & without children under 18 years												
1992	57,858	5,160	8.9	47,601	2,631	5.5	2,409	326	13.6	7,848	2,202	28.1
1991	57,224	5,022	8.8	47,124	2,573	5.5	2,374	257	10.8	7,726	2,192	28.4
1990	56,803	4,622	8.1	47,014	2,386	5.1	2,277	226	9.9	7,512	2,010	26.8
1989	56,590	4,409	7.8	46,981	2,329	5.0	2,303	223	9.7	7,306	1,858	25.4
1988	56,492	4,471	7.9	46,877	2,294	4.9	2,274	231	10.2	7,342	1,945	26.5
1987	56,086	4,567	8.1	46,510	2,382	5.1	2,279	224	9.8	7,297	1,961	26.9
1986	55,676	4,811	8.6	46,410	2,591	5.6	2,038	179	8.8	7,227	2,041	28.2
1985	54,991	4,983	9.1	45,924	2,815	6.1	1,956	218	11.2	7,111	1,950	27.4
1984	54,400	4,925	9.1	45,643	2,858	6.3	1,816	189	10.4	6,941	1,878	27.1
1983	53,890	5,220	9.7	45,470	3,125	6.9	1,624	168	10.4	6,796	1,926	28.3
1982	53,407	5,118	9.6	45,252	3,104	6.9	1,648	201	12.2	6,507	1,813	27.9
1981	53,269	4,670	8.8	45,007	2,712	6.0	1,642	145	8.8	6,620	1,814	27.4
1980	52,710	4,195	8.0	44,860	2,437	5.4	1,584	149	9.4	6,266	1,609	25.7
1979	52,243	3,581	6.9	44,751	2,099	4.7	1,441	132	9.2	6,052	1,350	22.3
1978	50,910	3,523	6.9	43,636	2,033	4.7	1,356	99	7.3	5,918	1,319	23.5
1977	50,530	3,540	7.0	43,423	2,028	4.7	1,279	112	8.8	5,828	1,400	24.0
1976	50,083	3,560	7.1	43,397	2,071	4.8	1,219	110	9.0	5,467	1,379	25.2
1975	49,873	3,838	7.7	43,311	2,363	5.5	1,182	81	6.9	5,380	1,394	25.9
1974	49,440	3,352	6.8	43,049	1,977	4.6	1,182	86	7.3	5,208	1,289	24.8
1973	48,919	3,219	6.6	43,805	2,306	5.3	(NA)	(NA)	(NA)	4,853	1,190	24.5

[Continued]

★ 604 ★

Families Living in Poverty, by Type of Family and Presence of Related Children, 1972-92

[Continued]

Year and characteristic	All families			Married-couple families			Male householder, no spouse present			Female householder, no spouse present		
	Total	Below poverty		Total	Below poverty		Total	Below poverty		Total	Below poverty	
		Number	Percent		Number	Percent		Number	Percent		Number	Percent
1972	48,477	3,441	7.1	42,585	(NA)	(NA)	1,220	(NA)	(NA)	4,672	1,135	24.3
With children under 18 years												
1992	28,709	3,926	13.7	22,406	1,706	7.6	1,243	240	19.3	5,060	1,980	39.1
1991	28,368	3,880	13.7	22,213	1,715	7.7	1,188	196	16.5	4,967	1,969	39.6
1990	28,117	3,553	12.6	22,289	1,572	7.1	1,042	167	16.0	4,786	1,814	37.9
1989	27,977	3,290	11.8	22,271	1,457	6.5	1,079	162	15.0	4,627	1,671	36.1
1988	27,999	3,321	11.9	22,435	1,434	6.4	1,011	147	14.5	4,553	1,740	38.2
1987	27,930	3,433	12.3	22,336	1,538	6.9	1,046	153	14.6	4,548	1,742	38.3
1986	27,929	3,637	13.0	22,466	1,692	7.5	911	132	14.5	4,552	1,812	39.8
1985	27,795	3,695	13.3	22,399	1,827	8.2	926	138	14.9	4,470	1,730	38.7
1984	27,380	3,679	13.4	22,181	1,879	8.5	862	117	13.6	4,337	1,682	38.8
1983	27,303	3,859	14.1	22,361	2,060	9.2	732	123	16.8	4,210	1,676	39.8
1982	27,118	3,709	13.7	22,390	2,005	9.0	692	120	17.4	4,037	1,584	39.3
1981	27,223	3,362	12.4	22,334	1,723	7.7	652	75	11.6	4,237	1,564	36.9
1980	27,416	3,078	11.2	22,793	1,544	6.8	628	100	16.0	3,995	1,433	35.9
1979	27,329	2,619	9.2	22,878	1,216	5.3	584	82	14.1	3,866	1,211	31.3
1978	26,907	2,513	9.3	22,601	1,185	5.2	526	60	11.4	3,780	1,268	33.5
1977	26,814	2,572	9.6	22,703	1,256	5.5	486	55	11.3	3,735	1,261	33.8
1976	26,812	2,566	9.6	22,872	1,242	5.4	484	64	13.2	3,456	1,260	36.4
1975	26,975	2,776	10.3	23,134	1,456	6.3	435	48	11.0	3,406	1,272	37.3
1974	26,890	2,430	9.0	(NA)	(NA)	(NA)	(NA)	(NA)	(NA)	3,244	1,180	36.4
1973	26,694	2,177	8.2	(NA)	(NA)	(NA)	(NA)	(NA)	(NA)	2,988	1,053	35.2
1972	26,763	2,238	8.4	(NA)	(NA)	(NA)	(NA)	(NA)	(NA)	2,748	970	35.3
BLACK												
With & without children under 18 years												
1992	7,888	2,435	30.9	3,748	486	13.0	460	114	24.7	3,680	1,835	49.8
1991	7,716	2,343	30.4	3,631	399	11.0	503	110	21.9	3,582	1,834	51.2
1990	7,471	2,193	29.3	3,569	448	12.6	472	97	20.6	3,430	1,648	48.1
1989	7,470	2,077	27.8	3,750	443	11.8	446	110	24.7	3,275	1,524	46.5
1988	7,409	2,089	28.2	3,722	421	11.3	464	88	18.9	3223	1,579	49.0
1987	7,202	2,117	29.4	3,681	439	11.9	432	101	23.4	3,089	1,577	51.1
1986	7,096	1,987	28.0	3,742	403	10.8	386	96	24.9	2,967	1,488	50.1
1985	6,921	1,983	28.7	3,680	447	12.2	368	84	22.9	2,874	1,452	50.5
1984	6,778	2,094	30.9	3,469	479	13.8	344	82	23.8	2,964	1,533	51.7
1983	6,681	2,161	32.3	3,454	535	15.5	355	85	24.0	2,871	1,541	53.7
1982	6,530	2,158	33.0	3,486	543	15.6	309	79	25.6	2,734	1,535	56.2
1981	6,413	1,972	30.8	3,535	543	15.4	273	52	19.1	2,605	1,377	52.9
1980	6,317	1,826	28.9	3,392	474	14.0	291	52	17.7	2,634	1,301	49.4
1979	6,184	1,722	27.8	3,433	453	13.2	256	35	13.7	2,495	1,234	49.4
1978	5,906	1,622	27.5	3,244	366	11.3	272	48	17.6	2,390	1,208	50.6
1977	5,806	1,637	28.2	3,260	429	13.1	269	46	17.1	2,277	1,162	51.0
1976	5,804	1,617	27.9	3,406	450	13.2	247	45	18.2	2,151	1,122	52.2
1975	5,586	1,513	27.1	3,352	479	14.3	230	30	13.0	2,004	1,004	50.1
1974	5,491	1,479	26.9	3,357	435	13.0	200	35	17.4	1,934	1,010	52.2
1973	5,440	1,527	28.1	3,360	(NA)	(NA)	231	(NA)	(NA)	1,849	974	52.7
1972	5,265	1,529	29.0	3,233	(NA)	(NA)	210	(NA)	(NA)	1,822	972	53.3
With children under 18 years												
1992	5,316	2,075	39.0	2,175	335	15.4	243	81	33.3	2,898	1,659	57.2
1991	5,143	2,016	39.2	2,129	263	12.4	243	77	31.7	2,771	1,676	60.5
1990	5,069	1,887	37.2	2,104	301	14.3	267	73	27.3	2,698	1,513	56.1
1989	5,031	1,783	35.4	2,179	291	13.3	228	77	33.8	2,624	1,415	53.9
1988	5,010	1,802	36.0	2,181	272	12.5	246	78	31.7	2,583	1,452	56.2
1987	4,880	1,788	36.6	2,205	290	13.2	222	61	27.5	2,453	1,437	58.6
1986	4,806	1,699	35.4	2,236	257	11.5	185	58	31.5	2,386	1,384	58.0
1985	4,636	1,670	36.0	2,185	281	12.9	182	53	29.0	2,269	1,336	58.9
1984	4,512	1,758	39.0	2,001	331	16.6	175	62	35.5	2,335	1,364	58.4
1983	4,482	1,789	39.9	2,052	369	18.0	186	58	31.1	2,244	1,362	60.7
1982	4,470	1,819	40.7	2,093	360	17.2	178	58	32.7	2,199	1,401	63.7
1981	4,455	1,652	37.1	2,202	357	16.2	135	34	25.0	2,118	1,261	59.5
1980	4,465	1,583	35.5	2,154	333	15.5	140	34	24.0	2,171	1,217	56.0
1979	4,297	1,441	33.5	2,095	286	13.7	139	26	18.4	2,063	1,129	54.7

[Continued]

★ 604 ★

Families Living in Poverty, by Type of Family and Presence of Related Children, 1972-92

[Continued]

Year and characteristic	All families			Married-couple families			Male householder, no spouse present			Female householder, no spouse present		
	Total	Below poverty		Total	Below poverty		Total	Below poverty		Total	Below poverty	
		Number	Percent		Number	Percent		Number	Percent		Number	Percent
1978	4,159	1,431	34.4	2,056	247	12.0	157	40	25.5	1,946	1,144	58.4
1977	4,107	1,406	34.2	2,088	295	14.1	141	30	21.3	1,878	1,081	57.5
1976	4,047	1,382	34.2	2,146	311	14.5	120	28	23.3	1,781	1,043	58.6
1975	3,878	1,314	33.9	2,119	349	16.5	108	16	14.8	1,651	949	57.5
1974	3,915	1,293	33.0	2,187	317	14.5	105	27	26.2	1,623	949	58.5
1973	3,831	1,280	33.4	(NA)	(NA)	(NA)	(NA)	(NA)	(NA)	1,538	905	58.8
1972	3,650	1,303	35.7	(NA)	(NA)	(NA)	(NA)	(NA)	(NA)	1,494	912	61.0
HISPANIC ORIGIN[1]												
With & without children under 18 years												
1992	5,318	1,395	26.2	3,674	680	18.5	406	111	27.3	1,238	604	48.8
1991	5,177	1,372	26.5	3,532	674	19.1	384	71	18.5	1,261	627	49.7
1990	4,981	1,244	25.0	3,454	605	17.5	341	66	19.4	1,186	573	48.3
1989	4,840	1,133	23.4	3,395	549	16.2	329	54	16.3	1,116	530	47.5
1988	4,823	1,141	23.7	3,398	547	16.1	314	48	15.2	1,112	546	49.1
1987	4,576	1,168	25.5	3,196	556	17.4	298	47	15.8	1,082	565	52.2
1986	4,403	1,085	24.7	3,118	518	16.6	253	39	15.5	1,032	528	51.2
1985	4,206	1,074	25.5	2,962	505	17.0	264	48	18.4	980	521	53.1
1984	3,939	991	25.2	2,824	469	16.6	210	39	18.4	905	483	53.4
1983	3,788	981	25.9	2,752	437	17.7	177	40	22.6	860	454	52.8
1982	3,369	916	27.2	2,448	465	19.0	153	26	17.0	767	425	55.4
1981	3,305	792	24.0	2,414	366	15.1	142	27	19.2	750	399	53.2
1980	3,235	751	23.2	2,365	363	15.3	164	26	16.0	706	362	51.3
1979	3,029	614	20.3	2,282	298	13.1	139	16	11.8	610	300	49.2
1978	2,741	559	20.4	2,089	248	11.9	110	23	20.9	542	288	53.1
1977	2,764	591	21.4	2,104	280	13.3	99	10	10.1	561	301	53.6
1976	2,583	598	23.1	1,978	312	15.8	88	11	12.5	517	275	53.1
1975	2,499	627	25.1	1,896	335	17.7	81	13	16.0	522	279	53.6
1974	2,475	526	21.2	1,926	278	14.4	87	19	21.6	462	229	49.6
1973	2,365	468	19.8	1,876	239	12.7	78	18	23.1	411	211	51.4
1972	2,312	477	20.6	(NA)	(NA)	(NA)	(NA)	(NA)	(NA)	(NA)	(NA)	(NA)
With children under 18 years												
1992	3,655	1,184	32.4	2,497	562	22.5	213	79	37.1	945	543	57.4
1991	3,621	1,219	33.7	2,445	575	23.5	204	60	29.4	972	584	60.1
1990	3,497	1,085	31.0	2,405	501	20.8	171	48	28.1	921	536	58.2
1989	3,314	966	29.8	2,309	453	19.6	157	42	26.8	848	491	57.9
1988	3,325	988	29.7	2,339	445	19.0	125	33	26.4	861	510	59.2
1987	3,201	1,022	31.9	2,197	460	20.9	139	35	25.2	865	527	60.9
1986	3,080	949	30.8	(NA)	(NA)	(NA)	(NA)	(NA)	(NA)	822	489	59.5
1985	2,973	955	32.1	(NA)	(NA)	(NA)	(NA)	(NA)	(NA)	771	493	64.0
1984	2,789	872	31.3	(NA)	(NA)	(NA)	(NA)	(NA)	(NA)	711	447	62.8
1983	2,697	867	32.1	(NA)	(NA)	(NA)	(NA)	(NA)	(NA)	660	418	63.4
1982	2,458	802	32.6	(NA)	(NA)	(NA)	(NA)	(NA)	(NA)	613	391	63.8
1981	2,428	692	28.5	(NA)	(NA)	(NA)	(NA)	(NA)	(NA)	622	374	60.0
1980	2,409	655	27.2	(NA)	(NA)	(NA)	(NA)	(NA)	(NA)	(NA)	(NA)	(NA)
1979	2,209	544	24.6	(NA)	(NA)	(NA)	(NA)	(NA)	(NA)	502	288	57.3
1978	2,0023	483	24.1	(NA)	(NA)	(NA)	(NA)	(NA)	(NA)	(NA)	(NA)	(NA)
1977	2,057	520	25.3	(NA)	(NA)	(NA)	(NA)	(NA)	(NA)	(NA)	(NA)	(NA)
1976	1,899	517	27.2	(NA)	(NA)	(NA)	(NA)	(NA)	(NA)	(NA)	(NA)	(NA)
1975	1,891	550	29.1	(NA)	(NA)	(NA)	(NA)	(NA)	(NA)	(NA)	(NA)	(NA)
1974	1,834	462	25.2	(NA)	(NA)	(NA)	(NA)	(NA)	(NA)	(NA)	(NA)	(NA)
1973	1,726	410	23.8	(NA)	(NA)	(NA)	(NA)	(NA)	(NA)	(NA)	(NA)	(NA)
1972	1,700	416	24.5	(NA)	(NA)	(NA)	(NA)	(NA)	(NA)	(NA)	(NA)	(NA)

Source: U.S. Bureau of the Census. *Poverty in the United States: 1992.* Current Population Reports, Series P60-185, U.S. Government Printing Office, Washington, D.C., 1993, pp. 6-9. *Notes:* NA stands for not available. Prior to 1979 unrelated subfamilies were included in all families. Beginning in 1979 unrelated subfamilies are excluded from all families. 1. Persons of Hispanic origin may be of any race.

★ 605 ★

Poverty

Families and Unrelated Individuals, by Size of Income Surplus or Deficit Above or Below Poverty Level, 1992

Numbers are shown in thousands.

Characteristic	Total	Size of deficit or surplus									
		Under $500	$500 to $999	$1,000 to $1,999	$2,000 to $2,999	$3,000 to $3,999	$4,000 to $4,999	$5,000 to $5,999	$6,000 to $6,999	$7,000 to $7,999	$8,000 or more
ALL RACES											
Below poverty level (Income deficit)											
All families	7,960	400	394	819	829	729	765	609	673	552	2,190
Number of related children under 18											
None	1,690	173	152	288	254	178	152	89	103	88	213
One or more	6,269	226	242	531	575	551	613	520	570	465	1,978
One	2,043	90	106	244	221	228	265	214	204	133	339
Two or more	4,227	137	136	287	354	323	348	306	366	332	1,638
Married-couple families	3,318	238	221	441	400	297	293	225	240	169	794
Number of related children under 18											
None	1,153	126	109	207	146	109	90	62	78	63	163
One or more	2,166	112	112	235	254	188	203	162	162	107	632
One	507	45	33	69	74	40	45	48	37	24	92
Two or more	1,658	67	79	166	180	147	159	114	124	83	540
Families with female householder no spouse present	4,171	136	153	318	378	375	420	362	400	368	1,262
Number of related children under 18											
None	410	39	32	54	91	45	55	23	22	25	23
One or more	3,761	96	121	264	287	330	365	339	378	342	1,239
One	1,339	33	68	148	125	163	187	159	151	100	205
Two or more	2,422	63	53	116	162	167	178	179	227	242	1,034
All unrelated subfamilies	368	11	14	35	25	27	28	26	37	23	144
Unrelated individuals	7,991	831	781	1,717	1,176	755	617	476	544	1,094	-
Male	3,103	303	247	568	402	296	285	196	256	549	-
Female	4,888	528	533	1,150	773	459	333	280	288	545	-
Above the poverty level (Income surplus)											
All families	60,184	476	524	979	928	1,065	1,000	1,080	1,079	1,032	52,021
Number of related children under 18											
None	30,961	180	188	436	426	512	533	512	536	533	27,105
One or more	29,223	296	336	544	501	553	467	568	543	499	24,916
One	12,684	149	145	255	242	265	207	269	233	199	10,720
Two or more	16,539	147	192	288	260	288	260	300	309	300	14,196
Married-couple families	49,852	258	326	604	594	699	710	741	733	749	44,437
Number of related children under 18											
None	26,304	134	149	313	327	404	427	409	413	417	23,312
One or more	23,548	124	178	292	267	295	283	332	320	332	21,126
One	9,407	51	64	107	103	124	99	132	109	115	8,502
Two or more	14,141	73	114	184	164	171	184	199	211	217	12,623
Families with female householder no spouse present	7,776	183	166	308	280	316	249	272	270	228	5,505
Number of related children under 18											
None	3,308	33	34	106	83	88	88	74	106	88	2,608
One or more	4,469	150	132	202	197	228	161	198	163	140	2,897
One	2,553	81	61	115	117	124	92	105	92	63	1,703
Two or more	1,915	69	71	87	80	104	69	93	71	77	1,194

[Continued]

★ 605 ★

Families and Unrelated Individuals, by Size of Income Surplus or Deficit Above or Below Poverty Level, 1992

[Continued]

Characteristic	Total	Size of deficit or surplus									
		Under $500	$500 to $999	$1,000 to $1,999	$2,000 to $2,999	$3,000 to $3,999	$4,000 to $4,999	$5,000 to $5,999	$6,000 to $6,999	$7,000 to $7,999	$8,000 or more
All unrelated subfamilies	340	19	27	12	23	21	21	25	21	12	159
Unrelated individuals	28,743	741	905	1,509	1,454	1,239	1,254	1,126	1,189	1,275	18,053
Male	14,175	246	367	595	597	489	538	519	562	596	9,664
Female	14,568	494	537	914	857	749	715	607	627	678	8,390
WHITE											
Below poverty level (Income deficit)											
All families	5,160	299	298	626	565	478	493	376	440	332	1,253
Number of related children under 18											
None	1,233	141	123	223	160	113	113	59	86	61	154
One or more	3,926	158	175	403	405	365	380	318	354	270	1,099
One	1,305	56	80	179	145	145	150	141	118	71	222
Two or more	2,621	102	95	223	260	220	230	177	236	200	878
Married-couple families	2,631	192	184	370	316	232	230	172	198	134	604
Number of related children under 18											
None	925	104	89	167	110	82	75	55	67	52	125
One or more	1,706	88	95	203	206	150	156	117	131	82	478
One	386	31	29	58	56	31	28	37	27	17	71
Two or more	1,320	57	66	145	150	119	128	80	104	85	407
Families with female householder no spouse present	2,202	88	101	210	212	210	224	191	220	188	559
Number of related children under 18											
None	222	29	26	38	37	20	30	4	18	10	11
One or more	1,980	59	75	172	175	190	194	187	202	178	548
One	788	19	47	99	74	97	100	101	81	48	122
Two or more	1,192	40	28	73	101	93	94	87	121	130	426
All unrelated subfamilies	306	10	9	27	22	23	24	18	30	16	126
Unrelated individuals	6,087	681	615	1,295	877	586	454	369	397	811	-
Male	2,229	234	169	414	293	221	202	132	179	383	-
Female	3,858	447	446	881	584	365	252	237	219	428	-
Above the poverty level (Income surplus)											
All families	52,698	346	391	754	743	829	818	861	866	855	46,237
Number of related children under 18											
None	27,916	128	145	351	363	416	461	429	468	473	24,681
One or more	24,782	218	246	403	379	412	357	432	397	382	21,556
One	10,560	103	114	170	174	199	158	210	165	161	9,105
Two or more	14,223	116	131	232	205	214	199	222	232	221	12,450
Married-couple families	44,970	208	269	504	529	590	621	6245	622	645	40,357
Number of related children under 18											
None	24,270	104	121	275	285	348	382	361	369	377	21,649
One or more	20,700	105	148	229	243	242	239	264	254	269	18,707
One	8,208	42	55	76	92	105	87	103	89	96	7,463
Two or more	12,492	63	93	152	151	136	152	161	165	173	11,245
Families with female householder no spouse present	5,645	110	97	207	171	196	165	181	189	165	4,163

[Continued]

★ 605 ★

Families and Unrelated Individuals, by Size of Income Surplus or Deficit Above or Below Poverty Level, 1992

[Continued]

Characteristic	Total	Size of deficit or surplus									
		Under $500	$500 to $999	$1,000 to $1,999	$2,000 to $2,999	$3,000 to $3,999	$4,000 to $4,999	$5,000 to $5,999	$6,000 to $6,999	$7,000 to $7,999	$8,000 or more
Number of related children under 18											
None	2,565	18	20	68	66	51	65	45	86	72	2,074
One or more	3,080	92	77	139	105	146	100	136	103	93	2,089
One	1,753	44	41	74	62	81	56	82	51	48	1,214
Two or more	1,328	47	36	65	43	65	45	54	52	45	876
All unrelated subfamilies	288	17	19	12	22	16	16	18	21	6	141
Unrelated individuals	25,089	641	732	1,309	1,264	1,071	1,071	940	1,054	1,098	15,909
Male	12,061	207	277	494	488	385	436	411	463	480	8,421
Female	13,028	434	455	815	776	686	636	529	591	618	7,488
BLACK											
Below poverty level (Income deficit)											
All families	2,435	85	79	156	236	2074	249	185	214	189	838
Number of related children under 18											
None	359	285	26	46	83	54	34	26	11	21	33
One or more	2,075	60	53	109	153	150	215	159	203	167	805
One	646	31	21	57	70	64	110	61	83	55	95
Two or more	1,430	29	32	53	83	86	106	98	120	113	710
Married-couple families	486	37	25	42	71	43	49	30	31	21	137
Number of related children under 18											
None	152	17	17	22	30	19	10	4	8	7	18
One or more	335	20	8	21	41	24	40	26	23	14	120
One	97	11	2	8	17	4	16	8	10	4	17
Two or more	238	8	6	13	23	20	24	18	13	10	103
Families with female householder no spouse present	1,835	43	48	100	155	144	187	147	176	166	668
Number of related children under 18											
None	176	8	6	16	51	25	24	18	4	14	10
One or more	1,659	35	42	84	104	119	163	129	172	152	658
One	496	14	18	45	46	53	83	49	68	51	70
Two or more	1,162	21	24	40	58	66	81	80	104	102	588
All unrelated subfamilies	50	-	5	7	2	1	2	8	4	5	15
Unrelated individuals	1,584	133	150	369	247	138	128	84	130	206	-
Male	708	62	72	127	91	60	70	48	68	111	-
Female	876	70	78	241	156	78	59	36	62	96	-
Above the poverty level (Income surplus)											
All families	5,453	104	113	181	159	208	142	177	174	147	4,048
Number of related children under 18											
None	2,212	45	36	68	51	90	47	65	49	55	1,706
One or more	3,241	60	77	113	108	119	95	111	125	92	2,343
One	1,585	35	25	72	58	57	41	46	53	23	1,176
Two or more	1,656	25	52	41	50	62	54	66	72	69	1,167
Married-couple families	3,262	33	42	72	51	86	58	84	82	81	2,675
Number of related children under 18											
None	1,422	24	24	28	35	49	27	33	30	39	1,133
One or more	1,840	9	18	44	16	36	31	51	52	42	1,542

[Continued]

★ 605 ★

Families and Unrelated Individuals, by Size of Income Surplus or Deficit Above or Below Poverty Level, 1992

[Continued]

Characteristic	Total	Size of deficit or surplus									
		Under $500	$500 to $999	$1,000 to $1,999	$2,000 to $2,999	$3,000 to $3,999	$4,000 to $4,999	$5,000 to $5,999	$6,000 to $6,999	$7,000 to $7,999	$8,000 or more
One	766	3	5	26	4	10	6	21	10	6	674
Two or more	1,074	6	12	18	12	26	25	29	42	36	868
Families with female householder no spouse present	1,846	65	66	89	102	116	75	82	71	59	1,121
Number of related children under 18											
None	607	15	12	35	15	38	16	27	16	15	418
One or more	1,239	50	54	54	86	78	59	55	55	44	702
One	717	31	19	34	52	42	36	19	37	13	434
Two or more	522	19	35	20	34	36	24	36	18	31	268
All unrelated subfamilies	38	2	5	-	1	4	4	6	-	4	11
Unrelated individuals	2,847	91	147	166	145	135	132	130	103	145	1,654
Male	1,629	35	76	93	75	80	62	75	78	95	960
Female	1,217	55	71	73	69	56	70	55	25	50	694
HISPANIC ORIGIN[1]											
Below poverty level (Income deficit)											
All families	1,395	56	78	136	156	143	118	93	149	88	378
Number of related children under 18											
None	211	16	25	37	32	27	17	7	17	5	28
One or more	1,184	40	53	99	124	116	101	86	132	84	350
One	292	13	14	37	46	36	30	27	37	14	38
Two or more	892	28	38	62	79	80	71	59	94	69	312
Married-couple families	680	37	53	82	80	57	54	46	68	31	173
Number of related children under 18											
None	118	10	16	23	18	10	8	7	12	1	15
One or more	562	28	37	60	62	47	47	39	56	29	157
One	114	10	8	20	23	5	7	9	14	7	11
Two or more	448	17	29	39	39	42	40	30	42	22	146
Families with female householder no spouse present	604	17	22	44	58	71	51	43	73	57	170
Number of related children under 18											
None	62	6	7	10	10	9	4	1	5	3	6
One or more	543	11	15	33	48	62	47	42	68	54	164
One	140	3	6	12	15	23	18	17	20	7	19
Two or more	403	9	9	21	33	38	29	25	48	46	145
All unrelated subfamilies	83	3	2	9	5	10	7	5	7	1	32
Unrelated individuals	777	43	54	142	117	55	71	37	50	209	-
Male	382	23	22	73	56	17	45	12	30	104	-
Female	396	19	33	68	62	37	26	25	20	105	-
Above the poverty level (Income surplus)											
All families	3,923	56	69	136	142	91	137	141	128	112	2,910
Number of related children under 18											
None	1,452	19	22	34	39	27	52	54	43	43	1,119
One or more	2,471	36	47	102	104	64	85	87	86	69	1,791
One	993	9	26	36	44	24	36	45	37	26	710
Two or more	1,477	28	21	66	60	40	49	42	49	42	1,081
Married-couple families	2,993	34	53	88	97	54	97	91	83	77	2,321

[Continued]

★ 605 ★

Families and Unrelated Individuals, by Size of Income Surplus or Deficit Above or Below Poverty Level, 1992

[Continued]

Characteristic	Total	Size of deficit or surplus									
		Under $500	$500 to $999	$1,000 to $1,999	$2,000 to $2,999	$3,000 to $3,999	$4,000 to $4,999	$5,000 to $5,999	$6,000 to $6,999	$7,000 to $7,999	$8,000 or more
Number of related children under 18											
None	1,058	13	18	27	31	8	37	31	25	23	846
One or more	1,935	21	35	60	65	46	61	59	58	54	1,475
One	719	6	17	19	31	13	23	31	23	16	540
Two or more	1,216	15	18	41	34	33	38	29	35	38	934
Families with female householder no spouse present	633	19	13	35	33	27	29	35	33	24	385
Number of related children under 18											
None	231	4	4	4	4	14	12	16	14	12	149
One or more	403	15	9	31	29	14	18	19	20	12	236
One	198	3	7	13	8	8	8	9	9	8	126
Two or more	204	12	3	18	21	6	10	10	10	4	110
All unrelated subfamilies	45	1	3	3	3	4	-	12	1	2	16
Unrelated individuals	1,500	56	76	109	114	77	60	56	53	93	808
Male	972	25	49	62	66	51	36	42	36	67	538
Female	528	31	27	47	47	26	24	14	17	26	270

Source: U.S. Bureau of the Census. *Poverty in the United States: 1992.* Current Population Reports, Series P60-185, U.S. Government Printing Office, Washington, D.C., 1993, pp. 144-146. *Note:* 1. Persons of Hispanic origin may be of any race.

★ 606 ★

Poverty

Persons 16 to 24 Years Old Living in Poverty, by Educational Status, Age Group, Sex, and Household Relationship, 1992

Numbers are shown in thousands.

Characteristic	All races			White			Black			Hispanic origin[1]		
	Total	Below poverty level		Total	Below poverty level		Total	Below poverty level		Total	Below poverty level	
		Number	Percent of total		Number	Percent of total		Number	Percent of total		Number	Percent of total
Both sexes												
Total	30,967	5,527	17.8	25,029	3,749	15.0	4,598	1,500	32.6	3,528	1,084	30.7
16 to 17 years old	6,657	1,160	17.4	5,319	725	13.6	1,067	379	35.5	718	240	33.6
Enrolled in school	6,256	999	16.0	4,978	600	12.1	1,019	350	34.3	602	184	30.5
Not enrolled	402	160	40.0	341	125	36.7	48	29	(B)	113	57	50.0
No high school diploma	364	151	41.5	307	119	38.6	46	29	(B)	105	55	52.5
18 to 21 years old	13,193	2,504	19.0	10,635	1,699	16.0	1,975	665	33.7	1,610	508	31.5
Enrolled in school	7,064	895	12.7	5,633	558	9.9	1,026	266	25.9	617	143	23.2
Not enrolled	6,129	1,609	26.2	5,002	1,141	22.8	949	399	42.0	993	365	36.7
No high school diploma	1,769	730	41.3	1,418	541	38.2	292	160	54.6	545	224	41.2
22 to 24 years old	11,117	1,863	16.8	9,076	1,324	14.6	1,556	456	29.3	1,203	336	27.9
Enrolled in school	2,721	353	13.0	2,228	259	11.6	300	65	21.7	181	23	12.6
Not enrolled	8,396	1,510	18.0	6,848	1,066	15.6	1,255	391	31.2	1,023	313	30.7
No high school diploma	1,479	589	39.8	1,166	435	37.3	264	134	50.7	468	202	43.2
Male												
Total	15,439	2,305	14.9	12,547	1,597	12.7	2,209	591	26.8	1,781	478	26.9
16 to 17 years old	3,390	591	17.4	2,726	376	13.8	539	187	34.7	363	118	32.6
Enrolled in school	3,182	512	16.1	2,557	322	12.6	510	166	32.5	306	90	29.5
Not enrolled	208	79	37.9	169	53	31.6	30	21	(B)	58	28	(B)

[Continued]

★ 606 ★

Persons 16 to 24 Years Old Living in Poverty, by Educational Status, Age Group, Sex, and Household Relationship, 1992

[Continued]

Characteristic	All races			White			Black			Hispanic origin[1]		
	Total	Below poverty level		Total	Below poverty level		Total	Below poverty level		Total	Below poverty level	
		Number	Percent of total		Number	Percent of total		Number	Percent of total		Number	Percent of total
No high school diploma	186	73	39.2	150	50	33.5	30	21	(B)	50	27	(B)
18 to 21 years old	6,554	999	15.2	5,310	682	12.8	936	256	27.4	822	221	26.9
Enrolled in school	3,498	397	11.3	2,782	2850	9.0	495	118	23.8	308	63	20.3
Not enrolled	3,055	602	19.7	2,527	432	17.1	441	138	31.3	514	158	30.8
No high school diploma	946	298	31.5	758	216	28.4	159	68	43.0	293	95	32.5
22 to 24 years old	5,496	715	13.0	4,512	539	11.9	733	148	20.2	595	139	23.4
Enrolled in school	1,410	168	11.9	1,170	131	11.2	129	24	18.6	80	8	9.9
Not enrolled	4,085	546	13.4	3,342	408	12.2	604	124	20.5	515	131	25.5
No high school diploma	804	225	28.0	647	171	26.5	133	47	35.6	254	85	33.5
Female												
Total	15,527	3,222	20.8	12,482	2,152	17.2	2,389	909	38.1	1,748	606	34.7
16 to 17 years old	3,267	569	17.4	2,593	350	3.5	527	192	36.5	352	122	34.7
Enrolled in school	3,073	487	15.9	2,421	278	11.5	509	184	36.2	296	94	31.6
Not enrolled	194	82	42.1	172	72	41.8	18	8	(B)	56	28	(B)
No high school diploma	178	78	43.9	157	68	43.4	17	8	(B)	54	28	(B)
18 to 21 years old	6,639	1,505	22.7	5,325	1,017	19.1	1,039	408	39.3	788	287	36.4
Enrolled in school	3,566	499	14.0	2,850	308	10.8	531	148	27.9	308	81	26.2
Not enrolled	3,073	1,006	32.7	2,475	709	28.6	508	260	51.2	480	206	43.0
No high school diploma	823	433	52.6	659	326	49.4	134	91	68.4	253	129	51.2
22 to 24 years old	5,621	1,148	20.4	4,564	786	17.2	823	308	37.5	608	197	32.4
Enrolled in school	1,311	185	14.1	1,058	128	12.1	171	41	24.1	100	15	14.8
Not enrolled	4,310	964	22.4	3,506	658	18.8	652	267	41.0	508	182	35.9
No high school diploma	674	364	53.9	619	264	50.8	131	86	66.1	214	117	54.8
Related children in families												
Total	19,330	2,029	10.5	15,460	1,138	7.4	3,076	778	25.3	1,827	436	23.9
16 to 17 years old	6,439	989	15.4	5,131	577	11.2	1,045	365	34.9	668	201	30.1
Enrolled in school	6,105	878	14.4	4,851	496	10.2	1,004	339	33.8	575	163	28.3
Not enrolled	334	112	33.5	279	81	28.9	42	25	(B)	93	39	41.5
No high school diploma	306	106	34.6	256	78	30.4	40	25	(B)	85	37	43.4
18 to 21 years old	8,801	814	9.2	7,138	455	6.4	1,321	308	23.3	843	185	22.0
Enrolled in school	5,811	422	7.3	4,714	224	4.8	820	166	20.3	473	99	21.0
Not enrolled	2,991	392	13.1	2,424	231	9.5	501	141	28.2	369	86	23.3
No high school diploma	760	209	27.5	573	137	24.0	161	3	39.1	158	54	34.2
22 to 24 years old	4,090	226	5.5	3,192	106	3.3	710	106	14.9	316	49	15.6
Enrolled in school	1,499	39	2.6	1,225	18	1.5	179	18	10.2	103	11	10.2
Not enrolled	2,591	187	7.2	1,967	88	4.5	531	88	16.5	213	39	18.2
No high school diploma	405	102	25.2	261	52	19.8	133	50	37.3	52	23	(B)
Related children in married-couple families												
Total	14,127	798	5.6	12,046	578	4.8	1,474	158	10.7	1,245	202	16.2
16 to 17 years old	4,609	384	8.3	3,948	297	7.5	463	67	14.5	433	91	21.1
Enrolled in school	4,425	346	7.8	3,777	261	6.9	456	65	14.2	390	74	18.9
Not enrolled	183	38	20.8	171	36	21.1	8	2	(B)	44	18	(B)
No high school diploma	163	35	21.5	151	33	21.7	6	2	(B)	37	16	(B)
18 to 21 years old	6,475	318	4.9	5,563	231	4.2	649	53	8.2	589	92	15.7
Enrolled in school	4,463	179	4.0	3,840	128	3.3	399	31	7.7	350	55	15.7
Not enrolled	2,012	140	6.9	1,723	103	6.0	250	23	9.1	239	38	15.8
No high school diploma	418	73	17.6	340	57	16.7	63	12	(B)	94	25	26.3
22 to 24 years old	3,044	96	3.1	2,535	49	1.9	361	37	10.2	223	18	8.0
Enrolled in school	1,222	16	1.3	1,035	7	.7	112	6	5.2	77	2	2.6
Not enrolled	1,822	80	4.4	1,501	42	2.8	250	31	12.5	146	16	10.9
No high school diploma	227	47	20.8	157	29	18.7	62	18	(B)	30	11	(B)
Related children in families with female householder, no spouse present												
Total	4,364	1,138	26.1	2,728	494	18.1	1,486	601	40.5	500	210	42.0
16 to 17 years old	1,572	566	36.0	976	256	26.2	540	286	52.9	205	101	49.3

[Continued]

★ 606 ★

Persons 16 to 24 Years Old Living in Poverty, by Educational Status, Age Group, Sex, and Household Relationship, 1992

[Continued]

Characteristic	All races			White			Black			Hispanic origin[1]		
	Total	Below poverty level		Total	Below poverty level		Total	Below poverty level		Total	Below poverty level	
		Number	Percent of total		Number	Percent of total		Number	Percent of total		Number	Percent of total
Enrolled in school	1,444	497	34.4	887	214	24.1	508	264	52.0	166	81	49.0
Not enrolled	128	69	54.2	89	43	47.9	33	22	(B)	39	20	(B)
No high school diploma	123	66)	53.9	87	43	48.9	33	22	(B)	38	20	(B)
18 to 21 years old	1,931	459	23.8	1,250	197	15.8	619	248	40.1	217	86	39.5
Enrolled in school	1,143	226	19.8	712	83	11.7	391	136	24.7	109	42	38.5
Not enrolled	788	232	29.5	539	114	21.2	228	113	49.5	108	44	40.6
No high school diploma	277	128	46.4	172	74	43.0	96	51	53.2	51	28	(B)
22 to 24 years old	862	114	13.2	501	41	8.2	327	67	20.6	78	23	29.7
Enrolled in school	224	20	8.9	142	7	5.1	66	12	(B)	22	7	(B)
Not enrolled	638	94	14.7	359	34	9.5	261	55	21.1	56	16	(B)
No high school diploma	148	53	35.8	76	20	26.6	69	32	(B)	19	10	(B)
Husbands in married-couple family												
Total	1,394	261	18.7	1,259	220	17.5	98	31	31.5	211	80	37.7
16 to 17 years old	-	-	(B)	-	-	(B)	-	-	(B)	-	-	(B)
Enrolled in school	-	-	(B)	-	-	(B)	-	-	(B)	-	-	(B)
Not enrolled	-	-	(B)	-	-	(B)	-	-	(B)	-	-	(B)
No high school diploma	-	-	(B)	-	-	(B)	-	-	(B)	-	-	(B)
18 to 21 years old	338	105	31.0	297	85	28.6	26	10	(B)	67	35	(B)
Enrolled in school	24	3	(B)	21	1	(B)	2	-	(B)	4	1	(B)
Not enrolled	314	102	32.5	276	84	30.3	24	10	(B)	63	34	(B)
No high school diploma	103	54	52.4	90	46	50.9	7	2	(B)	43	24	(B)
22 to 24 years old	1,055	157	14.8	962	135	14.0	73	21	(B)	144	45	31.0
Enrolled in school	130	20	15.2	118	17	14.2	9	3	(B)	9	1	(B)
Not enrolled	926	137	14.8	844	118	14.0	64	18	(B)	135	44	32.5
No high school diploma	183	50	27.4	175	44	25.0	6	6	(B)	68	31	(B)
Wives in married-couple family												
Total	2,617	435	16.6	2,351	372	15.8	176	50	28.7	371	117	31.5
16 to 17 years old	32	17	(B)	30	14	(B)	2	2	(B)	8	4	(B)
Enrolled in school	6	-	(B)	6	-	(B)	-	-	9B)	3	-	(B)
Not enrolled	26	16	(B)	24	14	(B)	2	2	(B)	5	4	(B)
No high school diploma	18	13	(B)	15	10	(B)	2	2	(B)	5	4	(B)
18 to 21 years old	834	190	22.8	739	162	21.9	70	22	(B)	140	52	37.4
Enrolled in school	116	21	17.8	108	17	15.7	6	2	(B)	11	3	(B)
Not enrolled	718	169	23.6	631	145	23.0	63	20	(B)	129	49	37.8
No high school diploma	201	78	39.0	175	72	40.9	18	5	(B)	79	32	40.6
22 to 24 years old	1,750	228	13.1	1,582	196	12.4	104	26	24.8	223	60	26.9
Enrolled in school	197	27	13.8	172	17	9.8	17	10	(B)	16	-	(B)
Not enrolled	1,553	201	13.0	1,410	179	12.7	86	16	18.5	207	60	28.9
No high school diploma	250	100	40.0	224	94	42.1	17	5	(B)	101	48	47.3
Women with children, spouse present												
Total	1,492	358	24.0	1,307	303	23.1	139	46	32.7	246	89	36.1
16 to 17 years old	14	6	(B)	12	4	(B)	2	2	(B)	3	2	(B)
Enrolled in school	1	-	(B)	1	-	(B)	-	-	9B)	-	-	(B)
Not enrolled	13	6	(B)	11	4	(B)	2	2	(B)	3	2	(B)
No high school diploma	10	6	(B)	7	4	(B)	2	2	(B)	3	2	(B)
18 to 21 years old	484	154	31.7	419	127	30.4	54	22	(B)	86	36	41.7
Enrolled in school	52	15	(B)	49	13	(B)	3	2	(B)	11	3	(B)
Not enrolled	432	138	32.0	370	114	30.8	51	20	(B)	75	32	43.1
No high school diploma	143	62	43.4	128	55	43.3	9	5	(B)	40	19	(B)
22 to 24 years old	994	199	20.0	877	171	19.5	83	21	25.2	157	51	32.3
Enrolled in school	80	21	26.3	66	13	(B)	13	7	(B)	4	-	(B)
Not enrolled	914	178	19.4	811	158	19.5	70	14	(B)	153	51	33.2
No high school diploma	208	91	43.6	186	88	47.1	14	2	(B)	80	41	51.0

[Continued]

★ 606 ★

Persons 16 to 24 Years Old Living in Poverty, by Educational Status, Age Group, Sex, and Household Relationship, 1992

[Continued]

Characteristic	All races			White			Black			Hispanic origin[1]		
	Total	Below poverty level		Total	Below poverty level		Total	Below poverty level		Total	Below poverty level	
		Number	Percent of total		Number	Percent of total		Number	Percent of total		Number	Percent of total
Women with children, no spouse present												
Total	900	700	77.8	514	387	75.2	356	290	81.6	132	100	75.7
16 to 17 years old	5	4	(B)	4	3	(B)	1	1	(B)	3	2	(B)
Enrolled in school	-	-	(B)	-	-	(B)	-	-	(B)	-	-	(B)
Not enrolled	5	4	(B)	4	3	(B)	1	1	(B)	3	2	(B)
No high school diploma	4	4	9B)	2	2	(B)	1	1	(B)	2	2	(B)
18 to 21 years old	359	301	83.6	205	163	79.7	143	129	90.3	56	44	(B)
Enrolled in school	72	52	(B)	43	27	(B)	26	25	(B)	8	1	(B)
Not enrolled	288	249	86.6	161	136	84.4	117	104	89.1	48	43	(B)
No high school diploma	121	110	91.2	77	68	88.3	43	42	(B)	38	35	(B)
22 to 24 years old	535	395	73.8	306	221	72.2	212	161	75.6	73	54	(B)
Enrolled in school	55	40	(B)	39	26	(B)	15	13	(B)	5	3	(B)
Not enrolled	480	355	74.0	266	194	73.0	197	147	74.9	67	51	(B)
No high school diploma	158	140	88.7	92	78	85.3	54	50	(B)	32	25	(B)
Employed persons												
Total	16,826	1,908	11.3	14,637	1,561	10.7	1,599	268	16.7	1,707	360	21.1
16 to 17 years old	1,776	164	9.2	1,610	137	8.5	117	21	18.1	120	33	27.4
Enrolled in school	1,651	125	7.6	1,496	104	7.0	113	19	17.3	79	15	19.2
Not enrolled	125	39	31.0	114	33	29.0	4	2	(B)	41	18	(B)
No high school diploma	106	36	33.8	100	33	33.2	3	2	(B)	35	18	(B)
18 to 21 years old	7,188	902	12.6	6,294	750	11.9	629	106	16.9	798	173	21.6
Enrolled in school	3,296	267	8.1	2,868	218	7.6	267	29	10.8	246	33	13.3
Not enrolled	3,892	635	16.3	3,425	532	15.5	362	77	21.3	552	140	25.4
No high school diploma	787	208	26.5	685	181	26.4	73	17	(B)	274	78	28.5
22 to 24 years old	7,863	843	10.7	6,734	673	10.0	853	141	16.5	789	154	19.5
Enrolled in school	1,606	140	8.7	1,366	108	7.9	156	26	16.7	1074	5	4.9
Not enrolled	6,257	702	11.2	5,368	565	10.5	696	115	16.4	686	149	21.7
No high school diploma	780	195	25.0	669	165	24.6	83	22	26.0	284	88	30.9
Unemployed persons												
Total	2,484	718	28.9	1,737	447	25.8	665	256	38.5	350	132	37.7
16 to 17 years old	576	119	20.7	464	83	18.0	95	32	33.7	80	29	36.6
Enrolled in school	495	92	18.6	393	62	15.7	88	27	30.7	56	18	(B)
Not enrolled	81	27	33.2	71	22	(B)	7	5	(B)	24	11	(B)
No high school diploma	76	25	33.2	66	20	(B)	7	5	(B)	21	10	(B)
18 to 21 years old	1,143	355	31.0	749	205	27.4	363	144	39.7	184	67	36.4
Enrolled in school	321	70	21.7	219	35	16.2	84	34	39.8	46	14	(B)
Not enrolled	822	285	34.7	530	170	32.1	279	111	39.7	138	53	38.9
No high school diploma	336	142	42.2	228	93	40.9	104	48	46.5	65	21	(B)
22 to 24 years old	765	244	31.9	524	159	30.3	207	80	38.5	86	36	41.4
Enrolled in school	127	36	28.2	104	27	25.8	12	9	(B)	9	3	(B)
Not enrolled	639	208	32.6	420	132	31.4	195	71	36.4	77	32	41.9
No high school diploma	180	77	43.0	127	56	43.8	52	21	(B)	42	23	(B)
Persons not in labor force												
Total	11,657	2,901	24.9	8,655	1,740	20.1	2,334	977	41.8	1,471	593	40.3
16 to 17 years old	4,306	877	20.4	3,245	505	15.6	855	326	38.1	516	178	34.6
Enrolled in school	4,110	782	19.0	3,089	434	14.1	819	303	37.1	468	151	32.2
Not enrolled	196	95	48.4	156	70	45.2	36	23	(B)	48	27	(B)
No high school diploma	182	90	49.6	142	66	46.4	36	23	(B)	48	27	(B)
18 to 21 years old	4,862	1,247	25.7	3,592	743	20.7	983	415	42.1	628	268	42.7
Enrolled in school	3,448	559	16.2	2,545	305	12.0	675	204	30.2	324	97	30.0
Not enrolled	1,414	688	48.7	1,047	439	41.9	308	211	68.3	303	171	56.4
No high school diploma	646	380	58.8	504	267	52.9	115	94.	81.8	206	125	60.8
22 to 24 years old	2,489	777	31.2	1,818	492	27.1	496	236	47.6	328	147	44.7
Enrolled in school	989	177	17.9	758	123	16.3	132	30	23.1	68	14	(B)

[Continued]

★ 606 ★

Persons 16 to 24 Years Old Living in Poverty, by Educational Status, Age Group, Sex, and Household Relationship, 1992

[Continued]

Characteristic	All races			White			Black			Hispanic origin[1]		
	Total	Below poverty level		Total	Below poverty level		Total	Below poverty level		Total	Below poverty level	
		Number	Percent of total		Number	Percent of total		Number	Percent of total		Number	Percent of total
Not enrolled	1,500	600	40.0	1,060	369	34.8	364	206	56.5	260	132	50.9
No high school diploma	519	316	61.0	370	215	58.0	129	91	70.8	141	91	64.5

Source: U.S. Bureau of the Census. *Poverty in the United States: 1992.* Current Population Reports, Series P60-185, U.S. Government Printing Office, Washington, D.C., 1993, pp. 74-76. *Notes:* A (B) indicates that the base was less than 75,000 or not applicable. 1. Persons of Hispanic origin may be of any race.

★ 607 ★

Poverty

Persons 25 Years Old and Older Living in Poverty, by Educational Status, Age Group, Sex, and Household Relationship, 1992

Numbers are shown in thousands.

Characteristic	All races			White			Black			Hispanic origin[1]		
	Total	Below poverty level		Total	Below poverty level		Total	Below poverty level		Total	Below poverty level	
		Number	Percent of total		Number	Percent of total		Number	Percent of total		Number	Percent of total
ALL EDUCATION LEVELS												
Both sexes												
Total	162,826	17,896	11.0	139,019	12,544	9.0	17,786	4,554	25.6	12,100	2,695	22.3
25 to 34 years	41,864	5,540	13.2	34,666	3,749	10.8	5,399	1,521	28.2	4,277	1,076	25.2
35 to 54 years	68,845	6,189	9.0	58,481	4,232	7.2	7,539	1,621	21.5	5,367	1,067	19.9
55 to 64 years	21,247	2,186	10.3	18,372	1,571	8.5	2,188	525	24.0	1,234	282	22.9
65 years and over	30,870	3,983	12.9	27,501	2,992	10.9	2,660	887	33.3	1,222	269	22.0
65 to 74 years	18,362	1,956	10.7	16,210	1,397	8.6	1,703	504	29.6	806	157	19.5
75 years and over	12,508	2,027	16.2	11,290	1,595	14.1	957	383	40.0	416	112	26.8
Male												
Total	77,644	6,643	8.6	66,797	4,763	7.1	7,953	1,515	19.1	6,003	1,156	19.3
25 to 34 years	20,856	2,050	9.8	17,408	1,477	8.5	2,487	441	17.7	2,237	467	20.9
35 to 54 years	33,751	2,611	7.7	29,057	1,860	6.4	3,399	608	17.9	2,717	498	18.3
55 to 64 years	10,205	840	8.2	8,888	616	6.9	987	176	17.8	541	103	19.0
65 years and over	12,832	1,142	8.9	11,443	809	7.1	1,081	290	26.9	508	88	17.4
65 to 74 years	8,114	657	8.1	7,187	465	6.5	742	173	23.3	345	57	16.7
75 years and over	4,718	485	10.3	4,256	344	8.1	338	118	34.8	163	31	18.8
Female												
Total	85,181	11,254	13.2	72,222	7,781	10.8	9,833	3,038	30.9	6,097	1,539	25.2
25 to 34 years	21,008	3,490	16.6	17,257	2,272	13.2	2,912	1,081	37.1	2,040	609	29.9
35 to 54 years	385,094	3,578	10.2	29,424	2,371	8.1	4,141	1,013	24.5	2,650	569	21.5
55 to 64 years	11,042	1,345	12.2	9,484	955	10.1	1,201	349	29.1	693	180	25.9
65 years and over	18,038	2,840	15.7	16,057	2,183	13.6	1,579	596	37.7	715	181	25.3
65 to 74 years	10,249	1,299	12.7	9,023	932	10.3	960	331	34.5	462	100	21.6
75 years and over	7,790	1,542	19.8	7,034	1,252	17.8	619	265	42.8	253	81	32.0
Household relationship												
In families	130,076	11,243	8.6	111,256	7,560	6.8	13,688	3,115	22.8	10,141	2,075	20.5
Householder	65,393	6,909	10.6	55,722	4,495	8.1	7,376	2,090	28.3	4,893	1,201	24.6
In families with related children under 18 years	62,193	7,822	12.6	51,237	5,111	10.0	7,981	2,338	29.3	6,558	1,664	25.4
Householder	33,622	5,288	15.7	27,369	3,317	12.1	4,853	1,740	35.9	3,341	1,010	30.2
In married couple families	108,854	6,365	5.8	96,663	4,984	5.2	7,958	983	12.4	7,774	1,294	16.6
Householder	51,707	3,054	5.9	46,288	2,414	5.2	3,634	448	12.3	3,468	608	17.5
Husband	51,797	3,069	5.9	46,320	2,411	5.2	3,678	465	12.6	3,489	619	17.8
Wife	50,589	2,894	5.7	45,182	2,284	5.1	3,464	426	12.3	3,456	565	16.3
In married couple families with related children under 18 years	51,447	4,025	7.8	44,427	3,131	7.0	4,431	647	14.6	5,204	1,075	20.6
Householder	24,910	1,952	7.8	21,714	1,534	7.1	2,087	301	14.4	2,357	506	21.4
Husband	24,959	1,964	7.9	21,726	1,533	7.1	2,113	312	14.8	2,368	516	21.8
Wife	24,221	1,807	7.5	21,111	1,415	6.7	1,949	278	14.3	2,339	464	19.9

[Continued]

★ 607 ★

Persons 25 Years Old and Older Living in Poverty, by Educational Status, Age Group, Sex, and Household Relationship, 1992

[Continued]

Characteristic	All races			White			Black			Hispanic origin[1]		
	Total	Below poverty level		Total	Below poverty level		Total	Below poverty level		Total	Below poverty level	
		Number	Percent of total		Number	Percent of total		Number	Percent of total		Number	Percent of total
In families with female householder, no spouse present	16,420	4,226	25.7	10,973	2,168	19.8	4,851	1,937	39.9	1,698	626	36.9
Householder	10,943	3,456	31.6	7,248	1,804	24.9	3,317	1,544	46.6	1,090	501	46.0
In families with female householder, no spouse present, with related children under 18 years	8,935	3,437	38.5	5,429	1,748	32.2	3,206	1,585	49.4	1,086	513	47.2
Householder	7,323	3,054	41.7	4,539	1,586	34.9	2,542	1,369	53.8	811	440	54.3
In unrelated subfamilies	614	276	44.9	514	231	45.0	73	35	(B)	103	58	56.1
Unrelated individuals	32,136	6,378	19.8	27,249	4,753	17.4	4,025	1,404	34.9	1,856	562	30.3
Male	14,892	2,367	15.9	12,266	1,631	13.3	2,134	620	29.0	1,116	275	24.7
Householder	10,970	1,489	13.6	9,246	1,058	11.4	1,397	366	26.2	596	121	20.3
Female	17,244	4,011	23.3	14,982	3,122	20.8	1,891	784	41.5	740	286	38.7
Householder	15,006	3,359	22.4	13,037	2,576	19.8	1,699	709	41.7	563	196	34.9
NO HIGH SCHOOL DIPLOMA												
Both sexes												
Total	32,195	8,228	25.6	25,668	5,635	22.0	5,261	2,249	42.7	5,677	1,836	32.4
25 to 34 years	5,497	1,998	36.3	4,334	1,365	31.5	908	548	60.3	1,694	659	38.9
35 to 54 years	8,965	2,454	27.4	6,904	1,644	23.8	1,627	665	40.9	2,342	716	30.6
55 to 64 years	5,464	1,184	21.7	4,329	809	18.7	945	332	35.1	742	230	31.0
65 years and over	12,268	2,592	21.1	10,102	1,817	18.0	1,781	704	39.5	898	231	25.7
65 to 74 years	6,272	1,154	18.4	4,998	741	14.8	1,046	372	35.6	553	129	23.4
75 years and over	5,995	1,438	24.0	5,104	1,076	21.1	736	332	45.1	345	102	29.5
Male												
Total	15,122	3,022	20.0	12,152	2,108	17.3	2,418	763	31.5	2,825	788	27.9
25 to 34 years	2,903	775	26.7	2,379	581	24.4	385	159	41.3	954	304	31.9
35 to 54 years	4,456	1,024	23.0	3,454	717	20.8	814	247	30.4	1,189	329	27.6
55 to 64 years	2,644	471	17.8	2,110	336	15.9	456	108	23.7	307	80	26.0
65 years and over	5,118	752	14.7	4,209	474	11.3	762	248	32.5	376	76	20.1
65 to 74 years	2,879	396	13.8	2,294	238	10.4	504	144	28.6	238	46	19.3
75 years and over	2,239	356	15.9	1,915	236	12.3	258	104	40.2	138	30	21.4
Female												
Total	17,072	5,206	30.5	13,516	3,527	26.1	2,843	1,486	52.3	2,851	1,048	36.8
25 to 34 years	2,594	1,223	47.2	1,955	784	40.1	523	389	74.4	741	355	47.9
35 to 54 years	4,509	1,430	31.7	3,450	927	26.9	812	417	51.4	1,153	388	33.6
55 to 64 years	2,820	713	25.3	2,219	473	21.3	489	224	45.8	436	150	34.5
65 years and over	7,149	1,840	25.7	5,893	1,343	22.8	1,019	456	44.8	522	155	29.8
65 to 74 years	3,393	758	22.3	2,703	503	18.6	542	228	42.1	316	83	26.4
75 years and over	3,757	1,082	28.8	3,190	840	26.3	477	228	47.8	207	72	34.9
Household relationship												
In families	24,412	5,050	20.7	19,558	3,373	17.2	3,773	1,424	37.7	4,754	1,425	30.0
Householder	12,610	3,035	24.1	9,991	1,932	19.3	2,186	965	44.2	2,279	809	35.5
In families with related children under 18 years	10,017	3,345	33.4	7,544	2,193	29.1	1,869	977	52.3	3,134	1,149	36.7
Householder	5,430	2,162	39.8	3,963	1,330	33.6	1,209	730	60.4	1,560	683	43.6
In married couple families	18,564	2,946	15.9	15,769	2,281	14.5	1,975	490	24.8	3,504	921	26.3
Householder	9,032	1,412	15.6	7,765	1,106	14.2	970	229	23.6	1,534	427	27.8
Husband	9,203	1,434	15.6	7,883	1,118	14.2	1,019	240	23.6	1,584	438	27.6
Wife	7,645	1,266	16.6	6,577	975	14.8	719	206	28.6	1,478	391	26.5
In married couple families with related children under 18 years	7,207	1,781	24.7	5,906	1,406	23.8	809	256	31.6	2,406	765	31.8
Householder	3,297	829	25.1	2,753	663	24.1	371	113	30.5	1,059	359	33.9
Husband	3,382	841	24.9	2,802	668	23.8	399	121	30.2	1,091	369	33.8
Wife	2,939	769	26.2	2,464	603	24.4	284	109	38.4	1,004	317	31.6
In families with female householder, no spouse present	4,511	1,793	39.8	2,816	904	32.1	1,512	837	55.4	870	408	46.9
Householder	2,917	1,456	49.9	1,740	713	41.0	1,072	695	64.8	577	331	57.4
In families with female householder, no spouse present, with related children under 18 years	2,352	1,405	59.7	1,308	679	51.9	960	679	70.8	577	335	58.1
Householder	1,822	1,218	66.8	986	584	59.3	771	591	76.6	421	287	68.2
In unrelated subfamilies	154	101	65.4	138	93	67.3	7	2	(B)	50	30	(B)
Unrelated individuals	7,629	3,077	40.3	5,972	2,169	36.3	1,481	822	55.5	873	382	43.7
Male	3,023	995	32.9	2,188	614	28.1	748	342	45.7	513	179	34.9
Householder	2,153	654	30.4	1,603	417	26.0	494	211	42.7	249	82	32.8
Female	4,606	2,082	45.2	3,785	1,555	41.1	733	481	65.5	360	203	56.3
Householder	4,231	1,855	43.9	3,475	1,370	39.4	684	448	65.5	274	142	51.8

[Continued]

★ 607 ★

Persons 25 Years Old and Older Living in Poverty, by Educational Status, Age Group, Sex, and Household Relationship, 1992

[Continued]

Characteristic	All races			White			Black			Hispanic origin[1]		
	Total	Below poverty level: Number	Below poverty level: Percent of total	Total	Below poverty level: Number	Below poverty level: Percent of total	Total	Below poverty level: Number	Below poverty level: Percent of total	Total	Below poverty level: Number	Below poverty level: Percent of total
HIGH SCHOOL DIPLOMA, NO COLLEGE												
Both sexes												
Total	57,589	5,989	10.4	49,538	4,198	8.5	6,451	1,588	24.6	3,242	538	16.6
25 to 34 years	15,036	2,239	14.9	12,344	1,493	12.1	2,234	663	29.7	1,310	268	20.4
35 to 54 years	23,928	2,120	8.9	20,248	1,391	6.9	2,930	650	22.2	1,494	215	14.4
55 to 64 years	8,058	626	7.8	7,109	475	6.7	740	133	17.9	266	30	11.2
65 years and over	10,567	1,004	9.5	9,838	838	8.5	547	143	26.1	171	26	15.1
65 to 74 years	3,879	589	8.6	6,339	466	7.4	420	111	26.4	132	20	15.4
75 years and over	3,688	415	11.3	3,498	372	10.6	127	32	25.2	40	6	(B)
Male												
Total	25,766	2,116	8.2	22,115	1,521	6.9	2,936	514	17.5	1,558	217	13.9
25 to 34 years	7,604	789	10.4	6,257	557	8.9	1,098	190	17.3	677	107	15.8
35 to 54 years	10,984	855	7.8	9,344	587	6.3	1,338	243	18.2	708	92	13.0
55 to 64 years	3,361	199	5.9	2,967	149	5.0	311	44	14.0	112	10	8.8
65 years and over	3,817	274	7.2	3,546	229	6.4	188	37	19.7	62	8	(B)
65 to 74 years	2,584	196	7.6	2,389	164	6.8	144	28	19.3	49	8	(B)
75 years and over	1,233	78	6.3	1,157	65	5.6	44	9	(B)	13	-	(B)
Female												
Total	31,823	3,873	12.2	27,423	2,677	9.8	3,516	1,074	30.6	1,683	321	19.1
25 to 34 years	7,432	1,450	19.5	6,087	936	15.4	1,136	473	41.7	633	161	25.4
35 to 54 years	12,944	1,265	9.8	10,903	804	7.4	1,592	406	25.5	785	122	15.6
55 to 64 years	4,697	427	9.1	4,142	327	7.9	429	89	20.7	155	20	12.9
65 years and over	6,750	731	10.8	6,291	610	9.7	359	106	29.5	110	17	15.9
65 to 74 years	4,295	393	9.2	3,950	303	7.7	275	83	30.1	83	12	14.3
75 years and over	2,455	338	13.8	2,341	307	13.1	83	23	27.4	27	6	(B)
Household relationship												
In families	47,311	4,000	8.5	40,743	2,672	6.6	5,181	1,169	22.6	2,789	424	15.2
Householder	22,205	2,446	11.0	18,917	1,590	8.4	2,707	769	28.4	1,292	251	19.4
In families with related children under 18 years	22,009	2,863	13.0	18,123	1,812	10.0	3,140	946	30.1	1,796	333	18.6
Householder	11,567	1,977	17.1	9,341	1,218	13.0	1,890	694	36.7	908	215	23.6
In married couple families	39,439	2,244	5.7	35,414	1,780	5.0	2,910	355	12.2	2,150	248	11.5
Householder	17,181	1,045	6.1	15,441	840	5.4	1,304	158	12.1	916	120	13.1
Husband	17,099	1,037	6.1	15,370	828	5.4	1,317	163	12.3	918	123	13.4
Wife	20,055	1,112	5.5	18,199	889	4.9	1,275	165	12.9	1,045	118	11.3
In married couple families with related children under 18 years	17,971	1,451	8.1	15,658	1,097	7.0	1,679	286	17.0	1,434	205	14.3
Householder	8,289	711	8.6	7,236	547	7.6	800	134	16.8	633	99	15.7
Husband	8,315	712	8.6	7,258	543	7.5	825	140	17.0	635	103	16.2
Wife	8,936	689	7.7	7,878	527	6.7	723	124	17.1	698	96	13.8
In families with female householder, no spouse present	6,125	1,562	25.5	4,024	758	18.9	1,933	762	39.5	466	142	30.4
Householder	4,020	1,266	31.5	2,667	653	24.5	1,244	580	46.7	283	110	38.7
In families with female householder, no spouse present, with related children under 18 years	3,358	1,293	38.5	1,939	627	32.4	1,335	635	47.6	294	112	37.9
Householder	2,720	1,159	42.6	1,649	592	35.9	1,003	537	53.5	222	99	44.6
In unrelated subfamilies	265	114	42.9	222	100	45.1	34	11	(B)	36	20	(B)
Unrelated individuals	10,013	1,875	18.7	8,573	1,426	16.6	1,236	408	33.0	417	94	22.6
Male	4,564	706	15.5	3,732	489	13.1	705	195	27.6	264	44	16.8
Householder	3,194	408	12.8	2,729	295	10.8	380	102	26.7	135	16	12.2
Female	5,449	1,170	21.5	4,842	936	19.3	531	214	40.2	153	50	32.5
Householder	4,704	935	19.9	4,192	736	17.6	459	186	40.4	112	33	29.7
SOME COLLEGE, LESS THAN BACHELOR'S DEGREE												
Both sexes												
Total	37,451	2,621	7.0	32,428	1,906	5.9	3,909	594	15.2	2,092	246	11.8
25 to 34 years	11,362	983	8.7	9,408	666	7.1	1,553	278	17.9	886	115	12.9
35 to 54 years	17,963	1,119	6.2	15,531	804	5.2	1,883	255	13.5	987	105	10.7
55 to 64 years	3,763	249	6.6	3,364	200	5.9	298	34	11.5	143	19	13.4
65 years and over	4,343	270	6.2	4,125	238	85.8	175	26	15.0	77	7	8.8
65 to 74 years	2,793	150	5.4	2,635	137	5.2	129	12	9.6	64	5	(B)
75 years and over	1,551	120	7.7	1,490	101	6.8	46	14	(B)	12	2	(B)

[Continued]

★ 607 ★

Persons 25 Years Old and Older Living in Poverty, by Educational Status, Age Group, Sex, and Household Relationship, 1992

[Continued]

Characteristic	All races			White			Black			Hispanic origin[1]		
	Total	Below poverty level		Total	Below poverty level		Total	Below poverty level		Total	Below poverty level	
		Number	Percent of total		Number	Percent of total		Number	Percent of total		Number	Percent of total
Male												
Total	17,522	943	5.4	15,358	711	4.6	1,650	187	11.3	1,049	114	10.9
25 to 34 years	5,309	317	6.0	4,406	217	4.9	698	87	12.5	426	42	9.8
35 to 54 years	8,624	482	5.6	7,601	366	4.8	776	89	11.5	520	60	11.6
55 to 64 years	1,753	82	4.7	1,597	68	4.3	110	9	8.2	70	10	(B)
65 years and over	1,835	63	3.4	1,755	60	3.4	66	2	(B)	32	2	(B)
65 to 74 years	1,210	38	3.1	1,154	38	3.3	50	-	(B)	30	2	(B)
75 years and over	625	25	4.0	601	22	3.7	16	2	(B)	2	-	(B)
Female												
Total	19,930	1,678	8.4	17,070	1,196	7.0	2,259	407	18.0	1,043	132	12.6
25 to 34 years	6,053	667	11.0	5,002	448	9.0	855	191	22.3	459	73	15.9
35 to 54 years	9,358	637	6.8	7,930	438	5.5	1,107	166	15.0	466	45	9.6
55 to 64 years	2,010	167	8.3	1,768	131	7.4	188	25	13.4	73	9	(B)
65 years and over	2,508	207	8.3	2,370	178	7.5	109	25	22.7	44	5	(B)
65 to 74 years	1,583	112	7.1	1,481	99	6.7	79	12	15.7	34	3	(B)
75 years and over	926	95	10.2	889	79	8.9	30	12	(B)	10	2	(B)
Household relationship												
In families	30,286	1,656	5.5	26,171	1,131	4.3	3,164	451	14.3	1,737	178	10.2
Householder	15,257	1,092	7.2	13,193	730	5.5	1,646	316	19.2	861	111	12.9
In families with related children under 18 years	16,157	1,276	7.9	13,481	854	6.3	2,083	368	17.7	1,138	141	12.4
Householder	8,655	920	10.6	7,140	599	8.4	1,226	282	23.0	602	89	14.8
In married couple families	25,489	812	3.2	22,765	645	2.8	1,950	120	6.1	1,390	95	6.8
Householder	11,968	389	3.3	10,825	313	2.9	835	51	6.1	644	46	7.2
Husband	11,794	384	3.3	10,641	305	2.9	836	52	6.3	621	44	7.1
Wife	12,278	375	3.1	10,987	309	2.8	930	50	5.3	617	42	6.9
In married couple families with related children under 18 years	13,427	576	4.3	11,632	456	3.9	1,298	90	6.9	933	77	8.2
Householder	6,380	291	4.6	5,569	228	4.1	596	46	7.8	445	35	8.0
Husband	6,239	291	4.7	5,441	226	4.2	578	44	7.7	426	33	7.8
Wife	6,777	261	3.9	5,913	215	3.6	637	39	6.1	444	38	8.5
In families with female householder, no spouse present	3,786	735	19.4	2,637	423	16.0	1,022	291	28.5	266	67	25.0
Householder	2,697	637	23.6	1,880	373	19.8	726	244	33.6	168	53	31.4
In families with female householder, no spouse present, with related children under 18 years	2,333	642	27.5	1,557	375	24.1	697	246	35.3	172	57	33.3
Householder	1,981	589	29.7	1,329	349	26.3	585	218	37.3	131	47	36.1
In unrelated subfamilies	152	52	34.2	122	31	25.7	25	19	(B)	14	6	(B)
Unrelated individuals	7,014	914	13.0	6,135	746	12.2	720	123	17.1	340	61	18.0
Male	3,403	380	11.2	2,932	303	10.3	392	61	15.6	210	40	19.1
Householder	2,555	240	9.4	2,214	193	8.7	282	35	12.3	123	13	10.6
Female	3,611	534	14.8	3,204	443	13.8	328	62	19.0	130	21	16.3
Householder	3,077	403	13.1	2,732	332	12.2	298	55	18.4	100	14	13.7
BACHELOR'S DEGREE OR MORE												
Both sexes												
Total	35,591	1,058	3.0	31,385	804	2.6	2,164	123	5.7	1,090	74	6.8
25 to 34 years	9,968	319	3.2	8,580	226	2.6	703	32	4.5	387	34	8.9
35 to 54 years	17,969	495	2.8	15,799	392	2.5	1,099	51	4.7	545	31	5.8
55 to 64 years	3,961	126	3.2	3,570	87	2.4	205	26	12.8	82	3	4.2
65 years and over	3,692	117	3.2	3,436	99	2.9	157	13	8.4	76	5	6.8
65 to 74 years	2,419	63	2.6	2,239	53	2.4	108	8	7.7	57	3	(B)
75 years and over	1,273	54	4.2	1,198	46	3.9	49	5	(B)	19	2	(B)
Male												
Total	19,234	561	2.9	17,173	422	2.5	949	51	5.4	570	36	6.4
25 to 34 years	5,040	170	3.4	4,367	122	2.8	306	4	1.3	180	14	7.8
35 to 54 years	9,687	249	2.6	8,658	189	2.2	470	29	6.1	300	17	5.7
55 to 64 years	2,447	88	3.6	2,215	63	2.8	109	15	13.9	53	3	(B)
65 years and over	2,061	54	2.6	1,933	47	2.4	64	4	(B)	38	2	(B)
65 to 74 years	1,441	27	1.9	1,350	27	2.0	44	1	(B)	28	1	(B)
75 years and over	621	26	4.3	583	21	3.5	20	3	(B)	10	1	(B)
Female												
Total	16,356	496	3.0	14,212	382	2.7	1,215	71	5.8	519	38	7.3

[Continued]

★ 607 ★

Persons 25 Years Old and Older Living in Poverty, by Educational Status, Age Group, Sex, and Household Relationship, 1992

[Continued]

Characteristic	All races			White			Black			Hispanic origin[1]		
	Total	Below poverty level		Total	Below poverty level		Total	Below poverty level		Total	Below poverty level	
		Number	Percent of total		Number	Percent of total		Number	Percent of total		Number	Percent of total
25 to 34 years	4,928	150	3.0	4,213	104	2.5	397	28	7.0	207	20	9.7
35 to 54 years	8,282	246	3.0	7,141	202	2.8	629	23	3.6	245	14	5.9
55 to 64 years	1,515	38	2.5	1,355	24	1.8	96	11	11.6	29	1	(B)
65 years and over	1,631	63	3.9	1,503	52	3.4	93	9	10.2	38	3	(B)
65 to 74 years	979	36	3.6	889	26	2.9	65	8	(B)	29	2	(B)
75 years and over	652	27	4.2	614	26	4.2	28	2	(B)	9	1	(B)
Household relationship												
In families	28,067	537	1.9	24,785	384	1.5	1,570	70	4.5	860	48	5.5
Householder	15,321	336	2.2	13,620	242	1.8	837	40	4.7	461	30	6.6
In families with related children under 18 years	14,010	338	2.4	12,089	251	2.1	890	47	5.3	491	41	8.3
Householder	7,971	229	2.9	6,926	171	2.5	528	34	6.5	271	23	8.5
In married couple families	25,362	363	1.4	22,715	277	1.2	1,124	18	1.6	730	30	4.2
Householder	13,527	207	1.5	12,257	155	1.3	524	10	2.0	375	15	4.0
Husband	13,701	213	1.6	12,426	161	1.3	507	10	1.9	366	15	4.1
Wife	10,611	141	1.3	9,420	111	1.2	540	6	1.1	314	13	4.2
In married couple families with related children under 18 years	12,842	217	1.7	11,231	172	1.5	644	16	2.4	432	27	6.2
Householder	6,944	121	1.7	6,155	96	1.6	319	7	2.3	220	11	5.1
Husband	7,022	120	1.7	6,226	95	1.5	311	7	2.1	216	11	5.2
Wife	5,569	88	1.6	4,855	70	1.5	304	6	2.0	193	13	6.9
In families with female householder, no spouse present	1,999	135	6.8	1,496	83	5.5	384	46	12.1	96	9	9.6
Householder	1,309	97	7.4	962	65	6.8	275	25	9.2	62	7	(B)
In families with female householder, no spouse present, with related children under 18 years	892	97	10.9	624	66	10.6	215	26	12.1	43	9	(B)
Householder	800	89	11.1	575	61	10.6	184	23	12.5	36	7	(B)
In unrelated subfamilies	43	9	(B)	32	7	(B)	7	2	(B)	4	2	(B)
Unrelated individuals	7,480	512	6.8	6,568	413	6.3	587	50	8.5	226	25	11.0
Male	3,902	285	7.3	3,416	225	6.6	289	22	7.7	130	12	9.4
Householder	3,068	187	6.1	2,700	153	5.7	241	18	7.7	89	10	10.8
Female	3,578	226	6.3	3,152	188	6.0	298	28	9.3	96	13	13.1
Householder	2,993	166	5.6	2,637	138	5.2	258	21	8.1	77	7	9.6

Source: U.S. Bureau of the Census. *Poverty in the United States: 1992.* Current Population Reports, Series P60-185, U.S. Government Printing Office, Washington, D.C., 1993, pp. 70-73. *Notes:* A (B) indicates that the base was less than 75,000 or not applicable. 1. Persons of Hispanic origin may be of any race.

★ 608 ★

Poverty

Persons 65 Years Old and Older Living Below Poverty Level, 1980-92

Data are shown in number of persons as of March of following year.

Race/ethnicity	Number below poverty level (000)				Percent below poverty level			
	1970	1990	1991	1992	1970	1990	1991	1992
Total[1]	4,793	3,658	3,781	3,983	24.6	12.2	12.4	12.9
White	4,011	2,707	2,802	2,992	22.6	10.1	10.3	10.9
Black	683	860	880	887	48.0	33.8	33.8	33.3
Hispanic[2]	(NA)	245	237	269	(NA)	22.5	20.8	22.0

Source: 1994 Statistical Abstract of the United States on CD-ROM [machine-readable datafiles]. CD-8A-94. Washington, DC: U.S. Department of Commerce, Economics and Statistics Administration, Bureau of the Census, Data User Services Division, January 1995. Primary source: U.S. Bureau of the Census, Current Population Reports, P60-185. *Notes:* NA stands for not available. 1. Beginning 1979, includes members of unrelated subfamilies not shown separately. For earlier years, unrelated subfamily members are included in the "In families" category. 2. Persons of Hispanic origin may be of any race.

★ 609 ★

Poverty

Persons 65 Years and Older Living Below the Poverty Level, 1989

The number, in thousands, and percent of elderly people living below the poverty level are shown, by race/ethnicity, sex, and living arrangements for 1989.

Race/ethnicity	Living arrangement of people below the poverty level							
	Number (thousands)				Percent			
	Total	Alone	With spouse	With others	Total	Alone	With spouse	With others
All races								
Men	965	339	525	101	7.8	17.4	5.6	10.4
Women	2,404	1,705	390	310	14.0	23.3	5.2	12.7
Total	3,369	2,044	915	411	11.4	22.0	5.4	12.0
Hispanic[1]								
Men	87	26	53	8	18.6	34.7	15.1	19.5
Women	124	62	33	29	22.4	41.9	12.4	20.4
Total	211	88	86	37	20.6	39.5	13.9	20.2
White								
Men	723	240	431	52	6.6	13.9	5.0	7.2
Women	1,819	1,339	318	162	11.8	20.0	4.6	8.5
Total	2,542	1,579	748	214	9.6	18.8	4.8	8.1
Black								
Men	221	96	80	46	22.1	48.2	13.7	21.0
Women	544	350	57	138	36.7	60.6	13.0	29.6
Total	766	445	137	183	30.8	57.3	13.4	26.6

Source: Aging America, Trends and Projections, 1991 Edition. Prepared by the U.S. Senate Special Committee on Aging, the American Association of Retired Persons, the Federal Council on the Aging, and the U.S. Administration on Aging, p. 53. Primary source: Unpublished date from the March 1990 *Current Population Survey*. *Note:* 1. Hispanic people may be of any race.

★ 610 ★

Poverty

Persons Living Below Poverty Level in U.S. Southwest Border States, 1980

Characteristic	United States	Total, border states	Border states			
			Border county areas		Non-border county areas	
			Hispanic	Non-Hispanic	Hispanic	Non-Hispanic
Total families	59,190,133	10,719,569	309,307	676,939	1,530,825	8,202,498
Families below poverty level	5,670,215	1,047,619	84,831	49,799	282,308	630,681
Percent						
Of total families below poverty level	9.6	9.8	27.4	7.4	18.4	7.7
With related children under 18 years	74.3	76.3	84.6	72.5	85.8	71.2

[Continued]

★ 610 ★

Persons Living Below Poverty Level in U.S. Southwest Border States, 1980

[Continued]

Characteristic	United States	Total, border states	Border states			
			Border county areas		Non-border county areas	
			Hispanic	Non-Hispanic	Hispanic	Non-Hispanic
Female householder with no husband present	43.8	39.1	30.3	42.1	34.6	42.1
Householder, 65 years and over	13.8	11.8	11.1	10.9	7.4	13.9

Source: U.S. Bureau of the Census, *The Hispanic Population of the Southwest Borderland.* Current Population Reports, Series P-23, No. 172, Washington, DC: U.S. Government Printing Office, 1991, p. 21. *Notes:* For the purposes of this report, the U.S. Census Bureau included the following counties: San Diego, and Imperial counties, in California; Cochise, Pima, Santa Cruz, and Yuma counties, in Arizona; Dona Ana, Hidalgo, and Luna counties, in New Mexico; El Paso, Hudspeth, Culberson, Jeff Davis, Presidio, Brewster, Terrell, Valverde, Kinney, Maverick, Dimmit, Webb, Zapata, Starr, Hidalgo, and Cameron counties, in Texas.

★ 611 ★

Poverty

Persons Living Below Poverty Level, by Hispanic Ethnicity and Major Age Group, 1991

Numbers are shown in thousands, except where noted.

Age group	Total population	Non-Hispanic population	Hispanic origin population	Mexican origin	Puerto Rican population	Cuban origin	Central and South American origin	Other Hispanic origin
Total persons[1]	33,585	27,578	6,006	3,764	966	178	748	350
Percent below poverty level[2]	13.5	12.1	28.1	28.1	40.6	16.9	25.4	21.5
Less than 18 years old	20.6	18.3	38.4	36.3	56.7	31.0	35.2	35.9
18-64 years old	10.7	9.7	22.5	23.2	31.2	12.0	21.1	15.6
65 years old and over	12.2	11.8	22.5	23.1	31.7	23.1	16.5	15.9
Percent[3]	100.0	100.0	100.0	100.0	100.0	100.0	100.0	100.0
Less than 18 years old	40.0	38.3	47.7	48.3	51.2	31.5	43.9	48.5
18-64 years old	49.1	49.3	48.2	48.1	45.2	48.4	54.2	44.9
65 years old and over	10.9	12.4	4.1	3.6	3.7	20.1	2.0	6.6

Source: U.S. Bureau of the Census, *The Hispanic Population in the United States: March 1991.* Current Population Reports, Series P-20, No. 455, Washington, DC: U.S. Government Printing Office, 1991, pp. 12-15. *Notes:* 1. Excludes unrelated individuals less than 15 years of age. 2. Percentages based on persons (for whom poverty status is determined) with specific characteristics and of specific origin. 3. Percent of all persons below the poverty level in 1990.

★ 612 ★

Poverty

Persons Living Below Poverty Level, by Race/Ethnicity and Definition of Income, 1992

Data are shown for persons as of March 1993.

Definition	Number below poverty level (000)				Percent below poverty level			
	All races[1]	White	Black	Hispanic[2]	All races[1]	White	Black	Hispanic[2]
All persons	253,969	211,820	31,916	22,720	(X)	(X)	(X)	(X)
INCOME BEFORE TAXES								
Income excluding capital gains[3]	36,880	24,523	10,613	6,655	14.5	11.6	33.3	29.3
Definition 1 less govt money transfers	57,287	41,630	13,357	8,320	22.6	19.7	41.9	36.6
Definition 2 plus capital gains	57,220	41,553	13,373	8,306	22.5	19.6	41.9	36.6
Definition 3 plus health insurance supplements to wage or salary income[4]	55,660	40,426	13,024	7,999	21.9	19.1	40.8	35.2
INCOME AFTER TAXES								
Definition 4 less Social Security payroll taxes	58,256	42,447	13,481	8,396	22.9	20.0	42.2	37.0
Definition 5 less Federal income taxes (excluding EITC)[5]	58,862	42,877	13,643	8,498	23.2	20.2	42.7	37.4
Definition 6 plus EITC[5]	56,940	41,432	13,264	8,137	22.4	19.6	41.6	35.8
Definition 7 less State income taxes	57,530	41,688	13,402	8,172	22.6	19.7	42.0	36.0
Definition 8 plus nonmeans-tested govt cash transfers[6]	39,481	26,124	11,458	7,045	15.5	12.3	35.9	31.0
Definition 9 plus value of Medicare	38,331	25,316	11,164	6,827	15.1	12.0	35.0	30.1
Definition 10 plus value of regular-price school lunches	38,316	25,310	11,156	6,819	15.1	11.9	35.0	30.0
Definition 11 plus means-tested govt cash transfers[7]	35,513	23,489	10,346	6,335	14.0	11.1	32.4	27.9
Definition 12 plus value of Medicaid	33,081	21,895	9,634	5,844	13.0	10.3	30.2	25.7
Definition 13 plus means-tested govt noncash transfers[8]	29,719	19,865	8,487	5,185	11.7	9.4	26.6	22.8
Definition 14 plus net imputed return on equity in own home[9]	26,533	17,375	7,896	4,883	10.4	8.2	24.7	21.5

Source: U.S. Bureau of the Census. *Statistical Abstract of the United States, 1994 on CD-ROM.* [machine-readable datafiles] Washington, DC: U.S. Government Printing Office, 1994. Primary source: U.S. Bureau of the Census, Current Population Reports, P60-186RD. *Notes:* An (X) stands for not applicable. 1. Includes other races not shown separately. 2. Persons of Hispanic origin may be of any race. 3. Official definition based on income before taxes and includes government cash transfers. 4. Employer contributions to the health insurance plans of employees. 5. Earned Income Tax Credit. 6. Includes Social Security and Railroad Retirement, veterans payments, unemployment and workers' compensation, Black Lung payments, Pell Grants, and other government educational assistance. 7. Includes AFDC and other public assistance or welfare payments, Supplemental Security Income, and veterans payments. Households must meet certain eligibility requirements in order to qualify for these benefits. 8. Includes Medicaid, food stamps, subsidies from free or reduced-price school lunches, and rent subsidies. 9. Estimated amount of income a household would receive if it chose to shift amount held as home equity into an interest bearing account.

★ 613 ★

Poverty

Persons Living in Poverty in the United States, by Type of Residence, Age Group, and Sex, 1992: Central Cities

Numbers are shown in thousands and refer to persons, families, and unrelated individuals, as of March of the following year.

Characteristic	All races			White			Black			Hispanic origin[1]		
	Total	Below poverty level		Total	Below poverty level		Total	Below poverty level		Total	Below poverty level	
		Number	Percent of total		Number	Percent of total		Number	Percent of total		Number	Percent of total
United States												
Central cities												
Both sexes												
Total	76,344	15,644	20.5	54.115	8,458	15.6	18,054	6,348	35.2	11,816	3,985	33.7
Under 18 years	19,734	6,411	32.5	12,629	3,078	24.4	5,915	2,979	50.4	4,080	1,864	45.7
18 to 24 years	8,172	1,976	24.2	5,700	1,224	21.5	1,981	638	32.2	1,536	499	32.5
25 to 34 years	13,892	2,395	17.2	9,958	1,336	13.4	3,104	927	29.8	2,204	610	27.7
35 to 44 years	11,481	1,619	14.2	8,337	874	10.5	2,500	653	26.1	1,623	420	25.9
45 to 54 years	7,936	952	12.0	5,849	551	9.4	1,677	346	20.6	1,072	240	22.4
55 to 59 years	2,983	402	13.5	2,122	243	11.4	693	142	20.5	357	90	25.2
60 to 64 years	3,041	384	12.6	2,298	231	10.0	629	135	21.4	275	84	30.6
65 years and over	9,106	1,495	16.4	7,221	922	12.8	1,554	529	34.0	669	178	26.6
65 to 74 years	5,293	781	14.8	4,099	450	11.0	978	306	31.3	408	92	22.4
75 years and over	3,813	714	18.7	3,122	472	15.1	576	223	38.7	260	86	33.1
Male												
Total	36,701	6,607	18.0	26,276	3,559	13.5	8,362	2,646	31.6	5,741	1,765	30.7
Under 18 years	9,937	3,183	32.0	6,348	1,460	23.0	2,989	1,542	51.6	1,979	887	44.8
18 to 24 years	4,035	768	19.0	2,847	507	17.8	926	215	23.2	750	217	28.9
25 to 34 years	6,933	865	12.5	5,080	546	10.7	1,416	254	18.0	1,132	242	21.4
35 to 44 years	5,579	652	11.7	4,160	371	8.9	1,100	229	20.8	812	189	23.2
45 to 54 years	3,797	419	11.0	2,889	241	8.3	721	150	20.9	551	119	21.6
55 to 59 years	1,395	148	10.6	1,013	98	9.6	318	45	14.3	146	30	20.3
60 to 64 years	1,393	133	9.5	1,053	84	8.0	291	38	13.2	110	30	27.2
65 years and over	3,633	440	12.1	2,886	252	8.7	602	171	28.4	262	52	19.9
65 to 74 years	2,279	266	11.7	1,764	143	8.1	420	114	27.1	165	31	18.8
75 years and over	1,354	174	12.8	1,122	109	9.7	182	57	31.4	97	21	21.6
Female												
Total	39,643	9,037	22.8	27,838	4,899	17.6	9,692	3,702	38.2	6,076	2,220	36.5
Under 18 years	9,797	3,228	32.9	6,282	1,618	25.8	2,926	1,436	49.1	2,101	977	46.5
18 to 24 years	4,136	1,208	29.2	2,853	717	25.1	1,055	423	40.1	786	282	35.9
25 to 34 years	6,959	1,531	22.0	4,878	790	16.2	1,688	672	39.8	1,073	368	34.3
35 to 44 years	5,902	976	16.5	4,177	504	12.1	1,400	424	30.3	811	231	28.5
45 to 54 years	4,139	534	12.9	2,959	309	10.5	956	195	20.4	521	122	23.3
55 to 59 years	1,588	254	16.0	1,110	145	13.1	375	97	25.8	212	61	28.6
60 to 64 years	1,648	252	15.3	1,244	147	11.8	339	96	28.4	166	54	32.8
65 years and over	5,474	1,054	19.3	4,336	670	15.5	952	358	37.6	407	126	30.9
65 to 74 years	3,014	514	17.1	2,336	307	13.1	558	192	34.5	244	61	24.9
75 years and over	2,459	540	22.0	2,000	363	18.2	394	166	42.1	163	65	40.0
Household relationship												
Total	76,344	15,644	20.5	54,115	8,458	15.6	18,054	6,348	35.2	11,816	3,985	33.7
65 years and over	9,106	1,495	16.4	7,221	922	12.8	1,554	529	34.0	669	178	26.6
In families	61,299	11,945	19.5	42,551	6,017	14.1	15,171	5,258	34.7	10,362	3,412	32.9
Householder	19,336	3,387	17.5	13,966	1,768	12.7	4,382	1,443	32.9	2,761	861	31.2
Under 65 years	16,278	3,055	18.8	11,561	1,593	13.8	3,842	1,297	33.8	2,526	814	32.2
65 years and over	3,057	332	10.9	2,405	175	7.3	539	146	27.1	236	46	19.7
Related children under 18 years	19,343	6,162	31.9	12,331	2,888	23.4	5,843	2,930	50.2	3,969	1,782	44.9
Under 6 years	7,423	2,679	36.1	4,750	1,270	26.7	2,218	1,276	57.5	1,512	746	49.4
6 to 17 years	11,921	3,483	29.2	7,581	1,618	21.3	3,625	1,655	45.7	2,457	1,035	42.1
Own children 18 years and over	6,516	849	13.0	3,994	361	9.0	2,194	463	21.1	1,023	235	23.0
In married-coupled families	42,840	4,263	10.0	33,276	2,983	9.0	6,763	864	12.8	6,992	1,679	24.0
Husbands	13,223	1,083	8.2	10,585	754	7.1	1,905	231	12.1	1,739	362	20.8
Under 65 years	10,823	873	8.1	8,602	621	7.2	1,572	159	10.1	1,582	336	21.2
65 years and over	2,400	210	8.7	1,983	133	6.7	332	72	21.6	158	26	16.5

[Continued]

★ 613 ★

Persons Living in Poverty in the United States, by Type of Residence, Age Group, and Sex, 1992: Central Cities

[Continued]

Characteristic	All races			White			Black			Hispanic origin[1]		
	Total	Below poverty level		Total	Below poverty level		Total	Below poverty level		Total	Below poverty level	
		Number	Percent of total		Number	Percent of total		Number	Percent of total		Number	Percent of total
Wives	13,223	1,083	8.2	10,602	777	7.3	1,836	217	11.8	1,797	354	19.7
Under 65 years	11,402	933	8.2	9,076	680	7.5	1,597	164	10.3	1,674	341	20.3
65 years and over	1,820	150	8.3	1,527	96	6.3	239	53	22.0	123	13	10.6
Related children under 18 years	11,810	1,753	14.8	8,966	1,214	13.5	1,956	340	17.4	2,498	790	31.6
Under 6 years	4,565	766	16.8	3,544	554	15.6	667	143	21.5	9499	341	35.9
6 to 17 years	7,245	987	13.6	5,422	659	12.2	1,289	197	15.3	1,549	449	29.0
Own children 18 years and over	3,596	213	5.9	2,496	137	5.5	859	59	6.8	603	87	14.4
In families with female householder, no spouse present	15,428	7,060	45.8	7,189	2,680	37.3	7,649	4,172	54.5	2,673	1,518	56.8
Householder	5,043	2,098	41.6	2,584	880	34.0	2,260	1,150	50.9	801	433	54.0
Under 65 years	4,463	1,981	44.4	2,207	834	37.8	2,076	1,082	52.1	738	412	55.8
65 years and over	580	117	20.2	377	45	12.0	184	68	36.9	64	21	B
Related children under 18 years	6,701	4,160	62.1	2,789	1,528	54.8	3,671	2,503	68.2	1,281	906	70.7
Under 6 years	2,537	1,809	71.3	994	661	66.5	1,462	1,093	74.7	476	370	77.7
6 to 17 years	4,164	2,351	56.5	1,795	868	48.3	2,209	1,410	63.8	805	537	66.6
Own children 18 years and over	2,522	567	22.5	1,232	192	15.5	1,216	369	30.3	364	130	35.9
In unrelated subfamilies	610	344	56.4	459	263	57.2	113	67	58.7	168	117	69.6
Under 18 years	328	204	62.1	245	153	62.6	65	41	B	85	63	74.1
Under 6 years	147	105	71.4	109	77	70.1	28	25	B	35	30	B
6 to 17 years	181	99	54.5	136	77	56.5	37	16	B	50	33	B
18 years and over	283	141	49.8	214	109	51.0	49	25	B	83	54	64.9
Unrelated individuals	14,435	3,354	23.2	11,104	2,178	19.6	2,770	1,024	37.0	1,286	456	35.5
Male	7,112	1,453	20.4	5,343	897	16.8	1,439	473	32.9	750	223	29.8
Under 65 years	6,244	1,252	20.1	4,662	788	16.9	1,266	386	30.5	698	202	28.9
Living alone	3,041	468	15.4	2,259	272	12.0	647	171	26.4	240	45	18.8
65 years and over	868	200	23.1	681	109	16.0	173	87	50.2	53	22	B
Living alone	757	169	22.3	596	95	16.0	150	68	45.5	45	21	B
Female	7,323	1,902	26.0	5,761	1,281	22.2	1,331	551	41.4	536	233	43.4
Under 65 years	4,791	1,164	24.3	3,697	786	21.3	906	325	35.9	406	160	39.4
Living alone	2,830	568	20.1	2,111	352	16.7	631	200	31.6	211	64	30.2
65 years and over	2,532	738	29.1	2,063	495	24.0	425	226	53.2	130	73	56.1
Living alone	2,433	698	28.7	1,986	464	23.4	409	220	53.9	117	63	54.1

Source: U.S. Bureau of the Census. *Poverty in the United States: 1992.* Current Population Reports, Series P60-185, U.S. Government Printing Office, Washington, D.C., 1993, p. 40. *Notes:* A (B) stands for base less than zero or not applicable. 1. Persons of Hispanic origin may be of any race.

★ 614 ★

Poverty

Persons Living in Poverty in the United States, by Type of Residence, Age Group, and Sex, 1992: Metropolitan Areas

Numbers are shown in thousands and refer to persons, families, and unrelated individuals, as of March of the following year.

Characteristic	All races			White			Black			Hispanic origin[1]		
	Total	Below poverty level		Total	Below poverty level		Total	Below poverty level		Total	Below poverty level	
		Number	Percent of total		Number	Percent of total		Number	Percent of total		Number	Percent of total
United States												
Metropolitan areas												
Both sexes												
Total	197,258	27,372	13.9	161,394	17,348	10.7	27,076	8,636	31.9	21,010	6,028	28.7
Under 18 years	51,381	10,979	21.4	39,580	6,365	16.0	8,889	4,043	45.5	7,159	2,808	39.2
18 to 24 years	19,213	3,380	17.6	15,196	2,243	14.8	3,068	948	30.9	2,609	763	29.2
25 to 34 years	33,762	4,229	12.5	27,492	2,757	10.0	4,699	1,255	26.7	3,980	970	24.4

[Continued]

★ 614 ★

Persons Living in Poverty in the United States, by Type of Residence, Age Group, and Sex, 1992: Metropolitan Areas

[Continued]

Characteristic	All races			White			Black			Hispanic origin[1]		
	Total	Below poverty level		Total	Below poverty level		Total	Below poverty level		Total	Below poverty level	
		Number	Percent of total		Number	Percent of total		Number	Percent of total		Number	Percent of total
35 to 44 years	3,655	2,875	9.1	26,264	1,833	7.0	3,875	859	22.2	3,097	674	21.8
45 to 54 years	22,415	1,664	7.4	18,878	1,104	5.8	2,598	469	18.0	1,900	322	16.9
55 to 59 years	8,134	712	8.8	6,800	492	7.2	1,002	193	19.3	635	126	19.8
60 to 64 years	7,966	759	9.5	6,841	528	7.7	877	191	21.8	503	128	25.4
65 years and over	22,732	2,774	12.2	20,075	2,025	10.1	2,068	678	32.8	1,126	238	21.1
65 to 74 years	13,550	1,372	10.1	11,837	927	7.8	1,341	407	30.3	733	134	18.2
75 years and over	9,182	1,403	15.3	8,238	1,098	13.3	727	271	37.3	392	104	26.6
Male												
Total	96,104	11,528	12.0	79,069	7,292	9.2	12,726	3,575	28.1	10,522	2,759	26.2
Under 18 years	29,192	5,449	20.8	20,416	3,124	15.3	4,486	2,032	45.3	3,623	1,389	38.3
18 to 24 years	9,533	1,315	13.8	7,589	897	11.8	1,444	341	23.6	1,320	327	24.8
25 to 34 years	16,871	1,558	9.2	13,829	1,083	7.8	2,202	368	16.7	2,065	409	19.8
35 to 44 years	15,573	1,145	7.4	13,104	776	5.9	1,747	292	16.7	1,581	307	19.4
45 to 54 years	10,849	713	6.6	9,272	463	5.0	1,158	207	17.9	971	160	16.5
55 to 59 years	3,907	286	7.3	3,301	213	6.5	455	62	13.6	268	47	17.5
60 to 64 years	3,882	268	6.9	3,354	199	5.9	398	46	11.6	228	43	19.0
65 years and over	9,297	793	8.5	8,204	537	6.6	837	228	27.2	465	77	16.5
65 to 74 years	5,903	464	7.9	5,155	300	5.8	587	149	25.4	313	48	15.3
75 years and over	3,394	329	9.7	3,048	238	7.8	250	79	31.4	151	29	19.2
Female												
Total	101,154	15,844	15.7	82,325	10,056	12.2	14,350	5,060	35.3	10,488	3,268	31.2
Under 18 years	25,189	5,529	22.0	19,434	3,241	16.7	4,403	2,011	45.7	3,537	1,419	40.1
18 to 24 years	9,680	2,065	21.3	7,607	1,346	17.7	1,624	606	37.3	1,289	436	33.8
25 to 34 years	16,892	2,671	15.8	13,663	1,674	12.3	2,497	887	35.5	1,915	561	29.3
35 to 44 years	16,083	1,730	10.8	13,159	1,057	8.0	2,128	568	26.7	1,515	367	24.2
45 to 54 years	11,566	951	8.2	9,605	641	6.7	1,441	262	18.2	929	162	17.4
55 to 59 years	4,227	426	10.1	3,499	279	8.0	548	132	24.1	367	79	21.6
60 to 64 years	4,084	491	12.0	3,486	329	9.4	479	145	30.3	275	84	30.6
65 years and over	13,435	1,981	14.7	11,871	1,488	12.5	1,231	450	36.6	661	161	24.4
65 to 74 years	7,647	908	11.9	6,681	628	9.4	754	258	34.2	420	86	20.4
75 years and over	5,788	1,073	18.5	5,190	860	16.6	477	192	40.4	241	75	31.3
Household relationship												
Total	197,258	27,372	13.9	161,394	17,348	10.7	27,076	8,636	31.9	21,010	6,028	28.7
65 years and over	22,732	2,774	12.2	20,075	2,025	10.1	2,068	678	32.8	1,126	238	21.1
In families	166,297	20,762	12.5	135,515	12,456	9.2	22,996	7,188	31.3	18,617	5,149	27.7
Householder	52,299	5,907	11.3	43,575	3,644	8.4	6,648	1,968	29.6	4,919	1,278	26.0
Under 65 years	44,183	5,297	12.0	36,389	3,243	8.9	5,893	1,776	30.1	4,515	1,215	26.9
65 years and over	8,117	610	7.5	7,186	401	5.6	755	192	25.4	404	63	15.5
Related children under 18 years	50,566	10,475	20.7	39,184	5,963	15.2	8,774	3,964	45.2	6,976	2,667	38.2
Under 6 years	18,344	4,476	24.4	14,119	2,590	18.3	3,263	1,693	51.9	2,639	1,101	41.7
6 to 17 years	32,222	5,999	18.6	25,065	3,374	13.5	5,511	2,270	41.2	4,337	1,566	36.1
Own children 18 years and over	16,961	1,384	8.2	13,055	673	5.2	3,207	654	20.4	1,792	318	17.7
In married-coupled families	130,631	8,679	6.6	113,007	6,589	5.8	11,319	1,402	12.4	13,390	2,775	20.7
Husbands	40,237	2,239	5.6	35,461	1,710	4.8	3,164	361	11.4	3,363	607	18.0
Under 65 years	33,498	1,816	5.4	29,328	1,397	4.8	2,698	262	9.7	3,072	565	18.4
65 years and over	6,739	423	6.3	6,133	313	5.1	466	99	21.3	291	42	14.3
Wives	40,237	2,239	5.6	35,428	1,728	4.9	3,051	346	11.3	3,464	590	17.0
Under 65 years	35,040	1,932	5.5	30,650	1,496	4.9	2,729	279	10.2	3,239	568	17.5
65 years and over	5,196	307	5.9	4,779	232	4.9	322	67	20.8	225	23	10.1
Related children under 18 years	36,780	3,557	9.7	31,289	2,715	8.7	3,400	539	15.9	4,785	1,320	27.6
Under 6 years	13,459	1,523	11.3	11,467	1,179	10.3	1,187	234	19.7	1,810	559	30.9
6 to 17 years	23,321	2,034	8.7	19,822	1,536	7.7	2,213	305	13.8	2,975	761	25.6
Own children 18 years and over	11,015	426	3.9	9,099	263	2.9	1,386	125	9.0	1,125	125	11.1
In families with female householder, no spouse present	28,984	11,027	38.0	17,446	5,196	29.8	10,499	5,486	52.3	4,028	2,052	50.9
Householder	9,671	3,321	34.3	6,206	1,699	27.4	3,122	1,517	48.6	1,187	579	48.8
Under 65 years	8,461	3,144	37.2	5,279	1,615	30.6	2,867	1,428	49.8	1,097	556	50.7
65 years and over	1,210	177	14.6	927	84	9.0	256	89	34.7	90	23	25.4
Related children under 18 years	11,978	6,484	54.1	6,508	2,961	45.5	5,047	3,308	65.5	1,868	1,219	65.3
Under 6 years	4,208	2,767	65.7	2,137	1,293	60.5	1,941	1,401	72.2	679	484	71.4
6 to 17 years	7,770	3,718	47.8	4,371	1,668	38.2	3,107	1,906	61.4	1,190	735	61.7
Own children 18 years and over	5,002	856	17.1	3,222	352	10.9	1,645	490	29.8	578	173	30.0
In unrelated subfamilies	1,277	661	51.7	1,043	525	50.3	183	113	61.4	281	183	65.2
Under 18 years	681	392	57.8	553	310	56.0	105	69	65.5	139	103	74.0
Under 6 years	296	203	68.4	236	154	65.3	47	42	B	64	53	B
6 to 17 years	385	190	49.3	317	156	49.1	58	27	B	75	50	66.3

[Continued]

★ 614 ★

Persons Living in Poverty in the United States, by Type of Residence, Age Group, and Sex, 1992: Metropolitan Areas

[Continued]

Characteristic	All races			White			Black			Hispanic origin[1]		
	Total	Below poverty level Number	Below poverty level Percent of total	Total	Below poverty level Number	Below poverty level Percent of total	Total	Below poverty level Number	Below poverty level Percent of total	Total	Below poverty level Number	Below poverty level Percent of total
18 years and over	597	269	45.0	490	215	43.9	78	44	55.9	142	80	56.6
Unrelated individuals	29,685	5,949	20.0	24,837	4,367	17.6	3,896	1,335	34.3	2,112	696	33.0
Male	14,152	2,409	17.0	11,518	1,655	14.4	2,066	618	29.9	1,271	348	27.4
Under 65 years	12,382	2,097	16.9	10,028	1,463	14.6	1,823	506	27.8	1,200	320	26.6
Living alone	6,090	771	12.7	4,951	510	10.3	908	217	24.0	384	68	17.7
65 years and over	1,770	312	17.6	1,490	192	12.9	243	112	46.1	70	29	B
Living alone	1,528	261	17.1	1,291	163	12.6	212	90	42.7	60	26	B
Female	15,533	3,540	22.8	13,319	2,712	20.4	1,830	716	39.1	841	348	41.4
Under 65 years	9,775	2,120	21.7	8,156	1,597	19.6	1,306	438	33.5	657	259	39.4
Living alone	5,698	964	16.9	4,629	664	14.3	929	278	29.9	319	95	29.7
65 years and over	5,758	1,419	24.7	5,163	1,115	21.6	524	279	53.2	184	89	48.3
Living alone	5,522	1,335	24.2	4,960	1,044	21.0	501	270	54.0	167	78	46.8

Source: U.S. Bureau of the Census. *Poverty in the United States: 1992.* Current Population Reports, Series P60-185, U.S. Government Printing Office, Washington, D.C., 1993, p. 39. *Notes:* A (B) stands for base less than 75,000 or not applicable. 1. Persons of Hispanic origin may be of any race.

★ 615 ★

Poverty

Persons Living in Poverty in the United States, by Type of Residence, Age Group, and Sex, 1992: Not in Central Cities

Numbers are shown in thousands and refer to persons, families, and unrelated individuals, as of March of the following year.

Characteristic	All races			White			Black			Hispanic origin[1]		
	Total	Below poverty level Number	Below poverty level Percent of total	Total	Below poverty level Number	Below poverty level Percent of total	Total	Below poverty level Number	Below poverty level Percent of total	Total	Below poverty level Number	Below poverty level Percent of total
United States												
Metropolitan, not in central cities												
Both sexes												
Total	120,914	11,728	9.7	107,280	8,890	8.3	9,022	2,288	25.4	9,193	2,043	22.2
Under 18 years	31,647	4,568	14.4	27,220	3,286	12.1	2,974	1,064	35.8	3,079	944	30.6
18 to 24 years	11,041	1,404	12.7	9,496	1,019	10.7	1,067	309	28.4	1,074	264	24.6
25 to 34 years	19,870	1,834	9.2	17,534	1,422	8.1	1,595	328	20.6	1,776	360	20.3
35 to 44 years	20,175	1,246	6.2	17,926	959	5.3	1,375	207	15.0	1,474	254	17.3
45 to 54 years	14,479	712	4.9	13,029	554	4.2	921	123	13.4	828	81	9.8
55 to 59 years	5,152	310	6.0	4,678	249	5.3	309	51	16.5	278	36	12.9
60 to 64 years	4,952	374	7.6	4,543	297	6.5	248	57	22.9	228	44	19.1
65 years and over	13,626	1,280	9.4	12,854	1,104	8.6	514	149	29.0	457	60	13.2
65 to 74 years	8,257	591	7.2	7,737	477	6.2	363	101	27.7	325	42	12.9
75 years and over	5,369	689	12.8	5,116	626	12.2	151	48	31.9	132	18	13.8
Male												
Total	59,403	4,921	8.3	52,793	3,733	7.1	4,363	929	21.3	4,781	995	20.8
Under 18 years	16,255	2,266	13.9	14,068	1,663	11.8	1,497	490	32.7	1,644	502	30.5
18 to 24 years	5,498	547	10.0	4,742	390	8.2	518	126	24.3	571	110	19.3
25 to 34 years	9,938	693	7.0	8,748	537	6.1	786	113	14.4	933	167	17.9
35 to 44 years	9,994	493	4.9	8,944	405	4.5	647	63	9.7	769	118	15.4
45 to 54 years	7,052	294	4.2	6,383	222	3.5	437	57	13.0	420	41	9.9
55 to 59 years	2,513	138	5.5	2,288	116	5.1	137	16	11.8	123	17	14.1
60 to 64 years	2,489	136	5.5	2,301	115	5.0	107	8	7.1	118	14	11.5
65 years and over	5,665	353	6.2	5,318	286	5.4	235	57	24.1	203	25	12.2
65 to 74 years	3,624	198	5.5	3,392	156	4.6	167	35	21.1	148	17	11.3
75 years and over	2,040	155	7.6	1,926	129	6.7	68	21	B	54	8	B
Female												
Total	61,511	6,807	11.1	54,487	5,157	9.5	4,658	1,358	29.2	4,412	1,049	23.8
Under 18 years	15,392	2,302	15.0	13,152	1,623	12.3	1,477	574	38.9	1,435	442	30.8
18 to 24 years	5,543	857	15.5	4,754	629	13.2	569	183	32.2	503	154	30.6
25 to 34 years	9,933	1,141	11.5	8,786	884	10.1	809	215	26.5	843	193	22.9

[Continued]

★ 615 ★

Persons Living in Poverty in the United States, by Type of Residence, Age Group, and Sex, 1992: Not in Central Cities

[Continued]

Characteristic	All races			White			Black			Hispanic origin[1]		
	Total	Below poverty level: Number	Below poverty level: Percent of total	Total	Below poverty level: Number	Below poverty level: Percent of total	Total	Below poverty level: Number	Below poverty level: Percent of total	Total	Below poverty level: Number	Below poverty level: Percent of total
35 to 44 years	10,180	753	7.4	8,982	554	6.2	728	144	19.8	705	136	19.3
45 to 54 years	7,427	418	5.6	6,646	332	5.0	484	66	13.7	408	40	9.8
55 to 59 years	2,639	172	6.5	2,389	134	5.6	172	35	20.3	155	19	12.0
60 to 64 years	2,436	239	9.8	2,242	182	8.1	140	49	34.9	109	30	27.4
65 years and over	7,961	927	11.6	7,536	818	10.9	278	92	33.1	254	35	13.9
65 to 74 years	4,633	393	8.5	4,346	321	7.4	196	65	33.4	176	25	14.3
75 years and over	3,329	533	16.0	3,190	497	15.6	83	27	32.3	78	10	13.1
Household relationship												
Total	120,914	11,728	9.7	107,280	8,890	8.3	9,022	2,288	25.4	9,193	2,043	22.2
65 years and over	13,626	1,280	9.4	12,854	1,104	8.6	514	149	29.0	457	60	13.2
In families	104,998	8,817	8.4	92,963	6,439	6.9	7,825	1,931	24.7	8,255	1,737	21.0
Householder	32,964	2,520	7.6	29,609	1,876	6.3	2,266	525	23.2	2,158	417	19.3
Under 65 years	27,904	2,242	8.0	24,829	1,650	6.6	2,050	479	23.4	1,989	401	20.2
65 years and over	5,059	277	5.5	4,780	226	4.7	216	46	21.2	168	16	9.7
Related children under 18 years	31,223	4,313	13.8	26,853	3,075	11.5	2,930	1,033	35.3	3,006	885	29.4
Under 6 years	10,922	1,797	16.5	9,369	1,320	14.1	1,045	418	40.0	1,127	354	31.5
6 to 17 years	20,301	2,516	12.4	17,484	1,755	10.0	1,886	616	32.6	1,879	531	28.2
Own children 18 years and over	10,445	535	5.1	9,061	312	3.4	1,013	192	18.9	769	83	10.8
In married-coupled families	87,791	4,415	5.0	79,731	3,606	4.5	4,556	538	11.8	6,398	1,096	17.1
Husbands	27,014	1,156	4.3	24,878	956	3.8	1,259	130	10.3	1,624	245	15.1
Under 65 years	22,675	943	4.2	20,726	776	3.7	1,126	103	9.1	1,490	230	15.4
65 years and over	4,339	213	4.9	4,150	180	4.3	133	27	20.6	133	16	11.7
Wives	27,014	1,156	4.3	24,826	951	3.8	1,215	129	10.6	1,666	237	14.2
Under 65 years	23,638	999	4.2	21,574	815	3.8	1,132	115	10.2	1,584	227	14.5
65 years and over	3,376	157	4.7	3,252	136	4.2	83	14	17.2	102	10	9.4
Related children under 18 years	24,970	1,803	7.2	22,323	1,501	6.7	1,444	199	13.8	2,287	530	23.2
Under 6 years	8,894	757	8.5	7,923	625	7.9	521	91	17.4	862	218	25.3
6 to 17 years	16,076	1,047	6.5	14,400	877	6.1	924	108	11.7	1,425	312	21.9
Own children 18 years and over	7,420	213	2.9	6,602	125	1.9	527	66	12.6	522	38	7.3
In families with female householder, no spouse present	13,556	3,966	29.3	10,256	2,516	24.5	2,851	1,315	46.1	1,355	534	39.4
Householder	4,628	1,223	26.4	3,623	819	22.6	862	367	42.6	386	146	37.9
Under 65 years	3,998	1,164	29.1	3,072	781	25.4	790	346	43.8	359	144	40.1
65 years and over	629	59	9.4	551	39	7.0	71	21	B	26	2	B
Related children under 18 years	5,277	2,324	44.0	3,719	1,433	38.5	1,376	805	58.5	587	313	53.3
Under 6 years	1,671	958	57.3	1,144	632	55.3	476	309	64.5	202	115	56.6
6 to 17 years	3,606	1,367	37.9	2,575	801	31.1	898	496	55.2	384	198	51.5
Own children 18 years and over	2,480	289	11.7	1,990	161	8.1	429	121	28.2	214	43	20.0
In unrelated subfamilies	667	316	47.5	583	262	44.9	70	46	B	113	66	58.6
Under 18 years	353	189	53.5	308	156	50.8	40	28	B	54	40	B
Under 6 years	149	97	65.5	126	77	61.1	19	17	B	29	23	B
6 to 17 years	204	91	44.7	182	79	43.6	21	11	B	25	17	B
18 years and over	314	128	40.7	275	106	38.4	30	18	B	59	27	B
Unrelated individuals	15,249	2,595	17.0	13,733	2,189	15.9	1,126	311	27.6	826	240	29.1
Male	7,040	957	13.6	6,175	758	12.3	627	145	23.2	521	125	24.0
Under 65 years	6,138	845	13.8	5,366	675	12.6	556	120	21.6	503	118	23.5
Living alone	3,049	303	9.9	2,693	238	8.9	260	47	17.9	144	23	15.9
65 years and over	902	111	12.4	809	83	10.3	70	25	B	18	7	B
Living alone	771	93	12.0	695	68	9.7	61	22	B	15	5	B
Female	8,210	1,638	20.0	7,558	1,431	18.9	500	166	33.1	305	115	37.7
Under 65 years	4,984	956	19.2	4,459	811	18.2	400	113	28.2	251	99	39.5
Living alone	2,868	396	13.8	2,518	312	12.4	298	79	26.4	108	31	28.9
65 years and over	3,226	682	21.1	3,099	620	20.0	99	53	53.2	54	16	B
Living alone	3,088	637	20.6	2,975	580	19.5	92	50	54.5	50	15	B

Source: U.S. Bureau of the Census. *Poverty in the United States: 1992.* Current Population Reports, Series P60-185, U.S. Government Printing Office, Washington, D.C., 1993, p. 41. *Notes:* A (B) stands for base less than 75,000 or not applicable. 1. Persons of Hispanic origin may be of any race.

★ 616 ★

Poverty

Persons Living in Poverty in the United States, by Type of Residence, Age Group, and Sex, 1992: Outside Metropolitan Areas

Numbers are shown in thousands and refer to persons, families, and unrelated individuals, as of March of the following year.

Characteristic	All races			White			Black			Hispanic origin[1]		
	Total	Below poverty level Number	Below poverty level Percent of total	Total	Below poverty level Number	Below poverty level Percent of total	Total	Below poverty level Number	Below poverty level Percent of total	Total	Below poverty level Number	Below poverty level Percent of total
United States												
Outside Metropolitan areas												
Both sexes												
Total	56,711	9,509	16.8	50,425	7,175	14.2	4,841	1,977	40.8	1,711	627	36.7
Under 18 years	15,453	3,638	23.5	13,240	2,591	19.6	1,710	895	52.3	648	309	47.7
18 to 24 years	5,096	987	19.4	4,515	780	17.3	463	174	37.5	204	81	39.8
25 to 34 years	8,101	1,310	16.2	7,174	992	13.8	700	266	38.0	297	106	35.8
35 to 44 years	8,687	1,069	12.3	7,712	808	10.5	755	218	28.8	233	45	19.1
45 to 54 years	6,087	581	9.5	5,627	486	8.6	312	76	24.3	137	27	19.8
55 to 59 years	2,584	361	14.0	2,390	278	11.6	142	69	48.4	44	11	B
60 to 64 years	2,563	353	13.8	2,341	272	11.6	167	72	42.9	51	17	B
65 years and over	8,138	1,208	14.8	7,426	967	13.0	592	209	35.3	97	31	31.8
65 to 74 years	4,813	584	12.1	4,374	470	10.7	361	97	26.8	73	24	B
75 years and over	3,325	624	18.8	3,052	497	16.3	230	112	48.5	23	7	B
Male												
Total	27,769	4,172	15.0	24,781	3,201	12.9	2,276	813	35.7	857	307	35.9
Under 18 years	7,988	1,894	23.7	6,816	1,385	20.3	893	436	48.8	335	162	48.4
18 to 24 years	2,516	399	15.8	2,232	324	14.5	226	63	28.0	97	33	34.1
25 to 34 years	3,985	492	12.3	3,580	395	11.0	285	73	25.5	172	58	33.6
35 to 44 years	4,331	502	11.6	3,872	390	10.1	362	96	26.5	101	21	20.7
45 to 54 years	2,998	251	8.4	2,809	232	8.3	132	14	10.4	64	10	B
55 to 59 years	1,214	157	12.9	1,127	115	10.2	61	32	B	24	6	B
60 to 64 years	1,202	129	10.7	1,106	89	8.0	73	36	B	21	6	B
65 years and over	3,534	349	9.9	3,240	272	8.4	243	63	25.8	43	11	B
65 to 74 years	2,211	193	8.7	2,032	166	8.2	155	24	15.3	32	10	B
75 years and over	1,323	156	11.8	1,208	106	8.8	88	39	44.4	11	2	B
Female												
Total	28,942	5,337	18.4	25,644	3,974	15.5	2,565	1,164	45.4	854	320	37.4
Under 18 years	7,465	1,744	23.4	6,425	1,205	18.8	817	459	56.2	312	147	46.9
18 to 24 years	2,580	589	22.8	2,282	457	20.0	238	110	46.5	107	48	44.9
25 to 34 years	4,116	818	19.9	3,594	598	16.6	415	194	46.7	125	48	38.8
35 to 44 years	4,356	567	13.0	3,841	418	10.9	392	122	31.0	133	24	17.9
45 to 54 years	3,089	330	10.7	2,819	254	9.0	180	62	34.5	73	17	B
55 to 59 years	1,370	204	14.9	1,263	163	12.9	81	37	45.3	20	5	B
60 to 64 years	1,361	225	16.5	1,235	183	14.8	94	35	37.6	30	11	B
65 years and over	4,603	859	18.7	4,186	695	16.6	348	146	41.9	54	19	B
65 to 74 years	2,602	391	15.0	2,342	304	13.0	206	73	35.5	42	14	B
75 years and over	2,002	468	23.4	1,844	391	21.2	142	73	51.1	12	5	B
Household relationship												
Total	56,711	9,509	16.8	50,425	7,175	14.2	4,841	1,977	40.8	1,711	627	36.7
65 years and over	8,138	1,208	14.8	7,426	967	13.0	592	209	35.3	97	31	31.8
In families	49,219	7,185	14.6	43,684	5,189	11.9	4,284	1,720	40.1	1,499	507	33.8
Householder	15,844	2,053	13.0	14,283	1,516	10.6	1,240	467	37.6	399	117	29.4
Under 65 years	12,700	1,785	14.1	11,422	1,320	11.6	1,009	412	40.9	365	108	29.7
65 years and over	3,144	269	8.5	2,861	196	6.9	231	54	23.5	34	9	B
Related children under 18 years	15,125	3,401	22.5	12,938	2,370	18.3	1,697	886	52.2	613	280	45.6
Under 6 years	4,785	1,305	27.3	4,121	937	22.7	502	307	61.2	231	122	52.8
6 to 17 years	10,340	2,096	20.3	8,817	1,433	16.2	1,195	580	48.5	382	157	41.2
Own children 18 years and over	4,130	449	10.9	3,517	277	7.9	499	148	29.8	96	15	16.0
In married-coupled families	40,884	4,151	10.2	37,709	3,464	9.2	2,236	540	24.2	1,235	362	29.3
Husbands	12,934	1,079	8.3	12,103	910	7.5	610	134	22.0	323	81	24.9
Under 65 years	10,221	894	8.7	9,564	762	8.0	468	106	22.6	292	73	24.8
65 years and over	2,713	185	6.8	2,538	148	5.8	142	29	20.4	31	8	B

[Continued]

★ 616 ★

Persons Living in Poverty in the United States, by Type of Residence, Age Group, and Sex, 1992: Outside Metropolitan Areas

[Continued]

Characteristic	All races			White			Black			Hispanic origin[1]		
	Total	Below poverty level		Total	Below poverty level		Total	Below poverty level		Total	Below poverty level	
		Number	Percent of total		Number	Percent of total		Number	Percent of total		Number	Percent of total
Wives	12,934	1,079	8.3	12,076	917	7.6	589	130	22.1	342	82	23.9
Under 65 years	10,904	964	8.8	10,170	820	8.1	494	115	23.3	323	80	24.9
65 years and over	2,030	115	5.7	1,906	98	5.1	94	15	15.7	19	2	B
Related children under 18 years	11,572	1,711	14.6	10,610	1,423	13.4	787	222	28.3	474	180	38.1
Under 6 years	3,720	675	18.1	3,417	569	16.6	188	74	39.1	177	82	46.1
6 to 17 years	8,032	1,036	12.9	7,193	854	11.9	599	149	24.9	297	99	33.3
Own children 18 years and over	2,851	213	7.5	2,566	158	6.2	214	43	19.9	68	12	B
In families with female householder, no spouse present	6,655	2,689	40.4	4,592	1,460	31.8	1,817	1,123	61.8	179	103	57.4
Householder	2,276	850	37.3	1,642	504	30.7	558	318	56.9	51	25	B
Under 65 years	1,893	778	41.1	1,358	463	34.1	475	293	61.8	45	24	B
65 years and over	383	71	18.6	284	41	14.4	83	24	29.0	5	1	B
Related children under 18 years	2,823	1,548	54.8	1,847	822	44.5	863	659	76.3	95	70	73.5
Under 6 years	844	564	66.9	511	309	60.5	292	231	79.1	32	25	B
6 to 17 years	1,979	984	49.7	1,335	512	38.4	571	428	74.9	64	45	B
Own children 18 years and over	1,064	212	20.0	770	100	12.9	264	106	40.2	25	4	B
In unrelated subfamilies	443	282	63.7	403	266	66.1	22	8	B	47	39	B
Under 18 years	261	177	67.9	240	167	69.5	10	6	B	29	24	B
Under 6 years	83	62	74.7	78	60	76.9	3	-	B	16	13	B
6 to 17 years	177	115	64.8	162	107	66.0	8	6	B	12	11	B
18 years and over	182	105	57.5	163	99	61.1	12	2	B	18	15	B
Unrelated individuals	7,049	2,042	29.0	6,338	1,720	27.1	535	250	46.6	166	81	49.1
Male	3,127	694	22.2	2,771	574	20.7	272	90	33.1	83	34	40.5
Under 65 years	2,542	568	22.4	2,258	475	21.0	206	65	31.5	74	30	B
Living alone	1,431	247	17.3	1,304	210	16.1	88	24	27.6	26	4	B
65 years and over	585	126	21.5	514	99	19.3	67	25	B	9	3	B
Living alone	477	95	20.0	422	72	17.0	50	22	B	9	3	B
Female	3,923	1,348	34.4	3,567	1,146	32.1	263	159	60.6	83	48	57.7
Under 65 years	1,994	707	35.4	1,784	609	34.1	136	64	45.8	62	33	B
Living alone	1,195	339	28.3	1,055	282	26.7	104	45	43.4	22	7	B
65 years and over	1,928	641	33.3	1,783	537	30.1	127	96	75.5	21	15	B
Living alone	1,861	619	33.2	1,724	522	30.3	120	89	74.1	21	15	B

Source: U.S. Bureau of the Census. *Poverty in the United States: 1992.* Current Population Reports, Series P60-185, U.S. Government Printing Office, Washington, D.C., 1993, p. 42. *Notes:* A (B) stands for base less than 75,000 or not applicable. 1. Persons of Hispanic origin may be of any race.

★ 617 ★

Poverty

Persons Living in Poverty in the Midwest Region, by Type of Residence, Age Group, and Sex, 1992: Central Cities

Numbers are shown in thousands and refer to person, families, and unrelated individuals, as of March of the following year.

Characteristic	All races			White			Black			Hispanic origin[1]		
	Total	Below poverty level		Total	Below poverty level		Total	Below poverty level		Total	Below poverty level	
		Number	Percent of total		Number	Percent of total		Number	Percent of total		Number	Percent of total
Midwest												
Central Cities												
Both sexes												
Total	17,194	3,655	21.3	11,624	1,589	13.7	5,054	1,930	38.2	1,053	302	28.6
Under 18 years	4,636	1,547	33.4	2,704	568	21.0	1,776	920	51.8	380	154	40.5

[Continued]

★ 617 ★

Persons Living in Poverty in the Midwest Region, by Type of Residence, Age Group, and Sex, 1992: Central Cities

[Continued]

Characteristic	All races			White			Black			Hispanic origin[1]		
	Total	Below poverty level		Total	Below poverty level		Total	Below poverty level		Total	Below poverty level	
		Number	Percent of total		Number	Percent of total		Number	Percent of total		Number	Percent of total
18 to 24 years	1,879	480	25.6	1,265	264	20.9	536	196	36.5	133	33	25.1
25 to 34 years	3,324	586	17.6	2,377	257	10.8	823	308	37.4	198	43	21.8
35 to 44 years	2,465	332	13.5	1,733	135	7.8	669	181	27.0	167	33	19.5
45 to 54 years	1,584	168	10.6	1,146	89	7.8	409	73	17.7	84	23	27.7
55 to 59 years	614	83	13.5	401	29	7.3	194	48	24.9	28	5	B
60 to 64 years	651	78	11.9	442	38	8.6	195	40	20.4	16	2	B
65 years and over	2,042	381	18.7	1,556	209	13.4	452	165	36.6	47	8	B
65 to 74 years	1,119	206	18.4	814	99	12.2	277	103	37.3	33	4	B
75 years and over	922	176	19.0	742	110	14.8	175	62	35.3	14	4	B
Male												
Total	8,173	1,515	18.5	5,611	651	11.6	2,294	799	34.8	533	144	27.1
Under 18 years	2,276	772	33.9	1,329	277	20.8	866	466	53.8	198	86	43.4
18 to 24 years	951	177	18.6	655	98	15.0	256	71	27.7	58	13	B
25 to 34 years	1,612	203	12.6	1,197	103	8.6	344	91	26.6	104	16	15.6
35 to 44 years	1,149	119	10.4	845	56	6.7	276	56	20.1	83	13	15.1
45 to 54 years	762	79	10.3	572	43	7.4	176	32	18.4	49	14	B
55 to 59 years	284	24	8.4	194	10	5.3	85	12	14.0	11	1	B
60 to 64 years	294	19	6.3	198	10	5.2	91	8	9.2	10	-	B
65 years and over	845	123	14.5	621	53	8.5	200	63	31.5	19	2	B
65 to 74 years	497	68	13.6	347	24	6.9	132	41	31.0	12	2	B
75 years and over	348	55	15.8	275	29	10.6	69	22	B	7	-	B
Female												
Total	9,020	2,140	23.7	6,013	938	15.6	2,760	1,131	41.0	520	158	30.3
Under 18 years	2,360	776	32.9	1,375	291	21.2	910	454	49.9	182	68	37.3
18 to 24 years	928	303	32.7	610	166	27.2	280	125	44.6	75	21	B
25 to 34 years	1,711	382	22.3	1,181	154	13.1	479	216	45.1	94	27	28.8
35 to 44 years	1,315	213	16.2	887	78	8.8	393	125	31.9	84	20	23.9
45 to 54 years	822	89	10.9	574	47	8.1	234	40	17.2	35	9	B
55 to 59 years	330	59	17.9	207	19	9.1	109	36	33.4	17	3	B
60 to 64 years	357	59	16.5	244	28	11.3	104	31	30.2	6	2	B
65 years and over	1,197	259	21.6	935	156	16.7	252	102	40.6	28	7	B
65 to 74 years	622	138	22.2	467	75	16.1	145	62	43.1	21	3	B
75 years and over	575	121	21.0	467	81	17.3	107	40	37.2	7	4	B
Household relationship												
Total	17,194	3,655	21.3	11,624	1,589	13.7	5,054	1,930	38.2	1,053	302	28.6
65 years and over	2,042	381	18.7	1,556	209	13.4	452	165	36.6	47	8	B
In families	13,651	2,772	20.3	8,972	1,050	11.7	4,272	1,628	38.1	947	275	29.1
Householder	4,309	792	18.4	2,971	319	10.7	1,226	449	36.7	244	64	26.2
Under 65 years	3,631	701	19.3	2,458	277	11.3	1,076	404	37.5	228	61	26.8
65 years and over	678	90	13.3	513	42	8.1	150	46	30.4	16	3	B
Related children under 18 years	4,555	1,485	32.6	2,656	536	20.2	1,750	897	51.2	375	152	40.5
Under 6 years	1,706	636	37.3	1,029	229	22.2	621	388	62.5	115	51	44.3
6 to 17 years	2,849	849	29.8	1,626	307	18.9	1,129	509	45.1	260	101	38.8
Own children 18 years and over	1,419	191	13.4	817	47	5.8	584	142	24.3	83	19	22.7
In married-coupled families	8,981	813	9.1	7,071	497	7.0	1,635	255	15.6	694	147	21.1
Husbands	2,768	200	7.2	2,252	121	5.4	448	65	14.5	169	30	18.0
Under 65 years	2,240	141	6.3	1,825	88	4.8	357	41	11.6	156	29	18.5
65 years and over	528	59	11.1	428	32	7.5	91	24	26.1	13	2	B
Wives	2,768	200	7.2	2,260	125	5.5	429	62	14.4	171	30	17.3
Under 65 years	2,379	156	6.6	1,929	100	5.2	377	43	11.4	161	29	18.1
65 years and over	389	44	11.3	331	25	7.4	53	19	B	10	-	B
Related children under 18 years	2,551	341	13.4	1,948	219	11.2	508	94	18.5	258	67	26.0
Under 6 years	963	149	15.4	777	94	12.1	143	40	28.3	77	21	27.2
6 to 17 years	1,588	193	12.1	1,171	124	10.6	364	53	14.6	181	46	25.5
Own children 18 years and over	723	47	6.5	523	21	3.9	186	25	13.4	63	11	B

[Continued]

★ 617 ★

Persons Living in Poverty in the Midwest Region, by Type of Residence, Age Group, and Sex, 1992: Central Cities

[Continued]

Characteristic	All races			White			Black			Hispanic origin[1]		
	Total	Below poverty level Number	Below poverty level Percent of total	Total	Below poverty level Number	Below poverty level Percent of total	Total	Below poverty level Number	Below poverty level Percent of total	Total	Below poverty level Number	Below poverty level Percent of total
In families with female householder, no spouse present	3,985	1,820	45.7	1,512	495	32.7	2,382	1,293	54.3	202	123	60.9
Householder	1,293	540	41.8	568	174	30.6	695	357	51.4	58	33	B
Under 65 years	1,182	514	43.5	504	166	33.0	648	339	52.3	56	31	B
65 years and over	111	26	23.3	64	8	B	46	18	B	3	1	B
Related children under 18 years	1,832	1,087	59.4	613	296	48.3	1,172	768	65.5	106	81	76.4
Under 6 years	668	466	69.6	217	128	59.2	439	331	75.3	35	29	B
6 to 17 years	1,163	622	53.5	396	167	42.3	733	437	59.6	71	52	B
Own children 18 years and over	601	127	21.2	221	19	8.5	375	109	29.0	20	8	B
In unrelated subfamilies	119	87	73.2	75	48	64.2	34	29	B	11	6	B
Under 18 years	73	57	B	44	31	B	23	20	B	6	2	B
Under 6 years	35	27	B	23	15	B	11	11	B	3	2	B
6 to 17 years	38	30	B	21	16	B	12	9	B	3	1	B
18 years and over	46	30	B	32	18	B	11	9	B	6	3	B
Unrelated individuals	3,424	796	23.2	2,576	491	19.0	747	273	36.6	95	21	21.6
Male	1,634	311	19.0	1,186	181	15.3	377	113	30.1	52	8	B
Under 65 years	1,419	257	18.1	1,040	163	15.7	310	78	25.1	48	8	B
Living alone	675	99	14.7	500	59	11.8	160	37	23.0	24	4	B
65 years and over	215	54	24.9	146	18	12.2	67	36	B	4	-	B
Living alone	187	42	22.6	128	15	11.4	59	28	B	4	-	B
Female	1,790	485	27.1	1,390	309	22.3	370	160	43.2	42	12	B
Under 65 years	1,182	304	25.7	912	190	20.8	240	98	40.9	32	7	B
Living alone	653	138	21.1	468	78	16.7	172	57	32.9	12	1	B
65 years and over	608	181	29.8	478	119	25.0	131	62	47.4	11	5	B
Living alone	583	170	29.1	455	108	23.7	128	62	48.2	9	3	B

Source: U.S. Bureau of the Census. *Poverty in the United States: 1992.* Current Population Reports, Series P60-185, U.S. Government Printing Office, Washington, D.C., 1993, p. 48. *Notes:* A (B) stands for base less than 75,000 or not applicable. 1. Persons of Hispanic origin may be of any race.

★ 618 ★

Poverty

Persons Living in Poverty in the Midwest Region, by Type of Residence, Age Group, and Sex, 1992: Metropolitan Areas

Numbers are shown in thousands and refer to persons, families, and unrelated individuals, as of March of the following year.

Characteristic	All races			White			Black			Hispanic origin[1]		
	Total	Below poverty level Number	Below poverty level Percent of total	Total	Below poverty level Number	Below poverty level Percent of total	Total	Below poverty level Number	Below poverty level Percent of total	Total	Below poverty level Number	Below poverty level Percent of total
Midwest												
Metropolitan areas												
Both sexes												
Total	43,309	5,510	12.7	36,095	3,133	8.7	6,347	2,217	34.9	1,548	422	27.2
Under 18 years	11,645	2,256	19.4	9,148	1,126	12.3	2,214	1,069	48.3	530	207	39.1
18 to 24 years	4,279	711	16.6	3,463	451	13.0	698	231	33.2	204	52	25.4
25 to 34 years	7,520	896	11.9	6,312	514	8.1	1,041	355	34.1	296	68	22.9
35 to 44 years	6,958	506	7.3	5,934	289	4.9	886	196	22.1	253	49	19.5
45 to 54 years	4,652	274	5.9	4,044	175	4.3	548	92	16.9	138	25	18.0
55 to 59 years	1,816	148	8.2	1,558	89	5.7	226	52	22.9	36	6	B
60 to 64 years	1,697	121	7.1	1,457	77	5.3	212	45	21.0	21	4	B
65 years and over	4,744	599	12.6	4,179	413	9.9	520	177	34.1	71	11	B
65 to 74 years	2,792	274	9.8	2,435	158	6.5	321	113	35.3	53	6	B

[Continued]

★ 618 ★

Persons Living in Poverty in the Midwest Region, by Type of Residence, Age Group, and Sex, 1992: Metropolitan Areas

[Continued]

Characteristic	All races			White			Black			Hispanic origin[1]		
	Total	Below poverty level Number	Below poverty level Percent of total	Total	Below poverty level Number	Below poverty level Percent of total	Total	Below poverty level Number	Below poverty level Percent of total	Total	Below poverty level Number	Below poverty level Percent of total
75 years and over	1,952	324	16.6	1,743	256	14.7	199	64	32.0	18	4	B
Male												
Total	20,991	2,272	10.8	17,623	1,273	7.2	2,913	919	31.5	792	206	26.0
Under 18 years	5,853	1,131	19.3	4,629	565	12.2	1,079	538	49.8	278	114	41.0
18 to 24 years	2,185	270	12.4	1,781	172	9.7	338	84	24.9	98	26	27.0
25 to 34 years	3,677	310	8.4	3,134	187	6.0	446	109	24.5	157	26	16.6
35 to 44 years	3,368	186	5.5	2,917	116	4.0	384	60	15.5	125	19	15.6
45 to 54 years	2,252	125	5.5	1,981	79	4.0	239	42	17.6	74	14	B
55 to 59 years	895	48	5.4	781	33	4.2	101	12	11.9	16	3	B
60 to 64 years	849	34	3.9	738	25	3.4	103	8	8.1	14	1	B
65 years and over	1,911	168	8.8	1,662	96	5.8	223	66	29.4	31	3	B
65 to 74 years	1,206	84	7.0	1,042	38	3.7	144	43	30.0	22	3	B
75 years and over	705	83	11.8	621	58	9.3	79	22	28.2	9	-	B
Female												
Total	22,319	3,238	14.5	18,472	1,860	10.1	3,434	1,299	37.8	756	215	28.5
Under 18 years	5,791	1,125	19.4	4,519	561	12.4	1,135	532	46.8	252	93	37.0
18 to 24 years	2,094	441	21.0	1,682	279	16.6	360	147	40.9	106	25	23.9
25 to 34 years	3,842	586	15.2	3,178	326	10.3	595	246	41.3	139	42	30.0
35 to 44 years	3,590	320	8.9	3,018	173	5.7	503	136	27.1	128	30	23.3
45 to 54 years	2,400	149	6.2	2,063	96	4.7	309	50	16.3	64	11	B
55 to 59 years	921	100	10.8	777	56	7.2	125	40	31.7	20	3	B
60 to 64 years	848	88	10.3	719	51	7.2	110	36	33.0	7	3	B
65 years and over	2,833	431	15.2	2,516	317	12.6	297	112	37.6	40	8	B
65 to 74 years	1,586	190	12.0	1,394	119	8.6	177	70	39.6	31	4	B
75 years and over	1,247	241	19.3	1,123	198	17.6	120	41	34.6	9	4	B
Household relationship												
Total	43,309	5,510	12.7	36,095	3,133	8.7	6,347	2,217	34.9	1,548	422	27.2
65 years and over	4,744	599	12.6	4,179	413	9.9	520	177	34.1	71	11	B
In families	36,351	4,057	11.2	30,204	2,061	6.8	5,434	1,893	34.8	1,382	387	28.0
Householder	11,472	1,177	10.3	9,713	627	6.5	1,567	523	33.4	376	97	25.9
Under 65 years	9,823	1,059	10.8	8,258	562	6.8	1,391	473	34.0	352	93	26.6
65 years and over	1,649	117	7.1	1,455	64	4.4	176	50	28.4	25	4	B
Related children under 18 years	11,483	2,147	18.7	9,019	1,046	11.6	2,188	1,046	47.8	524	204	39.0
Under 6 years	4,007	947	23.6	3,154	477	15.1	762	450	59.0	180	73	40.4
6 to 17 years	7,476	1,199	16.0	5,865	570	9.7	1,426	596	41.8	344	132	38.3
Own children 18 years and over	3,603	246	6.8	2,831	85	3.0	730	158	21.7	111	21	18.5
In married-coupled families	28,506	1,445	5.1	25,663	1,043	4.1	2,300	337	14.7	1,033	224	21.7
Husbands	8,782	357	4.1	8,015	261	3.3	631	80	12.7	265	47	17.9
Under 65 years	7,388	274	3.7	6,742	207	3.1	522	54	10.4	244	45	18.4
65 years and over	1,394	83	5.9	1,273	54	4.2	108	26	24.1	20	3	B
Wives	8,782	357	4.1	8,038	265	3.3	605	77	12.7	260	48	18.4
Under 65 years	7,741	298	3.8	7,069	225	3.2	541	58	10.7	247	46	18.7
65 years and over	1,041	59	5.7	970	40	4.1	64	19	B	13	2	B
Related children under 18 years	8,313	627	7.5	7,366	463	6.3	742	135	18.2	381	106	27.9
Under 6 years	2,893	271	9.4	2,619	202	7.7	197	55	28.0	127	36	28.1
6 to 17 years	5,421	355	6.6	4,747	261	5.5	544	79	14.6	254	71	27.8
Own children 18 years and over	2,312	67	2.9	2,044	37	1.8	234	28	11.9	84	11	12.6
In families with female householder, no spouse present	6,503	2,387	36.7	3,560	889	25.0	2,823	1,465	51.9	258	138	53.6
Householder	2,178	731	33.6	1,313	314	23.9	826	409	49.5	82	40	49.3
Under 65 years	1,955	700	35.8	1,152	304	26.4	766	386	50.4	78	39	49.6
65 years and over	223	32	14.2	161	9	5.7	61	23	B	3	1	B
Related children under 18 years	2,823	1,423	50.4	1,392	526	37.8	1,370	873	63.7	119	86	72.2
Under 6 years	980	630	64.3	442	248	56.2	524	375	71.6	40	31	B
6 to 17 years	1,843	792	43.0	950	277	29.2	846	498	58.8	79	55	69.5
Own children 18 years and over	1,076	158	14.7	611	36	5.9	459	122	26.6	27	10	B

[Continued]

★ 618 ★

Persons Living in Poverty in the Midwest Region, by Type of Residence, Age Group, and Sex, 1992: Metropolitan Areas

[Continued]

Characteristic	All races			White			Black			Hispanic origin[1]		
	Total	Below poverty level		Total	Below poverty level		Total	Below poverty level		Total	Below poverty level	
		Number	Percent of total		Number	Percent of total		Number	Percent of total		Number	Percent of total
In unrelated subfamilies	249	154	61.9	203	116	56.8	34	29	B	13	7	B
Under 18 years	143	95	66.8	113	69	60.7	23	20	B	6	3	B
Under 6 years	54	37	B	41	25	B	11	11	B	3	2	B
6 to 17 years	89	58	65.7	72	44	B	12	9	B	3	1	B
18 years and over	106	59	55.2	90	47	51.9	11	9	B	7	4	B
Unrelated individuals	6,710	1,299	19.4	5,688	957	16.8	879	295	33.6	153	27	17.9
Male	3,083	468	15.2	2,550	318	12.5	436	122	27.9	87	9	10.1
Under 65 years	2,708	394	14.6	2,247	281	12.5	367	86	23.4	79	9	11.1
Living alone	1,387	150	10.8	1,164	103	8.8	194	38	19.7	35	4	B
65 years and over	375	73	19.6	303	38	12.4	69	36	B	7	-	B
Living alone	333	61	18.5	272	34	12.4	61	28	B	6	-	B
Female	3,626	831	22.9	3,138	639	20.4	443	173	39.2	67	19	B
Under 65 years	2,251	502	22.3	1,908	376	19.7	298	108	36.4	54	13	B
Living alone	1,301	224	17.2	1,055	153	14.5	222	67	30.2	24	2	B
65 years and over	1,376	329	23.9	1,230	263	21.4	144	65	45.1	13	5	B
Living alone	1,314	309	23.5	1,171	243	20.7	142	65	45.8	11	3	B

Source: U.S. Bureau of the Census. *Poverty in the United States: 1992.* Current Population Reports, Series P60-185, U.S. Government Printing Office, Washington, D.C., 1993, p. 47. *Notes:* A dash (-) stands for zero or rounds to zero. A (B) stands for base less than 75,000 or not applicable. 1. Persons of Hispanic origin may be of any race.

★ 619 ★

Poverty

Persons Living in Poverty in the Midwest Region, by Type of Residence, Age Group, and Sex, 1992: Not in Central Cities

Numbers are shown in thousands and refer to persons, families, and unrelated individuals, as of March of the following year.

Characteristic	All races			White			Black			Hispanic origin[1]		
	Total	Below poverty level		Total	Below poverty level		Total	Below poverty level		Total	Below poverty level	
		Number	Percent of total		Number	Percent of total		Number	Percent of total		Number	Percent of total
Midwest												
Not in Central Cities												
Both sexes												
Total	26,116	1,855	7.1	24,472	1,544	6.3	1,293	287	22.2	495	120	24.2
Under 18 years	7,009	709	10.1	6,444	557	8.7	439	149	34.0	149	53	35.6
18 to 24 years	2,400	231	9.6	2,198	188	8.5	162	36	22.1	71	18	B
25 to 34 years	4,196	310	7.4	3,934	256	6.5	219	47	21.7	98	25	25.0
35 to 44 years	4,493	174	3.9	4,202	155	3.7	217	15	7.0	86	17	19.5
45 to 54 years	3,068	106	3.4	2,898	86	3.0	139	20	14.4	54	2	B
55 to 59 years	1,202	65	5.4	1,157	59	5.1	32	3	B	8	2	B
60 to 64 years	1,045	44	4.2	1,015	39	3.8	18	5	B	5	2	B
65 years and over	2,703	218	8.0	2,622	204	7.8	68	12	B	24	2	B
65 to 74 years	1,673	69	4.1	1,621	59	3.6	45	10	B	20	2	B
75 years and over	1,030	149	14.4	1,001	145	14.5	23	2	B	4	-	B
Male												
Total	12,817	757	5.9	12,012	622	5.2	619	119	19.3	260	62	23.9
Under 18 years	3,578	360	10.0	3,300	288	8.7	213	72	33.7	80	28	35.1
18 to 24 years	1,234	93	7.6	1,127	74	6.6	82	14	16.5	40	14	B
25 to 34 years	2,065	107	5.2	1,937	84	4.3	102	18	17.4	53	10	B
35 to 44 years	2,218	66	3.0	2,072	60	2.9	107	4	3.7	42	7	B
45 to 54 years	1,490	46	3.1	1,409	36	2.6	64	10	B	26	-	B

[Continued]

★ 619 ★

Persons Living in Poverty in the Midwest Region, by Type of Residence, Age Group, and Sex, 1992: Not in Central Cities

[Continued]

Characteristic	All races Total	All races Below poverty level Number	All races Below poverty level Percent of total	White Total	White Below poverty level Number	White Below poverty level Percent of total	Black Total	Black Below poverty level Number	Black Below poverty level Percent of total	Hispanic origin[1] Total	Hispanic origin[1] Below poverty level Number	Hispanic origin[1] Below poverty level Percent of total
55 to 59 years	611	24	4.0	587	22	3.8	15	-	B	5	2	B
60 to 64 years	555	15	2.7	540	15	2.8	12	-	B	3	1	B
65 years and over	1,066	45	4.2	1,041	43	4.1	23	2	B	12	1	B
65 to 74 years	709	17	2.4	695	14	2.1	13	2	B	10	1	B
75 years and over	358	28	7.9	346	28	8.2	10	-	B	2	-	B
Female												
Total	13,298	1,098	8.3	12,460	922	7.4	674	168	24.9	236	58	24.6
Under 18 years	3,431	349	10.2	3,144	270	8.6	225	77	34.3	70	25	B
18 to 24 years	1,166	137	11.8	1,072	114	10.6	80	22	27.8	31	5	B
25 to 34 years	2,131	203	9.5	1,997	172	8.6	116	30	25.4	45	15	B
35 to 44 years	2,275	107	4.7	2,130	95	4.5	110	11	10.1	44	10	B
45 to 54 years	1,578	60	3.8	1,489	49	3.3	75	10	13.4	29	2	B
55 to 59 years	591	41	6.9	571	37	6.5	16	3	B	3	-	B
60 to 64 years	491	29	5.9	475	24	5.0	6	5	B	2	1	B
65 years and over	1,636	172	10.5	1,582	161	10.2	45	9	B	12	1	B
65 to 74 years	964	52	5.4	926	44	4.8	32	8	B	10	1	B
75 years and over	672	120	17.9	655	117	17.9	13	2	B	2	-	B
Household relationship												
Total	26,116	1,855	7.1	24,472	1,544	6.3	1,293	287	22.2	495	120	24.2
65 years and over	2,703	218	8.0	2,622	204	7.8	68	12	B	24	2	B
In families	22,700	1,285	5.7	21,231	1,010	4.8	1,162	266	22.9	435	112	25.7
Householder	7,163	385	5.4	6,742	308	4.6	341	74	21.6	132	33	25.3
Under 65 years	6,193	358	5.8	5,800	285	4.9	315	69	22.0	124	32	26.1
65 years and over	971	27	2.8	942	23	2.4	26	4	B	8	1	B
Related children under 18 years	6,928	662	9.5	6,363	510	8.0	439	149	34.0	149	53	35.3
Under 6 years	2,301	311	13.5	2,125	248	11.7	142	62	43.8	64	22	B
6 to 17 years	4,627	351	7.6	4,239	262	6.2	297	87	29.3	84	31	36.7
Own children 18 years and over	2,183	56	2.5	2,015	38	1.9	146	16	11.1	28	2	B
In married-coupled families	19,524	632	3.2	18,593	547	2.9	665	82	12.4	339	77	22.7
Husbands	6,014	157	2.6	5,763	140	2.4	183	15	8.4	95	17	17.9
Under 65 years	5,148	133	2.6	4,918	119	2.4	165	13	7.8	88	16	18.2
65 years and over	865	24	2.7	845	21	2.5	18	2	B	7	1	B
Wives	6,014	157	2.6	5,778	140	2.4	176	15	8.7	89	18	20.5
Under 65 years	5,362	142	2.6	5,140	125	2.4	165	15	9.3	86	17	19.9
65 years and over	652	15	2.3	638	15	2.3	11	-	B	3	1	B
Related children under 18 years	5,762	285	5.0	5,418	244	4.5	234	41	17.4	124	40	32.0
Under 6 years	1,930	123	6.4	1,843	108	5.9	54	15	B	50	15	B
6 to 17 years	3,833	163	4.2	3,575	136	3.8	180	26	14.5	73	25	B
Own children 18 years and over	1,589	20	1.2	1,521	17	1.1	48	3	B	21	-	B
In families with female householder, no spouse present	2,518	567	22.5	2,048	395	19.3	442	172	38.9	56	15	B
Householder	885	191	21.6	745	140	18.7	132	52	39.4	23	8	B
Under 65 years	774	186	24.0	648	138	21.3	117	47	40.5	22	8	B
65 years and over	112	6	5.2	97	1	1.4	14	4	B	1	-	B
Related children under 18 years	991	335	33.8	779	230	29.5	198	105	53.1	13	5	B
Under 6 years	311	165	52.9	225	120	53.3	85	44	52.4	5	2	B
6 to 17 years	680	171	25.1	554	110	19.8	113	61	53.6	8	3	B
Own children 18 years and over	475	30	6.4	390	17	4.4	83	13	15.7	7	2	B
In unrelated subfamilies	130	67	51.5	128	67	52.4	-	-	B	2	1	B
Under 18 years	70	38	B	70	38	B	-	-	B	1	1	B
Under 6 years	18	10	B	18	10	B	-	-	B	1	1	B
6 to 17 years	51	29	B	51	29	B	-	-	B	-	-	B
18 years and over	61	29	B	58	29	B	-	-	B	2	1	B
Unrelated individuals	3,285	503	15.3	3,112	467	15.0	131	22	16.7	58	7	B
Male	1,449	157	10.8	1,364	137	10.0	59	8	B	34	1	B
Under 65 years	1,289	137	10.6	1,206	117	9.7	57	8	B	31	1	B

[Continued]

★ 619 ★

Persons Living in Poverty in the Midwest Region, by Type of Residence, Age Group, and Sex, 1992: Not in Central Cities

[Continued]

Characteristic	All races			White			Black			Hispanic origin[1]		
	Total	Below poverty level		Total	Below poverty level		Total	Below poverty level		Total	Below poverty level	
		Number	Percent of total		Number	Percent of total		Number	Percent of total		Number	Percent of total
Living alone	712	50	7.1	664	44	6.6	34	2	B	11	-	B
65 years and over	160	20	12.5	158	20	12.6	2	-	B	3	-	B
Living alone	145	19	13.1	144	19	13.2	2	-	B	2	-	B
Female	1,836	346	18.9	1,748	330	18.9	72	14	B	24	6	B
Under 65 years	1,069	198	18.5	996	186	18.7	59	11	B	22	6	B
Living alone	648	86	13.3	587	75	12.7	50	11	B	12	2	B
65 years and over	768	148	19.3	752	144	19.1	14	3	B	2	-	B
Living alone	731	139	19.1	715	135	18.8	14	3	B	2	-	B

Source: U.S. Bureau of the Census. *Poverty in the United States: 1992.* Current Population Reports, Series P60-185, U.S. Government Printing Office, Washington, D.C., 1993, p. 49. *Notes:* A dash (-) stands for zero or rounds to zero. A (B) stands for base less than 75,000 or not applicable. 1. Persons of Hispanic origin may be of any race.

★ 620 ★

Poverty

Persons Living in Poverty in the Midwest Region, by Type of Residence, Age Group, and Sex, 1992: Outside Metropolitan Areas

Numbers are shown in thousands and refer to persons, families, and unrelated individuals, as of March of the following year.

Characteristic	All races			White			Black			Hispanic origin[1]		
	Total	Below poverty level		Total	Below poverty level		Total	Below poverty level		Total	Below poverty level	
		Number	Percent of total		Number	Percent of total		Number	Percent of total		Number	Percent of total
Midwest												
Outside Metropolitan areas												
Both sexes												
Total	17,621	2,473	14.0	17,114	2,255	13.2	210	122	58.1	110	30	27.6
Under 18 years	4,870	962	19.7	4,650	853	18.3	91	57	62.4	31	12	B
18 to 24 years	1,632	286	17.5	1,585	263	16.6	25	18	B	18	5	B
25 to 34 years	2,593	392	15.1	2,502	345	13.8	46	28	B	26	7	B
35 to 44 years	2,567	256	10.0	2,511	241	9.6	17	5	B	17	2	B
45 to 54 years	1,856	137	7.4	1,820	133	7.3	11	2	B	7	1	B
55 to 59 years	806	100	12.5	787	91	11.5	5	5	B	4	3	B
60 to 64 years	850	85	10.0	837	80	9.5	5	2	B	4	-	B
65 years and over	2,448	255	10.4	2,423	249	10.3	10	5	B	2	1	B
65 to 74 years	1,457	113	7.8	1,444	112	7.7	-	-	B	2	1	B
75 years and over	991	142	14.3	978	137	14.0	10	5	B	-	-	B
Male												
Total	8,658	1,073	12.4	8,438	989	11.7	85	47	55.5	53	10	B
Under 18 years	2,487	504	20.3	2,383	457	19.2	40	27	B	17	4	B
18 to 24 years	787	111	14.1	772	104	13.5	5	5	B	12	3	B
25 to 34 years	1,310	133	10.2	1,267	117	9.2	20	8	B	11	2	B
35 to 44 years	1,337	134	10.1	1,312	127	9.7	9	5	B	5	1	B
45 to 54 years	904	69	7.6	884	66	7.5	8	2	B	3	-	B
55 to 59 years	371	33	8.9	366	32	8.6	-	-	B	-	-	B
60 to 64 years	399	32	8.1	399	32	8.1	-	-	B	2	-	B
65 years and over	1,064	56	5.3	1,055	55	5.2	2	-	B	1	-	B
65 to 74 years	672	31	4.6	666	30	4.5	-	-	B	1	-	B
75 years and over	391	25	6.4	388	25	6.5	2	-	B	-	-	B
Female												
Total	8,963	1,401	15.6	8,677	1,266	14.6	125	75	60.0	58	21	B

[Continued]

★ 620 ★

Persons Living in Poverty in the Midwest Region, by Type of Residence, Age Group, and Sex, 1992: Outside Metropolitan Areas

[Continued]

Characteristic	All races			White			Black			Hispanic origin[1]		
	Total	Below poverty level: Number	Below poverty level: Percent of total	Total	Below poverty level: Number	Below poverty level: Percent of total	Total	Below poverty level: Number	Below poverty level: Percent of total	Total	Below poverty level: Number	Below poverty level: Percent of total
Under 18 years	2,383	458	19.2	2,267	396	17.5	51	30	B	14	7	B
18 to 24 years	845	176	20.8	813	159	19.5	20	13	B	6	3	B
25 to 34 years	1,283	259	20.2	1,235	229	18.5	26	20	B	15	5	B
35 to 44 years	1,230	122	9.9	1,199	115	9.6	8	-	B	12	1	B
45 to 54 years	952	68	7.1	935	67	7.2	2	-	B	4	1	B
55 to 59 years	434	67	15.5	422	59	14.0	5	5	B	4	3	B
60 to 64 years	451	53	11.7	438	48	10.9	5	2	B	2	-	B
65 years and over	1,385	199	14.4	1,368	194	14.2	8	5	B	2	1	B
65 to 74 years	785	82	10.4	778	82	10.5	-	-	B	2	1	B
75 years and over	600	117	19.5	590	112	19.0	8	5	B	-	-	B
Household relationship												
Total	17,621	2,473	14.0	17,114	2,255	13.2	210	122	58.1	110	30	27.6
65 years and over	2,448	255	10.4	2,423	249	10.3	10	5	B	2	1	B
In families	15,119	1,748	11.6	14,687	1,567	10.7	178	107	60.0	83	15	17.7
Householder	4,854	493	10.2	4,742	437	9.2	55	38	B	24	5	B
Under 65 years	3,919	447	11.4	3,817	392	10.3	53	38	B	24	5	B
65 years and over	935	47	5.0	925	45	4.9	2	-	B	-	-	B
Related children under 18 years	4,742	873	18.4	4,526	766	16.9	91	57	62.4	26	7	B
Under 6 years	1,519	360	23.7	1,434	304	21.2	46	33	B	15	4	B
6 to 17 years	3,223	513	15.9	3,092	462	14.9	45	24	B	10	3	B
Own children 18 years and over	1,243	86	7.0	1,206	86	7.2	12	-	B	5	1	B
In married-coupled families	12,842	1,027	8.0	12,591	975	7.7	66	20	B	70	9	B
Husbands	4,045	261	6.5	3,988	244	6.1	17	8	B	17	3	B
Under 65 years	3,206	228	7.1	3,156	213	6.7	16	8	B	17	3	B
65 years and over	840	33	3.9	833	32	3.8	2	-	B	-	-	B
Wives	4,045	261	6.5	3,986	249	6.3	15	7	B	23	2	B
Under 65 years	3,411	236	6.9	3,359	224	6.7	14	7	B	23	2	B
65 years and over	634	25	4.0	627	25	4.0	2	-	B	-	-	B
Related children under 18 years	3,775	455	12.1	3,660	432	11.8	30	5	B	22	4	B
Under 6 years	1,177	178	15.1	1,145	166	14.5	9	-	B	12	3	B
6 to 17 years	2,598	277	10.7	2,515	266	10.6	21	5	B	9	2	B
Own children 18 years and over	907	41	4.5	887	41	4.6	3	-	B	3	-	B
In families with female householder, no spouse present	1,758	636	36.2	1,593	510	32.0	107	86	81.0	9	6	B
Householder	608	198	32.6	559	160	28.6	35	30	B	5	2	B
Under 65 years	528	185	35.0	482	147	30.4	35	30	B	5	2	B
65 years and over	80	13	16.7	77	13	17.3	-	-	B	-	-	B
Related children under 18 years	770	378	49.1	675	296	43.9	58	52	B	3	3	B
Under 6 years	244	160	65.8	193	117	60.7	36	33	B	2	2	B
6 to 17 years	526	218	41.4	482	179	37.2	22	19	B	1	1	B
Own children 18 years and over	284	40	14.0	270	40	14.8	9	-	B	1	1	B
In unrelated subfamilies	170	108	63.3	165	105	63.7	-	-	B	8	6	B
Under 18 years	104	69	65.9	101	67	66.5	-	-	B	3	2	B
Under 6 years	30	19	B	28	18	B	-	-	B	2	2	B
6 to 17 years	74	50	B	73	49	B	-	-	B	1	-	B
18 years and over	66	39	B	65	38	B	-	-	B	5	4	B
Unrelated individuals	2,332	617	26.5	2,262	583	25.8	32	15	B	19	9	B
Male	1,077	210	19.5	1,038	194	18.7	22	9	B	8	2	B
Under 65 years	901	187	20.7	864	171	19.8	22	9	B	7	2	B
Living alone	479	61	12.7	469	58	12.3	1	-	B	2	-	B
65 years and over	176	23	13.1	174	23	13.2	-	-	B	1	-	B
Living alone	150	19	12.9	148	19	13.0	-	-	B	1	-	B
Female	1,256	408	32.5	1,224	389	31.8	10	6	B	11	8	B
Under 65 years	646	252	39.0	619	236	38.2	5	3	B	10	7	B
Living alone	353	110	31.1	342	105	30.7	2	-	B	2	1	B

[Continued]

★ 620 ★

Persons Living in Poverty in the Midwest Region, by Type of Residence, Age Group, and Sex, 1992: Outside Metropolitan Areas

[Continued]

Characteristic	All races			White			Black			Hispanic origin[1]		
	Total	Below poverty level		Total	Below poverty level		Total	Below poverty level		Total	Below poverty level	
		Number	Percent of total		Number	Percent of total		Number	Percent of total		Number	Percent of total
65 years and over	610	155	25.5	605	153	25.2	4	3	B	1	1	B
Living alone	593	154	25.9	588	151	25.6	4	3	B	1	1	B

Source: U.S. Bureau of the Census. *Poverty in the United States: 1992.* Current Population Reports, Series P60-185, U.S. Government Printing Office, Washington, D.C., 1993, p. 50. *Notes:* A dash (-) stands for zero or rounds to zero. A (B) stands for base less than 75,000 or not applicable. 1. Persons of Hispanic origin may be of any race.

★ 621 ★

Poverty

Persons Living in Poverty in the Northeast Region, by Type of Residence, Age Group, and Sex, 1992: Central Cities

Numbers are shown in thousands and refer to persons, families, and unrelated individuals, as of March of the following year.

Characteristic	All races			White			Black			Hispanic origin[1]		
	Total	Below poverty level		Total	Below poverty level		Total	Below poverty level		Total	Below poverty level	
		Number	Percent of total		Number	Percent of total		Number	Percent of total		Number	Percent of total
Northeast												
Central Cities												
Both sexes												
Total	15,762	3,455	21.9	11,085	1,920	17.3	3,802	1,366	35.9	2,497	1,002	40.1
Under 18 years	3,897	1,409	36.1	2,397	730	30.5	1,250	625	50.0	881	503	57.1
18 to 24 years	1,542	338	21.9	1,071	177	16.5	382	138	36.1	264	93	35.3
25 to 34 years	2,841	477	16.8	1,980	275	13.9	677	170	25.2	466	154	33.1
35 to 44 years	2,281	369	16.2	1,637	196	12.0	498	147	29.6	353	103	29.3
45 to 54 years	1,686	275	16.3	1,207	156	12.9	386	112	29.0	257	64	25.0
55 to 59 years	674	113	16.8	501	68	13.6	143	43	29.8	79	22	27.7
60 to 64 years	684	92	13.4	527	53	10.1	137	35	25.8	62	20	B
65 years and over	2,156	382	17.7	1,765	266	15.1	329	96	29.2	134	42	31.6
65 to 74 years	1,232	194	15.7	986	122	12.4	204	60	29.4	86	25	29.1
75 years and over	924	188	20.4	779	144	18.4	124	36	28.9	48	17	B
Male												
Total	7,367	1,381	18.7	5,205	757	14.5	1,704	539	31.6	1,161	408	35.2
Under 18 years	1,983	696	35.1	1,206	355	29.4	629	311	49.5	452	252	55.7
18 to 24 years	737	113	15.4	526	62	11.7	163	43	26.1	119	30	24.9
25 to 34 years	1,380	138	10.0	994	95	9.5	297	23	7.8	215	52	24.4
35 to 44 years	1,080	126	11.7	779	55	7.0	217	57	26.4	146	23	15.6
45 to 54 years	746	123	16.5	546	66	12.2	156	51	32.6	123	25	20.7
55 to 59 years	319	39	12.1	227	23	10.0	75	16	21.3	34	7	B
60 to 64 years	304	34	11.3	243	23	9.4	52	10	B	20	6	B
65 years and over	818	111	13.6	684	79	11.5	115	27	23.7	52	14	B
65 to 74 years	510	74	14.5	413	49	11.9	85	23	26.7	35	10	B
75 years and over	308	37	12.1	270	30	10.9	31	5	B	16	3	B
Female												
Total	8,394	2,074	24.7	5,879	1,163	19.8	2,098	828	39.4	1,336	594	44.5
Under 18 years	1,914	713	37.2	1,191	375	31.5	620	313	50.5	429	251	58.6
18 to 24 years	805	224	27.9	545	115	21.2	219	96	43.6	145	64	43.8
15 to 34 years	1,462	339	23.2	986	180	18.2	381	147	38.6	251	102	40.6
35 to 44 years	1,201	243	20.2	858	141	16.5	281	90	32.0	207	81	38.9
45 to 54 years	940	152	16.2	662	89	13.5	231	61	26.5	134	39	29.1
55 to 59 years	355	74	21.0	274	45	16.6	68	27	B	46	15	B

[Continued]

★ 621 ★

Persons Living in Poverty in the Northeast Region, by Type of Residence, Age Group, and Sex, 1992: Central Cities

[Continued]

Characteristic	All races			White			Black			Hispanic origin[1]		
	Total	Below poverty level		Total	Below poverty level		Total	Below poverty level		Total	Below poverty level	
		Number	Percent of total		Number	Percent of total		Number	Percent of total		Number	Percent of total
60 to 64 years	380	57	15.1	284	30	10.7	85	25	29.8	42	14	B
65 years and over	1,338	271	20.3	1,081	187	17.3	213	69	32.2	83	29	35.0
65 to 74 years	722	120	16.6	573	73	12.7	120	37	31.3	51	15	B
75 years and over	615	151	24.5	508	114	22.4	94	31	33.4	32	14	B
Household relationship												
Total	15,762	3,455	21.9	11,085	1,920	17.3	3,802	1,366	35.9	2,497	1,002	40.1
65 years and over	2,156	382	17.7	1,765	266	15.1	329	96	29.2	134	42	31.6
In families	12,597	2,660	21.1	8,715	1,435	16.5	3,143	1,109	35.3	2,167	878	40.5
Householder	3,990	773	19.4	2,884	446	15.5	896	292	32.6	648	254	39.2
Under 65 years	3,326	708	21.3	2,343	408	17.4	791	273	34.4	611	249	40.7
65 years and over	664	65	9.8	540	38	7.0	105	19	18.5	37	5	B
Related children under 18 years	3,850	1,385	36.0	2,365	714	30.2	1,237	619	50.0	869	495	57.0
Under 6 years	1,478	573	38.8	922	294	31.9	458	259	56.6	329	201	61.0
6 to 17 years	2,372	812	34.2	1,443	420	29.1	778	359	46.2	539	295	54.6
Own children 18 years and over	1,618	223	13.8	1,087	92	8.5	468	127	27.1	219	58	26.5
In married-coupled families	8,309	827	10.0	6,354	541	8.5	1,374	212	15.4	1,086	222	20.5
Husbands	2,575	224	8.7	2,037	149	7.3	390	55	14.1	303	54	17.9
Under 65 years	2,066	175	8.5	1,600	113	7.1	326	44	13.5	282	50	17.8
65 years and over	509	49	9.6	437	35	8.1	65	11	B	21	4	B
Wives	2,575	224	8.7	2,051	156	7.6	373	49	13.1	307	52	17.0
Under 65 years	2,163	189	8.8	1,702	130	7.7	320	41	12.8	289	51	17.7
65 years and over	412	35	8.4	350	25	7.3	54	8	B	18	1	B
Related children under 18 years	2,138	325	15.2	1,534	201	13.1	403	94	23.4	359	108	30.2
Under 6 years	852	137	16.1	627	89	14.2	143	40	27.8	155	58	37.2
6 to 17 years	1,286	187	14.6	907	112	12.4	261	55	21.0	204	50	24.8
Own children 18 years and over	860	40	4.6	640	24	3.8	179	14	7.6	83	4	5.1
In families with female householder, no spouse present	3,675	1,750	47.6	1,948	839	43.0	1,623	880	54.2	972	622	64.0
Householder	1,193	518	43.4	690	275	39.9	470	233	49.6	305	186	60.9
Under 65 years	1,052	502	47.7	596	270	45.4	430	225	52.3	294	185	62.7
65 years and over	141	16	11.6	93	4	4.6	40	9	B	11	1	B
Related children under 18 years	1,558	1,024	65.7	740	490	66.2	779	516	66.2	488	374	76.7
Under 6 years	578	421	72.8	264	198	75.2	302	215	71.3	169	140	82.7
6 to 17 years	980	603	61.6	476	291	61.2	477	301	63.0	319	234	73.5
Own children 18 years and over	682	176	25.8	378	61	16.2	288	113	39.3	123	54	43.8
In unrelated subfamilies	93	40	43.1	55	25	B	32	13	B	18	12	B
Under 18 years	44	21	B	30	14	B	13	6	B	10	6	B
Under 6 years	14	11	B	5	5	B	7	4	B	3	2	B
6 to 17 years	30	10	B	24	9	B	6	1	B	8	4	B
18 years and over	50	19	B	26	11	B	20	7	B	8	6	B
Unrelated individuals	3,071	755	24.6	2,314	460	19.9	627	245	39.1	312	112	36.0
Male	1,393	313	22.4	1,015	174	17.2	305	109	35.6	169	50	29.4
Under 65 years	1,163	255	21.9	828	132	16.0	264	94	35.6	150	40	26.6
Living alone	638	125	19.6	450	73	16.3	159	47	29.5	65	21	B
65 years and over	230	57	25.0	187	42	22.4	41	15	B	19	10	B
Living alone	197	52	26.1	160	39	24.1	35	12	B	17	9	B
Female	1,678	442	26.3	1,300	286	22.0	322	136	42.4	143	63	43.8
Under 65 years	1,004	234	23.3	746	139	18.6	218	84	38.6	107	42	38.9
Living alone	676	157	23.2	491	89	18.2	164	63	38.4	73	28	B
65 years and over	675	208	30.8	553	147	26.5	103	52	50.3	36	21	B
Living alone	652	203	31.2	537	143	26.7	99	51	51.2	34	19	B

Source: U.S. Bureau of the Census. *Poverty in the United States: 1992.* Current Population Reports, Series P60-185, U.S. Government Printing Office, Washington, D.C., 1993, p. 44. *Notes:* A (B) stands for base less than 75,000 or not applicable. 1. Persons of Hispanic origin may be of any race.

★ 622 ★

Poverty

Persons Living in Poverty in the Northeast Region, by Type of Residence, Age Group, and Sex, 1992: Metropolitan Areas

Numbers are shown in thousands and refer to persons, families, and unrelated individuals, as of March of the following year.

Characteristic	All races			White			Black			Hispanic origin[1]		
	Total	Below poverty level		Total	Below poverty level		Total	Below poverty level		Total	Below poverty level	
		Number	Percent of total		Number	Percent of total		Number	Percent of total		Number	Percent of total
Northeast												
Metropolitan areas												
Both sexes												
Total	44,459	5,488	12.3	37,629	3,619	9.6	5,204	1,637	31.5	3,330	1,148	34.5
Under 18 years	10,734	2,126	19.8	8,547	1,304	15.3	1,664	747	44.9	1,121	572	51.0
18 to 24 years	4,194	552	13.2	3,470	334	9.6	576	188	32.6	349	112	32.0
25 to 34 years	7,420	777	10.5	6,209	518	8.3	923	212	23.0	638	178	27.9
35 to 44 years	6,980	598	8.6	5,995	389	6.5	681	171	25.2	497	117	23.6
45 to 54 years	5,254	413	7.9	4,525	270	6.0	555	131	23.6	351	71	20.2
55 to 59 years	1,922	159	8.3	1,669	106	6.4	198	48	24.0	107	22	20.5
60 to 64 years	1,991	172	8.6	1,763	131	7.4	190	38	20.1	89	24	26.6
65 years and over	5,965	690	11.6	5,451	567	10.4	417	103	24.6	177	52	29.5
65 to 74 years	3,474	335	9.6	3,146	258	8.2	271	65	24.0	114	30	26.3
75 years and over	2,491	355	14.3	2,305	309	13.4	147	38	25.7	63	22	B
Male												
Total	21,371	2,236	10.5	18,125	1,454	8.0	2,419	666	27.5	1,579	471	29.8
Under 18 years	5,474	1,091	19.9	4,349	670	15.4	847	384	45.3	586	292	49.8
18 to 24 years	2,054	199	9.7	1,710	125	7.3	263	59	22.6	159	36	23.0
25 to 34 years	3,724	248	6.7	3,171	178	5.6	415	39	9.4	299	59	19.6
35 to 44 years	3,402	221	6.5	2,931	135	4.6	312	68	21.9	224	29	12.8
45 to 54 years	2,484	171	6.9	2,156	103	4.8	240	61	25.4	166	26	15.6
55 to 59 years	910	59	6.4	778	40	5.2	99	16	16.2	45	7	B
60 to 64 years	939	73	7.8	847	61	7.3	75	10	B	30	6	B
65 years and over	2,385	174	7.3	2,182	140	6.4	167	29	17.3	71	17	B
65 to 74 years	1,507	115	7.6	1,365	89	6.5	125	24	19.4	48	12	B
75 years and over	877	58	6.7	818	51	6.2	42	5	B	23	5	B
Female												
Total	23,088	3,252	14.1	19,503	2,166	11.1	2,785	971	34.9	1,750	677	38.7
Under 18 years	5,260	1,035	19.7	4,198	634	15.1	816	363	44.5	534	280	52.4
18 to 24 years	2,140	354	16.5	1,760	209	11.9	313	128	41.0	190	75	39.5
25 to 34 years	3,696	530	14.3	3,038	340	11.2	508	173	34.1	340	120	35.2
35 to 44 years	3,578	377	10.5	3,063	253	8.3	369	103	28.0	273	89	32.4
45 to 54 years	2,770	241	8.7	2,369	167	7.0	315	70	22.2	185	45	24.4
55 to 59 years	1,012	100	9.9	890	66	7.4	99	31	31.8	62	15	B
60 to 64 years	1,052	99	9.4	916	69	7.5	115	28	24.4	59	18	B
65 years and over	3,581	517	14.4	3,269	428	13.1	250	74	29.5	107	35	33.2
65 to 74 years	1,967	220	11.2	1,782	170	9.5	146	41	28.0	66	18	B
75 years and over	1,614	297	18.4	1,487	258	17.4	104	33	31.6	41	17	B
Household relationship												
Total	44,459	5,488	12.3	37,629	3,619	9.6	5,204	1,637	31.5	3,330	1,148	34.5
65 years and over	5,965	690	11.6	5,451	567	10.4	417	103	24.6	177	52	29.5
In families	37,562	4,088	10.9	31,801	2,608	8.2	4,332	1,320	30.5	2,903	995	34.3
Householder	11,758	1,203	10.2	10,145	807	8.0	1,233	350	28.4	869	286	32.9
Under 65 years	9,721	1,090	11.2	8,274	724	8.7	1,092	328	30.0	816	279	34.2
65 years and over	2,037	113	5.6	1,871	83	4.4	141	22	16.0	53	7	B
Related children under 18 years	10,622	2,066	19.4	8,460	1,258	14.9	1,642	736	44.8	1,103	558	50.7
Under 6 years	3,883	876	22.6	3,076	533	17.3	611	316	51.7	413	230	55.7
6 to 17 years	6,740	1,189	17.6	5,384	725	13.5	1,031	420	40.7	689	329	47.6
Own children 18 years and over	4,799	331	6.9	4,024	176	4.4	658	147	22.4	292	66	22.7
In married-coupled families	29,397	1,467	5.0	26,113	1,122	4.3	2,080	241	11.6	1,621	263	16.2
Husbands	8,981	402	4.5	8,100	314	3.9	584	61	10.4	462	66	14.3
Under 65 years	7,318	318	4.3	6,539	243	3.7	497	49	10.0	425	59	14.0
65 years and over	1,662	84	5.0	1,562	70	4.5	88	11	12.7	37	7	B

[Continued]

★ 622 ★

Persons Living in Poverty in the Northeast Region, by Type of Residence, Age Group, and Sex, 1992: Metropolitan Areas

[Continued]

Characteristic	All races			White			Black			Hispanic origin[1]		
	Total	Below poverty level		Total	Below poverty level		Total	Below poverty level		Total	Below poverty level	
		Number	Percent of total		Number	Percent of total		Number	Percent of total		Number	Percent of total
Wives	8,981	402	4.5	8,110	319	3.9	562	54	9.7	464	61	13.2
Under 65 years	7,698	340	4.4	6,905	266	3.8	493	46	9.4	437	59	13.4
65 years and over	1,282	62	4.8	1,205	53	4.4	69	8	B	27	3	B
Related children under 18 years	7,697	560	7.3	6,661	414	6.2	587	104	17.7	509	124	24.4
Under 6 years	2,866	240	8.4	2,478	181	7.3	217	44	20.1	208	65	31.2
6 to 17 years	4,831	320	6.6	4,183	232	5.6	370	60	16.2	301	59	19.7
Own children 18 years and over	3,230	85	2.6	2,850	61	2.1	302	22	7.3	133	7	5.4
In families with female householder, no spouse present	6,652	2,442	36.7	4,472	1,354	30.3	2,025	1,043	51.5	1,141	699	61.3
Householder	2,236	741	33.1	1,599	449	28.0	588	279	47.5	357	207	58.0
Under 65 years	1,914	715	37.3	1,334	436	32.7	540	269	49.8	345	205	59.5
65 years and over	322	26	8.2	266	13	4.9	48	10	B	12	2	B
Related children under 18 years	2,539	1,427	56.2	1,500	783	52.2	981	618	63.0	566	421	74.3
Under 6 years	881	606	68.8	485	329	67.8	378	268	71.0	197	161	81.9
6 to 17 years	1,658	821	49.5	1,015	455	44.8	604	350	58.0	369	260	70.3
Own children 18 years and over	1,341	227	16.9	963	99	10.3	346	123	35.7	143	59	41.2
In unrelated subfamilies	197	85	43.3	146	65	44.8	45	17	B	25	19	B
Under 18 years	96	46	48.3	75	37	48.8	19	8	B	14	10	B
Under 6 years	35	24	B	24	16	B	9	7	B	6	5	B
6 to 17 years	61	22	B	51	21	B	10	1	B	8	4	B
18 years and over	101	39	38.5	70	29	B	26	9	B	12	9	B
Unrelated individuals	6,701	1,315	19.6	5,682	946	16.6	828	300	36.2	401	133	33.2
Male	2,994	507	17.0	2,441	321	13.1	440	144	32.8	223	55	24.9
Under 65 years	2,509	426	17.0	2,020	255	12.6	381	130	34.0	204	45	22.2
Living alone	1,334	185	13.9	1,091	122	11.2	201	56	28.0	82	22	26.7
65 years and over	485	81	16.7	421	65	15.5	58	15	B	19	10	B
Living alone	431	75	17.5	372	62	16.7	52	12	B	17	10	B
Female	3,707	808	21.8	3,242	625	19.3	388	155	40.0	178	78	43.8
Under 65 years	2,074	397	19.1	1,740	279	16.0	276	100	36.1	135	52	38.7
Living alone	1,323	237	18.0	1,090	158	14.5	199	72	36.3	89	34	37.8
65 years and over	1,633	411	25.2	1,501	346	23.1	112	56	49.6	43	25	B
Living alone	1,580	402	25.4	1,455	338	23.2	107	55	50.8	40	23	B

Source: U.S. Bureau of the Census. *Poverty in the United States: 1992.* Current Population Reports, Series P60-185, U.S. Government Printing Office, Washington, D.C., 1993, p. 43. *Notes:* A (B) stands for base less than 75,000 or not applicable. 1. Persons of Hispanic origin may be of any race.

★ 623 ★

Poverty

Persons Living in Poverty in the Northeast Region, by Type of Residence, Age Group, and Sex, 1992: Not in Central Cities

Numbers are shown in thousands and refer to persons, families, and unrelated individuals, as of March of the following year.

Characteristic	All races			White			Black			Hispanic origin[1]		
	Total	Below poverty level		Total	Below poverty level		Total	Below poverty level		Total	Below poverty level	
		Number	Percent of total		Number	Percent of total		Number	Percent of total		Number	Percent of total
Northeast												
Metropolitan, not in Central Cities												
Both sexes												
Total	28,698	2,033	7.1	26,544	1,699	6.4	1,403	271	19.3	833	145	17.5
Under 18 years	6,837	718	10.5	6,150	574	9.3	414	122	29.4	240	69	28.8

[Continued]

★ 623 ★

Persons Living in Poverty in the Northeast Region, by Type of Residence, Age Group, and Sex, 1992: Not in Central Cities

[Continued]

Characteristic	All races			White			Black			Hispanic origin[1]		
	Total	Below poverty level		Total	Below poverty level		Total	Below poverty level		Total	Below poverty level	
		Number	Percent of total		Number	Percent of total		Number	Percent of total		Number	Percent of total
18 to 24 years	2,652	215	8.1	2,399	157	6.6	194	49	25.5	85	18	21.7
25 to 34 years	4,579	301	6.6	4,229	243	5.7	245	42	16.9	172	24	13.8
35 to 44 years	4,699	229	4.9	4,358	193	4.4	183	24	13.3	144	14	9.6
45 to 54 years	3,568	137	3.8	3,318	115	3.5	169	19	11.3	94	7	7.1
55 to 59 years	1,248	45	3.6	1,167	38	3.3	55	5	B	28	-	B
60 to 64 years	1,307	80	6.1	1,237	78	6.3	53	3	B	26	4	B
65 years and over	3,810	308	8.1	3,686	302	8.2	89	7	7.4	43	10	B
65 to 74 years	2,242	141	6.3	2,160	136	6.3	66	5	B	28	5	B
75 years and over	1,568	167	10.7	1,526	165	10.8	22	2	B	15	5	B
Male												
Total	14,004	855	6.1	12,920	697	5.4	716	127	17.8	418	63	15.0
Under 18 years	3,491	395	11.3	3,143	315	10.0	218	72	33.1	134	40	30.0
18 to 24 years	1,316	85	6.5	1,184	64	5.4	101	17	16.8	40	7	B
25 to 34 years	2,344	110	4.7	2,177	83	3.8	118	16	13.2	84	6	7.3
35 to 44 years	2,322	95	4.1	2,153	81	3.7	95	11	11.5	77	6	7.4
45 to 54 years	1,738	48	2.8	1,611	37	2.3	85	10	12.1	43	-	B
55 to 59 years	591	20	3.4	551	18	3.2	24	-	B	11	-	B
60 to 64 years	635	39	6.1	604	39	6.4	23	-	B	10	-	B
65 years and over	1,567	62	4.0	1,498	61	4.1	52	2	B	19	3	B
65 to 74 years	997	41	4.1	951	40	4.2	40	2	B	13	1	B
75 years and over	569	21	3.7	547	21	3.9	12	-	B	6	2	B
Female												
Total	14,694	1,178	8.0	13,624	1,003	7.4	687	143	20.8	414	83	19.9
Under 18 years	3,346	322	9.6	3,007	259	8.6	196	50	25.3	106	29	27.2
18 to 24 years	1,335	129	9.7	1,216	94	7.7	93	33	34.9	45	12	B
25 to 34 years	2,234	191	8.5	2,052	160	7.8	127	26	20.4	88	18	20.0
35 to 44 years	2,377	134	5.6	2,205	112	5.1	88	13	15.2	67	8	B
45 to 54 years	1,830	89	4.9	1,707	78	4.6	84	9	10.5	51	6	B
55 to 59 years	657	26	3.9	617	21	3.3	31	5	B	16	-	B
60 to 64 years	672	42	6.2	632	39	6.1	30	3	B	17	4	B
65 years and over	2,243	246	11.0	2,188	241	11.0	37	5	B	24	7	B
65 to 74 years	1,245	100	8.0	1,209	97	8.0	26	3	B	16	4	B
75 years and over	998	146	14.6	979	144	14.7	11	2	B	9	3	B
Household relationship												
Total	28,698	2,033	7.1	26,544	1,699	6.4	1,403	271	19.3	833	145	17.5
65 years and over	3,810	308	8.1	3,686	302	8.2	89	7	7.4	43	10	B
In families	24,965	1,428	5.7	23,085	1,173	5.1	1,189	212	17.8	737	118	16.0
Householder	7,768	429	5.5	7,262	361	5.0	336	58	17.3	222	32	14.5
Under 65 years	6,395	381	6.0	5,931	315	5.3	301	55	18.3	206	30	14.6
65 years and over	1,373	48	3.5	1,331	45	3.4	35	3	B	16	2	B
Related children under 18 years	6,772	681	10.1	6,096	544	8.9	405	117	29.0	234	63	27.0
Under 6 years	2,405	303	12.6	2,154	239	11.1	153	57	37.2	84	29	34.8
6 to 17 years	4,368	377	8.6	3,942	305	7.7	252	61	24.0	150	34	22.6
Own children 18 years and over	3,181	107	3.4	2,937	84	2.8	190	21	10.8	73	8	B
In married-coupled families	21,088	640	3.0	19,759	580	2.9	706	29	4.1	534	41	7.6
Husbands	6,406	178	2.8	6,063	165	2.7	194	5	2.8	159	12	7.4
Under 65 years	5,252	143	2.7	4,939	130	2.6	171	5	3.2	143	9	6.3
65 years and over	1,154	35	3.0	1,124	35	3.1	23	-	B	16	3	B
Wives	6,406	178	2.8	6,059	163	2.7	189	5	2.9	157	9	5.8
Under 65 years	5,535	150	2.7	5,203	135	2.6	174	5	3.1	149	8	5.2
65 years and over	870	28	3.2	855	28	3.2	15	-	B	9	1	B
Related children under 18 years	5,559	236	4.2	5,127	213	4.1	184	9	5.1	151	16	10.8
Under 6 years	2,014	103	5.1	1,851	93	5.0	74	4	B	54	7	B
6 to 17 years	3,545	133	3.8	3,276	120	3.7	109	5	4.9	97	9	9.0
Own children 18 years and over	2,370	45	1.9	2,211	37	1.7	123	9	7.0	50	3	B

[Continued]

★ 623 ★

Persons Living in Poverty in the Northeast Region, by Type of Residence, Age Group, and Sex, 1992: Not in Central Cities

[Continued]

Characteristic	All races			White			Black			Hispanic origin[1]		
	Total	Below poverty level		Total	Below poverty level		Total	Below poverty level		Total	Below poverty level	
		Number	Percent of total		Number	Percent of total		Number	Percent of total		Number	Percent of total
In families with female householder, no spouse present	2,977	692	23.2	2,524	516	20.4	402	164	40.7	168	77	45.6
Householder	1,043	223	21.4	910	174	19.1	118	46	39.0	52	21	B
Under 65 years	862	213	24.7	738	165	22.4	111	45	40.4	50	20	B
65 years and over	181	10	5.6	172	9	5.0	8	1	B	1	1	B
Related children under 18 years	980	402	41.0	760	294	38.6	203	102	50.6	78	47	59.8
Under 6 years	303	185	61.0	221	130	58.9	76	53	69.6	28	22	B
6 to 17 years	677	217	32.1	539	163	30.3	127	50	39.2	50	25	B
Own children 18 years and over	659	51	7.7	585	38	6.4	58	10	B	20	5	B
In unrelated subfamilies	103	45	43.5	90	41	44.9	13	4	B	7	7	B
Under 18 years	52	25	B	46	23	B	7	2	B	3	3	B
Under 6 years	21	13	B	19	11	B	2	2	B	3	3	B
6 to 17 years	31	12	B	27	12	B	4	-	B	-	-	B
18 years and over	51	19	B	45	18	B	6	2	B	4	4	B
Unrelated individuals	3,629	560	15.4	3,368	486	14.4	201	55	27.2	89	21	23.5
Male	1,601	195	12.2	1,426	147	10.3	135	36	26.6	55	6	B
Under 65 years	1,345	171	12.7	1,192	123	10.3	117	36	30.5	54	5	B
Living alone	696	59	8.5	641	49	7.6	42	9	B	17	1	B
65 years and over	255	24	9.2	234	24	10.1	17	-	B	1	1	B
Living alone	233	24	10.1	212	24	11.1	17	-	B	1	1	B
Female	2,029	366	18.0	1,942	339	17.5	66	19	B	35	15	B
Under 65 years	1,071	162	15.2	994	140	14.0	57	15	B	28	11	B
Living alone	647	80	12.4	599	69	11.4	36	10	B	16	5	B
65 years and over	958	203	21.2	948	200	21.1	9	4	B	7	5	B
Living alone	928	199	21.4	919	195	21.2	8	4	B	6	5	B

Source: U.S. Bureau of the Census. *Poverty in the United States: 1992.* Current Population Reports, Series P60-185, U.S. Government Printing Office, Washington, D.C., 1993, pp. 45. *Notes:* A dash (-) stands for zero or rounds to zero. A (B) stands for base less than 75,000 or not applicable. 1. Persons of Hispanic origin may be of any race.

★ 624 ★

Poverty

Persons Living in Poverty in the Northeast Region, by Type of Residence, Age Group, and Sex, 1992: Outside Metropolitan Areas

Numbers are shown in thousands and refer to persons, families, and unrelated individuals, as of March of the following year.

Characteristic	All races			White			Black			Hispanic origin[1]		
	Total	Below poverty level		Total	Below poverty level		Total	Below poverty level		Total	Below poverty level	
		Number	Percent of total		Number	Percent of total		Number	Percent of total		Number	Percent of total
Northeast												
Outside Metropolitan areas												
Both sexes												
Total	6,195	739	11.9	6,060	700	11.6	57	27	B	53	20	B
Under 18 years	1,509	269	17.8	1,455	241	16.6	30	21	B	21	10	B
18 to 24 years	608	78	12.8	598	74	12.4	4	2	B	3	1	B
25 to 34 years	926	94	10.1	902	91	10.1	10	2	B	11	4	B
35 to 44 years	998	104	10.4	968	102	10.5	12	2	B	11	2	B
45 to 54 years	714	52	7.2	707	50	7.1	1	-	B	4	2	B
55 to 59 years	276	28	10.2	275	28	10.3	-	-	B	2	1	B
60 to 64 years	309	23	7.5	308	23	7.5	-	-	B	-	-	B
65 years and over	855	92	10.8	848	91	10.7	-	-	B	3	1	B
65 to 74 years	510	47	9.3	503	46	9.2	-	-	B	2	1	B

[Continued]

★ 624 ★

Persons Living in Poverty in the Northeast Region, by Type of Residence, Age Group, and Sex, 1992: Outside Metropolitan Areas

[Continued]

Characteristic	All races			White			Black			Hispanic origin[1]		
	Total	Below poverty level		Total	Below poverty level		Total	Below poverty level		Total	Below poverty level	
		Number	Percent of total		Number	Percent of total		Number	Percent of total		Number	Percent of total
75 years and over	345	45	13.0	345	45	13.0	-	-	B	-	-	B
Male												
Total	3,056	334	10.9	2,994	318	10.6	30	11	B	29	10	B
Under 18 years	785	138	17.6	763	128	16.7	13	8	B	12	6	B
18 to 24 years	306	37	12.0	300	33	11.2	2	2	B	2	1	B
25 to 34 years	459	34	7.5	447	33	7.4	6	1	B	4	1	B
35 to 44 years	495	46	9.2	477	46	9.6	8	-	B	6	1	B
45 to 54 years	361	19	5.2	360	18	5.0	-	-	B	2	1	B
55 to 59 years	131	14	10.6	131	14	10.6	-	-	B	1	-	B
60 to 64 years	145	6	3.9	145	6	3.9	-	-	B	-	-	B
65 years and over	375	41	10.8	372	41	10.9	-	-	B	2	1	B
65 to 74 years	239	28	11.8	236	28	12.0	-	-	B	2	1	B
75 years and over	136	12	9.1	136	12	9.1	-	-	B	-	-	B
Female												
Total	3,139	406	12.9	3,067	382	12.5	27	16	B	24	9	B
Under 18 years	724	131	18.0	692	114	16.5	17	13	B	9	4	B
18 to 24 years	302	41	13.5	298	41	13.7	2	-	B	1	-	B
25 to 34 years	467	60	12.8	455	58	12.7	4	1	B	7	3	B
35 to 44 years	503	58	11.6	492	56	11.4	4	2	B	5	1	B
45 to 54 years	353	33	9.3	348	32	9.2	1	-	B	2	1	B
55 to 59 years	145	14	9.8	143	14	9.9	-	-	B	1	1	B
60 to 64 years	164	17	10.6	164	17	10.7	-	-	B	-	-	B
65 years and over	480	52	10.7	476	50	10.5	-	-	B	-	-	B
65 to 74 years	271	19	7.1	267	18	6.7	-	-	B	-	-	B
75 years and over	209	32	15.4	209	32	15.4	-	-	B	-	-	B
Household relationship												
Total	6,195	739	11.9	6,060	700	11.6	57	27	B	53	20	B
65 years and over	855	92	10.8	848	91	10.7	-	-	B	3	1	B
In families	5,315	530	10.0	5,199	492	9.5	46	27	B	51	18	B
Householder	1,720	166	9.6	1,694	161	9.5	9	3	B	14	3	B
Under 65 years	1,375	144	10.5	1,352	139	10.3	9	3	B	12	2	B
65 years and over	346	22	6.4	342	22	6.5	-	-	B	2	1	B
Related children under 18 years	1,473	248	16.9	1,419	221	15.6	30	21	B	21	10	B
Under 6 years	463	86	18.5	452	78	17.3	7	6	B	5	3	B
6 to 17 years	1,010	163	16.1	967	143	14.8	23	14	B	15	6	B
Own children 18 years and over	580	22	3.7	574	18	3.2	2	2	B	2	1	B
In married-coupled families	4,478	304	6.8	4,392	293	6.7	27	8	B	47	16	B
Husbands	1,410	85	6.0	1,387	83	6.0	8	1	B	15	4	B
Under 65 years	1,132	67	5.9	1,112	65	5.8	8	1	B	13	3	B
65 years and over	278	18	6.5	275	18	6.6	-	-	B	2	1	B
Wives	1,410	85	6.0	1,387	83	6.0	5	1	B	12	3	B
Under 65 years	1,200	73	6.1	1,177	71	6.0	5	1	B	12	3	B
65 years and over	210	12	5.6	210	12	5.6	-	-	B	-	-	B
Related children under 18 years	1,190	118	9.9	1,157	112	9.7	15	5	B	18	8	B
Under 6 years	375	39	10.4	370	37	10.0	3	2	B	5	3	B
6 to 17 years	815	79	9.7	787	74	9.5	12	4	B	13	5	B
Own children 18 years and over	422	12	2.9	418	11	2.7	-	-	B	1	1	B
In families with female householder, no spouse present	660	199	30.1	635	176	27.7	19	19.9	B	4	2	B
Householder	241	72	30.0	238	70	29.4	2	2	B	1	-	B
Under 65 years	180	68	37.9	178	66	37.0	2	2	B	1	-	B
65 years and over	60	4	B	60	4	B	-	-	B	-	-	B
Related children under 18 years	231	114	49.3	213	96	45.0	15	15	B	3	2	B
Under 6 years	61	39	B	57	34	B	4	4	B	-	-	B
6 to 17 years	170	75	44.4	156	62	39.5	11	11	B	2	2	B
Own children 18 years and over	128	9	7.3	126	7	5.7	2	2	B	1	-	B

[Continued]

★ 624 ★

Persons Living in Poverty in the Northeast Region, by Type of Residence, Age Group, and Sex, 1992: Outside Metropolitan Areas

[Continued]

Characteristic	All races			White			Black			Hispanic origin[1]		
	Total	Below poverty level		Total	Below poverty level		Total	Below poverty level		Total	Below poverty level	
		Number	Percent of total		Number	Percent of total		Number	Percent of total		Number	Percent of total
In unrelated subfamilies	49	19	B	48	19	B	-	-	B	1	1	B
Under 18 years	27	12	B	26	12	B	-	-	B	-	-	B
Under 6 years	7	5	B	7	5	B	-	-	B	-	-	B
6 to 17 years	20	7	B	19	7	B	-	-	B	-	-	B
18 years and over	22	8	B	22	8	B	-	-	B	1	1	B
Unrelated individuals	832	190	22.8	813	189	23.2	10	-	B	1	1	B
Male	374	79	21.2	366	79	21.7	7	-	B	-	-	B
Under 65 years	316	61	19.4	307	61	20.0	7	-	B	-	-	B
Living alone	162	24	15.0	160	24	15.2	2	-	B	-	-	B
65 years and over	58	18	B	58	18	B	-	-	B	-	-	B
Living alone	37	7	B	37	7	B	-	-	B	-	-	B
Female	458	111	24.2	448	109	24.4	4	-	B	1	1	B
Under 65 years	279	75	26.9	272	75	27.5	4	-	B	1	1	B
Living alone	139	25	18.0	135	25	18.6	2	-	B	-	-	B
65 years and over	179	36	19.9	176	34	19.5	-	-	B	-	-	B
Living alone	168	34	20.0	166	34	20.2	-	-	B	-	-	B

Source: U.S. Bureau of the Census. *Poverty in the United States: 1992.* Current Population Reports, Series P60-185, U.S. Government Printing Office, Washington, D.C., 1993, p. 46. *Notes:* A dash (-) stands for zero or rounds to zero. A (B) stands for base less than 75,000 or not applicable. 1. Persons of Hispanic origin may be of any race.

★ 625 ★

Poverty

Persons Living in Poverty in the South Region, by Type of Residence, Age Group, and Sex, 1992: Central Cities

Numbers are shown in thousands and refer to persons, families, and unrelated individuals, as of March of the following year.

Characteristic	All races			White			Black			Hispanic origin[1]		
	Total	Below poverty level		Total	Below poverty level		Total	Below poverty level		Total	Below poverty level	
		Number	Percent of total		Number	Percent of total		Number	Percent of total		Number	Percent of total
South												
Central Cities												
Both sexes												
Total	24,318	5,143	21.2	15,909	2,277	14.3	7,772	2,724	35.0	3,654	1,124	30.8
Under 18 years	6,266	2,088	33.3	3,632	730	20.1	2,464	1,302	52.8	1,128	455	40.4
18 to 24 years	2,697	656	24.3	1,688	349	20.7	923	286	31.0	477	149	31.2
25 to 34 years	4,351	763	17.5	2,865	361	12.6	1,346	379	28.1	657	162	24.7
35 to 44 years	3,696	549	14.9	2,475	256	10.3	1,109	273	24.6	465	120	25.9
45 to 54 years	2,554	297	11.6	1,776	146	8.2	719	141	19.6	379	73	19.3
55 to 59 years	993	143	14.4	658	86	13.0	310	50	16.1	140	41	29.2
60 to 64 years	900	119	13.2	633	64	10.1	259	54	20.8	111	39	35.1
65 years and over	2,861	529	18.5	2,182	285	13.1	643	239	37.2	296	84	28.4
65 to 74 years	1,708	269	15.7	1,282	145	11.3	404	121	30.0	162	37	22.7
75 years and over	1,152	260	22.6	900	140	15.6	238	118	49.6	134	47	35.2
Male												
Total	11,671	2,175	18.6	7,672	957	12.5	3,699	1,148	31.0	1,748	509	29.1
Under 18 years	3,119	1,044	33.5	1,774	329	18.5	1,274	690	54.2	495	200	40.4
18 to 24 years	1,311	269	20.5	826	168	20.3	438	90	20.6	238	80	33.7
25 to 34 years	2,205	275	12.5	1,488	153	10.3	644	112	17.4	359	68	19.0
35 to 44 years	1,842	224	12.2	1,274	117	9.2	516	92	17.8	237	66	27.9
45 to 54 years	1,234	123	10.0	870	56	6.4	333	64	19.4	205	37	18.2

[Continued]

★ 625 ★

Persons Living in Poverty in the South Region, by Type of Residence, Age Group, and Sex, 1992: Central Cities

[Continued]

Characteristic	All races			White			Black			Hispanic origin[1]		
	Total	Below poverty level: Number	Below poverty level: Percent of total	Total	Below poverty level: Number	Below poverty level: Percent of total	Total	Below poverty level: Number	Below poverty level: Percent of total	Total	Below poverty level: Number	Below poverty level: Percent of total
55 to 59 years	432	56	13.0	292	36	12.5	143	18	13.0	44	12	B
60 to 64 years	407	39	9.7	269	19	7.2	133	18	13.9	47	14	B
65 years and over	1,123	145	12.9	878	78	8.9	228	63	27.5	123	31	25.5
65 to 74 years	715	87	12.2	560	49	8.8	152	36	23.5	73	17	B
75 years and over	407	58	14.2	317	29	9.1	76	27	35.6	50	15	B
Female												
Total	12,646	2,968	23.5	8,237	1,321	16.0	4,073	1,576	38.7	1,907	615	32.3
Under 18 years	3,147	1,045	33.2	1,858	401	21.6	1,190	612	51.4	634	256	40.3
18 to 24 years	1,386	387	27.9	861	181	21.1	486	196	40.3	240	69	28.7
25 to 34 years	2,147	488	22.7	1,377	208	15.1	701	266	38.0	297	94	31.5
35 to 44 years	1,854	325	17.5	1,201	139	11.6	593	181	30.6	229	54	23.8
45 to 54 years	1,320	174	13.2	905	91	10.0	387	77	19.9	174	36	20.7
55 to 59 years	561	87	15.5	366	49	13.5	176	32	18.4	96	29	29.8
60 to 64 years	493	80	16.2	364	44	12.2	126	35	28.1	64	25	B
65 years and over	1,738	384	22.1	1,305	207	15.9	415	177	42.6	173	53	30.4
65 to 74 years	993	181	18.3	722	96	13.3	253	86	33.9	89	20	22.6
75 years and over	745	202	27.2	583	111	19.1	162	91	56.2	85	33	38.6
Household relationship												
Total	24,318	5,143	21.2	15,909	2,277	14.3	7,772	2,724	35.0	3,654	1,124	30.8
65 years and over	2,861	529	18.5	2,182	285	13.1	643	239	37.2	296	84	28.4
In families	19,891	4,045	20.3	12,764	1,649	12.9	6,581	2,279	34.6	3,217	947	29.4
Householder	6,305	1,153	18.3	4,255	495	11.6	1,907	627	32.9	865	235	27.2
Under 65 years	5,283	1,017	19.2	3,487	432	12.4	1,661	554	33.4	749	212	28.4
65 years and over	1,022	136	13.3	768	63	8.3	246	73	29.5	116	23	19.6
Related children under 18 years	6,151	2,028	33.0	3,541	684	19.3	2,441	1,288	52.8	1,090	428	39.3
Under 6 years	2,365	905	38.3	1,305	295	22.6	999	586	58.7	409	174	42.4
6 to 17 years	3,786	1,123	29.7	2,236	390	17.4	1,443	702	48.6	681	255	37.4
Own children 18 years and over	2,197	307	14.0	1,153	122	10.6	992	182	18.3	372	81	21.7
In married-coupled families	13,960	1,390	10.0	10,424	974	9.3	3,109	355	11.4	2,430	616	25.4
Husbands	4,388	382	8.7	3,394	271	8.0	877	93	10.6	626	140	22.4
Under 65 years	3,585	302	8.4	2,740	219	8.0	735	64	8.8	538	122	22.7
65 years and over	803	81	10.0	654	52	7.9	142	29	20.3	87	18	20.4
Wives	4,388	382	8.7	3,382	273	8.1	863	95	11.1	659	139	21.2
Under 65 years	3,780	324	8.6	2,890	234	8.1	757	76	10.0	598	129	21.5
65 years and over	608	58	9.5	492	39	7.9	106	19	18.3	61	11	B
Related children under 18 years	3,707	517	13.9	2,732	349	12.8	854	142	16.6	803	267	33.3
Under 6 years	1,407	241	17.1	1,049	165	15.7	311	61	19.5	302	115	38.0
6 to 17 years	2,300	276	12.0	1,683	185	11.0	544	81	14.9	501	153	30.5
Own children 18 years and over	1,199	71	6.0	738	50	6.8	426	20	4.7	243	39	15.9
In families with female householder, no spouse present	5,130	2,456	47.9	1,875	602	32.1	3,168	1,810	57.1	613	268	43.7
Householder	1,640	711	43.4	669	195	29.2	944	503	53.3	180	75	41.9
Under 65 years	1,441	658	45.7	559	183	32.7	855	463	54.1	156	70	45.2
65 years and over	199	53	26.7	110	13	11.5	89	41	45.5	24	5	B
Related children under 18 years	2,233	1,451	65.0	673	312	46.3	1,513	1,109	73.3	248	146	58.7
Under 6 years	881	640	72.6	214	123	57.7	653	508	77.7	87	53	61.6
6 to 17 years	1,351	811	60.0	459	188	41.0	860	601	69.9	162	92	57.1
Own children 18 years and over	849	199	23.4	359	62	17.3	479	135	28.2	106	32	30.5
In unrelated subfamilies	155	67	43.2	123	50	40.8	29	16	B	50	30	B
Under 18 years	90	41	45.7	69	30	B	20	11	B	29	19	B
Under 6 years	34	19	B	28	13	B	6	6	B	8	7	B
6 to 17 years	56	22	B	41	16	B	14	5	B	21	12	B
18 years and over	65	26	B	55	21	B	10	4	B	21	11	B
Unrelated individuals	4,271	1,031	24.1	3,022	578	19.1	1,162	429	36.9	387	147	37.8
Male	2,139	436	20.4	1,462	224	15.3	627	200	31.8	226	66	29.3
Under 65 years	1,919	385	20.0	1,293	201	15.6	580	173	29.9	210	56	26.8

[Continued]

★ 625 ★

Persons Living in Poverty in the South Region, by Type of Residence, Age Group, and Sex, 1992: Central Cities

[Continued]

Characteristic	All races			White			Black			Hispanic origin[1]		
	Total	Below poverty level		Total	Below poverty level		Total	Below poverty level		Total	Below poverty level	
		Number	Percent of total		Number	Percent of total		Number	Percent of total		Number	Percent of total
Living alone	948	144	15.2	658	65	9.9	266	75	28.4	82	10	11.8
65 years and over	219	52	23.6	169	22	13.1	47	26	B	17	10	B
Living alone	207	46	22.4	162	21	13.2	42	22	B	15	10	B
Female	2,133	595	27.9	1,560	355	22.7	535	229	42.9	161	80	49.8
Under 65 years	1,377	341	24.8	981	209	21.3	360	121	33.6	108	48	44.4
Living alone	858	160	18.7	615	96	15.7	227	62	27.4	54	17	B
65 years and over	756	254	33.6	579	145	25.1	175	108	61.9	53	32	B
Living alone	730	243	33.3	563	139	24.8	165	104	62.9	50	31	B

Source: U.S. Bureau of the Census. *Poverty in the United States: 1992.* Current Population Reports, Series P60-185, U.S. Government Printing Office, Washington, D.C., 1993, p. 52. *Notes:* A (B) stands for base less than 75,000 or not applicable. 1. Persons of Hispanic origin may be of any race.

★ 626 ★

Poverty

Persons Living in Poverty in the South Region, by Type of Residence, Age Group, and Sex, 1992: Metropolitan Areas

Numbers are shown in thousands and refer to persons, families, and unrelated individuals, as of March of the following year.

Characteristic	All races			White			Black			Hispanic origin[1]		
	Total	Below poverty level		Total	Below poverty level		Total	Below poverty level		Total	Below poverty level	
		Number	Percent of total		Number	Percent of total		Number	Percent of total		Number	Percent of total
South												
Metropolitan areas												
Both sexes												
Total	62,746	9,688	15.4	48,084	5,429	10.9	13,009	4,170	32.1	6,224	1,652	26.5
Under 18 years	16,325	3,903	23.9	11,608	1,820	15.7	4,236	1,977	46.7	1,944	684	35.2
18 to 24 years	6,211	1,179	19.0	4,476	680	15.2	1,542	468	30.4	752	208	27.7
25 to 34 years	10,784	1,450	13.4	8,211	832	10.1	2,250	574	25.5	1,138	272	23.9
35 to 44 years	10,068	977	9.7	7,832	527	6.7	1,927	412	21.4	856	169	19.8
45 to 54 years	7,292	599	8.2	5,895	365	6.2	1,227	216	17.6	664	109	16.4
55 to 59 years	2,605	250	9.6	2,054	158	7.7	481	83	17.2	228	50	22.0
60 to 64 years	2,429	267	11.0	1,999	167	8.4	405	92	22.8	168	49	29.3
65 years and over	7,033	1,064	15.1	6,010	699	11.6	942	348	37.0	475	110	23.2
65 to 74 years	4,234	521	12.3	3,562	322	9.1	617	192	31.0	291	57	19.7
75 years and over	2,799	543	19.4	2,448	377	15.4	325	157	48.3	184	53	28.7
Male												
Total	30,403	3,973	13.1	23,454	2,153	9.2	6,159	1,696	27.5	3,074	778	25.3
Under 18 years	8,234	1,876	22.8	5,877	856	14.6	2,145	976	45.5	923	320	34.7
18 to 24 years	3,039	474	15.6	2,214	298	13.5	715	161	22.6	397	110	27.7
25 to 34 years	5,379	520	9.7	4,127	320	7.8	1,078	176	16.4	616	129	21.0
35 to 44 years	4,969	380	7.7	3,937	231	5.9	896	131	14.6	425	89	20.9
45 to 54 years	3,544	243	6.9	2,897	142	4.9	565	93	16.5	363	58	16.0
55 to 59 years	1,187	91	7.6	964	59	6.1	202	29	14.4	78	15	18.6
60 to 64 years	1,178	77	6.5	968	51	5.3	191	21	11.0	74	15	B
65 years and over	2,874	313	10.9	2,471	195	7.9	368	108	29.5	198	43	21.7
65 to 74 years	1,789	174	9.7	1,517	104	6.9	254	64	25.2	128	24	18.9
75 years and over	1,085	139	12.8	954	91	9.5	114	44	38.9	71	19	B
Female												
Total	32,343	5,715	17.7	24,631	3,096	12.6	6,851	2,473	36.1	3,150	874	27.7

[Continued]

★ 626 ★

Persons Living in Poverty in the South Region, by Type of Residence, Age Group, and Sex, 1992: Metropolitan Areas

[Continued]

Characteristic	All races			White			Black			Hispanic origin[1]		
	Total	Below poverty level		Total	Below poverty level		Total	Below poverty level		Total	Below poverty level	
		Number	Percent of total		Number	Percent of total		Number	Percent of total		Number	Percent of total
Under 18 years	8,092	2,027	25.1	5,731	965	16.8	2,091	1,001	47.9	1,021	364	35.6
18 to 24 years	3,171	705	22.2	2,263	382	16.9	826	307	37.1	355	98	27.7
25 to 34 years	5,405	931	17.2	4,084	512	12.5	1,173	397	33.9	522	143	27.3
35 to 44 years	5,099	597	11.7	3,895	295	7.6	1,031	281	27.2	430	80	18.7
45 to 54 years	3,748	355	9.5	2,997	224	7.5	662	123	18.5	301	51	16.9
55 to 59 years	1,418	159	11.2	1,091	99	9.1	279	54	19.2	149	36	23.8
60 to 64 years	1,251	190	15.2	1,031	116	11.2	214	71	33.3	94	35	36.9
65 years and over	4,159	751	18.1	3,539	504	14.2	574	240	41.8	276	67	24.3
65 to 74 years	2,445	347	14.2	2,045	218	10.7	364	128	35.1	163	33	20.4
75 years and over	1,714	404	23.6	1,494	286	19.1	211	112	53.3	113	34	29.9
Household relationship												
Total	62,746	9,688	15.4	48,084	5,249	10.9	13,009	4,170	32.1	6,224	1,652	26.5
65 years and over	7,033	1,064	15.1	6,010	699	11.6	942	348	37.0	475	110	23.2
In families	53,430	7,595	14.2	40,805	3,886	9.5	11,138	3,492	31.4	5,564	1,396	25.1
Householder	17,068	2,182	12.8	13,474	1,172	8.7	3,216	952	29.6	1,501	341	22.7
Under 65 years	14,447	1,924	13.3	11,247	1,016	9.0	2,843	852	29.9	1,319	311	23.6
65 years and over	2,621	259	9.9	2,227	157	7.0	373	100	26.9	181	30	16.4
Related children under 18 years	16,077	3,766	23.4	11,418	1,724	15.1	4,179	1,938	46.4	1,896	649	34.2
Under 6 years	5,907	1,625	27.5	4,132	745	18.0	1,608	845	52.6	700	258	36.8
6 to 17 years	10,170	2,141	21.1	7,287	979	13.4	2,571	1,092	42.5	1,196	392	32.8
Own children 18 years and over	5,262	538	10.2	3,552	221	6.2	1,573	310	19.7	600	105	17.5
In married-coupled families	41,681	3,138	7.5	34,755	2,301	6.6	5,746	722	12.6	4,352	962	22.1
Husbands	13,153	859	6.5	11,255	641	5.7	1,598	184	11.5	1,126	220	19.5
Under 65 years	10,995	675	6.1	9,338	508	5.4	1,375	135	9.8	990	195	19.7
65 years and over	2,158	184	8.5	1,917	133	6.9	223	49	21.9	136	25	18.4
Wives	13,153	859	6.5	11,219	647	5.8	1,564	186	11.9	1,176	222	18.9
Under 65 years	11,463	719	6.3	9,700	539	5.6	1,406	156	11.1	1,076	205	19.1
65 years and over	1,690	140	8.3	1,519	108	7.1	158	30	18.8	100	17	16.5
Related children under 18 years	11,389	1,197	10.5	9,329	876	9.4	1,695	273	16.1	1,477	434	29.4
Under 6 years	4,211	521	12.4	3,452	371	10.8	617	125	20.3	562	186	33.1
6 to 17 years	7,178	675	9.4	5,877	505	8.6	1,078	147	13.6	914	248	27.1
Own children 18 years and over	3,296	162	4.9	2,458	88	3.6	735	71	9.6	397	47	11.8
In families with female householder, no spouse present	9,990	4,171	41.7	4,912	1,469	29.9	4,873	2,620	53.8	923	361	39.0
Householder	3,286	1,237	37.6	1,764	488	27.7	1,460	727	49.8	274	100	36.4
Under 65 years	2,879	1,164	40.4	1,485	465	31.3	1,336	677	50.7	236	95	40.1
65 years and over	407	73	17.9	280	23	8.2	124	50	39.9	37	5	B
Related children under 18 years	4,249	2,476	58.3	1,794	805	44.9	2,349	1,615	68.7	353	195	55.3
Under 6 years	1,546	1,070	69.2	586	364	62.2	934	695	74.4	111	66	59.1
6 to 17 years	2,703	1,405	52.0	1,209	441	36.5	1,415	919	65.0	242	129	53.6
Own children 18 years and over	1,664	329	19.8	919	117	12.7	720	210	29.1	164	46	28.1
In unrelated subfamilies	374	171	45.8	282	113	39.9	87	57	66.1	67	37	B
Under 18 years	209	107	51.1	154	70	45.5	54	36	B	35	22	B
Under 6 years	89	56	62.9	66	35	B	22	20	B	12	9	B
6 to 17 years	120	51	42.4	88	35	39.5	31	16	B	23	13	B
18 years and over	165	64	38.9	128	43	33.2	33	21	B	31	15	B
Unrelated individuals	8,942	1,922	21.5	6,997	1,251	17.9	1,785	620	34.7	594	219	36.8
Male	4,287	730	17.0	3,237	432	13.3	955	274	28.7	356	112	31.4
Under 65 years	3,792	624	16.5	2,839	382	13.5	864	224	26.0	335	99	29.4
Living alone	1,911	252	13.2	1,468	142	9.7	403	103	25.6	118	17	14.2
65 years and over	495	106	21.3	398	50	12.5	91	50	54.5	22	13	B
Living alone	449	90	20.0	366	42	11.5	77	42	54.2	20	13	B
Female	4,655	1,192	25.6	3,760	819	21.8	829	346	41.7	237	107	44.9
Under 65 years	2,986	680	22.8	2,337	464	19.8	591	193	32.7	168	68	40.6
Living alone	1,858	320	17.2	1,438	211	14.7	402	107	26.7	84	26	30.6

[Continued]

★ 626 ★

Persons Living in Poverty in the South Region, by Type of Residence, Age Group, and Sex, 1992: Metropolitan Areas

[Continued]

Characteristic	All races Total	All races Below poverty level Number	All races Below poverty level Percent of total	White Total	White Below poverty level Number	White Below poverty level Percent of total	Black Total	Black Below poverty level Number	Black Below poverty level Percent of total	Hispanic origin[1] Total	Hispanic origin[1] Below poverty level Number	Hispanic origin[1] Below poverty level Percent of total
65 years and over	1,669	511	30.6	1,423	355	25.0	239	152	63.8	69	38	B
Living alone	1,609	480	29.8	1,377	331	24.0	225	145	64.6	66	37	B

Source: U.S. Bureau of the Census. *Poverty in the United States: 1992.* Current Population Reports, Series P60-185, U.S. Government Printing Office, Washington, D.C., 1993, p. 51. *Notes:* A (B) stands for base less than 75,000 or not applicable. 1. Persons of Hispanic origin may be of any race.

★ 627 ★

Poverty

Persons Living in Poverty in the South Region, by Type of Residence, Age Group, and Sex, 1992: Not in Central Cities

Numbers are shown in thousands and refer to persons, families, and unrelated individuals, as of March of the following year.

Characteristic	All races Total	All races Below poverty level Number	All races Below poverty level Percent of total	White Total	White Below poverty level Number	White Below poverty level Percent of total	Black Total	Black Below poverty level Number	Black Below poverty level Percent of total	Hispanic origin[1] Total	Hispanic origin[1] Below poverty level Number	Hispanic origin[1] Below poverty level Percent of total
South												
Not in Central Cities												
Both sexes												
Total	38,429	4,545	11.8	32,175	2,972	9.2	5,238	1,446	27.6	2,570	528	20.6
Under 18 years	10,059	1,815	18.0	7,976	1,090	13.7	1,772	675	38.1	816	228	28.0
18 to 24 years	3,514	523	14.9	2,788	330	11.9	618	182	29.5	275	60	21.7
25 to 34 years	6,433	688	10.7	5,345	471	8.8	905	195	21.6	481	110	22.9
35 to 44 years	6,372	428	6.7	5,357	271	5.1	818	139	17.0	390	49	12.6
45 to 54 years	4,738	302	6.4	4,119	219	5.3	507	74	14.7	285	36	12.5
55 to 59 years	1,612	107	6.6	1,397	72	5.2	171	33	19.2	87	9	10.4
60 to 64 years	1,529	148	9.6	1,366	103	7.6	146	39	26.4	58	11	B
65 years and over	4,172	535	12.8	3,827	414	10.8	300	109	36.4	178	26	14.6
65 to 74 years	2,525	252	10.0	2,280	177	7.8	213	71	33.1	129	221	16.0
75 years and over	1,647	283	17.2	1,547	236	15.3	86	39	44.5	49	5	B
Male												
Total	18,732	1,798	9.6	15,781	1,196	7.6	2,460	548	22.3	1,326	269	20.3
Under 18 years	5,115	832	16.3	4,102	526	12.8	871	286	32.8	428	120	28.0
18 to 24 years	1,729	205	11.9	1,387	130	9.4	278	71	25.6	159	30	18.8
25 to 34 years	3,174	245	7.7	2,639	167	6.3	434	64	14.8	256	61	23.8
35 to 44 years	3,127	156	5.0	2,662	115	4.3	380	39	10.3	189	23	12.2
45 to 54 years	2,310	120	5.2	2,027	86	4.3	232	29	12.3	158	21	13.1
55 to 59 years	755	34	4.6	672	23	3.4	67	12	B	34	2	B
60 to 64 years	771	37	4.8	699	32	4.6	58	3	B	27	1	B
65 years and over	1,752	168	9.6	1,593	117	7.3	140	46	32.6	75	12	15.4
65 to 74 years	1,073	86	8.1	957	55	5.7	102	29	27.9	54	7	B
75 years and over	678	81	12.0	637	62	9.7	38	17	B	21	4	B
Female												
Total	19,697	2,747	13.9	16,394	1,776	10.8	2,778	898	32.3	1,244	259	20.8
Under 18 years	4,944	983	19.9	3,873	564	14.6	901	389	43.2	388	108	27.9
18 to 24 years	1,786	318	17.8	1,401	201	14.3	341	111	32.6	116	30	25.8
25 to 34 years	3,258	443	13.6	2,707	304	11.2	471	131	27.8	225	49	21.8
35 to 44 years	3,245	272	8.4	2,694	156	5.8	438	100	22.7	202	26	12.9
45 to 54 years	2,428	181	7.5	2,092	133	6.4	275	46	16.6	127	15	11.8
55 to 59 years	857	73	8.5	725	50	6.8	104	21	20.6	53	7	B

[Continued]

★ 627 ★

Persons Living in Poverty in the South Region, by Type of Residence, Age Group, and Sex, 1992: Not in Central Cities

[Continued]

Characteristic	All races			White			Black			Hispanic origin[1]		
	Total	Below poverty level Number	Below poverty level Percent of total	Total	Below poverty level Number	Below poverty level Percent of total	Total	Below poverty level Number	Below poverty level Percent of total	Total	Below poverty level Number	Below poverty level Percent of total
60 to 64 years	758	110	14.5	667	72	10.7	88	36	40.8	31	10	B
65 years and over	2,420	367	15.2	2,234	297	13.3	160	63	39.7	103	14	13.9
65 to 74 years	1,452	166	11.4	1,323	122	9.3	111	42	37.9	75	13	B
75 years and over	968	202	20.8	911	174	19.2	49	21	B	28	1	B
Household relationship												
Total	38,429	4,545	11.8	32,175	2,972	9.2	5,238	1,446	27.6	2,570	528	20.6
65 years and over	4,172	535	12.8	3,827	414	10.8	300	109	36.4	178	26	14.6
In families	33,539	3,550	10.6	28,041	2,237	8.0	4,558	1,213	26.6	2,347	449	19.1
Householder	10,763	1,030	9.6	9,220	677	7.3	1,310	325	24.8	636	106	16.7
Under 65 years	9,164	907	9.9	7,760	584	7.5	1,182	297	25.2	570	99	17.3
65 years and over	1,599	123	7.7	1,460	93	6.4	127	28	21.7	66	7	B
Related children under 18 years	9,926	1,738	17.5	7,878	1,039	13.2	1,738	649	37.4	806	221	27.4
Under 6 years	3,543	720	20.3	2,827	450	15.9	609	259	42.5	291	84	28.8
6 to 17 years	6,384	1,018	15.9	5,051	589	11.7	1,129	390	34.6	515	137	26.6
Own children 18 years and over	3,065	231	7.5	2,399	99	4.1	581	128	22.0	228	24	10.6
In married-coupled families	27,721	1,748	6.3	24,332	1,327	5.5	2,637	367	13.9	1,922	345	18.0
Husbands	8,765	476	5.4	7,860	370	4.7	720	90	12.5	500	80	15.9
Under 65 years	7,411	373	5.0	6,598	289	4.4	639	70	11.0	451	73	16.1
65 years and over	1,355	103	7.6	1,263	81	6.4	81	20	24.6	49	7	B
Wives	8,765	476	5.4	7,837	374	4.8	701	90	12.9	517	83	16.0
Under 65 years	7,683	395	5.1	6,810	305	4.5	649	80	12.3	478	77	16.0
65 years and over	1,082	81	7.5	1,027	69	6.7	52	10	B	39	6	B
Related children under 18 years	7,682	680	8.8	6,597	527	8.0	841	131	15.6	674	167	24.7
Under 6 years	2,804	280	10.0	2,403	207	8.6	306	65	21.2	261	72	27.4
6 to 17 years	4,878	399	8.2	4,194	320	7.6	535	66	12.3	414	95	23.0
Own children 18 years and over	2,097	91	4.3	1,720	38	2.2	309	50	16.3	154	8	5.4
In families with female householder, no spouse present	4,860	1,715	35.3	3,037	867	28.6	1,705	811	47.6	310	92	29.8
Householder	1,646	525	31.9	1,095	293	26.7	517	224	43.4	94	24	25.9
Under 65 years	1,438	506	35.2	925	282	30.5	481	215	44.7	81	24	30.2
65 years and over	208	19	9.4	169	10	6.1	35	9	B	13	-	B
Related children under 18 years	2,016	1,025	50.8	1,121	494	44.0	836	506	60.5	105	50	47.4
Under 6 years	665	430	64.8	372	241	64.8	281	187	66.7	25	12	B
6 to 17 years	1,352	595	44.0	750	253	33.7	555	318	57.4	80	37	46.5
Own children 18 years and over	815	130	16.0	559	54	9.7	242	74	30.7	58	14	B
In unrelated subfamilies	219	104	47.6	159	62	39.3	57	42	B	17	7	B
Under 18 years	119	66	55.2	85	40	47.3	34	25	B	7	4	B
Under 6 years	55	37	B	38	22	B	17	15	B	4	2	B
6 to 17 years	64	29	B	47	18	B	17	11	B	3	1	B
18 years and over	100	39	38.5	74	22	B	24	16	B	10	4	B
Unrelated individuals	4,671	890	19.1	3,975	672	16.9	623	191	30.7	206	72	34.9
Male	2,149	294	13.7	1,774	208	11.7	328	75	22.8	130	46	35.1
Under 65 years	1,873	240	12.8	1,546	181	11.7	284	51	18.1	125	42	33.8
Living alone	964	108	11.2	810	77	9.5	137	28	20.2	36	7	B
65 years and over	276	54	19.6	229	28	12.1	44	23	B	5	3	B
Living alone	242	44	18.0	204	21	10.2	35	30	B	5	3	B
Female	2,523	597	23.7	2,201	464	21.1	295	116	39.5	76	26	34.5
Under 65 years	1,609	339	21.1	1,356	254	18.7	231	72	31.4	59	20	B
Living alone	1,000	160	16.0	823	115	13.9	174	45	25.9	30	9	B
65 years and over	913	258	28.2	844	210	24.9	64	44	B	17	6	B
Living alone	879	237	26.9	814	191	23.5	60	41	B	16	6	B

Source: U.S. Bureau of the Census. *Poverty in the United States: 1992*. Current Population Reports, Series P60-185, U.S. Government Printing Office, Washington, D.C., 1993, p. 53. *Notes:* A dash (-) stands for zero or rounds to zero. A (B) stands for base less than 75,000 or not applicable. 1. Persons of Hispanic origin may be of any race.

★ 628 ★

Poverty

Persons Living in Poverty in the South Region, by Type of Residence, Age Group, and Sex, 1992: Outside Metropolitan Areas

Numbers are shown in thousands and refer to persons, families, and unrelated individuals, as of March of the following year.

Characteristic	All races			White			Black			Hispanic origin[1]		
	Total	Below poverty level		Total	Below poverty level		Total	Below poverty level		Total	Below poverty level	
		Number	Percent of total		Number	Percent of total		Number	Percent of total		Number	Percent of total
South												
Outside Metropolitan areas												
Both sexes												
Total	24,676	5,075	20.6	19,740	3,184	16.1	4,489	1,806	40.2	790	345	43.7
Under 18 years	6,723	1,894	28.2	5,028	1,057	21.0	1,565	808	51.6	307	169	55.1
18 to 24 years	2,207	490	22.2	1,759	337	19.2	416	145	34.8	118	50	42.5
25 to 34 years	3,485	658	18.9	2,768	411	14.8	639	234	36.6	122	59	48.3
35 to 44 years	3,753	550	14.6	2,966	329	11.1	716	211	29.4	85	16	18.7
45 to 54 years	2,629	328	12.5	2,275	253	11.1	294	73	24.7	66	18	B
55 to 59 years	1,142	204	17.8	992	136	13.7	132	63	47.9	17	5	B
60 to 64 years	1,069	213	19.9	893	139	15.6	157	69	44.3	22	9	B
65 years and over	3,668	738	20.1	3,060	523	17.1	572	204	35.6	53	19	B
65 to 74 years	2,145	363	16.9	1,777	261	14.7	351	97	27.6	37	14	B
75 years and over	1,523	376	24.7	1,283	262	20.4	220	107	48.5	17	5	B
Male												
Total	11,935	2,214	18.6	9,588	1,424	14.8	2,121	746	35.2	382	165	43.1
Under 18 years	3,483	996	28.6	2,574	581	22.6	829	398	48.0	143	81	56.6
18 to 24 years	1,113	197	17.7	888	141	15.9	208	53	25.2	54	19	B
25 to 34 years	1,651	256	15.5	1,354	186	13.7	254	62	24.2	79	37	46.6
35 to 44 years	1,821	246	13.5	1,451	150	10.3	342	92	26.8	33	7	B
45 to 54 years	1,290	136	10.5	1,143	124	10.9	122	12	9.4	30	7	B
55 to 59 years	551	97	17.6	480	62	12.8	61	32	B	11	4	B
60 to 64 years	491	79	16.1	412	40	9.8	68	36	B	9	3	B
65 years and over	1,536	207	13.5	1,285	140	10.9	237	63	26.6	22	7	B
65 to 74 years	963	109	11.3	811	85	10.5	150	24	15.8	15	5	B
75 years and over	572	99	17.2	473	55	11.6	86	39	45.4	7	2	B
Female												
Total	12,741	2,861	22.5	10,152	1,761	17.3	2,368	1,060	44.8	408	180	44.2
Under 18 years	3,240	899	27.7	2,454	476	19.4	736	410	55.7	164	88	53.9
18 to 24 years	1,094	293	26.7	870	196	22.5	207	92	44.4	64	31	B
25 to 34 years	1,835	403	21.9	1,413	225	15.9	385	172	44.8	42	22	B
35 to 44 years	1,932	303	15.7	1,515	179	11.8	374	119	31.9	52	9	B
45 to 54 years	1,338	192	14.4	1,132	129	11.3	172	61	35.5	35	10	B
55 to 59 years	591	106	18.0	511	74	14.5	71	31	B	6	2	B
60 to 64 years	578	134	23.1	481	99	20.6	88	33	37.6	13	5	B
65 years and over	2,133	531	24.9	1,775	383	21.5	335	141	42.1	31	12	B
65 to 74 years	1,182	254	21.5	966	176	18.2	201	73	36.4	22	9	B
75 years and over	950	277	29.2	809	207	25.6	134	68	50.5	9	4	B
Household relationship												
Total	24,676	5,075	20.6	19,740	3,184	16.1	4,489	1,806	40.2	790	345	43.7
65 years and over	3,668	738	20.1	3,060	523	17.1	572	204	35.6	53	19	B
In families	21,690	3,988	18.4	17,318	2,354	13.6	3,979	1,565	39.3	681	272	40.0
Householder	6,972	1,137	16.3	5,709	698	12.2	1,145	416	36.3	176	63	35.8
Under 65 years	5,569	971	17.4	4,546	595	13.1	920	361	39.3	157	59	37.5
65 years and over	1,404	166	11.8	1,163	103	8.9	225	54	24.1	18	4	B
Related children under 18 years	6,595	1,794	27.2	4,917	967	19.7	1,551	799	51.5	286	152	53.1
Under 6 years	2,055	669	32.6	1,577	401	25.4	433	258	59.5	118	77	65.5
6 to 17 years	4,540	1,125	24.8	3,341	566	16.9	1,118	541	48.4	168	75	44.5
Own children 18 years and over	1,889	306	16.2	1,388	155	11.2	474	145	30.5	45	4	B
In married-coupled families	17,529	2,268	12.9	15,120	1,716	11.4	2,095	506	24.2	554	204	36.9
Husbands	5,551	599	10.8	4,898	462	9.4	567	122	21.6	140	45	32.0
Under 65 years	4,382	489	11.2	3,874	386	10.0	432	93	21.6	123	41	33.5
65 years and over	1,168	110	9.4	1,024	77	7.5	135	29	21.3	18	4	B

[Continued]

★ 628 ★

Persons Living in Poverty in the South Region, by Type of Residence, Age Group, and Sex, 1992: Outside Metropolitan Areas

[Continued]

Characteristic	All races			White			Black			Hispanic origin[1]		
	Total	Below poverty level		Total	Below poverty level		Total	Below poverty level		Total	Below poverty level	
		Number	Percent of total		Number	Percent of total		Number	Percent of total		Number	Percent of total
Wives	5,551	599	10.8	4,895	467	9.5	554	122	22.1	146	44	30.1
Under 65 years	4,688	534	11.4	4,127	417	10.1	467	107	23.0	135	43	31.8
65 years and over	863	65	7.6	768	50	6.6	87	15	17.0	11	1	B
Related children under 18 years	4,959	874	17.6	4,127	652	15.8	731	209	28.6	219	106	48.3
Under 6 years	1,588	364	22.9	1,374	287	20.9	172	69	40.0	84	51	61.4
6 to 17 years	3,371	510	15.1	2,752	364	13.2	558	140	25.1	135	54	40.2
Own children 18 years and over	1,218	143	11.7	994	94	9.5	207	43	20.5	33	3	B
In families with female householder, no spouse present	3,450	1,547	44.8	1,721	521	30.3	1,659	1,002	60.4	88	48	54.6
Householder	1,160	476	41.0	623	190	30.5	509	279	54.7	23	11	B
Under 65 years	950	428	45.1	503	170	33.9	426	254	59.8	21	11	B
65 years and over	210	48	22.8	120	20	16.3	83	24	29.0	2	-	B
Related children under 18 years	1,450	869	59.9	649	269	41.4	778	585	75.2	48	35	B
Under 6 years	411	284	69.2	166	96	57.6	241	187	77.4	20	16	B
6 to 17 years	1,039	584	56.3	483	173	35.9	536	398	74.3	28	19	B
Own children 18 years and over	559	149	26.6	306	47	15.2	246	102	41.6	12	1	B
In unrelated subfamilies	166	115	69.1	143	107	74.8	21	8	B	26	21	B
Under 18 years	97	72	74.5	85	67	78.4	10	6	B	18	16	B
Under 6 years	40	32	B	37	32	B	3	-	B	10	7	B
6 to 17 years	57	41	B	48	35	B	8	6	B	9	9	B
18 years and over	69	43	B	58	40	B	10	2	B	8	5	B
Unrelated individuals	2,820	972	34.5	2,279	723	31.7	490	233	47.7	83	52	62.3
Male	1,136	291	25.6	873	201	23.1	240	80	33.4	41	23	B
Under 65 years	899	222	24.6	703	157	22.4	173	55	31.6	38	20	B
Living alone	548	113	20.7	454	86	18.9	81	24	29.3	9	1	B
65 years and over	237	69	29.2	170	44	25.8	67	25	B	3	3	B
Living alone	200	58	28.8	150	36	23.9	50	22	B	3	3	B
Female	1,684	681	40.4	1,406	522	37.1	250	153	61.4	42	29	B
Under 65 years	762	289	37.9	613	226	36.9	127	60	47.5	29	19	B
Living alone	523	163	31.3	411	118	28.8	101	45	44.9	10	4	B
65 years and over	923	392	42.5	793	296	37.3	122	93	75.9	13	10	B
Living alone	893	377	42.2	770	288	37.4	116	86	74.5	13	10	B

Source: U.S. Bureau of the Census. *Poverty in the United States: 1992.* Current Population Reports, Series P60-185, U.S. Government Printing Office, Washington, D.C., 1993, p. 54. *Notes:* A dash (-) stands for zero or rounds to zero. A (B) stands for base less than 75,000 or not applicable. 1. Persons of Hispanic origin may be of any race.

★ 629 ★

Poverty

Persons Living in Poverty in the West Region, by Type of Residence, Age Group, and Sex, 1992: Central Cities

Numbers are shown in thousands and refer to persons, families, and unrelated individuals, as of March of the following year.

Characteristic	All races			White			Black			Hispanic origin[1]		
	Total	Below poverty level		Total	Below poverty level		Total	Below poverty level		Total	Below poverty level	
		Number	Percent of total		Number	Percent of total		Number	Percent of total		Number	Percent of total
West												
Central Cities												
Both sexes												
Total	19,071	3,391	17.8	15,497	2,672	17.2	1,427	328	23.0	4,612	1,557	33.8
Under 18 years	4,934	1,366	27.7	3,897	1,050	26.9	426	132	30.9	1,690	751	44.5

[Continued]

★ 629 ★

Persons Living in Poverty in the West Region, by Type of Residence, Age Group, and Sex, 1992: Central Cities

[Continued]

Characteristic	All races			White			Black			Hispanic origin[1]		
	Total	Below poverty level		Total	Below poverty level		Total	Below poverty level		Total	Below poverty level	
		Number	Percent of total		Number	Percent of total		Number	Percent of total		Number	Percent of total
18 to 24 years	2,054	502	24.5	1,676	434	25.9	139	19	13.5	662	223	33.8
25 to 34 years	3,376	570	16.9	2,735	442	16.2	259	70	27.1	883	250	28.3
35 to 44 years	3,040	379	12.5	2,492	288	11.6	224	52	23.0	638	163	25.6
45 to 54 years	2,112	212	10.0	1,720	160	9.3	162	20	12.3	351	79	22.6
55 to 59 years	701	62	8.9	563	60	10.7	46	2	B	110	23	20.5
60 to 64 years	806	96	11.9	696	76	11.0	39	6	B	86	23	27.1
65 years and over	2,048	203	9.9	1,718	162	9.4	131	28	21.6	191	43	22.4
65 to 74 years	1,233	113	9.1	1,017	84	8.2	93	22	23.2	127	26	20.2
75 years and over	815	90	11.0	701	78	11.1	38	7	B	64	17	B
Male												
Total	9,489	1,536	16.2	7,788	1,194	15.3	666	160	24.1	2,299	703	30.6
Under 18 years	2,559	672	26.3	2,038	499	24.5	220	75	33.9	834	349	41.9
18 to 24 years	1,037	209	20.1	840	179	21.4	70	12	B	335	94	28.2
25 to 34 years	1,736	248	14.3	1,401	194	13.9	132	27	20.9	453	105	23.1
35 to 44 years	1,508	183	12.1	1,261	143	11.3	91	24	26.9	346	87	25.2
45 to 54 years	1,054	93	8.9	902	77	8.5	57	3	B	174	42	24.3
55 to 59 years	359	29	8.1	299	28	9.4	23	-	B	57	9	B
60 to 64 years	389	40	10.3	343	32	9.3	15	2	B	32	10	B
65 years and over	847	61	7.2	703	42	5.9	58	18	B	68	6	B
65 to 74 years	556	37	6.7	443	21	4.7	52	15	B	44	2	B
75 years and over	291	24	8.2	259	21	8.0	7	3	B	24	3	B
Female												
Total	9,582	1,855	19.4	7,709	1,477	19.2	761	168	22.0	2,313	853	36.9
Under 18 years	2,375	694	29.2	1,858	551	29.6	206	57	27.7	857	402	46.9
18 to 24 years	1,018	294	28.8	836	254	30.4	69	7	B	327	129	39.5
25 to 34 years	1,639	322	19.7	1,334	248	18.6	127	43	33.6	430	145	33.8
35 to 44 years	1,532	196	12.8	1,231	145	11.8	133	27	20.4	291	76	26.0
45 to 54 years	1,058	119	11.2	818	83	10.2	106	17	16.3	177	37	21.0
55 to 59 years	342	33	9.8	263	32	12.0	23	2	B	53	13	B
60 to 64 years	417	56	13.4	353	44	12.6	24	4	B	55	13	B
65 years and over	1,201	141	11.8	1,015	120	11.8	73	11	B	123	37	30.4
65 to 74 years	677	75	11.1	574	63	11.0	41	7	B	83	23	28.0
75 years and over	524	66	12.6	441	57	12.9	32	4	B	40	14	B
Household relationship												
Total	19,071	3,391	17.8	15,497	2,672	17.2	1,427	328	23.0	4,612	1,557	33.8
65 years and over	2,048	203	9.9	1,718	162	9.4	131	28	21.6	191	43	22.4
In families	15,160	2,468	16.3	12,100	1,883	15.6	1,175	242	20.6	4,031	1,311	32.5
Householder	4,731	669	14.1	3,857	508	13.2	353	75	21.3	1,004	308	30.7
Under 65 years	4,038	628	15.5	3,272	475	14.5	314	66	21.1	938	292	31.1
65 years and over	693	42	6.0	584	32	5.5	39	9	B	67	16	B
Related children under 18 years	4,788	1,264	26.4	3,770	954	25.3	416	127	30.6	1,635	706	43.2
Under 6 years	1,874	565	30.1	1,494	453	30.3	141	42	29.9	658	321	48.7
6 to 17 years	2,913	699	24.0	2,276	501	22.0	275	85	30.9	977	385	39.4
Own children 18 years and over	1,281	127	9.9	937	99	10.6	149	12	7.9	349	77	22.2
In married-coupled families	11,590	1,233	10.6	9,427	971	10.3	645	43	6.6	2,781	693	24.9
Husbands	3,492	277	7.9	2,902	214	7.4	189	17	9.2	641	137	21.3
Under 65 years	2,932	255	8.7	2,438	200	8.2	154	10	6.2	605	134	22.2
65 years and over	560	22	3.9	464	14	3.0	355	8	B	36	3	B
Wives	3,492	277	7.9	2,909	223	7.7	171	11	6.2	660	133	20.1
Under 65 years	3,081	263	8.5	2,555	216	8.4	144	4	3.1	627	132	21.0
65 years and over	411	14	3.4	354	8	2.2	27	6	B	34	1	B
Related children under 18 years	3,414	571	16.7	2,752	445	16.2	190	10	5.5	1,079	348	32.2
Under 6 years	1,343	239	17.8	1,091	207	18.9	70	3	B	415	148	35.5
6 to 17 years	2,070	332	16.0	1,660	238	14.3	121	8	6.4	664	200	30.1
Own children 18 years and over	814	55	6.7	596	42	7.1	68	-	B	214	34	15.8

[Continued]

★ 629 ★

Persons Living in Poverty in the West Region, by Type of Residence, Age Group, and Sex, 1992: Central Cities

[Continued]

Characteristic	All races			White			Black			Hispanic origin[1]		
	Total	Below poverty level		Total	Below poverty level		Total	Below poverty level		Total	Below poverty level	
		Number	Percent of total		Number	Percent of total		Number	Percent of total		Number	Percent of total
In families with female householder, no spouse present	2,637	1,035	39.2	1,854	745	40.2	475	189	39.9	886	504	56.9
Householder	917	329	35.9	657	235	35.8	152	57	37.3	258	139	53.9
Under 65 years	789	307	38.9	547	215	39.3	143	56	39.1	231	125	54.2
65 years and over	128	22	17.0	110	20	18.6	9	1	B	27	14	B
Related children under 18 years	1,078	598	55.4	763	431	56.5	207	111	53.4	439	305	69.6
Under 6 years	409	283	69.1	299	210	70.4	68	39	B	186	148	79.4
6 to 17 years	669	315	47.1	464	221	47.5	139	72	51.5	253	158	62.4
Own children 18 years and over	390	65	16.7	275	49	17.9	74	12	B	114	36	31.5
In unrelated subfamilies	243	150	61.8	205	139	67.8	18	9	B	89	69	77.7
Under 18 years	121	84	69.7	103	79	76.9	10	4	B	40	36	B
Under 6 years	64	48	B	53	44	B	4	4	B	21	19	B
6 to 17 years	57	36	B	50	36	B	5	-	B	19	16	B
18 years and over	122	66	54.0	103	60	58.7	8	5	B	48	33	B
Unrelated individuals	3,668	773	21.1	3,192	649	20.3	234	77	32.8	492	177	35.9
Male	1,946	393	20.2	1,680	318	18.9	129	51	39.5	303	99	32.8
Under 65 years	1,742	355	20.4	1,501	291	19.4	113	41	36.8	290	97	33.5
Living alone	780	99	12.6	650	74	11.5	63	12	B	69	11	B
65 years and over	204	38	18.4	180	27	15.0	17	10	B	13	2	B
Living alone	166	28	17.1	146	21	14.2	14	7	B	9	2	B
Female	1,722	380	22.1	1,512	331	21.9	104	25	24.5	189	77	41.0
Under 65 years	1,228	285	23.2	1,058	247	23.4	88	22	24.6	158	63	39.6
Living alone	643	114	17.7	537	88	16.5	68	18	B	71	18	B
65 years and over	494	95	19.3	454	84	18.5	16	4	B	31	15	B
Living alone	467	82	17.5	431	73	17.0	16	4	B	24	10	B

Source: U.S. Bureau of the Census. *Poverty in the United States: 1992.* Current Population Reports, Series P60-185, U.S. Government Printing Office, Washington, D.C., 1993, p. 56. *Notes:* A dash (-) stands for zero or rounds to zero. A (B) stands for base less than 75,000 or not applicable. 1. Persons of Hispanic origin may be of any race.

★ 630 ★

Poverty

Persons Living in Poverty in the West Region, by Type of Residence, Age Group, and Sex, 1992: Metropolitan Areas

Numbers are shown in thousands and refer to persons, families, and unrelated individuals, as of March of the following year.

Characteristic	All races			White			Black			Hispanic origin[1]		
	Total	Below poverty level		Total	Below poverty level		Total	Below poverty level		Total	Below poverty level	
		Number	Percent of total		Number	Percent of total		Number	Percent of total		Number	Percent of total
West												
Metropolitan areas												
Both sexes												
Total	46,743	6,686	14.3	39,586	5,346	13.5	2,515	612	24.3	9,907	2,806	28.3
Under 18 years	12,677	2,693	21.2	10,548	2,115	20.0	775	250	32.3	3,565	1,345	37.7
18 to 24 years	4,530	938	20.7	3,787	778	20.5	252	60	24.0	1,305	392	30.0
25 to 34 years	8,039	1,106	13.8	6,761	894	13.2	485	114	23.6	1,908	451	23.7
35 to 44 years	7,651	794	10.4	6,502	628	9.7	380	80	21.0	1,491	338	22.7
45 to 54 years	5,218	379	7.3	4,414	294	6.7	268	30	11.0	746	117	15.7
55 to 59 years	1,791	158	8.7	1,519	139	9.2	97	12	11.9	265	48	18.1
60 to 64 years	1,850	199	10.8	1,621	154	9.5	69	16	B	225	51	22.6
65 years and over	4,990	422	8.5	4,435	346	7.8	188	50	26.3	403	65	16.1
65 to 74 years	3,050	242	7.9	2,693	189	7.0	131	37	27.9	275	40	14.4

[Continued]

★ 630 ★

Persons Living in Poverty in the West Region, by Type of Residence, Age Group, and Sex, 1992: Metropolitan Areas

[Continued]

Characteristic	All races			White			Black			Hispanic origin[1]		
	Total	Below poverty level		Total	Below poverty level		Total	Below poverty level		Total	Below poverty level	
		Number	Percent of total		Number	Percent of total		Number	Percent of total		Number	Percent of total
75 years and over	1,940	180	9.3	1,742	157	9.0	56	13	B	128	25	19.8
Male												
Total	23,339	3,047	13.1	19,867	2,412	12.1	1,235	294	23.8	5,076	1,304	25.7
Under 18 years	6,630	1,351	20.4	5,561	1,033	18.6	414	135	32.6	1,836	663	36.1
18 to 24 years	2,255	372	16.5	1,884	302	16.0	127	36	28.4	667	154	23.1
25 to 34 years	4,090	481	11.7	3,397	397	11.7	263	43	16.5	994	195	19.6
35 to 44 years	3,835	358	9.3	3,319	293	8.8	156	33	21.1	807	170	21.0
45 to 54 years	2,569	173	6.7	2,238	139	6.2	113	11	9.6	368	62	17.0
55 to 59 years	915	89	9.7	778	81	10.4	53	5	B	129	23	17.8
60 to 64 years	917	85	9.3	800	61	7.7	29	7	B	110	22	20.0
65 years and over	2,127	139	6.5	1,888	107	5.7	79	25	31.3	165	14	8.7
65 to 74 years	1,401	91	6.5	1,233	68	5.5	64	17	B	116	9	8.0
75 years and over	726	48	6.7	656	39	5.9	15	7	B	49	5	B
Female												
Total	23,404	3,639	15.5	19,719	2,934	14.9	1,280	317	24.8	4,832	1,503	31.1
Under 18 years	6,046	1,342	22.2	4,986	1,082	21.7	361	115	31.8	1,729	682	39.4
18 to 24 years	2,274	566	24.9	1,902	476	25.0	125	24	19.5	638	237	37.2
25 to 34 years	3,948	626	15.8	3,364	497	14.8	221	71	32.0	914	257	28.1
35 to 44 years	3,816	436	11.4	3,183	336	10.5	225	47	21.0	684	168	24.6
45 to 54 years	2,648	206	7.8	2,176	155	7.1	155	19	12.1	378	54	14.4
55 to 59 years	876	67	7.6	740	58	7.8	44	7	B	136	25	18.4
60 to 64 years	933	114	12.2	820	93	11.3	40	10	B	115	29	25.2
65 years and over	2,862	283	9.9	2,547	239	9.4	109	25	22.8	238	51	21.3
65 to 74 years	1,649	151	9.2	1,461	121	8.3	67	19	B	159	30	19.0
75 years and over	1,214	132	10.8	1,086	118	10.9	42	6	B	79	20	25.8
Household relationship												
Total	46,743	6,686	14.3	39,586	5,346	13.5	2,515	612	24.3	9,907	2,806	28.3
65 years and over	4,990	422	8.5	4,436	346	7.8	188	50	26.3	403	65	16.1
In families	38,954	5,022	12.9	32,706	3,902	11.9	2,092	482	23.1	8,768	2,370	27.0
Householder	12,001	1,345	11.2	10,243	1,038	10.1	632	143	22.6	2,173	554	25.5
Under 65 years	10,190	1,224	12.0	8,610	941	10.9	566	124	21.9	2,028	532	26.2
65 years and over	1,811	121	6.7	1,633	97	5.9	66	19	B	145	22	15.0
Related children under 18 years	12,384	2,497	20.2	10,286	1,936	18.8	765	245	32.0	3,454	1,255	36.3
Under 6 years	4,547	1,027	22.6	3,757	836	22.2	281	82	29.1	1,346	541	40.2
6 to 17 years	7,836	1,469	18.7	6,529	1,100	16.9	483	163	33.7	2,108	714	33.9
Own children 18 years and over	3,297	269	8.2	2,648	191	7.2	246	39	16.0	790	126	16.0
In married-coupled families	31,048	2,629	8.5	26,474	2,123	8.0	1,193	102	8.5	6,383	1,327	20.8
Husbands	9,321	622	6.7	8,091	494	6.1	351	37	10.4	1,511	273	18.1
Under 65 years	7,797	549	7.0	6,709	438	6.5	305	24	7.8	1,413	266	18.8
65 years and over	1,525	73	4.8	1,381	56	4.1	46	13	B	97	7	7.6
Wives	9,321	622	6.7	8,061	498	6.2	320	29	9.1	1,564	259	16.6
Under 65 years	8,138	575	7.1	6,976	465	6.7	288	19	6.5	1,478	257	17.4
65 years and over	1,183	47	4.0	1,085	32	3.0	32	10	B	85	2	2.5
Related children under 18 years	9,381	1,173	12.5	7,933	962	12.1	376	28	7.5	2,418	655	27.1
Under 6 years	3,490	490	14.0	2,918	424	14.5	156	10	6.3	912	272	29.8
6 to 17 years	5,890	683	11.6	5,015	538	10.7	220	18	8.3	1,505	383	25.5
Own children 18 years and over	2,178	112	5.2	1,746	76	4.4	115	4	3.6	511	61	11.9
In families with female householder, no spouse present	5,839	2,027	34.7	4,502	1,484	33.0	777	358	46.1	1,706	854	50.0
Householder	1,970	612	31.1	1,529	449	29.3	247	102	41.2	474	232	48.9
Under 65 years	1,713	566	33.1	1,308	410	31.3	225	95	42.4	437	217	49.8
65 years and over	257	46	17.8	221	39	17.5	23	6	B	37	15	B
Related children under 18 years	2,367	1,159	49.0	1,822	847	46.5	347	202	58.2	830	517	62.3
Under 6 years	801	460	57.5	625	352	56.3	105	63	60.2	331	227	68.5
6 to 17 years	1,566	699	44.6	1,197	495	41.4	242	139	57.4	499	290	58.2
Own children 18 years and over	921	142	15.5	729	101	13.8	121	35	29.1	242	58	23.9

[Continued]

★ 630 ★

Persons Living in Poverty in the West Region, by Type of Residence, Age Group, and Sex, 1992: Metropolitan Areas

[Continued]

Characteristic	All races			White			Black			Hispanic origin[1]		
	Total	Below poverty level		Total	Below poverty level		Total	Below poverty level		Total	Below poverty level	
		Number	Percent of total		Number	Percent of total		Number	Percent of total		Number	Percent of total
In unrelated subfamilies	457	251	54.8	411	231	56.2	18	9	B	176	120	68.2
Under 18 years	233	144	61.7	210	134	63.8	10	4	B	84	68	81.3
Under 6 years	118	86	72.4	104	78	75.1	4	4	B	42	36	B
6 to 17 years	114	58	50.6	106	56	52.6	5	-	B	41	32	B
18 years and over	225	107	47.6	201	97	48.3	8	5	B	92	52	56.4
Unrelated individuals	7,332	1,414	19.3	6,469	1,214	18.8	405	120	29.6	964	317	32.9
Male	3,788	704	18.6	3,291	584	17.7	235	78	33.2	605	172	28.5
Under 65 years	3,373	652	19.3	2,922	545	18.7	211	66	31.4	582	167	28.7
Living alone	1,458	184	12.6	1,228	143	11.7	110	20	18.1	149	26	17.2
65 years and over	415	52	12.4	368	39	10.6	24	12	B	22	5	B
Living alone	316	35	11.0	282	25	8.9	21	9	B	17	3	B
Female	3,544	709	20.0	3,179	630	19.8	170	42	24.6	359	145	40.3
Under 65 years	2,464	542	22.0	3,170	479	22.1	142	36	25.6	300	125	41.6
Living alone	1,216	183	15.0	1,045	143	13.7	106	31	29.6	122	33	27.2
65 years and over	1,081	168	15.5	1,009	151	15.0	29	6	B	59	20	B
Living alone	1,019	144	14.1	957	132	13.8	27	6	B	50	14	B

Source: U.S. Bureau of the Census. *Poverty in the United States: 1992.* Current Population Reports, Series P60-185, U.S. Government Printing Office, Washington, D.C., 1993, p. 55. *Notes:* A dash (-) stands for zero or rounds to zero. A (B) stands for base less than 75,000 or not applicable. 1. Persons of Hispanic origin may be of any race.

★ 631 ★

Poverty

Persons Living in Poverty in the West Region, by Type of Residence, Age Group, and Sex, 1992: Not in Central Cities

Numbers are shown in thousands and refer to persons, families, and unrelated individuals, as of March of the following year.

Characteristic	All races			White			Black			Hispanic origin[1]		
	Total	Below poverty level		Total	Below poverty level		Total	Below poverty level		Total	Below poverty level	
		Number	Percent of total		Number	Percent of total		Number	Percent of total		Number	Percent of total
West												
Metropolitan, not in Central Cities												
Both sexes												
Total	27,672	3,295	11.9	24,090	2,675	11.1	1,088	284	26.1	5,295	1,250	23.6
Under 18 years	7,742	1,327	17.1	6,651	1,065	16.0	350	119	33.9	1,874	593	31.7
18 to 24 years	2,476	435	17.6	2,110	344	16.3	113	42	37.0	643	168	26.1
25 to 34 years	4,663	536	11.5	4,025	451	11.2	226	44	19.5	1,024	201	19.7
35 to 44 years	4,611	416	9.0	4,010	340	8.5	156	28	18.2	854	175	20.5
45 to 54 years	3,106	167	5.4	2,694	134	5.0	106	10	9.1	395	37	9.5
55 to 59 years	1,090	93	8.6	956	79	8.3	51	10	B	155	25	16.3
60 to 64 years	1,044	103	9.9	925	77	8.4	31	10	B	139	28	19.8
65 years and over	2,941	219	7.4	2,718	184	6.8	57	21	B	212	22	10.4
65 to 74 years	1,817	129	7.1	1,676	105	6.3	38	15	B	148	14	9.4
75 years and over	1,125	90	8.0	1,042	79	7.6	18	6	B	64	8	B
Male												
Total	13,850	1,511	10.9	12,079	1,218	10.1	569	134	23.5	2,777	600	21.6
Under 18 years	4,071	679	16.7	3,523	534	15.1	195	61	31.1	1,002	314	31.3
18 to 24 years	1,219	163	13.4	1,045	123	11.8	57	24	B	332	60	18.0
25 to 34 years	2,354	232	9.9	1,995	203	10.2	132	16	12.1	540	90	16.7
35 to 44 years	2,327	175	7.5	2,058	150	7.3	65	8	B	461	82	17.9
45 to 54 years	1,515	80	5.3	1,336	62	4.7	56	8	B	194	20	10.5

[Continued]

★ 631 ★

Persons Living in Poverty in the West Region, by Type of Residence, Age Group, and Sex, 1992: Not in Central Cities

[Continued]

Characteristic	All races: Total	All races: Below poverty level Number	All races: Below poverty level Percent of total	White: Total	White: Below poverty level Number	White: Below poverty level Percent of total	Black: Total	Black: Below poverty level Number	Black: Below poverty level Percent of total	Hispanic origin[1]: Total	Hispanic origin[1]: Below poverty level Number	Hispanic origin[1]: Below poverty level Percent of total
55 to 59 years	556	60	10.8	479	53	11.0	30	5	B	72	13	B
60 to 64 years	528	45	8.5	457	29	6.4	14	5	B	78	12	15.1
65 years and over	1,280	78	6.1	1,186	65	5.5	20	7	B	97	9	9.0
65 to 74 years	845	53	6.3	789	47	6.0	12	3	B	71	7	B
75 years and over	435	25	5.6	396	18	4.5	8	4	B	25	2	B
Female												
Total	13,822	1,784	12.9	12,020	1,457	12.1	519	150	28.8	2,519	649	25.8
Under 18 years	3,671	648	17.6	3,128	531	17.0	155	58	37.4	872	280	32.1
18 to 24 years	1,257	272	21.7	1,066	221	20.8	55	17	B	311	108	34.8
25 to 34 years	2,309	303	13.1	2,030	248	12.2	94	28	29.8	484	111	23.0
35 to 44 years	2,284	241	10.5	1,953	191	9.8	91	20	21.8	393	92	23.5
45 to 54 years	1,590	87	5.5	1,357	72	5.3	49	2	B	201	17	8.5
55 to 59 years	533	33	6.2	477	26	5.5	21	5	B	83	12	14.3
60 to 64 years	516	58	11.3	468	48	10.3	16	5	B	60	16	B
65 years and over	1,661	141	8.5	1,532	119	7.8	37	14	B	115	13	11.6
65 to 74 years	972	76	7.8	887	58	6.5	26	12	B	76	7	9.2
75 years and over	690	65	9.5	645	61	9.5	10	2	B	39	6	B
Household relationship												
Total	27,672	3,295	11.9	24,090	2,675	11.1	1,088	284	26.1	5,295	1,250	23.6
65 years and over	2,941	219	7.4	2,718	184	6.8	57	21	B	212	22	10.4
In families	23,794	2,554	10.7	20,606	2,019	9.8	917	240	26.2	4,737	1,059	22.4
Householder	7,270	676	9.3	6,386	530	8.3	279	68	24.4	1,168	246	21.0
Under 65 years	6,152	597	9.7	5,338	466	8.7	252	58	22.8	1,090	240	22.0
65 years and over	1,117	79	7.1	1,048	65	6.2	27	11	B	78	6	7.6
Related children under 18 years	7,596	1,233	16.2	6,516	982	15.1	349	118	33.7	1,818	548	30.2
Under 6 years	2,673	463	17.3	2,263	383	16.9	141	40	28.3	688	220	31.9
6 to 17 years	4,923	770	15.6	4,253	599	14.1	208	78	37.4	1,130	329	29.1
Own children 18 years and over	2,016	142	7.0	1,711	92	5.4	96	27	28.5	440	49	11.1
In married-coupled families	19,458	1,396	7.2	17,047	1,152	6.8	548	59	10.8	3,602	633	17.6
Husbands	5,829	345	5.9	5,189	281	5.4	162	19	11.8	869	137	15.7
Under 65 years	4,864	294	6.0	4,271	238	5.6	151	14	9.4	808	132	16.3
65 years and over	965	51	5.3	918	42	4.6	11	5	B	61	5	B
Wives	5,829	345	5.9	5,152	274	5.3	150	18	12.3	903	127	14.0
Under 65 years	5,058	312	6.2	4,421	250	5.7	144	14	9.8	852	125	14.7
65 years and over	771	33	4.3	731	24	3.3	6	4	B	52	1	B
Related children under 18 years	5,967	602	10.1	5,181	518	10.0	186	18	9.5	1,338	308	23.0
Under 6 years	2,147	251	11.7	1,826	217	11.9	86	7	8.2	497	125	25.0
6 to 17 years	3,820	352	9.2	3,355	300	9.0	100	11	10.6	841	183	21.8
Own children 18 years and over	1,364	58	4.2	1,150	34	3.0	47	4	B	297	27	9.1
In families with female householder, no spouse present	3,202	992	31.0	2,648	738	27.9	302	169	55.8	820	349	42.6
Householder	1,053	283	26.9	873	213	24.4	95	45	47.3	217	93	42.9
Under 65 years	924	259	28.1	761	195	25.6	81	39	48.3	206	92	44.5
65 years and over	129	24	18.6	112	18	16.3	14	6	B	11	1	B
Related children under 18 years	1,289	561	43.6	1,058	416	39.3	140	91	65.3	391	211	54.1
Under 6 years	391	177	45.3	326	141	43.4	37	24	B	145	79	54.5
6 to 17 years	897	384	42.8	733	275	37.5	103	67	65.2	246	132	53.8
Own children 18 years and over	531	77	14.6	455	51	11.3	46	23	B	128	22	17.1
In unrelated subfamilies	214	100	46.8	206	92	44.7	-	-	B	87	51	58.6
Under 18 years	112	59	53.0	107	55	51.1	-	-	B	43	32	B
Under 6 years	54	38	B	51	35	B	-	-	B	21	17	B
6 to 17 years	58	22	B	56	20	B	-	-	B	22	15	B
18 years and over	102	41	40.0	99	37	37.6	-	-	B	44	19	B
Unrelated individuals	3,664	641	17.5	3,278	564	17.2	172	43	25.2	472	140	29.7
Male	1,842	311	16.9	1,610	266	16.5	105	27	25.4	302	73	24.1
Under 65 years	1,631	297	18.2	1,422	254	17.9	98	25	25.2	292	70	23.9

[Continued]

★ 631 ★

Persons Living in Poverty in the West Region, by Type of Residence, Age Group, and Sex, 1992: Not in Central Cities

[Continued]

Characteristic	All races			White			Black			Hispanic origin[1]		
	Total	Below poverty level		Total	Below poverty level		Total	Below poverty level		Total	Below poverty level	
		Number	Percent of total		Number	Percent of total		Number	Percent of total		Number	Percent of total
Living alone	678	86	12.6	579	69	11.9	47	8	B	80	15	18.4
65 years and over	211	14	6.7	189	12	6.4	7	2	B	9	3	B
Living alone	150	6	4.2	136	4	3.2	7	2	B	7	1	B
Female	1,822	330	18.1	1,667	298	17.9	66	16	B	170	67	39.6
Under 65 years	1,235	257	20.8	1,112	231	20.8	54	15	B	142	62	43.9
Living alone	573	69	12.1	509	54	10.7	37	13	B	50	15	B
65 years and over	587	73	12.4	555	67	12.1	13	2	B	28	5	B
Living alone	551	62	11.2	527	59	11.2	11		B	26	4	B

Source: U.S. Bureau of the Census. *Poverty in the United States: 1992.* Current Population Reports, Series P60-185, U.S. Government Printing Office, Washington, D.C., 1993, p. 57. *Notes:* A dash (-) stands for zero or rounds to zero. A (B) stands for base less than 75,000 or not applicable. 1. Persons of Hispanic origin may be of any race.

★ 632 ★

Poverty

Persons Living in Poverty in the West Region, by Type of Residence, Age Group, and Sex, 1992: Outside Metropolitan Areas

Numbers are shown in thousands and refer to persons, families, and unrelated individuals, as of March of the following year.

Characteristic	All races			White			Black			Hispanic origin[1]		
	Total	Below poverty level		Total	Below poverty level		Total	Below poverty level		Total	Below poverty level	
		Number	Percent of total		Number	Percent of total		Number	Percent of total		Number	Percent of total
West												
Outside Metropolitan areas												
Both sexes												
Total	8,218	1,221	14.9	7,510	1,035	13.8	84	22	26.5	758	232	30.6
Under 18 years	2,352	514	21.8	2,107	440	20.9	24	10	B	289	118	40.9
18 to 24 years	650	134	20.5	573	106	18.5	19	9	B	65	25	B
25 to 34 years	1,097	166	15.1	1,002	145	14.5	5	2	B	138	37	26.4
35 to 44 years	1,369	159	11.6	1,267	136	10.7	11	1	B	121	25	20.7
45 to 54 years	888	65	7.3	825	50	6.1	5	1	B	61	7	B
55 to 59 years	360	29	8.1	336	24	7.1	4	-	B	21	2	B
60 to 64 years	336	33	9.7	303	30	9.8	5	-	B	26	9	B
65 years and over	1,166	123	10.5	1,096	104	9.5	10	-	B	38	10	B
65 to 74 years	700	61	8.7	649	51	7.9	10	-	B	32	8	B
75 years and over	466	62	13.3	446	53	12.0	-	-	B	6	2	B
Male												
Total	4,119	551	13.4	3,761	470	12.5	40	9	B	393	123	31.2
Under 18 years	1,233	257	20.8	1,095	220	20.1	11	4	B	163	71	43.6
18 to 24 years	311	54	17.2	272	45	16.4	10	3	B	28	11	B
25 to 34 years	566	68	12.1	511	59	11.6	5	2	B	77	18	23.3
35 to 44 years	679	75	11.1	632	68	10.7	3	-	B	56	12	B
45 to 54 years	443	28	6.3	422	24	5.6	1	-	B	29	2	B
55 to 59 years	160	13	8.0	149	8	5.3	-	-	B	12	2	B
60 to 64 years	167	12	7.1	150	10	7.0	5	-	B	10	3	B
65 years and over	560	45	8.0	529	36	6.8	5	-	B	18	4	B
65 to 74 years	337	25	7.4	318	23	7.1	5	-	B	14	4	B
75 years and over	224	20	8.9	211	13	6.3	-	-	B	4	-	B
Female												
Total	4,099	670	16.3	3,749	565	15.1	44	13	B	365	110	30.0

[Continued]

★ 632 ★

Persons Living in Poverty in the West Region, by Type of Residence, Age Group, and Sex, 1992: Outside Metropolitan Areas

[Continued]

Characteristic	All races			White			Black			Hispanic origin[1]		
	Total	Below poverty level		Total	Below poverty level		Total	Below poverty level		Total	Below poverty level	
		Number	Percent of total		Number	Percent of total		Number	Percent of total		Number	Percent of total
Under 18 years	1,119	257	23.0	1,012	219	21.7	13	6	B	125	47	37.3
18 to 24 years	339	80	23.6	301	61	20.3	9	6	B	37	14	B
25 to 34 years	532	98	18.4	491	86	17.5	1	-	B	61	19	B
35 to 44 years	690	84	12.1	635	68	10.7	7	1	B	64	13	B
45 to 54 years	445	37	8.2	403	27	6.6	4	1	B	32	5	B
55 to 59 years	200	16	8.2	187	16	8.4	4	-	B	9	-	B
60 to 64 years	169	21	12.3	153	19	12.6	-	-	B	16	6	B
65 years and over	606	78	12.8	567	69	12.1	5	-	B	21	6	B
65 to 74 years	364	36	9.9	331	28	8.6	5	-	B	18	4	B
75 years and over	242	42	17.3	235	40	17.1	-	-	B	3	2	B
Household relationship												
Total	8,218	1,221	14.9	7,510	1,035	13.8	84	22	26.5	758	232	30.6
65 years and over	1,166	123	10.5	1,096	104	9.5	10	-	B	38	10	B
In families	7,096	918	12.9	6,480	775	12.0	80	22	26.9	684	202	29.5
Householder	2,298	257	11.2	2,138	219	10.2	31	10	B	185	46	25.0
Under 65 years	1,838	223	12.1	1,707	194	11.3	26	10	B	171	42	24.6
65 years and over	460	34	7.3	431	25	5.9	5	-	B	14	4	B
Related children under 18 years	2,314	485	21.0	2,076	415	20.0	24	10	B	280	110	39.4
Under 6 years	747	190	25.5	659	153	23.3	15	10	B	93	37	40.2
6 to 17 years	1,567	295	18.8	1,417	262	18.5	10	-	B	187	73	39.0
Own children 18 years and over	419	35	8.4	349	18	5.1	11	2	B	44	10	B
In married-coupled families	6,034	552	9.1	5,606	480	8.6	48	6	B	564	132	23.5
Husbands	1,927	134	7.0	1,829	121	6.6	18	3	B	151	29	19.1
Under 65 years	1,501	110	7.3	1,423	99	7.0	13	3	B	140	25	18.2
65 years and over	426	24	5.7	407	21	5.3	5	-	B	11	3	B
Wives	1,927	134	7.0	1,808	118	6.5	14	-	B	161	33	20.4
Under 65 years	1,605	121	7.6	1,507	108	7.2	9	-	B	153	32	21.2
65 years and over	323	13	4.0	301	10	3.3	5	-	B	8	-	B
Related children under 18 years	1,827	264	14.5	1,665	228	13.7	12	3	B	215	63	29.1
Under 6 years	580	94	16.3	527	79	15.0	4	3	B	76	24	32.0
6 to 17 years	1,248	170	13.6	1,138	149	13.1	7	-	B	139	38	27.6
Own children 18 years and over	303	17	5.5	266	12	4.4	4	-	B	30	8	B
In families with female householder, no spouse present	788	307	39.0	644	253	39.3	32	16	B	78	47	60.2
Householder	267	103	38.5	222	84	37.9	13	7	B	22	12	B
Under 65 years	235	97	41.2	195	80	41.0	13	7	B	19	11	B
65 years and over	32	6	B	27	4	B	-	-	B	3	1	B
Related children under 18 years	372	187	50.3	310	161	51.9	13	7	B	42	31	B
Under 6 years	127	81	63.4	95	62	65.5	10	7	B	9	8	B
6 to 17 years	245	107	43.6	215	98	45.9	2	-	B	32	23	B
Own children 18 years and over	93	15	15.8	68	6	B	7	2	B	11	2	B
In unrelated subfamilies	57	40	B	46	35	B	1	-	B	11	11	B
Under 18 years	33	25	B	28	22	B	-	-	B	7	6	B
Under 6 years	7	7	B	6	6	B	-	-	B	4	4	B
6 to 17 years	26	18	B	23	16	B	-	-	B	3	2	B
18 years and over	24	15	B	18	13	B	1	-	B	5	5	B
Unrelated individuals	1,065	263	24.7	984	225	22.8	3	1	B	63	20	B
Male	541	114	21.1	495	99	20.1	3	1	B	33	9	B
Under 65 years	427	99	23.1	384	85	22.2	3	1	B	28	8	B
Living alone	242	49	20.0	221	42	19.1	3	1	B	14	4	B
65 years and over	114	16	13.8	111	14	12.7	-	-	B	5	1	B
Living alone	90	11	12.6	87	10	11.2	-	-	B	5	1	B
Female	525	149	28.3	489	125	25.6	-	-	B	29	10	B
Under 65 years	308	91	29.4	280	71	25.5	-	-	B	21	6	B
Living alone	180	40	22.4	168	34	20.3	-	-	B	10	1	B

[Continued]

★ 632 ★

Persons Living in Poverty in the West Region, by Type of Residence, Age Group, and Sex, 1992: Outside Metropolitan Areas

[Continued]

Characteristic	All races			White			Black			Hispanic origin[1]		
	Total	Below poverty level		Total	Below poverty level		Total	Below poverty level		Total	Below poverty level	
		Number	Percent of total		Number	Percent of total		Number	Percent of total		Number	Percent of total
65 years and over	217	58	26.8	209	54	25.8	-	-	B	8	5	B
Living alone	207	54	26.2	200	50	25.2	-	-	B	7	5	B

Source: U.S. Bureau of the Census. *Poverty in the United States: 1992.* Current Population Reports, Series P60-185, U.S. Government Printing Office, Washington, D.C., 1993, p. 58. *Notes:* A dash (-) stands for zero or rounds to zero. A (B) stands for base less than 75,000 or not applicable. 1. Persons of Hispanic origin may be of any race.

★ 633 ★

Poverty

Persons Living in Poverty, by Age Group, 1973-1992

Numbers are shown in thousands.

Year and characteristic	Under 18 years						18 to 64 years			65 years and over		
	All persons			Related children in families			Total	Below poverty		Total	Below poverty	
	Total	Below poverty		Total	Below poverty							
		Number	Percent		Number	Percent		Number	Percent		Number	Percent
All races												
1992	66,834	14,617	21.9	65,691	13,876	21.1	156,265	18,281	11.7	30,870	3,983	12.9
1991	65,918	14,341	21.8	64,800	13,658	21.1	154,671	17,585	11.4	30,590	3,781	12.4
1990	65,049	13,431	20.6	63,908	12,715	19.9	153,502	16,496	10.7	30,093	3,658	12.2
1989	64,144	12,590	19.6	63,225	12,001	19.0	152,282	15,575	10.2	29,566	3,363	11.4
1988	63,747	12,455	19.5	62,906	11,935	19.0	150,761	15,809	10.5	29,022	3,481	12.0
1987	63,294	12,843	20.3	62,423	12,275	19.7	149,201	15,815	10.6	28,487	3,563	12.5
1986	62,948	12,876	20.5	62,009	12,257	19.8	147,631	16,017	10.8	27,975	3,477	12.4
1985	62,876	13,010	20.7	62,019	12,483	20.1	146,396	16,598	11.3	27,322	3,456	12.6
1984	62,447	13,420	21.5	61,681	12,929	21.0	144,551	16,952	11.7	26,818	3,330	12.4
1983	62,334	13,911	22.3	61,578	13,427	21.8	143,052	17,767	12.4	26,313	3,625	13.8
1982	62,345	13,647	21.9	61,565	13,139	21.3	141,328	17,000	12.0	25,738	3,751	14.6
1981	62,449	12,505	20.0	61,756	12,068	19.5	139,477	15,464	11.1	25,231	3,853	15.3
1980	62,914	11,543	18.3	62,168	11,114	17.9	137,428	13,858	10.1	24,686	3,871	15.7
1979	63,375	10,377	16.4	62,646	9,993	16.0	135,333	12,014	8.9	24,194	3,682	15.2
1978	62,311	9,931	15.9	61,987	9,722	15.7	130,169	11,332	8.7	23,175	3,233	14.0
1977	63,137	10,288	16.2	62,823	10,028	16.0	128,262	11,316	8.8	22,468	3,177	14.1
1976	64,028	10,273	16.0	63,729	10,081	15.8	126,175	11,389	9.0	22,100	3,313	15.0
1975	65,079	11,104	17.1	64,750	10,882	16.8	124,122	11,456	9.2	21,662	3,317	15.3
1974	66,134	10,156	15.4	65,802	9,967	15.1	122,101	10,132	8.3	21,127	3,085	14.6
1973	66,959	9,642	14.4	66,626	9,453	14.2	120,060	9,977	8.3	20,602	3,354	16.3
White												
1992	53,090	8,955	16.9	52,122	8,333	16.0	131,230	12,575	9.6	27,501	2,992	10.9
1991	52,523	8,848	16.8	51,627	8,316	16.1	130,300	12,098	9.3	27,297	2,802	10.3
1990	51,929	8,232	15.9	51,028	7,696	15.1	129,784	11,387	8.8	26,898	2,707	10.1
1989	51,400	7,599	14.8	50,704	7,164	14.1	128,974	10,647	8.3	26,479	2,539	9.6
1988	51,203	7,435	14.5	50,590	7,095	14.0	128,031	10,687	8.3	26,001	2,593	10.0
1987	51,012	7,788	15.3	50,360	7,398	14.7	126,991	10,703	8.4	25,602	2,704	10.6
1986	51,111	8,209	16.1	50,356	7,714	15.3	125,998	11,285	9.0	25,173	2,689	10.7
1985	51,031	8,253	16.2	50,358	7,838	15.6	125,258	11,909	9.5	24,629	2,698	11.0

[Continued]

★ 633 ★

Persons Living in Poverty, by Age Group, 1973-1992

[Continued]

Year and characteristic	Under 18 years - All persons - Total	Under 18 years - All persons - Below poverty - Number	Under 18 years - All persons - Below poverty - Percent	Under 18 years - Related children in families - Total	Under 18 years - Related children in families - Below poverty - Number	Under 18 years - Related children in families - Below poverty - Percent	18 to 64 years - Total	18 to 64 years - Below poverty - Number	18 to 64 years - Below poverty - Percent	65 years and over - Total	65 years and over - Below poverty - Number	65 years and over - Below poverty - Percent
1984	50,814	8,472	16.7	50,192	8,086	16.1	123,922	11,904	9.6	24,206	2,579	10.7
1983	50,726	8,862	17.5	50,183	8,534	17.0	123,014	12,347	10.0	23,754	2,776	11.7
1982	50,920	8,678	17.0	50,305	8,282	16.5	121,766	11,971	9.8	23,234	2,870	12.4
1981	51,140	7,785	15.2	50,553	7,429	14.7	120,574	10,790	8.9	22,791	2,978	13.1
1980	51,653	7,181	13.9	51,002	6,817	13.4	118,935	9,478	8.0	22,325	3,042	13.6
1979	52,262	6,193	11.8	51,687	5,909	11.4	117,583	8,110	6.9	21,898	2,911	13.3
1978	51,669	5,831	11.3	51,409	5,674	11.0	113,832	7,897	6.9	20,950	2,530	12.1
1977	52,563	6,097	11.6	52,299	5,943	11.4	112,374	7,893	7.0	20,316	2,426	11.9
1976	53,428	6,189	11.6	53,167	6,034	11.3	110,717	7,890	7.1	20,020	2,633	13.2
1975	54,405	6,927	12.7	54,126	6,748	12.5	109,105	8,210	7.5	19,654	2,634	13.4
1974	55,590	6,223	11.2	55,320	6,079	11.0	107,579	7,053	6.6	19,206	2,460	12.8
1973	(NA)	(NA)	(NA)	56,211	5,462	9.7	(NA)	(NA)	(NA)	(NA)	2,698	14.4
Black												
1992	10,599	4,938	46.6	10,471	4,850	46.3	18,657	4,788	25.7	2,660	887	33.3
1991	10,350	4,755	45.9	10,178	4,637	45.6	18,355	4,607	25.1	2,606	880	33.8
1990	10,162	4,550	44.8	9,980	4,412	44.2	18,097	4,427	24.5	2,547	860	33.8
1989	10,012	4,375	43.7	9,847	4,257	43.2	17,833	4,164	23.3	2,487	763	30.7
1988	9,865	4,296	43.5	9,681	4,148	42.8	17,548	4,275	24.4	2,436	785	32.2
1987	9,730	4,385	45.1	9,546	4,234	44.4	17,245	4,361	25.3	2,387	774	32.4
1986	9,629	4,148	43.1	9,467	4,037	42.7	16,911	4,113	24.3	2,331	722	31.0
1985	9,545	4,157	43.6	9,405	4,057	43.1	16,667	4,052	24.3	2,273	717	31.5
1984	9,480	4,413	46.6	9,356	4,320	46.2	16,369	4,368	26.7	2,238	710	31.7
1983	9,417	4,398	46.7	9,245	4,273	46.2	16,065	4,694	29.2	2,197	791	36.0
1982	9,400	4,472	47.6	9,269	4,388	47.3	15,692	4,415	28.1	2,124	811	38.2
1981	9,374	4,237	45.2	9,291	4,170	44.9	15,358	4,117	26.8	2,102	820	39.0
1980	9,368	3,961	42.3	9,287	3,906	42.1	14,987	3,835	25.6	2,054	783	38.1
1979	9,307	3,833	41.2	9,172	3,745	40.8	14,596	3,478	23.8	2,040	740	36.2
1978	9,229	3,830	41.5	9,168	3,781	41.2	13,774	3,133	22.7	1,954	662	33.9
1977	9,296	3,888	41.8	9,253	3,850	41.6	13,483	3,137	23.3	1,930	701	36.3
1976	9,322	3,787	40.6	9,291	3,758	40.4	13,224	3,163	23.9	1,852	644	34.8
1975	9,421	3,925	41.7	9,374	3,884	41.4	12,872	2,968	23.1	1,795	652	36.3
1974	9,439	3,755	39.8	9,384	3,713	39.6	12,539	2,836	22.6	1,721	591	34.3
1973	(NA)	(NA)	(NA)	9,405	3,822	40.6	(NA)	(NA)	(NA)	1,672	620	37.1
Hispanic origin[1]												
1992	7,807	3,116	39.9	7,589	2,946	38.8	13,691	3,270	23.9	1,222	269	22.0
1991	7,648	3,094	40.4	7,473	2,977	39.8	13,279	3,009	22.7	1,143	237	20.8
1990	7,457	2,865	38.4	7,300	2,750	37.7	12,857	2,896	22.5	1,091	245	22.5
1989	7,186	2,603	36.2	7,040	2,496	35.5	12,536	2,616	20.9	1,024	211	20.6
1988	7,003	2,631	37.6	6,908	2,576	37.3	12,056	2,501	20.7	1,005	225	22.4
1987	6,792	2,670	39.3	6,692	2,606	38.9	11,718	2,509	21.4	885	243	27.5
1986	6,646	2,507	37.7	6,511	2,413	37.1	11,206	2,406	21.5	906	204	22.5
1985	6,475	2,606	40.3	6,346	2,512	39.6	10,685	2,411	22.6	915	219	23.9
1984	6,068	2,376	39.2	5,982	2,317	38.7	10,029	2,254	22.5	819	176	21.5
1983	6,066	2,312	38.1	5,977	2,251	37.7	9,697	2,148	22.5	782	173	22.1
1982	5,527	2,181	39.5	5,436	2,117	38.9	8,262	1,963	23.8	596	159	26.6
1981	5,369	1,925	35.9	5,291	1,874	35.4	8,084	1,642	20.3	568	146	25.7
1980	5,276	1,749	33.2	5,211	1,718	33.0	7,740	1,563	20.2	582	179	30.8
1979	5,483	1,535	28.0	5,426	1,505	27.7	7,314	1,232	16.8	574	154	26.8

[Continued]

★ 633 ★

Persons Living in Poverty, by Age Group, 1973-1992

[Continued]

Year and characteristic	Under 18 years						18 to 64 years			65 years and over		
	All persons			Related children in families			Total	Below poverty		Total	Below poverty	
	Total	Below poverty		Total	Below poverty			Number	Percent		Number	Percent
		Number	Percent		Number	Percent						
1978	5,012	1,384	27.6	4,972	1,354	27.2	6,527	1,098	16.8	539	125	23.2
1977	5,028	1,422	28.3	5,000	1,402	28.0	6,500	1,164	17.9	518	113	21.9
1976	4,771	1,443	30.2	4,736	1,424	30.1	6,034	1,212	20.1	464	128	27.7
1975	(NA)	(NA)	(NA)	4,896	1,619	33.1	(NA)	(NA)	(NA)	(NA)	137	32.6
1974	(NA)	(NA)	(NA)	4,939	1,414	28.6	(NA)	(NA)	(NA)	(NA)	117	28.9
1973	(NA)	(NA)	(NA)	4,910	1,364	27.8	(NA)	(NA)	(NA)	(NA)	95	24.9

Source: U.S. Bureau of the Census. *Poverty in the United States: 1992.* Current Population Reports, Series P60-185, U.S. Government Printing Office, Washington, D.C., 1993, pp. 4-5. *Notes:* An (NA) indicates data were not available. 1. Persons of Hispanic origin may be of any race.

★ 634 ★

Poverty

Persons Living in Poverty, by Age, Sex, and Household Relationship, 1992 - I

Numbers are shown in thousands and refer to persons, families, and unrelated individuals, as of March of the following year.

Characteristic	All races			White			Black			Hispanic origin[1]		
	Total	Below poverty level		Total	Below poverty level		Total	Below poverty level		Total	Below poverty level	
		Number	Percent of total		Number	Percent of total		Number	Percent of total		Number	Percent of total
All PERSONS												
Both sexes												
Total	253,969	36,880	14.5	211,820	24,523	11.6	31,916	10,613	33.3	22,720	6,655	29.3
Under 18 years	66,834	14,617	21.9	53,090	8,955	16.9	10,599	4,938	46.6	7,807	3,116	39.9
18 to 24 years	24,309	4,367	18.0	19,711	3,023	15.3	3,531	1,121	31.7	2,813	844	30.0
25 to 34 years	41,864	5,540	13.2	34,666	3,749	10.8	5,399	1,521	28.2	4,277	1,076	25.2
35 to 44 years	40,342	3,944	9.8	33,976	2,641	7.8	4,629	1,077	23.3	3,330	719	21.6
45 to 54 years	28,503	2,245	7.9	24,505	1,591	6.5	2,910	544	18.7	2,037	349	17.1
55 to 59 years	10,718	1,073	10.0	9,190	771	8.4	1,144	262	22.9	680	137	20.2
60 to 64 years	10,529	1,112	10.6	9,182	800	8.7	1,044	263	25.2	554	145	26.2
65 years and over	30,870	3,983	12.9	27,501	2,992	10.9	2,660	887	33.3	1,222	269	22.0
65 to 74 years	18,362	1,956	10.7	16,210	1,397	8.6	1,703	504	29.6	806	157	19.5
75 years and over	12,508	2,027	16.2	11,290	1,595	14.1	957	383	40.0	416	112	26.8
Male												
Total	123,873	15,700	12.7	103,850	10,493	10.1	15,001	4,388	29.3	11,378	3,067	27.0
Under 18 years	34,180	7,343	21.5	27,231	4,509	16.6	5,379	2,468	45.9	3,958	1,551	39.2
18 to 24 years	12,049	1,714	14.2	9,821	1,221	12.4	1,669	404	24.2	1,417	360	25.4
25 to 34 years	20,856	2,050	9.8	17,408	1,477	8.5	2,487	441	17.7	2,237	467	20.9
35 to 44 years	19,904	1,647	8.3	16,976	1,166	6.9	2,109	388	18.4	1,682	328	19.5
45 to 54 years	13,847	964	7.0	12,081	695	5.7	1,289	221	17.1	1,035	170	16.5
55 to 59 years	5,122	443	8.7	4,428	328	7.4	516	94	18.2	292	53	18.1
60 to 64 years	5,084	397	7.8	4,460	288	6.4	471	82	17.5	249	50	19.9
65 years and over	12,832	1,142	8.9	11,443	809	7.1	1,081	290	26.9	508	88	17.4
65 to 74 years	8,114	657	8.1	7,187	465	6.5	742	173	23.3	345	57	16.7
75 years and over	4,718	485	10.3	4,256	344	8.1	338	118	34.8	163	31	18.8
Female												
Total	130,096	21,180	16.3	107,970	14,030	13.0	16,915	6,225	36.8	11,342	3,588	31.6
Under 18 years	32,654	7,273	22.3	25,859	4,446	17.2	5,220	2,470	47.3	3,849	1,565	40.7
18 to 24 years	12,260	2,653	21.6	9,889	1,802	18.2	1,862	717	38.5	1,396	484	34.7
25 to 34 years	21,008	3,490	16.6	17,257	2,272	13.2	2,912	1,081	37.1	2,040	609	29.9
35 to 44 years	20,438	2,297	11.2	17,000	1,475	8.7	2,520	689	27.3	1,648	391	23.7

[Continued]

★ 634 ★

Persons Living in Poverty, by Age, Sex, and Household Relationship, 1992 - I

[Continued]

Characteristic	All races			White			Black			Hispanic origin[1]		
	Total	Below poverty level Number	Below poverty level Percent of total	Total	Below poverty level Number	Below poverty level Percent of total	Total	Below poverty level Number	Below poverty level Percent of total	Total	Below poverty level Number	Below poverty level Percent of total
45 to 54 years	14,655	1,281	8.7	12,424	896	7.2	1,620	323	20.0	1,002	178	17.8
55 to 59 years	5,597	630	11.3	4,762	443	9.3	628	168	26.8	387	84	21.7
60 to 64 years	5,445	715	13.1	4,721	512	10.8	573	181	31.5	305	96	31.3
65 years and over	18,038	2,840	15.7	16,057	2,183	13.6	1,579	596	37.7	715	181	25.3
65 to 74 years	10,249	1,299	12.7	9,023	932	10.3	960	331	34.5	462	100	21.6
75 years and over	7,790	1,542	19.8	7,034	1,252	17.8	619	265	42.8	253	81	32.0
PERSONS IN FAMILIES												
Both sexes												
Total	215,515	27,947	13.0	179,199	17,645	9.8	27,280	8,908	32.7	20,116	5,655	28.1
Under 18 years	65,748	13,911	21.2	52,172	8,361	16.0	10,476	4,856	46.4	7,606	2,958	38.9
18 to 24 years	19,692	2,793	14.2	15,771	1,724	10.9	3,116	937	30.1	2,368	623	26.3
25 to 34 years	33,065	4,100	12.4	27,316	2,677	9.8	4,326	1,243	28.7	3,492	862	24.7
35 to 44 years	34,393	2,958	8.6	29,092	1,933	6.6	3,779	851	22.5	2,894	585	20.2
45 to 54 years	24,350	1,507	6.2	21,055	1,077	5.1	2,292	338	14.8	1,770	285	16.1
55 to 59 years	8,915	606	6.8	7,721	423	5.5	853	158	18.5	593	108	18.1
60 to 64 years	8,528	588	6.9	7,525	400	5.3	739	150	20.3	456	102	22.4
65 years and over	20,825	1,484	7.1	18,547	1,050	5.7	1,700	375	22.0	935	133	14.2
65 to 74 years	13,652	876	6.4	12,118	616	5.1	1,159	231	20.0	641	86	13.4
75 years and over	7,172	609	8.5	6,429	434	6.8	541	143	26.5	294	47	15.9
Male												
Total	105,968	12,303	11.6	89,054	8,024	9.0	12,594	3,639	28.9	9,899	2,608	26.4
Under 18 years	33,659	7,028	20.9	26,792	4,251	15.9	5,325	2,431	45.7	3,865	1,485	38.4
18 to 24 years	9,700	1,023	10.5	7,831	659	8.4	1,463	318	21.8	1,175	251	21.3
25 to 34 years	15,548	1,310	8.4	13,056	969	7.4	1,801	274	15.2	1,715	355	20.7
35 to 44 years	16,205	1,073	6.6	13,970	763	5.5	1,535	240	15.7	1,384	242	17.5
45 to 54 years	11,750	640	5.4	10,340	478	4.6	972	121	12.5	863	137	15.9
55 to 59 years	4,350	270	6.2	3,795	208	5.5	394	48	12.2	252	42	16.6
60 to 64 years	4,301	255	5.9	3,833	178	4.6	333	54	16.1	217	41	18.7
65 years and over	10,475	705	6.7	9,437	518	5.5	771	153	19.9	427	56	13.2
65 to 74 years	6,841	413	6.0	6,125	309	5.0	557	92	16.6	291	38	13.2
75 years and over	3,633	292	8.0	3,312	210	6.3	214	61	28.5	135	18	13.2
Female												
Total	109,527	15,643	14.3	90,145	9,621	10.7	14,686	5,269	35.9	10,217	3,047	29.8
Under 18 years	32,089	6,883	21.4	25,379	4,110	16.2	5,151	2,425	47.1	3,741	1,473	39.4
18 to 24 years	9,992	1,771	17.7	7,940	1,066	13.4	1,653	619	37.4	1,194	373	31.2
25 to 34 years	17,516	2,790	15.9	14,260	1,709	12.0	2,525	969	38.4	1,776	507	28.6
35 to 44 years	18,188	1,885	10.4	15,122	1,170	7.7	2,244	611	27.2	1,510	342	22.7
45 to 54 years	12,600	867	6.9	10,715	598	5.6	1,319	217	16.5	907	148	16.3
55 to 59 years	4,565	336	7.4	3,926	215	5.5	459	110	24.0	341	66	19.3
60 to 64 years	4,227	333	7.9	3,693	222	6.0	406	97	23.8	239	61	25.7
65 years and over	10,350	780	7.5	9,110	531	5.8	929	222	23.9	509	77	15.1
65 to 74 years	6,811	463	6.8	5,993	307	5.1	602	139	23.1	350	48	13.7
75 years and over	3,539	317	9.0	3,117	225	7.2	327	82	25.2	159	29	18.3
Householder												
Total	68,144	7,960	11.7	57,858	5,160	8.9	7,888	2,435	30.9	5,318	1,395	26.2
Under 18 years	23	20	B	18	16	B	3	3	B	10	7	B
18 to 24 years	2,728	1,031	37.8	2,118	649	30.7	508	342	67.2	416	187	45.0
25 to 34 years	14,376	2,567	17.9	11,769	1,605	13.6	2,039	855	41.9	1,507	481	31.9
35 to 44 years	17,569	1,904	10.8	14,699	1,237	8.4	2,142	567	26.5	1,453	367	25.3
45 to 54 years	13,069	901	6.9	11,288	633	5.6	1,295	225	17.4	935	168	18.0
55 to 59 years	4,663	338	7.3	4,015	216	5.4	484	108	22.2	310	61	19.8
60 to 64 years	4,454	321	7.2	3,905	207	5.3	429	88	20.6	249	52	20.9
65 years and over	11,261	878	7.8	10,046	597	5.9	986	246	24.9	438	72	16.3
65 to 74 years	7,350	496	6.7	6,522	337	5.2	683	145	21.2	305	48	15.7
75 years and over	3,911	383	9.8	3,524	260	7.4	303	101	33.4	133	24	17.9

[Continued]

★ 634 ★

Persons Living in Poverty, by Age, Sex, and Household Relationship, 1992 - I

[Continued]

Characteristic	All races			White			Black			Hispanic origin[1]		
	Total	Below poverty level Number	Below poverty level Percent of total	Total	Below poverty level Number	Below poverty level Percent of total	Total	Below poverty level Number	Below poverty level Percent of total	Total	Below poverty level Number	Below poverty level Percent of total
Related children												
Under 18 years	65,691	13,876	21.1	52,122	8,333	16.0	10,471	4,850	46.3	7,589	2,946	38.8
Under 6 years	23,129	5,781	25.0	18,240	3,527	19.3	3,765	2,000	53.1	2,870	1,223	42.6
6 to 17 years	42,562	8,095	19.0	33,882	4,806	14.2	6,706	2,850	42.5	4,719	1,723	36.5
Own children												
Under 18 years	61,184	12,422	20.3	49,521	7,701	15.6	8,782	4,068	46.3	6,738	2,642	39.2
Under 6 years	21,019	5,105	24.3	17,010	3,232	19.0	2,989	1,633	54.6	2,469	1,080	43.7
6 to 17 years	40,165	7,317	18.2	32,511	4,469	13.7	5,793	2,436	42.0	4,270	1,562	36.6
18 years and over	21,091	1,833	8.7	16,572	950	5.7	3,705	803	21.7	1,888	333	17.7
PERSONS IN FAMILIES WITH RELATED CHILDREN UNDER 18												
Both sexes												
Total	137,988	24,008	17.4	111,044	14,867	13.4	20,461	7,983	39.0	15,780	5,147	32.6
Under 18 years	65,724	13,897	21.1	52,148	8,348	16.0	10,476	4,856	46.4	7,601	2,955	38.9
18 to 24 years	10,071	2,288	22.7	7,659	1,409	18.4	2,004	790	39.4	1,621	528	32.6
25 to 34 years	22,570	3,719	16.5	18,474	2,451	13.3	3,193	1,126	35.3	2,691	796	29.6
35 to 44 years	26,189	2,554	9.8	22,180	1,687	7.6	2,827	718	25.4	2,346	527	22.5
45 to 54 years	9,621	887	9.2	7,999	618	7.7	1,092	226	20.7	955	194	20.4
55 to 59 years	1,370	226	16.5	981	137	14.0	288	77	26.8	236	58	24.4
60 to 64 years	890	156	17.5	602	86	14.4	215	62	28.9	127	42	33.3
65 years and over	1,553	280	18.0	1,000	131	13.1	365	128	35.0	204	47	23.2
65 to 74 years	1,106	207	18.8	700	100	14.3	274	94	34.4	147	37	24.9
75 years and over	447	73	16.3	300	31	10.4	91	34	36.8	57	11	B

Source: U.S. Bureau of the Census. *Poverty in the United States: 1992.* Current Population Reports, Series P60-185, U.S. Government Printing Office, Washington, D.C., 1993, pp. 10-11. *Notes:* A dash (-) stands for zero or rounds to zero. A (B) stands for base less than 75,000 or not applicable. 1. Persons of Hispanic origin may be of any race.

★ 635 ★

Poverty

Persons Living in Poverty, by Age, Sex, and Household Relationship, 1992 - II

Numbers are shown in thousands and refer to persons, families, and unrelated individuals, as of March of the following year.

Characteristic	All races			White			Black			Hispanic origin[1]		
	Total	Below poverty level Number	Below poverty level Percent of total	Total	Below poverty level Number	Below poverty level Percent of total	Total	Below poverty level Number	Below poverty level Percent of total	Total	Below poverty level Number	Below poverty level Percent of total
PERSONS IN FAMILIES WITH RELATED CHILDREN UNDER 18 (continued)												
Male												
Total	66,516	10,335	15.5	54,383	6,624	12.2	9,035	3,185	35.2	7,611	2,346	30.8
Under 18 years	33,658	7,028	20.9	26,792	4,251	15.9	5,325	2,431	45.7	3,865	1,485	38.4
18 to 24 years	4,461	754	16.9	3,454	479	13.9	805	242	30.0	765	198	25.9
25 to 34 years	9,261	1,059	11.4	7,814	811	10.4	1,064	200	18.8	1,171	306	26.1
35 to 44 years	11,988	860	7.2	10,461	640	6.1	1,004	166	16.5	1,049	201	19.1
45 to 54 years	5,256	381	7.2	4,522	284	6.3	464	73	15.8	498	101	20.2
55 to 59 years	757	88	11.7	572	69	12.1	137	14	9.9	115	23	20.2
60 to 64 years	460	49	10.6	323	33	10.2	87	10	11.9	58	14	B
65 years and over	675	116	17.2	444	57	12.8	150	48	32.2	89	19	20.7

[Continued]

★ 635 ★

Persons Living in Poverty, by Age, Sex, and Household Relationship, 1992 - II

[Continued]

Characteristic	All races			White			Black			Hispanic origin[1]		
	Total	Below poverty level		Total	Below poverty level		Total	Below poverty level		Total	Below poverty level	
		Number	Percent of total		Number	Percent of total		Number	Percent of total		Number	Percent of total
65 to 74 years	499	88	17.5	330	47	14.2	115	35	30.5	61	15	B
75 years and over	175	29	16.4	114	10	8.6	34	13	B	28	4	B
Female												
Total	71,472	13,673	19.1	56,661	8,244	14.5	11,426	4,799	42.0	8,170	2,801	34.3
Under 18 years	32,066	6,869	21.4	25,356	4,097	16.2	5,151	2,425	47.1	3,736	1,470	39.3
18 to 24 years	5,611	1,534	27.3	4,205	929	22.1	1,199	548	45.7	856	330	38.5
25 to 34 years	13,309	2,660	20.0	10,660	1,640	15.4	2,129	926	43.5	1,520	490	32.3
35 to 44 years	14,201	1,695	11.9	11,719	1,047	8.9	1,823	552	30.3	1,296	326	25.1
45 to 54 years	4,366	506	11.6	3,477	334	9.6	629	153	24.3	457	94	20.5
55 to 59 years	613	137	22.4	409	68	16.7	150	64	42.3	121	34	28.5
60 to 64 years	429	107	25.0	279	54	19.2	128	52	40.4	69	28	B
65 years and over	878	164	18.7	556	75	13.4	215	80	36.9	114	29	25.2
65 to 74 years	606	120	19.8	369	53	14.4	158	59	37.2	85	22	25.6
75 years and over	272	44	16.2	187	21	11.4	57	21	B	29	7	B
Householder												
Total	35,492	6,269	17.7	28,709	3,926	13.7	5,316	2,075	39.0	3,655	1,184	32.4
Under 18 years	19	17	B	15	13	B	3	3	B	9	6	B
18 to 24 years	1,851	965	52.1	1,325	596	45.0	460	332	72.1	305	168	55.0
25 to 34 years	11,117	2,459	22.1	8,914	1,535	17.2	1,808	834	46.1	1,248	458	36.7
35 to 44 years	14,375	1,770	12.3	11,999	1,154	9.6	1,780	526	29.6	1,259	346	27.5
45 to 54 years	6,013	622	10.3	5,024	420	8.4	699	173	24.8	566	127	22.4
55 to 59 years	893	155	17.4	630	83	13.2	215	65	30.1	128	34	26.4
60 to 64 years	509	117	23.0	345	53	15.4	134	59	43.9	60	21	B
65 years and over	716	165	23.1	458	71	15.6	217	84	38.6	79	24	30.5
65 to 74 years	555	119	21.5	358	57	15.8	169	59	35.3	65	22	B
75 years and over	161	46	28.6	101	15	14.8	49	24	B	14	2	B
Related children												
Under 18 years	65,691	13,876	21.1	52,122	8,333	16.0	10,471	4,850	46.3	7,589	2,,946	38.8
Under 6 years	23,129	5,781	25.0	18,240	3,527	19.3	3,785	2,000	53.1	2,870	1,223	42.6
6 to 17 years	42,562	8,095	19.0	33,882	4,806	14.2	6,706	2,850	42.5	4,719	1,723	36.5
Own children												
Under 18 years	61,184	12,422	20.3	49,521	7,701	15.6	8,782	4,068	46.3	6,738	2,642	39.2
Under 6 years	21,019	5,105	24.3	17,010	3,232	19.0	2,989	1,633	54.6	2,469	1,080	43.7
6 to 17 years	40,165	7,317	18.2	32,511	4,469	13.7	5,793	2,436	42.0	4,270	1,582	36.6
18 years and over	8,014	1,120	14.0	5,758	538	9.3	1,890	538	28.5	1,041	239	22.9
PERSONS IN MARRIED-COUPLE FAMILIES												
Both sexes												
Total	171,514	12,830	7.5	150,715	10,053	6.7	13,555	1,942	14.3	14,624	3,136	21.4
Under 18 years	48,567	5,284	10.9	41,932	4,152	9.9	4,190	764	18.2	5,266	1,505	28.6
18 to 24 years	14,094	1,181	8.4	12,120	917	7.6	1,407	195	13.8	1,584	338	21.3
25 to 34 years	26,275	2,026	7.7	23,027	1,614	7.0	2,112	296	14.0	2,669	543	20.3
35 to 44 years	28,633	1,496	5.2	25,184	1,150	4.6	2,182	230	10.5	2,228	347	15.6
45 to 54 years	20,988	964	4.6	18,596	754	4.1	1,520	137	9.0	1,374	181	13.2
55 to 59 years	7,755	380	4.9	6,906	312	4.5	564	51	9.0	472	71	15.0
60 to 64 years	7,498	406	5.4	6,794	318	4.7	478	55	11.5	353	67	18.9
65 years and over	17,704	1,093	6.2	16,156	838	5.2	1,103	216	19.6	679	86	12.7
65 to 74 years	11,973	681	5.7	10,863	516	4.8	818	147	17.9	488	60	12.3
75 years and over	5,731	412	7.2	5,292	321	6.1	285	69	24.3	191	26	13.6
Male												
Total	87,646	6,570	7.5	77,003	5,148	6.7	7,082	1,005	14.2	7,483	1,599	21.4
Under 18 years	24,947	2,721	10.9	21,595	2,165	10.0	2,137	372	17.4	2,728	771	28.3

[Continued]

★ 635 ★

Persons Living in Poverty, by Age, Sex, and Household Relationship, 1992 - II

[Continued]

Characteristic	All races			White			Black			Hispanic origin[1]		
	Total	Below poverty level		Total	Below poverty level		Total	Below poverty level		Total	Below poverty level	
		Number	Percent of total		Number	Percent of total		Number	Percent of total		Number	Percent of total
18 to 24 years	7,005	520	7.4	5,987	391	6.5	731	102	14.0	778	139	17.9
25 to 34 years	12,879	991	7.7	11,238	789	7.0	1,084	148	13.7	1,347	278	20.6
35 to 44 years	14,335	801	5.6	12,587	610	4.8	1,144	134	11.7	1,122	191	17.0
45 to 54 years	10,755	504	4.7	9,566	396	4.1	783	71	9.1	714	101	14.1
55 to 59 years	3,989	198	5.0	3,544	161	4.5	304	28	9.2	237	34	14.2
60 to 64 years	3,956	196	4.9	3,572	153	4.3	263	19	7.4	194	34	17.4
65 years and over	9,780	639	6.5	8,915	482	5.4	637	130	20.5	363	52	14.4
65 to 74 years	6,418	376	5.9	5,816	286	4.9	467	81	17.2	253	36	14.2
75 years and over	3,362	263	7.8	3,099	196	6.3	169	50	29.4	110	16	14.6
Female												
Total	83,868	6,260	7.5	73,712	4,905	6.7	6,473	937	14.5	7,141	1,537	21.5
Under 18 years	23,621	2,563	10.9	20,337	1,987	9.8	2,053	392	19.1	2,538	733	28.9
18 to 24 years	7,089	662	9.3	6,134	527	8.6	675	92	13.7	805	199	24.7
25 to 34 years	13,396	1,034	7.7	11,789	824	7.0	1,028	148	14.3	1,321	265	20.1
35 to 44 years	14,298	695	4.9	12,597	540	4.3	1,038	96	9.2	1,106	156	14.1
45 to 54 years	10,233	461	4.5	9,030	357	4.0	737	66	8.9	661	80	12.1
55 to 59 years	3,766	181	4.8	3,362	150	4.5	261	23	8.7	235	37	15.9
60 to 64 years	3,542	210	5.9	3,222	164	5.1	215	35	16.4	159	33	20.6
65 years and over	7,924	454	5.7	7,241	355	4.9	466	86	18.4	315	34	10.6
65 to 74 years	5,555	304	5.5	5,047	230	4.6	351	66	18.9	235	24	10.3
75 years and over	2,369	150	6.3	2,193	125	5.7	115	19	16.8	81	10	12.1
Householder												
Total	53,171	3,318	6.2	47,601	2,631	5.5	3,748	486	13.0	3,674	680	18.5
Under 18 years	2	2	B	2	2	B	-	-	B	-	-	B
18 to 24 years	1,462	263	18.0	1,311	215	16.4	114	38	33.6	206	72	35.2
25 to 34 years	10,655	881	8.3	9,440	711	7.5	794	119	15.0	1,058	236	22.3
35 to 44 years	13,522	722	5.3	11,959	577	4.8	997	89	9.0	1,028	172	16.7
45 to 54 years	10,550	469	4.4	9,426	368	3.9	735	69	9.4	669	92	13.7
55 to 59 years	3,883	187	4.8	3,456	148	4.3	293	29	10.0	215	28	13.1
60 to 64 years	3,791	207	5.5	3,451	157	4.6	234	25	10.5	187	33	17.6
65 years and over	9,307	589	6.3	8,557	453	5.3	581	117	20.1	310	48	15.4
65 to 74 years	6,223	355	5.7	5,681	273	4.8	440	76	17.3	221	33	14.9
75 years and over	3,084	234	7.6	2,875	180	6.3	141	41	28.9	89	15	16.6
Related children												
Under 18 years	48,532	5,268	10.9	41,898	4,138	9.9	4,187	762	18.2	5,259	1,500	28.5
Under 6 years	17,180	2,198	12.8	14,884	1,748	11.7	1,375	308	22.4	1,988	641	32.2
6 to 17 years	31,352	3,070	9.8	27,015	2,390	8.8	2,812	454	16.1	3,271	860	26.3
Own children												
Under 18 years	46,476	4,862	10.5	40,426	3,864	9.6	3,727	642	17.2	4,780	1,351	28.3
Under 6 years	16,222	2,015	12.4	14,187	1,621	11.4	1,181	258	21.9	1,764	570	32.3
6 to 17 years	30,254	2,848	9.4	26,239	2,243	8.5	2,547	384	15.1	3,017	780	25.9
18 years and over	13,866	639	4.6	11,664	421	3.6	1,599	167	10.5	1,194	137	11.5
PERSONS IN MARRIED-COUPLE FAMILIES WITH RELATED CHILDREN UNDER 18												
Both sexes												
Total	107,107	10,247	9.6	92,257	8,018	8.7	9,504	1,572	16.5	11,591	2,865	24.7
Under 18 years	48,547	5,274	10.9	41,911	4,142	9.9	4,190	764	18.2	5,262	1,503	28.6
18 to 24 years	7,112	948	13.3	5,919	745	12.6	884	161	18.2	1,125	288	25.6
25 to 34 years	18,271	1,857	10.2	15,907	1,496	9.4	1,593	270	17.0	2,139	522	24.4
35 to 44 years	22,259	1,296	5.8	19,585	1,008	5.1	1,631	186	11.4	1,889	331	17.5
45 to 54 years	8,173	543	6.6	6,974	417	6.0	728	96	13.1	765	134	17.5
55 to 59 years	1,045	114	10.9	792	86	10.8	163	21	12.8	178	37	20.7

[Continued]

★ 635 ★

Persons Living in Poverty, by Age, Sex, and Household Relationship, 1992 - II

[Continued]

Characteristic	All races			White			Black			Hispanic origin[1]		
	Total	Below poverty level		Total	Below poverty level		Total	Below poverty level		Total	Below poverty level	
		Number	Percent of total		Number	Percent of total		Number	Percent of total		Number	Percent of total
60 to 64 years	668	68	10.2	474	49	10.3	128	14	11.2	94	25	26.2
65 years and over	1,031	147	14.3	695	76	11.0	187	60	31.8	140	27	19.2
65 to 74 years	758	123	16.2	499	68	13.5	154	48	31.2	107	23	21.5
75 years and over	273	25	9.0	197	9	4.5	33	11	B	32	4	B
Male												
Total	54,415	5,245	9.6	46,874	4,108	8.8	4,898	804	16.4	5,915	1,466	24.8
Under 18 years	24,947	2,721	10.9	21,594	2,165	10.0	2,137	372	17.4	2,728	771	28.3
18 to 24 years	3,340	411	12.3	2,746	303	11.0	432	87	20.2	551	118	21.4
25 to 34 years	8,343	885	10.6	7,221	712	9.9	766	132	17.2	1,020	264	25.8
35 to 44 years	11,191	706	6.3	9,858	552	5.6	840	103	12.3	939	180	19.2
45 to 54 years	4,925	322	6.5	4,253	246	5.8	416	54	13.1	439	82	18.6
55 to 59 years	682	67	9.9	524	52	10.0	112	10	9.3	109	20	18.6
60 to 64 years	418	39	9.4	294	26	9.0	77	8	10.1	51	13	B
65 years and over	569	95	16.7	383	51	13.3	118	38	31.9	79	18	22.3
65 to 74 years	431	75	17.5	293	45	15.3	94	27	29.1	57	15	B
75 years and over	138	20	14.2	90	6	7.0	24	10	B	22	3	B

Source: U.S. Bureau of the Census. *Poverty in the United States: 1992.* Current Population Reports, Series P60-185, U.S. Government Printing Office, Washington, D.C., 1993, pp. 11-13. *Notes:* A dash (-) stands for zero or rounds to zero. A (B) stands for base less than 75,000 or not applicable. 1. Persons of Hispanic origin may be of any race.

★ 636 ★

Poverty

Persons Living in Poverty, by Age, Sex, and Household Relationship, 1992 - III

Numbers are shown in thousands.

Characteristic	All races			White			Black			Hispanic origin[1]		
	Total	Below poverty level		Total	Below poverty level		Total	Below poverty level		Total	Below poverty level	
		Number	Percent of total		Number	Percent of total		Number	Percent of total		Number	Percent of total
PERSONS IN MARRIED-COUPLE FAMILIES WITH RELATED CHILDREN UNDER 18 (continued)												
Female												
Total	52,692	5,002	9.5	45,382	3,910	8.6	4,606	768	16.7	5,676	1,399	24.7
Under 18 years	23,601	2,553	10.8	20,317	1,977	9.7	2,053	392	19.1	2,534	731	28.9
18 to 24 years	3,772	538	14.3	3,172	442	13.9	452	73	16.2	574	170	29.7
25 to 34 years	9,929	972	9.8	8,685	784	9.0	827	139	16.8	1,119	259	23.1
35 to 44 years	11,068	590	5.3	9,727	456	4.7	791	83	10.5	951	151	15.8
45 to 54 years	3,247	222	6.8	2,720	170	6.3	312	41	13.2	326	52	15.9
55 to 59 years	363	47	12.8	268	34	12.6	51	10	B	69	17	B
60 to 64 years	250	29	11.5	180	22	12.3	51	7	B	42	11	B
65 years and over	462	52	11.3	312	25	8.1	69	22	B	61	9	B
65 to 74 years	327	47	14.5	206	23	11.0	61	21	B	50	8	B
75 years and over	135	5	3.7	106	3	2.3	9	1	B	11	1	B
Householder												
Total	25,714	2,166	8.4	22,406	1,706	7.6	2,175	335	15.4	2,497	562	22.5
Under 18 years	2	2	B	2	2	B	-	-	B	-	-	B
18 to 24 years	803	212	26.4	690	170	24.6	88	34	38.2	139	56	40.5
25 to 34 years	7,856	829	10.6	6,893	671	9.7	666	118	17.7	871	228	26.2
35 to 44 years	10,991	652	5.9	9,721	528	5.4	789	78	9.8	899	165	18.4
45 to 54 years	4,738	302	6.4	4,117	228	5.5	378	55	14.5	409	70	17.1

[Continued]

★ 636 ★

Persons Living in Poverty, by Age, Sex, and Household Relationship, 1992 - III

[Continued]

Characteristic	All races			White			Black			Hispanic origin[1]		
	Total	Below poverty level		Total	Below poverty level		Total	Below poverty level		Total	Below poverty level	
		Number	Percent of total		Number	Percent of total		Number	Percent of total		Number	Percent of total
55 to 59 years	634	63	10.0	483	47	9.7	114	13	11.4	88	17	19.0
60 to 64 years	334	41	12.2	251	25	9.9	56	11	B	45	12	B
65 years and over	357	65	18.2	249	35	14.0	84	27	32.2	46	14	B
65 to 74 years	303	55	18.1	210	33	15.8	76	22	28.3	38	12	B
75 years and over	54	10	B	40	2	B	8	6	B	8	2	B
Related children												
Under 18 years	48,532	5,268	10.9	41,898	4,138	9.9	4,187	762	18.2	5,259	1,500	28.5
Under 6 years	17,180	2,198	12.8	14,884	1,748	11.7	1,375	308	22.4	1,988	641	32.2
6 to 17 years	31,352	3,070	9.8	27,015	2,390	8.8	2,812	454	16.1	3,271	860	26.3
Own children												
Under 18 years	46,476	4,862	10.5	40,426	3,864	9.6	3,727	642	17.2	4,780	1,351	28.3
Under 6 years	16,222	2,015	12.4	14,187	1,621	11.4	1,181	258	21.9	1,764	570	32.3
6 to 17 years	30,254	2,848	9.4	26,239	2,243	8.5	2,547	384	15.1	3,017	780	25.9
18 years and over	5,501	423	7.7	4,376	284	6.5	835	114	13.6	706	120	16.9
PERSONS IN FAMILIES WITH FEMALE HOUSEHOLDER, NO SPOUSE PRESENT												
Both sexes												
Total	35,639	13,716	38.5	22,037	6,656	30.2	12,316	6,609	53.7	4,207	2,154	51.2
Under 18 years	14,816	8,047	54.3	8,369	3,796	45.4	5,912	3,968	67.1	1,970	1,295	65.7
18 to 24 years	4,404	1,443	32.8	2,695	692	25.7	1,553	704	45.4	540	234	43.4
25 to 34 years	5,213	1,868	35.8	3,171	928	29.3	1,871	895	47.8	571	268	47.0
35 to 44 years	4,561	1,266	27.8	2,995	663	22.1	1,390	561	40.4	498	191	38.4
45 to 54 years	2,556	452	17.7	1,792	256	14.3	669	184	27.5	269	75	27.9
55 to 59 years	910	184	20.2	648	87	13.4	225	92	40.8	101	28	28.0
60 to 64 years	770	139	18.1	530	63	11.9	215	73	34.0	79	26	33.0
65 years and over	2,411	318	13.2	1,837	171	9.3	482	132	27.5	179	37	20.6
Householder												
Total	11,947	4,171	34.9	7,848	2,202	28.1	3,680	1,835	49.8	1,238	604	48.8
Under 18 years	15	14	B	14	13	B	1	1	B	6	6	B
18 to 24 years	989	701	70.8	585	385	65.8	362	289	79.9	141	98	69.2
25 to 34 years	2,946	1,549	52.6	1,760	804	45.7	1,093	703	64.3	327	208	63.7
35 to 44 years	3,269	1,059	32.4	2,100	567	27.0	1,041	451	43.3	337	171	50.9
45 to 54 years	1,957	370	18.9	1,370	217	15.9	504	141	28.0	196	58	29.3
55 to 59 years	640	131	20.5	458	53	11.6	159	75	47.2	84	25	29.6
60 to 64 years	539	99	18.5	350	38	10.9	180	61	34.0	51	15	B
65 years and over	1,592	248	15.6	1,211	125	10.3	339	113	33.3	95	24	25.1
Related children												
Under 18 years	14,801	8,032	54.3	8,355	3,783	45.3	5,911	3,967	67.1	1,963	1,289	65.7
Under 6 years	5,051	3,331	65.9	2,648	1,602	60.5	2,233	1,633	73.1	710	510	71.8
6 to 17 years	9,749	4,702	48.2	5,706	2,181	38.2	3,678	2,334	63.5	1,253	779	62.2
Own children												
Under 18 years	12,746	7,092	55.6	7,483	3,490	46.6	4,797	3,340	69.6	1,704	1,177	69.1
Under 6 years	4,075	2,881	70.7	2,240	1,460	65.2	1,698	1,333	78.5	578	452	78.2
6 to 17 years	8,671	4,211	48.6	5,243	2,031	38.7	3,099	2,008	64.8	1,126	725	64.4
18 years and over	6,066	1,069	17.6	3,992	452	11.3	1,909	596	31.2	603	177	29.3

[Continued]

★ 636 ★

Persons Living in Poverty, by Age, Sex, and Household Relationship, 1992 - III

[Continued]

Characteristic	All races			White			Black			Hispanic origin[1]		
	Total	Below poverty level		Total	Below poverty level		Total	Below poverty level		Total	Below poverty level	
		Number	Percent of total		Number	Percent of total		Number	Percent of total		Number	Percent of total
PERSONS IN FAMILIES WITH FEMALE HOUSEHOLDER, NO SPOUSE PRESENT, WITH RELATED CHILDREN UNDER 18												
Both sexes												
Total	26,283	12,707	48.3	15,191	6,128	40.3	10,182	6,154	60.4	3,436	2,009	58.5
Under 18 years	14,813	8,044	54.3	8,366	3,793	45.3	5,912	3,968	67.1	1,969	1,294	65.7
18 to 24 years	2,535	1,226	48.4	1,396	587	42.1	1,064	601	56.5	381	202	53.1
25 to 34 years	3,632	1,731	47.6	2,086	867	41.6	1,443	821	56.9	446	244	54.7
35 to 44 years	3,276	1,129	34.4	2,063	592	28.7	1,100	495	45.0	374	174	46.6
45 to 54 years	1,138	294	25.9	772	170	22.0	321	115	35.9	137	44	32.3
55 to 59 years	272	95	35.1	151	42	27.6	112	51	45.5	52	18	B
60 to 64 years	186	74	40.0	99	27	27.6	85	45	53.4	25	12	B
65 years and over	430	113	26.4	258	50	19.5	146	58	39.5	51	20	B
Householder												
Total	8,230	3,761	45.7	5,060	1,980	39.1	2,898	1,659	57.2	945	543	57.4
Under 18 years	12	11	B	11	10	B	1	1	B	5	5	B
18 to 24 years	895	696	77.8	510	384	75.2	355	289	81.5	129	98	75.7
25 to 34 years	2,796	1,528	54.6	1,671	796	47.6	1,042	689	66.1	313	203	64.9
35 to 44 years	2,859	1,024	35.8	1,821	549	30.1	939	434	46.3	305	164	53.9
45 to 54 years	1,008	275	27.2	683	160	23.4	285	105	36.9	114	41	35.6
55 to 59 years	217	79	36.3	117	27	23.2	90	48	53.6	38	14	B
60 to 64 years	149	67	44.9	73	22	B	76	45	59.8	14	8	B
65 years and over	293	82	27.9	173	32	18.5	110	46	42.2	28	10	B
Related children												
Under 18 years	14,801	8,032	54.3	8,355	3,783	45.3	5,911	3,967	67.1	1,963	1,289	65.7
Under 6 years	5,051	3,331	65.9	2,648	1,602	60.5	2,233	1,633	73.1	710	510	71.8
6 to 17 years	9,749	4,702	48.2	5,706	2,181	38.2	3,678	2,334	63.5	1,253	779	62.2
Own children												
Under 18 years	12,746	7,092	55.6	7,483	3,490	46.6	4,797	3,340	69.6	1,704	1,177	69.1
Under 6 years	4,075	2,881	70.7	2,240	1,460	65.2	1,698	1,333	78.5	578	452	78.2
6 to 17 years	8,671	4,211	48.6	5,243	2,031	38.7	3,099	2,008	64.8	1,126	725	64.4
18 years and over	2,209	625	28.3	1,169	220	18.8	985	390	39.6	299	105	35.2
UNRELATED INDIVIDUALS												
Both sexes												
Total	36,734	7,991	21.8	31,176	6,087	19.5	4,431	1,584	35.8	2,278	777	34.1
Under 18 years	145	137	94.3	125	118	94.0	8	8	B	33	32	B
18 to 24 years	4,453	1,476	33.2	3,801	1,216	32.0	398	173	43.3	388	184	47.4
25 to 34 years	8,385	1,231	14.7	7,002	892	12.7	1,026	254	24.8	712	172	24.1
35 to 44 years	5,784	926	16.0	4,744	663	14.0	831	216	26.0	415	120	29.0
45 to 54 years	4,125	731	17.7	3,428	507	14.8	615	205	33.3	260	61	23.6
55 to 59 years	1,800	468	26.0	1,469	348	23.7	289	104	36.1	87	30	34.3
60 to 64 years	2,001	525	26.2	1,656	400	24.1	305	113	37.0	98	43	43.9
65 years and over	10,041	2,498	24.9	8,949	1,943	21.7	960	512	53.3	285	136	47.6
65 to 74 years	4,709	1,080	22.9	4,091	781	19.1	544	272	50.1	165	71	43.0
75 years and over	5,332	1,418	26.6	4,858	1,161	23.9	417	240	57.5	120	65	54.1
Male												
Total	17,278	3,103	18.0	14,290	2,229	15.6	2,338	708	30.3	1,354	382	28.2
Under 18 years	65	61	B	54	51	B	3	3	B	11	10	B
18 to 24 years	2,321	675	29.1	1,969	547	27.8	201	86	42.7	227	97	42.6
25 to 34 years	5,232	722	13.8	4,297	497	11.6	674	161	23.9	501	106	21.1

[Continued]

★ 636 ★

Persons Living in Poverty, by Age, Sex, and Household Relationship, 1992 - III

[Continued]

Characteristic	All races			White			Black			Hispanic origin[1]		
	Total	Below poverty level		Total	Below poverty level		Total	Below poverty level		Total	Below poverty level	
		Number	Percent of total		Number	Percent of total		Number	Percent of total		Number	Percent of total
35 to 44 years	3,670	570	15.5	2,977	400	13.4	574	147	25.7	296	85	28.9
45 to 54 years	2,081	321	15.4	1,727	213	12.3	317	100	31.4	168	32	19.3
55 to 59 years	771	173	22.5	633	120	19.0	122	46	37.5	40	11	B
60 to 64 years	783	142	18.1	627	110	17.5	138	29	20.7	32	9	B
65 years and over	2,355	438	18.6	2,004	291	14.5	309	137	44.4	80	32	39.9
65 to 74 years	1,273	244	19.2	1,062	157	14.8	185	80	43.5	53	19	B
75 years and over	1,082	193	17.9	942	134	14.2	125	57	45.8	26	13	B
Female												
Total	19,456	4,888	25.1	16,886	3,858	22.8	2,093	876	41.8	924	396	42.8
Under 18 years	80	76	94.4	71	67	B	5	5	B	23	22	B
18 to 24 years	2,132	801	37.6	1,832	669	36.5	197	87	43.9	161	87	54.2
25 to 34 years	3,154	508	16.1	2,704	394	14.6	352	93	26.5	212	66	31.2
35 to 44 years	2,114	356	16.8	1,767	264	14.9	257	68	26.7	119	35	29.3
45 to 54 years	2,044	410	20.1	1,700	294	17.3	298	106	35.4	91	29	31.6
55 to 59 years	1,028	294	28.4	836	228	27.2	167	58	35.0	47	19	B
60 to 64 years	1,218	383	31.4	1,029	290	28.2	167	84	50.5	66	34	B
65 years and over	7,686	2,061	26.8	6,946	1,652	23.8	651	374	57.5	205	104	50.7
65 to 74 years	3,437	836	24.3	3,029	625	20.6	359	192	53.5	112	52	46.5
75 years and over	4,250	1,225	28.8	3,916	1,027	26.2	292	183	62.5	93	52	55.7
PERSONS IN UNRELATED SUB-FAMILIES												
Both sexes												
Total	1,720	943	54.8	1,445	791	54.7	205	121	58.9	327	222	67.9
Under 18 years	941	569	60.5	793	477	60.1	115	75	64.6	167	127	76.0
18 years and over	778	373	47.9	652	315	48.2	90	46	51.5	160	95	59.5
Male	607	293	48.3	506	240	47.4	70	40	B	125	77	61.1
Female	1,113	649	58.4	939	551	58.7	135	80	59.3	202	146	72.2
Children												
Under 18 years	928	556	59.9	784	467	59.6	112	71	63.4	163	123	75.4
Under 6 years	379	265	69.8	313	214	68.2	50	42	B	80	66	83.0
6 to 17 years	549	291	53.1	470	253	53.9	62	29	B	83	57	68.1

Source: U.S. Bureau of the Census. *Poverty in the United States: 1992.* Current Population Reports, Series P60-185, U.S. Government Printing Office, Washington, D.C., 1993, pp. 13-15. *Notes:* A dash (-) stands for zero or rounds to zero. A (B) stands for base less than 75,000 or not applicable. 1. Persons of Hispanic origin may be of any race.

★ 637 ★

Poverty

Persons Living in Poverty, by Ratio of Income to Poverty Level, Age Group, and Sex, 1992 - I

Numbers are shown in thousands and refer to persons, families, and unrelated individuals, as of March of the following year.

Characteristic	Total	Under .50		Under 1.00		Under 1.25	
		Number	Percent of total	Number	Percent of total	Number	Percent of total
ALL PERSONS							
Both sexes							
Total	253,969	15,020	5.9	36,880	14.5	49,168	19.4
Under 18 years	66,834	6,849	10.2	14,617	21.9	18,303	27.4
18 to 24 years	24,309	1,990	8.2	4,367	18.0	5,728	23.6
25 to 34 years	41,864	2,305	5.5	5,540	13.2	7,355	17.6
35 to 44 years	40,342	1,593	3.9	3,944	9.8	5,328	13.2
45 to 54 years	28,503	863	3.0	2,245	7.9	3,124	11.0
55 to 59 years	10,718	376	3.5	1,073	10.0	1,423	13.3
60 to 64 years	10,529	335	3.2	1,112	10.6	1,601	15.2
65 years and over	30,870	708	2.3	3,983	12.9	6,307	20.4
65 to 74 years	18,362	386	2.1	1,956	10.7	3,076	16.8
75 years and over	12,508	321	2.6	2,027	16.2	3,230	25.8
Male							
Total	123,873	6,398	5.2	15,700	12.7	21,323	17.2
Under 18 years	34,180	3,445	10.1	7,343	21.5	9,238	27.0
18 to 24 years	12,049	710	5.9	1,714	14.2	2,440	20.2
25 to 34 years	20,856	733	3.5	2,050	9.8	2,942	14.1
35 to 44 years	19,904	641	3.2	1,647	8.3	2,286	11.5
45 to 54 years	13,847	343	2.5	964	7.0	1,359	9.8
55 to 59 years	5,122	158	3.1	443	8.7	585	11.4
60 to 64 years	5,084	129	2.5	397	7.8	610	12.0
65 years and over	12,832	239	1.9	1,142	8.9	1,863	14.5
65 to 74 years	8,114	147	1.8	657	8.1	1,070	13.2
75 years and over	4,718	92	1.9	485	10.3	793	16.8
Female							
Total	130,096	8,622	6.6	21,180	16.3	27,845	21.4
Under 18 years	32,654	3,404	10.4	7,273	22.3	9,064	27.8
18 to 24 years	12,260	1,281	10.4	2,653	21.6	3,289	26.8
25 to 34 years	21,008	1,572	7.5	3,490	16.6	4,412	21.0
35 to 44 years	20,438	953	4.7	2,297	11.2	3,042	14.9
45 to 54 years	14,655	521	3.6	1,281	8.7	1,765	12.0
55 to 59 years	5,597	218	3.9	630	11.3	838	15.0
60 to 64 years	5,445	206	3.8	715	13.1	991	18.2
65 years and over	18,038	468	2.6	2,840	15.7	4,444	24.6
65 to 74 years	10,249	239	2.3	1,299	12.7	2,006	19.6
75 years and over	7,790	229	2.9	1,542	19.8	2,437	31.3

[Continued]

★637★

Persons Living in Poverty, by Ratio of Income to Poverty Level, Age Group, and Sex, 1992 - I

[Continued]

Characteristic	Total	Under .50		Under 1.00		Under 1.25	
		Number	Percent of total	Number	Percent of total	Number	Percent of total
WHITE							
Both sexes							
Total	211,820	9,095	4.3	24,523	11.6	34,012	16.1
Under 18 years	53,090	3,672	6.9	8,955	16.9	11,762	22.2
18 to 24 years	19,711	1,314	6.7	3,023	15.3	4,041	20.5
25 to 34 years	34,666	1,436	4.1	3,749	10.8	5,128	14.8
35 to 44 years	33,976	1,022	3.0	2,641	7.8	3,703	10.9
45 to 54 years	24,505	594	2.4	1,591	6.5	2,244	9.2
55 to 59 years	9,190	267	2.9	771	8.4	1,029	11.2
60 to 64 years	9,182	249	2.7	800	8 7	1,162	12.7
65 years and over	27,501	542	2.0	2,992	10.9	4,943	18.0
65 to 74 years	16,210	283	1.7	1,397	8.6	2,285	14.1
75 years and over	11,290	258	2.3	1,595	14.1	2,658	23.5
Male							
Total	103,850	3,875	3.7	10,493	10.1	14,829	14.3
Under 18 years	27,231	1,825	6.7	4,509	16.6	5,970	21.9
18 to 24 years	9,821	466	4.7	1,221	12.4	1,744	17.8
25 to 34 years	17,408	500	2.9	1,477	8.5	2,142	12.3
35 to 44 years	16,976	452	2.7	1,166	6.9	1,688	9.9
45 to 54 years	12,081	228	1.9	695	5.7	1,004	8.3
55 to 59 years	4,428	119	2.7	328	7.4	439	9.9
60 to 64 years	4,460	101	2.3	288	6.4	442	9.9
65 years and over	11,443	184	1.6	809	7.1	1,400	12.2
65 to 74 years	7,187	108	1.5	465	6.5	784	10.9
75 years and over	4,256	76	1.8	344	8.1	616	14.5
Female							
Total	107,970	5,220	4.8	14,030	13.0	19,183	17.8
Under 18 years	25,859	1,847	7.1	4,446	17.2	5,792	22.4
18 to 24 years	9,889	849	8.6	1,802	18.2	2,297	23.2
25 to 34 years	17,257	936	5.4	2,272	13.2	2,986	17.3
35 to 44 years	17,000	570	3.4	1,475	8.7	2,015	11.9
45 to 54 years	12,424	366	2.9	896	7.2	1,240	10.0
55 to 59 years	4,762	148	3.1	443	9.3	591	12.4
60 to 64 years	4,721	147	3.1	512	10.8	720	15.2
65 years and over	16,057	358	2.2	2,183	13.6	3,543	22.1
65 to 74 years	9,023	175	1.9	932	10.3	1,501	16.6
75 years and over	7,034	183	2.6	1,252	17.8	2,041	29.0

[Continued]

★637★

Persons Living in Poverty, by Ratio of Income to Poverty Level, Age Group, and Sex, 1992 - I

[Continued]

Characteristic	Total	Under .50		Under 1.00		Under 1.25	
		Number	Percent of total	Number	Percent of total	Number	Percent of total
BLACK							
Both sexes							
Total	31,916	5,210	16.3	10,613	33.3	12,840	40.2
Under 18 years	10,599	2,875	27.1	4,938	46.6	5,622	53.0
18 to 24 years	3,531	573	16.2	1,121	31.7	1,388	39.3
25 to 34 years	5,399	763	14.1	1,521	28.2	1,867	34.6
35 to 44 years	4,629	483	10.4	1,077	23.3	1,331	28.7
45 to 54 years	2,910	228	7.8	544	18.7	722	24.8
55 to 59 years	1,144	89	7.8	262	22.9	339	29.7
60 to 64 years	1,044	60	5.7	263	25.2	365	35.0
65 years and over	2,660	138	5.2	887	33.3	1,206	45.3
65 to 74 years	1,703	86	5.0	504	29.6	695	40.8
75 years and over	957	52	5.5	383	40.0	511	53.4
Male							
Total	15,001	2,169	14.5	4,388	29.3	5,394	36.0
Under 18 years	5,379	1,451	27.0	2,468	45.9	2,799	52.0
18 to 24 years	1,669	197	11.8	404	24.2	558	33.4
25 to 34 years	2,487	174	7.0	441	17.7	623	25.0
35 to 44 years	2,109	162	7.7	388	18.4	477	22.6
45 to 54 years	1,289	97	7.5	221	17.1	287	22.3
55 to 59 years	516	31	6.0	94	18.2	122	23.6
60 to 64 years	471	14	2.9	82	17.5	130	27.5
65 years and over	1,081	44	4.1	290	26.9	399	36.9
65 to 74 years	742	34	4.6	173	23.3	248	33.4
75 years and over	338	10	2.9	118	34.8	151	44.6
Female							
Total	16,915	3,041	18.0	6,225	36.8	7,447	44.0
Under 18 years	5,220	1,424	27.3	2,470	47.3	2,822	54.1
18 to 24 years	1,862	376	20.2	717	38.5	830	44.6
25 to 34 years	2,912	589	20.2	1,081	37.1	1,245	42.7
35 to 44 years	2,520	321	12.7	689	27.3	854	33.9
45 to 54 years	1,620	131	8.1	323	20.0	435	26.9
55 to 59 years	628	58	9.3	168	26.8	218	34.6
60 to 64 years	573	46	8.0	181	31.5	236	41.1
65 years and over	1,579	94	6.0	596	37.7	807	51.1
65 to 74 years	960	52	5.4	331	34.5	446	46.5
75 years and over	619	42	6.9	265	42.8	361	58.3

[Continued]

★ 637 ★

Persons Living in Poverty, by Ratio of Income to Poverty Level, Age Group, and Sex, 1992 - I

[Continued]

Characteristic	Total	Under .50		Under 1.00		Under 1.25	
		Number	Percent of total	Number	Percent of total	Number	Percent of total
HISPANIC ORIGIN[1]							
Both sexes							
Total	22,720	2,479	10.9	6,655	29.3	8,688	38.2
Under 18 years	7,807	1,218	15.6	3,116	39.9	3,928	50.3
18 to 24 years	2,813	355	12.6	844	30.0	1,081	38.4
25 to 34 years	4,277	414	9.7	1,076	25.2	1,417	33.1
35 to 44 years	3,330	250	7.5	719	21.6	980	29.4
45 to 54 years	2,037	109	5.3	349	17.1	482	23.7
55 to 59 years	680	51	7.5	137	20.2	185	27.2
60 to 64 years	554	40	7.2	145	26.2	195	35.2
65 years and over	1,222	44	3.6	269	22.0	419	34.3
65 to 74 years	806	31	3.9	157	19.5	255	31.7
75 years and over	416	13	3.0	112	26.8	164	39.4
Male							
Total	11,378	1,106	9.7	3,067	27.0	4,090	35.9
Under 18 years	3,958	587	14.8	1,551	39.2	1,971	49.8
18 to 24 years	1,417	142	10.0	360	25.4	493	34.8
25 to 34 years	2,237	169	7.6	467	20.9	634	28.3
35 to 44 years	1,682	117	6.9	328	19.5	461	27.4
45 to 54 years	1,035	46	4.4	170	16.5	238	23.0
55 to 59 years	292	21	7.0	53	18.1	74	25.4
60 to 64 years	249	10	4.0	50	19.9	73	29.3
65 years and over	508	15	2.9	88	17.4	146	28.7
65 to 74 years	345	12	3.3	57	16.7	94	27.2
75 years and over	163	3	1.9	31	18.8	52	31.9
Female							
Total	11,342	1,373	12.1	3,588	31.6	4,598	40.5
Under 18 years	3,849	631	16.4	1,565	40.7	1,957	50.8
18 to 24 years	1,396	212	15.2	484	34.7	589	42.2
25 to 34 years	2,040	244	12.0	609	29.9	783	38.4
35 to 44 years	1,648	133	8.1	391	23.7	519	31.5
45 to 54 years	1,002	63	6.3	178	17.8	244	24.3
55 to 59 years	387	30	7.9	84	21.7	111	28.6
60 to 64 years	305	30	9.8	96	31.3	122	39.9
65 years and over	715	29	4.1	181	25.3	274	38.3
65 to 74 years	462	20	4.2	100	21.6	162	35.0
75 years and over	253	9	3.7	81	32.0	112	44.3

Source: U.S. Bureau of the Census. Current Population Reports, Series P60-185, *Poverty in the United States: 1992*. Washington, D.C., U.S. Government Printing Office, 1993, pp. 16-19. *Note:* 1. Persons of Hispanic origin may be of any race.

★ 638 ★

Poverty

Persons Living in Poverty, by Ratio of Income to Poverty Level, Age Group, and Sex, 1992 - II

Numbers are shown in thousands and refer to persons, families, and unrelated individuals, as of March of the following year.

Characteristic	Under 1.50		Under 1.75		Under 2.00	
	Number	Percent of total	Number	Percent of total	Number	Percent of total
ALL PERSONS						
Both sexes						
Total	61,237	24.1	73,465	28.9	86,233	34.0
Under 18 years	21,904	32.8	25,409	38.0	29,178	43.7
18 to 24 years	6,978	28.7	8,348	34.3	9,625	39.6
25 to 34 years	9,222	22.0	11,177	26.7	13,163	31.4
35 to 44 years	6,797	16.8	8,381	20.8	10,041	24.9
45 to 54 years	3,927	13.8	4,790	16.8	5,827	20.4
55 to 59 years	1,776	16.6	2,124	19.8	2,517	23.5
60 to 64 years	2,100	19.9	2,587	24.6	3,078	29.2
65 years and over	8,533	27.6	10,651	34.5	12,805	41.5
65 to 74 years	4,136	22.5	5,243	28.6	6,461	35.2
75 years and over	4,397	35.2	5,408	43.2	6,343	50.7
Male						
Total	26,887	21.7	32,591	26.3	38,860	31.4
Under 18 years	11,095	32.5	12,865	37.6	14,806	43.3
18 to 24 years	3,031	25.2	3,658	30.4	4,327	35.9
25 to 34 years	3,824	18.3	4,810	23.1	5,841	28.0
35 to 44 years	3,008	15.1	3,761	18.9	4,582	23.0
45 to 54 years	1,734	12.5	2,131	15.4	2,609	18.8
55 to 59 years	735	14.3	869	17.0	1,043	20.4
60 to 64 years	837	16.5	1,023	20.1	1,279	25.1
65 years and over	2,624	20.5	3,474	27.1	4,373	34.1
65 to 74 years	1,476	18.2	1,941	23.9	2,458	30.3
75 years and over	1,148	24.3	1,533	32.5	1,914	40.6
Female						
Total	34,350	26.4	40,875	31.4	47,373	36.4
Under 18 years	10,808	33.1	12,544	38.4	14,372	44.0
18 to 24 years	3,947	32.2	4,690	38.3	5,298	43.2
25 to 34 years	5,398	25.7	6,367	30.3	7,322	34.9
35 to 44 years	3,789	18.5	4,619	22.6	5,459	26.7
45 to 54 years	2,193	15.0	2,659	18.1	3,218	22.0
55 to 59 years	1,041	18.6	1,255	22.4	1,474	26.3
60 to 64 years	1,264	23.2	1,563	28.7	1,799	33.0
65 years and over	5,909	32.8	7,177	39.8	8,432	46.7
65 to 74 years	2,659	25.9	3,302	32.2	4,003	39.1
75 years and over	3,249	41.7	3,875	49.7	4,429	56.9

[Continued]

★ 638 ★

Persons Living in Poverty, by Ratio of Income to Poverty Level, Age Group, and Sex, 1992 - II

[Continued]

Characteristic	Under 1.50		Under 1.75		Under 2.00	
	Number	Percent of total	Number	Percent of total	Number	Percent of total
WHITE						
Both sexes						
Total	43,569	20.6	53,425	25.2	63,983	30.2
Under 18 years	14,485	27.3	17,223	32.4	20,283	38.2
18 to 24 years	5,014	25.4	6,097	30.9	7,136	36.2
25 to 34 years	6,606	19.1	8,171	23.6	9,788	28.2
35 to 44 years	4,823	14.2	6,042	17.8	7,384	21.7
45 to 54 years	2,872	11.7	3,581	14.6	4,420	18.0
55 to 59 years	1,287	14.0	1,557	16.9	1,890	20.6
60 to 64 years	1,572	17.1	1,965	21.4	2,375	25.9
65 years and over	6,909	25.1	8,789	32.0	10,707	38.9
65 to 74 years	3,198	19.7	4,147	25.6	5,210	32.1
75 years and over	3,711	32.9	4,642	41.1	5,496	48.7
Male						
Total	19,214	18.5	23,807	22.9	28,915	27.8
Under 18 years	7,381	27.1	8,776	32.2	10,321	37.9
18 to 24 years	2,215	22.6	2,713	27.6	3,256	33.2
25 to 34 years	2,856	16.4	3,647	21.0	4,474	25.7
35 to 44 years	2,243	13.2	2,818	16.6	3,478	20.5
45 to 54 years	1,301	10.8	1,636	13.5	2,034	16.8
55 to 59 years	545	12.3	647	14.6	797	18.0
60 to 64 years	623	14.0	768	17.2	966	21.7
65 years and over	2,050	17.9	2,802	24.5	3,589	31.4
65 to 74 years	1,119	15.6	1,517	21.1	1,962	27.3
75 years and over	932	21.9	1,285	30.2	1,626	38.2
Female						
Total	24,355	22.6	29,618	27.4	35,068	32.5
Under 18 years	7,104	27.5	8,447	32.7	9,962	38.5
18 to 24 years	2,799	28.3	3,384	34.2	3,880	39.2
25 to 34 years	3,750	21.7	4,523	26.2	5,314	30.8
35 to 44 years	2,580	15.2	3,224	19.0	3,906	23.0
45 to 54 years	1,572	12.6	1,945	15.7	2,386	19.2
55 to 59 years	742	15.6	910	19.1	1,903	23.0
60 to 64 years	949	20.1	1,198	25.4	1,409	29.8
65 years and over	4,858	30.3	5,987	37.3	7,118	44.3
65 to 74 years	2,079	23.0	2,630	29.1	3,248	36.0
75 years and over	2,779	39.5	3,357	47.7	3,870	55.0

[Continued]

★ 638 ★

Persons Living in Poverty, by Ratio of Income to Poverty Level, Age Group, and Sex, 1992 - II

[Continued]

Characteristic	Under 1.50		Under 1.75		Under 2.00	
	Number	Percent of total	Number	Percent of total	Number	Percent of total
BLACK						
Both sexes						
Total	14,867	46.6	16,714	52.4	18,517	58.0
Under 18 years	6,353	59.9	6,960	65.7	7,526	71.0
18 to 24 years	1,584	44.9	1,793	50.8	1,991	56.4
25 to 34 years	2,201	40.8	2,490	46.1	2,788	51.6
35 to 44 years	1,609	34.7	1,899	41.0	2,154	46.5
45 to 54 years	853	29.3	966	33.2	1,144	39.3
55 to 59 years	415	36.3	475	41.5	520	45.5
60 to 64 years	435	41.6	507	48.6	577	55.3
65 years and over	1,418	53.3	1,624	61.1	1,816	68.3
65 to 74 years	818	48.1	956	56.3	1,088	63.9
75 years and over	599	62.6	666	69.6	728	76.1
Male						
Total	6,328	42.2	7,163	47.7	8,125	54.2
Under 18 years	3,176	59.0	3,470	64.5	3,791	70.5
18 to 24 years	629	37.7	711	42.6	821	49.2
25 to 34 years	761	30.6	899	36.1	1,064	42.8
35 to 44 years	604	28.6	746	35.4	877	41.6
45 to 54 years	349	27.1	392	30.4	468	36.3
55 to 59 years	157	30.4	181	35.1	199	38.6
60 to 64 years	164	34.9	196	41.7	244	51.9
65 years and over	488	45.2	589	52.7	660	61.0
65 to 74 years	310	41.8	364	49.1	425	57.3
75 years and over	177	52.4	205	60.5	235	69.4
Female						
Total	8,540	50.5	9,551	56.8	10,392	61.4
Under 18 years	3,177	60.9	3,490	66.9	3,735	71.5
18 to 24 years	955	51.3	1,082	58.1	1,170	62.8
25 to 34 years	1,441	49.5	1,592	54.7	1,724	59.2
35 to 44 years	1,005	39.9	1,153	45.7	1,277	50.7
45 to 54 years	504	31.1	574	35.5	676	41.7
55 to 59 years	258	41.1	294	46.8	321	51.0
60 to 64 years	270	47.1	311	54.2	333	58.1
65 years and over	930	58.9	1,055	66.8	1,156	73.2
65 to 74 years	508	52.9	594	61.9	663	69.0
75 years and over	422	68.2	461	74.5	494	79.7

[Continued]

★ 638 ★

Persons Living in Poverty, by Ratio of Income to Poverty Level, Age Group, and Sex, 1992 - II

[Continued]

Characteristic	Under 1.50		Under 1.75		Under 2.00	
	Number	Percent of total	Number	Percent of total	Number	Percent of total
HISPANIC ORIGIN[1]						
Both sexes						
Total	10,474	46.1	12,118	53.3	13,500	59.4
Under 18 years	4,544	58.2	5,060	64.8	5,536	70.9
18 to 24 years	1,351	48.0	1,574	55.9	1,770	62.9
25 to 34 years	1,738	40.6	2,047	47.8	2,299	53.7
35 to 44 years	1,218	36.6	1,471	44.2	1,642	49.3
45 to 54 years	631	31.0	773	38.0	924	45.4
55 to 59 years	223	32.8	262	38.5	303	44.6
60 to 64 years	238	42.9	272	49.0	297	53.6
65 years and over	531	43.4	661	54.0	728	59.6
65 to 74 years	321	39.8	403	50.0	447	55.4
75 years and over	210	50.4	257	61.9	282	67.7
Male						
Total	4,974	43.7	5,801	51.0	6,540	57.5
Under 18 years	2,285	57.7	2,549	64.4	2,801	70.8
18 to 24 years	629	44.4	730	51.5	846	59.7
25 to 34 years	808	36.1	970	43.4	1,125	50.3
35 to 44 years	577	34.3	713	42.4	795	47.3
45 to 54 years	310	30.0	390	37.7	465	45.0
55 to 59 years	90	30.6	104	35.5	116	39.6
60 to 64 years	90	36.1	99	39.8	114	45.7
65 years and over	185	36.5	245	48.3	277	54.6
65 to 74 years	115	33.3	155	44.9	173	50.2
75 years and over	71	43.4	90	55.6	104	63.9
Female						
Total	5,500	48.5	6,317	55.7	6,961	61.4
Under 18 years	2,259	58.7	2,510	65.2	2,734	71.0
18 to 24 years	723	51.8	844	60.5	924	66.2
25 to 34 years	930	45.6	1,076	52.8	1,173	57.5
35 to 44 years	640	38.9	758	46.0	847	51.4
45 to 54 years	321	32.0	382	38.2	459	45.8
55 to 59 years	134	34.5	158	40.8	188	48.4
60 to 64 years	148	48.4	173	56.5	183	60.0
65 years and over	346	48.3	415	58.1	451	63.2
65 to 74 years	206	44.7	248	53.8	274	59.3
75 years and over	139	55.0	167	65.9	178	70.2

Source: U.S. Bureau of the Census. *Poverty in the United States: 1992.* Current Population Reports, Series P60-185, U.S. Government Printing Office, Washington, D.C., 1993, pp. 16-19. *Note:* 1. Persons of Hispanic origin may be of any race.

★ 639 ★

Poverty

Persons Living in Poverty, by Ratio of Income to Poverty Level, Household Relationship, Age Group, and Sex, 1992 - I

Numbers are shown in thousands and refer to persons, families, and unrelated individuals, as of March of the following year.

Characteristic	Total	Under .50		Under 1.00		Under 1.25	
		Number	Percent of total	Number	Percent of total	Number	Percent of total
ALL PERSONS							
Household relationship							
Total	253,969	15,020	5.9	36,880	14.5	49,168	19.4
65 years and over	30,870	708	2.3	3,983	12.9	6,307	20.4
In families	212,515	11,469	5.3	27,947	13.0	37,244	17.3
Householder	68,144	3,269	4.8	7,960	11.7	10,736	15.8
Under 65 years	56,883	3,034	5.3	7,081	12.4	9,323	16.4
65 years and over	11,261	235	2.1	878	7.8	1,413	12.5
Related children under 18 years	65,691	6,365	9.7	13,876	21.1	17,475	26.6
Under 6 years	23,129	2,754	11.9	5,781	25.0	7,077	30.6
6 to 17 years	42,582	3,612	8.5	8,095	19.0	10,399	24.4
Own children 18 years and over	21,091	575	2.7	1,833	8.7	2,611	12.4
In married-couple families	171,514	3,862	2.3	12,830	7.5	19,045	11.1
Husbands	53,171	1,006	1.9	3,318	6.2	5,057	9.5
Under 65 years	43,719	840	1.9	2,710	6.2	4,042	9.2
65 years and over	9,451	167	1.8	608	6.4	1,016	10.7
Wives	53,171	1,006	1.9	3,318	6.2	5,057	9.5
Under 65 years	45,944	884	1.9	2,896	6.3	4,328	9.4
65 years and over	7,227	122	1.7	423	5.8	729	10.1
Related children under 18 years	48,532	1,617	3.3	5,268	10.9	7,533	15.5
Under 6 years	17,180	676	3.9	2,198	12.8	3,026	17.6
6 to 17 years	31,352	940	3.0	3,070	9.8	4,506	14.4
Own children 18 years and over	13,866	173	1.2	639	4.6	987	7.1
In families with female householder, no spouse present	35,639	7,048	19.8	13,716	38.5	16,276	45.7
Householder	11,947	2,073	17.4	4,171	34.9	5,025	42.1
Under 65 years	10,355	2,016	19.5	3,923	37.9	4,660	45.0
65 years and over	1,592	57	3.6	248	15.6	365	22.9
Related children under 18 years	14,801	4,479	30.3	8,032	54.3	9,151	61.8
Under 6 years	5,051	1,965	38.9	3,331	65.9	3,691	73.1
6 to 17 years	9,749	2,515	25.8	4,702	48.2	5,460	56.0
Own children 18 years and over	6,066	364	6.0	1,069	17.6	1,453	23.9
In unrelated subfamilies	1,720	548	31.9	943	54.8	1,113	64.7
Under 18 years	941	339	36.1	569	60.5	654	69.5
Under 6 years	379	156	41.1	265	69.8	285	75.2
6 to 17 years	562	183	32.6	305	54.2	369	65.6
18 years and over	778	209	26.6	373	47.9	459	59.0
Unrelated individuals	36,734	3,003	8.2	7,991	21.8	10,810	29.4

[Continued]

★ 639 ★

Persons Living in Poverty, by Ratio of Income to Poverty Level, Household Relationship, Age Group, and Sex, 1992 - I

[Continued]

Characteristic	Total	Under .50		Under 1.00		Under 1.25	
		Number	Percent of total	Number	Percent of total	Number	Percent of total
Male	17,278	1,379	8.0	3,103	18.0	4,208	24.4
Under 65 years	14,923	1,321	8.9	2,666	17.9	3,507	23.5
Living alone	7,521	394	5.2	1,018	13.5	1,359	18.1
65 years and over	2,355	58	2.5	438	18.6	700	29.7
Living alone	2,005	38	1.9	356	17.8	573	28.6
Female	19,456	1,624	8.3	4,888	25.1	6,603	33.9
Under 65 years	11,769	1,363	11.6	2,827	24.0	3,449	29.3
Living alone	6,893	464	6.7	1,303	18.9	1,635	23.7
65 years and over	7,686	261	3.4	2,061	26.8	3,154	41.0
Living alone	7,382	242	3.3	1,953	26.5	3,008	40.7
WHITE							
Household relationship							
Total	211,820	9,095	4.3	24,523	11.6	34,012	16.1
65 years and over	27,501	542	2.0	2,992	10.9	4,943	18.0
In families	179,199	6,386	3.6	17,645	9.8	24,613	13.7
Householder	57,858	1,920	3.3	5,160	8.9	7,266	12.6
Under 65 years	47,811	1,752	3.7	4,562	9.5	6,258	13.1
65 years and over	10,046	167	1.7	597	5.9	1,008	10.0
Related children under 18 years	52,122	3,263	6.3	8,333	16.0	11,065	21.2
Under 6 years	18,240	1,453	8.0	3,527	19.3	4,519	24.8
6 to 17 years	33,882	1,811	5.3	4,806	14.2	6,546	19.3
Own children 18 years and over	16,572	274	1.7	950	5.7	1,371	8.3
In married-couple families	150,715	2,954	2.0	10,053	6.7	15,182	10.1
Husbands	47,563	785	1.7	2,620	5.5	4,076	8.6
Under 65 years	38,892	648	1.7	2,159	5.6	3,287	8.5
65 years and over	8,671	137	1.6	461	5.3	789	9.1
Wives	47,504	803	1.7	2,645	5.6	4,090	8.6
Under 65 years	40,820	698	1.7	2,315	5.7	3,507	8.6
65 years and over	6,685	105	1.6	330	4.9	584	8.7
Related children under 18 years	41,898	1,205	2.9	4,138	9.9	6,037	14.4
Under 6 years	14,884	511	3.4	1,748	11.7	2,451	16.5
6 to 17 years	27,015	694	2.6	2,390	8.8	3,586	13.3
Own children 18 years and over	11,664	112	1.0	421	3.6	655	5.6
In families with female householder, no spouse present	22,037	3,067	13.9	6,656	30.2	8,135	36.9
Householder	7,848	1,005	12.8	2,202	28.1	2,726	34.7
Under 65 years	6,637	983	14.8	2,078	31.3	2,528	38.1
65 years and over	1,211	21	1.8	125	10.3	198	16.4
Related children under 18 years	8,355	1,874	22.4	3,783	45.3	4,454	53.3
Under 6 years	2,648	869	32.8	1,602	60.5	1,809	68.3

[Continued]

★ 639 ★

Persons Living in Poverty, by Ratio of Income to Poverty Level, Household Relationship, Age Group, and Sex, 1992 - I

[Continued]

Characteristic	Total	Under .50 Number	Under .50 Percent of total	Under 1.00 Number	Under 1.00 Percent of total	Under 1.25 Number	Under 1.25 Percent of total
6 to 17 years	5,706	1,004	17.6	2,181	38.2	2,645	46.4
Own children 18 years and over	3,992	136	3.4	452	11.3	610	15.3
In unrelated subfamilies	1,445	469	32.5	791	54.7	936	64.7
Under 18 years	793	288	36.3	477	60.1	549	69.2
Under 6 years	313	129	41.2	214	68.2	234	74.8
6 to 17 years	480	159	33.1	263	54.8	314	65.6
18 years and over	652	181	27.8	315	48.2	387	59.3
Unrelated individuals	31,176	2,239	7.2	6,087	19.5	8,484	27.1
Male	14,290	963	6.7	2,229	15.6	3,118	21.8
Under 65 years	12,286	923	7.5	1,938	15.8	2,602	21.2
Living alone	6,256	259	4.1	720	11.5	1,000	16.0
65 years and over	2,004	40	2.0	291	14.5	516	25.7
Living alone	1,713	29	1.7	235	13.7	414	24.2
Female	16,886	1,276	7.6	3,858	22.8	5,346	31.7
Under 65 years	9,940	1,065	10.7	2,206	22.2	2,715	27.3
Living alone	5,684	324	5.7	946	16.6	1,215	21.4
65 years and over	6,946	211	3.0	1,652	23.8	2,631	37.9
Living alone	6,684	196	2.9	1,567	23.4	2,512	37.6
BLACK							
Household relationship							
Total	31,916	5,210	16.3	10,613	33.3	12,840	40.2
65 years and over	2,660	138	5.2	887	33.3	1,206	45.3
In families	27,280	4,547	16.7	8,908	32.7	10,735	39.4
Householder	7,888	1,206	15.3	2,435	30.9	2,978	37.8
Under 65 years	6,902	1,149	16.6	2,188	31.7	2,629	38.1
65 years and over	986	57	5.8	246	24.9	348	35.3
Related children under 18 years	10,471	2,824	27.0	4,850	46.3	5,524	52.8
Under 6 years	3,765	1,222	32.5	2,000	53.1	2,235	59.4
6 to 17 years	6,706	1,602	23.9	2,850	42.5	3,290	49.1
Own children 18 years and over	3,705	270	7.3	803	21.7	1,094	29.5
In married-couple families	13,555	673	5.0	1,942	14.3	2,655	19.6
Husbands	3,774	162	4.3	496	13.1	693	18.4
Under 65 years	3,165	135	4.3	368	11.6	507	16.0
65 years and over	607	27	4.5	128	21.1	186	30.7
Wives	3,640	149	4.1	476	13.1	673	18.5
Under 65 years	3,223	133	4.1	394	12.2	553	17.1
65 years and over	417	16	3.8	82	19.6	120	28.8
Related children under 18 years	4,187	310	7.4	762	18.2	992	23.7
Under 6 years	1,375	127	9.3	308	22.4	382	27.7

[Continued]

★ 639 ★

Persons Living in Poverty, by Ratio of Income to Poverty Level, Household Relationship, Age Group, and Sex, 1992 - I

[Continued]

Characteristic	Total	Under .50		Under 1.00		Under 1.25	
		Number	Percent of total	Number	Percent of total	Number	Percent of total
6 to 17 years	2,812	183	6.5	454	16.1	610	21.7
Own children 18 years and over	1,599	45	2.8	167	10.5	234	14.6
In families with female householder, no spouse present	12,316	3,736	30.3	6,609	53.7	7,590	61.6
Householder	3,680	1,001	27.2	1,835	49.8	2,136	58.0
Under 65 years	3,341	970	29.0	1,722	51.5	1,980	59.3
65 years and over	339	31	9.1	113	33.3	156	46.0
Related children under 18 years	5,911	2,449	41.4	3,967	67.1	4,361	73.8
Under 6 years	2,233	1,058	47.4	1,633	73.1	1,769	79.2
6 to 17 years	3,678	1,390	37.8	2,334	63.5	2,592	70.5
Own children 18 years and over	1,909	217	11.4	596	31.2	811	42.5
In unrelated subfamilies	205	61	29.6	121	58.9	139	67.9
Under 18 years	115	39	34.0	75	64.6	84	73.2
Under 6 years	50	22	B	42	B	42	B
6 to 17 years	66	17	B	32	B	42	B
18 years and over	90	21	23.9	46	51.5	55	61.2
Unrelated individuals	4,431	602	13.6	1,584	35.8	1,966	44.4
Male	2,338	318	13.6	708	30.3	900	38.5
Under 65 years	2,028	303	14.9	571	28.1	725	35.8
Living alone	996	109	10.9	242	24.3	297	29.8
65 years and over	309	15	4.8	137	44.4	174	56.3
Living alone	262	6	2.4	112	42.8	149	56.9
Female	2,093	284	13.6	876	41.8	1,066	50.9
Under 65 years	1,443	240	16.7	502	34.8	591	41.0
Living alone	1,033	125	12.1	323	31.3	378	36.6
65 years and over	651	44	6.8	374	57.5	475	73.0
Living alone	621	44	7.1	359	57.9	455	73.3
HISPANIC ORIGIN[1]							
Household relationship							
Total	22,720	2,479	10.9	6,655	29.3	8,688	38.2
65 years and over	1,222	44	3.6	269	22.0	419	34.3
In families	20,116	1,977	9.8	5,655	28.1	7,446	37.0
Householder	5,318	499	9.4	1,395	26.2	1,825	34.3
Under 65 years	4,880	482	9.9	1,324	27.1	1,712	35.1
65 years and over	438	17	3.9	72	16.3	113	25.8
Related children under 18 years	7,589	1,114	14.7	2,946	38.8	3,753	49.5
Under 6 years	2,870	488	17.0	1,223	42.6	1,518	52.9
6 to 17 years	4,719	626	13.3	1,723	36.5	2,235	47.4
Own children 18 years and over	1,888	103	5.5	333	17.7	456	24.1

[Continued]

★ 639 ★

Persons Living in Poverty, by Ratio of Income to Poverty Level, Household Relationship, Age Group, and Sex, 1992 - I

[Continued]

Characteristic	Total	Under .50		Under 1.00		Under 1.25	
		Number	Percent of total	Number	Percent of total	Number	Percent of total
In married-couple families	14,624	892	6.1	3,136	21.4	4,489	30.7
Husbands	3,686	192	5.2	687	18.6	992	26.9
Under 65 years	3,364	182	5.4	638	19.0	908	27.0
65 years and over	322	11	3.4	50	15.4	84	26.1
Wives	3,806	188	4.9	672	17.7	985	25.9
Under 65 years	3,561	185	5.2	648	18.2	934	26.2
65 years and over	245	3	1.1	24	9.9	51	20.9
Related children under 18 years	5,259	447	8.5	1,500	28.5	2,088	39.7
Under 6 years	1,968	201	10.1	641	32.2	848	42.7
6 to 17 years	3,271	246	7.5	860	26.3	1,240	37.9
Own children 18 years and over	1,194	36	3.0	137	11.5	216	18.1
In families with female householder, no spouse present	4,207	945	22.5	2,154	51.2	2,506	59.6
Householder	1,238	264	21.3	604	48.8	704	56.9
Under 65 years	1,142	258	22.6	580	50.8	674	59.0
65 years and over	95	6	6.2	24	25.1	30	31.6
Related children under 18 years	1,963	595	30.3	1,289	65.7	1,468	74.8
Under 6 years	710	259	36.4	510	71.8	570	80.2
6 to 17 years	1,253	336	26.8	779	62.2	898	71.7
Own children 18 years and over	603	64	10.5	177	29.3	217	35.9
In unrelated subfamilies	327	110	33.5	222	67.9	240	73.3
Under 18 years	167	68	40.5	127	76.0	131	78.6
Under 6 years	80	35	43.5	66	83.0	67	84.2
6 to 17 years	87	33	37.8	61	69.7	64	73.5
18 years and over	160	42	26.2	95	59.5	109	67.8
Unrelated individuals	2,278	392	17.2	777	34.1	1,002	44.0
Male	1,354	203	15.0	382	28.2	512	37.8
Under 65 years	1,274	199	15.6	350	27.5	465	36.5
Living alone	410	31	7.6	72	17.6	102	24.8
65 years and over	80	4	4.6	32	39.9	47	58.9
Living alone	70	3	B	29	B	39	B
Female	924	189	20.5	396	42.8	490	53.1
Under 65 years	719	178	24.7	292	40.6	337	46.9
Living alone	340	37	10.8	102	29.8	130	38.2
65 years and over	205	12	5.8	104	50.7	153	74.7
Living alone	188	6	3.3	93	49.6	137	73.1

Source: U.S. Bureau of the Census. *Poverty in the United States: 1992.* Current Population Reports, Series P60-185, U.S. Government Printing Office, Washington, D.C., 1993, pp. 16-19. *Notes:* A (B) stands for base less than 75,000 or not applicable. 1. Persons of Hispanic origin may be of any race.

★ 640 ★

Poverty

Persons Living in Poverty, by Ratio of Income to Poverty Level, Household Relationship, Age Group, and Sex, 1992 - II

Numbers are shown in thousands and refer to persons, families, and unrelated individuals, as of March of the following year.

Characteristic	Under 1.50		Under 1.75		Under 2.00	
	Number	Percent of total	Number	Percent of total	Number	Percent of total
ALL PERSONS						
Household relationship						
Total	61,237	24.1	73,465	28.9	86,233	34.0
65 years and over	8,533	27.6	10,651	34.5	12,805	41.5
In families	46,861	21.7	56,746	26.3	67,369	31.3
Householder	13,639	20.0	16,639	24.4	19,820	29.1
Under 65 years	11,579	20.4	13,884	24.4	16,328	28.7
65 years and over	2,059	18.3	2,755	24.5	3,493	31.0
Related children under 18 years	21,015	32.0	24,463	37.2	28,203	42.9
Under 6 years	8,364	36.2	9,575	41.4	10,832	46.8
6 to 17 years	12,651	29.7	14,888	35.0	17,371	40.8
Own children 18 years and over	3,331	15.8	4,219	20.0	5,101	24.2
In married-couple families	26,083	15.2	33,459	19.5	41,498	24.2
Husbands	7,075	13.3	9,217	17.3	11.522	21.7
Under 65 years	5,541	12.7	7,096	16.2	8,815	20.2
65 years and over	1,534	16.2	2,121	22.4	2,708	28.6
Wives	7,075	13.3	9,217	17.3	11,522	21.7
Under 65 years	5,927	12.9	7,607	16.6	9,441	20.5
65 years and over	1,148	15.9	1,610	22.3	2,081	28.8
Related children under 18 years	10,061	20.7	12,562	25.9	15,343	31.6
Under 6 years	3,996	23.3	4,941	28.8	5,925	34.5
6 to 17 years	6,065	19.3	7,621	24.3	9,418	30.0
Own children 18 years and over	1,342	9.7	1,794	12.9	2,257	16.3
In families with female householder, no spouse present	18,468	51.8	20,589	57.8	22,574	63.3
Householder	5,780	48.4	6,495	54.4	7,179	60.1
Under 65 years	5,300	51.2	5,914	57.1	6,465	62.4
65 years and over	480	30.1	581	36.5	714	44.9
Related children under 18 years	10,028	67.8	10,850	73.3	11,585	78.3
Under 6 years	3,958	78.4	4,160	82.4	4,369	86.5
6 to 17 years	6,070	62.3	6,689	68.6	7,215	74.0
Own children 18 years and over	1,786	29.4	2,183	36.0	2,555	42.1
In unrelated subfamilies	1,221	71.0	1,341	78.0	1,387	80.6
Under 18 years	706	75.0	762	81.0	785	83.5
Under 6 years	302	79.5	324	85.3	329	86.8
6 to 17 years	405	72.0	439	78.0	457	81.3
18 years and over	514	66.0	579	74.4	601	77.2
Unrelated individuals	13,155	35.8	15,378	41.9	17,478	47.6

[Continued]

★ 640 ★

Persons Living in Poverty, by Ratio of Income to Poverty Level, Household Relationship, Age Group, and Sex, 1992 - II

[Continued]

Characteristic	Under 1.50		Under 1.75		Under 2.00	
	Number	Percent of total	Number	Percent of total	Number	Percent of total
Male	5,153	29.8	6,091	35.3	7,103	41.1
Under 65 years	4,263	28.6	5,000	33.5	5,780	38.7
Living alone	1,679	22.3	2,004	26.6	2,377	31.6
65 years and over	889	37.8	1,091	46.3	1,323	56.2
Living alone	751	37.5	937	46.7	1,129	56.3
Female	8,003	41.1	9,287	47.7	10,375	53.3
Under 65 years	3,998	34.0	4,670	39.7	5,187	44.1
Living alone	1,946	28.2	2,301	33.4	2,573	37.3
65 years and over	4,005	52.1	4,617	60.1	5,188	67.5
Living alone	3,828	51.8	4,432	60.0	4,985	67.5
WHITE						
Household relationship						
Total	43,569	20.6	53,425	25.2	63,983	30.2
65 years and over	6,909	25.1	8,789	32.0	10,707	38.9
In families	32,063	17.9	39,897	22.3	48,624	27.1
Householder	9,553	16.5	11,971	20.7	14,632	25.3
Under 65 years	7,999	16.7	9,812	20.5	11,816	24.7
65 years and over	1,553	15.5	2,159	21.5	2,816	28.0
Related children under 18 years	13,745	26.4	16,432	31.5	19,467	37.3
Under 6 years	5,493	30.1	6,421	35.2	7,463	40.9
6 to 17 years	8,252	24.4	10,011	29.5	12,004	35.4
Own children 18 years and over	1,876	11.3	2,505	15.1	3,163	19.1
In married-couple families	20,973	13.9	27,046	17.9	34,019	22.6
Husbands	5,768	12.1	7,577	15.9	9,608	20.2
Under 65 years	4,524	11.6	5,811	14.9	7,315	18.8
65 years and over	1,244	14.3	1,766	20.4	2,293	26.4
Wives	5,777	12.2	7,597	16.0	9,628	20.3
Under 65 years	4,824	11.8	6,231	15.3	7,836	19.2
65 years and over	954	14.3	1,366	20.4	1,792	26.8
Related children under 18 years	8,081	19.3	10,126	24.2	12,535	29.9
Under 6 years	3,236	21.7	3,999	26.9	4,873	32.7
6 to 17 years	4,845	17.9	6,127	22.7	7,662	28.4
Own children 18 years and over	929	8.0	1,251	10.7	1,626	13.9
In families with female householder, no spouse present	9,525	43.2	10,992	49.9	12,271	55.7
Householder	3,219	41.0	3,715	47.3	4,185	53.3
Under 65 years	2,937	44.2	3,357	50.6	3,714	56.0
65 years and over	282	23.3	358	29.6	471	38.9
Related children under 18 years	4,992	59.8	5,541	66.3	5,984	71.6
Under 6 years	1,954	73.8	2,075	78.4	2,193	82.8

[Continued]

★ 640 ★

Persons Living in Poverty, by Ratio of Income to Poverty Level, Household Relationship, Age Group, and Sex, 1992 - II

[Continued]

Characteristic	Under 1.50		Under 1.75		Under 2.00	
	Number	Percent of total	Number	Percent of total	Number	Percent of total
6 to 17 years	3,038	53.2	3,466	60.7	3,791	66.4
Own children 18 years and over	820	20.5	1,097	27.5	1,344	33.7
In unrelated subfamilies	1,010	69.9	1,116	77.2	1,151	79.6
Under 18 years	583	73.6	633	79.8	653	82.4
Under 6 years	247	78.7	269	85.8	272	86.9
6 to 17 years	337	70.2	364	75.9	381	79.4
18 years and over	427	65.4	483	74.1	498	76.3
Unrelated individuals	10,496	33.7	12,412	39.8	14,208	45.6
Male	3,876	27.1	4,636	32.4	5,449	38.1
Under 65 years	3,197	26.0	3,780	30.8	4,393	35.8
Living alone	1,241	19.8	1,501	24.0	1,791	28.6
65 years and over	678	33.9	855	42.7	1,056	52.7
Living alone	566	33.0	732	42.7	897	52.3
Female	6,621	39.2	7,776	46.0	8,758	51.9
Under 65 years	3,189	32.1	3,764	37.9	4,217	42.4
Living alone	1,475	25.9	1,768	31.1	2,002	35.2
65 years and over	3,431	49.4	4,012	57.8	4,542	65.4
Living alone	3,286	49.2	3,859	57.7	4,372	65.4
BLACK						
Household relationship						
Total	14,867	46.6	16,714	52.4	18,517	58.0
65 years and over	1,418	53.3	1,624	61.1	1,816	68.3
In families	12,490	45.6	14,109	51.7	15,668	57.4
Householder	3,486	44.2	3,950	50.1	4,385	55.6
Under 65 years	3,052	44.2	3,434	49.8	3,798	55.0
65 years and over	434	44.0	516	52.3	586	59.5
Related children under 18 years	6,242	59.6	6,843	65.4	7,405	70.7
Under 6 years	2,488	66.1	2,704	71.8	2,866	76.1
6 to 17 years	3,754	56.0	4,138	61.7	4,539	67.7
Own children 18 years and over	1,276	34.4	1,500	40.5	1,702	45.9
In married-couple families	3,576	26.4	4,532	33.4	5,353	39.5
Husbands	935	24.8	1,181	31.3	1,402	37.1
Under 65 years	697	22.0	886	28.0	1,058	33.4
65 years and over	238	39.2	295	48.6	344	56.7
Wives	907	24.9	1,140	31.3	1,351	37.1
Under 65 years	752	23.3	942	29.2	1,115	34.6
65 years and over	155	37.2	199	47.7	236	56.7
Related children under 18 years	1,360	32.5	1,684	40.2	1,959	46.8
Under 6 years	512	37.3	642	46.7	713	51.8

[Continued]

★ 640 ★

Persons Living in Poverty, by Ratio of Income to Poverty Level, Household Relationship, Age Group, and Sex, 1992 - II

[Continued]

Characteristic	Under 1.50		Under 1.75		Under 2.00	
	Number	Percent of total	Number	Percent of total	Number	Percent of total
6 to 17 years	848	30.2	1,042	37.0	1,247	44.3
Own children 18 years and over	288	18.0	394	24.6	472	29.5
In families with female householder, no spouse present	8,332	67.7	8,914	72.4	9,551	77.6
Householder	2,382	64.7	2,573	69.9	2,762	75.1
Under 65 years	2,196	65.7	2,363	70.7	2,532	75.8
65 years and over	186	54.8	210	61.9	230	67.9
Related children under 18 years	4,678	79.1	4,927	83.4	5,184	87.7
Under 6 years	1,886	84.5	1,956	87.6	2,038	91.3
6 to 17 years	2,792	75.9	2,970	80.8	3,146	85.5
Own children 18 years and over	929	48.7	1,037	54.3	1,158	60.6
In unrelated subfamilies	166	80.9	178	86.6	185	90.4
Under 18 years	98	85.0	104	90.3	108	93.4
Under 6 years	45	B	45	B	47	B
6 to 17 years	53	B	59	B	61	B
18 years and over	68	75.6	73	81.8	78	86.6
Unrelated individuals	2,212	49.9	2,427	54.8	2,663	60.1
Male	1,039	44.5	1,145	49.0	1,304	55.8
Under 65 years	840	41.4	928	45.8	1,066	52.6
Living alone	363	36.5	404	40.6	474	47.6
65 years and over	199	64.5	217	70.1	238	76.9
Living alone	174	66.5	190	72.8	209	79.9
Female	1,172	56.0	1,282	61.2	1,359	64.9
Under 65 years	653	45.3	733	50.8	781	54.1
Living alone	424	41.0	477	46.2	509	49.3
65 years and over	519	79.7	549	84.3	578	88.9
Living alone	495	79.7	525	84.5	554	89.3
HISPANIC ORIGIN[1]						
Household relationship						
Total	10,474	46.1	12,118	53.3	13,500	59.4
65 years and over	531	43.4	661	54.0	728	59.6
In families	9,055	45.0	10,545	52.4	11,814	58.7
Householder	2,224	41.8	2,611	49.1	2,931	55.1
Under 65 years	2,071	42.4	2,402	49.2	2,691	55.1
65 years and over	153	35.0	210	47.9	240	54.7
Related children under 18 years	4,361	57.5	4,867	64.1	5,339	70.4
Under 6 years	1,729	60.3	1,917	66.8	2,085	72.6
6 to 17 years	2,632	55.8	2,950	62.5	3,254	69.0
Own children 18 years and over	629	33.3	786	41.6	899	47.6

[Continued]

★640★

Persons Living in Poverty, by Ratio of Income to Poverty Level, Household Relationship, Age Group, and Sex, 1992 - II

[Continued]

Characteristic	Under 1.50		Under 1.75		Under 2.00	
	Number	Percent of total	Number	Percent of total	Number	Percent of total
In married-couple families	5,710	39.0	6,757	46.2	7,757	53.0
Husbands	1,273	34.5	1,531	41.5	1,769	48.0
Under 65 years	1,165	34.6	1,386	41.2	1,603	47.6
65 years and over	107	33.4	145	45.0	166	51.5
Wives	1,271	33.4	1,548	40.7	1,794	47.1
Under 65 years	1,196	33.6	1,443	40.5	1,673	47.0
65 years and over	75	30.7	105	42.7	121	49.4
Related children under 18 years	2,570	48.9	2,953	56.2	3,339	63.5
Under 6 years	1,022	51.4	1,167	58.7	1,306	65.7
6 to 17 years	1,548	47.3	1,787	54.6	2,033	62.2
Own children 18 years and over	324	27.2	408	34.1	484	40.5
In families with female householder, no spouse present	2,802	66.6	3,123	74.2	3,275	77.9
Householder	790	63.9	886	71.6	936	75.7
Under 65 years	744	65.2	824	72.2	869	76.1
65 years and over	46	48.3	62	64.6	67	70.4
Related children under 18 years	1,565	79.7	1,661	84.6	1,717	87.5
Under 6 years	593	83.5	624	87.8	644	90.6
6 to 17 years	972	77.5	1,038	82.8	1,074	85.7
Own children 18 years and over	280	46.4	337	55.9	364	60.4
In unrelated subfamilies	253	77.4	286	87.4	290	88.7
Under 18 years	134	80.3	144	86.3	147	88.1
Under 6 years	69	86.1	77	96.6	77	96.6
6 to 17 years	65	75.0	67	76.9	70	80.4
18 years and over	119	74.4	142	88.6	143	89.3
Unrelated individuals	1,165	51.2	1,286	56.5	1,396	61.3
Male	604	44.6	685	50.6	766	56.6
Under 65 years	550	43.2	625	49.0	700	55.0
Living alone	123	29.9	145	35.4	162	39.5
65 years and over	54	67.4	61	76.3	65	81.8
Living alone	46	B	52	B	56	B
Female	562	60.8	601	65.1	631	68.3
Under 65 years	399	55.5	430	59.9	454	63.2
Living alone	163	47.9	182	53.5	191	56.1
65 years and over	163	79.4	171	83.2	176	86.0
Living alone	147	78.3	155	82.4	160	85.4

Source: U.S. Bureau of the Census. *Poverty in the United States: 1992.* Current Population Reports, Series P60-185, U.S. Government Printing Office, Washington, D.C., 1993, pp. 16-19. *Notes:* A (B) stands for base less than 75,000 or not applicable. 1. Persons of Hispanic origin may be of any race.

★ 641 ★

Poverty

Persons Living in Poverty, by Sex and Number of Children, 1992

Numbers are shown in thousands.

Characteristic	16 years and over			16 to 24 years			25 to 34 years			35 years and over		
	Total	Below poverty level		Total	Below poverty level		Total	Below poverty level		Total	Below poverty level	
		Number	Percent of total		Number	Percent of total		Number	Percent of total		Number	Percent of total
WHITE												
Both sexes												
Total	132,885	10,218	7.7	21,115	2,427	11.5	27,664	2,858	10.3	84,106	4,933	5.9
No own children under 18 years	72,412	3,357	4.6	9,104	487	5.3	9,651	310	3.2	53,657	2,559	4.8
One or more own children under 18 years	60,473	6,861	11.3	12,011	1,940	16.2	18,013	2,547	14.1	30,449	2,374	7.8
One	25,381	2,261	8.9	6,495	860	13.2	6,443	598	9.3	12,443	803	6.5
Two or more	35,092	4,600	13.1	5,517	1,080	19.6	11,570	1,949	16.8	18,005	1,571	8.7
One or more own children under 6 years	24,960	3,754	15.0	3,519	1,179	33.5	13,128	1,823	13.9	8,313	753	9.1
One	16,991	2,200	12.9	2,449	698	28.5	8,411	988	11.7	6,131	514	8.4
Two or more	7,969	1,554	19.5	1,070	481	44.9	4,717	835	17.7	2,182	239	10.9
Male												
Total	65,063	4,139	6.4	10,533	1,008	9.6	13,111	980	7.5	41,419	2,151	5.2
No own children under 18 years	36,431	1,602	4.4	4,774	245	5.1	5,589	185	3.3	26,068	1,172	4.5
One or more own children under 18 years	28,632	2,537	8.9	5,759	763	13.2	7,522	795	10.6	15,351	979	6.4
One	11,949	786	6.6	3,048	318	10.4	2,906	178	6.1	5,995	290	4.8
Two or more	16,683	1,752	10.5	2,710	445	16.4	4,616	617	13.4	9,356	690	7.4
One or more own children under 6 years	11,761	1,320	11.2	1,262	329	26.1	5,759	637	11.1	4,740	354	7.5
One	7,978	742	9.3	892	197	22.1	3,669	313	8.5	3,417	232	6.8
Two or more	3,784	578	15.3	370	132	35.6	2,090	324	15.5	1,323	123	9.3
Female												
Total	67,822	6,079	9.0	10,582	1,419	13.4	14,553	1,878	12.9	42,687	2,782	6.5
No own children under 18 years	35,981	1,755	4.9	4,330	242	5.6	4,062	126	3.1	27,589	1,387	5.0
One or more own children under 18 years	31,841	4,324	13.6	6,253	1,177	18.8	10,490	1,752	16.7	15,098	1,394	9.2
One	13,432	1,475	11.0	3,446	542	15.7	3,537	420	11.9	6,449	513	8.0
Two or more	18,409	2,848	15.5	2,806	635	22.6	6,954	1,332	19.2	8,649	881	10.2
One or more own children under 6 years	13,199	2,434	18.4	2,258	850	37.6	7,369	1,186	16.1	3,572	398	11.2
One	9,013	1,458	16.2	1,557	501	32.1	4,742	675	14.2	2,714	283	10.4
Two or more	4,185	976	23.3	700	349	49.9	2,627	511	19.5	858	116	13.5
BLACK												
Both sexes												
Total	17,955	4,472	24.9	4,194	1,323	31.5	4,373	1,267	29.0	9,388	1,883	20.1
No own children under 18 years	9,103	1,678	18.4	1,686	377	22.4	1,650	249	15.1	5,768	1,052	18.2
One or more own children under 18 years	8,852	2,794	31.6	2,509	945	37.7	2,724	1,018	37.4	3,620	831	23.0
One	3,9812	900	22.6	1,238	327	26.5	1,019	269	26.4	1,726	304	17.6
Two or more	4,869	1,895	38.9	1,271	618	48.6	1,705	749	44.0	1,894	527	27.8
One or more own children under 6 years	3,580	1,466	40.9	896	504	56.3	1,708	669	39.1	976	293	30.0
One	2,388	840	35.2	561	262	46.7	1,072	357	33.3	755	221	29.2
Two or more	1,192	626	52.5	335	242	72.2	636	312	49.0	221	72	32.8
Male												
Total	7,826	1,400	17.9	2,007	505	25.1	1,813	279	15.4	4,006	616	15.4
No own children under 18 years	4,420	705	15.9	902	172	19.1	951	111	11.7	2,568	421	16.4
One or more own children under 18 years	3,405	696	20.4	1,105	332	30.1	863	169	19.5	1,437	195	13.6
One	1,623	242	14.9	595	106	17.8	375	64	17.1	653	72	11.0
Two or more	1,783	454	25.5	511	226	44.4	488	104	21.4	784	123	15.7
One or more own children under 6 years	1,249	303	24.3	241	104	43.2	546	101	18.5	462	98	21.2
One	875	196	22.5	178	72	40.7	344	51	14.7	352	73	20.8
Two or more	375	107	28.5	63	32	B	201	50	25.1	110	25	22.2
Female												
Total	10,129	3,072	30.3	2,187	818	37.4	2,560	987	38.6	5,382	1,267	23.5
No own children under 18 years	4,683	973	20.8	784	205	26.1	699	138	19.7	3,200	631	19.7
One or more own children under 18 years	5,446	2,099	38.5	1,403	613	43.7	1,861	849	45.6	2,182	636	29.2
One	2,360	658	27.9	643	222	34.5	644	205	31.8	1,073	232	21.6
Two or more	3,087	1,441	46.7	760	391	51.5	1,217	645	53.0	1,109	404	36.5
One or more own children under 6 years	2,331	1,163	49.9	655	400	61.1	1,162	567	48.8	513	195	38.0
One	1,514	643	42.5	383	190	49.6	728	306	42.1	403	147	36.6
Two or more	817	520	63.6	272	210	77.4	435	261	60.1	110	48	43.3

[Continued]

★ 641 ★

Persons Living in Poverty, by Sex and Number of Children, 1992

[Continued]

Characteristic	16 years and over			16 to 24 years			25 to 34 years			35 years and over		
	Total	Below poverty level		Total	Below poverty level		Total	Below poverty level		Total	Below poverty level	
		Number	Percent of total		Number	Percent of total		Number	Percent of total		Number	Percent of total
HISPANIC ORIGIN[1]												
Both sexes												
Total	13,358	3,008	22.5	3,114	875	28.1	3,565	904	25.4	6,679	1,228	18.4
No own children under 18 years	5,369	743	13.8	1,050	181	17.2	1,016	100	9.9	3,303	462	14.0
One or more own children under 18 years	7,989	2,265	28.4	2,064	695	33.7	2,549	804	31.6	3,376	766	22.7
One	3,041	620	20.4	966	254	26.3	828	164	19.8	1,247	202	16.2
Two or more	4,948	1,645	33.2	1,098	441	40.1	1,721	640	37.2	2,129	654	26.5
One or more own children under 6 years	3,970	1,372	34.6	951	430	45.2	1,860	628	33.8	1,159	314	27.1
One	2,661	799	30.0	648	263	40.6	1,140	320	28.1	873	216	24.7
Two or more	1,309	573	43.8	303	167	55.2	720	308	42.8	286	98	34.3
Male												
Total	6,433	1,256	19.5	1,547	376	24.3	1,736	361	20.8	3,150	519	16.5
No own children under 18 years	2,750	359	13.1	549	91	16.5	657	67	10.2	1,545	202	13.1
One or more own children under 18 years	3,683	897	24.4	997	285	28.6	1,080	294	27.3	1,606	318	19.8
One	1,424	248	17.4	449	99	22.0	399	72	18.1	575	77	13.4
Two or more	2,259	649	28.7	548	186	33.9	680	222	32.7	1,031	241	23.4
One or more own children under 6 years	1,818	537	29.5	386	150	38.9	819	246	30.0	614	141	23.0
One	1,214	308	25.4	270	101	37.6	496	119	24.0	448	88	19.6
Two or more	605	229	37.8	116	49	41.9	323	127	39.2	166	53	32.1
Female												
Total	6,925	1,752	25.3	1,568	500	31.9	1,828	543	29.7	3,529	709	20.1
No own children under 18 years	2,619	384	14.7	501	90	18.0	360	33	9.3	1,758	260	14.8
One or more own children under 18 years	4,306	1,368	31.8	1,066	410	38.4	1,469	510	34.7	1,771	449	25.3
One	1,618	372	23.0	516	155	30.0	429	92	21.4	673	126	18.7
Two or more	2,688	996	37.0	550	255	46.3	1,040	418	40.2	1,098	323	29.4
One or more own children under 6 years	2,151	835	38.8	566	280	49.5	1,041	382	36.7	545	173	31.7
One	1,448	491	33.9	379	161	42.7	644	201	31.2	425	128	30.2
Two or more	704	345	49.0	187	119	63.5	396	181	45.7	120	45	37.2

Source: U.S. Bureau of the Census. *Poverty in the United States: 1992.* Current Population Reports, Series P60-185, U.S. Government Printing Office, Washington, D.C., 1993, pp. 82-83. *Notes:* A B indicates that the base was less than 75,000 or not applicable. 1. Persons of Hispanic origin may be of any race.

★ 642 ★

Poverty

Persons and Families Living in Poverty, 1990-1991

Numbers are shown in thousands.

Characteristic	1991			1990			1991-90 difference	
	Total	Number below poverty level	Poverty rate	Total	Number below poverty level	Poverty rate	Number below poverty level	Poverty rate
PERSONS								
All persons	251,179	35,708	14.2	246,644	33,585	13.5	2,123[1]	.7[1]
Race and Hispanic origin								
Hispanic origin[2]	22,068	6,339	28.7	21,405	6,006	28.1	333[1]	.7[1]
Related children under 18	7,473	2,977	39.8	7,300	2,750	37.7	227[1]	2.2
White	210,121	23,747	11.3	208,611	22,326	10.7	1,421[1]	.6[1]

[Continued]

★ 642 ★

Persons and Families Living in Poverty, 1990-1991

[Continued]

Characteristic	1991			1990			1991-90 difference	
	Total	Number below poverty level	Poverty rate	Total	Number below poverty level	Poverty rate	Number below poverty level	Poverty rate
Related children under 18	51,631	8,321	16.1	51,028	7,696	15.1	624[1]	1.0[1]
Black	31,312	10,242	32.7	30,806	9,837	31.9	405	.8[1]
Related children under 18	10,178	4,637	45.6	9,980	4,412	44.2	225	1.4
FAMILIES								
Race and Hispanic origin[2] of householder								
All families	67,173	7,712	11.5	66,322	7,098	10.7	613[1]	8[1]
Married-couple families	52,457	3,158	6.0	52,147	2,981	5.7	177[1]	.3
Male householder, no wife present	3,025	392	13.0	2,907	349	12.0	43	.9
Female householder, no husband present	11,692	4,161	35.6	11,266	3,768	33.4	393[1]	2.2[1]
Hispanic origin families[2]	5,177	1,372	26.5	4,981	1,244	25.0	129[1]	1.5
Married-couple families	3,532	674	19.1	3,4454	605	17.5	70[1]	1.6
Male householder, no wife present	383	71	18.6	342	66	19.4	5	-.8[1]
Female householder, no husband present	1,261	627	49.7	1,186	573	48.3	54	1.4
White families	57,224	5,022	8.8	56,803	4,622	8.1	400[1]	.6[1]
Married-couple families	47,124	2,573	5.5	47,014	2,386	5.1	187[1]	.4[1]
Male householder, no wife present	2,374	257	10.8	2,276	226	9.9	30	.9
Female householder, no husband present	7,726	2,192	28.4	7,512	2,010	26.8	183[1]	1.6
Black families	7,716	2,343	30.4	7,471	2,193	29.3	150[1]	1.0
Married-couple families	3,631	399	11.0	3,569	448	12.6	-49	-1.6
Male householder, no wife present	504	109	21.7	472	96	20.4	13	1.3
Female householder, no husband present	3,582	1,834	51.2	3,430	1,648	48.1	186[1]	3.2

Source: U.S. Bureau of the Census. *Poverty in the United States: 1991.* Current Population Reports, Series P60-181, U.S. Government Printing Office, Washington, D.C., 1992, p. 1. *Notes:* 1. Number and poverty rate difference indicate statistically significant change at the 90-percent confidence level. 2. Persons of Hispanic origin may be of any race.

★ 643 ★

Poverty

Persons of Hispanic Origin Living in Poverty Areas, by Poverty Status and Selected Social Characteristics, 1992

Numbers are shown in thousands and refer to persons, families, or unrelated individuals, as of March of the following year. Poverty areas or neighborhoods are defined as census tracts and minor civil divisions outside tracted areas with a poverty rate of 20 percent or more based on the 1980 census.

Characteristic	All areas			Living in poverty areas			Living outside poverty areas		
	Total	Currently below poverty level		Total	Currently below poverty level		Total	Currently below poverty level	
		Number	Percent		Number	Percent		Number	Percent
HISPANIC ORIGIN[1]									
Both sexes									
Total	22,720	6,655	29.3	6,932	2,862	41.3	15,788	3,793	24.0
Under 18 years	7,807	3,116	39.9	2,531	1,359	53.7	5,276	1,757	33.3
18 to 24 years	2,813	844	30.0	875	350	40.0	1,938	494	25.5
25 to 34 years	4,277	1,076	25.2	1,151	421	36.5	3,126	655	21.0
35 to 44 years	3,330	719	21.6	853	272	31.9	2,477	447	18.0
45 to 54 years	2,037	349	17.1	625	177	28.4	1,411	171	12.1
55 to 59 years	680	137	20.2	243	76	31.2	437	62	14.1
60 to 64 years	554	145	26.2	197	74	37.6	357	71	19.9
65 years and over	1,222	269	22.0	457	134	29.3	765	135	17.6
65 to 74 years	806	157	19.5	291	71	24.5	516	86	16.7
75 years and over	416	112	26.8	167	63	37.7	249	49	19.6
Male									
Total	11,378	3,067	27.0	3,379	1,274	37.7	8,000	1,793	22.4
Under 18 years	3,958	1,551	39.2	1,265	666	52.7	2,693	885	32.9
18 to 24 years	1,417	360	25.4	428	141	33.0	990	219	22.1
25 to 34 years	2,237	467	20.9	593	180	30.4	1,644	287	17.4
35 to 44 years	1,682	328	19.5	416	108	25.9	1,265	220	17.4
45 to 54 years	1,035	170	16.5	320	84	26.3	715	86	12.1
55 to 59 years	292	53	18.1	94	24	25.4	198	29	14.7
60 to 64 years	249	50	19.9	87	27	30.9	162	23	14.0
65 years and over	508	88	17.4	175	43	24.6	332	45	13.5
65 to 74 years	345	57	16.7	116	25	22.0	229	32	13.9
75 years and over	163	31	18.8	60	18	(B)	103	13	12.6
Female									
Total	11,342	3,588	31.6	3,554	1,589	44.7	7,788	1,999	25.7
Under 18 years	3,849	1,565	40.7	1,266	693	54.7	2,583	872	33.8
18 to 24 years	1,396	484	34.7	447	209	46.7	949	275	29.0
25 to 34 years	2,040	609	29.9	559	241	43.1	1,482	369	24.9
35 to 44 years	1,648	391	23.7	437	164	37.5	1,211	227	18.7
45 to 54 years	1,002	178	17.8	305	93	30.5	696	85	12.2
55 to 59 years	387	84	21.7	149	52	34.8	239	33	13.6
60 to 64 years	305	96	31.3	110	47	43.0	196	48	24.7
65 years and over	715	181	25.3	282	91	32.2	433	90	20.8
65 to 74 years	462	100	21.6	175	46	26.1	287	54	18.9
75 years and over	253	81	32.0	107	45	42.2	146	36	24.5
Household relationship									
Total	22,720	6,655	29.3	6,932	2,862	41.3	15,788	3,793	24.0
65 years and over	1,222	269	22.0	457	134	29.3	765	135	17.6
In families	20,116	5,655	28.1	6,210	2,495	40.2	13,906	3,161	22.7
Householder	5,318	1,395	26.2	1,619	626	38.7	3,700	769	20.8
Under 65 years	4,880	1,324	27.1	1,442	591	41.0	3,438	733	21.3

[Continued]

★ 643 ★

Persons of Hispanic Origin Living in Poverty Areas, by Poverty Status and Selected Social Characteristics, 1992

[Continued]

Characteristic	All areas			Living in poverty areas			Living outside poverty areas		
	Total	Currently below poverty level		Total	Currently below poverty level		Total	Currently below poverty level	
		Number	Percent		Number	Percent		Number	Percent
65 years and over	438	72	16.3	177	35	19.7	261	37	14.1
Related children under 18 years	7,589	2,946	38.8	2,462	1,299	52.8	5,126	1,647	32.1
Under 6 years	2,870	1,223	42.6	914	534	58.5	1,956	688	35.2
6 to 17 years	4,719	1,723	36.5	1,549	765	49.4	3,170	958	30.2
Own children 18 years and over	1,888	333	17.7	677	178	26.4	1,212	155	12.8
In married-couple families	14,624	3,136	21.4	3,987	1,250	31.4	10,637	1,886	17.7
Husbands	3,686	687	18.6	963	276	28.7	2,724	411	15.1
Under 65 years	3,364	638	19.0	855	255	29.8	2,509	383	15.3
65 years and over	322	50	15.4	107	21	20.0	214	28	13.1
Wives	3,806	672	17.7	980	273	27.9	2,826	399	14.1
Under 65 years	3,561	648	18.2	900	263	29.2	2,661	385	14.5
65 years and over	245	24	9.9	80	10	12.3	165	14	8.7
Related children under 18 years	5,259	1,500	28.5	1,470	581	39.5	3,789	920	24.3
Under 6 years	1,988	641	32.2	547	249	45.6	1,441	391	27.2
6 to 17 years	3,271	860	26.3	923	331	35.9	2,348	529	22.5
Own children 18 years and over	1,194	137	11.5	377	73	19.4	816	64	7.8
In families with female householder, no spouse present	4,207	2,154	51.2	1,794	1,111	61.9	2,413	1,044	43.2
Householder	1,238	604	48.8	520	307	59.1	718	297	41.4
Under 65 years	1,142	580	50.8	466	293	63.0	677	287	42.4
65 years and over	95	24	25.1	54	14	(B)	41	10	(B)
Related children under 18 years	1,963	1,289	65.7	871	665	76.4	1,093	624	57.1
Under 6 years	710	510	71.8	315	261	82.6	395	249	63.1
6 to 17 years	1,253	779	62.2	555	404	72.8	698	375	53.7
Own children 18 years and over	603	177	29.3	268	100	37.3	335	77	23.0
Unrelated individuals	2,278	777	34.1	63	293	46.2	1,644	485	29.5
Male	1,354	382	28.2	348	127	36.6	1,006	255	25.3
Under 65 years	1,274	350	27.5	317	110	34.5	957	240	25.1
Living alone	410	72	17.6	119	38	31.6	291	35	11.9
65 years and over	80	32	39.9	30	18	(B)	49	14	(B)
Living alone	70	29	(B)	25	17	(B)	44	12	(B)
Female	924	396	42.8	286	166	58.0	638	230	36.0
Under 65 years	719	292	40.6	193	110	57.0	525	181	34.5
Living alone	340	102	29.8	100	50	49.5	240	52	21.6
65 years and over	205	104	50.7	92	55	60.0	113	48	43.0
Living alone	188	93	49.6	85	52	61.0	102	41	40.1
Residence and Region									
United States									
Metropolitan	21,010	6,028	28.7	6,346	2,593	40.9	14,663	3,435	23.4
Central city	11,816	3,985	33.7	5,165	2,184	42.3	6,651	1,800	27.1
Not central city	9,193	2,043	22.2	1,181	409	34.6	8,013	1,635	20.4
Not metropolitan	1,711	627	36.7	586	269	45.9	1,124	358	31.8
Northeast	3,383	1,167	34.5	1,714	812	47.4	1,669	355	21.3
Midwest	1,658	452	27.3	361	110	30.5	1,298	342	26.4

[Continued]

★ 643 ★

Persons of Hispanic Origin Living in Poverty Areas, by Poverty Status and Selected Social Characteristics, 1992

[Continued]

Characteristic	All areas			Living in poverty areas			Living outside poverty areas		
	Total	Currently below poverty level		Total	Currently below poverty level		Total	Currently below poverty level	
		Number	Percent		Number	Percent		Number	Percent
South	7,014	1,997	28.5	2,250	904	40.2	4,764	1,093	22.9
West	10,665	3,039	28.5	2,608	1,036	39.7	8,057	2,002	24.9
Receipt of Assistance									
In household that received means-tested assistance	11,405	5,465	47.9	4,663	2,536	54.4	6,742	2,929	43.4
Cash assistance	4,478	2,642	59.0	2,089	1,373	65.7	2,388	1,269	53.1
Noncash assistance	11,327	5,456	48.2	4,640	2,534	54.6	6,688	2,922	43.7
Food stamps	4,922	3,417	69.4	2,213	1,678	75.8	2,708	1,739	64.2
Free or reduced price school lunches only	2,821	883	31.3	1,096	342	31.2	1,726	542	31.4
In households that did not receive assistance	11,315	1,190	10.5	2,270	327	14.4	9,046	863	9.5
Years of school completed									
Persons 16 to 24 years	3,528	1,084	30.7	1,114	461	41.4	2,414	623	25.8
Enrolled in school	1,399	350	25.0	418	162	38.7	981	188	19.2
Not enrolled	2,129	735	34.5	696	300	43.0	1,433	435	30.4
No high school diploma	1,117	481	43.1	410	201	49.0	708	281	39.7
Persons 25 and over	12,100	2,695	22.3	3,527	1,154	32.7	8,573	1,541	18.0
No high school diploma	5,677	1,836	32.4	2,245	850	37.9	3,431	986	28.7
High school diploma or more	6,424	858	13.4	1,282	303	23.7	5,142	555	10.8
No college	3,242	538	16.6	816	216	26.4	2,425	322	13.3
Some college, less than Bachelor's degree	2,092	246	11.8	353	77	21.7	1,739	169	9.7
Bachelor's degree or more	1,090	74	6.8	112	11	9.7	977	63	6.5
Work experience									
Male									
Under 16 years	3,595	1,433	39.9	1,153	616	53.4	2,442	817	33.5
16 to 64 years	7,276	1,546	21.2	2,050	615	30.0	5,226	931	17.8
Worked during year	6,066	1,007	16.6	1,563	351	22.5	4,503	656	14.6
Year-round, full-time	3,719	317	8.5	898	117	13.0	2,822	200	7.1
Not year round, full-time	2,346	690	29.4	665	234	35.2	1,682	456	27.1
Did not work	1,210	539	44.5	487	264	54.1	723	275	38.1
65 years and over	508	88	17.4	175	43	24.6	332	45	13.5
Worked during year	86	8	9.3	25	4	(B)	61	4	(B)
Year-round, full-time	30	1	(B)	7	-	(B)	23	1	(B)
Not year round, full-time	56	7	(B)	18	4	(B)	38	3	(B)
Did not work	421	80	19.0	150	39	25.9	271	41	15.2
Female									
Under 16 years	3,497	1,443	41.3	1,138	632	55.5	2,359	811	34.4
16 to 24 years	7,130	1,964	27.5	2,133	866	40.6	4,997	1,098	22.0
Worked during year	4,170	645	15.5	1,009	241	23.9	3,162	405	12.8
Year-round, full-time	2,131	130	6.1	483	48	9.9	1,648	82	5.0
Not year round, full-time	2,040	516	25.3	526	193	36.7	1,514	323	21.3
Did not work	2,960	1,319	44.6	1,125	625	55.6	1,835	693	37.8

[Continued]

★ 643 ★

Persons of Hispanic Origin Living in Poverty Areas, by Poverty Status and Selected Social Characteristics, 1992

[Continued]

Characteristic	All areas			Living in poverty areas			Living outside poverty areas		
	Total	Currently below poverty level		Total	Currently below poverty level		Total	Currently below poverty level	
		Number	Percent		Number	Percent		Number	Percent
65 years and over	715	181	25.3	282	91	32.2	433	90	20.8
Worked during year	61	6	(B)	22	3	(B)	39	3	(B)
Year-round, full-time	25	-	(B)	10	-	(B)	16	-	(B)
Not year-round, full-time	35	6	(B)	12	3	(B)	23	3	(B)
Did not work	654	175	26.7	260	88	33.7	394	87	22.0

Source: U.S. Bureau of the Census. *Poverty in the United States: 1992.* Current Population Reports, Series P60-185, U.S. Government Printing Office, Washington, D.C., 1993, pp. 64-65. *Notes:* A dash (-) represents zero or rounds to zero. A (B) stands for base less than 75,000. 1. Hispanics may be of any race.

★ 644 ★

Poverty

Poverty Rates, by Hispanic Origin

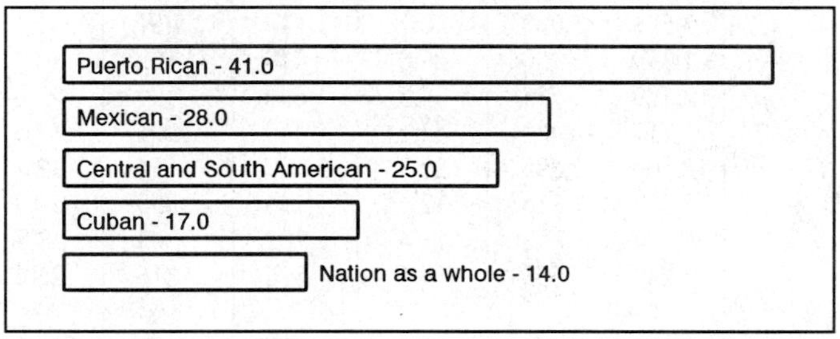

Hispanic origin	Poverty rate
Mexican	28.0
Central and South American	25.0
Puerto Rican	41.0
Cuban	17.0
Nation as a whole	14.0

Source: Tharp, Mike, David Whitman, and Betsy Streisand. "Hispanics' tale of two cities." *U.S. News & World Report* (25 May 1992), p. 40. U.S. Bureau of the Census.

Public Assistance

★ 645 ★

Child Recipients of Welfare Benefits

These data show percent distribution by race/ethnicity of the more than 8.5 million children who received welfare benefits in the year ended September 1991.

Race/ethnicity	Percent
Black	40.1
White	33.5
Hispanic	18.5
Asian	3.7
Native American	1.3
Unknown	2.9

Source: Chavez, Linda. "Why make it easier to receive welfare?" *USA TODAY* (8 June 1994), p. 11A. Department of Health and Human Services.

★ 646 ★

Public Assistance

Distribution of Government Social Programs, by Race/Ethnicity, 1991

Entitlement	Hispanics[1] (percent)	Non-Hispanic	
		Whites (percent)	Blacks (percent)
Welfare	15.0	48.0	32.0
Food stamps	17.0	46.0	33.0
Medicaid	17.0	47.0	31.0
Housing	14.0	38.0	43.0
Programs available for all income levels			
Social security	4.0	85.0	10.0
Medicare	4.0	84.0	20.0
Jobless insurance	7.0	77.0	15.0

Source: Usdansky, Margaret L. "Poor whites get more help than others." *USA TODAY* (9 October 1992), p. 3A. Primary source: Center on Budget and Policy Priorities, based on 1991 Census data. *Note:* 1. Hispanics can be of any race.

★ 647 ★

Public Assistance

Length of Welfare Benefits Received, by Race/Ethnicity

Distribution of persons receiving Aid to Families with Dependent Children is shown for 1979 to 1989.

Race/ethnicity	More than five years	Less than two years
White and other	43.0	65.0
Black	34.0	23.0
Hispanic	23.0	13.0

Source: Duggan, Celia W. "Iowa cuts off the cash, pushing some to work, and some over the edge." *The New York Times* (7 April 95), sec. A, p. 1. Primary source: LaDonna Pavetti, The Urban Institute.

★ 648 ★

Public Assistance

Parental Recipients of Welfare Benefits

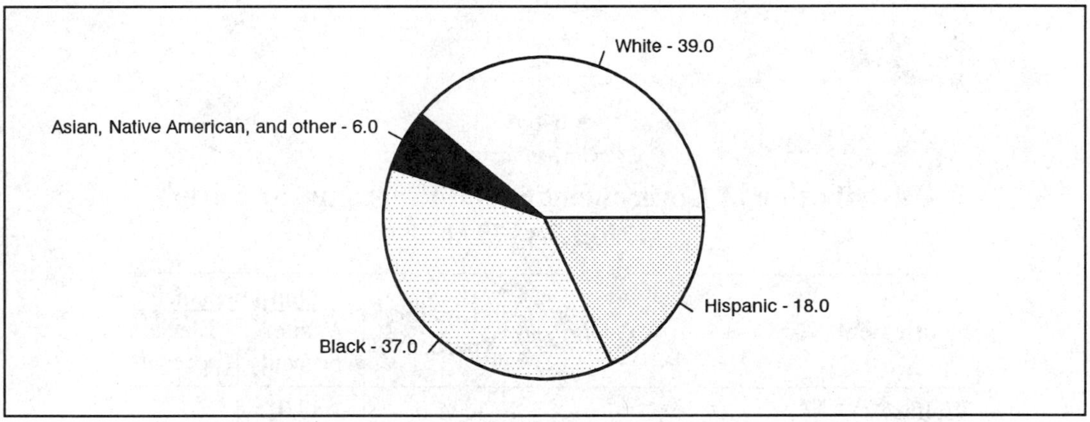

Data show percent distribution by race/ethnicity of parents who receive welfare benefits.

Race/ethnicity	Percent
White	39.0
Black	37.0
Hispanic	18.0
Asian, Native American, and other	6.0

Source: Usdansky, Margaret L. "Women on welfare: reality vs. stereotype." *USA TODAY* (26 October 1994), p. 9A. Primary source: Aid to Families for Dependent Children.

★ 649 ★

Public Assistance

Special Supplemental Food Program for Women, Infants, and Children (WIC): Racial Participation

Percentages are for April 1991.

Race and ethnicity	Percent
Hispanic	23.0
White	44.0
Black	28.0
Asian	2.0
Indian	2.0

Source: Special Supplemental Food Program for Women, Infants, and Children (WIC) Racial Participation, April 1991. Food and Nutrition Service Financial Management Program Information Division Data Base, Monitoring Branch, November, 1991.

★ 650 ★

Public Assistance

Special Supplemental Food Program for Women, Infants, and Children: Participation, by Race/Ethnicity

Number of participants is shown by race/ethnicity for April 1990 and 1991.

Race/ethnicity	April 1990	April 1991	Difference (+/-)
Hispanic			
Women	249,836	294,230	44,394
Infants	335,669	398,330	62,661
Children	414,569	435,500	20,931
Total	1,000,074	1,128,060	127,986
American Indian or Alaska Native			
Women	18,867	19,663	796
Infants	23,848	24,840	992
Children	52,018	52,710	692
Total	94,733	97,213	2,480
Black			
Women	268,503	276,383	7,880
Infants	427,196	456,772	29,576
Children	623,870	650,913	27,043
Total	1,319,569	1,384,068	64,499
Asian or Pacific			
Women	24,231	25,958	1,727
Infants	36,507	39,278	2,771
Children	50,875	50,035	-840
Total	111,613	115,271	3,658

[Continued]

★ 650 ★

Special Supplemental Food Program for Women, Infants, and Children: Participation, by Race/Ethnicity

[Continued]

Race/ethnicity	April 1990	April 1991	Difference (+/-)
White			
Women	485,155	507,549	22,394
Infants	598,518	653,559	55,041
Children	973,950	994,542	20,592
Total	2,057,623	2,155,650	98,027
All groups			
Women	1,046,592	1,123,783	77,191
Infants	1,421,738	1,572,779	151,041
Children	2,115,282	2,183,700	68,418
Total	4,583,612	4,880,262	296,650

Source: Special Supplemental Food Program for Women, Infants, and Children (WIC) Racial Participation, April 1991. Food and Nutrition Service Financial Management Program Information Division Data Base, Monitoring Branch, November 1991.

★ 651 ★

Public Assistance

Special Supplemental Food Program for Women, Infants, and Children: Participation, by Race/ Ethnicity and Area - I

Number of participants is shown as of April 1991.

Region/State	Hispanic			American Indian			White		
	Women	Infants	Children	Women	Infants	Children	Women	Infants	Children
Northeast Region									
Connecticut	3,176	4,055	12,572	51	58	95	3,673	4,702	11,623
Pleasant Pt., ME	0	0	0	22	20	65	0	0	0
Ind. Twnshp., ME	0	0	0	23	14	61	2	0	0
Maine	29	28	84	20	18	61	5,303	5,663	13,420
Massachusetts	4,463	5,940	11,842	23	19	38	6,774	10,982	17,493
New Hampshire	41	57	143	1	4	7	2,751	4,010	8,264
New York	21,636	34,507	52,144	183	280	429	23,214	32,272	56,947
Seneca Nation Ind., NY	0	0	0	48	41	188	5	5	12
Rhode Island	8	5	24	7	7	16	1,888	2,831	5,716
Vermont	8	5	24	6	5	6	3,482	2,931	10,352
Regional total	30,080	45,722	78,941	384	466	966	47,092	63,396	123,828
Mid-Atlantic Region									
Delaware	167	244	429	3	2	6	945	1,653	2,165
District of Columbia	538	700	837	3	3	3	46	49	3,045
Maryland	717	1,123	1,307	6	12	25	5,109	7,390	9,336
New Jersey	7,661	10,013	19,428	37	78	148	5,416	7,084	12,731
Pennsylvania	2,104	3,525	9,675	40	41	143	21,288	32,119	80,764

[Continued]

★651★

Special Supplemental Food Program for Women, Infants, and Children: Participation, by Race/ Ethnicity and Area - I

[Continued]

Region/State	Hispanic			American Indian			White		
	Women	Infants	Children	Women	Infants	Children	Women	Infants	Children
Puerto Rico	30,482	46,285	47,576	0	0	0	0	0	0
Virginia	1,220	1,834	1,687	69	81	85	8,301	14,132	18,131
Virgin Islands	132	201	348	1	0	1	24	10	17
West Virginia	12	34	71	6	6	14	7,307	10,496	17,604
Regional total	43,033	63,959	81,358	165	223	425	48,424	72,930	140,797
Southeast Region									
Alabama	269	71	159	29	37	111	11,752	15,935	20,141
Seminole Indian, FL	0	0	0	28	51	107	1	1	2
Miccosukee Ind., FL	0	0	0	12	12	21	0	0	0
Florida	8,477	13,278	15,098	50	57	81	24,844	29,034	35,843
Georgia	1,200	1,486	2,279	33	36	52	20,179	33,720	35,148
Kentucky	60	97	189	21	30	52	17,272	22,807	41,759
Choctaw Indian, MS	0	0	0	103	158	412	2	0	0
Mississippi	27	22	40	5	2	3	8,501	11,363	15,409
E. Cherokee Ind., NC	0	0	0	138	148	422	11	0	0
North Carolina	743	975	1,377	594	948	1,110	16,727	20,304	25,189
South Carolina	216	200	376	28	31	36	11,801	12,232	15,652
Tennessee	61	99	87	56	61	62	20,498	27,708	32,710
Regional total	11,053	16,228	19,605	1,097	1,571	2,469	127,376	159,563	220,425
Midwest Region									
Illinois	8,288	15,761	20,032	30	71	114	14,880	23,853	32,016
Indiana	594	931	1,654	12	9	37	20,917	26,907	43,506
Michigan	1,963	2,515	5,237	214	242	547	23,394	28,509	49,267
Minnesota	389	594	1,546	533	980	2,325	9,322	12,407	33,898
Ohio	912	1,532	2,007	35	52	50	31,141	47,292	59,255
Wisconsin	891	1,331	2,383	332	547	1,207	8,040	12,307	19,814
Regional total	13,037	22,664	32,859	1,156	1,901	4,280	107,694	151,275	287,756
Southwest Region									
Arkansas	178	161	224	41	33	51	11,112	11,155	15,385
Louisiana	332	236	665	169	107	380	12,316	13,046	20,341
Eight Pueblo Ind., NM	5	0	0	82	100	332	3	0	0
Isleta Pueblo Ind., NM	0	0	0	78	125	271	1	0	0
Zuni Pueblo Ind., NM	0	0	0	178	187	342	0	0	0
Five Sandoval Ind., NM	0	0	0	59	62	243	0	0	0
Santa Domingo Ind., NM	0	0	0	46	49	199	0	0	0
San Felipe Ind., NM	0	0	0	54	46	214	0	0	0
ALC., NM	1	0	0	93	135	328	0	0	0
New Mexico	5,559	7,707	6,515	373	511	406	2,041	2,716	2,427
Choctaw Nation Ind., OK	0	0	0	175	500	1,031	99	181	220
Chickasaw Nation Ind., OK	5	5	8	261	323	494	148	114	152
Cherokee Nation Ind., OK	1	0	1	1,077	1,608	2,704	118	14	30
Potawatomi Ind., OK	0	4	1	133	280	431	22	6	6
Inter-Tribal Council Inc., OK	2	0	0	57	90	29	15	0	0
WCD Enterprises Ind., OK	0	0	0	324	451	834	22	0	0
Oklahoma	723	1,055	968	419	816	923	9,142	11,881	12,404

[Continued]

★ 651 ★

Special Supplemental Food Program for Women, Infants, and Children: Participation, by Race/ Ethnicity and Area - I

[Continued]

Region/State	Hispanic			American Indian			White		
	Women	Infants	Children	Women	Infants	Children	Women	Infants	Children
Oklahoma	0	0	0	96	187	383	40	0	0
Texas	55,069	67,311	118,298	156	185	368	18,729	21,416	28,953
Regional total	61,879	76,479	126,680	3,871	5,795	9,963	53,808	60,529	79,918
Mountain Plains Region									
Ute Mt. Tribe Ind., CO	0	0	0	30	33	83	2	0	0
Colorado	3,130	3,627	7,574	92	109	185	6,410	6,670	13,737
Iowa	194	289	712	36	71	230	6,996	10,010	25,699
Kansas	960	1,304	2,005	109	143	225	6,744	8,548	14,718
Missouri	177	404	441	33	39	55	13,644	21,039	22,051
Montana	51	106	224	645	986	2,854	2,316	2,944	6,593
Nebraska	382	501	853	131	145	282	4,625	5,260	9,757
Nebr. IIIIDC Ind., NE	0	0	0	130	122	391	0	0	0
Standing Rock Sioux Ind., ND	0	0	0	195	176	702	1	0	0
Ft. Berthold, ND	0	0	0	102	95	306	4	0	0
North Dakota	60	61	203	464	455	1,550	2,652	2,416	7,361
Cheyenne River Sioux, SD	0	0	0	124	129	452	0	0	0
Rosebud Sioux Tr. Ind., SD	0	1	0	247	265	801	6	5	14
South Dakota	41	21	88	938	980	2,647	2,778	2,938	6,786
Utah	1,079	1,246	2,237	342	463	972	8,955	9,058	15,090
Shoshone-Arapahoe Ind., WY	1	3	8	135	171	484	5	3	7
Wyoming	194	285	564	27	52	106	1,669	2,151	3,329
Regional total	6,269	7,848	14,909	3,780	1,434	12,325	56,807	71,042	125,142
Western Region									
Mauneluk, AK	0	0	0	69	104	196	0	0	0
Alaska	89	127	100	1,038	1,208	1,688	1,480	1,605	1,509
Navajo Tribe, AZ	7	2	7	3,626	4,051	10,598	12	6	21
Inter Tribal Council, AZ	78	80	145	1,371	1,538	3,171	31	34	59
Arizona	7,611	9,351	9,426	606	639	1,396	5,705	6,068	7,399
California	118,409	146,211	61,272	925	956	1,818	24,328	28,861	18,315
Guam	5	4	6	0	0	0	69	117	162
Hawaii	141	184	196	34	45	47	965	1,249	1,335
Idaho	971	1,281	2,242	163	231	443	4,628	5,392	8,993
Inter-Tribe Council Ind., NV	1	0	0	205	228	653	6	0	0
Nevada	1,071	1,682	1,692	31	27	62	2,082	2,608	2,994
Oregon	2,148	2,086	3,130	309	256	537	12,383	10,295	15,950
Washington	3,348	4,472	2,932	833	1,167	1,673	14,659	18,589	9,939
Regional total	128,879	165,430	81,148	9,210	10,450	22,282	66,348	74,824	66,676
U.S. total	294,230	398,330	435,500	19,663	24,840	52,710	507,549	653,559	994,542

Source: Special Supplemental Food Program for Women, Infants, and Children (WIC) Racial Participation, April 1991. Food and Nutrition Service Financial Management Program Information Division Data Base, Monitoring Branch, November 1991, pp. 4-11.

★ 652 ★

Public Assistance

Special Supplemental Food Program for Women, Infants, and Children: Participation, by Race/ Ethnicity and Area - II

Number of participants is shown as of April 1991.

Region/State	Black			Asian/Pacific Islanders			Total participants			Total
	Women	Infants	Children	Women	Infants	Children	Women	Infants	Children	
Northeast Region										
Connecticut	2,717	4,056	10,768	111	145	364	9,728	13,016	35,422	58,166
Pleasant Pt., ME	0	0	0	0	0	0	22	20	65	107
Ind. Twnshp., ME	0	0	0	0	0	0	25	14	62	101
Maine	32	46	143	29	35	108	5,413	5,790	13,816	25,019
Massachusetts	3,162	4,970	8,644	775	1,512	3,375	15,197	23,423	41,392	80,012
New Hampshire	32	45	132	8	21	46	2,833	4,137	8,592	15,562
New York	21,693	38,080	55,129	2,344	4,200	6,581	69,070	109,339	171,230	349,639
Seneca Nation Ind., NY	0	0	0	0	0	0	53	46	200	299
Rhode Island	535	806	1,504	157	245	538	3,314	5,019	9,906	18,239
Vermont	17	19	74	17	12	31	3,530	2,972	10,487	16,989
Regional total	28,188	48,022	76,394	3,441	6,170	11,043	109,185	163,776	291,172	564,133
Mid-Atlantic Region										
Delaware	938	1,967	3,143	6	10	5	2,059	3,876	5,748	11,683
District of Columbia	2,433	4,354	5,595	37	40	49	3,045	5,143	6,533	14,721
Maryland	5,845	11,611	10,871	136	277	363	11,813	20,413	21,902	54,128
New Jersey	8,729	13,720	23,803	522	690	1,221	22,365	31,585	57,331	111,281
Pennsylvania	7,385	14,869	31,118	389	767	1,869	31,206	51,321	123,569	206,096
Puerto Rico	0	0	0	0	0	0	30,482	46,285	47,576	124,343
Virginia	6,957	16,095	23,184	257	449	521	16,804	32,591	43,608	93,003
Virgin Islands	771	1,388	2,754	0	1	1	928	1,600	3,121	5,649
West Virginia	556	919	1,993	32	37	57	7,913	11,492	19,739	39,144
Regional total	33,614	64,923	102,461	1,379	2,271	4,086	126,615	204,306	329,127	660,048
Southeast Region										
Alabama	12,353	18,789	29,860	106	117	134	24,509	34,949	50,405	109,863
Seminole Indian, FL	0	0	0	0	0	0	29	52	109	190
Miccosukee Ind., FL	0	0	0	0	0	0	12	12	21	45
Florida	17,318	27,865	35,292	405	398	744	51,094	70,632	87,058	208,784
Georgia	17,647	29,446	55,892	296	405	706	35,148	51,552	92,649	179,349
Kentucky	2,190	3,731	5,868	63	82	121	19,606	26,747	47,989	94,342
Choctaw Indian, MS	0	0	0	0	0	0	105	158	412	675
Mississippi	13,996	19,074	40,788	105	148	276	22,634	30,609	56,516	109,759
E. Cherokee Ind., NC	0	0	0	0	0	0	149	148	422	719
North Carolina	14,628	22,988	30,405	191	229	359	32,883	45,444	58,440	136,767
South Carolina	15,126	17,895	30,234	127	113	149	27,298	30,471	46,447	104,216
Tennessee	7,654	14,999	12,088	127	180	140	28,391	48,047	45,087	116,525
Regional total	100,912	154,787	240,427	1,420	1,672	2,620	241,858	333,821	485,555	1,061,234
Midwest Region										
Illinois	14,859	32,691	42,338	486	989	1,330	38,543	73,365	95,830	207,738
Indiana	4,968	8,070	11,045	155	154	303	26,646	36,071	56,545	119,262
Michigan	9,561	19,407	24,627	318	411	823	35,450	51,084	80,501	167,035
Minnesota	1,151	2,430	4,205	814	1,476	4,666	12,209	17,887	46,640	76,736
Ohio	11,486	22,687	26,234	341	592	794	43,915	72,155	88,340	204,410
Wisconsin	2,546	5,496	7,688	758	1,256	2,900	12,567	20,937	33,992	67,496
Regional total	44,571	80,781	116,137	2,872	4,878	10,816	169,330	271,499	401,848	842,677
Southwest Region										
Arkansas	5,575	6,492	10,952	42	57	92	16,948	17,898	26,704	61,550
Louisiana	17,739	20,792	36,455	340	287	675	30,896	34,468	58,516	123,880
Eight Pueblo Ind., NM	0	0	0	0	0	0	89	100	332	521
Isleta Pueblo Ind., NM	0	0	0	0	0	0	84	125	271	480

[Continued]

★652★

Special Supplemental Food Program for Women, Infants, and Children: Participation, by Race/ Ethnicity and Area - II

[Continued]

Region/State	Black			Asian/Pacific Islanders			Total participants			Total
	Women	Infants	Children	Women	Infants	Children	Women	Infants	Children	
Zuni Pueblo Ind., NM	0	0	0	0	0	0	178	187	342	707
Five Sandoval Ind., NM	0	0	0	0	0	0	59	62	423	364
Santa Domingo Ind., NM	0	0	0	0	0	0	46	49	199	294
San Felipe Ind., NM	0	0	0	0	0	0	54	46	214	314
ALC., NM	0	0	0	0	0	0	94	135	328	557
New Mexico	223	312	272	58	73	65	8,254	11,319	9,685	29,258
Choctaw Nation Ind., OK	10	38	30	0	0	0	284	719	1,281	2,284
Chickasaw Nation Ind., OK	9	6	4	0	0	0	423	448	658	1,529
Cherokee Nation Ind., OK	0	1	2	0	0	1	1,196	1,623	2,738	5,557
Potawatomi Ind., OK	1	1	0	0	0	0	156	291	438	885
Inter-Tribal Council Inc., OK	0	0	0	0	0	0	74	90	29	193
WCD Enterprises Ind., OK	2	0	0	1	0	0	349	451	834	1,634
Oklahoma	1,738	3,163	2,167	52	109	41	12,074	17,024	16,503	45,601
Oklahoma	0	0	0	0	0	0	136	187	383	706
Texas	15,266	21,933	29,649	620	825	1,087	89,840	111,670	178,355	379,865
Regional total	40,563	52,738	79,531	1,113	1,351	1,961	161,284	196,892	298,053	656,179
Mountain Plains Region										
Ute Mt Tribe Ind., CO	0	0	0	0	0	0	32	33	83	148
Colorado	760	1,162	1,823	184	235	469	10,576	11,803	23,788	46,167
Iowa	467	924	2,197	169	202	533	7,862	11,496	29,371	48,729
Kansas	1,475	2,351	3,255	159	239	381	9,447	12,585	20,584	42,616
Missouri	4,641	9,466	8,167	133	211	255	18,628	31,159	30,969	80,756
Montana	14	24	58	19	25	68	3,045	4,085	9,797	16,927
Nebraska	715	1,008	1,954	87	74	136	5,940	6,988	12,982	25,910
Nebr. IIIIDC Ind., NE	0	0	0	0	0	0	130	122	391	643
Standing Rock Sioux Ind., ND	0	0	0	0	0	0	196	176	702	1,074
Ft. Berthold, ND	0	0	0	0	0	0	106	95	306	507
North Dakota	41	54	202	32	26	96	3,249	3,012	9,412	15,673
Cheyenne River Sioux, SD	0	0	0	0	0	0	124	129	452	705
Rosebud Sioux Tr. Ind., SD	0	2	2	0	0	0	253	273	817	1,343
South Dakota	24	50	96	28	27	64	3,809	4,016	9,681	17,506
Utah	102	162	239	349	398	618	10,827	11,327	19,156	41,310
Shoshone-Arapahoe Ind., WY	0	0	0	0	0	0	141	177	499	817
Wyoming	20	51	80	8	9	29	1,918	2,548	4,108	8,574
Regional total	8,250	15,254	18,073	1,168	1,446	2,649	76,283	100,024	173,098	349,405
Western Region										
Mauneluk, AK	0	0	0	0	0	0	69	104	196	369
Alaska	171	268	245	-	77	88	2,829	3,285	3,630	9,744
Navajo Tribe, AZ	0	0	0	-	2	4	3,648	4,061	10,630	18,339
Inter Tribal Council, AZ	2	2	11	0	0	3	1,482	1,654	3,389	6,525
Arizona	730	1,112	1,184	150	168	165	14,802	17,338	19,570	51,710
California	16,589	24,608	12,555	9,510	14,597	9,397	164,761	215,233	103,357	483,351
Guam	23	31	28	733	870	1,507	830	1,022	1,703	3,555
Hawaii	228	296	323	2,683	3,710	3,807	4,051	5,484	5,708	15,243
Idaho	21	55	96	44	56	96	5,827	7,015	11,870	24,712
Inter-Tribe Council Ind., NV	0	0	0	0	0	0	212	228	653	1,093
Nevada	572	988	1,081	68	106	80	3,824	5,411	5,909	15,144
Oregon	635	677	958	379	386	699	15,854	13,650	21,274	50,778
Washington	1,305	2,230	1,409	944	1,518	1,005	21,089	27,976	16,958	66,023

[Continued]

★652★

Special Supplemental Food Program for Women, Infants, and Children: Participation, by Race/ Ethnicity and Area - II

[Continued]

Region/State	Black			Asian/Pacific Islanders			Total participants			Total
	Women	Infants	Children	Women	Infants	Children	Women	Infants	Children	
Regional total	20,276	30,267	17,890	14,565	21,490	16,851	239,278	302,461	204,847	746,586
U.S. total	276,383	456,772	650,913	25,958	39,278	50,035	1,123,783	1,572,779	2,183,700	4,880,262

Source: Special Supplemental Food Program for Women, Infants, and Children (WIC) Racial Participation, April 1991. Food and Nutrition Service Financial Management Program Information Division Data Base, Monitoring Branch, November 1991, pp. 4-11.

Support Networks

★653★

Living Arrangements of Adults Supported Outside the Provider's Household, by Relationship to Provider

Persons are shown in thousands.

Characteristic of provider	Total supported[1]	In private home	In nursing home	Other arrangement
Total	2,726	2,294	167	265
Race				
White	2,243	1,946	154	143
Black	224	185	6	33
Other	259	164	6	89
Hispanic origin				
Non-Hispanic	2,503	2,104	167	232
Hispanic	223	190	-	33

Source: U.S. Bureau of the Census. *Household Economic Studies, Who's Helping Out?: Support Networks Among American Families*. Current Population Reports, Series P-70, No. 13, p. 20. *Notes:* A dash (-) represents zero or figure that is too small to show derived measures. 1. Includes 138,000 persons for whom relationship was not ascertained.

★ 654 ★

Support Networks

Relationship of Adults Supported Outside the Provider's Household, by Selected Characteristics of the Provider

Numbers are shown in thousands.

Race/ethnicity	Number of providers	Adults supported						
		Total[1]	Parent	Spouse	Ex-spouse	Child 21 and over	Other relative	Nonrelative
Total	2,316	2,726	918	202	412	495	568	130
Race								
White	1,970	2,243	678	176	403	462	407	117
Black	188	224	93	18	9	21	69	13
Other	158	259	147	8	-	12	92	-
Hispanic origin								
Non-Hispanic	2,144	2,503	809	181	411	495	497	109
Hispanic	172	223	110	22	1	-	70	20

Source: U.S. Bureau of the Census. *Household Economic Studies, Who's Helping Out?: Support Networks Among American Families*. Current Population Reports, Series P-70, No. 13, p. 18. *Notes:* A dash (-) represents zero or a figure that is too small to show derived measure. 1. Excludes 138,000 persons for whom relationship was not ascertained.

★ 655 ★

Support Networks

Selected Characteristics of Women Receiving Child Support Payments, 1985

Persons are shown in thousands.

Characteristic of women receiving child support payments	Number of women	Annl. child support payments ($)		Annl. family income ($)	
		Mean	Standard error	Mean	Standard error
Women 18 to 64 years old	89,602	(X)	(X)	29,925	376
Supposed to receive child support	5,179	(X)	(X)	23,020	918
Actually received child support	4,017	2,506	117	23,545	1,111
Race and Hispanic origin					
White	3,406	2,682	134	24,948	1,277
Black	563	1,429	144	15,254	1,430
Hispanic origin[1]	208	2,088	435	21,224	4,991

Source: U.S. Bureau of the Census. *Household Economic Studies, Who's Helping Out?: Support Networks Among American Families*. Current Population Reports, Series P-70, No. 13, p. 19. *Notes:* (X) means not applicable. 1. Persons of Hispanic origin may be of any race.

Unemployment

★ 656 ★

Unemployment Rates

Date	Hispanic	White	Black
May 1991	9.7	6.0	12.8
April 1992	10.3	6.3	13.9
May 1992	11.3	6.5	14.7

Source: "Employment in the USA." *USA TODAY* (8 June 1992), p. 4B. Primary source: Bureau of Labor Statistics.

★ 657 ★

Unemployment

Unemployment Rates, by Duration of Unemployment, for Selected States, 1993

Data show the annual average percent distribution of unemployed persons in 1993.

Population group and State	Total unemployed		Duration of unemployment				
	Number (000)	%	Less than 5 weeks	5 to 14 weeks	15 weeks and over	27 weeks and over	52 weeks and over
TOTAL							
California	1,407	100.0	32.9	28.2	38.9	23.3	14.1
Florida	462	100.0	35.5	30.6	33.9	20.3	10.2
Illinois	444	100.0	35.9	27.5	36.6	22.2	12.8
New Jersey	295	100.0	25.6	27.9	46.4	28.4	17.1
New York	664	100.0	28.0	27.6	44.3	28.2	17.3
Texas	642	100.0	42.4	29.2	28.4	16.8	8.3
White							
California	1,139	100.0	33.7	28.5	37.8	22.2	13.2
Florida	337	100.0	34.9	30.2	35.0	21.1	10.7
Illinois	298	100.0	35.5	28.2	36.3	21.6	11.7
New Jersey	215	100.0	26.9	27.0	46.1	28.4	16.3
New York	475	100.0	30.2	27.7	42.1	26.2	15.7
Texas	471	100.0	43.8	29.4	26.8	15.6	7.4
Black							
California	123	100.0	28.9	26.4	44.7	28.7	19.8
Florida	116	100.0	38.3	30.5	31.2	18.0	9.0
Illinois	130	100.0	35.9	26.3	37.8	23.3	15.0
New Jersey	67	100.0	21.1	29.3	49.6	29.3	20.1
New York	157	100.0	21.9	27.7	50.4	34.2	22.4

[Continued]

★ 657 ★

Unemployment Rates, by Duration of Unemployment, for Selected States, 1993

[Continued]

Population group and State	Total unemployed Number (000)	%	Duration of unemployment Less than 5 weeks	5 to 14 weeks	15 weeks and over	27 weeks and over	52 weeks and over
Texas	148	100.0	37.4	29.6	33.0	20.8	10.0
Hispanic origin							
California	468	100.0	37.6	28.5	33.9	19.0	11.0
Florida	82	100.0	36.6	30.8	32.6	18.6	9.4
Illinois	35	100.0	43.1	29.9	27.0	14.7	4.2
New Jersey	46	100.0	25.9	28.5	45.6	24.9	13.6
New York	105	100.0	27.7	27.2	45.1	28.0	16.9
Texas	189	100.0	49.4	25.9	24.7	12.0	6.3

Source: U.S. Bureau of Labor Statistics. U.S. Department of Labor. *Geographic Profile of Employment and Unemployment, 1993* (Bulletin 2446). Washington, DC: U.S. Government Printing Office, September 1994, pp. 88-91. *Notes:* Data for demographic groups are not shown when they do not meet Bureau of Labor Statistics publication standards of reliability for the particular area based on the sample in that area. Items may not add to totals or compute to displayed percentages because of rounding. Detail for race and Hispanic origin groups will not add to totals because data for the "other races" group are not presented and Hispanics are included in both the white and black population groups.

★ 658 ★

Unemployment

Unemployment Rates, by Race/Ethnicity, 1991 and 1992

Data are shown for the month of November for both years.

Race/ethnicity	Percent unemployed 1991	1992
Hispanic	10.2	12.0
White	6.2	6.3
Black	12.3	13.8

Source: Mullins, Marcy E. "Employment in the USA." *USA TODAY* (7 December 1992), p. 4B. Primary source: Bureau of Labor Statistics.

★ 659 ★

Unemployment

Unemployment Rates, by Reason for Unemployment, in Selected States, 1993

Data show the annual average percent distribution of unemployed persons in 1993.

Population group and State	Total unemployed		Reason for unemployment				
	Number (000)	%	Job losers		Job leavers	Re-entrants	New entrants
			Total	On layoff			
TOTAL							
California	1,407	100.0	59.0	9.3	8.0	21.9	11.1
Florida	462	100.0	53.0	7.2	9.6	27.5	10.0
Illinois	444	100.0	53.4	10.9	11.4	23.4	11.8
New Jersey	295	100.0	66.9	13.9	7.6	18.9	6.5
New York	664	100.0	62.0	11.9	7.3	21.2	9.5
Texas	642	100.0	46.4	5.4	14.5	28.3	10.8
White							
California	1,139	100.0	59.8	10.2	7.8	21.7	10.8
Florida	337	100.0	55.9	7.4	10.3	25.2	8.6
Illinois	298	100.0	56.8	13.3	13.3	20.3	9.7
New Jersey	215	100.0	68.0	15.6	8.3	18.0	5.8
New York	475	100.0	62.2	14.1	7.3	21.5	9.0
Texas	471	100.0	44.8	5.8	16.3	27.5	11.5
Black							
California	123	100.0	56.7	5.5	8.5	25.0	9.8
Florida	116	100.0	45.4	7.0	7.6	33.7	13.4
Illinois	130	100.0	48.0	5.7	7.2	29.2	15.6
New Jersey	67	100.0	65.4	9.0	5.6	21.5	7.6
New York	157	100.0	62.8	6.1	6.9	20.4	10.0
Texas	148	100.0	52.3	4.4	9.2	30.5	8.0
Hispanic origin							
California	468	100.0	62.3	11.3	7.1	18.5	12.2
Florida	82	100.0	61.2	4.7	10.4	17.1	11.3
Illinois	35	100.0	59.8	11.1	13.5	12.8	13.8
New Jersey	46	100.0	78.6	15.2	5.7	9.9	5.8
New York	105	100.0	68.1	10.4	6.5	15.8	9.6
Texas	189	100.0	43.7	4.1	19.1	22.9	14.3

Source: U.S. Bureau of Labor Statistics. U.S. Department of Labor. *Geographic Profile of Employment and Unemployment, 1993* (Bulletin 2446). Washington, DC: U.S. Government Printing Office, September 1994, pp. 84-87. *Notes:* Data for demographic groups are not shown when they do not meet Bureau of Labor Statistics publication standards of reliability for the particular area based on the sample in that area. Items may not add to totals or compute to displayed percentages because of rounding. Detail for race and Hispanic origin groups will not add to totals because data for the "other races" group are not presented and Hispanics are included in both the white and black population groups.

★ 660 ★

Unemployment

Unemployment Rates, by U.S. Region and Duration of Unemployment, 1993

Average annual unemployment rates are shown for 1993.

Population group and area	Total unemployed		Duration of unemployment						
	Number (000)	%	Less than 5 weeks	5 to 14 weeks	15 weeks and over	15 to 26 weeks	27 weeks and over	27 to 51 weeks	52 weeks and over
TOTAL									
Northeast	1,848	100.0	28.9	27.9	43.2	15.8	27.4	10.5	16.8
New England	475	100.0	27.9	27.2	44.9	16.3	28.6	10.5	18.1
Middle Atlantic	1,372	100.0	29.2	28.2	42.6	15.7	26.9	10.5	16.4
Midwest	1,883	100.0	39.0	28.9	32.0	14.4	17.6	8.0	9.6
East North Central	1,414	100.0	38.4	28.7	32.9	14.4	18.5	8.0	10.5
West North Central	469	100.0	40.9	29.7	29.5	14.3	15.2	8.3	6.9
South	2,857	100.0	39.6	29.4	31.0	13.6	17.4	8.2	9.2
South Atlantic	1,436	100.0	36.9	29.6	33.5	14.5	18.9	8.5	10.4
East South Central	478	100.0	42.2	30.0	27.8	13.7	14.1	6.3	7.8
West South Central	943	100.0	42.3	28.8	28.9	12.2	16.8	8.8	8.0
West	2,202	100.0	35.6	29.0	35.5	14.9	20.6	8.4	12.2
Mountain	430	100.0	41.9	29.9	28.2	13.9	14.3	5.7	8.5
Pacific	1,772	100.0	34.1	28.7	37.2	15.1	22.1	9.0	13.1
White									
Northeast	1,465	100.0	30.1	27.9	42.1	15.6	26.4	10.5	15.9
New England	428	100.0	28.3	27.6	44.1	16.5	27.6	10.5	17.1
Middle Atlantic	1,037	100.0	30.8	28.0	41.2	15.2	26.0	10.6	15.4
Midwest	1,446	100.0	39.1	29.1	31.8	14.8	17.0	8.3	8.7
East North Central	1,060	100.0	38.4	28.7	32.9	14.9	18.0	8.3	9.6
West North Central	386	100.0	41.3	30.0	28.7	14.4	14.3	8.0	6.3
South	1,847	100.0	40.9	29.3	29.8	13.1	16.6	8.1	8.5
South Atlantic	887	100.0	38.5	29.3	32.3	13.8	18.5	8.6	9.9
East South Central	298	100.0	43.0	29.7	27.3	13.9	13.4	6.2	7.3
West South Central	662	100.0	43.1	29.2	27.6	12.0	15.6	8.4	7.2
West	1,829	100.0	36.0	29.3	34.6	15.0	19.7	8.1	11.5
Mountain	377	100.0	41.5	30.0	28.5	14.4	14.1	5.8	8.2
Pacific	1,452	100.0	34.6	29.2	36.2	15.1	21.1	8.7	12.4
Black									
Northeast	319	100.0	23.4	28.1	48.5	16.7	31.8	10.9	20.9
New England	38	100.0	24.2	22.1	53.7	13.9	39.8	11.4	28.4
Middle Atlantic	281	100.0	23.3	28.9	47.8	17.1	30.7	10.8	19.9
Midwest	390	100.0	37.8	28.5	33.7	13.3	20.4	7.5	12.9
East North Central	320	100.0	37.8	28.8	33.4	13.2	20.2	6.9	13.4
West North Central	70	100.0	37.9	27.1	35.0	14.1	20.9	10.2	10.7

[Continued]

★ 660 ★

Unemployment Rates, by U.S. Region and Duration of Unemployment, 1993

[Continued]

Population group and area	Total unemployed: Number (000)	Total unemployed: %	Less than 5 weeks	5 to 14 weeks	15 weeks and over	15 to 26 weeks	27 weeks and over	27 to 51 weeks	52 weeks and over
South	938	100.0	36.9	29.8	33.3	14.8	18.5	8.4	10.1
South Atlantic	516	100.0	34.5	30.0	35.5	16.3	19.2	8.2	11.0
East South Central	178	100.0	40.6	30.7	28.8	13.6	15.1	6.6	8.5
West South Central	244	100.0	39.4	28.7	31.9	12.6	19.4	10.1	9.3
West	163	100.0	31.5	25.6	42.9	15.1	27.8	10.1	17.7
Mountain	137	100.0	29.1	25.8	45.1	15.5	29.6	10.7	19.0
Pacific									
Hispanic origin									
Northeast	190	100.0	28.0	27.0	45.0	17.3	27.7	10.6	17.1
Middle Atlantic	164	100.0	27.2	27.1	45.1	18.0	27.1	11.0	16.1
Midwest	62	100.0	42.3	29.5	28.3	15.5	12.8	8.3	4.5
East North Central	50	100.0	43.8	28.3	27.9	13.9	14.0	9.1	4.9
South	298	100.0	46.1	26.8	27.1	13.2	13.8	6.5	7.3
South Atlantic	104	100.0	38.8	29.3	31.9	14.7	17.2	8.1	9.1
West South Central	192	100.0	50.2	25.5	24.4	12.5	11.9	5.7	6.2
West	564	100.0	38.3	29.0	32.7	14.5	18.2	7.8	10.4
Mountain	75	100.0	44.1	29.0	26.9	11.7	15.1	7.3	7.8
Pacific	489	100.0	37.4	29.0	33.6	15.0	18.6	7.8	10.8

Source: U.S. Bureau of Labor Statistics. U.S. Department of Labor. *Geographic Profile of Employment and Unemployment, 1993* (Bulletin 2446). Washington, DC: U.S. Government Printing Office, September 1994, pp. 33-34. *Notes:* Items may not add to totals or compute to displayed percentages because of rounding. Detail for race and Hispanic origin groups will not add to totals because data for the "other races" group are not presented and Hispanics are included in both the white and black population groups.

★ 661 ★

Unemployment

Unemployment Rates, by U.S. Region and Reason for Unemployment, 1993

Average annual unemployment rates are shown for 1993.

Population group and area	Total unemployed: Number (000)	Total unemployed: %	Job losers: Total	Job losers: On layoff	Job leavers	Re-entrants	New entrants
TOTAL							
Northeast	1,848	100.0	62.1	15.4	8.0	21.6	8.3
New England	475	100.0	65.0	15.6	8.2	20.2	6.5
Middle Atlantic	1,372	100.0	61.0	15.3	7.9	22.1	9.0
Midwest	1,883	100.0	53.5	17.1	11.5	24.8	10.3
East North Central	1,414	100.0	54.0	17.6	10.9	24.3	10.9

[Continued]

★ 661 ★

Unemployment Rates, by U.S. Region and Reason for Unemployment, 1993

[Continued]

Population group and area	Total unemployed		Reason for unemployment				
	Number (000)	%	Job losers		Job leavers	Re-entrants	New entrants
			Total	On layoff			
West North Central	469	100.0	52.1	15.4	13.3	26.1	8.4
South	2,857	100.0	49.2	9.5	12.9	26.8	11.1
South Atlantic	1,436	100.0	51.1	9.7	12.3	25.9	10.7
East South Central	478	100.0	48.9	13.9	12.6	25.7	12.7
West South Central	943	100.0	46.4	6.9	14.0	28.5	11.0
West	2,202	100.0	56.1	10.6	10.0	24.1	9.8
Mountain	430	100.0	47.4	10.4	14.9	29.0	8.7
Pacific	1,772	100.0	58.3	10.7	8.9	22.9	10.0
White							
Northeast	1,465	100.0	62.8	17.3	8.2	21.2	7.8
New England	428	100.0	65.7	16.6	8.2	20.1	6.0
Middle Atlantic	1,037	100.0	61.7	17.5	8.2	21.6	8.5
Midwest	1,446	100.0	56.3	19.4	12.1	22.8	8.8
East North Central	1,060	100.0	57.3	20.2	11.6	21.8	9.3
West North Central	386	100.0	53.4	17.1	13.7	25.4	7.5
South	1,847	100.0	50.2	10.5	14.3	26.0	9.4
South Atlantic	887	100.0	52.9	11.0	13.1	25.3	8.6
East South central	298	100.0	51.2	16.1	15.3	25.0	8.6
West South Central	662	100.0	46.2	7.4	15.5	27.4	10.9
West	1,829	100.0	57.0	11.4	10.1	23.6	9.3
Mountain	377	100.0	49.4	10.9	14.5	27.5	8.5
Pacific	1,452	100.0	58.9	11.5	8.9	22.6	9.5
Black							
Northeast	319	100.0	59.9	8.1	6.5	23.5	10.1
New England	38	100.0	58.8	5.0	8.8	21.1	11.4
Middle Atlantic	281	100.0	60.1	8.5	6.2	23.8	9.9
Midwest	390	100.0	45.6	9.8	9.1	30.8	14.5
East North Central	320	100.0	44.9	10.2	8.8	31.4	14.9
West North Central	70	100.0	49.0	7.5	10.5	27.9	12.7
South	938	100.0	47.7	7.7	10.1	28.2	14.0
South Atlantic	516	100.0	48.9	7.8	10.9	26.7	13.5
East South Central	178	100.0	44.9	9.8	8.1	27.2	19.7
West South Central	244	100.0	47.2	6.0	9.9	32.2	10.8
West	163	100.0	53.0	6.5	9.9	28.1	9.1
Pacific	137	100.0	57.0	6.8	8.3	25.5	9.2

[Continued]

★ 661 ★

Unemployment Rates, by U.S. Region and Reason for Unemployment, 1993

[Continued]

Population group and area	Total unemployed		Reason for unemployment				
	Number (000)	%	Job losers		Job leavers	Re-entrants	New entrants
			Total	On layoff			
Hispanic origin							
Northeast	190	100.0	69.2	12.5	6.7	15.2	8.9
Middle Atlantic	164	100.0	69.3	12.0	6.7	14.8	9.2
Midwest	62	100.0	55.0	12.8	11.1	23.2	10.6
East North Central	50	100.0	55.8	12.6	11.5	20.4	12.3
South	298	100.0	47.9	4.4	16.4	21.9	13.8
South Atlantic	104	100.0	55.8	4.9	11.8	20.3	12.0
West South Central	192	100.0	43.3	4.1	19.0	22.9	14.8
West	564	100.0	60.4	11.2	8.4	19.3	12.0
Mountain	75	100.0	49.6	8.7	15.1	25.1	10.2
Pacific	489	100.0	62.0	11.6	7.4	18.4	12.2

Source: U.S. Bureau of Labor Statistics. U.S. Department of Labor. *Geographic Profile of Employment and Unemployment, 1993* (Bulletin 2446). Washington, DC: U.S. Government Printing Office, September 1994, pp. 31-32. *Notes:* Items may not add to totals or compute to displayed percentages because of rounding. Detail for race and Hispanic origin groups will not add to totals because data for the "other races" group are not presented and Hispanics are included in both the white and black population groups.

★ 662 ★

Unemployment

Unemployment Trends of Persons 16 to 24 Years Old

Data are shown in thousands, except as indicated, for the civilian noninstitutional population 16 age years and older, as annual averages of monthly figures.

Age and race/ethnicity	1980	1985	1986	1987	1988	1989	1990	1991	1992	1993
Total unemployed[1]	7,637	8,312	8,237	7,425	6,701	6,528	6,874	8,426	9,384	8,734
16 to 19 years old	1,669	1,468	1,454	1,347	1,226	1,194	1,149	1,290	1,352	1,296
20 to 24 years old	1,835	1,738	1,651	1,453	1,261	1,218	1,221	1,477	1,546	1,421
25 to 44 years old	2,964	3,681	3,761	3,410	3,095	3,010	3,273	4,106	4,603	4,220
45 to 64 years old	1,075	1,331	1,279	1,135	1,032	1,016	1,124	1,437	1,748	1,686
65 years and over	94	93	91	78	87	91	107	116	135	111
White[2]	5,884	6,191	6,140	5,501	4,944	4,770	5,091	6,447	7,047	6,547
16 to 19 years old	1,291	1,074	1,070	995	910	863	856	977	983	943
20 to 24 years old	1,364	1,235	1,149	1,017	874	856	844	1,063	1,084	991
Black[2]	1,553	1,864	1,840	1,684	1,547	1,544	1,527	1,679	1,958	1,796
16 to 19 years old	343	357	347	312	288	300	258	270	313	302
20 to 24 years old	426	455	453	397	349	322	335	362	401	371
Hispanic[3]	620	811	857	751	732	750	769	963	1,160	1,104

[Continued]

★ 662 ★

Unemployment Trends of Persons 16 to 24 Years Old

[Continued]

Age and race/ethnicity	1980	1985	1986	1987	1988	1989	1990	1991	1992	1993
16 to 19 years old	145	141	141	136	148	132	131	149	185	173
20 to 24 years old	138	171	183	152	145	158	135	172	193	191

Source: 1994 Statistical Abstract of the United States on CD-ROM [machine-readable datafiles]. CD-8A-94. Washington, DC: U.S. Department of Commerce, Economics and Statistics Administration, Bureau of the Census, Data User Services Division, January 1995. Primary source: U.S. Bureau of Labor Statistics, Employment and Earnings, January issues; and unpublished data. *Notes:* NA stands for not available. 1. Includes other races, not shown separately. 2. Includes other ages, not shown separately. 3. Persons of Hispanic origin may be of any race.

★ 663 ★

Unemployment

Unemployment: Selected Indicators - Part I

Unemployment rates are shown, by sex and race/ethnicity, for 1992 and 1993.

Selected categories	Annual average		1993	
	1992	1993	Nov.	Dec.
Total, all workers	7.4	6.8	6.5	6.4
Both sexes, 16 to 19 years	20.0	19.0	18.3	17.8
Men, 20 years and over	7.0	6.4	5.9	5.8
Women, 20 years and over	6.3	5.9	5.7	5.7
White, total	6.5	6.0	5.6	5.6
Both sexes, 16 to 19 years	17.1	16.2	15.6	15.2
Men, 16 to 19 years	18.4	17.6	17.7	16.9
Women, 16 to 19 years	15.7	14.6	13.3	13.4
Men, 20 years and over	6.3	5.6	5.0	5.2
Women, 20 years and over	5.4	5.1	5.1	4.9
Black, total	14.1	12.9	12.5	11.5
Both sexes, 16 to 19 years	39.8	38.9	39.5	37.0
Men, 16 to 19 years	42.0	40.1	39.2	38.8
Women, 16 to 19 years	37.2	37.5	39.7	35.2
Men, 20 years and over	13.4	12.1	12.3	10.5
Women, 20 years and over	11.7	10.6	9.7	9.7
Hispanic origin, total	11.4	10.6	10.4	10.5

Source: U.S. Bureau of Labor Statistics. U.S. Department of Labor. *Monthly Labor Review* (January 1995), p. 82. *Notes:* Data for 1994 (see part II) are not directly comparable with data for 1993 and earlier years.

★ 664 ★

Unemployment

Unemployment: Selected Indicators - Part II

Unemployment rates are shown, by sex and race/ethnicity, for January through November of 1994.

Selected categories	1994										
	Jan.	Feb.	Mar.	Apr.	May	June	July	Aug.	Sept.	Oct.	Nov.
Total, all workers	6.7	6.5	6.5	6.4	6.0	6.0	6.1	6.1	5.9	5.8	5.6
Both sexes, 16 to 19 years	18.4	17.9	17.8	19.9	18.3	16.9	17.7	17.5	17.0	17.3	15.3
Men, 20 years and over	5.9	6.0	5.8	5.6	5.2	5.3	5.6	5.4	5.1	5.1	4.9
Women, 20 years and over	6.0	5.7	6.0	5.6	5.4	5.4	5.3	5.4	5.3	5.0	5.0
White, total	5.8	5.6	5.7	5.6	5.2	5.3	5.4	5.3	5.1	5.0	4.8
Both sexes, 16 to 19 years	16.4	15.8	15.6	17.5	15.5	14.1	14.4	14.5	14.9	14.3	12.9
Men, 16 to 19 years	18.5	16.7	16.7	19.0	17.3	14.7	16.1	15.1	16.4	14.8	13.8
Women, 16 to 19 years	14.0	14.7	14.6	16.0	13.5	13.5	12.6	13.8	13.1	13.9	12.0
Men, 20 years and over	5.3	5.2	5.2	5.0	4.6	4.6	4.9	4.7	4.4	4.5	4.2
Women, 20 years and over	5.1	4.8	5.0	4.7	4.5	4.8	4.7	4.7	4.6	4.4	4.4
Black, total	13.1	12.9	12.5	11.8	11.5	11.2	11.2	11.5	10.7	11.4	10.5
Both sexes, 16 to 19 years	31.7	35.3	34.0	36.2	39.9	37.6	38.1	36.8	30.9	37.5	31.7
Men, 16 to 19 years	38.1	40.1	37.5	40.8	42.8	40.0	43.0	42.3	29.1	35.9	29.2
Women, 16 to 19 years	25.5	30.5	30.2	31.3	36.5	34.9	32.3	30.4	32.8	39.2	34.4
Men, 20 years and over	12.3	12.1	10.2	10.0	9.9	9.7	10.5	10.5	10.0	9.8	9.5
Women, 20 years and over	11.5	11.0	12.1	10.6	9.9	9.4	8.6	9.4	8.9	9.4	8.8
Hispanic origin, total	10.6	10.0	10.0	10.8	9.5	10.3	10.1	10.2	10.2	9.4	8.6

Source: U.S. Bureau of Labor Statistics, U.S. Department of Labor, *Monthly Labor Review* (January 1995), p. 82. *Notes:* Data for 1994 are not directly comparable with data for 1993 (see Part I) and earlier years.

Chapter 7
BUSINESS AND INDUSTRY

Businesses

★ 665 ★

MBDA Assistance, by Race/Ethnicity, 1993

The Minority Business Development Agency (MBDA) is a part of the U.S. Department of Commerce that was developed to assist in problems encountered by minority-owned businesses in order to help them fully compete in industry. This table shows the number of clients assisted by the MBDA in fiscal year 1993 and the percent distribution of those clients, by race/ethnicity.

	Clients assisted	Pct. of of total
Black	8,128	50.0
Hispanic	4,629	29.0
Native American	1,116	7.0
Asian American	1,513	9.0
Other minority	625	4.0
Non-minority disadvantaged	190	1.0

Source: Minority Business Development Agency. U.S. Department of Commerce. *Annual Business Assistance Report, Fiscal Year 1993.* Washington, DC: U.S. Department of Commerce, 1994, p. I-5.

★ 666 ★

Businesses

MBDA Contracts Awarded, by Race/Ethnicity, 1993

The Minority Business Development Agency (MBDA) is a part of the U.S. Department of Commerce that was developed to assist in problems encountered by minority-owned businesses in order to help them fully compete in industry. This table shows minority contracts awarded in fiscal year 1993 and the percent distribution of those contracts among clients, by race/ethnicity.

	Contracts		Value of contracts	
	Number	% of total	($ mil.)	% of total
Black	1,552	50.0	288.3	44.0
Hispanic	831	27.0	267.5	41.0
Native American	250	8.0	40.7	6.0
Asian American	168	5.0	45.3	7.0
Other minority	308	10.0	14.8	2.0
Non-minority disadvantaged	16	1.0	1.4	0.0

Source: Minority Business Development Agency. U.S. Department of Commerce. *Annual Business Assistance Report, Fiscal Year 1993.* Washington, DC: U.S. Department of Commerce, 1994, p. I-5.

★ 667 ★

Businesses

MBDA Financial Packages Awarded, by Race/Ethnicity, 1993

The Minority Business Development Agency (MBDA) is a part of the U.S. Department of Commerce that was developed to assist in problems encountered by minority-owned businesses in order to help them fully compete in industry. This table shows financial packages awarded in fiscal year 1993 and the percent distribution of those awards among clients, by race/ethnicity.

	Financial packages		Value of packages	
	Number	% of total	($ mil.)	% of total
Black	754	46.0	126.1	38.0
Hispanic	430	26.0	101.0	30.0
Native American	106	7.0	33.5	10.0
Asian American	233	14.0	54.5	16.0
Other minority	66	4.0	10.3	3.0
Non-minority disadvantaged	39	2.0	6.0	2.0

Source: Minority Business Development Agency. U.S. Department of Commerce. *Annual Business Assistance Report, Fiscal Year 1993.* Washington, DC: U.S. Department of Commerce, 1994, p. I-5.

★ 668 ★

Businesses

Management & Technical Assistance, by Race/ Ethnicity, 1993

The Minority Business Development Agency (MBDA) is a part of the U.S. Department of Commerce that was developed to assist in problems encountered by minority-owned businesses in order to help them fully compete in industry. This table shows the number of hours of management and technical assistance provided in fiscal year 1993 and the percent distribution of those hours among clients, by race/ethnicity.

	Hours of assistance	Pct. of of total
Black	131,623.6	47.0
Hispanic	83,106.9	29.0
Native American	24,294.3	9.0
Asian American	27,642.0	10.0
Other minority	13,174.7	5.0
Non-minority disadvantaged	3,154.9	1.0

Source: Minority Business Development Agency. U.S. Department of Commerce. *Annual Business Assistance Report, Fiscal Year 1993.* Washington, DC: U.S. Department of Commerce, 1994, p. I-5.

★ 669 ★

Businesses

U.S. Exports, Imports, and Merchandise Trade Balance, by Selected Country, 1990-92

Data are shown in millions of dollars and include silver ore and bullion. Country totals include exports of special category commodities, if any. Data include nonmonetary gold and trade of Virgin Islands with foreign countries. A minus sign (-) denotes an excess of imports over exports.

Area	Exports, domestic and foreign[1]				General imports[1]				Merchandise trade balance			
	1990	1991	1992	1993	1990	1991	1992	1993	1990	1991	1992	1993
Total[2]	393,592	421,730	448,164	464,767	495,311	487,129	532,665	580,511	(101,718)	(65,399)	(84,501)	(115,744)
Argentina	1,179	2,045	3,223	3,772	1,511	1,287	1,256	1,206	(333)	758	1,967	2,566
Bolivia	138	192	222	216	203	209	162	191	(65)	(17)	60	25
Chile	1,664	1,839	2,466	2,605	1,313	1,302	1,388	1,462	351	537	1,078	1,143
Colombia	2,029	1,952	3,286	3,229	3,168	2,736	2,837	3,033	(1,139)	(784)	449	196
Costa Rica	986	1,034	1,357	1,547	1,005	1,154	1,411	1,542	(19)	(120)	(54)	5
Cuba	1	1	1	3	(Z)	(Z)	(X)	(-)	1	1	1	3
Dominican Republic	1,656	1,743	2,100	2,350	1,752	2,008	2,372	2,672	(96)	(265)	(273)	(323)
Ecuador	678	948	999	1,098	1,376	1,327	1,343	1,399	(697)	(379)	(344)	(301)
El Salvador	554	534	742	869	238	303	384	488	316	231	358	381
Guatemala	764	945	1,205	1,310	794	899	1,081	1,195	(31)	46	124	115
Honduras	564	625	811	898	491	557	783	915	73	68	28	(17)
Mexico	28,279	33,277	40,592	41,636	30,157	31,130	35,211	39,930	(1,878)	2,147	5,381	1,706
Nicaragua	68	150	185	150	15	60	69	126	52	91	117	24
Panama	869	978	1,103	1,191	234	269	254	281	635	709	850	910
Paraguay	307	374	415	521	51	43	35	50	256	331	380	471
Peru	772	840	1,005	1,069	802	776	739	754	(30)	64	267	315
Spain	5,213	5,474	5,537	4,181	3,311	2,848	3,002	2,813	1,901	2,626	2,535	1,368

[Continued]

★ 669 ★

U.S. Exports, Imports, and Merchandise Trade Balance, by Selected Country, 1990-92

[Continued]

Area	Exports, domestic and foreign[1]				General imports[1]				Merchandise trade balance			
	1990	1991	1992	1993	1990	1991	1992	1993	1990	1991	1992	1993
Uruguay	144	216	231	253	206	237	266	266	(62)	(21)	(35)	(13)
Venezuela	3,108	4,656	5,444	4,599	9,480	8,179	8,181	8,140	(6,371)	(3,523)	(2,737)	(3,541)

Source: 1994 Statistical Abstract of the United States on CD-ROM [machine-readable datafiles]. CD-8A-94. Washington, DC: U.S. Department of Commerce, Economics and Statistics Administration, Bureau of the Census, Data User Services Division, January 1995. Primary source: U.S. Bureau of the Census, U.S. Merchandise Trade, series FT 900, December issues. *Notes:* A (Z) stands for less than $500,000. 1. Imports: 1980, f.a.s. basis; other years, customs value basis. Exports are f.a.s. value. 2. Includes non-Hispanic countries. Includes revisions not carried to area values; therefore, area values will not add to total.

Consumer Affairs

★ 670 ★

Cake Mix Brands Purchased Most Often

Percentages are shown, by brand name and by consumers' ethnicity. Answers include multiple preferences.

Brand	Hispanic	Non-Hispanic
Betty Crocker	37.1	34.9
Duncan Hines	33.3	61.7
Pillsbury	15.7	27.2
Store	1.3	3.2
Other	2.9	2.8
Don't know/can't recall	20.0	3.8

Source: Grocery Marketing (24 November 1991), p. 12. Primary source: Telemundo Product Usage Study, 1991.

★ 671 ★

Consumer Affairs

Canned Vegetable Brands Purchased Most Often

Percentages of brands usually purchased are shown by consumers' ethnicity.

Type	Hispanic	Non-Hispanic
Del Monte	66.0	58.0
Green Giant	23.0	34.0
Goya	12.0	-
Libby's	9.0	8.0
Hunt's	2.0	2.0

Source: *Grocery Marketing* (24 November 1991), p. 12. Primary source: Telemundo Product Usage Study, 1991.

★ 672 ★

Consumer Affairs

Cookie Brands Purchased Most Often

Percentages are shown for brands with a Hispanic market share of 2% or more.

Type	Hispanic	Non-Hispanic
Gamesa (Marie)	27.0	-
Nabisco Vanilla Wafers	15.0	8.0
Oreo	14.0	29.0
Chips Ahoy	14.0	25.0
Oreo Fudge-Covered Sandwich	7.0	3.0
Chips Deluxe	3.0	0.0
Murray Chocolate Chip	2.0	1.0
Mothers	2.0	10.0

Source: *Grocery Marketing* (24 November 1991), p. 13. Primary source: Telemundo Product Usage Study, 1991.

★ 673 ★

Consumer Affairs

Coupon Use by Hispanics, by Language

Figures show percentage of persons surveyed using coupons in each language.

	Percent
English	52.0
Spanish	15.0
Both	33.0

Source: Alonzo, Vincent. "Muy grande!" *Incentive* (January 1994), p. 31. Primary source: The 1993 MSR Minority Market Research Report, Market Segment Research, Inc.

★ 674 ★

Consumer Affairs

Cracker Preferences

Percentages are shown, by product type and consumers' ethnicity. Answers include multiple preferences.

Type	Hispanic	Non-Hispanic
Saltines	91.0	78.0
Wheat crackers	15.0	36.0
Butter crackers	14.0	17.0
Cheese crackers	10.0	26.0
Graham crackers	8.0	32.0
Water crackers	8.0	8.0

Source: *Grocery Marketing* (24 November 1991), p. 13. Primary source: Telemundo Product Usage Study, 1991.

★ 675 ★

Consumer Affairs

Electronic Product Ownership, by Selected Minority

Percent who own a...	Hispanics	African-Americans	Asian-Americans
VCR	73.1	73.5	89.4
Camera	58.7	67.6	89.4
Microwave	62.3	66.8	79.1
Answering machine	27.5	47.2	50.0
Videogame system	39.8	42.3	41.8
Dishwasher	26.1	34.6	46.9

[Continued]

★ 675 ★

Electronic Product Ownership, by Selected Minority

[Continued]

Percent who own a...	Hispanics	African-Americans	Asian-Americans
Compact disc player	26.7	31.9	45.5
Personal computer	9.6	19.8	30.5
Beeper	14.0	16.9	19.5
Camcorder	17.1	15.0	35.6
Cellular phone	6.7	10.3	24.3

Source: Fisher, Christy. "Poll: Hispanics stick to brands: Asian-Americans shop for good price and African-Americans look for quality." *Advertising Age* (15 February 1993), p. 6. Market Segment Research.

★ 676 ★

Consumer Affairs

Frozen Vegetable Brands Purchased Most Often

Percentages of brands usually purchased are shown by brand name and consumers' ethnicity.

Type	Hispanic	Non-Hispanic
Green Giant	27.0	24.0
Bird's Eye	13.0	42.0
Goya	5.0	-
Libby's	4.0	2.0

Source: *Grocery Marketing* (24 November 1991), p. 12. Primary source: Telemundo Product Usage Study, 1991.

★ 677 ★

Consumer Affairs

Hispanic Shares of the Dallas-Fort Worth Bank Market

Data show results of a 1994 consumer survey conducted by Rincon & Associates. Market shares are shown in percent.

Bank	Share
Bank One	22.3
Credit Union	11.2
NationsBank	9.8
Texas Commerce Bank	5.2
Bank of America	3.7

[Continued]

★ 677 ★

Hispanic Shares of the Dallas-Fort Worth Bank Market

[Continued]

Bank	Share
All other	18.5
Don't know	6.7

Source: Castaneda, Laura. "Banking on opportunity: Bank One leads survey of Hispanics; 22% lack accounts." *Dallas Morning News* (16 July 1994), p. 1F. Primary source: Rincon & Associates, 1994 Dallas-Fort Worth Hispanic Consumer Survey.

★ 678 ★

Consumer Affairs

Purchase Incentives Preferred by Hispanics

Data show percentage of persons surveyed who would either definitely or probably respond to each type of marketing incentive.

	Percent
Buy one/get one free	57.0
Cents-off coupon	46.0
In-store samples	42.0
Rebates	37.0
Sweepstakes	25.0

Source: Alonzo, Vincent. "Muy grande!" *Incentive* (January 1994), p. 31. Primary source: The 1993 MSR Minority Market Research Report, Market Segment Research, Inc.

★ 679 ★

Consumer Affairs

Purchasing Characteristics of Hispanics

Percentage show results of a 1992 survey of 1,200 Hispanic consumers.

	1988	1990	1992
"I would be more inclined to purchase brands which are advertised in Spanish."	NA	46	56
"It is preferable to buy brands and products that others are buying."	41	35	41
"One ought to keep up with the latest fads and trends."	54	70	75
"Frequently store brands are better than well-known nationally advertised brands."	49	58	57

[Continued]

★ 679 ★

Purchasing Characteristics of Hispanics

[Continued]

	1988	1990	1992
"Of the products I know, I prefer to buy products made by well-established companies."	75	77	74

Source: "Surveys point to group differences." *Brandweek* (18 July 1994), p. 32. Primary source: Yankelovich Partners and Market Development.

★ 680 ★

Consumer Affairs

Reported Purchases of Selected Grocery Store Items Within a 30-Day Period, by Selected Minority

Percent who purchased...	Hispanics	African-Americans	Asian-Americans
Regular coffee	72.0	54.0	49.0
Decaffeinated coffee	20.0	19.0	13.0
Regular carbonated soft drinks	77.0	71.0	70.0
Diet carbonated soft drinks	20.0	23.0	12.0
Powdered drink mix	35.0	35.0	14.0
Fruit juice/nectar	78.0	68.0	73.0
Beer	38.0	31.0	44.0
Wine	10.0	11.0	16.0
Ready-to-eat cereal	78.0	72.0	44.0
Hot cereal	21.0	42.0	22.0
Shampoo	93.0	76.0	89.0
Conditioner	61.0	52.0	59.0
Hair spray	27.0	15.0	29.0
Gel	16.0	14.0	14.0
Mousse	17.0	6.0	22.0
Toothpaste	95.0	92.0	93.0
Denture cleaner	4.0	13.0	8.0
Ready-to-eat frozen entrees	8.0	18.0	11.0
Latin frozen entrees	3.0	2.0	6.0
Chinese frozen entrees	1.0	3.0	8.0
Frozen breakfast foods	2.0	9.0	6.0
Frozen vegetables	21.0	40.0	17.0
Bath soaps	97.0	95.0	89.0
Deodorants	89.0	84.0	26.0
Dishwashing detergent	88.0	86.0	79.0
Baby food	11.0	6.0	7.0
Powdered soups	16.0	17.0	13.0
Canned soups	32.0	53.0	36.0
Canned vegetables	42.0	44.0	17.0
Canned fruits	42.0	35.0	28.0
Solid air fresheners	12.0	24.0	13.0
Aerosol air fresheners	35.0	34.0	20.0

[Continued]

★ 680 ★

Reported Purchases of Selected Grocery Store Items Within a 30-Day Period, by Selected Minority

[Continued]

Percent who purchased...	Hispanics	African-Americans	Asian-Americans
Powdered cleaners	53.0	57.0	46.0
Fabric softener	81.0	67.0	51.0
Liquid cleaners	57.0	61.0	43.0
Toilet paper	95.0	95.0	93.0
Disposable diapers	16.0	7.0	9.0
Cloth diapers	1.0	1.0	1.0
Chocolate bars	23.0	33.0	36.0
Non-chocolate candy	9.0	11.0	17.0
Chewing gum	26.0	35.0	39.0
Bleach	73.0	76.0	57.0
Artificial sweeteners	12.0	16.0	17.0
Diet frozen entrees	1.0	3.0	1.0
Diet frozen desserts	1.0	3.0	1.0
White rice	89.0	73.0	90.0
Packaged cheese	65.0	53.0	39.0
Yogurt	25.0	23.0	28.0
Packaged sliced meats	55.0	39.0	43.0
Potato chips	36.0	52.0	41.0
Microwave popcorn	16.0	23.0	18.0
Insecticide spray	30.0	28.0	31.0
Dried fruit products	14.0	14.0	17.0
Underwear	66.0	63.0	66.0
Non-menthol cigarettes	14.0	12.0	22.0
Menthol cigarettes	5.0	16.0	4.0
Cat food	7.0	10.0	5.0
Dog food	14.0	14.0	10.0
Packaged cookies	42.0	46.0	44.0
Cake mixes	9.0	24.0	14.0
Sunscreen	5.0	3.0	9.0
Analgesics/headache remedies	80.0	60.0	48.0
Antacids	29.0	20.0	13.0
Laxatives	11.0	14.0	7.0
Cough syrup	50.0	41.0	28.0
Cold remedies	37.0	38.0	42.0
Stomach remedies	35.0	32.0	18.0
Condoms	9.0	16.0	12.0
Jams & jellies	36.0	28.0	37.0
Peanut butter	31.0	54.0	51.0
Ice cream	43.0	35.0	43.0
Ice cream toppings	4.0	6.0	6.0

Source: Fisher, Christy. "Poll: Hispanics stick to brands: Asian-Americans shop for good price and African-Americans look for quality." *Advertising Age* (15 February 1993), p. 6. Market Segment Research, Miami.

★ 681 ★

Consumer Affairs

Salad Dressing Used Most Often

Percentages are shown by the consumers' country of origin.

Type	Mexico	Puerto Rico	Cuba	Central America	Other
Italian	37.0	62.0	62.0	35.0	58.0
Ranch	36.0	8.0	21.0	32.0	18.0
Thousand Island	28.0	22.0	20.0	12.0	17.0
French	15.0	38.0	22.0	10.0	14.0
Blue Cheese	17.0	5.0	13.0	18.0	8.0
Oil/Vinegar	10.0	16.0	9.0	13.0	13.0
Russian	5.0	2.0	2.0	2.0	9.0
Other	2.0	6.0	8.0	5.0	-
Don't know/don't recall	1.0	1.0	2.0	4.0	1.0

Source: Grocery Marketing (24 November 1991), p. 12. Primary source: Telemundo Product Usage Study, 1991.

★ 682 ★

Consumer Affairs

Sales Contributions to Regional Malls

Percent of sales contributions, by race/ethnicity of consumer, per shopping trip.

Store type	Hispanic	White	Black	Asian
Conventional department stores	31.00	33.85	30.80	41.67
National department stores[1]	15.11	15.33	12.07	8.98
Women's apparel	10.19	9.75	13.02	9.13
Shoes	6.01	4.93	10.27	4.17
Jewelry	4.39	4.49	9.18	2.65
Men's apparel	2.94	2.70	6.80	4.36
Discount department stores	1.61	2.27	2.08	0.09
Children's apparel	0.91	0.49	0.57	0.09
Specialty department stores	0.03	0.40	0.31	0.36
All other	27.89	25.80	8.09	28.61

Source: Chain Store Age Executive, May 1992, p. 55. Primary source: 1992 Stillerman Jones & Co. National Benchmarks. *Notes:* Because of rounding, numbers may not add to 100%. 1. Sears, Roebuck; J.C. Penney; Montgomery Ward.

★ 683 ★

Consumer Affairs

Soft Drink Brands Purchased Most Often, 1991

Market shares and yields per case are shown, by company brand.

Brand	Rank	Share	Yield per case
Coca-Cola classic	1	27.1	1.32
Pepsi-Cola	2	15.5	1.54
Diet Coke	3	9.6	1.18
Seven-Up (All)	4	7.1	1.26
Diet Pepsi	5	4.7	1.22
Dr Pepper (All)	6	4.7	1.03
Sprite (All)	7	4.4	1.26
CF diet Coke	8	2.5	1.06
Royal Crown	9	1.7	1.26
Mountain Dew	10	1.2	1.41

Source: "Hispanic market? Definitely Coke!" *Beverage World*, December 1991, p. 135.

★ 684 ★

Consumer Affairs

Soft Drinks Brands Purchased Most Often, by Container Size, 1991

Market shares and yields per case are shown, by company brand.

Brand	Yield per case	Total share	Shares, by container size			
			2-L	6-pack	12-pack	24-pack
Pepsi-Cola	1.45	26.5	5.6	14.5	4.6	0.7
Coca-Cola	1.25	49.8	9.3	21.4	15.9	0.3
Seven-Up	1.26	7.1	2.2	3.8	0.8	0.1
Royal Crown	1.38	2.7	0.7	1.4	0.3	0.1
Dr. Pepper	1.03	4.7	0.6	1.9	1.8	0.0
All Other	1.51	9.3	2.6	4.8	0.7	0.0

Source: Phillips, Kent. "Hispanic market? Definitely Coke!" *Beverage World* (December 1991), p. 135.

★ 685 ★

Consumer Affairs

Yogurt Brands Purchased Most Often

Percentages of all brands usually purchased are shown.

Type	Hispanic	Non-Hispanic
Dannon	29.0	46.0
Yoplait	17.0	15.0
Light N Lively	8.0	3.0
Breyers	4.0	4.0
La Yogurt	3.0	0.0
Weight Watchers	1.0	2.0
Borden's	1.0	0.0
Other	16.0	23.0
Don't Know/can't recall	21.0	7.0

Source: Grocery Marketing (24 November 1991), p. 13. Primary source: Telemundo Product Usage Study, 1991.

Hispanic-Owned Firms

★ 686 ★

Characteristics of Hispanic-Owned Businesses

Data show selected results of a poll of 508 Hispanic business owners and Hispanic executives.

Among the poll's major findings:
—89 percent "... are confident doing business outside their own ethnic group."
—73 percent said English is their workplace language, 21 percent use Spanish and 4 percent use both.
—49 percent said doing business was tougher for Hispanics than non-Hispanics.
—More than 80 percent of Hispanic business owners believe they get the same service and price from their suppliers as non-Hispanic companies.
—56 percent believe Hispanic firms are "more family-like" than other businesses.
—40 percent said Hispanic firms are more likely to base business dealings on personal relationships than non-Hispanics.
—Hispanic firms employ an average of two family members per company.
—53 percent said they are more customer-service oriented than non-Hispanic firms and 39 percent said Hispanic businesses are more loyal to suppliers.
—33 percent of Hispanic businesses regularly import or export products.

Source: Flannery, William. "Hispanic-owned small businesses taking off, poll finds." *St. Louis-Dispatch* (16 May 94), p. 3. Primary source: Gallup Organization poll for MCI Communications.

★ 687 ★

Hispanic-Owned Firms

Counties with 100 or More Hispanic-Owned Firms, by State, 1987: Alaska - Florida

Geographic area	All firms		Firms with paid employees				Relative standard error of estimate (%) for column			
	Firms (number) A	Sales and receipts ($000) B	Firms (number) C	Sales and receipts ($000) D	Employees (number) E	Annual payroll ($000) F	A	B	C	D
Alaska										
Anchorage	238	13,375	38	9,720	153	2,583	6	1	4	-
Arizona										
Cochise	539	18,061	143	12,302	321	2,475	11	13	16	15
Coconino	259	16,713	55	11,989	160	1,729	15	9	18	6
Gila	102	3,984	22	2,980	100	565	23	10	-	-

[Continued]

★ 687 ★

Counties with 100 or More Hispanic-Owned Firms, by State, 1987: Alaska - Florida

[Continued]

Geographic area	All firms: Firms (number) A	All firms: Sales and receipts ($000) B	Firms with paid employees: Firms (number) C	Firms with paid employees: Sales and receipts ($000) D	Firms with paid employees: Employees (number) E	Firms with paid employees: Annual payroll ($000) F	Relative standard error of estimate (%) for column A	B	C	D
Maricopa	4,507	223,471	982	156,429	3,141	37,432	3	3	6	2
Navajo	142	7,081	25	5,223	168	656	21	10	38	1
Pima	2,430	112,126	498	85,214	2,087	17,481	4	2	7	2
Pinal	404	15,373	86	11,793	305	2,262	12	6	16	6
Santa Cruz	487	58,523	109	50,627	385	4,811	11	3	11	2
Yavapai	182	6,504	48	4,458	104	969	19	12	28	7
Yuma[1]	544	36,315	170	30,908	1,982	8,270	11	5	14	5
California										
Alameda	3,892	221,158	770	164,010	2,035	30,225	4	3	7	4
Butte	266	10,671	65	8,075	193	1,676	16	9	19	8
Contra Costa	2,154	132,560	376	91,723	1,335	17,871	6	4	9	3
El Dorado	176	10,122	54	8,352	89	1,336	18	9	26	9
Fresno	3,039	319,370	848	269,819	4,199	50,566	4	2	6	2
Humboldt	119	3,886	21	3,117	96	885	24	23	46	28
Imperial	1,337	103,226	304	79,512	1,313	13,813	7	4	11	4
Kern	2,073	148,144	536	111,373	2,380	25,192	6	4	8	4
Kings	408	20,602	110	14,461	304	2,669	13	11	19	13
Los Angeles	56,679	3,346,076	10,339	2,260,478	36,463	447,029	1	1	2	1
Madera	451	32,600	86	26,258	313	3,521	12	6	17	5
Marin	562	32,635	116	16,996	250	3,198	11	9	19	13
Merced	451	50,333	145	41,412	856	8,455	10	5	11	4
Monterey	1,365	98,610	311	78,475	1,464	15,895	7	4	10	4
Napa	177	10,194	60	8,059	140	1,159	17	8	24	9
Orange	9,683	650,604	1,997	460,487	5,667	88,163	3	2	5	2
Placer	344	23,928	102	18,204	315	4,075	13	10	21	11
Riverside	4,680	246,509	1,076	180,500	2,816	37,316	4	3	6	3
Sacramento	2,136	104,049	412	73,663	1,290	15,879	6	4	8	4
San Benito	329	20,613	89	14,166	197	2,576	15	11	23	12
San Bernardino	5,515	330,028	1,440	248,245	3,062	43,583	4	3	6	3
San Diego	10,373	559,444	2,007	401,549	6,384	79,028	3	2	4	2
San Francisco	2,787	244,974	488	198,369	2,178	36,138	5	2	6	2
San Joaquin	1,643	99,035	416	76,342	1,337	18,108	6	4	9	5
San Luis Obispo	538	26,102	73	17,133	323	3,085	11	6	17	7
San Mateo	3,123	153,723	519	94,296	1,363	18,321	5	4	9	4
Santa Barbara	1,882	108,657	470	79,797	1,314	15,551	6	4	9	4
Santa Clara	6,188	314,063	1,301	205,582	3,339	43,587	3	3	6	3
Santa Cruz	821	57,293	215	44,504	800	8,139	9	6	12	7
Shasta	149	69,628	47	67,510	319	7,941	20	2	29	1
Solano	589	40,394	158	30,869	649	7,336	10	10	15	10
Sonoma	844	36,696	164	24,286	379	4,601	9	9	14	11
Stanislaus	1,129	76,882	273	58,046	1,219	14,110	8	6	11	7
Tulare	1,567	107,366	395	82,170	1,631	19,753	6	4	10	5

[Continued]

★ 687 ★

Counties with 100 or More Hispanic-Owned Firms, by State, 1987: Alaska - Florida

[Continued]

Geographic area	All firms		Firms with paid employees				Relative standard error of estimate (%) for column			
	Firms (number) A	Sales and receipts ($000) B	Firms (number) C	Sales and receipts ($000) D	Employees (number) E	Annual payroll ($000) F	A	B	C	D
Ventura	3,297	216,836	726	156,851	2,328	30,972	4	3	7	3
Yolo	484	37,049	118	29,017	369	4,585	12	6	16	4
Colorado										
Adams	1,110	36,170	168	23,502	416	5,326	7	7	13	6
Alamosa	164	(D)	47	6,914	120	1,149	17	(D)	21	10
Arapahoe	533	53,504	88	(D)	(D)	(D)	10	4	17	(D)
Boulder	279	9,293	65	5,842	94	1,279	14	14	24	17
Conejos	174	5,285	64	4,363	25	453	19	20	29	24
Costilla	100	1,925	6	1,176	9	116	24	8	-	-
Denver	2,148	87,898	370	64,960	929	15,161	5	3	9	3
Eagle	122	2,616	15	1,297	41	318	23	20	56	25
El Paso	608	24,501	104	18,281	367	3,831	9	6	10	8
Fremont	105	1,195	5	558	10	82	24	23	29	27
Jefferson	894	34,184	176	23,525	357	4,689	8	6	14	7
Larimer	350	19,121	78	15,521	259	3,745	14	12	20	14
Las Animas	114	2,654	20	1,587	30	209	20	16	14	6
Mesa	165	5,527	26	4,153	107	801	19	9	11	8
Pueblo	808	29,382	216	22,962	588	4,531	8	8	12	10
Rio Grande	140	2,877	23	1,369	44	315	23	28	39	17
Weld	518	22,932	122	13,475	226	3,177	11	10	18	9
Connecticut										
Fairfield	1,041	61,816	173	35,592	433	5,486	5	3	7	2
Hartford	432	32,605	92	18,819	239	4,922	7	5	10	5
New Haven	509	68,865	89	55,769	826	7,813	7	2	11	2
Delaware										
New Castle	138	4,575	21	1,915	45	526	2	1	-	-
District of Columbia										
District of Columbia	762	63,948	128	53,255	725	12,584	2	-	3	-
Florida										
Alachua	167	7,459	33	(D)	(D)	(D)	21	10	17	(D)
Brevard	352	18,327	84	11,892	184	2,004	13	9	21	11
Broward	3,570	225,621	567	159,319	2,370	31,850	4	2	7	2
Collier	603	31,435	125	18,962	279	3,959	11	10	21	14
Dade	47,725	3,771,247	6,528	2,904,141	30,069	404,141	1	-	2	-
Duval[2]	348	51,748	55	(D)	(D)	(D)	13	2	9	(D)
Hardee	111	3,509	25	3,085	17	1,512	23	43	43	48
Hillsborough	3,539	287,151	753	202,632	2,774	36,978	4	2	6	2
Lee	238	16,181	54	10,570	121	2,084	17	10	26	7

[Continued]

★ 687 ★

Counties with 100 or More Hispanic-Owned Firms, by State, 1987: Alaska - Florida

[Continued]

Geographic area	All firms: Firms (number) A	All firms: Sales and receipts ($000) B	Firms with paid employees: Firms (number) C	Firms with paid employees: Sales and receipts ($000) D	Firms with paid employees: Employees (number) E	Firms with paid employees: Annual payroll ($000) F	Relative standard error of estimate (%) for column: A	B	C	D
Manatee	230	7,757	39	5,339	83	2,501	24	24	37	31
Marion	189	13,404	47	9,641	184	2,305	17	9	22	8
Monroe	457	29,606	101	20,313	314	2,879	11	9	18	12
Orange	1,330	85,897	264	68,462	1,076	12,830	7	4	10	4
Osceola	125	9,471	34	5,749	51	537	21	7	40	11
Palm Beach	1,870	157,607	307	112,105	1,509	20,384	6	3	8	3
Pasco	212	7,149	42	4,114	51	755	18	15	34	20
Pinellas	704	44,515	155	32,805	494	5,839	10	4	14	3
Polk	408	24,429	121	17,061	510	3,941	13	10	19	12
St. Lucie	112	6,088	21	3,714	58	669	26	24	38	35
Sarasota	259	20,555	86	17,188	331	3,967	15	9	18	10
Seminole	489	31,760	88	15,508	189	2,326	12	6	22	4
Volusia	247	12,037	63	6,225	111	1,239	16	15	23	16

Source: 1987 Economic Censuses, Survey of Minority-Owned Business Enterprises: Hispanics, U.S. Department of Commerce, Bureau of the Census, MB-87-2, 1991, pp. 71-76. *Notes:* A dash (-) represents zero. A (D) stands for data withheld to avoid disclosing data for individual companies; data are included in higher level totals. 1. Yuma County was divided to create La Paz County in January 1983. 2. Jacksonville comprises all of Duval County, but the semi-independent municipalities of Atlantic Beach, Jacksonville Beach, and Neptune Beach are tabulated separately. The semi-independent town of Baldwin is not populous enough for separate tabulation.

★ 688 ★

Hispanic-Owned Firms

Counties with 100 or More Hispanic-Owned Firms, by State, 1987: Georgia - New Jersey

Geographic area	All firms: Firms (number) A	All firms: Sales and receipts ($000) B	Firms with paid employees: Firms (number) C	Firms with paid employees: Sales and receipts ($000) D	Firms with paid employees: Employees (number) E	Firms with paid employees: Annual payroll ($000) F	Relative standard error of estimate (%) for column: A	B	C	D
Georgia										
Cobb	253	20,441	73	17,210	183	2,728	10	4	16	4
De Kalb	397	42,647	106	36,675	887	12,058	7	2	12	2
Fulton	291	25,266	78	20,845	258	3,579	8	1	10	1
Gwinnett	243	11,048	40	7,330	114	1,562	11	4	19	3
Hawaii										
Hawaii	202	4,151	26	2,578	38	384	11	6	20	7
Honolulu[1]	727	43,676	113	33,295	377	4,665	5	2	8	3
Kauai	103	3,486	15	2,193	31	297	21	5	-	-
Maui	194	6,785	23	3,772	96	577	11	6	16	8

[Continued]

★ 688 ★

Counties with 100 or More Hispanic-Owned Firms, by State, 1987: Georgia - New Jersey

[Continued]

Geographic area	All firms: Firms (number) A	All firms: Sales and receipts ($000) B	Firms with paid employees: Firms (number) C	Firms with paid employees: Sales and receipts ($000) D	Firms with paid employees: Employees (number) E	Firms with paid employees: Annual payroll ($000) F	Relative standard error of estimate (%) for column A	B	C	D
Idaho										
Ada	168	5,187	36	3,474	39	578	9	4	14	2
Canyon	201	6,897	35	4,595	58	933	9	2	19	2
Illinois										
Cook	7,105	474,322	1,172	337,188	4,138	52,094	2	1	4	1
Du Page	632	29,404	129	19,429	315	4,661	8	6	13	6
Kane	361	(D)	62	9,343	147	1,221	11	(D)	19	12
Lake	353	16,360	71	10,903	160	2,050	11	7	12	9
McHenry	111	2,667	7	1,312	27	332	20	11	-	-
Rock Island	113	4,543	27	(D)	(D)	(D)	18	11	21	(D)
Will	183	8,645	41	(D)	(D)	(D)	14	9	24	(D)
Indiana										
Allen	129	4,830	22	3,653	133	1,024	12	6	6	1
Lake	520	32,090	107	24,537	476	3,463	5	2	6	1
Marion[3]	196	37,265	47	(D)	(D)	(D)	8	1	10	(D)
Iowa										
Polk	129	6,426	27	(D)	(D)	(D)	6	1	5	(D)
Kansas										
Johnson	208	7,018	45	(D)	(D)	(D)	13	6	18	(D)
Sedgwick	306	10,340	66	6,378	181	1,570	9	4	11	1
Shawnee	169	5,365	33	3,841	116	898	13	3	6	2
Wyandotte	117	(D)	14	(D)	(D)	(D)	16	(D)	-	(D)
Kentucky										
Jefferson	122	6,516	28	(D)	(D)	(D)	5	1	11	(D)
Louisiana										
East Baton Rouge	229	14,714	36	11,466	127	1,864	6	2	8	-
Jefferson	904	37,193	166	24,046	299	4,231	3	2	5	2
Orleans	482	35,745	111	24,987	573	6,021	4	1	4	1
St. Bernard	173	6,177	26	3,864	30	473	7	3	11	2
St. Tammany	112	4,879	24	3,076	44	730	8	6	12	7
Maryland										
Anne Arundel	160	16,390	34	13,963	21	440	9	2	29	2
Baltimore	229	(D)	66	(D)	(D)	(D)	6	(D)	13	(D)
Montgomery	1,465	70,249	214	42,267	549	11,275	2	1	4	1
Prince Georges	635	37,376	94	29,436	383	7,244	4	2	6	1
Baltimore (IC)	142	13,864	32	11,838	171	3,037	7	-	8	-

[Continued]

★ 688 ★

Counties with 100 or More Hispanic-Owned Firms, by State, 1987: Georgia - New Jersey

[Continued]

Geographic area	All firms: Firms (number) A	All firms: Sales and receipts ($000) B	Firms with paid employees: Firms (number) C	Firms with paid employees: Sales and receipts ($000) D	Firms with paid employees: Employees (number) E	Firms with paid employees: Annual payroll ($000) F	Relative standard error of estimate (%) for column A	B	C	D
Massachusetts										
Bristol	286	13,826	44	7,063	99	957	5	4	11	6
Essex	276	33,296	46	24,891	136	2,419	5	2	10	2
Hampden	219	27,679	29	23,794	125	2,780	6	1	12	1
Middlesex	562	27,872	80	18,614	393	5,472	4	3	10	3
Norfolk	223	9,224	25	4,568	58	892	6	9	13	7
Plymouth	120	4,943	24	3,357	35	461	11	6	16	5
Suffolk	542	32,383	100	19,108	259	2,587	4	4	6	2
Worcester	242	17,476	29	11,922	163	3,257	7	6	12	2
Michigan										
Genesee	125	2,801	13	1,323	25	381	9	7	11	-
Ingham	163	6,744	19	4,881	46	2,211	8	3	13	1
Kent	139	5,616	27	3,809	56	493	8	6	25	6
Macomb	144	11,504	31	9,576	243	2,656	8	1	11	1
Oakland	349	26,687	42	20,137	281	6,651	5	2	8	1
Saginaw	150	8,003	39	6,155	98	910	7	3	8	1
Wayne	677	32,063	123	20,543	372	3,605	3	3	5	3
Minnesota										
Hennepin	229	7,440	31	4,994	53	704	6	2	11	1
Ramsey	143	8,147	28	6,377	129	1,358	7	1	9	-
Missouri										
Jackson	422	13,194	79	9,064	278	2,772	6	2	9	2
St. Louis	281	13,148	53	7,511	211	2,020	7	5	9	6
St. Louis (IC)	103	5,148	22	3,534	56	966	11	3	15	1
Nebraska										
Douglas	181	(D)	31	2,993	95	1,180	6	(D)	8	2
Scotts Bluff	128	4,526	33	3,280	100	721	9	4	10	5
Nevada										
Clark	1,084	84,518	237	66,095	1,353	17,368	4	1	7	1
Washoe	377	33,760	83	26,288	677	6,451	8	2	8	1
New Hampshire										
Hillsborough	101	6,290	19	4,257	63	749	6	3	11	2
New Jersey										
Atlantic	109	6,295	20	3,614	65	988	12	10	14	4
Bergen	1,451	94,103	212	56,031	642	11,930	3	3	7	3
Burlington	155	8,020	37	5,348	44	560	10	14	16	18

[Continued]

★ 688 ★

Counties with 100 or More Hispanic-Owned Firms, by State, 1987: Georgia - New Jersey

[Continued]

Geographic area	All firms: Firms (number) A	All firms: Sales and receipts ($000) B	Firms with paid employees: Firms (number) C	Firms with paid employees: Sales and receipts ($000) D	Firms with paid employees: Employees (number) E	Firms with paid employees: Annual payroll ($000) F	Relative standard error of estimate (%) for column: A	B	C	D
Camden	305	20,697	46	11,623	221	1,850	8	6	16	6
Cumberland	138	6,362	33	3,604	49	412	11	9	20	8
Essex	1,267	116,923	282	89,315	856	11,386	4	2	6	2
Hudson	3,949	294,372	679	193,472	1,642	20,207	2	1	4	1
Mercer	209	12,284	50	8,320	145	1,500	9	11	14	13
Middlesex	836	75,668	117	(D)	(D)	(D)	5	2	9	(D)
Monmouth	432	31,672	90	23,318	184	3,818	6	4	9	3
Morris	342	25,352	94	14,559	191	2,035	7	5	11	5
Ocean	253	26,925	55	21,808	307	4,900	8	3	14	2
Passaic	1,020	65,642	192	36,405	478	7,305	4	4	7	5
Somerset	169	9,196	35	(D)	(D)	(D)	11	11	16	(D)
Union	1,185	87,859	223	59,742	579	8,633	4	3	6	3

Source: 1987 Economic Censuses, Survey of Minority-Owned Business Enterprises: Hispanics, U.S. Department of Commerce, Bureau of the Census, MB-87-2, 1991, pp. 71-76. *Notes:* A dash (-) represents zero. A (D) stands for data withheld to avoid disclosing data for individual companies; data are included in higher level totals. 1. Honolulu County is coextensive with Honolulu city which is not recognized for the economic censuses; however, Honolulu CDP is recognized for the economic censuses. 2. Maui County consists of four islands. The state requested that two of the islands, Lanai and Molokai, be recognized as "places" for the economic censuses. Included on the island of Molokai is the nonfunctioning county of Kalawao. 3. Indianapolis comprises all of Marion County except for independent municipalities: Beech Grove, Lawrence, Southport, and Speedway. Thirteen of the fourteen semi-independent municipalities are not populous enough for separate tabulation; Cumberland, which is partially in Hancock County, is tabulated separately.

★ 689 ★

Hispanic-Owned Firms

Counties with 100 or More Hispanic-Owned Firms, by State, 1987: New Mexico - Tennessee

Geographic area	All firms: Firms (number) A	All firms: Sales and receipts ($000) B	Firms with paid employees: Firms (number) C	Firms with paid employees: Sales and receipts ($000) D	Firms with paid employees: Employees (number) E	Firms with paid employees: Annual payroll ($000) F	Relative standard error of estimate (%) for column: A	B	C	D
New Mexico										
Bernalillo	4,579	228,683	1,213	172,162	3,810	34,536	3	2	4	2
Chaves	364	11,630	83	7,446	174	1,372	11	6	14	7
Cibola	126	6,033	41	4,930	63	541	18	24	29	30
Colfax	145	5,534	49	4,075	69	574	20	12	35	15
Curry	122	3,950	31	2,879	52	508	20	12	29	15
Dona Ana	1,578	73,216	438	57,762	1,436	14,784	5	4	7	4
Eddy	264	10,118	96	8,113	174	1,659	12	16	18	19
Grant	301	9,832	73	7,320	193	1,551	12	10	18	13
Guadalupe	128	10,131	37	7,920	128	961	18	9	18	2
Lea	254	6,888	37	4,621	91	882	13	8	9	8

[Continued]

★ 689 ★

Counties with 100 or More Hispanic-Owned Firms, by State, 1987: New Mexico - Tennessee

[Continued]

Geographic area	All firms		Firms with paid employees				Relative standard error of estimate (%) for column			
	Firms (number) A	Sales and receipts ($000) B	Firms (number) C	Sales and receipts ($000) D	Employees (number) E	Annual payroll ($000) F	A	B	C	D
Lincoln	125	3,845	43	2,807	27	370	20	18	27	22
Luna	177	8,452	34	5,649	116	927	16	5	20	6
McKinley	254	16,782	94	14,251	328	2,428	13	6	13	6
Mora	164	5,224	12	1,165	7	93	17	19	47	8
Otero	285	11,411	72	7,785	143	1,016	13	13	21	6
Rio Arriba	764	32,739	158	22,364	399	3,396	7	4	11	4
Sandoval	480	25,123	114	19,452	357	3,109	9	4	13	3
San Juan	264	15,902	59	12,462	179	1,915	12	5	12	5
San Miguel	505	32,154	160	26,212	356	2,909	9	5	11	5
Santa Fe	1,528	81,514	332	61,243	1,262	12,587	5	3	5	2
Socorro	173	12,345	47	10,280	185	1,138	16	9	23	10
Taos	568	22,010	157	14,553	248	2,945	9	8	12	8
Valencia	662	41,582	196	32,736	453	4,227	8	5	11	5
New York										
Bronx[1]	3,527	182,774	530	105,097	1,418	16,770	3	3	6	3
Dutchess	128	7,673	20	4,099	52	680	17	15	17	12
Erie	213	11,426	51	8,444	130	1,517	13	14	15	16
Kings[1]	3,726	222,399	530	129,252	2,018	27,042	3	3	7	3
Monroe	268	22,978	39	(D)	(D)	(D)	12	8	21	(D)
Nassau	1,721	104,011	383	69,137	907	14,463	5	4	8	4
New York[1]	5,437	367,913	974	260,996	3,374	54,238	3	2	4	2
Orange[1]	292	11,971	63	6,485	125	1,381	11	9	19	9
Queens[1]	7,783	308,006	855	133,735	1,637	22,835	2	2	6	3
Richmond[1]	472	33,499	76	24,040	277	5,158	9	5	17	3
Rockland	350	25,602	73	15,963	153	1,181	10	7	15	7
Suffolk	1,592	110,647	297	75,133	922	14,974	5	4	9	3
Ulster	178	6,683	21	3,412	33	299	15	24	30	41
Westchester	1,644	96,250	233	65,052	1,139	16,369	5	3	9	4
North Carolina										
Cumberland	118	2,941	17	2,045	29	183	12	3	14	2
Mecklenburg	102	35,972	18	(D)	(D)	(D)	11	-	-	(D)
Ohio										
Cuyahoga	377	13,721	80	8,079	166	1,661	10	6	17	5
Franklin	224	12,136	63	10,001	217	2,787	12	9	22	11
Hamilton	162	10,765	28	8,336	66	1,404	15	6	12	2

[Continued]

★ 689 ★

Counties with 100 or More Hispanic-Owned Firms, by State, 1987: New Mexico - Tennessee

[Continued]

Geographic area	All firms		Firms with paid employees				Relative standard error of estimate (%) for column			
	Firms (number) A	Sales and receipts ($000) B	Firms (number) C	Sales and receipts ($000) D	Employees (number) E	Annual payroll ($000) F	A	B	C	D
Lorain	118	5,233	20	2,820	76	615	16	8	7	1
Lucas	169	4,448	23	(D)	(D)	(D)	15	15	14	(D)
Mahoning	127	2,578	8	1,178	16	103	21	20	18	16
Oklahoma										
Oklahoma	442	12,071	62	6,732	161	1,469	6	3	8	1
Tulsa	266	10,630	45	(D)	(D)	(D)	8	2	5	(D)
Oregon										
Clackamas	116	3,877	32	2,531	82	652	14	9	25	4
Lane	151	9,237	32	7,721	224	1,859	13	3	-	-
Marion	171	9,233	44	7,276	109	1,201	12	6	19	7
Multnomah	288	26,037	63	21,650	320	4,564	8	1	-	-
Washington	185	8,393	45	5,844	74	854	12	6	19	3
Pennsylvania										
Allegheny	250	16,293	54	10,502	155	1,713	13	15	19	6
Berks	133	3,777	20	1,664	31	270	9	10	16	10
Bucks	175	8,117	23	5,025	90	1,204	7	5	11	5
Chester	113	6,454	24	4,867	71	1,116	11	3	12	2
Delaware	115	7,609	24	5,183	58	693	10	6	12	5
Lancaster	112	5,261	21	2,630	54	433	8	8	13	8
Lehigh	116	4,207	22	(D)	(D)	(D)	9	10	17	(D)
Montgomery	195	20,285	45	15,710	164	2,482	6	3	9	3
Northampton	104	5,861	23	(D)	(D)	(D)	9	7	15	(D)
Philadelphia	787	127,032	139	102,117	710	14,819	3	2	5	1
Rhode Island										
Providence	302	21,094	74	11,645	194	2,558	3	1	4	-
Tennessee										
Davidson[2]	139	12,264	38	6,322	87	1,173	7	3	8	2

Source: 1987 Economic Censuses: Survey of Minority-Owned Business Enterprises: Hispanics, U.S. Department of Commerce, Bureau of the Census, MB-87-2, 1991, pp. 71-76. *Notes:* A dash (-) represents zero. A (D) stands for data withheld to avoid disclosing data for individual companies; data are included in higher level totals. 1. New York is in Bronx, Kings, New York, Queens, and Richmond Counties. 2. Goodlettsville is in Davidson and Summer Counties.

★ 690 ★

Hispanic-Owned Firms

Counties with 100 or More Hispanic-Owned Firms, by State, 1987: Texas - Wyoming

Geographic area	All firms		Firms with paid employees				Relative standard error of estimate (%) for column			
	Firms (number) A	Sales and receipts ($000) B	Firms (number) C	Sales and receipts ($000) D	Employees (number) E	Annual payroll ($000) F	A	B	C	D
Texas										
Aransas	183	(D)	29	1,967	63	572	20	(D)	46	42
Atascosa	360	(D)	64	4,923	57	1,144	13	(D)	26	31
Bastrop	114	(D)	8	595	14	126	25	(D)	25	39
Bee	350	(D)	93	7,172	132	1,104	14	(D)	23	10
Bell	314	6,941	40	4,579	76	834	15	16	26	20
Bexar	14,639	635,092	3,436	461,454	8,760	93,822	2	2	3	2
Brazoria	686	20,617	95	13,091	184	2,151	10	6	16	7
Brazos	301	13,216	76	10,201	235	1,945	17	14	33	17
Brooks	230	10,923	43	6,794	89	770	17	22	32	32
Caldwell	209	3,493	41	1,766	35	324	18	15	34	13
Calhoun	253	4,783	38	2,828	83	642	17	17	36	21
Cameron	4,413	218,948	1,011	159,324	2,855	25,265	3	2	5	2
Colin	498	21,274	115	13,739	126	2,655	13	13	22	10
Comal	275	9,806	72	7,621	127	1,237	16	17	26	21
Coryell	100	531	5	186	8	80	29	32	28	19
Dallas	5,530	240,942	1,095	170,733	2,975	41,920	4	3	6	3
Dawson	237	5,079	35	2,336	70	458	19	23	44	24
Deaf Smith	214	12,005	26	8,239	69	626	18	10	26	8
Denton	447	12,838	75	7,176	186	1,708	13	11	26	11
De Witt	148	1,801	8	597	15	128	21	30	31	31
Dimmit	225	6,724	68	4,847	64	871	18	19	28	24
Duval	395	15,367	73	9,239	143	1,040	13	12	19	10
Ector	1,013	24,683	168	15,112	180	3,808	9	11	19	14
Ellis	198	11,772	55	7,369	167	2,337	20	23	33	32
El Paso	8,214	450,840	2,155	345,530	6,983	67,348	3	2	4	2
Fort Bend	887	28,238	176	16,882	239	4,815	10	12	19	16
Frio	296	6,930	52	4,184	90	680	15	8	27	4
Galveston	627	22,590	96	11,707	296	2,453	11	11	19	8
Gonzales	123	4,388	40	3,170	86	691	22	18	34	15
Grayson	107	3,559	6	(D)	(D)	(D)	31	19	23	(D)
Guadalupe	327	12,276	70	8,116	229	1,731	14	13	17	11
Hale	143	6,769	40	5,123	113	1,624	20	25	33	32
Harris	14,810	538,768	2,843	318,263	3,817	76,587	2	2	4	3
Hays	277	11,010	85	7,343	164	1,490	15	16	23	12
Hidalgo	7,847	457,977	1,959	343,015	5,397	51,698	3	2	4	2
Hockley	225	2,502	24	1,004	31	333	18	27	42	32
Howard	168	5,672	17	3,138	89	893	20	16	19	9
Jefferson	325	15,869	85	(D)	(D)	(D)	14	15	23	(D)
Jim Hogg	158	9,241	41	7,967	91	748	18	7	25	8
Jim Wells	735	38,495	236	30,423	437	4,084	9	6	13	7
Johnson	189	6,091	65	4,596	56	1,164	22	31	33	41
Karnes	158	4,892	27	3,018	65	462	19	22	36	31
Kerr	172	3,939	28	2,200	34	411	21	22	35	23

[Continued]

★ 690 ★

Counties with 100 or More Hispanic-Owned Firms, by State, 1987: Texas - Wyoming

[Continued]

Geographic area	All firms		Firms with paid employees				Relative standard error of estimate (%) for column			
	Firms (number) A	Sales and receipts ($000) B	Firms (number) C	Sales and receipts ($000) D	Employees (number) E	Annual payroll ($000) F	A	B	C	D
Kleberg	428	13,461	94	10,261	230	1,565	12	8	18	10
Lamb	122	1,346	10	597	8	87	23	17	14	4
La Salle	101	3,589	12	884	10	60	21	36	20	27
Live Oak	160	4,827	31	3,179	69	450	20	32	36	40
Lubbock	1,055	36,036	199	26,062	477	4,863	8	8	15	10
McLennan	297	12,882	109	10,187	181	1,869	15	10	21	12
Matagorda	168	9,125	40	4,135	69	731	20	13	34	11
Maverick	691	38,779	182	25,357	345	3,723	9	8	14	7
Medina	296	16,500	49	12,361	161	1,474	15	13	22	16
Midland	662	18,653	121	12,204	216	2,551	11	10	23	8
Montgomery	209	15,281	26	11,224	85	1,708	16	4	12	3
Nolan	109	1,697	7	(D)	(D)	(D)	25	14	-	(D)
Nueces	3,586	142,072	814	95,309	1,949	20,078	4	4	7	4
Pecos	180	6,263	40	4,887	84	722	20	12	28	14
Potter	198	8,934	36	4,950	131	743	19	21	29	20
Presidio	152	5,009	31	3,517	27	255	20	14	32	15
Randall	144	(D)	33	(D)	(D)	(D)	20	(D)	32	(D)
Reeves	216	7,418	36	4,893	128	703	17	11	14	6
San Patricio	586	17,520	120	9,844	181	1,407	11	10	20	12
Scurry	112	2,640	29	1,562	45	339	25	11	47	9
Starr	1,385	77,439	331	58,732	627	5,965	7	5	11	5
Tarrant	2,197	85,798	496	60,919	1,196	14,746	6	6	9	7
Taylor	339	(D)	62	(D)	(D)	(D)	14	(D)	28	(D)
Tom Green	427	14,829	137	11,126	244	1,947	13	8	18	8
Travis	2,650	99,109	495	72,294	1,516	18,002	5	4	8	4
Uvalde	458	17,601	105	11,795	280	2,783	12	12	21	17
Val Verde	520	22,654	117	13,942	295	2,228	11	7	15	7
Victoria	836	20,976	141	13,041	287	2,681	9	9	17	9
Webb	2,768	236,734	803	190,400	2,817	28,043	5	2	6	2
Wharton	241	6,537	48	3,347	55	746	17	10	35	13
Wichita	206	9,535	21	7,308	301	2,993	18	7	15	3
Willacy	346	14,997	83	11,390	198	1,751	13	10	19	13
Williamson	439	12,078	96	8,414	92	1,350	13	19	24	26
Wilson	185	4,709	27	2,985	64	651	19	12	36	12
Yoakum	107	2,071	9	1,125	21	185	28	25	31	34
Zapata	168	11,553	38	6,195	97	755	17	16	28	6
Zavala	156	6,686	46	5,367	43	981	21	17	30	20
Utah										
Salt Lake	762	31,499	144	20,802	416	4,310	6	2	10	1
Utah	107	3,737	19	3,016	113	589	17	3	7	1
Weber	125	4,037	25	2,947	22	314	18	6	27	4

[Continued]

★ 690 ★

Counties with 100 or More Hispanic-Owned Firms, by State, 1987: Texas - Wyoming

[Continued]

Geographic area	All firms		Firms with paid employees				Relative standard error of estimate (%) for column			
	Firms (number) A	Sales and receipts ($000) B	Firms (number) C	Sales and receipts ($000) D	Employees (number) E	Annual payroll ($000) F	A	B	C	D
Virginia										
Arlington	423	10,597	61	5,669	72	1,162	5	5	17	5
Fairfax	1,076	64,915	172	49,560	722	17,127	3	1	5	1
Prince William	122	2,490	12	940	32	277	8	5	12	1
Alexandria (IC)	197	12,172	31	10,022	113	1,888	6	1	11	1
Virginia Beach (IC)	150	7,872	31	5,007	50	506	7	2	10	2
Washington										
Adams	122	(D)	18	2,049	24	358	8	(D)	11	4
Franklin	112	4,555	29	3,714	68	534	11	3	14	2
Grant	106	5,384	33	4,044	94	783	7	3	10	3
King	865	48,589	160	36,384	832	7,965	3	1	3	1
Pierce	217	10,495	42	8,036	219	1,570	8	3	7	3
Snohomish	169	6,592	38	4,952	117	875	7	3	6	1
Yakima	310	17,550	67	14,027	202	2,349	5	1	5	1
Wisconsin										
Milwaukee	401	48,364	82	(D)	(D)	(D)	5	1	8	(D)
Wyoming										
Laramie	174	5,353	37	3,636	139	991	5	1	8	1

Source: 1987 Economic Censuses, Survey of Minority-Owned Business Enterprises: Hispanics, U.S. Department of Commerce, Bureau of the Census, MB-87-2, 1991, pp. 71-76. *Notes:* A dash (-) represents zero. A (D) stands for data withheld to avoid disclosing data for individual companies; data are included in higher level totals.

★ 691 ★

Hispanic-Owned Firms

Hispanic-Owned Firms and Receipts as a Percent of All U.S. Firms and Receipts, by Industry, 1987

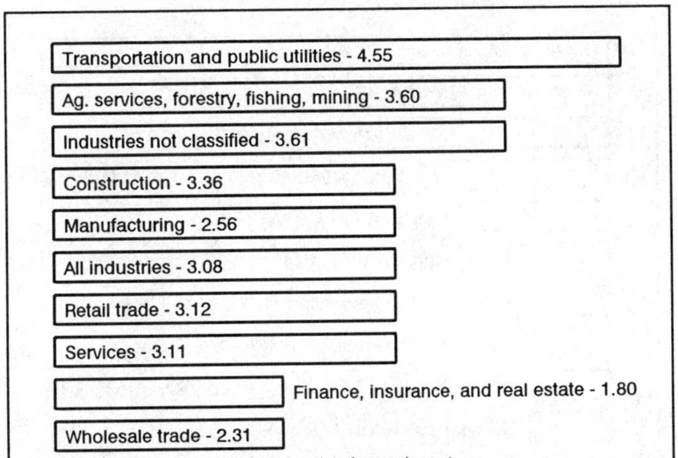

Chart shows data from column 1.

Industry	Firms (%)	Receipts (%)
All industries	3.08	1.24
Ag. services, forestry, fishing, mining	3.60	2.03
Construction	3.36	1.48
Manufacturing	2.56	0.64
Transportation and public utilities	4.55	1.81
Wholesale trade	2.31	0.82
Retail trade	3.12	1.40
Finance, insurance, and real estate	1.80	0.70
Services	3.11	1.45
Industries not classified	3.61	1.89

Source: 1987 Economic Censuses, Survey of Minority-Owned Business Enterprises: Hispanics, U.S. Department of Commerce, Bureau of the Census, MB-87-2, 1991, p. 7.

★ 692 ★

Hispanic-Owned Firms

Hispanic-Owned Firms and Receipts for 10 Largest Metropolitan Statistical Areas, 1987

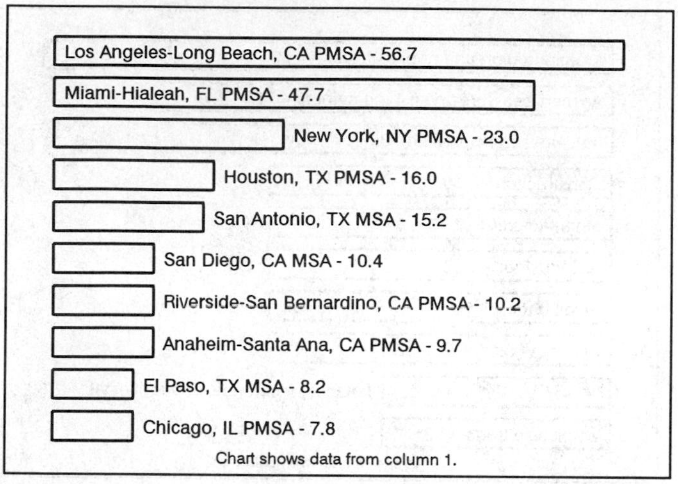

Number of firms is shown in thousands.

Metropolitan area	Number of firms (thous.)	Receipts ($ mil.)
Los Angeles-Long Beach, CA PMSA	56.7	3,346
Miami-Hialeah, FL PMSA	47.7	3,771
New York, NY PMSA	23.0	1,240
Houston, TX PMSA	16.0	584
San Antonio, TX MSA	15.2	657
San Diego, CA MSA	10.4	559
Riverside-San Bernardino, CA PMSA	10.2	577
Anaheim-Santa Ana, CA PMSA	9.7	651
El Paso, TX MSA	8.2	451
Chicago, IL PMSA	7.8	506

Source: 1987 Economic Censuses, Survey of Minority-Owned Business Enterprises: Hispanics, U.S. Department of Commerce, Bureau of the Census, MB-87-2, 1991, p. 7.

★ 693 ★

Hispanic-Owned Firms

Hispanic-Owned Firms, by Industry Division and Employment Size of Firm, 1987

This table is based on the 1972 Standard Industrial Classification (SIC) system.

Industry division and employment size	Firms (number) A	Sales and receipts ($000) B	Employees (number) C	Annual payroll ($000) D	Relative standard error of estimate (percent) for column -- A	B
All industries	422,373	24,731,600	264,846	3,243,342	-	-
With no paid employees	339,465	7,002,168	-	-	-	1
With paid employees	82,908	17,729,432	264,846	3,243,342	1	-
No employees[1]	33,717	2,300,522	-	457,870	1	1
1 to 4 employees	35,239	5,208,198	68,367	396,933	1	-
5 to 9 employees	8,221	3,075,801	53,181	526,090	1	-
10 to 19 employees	3,671	2,433,738	48,330	491,931	1	-
20 to 49 employees	1,582	2,126,435	46,142	477,564	1	-
50 to 99 employees	349	1,370,194	23,335	269,919	-	-
100 employees or more	129	1,214,544	25,491	323,035	-	-
Agricultural services, forestry, fishing, and mining	17,194	724,773	14,781	168,841	1	1
With no paid employees	13,791	226,617	-	-	1	3
With paid employees	3,403	498,156	14,781	168,8941	3	2
No employees[1]	1,918	126,766	-	49,556	5	6
1 to 4 employees	954	103,541	1,855	19,000	4	3
5 to 9 employees	210	52,022	1,386	13,128	9	5
10 to 19 employees	155	65,145	2,214	20,545	8	4
20 to 49 employees	115	77,928	3,328	29,506	7	2
50 to 99 employees	36	46,548	2,493	19,884	-	-
100 employees or more	15	26,206	3,505	17,222	-	-
Construction	55,516	3,438,708	34,684	631,477	-	1
With no paid employees	40,799	792,464	-	-	1	2
With paid employees	14,717	2,646,244	34,684	631,477	2	1
No employees[1]	8,390	557,276	-	155,059	3	3
1 to 4 employees	4,266	624,094	8,405	105,241	2	2
5 to 9 employees	1,204	379,992	7,853	90,610	2	2
10 to 19 employees	593	389,783	7,665	97,923	3	1
20 to 49 employees	210	378,935	6,099	91,137	-	-
50 to 99 employees	45	233,745	2,874	58,863	-	-
100 employees or more	9	82,419	1,788	32,644	-	-
Manufacturing	11,090	1,449,913	26,261	333,969	1	-
With no paid employees	7,330	141,789	-	-	1	3
With paid employees	3,760	1,308,124	26,261	333,969	2	-
No employees[1]	1,174	74,375	-	15,433	5	5
1 to 4 employees	1,354	174,156	2,898	33,132	2	2
5 to 9 employees	558	174,564	3,738	41,184	4	2
10 to 19 employees	361	197,730	4,961	53,599	2	1
20 to 49 employees	240	236,753	7,226	73,192	-	-
50 to 99 employees	49	155,422	3,251	42,919	-	-
100 employees or more	24	295,124	4,187	74,510	-	-
Transportation and public utilities	26,955	1,380,981	8,006	135,592	1	1
With no paid employees	22,966	655,497	-	-	1	2
With paid employees	3,989	725,484	8,006	135,592	3	1
No employees[1]	2,250	139,853	-	25,908	5	5
1 to 4 employees	1,285	236,126	2,362	27,840	4	2

[Continued]

★ 693 ★

Hispanic-Owned Firms, by Industry Division and Employment Size of Firm, 1987

[Continued]

Industry division and employment size	Firms (number) A	Sales and receipts ($000) B	Employees (number) C	Annual payroll ($000) D	Relative standard error of estimate (percent) for column -- A	B
5 to 9 employees	236	106,196	1,527	18,667	1	-
10 to 19 employees	164	140,384	2,149	29,099	-	-
20 to 49 employees	47	77,389	1,352	22,625	-	-
50 to 99 employees	5	(D)	(D)	(D)	-	(D)
100 employees or more	2	(D)	(D)	(D)	-	(D)
Wholesale trade	10,154	2,445,416	9,119	157,537	1	-
With no paid employees	7,845	453,680	-	-	1	2
With paid employees	2,309	1,991,736	9,119	157,537	2	-
No employees[1]	590	115,408	-	6,998	6	3
1 to 4 employees	1,188	490,692	2,335	32,611	2	1
5 to 9 employees	314	405,235	2,030	30,369	2	1
10 to 19 employees	141	368,320	1,833	32,626	1	1
20 to 49 employees	60	327,678	1,713	31,130	-	-
50 to 99 employees	14	(D)	(D)	(D)	-	(D)
100 employees or more	2	(D)	(D)	(D)	-	(D)
Retail trade	69,911	7,643,850	90,584	745,662	-	-
With no paid employees	49,563	1,547,960	-	-	1	1
With paid employees	20,348	6,095,890	90,584	745,662	1	-
No employees[1]	5,011	518,212	-	45,980	3	3
1 to 4 employees	10,196	1,779,355	20,205	156,164	1	1
5 to 9 employees	2,975	1,224,157	19,493	141,206	1	1
10 to 19 employees	1,388	834,536	18,350	128,986	1	-
20 to 49 employees	604	744,509	17,749	132,940	-	-
50 to 99 employees	140	629,856	9,471	85,406	-	-
100 employees or more	34	365,265	5,316	54,980	-	-
Finance, insurance, and real estate	22,106	864,282	4,960	80,882	1	1
With no paid employees	19,870	430,431	-	-	1	2
With paid employees	2,236	433,851	4,960	80,882	2	1
No employees[1]	869	48,464	-	5,859	5	6
1 to 4 employees	1,157	154,132	2,000	26,950	3	2
5 to 9 employees	135	50,346	851	12,831	2	2
10 to 19 employees	49	72,433	640	10,422	-	-
20 to 49 employees	18	(D)	(D)	(D)	-	(D)
50 to 99 employees	4	16,937	277	4,764	-	-
100 employees or more	4	(D)	(D)	(D)	-	(D)
Services	184,372	6,031,406	74,427	941,588	-	-
With no paid employees	154,622	2,257,289	-	-	-	1
With paid employees	29,750	3,774,117	74,427	941,588	1	1
No employees[1]	11,790	580,832	-	126,431	2	3
1 to 4 employees	14,274	1,569,570	27,319	285,134	1	1
5 to 9 employees	2,511	660,644	15,848	173,481	2	1
10 to 19 employees	801	353,891	10,276	116,137	1	1
20 to 49 employees	281	236,423	7,952	84,323	1	-
50 to 99 employees	54	81,874	3,564	33,968	-	-
100 employees or more	39	290,883	9,468	122,114	-	-

[Continued]

★ 693 ★

Hispanic-Owned Firms, by Industry Division and Employment Size of Firm, 1987

[Continued]

Industry division and employment size	Firms (number) A	Sales and receipts ($000) B	Employees (number) C	Annual payroll ($000) D	Relative standard error of estimate (percent) for column -- A	B
Industries not classified	25,075	752,271	2,024	47,794	1	2
With no paid employees	22,679	496,441	-	-	1	2
With paid employees	2,396	255,830	2,024	47,794	4	3
No employees[1]	1,725	139,336	-	26,646	6	5
1 to 4 employees	565	76,532	988	10,861	7	6
5 to 9 employees	78	22,645	455	4,614	21	12
10 to 19 employees	19	11,516	242	2,594	-	-
20 to 49 employees	7	(D)	(D)	(D)	-	(D)
50 to 99 employees	2	(D)	(D)	(D)	-	(D)
100 employees or more	-	-	-	-	-	-

Source: *1987 Economic Censuses, Survey of Minority-Owned Business Enterprises: Hispanics*, U.S. Department of Commerce, Bureau of the Census, MB-87-2, 1991, pp. 86-87. *Notes:* A dash (-) represents zero. (D) stands for data withheld to avoid disclosing data for individual companies; data are included in higher-level totals. Detail may not add to total due to rounding. 1. Firms reported annual payroll, but did not report any employees on their payroll during specified period in 1987.

★ 694 ★

Hispanic-Owned Firms

Hispanic-Owned Firms, by Major Industry Group and Ethnicity, 1987 - I

This table is based on the 1972 Standard Industrial Classification (SIC) system.

Major industry group and minority	SIC code	All firms: Firms (number) A	All firms: Sales and receipts ($000) B	Firms with paid employees: Firms (number) C	Sales and receipts ($000) D	Employees (number) E	Annual payroll ($000) F	Relative standard error estimate (percent) for column A	B	C	D
All industries		422,373	24,731,600	82,908	17,729,432	264,846	3,243,342	-	-	1	-
Mexican		229,706	11,835,080	49,078	8,403,796	148,008	1,687,401	-	-	1	-
Puerto Rican		27,697	1,447,680	4,629	903,848	13,231	179,379	1	1	2	1
Cuban		61,470	5,481,974	10,768	4,227,065	47,266	638,459	1	-	1	-
Other Central or South American		66,356	3,202,238	10,793	2,031,768	27,386	343,039	1	1	2	1
European Spanish		24,755	2,054,537	5,299	1,628,133	21,196	293,976	1	1	2	1
Other Hispanic		12,389	710,091	2,341	534,822	7,759	101,088	2	1	4	1
Agricultural services, forestry, and fishing		16,365	694,937	3,331	479,658	14,449	163,569	1	1	3	2
Mexican		11,991	536,546	2,571	385,088	12,233	136,355	1	2	4	2
Puerto Rican		506	19,841	109	12,275	552	3,415	8	8	14	8
Cuban		1,550	50,608	193	26,424	502	7,606	4	6	13	9
Other Central or South American		1,281	38,396	221	22,442	617	7,867	6	9	12	12
European Spanish		706	36,964	165	24,394	437	5,854	7	8	13	10
Other Hispanic		331	12,582	72	9,035	108	2,472	12	10	23	13
Agricultural services	07	14,752	648,290	3,210	464,607	14,197	160,618	1	2	3	2
Mexican		11,182	509,845	2,488	374,531	12,020	133,933	1	2	4	2
Puerto Rican		454	19,123	107	(D)	(D)	(D)	9	8	14	(D)
Cuban		1,137	41,672	178	(D)	(D)	(D)	5	7	14	(D)
Other Hispanic		1,979	77,650	437	53,339	1,129	15,885	5	6	9	7
Forestry	08	184	8,263	45	6,065	195	1,882	-	-	-	-
Mexican		121	7,067	37	5,422	180	1,776	-	-	-	-
Puerto Rican		4	(D)	1	(D)	(D)	(D)	-	(D)	-	(D)
Cuban		12	256	3	(D)	(D)	(D)	-	-	-	(D)
Other Hispanic		47	(D)	4	371	11	62	-	(D)	-	-
Fishing, hunting, and trapping	09	1,429	38,384	76	8,986	57	1,069	3	3	13	4
Mexican		688	19,634	46	5,135	33	646	5	5	21	7

[Continued]

★ 694 ★

Hispanic-Owned Firms, by Major Industry Group and Ethnicity, 1987 - I

[Continued]

Major industry group and minority	SIC code	All firms: Firms (number) A	All firms: Sales and receipts ($000) B	Firms with paid employees: Firms (number) C	Firms with paid employees: Sales and receipts ($000) D	Firms with paid employees: Employees (number) E	Firms with paid employees: Annual payroll ($000) F	Relative standard error estimate (percent) for column A	B	C	D
Puerto Rican		48	(D)	1	(D)	(D)	(D)	27	(D)	-	(D)
Cuban		401	8,680	12	(D)	(D)	(D)	8	10	-	(D)
Other Hispanic		292	(D)	17	2,161	22	246	9	(D)	12	3
Mining		829	29,836	72	18,498	332	5,272	4	4	6	3
Mexican		578	22,556	59	16,165	309	4,895	5	3	7	3
Puerto Rican		34	1,479	-	-	-	-	31	66	-	-
Cuban		33	404	-	-	-	-	22	25	-	-
Other Central or South American		58	1,098	3	(D)	(D)	(D)	12	6	-	(D)
European Spanish		89	2,910	7	885	6	163	9	5	21	8
Other Hispanic		37	1,389	3	(D)	(D)	(D)	19	1	-	(D)
Metal mining	10	16	244	1	(D)	(D)	(D)	-	-	-	(D)
Mexican		6	(D)	-	-	-	-	-	(D)	-	-
Puerto Rican		-	-	-	-	-	-	-	-	-	-
Cuban		-	-	-	-	-	-	-	-	-	-
Other Hispanic		10	(D)	1	(D)	(D)	(D)	-	(D)	-	(D)
Anthracite mining	11	-	-	-	-	-	-	-	-	-	-
Mexican		-	-	-	-	-	-	-	-	-	-
Puerto Rican		-	-	-	-	-	-	-	-	-	-
Cuban		-	-	-	-	-	-	-	-	-	-
Other Hispanic		-	-	-	-	-	-	-	-	-	-
Bituminous coal and lignite mining	12	4	58	1	(D)	(D)	(D)	-	-	-	(D)
Mexican		2	(D)	-	-	-	-	-	(D)	-	-
Puerto Rican		-	-	-	-	-	-	-	-	-	-
Cuban		-	-	-	-	-	-	-	-	-	-
Other Hispanic		2	(D)	1	(D)	(D)	(D)	-	(D)	-	(D)
Oil and gas extraction	13	763	22,917	57	12,283	257	4,098	5	5	8	4
Mexican		538	17,536	50	11,559	252	3,941	6	4	8	4
Puerto Rican		32	(D)	-	-	-	-	33	(D)	-	-
Cuban		32	(D)	-	-	-	-	23	(D)	-	-
Other Hispanic		161	3,556	7	724	5	157	8	4	21	10
Nonmetallic minerals, except fuels	14	46	6,617	13	(D)	(D)	(D)	-	-	-	(D)
Mexican		32	4,952	9	4,606	57	954	-	-	-	-
Puerto Rican		2	(D)	-	-	-	-	-	(D)	-	-
Cuban		1	(D)	-	-	-	-	-	(D)	-	-
Other Hispanic		11	1,607	4	(D)	(D)	(D)	-	-	-	(D)
Construction		55,516	3,438,708	14,717	2,646,244	34,684	631,477	-	1	2	1
Mexican		34,143	1,929,246	9,958	1,496,811	21,499	375,221	1	1	2	1
Puerto Rican		2,671	152,982	597	106,373	1,161	27,306	4	2	7	2
Cuban		7,336	667,621	1,292	522,316	5,948	109,272	2	1	5	1
Other Central or South American		6,618	288,343	1,512	198,347	2,339	49,957	3	2	5	3
European Spanish		3,030	268,992	885	216,333	2,429	46,231	4	2	6	2
Other Hispanic		1,718	131,524	473	106,064	1,308	23,490	6	3	9	4
General building contractors	15	7,990	860,943	2,522	689,809	7,271	138,470	1	1	3	1
Mexican		4,661	381,109	1,493	300,704	3,570	67,311	2	2	5	2
Puerto Rican		444	42,644	125	29,050	299	7,031	8	4	9	4
Cuban		1,061	228,395	324	185,482	1,807	34,192	5	2	9	1
Other Hispanic		1,824	208,795	580	174,573	1,595	29,936	5	2	7	2
Heavy construction contractors	16	859	205,100	318	192,606	2,137	39,942	2	1	5	1
Mexican		614	102,146	235	94,812	1,207	20,973	4	1	6	1
Puerto Rican		15	5,020	5	(D)	(D)	(D)	-	-	-	(D)
Cuban		71	50,959	24	49,229	584	9,142	11	-	-	-
Other Hispanic		159	46,975	54	(D)	(D)	(D)	10	2	12	(D)
Special trade contractors	17	46,383	2,266,204	11,803	1,691,285	25,032	446,520	1	1	2	1
Mexican		28,715	1,415,907	8,205	1,086,326	16,662	285,203	1	1	2	1

[Continued]

★ 694 ★

Hispanic-Owned Firms, by Major Industry Group and Ethnicity, 1987 - I

[Continued]

Major industry group and minority	SIC code	All firms: Firms (number) A	All firms: Sales and receipts ($000) B	Firms with paid employees: Firms (number) C	Firms with paid employees: Sales and receipts ($000) D	Firms with paid employees: Employees (number) E	Firms with paid employees: Annual payroll ($000) F	Relative standard error estimate (percent) for column: A	B	C	D
Puerto Rican		2,195	103,036	463	72,101	849	19,384	5	3	9	3
Cuban		6,154	328,837	914	237,062	3,417	61,858	2	2	6	2
Other Hispanic		9,319	418,424	2,221	295,796	4,104	80,075	2	2	4	3
Subdividers and developers, n.e.c.	6552	284	106,461	74	72,544	244	6,545	2	1	4	1
Mexican		153	30,084	25	14,969	60	1,734	4	3	6	3
Puerto Rican		17	2,282	4	(D)	(D)	(D)	9	1	-	(D)
Cuban		50	59,430	30	50,543	140	4,080	6	1	8	-
Other Hispanic		64	14,665	15	(D)	(D)	(D)	3	2	-	(D)
Manufacturing		11,090	1,449,913	3,760	1,308,124	26,261	333,969	1	-	2	-
Mexican		5,969	576,508	2,040	502,304	12,069	138,936	2	1	3	1
Puerto Rican		662	120,443	226	111,798	1,559	22,864	5	2	7	2
Cuban		1,545	393,819	549	374,019	6,345	88,061	3	1	4	-
Other Central or South American		1,794	170,141	615	148,306	4,198	44,353	4	2	5	2
European Spanish		753	151,016	250	140,899	1,595	32,470	5	1	6	1
Other Hispanic		367	37,986	80	30,798	495	7,285	9	3	8	2

Source: *1987 Economic Censuses, Survey of Minority-Owned Business Enterprises: Hispanics*, U.S. Department of Commerce, Bureau of the Census, MB-87-2, 1991, pp. 12-17. *Notes:* A dash (-) represents zero. A (D) stands for data withheld to avoid disclosing data for individual companies; data are included in higher level totals.

★ 695 ★

Hispanic-Owned Firms

Hispanic-Owned Firms, by Major Industry Group and Ethnicity, 1987 - II

This table is based on the 1972 Standard Industrial Classification (SIC) system.

Major industry group and minority	SIC code	All firms: Firms (number) A	All firms: Sales and receipts ($000) B	Firms with paid employees: Firms (number) C	Firms with paid employees: Sales and receipts ($000) D	Firms with paid employees: Employees (number) E	Firms with paid employees: Annual payroll ($000) F	Relative standard error estimate (percent) for column: A	B	C	D
Food and kindred products	20	589	151,632	240	140,141	2,100	23,442	3	1	2	1
Mexican		386	83,839	173	75,567	1,465	14,557	4	2	4	1
Puerto Rican		15	1,693	3	(D)	(D)	(D)	13	1	-	(D)
Cuban		52	51,969	23	50,818	367	6,714	9	-	6	-
Other Hispanic		136	14,131	41	(D)	(D)	(D)	10	1	10	(D)
Tobacco manufacturers	21	7	860	7	860	32	180	-	-	-	-
Mexican		-	-	-	-	-	-	-	-	-	-
Puerto Rican		-	-	-	-	-	-	-	-	-	-
Cuban		7	860	7	860	32	180	-	-	-	-
Other Hispanic		-	-	-	-	-	-	-	-	-	-
Textile mill products	22	188	21,361	56	18,894	437	5,229	1	-	-	-
Mexican		60	3,203	16	2,455	47	727	-	-	-	-
Puerto Rican		15	3,090	5	(D)	(D)	(D)	-	-	-	(D)
Cuban		52	7,064	16	6,663	193	2,203	-	-	-	-
Other Hispanic		61	8,004	19	(D)	(D)	(D)	2	-	-	(D)
Apparel and other textile products	23	1,713	278,810	833	267,198	10,294	84,350	2	1	4	1
Mexican		707	81,948	370	77,878	4,158	30,589	5	3	7	3
Puerto Rican		87	55,583	44	54,824	573	7,667	14	-	5	-
Cuban		413	72,963	190	70,049	2,679	22,376	7	2	7	2
Other Hispanic		506	68,316	229	64,447	2,884	23,718	8	4	8	4
Lumber and wood products	24	840	86,082	250	74,287	1,410	17,883	3	2	5	2
Mexican		507	43,967	158	36,128	716	7,492	4	3	8	4
Puerto Rican		40	7,630	20	7,327	159	2,714	10	1	14	1

[Continued]

★ 695 ★

Hispanic-Owned Firms, by Major Industry Group and Ethnicity, 1987 - II

[Continued]

Major industry group and minority	SIC code	All firms: Firms (number) A	All firms: Sales and receipts ($000) B	Firms with paid employees: Firms (number) C	Firms with paid employees: Sales and receipts ($000) D	Firms with paid employees: Employees (number) E	Firms with paid employees: Annual payroll ($000) F	Relative standard error estimate (percent) for column A	B	C	D
Cuban		63	12,928	23	11,558	216	3,294	10	1	-	-
Other Hispanic		230	21,557	49	19,274	319	4,383	8	1	9	1
Furniture and fixtures	25	657	88,946	249	80,165	1,617	19,810	3	1	5	1
Mexican		336	48,915	112	44,168	926	9,773	6	2	8	1
Puerto Rican		31	3,572	11	3,090	60	644	19	4	-	-
Cuban		141	22,738	60	20,494	406	5,681	9	4	10	4
Other Hispanic		149	13,721	66	12,413	225	3,712	9	5	13	6
Paper and allied products	26	87	11,499	19	10,553	111	1,742	-	-	-	-
Mexican		50	1,833	10	1,297	30	287	-	-	-	-
Puerto Rican		5	(D)	1	(D)	(D)	(D)	-	(D)	-	(D)
Cuban		13	4,870	4	(D)	(D)	(D)	-	-	-	(D)
Other Hispanic		19	(D)	4	(D)	(D)	(D)	-	(D)	-	(D)
Printing and publishing	27	1,886	179,062	575	158,977	2,409	41,942	3	2	5	2
Mexican		1,065	101,581	313	91,953	1,456	26,515	5	3	8	3
Puerto Rican		147	15,881	50	13,329	171	2,850	13	12	20	14
Cuban		256	26,663	64	23,478	381	6,218	9	3	6	2
Other Hispanic		418	34,937	148	30,217	401	6,359	8	3	8	4
Chemicals and allied products	28	72	20,157	28	19,432	179	3,135	-	-	-	-
Mexican		26	(D)	10	5,027	96	1,762	-	(D)	-	-
Puerto Rican		3	(D)	1	(D)	(D)	(D)	-	(D)	-	(D)
Cuban		18	6,555	8	6,373	38	511	-	-	-	-
Other Hispanic		25	6,747	9	(D)	(D)	(D)	-	-	-	(D)
Petroleum and coal products	29	3	(D)	2	(D)	(D)	(D)	-	(D)	-	(D)
Mexican		-	-	-	-	-	-	-	-	-	-
Puerto Rican		1	(D)	-	-	-	-	-	(D)	-	-
Cuban		1	(D)	1	(D)	(D)	(D)	-	(D)	-	(D)
Other Hispanic		1	(D)	1	(D)	(D)	(D)	-	(D)	-	(D)
Rubber and miscellaneous plastics products	30	176	50,765	62	48,960	698	12,891	-	-	-	-
Mexican		101	(D)	30	7,743	177	2,586	-	(D)	-	-
Puerto Rican		8	(D)	4	(D)	(D)	(D)	-	(D)	-	(D)
Cuban		26	31,460	12	31,205	353	7,721	-	-	-	-
Other Hispanic		41	7,087	16	(D)	(D)	(D)	-	-	-	(D)
Leather and leather products	31	194	22,108	53	20,053	362	5,038	-	-	-	-
Mexican		102	3,424	31	2,435	65	685	-	-	-	-
Puerto Rican		11	454	2	(D)	(D)	(D)	-	-	-	(D)
Cuban		23	(D)	6	(D)	(D)	(D)	-	(D)	-	(D)
Other Hispanic		58	(D)	14	(D)	(D)	(D)	-	(D)	-	(D)
Stone, clay, and glass products	32	400	38,880	106	33,782	370	7,203	3	1	5	1
Mexican		249	17,237	66	14,098	222	3,222	5	3	6	1
Puerto Rican		25	717	5	(D)	(D)	(D)	12	12	28	(D)
Cuban		38	3,792	10	(D)	(D)	(D)	10	2	19	(D)
Other Hispanic		88	17,134	25	15,895	95	3,033	6	1	-	-
Primary metal industries	33	104	53,897	32	(D)	(D)	(D)	-	-	-	(D)
Mexican		72	(D)	23	2,707	33	506	-	(D)	-	-
Puerto Rican		1	(D)	-	-	-	-	-	(D)	-	-
Cuban		7	(D)	1	(D)	(D)	(D)	-	(D)	-	(D)
Other Hispanic		24	(D)	8	(D)	(D)	(D)	-	(D)	-	(D)
Fabricated metal products	34	1,140	107,976	386	91,969	1,792	28,303	2	2	7	2
Mexican		734	60,571	232	50,450	1,022	15,411	5	3	9	3
Puerto Rican		61	9,470	31	9,206	138	2,488	22	5	30	5
Cuban		66	8,849	20	8,014	196	3,429	17	2	-	-
Other Hispanic		279	29,086	103	24,299	436	6,975	10	5	15	3

[Continued]

★ 695 ★

Hispanic-Owned Firms, by Major Industry Group and Ethnicity, 1987 - II

[Continued]

Major industry group and minority	SIC code	All firms: Firms (number) A	All firms: Sales and receipts ($000) B	Firms with paid employees: Firms (number) C	Firms with paid employees: Sales and receipts ($000) D	Firms with paid employees: Employees (number) E	Firms with paid employees: Annual payroll ($000) F	Relative standard error estimate (percent) for column: A	B	C	D
Machinery, except electrical	35	1,148	120,136	420	104,482	1,521	27,146	3	2	7	2
Mexican		704	48,105	264	38,081	651	10,350	5	4	10	3
Puerto Rican		37	7,471	17	6,974	191	3,036	13	1	-	-
Cuban		85	34,128	32	33,250	306	5,846	15	1	24	1
Other Hispanic		322	30,432	107	26,177	373	7,914	9	5	12	5
Electric and electronic equipment	36	295	39,990	67	37,233	670	13,168	1	-	-	-
Mexican		148	22,595	35	21,225	483	7,833	2	-	-	-
Puerto Rican		26	1,291	3	(D)	(D)	(D)	-	-	-	(D)
Cuban		31	13,486	11	(D)	(D)	(D)	-	-	-	(D)
Other Hispanic		90	2,618	18	1,838	23	331	3	2	-	-
Transportation equipment	37	129	74,747	66	70,875	938	17,821	-	-	-	-
Mexican		57	7,858	31	7,103	147	1,938	-	-	-	-
Puerto Rican		9	1,042	4	890	16	173	-	-	-	-
Cuban		35	40,987	17	40,738	422	8,871	-	-	-	-
Other Hispanic		28	24,860	14	22,144	353	6,839	-	-	-	-
Instruments and related products	38	68	5,581	21	(D)	(D)	(D)	-	-	-	(D)
Mexican		26	2,994	10	2,695	31	486	-	-	-	-
Puerto Rican		8	509	2	(D)	(D)	(D)	-	-	-	(D)
Cuban		8	309	3	(D)	(D)	(D)	-	-	-	(D)
Other Hispanic		26	1,769	6	1,247	17	202	-	-	-	-
Miscellaneous manufacturing industries	39	1,394	(D)	288	53,451	858	11,821	3	(D)	7	3
Mexican		639	30,660	156	21,294	344	4,217	6	5	11	6
Puerto Rican		132	6,041	23	4,392	85	1,167	15	7	23	4
Cuban		210	16,184	41	12,016	214	2,431	12	10	18	2
Other Hispanic		413	(D)	68	15,749	215	4,006	9	(D)	14	4

Source: 1987 Economic Censuses, Survey of Minority-Owned Business Enterprises: Hispanics, U.S. Department of Commerce, Bureau of the Census, MB-87-2, 1991, pp. 12-17. *Notes:* A dash (-) represents zero. A (D) stands for data withheld to avoid disclosing data for individual companies; data are included in higher level totals.

★ 696 ★

Hispanic-Owned Firms

Hispanic-Owned Firms, by Major Industry Group and Ethnicity, 1987 - III

This table is based on the 1972 Standard Industrial Classification (SIC) system.

Major industry group and minority	SIC code	All firms: Firms (number) A	All firms: Sales and receipts ($000) B	Firms with paid employees: Firms (number) C	Firms with paid employees: Sales and receipts ($000) D	Firms with paid employees: Employees (number) E	Firms with paid employees: Annual payroll ($000) F	Relative standard error estimate (percent) for column: A	B	C	D
Transportation and public utilities		26,955	1,380,981	3,989	725,484	8,006	135,592	1	1	3	1
Mexican		13,131	669,222	2,514	362,112	4,258	71,409	1	2	4	2
Puerto Rican		2,131	110,127	222	61,070	690	11,819	4	3	10	2
Cuban		4,545	248,410	403	128,298	1,390	24,011	2	2	8	2
Other Central or South American		5,468	246,841	578	109,745	774	14,853	3	3	8	3
European Spanish		1,073	79,050	151	49,751	698	10,854	6	3	9	2
Other Hispanic		607	27,331	121	14,508	196	2,646	9	7	18	5
Local and interurban passenger transit	41	4,522	105,763	260	20,340	744	6,188	2	2	10	3
Mexican		996	24,481	105	8,126	330	2,781	5	4	15	4
Puerto Rican		733	17,385	30	(D)	(D)	(D)	7	7	28	(D)
Cuban		734	13,893	35	(D)	(D)	(D)	6	7	29	(D)
Other Hispanic		2,059	50,004	90	7,818	251	2,274	4	4	17	6

[Continued]

★ 696 ★

Hispanic-Owned Firms, by Major Industry Group and Ethnicity, 1987 - III

[Continued]

Major industry group and minority	SIC code	All firms: Firms (number) A	All firms: Sales and receipts ($000) B	Firms with paid employees: Firms (number) C	Firms with paid employees: Sales and receipts ($000) D	Firms with paid employees: Employees (number) E	Firms with paid employees: Annual payroll ($000) F	Relative standard error estimate (percent) for column A	B	C	D
Trucking and warehousing	42	17,304	906,583	2,936	426,794	4,499	85,692	1	1	4	2
Mexican		9,994	521,556	2,060	266,971	2,832	52,775	1	2	5	3
Puerto Rican		926	47,260	109	19,930	307	6,416	7	5	16	5
Cuban		2,885	147,486	223	53,247	500	8,777	3	4	13	4
Other Hispanic		3,499	190,281	544	86,646	860	17,724	4	3	9	4
Water transportation	44	156	19,598	40	17,539	327	4,223	3	-	-	-
Mexican		66	6,051	13	4,863	83	958	5	1	-	-
Puerto Rican		11	1,930	5	(D)	(D)	(D)	-	-	-	(D)
Cuban		33	(D)	9	(D)	(D)	(D)	-	(D)	-	(D)
Other Hispanic		46	(D)	13	2,530	19	239	5	(D)	-	-
Transportation, by air	45	222	10,895	23	4,022	67	1,116	2	-	-	-
Mexican		69	1,690	8	606	13	109	-	-	-	-
Puerto Rican		26	234	-	-	-	-	-	-	-	-
Cuban		51	3,205	8	2,390	37	882	-	-	-	-
Other Hispanic		76	5,766	7	1,026	17	125	5	-	-	-
Pipelines, except natural gas	46	-	-	-	-	-	-	-	-	-	-
Mexican		-	-	-	-	-	-	-	-	-	-
Puerto Rican		-	-	-	-	-	-	-	-	-	-
Cuban		-	-	-	-	-	-	-	-	-	-
Other Hispanic		-	-	-	-	-	-	-	-	-	-
Transportation services	47	3,617	284,684	542	219,512	1,683	25,970	2	1	4	1
Mexican		1,385	85,788	203	61,945	589	9,142	4	2	8	2
Puerto Rican		337	37,736	59	32,427	165	2,394	8	2	12	2
Cuban		674	63,801	103	53,167	463	7,297	5	2	7	2
Other Hispanic		1,221	97,359	177	71,973	466	7,137	4	2	7	1
Communication	48	756	38,852	115	28,851	533	10,451	4	2	16	1
Mexican		371	18,528	64	13,408	284	4,028	8	4	20	3
Puerto Rican		81	5,314	17	4,509	93	1,953	19	2	47	1
Cuban		131	10,752	24	8,948	120	3,882	13	2	43	2
Other Hispanic		173	4,258	10	1,986	36	588	14	4	-	-
Electric, gas, and sanitary services	49	378	14,606	73	8,426	153	1,952	4	3	11	4
Mexican		250	11,128	61	6,193	127	1,616	4	4	13	5
Puerto Rican		17	268	2	(D)	(D)	(D)	25	2	-	(D)
Cuban		37	(D)	1	(D)	(D)	(D)	14	(D)	-	(D)
Other Hispanic		74	(D)	9	2,025	19	266	15	(D)	-	-
Wholesale trade		10,154	2,445,416	2,309	1,991,736	9,119	157,537	1	-	2	-
Mexican		4,467	835,716	1,103	649,209	3,928	58,189	2	1	3	1
Puerto Rican		650	92,259	108	57,653	297	4,524	6	4	8	3
Cuban		2,376	969,712	580	855,883	3,065	62,267	2	1	3	1
Other Central or South American		1,720	287,656	299	209,373	874	15,030	4	2	6	2
European Spanish		651	187,654	154	158,584	671	12,867	6	1	6	1
Other Hispanic		290	72,419	65	61,034	284	4,660	9	2	12	1
Wholesale trade - durable goods	50	5,080	1,056,969	1,218	851,385	4,744	84,530	1	1	2	1
Mexican		2,261	324,766	603	246,216	1,974	30,863	3	1	4	1
Puerto Rican		296	35,765	58	20,042	169	2,960	8	6	12	9
Cuban		1,117	424,380	307	373,488	1,645	32,935	4	1	5	1
Other Hispanic		1,406	272,058	250	211,639	956	17,772	4	1	5	1
Wholesale trade - nondurable goods	51	5,074	1,388,447	1,091	1,140,351	4,375	73,007	1	1	3	-
Mexican		2,206	510,950	500	402,993	1,954	27,326	2	1	4	1
Puerto Rican		354	56,494	50	37,611	128	1,564	8	4	11	2
Cuban		1,259	545,332	273	482,395	1,420	29,332	3	1	4	1
Other Hispanic		1,255	275,671	268	217,352	873	14,785	4	2	6	2
Retail trade		69,911	7,643,850	20,348	6,095,890	90,584	745,662	-	-	1	-
Mexican		40,900	3,793,339	12,495	3,000,839	54,510	408,017	1	1	1	1

[Continued]

★ 696 ★

Hispanic-Owned Firms, by Major Industry Group and Ethnicity, 1987 - III

[Continued]

Major industry group and minority	SIC code	All firms		Firms with paid employees				Relative standard error estimate (percent) for column			
		Firms (number) A	Sales and receipts ($000) B	Firms (number) C	Sales and receipts ($000) D	Employees (number) E	Annual payroll ($000) F	A	B	C	D
Puerto Rican		5,044	452,868	1,244	283,108	3,744	31,886	2	2	3	2
Cuban		8,940	1,621,807	2,515	1,384,101	14,575	142,378	2	1	2	1
Other Central or South American		9,504	910,552	2,251	669,556	8,147	71,535	2	1	3	1
European Spanish		3,571	680,111	1,269	610,022	7,149	73,195	3	1	4	1
Other Hispanic		1,952	185,173	574	148,264	2,459	18,651	5	3	6	3
Building materials and garden supplies	52	1,331	160,841	468	132,177	1,341	16,137	2	2	4	2
Mexican		776	84,154	268	69,990	761	8,751	4	3	5	2
Puerto Rican		82	7,596	32	5,913	66	753	15	6	11	3
Cuban		228	46,299	79	38,882	346	4,712	9	3	5	2
Other Hispanic		245	22,792	89	17,392	168	1,921	10	8	14	10
General merchandise stores	53	1,152	54,795	146	30,974	406	3,237	3	2	10	2
Mexican		523	23,870	71	14,102	244	1,396	7	4	13	3
Puerto Rican		131	6,581	21	2,999	36	288	14	4	25	2
Cuban		182	10,893	27	6,383	75	1,000	13	5	35	3
Other Hispanic		316	13,451	27	7,490	51	553	11	4	10	1
Food stores	54	9,599	1,835,802	3,569	1,383,998	14,010	118,064	1	1	2	1
Mexican		4,987	916,889	2,042	718,779	7,483	60,646	2	1	3	1
Puerto Rican		1,450	176,218	367	86,356	854	7,935	4	3	7	3
Cuban		1,237	422,727	490	361,021	3,440	31,380	4	1	4	1
Other Hispanic		1,925	319,968	670	217,842	2,233	18,103	4	2	5	2
Automotive dealers and service stations	55	5,627	2,100,213	2,475	1,853,478	9,378	128,153	1	-	2	-
Mexican		3,323	801,203	1,394	652,148	4,100	45,491	2	1	3	1
Puerto Rican		309	86,561	141	70,069	403	4,106	7	3	7	3
Cuban		845	527,209	437	496,802	2,218	30,272	4	1	3	1
Other Hispanic		1,150	685,240	503	634,459	2,657	48,284	4	1	4	1
Apparel and accessory stores	56	3,472	230,806	1,021	165,431	2,651	21,258	2	2	3	2
Mexican		1,834	101,954	549	71,745	1,318	9,190	3	3	4	3
Puerto Rican		193	10,666	58	6,252	107	958	10	7	14	10
Cuban		572	61,262	176	49,388	598	6,037	5	3	6	3
Other Hispanic		873	56,924	238	38,046	628	5,073	5	3	6	3
Furniture and home furnishings stores	57	2,992	349,024	979	279,512	2,771	34,466	1	1	3	1
Mexican		1,632	162,942	507	124,159	1,319	14,948	2	2	4	2
Puerto Rican		228	20,609	63	15,325	179	2,132	7	6	11	6
Cuban		438	88,206	170	79,665	751	10,531	5	2	7	2
Other Hispanic		694	77,267	239	60,363	522	6,855	5	3	6	3
Eating and drinking places	58	14,003	1,645,412	7,872	1,449,268	50,662	330,987	1	1	1	1
Mexican		9,594	1,094,667	5,555	971,182	34,334	221,509	1	1	2	1
Puerto Rican		682	63,824	303	50,639	1,654	10,535	6	3	7	3
Cuban		1,104	192,338	570	166,609	5,374	37,861	5	2	6	2
Other Hispanic		2,623	294,583	1,444	260,838	9,300	61,082	3	2	4	2
Miscellaneous retail	59	31,735	1,266,957	3,818	801,052	9,365	93,360	1	1	3	1
Mexican		18,231	607,660	2,109	378,734	4,951	46,086	1	2	4	2
Puerto Rican		1,969	80,813	259	45,555	445	5,179	4	6	8	9
Cuban		4,334	272,873	566	185,351	1,773	20,585	3	2	5	3
Other Hispanic		7,201	305,611	884	191,412	2,196	21,510	3	3	6	3

Source: *1987 Economic Censuses, Survey of Minority-Owned Business Enterprises: Hispanics*, U.S. Department of Commerce, Bureau of the Census, MB-87-2, 1991, pp. 12-17. *Notes:* A dash (-) represents zero. A (D) stands for data withheld to avoid disclosing data for individual companies; data are included in higher level totals.

★ 697 ★

Hispanic-Owned Firms

Hispanic-Owned Firms, by Major Industry Group and Ethnicity, 1987 - IV

This table is based on the 1972 Standard Industrial Classification (SIC) system.

Major industry group and minority	SIC code	All firms: Firms (number)	All firms: Sales and receipts ($000)	Firms with paid employees: Firms (number)	Firms with paid employees: Sales and receipts ($000)	Firms with paid employees: Employees (number)	Firms with paid employees: Annual payroll ($000)	Relative standard error estimate (percent) for column			
		A	B	C	D	E	F	A	B	C	D
Finance, insurance, and real estate		22,106	864,282	2,236	433,851	4,960	80,882	1	1	2	1
Mexican		10,271	301,681	1,050	131,716	1,940	25,001	1	2	4	2
Puerto Rican		1,758	55,465	150	25,257	313	6,325	4	3	9	4
Cuban		4,077	275,026	482	167,067	1,416	22,048	2	1	5	1
Other Central or South American		3,309	115,681	265	45,928	349	8,023	3	3	8	4
European Spanish		2,021	100,022	249	58,143	864	18,493	4	3	9	2
Other Hispanic		670	16,407	40	5,740	78	992	7	7	14	8
Banking	60	34	13,858	31	(D)	(D)	(D)	-	-	-	(D)
Mexican		18	5,617	17	(D)	(D)	(D)	-	-	-	(D)
Puerto Rican		9	7,058	7	(D)	(D)	(D)	-	-	-	(D)
Cuban		2	(D)	2	(D)	(D)	(D)	-	(D)	-	(D)
Other Hispanic		5	(D)	5	(D)	(D)	(D)	-	(D)	-	(D)
Credit agencies, other than banks	61	91	10,925	78	10,507	175	2,595	-	-	-	-
Mexican		40	4,585	36	(D)	(D)	(D)	-	-	-	(D)
Puerto Rican		7	(D)	4	(D)	(D)	(D)	-	(D)	-	(D)
Cuban		33	4,386	30	4,343	65	1,012	-	-	-	-
Other Hispanic		11	(D)	8	1,295	10	162	-	(D)	-	-
Security commodity brokers and services	62	525	89,792	67	69,857	173	12,707	4	1	12	1
Mexican		207	6,247	31	(D)	(D)	(D)	7	9	15	(D)
Puerto Rican		63	(D)	4	(D)	(D)	(D)	15	(D)	-	(D)
Cuban		91	(D)	12	(D)	(D)	(D)	11	(D)	21	(D)
Other Hispanic		164	31,952	20	27,108	118	10,802	10	2	30	-
Insurance carriers	63	33	5,086	15	4,567	71	1,115	-	-	-	-
Mexican		5	(D)	4	427	9	105	-	(D)	-	-
Puerto Rican		1	(D)	1	(D)	(D)	(D)	-	(D)	-	(D)
Cuban		22	3,208	5	(D)	(D)	(D)	-	-	-	(D)
Other Hispanic		5	944	5	944	29	461	-	-	-	-
Insurance agents, brokers, and service	64	6,013	209,229	926	122,195	1,668	24,434	2	2	4	2
Mexican		3,107	96,483	487	53,829	856	11,303	3	3	5	3
Puerto Rican		400	14,104	46	7,357	65	1,279	8	8	18	8
Cuban		945	44,139	166	29,965	426	6,588	5	4	8	5
Other Hispanic		1,561	54,503	227	31,044	321	5,264	5	5	11	5
Real estate[1]	65	12,872	472,278	971	203,480	2,611	35,073	1	1	3	1
Mexican		5,752	160,688	391	58,153	842	9,880	2	2	6	3
Puerto Rican		1,068	26,509	80	10,706	156	2,744	5	5	12	7
Cuban		2,506	160,113	248	88,832	839	12,422	3	2	7	2
Other Hispanic		3,546	124,968	252	45,789	774	10,027	3	3	7	3
Combined real estate, insurance, etc.	66	2,509	59,371	142	9,570	99	1,695	2	3	11	9
Mexican		1,127	24,961	82	5,765	69	1,067	4	5	16	13
Puerto Rican		209	4,865	8	323	-	36	8	12	43	16
Cuban		471	12,607	17	1,220	10	235	6	8	25	6
Other Hispanic		702	16,938	35	2,262	20	357	5	6	20	18
Holding and other investment offices[2]	67	29	3,743	6	(D)	(D)	(D)	-	-	-	(D)
Mexican		15	(D)	2	(D)	(D)	(D)	-	(D)	-	(D)
Puerto Rican		1	(D)	-	-	-	-	-	(D)	-	-
Cuban		7	469	2	(D)	(D)	(D)	-	-	-	(D)
Other Hispanic		6	(D)	2	(D)	(D)	(D)	-	(D)	-	(D)
Services		184,372	6,031,406	29,750	3,774,117	74,427	941,588	-	-	1	1
Mexican		95,683	2,782,169	15,825	1,707,680	36,051	438,731	1	1	1	1
Puerto Rican		12,508	397,097	1,835	233,389	4,786	69,147	2	2	4	2
Cuban		27,033	1,120,069	4,456	729,996	13,713	176,407	1	1	2	1
Other Central or South American		32,004	1,018,906	4,773	601,461	9,901	127,264	1	1	3	2
European Spanish		11,577	509,688	2,066	355,871	7,232	92,119	2	2	4	2
Other Hispanic		5,567	203,477	795	145,720	2,744	37,920	3	2	6	2

[Continued]

★ 697 ★

Hispanic-Owned Firms, by Major Industry Group and Ethnicity, 1987 - IV

[Continued]

Major industry group and minority	SIC code	All firms: Firms (number) A	All firms: Sales and receipts ($000) B	Firms with paid employees: Firms (number) C	Firms with paid employees: Sales and receipts ($000) D	Firms with paid employees: Employees (number) E	Firms with paid employees: Annual payroll ($000) F	Relative standard error estimate (percent) for column A	B	C	D
Hotels and lodging places	70	973	112,551	315	92,996	2,284	23,342	4	1	6	1
Mexican		486	39,012	155	29,796	970	7,238	5	3	7	2
Puerto Rican		49	4,318	19	3,647	96	952	14	8	27	9
Cuban		125	6,193	26	4,557	106	809	11	3	-	-
Other Hispanic		313	63,028	115	54,996	1,112	14,343	8	2	12	2
Personal services	72	44,872	893,064	6,111	430,645	13,688	129,379	1	1	2	2
Mexican		25,406	518,239	3,647	259,525	8,331	79,785	1	2	3	2
Puerto Rican		2,739	53,872	364	23,123	777	7,374	4	5	8	8
Cuban		6,034	115,381	707	53,972	1,647	15,538	2	3	6	3
Other Hispanic		10,693	205,572	1,393	94,025	2,933	26,682	2	3	5	3
Business services	73	59,948	1,419,790	6,716	747,056	18,979	235,949	1	1	2	1
Mexican		30,377	660,982	3,838	343,627	8,707	103,138	1	2	3	2
Puerto Rican		4,104	114,007	447	64,259	1,812	28,946	3	3	9	3
Cuban		8,112	252,790	700	142,144	3,682	44,329	2	2	5	2
Other Hispanic		17,355	392,011	1,731	197,026	4,778	59,536	2	2	5	3
Auto repair, services, and garages	75	15,824	836,738	4,522	622,052	9,749	139,178	1	1	2	1
Mexican		9,391	507,104	2,928	387,859	6,357	92,383	2	2	3	2
Puerto Rican		803	36,304	185	24,301	326	4,450	7	6	12	8
Cuban		2,083	92,017	429	63,865	1,032	13,123	4	3	6	3
Other Hispanic		3,547	201,313	980	146,027	2,034	29,222	4	3	6	3
Miscellaneous repair services	76	8,337	302,456	1,837	193,150	3,130	43,812	1	2	4	2
Mexican		4,842	173,335	1,126	111,280	1,802	24,273	2	3	5	4
Puerto Rican		498	17,879	120	10,369	170	2,676	8	8	15	10
Cuban		1,170	51,211	247	34,333	607	8,169	5	5	11	5
Other Hispanic		1,827	60,031	344	37,168	551	8,694	5	4	10	5
Motion pictures	78	694	24,880	107	14,278	344	2,877	3	3	7	2
Mexican		318	11,741	59	7,544	147	1,181	6	4	9	3
Puerto Rican		58	2,083	6	1,297	33	408	13	7	-	-
Cuban		98	2,689	11	922	20	267	9	11	22	5
Other Hispanic		220	8,367	31	4,515	144	1,021	7	7	14	3

Source: 1987 Economic Censuses, Survey of Minority-Owned Business Enterprises: Hispanics, U.S. Department of Commerce, Bureau of the Census, MB-87-2, 1991, pp. 12-17. *Notes:* A dash (-) represents zero. A (D) stands for data withheld to avoid disclosing data for individual companies; data are included in higher level totals. 1. Excludes 6552 which is included in construction industries. 2. Excludes 673 (Trusts) and 679 (Miscellaneous investing).

★ 698 ★

Hispanic-Owned Firms

Hispanic-Owned Firms, by Major Industry Group and Ethnicity, 1987 - V

This table is based on the 1972 Standard Industrial Classification (SIC) system.

Major industry group and minority	SIC code	All firms: Firms (number) A	All firms: Sales and receipts ($000) B	Firms with paid employees: Firms (number) C	Firms with paid employees: Sales and receipts ($000) D	Firms with paid employees: Employees (number) E	Firms with paid employees: Annual payroll ($000) F	Relative standard error estimate (percent) for column A	B	C	D
Amusement and recreation services	79	9,528	203,812	800	89,891	1,518	19,948	2	3	8	4
Mexican		5,295	90,083	455	32,857	678	7,764	2	3	11	6
Puerto Rican		855	26,316	98	16,931	214	3,793	7	7	25	10
Cuban		1,021	38,466	78	22,065	231	3,715	7	7	20	8
Other Hispanic		2,357	48,947	169	18,038	395	4,676	5	7	14	10
Health services	80	16,322	1,326,215	5,089	999,789	13,982	197,965	1	1	2	1
Mexican		5,424	384,362	1,531	284,654	4,143	59,023	3	2	4	3

[Continued]

★ 698 ★

Hispanic-Owned Firms, by Major Industry Group and Ethnicity, 1987 - V

[Continued]

Major industry group and minority	SIC code	All firms: Firms (number) A	All firms: Sales and receipts ($000) B	Firms with paid employees: Firms (number) C	Firms with paid employees: Sales and receipts ($000) D	Firms with paid employees: Employees (number) E	Firms with paid employees: Annual payroll ($000) F	Relative standard error estimate (percent) for column A	B	C	D
Puerto Rican		314	20,105	102	13,529	149	2,675	7	6	9	7
Cuban		589	55,445	248	46,336	547	9,528	4	3	5	3
Other Hispanic		891	63,740	282	45,883	504	9,128	4	4	6	4
Legal services	81	3,690	286,713	1,356	216,577	2,545	41,187	1	1	2	2
Mexican		1,896	147,423	724	110,829	1,345	19,856	2	2	3	2
Puerto Rican		314	20,105	102	13,529	149	2,675	7	6	9	7
Cuban		589	55,445	248	46,336	547	9,528	4	3	5	3
Other Hispanic		891	63,740	282	45,883	504	9,128	4	4	6	4
Educational services	82	2,797	54,119	157	36,409	975	10,684	2	1	6	1
Mexican		1,256	18,216	73	10,874	169	2,075	3	2	10	1
Puerto Rican		272	2,572	12	702	20	222	9	8	-	-
Cuban		391	23,077	18	(D)	(D)	(D)	6	1	-	(D)
Other Hispanic		878	10,254	54	(D)	(D)	(D)	4	4	12	(D)
Social services	83	8,840	100,321	697	45,344	1,886	13,215	2	2	7	4
Mexican		5,496	56,772	427	24,708	1,011	7,109	3	4	10	6
Puerto Rican		535	5,310	22	1,528	58	408	8	7	9	7
Cuban		589	11,481	62	(D)	(D)	(D)	9	4	6	(D)
Other Hispanic		2,220	26,758	186	(D)	(D)	(D)	5	5	14	(D)
Museums, botanical, zoological gardens	84	-	-	-	-	-	-	-	-	-	-
Mexican		-	-	-	-	-	-	-	-	-	-
Puerto Rican		-	-	-	-	-	-	-	-	-	-
Cuban		-	-	-	-	-	-	-	-	-	-
Other Hispanic		-	-	-	-	-	-	-	-	-	-
Miscellaneous services	89	12,547	470,747	2,043	285,930	5,347	84,052	1	1	3	1
Mexican		5,496	174,900	862	104,127	2,391	34,906	2	2	6	2
Puerto Rican		739	28,896	116	16,778	266	6,142	7	10	13	6
Cuban		2,816	130,903	561	82,921	1,514	24,050	3	3	5	3
Other Hispanic		3,496	136,048	504	82,104	1,176	18,954	3	3	7	3
Industries not classified		25,075	752,271	2,396	255,830	2,024	47,794	1	2	4	3
Mexican		12,573	388,097	1,463	151,872	1,211	30,647	2	3	6	5
Puerto Rican		1,733	45,119	138	12,925	129	2,093	5	5	15	10
Cuban		4,035	134,498	298	38,961	312	6,409	3	4	12	7
Other Central or South American		4,600	124,624	276	26,423	185	4,119	3	4	11	6
European Spanish		1,284	38,130	103	13,251	115	1,730	7	8	17	15
Other Hispanic		850	21,803	118	12,398	72	2,796	9	10	24	17

Source: 1987 Economic Censuses, Survey of Minority-Owned Business Enterprises: Hispanics, U.S. Department of Commerce, Bureau of the Census, MB-87-2, 1991, pp. 12-17. *Notes:* A dash (-) represents zero. A (D) stands for data withheld to avoid disclosing data for individual companies; data are included in higher level totals.

★ 699 ★

Hispanic-Owned Firms

Hispanic-Owned Firms, by Major Industry Group, 1982 and 1987 - I

This table is based on the 1972 Standard Industrial Classification (SIC) system.

Major industry group	SIC code	All firms				Firms with paid employees			
		Firms (number)		Sales and receipts ($000)		Firms (number)		Sales and receipts ($000)	
		1982	1987	1982	1987	1982	1987	1982	1987
All industries		233,975	422,373	11,759,133	24,731,600	39,272	82,908	7,435,664	17,729,432
Agricultural services, forestry, and fishing		6,976	16,365	(D)	694,937	752	3,331	(D)	479,658
Agricultural services	07	5,952	14,752	(D)	648,290	695	3,210	(D)	464,607
Forestry	08	104	184	3,547	8,263	14	45	2,300	6,065
Fishing, hunting, and trapping	09	921	1,429	24,673	38,384	43	76	5,832	8,986
Mining		387	829	34,765	29,836	55	72	20,368	18,498
Metal mining	10	12	16	(D)	244	2	1	(D)	(D)
Anthracite mining	11	6	-	(D)	-	-	-	-	-
Bituminous coal and lignite mining	12	1	4	(D)	58	-	1	-	(D)
Oil and gas extraction	13	336	763	(D)	22,917	45	57	(D)	12,283
Nonmetallic minerals, except fuels	14	32	46	(D)	6,617	8	13	(D)	(D)
Construction		26,298	55,516	1,294,800	3,438,708	5,060	14,717	756,100	2,646,244
General building contractors	15	3,938	7,990	274,486	860,943	850	2,522	162,293	689,809
Heavy construction contractors	16	578	859	(D)	205,100	130	318	(D)	192,606
Special trade contractors	17	21,687	46,383	960,681	2,266,204	4,053	11,803	557,683	1,691,285
Subdividers and developers, n.e.c.	6552	97	284	(D)	106,461	27	74	(D)	72,544
Manufacturing		3,938	11,090	480,333	1,449,913	1,305	3,760	412,021	1,308,124
Food and kindred products	20	161	589	79,846	151,632	99	240	75,730	140,141
Tobacco manufacturers	21	2	7	(D)	860	2	7	(D)	860
Textile mill products	22	43	188	3,068	21,361	16	56	2,661	18,894
Apparel and other textile products	23	448	1,713	73,639	278,810	271	833	68,911	267,198
Lumber and wood products	24	285	840	(D)	86,082	66	250	(D)	74,287
Furniture and fixtures	25	245	657	(D)	88,946	101	249	(D)	80,165
Paper and allied products	26	9	87	(D)	11,499	7	19	(D)	10,553
Printing and publishing	27	871	1,886	69,864	179,062	214	575	55,335	158,977
Chemicals and allied products	28	25	72	5,174	20,157	8	28	4,457	19,432
Petroleum and coal products	29	2	3	(D)	(D)	2	2	(D)	(D)
Rubber and miscellaneous plastics products	30	27	176	9,936	50,765	21	62	9,768	48,960
Leather and leather products	31	39	194	(D)	22,108	13	53	(D)	20,053
Stone, clay, and glass products	32	226	400	15,580	38,880	27	106	12,423	33,782
Primary metal industries	33	99	104	(D)	53,897	21	32	(D)	(D)
Fabricated metal products	34	210	1,140	26,196	107,976	83	386	20,984	91,969
Machinery, except electrical	35	274	1,148	27,932	120,136	112	420	23,351	104,482
Electric and electronic equipment	36	90	295	10,540	39,990	22	67	8,455	37,233
Transportation equipment	37	28	129	8,503	74,747	14	66	5,445	70,875
Instruments and related products	38	9	68	(D)	5,581	9	21	(D)	(D)
Miscellaneous manufacturing industries	39	846	1,394	(D)	(D)	196	288	(D)	53,451
Transportation and public utilities		12,957	26,955	566,877	1,380,981	1,340	3,989	259,048	725,484
Local and interurban passenger transit	41	1,838	4,522	32,806	105,763	87	260	8,197	20,340
Trucking and warehousing	42	9,131	17,304	404,465	906,583	927	2,936	157,569	426,794
Water transportation	44	29	156	(D)	19,598	13	40	(D)	17,539
Transportation by air	45	54	222	4,781	10,895	8	23	3,676	4,022
Pipelines, except natural gas	46	-	-	-	-	-	-	-	-
Transportation services	47	1,379	3,617	90,664	284,684	224	542	66,115	219,512
Communication	48	82	756	(D)	38,852	17	115	(D)	28,851
Electric, gas, and sanitary services	49	445	378	(D)	14,606	64	73	(D)	8,426

[Continued]

★ 699 ★

Hispanic-Owned Firms, by Major Industry Group, 1982 and 1987 - I

[Continued]

Major industry group	SIC code	All firms: Firms (number) 1982	All firms: Firms (number) 1987	All firms: Sales and receipts ($000) 1982	All firms: Sales and receipts ($000) 1987	Firms with paid employees: Firms (number) 1982	Firms with paid employees: Firms (number) 1987	Firms with paid employees: Sales and receipts ($000) 1982	Firms with paid employees: Sales and receipts ($000) 1987
Wholesale trade		3,359	10,154	766,654	2,445,416	786	2,309	635,154	1,991,736
Wholesale trade - durable goods	50	1,231	5,080	266,247	1,056,969	363	1,218	221,142	851,385
Wholesale trade - nondurable goods	51	2,129	5,074	500,407	1,388,447	424	1,091	414,012	1,140,351
Retail trade		53,334	69,911	4,408,413	7,643,850	13,169	20,348	3,154,389	6,095,890
Building materials and garden supplies	52	934	1,331	(D)	160,841	233	468	(D)	132,177
General merchandise stores	53	518	1,152	(D)	54,795	80	146	(D)	30,974
Food stores	54	7,634	9,599	1,027,021	1,835,802	2,190	3,569	664,479	1,383,998
Automotive dealers and service stations	55	3,668	5,627	1,067,634	2,100,213	1,598	2,475	842,994	1,853,478
Apparel and accessory stores	56	2,160	3,472	157,294	230,806	478	1,021	78,187	165,431
Furniture and home furnishings stores	57	2,371	2,992	150,527	349,024	523	979	100,246	279,512
Eating and drinking places	58	10,671	14,003	997,548	1,645,412	5,312	7,872	826,197	1,449,268
Miscellaneous retail	59	25,400	31,735	898,975	1,266,957	2,755	3,818	565,846	801,052
Finance, insurance, and real estate		10,284	22,106	302,190	864,282	900	2,236	143,140	433,851
Banking	60	154	34	7,865	13,858	17	31	4,024	(D)
Credit agencies other than banks	61	43	91	3,700	10,925	31	78	3,325	10,507
Security commodity brokers and services	62	109	525	12,253	89,792	11	67	998	69,857
Insurance carriers	63	23	33	(D)	5,086	4	15	(D)	4,567
Insurance agents, brokers, and service	64	2,861	6,013	(D)	209,229	402	926	(D)	122,195
Real estate[1]	65	7,021	12,872	(D)	472,278	427	971	(D)	203,480
Combined real estate, insurance, etc.	66	50	2,509	(D)	59,371	4	142	(D)	9,570
Holding and other investment offices[2]	67	27	29	(D)	3,743	5	6	(D)	(D)
Services		92,759	184,372	2,983,923	6,031,406	14,521	29,750	1,769,648	3,774,117
Hotels and lodging places	70	624	973	(D)	112,551	212	315	(D)	92,996
Personal services	72	21,545	44,872	(D)	893,064	3,332	6,111	(D)	430,645
Business services	73	NA	59,948	NA	1,419,790	2,075	6,716	292,615	747,979
Auto repair, services, and garages	75	6,753	15,824	355,891	836,738	1,816	4,522	243,977	622,052
Miscellaneous repair services	76	5,034	8,337	151,647	302,456	782	1,837	80,519	193,150
Motion pictures	78	237	694	(D)	24,880	57	107	(D)	14,278
Amusement and recreation services	79	3,848	9,528	(D)	203,812	270	800	(D)	89,891
Health services	80	8,230	16,322	544,899	1,326,215	2,630	5,089	396,541	999,789
Legal services	81	1,950	3,690	104,522	286,713	642	1,356	72,847	216,577
Educational services	82	1,755	2,797	21,805	54,119	135	157	10,377	36,409
Social services	83	59	8,840	(D)	100,321	56	697	(D)	45,344
Museums, botanical, zoological gardens	84	-	-	-	-	-	-	-	-
Miscellaneous services	89	NA	12,547	NA	470,747	2,514	2,043	(D)	285,930
Industries not classified		23,679	25,075	(D)	752,271	1,384	2,396	(D)	255,830

Source: *1987 Economic Censuses, Survey of Minority-Owned Business Enterprises: Hispanics*, U.S. Department of Commerce, Bureau of the Census, MB-87-2, 1991, pp. 8-11. *Notes:* (NA) stands for not available. A dash (-) represents zero. A (D) stands for data withheld to avoid disclosing data for individual companies; data are included in higher level totals. 1. Excludes 6552 which is included in construction industries. 2. Excludes 673 (Trusts) and 679 (Miscellaneous investing).

★ 700 ★

Hispanic-Owned Firms

Hispanic-Owned Firms, by Major Industry Group, 1982 and 1987 - II

This table is based on the 1972 Standard Industrial Classification (SIC) system.

Major industry group	SIC code	Firms with paid employees			
		Employees (number)		Annual payroll ($000)	
		1982	1987	1982	1987
All industries		154,791	264,846	1,139,933	3,243,342
Agricultural services, forestry, and fishing		(D)	14,449	(D)	163,569
Agricultural services	07	(D)	14,197	(D)	160,618
Forestry	08	266	195	917	1,882
Fishing, hunting, and trapping	09	115	57	1,054	1,069
Mining		257	332	2,966	5,272
Metal mining	10	(D)	(D)	(D)	(D)
Anthracite mining	11	-	-	-	-
Bituminous coal and lignite mining	12	-	(D)	-	(D)
Oil and gas extraction	13	(D)	257	(D)	4,098
Nonmetallic minerals, except fuels	14	(D)	(D)	(D)	(D)
Construction		19,367	34,684	183,990	631,477
General building contractors	15	3,793	7,271	36,964	138,470
Heavy construction contractors	16	(D)	2,137	(D)	39,942
Special trade contractors	17	14,990	25,032	140,126	446,520
Subdividers and developers, n.e.c.	6552	(D)	244	(D)	6,545
Manufacturing		11,338	26,261	106,217	333,969
Food and kindred products	20	1,780	2,100	14,809	23,442
Tobacco manufacturers	21	(D)	32	(D)	180
Textile mill products	22	83	437	731	5,229
Apparel and other textile products	23	3,800	10,294	29,019	84,350
Lumber and wood products	24	(D)	1,410	(D)	17,883
Furniture and fixtures	25	(D)	1,617	(D)	19,810
Paper and allied products	26	(D)	111	(D)	1,742
Printing and publishing	27	970	2,409	11,432	41,942
Chemicals and allied products	28	50	179	460	3,135
Petroleum and coal products	29	(D)	(D)	(D)	(D)
Rubber and miscellaneous plastics products	30	157	698	1,625	12,891
Leather and leather products	31	(D)	362	(D)	5,038
Stone, clay, and glass products	32	157	370	2,288	7,203
Primary metal industries	33	(D)	(D)	(D)	(D)
Fabricated metal products	34	525	1,792	6,607	28,303
Machinery, except electrical	35	467	1,521	5,787	27,146
Electric and electronic equipment	36	157	670	2,014	13,168
Transportation equipment	37	178	938	1,646	17,821
Instruments and related products	38	(D)	(D)	(D)	(D)
Miscellaneous manufacturing industries	39	(D)	858	(D)	11,821

[Continued]

★ 700 ★

Hispanic-Owned Firms, by Major Industry Group, 1982 and 1987 - II

[Continued]

Major industry group	SIC code	Firms with paid employees: Employees (number) 1982	Employees (number) 1987	Annual payroll ($000) 1982	Annual payroll ($000) 1987
Transportation and public utilities		4,560	8,006	52,172	135,592
Local and interurban passenger transit	41	421	744	2,669	6,188
Trucking and warehousing	42	2,760	4,499	33,828	85,692
Water transportation	44	(D)	327	(D)	4,223
Transportation by air	45	58	67	1,290	1,116
Pipelines, except natural gas	46	-	-	-	-
Transportation services	47	753	1,683	9,207	25,970
Communication	48	(D)	533	(D)	10,451
Electric, gas, and sanitary services	49	(D)	153	(D)	1,952
Wholesale trade		3,321	9,119	38,836	157,537
Wholesale trade - durable goods	50	1,456	4,744	20,006	84,530
Wholesale trade - nondurable goods	51	1,865	4,375	18,800	73,007
Retail trade		60,086	90,584	372,894	745,662
Building materials and garden supplies	52	(D)	1,341	(D)	16,137
General merchandise stores	53	(D)	406	(D)	3,237
Food stores	54	7,674	14,010	52,436	118,064
Automotive dealers and service stations	55	5,128	9,378	44,242	128,153
Apparel and accessory stores	56	1,759	2,651	11,895	21,258
Furniture and home furnishings stores	57	1,303	2,771	12,032	34,466
Eating and drinking places	58	34,089	50,662	179,633	330,987
Miscellaneous retail	59	9,197	9,365	64,985	93,360
Finance, insurance, and real estate		2,746	4,960	27,594	80,882
Banking	60	86	(D)	1,008	(D)
Credit agencies other than banks	61	74	175	632	2,595
Security commodity brokers and services	62	10	173	204	12,707
Insurance carriers	63	(D)	71	(D)	1,115
Insurance agents, brokers, and service	64	(D)	1,668	(D)	24,434
Real estate[1]	65	(D)	2,611	(D)	35,073
Combined real estate, insurance, etc.	66	(D)	99	(D)	1,695
Holding and other investment offices[2]	67	(D)	(D)	(D)	(D)
Services		47,402	74,427	403,732	941,588
Hotels and lodging places	70	(D)	2,284	(D)	23,342
Personal services	72	(D)	13,688	(D)	129,379
Business services	73	8,960	18,979	74,304	235,949
Auto repair, services, and garages	75	4,869	9,749	48,955	139,178
Miscellaneous repair services	76	1,771	3,130	16,508	43,812

[Continued]

★ 700 ★

Hispanic-Owned Firms, by Major Industry Group, 1982 and 1987 - II

[Continued]

Major industry group	SIC code	Firms with paid employees: Employees (number) 1982	Employees (number) 1987	Annual payroll ($000) 1982	Annual payroll ($000) 1987
Motion pictures	78	(D)	344	(D)	2,877
Amusement and recreation services	79	(D)	1,518	(D)	19,948
Health services	80	7,747	13,982	76,239	197,965
Legal services	81	1,056	2,545	12,589	41,187
Educational services	82	449	975	2,614	10,684
Social services	83	(D)	1,886	(D)	13,215
Museums, botanical, zoological gardens	84	-	-	-	-
Miscellaneous services	89	(D)	5,347	(D)	84,052
Industries not classified		(D)	2,024	(D)	47,794

Source: 1987 Economic Censuses, Survey of Minority-Owned Business Enterprises: Hispanics, U.S. Department of Commerce, Bureau of the Census, MB-87-2, 1991, pp. 8-11. *Notes:* A dash (-) represents zero. A (D) stands for data withheld to avoid disclosing data for individual companies; data are included in higher level totals. 1. Excludes 6552 which is included in construction industries. 2. Excludes 673 (Trusts) and 679 (Miscellaneous investing).

★ 701 ★

Hispanic-Owned Firms

Hispanic-Owned Firms, by Metropolitan Statistical Area With 100 or More Hispanic-Owned Firms: Abilene - Baton Rouge

Geographic area and minority	All firms: Firms (number) A	All firms: Sales and receipts ($000) B	Firms with paid employees: Firms (number) C	Sales and receipts ($000) D	Employees (number) E	Annual payroll ($000) F	Relative standard error of estimate (percent) for column - A	B	C	D
Abilene, TX MSA	339	(D)	62	(D)	(D)	(D)	14	(D)	28	(D)
Mexican	314	(D)	58	(D)	(D)	(D)	15	(D)	29	(D)
Puerto Rican	4	(D)	4	(D)	(D)	(D)	87	(D)	87	(D)
Cuban	-	-	-	-	-	-	-	-	-	-
Other Central or South American	1	(D)	-	-	-	-	-	(D)	-	-
European Spanish	-	-	-	-	-	-	-	-	-	-
Other Hispanic	20	(D)	-	-	-	-	67	(D)	-	-
Albany-Schenectady-Troy, NY MSA	254	(D)	49	9,016	124	1,697	12	(D)	17	5
Mexican	16	(D)	4	(D)	(D)	(D)	50	(D)	50	(D)
Puerto Rican	87	(D)	6	1,721	23	235	21	(D)	24	5
Cuban	51	(D)	17	(D)	(D)	(D)	27	(D)	46	(D)
Other Central or South American	52	(D)	7	(D)	(D)	(D)	25	(D)	29	(D)
European Spanish	44	(D)	14	(D)	(D)	(D)	26	(D)	-	(D)
Other Hispanic	4	(D)	1	(D)	(D)	(D)	35	(D)	-	(D)
Albuquerque, NM MSA	4,579	228,683	1,213	172,162	3,810	34,356	3	2	4	2
Mexican	2,527	136,286	649	104,555	2,212	20,268	4	2	6	2
Puerto Rican	19	(D)	5	(D)	(D)	(D)	40	(D)	41	(D)

[Continued]

★ 701 ★

Hispanic-Owned Firms, by Metropolitan Statistical Area With 100 or More Hispanic-Owned Firms: Abilene - Baton Rouge

[Continued]

Geographic area and minority	All firms		Firms with paid employees				Relative standard error of estimate (percent) for column -			
	Firms (number) A	Sales and receipts ($000) B	Firms (number) C	Sales and receipts ($000) D	Employees (number) E	Annual payroll ($000) F	A	B	C	D
Cuban	51	(D)	3	(D)	(D)	(D)	29	(D)	-	(D)
Other Central or South American	352	15,597	67	11,678	176	1,716	10	8	16	9
European Spanish	930	45,338	284	34,373	962	8,043	7	5	10	5
Other Hispanic	700	29,992	205	20,794	452	4,344	8	7	12	9
Allentown-Bethlehem, PA-NJ MSA	280	15,269	64	10,950	195	1,420	6	4	11	5
Mexican	37	883	11	652	28	146	17	23	26	29
Puerto Rican	107	5,804	30	4,814	48	554	9	9	15	10
Cuban	40	3,942	7	(D)	(D)	(D)	17	5	49	(D)
Other Central or South American	60	2,307	9	898	39	167	13	12	21	3
European Spanish	31	2,132	6	(D)	(D)	(D)	19	4	34	(D)
Other Hispanic	5	201	1	(D)	(D)	(D)	40	57	-	(D)
Amarillo, TX MSA	342	(D)	69	(D)	(D)	(D)	14	(D)	21	(D)
Mexican	266	(D)	51	6,561	185	1,222	15	(D)	22	18
Puerto Rican	6	(D)	1	(D)	(D)	(D)	41	(D)	-	(D)
Cuban	1	(D)	1	(D)	(D)	(D)	-	(D)	-	(D)
Other Central or South American	42	(D)	12	(D)	(D)	(D)	55	(D)	80	(D)
European Spanish	14	(D)	3	1,456	40	284	68	(D)	-	-
Other Hispanic	13	(D)	1	(D)	(D)	(D)	73	(D)	-	(D)
Anaheim-Santa Ana, CA PMSA	9,683	650,604	1,997	460,487	5,667	88,163	3	2	5	2
Mexican	7,169	444,501	1,481	(D)	(D)	(D)	3	2	5	(D)
Puerto Rican	169	(D)	27	(D)	(D)	(D)	21	(D)	36	(D)
Cuban	325	(D)	67	(D)	(D)	(D)	13	(D)	23	(D)
Other Central or South American	1,158	(D)	269	(D)	(D)	(D)	8	(D)	14	(D)
European Spanish	636	38,056	118	(D)	(D)	(D)	11	8	17	(D)
Other Hispanic	226	(D)	35	(D)	(D)	(D)	19	(D)	31	(D)
Anchorage, AK MSA	238	13,375	38	9,720	153	2,583	6	1	4	-
Mexican	118	8,924	24	97	1,948	7	1	6	-	
Puerto Rican	10	232	2	(D)	(D)	(D)	20	7	-	(D)
Cuban	6	(D)	2	(D)	(D)	(D)	23	(D)	-	(D)
Other Central or South American	59	1,947	7	1,012	25	260	11	5	-	-
European Spanish	24	675	3	(D)	(D)	(D)	16	3	-	(D)
Other Hispanic	21	(D)	-	-	-	-	45	(D)	-	-
Atlanta, GA MSA	1,424	110,492	364	90,749	1,563	21,348	3	1	6	1
Mexican	298	27,270	94	23,774	491	6,037	8	2	11	2
Puerto Rican	212	8,543	50	(D)	(D)	(D)	11	7	21	(D)
Cuban	322	39,976	68	34,001	717	10,075	8	1	12	1
Other Central or South American	442	19,146	114	13,160	185	2,565	7	4	12	4
European Spanish	103	14,618	33	13,009	103	1,558	13	3	22	3
Other Hispanic	47	939	5	(D)	(D)	(D)	23	6	-	(D)
Atlantic City, NJ MSA	124	6,891	23	3,745	67	1,022	11	10	14	4
Mexican	19	(D)	3	(D)	(D)	(D)	31	(D)	48	(D)

[Continued]

★ 701 ★

Hispanic-Owned Firms, by Metropolitan Statistical Area With 100 or More Hispanic-Owned Firms: Abilene - Baton Rouge

[Continued]

Geographic area and minority	All firms: Firms (number) A	All firms: Sales and receipts ($000) B	Firms with paid employees: Firms (number) C	Firms with paid employees: Sales and receipts ($000) D	Firms with paid employees: Employees (number) E	Firms with paid employees: Annual payroll ($000) F	Relative standard error of estimate (percent) for column - A	B	C	D
Puerto Rican	59	2,818	10	1,163	31	285	16	17	20	7
Cuban	12	(D)	4	(D)	(D)	(D)	34	(D)	35	(D)
Other Central or South American	25	569	4	(D)	(D)	(D)	25	17	35	(D)
European Spanish	7	(D)	1	(D)	(D)	(D)	41	(D)	-	(D)
Other Hispanic	2	(D)	1	(D)	(D)	(D)	-	(D)	-	(D)
Aurora-Elgin, IL PMSA	364	(D)	65	9,932	161	1,337	11	(D)	18	12
Mexican	282	(D)	55	8,496	136	1,117	12	(D)	21	13
Puerto Rican	40	(D)	4	691	7	47	32	(D)	-	-
Cuban	9	(D)	3	217	2	26	63	(D)	47	69
Other Central or South American	28	(D)	3	528	16	147	39	(D)	-	-
European Spanish	4	(D)	-	-	-	-	86	(D)	-	-
Other Hispanic	1	(D)	-	-	-	-	-	(D)	-	-
Austin, TX MSA	3,366	122,197	676	88,051	1,772	20,842	5	4	7	4
Mexican	2,905	(D)	625	(D)	(D)	(D)	5	(D)	8	(D)
Puerto Rican	42	(D)	1	(D)	(D)	(D)	45	(D)	-	(D)
Cuban	18	(D)	-	-	-	-	57	(D)	-	-
Other Central or South American	187	3,574	29	(D)	(D)	(D)	21	20	48	(D)
European Spanish	151	4,870	10	2,971	26	366	24	17	24	17
Other Hispanic	63	2,859	11	2,453	32	347	34	22	26	24
Bakersfield, CA MSA	2,073	148,144	536	111,373	2,380	25,192	6	4	8	4
Mexican	1,742	124,982	442	(D)	(D)	(D)	6	4	9	(D)
Puerto Rican	8	(D)	2	(D)	(D)	(D)	18	(D)	71	(D)
Cuban	18	(D)	2	(D)	(D)	(D)	53	(D)	-	(D)
Other Central or South American	121	(D)	37	(D)	(D)	(D)	22	(D)	28	(D)
European Spanish	105	7,137	19	(D)	(D)	(D)	24	18	17	(D)
Other Hispanic	79	5,604	34	5,241	15	849	31	33	46	35
Baltimore, MD MSA	680	70,588	164	60,323	428	6,505	3	2	8	2
Mexican	113	(D)	29	(D)	(D)	(D)	11	(D)	34	(D)
Puerto Rican	125	(D)	28	(D)	(D)	(D)	7	(D)	11	(D)
Cuban	97	(D)	34	(D)	(D)	(D)	11	(D)	23	(D)
Other Central or South American	234	32,687	49	28,541	157	2,262	6	1	7	1
European Spanish	84	(D)	21	(D)	(D)	(D)	8	(D)	7	(D)
Other Hispanic	27	(D)	3	(D)	(D)	(D)	18	(D)	-	(D)
Baton Rouge, LA MSA	273	16,305	46	12,177	143	1,998	5	2	8	1
Mexican	46	1,347	9	752	13	181	12	6	16	4
Puerto Rican	24	812	1	(D)	(D)	(D)	28	31	-	(D)
Cuban	40	1,218	6	(D)	(D)	(D)	13	8	33	(D)
Other Central or South American	92	2,415	12	986	22	124	9	9	12	2
European Spanish	61	10,447	18	9,649	93	1,475	11	2	11	2
Other Hispanic	10	66	-	-	-	-	28	42	-	-

Source: 1987 Economic Censuses, Survey of Minority-Owned Business Enterprises: Hispanics, U.S. Department of Commerce, Bureau of the Census, MB-87-2, 1991, pp. 55-70. *Notes:* A dash (-) represents zero. (D) stands for data withheld to avoid disclosing data for individual companies; data are included in higher-level totals.

★ 702 ★

Hispanic-Owned Firms

Hispanic-Owned Firms, by Metropolitan Statistical Area With 100 or More Hispanic-Owned Firms: Beaumont/Port Arthur - Cheyenne

Geographic area and minority	All firms		Firms with paid employees				Relative standard error of estimate (percent) for column -			
	Firms (number) A	Sales and receipts ($000) B	Firms (number) C	Sales and receipts ($000) D	Employees (number) E	Annual payroll ($000) F	A	B	C	D
Beaumont-Port Arthur, TX MSA	385	19,825	104	12,152	178	1,989	13	13	21	14
Mexican	336	14,089	88	9,251	152	1,650	14	17	25	17
Puerto Rican	14	925	3	367	5	47	69	54	47	34
Cuban	4	1,215	3	(D)	(D)	(D)	35	49	47	(D)
Other Central or South American	5	(D)	1	(D)	(D)	(D)	49	(D)	-	(D)
European Spanish	21	3,276	4	1,234	4	72	49	18	-	-
Other Hispanic	5	(D)	5	(D)	(D)	(D)	40	(D)	40	(D)
Bergen-Passaic, NJ PMSA	2,471	159,745	404	92,436	1,120	19,235	3	2	5	2
Mexican	51	5,425	4	(D)	(D)	(D)	18	5	35	(D)
Puerto Rican	558	35,613	98	22,735	396	6,628	5	4	10	4
Cuban	711	51,411	124	28,165	243	4,421	5	4	9	5
Other Central or South American	946	55,807	141	30,771	323	4,403	4	4	8	4
European Spanish	151	8,682	31	(D)	(D)	(D)	11	13	19	(D)
Other Hispanic	54	2,807	6	(D)	(D)	(D)	20	23	24	(D)
Birmingham, AL MSA	105	3,698	22	2,423	43	526	6	4	9	2
Mexican	30	(D)	10	672	12	170	12	(D)	20	6
Puerto Rican	7	(D)	-	-	-	-	20	(D)	-	-
Cuban	26	882	6	505	9	126	14	12	-	-
Other Central or South American	20	828	3	507	8	98	12	1	-	-
European Spanish	21	991	3	739	14	132	13	7	-	-
Other Hispanic	1	(D)	-	-	-	-	-	(D)	-	-
Boise City, ID MSA	168	5,187	36	3,474	39	578	9	4	14	2
Mexican	99	3,509	27	2,339	33	427	11	6	18	3
Puerto Rican	2	(D)	-	-	-	-	-	(D)	-	-
Cuban	4	(D)	-	-	-	-	86	(D)	-	-
Other Central or South American	12	221	1	(D)	(D)	(D)	40	12	-	(D)
European Spanish	46	1,217	7	(D)	(D)	(D)	20	4	-	(D)
Other Hispanic	5	(D)	1	(D)	(D)	(D)	-	(D)	-	(D)
Boston, MA PMSA	1,420	72,072	226	(D)	(D)	(D)	3	2	5	(D)
Mexican	140	(D)	18	(D)	(D)	(D)	8	(D)	19	(D)
Puerto Rican	273	(D)	47	(D)	(D)	(D)	6	(D)	9	(D)
Cuban	233	(D)	37	(D)	(D)	(D)	6	(D)	11	(D)
Other Central or South American	530	(D)	86	(D)	(D)	(D)	5	(D)	9	(D)
European Spanish	166	(D)	30	(D)	(D)	(D)	8	(D)	12	(D)
Other Hispanic	78	(D)	8	(D)	(D)	(D)	13	(D)	25	(D)
Boulder-Longmont, CO PMSA	279	9,293	65	5,842	94	1,279	14	14	24	17
Mexican	203	6,609	53	4,173	68	983	17	19	29	24
Puerto Rican	1	(D)	1	(D)	(D)	(D)	-	(D)	-	(D)
Cuban	-	-	-	-	-	-	-	-	-	-
Other Central or South American	25	(D)	1	(D)	(D)	(D)	42	(D)	-	(D)
European Spanish	34	1,385	7	(D)	(D)	(D)	37	16	21	(D)
Other Hispanic	16	685	3	(D)	(D)	(D)	57	11	46	(D)
Bradenton, FL MSA	230	7,757	39	5,339	83	2,501	24	24	37	31
Mexican	83	(D)	22	4,065	35	2,040	40	(D)	49	40
Puerto Rican	16	(D)	-	-	-	-	58	(D)	-	-
Cuban	98	(D)	15	(D)	(D)	(D)	37	(D)	65	(D)
Other Central or South American	12	(D)	1	(D)	(D)	(D)	79	(D)	-	(D)
European Spanish	21	(D)	1	(D)	(D)	(D)	90	(D)	-	(D)
Other Hispanic	-	-	-	-	-	-	-	-	-	-

[Continued]

★ 702 ★

Hispanic-Owned Firms, by Metropolitan Statistical Area With 100 or More Hispanic-Owned Firms: Beaumont/Port Arthur - Cheyenne

[Continued]

Geographic area and minority	All firms		Firms with paid employees				Relative standard error of estimate (percent) for column -			
	Firms (number) A	Sales and receipts ($000) B	Firms (number) C	Sales and receipts ($000) D	Employees (number) E	Annual payroll ($000) F	A	B	C	D
Brazoria, TX PMSA	686	20,617	95	13,091	184	2,151	10	6	16	7
Mexican	613	16,085	76	9,460	138	1,752	11	8	16	9
Puerto Rican	-	-	-	-	-	-	-	-	-	-
Cuban	4	(D)	3	530	6	62	36	(D)	47	39
Other Central or South American	26	828	2	(D)	(D)	(D)	52	34	-	(D)
European Spanish	31	2,749	12	2,388	17	218	53	14	79	10
Other Hispanic	12	(D)	2	(D)	(D)	(D)	79	(D)	-	(D)
Bridgeport-Milford, CT PMSA	439	34,559	95	22,343	447	3,419	7	3	7	2
Mexican	18	(D)	3	490	7	71	34	(D)	-	-
Puerto Rican	240	(D)	51	7,888	130	1,476	10	(D)	11	5
Cuban	62	(D)	12	(D)	(D)	(D)	16	(D)	-	(D)
Other Central or South American	79	(D)	17	3,026	33	481	17	(D)	26	7
European Spanish	32	(D)	9	3,772	33	318	23	(D)	-	-
Other Hispanic	8	(D)	3	(D)	(D)	(D)	18	(D)	-	(D)
Brownsville-Harlingen, TX MSA	4,413	218,948	1,011	159,324	2,855	25,265	3	2	5	2
Mexican	4,000	197,491	925	144,904	2,619	22,728	4	2	5	2
Puerto Rican	10	20	-	-	-	-	95	95	-	-
Cuban	38	894	7	547	8	80	38	23	20	21
Other Central or South American	211	12,135	48	9,210	126	1,684	17	9	23	11
European Spanish	55	3,255	14	2,179	48	401	29	25	20	23
Other Hispanic	99	5,153	17	2,484	54	372	29	8	26	9
Bryan-College Station, TX MSA	301	13,216	76	10,201	235	1,945	17	14	33	17
Mexican	249	8,643	69	6,757	138	1,379	19	21	37	26
Puerto Rican	-	-	-	-	-	-	-	-	-	-
Cuban	3	(D)	-	-	-	-	-	(D)	-	-
Other Central or South American	37	2,140	5	(D)	(D)	(D)	58	17	28	(D)
European Spanish	11	(D)	1	(D)	(D)	(D)	87	(D)	-	(D)
Other Hispanic	1	(D)	1	(D)	(D)	(D)	-	(D)	-	(D)
Buffalo, NY PMSA	213	11,426	51	8,444	130	1,517	13	14	15	16
Mexican	28	(D)	8	(D)	(D)	(D)	40	(D)	25	(D)
Puerto Rican	54	2,216	8	927	37	294	24	34	25	14
Cuban	35	3,777	8	3,152	48	719	31	24	25	27
Other Central or South American	52	2,224	16	1,870	25	263	25	11	25	7
European Spanish	38	1,894	10	1,541	4	105	38	56	55	68
Other Hispanic	6	(D)	1	(D)	(D)	(D)	58	(D)	-	(D)
Charlotte-Gastonia-Rock Hill, NC-SC MSA	145	54,269	25	50,770	279	6,527	8	-	-	-
Mexican	25	(D)	3	(D)	(D)	(D)	18	(D)	-	(D)
Puerto Rican	17	(D)	1	(D)	(D)	(D)	33	(D)	-	(D)
Cuban	27	(D)	6	(D)	(D)	(D)	20	(D)	-	(D)
Other Central or South American	55	18,133	10	(D)	(D)	(D)	13	-	-	(D)
European Spanish	15	(D)	5	914	25	187	13	(D)	-	-
Other Hispanic	6	(D)	-	-	-	-	41	(D)	-	-
Cheyenne, WY MSA	174	5,353	37	3,636	139	991	5	1	8	1
Mexican	128	3,846	24	2,591	93	735	6	2	8	1
Puerto Rican	5	(D)	-	-	-	-	40	(D)	-	-
Cuban	2	(D)	2	(D)	(D)	(D)	72	(D)	72	(D)
Other Central or South American	8	(D)	-	-	-	-	26	(D)	-	-

[Continued]

★ 702 ★

Hispanic-Owned Firms, by Metropolitan Statistical Area With 100 or More Hispanic-Owned Firms: Beaumont/Port Arthur - Cheyenne

[Continued]

Geographic area and minority	All firms: Firms (number) A	All firms: Sales and receipts ($000) B	Firms with paid employees: Firms (number) C	Firms with paid employees: Sales and receipts ($000) D	Firms with paid employees: Employees (number) E	Firms with paid employees: Annual payroll ($000) F	Relative standard error of estimate (percent) for column - A	B	C	D
European Spanish	15	481	5	(D)	(D)	(D)	9	1	-	(D)
Other Hispanic	16	(D)	6	(D)	(D)	(D)	20	(D)	24	(D)

Source: 1987 Economic Censuses, Survey of Minority-Owned Business Enterprises: Hispanics, U.S. Department of Commerce, Bureau of the Census, MB-87-2, 1991, pp. 55-70. *Notes:* A dash (-) represents zero. (D) stands for data withheld to avoid disclosing data for individual companies; data are included in higher-level totals.

★ 703 ★

Hispanic-Owned Firms

Hispanic-Owned Firms, by Metropolitan Statistical Area With 100 or More Hispanic-Owned Firms: Chicago - Des Moines

Geographic area and minority	All firms: Firms (number) A	All firms: Sales and receipts ($000) B	Firms with paid employees: Firms (number) C	Firms with paid employees: Sales and receipts ($000) D	Firms with paid employees: Employees (number) E	Firms with paid employees: Annual payroll ($000) F	Relative standard error of estimate (percent) for column - A	B	C	D
Chicago, IL PMSA	7,848	506,393	1,308	357,929	4,480	57,087	2	1	4	1
Mexican	4,413	257,125	714	172,380	2,303	26,899	3	2	5	1
Puerto Rican	1,083	48,612	129	(D)	(D)	(D)	6	5	12	(D)
Cuban	675	75,533	191	60,997	749	8,329	7	4	8	3
Other Central or South American	1,255	64,200	218	(D)	(D)	(D)	5	4	9	(D)
European Spanish	265	55,309	33	(D)	(D)	(D)	12	1	17	(D)
Other Hispanic	157	5,614	23	(D)	(D)	(D)	15	8	19	(D)
Chico, CA MSA	266	10,671	65	8,075	193	1,676	16	9	19	8
Mexican	180	6,182	47	4,926	119	1,119	20	11	26	12
Puerto Rican	22	617	2	(D)	(D)	(D)	61	18	-	(D)
Cuban	-	-	-	-	-	-	-	-	-	-
Other Central or South American	34	1,320	3	(D)	(D)	(D)	47	40	47	(D)
European Spanish	13	2,002	8	1,977	17	283	33	11	31	11
Other Hispanic	17	550	5	(D)	(D)	(D)	58	27	40	(D)
Cincinnati, OH-KY-IN PMSA	210	18,730	37	15,299	163	2,691	12	4	9	1
Mexican	47	1,645	3	(D)	(D)	(D)	26	33	-	(D)
Puerto Rican	13	775	2	(D)	(D)	(D)	11	-	-	(D)
Cuban	36	9,680	7	9,537	108	2,115	26	-	-	-
Other Central or South American	75	4,547	13	3,539	33	326	24	9	-	-
European Spanish	33	1,789	10	1,390	13	162	26	11	35	12
Other Hispanic	6	294	2	(D)	(D)	(D)	41	2	-	(D)
Cleveland, OH PMSA	433	18,784	89	12,457	488	4,685	9	4	16	3
Mexican	52	5,350	10	4,668	348	3,243	19	2	-	-
Puerto Rican	154	4,786	28	1,998	20	278	14	10	34	16
Cuban	57	1,905	15	1,037	22	285	25	36	29	21
Other Central or South American	99	3,497	26	2,521	76	522	20	5	35	5
European Spanish	53	3,181	10	2,233	22	357	21	1	-	-
Other Hispanic	18	65	-	-	-	-	72	40	-	-
Colorado Springs, CO MSA	608	24,501	104	18,281	367	3,831	9	6	10	8
Mexican	409	(D)	72	12,146	270	2,547	11	(D)	13	11

[Continued]

★ 703 ★

Hispanic-Owned Firms, by Metropolitan Statistical Area With 100 or More Hispanic-Owned Firms: Chicago - Des Moines

[Continued]

Geographic area and minority	All firms		Firms with paid employees				Relative standard error of estimate (percent) for column -			
	Firms (number) A	Sales and receipts ($000) B	Firms (number) C	Sales and receipts ($000) D	Employees (number) E	Annual payroll ($000) F	A	B	C	D
Puerto Rican	13	(D)	4	(D)	(D)	(D)	68	(D)	60	(D)
Cuban	12	(D)	1	(D)	(D)	(D)	71	(D)	-	(D)
Other Central or South American	20	(D)	5	644	12	140	43	(D)	28	8
European Spanish	97	4,599	14	3,732	45	517	24	5	18	2
Other Hispanic	57	1,905	8	1,590	38	589	33	6	-	-
Columbia, SC MSA	116	(D)	16	2,085	52	486	11	(D)	23	1
Mexican	23	(D)	2	(D)	(D)	(D)	44	(D)	-	(D)
Puerto Rican	31	669	7	341	13	171	16	15	49	6
Cuban	20	1,275	4	(D)	(D)	(D)	16	3	35	(D)
Other Central or South American	31	(D)	-	-	-	-	13	(D)	-	-
European Spanish	10	322	2	(D)	(D)	(D)	14	17	-	(D)
Other Hispanic	1	(D)	1	(D)	(D)	(D)	-	(D)	-	(D)
Columbus, OH MSA	260	12,927	66	10,568	232	2,881	12	8	21	10
Mexican	51	3,554	18	(D)	(D)	(D)	23	12	36	(D)
Puerto Rican	42	(D)	11	325	4	83	29	(D)	59	10
Cuban	55	1,881	4	(D)	(D)	(D)	25	7	-	(D)
Other Central or South American	71	1,786	14	1,413	5	410	29	30	46	38
European Spanish	40	4,985	19	4,655	85	1,298	28	17	41	18
Other Hispanic	1	(D)	-	-	-	-	-	(D)	-	-
Corpus Christi, TX MSA	4,172	159,592	934	105,153	2,130	21,485	4	4	6	4
Mexican	3,776	140,034	816	90,954	1,939	19,205	4	4	7	4
Puerto Rican	11	183	2	(D)	(D)	(D)	34	32	71	(D)
Cuban	21	3,488	6	(D)	(D)	(D)	46	4	33	(D)
Other Central or South American	213	8,902	48	5,447	95	1,127	18	18	28	11
European Spanish	60	5,003	38	3,917	62	841	29	18	36	23
Other Hispanic	91	1,982	24	(D)	(D)	(D)	30	40	57	(D)
Dallas, TX PMSA	6,747	294,403	1,351	204,878	3,531	49,319	3	3	6	3
Mexican	5,651	224,518	1,122	152,095	2,691	39,867	4	3	7	3
Puerto Rican	61	5,049	15	(D)	(D)	(D)	27	8	16	(D)
Cuban	188	20,669	22	15,748	277	2,003	19	3	9	2
Other Central or South American	508	22,297	128	16,516	271	3,941	13	7	19	7
European Spanish	202	7,667	38	5,071	29	766	19	13	36	16
Other Hispanic	137	14,203	26	(D)	(D)	(D)	22	7	47	(D)
Danbury, CT PMSA	159	7,444	28	4,972	79	1,029	12	6	16	-
Mexican	9	358	2	(D)	(D)	(D)	49	48	-	(D)
Puerto Rican	27	669	2	(D)	(D)	(D)	38	37	-	(D)
Cuban	31	1,176	3	770	10	122	26	12	-	-
Other Central or South American	71	4,121	16	3,398	51	660	19	6	28	-
European Spanish	15	450	1	(D)	(D)	(D)	28	29	-	(D)
Other Hispanic	6	670	4	(D)	(D)	(D)	-	-	-	(D)
Davenport-Rock Island-Moline, IA-IL MSA	197	8,248	45	7,234	218	1,642	11	6	13	7
Mexican	161	7,221	39	6,516	202	1,522	12	7	15	7
Puerto Rican	4	(D)	1	(D)	(D)	(D)	-	(D)	-	(D)
Cuban	3	337	3	337	7	34	-	-	-	-
Other Central or South American	13	371	1	(D)	(D)	(D)	44	6	-	(D)
European Spanish	7	(D)	-	-	-	-	29	(D)	-	-
Other Hispanic	9	182	1	(D)	(D)	(D)	61	24	-	(D)

[Continued]

★ 703 ★

Hispanic-Owned Firms, by Metropolitan Statistical Area With 100 or More Hispanic-Owned Firms: Chicago - Des Moines

[Continued]

Geographic area and minority	All firms: Firms (number) A	All firms: Sales and receipts ($000) B	Firms with paid employees: Firms (number) C	Firms with paid employees: Sales and receipts ($000) D	Firms with paid employees: Employees (number) E	Firms with paid employees: Annual payroll ($000) F	Relative standard error of estimate (percent) for column - A	B	C	D
Daytona Beach, FL MSA	247	12,037	63	6,225	111	1,239	16	15	23	16
Mexican	23	(D)	8	821	13	117	45	(D)	31	27
Puerto Rican	70	(D)	25	2,464	48	374	28	(D)	40	38
Cuban	90	(D)	8	1,090	14	321	28	(D)	18	11
Other Central or South American	34	(D)	6	921	19	187	41	(D)	24	12
European Spanish	19	(D)	5	(D)	(D)	(D)	51	(D)	28	(D)
Other Hispanic	11	(D)	11	(D)	(D)	(D)	86	(D)	86	(D)
Denver, CO PMSA	4,760	221,956	834	168,209	2,189	32,591	3	2	6	2
Mexican	3,211	173,474	588	137,249	1,692	26,166	4	2	7	2
Puerto Rican	87	2,544	25	(D)	(D)	(D)	26	17	48	(D)
Cuban	81	1,172	6	(D)	(D)	(D)	24	12	-	(D)
Other Central or South American	282	6,848	30	4,675	96	900	14	8	9	7
European Spanish	664	20,177	100	11,955	192	2,376	10	5	18	6
Other Hispanic	435	17,741	85	12,299	169	2,801	12	11	22	12
Des Moines, IA MSA	135	6,618	29	5,686	151	1,123	6	1	5	1
Mexican	106	5,956	25	5,297	139	1,029	7	1	6	2
Puerto Rican	5	(D)	-	-	-	-	28	(D)	-	-
Cuban	3	(D)	2	(D)	(D)	(D)	-	(D)	-	(D)
Other Central or South American	8	179	1	(D)	(D)	(D)	30	15	-	(D)
European Spanish	11	124	1	(D)	(D)	(D)	18	3	-	(D)
Other Hispanic	2	(D)	-	-	-	-	72	(D)	-	-

Source: 1987 Economic Censuses, Survey of Minority-Owned Business Enterprises: Hispanics, U.S. Department of Commerce, Bureau of the Census, MB-87-2, 1991, pp. 55-70. *Notes:* A dash (-) represents zero. (D) stands for data withheld to avoid disclosing data for individual companies; data are included in higher-level totals.

★ 704 ★

Hispanic-Owned Firms

Hispanic-Owned Firms, by Metropolitan Statistical Area With 100 or More Hispanic-Owned Firms: Detroit - Galveston/Texas City

Geographic area and minority	All firms: Firms (number) A	All firms: Sales and receipts ($000) B	Firms with paid employees: Firms (number) C	Firms with paid employees: Sales and receipts ($000) D	Firms with paid employees: Employees (number) E	Firms with paid employees: Annual payroll ($000) F	Relative standard error of estimate (percent) for column - A	B	C	D
Detroit, MI PMSA	1,288	74,642	222	53,122	960	13,370	2	1	4	1
Mexican	758	43,776	128	30,419	611	8,494	3	1	5	1
Puerto Rican	104	3,448	10	1,436	12	121	8	15	20	34
Cuban	59	2,890	14	2,360	33	516	11	4	14	4
Other Central or South American	172	6,645	25	3,564	116	718	6	8	10	10
European Spanish	142	8,114	36	6,346	86	1,259	8	2	10	1
Other Hispanic	53	9,769	9	8,997	102	2,262	11	1	-	-
El Paso, TX MSA	8,214	450,840	2,155	345,530	6,983	67,348	3	2	4	2
Mexican	7,589	407,044	1,970	310,151	6,367	61,377	3	2	4	2

[Continued]

★ 704 ★

Hispanic-Owned Firms, by Metropolitan Statistical Area With 100 or More Hispanic-Owned Firms: Detroit - Galveston/Texas City

[Continued]

Geographic area and minority	All firms		Firms with paid employees				Relative standard error of estimate (percent) for column -			
	Firms (number) A	Sales and receipts ($000) B	Firms (number) C	Sales and receipts ($000) D	Employees (number) E	Annual payroll ($000) F	A	B	C	D
Puerto Rican	51	1,893	13	880	9	121	38	45	74	74
Cuban	69	4,662	33	2,017	36	359	26	17	38	22
Other Central or South American	266	19,675	56	17,205	331	2,476	16	5	25	5
European Spanish	123	7,651	52	6,514	99	1,021	21	17	28	20
Other Hispanic	116	9,915	31	8,763	141	1,994	23	8	33	6
Eugene-Springfield, OR MSA	151	9,237	32	7,721	224	1,859	13	3	-	-
Mexican	93	5,048	22	4,525	99	1,130	18	2	-	-
Puerto Rican	12	(D)	2	(D)	(D)	(D)	46	(D)	-	(D)
Cuban	2	(D)	1	(D)	(D)	(D)	-	(D)	-	(D)
Other Central or South American	11	1,199	3	(D)	(D)	(D)	-	-	-	(D)
European Spanish	19	549	3	(D)	(D)	(D)	32	9	-	(D)
Other Hispanic	14	(D)	1	(D)	(D)	(D)	56	(D)	-	(D)
Fayetteville, NC MSA	118	2,941	17	2,045	29	183	12	3	14	2
Mexican	54	2,000	9	(D)	(D)	(D)	19	3	-	(D)
Puerto Rican	27	329	2	(D)	(D)	(D)	21	10	-	(D)
Cuban	15	(D)	1	(D)	(D)	(D)	32	(D)	-	(D)
Other Central or South American	6	(D)	2	(D)	(D)	(D)	24	(D)	-	(D)
European Spanish	12	193	3	(D)	(D)	(D)	46	37	82	(D)
Other Hispanic	4	(D)	-	-	-	-	61	(D)	-	-
Flint, MI MSA	125	2,801	13	1,323	25	381	9	7	11	-
Mexican	92	1,777	10	(D)	(D)	(D)	11	8	14	(D)
Puerto Rican	3	(D)	1	(D)	(D)	(D)	47	(D)	-	(D)
Cuban	12	(D)	-	-	-	-	24	(D)	-	-
Other Central or South American	9	462	1	(D)	(D)	(D)	27	29	-	(D)
European Spanish	5	10	-	-	-	-	40	32	-	-
Other Hispanic	4	(D)	1	(D)	(D)	(D)	36	(D)	-	(D)
Fort Collins-Loveland, CO MSA	350	19,121	78	15,521	259	3,745	14	12	20	14
Mexican	180	7,502	30	5,965	212	1,831	19	6	13	5
Puerto Rican	12	(D)	2	(D)	(D)	(D)	71	(D)	-	(D)
Cuban	14	2,289	10	(D)	(D)	(D)	63	90	84	(D)
Other Central or South American	35	(D)	14	(D)	(D)	(D)	42	(D)	62	(D)
European Spanish	101	2,394	15	(D)	(D)	(D)	29	29	60	(D)
Other Hispanic	8	(D)	7	(D)	(D)	(D)	24	(D)	28	(D)
Fort Lauderdale-Hollywood-Pompano Beach, FL PMSA	3,570	225,621	567	159,319	2,370	31,850	4	2	7	2
Mexican	174	6,506	10	3,787	35	466	23	16	20	11
Puerto Rican	496	20,458	95	14,035	216	2,789	12	9	21	11
Cuban	1,704	144,156	292	109,344	1,650	21,495	6	2	10	2
Other Central or South American	966	44,099	126	25,414	352	5,539	8	7	10	6
European Spanish	170	7,942	38	5,577	82	1,090	18	10	27	12
Other Hispanic	60	2,460	6	1,162	35	471	36	18	33	15

[Continued]

★ 704 ★

Hispanic-Owned Firms, by Metropolitan Statistical Area With 100 or More Hispanic-Owned Firms: Detroit - Galveston/Texas City

[Continued]

Geographic area and minority	All firms: Firms (number) A	All firms: Sales and receipts ($000) B	Firms with paid employees: Firms (number) C	Firms with paid employees: Sales and receipts ($000) D	Firms with paid employees: Employees (number) E	Firms with paid employees: Annual payroll ($000) F	Relative standard error of estimate (percent) for column - A	B	C	D
Fort Myers-Cape Coral, FL MSA	238	16,181	54	10,570	121	2,084	17	10	26	7
Mexican	34	2,370	11	(D)	(D)	(D)	42	48	86	(D)
Puerto Rican	36	1,408	7	1,162	4	170	38	39	35	46
Cuban	67	6,097	14	4,004	69	1,188	28	12	20	8
Other Central or South American	68	1,375	6	(D)	(D)	(D)	38	30	24	(D)
European Spanish	8	2,146	5	1,717	17	241	18	14	-	-
Other Hispanic	25	2,785	11	(D)	(D)	(D)	51	11	86	(D)
Fort Pierce, FL MSA	154	9,604	30	4,482	72	816	21	24	28	29
Mexican	31	1,396	2	(D)	(D)	(D)	42	47	70	(D)
Puerto Rican	19	596	3	(D)	(D)	(D)	52	9	48	(D)
Cuban	40	4,363	13	1,551	30	244	28	39	24	32
Other Central or South American	30	2,731	11	1,793	31	312	44	49	68	67
European Spanish	3	17	-	-	-	-	47	25	-	-
Other Hispanic	31	501	1	(D)	(D)	(D)	68	18	-	(D)
Fort Wayne, IN MSA	139	4,982	22	3,653	133	1,024	11	6	6	1
Mexican	91	4,043	16	3,301	119	910	14	4	-	-
Puerto Rican	19	523	3	157	8	71	35	46	47	34
Cuban	4	(D)	1	(D)	(D)	(D)	-	(D)	-	(D)
Other Central or South American	15	263	2	(D)	(D)	(D)	33	20	-	(D)
European Spanish	2	(D)	-	-	-	-	-	(D)	-	-
Other Hispanic	8	(D)	-	-	-	-	60	(D)	-	-
Fort Worth-Arlington, TX PMSA	2,449	94,272	577	67,567	1,261	16,235	5	5	9	7
Mexican	2,021	76,170	487	53,751	992	13,878	6	6	10	8
Puerto Rican	66	1,091	2	(D)	(D)	(D)	41	17	-	(D)
Cuban	66	2,222	8	1,141	13	177	37	15	25	24
Other Central or South American	179	9,416	55	8,337	129	1,357	20	23	32	26
European Spanish	46	4,013	14	2,526	69	476	33	11	30	18
Other Hispanic	71	1,360	11	(D)	(D)	(D)	47	40	29	(D)
Fresno, CA MSA	3,039	319,370	848	269,819	4,199	50,566	4	2	6	2
Mexican	2,665	218,132	746	172,052	3,540	40,445	5	3	7	3
Puerto Rican	44	1,579	6	1,196	29	168	38	12	33	12
Cuban	29	2,078	6	1,862	47	251	47	13	24	13
Other Central or South American	168	15,427	53	13,479	194	1,494	19	10	32	9
European Spanish	86	79,888	20	79,244	361	7,759	27	1	10	-
Other Hispanic	47	2,266	17	1,986	28	449	39	30	58	34
Gainesville, FL MSA	172	8,254	35	5,896	122	981	20	12	16	14
Mexican	2	(D)	-	-	-	-	71	(D)	-	-
Puerto Rican	14	2,354	8	2,294	33	246	30	20	31	21
Cuban	61	1,491	8	(D)	(D)	(D)	32	20	25	(D)
Other Central or South American	93	4,001	17	2,427	56	445	30	19	26	26
European Spanish	2	(D)	2	(D)	(D)	(D)	71	(D)	71	(D)
Other Hispanic	-	-	-	-	-	-	-	-	-	-

[Continued]

★ 704 ★

Hispanic-Owned Firms, by Metropolitan Statistical Area With 100 or More Hispanic-Owned Firms: Detroit - Galveston/Texas City

[Continued]

Geographic area and minority	All firms		Firms with paid employees				Relative standard error of estimate (percent) for column -			
	Firms (number) A	Sales and receipts ($000) B	Firms (number) C	Sales and receipts ($000) D	Employees (number) E	Annual payroll ($000) F	A	B	C	D
Galveston-Texas City, TX PMSA	627	22,590	96	11,707	296	2,453	11	11	19	8
Mexican	527	18,419	73	9,850	265	2,072	12	11	19	7
Puerto Rican	1	(D)	-	-	-	-	-	(D)	-	-
Cuban	1	(D)	-	-	-	-	-	(D)	-	-
Other Central or South American	43	1,667	2	(D)	(D)	(D)	41	66	71	(D)
European Spanish	41	2,313	21	(D)	(D)	(D)	54	34	55	(D)
Other Hispanic	14	(D)	-	-	-	-	72	(D)	-	-

Source: *1987 Economic Censuses, Survey of Minority-Owned Business Enterprises: Hispanics*, U.S. Department of Commerce, Bureau of the Census, MB-87-2, 1991, pp. 55-70. *Notes:* A dash (-) represents zero. (D) stands for data withheld to avoid disclosing data for individual companies; data are included in higher-level totals.

★ 705 ★

Hispanic-Owned Firms

Hispanic-Owned Firms, by Metropolitan Statistical Area With 100 or More Hispanic-Owned Firms: Gary/Hammond - Lake County

Geographic area and minority	All firms		Firms with paid employees				Relative standard error of estimate (percent) for column -			
	Firms (number) A	Sales and receipts ($000) B	Firms (number) C	Sales and receipts ($000) D	Employees (number) E	Annual payroll ($000) F	A	B	C	D
Gary-Hammond, IN PMSA	580	34,840	121	26,628	498	3,733	5	2	5	1
Mexican	390	(D)	75	17,585	377	2,674	6	(D)	6	1
Puerto Rican	104	5,191	18	2,937	27	324	13	8	19	4
Cuban	6	(D)	3	(D)	(D)	(D)	25	(D)	-	(D)
Other Central or South American	44	1,875	7	1,077	29	186	19	13	-	-
European Spanish	30	4,842	17	4,371	48	465	13	3	20	4
Other Hispanic	6	(D)	1	(D)	(D)	(D)	41	(D)	-	(D)
Grand Rapids, MI MSA	205	7,409	36	4,709	71	631	6	5	19	5
Mexican	144	5,573	31	3,794	55	495	8	6	23	6
Puerto Rican	23	1,069	3	(D)	(D)	(D)	18	16	-	(D)
Cuban	14	(D)	-	-	-	-	23	(D)	-	-
Other Central or South American	14	238	-	-	-	-	20	26	-	-
European Spanish	7	(D)	1	(D)	(D)	(D)	29	(D)	-	(D)
Other Hispanic	3	(D)	1	(D)	(D)	(D)	47	(D)	-	(D)
Greeley, CO MSA	518	22,932	122	13,475	226	3,177	11	10	18	9
Mexican	445	20,633	98	(D)	(D)	(D)	12	11	20	(D)
Puerto Rican	6	(D)	5	(D)	(D)	(D)	58	(D)	69	(D)
Cuban	9	(D)	-	-	-	-	95	(D)	-	-
Other Central or South American	30	338	3	(D)	(D)	(D)	49	55	46	(D)
European Spanish	18	(D)	16	(D)	(D)	(D)	49	(D)	55	(D)
Other Hispanic	10	(D)	-	-	-	-	84	(D)	-	-

[Continued]

★ 705 ★

Hispanic-Owned Firms, by Metropolitan Statistical Area With 100 or More Hispanic-Owned Firms: Gary/Hammond - Lake County

[Continued]

Geographic area and minority	All firms: Firms (number) A	All firms: Sales and receipts ($000) B	Firms with paid employees: Firms (number) C	Firms with paid employees: Sales and receipts ($000) D	Firms with paid employees: Employees (number) E	Firms with paid employees: Annual payroll ($000) F	Relative standard error of estimate (percent) for column - A	B	C	D
Greensboro-Winston-Salem-High Point, NC MSA	110	4,536	20	3,197	60	453	9	2	-	-
Mexican	23	651	5	(D)	(D)	(D)	15	1	-	(D)
Puerto Rican	14	(D)	1	(D)	(D)	(D)	32	(D)	-	(D)
Cuban	26	(D)	9	2,017	20	180	19	(D)	-	-
Other Central or South American	37	1,076	3	(D)	(D)	(D)	16	5	-	(D)
European Spanish	6	(D)	-	-	-	-	-	(D)	-	-
Other Hispanic	4	(D)	2	(D)	(D0	(D)	35	(D)	-	(D)
Hartford, CT PMSA	373	27,655	71	14,765	192	3,842	8	5	11	7
Mexican	17	551	-	-	-	-	40	52	-	-
Puerto Rican	130	9,559	28	7,140	79	2,234	13	9	17	11
Cuban	64	7,829	15	2,865	43	561	15	12	-	-
Other Central or South American	101	4,667	11	1,881	28	404	15	8	-	-
European Spanish	43	4,622	15	(D)	(D)	(D)	24	14	42	(D)
Other Hispanic	18	427	2	(D)	(D)	(D)	55	29	-	(D)
Honolulu, HI MSA	727	43,676	113	33,295	377	4,665	5	2	8	3
Mexican	181	24,019	25	(D)	(D)	(D)	9	3	8	(D)
Puerto Rican	179	5,996	25	3,682	69	775	10	7	8	7
Cuban	39	492	4	(D)	(D)	(D)	18	10	-	(D)
Other Central or South American	61	2,445	10	1,339	23	165	11	4	14	7
European Spanish	138	5,702	36	3,877	85	747	12	7	22	7
Other Hispanic	129	5,022	13	2,846	38	349	16	7	19	1
Houston, TX PMSA	15,967	584,356	3,053	347,901	4,183	83,399	2	2	4	3
Mexican	12,793	452,752	2,530	267,934	3,281	65,736	2	3	5	3
Puerto Rican	230	9,056	35	(D)	(D)	(D)	19	20	43	(D)
Cuban	641	38,801	102	22,760	339	4,986	10	7	14	8
Other Central or South American	1,671	56,816	285	36,351	282	7,312	7	7	15	9
European Spanish	365	17,186	49	(D)	(D)	(D)	14	9	26	(D)
Other Hispanic	267	9,745	52	6,850	98	1,554	17	15	37	19
Indianapolis, IN MSA	248	38,600	55	33,630	344	5,987	8	1	8	1
Mexican	123	28,337	28	26,550	282	5,120	11	1	5	-
Puerto Rican	29	2,293	8	(D)	(D)	(D)	20	7	45	(D)
Cuban	6	(D)	3	(D)	(D)	(D)	-	(D)	-	(D)
Other Central or South American	48	2,220	12	1,581	25	267	20	8	20	7
European Spanish	37	(D)	3	(D)	(D)	(D)	24	(D)	-	(D)
Other Hispanic	5	(D)	1	(D)	(D)	(D)	-	(D)	-	(D)
Jacksonville, FL MSA	444	57,052	64	47,727	439	6,737	12	2	8	1
Mexican	87	1,646	2	(D)	(D)	(D)	28	25	-	(D)
Puerto Rican	40	(D)	4	678	7	89	36	(D)	35	26
Cuban	176	47,273	38	42,393	276	5,583	19	2	11	1
Other Central or South American	96	3,729	11	2,041	68	473	26	13	18	9
European Spanish	43	2,513	7	1,401	58	313	36	18	20	24

[Continued]

★ 705 ★

Hispanic-Owned Firms, by Metropolitan Statistical Area With 100 or More Hispanic-Owned Firms: Gary/Hammond - Lake County

[Continued]

Geographic area and minority	All firms: Firms (number) A	All firms: Sales and receipts ($000) B	Firms with paid employees: Firms (number) C	Firms with paid employees: Sales and receipts ($000) D	Firms with paid employees: Employees (number) E	Firms with paid employees: Annual payroll ($000) F	Relative standard error of estimate (percent) for column - A	B	C	D
Other Hispanic	2	(D)	2	(D)	(D)	(D)	-	(D)	-	(D)
Jersey City, NJ PMSA	3,949	294,372	679	193,472	1,642	20,207	2	1	4	1
Mexican	97	5,504	7	1,867	21	188	13	15	20	26
Puerto Rican	612	28,746	100	13,977	224	2,913	5	5	10	6
Cuban	1,998	210,922	389	153,715	1,037	13,237	3	1	4	1
Other Central or South American	987	35,334	134	14,347	262	2,471	4	5	10	8
European Spanish	181	10,163	33	6,627	66	995	10	6	17	5
Other Hispanic	74	3,703	16	2,939	32	403	18	16	25	15
Joliet, IL PMSA	212	9,009	55	5,736	102	1,132	13	9	23	9
Mexican	187	7,312	44	4,336	74	965	15	9	25	6
Puerto Rican	1	(D)	-	-	-	-	-	(D)	-	-
Cuban	4	706	3	(D)	(D)	(D)	-	-	-	(D)
Other Central or South American	3	(D)	1	(D)	(D)	(D)	-	(D)	-	(D)
European Spanish	12	724	7	629	3	42	60	63	79	71
Other Hispanic	5	(D)	-	-	-	-	69	(D)	-	-
Kansas City, MO-KS MSA	834	30,054	161	20,608	411	4,436	5	2	7	1
Mexican	611	20,617	114	13,987	317	3,506	6	2	8	1
Puerto Rican	12	326	2	(D)	(D)	(D)	58	40	-	(D)
Cuban	36	5,087	13	4,471	44	517	23	5	19	-
Other Central or South American	79	2,135	17	877	21	174	19	12	38	26
European Spanish	65	1,490	9	918	17	133	20	4	15	1
Other Hispanic	31	399	6	(D)	(D)	(D)	30	11	56	(D)
Killeen-Temple, TX MSA	414	7,472	45	4,765	84	914	13	15	23	19
Mexican	368	6,845	37	(D)	(D)	(D)	14	17	27	(D)
Puerto Rican	9	107	4	44	4	16	45	53	50	68
Cuban	6	(D)	2	(D)	(D)	(D)	62	(D)	71	(D)
Other Central or South American	2	(D)	-	-	-	-	-	(D)	-	-
European Spanish	29	410	2	(D)	(D)	(D)	50	7	-	(D)
Other Hispanic	-	-	-	-	-	-	-	-	-	-
Lake County, IL PMSA	353	16,360	71	10,903	160	2,050	11	7	12	9
Mexican	179	8,152	48	6,313	96	1,204	14	13	17	16
Puerto Rican	30	1,040	3	(D)	(D)	(D)	30	16	-	(D)
Cuban	32	2,171	8	1,791	19	502	39	11	25	11
Other Central or South American	72	2,741	7	1,300	29	179	26	10	-	-
European Spanish	29	2,142	5	(D)	(D)	(D)	44	18	-	(D)
Other Hispanic	11	114	-	-	-	-	58	38	-	-

Source: 1987 Economic Censuses, Survey of Minority-Owned Business Enterprises: Hispanics, U.S. Department of Commerce, Bureau of the Census, MB-87-2, 1991, pp. 55-70. *Notes:* A dash (-) represents zero. (D) stands for data withheld to avoid disclosing data for individual companies; data are included in higher-level totals.

★706★

Hispanic-Owned Firms

Hispanic-Owned Firms, by Metropolitan Statistical Area With 100 or More Hispanic-Owned Firms: Lakeland/Winter Haven - Melbourne/Titusville/Palm Bay

Geographic area and minority	All firms		Firms with paid employees				Relative standard error of estimate (percent) for column -			
	Firms (number) A	Sales and receipts ($000) B	Firms (number) C	Sales and receipts ($000) D	Employees (number) E	Annual payroll ($000) F	A	B	C	D
Lakeland-Winter Haven, FL MSA	408	24,429	121	17,061	510	3,941	13	10	19	12
Mexican	125	5,286	27	4,105	95	1,467	23	24	45	31
Puerto Rican	43	1,794	6	(D)	(D)	(D)	40	20	32	(D)
Cuban	133	10,643	63	8,031	89	1,738	22	15	29	16
Other Central or South American	70	5,433	23	3,513	37	385	30	28	23	21
European Spanish	17	1,003	2	(D)	(D)	(D)	59	4	-	(D)
Other Hispanic	20	270	-	-	-	-	67	67	-	-
Lancaster, PA MSA	112	5,261	21	2,630	54	433	8	8	13	8
Mexican	14	1,456	6	1,139	24	191	20	14	24	3
Puerto Rican	49	1,478	8	(D)	(D)	(D)	13	5	25	(D)
Cuban	5	(D)	1	(D)	(D)	(D)	28	(D)	-	(D)
Other Central or South American	35	1,550	5	847	8	86	14	21	28	23
European Spanish	5	(D)	1	(D)	(D)	(D)	-	(D)	-	(D)
Other Hispanic	4	(D)	-	-	-	-	50	(D)	-	-
Lansing-East Lansing, MI MSA	211	8,815	31	6,560	96	2,485	7	3	14	2
Mexican	147	6,882	16	5,255	73	2,313	8	3	13	1
Puerto Rican	6	142	2	(D)	(D)	(D)	41	47	71	(D)
Cuban	16	105	-	-	-	-	22	16	-	-
Other Central or South American	17	425	9	(D)	(D)	(D)	26	32	42	(D)
European Spanish	17	1,223	4	864	12	85	17	1	-	-
Other Hispanic	8	38	-	-	-	-	35	45	-	-
Laredo, TX MSA	2,768	236,734	803	190,400	2,817	28,043	5	2	6	2
Mexican	2,557	225,669	760	183,420	2,714	27,093	5	2	7	2
Puerto Rican	1	(D)	1	(D)	(D)	(D)	-	(D)	-	(D)
Cuban	7	(D)	3	120	7	20	20	(D)	47	57
Other Central or South American	122	7,978	31	4,833	65	688	22	13	32	14
European Spanish	21	1,977	6	(D)	(D)	(D)	49	14	24	(D)
Other Hispanic	60	638	2	(D)	(D)	(D)	38	47	71	(D)
Las Cruces, NM MSA	1,578	73,216	438	57,762	1,436	14,784	5	4	7	4
Mexican	1,309	62,517	384	50,709	1,243	13,001	5	4	8	5
Puerto Rican	8	(D)	1	(D)	(D)	(D)	81	(D)	-	(D)
Cuban	10	(D)	1	(D)	(D)	(D)	64	(D)	-	(D)
Other Central or South American	50	2,349	15	(D)	(D)	(D)	25	11	19	(D)
European Spanish	140	3,149	27	1,971	84	382	21	14	29	7
Other Hispanic	61	3,344	10	2,395	50	768	25	5	14	5
Las Vegas, NV MSA	1,084	84,518	237	66,095	1,353	17,368	4	1	7	1
Mexican	616	33,272	143	25,397	475	5,462	6	2	8	1
Puerto Rican	25	(D)	8	(D)	(D)	(D)	10	(D)	-	(D)
Cuban	140	(D)	19	(D)	(D)	(D)	14	(D)	34	(D)
Other Central or South American	168	11,654	31	6,061	110	1,379	13	2	17	4
European Spanish	111	30,393	27	(D)	(D)	(D)	17	1	25	(D)
Other Hispanic	24	1,102	9	(D)	(D)	(D)	41	23	72	(D)

[Continued]

★ 706 ★

Hispanic-Owned Firms, by Metropolitan Statistical Area With 100 or More Hispanic-Owned Firms: Lakeland/Winter Haven - Melbourne/Titusville/Palm Bay

[Continued]

Geographic area and minority	All firms		Firms with paid employees				Relative standard error of estimate (percent) for column -			
	Firms (number) A	Sales and receipts ($000) B	Firms (number) C	Sales and receipts ($000) D	Employees (number) E	Annual payroll ($000) F	A	B	C	D
Lawrence-Haverhill, MA-NH PMSA	207	12,586	34	4,776	61	637	6	4	10	6
Mexican	20	832	3	313	18	120	17	7	-	-
Puerto Rican	55	2,284	10	889	16	188	12	13	24	32
Cuban	33	1,718	1	(D)	(D)	(D)	13	16	-	(D)
Other Central or South American	75	5,155	15	3,199	23	264	10	6	13	2
European Spanish	7	171	3	52	-	16	29	39	48	47
Other Hispanic	17	2,426	2	(D)	(D)	(D)	20	7	-	(D)
Longview-Marshall, TX MSA	100	3,092	30	(D)	(D)	(D)	27	29	46	(D)
Mexican	99	(D)	30	(D)	(D)	(D)	27	(D)	46	(D)
Puerto Rican	-	-	-	-	-	-	-	-	-	-
Cuban	-	-	-	-	-	-	-	-	-	-
Other Central or South American	-	-	-	-	-	-	-	-	-	-
European Spanish	1	(D)	-	-	-	-	-	(D)	-	-
Other Hispanic	-	-	-	-	-	-	-	-	-	-
Lorain-Elyria, OH PMSA	118	5,233	20	2,820	76	615	16	8	7	1
Mexican	40	2,229	5	(D)	(D)	(D)	31	13	-	(D)
Puerto Rican	63	2,403	10	576	10	81	19	13	-	-
Cuban	2	(D)	1	(D)	(D)	(D)	-	(D)	-	(D)
Other Central or South American	11	(D)	2	(D)	(D)	(D)	60	(D)	71	(D)
European Spanish	2	(D)	2	(D)	(D)	(D)	-	(D)	-	(D)
Other Hispanic	-	-	-	-	-	-	-	-	-	-
Los Angeles-Long Beach, CA PMSA	56,679	3,346,076	10,339	2,260,478	36,463	447,029	1	1	2	1
Mexican	38,505	2,275,663	7,030	1,530,376	24,788	304,292	1	1	2	1
Puerto Rican	1,202	103,444	243	84,095	738	10,906	8	4	14	4
Cuban	2,617	239,111	591	178,397	2,864	33,882	5	2	7	2
Other Central or South American	11,056	534,843	1,914	329,881	5,173	59,028	3	2	5	3
European Spanish	2,117	127,060	374	86,228	1,883	24,838	6	4	10	4
Other Hispanic	1,182	65,955	187	51,501	1,017	14,083	8	5	17	5
Louisville, KY-IN MSA	145	8,307	35	4,451	91	960	5	1	9	1
Mexican	38	3,181	6	645	16	105	9	1	24	1
Puerto Rican	14	1,106	3	(D)	(D)	(D)	18	2	-	(D)
Cuban	22	533	7	(D)	(D)	(D)	11	7	29	(D)
Other Central or South American	42	2,121	13	(D)	(D)	(D)	9	2	15	(D)
European Spanish	23	1,317	6	(D)	(D)	(D)	16	1	-	(D)
Other Hispanic	6	49	-	-	-	-	47	69	-	-
Lubbock, TX MSA	1,055	36,036	199	26,062	477	4,863	8	8	15	10
Mexican	901	27,609	166	19,879	343	3,409	9	10	17	13
Puerto Rican	2	(D)	2	(D)	(D)	(D)	-	(D)	-	(D)
Cuban	26	(D)	6	206	14	54	52	(D)	41	46
Other Central or South American	57	1,546	6	(D)	(D)	(D)	30	21	41	(D)
European Spanish	30	4,555	7	4,399	93	1,053	46	15	20	15
Other Hispanic	39	1,802	12	404	8	112	42	43	80	62

[Continued]

★ 706 ★

Hispanic-Owned Firms, by Metropolitan Statistical Area With 100 or More Hispanic-Owned Firms: Lakeland/Winter Haven - Melbourne/Titusville/Palm Bay

[Continued]

Geographic area and minority	All firms		Firms with paid employees				Relative standard error of estimate (percent) for column -			
	Firms (number) A	Sales and receipts ($000) B	Firms (number) C	Sales and receipts ($000) D	Employees (number) E	Annual payroll ($000) F	A	B	C	D
McAllen-Edinburg-Mission, TX MSA	7,847	457,977	1,959	343,015	5,397	51,698	3	2	4	2
Mexican	7,191	425,606	1,838	316,713	5,098	48,842	3	2	4	2
Puerto Rican	8	3,711	5	(D)	(D)	(D)	-	-	-	(D)
Cuban	89	2,109	10	(D)	(D)	(D)	30	21	28	(D)
Other Central or South American	296	17,417	68	13,716	145	1,378	15	9	21	6
European Spanish	98	4,487	15	3,581	65	509	29	19	21	23
Other Hispanic	165	4,647	23	3,945	56	557	24	21	43	23
Melbourne-Titusville-Palm Bay, FL MSA	352	18,327	84	11,892	184	2,004	13	9	21	11
Mexican	26	825	1	(D)	(D)	(D)	52	42	-	(D)
Puerto Rican	55	2,902	18	2,366	31	261	32	20	54	21
Cuban	155	10,816	38	6,613	95	1,182	19	12	29	16
Other Central or South American	66	2,924	11	2,182	42	323	30	25	26	29
European Spanish	35	630	14	(D)	(D)	(D)	43	43	69	(D)
Other Hispanic	15	230	2	(D)	(D)	(D0	66	51	71	(D)

Source: *1987 Economic Censuses: Survey of Minority-Owned Business Enterprises: Hispanics*, U.S. Department of Commerce, Bureau of the Census, MB-87-2, 1991, pp. 55-70. *Notes:* A dash (-) represents zero. (D) stands for data withheld to avoid disclosing data for individual companies; data are included in higher-level totals.

★ 707 ★

Hispanic-Owned Firms

Hispanic-Owned Firms, by Metropolitan Statistical Area With 100 or More Hispanic-Owned Firms: Memphis - New Haven/Meriden

Geographic area and minority	All firms		Firms with paid employees				Relative standard error of estimate (percent) for column -			
	Firms (number) A	Sales and receipts ($000) B	Firms (number) C	Sales and receipts ($000) D	Employees (number) E	Annual payroll ($000) F	A	B	C	D
Memphis, TN-AR-MS MSA	104	4,707	23	3,252	104	734	6	2	6	1
Mexican	31	1,607	6	954	14	193	11	3	23	4
Puerto Rican	11	(D)	-	-	-	-	22	(D)	-	-
Cuban	25	880	8	(D)	(D)	(D)	11	2	-	(D)
Other Central or South American	21	1,051	6	868	19	160	13	2	-	-
European Spanish	14	740	3	(D)	(D)	(D)	14	1	-	(D)
Other Hispanic	2	(D)	-	-	-	-	70	(D)	-	-
Merced, CA MSA	451	50,333	145	41,412	856	8,455	10	5	11	4
Mexican	397	45,145	133	37,328	763	7,638	11	5	12	5
Puerto Rican	6	940	4	(D)	(D)	(D)	33	7	35	(D)
Cuban	4	(D)	3	(D)	(D)	(D)	35	(D)	47	(D)
Other Central or South American	26	1,518	3	973	70	607	52	21	-	-
European Spanish	17	592	1	(D)	(D)	(D)	62	25	-	(D)
Other Hispanic	1	(D)	1	(D)	(D)	(D)	-	(D)	-	(D)
Miami-Hialeah, FL PMSA	47,725	3,771,247	6,528	2,904,141	30,069	404,141	1	-	2	-
Mexican	1,190	48,308	165	29,342	557	7,915	8	8	16	10
Puerto Rican	2,149	84,933	226	47,400	671	7,612	6	6	11	5

[Continued]

★ 707 ★

Hispanic-Owned Firms, by Metropolitan Statistical Area With 100 or More Hispanic-Owned Firms: Memphis - New Haven/Meriden

[Continued]

Geographic area and minority	All firms		Firms with paid employees				Relative standard error of estimate (percent) for column -			
	Firms (number) A	Sales and receipts ($000) B	Firms (number) C	Sales and receipts ($000) D	Employees (number) E	Annual payroll ($000) F	A	B	C	D
Cuban	34,771	3,146,999	5,205	2,489,927	25,117	345,023	1	1	2	-
Other Central or South American	7,934	354,972	735	229,484	2,465	29,923	3	2	6	2
European Spanish	1,286	105,684	169	83,518	1,083	12,069	8	3	13	2
Other Hispanic	395	30,351	28	24,470	176	1,599	14	4	14	3
Middlesex-Somerset-Hunterdon, NJ PMSA	1,039	90,759	160	61,338	636	10,519	4	2	8	1
Mexican	33	796	6	441	14	235	21	31	47	52
Puerto Rican	322	16,420	50	8,801	199	2,446	8	6	14	4
Cuban	256	30,004	34	19,485	116	1,469	8	4	16	2
Other Central or South American	275	28,440	42	20,934	167	2,934	9	4	16	3
European Spanish	118	12,933	21	9,879	122	3,012	12	5	21	2
Other Hispanic	35	2,166	7	1,798	18	423	21	11	20	9
Midland, TX MSA	662	18,653	121	12,204	216	2,551	11	10	23	8
Mexican	602	17,330	116	(D)	(D)	(D)	12	10	23	(D)
Puerto Rican	10	210	-	-	-	-	95	95	-	-
Cuban	10	60	-	-	-	-	95	95	-	-
Other Central or South American	8	147	3	(D)	(D)	(D)	47	41	48	(D)
European Spanish	-	-	-	-	-	-	-	-	-	-
Other Hispanic	32	906	2	(D)	(D)	(D)	51	8	-	(D)
Milwaukee, WI PMSA	496	50,854	103	43,712	277	3,705	4	1	7	1
Mexican	301	37,972	61	(D)	(D)	(D)	6	1	11	(D)
Puerto Rican	72	3,060	8	(D)	(D)	(D)	11	6	30	(D)
Cuban	18	1,481	4	(D)	(D)	(D)	19	1	-	(D)
Other Central or South American	57	3,634	9	(D)	(D)	(D)	12	2	-	(D)
European Spanish	41	4,328	18	4,053	46	868	26	3	19	3
Other Hispanic	7	379	3	(D)	(D)	(D)	-	-	-	(D)
Minneapolis-St. Paul, MN-WI MSA	568	23,278	81	16,608	242	3,081	4	1	5	-
Mexican	364	16,324	55	12,447	196	2,452	5	1	6	-
Puerto Rican	28	550	2	(D)	(D)	(D)	18	7	-	(D)
Cuban	28	851	4	633	4	52	18	7	-	-
Other Central or South American	81	2,647	14	1,845	18	298	11	3	18	-
European Spanish	46	1,804	4	359	6	65	11	3	-	-
Other Hispanic	21	1,102	2	(D)	(D)	(D)	26	1	-	(D)
Modesto, CA MSA	1,129	76,882	273	58,046	1,219	14,110	8	6	11	7
Mexican	843	65,229	228	50,338	1,087	12,978	9	6	12	7
Puerto Rican	68	4,180	22	2,890	32	404	35	48	61	65
Cuban	29	781	2	(D)	(D)	(D)	42	17	-	(D)
Other Central or South American	101	3,380	12	2,205	69	418	24	24	26	32
European Spanish	61	1,911	2	(D)	(D)	(D)	35	23	-	(D)
Other Hispanic	27	1,401	7	1,351	24	172	46	35	29	37
Monmouth-Ocean, NJ PMSA	685	58,597	145	45,126	491	8,718	5	2	8	2
Mexican	30	1,034	5	588	8	128	22	27	28	14
Puerto Rican	276	18,536	48	12,512	214	3,230	8	5	15	5
Cuban	132	12,273	32	9,122	67	1,415	10	5	15	2
Other Central or South American	126	11,555	35	9,419	147	1,758	12	5	17	5
European Spanish	79	11,128	15	9,735	46	905	15	3	19	2
Other Hispanic	42	4,071	10	3,750	9	1,282	20	6	37	7

[Continued]

★ 707 ★

Hispanic-Owned Firms, by Metropolitan Statistical Area With 100 or More Hispanic-Owned Firms: Memphis - New Haven/Meriden

[Continued]

Geographic area and minority	All firms: Firms (number) A	All firms: Sales and receipts ($000) B	Firms with paid employees: Firms (number) C	Firms with paid employees: Sales and receipts ($000) D	Firms with paid employees: Employees (number) E	Firms with paid employees: Annual payroll ($000) F	Relative standard error of estimate (percent) for column - A	B	C	D
Naples, FL MSA	603	31,435	125	18,962	279	3,959	11	10	21	14
Mexican	179	9,516	33	6,346	122	1,227	20	24	37	33
Puerto Rican	33	(D)	-	-	-	-	47	(D)	-	-
Cuban	287	14,765	75	8,803	111	2,018	16	15	29	16
Other Central or South American	84	2,242	5	(D)	(D)	(D)	34	20	28	(D)
European Spanish	18	2,983	10	(D)	(D)	(D)	52	23	75	(D)
Other Hispanic	2	(D)	2	(D)	(D)	(D)	71	(D)	71	(D)
Nashville, TN MSA	214	16,234	57	9,220	114	1,695	5	2	6	2
Mexican	62	3,287	29	2,689	41	801	8	3	10	3
Puerto Rican	26	2,790	8	(D)	(D)	(D)	15	4	17	(D)
Cuban	32	(D)	4	395	21	84	18	(D)	-	-
Other Central or South American	65	3,561	7	(D)	(D)	(D)	9	3	20	(D)
European Spanish	23	1,501	6	1,390	26	397	14	2	-	-
Other Hispanic	6	(D)	3	(D)	(D)	(D)	-	(D)	-	(D)
Nassau-Suffolk, NY PMSA	3,313	214,658	680	144,270	1,829	29,437	3	3	6	3
Mexican	185	7,869	37	4,324	88	1,304	15	17	31	25
Puerto Rican	1,032	62,665	199	41,442	623	8,477	6	4	9	4
Cuban	413	42,877	112	32,209	364	5,976	9	5	15	5
Other Central or South American	1,205	62,132	232	41,072	469	7,522	6	6	12	6
European Spanish	357	34,402	84	23,333	245	5,263	11	7	18	6
Other Hispanic	121	4,713	16	1,890	40	895	18	14	23	26
New Bedford, MA MSA	148	5,131	15	2,621	38	255	7	6	13	5
Mexican	7	129	1	(D)	(D)	(D)	29	44	-	(D)
Puerto Rican	28	478	2	(D)	(D)	(D)	18	27	71	(D)
Cuban	22	741	1	(D)	(D)	(D)	19	16	-	(D)
Other Central or South American	33	1,946	8	1,497	21	138	15	7	18	4
European Spanish	23	569	1	(D)	(D0	(D)	17	13	-	(D)
Other Hispanic	35	1,268	2	(D)	(D)	(D)	16	17	-	(D)
New Haven-Meriden, CT MSA	357	55,054	57	46,826	530	5,689	9	2	16	2
Mexican	28	470	7	(D)	(D)	(D)	39	17	63	(D)
Puerto Rican	136	7,877	24	(D)	(D)	(D)	14	15	26	(D)
Cuban	66	36,355	9	(D)	(D)	(D)	21	1	-	(D)
Other Central or South American	76	7,288	7	(D)	(D)	(D)	19	5	-	(D)
European Spanish	30	972	7	(D)	(D)	(D)	32	23	64	(D)
Other Hispanic	21	2,092	3	(D)	(D)	(D)	35	11	-	(D)

Source: 1987 Economic Censuses: Survey of Minority-Owned Business Enterprises: Hispanics, U.S. Department of Commerce, Bureau of the Census, MB-87-2, 1991, pp. 55-70. *Notes:* A dash (-) represents zero. (D) stands for data withheld to avoid disclosing data for individual companies; data are included in higher-level totals.

★ 708 ★

Hispanic-Owned Firms

Hispanic-Owned Firms, by Metropolitan Statistical Area With 100 or More Hispanic-Owned Firms: New London/Norwich - Oxnard/Ventura

Geographic area and minority	All firms		Firms with paid employees				Relative standard error of estimate (percent) for column -			
	Firms (number) A	Sales and receipts ($000) B	Firms (number) C	Sales and receipts ($000) D	Employees (number) E	Annual payroll ($000) F	A	B	C	D
New London-Norhich, CT-RI MSA	101	4,579	14	2,300	57	700	15	6	25	9
Mexican	9	257	1	(D)	(D)	(D)	38	23	-	(D)
Puerto Rican	21	1,426	3	(D)	(D)	(D)	33	5	-	(D)
Cuban	14	156	1	(D)	(D)	(D)	46	57	-	(D)
Other Central or South American	29	404	1	(D)	(D)	(D)	32	23	-	(D)
European Spanish	18	834	2	(D)	(D)	(D)	38	12	-	(D)
Other Hispanic	10	1,502	6	(D)	(D)	(D)	38	14	58	(D)
New Orleans, LA MSA	1,719	86,143	334	57,194	987	11,691	2	1	3	1
Mexican	240	8,351	49	5,222	105	1,020	5	3	10	3
Puerto Rican	102	5,974	25	4,496	163	1,178	8	5	11	4
Cuban	344	13,845	50	7,822	76	894	5	3	8	3
Other Central or South American	711	31,757	126	19,383	254	3,599	3	2	6	2
European Spanish	274	23,797	72	19,158	370	4,745	5	1	5	1
Other Hispanic	48	2,419	12	1,113	19	255	12	9	17	12
New York, NY PMSA	23,014	1,239,513	3,298	735,866	10,043	144,654	1	1	3	1
Mexican	902	35,145	137	18,827	323	4,690	7	7	14	9
Puerto Rican	7,046	389,747	1,083	232,376	3,165	48,540	2	2	4	2
Cuban	2,920	221,545	524	150,220	2,541	30,242	4	2	6	2
Other Central or South American	10,504	481,763	1,293	254,905	3,153	46,266	2	2	4	2
European Spanish	1,227	90,755	201	65,731	681	12,164	6	3	11	2
Other Hispanic	415	20,558	60	13,807	180	2,752	10	8	18	9
Newark, NJ PMSA	2,877	235,415	619	167,868	1,674	22,703	2	2	4	2
Mexican	97	5,302	18	3,408	43	611	12	8	18	5
Puerto Rican	568	41,994	136	26,444	313	4,246	5	5	9	6
Cuban	932	93,420	213	72,229	752	9,877	4	2	6	2
Other Central or South American	927	44,180	177	22,415	274	3,103	4	5	8	6
European Spanish	245	47,483	67	42,944	290	4,695	8	3	9	3
Other Hispanic	108	3,036	8	428	2	171	16	21	43	47
Norfolk-Virginia Beach-Newport News, VA MSA	364	16,446	90	11,724	234	2,424	5	2	5	2
Mexican	93	3,162	19	2,082	42	439	9	4	17	3
Puerto Rican	66	2,032	11	(D)	(D)	(D)	11	8	18	(D)
Cuban	40	1,269	11	891	50	305	13	10	18	13
Other Central or South American	102	4,536	33	3,485	77	848	9	5	7	4
European Spanish	52	4,713	14	3,300	35	349	13	1	-	-
Other Hispanic	11	734	2	(D)	(D)	(D)	22	8	-	(D)
Norwalk, CT PMSA	148	10,588	20	5,729	84	1,323	12	6	7	1
Mexican	3	(D)	1	(D)	(D)	(D)	-	(D)	-	(D)
Puerto Rican	18	(D)	3	(D)	(D)	(D)	35	(D)	-	(D)
Cuban	23	(D)	3	(D)	(D)	(D)	29	(D)	-	(D)
Other Central or South American	87	3,968	7	1,090	23	397	16	17	20	5
European Spanish	13	2,540	3	(D)	(D)	(D)	36	5	-	(D)
Other Hispanic	4	(D)	3	(D)	(D)	(D)	-	(D)	-	(D)
Oakland, CA PMSA	6,046	353,718	1,146	255,733	3,370	48,096	3	3	6	3
Mexican	3,771	203,054	653	141,624	2,347	29,330	4	3	7	4
Puerto Rican	276	10,722	45	7,211	127	1,677	16	14	28	15
Cuban	116	7,953	28	6,374	92	868	22	20	17	23
Other Central or South American	937	73,432	218	60,136	362	8,927	9	6	17	6
European Spanish	638	46,042	150	32,622	314	5,700	10	7	16	6
Other Hispanic	308	12,515	52	7,766	128	1,594	18	6	23	6

[Continued]

★ 708 ★

Hispanic-Owned Firms, by Metropolitan Statistical Area With 100 or More Hispanic-Owned Firms: New London/Norwich - Oxnard/Ventura

[Continued]

Geographic area and minority	All firms		Firms with paid employees				Relative standard error of estimate (percent) for column -			
	Firms (number) A	Sales and receipts ($000) B	Firms (number) C	Sales and receipts ($000) D	Employees (number) E	Annual payroll ($000) F	A	B	C	D
Ocala, FL MSA	189	13,404	47	9,641	184	2,305	17	9	22	8
Mexican	20	(D)	-	-	-	-	60	(D)	-	-
Puerto Rican	34	2,299	9	(D)	(D)	(D)	32	18	16	(D)
Cuban	64	7,125	18	5,555	111	999	29	10	17	4
Other Central or South American	62	1,504	17	(D)	(D)	(D)	35	26	57	(D)
European Spanish	7	1,746	3	(D)	(D)	(D)	40	36	47	(D)
Other Hispanic	2	(D)	-	-	-	-	71	(D)	-	-
Odessa, TX MSA	1,013	24,683	168	15,112	180	3,808	9	11	19	14
Mexican	899	20,947	152	11,880	151	2,965	10	11	20	15
Puerto Rican	-	-	-	-	-	-	-	-	-	-
Cuban	25	1,090	4	(D)	(D)	(D)	54	21	35	(D)
Other Central or South American	41	1,565	8	1,452	8	64	42	81	71	87
European Spanish	16	(D)	2	(D)	(D)	(D)	51	(D)	-	(D)
Other Hispanic	32	(D)	2	(D)	(D)	(D)	51	(D)	-	(D)
Oklahoma City, OK MSA	574	15,717	95	9,114	220	1,965	5	3	8	1
Mexican	417	10,776	68	6,297	141	1,349	7	3	10	2
Puerto Rican	34	2,254	10	1,746	47	321	20	2	-	-
Cuban	22	568	5	(D)	(D)	(D)	17	5	-	(D)
Other Central or South American	52	1,373	8	730	25	222	19	13	55	12
European Spanish	38	525	3	(D)	(D)	(D)	18	21	-	(D)
Other Hispanic	11	221	1	(D)	(D)	(D)	41	47	-	(D)
Omaha, NE-IA MSA	243	6,347	43	4,697	153	1,537	6	2	7	1
Mexican	206	5,072	37	(D)	(D)	(D)	6	3	8	(D)
Puerto Rican	6	(D)	1	(D)	(D)	(D)	47	(D)	-	(D)
Cuban	4	(D)	-	-	-	-	60	(D)	-	-
Other Central or South American	16	(D)	1	(D)	(D)	(D)	28	(D)	-	(D)
European Spanish	9	498	3	472	16	182	17	-	-	-
Other Hispanic	2	(D)	1	(D)	(D)	(D)	-	(D)	-	(D)
Orange County, NY PMSA	292	11,971	63	6,485	125	1,381	11	9	19	9
Mexican	26	1,693	1	(D)	(D)	(D)	36	26	-	(D)
Puerto Rican	134	3,838	28	1,312	37	442	18	12	34	21
Cuban	19	2,231	8	1,517	30	355	31	29	25	21
Other Central or South American	46	2,195	16	1,488	10	142	25	11	40	13
European Spanish	54	1,879	10	(D)	(D)	(D)	26	21	32	(D)
Other Hispanic	13	135	-	-	-	-	60	15	-	-
Orlando, FL MSA	1,944	127,128	386	89,719	1,316	15,693	6	3	9	3
Mexican	124	14,709	16	12,549	116	1,595	22	5	13	3
Puerto Rican	539	27,136	106	17,175	249	2,235	11	6	20	7
Cuban	733	49,378	177	39,571	619	7,154	9	4	12	3
Other Central or South American	406	22,018	61	11,721	259	3,472	13	11	27	17
European Spanish	106	12,519	20	8,175	69	1,123	26	9	49	5
Other Hispanic	36	1,368	6	528	4	114	47	58	62	61
Oxnard-Ventura, CA PMSA	3,297	216,836	726	156,851	2,328	30,972	4	3	7	3
Mexican	2,548	174,651	583	127,303	1,977	25,512	5	3	8	3
Puerto Rican	128	3,612	9	1,866	33	515	26	18	27	17
Cuban	85	4,871	21	3,278	48	559	28	33	47	40
Other Central or South American	332	13,892	68	8,875	80	1,076	14	8	22	10

[Continued]

★ 708 ★

Hispanic-Owned Firms, by Metropolitan Statistical Area With 100 or More Hispanic-Owned Firms: New London/Norwich - Oxnard/Ventura

[Continued]

Geographic area and minority	All firms		Firms with paid employees				Relative standard error of estimate (percent) for column -			
	Firms (number) A	Sales and receipts ($000) B	Firms (number) C	Sales and receipts ($000) D	Employees (number) E	Annual payroll ($000) F	A	B	C	D
European Spanish	144	8,561	28	5,276	59	1,357	23	24	36	29
Other Hispanic	60	11,249	17	10,253	131	1,953	33	16	56	17

Source: 1987 Economic Censuses, Survey of Minority-Owned Business Enterprises: Hispanics, U.S. Department of Commerce, Bureau of the Census, MB-87-2, 1991, pp. 55-70. *Notes:* A dash (-) represents zero. (D) stands for data withheld to avoid disclosing data for individual companies; data are included in higher-level totals.

★ 709 ★

Hispanic-Owned Firms

Hispanic-Owned Firms, by Metropolitan Statistical Area With 100 or More Hispanic-Owned Firms: Pawtucket/Woonsocket/Attleboro - Reno

Geographic area and minority	All firms		Firms with paid employees				Relative standard error of estimate (percent) for column -			
	Firms (number) A	Sales and receipts ($000) B	Firms (number) C	Sales and receipts ($000) D	Employees (number) E	Annual payroll ($000) F	A	B	C	D
Pawtucket-Woonsocket-Attleboro, RI-MA PMSA	129	6,165	29	3,470	24	395	7	6	14	5
Mexican	10	298	-	-	-	-	32	14	-	-
Puerto Rican	15	623	3	(D)	(D)	(D)	25	15	47	(D)
Cuban	14	826	8	(D)	(D)	(D)	20	19	35	(D)
Other Central or South American	48	1,797	7	587	11	139	9	7	20	1
European Spanish	22	2,170	6	(D)	(D)	(D)	14	12	24	(D)
Other Hispanic	20	451	5	310	2	117	16	12	28	16
Pensacola, FL MSA	151	6,928	62	5,793	123	1,028	21	16	25	18
Mexican	53	1,343	11	(D)	(D)	(D)	42	19	22	(D)
Puerto Rican	10	1,369	5	(D)	(D)	(D)	40	39	40	(D)
Cuban	51	2,202	21	1,560	25	237	30	26	47	34
Other Central or South American	19	723	8	694	6	78	58	55	71	57
European Spanish	14	749	13	(D)	(D)	(D)	68	63	73	(D)
Other Hispanic	4	542	4	542	14	78	50	63	50	63
Philadelphia, PA-NJ PMSA	1,930	202,374	351	151,471	1,369	23,161	2	1	4	1
Mexican	154	9,186	30	6,511	81	928	9	2	15	2
Puerto Rican	742	57,532	129	33,502	444	4,408	4	4	7	3
Cuban	312	40,060	67	32,525	357	9,074	6	2	9	1
Other Central or South American	484	28,534	81	17,687	180	2,785	5	5	8	4
European Spanish	169	61,184	30	(D)	(D)	(D)	9	1	9	(D)
Other Hispanic	69	5,878	14	(D)	(D)	(D)	12	8	20	(D)
Phoenix, AZ MSA	4,507	223,471	982	156,429	3,141	37,432	3	3	6	2
Mexican	3,685	184,842	842	131,109	2,799	32,436	4	3	6	3
Puerto Rican	113	(D)	22	(D)	(D)	(D)	25	(D)	44	(D)
Cuban	84	3,729	10	(D)	(D)	(D)	27	30	37	(D)
Other Central or South American	284	8,096	49	3,143	101	674	16	12	34	17
European Spanish	230	17,592	32	14,024	111	2,336	18	6	30	2
Other Hispanic	111	(D)	27	(D)	(D)	(D)	22	(D)	17	(D)
Pittsburgh, PA PMSA	318	21,659	75	13,812	222	2,231	10	11	14	5
Mexican	73	5,702	18	2,469	71	699	40	41	53	22

[Continued]

★ 709 ★

Hispanic-Owned Firms, by Metropolitan Statistical Area With 100 or More Hispanic-Owned Firms: Pawtucket/Woonsocket/Attleboro - Reno

[Continued]

Geographic area and minority	All firms: Firms (number) A	All firms: Sales and receipts ($000) B	Firms with paid employees: Firms (number) C	Firms with paid employees: Sales and receipts ($000) D	Firms with paid employees: Employees (number) E	Firms with paid employees: Annual payroll ($000) F	Relative standard error of estimate (percent) for column - A	B	C	D
Puerto Rican	45	1,359	10	(D)	(D)	(D)	13	18	28	(D)
Cuban	32	2,540	7	(D)	(D)	(D)	17	10	29	(D)
Other Central or South American	78	4,706	16	3,565	33	357	13	8	18	9
European Spanish	74	5,919	18	3,868	62	663	9	5	11	2
Other Hispanic	16	1,433	6	(D)	(D)	(D)	20	20	24	(D)
Portland, OR PMSA	625	59,327	154	50,754	564	7,424	6	1	8	1
Mexican	345	43,568	84	38,893	354	5,429	8	1	11	1
Puerto Rican	38	1,723	11	1,170	22	288	30	23	50	2
Cuban	46	1,787	10	825	17	182	27	18	24	15
Other Central or South American	85	2,222	19	1,406	40	331	17	5	29	1
European Spanish	89	8,270	24	6,808	101	938	12	3	10	1
Other Hispanic	22	1,757	6	1,652	30	256	35	2	-	-
Poughkeepsie, NY MSA	128	7,673	20	4,099	52	680	17	15	17	12
Mexican	10	(D)	-	-	-	-	56	(D)	-	-
Puerto Rican	33	1,730	5	757	6	146	33	38	39	40
Cuban	20	2,395	4	1,364	10	132	39	25	35	22
Other Central or South American	39	1,689	6	566	22	116	35	37	33	32
European Spanish	24	1,323	4	(D)	(D)	(D)	37	25	36	(D)
Other Hispanic	2	(D)	1	(D)	(D)	(D)	-	(D)	-	(D)
Providence, RI PMSA	299	27,504	74	16,492	228	2,933	3	1	4	1
Mexican	22	(D)	4	(D)	(D)	(D)	13	(D)	-	(D)
Puerto Rican	38	(D)	7	(D)	(D)	(D)	7	(D)	-	(D)
Cuban	34	(D)	13	(D)	(D)	(D)	9	(D)	-	(D)
Other Central or South American	140	17,162	33	9,688	142	1,450	4	1	7	1
European Spanish	36	1,534	12	(D)	(D)	(D)	9	5	17	(D)
Other Hispanic	29	3,799	5	(D)	(D)	(D)	14	2	-	(D)
Provo-Orem, UT MSA	107	3,737	19	3,016	113	589	17	3	7	1
Mexican	60	2,503	12	2,140	76	327	22	3	11	2
Puerto Rican	8	(D)	-	-	-	-	82	(D)	-	-
Cuban	-	-	-	-	-	-	-	-	-	-
Other Central or South American	16	693	4	(D)	(D)	(D)	41	8	-	(D)
European Spanish	21	522	3	(D)	(D)	(D)	44	7	-	(D)
Other Hispanic	2	(D)	-	-	-	-	-	(D)	-	-
Pueblo, CO MSA	808	29,382	216	22,962	588	4,531	8	8	12	10
Mexican	609	20,875	140	16,302	375	3,124	10	6	14	5
Puerto Rican	-	-	-	-	-	-	-	-	-	-
Cuban	1	(D)	-	-	-	-	-	(D)	-	-
Other Central or South American	54	3,760	23	3,619	101	784	32	53	53	55
European Spanish	100	2,989	26	1,807	76	373	24	19	35	12
Other Hispanic	44	(D)	27	1,234	36	250	31	(D)	35	27
Raleigh-Durham, NC MSA	130	5,853	28	4,019	115	971	8	4	5	-
Mexican	24	1,197	5	(D)	(D)	(D)	10	6	-	(D)
Puerto Rican	19	721	4	497	15	97	20	6	-	-
Cuban	14	(D)	4	(D)	(D)	(D)	18	(D)	-	(D)
Other Central or South American	55	2,110	11	(D)	(D)	(D)	14	7	13	(D)
European Spanish	14	838	3	(D)	(D)	(D)	30	17	-	(D)
Other Hispanic	4	(D)	1	(D)	(D)	(D)	61	(D)	-	(D)

[Continued]

★ 709 ★

Hispanic-Owned Firms, by Metropolitan Statistical Area With 100 or More Hispanic-Owned Firms: Pawtucket/Woonsocket/Attleboro - Reno

[Continued]

Geographic area and minority	All firms		Firms with paid employees				Relative standard error of estimate (percent) for column -			
	Firms (number) A	Sales and receipts ($000) B	Firms (number) C	Sales and receipts ($000) D	Employees (number) E	Annual payroll ($000) F	A	B	C	D
Reading, PA MSA	133	3,777	20	1,664	31	270	9	10	16	10
Mexican	9	(D)	2	(D)	(D)	(D)	27	(D)	-	(D)
Puerto Rican	76	2,302	13	(D)	(D)	(D)	11	14	22	(D)
Cuban	12	503	1	(D)	(D)	(D)	26	8	-	(D)
Other Central or South American	27	414	2	(D)	(D)	(D)	29	24	69	(D)
European Spanish	8	(D)	1	(D)	(D)	(D)	31	(D)	-	(D)
Other Hispanic	1	(D)	1	(D)	(D)	(D)	-	(D)	-	(D)
Redding, CA MSA	149	69,628	47	67,510	319	7,941	20	2	29	1
Mexican	113	5,159	34	3,393	60	570	23	18	40	13
Puerto Rican	-	-	-	-	-	-	-	-	-	-
Cuban	-	-	-	-	-	-	-	-	-	-
Other Central or South American	2	(D)	2	(D)	(D)	(D)	70	(D)	70	(D)
European Spanish	31	61,917	9	(D)	(D)	(D)	44	1	22	(D)
Other Hispanic	3	(D)	2	(D)	(D)	(D)	-	(D)	-	(D)
Reno, NV MSA	377	33,760	83	26,288	677	6,451	8	2	8	1
Mexican	210	19,268	44	16,285	523	4,640	11	2	-	-
Puerto Rican	16	433	3	(D)	(D)	(D)	22	1	-	(D)
Cuban	17	514	-	-	-	-	42	85	-	-
Other Central or South American	69	3,123	7	(D)	(D)	(D)	24	8	-	(D)
European Spanish	53	8,374	27	(D)	(D)	(D)	36	3	-	(D)
Other Hispanic	12	2,048	2	(D)	(D)	(D)	36	3	-	(D)

Source: 1987 Economic Censuses, Survey of Minority-Owned Business Enterprises: Hispanics, U.S. Department of Commerce, Bureau of the Census, MB-87-2, 1991, pp. 55-70. *Notes:* A dash (-) represents zero. (D) stands for data withheld to avoid disclosing data for individual companies; data are included in higher-level totals.

★ 710 ★

Hispanic-Owned Firms

Hispanic-Owned Firms, by Metropolitan Statistical Area With 100 or More Hispanic-Owned Firms: Richland/Kennewick/Pasco - San Diego

Geographic area and minority	All firms		Firms with paid employees				Relative standard error of estimate (percent) for column -			
	Firms (number) A	Sales and receipts ($000) B	Firms (number) C	Sales and receipts ($000) D	Employees (number) E	Annual payroll ($000) F	A	B	C	D
Richland-Kennewick-Pasco, WA MSA	202	8,225	51	6,439	142	1,160	9	2	9	2
Mexican	161	6,470	42	5,043	129	1,039	10	2	9	2
Puerto Rican	1	(D)	-	-	-	-	-	(D)	-	-
Cuban	3	(D)	1	(D)	(D)	(D)	47	(D)	-	(D)
Other Central or South American	14	(D)	2	(D)	(D)	(D)	23	(D)	71	(D)
European Spanish	17	1,242	6	(D)	(D)	(D)	21	5	24	(D)
Other Hispanic	6	(D)	-	-	-	-	41	(D)	-	-
Richmond-Petersburg, VA MSA	160	10,325	36	8,664	124	1,319	7	3	10	3
Mexican	32	1,818	9	(D)	(D)	(D)	12	15	16	(D)

[Continued]

★ 710 ★

Hispanic-Owned Firms, by Metropolitan Statistical Area With 100 or More Hispanic-Owned Firms: Richland/Kennewick/Pasco - San Diego

[Continued]

Geographic area and minority	All firms		Firms with paid employees				Relative standard error of estimate (percent) for column -			
	Firms (number) A	Sales and receipts ($000) B	Firms (number) C	Sales and receipts ($000) D	Employees (number) E	Annual payroll ($000) F	A	B	C	D
Puerto Rican	27	1,133	11	(D)	(D)	(D)	16	10	18	(D)
Cuban	11	(D)	1	(D)	(D)	(D)	22	(D)	-	(D)
Other Central or South American	71	1,332	9	826	25	208	12	9	16	3
European Spanish	14	(D)	6	(D)	(D)	(D)	25	(D)	33	(D)
Other Hispanic	5	(D)	-	-	-	-	56	(D)	-	-
Riverside-San Bernardino, CA PMSA	10,195	576,537	2,516	428,745	5,878	80,899	3	2	4	2
Mexican	8,079	459,280	2,004	343,095	4,823	65,954	3	2	5	2
Puerto Rican	224	8,424	65	6,005	79	957	17	12	27	12
Cuban	273	25,886	78	19,742	222	2,734	17	7	20	5
Other Central or South American	890	38,581	233	26,384	365	5,328	9	8	16	8
European Spanish	383	26,081	70	19,505	198	3,369	14	9	23	8
Other Hispanic	346	18,285	66	14,014	191	2,557	15	9	30	9
Rochester, NY MSA	303	23,562	47	16,454	104	3,290	11	7	18	4
Mexican	22	1,908	6	(D)	(D)	(D)	29	2	24	(D)
Puerto Rican	139	6,477	13	2,135	25	180	16	26	19	26
Cuban	43	(D)	7	(D)	(D)	(D)	32	(D)	78	(D)
Other Central or South American	74	(D)	16	(D)	(D)	(D)	22	(D)	37	(D)
European Spanish	12	1,351	5	(D)	(D)	(D)	36	24	-	(D)
Other Hispanic	13	(D)	-	-	-	-	60	(D)	-	-
Rockford, IL MSA	110	3,768	15	2,378	56	409	18	10	9	2
Mexican	86	3,118	13	(D)	(D)	(D)	21	10	11	(D)
Puerto Rican	6	(D)	-	-	-	-	91	(D)	-	-
Cuban	2	(D)	-	-	-	-	70	(D)	-	-
Other Central or South American	15	360	1	(D)	(D)	(D)	51	63	-	(D)
European Spanish	1	(D)	1	(D)	(D)	(D)	-	(D)	-	(D)
Other Hispanic	-	-	-	-	-	-	-	-	-	-
Sacramento, CA MSA	3,140	175,148	686	129,236	2,063	25,875	5	3	7	3
Mexican	2,273	118,404	487	84,484	1,539	17,860	5	4	8	4
Puerto Rican	96	3,503	10	2,890	36	589	27	9	24	9
Cuban	77	2,591	3	376	8	82	31	57	47	24
Other Central or South American	276	13,788	74	9,437	69	2,386	15	12	23	14
European Spanish	340	32,117	99	28,380	349	4,082	13	5	19	5
Other Hispanic	78	4,745	13	3,669	62	876	26	12	22	8
Saginaw-Bay City-Midland, MI MSA	196	9,895	51	7,812	136	1,354	6	2	7	1
Mexican	154	7,931	41	6,457	115	1,045	7	2	7	1
Puerto Rican	7	(D)	-	-	-	-	35	(D)	-	-
Cuban	8	157	3	(D)	(D)	(D)	31	15	47	(D)
Other Central or South American	14	687	5	(D)	(D)	(D)	27	12	28	(D)
European Spanish	5	(D)	2	(D)	(D)	(D)	28	(D)	-	(D)
Other Hispanic	8	(D)	-	-	-	-	36	(D)	-	-

[Continued]

★ 710 ★

Hispanic-Owned Firms, by Metropolitan Statistical Area With 100 or More Hispanic-Owned Firms: Richland/Kennewick/Pasco - San Diego

[Continued]

Geographic area and minority	All firms		Firms with paid employees				Relative standard error of estimate (percent) for column -			
	Firms (number) A	Sales and receipts ($000) B	Firms (number) C	Sales and receipts ($000) D	Employees (number) E	Annual payroll ($000) F	A	B	C	D
St. Louis, MO-IL MSA	604	31,449	121	21,912	745	5,732	6	3	7	3
Mexican	287	12,844	62	7,761	230	1,752	9	4	12	5
Puerto Rican	39	3,321	9	3,075	47	783	21	2	-	-
Cuban	38	1,315	7	752	25	154	21	12	20	15
Other Central or South American	102	5,672	23	4,004	106	1,091	12	8	14	10
European Spanish	108	6,590	14	4,955	267	1,324	14	8	-	-
Other Hispanic	30	1,707	6	1,365	70	628	40	2	-	-
Salem, OR MSA	215	11,114	57	8,994	141	1,468	10	5	15	5
Mexican	154	8,456	42	7,167	110	1,012	12	4	15	4
Puerto Rican	9	647	7	(D)	(D)	(D)	61	56	78	(D)
Cuban	-	-	-	-	-	-	-	-	-	-
Other Central or South American	14	337	2	(D)	(D)	(D)	41	17	-	(D)
European Spanish	30	1,563	4	(D)	(D)	(D)	27	14	-	(D)
Other Hispanic	8	111	2	(D)	(D)	(D)	68	25	-	(D)
Salinas-Seaside-Monterey, CA MSA	1,365	98,610	311	78,475	1,464	15,895	7	4	10	4
Mexican	1,003	78,749	246	63,579	1,200	12,045	8	5	11	4
Puerto Rican	53	420	1	(D)	(D)	(D)	47	35	-	(D)
Cuban	17	1,426	11	(D)	(D)	(D)	22	12	26	(D)
Other Central or South American	118	7,009	12	5,864	166	1,304	27	15	24	12
European Spanish	123	7,403	20	4,679	59	649	23	10	39	8
Other Hispanic	51	3,603	21	3,271	12	1,713	39	48	58	52
Salt Lake City-Ogden, UT MSA	982	37,497	178	24,949	445	4,742	5	2	9	1
Mexican	621	24,912	123	16,651	333	3,480	7	2	12	1
Puerto Rican	16	621	4	(D)	(D)	(D)	41	25	-	(D)
Cuban	27	1,005	2	(D)	(D)	(D)	35	18	-	(D)
Other Central or South American	112	4,675	14	(D)	(D)	(D)	18	7	-	(D)
European Spanish	125	4,240	26	3,276	57	663	15	8	26	7
Other Hispanic	81	2,044	9	(D)	(D)	(D)	22	9	24	(D)
San Angelo, TX MSA	427	14,829	137	11,126	244	1,947	13	8	18	8
Mexican	411	13,503	134	(D)	(D)	(D)	13	9	18	(D)
Puerto Rican	2	(D)	2	(D)	(D)	(D)	71	(D)	71	(D)
Cuban	-	-	-	-	-	-	-	-	-	-
Other Central or South American	12	36	-	-	-	-	79	79	-	-
European Spanish	2	(D)	1	(D)	(D)	(D)	-	(D)	-	(D)
Other Hispanic	-	-	-	-	-	-	-	-	-	-
San Antonio, TX MSA	15,241	657,174	3,578	477,191	9,116	96,790	2	2	3	2
Mexican	13,575	589,682	3,219	427,545	8,338	86,667	2	2	3	2
Puerto Rican	108	5,907	22	5,090	34	836	24	9	45	10
Cuban	138	11,784	48	10,614	212	2,128	23	16	29	17
Other Central or South American	637	23,250	129	11,800	231	2,254	10	9	17	12
European Spanish	405	13,115	74	10,924	178	1,805	14	15	20	16
Other Hispanic	378	13,436	86	11,218	123	3,100	15	21	27	25

[Continued]

★ 710 ★

Hispanic-Owned Firms, by Metropolitan Statistical Area With 100 or More Hispanic-Owned Firms: Richland/Kennewick/Pasco - San Diego

[Continued]

Geographic area and minority	All firms: Firms (number) A	All firms: Sales and receipts ($000) B	Firms with paid employees: Firms (number) C	Firms with paid employees: Sales and receipts ($000) D	Firms with paid employees: Employees (number) E	Firms with paid employees: Annual payroll ($000) F	Relative standard error of estimate (percent) for column - A	B	C	D
San Diego, CA MSA	10,373	559,444	2,007	401,549	6,384	79,028	3	2	4	2
Mexican	8,397	450,676	1,671	323,122	5,550	64,990	3	2	5	2
Puerto Rican	213	9,350	29	7,445	74	2,526	18	8	34	5
Cuban	221	11,069	24	7,974	133	1,143	17	11	16	11
Other Central or South American	879	57,340	170	39,367	393	6,012	9	7	17	8
European Spanish	425	25,622	87	21,501	214	3,654	13	7	20	8
Other Hispanic	238	5,387	26	2,140	20	703	19	23	52	35

Source: *1987 Economic Censuses, Survey of Minority-Owned Business Enterprises: Hispanics*, U.S. Department of Commerce, Bureau of the Census, MB-87-2, 1991, pp. 55-70. *Notes:* A dash (-) represents zero. (D) stands for data withheld to avoid disclosing data for individual companies; data are included in higher-level totals.

★ 711 ★

Hispanic-Owned Firms

Hispanic-Owned Firms, by Metropolitan Statistical Area With 100 or More Hispanic-Owned Firms: San Francisco - Syracuse

Geographic area and minority	All firms: Firms (number) A	All firms: Sales and receipts ($000) B	Firms with paid employees: Firms (number) C	Firms with paid employees: Sales and receipts ($000) D	Firms with paid employees: Employees (number) E	Firms with paid employees: Annual payroll ($000) F	Relative standard error of estimate (percent) for column - A	B	C	D
San Francisco, CA PMSA	6,472	431,332	1,123	309,661	3,791	57,657	3	2	5	2
Mexican	3,086	191,454	524	132,010	2,025	29,990	5	3	7	3
Puerto Rican	252	11,391	43	6,746	113	1,233	15	10	25	13
Cuban	240	13,806	62	10,230	148	2,401	16	14	24	17
Other Central or South American	2,051	96,607	334	62,459	769	9,543	6	4	10	4
European Spanish	574	91,690	117	77,879	588	12,728	10	3	17	2
Other Hispanic	269	26,384	43	20,337	148	1,762	16	6	23	5
San Jose, CA PMSA	6,188	314,063	1,301	205,582	3,339	43,587	3	3	6	3
Mexican	4,487	220,978	961	142,738	2,323	29,862	4	4	7	4
Puerto Rican	171	8,856	31	5,876	71	831	22	13	34	10
Cuban	151	14,072	43	9,492	173	1,803	21	16	24	6
Other Central or South American	711	30,337	145	19,625	345	4,293	10	7	18	9
European Spanish	409	32,499	112	26,241	379	6,436	12	6	18	6
Other Hispanic	259	7,321	9	1,610	48	362	17	16	27	17
Santa Barbara-Santa Maria-Lompoc, CA MSA	1,882	108,657	470	79,797	1,314	15,551	6	4	9	4
Mexican	1,548	90,066	417	67,172	1,057	13,132	6	4	10	5
Puerto Rican	4	(D)	1	(D)	(D)	(D)	-	(D)	-	(D)
Cuban	30	(D)	10	(D)	(D)	(D)	51	(D)	76	(D)
Other Central or South American	159	7,133	24	4,948	108	1,046	24	13	40	9
European Spanish	82	8,219	10	5,270	125	1,062	27	5	14	2
Other Hispanic	59	2,478	8	1,902	24	246	33	32	35	39
Santa Cruz, CA PMSA	821	57,293	215	44,504	800	8,139	9	6	12	7
Mexican	624	43,903	169	33,293	597	5,543	10	7	14	8
Puerto Rican	17	(D)	3	(D)	(D)	(D)	45	(D)	47	(D)

[Continued]

★ 711 ★

Hispanic-Owned Firms, by Metropolitan Statistical Area With 100 or More Hispanic-Owned Firms: San Francisco - Syracuse

[Continued]

Geographic area and minority	All firms: Firms (number) A	All firms: Sales and receipts ($000) B	Firms with paid employees: Firms (number) C	Firms with paid employees: Sales and receipts ($000) D	Firms with paid employees: Employees (number) E	Firms with paid employees: Annual payroll ($000) F	Relative standard error of estimate (percent) for column - A	B	C	D
Cuban	16	2,743	12	(D)	(D)	(D)	60	64	80	(D)
Other Central or South American	77	2,659	13	2,076	58	369	29	11	15	4
European Spanish	83	4,078	15	3,346	60	793	33	14	28	13
Other Hispanic	4	(D)	3	(D)	(D)	(D)	35	(D)	47	(D)
Santa Fe, NM MSA	1,606	84,968	356	63,996	1,331	12,958	5	2	5	2
Mexican	746	36,839	168	28,473	491	5,270	7	3	8	4
Puerto Rican	7	(D)	5	(D)	(D)	(D)	21	(D)	29	(D)
Cuban	9	(D)	-	-	-	-	73	(D)	-	-
Other Central or South American	119	5,000	22	(D)	(D)	(D)	20	7	11	(D)
European Spanish	460	27,665	102	21,293	536	5,536	9	4	7	2
Other Hispanic	265	14,897	59	10,308	226	1,609	12	8	14	7
Santa Rosa-Petaluma, CA PMSA	844	36,696	164	24,286	379	4,601	9	9	14	11
Mexican	538	26,439	124	19,216	252	3,650	12	11	18	13
Puerto Rican	30	1,718	3	(D)	(D)	(D)	45	24	-	(D)
Cuban	19	454	2	(D)	(D)	(D)	53	23	-	(D)
Other Central or South American	130	3,484	16	1,170	36	140	24	25	22	29
European Spanish	95	3,818	18	2,654	66	552	24	21	30	23
Other Hispanic	32	783	1	(D)	(D)	(D)	47	63	-	(D)
Sarasota, FL MSA	259	20,555	86	17,188	331	3,967	15	9	18	10
Mexican	39	1,046	3	(D)	(D)	(D)	40	17	-	(D)
Puerto Rican	13	7,960	11	(D)	(D)	(D)	19	2	22	(D)
Cuban	82	6,764	42	6,087	66	966	21	24	23	26
Other Central or South American	61	1,176	2	(D)	(D)	(D)	35	36	-	(D)
European Spanish	49	2,554	26	(D)	(D)	(D)	46	26	46	(D)
Other Hispanic	15	1,055	2	(D)	(D)	(D)	41	37	71	(D)
Scranton-Wilkes-Barre, PA MSA	111	5,687	22	3,844	78	906	10	4	9	3
Mexican	8	450	2	(D)	(D)	(D)	25	20	-	(D)
Puerto Rican	40	739	6	(D)	(D)	(D)	23	28	33	(D)
Cuban	13	792	2	(D)	(D)	(D)	22	2	-	(D)
Other Central or South American	30	2,293	5	1,615	32	316	14	3	-	-
European Spanish	8	1,009	5	910	18	109	18	5	-	-
Other Hispanic	12	404	2	(D)	(D)	(D)	26	14	-	(D)
Seattle, WA PMSA	1,034	55,181	198	41,336	949	8,840	3	1	3	1
Mexican	595	33,287	130	25,458	596	5,195	4	1	4	1
Puerto Rican	42	937	4	(D)	(D)	(D)	16	8	-	(D)
Cuban	36	1,555	4	(D)	(D)	(D)	15	8	-	(D)
Other Central or South American	164	8,874	33	7,217	160	1,806	7	3	6	3
European Spanish	147	7,863	17	5,167	80	1,196	10	4	11	2
Other Hispanic	50	2,665	10	1,875	92	463	11	2	-	-
Sherman-Denison, TX MSA	107	3,559	6	(D)	(D)	(D)	31	19	23	(D)
Mexican	96	(D)	5	(D)	(D)	(D)	33	(D)	28	(D)
Puerto Rican	10	(D)	-	-	-	-	95	(D)	-	-
Cuban	-	-	-	-	-	-	-	-	-	-
Other Central or South American	1	(D)	1	(D)	(D)	(D)	-	(D)	-	(D)
European Spanish	-	-	-	-	-	-	-	-	-	-
Other Hispanic	-	-	-	-	-	-	-	-	-	-

[Continued]

★ 711 ★

Hispanic-Owned Firms, by Metropolitan Statistical Area With 100 or More Hispanic-Owned Firms: San Francisco - Syracuse

[Continued]

Geographic area and minority	All firms: Firms (number) A	All firms: Sales and receipts ($000) B	Firms with paid employees: Firms (number) C	Firms with paid employees: Sales and receipts ($000) D	Firms with paid employees: Employees (number) E	Firms with paid employees: Annual payroll ($000) F	Relative standard error of estimate (percent) for column - A	B	C	D
Springfield, MA MSA	235	28,204	31	(D)	(D)	(D)	6	1	11	(D)
Mexican	12	(D)	-	-	-	-	26	(D)	-	-
Puerto Rican	123	4,317	15	(D)	(D)	(D)	9	9	19	(D)
Cuban	24	(D)	3	(D)	(D)	(D)	13	(D)	-	(D)
Other Central or South American	42	(D)	6	(D)	(D)	(D)	13	(D)	-	(D)
European Spanish	18	(D)	5	(D)	(D)	(D)	25	6	-	(D)
Other Hispanic	16	479	2	(D)	(D)	(D)	25	6	-	(D)
Stamford, CT PMSA	357	15,541	46	8,207	82	1,140	8	7	17	6
Mexican	12	151	-	-	-	-	37	18	-	-
Puerto Rican	74	2,651	6	1,095	8	105	19	20	-	-
Cuban	46	2,255	10	1,768	15	310	21	4	20	3
Other Central or South American	172	7,612	20	3,196	32	365	13	13	31	14
European Spanish	45	2,802	10	2,148	27	360	25	7	44	6
Other Hispanic	8	70	-	-	-	-	59	32	-	-
Stockton, CA MSA	1,643	99,035	416	76,342	1,337	18,108	6	4	9	5
Mexican	1,328	84,696	361	65,815	1,047	15,559	7	5	10	6
Puerto Rican	38	1,367	11	(D)	(D)	(D)	45	56	86	(D)
Cuban	22	672	2	(D)	(D)	(D)	61	64	70	(D)
Other Central or South American	82	2,917	11	2,057	42	432	29	19	26	21
European Spanish	128	6,890	27	4,824	143	1,294	23	15	37	15
Other Hispanic	45	2,493	4	2,083	50	419	38	6	-	-
Syracuse, NY MSA	124	4,697	37	3,516	76	748	17	19	28	24
Mexican	7	655	4	533	22	135	20	13	-	-
Puerto Rican	23	303	4	(D)	(D)	(D)	42	53	50	(D)
Cuban	11	377	2	(D)	(D)	(D)	53	47	72	(D)
Other Central or South American	28	1,313	9	1,164	23	166	38	54	72	60
European Spanish	37	1,881	12	1,449	19	357	31	26	47	32
Other Hispanic	18	168	6	(D)	(D)	(D)	53	53	91	(D)

Source: 1987 Economic Censuses, Survey of Minority-Owned Business Enterprises: Hispanics, U.S. Department of Commerce, Bureau of the Census, MB-87-2, 1991, pp. 55-70. *Notes:* A dash (-) represents zero. (D) stands for data withheld to avoid disclosing data for individual companies; data are included in higher-level totals.

★ 712 ★

Hispanic-Owned Firms

Hispanic-Owned Firms, by Metropolitan Statistical Area With 100 or More Hispanic-Owned Firms: Tacoma - Waterbury

Geographic area and minority	All firms: Firms (number) A	All firms: Sales and receipts ($000) B	Firms with paid employees: Firms (number) C	Firms with paid employees: Sales and receipts ($000) D	Firms with paid employees: Employees (number) E	Firms with paid employees: Annual payroll ($000) F	Relative standard error of estimate (percent) for column - A	B	C	D
Tacoma, WA PMSA	217	10,495	42	8,036	219	1,570	8	3	7	3
Mexican	135	7,472	31	5,714	128	1,053	9	4	8	4
Puerto Rican	24	867	4	638	18	84	18	8	-	-
Cuban	13	(D)	1	(D)	(D)	(D)	29	(D)	-	(D)
Other Central or South American	30	1,057	5	(D)	(D)	(D)	29	9	28	(D)

[Continued]

★ 712 ★

Hispanic-Owned Firms, by Metropolitan Statistical Area With 100 or More Hispanic-Owned Firms: Tacoma - Waterbury

[Continued]

Geographic area and minority	All firms		Firms with paid employees				Relative standard error of estimate (percent) for column -			
	Firms (number) A	Sales and receipts ($000) B	Firms (number) C	Sales and receipts ($000) D	Employees (number) E	Annual payroll ($000) F	A	B	C	D
European Spanish	11	930	1	(D)	(D)	(D)	22	8	-	(D)
Other Hispanic	4	(D)	-	-	-	-	50	(D)	-	-
Tampa-St. Petersburg-Clearwater, FL MSA	4,513	342,083	961	242,328	3,390	44,100	4	2	5	2
Mexican	244	12,142	44	7,759	115	1,414	17	16	24	22
Puerto Rican	671	22,984	126	12,773	225	3,373	10	8	17	9
Cuban	1,986	157,461	449	105,712	1,174	14,251	5	3	8	4
Other Central or South American	626	37,172	142	27,567	469	4,829	10	6	14	6
European Spanish	875	104,870	183	82,150	1,309	19,081	9	4	12	2
Other Hispanic	111	7,454	17	6,367	98	1,152	27	5	17	1
Toledo, OH MSA	226	6,772	35	3,248	60	734	13	11	18	13
Mexican	149	4,849	22	2,366	45	631	15	12	25	17
Puerto Rican	21	232	4	130	3	18	45	28	61	47
Cuban	5	(D)	2	(D)	(D)	(D)	56	(D)	69	(D)
Other Central or South American	32	1,158	5	449	8	36	35	43	28	31
European Spanish	5	(D)	2	(D)	(D)	(D)	-	(D)	-	(D)
Other Hispanic	14	210	-	-	-	-	65	89	-	-
Topeka, KS MSA	169	5,365	33	3,841	116	898	13	3	6	2
Mexican	136	4,295	27	(D)	(D)	(D)	15	4	5	(D)
Puerto Rican	7	222	2	(D)	(D)	(D)	20	19	71	(D)
Cuban	2	(D)	1	(D)	(D)	(D)	-	(D)	-	(D)
Other Central or South American	9	(D)	2	(D)	(D)	(D)	60	(D)	-	(D)
European Spanish	8	(D)	1	(D)	(D)	(D)	70	(D)	-	(D)
Other Hispanic	7	(D)	-	-	-	-	80	(D)	-	-
Trenton, NJ PMSA	209	12,284	50	8,320	145	1,500	9	11	14	13
Mexican	12	141	2	(D)	(D)	(D)	37	58	71	(D)
Puerto Rican	74	1,675	8	646	17	142	16	24	35	25
Cuban	28	1,915	11	1,435	18	226	25	33	37	38
Other Central or South American	74	6,153	24	(D)	(D)	(D)	14	17	20	(D)
European Spanish	12	906	3	(D)	(D)	(D)	29	11	-	(D)
Other Hispanic	9	1,494	2	(D)	(D)	(D)	31	10	-	(D)
Tucson, AZ MSA	2,430	112,126	498	85,214	2,087	17,481	4	2	7	2
Mexican	1,976	96,341	450	73,155	1,874	15,399	5	2	7	3
Puerto Rican	96	1,280	7	313	10	93	30	28	35	44
Cuban	44	2,413	4	1,829	17	194	39	13	35	12
Other Central or South American	166	3,128	14	2,100	78	557	20	11	17	11
European Spanish	87	7,460	15	6,488	81	957	23	5	21	3
Other Hispanic	61	1,504	8	1,329	27	281	32	13	18	14
Tulsa, OK MSA	319	12,231	58	8,550	147	1,823	8	3	11	1
Mexican	220	8,726	37	6,133	83	1,021	11	3	14	1
Puerto Rican	15	802	7	(D)	(D)	(D)	28	5	50	(D)
Cuban	18	(D)	4	(D)	(D)	(D)	35	(D)	-	(D)
Other Central or South American	39	720	3	189	2	48	21	14	-	-
European Spanish	23	548	7	(D)	(D)	(D)	28	22	-	(D)
Other Hispanic	4	(D)	-	-	-	-	61	(D)	-	-
Vallejo-Fairfield-Napa, CA PMSA	766	50,588	218	38,928	789	8,495	9	8	13	8
Mexican	542	38,866	174	30,790	676	7,375	11	10	15	10
Puerto Rican	12	(D)	1	(D)	(D)	(D)	79	(D)	-	(D)

[Continued]

★ 712 ★

Hispanic-Owned Firms, by Metropolitan Statistical Area With 100 or More Hispanic-Owned Firms: Tacoma - Waterbury

[Continued]

Geographic area and minority	All firms: Firms (number) A	All firms: Sales and receipts ($000) B	Firms with paid employees: Firms (number) C	Firms with paid employees: Sales and receipts ($000) D	Firms with paid employees: Employees (number) E	Firms with paid employees: Annual payroll ($000) F	Relative standard error of estimate (percent) for column - A	B	C	D
Cuban	6	(D)	2	(D)	(D)	(D)	24	(D)	-	(D)
Other Central or South American	41	1,755	10	(D)	(D)	(D)	34	19	28	(D)
European Spanish	93	8,916	27	5,935	66	768	24	16	36	12
Other Hispanic	72	475	4	90	2	20	36	30	50	55
Victoria, TX MSA	836	20,976	141	13,041	287	2,681	9	9	17	9
Mexican	784	18,386	125	11,978	266	2,497	10	8	19	10
Puerto Rican	-	-	-	-	-	-	-	-	-	-
Cuban	4	(D)	2	(D)	(D)	(D)	50	(D)	71	(D)
Other Central or South American	18	721	13	(D)	(D)	(D)	27	32	38	(D)
European Spanish	1	(D)	1	(D)	(D)	(D)	-	(D)	-	(D)
Other Hispanic	29	1,417	-	-	-	-	51	92	-	-
Vineland-Millville-Bridgeton, NJ PMSA	138	6,362	33	3,604	49	412	11	9	20	8
Mexican	3	(D)	2	(D)	(D)	(D)	-	(D)	-	(D)
Puerto Rican	107	4,141	26	(D)	(D)	(D)	12	13	24	(D)
Cuban	12	1,056	2	(D)	(D)	(D)	31	4	-	(D)
Other Central or South American	7	234	-	-	-	-	50	72	-	-
European Spanish	7	(D)	1	(D)	(D)	(D)	50	(D)	-	(D)
Other Hispanic	2	(D)	2	(D)	(D)	(D)	71	(D)	71	(D)
Visalia-Tulare-Porterville, CA MSA	1,567	107,366	395	82,170	1,631	19,753	6	4	10	5
Mexican	1,392	97,144	373	74,458	1,505	18,326	7	5	10	5
Puerto Rican	5	(D)	3	128	-	11	28	(D)	47	55
Cuban	2	(D)	2	(D)	(D)	(D)	-	(D)	-	(D)
Other Central or South American	93	(D)	4	(D)	(D)	(D)	29	(D)	35	(D)
European Spanish	60	3,390	7	1,927	31	471	34	20	20	11
Other Hispanic	15	2,911	6	(D)	(D)	(D)	40	20	33	(D)
Waco, TX MSA	297	12,882	109	10,187	181	1,869	15	10	21	12
Mexican	272	12,546	105	9,949	171	1,822	15	11	21	12
Puerto Rican	-	-	-	-	-	-	-	-	-	-
Cuban	-	-	-	-	-	-	-	-	-	-
Other Central or South American	25	336	4	238	10	47	54	30	35	33
European Spanish	-	-	-	-	-	-	-	-	-	-
Other Hispanic	-	-	-	-	-	-	-	-	-	
Washington, DC-MD-VA MSA	4,868	269,635	752	196,504	2,665	52,485	1	1	2	-
Mexican	581	18,565	89	10,550	120	1,878	3	2	5	2
Puerto Rican	502	43,636	66	35,304	535	14,649	4	1	6	1
Cuban	603	70,188	129	62,263	726	16,624	4	1	5	1
Other Central or South American	2,722	99,991	395	59,292	899	12,509	2	1	4	1
European Spanish	337	29,454	48	23,854	303	5,978	6	1	6	1
Other Hispanic	123	7,801	25	5,241	82	847	8	4	8	5
Waterbury, CT MSA	126	8,858	24	4,443	59	942	15	10	19	1
Mexican	7	557	1	(D)	(D)	(D)	63	68	-	(D)
Puerto Rican	67	3,966	7	1,865	12	378	21	21	21	3
Cuban	13	1,191	5	(D)	(D)	(D)	11	3	-	(D)
Other Central or South American	17	1,036	8	630	11	182	37	5	56	4

[Continued]

★ 712 ★

Hispanic-Owned Firms, by Metropolitan Statistical Area With 100 or More Hispanic-Owned Firms: Tacoma - Waterbury

[Continued]

Geographic area and minority	All firms: Firms (number) A	All firms: Sales and receipts ($000) B	Firms with paid employees: Firms (number) C	Firms with paid employees: Sales and receipts ($000) D	Firms with paid employees: Employees (number) E	Firms with paid employees: Annual payroll ($000) F	Relative standard error of estimate (percent) for column - A	B	C	D
European Spanish	20	(D)	2	(D)	(D)	(D)	50	(D)	-	(D)
Other Hispanic	2	(D)	1	(D)	(D)	(D)	-	(D)	-	(D)

Source: *1987 Economic Censuses, Survey of Minority-Owned Business Enterprises: Hispanics*, U.S. Department of Commerce, Bureau of the Census, MB-87-2, 1991, pp. 55-70. *Notes:* A dash (-) represents zero. (D) stands for data withheld to avoid disclosing data for individual companies; data are included in higher-level totals.

★ 713 ★

Hispanic-Owned Firms

Hispanic-Owned Firms, by Metropolitan Statistical Area With 100 or More Hispanic-Owned Firms: West Palm Beach/Boca Raton/Delray Beach - Yuba City

Geographic area and minority	All firms: Firms (number) A	All firms: Sales and receipts ($000) B	Firms with paid employees: Firms (number) C	Firms with paid employees: Sales and receipts ($000) D	Firms with paid employees: Employees (number) E	Firms with paid employees: Annual payroll ($000) F	Relative standard error of estimate (percent) for column - A	B	C	D
West Palm Beach-Boca Raton-Delray Beach, FL MSA	1,870	157,607	307	112,105	1,509	20,384	6	3	8	3
Mexican	117	11,041	29	7,490	237	2,518	22	13	34	9
Puerto Rican	191	10,879	43	(D)	(D)	(D)	18	8	32	(D)
Cuban	1,012	95,393	142	69,187	730	8,705	8	3	8	3
Other Central or South American	432	23,398	68	12,872	155	2,483	12	14	22	18
European Spanish	75	14,821	23	13,145	174	3,874	24	4	16	4
Other Hispanic	43	2,075	2	(D)	(D)	(D)	39	22	-	(D)
Wichita, KS MSA	357	12,189	77	7,717	218	1,790	8	3	10	1
Mexican	272	7,829	57	4,996	163	1,185	9	4	13	2
Puerto Rican	2	(D)	2	(D)	(D)	(D)	-	(D)	-	(D)
Cuban	21	1,700	5	(D)	(D)	(D)	26	11	-	(D)
Other Central or South American	22	1,705	7	1,110	23	243	15	3	-	-
European Spanish	19	557	3	(D)	(D)	(D)	41	4	-	(D)
Other Hispanic	21	(D)	3	(D)	(D)	(D)	40	(D)	-	(D)
Wichita Falls, TX MSA	206	9,535	21	7,308	301	2,993	18	7	15	3
Mexican	189	8,236	17	6,032	259	2,590	19	8	17	2
Puerto Rican	4	(D)	1	(D)	(D)	(D)	35	(D)	-	(D)
Cuban	-	-	-	-	-	-	-	-	-	-
Other Central or South American	10	10	-	-	-	-	95	95	-	-
European Spanish	1	(D)	1	(D)	(D)	(D)	-	(D)	-	(D)
Other Hispanic	2	(D)	2	(D)	(D)	(D)	71	(D)	71	(D)
Wilmington, DE-NJ-MD PMSA	164	5,551	26	2,339	56	648	6	3	5	2
Mexican	17	1,262	3	916	24	297	-	-	-	-
Puerto Rican	64	1,970	9	468	3	119	4	4	-	-
Cuban	33	626	4	(D)	(D)	(D)	29	24	-	(D)
Other Central or South American	38	1,221	9	726	26	211	9	5	16	6
European Spanish	9	(D)	1	(D)	(D)	(D)	-	(D)	-	(D)
Other Hispanic	3	(D)	-	-	-	-	-	(D)	-	-
Worcester, MA MSA	153	14,478	15	11,009	150	3,105	9	6	9	-
Mexican	7	(D)	1	(D)	(D)	(D)	35	(D)	-	(D)

[Continued]

★ 713 ★

Hispanic-Owned Firms, by Metropolitan Statistical Area With 100 or More Hispanic-Owned Firms: West Palm Beach/Boca Raton/Delray Beach - Yuba City

[Continued]

Geographic area and minority	All firms		Firms with paid employees				Relative standard error of estimate (percent) for column -			
	Firms (number) A	Sales and receipts ($000) B	Firms (number) C	Sales and receipts ($000) D	Employees (number) E	Annual payroll ($000) F	A	B	C	D
Puerto Rican	72	(D)	5	(D)	(D)	(D)	12	(D)	28	(D)
Cuban	19	(D)	3	(D)	(D)	(D)	25	(D)	-	(D)
Other Central or South American	41	(D)	4	(D)	(D)	(D)	18	(D)	-	(D)
European Spanish	7	(D)	2	(D)	(D)	(D)	28	(D)	-	(D)
Other Hispanic	7	(D)	-	-	-	-	45	(D)	-	-
Yakima, WA	310	17,550	67	14,027	202	2,349	5	1	5	1
Mexican	267	15,662	57	12,755	175	2,048	5	1	5	1
Puerto Rican	2	(D)	-	-	-	-	70	(D)	-	-
Cuban	3	(D)	3	(D)	(D)	(D)	47	(D)	47	(D)
Other Central or South American	11	195	1	(D)	(D)	(D)	29	11	-	(D)
European Spanish	18	1,096	5	964	11	233	27	12	28	14
Other Hispanic	9	(D)	1	(D)	(D)	(D)	22	(D)	-	(D)
Youngstown-Warren, OH MSA	150	5,249	25	3,739	66	544	18	11	27	9
Mexican	20	(D)	8	(D)	(D)	(D)	46	(D)	81	(D)
Puerto Rican	71	1,313	3	401	2	16	28	36	47	48
Cuban	12	(D)	2	(D)	(D)	(D)	54	(D)	-	(D)
Other Central or South American	34	1,144	6	787	17	93	46	21	24	18
European Spanish	13	1,036	6	(D)	(D)	(D)	11	1	-	(D)
Other Hispanic	-	-	-	-	-	-	-	-	-	-
Yuba City, CA MSA	131	8,779	36	7,000	154	1,445	19	11	16	12
Mexican	115	7,136	25	5,529	136	1,192	21	13	13	14
Puerto Rican	1	(D)	-	-	-	-	-	(D)	-	-
Cuban	2	(D)	2	(D)	(D)	(D)	71	(D)	71	(D)
Other Central or South American	4	240	3	(D)	(D)	(D)	35	28	47	(D)
European Spanish	7	1,143	6	(D)	(D)	(D)	64	18	75	(D)
Other Hispanic	2	(D)	-	-	-	-	71	(D)	-	-

Source: *1987 Economic Censuses, Survey of Minority-Owned Business Enterprises: Hispanics,* U.S. Department of Commerce, Bureau of the Census, MB-87-2, 1991, pp. 55-70.
Notes: A dash (-) represents zero. (D) stands for data withheld to avoid disclosing data for individual companies; data are included in higher-level totals.

★ 714 ★

Hispanic-Owned Firms

Hispanic-Owned Firms, by State and Ethnicity, 1987: Alaska - Illinois

Geographic area and minority	All firms		Firms with paid employees				Relative standard error of estimate (percent) for column			
	Firms (number) A	Sales and receipts ($000) B	Firms (number) C	Sales and receipts ($000) D	Employees (number) E	Annual payroll ($000) F	A	B	C	D
United States	422,373	24,731,600	82,908	17,729,432	264,846	3,243,342	-	-	1	-
Mexican	229,706	11,835,080	49,078	8,403,796	148,008	1,687,401	-	-	1	-
Puerto Rican	27,697	1,447,680	4,629	903,848	13,231	179,379	1	1	2	1
Cuban	61,470	5,481,974	10,768	4,227,065	47,266	638,459	1	-	1	-
Other Central or South American	66,356	3,202,238	10,793	2,031,768	27,386	343,039	1	1	2	1
European Spanish	24,755	2,054,537	5,299	1,628,133	21,196	293,976	1	1	2	1

[Continued]

★ 714 ★

Hispanic-Owned Firms, by State and Ethnicity, 1987: Alaska - Illinois

[Continued]

Geographic area and minority	All firms		Firms with paid employees				Relative standard error of estimate (percent) for column			
	Firms (number) A	Sales and receipts ($000) B	Firms (number) C	Sales and receipts ($000) D	Employees (number) E	Annual payroll ($000) F	A	B	C	D
Other Hispanic	12,389	710,091	2,341	534,822	7,759	101,088	2	1	4	1
Alabama	397	30,006	97	23,366	647	4,855	3	1	3	-
Mexican	113	9,927	30	8,629	395	2,145	5	1	7	-
Puerto Rican	66	7,026	17	5,819	90	910	7	1	9	1
Cuban	68	6,074	17	3,906	71	884	7	2	-	-
Other Central or South American	75	3,602	16	2,459	51	402	7	4	-	-
European Spanish	60	3,278	17	2,553	40	514	6	2	-	-
Other Hispanic	15	99	-	-	-	-	30	30	-	-
Alaska	502	27,412	86	18,099	282	3,926	5	3	11	2
Mexican	257	15,927	56	11,023	166	2,696	6	4	17	3
Puerto Rican	35	1,459	4	(D)	(D)	(D)	29	7	-	(D)
Cuban	32	2,050	3	1,685	18	303	42	7	-	-
Other Central or South American	96	4,153	14	2,449	32	373	8	3	-	-
European Spanish	51	3,162	7	1,922	50	477	10	1	-	-
Other Hispanic	31	661	2	(D)	(D)	(D)	31	5	-	(D)
Arizona	9,845	513,125	2,206	384,281	8,969	78,329	1	1	3	1
Mexican	8,246	420,141	1,941	310,359	8,016	67,871	2	2	4	2
Puerto Rican	230	5,225	33	2,837	30	457	18	15	31	13
Cuban	155	6,846	20	3,770	52	613	20	17	22	7
Other Central or South American	559	16,368	81	9,855	233	1,644	11	7	23	8
European Spanish	433	42,993	75	37,663	441	4,963	12	3	14	1
Other Hispanic	222	21,552	56	19,797	197	2,781	16	4	19	2
Arkansas	324	13,808	73	10,271	289	2,961	3	1	4	1
Mexican	198	7,666	45	5,705	230	2,178	4	1	6	1
Puerto Rican	26	585	4	(D)	(D)	(D)	14	4	-	(D)
Cuban	14	902	6	870	15	162	19	1	-	-
Other Central or South American	31	1,183	4	635	2	69	9	4	35	8
European Spanish	35	2,311	12	1,983	33	410	6	-	-	-
Other Hispanic	20	1,161	2	(D)	(D)	(D)	21	6	-	(D)
California	132,212	8,119,853	26,886	5,786,143	89,722	1,136,230	-	-	1	-
Mexican	94,548	5,680,635	19,654	4,014,205	66,832	823,746	1	1	1	1
Puerto Rican	3,120	187,979	570	138,519	1,596	22,712	5	3	8	3
Cuban	4,371	366,733	987	273,710	4,108	49,970	4	2	6	2
Other Central or South American	19,638	997,855	3,661	652,649	8,920	110,670	2	2	4	2
European Spanish	6,999	650,765	1,438	520,185	5,776	91,775	3	1	5	1
Other Hispanic	3,536	235,886	576	186,875	2,490	37,357	5	2	9	3
Colorado	9,516,	394,410	1,813	290,756	4,601	56,903	2	2	4	2
Mexican	6,394	288,878	1,229	218,406	3,400	42,381	2	2	5	2
Puerto Rican	135	8,606	39	7,613	40	1,747	20	6	33	5
Cuban	162	4,873	21	3,282	24	298	20	43	40	62
Other Central or South American	611	16,557	97	11,588	248	2,302	10	13	18	18
European Spanish	1,362	44,227	241	27,978	510	5,302	7	4	11	4
Other Hispanic	852	31,269	186	21,889	379	4,973	9	9	14	10

[Continued]

★ 714 ★

Hispanic-Owned Firms, by State and Ethnicity, 1987: Alaska - Illinois

[Continued]

Geographic area and minority	All firms: Firms (number) A	All firms: Sales and receipts ($000) B	Firms with paid employees: Firms (number) C	Firms with paid employees: Sales and receipts ($000) D	Firms with paid employees: Employees (number) E	Firms with paid employees: Annual payroll ($000) F	Relative standard error of estimate (percent) for column A	B	C	D
Connecticut	2,235	175,520	397	118,141	1,610	19,580	3	2	5	1
Mexican	119	3,639	19	1,575	25	302	15	15	23	1
Puerto Rican	792	47,294	138	27,314	346	6,143	5	4	8	5
Cuban	335	58,722	64	46,825	420	5,222	8	2	6	-
Other Central or South American	661	35,230	97	19,401	272	3,508	6	4	11	2
European Spanish	230	19,718	54	14,996	166	2,328	10	4	17	4
Other Hispanic	98	10,917	25	8,030	381	2,077	17	4	14	3
Delaware	184	6,230	30	3,135	67	740	2	1	-	-
Mexican	23	797	2	(D)	(D)	(D)	-	-	-	(D)
Puerto Rican	74	2,371	12	800	7	182	-	-	-	-
Cuban	36	1,194	7	693	11	120	-	-	-	-
Other Central or South American	35	1,291	7	763	29	213	8	3	-	-
European Spanish	13	(D)	2	(D)	(D)	(D)	-	(D)	-	(D)
Other Hispanic	3	(D)	-	-	-	-	-	(D)	-	-
District of Columbia	762	63,948	128	53,255	725	12,584	2	-	3	-
Mexican	83	2,398	12	(D)	(D)	(D)	8	2	-	(D)
Puerto Rican	72	8,158	14	6,716	70	1,885	9	1	-	-
Cuban	98	14,519	23	13,318	294	4,261	9	1	-	-
Other Central or South American	404	20,113	61	14,627	155	1,929	4	1	6	-
European Spanish	78	17,719	13	16,551	174	4,099	10	-	-	-
Other Hispanic	27	1,041	5	(D)	(D)	(D)	21	5	-	(D)
Florida	64,413	4,949,151	9,924	3,743,959	42,375	563,088	-	-	1	-
Mexican	2,821	140,765	431	89,446	1,729	24,007	5	4	9	5
Puerto Rican	4,556	201,104	742	125,408	2,288	24,062	4	3	7	3
Cuban	42,162	3,760,811	6,783	2,942,565	30,734	417,879	1	-	2	-
Other Central or South American	11,228	522,971	1,317	335,537	4,187	51,643	2	2	4	2
European Spanish	2,853	271,885	555	210,952	3,033	40,979	5	2	7	2
Other Hispanic	793	51,615	96	40,051	404	4,518	10	3	16	3
Georgia	1,931	145,252	480	115,841	2,375	27,796	3	1	5	1
Mexican	439	35,135	135	29,679	676	7,521	7	2	9	2
Puerto Rican	311	11,686	65	7,849	102	1,291	9	6	16	7
Cuban	414	51,733	94	43,937	1,176	12,825	7	1	10	1
Other Central or South American	558	25,256	133	16,217	245	2,995	6	4	10	3
European Spanish	150	19,823	46	16,996	164	2,922	10	3	16	2
Other Hispanic	59	1,619	7	1,163	12	242	19	21	21	29
Hawaii	1,226	58,098	177	41,838	542	5,923	4	2	6	2
Mexican	286	27,604	47	23,333	187	2,888	7	3	9	3
Puerto Rican	364	9,717	38	4,960	89	991	9	5	9	6
Cuban	48	1,452	7	1,170	11	130	16	3	-	-
Other Central or South American	114	3,472	14	1,872	24	217	10	4	10	5
European Spanish	228	9,500	49	6,733	181	1,182	10	5	17	4
Other Hispanic	186	6,353	22	3,770	50	515	13	7	20	8

[Continued]

★714★

Hispanic-Owned Firms, by State and Ethnicity, 1987: Alaska - Illinois

[Continued]

Geographic area and minority	All firms		Firms with paid employees				Relative standard error of estimate (percent) for column			
	Firms (number) A	Sales and receipts ($000) B	Firms (number) C	Sales and receipts ($000) D	Employees (number) E	Annual payroll ($000) F	A	B	C	D
Idaho	974	30,594	187	20,880	270	4,008	3	1	7	1
Mexican	724	19,744	147	12,923	195	2,608	3	2	8	2
Puerto Rican	18	579	4	(D)	(D)	(D)	26	7	-	(D)
Cuban	5	9	-	-	-	-	69	38	-	-
Other Central or South American	58	2,370	3	(D)	(D)	(D)	20	4	-	(D)
European Spanish	144	7,179	28	5,697	51	662	9	1	12	-
Other Hispanic	25	713	5	372	7	53	25	9	-	-
Illinois	9,636	588,646	1,712	416,569	5,890	68,893	1	1	3	1
Mexican	5,637	310,124	1,006	211,267	3,120	34,775	2	2	4	1
Puerto Rican	1,195	52,137	142	26,934	389	4,505	6	5	11	4
Cuban	740	80,773	215	65,148	830	9,194	7	4	8	3
Other Central or South American	1,503	74,695	258	49,944	748	7,861	5	4	8	5
European Spanish	366	64,459	65	58,581	655	11,311	10	2	15	1
Other Hispanic	195	6,458	26	4,695	148	1,247	14	7	17	7

Source: 1987 Economic Censuses: Survey of Minority-Owned Business Enterprises: Hispanics, U.S. Department of Commerce, Bureau of the Census, MB-87-2, 1991, pp. 28-32. *Notes:* A dash (-) represents zero. A (D) stands for data withheld to avoid disclosing data for individual companies; data are included in higher level totals.

★715★

Hispanic-Owned Firms

Hispanic-Owned Firms, by State and Ethnicity, 1987: Indiana - Nevada

Geographic area and minority	All firms		Firms with paid employees				Relative standard error of estimate (percent) for column			
	Firms (number) A	Sales and receipts ($000) B	Firms (number) C	Sales and receipts ($000) D	Employees (number) E	Annual payroll ($000) F	A	B	C	D
Indiana	1,427	106,111	300	85,099	1,455	16,541	3	1	3	-
Mexican	886	69,646	178	58,587	1,033	10,759	4	1	4	-
Puerto Rican	195	8,875	40	3,983	50	568	9	6	15	6
Cuban	36	2,144	11	1,882	40	249	14	3	-	-
Other Central or South American	170	9,092	37	6,312	154	1,343	10	3	12	2
European Spanish	113	8,501	28	6,861	123	1,227	141	3	12	2
Other Hispanic	27	7,853	6	7,474	55	2,395	22	-	-	-
Iowa	475	20,210	111	16,662	489	3,534	3	1	3	1
Mexican	365	15,806	85	13,227	367	2,634	3	1	3	1
Puerto Rican	15	179	1	(D)	(D)	(D)	19	5	-	(D)
Cuban	13	1,465	8	(D)	(D)	(D)	-	-	-	(D)
Other Central or South American	40	1,650	8	1,106	21	398	14	3	-	-
European Spanish	33	1,009	6	(D)	(D)	(D)	8	1	-	(D)
Other Hispanic	9	101	3	(D)	(D)	(D)	22	14	48	(D)
Kansas	1,541	62,275	335	43,035	1,027	9,405	3	1	4	1
Mexican	1,187	40,488	252	26,676	690	5,104	4	2	5	1

[Continued]

★ 715 ★

Hispanic-Owned Firms, by State and Ethnicity, 1987: Indiana - Nevada

[Continued]

Geographic area and minority	All firms		Firms with paid employees				Relative standard error of estimate (percent) for column			
	Firms (number)	Sales and receipts ($000)	Firms (number)	Sales and receipts ($000)	Employees (number)	Annual payroll ($000)				
	A	B	C	D	E	F	A	B	C	D
Puerto Rican	21	755	9	522	11	93	10	6	16	8
Cuban	65	7,105	16	5,277	68	684	18	6	15	-
Other Central or South American	96	5,688	25	3,793	54	791	15	4	22	6
European Spanish	108	6,637	23	5,629	185	2,594	15	1	14	1
Other Hispanic	64	1,602	10	1,138	19	139	21	8	14	5
Kentucky	359	16,562	68	9,319	153	1,354	3	1	5	1
Mexican	98	4,745	13	1,239	26	177	7	2	15	5
Puerto Rican	43	1,879	5	862	8	97	9	3	-	-
Cuban	60	2,292	14	1,790	20	137	8	3	14	2
Other Central or South American	96	3,265	20	1,819	49	337	7	3	10	3
European Spanish	40	3,324	11	2,752	35	404	5	1	-	-
Other Hispanic	22	1,057	5	857	15	202	18	11	28	13
Louisiana	2,697	136,083	505	91,532	1,434	17,406	2	1	3	1
Mexican	520	19,122	94	12,424	187	2,246	4	2	7	2
Puerto Rican	163	10,721	39	8,235	197	1,831	7	4	10	4
Cuban	464	17,525	70	9,946	128	1,459	4	3	7	2
Other Central or South American	926	39,337	157	22,482	310	4,038	3	2	5	2
European Spanish	525	43,472	125	34,459	564	7,086	4	1	4	1
Other Hispanic	99	5,906	20	3,986	48	746	8	4	10	3
Maine	139	12,061	42	9,504	173	1,768	2	-	3	-
Mexican	19	1,591	2	(D)	(D)	(D)	-	-	-	(D)
Puerto Rican	26	1,369	5	(D)	(D)	(D)	9	1	-	(D)
Cuban	21	3,808	9	(D)	(D)	(D)	7	1	16	(D)
Other Central or South American	33	1,186	8	984	14	188	-	-	-	-
European Spanish	28	3,338	15	2,600	37	549	-	-	-	-
Other Hispanic	12	769	3	(D)	(D)	(D)	-	-	-	(D)
Maryland	2,931	185,308	509	137,111	1,431	25,929	1	1	3	-
Mexican	361	12,299	63	7,420	110	1,497	5	4	16	6
Puerto Rican	369	25,784	65	20,075	125	1,715	4	2	7	1
Cuban	400	47,876	94	42,139	414	10,973	5	1	10	1
Other Central or South American	1,481	76,440	227	51,022	522	7,697	2	1	4	1
European Spanish	253	17,217	46	12,868	199	3,447	6	2	6	1
Other Hispanic	67	5,692	14	3,587	61	600	10	5	10	7
Massachusetts	2,636	173,969	411	118,907	1,346	19,736	2	1	3	1
Mexican	215	5,622	31	2,353	54	458	7	14	13	10
Puerto Rican	685	25,882	97	13,301	200	1,872	4	4	7	4
Cuban	382	44,818	57	33,814	338	5,787	5	3	9	1
Other Central or South American	829	48,224	137	31,207	414	6,013	4	3	6	2
European Spanish	301	20,200	58	14,746	191	3,051	5	3	9	3
Other Hispanic	224	29,223	31	23,486	149	2,555	7	2	11	2
Michigan	2,654	126,046	464	87,743	1,560	20,945	1	1	3	1
Mexican	1,704	78,588	296	55,122	1,031	14,142	2	1	4	1
Puerto Rican	196	6,870	27	3,643	28	480	6	10	12	16

[Continued]

★715★

Hispanic-Owned Firms, by State and Ethnicity, 1987: Indiana - Nevada

[Continued]

Geographic area and minority	All firms: Firms (number) A	All firms: Sales and receipts ($000) B	Firms with paid employees: Firms (number) C	Firms with paid employees: Sales and receipts ($000) D	Firms with paid employees: Employees (number) E	Firms with paid employees: Annual payroll ($000) F	Relative standard error of estimate (percent) for column A	B	C	D
Cuban	131	4,188	20	2,900	47	654	8	4	12	4
Other Central or South American	293	11,922	52	6,629	179	1,234	5	5	9	7
European Spanish	218	12,160	49	9,003	145	1,773	6	3	7	1
Other Hispanic	112	12,318	20	10,446	130	2,662	8	2	10	-
Minnesota	751	29,061	122	20,341	299	3,598	3	1	5	-
Mexican	470	20,108	81	15,056	243	2,871	4	1	5	-
Puerto Rican	41	665	6	(D)	(D)	(D)	18	10	42	(D)
Cuban	41	1,749	9	1,194	6	66	18	9	28	1
Other Central or South American	116	3,311	19	2,331	25	370	10	3	13	-
European Spanish	58	2,047	5	375	6	67	9	3	-	-
Other Hispanic	25	1,181	2	(D)	(D)	(D)	23	1	-	(D)
Mississippi	308	12,490	70	6,509	147	1,073	3	2	5	3
Mexican	87	4,226	21	2,264	47	409	7	4	15	7
Puerto Rican	26	524	7	292	7	41	11	8	20	14
Cuban	37	1,191	10	756	14	149	7	1	-	-
Other Central or South American	85	3,290	19	2,014	62	305	6	3	-	-
European Spanish	60	2,691	10	650	5	87	8	3	14	8
Other Hispanic	13	568	3	533	12	82	15	1	-	-
Missouri	1,247	49,677	258	32,830	765	8,022	3	2	5	2
Mexican	767	30,149	165	19,332	464	4,876	4	2	6	1
Puerto Rican	48	3,921	14	3,539	62	865	19	4	-	-
Cuban	55	1,525	12	(D)	(D)	(D)	15	8	-	(D)
Other Central or South American	179	7,512	41	4,981	143	1,270	8	6	14	9
European Spanish	147	3,793	16	2,048	37	410	11	3	-	-
Other Hispanic	51	2,777	10	(D)	(D)	(D)	19	2	34	(D)
Montana	304	10,107	61	6,416	114	995	2	1	-	-
Mexican	212	7,190	44	5,106	88	693	2	-	-	-
Puerto Rican	13	125	-	-	-	-	-	-	-	-
Cuban	12	232	1	(D)	(D)	(D)	-	-	-	(D)
Other Central or South American	11	233	3	(D)	(D)	(D)	-	-	-	(D)
European Spanish	37	1,572	11	1,053	16	226	9	6	-	-
Other Hispanic	19	755	2	(D)	(D)	(D)	-	-	-	(D)
Nebraska	619	19,391	122	14,557	413	3,414	3	1	3	1
Mexican	523	15,441	101	11,147	350	2,727	3	2	4	1
Puerto Rican	12	(D)	1	(D)	(D)	(D)	24	(D)	-	(D)
Cuban	16	(D)	1	(D)	(D)	(D)	27	(D)	-	(D)
Other Central or South American	33	1,133	8	(D)	(D)	(D)	16	4	-	(D)
European Spanish	25	1,754	8	1,621	29	290	15	1	-	-
Other Hispanic	10	631	3	(D)	(D)	(D)	25	1	-	(D)
Nevada	1,767	141,608	385	109,257	2,250	26,056	3	1	5	-
Mexican	1,018	63,889	221	50,852	1,113	11,136	4	1	5	1
Puerto Rican	53	2,661	12	1,443	47	137	15	3	-	-
Cuban	159	7,070	20	4,433	64	1,182	13	7	32	1

[Continued]

★ 715 ★

Hispanic-Owned Firms, by State and Ethnicity, 1987: Indiana - Nevada

[Continued]

Geographic area and minority	All firms: Firms (number) A	All firms: Sales and receipts ($000) B	Firms with paid employees: Firms (number) C	Firms with paid employees: Sales and receipts ($000) D	Firms with paid employees: Employees (number) E	Firms with paid employees: Annual payroll ($000) F	Relative standard error of estimate (percent) for column A	B	C	D
Other Central or South American	250	15,154	40	7,372	130	1,662	11	2	13	3
European Spanish	227	49,024	73	43,117	851	11,441	10	1	13	-
Other Hispanic	60	3,810	19	2,040	45	498	25	7	44	13

Source: 1987 Economic Censuses, Survey of Minority-Owned Business Enterprises: Hispanics, U.S. Department of Commerce, Bureau of the Census, MB-87-2, 1991, pp. 28-32. *Notes:* A dash (-) represents zero. A (D) stands for data withheld to avoid disclosing data for individual companies; data are included in higher level totals.

★ 716 ★

Hispanic-Owned Firms

Hispanic-Owned Firms, by State and Ethnicity, 1987: New Hampshire - Wyoming

Geographic area and minority	All firms: Firms (number) A	All firms: Sales and receipts ($000) B	Firms with paid employees: Firms (number) C	Firms with paid employees: Sales and receipts ($000) D	Firms with paid employees: Employees (number) E	Firms with paid employees: Annual payroll ($000) F	Relative standard error of estimate (percent) for column A	B	C	D
New Hampshire	244	12,818	49	8,248	120	1,333	4	2	5	2
Mexican	37	1,765	6	1,156	27	327	11	3	-	-
Puerto Rican	51	2,525	13	1,136	13	198	8	6	15	13
Cuban	38	3,952	8	(D)	(D)	(D)	10	2	-	(D)
Other Central or South American	56	2,645	9	1,305	25	386	7	5	-	-
European Spanish	53	1,477	10	(D)	(D)	(D)	12	9	14	(D)
Other Hispanic	9	454	3	(D)	(D)	(D)	22	1	-	(D)
New Jersey	12,094	902,004	2,226	598,775	6,167	87,642	1	1	2	1
Mexican	381	20,631	54	11,985	184	3,999	7	5	12	5
Puerto Rican	2,837	167,272	527	98,376	1,636	21,866	2	2	4	2
Cuban	4,188	410,798	838	291,729	2,316	31,776	2	1	3	1
Other Central or South American	3,489	187,925	571	105,162	1,283	15,702	2	2	4	2
European Spanish	852	95,821	180	79,034	622	11,364	4	2	6	2
Other Hispanic	347	19,557	56	12,489	126	2,935	8	6	13	5
New Mexico	14,299	702,098	3,716	529,176	10,680	97,036	1	1	2	1
Mexican	8,656	426,164	2,249	322,657	6,366	58,714	2	1	3	1
Puerto Rican	47	1,822	15	1,353	21	229	23	16	19	15
Cuban	102	4,607	18	3,299	43	451	20	7	37	9
Other Central or South American	950	38,694	180	26,083	471	4,370	6	5	8	5
European Spanish	2,668	135,440	746	105,015	2,431	21,018	4	2	5	2
Other Hispanic	1,876	95,371	508	70,769	1,348	12,254	5	3	7	3
New York	28,254	1,555,801	4,334	944,513	12,745	186,100	1	1	2	1
Mexican	1,244	53,397	207	30,142	514	7,223	6	5	11	7
Puerto Rican	8,762	478,866	1,381	284,308	4,010	58,899	2	2	4	2
Cuban	3,587	279,883	689	192,084	3,040	38,261	3	2	6	2
Other Central or South American	12,143	572,351	1,613	318,038	3,788	57,758	2	2	4	2
European Spanish	1,881	142,846	353	102,294	1,134	19,805	5	3	8	2

[Continued]

★ 716 ★

Hispanic-Owned Firms, by State and Ethnicity, 1987: New Hampshire - Wyoming

[Continued]

Geographic area and minority	All firms: Firms (number) A	All firms: Sales and receipts ($000) B	Firms with paid employees: Firms (number) C	Firms with paid employees: Sales and receipts ($000) D	Firms with paid employees: Employees (number) E	Firms with paid employees: Annual payroll ($000) F	Relative standard error of estimate (percent) for column A	B	C	D
Other Hispanic	637	28,458	91	17,647	259	4,154	8	7	14	8
North Carolina	918	92,903	179	80,052	695	10,751	3	1	5	1
Mexican	239	7,724	40	4,776	122	822	7	2	-	-
Puerto Rican	148	3,848	21	(D)	(D)	(D)	9	2	12	(D)
Cuban	142	42,693	35	40,325	212	6,002	8	-	7	-
Other Central or South American	263	25,951	53	22,151	198	1,982	8	3	13	2
European Spanish	92	6,109	21	4,012	67	954	10	3	12	1
Other Hispanic	34	6,578	9	(D)	(D)	(D)	18	1	27	(D)
North Dakota	88	2,167	14	1,279	35	315	2	-	-	-
Mexican	60	1,413	10	745	24	222	2	-	-	-
Puerto Rican	3	(D)	-	-	-	-	-	(D)	-	-
Cuban	1	(D)	-	-	-	-	-	(D)	-	-
Other Central or South American	10	257	1	(D)	(D)	(D)	-	-	-	(D)
European Spanish	7	(D)	1	(D)	(D)	(D)	-	(D)	-	(D)
Other Hispanic	7	(D)	2	(D)	(D)	(D)	-	(D)	-	(D)
Ohio	1,989	191,797	420	164,503	2,263	31,382	4	1	6	1
Mexican	640	26,812	124	19,103	635	6,046	7	5	13	6
Puerto Rican	449	12,744	78	5,259	66	735	9	7	18	9
Cuban	224	47,555	45	44,707	558	10,241	12	2	10	1
Other Central or South American	378	38,196	87	34,206	456	4,751	11	2	13	2
European Spanish	221	63,848	71	59,986	517	9,278	9	1	12	1
Other Hispanic	77	2,642	15	1,242	31	331	27	32	43	18
Oklahoma	1,516	50,409	243	33,883	725	6,958	3	1	5	-
Mexican	1,059	34,477	168	23,413	518	4,903	4	2	5	-
Puerto Rican	72	3,468	19	2,567	96	770	13	2	18	1
Cuban	60	2,296	10	1,557	32	459	20	5	-	1
Other Central or South American	166	5,718	26	4,199	49	582	11	4	24	2
European Spanish	107	3,440	16	2,085	30	240	13	5	-	-
Other Hispanic	52	1,010	4	62	-	4	23	13	61	67
Oregon	1,598	109,642	403	89,053	1,445	15,363	3	1	5	1
Mexican	980	79,893	253	67,426	1,016	11,329	4	1	5	1
Puerto Rican	65	3,015	23	1,898	31	527	21	20	34	19
Cuban	69	4,544	13	2,910	111	747	21	9	19	4
Other Central or South American	188	5,588	45	3,502	97	935	11	5	19	3
European Spanish	231	13,523	57	10,738	153	1,483	9	3	11	2
Other Hispanic	65	3,079	12	2,579	37	342	20	2	-	-
Pennsylvania	2,650	247,081	531	182,890	1,880	27,091	2	1	3	1
Mexican	339	18,764	75	(D)	(D)	(D)	10	13	15	(D)
Puerto Rican	888	55,649	170	33,138	387	4,166	3	4	5	2
Cuban	344	41,642	61	32,860	414	9,577	5	1	7	1
Other Central or South American	679	37,841	126	24,396	295	3,722	4	3	6	9
European Spanish	300	86,482	73	76,292	474	6,762	6	1	6	1
Other Hispanic	100	6,703	26	(D)	(D)	(D)	9	8	13	(D)

[Continued]

★ 716 ★

Hispanic-Owned Firms, by State and Ethnicity, 1987: New Hampshire - Wyoming

[Continued]

Geographic area and minority	All firms		Firms with paid employees				Relative standard error of estimate (percent) for column			
	Firms (number) A	Sales and receipts ($000) B	Firms (number) C	Sales and receipts ($000) D	Employees (number) E	Annual payroll ($000) F	A	B	C	D
Rhode Island	426	40,471	97	27,116	292	3,503	2	1	4	1
Mexican	29	1,017	5	(D)	(D)	(D)	11	4	-	(D)
Puerto Rican	48	2,844	8	1,461	18	183	7	2	-	-
Cuban	50	9,926	17	9,316	50	302	6	1	-	-
Other Central or South American	194	19,175	40	10,430	155	1,606	4	1	7	1
European Spanish	63	3,441	20	(D)	(D)	(D)	6	2	12	(D)
Other Hispanic	42	4,068	7	3,322	29	1,039	11	2	-	-
South Carolina	393	15,997	79	9,294	216	1,932	4	2	6	1
Mexican	82	1,547	11	(D)	(D)	(D)	14	12	13	(D)
Puerto Rican	77	4,551	19	1,926	46	429	9	2	20	2
Cuban	73	(D)	16	2,750	56	485	8	(D)	12	-
Other Central or South American	111	4,552	22	2,796	73	710	6	2	-	-
European Spanish	47	1,679	10	964	11	133	8	4	14	1
Other Hispanic	3	(D)	1	(D)	(D)	(D)	-	(D)	-	(D)
South Dakota	109	4,262	27	3,071	43	506	1	-	-	-
Mexican	71	2,619	17	1,867	20	212	2	-	-	-
Puerto Rican	2	(D)	-	-	-	-	-	(D)	-	-
Cuban	3	(D)	1	(D)	(D)	(D)	-	(D)	-	(D)
Other Central or South American	15	794	5	(D)	(D)	(D)	-	-	-	(D)
European Spanish	8	(D)	1	(D)	(D)	(D)	-	(D)	-	(D)
Other Hispanic	10	453	3	(D)	(D)	(D)	-	-	-	(D)
Tennessee	554	35,187	134	21,055	345	3,954	3	1	3	1
Mexican	149	7,314	50	5,142	94	1,319	5	2	6	2
Puerto Rican	65	(D)	11	2,428	27	353	9	(D)	13	5
Cuban	102	4,888	19	2,679	45	430	8	6	8	2
Other Central or South American	150	7,205	30	4,755	47	452	5	2	5	-
European Spanish	70	6,729	17	5,523	124	1,309	7	1	-	-
Other Hispanic	18	(D)	7	528	8	91	14	(D)	-	-
Texas	94,754	4,108,076	20,845	2,886,579	49,942	555,868	-	1	1	1
Mexican	83,380	3,591,462	18,552	2,523,300	44,563	489,908	-	1	1	1
Puerto Rican	686	31,032	114	21,614	289	3,780	10	7	18	9
Cuban	1,455	93,847	297	63,326	1,022	11,307	7	4	9	4
Other Central or South American	5,367	212,531	1,077	146,346	2,095	25,515	4	3	6	4
European Spanish	1,996	100,701	435	73,486	1,116	13,340	6	4	9	5
Other Hispanic	1,870	78,503	370	58,507	857	12,018	7	6	12	6
Utah	1,300	47,255	228	31,506	657	6,056	3	2	7	1
Mexican	796	31,146	150	20,893	455	4,235	5	2	10	1
Puerto Rican	31	644	4	(D)	(D)	(D)	37	24	-	(D)
Cuban	31	1,028	2	(D)	(D)	(D)	31	17	-	(D)
Other Central or South American	149	6,074	22	4,267	60	409	15	5	-	-
European Spanish	201	5,960	38	4,433	118	1,044	12	6	17	5
Other Hispanic	92	2,403	12	1,354	20	318	19	8	18	7

[Continued]

★ 716 ★

Hispanic-Owned Firms, by State and Ethnicity, 1987: New Hampshire - Wyoming

[Continued]

Geographic area and minority	All firms		Firms with paid employees				Relative standard error of estimate (percent) for column			
	Firms (number)	Sales and receipts ($000)	Firms (number)	Sales and receipts ($000)	Employees (number)	Annual payroll ($000)				
	A	B	C	D	E	F	A	B	C	D
Vermont	118	5,383	24	3,367	48	569	-	-	-	-
Mexican	11	494	5	(D)	(D)	(D)	-	-	-	(D)
Puerto Rican	16	504	3	(D)	(D)	(D)	-	-	-	(D)
Cuban	12	(D)	1	(D)	(D)	(D)	-	(D)	-	(D)
Other Central or South American	18	1,144	4	1,004	15	144	-	-	-	-
European Spanish	58	2,596	11	1,395	12	130	-	-	-	-
Other Hispanic	3	(D)	-	-	-	-	-	(D)	-	-
Virginia	2,716	140,917	483	103,186	1,605	28,485	2	1	3	1
Mexican	439	21,312	90	14,756	170	2,398	4	2	6	2
Puerto Rican	327	32,733	47	28,184	525	12,685	5	1	6	-
Cuban	322	20,026	76	16,096	194	3,053	4	2	7	2
Other Central or South American	1,340	49,059	217	31,086	582	8,612	3	2	6	2
European Spanish	201	14,459	40	(D)	(D)	(D)	8	2	8	(D)
Other Hispanic	87	3,328	13	(D)	(D)	(D)	10	5	11	(D)
Washington	2,686	141,196	553	108,472	2,333	21,424	2	1	2	-
Mexican	1,792	88,175	393	66,731	1,465	13,212	2	1	2	1
Puerto Rican	105	2,553	16	1,445	24	182	10	6	15	5
Cuban	81	2,365	12	1,781	44	281	10	6	12	1
Other Central or South American	293	21,850	55	18,983	283	3,273	6	1	5	1
European Spanish	300	20,982	53	15,895	388	3,659	6	2	6	1
Other Hispanic	115	5,271	24	3,637	129	817	8	4	10	5
West Virginia	177	13,847	46	10,323	126	1,417	1	-	-	-
Mexican	34	2,387	13	(D)	(D)	(D)	-	-	-	(D)
Puerto Rican	18	(D)	-	-	-	-	-	(D)	-	-
Cuban	16	(D)	-	-	-	-	-	(D)	-	-
Other Central or South American	45	4,681	18	3,559	59	656	3	-	-	-
European Spanish	57	5,585	14	4,410	32	421	-	-	-	-
Other Hispanic	7	(D)	1	(D)	(D)	(D)	-	(D)	-	(D)
Wisconsin	894	73,541	184	61,897	683	6,919	3	1	4	1
Mexican	557	49,099	116	42,627	372	3,759	4	1	6	1
Puerto Rican	93	4,168	10	(D)	(D)	(D)	8	4	24	(D)
Cuban	32	7,757	8	(D)	(D)	(D)	18	-	-	(D)
Other Central or South American	110	6,835	22	5,617	75	891	8	1	-	-
European Spanish	82	5,016	23	4,542	52	938	15	3	15	3
Other Hispanic	20	666	5	(D)	(D)	(D)	21	11	-	(D)
Wyoming	584	21,736	134	15,838	381	3,146	2	1	3	-
Mexican	411	15,178	89	11,449	267	2,185	2	1	3	1
Puerto Rican	7	(D)	-	-	-	-	35	(D)	-	-
Cuban	6	(D)	3	(D)	(D)	(D)	34	(D)	48	(D)
Other Central or South American	33	619	6	(D)	(D)	(D)	8	4	-	(D)

[Continued]

★ 716 ★

Hispanic-Owned Firms, by State and Ethnicity, 1987: New Hampshire - Wyoming

[Continued]

Geographic area and minority	All firms		Firms with paid employees				Relative standard error of estimate (percent) for column			
	Firms (number) A	Sales and receipts ($000) B	Firms (number) C	Sales and receipts ($000) D	Employees (number) E	Annual payroll ($000) F	A	B	C	D
European Spanish	85	3,578	23	2,565	53	537	6	1	6	1
Other Hispanic	42	2,057	13	1,225	47	269	10	2	11	1

Source: 1987 Economic Censuses: Survey of Minority-Owned Business Enterprises: Hispanics, U.S. Department of Commerce, Bureau of the Census, MB-87-2, 1991, pp. 28-32. *Notes:* A dash (-) represents zero. A (D) stands for data withheld to avoid disclosing data for individual companies; data are included in higher level totals.

★ 717 ★

Hispanic-Owned Firms

Hispanic-Owned Firms: Average Receipts per Firm, by Industry Division, 1987

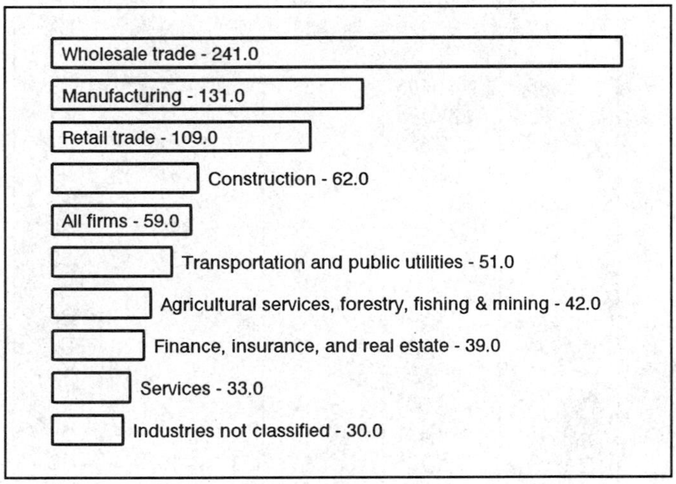

Average receipts per firm are shown in thousands of dollars.

Industry	Receipts ($ thous.)
All firms	59.0
Agricultural services, forestry, fishing & mining	42.0
Construction	62.0
Manufacturing	131.0
Transportation and public utilities	51.0
Wholesale trade	241.0
Retail trade	109.0
Finance, insurance, and real estate	39.0
Services	33.0
Industries not classified	30.0

Source: 1987 Economic Censuses, Survey of Minority-Owned Business Enterprises: Hispanics, U.S. Department of Commerce, Bureau of the Census, MB-87-2, 1991, p. 6.

★ 718 ★

Hispanic-Owned Firms

Hispanic-Owned Firms: Comparison to U.S. and Minority-Owned Firms, 1987

Industry	Hispanic-owned firms		Hispanic as percent of minority firms		Hispanic as percent of all U.S. firms	
	Number of of firms	Sales and receipts ($000)	Firms	Sales and receipts	Firms	Sales and receipts
All industries	422,373	24,731,600	34.8	33.0	3.0	1.2
Agriculture, forestry, and fishing	16,365	694,937	44.4	50.7	4.6	33.8
Mining	829	29,836	51.4	23.0	0.7	0.2
Construction	55,516	3,438,708	51.6	49.8	33.6	1.6
Manufacturing	11,090	1,449,913	37.1	36.6	2.6	0.3
Transportation, communications, and utilities	26,955	1,380,981	35.4	37.7	4.5	1.8
Wholesale	10,154	2,445,416	38.4	30.8	2.3	0.8
Retail	69,911	7,643,850	30.9	28.4	3.1	1.4
Finance, insurance, and real estate	22,106	864,282	28.9	31.3	1.8	0.7
Services	184,372	6,031,406	32.8	27.4	3.1	1.4
Industries not classified	25,075	752,271	35.9	33.7	3.6	1.9

Source: Derived from *1987 Economic Census: Survey of Minority-Owned Business Enterprises: Summary*, U.S. Department of Commerce, Bureau of the Census, MB87-4, 1991. *Note:* Percentages rounded to nearest tenth. Detail may not add to 100%.

★ 719 ★

Hispanic-Owned Firms

Hispanic-Owned Firms: Percent Distribution by Industry

Industry	Number of firms	Share of firms (percent)	Sales and receipts ($000)	Share of sales (percent)
All industries	422,373	100.0	24,731,600	100.0
Agriculture, forestry, and fishing	16,365	3.9	694,937	2.8
Mining	829	0.2	29,836	0.1
Construction	55,516	13.1	3,438,708	13.9
Manufacturing	11,090	2.6	1,449,913	5.9
Transportation, communications, and utilities	26,955	6.4	1,380,981	5.6
Wholesale	10,154	2.4	2,445,416	9.9
Retail	69,911	16.6	7,643,850	30.9
Finance, insurance, and real estate	22,106	5.2	864,282	3.5
Services	184,372	43.7	6,031,406	24.4
Industries not classified	25,075	5.9	752,271	3.0

Source: Derived from *1987 Economic Census: Survey of Minority-Owned Business Enterprises: Summary*, U.S. Department of Commerce, Bureau of the Census, MB87-4, 1991. *Notes:* Percentages rounded to nearest tenth. Detail may not add to 100% .

★ 720 ★

Hispanic-Owned Firms

Largest Hispanic-Owned Businesses in the Denver Area

The largest Hispanic businesses in the Denver, Colorado, area are ranked by 1991 revenues. These firms are also the largest area minority businesses—however, Jose Garcia Construction Inc. actually ranks 11th among all minority businesses.

Name and address	Revenues for 1991/1990 (000)	No. of employees/ percentage of minority employees	Percentage of work from government contracts	Major clients or contacts	Description of business	Name of owner(s)	Year founded
Lucero Computer Products 7100 N. Broadway, Suite 1-G Denver, CO 80221 426-8582	10,000/9,000	21/33	60	Bell Aerospace, AT&T, EG&G Idaho IHS, NREL	Personal computer hardware and software reseller	Yvonne Lucero	1966
ProServe Corp. 730 17th St., Suite 617 Denver, CO 80202 571-0900	8,274/7,209	393/68	100	Lowry Air Force Base, Buckley Air National Guard, U.S. Air Force Academy, Grand Forks Air	Food service management	Joseph Aragon	1964
Chavez Sheet Metal 1001 W. 42nd Ave. Denver, CO 80211 455-9387	7,500/8,500	115/40	80	City and County of Denver, IBM, Coors	Sheet metal contractors, HVAC fabrication and installation	Robert Chavez	1960
Greenbar Corp. 1230 N. Grant St. Thornton, CO 80241 450-7575	6,722/4,535	30/30	30	Coors, US WEST, National Park Service, Woodward-Clyde	Computer services including needs assessment, network integration, hardware software, peripherals, training, project management	Gary Solis	1964
Martinez Construction and Development Co. 12335 E. Bates Circle Aurora, CO 80014 750-9199	6,501/3,116	25/6	60	Hanging Lake Tunnel, ADAL Academic Bulking at Lowry Air Force Base, Shoshone Dam Interchange	General contractor, manufacture and supply ready-mixed concrete	L.E. Martinez	1976
Wayne Gomez Demolition & Excavating Inc. 4304 E. 60th Ave. Commerce City, CO 80022 287-5555	5,800/4,900	25/30	20	Removal of underground storage tanks for Denver, demolition of Westland Shopping Center, upgrade of RTD's storage tanks	Demolition, trucking, concrete/asphalt recycling environmental services, site remediation, tank removal, hazardous materials removal	Wayne Gomez	1963
The Solis Group 1350 17th St., Suite 200 Denver, CO 80202 629-9090	5,800/4,100[1]	21/50	NA	NA	Advertising firm	Frank Solis	1967
Uniglobe Advance Travel 50 S. Steele St., Suite 100 Denver, CO 80206 355-7926	5,500/5,000	10/50	.01	US WEST, Coors, Pepsi, Frito Lay, Allied Signal, RTC	Full-service travel agency	Sarah Barela, Ramona Martinez	1986
CEI Automation 15250 E. 33rd Place Aurora, CO 80011 375-0050	4,135/3,486	40/17	3	TRW, Atlantic Research, Dow Chemical, Coors, Miller Brewing, NIST, RTA-Chicago	Automated production, assembly and test equipment, automated controls	Carlos de Moraes[2]	1975
Jose Garcia Construction Inc. 2963 W. 91st Place Denver, CO 80221 429-3209	3,847/3,330	20-40/ 80	80	Army National Guard, Dept. of Energy, Dept. of the Army, U.S. Postal Service, US WEST, Dept. of Commerce	General contracting specializing in commercial and industrial buildings, additions, remodeling	Jose Garcia	1978

Source: "Largest Denver-area minority-owned businesses." *Denver Business Journal* (2-8 October 1992), p. 16. *Notes:* Information was compiled from mailed questionnaires and telephone interviews. In case of ties, companies were rated by 1990 revenues. NA stands for not available. 1. Billings. 2. Has a 55 percent interest and four other partners.

★ 721 ★

Hispanic-Owned Firms

Top 10 Hispanic-Owned Businesses in Southern Florida

Shown are the top 10 businesses, ranked by 1992 revenues.

Company	Phone/ Fax	Rank	Last year's rank	1992 revenues (in mil.)	No. of employees	Year founded	Top executive	Type of business
Sedano's Supermarkets 840 E. 41st St. Hialeah 33013	(305)696-0928 Fax (305)696-0949	1	2	224.56	1,500	1962	Manuel A. Herran	Supermarket chain
Capital Bancorp 1221 Brickell Ave. Miami 33131	(305)536-1500 Fax (305)536-1776	2	3	114.17	632	1974	Abel Holtz	Financial services
CareFlorida Inc. 7950 NW 53rd St. Miami 33166	(305)591-3311 Fax (305)470-1996	3	7	110.6	194	1986	Paul L. Cejas	Health care services
Eagle Brands, Inc. 3201 NW 72nd. Ave. Miami 33122	(305)599-2337 Fax (305)477-6162	4	5	97.95	200	1984	Carlos M. de la Cruz Sr.	Beer distributor
Precision Trading Corp. 1401 NW 88th Ave. Miami 33172	(305)592-4500 Fax (305)593-6169	5	4	96	35	1979	Israel Lapiuc	Consumer electronics
The Vincam Group 9040 Sunset Drive Miami 33173	(305)271-9920 Fax (305)598-4845	6	16	85.3	6,500	1985	Carlos A. Saladrigas	Employee leasing
Pan American Hospital 5959 NW Seventh St. Miami 33126	(305)264-1000 Fax (305)264-4565	7	8	76	600	1963	Carolina Calderin	Health care services
Miami Honda & Central Hyundai 3100 NW 36th St. Miami 33142	(305)638-4800 Fax (305)634-3676	8	14	66.38	145	1990	Carlos de la Cruz Sr.	Automotive sales and services
Gator Industries Inc. 1000 SE Eighth St. Miami 33010	(305)888-5000 Fax (305)885-3869	9	9	65	989	1970	Guillermo Miranda Jr.	Shoe manufacturing
Avanti Press Inc 13449 NW 42nd Ave. Miami 33054	(305)685-7381 Fax (305)685-3448	10	10	60.8	400	1965	Joe Arriola	Web offset printing services

Source: "Top 25 Hispanic-owned businesses." *South Florida Business Journal* (11- 17 June 1993), p. 24.

Industry Employment

★ 722 ★

Private Industry Employment by Occupation: United States

Data are shown for all industries, by race/ethnicity and sex, in 1993. Data do not include Hawaii.

	Total employment	Officials and managers	Professionals	Technicians	Sales workers	Office & clerical workers	Craft workers	Operatives	Laborers	Service workers
	Number of persons									
All employers	36,321,236	3,976,608	5,251,884	2,224,637	3,849,873	5,578,787	3,360,333	5,534,879	2,652,578	3,891,657
Male	19,425,287	2,789,118	2,613,254	1,182,134	1,675,551	959,091	2,975,681	3,750,207	1,740,266	1,739,985
Female	16,895,949	1,187,490	2,638,630	1,042,503	2,174,322	4,619,696	384,652	1,784,672	912,312	2,151,672
White	27,775,606	3,548,244	4,499,412	1,781,941	3,078,474	4,255,981	2,758,689	3,892,354	1,632,347	2,328,164
Male	15,053,016	2,520,475	2,274,476	969,838	1,363,715	683,719	2,470,132	2,720,268	1,075,082	975,311
Female	12,722,590	1,027,769	2,224,936	812,103	1,714,759	3,572,262	288,557	1,172,086	557,265	1,352,853
Minority	8,545,630	428,634	752,472	442,696	771,399	1,322,806	601,644	642,525	1,020,231	1,563,493
Male	4,372,271	268,643	338,778	212,296	311,836	275,372	505,549	1,029,939	665,184	764,674
Female	4,173,359	159,721	413,694	230,400	459,563	1,047,434	96,095	612,586	355,047	798,819
Black	4,603,282	209,045	291,045	233,294	409,174	779,365	310,167	949,143	496,476	925,573
Male	2,161,798	118,906	101,796	90,516	150,986	140,853	254,822	577,459	317,592	408,968
Female	2,441,484	90,139	189,249	142,778	258,188	638,612	55,345	371,684	178,884	516,605
Hispanic	2,630,746	121,908	141,708	105,293	262,685	357,871	218,759	507,227	432,335	482,960
Male	1,530,555	82,700	71,806	62,132	117,312	83,881	192,033	346,315	294,129	280,247
Female	1,100,191	39,208	69,902	43,161	145,373	273,990	26,726	160,912	138,206	202,713
Asian/Pacific Islander	1,134,536	84,561	303,279	94,572	80,155	162,276	53,609	152,509	71,411	131,153
Male	579,873	57,992	155,971	54,314	35,381	45,219	41,614	84,161	40,906	64,315
Female	554,663	26,569	147,308	40,258	44,774	117,057	11,995	68,348	31,516	66,838
American Indian/Alaskan Native	177,066	12,850	16,440	9,537	19,385	23,294	19,109	33,646	18,998	23,807
Male	100,045	9,045	9,205	5,334	8,157	5,519	17,080	22,004	12,557	11,144
Female	77,021	3,805	7,235	4,203	11,228	17,775	2,029	11,642	6,441	12,663
	Participation rate									
All employers	100.0	100.0	100.0	100.0	100.0	100.0	100.0	100.0	100.0	100.0
Male	53.5	70.1	49.8	53.1	43.5	17.2	88.6	67.8	65.6	44.7
Female	46.5	39.9	50.2	46.9	56.5	82.8	11.4	32.2	34.4	55.3
White	76.5	89.2	85.7	80.1	80.0	76.3	82.1	70.3	61.5	59.8
Male	41.4	63.4	43.3	43.6	35.4	12.3	73.5	49.1	40.5	25.1
Female	35.0	25.8	42.4	36.5	44.5	64.0	8.6	21.2	21.0	34.8
Minority	23.5	10.8	14.3	19.9	20.0	23.7	17.9	29.7	38.5	40.2
Male	12.0	6.8	6.5	9.5	8.1	4.9	15.0	18.6	25.1	19.6
Female	11.5	4.0	7.9	10.4	11.9	18.8	2.9	11.1	13.4	20.5
Black	12.7	5.3	5.5	10.5	10.6	14.0	9.2	17.1	18.7	23.8
Male	6.0	3.0	1.9	4.1	3.9	2.5	7.6	10.4	12.0	10.5
Female	6.7	2.3	3.6	6.4	6.7	11.4	1.6	6.7	6.7	13.3
Hispanic	7.2	3.1	2.7	4.7	6.8	6.4	6.5	9.2	16.3	12.4
Male	4.2	2.1	1.4	2.8	3.0	1.5	5.7	6.3	11.1	7.2
Female	3.0	1.0	1.3	1.9	3.8	4.9	0.8	2.9	5.2	5.2
Asian/Pacific Islander	3.1	2.1	5.8	4.3	2.1	2.9	1.6	2.8	2.7	3.4
Male	1.6	1.5	3.0	2.4	0.9	0.8	1.2	1.5	1.5	1.7
Female	1.5	0.7	2.8	1.8	1.2	2.1	0.4	1.2	1.2	1.7
American Indian/Alaskan Native	0.5	0.3	0.3	0.4	0.5	0.4	0.6	0.6	0.7	0.6
Male	0.3	0.2	0.2	0.2	0.2	0.1	0.5	0.4	0.5	0.3
Female	0.2	0.1	0.1	0.2	0.3	0.3	0.1	0.2	0.2	0.3

Source: U.S. Equal Employment Opportunity Commission. *Job Patterns for Minorities and Women in Private Industry, 1993.* Washington, DC: U.S. Government Printing Office, 1994, p. 1.

★ 723 ★

Industry Employment

Private Industry Employment: Agriculture, Forestry, and Fishing

Number of persons employed in each occupation is shown, by race/ethnicity, in 1993. Data do not include Hawaii.

	Total employment	Officials and managers	Professionals	Technicians	Sales workers	Office & clerical workers	Craft workers	Operatives	Laborers	Service workers
All employers	128,647	11,923	4,601	3,672	2,679	8,868	14,262	25,078	55,365	2,199
White	66,764	10,066	4,180	3,048	2,532	7,466	10,232	12,938	15,014	1,288
Minority	61,882	1,857	421	624	147	1,402	4,030	12,140	40,351	911
Black	14,136	476	114	208	11	473	1,156	3,144	8,102	452
Hispanic	44,166	1,136	148	300	96	759	2,581	8,348	30,367	431
Asian/Pacific Islander	2,517	203	146	98	34	141	138	329	1,400	28
American Indian/Alaskan Native	1,064	42	13	18	6	29	155	319	482	0

Source: U.S. Equal Employment Opportunity Commission. *Job Patterns for Minorities and Women in Private Industry, 1993.* Washington, DC: U.S. Government Printing Office, 1994, p. 2.

★ 724 ★

Industry Employment

Private Industry Employment: Air Transport Industry

Number of persons employed in each occupation is shown, by race/ethnicity, in 1993. Data are shown for selected industry sectors and do not include Hawaii.

	Total employment	Officials and managers	Professionals	Technicians	Sales workers	Office & clerical workers	Craft workers	Operatives	Laborers	Service workers
Scheduled air transportation										
All employers	370,707	23,814	54,981	6,117	39,366	53,482	65,335	27,522	14,124	85,966
White	298,260	20,690	51,835	5,382	29,650	41,962	54,041	19,864	7,301	67,535
Minority	72,447	3,124	3,146	735	9,716	11,520	11,294	7,658	6,823	18,431
Black	35,359	1,576	1,037	374	5,188	6,227	4,748	3,909	3,335	8,965
Hispanic	21,069	767	1,024	150	2,467	3,111	3,753	2,419	1,918	5,460
Asian/Pacific Islander	14,500	697	865	177	1,861	1,968	2,572	1,122	1,530	3,708
American Indian/Alaskan Native	1,519	84	220	34	200	214	221	208	40	298
Nonscheduled air transportation										
All employers	5,562	697	1,351	419	205	847	834	526	323	360
White	4,635	630	1,295	389	165	679	710	312	200	255
Minority	927	67	56	30	40	168	124	214	123	105
Black	368	18	15	11	14	82	29	102	58	39
Hispanic	416	41	25	11	17	66	80	77	40	59
Asian/Pacific Islander	125	6	10	7	9	19	9	35	23	7
American Indian/Alaskan Native	18	2	6	1	0	1	6	0	2	0

Source: U.S. Equal Employment Opportunity Commission. *Job Patterns for Minorities and Women in Private Industry, 1993.* Washington, DC: U.S. Government Printing Office, 1994, p. 26-27.

★ 725 ★

Industry Employment

Private Industry Employment: Apparel Industry

Number of persons employed in each occupation is shown, by race/ethnicity, in 1993. Data are shown for selected industry sectors and do not include Hawaii.

	Total employ-ment	Officials and managers	Profes-sionals	Techni-cians	Sales workers	Office & clerical workers	Craft workers	Opera-tives	Laborers	Service workers
Men's and boys' furnishings										
All employers	194,924	10,176	3,457	2,016	2,537	12,046	16,125	133,926	12,200	2,441
White	120,100	8,389	2,679	1,444	2,320	8,740	11,272	76,258	7,334	1,664
Minority	74,824	1,787	778	572	217	3,306	4,853	57,668	4,866	777
Black	40,979	731	206	173	127	1,326	3,010	31,942	2,928	536
Hispanic	28,570	818	276	338	61	1,560	1,442	22,123	1,733	219
Asian/Pacific Islander	3,967	199	285	57	24	385	354	2,527	124	12
American Indian/Alaskan Native	1,308	39	11	4	5	35	47	1,076	81	10
Women's and misses' outerwear										
All employers	56,090	3,810	1,776	868	3,831	6,392	6,356	26,655	5,548	854
White	38,721	3,332	1,516	674	3,411	4,622	4,554	16,804	3,212	596
Minority	17,369	478	260	194	420	1,770	1,802	9,851	2,336	258
Black	6,628	136	69	58	204	511	693	4,235	593	129
Hispanic	7,477	257	76	79	148	929	632	3,920	1,327	109
Asian/Pacific Islander	3,078	81	110	56	63	319	464	1,565	405	15
American Indian/Alaskan Native	186	4	5	1	5	11	13	131	11	5

Source: U.S. Equal Employment Opportunity Commission. *Job Patterns for Minorities and Women in Private Industry, 1993.* Washington, DC: U.S. Government Printing Office, 1994, p. 9.

★ 726 ★

Industry Employment

Private Industry Employment: Auto Sales

Number of persons employed in each occupation is shown, by race/ethnicity, in 1993. Data do not include Hawaii.

	Total employ-ment	Officials and managers	Profes-sionals	Techni-cians	Sales workers	Office & clerical workers	Craft workers	Opera-tives	Laborers	Service workers
All employers	78,460	9,114	2,574	4,820	18,384	11,135	10,504	12,421	6,661	2,847
White	63,058	8,318	2,035	3,838	14,796	9,569	8,571	10,127	4,040	1,764
Minority	15,402	796	539	982	3,588	1,566	1,933	2,294	2,621	1,083
Black	6,290	219	92	255	1,687	439	545	1,196	1,356	501
Hispanic	7,138	401	46	559	1,521	875	1,124	938	1,134	540
Asian/Pacific Islander	1,670	145	397	126	331	178	217	140	103	33
American Indian/Alaskan Native	304	31	4	42	49	74	47	20	28	9

Source: U.S. Equal Employment Opportunity Commission. *Job Patterns for Minorities and Women in Private Industry, 1993.* Washington, DC: U.S. Government Printing Office, 1994, p. 32.

★ 727 ★

Industry Employment

Private Industry Employment: Business Services

Number of persons employed in each occupation is shown, by race/ethnicity, in 1993. Data are shown for selected industry sectors and do not include Hawaii.

	Total employment	Officials and managers	Professionals	Technicians	Sales workers	Office & clerical workers	Craft workers	Operatives	Laborers	Service workers
Services to buildings										
All employers	228,765	11,601	2,763	2,528	4,683	8,347	11,635	9,607	11,375	166,226
White	92,592	8,275	2,236	2,046	3,713	6,485	8,399	5,938	4,089	51,411
Minority	136,173	3,326	527	482	970	1,862	3,236	3,669	7,286	114,815
Black	62,730	1,687	248	206	461	970	1,541	1,628	3,669	52,320
Hispanic	66,483	1,391	158	199	365	652	1,451	1,634	3,274	57,359
Asian/Pacific Islander	6,067	204	104	54	129	192	170	367	293	4,554
American Indian/Alaskan Native	893	44	17	23	15	48	74	40	50	582
Miscellaneous business services										
All employers	928,206	101,785	140,366	51,325	46,823	158,432	46,496	86,780	35,941	260,258
White	679,516	91,096	121,366	42,046	36,032	120,792	37,846	57,447	19,915	152,976
Minority	248,690	10,689	19,000	9,279	10,791	37,640	8,650	29,333	16,026	107,282
Black	148,827	5,048	6,758	4,293	6,492	21,636	4,012	14,855	8,018	77,715
Hispanic	60,986	2,721	3,597	2,344	3,379	9,606	3,258	8,891	5,959	21,231
Asian/Pacific Islander	35,084	2,618	8,187	2,411	763	5,826	1,060	5,134	1,851	7,234
American Indian/Alaskan Native	3,793	302	458	231	157	572	320	453	198	1,102

Source: U.S. Equal Employment Opportunity Commission. *Job Patterns for Minorities and Women in Private Industry, 1993.* Washington, DC: U.S. Government Printing Office, 1994, p. 35.

★ 728 ★

Industry Employment

Private Industry Employment: Chemicals & Allied Products

Number of persons employed in each occupation is shown, by race/ethnicity, in 1993. Data are shown for selected industry sectors and do not include Hawaii.

	Total employment	Officials and managers	Professionals	Technicians	Sales workers	Office & clerical workers	Craft workers	Operatives	Laborers	Service workers
Industrial organic chemicals										
All employers	155,221	27,258	31,545	12,356	4,804	17,590	25,404	28,829	3,746	3,689
White	128,597	24,810	27,795	10,276	4,431	14,575	20,899	20,624	2,568	2,619
Minority	26,624	2,448	3,750	2,080	373	3,015	4,505	8,205	1,178	1,070
Black	16,421	1,278	1,503	1,289	204	2,130	2,845	5,528	827	817
Hispanic	6,615	615	642	433	113	636	1,416	2,302	266	192
Asian/Pacific Islander	3,025	471	1,528	323	44	204	125	240	42	48
American Indian/Alaskan Native	563	84	77	35	12	45	119	135	43	13
Plastics materials and synthetics										
All employers	190,815	22,003	28,619	16,158	3,056	14,789	45,241	48,266	10,557	2,126
White	158,062	20,072	25,196	13,790	2,832	12,768	38,613	36,232	6,898	1,661
Minority	32,753	1,931	3,423	2,368	224	2,021	6,628	12,034	3,659	465
Black	21,546	1,165	1,332	1,586	119	1,311	4,918	8,928	1,861	326
Hispanic	7,431	363	529	476	50	521	1,411	2,453	1,525	103

[Continued]

★ 728 ★

Private Industry Employment: Chemicals & Allied Products

[Continued]

	Total employ-ment	Officials and managers	Profes-sionals	Techni-cians	Sales workers	Office & clerical workers	Craft workers	Opera-tives	Laborers	Service workers
Asian/Pacific Islander	3,227	342	1,509	256	47	140	170	489	246	28
American Indian/Alaskan Native	549	61	53	50	8	49	129	164	27	8
Drugs										
All employers	259,664	44,873	60,146	17,745	39,624	33,317	18,267	34,833	5,831	5,028
White	206,929	39,955	49,185	13,590	34,351	26,985	14,631	21,821	3,310	3,101
Minority	52,735	4,918	10,961	4,155	5,273	6,332	3,636	13,012	2,521	1,927
Black	25,212	1,867	2,981	2,192	2,645	4,025	2,069	7,281	862	1,290
Hispanic	12,025	1,003	1,503	777	1,426	1,418	1,121	3,390	967	420
Asian/Pacific Islander	14,593	1,918	6,361	1,120	1,018	809	391	2,096	676	204
American Indian/Alaskan Native	905	130	116	66	184	80	55	245	16	13
Soaps, cleaners, and toilet goods										
All employers	125,628	20,970	13,713	5,657	13,997	18,961	10,256	23,796	16,616	1,662
White	96,222	18,616	11,612	4,591	12,868	15,622	8,159	15,635	8,048	1,071
Minority	29,406	2,354	2,101	1,066	1,129	3,339	2,097	8,161	8,568	591
Black	16,047	1,277	798	637	479	2,035	1,154	4,778	4,533	356
Hispanic	9,482	501	392	207	426	958	711	2,680	3,403	204
Asian/Pacific Islander	3,511	542	887	208	190	302	178	612	565	27
American Indian/Alaskan Native	366	34	24	14	34	44	54	91	67	4

Source: U.S. Equal Employment Opportunity Commission. *Job Patterns for Minorities and Women in Private Industry, 1993.* Washington, DC: U.S. Government Printing Office, 1994, pp. 13-14.

★ 729 ★

Industry Employment

Private Industry Employment: Commercial Banking

Number of persons employed in each occupation is shown, by race/ethnicity, in 1993. Data do not include Hawaii.

	Total employ-ment	Officials and managers	Profes-sionals	Techni-cians	Sales workers	Office & clerical workers	Craft workers	Opera-tives	Laborers	Service workers
All employers	1,002,942	211,534	165,360	24,625	23,017	554,566	3,062	7,817	982	11,979
White	761,242	185,651	136,539	18,482	18,973	385,249	2,516	4,953	661	8,218
Minority	241,700	25,883	28,821	6,143	4,044	169,317	546	2,864	321	3,761
Black	130,250	11,913	13,321	3,044	2,712	95,197	279	1,486	204	2,634
Hispanic	61,279	7,374	6,667	1,482	1,138	42,717	199	705	92	905
Asian/Pacific Islander	46,759	6,123	8,421	1,541	657	29,156	55	614	20	172
American Indian/Alaskan Native	3,412	473	412	76	77	2,247	13	59	5	50

Source: U.S. Equal Employment Opportunity Commission. *Job Patterns for Minorities and Women in Private Industry, 1993.* Washington, DC: U.S. Government Printing Office, 1994, p. 33.

★ 730 ★

Industry Employment

Private Industry Employment: Construction

Number of persons employed in each occupation is shown, by race/ethnicity, in 1993. Data do not include Hawaii.

	Total employ-ment	Officials and managers	Profes-sionals	Techni-cians	Sales workers	Office & clerical workers	Craft workers	Opera-tives	Laborers	Service workers
All employers	534,603	49,467	30,259	16,709	11,095	40,634	191,651	103,670	78,179	12,939
White	429,581	46,691	27,769	14,878	9,799	35,478	160,029	77,712	48,246	8,979
Minority	105,022	2,776	2,490	1,831	1,296	5,156	31,622	25,958	29,933	3,960
Black	48,581	1,012	734	714	808	2,405	12,929	12,841	14,566	2,572
Hispanic	45,878	1,110	744	740	368	1,915	15,253	10,925	13,804	1,019
Asian/Pacific Islander	5,146	428	898	298	98	623	1,191	876	456	278
American Indian/Alaskan Native	5,417	226	114	79	22	213	2,249	1,316	1,107	91

Source: U.S. Equal Employment Opportunity Commission. *Job Patterns for Minorities and Women in Private Industry, 1993.* Washington, DC: U.S. Government Printing Office, 1994, p. 2.

★ 731 ★

Industry Employment

Private Industry Employment: Department & Variety Stores

Number of persons employed in each occupation is shown, by race/ethnicity, in 1993. Data do not include Hawaii.

	Total employ-ment	Officials and managers	Profes-sionals	Techni-cians	Sales workers	Office & clerical workers	Craft workers	Opera-tives	Laborers	Service workers
Department stores										
All employers	1,814,586	141,520	22,358	13,707	1,041,609	206,719	61,487	54,614	185,530	87,042
White	1,400,963	123,873	19,832	11,062	801,625	161,762	49,847	40,537	130,542	61,883
Minority	413,623	17,647	2,526	2,645	239,984	44,957	11,640	14,077	54,988	25,159
Black	230,446	9,850	1,080	1,565	132,434	26,438	5,495	6,871	31,852	14,861
Hispanic	136,245	5,549	646	716	78,312	13,900	4,652	5,256	19,003	8,211
Asian/Pacific Islander	38,335	1,877	710	328	23,853	3,836	1,267	1,655	3,101	1,708
American Indian/Alaskan Native	8,597	371	90	36	5,385	783	226	295	1,032	379
Variety stores										
All employers	120,566	12,384	1,025	957	64,858	11,268	7,452	2,365	15,706	4,551
White	98,989	11,174	953	857	52,236	9,982	6,732	2,031	12,501	2,523
Minority	21,577	1,210	72	100	12,622	1,286	720	334	3,205	2,028
Black	14,162	646	31	60	8,481	771	532	176	2,383	1,082
Hispanic	4,967	394	15	20	2,549	333	110	140	557	849
Asian/Pacific Islander	1,592	136	23	19	1,041	139	21	10	116	87
American Indian/Alaskan Native	856	34	3	1	551	43	57	8	149	10

Source: U.S. Equal Employment Opportunity Commission. *Job Patterns for Minorities and Women in Private Industry, 1993.* Washington, DC: U.S. Government Printing Office, 1994, p. 31.

★ 732 ★

Industry Employment

Private Industry Employment: Drugstores & Proprietary Stores

Number of persons employed in each occupation is shown, by race/ethnicity, in 1993. Data do not include Hawaii.

	Total employ-ment	Officials and managers	Profes-sionals	Techni-cians	Sales workers	Office & clerical workers	Craft workers	Opera-tives	Laborers	Service workers
All employers	57,663	6,796	4,675	2,456	22,172	7,422	1,095	6,671	5,285	1,091
White	43,394	5,926	3,820	1,944	15,494	6,107	892	4,670	3,757	784
Minority	14,269	870	855	512	6,678	1,315	203	2,001	1,528	307
Black	6,277	351	225	201	2,473	668	110	1,266	851	132
Hispanic	5,002	299	113	145	2,900	362	60	577	413	133
Asian/Pacific Islander	2,692	199	506	155	1,136	260	32	130	242	32
American Indian/Alaskan Native	298	21	11	11	169	25	1	28	22	10

Source: U.S. Equal Employment Opportunity Commission. *Job Patterns for Minorities and Women in Private Industry, 1993.* Washington, DC: U.S. Government Printing Office, 1994, p. 33.

★ 733 ★

Industry Employment

Private Industry Employment: Electronic/Electrical Equipment Industry

Number of persons employed in each occupation is shown, by race/ethnicity, in 1993. Data are shown for selected industry sectors and do not include Hawaii.

	Total employ-ment	Officials and managers	Profes-sionals	Techni-cians	Sales workers	Office & clerical workers	Craft workers	Opera-tives	Laborers	Service workers
Electric distributing equipment										
All employers	88,806	8,568	10,831	6,201	1,851	6,751	13,511	34,362	6,279	452
White	73,351	7,999	9,806	5,377	1,762	5,723	11,252	26,598	4,509	325
Minority	15,455	569	1,025	824	89	1,028	2,259	7,764	1,770	127
Black	8,292	227	286	292	36	570	1,383	4,889	541	68
Hispanic	4,254	155	177	196	29	260	572	1,784	1,042	39
Asian/Pacific Islander	2,576	162	530	315	19	164	262	958	147	19
American Indian/Alaskan Native	333	25	32	21	5	34	42	133	40	1
Electrical industrial apparatus										
All employers	134,342	12,862	17,270	8,601	3,256	9,184	20,706	49,478	12,064	921
White	113,133	12,069	15,925	7,675	3,102	8,075	17,684	38,436	9,422	745
Minority	21,209	793	1,345	926	154	1,109	3,022	11,042	2,642	176
Black	11,141	292	389	352	53	533	1,684	6,493	1,230	115
Hispanic	6,168	225	328	252	62	383	873	2,982	1,016	47
Asian/Pacific Islander	3,019	210	586	280	31	147	350	1,191	218	6
American Indian/Alaskan Native	881	66	42	42	8	46	115	376	178	8
Household appliances										
All employers	102,699	8,090	6,656	2,789	1,469	6,763	10,467	45,624	20,017	824
White	85,022	7,632	6,231	2,554	1,403	6,007	9,206	35,119	16,177	693
Minority	17,677	458	425	235	66	756	1,261	10,505	3,840	131
Black	12,869	236	204	150	27	498	864	8,346	2,457	87
Hispanic	3,491	120	78	61	31	200	283	1,722	953	43
Asian/Pacific Islander	1,016	76	125	21	7	48	73	301	365	0
American Indian/Alaskan Native	301	26	18	3	1	10	41	136	65	1
Electric lighting and wiring equipment										
All employers	86,820	7,936	5,410	2,887	2,326	6,412	13,943	33,279	13,934	693
White	63,667	7,261	4,880	2,401	2,184	5,248	11,537	22,047	7,660	449

[Continued]

★ 733 ★

Private Industry Employment: Electronic/Electrical Equipment Industry

[Continued]

	Total employ-ment	Officials and managers	Profes-sionals	Techni-cians	Sales workers	Office & clerical workers	Craft workers	Opera-tives	Laborers	Service workers
Minority	23,153	675	530	486	142	1,164	2,406	11,232	6,274	244
Black	11,999	272	162	189	82	491	1,095	6,265	3,308	135
Hispanic	8,032	233	121	106	44	435	1,014	3,826	2,166	87
Asian/Pacific Islander	2,759	143	232	182	13	182	265	1,049	673	20
American Indian/Alaskan Native	363	27	15	9	3	56	32	92	127	2
Communications equipment										
All employers	318,707	46,327	108,398	35,338	6,183	40,422	20,263	53,848	5,253	2,675
White	256,303	41,910	93,400	28,218	5,455	30,908	16,696	34,754	3,110	1,852
Minority	62,404	4,417	14,998	7,120	728	9,514	3,567	19,094	2,143	823
Black	28,395	1,743	4,647	3,115	318	5,971	1,780	9,414	966	441
Hispanic	14,730	1,044	2,666	1,684	163	2,183	887	5,253	558	292
Asian/Pacific Islander	17,706	1,476	7,396	2,138	218	1,160	794	4,027	420	77
American Indian/Alaskan Native	1,573	154	289	183	29	200	106	400	199	13
Electronic components and accessories										
All employers	548,716	72,230	134,942	60,448	9,104	52,288	46,440	147,005	20,265	5,994
White	394,780	62,289	106,405	43,480	8,404	39,155	33,763	85,645	11,920	3,719
Minority	153,936	9,941	28,537	16,968	700	13,133	12,677	61,360	8,345	2,275
Black	38,230	1,993	4,383	3,981	180	4,334	3,618	15,617	3,021	1,103
Hispanic	49,733	2,659	5,492	5,006	239	5,105	5,037	21,920	3,333	942
Asian/Pacific Islander	63,047	5,012	18,231	7,683	251	3,405	3,735	22,643	1,900	187
American Indian/Alaskan Native	2,926	277	431	298	30	289	287	1,180	91	43
Misc. electrical equipment and supplies										
All employers	81,105	8,630	10,887	7,455	2,667	6,329	8,888	28,675	6,675	899
White	65,241	7,951	9,652	6,318	2,491	5,455	7,443	21,163	4,117	651
Minority	15,864	679	1,235	1,137	176	874	1,445	7,512	2,558	248
Black	7,620	236	314	402	77	408	839	3,987	1,187	170
Hispanic	4,287	177	246	308	50	278	381	1,876	925	46
Asian/Pacific Islander	3,317	227	646	380	42	155	167	1,433	254	13
American Indian/Alaskan Native	640	39	29	47	7	33	58	216	192	19

Source: U.S. Equal Employment Opportunity Commission. *Job Patterns for Minorities and Women in Private Industry, 1993.* Washington, DC: U.S. Government Printing Office, 1994, pp. 21-23.

★ 734 ★

Industry Employment

Private Industry Employment: Fabricated Metals Industry

Number of persons employed in each occupation is shown, by race/ethnicity, in 1993. Data are shown for selected industry sectors and do not include Hawaii.

	Total employ-ment	Officials and managers	Profes-sionals	Techni-cians	Sales workers	Office & clerical workers	Craft workers	Opera-tives	Laborers	Service workers
Metal cans and shipping containers										
All employers	40,849	4,896	1,477	630	896	2,491	10,741	14,541	4,923	254
White	31,408	4,502	1,360	566	766	2,181	8,907	9,836	3,086	204
Minority	9,441	394	117	64	130	310	1,834	4,705	1,837	50
Black	4,599	202	41	26	61	166	868	2,639	838	28
Hispanic	4,028	124	32	27	56	100	784	1,980	909	16
Asian/Pacific Islander	605	47	42	10	10	29	143	253	65	6
American Indian/Alaskan Native	209	21	2	1	3	15	39	103	25	0
Cutlery, hand tools, and hardware										
All employers	65,268	6,298	3,501	2,236	2,457	4,950	10,372	27,301	7,495	658
White	50,054	5,879	3,203	1,961	2,315	4,244	8,494	18,797	4,688	473

[Continued]

★ 734 ★

Private Industry Employment: Fabricated Metals Industry

[Continued]

	Total employ-ment	Officials and managers	Profes-sionals	Techni-cians	Sales workers	Office & clerical workers	Craft workers	Opera-tives	Laborers	Service workers
Minority	15,214	419	298	275	142	706	1,878	8,504	2,807	185
Black	6,970	177	101	91	63	318	903	4,161	1,068	88
Hispanic	6,257	138	85	114	61	288	706	3,276	1,507	82
Asian/Pacific Islander	1,627	87	108	62	13	85	228	846	191	7
American Indian/Alaskan Native	360	17	4	8	5	15	41	221	41	8
Fabricated structural metal products										
All employers	190,091	18,947	15,656	10,285	4,652	13,769	41,316	57,625	25,585	2,256
White	150,805	17,685	13,843	9,228	4,481	12,003	33,488	41,496	17,019	1,562
Minority	39,286	1,262	1,813	1,057	171	1,766	7,828	16,129	8,566	694
Black	18,091	477	345	430	45	854	3,782	8,034	3,676	448
Hispanic	16,079	434	414	362	96	632	3,178	6,627	4,124	212
Asian/Pacific Islander	4,025	273	1,024	224	18	220	602	1,113	526	25
American Indian/Alaskan Native	1,091	78	30	41	12	60	266	355	240	9
Metal forgings and stampings										
All employers	108,440	9,349	5,030	3,900	1,366	5,891	23,126	44,086	14,559	1,133
White	89,168	8,667	4,633	3,588	1,326	5,276	20,407	33,597	10,869	805
Minority	19,272	682	397	312	40	615	2,719	10,489	3,690	328
Black	11,593	336	143	106	12	328	1,438	6,710	2,256	264
Hispanic	5,658	159	61	92	16	181	962	2,896	1,235	56
Asian/Pacific Islander	1,677	161	181	101	10	77	257	727	155	8
American Indian/Alaskan Native	344	26	12	13	2	29	62	156	44	0
Misc. fabricated metal products										
All employers	150,605	15,724	9,320	7,180	4,885	11,874	30,146	55,561	14,664	1,251
White	123,794	14,844	8,603	6,356	4,565	10,586	25,573	42,383	9,908	976
Minority	26,811	880	717	824	320	1,288	4,573	13,178	4,756	275
Black	12,302	330	178	282	163	592	1,924	6,862	1,796	175
Hispanic	10,343	299	158	303	104	502	1,848	4,555	2,497	77
Asian/Pacific Islander	3,655	190	361	219	47	151	705	1,560	404	18
American Indian/Alaskan Native	511	61	20	20	6	43	96	201	59	5

Source: U.S. Equal Employment Opportunity Commission. *Job Patterns for Minorities and Women in Private Industry, 1993.* Washington, DC: U.S. Government Printing Office, 1994, pp. 17-18.

★ 735 ★

Industry Employment

Private Industry Employment: Finance, Insurance, and Real Estate

Number of persons employed in each occupation is shown, by race/ethnicity, in 1993. Data do not include Hawaii.

	Total employ-ment	Officials and managers	Profes-sionals	Techni-cians	Sales workers	Office & clerical workers	Craft workers	Opera-tives	Laborers	Service workers
All employers	2,911,748	514,605	585,991	176,261	153,743	1,360,242	19,628	26,474	15,693	59,111
White	2,293,247	459,660	494,930	139,688	135,516	985,145	15,401	16,900	8,745	37,262
Minority	618,501	54,945	91,061	36,573	18,227	375,097	4,227	9,574	6,948	21,848
Black	346,427	27,275	45,621	21,548	8,324	219,187	2,074	5,400	3,292	13,726
Hispanic	154,921	14,374	19,437	7,239	5,747	93,454	1,779	2,839	3,241	6,811
Asian/Pacific Islander	107,264	12,119	24,588	7,249	3,662	56,736	308	1,170	367	1,065
American Indian/Alaskan Native	9,889	1,177	1,415	557	494	5,720	66	165	48	247

Source: U.S. Equal Employment Opportunity Commission. *Job Patterns for Minorities and Women in Private Industry, 1993.* Washington, DC: U.S. Government Printing Office, 1994, p. 4.

★ 736 ★

Industry Employment

Private Industry Employment: Food & Kindred Products

Number of persons employed in each occupation is shown, by race/ethnicity, in 1993. Data are shown for selected industry sectors and do not include Hawaii.

	Total employment	Officials and managers	Professionals	Technicians	Sales workers	Office & clerical workers	Craft workers	Operatives	Laborers	Service workers
Meat products										
All employers	349,827	24,987	5,653	6,487	5,288	12,730	27,896	90,204	170,094	6,488
White	186,156	21,527	5,035	5,211	4,785	10,825	19,742	41,153	74,329	3,549
Minority	163,671	3,460	618	1,276	503	1,905	8,154	49,051	95,765	2,939
Black	79,293	2,089	340	695	354	1,209	4,781	25,397	42,650	1,778
Hispanic	67,536	1,066	148	417	105	548	2,750	18,591	42,961	950
Asian/Pacific Islander	13,253	186	105	112	32	83	422	4,345	7,852	116
American Indian/Alaskan Native	3,589	119	25	52	12	65	201	718	2,302	95
Dairy products										
All employers	109,338	11,921	3,918	3,414	8,329	11,086	13,248	32,555	22,194	2,673
White	91,177	11,029	3,632	2,962	7,274	9,623	11,281	26,410	16,769	2,197
Minority	18,161	892	286	452	1,055	1,463	1,967	6,145	5,425	476
Black	8,463	407	112	204	568	718	932	2,978	2,308	236
Hispanic	7,482	311	58	124	388	438	816	2,598	2,617	132
Asian/Pacific Islander	1,777	139	107	106	70	253	172	425	414	91
American Indian/Alaskan Native	439	35	9	18	29	54	47	144	86	17
Preserved fruits & vegetables										
All employers	163,573	14,533	6,448	4,084	2,935	10,548	20,982	41,029	59,990	3,024
White	102,369	13,080	5,719	3,170	2,689	8,992	16,421	25,827	24,727	1,744
Minority	61,204	1,453	729	914	246	1,556	4,561	15,202	35,263	1,280
Black	12,687	452	304	270	104	515	1,032	4,346	5,351	313
Hispanic	43,065	674	183	531	106	791	3,141	9,887	26,875	877
Asian/Pacific Islander	4,166	244	222	92	21	202	204	630	2,502	49
American Indian/Alaskan Native	1,286	83	20	21	15	48	184	339	535	41
Grain mill products										
All employers	77,874	12,230	6,314	3,365	4,392	8,602	9,024	22,263	10,620	1,064
White	64,274	11,385	5,663	2,952	4,241	7,394	7,799	17,130	6,880	830
Minority	13,600	845	651	413	151	1,208	1,225	5,133	3,740	234
Black	8,235	455	331	251	68	759	671	3,394	2,140	166
Hispanic	4,041	205	121	85	59	313	443	1,387	1,375	53
Asian/Pacific Islander	985	147	191	63	16	105	61	247	142	13
American Indian/Alaskan Native	339	38	8	14	8	31	50	105	83	2
Bakery products										
All employers	137,286	14,836	1,707	1,334	18,891	7,431	17,955	38,320	30,482	6,330
White	94,607	12,995	1,506	1,036	16,345	5,985	12,600	24,505	16,338	3,297
Minority	42,679	1,841	201	298	2,546	1,446	5,355	13,815	14,144	3,033
Black	24,501	1,047	103	175	1,251	833	2,953	8,374	8,091	1,674
Hispanic	14,803	551	44	76	1,102	429	1,972	4,572	4,923	1,134
Asian/Pacific Islander	2,790	188	53	43	134	161	347	710	964	190
American Indian/Alaskan Native	585	55	1	4	59	23	83	159	166	35
Beverages										
All employers	181,381	24,974	12,427	4,400	31,135	20,099	17,004	46,612	18,646	6,084
White	137,362	22,109	10,637	3,309	25,147	15,852	13,994	32,525	10,172	3,617
Minority	44,019	2,865	1,790	1,091	5,988	4,247	3,010	14,087	8,474	2,467
Black	24,012	1,567	939	549	3,410	2,466	1,346	8,305	3,684	1,746
Hispanic	16,494	906	481	393	2,131	1,329	1,387	5,119	4,301	447

[Continued]

★ 736 ★

Private Industry Employment: Food & Kindred Products

[Continued]

	Total employment	Officials and managers	Professionals	Technicians	Sales workers	Office & clerical workers	Craft workers	Operatives	Laborers	Service workers
Asian/Pacific Islander	2,543	324	347	134	288	345	200	465	360	80
American Indian/Alaskan Native	970	68	23	15	159	107	77	198	129	194

Source: U.S. Equal Employment Opportunity Commission. *Job Patterns for Minorities and Women in Private Industry, 1993.* Washington, DC: U.S. Government Printing Office, 1994, p. 6-7.

★ 737 ★

Industry Employment

Private Industry Employment: Freight Transport Industry

Number of persons employed in each occupation is shown, by race/ethnicity, in 1993. Data are shown for selected industry sectors and do not include Hawaii.

	Total employment	Officials and managers	Professionals	Technicians	Sales workers	Office & clerical workers	Craft workers	Operatives	Laborers	Service workers
Trucking and courier services										
All employers	691,347	73,783	27,378	7,575	25,761	78,037	37,872	271,469	136,424	33,048
White	540,586	63,014	25,330	6,633	19,769	61,010	32,120	213,796	92,354	26,560
Minority	150,761	10,769	2,048	942	5,992	17,027	5,752	57,673	44,070	6,488
Black	94,619	6,351	939	405	2,954	10,673	3,024	37,753	28,550	3,970
Hispanic	43,024	3,057	582	243	2,340	4,606	1,952	15,825	12,519	1,900
Asian/Pacific Islander	10,191	1,080	459	263	620	1,460	577	2,699	2,502	531
American Indian/Alaskan Native	2,927	281	68	31	78	288	199	1,396	499	87
Trucking terminal facilities										
All employers	5,195	375	195	248	81	468	220	3,137	392	79
White	4,574	360	177	225	81	434	186	2,762	278	71
Minority	621	15	18	23	0	34	34	375	114	8
Black	425	8	3	18	0	16	7	294	76	3
Hispanic	141	3	1	2	0	12	18	70	31	4
Asian/Pacific Islander	33	4	13	3	0	1	6	1	4	1
American Indian/Alaskan Native	22	0	1	0	0	5	3	10	3	0

Source: U.S. Equal Employment Opportunity Commission. *Job Patterns for Minorities and Women in Private Industry, 1993.* Washington, DC: U.S. Government Printing Office, 1994, p. 26.

★ 738 ★

Industry Employment

Private Industry Employment: Furniture and Home Furnishings Stores

Number of persons employed in each occupation is shown, by race/ethnicity, in 1993. Data do not include Hawaii.

	Total employment	Officials and managers	Professionals	Technicians	Sales workers	Office & clerical workers	Craft workers	Operatives	Laborers	Service workers
All employers	41,847	5,259	1,368	546	8,826	9,944	2,237	6,791	5,834	1,042
White	30,750	4,697	1,233	422	6,707	7,436	1,497	4,234	3,875	649
Minority	11,097	562	135	124	2,119	2,508	740	2,557	1,959	393
Black	5,414	256	43	51	1,003	1,205	290	1,252	1,175	139
Hispanic	4,236	223	50	52	783	998	365	887	645	233
Asian/Pacific Islander	1,263	77	40	20	310	283	60	344	113	16
American Indian/Alaskan Native	184	6	2	1	23	22	25	74	26	5

Source: U.S. Equal Employment Opportunity Commission. *Job Patterns for Minorities and Women in Private Industry, 1993.* Washington, DC: U.S. Government Printing Office, 1994, p. 32.

★ 739 ★

Industry Employment

Private Industry Employment: Grocery Stores

Number of persons employed in each occupation is shown, by race/ethnicity, in 1993. Data do not include Hawaii.

	Total employment	Officials and managers	Professionals	Technicians	Sales workers	Office & clerical workers	Craft workers	Operatives	Laborers	Service workers
All employers	1,601,271	140,778	16,018	7,706	1,052,123	60,504	54,060	96,288	96,082	77,712
White	1,249,802	124,389	13,614	6,251	813,468	50,867	44,417	71,148	68,385	57,263
Minority	351,469	16,389	2,404	1,455	238,655	9,637	9,643	25,140	27,697	20,449
Black	174,268	7,554	651	421	124,937	4,419	3,926	10,713	12,448	9,199
Hispanic	139,253	6,629	850	819	88,801	3,988	4,542	12,162	12,584	8,878
Asian/Pacific Islander	27,159	1,736	804	155	17,948	924	905	1,237	1,523	1,927
American Indian/Alaskan Native	10,789	470	99	60	6,969	306	270	1,028	1,142	445

Source: U.S. Equal Employment Opportunity Commission. *Job Patterns for Minorities and Women in Private Industry, 1993.* Washington, DC: U.S. Government Printing Office, 1994, p. 31.

★ 740 ★

Industry Employment

Private Industry Employment: Health Care Industry

Number of persons employed in each occupation is shown, by race/ethnicity, in 1993. Data are shown for selected industry sectors and do not include Hawaii.

	Total employ-ment	Officials and managers	Profes-sionals	Techni-cians	Sales workers	Office & clerical workers	Craft workers	Opera-tives	Laborers	Service workers
Nursing and personal care facilities										
All employers	845,204	50,273	133,040	100,220	2,087	67,484	11,270	17,916	13,510	449,404
White	561,013	43,955	108,040	73,045	1,863	53,386	7,789	11,797	7,530	253,608
Minority	284,191	6,318	25,000	27,175	224	14,098	3,481	6,119	5,980	195,796
Black	198,943	3,817	11,604	18,902	157	8,777	2,262	4,104	3,844	145,476
Hispanic	48,287	1,224	2,639	3,602	43	3,421	808	1,343	1,596	33,611
Asian/Pacific Islander	33,174	1,140	10,357	4,216	20	1,679	357	547	488	14,370
American Indian/Alaskan Native	3,787	137	400	455	4	221	54	125	52	2,339
Hospitals										
All employers	3,436,239	234,537	1,298,175	555,455	6,031	610,988	47,066	37,243	21,944	627,800
White	2,655,559	207,103	1,105,821	425,508	4,659	468,816	37,910	25,828	13,458	366,456
Minority	780,680	27,434	192,354	126,947	1,372	142,172	9,156	11,415	8,486	261,344
Black	467,090	15,159	77,566	76,607	802	92,767	5,201	7,528	5,790	185,670
Hispanic	158,257	6,000	29,617	25,876	284	35,560	2,753	2,769	2,068	53,330
Asian/Pacific Islander	142,881	5,767	80,077	22,438	266	12,133	1,032	967	519	19,682
American Indian/Alaskan Native	12,452	508	5,094	2,026	20	1,712	170	151	109	2,662

Source: U.S. Equal Employment Opportunity Commission. *Job Patterns for Minorities and Women in Private Industry, 1993.* Washington, DC: U.S. Government Printing Office, 1994, p. 36.

★ 741 ★

Industry Employment

Private Industry Employment: Household Furniture Production

Number of persons employed in each occupation is shown, by race/ethnicity, in 1993. Data are shown for selected industry sectors and do not include Hawaii.

	Total employ-ment	Officials and managers	Profes-sionals	Techni-cians	Sales workers	Office & clerical workers	Craft workers	Opera-tives	Laborers	Service workers
All employers	177,047	12,146	3,152	2,210	6,243	11,369	38,390	71,868	29,521	2,148
White	138,109	11,255	2,953	2,044	5,555	10,177	31,656	53,280	19,729	1,460
Minority	38,938	891	199	166	688	1,192	6,734	18,588	9,792	688
Black	25,571	411	64	77	374	517	4,713	12,820	6,055	540
Hispanic	10,958	315	32	56	220	468	1,595	4,774	3,376	122
Asian/Pacific Islander	1,639	64	42	24	79	96	313	752	253	16
American Indian/Alaskan Native	770	101	61	9	15	111	113	242	108	10

Source: U.S. Equal Employment Opportunity Commission. *Job Patterns for Minorities and Women in Private Industry, 1993.* Washington, DC: U.S. Government Printing Office, 1994, p. 10.

★ 742 ★

Industry Employment

Private Industry Employment: Instrumentation Industry

Number of persons employed in each occupation is shown, by race/ethnicity, in 1993. Data are shown for selected industry sectors and do not include Hawaii.

	Total employ-ment	Officials and managers	Profes-sionals	Techni-cians	Sales workers	Office & clerical workers	Craft workers	Opera-tives	Laborers	Service workers
Measuring and controlling devices										
All employers	191,391	25,978	42,184	21,446	5,732	22,248	21,086	42,733	7,049	2,935
White	159,120	24,092	37,487	17,855	5,383	18,861	17,564	30,351	5,171	2,356
Minority	32,271	1,886	4,697	3,591	349	3,387	3,522	12,382	1,878	579
Black	10,718	491	851	1,005	119	1,368	1,306	4,606	706	266
Hispanic	10,805	557	1,006	1,015	122	1,296	1,345	4,188	995	281
Asian/Pacific Islander	9,929	739	2,691	1,481	93	604	795	3,355	148	23
American Indian/Alaskan Native	819	99	149	90	15	119	76	233	29	9
Medical instruments and supplies										
All employers	225,297	29,627	33,690	19,824	15,050	28,606	17,278	63,077	15,704	2,441
White	168,912	26,940	28,580	14,994	14,101	23,214	13,258	38,176	7,951	1,698
Minority	56,385	2,687	5,110	4,830	949	5,392	4,020	24,901	7,753	743
Black	17,304	862	1,074	1,232	439	1,992	1,270	7,569	2,553	313
Hispanic	22,731	967	1,476	1,697	343	2,459	1,866	10,256	3,291	376
Asian/Pacific Islander	15,423	780	2,465	1,819	135	833	827	6,716	1,808	40
American Indian/Alaskan Native	927	78	95	82	32	108	57	360	101	14

Source: U.S. Equal Employment Opportunity Commission. *Job Patterns for Minorities and Women in Private Industry, 1993.* Washington, DC: U.S. Government Printing Office, 1994, p. 25.

★ 743 ★

Industry Employment

Private Industry Employment: Insurance Industry

Number of persons employed in each occupation is shown, by race/ethnicity, in 1993. Data are shown for selected industry sectors and do not include Hawaii.

	Total employ-ment	Officials and managers	Profes-sionals	Techni-cians	Sales workers	Office & clerical workers	Craft workers	Opera-tives	Laborers	Service workers
Life insurance										
All employers	327,518	50,277	71,190	40,774	33,559	125,698	1,566	1,260	338	2,856
White	267,361	45,701	60,721	32,692	29,125	95,135	1,259	859	256	1,613
Minority	60,157	4,576	10,469	8,082	4,434	30,563	307	401	82	1,243
Black	36,993	2,576	5,877	5,014	1,946	20,280	189	251	59	801
Hispanic	13,113	939	2,040	1,650	1,035	6,907	100	96	18	328
Asian/Pacific Islander	9,143	971	2,396	1,323	1,261	3,018	15	50	3	106
American Indian/Alaskan Native	908	90	156	95	192	358	3	4	2	8
Health insurance and medical service plans										
All employers	262,904	34,370	65,717	35,708	10,236	111,456	1,197	1,038	228	2,954
White	203,938	30,441	55,300	27,168	9,057	78,478	925	626	141	1,802
Minority	58,966	3,929	10,417	8,540	1,179	32,978	272	412	87	1,152
Black	40,386	2,528	6,158	6,610	693	23,090	185	268	61	793
Hispanic	9,481	718	1,700	810	348	5,439	51	112	22	281
Asian/Pacific Islander	8,111	580	2,401	993	107	3,908	26	28	2	66
American Indian/Alaskan Native	988	103	158	127	31	541	10	4	2	12

[Continued]

★ 743 ★

Private Industry Employment: Insurance Industry

[Continued]

	Total employ-ment	Officials and managers	Profes-sionals	Techni-cians	Sales workers	Office & clerical workers	Craft workers	Opera-tives	Laborers	Service workers
Fire, marine, and casualty insurance										
All employers	392,918	59,584	117,762	35,062	11,991	161,186	1,985	2,279	524	2,545
White	324,628	54,076	101,901	29,455	9,987	124,424	1,694	1,665	366	1,870
Minority	68,290	5,508	16,671	5,607	2,004	36,762	291	614	158	675
Black	38,894	3,246	9,593	2,990	805	21,280	108	322	73	477
Hispanic	17,499	1,242	3,770	1,297	1,022	9,571	160	225	75	137
Asian/Pacific Islander	10,715	857	3,014	1,243	150	5,315	21	51	8	56
American Indian/Alaskan Native	1,182	163	294	77	27	596	2	16	2	5

Source: U.S. Equal Employment Opportunity Commission. *Job Patterns for Minorities and Women in Private Industry, 1993.* Washington, DC: U.S. Government Printing Office, 1994, pp. 33-34.

★ 744 ★

Industry Employment

Private Industry Employment: Laundry, Cleaning & Garment Services

Number of persons employed in each occupation is shown, by race/ethnicity, in 1993. Data do not include Hawaii.

	Total employ-ment	Officials and managers	Profes-sionals	Techni-cians	Sales workers	Office & clerical workers	Craft workers	Opera-tives	Laborers	Service workers
All employers	82,069	7,629	539	610	9,580	5,229	4,052	28,872	22,636	2,992
White	45,637	6,762	490	515	8,282	4,131	2,704	12,820	8,368	1,565
Minority	36,432	867	49	95	1,298	1,098	1,348	16,052	14,268	1,357
Black	17,658	419	25	50	589	604	597	8,128	6,543	703
Hispanic	16,580	401	16	27	651	405	670	6,860	7,003	547
Asian/Pacific Islander	1,898	41	7	16	48	78	68	942	606	92
American Indian/Alaskan Native	296	6	1	2	10	11	13	122	116	15

Source: U.S. Equal Employment Opportunity Commission. *Job Patterns for Minorities and Women in Private Industry, 1993.* Washington, DC: U.S. Government Printing Office, 1994, p. 35.

★ 745 ★

Industry Employment

Private Industry Employment: Leather Footwear Industry

Number of persons employed in each occupation is shown, by race/ethnicity, in 1993. Data do not include Hawaii.

	Total employ-ment	Officials and managers	Profes-sionals	Techni-cians	Sales workers	Office & clerical workers	Craft workers	Opera-tives	Laborers	Service workers
All employers	59,638	5,729	2,408	801	4,080	4,777	7,448	23,937	9,725	733
White	47,316	5,197	2,172	713	3,477	4,102	5,997	18,978	6,081	599
Minority	12,322	532	236	88	603	675	1,451	4,959	3,644	134
Black	3,906	133	67	21	239	268	341	1,975	809	53

[Continued]

★ 745 ★

Private Industry Employment: Leather Footwear Industry

[Continued]

	Total employment	Officials and managers	Professionals	Technicians	Sales workers	Office & clerical workers	Craft workers	Operatives	Laborers	Service workers
Hispanic	6,876	303	70	46	267	319	979	2,397	2,427	68
Asian/Pacific Islander	728	59	88	15	78	61	78	277	60	12
American Indian/Alaskan Native	812	37	11	6	19	27	53	310	348	1

Source: U.S. Equal Employment Opportunity Commission. *Job Patterns for Minorities and Women in Private Industry, 1993.* Washington, DC: U.S. Government Printing Office, 1994, p. 15.

★ 746 ★

Industry Employment

Private Industry Employment: Lodging Industry

Number of persons employed in each occupation is shown, by race/ethnicity, in 1993. Data are shown for the hotel and motel sectors and do not include Hawaii.

	Total employment	Officials and managers	Professionals	Technicians	Sales workers	Office & clerical workers	Craft workers	Operatives	Laborers	Service workers
All employers	653,316	60,152	12,268	4,989	21,550	80,957	33,248	23,583	23,993	395,576
White	364,413	49,335	9,711	3,950	16,945	55,472	22,425	10,642	9,921	186,012
Minority	288,903	10,817	2,557	1,039	4,605	25,485	10,823	9,941	14,072	209,564
Black	116,857	4,629	1,027	389	2,242	12,736	3,710	4,018	5,365	82,731
Hispanic	127,280	3,826	708	442	1,379	7,994	4,457	4,400	7,547	96,527
Asian/Pacific Islander	41,552	2,161	756	192	883	4,358	2,503	1,381	1,014	28,304
American Indian/Alaskan Native	3,214	191	66	16	101	397	153	142	146	2,002

Source: U.S. Equal Employment Opportunity Commission. *Job Patterns for Minorities and Women in Private Industry, 1993.* Washington, DC: U.S. Government Printing Office, 1994, p. 34.

★ 747 ★

Industry Employment

Private Industry Employment: Lumber & Wood Products

Number of persons employed in each occupation is shown, by race/ethnicity, in 1993. Data are shown for selected industry sectors and do not include Hawaii.

	Total employment	Officials and managers	Professionals	Technicians	Sales workers	Office & clerical workers	Craft workers	Operatives	Laborers	Service workers
Sawmills and planing mills										
All employers	71,981	6,532	3,381	1,498	991	4,044	15,363	22,550	16,941	681
White	56,419	6,200	3,172	1,317	934	3,495	13,272	16,223	11,277	529
Minority	15,562	332	209	181	57	549	2,091	6,327	5,664	152
Black	11,459	179	115	113	39	437	1,431	5,005	4,011	129
Hispanic	2,570	60	25	20	12	59	342	823	1,218	11

[Continued]

★ 747 ★

Private Industry Employment: Lumber & Wood Products

[Continued]

	Total employment	Officials and managers	Professionals	Technicians	Sales workers	Office & clerical workers	Craft workers	Operatives	Laborers	Service workers
Asian/Pacific Islander	429	37	58	32	3	27	51	108	113	0
American Indian/Alaskan Native	1,104	56	11	16	3	26	267	391	322	12
Millwork, plywood & structural members										
All employers	99,618	7,173	2,021	1,786	2,335	5,475	20,304	32,951	26,819	754
White	80,885	6,738	1,919	1,668	2,270	5,024	17,415	25,283	19,920	648
Minority	18,733	435	102	118	65	451	2,889	7,668	6,899	106
Black	12,304	245	35	44	19	262	1,910	5,246	4,491	52
Hispanic	4,942	114	23	49	35	138	741	1,923	1,883	36
Asian/Pacific Islander	938	39	42	19	7	40	121	325	333	12
American Indian/Alaskan Native	549	37	2	6	4	11	117	174	192	6

Source: U.S. Equal Employment Opportunity Commission. *Job Patterns for Minorities and Women in Private Industry, 1993.* Washington, DC: U.S. Government Printing Office, 1994, pp. 9-10.

★ 748 ★

Industry Employment

Private Industry Employment: Machinery and Computer Equipment Industry

Number of persons employed in each occupation is shown, by race/ethnicity, in 1993. Data are shown for selected industry sectors and do not include Hawaii.

	Total employment	Officials and managers	Professionals	Technicians	Sales workers	Office & clerical workers	Craft workers	Operatives	Laborers	Service workers
Farm and garden machinery										
All employers	54,398	5,169	3,648	3,140	1,422	4,802	9,232	17,714	7,999	1,272
White	45,302	4,913	3,484	2,943	1,392	4,359	8,159	13,924	5,015	1,113
Minority	9,096	256	164	197	30	443	1,073	3,790	2,984	159
Black	6,111	137	73	133	9	287	707	2,739	1,908	118
Hispanic	2,489	80	38	38	18	124	287	892	975	37
Asian/Pacific Islander	325	25	47	21	2	20	41	102	66	1
American Indian/Alaskan Native	171	14	6	5	1	12	38	57	35	3
Construction and related machinery										
All employers	143,649	16,660	16,707	10,217	3,702	12,999	31,661	41,716	8,480	1,507
White	126,989	15,857	15,677	9,459	3,538	11,620	27,797	35,494	6,233	1,314
Minority	16,660	803	1,030	758	164	1,379	3,864	6,222	2,247	193
Black	8,610	324	340	340	44	807	1,737	3,742	1,157	119
Hispanic	5,414	190	201	221	83	379	1,499	1,841	942	58
Asian/Pacific Islander	1,785	219	439	154	20	135	370	371	65	12
American Indian/Alaskan Native	851	70	50	43	17	58	258	268	83	4
Metalworking machinery										
All employers	101,385	10,840	7,964	6,340	4,039	7,875	27,772	30,656	5,127	772
White	86,645	10,272	7,444	5,825	3,910	7,121	24,397	23,202	3,918	556
Minority	14,740	568	520	515	129	754	3,375	7,454	1,209	216
Black	6,543	191	136	185	41	372	1,486	3,344	644	144
Hispanic	5,714	176	96	174	60	264	1,280	3,170	429	65
Asian/Pacific Islander	2,164	168	261	139	20	86	527	835	124	4
American Indian/Alaskan Native	319	33	27	17	8	32	82	105	12	3
Special industry machinery										
All employers	118,436	13,875	14,057	8,979	4,173	11,567	26,271	30,145	8,448	921
White	102,301	13,204	13,101	8,006	3,992	10,396	23,537	23,623	5,761	681
Minority	16,135	671	956	973	181	1,171	2,734	6,522	2,687	240
Black	7,706	257	245	291	38	597	1,263	3,603	1,268	144
Hispanic	5,297	192	218	378	98	386	1,019	1,868	1,068	70

[Continued]

★ 748 ★

Private Industry Employment: Machinery and Computer Equipment Industry

[Continued]

	Total employ-ment	Officials and managers	Profes-sionals	Techni-cians	Sales workers	Office & clerical workers	Craft workers	Opera-tives	Laborers	Service workers
Asian/Pacific Islander	2,533	179	463	259	34	125	349	808	292	24
American Indian/Alaskan Native	599	43	30	45	11	63	103	243	59	2
General industry machinery										
All employers	195,179	23,313	23,177	12,513	5,804	17,318	40,469	58,240	12,930	1,415
White	168,706	22,089	21,196	11,537	5,598	15,598	35,245	46,541	9,819	1,083
Minority	26,473	1,224	1,981	976	206	1,720	5,224	11,699	3,111	332
Black	14,625	455	498	388	59	968	2,617	7,581	1,827	232
Hispanic	7,402	344	471	331	90	492	1,677	2,888	1,026	83
Asian/Pacific Islander	3,579	326	944	220	44	183	675	973	200	14
American Indian/Alaskan Native	867	99	68	37	13	77	255	257	58	3
Computer and office equipment										
All employers	356,139	47,336	131,952	43,079	21,889	36,046	18,885	50,352	5,213	1,387
White	282,638	41,804	110,766	34,414	18,654	28,286	14,985	30,273	2,439	1,017
Minority	73,501	5,532	21,186	8,665	3,235	7,760	3,900	20,079	2,774	370
Black	25,391	2,023	5,776	3,027	1,626	3,942	1,683	6,292	884	138
Hispanic	18,155	1,147	3,483	2,392	651	2,409	1,298	5,444	1,146	185
Asian/Pacific Islander	28,715	2,235	11,618	3,048	875	1,245	851	8,094	716	33
American Indian/Alaskan Native	1,240	127	309	198	83	164	68	249	28	14
Refrigeration and service machinery										
All employers	110,099	10,913	8,524	5,559	2,078	8,356	18,851	45,868	8,969	981
White	88,345	10,159	7,880	5,052	1,995	7,429	15,758	33,328	5,952	792
Minority	21,754	754	644	507	83	927	3,093	12,540	3,017	189
Black	12,678	318	211	227	17	464	1,785	8,184	1,348	124
Hispanic	6,555	234	142	137	49	334	1,000	3,218	1,392	49
Asian/Pacific Islander	2,055	165	266	122	11	109	219	916	236	11
American Indian/Alaskan Native	466	37	25	21	6	20	89	222	41	5
Misc. industrial and commercial machinery										
All employers	30,134	3,038	1,987	1,661	993	2,366	6,551	11,063	2,118	357
White	24,714	2,858	1,822	1,500	958	2,087	5,624	8,165	1,457	243
Minority	5,420	180	165	161	35	279	927	2,898	661	114
Black	2,311	55	31	62	8	142	346	1,295	324	48
Hispanic	2,176	63	28	51	20	95	388	1,192	275	64
Asian/Pacific Islander	820	54	101	42	3	26	168	367	57	2
American Indian/Alaskan Native	113	8	5	6	4	16	25	44	5	0

Source: U.S. Equal Employment Opportunity Commission. *Job Patterns for Minorities and Women in Private Industry, 1993.* Washington, DC: U.S. Government Printing Office, 1994, pp. 19-21.

★ 749 ★

Industry Employment

Private Industry Employment: Manufacturing-Durable Goods

Number of persons employed in each occupation is shown, by race/ethnicity, in 1993. Data do not include Hawaii.

	Total employ-ment	Officials and managers	Profes-sionals	Techni-cians	Sales workers	Office & clerical workers	Craft workers	Opera-tives	Laborers	Service workers
All employers	7,006,445	761,229	1,032,890	438,816	174,769	562,111	1,168,232	2,196,122	591,274	81,002
White	5,611,529	695,966	896,732	367,045	160,194	470,380	973,132	1,585,636	403,744	58,700
Minority	1,394,916	65,263	136,158	71,771	14,575	91,731	195,100	610,486	187,530	22,302
Black	693,710	26,595	37,062	25,494	6,583	45,377	102,889	339,690	95,531	14,489
Hispanic	423,304	17,521	27,074	20,714	4,828	30,353	65,229	179,006	72,295	6,284

[Continued]

★ 749 ★

Private Industry Employment: Manufacturing-Durable Goods

[Continued]

	Total employ-ment	Officials and managers	Profes-sionals	Techni-cians	Sales workers	Office & clerical workers	Craft workers	Opera-tives	Laborers	Service workers
Asian/Pacific Islander	246,219	18,330	68,997	23,627	2,654	13,441	21,544	80,290	16,160	1,176
American Indian/Alaskan Native	31,683	2,817	3,025	1,936	510	2,560	5,438	11,500	3,544	353

Source: U.S. Equal Employment Opportunity Commission. *Job Patterns for Minorities and Women in Private Industry, 1993.* Washington, DC: U.S. Government Printing Office, 1994, p. 3.

★ 750 ★

Industry Employment

Private Industry Employment: Manufacturing-Nondurable Goods

Number of persons employed in each occupation is shown, by race/ethnicity, in 1993. Data do not include Hawaii.

	Total employ-ment	Officials and managers	Profes-sionals	Techni-cians	Sales workers	Office & clerical workers	Craft workers	Opera-tives	Laborers	Service workers
All employers	5,246,093	574,009	422,940	184,624	331,153	502,148	730,248	1,614,351	768,957	117,663
White	3,937,953	519,238	372,275	153,445	287,765	413,955	593,078	1,082,269	435,175	80,753
Minority	1,308,140	54,771	50,665	31,179	43,388	88,193	137,170	532,082	333,782	36,910
Black	726,528	28,248	19,702	17,131	22,535	51,243	79,468	333,276	152,617	22,308
Hispanic	434,151	15,735	10,049	7,938	14,816	25,360	44,877	154,648	149,394	11,334
Asian/Pacific Islander	120,505	8,954	19,894	5,356	4,880	9,773	9,390	33,975	25,746	2,537
American Indian/Alaskan Native	26,956	1,834	1,020	754	1,157	1,817	3,435	10,183	6,025	731

Source: U.S. Equal Employment Opportunity Commission. *Job Patterns for Minorities and Women in Private Industry, 1993.* Washington, DC: U.S. Government Printing Office, 1994, p. 3.

★ 751 ★

Industry Employment

Private Industry Employment: Mining

Number of persons employed in each occupation is shown, by race/ethnicity, in 1993. Data do not include Hawaii.

	Total employ-ment	Officials and managers	Profes-sionals	Techni-cians	Sales workers	Office & clerical workers	Craft workers	Opera-tives	Laborers	Service workers
All employers	337,741	47,557	53,243	19,798	7,090	32,878	71,411	74,434	26,426	4,904
White	281,928	44,247	47,263	16,361	5,977	25,803	59,447	59,259	20,523	3,048
Minority	55,813	3,310	5,980	3,437	1,113	7,075	11,964	15,175	5,903	1,856
Black	22,191	1,104	2,007	1,412	521	3,867	4,002	5,911	2,347	1,020
Hispanic	24,624	1,384	1,623	1,254	448	2,389	6,079	7,682	3,073	692
Asian/Pacific Islander	4,516	439	2,068	526	92	492	325	370	123	81
American Indian/Alaskan Native	4,482	383	282	245	52	327	1,558	1,212	360	63

Source: U.S. Equal Employment Opportunity Commission. *Job Patterns for Minorities and Women in Private Industry, 1993.* Washington, DC: U.S. Government Printing Office, 1994, p. 2.

★ 752 ★

Industry Employment

Private Industry Employment: Paper and Allied Products

Number of persons employed in each occupation is shown, by race/ethnicity, in 1993. Data are shown for selected industry sectors and do not include Hawaii.

	Total employment	Officials and managers	Professionals	Technicians	Sales workers	Office & clerical workers	Craft workers	Operatives	Laborers	Service workers
Pulp mills										
All employers	25,911	3,076	1,698	915	273	1,395	6,853	8,645	2,760	296
White	22,441	2,932	1,609	815	264	1,249	6,155	6,942	2,232	243
Minority	3,470	144	89	100	9	146	698	1,703	528	53
Black	2,694	83	45	66	5	119	559	1,398	381	38
Hispanic	296	28	13	13	1	14	38	126	57	6
Asian/Pacific Islander	162	16	28	14	1	5	21	54	22	1
American Indian/Alaskan Native	318	17	3	7	2	8	80	125	68	8
Paper mills, except building paper										
All employers	158,856	17,236	13,760	4,925	2,869	10,723	39,561	51,318	16,908	1,556
White	137,619	16,265	12,807	4,483	2,654	9,511	35,578	41,625	13,423	1,273
Minority	21,237	971	953	442	215	1,212	3,983	9,693	3,485	283
Black	15,757	585	513	335	132	879	2,920	7,726	2,440	227
Hispanic	3,471	184	121	58	62	222	712	1,291	787	34
Asian/Pacific Islander	1,021	142	274	28	16	53	114	252	128	14
American Indian/Alaskan Native	988	60	45	21	5	58	237	424	130	8
Paperboard mills										
All employers	29,433	3,547	1,367	777	387	1,775	9,254	8,376	3,738	212
White	24,306	3,376	1,297	673	375	1,561	7,748	6,396	2,735	145
Minority	5,127	171	70	104	12	214	1,506	1,980	1,003	67
Black	3,886	108	38	90	3	167	1,157	1,587	678	58
Hispanic	908	37	14	8	6	29	262	292	254	6
Asian/Pacific Islander	158	14	14	4	1	11	36	40	37	1
American Indian/Alaskan Native	175	12	4	2	2	7	51	61	34	2
Paperboard containers and boxes										
All employers	112,176	11,893	3,130	1,694	4,107	7,864	23,442	37,865	21,495	686
White	85,962	10,963	2,849	1,519	3,961	6,913	18,558	26,586	14,086	527
Minority	26,214	930	281	175	146	951	4,884	11,279	7,409	159
Black	14,332	464	120	76	61	508	2,682	6,433	3,888	100
Hispanic	9,784	340	68	60	51	306	1,849	4,163	2,896	51
Asian/Pacific Islander	1,444	74	83	29	9	89	226	460	472	2
American Indian/Alaskan Native	654	52	10	10	25	48	127	223	153	6
Converted paper and paperboard products										
All employers	180,308	19,604	14,540	5,176	8,068	15,430	32,400	55,508	27,765	1,817
White	143,564	18,285	13,371	4,514	7,571	13,821	26,879	40,178	17,597	1,348
Minority	36,744	1,319	1,169	662	497	1,609	5,521	15,330	10,168	469
Black	20,827	641	402	311	253	934	3,014	9,174	5,806	292
Hispanic	11,986	387	206	234	169	455	1,915	4,916	3,553	151
Asian/Pacific Islander	3,248	238	517	100	51	165	470	1,022	665	20
American Indian/Alaskan Native	683	53	44	17	24	55	122	218	144	6

Source: U.S. Equal Employment Opportunity Commission. *Job Patterns for Minorities and Women in Private Industry, 1993.* Washington, DC: U.S. Government Printing Office, 1994, pp. 11-12.

★ 753 ★

Industry Employment

Private Industry Employment: Petroleum Refining

Number of persons employed in each occupation is shown, by race/ethnicity, in 1993. Data do not include Hawaii.

	Total employ-ment	Officials and managers	Profes-sionals	Techni-cians	Sales workers	Office & clerical workers	Craft workers	Opera-tives	Laborers	Service workers
All employers	111,375	18,095	21,800	6,188	5,543	12,435	33,430	11,316	1,894	674
White	89,415	16,111	18,615	4,923	4,341	9,184	25,895	8,544	1,339	463
Minority	21,960	1,984	3,185	1,265	1,202	3,251	7,535	2,772	555	211
Black	11,816	1,047	1,200	644	869	1,711	4,379	1,556	277	133
Hispanic	6,531	581	781	315	210	883	2,504	960	241	56
Asian/Pacific Islander	2,714	266	1,074	239	54	507	409	143	9	13
American Indian/Alaskan Native	899	90	130	67	69	150	243	113	28	9

Source: U.S. Equal Employment Opportunity Commission. *Job Patterns for Minorities and Women in Private Industry, 1993.* Washington, DC: U.S. Government Printing Office, 1994, p. 14.

★ 754 ★

Industry Employment

Private Industry Employment: Primary Metals Industry

Number of persons employed in each occupation is shown, by race/ethnicity, in 1993. Data are shown for selected industry sectors and do not include Hawaii.

	Total employ-ment	Officials and managers	Profes-sionals	Techni-cians	Sales workers	Office & clerical workers	Craft workers	Opera-tives	Laborers	Service workers
Iron and steel foundries										
All employers	189,101	20,359	10,834	5,634	3,145	11,691	57,346	60,793	17,454	1,826
White	153,907	18,870	10,063	5,023	2,900	10,230	48,053	45,608	11,755	1,405
Minority	35,194	1,489	771	630	245	1,461	9,293	15,185	5,699	421
Black	23,352	828	322	334	148	945	6,372	10,489	3,625	289
Hispanic	9,832	397	165	235	65	435	2,708	3,800	1,903	124
Asian/Pacific Islander	1,563	221	236	49	20	58	133	749	91	6
American Indian/Alaskan Native	447	43	48	12	12	23	80	147	80	2
Rolling and drawing										
All employers	94,370	9,839	3,880	3,172	1,300	5,312	18,693	39,813	11,192	1,169
White	70,889	9,003	3,597	2,649	1,231	4,613	15,302	26,070	7,538	886
Minority	23,481	836	283	523	69	699	3,391	13,743	3,654	283
Black	15,526	502	143	275	32	447	2,061	9,398	2,446	222
Hispanic	6,950	239	48	181	26	185	1,156	3,965	1,101	49
Asian/Pacific Islander	721	71	80	52	10	46	107	282	67	6
American Indian/Alaskan Native	284	24	12	15	1	21	67	98	40	6
All employers	85,986	9,631	5,099	2,963	1,455	4,990	17,954	36,130	6,961	803
White	70,487	8,920	4,694	2,604	1,402	4,416	15,449	27,767	4,596	639
Minority	15,499	711	405	359	53	574	2,505	8,363	2,365	164
Black	9,046	361	132	185	21	298	1,475	5,247	1,208	119
Hispanic	4,685	196	86	105	22	212	837	2,326	867	34

[Continued]

★ 754 ★

Private Industry Employment: Primary Metals Industry

[Continued]

	Total employment	Officials and managers	Professionals	Technicians	Sales workers	Office & clerical workers	Craft workers	Operatives	Laborers	Service workers
Asian/Pacific Islander	1,444	124	175	48	6	52	129	636	268	6
American Indian/Alaskan Native	324	30	12	21	4	12	64	154	22	5

Source: U.S. Equal Employment Opportunity Commission. *Job Patterns for Minorities and Women in Private Industry, 1993.* Washington, DC: U.S. Government Printing Office, 1994, pp. 16-17.

★ 755 ★

Industry Employment

Private Industry Employment: Printing & Publishing

Number of persons employed in each occupation is shown, by race/ethnicity, in 1993. Data are shown for selected industry sectors and do not include Hawaii.

	Total employment	Officials and managers	Professionals	Technicians	Sales workers	Office & clerical workers	Craft workers	Operatives	Laborers	Service workers
Newspapers										
All employers	292,850	36,117	47,417	8,795	36,332	48,174	38,156	41,591	29,090	7,178
White	236,687	32,603	42,200	7,463	30,421	37,665	33,084	30,251	18,608	4,392
Minority	56,163	3,514	5,217	1,332	5,911	10,509	5,072	11,340	10,482	2,786
Black	33,423	1,833	2,669	649	3,600	6,560	2,585	6,783	6,800	1,944
Hispanic	15,838	1,175	1,470	389	1,673	2,797	1,856	3,251	2,620	607
Asian/Pacific Islander	5,767	373	954	251	512	991	466	1,108	906	206
American Indian/Alaskan Native	1,135	133	124	43	126	161	165	198	156	29
Commercial printing										
All employers	176,521	15,292	8,297	5,808	7,982	20,264	46,162	38,315	32,574	1,827
White	149,943	14,492	7,729	5,294	7,554	17,901	40,492	30,289	24,918	1,274
Minority	26,578	800	568	514	428	2,363	5,670	8,026	7,656	553
Black	12,966	344	247	216	266	1,149	2,574	4,001	3,847	322
Hispanic	10,129	291	145	156	101	811	2,336	3,156	2,946	187
Asian/Pacific Islander	2,988	137	158	124	48	338	640	741	763	39
American Indian/Alaskan Native	495	28	18	18	13	65	120	128	100	5

Source: U.S. Equal Employment Opportunity Commission. *Job Patterns for Minorities and Women in Private Industry, 1993.* Washington, DC: U.S. Government Printing Office, 1994, p. 12.

★ 756 ★

Industry Employment

Private Industry Employment: Retail Trade

Number of persons employed in each occupation is shown, by race/ethnicity, in 1993. Data do not include Hawaii.

	Total employ-ment	Officials and managers	Profes-sionals	Techni-cians	Sales workers	Office & clerical workers	Craft workers	Opera-tives	Laborers	Service workers
All employers	5,677,285	509,620	85,264	52,753	2,586,528	475,842	171,095	269,811	430,656	1,095,716
White	4,298,787	445,756	73,900	42,615	2,002,117	375,935	136,498	197,093	293,069	731,804
Minority	1,378,498	63,864	11,364	10,138	584,411	99,907	34,597	72,718	137,587	363,912
Black	717,411	32,387	4,206	4,515	311,461	55,011	14,122	35,208	71,630	188,871
Hispanic	496,266	22,072	2,996	3,624	202,212	32,301	15,934	29,609	53,891	133,627
Asian/Pacific Islander	129,065	7,826	3,836	1,765	55,692	10,555	3,752	5,872	8,873	30,894
American Indian/Alaskan Native	35,756	1,579	326	234	15,046	2,040	789	2,029	3,193	10,520

Source: U.S. Equal Employment Opportunity Commission. *Job Patterns for Minorities and Women in Private Industry, 1993.* Washington, DC: U.S. Government Printing Office, 1994, p. 4.

★ 757 ★

Industry Employment

Private Industry Employment: Rubber & Plastics Products

Number of persons employed in each occupation is shown, by race/ethnicity, in 1993. Data are shown for selected industry sectors and do not include Hawaii.

	Total employ-ment	Officials and managers	Profes-sionals	Techni-cians	Sales workers	Office & clerical workers	Craft workers	Opera-tives	Laborers	Service workers
Tires and inner tubes										
All employers	73,238	7,872	5,964	2,969	920	2,915	8,600	40,493	2,561	944
White	61,253	7,252	5,441	2,607	865	2,590	7,813	32,052	1,896	737
Minority	11,985	620	523	362	55	325	787	8,441	665	207
Black	9,968	432	264	302	31	274	602	7,431	447	185
Hispanic	989	76	52	35	19	39	78	480	199	11
Asian/Pacific Islander	505	72	194	10	4	6	39	164	13	3
American Indian/Alaskan Native	523	40	13	15	1	6	68	366	6	8
Miscellaneous plastics products										
All employers	315,102	29,005	14,230	11,295	6,172	19,851	47,991	126,866	57,259	2,433
White	241,716	26,619	13,063	9,969	5,918	17,573	40,035	90,353	36,469	1,717
Minority	73,386	2,386	1,167	1,326	254	2,278	7,956	36,513	20,790	716
Black	33,648	946	368	568	98	1,059	3,377	18,120	8,765	347
Hispanic	30,490	901	300	486	116	936	3,536	14,277	9,627	311
Asian/Pacific Islander	8,145	454	475	234	35	239	874	3,665	2,115	54
American Indian/Alaskan Native	1,103	85	24	38	5	44	169	451	283	4

Source: U.S. Equal Employment Opportunity Commission. *Job Patterns for Minorities and Women in Private Industry, 1993.* Washington, DC: U.S. Government Printing Office, 1994, pp. 14-15.

★ 758 ★

Industry Employment

Private Industry Employment: Services

Number of persons employed in each occupation is shown, by race/ethnicity, in 1993. Data do not include Hawaii.

	Total employment	Officials and managers	Professionals	Technicians	Sales workers	Office & clerical workers	Craft workers	Operatives	Laborers	Service workers
All employers	9,613,652	861,552	2,557,136	1,081,360	205,482	1,679,543	288,963	354,675	258,750	2,326,191
White	7,036,286	759,028	2,166,066	836,946	163,962	1,260,490	221,318	223,616	137,136	1,267,724
Minority	2,577,366	102,524	391,070	244,414	41,520	419,053	67,645	131,059	121,614	1,058,467
Black	1,433,980	50,386	155,901	141,203	22,120	252,409	31,059	68,848	61,170	650,884
Hispanic	695,237	26,723	65,062	51,026	13,159	110,150	26,865	44,144	50,601	307,507
Asian/Pacific Islander	410,304	23,063	161,527	47,859	5,583	50,199	8,255	16,273	8,450	89,095
American Indian/Alaskan Native	37,845	2,352	8,580	4,326	658	6,295	1,466	1,794	1,393	10,981

Source: U.S. Equal Employment Opportunity Commission. *Job Patterns for Minorities and Women in Private Industry, 1993.* Washington, DC: U.S. Government Printing Office, 1994, p. 5.

★ 759 ★

Industry Employment

Private Industry Employment: Stone, Clay, and Glass Industry

Number of persons employed in each occupation is shown, by race/ethnicity, in 1993. Data are shown for selected industry sectors and do not include Hawaii.

	Total employment	Officials and managers	Professionals	Technicians	Sales workers	Office & clerical workers	Craft workers	Operatives	Laborers	Service workers
Glass and glassware, pressed or blown										
All employers	70,025	6,540	3,565	1,942	459	3,602	15,454	23,307	14,539	617
White	57,536	6,058	3,225	1,765	424	3,300	13,660	17,894	10,715	495
Minority	12,489	482	340	177	35	302	1,794	5,413	3,824	122
Black	7,627	276	193	87	13	174	1,039	3,568	2,205	72
Hispanic	3,572	88	40	63	11	92	565	1,439	1,235	39
Asian/Pacific Islander	982	91	98	21	5	27	102	284	345	9
American Indian/Alaskan Native	308	27	9	6	6	9	88	122	39	2
Misc. nonmetallic mineral products										
All employers	70,430	7,316	5,150	2,730	3,754	5,053	10,421	26,171	9,331	504
White	57,179	6,829	4,731	2,431	3,317	4,216	8,726	19,947	6,590	392
Minority	13,251	487	419	299	437	837	1,695	6,224	2,741	112
Black	7,682	224	148	156	207	431	919	3,981	1,545	71
Hispanic	4,160	151	75	89	128	330	590	1,750	1,015	32
Asian/Pacific Islander	1,220	100	189	49	94	69	144	408	160	7
American Indian/Alaskan Native	189	12	7	5	8	7	42	85	21	2

Source: U.S. Equal Employment Opportunity Commission. *Job Patterns for Minorities and Women in Private Industry, 1993.* Washington, DC: U.S. Government Printing Office, 1994, pp. 15-16.

★ 760 ★

Industry Employment

Private Industry Employment: Telephone Communications

Number of persons employed in each occupation is shown, by race/ethnicity, in 1993. Data do not include Hawaii.

	Total employment	Officials and managers	Professionals	Technicians	Sales workers	Office & clerical workers	Craft workers	Operatives	Laborers	Service workers
All employers	771,874	153,416	63,937	40,966	57,425	277,663	157,867	15,620	1,695	3,285
White	586,713	127,107	51,657	33,935	40,560	188,577	131,358	10,176	1,332	2,011
Minority	185,161	26,309	12,280	7,031	16,865	89,086	26,509	5,444	363	1,274
Black	119,424	15,595	5,106	4,180	10,160	64,196	15,625	3,334	232	996
Hispanic	44,786	6,416	2,045	1,623	5,153	18,899	8,656	1,653	106	235
Asian/Pacific Islander	17,577	3,710	4,918	1,086	1,252	4,630	1,543	395	11	32
American Indian/Alaskan Native	3,374	588	211	142	300	1,361	685	62	14	11

Source: U.S. Equal Employment Opportunity Commission. *Job Patterns for Minorities and Women in Private Industry, 1993.* Washington, DC: U.S. Government Printing Office, 1994, p. 27.

★ 761 ★

Industry Employment

Private Industry Employment: Textile Mill Products

Number of persons employed in each occupation is shown, by race/ethnicity, in 1993. Data are shown for selected industry sectors and do not include Hawaii.

	Total employment	Officials and managers	Professionals	Technicians	Sales workers	Office & clerical workers	Craft workers	Operatives	Laborers	Service workers
Weaving mills, cotton										
All employers	98,048	6,758	1,738	2,083	528	5,236	14,706	54,308	10,770	1,921
White	66,151	6,171	1,630	1,755	489	4,433	11,590	32,624	6,291	1,168
Minority	31,897	587	108	328	39	803	3,116	21,684	4,479	753
Black	29,854	541	85	307	25	748	2,925	20,259	4,236	728
Hispanic	1,172	24	8	12	11	38	113	767	186	13
Asian/Pacific Islander	793	19	13	5	3	10	66	616	49	12
American Indian/Alaskan Native	78	3	2	4	0	7	12	42	8	0
Knitting mills										
All employers	87,346	5,538	1,254	1,965	1,086	4,858	10,313	52,597	8,730	1,005
White	59,905	4,944	1,096	1,686	1,008	4,214	7,847	33,314	5,102	694
Minority	27,441	594	158	279	78	644	2,466	19,283	3,628	311
Black	20,158	414	59	201	37	473	1,542	14,824	2,332	276
Hispanic	4,722	97	63	38	21	104	673	2,626	1,078	22
Asian/Pacific Islander	1,453	60	31	32	19	41	155	1,003	105	7
American Indian/Alaskan Native	1,108	23	5	8	1	26	96	830	113	6
Yarn and thread mills										
All employers	93,437	7,007	1,776	2,361	617	5,010	15,493	51,988	7,349	1,836
White	66,074	6,434	1,665	1,884	602	4,306	12,375	33,418	4,075	1,315
Minority	27,363	573	111	477	15	704	3,118	18,570	3,274	521
Black	24,012	465	58	377	6	631	2,785	16,413	2,803	474
Hispanic	1,544	38	7	61	5	35	132	997	254	15

[Continued]

★ 761 ★

Private Industry Employment: Textile Mill Products

[Continued]

	Total employ-ment	Officials and managers	Profes-sionals	Techni-cians	Sales workers	Office & clerical workers	Craft workers	Opera-tives	Laborers	Service workers
Asian/Pacific Islander	1,292	42	42	33	4	19	123	828	180	21
American Indian/Alaskan Native	515	28	4	6	0	19	78	332	37	11

Source: U.S. Equal Employment Opportunity Commission. *Job Patterns for Minorities and Women in Private Industry, 1993.* Washington, DC: U.S. Government Printing Office, 1994, p. 8.

★ 762 ★

Industry Employment

Private Industry Employment: Toys & Sporting Goods Industry

Number of persons employed in each occupation is shown, by race/ethnicity, in 1993. Data do not include Hawaii.

	Total employ-ment	Officials and managers	Profes-sionals	Techni-cians	Sales workers	Office & clerical workers	Craft workers	Opera-tives	Laborers	Service workers
All employers	58,259	5,890	3,587	2,078	2,175	5,603	5,862	23,943	8,431	690
White	44,404	5,376	3,223	1,789	1,998	4,824	4,767	16,399	5,598	430
Minority	13,855	514	364	289	177	779	1,095	7,544	2,833	260
Black	4,632	122	83	106	73	276	349	2,465	1,096	62
Hispanic	6,152	250	97	117	81	331	566	3,351	1,179	180
Asian/Pacific Islander	2,749	128	172	61	18	160	156	1,528	516	10
American Indian/Alaskan Native	322	14	12	5	5	12	24	200	42	8

Source: U.S. Equal Employment Opportunity Commission. *Job Patterns for Minorities and Women in Private Industry, 1993.* Washington, DC: U.S. Government Printing Office, 1994, p. 25.

★ 763 ★

Industry Employment

Private Industry Employment: Transportation Equipment Industry

Number of persons employed in each occupation is shown, by race/ethnicity, in 1993. Data are shown for selected industry sectors and do not include Hawaii.

	Total employ-ment	Officials and managers	Profes-sionals	Techni-cians	Sales workers	Office & clerical workers	Craft workers	Opera-tives	Laborers	Service workers
Motor vehicles and equipment										
All employers	864,525	70,927	81,811	27,273	8,842	34,123	143,999	420,636	61,476	15,438
White	693,921	63,231	71,995	24,257	7,865	28,996	127,642	312,847	45,908	11,180
Minority	170,604	7,696	9,816	3,016	977	5,127	16,357	107,789	15,568	4,258
Black	128,665	5,103	4,937	1,721	433	3,449	11,582	87,541	10,269	3,630
Hispanic	27,464	1,107	1,229	674	414	1,201	3,487	15,265	3,562	525
Asian/Pacific Islander	11,713	1,233	3,437	493	101	357	751	3,783	1,501	57
American Indian/Alaskan Native	2,762	253	213	128	29	120	537	1,200	236	46

[Continued]

★ 763 ★

Private Industry Employment: Transportation Equipment Industry

[Continued]

	Total employ-ment	Officials and managers	Profes-sionals	Techni-cians	Sales workers	Office & clerical workers	Craft workers	Opera-tives	Laborers	Service workers
Aircraft and parts										
All employers	439,549	54,742	126,328	36,093	1,169	40,080	105,957	62,887	7,061	5,232
White	365,726	50,589	110,966	30,960	1,055	32,949	86,215	44,532	4,844	3,616
Minority	73,823	4,153	15,362	5,133	114	7,131	19,742	18,355	2,217	1,616
Black	30,890	1,562	4,384	1,909	30	3,629	8,999	8,441	987	949
Hispanic	23,694	1,293	3,592	1,473	58	2,223	7,462	6,321	757	515
Asian/Pacific Islander	16,945	1,002	6,961	1,516	18	1,019	2,711	3,154	430	134
American Indian/Alaskan Native	2,294	296	425	235	8	260	570	439	43	18
Ship and boat building and repairing										
All employers	79,556	8,323	6,900	3,350	282	3,357	37,909	13,165	5,426	844
White	62,138	7,662	6,345	3,123	273	2,895	28,228	9,585	3,391	636
Minority	17,418	661	555	227	9	462	9,681	3,580	2,035	208
Black	11,412	425	371	109	3	324	6,543	2,005	1,471	161
Hispanic	4,198	164	75	61	5	85	2,100	1,201	473	34
Asian/Pacific Islander	1,528	48	96	50	1	45	884	326	70	8
American Indian/Alaskan Native	280	24	13	7	0	8	154	48	21	5

Source: U.S. Equal Employment Opportunity Commission. *Job Patterns for Minorities and Women in Private Industry, 1993.* Washington, DC: U.S. Government Printing Office, 1994, p. 24.

★ 764 ★

Industry Employment

Private Industry Employment: Transportation & Public Utilities

Number of persons employed in each occupation is shown, by race/ethnicity, in 1993. Data do not include Hawaii.

	Total employ-ment	Officials and managers	Profes-sionals	Techni-cians	Sales workers	Office & clerical workers	Craft workers	Opera-tives	Laborers	Service workers
All employers	3,501,987	461,370	356,493	178,271	176,257	704,444	609,308	590,848	258,933	166,063
White	2,731,421	399,508	309,931	143,884	131,969	507,749	511,162	438,601	163,191	120,426
Minority	770,566	61,862	46,562	29,387	44,288	196,695	98,146	152,247	95,742	45,637
Black	461,643	34,680	20,011	15,603	25,584	129,366	54,678	97,923	57,090	26,708
Hispanic	217,880	16,820	11,077	8,478	13,243	48,837	32,800	43,435	30,417	12,773
Asian/Pacific Islander	72,381	8,542	14,199	4,266	4,601	14,969	7,145	7,064	6,144	5,451
American Indian/Alaskan Native	18,662	1,820	1,275	1,040	860	3,523	3,523	3,825	2,091	705

Source: U.S. Equal Employment Opportunity Commission. *Job Patterns for Minorities and Women in Private Industry, 1993.* Washington, DC: U.S. Government Printing Office, 1994, p. 3.

★ 765 ★

Industry Employment

Private Industry Employment: Utilities

Number of persons employed in each occupation is shown, by race/ethnicity, in 1993. Data are shown for selected industry sectors and do not include Hawaii.

	Total employment	Officials and managers	Professionals	Technicians	Sales workers	Office & clerical workers	Craft workers	Operatives	Laborers	Service workers
Electric services										
All employers	344,011	52,206	67,180	30,270	1,915	58,873	91,697	29,658	7,915	4,297
White	295,120	48,467	59,843	26,505	1,586	45,653	80,522	23,524	6,057	2,963
Minority	48,891	3,739	7,337	3,765	329	13,220	11,175	6,134	1,858	1,334
Black	30,934	2,142	3,318	2,160	276	9,036	7,527	4,344	1,166	965
Hispanic	12,320	1,040	1,830	1,092	31	3,290	2,795	1,434	527	281
Asian/Pacific Islander	3,835	372	2,017	346	7	529	279	169	80	36
American Indian/Alaskan Native	1,802	185	172	167	15	365	574	187	85	52
Gas production and distribution										
All employers	110,263	17,259	16,372	7,995	2,443	25,598	25,416	11,241	2,437	1,502
White	86,289	15,465	13,827	6,532	2,211	17,499	19,852	8,077	1,722	1,104
Minority	23,974	1,794	2,545	1,463	232	8,099	5,564	3,164	715	398
Black	13,447	1,010	1,116	512	101	4,832	3,146	1,993	479	258
Hispanic	8,201	537	767	651	102	2,677	2,088	1,064	198	117
Asian/Pacific Islander	1,619	173	595	203	14	425	147	43	13	6
American Indian/Alaskan Native	707	74	67	97	15	165	183	64	25	17
Combination utility services										
All employers	183,491	26,394	32,867	16,955	591	35,465	51,421	13,818	4,307	1,673
White	150,355	23,931	28,330	14,341	524	25,779	43,305	9,884	3,070	1,191
Minority	33,136	2,463	4,537	2,614	67	9,686	8,116	3,934	1,237	482
Black	18,055	1,153	1,716	1,291	37	6,095	4,448	2,274	696	345
Hispanic	9,152	711	979	799	26	2,313	2,755	1,147	329	93
Asian/Pacific Islander	4,242	480	1,700	419	2	1,001	399	139	86	16
American Indian/Alaskan Native	1,687	119	142	105	2	277	514	374	126	28

Source: U.S. Equal Employment Opportunity Commission. *Job Patterns for Minorities and Women in Private Industry, 1993.* Washington, DC: U.S. Government Printing Office, 1994, pp. 27-28.

★ 766 ★

Industry Employment

Private Industry Employment: Wholesale Trade

Number of persons employed in each occupation is shown, by race/ethnicity, in 1993. Data do not include Hawaii.

	Total employment	Officials and managers	Professionals	Technicians	Sales workers	Office & clerical workers	Craft workers	Operatives	Laborers	Service workers
All employers	1,363,035	185,276	123,067	72,373	201,077	212,077	95,535	279,416	168,345	25,869
White	1,088,110	168,084	106,366	59,031	178,643	173,580	78,392	198,330	107,504	18,180
Minority	274,925	17,192	16,701	13,342	22,434	38,497	17,143	81,086	60,841	7,689
Black	138,675	6,882	5,687	5,486	11,227	20,027	7,790	46,902	30,131	4,543
Hispanic	94,319	5,033	3,498	3,980	7,768	12,353	7,362	26,591	25,252	2,482

[Continued]

★ 766 ★

Private Industry Employment: Wholesale Trade

[Continued]

	Total employ-ment	Officials and managers	Profes-sionals	Techni-cians	Sales workers	Office & clerical workers	Craft workers	Opera-tives	Laborers	Service workers
Asian/Pacific Islander	36,619	4,657	7,126	3,528	2,859	5,347	1,561	6,290	4,703	548
American Indian/Alaskan Native	5,312	620	390	348	580	770	430	1,303	755	116

Source: U.S. Equal Employment Opportunity Commission. *Job Patterns for Minorities and Women in Private Industry, 1993.* Washington, DC: U.S. Government Printing Office, 1994, p. 4.

★ 767 ★

Industry Employment

Private Industry Employment: Wholesale - Durable Goods

Number of persons employed in each occupation is shown, by race/ethnicity, in 1993. Data are shown for selected industry sectors and do not include Hawaii.

	Total employ-ment	Officials and managers	Profes-sionals	Techni-cians	Sales workers	Office & clerical workers	Craft workers	Opera-tives	Laborers	Service workers
Motor vehicles & automotive equipment										
All employers	115,578	15,209	11,658	3,031	7,748	17,017	9,293	33,586	15,235	2,801
White	93,663	13,884	9,919	2,714	7,187	13,985	8,040	25,507	10,672	1,755
Minority	21,915	1,325	1,739	317	561	3,032	1,253	8,079	4,563	1,046
Black	12,423	500	615	137	245	1,652	623	5,626	2,319	706
Hispanic	6,208	301	300	79	237	828	500	1,966	1,731	266
Asian/Pacific Islander	2,913	482	790	98	57	494	119	347	466	60
American Indian/Alaskan Native	371	42	34	3	22	58	11	140	47	14
Electrical goods										
All employers	105,431	18,667	18,158	8,046	9,208	18,827	5,987	19,693	5,775	1,070
White	80,441	16,162	15,159	6,187	8,331	14,302	4,828	11,527	3,267	678
Minority	24,990	2,505	2,999	1,859	877	4,525	1,159	8,166	2,508	392
Black	9,822	595	735	478	331	1,945	639	3,816	1,062	221
Hispanic	7,864	593	665	538	276	1,565	324	2,545	1,241	117
Asian/Pacific Islander	6,913	1,258	1,555	809	250	935	180	1,696	180	50
American Indian/Alaskan Native	391	59	44	34	20	80	16	109	25	4
Machinery, equipment, and vehicles										
All employers	218,563	30,913	34,004	27,310	24,194	36,687	25,125	26,501	11,500	2,329
White	180,175	27,992	29,285	22,116	21,707	29,683	21,306	18,881	7,699	1,506
Minority	38,388	2,921	4,719	5,194	2,487	7,004	3,819	7,620	3,801	823
Black	18,367	1,311	1,744	2,294	1,223	4,001	1,501	3,700	2,010	583
Hispanic	12,443	721	1,009	1,568	841	2,081	1,692	2,765	1,593	173
Asian/Pacific Islander	6,575	744	1,864	1,174	352	782	473	975	151	60
American Indian/Alaskan Native	1,003	145	102	158	71	140	153	180	47	7
Miscellaneous durable goods										
All employers	39,638	5,481	3,071	1,243	4,235	7,336	3,495	6,696	6,726	1,355
White	29,981	4,810	2,594	981	3,547	5,744	2,933	4,716	3,735	921
Minority	9,657	671	477	262	688	1,592	562	1,980	2,991	434
Black	4,625	203	140	113	383	733	241	1,206	1,478	128
Hispanic	3,038	148	100	82	185	528	225	528	1,049	193
Asian/Pacific Islander	1,843	300	233	63	106	308	81	216	437	99
American Indian/Alaskan Native	151	20	4	4	14	23	15	30	27	14

Source: U.S. Equal Employment Opportunity Commission. *Job Patterns for Minorities and Women in Private Industry, 1993.* Washington, DC: U.S. Government Printing Office, 1994, pp. 28-29.

★ 768 ★

Industry Employment

Private Industry Employment: Wholesale - Nondurable Goods

Number of persons employed in each occupation is shown, by race/ethnicity, in 1993. Data are shown for selected industry sectors and do not include Hawaii.

	Total employment	Officials and managers	Professionals	Technicians	Sales workers	Office & clerical workers	Craft workers	Operatives	Laborers	Service workers
Drugs, proprietaries, and sundries										
All employers	88,328	13,167	11,003	4,448	24,277	12,765	2,806	12,012	6,406	1,444
White	72,373	11,880	9,390	3,493	20,945	10,549	2,133	8,155	4,846	982
Minority	15,955	1,287	1,613	955	3,332	2,216	673	3,857	1,560	462
Black	8,111	564	479	390	1,996	1,298	240	2,036	885	223
Hispanic	4,816	403	235	219	858	614	352	1,458	488	189
Asian/Pacific Islander	2,744	287	883	336	359	268	76	322	164	49
American Indian/Alaskan Native	284	33	16	10	119	36	5	41	23	1
Groceries and related products										
All employers	293,475	35,124	8,890	4,750	49,772	33,473	13,850	79,497	61,473	6,646
White	233,684	32,192	8,013	4,072	44,539	28,507	10,957	59,052	41,490	4,862
Minority	59,791	2,932	877	678	5,233	4,966	2,893	20,445	19,983	1,784
Black	30,524	1,332	321	268	2,180	2,255	1,298	11,011	10,865	994
Hispanic	23,558	1,125	259	273	2,334	1,986	1,399	8,174	7,351	657
Asian/Pacific Islander	4,641	378	263	117	601	625	135	924	1,486	112
American Indian/Alaskan Native	1,068	97	34	20	118	100	61	336	281	21
Chemicals and allied products										
All employers	23,632	4,015	2,758	1,221	2,768	3,553	2,038	4,795	2,320	164
White	19,280	3,714	2,424	1,026	2,607	3,030	1,633	3,650	1,095	101
Minority	4,352	301	334	195	161	523	405	1,145	1,225	63
Black	2,471	144	111	77	76	305	252	786	683	37
Hispanic	1,331	77	67	83	48	153	131	281	470	21
Asian/Pacific Islander	468	68	147	32	27	51	17	54	67	5
American Indian/Alaskan Native	82	12	9	3	10	14	5	24	5	0

Source: U.S. Equal Employment Opportunity Commission. *Job Patterns for Minorities and Women in Private Industry, 1993.* Washington, DC: U.S. Government Printing Office, 1994, p. 30.

★ 769 ★

Industry Employment

Private Industry Employment: Women's Apparel Stores

Number of persons employed in each occupation is shown, by race/ethnicity, in 1993. Data do not include Hawaii.

	Total employment	Officials and managers	Professionals	Technicians	Sales workers	Office & clerical workers	Craft workers	Operatives	Laborers	Service workers
All employers	21,144	3,560	895	387	5,463	3,746	918	2,365	2,572	1,238
White	15,497	3,212	807	315	4,388	2,592	649	1,566	1,123	845
Minority	5,647	348	88	75	1,075	1,154	269	799	1,449	393
Black	3,034	156	44	38	704	591	75	654	596	176
Hispanic	1,858	120	18	17	238	427	132	105	637	164

[Continued]

★ 769 ★

Private Industry Employment: Women's Apparel Stores

[Continued]

	Total employ-ment	Officials and managers	Profes-sionals	Techni-cians	Sales workers	Office & clerical workers	Craft workers	Opera-tives	Laborers	Service workers
Asian/Pacific Islander	702	67	25	17	123	127	62	38	198	45
American Indian/Alaskan Native	53	5	1	0	10	9	0	2	18	8

Source: U.S. Equal Employment Opportunity Commission. *Job Patterns for Minorities and Women in Private Industry, 1993.* Washington, DC: U.S. Government Printing Office, 1994, p. 32.

Minority-Owned Firms

★ 770 ★

Minority Business Characteristics

Data are shown for 1987.

Industry division, legal form of organization, and minority	All firms		Firms with paid employees				Relative standard error of estimate (%) for column -			
	Firms (number) A	Sales and receipts ($1,000) B	Firms (number) C	Sales and receipts ($1,000) D	Employees (number) E	Annual payroll ($1,000) F	A	B	C	D
All industries	1,213,750	77,839,943	248,149	56,463,624	836,483	9,508,592	-	-	-	-
Subchapter S corporations	42,212	23,300,949	30,783	22,137,767	291,319	4,056,980	-	-	-	-
Minority men	25,528	15,658,873	18,740	14,905,851	188,706	2,692,533	-	-	-	-
Minority women	16,684	7,642,076	12,043	7,231,916	102,613	1,364,447	-	-	-	-
Hispanic	13,374	7,265,356	9,628	6,871,684	85,102	1,239,896	-	-	1	-
Black	12,565	7,741,387	8,669	7,389,781	102,504	1,498,206	-	-	-	-
American Indian and Alaska Native	360	138,126	242	128,463	2,088	27,654	3	1	3	1
Asian and Pacific Islander	16,475	8,402,698	12,656	7,977,348	105,402	1,347,721	-	-	-	-
Individual proprietorships	1,129,705	46,164,026	196,600	27,818,283	426,636	4,406,130	-	-	-	-
Minority men	773,846	38,282,773	157,353	23,971,930	353,914	3,756,446	-	-	-	-
Minority women	355,859	7,881,253	39,247	3,846,353	72,722	649,684	-	-	1	1
Hispanic	396,769	15,169,291	67,552	9,112,214	147,544	1,705,000	-	-	1	-
Black	400,339	10,056,751	57,398	5,210,241	91,671	986,628	-	-	-	-
American Indian and Alaska Native	20,454	674,173	3,247	396,429	5,864	71,237	1	1	3	2
Asian and Pacific Islander	320,161	20,570,018	69,663	13,276,736	185,065	1,677,348	-	-	1	-
Partnerships	41,833	8,374,968	20,766	6,507,574	118,528	1,045,482	-	-	-	-
Minority men	26,067	5,905,347	13,428	4,610,225	80,807	731,690	-	-	1	-
Minority women	15,766	2,469,621	7,338	1,897,319	37,721	313,792	-	-	1	1
Hispanic	12,230	2,296,953	5,728	1,745,534	32,200	298,446	1	-	1	-
Black	11,261	1,964,738	4,748	1,530,398	26,292	276,271	-	-	-	-

[Continued]

★ 770 ★

Minority Business Characteristics

[Continued]

Industry division, legal form of organization, and minority	All firms		Firms with paid employees				Relative standard error of estimate (%) for column -			
	Firms (number) A	Sales and receipts ($1,000) B	Firms (number) C	Sales and receipts ($1,000) D	Employees (number) E	Annual payroll ($1,000) F	A	B	C	D
American Indian and Alaska Native	566	98,980	250	77,897	1,004	10,380	2	2	3	2
Asian and Pacific Islander	18,695	4,151,610	10,399	3,247,254	60,878	476,848	-	-	1	-

Source: 1987 Economic Censuses, Survey of Minority-Owned Business Enterprises: Summary, U.S. Department of Commerce, Bureau of the Census, 1991, p. 80. *Notes:* Detail may not add to total because of rounding and because a firm may be included in more than one minority group. This table is based on the 1972 SIC system.

★ 771 ★

Minority-Owned Firms

Minority Business Distribution, by Industry

Data are shown for 1987.

Industry	Hispanic	Black	Asian and Pacific Islander	American Indian and Alaskan Native
Agricultural services, forestry, fishing, and mining	45.0	20.0	26.0	10.0
Construction	52.0	34.0	12.0	3.0
Manufacturing	37.0	27.0	34.0	3.0
Transportation and public utilities	35.0	48.0	16.0	1.0
Wholesale trade	38.0	21.0	40.0	1.0
Retail trade	31.0	29.0	39.0	1.0
Finance, insurance, and real estate	29.0	35.0	36.0	1.0
Services	33.0	37.0	29.0	1.0
Industries not classified	36.0	38.0	25.0	2.0

Source: "Minority-Owned Firms by Industry Division: 1987." *Minority-Owned Businesses*, p. 8. Primary source: 1987 Survey of Minority-Owned Businesses. *Minority-Owned Businesses*. Washington, D.C.: U.S. Government Printing Office, 1990. Percent distributions may not add to 100, since duplication of firms exists among minority groups.

★ 772 ★

Minority-Owned Firms

Minority Business Employment Size

Employment size and minority	Firms (number) A	Sales and receipts ($1,000) B	Employees (number) C	Annual payroll ($1,000) D	Relative standard error of estimate (%) for column A	B
All industries	1,213,750	77,839,943	836,483	9,508,592	-	-
With no paid employees	965,601	21,376,319	-	-	-	-
Minority men	635,920	16,358,957	-	-	-	-
Minority women	329,681	5,017,362	-	-	-	1
Hispanic	339,465	7,002,168	-	-	-	1
Black	353,350	5,632,	456	-	-	-
American Indian and Alaska Native	17,641	308,490	-	-	1	2
Asian and Pacific Islander	262,613	8,622,988	-	-	-	-
With paid employees	248,149	56,463,624	836,483	9,508,592	-	-
Minority men	189,521	43,488,036	623,427	7,180,669	-	-
Minority women	58,628	12,975,588	213,056	2,327,923	1	-
Hispanic	82,908	17,729,432	264,846	3,243,342	1	-
Black	70,815	14,130,420	220,467	2,761,105	-	-
American Indian and Alaska Native	3,739	602,789	8,956	109,271	3	1
Asian and Pacific Islander	92,718	24,501,338	351,345	3,501,917	-	-
No employees[1]	90,794	6,324,443	-	1,055,951	1	1
Minority men	71,210	5,275,213	-	893,258	1	1
Minority women	19,584	1,049,230	-	162,693	1	1
Hispanic	33,717	2,300,522	-	457,870	1	1
Black	31,414	1,495,861	-	295,167	-	-
American Indian and Alaska Native	1,894	103,948	-	19,252	5	4
Asian and Pacific Islander	24,372	2,461,292	-	290,507	1	1
1 to 4 employees	113,295	17,677,566	218,776	2,128,328	-	-
Minority men	85,291	13,901,557	165,046	1,648,380	-	-
Minority women	28,004	3,776,009	53,730	479,948	1	1
Hispanic	35,239	5,208,198	68,367	696,933	1	-
Black	29,238	3,565,200	54,936	541,404	-	-
American Indian and Alaska Native	1,365	190,813	2,646	25,810	3	2
Asian and Pacific Islander	48,466	8,867,263	94,757	883,105	-	-
5 to 9 employees	26,114	9,887,070	168,495	1,571,332	-	-
Minority men	19,626	7,652,265	126,728	1,192,794	-	-
Minority women	6,488	2,234,805	41,767	378,538	1	1
Hispanic	8,221	3,075,801	53,181	526,090	1	-
Black	6,060	1,984,302	38,851	385,923	-	-
American Indian and Alaska Native	286	112,284	1,870	20,160	3	1

[Continued]

★ 772 ★

Minority Business Employment Size

[Continued]

Employment size and minority	Firms (number) A	Sales and receipts ($1,000) B	Employees (number) C	Annual payroll ($1,000) D	Relative standard error of estimate (%) for column A	B
Asian and Pacific Islander	11,788	4,801,877	76,139	654,046	1	-
10 to 19 employees	11,566	7,430,113	151,985	1,407,438	-	-
Minority men	8,697	5,748,744	114,252	1,063,083	-	-
Minority women	2,869	1,681,369	37,733	344,355	1	-
Hispanic	3,671	2,433,738	48,330	491,931	1	-
Black	2,443	1,650,580	31,978	338,183	-	-
American Indian and Alaska Native	136	91,447	1,755	16,654	-	-
Asian and Pacific Islander	5,419	3,316,649	71,301	573,764	1	-
20 to 49 employees	4,914	6,671,271	142,516	1,442,486	-	-
Minority men	3,636	4,902,599	105,178	1,054,968	-	-
Minority women	1,278	1,768,672	37,338	387,518	-	-
Hispanic	1,582	2,126,435	46,142	477,564	1	-
Black	1,143	1,933,049	33,630	415,857	-	-
American Indian and Alaska Native	49	70,164	1,396	15,979	-	-
Asian and Pacific Islander	2,187	2,601,780	62,820	552,254	-	-
50 to 99 employees	1,033	4,103,812	69,809	824,387	-	-
Minority men	745	2,968,384	50,200	572,507	1	-
Minority women	288	1,135,428	19,609	251,880	-	-
Hispanic	349	1,370,194	23,335	269,919	-	-
Black	328	1,493,038	22,363	306,820	-	-
American Indian and Alaska Native	4	7,743	271	2,482	-	-
Asian and Pacific Islander	368	1,296,402	24,885	262,097	1	-
100 employees or more	433	4,369,349	84,902	1,078,670	-	-
Minority men	316	3,039,274	62,023	755,679	-	-
Minority women	117	1,330,075	22,879	322,991	-	-
Hispanic	129	1,214,544	25,491	323,035	-	-
Black	189	2,008,390	38,709	477,751	-	-
American Indian and Alaska Native	5	26,390	1,018	8,934	-	-
Asian and Pacific Islander	118	1,156,075	21,443	286,144	-	-

Source: 1987 Economic Censuses, Survey of Minority-Owned Business Enterprises: Summary, U.S. Department of Commerce, Bureau of the Census, 1991, pp. 82- 83. *Notes:* Detail may not add to total because of rounding and because a firm may be included in more than one minority group. 1. Firms reported annual payroll but did not report any employees on their payroll during specified period in 1987.

★ 773 ★

Minority-Owned Firms

Minority Business Ownership, 1987

Minority	Firms (number)			Sales and receipts ($1,000,000)		
	1982	1987	% change	1982	1987	% change
All minorities	741,640	1,213,750	63.7	34,454	77,454	125.9
Hispanic	233,975	422,373	80.5	11,759	24,732	110.3
Black	308,260	424,165	37.6	9,619	19,763	105.5
American Indian and Alaska Native	13,573	21,380	57.5	495	911	84.4
Asian and Pacific Islander	187,691	355,331	89.3	12,654	33,124	161.8

Source: "Comparison of Business Ownership by Minority Group: 1987 and 1982," *Minority-Owned Businesses*, p. 2. Primary source: 1987 Survey of Minority-Owned Businesses, *Minority-Owned Businesses*. Washington, D.C.: U.S. Government Printing Office, 1990. *Notes:* Detail in this table does not add to total because of duplication of some firms. Firms that were owned equally by 2 or more minorities are in the data for each minority group but counted only once at total levels. Figures for 1982 have been adjusted for comparability to 1987 data.

★ 774 ★

Minority-Owned Firms

Minority Business Ownership, 1982 and 1987

Ethnicity	1982	1987
Korean	6.8	10.2
Asian Indian	6.6	7.6
Japanese	5.9	6.6
Chinese	4.9	6.3
Cuban	4.1	6.3
Vietnamese	1.5	4.9
Filipino	2.6	3.3
Other Hispanic	1.4	2.3
Hawaiian	1.7	2.2
Mexican	1.4	1.9
Black	1.1	1.5
Puerto Rican	0.6	1.1

Source: Noah, Timothy. "Asian-Americans take lead in starting U.S. businesses." *Wall Street Journal* (2 August 1991), p. B2. Primary source: U.S. Census Bureau and William O'Hare of the University of Louisville.

★775★

Minority-Owned Firms

Minority Business Ownership and Receipts, 1982 and 1987

Percentages may not add to 100 since duplication of firms exists among minority groups.

Characteristic	Firms		Receipts	
	1982	1987	1982	1987
Hispanic	30.0	35.0	33.0	32.0
Black	40.0	35.0	27.0	25.0
Asian and Pacific Islander	29.0	29.0	38.0	43.0
American Indian and Alaska Native	2.0	2.0	1.0	1.0

Source: 1987 Economic Censuses, Survey of Minority-Owned Business Enterprises: Summary, U.S. Department of Commerce, Bureau of the Census, 1991, p. 6.

★776★

Minority-Owned Firms

Minority Business Ownership per 1,000 Population, 1982-87

The number of firms owned, per 1,000 population, is shown, by race/ethnicity.

Race/ethnicity	1982	1987	Percent change 1982-87
Hispanics	14.3	20.9	46.2
Mexican	13.7	18.8	37.2
Puerto Rican	6.3	10.9	73.0
Cuban	41.4	62.9	51.9
Other Hispanic	14.2	22.9	61.3
Blacks	11.3	14.6	29.2
Asian	43.2	57.0	31.9
Asian Indian	51.3	75.7	47.6
Chinese	49.1	63.4	29.1
Japanese	59.3	66.1	11.5
Korean	68.0	102.4	50.6
Vietnamese	14.6	49.6	239.7
Filipino	25.5	32.8	28.6
Hawaiian	16.6	21.5	29.5
American Indian	8.8	11.8	34.1
Aleut	58.5	54.0	7.7
Eskimo	36.8	44.4	20.7

[Continued]

★ 776 ★

Minority Business Ownership per 1,000 Population, 1982-87

[Continued]

Race/ethnicity	1982	1987	Percent change 1982-87
Native American	7.4	10.3	39.2
Nonminority	61.9	67.1	8.4

Source: American Demographics (January 1992), p. 34. Primary source: Bureau of the Census, 1982 and 1987 Economic Census and population estimates. *Note:* 1. Data include Pacific Islanders.

★ 777 ★

Minority-Owned Firms

Minority Business Ownership Trends, 1982-87

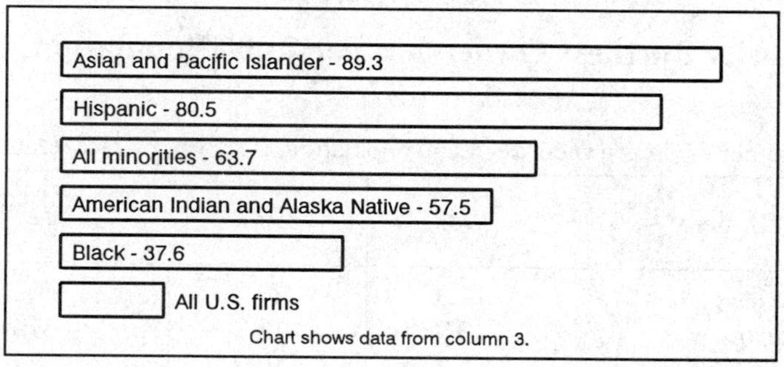

The number of firms owned and the percent change, from 1982 to 1987, is shown, by race/ethnicity.

Race/ethnicity	Number of firms		Percent change
	1982	1987	
Hispanic	233,975	422,373	80.5
Black	308,260	424,165	37.6
American Indian and Alaska Native	13,573	21,380	57.5
Asian and Pacific Islander	187,691	355,331	89.3
All minorities	741,640	1,213,750	63.7
All U.S. firms (incl. minorities)	12,000,000	13,700,000	14.2

Source: "Black entrepreneurship." *Wall Street Journal* (3 April 1992), p. R4. Primary source: Bureau of the Census.

★ 778 ★

Minority-Owned Firms

Minority Business Ownership, by Sex

Data are shown for 1987.

Minority	Firms (number)	Sales and receipts ($ mil)	% of all minority-owned firms by gender	
			Firms	Sales and receipts
All minority firms	1,213,750	77,840	100.0	100.0
Men	825,443	59,847	100.0	100.0
Hispanic	307,348	20,442	36.9	33.8
Black	265,889	13,377	32.0	22.1
American Indian and Alaska Native	15,072	711	1.8	1.2
Asian and Pacific Islander	243,442	25,988	29.3	42.9
Women	388,309	17,993	100.0	100.0
Hispanic	115,025	4,328	29.4	23.8
Black	158,278	6,531	40.4	35.9
American Indian and Alaskan Native	6,308	200	1.6	1.1
Asian and Pacific Islander	111,889	7,136	28.6	39.2

Source: "Minority-Owned Firms by Gender." *Minority-Owned Businesses,* p. 2. Primary source: 1987 Survey of Minority-Owned Businesses, *Minority-Owned Businesses,* Washington, D.C.: U.S. Government Printing Office, 1990. *Notes:* Detail in this table does not add to total because of duplication of some firms. Firms that were owned equally by two or more minorities are included in the data for each minority group but counted only once at total levels.

★ 779 ★

Minority-Owned Firms

Minority Business Receipts Per Firm, by Race/Ethnicity and Gender, 1987

Figures are shown in thousands of dollars.

Characteristic	Ave. receipts ($ thous.)	
	Men	Women
Hispanic	66	38
White	189	70
Black	50	41
Asian and Pacific Islander	107	64
American Indian and Alaska Native	47	32

Source: 1987 Economic Censuses, Survey of Minority-Owned Business Enterprises: Summary, U.S. Department of Commerce, Bureau of the Census, 1991, p. 6.

★ 780 ★

Minority-Owned Firms

Minority Business Sales and Receipts

Data are shown for 1987.

Receipts size and minority	All firms		Firms with paid employees				Relative standard error of estimate (%) for column			
	Firms (number) A	Sales and receipts ($1,000) B	Firms (number) C	Sales and receipts ($1,000) D	Employees (number) E	Annual payroll ($1,000) F	A	B	C	D
All industries	1,213,750	77,839,943	248,149	56,463,624	836,483	9,508,592	-	-	-	-
Less than $5,000	357,180	767,373	6,191	18,018	1,356	13,264	-	-	2	2
Minority men	212,340	459,143	4,010	11,738	875	8,714	-	-	3	3
Minority women	144,840	308,230	2,181	6,280	481	4,550	-	1	4	4
Hispanic	120,717	261,704	2,030	6,067	406	4,273	1	1	5	6
Black	149,446	316,631	2,812	8,051	501	5,674	-	-	-	-
American Indian and Alaska Native	7,621	16,163	94	287	14	150	2	3	24	29
Asian and Pacific Islander	81,973	178,337	1,286	3,701	446	3,212	1	1	6	6
$5,000 to $9,999	202,669	1,365,675	11,094	77,435	2,208	27,831	-	-	2	2
Minority men	126,505	856,227	7,588	52,934	1,431	18,970	1	1	2	2
Minority women	76,164	509,448	3,506	24,501	777	8,861	1	1	3	3
Hispanic	74,711	504,776	3,555	24,696	674	8,879	1	1	4	4
Black	77,874	524,276	4,860	33,893	830	12,377	-	-	-	-
American Indian and Alaska Native	3,971	26,520	318	2,178	28	757	3	4	13	13
Asian and Pacific Islander	47,618	320,333	2,446	17,283	702	6,092	1	1	4	4
$10,000 to $24,999	251,749	3,920,362	30,368	510,301	12,744	136,941	-	-	1	1
Minority men	172,921	2,719,467	21,981	371,110	8,370	99,747	-	-	1	1
Minority women	78,828	1,200,895	8,387	139,191	4,374	37,194	1	1	2	2
Hispanic	92,386	1,430,591	10,742	180,700	3,876	49,395	1	1	2	2
Black	91,566	1,416,051	12,445	206,391	4,901	56,803	-	-	-	-
American Indian and Alaska Native	4,153	63,104	651	10,834	173	2,754	3	3	8	8
Asian and Pacific Islander	65,521	1,039,524	6,771	116,147	3,884	176,848	1	1	2	2
$25,000 to $49,999	147,247	5,162,808	39,875	1,452,814	33,125	338,811	-	-	1	1
Minority men	111,523	9,918,201	29,829	1,089,678	22,616	255,013	1	1	1	1
Minority women	35,724	1,244,607	10,046	363,136	10,509	83,798	1	1	1	1
Hispanic	52,737	1,849,069	14,686	535,844	11,180	129,340	1	1	2	2
Black	46,583	1,616,585	13,807	496,718	11,582	121,062	-	-	-	-
American Indian and Alaska Native	2,085	72,868	635	22,976	507	5,307	4	4	7	7
Asian and Pacific Islander	47,112	1,667,594	11,031	407,377	10,197	85,360	1	1	2	2
$50,000 to $99,999	109,235	7,672,302	50,833	3,672,971	78,494	746,614	-	-	1	1
Minority men	85,576	6,014,686	38,962	2,818,375	55,505	569,968	1	1	1	1
Minority women	23,659	1,657,616	11,871	854,596	22,989	176,646	1	1	1	1
Hispanic	36,589	2,554,350	17,642	1,266,051	25,711	277,329	1	1	1	1
Black	29,482	2,044,481	14,353	1,019,898	23,194	231,730	-	-	-	-
American Indian and Alaska Native	1,848	127,880	791	54,899	1,060	13,011	5	5	5	5
Asian and Pacific Islander	42,235	3,011,371	18,446	1,360,951	29,192	230,816	1	1	1	1

[Continued]

★ 780 ★

Minority Business Sales and Receipts

[Continued]

Receipts size and minority	All firms: Firms (number) A	All firms: Sales and receipts ($1,000) B	Firms with paid employees: Firms (number) C	Firms with paid employees: Sales and receipts ($1,000) D	Firms with paid employees: Employees (number) E	Firms with paid employees: Annual payroll ($1,000) F	Relative standard error of estimate (%) for column A	B	C	D
$100,000 to $199,999	75,530	10,575,649	50,825	7,223,250	144,597	1,344,961	1	1	1	1
Minority men	60,282	8,437,235	40,166	5,708,013	107,865	1,050,795	1	1	1	1
Minority women	15,248	2,138,414	10,659	1,515,237	36,732	294,166	1	1	1	1
Hispanic	23,711	3,308,844	15,927	2,251,181	43,490	467,072	1	1	1	1
Black	15,942	2,201,517	11,086	1,552,069	33,591	330,816	-	-	-	-
American Indian and Alaska Native	957	132,186	628	87,231	1,575	17,173	5	5	5	5
Asian and Pacific Islander	35,671	5,039,149	23,670	3,401,617	67,305	543,159	1	1	1	1
$200,000 to $249,999	16,738	3,726,447	13,087	2,916,812	54,561	537,175	1	1	1	1
Minority men	13,576	3,023,041	10,507	2,342,444	41,677	424,906	1	1	1	1
Minority women	3,162	703,406	2,580	574,368	12,884	112,269	2	2	2	2
Hispanic	5,105	1,137,501	4,052	902,989	16,715	190,127	2	2	2	2
Black	3,116	693,241	2,491	554,446	10,752	115,103	-	-	-	-
American Indian and Alaska Native	154	34,425	124	27,711	455	5,623	6	6	7	7
Asian and Pacific Islander	8,484	1,888,270	6,511	1,452,094	26,986	229,835	2	2	2	2
$250,000 to $499,999	32,089	11,012,084	26,713	9,216,396	160,815	1,636,006	-	-	-	-
Minority men	25,873	8,870,936	21,398	7,375,467	122,942	1,280,040	-	-	-	-
Minority women	6,216	2,141,148	5,315	1,840,929	37,873	355,966	1	1	1	1
Hispanic	9,581	3,290,917	8,078	2,789,838	50,969	566,462	1	1	1	1
Black	5,843	2,009,503	4,994	1,727,663	30,931	342,475	-	-	-	-
American Indian and Alaska Native	355	124,565	277	97,409	1,604	17,723	1	1	2	2
Asian and Pacific Islander	16,584	5,683,919	13,595	4,683,806	78,949	725,621	-	-	-	-
$500,000 to $999,999	13,164	9,041,044	11,697	8,051,763	126,253	1,333,349	-	-	-	-
Minority men	10,570	7,257,529	9,358	6,442,079	98,296	1,038,699	-	-	-	-
Minority women	2,594	1,783,515	2,339	1,609,684	27,957	294,650	1	1	1	1
Hispanic	4,292	2,933,649	3,843	2,635,973	41,930	474,069	-	-	-	-
Black	2,366	1,636,463	2,134	1,474,381	25,295	290,403	-	-	-	-
American Indian and Alaska Native	154	105,787	143	98,922	1,317	16,037	1	1	1	1
Asian and Pacific Islander	6,476	4,448,267	5,687	3,916,417	58,886	565,818	-	-	-	1
$1,000,000 or more	8,149	24,596,199	7,466	23,323,864	222,330	3,393,640	-	-	-	-
Minority men	6,275	18,290,528	5,722	17,276,198	163,850	2,433,817	-	-	-	-
Minority women	1,874	6,305,671	1,744	6,047,666	58,480	959,823	-	-	-	-
Hispanic	2,544	7,460,199	2,353	7,136,093	69,895	1,076,396	-	-	-	-
Black	1,947	7,304,128	1,833	7,056,910	78,890	1,254,662	-	-	-	-
American Indian and Alaska Native	82	207,781	78	200,342	2,223	30,736	-	-	-	-
Asian and Pacific Islander	3,657	9,847,562	3,275	9,141,945	74,798	1,083,042	-	-	-	-

Source: 1987 Economic Censuses, Survey of Minority-Owned Business Enterprises: Summary, U.S. Department of Commerce, Bureau of the Census, 1991, p. 81. *Notes:* Detail may not add to total because of rounding and because a firm may be included in more than one minority group.

★ 781 ★

Minority-Owned Firms

Minority Business Sales Trends, 1982-87

Firm sales and the percent change, from 1982 to 1987, are shown, by race/ ethnicity.

Race/ethncity	Total sales (in millions of dollars)		Percent change
	1982	1987	
Hispanic	11,759	24,732	110.3
Black	9,619	19,763	105.5
American Indian and Alaska Native	495	911	84.0
Asian and Pacific Islander	12,654	33,124	161.8
All minorities	34,454	77,840	125.9
All U.S. firms (including minorities)	967,500	1,994,800	106.2

Source: "Black entrepreneurship." *Wall Street Journal* (3 April 1992), p. R4. Primary source: Bureau of the Census.

★ 782 ★

Minority-Owned Firms

Minority-Owned Firms, 1992

A minority business is a company that is at least 51 percent owned, managed and controlled by one or more minority persons. Figures are shown for 1992, by race/ethnicity.

Ethnic group	Percentage of firms
Black	56.0
Hispanic	23.0
Asian Indian	7.0
Asian Pacific	7.0
Native American	6.0
Other	1.0

Source: "'Do good' won't do it on the supply front." *Purchasing* (16 February 1995) p. 87. Primary source: National Minority Supplier Development Council.

★ 783 ★

Minority-Owned Firms

Minority-Owned Firms: Midwestern States

Data are shown for 1987.

Geographic area and minority	All firms		Firms with paid employees				Relative standard error of estimate % for column			
	Firms (number) A	Sales and receipts ($1,000) B	Firms (number) C	Sales and receipts ($1,000) D	Employees (number) E	Annual payroll ($1,000) F	A	B	C	D
Illinois	43,247	3,106,646	8,631	2,271,936	30,662	356,981	-	-	1	-
Minority men	28,696	2,204,476	6,417	1,585,935	21,731	242,495	1	1	1	-
Minority women	14,551	902,170	2,214	686,001	8,931	114,486	1	1	2	1
Hispanic	9,636	588,646	1,712	416,569	5,890	68,893	1	1	3	1
Men	6,778	422,253	1,338	288,645	4,463	47,511	2	1	3	1
Women	2,858	166,393	374	127,924	1,427	21,382	3	2	7	2
Black	19,011	1,100,204	3,014	816,022	10,655	138,699	-	-	-	-
Men	11,608	693,830	2,146	495,536	6,799	81,077	-	-	-	-
Women	7,403	406,374	868	320,486	3,856	57,622	-	-	-	-
American Indian and Alaska Native	193	7,213	48	(D)	(D)	(D)	14	10	26	(D)
Men	122	6,033	33	3,564	31	527	18	12	30	15
Women	71	1,180	15	(D)	(D)	(D)	24	17	53	(D)
Asian and Pacific Islander	14,679	1,437,700	3,904	(D)	(D)	(D)	1	1	2	(D)
Men	10,352	1,099,540	2,931	812,551	10,574	114,746	1	1	2	1
Women	4,327	338,160	973	(D)	(D)	(D)	3	2	4	(D)
Indiana	9,063	660,646	2,111	534,487	9,871	102,775	1	-	1	-
Minority men	5,744	493,768	1,526	402,946	6,991	74,615	1	-	1	-
Minority women	3,319	166,878	585	131,541	2,880	28,160	1	1	2	1
Hispanic	1,427	106,111	300	85,099	1,455	16,541	3	1	3	-
Men	1,016	93,216	250	77,746	1,310	15,111	3	1	4	-
Women	411	12,895	50	7,353	145	1,430	6	2	10	-
Black	5,867	349,643	1,110	281,611	4,715	53,703	-	-	-	-
Men	3,563	241,909	761	195,440	2,882	33,585	-	-	-	-
Women	2,304	107,734	349	86,171	1,833	20,118	-	-	-	-
American Indian and Alaska Native	90	3,221	15	2,361	33	331	12	5	16	-
Men	57	2,788	10	2,100	23	246	14	5	24	-
Women	33	433	5	261	10	85	21	10	-	-
Asian and Pacific Islander	1,718	205,485	699	168,918	3,744	33,100	2	1	2	1
Men	1,132	157,786	512	129,413	2,814	26,189	2	1	2	1
Women	586	47,699	187	39,505	930	6,911	4	3	5	2
Iowa	1,785	119,792	490	101,511	2,344	18,255	1	1	2	1
Minority men	1,129	84,799	345	72,466	1,448	11,874	2	1	3	1
Minority women	656	34,993	145	29,045	896	6,381	3	1	4	1
Hispanic	475	20,210	111	16,662	489	3,534	3	1	3	1
Men	308	12,403	77	9,715	328	2,216	3	1	4	1
Women	167	7,807	34	6,947	161	1,318	6	1	-	-
Black	703	44,795	142	38,013	722	7,158	-	-	-	-
Men	449	31,835	104	27,027	327	4,039	-	-	-	-
Women	254	12,960	38	10,986	395	3,119	-	-	-	-
American Indian and Alaska Native	43	1,302	8	764	11	110	17	19	18	18
Men	25	687	4	485	2	53	20	3	-	-
Women	18	615	4	279	9	57	30	40	37	50
Asian and Pacific Islander	574	53,931	232	46,453	1,136	7,544	4	2	4	2

[Continued]

★ 783 ★

Minority-Owned Firms: Midwestern States

[Continued]

Geographic area and minority	All firms		Firms with paid employees				Relative standard error of estimate % for column			
	Firms (number) A	Sales and receipts ($1,000) B	Firms (number) C	Sales and receipts ($1,000) D	Employees (number) E	Annual payroll ($1,000) F	A	B	C	D
Men	350	40,062	161	35,412	796	5,622	5	2	5	3
Women	224	13,869	71	11,041	338	1,922	7	3	7	2
Kansas	5,164	300,722	1,166	237,248	4,627	48,993	1	-	2	-
Minority men	3,351	232,133	889	186,913	3,471	38,034	2	1	3	-
Minority women	1,813	68,589	277	50,335	1,156	10,959	3	1	4	1
Hispanic	1,541	62,275	335	43,035	1,027	9,405	3	1	4	1
Men	1,088	44,752	265	29,071	575	5,457	4	2	6	1
Women	453	17,523	70	13,964	452	3,948	7	2	3	-
Black	2,323	154,448	403	127,424	2,132	28,094	-	-	-	-
Men	1,451	122,595	307	104,092	1,893	24,081	-	-	-	-
Women	872	31,853	96	23,332	239	4,013	-	-	-	-
American Indian and Alaska Native	231	(D)	33	5,426	79	631	14	(D)	23	2
Men	135	6,474	27	4,955	53	570	16	5	28	2
Women	96	(D)	6	471	26	61	21	(D)	-	-
Asian and Pacific Islander	1,135	(D)	406	62,750	1,437	11,146	4	(D)	5	1
Men	721	59,768	299	49,940	979	8,172	6	2	5	1
Women	414	(D)	107	12,810	458	2,974	8	(D)	11	3
Michigan	21,032	1,230,777	4,131	922,413	15,975	170,356	-	-	-	-
Minority men	12,992	904,046	2,982	691,324	11,120	125,797	1	1	1	1
Minority women	8,040	326,731	1,149	231,089	4,855	44,559	1	1	2	1
Hispanic	2,654	126,046	464	87,743	1,560	20,945	1	1	3	1
Men	1,788	104,064	354	75,333	1,260	18,420	2	1	3	1
Women	866	21,982	110	12,410	300	2,525	3	3	8	4
Black	13,708	701,335	2,241	524,583	8,485	91,991	-	-	-	-
Men	8,112	489,595	1,553	372,031	5,561	63,416	-	-	-	-
Women	5,596	211,740	688	152,552	2,924	28,575	-	-	-	-
American Indian and Alaska Native	305	(D)	42	(D)	(D)	(D)	10	(D)	13	(D)
Men	214	6,909	29	4,915	62	844	12	5	15	4
Women	91	(D)	13	(D)	(D)	(D)	21	(D)	27	(D)
Asian and Pacific Islander	4,424	(D)	1,402	(D)	(D)	(D)	2	(D)	3	(D)
Men	2,916	313,276	1,058	248,593	4,347	44,348	3	2	3	2
Women	1,508	(D)	344	(D)	(D)	(D)	5	(D)	6	(D)
Minnesota	4,188	324,316	906	260,880	5,098	53,716	1	-	1	-
Minority men	2,690	226,943	625	179,651	3,068	34,980	1	-	2	-
Minority women	1,498	97,373	281	81,229	2,030	18,736	2	1	4	1
Hispanic	751	29,061	122	20,341	299	3,598	3	1	5	-
Men	528	17,745	87	10,694	178	2,148	4	2	4	1
Women	223	11,316	35	9,647	121	1,450	7	1	12	1
Black	1,448	124,915	224	101,434	1,727	21,557	-	-	-	-
Men	926	77,179	163	61,213	859	10,576	-	-	-	-
Women	522	47,736	61	40,221	868	10,981	-	-	-	-
American Indian and Alaska Native	340	18,054	56	13,088	248	2,773	6	2	8	1
Men	227	14,003	39	9,981	186	2,295	7	2	9	1

[Continued]

★ 783 ★

Minority-Owned Firms: Midwestern States

[Continued]

Geographic area and minority	All firms: Firms (number) A	All firms: Sales and receipts ($1,000) B	Firms with paid employees: Firms (number) C	Firms with paid employees: Sales and receipts ($1,000) D	Firms with paid employees: Employees (number) E	Firms with paid employees: Annual payroll ($1,000) F	Relative standard error of estimate % for column A	B	C	D
Women	113	4,051	17	3,107	62	478	11	3	16	2
Asian and Pacific Islander	1,684	153,953	509	126,937	2,842	25,965	2	1	2	1
Men	1,026	118,957	338	96,232	1,852	20,059	3	1	3	1
Women	658	34,996	171	28,705	990	5,906	4	2	5	2
Missouri	11,215	549,921	2,388	400,435	8,348	79,486	-	-	1	-
Minority men	7,111	404,289	1,729	301,724	6,018	61,214	1	1	1	1
Minority women	4,104	145,632	659	98,711	2,330	18,272	1	1	2	1
Hispanic	1,247	49,677	258	32,830	765	8,022	3	2	5	2
Men	852	37,905	194	24,350	545	5,714	4	2	5	2
Women	395	11,772	64	8,480	220	2,308	7	2	9	1
Black	7,832	336,094	1,306	239,602	4,831	50,354	-	-	-	-
Men	4,848	240,162	929	179,274	3,430	39,526	-	-	-	-
Women	2,984	95,932	377	60,328	1,401	10,828	-	-	-	-
American Indian and Alaska Native	137	2,145	16	994	34	282	11	11	28	15
Men	94	1,485	11	563	18	179	13	14	39	23
Women	43	660	5	431	16	103	19	15	29	15
Asian and Pacific Islander	2,056	164,617	824	129,157	2,757	21,347	2	1	2	1
Men	1,354	125,975	605	98,370	2,037	15,884	2	2	3	2
Women	702	38,642	219	30,787	720	5,463	4	2	5	2
Nebraska	1,921	81,448	423	63,608	1,555	12,345	1	-	2	-
Minority men	1,204	60,507	307	47,160	1,094	9,246	2	1	2	1
Minority women	717	20,941	116	16,448	461	3,099	3	1	1	-
Hispanic	619	19,391	122	14,557	413	3,414	3	1	3	1
Men	421	16,759	104	12,907	343	3,054	3	1	4	1
Women	198	2,632	18	1,650	70	360	7	3	-	-
Black	863	30,826	160	24,289	612	4,832	-	-	-	-
Men	483	21,338	104	16,984	451	3,738	-	-	-	-
Women	380	9,488	56	7,305	161	1,094	-	-	-	-
American Indian and Alaska Native	66	1,611	18	947	18	204	11	9	21	16
Men	44	1,288	13	720	15	167	13	11	29	20
Women	22	323	5	227	3	37	20	3	-	-
Asian and Pacific Islander	385	29,776	125	23,893	513	3,905	5	1	3	-
Men	261	21,220	87	16,588	286	2,288	6	1	5	1
Women	124	8,556	38	7,305	227	1,617	11	1	4	1
North Dakota	472	31,545	123	26,048	395	3,752	2	-	2	-
Minority men	344	19,866	95	15,327	299	2,413	2	-	-	-
Minority women	128	11,679	28	10,721	96	1,339	4	-	9	-
Hispanic	88	2,167	14	1,279	35	315	2	-	-	-
Men	66	(D)	12	(D)	(D)	(D)	2	(D)	-	(D)
Women	22	(D)	2	(D)	(D)	(D)	-	(D)	-	(D)
Black	57	1,207	9	670	8	96	-	-	-	-
Men	37	(D)	7	(D)	(D)	(D)	-	(D)	-	(D)
Women	20	(D)	2	(D)	(D)	(D)	-	(D)	-	(D)

[Continued]

★ 783 ★

Minority-Owned Firms: Midwestern States

[Continued]

Geographic area and minority	All firms: Firms (number) A	All firms: Sales and receipts ($1,000) B	Firms with paid employees: Firms (number) C	Firms with paid employees: Sales and receipts ($1,000) D	Firms with paid employees: Employees (number) E	Firms with paid employees: Annual payroll ($1,000) F	Relative standard error of estimate % for column A	B	C	D
American Indian and Alaska Native	210	(D)	57	(D)	(D)	(D)	3	(D)	4	(D)
Men	151	8,686	40	(D)	(D)	(D)	3	1	-	(D)
Women	59	(D)	17	9,159	35	960	8	(D)	15	-
Asian and Pacific Islander	119	(D)	43	(D)	(D)	(D)	5	(D)	-	(D)
Men	91	8,250	36	6,670	181	1,265	5	-	-	-
Women	28	(D)	7	(D)	(D)	(D)	11	(D)	-	(D)
Ohio	21,902	1,207,885	4,360	907,907	16,847	180,419	1	1	1	1
Minority men	13,762	909,518	3,214	698,066	11,518	130,162	1	1	1	1
Minority women	8,140	298,367	1,146	209,841	5,329	50,257	1	1	2	1
Hispanic	1,989	191,797	420	164,503	2,263	31,382	4	1	6	1
Men	1,379	178,534	363	157,745	2,092	30,171	4	1	7	1
Women	592	13,263	57	6,758	171	1,211	8	7	17	8
Black	15,983	625,665	2,548	439,841	8,888	96,243	-	-	-	-
Men	9,715	430,099	1,842	300,745	5,142	58,637	-	-	-	-
Women	6,268	195,566	706	139,096	3,746	37,606	-	-	-	-
American Indian and Alaska Native	152	(D)	22	(D)	(D)	(D)	15	(D)	9	(D)
Men	87	4,370	11	3,341	35	360	18	4	-	-
Women	65	(D)	11	(D)	(D)	(D)	24	(D)	18	(D)
Asian and Pacific Islander	3,859	(D)	1,392	(D)	(D)	(D)	2	(D)	2	(D)
Men	2,618	299,921	1,017	238,830	4,297	41,463	3	2	3	2
Women	1,241	(D)	375	(D)	(D)	(D)	5	(D)	6	(D)
South Dakota	539	25,488	153	19,858	328	2,798	2	-	2	-
Minority men	380	18,356	108	13,593	254	2,141	2	-	2	-
Minority women	159	7,132	45	6,265	74	657	4	1	5	1
Hispanic	109	4,262	27	3,071	43	506	1	-	-	-
Men	86	(D)	19	(D)	(D)	(D)	2	(D)	-	(D)
Women	23	(D)	8	(D)	(D)	(D)	-	(D)	-	(D)
Black	63	4,832	14	4,391	35	418	-	-	-	-
Men	41	(D)	10	(D)	(D)	(D)	-	(D)	-	(D)
Women	22	(D)	4	(D)	(D)	(D)	-	(D)	-	(D)
American Indian and Alaska Native	267	11,166	75	8,240	153	1,366	3	1	3	-
Men	199	9,106	57	6,528	126	1,181	4	1	3	-
Women	68	2,060	18	1,712	27	185	8	2	8	1
Asian and Pacific Islander	108	5,714	39	4,607	110	707	6	1	5	1
Men	62	4,443	24	3,638	88	534	6	1	-	-
Women	46	1,271	15	969	22	173	10	3	13	3
Wisconsin	4,689	417,655	1,154	343,643	5,921	58,166	1	1	2	1
Minority men	3,043	313,228	833	255,633	3,825	36,610	2	1	2	1
Minority women	1,646	104,427	321	88,010	2,096	21,556	3	1	5	1
Hispanic	894	73,541	184	61,897	683	6,919	3	1	4	1
Men	612	61,712	136	52,099	548	5,624	3	1	5	1
Women	282	11,829	48	9,798	135	1,295	7	3	10	2
Black	2,381	190,696	477	159,597	2,552	28,726	-	-	-	-

[Continued]

★ 783 ★

Minority-Owned Firms: Midwestern States

[Continued]

Geographic area and minority	All firms: Firms (number) A	All firms: Sales and receipts ($1,000) B	Firms with paid employees: Firms (number) C	Firms with paid employees: Sales and receipts ($1,000) D	Firms with paid employees: Employees (number) E	Firms with paid employees: Annual payroll ($1,000) F	Relative standard error of estimate % for column A	B	C	D
Men	1,474	124,027	334	101,710	1,066	11,860	-	-	-	-
Women	907	66,669	143	57,887	1,486	16,866	-	-	-	-
American Indian and Alaska Native	307	(D)	89	18,280	520	3,808	10	(D)	14	5
Men	219	17,325	64	14,925	488	3,561	10	5	14	6
Women	88	(D)	25	3,355	32	247	24	(D)	37	2
Asian and Pacific Islander	1,144	(D)	417	105,222	2,198	18,928	4	(D)	5	2
Men	766	111,350	309	87,632	1,745	15,743	5	2	5	2
Women	378	(D)	108	17,590	453	3,185	10	(D)	13	5

Source: 1987 Economic Censuses, Survey of Minority-Owned Business Enterprises: Summary, U.S. Department of Commerce, Bureau of the Census, 1991, pp. 18- 28. Primary source: 1987 Survey of Minority-Owned Businesses, *Minority-Owned Businesses*, Washington, D.C., U.S. Government Printing Office, 1990. Arranged by the editors. *Notes:* A dash (-) represents zero. Details may not add to total because of rounding and because a firm may be included in more than one minority group. (D) stands for data withheld to avoid disclosure of competitive information.

★ 784 ★

Minority-Owned Firms

Minority-Owned Firms: Northeastern States

Data are shown for 1987.

Geographic area and industry division	All firms: Firms (number) A	All firms: Sales and receipts ($1,000) B	Firms with paid employees: Firms (number) C	Firms with paid employees: Sales and receipts ($1,000) D	Firms with paid employees: Employees (number) E	Firms with paid employees: Annual payroll ($1,000) F	Relative standard error of estimate % for column A	B	C	D
Connecticut	8,236	620,841	1,765	449,393	5,626	76,850	1	1	1	-
Minority men	5,421	465,269	1,307	333,261	4,131	54,660	1	1	2	-
Minority women	2,815	155,572	458	116,132	1,495	22,190	2	1	3	1
Hispanic	2,235	175,520	397	118,141	1,610	19,580	3	2	5	1
Men	1,603	148,314	319	100,913	1,307	14,379	3	2	5	1
Women	632	27,206	78	17,228	303	5,201	6	5	11	7
Black	4,061	225,718	724	162,610	1,936	28,798	-	-	-	-
Men	2,493	157,903	503	113,908	1,275	18,826	-	-	-	-
Women	1,568	67,815	221	48,702	661	9,972	-	-	-	-
American Indian and Alaska Native	88	(D)	9	785	13	155	14	(D)	23	19
Men	68	1,522	7	(D)	(D)	(D)	15	16	29	(D)
Women	20	(D)	2	(D)	(D)	(D)	30	(D)	-	(D)
Asian and Pacific Islander	1,963	(D)	650	171,402	2,123	29,085	2	(D)	3	1
Men	1,314	160,687	489	(D)	(D)	(D)	3	1	3	(D)
Women	649	(D)	161	(D)	(D)	(D)	5	(D)	6	(D)
Maine	496	43,772	143	33,339	811	7,736	2	-	1	-
Minority men	330	38,286	104	29,650	714	6,894	2	-	1	-
Minority women	168	5,486	39	3,689	97	842	3	1	-	-
Hispanic	139	12,061	42	9,504	173	1,768	2	-	3	-

[Continued]

★ 784 ★

Minority-Owned Firms: Northeastern States

[Continued]

Geographic area and industry division	All firms: Firms (number) A	All firms: Sales and receipts ($1,000) B	Firms with paid employees: Firms (number) C	Firms with paid employees: Sales and receipts ($1,000) D	Firms with paid employees: Employees (number) E	Firms with paid employees: Annual payroll ($1,000) F	Relative standard error of estimate % for column A	B	C	D
Men	98	11,409	31	9,145	165	1,631	3	-	5	-
Women	41	652	11	359	8	137	-	-	-	-
Black	131	5,151	31	3,706	80	675	-	-	-	-
Men	77	2,831	20	2,130	47	415	-	-	-	-
Women	54	2,320	11	1,576	33	260	-	-	-	-
American Indian and Alaska Native	68	3,956	16	3,012	46	541	7	1	-	-
Men	43	2,724	10	2,194	23	350	6	-	-	-
Women	25	1,232	6	818	23	191	15	4	-	-
Asian and Pacific Islander	165	22,786	56	17,260	514	4,772	3	-	-	-
Men	116	21,403	44	16,223	480	4,515	4	-	-	-
Women	49	1,383	12	1,037	34	257	7	2	-	-
Massachusetts	11,180	714,391	1,856	502,212	7,186	99,228	1	1	2	1
Minority men	7,041	505,79	1,359	346,994	4,662	69,567	1	1	2	1
Minority women	4,139	208,602	497	155,218	2,524	29,661	2	1	3	1
Hispanic	2,636	173,969	411	118,907	1,346	19,736	2	1	3	1
Men	1,756	154,291	329	109,913	1,201	18,425	2	1	4	1
Women	880	19,678	82	8,994	145	1,311	3	6	8	4
Black	4,761	251,946	628	182,043	2,683	41,186	-	-	-	-
Men	2,886	154,712	465	104,940	1,512	26,367	-	-	-	-
Women	1,875	97,234	163	77,103	1,171	14,819	-	-	-	-
American Indian and Alaska Native	132	4,557	24	(D)	(D)	(D)	13	7	23	(D)
Men	102	3,907	20	2,433	42	742	15	7	27	6
Women	30	650	4	(D)	(D)	(D)	27	21	34	(D)
Asian and Pacific Islander	3,784	292,291	803	(D)	(D)	(D)	2	1	3	(D)
Men	2,371	199,744	552	133,140	1,950	26,141	3	2	4	2
Women	1,413	92,547	251	(D)	(D)	(D)	4	2	6	(D)
New Hampshire	801	84,946	174	68,166	688	10,050	2	-	2	-
Minority men	523	51,037	126	38,082	431	5,862	3	1	3	-
Minority women	278	33,909	48	30,086	257	4,188	4	1	-	-
Hispanic	244	12,818	49	8,248	120	1,333	4	2	5	2
Men	167	9,001	41	5,199	80	1,100	5	2	6	3
Women	77	3,817	8	3,049	40	233	8	4	-	-
Black	229	31,198	49	27,295	246	4,179	-	-	-	-
Men	141	6,918	26	4,385	77	935	-	-	-	-
Women	88	24,280	23	22,910	169	3,244	-	-	-	-
American Indian and Alaska Native	29	(D)	3	625	2	54	11	(D)	-	-
Men	24	1,254	3	625	2	54	13	1	-	-
Women	5	(D)	-	-	-	-	-	(D)	-	-
Asian and Pacific Islander	304	(D)	74	32,034	320	4,485	5	(D)	4	-
Men	196	34,452	57	27,909	272	3,774	6	1	5	-
Women	108	(D)	17	4,125	48	711	10	(D)	-	-
New Jersey	38,914	3,075,652	7,181	2,119,310	22,765	326,973	-	-	1	-
Minority men	26,511	2,158,010	5,233	1,424,051	14,948	206,961	1	1	1	1
Minority women	12,403	917,642	1,948	695,259	7,817	120,012	1	1	2	1

[Continued]

★ 784 ★

Minority-Owned Firms: Northeastern States

[Continued]

Geographic area and industry division	All firms: Firms (number) A	All firms: Sales and receipts ($1,000) B	Firms with paid employees: Firms (number) C	Firms with paid employees: Sales and receipts ($1,000) D	Firms with paid employees: Employees (number) E	Firms with paid employees: Annual payroll ($1,000) F	Relative standard error of estimate % for column A	B	C	D
Hispanic	12,094	902,004	2,226	598,775	6,167	87,642	1	1	2	1
Men	8,991	733,236	1,714	481,002	4,618	67,051	1	1	2	1
Women	3,103	168,768	512	117,773	1,549	20,591	2	2	4	2
Black	14,556	995,614	2,169	731,490	8,969	138,762	-	-	-	-
Men	9,123	514,016	1,500	330,719	4,882	64,672	-	-	-	-
Women	5,433	481,598	669	400,771	4,087	74,090	-	-	-	-
American Indian and Alaska Native	135	(D)	17	5,467	42	328	15	(D)	19	8
Men	68	7,455	9	5,154	32	260	18	7	16	9
Women	67	(D)	8	313	10	68	23	(D)	35	24
Asian and Pacific Islander	12,530	(D)	2,846	804,173	7,828	103,840	1	(D)	2	1
Men	8,593	921,973	2,061	617,690	5,536	76,368	1	1	2	1
Women	3,937	(D)	785	186,483	2,292	27,472	3	(D)	4	2
New York	99,148	6,553,732	15,658	4,377,469	49,823	720,487	-	-	1	-
Minority men	64,353	4,721,673	11,233	3,105,769	34,884	503,172	1	1	1	1
Minority women	34,795	1,832,059	4,425	1,271,700	14,939	217,315	1	1	2	1
Hispanic	28,254	1,555,801	4,334	944,513	12,745	186,100	1	1	2	1
Men	20,222	1,245,276	3,279	755,775	9,507	145,512	1	1	3	1
Women	8,032	310,525	1,055	188,738	3,238	40,588	2	2	4	3
Black	36,289	1,886,038	4,438	1,315,458	16,799	258,234	-	-	-	-
Men	20,834	1,184,246	3,025	796,586	10,321	151,197	-	-	-	-
Women	15,455	701,792	1,413	518,872	6,478	107,037	-	-	-	-
American Indian and Alaska Native	445	25,008	95	15,048	251	3,663	11	10	20	11
Men	273	20,352	69	11,903	206	2,880	13	11	23	11
Women	172	4,656	26	3,145	45	783	20	23	39	31
Asian and Pacific Islander	35,812	3,192,830	7,061	2,167,260	21,367	287,376	1	1	2	1
Men	24,118	2,337,569	5,035	1,576,506	15,583	211,006	1	1	2	1
Women	11,694	855,261	2,026	590,754	5,784	76,370	2	2	4	2
Pennsylvania	21,464	1,920,686	4,711	1,461,277	17,475	210,076	1	-	1	-
Minority men	14,191	1,372,696	3,561	1,026,754	12,252	148,701	1	1	2	1
Minority women	7,273	547,990	1,150	434,523	5,223	61,375	1	1	3	-
Hispanic	2,650	247,081	531	182,890	1,880	27,091	2	1	3	1
Men	1,897	214,586	423	160,928	1,561	24,047	3	2	4	1
Women	753	32,495	108	21,962	319	3,044	4	3	6	2
Black	11,728	747,417	1,970	568,904	7,325	93,781	-	-	-	-
Men	7,352	493,809	1,399	364,807	4,782	58,317	-	-	-	-
Women	4,376	253,608	571	204,097	2,543	35,464	-	-	-	-
American Indian and Alaska Native	140	(D)	34	(D)	(D)	(D)	24	(D)	31	(D)
Men	70	3,089	25	992	31	176	25	39	41	19
Women	70	(D)	9	(D)	(D)	(D)	31	(D)	16	(D)
Asian and Pacific Islander	7,049	(D)	2,193	(D)	(D)	(D)	2	(D)	3	(D)
Men	4,932	665,353	1,728	502,726	5,934	66,701	2	1	3	1
Women	2,117	(D)	465	(D)	(D)	(D)	5	(D)	6	(D)
Rhode Island	1,353	98,188	292	69,396	1,350	11,434	2	-	1	-
Minority men	937	75,194	212	52,487	997	7,633	2	-	2	-

[Continued]

★ 784 ★

Minority-Owned Firms: Northeastern States

[Continued]

Geographic area and industry division	All firms: Firms (number) A	All firms: Sales and receipts ($1,000) B	Firms with paid employees: Firms (number) C	Firms with paid employees: Sales and receipts ($1,000) D	Firms with paid employees: Employees (number) E	Firms with paid employees: Annual payroll ($1,000) F	Relative standard error of estimate % for column A	B	C	D
Minority women	416	22,994	80	16,909	353	3,801	3	1	-	-
Hispanic	426	40,471	97	27,116	292	3,503	2	1	4	1
Men	322	32,427	78	21,218	182	1,786	3	1	5	1
Women	104	8,044	19	5,898	110	1,717	6	2	-	-
Black	489	18,209	70	11,988	356	2,957	-	-	-	-
Men	322	13,306	49	(D)	(D)	(D)	-	-	-	(D)
Women	167	4,903	21	(D)	(D)	(D)	-	-	-	(D)
American Indian and Alaska Native	36	(D)	3	278	4	40	15	(D)	-	-
Men	22	964	2	(D)	(D)	(D)	19	12	-	(D)
Women	14	(D)	1	(D)	(D)	(D)	24	(D)	-	(D)
Asian and Pacific Islander	436	(D)	129	30,581	706	5,032	4	(D)	-	-
Men	298	29,999	90	23,121	550	3,925	5	1	-	-
Women	138	(D)	39	7,460	156	1,107	9	(D)	-	-
Vermont	326	24,679	93	19,572	324	3,903	-	-	-	-
Minority men	209	18,806	65	14,655	227	3,026	-	-	-	-
Minority women	117	5,873	28	4,917	97	877	-	-	-	-
Hispanic	118	5,383	24	3,367	48	569	-	-	-	-
Men	83	4,917	21	(D)	(D)	(D)	-	-	-	(D)
Women	35	466	3	(D)	(D)	(D)	-	-	-	(D)
Black	98	6,682	27	5,626	84	1,076	-	-	-	-
Men	64	6,358	16	(D)	(D)	(D)	-	-	-	(D)
Women	34	3,324	11	(D)	(D)	(D)	-	-	-	(D)
American Indian and Alaska Native	9	(D)	-	-	-	-	-	(D)	-	-
Men	6	120	-	-	-	-	-	-	-	-
Women	3	(D)	-	-	-	-	-	(D)	-	-
Asian and Pacific Islander	102	(D)	42	10,579	192	2,258	-	(D)	-	-
Men	57	10,421	28	8,868	144	1,979	-	-	-	-
Women	45	(D)	14	1,711	48	279	-	(D)	-	-

Source: *1987 Economic Censuses, Survey of Minority-Owned Business Enterprises: Summary,* U.S. Department of Commerce, Bureau of the Census, 1991, pp. 18-28. *Notes:* Details may not add to total because of rounding and because a firm may be included in more than one minority group. (D) stands for data withheld to avoid disclosure of competitive information. A dash (-) represents zero.

★ 785 ★

Minority-Owned Firms

Minority-Owned Firms: Southern States

Data are shown for 1987.

Geographic area and minority	All firms: Firms (number) A	All firms: Sales and receipts ($1,000) B	Firms with paid employees: Firms (number) C	Firms with paid employees: Sales and receipts ($1,000) D	Firms with paid employees: Employees (number) E	Firms with paid employees: Annual payroll ($1,000) F	Relative standard error of estimate % for column A	B	C	D
Alabama	11,458	599,258	2,870	454,103	7,913	79,622	-	-	1	-
Minority men	7,654	454,182	2,187	351,113	5,677	56,020	-	-	-	-
Minority women	3,804	145,076	683	102,990	2,236	23,602	1	1	2	-
Hispanic	397	30,006	97	23,366	647	4,855	3	1	3	-
Men	259	24,650	81	21,079	586	4,454	3	1	3	-
Women	138	5,356	16	2,287	61	401	6	3	-	-
Black	10,085	439,966	2,337	320,594	5,562	59,450	-	-	-	-
Men	6,709	326,577	1,784	241,576	3,892	41,089	-	-	-	-
Women	3,376	113,389	553	79,018	1,670	18,361	-	-	-	-
American Indian and Alaska Native	90	5,053	26	3,830	36	882	15	11	18	3
Men	70	4,898	22	3,730	32	859	19	11	20	3
Women	20	155	4	100	4	23	15	8	35	10
Asian and Pacific Islander	917	125,771	417	107,553	1,691	14,642	5	1	4	1
Men	637	98,549	303	84,975	1,174	9,685	5	1	5	1
Women	280	27,222	114	22,578	517	4,957	10	3	9	2
Arkansas	5,371	284,537	1,181	215,133	3,648	36,982	-	-	1	-
Minority men	3,686	202,968	917	149,044	2,774	28,371	1	-	1	-
Minority women	1,685	81,569	264	66,089	874	8,611	1	-	2	-
Hispanic	324	13,808	73	10,271	289	2,961	3	1	4	1
Men	230	11,007	59	(D)	(D)	(D)	4	1	5	(D)
Women	94	2,801	14	(D)	(D)	(D)	7	2	10	(D)
Black	4,392	214,596	844	161,034	2,304	26,772	-	-	-	-
Men	2,953	146,669	658	105,938	1,685	19,912	-	-	-	-
Women	1,439	67,927	186	55,096	619	6,860	-	-	-	-
American Indian and Alaska Native	91	3,141	11	1,694	32	219	12	4	14	6
Men	75	2,085	9	(D)	(D)	(D)	18	2	-	(D)
Women	16	1,056	2	(D)	(D)	(D)	18	2	-	(D)
Asian and Pacific Islander	567	53,064	253	42,134	1,023	7,030	3	1	3	1
Men	430	43,256	191	34,145	862	5,818	4	1	4	1
Women	137	9,808	62	7,989	161	1,212	9	3	8	1
Delaware	2,039	127,249	478	93,477	1,950	19,585	1	-	-	-
Minority men	1,286	79,062	328	54,504	1,077	10,792	1	-	-	-
Minority women	753	48,187	150	38,973	873	8,793	1	-	1	-
Hispanic	184	6,230	30	3,135	67	740	2	1	-	-
Men	130	4,728	24	2,218	33	482	-	-	-	-
Women	54	1,502	6	917	34	258	5	2	-	-
Black	1,399	77,701	290	58,971	1,189	13,547	-	-	-	-
Men	869	43,060	198	29,012	559	6,598	-	-	-	-
Women	530	34,641	92	29,959	630	6,949	-	-	-	-
American Indian and Alaska Native	43	(D)	7	664	13	178	11	(D)	-	-
Men	29	770	6	(D)	(D)	(D)	10	2	-	(D)
Women	14	(D)	1	(D)	(D)	(D)	25	(D)	-	(D)
Asian and Pacific Islander	436	(D)	155	31,477	699	5,383	2	(D)	1	-

[Continued]

★ 785 ★

Minority-Owned Firms: Southern States

[Continued]

Geographic area and minority	All firms: Firms (number) A	All firms: Sales and receipts ($1,000) B	Firms with paid employees: Firms (number) C	Firms with paid employees: Sales and receipts ($1,000) D	Firms with paid employees: Employees (number) E	Firms with paid employees: Annual payroll ($1,000) F	Relative standard error of estimate % for column: A	B	C	D
Men	273	31,177	102	(D)	(D)	(D)	3	-	-	(D)
Women	163	(D)	53	(D)	(D)	(D)	5	(D)	3	(D)
District of Columbia	9,722	602,789	1,412	478,635	6,046	89,017	-	-	-	-
Minority men	5,922	410,338	983	330,141	4,375	65,216	-	-	-	-
Minority women	3,850	192,451	429	148,494	1,671	23,801	-	-	1	-
Hispanic	762	63,948	128	53,255	725	12,584	2	-	3	-
Men	446	50,703	91	43,328	611	10,857	3	-	3	-
Women	316	13,245	37	9,927	114	1,727	5	1	7	-
Black	8,275	411,941	956	309,028	4,085	61,239	-	-	-	-
Men	5,021	272,015	666	205,493	2,952	44,429	-	-	-	-
Women	3,254	139,926	290	103,535	1,133	16,810	-	-	-	-
American Indian and Alaska Native	28	865	2	(D)	(D)	(D)	21	5	-	(D)
Men	16	803	2	(D)	(D)	(D)	27	5	-	(D)
Women	12	62	-	-	-	-	35	34	-	-
Asian and Pacific Islander	779	132,546	337	(D)	(D)	(D)	2	-	1	(D)
Men	484	91,897	229	(D)	(D)	(D)	3	-	-	(D)
Women	295	40,649	108	36,138	447	5,472	4	-	2	-
Florida	97,961	7,085,085	17,335	5,306,895	66,757	826,522	-	-	1	-
Minority men	69,121	5,541,004	12,741	4,127,260	48,311	627,190	-	-	1	-
Minority women	28,840	1,544,081	4,594	1,179,635	18,446	199,332	1	1	1	1
Hispanic	64,413	4,949,151	9,924	3,743,959	42,375	563,088	-	-	1	-
Men	47,832	4,035,364	7,462	3,033,185	31,806	442,897	1	-	2	-
Women	16,581	913,787	2,462	710,774	10,569	120,191	2	1	2	1
Black	25,527	1,211,648	4,919	829,865	13,583	161,949	-	-	-	-
Men	15,976	766,466	3,502	502,475	8,538	106,221	-	-	-	-
Women	9,551	445,182	1,417	327,390	5,045	55,728	-	-	-	-
American Indian and Alaska Native	349	(D)	72	(D)	(D)	(D)	11	(D)	20	(D)
Men	184	11,893	38	9,857	103	1,148	15	6	28	6
Women	165	(D)	34	(D)	(D)	(D)	16	(D)	29	(D)
Asian and Pacific Islander	8,553	(D)	2,670	(D)	(D)	(D)	2	(D)	2	(D)
Men	5,722	771,264	1,909	612,066	8,593	86,309	2	1	3	1
Women	2,831	(D)	761	(D)	(D)	(D)	3	(D)	4	(D)
Georgia	27,350	1,789,953	6,103	1,396,438	19,888	235,494	-	-	1	-
Minority men	17,974	1,322,369	4,639	1,035,932	15,254	179,657	-	-	1	-
Minority women	9,376	467,584	1,464	360,506	4,634	55,837	1	-	1	-
Hispanic	1,931	145,252	480	115,841	2,375	27,796	3	1	5	1
Men	1,343	124,175	377	100,623	2,028	24,533	3	1	5	1
Women	588	21,077	103	15,218	347	3,263	6	3	12	3
Black	21,283	1,179,730	4,079	916,426	12,306	163,527	-	-	-	-
Men	13,682	828,199	3,062	642,456	9,162	119,503	-	-	-	-
Women	7,601	351,531	1,017	273,970	3,144	44,024	-	-	-	-
American Indian and Alaska Native	129	5,715	39	(D)	(D)	(D)	13	7	21	(D)
Men	97	4,229	30	2,126	42	638	16	10	26	14

[Continued]

★ 785 ★

Minority-Owned Firms: Southern States

[Continued]

Geographic area and minority	All firms: Firms (number) A	All firms: Sales and receipts ($1,000) B	Firms with paid employees: Firms (number) C	Firms with paid employees: Sales and receipts ($1,000) D	Firms with paid employees: Employees (number) E	Firms with paid employees: Annual payroll ($1,000) F	Relative standard error of estimate % for column A	B	C	D
Women	32	1,486	9	(D)	(D)	(D)	21	7	27	(D)
Asian and Pacific Islander	4,092	463,354	1,533	(D)	(D)	(D)	2	1	2	(D)
Men	2,916	368,263	1,190	292,615	4,063	35,346	2	1	2	1
Women	1,176	95,091	343	(D)	(D)	(D)	4	2	5	(D)
Kentucky	4,979	233,007	1,010	174,534	3,518	33,088	1	1	1	-
Minority men	3,145	166,903	712	123,435	2,485	24,286	1	1	1	-
Minority women	1,834	66,104	298	51,099	1,033	8,802	2	1	3	1
Hispanic	359	16,562	68	9,319	153	1,354	3	1	5	1
Men	249	12,326	54	(D)	(D)	(D)	4	1	6	(D)
Women	110	4,236	14	(D)	(D)	(D)	6	2	10	(D)
Black	3,738	120,201	617	85,628	1,706	17,882	-	-	-	-
Men	2,330	73,993	418	48,960	1,084	11,888	-	-	-	-
Women	1,408	46,208	199	36,668	622	5,994	-	-	-	-
American Indian and Alaska Native	24	1,705	7	1,575	17	203	10	1	-	-
Men	19	1,629	6	(D)	(D)	(D)	11	-	-	(D)
Women	5	76	1	(D)	(D)	(D)	28	17	-	(D)
Asian and Pacific Islander	875	95,656	324	78,987	1,660	13,882	4	1	3	1
Men	557	79,485	237	66,076	1,276	11,.297	5	2	2	1
Women	318	16,171	87	12,911	384	2,858	10	3	11	3
Louisiana	20,766	841,624	3,868	554,426	8,662	96,918	-	-	1	1
Minority men	14,672	598,995	2,983	376,639	6,008	65,637	-	1	1	1
Minority women	6,094	242,629	885	177,787	2,654	31,281	1	-	1	-
Hispanic	2,697	136,083	505	91,532	1,434	17,406	2	1	3	1
Men	1,983	108,285	414	71,688	1,004	12,519	2	1	3	1
Women	714	27,798	91	19,844	430	4,887	3	1	6	1
Black	15,331	531,548	2,611	346,946	5,259	62,283	-	-	-	-
Men	10,585	348,017	1,948	210,202	3,431	39,018	-	-	-	-
Women	4,766	183,531	663	136,744	1,828	23,265	-	-	-	-
American Indian and Alaska Native	225	(D)	50	(D)	(D)	(D)	12	(D)	25	(D)
Men	182	6,658	38	3,802	37	909	13	20	29	30
Women	43	(D)	12	(D)	(D)	(D)	24	(D)	47	(D)
Asian and Pacific Islander	2,583	(D)	717	(D)	(D)	(D)	3	(D)	5	(D)
Men	1,988	139,325	594	93,607	1,569	13,27	3	3	5	3
Women	595	(D)	123	(D)	(D)	(D)	7	(D)	9	(D)
Maryland	32,445	1,605,358	5,352	1,086,549	15,505	197,205	-	1	1	1
Minority men	19,751	1,122,431	3,894	758,975	10,876	133,767	1	1	1	1
Minority women	12,694	482,927	1,458	327,574	4,629	63,438	1	1	3	1
Hispanic	2,931	185,308	509	137,111	1,431	25,929	1	1	3	-
Men	1,882	117,413	389	84,162	991	15,451	2	1	3	1
Women	1,049	67,895	120	52,949	440	10,478	3	1	11	1
Black	21,678	719,715	2,689	451,643	7,248	92,740	-	-	-	-
Men	12,383	508,379	1,920	334,432	5,152	69,185	-	-	-	-
Women	9,295	211,336	769	117,211	2,096	23,555	-	-	-	-

[Continued]

★ 785 ★

Minority-Owned Firms: Southern States

[Continued]

Geographic area and minority	All firms: Firms (number) A	All firms: Sales and receipts ($1,000) B	Firms with paid employees: Firms (number) C	Firms with paid employees: Sales and receipts ($1,000) D	Firms with paid employees: Employees (number) E	Firms with paid employees: Annual payroll ($1,000) F	Relative standard error of estimate % for column A	B	C	D
American Indian and Alaska Native	123	9,411	25	8,035	96	1,451	18	5	11	4
Men	73	7,589	19	6,605	86	1,348	22	5	15	5
Women	50	1,822	6	1,430	10	103	32	11	-	-
Asian and Pacific Islander	7,831	701,690	2,172	498,724	6,817	78,945	2	1	3	1
Men	5,492	495,143	1,600	338,639	4,691	48,410	2	2	3	2
Women	2,339	206,547	572	160,085	2,126	30,535	4	3	7	2
Mississippi	11,122	683,679	2,871	528,060	8,291	76,249	-	-	1	1
Minority men	7,849	506,013	2,203	388,563	6,056	54,992	-	1	1	1
Minority women	3,273	177,666	668	139,497	2,235	21,257	1	1	2	1
Hispanic	308	12,490	70	6,509	147	1,073	3	2	5	3
Men	228	10,442	58	(D)	(D)	(D)	3	2	6	(D)
Women	80	2,048	12	(D)	(D)	(D)	7	3	12	(D)
Black	9,667	531,929	2,249	410,481	5,760	60,171	-	-	-	-
Men	6,743	385,089	1,712	295,171	4,080	42,141	-	-	-	-
Women	2,924	146,840	537	115,310	1,680	18,030	-	-	-	-
American Indian and Alaska Native	50	(D)	10	1,666	13	152	24	(D)	37	12
Men	42	1,207	7	(D)	(D)	(D)	28	13	50	(D)
Women	8	(D)	3	(D)	(D)	(D)	24	(D)	45	(D)
Asian and Pacific Islander	1,128	(D)	551	110,700	2,404	15,069	3	(D)	5	3
Men	858	110,221	431	87,470	1,873	11.945	4	3	6	3
Women	270	(D)	120	23,230	531	3,124	11	(D)	13	6
North Carolina	24,149	1,136,114	5,394	839,087	16,531	165,884	-	-	1	-
Minority men	16,399	815,151	4,146	600,512	12,011	120,145	-	1	1	1
Minority women	7,750	320,963	1,248	238,575	4,520	45,739	1	1	2	-
Hispanic	918	92,903	179	80,052	695	10,751	3	1	5	1
Men	614	65,503	128	56,796	466	8,574	4	1	6	1
Women	304	27,400	51	23,256	229	2,177	6	1	7	-
Black	19,487	746,112	3,843	529,118	10,930	114,331	-	-	-	-
Men	13,079	505,561	2,930	349,987	7,866	78,968	-	-	-	-
Women	6,408	240,551	913	179,131	3,064	35,363	-	-	-	-
American Indian and Alaska Native	1,758	(D)	547	63,434	1,151	14,140	4	(D)	6	3
Men	1,373	79,362	467	58,486	1,016	13,075	4	3	6	3
Women	385	(D)	80	4,948	135	1,065	10	(D)	17	10
Asian and Pacific Islander	2,069	(D)	855	168,937	3,807	27,024	3	(D)	3	2
Men	1,385	166,700	638	136,563	2,692	19,728	4	2	4	2
Women	684	(D)	217	32,374	1,115	7,296	7	(D)	7	3
Oklahoma	8,659	299,270	1,431	195,387	4,248	39,143	1	1	2	1
Minority men	5,804	227,772	1,072	147,600	3,052	27,873	1	1	2	1
Minority women	2,855	71,498	359	47,787	1,196	11,270	2	2	4	2
Hispanic	1,516	50,409	243	33,883	725	6,958	3	1	5	-
Men	1,087	40,004	190	27,186	493	5,002	3	1	5	1
Women	429	10,405	53	6,697	232	1,956	7	4	12	1
Black	3,461	93,903	489	58,677	1,423	14,730	-	-	-	-

[Continued]

★ 785 ★

Minority-Owned Firms: Southern States

[Continued]

Geographic area and minority	All firms		Firms with paid employees				Relative standard error of estimate % for column			
	Firms (number) A	Sales and receipts ($1,000) B	Firms (number) C	Sales and receipts ($1,000) D	Employees (number) E	Annual payroll ($1,000) F	A	B	C	D
Men	2,187	63,532	361	37,334	882	8,805	-	-	-	-
Women	1,274	30,371	128	21,343	541	5,925	-	-	-	-
American Indian and Alaska Native	2,051	57,294	268	33,812	456	5,489	3	2	6	3
Men	1,501	47,875	225	27,963	353	4,549	3	3	7	4
Women	550	9,419	43	5,849	103	940	7	4	11	2
Asian and Pacific Islander	1,700	98,174	440	69,191	1,645	12,007	3	2	4	2
Men	1,087	76,804	300	55,239	1,325	9,537	4	2	5	2
Women	613	21,370	140	13,952	320	2,470	6	6	9	7
South Carolina	14,155	546,465	3,039	372,719	8,765	78,842	-	-	-	-
Minority men	9,612	412,355	2,373	283,381	6,885	61,198	-	-	-	-
Minority women	4,543	134,110	666	89,338	1,880	17,644	1	1	2	1
Hispanic	393	15,997	79	9,294	216	1,932	4	2	6	1
Men	252	12,408	57	(D)	(D)	(D)	4	1	7	(D)
Women	141	3,589	22	(D)	(D)	(D)	9	6	9	(D)
Black	12,815	444,201	2,567	290,463	6,888	65,975	-	-	-	-
Men	8,720	335,572	2,025	221,207	5,478	51,753	-	-	-	-
Women	4,095	108,629	542	69,256	1,410	14,222	-	-	-	-
American Indian and Alaska Native	47	3,832	15	3,049	79	568	11	2	9	2
Men	41	3,108	11	(D)	(D)	(D)	13	2	12	(D)
Women	6	724	4	(D)	(D)	(D)	-	-	-	(D)
Asian and Pacific Islander	918	83,892	386	71,316	1,621	10,653	4	2	3	2
Men	607	62,411	285	53,976	1,227	7,665	5	1	3	1
Women	311	21,481	101	17,340	394	2,988	8	5	10	5
Tennessee	12,606	600,234	2,785	427,083	8,381	74,766	-	-	1	-
Minority men	8,322	442,295	2,099	313,495	6,451	56,827	-	1	1	1
Minority women	4,284	157,939	686	113,588	1,930	17,939	1	1	1	1
Hispanic	554	35,187	134	21,055	345	3,954	3	1	3	1
Men	415	30,985	110	18,866	304	3,528	3	1	3	1
Women	139	4,202	24	2,189	41	426	6	3	8	5
Black	10,423	386,078	1,929	260,582	4,902	50,139	-	-	-	-
Men	6,712	263,319	1,425	173,859	3,676	36,463	-	-	-	-
Women	3,711	122,759	504	86,723	1,226	13,676	-	-	-	-
American Indian and Alaska Native	90	(D)	18	2,314	30	240	12	(D)	21	9
Men	64	3,119	15	2,239	27	228	13	7	19	8
Women	26	(D)	3	75	3	12	24	(D)	81	81
Asian and Pacific Islander	1,574	(D)	713	144,233	3,125	20,648	2	(D)	2	1
Men	1,161	146,014	556	119,174	2,456	16,760	2	2	3	2
Women	413	(D)	157	25,059	669	3,888	5	(D)	6	3
Texas	152,409	6,961,063	32,113	4,835,241	77,983	851,079	-	-	1	-
Minority men	109,456	5,702,720	25,603	4,008,148	62,070	703,712	-	-	1	-
Minority women	42,953	1,258,343	6,510	827,093	15,913	147,367	1	1	2	1
Hispanic	94,754	4,108,076	20,845	2,886,579	49,942	555,868	-	1	1	1
Men	71,996	3,495,544	17,278	2,478,732	41,125	479,386	1	1	1	1

[Continued]

★ 785 ★

Minority-Owned Firms: Southern States

[Continued]

Geographic area and minority	All firms: Firms (number) A	All firms: Sales and receipts ($1,000) B	Firms with paid employees: Firms (number) C	Firms with paid employees: Sales and receipts ($1,000) D	Firms with paid employees: Employees (number) E	Firms with paid employees: Annual payroll ($1,000) F	Relative standard error of estimate % for column A	B	C	D
Women	22,758	612,532	3,567	407,847	8,817	76,482	1	2	3	2
Black	35,725	1,084,014	5,570	679,204	12,374	137,101	-	-	-	-
Men	22,946	798,775	4,099	504,496	9,059	103,415	-	-	-	-
Women	12,779	285,239	1,471	174,708	3,315	33,686	-	-	-	-
American Indian and Alaska Native	929	28,116	167	(D)	(D)	(D)	8	5	14	(D)
Men	618	21,619	130	14,679	337	3,199	9	6	16	6
Women	311	6,497	37	(D)	(D)	(D)	13	11	27	(D)
Asian and Pacific Islander	21,753	1,787,067	5,704	(D)	(D)	(D)	1	1	2	(D)
Men	14,408	1,420,025	4,234	1,038,064	12,591	126,550	1	1	2	1
Women	7,345	367,042	1,470	(D)	(D)	(D)	2	2	4	(D)
Virginia	29,555	1,549,881	6,237	1,161,164	19,866	251,178	-	1	1	1
Minority men	19,503	1,137,589	4,688	839,131	12,900	167,215	1	1	1	1
Minority women	10,052	412,292	1,549	322,033	6,966	83,963	1	1	3	1
Hispanic	2,716	140,917	483	103,186	1,605	28,485	2	1	3	1
Men	1,735	104,832	375	76,429	1,175	22,418	2	1	3	1
Women	981	36,085	108	26,757	430	6,067	3	1	10	1
Black	18,781	810,569	3,530	610,435	11,094	143,513	-	-	-	-
Men	12,188	587,934	2,725	439,327	7,178	92,927	-	-	-	-
Women	6,593	222,635	805	171,108	3,916	50,586	-	-	-	-
American Indian and Alaska Native	190	(D)	42	(D)	(D)	(D)	16	(D)	25	(D)
Men	68	4,886	22	3,885	44	1,154	15	16	19	20
Women	122	(D)	20	(D)	(D)	(D)	24	(D)	48	(D)
Asian and Pacific Islander	7,973	(D)	2,209	(D)	(D)	(D)	2	(D)	3	(D)
Men	5,580	451,185	1,584	330,230	4,604	53,310	2	2	3	2
Women	2,393	(D)	625	(D)	(D)	(D)	4	(D)	6	(D)
West Virginia	1,446	127,700	428	109,604	1,391	14,994	1	1	1	1
Minority men	941	108,673	331	95,580	1,100	12,686	1	1	2	1
Minority women	505	19,027	97	14,024	291	2,308	2	2	3	2
Hispanic	177	13,847	46	10,323	126	1,417	1	-	-	-
Men	130	12,960	40	(D)	(D)	(D)	1	-	-	(D)
Women	47	887	6	(D)	(D)	(D)	-	-	-	(D)
Black	727	38,930	107	32,959	264	4,130	-	-	-	-
Men	430	33,090	82	29,124	196	3,521	-	-	-	-
Women	297	5,840	25	3,835	68	609	-	-	-	-
American Indian and Alaska Native	28	1,438	8	1,015	15	144	15	1	-	-
Men	16	1,139	5	(D)	(D)	(D)	-	-	-	(D)
Women	12	299	3	(D)	(D)	(D)	36	3	-	(D)
Asian and Pacific Islander	523	74,821	271	66,568	995	9,470	3	2	2	2
Men	369	62,653	207	56,939	783	7,850	4	2	3	2
Women	154	12,168	64	9,629	212	1,620	7	3	5	3

Source: *1987 Economic Censuses, Survey of Minority-Owned Business Enterprises: Summary*, U.S. Department of Commerce, Bureau of the Census, 1991, pp. 16-17. Primary source: 1987 Survey of Minority-Owned Businesses, *Minority-Owned Businesses*, Washington, D.C., U.S. Government Printing Office, 1990. Arranged by the editors. *Notes:* A dash (-) represents zero. Details may not add to total because of rounding and because a firm may be included in more than one minority group. (D) stands for data withheld to avoid disclosure of competitive information.

★ 786 ★

Minority-Owned Firms

Minority-Owned Firms: Western States

Data are shown for 1987.

Geographic area and minority	All firms: Firms (number) A	All firms: Sales and receipts ($1,000) B	Firms with paid employees: Firms (number) C	Firms with paid employees: Sales and receipts ($1,000) D	Firms with paid employees: Employees (number) E	Firms with paid employees: Annual payroll ($1,000) F	Relative standard error of estimate % for column A	B	C	D
Alaska	6,011	236,742	818	118,135	1,756	23,894	2	2	6	2
Minority men	4,553	193,273	636	99,240	1,451	20,670	2	2	8	2
Minority women	1,458	43,469	182	18,895	305	3,224	5	7	12	3
Hispanic	502	27,412	86	18,099	282	3,926	5	3	11	2
Men	316	19,498	48	13,976	216	3,176	6	1	3	-
Women	186	7,914	38	4,123	66	750	9	9	25	8
Black	507	14,444	81	9,050	200	2,181	-	-	-	-
Men	285	10,461	57	6,925	158	1,747	-	-	-	-
Women	222	3,983	24	2,125	42	434	-	-	-	-
American Indian and Alaska Native	4,006	117,726	405	37,182	320	6,229	3	4	11	5
Men	3,256	98,566	325	30,933	257	5,465	3	4	13	6
Women	750	19,160	80	6,249	63	764	9	13	23	5
Asian and Pacific Islander	1,028	78,378	250	54,286	957	11,591	7	3	10	1
Men	711	65,501	208	47,747	822	10,298	8	3	12	2
Women	317	12,877	42	6,539	135	1,293	14	12	-	-
Arizona	14,960	904,314	3,384	679,621	15,025	126,476	1	1	2	1
Minority men	10,191	714,866	2,721	535,350	12,055	101,134	1	1	3	1
Minority women	4,769	189,448	663	144,271	2,970	25,342	3	2	5	1
Hispanic	9,845	513,125	2,206	384,281	8,969	78,329	1	1	3	1
Men	6,802	423,294	1,834	320,696	7,304	63,870	2	1	4	1
Women	3,043	89,831	372	63,585	1,665	14,459	4	3	7	2
Black	1,811	91,439	319	68,032	1,601	14,161	-	-	-	-
Men	1,154	56,333	241	38,594	1,196	9,901	-	-	-	-
Women	657	35,106	78	29,438	405	4,260	-	-	-	-
American Indian and Alaska Native	872	50,276	165	41,613	491	4,364	5	3	11	3
Men	648	38,471	132	31,381	417	3,521	6	3	13	2
Women	224	11,805	33	10,232	74	843	11	8	19	8
Asian and Pacific Islander	2,526	253,109	736	187,903	3,988	867	2	1	2	1
Men	1,658	200,048	554	146,733	3,161	24,081	3	1	3	1
Women	868	53,061	182	41,170	827	5,786	5	3	5	2
California	324,584	25,022,349	72,765	18,244,209	264,410	2,953,274	-	-	1	-
Minority men	226,601	20,201,916	57,261	14,890,888	207,144	2,355,317	-	-	1	-
Minority women	97,983	4,820,433	15,504	3,353,321	57,266	597,957	1	1	1	1
Hispanic	132,212	8,119,853	26,886	5,786,143	89,722	1,136,230	-	-	1	-
Men	95,254	6,772,518	22,127	4,886,061	72,588	939,893	1	-	1	1
Women	36,958	1,347,335	4,759	900,082	17,134	196,337	1	1	3	1
Black	47,728	2,364,024	7,614	1,618,988	22,631	340,281	-	-	-	-
Men	29,627	1,621,645	5,466	1,103,238	16,174	238,186	-	-	-	-
Women	18,101	742,379	2,148	515,750	6,457	102,095	-	-	-	-
American Indian and Alaska Native	3,280	162,179	631	109,621	1,572	21,332	5	4	8	4
Men	2,173	126,118	501	87,086	1,213	17,417	5	5	10	5
Women	1,107	36,061	130	22,535	359	3,915	8	6	16	6
Asian and Pacific Islander	144,353	14,620,377	38,273	10,907,652	153,519	1,490,434	-	-	1	-

[Continued]

★ 786 ★

Minority-Owned Firms: Western States

[Continued]

Geographic area and minority	All firms: Firms (number) A	All firms: Sales and receipts ($1,000) B	Firms with paid employees: Firms (number) C	Firms with paid employees: Sales and receipts ($1,000) D	Firms with paid employees: Employees (number) E	Firms with paid employees: Annual payroll ($1,000) F	Relative standard error of estimate % for column A	B	C	D
Men	101,562	11,871,690	29,653	8,957,609	119,360	1,187,089	1	-	1	-
Women	42,791	2,748,687	8,620	1,950,043	34,159	303,345	1	1	2	1
Colorado	15,762	725,030	3,196	530,568	9,704	103,027	1	1	2	1
Minority men	10,314	546,308	2,372	397,272	7,080	77,051	1	1	3	1
Minority women	5,448	178,722	824	133,296	2,624	25,976	2	2	4	2
Hispanic	9,516	394,410	1,813	290,756	4,601	56,903	2	2	4	2
Men	6,381	305,643	1,402	226,079	3,480	42,751	2	2	4	2
Women	3,135	88,767	411	64,677	1,121	14,152	4	4	8	4
Black	2,871	105,849	414	69,259	1,051	15,794	-	-	-	-
Men	1,751	70,180	291	44,068	715	11,906	-	-	-	-
Women	1,120	35,669	123	25,191	336	3,888	-	-	-	-
American Indian and Alaska Native	351	14,084	38	(D)	(D)	(D)	12	4	17	(D)
Men	226	12,332	31	9,770	104	1,087	14	5	21	1
Women	125	1,752	7	(D)	(D)	(D)	19	17	-	(D)
Asian and Pacific Islander	3,192	215,875	952	(D)	(D)	(D)	2	2	3	(D)
Men	2,066	162,137	665	119,259	2,859	21,769	3	2	4	2
Women	1,126	53,738	287	(D)	(D)	(D)	4	3	6	(D)
Hawaii	32,705	1,721,407	4,618	1,157,349	15,671	184,967	-	1	2	1
Minority men	21,137	1,284,297	3,309	876,968	10,875	139,234	1	1	2	1
Minority women	11,568	437,110	1,309	280,381	4,796	45,753	2	2	3	2
Hispanic	1,226	58,098	177	41,838	542	5,923	4	2	6	2
Men	822	50,190	135	37,597	459	5,200	5	2	8	2
Women	404	7,908	42	4,241	83	723	8	6	9	7
Black	399	12,310	52	7,429	147	1,286	-	-	-	-
Men	254	8,125	41	(D)	(D)	(D)	-	-	-	(D)
Women	145	4,185	11	(D)	(D)	(D)	-	-	-	(D)
American Indian and Alaska Native	106	6,239	16	5,512	48	675	21	3	15	2
Men	81	5,897	15	(D)	(D)	(D)	23	3	16	(D)
Women	25	342	1	(D)	(D)	(D)	54	10	-	(D)
Asian and Pacific Islander	31,300	1,656,030	4,427	1,109,366	15,046	178,004	-	1	2	1
Men	20,186	1,228,047	3,158	833,809	10,367	133,163	1	1	2	1
Women	11,114	427,983	1,269	275,557	4,479	44,841	2	2	4	2
Idaho	1,541	70,760	362	53,922	1,173	10,286	2	1	4	1
Minority men	1,121	60,989	297	47,283	1,032	9,114	3	1	4	1
Minority women	420	9,771	65	6,639	141	1,172	5	3	8	3
Hispanic	974	30,594	187	20,880	270	4,008	3	1	7	1
Men	731	26,000	153	17,965	220	3,564	3	1	8	1
Women	243	4,594	34	2,915	50	444	7	4	11	2
Black	94	4,776	26	3,583	98	630	-	-	-	-
Men	67	3,026	16	1,981	69	352	-	-	-	-
Women	27	1,750	10	1,602	29	278	-	-	-	-
American Indian and Alaska Native	80	6,965	17	(D)	(D)	(D)	11	-	-	(D)
Men	61	5,801	13	5,011	42	843	12	-	-	-

[Continued]

★ 786 ★

Minority-Owned Firms: Western States

[Continued]

Geographic area and minority	All firms: Firms (number) A	All firms: Sales and receipts ($1,000) B	Firms with paid employees: Firms (number) C	Firms with paid employees: Sales and receipts ($1,000) D	Firms with paid employees: Employees (number) E	Firms with paid employees: Annual payroll ($1,000) F	Relative standard error of estimate % for column A	B	C	D
Women	19	1,164	4	(D)	(D)	(D)	25	2	-	(D)
Asian and Pacific Islander	433	30,671	143	(D)	(D)	(D)	5	1	4	(D)
Men	286	27,365	118	23,096	714	4,503	5	1	3	1
Women	147	3,306	25	(D)	(D)	(D)	10	6	20	(D)
Montana	989	46,819	236	36,276	763	6,238	2	1	2	-
Minority men	674	37,159	183	28,988	569	4,746	3	1	2	-
Minority women	315	9,660	53	7,288	194	1,492	5	1	7	-
Hispanic	304	10,107	61	6,416	114	995	2	1	-	-
Men	215	9,026	53	5,951	95	890	2	1	-	-
Women	89	1,081	8	465	19	105	4	2	-	-
Black	77	6,944	21	6,255	123	1,027	-	-	-	-
Men	45	4,054	15	3,798	61	403	-	-	-	-
Women	32	2,890	6	2,457	62	624	-	-	-	-
American Indian and Alaska Native	405	16,510	83	12,619	157	1,609	5	2	7	-
Men	281	13,163	62	10,147	119	1,220	5	2	7	1
Women	124	3,347	21	2,472	38	389	10	4	18	1
Asian and Pacific Islander	207	13,317	72	11,020	371	2,613	6	1	-	-
Men	135	10,953	54	9,126	296	2,239	6	1	-	-
Women	72	2,364	18	1,894	75	374	14	1	-	-
Nevada	4,116	271,038	915	201,131	4,072	42,892	1	-	2	-
Minority men	2,741	216,537	686	162,556	6,300	35,970	2	1	3	-
Minority women	1,375	54,501	229	38,575	772	6,922	3	1	4	1
Hispanic	1,767	141,608	385	109,257	2,250	26,056	3	1	5	-
Men	1,274	124,395	322	97,961	2,017	23,858	3	1	6	-
Women	493	17,213	63	11,296	233	2,198	7	3	5	1
Black	1,002	38,608	182	27,916	592	4,925	-	-	-	-
Men	591	24,798	120	18,124	427	3,274	-	-	-	-
Women	411	13,810	62	9,792	165	1,651	-	-	-	-
American Indian and Alaska Native	150	8,712	33	6,967	75	897	11	2	11	2
Men	101	6,289	20	4,952	31	492	14	3	18	2
Women	49	2,423	13	2,015	44	405	19	3	-	-
Asian and Pacific Islander	1,245	83,915	320	58,251	1,197	11,264	3	1	4	1
Men	818	62,405	228	42,418	855	8,536	4	1	4	1
Women	427	21,510	92	15,833	342	2,728	7	2	10	1
New Mexico	16,963	828,247	4,279	625,462	12,868	114,331	1	1	2	1
Minority men	12,174	688,118	3,523	529,463	10,273	94,535	1	1	2	1
Minority women	4,789	140,129	756	95,999	2,595	19,796	2	2	5	2
Hispanic	14,299	702,098	3,716	529,176	10,680	97,036	1	1	2	1
Men	10,450	600,900	3,126	463,471	8,776	82,502	1	1	2	1
Women	3,849	101,198	590	65,705	1,904	14,534	3	3	6	2
Black	587	27,133	110	20,762	481	4,284	-	-	-	-
Men	374	14,437	76	10,733	246	2,161	-	-	-	-
Women	213	12,696	34	10,029	235	2,123	-	-	-	-

[Continued]

★ 786 ★

Minority-Owned Firms: Western States

[Continued]

Geographic area and minority	All firms: Firms (number) A	All firms: Sales and receipts ($1,000) B	Firms with paid employees: Firms (number) C	Firms with paid employees: Sales and receipts ($1,000) D	Firms with paid employees: Employees (number) E	Firms with paid employees: Annual payroll ($1,000) F	Relative standard error of estimate % for column A	B	C	D
American Indian and Alaska Native	1,258	37,474	151	(D)	(D)	(D)	5	3	11	(D)
Men	782	25,051	98	17,916	276	3,378	7	3	9	3
Women	476	12,423	53	(D)	(D)	(D)	9	5	26	(D)
Asian and Pacific Islander	897	66,611	330	(D)	(D)	(D)	5	2	4	(D)
Men	619	50,911	242	40,108	1,025	6,898	6	3	5	4
Women	278	15,700	88	(D)	(D)	(D)	11	3	8	(D)
Oregon	5,725	476,830	1,575	379,657	6,651	57,417	1	1	2	1
Minority men	3,735	372,305	1,178	299,810	4,897	43,763	2	1	2	1
Minority women	1,990	104,525	397	79,847	1,754	13,654	3	2	3	1
Hispanic	1,598	109,642	403	89,053	1,445	15,363	3	1	5	1
Men	1,118	84,628	325	68,964	1,194	12,859	4	1	5	1
Women	480	25,014	78	20,089	251	2,504	7	2	9	-
Black	848	34,136	134	24,189	448	4,456	-	-	-	-
Men	510	20,417	85	13,982	279	2,805	-	-	-	-
Women	338	13,719	49	10,207	169	1,651	-	-	-	-
American Indian and Alaska Native	333	19,200	47	14,242	217	2,790	8	4	13	1
Men	187	15,781	32	12,751	189	2,608	10	2	16	1
Women	146	3,419	15	1,491	28	182	13	19	25	7
Asian and Pacific Islander	3,007	331,950	1,002	269,264	4,644	37,664	2	1	2	1
Men	1,962	269,254	744	221,050	3,328	28,302	2	1	3	1
Women	1,045	62,696	258	48,214	1,316	9,362	4	2	4	2
Utah	2,722	125,866	543	89,343	1,987	16,101	2	1	4	1
Minority men	1,718	104,670	448	77,636	1,578	13,930	3	1	4	1
Minority women	1,004	21,196	95	11,707	409	2,171	6	3	9	2
Hispanic	1,300	47,255	228	31,506	657	6,056	3	2	7	1
Men	842	40,578	204	28,612	497	5,471	4	1	8	1
Women	458	6,677	24	2,894	160	585	8	7	-	-
Black	202	8,615	35	5,619	110	1,212	-	-	-	-
Men	125	5,109	23	3,829	79	987	-	-	-	-
Women	77	3,506	12	1,790	31	225	-	-	-	-
American Indian and Alaska Native	110	(D)	16	2,648	40	615	15	(D)	25	2
Men	66	3,066	12	2,544	40	596	17	2	31	2
Women	44	(D)	4	104	-	19	29	(D)	35	38
Asian and Pacific Islander	1,129	(D)	270	50,313	1,196	8,338	4	(D)	5	1
Men	697	56,765	215	43,394	978	6,996	5	1	5	1
Women	432	(D)	55	6,919	218	1,342	10	(D)	16	4
Washington	13,408	1,103,835	3,413	899,335	14,242	141,891	1	1	2	-
Minority men	8,838	869,808	2,571	716,871	11,219	109,176	1	1	2	1
Minority women	4,570	234,027	842	182,464	3,023	32,715	2	1	4	1
Hispanic	2,686	141,196	553	108,472	2,333	21,424	2	1	2	-
Men	1,859	122,980	463	96,785	1,988	19,009	2	1	2	1
Women	827	18,216	90	11,687	345	2,415	4	2	4	1
Black	2,583	175,671	436	148,082	2,212	29,085	-	-	-	-

[Continued]

★ 786 ★

Minority-Owned Firms: Western States

[Continued]

Geographic area and minority	All firms: Firms (number) A	All firms: Sales and receipts ($1,000) B	Firms with paid employees: Firms (number) C	Firms with paid employees: Sales and receipts ($1,000) D	Firms with paid employees: Employees (number) E	Firms with paid employees: Annual payroll ($1,000) F	Relative standard error of estimate % for column A	B	C	D
Men	1,561	99,348	301	81,986	1,518	17,708	-	-	-	-
Women	1,022	76,323	135	66,096	694	11,377	-	-	-	-
American Indian and Alaska Native	682	47,803	126	36,180	314	6,057	9	4	19	3
Men	442	34,572	93	24,825	211	3,380	10	5	23	3
Women	240	13,231	33	11,355	103	2,677	17	5	31	4
Asian and Pacific Islander	7,559	744,585	2,322	611,190	9,455	86,223	2	1	2	1
Men	5,042	617,577	1,731	517,630	7,569	69,939	2	1	3	1
Women	2,517	127,008	591	93,560	1,886	16,284	4	3	6	2
Wyoming	885	39,712	229	29,973	799	6,431	1	-	2	-
Minority men	585	27,238	167	19,817	509	4,388	2	-	2	-
Minority women	300	12,474	62	10,156	290	2,043	3	-	3	-
Hispanic	584	21,736	134	15,838	381	3,146	2	1	3	-
Men	394	13,909	94	9,307	207	2,034	2	1	3	1
Women	190	7,827	40	6,531	174	1,112	5	1	5	-
Black	81	3,512	11	2,605	56	785	-	-	-	-
Men	51	1,776	8	1,006	15	224	-	-	-	-
Women	30	1,736	3	1,599	41	561	-	-	-	-
American Indian and Alaska Native	79	(D)	17	2,273	61	666	3	(D)	-	-
Men	50	2,649	12	1,816	48	564	4	-	-	-
Women	29	(D)	5	457	13	102	-	(D)	-	-
Asian and Pacific Islander	154	(D)	68	9,361	307	1,850	1	(D)	-	-
Men	102	9,319	54	7,792	245	1,582	-	-	-	-
Women	52	(D)	14	1,569	62	268	4	(D)	-	-

Source: 1987 Economic Censuses, Survey of Minority-Owned Business Enterprises: Summary, U.S. Department of Commerce, Bureau of the Census, 1991, pp. 18- 28. Primary source: 1987 Survey of Minority-Owned Businesses, *Minority-Owned Businesses,* Washington, D.C., U.S. Government Printing Office, 1990. Arranged by the editors. *Notes:* A dash (-) represents zero. Details may not add to total because of rounding and because a firm may be included in more than one minority group. (D) stands for data withheld to avoid disclosure of competitive information.

★ 787 ★

Minority-Owned Firms

Minority-Owned Firms, by Industry Division, 1987

Percentages may not add to 100 since duplication of firms exists among minority groups.

Industry	Hispanic	Black	Asian and Pacific Islander American Indian and Alaska Native
Agricultural services, forestry, fishing, and mining	45.0	20.0	26.0
Construction	52.0	34.0	12.0
Manufacturing	37.0	27.0	34.0
Transportation and public utilities	35.0	48.0	16.0
Wholesale trade	38.0	21.0	40.0
Retail trade	31.0	29.0	39.0
Finance, insurance, and real estate	29.0	35.0	36.0
Services	33.0	37.0	29.0
Industries not classified	36.0	38.0	25.0

Source: 1987 Economic Censuses, Survey of Minority-Owned Business Enterprises: Summary, U.S. Department of Commerce, Bureau of the Census, 1991, p. 8.

★ 788 ★

Minority-Owned Firms

Minority-Owned Firms: All Industries

The number of firms, employees, sales and receipts, and annual payroll are shown for all industries, by sex and race/ethnicity, for 1987. Dollars are shown in thousands.

Characteristic	All firms		Firms with paid employees				Relative standard error of estimate % for column			
	Firms (number) A	Sales and receipts ($1,000) B	Firms (number) C	Sales and receipts ($1,000) D	Employees (number) E	Annual payroll ($1,000) F	A	B	C	D
All industries	1,213,750	77,839,943	248,149	56,463,624	836,483	9,506,592	-	-	-	-
Minority men	825,441	59,846,993	189,521	43,488,036	623,427	7,180,669	-	-	-	-
Minority women	388,309	17,992,950	58,628	12,975,588	213,056	2,327,923	-	-	1	-
Hispanic	422,373	24,731,600	82,908	17,729,432	264,846	3,243,342	-	-	1	-
Men	307,348	20,403,191	66,907	14,715,111	210,749	2,653,099	-	-	1	-
Women	115,025	4,328,409	16,001	3,014,321	54,097	590,243	1	1	1	1
Black	424,165	19,762,876	70,815	14,130,420	220,467	2,761,105	-	-	-	-
Men	265,887	13,232,364	51,518	9,289,084	147,520	1,820,396	-	-	-	-
Women	158,278	6,530,512	19,297	4,841,336	72,947	940,709	-	-	-	-
American Indian and Alaska Native	21,380	911,279	3,739	602,789	8,956	109,271	1	1	3	1
Men	15,072	711,166	2,881	468,016	6,660	85,144	1	1	3	1
Women	6,306	200,113	858	134,773	2,296	24,127	3	20	5	2
Asian and Pacific Islander	355,331	33,124,326	92,718	24,501,338	351,345	3,501,917	-	-	-	-

[Continued]

★ 788 ★

Minority-Owned Firms: All Industries

[Continued]

Characteristic	All firms: Firms (number) A	All firms: Sales and receipts ($1,000) B	Firms with paid employees: Firms (number) C	Firms with paid employees: Sales and receipts ($1,000) D	Firms with paid employees: Employees (number) E	Firms with paid employees: Annual payroll ($1,000) F	Relative standard error of estimate % for column A	B	C	D
Men	243,442	25,988,493	69,675	19,370,068	264,873	2,698,681	-	-	-	-
Women	111,889	7,135,833	23,043	5,131,270	86,472	803,236	1	-	1	-

Source: *1987 Economic Censuses, Survey of Minority-Owned Business Enterprises: Summary*, U.S. Department of Commerce, Bureau of the Census, 1991, p. 9. Primary source: 1987 Survey of Minority-Owned Businesses, *Minority-Owned Businesses*, Washington, D.C.: U.S. Government Printing Office, 1990. *Notes:* Details may not add to total because of rounding and because a firm may be included in more than one minority group.

★ 789 ★

Minority-Owned Firms

Minority-Owned Firms: Agricultural Services

Data are shown for 1987. Trade groups are based on the 1972 Standard Industrial Classification (SIC) system.

Industry group and minority	All firms: Firms (number) A	All firms: Sales and receipts ($1,000) B	Firms with paid employees: Firms (number) C	Firms with paid employees: Sales and receipts ($1,000) D	Firms with paid employees: Employees (number) E	Firms with paid employees: Annual payroll ($1,000) F	Relative standard error of estimate (%) for column - A	B	C	D
Agricultural services, forestry, and fishing	36,864	1,372,297	7,087	858,401	21,706	260,062	-	1	2	1
Minority men	33,861	1,238,555	6,497	770,464	19,701	235,241	1	1	2	1
Minority women	3,003	133,742	590	87,937	2,005	24,821	4	4	6	4
Hispanic	16,365	694,937	3,331	479,658	14,449	163,569	1	1	3	2
Men	15,211	645,694	3,096	446,248	13,309	150,316	1	1	3	2
Women	1,154	49,243	235	33,410	1,140	13,253	6	7	11	9
Black	7,316	216,742	1,662	144,276	3,078	38,046	-	-	-	-
Men	6,645	176,988	1,482	112,995	2,564	31,652	-	-	-	-
Women	671	39,754	180	31,281	514	6,394	-	-	-	-
American Indian and Alaska Native	3,661	104,446	371	30,109	486	8,950	2	5	12	8
Men	3,204	93,986	329	28,357	460	8,480	3	5	13	8
Women	457	10,460	42	1,752	26	470	12	23	39	19
Asian and Pacific Islander	9,726	365,309	1,760	211,467	3,976	52,155	1	2	4	3
Men	8,975	330,533	1,622	189,712	3,635	47,386	1	2	4	3
Women	751	34,776	138	21,755	341	4,769	8	8	15	8
Agricultural services (SIC 07)	27,366	1,098,190	5,818	766,864	21,083	241,874	1	1	2	1
Minority men	25,241	994,220	5,363	689,959	19,131	218,459	1	1	2	1
Minority women	2,125	103,970	455	76,905	1,952	23,415	4	3	6	4
Hispanic	14,752	648,290	3,210	464,607	14,197	160,618	1	2	3	2
Black	6,155	189,980	1,474	134,886	2,984	36,210	-	-	-	-
American Indian and Alaska Native	444	19,081	75	12,534	339	4,120	9	2	14	2
Asian and Pacific Islander	6,184	248,865	1,093	161,548	3,836	43,482	2	2	4	3
Forestry (SIC 08)	728	21,520	186	13,316	317	3,486	-	-	-	-
Minority men	665	20,100	172	12,724	309	3,378	-	-	-	-

[Continued]

★ 789 ★

Minority-Owned Firms: Agricultural Services

[Continued]

Industry group and minority	All firms: Firms (number) A	All firms: Sales and receipts ($1,000) B	Firms with paid employees: Firms (number) C	Firms with paid employees: Sales and receipts ($1,000) D	Firms with paid employees: Employees (number) E	Firms with paid employees: Annual payroll ($1,000) F	Relative standard error of estimate (%) for column - A	B	C	D
Minority women	63	1,420	14	592	8	108	-	-	-	-
Hispanic	184	8,263	45	6,065	195	1,882	-	-	-	-
Black	417	11,416	119	6,129	85	1,274	-	-	-	-
American Indian and Alaska Native	89	1,368	12	803	30	266	-	-	-	-
Asian and Pacific Islander	43	861	11	664	17	160	-	-	-	-
Fishing, hunting, and trapping (SIC 09)	8,770	252,587	1,083	78,221	306	14,702	1	3	7	6
Minority men	7,955	224,235	962	67,781	261	13,404	1	3	7	7
Minority women	815	28,352	121	10,440	45	1,298	8	12	23	16
Hispanic	1,429	38,384	76	8,986	57	1,069	3	3	13	4
Black	744	15,346	69	3,261	9	562	-	-	-	-
American Indian and Alaska Native	3,128	83,997	284	16,772	117	4,564	3	6	16	14
Asian and Pacific Islander	3,499	115,583	656	49,255	123	8,513	2	5	8	9

Source: 1987 Economic Censuses, Survey of Minority-Owned Business Enterprises: Summary, U.S. Department of Commerce, Bureau of the Census, 1991, p. 9. *Notes:* Details may not add to total because of rounding and because a firm may be included in more than one minority group. A dash (-) represents zero.

★ 790 ★

Minority-Owned Firms

Minority-Owned Firms: Construction

Data are shown for 1987. Trade groups are based on the 1972 Standard Industrial Classification (SIC) system.

Industry group and minority	SIC code	All firms: Firms (number) A	All firms: Sales and receipts ($1,000) B	Firms with paid employees: Firms (number) C	Firms with paid employees: Sales and receipts ($1,000) D	Firms with paid employees: Employees (number) E	Firms with paid employees: Annual payroll ($1,000) F	Relative standard error of estimate % for column A	B	C	D
Construction		107,650	6,903,022	29,721	5,196,718	69,878	1,222,932	-	-	1	-
Minority men		101,791	5,933,726	27,594	4,384,423	59,918	1,037,318	-	-	1	-
Minority women		5,859	969,296	2,127	812,295	9,960	185,614	2	1	2	-
Hispanic		55,516	3,438,706	14,717	2,646,244	34,684	631,477	-	1	2	1
Men		53,092	3,117,491	13,901	2,365,673	31,241	565,954	1	1	2	1
Women		2,424	321,217	816	280,571	3,443	65,523	5	2	6	1
Black		36,763	2,174,399	11,081	1,668,952	27,427	424,665	-	-	-	-
Men		34,455	1,697,563	10,078	1,266,771	21,966	325,833	-	-	-	-
Women		2,308	476,836	1,003	402,181	5,461	98,832	-	-	-	-
American Indian and Alaska Native		2,832	155,784	835	(D)	(D)	(D)	3	2	5	(D)
Men		2,606	132,389	769	102,303	1,445	25,038	3	3	5	3
Women		226	23,395	66	(D)	(D)	(D)	10	5	11	(D)
Asian and Pacific Islander		13,391	1,224,190	3,330	(D)	(D)	(D)	1	1	2	(D)
Men		12,419	1,067,003	3,067	720,819	5,995	137,159	1	1	2	1
Women		972	157,187	263	(D)	(D)	(D)	5	1	7	(D)

[Continued]

★ 790 ★

Minority-Owned Firms: Construction

[Continued]

Industry group and minority	SIC code	All firms: Firms (number) A	All firms: Sales and receipts ($1,000) B	Firms with paid employees: Firms (number) C	Firms with paid employees: Sales and receipts ($1,000) D	Firms with paid employees: Employees (number) E	Firms with paid employees: Annual payroll ($1,000) F	Relative standard error of estimate % for column A	B	C	D
General building contractors	15	17,236	1,981,974	5,846	1,575,624	14,984	280,998	1	1	2	1
Minority men		16,074	1,618,344	5,311	1,367,321	12,821	235,519	1	1	2	1
Minority women		1,162	363,630	535	308,303	2,163	45,479	4	1	4	1
Hispanic		7,990	860,943	2,522	689,809	7,271	138,470	1	1	3	1
Black		6,285	635,702	2,291	516,768	5,227	92,940	-	-	-	-
American Indian and Alaska Native		461	34,219	175	28,153	251	5,269	6	5	11	5
Asian and Pacific Islander		2,632	486,113	909	374,588	2,491	51,694	2	1	3	1
Heavy construction contractors	16	1,683	389,244	668	361,861	4,582	79,241	1	-	2	-
Minority men		1,546	357,742	588	331,703	4,216	70,387	2	-	2	-
Minority women		137	31,502	80	30,158	366	8,854	8	1	8	1
Hispanic		859	205,100	318	192,606	2,137	39,942	2	1	5	1
Black		638	155,949	275	144,259	2,118	32,911	-	-	-	-
American Indian and Alaska Native		93	(D)	38	15,549	178	3,902	3	(D)	-	-
Asian and Pacific Islander		107	(D)	40	15,996	208	3,746	10	(D)	4	2
Special trade contractors	17	87,920	4,209,682	23,008	3,102,746	49,530	844,885	-	-	1	1
Minority men		83,514	3,700,436	21,538	2,658,510	42,296	718,565	-	1	1	1
Minority women		4,406	509,246	1,470	444,236	7,234	126,320	3	1	3	1
Hispanic		46,383	2,266,204	11,803	1,691,285	25,032	446,520	1	1	2	1
Black		29,631	1,313,819	8,462	972,180	19,817	292,741	-	-	-	-
American Indian and Alaska Native		2,268	97,410	619	72,247	1,166	19,299	3	3	6	4
Asian and Pacific Islander		10,331	579,278	2,308	404,939	4,035	95,933	1	1	33	1
Subdividers and developers, n.e.c.	6552	811	322,122	199	156,487	782	17,808	2	-	2	-
Minority men		657	257,204	157	126,889	585	12,847	1	1	2	-
Minority women		154	64,918	42	29,598	197	4,961	6	-	3	1
Hispanic		284	106,461	74	72,544	244	6,545	2	1	4	1
Black		209	68,929	53	35,745	265	6,073	-	-	-	-
American Indian and Alaska Native		10	(D)	3	(D)	(D)	(D)	-	(D)	-	(D)
Asian and Pacific Islander		321	(D)	73	(D)	(D)	(D)	3	(D)	4	(D)

Source: 1987 Economic Censuses, Survey of Minority-Owned Business Enterprises: Summary, U.S. Department of Commerce, Bureau of the Census, 1991, pp. 16-17. *Notes:* (D) stands for data withheld to avoid disclosure of competitive information. Details may not add to total because of rounding and because a firm may be included in more than one minority group. A dash (-) represents zero.

★ 791 ★

Minority-Owned Firms

Minority-Owned Firms: Finance, Insurance, and Real Estate

Data are shown for 1987. Trade groups are based on the 1972 Standard Industrial Classification (SIC) system.

Major industry group and minority	SIC code	All firms: Firms (number) A	All firms: Sales and receipts ($1,000) B	Firms with paid employees: Firms (number) C	Firms with paid employees: Sales and receipts ($1,000) D	Firms with paid employees: Employees (number) E	Firms with paid employees: Annual payroll ($1,000) F	Relative standard error of estimate % for column A	B	C	D
Finance, insurance, and real estate		76,442	2,759,980	7,340	1,364,515	17,066	252,776	-	-	1	-
Minority men		47,936	1,942,427	5,388	997,955	12,337	179,468	1	1	1	1
Minority women		28,506	817,553	1,952	366,560	4,729	73,308	1	1	3	1
Hispanic		22,106	864,282	2,236	433,851	4,960	80,882	1	1	2	1
Men		14,565	673,894	1,702	361,560	3,977	67,008	1	1	3	1
Women		7,541	190,388	534	72,291	983	13,874	2	2	5	3
Black		26,989	804,252	2,514	464,389	5,938	94,718	-	-	-	-
Men		15,971	478,540	1,783	267,282	3,607	51,137	-	-	-	-
Women		11,018	325,712	731	197,107	2,331	43,581	-	-	-	-
American Indian and Alaska Native		614	20,192	71	(D)	(D)	(D)	7	7	19	(D)
Men		389	11,508	44	4,420	167	2,021	9	11	21	6
Women		225	8,684	27	(D)	(D)	(D)	13	7	37	(D)
Asian and Pacific Islander		27,297	1,086,855	2,558	(D)	(D)	(D)	1	1	3	(D)
Men		17,340	787,749	1,887	369,408	4,639	60,104	1	1	3	1
Women		9,957	299,106	671	(D)	(D)	(D)	2	2	6	(D)
Banking	60	86	(D)	82	88,897	881	14,146	-	(D)	-	-
Minority men		56	71,995	54	(D)	(D)	(D)	-	-	-	(D)
Minority women		30	(D)	28	(D)	(D)	(D)	-	(D)	-	(D)
Hispanic		34	13,858	31	(D)	(D)	(D)	-	-	-	(D)
Black		35	17,402	34	(D)	(D)	(D)	-	-	-	(D)
American Indian and Alaska Native		1	(D)	1	(D)	(D)	(D)	-	(D)	-	(D)
Asian and Pacific Islander		18	(D)	18	(D)	(D)	(D)	-	(D)	-	(D)
Credit agencies other than banks	61	175	(D)	141	30,116	624	9,775	-	(D)	-	-
Minority men		114	21,509	91	20,568	438	5,945	-	-	-	-
Minority women		61	(D)	50	9,548	186	3,830	-	(D)	-	-
Hispanic		91	10,925	78	10,507	175	2,595	-	-	-	-
Black		45	13,429	35	12,926	283	5,015	-	-	-	-
American Indian and Alaska Native		1	(D)	1	(D)	(D)	(D)	-	(D)	-	(D)
Asian and Pacific Islander		40	6,852	27	(D)	(D)	(D)	-	-	-	(D)
Security, commodity brokers and services	62	1,981	165,577	192	112,452	394	22,174	2	1	6	-
Minority men		1,521	147,545	153	101,256	334	19,776	2	1	8	-
Minority women		460	18,032	39	11,196	60	2,398	6	7	6	1
Hispanic		525	89,792	67	69,857	173	12,707	4	1	12	1
Black		711	22,723	62	11,031	77	2,856	-	-	-	-
American Indian and Alaska Native		30	(D)	12	369	3	54	34	(D)	58	35
Asian and Pacific Islander		733	(D)	52	31,234	142	6,559	4	(D)	13	-
Insurance carriers	63	78	13,132	38	(D)	(D)	(D)	-	-	-	(D)
Minority men		49	6,472	21	5,516	99	1,523	-	-	-	-
Minority women		29	6,660	17	(D)	(D)	(D)	-	-	-	(D)
Hispanic		33	5,086	15	4,567	71	1,115	-	-	-	-
Black		36	6,220	16	4,532	52	611	-	-	-	-
American Indian and Alaska Native		-	-	-	-	-	-	-	-	-	-
Asian and Pacific Islander		9	1,826	7	(D)	(D)	(D)	-	-	-	(D)
Insurance agents, brokers, and services		64	20,793	576,848	305,429	3,979	62,749	1	1	2	1
Minority men		16,220	461,412	2,119	235,115	3,075	45,780	1	1	2	1

[Continued]

★ 791 ★

Minority-Owned Firms: Finance, Insurance, and Real Estate

[Continued]

Major industry group and minority	SIC code	All firms: Firms (number) A	All firms: Sales and receipts ($1,000) B	Firms with paid employees: Firms (number) C	Firms with paid employees: Sales and receipts ($1,000) D	Firms with paid employees: Employees (number) E	Firms with paid employees: Annual payroll ($1,000) F	Relative standard error of estimate % for column A	B	C	D
Minority women		4,573	115,436	457	70,314	904	16,969	2	2	6	2
Hispanic		6,013	209,229	926	122,195	1,668	24,434	2	2	4	2
Black		7,956	188,690	992	112,760	1,454	24,998	-	-	-	-
American Indian and Alaska Native		152	5,051	20	2,321	40	500	15	21	27	1
Asian and Pacific Islander		6,829	175,748	646	68,808	830	13,009	2	3	6	4
Real estate	65 pt.	46,253	1,671,457	3,864	772,820	10,604	133,755	-	1	2	1
Minority men		24,561	1,072,191	2,596	529,643	7,440	90,765	1	1	2	1
Minority women		20,692	599,266	1,268	243,177	3,164	42,990	1	1	3	1
Hispanic		12,872	472,278	971	203,480	2,611	35,073	1	1	3	1
Black		15,552	505,936	1,182	292,454	3,662	54,274	-	-	-	-
American Indian and Alaska Native		370	12,746	33	7,710	150	1,668	10	7	31	7
Asian and Pacific Islander		16,794	692,242	1,704	273,705	4,224	43,195	1	1	3	2
Combined real estate, insurance, etc.	66	7,959	189,043	430	35,734	333	6,138	1	2	5	3
Minority men		5,335	144,625	344	28,356	256	4,541	2	2	5	4
Minority women		2,624	44,418	86	7,378	77	1,597	3	5	10	9
Hispanic		2,509	59,371	142	9,570	99	1,695	2	3	11	9
Black		2,624	47,360	190	12,893	128	2,533	-	-	-	-
American Indian and Alaska Native		59	1,212	4	411	9	96	21	34	-	-
Asian and Pacific Islander		2,815	81,980	96	13,195	104	1,894	2	4	14	6
Holding and other investment offices	67 pt.	117	21,487	17	(D)	(D)	(D)	2	3	-	(D)
Minority men		80	16,678	10	(D)	(D)	(D)	4	3	-	(D)
Minority women		37	4,809	7	936	10	231	5	1	-	-
Hispanic		29	3,743	6	(D)	(D)	(D)	-	-	-	(D)
Black		30	2,492	3	(D)	(D)	(D)	-	-	-	(D)
American Indian and Alaska Native		1	(D)	-	-	-	-	-	(D)	-	-
Asian and Pacific Islander		59	(D)	8	(D)	(D)	(D)	4	(D)	-	(D)

Source: 1987 Economic Censuses, Survey of Minority-Owned Business Enterprises: Summary, U.S. Department of Commerce, Bureau of the Census, 1991, pp. 15- 16. *Notes:* Pt. stands for part. (D) stands for data withheld to avoid disclosures of competitive information. Details may not add to total because of rounding and because a firm may be included in more than one minority group. A dash (-) represents zero.

★ 792 ★

Minority-Owned Firms

Minority-Owned Firms: Manufacturing

Data are shown for 1987. Trade groups are based on the 1972 Standard Industrial Classification (SIC) system.

Industry group and minority	SIC code	All firms: Firms (number) A	All firms: Sales and receipts ($1,000) B	Firms with paid employees: Firms (number) C	Firms with paid employees: Sales and receipts ($1,000) D	Firms with paid employees: Employees (number) E	Firms with paid employees: Annual payroll ($1,000) F	Relative standard error of estimate % for column A	B	C	D
Manufacturing		29,879	3,961,128	10,126	3,584,420	76,741	946,089	-	-	1	-
Minority men		21,464	2,885,678	7,677	2,590,911	53,640	661,987	1	-	1	-
Minority women		8,415	1,075,450	2,449	993,509	23,101	284,102	1	-	2	-
Hispanic		11,090	1,449,913	3,760	1,308,124	26,261	333,969	1	-	2	-
Men		8,358	1,085,513	2,890	967,467	18,468	242,123	1	1	2	1
Women		2,732	361,400	870	340,657	7,793	91,846	3	1	4	1
Black		8,004	1,023,104	2,612	927,105	13,684	244,038	-	-	-	-
Men		6,349	639,407	2,111	563,806	8,719	146,829	-	-	-	-
Women		1,655	383,697	501	363,299	4,965	97,209	-	-	-	-
American Indian and Alaska Native		911	63,563	148	(D)	(D)	(D)	4	1	5	(D)
Men		666	44,690	125	37,721	922	10,231	4	1	6	1
Women		245	18,873	23	(D)	(D)	(D)	10	3	6	(D)
Asian and Pacific Islander		10,121	1,461,396	3,701	(D)	(D)	(D)	1	-	1	(D)
Men		6,253	1,135,387	2,616	1,041,615	26,077	269,851	1	-	2	-
Women		3,868	326,009	1,085	(D)	(D)	(D)	2	1	3	(D)
Food and kindred products	20	1,326	318,238	479	293,678	4,124	47,078	1	-	2	-
Minority men		871	252,347	360	233,092	3,200	35,092	2	1	2	-
Minority women		457	65,891	119	60,586	924	11,986	4	-	4	-
Hispanic		589	151,632	240	140,141	2,100	23,442	3	1	3	1
Black		286	60,595	70	57,181	699	11,019	-	-	-	-
American Indian and Alaska Native		9	314	2	(D)	(D)	(D)	-	-	-	(D)
Asian and Pacific Islander		459	110,276	170	(D)	(D)	(D)	2	-	-	(D)
Tobacco manufactures	21	7	860	7	860	32	180	-	-	-	-
Minority men		7	860	7	860	32	180	-	-	-	-
Minority women		-	-	-	-	-	-	-	-	-	-
Hispanic		7	860	7	860	32	180	-	-	-	-
Black		-	-	-	-	-	-	-	-	-	-
American Indian and Alaska Native		-	-	-	-	-	-	-	-	-	-
Asian and Pacific Islander		-	-	-	-	-	-	-	-	-	-
Textile mill products	22	477	53,088	126	47,306	1,000	12,328	1	-	-	-
Minority men		225	35,093	72	31,285	581	6,852	-	-	-	-
Minority women		252	17,995	54	16,021	419	5,476	2	-	-	-
Hispanic		188	21,361	56	18,894	437	5,229	1	-	-	-
Black		74	9,954	25	9,384	115	3,070	-	-	-	-
American Indian and Alaska Native		13	262	2	(D)	(D)	(D)	-	-	-	(D)
Asian and Pacific Islander		208	22,337	47	(D)	(D)	(D)	3	-	-	(D)
Apparel and other textile products	23	6,536	847,492	2,720	794,509	36,611	278,739	1	1	2	1
Minority men		2,913	496,559	1,540	469,085	22,578	170,394	2	1	2	1
Minority women		3,623	350,933	1,180	325,424	14,033	108,345	2	1	3	1
Hispanic		1,713	278,810	833	267,198	10,294	84,350	2	1	4	1
Black		552	64,671	146	60,859	1,360	16,392	-	-	-	-
American Indian and Alaska Native		76	(D)	6	(D)	(D)	(D)	14	(D)	24	(D)
Asian and Pacific Islander		4,265	(D)	1,781	(D)	(D)	(D)	1	(D)	2	(D)
Lumber and wood products	24	5,046	344,167	1,838	278,091	5,056	68,168	1	-	1	1
Minority men		4,697	294,054	1,703	234,657	4,234	55,632	1	1	1	1

[Continued]

★ 792 ★

Minority-Owned Firms: Manufacturing

[Continued]

Industry group and minority	SIC code	All firms: Firms (number) A	All firms: Sales and receipts ($1,000) B	Firms with paid employees: Firms (number) C	Firms with paid employees: Sales and receipts ($1,000) D	Firms with paid employees: Employees (number) E	Firms with paid employees: Annual payroll ($1,000) F	Relative standard error of estimate % for column A	B	C	D
Minority women		349	50,113	135	43,434	822	12,536	4	1	6	1
Hispanic		840	86,082	250	74,287	1,410	17,883	3	2	5	2
Black		3,720	211,281	1,438	163,852	2,932	41,362	-	-	-	-
American Indian and Alaska Native		274	22,230	78	18,796	407	5,155	7	2	10	1
Asian and Pacific Islander		228	25,214	77	21,654	314	3,848	8	3	17	3
Furniture and fixtures	25	1,090	146,586	386	132,487	2,490	32,053	2	1	3	1
Minority men		931	127,483	340	114,921	2,151	26,779	2	1	4	1
Minority women		159	19,103	46	17,566	339	5,274	10	1	7	-
Hispanic		657	88,946	249	80,165	1,617	19,810	3	1	5	1
Black		226	29,812	65	27,429	545	7,960	-	-	-	-
American Indian and Alaska Native		21	702	2	(D)	(D)	(D)	19	17	-	(D)
Asian and Pacific Islander		202	28,309	73	(D)	(D)	(D)	3	-	-	(D)
Paper and allied products	26	195	(D)	51	(D)	(D)	(D)	-	(D)	-	(D)
Minority men		140	65,742	42	64,389	657	12,621	-	-	-	-
Minority women		55	(D)	9	(D)	(D)	(D)	-	(D)	-	(D)
Hispanic		87	11,499	19	10,553	111	1,742	-	-	-	-
Black		55	26,230	17	25,666	287	5,154	-	-	-	-
American Indian and Alaska Native		2	(D)	-	-	-	-	-	(D)	-	-
Asian and Pacific Islander		55	(D)	15	(D)	(D)	(D)	-	(D)	-	(D)
Printing and publishing	27	4,823	523,128	1,626	462,676	6,394	115,930	1	1	3	1
Minority men		3,652	359,175	1,246	314,458	4,551	76,998	2	1	3	1
Minority women		1,171	163,953	380	148,218	1,843	38,932	4	2	6	2
Hispanic		1,886	179,062	575	158,977	2,409	41,942	3	2	5	2
Black		1,394	126,488	360	109,971	1,629	35,538	-	-	-	-
American Indian and Alaska Native		50	2,501	11	2,192	58	680	19	1	-	-
Asian and Pacific Islander		1,532	226,151	690	202,036	2,474	41,491	3	2	5	2
Chemicals and allied products	28	241	96,977	89	91,600	890	17,021	1	-	-	-
Minority men		195	87,925	74	83,257	806	14,815	2	-	-	-
Minority women		46	9,052	15	8,343	84	2,206	-	-	-	-
Hispanic		72	20,157	28	19,432	179	3,135	-	-	-	-
Black		65	57,468	23	56,511	498	10,329	-	-	-	-
American Indian and Alaska Native		4	146	2	(D)	(D)	(D)	-	-	-	(D)
Asian and Pacific Islander		100	19,206	36	(D)	(D)	(D)	3	-	-	(D)
Petroleum and coal products	29	8	(D)	6	(D)	(D)	(D)	-	(D)	-	(D)
Minority men		6	(D)	4	(D)	(D)	(D)	-	(D)	-	(D)
Minority women		2	(D)	2	(D)	(D)	(D)	-	(D)	-	(D)
Hispanic		3	(D)	2	(D)	(D)	(D)	-	(D)	-	(D)
Black		1	(D)	-	-	-	-	-	(D)	-	-
American Indian and Alaska Native		-	-	-	-	-	-	-	-	-	-
Asian and Pacific Islander		4	(D)	4	(D)	(D)	(D)	-	(D)	-	(D)
Rubber and miscellaneous plastics products	30	350	91,535	129	88,197	1,190	21,539	-	-	-	-
Minority men		260	74,426	101	71,610	870	16,501	-	-	-	-
Minority women		90	17,109	28	16,587	320	5,038	-	-	-	-

[Continued]

★ 792 ★

Minority-Owned Firms: Manufacturing

[Continued]

Industry group and minority	SIC code	All firms: Firms (number) A	All firms: Sales and receipts ($1,000) B	Firms with paid employees: Firms (number) C	Firms with paid employees: Sales and receipts ($1,000) D	Firms with paid employees: Employees (number) E	Firms with paid employees: Annual payroll ($1,000) F	Relative standard error of estimate % for column: A	B	C	D
Hispanic		176	50,765	62	48,960	698	12,891	-	-	-	-
Black		71	11,844	29	11,383	214	4,231	-	-	-	-
American Indian and Alaska Native		5	251	1	(D)	(D)	(D)	-	-	-	(D)
Asian and Pacific Islander		101	30,244	38	(D)	(D)	(D)	-	-	-	(D)
Leather and leather products	31	362	35,834	92	31,313	590	7,701	3	-	-	-
Minority men		248	28,972	73	25,335	460	5,665	3	1	-	-
Minority women		114	6,862	19	5,978	130	2,036	6	-	-	-
Hispanic		194	22,108	53	20,053	362	5,038	-	-	-	-
Black		42	5,187	10	4,860	117	1,503	-	-	-	-
American Indian and Alaska Native		18	212	2	(D)	(D)	(D)	-	-	-	(D)
Asian and Pacific Islander		112	8,497	29	(D)	(D)	(D)	9	2	-	(D)
Stone, clay, and glass products	32	909	93,326	208	83,612	922	17,061	2	1	2	-
Minority men		595	63,485	172	56,673	654	11,906	3	1	3	-
Minority women		314	29,841	36	26,939	268	5,155	3	1	4	-
Hispanic		400	38,880	106	33,782	370	7,203	3	1	5	1
Black		193	30,428	61	29,637	349	5,742	-	-	-	-
American Indian and Alaska Native		60	2,040	7	1,493	16	225	12	2	-	-
Asian and Pacific Islander		263	22,175	35	18,717	187	3,897	9	1	-	-
Primary metal industry	33	219	97,553	66	(D)	(D)	(D)	4	-	-	(D)
Minority men		187	(D)	48	37,065	799	8,784	5	(D)	-	-
Minority women		32	(D)	18	(D)	(D)	(D)	-	(D)	-	(D)
Hispanic		104	53,897	32	(D)	(D)	(D)	-	-	-	(D)
Black		54	8,122	12	7,420	76	772	-	-	-	-
American Indian and Alaska Native		10	(D)	2	(D)	(D)	(D)	-	(D)	-	(D)
Asian and Pacific Islander		51	(D)	20	(D)	(D)	(D)	19	(D)	-	(D)
Fabricated metal products	34	1,835	285,963	591	259,079	3,714	75,695	2	1	5	1
Minority men		1,563	189,915	485	166,400	2,527	44,356	2	1	5	1
Minority women		272	96,048	106	92,679	1,187	31,339	9	1	14	1
Hispanic		1,140	107,976	386	91,969	1,792	28,303	2	2	7	2
Black		338	116,191	106	111,785	1,271	33,167	-	-	-	-
American Indian and Alaska Native		91	2,153	6	1,356	16	239	10	3	-	-
Asian and Pacific Islander		275	60,548	94	54,614	651	14,166	3	1	5	1
Machinery, except electrical	35	2,003	249,327	701	222,707	3,074	63,193	2	1	4	1
Minority men		1,774	218,975	612	194,888	2,534	52,772	2	1	5	1
Minority women		229	30,352	89	27,819	540	10,421	10	2	9	2
Hispanic		1,148	120,136	420	104,482	1,521	27,146	3	2	7	2
Black		271	45,711	95	42,566	672	15,800	-	-	-	-
American Indian and Alaska Native		34	4,090	8	3,635	44	1,042	11	6	17	6
Asian and Pacific Islander		562	82,936	188	75,561	899	20,320	4	2	6	2
Electric and electronic equipment	36	1,037	314,557	250	298,577	4,333	79,415	1	-	3	-
Minority men		700	224,892	204	211,605	3,455	59,544	2	1	4	-
Minority women		337	89,665	46	86,972	878	19,871	5	-	3	-
Hispanic		295	39,990	67	37,233	670	13,168	1	-	-	-
Black		136	113,567	34	112,422	1,594	26,054	-	-	-	-

[Continued]

★ 792 ★

Minority-Owned Firms: Manufacturing

[Continued]

Industry group and minority	SIC code	All firms: Firms (number) A	All firms: Sales and receipts ($1,000) B	Firms with paid employees: Firms (number) C	Firms with paid employees: Sales and receipts ($1,000) D	Firms with paid employees: Employees (number) E	Firms with paid employees: Annual payroll ($1,000) F	Relative standard error of estimate % for column A	B	C	D
American Indian and Alaska Native		8	4,250	3	4,236	59	630	31	-	-	-
Asian and Pacific Islander		601	156,903	147	144,768	2,011	39,582	3	1	5	1
Transportation equipment	37	236	161,229	113	156,009	2,063	39,334	-	-	-	-
Minority men		197	146,418	89	141,533	1,761	34,806	-	-	-	-
Minority women		39	14,811	24	14,476	302	4,528	-	-	-	-
Hispanic		129	74,747	66	70,875	938	17,821	-	-	-	-
Black		57	69,685	24	68,917	902	18,396	-	-	-	-
American Indian and Alaska Native		7	694	4	(D)	(D)	(D)	-	-	-	(D)
Asian and Pacific Islander		48	17,023	22	(D)	(D)	(D)	-	-	-	(D)
Instruments and related products	38	187	26,979	78	(D)	(D)	(D)	-	-	-	(D)
Minority men		156	21,765	65	(D)	(D)	(D)	-	-	-	(D)
Minority women		31	5,214	13	4,706	59	1,082	-	-	-	-
Hispanic		68	5,581	21	(D)	(D)	(D)	-	-	-	(D)
Black		31	11,291	12	10,829	122	3,391	-	-	-	-
American Indian and Alaska Native		3	14	-	-	-	-	-	-	-	-
Asian and Pacific Islander		86	10,096	45	9,258	135	2,077	-	-	-	-
Miscellaneous manufacturing industries	39	2,990	170,602	570	124,418	1,920	27,606	2	2	4	1
Minority men		2,147	129,528	440	93,440	1,460	20,545	3	2	5	1
Minority women		843	41,074	130	30,978	460	7,061	5	2	9	1
Hispanic		1,394	(D)	288	53,451	858	11,821	3	(D)	7	3
Black		438	(D)	85	16,433	302	4,158	-	(D)	-	-
American Indian and Alaska Native		226	4,266	12	2,320	57	530	9	14	-	-
Asian and Pacific Islander		969	68,340	190	54,365	741	11,650	4	2	7	1

Source: *1987 Economic Censuses, Survey of Minority-Owned Business Enterprises: Summary*, U.S. Department of Commerce, Bureau of the Census, 1991, pp. 16-17. *Notes:* A dash (-) represents zero. (D) stands for data withheld to avoid disclosure of competitive information. Details may not add to total because of rounding and because a firm may be included in more than one minority group.

★ 793 ★

Minority-Owned Firms

Minority-Owned Firms: Mining

Data are shown for 1987. Trade groups are based on the 1972 Standard Industrial Classification (SIC) system.

Major industry group and minority	All firms: Firms (number) A	All firms: Sales and receipts ($1,000) B	Firms with paid employees: Firms (number) C	Firms with paid employees: Sales and receipts ($1,000) D	Firms with paid employees: Employees (number) E	Firms with paid employees: Annual payroll ($1,000) F	Relative standard error of estimate % for column A	B	C	D
Mining	1,613	103,075	147	76,961	859	14,532	3	1	3	1
Minority men	1,289	80,189	111	58,331	621	10,451	3	2	3	1
Minority women	324	22,886	36	18,630	238	4,081	7	1	7	-
Hispanic	829	29,836	72	18,498	332	5,272	4	4	6	3
Men	684	25,109	62	15,763	291	4,678	4	5	6	3

[Continued]

★ 793 ★

Minority-Owned Firms: Mining

[Continued]

Major industry group and minority	All firms: Firms (number) A	All firms: Sales and receipts ($1,000) B	Firms with paid employees: Firms (number) C	Firms with paid employees: Sales and receipts ($1,000) D	Firms with paid employees: Employees (number) E	Firms with paid employees: Annual payroll ($1,000) F	Relative standard error of estimate % for column A	B	C	D
Women	145	4,727	10	2,735	41	594	13	5	24	1
Black	322	54,071	48	46,013	401	7,003	-	-	-	-
Men	221	38,462	29	31,906	222	3,750	-	-	-	-
Women	101	15,609	19	14,107	179	3,253	-	-	-	-
American Indian and Alaska Native	106	4,062	8	1,882	28	522	11	5	-	-
Men	82	3,491	7	(D)	(D)	(D)	11	1	-	(D)
Women	24	571	1	(D)	(D)	(D)	31	37	-	(D)
Asian and Pacific Islander	360	15,114	19	10,568	98	1,735	7	3	-	-
Men	303	13,128	13	(D)	(D)	(D)	8	4	-	(D)
Women	57	1,986	6	(D)	(D)	(D)	16	4	-	(D)
Metal mining	41	(D)	8	359	15	75	-	(D)	-	-
Minority men	38	(D)	7	(D)	(D)	(D)	-	(D)	-	(D)
Minority women	3	14	1	(D)	(D)	(D)	-	-	-	(D)
Hispanic	16	244	1	(D)	(D)	(D)	-	-	-	(D)
Black	6	75	3	52	2	13	-	-	-	-
American Indian and Alaska Native	11	(D)	2	(D)	(D)	(D)	-	(D)	-	(D)
Asian and Pacific Islander	9	274	2	(D)	(D)	(D)	-	-	-	(D)
Anthracite mining	3	23	-	-	-	-	-	-	-	-
Minority men	1	(D)	-	-	-	-	-	(D)	-	-
Minority women	2	(D)	-	-	-	-	-	(D)	-	-
Hispanic	-	-	-	-	-	-	-	-	-	-
Black	3	23	-	-	-	-	-	-	-	-
American Indian and Alaska Native	-	-	-	-	-	-	-	-	-	-
Asian and Pacific Islander	-	-	-	-	-	-	-	-	-	-
Bituminous coal and lignite mining	19	(D)	9	5,074	87	1,447	-	(D)	-	-
Minority men	16	4,311	6	(D)	(D)	(D)	-	-	-	(D)
Minority women	3	(D)	3	(D)	(D)	(D)	-	(D)	-	(D)
Hispanic	4	58	1	(D)	(D)	(D)	-	-	-	(D)
Black	9	3,968	6	(D)	(D)	(D)	-	-	-	(D)
American Indian and Alaska Native	3	(D)	-	-	-	-	-	(D)	-	-
Asian and Pacific Islander	3	(D)	2	(D)	(D)	(D)	-	(D)	-	(D)
Oil and gas extraction	1,448	73,870	100	54,299	543	9,737	3	2	4	1
Minority men	1,149	54,774	75	39,274	361	6,326	3	2	5	1
Minority women	299	19,096	25	15,025	182	3,411	7	2	10	-
Hispanic	763	22,917	57	12,283	257	4,098	5	5	8	4
Black	270	39,946	26	36,922	241	5,089	-	-	-	-
American Indian and Alaska Native	80	2,441	5	(D)	(D)	(D)	14	9	-	(D)
Asian and Pacific Islander	338	8,573	12	(D)	(D)	(D)	7	6	-	(D)
Nonmetallic minerals, except fuels	102	22,382	30	17,229	214	3,273	-	-	-	-
Minority men	85	(D)	23	(D)	(D)	(D)	-	(D)	-	(D)

[Continued]

★ 793 ★

Minority-Owned Firms: Mining

[Continued]

Major industry group and minority	All firms: Firms (number) A	All firms: Sales and receipts ($1,000) B	Firms with paid employees: Firms (number) C	Firms with paid employees: Sales and receipts ($1,000) D	Firms with paid employees: Employees (number) E	Firms with paid employees: Annual payroll ($1,000) F	Relative standard error of estimate % for column A	B	C	D
Minority women	17	(D)	7	(D)	(D)	(D)	-	(D)	-	(D)
Hispanic	46	6,617	13	(D)	(D)	(D)	-	-	-	(D)
Black	34	10,039	13	(D)	(D)	(D)	-	-	-	(D)
American Indian and Alaska Native	12	(D)	1	(D)	(D)	(D)	-	(D)	-	(D)
Asian and Pacific Islander	10	(D)	3	(D)	(D)	(D)	-	(D)	-	(D)

Source: 1987 Economic Censuses, Survey of Minority-Owned Business Enterprises: Summary, U.S. Department of Commerce, Bureau of the Census, 1991, pp. 9-10. *Notes:* A dash (-) represents zero. Details may not add to total because of rounding and because a firm may be included in more than one minority group. (D) stands for data withheld to avoid disclosure of competitive information.

★ 794 ★

Minority-Owned Firms

Minority-Owned Firms: Retail Trade

Data are shown for 1987. Trade groups are based on the 1972 Standard Industrial Classification (SIC) system.

Industry group and minority	SIC code	All firms: Firms (number) A	All firms: Sales and receipts ($1,000) B	Firms with paid employees: Firms (number) C	Firms with paid employees: Sales and receipts ($1,000) D	Firms with paid employees: Employees (number) E	Firms with paid employees: Annual payroll ($1,000) F	Relative standard error of estimate % for column A	B	C	D
Retail trade		226,140	26,903,914	72,310	21,614,740	319,048	2,522,579	-	-	-	-
Minority men		144,463	20,599,037	51,973	16,584,089	233,254	1,849,591	-	-	-	-
Minority women		81,677	6,304,877	20,337	5,030,651	85,794	672,988	1	-	1	-
Hispanic		69,911	7,643,850	20,348	6,095,890	90,584	745,662	-	-	1	-
Men		46,179	6,216,518	15,114	5,011,191	70,394	590,518	1	-	1	-
Women		23,732	1,427,332	5,234	1,084,699	20,190	155,144	1	1	2	1
Black		66,229	5,889,654	14,293	4,861,485	62,530	571,450	-	-	-	-
Men		36,389	3,812,061	9,274	3,124,476	39,383	350,570	-	-	-	-
Women		29,840	2,077,593	5,019	1,737,009	23,147	220,880	-	-	-	-
American Indian and Alaska Native		3,090	268,086	837	210,191	2,427	20,170	3	2	4	1
Men		1,683	202,941	534	163,835	1,730	14,722	4	2	5	2
Women		1,407	65,145	303	46,356	697	5,448	6	4	8	3
Asian and Pacific Islander		88,761	13,315,753	37,399	10,613,682	165,865	1,204,132	-	-	1	-
Men		61,356	10,514,603	27,390	8,398,758	123,261	905,725	1	-	1	-
Women		27,405	2,801,150	10,009	2,214,924	42,604	298,407	1	-	1	-
Building materials and garden supplies	52	2,690	467,932	971	407,114	3,737	49,022	1	1	2	1
Minority men		2,235	319,659	774	269,565	2,358	29,695	2	1	3	1
Minority women		455	148,273	197	137,549	1,379	19,327	5	1	3	1
Hispanic		1,331	160,841	468	132,177	1,341	16,137	2	2	4	2
Black		650	190,291	249	180,137	1,592	23,695	-	-	-	-
American Indian and Alaska Native		61	5,578	17	4,509	35	733	13	4	8	5
Asian and Pacific Islander		687	120,497	255	99,097	837	9,432	3	2	5	2
General merchandise stores	53	4,792	313,788	840	175,190	1,820	16,640	1	1	3	1
Minority men		3,359	219,268	607	113,058	1,129	9,512	2	2	4	1
Minority women		1,433	94,520	233	62,132	691	7,128	4	2	6	2

[Continued]

★ 794 ★

Minority-Owned Firms: Retail Trade

[Continued]

Industry group and minority	SIC code	All firms: Firms (number) A	All firms: Sales and receipts ($1,000) B	Firms with paid employees: Firms (number) C	Firms with paid employees: Sales and receipts ($1,000) D	Firms with paid employees: Employees (number) E	Firms with paid employees: Annual payroll ($1,000) F	Relative standard error of estimate % for column A	B	C	D
Hispanic		1,152	54,795	146	30,974	406	3,237	3	2	10	2
Black		1,064	44,343	194	26,097	306	2,569	-	-	-	-
American Indian and Alaska Native		72	8,394	29	6,658	47	385	15	7	15	9
Asian and Pacific Islander		2,564	210,192	481	113,638	1,080	10,612	2	2	5	2
Food stores	54	35,747	6,617,891	13,650	4,915,955	47,917	388,722	-	-	1	-
Minority men		27,146	5,288,873	10,467	3,923,594	37,116	301,489	1	-	1	-
Minority women		8,601	1,329,018	3,183	992,361	10,801	87,233	1	1	2	1
Hispanic		9,599	1,835,802	3,569	1,383,998	14,010	1418,064	1	1	2	1
Black		8,952	1,001,462	2,664	719,575	7,946	65,389	-	-	-	-
American Indian and Alaska Native		301	54,320	108	42,230	356	2,526	9	4	5	2
Asian and Pacific Islander		17,263	3,785,579	7,430	2,810,796	26,075	206,260	1	1	1	1
Automotive dealers and service stations	55	12,275	6,156,369	6,027	5,646,224	26,348	379,555	1	-	1	-
Minority men		10,982	5,122,074	5,329	4,654,304	21,890	304,893	1	-	1	-
Minority women		1,293	1,034,295	698	991,920	4,458	74,662	3	-	3	-
Hispanic		5,627	2,100,213	2,475	1,853,478	9,378	128,153	1	-	2	-
Black		3,690	2,155,680	1,689	2,041,434	9,370	160,026	-	-	-	-
American Indian and Alaska Native		222	65,257	88	55,793	330	3,754	8	1	5	1
Asian and Pacific Islander		2,831	1,880,502	1,825	1,735,791	7,540	90,595	1	-	1	-
Apparel and accessory stores	56	12,687	1,043,144	4,026	754,812	11,225	85,000	1	1	2	1
Minority men		7,416	702,997	2,420	508,514	7,176	54,025	1	1	2	1
Minority women		5,271	340,147	1,606	246,298	4,049	30,975	2	2	3	2
Hispanic		3,472	230,806	1,021	165,431	2,651	21,258	2	2	3	2
Black		3,061	140,187	771	103,529	1,743	14,959	-	-	-	-
American Indian and Alaska Native		85	5,994	36	4,992	88	516	11	4	14	4
Asian and Pacific Islander		6,208	677,045	2,242	489,078	6,847	49,087	1	1	2	1
Furniture and home furnishings stores	57	7,536	961,045	2,399	756,200	6,338	79,599	1	1	1	1
Minority men		5,629	719,876	1,792	551,983	4,677	57,735	1	1	2	1
Minority women		1,907	241,169	607	204,217	1,661	21,864	3	1	3	1
Hispanic		2,992	349,024	979	279,512	2,771	34,466	1	1	3	1
Black		2,106	187,063	620	152,601	1,452	20,005	-	-	-	-
American Indian and Alaska Native		86	7,915	32	6,373	63	792	10	11	13	13
Asian and Pacific Islander		2,421	428,044	790	327,452	2,111	24,914	2	1	3	1
Eating and drinking places	58	52,202	6,324,180	30,586	5,620,474	186,687	1,198,209	-	-	1	-
Minority men		36,015	4,622,949	21,451	4,106,449	134,485	865,079	1	-	1	-
Minority women		16,187	1,701,231	9,135	1,514,025	52,202	333,130	1	1	1	1
Hispanic		14,003	1,645,412	7,872	1,449,268	50,662	330,987	1	1	1	1
Black		11,834	1,084,468	4,747	918,321	32,343	204,696	-	-	-	-
American Indian and Alaska Native		464	35,251	286	29,492	1,083	6,224	8	7	9	6
Asian and Pacific Islander		26,280	3,599,887	17,887	3,258,630	103,743	663,861	-	-	1	1
Miscellaneous retail	59	98,211	5,019,565	13,811	3,338,771	34,976	325,832	-	1	1	1
Minority men		51,681	3,603,341	9,133	2,456,622	24,423	227,163	1	1	1	1
Minority women		46,530	1,416,224	4,678	882,149	10,553	98,669	1	1	2	1
Hispanic		31,735	1,266,957	3,818	801,052	9,365	93,360	1	1	3	1
Black		34,870	1,086,160	3,359	719,791	7,778	80,111	-	-	-	-

[Continued]

★ 794 ★

Minority-Owned Firms: Retail Trade

[Continued]

Industry group and minority	SIC code	All firms: Firms (number) A	All firms: Sales and receipts ($1,000) B	Firms with paid employees: Firms (number) C	Firms with paid employees: Sales and receipts ($1,000) D	Firms with paid employees: Employees (number) E	Firms with paid employees: Annual payroll ($1,000) F	Relative standard error of estimate % for column A	B	C	D
American Indian and Alaska Native		1,799	85,377	241	60,144	425	5,240	5	4	10	3
Asian and Pacific Islander		30,507	2,614,007	6,489	1,779,200	17,632	149,371	1	1	2	1

Source: 1987 Economic Censuses, Survey of Minority-Owned Business Enterprises: Summary, U.S. Department of Commerce, Bureau of the Census, 1991, pp. 14-15. *Notes:* A dash (-) represents zero. Details may not add to total because of rounding and because a firm may be included in more than one minority group. (D) stands for data withheld to avoid disclosure of competitive information.

★ 795 ★

Minority-Owned Firms

Minority-Owned Firms: Services

Detail may not add to total because of rounding and because a firm may be included in more than one minority group. This table is based on the 1972 SIC system.

Industry group and minority	All firms: Firms (number) A	All firms: Sales and receipts ($1,000) B	Firms with paid employees: Firms (number) C	Firms with paid employees: Sales and receipts ($1,000) D	Firms with paid employees: Employees (number) E	Firms with paid employees: Annual payroll ($1,000) F	Relative standard error of estimate (%) for column A	B	C	D
Services	562,559	21,990,719	98,110	14,577,051	280,181	3,384,329	-	-	-	-
Minority men	337,630	16,279,824	71,314	11,152,064	205,861	2,520,901	-	-	-	-
Minority women	224,929	5,710,895	26,796	3,424,987	74,320	863,428	-	-	1	-
Hispanic	184,372	6,031,406	29,750	3,774,117	74,427	941,588	-	-	1	1
Men	118,156	4,793,242	22,738	3,109,238	57,664	754,106	1	1	1	1
Women	66,216	1,238,164	7,012	664,879	16,763	187,482	1	1	2	1
Black	209,547	6,120,084	29,963	3,888,212	89,700	1,077,437	-	-	-	-
Men	111,576	3,862,054	19,783	2,521,990	58,855	702,653	-	-	-	-
Women	97,971	2,258,030	10,180	1,366,222	30,845	374,784	-	-	-	-
American Indian and Alaska Native	7,604	178,165	1,073	108,396	2,297	24,390	2	2	5	2
Men	4,422	121,878	744	76,074	1,409	16,262	3	3	6	3
Women	3,182	56,287	329	32,322	888	8,128	4	4	9	4
Asian and Pacific Islander	165,342	9,880,868	38,176	6,962,276	117,946	1,387,293	-	-	1	-
Men	106,053	7,653,846	28,671	5,551,402	90,947	1,080,001	1	-	1	-
Women	59,289	2,227,022	9,505	1,410,874	26,999	307,292	1	1	2	1
Hotels and other lodging places	10,499	1,588,435	5,345	1,346,880	32,345	234,823	1	-	1	1
Minority men	7,498	1,245,764	4,134	1,060,050	25,073	180,130	1	1	1	1
Minority women	3,001	342,671	1,211	286,830	7,272	54,693	2	1	2	1
Hispanic	973	112,551	315	92,996	2,284	23,342	4	1	6	1
Black	1,734	128,256	553	94,028	2,698	22,334	-	-	-	-
American Indian and Alaska Native	102	5,734	34	5,090	98	788	15	3	10	3
Asian and Pacific Islander	7,809	1,366,121	4,507	1,177,169	27,682	192,406	1	1	1	1
Personal services	138,765	3,162,616	20,732	1,669,271	46,675	427,226	-	1	1	1
Minority men	68,771	1,927,822	12,067	1,097,981	29,342	270,185	1	1	1	1
Minority women	69,994	1,234,794	8,665	571,290	17,333	157,041	1	1	2	1
Hispanic	44,872	893,064	6,111	430,645	13,688	129,379	1	1	2	2
Black	56,772	959,696	6,246	427,283	12,108	109,773	-	-	-	-
American Indian and Alaska Native	1,719	26,547	223	14,128	519	4,388	5	6	11	9
Asian and Pacific Islander	36,392	1,318,400	8,304	819,467	21,249	190,277	1	1	2	1

[Continued]

★ 795 ★

Minority-Owned Firms: Services

[Continued]

Industry group and minority	All firms		Firms with paid employees				Relative standard error of estimate (%) for column			
	Firms (number) A	Sales and receipts ($1,000) B	Firms (number) C	Sales and receipts ($1,000) D	Employees (number) E	Annual payroll ($1,000) F	A	B	C	D
Business services	166,666	4,510,917	19,755	2,592,828	63,552	799,677	-	-	1	1
Minority men	107,207	3,232,646	14,513	1,832,968	46,225	574,717	-	1	1	1
Minority women	59,459	1,278,271	5,242	759,860	17,327	224,960	1	1	2	1
Hispanic	59,948	1,419,790	6,716	747,056	18,979	235,949	1	1	2	1
Black	59,177	1,570,161	8,021	1,047,390	32,636	373,456	-	-	-	-
American Indian and Alaska Native	2,532	48,601	319	23,585	545	6,238	5	5	12	5
Asian and Pacific Islander	46,066	1,523,290	4,847	814,432	12,913	202,894	1	1	3	1
Auto repair, services, and garages	32,861	1,765,545	9,328	1,302,474	19,942	270,583	-	1	1	1
Minority men	30,814	1,580,288	8,503	1,142,551	17,218	230,066	1	1	1	1
Minority women	2,047	185,257	825	159,923	2,724	40,517	3	2	4	2
Hispanic	15,824	836,738	4,522	622,052	9,749	139,178	1	1	2	1
Black	11,801	426,584	2,767	271,836	4,543	57,223	-	-	-	-
American Indian and Alaska Native	538	20,704	134	14,111	226	2,710	8	7	11	8
Asian and Pacific Islander	5,072	499,491	2,022	405,607	5,592	74,176	2	1	2	1
Miscellaneous repair services	17,321	623,735	3,431	394,622	6,736	89,471	1	1	2	1
Minority men	15,834	557,412	3,050	344,546	5,839	76,923	1	1	3	1
Minority women	1,487	66,323	381	50,076	897	12,548	4	3	6	3
Hispanic	8,337	302,456	1,837	193,150	3,130	43,812	1	2	4	2
Black	5,197	154,027	895	101,433	1,827	25,996	-	-	-	-
American Indian and Alaska Native	300	11,105	53	8,023	103	1,144	9	5	12	6
Asian and Pacific Islander	3,601	163,272	685	97,614	1,786	19,569	2	2	5	2
Motion pictures	1,939	109,396	263	76,501	882	14,296	2	1	4	1
Minority men	1,371	78,202	188	52,916	712	9,050	2	1	5	1
Minority women	568	31,194	75	23,585	170	5,246	5	2	7	1
Hispanic	694	24,880	107	14,278	344	2,877	3	3	7	2
Black	733	61,911	72	48,867	358	9,006	-	-	-	-
American Indian and Alaska Native	34	1,691	5	(D)	(D)	(D)	20	9	-	(D)
Asian and Pacific Islander	505	22,730	82	(D)	(D)	(D)	5	4	10	(D)
Amusement and recreation services	28,430	858,082	2,256	484,502	5,451	99,085	1	1	3	1
Minority men	21,653	619,237	1,729	316,275	4,079	72,178	1	1	3	1
Minority women	6,777	238,845	527	168,227	1,372	26,907	2	1	6	-
Hispanic	9,528	203,812	800	89,891	1,518	19,948	2	3	8	4
Black	13,250	502,847	965	316,336	2,021	62,094	-	-	-	-
American Indian and Alaska Native	556	15,698	57	11,602	212	1,663	8	3	23	2
Asian and Pacific Islander	5,307	142,451	467	70,229	1,736	16,188	2	3	7	3
Health services	80,753	6,399,878	23,508	4,727,372	66,568	889,621	-	-	1	1
Minority men	42,337	5,006,101	18,591	3,912,273	53,320	719,672	1	1	1	1
Minority women	38,416	1,393,777	4,917	815,099	13,248	169,949	1	1	2	1
Hispanic	16,322	1,326,215	5,089	999,789	13,982	197,965	1	1	2	1
Black	30,026	1,350,606	5,251	924,048	18,078	216,304	-	-	-	-
American Indian and Alaska Native	488	20,840	91	13,417	205	2,293	10	11	18	11
Asian and Pacific Islander	34,590	3,754,983	13,292	2,830,922	34,917	481,271	1	1	1	1
Legal services	10,887	809,756	3,572	608,052	7,121	120,514	1	1	1	1
Minority men	7,787	653,896	2,890	501,305	5,664	99,312	1	1	1	1
Minority women	3,100	155,860	682	106,747	1,457	21,202	2	1	3	2
Hispanic	3,690	286,713	1,356	216,577	2,545	41,187	1	1	2	2
Black	4,920	336,218	1,541	253,249	3,040	51,576	-	-	-	-
American Indian and Alaska Native	169	11,153	52	8,400	105	1,916	8	4	10	2
Asian and Pacific Islander	2,186	179,585	635	131,954	1,406	26,223	2	1	3	2

[Continued]

★ 795 ★

Minority-Owned Firms: Services

[Continued]

Industry group and minority	All firms		Firms with paid employees				Relative standard error of estimate (%) for column			
	Firms (number) A	Sales and receipts ($1,000) B	Firms (number) C	Sales and receipts ($1,000) D	Employees (number) E	Annual payroll ($1,000) F	A	B	C	D
Educational services	10,124	173,474	574	104,556	2,764	34,429	1	1	3	-
Minority men	4,436	70,581	280	32,864	875	9,822	2	2	5	1
Minority women	5,688	102,893	294	71,692	1,889	24,607	2	1	5	-
Hispanic	2,797	54,119	157	36,409	975	10,684	2	1	6	1
Black	3,561	64,545	216	43,466	1,120	16,839	-	-	-	-
American Indian and Alaska Native	210	1,051	3	214	4	38	12	7	-	-
Asian and Pacific Islander	3,662	54,389	199	24,526	669	6,892	2	2	8	1
Social services	26,356	410,281	3,480	244,196	10,095	77,449	1	1	1	1
Minority men	4,121	128,058	844	95,455	3,916	31,745	3	1	3	1
Minority women	22,235	282,223	2,636	148,741	6,179	45,704	1	1	2	1
Hispanic	8,840	100,321	697	45,344	1,886	13,215	2	2	7	4
Black	13,210	224,137	2,229	139,407	6,005	47,262	-	-	-	-
American Indian and Alaska Native	451	3,842	28	1,413	85	545	10	8	-	-
Asian and Pacific Islander	4,038	84,553	549	59,699	2,225	17,039	3	2	4	1
Museums, botanical, zoological gardens	-	-	-	-	-	-	-	-	-	-
Minority men	-	-	-	-	-	-	-	-	-	-
Minority women	-	-	-	-	-	-	-	-	-	-
Hispanic	-	-	-	-	-	-	-	-	-	-
Black	-	-	-	-	-	-	-	-	-	-
American Indian and Alaska Native	-	-	-	-	-	-	-	-	-	-
Asian and Pacific Islander	-	-	-	-	-	-	-	-	-	-
Miscellaneous services	37,958	1,576,604	5,866	1,025,797	18,050	327,155	1	1	2	1
Minority men	25,801	1,179,817	4,525	762,880	13,598	247,101	1	1	2	1
Minority women	12,157	398,787	1,341	262,917	4,452	80,054	2	1	4	1
Hispanic	12,547	470,747	2,043	285,930	5,347	84,052	1	1	3	1
Black	9,166	341,096	1,207	220,869	5,266	85,574	-	-	-	-
American Indian and Alaska Native	505	11,199	74	(D)	(D)	(D)	9	8	21	(D)
Asian and Pacific Islander	16,114	771,603	2,587	(D)	(D)	(D)	1	1	3	(D)

Source: 1987 Economic Censuses, Survey of Minority-Owned Business Enterprises: Summary, U.S. Department of Commerce, Bureau of the Census, 1991, pp. 16-17. *Note:* A dash (-) represents zero.

★ 796 ★

Minority-Owned Firms

Minority-Owned Firms: Transportation and Utilities

Data are shown for 1987. Trade groups are based on the 1972 Standard Industrial Classification (SIC) system.

Industry group and minority	All firms		Firms with paid employees				Relative standard error of estimate % for column			
	Firms (number) A	Sales and receipts ($1,000) B	Firms (number) C	Sales and receipts ($1,000) D	Employees (number) E	Annual payroll ($1,000) F	A	B	C	D
Transportation and public utilities	76,229	3,665,682	10,223	1,955,168	20,795	335,242	-	-	1	-
Minority men	68,052	3,052,314	8,710	1,482,705	15,900	262,551	-	-	1	1
Minority women	8,177	613,368	1,513	472,463	4,895	72,691	2	1	3	1
Hispanic	26,955	1,380,981	3,989	725,484	8,006	135,592	1	1	3	1

[Continued]

★ 796 ★

Minority-Owned Firms: Transportation and Utilities

[Continued]

Industry group and minority	All firms: Firms (number) A	All firms: Sales and receipts ($1,000) B	Firms with paid employees: Firms (number) C	Firms with paid employees: Sales and receipts ($1,000) D	Firms with paid employees: Employees (number) E	Firms with paid employees: Annual payroll ($1,000) F	Relative standard error of estimate % for column A	B	C	D
Men	24,230	1,207,449	3,459	597,628	6,437	111,669	1	1	3	1
Women	2,725	173,532	530	127,856	1,569	23,923	4	2	7	2
Black	36,958	1,573,342	4,987	786,091	9,910	153,959	-	-	-	-
Men	33,165	1,279,210	4,295	554,535	7,305	115,165	-	-	-	-
Women	3,793	294,132	692	231,556	2,605	38,794	-	-	-	-
American Indian and Alaska Native	917	44,286	161	22,979	280	3,990	5	4	9	4
Men	764	38,602	136	19,981	241	3,490	5	4	10	4
Women	153	5,684	25	2,998	39	500	12	8	15	2
Asian and Pacific Islander	11,940	691,480	1,154	432,638	2,750	45,784	1	1	3	1
Men	10,359	545,809	878	318,035	2,032	35,732	1	1	4	1
Women	1,581	145,671	276	114,603	718	10,052	4	2	6	1
Local and interurban passenger transit	22,037	454,980	1,106	86,151	2,722	23,571	1	1	3	1
Minority men	20,072	411,789	863	68,298	2,109	18,678	1	1	3	1
Minority women	1,965	43,191	243	17,853	613	4,893	3	3	6	3
Hispanic	4,522	105,763	260	20,340	744	6,188	2	2	10	3
Black	11,566	218,209	700	53,266	1,746	14,621	-	-	-	-
American Indian and Alaska Native	95	2,941	13	1,357	40	265	13	12	26	-
Asian and Pacific Islander	6,049	132,832	159	12,092	235	2,770	2	2	15	5
Trucking and warehousing	39,556	2,060,753	7,044	966,322	10,952	196,536	-	1	2	1
Minority men	37,005	1,842,679	6,372	811,677	8,818	161,792	-	1	2	1
Minority women	2,551	218,074	672	154,645	2,134	36,744	3	2	5	1
Hispanic	17,304	906,583	2,936	426,794	4,499	85,692	1	1	4	2
Black	19,663	1,010,229	3,632	465,617	5,504	98,309	-	-	-	-
American Indian and Alaska Native	590	32,189	125	15,359	185	2,900	6	5	11	6
Asian and Pacific Islander	2,214	121,853	377	61,832	786	12,228	3	2	6	3
Water transportation	339	37,000	89	31,814	572	7,820	1	-	-	-
Minority men	286	30,222	69	26,035	512	7,020	1	-	-	-
Minority women	53	6,778	20	5,779	60	800	7	1	-	-
Hispanic	156	19,598	40	17,539	327	4,223	3	-	-	-
Black	83	9,042	26	7,687	160	2,307	-	-	-	-
American Indian and Alaska Native	12	695	3	452	10	127	-	-	-	-
Asian and Pacific Islander	91	7,836	22	6,282	77	1,198	-	-	-	-
Transportation by air	462	29,332	51	15,919	239	4,279	3	-	-	-
Minority men	395	16,523	39	7,404	100	1,697	3	-	-	-
Minority women	67	12,809	12	8,515	139	2,582	5	-	-	-
Hispanic	222	10,895	23	4,022	67	1,116	2	-	-	-
Black	117	11,485	12	7,860	121	2,447	-	-	-	-
American Indian and Alaska Native	30	865	6	414	4	63	31	6	-	-
Asian and Pacific Islander	101	6,154	10	3,623	47	653	8	-	-	-

[Continued]

★ 796 ★

Minority-Owned Firms: Transportation and Utilities

[Continued]

Industry group and minority	All firms		Firms with paid employees				Relative standard error of estimate % for column			
	Firms (number) A	Sales and receipts ($1,000) B	Firms (number) C	Sales and receipts ($1,000) D	Employees (number) E	Annual payroll ($1,000) F	A	B	C	D
Pipe lines, except natural gas	1	(D)	-	-	-	-	-	(D)	-	-
Minority men	1	(D)	-	-	-	-	-	(D)	-	-
Minority women	-	-	-	-	-	-	-	-	-	-
Hispanic	-	-	-	-	-	-	-	-	-	-
Black	-	-	-	-	-	-	-	-	-	-
American Indian and Alaska Native	-	-	-	-	-	-	-	-	-	-
Asian and Pacific Islander	1	(D)	-	-	-	-	-	(D)	-	-
Transportation services	10,665	895,539	1,479	706,588	4,018	62,172	1	-	2	-
Minority men	7,757	587,323	990	439,876	2,513	41,317	1	1	3	1
Minority women	2,908	308,216	489	266,712	1,505	20,855	2	1	3	1
Hispanic	3,617	284,684	542	219,512	1,683	25,970	2	1	4	1
Black	4,053	222,757	405	166,710	920	14,303	-	-	-	-
American Indian and Alaska Native	134	6,296	8	4,711	34	494	13	3	-	-
Asian and Pacific Islander	2,959	387,708	536	320,159	1,419	22,289	2	1	4	1
Communication	2,062	150,568	274	125,340	1,992	35,207	2	1	7	-
Minority men	1,537	130,548	219	109,567	1,583	28,928	2	1	8	-
Minority women	525	20,020	55	15,773	409	6,279	5	2	13	-
Hispanic	756	38,852	115	28,851	533	10,451	4	2	16	1
Black	896	81,785	118	71,953	1,334	20,779	-	-	-	-
American Indian and Alaska Native	36	682	2	(D)	(D)	(D)	9	13	-	(D)
Asian and Pacific Islander	385	32,355	40	(D)	(D)	(D)	5	1	5	(D)
Electric, gas, and sanitary services	1,107	(D)	180	23,034	300	3,657	2	(D)	5	1
Minority men	999	(D)	158	19,848	265	3,119	2	(D)	5	2
Minority women	108	4,280	22	3,186	35	538	6	4	16	5
Hispanic	378	14,606	73	8,426	153	1,952	4	3	11	4
Black	580	19,835	94	12,998	125	1,466	-	-	-	-
American Indian and Alaska Native	20	618	4	(D)	(D)	(D)	-	-	-	(D)
Asian and Pacific Islander	140	(D)	10	(D)	(D)	(D)	10	(D)	-	(D)

Source: 1987 Economic Censuses, Survey of Minority-Owned Business Enterprises: Summary, U.S. Department of Commerce, Bureau of the Census, 1991, p. 13. *Notes:* A dash (-) represents zero. Details may not add to total because of rounding and because a firm may be included in more than one minority group. (D) stands for data withheld to avoid disclosure of competitive information.

★ 797 ★

Minority-Owned Firms

Minority-Owned Firms: Wholesale Trade

Data are shown for 1987. Trade groups are based on the 1972 Standard Industrial Classification (SIC) system.

Industry group and minority	All firms		Firms with paid employees				Relative standard error of estimate % for column			
	Firms (Number) A	Sales and receipts ($1,000) B	Firms (Number) C	Sales and receipts ($1,000) D	Employees (Number) E	Annual payroll ($1,000) F	A	B	C	D
Wholesale trade	26,432	7,950,013	6,216	6,216	6,489,777	24,455	1	-	1	-
Minority men	20,685	6,087,858	4,812	4,844,929	17,588	323,063	1	-	1	-
Minority women	5,747	1,862,155	1,404	1,644,845	6,867	127,794	2	-	2	-
Hispanic	10,154	2,445,416	2,309	1,991,736	9,119	157,537	1	-	2	-
Men	8,292	2,011,404	1,888	1,616,146	7,204	123,920	1	-	2	-
Women	1,862	434,012	421	375,590	1,915	33,617	4	1	4	1
Black	5,519	1,327,479	1,256	1,169,608	6,156	115,944	-	-	-	-
Men	4,016	821,228	850	702,267	3,589	64,940	-	-	-	-
Women	1,503	506,251	406	467,341	2,567	51,004	-	-	-	-
American Indian and Alaska Native	360	36,058	93	26,490	192	2,755	8	3	16	2
Men	292	29,709	75	20,846	159	2,283	10	3	20	3
Women	68	6,349	18	5,644	33	472	16	2	19	1
Asian and Pacific Islander	10,654	4,188,852	2,622	3,337,014	9,192	177,221	1	-	2	-
Men	8,259	3,251,019	2,031	2,524,919	6,727	133,214	1	-	2	-
Women	2,395	937,833	591	812,095	2,465	44,007	4	1	3	1
Wholesale trade - durable goods	13,219	3,463,935	3,281	2,784,804	11,909	231,471	1	-	2	-
Minority men	10,513	2,673,962	2,519	2,100,024	8,764	169,669	1	-	2	-
Minority women	2,706	789,973	762	684,780	3,145	61,802	3	1	3	1
Hispanic	5,080	1,056,969	1,218	851,385	4,744	84,530	1	1	2	1
Black	2,792	628,729	731	559,469	3,309	63,196	-	-	-	-
American Indian and Alaska Native	247	24,294	60	18,867	158	2,251	11	3	20	2
Asian and Pacific Islander	5,238	1,775,057	1,305	1,367,633	3,789	82,773	2	1	3	1
Wholesale trade - nondurable goods	13,213	4,486,078	2,935	3,704,973	12,546	219,386	1	-	1	-
Minority men	10,172	3,413,896	2,293	2,744,905	8,824	153,394	1	-	2	-
Minority women	3,041	1,072,182	642	960,068	3,722	65,992	2	1	2	1
Hispanic	5,074	1,388,447	1,091	1,140,351	4,375	73,007	1	1	3	-
Black	2,727	698,750	525	610,139	2,847	52,748	-	-	-	-
American Indian and Alaska Native	113	11,764	33	7,623	34	504	12	5	27	6
Asian and Pacific Islander	5,416	2,413,795	1,317	1,969,381	5,403	94,448	1	-	2	-

Source: *1987 Economic Censuses, Survey of Minority-Owned Business Enterprises: Summary,* U.S. Department of Commerce, Bureau of the Census, 1991, pp. 13- 14. *Note:* A dash (-) represents zero.

★ 798 ★

Minority-Owned Firms

Minority-Owned Firms: Unclassified Firms

Data are shown for 1987.

Industry group and minority	All firms: Firms (number) A	All firms: Sales and receipts ($1,000) B	Firms with paid employees: Firms (number) C	Firms with paid employees: Sales and receipts ($1,000) D	Firms with paid employees: Employees (number) E	Firms with paid employees: Annual payroll ($1,000) F	Relative standard error of estimate % for column: A	B	C	D
Industries not classified	69,942	2,230,113	6,869	745,873	5,754	119,194	-	1	2	2
Minority men	48,270	1,747,385	5,445	622,165	4,607	100,098	1	1	2	2
Minority women	21,672	482,728	1,424	123,708	1,147	19,096	1	2	4	4
Hispanic	25,075	752,271	2,396	255,830	2,024	47,794	1	2	4	3
Men	18,581	623,877	2,057	224,197	1,764	42,807	1	2	5	4
Women	6,494	128,394	339	31,633	260	4,987	3	4	12	12
Black	26,518	579,749	2,399	174,289	1,643	33,845	-	-	-	-
Men	17,100	426,851	1,833	143,056	1,310	27,867	-	-	-	-
Women	9,418	152,898	566	31,233	333	5,978	-	-	-	-
American Indian and Alaska Native	1,285	36,637	142	14,001	119	2,353	5	9	18	12
Men	964	31,972	118	(D)	(D)	(D)	7	10	19	(D)
Women	321	4,665	24	(D)	(D)	(D)	12	11	46	(D)
Asian and Pacific Islander	17,739	894,509	1,999	306,801	2,028	36,011	1	1	4	3
Men	12,125	689,416	1,500	(D)	(D)	(D)	2	2	5	(D)
Women	5,614	205,093	499	(D)	(D)	(D)	3	3	9	(D)

Source: *1987 Economic Censuses, Survey of Minority-Owned Business Enterprises: Summary*, U.S. Department of Commerce, Bureau of the Census, 1991, p. 17. *Notes:* A dash (-) represents zero. Details may not add to total because of rounding and because a firm may be included in more than one minority group. (D) stands for data withheld to avoid disclosure of competitive information.

Puerto Rico

★ 799 ★

Establishments Engaged in Retail Trade in Puerto Rico, by Type of Business and Selected Characteristics, 1987

This table is based on the 1972 Standard Industrial Classification (SIC) code. Data are based on samples.

Type of business	SIC code	All establishments: Number	All establishments: Sales ($1,000)	All establishments: Proprietors and partners (number)	All establishments: Unpaid family workers (number)	Establishments with payroll: Number	Establishments with payroll: Sales ($1,000)	Establishments with payroll: Annual payroll ($1,000)	Establishments with payroll: First quarter payroll ($1,000)	Establishments with payroll: Paid employees for pay period including Mar. 12 (number)
RETAIL TRADE		31,821	8,590,872	25,310	12,025	11,451	8,143,608	704,083	166,049	88,530
Building materials and garden supplies	52	1,449	525,752	1,011	409	766	507,780	43,890	9,970	4,866
Lumber and other building materials	521	230	165,252	159	30	117	163,568	12,324	2,653	1,341
Paint, glass, and wall paper stores	523	119	28,047	62	31	77	27,165	2,904	676	240
Hardware stores	525	917	323,646	623	312	541	309,234	27,737	6,429	3,139

[Continued]

★ 799 ★

Establishments Engaged in Retail Trade in Puerto Rico, by Type of Business and Selected Characteristics, 1987

[Continued]

Type of business	SIC code	All establishments				Establishments with payroll				
		Number	Sales ($1,000)	Proprietors and partners (number)	Unpaid family workers (number)	Number	Sales ($1,000)	Annual payroll ($1,000)	First quarter payroll ($1,000)	Paid employees for pay period including Mar. 12 (number)
Retail nurseries and garden stores	526	180	(D)	(D)	(D)	31	7,813	925	212	146
Mobile home dealers	527	3	(D)	(D)	(D)	-	-	-	-	-
General merchandise stores	53	651	887,724	411	342	878,167	100,920	23,949	11,222	
Department stores[1]	531	40	557,775	-	-	40	557,775	67,630	16,197	6,925
Variety stores	533	158	92,001	104	96	86	90,104	12,528	2,811	1,517
Miscellaneous general merchandise stores	539	453	237,948	307	161	216	230,288	20,762	4,941	2,780
Food stores	54	9,847	2,150,487	9,224	4,687	1,696	1,965,601	123,911	30,825	17,265
Grocery stores	541	7,005	1,997,568	6,492	3,576	1,249	1,843,471	111,436	27,724	15,114
Grocery stores	5411 pt.	6,288	464,134	6,012	3,182	827	323,480	20,293	5,462	2,271
Supermarkets	5411 pt.	628	1,307,934	413	340	363	1,295,768	80,136	19,682	11,361
Cash and carry	5411 pt.	89	225,500	67	54	59	224,223	11,007	2,580	1,482
Meat and fish markets	542	289	36,615	301	83	87	29,999	1,832	432	258
Fruit and vegetable markets	543	383	9,622	375	78	29	5,866	561	115	90
Candy, nut, and confectionery stores	544	933	13,448	919	383	30	8,691	555	135	149
Dairy products stores	545	27	1,906	24	12	4	1,623	111	23	16
Retail bakeries	546	512	71,400	417	257	243	64,601	8,225	2,049	1,418
Miscellaneous food stores	549	698	19,928	696	298	54	11,350	1,191	347	220
Automotive dealers, excluding gasoline service stations	55, exc. 554	1,221	1,254,260	606	235	867	1,239,237	65,932	14,987	6,244
New and used car dealers	551	256	929,262	14	3	249	928,042	38,731	8,686	3,074
Used car dealers	552	62	44,802	25	11	43	44,525	1,402	334	162
Auto and home supply stores	553	863	262,079	546	219	551	249,557	24,729	5,717	2,915
Boat dealers	555	17	10,041	6	2	13	9,997	720	163	53
Recreational vehicle dealers	556	20	6,057	14	-	8	5,097	276	62	21
Automotive dealers, n.e.c.	559	3	2,019	1	-	3	2,019	74	25	19
Gasoline service stations	554	1,219	585,991	789	370	984	559,198	22,910	5,538	3,244
Apparel and accessory stores	56	2,630	841,250	1,378	491	1,704	817,040	96,017	21,453	13,166
Men's and boys' clothing stores	561	411	145,096	214	58	308	141,519	15,767	3,156	1,881
Women's clothing stores	562	640	244,847	297	97	430	238,539	26,380	6,228	4,444
Women's accessory and specialty stores	563	131	11,390	107	43	51	9,456	1,056	249	190
Children's and infants' wear stores	564	105	9,894	72	29	50	8,634	865	208	130
Family clothing stores	565	551	161,444	314	136	388	156,034	19,377	4,240	2,515
Shoe stores	566	507	240,308	119	56	423	238,191	30,513	6,894	3,819
Miscellaneous apparel and accessory stores	569	285	28,271	255	72	54	24,667	2,059	478	187
Furniture and homefurnishings stores	57	1,224	458,416	661	317	802	445,021	39,718	9,241	4,470
Furniture and homefurnishings stores	571	841	349,353	422	173	598	341,317	31,256	7,246	3,564
Furniture stores	5712	627	314,764	262	104	528	309,214	27,740	6,464	3,219
Floor covering stores	5713	28	14,777	5	-	23	14,717	1,639	383	131
Drapery and upholstery stores	5714	82	6,450	70	42	12	5,119	587	133	94
Miscellaneous homefurnishings stores	5719	104	13,362	85	27	35	12,267	1,290	266	120
Household appliance stores	572	108	36,260	56	30	80	35,878	3,337	800	385
Radio, television, and computer stores	573	275	72,803	183	114	124	67,826	5,125	1,195	521
Radio, television, and electronic stores	5731	85	17,645	61	34	36	16,395	1,344	293	145
Computer and software stores	5734	47	27,944	23	8	31	27,475	1,800	390	175
Record and prerecorded tape stores	5735	110	20,586	72	46	48	18,687	1,362	343	139
Musical instrument stores	5736	33	6,628	27	26	9	5,269	619	169	62
Eating and drinking places	58	8,238	888,790	7,256	3,446	2,007	795,052	106,480	25,860	15,509
Eating places	5812	3,213	796,251	2,231	1,368	1,907	774,778	104,194	25,300	15,146
Cafeteria	5812 pt.	509	71,285	464	183	509	71,285	13,389	3,722	2,085
Restaurant	5812 pt.	907	440,363	307	258	788	436,445	42,590	10,609	4,795
Refreshment	5812 pt.	833	32,919	818	567	169	21,981	3,702	865	619
Fast food	5812 pt.	575	236,498	266	155	368	233,120	42,415	9,5887	7,169
Other eating places	5812 pt.	389	15,186	376	205	73	11,947	2,098	517	478

[Continued]

★ 799 ★

Establishments Engaged in Retail Trade in Puerto Rico, by Type of Business and Selected Characteristics, 1987

[Continued]

Type of business	SIC code	All establishments				Establishments with payroll				
		Number	Sales ($1,000)	Proprietors and partners (number)	Unpaid family workers (number)	Number	Sales ($1,000)	Annual payroll ($1,000)	First quarter payroll ($1,000)	Paid employees for pay period including Mar. 12 (number)
Drinking places	5813	5,025	92,539	5,025	2,078	100	20,274	2,286	560	363
Drug stores and proprietary stores	591	844	396,508	464	192	711	389,332	40,377	9,896	4,641
Miscellaneous retail	59 ex. 591	4,498	601,694	3,510	1,621	1,572	547,180	63,928	14,330	7,903
Liquor stores	592	664	46,411	630	227	80	35,994	4,212	384	279
Used merchandise stores	593	88	2,503	87	111	4	428	56	14	11
Miscellaneous shopping goods stores	594	1,706	303,187	1,153	570	790	285,595	30,957	7,202	4,318
Sporting goods and bicycle shops	5941	212	37,598	149	70	91	35,353	3,379	468	420
Book stores	5942	144	35,634	83	64	69	33,658	3,150	687	332
Stationery stores	5943	287	43,574	230	124	90	40,953	3,540	858	397
Jewelry stores	5944	370	95,995	186	84	258	92,250	10,689	2,700	1,317
Hobby, toy, and game shops	5945	53	14,479	26	19	29	14,087	1,311	300	175
Camera and photographic supply store	5946	86	(D)	(D)	(D)	40	(D)	(D)	(D)	(D)
Gift, novelty, and souvenir shops	5947	329	25,242	276	116	101	21,632	2,680	747	380
Luggage and leather goods stores	5948	6	(D)	(D)	(D)	3	(D)	(D)	(D)	(D)
Sewing, needlework, and piece goods	5949	219	34,249	152	58	109	32,551	4,561	1,039	994
Nonstore retailers	596	33	13,056	18	3	29	12,932	1,274	305	213
Catalog and mail-order houses	5961	5	(D)	(D)	(D)	1	(D)	(D)	(D)	(D)
Merchandising machine operators	5962	6	(D)	(D)	-	6	(D)	(D)	(D)	(D)
Direct selling establishments	5963	22	6,397	12	1	22	6,397	682	160	152
Fuel dealers	598	147	19,425	125	29	87	17,876	1,939	473	238
Retail stores, n.e.c.	599	1,860	217,112	1,497	681	582	194,355	25,490	5,952	2,844
Florists	5992	532	16,507	502	247	98	12,129	1,796	458	299
Tobacco stores and stands	5993	9	189	8	-	1	(D)	(D)	(D)	(D)
News dealers and newsstands	5994	7	982	4	1	3	(D)	(D)	(D)	(D)
Optical goods stores	5995	138	34,689	58	25	105	34,176	8,137	2,075	580
Miscellaneous retail stores, n.e.c.	5999	1,174	164,745	925	408	375	147,048	15,477	3,399	1,956

Source: 1987 Economic Census of Outlying Areas, Puerto Rico: Geographic Area Statistics, Wholesale Trade, Retail Trade, Service Industries. U.S. Department of Commerce, Bureau of the Census, OA87-E-1, 1990, pp. 10-11. *Notes:* Pt. stands for part. A dash (-) represents zero. A (D) stands for data withheld to avoid disclosure of information; (n.e.c.) stands for not elsewhere classified. 1. Includes sales from catalog order desks.

★ 800 ★

Puerto Rico

Establishments Engaged in Wholesale Trade in Puerto Rico, by Type of Business and Selected Characteristics, 1987

This table is based on the 1972 Standard Industrial Classification (SIC) code. Data are based on samples.

Type of operation and kind of business	SIC code	Establishments (number)	Sales ($1,000)	End-of-year inventories ($1,000)	Operating expenses ($1,000)	Annual payroll ($1,000)	First quarter payroll ($1,000)	Paid employees for pay period including Mar. 12 (number)	Proprietors and partners (number)	Unpaid family workers (number)
Wholesale trade		2,596	9,591,048	1,465,137	1,828,736	546,807	130,578	37,655	342	139
Merchant wholesalers		2,302	7,804,565	1,301,081	1,505,735	425,569	99,924	30,852	322	132
Other operating types		294	1,786,483	164,056	323,001	121,238	30,654	6,803	20	7
Durable goods	50	1,301	3,582,760	741,157	770,087	246,804	57,389	16,178	148	44
Motor vehicles, parts, and supplies	501	157	771,669	178,627	121,287	31,765	7,603	2,239	50	8
Furniture and homefurnishings	502	60	153,960	20,156	31,282	9,167	2,151	729	3	1
Lumber and construction materials	503	122	280,295	51,801	45,019	14,650	3,598	1,326	8	5
Professional and commercial equipment	504	257	658,879	131,696	164,522	68,126	16,322	3,748	19	3
Photographic equipment and supplies	5043	14	81,106	16,797	18,990	5,081	1,257	255	-	-
Office equipment	5044	91	194,548	46,637	52,856	22,133	5,230	1,334	8	2
Computers, peripherals, and software	5045	30	86,560	11,434	18,906	13,771	3,325	691	-	-
Commercial equipment, n.e.c.	5046	16	19,814	2,139	4,683	1,749	427	125	-	-
Medical and hospital equipment	5047	88	252,434	50,803	61,976	23,107	5,559	1,187	8	1
Ophthalmic goods	5048	3	(D)	(D)	(D)	(D)	(D)	(D)	(D)	-
Professional equipment, n.e.c.	5049	15	(D)	(D)	(D)	(D)	(D)	(D)	(D)	-
Metals and minerals, except petroleum	505	30	139,550	10,974	16,422	3,280	851	268	4	6
Electrical goods	506	168	453,224	95,184	110,244	37,906	8,333	1,843	12	4
Electrical apparatus and equipment	5063	75	172,390	24,635	33,402	13,675	3,098	859	5	1
Electrical appliances, televisions, and radios	5064	34	195,953	60,455	56,619	14,613	2,819	460	3	3
Electronic parts and equipment	5065	59	84,881	10,094	20,223	9,618	2,416	524	4	-
Hardware, plumbing, and heating equipment	507	129	262,468	60,844	67,705	18,357	4,208	1,409	15	5
Hardware	5072	69	134,544	29,657	32,481	9,984	2,373	816	13	3
Plumbing and hydronic heating supplies	5074	23	69,183	20,169	18,271	3,854	820	256	-	-
Warm air heating and air-conditioning	5075	9	17,173	4,639	4,828	1,079	233	54	-	-
Refrigeration equipment and supplies	5078	28	41,568	6,379	12,125	3,440	782	283	2	2
Machinery, equipment, and supplies	508	273	685,970	161,405	174,030	52,868	11,943	3,641	22	4
Construction and mining machinery	5082	24	93,813	19,257	16,219	6,873	1,486	412	1	-
Farm and garden machinery	5083	14	21,782	3,137	3,903	1,730	401	151	1	1
Industrial machinery and equipment	5084	109	147,789	32,876	41,146	13,531	3,186	1,012	8	1
Industrial supplies	5085	48	145,324	46,231	45,240	9,226	2,146	506	7	-
Service establishment equipment	5087	69	256,561	55,237	61,444	20,489	4,501	1,497	5	2
Transportation equipment and supplies	5088	9	20,701	4,667	6,078	1,019	223	63	-	-
Miscellaneous durable goods	509	105	176,745	30,470	39,576	10,685	2,380	975	15	8
Sporting and recreational goods	5091	9	16,672	3,258	4,482	1,075	247	97	1	1
Toys and hobby goods and supplies	5092	12	30,203	4,099	7,796	1,489	323	117	5	3
Scrap and waste materials	5093	19	32,705	3,680	6,949	1,908	399	160	2	2
Jewelry and precious stones	5094	43	57,318	7,567	8,616	3,906	820	346	7	2
Durable goods, n.e.c.	5099	22	39,847	11,866	11,733	2,307	591	255	-	-
Nondurable goods	51	1,295	6,008,288	723,980	1,058,649	300,003	73,189	21,477	194	95
Paper and paper products	511	58	218,254	38,717	56,524	14,818	3,527	769	10	3
Drugs, proprietaries, and sundries	512	122	821,309	162,455	244,207	75,297	19,850	3,646	8	3
Apparel, piece goods, and notions	513	168	216,877	39,122	43,000	15,567	3,729	1,408	25	3
Groceries and related products	514	410	2,286,339	261,865	358,453	93,987	22,546	8,308	59	25
Farm-product raw materials	515	17	52,271	4,575	9,659	3,375	813	215	6	3
Chemicals and allied products	516	98	171,224	32,688	41,061	41,082	3,544	950	3	4
Petroleum and petroleum products	517	95	855,161	47,920	68,580	18,129	4,050	907	3	1
Beer, wine, and distilled beverages	518	36	615,707	47,180	101,771	24,036	5,329	1,292	11	6
Miscellaneous nondurable goods	519	291	771,146	89,458	135,394	40,712	9,801	3,982	69	47
Farm supplies	5191	27	25,616	3,243	3,784	1,684	402	224	7	6

[Continued]

★ 800 ★

Establishments Engaged in Wholesale Trade in Puerto Rico, by Type of Business and Selected Characteristics, 1987

[Continued]

Type of operation and kind of business	SIC code	Establishments (number)	Sales ($1,000)	End-of-year inventories ($1,000)	Operating expenses ($1,000)	Annual payroll ($1,000)	First quarter payroll ($1,000)	Paid employees for pay period including Mar. 12 (number)	Proprietors and partners (number)	Unpaid family workers (number)
Books, periodicals, and newspapers	5192	50	51,583	9,387	11,842	5,593	1,320	469	1	1
Flowers and florists' supplies	5193	13	14,183	1,529	3,717	1,174	247	91	6	-
Tobacco and tobacco products	5194	5	(D)	(D)	(D)	(D)	(D)	(D)	(D)	(D)
Paints, varnishes, and supplies	5198	28	36,344	6,133	6,058	2,939	718	192	1	-
Nondurable goods, n.e.c.	5199	168	(D)	(D)	(D)	(D)	(D)	(D)	(D)	(D)

Source: 1987 Economic Census of Outlying Areas, Puerto Rico: Geographic Area Statistics, Wholesale Trade, Retail Trade, Service Industries. U.S. Department of Commerce, Bureau of the Census, OA87-E-1, 1990, p. 2. *Notes:* A dash (-) represents zero. A (D) stands for data withheld to avoid disclosure of information; (n.e.c.) stands for not elsewhere classified.

★ 801 ★

Puerto Rico

Establishments in Service Industries in Puerto Rico, by Type of Business and Selected Characteristics - I

This table is based on the 1972 Standard Industrial Classification (SIC) code. Data are based on a sample.

Type of business	SIC code	All establishments				Establishments with payroll				
		Number	Receipts ($1,000)	Proprietors and partners (number)	Unpaid family workers (number)	Number	Receipts ($1,000)	Annual payroll ($1,000)	First quarter payroll ($1,000)	Paid employees for pay period including Mar. 12 (number)
SERVICE INDUSTRIES[1]		27,670	2,123,328	9,349	2,374	4,774	1,939,234	545,481	132,043	50,757
Passenger transportation arrangement	472	339	69,790	166	112	210	59,511	8,265	1,922	715
Travel agencies	4724	303	63,587	140	87	200	53,966	7,154	1,657	615
Tour operators	4725	7	(D)	-	-	7	(D)	(D)	(D)	(D)
Passenger transport arrangement, n.e.c.	4729	29	(D)	(D)	(D)	3	(D)	(D)	(D)	(D)
Hotels and other lodging places	70, exc. 702, 704	242	328,537	149	53	139	327,491	96,150	22,591	7,660
Hotels and motels	701	235	328,228	144	51	135	327,200	96,090	22,576	7,646
Hotels	7011 pt.	197	317,190	131	48	97	316,162	92,433	21,680	7,128
100 guest rooms or more	7011 pt.	17	282,301	1	-	17	282,301	83,385	19,445	6,026
25 to 99 guest rooms	7011 pt.	69	29,954	33	6	50	29,840	8,091	2,001	921
Less than 25 guest rooms	7011 pt.	111	4,935	97	42	30	4,021	957	234	181
Motels and guest houses	7011 pt.	28	7,169	12	3	28	7,169	2,459	590	349
Tourist villas and paradores	7011 pt.	10	3,869	1	-	10	3,869	1,198	306	169
Camps and recreational vehicle parks	703	7	309	5	2	4	291	60	15	14
Personal services	72	2,894	128,982	2,632	520	733	108,195	28,422	6,561	3,665
Laundry, cleaning, and garment services	721	406	34,661	311	98	197	33,294	10,828	2,493	1,388
Power laundries, family and commercial	7211	58	8,519	30	10	48	8,462	3,023	708	552
Garment pressing and cleaners' agents	7212	93	4,956	81	50	57	4,610	1,443	315	224
Linen supply	7213	5	(D)	-	-	5	(D)	(D)	(D)	(D)
Coin-operated laundries and cleaning	7215	36	(D)	(D)	(D)	12	(D)	(D)	(D)	(D)
Drycleaning plants, except rug	7216	55	5,142	22	10	39	4,911	1,616	448	232
Carpet and upholstery cleaning	7217	53	1,013	43	3	12	833	214	51	28
Laundry and garment services, n.e.c.	7219	106	1,780	102	16	24	1,438	279	58	65
Photographic studios, portrait	722	70	8,929	39	11	40	8,295	1,557	408	211
Beauty shops	723	1,005	32,097	860	98	287	26,752	8,338	1,824	1,138

[Continued]

★ 801 ★

Establishments in Service Industries in Puerto Rico, by Type of Business and Selected Characteristics - I

[Continued]

Type of business	SIC code	All establishments				Establishments with payroll				
		Number	Receipts ($1,000)	Proprietors and partners (number)	Unpaid family workers (number)	Number	Receipts ($1,000)	Annual payroll ($1,000)	First quarter payroll ($1,000)	Paid employees for pay period including Mar. 12 (number)
Barber shops	724	655	4,921	766	45	30	1,372	512	124	85
Shoe repair and shoeshine parlors	725	126	2,253	113	29	21	1,516	338	86	64
Funeral service and crematories	726	183	31,958	121	80	107	28,196	4,630	1,130	526
Miscellaneous personal services	729	449	14,163	422	159	51	8,770	2,219	496	253
Tax return preparation services	7291	37	974	35	4	6	421	125	30	17
Miscellaneous personal services, n.e.c.	7299	412	13,189	387	155	45	8,349	2,094	466	236
Business services	73	1,401	642,353	679	198	874	624,219	218,873	50,398	24,788
Advertising	731	134	99,045	39	3	112	98,851	23,705	5,754	1,425
Advertising agencies	7311	90	87,611	15	3	83	87,513	21,424	5,171	1,184
Advertising, n.e.c.	7319	44	11,434	24	-	29	11,338	2,281	583	241
Credit reporting and collection	732	36	23,848	1	-	36	23,848	6,215	1,322	504
Adjustment and collection services	7322	26	7,920	1	-	26	7,920	2,632	476	228
Credit reporting services	7323	10	15,928	-	-	10	15,928	3,583	846	276
Mailing, reproduction, stenographic	733	138	15,091	110	24	41	14,225	2,392	531	191
Direct mail advertising services	7331	2	(D)	(D)	-	2	(D)	(D)	(D)	(D)
Photocopying and duplicating services	7334	20	1,743	12	7	10	1,610	318	75	37
Commercial photography	7335	61	2,128	57	8	7	1,786	425	120	11
Commercial art and graphic design	7336	41	10,234	29	9	16	9,884	1,396	280	117
Secretarial and court reporting	7338	14	(D)	(D)	-	6	(D)	(D)	(D)	(D)
Services to buildings	734	162	67,417	62	17	127	57,717	24,535	5,890	3,456
Disinfecting and pest control services	7342	68	17,573	41	4	36	7,882	2,488	659	301
Building maintenance services, n.e.c.	7349	94	49,844	21	13	91	49,835	22,047	5,231	3,155
Miscellaneous equipment rental and leasing	735	198	87,658	77	41	143	86,431	18,784	4,292	1,342
Medical equipment rental	7352	24	13,658	6	5	19	13,524	2,516	514	206
Heavy construction equipment rental	7353	115	54,433	44	33	85	53,710	12,066	2,828	706
Equipment rental and leasing, n.e.c.	7359	59	19,567	27	3	39	19,197	4,202	950	430
Personnel supply services	736	69	88,583	8	2	67	88,570	49,909	10,886	5,523
Employment agencies	7361	26	37,137	-	-	26	37,137	17,243	3,290	1,469
Help supply services	7363	43	51,446	8	2	41	51,433	32,666	7,596	4,054
Computer and data processing services	737	78	27,166	4	2	78	27,166	9,684	2,068	679
Computer programming services	7371	26	11,132	3,833	757	186				
Information retrieval services	7375	35	13,646	-	-	35	13,646	4,912	1,086	388
Computer rental and leasing	7377	17	2,388	-	-	17	2,388	939	225	105
Miscellaneous business services	738	586	233,545	378	109	270	227,411	83,649	19,655	11,668
Detective and armored car services	7381	84	79,904	5	3	84	79,904	37,896	9,342	5,845
Security systems services	7382	49	27,171	15	4	41	27,091	15,340	3,630	2,321
News syndicates	7383	2	(D)	-	-	2	(D)	9D)	(D)	(D)
Photofinishing laboratories	7384	53	(D)	(D)	(D)	9	(D)	(D)	(D)	(D)
Business services, n.e.c.	7389	398	120,338	309	71	134	115,164	28,999	6,385	3,372
Auto repair, services, and parking	75	3,005	180,435	2,681	651	665	152,264	21,212	5,101	2,654
Automotive rentals, no drivers	751	29	58,936	4	-	27	58,932	4,666	1,017	364
Passenger car rental	7514	21	16,033	4	-	19	16,029	2,186	455	201
Passenger car leasing	7515	8	42,903	-	-	8	42,903	2,480	562	163
Automobile parking	752	78	12,163	25	5	58	11,997	2,300	560	410
Automotive repair shops	753	2,591	96,033	2,364	629	542	71,637	13,125	3,218	1,689
Top and body repair and paint shops	7532	795	21,266	791	227	90	12,686	1,875	500	300

[Continued]

★ 801 ★

Establishments in Service Industries in Puerto Rico, by Type of Business and Selected Characteristics - I

[Continued]

Type of business	SIC code	All establishments				Establishments with payroll				
		Number	Receipts ($1,000)	Proprie-tors and partners (number)	Unpaid family workers (number)	Number	Receipts ($1,000)	Annual payroll ($1,000)	First quarter payroll ($1,000)	Paid employees for pay period including Mar. 12 (number)
Auto exhaust system repair shops	7533	193	10,330	121	28	95	7,710	1,600	399	216
Automotive glass replacement shops	7536	27	1,976	25	24	7	1,684	209	48	28
Automotive transmission repair shops	7537	179	3,554	167	13	28	2,483	485	119	69
General automotive repair shops	7538	69	4,976	-	-	69	4,976	1,244	321	119
Automotive repair shops, n.e.c.	7539	1,328	53,931	1,260	337	253	42,098	7,712	1,831	957
Automotive services, except repair	754	307	13,303	288	17	38	9,698	1,121	306	191
Car washes	7542	93	4,947	81	4	15	4,036	522	146	92
Automotive services, n.e.c.	7549	214	8,356	207	13	23	5,662	599	160	99

Source: 1987 Economic Census of Outlying Areas, Puerto Rico: Geographic Area Statistics, Wholesale Trade, Retail Trade, Service Industries. U.S. Department of Commerce, Bureau of the Census, OA87-E-1, pp. 26-27. *Notes:* A dash (-) represents zero. (D) stands for data withheld to avoid disclosure of information; (n.e.c.) stands for not elsewhere classified. 1. For establishments with payroll, data do not include horserace betting agencies.

★ 802 ★

Puerto Rico

Establishments in Service Industries in Puerto Rico, by Type of Business and Selected Characteristics - II

This table is based on the 1972 Standard Industrial Classification (SIC) code. Data are based on a sample.

Type of business	SIC code	All establishments				Establishments with payroll				
		Number	Receipts ($1,000)	Proprie-tors and partners (number)	Unpaid family workers (number)	Number	Receipts ($1,000)	Annual payroll ($1,000)	First quarter payroll ($1,000)	Paid employees for pay period including Mar. 12 (number)
Miscellaneous repair services	76	1,255	97,834	1,081	216	279	88,620	15,914	3,518	1,558
Electrical repair shops	762	589	58,279	493	75	164	54,286	9,651	2,119	973
Radio and television repair	7622	203	6,339	178	24	36	4,790	1,300	276	150
Refrigeration service and repair	7623	188	41,095	143	33	86	40,038	5,647	1,261	593
Electrical repair shops, n.e.c.	7629	198	10,845	172	18	42	9,458	2,704	582	230
Watch, clock, and jewelry repair	763	65	1,803	64	11	2	(D)	(D)	(D)	(D)
Reupholstery and furniture repair	764	178	1,871	169	32	17	(D)	(D)	(D)	(D)
Miscellaneous repair shops	769	423	35,881	355	98	96	32,939	5,815	1,304	534
Welding repair	7692	239	2,867	230	68	12	1,115	336	65	32
Armature rewinding shops	7694	16	1,922	12	7	11	1,722	452	452	104
Repair services, n.e.c.	7699	168	31,092	113	23	73	30,102	5,027	1,135	444
Motion pictures	78	381	46,694	334	228	97	41,603	6,074	1,375	563
Motion picture production and services	781	7	10,302	-	-	7	10,302	1,843	433	127
Motion picture distribution and services	782	26	16,124	14	-	13	16,038	1,729	315	72
Motion picture theatres	783	25	10,513	7	6	19	10,258	1,475	365	221
Video tape rental	784	323	9,755	313	222	58	5,005	1,027	262	143
Amusement and recreation services	79	16,280	256,543	385	166	307	174,261	42,892	16,803	1,694
Dance studios, schools, and halls	791	39	2,073	35	26	8	1,900	375	94	56
Producers, orchestras, entertainers	792	22	8,097	6	3	19	8,088	2,003	532	170
Bowling centers	793	5	4,815	-	-	5	4,815	912	212	106
Commercial sports	794	19	5,705	7	-	13	5,662	645	283	90

[Continued]

★ 802 ★

Establishments in Service Industries in Puerto Rico, by Type of Business and Selected Characteristics - II

[Continued]

Type of business	SIC code	All establishments				Establishments with payroll				
		Number	Receipts ($1,000)	Proprietors and partners (number)	Unpaid family workers (number)	Number	Receipts ($1,000)	Annual payroll ($1,000)	First quarter payroll ($1,000)	Paid employees for pay period including Mar. 12 (number)
Miscellaneous amusement, recreation services	799	16,195	235,853	337	137	262	153,796	38,957	15,682	1,272
Physical fitness facilities	7991	75	2,870	49	1	30	2,741	713	197	98
Public golf course	7992	2	(D)	(D)	-	2	(D)	(D)	(D)	(D)
Coin-operated amusement devices	7993	7	2,470	-	-	7	2,470	597	162	54
Amusement parks	7996	2	(D)	-	-	2	(D)	(D)	(D)	(D)
Membership sports and recreation clubs	7997	29	4,560	41	-	16	4,500	1,490	345	152
Lottery agencies	799 pt.	15,063	68,625	-	-	-	-	-	-	-
Betting agencies	799 pt.	597	10,616	-	-	-	-	-	-	-
Cockfight arenas	799 pt.	61	991	67	49	2	(D)	(D)	(D)	(D)
Amusement and recreation, n.e.c.	Other 7999	359	145,062	179	87	203	143,236	35,985	14,923	943
Dental laboratories	8072	52	(D)	(D)	(D)	23	3,299	1,011	216	117
Legal, services	81	1,249	147,895	892	166	948	142,030	41,826	8,250	2,475
Botanical and zoological gardens	5	(D)	(D)	(D)	-	-	-	-	-	-
Engineering and management services	87, ex. 872	567	220,015	299	58	499	217,741	64,842	15,308	4,868
Engineering and architectural services	871	339	109,024	245	47	295	107,584	25,559	6,268	2,076
Engineering services	8711	247	88,731	180	38	217	87,871	23,975	5,228	1,743
Architectural services	8712	71	19,059	48	6	67	18,592	4,217	920	286
Surveying services	8713	21	1,234	17	3	11	1,121	367	120	47
Research and testing services	873, ex. 8733	43	8,373	21	4	33	8,070	2,279	485	177
Commercial physical research	8731	17	2,602	9	1	10	2,350	787	143	60
Commercial nonphysical research	8732	13	3,445	4	-	13	3,445	739	169	59
Testing laboratories	8734	13	2,326	8	3	10	2,275	753	173	58
Management and public relations	874	185	102,618	33	7	171	102,087	34,004	8,555	2,615
Management services	8741	72	52,620	9	-	67	52,445	17,807	4,786	1,502
Management consulting services	8742	25	7,133	5	4	25	7,133	3,047	745	149
Public relations services	8743	20	22,472	3	-	20	22,472	6,132	1,411	232
Facilities support services	8744	20	3,055	1	-	20	3,055	1,569	333	151
Business consulting, n.e.c.	8748	48	17,338	15	3	39	16,982	5,449	1,280	581

Source: 1987 Economic Census of Outlying Areas, Puerto Rico: Geographic Area Statistics, Wholesale Trade, Retail Trade, Service Industries. U.S. Department of Commerce, Bureau of the Census, OA87-E-1, 1990, pp. 26-27. *Notes:* A dash (-) represents zero. (D) stands for data withheld to avoid disclosure of information; (n.e.c.) stands for not elsewhere classified.

Chapter 8
GOVERNMENT AND POLITICS

Foreign Affairs

★ 803 ★

U.S. Foreign Military Aid Given to Selected Countries

Data are shown in millions of dollars for years ending Sept. 30. Military aid data include Military Assistance Program (MAP) grants, foreign military credit sales, International Military Education and Training, and excess defense articles.

Country	1984	1985	1986	1987	1988	1989	1990	1991
Total	6,486	5,801	5,839	5,102	4,831	4,828	4,893	4,783
Spain	403	403	385	108	2	2	2	2
Latin America[1]	359	269	238	215	144	164	234	237
Colombia	25	1	4	5	4	8	73	50
Costa Rica	9	11	3	2	(Z)	(Z)	0	0
Dominican Rep	6	9	5	3	1	1	2	2
Ecuador	7	7	5	5	1	5	1	3
El Salvador	197	136	122	112	82	81	81	67
Haiti	1	1	2	1	(Z)	(Z)	1	2
Honduras	77	67	61	61	41	41	21	34
Jamaica	4	8	8	3	(Z)	4	1	2
Panama	14	11	8	4	0	0	0	0
Peru	11	9	1	(Z)	(Z)	3	2	25

Source: 1994 Statistical Abstract of the United States on CD-ROM [machine-readable datafiles]. CD-8A-94. Washington, DC: U.S. Department of Commerce, Economics and Statistics Administration, Bureau of the Census, Data User Services Division, January 1995. Primary source: U.S. Agency for International Development, U.S. Overseas Loans and Grants and Assistance from International Organizations, annual. *Notes:* A (Z) stands for less than $500,000. 1. Includes amounts not shown separately.

★ 804 ★

Foreign Affairs

U.S. Government Foreign Grants and Credits, in the Western Hemisphere, by Country

Data are shown in millions of dollars. Negative figures (-) occur when the total of grant returns, principal repayments, and/or foreign currencies disbursed by the U.S. Government exceeds new grants and new credits utilized and/or acquisitions of foreign currencies through new sales of farm products.

Country	1946-1955, total	1956-1965, total	1966-1975, total	1976-1985, total	1986	1987	1988	1989	1990	1991	1992 prel.
Total, net	51,509	49,723	70,368	104,188	15,015	9,403	8,081	10,041	14,297	(31,897)	16,624
Western Hemisphere	1,248	5,181	6,816	9,860	1,812	2,100	1,448	1,194	2,034	1,976	2,244
Argentina	86	342	34	21	85	27	16	(6)	64	87	90
Bolivia	77	288	270	413	111	124	82	131	116	197	174
Brazil	509	1,400	1,518	399	7	34	(Z)	(202)	260	(21)	494
Canada	(1)	4	272	317	(61)	(158)	(50)	(30)	(41)	(50)	(38)
Chile	100	740	724	(565)	56	26	11	(46)	(32)	(40)	(56)
Colombia	43	446	846	298	63	22	(23)	29	(29)	19	(77)
Costa Rica	15	83	103	687	136	159	107	143	108	63	23
Dominican Republic	2	184	360	550	230	78	52	52	28	25	3
Ecuador	32	131	144	153	59	60	47	24	62	26	26
El Salvador	3	56	93	1,681	376	418	405	406	303	309	288
Guatemala	23	146	160	270	91	159	142	161	96	82	105
Guyana	(Z)	7	71	36	2	8	5	8	42	11	9
Haiti	27	75	42	370	87	94	41	76	53	69	40
Honduras	6	53	113	801	224	212	194	133	223	194	126
Jamaica	16	3	120	643	121	92	95	148	108	111	83
Mexico	225	178	305	1,162	(29)	543	62	(100)	141	38	(172)
Nicaragua	8	67	150	197	(Z)	(Z)	(Z)	(Z)	100	395	205
Panama	10	103	210	205	24	10	13	8	102	152	193
Paraguay	4	67	86	22	(Z)	(Z)	(Z)	1	(Z)	1	(Z)
Peru	55	304	274	757	98	74	67	36	87	139	607
Trinidad and Tobago	0	35	21	151	(32)	(33)	(11)	16	5	5	(10)
Uruguay	8	90	116	(9)	11	(3)	9	(6)	(4)	(5)	(3)
Venezuela	6	156	115	(35)	(31)	(38)	(28)	(21)	(18)	(14)	(3)

Source: 1994 Statistical Abstract of the United States on CD-ROM [machine-readable datafiles]. CD-8A-94. Washington, DC: U.S. Department of Commerce, Economics and Statistics Administration, Bureau of the Census, Data User Services Division, January 1995. Primary source: U.S. Bureau of Economic Analysis, press releases, and unpublished data. *Note:* A (Z) stands for less than $500,000.

Government Employment

★ 805 ★

Employment in Key Federal Jobs, by Race/Ethnicity

Data show numbers of white and minority men and women employed in key jobs at 25 federal agencies, by race/ethnicity and general schedule (GS) pay level. Figures are for fiscal years 1984 and 1990.

Year and grade	White		Black		Hispanic		Asian		Native American	
	Men	Women	Men	Women	Men	Women	Men	Women	Men	Women
1984										
<11	76,469	51,791	8,384	13,857	4,967	2,867	1,882	2,029	1,558	2,254
11	46,159	19,208	3,085	4,556	1,705	644	1,430	983	456	282
12	49,518	8,728	2,788	2,260	1,423	243	1,792	281	375	115
13	35,414	4,060	1,697	805	721	118	873	134	228	32
14	21,001	1,861	991	275	369	47	464	84	127	12
15	14,170	1,231	463	92	336	42	671	202	51	4
Total	242,731	86,879	17,408	21,845	9,521	3,961	7,112	3,713	2,795	2,699
1990										
<11	68,174	52,800	8,290	15,665	5,670	3,952	2,407	2,490	1,589	1,932
11	47,132	27,033	3,991	6,810	2,641	1,495	2,173	2,315	590	459
12	53,598	15,954	3,581	4,134	2,391	639	2,668	783	503	204
13	40,404	8,399	2,304	1,716	1,261	266	1,394	337	281	78
14	26,359	3,950	1,265	570	618	119	638	135	203	37
15	16,057	2,044	615	196	454	68	997	366	67	12
Total	251,724	110,180	20,046	29,091	13,035	6,539	10,277	6,426	3,233	2,722

Source: U.S. General Accounting Office. *Affirmative Employment: Assessing Progress of EEO Groups in Key Federal Jobs Can Be Improved*, GAO/GGD-93-65. Washington, DC: U.S. GAO, March 1993, p. 59. Primary source: Office of Personnel Management.

★ 806 ★

Government Employment

Federal and Civilian Employment, 1992

This table shows percent distribution of workers in each sector by race/ethnicity.

Group	All federal workers	U.S. civilian workers
White	71.8	77.0
Male	43.8	42.1
Female	28.0	34.9
Black	17.2	10.6
Male	6.7	5.2
Female	10.5	5.4
Hispanic	5.6	8.9

[Continued]

★ 806 ★

Federal and Civilian Employment, 1992

[Continued]

Group	All federal workers	U.S. civilian workers
Male	3.3	5.4
Female	2.3	3.5
Asian/Pacific	3.5	2.6
Male	2.1	1.4
Female	1.4	1.2
Native American	1.9	0.9
Male	0.9	0.5
Female	1.0	0.4
Total	100.0	100.0

Source: "Minorities in government." *Manpower Comments* (April/May 1994), p. 20. Primary source: U.S. Merit Systems Protection Board and *Career Opportunity News* (March/April 1994).

★ 807 ★

Government Employment

Hispanic Distribution in Federal Public Service

These data show percent distribution of Hispanic employees by general schedule (GS) wage range and by occupational area. SES stands for Senior Executive Service. Figures are shown for 1982-89.

	1982	1983	1984	1985	1986	1987	1988	1989
GS 1-4	21.97	21.66	21.16	20.22	18.95	16.92	15.73	14.41
GS 5-8	35.52	35.27	34.87	35.79	35.69	35.50	35.62	35.48
GS 9-12	34.41	34.95	35.71	35.60	36.83	38.38	38.94	39.63
GS/GM 13-15	7.19	7.00	7.14	7.15	7.28	7.82	8.17	8.52
SES	0.11	0.13	0.13	0.12	0.13	0.11	0.14	0.15
White collar								
Male	2.1	2.2	2.2	2.3	2.3	2.3	2.4	2.4
Female	1.7	1.8	1.9	2.0	2.1	2.1	2.2	2.3
Blue collar								
Male	6.4	6.5	6.5	6.5	6.6	6.6	6.7	6.7
Female	0.4	0.4	0.4	0.5	0.5	0.5	0.5	0.5
Government-wide								
Male	3.0	3.1	3.1	3.1	3.2	3.2	3.2	3.2
Female	1.4	1.5	1.6	1.7	1.8	1.8	1.9	2.0

Source: Sisneros, Antonio. "Hispanics in the public service in the late twentieth century." *Public Administration Review* 53 no. 1 (January/February 1993), p. 2. Primary source: U.S. Equal Employment Opportunity Commission, *Annual Report on the Employment of Minorities, Women & People with Disabilities in the Federal Government Fiscal Year 1989*, Tables 1-11 and 1-12, pp. 123-125.

★ 808 ★

Government Employment

Hispanic Men in Key Federal Jobs

These data show the number of Hispanic males per 1,000 white males at each general schedule (GS) pay level in fiscal years 1984 and 1990. Figures refer to employment in 25 federal agencies.

GS level	Hispanic men per 1,000 white men		Ratio
	1984	1990	
<11	65	83	1.28
11	37	56	1.51
12	29	45	1.55
13	20	31	1.55
14	18	23	1.28
15	24	28	1.17

Source: U.S. General Accounting Office. *Affirmative Employment: Assessing Progress of EEO Groups in Key Federal Jobs Can Be Improved*, GAO/GGD-93-65. Washington, DC: U.S. GAO, March 1993, p. 31. Primary source: Office of Personnel Management.

★ 809 ★

Government Employment

Hispanic Women in Key Federal Jobs

These data show the number of Hispanic women per 1,000 white men at each general schedule (GS) pay level in fiscal years 1984 and 1990. Figures refer to employment in 25 federal agencies.

GS level	Hispanic women per 1,000 white men		Ratio
	1984	1990	
<11	37	58	1.57
11	14	32	2.29
12	5	12	2.4
13	3	7	2.33
14	2	5	2.5
15	3	4	1.33

Source: U.S. General Accounting Office. *Affirmative Employment: Assessing Progress of EEO Groups in Key Federal Jobs Can Be Improved*, GAO/GGD-93-65. Washington, DC: U.S. GAO, March 1993, p. 32. Primary source: Office of Personnel Management.

★810★

Government Employment

Hispanics Employed, Hired, and Separated From Key Federal Jobs

These data show numbers of Hispanic men and women per 1,000 white men employed, hired, and separated from key federal jobs in fiscal years 1984 and 1990.

	Hispanic men per 1,000 white men		Hispanic women per 1,000 white men	
	1984	1990	1984	1990
Hired	58	60	20	28
Employed	39	52	16	26
Separated	38	47	18	27

Source: U.S. General Accounting Office. *Affirmative Employment: Assessing Progress of EEO Groups in Key Federal Jobs Can Be Improved,* GAO/GGD-93-65. Washington, DC: U.S. GAO, March 1993, p. 41. Primary source: Office of Personnel Management.

★811★

Government Employment

Number of Full-Time Government Employees, by Sex and Income Level, 1990: U.S. Summary

Annual salary	Total		Hispanic		White		Black		Asian		American Indian/ Alaska Native	
	Number	%	Number	%	Number	%	Number	%	Number	%	Number	%
Male												
$100-$7,900	18,886	49.8	920	2.4	14,733	38.8	2,970	7.8	114	0.3	149	0.4
$800-$11,900	69,181	37.9	5,945	3.3	39,724	21.8	22,740	12.5	274	0.2	498	0.3
$12,000-$15,900	229,659	39.5	17,884	3.1	146,625	25.2	61,961	10.7	1,255	0.2	1,934	0.3
$16,000-$19,900	406,326	46.5	28,324	3.2	284,873	32.6	86,471	9.9	3,474	0.4	3,184	0.4
$20,000-$32,900	583,235	51.9	36,948	3.3	435,728	38.8	99,904	8.9	7,233	0.6	3,422	0.3
$33,000-$42,900	786,335	62.6	46,865	3.7	609,236	48.5	112,876	9.0	13,396	1.1	3,962	0.3
$43,000 and over	374,137	78.6	17,885	3.8	311,370	65.4	29,563	6.2	14,083	3.0	1,236	0.3
Total	3,071,354	57.2	191,728	3.6	2,325,539	43.3	482,170	9.0	54,825	1.0	17,092	0.3
Female												
$100-$7,900	19,069	50.2	762	2.0	14,586	38.4	3,520	9.3	101	0.3	100	0.3
$800-$11,900	113,129	62.1	6,249	3.4	75,196	41.2	30,540	16.8	524	0.3	620	0.3
$12,000-$15,900	351,550	60.5	20,084	3.5	241,407	41.5	85,723	14.7	2,135	0.4	2,201	0.4
$16,000-$19,900	467,700	53.5	29,602	3.4	318,643	36.5	111,412	12.7	5,381	0.6	2,662	0.3
$20,000-$32,900	540,928	48.1	34,273	3.0	365,502	32.5	127,721	11.4	10,838	1.0	2,594	0.2
$33,000-$42,900	239,252	28.4	13,122	1.6	170,135	20.2	43,104	5.1	12,021	1.4	870	0.1
$43,000 and over	101,901	21.4	4,567	1.0	74,165	15.6	15,954	3.4	6,830	1.4	385	0.1
Total	2,302,412	42.8	135,030	2.5	1,592,758	29.6	511,587	9.5	51,401	1.0	11,636	0.2
Total												
$100-$7,900	37,955	100.0	1,682	4.4	29,319	77.2	6,490	17.1	215	0.6	249	0.7

[Continued]

★811★

Number of Full-Time Government Employees, by Sex and Income Level, 1990: U.S. Summary

[Continued]

Annual salary	Total		Hispanic		White		Black		Asian		American Indian/ Alaska Native	
	Number	%	Number	%	Number	%	Number	%	Number	%	Number	%
$800-$11,900	182,310	100.0	12,194	6.7	114,920	63.0	53,280	29.2	798	0.4	1,118	0.6
$12,000-$15,900	581,209	100.0	37,968	6.5	388,032	66.8	147,684	25.4	3,390	0.6	4,135	0.7
$16,000-$19,900	874,026	100.0	57,926	6.6	603,516	69.1	197,883	22.6	8,855	1.0	5,846	0.7
$20,000-$32,900	1,124,163	100.0	71,221	6.3	801,230	71.3	227,625	20.2	18,071	1.6	6,016	0.5
$33,000-$42,900	842,847	100.0	50,079	5.9	653,385	77.5	108,789	12.9	27,017	3.2	3,577	0.4
$43,000 and over	476,038	100.0	22,452	4.7	385,535	81.0	45,517	9.6	20,913	4.4	1,621	0.3
Total	5,373,766	100.0	326,758	6.1	3,918,297	72.9	993,757	18.5	106,226	2.0	28,728	0.5

Source: U.S. Equal Employment Opportunity Commission. *Job Patterns for Minorities and Women in State and Local Government, 1990.* Washington, DC: U.S. Government Printing Office, 1991, p. 1.

★812★

Government Employment

Number of Full-Time Local Government Employees, by Sex and Income Level, 1990: Cities

Annual salary	Total		Hispanic		White		Black		Asian		American Indian/ Alaska Native	
	Number	%	Number	%	Number	%	Number	%	Number	%	Number	%
Male												
$100-$7,900	5,732	56.0	292	2.9	4,261	41.6	1,081	10.6	25	0.2	73	0.7
$8,000-$11,900	22,655	59.7	2,617	6.9	10,596	27.9	9,228	24.3	53	0.1	161	0.4
$12,000-$15,900	74,004	60.3	8,292	6.8	41,058	33.4	23,853	19.4	309	0.3	492	0.4
$16,000-$19,900	145,888	61.8	13,633	5.8	90,394	38.3	39,933	16.9	1,075	0.5	853	0.4
$20,000-$24,900	210,384	64.7	17,580	5.4	143,760	44.2	45,441	14.0	2,588	0.8	1,015	0.3
$25,000-$32,900	300,364	76.4	22,403	5.7	222,911	56.7	48,139	12.2	5,574	1.4	1,337	0.3
$33,000-$42,900	249,284	82.7	17,646	5.9	194,102	64.4	30,294	10.0	6,264	2.1	978	0.3
$43,000 plus	137,875	85.5	8,320	5.2	112,563	69.8	11,846	7.3	4,652	2.9	494	0.3
Total	1,146,186	72.2	90,783	5.7	819,645	51.6	209,815	13.2	20,540	1.3	5,403	0.3
Female												
$100-$7,900	4,501	44.0	190	1.9	3,044	29.7	1,231	12.0	15	0.1	21	0.2
$8,000-$11,900	15,273	40.3	1,083	2.9	9,164	24.2	4,886	12.9	54	0.1	86	0.2
$12,000-$15,900	48,776	39.7	3,609	2.9	32,403	26.4	12,249	10.0	220	0.2	295	0.2
$16,000- $19,900	90,017	38.2	7,775	3.3	51,675	21.9	29,141	12.4	980	0.4	446	0.2
$20,000-$24,900	114,987	35.3	9,754	3.0	60,366	18.6	41,698	12.8	2,663	0.8	506	0.2
$25,000-$32,900	92,670	23.6	7,222	1.8	55,592	14.1	25,112	6.4	4,289	1.1	455	0.1
$33,000-$42,900	52,255	17.3	3,678	1.2	30,728	10.2	14,308	4.7	3,324	2.8	506	0.1
$43,000 plus	23,337	14.5	1,389	0.9	14,965	9.3	4,918	3.1	1,969	1.2	96	0.1
Total	441,816	27.8	34,709	2.2	257,937	16.2	133,543	8.4	13,514	0.9	2,113	0.1
Total												
$100-$7,900	10,233	100.0	482	4.7	7,305	71.4	2,312	22.6	40	0.4	94	0.9
$8,000-$11,900	37,928	100.0	3,700	9.8	19,760	52.1	14,114	37.2	107	0.3	247	0.7

[Continued]

★ 812 ★

Number of Full-Time Local Government Employees, by Sex and Income Level, 1990: Cities

[Continued]

Annual salary	Total		Hispanic		White		Black		Asian		American Indian/ Alaska Native	
	Number	%	Number	%	Number	%	Number	%	Number	%	Number	%
$12,000-$15,900	122,780	100.0	11,901	9.7	73,461	59.8	36,102	29.4	529	0.4	787	0.6
$16,000-$19,900	235,905	100.0	21,408	9.1	142,069	60.2	69,074	29.3	2,055	0.9	1,299	0.6
$20,000-$24,900	325,371	100.0	27,334	8.4	204,126	62.7	87,139	26.8	5,251	1.6	1,521	0.5
$25,000-$32,900	393,034	100.0	29,625	7.5	278,503	70.9	73,251	18.6	9,863	2.5	1,792	0.5
$33,000-$42,900	301,539	100.0	21,333	7.1	224,830	74.6	44,602	14.8	9,588	3.2	1,186	0.4
$43,000 plus	161,212	100.0	9,709	6.0	127,528	79.1	16,764	10.4	6,621	4.1	590	0.4
Total	1,588,002	100.0	125,492	7.9	1,077,582	67.9	343,358	21.6	34,054	2.1	7,516	0.5

Source: U.S. Equal Employment Opportunity Commission. *Job Patterns for Minorities and Women in State and Local Government, 1990.* Washington, DC: U.S. Government Printing Office, 1991, p. 18.

★ 813 ★

Government Employment

Number of Full-Time Local Government Employees, by Sex and Income Level, 1990: Counties

Annual salary	Total		Hispanic		White		Black		Asian		American Indian/ Alaska Native	
	Number	%	Number	%	Number	%	Number	%	Number	%	Number	%
Male												
$100-$7,900	9,303	46.0	397	2.0	7,597	37.6	1,213	6.0	45	0.2	51	0.3
$8,000-$11,900	22,698	32.3	1,451	2.1	15,844	22.6	5,116	7.3	81	0.1	206	0.3
$12,000-$15,900	65,587	33.9	3,969	2.1	49,090	25.4	11,579	6.0	327	0.2	622	0.3
$16,000-$19,900	100,803	41.8	6,144	2.5	79,383	32.9	13,658	5.7	995	0.4	623	0.3
$20,000-$24,900	121,749	47.3	7,538	2.9	96,663	37.6	15,006	5.8	1,860	0.7	682	0.3
$25,000-$32,900	123,477	53.1	7,813	3.4	98,827	42.5	13,811	5.9	2,349	1.0	677	0.3
$33,000-$42,900	86,811	58.7	5,766	3.9	70,430	47.6	7,710	5.2	2,489	1.7	416	0.3
$43,000 plus	71,248	71.2	3,977	4.0	60,346	60.3	4,337	4.3	2,300	2.3	288	0.3
Total	601,676	47.6	37,055	2.9	478,180	37.9	72,430	5.7	10,446	0.8	3,565	0.3
Female												
$100-$7,900	10,916	54.0	494	2.4	8,929	44.2	1,366	6.8	59	0.3	68	0.3
$8,000-$11,900	47,468	67.7	2,364	3.4	36,419	51.9	8,283	11.8	190	0.3	212	0.3
$12,000-$15,900	127,950	66.1	6,964	3.6	100,510	51.9	19,003	9.8	726	0.4	747	0.4
$16,000- $19,900	140,565	58.2	9,929	4.1	104,572	43.3	23,469	9.7	1,910	0.8	685	0.3
$20,000-$24,900	135,381	52.7	11,432	4.4	95,344	37.1	24,535	9.5	3,474	1.4	596	0.2
$25,000-$32,900	109,069	46.9	7,503	3.2	80,673	34.7	17,319	7.4	3,121	1.3	453	0.2
$33,000-$42,900	61,198	41.3	4,446	3.0	43,233	29.2	9,105	6.2	4,170	2.8	244	0.2
$43,000 plus	28,846	28.8	1,637	1.6	21,556	21.5	3,551	3.5	2,003	2.0	99	0.1
Total	661,393	52.4	44,769	3.5	491,236	38.9	106,631	8.4	15,653	1.2	3,104	0.2
Total												
$100-$7,900	20,219	100.0	891	4.4	16,526	81.7	2,579	12.8	104	0.5	119	0.6
$8,000-$11,900	70,166	100.0	3,815	5.4	52,263	74.5	13,399	19.1	271	0.4	418	0.6

[Continued]

★813★

Number of Full-Time Local Government Employees, by Sex and Income Level, 1990: Counties

[Continued]

Annual salary	Total		Hispanic		White		Black		Asian		American Indian/ Alaska Native	
	Number	%	Number	%	Number	%	Number	%	Number	%	Number	%
$12,000-$15,900	193,537	100.0	10,933	5.6	149,600	77.3	30,582	15.8	1,053	0.5	1,369	0.7
$16,000-$19,900	241,368	100.0	16,073	6.7	183,955	76.2	37,127	15.4	2,905	1.2	1,308	0.5
$20,000-$24,900	257,130	100.0	18,970	7.4	192,007	74.7	39,541	15.4	5,334	2.1	1,278	0.5
$25,000-$32,900	232,546	100.0	15,316	6.6	179,500	77.2	31,130	13.4	5,470	2.4	1,130	0.5
$33,000-$42,900	148,009	100.0	10,212	6.9	113,663	76.8	16,815	11.4	6,659	4.5	660	0.4
$43,000 plus	100,094	100.0	5,614	5.6	81,902	81.8	7,888	7.9	4,303	4.3	387	0.4
Total	1,263,069	100.0	81,824	6.5	969,416	76.8	179,061	14.2	26,099	2.1	6,669	0.5

Source: U.S. Equal Employment Opportunity Commission. *Job Patterns for Minorities and Women in State and Local Government, 1990.* Washington, DC: U.S. Government Printing Office, 1991, p. 15.

★814★

Government Employment

Number of Full-Time Local Government Employees, by Sex and Income Level, 1990: Special Districts

Annual salary	Total		Hispanic		White		Black		Asian		American Indian/ Alaska Native	
	Number	%	Number	%	Number	%	Number	%	Number	%	Number	%
Male												
$100-$7,900	975	42.7	205	9.0	533	23.4	202	8.9	27	1.2	8	0.4
$8,000-$11,900	5,390	25.7	1,004	4.8	1,969	9.4	2,343	11.2	62	0.3	12	0.1
$12,000-$15,900	9,800	25.6	1,228	3.2	4,517	11.8	3,885	10.1	144	0.4	26	0.1
$16,000-$19,900	13,550	33.1	1,268	3.1	7,133	17.4	4,870	11.9	215	0.5	64	0.2
$20,000-$24,900	25,352	47.6	2,366	4.4	15,382	28.9	6,964	13.1	466	0.9	174	0.3
$25,000-$32,900	66,905	62.7	5,053	4.7	41,296	36.7	18,912	17.7	1,293	1.2	351	0.3
$33,000-$42,900	44,961	68.1	3,416	5.2	32,404	49.1	7,329	11.1	1,315	2.0	497	0.8
$43,000 plus	33,190	79.0	1,310	3.1	24,112	57.4	6,147	14.6	1,451	3.5	170	0.4
Total	200,123	54.0	15,850	4.3	127,346	34.4	50,652	13.7	4,973	1.3	1,302	0.4
Female												
$100-$7,900	1,307	57.3	62	2.7	875	38.3	353	15.5	10	0.4	7	0.3
$8,000-$11,900	15,565	74.3	1,384	6.6	8,678	41.4	5,395	25.7	77	0.4	31	0.1
$12,000-$15,900	28,540	74.4	1,997	5.2	16,077	41.9	10,089	26.3	314	0.8	63	0.2
$16,000- $19,900	27,445	66.9	1,647	4.0	16,869	41.1	8,529	20.8	324	0.8	76	0.2
$20,000-$24,900	27,906	52.4	1,524	2.9	19,052	35.8	6,611	12.4	570	1.1	149	0.3
$25,000-$32,900	39,812	37.3	1,910	1.8	27,783	26.0	8,700	8.2	1,269	1.2	150	0.1
$33,000-$42,900	21,047	31.9	778	1.2	15,672	23.7	3,398	5.1	1,105	1.7	94	0.1
$43,000 plus	8,844	21.0	247	0.6	6,294	15.0	1,800	4.3	463	1.1	40	0.1
Total	170,466	46.0	9,549	2.6	111,300	30.0	44,875	12.1	4,132	1.1	610	0.2
Total												
$100-$7,900	2,282	100.0	267	11.7	1,408	61.7	555	24.3	37	1.6	15	0.7

[Continued]

★814★

Number of Full-Time Local Government Employees, by Sex and Income Level, 1990: Special Districts

[Continued]

Annual salary	Total		Hispanic		White		Black		Asian		American Indian/ Alaska Native	
	Number	%	Number	%	Number	%	Number	%	Number	%	Number	%
$8,000-$11,900	20,955	100.0	2,388	11.4	10,647	50.8	7,738	36.9	139	0.7	43	0.2
$12,000-$15,900	38,340	100.0	3,225	8.4	20,594	53.7	13,974	36.4	458	1.2	89	0.2
$16,000-$19,900	40,995	100.0	2,915	7.1	24,002	58.5	13,399	32.7	539	1.3	140	0.3
$20,000-$24,900	53,258	100.0	3,890	7.3	34,434	64.7	13,575	25.5	1,036	1.9	323	0.6
$25,000-$32,900	106,717	100.0	6,963	6.5	69,079	64.7	27,612	25.9	2,562	2.4	501	0.5
$33,000-$42,900	66,008	100.0	4,194	6.4	48,076	72.8	10,727	16.3	2,420	3.7	591	0.9
$43,000 plus	42,034	100.0	1,557	3.7	30,406	72.3	7,947	18.9	1,914	4.6	210	0.5
Total	370,589	100.0	25,399	6.9	238,646	64.4	95,527	25.8	9,105	2.5	1,912	0.5

Source: U.S. Equal Employment Opportunity Commission. *Job Patterns for Minorities and Women in State and Local Government, 1990.* Washington, DC: U.S. Government Printing Office, 1991, p. 24.

★815★

Government Employment

Number of Full-Time Local Government Employees, by Sex and Income Level, 1990: Towns

Annual salary	Total		Hispanic		White		Black		Asian		American Indian/ Alaska Native	
	Number	%	Number	%	Number	%	Number	%	Number	%	Number	%
Male												
$100-$7,900	619	60.7	1	0.1	608	59.6	10	1.0	0	0.0	0	0.0
$8,000-$11,900	367	39.6	3	0.3	350	37.8	10	1.1	1	0.1	3	0.3
$12,000-$15,900	1,477	34.2	27	0.6	1,355	31.4	92	2.1	0	0.0	3	0.1
$16,000-$19,900	4,904	43.8	62	0.6	4,593	41.1	229	2.0	7	0.1	13	0.1
$20,000-$24,900	13,968	66.1	124	0.6	13,269	62.8	541	2.6	12	0.1	22	0.1
$25,000-$32,900	25,120	83.4	200	0.7	24,221	80.5	627	2.1	33	0.1	39	0.1
$33,000-$42,900	16,599	89.4	102	0.5	16,145	87.0	313	1.7	16	0.1	23	0.1
$43,000 plus	6,726	92.4	23	0.3	6,607	90.8	75	1.0	11	0.2	10	0.1
Total	69,780	73.8	542	0.6	67,148	71.0	1,897	2.0	80	0.1	113	0.1
Female												
$100-$7,900	401	39.3	1	0.1	397	38.9	2	0.3	0	0.0	1	0.1
$8,000-$11,900	559	60.4	12	1.3	532	57.5	12	1.3	3	0.3	0	0.0
$12,000-$15,900	2,839	65.8	25	0.6	2,712	62.8	94	2.2	4	0.1	4	0.1
$16,000- $19,900	6,284	56.2	46	0.4	6,067	54.2	146	1.3	21	0.2	4	0.0
$20,000-$24,900	7,167	33.9	52	0.2	6,842	32.4	249	1.2	17	0.1	7	0.0
$25,000-$32,900	4,985	16.6	33	0.1	4,776	15.9	149	0.5	18	0.1	9	0.0
$33,000-$42,900	1,961	10.6	7	0.0	1,902	10.2	48	0.3	3	0.0	1	0.0
$43,000 plus	553	7.6	6	0.1	523	7.2	18	0.2	6	0.1	0	0.0
Total	24,749	26.2	182	0.2	23,751	25.1	718	0.8	72	0.1	26	0.0

[Continued]

★ 815 ★

Number of Full-Time Local Government Employees, by Sex and Income Level, 1990: Towns

[Continued]

Annual salary	Total		Hispanic		White		Black		Asian		American Indian/ Alaska Native	
	Number	%	Number	%	Number	%	Number	%	Number	%	Number	%
Total												
$100-$7,900	1,020	100.0	2	0.2	1,005	98.5	12	1.2	0	0.0	1	0.1
$8,000-$11,900	926	100.0	15	1.6	882	95.2	22	2.4	4	0.4	3	0.3
$12,000-$15,900	4,316	100.0	52	1.2	4,067	94.2	186	4.3	4	0.1	7	0.2
$16,000-$19,900	11,188	100.0	108	1.0	10,660	95.3	375	3.4	28	0.3	17	0.2
$20,000-$24,900	21,135	100.0	176	0.8	20,111	95.2	790	3.7	29	0.1	29	0.1
$25,000-$32,900	30,105	100.0	233	0.8	28,997	96.3	776	2.6	51	0.2	48	0.2
$33,000-$42,900	18,560	100.0	109	0.6	18,047	97.2	361	1.9	19	0.1	24	0.1
$43,000 plus	7,279	100.0	29	0.4	7,130	98.0	93	1.3	17	0.2	10	0.1
Total	94,529	100.0	724	0.8	90,899	96.2	2,615	2.8	152	0.2	139	0.1

Source: U.S. Equal Employment Opportunity Commission. *Job Patterns for Minorities and Women in State and Local Government, 1990.* Washington, DC: U.S. Government Printing Office, 1991, p. 21.

★ 816 ★

Government Employment

Number of Full-Time State and Local Government Employees, by Sex and Income Level, 1990: Officials and Administrators

Annual salary	Total		Hispanic		White		Black		Asian		American Indian/ Alaska Native	
	Number	%	Number	%	Number	%	Number	%	Number	%	Number	%
Male												
$100-$7,900	2,401	77.6	30	1.0	2,239	72.4	125	4.0	6	0.2	1	0.0
$8,000-$11,900	1,366	56.1	36	1.5	1,182	48.6	140	5.8	4	0.2	4	0.2
$12,000-$15,900	2,114	42.5	88	1.8	1,821	36.6	186	3.7	11	0.2	8	0.2
$16,000-$19,900	4,921	49.6	210	2.1	4,280	43.1	401	4.0	11	0.1	19	0.2
$20,000-$24,900	11,637	56.5	388	1.9	10,287	49.9	882	4.3	37	0.2	43	0.2
$25,000-$32,900	31,735	57.9	1,090	2.0	27,559	50.3	2,773	5.1	186	0.3	127	0.2
$33,000-$42,900	51,491	66.7	1,557	2.0	45,336	58.7	3,883	5.0	483	0.6	232	0.3
$43,000 plus	100,076	79.1	2,941	2.3	88,209	69.8	6,900	5.5	1,722	1.4	304	0.2
Total	205,741	68.7	6,340	2.1	180,913	60.4	15,290	5.1	2,460	0.8	738	0.2
Female												
$100-$7,900	693	22.4	5	0.2	641	20.7	42	1.4	3	0.1	2	0.1
$8,000-$11,900	1,067	43.9	31	1.3	941	38.7	71	2.9	2	0.1	22	0.9
$12,000-$15,900	2,856	57.5	86	1.7	2,542	51.1	209	4.2	7	0.1	12	0.2
$16,000- $19,900	5,000	50.4	151	1.5	4,339	43.7	464	4.7	15	0.2	31	0.3
$20,000-$24,900	8,960	43.5	384	1.9	7,578	36.8	923	4.5	28	0.1	47	0.2
$25,000-$32,900	23,046	42.1	1,252	2.3	16,491	30.1	5,016	9.2	192	0.4	95	0.2
$33,000-$42,900	25,718	33.3	982	1.3	20,015	25.9	4,281	5.5	334	0.4	106	0.1
$43,000 plus	26,360	20.9	846	0.7	20,550	16.3	4,187	3.3	734	0.6	63	0.0
Total	93,720	31.3	3,737	1.2	73,097	24.4	15,193	5.1	1,315	0.4	378	0.1

[Continued]

★816★

Number of Full-Time State and Local Government Employees, by Sex and Income Level, 1990: Officials and Administrators

[Continued]

Annual salary	Total		Hispanic		White		Black		Asian		American Indian/ Alaska Native	
	Number	%	Number	%	Number	%	Number	%	Number	%	Number	%
Total												
$100-$7,900	3,094	100.0	35	1.1	2,880	93.1	167	5.4	9	0.3	3	0.1
$8,000-$11,900	2,433	100.0	67	2.8	2,123	87.3	211	8.7	6	0.2	26	1.1
$12,000-$15,900	4,970	100.0	174	3.5	4,363	87.8	395	7.9	18	0.4	20	0.4
$16,000-$19,900	9,921	100.0	361	3.6	8,619	86.9	865	8.7	26	0.3	50	0.5
$20,000-$24,900	20,597	100.0	772	3.7	17,865	86.7	1,805	8.8	65	0.3	90	0.4
$25,000-$32,900	54,781	100.0	2,342	4.3	44,050	80.4	7,789	14.2	378	0.7	222	0.4
$33,000-$42,900	77,209	100.0	2,539	3.3	65,351	84.6	8,164	10.6	817	1.1	338	0.4
$43,000 plus	126,456	100.0	3,787	3.0	108,759	86.0	11,087	8.8	2,456	1.9	367	0.3
Total	299,461	100.0	10,077	3.4	254,010	84.8	30,483	10.2	3,775	1.3	1,116	0.4

Source: U.S. Equal Employment Opportunity Commission. *Job Patterns for Minorities and Women in State and Local Government, 1990.* Washington, DC: U.S. Government Printing Office, 1991, p. 4.

★817★

Government Employment

Number of Full-Time State and Local Government Employees, by Sex and Income Level, 1990: Professionals

Annual salary	Total		Hispanic		White		Black		Asian		American Indian/ Alaska Native	
	Number	%	Number	%	Number	%	Number	%	Number	%	Number	%
Male												
$100-$7,900	1,866	54.0	57	1.6	1,656	47.9	110	3.2	32	0.9	11	0.3
$8,000-$11,900	1,265	39.2	21	0.7	1,095	33.9	128	4.0	16	0.5	5	0.2
$12,000-$15,900	5,035	32.4	251	1.6	3,900	25.1	827	5.3	25	0.2	32	0.2
$16,000-$19,900	24,557	35.8	1,162	1.7	19,063	27.8	3,943	5.8	216	0.3	173	0.3
$20,000-$24,900	72,267	38.6	3,346	1.8	56,607	30.2	10,663	5.7	1,039	0.6	612	0.3
$25,000-$32,900	163,673	43.8	7,025	1.9	134,457	36.0	17,067	4.6	4,192	1.1	932	0.2
$33,000-$42,900	181,345	54.3	7,519	2.3	150,791	45.2	14,839	4.4	7,449	2.2	747	0.2
$43,000 plus	147,867	71.7	5,745	2.8	124,245	60.2	8,008	3.9	9,472	4.6	397	0.2
Total	597,875	50.2	25,126	2.1	491,814	41.3	55,585	4.7	22,441	1.9	2,909	0.2
Female												
$100-$7,900	1,589	46.0	47	1.4	1,271	36.8	245	7.1	26	0.8	0	0.0
$8,000-$11,900	1,961	60.8	44	1.4	1,521	47.1	373	11.6	16	0.5	7	0.2
$12,000-$15,900	10,499	67.6	509	3.3	7,848	50.5	2,002	12.9	67	0.4	73	0.5
$16,000- $19,900	43,966	64.2	2,067	3.0	32,443	47.3	8,853	12.9	280	0.4	323	0.5
$20,000-$24,900	114,876	61.4	4,868	2.6	85,927	45.9	22,299	11.9	1,143	0.6	639	0.3
$25,000-$32,900	210,247	56.2	8,246	2.2	160,725	43.0	34,996	9.4	5,365	1.4	915	0.2
$33,000-$42,900	152,582	45.7	6,739	2.0	111,248	33.3	24,756	7.4	9,349	2.8	490	0.1
$43,000 plus	58,372	28.3	2,656	1.3	41,736	20.2	8,150	4.0	5,618	2.7	212	0.1

[Continued]

★ 817 ★

Number of Full-Time State and Local Government Employees, by Sex and Income Level, 1990: Professionals

[Continued]

Annual salary	Total		Hispanic		White		Black		Asian		American Indian/ Alaska Native	
	Number	%	Number	%	Number	%	Number	%	Number	%	Number	%
Total	594,092	49.8	25,176	2.1	442,719	37.1	101,674	8.5	21,864	1.8	2,659	0.2
Total												
$100-$7,900	3,455	100.0	104	3.0	2,927	84.7	355	10.3	58	1.7	11	0.3
$8,000-$11,900	3,226	100.0	65	2.0	2,616	81.1	501	15.5	32	1.0	12	0.4
$12,000-$15,900	15,534	100.0	760	4.9	11,748	75.6	2,829	18.2	92	0.6	105	0.7
$16,000-$19,900	68,523	100.0	3,229	4.7	51,506	75.2	12,796	18.7	496	0.7	496	0.7
$20,000-$24,900	187,143	100.0	8,214	4.4	142,534	76.2	32,962	17.6	2,182	1.2	1,251	0.7
$25,000-$32,900	373,920	100.0	125,271	4.1	295,182	78.9	52,063	13.9	9,557	2.6	1,847	0.5
$33,000-$42,900	333,927	100.0	14,258	4.3	262,039	78.5	39,595	11.9	16,798	5.0	1,237	0.4
$43,000 plus	206,239	100.0	8,401	4.1	165,981	80.5	16,158	7.8	15,090	7.3	609	0.3
Total	1,191,967	100.0	50,302	4.2	934,533	78.4	157,259	13.2	44,305	3.7	5,568	0.5

Source: U.S. Equal Employment Opportunity Commission. *Job Patterns for Minorities and Women in State and Local Government, 1990.* Washington, DC: U.S. Government Printing Office, 1991, p. 5.

★ 818 ★

Government Employment

Number of Full-Time State and Local Government Employees, by Sex and Income Level, 1990: Protective Service

Annual salary	Total		Hispanic		White		Black		Asian		American Indian/ Alaska Native	
	Number	%	Number	%	Number	%	Number	%	Number	%	Number	%
Male												
$100-$7,900	3,541	63.1	145	2.6	2,842	50.6	478	8.5	15	0.3	61	1.1
$8,000-$11,900	6,512	68.2	364	3.8	4,921	51.5	1,148	12.0	23	0.2	56	0.6
$12,000-$15,900	35,914	75.8	1,523	3.2	26,288	55.5	7,741	16.3	109	0.2	253	0.5
$16,000-$19,900	98,924	82.7	4,963	4.1	76,332	63.8	16,400	13.7	269	0.2	960	0.8
$20,000-$24,900	146,292	84.8	6,881	4.0	115,610	67.0	22,569	13.1	492	0.3	740	0.4
$25,000-$32,900	226,986	8.9	11,719	4.6	183,608	71.9	29,483	11.6	1,214	0.5	962	0.4
$33,000-$42,900	196,812	90.7	15,285	7.0	155,404	71.6	23,060	10.6	2,405	1.1	658	0.3
$43,000 plus	52,641	92.3	4,539	8.0	42,809	75.1	4,305	7.6	822	1.4	166	0.3
Total	767,622	86.8	45,419	5.1	607,814	68.8	105,184	11.9	5,349	0.6	3,856	0.4
Female												
$100-$7,900	2,073	36.9	107	1.9	1,348	24.0	602	10.7	4	0.1	12	0.2
$8,000-$11,900	3,039	31.8	149	1.6	2,243	23.5	628	6.6	4	0.0	15	0.2
$12,000-$15,900	11,449	24.2	381	0.8	7,524	15.9	3,442	7.3	24	0.1	78	0.2
$16,000- $19,900	20,667	17.3	918	0.8	13,872	11.6	5,634	4.7	58	0.0	185	0.2
$20,000-$24,900	26,222	15.2	1,132	0.7	16,756	9.7	8,110	4.7	60	0.0	164	0.1
$25,000-$32,900	28,268	11.1	1,758	0.7	16,888	6.6	9,287	3.6	195	0.1	140	0.1

[Continued]

★ 818 ★

Number of Full-Time State and Local Government Employees, by Sex and Income Level, 1990: Protective Service

[Continued]

Annual salary	Total		Hispanic		White		Black		Asian		American Indian/ Alaska Native	
	Number	%	Number	%	Number	%	Number	%	Number	%	Number	%
$33,000-$42,900	20,274	9.3	2,047	0.9	11,393	5.2	6,475	3.0	294	0.1	65	0.0
$43,000 plus	4,363	7.7	4884	0.8	2,813	4.9	971	1.7	82	0.1	13	0.0
Total	116,355	13.2	6,976	0.8	72,837	8.2	35,149	4.0	721	0.1	672	0.1
Total												
$100-$7,900	5,614	100.0	252	4.5	4,190	74.6	1,080	19.2	19	0.3	73	1.3
$8,000-$11,900	9,551	100.0	513	5.4	7,164	75.0	1,776	18.6	27	0.3	71	0.7
$12,000-$15,900	47,363	100.0	1,904	4.0	33,812	71.4	11,183	23.6	133	0.3	331	0.7
$16,000-$19,900	119,591	100.0	5,881	4.9	90,204	75.4	22,034	18.4	327	0.3	1,145	1.0
$20,000-$24,900	172,514	100.0	8,013	4.6	132,366	76.7	30,679	17.8	552	0.3	904	0.5
$25,000-$32,900	255,254	100.0	13,477	5.3	200,496	78.5	38,770	15.2	1,409	0.6	1,102	0.4
$33,000-$42,900	217,086	100.0	17,332	8.0	166,797	76.8	29,535	13.6	2,699	1.2	723	0.3
$43,000 plus	57,004	100.0	5,023	8.8	45,622	80.0	5,276	9.3	904	1.6	179	0.3
Total	883,977	100.0	52,395	5.9	680,651	77.0	140,333	15.9	6,070	0.7	4,528	0.5

Source: U.S. Equal Employment Opportunity Commission. *Job Patterns for Minorities and Women in State and Local Government, 1990.* Washington, DC: U.S. Government Printing Office, 1991, p. 7.

★ 819 ★

Government Employment

Number of Full-Time State and Local Government Employees, by Sex and Income Level, 1990: Technicians

Annual salary	Total		Hispanic		White		Black		Asian		American Indian/ Alaska Native	
	Number	%	Number	%	Number	%	Number	%	Number	%	Number	%
Male												
$100-$7,900	701	43.7	25	1.6	597	37.2	70	4.4	8	0.5	1	0.1
$8,000-$11,900	2,760	36.0	240	3.1	2,096	27.3	402	5.2	10	0.1	12	0.2
$12,000-$15,900	14,966	38.0	998	2.5	11,114	28.2	2,638	6.7	89	0.2	127	0.3
$16,000-$19,900	35,024	43.5	2,028	2.5	27,465	34.1	4,828	6.0	385	0.5	318	0.4
$20,000-$24,900	61,716	50.3	3,525	2.9	49,090	40.0	7,505	6.1	1,178	1.0	418	0.3
$25,000-$32,900	89,203	63.9	4,728	3.4	73,108	52.3	8,617	6.2	2,347	1.7	403	0.3
$33,000-$42,900	61,736	82.1	2,984	4.0	52,071	69.2	4,726	6.3	1,706	2.3	249	0.3
$43,000 plus	31,438	90.1	1,829	5.2	26,462	75.8	2,202	6.3	835	2.4	110	0.3
Total	297,544	59.3	16,357	3.3	242,003	48.2	30,988	6.2	6,558	1.3	1,638	0.3
Female												
$100-$7,900	902	56.3	24	7.6	738	46.0	122	7.6	12	0.7	6	0.4
$8,000-$11,900	4,917	64.0	440	5.7	3,491	45.5	930	12.1	27	0.4	29	0.4
$12,000-$15,900	24,413	62.0	1,223	3.1	17,134	43.5	5,795	14.7	146	0.4	115	0.3
$16,000- $19,900	45,568	56.5	2,325	2.9	32,376	40.2	10,098	12.5	503	0.6	266	0.3

[Continued]

★ 819 ★

Number of Full-Time State and Local Government Employees, by Sex and Income Level, 1990: Technicians

[Continued]

Annual salary	Total		Hispanic		White		Black		Asian		American Indian/ Alaska Native	
	Number	%	Number	%	Number	%	Number	%	Number	%	Number	%
$20,000-$24,900	61,063	49.7	3,708	3.0	40,956	33.4	14,389	11.7	1,735	1.4	275	0.2
$25,000-$32,900	50,471	36.1	3,649	2.6	34,734	24.9	9,414	6.7	2,466	1.8	208	0.1
$33,000-$42,900	13,495	17.9	1,012	1.3	9,535	12.7	2,099	2.8	789	1.0	60	0.1
$43,000 plus	3,453	9.9	202	0.6	2,521	7.2	499	1.4	219	0.6	12	0.0
Total	204,282	40.7	12,583	2.5	141,485	28.2	43,346	8.6	5,897	1.2	971	0.2
Total												
$100-$7,900	1,603	100.0	49	3.1	1,335	83.3	192	12.0	20	1.2	7	0.4
$8,000-$11,900	7,677	100.0	680	8.9	5,587	72.8	1,332	17.4	37	0.5	41	0.5
$12,000-$15,900	39,379	100.0	2,221	5.6	28,248	71.7	8,433	21.4	235	0.6	242	0.6
$16,000-$19,900	80,592	100.0	4,353	5.4	59,841	74.3	14,926	18.5	888	1.1	584	0.7
$20,000-$24,900	122,779	100.0	7,233	5.9	90,046	73.3	21,894	17.8	2,913	2.4	693	0.6
$25,000-$32,900	139,674	100.0	8,377	6.0	107,842	77.2	18,031	12.9	4,813	3.4	611	0.4
$33,000-$42,900	75,231	100.0	3,996	5.3	61,606	81.9	6,825	9.1	2,495	3.3	309	0.4
$43,000 plus	34,891	100.0	2,031	5.8	28,983	83.1	2,701	7.7	1,054	3.0	122	0.3
Total	501,826	100.0	28,940	5.8	383,488	76.4	74,334	14.8	12,455	2.5	2,609	0.5

Source: U.S. Equal Employment Opportunity Commission. *Job Patterns for Minorities and Women in State and Local Government, 1990.* Washington, DC: U.S. Government Printing Office, 1991, p. 6.

★ 820 ★

Government Employment

Number of Part-Time State and Local Government Employees, by Job Category, 1990

Job category	Total		Hispanic		White		Black		Asian		American Indian/ Alaska Native	
	Number	%	Number	%	Number	%	Number	%	Number	%	Number	%
Male												
Officials/administrators	14,052	60.7	558	2.4	12,159	52.5	999	4.3	284	1.2	52	0.2
Professionals	50,679	31.9	2,020	1.3	41,006	25.8	4,780	3.0	2,628	1.7	245	0.2
Technicians	29,642	40.3	1,689	2.3	23,849	32.5	2,762	3.8	1,109	1.5	233	0.3
Protective service workers	71,537	70.0	2,737	2.7	62,879	61.6	5,067	5.0	506	0.5	348	0.3
Paraprofessionals	73,755	36.4	5,750	2.8	53,124	26.2	12,698	6.3	1,802	0.9	381	0.2
Administrative support	48,840	22.4	3,171	1.5	35,654	16.3	7,119	3.3	1,953	0.9	943	0.4
Skilled craft workers	26,333	68.4	1,698	4.4	20,098	52.2	3,934	10.2	346	0.9	257	0.7
Service-maintenance	180,025	61.0	12,073	4.1	133,741	45.3	30,469	10.3	2,421	0.8	1,321	0.4
Total	494,863	44.5	29,696	2.7	382,510	34.4	67,828	6.1	11,049	1.0	3,780	0.3
Female												
Officials/administrators	9,108	39.3	688	3.0	7,062	30.5	1,089	4.7	235	1.0	34	0.1
Professionals	108,057	68.1	3,174	2.0	92,059	58.0	8,575	5.4	3,869	2.4	380	0.2
Technicians	43,828	59.7	2,338	3.2	34,719	47.3	5,284	7.2	1,278	1.7	209	0.3
Protective service workers	30,605	30.0	1,070	1.0	24,516	24.0	4,733	4.6	141	0.1	145	0.1
Paraprofessionals	128,628	63.6	7,264	3.6	97,163	48.0	21,553	10.6	1,995	1.0	653	0.3

[Continued]

★ 820 ★

Number of Part-Time State and Local Government Employees, by Job Category, 1990

[Continued]

Job category	Total		Hispanic		White		Black		Asian		American Indian/ Alaska Native	
	Number	%	Number	%	Number	%	Number	%	Number	%	Number	%
Administrative support	169,596	77.6	10,265	4.7	131,857	60.4	22,502	10.3	4,061	1.9	911	0.4
Skilled craft workers	12,151	31.6	537	1.4	9,649	25.1	1,781	4.6	115	0.3	69	0.2
Service-maintenance	115,018	39.0	6,253	2.1	86,117	29.2	20,292	6.9	1,588	0.5	768	0.3
Total	616,991	55.5	31,589	2.8	483,142	43.5	85,809	7.7	13,282	1.2	3,169	0.3
Total												
Officials/administrators	23,160	100.0	1,246	5.4	19,221	83.0	2,088	9.0	519	2.2	86	0.4
Professionals	158,736	100.0	5,194	3.3	133,065	83.8	13,355	8.4	6,497	4.1	625	0.4
Technicians	73,470	100.0	4,027	5.5	58,568	79.7	8,046	11.0	2,387	3.2	442	0.6
Protective service workers	102,142	100.0	3,807	3.7	87,395	85.6	9,800	9.6	647	0.6	493	0.5
Paraprofessionals	202,383	100.0	13,014	6.4	150,287	74.3	34,251	16.9	3,797	1.9	1,034	0.5
Administrative support	218,436	100.0	13,436	6.2	167,511	76.7	29,621	13.6	6,014	2.8	1,854	0.8
Skilled craft workers	38,484	100.0	2,235	5.8	29,747	77.3	5,715	14.9	461	1.2	326	0.8
Service-maintenance	295,043	100.0	18,326	6.2	219,858	74.5	50,761	17.2	4,009	1.4	2,089	0.7
Total	1,111,854	100.0	61,285	5.5	865,652	77.9	153,637	13.8	24,331	2.2	6,949	0.6

Source: U.S. Equal Employment Opportunity Commission. *Job Patterns for Minorities and Women in State and Local Government, 1990.* Washington, DC: U.S. Government Printing Office, 1991, p. 2.

★ 821 ★

Government Employment

White Collar Federal Employment, by Race/Ethnicity

Data show percent distribution of employees by race/ethnicity for each general schedule (GS) pay level. SES stands for Senior Executive Service.

Race/ethnicity	GS 1-10	GS 11-13	GS 14-15	SES
White	65.0	81.0	88.0	92.0
Black	24.0	11.0	6.0	5.0
Hispanic	6.0	4.0	2.0	2.0
Native American	2.0	1.0	1.0	1.0
Asian/Pacific Islander	3.0	4.0	3.0	1.0

Source: "Federal diversity." *Manpower Comments* (January/February 1994), p. 28. Primary source: Merit Systems Protection Board and *The Washington Post.*

Government Representatives

★ 822 ★

Dependent School System Board Members and Other Elected Officials, by Race/Ethnicity, 1987

Race/ethnicity	Total elected officials			Members of systems boards			Other elected officials			Exhibit: nonelected members of systems boards		
	Total	Male	Female	Total	Male	Female	Total	Male	Female	Total	Male	Female
United States, total	6,605	3,555	2,144	6,090	3,237	1,949	515	318	195	2,989	1,979	721
Hispanic	66	34	32	28	14	14	38	20	18	28	19	9
White	62	30	32	24	10	14	38	20	18	23	16	7
Black	4	4	-	4	4	-	-	-	-	5	3	2
White, not Hispanic	5,078	3,175	1,903	4,827	3,013	1,814	251	162	89	2,279	1,699	580
Black, not Hispanic	302	204	98	202	124	78	100	80	20	385	257	128
American Indian/Alaska Native	238	130	108	114	74	40	124	56	68	6	3	3
Asian/Pacific Islander	15	12	3	15	12	3	-	-	-	2	1	1
Not reported	906	-	-	904	-	-	2	-	-	289	-	-

Source: Popularly Elected Officials in 1987, (GC87(1)- 2), Bureau of the Census, U.S. Department of Commerce, p. 24. *Notes:* A dash (-) represents zero; details may not add to totals due to nonresponse.

★ 823 ★

Government Representatives

Elected Officials of County Governments, by Race/Ethnicity, 1987

Race/ethnicity	Total elected officials			Members of governing boards			Members of other elected boards			Other elected officials		
	Total	Male	Female	Total	Male	Female	Total	Male	Female	Total	Male	Female
United States	55,500	45,862	9,560	17,014	15,455	1,557	9,563	8,238	1,259	28,923	22,169	6,744
Hispanic	832	689	143	176	162	14	30	18	12	626	509	117
White	827	685	142	175	162	13	30	18	12	622	505	117
Black	5	4	1	1	-	1	-	-	-	4	4	-
White, not Hispanic	52,887	43,762	9,125	16,054	14,597	1,457	9,159	8,007	1,152	27,674	21,158	6,516
Black, not Hispanic	1,504	1,258	246	690	617	73	270	187	83	544	454	90
American Indian/Alaska Native	144	106	38	64	54	10	36	25	11	44	27	17
Asian/Pacific Islander	55	47	8	28	25	3	2	1	1	25	21	4
Not reported	78	-	-	2	-	-	66	-	-	10	-	-

Source: Popularly Elected Officials in 1987, (GC87(1)- 2), Bureau of the Census, U.S. Department of Commerce, p. 20. *Notes:* A dash (-) represents zero; details may not add to totals due to nonresponse.

★ 824 ★

Government Representatives

Elected Officials of Local Governments, by Sex and State, 1987

Geographic area	Total	Male elected officials				Female elected officials				Not reported
		Total	Hispanics		Non-Hispanic	Total	Hispanics		Non-Hispanic	
			Number	% of men			Number	% of women		
United States	479,021	335,335	3,837	1.14	331,498	83,739	867	1.04	82,872	59,947
Alabama	3,892	3,070	8	0.26	3,062	448	-	0.00	448	374
Alaska	1,509	915	2	0.22	913	358	3	0.84	355	236
Arizona	2,968	1,901	190	9.99	1,711	638	67	10.50	571	429
Arkansas	8,021	6,063	16	0.26	6,047	1,210	5	0.41	1,205	748
California	19,021	12,101	581	4.80	11,520	3,842	160	4.16	3,682	3,078
Colorado	7,770	4,989	204	4.09	4,785	1,046	50	4.78	996	1,735
Connecticut	8,156	5,193	21	0.40	5,172	2,304	8	0.35	2,296	659
Delaware	1,147	667	2	0.30	665	160	-	0.00	160	320
District of Columbia	325	184	-	0.00	184	141	-	0.00	141	-
Florida	4,439	3,340	40	1.20	3,300	720	9	1.25	711	379
Georgia	6,109	4,732	11	0.23	4,721	919	4	0.44	915	458
Hawaii	69	60	3	5.00	57	9	-	0.00	9	-
Idaho	4,509	2,977	14	0.47	2,963	658	9	1.37	649	874
Illinois	38,310	26,459	68	0.26	26,391	6,553	12	0.18	6,541	5,298
Indiana	10,880	7,651	23	0.30	7,628	2,034	5	0.25	2,029	1,195
Iowa	16,734	13,523	23	0.17	13,500	2,317	2	0.09	2,315	894
Kansas	16,066	11,066	38	0.34	11,028	1,949	9	0.46	1,940	3,051
Kentucky	6,828	5,409	21	0.39	5,388	797	7	0.88	790	622
Louisiana	4,380	3,613	12	0.33	3,601	402	1	0.25	401	365
Maine	6,791	4,231	4	0.09	4,227	1,762	3	0.17	1,759	798
Maryland	1,598	1,105	3	0.27	1,102	294	1	0.34	293	199
Massachusetts	13,407	8,888	14	0.16	8,874	3,530	10	0.28	3,520	989
Michigan	18,670	12,380	27	0.22	12,353	4,779	10	0.21	4,769	1,511
Minnesota	18,308	13,978	40	0.29	13,938	2,759	9	0.33	2,750	1,571
Mississippi	4,650	3,733	12	0.32	3,721	504	2	0.40	502	413
Missouri	16,122	10,950	25	0.23	10,925	2,490	7	0.28	2,483	2,682
Montana	5,446	3,231	16	0.50	3,215	783	2	0.26	781	1,432
Nebraska	14,876	9,457	32	0.34	9,425	1,668	9	0.54	1,659	3,751
Nevada	1,047	630	8	1.27	622	184	1	0.54	183	233
New Hampshire	6,291	3,182	1	0.03	3,181	2,123	2	0.09	2,121	986
New Jersey	9,224	5,907	32	0.54	5,875	1,968	17	0.86	1,951	1,349
New Mexico	1,903	1,321	484	36.64	837	294	81	27.55	213	288
New York	25,073	17,873	61	0.34	17,812	4,265	27	0.63	4,238	2,935
North Carolina	4,982	3,947	-	0.00	3,947	700	-	0.00	700	335
North Dakota	14,937	10,385	34	0.33	10,351	1,715	13	0.76	1,702	2,837
Ohio	19,526	14,545	56	0.39	14,489	3,455	12	0.35	3,443	1,526
Oklahoma	8,939	5,853	63	1.08	5,790	1,448	11	0.76	1,437	1,638
Oregon	8,075	5,351	28	0.52	5,323	1,439	12	0.83	1,427	1,285
Pennsylvania	28,404	19,784	25	0.13	19,759	6,641	6	0.09	6,635	1,979
Rhode Island	965	636	1	0.16	635	210	-	0.00	210	119
South Carolina	3,497	2,730	14	0.51	2,716	481	1	0.21	480	286
South Dakota	9,093	6,293	15	0.24	6,278	824	1	0.12	823	1,976
Tennessee	6,519	5,535	-	0.00	5,535	647	-	0.00	647	337
Texas	26,135	19,151	1,452	7.58	17,699	3,522	237	6.73	3,285	3,462
Utah	2,429	1,894	7	0.37	1,887	249	4	1.61	245	286
Vermont	7,835	4,586	26	0.57	4,560	2,219	13	0.59	2,206	1,030
Virginia	2,969	2,435	-	0.00	2,435	364	-	0.00	364	170

[Continued]

★ 824 ★

Elected Officials of Local Governments, by Sex and State, 1987

[Continued]

Geographic area	Total	Male elected officials				Female elected officials				Not reported
		Total	Hispanics		Non-Hispanic	Total	Hispanics		Non-Hispanic	
			Number	% of men			Number	% of women		
Washington	7,449	4,963	25	0.50	4,938	1,290	8	0.62	1,282	1,196
West Virginia	2,633	1,954	-	0.00	1,954	485	1	0.21	484	194
Wisconsin	17,876	13,084	49	0.37	13,035	3,794	12	0.32	3,782	998
Wyoming	2,219	1,430	6	0.42	1,424	348	4	1.15	344	441

Source: Popularly Elected Officials in 1987, (GC87(1)- 2), Bureau of the Census, U.S. Department of Commerce, p. 19. *Note:* A dash (-) represents zero.

★ 825 ★

Government Representatives

Elected Officials of Municipal Governments, by Race/Ethnicity, 1987

Race/ethnicity	Total elected officials			Members of governing boards			Members of other elected boards			Other elected officials		
	Total	Male	Female	Total	Male	Female	Total	Male	Female	Total	Male	Female
United States	137,542	102,547	23,194	106,791	82,239	15,583	4,179	2,642	1,295	26,572	17,666	6,316
Hispanic	1,577	1,285	292	1,362	1,137	225	21	12	9	194	136	58
White	1,526	1,241	285	1,323	1,102	221	18	10	8	185	129	56
Black	51	44	7	39	35	4	3	2	1	9	7	2
White, not Hispanic	119,114	97,337	21,777	92,414	77,861	14,553	3,516	2,406	1,110	23,184	17,070	6,114
Black, not Hispanic	4,100	3,230	870	3,262	2,653	609	357	202	155	481	375	106
American Indian/Alaska Native	856	622	234	710	529	181	41	20	21	105	73	32
Asian/Pacific Islander	94	73	21	74	59	15	2	2	-	18	12	6
Not reported	11,801	-	-	8,969	-	-	242	-	-	2,590	-	-

Source: Popularly Elected Officials in 1987, (GC87(1)- 2), Bureau of the Census, U.S. Department of Commerce, p. 21. *Notes:* A dash (-) represents zero; details may not add to totals due to nonresponse.

★ 826 ★

Government Representatives

Elected Officials of Special District Governments, by Race/Ethnicity, 1987

Race/ethnicity	Total elected officials			Members of governing boards			Members of other elected boards			Other elected officials		
	Total	Male	Female	Total	Male	Female	Total	Male	Female	Total	Male	Female
United States	80,538	49,510	6,454	79,190	48,812	6,141	1,348	698	313	67,995	38,595	7,676
Hispanic	680	606	74	675	604	71	5	2	3	719	543	176
White	673	601	72	668	599	69	5	2	3	707	535	172
Black	7	5	2	7	5	2	-	-	-	12	8	4
White, not Hispanic	54,671	48,415	6,256	53,674	47,724	5,950	997	691	306	43,306	36,501	6,805
Black, not Hispanic	360	279	81	352	274	78	8	5	3	1,919	1,339	580
American Indian/Alaska Native	154	128	26	154	128	26	-	-	-	257	154	103
Asian/Pacific Islander	99	82	17	98	82	16	1	-	1	70	58	12
Not reported	24,574	-	-	24,237	-	-	337	-	-	21,724	-	-

Source: Popularly Elected Officials in 1987, (GC87(1)- 2), Bureau of the Census, U.S. Department of Commerce, p. 25. *Notes:* A dash (-) represents zero; details may not add to totals due to nonresponse.

★ 827 ★

Government Representatives

Elected Officials of Township Governments, by Race/Ethnicity, 1987

Race/ethnicity	Total elected officials			Members of governing boards			Members of other elected boards			Other elected officials		
	Total	Male	Female	Total	Male	Female	Total	Male	Female	Total	Male	Female
United States	118,669	80,242	23,883	41,390	33,803	3,211	26,030	17,144	6,235	51,249	29,295	14,437
Hispanic	200	156	44	80	73	7	37	30	7	83	53	30
White	195	152	43	79	73	6	33	26	7	83	53	30
Black	5	4	1	1	-	1	4	4	-	-	-	-
White, not Hispanic	103,456	79,719	23,737	36,747	33,575	3,172	23,195	17,004	6,191	43,514	29,140	14,374
Black, not Hispanic	392	312	80	143	119	24	140	104	36	109	89	20
American Indian/Alaska Native	68	48	20	40	32	8	3	3	-	25	13	12
Asian/Pacific Islander	9	7	2	4	4	-	4	3	1	1	-	1
Not reported	14,544	-	-	4,376	-	-	2,651	-	-	7,517	-	-

Source: Popularly Elected Officials in 1987, (GC87(1)- 2), Bureau of the Census, U.S. Department of Commerce, p. 22. *Notes:* A dash (-) represents zero; details may not add to totals due to nonresponse.

★ 828 ★

Government Representatives

Hispanics and Blacks in Congress, 1931-1991

Race/ethnicity	1931	1941	1951	1961	1971	1981	1991
Hispanics[1]	2	2	2	3	6	6	11
Blacks	1	2	2	3	13	17	25

Source: Wolf, Richard. "Redistricting to change the face of Congress." *USA TODAY* (22 October 1992), p. 8A. Primary source: American Enterprise Institute. *Note:* 1. Hispanics may be of any race.

★ 829 ★

Government Representatives

Hispanics and Blacks in Congress, 1992-93

Race/ethnicity	102nd Congress		103rd Congress	
	House	Senate	House	Senate
Hispanic	10	0	17	0
Black	25	0	38	1
Other	393	100	387	99

Source: Krauss, Clifford. "Democrats retreat on strengthening votes of non-state delegates." *The New York Times* (5 January 1993), p. A7.

★ 830 ★

Government Representatives

Hispanics, Women, and Other Minorities in Congress, 1991-93

Data include non-voting delegates.

Group	1991	1993
Women	31	54
Blacks	25	39
Hispanics	14	19
Asians	6	9
Native American	1	1

Source: Wolf, Richard. "Speaker Foley's back and in top form." *USA TODAY* (7 December 1992), p. 10A. Primary source: *USA TODAY* research.

★ 831 ★

Government Representatives

Local Elected Officials of Hispanic Origin, 1987

Type of government	Total	Hispanic	Non-Hispanic	Not reported	Percent of reported		
					Total	Hispanic	Non-Hispanic
Local governments	479,021	4,704	414,370	59,947	100.0	1.1	98.9
County	55,500	832	54,590	78	100.0	1.5	98.5
Municipal	137,542	1,577	124,164	11,801	100.0	1.3	98.7
Township	118,669	200	103,925	14,544	100.0	.2	99.8
School district	86,772	1,415	76,407	8,950	100.0	1.8	98.2
Special district	80,538	680	55,284	24,574	100.0	1.2	98.8

Source: Popularly Elected Officials in 1987, (GC87(1)- 2), Bureau of the Census, U.S. Department of Commerce, p. XII.

★ 832 ★

Government Representatives

School District Board Members and Other Elected Officials, by Race/Ethnicity, 1987

Race/ethnicity	Total elected officials			Members of district boards			Other elected officials			Exhibit: Nonelected members of district boards		
	Total	Male	Female	Total	Male	Female	Total	Male	Female	Total	Male	Female
United States	86,772	57,174	20,648	86,015	56,741	20,421	757	433	227	2,574	1,635	478
Hispanic	1,415	1,101	314	1,412	1,098	314	3	3	-	34	24	10
White	1,397	1,088	309	1,395	1,086	309	2	2	-	30	21	9
Black	18	13	5	17	12	5	1	1	-	4	3	1
White, not Hispanic	74,003	54,380	19,623	73,361	53,962	19,399	642	418	224	1,777	1,396	381
Black, not Hispanic	1,825	1,276	549	1,811	1,265	546	14	11	3	270	193	77
American Indian/Alaska Native	488	347	141	487	346	141	1	1	-	17	15	2

[Continued]

★ 832 ★

School District Board Members and Other Elected Officials, by Race/Ethnicity, 1987

[Continued]

Race/ethnicity	Total elected officials			Members of district boards			Other elected officials			Exhibit: Nonelected members of district boards		
	Total	Male	Female	Total	Male	Female	Total	Male	Female	Total	Male	Female
Asian/Pacific Islander	91	70	21	91	70	21	-	-	-	15	7	8
Not reported	8,950	-	-	8,853	-	-	97	-	-	461	-	-

Source: Popularly Elected Officials in 1987, (GC87(1)- 2), Bureau of the Census, U.S. Department of Commerce, p. 23. *Notes:* A dash (-) represents zero; details may not add to totals due to nonresponse.

★ 833 ★

Government Representatives

Where Hispanic Elected Officials Serve

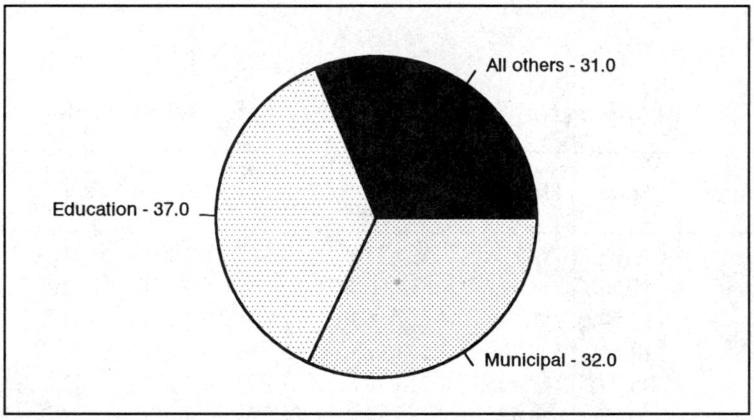

Type of service	Percent
Education	37.0
Municipal	32.0
All others	31.0

Source: Vargas, Arturo. "Redistricting: route to Latino empowerment." *USA TODAY* (3 March 1992), p. 13A. Primary source: Census Bureau; National Association of Latino Elected and Appointed Officials.

Judicial Appointments

★ 834 ★

Appointment of Judges to U.S. Court of Appeals, 1963-92

Race and ethnicity	President Johnson's appointees 1963-68 (N=40)	President Nixon's appointees 1969-74 (N=45)	President Ford's appointees 1974-76 (N=12)	President Carter's appointees 1977-80 (N=56)	President Reagan's first term appointees 1981-84 (N=31)	President Reagan's second term appointees 1985-88 (N=47)	President Bush's appointees 1989-92 (N=37)
White	95.0	97.8	100.0	78.6	93.5	100.0	89.2
Black	5.0	0.0	0.0	16.1	3.2	0.0	5.4
Hispanic	0.0	0.0	0.0	3.6	3.2	0.0	5.4
Asian	0.0	2.2	0.0	1.8	0.0	0.0	0.0

Source: Maguire, Kathleen and Ann L. Pastore (eds.). U.S. Department of Justice. U.S. Bureau of Justice Statistics. *Sourcebook of Criminal Justice Statistics 1993.* Washington, DC: U.S. Government Printing Office, 1994, p. 71. Primary source: Sheldon Goldman, "Reagan's Judicial Legacy: Completing the Puzzle and Summing Up," *Judicature* 76 (April-May 1993), pp. 323,324, Table 3; and "Bush's Judicial Legacy: The Final Imprint," *Judicature* 76 (April-May 1993), p. 293. Table adapted by *Sourcebook* staff. *Notes:* These data were compiled from a variety of sources. Primarily used were questionnaires completed by judicial nominees for the U.S. Senate Judiciary Committee, transcripts of the confirmation hearing conducted by the Committee, and personal interviews. In addition, an investigation was made of various biographical directories including *The American Bench* (Sacramento: R.B. Forster), *Who's Who in American Politics* (New York: Bowker), *Martindale-Hubbell Law Directory* (Summit, NJ: Martindale-Hubbell, Inc.), national and regional editions of *Who's Who, The Judicial Staff directory* (1992 edition), and local newspaper articles.

★ 835 ★

Judicial Appointments

Federal Bench Appointments by Sex and Race/Ethnicity, 1969-93

These data show appointments made by U.S. presidents throughout the last six administrations.

	Total	White		African American		Hispanic American		Asian American	
		Males	Females	Males	Females	Males	Females	Males	Females
Clinton 1993	28	11	10	6	0	0	1	0	0
Percent		39.3	35.7	21.4			3.6		
Bush 1989-1992	192	141	31	9	2	5	3	1	0
Percent		73.4	16.2	4.7	1.0	2.6	1.6	0.5	
Reagan 1981-1988	378	328	28	6	1	11	2	2	0
Percent		86.8	7.4	1.6	0.3	2.9	0.5	0.5	
Carter 1977-1980	258	170	33	30	7	15	1	2	0
Percent		65.9	12.8	11.7	2.7	5.8	0.3	0.8	
Ford 1974-1976	65	58	1	3	0	1	0	2	0
Percent		89.3	1.5	4.6		1.5		3.1	
Nixon 1969-1974	227	217	1	6	0	2	0	1	0
Percent		95.6	0.4	2.7		0.9		0.4	

Source: Reske, Henry J. "A report card on Clinton's judges: President's picks are diverse in look and legal background but not in wealth." *ABA Journal* (April 1994), p. 16. Primary source: Alliance for Justice Judicial Selection Project.

★ 836 ★

Judicial Appointments

Federal Judges, With Selected Characteristics, 1992

There are a total of 846 federal judgeships.

Group	Number of judges
Women[1]	76
Black	44
Hispanic[2]	30
Asian	4
Disabled[1]	2

Source: Mauro, Tony. "Death penalty may help kill nomination." *USA TODAY* (7 May 1992), p. 8A. Primary source: Administrative Office of U.S. Courts, Alliance for Justice. *Notes:* 1. Ethnic categories include women and the disabled. 2. Hispanics can be of any race.

Politics

★ 837 ★

Hispanic Party Affiliation, by Ethnicity, 1992

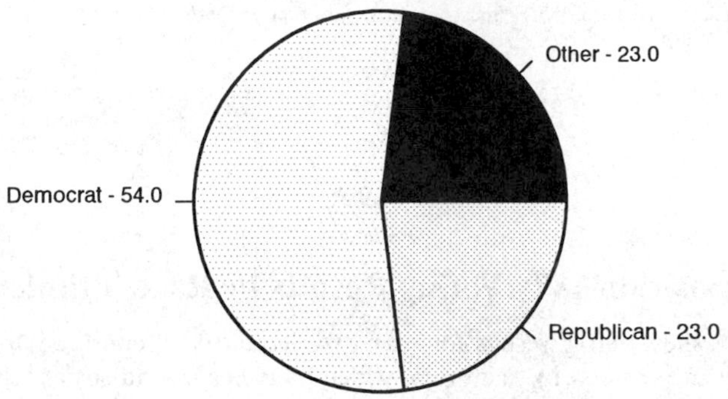

Chart shows data from column 1.

Numbers are shown as percentages. Chart shows Hispanic totals.

Political Party	Hispanic				White
	Total	Mexican	Puerto Rican	Cuban	
Democrat	54.0	59.6	63.6	19.5	43.7
Republican	23.0	16.0	13.9	64.0	29.1
Other	23.0	24.4	22.5	16.5	27.2

Source: Arocha, Zita. "Parties: don't take Hispanic voters for granted." *USA TODAY* (28 July 1992), p. 11A; Benedetto, Richard. "Hispanics feeling at home: survey shows a solid fit in mainstream." *USA TODAY* (16 December 1992), p. 5A. Primary source: Gallup organization and Latino National Political Survey.

★ 838 ★

Politics

Percentage of Selected Groups Who Voted Republican in the Presidential Elections of 1988 and 1992

Characteristic	1988	1992
Republican	92.0	73.0
Conservatives	81.0	64.0
Men	58.0	38.0
Women	51.0	37.0
White	60.0	40.0

[Continued]

★ 838 ★

Percentage of Selected Groups Who Voted Republican in the Presidential Elections of 1988 and 1992

[Continued]

Characteristic	1988	1992
Black	11.0	10.0
Hispanics	30.0	25.0

Source: Benedetto, Richard. "GOP must regain its position as 'party of ideas'." *USA TODAY* (3 March 1993), p. 13A.

★ 839 ★

Politics

Proposition 187 - Voting Results by Race/Ethnicity

These data show voting results for each race/ethnicity. Proposition 187 was a ballot measure, passed in California, which bans health and social services to illegal aliens.

Race/ethnicity	Percent	
	Yes	No
White	56.0	44.0
Black	51.0	49.0
Hispanic[1]	20.0	80.0

Source: Puente, Maria. "Bitter battle over Prop. 187 down to wire." *USA TODAY* (9 November 94), p. 2A. Primary source: Voter News Service exit polls *Note:* 1. Hispanics can be of any race.

U.S. Military Personnel

★ 840 ★

Active-Duty Air Force Personnel, by Race/Ethnicity, 1994

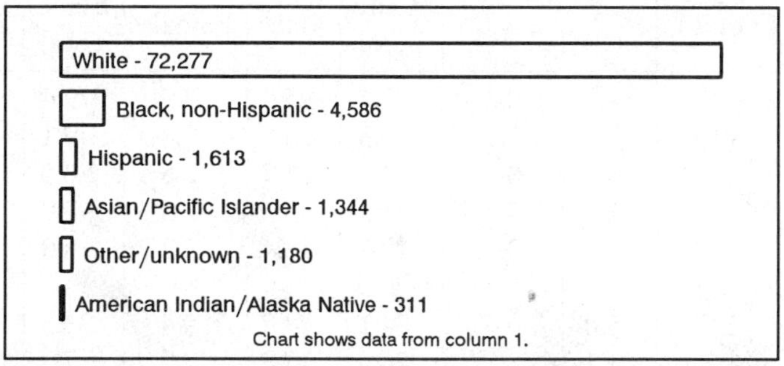

Figures show number of persons serving as enlisted personnel or as officers, as of May 1994.

	Officer	Enlisted
American Indian/Alaska Native	311	2,102
Asian/Pacific Islander	1,344	6,545
Black, non-Hispanic	4,586	58,439
Hispanic	1,613	13,491
White	72,277	264,294
Other/unknown	1,180	2,885

Source: Airman - The Book '94 (September 1994), p. 31.

★ 841 ★

U.S. Military Personnel

Estimates of the Number of Persons in the Armed Forces Overseas, by Age, Sex, and Race/Ethnicity, 1991 - I

Numbers are shown in thousands; estimates are for July 1, 1991.

Age	Hispanic origin Total	Male	Female	Race, not of Hispanic origin					
				White Total	Male	Female	Black Total	Male	Female
All ages	23.5	21.2	2.3	346.5	312.1	34.4	127.4	106.1	21.2
Under 20	1.8	1.6	0.2	25.3	22.6	2.6	9.0	7.4	1.5
17	0.0	0.0	0.0	0.1	0.1	0.0	0.0	0.0	0.0
18	0.4	0.3	0.1	5.6	5.0	0.6	2.2	1.7	0.4
19	1.4	1.3	0.2	19.6	17.5	2.0	6.8	5.7	1.1
20-24	8.1	7.2	0.9	123.1	110.5	12.6	42.8	35.3	7.4

[Continued]

★ 841 ★

Estimates of the Number of Persons in the Armed Forces Overseas, by Age, Sex, and Race/Ethnicity, 1991 - I

[Continued]

Age	Hispanic origin Total	Male	Female	Race, not of Hispanic origin					
				White Total	Male	Female	Black Total	Male	Female
20	1.9	1.7	0.2	28.4	25.5	2.9	9.4	7.8	1.6
21	1.9	1.7	0.2	28.3	25.5	2.8	9.1	7.6	1.5
22	1.6	1.5	0.2	24.2	21.7	2.5	8.3	6.9	1.4
23	1.3	1.2	0.2	21.6	19.3	2.3	7.9	6.4	1.4
24	1.2	1.1	0.1	20.7	18.4	2.2	8.0	6.6	1.5
25-29	5.5	5.0	0.6	84.1	74.7	9.4	33.5	27.1	6.3
25	1.2	1.1	0.1	20.0	17.8	2.2	7.7	6.3	1.4
26	1.2	1.1	0.1	18.6	16.5	2.1	7.2	5.9	1.3
27	1.1	1.0	0.1	16.6	14.7	1.9	6.4	5.2	1.2
28	1.1	0.9	0.1	15.2	13.4	1.7	6.1	4.9	1.2
29	1.0	0.9	0.1	13.7	12.2	1.5	6.0	4.8	1.1
30-34	4.1	3.8	0.4	52.8	47.1	5.6	23.7	19.8	3.9
20	0.9	0.8	0.1	12.4	11.1	1.3	5.6	4.5	1.0
31	0.9	0.8	0.1	11.2	10.0	1.3	5.1	4.3	0.8
32	0.8	0.7	0.1	10.6	9.4	1.2	4.7	4.0	0.7
33	0.8	0.7	0.1	9.5	8.5	1.0	4.3	3.7	0.7
34	0.7	0.7	0.1	9.0	8.1	0.9	3.9	3.3	0.6
35-39	2.7	2.6	0.2	36.8	33.7	3.0	13.1	11.5	1.6
35	0.6	0.6	0.0	8.6	7.8	0.8	3.5	3.0	0.5
36	0.6	0.6	0.0	8.2	7.5	0.7	3.0	2.6	0.4
37	0.6	0.5	0.0	7.7	7.0	0.7	2.6	2.3	0.3
38	0.5	0.5	0.0	6.6	6.1	0.5	2.2	2.0	0.2
39	0.4	0.4	0.0	5.7	5.3	0.4	1.8	1.6	0.2
40-44	1.0	0.9	0.1	18.5	17.6	0.9	4.3	3.9	0.4
40	0.3	0.3	0.0	5.1	4.8	0.2	1.4	1.3	0.1
41	0.2	0.2	0.0	4.3	4.1	0.2	1.1	1.0	0.1
42	0.2	0.2	0.0	3.9	3.7	0.2	0.8	0.7	0.1
43	0.1	0.1	0.0	3.3	3.2	0.1	0.6	0.5	0.1
44	0.1	0.1	0.0	1.8	1.8	0.1	0.4	0.4	0.0
45-49	0.2	0.2	0.0	4.9	4.7	0.2	0.9	0.9	0.1
45	0.1	0.1	0.0	1.5	1.5	0.0	0.3	0.3	0.0
46	0.1	0.1	0.0	1.3	1.2	0.1	0.2	0.2	0.0
47	0.0	0.0	0.0	1.0	1.0	0.0	0.2	0.2	0.0
48	0.0	0.0	0.0	0.7	0.6	0.0	0.1	0.1	0.0

[Continued]

★ 841 ★

Estimates of the Number of Persons in the Armed Forces Overseas, by Age, Sex, and Race/Ethnicity, 1991 - I

[Continued]

Age	Hispanic origin Total	Male	Female	Race, not of Hispanic origin					
				White Total	Male	Female	Black Total	Male	Female
49	0.0	0.0	0.0	0.5	0.4	0.0	0.1	0.1	0.0
50-64	0.0	0.0	0.0	1.2	1.2	0.0	0.1	0.1	0.0

Source: U.S. Bureau of the Census. *Estimates of the Armed Forces Overseas, by Age, Sex, Race, and Hispanic Origin.*

★ 842 ★

U.S. Military Personnel

Estimates of the Number of Persons in the Armed Forces Overseas, by Age, Sex, and Race/Ethnicity, 1991 - II

Numbers are shown in thousands; estimates are for July 1, 1991.

Age	Race, not of Hispanic origin					
	American Indian, Eskimo, and Aleut Total	Male	Female	Asian and Pacific Islander Total	Male	Female
All ages	2.6	2.2	0.4	11.6	10.6	1.0
Under 20	0.2	0.2	0.0	0.5	0.4	0.1
17	0.0	0.0	0.0	0.0	0.0	0.0
18	0.0	0.0	0.0	0.1	0.1	0.0
19	0.2	0.2	0.0	0.4	0.3	0.0
20-24	0.9	0.7	0.2	2.6	2.3	0.3
20	0.2	0.2	0.0	0.5	0.5	0.1
21	0.2	0.2	0.0	0.6	0.5	0.1
22	0.2	0.2	0.0	0.5	0.5	0.1
23	0.1	0.1	0.0	0.5	0.4	0.1
24	0.1	0.1	0.0	0.5	0.5	0.1
25-29	0.5	0.4	0.1	2.6	2.4	0.3
25	0.1	0.1	0.0	0.5	0.5	0.1
26	0.1	0.1	0.0	0.5	0.5	0.1
27	0.1	0.1	0.0	0.5	0.5	0.0
28	0.1	0.1	0.0	0.5	0.5	0.0
29	0.1	0.1	0.0	0.5	0.4	0.1
30-34	0.4	0.3	0.1	2.3	2.1	0.2
30	0.1	0.1	0.0	0.5	0.5	0.0

[Continued]

★ 842 ★

Estimates of the Number of Persons in the Armed Forces Overseas, by Age, Sex, and Race/Ethnicity, 1991 - II

[Continued]

Age	Race, not of Hispanic origin					
	American Indian, Eskimo, and Aleut Total	Male	Female	Asian and Pacific Islander Total	Male	Female
31	0.1	0.1	0.0	0.5	0.4	0.0
32	0.1	0.1	0.0	0.4	0.4	0.0
33	0.1	0.1	0.0	0.5	0.4	0.0
34	0.1	0.1	0.0	0.5	0.4	0.0
35-39	0.4	0.3	0.0	2.2	2.1	0.1
35	0.1	0.1	0.0	0.5	0.4	0.0
36	0.1	0.1	0.0	0.5	0.4	0.0
37	0.1	0.1	0.0	0.5	0.5	0.0
38	0.1	0.1	0.0	0.4	0.4	0.0
39	0.1	0.1	0.0	0.4	0.3	0.0
40-44	0.2	0.2	0.0	1.0	1.0	0.0
40	0.0	0.0	0.0	0.3	0.3	0.0
41	0.0	0.0	0.0	0.2	0.2	0.0
42	0.0	0.0	0.0	0.2	0.0	0.0
43	0.0	0.0	0.2	0.2	0.0	0.0
44	0.0	0.0	0.0	0.1	0.1	0.0
45-49	0.0	0.0	0.0	0.3	0.3	0.0
45	0.0	0.0	0.0	0.1	0.1	0.0
46	0.0	0.0	0.0	0.1	0.1	0.0
47	0.0	0.0	0.0	0.1	0.1	0.0
48	0.0	0.0	0.0	0.0	0.0	0.0
49	0.0	0.0	0.0	0.0	0.0	0.0
50-64	0.0	0.0	0.0	0.1	0.1	0.0

Source: U.S. Bureau of the Census. *Estimates of the Armed Forces Overseas, by Age, Sex, Race, and Hispanic Origin.*

★ 843 ★

U.S. Military Personnel

Women in the Military, by Race/Ethnicity

Data show number of women in active duty at the beginning of fiscal year 1994. Nearly thirty percent of women were minorities.

Race/ethnicity	Number
White	120,442
Black	60,264
Hispanic[1]	9,586
Other	8,751

Source: Komarow, Steve. "Door opens for women, but not all the way." *USA TODAY* (28 July 1994), p. 11A. Primary source: Department of Defense. *Note:* 1. Hispanics can be of any race.

Veterans

★ 844 ★

GI Bill Utilization, by Race/Ethnicity

Percent of veterans of each race/ethnicity using the GI Bill (Public Law 345) as an educational benefit is shown for veterans in 1987.

Race/ethnicity	Percent using benefits
Hispanic	48.0
Black	43.0
White	38.0

Source: U.S. Department of Veterans Affairs. National Center for Veteran Analysis and Statistics. *Facts About Hispanic Veterans.* Washington, DC: Department of Veterans Affairs, September 1994, n.p. Primary source: U.S. Bureau of the Census.

★ 845 ★

Veterans

State Ranking by Number of Hispanic Veterans

State	Hispanic veteran pop.
Largest population	
California	273,700
Texas	196,400
New York	75,200
Florida	55,800
New Mexico	46,500
Smallest population	
Maine	700
West Virginia	670
South Dakota	390
Vermont	340
North Dakota	280

Source: U.S. Department of Veterans Affairs. National Center for Veteran Analysis and Statistics. *Facts About Hispanic Veterans*. Washington, DC: Department of Veterans Affairs, September 1994, n.p. Primary source: U.S. Bureau of the Census.

★ 846 ★

Veterans

State Ranking by Percentage of Hispanic Veterans

State	Percent Hispanic veteran pop.
New Mexico	26.0
Texas	12.0
California	9.0
Arizona	8.0
Colorado	8.0

Source: U.S. Department of Veterans Affairs. National Center for Veteran Analysis and Statistics. *Facts About Hispanic Veterans*. Washington, DC: Department of Veterans Affairs, September 1994, n.p. Primary source: U.S. Bureau of the Census.

★ 847 ★

Veterans

VA Hospital Utilization Rate, by Race/Ethnicity

Utilization of VA (Veterans Administration) hospitals is shown for fiscal 1993, as rate per 1,000 veterans.

Race/ethnicity	Rate per 1,000 veterans
Black	81.9
Hispanic	31.5
White	28.7

Source: U.S. Department of Veterans Affairs. National Center for Veteran Analysis and Statistics. *Facts About Hispanic Veterans*. Washington, DC: Department of Veterans Affairs, September 1994, n.p. Primary source: U.S. Bureau of the Census.

★ 848 ★

Veterans

VA Hospital Utilization Rate, by Race/Ethnicity and Age Group

Utilization of VA (Veterans Administration) hospitals is shown for fiscal 1993, as rate per 1,000 veterans.

Race/ethnicity	Rate per 1,000 veterans
White	
Less than 45	17.6
45 to 64	24.3
65 and older	47.9
Black	
Less than 45	64.5
45 to 64	74.0
65 and older	144.2
Hispanic	
Less than 45	19.4
45 to 64	32.5
65 and older	73.6

Source: U.S. Department of Veterans Affairs. National Center for Veteran Analysis and Statistics. *Facts About Hispanic Veterans*. Washington, DC: Department of Veterans Affairs, September 1994, n.p. Primary source: U.S. Bureau of the Census.

Voting

★ 849 ★

Hispanic Voting in Presidential Elections

Election	Percent
1980 (2% of all voters)	
Jimmy Carter	55.0
Ronald Reagan	37.0
John Anderson	7.0
1984 (3% of all voters)	
Walter Mondale	56.0
Ronald Reagan	44.0
1988 (3% of all voters)	
Michael Dukakis	66.0
George Bush	33.0

Source: Colton, David. "Hispanic voters." *USA TODAY* (2 July 1992), p. 4A. Primary source: ABC News.

★ 850 ★

Voting

Reported Voter Registration in Presidential Elections, 1968-92

The number of voting age persons, in thousands, and the percentage who reported registered are shown, by race/ethnicity, for presidential election years. Numbers are shown in thousands for the civilian noninstitutional population.

Race/ethnicity	Presidential elections						
	1992	1988	1984	1980	1976	1972	1968
Total, voting age	185,684	178,098	169,963	157,085	146,548	136,203	116,535
Percent registered	68.2	66.6	68.3	66.9	66.7	72.3	74.3
White	70.1	67.9	69.6	68.4	68.3	73.4	75.4
Black	63.9	64.5	66.3	60.0	58.5	65.5	66.2
Hispanic origin[1]	35.0	35.5	40.1	36.3	37.8	44.4	NA

Source: U.S. Bureau of the Census. *Voting and Registration in the Election of November 1992*, Current Population Reports, P20-466. Washington, DC, U.S. GPO, 1993, p. vi. Current Population Reports, Series P-20, Nos. 192, 253, 293, 322, 344, 370, 383, 405, 414, 440, and Table 2 of source. *Notes:* NA stands for not available. 1. Persons of Hispanic origin may be of any race.

★ 851 ★

Voting

Reported Voter Turnout in Presidential Elections, 1964-92

The number of voting age persons, in thousands, and the percentage who reported having voted are shown, by race/ethnicity, for presidential election years. Numbers are shown in thousands for the civilian noninstitutional population.

Race/ethnicity	Presidential elections							
	1992	1988	1984	1980	1976	1972	1968	1964
Total, voting age	185,684	178,098	169,963	157,085	146,548	136,203	116,535	110,604
Percent voted	61.3	57.4	59.9	59.2	59.2	63.0	67.8	69.3
White	63.6	59.1	61.4	60.9	60.9	64.5	69.1	70.7
Black	54.0	51.5	55.8	50.5	48.7	52.1	57.6	58.5[2]
Hispanic origin[1]	28.9	28.8	32.6	29.9	31.8	37.5	NA	NA

Source: U.S. Bureau of the Census. *Voting and Registration in the Election of November 1992*, Current Population Reports, P20-466. Washington, DC, U.S. GPO, 1993, p. v. Current Population Reports, Series P-20, Nos. 174, 228, 293, 344, 383, 414, 440 and Table 2 of source. *Notes:* NA stands for not available. 1. Persons of Hispanic origin may be of any race. 2. Black and other races in 1964.

★ 852 ★

Voting

Reported Voting and Registration in the United States, by Race/Ethnicity, Age and Sex, 1992

Data for November 1992 are shown in thousands and as percent of total in each voting status category.

Race, Hispanic origin, sex, and age	All persons	Reported registered		Reported voted		Reported that they did not vote[1]				
						Total	Registered	Not registered		
		Number	Percent	Number	Percent			Total[2]	Not a U.S. citizen	Do not know and not reported on registration[3]
All Races										
Both Sexes										
Total, 18 years and over	185,684	126,578	68.2	113,866	61.3	71,818	12,712	59,106	11,900	10,638
18 to 20 years	9,727	4,696	48.3	3,749	38.5	5,979	947	5,032	857	821
21 to 24 years	14,644	8,091	55.3	6,693	45.7	7,951	1,398	6,553	1,288	1,075
25 to 34 years	41,603	25,223	60.6	22,120	53.2	19,483	3,103	16,380	3,675	2,223
35 to 44 years	39,716	27,503	69.2	25,269	63.6	14,447	2,234	12,213	2,800	2,144
45 to 54 years	28,058	20,785	74.1	19,292	68.8	8,766	1,493	7,273	1,435	1,466
55 to 64 years	21,089	16,231	77.0	15,107	71.6	5,982	1,124	4,858	955	1,107
65 to 74 years	18,445	14,685	79.6	13,607	73.8	4,839	1,078	3,760	538	952
75 years and over	12,401	9,364	75.5	8,030	64.8	4,371	1,334	3,037	352	850
Male										
Total, 18 years and over	88,557	59,254	66.9	53,312	60.2	35,245	5,942	29,303	6,065	5,327
18 to 20 years	4,876	2,274	46.6	1,786	36.6	3,090	488	2,602	444	405
21 to 24 years	7,158	3,797	53.0	3,086	43.1	4,072	711	3,361	722	597
25 to 34 years	20,465	11,869	58.0	10,324	50.4	10,141	1,545	8,597	2,031	1,251
35 to 44 years	19,509	13,153	67.4	11,995	61.5	7,514	1,158	6,357	1,444	1,059
45 to 54 years	13,608	9,956	73.2	9,287	68.2	4,321	668	3,652	697	799
55 to 64 years	10,012	7,725	77.2	7,203	71.9	2,809	522	2,287	396	527
65 to 74 years	8,289	6,745	81.4	6,318	76.2	1,971	427	1,544	218	410
75 years and over	4,640	3,736	80.5	3,313	71.4	1,327	424	904	113	279

[Continued]

★852★

Reported Voting and Registration in the United States, by Race/Ethnicity, Age and Sex, 1992

[Continued]

Race, Hispanic origin, sex, and age	All persons	Reported registered		Reported voted		Reported that they did not vote[1]				
						Total	Registered	Not registered		
								Total[2]	Not a U.S. citizen	Do not know and not reported on registration[3]
		Number	Percent	Number	Percent					
Female										
Total, 18 years and over	97,126	67,324	69.3	60,554	62.3	36,573	6,770	29,803	5,834	5,311
18 to 20 years	4,851	2,421	49.9	1,962	40.5	2,889	459	2,430	413	416
21 to 24 years	7,486	4,394	57.4	3,607	48.2	3,879	687	3,192	566	478
25 to 34 years	21,138	13,354	63.2	11,795	55.8	9,342	1,558	7,784	1,645	972
35 to 44 years	20,207	14,350	71.0	13,274	65.7	6,933	1,076	5,856	1,356	1,085
45 to 54 years	14,450	10,829	74.9	10,005	69.2	4,445	825	3,620	738	667
55 to 64 years	11,077	8,506	76.8	7,904	71.4	3,173	602	2,571	558	580
65 to 74 years	10,157	7,940	78.2	7,289	71.8	2,868	652	2,216	320	541
75 years and over	7,761	5,628	72.5	4,717	60.8	3,044	911	2,133	240	571
White										
Both Sexes										
Total, 18 years and over	157,837	110,684	70.1	100,405	63.6	57,432	10,279	47,153	8,284	8,289
18 to 20 years	7,743	3,938	50.9	3,187	41.2	4,555	750	3,805	566	585
21 to 24 years	11,9939	6,808	57.0	5,745	48.1	6,194	1,064	5,130	912	787
25 to 34 years	34,640	21,631	62.4	19,193	55.4	15,447	2,437	13,010	2,596	1,633
35 to 44 years	33,644	23,964	71.2	22,186	65.9	11,459	1,778	9,680	1,901	1,643
45 to 54 years	24,071	18,243	75.8	17,013	70.7	7,058	1,230	5,829	963	1,156
55 to 64 years	18,208	14,270	78.4	13,357	73.4	4,851	913	3,938	706	887
65 to 74 years	16,400	13,281	81.0	12,365	75.4	4,035	916	3,119	382	836
75 years and over	11,192	8,550	76.4	7,360	65.8	3,832	1,190	2,642	257	762
Male										
Total, 18 years and over	75,915	52,383	69.0	47,552	62.6	28,364	4,831	23,533	4,296	4,116
18 to 20 years	3,876	1,897	48.9	1,510	39.0	2,366	387	1,979	302	279
21 to 24 years	5,874	3,238	55.1	2,710	46.1	3,164	528	2,637	527	435
25 to 34 years	17,286	10,360	59.9	9,130	52.8	8,156	1,230	6,927	1,460	933
35 to 44 years	16,752	11,617	69.3	10,677	63.7	6,075	940	5,135	1,006	809
45 to 54 years	11,826	8,886	75.1	8,315	70.3	3,511	571	2,940	470	633
55 to 64 years	8,706	6,859	78.8	6,428	73.8	2,278	432	1,846	292	406
65 to 74 years	7,385	6,115	82.8	5,754	77.9	1,631	360	1,271	156	364
75 years and over	4,210	3,411	81.0	3,029	71.9	1,181	383	798	85	258
Female										
Total, 18 years and over	81,922	58,301	71.2	52,853	64.5	29,068	5,448	23,621	3,966	4,173
18 to 20 years	3,867	2,041	52.8	1,677	43.4	2,190	364	1,826	264	305
21 to 24 years	6,064	3,571	58.9	3,035	50.0	3,029	536	2,494	385	352
25 to 34 years	17,354	11,271	64.9	10,063	58.0	7,291	1,208	6,083	1,136	701
35 to 44 years	16,892	12,347	73.1	11,509	68.1	5,383	838	4,545	896	834
45 to 54 years	12,245	9,356	76.4	8,698	71.0	3,548	658	2,889	493	523
55 to 64 years	9,502	7,411	78.0	6,929	72.9	2,573	481	2,091	414	482
65 to 74 years	9,015	7,166	79.5	6,610	73.3	2,404	556	1,848	226	472
75 years and over	6,982	5,139	73.6	4,331	62.0	2,651	807	1,844	173	504
Black										
Both Sexes										
Total, 18 years and over	21,039	13,442	63.9	11,371	54.0	9,668	2,070	7,598	1,044	1,870
18 to 20 years	1,501	638	42.5	474	31.6	1,027	164	863	103	176
21 to 24 years	2,042	1,106	54.2	821	40.2	1,221	284	936	116	230
25 to 34 years	5,295	3,107	58.7	2,518	47.6	2,777	589	2,188	348	479
35 to 44 years	4,515	2,976	65.9	2,589	57.3	1,926	387	1,538	274	419
45 to 54 years	2,861	2,040	71.3	1,821	63.7	1,040	219	821	118	235
55 to 64 years	2,181	1,611	73.9	1,452	66.6	729	159	570	52	170

[Continued]

★ 852 ★

Reported Voting and Registration in the United States, by Race/Ethnicity, Age and Sex, 1992

[Continued]

Race, Hispanic origin, sex, and age	All persons	Reported registered		Reported voted		Reported that they did not vote[1]				
						Total	Registered	Not registered		
								Total[2]	Not a U.S. citizen	Do not know and not reported on registration[3]
		Number	Percent	Number	Percent					
65 to 74 years	1,634	1,219	74.6	1,083	66.3	551	137	415	17	94
75 years and over	1,010	744	73.7	613	60.7	397	131	266	16	68
Male										
Total, 18 years and over	9,425	5,727	60.8	4,786	50.8	4,639	941	3,698	548	965
18 to 20 years	745	307	41.2	218	29.2	527	89	438	47	96
21 to 24 years	940	471	50.1	319	33.9	621	152	469	60	134
25 to 34 years	2,388	1,283	53.7	1,009	42.2	1,379	274	1,105	216	260
35 to 44 years	2,027	1,295	63.9	1,113	54.9	914	181	732	138	207
45 to 54 years	1,267	838	66.2	757	59.7	510	82	428	59	125
55 to 64 years	984	710	72.1	640	65.0	344	70	274	18	94
65 to 74 years	724	533	73.7	475	65.6	249	58	190	8	37
75 years and over	350	290	82.7	256	73.0	95	34	61	2	12
Female										
Total, 18 years and over	11,614	7,715	66.4	6,585	56.7	5,029	1,129	3,899	496	905
18 to 20 years	756	331	43.8	256	33.9	500	75	425	56	79
21 to 24 years	1,102	635	57.6	503	45.6	599	132	467	56	96
25 to 34 years	2,907	1,824	62.7	1,509	51.9	1,398	315	1,083	133	219
35 to 44 years	2,488	1,682	67.6	1,476	59.3	1,012	206	806	136	212
45 to 54 years	1,595	1,202	75.4	1,065	66.8	530	137	393	59	110
55 to 64 years	1,197	901	75.3	812	67.8	385	89	296	34	75
65 to 74 years	910	686	75.3	608	66.8	303	78	225	9	57
75 years and over	659	454	68.9	357	54.2	302	97	205	14	56
Hispanic[4]										
Both Sexes										
Total, 18 years and over	14,688	5,137	35.0	4,238	26.9	10,450	899	9,551	5,910	995
18 to 20 years	1,159	267	23.1	183	15.8	976	85	891	483	93
21 to 24 years	1,636	429	26.2	310	18.9	1,327	119	1,207	722	120
25 to 34 years	4,177	1,239	29.7	1,000	23.9	3,177	239	2,938	1,930	237
35 to 44 years	3,322	1,160	34.9	979	29.5	2,343	181	2,162	1,353	251
45 to 54 years	1,954	851	43.5	731	37.4	1,223	120	1,103	678	143
55 to 64 years	1,257	624	49.6	566	45.0	691	58	633	401	72
65 to 74 years	767	385	50.3	319	41.6	447	66	391	199	54
75 years and over	417	182	43.6	151	36.1	267	31	235	145	26
Male										
Total, 18 years and over	7,273	2,337	32.1	1,946	26.8	5,327	391	4,936	3,132	519
18 to 20 years	563	110	19.5	72	12.5	491	38	454	259	46
21 to 24 years	855	178	20.8	124	14.5	731	54	677	413	82
25 to 34 years	2,182	562	25.8	464	21.3	1,717	98	1,619	1,100	121
35 to 44 years	1,669	540	32.4	447	26.8	1,222	93	1,129	722	127
45 to 54 years	983	416	42.4	363	36.9	620	53	566	354	78
55 to 64 years	535	276	51.6	252	47.1	283	24	59	164	37
65 to 74 years	340	186	54.8	159	46.7	181	27	154	71	18
75 years and over	147	69	46.8	66	44.9	81	3	78	49	10
Female										
Total, 18 years and over	7,415	2,800	37.8	2,291	30.9	5,124	508	4,615	2,778	476
18 to 20 years	595	158	26.5	111	18.6	485	47	438	224	47
21 to 24 years	781	250	32.1	186	23.8	596	65	531	309	38
25 to 34 years	1,995	676	33.9	535	26.8	1,460	141	1,319	830	116
35 to 44 years	1,654	620	37.5	533	32.2	1,121	87	1,033	631	123

[Continued]

★ 852 ★

Reported Voting and Registration in the United States, by Race/Ethnicity, Age and Sex, 1992

[Continued]

Race, Hispanic origin, sex, and age	All persons	Reported registered		Reported voted		Reported that they did not vote[1]				
						Total	Registered	Not registered		
		Number	Percent	Number	Percent			Total[2]	Not a U.S. citizen	Do not know and not reported on registration[3]
45 to 54 years	971	435	44.7	368	37.9	603	67	537	324	65
55 to 64 years	722	348	48.2	314	43.5	408	34	374	237	35
65 to 74 years	427	199	46.7	161	37.6	266	39	227	128	35
75 years and over	270	113	41.8	85	31.3	186	29	157	96	16

Source: U.S. Bureau of the Census. *Voting and Registration in the Election of November 1992*, Current Population Reports, P20-466. Washington, DC, U.S. GPO, 1993, pp. 4-5. *Notes:* 1. Includes persons reported as "did not know," and "not reported" on voting. 2. In addition to those reported as "not registered," total includes those "not a U.S. citizen," and "do not know" and "not reported" on registration. 3. Includes "do not know" and "not reported" on citizenship. 4. Persons of Hispanic origin may be of any race.

★ 853 ★

Voting

Reported Voting and Registration in Selected States, 1992

The number, in thousands, and percent of reported voter registration, reported voting are shown, by race/ethnicity for selected states in November 1992.

State, race, sex, and Hispanic origin	All persons[1]	Reported registered			Reported voted		
		Total	Percent	Standard error	Total	Percent	Standard error
United States							
Total	185,684	126,578	68.2	.19	113,866	61.3	.20
Percent							
White	157,837	110,684	70.1	.20	100,405	63.6	.21
Black	21,039	13,442	63.9	.70	11,371	54.0	.72
Hispanic origin[1]	14,688	5,137	35.0	1.07	4,238	28.9	1.02
Arizona							
Total	2,671	1,882	70.5	1.57	1,728	64.7	1.65
Percent							
White	2,549	1,831	71.8	1.59	1,684	66.1	1.67
Black	58	28	(B)	(B)	28	(B)	(B)
Hispanic origin[1]	442	197	44.7	6.62	156	35.3	6.37
California							
Total	22,340	12,864	57.6	.64	11,789	52.8	.65
Percent							
White	18,759	11,349	60.5	.69	10,482	55.9	.70
Black	1,268	812	64.0	3.16	712	56.1	3.27
Hispanic origin[1]	5,443	1,384	2.4	1.80	1,135	20.9	1.68
Colorado							
Total	2,451	1,831	74.7	1.57	1,688	68.8	1.67
Percent							
White	2,221	1,715	77.2	1.59	1,589	71.5	1.71
Black	119	75	63.0	9.53	64	53.4	9.85
Hispanic origin[1]	218	145	66.5	8.95	136	62.2	9.20

[Continued]

★ 853 ★

Reported Voting and Registration in Selected States, 1992

[Continued]

State, race, sex, and Hispanic origin	All persons[1]	Reported registered			Reported voted		
		Total	Percent	Standard error	Total	Percent	Standard error
Connecticut							
Total	2,428	1,863	76.8	1.63	1,740	71.7	1.74
Percent							
White	2,170	1,735	80.0	1.63	1,628	75.0	1.76
Black	222	115	51.5	7.69	100	45.1	7.66
Hispanic origin[1]	127	63	49.7	13.24	54	42.8	13.10
Florida							
Total	10,342	6,486	62.7	.78	5,772	55.8	.80
Percent							
White	8,742	5,643	64.5	.84	5,062	57.9	.87
Black	1,410	772	54.7	2.63	652	46.3	2.64
Hispanic origin[1]	1,349	472	35.0	3.35	411	30.5	3.23
Illinois							
Total	8,676	6,251	72.1	.81	5,650	65.1	.86
Percent							
White	7,197	5,237	72.8	.88	4,775	66.3	.93
Black	1,202	903	75.2	2.52	784	65.3	2.78
Hispanic origin[1]	646	223	34.6	4.91	171	26.4	4.55
Massachusetts							
Total	4,501	3,262	72.5	.81	2,960	65.8	.86
Percent							
White	4,233	3,141	74.2	.82	2,854	67.4	.87
Black	184	95	.851.7	5.41	83	45.3	5.39
Hispanic origin[1]	124	28	22.7	7.17	18	14.4	6.01
Michigan							
Total	6,811	5,078	74.6	.78	4,486	65.9	.85
Percent							
White	5,812	4,374	75.3	.84	63,882	66.8	.92
Black	867	659	76.0	2.61	569	65.6	2.90
Hispanic origin[1]	111	58	52.5	11.08	48	43.3	11.00
New Jersey							
Total	5,838	3,972	68.0	.82	3,572	61.2	.86
Percent							
White	4,837	3,436	71.0	.88	3,150	65.1	.93
Black	769	482	62.7	2.85	381	49.6	2.95
Hispanic origin[1]	564	207	36.8	4.31	173	30.6	4.12
New Mexico							
Total	1,079	724	67.1	1.59	675	62.6	1.64
Percent							
White	970	660	68.0	1.67	618	63.8	1.72
Black	23	16	(B)	(B)	13	(B)	(B)
Hispanic origin[1]	334	190	56.8	4.73	172	51.3	4.78
New York							
Total	13,401	8,314	62.0	.65	7,613	56.8	.66

[Continued]

★853★

Reported Voting and Registration in Selected States, 1992

[Continued]

State, race, sex, and Hispanic origin	All persons[1]	Reported registered Total	Reported registered Percent	Reported registered Standard error	Reported voted Total	Reported voted Percent	Reported voted Standard error
Percent							
White	10,790	7,136	66.1	.71	6,590	61.1	.73
Black	2,052	1,020	49.7	2.08	890	43.4	2.06
Hispanic origin[1]	1,172	449	38.3	3.47	382	32.6	3.34
Pennsylvania							
Total	9,170	5,967	65.1	.82	5,491	59.9	.84
Percent							
White	8,257	5,426	65.7	.86	5,033	61.0	.88
Black	767	507	66.1	3.40	436	56.9	3.55
Hispanic origin[1]	107	52	48.5	12.48	39	36.5	12.02
Texas							
Total	12,267	7,956	64.9	.84	6,817	55.6	.87
Percent							
White	10,597	7,001	66.1	.90	6,066	57.2	.94
Black	1,361	864	63.5	3.07	682	50.1	3.19
Hispanic origin[1]	2,806	1,203	42.9	2.86	927	3.1	2.71

Source: U.S. Bureau of the Census. *Voting and Registration in the Election of November 1992,* Current Population Reports, P20-466. Washington, DC, U.S. GPO, 1993, pp. 23-30. *Notes:* A (B) stands for base less than 75,000. 1. Hispanics may be of any race.

★854★

Voting

Reported Voting and Registration in the Midwest, by Race/Ethnicity, Age and Sex, 1992

Data for November 1992 are shown in thousands and as percent of total in each voting status category.

Race, Hispanic origin, sex, and age	All persons	Reported registered Number	Reported registered Percent	Reported voted Number	Reported voted Percent	Reported that they did not vote[1] Total	Registered	Not registered Total[2]	Not a U.S. citizen	Do not know and not reported on registration[3]
All Races										
Both Sexes										
Total, 18 years and over	44,410	33,137	74.6	29,830	67.2	14,580	3,307	11,272	1,098	2,610
18 to 20 years	2,429	1,343	55.3	1,068	44.0	1,361	275	1,086	80	219
21 to 24 years	3,591	2,318	64.6	1,946	54.2	1,645	372	1,273	117	275
25 to 34 years	9,793	6,744	68.9	5,863	59.9	3,929	881	3,049	327	534
35 to 44 years	9,339	7,120	76.2	6,593	70.6	2,745	526	2,219	260	537
45 to 54 years	6,670	5,338	80.0	4,990	74.8	1,680	348	1,332	146	334
55 to 64 years	4,876	3,994	81.9	3,734	76.6	1,143	260	882	81	249
65 to 74 years	4,397	3,646	82.9	3,403	77.4	994	243	751	62	226
75 years and over	3,315	2,635	79.5	2,233	67.4	1,062	402	680	25	236
Male										
Total, 18 years and over	21,187	15,561	73.4	13,971	65.9	7,217	1,591	5,626	573	1,309
18 to 20 years	1,253	678	54.1	523	41.8	730	155	575	44	118
21 to 24 years	1,754	1,118	63.7	928	52.9	826	190	636	60	146

[Continued]

★854★

Reported Voting and Registration in the Midwest, by Race/Ethnicity, Age and Sex, 1992

[Continued]

Race, Hispanic origin, sex, and age	All persons	Reported registered		Reported voted		Reported that they did not vote[1]				
						Total	Registered	Not registered		
								Total[2]	Not a U.S. citizen	Do not know and not reported on registration[3]
		Number	Percent	Number	Percent					
25 to 34 years	4,819	3,194	66.3	2,744	57.0	2,074	450	1,625	177	306
35 to 44 years	4,617	3,433	74.4	3,151	68.3	1,465	282	1,184	147	270
45 to 54 years	3,218	2,534	78.7	2,373	73.78	846	161	685	74	183
55 to 64 years	2,356	1,938	82.2	1,822	77.3	535	116	419	38	113
65 to 74 years	1,951	1,654	84.8	1,535	78.7	415	118	297	26	91
75 years and over	1,220	1,013	83.1	894	73.3	326	120	207	7	82
Female										
Total, 18 years and over	23,222	17,576	75.7	15,859	68.3	7,363	1,717	5,646	525	1,301
18 to 20 years	1,176	665	56.5	544	46.3	631	121	511	36	101
21 to 24 years	1,837	1,200	65.3	1,018	55.4	819	182	637	57	129
25 to 34 years	4,974	3,550	71.4	3,119	62.7	1,855	431	1,424	150	228
35 to 44 years	4,722	3,687	78.1	3,442	72.9	1,260	245	1,036	113	267
45 to 54 years	3,452	2,804	81.2	2,617	75.8	835	187	648	72	151
55 to 64 years	2,520	2,056	81.6	1,912	75.9	608	144	464	43	137
65 to 74 years	2,447	1,993	81.4	1,868	76.4	578	124	454	36	135
75 years and over	2,095	1,621	77.4	1,339	63.9	756	282	473	19	154
White										
Both Sexes										
Total, 18 years and over	39,607	29,964	75.7	27,136	68.5	12,471	2,828	9,643	770	2,164
18 to 20 years	2,080	1,190	57.2	955	45.9	1,124	235	890	58	171
21 to 24 years	3,062	2,023	66.1	1,702	55.6	1,360	321	1,039	77	205
25 to 34 years	8,590	6,037	70.3	5,310	61.8	3,260	726	2,554	201	422
35 to 44 years	8,346	6,446	77.2	6,005	72.0	2,341	441	1,899	187	451
45 to 54 years	6,038	4,853	80.4	4,545	75.3	1,494	309	1,185	107	270
55 to 64 years	4,384	3,606	82.3	3,382	77.2	1,002	224	778	67	220
65 to 74 years	4,037	3,358	83.2	3,149	78.0	888	209	679	51	206
75 years and over	3,070	2,451	79.9	2,087	68.0	963	364	619	22	218
Male										
Total, 18 years and over	19,036	14,221	74.7	12,846	67.5	6,190	1,375	4,815	394	1,097
18 to 20 years	1,079	606	56.1	472	43.7	607	134	474	30	95
21 to 24 years	1,505	988	645.6	830	55.1	676	158	518	39	106
25 to 34 years	4,278	2,908	68.0	2,523	59.0	1,755	385	1,371	108	255
35 to 44 years	4,168	3,162	75.9	2,923	70.1	1,245	239	1,007	98	227
45 to 54 years	2,959	2,342	79.1	2,197	74.3	761	144	617	55	155
55 to 64 years	2,142	1,766	82.4	1,657	77.4	484	108	376	35	93
65 to 74 years	1,780	1,515	85.1	1,415	79.5	366	100	265	25	85
75 years and over	1,124	936	83.3	829	73.8	295	107	188	3	82
Female										
Total, 18 years and over	20,571	15,743	76.5	14,289	69.5	6,261	1,453	4,828	376	1,067
18 to 20 years	1,000	584	58.4	483	48.3	517	101	416	27	76
21 to 24 years	1,556	1,035	66.5	872	56.0	584	163	522	38	99
25 to 34 years	4,312	3,129	72.6	2,787	64.6	1,525	342	1,183	93	167
35 to 44 years	4,177	3,285	78.6	3,082	73.8	1,095	203	893	89	224
45 to 54 years	3,080	2,512	81.6	2,347	76.2	732	164	568	52	115
55 to 64 years	2,242	1,840	82.1	1,725	76.9	517	115	402	33	127
65 to 74 years	2,257	1,843	81.6	1,734	76.8	523	109	414	26	123
75 years and over	1,945	1,515	77.9	1,258	64.7	688	257	430	19	136

[Continued]

★ 854 ★

Reported Voting and Registration in the Midwest, by Race/Ethnicity, Age and Sex, 1992

[Continued]

Race, Hispanic origin, sex, and age	All persons	Reported registered		Reported voted		Reported that they did not vote[1]				
						Total	Registered	Not registered		
		Number	Percent	Number	Percent			Total[2]	Not a U.S. citizen	Do not know and not reported on registration[3]
Black										
Both Sexes										
Total, 18 years and over	3,943	2,809	71.2	2,393	60.7	1,550	415	1,135	50	389
18 to 20 years	278	128	46.0	95	34.2	183	33	150	2	41
21 to 24 years	441	267	60.5	222	50.4	219	45	174	11	63
25 to 34 years	977	642	65.8	503	51.4	474	140	334	24	97
35 to 44 years	799	588	73.6	513	64.1	287	75	211	10	78
45 to 54 years	495	413	83.5	378	76.3	117	35	82	1	49
55 to 64 years	411	335	81.5	307	74.6	105	28	76	2	27
65 to 74 years	309	259	83.7	236	76.4	73	23	50	-	17
75 years and over	232	176	75.7	140	60.3	92	36	56	-	18
Male										
Total, 18 years and over	1,723	1,168	67.8	974	56.6	748	193	555	34	183
18 to 20 years	131	58	44.0	40	30.7	91	18	74	2	20
21 to 24 years	196	112	57.3	84	42.9	112	28	84	5	35
25 to 34 years	431	257	59.6	199	46.1	232	58	174	19	45
35 to 44 years	359	240	67.0	198	55.2	161	42	118	9	42
45 to 54 years	184	152	82.5	139	75.2	46	13	32	-	18
55 to 64 years	185	153	82.8	145	78.5	40	8	32	-	19
65 to 74 years	148	121	81.7	107	72.1	41	14	27	-	5
75 years and over	87	74	84.4	62	71.5	25	11	14	-	-
Female										
Total, 18 years and over	2,221	1,641	73.9	1,419	63.9	802	222	580	16	206
18 to 20 years	147	70	47.8	55	37.3	92	15	77	-	22
21 to 24 years	245	154	63.0	138	56.4	107	16	90	6	28
25 to 34 years	546	385	70.6	304	55.7	242	82	160	5	52
35 to 44 years	440	348	79.0	315	71.4	126	33	93	2	36
45 to 54 years	311	261	84.1	239	77.0	72	22	49	1	31
55 to 64 years	226	182	80.4	161	71.4	65	20	44	2	8
65 to 74 years	161	138	85.5	130	80.3	32	8	23	-	12
75 years and over	145	102	70.5	78	53.6	67	25	43	-	18
Hispanic[4]										
Both Sexes										
Total, 18 years and over	1,104	439	39.8	354	32.1	750	85	665	367	105
18 to 20 years	86	20	23.5	14	16.8	72	6	66	27	16
21 to 24 years	110	29	26.6	19	17.3	91	10	81	39	15
25 to 34 years	312	103	33.0	74	23.9	237	28	209	120	35
35 to 44 years	312	120	38.5	109	34.8	204	11	192	99	31
45 to 54 years	132	68	51.8	59	44.8	73	9	64	55	6
55 to 64 years	74	50	(B)	40	(B)	34	10	24	14	-
65 to 74 years	60	47	(B)	37	(B)	23	10	12	3	3
75 years and over	19	2	(B)	2	(B)	17	-	17	10	-
Male										
Total, 18 years and over	550	204	37.1	170	30.8	380	34	346	204	57
18 to 20 years	38	7	(B)	3	(B)	35	4	31	13	7
21 to 24 years	54	12	(B)	7	(B)	47	5	42	24	11
25 to 34 years	149	43	28.8	32	21.2	117	11	106	62	16
35 to 44 years	151	44	29.3	43	28.2	109	2	107	60	19
45 to 54 years	75	36	48.0	34	45.2	41	2	39	36	3

[Continued]

★ 854 ★

Reported Voting and Registration in the Midwest, by Race/Ethnicity, Age and Sex, 1992

[Continued]

Race, Hispanic origin, sex, and age	All persons	Reported registered		Reported voted		Reported that they did not vote[1]				
						Total	Registered	Not registered		
								Total[2]	Not a U.S. citizen	Do not know and not reported on registration[3]
		Number	Percent	Number	Percent					
55 to 64 years	44	28	(B)	23	(B)	21	6	15	9	-
65 to 74 years	36	32	(B)	27	(B)	8	5	3	-	2
75 years and over	4	2	(B)	2	(B)	2	-	2	-	-
Female										
Total, 18 years and over	554	235	42.4	185	33.3	370	51	319	163	48
18 to 20 years	48	14	(B)	12	(B)	37	2	35	14	9
21 to 24 years	55	17	(B)	12	(B)	43	5	38	15	4
25 to 34 years	163	60	36.9	43	26.3	120	17	103	58	19
35 to 44 years	161	76	47.1	66	41.0	95	10	85	39	12
45 to 54 years	57	32	(B)	25	(B)	32	7	25	19	3
55 to 64 years	30	21	(B)	17	(B)	13	4	9	5	-
65 to 74 years	24	15	(B)	10	(B)	15	5	9	3	2
75 years and over	15	-	(B)	-	(B)	15	-	15	10	-

Source: U.S. Bureau of the Census. *Voting and Registration in the Election of November 1992*, Current Population Reports, P20-466. Washington, DC, U.S. GPO, 1993, pp. 8-9. *Notes:* A dash stands for zero or rounds to zero. A (B) stands for base less than 75,000. 1. Includes persons reported as "did not know," and "not reported" on voting. 2. In addition to those reported as "not registered," total includes those "not a U.S. citizen," and "do not know" and "not reported" on registration. 3. Includes "do not know" and "not reported" on citizenship. 4. Persons of Hispanic origin may be of any race.

★ 855 ★

Voting

Reported Voting and Registration in the Northeast, by Race/Ethnicity, Age and Sex, 1992

Data for November 1992 are shown in thousands and as percent of total in each voting status category.

Race, Hispanic origin, sex, and age	All persons	Reported registered		Reported voted		Reported that they did not vote[1]				
						Total	Registered	Not registered		
								Total[2]	Not a U.S. citizen	Do not know and not reported on registration[3]
		Number	Percent	Number	Percent					
All Races										
Both Sexes										
Total, 18 years and over	38,329	25,673	67.0	23,448	61.2	14,881	2,225	12,656	2,568	2,630
18 to 20 years	1,858	858	46.2	686	36.9	1,172	172	999	137	194
21 to 24 years	2,840	1,560	54.9	1,358	47.8	1,482	203	1,280	263	238
25 to 34 years	8,491	5,088	59.9	4,580	53.9	3,911	508	3,403	789	531
35 to 44 years	8,154	5,587	68.5	5,183	63.6	2,972	404	2,568	615	461
45 to 54 years	5,687	4,090	71.9	3,849	67.7	1,838	242	1,597	335	350
55 to 64 years	4,525	3,431	75.8	3,240	71.6	1,285	191	1,094	217	319
65 to 74 years	4,063	3,085	75.9	2,869	70.6	1,194	216	978	123	285
75 years and over	2,711	1,974	72.8	1,684	62.1	1,027	290	737	89	252
Male										
Total, 18 years and over	18,106	11,979	66.2	10,966	60.6	7,141	1,014	6,127	1,257	1,286
18 to 20 years	913	404	44.3	320	35.0	593	84	509	70	97
21 to 24 years	1,422	776	54.6	666	45.8	756	110	645	134	123
25 to 34 years	4,149	2,427	58.5	2,159	52.0	1,990	268	1,722	408	289
35 to 44 years	3,985	2,658	66.7	2,460	61.7	1,525	198	1,327	317	247

[Continued]

★ 855 ★

Reported Voting and Registration in the Northeast, by Race/Ethnicity, Age and Sex, 1992

[Continued]

Race, Hispanic origin, sex, and age	All persons	Reported registered		Reported voted		Reported that they did not vote[1]				
						Total	Registered	Not registered		
		Number	Percent	Number	Percent			Total[2]	Not a U.S. citizen	Do not know and not reported on registration[3]
45 to 54 years	2,752	1,960	71.2	1,864	67.8	887	96	792	160	176
55 to 64 years	2,105	1,601	76.1	1,515	72.0	590	86	504	91	141
65 to 74 years	1,846	1,422	77.0	1,335	72.3	511	87	424	47	135
75 years and over	935	732	78.3	647	69.2	288	85	203	29	78
Female										
Total, 18 years and over	20,223	13,694	67.7	12,483	61.7	7,740	1,211	6,529	1,311	1,344
18 to 20 years	945	454	48.1	367	38.8	578	88	490	67	96
21 to 24 years	1,419	784	55.3	692	48.8	727	93	634	129	115
25 to 34 years	4,342	2,661	61.3	2,421	55.8	1,921	240	1,681	380	242
35 to 44 years	4,169	2,929	70.2	2,723	65.3	1,446	206	1,240	298	214
45 to 54 years	2,935	2,131	72.6	1,985	67.6	951	146	805	174	174
55 to 64 years	2,420	1,830	75.6	1,725	71.3	695	105	590	125	178
65 to 74 years	2,217	1,663	75.0	1,534	69.2	683	129	554	77	150
75 years and over	1,775	1,241	69.9	1,037	58.4	739	205	534	60	174
White										
Both Sexes										
Total, 18 years and over	33,206	23,138	69.7	21,305	64.2	11,900	1,833	10,068	1,467	2,129
18 to 20 years	1,482	749	50.5	613	41.4	868	135	733	49	141
21 to 24 years	2,337	1,358	58.1	1,203	51.5	1,134	154	980	135	173
25 to 34 years	7,266	4,533	62.4	4,112	56.6	3,154	422	2,732	461	421
35 to 44 years	6,956	4,977	71.5	4,647	66.8	2,310	330	1,979	337	356
45 to 54 years	4,953	3,689	74.5	3,499	70.6	1,455	191	1,264	184	287
55 to 64 years	3,986	3,094	77.6	2,942	73.8	1,044	151	893	152	269
65 to 74 years	3,718	2,895	77.9	2,711	72.9	1,007	184	823	89	244
75 years and over	2,507	1,843	73.5	1,579	63.0	928	265	664	60	237
Male										
Total, 18 years and over	15,762	10,894	69.1	10,047	63.7	5,715	847	4,868	723	1,015
18 to 20 years	729	343	47.1	279	38.2	450	65	385	31	67
21 to 24 years	1,176	671	57.1	588	50.0	588	83	505	79	86
25 to 34 years	3,582	2,197	61.3	1,971	55.0	1,611	226	1,385	242	232
35 to 44 years	3,431	2,415	70.4	2,243	65.4	1,187	171	1,016	170	184
45 to 54 years	2,396	1,770	73.9	1,691	70.6	705	79	626	86	143
55 to 64 years	1,878	1,466	78.1	1,397	74.4	481	69	412	61	117
65 to 74 years	1,696	1,344	79.2	1,269	74.8	427	74	352	33	114
75 years and over	875	689	78.7	609	69.6	266	80	186	21	74
Female										
Total, 18 years and over	17,444	12,244	70.2	11,259	64.5	6,185	985	5,200	744	1,113
18 to 20 years	753	406	53.9	335	44.5	418	71	347	18	74
21 to 24 years	1,161	687	59.1	616	53.0	546	71	475	56	87
25 to 34 years	3,683	2,336	63.4	2,140	58.1	1,543	196	1,347	219	189
35 to 44 years	3,526	2,562	72.7	2,403	68.2	1,122	159	963	167	173
45 to 54 years	2,558	1,920	75.1	1,808	70.7	750	112	638	98	144
55 to 64 ycars	2,108	1,627	77.2	1,546	73.3	563	82	481	92	152
65 to 74 years	2,022	1,551	76.7	1,441	71.3	580	110	471	56	130
75 years and over	1,632	1,155	70.7	970	59.4	663	185	478	39	163
Black										
Both Sexes										
Total, 18 years and over	4,033	2,239	55.5	1,905	47.2	2,128	334	1,794	578	423

[Continued]

★ 855 ★

Reported Voting and Registration in the Northeast, by Race/Ethnicity, Age and Sex, 1992

[Continued]

Race, Hispanic origin, sex, and age	All persons	Reported registered		Reported voted		Reported that they did not vote[1]				
						Total	Registered	Not registered		
		Number	Percent	Number	Percent			Total[2]	Not a U.S. citizen	Do not know and not reported on registration[3]
18 to 20 years	304	94	31.0	60	19.9	243	34	210	58	41
21 to 24 years	378	174	46.1	138	36.7	239	36	203	71	48
25 to 34 years	969	509	52.5	426	43.9	544	83	461	176	99
35 to 44 years	931	529	56.8	462	49.6	469	67	402	144	94
45 to 54 years	550	332	60.4	295	53.6	255	37	218	78	52
55 to 64 years	445	302	67.7	271	60.8	174	31	144	32	42
65 to 74 years	287	175	60.8	151	52.4	137	24	113	13	35
75 years and over	169	125	74.2	103	60.9	66	22	44	7	11
Male										
Total, 18 years and over	1,833	950	51.8	806	44.0	1,027	144	883	285	227
18 to 20 years	150	50	33.2	31	2.9	119	18	100	27	24
21 to 24 years	185	88	47.4	68	36.9	117	19	97	30	28
25 to 34 years	446	210	47.2	170	38.2	275	40	235	93	51
35 to 44 years	427	215	50.3	191	44.8	236	24	212	77	55
45 to 54 years	268	155	57.7	1742	52.8	126	13	113	38	28
55 to 64 years	181	120	66.3	106	58.5	75	14	61	12	18
65 to 74 years	125	70	55.7	60	48.0	65	10	55	7	19
75 years and over	51	43	(B)	38	(B)	14	6	8	2	5
Female										
Total, 18 years and over	2,200	1,290	58.6	1,100	50.0	1,101	190	911	292	195
18 to 20 years	154	44	28.8	29	18.9	125	15	109	31	17
21 to 24 years	192	86	44.9	70	36.4	122	16	106	40	20
25 to 34 years	524	299	57.0	256	48.8	268	43	225	73	47
35 to 44 years	504	314	62.3	271	53.7	233	43	190	66	39
45 to 54 years	282	177	62.9	153	54.3	129	24	105	40	24
55 to 64 years	264	182	68.8	165	62.4	99	17	83	20	25
65 to 74 years	162	105	64.8	91	55.8	72	15	57	6	17
75 years and over	118	82	70.0	66	55.7	52	17	35	5	7
Hispanic[4]										
Both Sexes										
Total, 18 years and over	2,123	808	38.1	675	31.8	1,448	133	1,314	674	190
18 to 20 years	132	34	25.6	32	24.0	100	2	98	28	13
21 to 24 years	229	85	37.1	60	26.4	169	25	144	73	22
25 to 34 years	576	196	34.0	153	26.6	423	43	380	227	34
35 to 44 years	485	201	41.4	182	37.4	304	20	284	157	33
45 to 54 years	320	138	43.1	122	38.1	198	16	182	73	40
55 to 64 years	186	91	49.1	80	43.1	106	11	94	59	14
65 to 74 years	118	34	29.1	26	21.7	912	9	84	36	17
75 years and over	76	29	38.1	20	26.4	56	9	47	22	15
Male										
Total, 18 years and over	959	323	33.7	280	29.2	679	43	636	337	87
18 to 20 years	69	13	(B)	12	(B)	57	1	56	23	8
21 to 24 years	110	29	26.5	17	15.9	92	12	81	38	14
25 to 34 years	259	70	26.9	56	21.7	203	13	189	125	13
35 to 44 years	231	92	39.6	84	36.2	148	8	140	73	15
45 to 54 years	152	60	39.3	55	36.1	97	5	92	38	23
55 to 64 years	64	34	(B)	33	(B)	31	2	30	19	5
65 to 74 years	53	20	(B)	18	(B)	36	3	33	8	6
75 years and over	21	6	(B)	6	(B)	16	-	16	11	4

[Continued]

★ 855 ★

Reported Voting and Registration in the Northeast, by Race/Ethnicity, Age and Sex, 1992

[Continued]

Race, Hispanic origin, sex, and age	All persons	Reported registered		Reported voted		Reported that they did not vote[1]				
						Total	Registered	Not registered		
		Number	Percent	Number	Percent			Total[2]	Not a U.S. citizen	Do not know and not reported on registration[3]
Female										
Total, 18 years and over	1,163	485	41.7	395	33.9	768	90	678	338	102
18 to 20 years	63	21	(B)	20	(B)	43	1	42	6	6
21 to 24 years	119	56	46.8	43	36.0	76	13	64	34	9
25 to 34 years	317	126	39.8	97	30.6	220	29	191	102	21
35 to 44 years	254	110	43.1	98	38.6	156	12	145	83	18
45 to 54 years	168	78	46.5	67	39.9	101	11	90	35	18
55 to 64 years	122	57	46.8	47	39.0	74	10	65	39	9
65 to 74 years	65	14	(B)	8	(B)	57	6	51	28	11
75 years and over	55	23	(B)	15	(B)	41	9	32	10	11

Source: U.S. Bureau of the Census. *Voting and Registration in the Election of November 1992*, Current Population Reports, P20-466. Washington, DC, U.S. GPO, 1993, pp. 6-7. *Notes:* A (B) stands for base less than 75,000. 1. Includes persons reported as "did not know," and "not reported" on voting. 2. In addition to those reported as "not registered," total includes those "not a U.S. citizen," and "do not know" and "not reported" on registration. 3. Includes "do not know" and "not reported" on citizenship. 4. Persons of Hispanic origin may be of any race.

★ 856 ★

Voting

Reported Voting and Registration in the South, by Race/Ethnicity, Age and Sex, 1992

Data for November 1992 are shown in thousands and as percent of total in each voting status category.

Race, Hispanic origin, sex, and age	All persons	Reported registered		Reported voted		Reported that they did not vote[1]				
						Total	Registered	Not registered		
		Number	Percent	Number	Percent			Total[2]	Not a U.S. citizen	Do not know and not reported on registration[3]
All Races										
Both Sexes										
Total, 18 years and over	63,659	42,762	67.2	37,590	59.0	26,068	5,172	20,896	2,838	3,229
18 to 20 years	3,321	1,586	47.8	1,223	36.8	2,099	363	1,735	192	221
21 to 24 years	4,993	2,682	53.7	2,140	42.9	2,852	541	2,311	273	355
25 to 34 years	14,025	8,235	58.7	7,043	50.2	6,982	1,193	5,790	876	686
35 to 44 years	13,421	9,132	68.0	8,212	61.2	5,209	920	4,289	661	684
45 to 54 years	9,775	7,143	73.1	6,490	66.4	3,285	653	2,631	340	494
55 to 64 years	7,528	5,718	76.0	5,201	69.1	2,327	517	1,810	227	342
65 to 74 years	6,520	5,181	79.5	4,689	71.9	1,831	492	1,339	137	256
75 years and over	4,076	3,084	75.7	2,592	63.6	1,484	492	992	115	191
Male										
Total, 18 years and over	30,100	19,870	66.0	17,470	58.0	12,630	2,401	10,229	1,459	1,656
18 to 20 years	1,670	760	45.5	566	33.9	1,104	194	910	104	101
21 to 24 years	2,377	1,179	49.6	892	37.5	1,485	288	1,197	141	223
25 to 34 years	6,763	3,769	55.7	3,202	47.3	3,561	567	2,994	517	402
35 to 44 years	6,500	4,340	66.8	3,874	59.6	2,627	467	2,160	341	325
45 to 54 years	4,748	3,426	72.2	3,138	66.1	1,611	289	1,322	175	285
55 to 64 years	3,556	2,724	76.6	2,479	69.7	1,077	245	832	86	168
65 to 74 years	2,907	2,373	81.7	2,185	75.2	722	189	533	58	101
75 years and over	1,578	1,298	82.3	1,134	71.9	443	164	280	38	50

[Continued]

★ 856 ★

Reported Voting and Registration in the South, by Race/Ethnicity, Age and Sex, 1992

[Continued]

Race, Hispanic origin, sex, and age	All persons	Reported registered		Reported voted		Reported that they did not vote[1]				
						Total	Registered	Not registered		
		Number	Percent	Number	Percent			Total[2]	Not a U.S. citizen	Do not know and not reported on registration[3]
Female										
Total, 18 years and over	33,559	22,892	68.2	20,121	60.0	13,438	2,771	10,667	1,379	1,573
18 to 20 years	1,651	826	50.0	657	39.8	994	169	825	88	121
21 to 24 years	2,616	1,503	57.4	1,249	47.7	1,367	254	1,113	132	132
25 to 34 years	7,262	4,467	61.5	3,841	52.9	3,421	626	2,795	377	284
35 to 44 years	6,921	4,792	69.2	4,338	62.7	2,583	454	2,129	320	358
45 to 54 years	5,026	3,717	74.0	3,352	66.7	1,674	364	1,309	165	210
55 to 64 years	3,972	2,994	75.4	2,722	68.5	1,250	272	978	141	174
65 to 74 years	3,613	2,807	77.7	2,504	69.3	1,109	303	806	79	155
75 years and over	2,496	1,786	71.5	1,458	58.4	1,040	328	713	77	141
White										
Both Sexes										
Total, 18 years and over	51,001	34,954	68.5	31,034	60.8	19,967	3,920	16,047	2,044	2,299
18 to 20 years	2,426	1,192	49.1	926	38.2	1,500	266	1,234	134	151
21 to 24 years	3,801	2,047	53.9	1,695	44.6	2,106	352	1,754	204	261
25 to 34 years	10,819	6,452	59.6	5,605	51.8	5,215	847	4,367	610	445
35 to 44 years	10,700	7,411	69.3	6,712	62.7	3,989	699	3,290	437	464
45 to 54 years	7,964	5,918	74.1	5,403	67.7	2,581	516	2,066	267	360
55 to 64 years	6,225	4,780	76.8	4,375	70.3	1,851	406	1,445	183	252
65 to 74 years	5,522	4,463	80.8	4,054	73.4	1,467	408	1,059	108	211
75 years and over	3,523	2,691	76.4	2,265	64.3	1,259	426	833	101	155
Male										
Total, 18 years and over	24,394	16,474	67.5	14,669	60.1	9,725	1,806	7,920	1,053	1,174
18 to 20 years	1,221	567	46.5	425	34.8	795	142	654	79	62
21 to 24 years	1,634	919	50.1	740	40.3	1,095	179	916	101	173
25 to 34 years	5,313	3,023	56.9	2,631	49.5	2,682	392	2,290	346	255
35 to 44 years	5,301	3,562	67.2	3,202	60.4	2,099	360	1,739	243	227
45 to 54 years	3,932	2,911	74.0	2,676	68.1	1,256	235	1,021	137	205
55 to 64 years	2,942	2,296	78.1	2,104	71.5	838	192	646	65	122
65 to 74 years	2,454	2,050	83.2	1,892	76.8	572	158	414	46	86
75 years and over	1,365	1,146	82.7	999	72.1	387	148	239	35	43
Female										
Total, 18 years and over	26,507	18,480	69.5	16,365	61.5	10,242	2,114	8,128	991	1,125
18 to 20 years	1,205	625	51.9	501	41.5	705	125	580	55	89
21 to 24 years	1,966	1,128	57.4	955	48.6	1,011	173	838	103	88
25 to 34 years	5,506	3,429	62.3	2,974	54.0	2,533	456	2,077	265	190
35 to 44 years	5,399	3,848	71.3	3,510	65.0	1,889	339	1,551	193	237
45 to 54 years	4,052	3,007	74.2	2,726	67.3	1,325	281	1,045	130	154
55 to 64 years	3,283	2,484	75.7	2,271	69.2	1,013	213	799	118	130
65 to 74 years	3,058	2,413	78.9	2,163	70.7	895	250	644	61	126
75 years and over	2,138	1,544	72.2	1,266	59.2	871	278	593	66	111
Black										
Both Sexes										
Total, 18 years and over	11,334	7,331	64.7	6,151	54.3	5,183	1,180	4,004	338	836
18 to 20 years	807	365	45.2	275	34.1	532	90	442	34	62
21 to 24 years	1,071	590	55.1	414	38.6	657	176	481	31	85
25 to 34 years	2,878	1,708	59.3	1,373	47.7	1,504	334	1,170	124	222
35 to 44 years	2,387	1,621	67.9	1,413	59.2	974	208	766	95	194
45 to 54 years	1,574	1,112	70.6	982	62.4	591	129	462	35	120

[Continued]

★ 856 ★

Reported Voting and Registration in the South, by Race/Ethnicity, Age and Sex, 1992

[Continued]

Race, Hispanic origin, sex, and age	All persons	Reported registered		Reported voted		Reported that they did not vote[1]				
						Total	Registered	Not registered		
		Number	Percent	Number	Percent			Total[2]	Not a U.S. citizen	Do not know and not reported on registration[3]
55 to 64 years	1,162	862	74.2	767	66.0	395	95	300	6	78
65 to 74 years	924	692	74.9	610	66.1	313	81	232	4	41
75 years and over	532	382	71.8	316	59.4	216	66	150	9	35
Male										
Total, 18 years and over	5,099	3,180	62.4	2,622	51.4	2,477	558	1,919	183	440
18 to 20 years	405	177	43.8	127	31.4	277	50	227	10	36
21 to 24 years	485	238	49.0	141	29.1	344	96	247	23	46
25 to 34 years	1,298	716	55.1	546	42.1	752	170	582	92	137
35 to 44 years	1,051	737	70.2	637	60.6	414	101	313	38	87
45 to 54 years	719	462	64.3	411	57.2	308	51	256	19	72
55 to 64 years	550	396	72.0	352	64.1	197	44	154	-	44
65 to 74 years	409	308	75.3	277	67.8	132	31	101	1	13
75 years and over	184	146	79.6	130	70.9	53	16	38	-	7
Female										
Total, 18 years and over	6,236	4,151	66.6	3,529	56.6	2,706	621	2,085	155	396
18 to 20 years	403	188	46.7	148	36.8	255	40	215	25	27
21 to 24 years	586	352	60.1	272	46.5	131	80	234	8	39
25 to 34 years	1,580	992	62.8	827	52.4	753	165	588	31	85
35 to 44 years	1,336	884	66.1	776	58.1	560	108	452	57	107
45 to 54 years	855	649	75.9	571	66.8	284	78	206	16	49
55 to 64 years	612	466	76.1	415	67.8	197	51	146	6	34
65 to 74 years	515	384	74.5	333	64.7	182	50	131	3	28
75 years and over	349	236	67.6	186	53.3	163	50	113	9	28
Hispanic[4]										
Both Sexes										
Total, 18 years and over	4,687	1,842	39.3	1,499	32.0	3,189	344	2,845	1,591	314
18 to 20 years	338	102	30.1	61	18.2	276	40	236	118	26
21 to 24 years	467	142	30.4	109	23.3	358	33	325	154	47
25 to 34 years	1,248	396	31.7	304	24.4	944	914	852	491	65
35 to 44 years	992	400	40.3	332	33.4	661	68	493	314	79
45 to 54 years	708	327	46.2	274	38.7	434	53	381	27	50
55 to 64 years	431	215	49.9	198	45.9	233	17	216	125	27
65 to 74 years	311	169	54.3	140	45.1	171	29	142	80	15
75 years and over	192	92	48.1	81	42.0	112	12	100	81	5
Male										
Total, 18 years and over	2,330	855	36.7	704	30.2	1,627	152	1,475	846	176
18 to 20 years	187	50	26.8	27	14.7	159	23	137	69	15
21 to 24 years	223	53	23.7	38	16.9	185	15	170	78	35
25 to 34 years	668	185	27.8	153	23.0	514	32	482	292	39
35 to 44 years	511	191	37.4	160	31.2	351	31	320	177	41
45 to 54 years	367	162	44.2	137	37.3	230	25	205	125	32
55 to 64 years	162	96	59.1	90	55.5	72	6	66	42	10
65 to 74 years	136	81	59.7	62	45.5	74	19	55	33	-
75 years and over	76	37	48.4	37	48.4	39	-	39	29	5
Female										
Total, 18 years and over	2,357	987	41.9	795	33.7	1,562	192	1,370	745	139
18 to 20 years	151	51	34.2	34	22.5	117	18	99	48	12
21 to 24 years	243	89	36.6	71	29.1	173	18	154	76	12
25 to 34 years	581	210	36.2	151	26.0	430	59	370	199	26

[Continued]

★ 856 ★

Reported Voting and Registration in the South, by Race/Ethnicity, Age and Sex, 1992

[Continued]

Race, Hispanic origin, sex, and age	All persons	Reported registered		Reported voted		Reported that they did not vote[1]				
						Total	Registered	Not registered		
								Total[2]	Not a U.S. citizen	Do not know and not reported on registration[3]
		Number	Percent	Number	Percent					
35 to 44 years	481	209	43.4	172	35.7	309	37	273	137	38
45 to 54 years	341	165	48.4	137	40.1	204	28	176	102	18
55 to 64 years	269	119	44.3	108	40.1	161	11	150	83	18
65 to 74 years	175	87	50.1	78	44.8	96	9	87	47	15
75 years and over	116	56	47.8	44	37.8	72	12	61	52	-

Source: U.S. Bureau of the Census. *Voting and Registration in the Election of November 1992*, Current Population Reports, P20-466. Washington, DC, U.S. GPO, 1993, pp. 10-11. *Notes:* A dash (-) stands for zero or rounds to zero. 1. Includes persons reported as "did not know," and "not reported" on voting. 2. In addition to those reported as "not registered," total includes those "not a U.S. citizen," and "do not know" and "not reported" on registration. 3. Includes "do not know" and "not reported" on citizenship. 4. Persons of Hispanic origin may be of any race.

★ 857 ★

Voting

Reported Voting and Registration in the West, by Race/Ethnicity, Age and Sex, 1992

Data for November 1992 are shown in thousands and as percent of total in each voting status category.

Race, Hispanic origin, sex, and age	All persons	Reported registered		Reported voted		Reported that they did not vote[1]				
						Total	Registered	Not registered		
								Total[2]	Not a U.S. citizen	Do not know and not reported on registration[3]
		Number	Percent	Number	Percent					
All Races										
Both Sexes										
Total, 18 years and over	39,286	25,005	63.6	22,997	58.5	16,289	2,006	14,281	5,396	2,169
18 to 20 years	2,119	906	42.9	772	36.4	1,348	136	1,211	448	187
21 to 24 years	3,220	1,531	47.6	1,249	38.8	1,971	262	1,689	635	207
25 to 34 years	9,294	5,155	55.5	4,633	49.9	4,661	522	4,139	1,666	472
35 to 44 years	8,801	5,664	64.4	5,281	60.0	3,520	383	3,137	1,263	463
45 to 54 years	5,926	4,214	71.1	3,963	66.9	1,963	250	1,712	614	287
55 to 64 years	4,160	3,088	74.2	2,932	70.5	1,227	155	1,072	431	197
65 to 74 years	3,466	2,773	80.0	2,645	76.3	820	128	692	216	185
75 years and over	2,299	1,672	72.7	1,521	66.1	778	151	627	123	171
Male										
Total, 18 years and over	19,164	11,843	61.8	10,907	56.9	8,257	936	7,321	2,777	1,076
18 to 20 years	1,040	432	41.6	377	36.3	663	55	608	227	89
21 to 24 years	1,606	724	45.1	600	37.4	1,006	124	882	387	105
25 to 34 years	4,735	2,479	52.4	2,219	46.9	2,516	260	2,256	928	254
35 to 44 years	4,407	2,722	61.8	2,510	57.0	1,897	212	1,685	639	217
45 to 54 years	2,890	2,036	70.4	1,913	66.2	977	123	854	288	156
55 to 64 years	1,994	1,462	73.3	1,387	69.5	608	75	532	183	105
65 to 74 years	1,586	1,296	81.7	1,263	79.6	323	33	290	87	82
75 years and over	906	692	76.4	637	70.3	269	55	214	39	68
Female										
Total, 18 years and over	20,122	13,163	65.4	12,091	60.1	8,031	1,072	6,960	2,619	1,093
18 to 20 years	1,079	476	44.1	395	36.6	685	81	603	221	98
21 to 24 years	1,614	807	50.0	649	40.2	966	159	807	248	103

[Continued]

★ 857 ★

Reported Voting and Registration in the West, by Race/Ethnicity, Age and Sex, 1992

[Continued]

Race, Hispanic origin, sex, and age	All persons	Reported registered		Reported voted		Reported that they did not vote[1]				
						Total	Registered	Not registered		
								Total[2]	Not a U.S. citizen	Do not know and not reported on registration[3]
		Number	Percent	Number	Percent					
25 to 34 years	4,559	2,676	58.7	2,414	53.0	2,145	262	1,883	738	218
35 to 44 years	4,395	2,943	67.0	2,771	63.1	1,624	172	1,452	624	246
45 to 54 years	3,036	2,178	71.7	2,050	67.5	986	127	858	327	131
55 to 64 years	2,165	1,626	75.1	1,546	71.4	620	80	540	248	91
65 to 74 years	1,880	1,477	78.6	1,382	73.5	498	95	403	128	102
75 years and over	1,393	980	70.4	884	63.4	509	96	413	84	103
White										
Both Sexes										
Total, 18 years and over	34,023	33,628	66.5	20,930	61.5	13,093	1,696	11,395	4,003	1,697
18 to 20 years	1,755	806	45.9	693	39.5	1,062	114	949	326	121
21 to 24 years	2,738	1,381	50.4	1,144	41.8	1,594	237	1,357	496	148
25 to 34 years	7,965	4,609	57.9	4,167	52.3	3,798	442	3,356	1,324	345
35 to 44 years	7,642	5,130	67.1	4,822	63.1	2,820	308	2,512	940	372
45 to 54 years	5,095	3,781	74.2	3,567	70.0	1,529	215	1,314	404	239
55 to 64 years	3,613	2,790	77.2	2,658	73.6	955	133	822	303	146
65 to 74 years	3,123	2,565	82.1	2,451	78.5	673	115	558	135	173
75 years and over	2,092	1,565	74.8	1,429	68.3	662	136	527	74	152
Male										
Total, 18 years and over	16,724	10,793	64.5	9,990	59.7	6,734	803	5,930	2,128	830
18 to 20 years	847	381	45.0	334	39.5	513	47	466	163	55
21 to 24 years	1,358	660	48.6	552	40.7	806	108	469	308	71
25 to 34 years	4,113	2,232	54.3	2,005	48.7	2,108	228	1,881	764	191
35 to 44 years	3,852	2,479	64.3	2,308	59.9	1,544	170	1,373	494	172
45 to 54 years	2,540	1,864	73.4	1,750	68.9	789	113	676	191	130
55 to 64 years	1,744	1,331	76.3	1,269	72.8	475	62	413	132	74
65 to 74 years	1,445	1,206	83.5	1,179	81.6	266	28	239	52	80
75 years and over	825	640	77.6	892	71.7	233	48	185	24	58
Female										
Total, 18 years and over	17,300	11,835	68.4	10,940	63.2	6,360	895	5,465	1,875	867
18 to 20 years	908	425	46.9	358	39.5	549	67	482	164	67
21 to 24 years	1,380	721	52.2	592	42.9	789	129	659	188	78
25 to 34 years	3,852	2,376	61.7	2,162	56.1	1,690	214	1,476	560	154
35 to 44 years	3,790	2,651	70.0	2,514	66.3	1,276	137	1,139	447	200
45 to 54 years	2,556	1,918	75.0	1,816	71.1	739	101	638	213	109
55 to 64 years	1,868	1,459	78.1	1,388	74.3	480	71	409	171	72
65 to 74 years	1,678	1,359	81.0	1,272	75.8	406	87	319	83	93
75 years and over	1,267	925	73.0	837	66.1	429	87	342	50	94
Black										
Both Sexes										
Total, 18 years and over	1,729	1,063	61.5	922	53.3	807	141	666	78	222
18 to 20 years	111	51	45.4	43	38.9	68	7	61	9	31
21 to 24 years	153	76	49.3	48	31.0	106	28	78	4	34
25 to 34 years	472	248	52.7	216	45.9	255	32	223	24	62
35 to 44 years	398	239	59.9	202	50.7	196	36	160	25	53
45 to 54 years	243	183	75.5	167	68.6	76	17	60	4	13
55 to 64 years	163	112	69.2	107	65.7	56	6	50	12	23
65 to 74 years	114	94	82.7	85	75.2	28	8	20	1	1
75 years and over	76	61	80.1	54	71.1	22	7	15	-	4

[Continued]

★ 857 ★

Reported Voting and Registration in the West, by Race/Ethnicity, Age and Sex, 1992

[Continued]

Race, Hispanic origin, sex, and age	All persons	Reported registered		Reported voted		Reported that they did not vote[1]				
						Total	Registered	Not registered		
		Number	Percent	Number	Percent			Total[2]	Not a U.S. citizen	Do not know and not reported on registration[3]
Male										
Total, 18 years and over	771	429	55.7	384	49.8	387	45	342	45	115
18 to 20 years	59	22	(B)	19	(B)	40	3	37	9	18
21 to 24 years	74	33	(B)	25	(B)	49	8	40	3	24
25 to 34 years	214	100	46.8	94	44.0	120	6	114	11	28
35 to 44 years	191	102	53.5	87	45.8	103	15	89	14	23
45 to 54 years	96	69	72.3	65	68.2	30	4	27	2	7
55 to 64 years	69	41	(B)	37	(B)	32	5	28	6	14
65 to 74 years	42	35	(B)	31	(B)	11	4	7	-	1
75 years and over	28	27	(B)	26	(B)	2	1	1	-	-
Female										
Total, 18 years and over	958	634	66.2	538	56.2	420	96	324	33	108
18 to 20 years	53	29	(B)	24	(B)	28	4	24	-	14
21 to 24 years	80	42	53.2	22	28.2	57	20	37	1	10
25 to 34 years	258	148	57.5	122	47.5	135	26	110	13	35
35 to 44 years	207	136	65.8	115	55.3	93	22	71	11	30
45 to 54 years	147	114	77.6	101	68.9	46	13	33	2	7
55 to 64 years	94	71	76.0	70	74.9	24	1	22	6	9
65 to 74 years	72	59	(B)	54	(B)	17	5	13	-	-
75 years and over	48	34	(B)	28	(B)	20	6	14	-	4
Hispanic[4]										
Both Sexes										
Total, 18 years and over	6,774	2,047	30.2	1,710	25.2	5,064	337	4,727	3,278	385
18 to 20 years	603	112	18.5	75	12.5	528	37	491	310	38
21 to 24 years	831	173	20.8	122	14.6	709	51	658	456	36
25 to 34 years	2,041	544	26.7	468	22.9	1,573	77	1,496	1,092	103
35 to 44 years	1,532	439	28.7	357	23.3	1,175	82	1,093	783	107
45 to 54 years	793	317	40.0	276	34.8	517	41	476	322	47
55 to 64 years	566	268	47.4	248	43.8	318	20	298	203	30
65 to 74 years	278	135	48.6	117	41.9	162	19	143	79	19
75 years and over	129	58	45.2	48	37.0	82	11	71	32	6
Male										
Total, 18 years and over	3,433	955	27.8	793	23.1	2,640	162	2,479	1,745	199
18 to 20 years	269	40	14.8	630	11.0	240	10	229	154	16
21 to 24 years	468	84	18.0	62	13.2	106	22	384	273	23
25 to 34 years	1,106	265	23.9	223	20.2	883	41	842	620	54
35 to 44 years	775	213	27.5	161	20.7	615	53	562	411	52
45 to 54 years	388	158	40.8	137	35.3	251	21	230	155	20
55 to 64 years	266	118	44.3	107	40.2	159	11	148	94	22
65 to 74 years	115	52	45.6	52	45.1	63	1	62	30	11
75 years and over	46	24	(B)	22	(B)	24	3	21	9	1
Female										
Total, 18 years and over	3,341	1,092	32.7	917	27.5	2,423	175	2,248	1,533	186
18 to 20 years	334	72	21.5	46	13.6	288	26	262	156	21
21 to 24 years	363	88	24.4	60	16.5	303	29	274	183	13
25 to 34 years	934	280	29.9	244	26.2	690	35	655	472	50
35 to 44 years	757	226	29.9	197	26.0	560	29	531	372	55
45 to 54 years	405	159	39.3	139	34.3	266	20	246	167	27
55 to 64 years	301	151	50.1	141	47.0	159	9	150	109	8

[Continued]

★ 857 ★

Reported Voting and Registration in the West, by Race/Ethnicity, Age and Sex, 1992

[Continued]

Race, Hispanic origin, sex, and age	All persons	Reported registered		Reported voted		Reported that they did not vote[1]				
						Total	Registered	Not registered		
								Total[2]	Not a U.S. citizen	Do not know and not reported on registration[3]
		Number	Percent	Number	Percent					
65 to 74 years	163	83	50.7	65	39.7	99	18	80	49	8
75 years and over	84	34	40.7	26	31.2	58	8	50	23	5

Source: U.S. Bureau of the Census. *Voting and Registration in the Election of November 1992*, Current Population Reports, P20-466. Washington, DC, U.S. GPO, 1993, pp. 12-13. *Notes:* A dash (-) stands for zero or rounds to zero. A (B) stands for base less than 75,000. 1. Includes persons reported as "did not know," and "not reported" on voting. 2. In addition to those reported as "not registered," total includes those "not a U.S. citizen," and "do not know" and "not reported" on registration. 3. Includes "do not know" and "not reported" on citizenship. 4. Persons of Hispanic origin may be of any race.

★ 858 ★

Voting

Reported Voting and Registration of Persons 18 to 24 Years Old, by Educational Status, Race/Ethnicity, Sex and Age, 1992

Data for November 1992 are shown in thousands and as percent of total in each voting status category.

Race, Hispanic origin, sex, age, and enrollment status	All persons	Reported registered		Reported voted		Reported that they did not vote[1]				
						Total	Registered	Not registered		
								Total[2]	Not a U.S. citizen	Do not know and not reported on registration[3]
		Number	Percent	Number	Percent					
All Races										
Both Sexes										
Total, 18 to 24 years old	24,371	12,787	52.5	10,442	42.8	13,930	2,346	11,584	2,145	1,896
Enrolled in school	9,450	5,996	63.4	5,050	53.4	4,400	946	3,454	755	778
18 to 20 years old	5,420	3,135	57.8	2,608	48.1	2,812	526	2,285	431	478
21 to 24 years old	4,030	2,861	71.0	2,442	60.6	1,588	419	1,169	324	300
In high school	1,399	527	37.7	436	31.2	963	91	872	184	121
In college	8,051	5,469	67.9	4,614	57.3	3,437	855	2,582	571	658
Full time	6,884	4,674	67.9	3,894	56.6	2,990	780	2,210	485	586
Part time	1,167	795	68.1	720	61.7	447	75	372	86	71
Not enrolled in school	14,922	6,791	45.5	5,391	36.1	9,530	1,400	8,130	1,391	1,118
18 to 20 years old	4,307	1,561	36.2	1,140	26.5	3,167	421	2,746	426	343
21 to 24 years old	10,614	5,230	49.3	4,251	40.1	6,363	979	5,384	965	775
Male										
Total, 18 to 24 years old	12,034	6,072	50.5	4,872	40.5	7,162	1,199	5,963	1,166	1,002
Enrolled in school	4,762	2,885	60.6	2,367	49.7	2,395	519	1,877	407	430
18 to 20 years old	2,731	1,485	54.4	1,213	44.4	1,518	273	1,246	220	250
21 to 24 years old	2,031	1,400	68.9	1,154	56.8	877	246	631	187	180
In high school	875	311	35.6	258	29.5	617	54	564	108	77
In college	3,887	2,574	66.2	2,109	54.3	1,778	465	1,313	300	352
Full time	3,369	2,223	66.0	1,791	53.2	1,577	432	1,146	273	317
Part time	518	351	67.7	317	61.2	201	33	168	27	35
Not enrolled in school	7,272	3,186	43.8	2,506	34.5	4,766	681	4,086	752	572
18 to 20 years old	2,145	789	36.8	573	26.7	1,572	216	1,356	224	156
21 to 24 years old	5,127	2,398	46.8	1,933	37.7	3,195	465	2,730	534	417
Female										
Total, 18 to 24 years old	12,337	6,716	54.4	5,569	445.1	6,768	1,146	5,622	979	894

[Continued]

★ 858 ★

Reported Voting and Registration of Persons 18 to 24 Years Old, by Educational Status, Race/ Ethnicity, Sex and Age, 1992

[Continued]

Race, Hispanic origin, sex, age, and enrollment status	All persons	Reported registered		Reported voted		Reported that they did not vote[1]				
						Total	Registered	Not registered		
								Total[2]	Not a U.S. citizen	Do not know and not reported on registration[3]
		Number	Percent	Number	Percent					
Enrolled in school	4,688	3,111	66.4	2,684	57.2	2,004	427	1,577	347	349
18 to 20 years old	2,689	1,649	61.3	1,395	51.9	1,293	254	1,039	211	228
21 to 24 years old	1,999	1,461	73.1	1,288	64.4	711	173	538	136	120
In high school	524	215	41.1	178	34.0	345	37	308	76	44
In college	4,164	2,895	69.5	2,505	60.2	1,659	390	1,269	271	305
Full time	3,515	2,451	69.7	2,102	59.8	1,413	349	1,064	212	269
Part time	649	444	68.5	403	62.1	246	41	205	50	36
Not enrolled in school	7,649	3,605	47.1	2,886	37.7	4,764	719	4,044	632	545
18 to 20 years old	2,163	772	35.7	567	26.2	1,596	205	1,390	201	187
21 to 24 years old	5,487	2,833	51.6	2,319	42.3	3,168	514	2,654	430	358
White										
Both Sexes										
Total, 18 to 24 years old	19,681	10,746	54.6	8,932	45.4	10,749	1,814	8,935	1,478	1,372
Enrolled in school	7,607	5,130	67.4	4,396	57.8	3,211	733	2,477	398	560
18 to 20 years old	4,340	2,679	61.7	2,281	52.6	2,058	398	1,660	235	339
21 to 24 years old	3,268	2,450	75.0	2,115	64.7	1,153	335	817	163	221
In high school	989	398	40.3	354	35.7	636	45	591	121	74
In college	6,618	4,731	71.5	4,043	61.1	2,575	689	1,887	276	485
Full time	5,639	4,042	71.7	3,413	60.5	2,226	629	1,597	232	430
Part time	979	690	70.4	630	64.3	350	60	290	44	55
Not enrolled in school	12,074	5,616	46.5	4,536	37.6	7,538	1,080	6,458	1,080	812
18 to 20 years old	3,403	1,258	37.0	906	26.6	2,497	352	2,145	331	246
21 to 24 years old	8,671	4,358	50.3	3,630	41.9	5,041	728	4,313	749	566
Male										
Total, 18 to 24 years old	9,750	5,134	52.7	4,220	43.3	5,530	915	4,616	830	714
Enrolled in school	3,841	2,501	65.1	2,107	54.9	1,733	394	1,339	225	293
18 to 20 years old	2,159	1,261	58.4	1,054	48.8	1,105	207	898	129	160
21 to 24 years old	1,681	1,240	73.8	1,053	62.7	628	187	441	95	132
In high school	611	235	38.5	204	33.4	407	31	376	71	41
In college	3,229	2,266	70.2	1,903	58.9	1,326	363	964	154	251
Full time	2,785	1,958	70.3	1,621	58.2	1,163	337	826	139	227
Part time	445	308	69.2	262	36.4	163	26	137	15	25
Not enrolled in school	5,909	2,633	44.6	2,112	35.7	3,797	521	3,276	605	421
18 to 20 years old	1,717	636	37.0	456	26.6	1,260	179	1,081	173	119
21 to 24 years old	4,193	1,997	47.6	1,656	39.5	2,537	341	2,195	432	302
Female										
Total, 18 to 24 years old	9,931	5,611	56.5	4,712	47.4	5,219	899	4,320	649	658
Enrolled in school	3,767	2,628	69.8	2,289	60.8	1,478	339	1,138	173	267
18 to 20 years old	2,180	1,418	65.0	1,227	56.3	953	191	762	106	179
21 to 24 years old	1,586	1,210	76.3	1,061	66.9	525	149	376	58	88
In high school	378	163	43.1	149	39.5	229	14	215	51	33
In college	3,389	2,466	72.8	2,140	63.1	1,249	326	923	123	234
Full time	2,854	2,083	73.0	1,792	62.8	1,062	292	771	83	203
Part time	535	382	71.5	348	65.1	187	34	153	30	30
Not enrolled in school	6,165	2,983	48.4	2,423	39.3	3,742	560	3,182	475	391
18 to 20 years old	1,687	622	36.9	450	26.7	1,237	173	1,064	158	127
21 to 24 years old	4,478	2,361	52.7	1,973	44.1	2,505	387	2,118	317	264

[Continued]

★ 858 ★

Reported Voting and Registration of Persons 18 to 24 Years Old, by Educational Status, Race/ Ethnicity, Sex and Age, 1992

[Continued]

Race, Hispanic origin, sex, age, and enrollment status	All persons	Reported registered		Reported voted		Reported that they did not vote[1]				
						Total	Registered	Not registered		
								Total[2]	Not a U.S. citizen	Do not know and not reported on registration[3]
		Number	Percent	Number	Percent					
Black										
Both Sexes										
Total, 18 to 24 years old	3,543	1,744	49.2	1,296	36.6	2,247	448	1,799	219	405
Enrolled in school	1,224	689	56.3	528	43.1	697	161	535	106	142
18 to 20 years old	758	370	48.9	265	35.0	492	105	387	65	93
21 to 24 years old	467	319	68.3	262	56.2	204	56	148	41	49
In high school	338	122	36.2	78	23.1	260	44	216	27	38
In college	886	567	63.9	450	50.8	436	117	320	79	104
Full time	764	482	63.0	373	48.8	391	109	282	89	90
Part time	122	85	69.6	77	63.0	45	8	37	10	14
Not enrolled in school	2,319	1,055	45.5	768	33.1	1,551	287	1,264	113	263
18 to 20 years old	743	268	36.0	209	28.1	534	59	476	38	83
21 to 24 years old	1,575	787	50.0	559	35.5	1,016	228	788	75	180
Male										
Total, 18 to 24 years old	1,685	778	46.2	537	31.8	1,148	241	907	107	230
Enrolled in school	590	283	47.9	191	32.4	399	92	307	53	98
18 to 20 years old	400	172	43.0	116	29.0	284	56	228	29	65
21 to 24 years old	190	111	58.2	76	39.7	115	35	80	24	34
In high school	223	72	32.2	51	22.8	172	21	151	20	28
In college	368	211	57.4	141	38.3	227	70	157	33	70
Full time	325	178	54.7	109	33.6	216	69	147	33	63
Part time	43	34	(B)	32	(B)	11	2	9	-	8
Not enrolled in school	1,095	495	45.2	345	31.5	749	150	600	54	132
18 to 20 years old	345	135	39.0	102	29.6	243	33	210	18	32
21 to 24 years old	749	360	48.0	243	32.4	506	117	389	36	100
Female										
Total, 18 to 24 years old	1,858	966	52.0	759	40.9	1,099	207	892	112	175
Enrolled in school	634	406	64.1	336	53.0	298	70	228	52	44
18 to 20 years old	358	198	55.4	149	41.8	208	49	160	36	28
21 to 24 years old	276	208	75.3	187	67.6	89	21	68	17	16
In high school	115	51	43.9	27	23.6	88	23	65	7	10
In college	518	355	68.6	309	59.6	209	46	163	45	34
Full time	439	304	69.2	264	60.0	176	40	135	35	28
Part time	79	51	64.9	45	57.1	34	6	28	10	6
Not enrolled in school	1,224	560	45.7	423	34.5	801	137	664	59	131
18 to 20 years old	396	133	33.4	107	26.9	291	26	265	20	51
21 to 24 years old	626	427	51.7	316	38.3	510	111	399	39	80
Hispanic[4]										
Both Sexes										
Total, 18 to 24 years old	2,795	696	24.9	492	17.6	2,303	204	2,099	1,206	213
Enrolled in school	742	287	38.6	223	30.1	519	63	455	237	71
18 to 20 years old	472	154	32.6	120	25.5	351	33	318	169	42
21 to 24 years old	270	133	49.2	103	38.1	167	30	137	68	28
In high school	207	29	14.1	25	11.8	183	5	178	99	22
In college	535	258	48.2	199	37.2	336	59	277	138	49
Full time	395	186	47.1	148	37.6	246	38	209	98	42
Part time	140	72	51.2	50	36.0	90	21	68	40	7
Not enrolled in school	2,053	409	19.9	269	13.1	1,784	140	1,644	969	142

[Continued]

★ 858 ★

Reported Voting and Registration of Persons 18 to 24 Years Old, by Educational Status, Race/ Ethnicity, Sex and Age, 1992

[Continued]

Race, Hispanic origin, sex, age, and enrollment status	All persons	Reported registered		Reported voted		Reported that they did not vote[1]				
						Total	Registered	Not registered		
		Number	Percent	Number	Percent			Total[2]	Not a U.S. citizen	Do not know and not reported on registration[3]
18 to 20 years old	687	114	16.5	62	9.1	625	51	573	315	51
21 to 24 years old	1,366	296	21.6	207	15.1	1,159	89	1,070	654	91
Male										
Total, 18 to 24 years old	1,418	288	20.3	196	13.8	1,222	92	1,130	673	128
Enrolled in school	354	110	31.2	82	23.3	271	28	243	114	40
18 to 20 years old	220	56	25.5	44	20.2	176	12	164	85	19
21 to 24 years old	133	54	40.7	38	28.4	95	16	79	29	20
In high school	116	12	10.7	10	8.4	106	3	104	52	15
In college	237	98	41.2	73	30.6	165	25	140	62	25
Full time	179	70	39.0	55	30.6	124	15	109	50	23
Part time	58	28	(B)	18	(B()	41	10	30	12	2
Not enrolled in school	1,065	178	16.7	114	10.7	51	64	887	558	88
18 to 20 years old	343	54	15.6	28	8.0	315	26	289	174	26
21 to 24 years old	722	124	17.2	86	11.9	636	38	598	384	62
Female										
Total, 18 to 24 years old	1,377	408	29.6	296	21.5	1,080	112	969	533	85
Enrolled in school	388	176	45.4	141	36.3	247	36	212	122	31
18 to 20 years old	251	98	38.8	76	30.2	175	22	154	83	23
21 to 24 years old	137	79	57.5	65	47.4	72	14	58	39	8
In high school	91	17	18.4	15	16.2	76	2	74	47	7
In college	297	160	53.7	126	42.4	171	34	138	76	24
Full time	216	116	53.8	94	43.4	122	23	100	48	19
Part time	82	44	53.4	33	39.9	49	11	38	28	5
Not enrolled in school	968	232	23.4	155	15.7	833	76	757	411	54
18 to 20 years old	344	60	17.4	35	10.1	310	25	284	141	24
21 to 24 years old	644	172	26.6	121	18.7	523	51	472	270	30

Source: U.S. Bureau of the Census. *Voting and Registration in the Election of November 1992,* Current Population Reports, P20-466. Washington, DC, U.S. GPO, 1993, pp. 32-33. *Notes:* 1. Includes persons reported as "did not know," and "not reported" on voting. 2. In addition to those reported as "not registered," total includes those "not a U.S. citizen," and "do not know" and "not reported" on registration. 3. Includes "do not know" and "not reported" on citizenship. 4. Persons of Hispanic origin may be of any race.

★ 859 ★

Voting

Reported Voting and Registration, by Educational Status, Race/Ethnicity, and Sex, 1992

Data for November 1992 are shown in thousands and as percent of total in each voting category.

Race, Hispanic origin, sex, and years of school completed	All persons	Reported registered		Reported voted		Reported that they did not vote[1]				
						Total	Registered	Not registered		
		Number	Percent	Number	Percent			Total[2]	Not a U.S. citizen	Do not know and not reported on registration[3]
ALL RACES										
Both Sexes										
Total	185,684	126,578	68.2	113,866	61.3	71,818	12,712	59,106	11,900	10,638

[Continued]

★ 859 ★

Reported Voting and Registration, by Educational Status, Race/Ethnicity, and Sex, 1992

[Continued]

Race, Hispanic origin, sex, and years of school completed	All persons	Reported registered		Reported voted		Reported that they did not vote[1]				
						Total	Registered	Not registered		
		Number	Percent	Number	Percent			Total[2]	Not a U.S. citizen	Do not know and not reported on registration[3]
Less than 5th grade	3,466	1,005	29.0	746	21.5	2,720	258	2,462	1,280	230
5th to 8th grade	11,925	5,745	48.2	4,660	39.1	7,265	1,085	6,179	2,160	812
9th to 12th grade, no diploma	20,970	10,575	50.4	8,638	41.2	12,332	1,937	10,395	1,729	1,533
High school graduate	65,281	42,355	64.9	37,517	57.5	27,765	4,839	22,926	2,896	4,180
Some college or associate degree	46,691	35,226	75.4	32,069	68.7	14,622	3,157	11,465	1,946	2,474
Bachelor's degree	25,055	21,055	84.0	20,009	79.9	5,046	1,047	3,999	1,169	963
Advanced degree	12,296	10,617	86.3	10,227	83.2	2,069	389	1,680	719	446
Male										
Total	88,557	59,254	66.9	53,312	60.2	35,245	5,942	29,303	6,065	5,327
Less than 5th grade	1,718	550	32.0	423	24.6	1,294	127	1,168	575	101
5th to 8th grade	5,710	2,737	47.9	2,284	40.0	3,427	453	2,974	1,118	402
9th to 12th grade, no diploma	9,867	4,754	48.2	3,910	39.6	5,956	844	5,113	923	827
High school graduate	29,336	18,244	62.2	16,047	54.7	13,289	2,197	11,092	1,350	2,035
Some college or associate degree	21,963	16,241	73.9	14,680	66.8	7,283	1,561	5,723	964	1,208
Bachelor's degree	12,701	10,526	80.9	9,991	78.7	2,709	534	2,175	654	486
Advanced degree	7,263	6,204	85.4	5,977	82.3	1,286	226	1,060	481	268
Female										
Total	97,126	67,324	69.3	60,554	62.3	36,573	6,770	29,803	5,834	5,311
Less than 5th grade	1,749	455	26.0	323	18.5	1,426	131	1,294	705	129
5th to 8th grade	6,214	3,009	48.4	2,376	38.2	3,838	632	3,206	1,042	410
9th to 12th grade, no diploma	11,103	5,821	52.4	4,728	42.6	6,376	1,094	5,282	806	706
High school graduate	35,945	24,112	67.1	21,470	59.7	14,475	2,642	11,834	1,547	2,145
Some college or associate degree	24,728	18,985	76.8	17,389	70.3	7,338	1,596	5,743	982	1,266
Bachelor's degree	12,354	10,530	85.2	10,017	81.1	2,337	513	1,824	515	477
Advanced degree	5,033	4,413	87.7	4,250	84.4	783	163	620	238	178
WHITE										
Both Sexes										
Total	157,837	110,684	70.1	100,405	63.6	57,432	10,279	47,153	8,284	8,289
Less than 5th grade	2,545	646	25.4	478	18.8	2,067	168	1,899	1,065	173
5th to 8th grade	9,894	4,681	47.3	3,798	38.4	6,096	883	5,213	1,814	670
9th to 12th grade, no diploma	16,398	8,324	50.8	6,861	41.8	9,537	1,463	8,074	1,316	1,083
High school graduate	55,728	36,921	66.3	32,998	59.2	22,730	3,923	18,807	1,950	3,280
Some college or associate degree	40,104	31,042	77.4	28,467	71.0	11,637	2,575	9,062	1,183	1,963
Bachelor's degree	22,304	19,346	8637	18,421	82.6	3,882	925	2,958	601	766
Advanced degree	10,865	9,724	89.5	9,382	86.4	1,783	342	1,140	354	354
Male										
Total	75,915	52,383	69.0	47,552	62.6	28,364	4,831	23,533	4,298	4,116
Less than 5th grade	1,296	346	26.7	268	20.7	1,028	78	950	506	80
5th to 8th grade	4,769	2,258	47.3	1,878	39.4	2,891	380	2,511	950	337
9th to 12th grade, no diploma	7,908	3,907	49.4	3,242	41.0	4,667	665	4,001	733	566
High school graduate	25,024	15,873	63.4	14,092	56.3	10,932	1,781	9,151	941	1,574
Some college or associate degree	18,991	14,427	76.0	13,180	69.4	5,812	1,248	4,564	581	959
Bachelor's degree	11,460	9,819	85.7	9,341	81.5	2,119	478	1,641	343	393
Advanced degree	6,466	5,753	89.0	5,552	85.9	915	201	713	245	207
Female										
Total	81,922	58,301	71.2	52,853	64.5	29,068	5,448	23,621	3,986	4,173
Less than 5th grade	1,249	300	24.0	210	16.8	1,039	90	949	559	92
5th to 8th grade	5,125	2,423	47.3	1,920	37.5	3,205	503	2,702	865	333
9th to 12th grade, no diploma	8,489	4,417	52.0	3,619	42.6	4,870	797	4,073	583	517

[Continued]

★ 859 ★

Reported Voting and Registration, by Educational Status, Race/Ethnicity, and Sex, 1992

[Continued]

Race, Hispanic origin, sex, and years of school completed	All persons	Reported registered		Reported voted		Reported that they did not vote[1]				
						Total	Registered	Not registered		
								Total[2]	Not a U.S. citizen	Do not know and not reported on registration[3]
		Number	Percent	Number	Percent					
High school graduate	30,704	21,048	68.6	18,906	61.6	11,798	2,142	9,656	1,009	1,706
Some college or associate degree	21,113	16,615	78.7	15,288	72.4	5,825	1,327	4,498	602	1,004
Bachelor's degree	10,844	9,527	87.9	9,080	83.7	1,763	447	1,316	258	373
Advanced degree	4,398	3,972	90.3	3,830	87.1	568	141	427	110	147
BLACK										
Both Sexes										
Total	21,039	13,442	63.9	11,371	54.0	9,668	2,070	7,598	1,044	1,870
Less than 5th grade	619	303	48.9	228	36.9	391	74	316	30	40
5th to 8th grade	1,562	951	60.9	775	49.6	788	177	611	126	101
9th to 12th grade, no diploma	3,911	2,105	53.8	1,669	42.7	2,242	436	1,805	153	394
High school graduate	7,719	4,746	61.5	3,944	51.1	3,775	802	2,973	360	783
Some college or associate degree	5,019	3,548	70.7	3,062	61.0	1,957	486	1,471	266	393
Bachelor's degree	1,481	1,182	79.8	1,116	75.3	365	67	299	71	104
Advanced degree	729	606	83.1	579	79.4	151	28	123	39	55
Male										
Total	9,425	5,727	60.8	4,786	50.8	4,639	941	3,696	548	965
Less than 5th grade	330	186	56.4	140	42.4	190	46	144	14	15
5th to 8th grade	743	436	58.7	373	50.1	370	64	307	68	43
9th to 12th grade, no diploma	1,657	781	47.2	618	37.3	1,038	163	875	78	227
High school graduate	3,488	2,055	58.9	1,694	48.6	1,795	362	1,433	171	409
Some college or associate degree	2,213	1,516	68.5	1,259	56.9	953	257	969	138	189
Bachelor's degree	629	473	75.1	438	69.5	192	35	157	45	47
Advanced degree	366	279	76.3	265	72.4	101	14	87	34	35
Female										
Total	11,614	7,715	66.4	6,585	56.7	5,029	1,129	3,899	496	905
Less than 5th grade	290	117	40.4	89	30.6	201	28	173	15	24
5th to 8th grade	819	515	62.9	402	49.1	417	113	304	58	57
9th to 12th grade, no diploma	2,254	1,324	58.7	1,051	46.6	1,203	273	930	75	167
High school graduate	4,231	2,691	63.6	2,250	53.2	1,981	441	1,540	189	374
Some college or associate degree	2,806	2,032	72.4	1,802	64.2	1,004	229	774	128	205
Bachelor's degree	851	709	83.3	678	79.6	173	31	142	26	57
Advanced degree	364	327	90.0	314	86.3	50	13	36	5	20
HISPANIC ORIGIN[4]										
Both Sexes										
Total	14,688	5,137	35.0	4,238	28.9	10,450	899	9,551	5,910	995
Less than 5th grade	1,488	263	17.7	186	12.5	1,302	77	1,225	970	90
5th to 8th grade	2,785	519	18.6	419	15.0	2,367	100	2,267	1,688	180
9th to 12th grade, no diploma	2,681	655	24.4	492	18.3	2,189	163	2,026	1,145	220
High school graduate	4,010	1,585	39.5	1,282	32.0	2,728	303	2,425	1,230	264
Some college or associate degree	2,584	1,427	55.2	1,218	47.1	1,366	209	1,157	576	185
Bachelor's degree	796	468	58.8	439	55.1	357	29	328	212	40
Advanced degree	343	220	64.0	202	59.0	141	17	124	91	15
Male										
Total	7,273	2,337	32.1	1,946	26.8	5,327	391	4,936	3,132	519
Less than 5th grade	715	100	14.0	84	11.7	632	16	615	478	39
5th to 8th grade	1,389	211	15.2	172	12.4	1,217	39	1,178	900	99
9th to 12th grade, no diploma	1,374	290	21.1	222	16.2	1,151	68	1,063	642	118
High school graduate	1,946	727	37.4	589	30.3	1,357	139	1,218	635	138

[Continued]

★ 859 ★

Reported Voting and Registration, by Educational Status, Race/Ethnicity, and Sex, 1992

[Continued]

Race, Hispanic origin, sex, and years of school completed	All persons	Reported registered		Reported voted		Reported that they did not vote[1]				
						Total	Registered	Not registered		
								Total[2]	Not a U.S. citizen	Do not know and not reported on registration[3]
		Number	Percent	Number	Percent					
Some college or associate degree	1,240	663	53.5	563	45.4	677	100	577	296	87
Bachelor's degree	397	225	56.7	210	52.8	188	16	172	114	23
Advanced degree	212	121	56.8	107	50.6	105	13	92	68	15
Female										
Total	7,415	2,800	37.8	2,291	30.9	5,124	508	4,515	2,778	476
Less than 5th grade	773	163	21.1	103	13.3	671	61	610	492	51
5th to 8th grade	1,396	308	22.1	247	17.7	1,150	61	1,88	788	81
9th to 12th grade, no diploma	1,307	365	27.9	269	20.6	1,038	95	943	503	102
High school graduate	2,064	857	41.5	693	33.6	1,371	164	1,206	595	125
Some college or associate degree	1,344	764	56.9	655	48.8	689	109	580	280	98
Bachelor's degree	399	243	60.8	229	57.4	170	14	156	98	18
Advanced degree	131	99	75.6	95	72.4	36	4	32	23	-

Source: U.S. Bureau of the Census. *Voting and Registration in the Election of November 1992*, Current Population Reports, P20-466. Washington, DC, U.S. GPO, 1993, pp. 39-40. *Notes:* 1. Includes persons reported as "did not know," and "not reported" on voting. 2. In addition to those reported as "not registered," total includes those "not a U.S. citizen," and "do not know" and "not reported" on registration. 3. Includes "do not know" and "not reported" on citizenship. 4. Persons of Hispanic origin may be of any race.

★ 860 ★

Voting

Reported Voting and Registration, by Employment Status, Race/Ethnicity, and Sex, 1992

Data for November 1992 are shown in thousands and as percent of total in each voting category.

Race, sex, Hispanic origin, employment status, and class of worker	All persons	Reported registered		Reported voted		Reported that they did not vote[1]				
						Total	Registered	Not registered		
								Total[2]	Not a U.S. citizen	Do not know and not reported on registration[3]
		Number	Percent	Number	Percent					
All Races										
Both Sexes										
Total	185,684	126,578	68.2	113,866	61.3	71,818	12,712	59,106	11,900	10,638
Civilian labor force	124,553	85,750	68.8	77,958	62.6	46,595	7,793	38,803	7,803	6,550
Employed	116,290	81,313	69.9	74,138	63.8	42,152	7,175	34,976	6,922	5,992
Agricultural industries	3,039	1,891	62.2	1,717	56.5	1,322	174	1,148	441	147
Self-employed workers[4]	1,472	1,181	80.2	1,084	73.6	388	97	291	55	72
Wage and salary workers	1,568	710	45.3	634	40.4	934	77	857	386	75
Nonagricultural industries	113,250	79,422	70.1	72,421	63.9	40,830	7,001	33,829	6,481	5,845
Private wage and salary workers	85,880	57,461	66.9	51,742	60.2	34,138	5,719	28,419	5,549	4,647
Government workers	18,383	15,322	83.4	14,460	78.7	3,924	863	3,061	449	719
Self-employed workers[4]	8,987	6,638	73.9	6,219	69.2	2,769	420	2,349	483	478
Unemployed	8,263	4,437	53.7	3,820	46.2	4,444	617	3,826	881	559
Not in labor force	61,131	40,828	66.8	36,908	58.7	25,223	4,920	20,303	4,096	4,088
Male										
Total	88,557	59,254	66.9	53,312	60.2	35,245	5,942	29,303	6,065	5,327
Civilian labor force	67,694	44,903	66.3	40,624	60.0	27,070	4,279	22,791	4,936	3,774
Employed	63,003	42,495	67.4	38,546	61.2	24,457	3,949	20,508	4,406	3,419

[Continued]

★ 860 ★

Reported Voting and Registration, by Employment Status, Race/Ethnicity, and Sex, 1992

[Continued]

Race, sex, Hispanic origin, employment status, and class of worker	All persons	Reported registered		Reported voted		Reported that they did not vote[1]				
						Total	Registered	Not registered		
								Total[2]	Not a U.S. citizen	Do not know and not reported on registration[3]
		Number	Percent	Number	Percent					
Agricultural industries	2,392	1,429	59.8	1,296	54.2	1,096	134	962	396	111
Self-employed workers[4]	1,152	923	80.2	851	73.9	301	72	229	49	51
Wage and salary workers	1,240	506	40.8	445	35.9	79	61	734	349	60
Nonagricultural industries	60,611	41,066	67.8	37,250	61.5	23,361	3,815	19,546	4,006	3,308
Private wage and salary workers	46,571	30,258	65.0	27,142	58.3	19,429	3,115	16,313	3,423	2,610
Government workers	8,296	6,731	81.1	6,313	76.1	1,984	419	1,565	246	343
Self-employed workers[4]	5,744	4,077	71.0	3,795	66.1	1,949	281	1,668	339	354
Unemployed	4,691	2,408	51.3	2,078	44.3	2,613	330	2,283	530	356
Not in labor force	20,863	14,351	68.8	12,688	60.8	8,175	1,663	6,512	1,129	1,553
Female										
Total	97,126	67,324	69.3	60,554	62.3	36,573	6,770	29,803	5,834	5,311
Civilian labor force	56,859	40,847	71.8	37,334	65.7	19,525	3,514	16,011	2,867	2,776
Employed	53,286	38,818	72.8	35,592	66.8	17,694	3,226	14,468	2,516	2,573
Agricultural industries	647	462	71.4	422	65.1	226	41	185	43	36
Self-employed workers[4]	320	258	80.6	233	72.8	87	25	62	6	21
Wage and salary workers	327	204	62.4	188	57.6	139	16	123	37	15
Nonagricultural industries	52,639	38,356	72.9	35,170	66.8	17,469	3,186	14,283	2,473	2,537
Private wage and salary workers	39,309	27,203	69.2	24,600	62.6	14,709	2,604	12,105	2,126	2,037
Government workers	10,087	8,591	85.2	6,147	80.8	1,940	444	1,496	203	376
Self-employed workers[4]	3,243	2,562	79.0	2,424	74.7	820	138	681	144	124
Unemployed	3,573	2,029	56.8	1,742	48.8	1,831	288	1,543	351	203
Not in labor force	40,268	26,477	65.8	23,220	57.7	17,048	3,256	13,791	2,967	2,534
White										
Both Sexes										
Total	157,837	110,684	70.1	100,405	63.6	57,432	10,279	47,153	8,284	8,289
Civilian labor force	106,314	74,977	70.5	68,621	64.5	37,692	6,356	31,336	5,474	5,086
Employed	100,200	71,617	71.5	65,678	65.5	34,522	5,940	28,582	4,833	4,735
Agricultural industries	2,840	1,791	63.1	1,628	57.3	1,212	163	1,049	419	131
Self-employed workers[4]	1,424	1,151	80.8	1,058	74.3	366	93	273	55	68
Wage and salary workers	1,416	640	45.2	570	40.3	846	70	776	364	63
Nonagricultural industries	97,360	69,827	71.7	64,050	65.8	33,310	5,777	27,533	4,413	4,604
Private wage and salary workers	74,164	50,843	68.6	46,122	62.2	28,042	4,721	23,320	3,848	3,675
Government workers	15,008	12,758	85.0	12,087	80.5	2,920	671	2,250	239	515
Self-employed workers[4]	8,188	6,225	76.0	5,840	71.3	2,348	385	1,963	327	414
Unemployed	6,114	3,360	55.0	2,944	48.1	3,170	416	2,754	641	351
Not in labor force	51,523	35,707	69.3	31,784	61.7	19,739	3,923	15,817	2,810	3,203
Male										
Total	75,915	52,383	69.0	47,552	62.6	28,364	4,831	23,533	4,298	4,116
Civilian labor force	58,477	39,863	68.2	36,364	62.2	22,113	3,499	18,614	3,591	2,930
Employed	54,894	37,956	69.1	34,694	63.2	20,201	3,263	16,938	3,191	2,710
Agricultural industries	2,227	1,350	60.6	1,226	55.0	1,001	124	877	380	95
Self-employed workers[4]	1,113	899	80.7	829	74.4	284	70	215	49	47
Wage and salary workers	1,114	451	40.5	397	35.6	717	54	663	330	48
Nonagricultural industries	52,667	36,606	69.5	33,468	63.5	19,199	3,139	16,060	2,811	2,614
Private wage and salary workers	40,554	27,072	66.8	24,518	60.5	16,037	2,554	13,482	2,452	2,058
Government workers	6,859	5,699	83.1	5,374	78.3	1,485	326	1,159	121	253
Self-employed workers[4]	5,254	3,835	73.0	3,375	68.1	1,678	259	1,419	238	303
Unemployed	3,582	1,907	53.2	1,670	46.6	1,912	237	1,676	401	221
Not in labor force	17,439	12,520	71.8	11,188	64.2	6,251	1,332	4,919	706	1,186

[Continued]

★ 860 ★

Reported Voting and Registration, by Employment Status, Race/Ethnicity, and Sex, 1992

[Continued]

Race, sex, Hispanic origin, employment status, and class of worker	All persons	Reported registered		Reported voted		Reported that they did not vote[1]				
						Total	Registered	Not registered		
		Number	Percent	Number	Percent			Total[2]	Not a U.S. citizen	Do not know and not reported on registration[3]
Female										
Total	81,922	58,301	71.2	52,853	64.5	29,068	5,448	23,621	3,986	4,173
Civilian labor force	47,837	35,114	73.4	32,257	67.4	15,579	2,857	12,723	1,882	2,156
Employed	45,306	33,661	74.3	30,984	68.4	14,322	2,677	11,644	1,642	2,025
Agricultural industries	613	441	72.0	402	65.6	211	39	172	39	36
Self-employed workers[4]	311	252	81.1	229	73.7	82	23	59	6	21
Wage and salary workers	302	189	62.5	173	57.3	129	16	113	34	15
Nonagricultural industries	44,693	33,220	74.3	30,582	68.4	14,111	2,638	11,473	1,602	1,990
Private wage and salary workers	33,609	23,771	70.7	21,604	64.3	12,005	2,167	9,838	1,396	1,617
Government workers	8,149	7,059	86.6	6,714	82.4	1,435	345	1,090	118	263
Self-employed workers[4]	2,934	2,390	81.5	2,264	77.1	670	127	544	88	110
Unemployed	2,531	1,453	57.4	1,273	50.3	1,258	180	1,078	241	131
Not in labor force	34,085	23,187	68.0	20,596	60.4	13,489	2,591	10,898	2,104	2,017
Black										
Both Sexes										
Total	21,039	13,442	63.9	11,371	54.0	9,668	2,070	7,598	1,044	1,870
Civilian labor force	13,629	8,993	66.0	7,771	57.0	5,857	1,221	4,636	745	1,152
Employed	11,851	8,042	67.9	7,001	59.1	4,851	1,042	3,809	636	966
Agricultural industries	144	70	48.6	65	44.9	79	5	74	9	12
Self-employed workers[4]	31	19	(B)	19	(B)	13	-	13	-	4
Wage and salary workers	113	51	45.5	46	40.9	67	5	61	9	9
Nonagricultural industries	11,708	7,972	68.1	6,936	59.2	4,772	1,036	3,735	627	954
Private wage and salary workers	8,588	5,514	64.2	4,660	54.3	3,928	853	3,074	537	743
Government workers	2,667	2,167	81.2	2,005	75.2	662	162	501	60	172
Self-employed workers[4]	452	292	64.6	271	59.9	181	21	160	30	38
Unemployed	1,777	950	53.5	771	43.4	1,006	180	827	110	186
Not in labor force	7,411	4,449	60.0	3,600	48.6	3,811	849	2,962	299	718
Male										
Total	9,425	5,727	60.8	4,786	50.8	4,639	941	3,696	548	965
Civilian labor force	6,737	4,155	61.7	3,490	51.8	3,247	665	2,582	438	662
Employed	5,836	3,713	63.6	3,135	53.7	2,702	578	2,123	378	544
Agricultural industries	129	61	47.8	56	43.7	72	5	67	7	12
Self-employed workers[4]	29	16	(B)	16	(B)	13	-	13	-	4
Wage and salary workers	100	45	45.5	40	40.2	60	5	54	7	9
Nonagricultural industries	5,708	3,651	64.0	3,079	53.9	2,629	573	2,056	372	532
Private wage and salary workers	4,321	2,628	60.8	2,144	49.6	2,177	483	1,693	308	420
Government workers	1,098	850	77.5	773	70.4	325	77	247	40	77
Self-employed workers[4]	289	174	60.1	161	55.8	128	12	115	23	35
Unemployed	901	442	49.1	355	39.4	545	87	458	60	117
Not in labor force	2,688	1,572	58.5	1,296	48.2	1,392	276	1,117	110	304
Female										
Total	11,614	7,715	66.4	6,585	56.7	5,029	1,129	3,899	496	905
Civilian labor force	6,892	4,4838	70.2	4,281	62.1	2,610	556	2,054	307	491
Employed	6,015	4,329	72.0	3,866	64.3	2,149	464	1,686	257	422
Agricultural industries	15	8	(B)	8	(B)	7	-	7	2	-
Self-employed workers[4]	2	2	(B)	2	(B)	-	-	-	-	-
Wage and salary workers	13	6	(B)	6	(B)	7	-	7	2	-
Nonagricultural industries	6,000	4,321	72.0	3,857	64.3	2,142	464	1,679	255	422
Private wage and salary workers	4,267	2,886	67.6	2,516	69.0	1,751	370	1,381	229	323
Government workers	1,570	1,317	83.9	1,232	78.5	338	85	253	20	96
Self-employed workers[4]	163	118	72.6	109	67.1	54	9	45	6	3

[Continued]

★ 860 ★

Reported Voting and Registration, by Employment Status, Race/Ethnicity, and Sex, 1992

[Continued]

Race, sex, Hispanic origin, employment status, and class of worker	All persons	Reported registered		Reported voted		Reported that they did not vote[1]				
						Total	Registered	Not registered		
		Number	Percent	Number	Percent			Total[2]	Not a U.S. citizen	Do not know and not reported on registration[3]
Unemployed	877	508	58.0	416	47.4	761	93	368	50	69
Not in labor force	4,722	2,877	60.9	2,304	48.8	2,418	573	1,845	189	414
Hispanic[5]										
Both Sexes										
Total	14,688	5,137	35.0	4,238	28.9	10,450	899	9,551	5,910	995
Civilian labor force	9,915	3,513	35.4	2,921	29.5	6,993	592	6,401	4,019	638
Employed	8,800	3,226	36.7	2,682	30.5	6,117	543	5,574	3,489	570
Agricultural industries	506	51	10.0	44	8.6	463	7	456	397	16
Self-employed workers[4]	70	16	(B)	10	(B)	60	6	54	43	8
Wage and salary workers	436	35	7.9	34	7.8	402	1	402	354	8
Nonagricultural industries	8,293	3,175	38.3	2,639	31.8	5,655	536	5,118	3,092	555
Private wage and salary workers	6,835	2,290	33.5	1,843	27.0	4,992	447	4,545	2,827	457
Government workers	1,013	699	69.0	641	63.3	372	58	314	90	61
Self-employed workers[4]	445	187	41.9	155	34.8	290	32	258	175	36
Unemployed	1,115	287	25.8	239	21.4	876	48	828	530	68
Not in labor force	4,773	1,624	34.0	1,316	27.6	3,457	308	3,150	1,891	357
Male										
Total	7,273	2,337	32.1	1,946	26.8	5,327	391	4,936	3,132	519
Civilian labor force	6,003	1,838	30.6	1,532	25.5	4,471	306	4,165	2,736	391
Employed	5,347	1,692	31.6	1,405	26.3	3,943	287	3,656	2,400	354
Agricultural industries	456	42	9.3	35	7.7	421	7	414	361	16
Self-employed workers[4]	66	16	(B)	10	(B)	56	6	50	39	8
Wage and salary workers	390	26	6.7	25	6.5	365	1	364	322	8
Nonagricultural industries	4,891	1,649	33.7	1,370	28.0	3,522	280	3,242	2,040	338
Private wage and salary workers	4,097	1,207	29.5	975	23.8	3,122	232	2,890	1,865	285
Government workers	490	329	67.1	303	61.8	187	26	161	41	25
Self-employed workers[4]	304	113	37.3	92	30.2	212	22	191	133	28
Unemployed	655	146	22.4	127	19.3	528	20	509	335	37
Not in labor force	1,271	499	39.3	415	32.7	856	84	771	396	126
Female										
Total	7,415	2,800	37.8	2,291	30.9	5,124	508	4,615	2,778	476
Civilian labor force	3,912	1,675	42.8	1,390	35.5	2,522	285	2,237	1,283	247
Employed	3,452	1,534	44.4	1,278	37.0	2,175	257	1,918	1,089	216
Agricultural industries	50	8	(B)	8	(B)	42	-	42	36	-
Self-employed workers[4]	4	-	(B)	-	(B)	4	-	4	4	-
Wage and salary workers	46	8	(B)	8	(B)	37	-	37	32	-
Nonagricultural industries	3,402	1,526	44.8	1,269	37.3	2,133	257	1,876	1,053	216
Private wage and salary workers	2,738	1,083	39.5	868	31.7	1,870	215	1,655	962	172
Government workers	523	370	70.7	338	64.7	185	32	153	49	36
Self-employed workers[4]	141	73	51.9	63	44.6	78	10	68	43	9
Unemployed	460	141	30.6	112	24.4	347	29	319	195	31
Not in labor force	3,503	1,124	32.1	901	25.7	2,602	223	2,379	1,495	229

Source: U.S. Bureau of the Census. *Voting and Registration in the Election of November 1992*, Current Population Reports, P20-466. Washington, DC, U.S. GPO, 1993, pp. 47-50. *Notes:* A dash (-) stands for zero or rounds to zero. A (B) stands for base less than 75,000. 1. Includes persons reported as "did not know," and "not reported" on voting. 2. In addition to those reported as "not registered," total includes those "not a U.S. citizen," and "do not know" and "not reported" on registration. 3. Includes "do not know" and "not reported" on citizenship. 4. Includes unpaid family workers. 5. Persons of Hispanic origin may be of any race.

★ 861 ★

Voting

Reported Voting and Registration, by Family Income and Race/Ethnicity, 1992

Data for November 1992 are shown in thousands and as percent of total in each voting category. Reported voting, and reported non-registered non- voters are shown, by family income and race/ethnicity, for November 1992.

Race/ethnicity and family income	All persons	Reported registered		Reported voted		Reported that they did not vote[1]				
						Total	Registered	Not registered		
		Number	Percent	Number	Percent			Total[2]	Not a U.S. citizen	Do not know and not reported on registration[3]
All races										
Total	148,286	102,071	68.8	92,492	62.4	55,794	9,580	46,214	9,973	8,007
Under $5,000	4,489	1,953	43.5	1,453	32.4	3,036	499	2,536	588	381
$5,000 to $9,999	9,420	4,640	49.3	3,722	39.5	5,699	919	4,780	1,148	616
$10,000 to $14,999	13,529	7,486	55.3	6,333	46.8	7,196	1,154	6,042	1,695	784
$15,000 to $19,999	22,974	14,500	63.1	12,790	55.7	10,184	1,710	8,474	1,979	1,037
$20,000 to $24,999	22,596	15,547	68.8	14,128	62.5	8,470	1,419	7,051	1,468	972
$25,000 to $34,999	26,259	19,713	75.1	18,245	69.5	8,013	1,468	6,546	1,107	1,085
$35,000 to $49,999	23,452	18,945	80.8	17,762	75.7	5,690	1,182	4,508	781	779
$50,000 and over	15,112	12,722	84.2	12,067	79.9	3,044	655	2,390	543	670
Income not reported	10,453	6,565	62.8	5,991	57.3	4,462	574	3,887	664	1,682
White										
Total	126,099	89,527	71.0	81,819	64.9	44,280	7,708	36,572	6,979	6,139
Under $5,000	2,683	1,129	42.1	867	32.3	1,815	261	1,554	426	190
$5,000 to $9,999	6,580	3,236	49.2	2,610	39.7	3,970	626	3,344	817	407
$10,000 to $14,999	10,662	5,890	55.2	5,074	47.6	5,587	816	4,771	1,312	549
$15,000 to $19,999	19,273	12,360	64.1	10,958	56.9	8,315	1,402	6,913	1,442	791
$20,000 to $24,999	19,688	13,837	70.3	12,629	64.1	7,060	1,208	5,852	1,047	761
$25,000 to $34,999	23,349	17,898	76.7	16,615	71.2	6,734	1,282	5,451	711	893
$35,000 to $49,999	21,322	17,528	82.2	16,482	77.3	4,840	1,046	3,794	503	648
$50,000 and over	13,945	12,016	86.2	11,413	81.8	2,531	602	1,929	331	564
Income not reported	8,596	5,634	65.5	5,170	60.1	3,428	464	2,964	391	1,336
Black										
Total	16,471	10,504	63.8	8,917	54.1	7,554	1,586	5,967	810	1,470
Under $5,000	1,568	758	48.3	541	34.5	1,026	217	810	47	169
$5,000 to $9,999	2,414	1,309	54.2	1,042	43.2	1,372	266	1,105	118	191
$10,000 to $14,999	2,348	1,475	62.8	1,172	49.9	1,176	303	873	118	202
$15,000 to $19,999	2,839	1,882	66.3	1,616	56.9	1,223	266	957	172	204
$20,000 to $24,999	2,165	1,475	68.1	1,296	59.9	869	179	690	122	149
$25,000 to $34,999	1,993	1,448	72.6	1,304	65.4	689	144	545	95	128
$35,000 to $49,999	1,225	995	81.2	903	73.7	322	92	230	33	63
$50,000 and over	472	368	78.0	339	71.9	133	29	104	10	51
Income not reported	1,447	795	54.9	703	48.6	743	91	652	95	311
Hispanic[4]										
Total	12,360	4,274	34.6	3,525	28.5	8,836	749	8,086	5,079	834
Under $5,000	794	200	25.1	108	13.7	686	91	595	349	79
$5,000 to $9,999	1,680	515	30.6	402	23.9	1,277	113	1,165	714	129
$10,000 to $14,999	2,138	433	20.2	322	15.1	1,816	111	1,706	1,178	138
$15,000 to $19,999	2,573	782	30.4	624	24.3	1,949	158	1,791	1,191	123
$20,000 to $24,999	1,768	676	38.3	605	34.2	1,163	72	1,091	712	97
$25,000 to $34,999	1,415	688	48.6	596	42.1	819	92	727	409	68
$35,000 to $49,999	1,073	570	53.2	509	47.5	564	61	503	237	86
$50,000 and over	429	263	61.3	235	54.7	194	28	166	85	39
Income not reported	490	147	30.1	123	25.1	367	24	343	204	75

Source: U.S. Bureau of the Census. *Voting and Registration in the Election of November 1992*, Current Population Reports, P20-466. Washington, DC, U.S. GPO, 1993, p. 56. *Notes:* 1. Includes persons reported as "did not vote," "do not know," and "not reported" on voting. 2. In addition to those reported as "not registered," total includes those "not a U.S. citizen," and "do not know" and "not reported" on registration. 3. Includes "do not know" and "not reported" on citizenship. 4. Persons of Hispanic origin may be of any race.

★ 862 ★

Voting

Reported Voting and Registration, by Metropolitan vs. Nonmetropolitan Residence, 1992

Data for November 1992 are shown in thousands and as percent of total in each voting status category.

Race, Hispanic origin, and residence	Reported registered			Reported voted		Reported that they did not vote[1]				
						Total	Registered	Not registered		
	All persons	Number	Percent	Number	Percent			Total[2]	Not a U.S. citizen	Do not know and not reported on registration[3]
All Races										
Total	185,684	126,578	68.2	113,866	61.3	71,818	12,712	59,106	11,900	10,638
Metropolitan	144,593	97,460	67.4	88,222	61.0	56,371	9,238	47,133	11,332	8,880
In central cities	55,855	36,118	64.7	32,301	57.8	23,554	3,817	19,736	6,024	3,696
Outside central cities	88,738	61,342	69.1	55,921	63.0	32,817	5,421	27,397	5,308	5,183
Nonmetropolitan	41,091	29,118	70.9	25,644	62.4	15,447	3,474	11,973	568	1,758
White										
Total	157,837	110,684	70.1	100,405	63.6	57,432	10,279	47,153	8,284	8,289
Metropolitan	120,848	84,094	69.6	76,807	63.6	44,041	7,287	36,755	7,811	6,800
In central cities	41,176	27,598	67.0	25,011	60.7	16,165	2,587	13,578	3,961	2,371
Outside central cities	79,672	56,495	70.9	51,796	65.0	27,876	4,699	23,177	3,850	4,429
Nonmetropolitan	36,988	26,590	71.9	23,598	63.8	13,391	2,992	10,399	473	1,489
Black										
Total	21,039	13,442	63.9	11,371	54.0	9,668	2,070	7,598	1,044	1,870
Metropolitan	17,677	11,341	64.2	9,703	54.9	7,974	1,637	6,337	1,018	1,638
In central cities	11,689	7,596	65.0	6,505	55.6	5,185	1,091	4,094	708	1,127
Outside central cities	5,968	3,745	62.5	3,199	53.4	2,789	546	2,243	310	510
Nonmetropolitan	3,362	2,101	62.5	1,668	49.6	1,694	433	1,261	26	233
Hispanic[4]										
Total	14,688	5,137	35.0	4,238	28.9	10,450	899	9,551	5,910	995
Metropolitan	13,569	4,655	34.3	3,855	28.4	9,714	800	8,914	5,655	944
In central cities	7,303	2,529	34.6	2,053	28.1	5,250	476	4,774	3,020	486
Outside central cities	6,266	2,126	33.9	1,802	28.8	4,464	325	4,140	2,635	459
Nonmetropolitan	1,119	481	43.0	383	34.2	736	99	637	256	51

Source: U.S. Bureau of the Census. *Voting and Registration in the Election of November 1992,* Current Population Reports, P20-466. Washington, DC, U.S. GPO, 1993, p. 31. *Notes:* 1. Includes persons reported as "did not know," and "not reported" on voting. 2. In addition to those reported as "not registered," total includes those "not a U.S. citizen," and "do not know" and "not reported" on registration. 3. Includes "do not know" and "not reported" on citizenship. 4. Persons of Hispanic origin may be of any race.

★ 863 ★

Voting

Reported Voting and Registration, of Employed Persons, by Major Occupation Group, Race/Ethnicity, and Sex, 1992

Data for November 1992 are shown in thousands and as percent of total in each voting status category.

Race, Hispanic Origin, sex, and major occupation group	All persons	Reported registered		Reported voted		Reported that they did not vote[1]				
						Total	Registered	Not registered		
								Total[2]	Not a U.S. citizen	Do not know and not reported on registration[3]
		Number	Percent	Number	Percent					
All Races										
Both Sexes										
Total employed	116,290	81,313	69.9	74,138	63.8	42,152	7,175	34,976	6,922	5,992
Managerial and professional	31,772	26,471	83.3	25,087	79.0	6,685	1,384	5,300	1,149	1,181
Executive, administrative, and managerial	14,967	12,182	81.4	11,506	76.9	3,461	676	2,785	493	603
Professional specialty	16,805	14,289	85.0	13,581	80.8	3,223	708	2,515	656	578
Technical, sales, and administrative support	36,056	26,584	73.7	24,503	68.0	11,553	2,080	9,472	1,407	1,722
Technicians and related support	4,221	3,187	75.5	2,957	70.1	1,264	230	1,034	173	149
Sales	13,451	9,452	70.3	8,657	64.4	4,794	795	3,998	636	754
Administrative support, include clerical	18,384	13,944	75.8	12,890	70.1	5,495	1,055	4,440	598	819
Service occupations	15,144	9,124	60.2	7,901	52.2	7,243	1,223	6,020	1,465	994
Private household	803	389	48.4	338	42.0	465	51	414	165	56
Service, except household	14,341	8,735	60.9	7,563	52.7	6,777	1,172	5,606	1,299	938
Farming, forestry, and fishing	3,203	1,935	60.4	1,734	54.2	1,468	201	1,268	476	165
Precision product, craft, and repair	13,180	7,970	60.5	7,061	53.6	6,119	909	5,210	871	764
Operators, fabricators, and laborers	16,936	9,229	54.5	7,851	46.4	9,084	1,378	7,706	1,555	1,166
Machine operators, assemblers, and inspectors	7,482	3,977	53.2	3,405	45.5	4,078	573	3,505	912	433
Transportation and material moving	4,981	2,966	59.5	2,550	51.2	2,431	416	2,015	268	330
Handlers, equipment cleaners, helpers, and laborers	4,473	2,286	51.1	1,897	42.4	2,576	389	2,187	375	403
Male										
Total employed	63,003	42,495	67.4	38,546	61.2	24,457	3,949	20,508	4,406	3,419
Managerial and professional	16,688	13,702	82.1	12,996	77.89	3,691	705	2,986	738	618
Executive, administrative, and managerial	8,724	7,068	81.0	6,699	76.8	2,025	368	1,657	326	331
Professional specialty	7,963	6,634	83.3	6,297	79.1	1,667	337	1,329	412	286
Technical, sales, and administrative support	13,021	9,480	72.8	8,793	67.5	4,228	687	3,541	669	637
Technicians and related support	2,183	1,669	76.4	1,549	71.0	634	120	514	96	73
Sales	7,014	5,096	72.7	4,737	67.5	2,277	358	1,918	361	386
Administrative support, include clerical	3,824	2,715	71.0	2,506	65.5	1,318	209	1,109	211	178
Service occupations	6,084	3,651	60.0	3,140	51.6	2,945	511	2,434	703	439
Private household	23	13	(B)	13	(B)	11	-	11	5	-
Service, except household	6,061	3,638	60.0	3,127	51.6	2,934	511	2,423	698	439
Farming, forestry, and fishing	2,656	1,562	58.8	1,396	52.6	1,260	166	1,094	422	139
Precision product, craft, and repair	11,978	7,236	60.4	6,406	53.5	5,572	830	4,742	789	693
Operators, fabricators, and laborers	12,576	6,865	54.6	5,816	46.2	6,761	1,049	5,711	1,085	893
Machine operators, assemblers, and inspectors	4,382	2,393	54.6	2,056	46.9	2,325	337	1,989	495	243
Transportation and material moving	4,528	2,649	58.5	2,254	49.8	2,274	395	1,879	263	290
Handlers, equipment cleaners, helpers, and laborers	3,666	1,823	49.7	1,505	41.1	2,161	317	1,844	326	361
Female										
Total employed	53,286	38,818	72.8	35,592	66.8	17,694	3,226	14,468	2,516	2,573
Managerial and professional	15,084	12,770	84.7	12,091	80.2	2,993	679	2,314	410	563
Executive, administrative, and managerial	6,243	5,115	81.9	4,807	77.0	1,436	308	1,128	166	271
Professional specialty	8,841	7,655	86.6	7,284	82.4	1,557	371	1,186	244	292
Technical, sales, and administrative support	23,035	17,104	74.3	15,711	68.2	7,324	1,393	5,931	738	1,085
Technicians and related support	2,038	1,518	74.5	1,408	69.1	630	111	520	76	76
Sales	6,436	4,357	67.7	3,919	60.9	2,517	437	2,080	274	369
Administrative support, include clerical	14,561	11,229	77.1	10,384	71.3	4,177	846	3,332	387	641
Service occupations	9,059	5,473	60.4	4,761	52.6	4,298	712	3,586	761	555
Private household	779	376	48.3	325	41.7	454	51	403	160	56
Service, except household	8,280	5,097	61.6	4,436	53.6	3,843	661	3,183	602	499
Farming, forestry, and fishing	547	373	68.2	339	61.9	208	34	174	54	26
Precision product, craft, and repair	1,202	734	61.1	655	54.5	547	80	467	82	71
Operators, fabricators, and laborers	4,359	2,364	54.2	2,036	46.7	2,324	329	1,995	470	273
Machine operators, assemblers, and inspectors	3,100	1,584	51.1	1,348	43.5	1,752	236	1,516	417	190
Transportation and material moving	452	316	69.9	296	65.4	157	21	136	5	41
Handlers, equipment cleaners, helpers, and laborers	807	464	57.5	392	48.6	415	72	343	49	42

[Continued]

★ 863 ★

Reported Voting and Registration, of Employed Persons, by Major Occupation Group, Race/ Ethnicity, and Sex, 1992

[Continued]

Race, Hispanic Origin, sex, and major occupation group	All persons	Reported registered		Reported voted		Reported that they did not vote[1]				
								Not registered		
		Number	Percent	Number	Percent	Total	Registered	Total[2]	Not a U.S. citizen	Do not know and not reported on registration[3]
White										
Both sexes										
Total employed	100,200	71,617	71.5	65,678	65.5	34,522	5,940	28,582	4,833	4,735
Managerial and professional	28,432	24,166	85.0	22,937	80.7	5,495	1,229	4,266	700	969
Executive, administrative, and managerial	13,584	11,231	82.7	10,610	78.1	2,974	621	2,353	328	512
Professional specialty	14,848	12,935	87.1	12,327	83.0	2,520	608	1,913	371	457
Technical, sales, and administrative support	31,522	23,789	75.5	22,014	69.8	9,508	1,776	7,732	799	1,423
Technicians and related support	3,624	2,802	77.3	2,617	72.2	1,007	185	822	92	121
Sales	12,092	8,756	72.4	8,061	66.7	4,031	695	3,336	375	650
Administrative support, include clerical	15,805	12,231	77.4	11,335	71.7	4,470	896	3,574	332	652
Service occupations	11,782	7,164	60.8	6,276	53.3	5,505	888	4,617	983	727
Private household	826	289	46.1	248	39.5	379	42	337	127	44
Service, except household	11,155	6,875	61.6	6,029	54.0	5,126	846	4,280	856	683
Farming, forestry, and fishing	2,922	1,796	61.5	1,613	55.2	1,308	183	1,126	445	137
Precision product, craft, and repair	11,738	7,150	60.9	6,348	54.1	5,390	802	4,588	693	622
Operators, fabricators, and laborers	13,805	7,552	54.7	6,490	47.0	7,315	1,062	6,253	1,213	857
Machine operators, assemblers, and inspectors	6,036	3,168	52.5	2,752	45.6	3,284	416	2,868	706	335
Transportation and material moving	4,167	2,514	50.3	2,168	52.0	1,999	346	1,653	216	244
Handlers, equipment cleaners, helpers, and laborers	3,602	1,869	51.9	1,570	43.6	2,032	300	1,733	292	278
Male										
Total employed	54,894	37,956	69.1	34,694	63.2	20,201	3,263	16,938	3,191	2,710
Managerial and professional	15,161	12,729	84.0	12,100	79.8	3,060	629	2,431	461	510
Executive, administrative, and managerial	8,026	6,602	82.3	6,258	78.0	1,768	343	1,424	222	283
Professional specialty	7,135	6,128	85.9	5,842	81.9	1,293	286	1,007	239	227
Technical, sales, and administrative support	11,485	8,657	75.4	8,077	70.3	3,409	580	2,826	355	559
Technicians and related support	1,897	1,492	78.6	1,400	73.8	497	92	406	52	67
Sales	6,451	4,840	75.0	4,518	70.0	1,934	323	1,611	196	355
Administrative support, include clerical	3,137	2,325	74.1	2,159	68.8	978	166	812	105	137
Service occupations	4,668	2,867	61.4	2,521	54.0	2,147	346	1,801	476	304
Private household	16	6	(B)	6	(B)	10	-	10	5	-
Service, except household	4,652	2,861	61.5	2,515	54.1	2,137	346	1,791	471	304
Farming, forestry, and fishing	2,418	1,445	59.8	1,295	53.6	1,123	150	973	398	111
Precision product, craft, and repair	10,787	6,564	60.6	5,822	54.0	4,965	741	4,223	643	571
Operators, fabricators, and laborers	10,376	5,695	54.9	4,879	47.0	5,497	816	4,661	854	654
Machine operators, assemblers, and inspectors	3,674	1,987	54.1	1,738	47.3	1,937	249	1,688	392	201
Transportation and material moving	3,779	2,237	59.2	1,912	50.6	1,867	325	1,542	213	207
Handlers, equipment cleaners, helpers, and laborers	2,922	1,470	50.3	1,229	42.1	1,693	241	1,452	253	246
Female										
Total employed	45,306	33,661	74.3	30,984	68.4	14,322	2,677	11,644	1,642	2,025
Managerial and professional	13,271	11,437	86.2	10,837	81.7	2,434	600	1,835	239	459
Executive, administrative, and managerial	5,558	4,630	83.3	4,352	78.3	1,207	278	929	106	228
Professional specialty	7,713	6,807	88.3	6,486	84.1	1,227	322	906	133	231
Technical, sales, and administrative support	20,036	15,133	75.5	13,937	69.6	6,099	1,196	4,904	444	864
Technicians and related support	1,726	1,310	75.9	1,217	70.5	509	93	416	40	54
Sales	5,5641	3,916	69.4	3,544	62.8	2,097	372	1,725	177	295
Administrative support, include clerical	12,669	9,906	78.2	9,176	72.4	3,493	730	2,762	227	515
Service occupations	7,114	4,297	60.4	3,755	52.8	3,359	542	2,816	507	422
Private household	610	283	46.4	242	39.6	369	42	327	122	44
Service, except household	6,503	4,014	61.7	3,514	54.0	2,990	501	2,489	385	379
Farming, forestry, and fishing	504	351	69.7	318	63.2	185	33	153	46	26
Precision product, craft, and repair	951	586	61.5	525	55.2	426	61	385	50	51
Operators, fabricators, and laborers	3,429	1,857	54.2	1,611	47.0	1,818	246	1,572	356	203
Machine operators, assemblers, and inspectors	2,361	1,181	50.0	1,014	42.9	1,347	167	1,180	312	134
Transportation and material moving	388	277	71.3	256	66.0	132	21	111	4	37
Handlers, equipment cleaners, helpers, and laborers	680	399	58.7	341	50.1	339	58	281	39	32
Black										
Both sexes										
Total employed	11,851	8,042	67.9	7,001	59.1	4,851	1,042	3,809	636	966
Managerial and professional	2,126	1,713	80.6	1,603	75.4	523	110	413	77	142

[Continued]

★ 863 ★

Reported Voting and Registration, of Employed Persons, by Major Occupation Group, Race/ Ethnicity, and Sex, 1992

[Continued]

Race, Hispanic Origin, sex, and major occupation group	All persons	Reported registered		Reported voted		Reported that they did not vote[1]				
								Not registered		
		Number	Percent	Number	Percent	Total	Registered	Total[2]	Not a U.S. citizen	Do not know and not reported on registration[3]
Executive, administrative, and managerial	896	724	80.8	683	76.2	213	41	172	32	55
Professional specialty	1,230	989	80.4	920	74.8	310	69	241	45	88
Technical, sales, and administrative support	3,169	2,257	71.2	2,019	63.7	1,150	238	912	137	212
Technicians and related support	383	288	75.1	248	64.8	135	40	95	11	20
Sales	855	535	62.5	462	54.1	393	72	320	58	75
Administrative support, include clerical	1,931	1,435	74.3	1,309	67.8	622	126	496	68	117
Service occupations	2,713	1,749	64.5	1,447	53.3	1,266	302	964	223	219
Private household	152	91	59.9	84	55.7	68	7	61	26	11
Service, except household	2,562	1,658	64.7	1,363	53.2	1,199	295	903	197	208
Farming, forestry, and fishing	222	115	51.9	103	46.5	119	12	107	12	25
Precision product, craft, and repair	1,067	684	64.1	594	55.6	474	90	384	69	104
Operators, fabricators, and laborers	2,555	1,525	59.7	1,235	48.3	1,320	290	1,030	117	264
Machine operators, assemblers, and inspectors	1,124	739	65.8	594	52.9	530	145	385	42	78
Transportation and material moving	709	415	58.5	349	49.2	361	66	295	29	75
Handlers, equipment cleaners, helpers, and laborers	722	371	51.4	292	40.5	430	79	351	45	111
Male										
Total employed	5,836	3,713	63.6	3,135	53.7	2,702	578	2,123	378	544
Managerial and professional	846	650	76.8	604	71.4	242	46	196	45	66
Executive, administrative, and managerial	430	344	80.1	330	76.7	100	15	85	14	31
Professional specialty	416	305	73.4	275	66.0	142	31	111	31	35
Technical, sales, and administrative support	964	642	66.5	559	58.0	405	82	323	68	44
Technicians and related support	175	132	75.5	108	61.7	67	24	43	5	3
Sales	302	185	61.1	160	53.1	142	24	118	35	19
Administrative support, include clerical	487	325	66.7	291	59.7	196	34	162	28	21
Service occupations	1,101	686	62.3	537	48.8	564	149	415	95	112
Private household	7	7	(B)	7	(B)	-	-	-	-	-
Service, except household	1,095	679	62.1	531	48.5	564	149	415	95	112
Farming, forestry, and fishing	197	102	51.7	90	45.6	107	12	95	10	25
Precision product, craft, and repair	891	564	63.3	489	54.9	402	75	327	66	89
Operators, fabricators, and laborers	1,837	1,070	58.2	855	46.6	982	215	767	94	209
Machine operators, assemblers, and inspectors	556	374	67.2	293	52.6	263	81	182	22	32
Transportation and material moving	653	380	58.2	314	48.1	339	66	273	29	72
Handlers, equipment cleaners, helpers, and laborers	627	316	50.3	248	39.6	379	68	312	42	105
Female										
Total employed	6,015	4,329	72.0	3,866	64.3	2,149	464	1,686	257	422
Managerial and professional	1,279	1,063	83.1	998	78.0	281	64	217	32	76
Executive, administrative, and managerial	466	379	81.5	353	75.8	113	26	86	18	24
Professional specialty	814	683	84.0	645	79.3	168	38	130	14	52
Technical, sales, and administrative support	2,205	1,616	73.3	1,460	66.2	745	155	589	69	168
Technicians and related support	208	156	74.8	140	67.4	68	15	53	6	17
Sales	553	350	63.3	302	54.6	251	48	203	23	56
Administrative support, include clerical	1,444	1,110	76.9	1,018	70.5	426	92	334	40	95
Service occupations	1,612	1,063	66.0	910	56.4	702	153	549	128	107
Private household	145	84	58.1	77	53.4	68	7	61	26	11
Service, except household	1,467	979	66.7	832	56.7	635	147	488	102	96
Farming, forestry, and fishing	24	13	(B)	13	(B)	11	-	11	2	-
Precision product, craft, and repair	177	120	67.9	105	59.4	72	15	57	3	15
Operators, fabricators, and laborers	718	455	63.4	380	52.9	338	75	263	23	55
Machine operators, assemblers, and inspectors	568	365	64.3	301	53.1	266	64	202	20	46
Transportation and material moving	56	35	(B)	35	(B)	21	-	21	-	3
Handlers, equipment cleaners, helpers, and laborers	94	55	58.7	44	46.5	50	11	39	3	6
Hispanic Origin[4]										
Both sexes										
Total employed	8,800	3,226	36.7	2,682	30.5	6,117	543	5,574	3,489	570
Managerial and professional	1,188	775	65.2	700	58.9	489	76	413	205	65
Executive, administrative, and managerial	636	375	58.9	333	52.4	303	42	261	120	48
Professional specialty	553	401	72.5	367	66.3	186	34	152	85	17
Technical, sales, and administrative support	2,137	1,116	52.2	925	43.3	1,212	191	1,021	434	147
Technicians and related support	203	109	53.9	102	50.4	101	7	94	47	4

[Continued]

★ 863 ★

Reported Voting and Registration, of Employed Persons, by Major Occupation Group, Race/ Ethnicity, and Sex, 1992

[Continued]

Race, Hispanic Origin, sex, and major occupation group	All persons	Reported registered		Reported voted		Reported that they did not vote[1]				
						Total	Registered	Not registered		
								Total[2]	Not a U.S. citizen	Do not know and not reported on registration[3]
		Number	Percent	Number	Percent					
Sales	755	336	44.5	265	35.1	490	71	419	199	68
Administrative support, include clerical	1,179	671	56.9	558	47.3	622	113	509	187	75
Service occupations	1,654	461	27.9	366	22.2	1,287	94	1,193	814	121
Private household	135	13	9.8	4	3.3	131	9	122	108	8
Service, except household	1,518	448	29.5	362	23.8	1,156	86	1,071	706	113
Farming, forestry, and fishing	558	57	10.3	42	7.5	516	16	500	421	24
Precision product, craft, and repair	1,209	338	28.0	266	22.0	943	72	871	547	94
Operators, fabricators, and laborers	2,054	478	23.3	383	18.7	1,671	95	1,576	1,068	119
Machine operators, assemblers, and inspectors	1,101	209	19.0	175	15.9	926	34	892	640	62
Transportation and material moving	421	131	31.2	111	26.3	310	20	290	176	21
Handlers, equipment cleaners, helpers, and laborers	532	138	26.0	98	18.4	434	40	394	253	35
Male										
Total employed	5,347	1,692	31.6	1,405	26.3	3,943	287	3,656	2,400	354
Managerial and professional	646	405	62.7	349	54.1	297	56	241	138	34
Executive, administrative, and managerial	379	225	59.3	194	51.1	186	31	154	89	22
Professional specialty	266	180	67.7	155	58.3	111	25	86	50	12
Technical, sales, and administrative support	776	361	46.5	314	40.5	462	47	415	217	49
Technicians and related support	100	56	56.7	54	53.8	46	3	43	29	4
Sales	359	147	40.9	128	35.7	231	19	212	106	32
Administrative support, include clerical	317	158	49.7	133	41.8	185	25	159	81	14
Service occupations	811	202	24.9	172	21.2	639	29	610	418	75
Private household	5	-	(B)	-	(B)	5	-	5	5	-
Service, except household	806	202	25.0	172	21.4	634	29	604	413	75
Farming, forestry, and fishing	499	55	10.9	39	7.8	460	16	444	375	24
Precision product, craft, and repair	1,094	299	27.3	231	21.1	863	68	795	504	81
Operators, fabricators, and laborers	1,522	370	24.3	299	19.7	1,222	71	1,152	748	90
Machine operators, assemblers, and inspectors	650	129	19.8	113	17.3	537	16	521	356	39
Transportation and material moving	401	124	30.9	105	26.1	296	19	277	172	17
Handlers, equipment cleaners, helpers, and laborers	471	118	25.0	82	17.4	389	35	354	220	33
Female										
Total employed	3,452	1,534	44.4	1,278	37.0	2,175	257	1,918	1,089	216
Managerial and professional	543	370	68.2	351	64.6	192	20	172	67	31
Executive, administrative, and managerial	265	150	58.5	139	54.3	117	11	106	31	26
Professional specialty	286	221	77.0	211	73.8	75	9	66	35	5
Technical, sales, and administrative support	1,361	755	5.5	611	44.9	750	144	606	217	98
Technicians and related support	103	53	51.1	49	47.1	55	4	50	18	-
Sales	396	189	47.9	137	34.7	258	52	206	93	36
Administrative support, include clerical	862	513	59.5	425	49.3	437	88	349	106	62
Service occupations	842	259	30.8	194	23.0	648	65	583	396	46
Private household	130	13	10.2	4	3.4	126	9	117	103	8
Service, except household	712	246	34.5	190	26.6	522	56	466	293	38
Farming, forestry, and fishing	59	3	(B)	3	(B)	56	-	56	46	-
Precision product, craft, and repair	114	39	33.9	35	30.4	80	4	76	43	13
Operators, fabricators, and laborers	533	108	20.3	84	15.8	449	24	425	320	29
Machine operators, assemblers, and inspectors	451	80	17.7	62	13.8	389	18	371	284	23
Transportation and material moving	20	8	(B)	6	(B)	14	1	13	4	4
Handlers, equipment cleaners, helpers, and laborers	61	20	(B)	16	(B)	45	5	41	33	1

Source: U.S. Bureau of the Census. *Voting and Registration in the Election of November 1992*, Current Population Reports, P20-466. Washington, DC, U.S. GPO, 1993, pp. 51-54. *Notes:* A dash (-) stands for zero or rounds to zero. A (B) stands for base less than 75,000. 1. Includes persons reported as "did not know," and "not reported" on voting. 2. In addition to those reported as "not registered," total includes those "not a U.S. citizen," and "do not know" and "not reported" on registration. 3. Includes "do not know" and "not reported" on citizenship. 4. Persons of Hispanic origin may be of any race.

★ 864 ★

Voting

Voter Participation of Persons Age 65 Years or Older, 1984-88

The percent of people who reported voting in elections is shown, by race/ethnicity, sex, and age, for 1984-1988.

Race/ethnicity and election year	65 to 74 years		75+	
	Men	Women	Men	Women
1984 Election				
Total	73.9	70.2	68.3	57.2
Hispanic[1]	49.7	44.6	30.3	29.2
White	75.0	71.2	69.6	57.8
Black	65.9	57.9	64.0	55.0
1986 Election				
Total	68.7	62.2	63.1	48.8
Hispanic[1]	43.7	35.8	32.6	30.9
White	70.1	63.3	64.2	49.5
Black	58.9	55.8	52.1	43.9
1988 Election				
Total	75.0	71.5	70.2	57.5
Hispanic[1]	52.0	48.2	53.1	29.1
White	75.9	72.1	71.9	58.7
Black	68.5	70.2	59.4	49.9

Source: Aging America, Trends and Projections, 1991 Edition. Prepared by the U.S. Senate Special Committee on Aging, the American Association of Retired Persons, the Federal Council on the Aging, and the U.S. Administration on Aging, p. 203. Primary source: U.S. Bureau of the Census. "Voting and Registration in the Election of November 1984." Current Population Reports Series P-20. No. 405 (March 1980). U.S. Bureau of the Census. "Voting and Registration in the Election of November 1986." Current Population Reports Series P-20. No. 414 (September 1987). U.S. Bureau of the Census. "Voting and Registration in the Election of November 1988. "Current Population Reports Series P-20. No. 440 (October 1989). *Note:* 1. People of Hispanic origin may be of any race.

★ 865 ★

Voting

Voting-Age Population, 1972-92

Data are shown as of November of each year and cover the civilian noninstitutional population age 18 years and older, including aliens. Figures are based on Current Population Survey and differ from those based on population estimates and official vote counts.

Race/ethnicity	Voting age population (millions)										
	1972	1974	1976	1978	1980	1982	1984	1986	1988	1990	1992
Total[1]	136.2	141.3	146.5	151.6	157.1	165.5	170.0	173.9	178.1	182.1	185.7
White	121.2	125.1	129.3	133.4	137.7	143.6	146.8	149.9	152.9	155.6	157.8
Black	13.5	14.2	14.9	15.6	16.4	17.6	18.4	19.0	19.7	20.4	21.0
Hispanic[2]	5.6	6.1	6.6	6.8	8.2	8.8	9.5	11.8	12.9	13.8	14.7

Source: 1994 Statistical Abstract of the United States on CD-ROM [machine-readable datafiles]. CD-8A-94. Washington, DC: U.S. Department of Commerce, Economics and Statistics Administration, Bureau of the Census, Data User Services Division, January 1995. Primary source: U.S. Bureau of the Census, Current Population Reports, P20-466, and earlier reports. *Notes:* 1. Includes other races not shown separately. 2. Hispanic persons may be of any race.

★ 866 ★

Voting

Voting-Age Population Reporting Registered, 1972-90

Data are shown as of November of each year and cover the civilian noninstitutional population age 18 years and older, including aliens. Figures are based on Current Population Survey and differ from those based on population estimates and official vote counts.

Race/ethnicity	Percent reporting registered										
	Presidential election years						Congressional election years				
	1972	1976	1980	1984	1988	1992	1974	1978	1982	1986	1990
Total[1]	72.3	66.7	66.9	68.3	66.6	68.2	62.2	62.6	64.1	64.3	62.2
White	73.4	68.3	68.4	69.6	67.9	70.1	63.5	63.8	65.6	65.3	63.8
Black	65.5	58.5	60.0	66.3	64.5	63.9	54.9	57.1	59.1	64.0	58.8
Hispanic[2]	44.4	37.8	36.3	40.1	35.5	35.0	34.9	32.9	35.3	35.9	32.3

Source: 1994 Statistical Abstract of the United States on CD-ROM [machine-readable datafiles]. CD-8A-94. Washington, DC: U.S. Department of Commerce, Economics and Statistics Administration, Bureau of the Census, Data User Services Division, January 1995. Primary source: U.S. Bureau of the Census, Current Population Reports, P20-466, and earlier reports. *Notes:* 1. Includes other races not shown separately. 2. Hispanic persons may be of any race.

★ 867 ★

Voting

Voting-Age Population Reporting Voted, 1972-92

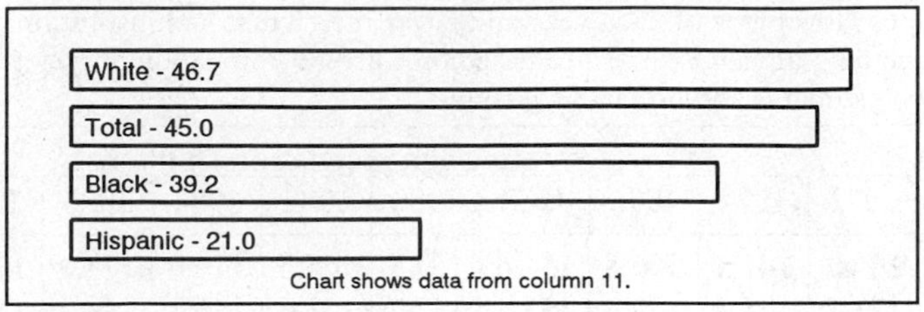

Data are shown as of November of each year and cover the civilian noninstitutional population age 18 years and older, including aliens. Figures are based on Current Population Survey and differ from those based on population estimates and official vote counts.

	Percent of registered voters reporting they voted										
	1972	1976	1980	1984	1988	1992	1974	1978	1982	1986	1990
Total[1]	63.0	59.2	59.2	59.9	57.4	61.3	44.7	45.9	48.5	46.0	45.0
White	64.5	60.9	60.9	61.4	59.1	63.6	46.3	47.3	49.9	47.0	46.7
Black	52.1	48.7	50.5	55.8	51.5	54.0	33.8	37.2	43.0	43.2	39.2
Hispanic[2]	37.5	31.8	29.9	32.6	28.8	28.9	22.9	23.5	25.3	24.2	21.0

Source: 1994 Statistical Abstract of the United States on CD-ROM [machine-readable datafiles]. CD-8A-94. Washington, DC: U.S. Department of Commerce, Economics and Statistics Administration, Bureau of the Census, Data User Services Division, January 1995. Primary source: U.S. Bureau of the Census, Current Population Reports, P20-466, and earlier reports. *Notes:* 1. Includes other races not shown separately. 2. Hispanic persons may be of any race.

Chapter 9
LAW AND LAW ENFORCEMENT

Crime Victims

★ 868 ★

Ages of Victims and Offenders in Violent Crime Victimizations, 1979-86

Figures are shown as percentages.

Age and race or ethnicity of victim	Perceived age of offenders						
	Total	Under 21	21-29	30 or over	Mixed ages	Not known or not ascertained	Number of offenders unknown
Crimes of violence							
Age under 21							
Hispanic	100.0	62.0	16.0	8.0	9.0	3.0	1.0
White	100.0	61.0	19.0	10.0	6.0	3.0	1.0
Black	100.0	60.0	18.0	10.0	7.0	5.0	1.0
Age 21-29							
Hispanic	100.0	21.0	38.0	21.0	14.0	4.0	1.0[1]
White	100.0	17.0	45.0	25.0	9.0	3.0	1.0
Black	100.0	13.0	48.0	23.0	10.0	5.0	1.0
Age 30 or over							
Hispanic	100.0	21.0	27.0	30.0	11.0	9.0	2.0
White	100.0	18.0	28.0	40.0	7.0	5.0	3.0
Black	100.0	17.0	22.0	40.0	10.0	9.0	2.0

Source: U.S. Department of Justice. Office of Justice Programs. Bureau of Justice Statistics. *Bureau of Justice Statistics, Special Report: Hispanic Victims*, NCJ-120507, Washington, DC: Bureau of Justice Statistics, January 1990, p. 9. *Notes:* Detail may not total 100% because of rounding. 1. Estimate is based on 10 or fewer sample cases.

★ 869 ★

Crime Victims

Homicides in New York City, by Race/Ethnicity of Victim

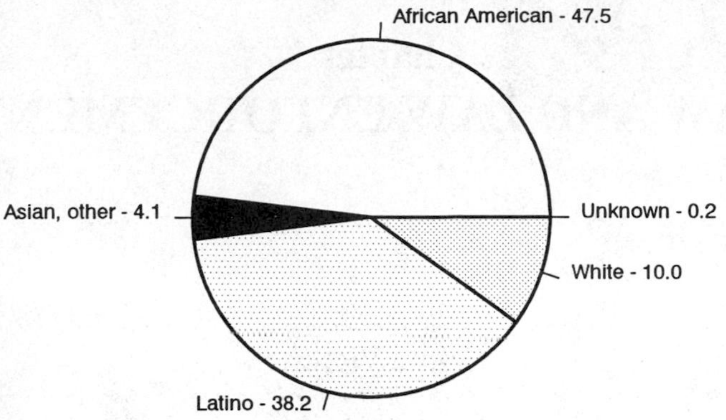

Chart shows data from column 2.

Data represent race and ethnic origin of all homicide victims in New York City from 1990-1991. Figures are based on files of the Chief Medical Examiner, which contained reports on a total of 4,468 homicides over the two-year period.

Race/ethnicity	Homicide victims	
	Number	Percent
African American	2,121	47.5
Latino	1,708	38.2
White	446	10.0
Asian, other	185	4.1
Unknown	8	0.2

Source: Tardiff, Kenneth, MD, MPH, and others. "A Profile of Homicides on the Streets and in the Homes of New York City." *Public Health Reports* 110, no. 1 (January-February 1995), p. 14.

★ 870 ★

Crime Victims

Homicides in New York City, by Race/Ethnicity of Victim and by Crime Location

Data represent race and ethnic origin of all homicide victims in New York City from 1990-1991. Figures are based on files of the Chief Medical Examiner, which contained reports on a total of 4,468 homicides over the two-year period. For all races, the majority of homicides were committed with firearms—shootings accounted for 80.3 percent of all street murders and 46.3% of all murders in homes. The most likely targets of street homicides were persons between the ages of 15 and 24 years.

Race/ethnicity	Home		Street	
	Number	Percent	Number	Percent
African American	397	46.1	1,189	53.2
Latino	315	36.6	816	36.5
White	121	14.1	169	7.6
Asian, other	28	3.3	60	2.2

Source: Tardiff MD, MPH, Kenneth and others. "A Profile of Homicides on the Streets and in the Homes of New York City." *Public Health Reports* 110, no. 1 (January-February 1995), p. 14.

★ 871 ★

Crime Victims

Number and Age of Offenders in Violent Crime Victimizations, 1979-86

Figures are shown as percentages.

Type of crime, number of offenders, and race or ethnicity of victim	Perceived age of offenders					
	Total	Under 21	21-29	30 or over	Mixed ages	Not known or not ascertained
Crimes of violence[1]						
Single offender						
Hispanic victims	100.0	32.0	36.0	29.0	na	3.0
White	100.0	29.0	36.0	32.0	na	2.0
Black	100.0	28.0	36.0	32.0	na	3.0
Two or more offenders						
Hispanic victims	100.0	43.0	15.0	6.0	28.0	9.0
White	100.0	41.0	17.0	6.0	28.0	8.0
Black	100.0	39.0	15.0	7.0	28.0	11.0
Robbery						
Single offender						
Hispanic victims	100.0	44.0	33.0	17.0	na	6.0
White	100.0	33.0	42.0	21.0	na	3.0
Black	100.0	33.0	39.0	20.0	na	8.0

[Continued]

★ 871 ★

Number and Age of Offenders in Violent Crime Victimizations, 1979-86

[Continued]

Type of crime, number of offenders, and race or ethnicity of victim	Perceived age of offenders					
	Total	Under 21	21-29	30 or over	Mixed ages	Not known or not ascertained
Two or more offenders						
Hispanic victims	100.0	43.0	18.0	4.0	25.0	9.0
White	100.0	40.0	19.0	6.0	25.0	10.0
Black	100.0	40.0	15.0	7.0	25.0	12.0
Aggravated assault						
Single offender						
Hispanic victims[2]	100.0	26.0	41.0	32.0	na	1.0
White	100.0	26.0	37.0	35.0	na	3.0
Black	100.0	25.0	35.0	39.0	na	2.0
Two or more offenders						
Hispanic victims	100.0	39.0	11.0	6.0	33.0	11.0
White	100.0	36.0	17.0	7.0	33.0	7.0
Black	100.0	29.0	14.0	8.0	34.0	14.0
Simple assault						
Single offender						
Hispanic victims	100.0	32.0	34.0	31.0	na	3.0
White	100.0	30.0	35.0	33.0	na	2.0
Black	100.0	30.0	36.0	32.0	na	3.0
Two or more offenders						
Hispanic victims	100.0	48.0	15.0	7.0	24.0	5.0
White	100.0	46.0	16.0	6.0	26.0	6.0
Black	100.0	46.0	16.0	4.0	26.0	8.0

Source: U.S. Department of Justice. Office of Justice Programs. Bureau of Justice Statistics. *Bureau of Justice Statistics, Special Report: Hispanic Victims*, NCJ-120507, Washington, DC: Bureau of Justice Statistics, January 1990, p. 9. *Notes:* (na) stands for not applicable. Detail may not total 100% because of rounding. 1. Include data on rape not shown as a separate category. 2. The estimate for "not known or ascertained" is based on 10 or fewer sample cases.

★ 872 ★

Crime Victims

Places Where Violent Crime Occurred, 1979-86

Type of crime and race or ethnicity of victim	The percent of violent crime that took place -							
	Total	On the street[1]	Near home[2]	At home[3]	In a parking lot	In school	On public transportation	Elsewhere or not ascertained
Crimes of violence[4]								
Hispanic	100.0	30.0	15.0	12.0	7.0	8.0	2.0	27.0
White	100.0	24.0	10.0	12.0	9.0	9.0	1.0	34.0
Black	100.0	35.0	14.0	15.0	5.0	6.0	2.0	23.0

[Continued]

★ 872 ★

Places Where Violent Crime Occurred, 1979-86

[Continued]

Type of crime and race or ethnicity of victim	The percent of violent crime that took place -							
	Total	On the street[1]	Near home[2]	At home[3]	In a parking lot	In school	On public transportation	Elsewhere or not ascertained
Robbery								
Hispanic	100.0	45.0	12.0	9.0	9.0	3.0	5.0	17.0
White	100.0	34.0	9.0	14.0	12.0	6.0	3.0	22.0
Black	100.0	51.0	12.0	11.0	6.0	4.0	2.0	14.0
Aggravated assault								
Hispanic	100.0	26.0	18.0	10.0	8.0	5.0	1.0	32.0
White	100.0	26.0	10.0	11.0	10.0	5.0	1.0	37.0
Black	100.0	30.0	14.0	14.0	6.0	4.0	1.0	30.0
Simple assault								
Hispanic	100.0	24.0	14.0	13.0	5.0	13.0	1.0	30.0
White	100.0	21.0	10.0	12.0	8.0	12.0	1.0	36.0
Black	100.0	26.0	15.0	19.0	4.0	11.0	2.0	24.0

Source: U.S. Department of Justice. Office of Justice Programs. Bureau of Justice Statistics. *Bureau of Justice Statistics, Special Report: Hispanic Victims*, NCJ-120507, Washington, DC: Bureau of Justice Statistics, January 1990, p. 6. *Notes:* Detail may not total 100% because of rounding. 1. "On the street" is defined as on the street other than immediately adjacent to one's own home or to a friend's, relative's, or neighbor's home. 2. "Near home" is defined as being near one's own home, yard, sidewalk, driveway, carport, or on a street immediately adjacent to one's own home, apartment, storage area, or laundry room. 3. "At home" is defined as being at or in one's own dwelling or attached garage or being at or in a detached building on one's own property. 4. Includes data on rape not shown as a separate category.

★ 873 ★

Crime Victims

Presence and Severity of Injuries Received in Violent Attacks, 1979-86

Type of crime and injury	Percent of attacks on victims who were		
	Hispanic	White	Black
Crimes of violence[1]			
Total	100.0	100.0	100.0
No injury	39.0	37.0	38.0
Injury	61.0	63.0	62.0
Serious	11.0	10.0	15.0
Minor	50.0	53.0	47.0
Robbery			
Total	100.0	100.0	100.0
No injury	41.0	36.0	44.0
Injury	59.0	64.0	56.0
Serious	12.0	14.0	13.0

[Continued]

★ 873 ★

Presence and Severity of Injuries Received in Violent Attacks, 1979-86

[Continued]

Type of crime and injury	Percent of attacks on victims who were		
	Hispanic	White	Black
Minor	47.0	50.0	42.0
Aggravated assault[2]			
Total	100.0	100.0	100.0
No injury	27.0	23.0	22.0
Injury	73.0	77.0	78.0
Serious	27.0	30.0	33.0
Minor	46.0	48.0	45.0

Source: U.S. Department of Justice. Office of Justice Programs. Bureau of Justice Statistics. *Bureau of Justice Statistics, Special Report: Hispanic Victims*, NCJ-120507, Washington, DC: Bureau of Justice Statistics, January 1990, p. 7. *Notes:* Subgroup percentages may not total to the overall category because of rounding. Figures exclude rape injuries, those victimizations in which the presence of injury was not ascertained, and violent victimizations involving threats but not attacks. Although some respondents may have reported more than one type of injury, victimizations have been classified according to the most serious injury received. Serious injury includes knife, gunshot, or bullet wounds; broken bones and teeth; internal injuries; being knocked unconscious; or other injuries requiring 2 or more days of hospitalization. Minor injuries include bruises, cuts, scratches, black eyes, swelling, or other injuries requiring less than 2 days of hospitalization. 1. Includes data on rape and simple assault not shown as separate categories. 2. Involves attack with a weapon or attack without a weapon which results in serious injury.

★ 874 ★

Crime Victims

Presence and Type of Medical Care Received by Victims of Violent Crime, 1979-86

Type of crime and medical care	Percent of injuries		
	Hispanic	White	Black
Crimes of violence[1]			
Total	100.0	100.0	100.0
No care received	49.0	54.0	39.0
Medical care received	51.0	46.0	61.0
Outside an emergency room or hospital	23.0	23.0	24.0
In an emergency room or hospital	28.0	23.0	37.0
Did not stay overnight	22.0	20.0	29.0
Stayed overnight	7.0	3.0	9.0
Robbery			
Total	100.0	100.0	100.0
No care received	53.0	52.0	42.0
Medical care received	47.0	48.0	58.0

[Continued]

★874★

Presence and Type of Medical Care Received by Victims of Violent Crime, 1979-86

[Continued]

Type of crime and medical care	Percent of injuries Hispanic	White	Black
Outside an emergency room or hospital	20.0	22.0	25.0
In an emergency room or hospital	27.0	26.0	33.0
Did not stay overnight	21.0	20.0	28.0
Stayed overnight	7.0	5.0	5.0
Aggravated assault[2]			
Total	100.0	100.0	100.0
No care received	33.0	40.0	25.0
Medical care received	67.0	60.0	75.0
Outside and emergency room or hospital	25.0	23.0	23.0
In an emergency room or hospital	43.0	37.0	52.0
Did not stay overnight	29.0	30.0	35.0
Stayed overnight	13.0	7.0	17.0

Source: U.S. Department of Justice. Office of Justice Programs. Bureau of Justice Statistics. *Bureau of Justice Statistics, Special Report: Hispanic Victims*, NCJ-120507, Washington, DC: Bureau of Justice Statistics, January 1990, p. 7. *Notes:* Subgroup percentages may not total to the overall category because of rounding. Although some respondents may have reported more than one type of medical treatment, victimizations have been classified according to a hierarchy based upon the most intensive treatment received. 1. Includes data on rape and simple assault not shown as separate categories. 2. Involves attack with a weapon or attack without a weapon which results in serious injury; thus, a large share of aggravated assaults result in some type of medical care being received.

★875★

Crime Victims

Presence and Type of Weapons in Violent Crimes, 1979-86

Type of crime, presence and type of weapon	Hispanic	White	Black
Crimes of violence[1]			
Total	100.0	100.0	100.0
No weapon	48.0	61.0	42.0
Weapon	45.0	32.0	49.0
Gun	15.0	10.0	20.0
Knife	15.0	8.0	14.0
Other	13.0	12.0	13.0

[Continued]

★ 875 ★

Presence and Type of Weapons in Violent Crimes, 1979-86

[Continued]

Type of crime, presence and type of weapon	Hispanic	White	Black
Weapon type unknown	2.0	2.0	2.0
Not known or not ascertained if armed	7.0	7.0	10.0
Robbery			
Total	100.0	100.0	100.0
No weapon	33.0	44.0	30.0
Weapon	57.0	43.0	57.0
Gun	19.0	16.0	29.0
Knife	25.0	15.0	16.0
Other	11.0	10.0	10.0
Weapon type unknown	2.0	2.0	2.0
Not known or not ascertained if armed	9.0	11.0	12.0
Aggravated assault[2]			
Total	100.0	100.0	100.0
No weapon	3.0	6.0	3.0
Weapon	97.0	94.0	97.0
Gun	32.0	29.0	36.0
Knife	27.0	22.0	27.0
Other	34.0	39.0	30.0
Weapon type unknown	4.0	4.0	3.0
Not known or not ascertained if armed	[3]	[3]	1.0

Source: U.S. Department of Justice. Office of Justice Programs. Bureau of Justice Statistics. *Bureau of Justice Statistics, Special Report: Hispanic Victims*, NCJ-120507, Washington, DC: Bureau of Justice Statistics, January 1990, p. 7. *Notes:* Detail may not total 100% because of rounding. Although some respondents may have reported more than one weapon present, victimizations have been classified according to a hierarchy of weapons use: any gun present, any knife present, other weapon present but type not ascertained, no weapon, and not known or not ascertained if weapon was present. A dash (-) indicates a figure less than 0.5%. 1. Includes data on rape and simple assault not shown as separate categories. 2. Involves attack with a weapon or attack without a weapon which results in serious injury. 3. Estimates for Hispanics and blacks are based on 10 or fewer sample cases.

★ 876 ★

Crime Victims

Rape Victims

The average annual rate of completed or attempted rape is shown per 1,000 women age 12 and older for the United States and the 1973-87 period.

Race/ethnicity	Total	Completed	Attempted
Total	1.6	0.6	1.1
Ethnicity			
Hispanic	1.5	0.5	1.0
Non-Hispanic	1.6	0.6	1.1
Race			
White	1.5	0.5	1.0
Black	2.7	1.2	1.5
Other	1.8	0.9	0.9

Source: Sourcebook of Criminal Justice Statistics - 1990, U.S. Department of Justice, Office of Justice Programs, Bureau of Justice Statistics, U.S. G.P.O., Washington, D.C., p. 270. Primary source: U.S. Department of Justice, Bureau of Justice Statistics, *Female Victims of Violent Crime,* Special Report NCJ-126826 (Washington, D.C.: U.S. Department of Justice, 1991), p. 8, Tables 15 and 16.

★ 877 ★

Crime Victims

Rate of Violent Offenses Against Females Age 12 and Older, 1987-91

Data show rate per 1,000 females age 12 years and older, by race/ethnicity of victim and relationship to offender.

	Victim-offender relationship			
	Intimate	Other relative	Acquaintance	Stranger
Total	5.4	1.1	7.6	5.4
Race				
White	5.4	1.2	7.2	5.1
Black	5.8	1.3	10.5	7.4
Other[1]	3.6	0.7[2]	6.2	5.3
Ethnicity				
Hispanic	5.5	1.3	6.3	7.2
Non-Hispanic	5.4	1.1	7.7	5.3

Source: Maguire, Kathleen and Ann L. Pastore (eds.). U.S. Department of Justice. U.S. Bureau of Justice Statistics. *Sourcebook of Criminal Justice Statistics 1993.* Washington, DC: U.S. Government Printing Office, 1994, p. 269. Primary source: U.S. Department of Justice, Bureau of Justice Statistics, *Violence Against Women,* NCJ-145325 (Washington, DC: U.S. Department of Justice, 1994), pp. 7, 8. *Notes:* These data include only violent victimizations involving single offenders. 1. Includes groups such as Asians and Native Americans. 2. Estimate is based on about 10 or fewer sample cases.

★ 878 ★

Crime Victims

Reasons for Not Reporting Victimizations to the Police, 1979-86

Figures are shown in percent for each race/ethnicity.

Type of crime and race or ethnicity of victim	Private matter	Not important enough to respondent	Lack of proof	Not important enough to police	Police would not do anything[1]	Fear of reprisal	Reported crime to some-one else	Other and not known
Crimes of violence[2]								
Hispanic	22.0	20.0	12.0	11.0	8.0	7.0	10.0	29.0
White	31.0	23.0	8.0	7.0	5.0	5.0	13.0	24.0
Black	26.0	20.0	11.0	10.0	8.0	4.0	11.0	26.0
Robbery								
Hispanic	9.0	12.0	21.0	12.0	14.0	8.0	6.0	42.0
White	20.0	17.0	18.0	9.0	9.0	6.0	9.0	36.0
Black	15.0	13.0	20.0	13.0	14.0	5.0	7.0	38.0
Aggravated assault								
Hispanic	29.0	18.0	9.0	12.0	9.0	9.0	8.0	27.0
White	33.0	19.0	9.0	7.0	5.0	6.0	10.0	27.0
Black	30.0	20.0	9.0	9.0	8.0	5.0	10.0	23.0
Simple assault								
Hispanic	26.0	26.0	8.0	10.0	5.0	5.0	14.0	22.0
White	33.0	26.0	5.0	7.0	3.0	5.0	14.0	21.0
Black	30.0	25.0	7.0	8.0	4.0	3.0	14.0	20.0
Crimes of theft								
Hispanic	3.0	27.0	20.0	10.0	4.0	1.0	20.0	37.0
White	4.0	32.0	21.0	7.0	3.0	-	21.0	35.0
Black	5.0	24.0	22.0	9.0	4.0	-	21.0	34.0
Household crimes								
Hispanic	6.0	28.0	19.0	12.0	8.0	1.0	4.0	42.0
White	8.0	33.0	22.0	10.0	5.0	1.0	4.0	39.0
Black	9.0	25.0	22.0	12.0	7.0	1.0	5.0	42.0

Source: U.S. Department of Justice. Office of Justice Programs. Bureau of Justice Statistics. *Bureau of Justice Statistics, Special Report: Hispanic Victims,* NCJ-120507, Washington, DC: Bureau of Justice Statistics, January 1990, p. 8. *Notes:* A dash (-) indicates a figure less than 0.5%. Some respondents may have cited more than one reason for not reporting victimizations to the police. Therefore, detail will not total 100%. 1. Includes reasons given by respondents such as: the police would be inefficient, ineffective, or insensitive. 2. Includes data on rape not shown as a separate category.

★ 879 ★

Crime Victims

Victim/Offender Relationship in Violent Crime Victimizations, 1979-86

Victim-offender relationship	Crimes of violence (%)		
	Hispanic	White	Black
Total	100.0	100.0	100.0
Nonstranger			
Total	32.0	38.0	42.0
Spouse	2.0	3.0	2.0
Ex-spouse	2.0	2.0	1.0
Parent	1	1.0	-
Child	1	-	-
Other relative	3.0	2.0	2.0
Casual acquaintance	12.0	13.0	14.0
Well known	12.0	17.0	22.0
Stranger	65.0	58.0	54.0
Relationship not known or not ascertained	4.0	4.0	5.0

Source: U.S. Department of Justice. Office of Justice Programs. Bureau of Justice Statistics. *Bureau of Justice Statistics, Special Report: Hispanic Victims*, NCJ-120507, Washington, DC: Bureau of Justice Statistics, January 1990, p. 6. *Notes:* Detail may not total 100% because of rounding. A dash (-) indicates a figure less than 0.5%. 1. Estimate is based on 10 or fewer sample cases.

★ 880 ★

Crime Victims

Victimization Rates for Personal and Household Crimes, 1979-86

Rates per 1,000 are shown for persons 12 years old and older.

Ethnicity	1979	1980	1981	1982	1983	1984	1985	1986
Hispanics								
Crimes of violence	44	45	43	45	43	39	31	29
Crimes of theft	84	78	88	88	74	66	61	66
Household crimes	299	278	291	279	253	262	240	237
Non-Hispanics								
Crimes of violence	38	36	39	38	34	34	32	31

[Continued]

★880★

Victimization Rates for Personal and Household Crimes, 1979-86

[Continued]

Ethnicity	1979	1980	1981	1982	1983	1984	1985	1986
Crimes of theft	95	85	87	84	79	74	71	69
Household crimes	242	233	231	213	194	181	177	172

Source: U.S. Department of Justice. Office of Justice Programs. Bureau of Justice Statistics. *Bureau of Justice Statistics, Special Report: Hispanic Victims*, NCJ-120507, Washington, DC: Bureau of Justice Statistics, January 1990, p. 2.

★881★

Crime Victims

Victimization Rates, by Type of Crime and Home Ownership, 1979-86

Characteristics of the victim are shown for crimes of violence and theft; characteristics of the head of household are shown for household crimes. Victimization rates are average annual victimization rates per 1,000 persons or households.

Type of crime and ethnicity	Households that	
	Owned	Rented
Crimes of violence[1]		
Hispanic	28.4	50.5
Non-Hispanic	23.8	63.2
Robbery		
Hispanic	5.6	15.4
Non-Hispanic	3.5	12.4
Aggravated assault		
Hispanic	9.2	14.7
Non-Hispanic	6.5	17.6
Simple assault		
Hispanic	13.3	19.2
Non-Hispanic	13.4	31.2
Crimes of theft		
Hispanic	69.6	80.0
Non-Hispanic	67.1	112.3
Personal larceny with contact		
Hispanic	3.2	7.0
Non-Hispanic	1.8	5.4
Personal larceny without contact		
Hispanic	66.5	73.0
Non-Hispanic	65.3	106.9

[Continued]

★ 881 ★

Victimization Rates, by Type of Crime and Home Ownership, 1979-86

[Continued]

Type of crime and ethnicity	Households that	
	Owned	Rented
Household crimes		
Hispanic	243.4	282.1
Non-Hispanic	171.0	266.9
Burglary		
Hispanic	78.9	107.8
Non-Hispanic	60.7	102.6
Household larceny		
Hispanic	140.1	146.7
Non-Hispanic	98.4	142.4
Motor vehicle theft		
Hispanic	24.3	27.7
Non-Hispanic	12.0	21.9

Source: U.S. Department of Justice. Office of Justice Programs. Bureau of Justice Statistics. *Bureau of Justice Statistics, Special Report: Hispanic Victims,* NCJ-120507, Washington, DC: Bureau of Justice Statistics, January 1990, p. 5. *Note:* 1. Includes data on rape not shown as a separate category.

★ 882 ★

Crime Victims

Victimization Rates, by Type of Crime and Location of Residence, 1979-86

Characteristics of the victim are shown for crimes of violence and theft; characteristics of the head of household are shown for household crimes. Victimization rates are average annual victimization rates per 1,000 persons or households.

Type of crime and ethnicity	Average annual crime rate of persons or households in		
	Central city	Suburbs	Nonmetropolitan area
Crimes of violence[1]			
Hispanic	45.7	34.1	32.3
Non-Hispanic	48.5	33.9	26.0
Robbery			
Hispanic	14.8	7.5	3.4
Non-Hispanic	11.7	5.0	2.7
Aggravated assault			
Hispanic	12.9	10.6	12.2
Non-Hispanic	13.1	9.1	7.7
Simple assault			
Hispanic	17.0	15.5	16.0
Non-Hispanic	22.2	19.0	14.9

[Continued]

★ 882 ★

Victimization Rates, by Type of Crime and Location of Residence, 1979-86

[Continued]

Type of crime and ethnicity	Average annual crime rate of persons or households in		
	Central city	Suburbs	Nonmetropolitan area
Crimes of theft			
Hispanic	78.1	75.6	62.1
Non-Hispanic	96.7	85.9	59.2
Personal larceny with contact			
Hispanic	7.5	3.3	1.0
Non-Hispanic	6.1	2.2	1.1
Personal larceny without contact			
Hispanic	70.5	72.3	61.1
Non-Hispanic	90.6	83.7	58.2
Household crimes			
Hispanic	277.0	259.1	239.8
Non-Hispanic	263.7	196.3	160.5
Burglary			
Hispanic	104.1	87.2	84.4
Non-Hispanic	99.3	68.8	61.6
Household larceny			
Hispanic	143.7	144.3	143.7
Non-Hispanic	140.8	112.0	91.2
Motor vehicle theft			
Hispanic	29.3	27.7	11.7
Non-Hispanic	23.6	15.6	7.7

Source: U.S. Department of Justice. Office of Justice Programs. Bureau of Justice Statistics. *Bureau of Justice Statistics, Special Report: Hispanic Victims*, NCJ-120507, Washington, DC: Bureau of Justice Statistics, January 1990, p. 5. *Note:* 1. Includes data on rape not shown as a separate category.

★ 883 ★

Crime Victims

Victimization Rates, by Type of Crime, 1979-86

Characteristics of the victim are used for crimes of violence and theft; characteristics of the head of household are used for household crimes. Victimization rates are average annual victimization rates per 1,000 persons or households.

Type of crime	Hispanic	Non-Hispanic
Crimes of violence	39.6	35.3
Rape	1.0	1.0
Robbery	10.5	6.1
Aggravated assault	12.0	9.7

[Continued]

★ 883 ★

Victimization Rates, by Type of Crime, 1979-86

[Continued]

Type of crime	Hispanic	Non-Hispanic
Simple assault	16.3	18.6
Crimes of theft	74.9	80.3
Personal larceny with contact	5.1	2.9
Personal larceny without contact	69.8	77.4
Household crimes	265.6	204.5
Burglary	95.4	75.3
Household larceny	143.9	113.8
Motor vehicle theft	26.2	15.4

Source: U.S. Department of Justice. Office of Justice Programs. Bureau of Justice Statistics. *Bureau of Justice Statistics, Special Report: Hispanic Victims*, NCJ-120507, Washington, DC: Bureau of Justice Statistics, January 1990, p. 3.

★ 884 ★

Crime Victims

Victimizations Reported to the Police, 1979-86

Type of crime	Percent of victimizations reported when victims were		
	Hispanic	White	Black
Crimes of violence	48.0	48.0	52.0
Rape	50.0	51.0	57.0
Robbery	47.0	57.0	55.0
Aggravated assault	62.0	57.0	59.0
Simple assault	38.0	41.0	43.0
Crimes of theft	24.0	27.0	24.0
Personal larceny			
With contact	31.0	37.0	35.0
Without contact	24.0	27.0	24.0
Household crimes	36.0	38.0	40.0
Burglary	48.0	49.0	52.0
Household larceny	23.0	27.0	23.0
Motor vehicle theft	67.0	69.0	75.0

Source: U.S. Department of Justice. Office of Justice Programs. Bureau of Justice Statistics. *Bureau of Justice Statistics, Special Report: Hispanic Victims*, NCJ-120507, Washington, DC: Bureau of Justice Statistics, January 1990, p. 8.

Drugs

★ 885 ★

Drug Testing of Arrestees in Major Cities, 1992

Data show percent of arrestees of each sex and race/ethnicity who tested positive for each drug, in 1992.

City	Any drug[1]			Marijuana			Cocaine			Heroin		
	Black	White	Hispanic	Black	White	Hispanic	Black	White	Hispanic	Black	White	Hispanic
Male												
Atlanta, GA	69.0	66.0	[2]	20.0	44.0	[2]	59.0	40.0	[2]	4.0	9.0	[2]
Birmingham, AL	64.0	62.0	[2]	19.0	31.0	[2]	53.0	31.0	[2]	2.0	5.0	[2]
Chicago, IL	70.0	66.0	66.0	28.0	18.0	25.0	57.0	54.0	53.0	21.0	14.0	11.0
Cleveland, OH	68.0	45.0	64.0	16.0	24.0	17.0	60.0	22.0	47.0	3.0	2.0	11.0
Dallas, TX	63.0	57.0	47.0	27.0	29.0	29.0	47.0	32.0	32.0	5.0	3.0	4.0
Denver, CO	68.0	52.0	58.0	30.0	32.0	42.0	52.0	27.0	28.0	1.0	2.0	2.0
Detroit, MI	58.0	50.0	60.0	28.0	19.0	25.0	38.0	24.0	40.0	8.0	9.0	5.0
Fort Lauderdale, FL	69.0	62.0	44.0	30.0	34.0	24.0	55.0	37.0	32.0	1.0	1.0	5.0
Houston, TX	66.0	59.0	46.0	22.0	30.0	22.0	49.0	38.0	27.0	3.0	2.0	4.0
Indianapolis, IN	54.0	49.0	[2]	32.0	39.0	[2]	35.0	8.0	[2]	5.0	3.0	[2]
Kansas City, MO	66.0	42.0	39.0	29.0	25.0	22.0	47.0	21.0	35.0	1.0	2.0	4.0
Los Angeles, CA	80.0	73.0	56.0	24.0	28.0	21.0	66.0	40.0	45.0	7.0	16.0	12.0
Manhattan, NY	82.0	75.0	70.0	23.0	17.0	22.0	71.0	57.0	51.0	12.0	24.0	26.0
Miami, FL	72.0	63.0	63.0	33.0	23.0	27.0	61.0	50.0	50.0	2.0	2.0	1.0
New Orleans, LA	63.0	49.0	[2]	18.0	26.0	[2]	54.0	23.0	[2]	4.0	7.0	[2]
Omaha, NE	52.0	46.0	40.0	37.0	41.0	29.0	28.0	5.0	15.0	2.0	2.0	0.0
Philadelphia, PA	80.0	74.0	74.0	25.0	26.0	35.0	67.0	50.0	57.0	7.0	24.0	23.0
Phoenix, AZ	63.0	44.0	45.0	23.0	22.0	20.0	49.0	19.0	28.0	3.0	4.0	8.0
Portland, OR	71.0	55.0	66.0	32.0	29.0	18.0	50.0	24.0	55.0	8.0	10.0	22.0
St. Louis, MO	63.0	66.0	[2]	18.0	40.0	[2]	52.0	36.0	[2]	8.0	5.0	[2]
San Antonio, TX	70.0	51.0	50.0	33.0	33.0	26.0	52.0	19.0	31.0	11.0	12.0	17.0
San Diego, CA	82.0	78.0	75.0	35.0	38.0	36.0	64.0	21.0	53.0	10.0	13.0	23.0
San Jose, CA	57.0	58.0	49.0	28.0	34.0	22.0	38.0	20.0	31.0	4.0	5.0	4.0
Washington, DC	62.0	30.0	[2]	21.0	9.0	[2]	45.0	21.0	[2]	11.0	9.0	[2]
Female												
Atlanta, GA	62.0	79.0	[2]	12.0	18.0	[2]	58.0	59.0	[2]	4.0	10.0	[2]
Birmingham, AL	59.0	62.0	[2]	12.0	14.0	[2]	52.0	32.0	[2]	2.0	10.0	[2]
Cleveland, OH	78.0	67.0	[2]	10.0	13.0	[2]	72.0	52.0	[2]	6.0	3.0	[2]
Dallas, TX	68.0	67.0	39.0	24.0	25.0	9.0	51.0	47.0	26.0	8.0	12.0	0.0
Denver, CO	71.0	53.0	57.0	15.0	18.0	27.0	66.0	39.0	42.0	3.0	6.0	7.0
Detroit, MI	72.0	74.0	[2]	11.0	11.0	[2]	61.0	67.0	[2]	15.0	15.0	[2]
Fort Lauderdale, FL	57.0	65.0	[2]	18.0	23.0	[2]	48.0	48.0	[2]	3.0	3.0	[2]
Houston, TX	59.0	54.0	33.0	10.0	16.0	13.0	51.0	43.0	18.0	3.0	6.0	2.0
Indianapolis, IN	51.0	50.0	[2]	25.0	28.0	[2]	35.0	14.0	[2]	4.0	12.0	[2]
Kansas City, MO	76.0	67.0	[2]	19.0	14.0	[2]	67.0	51.0	[2]	4.0	3.0	[2]
Los Angeles, CA	84.0	78.0	46.0	15.0	16.0	6.0	75.0	54.0	37.0	7.0	17.0	18.0
Manhattan, NY	87.0	77.0	84.0	14.0	17.0	8.0	76.0	60.0	72.0	14.0	36.0	39.0
New Orleans, LA	52.0	56.0	[2]	7.0	17.0	[2]	47.0	33.0	[2]	5.0	9.0	[2]
Philadelphia, PA	77.0	78.0	84.0	14.0	18.0	18.0	70.0	54.0	74.0	5.0	22.0	29.0
Phoenix, AZ	75.0	66.0	53.0	12.0	17.0	12.0	70.0	48.0	39.0	7.0	19.0	14.0
Portland, OR	74.0	74.0	[2]	15.0	20.0	[2]	64.0	51.0	[2]	9.0	28.0	[2]
St. Louis, MO	65.0	82.0	[2]	7.0	21.0	[2]	61.0	65.0	[2]	5.0	12.0	[2]
San Antonio, TX	54.0	54.0	40.0	20.0	19.0	14.0	41.0	32.0	20.0	7.0	19.0	14.0
San Diego, CA	70.0	76.0	66.0	20.0	30.0	16.0	57.0	24.0	45.0	9.0	18.0	26.0

[Continued]

★ 885 ★

Drug Testing of Arrestees in Major Cities, 1992

[Continued]

City	Any drug[1]			Marijuana			Cocaine			Heroin		
	Black	White	Hispanic	Black	White	Hispanic	Black	White	Hispanic	Black	White	Hispanic
San Jose, CA	69.0	60.0	49.0	22.0	21.0	15.0	58.0	53.0	27.0	8.0	14.0	6.0
Washington, DC	72.0	73.0	2	9.0	6.0	2	65.0	64.0	2	18.0	33.0	2

Source: Maguire, Kathleen and Ann L. Pastore (eds.). U.S. Department of Justice. U.S. Bureau of Justice Statistics. *Sourcebook of Criminal Justice Statistics 1993.* Washington, DC: U.S. Government Printing Office, 1994, p. 462. Primary source: U.S. Department*p+10Xof Justice, National Institute of Justice, *Drug Use Forecasting 1992 Annual Report*, NCJ-142973 (Washington, DC: U.S. Department of Justice, 1993), pp. 6-29. Table adapted by *Sourcebook* staff. *Notes:* 1. Includes cocaine, opiates, marijuana, phencyclidine (PCP), methadone, benzodiazepines, methaqualone, propoxyphene, barbiturates, and amphetamines. 2. Less than 20 cases.

Hate Crimes

★ 886 ★

Bias Motivations in Reported Hate Crimes, 1991 and 1992

Number and percent distribution of crimes are shown, by race/ethnicity, religion, and sexual orientation.

	1991		1992	
	Number	Percent[1]	Number	Percent[1]
Total	4,755	100.0	8,075	100.0
Race	2,963	62.3	5,050	62.5
Anti-white	888	18.7	1,664	20.6
Anti-black	1,689	35.5	2,884	35.7
Anti-American Indian/Alaskan Native	11	0.2	31	0.4
Anti-Asian/Pacific Islander	287	6.0	275	3.4
Anti-multi-racial group	88	1.9	198	2.5
Ethnicity	450	9.5	841	10.4
Ant-Hispanic	242	5.1	498	6.2
Anti-other ethnicity/national origin	208	4.4	343	4.2
Religion	917	19.3	1,240	15.4
Anti-Jewish	792	16.7	1,084	13.4
Anti-Catholic	23	0.5	18	0.2
Anti-Protestant	26	0.5	29	0.4
Anti-Islamic (Moslem)	10	0.2	17	0.2
Anti-other religion	51	11.1	77	1.0
Anti-multi-religious group	11	0.2	14	0.2
Anti-atheism/agnosticism/etc.	4	0.1	1	2
Sexual orientation	425	8.9	944	11.7
Anti-homosexual	421	8.9	928	11.5

[Continued]

★ 886 ★

Bias Motivations in Reported Hate Crimes, 1991 and 1992

[Continued]

	1991		1992	
	Number	Percent[1]	Number	Percent[1]
Anti-heterosexual	3	0.1	13	0.2
Anti-bisexual	1	0.0	3	[2]

Source: Maguire, Kathleen and Ann L. Pastore (eds.). U.S. Department of Justice. U.S. Bureau of Justice Statistics. *Sourcebook of Criminal Justice Statistics 1993.* Washington, DC: U.S. Government Printing Office, 1994, p. 375. Primary source: Table provided to *Sourcebook* staff by the U.S. Department of Justice, Federal Bureau of Investigation. *Notes:* The data were obtained from the Federal Bureau of Investigation's statistical program on hate crimes. Data for 1991 were supplied by 2,771 law enforcement agencies in 32 states. Data for 1992 were supplied by 6,180 law enforcement agencies in 41 states and the District of Columbia. 1. Because of rounding, percents may not add to totals. 2. Less than 0.05 percent.

Jails

★ 887 ★

Jail Inmates, by Race/Ethnicity, 1990 and 1991

Data show number of inmates, by race and Hispanic origin, for the United States in 1991 and 1992.

	Percent of inmates[1]	
	1991	1992
Total	100.0	100.0
White, non-Hispanic	41.1	40.1
Black, non-Hispanic	43.4	44.1
Hispanic	14.2	14.5
Other[2]	1.2	1.3

Source: Maguire, Kathleen and Ann L. Pastore (eds.). U.S. Department of Justice. U.S. Bureau of Justice Statistics. *Sourcebook of Criminal Justice Statistics 1993.* Washington, DC: U.S. Government Printing Office, 1994, p. 592. Primary source: U.S. Department of Justice, Bureau of Justice Statistics, *Jail Inmates 1992,* Bulletin NCJ-143284 (Washington, DC: U.S. Department of Justice, August 1993), p. 2, Table 4. *Notes:* Data are for June 28, 1991 and June 30, 1992. Race was reported for 99 percent of the inmates in 1991 and for 98 percent in 1992. 1. Percents may not add to total because of rounding. 2. Native Americans, Aleuts, Alaska Natives, and Pacific Islanders.

Juveniles

★ 888 ★

Delinquents: Runaway and Homeless Centers

Use of runaway and homeless centers by youths is shown for fiscal year 1989. Data are shown, by race/ethnicity and by sex, for the U.S.

Race, ethnicity	Total (N=34,819)	Female (N=19,670)	Male (N=15,149)
Hispanic	9.4	9.3	9.4
American Indian or Alaskan Native	2.6	2.8	2.4
Asian or Pacific Islander	3.7	4.0	3.4
Black, non-Hispanic	19.5	18.8	20.5
White, non-Hispanic	64.8	65.1	64.4

Source: U.S. Department of Justice. Office of Justice Programs. Bureau of Justice Statistics. *Sourcebook of Criminal Justice Statistics, 1990*. Washington, DC: U.S. Government Printing Office, 1991, p. 577. Primary source: U.S. Department of Health and Human Services, Office of Human Development Services, "Annual Report to the Congress on the Runaway and Homeless Youth Program, Fiscal Year 1989," pp. 56, 57, 59. Washington, DC: U.S. Department of Health and Human Services. (Mimeographed). Table adapted by *Sourcebook* staff.

★ 889 ★

Juveniles

Juvenile Facility Inmates, 1987-89

The number of juveniles held in juvenile facilities is shown, by race/ethnicity, for selected years.

Race/ethnicity	1987	1989	% change 1987-89
Total juveniles	53,503	56,123	5.0
Hispanic[1]	7,887	8,671	10.0
White[2]	23,375	22,201	-5.0
Black[3]	20,898	23,836	14.0
Other	1,343	1,415	5.0

Source: U.S. Department of Justice. Bureau of Justice Statistics. *Sourcebook of Criminal Justice Statistics 1990*. Washington, DC: U.S. Government Printing Office, 1991, p. 572. Primary source: U.S. Department of Justice, Office of Juvenile Justice and Delinquency Prevention, *Children in Custody 1989*, NCJ-127189 (Washington, DC, U.S. Department of Justice, January 1991), p. 3. *Notes:* 1. Includes both whites and blacks of Hispanic origin. 2. Includes whites not of Hispanic origin. 3. Includes blacks not of Hispanic origin.

★ 890 ★

Juveniles

Juvenile Facility Inmates, by Race/Ethnicity, and Type of Facility, 1991

Data show the number of juveniles in each type of private facility, for the United States in 1991.

	Total	Detention center	Shelter	Recreation center	Training school	Ranch/ camp	Halfway house
Population	36,190	480	2,783	317	7,135	3,676	21,799
White	20,524	207	1,670	170	2,993	2,079	13,405
Black	11,555	190	785	95	3,459	1,143	5,883
Hispanic	3,136	66	210	43	610	367	1,840
Other	975	17	118	9	73	87	671

Source: Maguire, Kathleen and Ann L. Pastore (eds.). U.S. Department of Justice. U.S. Bureau of Justice Statistics. *Sourcebook of Criminal Justice Statistics 1993.* Washington, DC: U.S. Government Printing Office, 1994, p. 586. Primary source: Data provided to *Sourcebook* staff by the U.S. Department of Justice, Office of Juvenile Justice and Delinquency Prevention.

Law Officers

★ 891 ★

Racial/Ethnic Representation in Law Enforcement Agencies, 1988

Chart shows representation of police officers.

Race/ethnicity	Police (%)	National (%)
Hispanic	6.4	8.0
White	80.3	76.9
Black	12.3	12.1
Other	1.0	3.0

Source: Carter, David L. and Sapp, Allen D. "College Education and Policing: Coming of Age." *FBI Law Enforcement Bulletin* (January 1992), p. 10.

★ 892 ★

Law Officers

Education Levels of Law Officers, by Race/Ethnicity

Race/ethnicity	Average level of education	No college (%)	Some undergraduate work (%)	Graduate degree (%)
Hispanic	13.3 years	27.0	68.0	5.0
White	13.7 years	34.0	62.0	4.0
Black	13.6 years	28.0	63.0	9.0
Other	13.8 years	19.0	73.0	8.0

Source: Carter, David L. and Allen D. Sapp, "College Education and Policing: Coming of Age." *FBI Law Enforcement Bulletin.* (January 1992), p. 11.

★ 893 ★

Law Officers

Hispanic Representation in Federal Law Enforcement Occupations, 1991

The estimated number of persons needed to reach full representation per capita population is shown, for selected groups.

Agency	Occupation series[1]	Hispanic		White		Black		Asian		American Indian	
		Men	Women	Men	Women	Men	Women	Men	Women	Men	Women
Drug Enforcement Administration	1811		10		101	23	56				3
Federal Bureau of Investigation	1811	45	36			476	206		4	34	6
U.S. Immigration and Naturalization Service	1801			19	37	13	.34	4	2	.82	2
	1802			200	155		.62	30	15		2
	1811			120	22	66	29			5	2
	1869			482	242	282	96	18	4	17	3
	2181	.37	.05		3	.96	.18		.03	.23	.01
U.S. Marshals Service	0082	11	3			39	16	3	2	3	.84
	1811	3	6		19	14	37	11	3		.89
Bureau of Alcohol, Tobacco and Firearms	1811		3		2	29	25	4		7	3
U.S. Customs Service	1801		6		42	15	15	.63	2	2	.65
	1811		6		20	171	65		3	5	4
	2181	.75	.26		8	3	.87	4	.14	2	.06
Internal Revenue Service	1811	72		69		128	7			5	3
U.S. Secret Service	0083	33	9		50			8	2	7	2
	1811	20	14		66	61	38		2	5	2
U.S. Postal Service	1811	39	11			27	12			6	2

Source: U.S. General Accounting Office. *Federal Affirmative Employment: Status of Women and Minority Representation in Federal Law Enforcement Occupations*, GAO/T-GGD-93-2. Washington, DC: U.S. GAO, October 1, 1992, p. 10. *Notes:* Except when the estimated number was less than 1 person, each fraction of a person was rounded to the next whole person; for example, 21.6 was rounded to 22 people. 1. Occupation series represent the following groups: 0082, U.S. Marshal; 0083, Police; 1801, General inspection, investigation, and compliance; 1802, Compliance inspection and support; 1811, Criminal investigation; 1896, Border Patrol Agent; 2181, Aircraft operation.

★ 894 ★

Law Officers

Assaults on Federal Officers, 1981-92

Data are shown by department and agency.

Department and agency	Number of officers assaulted											
	1981	1982	1983	1984	1985	1986	1987	1988	1989	1990	1991	1992
Total	728	712	580	672	808	628	690	880	751[1]	1,1254[1]	63[1]	661[1]
U.S. Department of the Interior	29	22	11	47	30	9	33	35	33	38	96	167
Bureau of Indian Affairs	22	19	7	20	6	6	9	9	8	5	[2]	110
National Park Service	7	3	4	27	24	3	24	26	25	33	96	57
U.S. Department of Justice	316	252	1743	143	211	192	310	312	570	968	404	376
Bureau of Prisons	111	115	59	60	51	61	33	146	161	185	[3]	[3]
Drug Enforcement Administration	95	63	18	32	92	53	80	70	77	65	47	66
Federal Bureau of Investigation	42	40	22	32	32	37	14	18	17	24	31	50
Immigration and Naturalization Service[4]	46	22	18	14	21	31	118	37	288	409	296	228[5]
U.S. and Assistant U.S. attorney	8	4	5	4	8	7	45	6	6	269[6]	[4]	[4]
U.S. Marshals Service	14	8	21	4	7	4	20	35	21	16	30	32
U.S. Department of the Treasury	333	395	396	438	524	369	270	647	99	73	127	89
Bureau of Alcohol, Tobacco, and Firearms	31	9	15	5	17	16	5	7	18	7	31	36
Internal Revenue Service	251	347	334	409	465	323	220	391	18[7]	3	1	9
U.S. Customs Service	25	15	19	3	15	4	21	51	21	35	66	7
U.S. Secret Service	26	24	28	21	27	26	24	18	42	28	29	37
Judicial branch	24	22	21	19	23	23	41	26	23	36	[4]	[4]
U.S. Capitol Police	NA	NA	NA	10	10	10	7	8	8	16	17	5
U.S. Postal Service	26	21	9	12	10	26	29	32	18	23	39	24
Postal Inspectors	4	6	2	1	5	5	10	13	7	6	[8]	[8]
Postal Security Police	22	15	7	11	5	21	19	19	11	17	[8]	[8]

Source: Maguire, Kathleen and Ann L. Pastore (eds.). U.S. Department of Justice. U.S. Bureau of Justice Statistics. *Sourcebook of Criminal Justice Statistics 1993.* Washington, DC: U.S. Government Printing Office, 1994, p. 398. Primary source: U.S. Department of Justice, Federal Bureau of Investigation, *Assaults on Federal Officers, 1979*, p. 7; *1981*, p. 4, Table 1, FBI Uniform Crime reports (Washington, DC: USGPO); *Law Enforcement Officers Killed and Assaulted, 1983*, FBI Uniform Crime reports (Washington, DC: USGPO, 1984), p. 49, Table 1; *Law Enforcement Officers Killed and Assaulted, 1985*, FBI Uniform Crime Reports (Washington, DC: U.S. Department of Justice, 1986), p. 52; and *Law Enforcement Officers Killed and Assaulted, 1987*, p. 51; *1989*, p. 61; *1990*, p.51; *1992*, p. 73, FBI Uniform Crime Reports (Washington, DC: USGPO). Table adapted by *Sourcebook* staff. *Notes:* NA stands for data not separately enumerated, tabulated or otherwise available. These data were compiled from reports of investigations conducted by the Federal Bureau of Investigation, the U.S. Department of Treasury, the U.S. Postal Service, and the U.S. Capitol Police. The Federal Bureau of Investigation is responsible for the investigation of assaults on personnel of the U.S. Department of the Interior, the U.S. Department of Justice, and the Federal judiciary. Customarily, the U.S. Department of the Treasury, the U.S. Postal Service, and the U.S. Capitol Police investigate assaults against officers assigned to their agencies. All assaults and threats of assault are included in the analysis even though no injury to an officer may have resulted, as are assaults that resulted in the death of an officer (Source, *1990*, p. 2). 1. Beginning in 1989, totals and subtotals may not be directly comparable due to modifications in reporting procedures, failures to report, or changes in Federal agencies included. 2. No report concerning assaults on Bureau of Indian Affairs officers was received for 1991. 3. Beginning in 1991, assault statistics from the Bureau of Prisons, U.S. and Assistant U.S. attorneys, and the judicial branch were no longer collected. 4. Beginning in 1989, the variation in Immigration and Naturalization Service figures is due to changes in reporting procedures. 5. Covers only Border Patrol Division. 6. Increase in U.S. and Assistant U.S. attorney figures due to change in reporting procedures. 7. Decrease in Internal Revenue Service figures due to change in reporting procedures. 8. Beginning in 1991, the U.S. Postal Service no longer differentiates between Inspectors and Security Police in its report.

★ 895 ★

Law Officers

Hispanic Police Representation in Major Cities, 1992 and 1993

Data are shown for the 50 largest U.S. cities.

City	Total number of officers		Hispanic officers				Index of Hispanic representation		
			1983		1992				
	1983	1992	Number	Percent	Number	Percent	1983	1992	Percent change
New York, NY	23,408	27,154	1,704	7.2	3,688	13.6	0.36	55.30	52.7
Los Angeles, CA	6,928	8,020	943	13.6	1,787	22.3	0.49	0.56	14.2
Chicago, IL	12,472	12,291	432	3.4	925	7.5	0.24	0.38	58.3
Houston, TX	3,629	4,056	314	8.6	506	12.5	0.49	0.44	-10.2
Philadelphia, PA	7,265	6,280	46	0.6	202	3.2	0.16	0.57	256.2
San Diego, CA	1,363	1,937	107	7.8	226	11.6	0.52	0.56	7.6
Detroit, MI	4,032	4,787	32	0.7	62	1.2	0.29	0.43	48.2
Dallas, TX	2,053	2,878	96	4.6	234	8.1	0.37	0.39	5.4
Phoenix, AZ	1,660	1,644	156	9.3	211	12.8	0.63	0.64	1.5
San Antonio, TX[1]	1,164	1,606	384	32.9	583	36.3	NA	0.65	NA
San Jose, CA	915	1,223	159	17.3	240	19.6	0.78	0.74	-5.1
Baltimore, MD	3,056	2,822	10	0.3	14	0.5	0.30	0.40	33.3
Indianapolis, IN	936	979	1	0.1	0	NA	0.11	0.00	-100.0
San Francisco, CA	1,957	1,818	159	8.1	189	10.4	0.66	0.74	12.1
Jacksonville, FL[1]	1,263	1,205	9	0.7	0	NA	0.38	0.00	-100.0
Columbus, OH	1,197	1,444	0	NA	1	0.1	0.00	0.05	0.0
Milwaukee, WI	1,438	1,971	66	4.5	109	5.5	1.09	0.87	-20.1
Memphis, TN	1,216	1,403	0	NA	0	NA	0.00	00.0	0.0
Washington, DC	3,851	4,396	40	1.0	132	3.0	0.36	0.56	55.5
Boston, MA	1,871	1,972	40	2.1	84	4.2	0.33	0.39	18.1
Seattle, WA	1,011	1,231	18	1.7	32	2.6	0.65	0.69	6.1
El Paso, TX	650	787	370	56.9	481	61.1	0.91	0.89	-2.1
Cleveland, OH	2,091	1,668	6	0.2	66	3.9	0.06	0.85	1,316.6
New Orleans, LA	1,317	1,551	26	1.9	25	1.6	0.56	0.46	-17.8
Nashville, TN	969	1,058	3	0.3	6	0.6	0.38	0.56	47.3
Denver, CO	1,379	1,348	180	13.0	122	9.1	0.69	0.40	-42.0
Austin, TX	607	830	73	12.0	123	14.8	0.64	0.64	0.0
Fort Worth, TX	766	967	51	6.6	85	8.8	0.52	0.45	-13.4
Oklahoma City, OK	622	932	5	0.7	16	1.7	0.25	0.34	36.0
Portland, OR	688	877	9	1.3	20	2.3	0.68	0.69	1.4
Kansas City, MO	1,140	1,166	18	1.5	32	2.7	0.45	0.69	53.3
Long Beach, CA	637	696	35	5.4	88	12.6	0.39	0.853	35.8
Tucson, AZ	549	771	95	17.3	151	19.6	0.69	0.67	-2.8
St. Louis, MO	1,763	1,552	0	NA	7	0.5	0.00	0.31	100.0
Charlotte, NC	644	872	0	NA	0	NA	0.00	0.00	0.0
Atlanta, GA	1,313	1,223	9	0.6	0	NA	0.43	0.00	-100.0
Virginia Beach, VA	NA	599	NA	NA	6	1.0	NA	0.32	NA
Albuquerque, NM	561	765	184	32.7	262	34.2	0.97	0.99	2.0

[Continued]

★ 895 ★

Hispanic Police Representation in Major Cities, 1992 and 1993

[Continued]

City	Total number of officers		Hispanic officers				Index of Hispanic representation		
			1983		1992				
	1983	1992	Number	Percent	Number	Percent	1983	1992	Percent change
Oakland, CA	636	549	59	9.2	61	11.1	0.96	0.80	16.6
Pittsburgh, PA	1,222	1,128	4	0.3	0	NA	0.38	0.00	-100.0
Sacramento, CA	NA	607	NA	NA	70	11.5	NA	0.71	NA
Minneapolis, MN	672	840	8	1.1	24	2.9	0.85	1.38	62.3
Tulsa, OK	695	718	4	0.5	2	0.3	0.29	0.08	-72.4
Honolulu, HI	1,557	1,870	4	0.2	30	1.6	0.04	.35	775.0
Cincinnati, OH	971	927	1	0.1	1	0.1	0.13	0.14	7.6
Miami, FL	1,051	1,032	413	39.2	487	47.2	0.70	0.75	7.1
Fresno, CA	NA	412	NA	NA	82	19.9	NA	0.67	NA
Omaha, NE	551	610	12	2.1	18	3.0	0.91	0.94	3.2
Toledo, OH	757	639	28	3.6	33	5.2	1.20	1.28	6.6
Buffalo, NY	1,018	963	21	2.0	64	6.6	0.74	1.35	82.4

Source: Maguire, Kathleen and Ann L. Pastore (eds.). U.S. Department of Justice. U.S. Bureau of Justice Statistics. *Sourcebook of Criminal Justice Statistics 1993.* Washington, DC: U.S. Government Printing Office, 1994, p. 54. Primary source: Samuel Walker, "Employment of Black and Hispanic Police Officers," *Review of Applied Urban Research* XI (October 1983), p. 3; and Samuel Walker and K.B. Turner, "A Decade of Modest Progress: Employment of Black and Hispanic Police Officers, 1983-1992," Department of Criminal Justice, University of Nebraska at Omaha, 1992. Table adapted by *Sourcebook* staff. *Notes:* NA stands for not applicable. The index of Hispanic representation is calculated by dividing the percent of Hispanic police officers in a department by the percent of Hispanics in the local population. An index approaching 1.0 indicates that a city is closer to achieving a representation of Hispanic police officers equal to their proportion in the local population. The Hispanic population of a city is derived from the 1990 census of the population. 1. Data for 1983 are based on 1980-81 information from the Police Executive Research Forum, *Survey of Operational and Administrative Practices 1981* (Washington, DC: Police Executive Research Forum, 1981).

★ 896 ★

Law Officers

Detroit and Los Angeles: Racial/Ethnic Distribution of Police Forces

Total population is 3,485,398 for Los Angeles and 1,027,974 for Detroit. Women constitute 20% of the police force in Detroit and 14% in Los Angeles.

Race/ethnicity	Detroit		Los Angeles	
	Percent of population	Percent of police force	Percent of population	Percent of police force
Hispanic[1]	3	1	40	22.7
White	21.6	45.2	52.8	59.4
Black	75.7	53.3	14	14.2
Asian	8	2	9.8	3.4
Other	1.9	-	23.4	-

Source: Edmonds, Patricia. "No violence, but Detroit bitter: efforts of police, city paying off." *USA TODAY* (11 November 1992), p. 3A. Primary source: U.S. Census Bureau; Detroit Police Department; Los Angeles Police Department. *Notes:* A dash (-) indicates data were not given. 1. Hispanics may be of any race.

★ 897 ★

Law Officers

New York City: Police Officers, by Race/Ethnicity and Rank

Data show distribution of personnel at each rank, by race/ethnicity.

Rank	White	Black	Hispanic	Asian/ Pacific Islander
Police officers and detectives	69.6	12.6	16.7	1.1
Sergeants	84.5	7.2	7.4	0.8
Lieutenants	88.1	5.8	5.6	0.5
Captains	98.4	0.3	1.0	0.3
Ranks above captain	93.3	3.9	2.8	0.0
Total	72.3	11.6	15.0	1.0

Source: Bray, Rosemary L. "Good cop, bad cop: what blacks think of white cops." *The New York Times* (11 July 1994), p. 33.

★ 898 ★

Law Officers

New York City: Police Officers, by Race/Ethnicity, 1992

Distribution of police officers is shown by race/ethnicity.

Race/ethnicity	Number of officers
Hispanic	3,688[1]
White	20,098
Black	3,121
Native American	28
Asian-Pacific Islander	219

Source: Frankel, Bruce. "Change looms large for troubled NYC police force." *USA TODAY* (7 October 1992), p. 8A. Primary source: *USA TODAY* research. *Note:* 1. Hispanics can be of any race.

Prisons

★ 899 ★

Average Sentence Length Imposed by U.S. District Courts, 1990

Average sentences are shown in months, by race/ethnicity of offender and nature of conviction.

Race and ethnicity[1]	Average sentence length for offenders convicted of:						
	All offenses	Violent offenses	Property offenses: Fraudulent	Property offenses: Other	Drug offenses	Public-order offenses: Regulatory	Public-order offenses: Other
All offenders[2]	57.2	89.2	21.9	22.4	80.9	26.7	28.5
Race							
White	53.9	84.9	19.2	20.4	73.7	28.9	26.3
Black	77.4	115.5	14.3	17.3	98.2	28.1	48.0
Other	53.8	64.9	10.6	15.0	80.1	22.2	22.1
Ethnicity							
Hispanic	53.1	105.8	15.1	19.6	71.4	42.1	15.6
Non-Hispanic	63.2	90.5	17.8	18.9	86.1	25.6	38.4

Source: Maguire, Kathleen and Ann L. Pastore (eds.). U.S. Department of Justice. U.S. Bureau of Justice Statistics. *Sourcebook of Criminal Justice Statistics 1993.* Washington, DC: U.S. Government Printing Office, 1994, p. 497. Primary source: U.S. Department of Justice, Bureau of Justice Statistics, *Compendium of Federal Justice Statistics, 1990*, NCJ-143499 (Washington, DC: U.S. Department of Justice, 1993), p. 43. *Notes:* Data exclude corporations, offenders sentenced to life sentences, and indeterminate sentences for youthful or drug offenders; and include prison portion of split or mixed sentences. 1. Offender characteristics are not directly comparable to prior years. 2. Includes offenders for whom these characteristics were unknown.

★ 900 ★

Prisons

Death Row Prisoners in California, by Race/Ethnicity, 1992

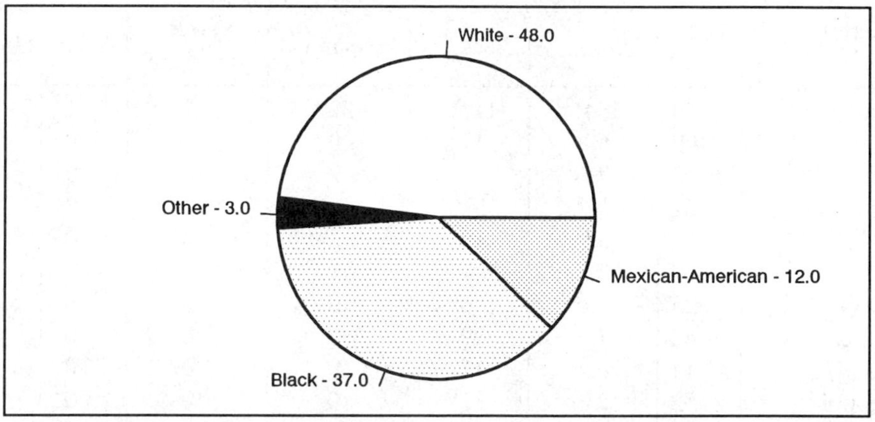

Race and ethnicity	Percent
Mexican-American	12.0
White	48.0
Black	37.0
Other	3.0

Source: "Death penalty: man by a window." *The Economist* (4 April 1992), p. 27. Primary source: California Corrections Department.

★ 901 ★

Prisons

Death Row Prisoners, by Race/Ethnicity and State, 1994

Data show the number of prisoners under sentence of death in each state, as of April 20, 1994.

Jurisdiction	Total	Race, ethnicity					
		White	Black	Hispanic	Native American	Asian	Unknown
United States[1]	2,848	1,423	1,138	208	50	20	9
Federal statutes	5	1	3	1	0	0	0
U.S. military	8	1	6	0	0	1	0
Alabama	122	68[2,3]	52[2,4]	1	0	1	0
Arizona	119	80[4,5,6]	14[7]	20[4,6]	4	0	1
Arkansas	41	24	15[6]	1	1[6]	0	0
California	383	166[2,8]	143[5]	54[5]	13	6	1
Colorado	3	2	0	1	0	0	0
Connecticut	5	3	2	0	0	0	0
Delaware	15	7	8	0	0	0	0

[Continued]

★ 901 ★

Death Row Prisoners, by Race/Ethnicity and State, 1994

[Continued]

Jurisdiction	Total	Race, ethnicity					
		White	Black	Hispanic	Native American	Asian	Unknown
Florida	330	184[7,9,10]	112[5]	32[5]	1	1	0
Georgia	109	60	49[11]	0	0	0	0
Idaho	23	21	0	2[6]	0	0	0
Illinois	161	52[5]	98[2,6]	8[5]	0	0	3
Indiana	51	31[6]	19[6,12]	1	0	0	0
Kansas	0	NA	NA	NA	NA	NA	NA
Kentucky	25	19[5]	6[4]	0	0	0	0
Louisiana	42	11	29	2	0	0	0
Maryland	14	3	11	0	0	0	0
Mississippi	52	21[4,5,6]	31[11]	0	0	0	0
Missouri	84	47[13]	33[6]	1[5]	1	1	1
Montana	8	6	0	0	2	0	0
Nebraska	10	6	3	0	1	0	0
Nevada	66	36	23[5,6]	7	0	0	0
New Hampshire	0	NA	NA	NA	NA	NA	NA
New Jersey	9	3[6]	5	1	0	0	0
New Mexico	2	2	0	0	0	0	0
North Carolina	132	71[9]	52[5]	1	4	1	3
Ohio	127	60	62	3	2	0	0
Oklahoma	118	72[4,6,13]	29[5]	2	13[6]	2	0
Oregon	14	12	0	1	1	0	0
Pennsylvania	170	60[5]	101[2,6,11]	7	0	2	0
South Carolina	55	27[4]	27[4]	0	1	0	0
South Dakota	1	1	0	0	0	0	0
Tennessee	100	65[5]	31[6]	1	2	1	0
Texas	386	167[4,13]	150[2,14]	60[10]	5	4	0
Utah	11	8	2	1	0	0	0
Virginia	46	24[4]	22[4]	0	0	0	0
Washington	13	9	3	0	0	1	0
Wyoming	0	NA	NA	NA	NA	NA	NA

Source: Maguire, Kathleen and Ann L. Pastore (eds.). U.S. Department of Justice. U.S. Bureau of Justice Statistics. *Sourcebook of Criminal Justice Statistics 1993.* Washington, DC: U.S. Government Printing Office, 1994, p. 666. Primary source: Table constructed by *Sourcebook* staff from data provided by the NAACP Legal Defense and Educational Fund, Inc. *Notes:* NA stands for not applicable. The NAACP Legal Defense and Educational Fund, Inc. periodically collects data on persons on death row. As of Apr. 20, 1994, 37 jurisdictions, the Federal Government, and the United States military had capital punishment laws; and 34 jurisdictions, the Federal Government, and the United States military had at least 1 prisoner under sentence of death. Between Jan. 1, 1973 and Apr. 20, 1994, an estimated 1,379 convictions or sentences, have been reversed or vacated on grounds other than constitutional. Between Jan. 1, 1973 and May 30, 1990, an estimated 558 death sentences have been vacated as unconstitutional. 1. Detail will not add to total because inmates sentenced to death in more than one state are listed in the respective state totals, but each is counted only once at the national level. 2. Includes two females. 3. Includes three males who were juveniles at the time of their offenses. 4. Includes one male who was a juvenile at the time of his offense. 5. Includes one female. 6. Includes one male sentenced to death in the state but serving another sentence in another state. 7. Includes two males sentenced to death in the state but serving another sentence in another state. 8. Includes three males sentenced to death in the state but serving another sentence in another state. 9. Includes four females. 10. Includes four males who were juveniles at the time of their offenses. 11. Includes two males who were juveniles at the time of their offenses. 12. Includes one female sentenced to death in the state but serving another sentence in another state. 13. Includes three females. 14. Includes six males who were juveniles at the time of their offenses.

★ 902 ★

Prisons

Death Row Prisoners, by Race/Ethnicity, 1992

Data show percent distribution of prisoners under sentence of death in the United States, as of December 31, 1992.

	Percent
Race	
White	58.6
Black	40.0
Other[1]	1.4
Ethnicity	
Hispanic	7.6
Non-Hispanic	92.4

Source: Maguire, Kathleen and Pastore, Ann L. (eds.). U.S. Department of Justice. U.S. Bureau of Justice Statistics. *Sourcebook of Criminal Justice Statistics 1993.* Washington, DC: U.S. Government Printing Office, 1994, p. 666. Primary source: U.S. Department of Justice, Bureau of Justice Statistics, *Capital Punishment 1992*, Bulletin NCJ-145031 (Washington DC: U.S. Department of Justice, December 1992). *Notes:* Thirty-six states and the Federal Government had death penalty statutes in effect on Dec. 31, 1992. Data on ethnicity were not reported for 142 prisoners; education, 315 prisoners; marital status, 186 prisoners; prior felony conviction history, 154 prisoners; legal status at time of capital offense, 296 prisoners. 1. Consists of 23 American Indians and 15 Asians.

★ 903 ★

Prisons

Drug Use History of State Prisoners, 1991

Data are shown by race/ethnicity of prisoner, for 1991.

Characteristic	Number of inmates	Percent who ever used drugs	Percent who used drugs in the month before the offense		Percent under the influence at the time of the offense
			At all	Daily	
All inmates	710,798	79.4	49.9	36.0	30.9
White, non-Hispanic	251,916	79.9	49.4	38.2	32.4
Black, non-Hispanic	323,677	78.9	49.0	33.7	28.8
Hispanic	16,748	76.6	48.4	36.1	32.3
Other	16,748	76.6	48.4	36.1	32.3

Source: U.S. Department of Justice. Office of Justice Programs. Bureau of Justice Statistics. *Correctional Populations in the United States, 1991* (NCJ-142729). Washington, DC: Bureau of Justice Statistics, August 1993, p. 31.

★ 904 ★

Prisons

Drug Use in State Prisons, 1991

Data show number and percent of inmates in each category, for the United States in 1991.

Race and ethnicity	Number of inmates	Drug use history (percent)			
		Ever used drugs	Used drugs in the month before the offense		Under the influence of drugs at time of offense
			At all	Daily	
All inmates	710,798	79.4	49.9	36.0	30.9
White, non-Hispanic	251,916	79.9	49.4	38.2	32.4
Black, non-Hispanic	323,677	78.9	49.0	33.7	28.8
Hispanic	118,457	80.1	53.6	37.8	33.6
Other[1]	16,748	76.6	48.4	36.1	32.3

Source: Maguire, Kathleen and Ann L. Pastore (eds.). U.S. Department of Justice. U.S. Bureau of Justice Statistics. *Sourcebook of Criminal Justice Statistics 1993.* Washington, DC: U.S. Government Printing Office, 1994, p. 620. Primary source: U.S. Department of Justice, Bureau of Justice Statistics, *Correctional Populations in the United States, 1991,* NCJ-142729 (Washington, DC: USGPO, 1993), p. 31. *Notes:* 1. Includes Asians, Pacific Islanders, American Indians, and other racial groups.

★ 905 ★

Prisons

Entries to Federal Parole Supervision, 1991

Data are shown by offense, sex, race, and Hispanic origin, for the United States in 1991.

Most serious offense	All entries[1]	Sex		Race[2]			Hispanic[4]
		Male	Female	White	Black	Other[3]	
Number of parole entries	7,219	6,644	575	5,111	1,919	189	1,260
	Percent						
All offenses	100.0	100.0	100.0	100.0	100.0	100.0	100.0
Violent offenses	14.5	15.2	7.0	10.0	23.4	47.1	5.4
Homicide	0.8	0.9	0.3	0.3	1.1	12.7	0.2
Kidnapping	0.5	0.5	0.5	0.6	0.3	0.0	0.6
Rape	0.4	0.5	0.0	0.2	0.7	5.8	0.1
Other sexual assault	0.3	0.3	0.0	0.1	0.2	7.4	0.0
Robbery	9.1	9.5	5.2	6.9	15.7	2.1	2.9
Assault	3.3	3.5	0.9	1.9	5.5	19.0	1.6
Other violent	0.1	0.1	0.0	0.1	0.0	0.0	0.0
Property offenses	22.4	21.3	34.6	21.5	25.4	16.4	5.5
Fraud offenses	15.1	14.2	25.2	15.5	14.4	9.0	3.7
Embezzlement	1.1	0.7	5.2	1.0	1.1	2.1	0.4
Fraud	11.7	11.3	15.8	12.6	9.6	6.9	2.4
Forgery	1.4	1.2	3.1	0.9	2.9	0.0	0.5

[Continued]

★ 905 ★

Entries to Federal Parole Supervision, 1991

[Continued]

Most serious offense	All entries[1]	Sex: Male	Sex: Female	Race[2]: White	Race[2]: Black	Race[2]: Other[3]	Hispanic[4]
Counterfeiting	0.9	0.9	1.0	1.0	0.7	0.0	0.5
Nonfraud offenses	7.3	7.1	9.4	5.9	10.9	7.4	1.7
Burglary	0.5	0.5	0.3	0.2	1.3	2.1	0.0
Larceny-theft	3.5	3.2	7.3	2.2	6.9	3.2	1.2
Arson	0.6	0.6	0.3	0.7	0.3	0.0	0.2
Motor vehicle theft	1.3	1.4	0.2	1.2	1.6	0.5	0.1
Other property	1.4	1.4	1.2	1.6	0.8	1.6	0.3
Drug offenses	48.6	48.5	50.1	52.3	41.0	28.0	77.1
Possession	0.1	0.1	0.2	0.2	0.1	0.5	0.2
Trafficking	26.2	26.0	28.3	28.2	21.7	16.4	45.6
Other drug	22.3	22.4	21.6	23.9	19.2	11.1	31.3
Public-order offenses	14.1	14.6	8.3	16.0	9.7	8.5	11.6
Regulatory offenses	0.9	0.9	0.9	1.1	0.5	0.0	0.6
Nonregulatory public-order	13.2	13.7	7.5	14.8	9.3	8.5	11.0
Weapons	4.5	4.8	1.0	4.3	5.2	2.6	3.7
Immigration	0.6	0.6	0.5	0.8	0.1	0.0	2.7
Tax law violations	2.0	2.0	1.2	2.5	0.8	0.0	0.5
Racketeering and extortion	3.5	3.6	2.3	4.4	1.2	2.1	2.1
Other public-order	2.6	2.6	2.4	2.8	2.0	3.7	2.0
Other offenses	0.3	0.3	0.0	.03	0.5	0.0	0.4

Source: Maguire, Kathleen and Ann L. Pastore (eds.). U.S. Department of Justice. U.S. Bureau of Justice Statistics. *Sourcebook of Criminal Justice Statistics 1993.* Washington, DC: U.S. Government Printing Office, 1994, p. 659. Primary source: U.S. Department of Justice, Bureau of Justice Statistics, *National Corrections Reporting Program 1991,* NCJ-145861 (Washington, DC: U.S. Department of Justice, 1994), p. 81. *Notes:* 1. Detail may not add to total because of rounding. 2. Includes persons of Hispanic origin. 3. Includes Asians, Pacific Islanders, Native Americans, and others. 4. Includes persons of all races.

★ 906 ★

Prisons

Family Characteristics of State Prisoners, 1991

Characteristic	All inmates	Race/Hispanic origin: White, non-Hispanic	Black, non-Hispanic	Hispanic	Other
Person(s) lived with most of time while growing up					
Both parents	43.1	56.2	31.9	46.1	41.1
Mother only	39.2	27.6	49.7	36.1	31.1
Father only	3.9	4.9	3.0	4.0	5.9
Grandparents	7.7	5.2	10.0	6.8	5.3
Other relatives	3.0	1.7	3.5	3.8	5.5
Other[1]	3.2	4.5	1.7	3.2	11.0

[Continued]

★ 906 ★

Family Characteristics of State Prisoners, 1991

[Continued]

Characteristic	All inmates	Race/Hispanic origin			
		White, non-Hispanic	Black, non-Hispanic	Hispanic	Other
Ever lived in foster home, agency, or institution while growing up					
No	82.7	76.9	86.9	85.8	65.8
Yes	17.3	23.1	13.1	14.2	34.2
Family member ever incarcerated					
No	62.6	66.9	58.4	65.3	59.8
Yes	37.4	33.1	41.6	34.7	40.2
Mother	1.6	1.9	1.5	1.1	2.9
Father	6.4	8.4	5.0	5.3	10.6
Brother	31.2	25.8	36.0	29.1	33.3
Sister	4.5	3.6	5.1	4.3	8.1
Child	0.3	0.3	0.3	0.5	0.1
Parent or guardian abused alcohol or drugs while inmate was growing up					
No	73.1	63.2	79.9	77.8	57.8
Yes	26.9	36.8	20.1	22.2	42.2
Alcohol	22.2	30.5	16.7	17.5	36.1
Drugs	0.8	0.7	0.7	1.3	0.2
Both	3.7	5.3	2.5	3.2	5.9

Source: U.S. Department of Justice. Office of Justice Programs. Bureau of Justice Statistics. *Correctional Populations in the United States, 1991* (NCJ-142729). Washington, DC: Bureau of Justice Statistics, August 1993, p. 30. *Note:* 1. Includes friends, foster home, agency, or institution.

★ 907 ★

Prisons

Family History of State Prisoners, by Race/Ethnicity

Data are shown for the United States in 1991.

Characteristic	Percent of female inmates				Percent of male inmates
	All[1]	White	Black	Hispanic	All[1]
Number of inmates	38,630	13,969	17,739	5,521	669,578
Person(s) inmates lived with most of time while growing up					
Both parents	42.0	55.1	31.9	40.3	43.1
Mother only	38.9	29.3	46.1	41.0	39.2
Father only	3.4	3.7	3.0	3.8	4.0
Grandparents	9.3	6.1	11.3	10.3	7.6
Other relatives	3.0	1.1	4.7	2.8	3.0
Friends	0.4	0.4	0.4	0.5	0.4

[Continued]

★ 907 ★

Family History of State Prisoners, by Race/Ethnicity

[Continued]

Characteristic	Percent of female inmates				Percent of male inmates
	All[1]	White	Black	Hispanic	All[1]
Foster home	1.8	2.7	1.5	0.8	1.5
Agency or institution	0.8	1.1	0.6	0.2	0.8
Other	0.5	0.5	0.5	0.2	0.5
Ever lived in a foster home, agency, or institution while growing up					
No	82.8	78.9	85.9	85.6	82.7
Yes	17.2	21.1	14.1	14.4	17.3
Family member ever incarcerated					
No	53.4	61.1	47.3	53.0	63.1
Yes[2]	46.6	38.9	52.7	47.0	36.9
Spouse	1.8	3.1	1.1	1.4	0.2
Mother	4.0	3.5	4.5	3.6	1.5
Father	7.8	10.9	5.4	6.7	6.3
Brother	35.1	26.1	42.0	35.9	30.9
Sister	10.0	5.6	12.4	14.6	4.2
Child	1.6	1.3	1.6	2.3	0.2
Parent/guardian abused alcohol or drugs					
No	66.4	57.7	74.0	67.1	73.5
Yes	33.6	42.3	26.0	32.9	26.5
Alcohol only	26.3	32.7	20.7	25.4	21.9
Drugs only	1.6	1.0	2.0	2.2	0.8
Both alcohol and drugs	5.7	8.6	3.2	5.2	3.6

Source: Maguire, Kathleen and Ann L. Pastore (eds.). U.S. Department of Justice. U.S. Bureau of Justice Statistics. *Sourcebook of Criminal Justice Statistics 1993.* Washington, DC: U.S. Government Printing Office, 1994, p. 616. Primary source: U.S. Department of Justice, Bureau of Justice Statistics, *Women in Prison*, Special Report NCJ-145321 (Washington, DC: U.S. Department of Justice, March 1994), p. 5, Table 7. *Notes:* These data were collected by the U.S. Bureau of the Census for the U.S. Department of Justice, Bureau of Justice Statistics through the 1991 Survey of Inmates in State Correctional Facilities. Similar surveys were conducted in 1974, 1979, and 1986. The sample for the 1991 survey was selected from the 1,239 state prisons that were enumerated in the 1990 Census of State and Federal Adult Correctional Facilities and those that were opened after completion of the census. The survey employed a stratified two-stage selection design. In the first stage, correctional facilities were separated into two sampling frames: one for prisons housing male inmates and one for prisons housing female inmates. Prisons housing both sexes were included on both lists. Within each frame, prisons were stratified into eight strata based on census region and facility type (confinement and community-based). All prisons with 1,950 or more men and all prisons with 380 or more women were selected. The remaining prisons in the male and female frames were grouped into strata. A systematic sample of prisons was then selected within strata with probabilities proportional to the size of each prison. In the second stage, interviewers visited each selected facility and systematically selected a sample of male and female inmates using predetermined procedures. In 1991, a total of 13,986 interviews were completed at 277 prisons for a response rate of 93.75 percent. In 1986, a total of 13,711 interviews were completed at 275 prisons from a sample of approximately 15,000. These data are estimates derived from a sample and therefore subject to sampling variation. Data for marital status were missing for 1.1 percent of the inmates; for education, 0.8 percent; and for military service, 0.2 percent. Excludes 3,435 inmates for whom information on family history was missing. 1. Includes Asians, Pacific Islanders, American Indians, Alaska Natives, and other racial groups. 2. Detail may add to more than total because more than one family member may have been incarcerated.

★ 908 ★

Prisons

HIV and Drug/Needle Use of State Prisoners, 1991

Data are shown for state prisoners reporting having tested positive for HIV (human immunodeficiency virus), as of 1991.

Race and ethnicity	Percent of state prisoners who reported testing positive and who:				
	Never used drugs	Ever used drugs	Used drugs in the month before offense	Used a needle to inject drugs	Shared a needle to inject drugs
All prisoners	0.8	2.5	2.8	4.9	7.1
White, non-Hispanic	0.3	1.2	1.5	2.4	3.7
Black, non-Hispanic	1.1	2.9	3.2	7.2	11.1
Hispanic	0.6	4.3	5.2	8.2	11.3

Source: Maguire, Kathleen and Ann L. Pastore (eds.). U.S. Department of Justice. U.S. Bureau of Justice Statistics. *Sourcebook of Criminal Justice Statistics 1993.* Washington, DC: U.S. Government Printing Office, 1994, p. 618. Primary source: U.S. Department of Justice, Bureau of Justice Statistics, *HIV in U.S. Prisons and Jails*, Special Report NCJ-143292 (Washington, DC: U.S. Department of Justice, September 1993), p. 5, Table 6. *Notes:* These data were collected by the U.S. Bureau of the Census for the Department of Justice, Bureau of Justice Statistics through the 1991 Survey of Inmates in State Correctional Facilities.

★ 909 ★

Prisons

HIV in State Prisons, 1991

Data number and percent distribution of prisoners ever having tested positive for HIV (human immunodeficiency virus), as of 1991.

Race and ethnicity	Percent of all inmates who were ever tested	Tested inmates who reported results	
		Number	Percent HIV positive
All prisoners	51.2	364,515	2.2
White, non-Hispanic	52.6	132,594	1.1
Black, non-Hispanic	52.1	168,873	2.6
Hispanic	46.0	54,563	3.7
Other	50.5	8,485	0.9

Source: Maguire, Kathleen and Ann L. Pastore (eds.). U.S. Department of Justice. U.S. Bureau of Justice Statistics. *Sourcebook of Criminal Justice Statistics 1993.* Washington, DC: U.S. Government Printing Office, 1994, p. 618. Primary source: U.S. Department of Justice, Bureau of Justice Statistics, *HIV in U.S. Prisons and Jails*, Special Report NCJ-143292 (Washington, DC: U.S. Department of Justice, September 1993), p. 5, Table 5. *Notes:* These data were collected by the U.S. Bureau of Census for the department of Justice. Bureau of Justice Statistics through the 1991 Survey of Inmates in State Correctional Facilities.

★910★

Prisons

Jail Inmate Percent Distribution, by Race/Ethnicity and Sex, 1984-90

Data for 1988 were not available in the original source.

Race/ethnicity	Percent of jail inmates[1]					
	June 30, 1984	June 30, 1985	June 30, 1986	June 30, 1987	June 30, 1989	June 29, 1990
Ethnicity[2]						
Hispanic	13.0	14.0	14.0	14.0	14.0	14.0
Male	12.0	13.0	13.0	13.0	13.0	13.0
Female	1.0	1.0	1.0	1.0	1.0	1.0
Non-Hispanic	87.0	86.0	86.0	86.0	86.0	86.0
Male	81.0	80.0	80.0	79.0	78.0	78.0
Female	6.0	7.0	7.0	7.0	8.0	8.0
Race[2]						
White	59.0	59.0	58.0	57.0	51.0	51.0
Male	55.0	55.0	54.0	53.0	46.0	46.0
Female	4.0	4.0	4.0	4.0	5.0	5.0
Black	40.0	40.0	41.0	42.0	47.0	47.0
Male	37.0	37.0	37.0	38.0	43.0	43.0
Female	3.0	3.0	3.0	4.0	4.0	4.0
Other[3]	1.0	1.0	1.0	1.0	2.0	2.0
Male	1.0	1.0	1.0	1.0	1.0	1.0
Female	[4]	[4]	[4]	[4]	[4]	[4]

Source: U.S. Department of Justice. Office of Justice Programs. Bureau of Justice Statistics. *Sourcebook of Criminal Justice Statistics, 1990.* Washington, DC: U.S. Government Printing Office, 1991, p. 587. Primary source: U.S. Department of Justice Bureau of Justice Statistics, Jail Inmates, 1985, NCJ-105586 (Washington, DC: USGPO, 1987), p. 6, Table 3; U.S. Department of Justice, Bureau of Justice Statistics, Jail Inmates 1987, Bulletin NCJ-114319, p. 2, Table 3; 1989, Bulletin NCJ-123264, p. 2, Table 3; and 1990, Bulletin BCJ-129756, p. 2, Table 3 (Washington DC: U.S. Department of Justice). Table adapted by Sourcebook staff. *Notes:* 1. Percentages may not add to total because of rounding. 2. Sex was reported for all inmates for all 6 years. Race and ethnicity were reported for 88 percent of the inmates in 1984, 80 percent in 1985, 97 percent in 1986, 93 percent in 1987, 91 percent in 1989, and 90 percent of the inmates in 1990. 3. Native Americans, Aleuts, Asians, and Pacific Islanders. 4. Less than 0.5 percent.

★ 911 ★

Prisons

Jail Inmates, by Race/Ethnicity, 1991 and 1992

Data are shown as of June 29, 1990 and June 28, 1991. Race was not reported for 4,214 inmates in 1990 and 3,808 inmates in 1991.

Characteristic	Number of jail inmates		Percent of jail inmates	
	1990	1991	1990	1991
Total	405,320	426,479	100.0	100.0
White, non-Hispanic	167,831	173,512	41.8	41.1
Black, non-Hispanic	170,505	183,639	42.5	43.4
Hispanic	57,449	60,129	14.3	14.2
Other[1]	5,321	5,391	1.3	1.2

Source: U.S. Department of Justice. Office of Justice Programs. Bureau of Justice Statistics. *Correctional Populations in the United States, 1991* (NCJ-142729). Washington, DC: Bureau of Justice Statistics, August 1993, p. 9. *Note:* 1. American Indians, Alaska Natives, Asians, and Pacific Islanders.

★ 912 ★

Prisons

Jail Population, 1989-91

Estimates of population, by race/ethnicity, and standard errors are shown for each year.

Characteristic	Estimate			Standard error		
	1989	1990	1991	1989	1990	1991
Total inmates	395,553	405,320	426,479	1,583	1,778	2,037
Adult inmates by race						
White, non-Hispanic	166,614	166,813	172,610	1,503	1,631	1,789
Black, non-Hispanic	166,763	169,414	182,487	1,169	1,309	1,494
Hispanic	56,678	57,350	60,007	586	650	569
Other non-Hispanic	5,380	5,228	5,217	390	298	320

Source: U.S. Department of Justice. Office of Justice Programs. Bureau of Justice Statistics. *Correctional Populations in the United States, 1991* (NCJ-142729). Washington, DC: Bureau of Justice Statistics, August 1993, p. 13.

★913★

Prisons

Most Serious Offenses of State Prisoners, 1991

Data show most serious offenses of state prison inmates, by race/ethnicity, for 1991. Figures exclude an estimated 7,462 prisoners whose offenses were unknown.

Most serious offense	Percent of prison inmates in 1991				
	Total	White, non-Hispanic	Black, non-Hispanic	Hispanic	Other
Violent offenses	46.6	49.0	47.2	38.6	53.6
Murder[1]	10.6	11.8	10.3	8.8	12.0
Negligent manslaughter	1.8	2.0	1.7	1.9	0.7
Kidnapping	1.2	1.5	1.0	0.8	1.8
Rape	3.5	4.8	3.1	1.7	6.3
Other sexual assault	5.9	10.45	2.9	4.3	5.9
Robbery	14.8	10.3	19.2	12.6	12.8
Assault	8.2	7.4	8.5	8.1	13.8
Other violent[2]	0.6	0.7	0.5	0.5	0.4
Property offenses	24.8	30.2	22.0	20.6	28.4
Burglary	12.4	15.3	10.5	11.6	11.9
Larceny/theft	4.9	5.4	5.0	3.5	4.3
Motor vehicle theft	2.2	2.4	1.9	2.3	2.3
Arson	0.7	1.1	0.4	0.5	0.9
Fraud	2.8	3.8	2.5	1.2	5.0
Stolen property	1.4	1.5	1.3	1.0	3.3
Other property[3]	0.4	0.5	0.4	0.4	0.6
Drug offenses	21.3	12.0	24.9	33.0	9.7
Possession	7.6	4.0	8.6	13.1	2.0
Trafficking	13.3	7.7	15.7	19.5	7.4
Other/unspecified	0.5	0.3	0.6	0.4	0.3
Public-order offenses	6.9	8.4	5.4	7.5	8.2
Weapons	1.8	1.2	2.2	2.0	1.1
Other public-order[4]	5.1	7.1	3.2	5.5	7.1
Other offenses[5]	0.4	0.5	0.4	0.3	0.1
Number of inmates	704,181	248,705	321,217	117,632	16,627

Source: U.S. Department of Justice. Office of Justice Programs. Bureau of Justice Statistics. *Correctional Populations in the United States, 1991* (NCJ-142729). Washington, DC: Bureau of Justice Statistics, August 1993, p. 27. *Notes:* 1. Includes nonnegligent manslaughter. 2. Includes blackmail, extortion, hit-and-run driving with bodily injury, child abuse, and criminal endangerment against a person. 3. Includes destruction of property, vandalism, criminal tampering, trespassing, entering without breaking, and possession of burglary tools. 4. Includes escape from custody, court offenses, obstruction, driving while intoxicated, other traffic offenses, drunkenness, disorderly conduct, morals and decency violations, commercialized vice, and liquor law violations. 5. Includes juvenile offenses and unspecified offenses.

★ 914 ★

Prisons

Prison Releases in Selected States, 1991

Data show number of first releases from prisons in 34 states, by offense, race/ethnicity, and time served, for the United States in 1991.

Most serious offense	Total			White[1]			Black[1]			Hispanic[2]		
	Percent of releases	Time served in prison (in months)		Percent of releases	Time served in prison (in months)		Percent of releases	Time served in prison (in months)		Percent of releases	Time served in prison (in months)	
		Median	Mean		Median	Mean		Median	Mean		Median	Mean
Number of releases	223,991	NA	NA	95,140	NA	NA	107,361	NA	NA	31,058	NA	NA
All offenses	100.0	13	22	100.0	13	21	100.0	14	22	100.0	14	20
Violent offenses	24.4	25	38	22.9	24	36	26.1	25	40	20.6	22	33
Homicide	2.8	47	64	2.8	39	58	2.6	54	70	2.4	44	57
Murder and nonnegligent manslaughter	1.6	68	84	1.5	68	82	1.7	70	86	1.7	60	69
Murder	1.2	78	93	1.1	76	91	1.3	85	97	1.1	64	76
Nonnegligent manslaughter	0.4	46	57	0.3	39	52	0.5	49	56	0.7	45	58
Negligent manslaughter	1.0	24	32	1.3	23	29	0.9	29	37	0.7	24	27
Unspecified homicide	0.1	73	84	0.1	69	83	0.1	78	86	[3]	[4]	[4]
Kidnapping	0.4	34	47	0.5	31	44	0.3	44	53	0.3	23	34
Rape	1.8	44	56	2.1	41	51	1.5	52	64	1.5	35	45
Other sexual assault	2.7	24	31	4.4	25	31	1.4	24	31	1.8	21	28
Robbery	10.0	27	40	6.4	27	39	13.1	28	41	8.9	21	32
Assault	6.2	15	23	5.8	16	22	6.7	15	23	5.3	16	22
Other violent	0.6	16	21	0.7	15	20	0.4	17	22	0.4	14	18
Property offenses	35.9	12	18	10.6	12	18	32.7	12	18	26.9	12	17
Burglary	16.1	15	22	18.8	14	22	13.5	15	23	15.1	13	21
Larceny-theft	9.5	9	14	9.8	9	14	9.9	10	15	6.0	9	13
Motor vehicle theft	2.5	11	14	2.6	11	15	2.3	11	14	2.6	10	12
Arson	0.6	18	26	0.9	18	26	0.4	18	25	0.4	16	26
Fraud	4.6	9	15	5.9	10	15	3.8	9	15	1.4	9	14
Stolen property	1.8	13	17	1.7	12	18	2.1	12	17	1.0	16	17
Other property	0.8	9	14	1.0	9	14	0.7	10	15	0.2	10	12
Drug offenses	29.3	12	16	22.3	12	15	33.7	12	15	42.3	14	18
Possession	8.5	10	14	5.2	10	13	10.9	9	13	8.2	12	18
Trafficking	16.4	14	17	12.2	14	17	18.2	14	16	28.8	16	19
Other drug	4.5	10	14	4.8	10	14	4.7	11	13	5.4	9	11
Public-order offenses	9.1	9	13	12.5	8	13	6.5	9	15	8.8	9	13
Weapons	1.8	13	18	1.3	12	17	2.1	12	18	1.8	17	22
Driving while intoxicated	3.5	8	9	6.4	8	10	1.1	5	7	5.8	8	9
Other public-order	3.8	9	15	4.8	8	15	3.3	9	15	1.1	11	16
Other offenses	1.2	11	17	1.7	11	17	0.9	11	17	1.4	10	13

Source: Maguire, Kathleen and Ann L. Pastore (eds.). U.S. Department of Justice. U.S. Bureau of Justice Statistics. *Sourcebook of Criminal Justice Statistics 1993.* Washington, DC: U.S. Government Printing Office, 1994, p. 650. Primary source: U.S. Department of Justice, Bureau of Justice Statistics, *National Corrections Reporting Program, 1991,* NCJ-145861 (Washington, DC: U.S. Department of Justice, 1994), pp. 26, 29. *Notes:* NA stands for not applicable. Data are based on the first releases with a sentence of more than a year for whom the most serious offense and time served in prison were reported. All data exclude persons released from prison by escape, death, transfer, appeal, or detainer. Detail may not add to total because of rounding. 1. Includes persons of Hispanic origin. 2. Includes persons of all races. 3. Less than 0.05 percent. 4. Figure not computed because there were fewer than 10 cases.

★915★

Prisons

Prisoners Sentenced to Incarceration by U.S. District Courts, 1990

Data show number of offenders and percent of those offenders incarcerated, by race/ethnicity, for the United States in 1990.

Race and ethnicity[1]	Total number of offenders	Of all offenders convicted in cases terminated in 1990, the percent who were incarcerated						
		All offenses	Violent offenses	Property offenses: Fraudulent	Property offenses: Other	Drug offenses	Public-order offenses: Regulatory	Public-order offenses: Other
All offenders[2]	47,543	60.4	87.2	44.1	41.0	86.4	38.9	44.3
Race								
White	14,978	76.6	92.6	53.6	48.7	91.1	52.3	77.1
Black	6,656	79.3	97.2	48.1	49.1	94.1	54.1	85.4
Other	1,025	74.8	92.9	40.1	44.8	90.9	61.2	74.4
Ethnicity								
Hispanic	4,817	86.0	95.0	52.3	54.9	94.6	63.2	83.2
Non-Hispanic	18,106	74.7	93.7	50.9	47.9	91.1	51.0	76.4

Source: Maguire, Kathleen and Ann L. Pastore (eds.). U.S. Department of Justice. U.S. Bureau of Justice Statistics. *Sourcebook of Criminal Justice Statistics 1993.* Washington, DC: U.S. Government Printing Office, 1994, p. 493. Primary source: U.S. Department of Justice, Bureau of Justice Statistics, *Compendium of Federal Justice Statistics, 1990,* NCJ-143499 (Washington, DC: U.S. Department of Justice, 1993), p. 42. *Notes:* Data exclude corporations. Offenders are classified by the most serious offense of conviction. 1. Offender characteristics are not directly comparable with prior years. 2. Includes offenders for whom these characteristics were unknown.

★916★

Prisons

Probation of Adult Offenders, by Hispanic Origin, 1989

Regions and jurisdictions	Probation population 12/31/89	Number of adults on probation: Hispanic	Non-Hispanic	Unknown
U.S. total	2,520,479	148,555	1,035,782	1,336,142
Federal	59,146	6,172	51,251	1,723
State	2,461,333	142,383	984,531	1,334,419
Northeast	443,794	25,758	144,942	273,094
Connecticut[1]	42,842	4,713	38,129	0
Maine[1]	6,851	25	6,826	0
Massachusetts	88,529	-	-	88,529
New Hampshire	2,991	20	2,971	0
New Jersey	66,753	-	-	66,753
New York	128,707	17,922	5,204	105,581
Pennsylvania	89,491	3,051	86,440	0
Rhode Island	12,231	-	-	0
Vermont[1]	5,399	27	5,372	0

[Continued]

★ 916 ★

Probation of Adult Offenders, by Hispanic Origin, 1989

[Continued]

Regions and jurisdictions	Probation population 12/31/89	Number of adults on probation		
		Hispanic	Non-Hispanic	Unknown
Midwest	542,765	6,578	187,207	348,980
Illinois	93,944	-	-	93,944
Indiana	61,861	-	-	61,861
Iowa	13,722	-	-	13,722
Kansas	22,525	972	21,410	143
Michigan	121,436	2,128	52,975	66,333
Minnesota	58,648	938	54,214	3,496
Missouri	45,251	-	-	42.251
Nebraska	12,627	554	11,743	330
North Dakota	1,652	19	1,633	0
Ohio	78,223	743	23,569	53,911
South Dakota	2,716	-	-	2,716
Wisconsin	30,160	1,224	21,663	7,273
South	986,508	95,897	558,246	332,365
Alabama[2]	26,475	-	3,047	23,428
Arkansas[2]	17,572	145	3,402	14,025
Delaware[2]	9,701	-	-	9,701
District of Columbia	10,351	120	10,231	0
Florida	192,495	12,469	171,645	8,381
Georgia	125,441	1,032	124,366	43
Kentucky	8,062	-	-	8,062
Louisiana	32,295	-	-	32,295
Maryland	84,456	-	-	84,456
Mississippi	7,333	12	7,321	0
North Carolina	72,325	-	-	72,325
Oklahoma	24,240	572	23,662	6
South Carolina	29,652	-	-	29,652
Tennessee	30,906	-	-	30,906
Texas	291,156	81,524	209,632	0
Virginia[1]	19,085	-	-	19,085
West Virginia	4,963	23	4,940	0
West	488,266	14,150	94,136	379,980
Alaska	3,335	54	3,281	0
Arizona	27,650	237	592	26,821
California	285,018	-	-	285,018
Colorado	26,378	4,629	16,059	5,690
Hawaii	11,377	-	-	11,377
Idaho	4,025	450	3,575	0
Montana	3,459	73	3,386	0
Nevada	7,324	414	6,910	0
New Mexico	5,660	2,639	2,964	57
Oregon	31,878	1,213	30,665	0
Utah	5,524	526	4,828	170

[Continued]

★916★

Probation of Adult Offenders, by Hispanic Origin, 1989

[Continued]

Regions and jurisdictions	Probation population 12/31/89	Number of adults on probation		
		Hispanic	Non-Hispanic	Unknown
Washington	74,254	3,915	21,876	48,463
Wyoming[1]	2,384	-	-	2,384

Source: U.S. Department of Justice. Office of Justice Programs. Bureau of Justice Statistics. *Correctional Populations in the United States, 1989,* NCJ-130445. Washington, DC: Bureau of Justice Statistics, October 1991, p. 32. *Notes:* A dash (-) indicates that data were not reported. 1. The state estimated all numbers in the detailed categories. 2. The state estimated all data.

★917★

Prisons

State Prisoners Who Have Children, 1991

Data show number and age of children and children's living arrangements, by race/ethnicity of prisoner, for the United States in 1991.

Characteristics	Percent of female inmates				Percent of male inmates
	All[1]	White	Black	Hispanic	All[1]
Number of inmates	38,658	13,983	17,754	5,521	669,732
Have children					
No	21.9	26.1	20.4	17.8	3.1
Yes	78.1	73.9	79.6	82.2	63.9
Under age 18	66.6	61.6	69.0	71.6	56.1
Adult only	11.4	12.3	10.6	10.6	7.6
Number of children under age 18[2]					
1	37.3	40.7	37.0	31.2	43.2
2	29.9	30.8	28.4	33.3	28.9
3	18.1	17.5	18.2	19.8	15.2
4	8.5	6.5	9.0	10.0	6.8
5 or more	6.1	4.5	7.4	5.7	5.9
Lived with child(ren) under 18 before entering prison[2]					
No	28.3	31.3	24.5	34.3	47.1
Yes	71.7	68.7	75.5	65.7	52.9
Where child(ren) under 18 live(s) now[2,3]					
Father/mother	25.4	35.2	18.7	24.4	89.7
Grandparent	50.6	40.6	56.7	54.9	9.9
Other relative	20.3	14.7	23.7	22.8	2.9
Friends	4.1	5.7	2.7	4.2	0.4
Foster home	8.6	12.6	5.8	6.5	1.7
Agency/institution	2.1	2.1	1.8	2.1	0.5

[Continued]

★ 917 ★

State Prisoners Who Have Children, 1991

[Continued]

Characteristics	Percent of female inmates				Percent of male inmates
	All[1]	White	Black	Hispanic	All[1]
Alone	2.0	1.9	2.3	1.5	1.1
Other	4.2	6.4	3.0	3.0	1.0

Source: Maguire, Kathleen and Ann L. Pastore (eds.). U.S. Department of Justice. U.S. Bureau of Justice Statistics. *Sourcebook of Criminal Justice Statistics 1993.* Washington, DC: U.S. Government Printing Office, 1994, p. 616. Primary source: U.S. Department of Justice, Bureau of Justice Statistics, *Women in Prison*, Special Report NCJ-145321 (Washington, DC: U.S. Department of Justice, March 1994), p. 6. *Notes:* These data were collected by the U.S. Bureau of the Census for the U.S. Department of Justice, Bureau of Justice Statistics through the 1991 Survey of Inmates in State Correctional Facilities. Similar surveys were conducted in 1974, 1979, and 1986. The sample for the 1991 survey was selected from the 1,239 state prisons that were enumerated in the 1990 Census of State and Federal Adult Correctional Facilities and those that were opened after completion of the census. The survey employed a stratified two-stage selection design. In the first stage, correctional facilities were separated into two sampling frames: one for prisons housing male inmates and one for prisons housing female inmates. Prisons housing both sexes were included on both lists. Within each frame, prisons were stratified into eight strata based on census region and facility type (confinement and community-based). All prisons with 1,950 or more men and all prisons with 380 or more women were selected. The remaining prisons in the male and female frames were grouped into strata. A systematic sample of prisons was then selected within strata with probabilities proportional to the size of each prison. In the second stage, interviewers visited each selected facility and systematically selected a sample of male and female inmates using predetermined procedures. In 1991, a total of 13,986 interviews were completed at 277 prisons for a response rate of 93.75 percent. In 1986, a total of 13,711 interviews were completed at 275 prisons from a sample of approximately 15,000. These data are estimates derived from a sample and therefore subject to sampling variation. Data for marital status were missing for 1.1 percent of the inmates; for education, 0.8 percent; and for military service, 0.2 percent. Excludes 3,435 inmates for whom information on family history was missing. Female prison inmates had an estimated 56,123 children and male inmates 770,841 children under the age of 18. 1. Includes Asians, Pacific Islanders, American Indians, Alaska Natives, and other racial groups. 2. Percents are based on those inmates with children under age 18. 3. Percents add to more than 100 because inmates with more than one child may have provided multiple responses.

★ 918 ★

Prisons

State Prisoners, by Sex and Race/Ethnicity, 1986 and 1991

Characteristic	Percent of prison inmates					
	1986			1991		
	Total[1]	Male	Female	Total	Male	Female
Number of inmates	450,416	430,604	19,812	711,643	672,847	38,796
White, non-Hispanic	39.6	39.6	39.7	35.4	35.4	36.2
Black, non-Hispanic	45.3	45.3	46.0	45.6	45.5	46.0

[Continued]

★918★

State Prisoners, by Sex and Race/Ethnicity, 1986 and 1991

[Continued]

Characteristic	Percent of prison inmates					
	1986			1991		
	Total[1]	Male	Female	Total	Male	Female
Hispanic	12.6	12.7	11.7	16.7	16.8	14.2
Other[2]	2.5	2.5	2.5	2.4	2.3	3.6

Source: Maguire, Kathleen and Ann L. Pastore (eds.). U.S. Department of Justice. U.S. Bureau of Justice Statistics. *Sourcebook of Criminal Justice Statistics 1993.* Washington, DC: U.S. Government Printing Office, 1994, p. 611. Primary source: U.S. Department of Justice, Bureau of Justice Statistics, *Correctional Populations in the United states, 1991,* NCJ-142729 (Washington, DC: USGPO, 1993), p. 26. *Notes:* These data were collected by the U.S. Bureau of the Census for the U.S. Department of Justice, Bureau of Justice Statistics through the 1991 Survey of Inmates in State Correctional Facilities. Similar surveys were conducted in 1974, 1979, and 1986. The sample for the 1991 survey was selected from the 1,239 state prisons hat were enumerated in the 1990 Census of State and Federal Adult Correctional Facilities and those that were opened after completion of the census. The survey employed a stratified two-stage selection design. In the first stage, correctional facilities were separated into two sampling frames: one for prisons housing male inmates and one for prisons housing female inmates. Prisons housing both sexes were included on both lists. Within each frame, prisons were stratified into eight strata based on census region and facility type (confinement and community-based). All prisons with 1,950 or more men and all prisons with 380 or more women were selected. The remaining prisons in the male and female frames were grouped into strata. A systematic sample of prisons was then selected within strata with probabilities proportional to the size of each prison. In the second stage, interviewers visited each selected facility and systematically selected a sample of male and female inmates using predetermined procedures. In 1991, a total of 13,986 interviews were completed at 277 prisons for a response rate of 93.75 percent. In 1986, a total of 13,711 interviews were completed at 275 prisons from a sample of approximately 15,000. These data are estimates derived from a sample and therefore subject to sampling variation. Data for marital status were missing for 1.1 percent of the inmates; for education, 0.8 percent; and for military service, 0.2 percent. 1. Percents may not add to 100 because of rounding. 2. Includes Asians, Pacific Islanders, American Indians, Alaska Natives, and other racial groups.

★919★

Prisons

State and Federal Prisoners, by State, 1991

Number of prisoners in each U.S. region and state jurisdiction is shown, by race and ethnicity, as of December 31, 1991.

Region and jurisdiction	Total	White	Black	American Indian or Alaska Native	Asian or Pacific Islander	Not known
United States, total	824,133	385,347	395,245	7,407	3,423	32,711
Federal institutions, total	71,608	46,868	22,727	1,222	791	0
State institutions, total	752,525	338,479	372,518	6,185	2,632	32,711
Northeast	131,866	56,815	66,442	214	338	8,057
Connecticut[1,2]	10,977	3,053	5,144	7	26	2,747
Maine	1,579	1,522	37	16	4	0
Massachusetts[2,3]	9,155	4,410	3,036	14	51	1,644
New Hampshire	1,533	1,443	80	5	5	0
New Jersey[2]	23,483	6,762	15,005	4	41	1,671
New York[4]	57,862	28,181	29,151	135	155	240
Pennsylvania[2]	23,388	8,470	13,090	28	45	1,755
Rhode Island[1]	2,771	1,856	899	5	11	0

[Continued]

★ 919 ★

State and Federal Prisoners, by State, 1991

[Continued]

Region and jurisdiction	Total	White	Black	American Indian or Alaska Native	Asian or Pacific Islander	Not known
Vermont[1,5]	1,118	1,118	NA	NA	NA	0
Midwest	155,917	71,227	79,217	1,394	130	3,949
Illinois[2,3]	29,115	8,055	18,306	49	28	2,677
Indiana[3]	13,008	8,000	4,971	30	7	0
Iowa[3]	4,145	3,089	940	69	15	32
Kansas[2]	5,903	3,329	2,145	81	33	315
Michigan[2,3]	36,423	14,586	20,985	137	25	690
Minnesota[2]	3,472	1,960	1,051	287	1	173
Missouri	15,897	8,547	7,317	30	3	0
Nebraska	2,495	1,564	830	95	0	6
North Dakota	492	397	4	88	3	0
Ohio[5]	35,744	16,433	19,311	0	0	0
South Dakota	1,374	992	32	350	NA	0
Wisconsin	7,849	4,275	3,325	178	15	56
South	301,866	104,969	181,341	1,249	374	13,933
Alabama[2]	16,760	5,958	10,793	6	2	1
Arkansas[2]	7,766	3,302	4,437	3	1	23
Delaware[1,2]	3,717	1,175	2,449	2	3	88
District of Columbia[1,5]	10,455	218	10,237	0	0	0
Florida[2,3]	46,533	18,383	27,185	0	105	860
Georgia[3]	23,644	7,613	15,931	20	6	74
Kentucky	9,799	6,672	3,123	2	0	2
Louisiana[6]	20,003	5,168	14,834	NA	NA	1
Maryland	19,291	4,581	14,638	6	0	66
Mississippi[2]	8,904	2,437	6,410	7	9	41
North Carolina	18,903	6,747	11,522	421	11	202
Oklahoma[2]	13,340	7,522	4,652	760	0	406
South Carolina	18,269	6,099	12,120	13	2	35
Tennessee[6]	11,474	5,857	5,503	NA	NA	114
Texas[2,3]	51,677	15,013	24,520	6	193	11,945
Virginia[2]	19,829	6,942	12,769	2	41	75
West Virginia	1,502	1,282	218	1	1	0
West	162,876	105,468	45,518	3,328	1,790	6,772
Alaska[1,5]	2,706	1,488	339	847	32	0
Arizona[3]	15,415	12,271	2,633	498	12	1
California[3]	101,808	61,594	35,205	662	NA	3,347
Colorado[5]	8,392	5,990	1,937	108	27	330
Hawaii[1,2,5]	2,700	642	155	34	1,470	399
Idaho[5]	2,143	1,997	32	94	15	5
Montana	1,478	1,189	20	269	0	0
Nevada[2]	5,503	3,141	1,719	77	50	516
New Mexico	3,119	2,680	316	97	4	22
Oregon	6,732	4,994	923	147	51	617
Utah	2,625	2,264	222	67	36	36

[Continued]

★ 919 ★

State and Federal Prisoners, by State, 1991

[Continued]

Region and jurisdiction	Total	White	Black	American Indian or Alaska Native	Asian or Pacific Islander	Not known
Washington	9,156	6,345	1,966	372	91	382
Wyoming[2,3]	1,099	873	51	56	2	117

Source: Maguire, Kathleen and Ann L. Pastore (eds.). U.S. Department of Justice. U.S. Bureau of Justice Statistics. *Sourcebook of Criminal Justice Statistics 1993.* Washington, DC: U.S. Government Printing Office, 1994, p. 606. Primary source: U.S. Department of Justice, Bureau of Justice Statistics, *Correctional Populations in the United States, 1991,* NCJ-142729 (Washington, DC: USGPO, 1993), p. 57. *Notes:* 1. Figures include both jail and prison inmates; jails and prisons are combined in one system. 2. Hispanic prisoners were classified as persons of unknown race. 3. All data for Arizona, California, Florida, Georgia, Illinois, Indiana, Iowa, Massachusetts, Michigan, Texas, and Wyoming are custody rather than jurisdiction counts. 4. Hispanic prisoners were classified as white. 5. Racial group membership of the population was estimated. 6. Louisiana and Tennessee reported persons whose race is neither black nor white under "other race," here reported under "unknown race."

★ 920 ★

Prisons

Status of Hispanic Prisoners on Death Row, 1991

Data show movement of Hispanic prisoners under sentence of death in 1991.

Characteristic	Hispanic prisoners under sentence of death				
	Under death sentence 12/31/90	Received from court in 1991	Executed in 1991	Death sentence removed in 1991[1]	Under death sentence 12/31/91
U.S. total	171	20	1	6	184
Federal	0	0	0	0	0
State	171	20	1	6	184
Northeast	3	0	0	1	2
Pennsylvania	3	0	0	1	2
Midwest	15	2	0	1	16
Illinois	8	0	0	0	8
Indiana	2	0	0	0	2
Missouri	0	1	0	0	1
Ohio	5	1	0	1	5
South	87	13	1	1	98
Arkansas	1	0	0	0	1
Florida	27	5	0	1	31
Georgia	1	0	0	0	1
Mississippi	1	0	0	0	1
North Carolina	1	1	0	0	2
Oklahoma	5	0	0	0	5
Tennessee	0	1	0	0	1
Texas	51	6	1	0	56
West	66	5	0	3	68
Arizona	19	2	0	2	19
California	37	2	0	1	38

[Continued]

★ 920 ★

Status of Hispanic Prisoners on Death Row, 1991

[Continued]

Characteristic	Hispanic prisoners under sentence of death				
	Under death sentence 12/31/90	Received from court in 1991	Executed in 1991	Death sentence removed in 1991[1]	Under death sentence 12/31/91
Colorado	1	0	0	0	1
Idaho	1	0	0	0	1
Nevada	6	1	0	0	7
Utah	2	0	0	0	2

Source: U.S. Department of Justice. Office of Justice Programs. Bureau of Justice Statistics. *Correctional Populations in the United States, 1991* (NCJ-142729). Washington, DC: Bureau of Justice Statistics, August 1993, p. 95. *Notes:* Hispanic prisoners may be of any race. States that do not appear had no Hispanic prisoners under a death sentence in 1991. 1. Dispositions of death sentences other than by execution included dismissal of indictment, reversal of judgment, commutation, resentencing, and order of a new trial.

★ 921 ★

Prisons

Status of Prisoners on Death Row, 1991

Data show number of death row prisoners in each category as of year end, 1991.

Characteristic	Present year end 1991	Received from court in 1991	Removed from death row in 1991	
			Executed	Removed by other means[1]
U.S. total	2,482	266	14	116
Race				
White	1,464	163	7	60
Black	982	101	7	52
Other[2]	36	2	0	4
Hispanic origin				
Hispanic	184	20	1	6
Non-Hispanic	2,109	232	11	102
Not known	189	14	2	8

Source: U.S. Department of Justice. Office of Justice Programs. Bureau of Justice Statistics. *Correctional Populations in the United States, 1991* (NCJ-142729). Washington, DC: Bureau of Justice Statistics, August 1993, p. 92. *Notes:* 1. Includes deceased from causes other than execution, commutation of sentence, sentence vacated, and conviction vacated. 2. "Other" race present at year end includes 23 American Indians and 13 Asians. "Other" race admitted includes 1 American Indian and 1 Asian inmate. Two American Indians and 2 Asians had their death sentences removed in 1991.

Listing of Sources

The following listing shows all sources under in *SRHA2* in the format in which the sources appear referenced under each table. In addition to these sources, the originators of the data frequently cited additional sources on which they based their work. Those sources are shown with each table but, because of the diversity of the citations, have not been extracted and included here.

1987 Economic Census of Outlying Areas, Puerto Rico: Geographic Area Statistics, Wholesale Trade, Retail Trade, Service Industries. U.S. Department of Commerce, Bureau of the Census, OA87-E-1, 1990. Tables: 799-802

1987 Economic Censuses, Survey of Minority-Owned Business Enterprises: Hispanics, U.S. Department of Commerce, Bureau of the Census, MB-87-2, 1991. Tables: 687-717

1987 Economic Censuses, Survey of Minority-Owned Business Enterprises: Summary, U.S. Department of Commerce, Bureau of the Census, 1991. Tables: 718-719, 770, 772, 775, 779-780, 783-798

1994 Statistical Abstract of the United States on CD-ROM [machine-readable datafiles]. CD-8A-94. Washington, DC: U.S. Department of Commerce, Economics and Statistics Administration, Bureau of the Census, Data User Services Division, January 1995. Tables: 82, 139, 164, 173, 181- 182, 243-244, 264, 289-290, 377, 381, 408, 412, 416, 474, 477, 485-486, 488-489, 492, 500, 521, 563-564, 586-587, 589-590, 593, 598, 608, 612, 662, 669, 803-804, 865-867

Aging America, Trends and Projections, 1991 Edition. Prepared by the U.S. Senate Special Committee on Aging, the American Association of Retired Persons, the Federal Council on the Aging, and the U.S. Administration on Aging. Tables: 145-146, 180, 241, 538-539, 580, 582, 585, 609, 864

Airman - The Book '94 (September 1994). Table: 840

Alaniz, Gabriela A. National Council of La Raza. Center for Health Promotion. *NCLR Health Fact Sheet: Childhood Immunization in the Hispanic Community*. Washington, DC: NCLR, June 1994. Tables: 389, 391-398

Alonzo, Vincent. "Muy grande!" *Incentive* (January 1994). Tables: 673, 678

American Demographics (December 1992). Table: 555

American Demographics (February 1993). Table: 124

American Demographics (January 1992). Table: 776

American Demographics (June 1992). Table: 502

American Demographics (October 1991). Table: 76

Anderson, D. Michael and Christenson, Gregory M. "Ethnic breakdown of AIDS related knowledge and attitudes from the National Adolescent Student Health Survey." *Journal of Health Education* vol. 22, no. 1, (January/February 1991). Tables: 365-367, 369

Arocha, Zita. "Parties: don't take Hispanic voters for granted." *USA TODAY* (28 July 1992), p. 11A; Benedetto, Richard. "Hispanics feeling at home: survey shows a solid fit in mainstream." *USA TODAY* (16 December 1992), p. 5A. Table: 837

Arocha, Zita. "Stop putting barriers in front of Hispanic kids." *USA TODAY* (22 September 1992). Table: 232

ASPIRA News: National Newsletter of the ASPIRA Association, Inc. Vol. 5, No. 4 (Winter 1991-92). Tables: 233-234, 262

Atkins, Elizabeth. "Racial bias still widespread in the media, study finds." *Detroit News* (24 July 1994). Tables: 505-507

Baumann, Marty. "USA Snapshots: Which students smoke most." *USA TODAY* (15 July 1992). Table: 460

Benedetto, Richard. "GOP must regain its position as 'party of ideas'." *USA TODAY* (3 March 1993). Table: 838

Benedetto, Richard. "Hispanics feeling at home: survey shows a solid fit in mainstream." *USA TODAY* (16 December 1992). Table: 352

Bennefield, Robert L. U.S. Bureau of the Census. *Dynamics of Economic Well-Being: Health Insurance, 1990 to 1992.* Current Population Reports, P70-37. Washington, DC: U.S. Government Printing Office, 1994. Tables: 402, 404, 413-414

Berger, Joseph. "New York's bilingual bureaucracy assailed as non-English programs cover more pupils." *The New York Times* (4 January 1993). Table: 347

"Black entrepreneurship." *Wall Street Journal* (3 April 1992). Tables: 777, 781

Brady, Erik. "Leagues have catching up to do off field." *USA TODAY* (3 August 1994). Table: 475

Bray, Rosemary L. "Good cop, bad cop: what blacks think of white cops." *The New York Times* (11 July 1994). Table: 897

Burciaga Valdez, PH.D., R. and others. "Insuring Latinos against the cost of illness." *JAMA* Vol. 269, No. 7. Tables: 403, 410

Business Horizons, (January/February 1990). Table: 501

Cage, Mary Crystal. "Fewer students get bachelor's degrees in 4 years, study finds." *Chronicle of Higher Education* (15 July 1992). Table: 237

"California's mix offers a look at the future." *USA TODAY* (4 December 1992). Table: 125

Campbell, Paul R. U.S. Bureau of the Census. *Population Projections for States, by Age, Race, and Sex: 1993 to 2020.* Current Population Reports, P25- 1111. Washington, DC: U.S. Government Printing Office, 1994. Table: 132

Carter, David L. and Allen D. Sapp, "College Education and Policing: Coming of Age." *FBI Law Enforcement Bulletin.* (January 1992). Tables: 891-892

Casper, Lynne M., Mary Hawkins, and Martin O'Connell. U.S. Bureau of the Census. *Who's Minding the Kids? Child Care Arrangements: Fall 1991*. Current Population Reports, P70-36. Washington, DC: U.S. Government Printing Office, 1994. Tables: 148-150, 152

Castaneda, Laura. "Banking on opportunity: Bank One leads survey of Hispanics; 22% lack accounts." *Dallas Morning News* (16 July 1994). Table: 677

Chain Store Age Executive, May 1992. Table: 682

"The changing face of foodservice: grappling with diversity in the workplace." *Nation's Restaurant News* (20 September 1993). Table: 493

Chavez, Linda. "Minimum Wage Hurts the Poor." *USA TODAY* (8 February 1994). Table: 588

Chavez, Linda. "Why make it easier to receive welfare?" *USA TODAY* (8 June 1994). Table: 645

Chronicle of Higher Education Almanac (1 September 1994). Table: 201

Chronicle of Higher Education Almanac (7 September 1994). Table: 185

Colton, David. "Hispanic voters." *USA TODAY* (2 July 1992). Table: 849

"Comparison of Business Ownership by Minority Group: 1987 and 1982," *Minority-Owned Businesses*. Table: 773

"Counting homelessness." *Social Science and the Citizen* (November/December, 1994). Table: 524

de Palomo, Frank B. National Council of La Raza. "CDC HIV/AIDS Surveillance Report Adds HIV Cases: Report Lacks Representative Hispanic Data." *NCLR AIDS/SIDA Network News* 5(3): (Fall 1994). Table: 368

De Witt, Karen. "The nation's schools learn a 4th: resegregation." *The New York Times* (19 January 1992). Table: 283

"Death penalty: man by a window." *The Economist* (4 April 1992). Table: 900

"'Do good' won't do it on the supply front." *Purchasing* (16 February 1995). Table: 782

Duggan, Celia W. "Iowa cuts off the cash, pushing some to work, and some over the edge." *The New York Times* (7 April 1995). Table: 647

Edmonds, Patricia. "No violence, but Detroit bitter: efforts of police, city paying off." *USA TODAY* (11 November 1992). Table: 896

Edmondson, Brad. "American diversity." *American Demographics Desk Reference*, July 1991. Table: 108

Edmondson, Brad. "Hispanic America." *American Demographics Desk Reference*, July 1991. Table: 119

"Employment in the USA." *USA TODAY* (8 June 1992). Table: 656

Estrich, Susan. "Positive signal for working women." *USA TODAY* (29 April 1992). Table: 583

"Fatalities decline." *Occupational Hazards* (July 1993). Table: 422

"Federal diversity." *Manpower Comments* (January/February 1994). Table: 821

"Firms try to improve Hispanic measurement." *Broadcasting* (20 May 91). Table: 349

Fisher, Christy. "Poll: Hispanics stick to brands: Asian- Americans shop for good price and African-Americans look for quality." *Advertising Age* (15 February 1993). Tables: 675, 680

Fisher, Helen S. (ed.). *Gale City & Metro Rankings Reporter*. Detroit, MI: Gale Research Inc., 1994. Published with permission. Tables: 96-107

Flannery, William. "Hispanic-owned small businesses taking off, poll finds." *St. Louis-Dispatch* (16 May 94). Table: 686

Frankel, Bruce. "Change looms large for troubled NYC police force." *USA TODAY* (7 October 1992). Table: 898

Furukawa, Stacy. U.S. Bureau of the Census. *The Diverse Living Arrangements of Children: Summer 1991*. Current Population Reports, Series P70, No. 38, Washington, DC: U.S. Government Printing Office, 1994. Tables: 153-163

Galifianakis, Nick. "USA Snaphots: The language of sports." *USA TODAY* (14 January 1993). Table: 359

Gonzalez, Davis. "What's the problem with 'Hispanic'? Just ask a 'Latino'." *The New York Times* (15 November 1992). Table: 354

Goodavage, Maria. "Curfew arrests fuel rage in L.A." *USA TODAY* (11 May 1992). Table: 113

Greenhouse, Steven. "The coming crisis of the American work force." *The New York Times* (7 June 1992). Table: 491

Grocery Marketing (24 November 1991). Tables: 670- 672, 674, 676, 681, 685

Hall, Cindy and Stephen Conley. "Choosing primary care careers." *USA TODAY* (22 November 1994). Table: 319

Hall, Mimi. ''Study zeros in on pregnant teens, parents: both sides say new report is a validation of positions.'' *USA TODAY* (20 October 1992). Table: 372

Hansen, Kristin A. U.S. Bureau of the Census. *Geographic Mobility: March 1991 to March 1992*. Current Population Reports, P20-473. Washington, DC: U.S. Government Printing Office, 1993. Tables: 2-3, 9

Harney, James and Deborah Sharp. "For farm workers, a harvest of danger." *USA TODAY* (25 February 1992). Table: 499

"Heterosexually Acquired AIDS - United States, 1993." *JAMA*, vol. 271, no. 13 (6 April 1994). Table: 371

Hispanic (December 1994). Table: 331

Hispanic (March 1995). Table: 320

Hollmann, Frederick W. U.S. Department of Commerce. Bureau of the Census. *United States Population Estimates, by Age, Sex, Race, and Hispanic Origin: 1980 to 1988*. Current Population Reports, Population Estimates and Projections, Series P-25, No. 1045. Washington, DC: The Bureau, January 1990. Tables: 43-44, 46, 57, 75, 78, 117- 118, 123

"How are we covered?" *Hispanic* (October 1994). Table: 355

"HS Science/Math." *Manpower Comments*, September 1993. Table: 193

"Issues 'too critical' for glib debate." *USA TODAY* (21 May 1992). Tables: 137-138, 177

Jones, Lee R., and others. *The 1990 Science Report Card: NAEP's Assessment of Fourth, Eighth, and Twelfth Graders*, Prepared by Educational Testing Service under contract with the National Center for Education Statistics, Office of Educational Research and Improvement, U.S. Department of Education, March 1992. Tables: 206-211, 213-226, 294

Kelly, Dennis. "When kids are fighting mad: curbing conflict becomes part of the curriculum." *USA TODAY* (18 November 1992). Table: 284

Kilborn, Peter T. "Extending jobless benefits is on the table, Reich says." *The New York Times* (28 January 1993). Table: 584

Kisker, Ellen Eliason and others. *A Profile of Child Care Settings: Early Education and Care in 1990, Volume 1*. Prepared under contract for the U.S. Department of Education by Mathematica Policy Research Inc., 1991, pp. 166-167. Table: 151

Komarow, Steve. "Door opens for women, but not all the way." *USA TODAY* (28 July 1994). Table: 843

Kominski, Robert and Andrea Adams. U.S. Bureau of the Census. *Educational Attainment in the United States: March 1993 and 1992*. Current Population Reports, P20- 476. Washington, DC: U.S. Government Printing Office, 1994. Tables: 242, 245-246, 249, 576-577

Krauss, Clifford. "Democrats retreat on strengthening votes of non-state delegates." *The New York Times* (5 January 1993). Table: 829

"Largest Denver-area minority-owned businesses." *Denver Business Journal* (2-8 October 1992). Table: 720

Leavitt, Paul. "Child poverty rates on the rise." *USA TODAY* (12 August 1992). Table: 602

Lewin, David. "Washington window: across the gender divide." *Mechanical Engineering* (October 1993). Table: 504

Lewin, Tamar. "Study points to increase in tolerance of ethnicity." *The New York Times* (8 January 1992). Table: 356

Lillie-Blanton, Dr. Marsha PH; James C. Anthony, PH.D.; Charles R. Schuster, PH.D. "Probing the meaning of racial/ethnic group comparisons in crack cocaine smoking." *JAMA* (24 February 1993) Vol. 269, No. 8. Table: 448

"Los Angeles schools hobbled and desperate." *The New York Times* (16 February 1993). Tables: 261, 286-287

Maguire, Kathleen and Ann L. Pastore (eds.). U.S. Department of Justice. U.S. Bureau of Justice Statistics. *Sourcebook of Criminal Justice Statistics 1993*. Washington, DC: U.S. Government Printing Office, 1994. Tables: 834, 877, 885-887, 890, 894-895, 899, 901-902, 904-905, 907-909, 914-915, 917-919

Manning, Anita. "Hispanics are at higher risk for diabetes." *USA TODAY* (10 February 1994), sec. D. Table: 387

Mauro, Tony. "Death penalty may help kill nomination." *USA TODAY* (7 May 1992). Table: 836

Meyer, Michael. "Los Angeles 2010: a Latino subcontinent." *Newsweek* (9 November 1992). Table: 115

Mide, Susan. "Healing the hurt of homeless kids." *USA TODAY* (23 November 1992). Table: 417

Miner, Betsy. "Tough times have people staying put." *USA TODAY* (18 November 1992). Table: 1

"Minorities in government." *Manpower Comments* (April/May 1994). Table: 806

Minority Business Development Agency. U.S. Department of Commerce. *Annual Business Assistance Report, Fiscal Year 1993*. Washington, DC: U.S. Department of Commerce, 1994. Tables: 665-668

"Minority customers to become a major marketing target." *Discount Store News* (18 May 1992). Table: 126

"Minority-Owned Firms by Gender." *Minority-Owned Businesses*. Table: 778

"Minority-Owned Firms by Industry Division: 1987." *Minority-Owned Businesses*. Table: 771

Montgomery, Patricia A. U.S. Bureau of the Census. *The Hispanic Population in the United States: March 1993*. Current Population Reports, Series P20-475. Washington, DC: U.S. Government Printing Office, 1994. Tables: 140, 142, 170, 179, 251, 548, 551, 566, 573

Mouat, Lucia. "New York City - a vibrant but troubled metropolis." *Christian Science Monitor* (6 November 1991). Table: 116

Mullins, Marcy E. "Employment in the USA." *USA TODAY* (7 December 1992),. Table: 658

"Multiple jobholders by age, marital status, race, Hispanic origin, and sex, May 1991." *Bureau of Labor Statistics News* (28 October 1991). Tables: 509, 511

"Multiple jobholders by selected characteristics and extent of work at home on secondary job, May 1991," *Bureau of Labor Statistics News* (28 October 1991). Table: 510

"Multiple jobholders by sex, marital status, race, Hispanic origin, and reason for working at more than one job," *Bureau of Labor Statistics News* (28 October 1991). Table: 508

National Center for Health Statistics. *Health, United States, 1993*. Hyattsville, MD: Public Health Service, May 1994. Tables: 362-364, 373-376, 378-380, 383, 429, 432-433, 436, 439, 446

National Center for Health Statistics. *Healthy People 2000 Review. Health, United States, 1992*. Hyattsville, MD: Public Health Service, 1993,. Tables: 361, 431

National Commission for Employment Policy. *Training Hispanics: Implications for the JTPA System: Special Report*. January 1990. Table: 345

National Science Board. *Science & Engineering Indicators—1993* (NSB 93-1). Washington, DC: U.S. Government Printing Office, 1993. Tables: 288, 321, 323- 324, 472-473, 494, 519

Noah, Timothy. "Asian-Americans take lead in starting U.S. businesses." *Wall Street Journal* (2 August 1991). Table: 774

Painter, Kim. "Lifestyles remain a major barrier to condom use." *USA TODAY* (7 July 1992). Table: 370

Park, C.H. and others. National Center for Health Statistics. *Health Conditions Among the Currently Employed: United States, 1988. Vital Health Statistics* 10 (186), 1993. Tables: 423-426, 462-463

Parker, Suzy. "USA Snapshots: Catholics in the USA." *USA TODAY* (20 November 1992). Table: 357

"Percent of conventional mortgages denied, 1990," *Time*, Vol. 138, No. 18 (4 November 1991). Table: 464

"Persistent gap: blacks can face a host of trying conditions in getting mortgages." *Wall Street Journal* (30 November 1992). Tables: 466-470

Phillips, Kent. "Hispanic market? Definitely Coke!" *Beverage World* (December 1991). Tables: 683-684

Piani, A., and C. Schoenborn. National Center for Health Statistics. *Health Promotion and Disease Prevention: United States, 1990. Vital and Health Statistics* 10(185), 1993. Tables: 385-386, 399-401, 419-421, 430, 461

Popularly Elected Officials in 1987, (GC87(1)-2), Bureau of the Census, U.S. Department of Commerce. Tables: 822-827, 831-832

Potter, Jerry. "Minorities try to forge link with golf." *USA TODAY* (21 October 1992). Table: 358

Puente, Maria. "Bitter battle over Prop. 187 down to wire." *USA TODAY* (9 November 94). Table: 839

"Ranking of total combined non-white population of states, 1990," *Black Issues in Higher Education*, (29 August 1991). Table: 80

"Rate of Down's syndrome highest among Hispanics, CDC finds." *Chicago Tribune* (26 August 1994). Table: 390

Reinhold, Robert. "A terrible chain of events reveals Los Angeles without its makeup." *The New York Times* (3 May 1992). Table: 114

"Report calls a third of U.S. adults obese." *St. Louis Post-Dispatch* (18 July 1994). Table: 382

Reske, Henry J. "A report card on Clinton's judges: President's picks are diverse in look and legal background but not in wealth." *ABA Journal* (April 1994). Table: 835

Richardson, Rod. "Blacks reluctant to donate organs." *Detroit News* (1 March 1993). Table: 427

Sanchez, Sandra. "Hispanics in L.A.: we suffered too." *USA TODAY* (7 May 1992). Table: 112

SCAN/INFO (September 1992). Table: 338

Schwenk, F.N. Family Economics Research Group. "Income and consumer expenditures of households headed by Hispanic and Black elderly women." *Family Economics Review* Vol. 7, no. 1 (1994). Table: 172

Shai, Donna. "Cancer Mortality in Cuba and Among the Cuban-Born in the United States: 1979-81." *Public Health Reports* Vol. 106, No. 1, (January-February 1991). Table: 384

Sharp, Deborah. "Miami's language gap widens: culturally rich but very divided." *USA TODAY* (3 April 1992). Table: 346

Sisneros, Antonio. "Hispanics in the public service in the late twentieth century." *Public Administration Review* 53 no. 1 (January/February 1993). Tables: 306, 807

Special Supplemental Food Program for Women, Infants, and Children (WIC) Racial Participation, April 1991. Food and Nutrition Service Financial Management Program Information Division Data Base, Monitoring Branch, November 1991. Tables: 649-652

Spencer, Gregory. U.S. Bureau of the Census. *Current Population Reports*, Series P-25, No. 995, *Projections of the Hispanic Population: 1983 to 2080.* Washington, D.C.: The Bureau, 1986. Table: 67

Staff Report on Homelessness in the United States, August 1990, p. 16. Prepared by the staff of the U.S. Commission on Security and Cooperation in Europe. Tables: 522-523

Stein, M.L. "Concerned about diversity: Hispanic journalists say the slightest percentage increase in the number of Hispanic editorial staffers at newspapers is 'insignificant'." *Editor and Publisher - the Fourth Estate* (9 May 1992). Tables: 476, 503

Suro, Robert. "Poll finds Hispanic desire to assimilate." *The New York Times* (15 December 1992). Tables: 339, 351, 353

Suro, Roberto. "Pollution-weary minorities try civil rights tack." *The New York Times* (11 January 1993). Table: 428

"Surveys point to group differences." *Brandweek* (18 July 1994). Tables: 344, 679

Sutterlin, Rebecca and Robert A. Kominski. U.S. Bureau of the Census. *Dollars for Scholars: Postsecondary Costs and Financing, 1990-1991.* Current Population Reports, P70-39, Washington, DC: U.S. Government Printing Office, 1994. Tables: 327-328

Tan, Evelyn D. "Immigrants may find more of a promised land." *USA TODAY* (17 November 1992). Table: 39

Tardiff, Kenneth, MD, MPH, and others. "A profile of homicides on the streets and in the homes of New York City." *Public Health Reports* 110, no. 1 (January-February 1995). Tables: 869-870

Tharp, Mike, David Whitman, and Betsy Streisand. "Hispanics' tale of two cities." *U.S. News & World Report* (25 May 1992). Tables: 147, 644

"Top 25 Hispanic-owned businesses." *South Florida Business Journal* (11- 17 June 1993). Table: 721

"Uninsured strain hospitals, hike costs: the working poor often delay treatment." *Detroit Free Press* (10 February 1993). Table: 415

U.S. Bureau of Labor Statistics. U.S. Department of Labor. *Geographic Profile of Employment and Unemployment, 1993* (Bulletin 2446). Washington, DC: U.S. Government Printing Office, September 1994. Tables: 479-481, 490, 495-498, 657, 659-661

U.S. Bureau of Labor Statistics. U.S. Department of Labor. *Monthly Labor Review* (January 1995). Tables: 487, 663-664

U.S. Bureau of the Census, *1990 Census of Population and Housing, Summary Tape File 1C on CD-ROM, United States Summary,* February, 1992. Tables: 84-86, 91-92, 528-530, 542

U.S. Bureau of the Census, *1990 Census of Population and Housing, Summary Tape File, STF-3A on CD-ROM, United States Summary*. Table: 343

U.S. Bureau of the Census. *The Condition of Hispanics in America Today*. Washington, DC: U.S. Government Printing Office, 1983. Table: 342

U.S. Bureau of the Census. *Educational Attainment in the United States: March 1989 and 1988.* Current Population Reports, Series P-20, No. 451, Washington, DC: U.S. Government Printing Office, 1991. Table: 248

U.S. Bureau of the Census. *Estimates of the Armed Forces Overseas, by Age, Sex, Race, and Hispanic Origin*. Tables: 841-842

U.S. Bureau of the Census, *The Hispanic Population in the United States: March 1991.* Current Population Reports, Series P-20, No. 455, Washington, DC: U.S. Government Printing Office, 1991. Tables: 79, 81, 171, 478, 537, 601, 611

U.S. Bureau of the Census. *The Hispanic Population of the Southwest Borderland.* Current Population Reports, Series P-23, No. 172, Washington, DC: U.S. Government Printing Office, 1991. Tables: 87-90, 93-94, 109, 133, 141, 168-169, 270, 340-341, 482-484, 610

U.S. Bureau of the Census. *Household Economic Studies, Who's Helping Out?: Support Networks Among American Families*. Current Population Reports, Series P-70, No. 13. Tables: 653-655

U.S. Bureau of the Census. *Job Creation During the Late 1980's (Data from the Survey of Income and Program Participation).* Current Population Reports, P70, No. 27. Washington, DC: U.S. Government Printing Office, 1992. Tables: 517, 562, 599

U.S. Bureau of the Census. *Marriage, Divorce, and Remarriage in the 1990's.* Current Population Reports, P23-180. Washington, DC: U.S. Government Printing Office, 1992. Tables: 165-166, 178

U.S. Bureau of the Census. *Money Income of Households, Families, and Persons in the United States: 1990.* Current Population Reports, P60-174, 1991. Tables: 556- 559, 565, 569-572, 581, 594-597

U.S. Bureau of the Census. *Poverty in the United States: 1991*. Current Population Reports, Series P60- 181, U.S. Government Printing Office, Washington, D.C., 1992. Tables: 174, 642

U.S. Bureau of the Census. *Poverty in the United States: 1992*. Current Population Reports, Series P60- 185, U.S. Government Printing Office, Washington, D.C., 1993. Tables: 4-7, 134-136, 405-407, 411, 567-568, 603- 607, 613-641, 643

U.S. Bureau of the Census. *Projections of the Hispanic Population: 1983 to 2080*. Current Population Reports, Series P-25, No. 995, Washington, DC: U.S. Government Printing Office, 1986. Tables: 127-131

U.S. Bureau of the Census. *Statistical Abstract of the United States: 1992*, (112th edition). Washington, DC: U.S. Government Printing Office, 1992. Tables: 83, 95, 110-111, 121, 253, 268, 527, 574

U.S. Bureau of the Census. *Voting and Registration in the Election of November 1992*, Current Population Reports, P20-466. Washington, DC, U.S. GPO, 1993. Tables: 850-863

U.S. Bureau of the Census. *What's it Worth? Educational Background and Economic Status: Spring 1990*. Current Population Reports, Series P70-32. Washington DC: U.S. Government Printing Office, 1992. Tables: 250, 318, 520, 575

U.S. Bureau of the Census. *Workers With Low Earnings: 1964 to 1990*. Current Population Reports, Series P-60, No. 178. Washington, DC: U.S. Government Printing Office, 1992. Tables: 143-144, 175-176, 515-516, 560-561, 591-592

U.S. Department of Education. National Center for Education Statistics. *Digest of Education Statistics 1991*. Washington, DC: U.S. Government Printing Office, November 1991. Tables: 336-337, 360

U.S. Department of Education. National Center for Education Statistics. Office of Educational Research and Improvement. *Digest of Education Statistics, 1994*. Lanham, MD: Bernan, November 1994. Tables: 186-190, 197- 198, 200, 204, 212, 227-228, 230, 235-236, 238-240, 247, 254-256, 258, 260, 267, 269, 273-276, 282, 285, 291-293, 295, 299-304, 308-310, 312, 315-317, 325-326, 332-335

U.S. Department of Education. National Center for Education Statistics. Office of Educational Research and Improvement. *The Condition of Education 1991, Volume 1, Elementary and Secondary Education*, 1991. Table: 266

U.S. Department of Education. National Center for Education Statistics. *The Condition of Education, 1992*. Washington, DC: U.S. Government Printing Office, 1992. Tables: 199, 203, 252, 278-281, 298, 348

U.S. Department of Education. National Center for Education Statistics. *The Condition of Education 1994*. Washington, DC: U.S. Government Printing Office, 1994. Tables: 191-192, 194-196, 202, 205, 229, 231, 257-259, 263, 265, 271-272, 277, 297, 329-330

U.S. Department of Education. National Center for Education Statistics. U.S. Department of Education. Office of Educational Research and Improvement. Postsecondary Education Statistics Division. *Trends in Racial/Ethnic Enrollment in Higher Education: Fall 1980 Through Fall 1990*. Washington, DC: U.S. Government Printing Office. Tables: 305, 307, 311, 313-314

U.S. Department of Health and Human Services. Center for Mental Health Services. *Mental Health, United States, 1994*. Manderscheid, R.W., and Sonnenschein, M.A., eds. DHHS Pub. No. (SMA)94-3000. Washington, DC: U.S. Government Printing Office, 1994. Table: 418

U.S. Department of Health and Human Services. Public Health Service. Alcohol, Drug Abuse, and Mental Health Administration. *National Household Survey on Drug Abuse: Population Estimates 1993*. DHHS Publication No. (SMA) 94-3017. Bethesda, MD: Department of Health and Human Services, 1994. Tables: 434-435, 437-438, 440-445, 447, 449-452, 459

U.S. Department of Health and Human Services. Public Health Service. Substance Abuse and Mental Health Services Administration. Office of Applied Studies. *National Drug and Alcoholism Treatment Unit Survey (NDATUS)*, 1991 Main Findings Report. DHHS Publication No. (SMA) 92- 2007, 1993. Tables: 454-455, 457-458

U.S. Department of Health and Human Services. Public Health Service. Substance Abuse and Mental Health Services Administration. Office of Applied Studies. *State Resources and Services Related to Alcohol and Other Drug Problems, Fiscal Year 1992: An Analysis of State Alcohol and Drug Abuse Profile Data*. Prepared by the National Association of State Alcohol and Drug Abuse Directors, Incorporated. DHHS Publication No. (SMA) 94-2092. Rockville, MD: Department of Health and Human Services, 1994. Tables: 453, 456

U.S. Department of Housing and Urban Development. Office of Policy Development and Research. *Current Housing Reports, American Housing Survey for the United States in 1991*, Washington, DC: U.S. Government Printing Office, April 1993. Tables: 8, 525-526, 531-536, 540-541, 543-547, 549-550, 552-554

U.S. Department of Justice. Office of Justice Programs. Bureau of Justice Statistics. *Bureau of Justice Statistics, Special Report: Hispanic Victims*, NCJ- 120507, Washington, DC: Bureau of Justice Statistics, January 1990. Tables: 868, 871-875, 878-884

U.S. Department of Justice. Office of Justice Programs. Bureau of Justice Statistics. *Correctional Populations in the United States, 1989* (NCJ-130445). Washington, DC: Bureau of Justice Statistics, October 1991. Table: 916

U.S. Department of Justice. Office of Justice Programs. Bureau of Justice Statistics. *Correctional Populations in the United States, 1991* (NCJ-142729). Washington, DC: Bureau of Justice Statistics, August 1993. Tables: 903, 906, 911-913, 920-921

U.S. Department of Justice. Office of Justice Programs. Bureau of Justice Statistics. *Sourcebook of Criminal Justice Statistics, 1990*. Washington, DC: U.S. Government Printing Office, 1991. Tables: 876, 888-889, 910

U.S. Department of Veterans Affairs. National Center for Veteran Analysis and Statistics. *Facts About Hispanic Veterans*. Washington, DC: Department of Veterans Affairs, September 1994. Tables: 844-848

U.S. Equal Employment Opportunity Commission. *Job Patterns for Minorities and Women in Private Industry, 1993*. Washington, DC: U.S. Government Printing Office, 1994. Tables: 722-769

U.S. Equal Employment Opportunity Commission. *Job Patterns for Minorities and Women in State and Local Government, 1990*. Washington, DC: U.S. Government Printing Office, 1991. Tables: 578-579, 811-820

U.S. General Accounting Office. *Affirmative Employment: Assessing Progress of EEO Groups in Key Federal Jobs Can Be Improved*, GAO/GGD-93-65. Washington, DC: U.S. GAO, March 1993. Tables: 805, 808-810

U.S. General Accounting Office. *Diabetes: Status of the Disease Among American Indians, Blacks and Hispanics*. Washington, DC: U.S. GAO, 1992. Table: 388

U.S. General Accounting Office. *Federal Affirmative Employment: Status of Women and Minority Representation in Federal Law Enforcement Occupations*, GAO/T-GGD-93-2. Washington, DC: U.S. GAO, October 1, 1992. Table: 893

U.S. General Accounting Office. Report to the Chairman Select Committee on Aging, House of Representatives, *Social Security Administration: Employment and Services to Hispanics*, GAO/HRD-89-35. Washington, DC: U.S. GAO, January 1989. Table: 350

U.S. Immigration and Naturalization Service, *Statistical Yearbook of the Immigration and Naturalization Service, 1993*, U.S. Government Printing Office, Washington, DC, 1994. Tables: 10-38, 40-42, 45, 47-56, 58-66, 68-74

USA TODAY (10 December 1992). Tables: 120, 296

Usdansky, Margaret L. "1990s' wedding bell blues: new report echoes trend of the '70s." *USA TODAY* (9 December 1992). Table: 167

Usdansky, Margaret L. "A new U.S. workforce evolves: job shifts reflect progress of Hispanics and women." *USA TODAY* (29 January 1993). Tables: 512-514, 518

Usdansky, Margaret L. "NYC in 'dumps' after losing gains of '80." *USA TODAY* (16 April 1992). Table: 122

Usdansky, Margaret L. "Old ethnic influences still play in cities." *USA TODAY* (4 August 1992). Table: 77

Usdansky, Margaret L. "Poor whites get more help than others." *USA TODAY* (9 October 1992). Table: 646

Usdansky, Margaret L. "Wedded to the single life: attitudes, economy delaying marriages." *USA TODAY* (17 July 1992). Tables: 183-184

Usdansky, Margaret L. "Women on welfare: reality vs. stereotype." *USA TODAY* (26 October 1994). Table: 648

Valdiserri, Ronald O., MD, MPH, et al. "Clients without health insurance at publicly funded HIV counseling and testing sites: implications for early intervention." *Public Health Reports* 110, no. 1 (January-February 1995). Table: 409

Vargas, Arturo. "Redistricting: route to Latino empowerment." *USA TODAY* (3 March 1992). Table: 833

"Weak economy may be hurting moves to fight mortgage bias, study finds." *Wall Street Journal* (28 October 1992). Table: 465

"Who's who among Hispanic Americans." *USA TODAY* (24 February 1993). Table: 600

Willette, Anne. "New rules help more people qualify." *USA TODAY* (15 November 1994). Table: 471

Wolf, Richard. "Redistricting to change the face of Congress." *USA TODAY* (22 October 1992). Table: 828

Wolf, Richard. "Speaker Foley's back and in top form." *USA TODAY* (7 December 1992). Table: 830

Keyword Index

The Keyword Index lists every topic, company or business, agency, organization, brand, or personal name mentioned in *Statistical Record of Hispanic Americans, 2nd Edition* tables. Citations are arranged alphabetically, word by word, then letter by letter. Each index citation is followed by page and table reference numbers. Page numbers are preceded by "p." or "pp." Page references do not necessarily identify the page on which a table begins. In cases where tables span two or more pages, references point to to the page on which the index term actually appears, which may be the second or subsequent page of a table. Table reference numbers appear in brackets ([ ]). This index, too, is extensively cross-referenced to direct users to related subjects or terms.

Numbers following p. or pp. are page references. Numbers in [ ] are table references.

Numbers following p. or pp. are page references. Numbers in [ ] are table references.

Numbers following p. or pp. are page references. Numbers in [ ] are table references.

Keyword Index

Numbers following p. or pp. are page references. Numbers in [ ] are table references.

Numbers following p. or pp. are page references. Numbers in [ ] are table references.

Numbers following p. or pp. are page references. Numbers in [ ] are table references.

Numbers following p. or pp. are page references. Numbers in [ ] are table references.

Keyword Index

Numbers following p. or pp. are page references. Numbers in [ ] are table references.

Numbers following p. or pp. are page references. Numbers in [ ] are table references.

Numbers following p. or pp. are page references. Numbers in [ ] are table references.

Keyword Index

Numbers following p. or pp. are page references. Numbers in [ ] are table references.

Numbers following p. or pp. are page references. Numbers in [ ] are table references.

Numbers following p. or pp. are page references. Numbers in [ ] are table references.

Keyword Index

Numbers following p. or pp. are page references. Numbers in [ ] are table references.

Numbers following p. or pp. are page references. Numbers in [ ] are table references.

Numbers following p. or pp. are page references. Numbers in [ ] are table references.

Keyword Index

Numbers following p. or pp. are page references. Numbers in [ ] are table references.

Numbers following p. or pp. are page references. Numbers in [ ] are table references.

Numbers following p. or pp. are page references. Numbers in [ ] are table references.

Numbers following p. or pp. are page references. Numbers in [ ] are table references.

Keyword Index

Numbers following p. or pp. are page references. Numbers in [ ] are table references.

Keyword Index

Numbers following p. or pp. are page references. Numbers in [ ] are table references.

Numbers following p. or pp. are page references. Numbers in [ ] are table references.

Numbers following p. or pp. are page references. Numbers in [ ] are table references.

Numbers following p. or pp. are page references. Numbers in [ ] are table references.

Numbers following p. or pp. are page references. Numbers in [ ] are table references.

Numbers following p. or pp. are page references. Numbers in [ ] are table references.

Keyword Index

Numbers following p. or pp. are page references. Numbers in [ ] are table references.

Numbers following p. or pp. are page references. Numbers in [ ] are table references.

Numbers following p. or pp. are page references. Numbers in [ ] are table references.

Numbers following p. or pp. are page references. Numbers in [ ] are table references.

Numbers following p. or pp. are page references. Numbers in [ ] are table references.

Numbers following p. or pp. are page references. Numbers in [ ] are table references.

Numbers following p. or pp. are page references. Numbers in [ ] are table references.

Numbers following p. or pp. are page references. Numbers in [ ] are table references.

Keyword Index

Numbers following p. or pp. are page references. Numbers in [ ] are table references.

Numbers following p. or pp. are page references. Numbers in [ ] are table references.

Numbers following p. or pp. are page references. Numbers in [ ] are table references.

Numbers following p. or pp. are page references. Numbers in [ ] are table references.

Numbers following p. or pp. are page references. Numbers in [ ] are table references.

Keyword Index

Numbers following p. or pp. are page references. Numbers in [ ] are table references.

Numbers following p. or pp. are page references. Numbers in [ ] are table references.

Numbers following p. or pp. are page references. Numbers in [ ] are table references.

Numbers following p. or pp. are page references. Numbers in [ ] are table references.

Keyword Index

Numbers following p. or pp. are page references. Numbers in [ ] are table references.

Numbers following p. or pp. are page references. Numbers in [ ] are table references.

Keyword Index

Numbers following p. or pp. are page references. Numbers in [ ] are table references.

Numbers following p. or pp. are page references. Numbers in [ ] are table references.

Numbers following p. or pp. are page references. Numbers in [ ] are table references.

Numbers following p. or pp. are page references. Numbers in [ ] are table references.

Numbers following p. or pp. are page references. Numbers in [ ] are table references.

Numbers following p. or pp. are page references. Numbers in [ ] are table references.

Numbers following p. or pp. are page references. Numbers in [ ] are table references.

Numbers following p. or pp. are page references. Numbers in [ ] are table references.

Numbers following p. or pp. are page references. Numbers in [ ] are table references.

Keyword Index

Numbers following p. or pp. are page references. Numbers in [ ] are table references.

Numbers following p. or pp. are page references. Numbers in [ ] are table references.

Numbers following p. or pp. are page references. Numbers in [ ] are table references.

Numbers following p. or pp. are page references. Numbers in [ ] are table references.

Keyword Index

Numbers following p. or pp. are page references. Numbers in [ ] are table references.

Numbers following p. or pp. are page references. Numbers in [ ] are table references.

Numbers following p. or pp. are page references. Numbers in [ ] are table references.

Numbers following p. or pp. are page references. Numbers in [ ] are table references.

Keyword Index

Numbers following p. or pp. are page references. Numbers in [ ] are table references.

Numbers following p. or pp. are page references. Numbers in [ ] are table references.

Keyword Index

Numbers following p. or pp. are page references. Numbers in [ ] are table references.

Numbers following p. or pp. are page references. Numbers in [ ] are table references.

Numbers following p. or pp. are page references. Numbers in [ ] are table references.

Numbers following p. or pp. are page references. Numbers in [ ] are table references.

Numbers following p. or pp. are page references. Numbers in [ ] are table references.

Numbers following p. or pp. are page references. Numbers in [ ] are table references.

Keyword Index

Numbers following p. or pp. are page references. Numbers in [ ] are table references.

Numbers following p. or pp. are page references. Numbers in [ ] are table references.

Keyword Index

Numbers following p. or pp. are page references. Numbers in [ ] are table references.

Numbers following p. or pp. are page references. Numbers in [ ] are table references.

Keyword Index

Numbers following p. or pp. are page references. Numbers in [ ] are table references.

Numbers following p. or pp. are page references. Numbers in [ ] are table references.

Numbers following p. or pp. are page references. Numbers in [ ] are table references.

Numbers following p. or pp. are page references. Numbers in [ ] are table references.

Keyword Index

Numbers following p. or pp. are page references. Numbers in [ ] are table references.

Numbers following p. or pp. are page references. Numbers in [ ] are table references.

Keyword Index

Numbers following p. or pp. are page references. Numbers in [ ] are table references.

Numbers following p. or pp. are page references. Numbers in [ ] are table references.

Keyword Index

Numbers following p. or pp. are page references. Numbers in [ ] are table references.

Numbers following p. or pp. are page references. Numbers in [ ] are table references.

Numbers following p. or pp. are page references. Numbers in [ ] are table references.

Numbers following p. or pp. are page references. Numbers in [ ] are table references.